Now the <u>program</u> designed to meet you

 ①

The Annotated Teacher's Edition

- integrates the unique components that make *A History of the United States* a total learning system

- includes cooperative learning, critical thinking, and other on-page teaching notes to enliven class discussion

 ②

Teacher's Resource File: Instructional Support Files

- conveniently organizes pre-reading, reading, skill review, skill application, and critical thinking activity sheets, and tests, chapter-by-chapter in file folders

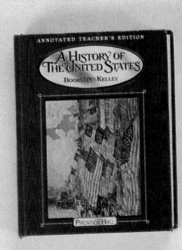

Core support materials reinforce chronology and historical concepts.

A History of the United States © 1996

The sixth edition.
A History of the United States ©1996

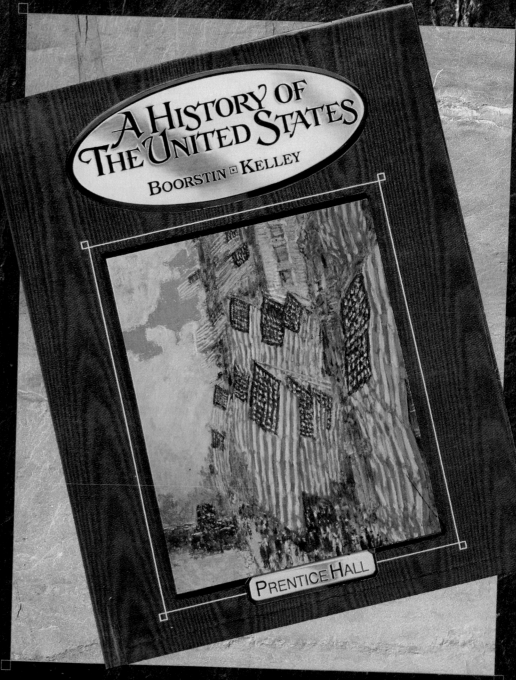

Consistently recognized as the book of choice
for its well-told story.

PRENTICE HALL

Teacher's Resource File: Enrichment Support Files

- unique enrichment
  - Literature selections
  - Primary Source readings
  - Geography in History essays
  - Biographies
  - Great Debates readings
  - Art lessons

- organized around central topics in American History

Perspectives: Readings on American History in the 20th Century

- offers several different points of view on ten key 20th-century topics

- points of view are illustrated in short essays by well-known historians and commentators

American History Transparencies

- designed with the diverse learning styles of today's students in mind

- complete package includes 110 full-color transparencies:
  - Multicultural transparencies
  - Cause and Effect charts
  - Historical maps
  - Geographic Setting maps
  - Fine Art
  - Time lines

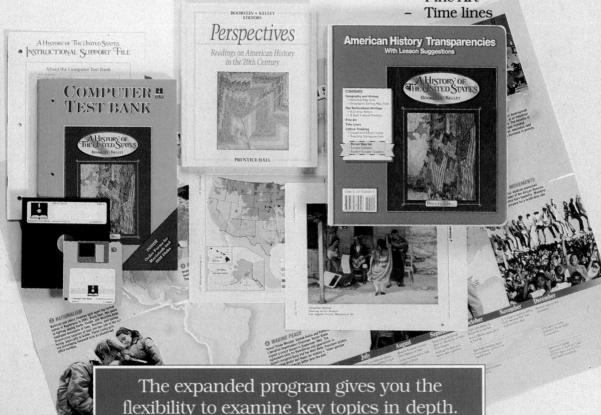

The expanded program gives you the flexibility to examine key topics in depth.

The p

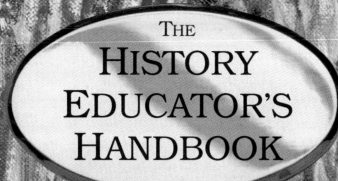

THE HISTORY EDUCATOR'S HANDBOOK

CONTENTS

"A Wrestler with the Angel"   T6
Themes in History   T8
Teaching Geography Through
  History   T10
Muliticultural Education:
  Valuing Differences   T12
Cooperative Learning   T14
Writing as a Process   T16
Critical Thinking: A Key to
  Understanding   T18
A Guided Tour of *A History
  of the United States*   T20
Lesson Plan Contents   T23

"A Wrestler with the Angel"

by Daniel J. Boorstin

The historian is both discoverer and creator. To the uniqueness of his role we have a clue in the very word "history," which means both the course of the past and the legible account of the past. The historian is always trying to reduce, or remove, that ambiguity. If he is successful, he leads his readers to take-or-mistake his account for what was really there.

The historian sets himself a dangerous, even an impossible, task. In the phrase of the great Dutch historian, J. H. Huizinga, he is "A Wrestler with the Angel." It is the angel of death who makes his work necessary yet destined never to be definitive. If man were not mortal, we would not be deprived of the living testimony of the actors, and so required to give new form to the receding infinity.

The Historian as Discoverer

The historian can rediscover the past only by the relics it has left for the present. Historians of all ages have worked under these limitations. Their mission requires that they make the most of whatever they can find. They try to convince us that the relics they have examined and interpreted in their narrative are a reliable sample of the experience that men really had. But how reliable are the remains of the past as clues to what was really there?

My own experience as a historian has brought me vivid reminders of how partial is the remaining evidence of the whole human past, how casual and how accidental is the survival of its relics.

The Law of the Survival of the Unread. If there is a natural and perhaps inevitable tendency toward the destruction and disappearance of the documents most widely used, this poses a discomfiting problem for the historian. For he inevitably relies heavily on the surviving printed matter. Is the historian, then, the victim of a diabolical solipsism? Is there an inverse relation between the probability of a document surviving and its value as evidence of the daily life of the age from which it survives?

Survival of the Collected and the Protected: What Goes in Government Files. We emphasize political history and government in the life of the past partly because governments keep records, while families and other informal groups seldom do. Yet informal groups were among the most remarkable and most characteristic of American communities. Much of the peculiarly American experience, which has had this voluntary, spontaneous character, has eluded historians.

Survival of the Victorious Point of View: The Success Bias. The history of inventions which we read today seems to have become the story of successful inventors. Eli Whitney, Isaac Merritt Singer, Henry Ford, Thomas A. Edison, and other lucky ones leave a vivid record. But the countless anonymous experimenters, the frustrated tinkers who nearly made it, disappear. How many of their efforts ought to be part of the story?

American history as a whole presents a spectacle of this bias. A dominant theme in the writing of American history has been the filling of the continent, the consolidating of a great nation. But the desire to secede, to move *away* from the larger political community might have become the leitmotif. Just as the Puritans came to America as seceders from Britain, so the westward movers in the nineteenth century were seceders from the heavily settled, increasingly urban Atlantic coastal nation. If the South had won the Civil War, if the Bear Flag Republic of 1846 had survived, if the Republic of Texas had remained independent, the earlier American settlers too would have continued to shine not as nation builders but as courageous seceders.

The preservative and disintegrating processes of time are vagrant. The randomness of our list suggests both the unpredictable effects of the toll of time and the bizarre miscellany which is our inheritance from our past.

It is the sheerest folly to believe that we, Wrestlers with the Angel, can ever know the extent of the boundaries of our ignorance. Or that we can conquer the biases of survival by some new technology.

The Historian as Creator

Historians are always writing about us. Not because they extrapolate "laws" of social science. But because they write for people about people, than whom nothing is more interesting or more inscrutable.

New temptations for the twentieth-century historian are the by-product of his new instruments of discovery. Biases of the social sciences can seduce the historian into attitudes at odds with his role as a literary artist. We are unwilling victims of the Biases of Survival, grateful for whatever the past happens to leave us.

While the discoverer focuses our vision anew on something already out there, the creator, of whom the historian is a peculiar breed, makes the object for us to see. He does it with words, and so is inhibited, guided, and fulfilled by language. But his limitations are at least as restricting as the hardness of the sculptor's marble.

While the poet and the novelist can hold off the reader's knowledge of how it all turned out, and entice him by the promise of telling, where the historian labors we already know the last chapter. His greatest challenge, while conforming to the facts as best determined in his age, is to provide his reader with a new access of surprise at how and why and when and who. The successful historian at his best demands and secures a willing suspension of knowledge. He asks the reader to pretend that he does not already know, so that the historian can add suspense to the true course of events. He can do this by his more vivid portrait in detail, by his network of surprising connections, and his array of unexpected consequences. The great historian, the historian-creator, adds a new drama to everything we thought we already knew. Everybody knew that the Roman Empire declined and fell. Gibbon made his readers feel that they had not really known.

The historian-creator refuses to be defeated by the Biases of Survival. For he chooses, defines, and shapes his subject to provide a reasonably truthful account from miscellaneous remains. Like other literary artists, creators in the world of the word, and unlike the advancing social

> ❝The successful historian at his best demands and secures a willing suspension of knowledge.❞

scientist, he is not engaged merely in correcting and revising his predecessors. He adds to our inheritance. At his best he is not accumulating knowledge which becomes obsolete, but creating a work with a life of its own. The truth which the historian in any age finds in the past becomes part of our literary treasure. Inevitably the historian is torn between his efforts to create anew what he sees was really there, and the urgent shifting demands of the living audience. His motto could be Saint Augustine's *Credo quia impossibilia,* I believe because it is impossible. At his best he remains a Wrestler with the Angel.

Excerpted from "A Wrestler with the Angel," Hidden History: Discovering Our Secret Past (New York: Harper & Row, 1987) Reprinted with permission of the author.

THEMES IN HISTORY

By Stephen L. Cox, Ph.D.

Adjunct Professor of History
University of New Hampshire

Staff Historian
New Hampshire Historical Society

Educators have begun to emphasize themes as a means to facilitate student comprehension of American history. In 1987 the Bradley Commission on History in the Schools was created "in response to widespread concern over the inadequecy, both in quantity and quality, of the history taught in American elementary and secondary classrooms." The Commission, consisting of eminent historians and innovative high school teachers, provided recommendations regarding how the study of history may be improved in the schools. The Commission noted that:

"We can be sure that students will experience enormous changes over their lifetimes. History is the discipline that can best help them to understand and deal with change, and at the same time to identify the deep continuities that link past and present . . . . [History] can satisfy young people's longing for a sense of identity and of their time and place in the human story. Well-taught, history and biography are naturally engaging to students by speaking to their individuality, to their possibilities for choice, and to their desire to control their lives."

One recommendation issued by the Bradley Commission noted that "historical study must often focus upon broad, significant themes and questions, rather than short-lived memorization of facts without context." And the Commission also noted that "narrative history must illuminate vital themes and significant questions, including but reaching beyond the acquisition of useful facts."

Few historians in the late twentieth century debate "facts," but most are concerned about what those facts mean in a broader sense. Indeed, most historians weave their material about history not so much around specific events, but around issues that place specific events in some thematic framework. For example, when analyzing the Constitution, historians are usually less concerned about when (1787) it was written than with the ideas and values that inspired the Framers, or the document's continued impact on American society.

How Do Historical Themes Help Us to Teach History?

By themselves, "facts" seldom provide the necessary framework for the study of history. However, by organizing information thematically, students are provided with the opportunity to analyze related information over time. In this way, one event in the past can help to shed light on those that follow, and on the present as well.

For example, knowing that the Supreme Court case *Brown* v. *Board of Education* came before the Court in 1954 and that it overturned an earlier case, *Plessy* v. *Ferguson*, are facts students should know. However, the *Brown* decision will be much more meaningful to students if they are familiar with other Supreme Court cases leading to *Brown*, as well as significant cases that followed.

A thematic approach in this instance will give students a context for understanding *Brown*, not only as a step forward in the struggle for civil rights in America, but as a significant event in our constitutional history.

Themes provide the context that students may use as a tool for really understanding and integrating the "facts" about historical events. Clearly, a thematic approach to the study of history will link the past with the present in a meaningful, integrated, and more engaging fashion. And of course, as teachers we want students to understand and become engaged by the material we present to them.

■

How Are Historical Themes Developed in *A History of the United States*?

Boorstin and Kelley's *A History of the United States* offers teachers several pedagogical "handles" that help students grasp the broad themes of American history.

At the beginning of the unit. To ensure comprehension of these broad themes, Boorstin and Kelley identify "Themes in American History" at the beginning of each unit. Written as summaries of main ideas, these themes alert students to the significant issues they will encounter throughout the unit. In the *Annotated Teacher's Edition* (ATE) unit openers, the following themes are categorized and labeled accordingly:

- Economics
- The Constitution
- Social Change
- Geography
- Science, Technology, and Society
- Government and Politics
- Ethics and Values
- Conflict

In the narrative. Boorstin and Kelley take a long view of our past, seeing American history as an unfolding story. Their narrative is interpretive, always seeking to connect events that occurred at different moments in our history. Thus, historical themes are naturally woven throughout the narrative. The ATE features on-page "Continuity and Change" notes that highlight content in the narrative that illustrates a unit theme. These teaching notes also provide links between issues and events from one period in American history with issues and events from another.

At the end of the unit. At the end of the unit, in the "Making Connections" feature, the unit themes are reinforced using a time line and critical thinking questions. The time-line callouts serve as clues to answering the critical thinking question for each theme. Thus, historical themes are introduced in the unit opener, highlighted in the narrative, and reinforced at the end of the unit.

These pedagogical "handles" help students to recognize change and "the deep continuities that link past and present." In short, Boorstin and Kelley put history in context and give students a reason to study our nation's past.

TEACHING GEOGRAPHY THROUGH HISTORY

Newspapers and magazines fill their education sections with stories documenting the lack of geographic knowledge among students. Few social studies educators dispute these findings. But teachers quickly point out that the social studies curriculum is filled with numerous and varied subjects, all of them worthy of attention. History–American and world–government, civics, sociology, psychology, political science, economics, and world cultures compete for attention with geography in a two- or three-year course of study. History teachers wonder how they can work in more instruction in geography without stealing time from their concentration on history.

History teachers have not ignored geography. In reality, most history teachers already teach some geography, and they have been doing this for some time. History teachers teach map skills and place location, and discuss geographic influences on places and events. But much of their instruction in geography has been sporadic and unfocused, largely because of the lack of an analytical framework that would enable geography and history to be integrated.

The Need for Analytical Framework in Geographic Education

In 1984 two professional organizations, the National Council for Geographic Education and the Association of American Geographers, addressed the need for an analytical framework for geographic education. In truth, geography has always been an analytical discipline, a study of *where* such things as landforms, resources, and human activities are located, *why* they are located in particular places, and *how* they relate to people, events, other places, and other things.

The two professional organizations issued the "Guidelines for Geographic Education." This document provided an easily understood framework for geographic education and described the five themes of geography, and their place in the social studies classroom. Since that time, professional geographic organizations have published additional documents that provide still more strategies for using the five themes in history classes.

In a nutshell, the five themes provide an organizing focus for geographic study. They are the tools that students use to analyze a place, to answer the *where, why,* and *how* questions that constitute geography, and to identify some of the *whos* and *whats* as well. The themes are known by their one-word names of *location, place, interaction, movement,* and *region.*

Defining the Five Themes of Geography

You will find many "Geography and History" notes on the pupil pages in the Annotated Teacher's Edition of *A History of the United States.* These annotations apply the five themes of geography in their historical context.

Location can be expressed in two ways, absolute and relative. Knowing the **absolute location** of places is like knowing the alphabet before you begin to read. If students know something about the climate of the earth, learning that the search for the Northwest Passage took explorers closer and closer to the North Pole becomes meaningful.

Each **place** differs from every other place in its physical and human characteristics. Asking students to describe the characteristics that make a place unique requires them to learn about geography. Students must consider landforms, water bodies, climate, and vegetation. They must also consider such human characteristics as the population, settlement patterns, culture, political systems, economic activities, and transportation and communication networks. Physical and human characteristics form "geographic signatures" that make a place unique.

Interaction focuses on the relationship between people and the environment. All places on earth have advantages and disadvantages for human settlement and survival. The more advantageous places usually have higher population densities than less advantageous places, such as deserts. In response to environmental shortcomings, human populations have learned to modify their environment. Interaction examines how people have changed the environment and the consequences of those changes.

Using the theme of **movement** helps students investigate the relationships between places. How one place is linked to another provides important clues to understanding the historical development of places. For example, the movement of ideas from Europe to the United States had a significant influence upon the American Revolution in the eighteenth century. In turn, the movement of American ideas to Europe and South America helped shape events in these places in the 1800s.

Particular **regions** are those with human or physical traits that distinguish them from other areas. Analyzing places in terms of region provides a context for making comparisons, and there are countless ways of identifying a region. For example, the regions of the North and the South are the main organizing themes in the historical analysis of the Civil War.

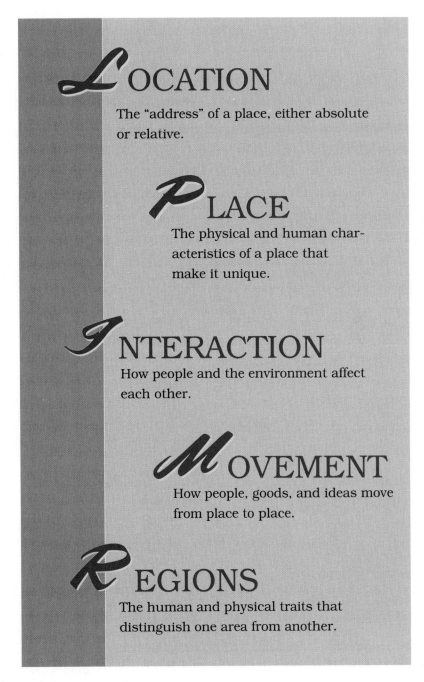

*L*OCATION
The "address" of a place, either absolute or relative.

*P*LACE
The physical and human characteristics of a place that make it unique.

*I*NTERACTION
How people and the environment affect each other.

*M*OVEMENT
How people, goods, and ideas move from place to place.

*R*EGIONS
The human and physical traits that distinguish one area from another.

MULTICULTURAL EDUCATION

Valuing
Differences

What is multicultural education? It is a curriculum and a way of teaching that acknowledges the cultural diversity of the United States and the world and sees this diversity as a positive fact of life. Multicultural education strives for more complex understanding and more sensitivity to issues of diversity. At its foundation is the recognition of the intrinsic worth of each individual, regardless of race, ethnic background, gender, religion, socioeconomic status, or physical or mental condition.

Multicultural education is slowly being incorporated in all content areas, especially in the social studies. This movement for educational reform is not without disagreements, however. Proponents of multicultural education differ greatly in their proposals for teaching and content reform.

The Melting Pot and the Salad Bowl

At the heart of the multicultural movement is the recognition that the United States is a multiracial, multiethnic, and multicultural society. This view contrasts sharply with the prevalent view in American education for many decades—the vision of the United States as a melting pot. This assimilationist view held that, over time, all nationalities and ethnicities would give up their original culture and mix in the American melting pot, producing a uniquely American culture. In the interest of serving this point of view, American educators intentionally ignored or devalued differences and sought to minimize their expression.

In the last few decades, however, social scientists have determined that the melting pot idea does not do a good job of describing American society. All ethnic and cultural groups have retained some aspects of their culture, even after moving into the American mainstream.

Thus, a different model was proposed to describe American society—that of cultural pluralism. In this view, ethnic groups retain many of their traditions, such as language and social customs. At the same time, ethnic groups adopt many aspects of the predominant Anglo-American culture, such as obedience to laws and participation in the mainstream political and economic systems. In the view of cultural pluralism, ethnic identification continues to be important to all Americans and is central both to self-identification and to group action.

The Debate Leads to Action

The debate between the melting pot theorists and the cultural pluralists would have been largely academic, except for evidence that educational practices based on the melting pot theory were negatively affecting students' performance. Educators noted that the failure to include diverse cultural perspectives—and to treat these perspectives with respect—could undermine the self-respect and motivation of minority students, resulting in high rates of failure and alienation from the school environment. Also, the narrow cultural focus in the curriculum meant that students from majority groups lacked the knowledge they needed to overcome prejudice and to participate in our multicultural society.

Proponents of multicultural education argue that educators must teach about the diverse nature of our society and our world to fulfill their mission. For, without sensitivity to and appreciation for ethnic, racial, and cultural differences, educational excellence and equality of opportunity cannot be achieved.

The multiculturalists' arguments have had a great effect on the educational community. Iowa and Minnesota have mandated that multicultural approaches be part of all content instruction. In California and New York, cultural pluralism and multicultural education have been placed at the core of the states' social studies instruction. In the cities, which have the greatest cultural diversity, the need for multicultural education is being addressed through changes in the curriculum, teacher awareness, and a search for new multicultural materials.

American History and Multiculturalism

American history is the story of many diverse cultural and ethnic groups. For many school districts, it is the core subject in the curriculum for the exploration of American diversity.

In *A History of the United States*, Drs. Boorstin and Kelley tell the story of American diversity well. They weave the varied stories of the American people—whom they call "the most miscellaneous people on earth"—into the story of our common nation. The achievements and sufferings of minorities, women, and the disadvantaged are not relegated to features and side columns, because they are not sidelights to American history. The struggle of a diverse people to achieve freedom and equality for all is told dynamically, as an enduring issue that has concerned Americans in the past and will continue to be a national goal for the future.

The Goals of *Multicultural Education*

Multicultural education is a broad educational reform movement and, therefore, seeks to achieve numerous goals. The list below draws upon many of the goals of state and local educational agencies as well as the writings of such multicultural educators as James A. Banks and Christine I. Bennett. *A History of the United States* uses these goals as guidelines for incorporating multicultural education into its program.

- To develop positive self-images by helping students understand their own cultures

- To help students gain greater self-understanding by viewing their cultures from the perspectives of other groups

- To help students develop an appreciation of individual and cultural differences

- To enrich students with the diverse historical, artistic, and literary contributions of other groups

- To provide students with the ability to function within other cultures

- To combat racism, prejudice, and discrimination

- To build social action skills and inspire students to participate in a culturally diverse nation and world

- To help students master essential content and skills

COOPERATIVE LEARNING

An Interview with **Robert Slavin**

Cooperative learning is being used now more than ever before. But what *is* cooperative learning, and why should you incorporate it into *your* classroom activities? For a clearer picture, we talked to Robert Slavin, Director of the Johns Hopkins University Center for Social Organization of Schools and one of the nation's leading researchers on the use of cooperative learning in the classroom.

What are we talking about when we say "cooperative learning"?

Cooperative learning actually refers to a wide range of different methods. What is common to all of them is the idea that kids of the same age are working together to help each other learn.

How does that happen? How does cooperative learning reinforce or expand learning?

One of the things that cooperative learning does is motivate students to be concerned about each other's learning, so that students feel that their peers are supporting their learning efforts.

Another thing is that students, in the process of discussing the material that the teacher has presented, get to voice their own current understanding, which helps them in the sense that people learn by teaching. It also helps other kids by filling in gaps—by kids' ability to explain ideas to each other that they may have only dimly understood at the end of the teacher's lesson.

Why should cooperative learning be used in the classroom? What are its benefits, for example?

The main benefit of cooperative learning is that it improves student achievement. Many studies that have compared it to traditional learning have found that cooperative learning improves the achievement of high achievers, of average achievers, and of low achievers in many different circumstances.

Cooperative learning also fosters improved intergroup relations, acceptance of mainstreamed academically handicapped kids, and self-esteem. Since kids enjoy working cooperatively, I think they would feel good about a class in which they are able to work together in this way.

Are there any drawbacks to using cooperative learning?

Well, I suppose some people would say that it's noisy. You've got to be prepared for some noise. Also, in many forms of cooperative learning there is scoring to be done, so there's some paperwork that may be involved, but not a great deal. Other than that, I'm not sure that there are any serious drawbacks.

Let's focus on the groups. What is the ideal group size?

I personally believe four is the ideal group size. It allows you to do some activities in pairs and some activities as a total team. Of course, then, five, if you have left-over kids.

How should groups be assigned?

I think they should be assigned by the teacher. Try to have a high achiever, a low achiever, and a couple of average achievers in each group, and be sure that there's some kind of balance of sex and ethnicity. The teacher should also take into account which kids are likely to work together—you know, which kids were dating but have now broken up, the personalities involved, etc.

*O*nce assigned to a group, how are individual roles decided?

Well, in our methods [at Johns Hopkins], there aren't individual roles. All the students have the same role, which is to be a learner and a teacher. In methods that do use roles, I think that they should be assigned randomly and then rotated over time.

*H*ow can cooperative learning be structured so that one student doesn't end up doing all the work?

There are many ways to do it. In our methods, the groups are working to earn certificates or other kinds of recognition based on the learning of all members of the group. . . . What this means is that the only way for the group to succeed is if everybody learns, so there's no way for one student to do all the work. You rarely want to give the group a single task, or a single activity that they all have to do, because then it is possible for one kid to do all the work.

*Y*ou've said that group success should depend on individual learning. How does that work?

It means that if you have some kind of assessment of individual learning, something that can be traced back to each individual student, then the sum of those individual assessments are used to determine teams that get certificates or special recognition, or bonus points on their grades, or something to indicate that the teacher values group performance. But

the success of the group is dependent on things that show the individual learning or the individual participation of the student.

*S*ome people are opposed to the idea of using rewards and certificates. How do you feel about that?

I think there are some kinds of objectives for which they may not be necessary, such as composition, because kids enjoy that anyway; but for most school subjects, some kind of a group reward is necessary. It doesn't have to be big, just something to communicate to the kids that the activity is important and valuable. Because without that, the students don't see as clearly the need to help each other. There has to be something that they're trying to work toward as a group. Most often, simple recognition is sufficient to tell the group that its success matters.

*H*ow often should cooperative learning be used?

It should be used pretty extensively. Even when you're using cooperative learning, the kids are not working in groups all day or all the time. There's a cycle of activities that includes instruction, individual assessment, and may include some individual work. I think that we certainly have many, many classrooms where cooperative learning is used essentially all year. But it also makes sense to use it for shorter periods, as long as you're not using it on, say, every other Thursday when it's raining. If you are going to use it, it's important to use it consistently for some period of time, maybe six weeks, rather than to do it just from time to time.

*S*hould the groups be constant over that period?

We recommend changing them after every six weeks, or thereabouts. But we definitely recommend against the use of ad hoc groups, of just saying, "Everybody find a partner." There's a major benefit to having a group that kids really identify with and think is important. If you're changing groups every day, then that's not going to happen.

HOW IT WORKS

To give you a wide range of options, cooperative learning activities are provided several times in a chapter. *You* are the best judge of how often to use them. These guidelines will help you get started:

◆ **Group Make-Up:** Combination of high, average, and low achievers, with a balance of sex, ethnicity, and personalities.

◆ **Duration of Groups:** Change after about six weeks.

◆ **Frequency of Use:** As often as practical; consistency is important.

◆ **Accountability:** Group success should depend on individual learning—measured by one evaluation, or by improvement over time.

◆ **Recognition**: Just something small to show you value group success—praise and public recognition are often enough; bonus points or small prizes such as stickers or pins are good, too.

WRITING AS A PROCESS

Today we think of writing as a complex process that involves the application of a wide range of thinking skills and language abilities. Thinking of the process as a series of steps, we can focus on the techniques and tools writers need, the knowledge they must develop, and the choices they must learn to make at each of these steps. From this understanding of what writers must be able to do, we can begin to devise some instructional strategies, some direct activities to teach appropriate skills and knowledge.

The process theory proposes that writers practice very different skills and undertake very different activities at each of the following three productive stages:

PREWRITING

Writers get warmed up, choose a focus, gather ideas and details, record, and begin to sort out their data, seeing how the data fit together in useful ways. This stage is a time of discovery and of invention. It is rich, productive, and extravagant.

WRITING

Writers need to get their ideas recorded in some sort of tentative, first-draft shape as easily and as quickly as possible. Fluency with written English is critical to this stage, as is the knowledge of what choices are available to writers and what factors influence their judgment about these options. Therefore, writers must learn how to turn streams of thoughts and ideas into coherent, organized written streams, and they need to have much experience in making the choices and in having their judgements work effectively in the written piece.

REVISING

From revision that is supported by the positive, informed response of outside readers and by the rethinking and revising by the writers themselves, writers learn that writing benefits from being scrutinized again (and again) after that first draft. This stage involves revising for sense and editing for word choice and sentence style. Writers need to learn how to review a draft with an eye to revision; they need to learn to be editors. In addition, they need to learn to proofread—to spot errors and make corrections in spelling, capitalization, punctuation, and grammar. These are complicated skills that require much learning and much teaching.

THE WRITING PROCESS

▶▶▶▶ PREWRITING ▶▶▶▶▶▶▶▶▶▶▶ WRITING ▶▶▶▶▶▶

Developing Ideas

Observing	Log-keeping
Mapping	Researching
Listening	Brainstorming
Cueing	Remembering
Imagining	Journal Writing
Clustering	Dramatizing
Outlining	Questioning
Reading	Free Writing

Organizing

Developing with details, reasons, examples, incidents, or arguments

Ordering by chronology, spatial order, importance, or other logic

Classifying

Deductive-Inductive order

Setting Rhetorical Stance

Voice

Audience

Purpose

Form

Making Linguistic Choices

Diction-choice of words

Phrase/clause structure

Sentence structure

Modification and subordination

Connections; transitions

Figurative language

▶▶▶▶▶ REVISING ▶▶▶▶▶ EVALUATING ▶▶ PUBLISHING

Editing

Peer Editing

Response Groups

Self-Revision

Yes-No

Questionnaire

Written Responses

Proofreading

Catching copy errors

Checking mechanics

Proofing spelling

Revising sentence structure

Grading

Correcting

Holistic Scoring

Primary-trait Scoring

Sharing

Posting

Filing

Dispatching

EVALUATING

After a student's final draft is turned in, there is still opportunity for teaching and learning to occur. Students may be involved in evaluating their writing and the writing of others by using scoring sheets or rubrics and by emphasizing one of several different methods of scoring.

PUBLISHING

A final step in the writing process is to give credibility and value to the act of writing and to its product. Although honoring student writing can be done quite simply, it seems to be overlooked in many classrooms. It really means to demonstrate to the student that the written piece (and indirectly its author) is valued by other people. Writing benefits when the classroom is a place where writing is valued as more than pointless exercise, where it is honored, put on display, kept in a student file, or presented in a classroom book.

BENEFITS

Following these steps can involve students deeply in a process in which they have a reasonably good chance of success. The steps teach them how to make the process useful and operational in their own writing experience.

Much of the information in "Writing as a Process" was adapted from The Writing Process in Action: A Handbook for Teachers *by Jackie Proett and Kent Gill, University of California, Davis. Copyright 1986 by the National Council of Teachers of English. Reprinted with permission.*

Critical Thinking:
A Key to Understanding

By Susan Feibelman
Program Specialist
Dallas Independent School District

On the afternoon of April 9, 1865 General Robert E. Lee rode to a small house in Appomattox Court House, Virginia. Spotlessly dressed in full uniform, Lee had come to arrange for the surrender of the Confederate Army. Ulysses S. Grant, dusty and unkempt, greeted Lee cordially, and then the two men negotiated the terms for surrender. Lee was relieved that his officers would be allowed to keep their swords as a symbol of honor, and that both officers and enlisted men could keep their horses as they would be needed for planting their first crops when they returned home.

Like clockwork, at the start of each school year, one student in my history classroom will raise his or her hand and ask about the number of dates I will require memorized over the term. Unfortunately, countless students have learned that the study of history is composed of an endless number of names and dates that must be committed to memory.

For a time students might remember that Lee surrendered to Grant on April 9, 1865 at Appomattox Court House. But this well-learned lesson precludes their engagement in any critical evaluation of that surrender. For example, what effect did Grant's disorderly appearance have on the meeting? Should Grant have been so generous with his terms of surrender? These are the types of questions that invite students to think critically and develop their own interpretations of history—which is, in large part, what the study of history is all about.

Trends and Developments

Over the past fifteen years educators have had constant reminders that they should be teaching for both convergent and divergent thinking. The 1989 report of the National Council for the Social Studies Task Force on Scope and Sequence was full of critical thinking strategies that should be a part of any social studies curriculum. Regional and national conferences for the social studies have been packed with "how-to" offerings for integrating critical thinking into the social studies classroom. Staff development sessions in local school districts have placed special emphasis on preparing students of all abilities to think critically in all content areas. And, social studies textbooks have highlighted critical thinking as a part of their instructional package.

Amidst all this discussion we risk losing our original focus—teaching students to think. We have regarded critical thinking as something else that must be added to our already overflowing instructional plate. The study of history has always been an exercise in critical thinking—teaching the process of critical thinking is the natural outgrowth of this study.

A Multi-Purpose Approach

A History of the United States, by Daniel J. Boorstin and Brooks Mather Kelley, provides teachers with a variety of critical thinking activities and questions.

Throughout the textbook students will be introduced to questions in three broad categories and seventeen subcategories. (See chart at right.)

In each instance the critical thinking approach is driven by the historical content. These activities and questions have been developed to offer an instructional focus for the unit of study, an extension to daily instruction, and as a process for achieving instructional closure.

By using these instructional materials teachers will be able to provide practice in the art and science of critical thinking. Only with practice do we actually build communication, organization, and leadership skills in our students. To prepare our students for participatory citizenship into the twenty-first century these will be invaluable skills to possess. We must then recognize the need to make sure that critical thinking is a key component of classroom instruction.

CRITICAL THINKING SKILLS

Skill	Definition

1. Identifying and Clarifying the Problem

Expressing problems clearly — To succinctly describe a complex situation or body of information.

Identifying central issues — To extract the critical idea(s) in a paragraph, lesson, or chapter.

Making comparisons — To identify how two or more ideas, objects, historical figures, or situations are alike and/or different.

Determining relevance — To decide if and how things are related to one another.

Formulating questions — To create questions that seek answers to specific objectives.

2. Judging Information Related to the Problem

Distinguishing fact from opinion — To separate those statements that can be proven to be true from those that reflect a personal viewpoint.

Checking consistency — To compare two or more items and determine whether they are in agreement or opposition.

Distinguishing false from accurate images — To examine a widely-held belief about a person, place, or thing and determine whether or not this belief is based in fact.

Identifying assumptions — To recognize unstated beliefs that may underlie a given set of statements, actions, or events.

Recognizing bias — To identify a stated or unstated viewpoint or slant of an author or historical figure.

Recognizing ideologies — To deduce underlying beliefs from actions or statements.

3. Solving Problems/Drawing Conclusions

Drawing conclusions — To find an answer or to form an opinion based on available information.

Recognizing cause and effect — To examine the causal links among given events or ideas.

Predicting consequences — To determine the logical effect of an event or action on the outcome of future events or actions.

Identifying alternatives — To identify one or several different methods to achieve a goal and to recognize the possibility of other goals.

Testing conclusions — To examine a statement and decide whether or not it is supported by known facts.

Demonstrating reasoned judgment — To present evidence that supports a given opinion or statement.

A GUIDED TOUR OF
A History of the United States

History of the United States © 1996, by Daniel J. Boorstin and Brooks Mather Kelley, is a unique and flexible program designed to meet your changing curriculum and classroom needs. The core program features the Student Edition, the <u>Annotated Teacher's Edition</u>, and the <u>Teacher's Resource File</u>. The expanded program includes *Perspectives: Readings on American History in the 20th Century* and <u>American History Transparencies</u>.

C O R E   P R O G R A M

Student Edition
A well-told, chronological story

- **Narrative.** *A History of the United States* is a unique United States history textbook. Boorstin and Kelley's well-told story is not disrupted by sidebars or boxed special features that would compete with the narrative for students' attention.
- **Review chapters.** For those teachers who prefer to concentrate their instruction on the Twentieth Century, we have included two review chapters "Beginnings to 1789" (See pgs. 126-147.) and "The United States, 1789-1898." (See pgs. 480-501.) These two chapters can be used in place of the first 18 chapters.
- **Fine Art.** The text begins with "A Note on American

Pictorial Art" that establishes the interplay of art and history. (See pgs. xvi-xvii.) To reinforce this link, all illustrations in the text are from the period under discussion.
- **Themes in American History.** Each unit begins with the identification of historical themes that will be explored in the unit. (See pg. 1.) These themes are written as statements of each chapter's main idea. At the end of the unit, in the "Making Connections" feature, the unit themes are reinforced with critical thinking questions. (See pg. 72.)
- **Section Reviews.** Each section concludes with a review of key terms, people, and places and main ideas. In addition, it contains a labeled critical thinking question. (See pg. 6.) The labels help students to rec-

ognize the kind of thinking skill that must be applied.
- **Chapter Reviews.** Each chapter concludes with a review that contains main-idea, regional history, map and chart skill, and labeled critical thinking questions. (See pg. 25.)
- **Appendixes.** The appendixes include an atlas, a list of presidents and vice-presidents, the Declaration of Independence, and the United States Constitution.

Annotated Teacher's Edition (ATE)

Supports instruction in today's heterogeneous classroom

- **Interleaf format.** Lesson plans are inserted in front of the text chapters they support. Each lesson plan begins with an "Identifying Chapter Materials" chart, which lists all the materials in the program that reinforce, review, and extend the lesson. (See pg. 2A.) This is followed by a "Providing In-Depth Coverage Chart," which lists the materials in the program that focus on a particular topic. (See pg. 2B.)
- **Lesson plans.** Lesson plans are organized section-by-section and follow a modified Madeline Hunter "Focus," "Instruct," "Close," "Extend" model. There is a "Cooperative Learning,"

"Writing Process," or "Independent" activity for every section. (See pgs. 2A–2F.)

- **Teaching notes.** There are six kinds of on-page notes:
  - **Continuity and Change** notes link past and present and reinforce important themes. (See pg. 3.)
  - **Critical Thinking Activity** notes suggest in-class and homework assignments to reinforce content and critical thinking skills. (See pg. 4.)
  - **Geography and History** notes apply the five themes in geography in their historical context. (See pg. 5.)
  - **Cooperative Learning** notes highlight content that is supported by a cooperative learning activity in the lesson plans. (See pg. 6.)
  - **More from Boorstin** notes offer quotes from other of the author's works. (See pg. 7.)

- **Writing Process** notes help develop students' writing skills through a step-by-step process. (See pg. 10.)

Icons link the notes to the content they support.

Teacher's Resource File:
Instructional Support Files

Chapter-by-chapter organization of instructional materials in file folders

- **Pre-Reading Activities** help establish learning goals before students read the chapter.
- **Reading Activities** help students reinforce main ideas as they read the chapter or review the content following the reading.
- **Skill Review Activities** develop students reading and social studies skills.
- **Skill Application Activities** help reinforce these same skills.
- **Critical Thinking Activities** develop and reinforce the critical thinking skills students are asked to apply in the text.
- **Chapter Tests** include key fact and terms, main idea, critical thinking, and essay questions in a four-page test. In addition to the ready-made test, there is also a bank of extra questions for each chapter.
- **Unit Tests** are formatted in the same way as "Chapter Tests."
- **Answer Keys** are included for all activities.

Teacher's Resource File:

Enrichment Support Files

Unique enrichment that enables you and your students to explore key topics in depth

The Enrichment Support Files consist of 40 file folders, each organized around a central topic. There is at least one folder for every text chapter. Each topic includes several of the following, as appropriate to the topic:

- **literature excerpts**
- **primary source readings**
- **geography in history essays**
- **biographies**
- **art lessons**
- **great debates**

Plus an overview essay, lesson suggestions, a simulation, a wrap-up activity, and answers.

Again, the file(s) that are appropriate to a chapter are identified in the ATE.

Perspectives

Readings on American History in the 20th Century

In-depth analysis of key 20th Century topics

Edited by Boorstin and Kelley, *Perspectives* is designed for the teacher who wants to explore key twentieth-century topics in depth. Boorstin and Kelley have selected 5–6 short articles for each of ten topics. The articles are written by well-known historians and commentators with different points of view. The editors preface each topic with an overview essay and provide a foreword and afterword for each article. Where appropriate, footnotes are included to explain important key concepts.

The topic appropriate to a particular student text chapter is identified on the "Providing In-Depth Coverage Chart" in the ATE.

American History Transparencies

Designed with the diverse learning styles of your students in mind

American History Transparencies features 110 full-color transparencies with overlays and lesson ideas:

- **Historical Period Maps**
- **Geographic Setting Maps**
- **A Diverse Nation Transparencies**
- **A Rich Cultural Tradition Transparencies**
- **Fine Art Transparencies**
- **Time Line Transparencies**
- **Cause and Effect Charts**
- **Teaching Transparencies**

All the transparencies in this package can be used to reinforce or extend the text lessons.

Transparencies are referenced in the "Identifying Chapter Materials" charts in the ATE.

LESSON PLAN

C O N T E N T S

Chapter 1	What Europeans Found: The American Surprise	2A - 2F
Chapter 2	An Assortment of Colonies	26A - 26H
Chapter 3	New Ways in a New World	50A - 50F
Chapter 4	The Road to Revolution and Victory	76A - 76F
Chapter 5	From Confederation to Nation	102A - 102F
REVIEW	Beginnings to 1789	126A - 126B
Chapter 6	The United States Begins	148A - 148F
Chapter 7	Jefferson in Power	176A - 176F
Chapter 8	Struggles of a Young Nation	198A - 198F
Chapter 9	The Jacksonian Era	222A - 222F
Chapter 10	The Flourishing Land	250A - 250F
Chapter 11	Reforming and Expanding	278A - 278F
Chapter 12	The Failure of the Politicians	304A - 304H
Chapter 13	The Civil War	332A - 332F
Chapter 14	To Punish or to Forgive?	360A - 360F
Chapter 15	The Passing of the Frontier	384A - 384F
Chapter 16	The Nation Transformed	412A - 412F
Chapter 17	The Challenge of the Cities	436A - 436H
Chapter 18	Politics in the Gilded Age	458A - 458F
REVIEW	The United States, 1789 – 1898	480A - 480B
Chapter 19	The United States and the World	504A - 504F
Chapter 20	The Progressive Era	520A - 520F
Chapter 21	The United States and World War I	546A - 546F
Chapter 22	Return to Normalcy, 1918–1929	576A - 576F
Chapter 23	The Coming of the Great Depression	598A - 598F
Chapter 24	"Nothing to fear but fear itself"	620A - 620F
Chapter 25	Reshaping American Life	642A - 642F
Chapter 26	Clouds of War	656A - 656F
Chapter 27	A World Conflict	674A - 674F
Chapter 28	Truman: Neither War nor Peace	706A - 706F
Chapter 29	Eisenhower, Moderate Republican	728A - 728F
Chapter 30	Mobile People and Magic Machines	750A - 750F
Chapter 31	Years of Hope and Promise	774A - 774F
Chapter 32	LBJ: From the Great Society to Vietnam	796A - 796F
Chapter 33	The Rise and Fall of Richard Nixon	816A - 816F
Chapter 34	In Pursuit of Civil Rights for All	844A - 844H
Chapter 35	Changing Leaders in Washington	876A - 876H
Chapter 36	The Emergence of a New World	906A - 906H

Annotated
Teacher's Edition

A History of
The United States

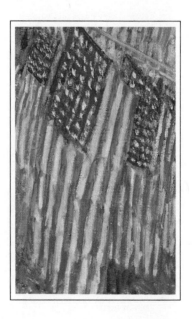

PRENTICE HALL
A Division of Simon & Schuster
Upper Saddle River, New Jersey 07458

ISBN   0–13–833815–9

Printed in the United States of America

2   3   4   5   6   7   8   9   02   01   00   99   98   97   96   95

CONTENTS

List of Maps   xiv

List of Charts and Graphs   xv

List of Primary Sources   xv

A Note on American Pictorial Art   xvi

Prologue   xix

1   The Making of Americans 1

Chapter 1   What Europeans Found:
The American Surprise   2

Christopher Columbus:
Who he was and why he came   3
Before discovery   6
Why Europeans went exploring   10
Spanish adventurers   12
French and English exploration   22

Chapter 2   An Assortment of Colonies   26

The Spanish Empire   27
A great and victorious England   30
The planting of Virginia   34
The Puritans come to New England   38
Other Europeans in North America   44
The proprietary colonies   46

Chapter 3   New Ways in a New World   50

Many kinds of Americans   51
The colonists govern themselves   61
Britain against France   66

MAKING CONNECTIONS   72

2 Forming a New Nation 1763–1800 75

Chapter 4   The Road to Revolution and Victory   **76**
The British take a collision course   77
Declaring independence   84
How British power was overthrown   90

Chapter 5   From Confederation to Nation   **102**
New state governments   103
The Continental Congress   106
A weak confederation   108
Writing a nation's constitution   115
The states ratify   121

REVIEW: BEGINNINGS TO 1789   **126**
The American discovery   127
The making of America   129
Forming a new nation, 1763–1789   135

Chapter 6   The United States Begins   **148**
The nation in the 1790s   149
George Washington sets the course   152
Foreign affairs for a new nation   159
John Adams and the rise of parties   165

MAKING CONNECTIONS   **172**

3 E pluribus unum: One Made from Many 1800–1840 175

Chapter 7   Jefferson in Power   **176**
The man and his policies   177
Buying Louisiana   182
Jefferson, Marshall, and the courts   189
Trouble on the seas   193

Chapter 8   Struggles of a Young Nation   **198**
The War of 1812   199
Madison and Monroe   209
The Missouri Compromise   214
The Monroe Doctrine   217
A national spirit   218

Chapter 9   The Jacksonian Era   **222**
A second Adams in the White House   223
The new politics   226
Jackson takes command   231
Banks and money   238

MAKING CONNECTIONS   **246**

4 A Nation Growing and Dividing 1800–1860 249

Chapter 10	The Flourishing Land	250
Drawing the people together		251
The Industrial Revolution		259
America's leading import: People		265
The rise of the West		269
The cotton kingdom		271

Chapter 11	Reforming and Expanding	278
An age of reform		279
The abolition movement		286
Westward ho!		288
Texas and Oregon		294
War with Mexico		299

Chapter 12	The Failure of the Politicians	304
The Compromise of 1850		305
How the compromise collapsed		312
The nation comes apart		317
The election of 1860		321

MAKING CONNECTIONS   328

5 The Rocky Road to Union 1860–1890 331

Chapter 13	The Civil War	332
A new kind of war		333
The first year: 1861–1862		341
The widening conflict		349
Gettysburg to Appomattox, 1863–1865		353

Chapter 14	To Punish or to Forgive?	360
"With malice toward none"		361
Andrew Johnson and the Radicals		365
"Black Reconstruction"		369
The North withdraws		375
The divided South		379

Chapter 15	The Passing of the Frontier	384
Indian wars and resettlement		385
Seeking gold and silver		391
The cattle kingdom		396
The farmers' frontier		401

MAKING CONNECTIONS   408

6

The New Industrial Age 1865–1900 411

Chapter 16	**The Nation Transformed**	**412**
	Railroads and big business	413
	Rock oil lights up the world	419
	City goods for country customers	422
	Buyers' Palaces	425
	Things by the millions	427
	Labor begins to organize	430

Chapter 17	**The Challenge of the Cities**	**436**
	The growth of an urban nation	437
	Reformers and self-helpers	444
	The spread of learning	446
	Bridge-building heroes	450
	Going up! elevators and skyscrapers	453
	New towns in the country	455

Chapter 18	**Politics in the Gilded Age**	**458**
	Parties in balance	459
	The Democrats come and go	463
	The farmers' revolt	468
	Our money: Gold versus silver	475

| | **MAKING CONNECTIONS** | 478 |

REVIEW: THE UNITED STATES, 1789–1898   **480**

	A new nation	481
	A nation expanding, reforming, and dividing	485
	The nation transformed	496

7

Democratic Reforms and World Power 1890–1920 503

Chapter 19	**The United States and the World**	**504**
	Looking outward	505
	Expanding on the seas	508
	War with Spain	510

Chapter 20	**The Progressive Era**	**520**
	Theodore Roosevelt's Square Deal	521
	Middle-class reformers	527
	Taft in the White House	532
	Woodrow Wilson and the New Freedom	536
	Seeking a world role	540

Chapter 21	**The United States and World War I**	**546**
	A spark ignites Europe	547
	Helping to win the war	556
	The home front	560
	Losing the peace	567

| | **MAKING CONNECTIONS** | 572 |

8

From Boom to Bust 1918–1932 575

Chapter 22   Return to Normalcy, 1918–1929   576
The postwar reaction   577
Searching for the good old days   583
"Keeping cool with Coolidge"   588
Life in the Jazz Age   592

**Chapter 23   The Coming of the
Great Depression   598**
A prosperous nation   599
The big crash   601
Foreign affairs in a gloomy world   609
The election of 1932   613

MAKING CONNECTIONS   616

9

Depression at Home and Aggression Abroad
1933–1945 619

Chapter 24   "Nothing to fear but fear itself"   620
Franklin D. Roosevelt's New Deal   621
From recovery to reform   631
The end of the New Deal   637

Chapter 25   Reshaping American Life   642
Problems on the farm   643
The problems of black Americans   646
The New Deal and women   649
The struggles of labor   652

Chapter 26   Clouds of War   656
Foreign Affairs, 1933–1939   657
The battlefield is everywhere   664
War comes to the United States   670

Chapter 27   A World Conflict   674
Mobilizing for defense   675
"The end of the beginning"—1942   679
Victory in Europe   685
The war in the Pacific   695

MAKING CONNECTIONS   702

10 Postwar Problems 1945–1960 705

Chapter 28   Truman: Neither War nor Peace   706
Beginnings of the cold war   707
Dealing with a new world   711
President in his own right   721

Chapter 29   Eisenhower, Moderate Republican   728
The Republicans return   729
Everybody's New Deal   734
The fight for equality   738
Difficulties abroad   742

Chapter 30   Mobile People and Magic Machines   750
A changing people   751
Everyday life transformed   756
Education and religion   763
Art and the machine   766

MAKING CONNECTIONS   770

11 Turbulent Times 1961–1974 773

Chapter 31   Years of Hope and Promise   774
John F. Kennedy wins   775
Learning hard lessons   778
Facing Communist challenges   783
A New Frontier   788
The tragic end   792

Chapter 32   LBJ: From the Great Society to Vietnam   796
Taking the reins   797
The Great Society   801
Black revolt and youth rebellion   804
Vietnam: "The most unpopular war"   809

Chapter 33   The Rise and Fall of Richard Nixon   816
Electing the President, 1968   817
Nixon's first term   820
The fall   830

MAKING CONNECTIONS   840

12 The United States Looks Ahead 843

Chapter 34   In Pursuit of Civil Rights for All   844
The two ideals   845
Dealing with racism   850
Women seek equality   855
Spanish-speaking peoples   860
New waves of immigration   865
The American Indians   867
New vistas of equality   870

Chapter 35   Changing Leaders in Washington 876
Gerald Ford becomes President   877
Carter: A campaigner as President   882
The United States and the world   888
New foreign initiatives by Carter   892
New directions   896
The changing economy   900

Chapter 36   The Emergence of a New World   906
Troubles abroad   907
Successes and failures   912
New problems for "the Teflon President"   917
The end of the Reagan years   921
The end of the cold war   924
A dangerous world   930
The State of the Nation   933
The Clinton Presidency   939

MAKING CONNECTIONS   946

Epilogue: The Mysterious Future   948

Appendixes

Atlas of Today's World   950

Presidents and Vice-Presidents
of the United States   958

The Declaration of Independence   959

The Constitution of the United States   965

Glossary   **1000**

Index   **1012**

LIST OF MAPS

The Voyages of Columbus	5
Major Indian Tribes of North America about 1500	9
Europe about 1500	11
Early Voyages of Discovery	15
Early New World Explorations	19
Spanish Borderlands about 1780	28
Colonial Settlement to 1775	54
Colonial Trade about 1750	57
New France and Louisiana before 1763	69
Results of the Peace of Paris	78
The American Revolution	93
The United States in 1783	98
Western Land Claims Ceded, 1784–1802	110
The Northwest Territory	112
Major Roads in 1800	150
Indian Land Cessions and Other Treaties, 1784–1810	163
The Barbary States	181
The Mississippi River Basin	183
Lewis and Clark and Pike Explore the West	187
Napoleonic Europe	195
Area of the Tecumseh Confederation	201
The War of 1812	203
Missouri Compromise, 1820	216
The Americas in 1823	219
Indian Removals, 1820–1840	237
Major Roads about 1851	252
Canals in the North about 1840	254
Railroads, 1850–1860	256
Trails to the Far West, 1835–1850	292
Coahuila-Texas	295
Oregon Boundary Settlement	298
The Mexican War, 1846–1848	299
Growth of the United States to 1853	301
Compromise of 1850	309
Kansas-Nebraska Act of 1854	314
The Election of 1860	324
The Confederacy	340
The Civil War, 1861–1865	342
The War in the West, 1862–1863	345
The War in the East, 1862	347
The War in the East, 1863	354
Final Phases of the War, 1863–1865	357
The Plains: Vegetation and Rainfall	386
Indian Reservations, 1875 and 1890	388
The Mining Frontier	394
Cattle Trails and Cow Towns	400
The Vanishing Western Frontier	405
Land Grants to Railroads	414
Railroad Growth, 1870–1890	414
Growth of Cities, 1870–1900	439
The Spanish-American War	511
Territory Acquired by the United States, 1857–1899	515
Spheres of Influence in the Far East about 1900	517
Relations with Our Southern Neighbors, 1898–1933	543
The Vote for Women by 1919	545
Europe in 1914	548
World War I, 1914–1917	557
World War I, The Western Front, 1918	559
Europe and the Near East after the Treaty of Versailles and Other Peace Settlements	568
The Tennessee Valley Authority	627
German and Italian Aggression, 1935–1939	661
Europe at the Peak of the Axis Power, 1942	671
World War II, The Mediterranean, 1942–1944	680
Japanese Conquests in Far East to August, 1942	684
World War II, European Theater, 1944–1945	693
World War II, Pacific Theater, 1942–1945	700
Europe after World War II	716
NATO	718
Korea, 1950–1953	725
Germany Divided	727
Trouble Spots of the Cold War, 1950s	746
United States Population Movement, 1955–1965	753
Standard Metropolitan Statistical Areas	755
United States Interstate Highway System	758
Vietnam	810
Indian Lands in the 1970s	862
OPEC, 1975	881
The Nations of Central America	907
The United States: Political	950
North and South America: Political	952
Africa: Political	953
Asia: Political	954
Europe: Political	955
The World: Political	956

List of Charts and Graphs

Indian Population of Central America	25
Founding of the Colonies	49
Ethnic Division of Colonial Population, 1775	71
Imports from Great Britain, 1763–1776	101
System of Federalism	125
Bank of the United States	171
American Foreign Trade, 1800–1812	197
Growth of Population by Region, 1800–1830	221
Election of 1824	245
Origin of Immigrants to the United States, 1820–1860	277
School Enrollment Rates, 1840–1870	303
Cotton Production and Slave Population, 1800–1860	327
Division of American Resources Between the North and South	359
Reconstruction	383
Indian Population of the United States, 1850–1900	407
Production and Value of Crude Petroleum, 1870–1900	435
United States Demographics, 1851–1900	457
Output and Price of Wheat, 1867–1900	477
American Foreign Trade, 1865–1915	519
Costs and Casualties of World War I for the Allies	571
Car Sales, 1920–1929	597
Unemployment, 1920–1933	615
Federal Income and Spending, 1928–1940	641
Labor Union Membership, 1900–1940	655
Comparative Military Strengths of Allies, 1939	673
Casualties in World War II	701
Median Family Income, 1940–1980	749
Homes with Television Sets/U.S. Population, 1948–1960	769
Americans Below the Poverty Level	795
American Voters	815
Troops in Vietnam, 1968–1973	839
Women Working Outside the Home	875
National Defense Budget, 1950–1999	905
The Federal Government Dollar—Where It Goes	941

Primary Sources

Within the narrative the authors have integrated more than 100 excerpts from primary sources, including the following:

John Winthrop, "A Modell of Christian Charity," 1630	41
Continental Congress, "Declaration of the Causes and Necessity of Taking Up Arms," July 6, 1775	86
Thomas Paine, *The Crisis*, No. 1, December 19, 1776	92
Thomas Jefferson in a letter to R.R. Livingston, April 18, 1802	183
Anthony Trollope, from *North America* (1862)	270
Ralph Waldo Emerson, from his *Journals*, June (?), 1846	279
Sojourner Truth, from her speech at the Ohio Women's Convention in Akron, Ohio, 1851	285
Abraham Lincoln, from his speech "A House Divided" at Springfield, Illinois, June 16, 1858	320
Louisa May Alcott, from a letter to her family in 1862, later published in her book *Hospital Sketches*	338
Abraham Lincoln, in a letter to Horace Greeley, August 22, 1862	349
William Tecumseh Sherman, from a telegram to Abraham Lincoln, December 22, 1864	357
Editorial on Jim Crow laws, Charleston, S.C., *News & Courier*, January 25, 1898	380
Chief Joseph, from his surrender speech, October 5, 1877	389
John D. Rockefeller, from an interview quoted in *God's Gold*, by J.T. Flynn (1932)	416
Louis Sullivan, from his book *The Autobiography of an Idea* (1924)	436
Mary Elizabeth Lease, from her campaign speeches in 1890	471
Abraham Lincoln, from his Second Inaugural Address, March 4, 1865	493
Henry Ford, from *My Life and Work*, by Henry Ford and Samuel Crowther (1922)	594
Herbert Hoover, from a speech during the 1928 election campaign	600
Edna St. Vincent Millay, the poem "First Fig," (1920)	616
Will Rogers, from "Bacon, Beans, and Limousines," *The Survey*, November 15, 1931	621
Martin Luther King, Jr., from his speech "I Have a Dream" at Washington, D.C., August 28, 1963	791
Lyndon Baines Johnson, from an interview with Doris Kearns, quoted in *Lyndon Johnson and the American Dream*, by Doris Kearns (1976)	797
Margaret Mead, from her article "The American Woman Today," in *The 1969 World Book Year Book*, pp. 78–95.	857

A Note on American Pictorial Art

The illustrations in this book not only show the American past. They are specially selected to introduce you to American art. In every chapter, the paintings, drawings, engravings, lithographs, and photographs come from or show objects from the very period described in that chapter. They are authentic witnesses of our art and history. To help you understand and enjoy these pictures, here is a thumbnail history of American art.

Most early settlers of our country had little time for the fine arts. Clearing the wilderness kept them busy enough. But as the 17th century advanced, some of these new Americans had the leisure to enjoy the arts, and the money to commission a portrait. Of course they could not be photographed, for that invention was still two centuries in the future!

Portraits were the main form of painting in the colonial era. Over the years, portrait painters became ever more skillful. Among the best in the 18th century were John Smibert, an English immigrant, Robert Feke, Joseph Badger, John Singleton Copley, Charles Willson Peale, Ralph Earl, Gilbert Stuart, and Benjamin West. Copley and West went to England, where they painted statesmen and wealthy aristocrats and won international reputations.

Benjamin West was one of the earliest American painters to focus on historical events. Following his example, John Trumbull painted a whole series on the American Revolution. Citizens sometimes commissioned a view of their harbor or their city for proud display in the town hall.

In the 19th century, American artists became increasingly aware of the peculiar charms of America. Between 1829 and 1838, George Catlin, fascinated by the handsome Indians, recorded their colorful costumes and dances, and painted 600 Indian portraits. The skilled brushes of Karl Bodmer, Alfred Jacob Miller, and others depicted the Native Americans at home, on the hunt, and at war. John James Audubon's stunning 4-volume *Birds of America* (1827–1838) beautifully portrays our birds.

Meanwhile some artists were captivated by the romantic beauty of the American wilderness. Thomas Cole, Asher B. Durand, and other brilliant landscape painters came to be called "The Hudson River School." They were followed by Thomas Moran and Thomas Hill, both born in England, and Albert Bierstadt, a German—who traveled all over the West. Their gigantic canvases capture the wild continent which was everywhere then.

After the Civil War, more American painters began to look to Europe, especially to the French Impressionists, for new ways of using color. Childe Hassam, Mary Cassatt, and others imported their techniques. Still Winslow Homer, Thomas Eakins, and Albert Pinkham Ryder resisted European influences and went their own American ways.

In the 20th century American painting has run the gamut from the photograph-like work of Andrew Wyeth and the pop art of Andy Warhol to the abstract expressionism of Willem de Kooning and Jackson Pollock. These range from the seamy realism of Edward Hopper and the regionalism of Thomas Hart Benton or Grant Wood to the elegant abstractions of Georgia O'Keeffe.

We should not forget, in even the briefest survey, the so-called "primitives." These were the amateur artists who lacked formal training. For this very reason they gave their work a naive charm and offered a fresh insight into the American past. Most of their names remain unknown. Two whose names do survive are Horace Pickens and Grandma Moses.

Painting, of course, is only one kind of pictorial art. In the days before photography, the engraving and (beginning about 1800) the lithograph provided inexpensive copies of political cartoons, propaganda, and advertising messages, romantic landscapes, battle scenes, and likenesses of George Washington for the home, the office, or the classroom. Nathaniel Currier and James M. Ives, for much of the 19th century, sold thousands of copies of colorful lithographs which recapture for us the pleasures of ice-skating, steamboat-riding, and horse-racing. Their works became less popular with the rise of photography.

The political cartoon has flourished ever

since colonial days. German-born Thomas Nast and Austrian-born Joseph Keppler brought here their sharp eye for caricature. Their hard-hitting attacks made corrupt politicians miserable. Other cartoonists, over the years, have used a variety of styles to deliver a political or moral message—or just to poke fun at us. Among the more influential have been Daniel Fitzpatrick, especially in the 1930s and 1940s, Bill Mauldin (famous for his "G.I. Joe") beginning in World War II, and Herblock (Herbert Block), whose caricatures of Joseph McCarthy and Richard Nixon became classics.

Photography was introduced into the United States with an assist from the versatile painter-inventor Samuel F. B. Morse. In 1840 he reported from France on the daguerreotype process by which (in half an hour!) a photographic image could be captured on silver-plated copper. Mathew Brady, the great Civil War photographer, first worked with daguerreotypes, but then learned the more flexible (but terribly complicated) wet-plate process. Brady and his team of photographers, wandering about in their "What-is-it?" buggies filled with chemicals for developing their pictures made the first photographic record of warfare. And they risked their lives, too, because mystified soldiers in the field thought the camera was a new kind of artillery.

Not until the 1880s with easy-to-use dry and flexible film invented by George Eastman, and his simple box camera, could photography go everywhere. Danish-born journalist-reformer Jacob Riis took his camera into alleys and tenements and then shocked Americans by his pictures of big-city slums. In the 1930s the power of the camera worked again—now through the photographs of the impoverished and the unemployed taken by Ben Shahn, Walker Evans, Dorothea Lange, and others under the auspices of the Farm Security Administration. World War II was brought home to the people of the United States by daring photographers like Robert Capa and Margaret Bourke-White. Capa lost his life to a land mine in 1954 while photographing the war in Vietnam.

Looking at pictures—paintings, drawings, photographs, even posters, advertisements and other commercial art—like reading or visiting museums and historic places, is a happy way of studying our past. We hope that the illustrations in this book and this note on American art will entice you to seek out and enjoy American artists, cartoonists, and photographers to open up vistas that you cannot find in words.

Thomas Moran, "The Grand Canyon of the Yellowstone," 1871.

National Museum of American Art, Smithsonian Institution, Washington, D.C.
U.S. Department of the Interior, National Park Service

Prologue

American history is the story of a magic transformation. How did people from everywhere join the American family? How did men and women from a tired Old World, where people thought they knew what to expect, become wide-eyed explorers of a New World?

Our history is the story of these millions in search of what it means to be an American. In the Old World people knew quite definitely whether they were English, French, or Spanish. But here it took time for them to discover that they really were Americans.

What does it mean to be an American? To answer that question we must shake hands with our earlier selves and try to become acquainted. We must discover what puzzled and interested and troubled earlier Americans.

What has been especially American about our ways of living and earning a living? Our ways of making war and making peace? Our ways of thinking and hoping and fearing, of worshiping God and fighting the Devil? Our ways of traveling and politicking, of importing people, of building houses and cities? These are some of the questions we try to answer in this book.

Discovering America is a way of discovering ourselves. This is a book about us.

⊙ Commerce, industry, and agriculture flourish under the protective wings of the American eagle in this 1844 political banner. The banner was painted by a signmaker from Auburn, New York.
New York State Historical Association

Unit 1

Writing About History and Art: Direct students' attention to the unit introduction, illustration, and list of themes on pages xx - 1. Have the introduction and unit themes read aloud. After a brief discussion of the subject matter of the unit, instruct students to write a brief paragraph explaining how the art:

—relates to the unit themes;
—exemplifies the unit title and illustrates the introduction; and
—is an appropriate choice for the unit.

The Making of Americans

The history of the United States begins in Europe before an America was known there, and in America before the Europeans came. In the Age of Columbus the peoples of Europe were discovering the world anew, reaching out to far and fabulous places. Columbus's wonderful, puzzling find enticed other adventurers to risk their lives for riches and empire.

The America they found already held millions of people, but these were spread thin across two continents. These Native Americans had neither the ships nor the science to reach out. Europeans first put them in touch with the world. What for Europe spelled empire and success, for most Native Americans spelled a losing fight to keep their lands and ways of life.

The hopes that people brought from the Old World to the New were as varied as their nations. Some came for gold or glory or adventure, some to worship in their own way, others to escape poverty, prison, or oppression. Some came without hope—to serve as slaves on plantations, and in mines and mills. Gradually life in America made them all into Americans.

THEMES IN HISTORY

- People leave Europe for the New World for a variety of reasons. GEOGRAPHY
- The success of Europeans in the New World spells disaster for most Native Americans. CONFLICT
- Shaped by their experiences in the New World, colonists begin to develop new ways of life. SOCIAL CHANGE

On this beautiful map, drawn in 1459 by Fra Mauro, an Italian monk, Europe, Africa, and Asia fill the whole planet. There is no room for America!
Art Resource, NY

Chapter 1
What Europeans Found: The American Surprise

Identifying Chapter Materials

Objectives	Basic Instructional Materials	Extension Materials
1 Christopher Columbus: Who He Was and Why He Came • Define Columbus's "Enterprise of the Indies" and explain his achievement. • Explain why Columbus was so successful while others were not.	**Annotated Teacher's Edition** • Lesson Plans, p. 2C **Instructional Support File** • Pre-Reading Activities, Unit 1, p. 1	**Documents of American History** • Privileges and Prerogatives Granted to Columbus, Vol. 1, p. 1 **American History Transparencies** • Our Multicultural Heritage, p. C35 • Fine Art, pp. D5, D9
2 Before Discovery • Identify the origin of the first Americans and describe some of their major cultural activities. • Locate the Mayas, Incas, Aztecs, and name distinctive aspects of each of their cultures. • Identify cultural features of the Southwestern and Eastern Woodlands Indians.	**Annotated Teacher's Edition** • Lesson Plans, pp. 2C–2D **Instructional Support File** • Skill Application Activity, Unit 1, p. 5	**Enrichment Support File** • The First Americans (See "In-Depth Coverage" at right.) **Suggested Secondary Sources** • See chart at right.
3 Why Europeans Went Exploring • Cite several reasons for European exploration in the 1400s and 1500s. • Explain how each of the following helped bring about the voyages of discovery: the printing press, the Crusades, the Renaissance, the rise of nation states, and Portugese navigators.	**Annotated Teacher's Edition** • Lesson Plans, pp. 2D–2E **Instructional Support File** • Critical Thinking Activity, Unit 1, p. 6	**Extension Activity** • Europeans in the Far East, Lesson Plans, p. 2E
4 Spanish Adventurers • Identify the Spanish explorers, name the main achievements of each, and explain the significance of those achievements. • Summarize the effects of Spanish conquest of the Aztecs.	**Annotated Teacher's Edition** • Lesson Plans, p. 2E **Instructional Support File** • Skill Review Activity, Unit 1, p. 4	**Documents of American History** • The Treaty of Tordesillas, Vol. 1, p. 4 **American History Transparencies** • Time Lines, p. E3
5 French and English Exploration • Identify the main achievements of Cabot, Verrazzano, and Cartier, and state their significance. • Explain the motives for English and French exploration.	**Annotated Teacher's Edition** • Lesson Plans, p. 2F **Instructional Support File** • Reading Activities, Unit 1, pp. 2–3 • Chapter Test, Unit 1, pp. 7–10 • Additional Test Questions, Unit 1, pp. 11–14	**Documents of American History** • Letters Patent to John Cabot, Vol. 1, p. 5 **American History Transparencies** • Critical Thinking, p. F3

Providing In-Depth Coverage

Perspectives on the First Americans

Columbus's discovery of North America is a major focus of Chapter 1 and provides a backdrop for an in-depth focus on Indian life in the Americas before European discovery.

In pre-Columbian times, the Indians of North America were as varied as the peoples of Europe. Spread all across the continent, they lived simple lives, the majority being hunters and gatherers, though a few tribes settled in one place and farmed the land.

The Indians of South America had made advances in areas such as architecture, government, and farming. However, their isolation made them vulnerable to outsiders.

Once European exploration began, the lives of the Indians would change forever.

A History of the United States as an instructional program provides two types of resources you can use to offer in-depth coverage of how pre-Columbian Indians lived: the *student text* and the *Enrichment Support File*. A list of *Suggested Secondary Sources* is also provided. The chart below shows the topics that are covered in each.

THE STUDENT TEXT. Boorstin and Kelley's

A History of the United States unfolds the chronology of events regarding the Indian nations before and after Columbus's discovery of North America.

AMERICAN HISTORY ENRICHMENT SUPPORT FILE. This collection of primary

source readings and classroom activities reveals aspects of Indian life before the discovery of North America.

SUGGESTED SECONDARY SOURCES.

This reference list of readings by well-known historians and other commentators provides an array of perspectives on aspects of Indian life before the discovery of North America.

Locating Instructional Materials

Detailed lesson plans for teaching the first Americans as a mini-course or to study one more elements of Indian culture in depth are offered in the following areas: in the *student text*, see individual lesson plans at the beginning of each chapter; in the *Enrichment Support File*, see page 3; for readings beyond the student text, see *Suggested Secondary Sources*.

	IN-DEPTH COVERAGE ON THE FIRST AMERICANS	
Student Text	**Enrichment Support File**	**Suggested Secondary Sources**
■ Early Indian Culture, pp. 6–9 ■ Cortes and the Aztecs, p. 17 ■ Pizarro and the Incas, p. 17–18 ■ Controlling the Indians, pp. 27–30 ■ Results of Spanish Conquests, p. 30	■ Lesson Suggestions ■ Multimedia Resources ■ Overview Essay/The First Americans ■ Literature in American History/"The Origin of the Buffalo and of Corn" ■ Primary Sources in American History/ Sioux Beliefs: A Journey of the Soul ■ Art in American History/Navajo Sand Paintings ■ Geography in American History/How Environment Shaped the Life of the Woodlands Indians ■ Simulation/Holding a Meeting of the Great Council of the Iroquois ■ Making Connections	■ *The Native Americans: Ethnology and Backgrounds of the North American Indians* by Jesse Jennings, et al., pp. 1–36. ■ *The Indian Heritage of America* by Alvin M. Josephy, pp. 37–56. ■ *Indian New England Before the Mayflower* by Howard S. Russell, pp. 19–42. ■ *American Indian Almanac* by John Upton Terrell, pp. 117–160.

Christopher Columbus: Who He Was and Why He Came

FOCUS

To introduce the lesson, ask students: What did Columbus hope to accomplish by making his voyage? Why did Spain finally fund Columbus's voyage? List responses on the chalkboard. Do countries continue to fund exploration today? What would be the modern equivalent of the "American surprise"?

Developing Vocabulary

The words listed in this chapter are essential terms for reading and understanding particular sections of the chapter. The page number after each term indicates the page of its first or most important appearance in this chapter. These terms are defined in the text Glossary (text pages 1000–1011).

latitude (page 5); **hemisphere** (page 6).

INSTRUCT

Explain

Columbus failed to reach his goal. His "Enterprise of the Indies" was misnamed. He made no money and he never reached the Indies. However, Columbus's voyages eventually made Spain the greatest nation in Europe. Today it is Columbus's daring and skill that are remembered, not his failures.

❀ Cooperative Learning Activity

Determining Relevance Explain that students will work in pairs to compile information for an obituary of Christopher Columbus. Based on information found in their text, assign one student in each pair to list Columbus's accomplishments and the other student to list events that led to his disgrace. Have partners discuss and revise lists. Then have each student write an obituary, including only information available at the time of Columbus's death. Have students refer to newspaper obituaries for style and organization. Bring the class together to read a sampling of students' work.

Section Review Answers

Section 1, page 6

1. a) Queen of Spain, financed Columbus's voyage. b) name Columbus gave to his plan to sail to Asia by heading directly west, a plan he expected to produce profits. c) Portugese navigator who rounded the Cape of Good Hope of Africa in 1488. d) what fifteenth-century Europeans called China. 2. Beijing is on the map on page 955, in northern China. Genoa is on the map on page 11, in northern Italy. Lisbon and Palos are shown on the map on page 5, in Spain. San Salvador is an island in the Bahamas, shown on the map on page 5. Hispaniola can be found on the map on page 19. 3. In Columbus's time Europeans called Asia "the Indies," and Columbus thought he had reached Asia. 4. Columbus realized that he first had to sail south from Europe in order to catch the winds that would carry him westward. On the return trip he first sailed north to catch the winds that brought him back to Europe. 5. Europeans wanted treasures such as silks, spices, tea, diamonds, rubies, and gold from Asia. 6. Besides returning to the islands he called the "Indies," Columbus skirted the shore of South America and explored the coast of Central America. 7. Since no one knew the risks of sailing from Europe to the coast of Asia, Columbus had difficulty convincing the advisers to Europe's monarchs that his planned expedition was viable.

CLOSE

To conclude the lesson, ask: What were the causes of exploration? Discuss and list the answers on the board. (Possible answers: national pride, search for wealth, curiousity about the uncharted world.)

Before Discovery

FOCUS

To introduce the lesson, direct students to open their books to the physical map of North America on page 948 of their texts. Have students locate the Bering Strait area. Explain that it is believed that North America and Asia were joined here by a land bridge during the last Ice Age, 25,000 to 40,000 years ago. Over that land bridge, the first humans traveled to America.

INSTRUCT

Explain

(1) Tell students that the authors use quotation marks around the word "discovered" on page 6 because there were flourishing civilizations and active cultures in the Americas before European explorers arrived; and (2) that archaeologists are still learning about the Mayas, Aztecs, Incas, and Indian groups of North America.

☑ Writing Process Activity

Drawing Conclusions Have students imagine they are members of a North American Indian tribe who visited an Aztec, Mayan, or Incan city. In preparation for creating a tale about their experience, have them brainstorm details about environment, lifestyle, economy, and culture of the people whose city they visited. As they write their tales, have them concentrate on capturing audience interest and on recreating their visit vividly. Students should revise for narrative impact and specific detail. After proofreading carefully, students can read their tales aloud as if they were delivering them at a campfire.

Section Review Answers

Section 2, page 10

1. a) an Indian civilization in Central America. b) an Indian civilization in what is now Central Mexico. They were great warriors, architects, and jewelers. c) an Indian civilization in what is now Peru, that developed a strong, very organized government, sophisticated farming techniques, and impressive roads. d) a loose association for defense formed by five tribes who lived in what is now upper New York State. e) Anasazi Indians of the American Southwest. The Spanish gave them the name "Pueblo" because they lived in pueblos, adobe houses built on top of each other. f) the body of water separating what is now Alaska and the Soviet Union. 2. South and Central American Indians such as the Incas, Aztecs, and Mayas lived in permanent settlements. On the whole, their political, social, and cultural life was more advanced that that of Indians living north of present-day Mexico. Most North American Indians, by contrast, were wandering hunters and gatherers, although some groups, such as the Anasazis, were farmers, living in permanent settlements.

CLOSE

To conclude the lesson, refer the students to the text where it states that the Indian civilizations of Central and South America were "ripe for conquest" (p. 8). Ask and discuss the following: What about their way of life made Indians vulnerable to European domination? What yardsticks might be used as a measure of a culture's advancement or sophistication. (Generally, only economic, technological, and scientific factors are considered. Be sure students understand that such cultural factors as religion and family structure cannot be considered "advanced" or "primitive.") Discuss why the Europeans had such a wide technological lead at this time. You might also want students to consider what other factors contributed to the European success.

Why Europeans Went Exploring

FOCUS

To introduce the lesson, have the class quickly compile a list of the feats in space exploration accomplished by the United States and the USSR. Then ask: Why has space exploration been attempted? Have there been any benefits? (Computers, miniaturization, military, etc.) Unexpected costs? (Deaths of astronauts on missions and in training.) Ask students to think about why people have engaged in exploration despite the costs and dangers as they read the section.

Developing Vocabulary

Renaissance (page 10); **longitude** (page 12); **caravel** (page 12).

INSTRUCT

Explain

Remind students of the importance of connections in history. A historical event never takes place in a vacuum. The reasons for European exploration are closely intertwined.

★ Independent Activity

Drawing Conclusions Explain to students that European exploration was spurred by events and discoveries made prior to even Columbus's voyage. List the following topics on the board: the Crusades, the Renaissance, Marco Polo, Portugese navigators. Have students select a topic and write a 500-word report based on their independent research. Students should include in their reports how their topic helped to inspire exploration.

Section Review Answers

Section 3, page 12

1. a) showed that the earth revolves around the sun. b) invented moveable type in Germany in 1456. c) a Venetian merchant, traveled to China in the thirteenth century, and two centuries later, descriptions of his adventures were printed. d) set up a school for explorers in the fifteenth century and pushed for explorations of the African coast. e) a three-masted, round-hulled, shallow draft ship that can sail against the wind. 2. The Portugese established a school that trained sailors and gathered all the new information about ships and voyages of exploration in one place so that it could be used to best advantage. They de-

1

2D

signed the caravel and explored the African coast. 3. Such things as the mass printing of books, the development of the science of astronomy and Copernicus's theory of Earth's movement around the sun, advances in navigation prompted by Prince Henry of Portugal, and the growth of modern nation states helped to shape the Age of Discovery.

CLOSE

To conclude the lesson, have students speculate on why other regions of the world did not embark on voyages of exploration before Europe. Correlate their answers to why other countries have not been able to match the Soviet and American space efforts. (Europeans had the capabilities and incentives simultaneously.)

Extension Activity

To extend the lesson, tell students that they will research and write a report on early interactions between Europeans and the Chinese or Japanese. Possible topics include the Eastern travels of the Polos or early Jesuit missionaries. In their reports, students should include how the Europeans were received in the Far East and the cultural contributions which they brought back to Europe.

Section 4 (pages 12–21)

Spanish Adventurers

FOCUS

To introduce the lesson, have students read the account of Cortes conquering the Aztecs on page 17 of the text. Ask: What kind of civilization did the Indians have before the arrival of Cortes? How did it compare with that of the Spaniards? Can you imagine yourself living in that time and place?

Developing Vocabulary

conquistadores (page 15); **Christendom** (page 16); **empire** (page 17).

INSTRUCT

Explain

England and France had no part in the Treaty of Tordesillas. How do students think those and other European nations reacted to the Treaty?

☑ Writing Process Activity

Identifying Central Issues Ask students to imagine they are Spanish explorers who must petition their government for permission and funds for making a voyage. Have students free-write about possible goals, such as conquering new territory for the glory of the crown, finding a shorter route, and so forth. After organizing their goals in order of importance, students should write a persuasive letter. Have them revise their letters for logic and clarity, and proofread to correct errors. Students can exchange letters and discuss the level of persuasiveness.

Section Review Answers

Section 4, page 21

1. a) a Norseman, sailed to Newfoundland in 1001. b) Italian navigator for whom the Americas were named. c) first European to see the Pacific Ocean. d) led the first circumnavigation of the world. e) king of Spain who became Holy Roman Emperor in 1519. f) conquered the Aztecs in 1519. g) conquered the Incas in 1531. h) discovered Florida. i) led an expedition to Florida. j) survived the Narváez expedition and described the horrors that destroyed it. k) also a survivor of the Narváez expedition, was an ex-slave who helped Fray Marcos look for the Seven Cities of Cibola. l) found the Grand Canyon. 2. Labrador is shown on the map on page 19. Greenland is at the top of the map on page 15. The Canary Islands are shown on the map on page 5. Panama and Newfoundland are shown on the map on page 19. Guam is on the map on page 953. 3. News of the Norse voyages did not spread beyond the Norse sagas and their discoveries had no significant effects. 4. When the treaty was signed, Brazil had not been discovered and the Spanish and Portugese thought the treaty's line fell in the middle of the Atlantic. 5. Magellan's journey proved that the world is round, larger than had been thought, and that Columbus had reached "new" lands. 6. The conquest of the Aztecs started a stampede to the New World by adventurers who hoped to plunder Indian gold and silver. 7. Their small armies had advanced weapons, horses, surprise, diseases for which the Indians had no defense, and unity of purpose. 8. The Northwest Passage was a hoped-for waterway through North America to Asia. 9. Each new discovery expanded the horizons of Europeans. Columbus's discovery of the Americas, followed by the conquests of Cortes and Pizarro, provided Europeans with images of riches and fame to be found across the Atlantic. The discovery of the Pacific Ocean and Magellan's voyage opened up new possibilities for trade and settlement.

CLOSE

To conclude the lesson, ask students how they, as Aztecs or Incas, would have reacted to the arrival of European explorers. Be sure students cite specific information from the text in their responses.

French and English Exploration

FOCUS

To introduce the lesson, remind students that the information found in their text on New World exploration is based on historical evidence, such as records of voyages and the reports of the explorers. Tell students that your school has one of the top win/loss records in the state in all sports. Ask: How would you decide if this statement is true? (Find out what evidence there is to support it: Check the record books for the various teams at your school and elsewhere in the state.)

INSTRUCT

Explain

French and English explorers claimed land for their nations in North America, but had not set up any lasting settlements by 1541.

❖ Cooperative Learning Activity

Drawing Conclusions Break the class into groups of four to six and explain that each group will complete a chart of New World explorations. Assign two students in each group to be recorders and two to be reporters. Have group members work together to list the names of explorers found on pages 22–24 in their texts. Have students divide the list and, for each name, write the dates of exploration, country sailed from, and one or two major consequences of the exploration. Have recorders prepare a chronological chart of the information. Then have group members discuss conclusions that can be drawn from the chart. Have reporters present the chart and conclusions to the class.

Section Review Answers

Section 5, page 24

1. a) English explorer who reached Newfoundland and claimed the land for England in 1497. b) French explorer of the east coast of North America (1524). c) French explorer of the St. Lawrence River. d) English king who authorized John Cabot's voyage. e) ruler of France who backed the voyages of Verrazzano and Cartier. f) Cabot's vessel. 2. Newfoundland, Verrazzano's route, Cartier's route, Florida, and the St. Lawrence River are shown on the map on page 19. Montreal and Quebec are shown on the map on page 949. 3. Cartier's settlement was attacked by

Indians. By the time relief came, he had decided to give up the settlement and return home. 4. Both France and England sought a new, shorter passage to the Indies. Although the Treaty of Tordesillas gave only Spain and Portugal the right to claim lands in the New World, France and England began claiming lands in North America for their respective crowns.

CLOSE

To conclude the lesson, have students read the material under the heading "Esteban and Fray Marcos" on page 20 of their texts and decide if any historical *evidence* is presented in it. (Yes, in the last sentence: "Father Marcos . . . reported . . .") Have students locate other examples of evidence from the text.

Chapter Review Answers

Focusing on Ideas

1. Columbus opened the New World, set up the first permanent settlement there, explored Central America's coast, and showed how to use winds to sail to America. 2. The rise of nation states; the invention of printing; advances in navigation; the spread of knowledge about the Near East; and advances in knowledge of astronomy. 3. Nationalism led Europeans to compete to explore the world and plant their country's flag abroad. 4. In the sixteenth century, Spain and England both claimed the North American continent. Portugal claimed Brazil. France made no claims until much later.

Taking a Critical Look

1. Many early sea explorations were to find a Northwest Passage, yet new landforms and waterways were discovered instead. Rumors of wealth tempted explorers. 2. **(a)** Their vast wealth; architecture, farming, science, math, and communication. **(b)** Europeans probably believed all innovations originated in Europe. 3. Use current encyclopedias of American history and world history to help students compile a list of events.

Your Region in History

1–3. Answers will vary depending on your region. Consult your local library or historical society for books on the early history of the area.

Historical Facts and Figures

(a) The Indian population declined from approximately 25 million in 1520 to about one million in 1610. **(b)** Students' paragraphs should note that the arrival of Spanish conquerors in Central America led to the rapid and steep decline of the Indian population.

Chapter 1

What Europeans Found: The American Surprise

The discovery of America was the world's greatest surprise. When the first Europeans came, their maps of the world left no place for America. They knew only three continents—Europe, Asia, and Africa. These seemed to be merged together into one huge "Island of the Earth." That big island was indented by lakes, and a few seas like the Mediterranean and the Western Ocean. The planet seemed covered mostly by land, and there was no room for another continent.

Columbus was not looking for a new continent. He thought he was on his way to China and India. Europeans were disappointed to find unexpected lands in their way. Still they insisted on calling the natives here the "Indians." So America was discovered by accident.

As more Europeans came and explored the unknown lands, their disappointment became surprise. They had found a world for new beginnings.

In the late 1500s Theodore De Bry's engravings showed Europeans the strange wonders of America.
John Carter Brown Library at Brown University.

See "Lesson Plan," p. 2C.

1. Christopher Columbus: Who he was and why he came

The adventure that Columbus had in mind was exciting enough. He aimed to sail westward from the shores of Europe until he reached the shores of Asia. Asia was then Europe's treasure-house. It supplied peppers and spices and tea for the table, silks and gold brocade for the dresses of noble ladies and for draperies in palaces, diamonds and rubies for rings and bracelets and necklaces. Until then the main way to the Orient had been the slow, long trek overland. From Venice it might take a year to reach Beijing. You would not arrive at all unless you survived the attacks of bandits, the high-mountain snows, and torrid desert heats. Even after you arrived in Asia, it was hard to bring your treasure back overland. For there were no wagon highways and you had to pack your treasure in caravans on the backs of donkeys, horses, and camels.

A direct westward voyage by sea would make all the difference. You could avoid bandits and mountains and deserts. The spacious hold of your ship would safely carry back your treasure. This was a simple and appealing idea. The wonder is why more people before Columbus did not try it.

Earlier in the 1400s a few sailors had tried. But they were not prepared for so long a voyage, and they did not know the winds. Some reached out into the Atlantic Ocean as far as the Azores and beyond. But the winds were against them and the seas rough. They all soon turned back for home.

As a determined young man Christopher Columbus decided that he would sail into the Western Ocean—to Asia and back. He had no doubt he could do it. He knew the sea, the winds, and the currents.

Early experiences. Columbus was born in 1451 in bustling Genoa, Italy, "that noble and powerful city by the sea." He was the son of a prosperous wool-weaver. For the first 22 years of his life he lived there. He saw ships bringing rich cargo from the eastern Mediterranean where the treasures of the Orient had been taken overland. When he went to sea, he sailed in all directions where ships went at the time. Once his cargo was wool and dried fish and wine carried from Iceland and northern Ireland to Lisbon and the islands of the Azores. Then he lived for a while in the Madeira Islands off the coast of Africa. He even sailed down the steaming African coast to distant Portuguese trading posts on the Gulf of Guinea.

When he left Genoa to settle in Lisbon, Portugal, that city was "the street corner of Europe." Its deep, sheltered harbor was the point of arrival and departure, a place of exchange, for the seaborne commerce of the whole western end of the continent. From there shipments went northward to the British Isles or the North Sea, southward for trade into Africa. And, why not westward—to Asia?

No portraits of Christopher Columbus are known to have been painted during his lifetime. This picture by an unknown artist, painted some 30 years after Columbus died, is considered his earliest and best likeness.

Civico Museo Storico, G. Garibaldi, Como

Continuity and Change: Geography Point out to students that other Europeans, the Norse, did reach North America before Columbus, and even attempted temporary settlement in what is now Newfoundland. But knowledge of the New World was lost, a matter only for tales and legends. Until the Renaissance, there was neither the need, technology, nor the curiosity, to find new lands. (See page 13.)

There in Lisbon the single-minded young Columbus laid his plans for his grand "Enterprise of the Indies." He called it an "enterprise" because he expected it to be not just a voyage of discovery but a money-making project. "The Indies" was the name for India and the other Asian lands of the Far East. Convinced that they had a great project to sell, Christopher and his brother Bartholomew made Lisbon their headquarters.

The "Enterprise of the Indies" would not be inexpensive. Ships would have to be bought or hired, crews found and paid. Food and other supplies had to be collected for the long voyage there and back. No ordinary merchant would have the wealth and the power needed. It would take a rich monarch. There was hope of great profit, but there was also great risk. Was there a ruler bold enough to take the big gamble?

No one knew exactly what the risks might be—or even how far it was from the coast of western Europe to the coasts of Asia. No one had ever made that trip before. The questions could not be answered from experience.

The learned men disagreed in their guesses. Some said it was about 2000 miles. Others said it was two or three times that long. The leading authority was the ancient Greek geographer Ptolemy. Columbus read the best geography books he could find. We still have some of them with his own marks. He underlined the passage that said, "this sea is navigable in a very few days if the wind be fair." He believed the writers who said the distance was short, and accordingly he made his plans.

Seeking support.

Christopher and his brother traveled to the capitals of Europe trying to sell their project. The monarchs shunned Columbus's grand Enterprise of the Indies. When in 1484 King John II of Portugal asked his committee of experts if Columbus could succeed, they said it was too far to Asia and told him not to take the risk. Instead King John sent daring sailors on the long way round Africa eastward to India. In 1488 Bartholomeu Dias succeeded in rounding the Cape of Good Hope, at the southern tip of Africa. Now the eastern route to India was open. Why risk the uncertain way west when there was a sea-path to the east?

Columbus then went next door to Spain, where Queen Isabella had a mind of her own. The bold mariner awakened her interest. To finance the trip she needed money from the royal treasury, but her committee of experts refused to approve the project. She kept the impatient Columbus waiting for six years. Finally, he gave up and prepared to take ship for France. At the last moment, the court treasurer convinced Isabella the gamble was worth the risk. She now became so enthusiastic she was even prepared to pawn her jewels to help Columbus. But that was not necessary. She was told the royal treasury could pay the cost. So Queen Isabella sent Columbus a promise of royal support. She also granted all his demands for noble titles and a 10 percent share of whatever wealth came from land he might discover.

Columbus formed his enterprise in the small port of Palos, which had done something illegal. As a penalty the Queen fined it two caravels— light, swift sailboats—to go with Columbus. The caravels were the *Niña* and the *Pinta.* The third vessel of the expedition was the biggest, the *Santa Maria*, which Columbus chartered. The crew was mostly from Palos and nearby, and they were courageous and expert sailors.

The great voyage.

With his three ships ⍟ Columbus set sail from the coast of Spain on August 3, 1492. In the next weeks he proved that he was the greatest mariner of the age.

Still, it is hard to be at sea for weeks when you are not sure what—if anything—is ahead. So Columbus's men grew rebellious and reached the verge of mutiny. But Columbus was a true leader. A man taller than most, blue eyed and red haired, he was respected by his followers. He altered the records of distances they had covered so the crew would not think they had gone too far from home. He convinced them to go on. Still, on October 9, Columbus agreed that if they did not find land in three days, he would turn back. But by then there were more and more signs of land—birds in the air, leaves and flowers floating in the water.

⍟ **Multicultural Connection:** According to some accounts of Columbus's first voyage, a Spanish-African pilot named Pedro Alonzo Niño was a member of the crew and, therefore, may have been the first African to see the Americas.

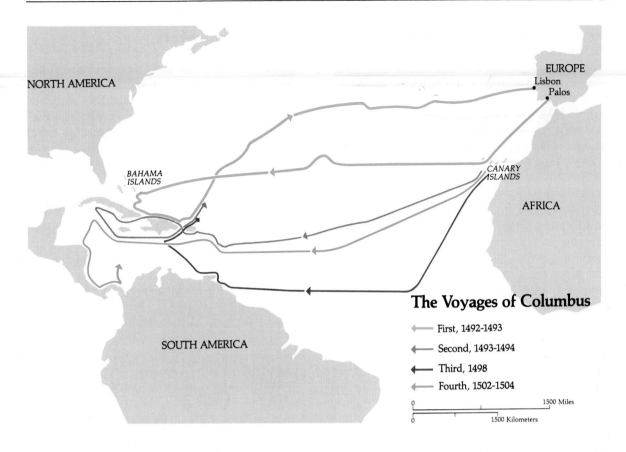

NORTH AMERICA

EUROPE
Lisbon
Palos

BAHAMA
ISLANDS

CANARY
ISLANDS

AFRICA

SOUTH AMERICA

The Voyages of Columbus

←— First, 1492-1493

←— Second, 1493-1494

←— Third, 1498

←— Fourth, 1502-1504

0   1500 Miles

0   1500 Kilometers

It was not enough to know the sea. The winds were the engine that took you there and back. Others had failed because they did not know how to use the winds. They had tried going straight west from Spain. That was their mistake. Instead Columbus first had sailed south to the Canary Islands off the coast of Africa, then sailed west from there. That was where the winds blowing from the east would carry his ships straight on to his destination. Also the Canaries were on the same latitude as Japan, so if he went due west he thought he would arrive where he wanted to be.

The winds blew just as Columbus expected. This, the most important sea voyage in history, had good weather and clear sailing. At 2 o'clock in the morning on October 12, 1492, after thirty-three days at sea, a lookout sighted the white cliffs of an island in the Bahamas. The natives called it Guanahani, and Columbus

named it San Salvador—Holy Savior. Columbus had discovered America—though he did not know it.

Columbus cruised about in the Caribbean Sea for several months. He landed on Cuba, which he thought and hoped might be Japan. After the *Santa Maria* was wrecked on a reef off Haiti, he built a fort on the island. They named the island Hispaniola (after Spain). He left about 40 men when he headed for home January 4, 1493. Columbus had found no great cities in his travels—but he had seen gold ornaments and found a little gold in a stream on Hispaniola. So he thought he had reached the outposts of the rich empire of Cathay (China).

By great luck Columbus did not try to sail back the way he had come. It would have been a mistake, for at that latitude the winds came from the east. Instead Columbus sailed north to

Geography and History: Location Tell students to look at the map above. Ask: What should you look at first on a map? (Title and key) Ask: Why did Columbus sail so far south? Why didn't he take the straightest route across the Atlantic? (Prevailing winds) In which voyage did he sail the farthest north? (First)

about 35° north latitude. There the prevailing winds from the west blew him back to Spain.

When he arrived on March 15, 1493, he had accomplished much more than he knew. He had discovered a new world. The king and queen loaded him with honors and made his two sons pages at the court. Meanwhile he had shown sailors how to sail and where to sail so the winds would carry them to America *and back!* This made it possible for countless other ships to follow.

Columbus's other voyages. Three times on later voyages Columbus returned to the islands that he called the "Indies," or lands of the East. On these trips he established the first permanent settlement of Europeans in the Western Hemisphere, he skirted the shore of South America, and he explored the coast of Central America. He was always trying to prove that he had found the treasure lands of the East. But he finally reaped only misfortune and disgrace. When he returned to Spain in 1504 after his last voyage, he found Queen Isabella dying and his friends, his influence, and his reputation

� gone. Two years later Columbus died still believing that he had sailed to the coast of Asia.

See "Section 1 Review answers," p. 2C.

Section 1 Review

1. Identify: Isabella, Enterprise of the Indies, Bartholomeu Dias, Cathay.

2. Locate: Beijing, Genoa, Lisbon, Palos, San Salvador, Hispaniola.

3. Why did Columbus call the islands he found "The Indies"?

4. What important discovery did Columbus make about the winds?

5. What did Europeans want from a trade relationship with the East?

6. What other areas did Columbus explore after his first voyage?

7. **Critical Thinking: Identifying Central Issues.** What obstacles did Columbus face when seeking support from European monarchs?

See "Lesson Plan," p. 2C.

2. Before discovery

If it hadn't been for Columbus, years might have passed before the people of Europe "discovered" America. But it was only for the people of Europe that America had to be "discovered." Millions of Native Americans were already here! For them, Columbus, and all the sailors, explorers, and settlers who came later, provided their "discovery" of Europe!

For Europeans the "discovery" of America offered vast lands, treasures of gold and silver and timber, places to build cities and places of refuge. For them this was a happy discovery. In the long run it would be a great discovery for the world. But for the millions of Native Americans already here their "discovery" of Europeans was not quite so happy. For some it meant the end of their Native American civilization. For some it meant slavery. For nearly all of them Europeans brought shock, disease, and change.

The first people to come to America were the ancestors of those who Columbus by mistake (p. 7) called Indians. No one knows when they came. A widely held theory is that sometime between 35,000 and 11,500 years ago during the last great ice age the first small groups arrived. They were people on the move. They had come from northern China and Siberia.

So much of the earth's water had frozen into ice that it lowered the level of the sea in the Bering Strait. Then as they tracked wild game they could walk across the 56 miles from Siberia to Alaska. Without knowing it, they had discovered two large continents that were completely empty of people but were full of wild game— huge mastodons and mammoths, giant ground sloths, camels, antelopes, and great long-horned bison. In the thousands of years afterwards many other groups followed. These small bands spread all across North and South America.

The high mountains and broad rivers separated the communities. There were hundreds of languages and many different styles of life. Some small bands of people had no fixed homes. They followed their quarry and lived the wandering life of hunters. Others settled down and after centuries built vast kingdoms with

---

✾ See "Lesson Plan," p. 2C for **Cooperative Learning Activity: Determining Relevance** relating to the life of Columbus.

flourishing cities, temples and palaces, and lively commerce.

Enrichment Support File Topic

Mayas, Incas, and Aztecs. The grandest of these Native American cultures astonished the Europeans. South of the present United States—from central Mexico to Peru—they found the Aztecs, the Mayas, and the Incas.

In the mountains, deserts, and rain forests of Guatemala, Belize, Honduras, and Mexico the Mayas had built temples and pyramids clustered about broad plazas. We can still climb them. The Mayas invented their own writing. Although they had no telescope, they built their own kind of observatory and made accurate calendars. Their "Indian corn" (maize) had never been seen in Europe. It was originally a wild grass, but would become a staple food for the world.

In Peru the Incas had constructed palaces surrounded by high walls, and had connected their mountain-towns with a network of roads. To farm their steep land they had built terraces. Where water was scarce, they had cut canals and erected stone aqueducts to irrigate their crops. The Incas gave us the potato and the tomato.

When European explorers came to Peru, they were amazed by the Incan government. They never expected to find such powerful rulers so well organized in the mountain wilderness. The Incas had succeeded even without a system of writing. No Americans were richer. In Cuzco, the mountain capital of the Incan empire, even the buildings were covered with gold!

The Aztecs were a warlike people who lived in central Mexico. They were clever architects. Like the Mayas, they too built grand temples and high pyramids. Their capital, where Mexico City is today, was a bustling metropolis. And they fashioned their gold into jewelry so ornate as to make European kings jealous.

The great pyramid at Chichén Itzá, Mexico, was part of a Mayan religious center.

Carl Frank/Photo Researchers, Inc.

More from Boorstin: "Columbus reported to his surprise and somewhat to his disappointment, that 'in these islands I have so far found no human monstrosities, as many expected, on the contrary, among all these peoples good looks are esteemed. . . . Thus I have neither found monsters nor any report of any, except . . . a people . . . who eat human flesh . . . they are no more malformed than the others.' These Indians, he reassured the Spanish sovereigns, were 'very well built, of very handsome bodies and fine faces.'" (From *The Discoverers*)

Tom Nebbia/Click/Chicago

Machu Picchu is located above the Urubamba River in Peru. This Incan center, with its terraces for farming, escaped destruction because of its inaccessible location.

These peoples had found their own ways of progress—different from the ways of Europe. They had never invented the wheel. They had no iron tools. Their beasts of burden were the dog and, in Peru, the llama. Unlike the peoples of Europe, they had not built ships to cross the oceans. They had not reached out to the world. In their isolation they found it hard to learn new ways. When the Spanish came, it seemed that the Incas, the Mayas, and the Aztecs had ceased to progress. They were ripe for conquest.

⊕ **North American Indians.** Of course there was no census of early America. But in 1500 the people in Mexico probably numbered about 12 million. Farther north in what is now the United States and Canada there were only some 4 million. The great empires of old America—of the Mayas, the Incas, and the Aztecs—were all in Mexico or south.

North of Mexico most of the people lived in wandering tribes and led a simple life. North American Indians were mainly hunters and gatherers of wild food. An exceptional few—in Arizona and New Mexico—settled in one place and became farmers.

The most advanced Indians of North America lived in the Southwest. The Anasazi came to be known as Pueblo Indians, after their style of building. A "pueblo" was a kind of apartment several stories tall, built of stone or adobe. The Anasazi also built cliff dwellings where they could defend themselves against enemy tribes. They and their descendants—the Hopi, Zuñi, and Acoma—made pottery, textiles, and baskets which we still admire.

When the Europeans came, the largest population of Indians north of Mexico was in California. They were a tenth of all the Indians in what is now the United States. They and the Indians of the Northwest lived by hunting and fishing and by gathering the plentiful nuts and berries.

Before Columbus and the Spanish came to America, there were not many Indians on the Great Plains. They walked for miles in pursuit of the herds of buffalo. The buffalo supplied them with skins to wear, meat to eat—and even (in dried buffalo chips) with fuel for their fires. Their only beast of burden was the dog. There were no horses in America until the Spanish brought them.

In the Eastern Woodlands the many tribes were mainly hunter-food gatherers, but they also did some farming. Some of them had joined in their own small version of a United Nations. Five tribes of Huron-Iroquois-speaking people—the Mohawk, Seneca, Oneida, Onondaga, and Cayuga—in upper New York State formed the Iroquois League. The council of chiefs who governed the league was chosen by certain women of high station. The council had no power to make war but planned defense. The powerful Chief Powhatan formed his own league (in Virginia), and there were others.

Down south in Mississippi the Natchez Indians seemed more like the Mexican Indians.

⊕ Geography and History: Interaction Refer students to the map on page 9. Have them locate all Indian tribes mentioned in Section 2. Ask: What do the colors on the map mean? (The colors signify culture areas.) Ask: Why would tribes living in particular areas share a similar culture? (Over time, people adapt to the conditions of their environments, and their cultures reflect these adaptations. Groups living within a particular geographic region would necessarily share certain cultural values, economic and political systems, and technologies.)

Major Indian Tribes of North America about 1500

Culture Areas

- Arctic
- Subarctic
- Northwest Coast
- California
- Plateau
- Great Basin
- Southwest
- Great Plains
- Northeast and Great Lakes
- Southeast
- Middle America

ESKIMO

KOYUKON
KUTCHIN
INGALIK
TANANA
ALEUT TANAINA HAN ESKIMO
NABESNA HARE
ATHENA BEAR LAKE
TUTCHONE ESKIMO
MOUNTAIN ESKIMO
YELLOWKNIFE
DOGRIB
TAHLTAN KASKA ESKIMO
TLINGIT SEKANI SLAVE
CHIPEWYAN
HAIDA
TSIMSHIAN
CARRIER
BELLA COOLA
KWAKIUTL SARSI
CHILCOTIN KAIGANI (BLOOD) CREE
SHUSWAP
NOOTKA LILLOOET
KUTENAI PLAINS CREE
SALISH SIKSIKA
PUYALLUP (BLACKFOOT)
SPOKANE COUER ASSINIBOIN OJIBWA
KLIKITAT D'ALENE
PALUS FLATHEAD OJIBWA (CHIPPEWA)
CHINOOK YAKIMA NEZ PERCÉ CROW HIDATSA
COOS TILLAMOOK CAYUSE MANDAN
KLAMATH WALLA WALLA ARIKARA MENOMINEE
SHASTA SHOSHONI—BANNOCK TETON DAKOTA SANTEE DAKOTA
YUROK MODOC NORTH CHEYENNE SAUK FOX
YUKI NORTH PAIUTE SIOUX YANKTON POTAWATOMI
YANA WASHO PONCA DAKOTA KICKAPOO
HUPA MAIDU OMAHA IOWA WEA
POMO MIWOK PAWNEE PEORIA MIAMI
COSTANOAN UTE ARAPAHO OTO
SALINAN SOUTH PAIUTE KANSA ILLINOIS
YOKUTS PUEBLO MISSOURI
CHUMASH SOUTH CHEYENNE SHAWNEE
CAHUILLA HOPI JICARILLA KIOWA OSAGE PIANKASAW
MOHAVE NAVAHO APACHE KIOWA APACHE QUAPAW
YUMA HAVASUPAI ZUNI WICHITA CHICKASAW
MARICOPA APACHE
PAPAGO PIMA COMANCHE CADDO ALABAMA
COCHIMI MESCALERO WACO NATCHEZ
OPATA APACHE TONKAWA CHOCTAW
SERI LIPAN APACHE CHITIMACHA
YAQUI CONCHO ATAKAPA
TARAHUMARA KARANKAWA
COAHUILTEC
WAICURI
PERICU ACAXEE TAMAULIPEC
TOLTEC HUICHOL HUASTEC
TLAXCALAN TOTONAC YUCATAN MAYA
TARASCAN AZTEC
MIXTEC
ZAPOTEC QUICHE MAYA

MONTAGNAIS NASKAPI BEOTHUK
MICMAC
ABNAKI MALECITE
PASSAMAQUODDY
OTTAWA HURON MOHICAN
MOHAWK PENOBSCOT
ONONDAGA PENNACOOK
CAYUGA
SENECA MAHICAN MASSACHUSET
NEUTRAL ONEIDA WAMPANOAG
WAPPINGER NARRAGANSET
ERIE SUSQUEHANNA PEQUOT
DELAWARE
NANTICOKE
POWHATAN
PAMUNKEY CHICKAHOMINY
NOTTOWAY MATTAPONY
TUTELO ALGONQUIN
CHEROKEE PAMLICO
CATAWBA
CREEK
HICHITI
APALACHEE
BILOXI TIMUCUA
SEMINOLE
CALUSA

ARCTIC OCEAN

PACIFIC OCEAN

HUDSON BAY

ATLANTIC OCEAN

GULF OF MEXICO

See "Geography and History," p. 8.

1000 Miles

1000 Kilometers

Paolo Koch/Photo Researchers, Inc.

Pueblo Indians built these cliff dwellings in Arizona.

Mainly farmers, they were divided into nobles and commoners, and were ruled by a man they called the Great Sun.

The Indians of North America were as varied as the peoples of Europe. There were countless tribes and hundreds of languages. Some tribes made elegant gold jewelry, but others were still in the Stone Age. Some wove handsome rugs and wore textiles of beautiful design. Others knew only skins and furs. Their meat depended on the place. Deer were nearly everywhere, and on the plains were herds of buffalo. The seashores and streams abounded in fish and shell food. The Indians planted corn, which made their bread, and beans, squashes, and many other crops. They knew where to find, and how to enjoy, the nuts and berries and mushrooms and other delights of the woods. They raised and smoked tobacco.

See the "Lesson Plan," p. 2D for **Writing Process Activity: Drawing Conclusions** relating to pre-Columbian Indians of North America.

Because the Indians lived so close to nature, most of them had religions in which natural things played a major role. The Indians saw and worshiped Nature. They had learned to know the stones, the animals, and the plants. They were adept at using what they found for food, shelter, and clothing.

See "Section 2 Review answers," p. 2D.

Section 2 Review

1. Identify and locate: Mayas, Aztecs, Incas, Iroquois League, Pueblo Indians, Bering Strait.
2. **Critical Thinking: Identifying Alternatives.** How did the lifestyles of South and Central American Indians differ from those living north of Mexico?

See "Lesson Plan," p. 2D.

3. Why Europeans went exploring

For centuries all these people and their cultures lay hidden from Europe: What happened to stir Europeans to reach out to this vast unknown?

The Renaissance, 1300–1600. Near the end of the Middle Ages, the Christians of western Europe launched crusades to take Jerusalem back from the Muslims. When thousands of Europeans traveled across the Mediterranean and reached the Holy Land, they discovered that they had much to learn from the East. Commerce grew and minds were opened. Scholars translated books of poetry, adventure, and science from Greek, Arabic, Hebrew, Persian, and other eastern languages. They revived the questioning spirit of the ancient Greeks. Ambitious princes led new city-states in Italy. They built palaces and churches in the style of Greece and Rome. For the first time artists discovered the science of perspective. Leonardo da Vinci and Michelangelo painted their masterpieces and kept notebooks of all the wonders of the world.

Of course there were books before there was printing. But those early books were all copied by hand. It would take six months to make one copy of a long book. Books were costly and few

Europe about 1500

people could read. Then Johann Gutenberg at Mainz in Germany invented movable type. Here was a way to make many copies of a book—and at much less cost. In 1456 he printed his first Bible and opened a new world for books. Within only fifty years 10 million copies of printed books appeared in Europe.

Modern astronomy was born. Copernicus showed that the earth revolved around the sun, and the word went everywhere in books.

⊕ **The rise of nation states.** At the same time, the modern nation state took shape. Strong kings conquered weak feudal lords. The na-

tion's laws, taxes, armies, and courts replaced those of the local nobles. People began to glory in the power of their king. They were proud to be French, English, Spanish, or Portuguese. For "king and country" they sought glory in war, riches in commerce, honor in the arts. And the more adventurous went out to plant their country's flag abroad. The wealth of the nation commanded by the new monarchs would outfit the ships to explore the world.

The lure of the East. The fabled Orient had a wonderful charm for the people of Europe. In 1271 the Venetian merchants Maffeo and Nicolo

Polo, and Nicolo's young son Marco, traveled to China. They spent seventeen years there in the service of the Khan. Upon the Polos' return, the people of Venice were astonished by the gold and silks and jewels they had brought back. Marco Polo's book about his adventures was printed two centuries later on the new presses. When Columbus read Marco Polo's book, it whetted his appetite for the East.

Meanwhile the rich people of Europe wanted more and more of the goods from the Orient. These had come partly overland by risky trails through mountain and desert and partly by sea. Much was lost to bandits or to shipwrecks. The rising monarchs began to think of finding a direct way to the East entirely by sea.

The techniques of discovery. In Columbus's time all educated people and most sailors believed that the earth was a sphere. They disagreed about the size of the globe, and about how much was land and how much water. The coast of Africa was only beginning to be explored.

Prince Henry "the Navigator" (1394–1460) had set up a school for explorers at Cape St. Vincent on the southwestern tip of Portugal. He began to push voyages of discovery along the coast of Africa. He trained the sailors and their captains, improved the design of ships, and gathered maps and charts. Within fifty years, his sailors made more progress exploring the west coast of Africa than Europeans had made in the thousand years before.

Since about 1200, sailors had had the compass to help them find their way. To figure latitude and see where they were on the map, they used other simple instruments—the astrolabe, the quadrant, and the cross-staff. They had no way to discover longitude. This meant that they could not figure exactly where they were east or west, or how wide was the Western Ocean.

During their African voyages of discovery the Portuguese designed a new kind of sailing ship—the "caravel." It was a lithe, but sturdy, three-masted or four-masted vessel that was excellent for exploration. Caravels had lateen sails that could be set to catch the wind so if they sailed somewhere with the wind they could still sail back, even with the wind against them.

National Maritime Museum, Greenwich, England

The astrolabe, first invented by the ancient Greeks, was used by mariners in the 15th, 16th, and even 17th centuries to try to find their latitude. This instrument was found off Ireland after the defeat of the Armada.

See "Section 3 Review answers," p. 2E.

Section 3 Review

1. Identify: Copernicus, Johann Gutenberg, Marco Polo, Prince Henry of Portugal, caravel.
2. Describe Portuguese explorers' contributions.
3. **Critical Thinking: Determining Relevance.** What developments set the stage for an age of discovery?

See "Lesson Plan," p. 2E.

4. Spanish adventurers

All the forces at work in western Europe and all the new knowledge, equipment, and techniques gathered by the Portuguese came together, as we have seen, in the most important seafaring voyage in history. Columbus opened a half-

The lateen sail, invented by the Arabs, enabled Portuguese sailors to tack into the wind.

century of Spanish exploration and conquest. For Europe the 1500s became the Age of Discovery and a time of grand adventure.

The Norse discoveries. In fact, Columbus was not the very first European to see America. From 800 to 1100 the best sailors in Europe came from Norway, Denmark, and Sweden. They sailed to Iceland by 870 and on to Greenland by about 985. They did not use the boats with big figureheads that we usually think of as "Viking," because those were warships. They crossed the ocean in heavy open boats without the aid of the compass.

The first Norseman to see America was probably Bjarni Herjulfson. He had set out for Greenland in 986, but missed it and came upon an unknown shore covered with woods. Bjarni did not land, but he saw Labrador and Baffin Island before sailing back to Greenland. His report of what he had seen led Leif Eriksson in 1001 to sail across and put a temporary settlement in Newfoundland. The Norse sagas tell of others who came to America, including one of Leif's brothers and his bold but quarrelsome half sister Freydis. When the Eskimos attacked one of these settlements, Freydis saved the day. Grabbing a sword, she rallied the frightened men and led them against the attackers. But the Norse people were too few, they did not know the frigid land, and they squabbled among themselves. They did not manage to stay.

The Norse voyages brought no feedback to Europe. Their tales were buried in the Norse sagas. Their actions led nowhere. Not until the first voyage of Columbus did Europe learn of America.

Amerigo Vespucci. Since Columbus discovered a New World, we might expect it to be called by his name. Instead, the name "America" comes from Amerigo Vespucci, an Italian navigator from Florence. Soon after Columbus, Vespucci made two voyages to the New World. Vespucci wrote a vivid account of the lands he saw. He called them a new continent—"what we may rightly call a New World."

Amerigo's name—America—first appeared on a map in 1507 because a French mapprinter, Waldseemüller, had read his account of the New World and was impressed. So he called the new continent "America." The printer later changed his mind. He thought maybe some other name would be better. In his next maps he left off the word. But by then it was too late. Printing presses had spread hundreds of copies over Europe. The name "America" stuck because people liked it, and it has been used ever since.

The Treaty of Tordesillas. The Christians in Europe believed that the Pope had the power to divide up all newly discovered "pagan" lands among the Christian monarchs. Columbus had sailed under the Spanish flag. When King John II of Portugal learned of Columbus's voyage, he protested to the Pope. He said that Columbus had sailed into lands reserved for Portugal. The Pope issued a series of new "bulls" (formal papal decrees) in 1493 that divided the

More from Boorstin: "Vespucci calculated how far west he had come. His astronomical method could eventually yield results far more accurate than the dead reckoning used by Columbus and others at the time, but, for lack of precision instruments, was not yet practical. Even so, during his calculations of the length of a degree, he improved the current figure and produced an estimate of the earth's equatorial circumference which was the most accurate until his time—only fifty miles short of the actual dimensions." (From *The Discoverers*)

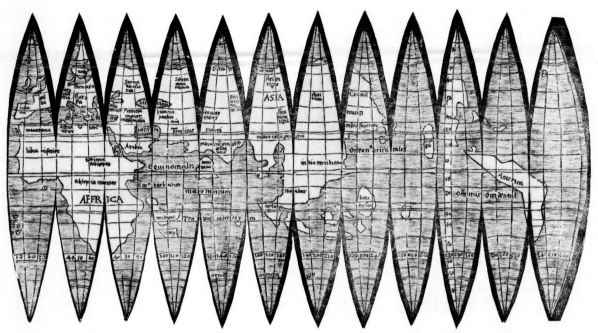

The name "America" was first used on this map made by Martin Waldseemüller in 1507. These segments were designed to fit together into the sphere of the earth. The label "America" is to the right, on what represents South America. Waldseemüller left a gap between North and South America and avoided delineating the unknown west coast of North America.

world along a line drawn down the Atlantic Ocean. Luckily for Spain, Pope Alexander VI was a Spaniard who owed his election to Ferdinand and Isabella. The line he drew just happened to be in Spain's favor. All lands discovered west of the line (where most of the new lands were) would belong to Spain, all lands to the east (including mostly Atlantic Ocean) would go to Portugal.

Portugal was not pleased with this papal line. And Spain was not sure that it could enforce the line if Portugal did not agree. So in 1494 the two seafaring powers signed the Treaty of Tordesillas. This moved the line farther west. The two nations still thought the line would fall in the middle of the Atlantic. Instead it cut off most of what is now Brazil. This explains why today the Brazilians speak Portuguese. The lands of Brazil were discovered by accident by a Portuguese sailor in 1500. Portugal's claim to the area dates back to this treaty.

Balboa. For Europeans wanting to sail west ✂ to Asia, the American continents were only an obstacle. How could they get through? In the first century after Columbus, explorers looked anxiously for a way through, around, or over America. Then they could reach the real Indies, where the treasure was!

At the time, nobody in Europe imagined there would be a Pacific Ocean. It, too, would be discovered by the good luck of courageous men. Vasco Núñez de Balboa, a Spaniard, had tried to be a planter on the island of Hispaniola in the Caribbean. When he failed, and was pursued by his creditors, he smuggled himself off the island in a cask. The ship he happened on was going to Panama, and Balboa joined the expedition.

In the new settlement in Panama the bold Balboa quickly rose to become governor. Darien (Santa Maria de l'Antigua) was the earliest permanent European settlement on the continent.

✂ **Critical Thinking Activity: Making Comparisons** How do the motivations of modern space explorers and Renaissance explorers compare? Have students construct a chart on the chalkboard. Across the top write "Motivations," "Renaissance Explorers," and "Modern Explorers." Under "Motivations," list possible reasons for exploration, such as religion, money, conquest, nationalism, and knowledge. Have students check off the motivations that apply to each group, and write a paragraph comparing the two.

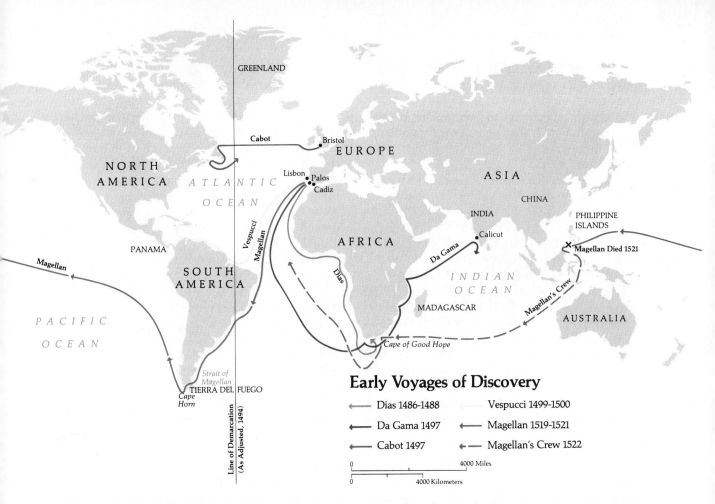

Early Voyages of Discovery

⟵ Dias 1486-1488	Vespucci 1499-1500
⟵ Da Gama 1497	⟵ Magellan 1519-1521
⟵ Cabot 1497	⟵-- Magellan's Crew 1522

0   4000 Miles

0   4000 Kilometers

Balboa married the daughter of an Indian chief. For Balboa's help in one of their wars, the Indians offered the Spaniards 4000 ounces of gold. The impatient Spaniards quarreled over the scales as the gold was weighed out. The Indian chief was disgusted. Since they seemed so greedy, he said, "I'll show you a region flowing with gold."

To find that fabulous land, Balboa set out across the Isthmus of Panama on September 1, 1513. With him were 190 Spaniards and several hundred Indians. There were 30 blacks with Balboa. He needed plenty of help, for the jungle was dense and dark. It took them four weeks to cover 45 miles. Finally, on September 29, Balboa, sword in hand, waded into the surf of the ocean that Europeans had never known. In the name of the king of Spain he claimed possession of the Sea of the South and all the coasts it touched.

Balboa's life ended in tragedy—the risk of every *conquistador* (Spanish for "conqueror"). When an enemy became governor of Darien, Balboa and four of his companions were falsely accused of treason. They were all beheaded in the Darien public square and their bodies thrown to the vultures.

Magellan. The Pacific Ocean which Balboa ⊕ had discovered was the largest ocean in the world. It was equal in area to all the lands of the planet. The man who unveiled the grandeur of the Pacific was Fernão de Magalhães, whom we call Ferdinand Magellan. A Portuguese noble and an expert sailor, he had already sailed eastward from Europe—even as far as the Spice Islands. Like Columbus, he believed that those islands could more easily be reached by sailing west. He proposed this round-the-world trip to his king, Manuel I. But by then King Manuel

was more interested in the route around Africa which the Portuguese Vasco da Gama had already taken all the way to India.

So Magellan went on to Spain. The 18-year-old king, Charles I, snapped up the idea and put Magellan in charge of five ships carrying 265 officers and men.

In September 1519 Magellan set out on a trip around the world—the longest sea voyage in history. First, he had to find a way around America. That took him over a year, during which he put down a mutiny and lost one of his vessels in a shipwreck. By October 1520 he had entered what we now call the Strait of Magellan. It took him five weeks (as long as it had taken Columbus to cross the Atlantic) to make his way through the perilous, twisting, mountain-lined waterway at the southern end of South America. During this frightening passage the crew of one of his ships mutinied and sailed back to Spain.

On November 28, 1520, Magellan entered the Pacific with three ships and 150 crewmen. With no idea of its size, they started across the world's greatest ocean. The optimistic Magellan believed that it was only a few hundred miles from Panama to Japan.

Instead, the Pacific stretched 10,000 miles! For three months Magellan and his three ships sailed on. They had so much fair weather that they decided to call this the "Pacific" (peaceful) Ocean. But they had no fresh provisions or fresh water. After devouring their last moldy biscuits which swarmed with worms, they chewed the leather of the rigging and they ate sawdust. They were glad to make a meal of the shipboard rats. Nineteen of the crew died of scurvy, caused by a lack of the vitamin C found in fresh fruit and vegetables. If they had been delayed by storms, they could not have survived. "Had not God and His blessed mother given us good weather," wrote Antonio Pigafetta, who accompanied Magellan, "we would all have died of hunger in that exceeding vast ocean."

On March 6, 1521, Magellan's fleet finally reached the island of Guam. There they resupplied for the next stage of their voyage—to the islands now called the Philippines (after King Philip of Spain). In the Philippines Magellan's slave Enrique, whom he had bought eleven years before at Malacca on the Malay peninsula, was able to communicate with the natives. Magellan made the fatal mistake of joining in the battles between the Philippine tribes. On the shore of a Philippine island in a petty skirmish over a cause he never understood, the great Magellan was hacked to death. He was denied the glory of completing that first trip around the world.

After his death in that trivial tribal fight, the remaining crew pushed on. One ship, no longer seaworthy, was left behind. Another was seized by the Portuguese. A further year of danger—completing three years at sea—at last brought one ship, the *Vittoria*, with eighteen sailors and three natives back home to Spain. Finally someone had circumnavigated the globe!

No other voyage has equaled Magellan's contribution to our knowledge of the earth. Now the notion that the world was round was no longer just a theory. Magellan fulfilled Columbus's dream of reaching the Indies by sailing west. The voyage began to show how much of the earth is covered by the sea. Even so, the extent of the Pacific would be underestimated for many years to come. Most important of all, Magellan's voyage—around America—revealed that the new lands were not part of Asia, not just a promontory of the Island of the Earth. The Americas were continents by themselves. The American continents would be called the Western Hemisphere—which filled a half of the sphere that was the earth.

Spain and America. For more than 50 years ☑ after Columbus, the Spaniards had the New World mostly to themselves. Who dared challenge Spain—the richest and most powerful nation in Europe? In 1519 King Charles I of Spain was elected Holy Roman Emperor and became Emperor Charles V. In theory the Holy Roman Empire covered all of Christendom. The emperor was supposed to rule it all. The armies of Charles V defeated the French, then the only serious rival power on the continent of Europe.

☑ See the "Lesson Plan," p. 2E for **Writing Process Activity: Identifying Central Issues** concerning the Spanish explorers.

His fleets controlled the Mediterranean. And his Council of the Indies at Seville was supposed to run the affairs of the whole New World.

The Spanish court gave charters to one adventurer after another. Ferdinand and Isabella had made Columbus the "Admiral of the Ocean Sea." Some went without permission. Brave conquistadores led expeditions to the mainland of America. There they set themselves up as viceroys, or governors, of new provinces. Most spent their lives searching for treasure that never existed. Some actually conquered native empires and fulfilled their dreams with the New World's treasure.

Hernando Cortes and the Aztecs. Perhaps the most courageous and successful conquistador was Hernando Cortes. In 1519, the same year Magellan set out on his voyage, the bold 34-year-old Cortes landed on the coast of Mexico with 550 soldiers, 16 horses, and 10 brass cannon. Within a year he had subdued the Aztec empire. He won by bravery, ruthlessness, skill, luck, and the help of imported European diseases which killed thousands of Indians. Cortes arrived in a ship larger than any seen there before. Riding on horses, the Spaniards seemed superhuman. Their guns killed at a distance with terrifying magic. No wonder the Aztecs thought they had been invaded by the gods!

From Mexico Cortes brought to the king of Spain the first rich cargoes from America. When the treasures of gold and silver reached the court of Charles V, Spaniards awoke to the fact that America was more than a mere obstacle to the Indies.

Pizarro and Peru. In Europe scores of other adventurers now hoped to find their fortune here. Early in 1531 another ambitious Spaniard, Francisco Pizarro, landed in Peru with a small force of 180 soldiers and 27 horses. In the splendid ancient city of Cajamarca he found the

This double-headed snake sculpture of turquoise mosaic was made by the Aztecs.

Skilled Incan artisans fashioned these exquisite cups of solid gold to hold offerings to the gods during special ceremonies.

new Inca, or emperor, who had just won a civil war. The Inca greeted Pizarro as a friend. In return, Pizarro seized him. The Inca offered to fill a room with treasure to win his release, and Pizarro agreed. Soon the room was bulging with a glittering pile of gold, silver, and precious gems. When the gold was weighed, it totaled 13,265 pounds and the silver 26,000 pounds. Pizarro melted it down to divide between himself and his men. Each cavalryman received 90 pounds of gold and 180 of silver. Infantrymen received less, but everyone had enough to be rich for life.

The Spanish were afraid to release the Inca for fear he would lead an uprising against them. So they used treachery. They accused the Inca of crimes he had never committed and executed him. Then they took the Incan capital at Cuzco, which brought down the whole Incan empire.

When the treasure flowed back to Spain, countless adventurous young men laid plans for their own expeditions to America. To find another Mexico or Peru, was it not worth risking your life? Reckless, ruthless conquistadores crossed the ocean to face fever, starvation, shipwreck, and hostile Indians. They stumbled their way through pathless woods, swamps, jungles, and deserts—hoping to win their gamble for a fortune.

Exploration in the present-day United States. (p. 19)
While some conquistadores explored southward from central Mexico, others were searching for gold—or something more precious—in North America. When Juan Ponce de León ventured to Florida in 1513, he was looking for an island named "Bimini." On that island there was said to be a fountain that would restore youth to all who bathed in it. Ponce de León named the mainland "Florida," either because of the flowers there or the fact that he arrived on or soon after Easter (Pascua Florida, or "Flowering Easter"). Unfortunately he never found the magic fountain.

Florida, a beautiful tropic land, attracted many others who were no more lucky. Pánfilo de Narváez, the enemy and rival of Cortes, hoped to find in Florida (a name the Spanish applied to all America north of the Gulf of Mexico between the Rocky Mountains and the Atlantic) wealth like that Cortes had found in Mexico. In 1527 he landed with 400 men and 80 horses on the gulf coast.

Nothing was heard of the expedition until nine years later. Then remnants of Narváez's crew—Cabeza de Vaca, Alonso del Castillo, Andrés Dorantes, and Dorantes's black slave Esteban—met a Spanish party seeking Indian slaves in the western desert. The survivors told a hair-raising story of Indian battles, of building boats and trying to sail to Mexico, of the loss of their boats one by one, and then the deaths of all the other hundreds in their party. For years they had been held by Indians until they escaped and made their way toward Mexico. The Indians had learned to distrust the warlike strangers. Still the Indians did not kill these

Multicultural Connection: The first European settlement founded in what is now the U.S. was San Miguel de Gualdape. It was founded by Lucas Vázquez de Ayllón. In 1526 he set out from Hispaniola with six ships and about 600 colonists. The group landed on the coast of Georgia near St. Catherine's Island. The settlement did not survive, because most of the colonists, including Ayllón, died of malaria. After a few months the survivors returned to Hispaniola.

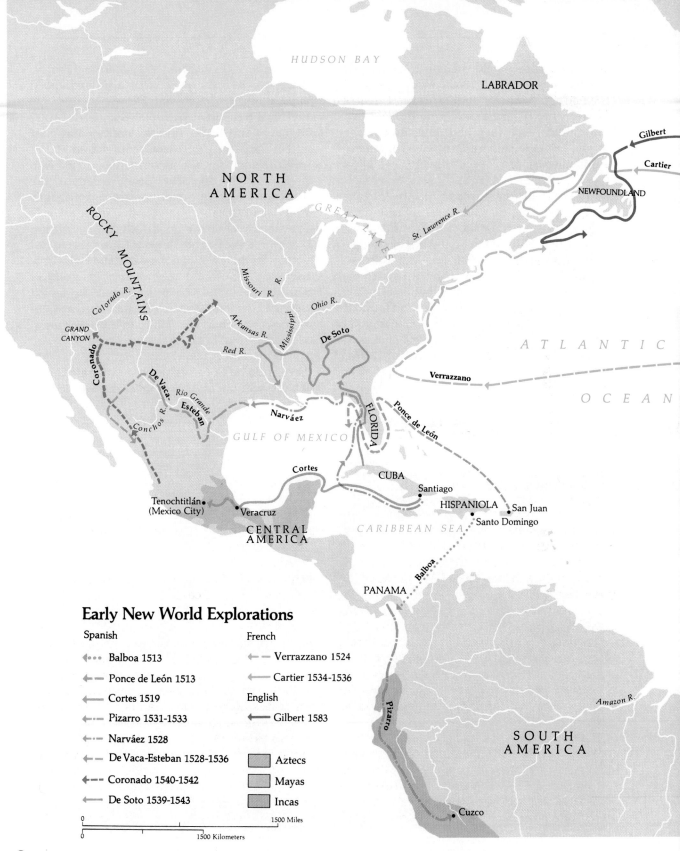

Early New World Explorations

HUDSON BAY

LABRADOR

NORTH
AMERICA

GREAT LAKES

NEWFOUNDLAND

Gilbert

Cartier

ROCKY MOUNTAINS

St. Lawrence R.

ATLANTIC

OCEAN

Missouri R.

Ohio R.

Colorado R.

GRAND
CANYON

Arkansas R.

Mississippi

Red R.

De Soto

Coronado

De Vaca-

Rio Grande

Verrazzano

Esteban

Narváez

FLORIDA

Ponce de León

Conchos R.

GULF OF MEXICO

Cortes

CUBA

Tenochtitlán
(Mexico City)

Veracruz

Santiago

HISPANIOLA

San Juan

CENTRAL
AMERICA

CARIBBEAN SEA

Santo Domingo

Balboa

PANAMA

SOUTH
AMERICA

Pizarro

Amazon R.

Cuzco

Spanish

⊷⊷⊷ Balboa 1513

◄─ ─ Ponce de León 1513

◄── Cortes 1519

◄─·─ Pizarro 1531-1533

◄─·─ Narváez 1528

◄── De Vaca-Esteban 1528-1536

◄─ ─ Coronado 1540-1542

◄── De Soto 1539-1543

French

◄─ ─ Verrazzano 1524

◄── Cartier 1534-1536

English

◄── Gilbert 1583

Aztecs

Mayas

Incas

0 ————————— 1500 Miles

0 ————————— 1500 Kilometers

⊕ **Geography and History: Movement** Have students refer to the map above. Ask: Who discovered Florida? (Ponce de León) Cuzco? Peru? (Pizarro) The Pacific Ocean? (Balboa) Tenochtitlan? (Cortes) The Rio Grande? (De Vaca-Esteban) The Colorado River? (Narváez) The St. Lawrence River? (Cartier) Which country sent the most expeditions to explore the New World in the 1500s? (Spain) For whom did Verazzano and Cartier sail? (The French) What English explorer sailed to Newfoundland? (Gilbert) Who explored the lands of the Aztecs and Mayas? (Cortes) The Incas? (Pizarro)

four because they were thought to be medicine men with powers to heal the sick.

When at last the four survivors reached Mexico, they reported the "hunchbacked cows" (the buffalo) that they had seen. And they repeated enticing rumors of cities with emerald-studded walls.

Esteban and Fray Marcos. Having had their fill of exploring, three of these plucky adventurers—de Vaca, Castillo, and Dorantes—were glad to return to Spain. Esteban, no longer a slave, was hired in 1539 by Fray Marcos, a Franciscan monk, to help find the cities with emerald-studded walls—the fabulous "Seven Cities of Cibola." This new expedition found the pueblos of the Zuñi Indians, which can still be seen in New Mexico. Esteban was killed by the Indians. Father Marcos, who had only heard of the pueblos from Esteban, reported that he had located the fabulous Seven Cities.

Coronado. On hearing Fray Marcos's report, Francisco de Coronado, with a well-equipped expedition, set out from Mexico to find the mythical treasures. With 300 Spaniards, 1000 Indians, and 1500 horses, mules, and beef cattle, the large party departed north in March 1540 to look for the Seven Cities. They also hoped to come upon the "Strait of Anian," the Northwest Passage which most people thought would lead through America and open the way to Asia. By amazing good luck the expedition discovered the Grand Canyon! Even this did not satisfy them. It would not make them rich. They saw the pueblos, and went all the way to central Kansas. But since he never found the fabled Seven Cities of Cibola, Coronado returned "in sadness" to report his failure to the governor of Mexico.

Hernando de Soto. The most elaborate Spanish expedition in the New World was led by

Coronado and his elaborate expedition in 1540 were the first Europeans to see the awesome Grand Canyon.

David Muench Photography

Richard Erdes

This Navajo painting of the arrival of the Spanish, including a Catholic priest, is on a wall in Canyon del Muerto, Arizona.

Hernando de Soto. He was already a wealthy man, since he had been a partner of Pizarro's in Peru. But he wanted to be even richer.

De Soto was in Spain when de Vaca returned there with his tall tales of the mysterious Seven Cities of Cibola. Upon hearing the news, de Soto thought this might be a chance to find another Incan empire. He went to Charles V for aid. The emperor agreed, since de Soto had lent him money. So Charles helped de Soto enlist hundreds of nobles and gentlemen along with carpenters, smiths, and priests.

De Soto's party of 570 men, 223 horses, a pack of dogs for hunting, and a herd of hogs for meat landed near the present Fort Myers, Florida, in May 1539. During the next four years the expedition wandered over what is now Georgia, Alabama, Mississippi, across Arkansas, and on to Oklahoma. Finally they gave up their fruitless quest for a new Incan empire. They made boats to sail down the Mississippi

and cross the gulf to Mexico, where they arrived in September 1543. Over half the party had died during those four years, including de Soto, who was buried in the Mississippi River.

New Spain. The Spanish settlers wanted gold. And at first they were not eager to settle in a land of disappointment. Still the Spanish actually claimed the entire North American continent. They settled only in the West Indies and Mexico. This realm, which they called New Spain, became a great overseas empire spreading into Central and South America. Not until the 1560s did they begin to plant permanent settlements in the present area of the United States. Then, when their settlements had pushed close to the Rio Grande, they conquered the Pueblo Indians and established the province of New Mexico. Santa Fe was founded in 1609, at about the same time as Jamestown.

See "Section 4 Review answers," p. 2E.

Section 4 Review

1. Identify: Leif Eriksson, Amerigo Vespucci, Vasco Núñez de Balboa, Ferdinand Magellan, Charles V, Hernando Cortes, Francisco Pizarro, Ponce de León, Pánfilo de Narváez, Cabeza de Vaca, Esteban, Francisco de Coronado.
2. Locate; Labrador, Greenland, Canary Islands, Panama, Newfoundland, Guam.
3. Why do we celebrate Columbus's discovery of America rather than the Vikings'?
4. What were the unexpected results of the Treaty of Tordesillas?
5. Why was Magellan's voyage important?
6. What effect did the conquest of the Aztecs have on Spain?
7. Why could the small armies of Cortes and Pizarro defeat the Aztecs and the Incas?
8. What is "the Northwest Passage"? Why did explorers want to find it?
9. **Critical Thinking: Drawing Conclusions.** How did the explorers' reports shape Europeans' views of the world?

See "Lesson Plan," p. 2E.

5. French and English exploration

For many years the Spanish dominated the New World, but they did not have it all to themselves. Despite the Papal Bull dividing the New World between Spain and Portugal, other nations wanted their share. King Francis I of France joked at the Pope's division of the earth. The ancestor of all mankind was Adam. But where in Adam's will, Francis asked, was the provision cutting out all the other nations in the world? By now England, too, had become a great seafaring nation, ready to ignore the Pope's decision.

John Cabot. The first successful attempt to break the Spanish and Portuguese monopoly was made by England. The capable but cautious King Henry VII had actually refused to finance Columbus's voyage. Since he had missed that chance, he was ready to listen when John Cabot (who, like Columbus, had been born in Genoa) approached him. Since everyone still believed that Columbus had reached the Indies, Cabot now proposed to find a better way to get there. He thought that sailing northwest was the answer.

Cabot offered to make the trip at his own cost, but he wanted royal approval. He manned his one small vessel, the *Mathew*, with a crew of only eighteen. On May 20, 1497, he sailed into the North Atlantic. Except for one gale just before he reached America, he had an easy crossing. Shortly after sunrise on the morning of June 24 Cabot reached Newfoundland. He was probably only a few miles from where Leif Eriksson had tried his settlement 500 years before.

Cabot—like Columbus before him—was looking for a way through to China. He turned south, probably because of ice. Then somewhere along the coast he entered a harbor (perhaps Griquet Harbor) and claimed the land for England. He coasted all along Newfoundland, but he did not stop again. Reaching the end of Newfoundland, Cabot sailed back to where he had first touched on the island and then headed for home. After an amazingly fast passage of fifteen days to Brittany he then sailed on to Bristol, where he had started. His whole trip

had taken only eleven weeks. It would be nearly a century before anyone would make a faster round trip to America.

When Henry VII received Cabot's report, he was delighted. Stingy as usual, he handed Cabot only £10. Then, to show his pleasure, he gave Cabot a pension of £20 a year. Others were more enthusiastic. Londoners paid him "vast honor" and "ran after him like mad people."

In February 1498, King Henry gave Cabot the power to impress four good-sized ships into his service for a new expedition. King Henry even supplied one vessel himself. These ships were loaded with goods to start a trading post—in Japan! Cabot sailed again from Bristol in May 1498. One ship had to turn back, but the other four sailed away, never to return. Nothing was ever heard again of them, or of Cabot. But for the next two centuries John Cabot's first voyage remained the basis of England's claim to the whole mainland of North America.

Giovanni da Verrazzano. The French also tried to find a passage through America toward the riches of the East. For the first half of the 1500s France was at war with Spain. In 1522, French corsairs seized a Spanish treasure ship that Cortes was sending home from Mexico. The riches on that ship must have encouraged Francis I.

Meanwhile, as early as 1503, French boats had started fishing on the Grand Banks of Newfoundland. In the next century French boats were active there and were drying their catch on the land.

At this time the geography of North America, between Newfoundland and Florida, was still a mystery. Why couldn't there be, somewhere along that coast, the long-sought water passage westward to Asia? Merchants in the French city of Lyon were eager for the profits of the China trade. With the approval of King Francis they hired the Italian explorer Giovanni da Verrazzano from Florence to seek the way.

On January 17, 1524, Verrazzano sailed for America. On March 1 he reached Cape Fear in what is now North Carolina. To avoid the Spaniards, he turned north. In the neighborhood of Cape Hatteras he looked across an isthmus only

Continuity and Change: Geography Point out to students that exploration has continued to be an arena of international competition in modern times, and was especially so during the "space race" of the 1950s between the United States and the Soviet Union. (See page 744.)

The New-York Historical Society

This delicately colored glazed terra cotta figure of Italian explorer Giovanni da Verrazzano was made sometime around the 1520s.

Nantucket Sound with its many shoals, rounded Cape Cod, crossed to Maine, and sailed on to Newfoundland. Then, when he realized that he had reached the land discovered by Cabot, he turned for home.

Verrazzano had done more than anyone before to fill in the map of east-coast North America. But he had not found the westward passage, and he had made no profits. The merchants of Lyon gave up, and King Francis turned to his endless wars with Spain.

Jacques Cartier. Francis I's interest in America was accidentally reawakened on a pilgrimage to Mont-St.-Michel, the magnificent abbey which we can still visit on the northern coast of France. There the abbot told the king that in the nearby town of Saint-Malo lived a sailor who would discover lands for the king in the New World. The wealthy abbot even offered to share the cost of the expedition. With the help of the abbot, and a new Pope who now agreed to let Francis claim lands in the New World, the French returned to explore North America.

Jacques Cartier, the sailor from Saint-Malo, made three voyages to the New World for the king. On his first voyage in 1534, Cartier discovered and explored the Gulf of St. Lawrence. So he began to open the great passage to the continent's interior.

Cartier's voyage the following spring penetrated the continent. Entering the St. Lawrence River itself, he sailed all the way to the site of Montreal, where there was a large Indian village. Since his boat could not pass the rapids, he returned to the site of what is now Quebec. There he spent a long, hard winter. When his men came down with scurvy, they finally were saved by a friendly Indian who showed them how to cure the disease by eating the crushed and cooked bark of the evergreen arbor-vitae (tree of life).

When Cartier returned to France in July 1536, he brought back with him an Indian chief. The chief told the king tall tales about the riches of Canada. In May 1541 Cartier set out again with five ships, some colonists (many were convicts), and a variety of animals. This time he aimed to start a permanent French

a mile wide. He thought he could see the Pacific Ocean. In fact, he was looking into Pamlico Sound. But he failed to find a way through the isthmus.

Verrazzano then sailed still farther north. He missed Chesapeake and Delaware bays but discovered the beautiful bay of New York. He anchored near the site of the present-day Verrazano Bridge. He did not stay long. Instead he sailed east along Long Island, discovered Block Island, entered Narragansett Bay and anchored at Newport Harbor. Since the Indians there were friendly, he stayed two weeks before again heading east. He passed through Vineyard Sound, crossed the dangerous waters of

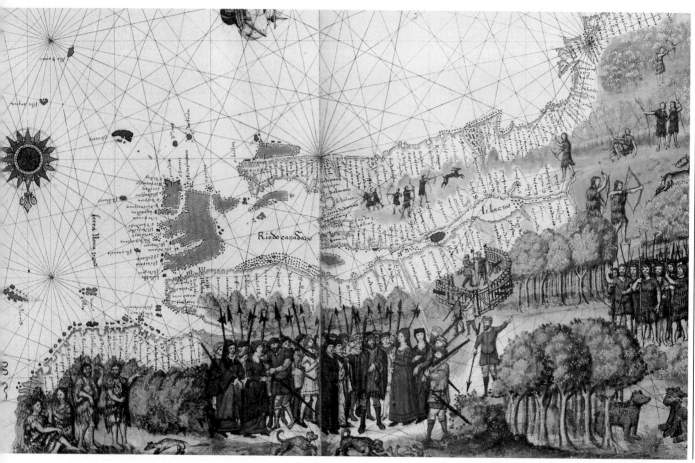

Nicolas Vallard's map of Canada in 1547 showed the arrival of Cartier and his party, including the surprising presence of several women. Cartier is in front center wearing a short cloak. Vallard also portrayed several groups of Indians.

colony in America. Near modern Quebec they did build a settlement. Indian attacks killed off 35 of the colonists. The next spring, when no help had come from home, Cartier decided to take all the colonists back to France. Just as they were departing, at St. John's, Newfoundland, they met the expedition sent to their aid. It was too late. Cartier's patience was worn thin, and he led his people home. The new arrivals, after a hard winter ashore, also gave up.

Hardy French adventurers kept coming back to Canada to fish and trade for fur. They also ❧ tried to establish colonies in South Carolina and Florida. But decades would pass before there was a New France in America.

See "Section 5 Review answers," p. 2F.

Section 5 Review

1. Identify: John Cabot, Giovanni da Verrazzano, Jacques Cartier, Henry VII, Francis I, the *Mathew*.

2. Locate: Newfoundland, Verrazzano's route, Cartier's route, Florida, St. Lawrence River, Montreal, Quebec.

3. Why did Cartier fail to establish a successful permanent settlement in Canada?

4. **Critical Thinking: Making Comparisons.** How did France's and England's explorational aims compare to those of Spain and Portugal?

❧ See "Lesson Plan" p. 2F for **Cooperative Learning Activity: Drawing Conclusions** relating to early explorations in North and South America.

Chapter 1 Review

See "Chapter Review answers," p. 2F.

Focusing on Ideas

1. Identify Columbus's most important navigational and geographic achievements and explain how they aided later explorations.

2. What developments in Europe contributed to interest in and support for exploration?

3. What role did rivalries between European nations play in the discovery and exploration of the New World?

4. What lands in the Western Hemisphere did Spain, Portugal, England, and France claim? On what was each of these claims based?

Taking a Critical Look

1. **Recognizing Cause and Effect.** The story of the first European explorations of the Western Hemisphere is full of "accidents" and rumors. How did accidents and rumors affect where exploration took place?

2. **Recognizing Bias.** The first encounters Europeans had with the advanced Indian cultures of the New World, such as the Aztecs and Incas, left Europeans astonished. What elements of these Indian civilizations were most surprising to the Europeans? How is this astonishment an example of ethnocentrism, the feeling that one's own ethnic group or race is superior to all others?

3. **Making Comparisons.** Within a span of only 35 years, Dias rounded the Cape of Good Hope, Columbus made his voyage to the New World, Balboa discovered the Pacific Ocean, and Magellan and his crew sailed around the world. All of these events fit easily into an average lifetime. What major world events have occurred so far in your lifetime? During your parents' lifetimes? How do these events compare with those of the sixteenth century?

Your Region in History

1. **Geography.** What European nation first laid claim to your locality? What evidence can you identify as to their presence?

2. **Culture.** What Indian groups lived in your region about the year 1500? What sort of culture did they have? What, if any, artifacts did they leave behind?

3. **Economics.** In what ways did the early adventurers profit from the exploration of your region?

Historical Facts and Figures

Formulating Hypotheses. Study the graph below to help answer the following questions: (a) What happened to the Indian population of Central America during the period 1520–1610? (b) Formulate a hypothesis, or educated guess, explaining the impact of Spain's arrival in the New World.

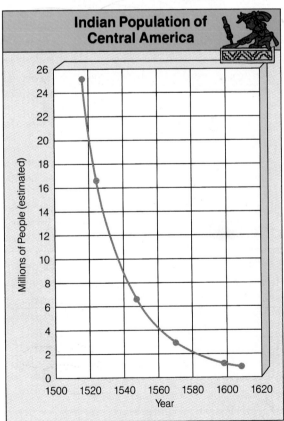

Source: *The Population of Latin America*, Nicolas Sanchez-Albornoz

Chapter 2
An Assortment of Colonies

Identifying Chapter Materials

Objectives	Basic Instructional Materials	Extension Materials
1 The Spanish Empire • Analyze the framework of Spanish colonial government. • Give examples of the influence of Catholicism and the missions. • Discuss ways in which the Spanish viewed Aztec culture.	**Annotated Teacher's Edition** • Lesson Plans, p. 26C **Instructional Support File** • Pre-Reading Activities, Unit 1, p. 15	**Extension Activity** • Hispanic Contributions to American Culture, Lesson Plans, p. 26C
2 A Great and Victorious England • Describe early English attempts to found a colony in North America.	**Annotated Teacher's Edition** • Lesson Plans, pp. 26C–26D	**Documents of American History** • Charter to Sir Walter Raleigh, Vol. 1, p. 6
3 The Planting of Virginia • List at least five reasons for English interest in forming colonies. • Name three important events of 1619 and tell the significance of each.	**Annotated Teacher's Edition** • Lesson Plans, pp. 26D–26E	**Documents of American History** • First Charter of Virginia, Vol. 1, p. 8
4 The Puritans Come to New England • Identify the Puritan colonies and give reasons for their success. • Distinguish between the Pilgrims and the Puritans, and indicate what role each group played in New England.	**Annotated Teacher's Edition** • Lesson Plans, p. 26E **Instructional Support File** • Skill Review Activity, Unit 1, p. 18 • Skill Application Activity, Unit 1, p. 19	**Enrichment Support File** • Settling the New World (See "In-Depth Coverage" at right.) **Suggested Secondary Sources** • See chart at right.
5 Other Europeans in North America • Describe the colonies of the French, Dutch, and Swedish. • Explain how the French and Dutch settlements differed from the English.	**Annotated Teacher's Edition** • Lesson Plans, p. 26F	**Extension Activity** • Theme Link, Lesson Plans, p. 26F **American History Transparencies** • Geography and History, pp. B3, B7 • Our Multicultural Heritage, p. C43
6 The Proprietary Colonies • Illustrate the effects of religious beliefs and idealism on the development of Pennsylvania and Georgia. • Define the term *proprietary colony*. • Discuss the role of William Penn and the Quakers in Pennsylvania.	**Annotated Teacher's Edition** • Lesson Plans, pp. 26F–26G **Instructional Support File** • Reading Activities, Unit 1, pp. 16–17 • Critical Thinking Activity, Unit 1, p. 20 • Chapter Test, Unit 1, pp. 21–24 • Additional Test Questions, Unit 1, pp. 25–28	**Documents of American History** • The Charter of Maryland, Vol. 1, p. 21 **American History Transparencies** • Geography and History, pp. B3, B7, B9 • Critical Thinking, p. F3

Providing In-Depth Coverage

Perspectives on the Settlement of the New World

Spain was the first European nation to establish successful colonies in the New World, but it was England that had the greatest influence on the development of the United States. Chapter 2 examines the strengths and weaknesses of the different European efforts to develop colonial empires in the New World, with emphasis placed on the English colonies. This provides a backdrop for an in-depth focus on the settlement of the Massachusetts and Virginia colonies.

A History of the United States as an instructional program provides two types of resources you can use to offer in-depth coverage of the settlement of the New World: the *student text* and the *Enrichment Support File*. A list of *Suggested Secondary Sources* is also provided. The chart below shows the topics that are covered in each.

THE STUDENT TEXT. Boorstin and Kelley's *A History of the United States* unfolds the chronology of events and the key players in the creation of New World colonies.

AMERICAN HISTORY ENRICHMENT SUPPORT FILE. This collection of primary source readings and classroom activities reveals the hardships of establishing the first American colonies.

SUGGESTED SECONDARY SOURCES. This reference list of readings by well-known historians and other commentators provides an array of perspectives on the hardships of establishing the first American colonies.

Locating Instructional Materials

Detailed lesson plans for teaching the settlement of the New World as a mini-course or to study one or more elements of the colonies in depth are offered in the following areas: in the *student text*, see individual lesson plans at the beginning of each chapter; in the *Enrichment Support File*, see page 3; for readings beyond the student text, see *Suggested Secondary Sources*.

IN-DEPTH COVERAGE OF THE SETTLEMENT OF THE NEW WORLD		
Student Text	**Enrichment Support File**	**Suggested Secondary Sources**
▪ Settlement of Virginia, pp. 35–38 ▪ John Smith, p. 37 ▪ John Rolfe, pp. 37–38 ▪ Coming to New England, pp. 38–40 ▪ The Mayflower Compact, p. 40 ▪ Creating the Colony, pp. 40–41 ▪ Fishing Industry, pp. 54–56 ▪ Education, p. 59 ▪ Communication with England, pp. 63–64	▪ Lesson Suggestions ▪ Multimedia Resources ▪ Overview Essay/Settling the New World ▪ Literature in American History/*Philip of Pokanoket* ▪ Songs in American History/Pilgrims Make Light of Their Lot ▪ Primary Sources in American History/Hard Times in Jamestown, Virginia ▪ Geography in American History/Place Names and the Geography of Settlement ▪ Simulation/A Meeting of the Virginia Company ▪ Making Connections	▪ *Pilgrim Colony: A History of New Plymouth, 1620–1691* by George Langdon, pp. 1–37. ▪ *American Slavery, American Freedom: The Ordeal of Colonial Virginia* by Edmund S. Morgan, pp. 71–91. ▪ *Winthrop's Boston: Portrait of a Puritan Town, 1630–1649* by Darrett Rutman, pp. 3–40. ▪ *American Genesis: Captain John Smith and the Founding of Virginia* by Alden Vaughan, pp. 1–21, 23–38.

Section 1 (pages 27–30)

The Spanish Empire

FOCUS

To introduce the lesson, ask students: What modern-day examples can you cite of the subjugation of one people by another? Why does this occur?

Developing Vocabulary

The words listed in this chapter are essential terms for reading and understanding particular sections of the chapter. The page number after each term indicates the page of its first or most important appearance in this chapter. These terms are defined in the text Glossary (text pages 1000–1011).

colony (page 27); *encomienda* (page 27); **hacienda** (page 28); **mercantilism** (page 28); **mestizo** (page 30)

INSTRUCT

Explain

In the borderlands the main form of landholding and Indian control was the missions. In most of the Spanish empire it was the encomienda and hacienda.

☑Writing Process Activity

Expressing Problems Clearly Tell students that as the Spanish king, they are concerned with governing their colonies in the New World. To prepare for writing a document explaining policy to the colonial viceroy, have them outline specific methods, such as mercantilism, the establishment of missions, and so forth. Have students begin their explanations with a topic sentence summarizing Spain's philosophy and the importance of the policies. Ask them to revise for clarity, completeness, and logical development. After proofreading their papers, pairs of students can compare their explanations.

Section Review Answers

Section 1, page 30

1. a) system by which the Spanish king "entrusted" a group of Indian families to a Spanish settler and the Indians then paid tribute to the settler. It was a system of forced labor that often came close to slavery. b) a large estate in Spanish America. c) a Spanish missionary who helped found a series of missions along the California coast and tried to protect the Indians from the Spanish army. d) the council in Spain through which the king ruled the Spanish colonies of America. 2. St. Augustine and the Spanish borderlands are shown on the map on page 28. 3. The Spanish aimed to convert the Indians to Catholicism.

Both the church and the king opposed enslavement of the Indians, but the Indians ended up with little freedom. 4. The aim of Spanish colonial policy was to make the colonies benefit Spain by producing goods that Spain needed and by buying Spanish goods. The policy was called *mercantilism*. 5. The wealth of the empire made Spain the richest nation of Europe, tempted Spanish kings to extend their empire and ignore domestic needs, and ultimately helped lead to the decline of Spain. 6. If the Indian population had not declined, it is possible that the slavery of blacks may never have been established in the Spanish colonies.

CLOSE

To conclude the lesson, ask students to write an essay in which they adopt the point of view of Father Serra to explain the importance of religion in settling the New World and the activities of missions there. Ask them to name at least three of the activities of the missions in the essay. (Religious services, education, farming, protection.)

Extension Activity

To extend the lesson, have each student compile a list of five contributions of Hispanics to North American culture. (Some possible responses include words, place names, architectural styles, foods, etc.) Students can share their lists with the rest of the class.

Section 2 (pages 30–33)

A Great and Victorious England

FOCUS

To introduce the lesson, ask students: What is a turning point in history? What makes it a turning point? List their answers on the chalkboard. When you have a number of answers, ask the students if there are any answers they would like to cross off or rephrase. (Answers should include a dramatic change in a country or countries.) Then ask students to list any information they find in their reading about the defeat of the Spanish Armada (pp. 31–32 in the text).

Developing Vocabulary

pioneers (page 32); **joint stock company** (page 33)

INSTRUCT

Explain

With the defeat of the Spanish Armada in 1588, England grew in power as Spain began a decline. The

English, however, were not able to set up a lasting colony in North America.

❧ Cooperative Learning Activity

Formulating Questions Break the class into small groups, and explain that each will design an interview with Queen Elizabeth I. Have students decide who in their group will lead the discussion, who will act as recorder, and who will present the interview questions to the class. Have students reach consensus on eight interview questions that can be answered using facts presented in the text. When all groups have recorded their questions, have each interviewer present a few of the group's questions to an empty chair, where Elizabeth is supposed to be sitting. Have students from other groups answer for Elizabeth, or have one student answer for Elizabeth.

Section Review Answers

Section 2, page 33

1. a) a group of strong English monarchs who united England and laid the foundation for its great empire. b) King of Spain who dispatched the Armada against England. c) urged Queen Elizabeth to establish English settlements in North America and received England's first colonial charter. d) vainly attempted to establish a colony in Virginia and was the first to try to finance colonies by forming a joint stock company. e) English geographer who collected accounts of exploration and published them to encourage efforts to establish English colonies. f) the word found written on a post at the settlement on Roanoke Island. g) the settlement established on Roanoke Island in 1587. When supply ships returned to the settlement in 1590, the settlers had disappeared. 2. Cadiz is on the map on page 15. The Netherlands and London are on the map on page 11. 3. A joint stock company was owned by a number of people, each of whom bought "shares" of stock. People could invest small sums, which increased the number of potential investors, and spread the risks of the enterprise among many people. 4. The defeat of the Armada marked the beginning of Spain's decline and England's rise as a major power.

CLOSE

To conclude the lesson, ask: Does the difference between what might have happened if Spain had defeated England and remained the greatest power in Europe and on the seas suggest that the defeat of the Armada was a turning point in history? (Yes: "one of the decisive battles of history," p. 32.) Ask students to write an essay of 100 to 200 words explaining why or why not they think the battle was a turning point in history.

Section 3 (pages 34–38)

The Planting of Virginia

FOCUS

Have students imagine that they are young men and women in England in 1606 when the Virginia Company began to recruit settlers for what would become the Jamestown Colony. Have students suggest the type of "sales pitch" from a Virginia Company recruiter that would appeal to them. What objections do students think they might have offered to a recruiter?

Developing Vocabulary

martial law (page 38); **House of Burgesses** (page 38); **staple crop** (page 38); **representative government** (page 38)

INSTRUCT

Explain

The Virginia Company made many mistakes in its rules for the Jamestown Colony. Some of the mistakes were the result of ignorance about Virginia, and some mistakes resulted from the Company's need for profits.

☑ Writing Process Activity

Distinguishing False from Accurate Images Tell students it is 1609, and advertising has persuaded them to leave England for Virginia. Before they write a diary entry about living in America, ask them to cluster the differences between what they heard about the New World and what their lives are actually like. Have them begin with a topic sentence summarizing the major differences. They should organize by presenting a rumor followed by a corresponding point about reality. After revising for unity and coherence, they should proofread. Students can publish their diary entries by making a bulletin board display.

Section Review Answers

Section 3, page 38

1. a) adventurer who took charge of the Jamestown settlement and saved the colony. b) married Pocahontas, discovered how to grow a popular kind of tobacco, which gave Virginia a staple crop. c) the bitter winter of 1609–1610 in Jamestown, when more than 400 settlers died. d) a person who agreed to work for someone for a certain number of years in return for passage to America. 2. Jamestown is on the map on page 54. 3. The English wanted to set up colonies in order to compete with Spain, to find raw materials and markets for its own products, to increase commerce, and to provide a place for its unemployed

2

26D

people. The English also hoped to find gold, silver, the Northwest Passage, and to convert the Indians. 4. The Jamestown settlers faced malaria and other diseases, Indian attacks, internal bickering, and starvation. 5. In 1619, Jamestown moved from martial law to a system that gave the settlers some freedom. That year blacks and unmarried women were brought to the settlement, and the House of Burgesses was created. Jamestown became a real community with the arrival of women. The House of Burgesses was the first elected legislative assembly in the Americas. 6. The purpose of the Spanish colonies was more simply mercantilistic than the purpose of the English colonies. The government of the Spanish colonies was tightly controlled by the king and centralized in Spain. The English crown gave the founders of its colonies considerable freedom in their charters. The Virginia Company, in turn, granted its settlers a voice in the government of the colony.

CLOSE

To conclude the lesson, ask students: Why did the English government want a colony in North America? Why did the Virginia Company want to start a colony? Why did most colonists want to settle in North America? Which of all those reasons was most important?

Section 4 (pages 38–44)

The Puritans Come to New England

FOCUS

To introduce the lesson, write two column headings on the board: Pilgrims and Puritans. In each column, have the students supply words and phrases for the following item as they read: Meaning of group's name; attitude toward Church of England; reason for leaving England; location of original land grant; growth of colony; prominent leaders; attitude toward religious freedom.

INSTRUCT

Explain

The Puritans believed that you must be prepared for disappointment, yet have faith in your goals and yourself. Many historians and social scientists think that these Puritan ideas and ideals still influence the United States today.

★ Independent Activity

Checking Consistency Have students read the material under the heading "Squanto to the rescue," on p. 40 of their texts. Ask them to identify and evaluate any evidence presented. They should recognize the last sentence of the second paragraph as evidence: "No wonder the Pilgrims called him a 'special instrument sent of God for their good beyond their expectation.'" Have students check facts independently, compare findings to the story presented in the text, and write a short report presenting these findings.

Section Review Answers

Section 4, page 44

1. a) Puritans who separated from the Church of England. b) wanted to "purify" the church of England and were persecuted for their beliefs. c) Separatists who founded Plymouth Colony in 1620. d) demanded religious conformity but gave Puritans a charter for Massachusetts Bay Colony. e) an Indian who helped the Pilgrims survive in New England. f) strong governor of Massachusetts Bay Colony. g) a pastor forced to leave Massachusetts because of his disagreements with the Puritans, founded Rhode Island in 1636. h) banished from Massachusetts for challenging the authority of the Puritan clergy. 2. All of these locations may be found on the map on page 43. 3. The Mayflower Compact, an agreement written by the Pilgrims before they settled in Plymouth, set up a government for the colony. It is often called the first American constitution and it worked well for the colony. 4. The Puritans had a sense of mission and a conviction that God would help them through all hazards. Their church provided a unity and organization that simplified the problems of organizing settlements. In addition, Puritan settlers were people of wealth and influence. 5. Roger Williams, banished from Massachusetts Bay Colony, founded Rhode Island as a colony that would welcome people of all religions, except Catholics. 6. Religion was a focus in Plymouth and Massachusetts Bay colonies, both of which were founded by dissenters from the Church of England. Rhode Island was founded to welcome religious diversity. The founders of New Haven Colony wanted stricter rules than were found in Massachusetts.

CLOSE

To conclude the lesson, discuss some of the myths about the Puritans. (For example, that they always wore black, prayed all the time, never drank, did not allow games or music, etc.) Ask: Where did these stereotypes of the Puritans come from? (From their fellow Englishmen at the time. If you want to show some of these sources to your students, use a concordance of Shakespeare's works to find all the references to Puritans in Shakespeare's plays, and read some of them to the class.)

Other Europeans in North America

FOCUS

To introduce the lesson, ask students: How are the Dutch presented in the text? Then read the following excerpt from the text: "If you had money or goods, the Dutch would trade with you. It didn't matter who you were or what you believed." How would you contrast the Dutch priorities with those of the Puritans?

INSTRUCT

Explain

The Dutch did little to attract small farmers to their colony; instead, they tried to set up large estates called *patroonships*. Only one patroonship was actually created, however.

☑ Writing Process Activity

Demonstrating Reasoned Judgment Tell students they will write an essay evaluating which of the colonies experienced the greatest initial success. With the class, create a chart for Massachusetts, New France, and New Netherland, including such information as leaders, purpose, types of settlers, and so forth. Tell students to use this chart to determine which colony to focus on. They should begin their essays with a thesis statement summarizing their main points about the colony. Have them revise for logical order and proofread for correct mechanics. Students can read their essays aloud and compare their evaluations.

Section Review Answers

Section 5, page 45

1. a) in 1608 he established the first permanent French settlement in America at Quebec. b) the Dutch governor of New Netherland (New York) when the British took over the colony. c) granted all the land between the Delaware River and the Connecticut River by his brother, King Charles II. 2. Louisbourg is on the map on page 69, in Nova Scotia. New Orleans is on the map on page 28. Albany, the Hudson River, and the Delaware River are on the map on page 54. New Sweden is shown by the area labeled "Swedes" on the map on page 54. 3. Dutch settlers were interested in making money, and they were quite tolerant because tolerance helped them to make profits. 4. The French colonies remained relatively small because only French Roman Catholics were allowed in the colony. The large tracts were granted to a few proprietors who rented out small strips in exchange for produce or for labor on their estates. Colonial officers were chosen in France and there was no representative assembly. In the courts there was no trial by jury. Dissenters were not allowed to become colonists.

CLOSE

To conclude the lesson, assign five students to play the parts of Dutch merchants discussing what their response should be to the Duke of York's call for the immediate surrender of the Dutch colony at Manhattan Island. What might be lost and what gained by a decision to yield to the English?

Extension Activity

To extend the lesson, have students review the list of themes on page 1 in their text. Ask students to write a paragraph or two identifying and explaining which theme they feel best represents this section of the chapter.

The Proprietary Colonies

FOCUS

To introduce the lesson, tell students that William Penn wished to create a "Holy Experiment" in Pennsylvania. Ask: What were Penn's goals for the colony? What were the goals of the proprietors of Georgia? What sort of colony did the proprietors of Maryland wish to create? Were any of these new colonies as successful in reaching their goals as the Massachusetts Bay Colony? Why or why not?

INSTRUCT

Explain

During the early years of the Pennsylvania colony, relations with the local Delaware Indians were quite friendly. Penn, who even learned the Delaware language, was careful that settlers did not seize land but instead bought it from the Indians. Nonetheless, by 1755 the western part of the colony was deep in war with the Indians.

❀ Cooperative Learning Activity

Making Comparisons Break the class into small groups. Tell students that they will prepare a report on the role of religion in the New World colonies using the information in Chapter 2 of their texts. Explain that reports will be divided into three sections: Spanish colonies, New England colonies, and proprietary colonies. Have group members decide who will prepare each section of their report. For each section, have students write four to eight paragraphs and prepare one visual aid, such as a map or time line. Have group members review the completed report and then discuss how well the group functioned in preparing it, what was done well, and what could be improved.

Section Review Answers

Section 6, page 48

1. a) Quaker founder of Pennsylvania. b) influential English philosopher. c) English soldier and reformer, founded Georgia. d) a Puritan sect that opposed the Church of England, rejected religious ceremony, and emphasized equality and pacifism. 2. A proprietary colony was one that the king had turned over to a proprietor, who was usually a friend of the king. The proprietor, not the king, then chose the governor, set up courts, collected a tax, and managed the province as a business venture. 3. Both the Quakers of Pennsylvania and the proprietors of Georgia found it difficult to govern their colonies because of their ideals. The Quakers' specific problem was their pacifism; they refused to fight, even after an Indian war disrupted the western part of their colony. The Georgia proprietors planned to settle criminals, debtors, and drunkards in their colony, giving them a chance for new life. The proprietors had a very detailed plan for the colony's economy and planned to maintain tight control over the settlers. However, the economic plan was not suited to actual conditions in Georgia. Both the Quakers and the Georgia proprietors were challenged by other groups in the colonies, and both groups eventually lost control of the colonies they had established.

CLOSE

To conclude the lesson, ask students: How did religion in Pennsylvania compare to religion in Massachusetts? Refer them to page 39. Discuss the disastrous effects of idealism on the frontier.

Chapter Review Answers
Focusing on Ideas

1. Use the text to compare the four items. 2. Rise of the strong Tudor rulers; the English "sea dogs"; persistence of English settlers despite enormous hardships; inflation in Spain resulting from the rapid increase of specie; the defeat of the Spanish Armada. 3. Good planning: Organization helped the Puritans of Massachusetts Bay and the Quakers in Pennsylvania. Bad planning: The Georgia colony; Locke's elaborate scheme of government for the Carolinas, etc. Good luck: The arrival of Squanto; help from Indians; Rolfe's finding of tobacco as a "money crop"; outstanding leaders; etc. Bad luck: Fight with Spain delaying help for Roanoke colony; swampy ground at Jamestown; outbreak of infectious diseases; hostility of Indians in some places; etc. 4. Royal colonies: martial law, strict discipline, governed by people sent by the founding company, comprised mostly of seekers of religious freedom. Proprietary colonies: managed as a business venture; "proprietors" appointed governor, set up laws and courts, and collected land tax from settlers; some self-government.

Taking a Critical Look

1. Settlers were recruited by false advertising. Rumors of dangers may have deterred others from leaving Europe. 2. Puritans escaped religious persecution, yet did not tolerate other religions. So Roger Williams founded Rhode Island for free thinkers. Connecticut's government allowed voting without church membership.

Your Region in History

1–2. Answers will vary depending on your region. Consult your local library or historical society for books on the early history of the area.

Historical Facts and Figures

Students' paragraphs will vary but should focus on one group of colonies and include the dates and reasons why the colonies were founded.

Chapter 2

Focusing the Chapter: Have students identify the chapter logo. Discuss what unit theme the logo might symbolize. Then ask students to skim the chapter to identify other illustrations or titles that relate to this theme.

An Assortment of Colonies

The first Europeans to settle in America were the Spaniards. It was nearly 100 years before other Europeans joined them on the North American continent. The Spanish pioneers came for God, gold, and glory. They created an American empire that lasted 300 years.

The nearer the Indians were to centers of Spanish settlement like Mexico City or Lima, the more their own cultures were replaced by the language, the religion, and the politics imported from Spain. But there were remote areas that the Spaniards did not reach for a long time. Until 1700, in the jungles of northern Guatemala Mayan priests worshiped undisturbed! In the Amazon basin today there are Indians still untouched by Western civilization. But the Spanish wanted to convert all the Indians to their Spanish ways. And, on the whole, they were surprisingly successful.

When the English came, they never tried to make Englishmen out of Indians. Instead they saw the Indians as part of the wilderness that they aimed to clear away. The English came for many reasons. To them the American colonies were an assortment of dreams and hopes and fears. English settlers thought anything was possible here, and they were not far wrong. Some came with definite plans, others with troubled consciences. Some came as charity cases, owing everything to a few rich people in London. Some came simply for profit. Others came seeking refuge. All would become Americans.

Besides the Spanish and the English, the French, the Dutch, and the Swedes all founded colonies in North America. Each of these differed from the others. Whether a settlement died or lived and how it grew depended on many things. Much depended on the climate and the soil and the animals and the Indians. Much depended on government policies. Much depended on whether the settlers had planned, and what they had planned, and how quickly they could learn what the continent had to teach. And much depended on luck.

Multicultural Connection: The Spanish brought the first Asian immigrants to the Americas— the Filipinos. In 1763 a group of Filipinos settled in the bayous of St. Malo near New Orleans, Louisiana. They jumped ship in Mexico to escape the harsh conditions aboard Spanish galleons and traveled northward to St. Malo. Others escaped directly from Spanish galleons headed for Louisiana.

This document which Indians sent to the Spanish court protested the burdens of the encomienda.

See "Lesson Plan," p. 26C.

1. The Spanish Empire

Vast stretches of what is now the United States were explored by the Spaniards. Their forts and missions dotted the Spanish borderlands which stretched from Florida, Georgia, and the Carolinas westward along the Gulf Coast, across Arizona and New Mexico and on into California. The first traders and settlers from the United States arrived in New Mexico and California in the 1820s. There they found a Spanish-American society that had existed for 200 years. And there the Spanish settlements have left their mark to this day.

The control of the Indians. The settlers, the church, and the crown all competed for power in the Spanish colonies. At first the conquistadores who had come from Spain ruled them all.

These men came to get rich quick. They enslaved the Indians, but both the church and the crown objected. So a new system was devised called the *encomienda* (from a Spanish word meaning to entrust). By the encomienda the king "entrusted" to a Spanish settler a group of Indian families. The Indians had to pay tribute to the Spanish settler. This tribute was either in the form of the crops they grew or in days of forced labor. Many times the encomienda was little better than slavery.

The kings of Spain feared that the lords of the encomiendas were becoming too rich and too independent. So over many years the crown slowly reduced the power of the encomiendas. Meanwhile diseases brought by the Europeans—smallpox, typhoid, and measles—were killing off the Indian population. At first there were about 50 million Indians in the areas the

Continuity and Change: Conflict Explain to students that the encomienda and hacienda are two types of economic systems that involved the control of, and were based upon, the labor of a specific population. Examples of similar systems include, the manorial system of the Middle Ages and the plantation system of the American South before the Civil War. These systems find their roots in the ancient Roman system of the *latifundia*. (See page 324.)

Spanish Borderlands about 1780

← Kino
← Serra
☦ Mission and Fort
✝ Mission

0 ————— 500 Miles
0 ————— 500 Kilometers

Spanish conquered. By 1700 this number fell to some 4 million Indians. The encomiendas naturally lost their value without Indians to work them.

As the encomienda system disappeared, its place was taken by another kind of forced labor on the large estates called *haciendas*. In theory, the Indians were not slaves, but they usually became indebted to the owner of the hacienda and were not allowed to leave. Still, the landowner had reason to keep the families well enough fed so they could do their work. The poor Indian farmer had become a "peon"— enslaved by debt.

Colonial government. The Spanish king thought of the colonies as his personal property. He ruled through the Supreme Council of the Indies, which remained in Spain. That Council had absolute power over colonial life. The head of the government in America was the viceroy.

Spanish policy aimed to make the colonies benefit the mother country. The colony was supposed to produce only what Spain needed and to buy everything that it needed from Spain. Thus the mother country profited both ways. This policy was called *mercantilism*. It was followed by all the countries that planted colonies in America. Unlike England, Spain strictly enforced this policy. The Council organized an elaborate system of control.

The Spanish king and Spanish churchmen believed it was their sacred duty to convert the Indians to the Roman Catholic church. To accomplish this, they organized missions. Each mission was a complete Indian settlement including a church, shops, farms, and livestock, all overseen by a few monks. Some missions, like the worst encomiendas, offered the Indians a kind of slavery. Others were sincere, saintly efforts to bring the Indians into a Christian community of brotherly love.

The church early declared itself against the

enslavement of the Indians but did not oppose the use of black slaves. As the Indian population declined—and in some areas disappeared—black slaves from Africa took their place. At the end of the colonial period, in the 1820s, in Spanish America there were 750,000 blacks in a total population of 17 million.

⊕ *Settling the Spanish borderlands.*

(p. 28) Since the Spanish feared that someone else would occupy the borderlands, they made it a point to settle there whenever it appeared another country might move in. They tried to hold the territory by setting up Catholic missions and army forts. The first Spanish settlement in the borderlands was built in 1565 at St. Augustine, Florida. At a fort there, a force of soldiers with their families was stationed. St. Augustine remained a Spanish settlement until 1821.

The Spanish moved into New Mexico mainly to convert the Indians. Missionaries were followed by the settlers who founded Santa Fe in 1609. When the Indians revolted in 1680, all the Europeans were forced to flee. They did not return until Spanish soldiers retook the area in the 1690s. Anglo-Americans, who came in the 1800s, remained a minority in New Mexico as late as 1928.

Missionaries, led by Father Eusebio Francisco Kino, entered Arizona in the late 1600s. In Texas, a mission was founded at El Paso in 1659. Six other missions and two forts were set up in Texas between 1712 and 1721. The Spanish advanced into California after Russian explorers and fur trappers began to show up there. Beginning in 1769 the Spanish built a string of missions and forts to protect California against the Russians.

The pioneer missionary was the brave and learned Father Junípero Serra. Born on the Spanish island of Mallorca, he became a Franciscan monk and was sent to Mexico City. He founded San Diego mission, the first of 21 missions on the California coast. Then he helped found missions at San Gabriel, San Luis Obispo, Santa Clara, and San Francisco. Father Serra was a living example of charity. He stood up for the Indians against the Spanish army ⍑

The Spanish mission and presidio at San Francisco were founded in 1776. Louis Choris, a Frenchman, made this lithograph of Indians dancing outside the California mission of San Francisco in 1813. He may have based his work on an earlier painting that has now disappeared. The priests watch from the left in front of the mission, a characteristically low building made of sun-dried bricks covered with stucco.

The Bancroft Library, University of California, Berkeley

⍑ Multicultural Connection: One of the best known of the 16th-century human rights advocates was Bartoloméde las Casas. He had come to Hispaniola in 1502 and later participated in the conquest of Cuba. Although he owned an *encomienda*, he later became a priest and denounced the harsh treatment of Indians by the *encomenderos*. In his several books and in his speeches, Father Las Casas documented abuses of the Native Americans and asked the king to protect them.

commanders. He walked the long miles from one mission to another to counsel the missionaries and to protect the Indians.

The Spanish settler. Nearly all Spaniards who came to America were men. Unmarried girls in Spain were strictly supervised by their families and were not allowed to come to America alone. The young Spanish settlers here married Indian women. And there grew up in the Spanish lands an interesting racially mixed society.

These Spanish and mestizo (mixed blood) communities that arose before 1800 in New Mexico, California, and Arizona were small. Far from the chief Spanish settlements in Mexico, they had little contact with the outside world. They lived on what they could raise, grow, or catch. By 1810 in New Mexico there were 35,000 Spanish and mestizos raising corn, onions, peas, beans, wheat, red peppers, and sheep. Many of them had become peons like those in Mexico.

In California, too, there were a few thousand Spanish and mestizos. They raised horses, cows, and sheep, and grew grapes, figs, oranges, and olives near the missions and the forts. In the missions, the Indians were taught Spanish ways of building, farming, and worshiping. But they were not allowed to leave these mission "schools." They were forever students of the friars. The economic growth of California would come only after Mexico declared independence from Spain in 1821.

📝 ***Results of the Spanish conquests.*** The Spanish cut off the development of the Indian civilizations. In place of Mayan, Aztec, and Incan culture the Spanish built European-style cities. In Mexico City and Lima they set up universities and printing presses. They published learned books. They erected beautiful cathedrals. Spain's achievements and the wealth sent back to Spain led other countries to start their own colonies.

In the 1500s this overseas empire made Spain the most powerful nation in Europe. The riches pouring in from overseas tempted Spanish kings to extend their empire across Europe. Glutted with gold and silver from abroad, the Spanish rulers overlooked what their people needed at home. The growth of Spain's overseas empire became a cause of the decline of Spain.

See "Section 1 Review answers," p. 26C.

Section 1 Review

1. Identify or explain: encomienda, hacienda, Father Serra, Supreme Council of the Indies.
2. Locate: St. Augustine, the Spanish borderlands.
3. Describe the Spanish policy toward the Indians.
4. What was the aim of Spanish colonial policy? What was this policy called?
5. How did wealth from the empire affect Spain?
6. **Critical Thinking: Predicting Consequences.** If the Indian population had not declined, would the African slave trade have developed?

See "Lesson Plan," p. 26C.

2. A great and victorious England

In the history of the United States the English colonies loomed larger than the colonies of other nations. Despite the early Spanish, Dutch, French, and Swedish settlements within the present borders of our nation, the English culture has dominated the land. Before England tried to rival Spain in America, England had to challenge Spain in Europe.

The Tudors transform England. A strong England needed a strong monarch. But until almost 1500 England was ruled by petty lords who fought with each other. The country was in a state of anarchy in 1485 when Henry Tudor (Henry VII) defeated Richard III in the battle at Bosworth. This began the reign of the Tudors, who unified the country and gave it great leaders. Tudor monarchs were intelligent, skillful, and ruthless. Henry VIII had many wives but a single love for England. Wishing to run the church himself, he left the Roman Catholic church and made himself head of a new English (Episcopal) church. His brilliant daughter, Queen Elizabeth I, made England a leader of the Protestant states of Europe.

📝 See "Lesson Plan," p. 26C for **Writing Process Activity: Expressing Problems Clearly** relating to the Spanish colonial experience in North America.

The "Armada Portrait" of Queen Elizabeth I, painted about 1588, emphasizes the power and wealth of the monarch whose navy has just gained supremacy on the sea. The English fleet sails by Elizabeth's right window. In the other window you can see the storm-tossed Spanish Armada.

Queen Elizabeth was unusually learned for a monarch in those days. She read Latin and wrote poetry. But she never neglected the defense of her country. She never married, and so was called the Virgin Queen. She was afraid that if, as was the custom, her husband was the king of another country, England would be less independent. She saw that sea-power would build a strong nation. The navy would open the way to world-power. So she sent England's traders sailing to every corner of the globe.

Elizabeth's "sea-dogs" looted the Spanish treasure ships. The boldest of her loyal pirates was Sir Francis Drake. On one voyage Drake took his ship around the world and returned laden with treasure. Elizabeth got her full share.

The grand test came when King Philip II of Spain decided to invade England. He was a proud and stubborn man. He worked hard at his job as ruler. He studied the products of his empire, and the weakening of his enemies. Philip was angered at the looting by English

More from Boorstin: "On his return to England, Drake and his cousin presented to Queen Elizabeth their own illustrated log. This top-security document with so much information useful to foreign competitors must have been locked in a safe place, but it has never turned up. There seems to have been an embargo on other accounts of the great voyage. How else explain that so grand an adventure was not reported in print for more than a decade? (From *The Discoverers*)

sea-dogs and by English support of a revolt against Spanish rule in the Netherlands. Since he had once been married to Mary Tudor, the Catholic queen of England, he believed that he and not Elizabeth should sit on the English throne. In 1587, when Philip was putting together his navy to invade England, Sir Francis Drake bravely sailed right into the harbor of Cadiz and burned a large part of the Spanish fleet. Philip still did not give up. He collected another fleet, and in 1588 the Spanish "Armada" (from the Spanish word for army or fleet), the largest ever assembled in Europe till then, set sail up the English Channel. Certain of success, the Spanish called it the "Invincible Armada."

England was ready and waiting. Every armed ship had been called into action. The British fleet fought the Spaniards as they moved through the channel and prevented them from reaching England. The Spanish sailors were well disciplined and well led. But they were far from home ports and could not get fresh supplies. The odds were against them. To cap it all, gale winds blew up to help the British defenders. The Armada was driven north and finally tried to reach home by sailing around Scotland and Ireland. In the end, only half the grand Spanish fleet limped home.

The defeat of the Spanish Armada in 1588 was one of the decisive battles of history. It marked the beginning of the decline of Spain and the rise of England. For only another century was Spain to remain a major power. In the
❧ last fifteen years of Elizabeth's reign, England still feared invasion. But England seized the opportunity to take the lead from Spain. England's trade was growing, and new industries (such as the manufacture of woolens) were prospering. Inspired by poets like William Shakespeare, the English set out to be heroes and pioneers—

This happy breed of men, this little world,
This precious stone set in the silver sea . . .

Gilbert, Raleigh, and Hakluyt. Patriots, dreamers, and adventurers, they went out to plant colonies overseas. Sir Humphrey Gilbert,
like many Elizabethans, was not only a man of action but a learned man as well. In 1566 he wrote *A Discourse of a Discoverie for a New Passage to Cataia* (Cathay) to persuade Queen Elizabeth to start settlements in the New World near the Northwest Passage to Asia. (They were sure the passage existed somewhere—but they never found it.) These settlements would extend England's trade and give jobs to the unemployed. Gilbert himself would lead the way, and he would pay for the expedition.

In 1578 the queen gave him England's first colonial charter. An expedition in 1578–1579 failed to establish a colony. In June 1583 Gilbert set forth with five ships to try his luck once again. Since he did not find a suitable place that summer, he decided to go home and try again the following year. But on the trip back to England his ship sank in a storm, and he and all the crew were lost. Gilbert had failed, but he was the pathfinder of the British Empire.

Gilbert's dream did not die with him. Others agreed that England must plant overseas colonies. And they found the ideal advertiser. A patriotic and industrious geographer, Richard Hakluyt, collected accounts of *The Principall Navigations, Voiages and Discoveries of the English Nation.* These three volumes told exciting tales of English heroes overseas. They encouraged others to serve their country by building an empire across the world.

Gilbert's half brother Walter Raleigh wanted to pursue the dream of a colony in America. The dashing, brilliant Raleigh was one of the most remarkable men of a remarkable generation. Educated at Oxford, he wrote good poetry and lively history. He even turned out a *History of the World.* And he too was a man of action if there ever was one. It is no wonder that he was a favorite of Queen Elizabeth's. In 1584 she granted him the right to start a settlement in America.

When Raleigh's men discovered Roanoke Island in Pamlico Sound, North Carolina, they said it was blessed with friendly Indians and fertile soil. It seemed perfect for an English colony. Raleigh then persuaded Hakluyt to write a *Discourse on Western Planting* to convince Queen Elizabeth to "plant" a royal colony there.

❧ See "Lesson Plan," p. 26D for **Cooperative Learning Activity: Formulating Questions** in which students "interview" Elizabeth I.

National Portrait Gallery, London

This portrait of Sir Walter Raleigh and his son Wat is dated 1602. A year later, on the death of Queen Elizabeth, Raleigh was imprisoned in the Tower of London.

The thrifty Elizabeth refused to risk her own money on the project, but she found less costly ways to please Raleigh. She knighted him and allowed him to name the settlement "Virginia" after her, the Virgin Queen.

In 1585 Sir Walter sent out his own expedition of about 100 men and boys to found his colony on Roanoke Island. After suffering through a terrible winter, the settlers gladly left when Sir Francis Drake with a fleet of 29 ships came by in the spring. Drake was on the way home after raids in the Spanish West Indies and at St. Augustine.

Still Raleigh did not give up. Having spent so much of his own fortune, now he had to enlist other people's money. He did this by the novel device of a "joint stock" company. He persuaded many people to buy "shares" of stock. In this way the risks in the venture could be divided. People without much money could still invest and have a share of the profit. Investors divided the profits (or losses) according to the number of shares they had bought.

With Hakluyt's help in advertising, Raleigh raised enough money to send out in 1587 a group of men, women, and children. Again they settled on Roanoke Island. The next year Raleigh and his fellow "adventurers" (as the investors were called) had a fleet of seven ships ready to take supplies to the colony. But they were stopped by the threat of the Spanish Armada. No supply ships went out in 1588, and none sailed the next year. Not until 1590 did help reach Roanoke. There they found an empty island and only the word CROATOAN written on a post and CRO on a tree. No one was sure what it meant. But the rescuers thought it was the name of the island to which the settlers had fled. Because of bad weather the relief expedition could not reach the island of Croatan. No one ever saw any of the Roanoke settlers again. They came to be called the "Lost Colony." Their true fate remained a mystery. But the Croatan Indians have a legend that the settlers became members of their tribe. Family names of 41 of the colonists survived within the tribe.

See "Section 2 Review answers," p. 26D.

Section 2 Review

1. Identify: the Tudors, Philip II, Humphrey Gilbert, Walter Raleigh, Richard Hakluyt, Croatoan, Lost Colony.
2. Locate: Cadiz, the Netherlands, London.
3. What was a joint stock company? Why was it used?
4. **Critical Thinking: Identifying Central Issues.** Why was the Spanish Armada's defeat important?

See "Lesson Plan," p. 26D.

3. The planting of Virginia

Much had been learned from the failure of the Roanoke colony. Raleigh and Gilbert, helped by Hakluyt's advertising, had laid the groundwork for a British Empire in America.

At the end of Elizabeth's reign, England had the power and the will to found colonies in the New World. In a great burst of activity from 1606 to 1637, England planted Virginia, Maryland, and New England as well as colonies in Bermuda and the British West Indies.

Reasons for colonies. There were many reasons why England wanted to establish colonies. There was the lure of gold and silver. English sailors hoped at last to find a water passage through the North American continent to the rich trade of China and the Indies. And, of course, there was the chance to challenge Spain in North America!

The English hoped, too, that they would find in the New World the staple raw materials that they were spending their precious gold and silver to buy from other European countries. England was using up its own forests, and timber was needed for the navy. The settlers in America would be a market for British goods, especially for woolens. Commerce with the colonies would support a growing navy and merchant marine.

In England the rise in sheep farming had forced many men and women off the land. These jobless displaced people were flocking to the cities and increasing the crime there. If they were sent overseas, they could make their own way. And they could help convert the Indians to Protestant Christianity.

The unknown land. Even with all these motives, most people still did not want to emigrate. Why should they leave their familiar homeland

John Visscher's 1616 engraving of London Bridge shows a crowded city with no grass or trees. Promoters of the colonies emphasized the healthy life and open space to be found in America.

The British Library

✂ Critical Thinking Activity: Distinguishing False from Accurate Images What did the average European think America might look like? Using a blank sheet of paper and pencils, have students create their own imaginary maps of America in the seventeenth century. Ask students what they had to consider when creating their maps. How do their ideas about America compare to those of settlers in the 1600s? Would their depiction of America have encouraged settlement or discouraged it?

for the dangers of an unknown America? Most of the facts they were told about the new country were wrong. Some of these imagined facts were printed because honest promoters did not know the truth. But much of what was printed was a sales pitch. The fantastic advertising brochures invented "facts" to help sell land in America. People who had invested in the American land knew that if nobody went out there it would remain a wilderness. And their land would be worthless.

So the promoters drew imaginary pictures, using ancient legends mixed with their wildest hopes and fondest dreams. The weather in America, they said, was always sunny. The oranges, lemons, apples, pears, peaches, and apricots were "so delicious that whoever tastes them will despise the insipid watery taste of those we have in England." The American venison was so juicy that English people would barely recognize it. The fish were large and easy to catch. In America there were no diseases—and no crowds. Everybody stayed young and everybody could live like a king. Come to this American paradise!

The real America was very different. Of course the Europeans heard rumors about the Indians, and what they heard was not encouraging. The "savages" of America, it was said, were not content merely to kill their victims. There were stories that they liked to torture their captives and even to eat them. Some Indian cruelties were supposed to be too horrible to tell.

It is surprising that English men and women dared to come to America at all. For in addition to all the real threats of a "hideous and desolate wilderness," they were haunted by horror stories and nightmares. Out there in Virginia the cheery advertising boasts were not much help. And it is still more surprising that, in spite of all their wrong "facts," the settlers in Virginia and elsewhere along the Atlantic Coast not only survived but managed to build lasting colonies.

Settling Jamestown.

The first successful colony that these English people founded was in Virginia. A joint stock company named the Virginia Company of London (often called the London Company) was granted all the westward-stretching land between what is now the northern end of New Jersey and the middle of South Carolina.

In 1603 King James I succeeded Queen Elizabeth on the throne. He was the son of Mary Queen of Scots, who had been executed by Queen Elizabeth. With his passion for theories, he was as different as possible from the practical Virgin Queen. He could not get along with Parliament and was known as "the most learned fool in Christendom."

James I gave the Virginia Company its grant in 1606. The company quickly sent out three ships. This time the settlers avoided Roanoke

Advertisements glowed with the wonders—real and imaginary—of the New World. Printers at this time often used a letter something like an "f" where we use an "s."

North Carolina Collection, University of North Carolina Library

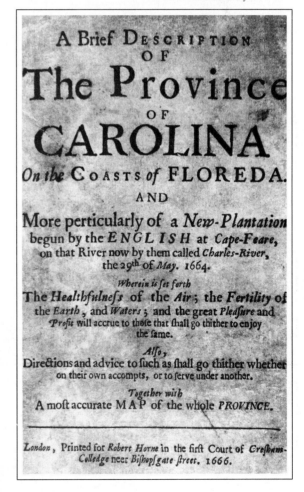

See "Lesson Plan," p. 26D for **Writing Process Activity: Distinguishing False from Accurate Images** relating to advertising and the New World.

THE INCONVENIENCIES
THAT HAVE HAPPENED TO SOME PER-
SONS WHICH HAVE TRANSPORTED THEMSELVES

from *England* to *Virginia*, vvithout prouisions necessary to suſtaine themſelues, hath greatly hindred the *Progreſſe of that noble Plantation*: For preuention of the like diſorders heereafter, that no man ſuffer, either through ignorance or miſinformation; it is thought re- quiſite to publiſh this ſhort declaration: wherein is contained a particular of ſuch neceſ- ſaries, as either priuate families or ſingle perſons ſhall haue cauſe to furniſh themſelues with, for their better ſupport at their firſt landing in Virginia; whereby alſo greater numbers may receiue in part directions how to prouide themſelues.

Apparrell.

	li.	s.	d.
One Monmouth Cap	∞	01	10
Three falling bands	—	01	03
Three ſhirts	—	07	c6
One waſte-coate	—	02	02
One ſuite of Canuaſe	—	07	06
One ſuite of Frize	—	10	00
One ſuite of Cloth	—	15	00
Three paire of Iriſh ſtockins	—	04	—
Foure paire of ſhooes	—	c8	08
One paire of garters	—	00	10
One doozen of points	—	00	03
One paire of Canuaſe ſheets	—	08	00
Seuen ells of Canuaſe, to make a bed and boulſter, to be filled in *Virginia* 8.s.			
One Rug for a bed 8.s. which with the bed ſeruing for two men, halfe is	c8	00	
Fiue ells coorſe Canuaſe, to make a bed at Sea for two men, to be filled with ſtraw, iiij.s.			
One coorſe Rug at Sea for two men, will coſt vj.s. is for one	05	00	
	04	00	00

Apparrell for one man, and ſo after the rate for more.

Victuall.

	li.	s.	d.
Eight buſhels of Meale	02	00	00
Two buſhels of peaſe at 3.s.	—	06	00
Two buſhels of Oatemeale 4.s. 6.d.	—	09	00
One gallon of *Aquauite*	—	02	06
One gallon of Oyle	—	03	06
Two gallons of Vineger 1.s.	—	02	00
	03	03	00

For a whole yeere for one man, and ſo for more after the rate.

Armes.

	li.	s.	d.
One Armour compleat, light	—	17	00
One long Peece, fiue foot or fiue and a halfe, neere Musket bore	01	02	—
One ſword	—	05	—
One belt	—	01	—
One bandaleere	—	01	06
Twenty pound of powder	—	18	00
Sixty pound of ſhot or lead, Piſtoll and Gooſe ſhot	—	05	00
	03	09	06

For one man, but if halfe of your men haue armour it is ſufficient ſo that all haue Peeces and ſwords.

Tooles.

	li.	s.	d.
Fiue broad howes at 2.s. a piece	—	10	—
Fiue narrow howes at 16.d. a piece	—	06	c8
Two broad Axes at 3.s. 8.d. a piece	—	07	c4
Fiue felling Axes at 18.d. a piece	—	07	06
Two ſteele hand ſawes at 16.d. a piece	—	02	08
Two two-hand ſawes at 5.s. a piece	—	10	—
One whip-ſaw, ſet and filed with box, file, and wreſt	—	10	—
Two hammers 12.d. a piece	—	02	00
Three ſhouels 18.d. a piece	—	04	06
Two ſpades at 18.d. a piece	—	03	—
Two augers 6.d. a piece	—	01	00
Sixe chiſſels 6.d. a piece	—	03	00
Two percers ſtocked 4.d. a piece	—	00	c8
Three gimlets 2.d. a piece	—	00	c6
Two hatchets 21.d. a piece	—	03	c6
Two froues to cleaue pale 18.d.	—	03	00
Two hand-bills 20. a piece	—	03	c4
One grindleſtone 4.s.	—	04	00
Nailes of all ſorts to the value of	02	00	—
Two Pickaxes	—	c3	—
	c6	02	08

For a family of 6. perſons and ſo after the rate for more.

Houſhold Implements.

	li.	s.	d.
One Iron Pot	—	00	07
One kettle	—	06	—
One large frying-pan	—	02	06
One gridiron	—	01	06
Two ſkillets	—	05	—
One ſpit	—	02	—
Platters, diſhes, ſpoones of wood	—	04	—
	01	c8	00

For a family of 6. perſons, and ſo for more or leſſe After the rate.

For Suger, Spice, and fruit, and at Sea for 6. men — ∞ 12 06

So the full charge of Apparrell, Victuall, Armes, Tooles, and houſhold ſtuffe, and after this rate for each perſon, will amount vnto about the ſumme of — 12 10 00

The paſſage of each man is — 06 00 00

The fraight of theſe prouiſions for a man, will bee about halfe a Tun, which is — 01 10 —

So the whole charge will amount to about — 20 00 00

Nets, hookes, lines, and a tent muſt be added, if the number of people be greater, as alſo ſome kine.

And this is the vſuall proportion that the Virginia *Company* doe beſtow vpon their Tenants which they ſend.

Whoſoeuer tranſports himſelfe or any other at his owne charge vnto *Virginia*, ſhall for each perſon ſo tranſported before Midſummer 1625. haue to him and his heires for euer fifty Acres of Land vpon a firſt, and fifty Acres vpon a ſecond diuiſion.

Imprinted at London by FELIX KYNGSTON. 1622.

This 1622 English handbill advises families leaving for America to take the necessary tools and supplies to avoid "inconveniencies."

Island and shallow Pamlico Sound and sailed instead into the broad, deep Chesapeake Bay. The settlers went up a river about 32 miles, landed on a peninsula, and began to build a town. Both the river and the town they named after their king.

In selecting the spot for Jamestown these settlers showed poor judgment. The site was low and swampy—just what the company had warned against. But the 104 men and boys who landed in this wilderness on May 23, 1607, somehow thought the site would be easy to defend against the Indians and the Spanish. From the swampy ground came mosquitoes carrying malaria, and from their well water came dysentery. They would have been better off if they had faced their enemies on dry and solid ground.

The council that governed the colony had no head. Members wasted time arguing, while no one had the power to make decisions. Disrupted by its squabbling council and weakened by disease, Jamestown was also menaced by Indian raids. These raids were brought on by rash acts of the colonists themselves.

Still, the colony was blessed with a remarkable leader, Captain John Smith. He had been a merchant's poor apprentice in England. But adventure was his middle name, so he had joined armies and fought in distant Hungary and Turkey. He had the bad luck to be made a slave in Turkey. But he escaped, returned to England, and joined the new Virginia Company.

Smith saved the settlers from themselves. With his courage and his wide experience he knew how to stop the settlers' quarreling. He worked to keep peace with the Indians. The Indians traded him the corn needed to feed the settlers till they could raise their own crops. Even then, more than half the colonists died of fever, starvation, or the arrows of Indians before the winter was over.

Fortunately, the company back in London was committed to make the colony succeed. In 1608 they sent out new recruits—men, women, and children—and supplies. In 1609 alone about 400 colonists arrived. But then the colony lost its leader when John Smith was in-

jured by a gunpowder explosion and was forced to return home. The woods were full of game and the soil was fertile for growing corn. But without their leader the colonists proved unable to feed themselves. The bitter winter of 1609–1610 was called "the Starving Time." There were ghastly tales of cannibalism. Only 60 of the 500 settlers were left when spring arrived.

Over the next years the company still poured in settlers and supplies. But the colony could not be self-supporting unless they could produce something they could sell. What they found was quite a surprise. Earlier, the Spanish had brought tobacco to Europe from America, and the English had quickly taken to smoking. They smoked not only because they enjoyed it. Doctors at the time said it would cure almost any disease. In 1612 John Rolfe, who later married the Indian princess Pocahontas, learned

This painting shows Pocahontas, also known as Matoaka, in English clothes. She married John Rolfe and died in England in 1617 just as she was about to return to America.

National Portrait Gallery, Smithsonian Institution

More from Boorstin: "It was claimed that smoking tobacco would heal gout and ague, cure hangovers, and reduce fatigue and hunger. The 'Jamestown Weed' (*datura stramonium*), which modern medicine has proved to be sedative and antispasmodic when taken in small doses, and narcotic and poisonous when taken in larger doses, was praised for its 'cooling' effect." (From *The Americans: The Colonial Experience*)

how to grow a kind of tobacco in Virginia that English people especially liked. Because the English were eager to buy this crop, the colony now finally had found a solid economic base.

A colony established. By 1619 the Virginia colony was well on its way to success. The company was sending out hundreds of craftsmen and laborers. New directors in London then decided to give the settlers more freedom. Up to then the colonists had lived under strict martial law. For example, every man and woman had to attend church twice daily and could be fined a full day's pay for one absence, whipped for a second, and put in jail six months for a third. Strict discipline helped the colony survive the early years. But it would scare away new settlers. The company sent out a new governor with orders to let the people work for themselves as well as for the company. The governor allowed the colonists to elect an assembly to help make their own laws. The House of Burgesses, as Virginians called it, met at Jamestown on July 30, 1619. It was the first elected legislative assembly in America.

That same year saw the arrival of two groups who played a leading role in the colony's future. Jamestown was changed from a military outpost into a full community when the Virginia Company sent out from London a group of "respectable maidens" who soon married men of their choice. About the same time a Dutch ship arrived carrying twenty blacks. These were probably not slaves but indentured servants (like many of the white settlers). An indentured servant was a person who had signed an "indenture," an agreement to serve a master for a certain number of years. (It was called an "indenture" because the two parts of each agreement—one for master, one for servant—were indented to fit together.) Outright slavery probably did not appear in the English colonies until later.

In the next few years the company sent many more settlers to Virginia—often without the needed supplies. Some 5000 arrived between 1619 and 1624. And yet by 1624 the total population in the colony had increased by only 200. Sickness killed most of the newcomers,

starvation took some, and others fell to the tomahawk. In 1622 the Indians attacked in an all-out try to drive the European invaders from their land. The colony lost 350 lives (including John Rolfe), and the settlers were pushed back close to Jamestown.

The men running the Virginia Company included some of King James's opponents in Parliament. He used the problems of the company to persuade his judges to annul the company charter. The settlement now became a *royal colony* with its governor appointed by the king. But after a brief pause the legislative assembly was allowed to continue.

The London Company had founded the first permanent English settlement in America. Tobacco—its staple crop—gave the colony a firm economic base. And the settlers in Virginia had set the pattern of representative government for future English colonies. All this had been done at fearful cost in money and lives. But the Virginia experience—the successes and the failures—would save lives and light the way for later settlers.

See "Section 3 Review answers," p. 26D.

Section 3 Review

1. Identify or explain: John Smith, John Rolfe, the Starving Time, indentured servant.
2. Locate Jamestown.
3. Why did England want colonies?
4. What problems faced the Jamestown settlers?
5. What significant events happened in Virginia in 1619? Why was each important?
6. **Critical Thinking: Making Comparisons.** Contrast Spain's and England's colonies.

See "Lesson Plan," p. 26E.

4. The Puritans come to New England

The settlement of Virginia was mostly a business enterprise. Settlers of New England also hoped to make money. But their lives and their hopes were ruled by religion. The people who went there were called "Puritans" because they wanted to purify the Church of England. They wanted to do away with the colorful robes of priests, with prayer books, and even with altars. Some Puritans remained inside the Church of England and worked for reform there. Others were known as "Independents" or "Separatists." They went out of the church— separated from it.

The Pilgrims. Three centuries ago kings and queens believed that the religion of their people helped keep them loyal and obedient. Subjects who were allowed to make up their own minds about religion might also make up their own minds about politics—and even about whether to obey the king! James I began his reign by declaring that his subjects had to "conform" in religion or he would "harry them out of the land."

The Separatist congregations of some little villages in the east of England were harried until in 1608 they took refuge in Holland. That was the only country in Europe where complete religious freedom was allowed. But after they had lived there for a few years, they began to fear that their children would forget the customs and speech of England. These Separatists decided to move on to the new land of America. They were given permission by the London Company to settle in Virginia.

They went back to England, where they set out from Plymouth in the *Mayflower* on September 16, 1620, with 102 passengers. After a seven-week voyage in cramped quarters, they first sighted land in early November. They looked for a suitable place and finally landed on December 21, 1620. The winter was harsher than anything they had known in England.

Their pilot brought them by mistake to Cape Cod. They had no right to own the land there, for that required a *patent*, or land grant. They

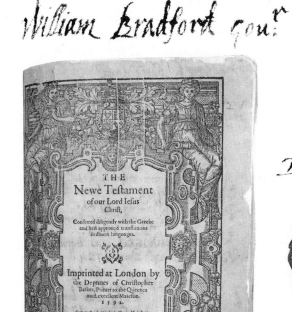

This New Testament title page (left) is from William Bradford's Bible. His autograph is above it. Bradford was one of the main leaders of the Pilgrims who settled in New England in 1620. Peregrine White, the first English child born in New England, slept in this cradle (below). His name and that of the Pilgrims comes from the Latin word meaning "to travel abroad."

Pilgrim Society, Plymouth, MA

had no power either to establish a government, for that required a charter.

But they had something far better. They had a plan to build a purified society, and they had a guide in the Bible. This was important, for in the mysterious New World you would surely be lost unless you had some plans of your own. If you had goals, they would guide and encourage you while you were discovering what America was really like. Your plans had to be definite, but not too definite. You had to be willing to change your plans when you ran into trouble, or when the New World did not offer what you expected. You had to be prepared for disappointment. Yet you had to have self-confidence, faith in your mission and in yourself. The Pilgrims and other Puritans had all this. They were equipped, too, with just the right combination of hopes and fears, optimism and pessimism, self-confidence and humility to be successful settlers. And this was one of the most fortunate coincidences in our history.

The Mayflower Compact.

When the Pilgrims reached Cape Cod, they were outside the boundaries where they had permission to settle. Some unruly passengers noticed this. They threatened "that when they came ashore they would use their own liberty, for none had power to command them, the patent they had being for Virginia." But the Mayflower leaders, anxious to land and begin their colony, could not tolerate a community without government. Why should their plans be spoiled by a few roughnecks?

So they decided on shipboard, then and there, to create a new government to serve their very special purposes. Their leaders included the steady William Bradford, who would be governor of Plymouth Colony for 31 years, and Captain Miles Standish, whom they had hired to head their militia. Like people making up rules for a club that already existed, they wrote out and signed an agreement, or covenant. This was the famous Mayflower Compact. In it they pledged allegiance to the king, combined themselves "into a civil body politic," and bound themselves to obey all the laws this new government might enact. They created an instant government. It worked surprisingly well for the infant colony, and later became the foundation for the state of Massachusetts.

Squanto to the rescue.

The Pilgrims and other Puritans thought God was on their side when they settled in the wilderness. And often it seemed that He was. The Pilgrims might all have died if a remarkable Indian had not come to help them.

Squanto was an Indian kidnapped a few years before by an English sea captain, who had sold him into slavery in Spain. He escaped to England, where he learned some English, and then returned to New England in 1619. There he found that his whole village had died of disease. Now, in March 1621, it was Squanto—of all the thousands of Indians in America—who happened to turn up in Plymouth! He knew enough English to act as an interpreter. And he showed the Pilgrims how to plant corn (which was not known in England), how to fertilize the soil, where to catch fish, and how to trap beaver. No wonder the Pilgrims called him a "special instrument sent of God for their good beyond their expectation."

The Plymouth Colony never grew very large, and in 1691 it was absorbed into the Massachusetts Bay Colony. But we still revere the Pilgrim Fathers as the first successful settlers of the New England shore, who began an American custom—finding a way of self-government for every occasion.

The Massachusetts Bay Colony.

Charles I's archbishop, William Laud, and other high officials within the established Church of England tried to force the Puritans to conform to the rules of the church. Many Puritans then made up their minds to leave England, and fortunately they had a place to go to. Some of them had received a charter from King James for a company that was allowed to create settlements in the Massachusetts Bay area in New England.

The most significant point about this charter was that it did not say where the company headquarters had to be. It did not say where the company should hold its meetings to admit new members, to select officers, or to make laws.

Enrichment Support File Topic

Continuity and Change: Conflict Tell students that by the early eighteenth century the friendly relationship between the colonists and the Indians was greatly eroded. This increasing conflict is illustrated by such events as King Philip's War (1675) and the Deerfield Massacre (1704). By 1810, the Indians of the northeast region of North America had lost nearly 48 million acres of territory to white settlers. (See pages 66 and 201.)

This meant that if the company headquarters was transferred from England to Massachusetts, the stockholders in Massachusetts would be able to run the company. Since they were settlers, it also meant that settlers would be governing themselves.

In 1629 the company members voted to transfer the company to Massachusetts Bay. Certain strong Puritans, leaders like John Winthrop, were now willing to go there. From the start, Massachusetts Bay was a self-governing colony.

One thousand settlers went out in the summer of 1630 and planted settlements around Massachusetts Bay. By the end of the first decade, 20,000 settlers had arrived. Among these, right from the start, were more people of means and influence than in any other group of colonists. When the settlers arrived, they soon founded settlements at Boston, Charlestown, Watertown, Lynn, Medford, Dorchester, and Roxbury.

The Puritan religion was admirably suited for settling the wilderness. A church (by which the Puritans meant the members of a congregation) would receive a grant of land from the Great and General Court (a meeting of the company). Then it would move as a group to a spot already selected and surveyed. There a village would be built around a meetinghouse with the fields scattered outside the village.

John Winthrop, whose portrait was painted by an unknown artist in England, provided strong leadership as governor of the Massachusetts Bay Colony.

American Antiquarian Society

A City upon a hill. The Puritans had a grand purpose in America. John Winthrop, who was to be their governor for many years, spoke to them on the boat coming over:

> We shall be as a City upon a hill, the eyes of all people are upon us; so that if we shall deal falsely with our god in this work we have undertaken and so cause him to withdraw his present help from us, we shall be made a story and a by-word through the world.

Winthrop was saying what many Americans then and since have felt. The American example could help shape the lives of people everywhere.

With their beliefs, it would have been difficult ✕ for the Puritans to fail. Even the Devil, who was a lively presence for them, could not really defeat them. Sooner or later, they knew, God always won. He would see that His own people were not destroyed. The troubles of this world—New England blizzards, Indian arrows, the plottings of enemies in England, or the crimes of their own people—never overwhelmed them. The Puritans were ready for what wilderness America demanded.

Rhode Island. The Puritans who settled Massachusetts Bay did not believe in religious freedom. They thought that they knew God's truth and that all reasonable men and women should be able to see that truth. If you disagreed with

✕ Critical Thinking Activity: Recognizing Ideologies What does John Winthrop's "City upon a hill" look like today? Have students list characteristics of the United States that they feel serve as a positive example to the rest of the world. Ask students to determine how closely their list comes to reflecting those qualities that John Winthrop envisioned in the seventeenth century.

them, you had the right to go away but not to stay in Massachusetts.

Roger Williams, the young pastor of the church in Salem, would not agree to the Puritan version of the truth, so he was banished from Massachusetts Bay. He made his way, in 1636, to Narragansett Bay. There he purchased a tract of land from the Indians and began the settlement we know as Rhode Island.

Rhode Island was a haven for independent thinkers. One who went there was the bright, brave, freethinking Anne Hutchinson. She had held meetings at her house in Boston to discuss the preacher's Sunday sermons. Then she had begun to put forth her own ideas. Soon she was disagreeing with some of the accepted doctrines of the churches of the Bay Colony and criticizing many of its ministers. So Mrs. Hutchinson was banished. She moved to Rhode Island. Later she settled in New York where, in 1643, she and all but one of her household were massacred by Indians.

The scornful Puritans in Massachusetts 📖 called the Rhode Island people "the Lord's debris." They sneered that if any man had lost his religion he would be sure to find it in some Rhode Island village. Still, Rhode Island grew and prospered as a refuge for liberty.

In the 1650s, Quakers (considered in Massachusetts the most dangerous of all Separatists) and Jews began to appear in the colony. The Jews formed their first congregation there in 1658. In 1763 they built the beautiful Touro Synagogue, which still stands in Newport. But Catholics were not welcomed even in Rhode Island. They were allowed to settle there but were not allowed to vote.

Other New England settlements. In 1636, men and women from several Massachusetts towns were granted permission to "transport themselves and their estates" westward to the Connecticut Valley, noted for its rich farmland. They were the first wave of the mighty overland movement to the West that marked American history for 200 years. In Connecticut the first settlers founded Hartford, Windsor, and Wethersfield.

Jack Spratt

Beautiful Touro Synagogue in Newport, Rhode Island, was designed by Peter Harrison.

📖 **More from Boorstin:** "The failure of New England Puritans to develop a theory of toleration, or even freely to examine the question, was not in all ways a weakness. It made their literature less rich and gave much of their writing a quaint and crabbed sound, but for a time at least, it was a source of strength. Theirs was not a philosophic enterprise; they were, first and foremost, community-builders." (From *The Americans: The Colonial Experience*)

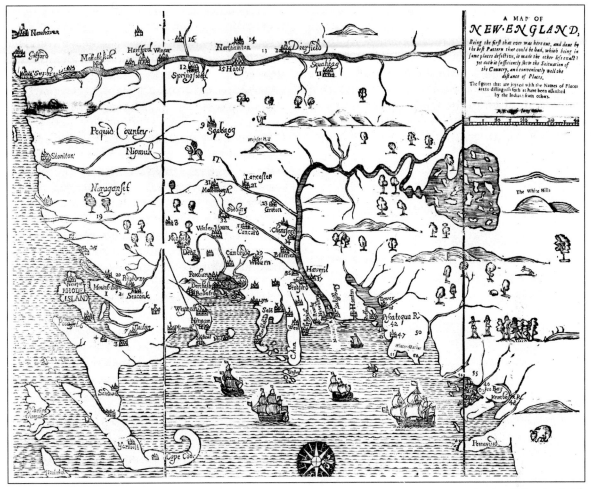

This 1677 woodcut by John Foster is the first such map made in the colonies. West is at the top. The map shows Puritan settlements stretching from Connecticut to Maine. The Merrimack River (center) and the Connecticut River (top) are featured.

In 1639 the Connecticut settlers adopted their own "Fundamental Orders." This was a frame of self-government with a governor, a legislative assembly, and courts. Voting was restricted to male property owners, as was customary at that time. To vote in Massachusetts Bay, you still had to be a member of the church, but not here. Features of the Fundamental Orders remained the basis of Connecticut's government long after it became a state.

Another group of settlers who left Massachusetts Bay founded the New Haven Colony. They had no real quarrel with the Bay Colony—except that it was not quite strict enough! They had come from England to start commerce here, and they could find no harbor to their taste in Massachusetts Bay. At New Haven they had the harbor they needed. They settled there in 1638. This colony attracted many of the wealthiest settlers who had yet come to America. But the location they had chosen was not as good as they had thought. The harbor was too shallow. And hemmed in by Connecticut, they lacked lands to produce goods to export. The New Haven Colony was absorbed by Connecticut in 1664.

Geography and History: Place Refer students to the map above. Ask: Which directions are at the bottom, the right, and the left of the map? (The bottom is east; right is north; left is south.) What feature seemed to be important to the founding of a colonial town? (Nearly all towns on the map are on the coast or on a river.) Why was this important? (Towns were founded on or near water to facilitate trade and communication; it took much longer to travel over land than over water in colonial America.)

Settlers also went north from the Massachusetts Bay Colony. Some moved into New Hampshire, which became a royal province in 1679. Others traveled to Maine where Sir Ferdinando Gorges had tried in vain to plant a colony. He wanted one, unlike Massachusetts Bay, that would be faithful to the king and the Anglican church. But Maine remained a province of Massachusetts until 1820.

See "Section 4 Review answers," p. 26E.

Section 4 Review

1. Identify or explain: Separatists, Puritans, Pilgrims, James I, Squanto, John Winthrop, Roger Williams, Anne Hutchinson.
2. Locate: Cape Cod, Plymouth, Rhode Island, Hartford, New Haven.
3. What was the Mayflower Compact? Why was it important?
4. What made the Puritans successful settlers?
5. Why was the Rhode Island Colony founded?
6. **Critical Thinking: Drawing Conclusions.** In which colonies were religious beliefs a central focus?

See "Lesson Plan," p. 26E.

5. Other Europeans in North America

Three centuries ago the kings and queens of Europe regarded as their own private property any lands that ships flying their flag discovered. They granted these lands as they pleased to settlers or trading companies. Vast tracts of land in America were sold for cash or given away to favorites by the States-General (parliament) of the Netherlands and by the English, French, and Swedish kings.

New France. Samuel de Champlain—expert navigator, student of science, brave explorer, earnest missionary—became the founder of New France in America. At Quebec in 1608 he planted the first permanent French settlement in the New World.

For the French that was only a foothold. From Quebec, their explorers, missionaries, fur trappers, and settlers moved up the St. Lawrence River, through the Great Lakes, and down the Mississippi. In time, they claimed an empire that stretched over a great arc—behind the English. The French Empire reached from New Orleans on the Gulf of Mexico to the powerful Canadian fortress, Louisbourg, on the Atlantic Ocean.

But while New France was vast in area, it remained small in population. The reasons are not hard to find. Only French Roman Catholics were allowed in the colony. The fierce Iroquois were a constant menace. Farming was difficult in this cold northern land. Though those who did migrate found that by hard work they could become comfortable and relatively prosperous, most French people did not want to leave home for this rugged, far-distant colony.

All of this still might not have stopped settlers from coming. But the French crown, unlike the English, did not allow those who were discontented at home to go abroad. The English monarchs wisely let their dissenters leave. The French rulers insisted on keeping their Protestants, called Huguenots, at home where they could be watched and punished. As a result, by 1700 the English population along the Atlantic seaboard had grown to a quarter of a million. Meanwhile, the French population in Canada had barely reached 18,000.

The Dutch colony on the Hudson. The best place on the Atlantic Coast for a trading colony was at the present site of New York City. Its grand natural harbor invited commerce from the whole world. At the same time a broad river provided a super-highway for furs from the interior. Not the English but the Dutch took possession of this choice region. In September 1609 Henry Hudson, an English captain in the service of the Dutch, sailed up the river that now bears his name. Like countless other mariners in those days, Hudson was searching for the Northwest Passage from Europe to Cathay.

After Hudson's voyage, the Dutch set up a trading post on the river near the present site of Albany. Later, in 1623, they settled at Manhattan for their marketplace. They bought the island with trading goods valued at 60 Dutch

This early engraving shows the little village of New Amsterdam and its protective fort about 1626.

guilders (about $24) from several Indian chiefs. Of course, in those days $24 was worth what several thousand dollars would be worth now. The Dutch called their colony New Netherland. But unlike the Puritans, the Dutch settlers were less interested in building "a City upon a hill," a model community as an example to the world, than in making money.

The Dutch were the merchants of the world. There on Manhattan Island they began the great American democracy of cash. If you had money or goods, the Dutch would trade with you. It didn't matter who you were or what you believed. The Dutch let in nearly everyone to New York—not so much because they believed in toleration, but simply because it meant profit.

The Dutch colony was a wedge between New England and the southern colonies. So in 1664, when England was on the verge of war with Holland, Charles II granted his brother James, Duke of York, all the land between the Connecticut and Delaware rivers, including New Netherland.

When a fleet sent out by the Duke of York arrived at the fort at the foot of Manhattan Island and called for the surrender of the colony, the stubborn Dutch Governor Peter Stuyvesant refused. But the leading citizens, hardheaded merchants, knew that resistance was hopeless. They finally persuaded Stuyvesant to yield, and

New Netherland fell without a blow. The English flag now waved over an unbroken coast ☑ from Canada to the Carolinas.

New Sweden. When New Netherland fell to England, so did the land that had once been New Sweden. This was a colony first settled by Swedes and Finns in 1638 on the western shore of the Delaware River where Wilmington now stands. But since the settlement was small and weak, it was easily seized by the Dutch in 1655.

New Sweden gave America the log cabin. In the cold Swedish forests farmers had learned to use rough logs to build a cozy weather-tight house. Clever Swedish builders brought here their skill with logs. And the log cabin became standard housing on the western frontier.

See "Section 5 Review answers," p. 26F.

Section 5 Review

1. Identify: Samuel de Champlain, Peter Stuyvesant, Duke of York.

2. Locate: Louisbourg, New Orleans, Albany.

3. What was distinctive about New Netherland in American history?

4. **Critical Thinking: Recognizing Cause and Effect.** Why did the French colonies stay relatively small?

☑ See "Lesson Plan," p. 26F for **Writing Process Activity: Demonstrating Reasoned Judgment** relating to the success of the colonies.

See "Lesson Plan," p. 26F.

6. The proprietary colonies

Of the thirteen colonies that later united to form the American nation, all except Virginia and the New England settlements had been founded as *proprietorships*. This was halfway between a royal province and a self-governing colony. The king let control out of his hands, but he did not give it to a company or to the colonists. Instead it went to a man or a group of men, usually the king's personal friends. The "proprietors" then appointed the governor, set up law courts, and collected land tax ("quitrent") from the settlers. They also offered bonuses to lure settlers to their lands. They managed their provinces as business ventures, under whatever rules the king had put in their charters.

The proprietors were also limited by elected assemblies. All the proprietors except the Duke of York (who finally agreed in 1683) allowed the people some form of self-government. They could not attract settlers on any other terms. Even the royal provinces had to allow assemblies.

Starting with Maryland in 1634 a series of proprietary colonies was founded: the Carolinas in 1663, New Jersey in 1664, Pennsylvania in 1681, Delaware in 1702 (with the Penns as governors), and Georgia, first settled in 1733. Each colony faced its own problems, enjoyed its own successes, suffered its own failures.

Maryland, a colony founded for Catholics, like Rhode Island allowed religious freedom from the first. It passed an Act of Toleration in 1649. This permitted religious freedom only for all who believed in the Trinity—God the Father, Jesus Christ, and the Holy Ghost. It was the first legislative act of religious toleration in the colonies.

The Carolina proprietors tried to rule their colony by an elaborate constitution called the "Grand Model" drawn up by English philosopher John Locke. But the philosopher's theories proved unfit for the problems of government in the wilderness.

Pennsylvania. Pennsylvania was founded by Quakers, who were a special kind of Puritan.

They rejected all ceremonies of worship and the authority of all priests, ministers, or bishops. They obeyed only the "inner light," which they said came to them direct from God. The Quakers believed in equality so strongly that they refused to bow or remove their hats in the presence of officials. It is not surprising, then, that royal officials became impatient with them and persecuted the Quakers for any reason they could think up. The Quakers were not welcome in England.

William Penn, who had been jailed in England for his religious beliefs, decided to found an American colony for his fellow Quakers. Penn's father, a rich British admiral who was not a Quaker, had loaned money to King Charles II.

That William Penn was more than just a visionary Quaker is apparent in this early portrait. The sternness, practicality, and pertinacity needed to found a successful colony all shine through.

Historical Society of Pennsylvania

❖ See "Lesson Plan," p. 26F for **Cooperative Learning Activity: Making Comparisons** relating to the role of religion in the colonies.

No doubt this helped young Penn, who was shrewd and persuasive, to secure a vast colonial grant from Charles. At the king's demand, the new land was called "Pennsylvania" in honor of Penn's father. There William Penn established religious toleration, and the colony soon became a haven for persecuted people from all over.

Back in England, the Quakers had been strict pacifists. They opposed war and refused to fight for any reason, even in self-defense. There they were nothing but a small group of peculiar people. If they refused to fight, the country could still be defended by others. It was quite different in Pennsylvania. Here at first they were the majority, but they ran the government until 1756, long after they had stopped being a majority. In Pennsylvania, if the Quakers refused to raise an army, the countryside was left defenseless. This is precisely what happened.

✿ For some time, by various dodges, the Quak-
(p. 46) ers did try to help defend the colony without violating their consciences. In one case they voted money "to feed and clothe the Indians" that they knew would go to defense instead. In another they voted "other grain" for a military garrison, even though they knew "other grain" really meant a not-very-nourishing grain called gunpowder.

But in 1755, dodges ceased to be enough. Total war broke out in western Pennsylvania. The Indians burned homes, ruined crops, and killed or captured men, women, and children. Panic gripped the land, and eastern towns were filled with refugees. The Quakers insisted on remaining pacifists even as western Pennsylvania ran red with blood.

At that time the Quakers, although numbering only one-quarter of the colony's population, still held over three-fourths of the seats in the legislature. And they would not vote funds for defense. They insisted they could not violate their consciences by helping to fight a war. Now, however, the non-Quakers had had enough. They forced the Quakers to give up their control of the government. The Quakers never ruled the colony again.

After that the Quakers became the gadflies and prophets of America. They remained paci-

fists, and spoke out against slavery and other forms of oppression. They were the voices of everybody's conscience. That was their strength and their weakness. They were not meant for governing a colony.

Georgia. If Pennsylvania faced problems because of the beliefs of its settlers, Georgia suffered because of its English founders' ignorance and idealism. The 21 men in England who secured a charter for Georgia in 1732 thought they were very practical. The best known of them was James Oglethorpe. He was a tough-minded soldier who combined a passion for building the British Empire with a passion for reform. Oglethorpe and his friends had their eyes not so much on the Bible or on their own consciences as on the practical problems of their day. In London they worried over the growing unemployment and the increasing crime.

The land south of the Carolinas was rumored to be a new paradise. There they would settle some of London's criminals and the drunken, idle poor. That also happened to be right where the empire needed to block the Spaniards, who were trying to push their settlements northward. In Georgia, named after King George II, these unlucky people could serve as a human barricade. At the same time in that tropical climate they could provide the exotic products needed at home in England.

The founders even knew what the colony ought to produce—silk. At that time Britain was spending a fortune in gold and silver to buy silk. If the English could grow silk themselves, they would save their gold and silver and also provide work for the unemployed. The London promoters therefore ordered every settler in Georgia to grow mulberry trees so the leaves would be food for silkworms. Unfortunately, the black mulberry trees that grew in Georgia were not the kind the silkworms liked. This was a little fact that the London promoters had not bothered to notice.

Plans bred more plans. The ill-informed trust- 📖 ees of Georgia, sitting in their easy chairs in London, went on drawing their plans. Not only did they require mulberry trees to be planted,

📖 **More from Boorstin:** "[The Trustees] investigated the moral character of applicants and the circumstances which accounted for their distress. They even advertised the names of prospective emigrants in London newspapers a fortnight before departure so that creditors and deserted wives might have ample warning. Very few, perhaps not over a dozen, imprisoned debtors were brought to Georgia. Even these were chosen because they showed promise of becoming sturdy colonists." (From *The Americans: The Colonial Experience*)

Methodist Collection of Drew University, Madison, New Jersey

This 1734 engraving by Pierre Fourdrinier was designed to attract settlers to Savannah, Georgia.

but they laid down rules on just where the people could live. They prohibited "Rum, Brandies, Spirits, or Strong Waters." They would not let the settlers own or sell the land they worked. The settlers could use the land only according to company rules. No black slaves were to be allowed.

Georgia was intended to be a charity colony. It was the only English colony whose founders did not expect to make a profit. Because the people who were sent out were charity cases, they were not allowed to govern themselves. Almost as if they were in a Spanish colony, the inhabitants of Georgia had everything decided for them.

✖ It is not surprising that colonial Georgia did not flourish. An empire builder's dream turned out to be a nightmare. The settlers rebelled, and the trustees who had founded the colony gave up. By the time of the American Revolution, Georgia—the spoiled child of charitable London—was the least prosperous and least populous of all the English colonies.

"The poor inhabitants of Georgia," a settler lamented, "are scattered over the face of the earth; her plantations a wild; her towns a desert; her villages in rubbish, her improvements a by-word, and her liberties a jest; an object of pity to friends, and of insult, contempt and ridicule to enemies."

See "Section 6 Review answers," p. 26G.

Section 6 Review

1. Identify: William Penn, John Locke, James Oglethorpe, Quakers.
2. Define a "proprietary" colony.
3. **Critical Thinking: Expressing Problems Clearly.** Why did both the Pennsylvania Quakers and Georgia's proprietors find it hard to rule their colonies?

✖ **Critical Thinking Activity: Checking Consistency** What factors contributed to the success of a colony in North America? Have students work in small groups to develop a checklist of items they feel would have contributed to the success of a colony. Have students combine their lists to make one class list. Are the items applicable to all colonies? Which colony would have been most successful according to these criteria? Where would students have wanted to live?

Many Kinds of Americans

FOCUS

To introduce the lesson, direct students to the portrait of Isaiah Thomas on page 53. Ask: How did Thomas come to America? (As an indentured servant.) What was his status at the time the portrait was made? (He was a successful printer and publisher.) What does this rise in status tell students about life in the colonies? (Social mobility was possible.)

Developing Vocabulary

The words listed in this chapter are essential terms for reading and understanding particular sections of the chapter. The page number after each term indicates the page of its first or most important appearance in this chapter. These terms are defined in the text Glossary (text pages 1000–1011).

immigration (page 51); **emigrant** (page 51); **indentured servant** (page 52); **plantation** (page 54)

INSTRUCT

Explain

The population of the English colonies increased rapidly in the 1700s. The main cause of this population explosion was immigration. People came to the New World for different reasons: Africans were brought to America against their will, Huguenots wanted the religious freedom that the French government denied them, and for others, the prospect of buying cheap land was a powerful attraction for the masses who had never even dreamed of owning land.

☑ Writing Process Activity

Predicting Consequences Ask students to imagine they are one of the slaves in the hold of the *Albatross* pictured on page 55. Have them freewrite about the experience of being torn from their home to work for a colonial planter. Using the details from their pre-writing, they should write a story about their lives for their ancestors. Ask them to include facts as well as feelings. Tell students to revise for specific detail and chronological order. After they proofread, ask them to read their stories aloud.

Section Review Answers

Section 1, page 61

1. a) silversmith; b) painter; c) printer, journalist; d) furniture maker; e) silversmith. 2. On ships sailing from Salem you could find seafood, salt, wine, oranges, grapes, rum, whale oil, and even iron. From Charleston the main exports would be tobacco, rice, and indigo. 3. The large amounts of land meant that unlike Europeans, all Americans could hope to own land. There was so much open land that there were not enough people to work it, so slaves were imported. 4. In the South the rivers provided a direct link between the interior plantations and the oceans. Since travel on land between the colonies was extremely difficult, it was easier for southerners to trade with England than with the other colonies. In New England the coast was not tied by navigable waterways to the interior, so New Englanders became fishermen, built ships, and developed worldwide commerce. In the Middle Colonies, too, merchants sold their goods, not just to England, but to the best markets they could find. 5. Colonial children had very little independence. Often their parents chose their careers and arranged their marriages. Colonial women were expected to do many things, but men monopolized economic, social, and political power. Women were not expected to have had any formal education, and usually they could not vote.

CLOSE

To conclude the lesson, tell students that there was abundant land in America, far more than in Europe. Ask them: How do you think inexpensive land affected population growth in the colonies? (Increased it. Enabled young people to support themselves earlier, and so to marry earlier; thus there were more children. Allowed colonists to produce more food per person. Sparked immigration of Europeans who wanted to take advantage of the greater farming opportunities.)

The Colonists Govern Themselves

FOCUS

To introduce the lesson, have students reread the first two paragraphs under the heading "The problems of governing," on page 63, and ask them to identify the main point of the passage. (The main point is stated in the first sentence.)

Developing Vocabulary

Parliament (page 61); **salutary neglect** (page 62)

INSTRUCT

Explain

Write the following listing of English rulers on the chalkboard to help students retain a time perspective:

Providing In-Depth Coverage

Perspectives on Religion in the Colonies

Centuries ago, rulers felt that if people were allowed to make up their own minds about religion, they would soon be making up their own minds about politics as well. By forcing religious conformity upon the people, rulers felt that their power was secure.

Many colonies in the New World were created by groups in search of religious freedom. The Plymouth Colony and the Massachusetts Bay Colony were founded by English Separatists. They practiced their own religion, yet were intolerant of other religions, hence the formation of the Rhode Island colony by Roger Williams. Maryland was founded for Catholics, the only religion not tolerated in Rhode Island.

Religion played a key role in the founding of these colonies, as well as in the colonies' government, education, and other aspects of day-to-day life.

A History of the United States as an instructional program provides two types of resources you can use to offer in-depth coverage of religion in colonial life: the *student text* and the *Enrichment Support File*. A list of *Suggested Secondary Sources* is also provided. The chart below shows the topics that are covered in each.

THE STUDENT TEXT.
Boorstin and Kelley's *A History of the United States* unfolds the chronology of events, the key players, and, as an interpretive history, religion in colonial life.

AMERICAN HISTORY ENRICHMENT SUPPORT FILE.
This collection of primary source readings and classroom activities reveals the role of religion in colonial life.

SUGGESTED SECONDARY SOURCES.
This reference list of readings by well-known historians and other commentators provides an array of perspectives on the role of religion in colonial life.

Locating Instructional Materials

Detailed lesson plans for teaching religion in colonial life as a mini-course or to study one or more elements of religion in the colonies in depth are offered in the following areas: in the *student text*, see individual lesson plans at the beginning of each chapter; in the *Enrichment Support File*, see page 3; for readings beyond the student text, see *Suggested Secondary Sources*.

IN-DEPTH COVERAGE ON RELIGION IN THE COLONIES

Student Text	Enrichment Support File	Suggested Secondary Sources
• Crusades Spur Exploration, p. 10 • Spanish Colonies, pp. 28–30 • New England Colonies, pp. 39–42 • Proprietary Colonies, pp. 46–48 • Quakers, pp. 46–47 • New France, p. 51 • Religion and Education, p. 59	• Lesson Suggestions • Multimedia Resources • Overview Essay/Reviving Religion: The Great Awakening • Literature in American History/"Sinners in the Hands of an Angry God" • Primary Sources in American History/ The Great Awakening Stirs the Soul of the Nation • Biography in American History/George Whitefield • Great Debates in American History/ The Old Lights *vs.* the New Lights • Making Connections	• *"What Must I do to be Saved?": The Great Awakening in Colonial America* by J.M. Bumstead and John E. Van de Wetering, pp. 71–91. • *The Great Awakening and the American Revolution: Colonial Thought in the 18th Century* by Cedric Cowing, pp. 40–74. • *The Great Awakening in New England* by E.S. Gausted, pp. 1–15. • *Religion and the American Mind: From the Great Awakening to the Revolution* by Alan Heimert, pp. 27–58.

Chapter 3
New Ways in a New World

Identifying Chapter Materials

Objectives	Basic Instructional Materials	Extension Materials
1 Many Kinds of Americans • Explain why so many different kinds of people came to the English colonies in North America. • Describe the pattern and limits of social mobility in America in the 1700s. • Compare the experience of settlement in the New World for blacks and whites.	**Annotated Teacher's Edition** • Lesson Plans, p. 50C **Instructional Support File** • Pre-Reading Activities, Unit 1, p. 29 • Skill Review Activity, Unit 1, p. 32 • Skill Application Activity, Unit 1, p. 33	**Enrichment Support File** • Reviving Religion: The Great Awakening (see "In-Depth Coverage" at right.) **Suggested Secondary Sources** • See chart at right. **American History Transparencies** • Our Multicultural Heritage, pp. C39, C47 • Fine Art, p. D13
2 The Colonists Govern Themselves • Trace the steps leading to colonial self-government. • Explain the reason for conflict between England and France.	**Annotated Teacher's Edition** • Lesson Plans, pp. 50C–50D **Instructional Support File** • Critical Thinking Activity, Unit 1, p. 34	**Documents of American History** • The Navigation Act of 1660, Vol. 1, p. 32
3 Britain against France • Describe the events that led up to the French and Indian War. • Relate highlights of the French and Indian War.	**Annotated Teacher's Edition** • Lesson Plans, pp. 50D–50E **Instructional Support File** • Reading Activities, Unit 1, pp. 30–31 • Chapter Test, Unit 1, pp. 35–38 • Additional Test Questions, Unit 1, pp. 39–42 • Unit Test, Unit 1, pp. 43–46	**Documents of American History** • The Albany Plan of Union, Vol. 1, p. 43 **American History Transparencies** • Our Multicultural Heritage, pp. C5, C63

Chapter 2 Review

See "Chapter Review answers," p. 26G.

Focusing on Ideas

1. Compare the Spanish and English colonies. Describe such things as the treatment of Indians; the population profile; and slavery.

2. What developments in the 1500s enabled England to challenge Spain in North America?

3. Both planning and luck were crucial to the settlements in America. Find two examples of good or bad planning and luck in the chapter.

4. Describe the key features of royal colonies and proprietary colonies.

Taking a Critical Look

1. **Recognizing Cause and Effect.** How did false advertising and rumors affect the settlement of the English colonies?

2. **Drawing Conclusions.** In what way did the founding of Connecticut and Rhode Island provide evidence of both religious intolerance and religious freedom in colonial America?

Your Region in History

1. **Culture.** How did the early settlers of your area carry on their Old World traditions? What evidence of Old World traditions can you find in foods, music, dance, speech, and other aspects of your region's culture?

2. **Economics.** How did the early settlers of your area earn a living? What environmental factors influenced their choices? What impact did the first settlers have on the environment?

Historical Facts and Figures

Synthesizing Information. Study the information about the American colonies on the chart below. Then write a brief paragraph summarizing the information presented in the chart about (a) the New England Colonies, (b) the Middle Colonies, or (c) the Southern Colonies. Include a discussion about the reasons for the founding of each colony and the events in Europe that may have affected its development.

Founding of the Colonies

	Colony	Date Founded	Reasons Founded
New England Colonies	Plymouth	1620	Escape religious persecution
	Massachusetts Bay	1630	Escape religious persecution
	New Hampshire	1679	Agriculture; trade; fishing
	Hartford	1636	Trade; escape religious/political persecution
	New Haven	1638	Religious freedom; trade
	Rhode Island	1636	Escape religious persecution
Middle Colonies	New York	1623	Trade
	Delaware	1702	Trade
	New Jersey	1664	Land sales; escape religious/political persecution
	Pennsylvania	1681	Land sales; trade; escape religious/political persecution
Southern Colonies	Virginia	1607	Trade and farming
	Maryland	1634	Land sales; escape religious/political persecution
	The Carolinas	1663	Trade; farming; religious freedom
	Georgia	1733	Land sales; home for debtors; buffer against Spanish Florida

Charles I	1625–1649
Council of State (dominated by Cromwell)	1649–1653
Protectorate	
Oliver Cromwell	1653–1658
Richard Cromwell	1658–1660
Charles II	1660–1685
James II	1685–1688
William III (of Orange) and Mary	1689–1702

Have students keep this framework in mind as they read.

★ Independent Activity

Recognizing Cause and Effect Have students list three steps that contributed to the formation of colonial self-government in the 150 years after the settlement of the first English colony. Have students complete their lists and answer the following questions independently: To what degree did the colonies benefit from events taking place in England during this period? (A number of wars and uprisings distracted England from the business of ruling its colony.) What role did distance and poor communication play in promoting a spirit of independence in the colonies? (Vast distances and slow communication reinforced the colonials' sense of separation from Britain.)

Section Review Answers

Section 2, page 66

1. a) a license from the government authorizing an individual to seize an enemy's ships. b) English king who was beheaded in 1649. c) led the forces that deposed Charles I and then ruled England for a decade. d) became king at Parliament's request, replacing Cromwell's son. e) Charles II's brother, came to power in 1685 and quickly managed to alienate everyone. f) invited to England to replace the unpopular James II in 1689. This began a new era of representative government. g) the first and last governor of the ill-fated Dominion of New England. 2. The Dominion of New England represented an attempt by James II to rule the northeastern colonies as one Dominion; representative local governments would be abolished. The colonists refused to accept this plan. So, local government was saved, and the colonists' defiance was a sign of things to come. 3. The Navigation Acts eventually required that all colonial trade be carried on English-built ships and go through English ports. Bribes and legal technicalities helped the colonists avoid punishment for violating these acts, and too many things were happening in Europe for the British to enforce them. 4. It was extremely difficult for England to govern the colonies because they were so far away, because the colonists were

used to considerable self-government, and because so many things were happening within Great Britain and Europe. 5. A system of salutary neglect, in which England did not enforce its regulations (particularly the Navigation Acts), and the colonies prospered. 6. The Glorious Revolution brought more representative government to England but also helped embroil England in a war against France that would stretch across the globe. As a result, the English were preoccupied, and the colonists were able to create a prosperous situation for themselves.

CLOSE

To conclude the lesson, ask students to write brief definitions of the following terms: *salutary neglect, mercantilism,* and *privateer.* Then ask students to suggest connections between these three terms. (Students should suggest that the colonists were unhappy when England tried to enforce trade laws [the policy of mercantilism] after the many years of salutary neglect, a time during which the colonists prospered. In defiance of these trade laws, licensed pirates [privateers] turned smuggling into a profitable business.)

Section 3 (pages 66–70)

Britain against France

FOCUS

To introduce the lesson, have students make a time line of the period of the French and Indian War. Have them place the following dates on the line: 1745, 1754, 1755, 1757, 1758, 1759, and 1763. Then ask them to record the events and results alongside the dates as they read the section.

INSTRUCT

Explain

As the English pushed westward, they moved closer and closer to French territory, causing tension that would eventually lead to war. Review with the students the definition of *empire.* Explain that the Seven Years' War was not a war of *conquest*—an attempt to overthrow the opponent's government and rule the country—but a war for *empire.*

☑ Writing Process Activity

Expressing Problems Clearly Have students imagine they are newspaper reporters sent to Albany, New York in June 1754. Using the journalist's questions (*who, what, where, when, why,* and *how*), they should take notes on what occurred. Suggest that they interview a representative or an Indian to get a specific point of view. Ask them to use these notes as the background for an article explaining what the colonial congress tried to accomplish and why it failed. Have them revise for logical explanation and proofread for mechanical errors. They can publish their articles in a class newspaper.

Section Review Answers

Section 3, page 70

1. a) British general who expected to fight in the European style but was surprised and defeated by the French and Indians at Fort Duquesne. b) British general who ingeniously captured Quebec from the French in 1759. c) French commander defeated at Quebec. d) powerful and effective prime minister of England who realized that British troops in America were fighting for worldwide empire. e) British general who fought alongside Wolfe in the recapture of Louisbourg. 2. Sault Ste. Marie, Vincennes, Natchez are shown on page 69. Great Meadows was near the fork of the Allegheny River and the Ohio River, as shown on page 69 (where Pittsburgh is today). Fort Pitt was known by the French as Fort Frontenac, on page 69, on Lake Ontario. Lake Champlain is the unlabeled body of water south of Montreal on page 69. The Plains of Abraham are outside Quebec, on page 69. Guadeloupe is one of the small, unlabeled Leeward Islands in the Caribbean, shown on page 948. 3. The Albany Plan of Union would meet annually, regulate Indian affairs, manage public lands and an army, pass laws, and levy taxes for the common defense; the king's agent would have veto power over the council. 4. According to the Peace of Paris, England gained Canada and all French lands between the Appalachian Mountains and the Mississippi. France regained Guadeloupe and Martinique from England and retained two tiny islands near Newfoundland. Spain gained the Louisiana region from France and got Havana and Manila back from England, but it ceded Florida to England. 5. As the English pushed farther to the west with their settlements, the French reacted by strengthening their own defenses. Prior to this time, the French and English had remained at enough of a distance to avoid conflict. Between 1689 and 1763, England and France were involved in a war for empire. The colonies were part of the stakes in that war, and English settlements were frequently attacked by the French and their Indian allies.

CLOSE

To conclude the lesson, ask students to research some of the Indian tribes that were involved in the French and Indian War, and to report to the class on the reasons several tribes allied themselves with either the French or the British.

Chapter Review Answers
Focusing on Ideas

1. Although determined to rule themselves, colonists had to answer to a governor appointed by the English king. 2. Indians could not be induced to supply labor; it was almost impossible to recruit workers from Europe. 3. As English colonies stretched west, French soldiers and Indian allies attacked outlying English settlements. The conflicts eventually led to the French and Indian war. 4. England intended to ensure that the colonies' economic policies would only benefit England. 5. People had to learn to accept change. The English language was enriched, and skills and customs were shared and adapted. 6. This turned out to be a system for not enforcing the Navigation Acts. 7. Artists painted portraits for family living rooms and town halls to preserve the faces of the people of the era.

Taking a Critical Look

1. Simple designs in furniture, silverware, etc., reflected that things were for use, not just to admire. 2. The colonies had economic and political independence by resisting the Navigation Acts, coining their own money, etc. Socially, American culture emerged. 3. Not enforcing the Navigation Acts and other aspects of the mercantile system permitted the colonies to thrive economically; England reaped the benefits. 4. (a) Colonists shared wars with England, France, and Spain. (b) Colonists had military and naval training; forts were set up; hostility toward Indians grew.

Your Region in History

1–3. Answers will vary depending on your region. Consult your local library or historical society for books on the early history of the area.

Historical Facts and Figures

(a) 48.7%; (b) No—a small percentage were free; (c) 5.3%—the rest of the population is accounted for.

Answers to "Making Connections"

(See "Using Making Connections" on p. 72.)

Answers will vary, but may include one or more of the following examples. Answers based on the time line callouts are in italics.

1. An examination of the motivations of early settlers bears out the assertion that some people came to America looking for situations while others were trying to escape situations. *Francisco Pizarro*, for example, was looking for a situation in which he could win fame and fortune when he *conquered Peru in 1531*. Many Spaniards came to the New World for similar reasons. (*Missionaries* such as the ones that *founded the Spanish mission at San Francisco in 1776* were an exception to this rule. They were seeking the op-

portunity to *convert Indians to Christianity*.) English colonists on the other hand tended to have more modest goals. *In 1606 King James granted the Virginia Company a charter.* Most of the people who joined up and settled there were happy to find the opportunity to run or work on prosperous plantations. One reason people were anxious to leave England was that *by 1616 London was so overcrowded that promoters looking for colonial immigrants simply advertised the natural beauty of America.* The *Separatist Puritans* had yet another reason for *heading to the New World in 1620.* They were running away from religious persecution in England. Many Georgia colonists, too, were running away from something. *Established in 1732 as a charity colony, Georgia was viewed as a second chance by the outcasts of London* who set sail to escape poverty and prison. 2. People who believe that Native Americans would be better off today if Europeans had not discovered America might point out that these newcomers brought European diseases with them. These diseases almost wiped out the Indians. It is estimated that *by 1700 the Indian population of Central and South America had dropped from 50 million to about 4 million.* It might also be pointed out that the con-

quistadors destroyed the mightiest Indian civilization in the Americas. Cortes razed the Aztec capital, Tenochtitlan, and *Pizarro* turned the once proud *Incas* into virtual slaves when he *conquered them in 1531.* People who believe the Native Americans are better off could point out the many beneficial things that the Europeans brought to the Americas—new types of animals, fruit, and vegetables; scientific and technological inventions; and the ideals of western civilization. 3. There is a great deal of evidence to suggest that American colonists had developed a thriving culture by the eighteenth century. One of the most convincing bits of evidence was the emphasis placed on higher education. *Harvard was founded in 1636*, not long after the colonists began to settle Massachusetts. It might also be pointed out that fine arts flourished in the colonies. *Painters such as* John Smibert, John Greenwood, and *John Singleton Copley received many commissions, often for portraits.* Artisans such as cabinetmaker John Goddard and *silversmiths Paul Revere* and Myer Myers were also in demand. Colonial writers included *Thomas Paine, who published "Common Sense" in 1776*, as well as theologicans such as Jonathan Edwards.

3

Chapter 3

New Ways in a New World

Focusing on the Chapter: Have students identify the chapter logo. Discuss what unit theme the logo might symbolize. Then ask students to skim the chapter to identify other illustrations or titles that relate to this theme.

During these early colonial years, American ways of life began to appear. They emerged from how Americans defended themselves in war and governed themselves in peace. Challenged by a New World, they developed their own ideas about government, law, and politics. Still, the British colonists in America considered themselves loyal Britons. In 1763, at the end of the French and Indian War, few people anywhere would have predicted the break that was to come. The next twenty years were a time of surprising change. Before the colonists could realize it, they had made themselves into a new, self-governing nation.

How did that happen? To understand how this New World novelty was created, we must look at the relations of Americans to each other, to England, and to the wars that France and England exported to America.

John Smibert, who was born in Scotland, painted this panorama of Boston as seen from a hill across the harbor in 1738. It is one of the first paintings of the city. The long wharf jutting out from the city (left of center in the painting) was a much-noted wonder of early America.

Childs Gallery, Boston

See "Lesson Plan," p. 50C.

1. Many kinds of Americans

During the seventeenth century the English settlements in America grew slowly. One hundred years after the landing at Jamestown the colonies still held only 250,000 people. Then the 1700s saw immigration and a high birthrate create the first American population explosion. The number of people more than doubled every 25 years. By 1765 they counted two and a quarter million. These were no longer just European emigrants, but a new breed of people, shaped by a New World.

A land of many peoples. The people who lived in the thirteen colonies at the end of the French and Indian War came from many lands. But the population was more English than it would ever be again. Since about 60 percent of all the white settlers had come from England, it is not surprising that the English language, English customs, English law, and English ways of government dominated the land. Pennsylvania had the most mixed population of all, but even there the English stock made up at least half of the population.

What transformed Britons into Americans was that here they had the challenges of living with Africans, Scots, Scotch-Irish, Irish, Portuguese Jews, Swedes, Finns, Swiss, and even a few Austrians and Italians. This made life here much more interesting than life back home. Of course it made some new problems, but it created new opportunities.

These many peoples had come for many different reasons. Most came because they wanted to, some because they were forced. Some, like the Swedes, learned English and became Americans quickly.

Others, like the Germans, tried to hold on to their own language and their own customs, even in this New World. Still others, like the indentured servants and many of the blacks from Africa, might have wanted to become full-fledged Americans but were not yet allowed that chance.

Black Americans had been brought here against their will. Most were slaves, but at an early date there were a few who were free. In 1765 the colonies held 400,000 blacks scattered from Massachusetts Bay to Georgia. Over half worked on the tobacco plantations in Virginia and Maryland. Only 40,000 were found farther north.

Besides colonists of English or of African descent, the largest group consisted of the Scots, the Irish, and the Scotch-Irish (the Scots who had tried to settle in Ireland). These hard-bitten, intelligent people took naturally to the frontier. They could usually be found in the "back country." This was a new American expression for the unsettled lands that stretched from Pennsylvania down through the mountains into the Carolinas.

A smaller number were the Germans, industrious and thrifty, who settled mainly in Pennsylvania. So many came in the mid-eighteenth century that the English settlers there feared that the whole colony would become German.

The Germans worked large farms on the rich limestone soil. Some of their descendants are still working the same lands today. They are often mistakenly referred to as Pennsylvania Dutch (from *Deutsch*, meaning German). They were ingenious and willing to try new ways. For hunting they replaced the old-fashioned musket with the accurate long rifle of frontier fame. For travel they built the sturdy Conestoga wagon, which took many pioneers west. And to warm their houses in the winters, which were much colder than those in Europe, they developed and improved the iron stove.

The French Protestants, a small group, had an influence all out of proportion to their numbers. These Huguenots came to America after 1685 when the French government deprived them of their religious freedom and their right to take part in government. An older French law, the Edict of Nantes, which had once given them religious liberty, was repealed. Now they joined the stream of refugees who, over the centuries, came here to escape persecution. It was against the law for them to leave France, but they came anyway. Their intelligence and their skills enriched the colonies.

One famous descendant of the French Huguenots was Paul Revere, who made the celebrated ride in 1775 to tell the people that British

Continuity and Change: Social Change Explain to students that although many Americans are proud of the United States as a "melting pot," immigrants have not always been welcome. Tell students that in the latter part of the nineteenth century, some Americans formed groups, such as the Immigration Restriction League, to try to stop the immigration of people from particular countries. Throughout their history, Americans would periodically support legislation to control the number and nationality of immigrants. The National Origins Act (1924) was one such piece of discriminatory legislation. (See pages 443, 580.)

Paul Revere's likeness was painted in 1765 by John Singleton Copley. It shows him in his silversmith's work clothes holding an elegant example of his craft.

troops were on their way to Concord and Lexington. Revere made his living as a silversmith, and his elegant work can be seen in many museums today.

Empty land creates opportunity. Most colonists found here a greater dignity and a better life than they had had before. At long last they could buy their own tract of land and run their own farm. The vote in all colonies was restricted to male landowners, but most adult white males did own land and thus could vote.

Even poor people could eventually own land in America. Many immigrants, either before or after they arrived in the colonies, hired themselves out as indentured servants—sometimes for as long as seven years—to someone already here. In a few cases indentured servants were treated no better than slaves. Some of them ran away. But if they worked out their full term, they usually received clothes and tools, and sometimes a little cash or even a piece of land to give them a new start in life. In America the shortage of labor and the abundance of land spelled opportunity—the chance to become a landowner.

Empty land creates slavery. To grow tobacco economically a planter needed a large estate and a sizable work force. It was easy to find the land, but hard to find the workers. Many indentured servants, once free, would go off and start their own farms. Why should they work for someone else? (p. 53)

Since the planters could not fill their labor needs with Europeans, they turned to slaves from Africa or the West Indies. The institution of slavery was ancient and familiar in western Europe and throughout Africa. People defeated in war, instead of being killed, were often enslaved. In Europe, with the passing centuries, slavery became reserved for people who were not Christians. They were called pagans. To justify the institution, slaveholders argued that they were helping pagans by making them into slaves so in time they could become Christians. When Jamestown was settled, slavery hardly existed in England. But English ships plied the slave trade between Africa and the Spanish colonies. And when the planters in the English colonies needed workers, they were supplied with African slaves.

Africans were not the only people who were brought to America by force. In England kidnappers seized unsuspecting poor people—children and adults—and then made a profit by selling them as indentured servants in the colonies. Political radicals, religious nonconformists—along with thieves and murderers—were "transported" to America as a punishment or simply to get them out of the way. When the term of their indenture was over, they were freed. But blacks, and sometimes Indians, were kept in slavery for life. Since Indians knew how to survive in the American wilderness, they could more easily run away. So southern

See "Lesson Plan," p. 50C for **Writing Process Activity: Predicting Consequences** relating to the experiences of Africans captured for the slave trade.

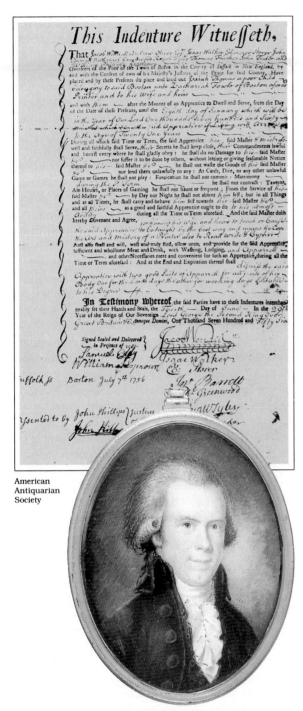

American Antiquarian Society

Worcester Art Museum

Isaiah Thomas's indenture papers apprenticed him to a printer. During the Revolution Thomas was the official printer for the Massachusetts patriots. Later he became a leading American publisher and founded the American Antiquarian Society.

planters turned more and more to using black slaves as their workers.

How the ocean tied some to England. The southern colonies, stretching from Maryland and Virginia down the seacoast to Georgia, were covered with plantations. In Maryland and Virginia the planters grew tobacco, and in the Carolinas and Georgia they grew rice and indigo (a blue dye used by English textile manufacturers). In all these colonies there were some small farmers growing whatever they could.

The great plantations set the tone for these southern colonies. To understand the plantation South, we must understand Virginia.

Virginia was a land of riverways. Viewed from Chesapeake Bay, Virginia had no solid seacoast but was a half-dozen outreaching fingers of land separated by inreaching fingers of water. These were the rich lowlands of "tidewater" Virginia, so called because the ocean tides reach there. The land and the sea seemed perfectly married. Deep navigable rivers—the Potomac, the Rappahannock, the York, and the James—divided Virginia into strips stretching southeastward. Each of these strips was nearly an island. Each in turn was veined by smaller rivers, many large enough to carry traffic to the ocean.

These riverways brought the whole world to the door of every great plantation. From the (p. 54) ocean came ships carrying slaves from Africa and the West Indies, and carrying muskets, hoes, clothing, furniture, and books from London. Down to the ocean went ships carrying large barrels (called hogsheads) of tobacco from the broad plantations of the Lees, the Carters, and the Byrds.

Every large plantation had its own dock. Goods arrived there direct from London. Virginians felt little need to have their own cities, for London was their shopping center.

Planters with riverways running direct to London from their door felt close to Old England. In those days before railroads, it was slow and expensive to carry anything across the land. It was easier at that time for a Virginia family to get all the way from London the products it needed than it was for someone living five miles outside of London. The ships that

Multicultural Connection: On August 20, 1619, John Rolfe of Jamestown recorded in his Journal the arrival of twenty Africans aboard a Dutch man-of-war. These first Africans in an English colony were not brought as slaves, but as indentured servants. Like white indentured servants, when their period of service was ended, they were free to buy land or leave the colony.

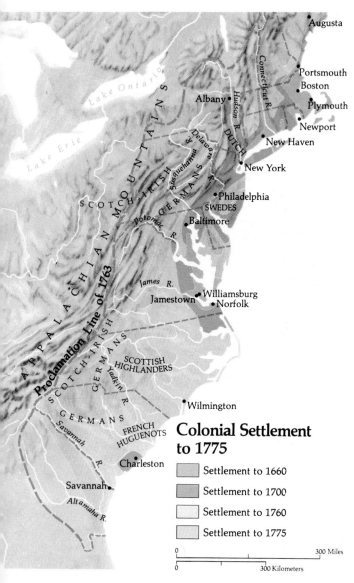

Colonial Settlement to 1775

Settlement to 1660
Settlement to 1700
Settlement to 1760
Settlement to 1775

0 ———————— 300 Miles

0 ———————— 300 Kilometers

arranged the English education of a planter's son or daughter. He reported this season's London styles and sent the latest market news. The London agent advised which recent books were worth reading, and he recounted court scandal or the latest trends in English politics. Sometimes he even helped a lonely bachelor-planter find a wife.

Virginia planters thought of themselves not so much as Americans, but as English country gentlemen who happened to live in America. They still relied on England for almost everything. The easiest way for them to send goods to Boston was to send the goods to London first, where they would be shipped out to Boston on an English vessel. Virginia Englishmen—including leaders of the American Revolution like George Washington and Thomas Jefferson—owed most of the furniture of their houses and of their minds to England.

The ocean that tied them to the English homeland helped them keep the habits and ideas of English gentry. With few exceptions they were moderate, sensible men and women. They would make no trouble and would stay loyal so long as they could prosper.

The colonies south of Chesapeake Bay also lived a tidewater life. This was true even though the Carolina and Georgia coast had shallow waterways which were harder to reach by ocean-going boat than the rivers in Virginia and Maryland. South Carolina's crops of rice and indigo were shipped to London from the deep harbor of the city of Charleston. Here many planters and their families would come to spend the summers away from the heat and malaria of their plantations. Charleston, one of the largest cities in America, had an active business life and more rich people for its size than any other city in the colonies. It was well known for its bustling, bubbling ways. It was a town full of people trying to rise, people trying to grow rich or richer. Most of Charleston's active trade was with England, so here too the ocean tied the people to the homeland.

How the ocean led others out to the world.
The same ocean that tied southern plantation owners to Mother England led the New

carried the large barrels of tobacco back to England were happy to have a cargo to carry to America. For very little cost they would bring furniture and carriages from London to the wealthy families of Virginia.

Planters could order from England almost everything they needed. Most purchases were made through an agent in London, generally the same man who helped sell the planter's tobacco there. The London agent ran a kind of mail-order shopping service. He supplied all sorts of things—a set of law books, a fancy bonnet, a case of wine, shoes for slaves. He

✂ Godfrey Meynall, an eyewitness, painted this watercolor of the hold of the slave ship *Albatross* in 1846. Similar conditions were the rule throughout the existence of the slave trade.

Englanders elsewhere. The rough and rocky coast of New England offered few gateways to the interior. There were sheltered bays and deep harbors—Salem, Boston, Plymouth, and many others. But New England rivers, with few exceptions, ran steeply downhill. Although they were good for turning a millwheel, most of them were one-way streets tumbling to the ocean. In New England you could not take an ocean vessel very far inland.

New England bays became havens for big ships that traveled the oceans of the world. On the rocky New England soil, covered by snowy winters far colder than those of Old England, there grew no single staple crop. There was little tobacco, no sugar or indigo or rice. New England found its wealth in the sea.

"The abundance of sea-fish are almost beyond believing," Francis Higginson wrote in 1630, "and sure I would scarce have believed it

with mine own eyes." There was seafood for every taste: mackerel, bass, salmon, lobster, herring, turbot, sturgeon, haddock, mullets, eels, crabs, mussels, clams, and oysters. A small quantity the New Englanders themselves ate. Most they dried, salted, and carried to far parts of the world. Some they sold to the Catholics of Europe, who ate much fish on Fridays. The scraps and leavings went to the Caribbean plantation owners as cheap food for their slaves.

Fishing became the main industry of Massachusetts Bay. In 1784 the Massachusetts House of Representatives voted "to hang up a representation of a codfish in the room where the House sit, as a memorial of the importance of the codfishery to the welfare of the Commonwealth." The codfish became the totem of the state. It hung over the Speaker's desk until the middle of the twentieth century.

✂ **Critical Thinking: Drawing Conclusions** What can be learned about history by studying a painting? Have students look at the painting above. Ask: What does this painting show about the conditions under which Africans were transported to the colonies on slave ships? How does it show how the artist felt about these conditions? Ask students to describe in words or phrases the atmosphere the artist has created with color and line.

A View of Mr Joshua Winsor's House &

Joshua Winsor was active in the mackerel and cod fishing industry. His house, built about 1768 in Duxbury, Massachusetts, was typical of seaside architecture. In the late 1700s Winsor's son-in-law, Dr. Rufus Hathaway, painted this picture showing the wharves, countinghouse, and fishing fleet. Winsor is in the foreground, on the right.

The New England fisheries actually helped bring on the Revolution. Deep-sea fishermen need ships, and the New Englanders began building their own fishing ships in large numbers. This worried the English. They wanted to be sure the trade of the New Englanders benefited the mother country. And this was one of the reasons why the English clamped the Navigation Acts on the colonies, telling them where they could sail their ships and limiting where they could carry some of the produce of the colonies. Over the years the English went on to tighten their senseless and unenforceable restrictions against colonial trading (p. 62). Faneuil Hall (which still stands in Boston), the meeting place of the Massachusetts rebels, was given to the city by Peter Faneuil, son of a French Huguenot immigrant and one of the many merchants who had become rich by shipping New England codfish to forbidden distant markets.

Why should bold and adventurous New England sailors obey boundaries marked off by a few English politicians? Even before the new United States was launched as a nation, New England sailors were showing their

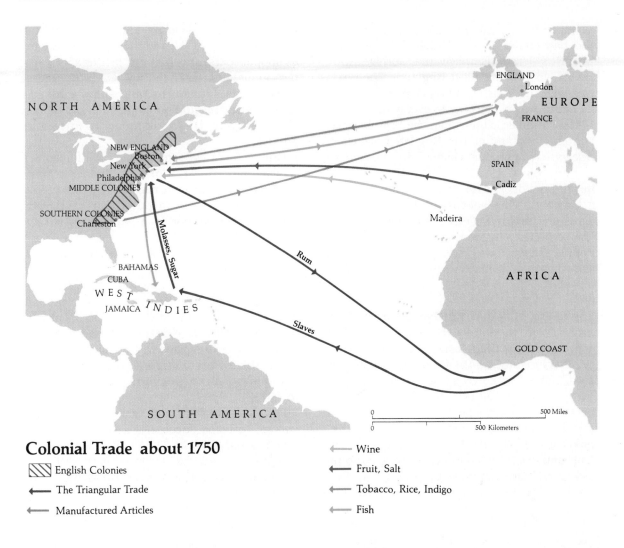

Colonial Trade about 1750

- 〰〰 English Colonies
- ← The Triangular Trade
- ← Manufactured Articles

- ← Wine
- ← Fruit, Salt
- ← Tobacco, Rice, Indigo
- ← Fish

independence. They were shipping whatever they could find or make—and to wherever they were attracted by whim or profit.

New England ships roamed the world. Their sailors went to Portugal, Spain, France, Syria, the West Indies, Brazil, Guinea, and Madagascar. They carried fish to trade for salt from Cadiz, wine from the Azores and Madeira, iron from Bilbao, grapes from Málaga, and oranges from Valencia to ports in England and the colonies. To get oil to burn in their lamps for light, whaling expeditions went out on long voyages from New Bedford and Nantucket south to the coast of Brazil and north to the Arctic Ocean. They took rum from New England ports to the west coast of Africa, where they traded it for

slaves whom they then took to the Caribbean and sold for sugar, which was then taken north to be made into more rum. This was called "the triangular trade." They were willing to "trye all ports," as they said, with all kinds of freight. Nothing was too small or too big for their commerce or their imaginations.

In the days before independence when English laws still hemmed them in, enterprising New Englanders had to be smugglers. For them, American independence would be a great relief. It would make them honest, law-abiding traders. But long before the American Revolution, the minds and hearts and pocketbooks of bold New Englanders were attached to the whole world.

⊕ **Geography and History: Interaction** Refer students to the map above. Ask: Did all the colonies trade the same goods? (No) Name three products of the southern colonies. (Tobacco, rice, indigo) Name two products of New England. (Fish, rum) Why do you think the products of the southern colonies and the New England colonies differed? (Answers should include such geographic factors as variations in climate, soil, and resources of each region.) What four "items" were bought and sold in the Triangular Trade? (Sugar, molasses, rum, and slaves)

The Dutch, Germans, Swedes, and Finns who had settled in the Middle Colonies (New York, New Jersey, Pennsylvania, and Delaware) had no special ties with England. Their relatives were in their own homelands. For them the ocean was a highway to everywhere.

These Middle Colonies had the best-balanced economies of any of the English colonies. A wide variety of products came from the rich soil of their farms. Unlike the southern planters they did not depend on a single staple crop sold in England. They sold their produce to merchants in the thriving cities of Philadelphia and New York. The city merchants in turn sent the produce overseas wherever they could find the best market—no matter what the Navigation Acts said.

Family life. Life in colonial America put heavy demands on the family. On the farm, where most Americans lived, labor was in short supply. Every member of the farm family had work to do. Women took care of the cows, hogs, and chickens, and made the butter and cheese. In the fields they were expected to sow, hoe, and reap the corn. They also sewed the clothes, cooked the food, and kept the simple houses clean and neat. A woman had to be a combination farmer, chef, and tailor!

In addition to all this the women bore many children. Families with 10 or 11 children were common, and 22 or more were not unheard of. From poor nutrition and lack of medical care the mortality rate was high. Many of the children died young. For the children who survived, in the back country where there were no schools the mother was their only teacher.

What doctors prescribed was more likely to kill than to cure the patient. A sensible person would try to stay out of the hands of a doctor. George Washington died in 1799 after he was bled of two quarts of blood by leeches and then "dosed to nausea and blistered to rawness." Even Washington's sturdy constitution could not survive that sort of treatment.

There were few things women were not expected to do in America. Most women married, and usually they helped their husbands on the farm or in the shop. After their husbands died, the women kept the farms and plantations running. Women also showed their versatile talents as shopkeepers, shoemakers, printers, newspaper publishers, teachers, lawyers, and even as blacksmiths, gunsmiths, and shipwrights. Although women could not hold office and usually could not vote, they took an active interest in politics.

One of the most remarkable colonial women was Margaret Brent. A large landholder in Maryland, she ran her own plantation and actually led a force of men to put down a rebellion against the governor in 1646. And when the governor died, she was made executor of his will. She ran his estates and collected his rents. She was also attorney for the proprietor, Lord Baltimore, to take care of his affairs in Maryland. Naturally, she thought all this ought to give her the right to vote in the colonial assembly. When the new governor refused to let her have her rightful place in the colonial government, she moved to Virginia, where she made a new home and ran great estates until her death in 1671.

Few women were rich enough and willful enough to be as successful as Margaret Brent was in a man's world. The English common law which governed the colonies gave few legal rights to women. Husbands controlled the family property.

In those days, unlike ours, children were not allowed to make up their own minds. Parents decided whether a boy would be apprenticed to a shoemaker or a blacksmith, or be educated to become a minister or a lawyer. If not bound out as an indentured servant, the child worked for his parents, on the farm or in the shop.

Usually parents arranged marriages for their children. But in the New World things began to change. In New England more young people were beginning to be allowed to select their own mates.

The colonial family, of course, had no cars, no electric lights, no radios or television sets, no running water, no heat in winter except from the fireplace or, after around 1740, the iron stove. They had to take care of themselves and one another. They looked to other family members not only for love and advice, for food,

Continuity and Change: Social Change Explain to students that it was not until 1920, with the passage of the Nineteenth Amendment to the Constitution, that women received the right to vote. (See page 582.)

Worcester Art Museum, Sarah E. Garver Fund

Worcester Art Museum, Gift of Mr. and Mrs. Albert Rice (detail)

These portraits of Boston merchant and lawyer John Freake and of his wife, Elizabeth, with their child Mary are the work of an unknown artist in the 1670s.

shelter, and clothing, but they also needed them for their education and entertainment.

Education in the colonies. Compared to Europeans in their time, the American colonists were a well-educated people. Most were Protestants who believed that all Christians should be able to read the Bible. Massachusetts Bay Colony passed a law requiring every town of 50 families or more to maintain a school to teach the boys reading, writing, and arithmetic. Every town of 100 families or more was to have a "grammar school" where boys could prepare for college. Girls had little formal education. Instead they were expected to learn the household arts of sewing, cooking, housekeeping, and childrearing. Books were not for them.

In 1636, only six years after the first settlers of Massachusetts Bay arrived in the New England wilderness, the people founded Harvard College. In the Old World, colleges and universities were ancient and honored institutions. Would it be possible to establish such an insti-

tution in the wilderness? The colonists said they needed Harvard College "to advance *Learning* and perpetuate it to Posterity; dreading to leave an illiterate Ministry to the Churches." Many farmers' sons went to Harvard to learn to serve as ministers or lawyers, judges or governors—or simply to be well educated.

Outside New England the colonies were not so quick to establish schools. Teachers lived with families while they taught the boys living nearby to read and write. Women opened "dame schools" to teach reading to young boys and sometimes even to girls. Where there were no schools, parents had to teach their children at home. On large southern plantations, private teachers were hired to live on the estate and instruct the children. Then the boys sometimes went back to England to attend college at Oxford or Cambridge. A few went to London or Edinburgh to study law or medicine.

By the time Yale was founded in Connecticut in 1701, there were only two other colleges: Harvard (1636) and William and Mary (1693) in

Enrichment Support File Topic

More from Boorstin "The primary aim of the American college was not to increase the continental stock of cultivated men, but rather to supply its particular region with knowledgeable ministers, lawyers, doctors, merchants, and political leaders. . . . It symbolized both the easy intercourse between American higher learning and the community as a whole and the identification of leading men with the special problems of their particular regions. (From *The Americans: The Colonial Experience*)

Virginia. But William and Mary remained little more than a grammar school for its first 35 years. Not until the 1740s were more colleges founded. Before that the colonies were too poor and the hardships and dangers of transportation too great. As the colonies flourished, new colleges appeared. Between 1746 and 1769, we see the founding of the College of New Jersey (Princeton), the University of Pennsylvania, King's College (Columbia) in New York, Rhode Island University (Brown), Queen's College (Rutgers) in New Jersey, and Dartmouth in New Hampshire. In 1784 Yale College, with its 270 students, had the largest student body. By the time of the American Revolution the colonies actually had a surprising number of institutions of higher learning. Of course they were not as well equipped—with libraries or scientific instruments—as their English counterparts. But for the remote New World colonies these colleges were a wondrous beginning.

Journalism and the arts and sciences.
Outside the cities, life in the colonies was simple. "Some few towns excepted," wrote John Dickinson on the eve of the Revolution, "we are all tillers of the soil from Nova Scotia to West Florida." The settlers, busy creating a new life in a New World, did not have much time for the arts or sciences.

The first successful newspaper did not appear until 1704, and as late as 1754 three of the colonies still had no newspaper. Despite their small numbers, American journalists pioneered in freedom. In 1733 a bold printer, John Peter Zenger, was arrested and tried for libel for printing articles critical of the governor of New York. But he went to court and won the right to print unpleasant political facts in his newspaper. This was a momentous step in establishing the freedom of the press in America. Gouverneur Morris later called the Zenger case "the morning star of that liberty which subsequently revolutionized America."

Colonial America, far from the Old World treasures of learning, produced a surprising number of original thinkers. Jonathan Edwards, though his writings are hard to understand, was a profound theologian who still has much to teach us. Benjamin Franklin won worldwide fame for his researches in electricity (he first suggested the lightning rod!) and his many practical inventions (he invented the Franklin stove). There were some others, too—other scientists, political philosophers, theologians, and historians.

Colonial goods ranged from homemade items like this needlepoint card table cover stitched by Mercy Otis Warren to heavy carved and painted chests like this one made by the Pilgrims.

© Sotheby Parke-Bernet; Agent: Art Resources

The Pilgrim Society, Plymouth, Massachusetts

Multicultural Connection: The first integrated public school North America was the St. Augustine School, founded in Spanish-controlled Florida in 1787. The school was opened with compulsory attendance for whites and optional attendance for blacks. The first teacher selected was Father Francisco Traconis, a native of Santiago de Cuba.

Some colonists made their living as cabinet-makers and silversmiths. The desks designed by John Goddard of Newport, Rhode Island, were equal to the best made in Europe. Handsome silver bowls, beakers, and candlesticks by Paul Revere in Boston, Myer Myers in New York, and others in Newport, Philadelphia, and Charleston, adorned colonial tables and churches.

In those days before the camera, colonial painters traveled the countryside. They painted lifelike portraits for the family living room and for town halls. John Smibert, the Englishman who designed Faneuil Hall in Boston, preserved the faces of sturdy New England families. John Greenwood went to Surinam, where he, portrayed the lonely sea captains away from home.

Most colonists, of course, could not afford fine furniture and silver or the price of a family portrait. At home they made what they needed. Their quilting, weaving, and needlework had a special simple charm. German gunsmiths in Pennsylvania turned out long rifles, which also were works of art.

American art reflected American lives. These were a practical people in search of a better life.

See "Section 1 Review answers," p. 50C.

Section 1 Review

1. Suppose Margaret Brent wanted to employ the following people: Paul Revere, John Smibert, John Peter Zenger, John Goddard, and Myer Myers. What products or services would each provide?

2. If you were to visit Salem and Charleston in colonial times, what kinds of products would you expect to see on the ships that sailed from these two ports?

3. How did the large amounts of open land affect those who came to America?

4. How did the ocean tie some colonies to England and others to the rest of the world?

5. **Critical Thinking: Predicting Consequences.** How would your life be different if you were a colonial man, woman, or child?

See "Lesson Plan," p. 50C.

2. The colonists govern themselves

For 150 years after the founding of the first English colony, new colonies were settled, and the English empire grew, with little attention from England. In the seventeenth century the English people had problems enough at home. They were moving from the medieval world of monarchy into a modern world of representative government. In England Parliament was demanding the power to govern the nation.

England from civil war to Glorious Revolution. In the 1640s the English suffered through wars between the king and Parliament. After King Charles I was beheaded in January 1649, for a decade England was ruled by the obstinate and courageous Oliver Cromwell, who had led Parliament's army against the king. When Oliver Cromwell died, his son tried to rule, but failed dismally. Parliament called Charles II to the throne. Then Charles's brother, the foolish James II, who inherited the throne in 1685, soon alienated everyone.

The next explosion came with the "Glorious Revolution" in 1688. Then the king's opponents summoned William and Mary (daughter of James II) from Holland to take the throne as joint monarchs and preserve the power of Parliament. James II fled to France. When William and Mary came to the throne in 1689, they opened a new era of representative government. Parliament had shown that it was supreme. The monarch owed power to the people's representatives in the House of Commons. Never again would there be an absolute ruler in England.

William of Orange, who came to the throne with Mary, was also the leader of the Dutch. They had been fighting against France for their independence. The French under Louis XIV had replaced Spain as the dominant power on the continent. So in 1689, William brought England into the battle against France. From then until 1763, England fought four wars against the French on battlefields that stretched across the world—from Europe to India to Egypt to the West Indies to Canada. Meanwhile—when the government in London was too busy to notice—

the American colonies were prospering. In 1763 England made peace with France. Then the government of England could turn its attention again to its colonies.

During these years of salutary (or helpful) neglect, the colonies developed their own institutions. These would make it difficult for England ever again to rule them. But now that peace had come, England intended to enforce the policy of mercantilism. This was the same policy that Spain had so long followed in its colonies (p. 28). Colonies were only servants of the mother country. It was the prosperity back home in England that was important. Colonists were not to be allowed to manufacture anything that competed with products at home. They must be encouraged to grow what England needed. They must not buy from anybody but the English; they must not ship their products to any country but England. To help the English shipbuilders, the colonists must use only English ships built in England or the colonies.

This was the theory. In fact, the policy was not enforced until after Cromwell took over. The Dutch had begun to trade with the colonists while England was embroiled in civil war. In this way the Dutch reaped profits that England wanted for itself. To bar the Dutch traders from America, Parliament passed a series of Navigation Acts. These laws, from the 1650s down to the 1770s, gave bounties to the colonists for growing certain crops and dictated what goods they could manufacture, in what ships they could transport their goods, where they could buy and sell.

Earlier laws listed only a few items that had to be bought directly from England. This list gradually grew longer. At first goods could be carried in any ships, provided these were *owned* by Englishmen, but by 1696, *all* trade between the colonies and England had to be carried in English-*built* (which included colonial-built) ships. *All* European goods for the colonies had to come from or through England. The principal colonial products could be exported only to England or to another British colony. Trade with the English or not at all!

It is not surprising that energetic people, who had crossed the ocean and were just beginning to explore the resources of a vast new world, would not let themselves be fenced in. They wanted to ship everywhere and buy everywhere.

Smugglers and pirates. But the Navigation Acts were not regularly enforced. In fact they couldn't be. The British navy, busy fighting France, had no time left for trying to catch smugglers.

Smuggling then became a wonderfully profitable business in the colonial period. Many famous old New England and New York families like the Cabots, the Hancocks, and the Livingstons built their fortunes on colonial smuggling. It was descendants of these same families who looked down their noses at later immigrants in the nineteenth century. They said that these new arrivals might not have enough respect for law and order.

A "privateer" was a legally licensed pirate. ✂ After the first Navigation Acts, the word came into use about 1664 to describe someone who had a "private" ship that he used for government purposes. The owner of a private vessel in time of war could get a license from his government (called a "letter of marque," after the old French word meaning *to seize*) allowing him to seize enemy ships. Since he helped the war effort by crippling the enemy, he was allowed by his own king to keep a share of the loot. But when a privateer with a letter of marque happened to find any ship carrying a rich cargo, he was tempted not to take too much trouble to find out its exact nationality.

Once a privateer (or "pirate," to use the less respectable name) had loaded his ship with treasure, he would hurry to an American port, such as New York. In port, he simply showed his letter of marque and explained that he had seized his rich cargo as a patriotic duty to help the war effort. New York merchants, who themselves found this trade profitable, did not want to know whether the goods were from enemy ships or whether they were actually stolen goods. They were only too glad to have the privateers deliver merchandise to them that they could not buy from England, and which they were forbidden to buy elsewhere.

The pirates found New York especially to their

This painting from the 1750s shows British privateers and captured French ships in New York Harbor.

taste. His Majesty's governor and officers were pleased to have them around. The pirates paid handsome "protection money" to the governor. He issued their letters of marque, and he protected them while they sold their booty. There were few other places in the world where the market for pirates' booty was so good. Prosperous New Yorkers were ready to pay high prices for all the glittering items—heavily carved and inlaid tables and chairs, filigreed daggers, feathered fans, ornate porcelain, and gold-embroidered cloth—that the pirates had captured from "enemy" ships trading with the Orient. In this way the unenforceable laws and the continuous wars of the British Empire transformed reckless pirates into respectable merchants.

The problems of governing.

Even if the American colonists had not already been independent minded and determined to govern themselves, the vast ocean would have made them so. In the days before the steamship or the transatlantic cable, the colonial office in London could not govern across three thousand miles of water. The ocean was the father of self-government.

When Charles II finally created the Lords of Trade in London in 1675 to manage colonial affairs, they had to do their business by mail. But in those days there was no regular mail service. Letters from London to Boston went by ships that depended on wind and weather and often took many weeks. If the mail-ship was captured by the French or Spanish, the letters were delivered to the bottom of the ocean.

Although each colony had its own representative assembly, the person who had the greatest power and the highest social prestige was the governor. In most colonies he came from

Massachusetts State Archives

Sir Edmund Andros was both an English aristocrat and a trained military man.

England, but wherever he came from he received his orders from London. The Lords of Trade depended on him for information about his colony. But it was hard for him to get his messages across the ocean. If no ship was sailing, no message could go. The governor of North Carolina, for example, normally received his communications by way of Virginia. In June 1745 the Board of Trade in London (successor to the Lords of Trade) wrote Governor Johnson of North Carolina complaining that it had had no letter from him in the past three years. A full year later he replied from North Carolina that their letter had only just reached him.

During the long New England winter when Boston Harbor was frozen or impassable, the whole colony received no word from the outside world. A letter that the governor of Massachusetts Bay wrote in late November was not likely to reach London before the following April or May. By that time the information it carried would be ancient history. Even if the mail actually reached an English port, there were more delays. It might take weeks or months for mail arriving at Bristol or Falmouth to be carried overland to London. Papers addressed to the Board of Trade were sometimes lost in the customshouse, or they might lie there for a year before anyone bothered to deliver them.

Still, the king did try, from time to time, to control the situation so he might rule his distant subjects. Of all his domains, New England was one of the most troublesome. With its rocky soil, it could grow few crops that England needed, and so it did not fit well into the mercantile system. Its adventurous seamen were always daring to trade in prohibited areas.

The people of Massachusetts Bay, the richest and most populous of the New England colonies, found countless ways to irritate their king and express their rebellious spirit. Determined to "obey God rather than man," they went their own way. They coined their own money. They left the king's name off their legal forms. They ignored the Navigation Acts. They banned the Anglican church. They gave the vote only to their own church members. They even hanged Mary Dyer and three other Quakers on Boston Common.

Charles II had no love for these Puritan relatives of the fanatics who had beheaded his father. When Charles II sent commissioners to find out what was going on in the colony, they were insulted and ignored. Finally, in 1684, the king accused his unruly subjects of disobeying English laws. He managed to have his judges nullify the Massachusetts Bay Colony charter. The colony then became, like Virginia, a royal colony with a governor and council appointed by the king.

The Dominion of New England. In 1685 📖 James II succeeded his brother Charles II on the throne. James had been the proprietor of New York and New Jersey, so when he became king they automatically became royal provinces. From that start, on the advice of the Board of Trade, James decided to unite New York and New Jersey with all the New England colonies

📖 **More from Boorstin** "To those crimes punishable by death under the laws of England, the colonists by 1648 had added a number of others, including . . . the cursing of a parent by a child over 16 years of age (Exod. 21.17), the offense of being a "rebellious son" (Deut. 20.20.21), and the third offense of burglary or highway robbery. . . . But before we attach too much significance to these deviations . . . in England the merciful fictions of "benefit of clergy" nullified the letter of the law; in New England the practice of public confession perhaps accomplished a similar result." (From *The Americans: The Colonial Experience*)

into one large Dominion of New England. It would be ruled by a single royal governor assisted by a council also appointed by the crown. Representative assemblies would be abolished. At last the king himself would really rule.

All of these changes were bad enough for the independent colonists. James II made matters worse by appointing as governor Edmund Andros, a faithful servant and honest man, who happened also to be harsh, narrow, and unbending. He quickly antagonized everyone. At first non-Puritans and some wealthy merchants who were tired of the "rule of the Saints" in Massachusetts welcomed Andros. But he soon lost their support, too, when he tried to stop their smuggling along with the privateering and the piracy that made them rich.

The colonists were saved from Andros and the Dominion of New England by the Glorious Revolution of 1688. Without even waiting to hear if it was a success, the people of Boston seized Governor Andros and threw him in jail. Then the separate colonies went back to running their own affairs.

England would not again try to combine colonies. It was just as well, because communication was too slow for the effective government of large areas from a single center. Anyway, each colony had become accustomed to governing itself.

William and Mary revise the colonial governments. At first, William and Mary had too many problems in England and Holland to worry about the colonies. But by 1696 the English merchants saw that they were losing large profits because the colonial merchants were flouting the mercantile laws. They complained to the king and demanded that he turn his attention to America. He then formed a new Board of Trade (its full title was "the Lords Commissioners of Trade and Plantations") to oversee colonial affairs. For each colony he provided a regular customs service and special Admiralty

This handsome manuscript (from the Latin word for "written by hand") is the charter given by James II for the Dominion of New England. The king's likeness is in the upper left-hand corner.

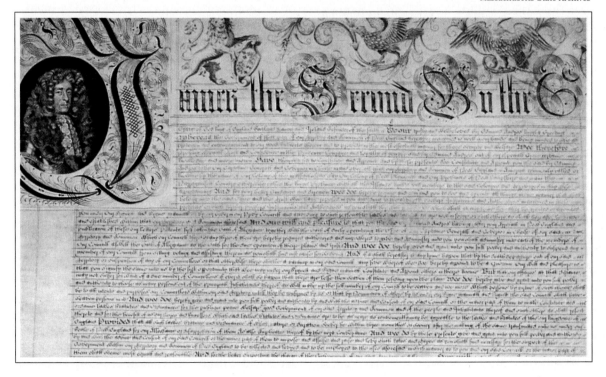

Courts (which had no juries) to catch and punish New England smugglers.

He imposed "royal" government on one colony after another. This meant rule by governors appointed by the king. In 1682 there were only two royal provinces, Virginia and New Hampshire. By 1729 all the colonies except Connecticut, Rhode Island, and Georgia had governors either named by the crown or appointed by proprietors subject to the king's approval (Pennsylvania, Delaware, and Maryland). Georgia became a royal colony in 1752.

The colonists did not really suffer much from these new efforts to enforce the Navigation Acts. Customs officers were glad to be bribed. The Admiralty Courts became tangled in all sorts of legal technicalities. The royal governors found that they could not govern without the agreement of the colonial assemblies.

This "Old Colonial System," as the years of salutary neglect were called, turned out to be a "system" for not enforcing the Navigation Acts. It seemed to work as long as everybody agreed to leave well enough alone. And so during the many years while England's wars kept the government busy, the population of the colonies grew and their wealth accumulated. Between 1700 and 1760 the foreign trade of the thirteen mainland colonies increased fivefold.

See "Section 2 Review answers," p. 50D.

Section 2 Review

1. Identify or explain: letter of marque, Charles I, Oliver Cromwell, Charles II, James II, William and Mary, Edmund Andros.
2. What was the Dominion of New England, and why was it important?
3. Summarize the provisions of the Navigation Acts. Why were they not strictly enforced?
4. Why was it difficult for Britain to govern America?
5. What was the Old Colonial System?
6. **Critical Thinking: Drawing Conclusions.** What impact did the Glorious Revolution have on British citizens living in the American colonies?

See "Lesson Plan," p. 50D.

3. Britain against France

The growth of the English colonies made a clash with France inevitable. From Louisbourg through Quebec, Montreal, Detroit, Sault Ste. Marie, Vincennes, and Natchez to New Orleans and Mobile a string of French forts tied together an immense, thinly settled empire.

For some time the French and English stayed far enough apart so that they did not bother each other. But the English were ever pushing westward. And after the Glorious Revolution when the energetic Dutch leader William of Orange and his popular wife, Mary, came to the English throne, it was not long before the two leading colonial powers of North America were at war.

America was a battlefield for European rivalries. A series of conflicts began as attacks by French soldiers and by their Indian allies upon outlying English settlements. King William's War (1689–1697), Queen Anne's War (1702–1713), and King George's War (1744–1748) climaxed in the French and Indian War proper (1754–1763). Life on the frontier became a nightmare. Unpredicted attacks by French regular troops and Indians were followed by massacres. Scalps were taken. Men, women, and children were kidnapped.

The Deerfield Massacre. One cold night in February 1704 the 300 inhabitants of the frontier village of Deerfield, Massachusetts, were sound asleep. Suddenly the silence was broken by French and Indian war cries. Within a few hours 50 settlers were dead and 17 of their houses burnt to the ground. One hundred and eleven settlers (including the town's minister, John Williams, his wife, Eunice, and one of his children) were taken prisoner. Eunice Williams, weakened by recent childbirth, could not keep up with the group as they were hastened north through the winter snow. She and others who fell behind were tomahawked and left to die.

Most of the tough New England settlers were more lucky. All but 17 of the 111 captives lived through the march to Canada. Finally, 60 of the Deerfield villagers, including John Williams

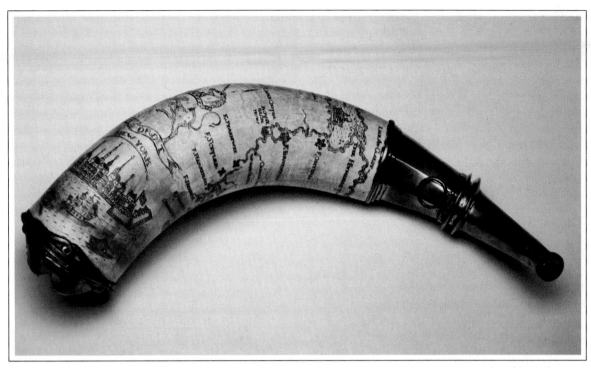

This powder horn of carved whalebone (scrimshaw) was made during the French and Indian wars. It shows a view of New York as well as Lake Ontario, right, and forts along the Mohawk River.

himself, returned to the English colonies. Of those who did not go home, some died, some married Canadians, some converted to Catholicism, and a few, including Williams's own daughter, married Indians and made a new life with their captors.

The colonial reaction. English colonists reacted to these raids by attacking Quebec or some other stronghold in New France. Once, in 1745, they captured Louisbourg, France's Gibraltar in the New World. When the English government returned Louisbourg in exchange for Madras in India, New Englanders were outraged. Their interests seemed to count for nothing when the government back home saw a chance to add a distant piece to the empire.

By 1750, English colonists were beginning to make their way through the Allegheny barrier into the valleys that led down to the Ohio and the Mississippi rivers. The governors of the English colonies called for forts to protect them against the French. The French, at the same time, moved vigorously to bolster their defenses. In one of the backwoods clashes, at Great Meadows near the forks of the Ohio where Pittsburgh now stands, a Virginia militia force was commanded by 22-year-old George Washington. There he won his first skirmish, but was soon forced to retreat to Virginia.

The Albany Plan of Union. The war that began at Great Meadows in 1754 was to continue until 1763. During these years battles were fought not only in America and in Europe, but even in India. This was truly a world war. Even before it had begun, American leaders had been calling for some union of the colonies. Now it seemed urgent against the bloody French and Indian menace.

In June 1754, just two weeks before Washington had to retreat from the French force, a colonial congress met at Albany, New York. Albany was then a small town on the Hudson River,

See "Lesson Plan," p. 50D for **Writing Process Activity: Expressing Problems Clearly** relating to the Albany Plan of Union.

sheltered from attack by a wooden stockade. The Iroquois in that area had long helped to protect the English from attacks down the Mohawk Valley because their traditional enemies, the Hurons, were allied with the French. The Albany meeting had been ordered by the British government to try to keep the Iroquois happy and firmly allied with the British.

The Albany Congress, attended by 150 Indians and representatives of seven colonies, renewed the alliance with the Iroquois. At the same time the colonial delegates voted to adopt a plan suggested by Benjamin Franklin for a new union of the colonies.

A Grand Council of 48 members (similar to that which the Iroquois used to govern their tribe) was to be chosen by the colonial legislatures. Meeting annually, this council would regulate Indian affairs, control a colonial army, manage the public lands, pass laws for the general good, and levy taxes for the common defense. A president-general appointed by the king would name the other high officials and could veto laws passed by the council.

But even the threats of war on their borders could not unite the colonies in this sensible common plan. The colonial legislatures turned it down. Each colony feared it would lose its power to govern itself. The king also rejected the plan because he feared that the union might give all the colonies together too much self-government.

The French and Indian War. At first the war that opened with Washington's skirmish at Great Meadows went badly for the English. To strengthen the defense of the colonies, in the summer of 1755 the British General Edward Braddock set out with 1400 British regular troops and 450 colonials to try to take Fort Duquesne. The French had built this fort at the point called "the forks of the Ohio," where the Allegheny and Monongahela rivers meet.

Braddock had been warned by Benjamin Franklin, who was shrewd also in military matters, to watch out for surprise attacks by the Indians. But Braddock did not listen. He expected the Indians to behave like troops in the orderly wars in Europe. Over there, battles were usually fought only in good weather, when small professional armies faced each other on open fields. But the French and Indians did not follow the etiquette of Old World warfare. They caught Braddock off guard when they attacked his army from behind rocks and trees. The general was killed, and 976 of his men were killed or wounded.

In 1757, when the brilliant and self-confident William Pitt came to power as prime minister of England, he declared, "I am sure that I can save the country, and that no one else can." He put new life into the nation's armies and its fleets spread over the globe. He was the architect of the first British Empire. He removed weak commanders, jumped young men over older ones into positions of command, and gave colonial officers their due rank. Pitt realized that the British troops in America were fighting for a worldwide empire and not just defending American colonists. When he assured the colonies that England would pay the costs of raising and supporting their armies, the colonists offered the British their manpower and their cooperation.

In the campaigns of 1758, the British and Americans working together were victorious against the French all along the line. The cold and capable 41-year-old General Jeffrey Amherst and General James Wolfe, a bad-tempered upstart of 30, both of whom Pitt had promoted to command, recaptured the stronghold at Louisbourg. Another Pitt appointee, Lt. Col. John Bradstreet, led an expedition of 3000 men through miles of wilderness waterways to take Fort Frontenac on Lake Ontario. Since this cut the French line of communication between Canada and Fort Duquesne, the French troops there soon had to be withdrawn. The English occupied the fort and renamed it Fort Pitt (later Pittsburgh) in honor of England's great leader.

The fall of Quebec. Pitt was now ready to carry out his grand strategy for the invasion of (p. 69) Canada. One army under General Amherst would go by natural valley through the mountains up the Hudson River–Lake George–Lake Champlain route to attack Montreal in the

Critical Thinking Activity: Identifying Alternatives What made Benjamin Franklin's Albany Plan so undesirable to the colonies? Offer a quick review of the events that led up to the plan. Ask students to critique the plan from the colonists' point of view. What was unacceptable in the proposal and what was appealing? Why would unification be destructive to the colonies? Finally, ask students to write an outline for an alternative plan that would offer solutions for the colonies that were being threatened by the French and Indians.

New France and Louisiana before 1763

French

English

Spanish

0	400 Miles
0	400 Kilometers

heart of French Canada. At the same time another force under general Wolfe would come by sea up the St. Lawrence to attack Quebec in the east. Wolfe's expedition reached Quebec in June 1759. But from then until September, while the British fleet lay in the river before the great rock of Quebec, Wolfe vainly sought an undefended landing place.

After a summer during which he was painfully weakened and often forced to keep to his bed by a mysterious disease, it seemed that Wolfe had failed. But he did not give up. Instead he devised an ingenious surprise attack. He shifted his forces one way to fool the French and then under cover of darkness slipped his men ashore at a point upriver where they were not

⊕ Geography and History: Regions Have students use the map on this page to examine the physical terrain and strategic position of the Ohio River valley in linking the French settlements in Canada to the Mississippi River. Have them identify the regions of North America that were claimed and controlled by England, France, and Spain.

expected. When daylight came, the French commander, the Marquis de Montcalm, was astonished to see the English redcoats (who were so named because of the color of their uniforms) forming their lines of battle on the high Plains of Abraham west of the city.

In a battle in the classic European style the two sides drew up ranks and faced each other on an open field. Since Wolfe had trained his men in marksmanship (which was unusual at a time when muskets could be aimed only crudely), the powerful volleys of the English soon broke the French and gave Britain the victory. Both opposing generals—Wolfe and Montcalm—were mortally wounded.

The French tried but failed to retake Quebec that winter. The next summer when British General Amherst marched into Montreal, the French and Indian War in America was brought to an end. Elsewhere, war continued for two more years. Spain made the mistake of joining the conflict and lost Havana in Cuba and Manila in the Philippines. The French and Spanish empires in North America had begun to dissolve. Britain's navy now controlled the seas, and the British Empire reached from India west to the Mississippi River.

The Peace of Paris. A peace treaty between Britain and France was signed in Paris in 1763. In the part of the treaty dealing with America, France ceded to England all of Canada and all French lands between the Mississippi and the Appalachian Mountains. France retained only two small islands south of Newfoundland—St. Pierre and Miquelon. These were not to be fortified and were only to be used for drying fish. England gave back to France the sugar islands— Guadeloupe and Martinique—it had seized in the West Indies. To its ally Spain, France ceded New Orleans and all its country west of the Mississippi, the land called Louisiana (after the French King Louis XIV). England kept Florida, but gave Havana and Manila back to Spain.

Before they sat down at the peace table, the English leaders saw that if they really wanted France to stop fighting they could not keep all the French lands taken during the war. They

had to choose. Canada was vast. But its cold climate resembled that of New England, and the land produced little that the homeland needed. At the same time, the tiny Caribbean tropical island of Guadeloupe was rich in sugar, which England desperately wanted. Some argued, too, that if the French menace was removed from the colonial frontiers, it would be harder to keep the American colonies in line. According to the mercantile theory, Guadeloupe was clearly more valuable than Canada. But William Pitt had a wider vision. He saw that Canada might be the bulwark of a grand new empire.

Benjamin Franklin, who was in London at the time as a colonial agent, wrote a persuasive pamphlet on the subject in his usual simple style. He predicted that Canada would become a populous and prosperous agricultural community. Then Canadians would buy English goods and enrich the merchants of the homeland. American colonists who saw the English flag flying from the arctic seas to the Gulf of Mexico would be proud of their Englishness and doubly loyal to the homeland. The English, he said, need not fear that the colonists would ever unite against their own nation. If they had not been able to unite against the French and Indians, surely they would never combine against the land of their beloved ancestors.

Franklin won his point. England took Canada from France and gave back Guadeloupe. Thirteen years later the colonies declared their independence.

See "Section 3 Review answers," p. 50E.

Section 3 Review

1. Identify: Edward Braddock, James Wolfe, Montcalm, William Pitt, Jeffrey Amherst.
2. Locate: Sault Ste. Marie, Vincennes, Natchez, Great Meadows, Fort Pitt, Lake Champlain, Plains of Abraham, Guadeloupe.
3. Describe the Albany Plan of Union.
4. Summarize the terms of the Peace of Paris.
5. **Critical Thinking: Identifying Central Issues.** In what sense was America an "unwilling battlefield" for European rivalries?

Chapter 3 Review

See "Chapter Review answers," p. 50E.

Focusing on Ideas

1. What problems did the colonists encounter in trying to govern themselves?

2. Why did plantation owners turn to using slaves to grow and harvest their crops?

3. How did conflict between France and England lead to the French and Indian War?

4. What was the goal of England's *mercantilist* policy?

5. By 1765 about 40 percent of the settlers in the English colonies were of non-English heritage. What were some effects of this mixture?

6. Describe Britain's "Old Colonial System."

7. Why did colonial artists specialize in painting portraits?

Taking a Critical Look

1. **Drawing Conclusions.** How did American colonial crafts reflect American lives?

2. **Testing Conclusions.** Do you think it is true that there was an American Revolution under way long before fighting broke out? What are your reasons?

3. **Recognizing Cause and Effect.** Britain's "Old Colonial System" worked best when it worked least. Why?

4. **Demonstrating Reasoned Judgment.** (a) To what extent was America involved in a "world war" from 1689 to 1763? (b) How did this war shape the future of the colonies?

Your Region in History

1. **Geography.** What countries had laid claim to your region by 1763?

2. **Culture.** What Indian or European settlements existed within 50 miles of your home by 1763? Describe how people lived in these settlements.

3. **Economics.** How, if at all, did the Peace of Paris affect the growth of the region where you live?

Historical Facts and Figures

Inferring Information. Some of the information in the graph below is very straightforward and can be gathered by simply reading the graph. Other information can be inferred. To *infer* means to draw a conclusion based on a careful analysis of the available data. Read the following questions and study the information in the graph. Then decide whether or not the answer can be inferred from the graph. If the answers need to be inferred, give the answer and explain how you derived it. (a) What percentage of the colonial population spoke English? (b) Were all Africans in the colonies slaves? (c) What is the largest percentage of the colonial population that could possibly have been Indians?

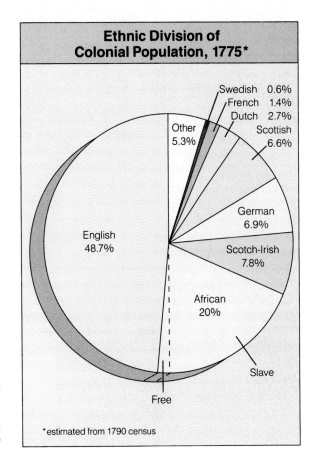

Ethnic Division of Colonial Population, 1775*

- Swedish 0.6%
- French 1.4%
- Dutch 2.7%
- Scottish 6.6%
- Other 5.3%
- German 6.9%
- English 48.7%
- Scotch-Irish 7.8%
- African 20%
- Slave
- Free

*estimated from 1790 census

71

MAKING CONNECTIONS

Unit 1

This unit began on page 1 with a brief but important observation:

In the Age of Columbus the peoples of Europe were discovering the world anew, reaching out to far and fabulous places.

This conclusion was supported by the three unit themes that are reprinted in **dark type** below. Use the time line and the information in Unit 1 to answer the questions that follow the unit themes.

THEMES IN HISTORY

Using "Making Connections": Have students look at the unit themes printed in dark type. Explain that each event on the time line relates to one of these themes. Ask students to decide which events are related to which theme. Students should use events from the time line in their answers and explain how events are related. You may also wish to have students go back through the text of Unit 1 to find other events related to the unit themes.

GEOGRAPHY

1. People leave Europe for the New World for a variety of reasons.
Evaluate the following opinion: "Immigration to America is the history of people trying to get *away* from some situations and trying to get *to* others." (Distinguishing False from Accurate Images)

2. The success of Europeans in the New World spells disaster for most Native Americans. CONFLICT
Some people believe that Native Americans would be better off today if Europeans had never discovered the Americas. Do you agree or disagree? List facts that support your conclusions. (Predicting Consequences)

3. Shaped by their experiences in the New World, colonists begin to develop new ways of life. SOCIAL CHANGE
Many people in eighteenth-century Europe believed the American colonists to be rough and uncivilized farmers. What facts contradict this opinion? (Distinguishing Fact from Opinion)

1606
The Virginia Company receives its charter from Britain's King James I.

Events in American History

1400	1450	1500	1550	1600

Events in World History

1456
The Gutenberg Bible is published in Mainz, Germany.

1494
Spain and Portugal sign the Treaty of Tordesillas.

1531
Pizarro conquers Peru, where the Incan center Machu Picchu still stands.

72

1616
Promoters of the colonies contrast overcrowded London with America's natural beauty.

1620
Separatist Puritans flee Britain for the New World.

1636
Harvard College is founded in Cambridge, Massachusetts.

1733
Georgia is established as a charity colony for London's outcasts.

1776
A Spanish mission is founded in San Francisco to convert Indians.

1776
Thomas Paine's *Common Sense*, urging American independence, is published.

| 1650 | 1700 | 1750 | 1800 | 1850 |

1700
The Indian population of Central and South America has dropped from 50 million to 4 million.

1789
The French Revolution begins.

Unit 2

Writing About History and Art: Direct students' attention to the unit introduction, illustration, and list of themes on pages 74–75. Have the introduction and unit themes read aloud. After a brief discussion of the subject matter of the unit, instruct students to write a brief paragraph explaining how the art:

—relates to the unit themes;
—exemplifies the unit title and illustrates the introduction; and
—is an appropriate choice for the unit.

Forming a New Nation 1763–1800

Winning the American Revolution, John Adams once said, was like trying to make thirteen clocks strike at once. The colonies were so different that they seldom had come to the same idea at the same time. Starting as colonies at different times and with different goals, they moved to independence in thirteen different ways. To bring the people of any single colony to agree was difficult enough. To lead thirteen different colonies to take common action seemed next to impossible. This was the main American problem in the War of Independence.

But the variety of the colonies turned out to be a secret weapon in the war. The colonies were like a monster with many heads. They could survive the loss of several of them. Nothing was more baffling to the British. Nothing did more to make it impossible for them to win the war. But after the war, this peculiarly American variety was a problem. Each new state wanted to act like an independent nation. They could not see that they ought to work together. During the early years, the Americans were still trying to find out what it meant to be the people of one nation.

THEMES IN HISTORY

- The British have trouble subduing the colonies because of the colonies' variety and lack of a critical center. CONFLICT

- The states' desire for self-rule and their fear of tyranny result in a weak central government under the Articles of Confederation. GOVERNMENT AND POLITICS

- The drafting and the ratification of a new constitution begin the process of binding Americans together into one nation. THE CONSTITUTION

◉ The American Revolution began on April 19, 1775, with the battles at Lexington and Concord. This engraving of the battle at the North Bridge in Concord was made by Amos Doolittle in 1775.
Print Collection, The New York Public Library, Astor, Lenox and Tilden Foundations

75

Chapter 4
The Road to Revolution and Victory

Identifying Chapter Materials

Objectives	Basic Instructional Materials	Extension Materials
1 The British Take a Collision Course • Describe the major events leading to the American Revolution. • Explain the economic pressures on England during the pre-Revolutionary War period. • Show how differing points of view affect the writing of history.	**Annotated Teacher's Edition** • Lesson Plans, p. 76C **Instructional Support File** • Pre-Reading Activities, Unit 2, p. 1 • Critical Thinking Activity, Unit 2, p. 6	**Documents of American History** • The Proclamation of 1763, Vol. 1, p. 47 • The Stamp Act, Vol. 1, p. 53 • Resolutions of the Stamp Act Congress, Vol. 1, p. 57 • The Declaratory Act, Vol. 1, p. 60 • The Townshend Revenue Act, Vol. 1, p. 63 • The Intolerable Acts, Vol. 1, p. 71 **American History Transparencies** • Geography and History, p. B31
2 Declaring Independence • Summarize the principles stated in the preamble to the Declaration of Independence, and list some accusations against the King in the Declaration. • Describe and explain the significance of the battles at Lexington, Concord, and Bunker Hill.	**Annotated Teacher's Edition** • Lesson Plans, pp. 76C–76D **Instructional Support File** • Skill Application Activity, Unit 2, p. 5	**Enrichment Support File** • To Arms! The Revolution Begins • Writing the Declaration of Independence (See "In-Depth Coverage" at right.) **Suggested Secondary Sources** • See chart at right. **American History Transparencies** • Fine Art, p. D17
3 How British Power Was Overthrown • Identify and describe the major events of the American Revolution. • Compare European and American styles of warfare in the 1770s. • Summarize the chief campaigns and battles of the Revolutionary War.	**Annotated Teacher's Edition** • Lesson Plans, pp. 76D–76E **Instructional Support File** • Reading Activities, Unit 2, pp. 2–3 • Skill Review Activity, Unit 2, p. 4 • Chapter Test, Unit 2, pp. 7–10 • Additional Test Questions, Unit 2, pp. 11–14	**Extension Activity** • Revolutionary War Battles, Lesson Plans, p. 76E **American History Transparencies** • Fine Art, p. D21 • Critical Thinking, p. F7

Providing In-Depth Coverage

Perspectives on the Declaration of Independence

In 1776 radicals in 13 British colonies along the east coast of North America declared that because of numerous acts on the part of the king of England they had no choice but to declare the colonies independent of England. The Declaration of Independence told the world that the colonists valued political equality and the rights of the governed, and that they thought the king had violated those rights.

Seven years later those rebels, whom the king had dismissed as traitors and rabble in arms, succeeded in creating a new nation. Chapter 4 focuses on this unlikely turn of events.

A History of the United States as an instructional program provides two types of resources you can use to offer in-depth coverage of the Declaration of Independence: the *student text* and the *Enrichment Support File*. A list of *Suggested Secondary Sources* is also provided. The chart below shows the topics that are covered in each.

THE STUDENT TEXT. Boorstin and Kelley's *A History of the United States* unfolds the chronology of events and the key players of the writing of the Declaration of Independence and the beginning of the Revolutionary War.

AMERICAN HISTORY ENRICHMENT SUPPORT FILE. This collection of primary source readings and classroom activities reveals details of the writing of the Declaration of Independence.

SUGGESTED SECONDARY SOURCES. This reference list of readings by well-known historians and other commentators provides an array of perspectives on the writing of the Declaration of Independence.

Locating Instructional Materials

Detailed lesson plans for teaching the writing of the Declaration of Independence as a mini-course or to study one or more elements of the Declaration in depth are offered in the following areas: in the *student text*, see individual lesson plans at the beginning of each chapter; in the *Enrichment Support File*, see page 3; for readings beyond the student text, see *Suggested Secondary Sources*.

IN-DEPTH COVERAGE ON THE DECLARATION OF INDEPENDENCE		
Student Text	**Enrichment Support File**	**Suggested Secondary Sources**
• Taxes imposed on colonists, pp. 77–79, 80–81, 83–84 • Benjamin Franklin, pp. 79–80, 84, 88 • Thomas Jefferson, pp. 82, 88–89, 96 • Continental Congresses, pp. 84, 85–86 • Thomas Paine, pp. 86–87 • Declaration of Independence, pp. 88–90	• Lesson Suggestions • Multimedia Resources • Overview Essay/Writing the Declaration of Independence • Primary Sources in American History/Declaring Independence • Art in American History/John Trumbull: Painter of History • Biography in American History/Thomas Jefferson • Great Debates in American History/The Debate Over Slavery in the Declaration of Independence • Making Connections	• *The Declaration of Independence: A Study in the History of Political Ideas* by Carl L. Becker, pp. 135–193. • *The Declaration of Independence and the Men Who Signed It* by David Freeman Hawke, pp. 140–175. • *Four Days in July: The Story Behind the Declaration of Independence* by Cornel Lengyel, pp. 233–314. • *Inventing America: Jefferson's Declaration of Independence* by Gary Wills, pp. 3–75.

The British Take a Collision Course

FOCUS

To introduce the lesson, ask students to think about the following questions as they read: Who caused the Revolution—the British or the colonists? Most students will probably say Britain, while some may object that neither side caused it—it was inevitable. One or two students may suggest that the British were not as bad as the colonists represented them to be.

INSTRUCT

Explain

Ask students to define the term *propaganda*. (The spreading of certain ideas or allegations in order to convince someone of a certain point of view or win someone over to a cause. Propaganda may be true.) Then ask what role propaganda played in leading the colonies to revolt.

❧ Cooperative Learning Activity

Making Comparisons Explain that students will work in pairs to write "opposing viewpoint" editorials. Have partners decide on an issue that divided the colonists and the British government. Then have partners decide who will write an editorial expressing the colonists' viewpoint and who will write for the British rulers. Have available newspaper editorials as examples of persuasive and expository writing. When all students have finished writing, have pairs identify the issue they chose and read their opposing editorials to the class.

Section Review Answers

Section 1, page 84

1. a) led the Ottawa Indians in their seige of Detroit. b) was not enforced, placed a duty on molasses imported from non-British islands. c) was meant to be enforced, placed a duty on molasses. d) secret society formed to stop the enforcement of the Stamp Act; became the center of the revolutionary movement. e) passed by Parliament after it repealed the Stamp Act, affirmed that Parliament did have the right to pass laws for the colonies. f) reorganized the colonial customs service and put a duty on many imports. g) an incident in which five Americans were killed by British soldiers. h) formed a network of colonists who communicated regularly to coordinate opposition to English efforts to impose taxes. 2. The Proclamation Line of 1763 was a British attempt to keep peace in the colonies. It prohibited settlement west of the Appalachian Mountains until an Indian policy could be implemented. 3. In the colonists' view, the Stamp Act did not deal with imports, and thus represented interference in internal affairs. Furthermore, if it worked, other taxes and other laws would surely follow. 4. The Intolerable Acts closed Boston's harbor, took away powers of the colonial legislature, prohibited the town meetings through which New England towns governed themselves, and declared that British troops could take over taverns and live for free in private homes. The British passed these laws to punish Boston for the Boston Tea Party. 5. A more astute English government would have attempted to set up a cooperative empire. Such a government would have seen that the colonists would not be ruled by others, but that they would compromise. The colonists would have been happy to have Parliament run their foreign affairs, while staying out of domestic affairs.

CLOSE

To conclude the lesson, tell students that everyone writes history from a frame of reference. Thus no history is absolute objective truth; rather, it is some historians' views (or interpretations) of events, based on the study of information and evidence, and the general knowledge and beliefs they bring to the task.

Declaring Independence

FOCUS

To introduce the lesson, point out that historians consider the question of who fired the first shot in any war important, because it allows them to know who was the aggressor and who the defender. For example, it was important to Abraham Lincoln, who wanted to *defend* the Union, that the South fire first at Fort Sumter.

Developing Vocabulary

The words listed in this chapter are essential terms for reading and understanding particular sections of this chapter. The page number after each term indicates the page of its first or most important appearance in this chapter. These terms are defined in the text Glossary (text pages 1000–1011).

mercenaries (page 86); **refugee** (page 87); **Loyalists** (page 87); **preamble** (page 88); **petition** (page 89); **revolution** (page 89)

INSTRUCT

Explain

Ask these questions to help students analyze the Declaration: To whom is the Declaration addressed? (The world.) What does Jefferson mean by self-evident? (Obvious.) What groups were excluded in Jefferson's time from the ideal that all men are created equal? (Slaves, American Indians, women.)

☑ Writing Process Activity

Recognizing Cause and Effect Have students imagine they are members of the militia during the Battle of Bunker Hill. Before writing a diary entry about their experiences, they should free-write about the facts of the battle as well as their feelings and reactions. Ask them to include an explanation of why this incident was a moral victory. Students should revise for specific detail and chronological order. After proofreading their entries, they can exchange papers and compare and contrast the variety of reactions to the same experience.

Section Review Answers

Section 2, page 90

1. Joseph Galloway and the First Continental Congress, because Galloway was a delegate to the Congress, where he attempted to revive the old Albany Plan. Paul Revere and William Dawes, because both rode through the Massachusetts countryside on the night of April 18, 1775, to warn that the British were on the march. *Common Sense* and Thomas Paine, because Paine wrote this pamphlet, in which he argued that it was "common sense" for the colonies to become independent. William Howe and Tories, because when Howe, a British general, retreated from Boston, he took with him many Tories (loyalists to the British government) as refugees. 2. The First Continental Congress agreed to end all trade with Britain, drew up a document that denied the right of Parliament to tax the colonies, and agreed to allow Britain to regulate trade as it had before 1763. 3. Americans considered the Battle of Bunker Hill a victory because it showed that the colonists could stand up to regular soldiers. British casualties were very high, much higher than American casualties. 4. America needed aid from France in order to obtain gunpowder, naval support, troops, and money. France was willing to help in order to obtain revenge and tear apart the British empire. 5. The Second Continental Congress adopted the Declaration of Independence in order to explain clearly to the colonists and the world why the colonies were in rebellion. This was necessary to secure domestic and overseas support. 6. The shot at Concord was heard around the world in the sense that it began a war for independence that would later influence movements for independence around the world.

CLOSE

To conclude the lesson, bring the class together for a discussion of who fired first. It is two witnesses against two witnesses. All have reasons to distort. One factor you might want to interject is the seriousness of an oath in the eighteenth century. The lesson here is the importance of interpreting evidence within the context of the time period. Impress upon the students that the important thing is the evaluation of evidence, not the question of who actually fired first. They are bound to ask you for the right answer. Have the students write an essay of 100 to 200 words proving that one side or the other fired first, based on the evidence presented in the handout.

Section 3 (pages 90–100)

How British Power Was Overthrown

FOCUS

To introduce the lesson, have students open their texts to the map on page 93. Point out that the map provides a rough time framework for tracing the course of the war, using the boldface numbers (1 through 7) and titles. Tell students to tally the number of American wins, British wins, and indecisive battles listed on the map. (British 8, American 11, Indecisive, 1.) Can they see any pattern? (Americans lose many battles, but are never decisively defeated. Whenever defeat seemed certain, the American rebel army and militia would rally for another round of engagements that kept them from losing the war.)

Developing Vocabulary

Hessians (page 90); **militia** (page 90); **guerrilla** (page 96)

INSTRUCT

Explain

Notice that the map "The American Revolution" on page 93 provides a rough time framework for tracing the course of the war. For a quick review, have students identify battles (and their significance) for each of the seven main titles on the map.

★ Independent Activity

Making Comparisons Read aloud to the class these two sentences from page 100 of the text: "Even today it is not easy to understand how the Americans managed to win. It is easier to explain why the British lost." Write two column headings on the board, European and American. To the left write these side headings: Rules of battles and styles of fighting; Casualty rates; Soldiers; Recruitment; Degree of patriotism; Dependability of armies. Have students work independently to complete the list with words or phrases, using the text as a guide. Below the chart have students write how the different positions on each helped or hurt the American cause.

Section Review Answers

Section 3, page 100

1. a) people who hire themselves out as soldiers to foreign governments. b) German mercenaries hired by the British in the American Revolution. c) pamphlet by Thomas Paine in which he urged the Americans not to give up. d) British general whose forces were captured in the concluding battle of Yorktown. e) British general defeated at Saratoga. f) French aristocrat commissioned as an officer in the American army. g) immigrated to America to help train the American army. h) helped lead the fight against the British in the South. i) commander of the French fleet in America. j) commander of the French troops in America. 2. All these locations can be found on the map on page 93. 3. In Europe the fighting was done by professional soldiers, on an open field, with clearly understood rules, and the war could be won by winning battles for the capital or a few major cities. In America the fighting often occurred in isolated areas, and winning a city could not win the war. Much of the fighting was done by militia soldiers fighting Indian-style. 4. a) Some farmers fought in the war; some prospered by selling their crops to armies of either side. b) Women had to take over men's jobs; some followed their husbands, going where the army went; some helped the wounded; some pretended to be men and joined the army. c) The British promised freedom to blacks who joined them and Congress eventually followed suit. Blacks fought on both sides to gain freedom. d) Some Loyalists fled when the war began; some fought against the rebels; some who stayed home were harassed by their neighbors. Many fled after the war, mostly to Canada. 5. The Treaty of Paris recognized the independence of the United States with boundaries that stretched from the Atlantic to the Mississippi River and from the Great Lakes to Florida. The Mississippi was declared open to both American and British shipping. 6. Poor planning on the part of the British did contribute to their defeat. They kept their headquarters in England, so communication lines had to span the ocean. They thought the Americans would be less prepared than reality proved, and they expected more help from the Loyalists than they received.

CLOSE

To conclude the lesson, ask students to help you compile a list on the board of things mentioned in the lesson that help explain how the colonists managed to win the war.

Extension Activity

To extend the lesson, have students research the battles of the Revolutionary War and create a time line based on their findings. Time line callouts should include the name of the battle, the approximate date, and the victor.

Chapter Review Answers
Focusing on Ideas

1. France nearly eliminated from North America; Spain expanded west; northwest disputed; British consider controlling migration. 2. First: Diverse opinions, no shared ideology. Second: understood needs of nationhood; prepared to use force and form army; urged "state" governments. 3. To rouse colonists against British rule. 4. Had to beg Congress for regular army; supplying, training, and sustaining troops throughout the war. 5. Non-English colonists adopted English laws, culture; became American; wanted independence for political and economic reasons.

Taking a Critical Look

1. Defend: British leader never visited the colonies; expected gratitude for military protection and acceptance of "justified" taxes. Challenge: Franklin warned Parliament about tax opposition; merchants noticed trade decline; leaders couldn't accept colonial spirit of self-government. 2. Agree: learned about colonial control; later war might have caused greater losses; strong U.S. ally a benefit in twentieth century. Disagree: would have been more dominant power longer; Napoleon might not have challenged Britain.

Your Region in History

1–3. Answers will vary depending on your region. Consult your local library or historical society.

Historical Facts and Figures

Answers should mention that colonial boycotts ended trade with Britain by 1776.

Chapter 4

The Road to Revolution and Victory

In 1763 few people in Great Britain's American colonies would have foreseen that in little more than a decade the colonists would declare their independence. Fewer people, still, would have predicted that in a revolutionary war the thirteen former colonies, which had never been able to cooperate on anything, would be able to defeat the most powerful nation in the world. Yet strangely enough, against all belief, that is exactly what happened.

John Trumbull, whose art brought him the title, painter of the Revolution, worked on this colorful oil, "Surrender of Lord Cornwallis at Yorktown," during the years 1787–1794. To be historically accurate, he drew many of the participants from life and also visited the site at Yorktown.

Yale University Art Gallery

See "Lesson Plan," p. 76C.

1. The British take a collision course

After its victory over the French in 1763 the British Empire was bigger than ever, which made the thirteen American colonies only a small part of the empire. To the north of the thirteen colonies the British had now added all of Canada, and to the west and south all the regions east of the Mississippi River, including Florida. The people living in these vast lands became new members of the British Empire.

The British situation in 1763. Between the Appalachian Mountains and the Mississippi River there lived 200,000 Indians who were now part of Britain's new empire. They had heard stories from the French that their new English masters were going to rob them of their hunting grounds. Indeed, in the spring of 1763 the Shawnee, Delaware, Seneca, and Ottawa were in the forefront leading the Indians of the West on the warpath.

By June the tribes had captured eight of the eleven British forts west of the mountains, and many settlers had died. Only Niagara, Fort Pitt, and Detroit remained, and Detroit was under siege by the Ottawa led by their able chieftain, Pontiac. This garrison was of such strategic importance that the British came to call the whole war "Pontiac's Conspiracy."

The British were so desperate that they even resorted to sending blankets infected with smallpox to the tribes. Many Indians died of the disease. Illness and British troops broke most Indian resistance by 1764, but not until the following year were Pontiac and his followers put down.

The English government came to the conclusion that it would take a standing army of 10,000 men to control the western Indians and to protect all the American colonies. This task they could not entrust to the colonists. The French in Canada did not like their conquerors. The Americans could not even unite to defend themselves. In fact, some of them had even aided the enemy by carrying on forbidden trade with the French and Spanish West Indies. So the government would have to send over an army to America. And it was decided the colonists ought to be made to pay part of the costs of this army sent to protect them.

The Proclamation Line of 1763. The trouble really began when the well-meaning men running the government in London decided in 1763 to set this far-flung empire in order. Their plans were much too simple and old-fashioned to work on a continent that was nearly all wilderness. To prevent fighting among the colonies, and to avoid war with the Indians, the officials in London decided to try to keep the colonists confined where they already were. Settlement of the new lands would have to wait until Indian relations and a land policy were worked out.

(p. 78)

The British thought that the Appalachian Mountains, which ran roughly parallel to the Atlantic coastline a few hundred miles inland, would be a useful barrier to keep the colonists separated from the Indians in the west. They proclaimed that for the time being the colonists should not settle on the western side of those mountains, and that the Indians should not go eastward.

This Proclamation Line of 1763 was a neat enough idea, but hardly designed to please Virginians. They were always looking for new tobacco land and were hoping also to make money from wilderness real estate. Virginians and other colonists wanted to go west now. Was not the continent theirs every bit as much as it was the Indians?

The Sugar Act of 1764. At the same time George Grenville, who was in charge of the British treasury (his title was "Chancellor of the Exchequer"), was desperately looking for ways to pay the bills left over from a century of wars. He was aware of how much the American colonists had eventually benefited from the successful outcome of the British wars against the enemies of the empire. In the backwoods, colonists had seen their homes burned and their families killed by the French and Indians. On the sea, colonial merchants had lost ships and goods to marauding French and Spanish and Dutch privateers. The empire had come to their aid and

---

More from Boorstin: "Perhaps the dominant fact about the relationship of the colonies to each other was this reluctance of any one colony to send its militia to join in the defense of its neighbor. . . . For a long time Virginia regularly sent a messenger to New York and New England to bring back word on the movements of the hostile French and the northern Indians —never to see whether help was needed in the North, but simply to be forewarned against a possible attack on themselves." (From *The Americans: The Colonial Experience*)

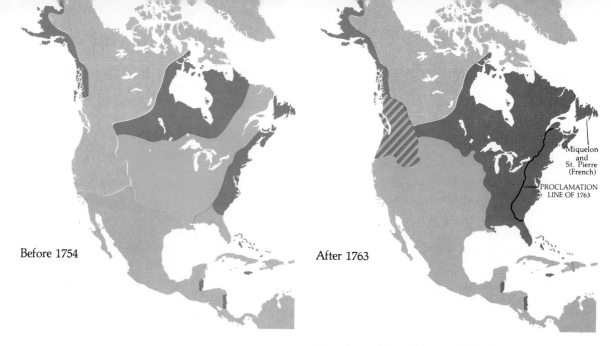

Before 1754

After 1763

Miquelon
and
St. Pierre
(French)

PROCLAMATION
LINE OF 1763

Results of the Peace of Paris

■ English ■ Spanish ▨ Disputed

■ French ■ Russian

ended all that. Why should not Americans now at last pay a fair share of the bills for keeping peace and defending the empire?

Grenville therefore persuaded Parliament to pass the Sugar Act in 1764. This act replaced the old Molasses Act of 1733, the only one of the Navigation Acts that might have caused real financial problems for the colonists. The Molasses Act had put a duty of sixpence per gallon on molasses imported from the French, Dutch, and Spanish islands of the West Indies into the ports of the American mainland. The molasses Americans imported was made into rum, which was sold in the colonies, used in the slave trade, and in trade with all the West Indies along with fish, lumber, horses, and wheat.

The Molasses Act would have made foreign molasses too expensive to buy. And the British West Indies, which the act was intended to help, did not produce enough molasses to supply the needs of New England merchants. New England's important rum trade would have been ruined. But the Molasses Act had not been enforced. Now, in the Sugar Act, Grenville lowered the duty on molasses to threepence a gallon, and he intended to collect it. Since the colonists had regularly paid a bribe of a penny and a

half per gallon to the customs officers, Grenville reckoned they could afford to pay the duty. Grenville's purpose was not so much to regulate colonial trade as to extract American money. In addition to taxing sugar, new or higher duties were also put on coffee and wines imported into the colonies.

The Stamp Act. Then, on top of taxing colonial imports, in the Stamp Act of March 1765 the British imposed on the colonies a kind of tax that had long been used in England. The British now put taxes on all sorts of everyday things that the American colonists used, even if they were not imported. To show that you had paid the tax, you had to buy specially stamped paper. A stamp had to be put on nearly every piece of printed matter in daily use—on newspapers, magazines, calendars, receipts, legal papers for buying and selling land, on ships' papers, on insurance policies, and even on playing cards. If your papers did not have stamps on them, they would be seized and you would be tried without a jury in an Admiralty Court, and be fined or jailed.

It was bad enough for an uninformed Parliament three thousand miles away to control

The hated Stamp Act of 1765 forced the colonists to buy paper bearing a stamp such as the above to show that they had paid the tax. After strong protests by the colonists, Parliament repealed the Stamp Act.

what came into the colonies. But many colonists still thought that might be a reasonable price to pay for preserving the empire and supporting the British navy. It was quite another matter—and far more serious—when the Parliament in London now started meddling inside the colonies. If Parliament taxed newspapers, then what couldn't they tax? If they could tax everything in the colonies, they could control all daily life. Where would it end?

In a new push to organize trade in the enlarged empire, and to improve business in England, Grenville now also decided to regulate the trade of the colonies more tightly than ever before. The old Navigation Acts restricting imports and exports had not been consistently enforced. Otherwise Americans would not have tolerated them. But Grenville intended that the new laws should be enforced. And to see that they were, he clarified the authority of the Admiralty Courts so they could try smugglers. These independent Americans would no longer be able to escape punishment by appealing to juries of their friends and neighbors, who seldom punished them.

The American reaction. If these new policies continued, Americans thought, they would no longer be American members of the British Empire with all the rights of freeborn Englishmen. They would simply be slaves of Parliament. Even in England, some people warned against the new policies.

The colonists quickly replied to what they considered British tyranny. They organized town meetings to protest. In order to punish British businessmen, colonists decided not to buy their goods. Some of the richest and most respectable Americans formed a secret society called the Sons of Liberty to terrorize the agents of the British who were trying to sell the hated tax stamps. They persuaded many of the British agents to resign. The Americans used all sorts of arguments, including brickbats and tar and feathers.

Hundreds of merchants in New York City, Philadelphia, and Boston agreed not to buy imported goods until the Stamp Act was repealed. Nine of the thirteen colonies sent official representatives from their colonial assemblies to a special Stamp Act Congress in New York City in October 1765, where they protested taxation by Parliament and the widening of the powers of the Admiralty Courts. They demanded the repeal of the Sugar and Stamp acts.

All this began to empty British pocketbooks. In a single year, 1765, British sales to America fell by £305,600, or more than 13 percent.

The London merchants began to worry. To save themselves, they demanded that Parliament repeal the Stamp Act. Benjamin Franklin, representing the colonies in London, went to the House of Commons and warned the British that they were on the road to ruin. If they did not change their policies, there would very likely be rebellion. The Americans, he explained, dearly loved their Mother England, but they loved their liberties even more.

The Declaratory Act. The rulers of Britain might still have saved the situation. If they had known the colonists better, they would have realized that Americans would not let their lives be run by others. A shrewder British government might have worked out a cooperative empire. Then there might never have been a War of Independence. But the rulers of Britain were shortsighted. They thought that government by Parliament had to be all-powerful or it would have no power at all. Unlike the Americans, they were not willing to compromise.

The colonists were practical people. They knew it was possible for Parliament to run their foreign relations and still permit Americans to have their own assemblies—in Massachusetts, in Virginia, and elsewhere—to govern inside the colonies.

The leaders in London did not see it that way. Even when they repealed the Stamp Act on March 18, 1766, they felt they had to pass a Declaratory Act that stated that Parliament still had power to make laws for the Americans "in all cases whatsoever." They did not realize that a new age had arrived. Two million people—one-fourth as many as in England—were now living in the thirteen colonies. And now they were beginning to be a new people—Americans.

The Townshend Acts. The British government continued on its collision course. The government still wanted money from the colonists, and Charles Townshend, who was now Chancellor of the Exchequer, thought he saw a way to collect it. To get rid of the stamp tax, Benjamin Franklin had told Parliament that the colonists opposed it because it was an internal tax but that they would accept external taxes, like the import duties. Franklin said this to bring about the repeal of the Stamp Act; but he knew it was not so, and his deception would make trouble. For in fact the colonies had made it very clear that they opposed any tax placed on them by a Parliament in which they were not represented. No taxation without representation!

Townshend chose to take Franklin at his word. He proposed duties on many items Americans imported: lead, glass, paper, paint, and tea. He also suggested that the colonial customs service be reorganized. Furthermore, he wanted the governor of New York to veto every act of the provincial assembly until New York provided the full amount of supplies to British troops stationed there—as it (and every) colony was supposed to do under the Billeting Act of 1765.

Glorious News,

Juft received from *Bofton*, brought by Meffrs. *Jonathan Lowder*, and *Thomas Brackett*.

BOSTON, Friday 11 o'Clock, 16th May, 1766.
THIS Inftant arrived here the Brig Harrifon, belonging to John Hancock, Efq; Captain Shubael Coffin, in 6 Weeks and 2 Days from LONDON, with important News, as follows.

From the London Gazette.

Weftminfter, March 18th, 1766.

THIS day his Majefty came to the Houfe of Peers, and being in his royal robes feated on the Throne with the ufual folemnity, Sir Francis Molineux, Gentleman Ufher of the Black Rod, was fent with a Meffage from his Majefty to the Houfe of Commons, commanding their attendance in the Houfe of Peers. The Commons being come thither accordingly, his Majefty was pleafed to give his royal affent to

An ACT to REPEAL an Act made in the laft Seffion of Parliament intituled, an Act for granting and applying certain Stamp-Duties and other Duties in the Britifh Colonies and Plantations in America, towards further defraying the Expences of defending, protefting and fecuring the fame, and for amending fuch parts of the feveral Acts of Parliament relating to the trade and revenues of the faid Colonies and Plantations, as direct the manner of determining and recovering the penalties and forfeitures therein mentioned.

Alfo ten public bills, and feventeen private ones.

Yefterday there was a meeting of the principal Merchants concerned in the American trade, at the King's Arms tavern in Cornhill, to confider of an Addrefs to his Majefty on the beneficial Repeal of the late Stamp-Act.

Yefterday morning about eleven o'clock a great number of North-American Merchants went in their coaches from the King's Arms tavern in Cornhill to the Houfe of Peers, to pay their duty to his Majefty, and to exprefs their fatisfaction at his figning the Bill for Repealing the American Stamp-Act, there was upwards of fifty coaches in the proceffion.

Laft night the faid gentlemen difpatched an exprefs for Falmouth with fifteen copies of the act for repealing the Stamp-Act, to be forwarded immediately for New-York.

Orders are given for feveral merchantmen in the river to proceed to fea immediately on their refpective voyages to North-America, fome of whom have been cleared fince the firft of November laft.

Yefterday meffengers were difpatched to Birmingham, Sheffield, Manchefter, and all the great manufacturing towns in England, with an account of the final decifion of an auguft affembly relating to the Stamp-Act.

When the KING went to the Houfe of Peers to give the Royal Affent, there was fuch a vaft Concourfe of People, huzzaing, clapping Hands, &c. that it was feveral Hours before his Majefty reached the Houfe.

Immediately on his Majefty's Signing the Royal Affent to the Repeal of the Stamp-Act the Merchants trading to America, difpatched a Veffel which had been waiting, to put into the firft Port on the Continent with the Account.

There were the greateft Rejoicings poffible in the City of London, by all Ranks of People, on the TOTAL Repeal of the Stamp-Act,----the Ships in the River difplayed all their Colours, Illuminations and Bonfires in many Parts. In fhort, the Rejoicings were as great as was ever known on any Occafion.

It is faid the Acts of Trade relating to America would be taken under Confideration, and all Grievances removed. The Friends to America are very powerful, and difpofed to affift us to the utmoft of their Ability.

It is impoffible to exprefs the Joy the Town is now in, on receiving the above great, glorious and important News.----The Bells in all the Churches were immediately fet a Ringing, and we hear the Day for a general Rejoicing will be the Beginning of next Week.

NEWPORT : Printed by S. Hall, for the Benefit of the Public in general, and his *good Cuftomers* in particular.

Mr. Lowder and Mr. Brackett, have rode all Night, in order to bring the above glorious Tidings, and it is not doubted all Sons of Liberty will be generous in helping to defray their Expences.----All Donations are defired to be left at the Printing-Office.

The news from London of the repeal of the Stamp Act was rushed to Boston. Then two men rode all night to deliver the message to Newport, Rhode Island, where the broadside shown here was printed. It notes that a ship owned by John Hancock had crossed the ocean with the report in six weeks and two days.

Critical Thinking Activity: Determining Relevance How did slogans help to enhance the revolutionary spirit? The revolutionary period of American history is chock-full of neatly constructed slogans, such as: "No taxation without representation"; "Join or die"; or "These are the times that try men's souls." Have students create their own slogans expressing the need for the colonies to unite. Have volunteers write their slogans on the chalkboard. Then lead a class discussion on the clarity, originality, and relevance of each slogan.

All these measures were contained in three acts passed by Parliament in 1767. The Townshend Acts, as they were called, created a fury of resistance in America. The act reorganizing the customs service was especially hated. The new officers who came to collect the various duties were little better than racketeers. Since they received one-third of the proceeds when a ship was seized and sold because it had broken the law, they used every trick possible to find an excuse to take possession of a vessel and its cargo.

❈ The chief method adopted for opposing the duties was to refuse to import British goods. By the spring of 1769 non-importation agreements had been made by the merchants of New York, Philadelphia, and Charleston. Within a year the value of British exports to the colonies fell nearly 40 percent.

Sam Adams and the Boston Massacre. In response to colonial non-importation, smuggling, opposition to the customs racketeers, and to the colonists' denials of Parliament's right to tax America, the government sent British troops to Boston. That simply increased colonial resistance.

One of the ablest organizers of colonial rebellion was Sam Adams of Boston. He was a strange man who always had trouble managing his own affairs, but could persuade others how to run theirs. He came from a well-known family and went to Harvard College, where he studied Latin and Greek. When his father set him up in business, he soon lost his father's money. Then when he became tax collector for the town of Boston, he got into trouble when he failed to hand over all the taxes he collected. He was always in debt, and many Bostonians considered him a shady character. But Adams made himself a master of propaganda and mob tactics. He was clever at creating a sensation out of every incident and blaming it all on the British. Two regiments of British troops sent to Boston in 1768 had been taunted for months by people there. Then late one March night in 1770 a small group of redcoats was jeered at and pelted with snowballs by a few restless unemployed workers. In their confusion, the British troops

Museum of Fine Arts, Boston

Samuel Adams fanned the flames of the colonists' outrage over British abuses in Boston.

fired and killed five colonists. The first to die was Crispus Attucks, a black man of giant stature who was the leader of the throng.

Sam Adams advertised this event as the "Boston Massacre" where bloodthirsty British soldiers slaughtered innocent Americans. Later, Sam's cousin, John Adams, defended the soldiers in court and was able to get them acquitted of murder. But most Americans still believed Sam Adams's portrayal of the event.

Britain backs down. In the face of American opposition and the boycott, which was severely injuring British trade, a new English ministry led by Lord North retreated. All the Townshend duties were repealed, except for a small tax on tea, which King George III insisted should be kept in order to prove that Parliament had the right to tax the colonies.

When England backed down, the colonists' scheme of non-importation collapsed. And many Americans, though it went against their

❈ See the "Lesson Plan," p. 76C for **Cooperative Learning Activity: Making Comparisons** relating to British and colonial views on issues leading to the Revolutionary War.

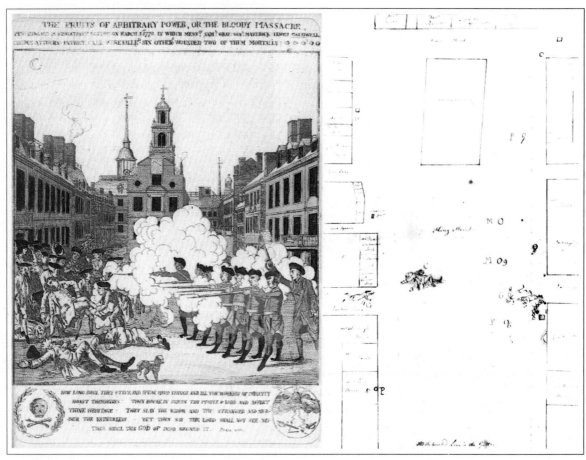

News of the Boston Massacre was spread by engravings like the one on the left which helped to arouse the colonists against British rule. The diagram showing the location of the bodies after the Massacre is thought to be the work of Paul Revere. The circles at the right represent British soldiers. Note the differences between the engraving and the diagram.

principles, paid the tea tax and the tax on molasses contained in the Sugar Act. They had won most of their points, and the threat of interference was much less. So the colonists traded and prospered.

Still, some energetic, freedom-loving colonists—including Sam Adams, Thomas Jefferson, and Patrick Henry—kept resistance alive. In 1772 Adams was the leader in organizing Committees of Correspondence in Massachusetts to consult on violations of the colonists' rights. The idea spread to other colonies, and in 1773 Virginia suggested that the committees in different states should work together.

The Boston Tea Party. The colonists were now ready to act as one, and at this point Lord North made a bad mistake. The British East India Company was in financial trouble. It had large amounts of tea stored in England. But the company could not sell the tea there because it did not have enough money to pay the customs taxes due. To help this huge business, which not only controlled the trade of India but even governed that land, the government decided to let the company sell the tea directly to the colonies without paying any duty in England. In this way the company, even if it actually paid the customs charges in the colonies, could sell the tea for less than the colonists were then paying for tea smuggled in to avoid the customs duties. Everybody, it seemed, would benefit. The East India Company would sell its tea, the crown would get the American duty, and the colonists would pay less for tea.

The colonists did not see it that way. Colonial merchants, who stood to lose their profitable trade in smuggled tea, led the resistance. They cried "monopoly" against the East India Company. They insisted that as soon as they went out of business the East India Company would raise the price of tea. Most of the colonies refused to buy any of the tea, which quickly became a symbol of British tyranny.

Boston, where it was easy to collect a crowd, became a center of agitation. On the night of December 16, 1773, a group of townspeople, organized by Sam Adams, enjoyed the most famous tea party in history. It was also a costume party because they put on the disguise of Mohawk Indians before they boarded the tea ships in Boston Harbor and threw overboard 342 chests of tea.

The Intolerable Acts and the Quebec Act.
Still the British rulers of the empire refused to retreat or to compromise. Instead the "Boston Tea Party" made them decide to use force. In a series of acts in 1774, called the "Coercive Acts" in Britain and the "Intolerable Acts" in America, they tried to punish Boston. They closed its port. They undermined the independence of the colonial government by taking from the Assembly the power to appoint the Governor's Council and giving that power to the king. They interfered with local government by forbidding towns to hold the meetings in which New England towns normally conducted their affairs. They declared that government officials and soldiers accused of crimes punishable by death could be tried in England or Nova Scotia. They gave British troops in America the power to

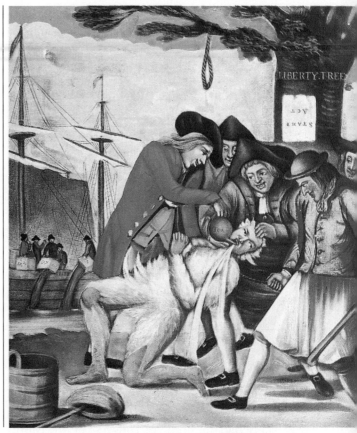

Courtesy of the John Carter Brown Library at Brown University

This British view of patriot activity shows colonists forcing a tarred and feathered tax collector to drink some tea. In the background, other colonists dump tea from a ship into the ocean.

take over taverns, and even to live free of charge in private homes.

To these measures Parliament foolishly added the Quebec Act, which seemed one more attack on the colonists' freedom. From the British point of view the Quebec Act was only an innocent attempt to organize into the empire the area taken from France in the French and Indian War. But when the act extended the province of Quebec southward to the Ohio River, it cut off the claims of Massachusetts, Connecticut, Virginia, and New York to their western lands. For that area the act set up a government without a representative assembly and gave special privileges to the Catholic church. The irritated and suspicious colonists saw the Quebec Act as a signal of what might happen to the thirteen colonies.

See "Section 1 Review answers," p. 76C.

Section 1 Review

1. Identify or explain: Pontiac, Molasses Act of 1733, Sugar Act of 1764, Sons of Liberty, Declaratory Act, Townshend Acts, Boston Massacre, Committees of Correspondence.
2. What was the Proclamation Line of 1763?
3. Why did the Americans oppose the Stamp Act?
4. What were the Intolerable Acts? Why were they passed?
5. **Critical Thinking: Identifying Alternatives.** How could England have successfully re-established its authority over the colonies?

See "Lesson Plan," p. 76C.

2. Declaring independence

Until the conflicts with the British government, the colonies had gone their separate ways. There had not been any congress or any central government where all thirteen colonies could meet and talk about their problems. Franklin and others had tried to persuade the colonies to join hands, but with very little success. Now within only a few years, the assertive politicians in London did more to push the colonies together than colonial statesmen had accomplished in over a century.

The First Continental Congress. In response to a call from Massachusetts to stop all trade with Great Britain, twelve of the colonies—all except Georgia—sent delegates (56 altogether) to Carpenters' Hall in Philadelphia on September 5, 1774. The meeting called itself the Continental Congress. It was not really the congress of any government, for there was no *American* government. It could be nothing more than a *continental* congress—a collection of delegates from the colonies that happened to be neighbors on the same continent.

At first each colony believed it had all the powers of a nation. Yet, because each had been part of the British Empire, many of the usual tasks of a national government—for example, building an army or navy, or conducting diplomacy—had been left to London. When the First Continental Congress met, then, it had to start from scratch.

The delegates to the Congress were men of widely varying views. Joseph Galloway, a conservative lawyer from Philadelphia, revived the Albany Plan that Benjamin Franklin had proposed twenty years before. Sam Adams and Patrick Henry desired outright independence. No one got his way entirely, but Sam Adams cleverly led the delegates along the radical path.

The Congress agreed to form a Non-Importation Association and cease all trade with Great Britain. Committees chosen in every county and town were to see that the boycott was obeyed.

The delegates also dealt with the difficult problem of the relationship of the colonies to Parliament. In a Declaration of Rights and Grievances written by John Adams, the Congress appealed to both the unchangeable "Laws of Nature" and the British constitution to deny any right of Parliament to tax the colonies. The colonists, they told the British government, could only be taxed by their own assemblies. To show that they were not unreasonable, however, they agreed to *allow* Parliament to regulate trade as it had in the Navigation Acts before 1763.

The battles of Lexington and Concord. Some Americans still hoped somehow to find their way back into the empire. But, in April 1775, within a few months after the First Continental Congress, dramatic events would put an end to their hopes. Massachusetts had been hardest hit by the British acts of force. And, without waiting for others, Massachusetts began to prepare for war by collecting military supplies in the little town of Concord, about twenty miles inland from Boston.

When the British Secretary of State for Colonies heard of this, he decided to act quickly to

Continuity and Change: Conflict Point out to students that, ideologically speaking, the impending war brought the colonies closer together than any other event in their short history. In later years, however, war would divide the country, as in 1812, when the South and the West sided against the Northeast over the impending war with Britain. (See p. 200.)

destroy that first supply base before the Americans were any better organized. Bostonians learned of the plan and on the night of April 18, 1775, sent Paul Revere and William Dawes on their celebrated ride to Lexington, which was on the road to Concord. They warned Americans to form ranks to stop the king's troops before they could reach and destroy the colony's Concord supply base.

Early the next morning when the 700 British troops reached Lexington, they found 70 American minutemen—militia who had agreed to be ready at a minute's warning—arrayed against them on the town common. The British killed eight and wounded ten Americans before hastening to Concord. As if by magic, the countryside sprang to arms. From nowhere appeared thousands of American militiamen. They har-

assed the British troops, who, before returning to their ships in Charlestown Harbor, suffered nearly 300 dead and wounded while the American losses were fewer than 100.

Now talk was at an end. War had begun. There was no turning back.

The Second Continental Congress. When delegates from twelve colonies (all but Georgia's, who arrived late) met again in their Second Continental Congress in the Philadelphia State House in May 1775, they were no longer American children pleading for better treatment from their British parent country. Instead they were armed colonists demanding their rights. George Washington was chosen commander in chief of the "Continental Army," which was drawn up around Boston. It could

This engraving of the Battle of Bunker Hill was made by Bernard Romans, an eyewitness, who was captain of a Pennsylvania artillery company. Later captured, he was taken to England.

Courtesy of the John Carter Brown Library at Brown University

not be called the Army of the United States, for there was yet no United States.

The Continental Congress quickly realized that they would need a navy. Following the old British example, the Congress, with their own letters of marque, began creating privateers. But now they were *American* privateers in hot pursuit of all British ships.

The Battle of Bunker Hill.

Sixteen thousand militiamen from New Hampshire, Connecticut, Rhode Island, and Massachusetts gathered around Boston after the battles of Lexington and Concord. Even before Washington could join his troops, these colonial militia met the English regulars in the bloodiest conflict that had ever taken place on the soil of British North America.

During the night of June 16, colonial militia under Colonel William Prescott were sent to fortify Bunker Hill across the water from Boston. By mistake, he and his men fortified Breed's Hill, and that was where a great battle was fought. But it was given the name of Bunker Hill—the hill where they should have been!

The next day the British decided to drive the Americans away from Breed's Hill. Twice the redcoats charged up the hill against Americans who were behind a rail fence stuffed with hay. Twice they were met with deadly fire and driven back with terrible losses. On the third attack the colonials, with powder gone, were forced from their position with bayonets.

But the American defeat in the Battle of Bunker Hill was a moral victory. It showed that the raw colonial troops could face regulars without flinching. When Washington heard of the battle, he said, "The country is safe." The British General Howe's loss of 1000 men was more than double that of the Americans. One-eighth of all the British officers killed in the Revolutionary War fell at Bunker Hill. "I wish we could sell them another hill at the same price," said one American officer.

The Americans offer peace and go to war.

After Bunker Hill the Continental Congress sent a petition, called the Olive Branch Petition, to King George. It asked the king to stop the efforts of Parliament to enslave them and said that they wanted peace and harmony with England. The king refused to receive the petition. But even before that, on July 6, 1775, Congress issued a spirited declaration of war:

> We are reduced to the alternative of choosing an unconditional submission to the tyranny of irritated ministers, or resistance by force. The latter is our choice. We have counted the cost of this contest, and find nothing so dreadful as voluntary slavery. . . . Our cause is just. Our union is perfect. . . . In defense of the freedom that is our birthright . . . we have taken up arms. We shall lay them down when hostility shall cease on the part of the aggressors.

Though Congress still said that it did not want to separate from Great Britain, the breach between the two sides deepened. The king hired 30,000 mercenary troops from the German princes of Brunswick, Hesse, and Anhalt to help put down the rebels. In America, royal governors took refuge on warships. Their legislatures were refusing to obey them and were converting themselves into popular conventions controlled by the radical leaders. Congress was laboring to increase Washington's army and provide it with food, clothing, and money.

Brave captains of speedy privateers were attacking British supply ships and seizing barrels of flour and gunpowder. Eighty yoke of oxen were dragging cannons, captured in May at Fort Ticonderoga by Ethan Allen and the Green Mountain Boys, over the December snow to Boston. Richard Montgomery and Benedict Arnold were leading American troops to invade Canada. On the last day of 1775, in the midst of a blinding snowstorm, Montgomery was killed and Arnold severely wounded in a vain attempt to capture the town of Quebec. So ended the patriot effort to conquer Canada.

Common Sense *stirs the colonies.*

On January 15, 1776, the most influential pamphlet ever to be published in America appeared. *Common Sense* was written by Thomas Paine, an Englishman who had come to America on

See the "Lesson Plan," p. 76D for **Writing Process Activity: Recognizing Cause and Effect** relating to the Battle of Bunker Hill.

COMMON SENSE;

ADDRESSED TO THE

INHABITANTS

OF

AMERICA,

On the following interesting

SUBJECTS.

I. Of the Origin and Design of Government in general, with concise Remarks on the English Constitution.

II. Of Monarchy and Hereditary Succession.

III. Thoughts on the present State of American Affairs.

IV. Of the present Ability of America, with some miscellaneous Reflections.

Man knows no Master save creating HEAVEN,
Or those whom choice and common good ordain.
THOMSON.

PHILADELPHIA;
Printed, and Sold, by R. BELL, in Third-Street.
MDCCLXXVI.

American Antiquarian Society

National Portrait Gallery, Smithsonian Institution, Washington, D.C.; on loan from the National Gallery of Art; Gift of Marion B. Maurice

Thomas Paine's 47-page pamphlet *Common Sense* roused the colonies against British rule. The painting of Paine is by John Wesley Jarvis, one of the leading portraitists of the time.

Franklin's advice to help the cause of freedom. Paine urged that it was simply "common sense" to stop recognizing the "royal brute," King George III. America should break all connection with Great Britain. This nation, he wrote, was destined to show the whole world how a people could rule themselves and be free of the tyranny of kings and nobles.

Common Sense swept the colonies. More than 100,000 copies were quickly sold. Many colonists agreed with George Washington that Paine's reasoning left no room for rebuttal. Edmund Randolph, a Virginia statesman, believed that, next to King George, Thomas Paine was the man most responsible for the declaration of our independence.

The British leave Boston. Washington brought the long siege of Boston to an end in March 1776 by seizing Dorchester Heights.

There the cannon brought from Fort Ticonderoga over the snow looked down upon the town and the British fleet in the harbor. This forced the British general, William Howe, to sail away with his troops to Halifax, Nova Scotia. With Howe went 1100 Tory refugees (Loyalists, the British called them) representing many of the "best families" of the colony.

Secret aid from France. What the Americans most needed was the aid of France with its great navy and, if possible, also the aid of Spain. So in March 1776 Silas Deane of Connecticut was sent to France to ask for help in men and money. To encourage this aid, the Continental Congress on April 6, 1776, at one stroke abolished a whole century's accumulation of Navigation Acts. They opened all American ports to all nations of the world, except Britain.

Meanwhile, fortunately for the Americans,

the French were already conspiring with the Spanish to use this opportunity to tear apart the British Empire. The French King Louis XVI secretly arranged to supply gunpowder to the American rebels. From the French the American armies received nearly all the gunpowder they used during the first two years of war. But this was only the start of French aid.

Enrichment Support File Topic

The Declaration of Independence. In May the Congress advised all the colonies to form their own governments. American independence was rapidly becoming a fact. The Americans had set up their own Congress, they had organized their own army, they were beginning to organize a navy. They had already plainly declared commercial independence by abolishing all the British laws of navigation. Then, on July 2, 1776, the Continental Congress adopted a short resolution "that these United Colonies are, and of right ought to be, free and independent states," and that all political connection with Great Britain was now broken.

With the resolution on July 2, Americans *announced* their independence. They gave out the news that a new nation was born, but they had not yet given out the reasons. Strictly speaking, American independence was not yet *declared.* ("Declare" comes from the Latin word meaning *to make clear.*) It was not the mere announcement, but the "declaration"—the explanation—of independence that Americans would always celebrate. For Americans were proud of the reasons for the birth of their nation. These reasons gave the new nation a purpose that it would not forget.

One of the remarkable things about the United States, which made it different from the older nations of Europe, was that it could actually point to the reasons why it had become a separate nation. These reasons were listed in a Declaration of Independence prepared and approved by the very men who made the nation independent.

Three weeks before the Continental Congress adopted its brief resolution announcing independence, it had named a committee to prepare a longer Declaration of Independence. Virginia's brilliant Thomas Jefferson, then only 33 years of age, was appointed chairman. Also on the committee were John Adams and Benjamin Franklin, but Jefferson did the writing and the others only changed a word here and there.

Jefferson did not try to be original in the Declaration; he only tried to state clearly what everybody already believed. He tried to write the common sense of the subject. He was speaking to the whole world. It was no good trying to persuade the world unless you started from what lots of people everywhere already believed. That is precisely what Jefferson did.

The opening part of the Declaration, usually called the "preamble," was cribbed from various books and declarations that Englishmen had written a hundred years before when, at the time of the Glorious Revolution, they removed James II and replaced him with William and Mary. The British then could not possibly deny Jefferson's words in his Declaration—that governments derive "their just powers from the consent of the governed." Nor "that whenever any form of government shall become destructive of these ends"—life, liberty, and the pursuit of happiness—"it is the right of the people to alter or to abolish it, and to institute new government . . . in such form as to them shall seem most likely to effect their safety and happiness." Their own British government, as they were repeatedly saying after 1688, was made by precisely that formula. You could hardly call an idea radical if it was the basis of the very respectable government of England.

After the common sense in the preamble there came a long list—"a long train of abuses and usurpations." Every item showed how the British king, George III, had disobeyed his own laws. The king aimed to reduce the colonists to "absolute despotism," to establish "an absolute tyranny over these states." His many crimes included "cutting off our trade with all parts of the world," "imposing taxes on us without our consent," and "quartering large bodies of armed troops among us." They also included the king's crimes against the very special rights of Englishmen—for example, taking away the right of trial by jury and violating the legal charters given to the colonies.

The colonists, Jefferson explained, had

The Second Continental Congress approves the Declaration of Independence. Benjamin Franklin is seated in the center.

shown great respect for their king and great love for their "British brethren." "In every stage of these oppressions we have petitioned for redress in the most humble terms: Our repeated petitions have been answered only by repeated injury." The king had proved himself a tyrant, "unfit to be the ruler of a free people." If the king would not respect the colonists' rights, the Americans had no choice. They had to set up their own government.

Jefferson's Declaration simply ignored the British Parliament. For, according to Jefferson, Parliament had no rights over the colonies. It was the king's duty to hold the empire together and to protect all his subjects. The Americans demanded nothing but their simple rights as British subjects. The king had denied those traditional rights. The law was on the side of the Americans. If Americans wondered why they were fighting, here was their simple answer.

On July 4, 1776, Jefferson's Declaration of Independence was approved by the Second Continental Congress, signed by John Hancock,

the president of the Congress, and certified by the secretary. Then copies were sent out to all the states. As new members arrived to represent colonies in Congress, they too signed the Declaration, even though they had not been there when Jefferson first presented it. One representative signed it as late as November (there were finally 56 signatures altogether). In this way, they showed that they believed in the 🏛 Revolution.

Jefferson had written an eloquent birth certificate of the new United States, which would inspire people all over the world. A few years after the American Revolution was won, when the French people decided to defend their own rights against their king, they found inspiration in Jefferson's words. In the 1820s, when colonists in South America separated from Spain, they turned to the same source. Jefferson's Declaration of Independence, like other documents that live and shape history, has had the magical power to be filled with new ideas. In the twentieth century, when colonists in Asia and Africa tried to explain to the world why they

🏛 **More from Boorstin:** "One explanation, given by Thomas McKean, a member of Congress from Pennsylvania who had been present on July 4, was that the purpose of the Declaration as finally signed was to provide a kind of public loyalty-oath, a pledge of allegiance to the course already taken. Or (as he put it), 'to prevent traitors or spies from worming themselves among us.' It seems to have been decided for security's sake that 'no person should have a seat in Congress during that year until he should have signed the declaration of independence.'" (From *The Americans: The National Experience*)

were fighting for their independence, they still recalled the Declaration of Independence of the thirteen American colonies.

See "Section 2 Review answers," p. 76D.

Section 2 Review

1. Match each of the following with another in the list: Joseph Galloway, Paul Revere, *Common Sense*, William Howe, William Dawes, Tories, First Continental Congress, Thomas Paine. Why should each pair go together?

2. Name three tasks the First Continental Congress accomplished.

3. Although losing at Bunker Hill, the patriots considered the battle a victory. Why?

4. Why did America need French aid? Why was France willing to help?

5. Why did the Second Continental Congress adopt a Declaration of Independence?

6. **Critical Thinking: Distinguishing False from Accurate Images.** The first shot fired at Concord has been called "the shot heard round the world." How does this image express the significance of the American Revolution?

See "Lesson Plan," p. 76D.

3. How British power was overthrown

America produced a new style of warfare. Here the skirmish, not the battle, was important. Communications did not exist, the land was vast. There was no way of directing operations from a center. Every man for himself! Colonists had learned to hide behind rocks and tree trunks.

"In our first war with the Indians," the Puritan missionary John Eliot noted back in 1677, "God pleased to show us the vanity of our military skill, in managing our arms, after the European mode. Now we are glad to learn the skulking way of war."

War in Europe in the 1700s. In Europe it was the Age of Limited Warfare. Armies fought according to certain definite rules, which made a battle in many ways like a football match.

Battles took place on open fields, in good weather. Each side set up its men in neat array. Each side knew what forces the other possessed, and each part of an army was expected to perform only certain maneuvers. To begin a battle before the heralds had sounded their fanfares, to use sneak tactics or unusual weapons, were generally frowned upon.

The only people who fought were the professionals out there on the battlefield. Officers came from the aristocracy. They knew the rules and were willing to abide by them. At nightfall, or when the weather was bad, officers from opposing armies would actually entertain one another at dinner parties, concerts, and balls. Then the next day they would take their places on the battlefield. The privates were human dregs who had been dragged out of jails and bars. The best-trained and most reliable soldiers often were mercenaries—like the Swiss or the Hessians—who made a living from hiring themselves out to the highest bidder.

Patriotism had very little to do with those battles. Armies were small. The men were seldom fighting to preserve their country, but more often for some secret purpose known only to the monarch and his few advisers. By modern standards, the casualties were few. Weapons were crude. The old-fashioned musket had a poor aim, was hard to reload, and would not fire at all in wet weather—so armies had the pleasant custom of going into winter quarters. Kings could have their battles, and yet interfere very little with the peaceful round of daily life. The people could leave the fighting to the professional soldiers.

The American soldier. In America, the Indian had never heard of the polite tradition of war-by-the-rules. The Indian conducted a primitive form of total war. And the colonists' only good protection was a primitive form of total defense. Colonists could not leave their defense to professional soldiers far away on some neat battlefield. Where everybody was a target, every man, woman, and child had to be a soldier. Here, then, grew a new and American kind of army. The colonists called it their "militia." The militia was not really an army at all, but only a name

This engraving by Amos Doolittle shows how British soldiers fought out in the open in neat rows and bright uniforms. From the Indians Americans had learned a different way of fighting. Here minutemen hiding behind a stone wall harass the British retreating from Concord in 1775.

for all the men who bore arms. Regular membership in the militia usually began at about 16 years of age, and might last till a man was 60. There was no uniform, not much discipline, and little of the colorful ritual of the European battlefields.

Still, against a professional army like that of the British Empire, the militia had some grave disadvantages. American militiamen often ran away or stopped fighting if they felt like it. The very idea of enlistment—which kept men in the army even when it was personally inconvenient— did not suit the militia. These were vexing problems for George Washington. His forces consisted largely of militiamen, but he could never be sure how many he could count on.

Militia were a home guard and not an imperial army. They did not like to travel far from home. But the American Revolution had to be fought wherever the battle required and against a large regular army. George Washington's first, and probably his greatest, achievement was somehow to create a Continental Army.

This Continental Army was made up of men who were enlisted and paid by the Continental Congress. It was a small regular army of the European sort, but it could always be helped by the militia. If it was hard to bring the militia together, that was because they were spread all over the continent. In vast and trackless America, that itself could be helpful. You did not have to transport all your soldiers. Wherever you

More from Boorstin: "All the American armies were competing against each other for men, for officers, for rank, and for glory. Privates from New England were being offered higher pay than those from the Middle States. Massachusetts even offered to pay its men by lunar rather than calendar months to secure a competitive advantage." (From *The Americans: The Colonial Experience*)

were, or wherever the enemy was, the militia was always there.

The major problem with the militia was that you could not depend on them. Forces of militia melted away whenever the men decided to go home to help bring in the harvest, or to be present at the birth of a child, or sometimes simply because they were tired of fighting. When General Washington begged Congress for a regular army organized in the European way, he complained that he had never seen a single instance of militia "being fit for the real business of fighting. I have found them useful as light parties to skirmish in the woods, but incapable of making or sustaining a serious attack."

So the militia were useful and useless. They were everywhere and nowhere. They might by their very presence keep an enemy from winning, but could a militia ever *win*?

🌐 ***Washington creates, and saves, an army.*** After the evacuation of Boston by the British troops, the military history of the American Revolution falls into two stages. The first part was the critical period from 1776 to 1778, when fighting took place in the North. During this time Washington's greatest tasks were to organize an army and then keep it in the field and prevent it from being destroyed by the British. The second stage of the war came in the years 1779 to 1781. Washington had proved in the first phase that he could not be easily defeated, so fighting moved to the South where the British hoped the Loyalists would rise to help them. If the southern colonies surrendered, the British expected that it would be easier to reconquer the North.

In the beginning of the first phase, Washington had to create a Continental Army and also fight the British. After the British left Boston, Washington moved to New York City and Long Island, where he expected the next attack. The British did not disappoint him. In July and August 1776, they poured men and equipment onto Staten Island until they had a force there of 32,000 soldiers. New York City in normal times contained only 25,000 people! Washington faced this great force with 23,000 men, most of whom were militia.

The British general, William Howe, crossed from Staten Island and landed 20,000 well-trained soldiers on Long Island during August 22–25, 1776. They attacked Washington's untrained troops on the 27th, inflicting heavy casualties. The American army retreated, and Colonel John Glover and his Massachusetts regiment of Marblehead fishermen ferried the army together with its horses, cannons, food, and equipment across the East River to Manhattan Island under the cover of fog. In this retreat, and again in the retreat from Manhattan Island that followed when Howe's redcoats crossed the river on September 15, the most important thing was for Washington to get his army away. Had Washington's army been trapped at that time, the rebellion might have been over. Cities the British could have, for there was no center in America whose loss would really matter. But if the American army was lost, all might be lost.

The British followed Washington out of New York and across the Hudson River. As he retreated through New Jersey in November 1776, the redcoats were close behind. This was the low point of the war for Washington and for the American cause. The militia drifted off to their homes. The regular troops were on one-year enlistments that would end on December 31. With the military situation looking so bleak, they would not re-enlist and new men were unlikely to take their places. Washington's army would just fade away.

On December 7, 1776, Washington crossed the Delaware River into Pennsylvania. The last boatloads were just crossing from Trenton when the British entered that town. On December 18 Washington informed his brother, "If every nerve is not strained to recruit the new army, . . . I think the game is pretty near up." Thomas Paine called this *The Crisis* and wrote:

> These are the times that try men's souls. The summer soldier and the sunshine patriot will, in this crisis, shrink from the service of their country; but he that stands it *now*, deserves the love and thanks of man and woman.

🌐 **Geography and History: Movement** Refer students to the map on the facing page. Point out that the map provides a rough time framework for tracing the course of the war, using boldface numbers (1 through 7) and titles. Have the students briefly discuss the significance of each battle shown on the map.

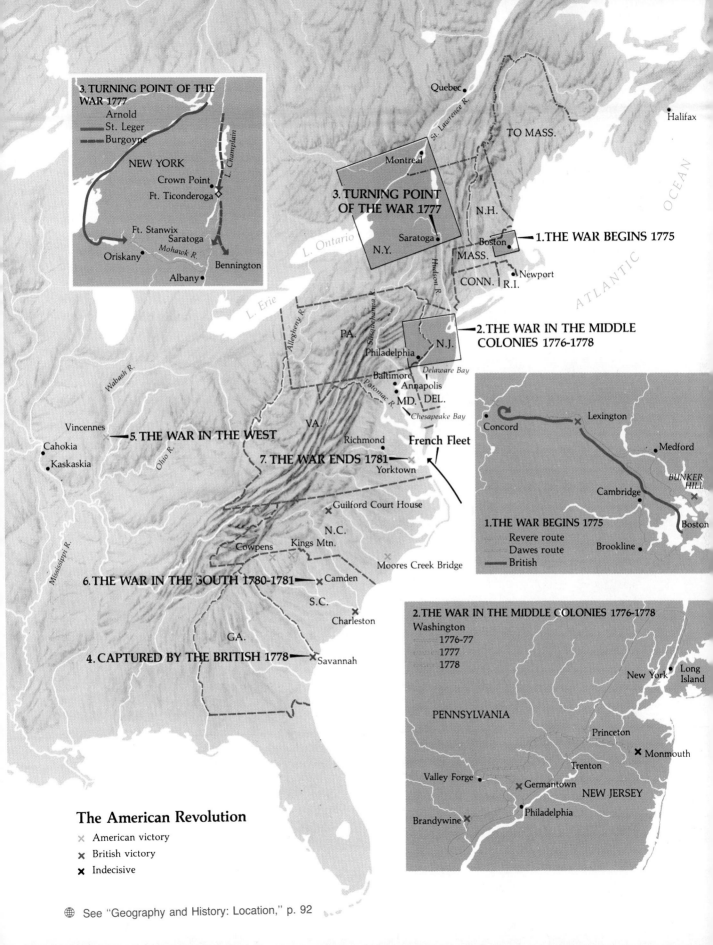

3. TURNING POINT OF THE WAR 1777
Arnold
St. Leger
Burgoyne

NEW YORK

Quebec
Halifax

TO MASS.

Montreal

L. Ontario

Crown Point
Ft. Ticonderoga

L. Champlain

Ft. Stanwix
Oriskany
Saratoga
Mohawk R.
Albany
Bennington

3. TURNING POINT OF THE WAR 1777

N.H.

N.Y.

Saratoga

Boston

1. THE WAR BEGINS 1775

MASS.

Hudson R.

CONN.
R.I.
Newport

L. Erie

Allegheny R.

Susquehanna R.

PA.

N.J.

Philadelphia

2. THE WAR IN THE MIDDLE COLONIES 1776-1778

Delaware Bay

Baltimore
Annapolis
Potomac R.
MD. DEL.

Chesapeake Bay

Wabash R.

Vincennes

5. THE WAR IN THE WEST

VA.

Richmond

French Fleet

Cahokia
Kaskaskia

Ohio R.

7. THE WAR ENDS 1781
Yorktown

Mississippi R.

Guilford Court House

Cowpens
Kings Mtn.
N.C.

Moores Creek Bridge

6. THE WAR IN THE SOUTH 1780-1781
Camden

S.C.

Charleston

GA.

4. CAPTURED BY THE BRITISH 1778
Savannah

ATLANTIC OCEAN

Concord
Lexington
Medford
BUNKER HILL
Cambridge
Boston
Brookline

1. THE WAR BEGINS 1775
Revere route
Dawes route
British

2. THE WAR IN THE MIDDLE COLONIES 1776-1778
Washington
1776-77
1777
1778

New York
Long Island

PENNSYLVANIA

Princeton
Monmouth

Valley Forge
Germantown
Trenton
NEW JERSEY
Brandywine
Philadelphia

The American Revolution

✗ American victory
✗ British victory
✗ Indecisive

See "Geography and History: Location," p. 92

Yale University Art Gallery, Gift of the Associates
in Fine Arts and Mrs. Henry F. Loomis in Memory
of Henry Bradford Loomis, BA 1875

This portrait of Washington at the Battle of Princeton
was painted three or four years after the fight by Charles
Willson Peale, who served as an officer in the American
army there. Although not a realistic battle scene, the
painting shows Washington's self-confidence and poise.
Peale set up one of the first museums in America.

Even after receiving reinforcements from other
units, and 2000 militia from Pennsylvania,
Washington had fewer than 8000 men. Nevertheless, he decided he must attack while he still
had some soldiers. So on the night of December
25, John Glover and the Marblehead men ferried Washington and 2400 of his troops across
the ice-filled Delaware River in a driving sleet
storm. On the next day they struck Trenton,
where Hessian mercenaries were sleeping off
their holiday celebration. The surprise was
complete. With a loss of only four men, the
Americans took 900 prisoners.

The victory at Trenton, and Washington's persuasive powers, encouraged many of his soldiers to re-enlist for a little longer. Then he
moved on the British again. He fooled General
Charles Cornwallis and the main British army
by marching away in the night from his burning campfires. Before Cornwallis had time to
react, Washington had routed the British rear
guard at Princeton.

After the battle at Princeton, the British evacuated New Jersey and returned to New York.
Then both armies went into winter quarters. In
a brilliant campaign of ten days Washington
had saved the cause of independence. American
morale shot up, enlistments increased, the war
would go on. Lord George Germain, the new
British Minister of War, sadly confessed that all
his hopes "were blasted by the unhappy affair at
Trenton."

Victory at Saratoga brings help from France.
The British drew up an elaborate plan for the
military campaigns of the summer of 1777.
Three armies were to invade New York and
unite at Albany. By controlling the Hudson
River they would shut off New England from the
other colonies. Pleasure-loving "Gentleman
Johnny" Burgoyne was to come down from
Montreal by way of Lake Champlain and the
upper Hudson. Lieutenant Colonel St. Leger
was to move eastward from Lake Ontario
through the Mohawk Valley, and General Howe
was to come up the Hudson. So the plan said.

This scheme showed how little the British
had learned from Braddock's defeat of twenty
years earlier. For it totally disregarded the conditions of travel in northern and western New
York. Had the forces succeeded in meeting at
Albany, it is doubtful they could have held the
land they had marched through. In addition the

British had come up with a plan that favored the American militia. The British tactics were perfect for Europe, where the people from the neighboring countryside did not take part in the war and where by capturing a town it was possible to dominate an area. In America none of that was true, as the British were soon bitterly to learn.

St. Leger was defeated before he got halfway to Albany. Howe, perhaps because Lord Germain forgot to send his instructions, sailed off to Chesapeake Bay and then captured Philadelphia. Burgoyne proceeded to walk into a trap. The farther he moved into the forests, the more the militia from the countryside swarmed around him. Finally, at Saratoga, New York, he was brought to bay. He surrendered his outnumbered army on October 17, 1777.

The American victory at Saratoga was a turning point in history. The French, who were already secretly helping the Americans, now openly proclaimed themselves allies. On February 7, 1778, the French signed a treaty of alliance with the new American nation. Now American independence seemed assured. The Revolution could hardly fail with the help of the money, supplies, troops, and (most important of all) the navy of one of the world's great powers.

Washington heard the welcome news of the French alliance at Valley Forge, where he and his army had spent a terrible winter. Still he had kept his army together, and Baron von Steuben, who became Washington's right-hand man, had drilled it into a better fighting force.

Von Steuben had come, as had other European officers, to help the American cause. From France came the aristocratic young Marquis de Lafayette, who was commissioned a major general in the American army at the age of twenty! From Germany, in addition to von Steuben, came "Baron" de Kalb, also to be a major general. From Poland came Count Casimir Pulaski (killed fighting in the South) and Thaddeus Kosciusko (who built the fortifications at West Point).

The nature of the war was about to change. The British had now decided to move the battle

By His EXCELLENCY
GEORGE WASHINGTON, Esquire,
GENERAL and COMMANDER in CHIEF of the Forces of the UNITED STATES of America.

BY Virtue of the Power and Direction to Me especially given, I hereby enjoin and require all Persons residing within seventy Miles of my Head Quarters to thresh one Half of their Grain by the 1st Day of February, and the other Half by the 1st Day of March next ensuing, on Pain, in Case of Failure, of having all that shall remain in Sheaves after the Period above mentioned, seized by the Commissaries and Quarter-Masters of the Army, and paid for as Straw.

G I V E N *under my Hand, at Head Quarters, near the Valley Forge, in Philadelphia County, this 20th Day of December,* 1777.

G. *W A S H I N G T O N.*
By His Excellency's Command,
ROBERT H. HARRISON, Sec'y.

LANCASTER; Printed by JOHN DUNLAP.

Historical Society of Pennsylvania

The winter that Washington's army spent at Valley Forge was bleak. Food, clothing, and fuel were scarce. In this broadside, Washington orders local farmers to thresh their grain. Then the army could buy it. Grain not threshed would be seized, and the farmers would be paid only for straw.

south, where they expected more help from the Loyalists. Also, the British army would then be closer to their colonies in the West Indies if the French attacked there.

With the decision to move south, General Clinton, who had succeeded Howe in the British command, abandoned Philadelphia. As Clinton marched back to New York, the British forces were attacked by Washington's army at Monmouth, New Jersey, on June 28, 1778. A fierce battle ensued, but the result was a draw. The British went on to New York and thereafter ventured out of that city only on raids. Monmouth was the last big battle of the war north of Virginia.

The pace of the war now slowed, and combat moved to the edges of the colonies. Out in the

Multicultural Connection: One of the most famous spies of the American Revolution was James Armistead LaFayette. At the age of twenty-one, Armistead, who was enslaved, became a spy for the Marquis de LaFayette, whose name he took, eventually doing intelligence work right in the camp of General Cornwallis. After the war, the Virginia legislature purchased Armistead's freedom in recognition of his service.

huge Ohio country west of the Appalachian Mountains in the summer of 1778, George Rogers Clark led a force of Kentucky frontiersmen across the trackless plains of southern Illinois to seize the British posts at Kaskaskia and Cahokia. And when, that winter, he heard that a British military unit had occupied Vincennes, he marched across icy swamps and flooded rivers to surprise the redcoats and force them to surrender in February 1779. That still did not end the British threat in the West, but Clark controlled the situation.

Defeat, then victory, in the South. The second—southern—phase of the Revolution now began. In December 1778, Savannah fell to the British, and swiftly they brought Georgia under their control. One year later, leaving a force to hold the city, Clinton sailed from New York with an army of 8500 men for the conquest of South Carolina. In May 1780, Charleston was captured with its entire defending American garrison. When the British defeated General Gates at Camden, South Carolina, on August 16, 1780, it seemed that the southern states were lost to the patriot cause.

But then on October 7, 1780, several regiments of backwoods militia caught a British force of 1200 Loyalists at King's Mountain, South Carolina, and killed or captured all of them in the bloodiest battle since Bunker Hill. The battle struck terror into the British army and aroused the patriots throughout the Carolinas. Guerrilla bands under Sumter, Pickens, and the "Swamp Fox" Marion struck the British at every turn.

The Continental Army under Nathanael Greene and Daniel Morgan, everywhere assisted by backwoods militia, now proceeded to pick to pieces the British army, under Lord Cornwallis. Finally, the British general decided to head for Virginia. He believed that if he could link up with a British force under Benedict Arnold, who for pride and pelf had turned traitor, he could conquer Virginia and thereby hold the Carolinas.

Cornwallis, outmaneuvered by American (p. 95) forces under the young Marquis de Lafayette, moved to the coast and fortified a position at Yorktown, Virginia. Now Washington saw a chance to trap Cornwallis's army at Yorktown, especially when he learned that a French fleet under Admiral de Grasse was on its way there. Moving swiftly, Washington marched his troops, strengthened by a French force under General Rochambeau, to the head of Chesapeake Bay. There they met de Grasse, who ferried them to the Yorktown peninsula.

Cut off from the British fleet by the French ships, surrounded on the land side by Washington and Rochambeau whose troops outnumbered his two to one, Cornwallis was caught. As the siege lines drew closer, the British army could find no way out. On October 19, 1781, Cornwallis surrendered his entire army of 7750 regulars, together with 850 sailors, 244 cannon, and all his military stores. When news of Yorktown reached England, Prime Minister Lord North exclaimed, "My God! it is all over."

(p. 97)

Wartime in America. The war affected every American in the thirteen colonies—patriot, loyalist, or indifferent; man, woman, or child; black, red, or white; slave, indentured, or free. Even in areas that never saw a redcoat, the war was felt, if in no other way than by inflation. To

Many women managed farms and other businesses while men were fighting. This detail from a commemorative handkerchief shows three southern women working the fields of their farm.

Concord Antiquarian Society

Critical Thinking Activity: Drawing Conclusions How were the colonists able to persevere and defeat the British? Write the word "persevere" on the chalkboard and ask students to list examples of colonial perseverance employed to defeat the British. Take a vote to see how many students think that perseverance was a crucial factor on winning the war. You may wish to extend the activity by having students write a brief paragraph explaining their reasons for voting.

finance the war the Continental Congress and the state governments printed money as fast as they could. The phrase "not worth a continental" soon showed what people thought of this money.

The war brought prosperity to many. Farmers included 90 percent of all Americans, and many of them prospered by selling their crops to both the British and the American armies. They sold to whichever side paid more. Washington's men were starving at Valley Forge in the winter of 1777–1778, while the British, only a few miles away, were being well fed from the rich farms of Pennsylvania and New Jersey. Washington could never forget the irony of his army lacking food in a country filled with farms. One army officer, bitter about profiteering, wrote, "I despise my countrymen. I wish I could say I was not born in America."

Women at war. The departure of men for war forced women to take up many jobs. Like women who were widowed, they operated the farms, ran the printing presses, served as artisans and shopkeepers—doing whatever needed to be done. Some women gathered their children and followed their husbands to the army. They went with the army wherever it moved, and they helped to nurse the wounded, make camp, cook, do the laundry, carry out clerical tasks, and, in battle, carry water and bullets to the soldiers, even load and fire muskets and cannons.

Margaret Corbin followed her husband to war from their home in Pennsylvania. When he was killed while commanding a cannon at the Battle of Fort Washington, New York (November 16, 1776), she filled his place until she was severely wounded. More famous, though no more courageous, was Mary (Molly) McCauley, known as Molly Pitcher for the pitcher of water she carried back and forth during the hot weather and hot fighting of the Battle of Monmouth, June 28, 1778. When her husband fell in the battle, she too took his place at a cannon till the battle was over.

We know of at least one woman, and there were probably more, who passed as a man and

New York State Historical Association, Cooperstown

Abigail Adams was a woman of many talents. Her vivid letters to her husband are some of the best sources for life in the age of the Revolution. This painting was made in 1800.

fought as a soldier. Deborah Sampson enlisted in the 4th Massachusetts Regiment in 1782 and served for more than a year.

Abigail Adams, brilliant wife of John Adams, played another kind of role. She ran the farm and business while her husband was away at the Continental Congress. She kept him aware of what was going on at home. She told him of the profiteering, of how the people felt, and she discussed ways to recruit soldiers and finance the war. Abigail tried to improve the lot of women in the new country, but John was not impressed: "Depend on it," he wrote, "we know better than to repeal our masculine systems."

≋ Continuity and Change: Conflict Point out to students that despite Britain's strength and military power, they could not defeat the colonies, a small group of ill-prepared, ill-outfitted farmers and merchants with no combat experience. The United States would realize this same type of frustration during the Vietnam War, when stronger U.S. forces were forced to withdraw while the less powerful Communist forces still occupied South Vietnam. (See p. 824)

Blacks in the Revolution. Many blacks were involved in the war right from the start. They were present at the battles of Lexington and Concord. At the Battle of Bunker Hill, Peter Salem and Salem Poor stood out for their bravery.

After George Washington took over the army, however, it was decided not to have blacks in the service any more. But this policy did not last long because the British promised freedom to all blacks who came to them. Whenever British armies appeared in the South, large numbers of slaves, seeking to be as free as white Americans, joined them. At war's end 14,000 sailed away with the British.

As blacks flocked to the British, George Washington, Congress, and all the states except South Carolina and Georgia changed their

minds. They enlisted blacks and promised slaves that they would receive their freedom after the war. Of course, slaves could not join without their masters' permission, so of the 5000 blacks who fought in the war, most were from the North. In general, they served in mixed units and were present at almost all the military actions of the war.

The Loyalists. A substantial number of Americans opposed the war and wanted to stay with Great Britain. The Loyalists came from every occupation and were of every degree of wealth. Many kept quiet about how they felt and were not bothered by the patriots. Some went to Canada or England. A few, like Jedediah Smith and Phineas Lyman of New England, took their families from comfortable homes and headed west to try to establish a new life in the wilderness—far from the problems of empire and freedom. About 60,000 became soldiers and fought on the British side.

Loyalists who did not leave their homes, but whose sentiments were known, often found themselves shunned by their neighbors. Some were tarred and feathered, and many lost their property by state confiscation or patriot plundering. Others were treated as traitors and were imprisoned or exiled to towns far from home.

During the course of the war, and at its end, thousands of Loyalists left America never to return. Most went to Canada. There they added a strongly British element to the largely French population. They became useful citizens, serving in the assemblies and as judges and governors.

The Treaty of Paris. Even after the Battle of Yorktown, King George III showed his usual misunderstanding of the American situation when he wanted to keep fighting. But from the British point of view conditions were hopeless. The American phase of the war was over. In March 1782 a new government came to power in England with the sole condition that there would be "no veto to the independence of America." Peace negotiations began in Paris the next month.

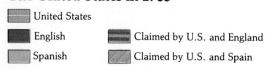

The United States in 1783

- United States
- English
- Spanish
- Claimed by U.S. and England
- Claimed by U.S. and Spain

ATLANTIC OCEAN

Gulf of Mexico

W. FLORIDA
E. FLORIDA

Multicultural Connection: Over 7,000 Hispanic soldiers fought in the American Revolution. One such soldier Jorge Farragut, who was born in Ciudadela, Minorca, and was the father of Civil War hero David G. Farragut. Jorge Farragut served as captain of a ship in the navy of South Carolina. At the end of the war, Jorge Farragut had attained the rank of major in the calvary.

Benjamin West began this painting of the negotiations that led to the Treaty of Paris in 1783. The Americans are (from left to right) John Jay, John Adams, Benjamin Franklin, Henry Laurens, and William Temple Franklin. West did not finish the painting because the British negotiators refused to pose.

The American delegates—Benjamin Franklin, John Adams, and John Jay—had been instructed by Congress to take no step "without the knowledge and agreements" of the French government. In spite of these instructions, thinking it more advantageous to act independently, they went ahead and concluded an agreement with the British without consulting Vergennes, the French minister of state.

In fact, Vergennes did not protest too much over American activities. After all, the treaty was only preliminary and would not go into effect until France had signed a treaty with England. This finally occurred on September 3, 1783, when peace treaties were signed between Great Britain and its enemies France, Spain, and the United States.

For America, the Treaty of Paris had the following provisions: England acknowledged the independence of the United States with approximately the present northern boundary, a western boundary set at the Mississippi River, and a southern border at Florida. The commissioners had tried to have Canada made part of the United States, but in this they failed. If Spain had had its way, however, America's western boundary would have been the Appalachian Mountains. The Mississippi River was to be open to the shipping of both America and Britain, and Americans were to be able to fish in

Geography and History: Place Refer students to the map on the facing page. Ask: What natural geographic features were used to form the borders between English territory and that of the United States? (The Great Lakes and part of the St. Lawrence River.) Were borders with Spain formed by natural features? (Some were: the Mississippi River, for example. Others, such as the southern border, were along a line of latitude. They are too straight and regular to be formed by a river or mountain.)

England's Newfoundland fisheries. No legal obstacles were to be placed in the way of British businessmen collecting debts owed them by American merchants.

Finally, there was the difficult problem of what to do about the Loyalists whose estates had been confiscated during the war. Feelings still ran too high for Congress to vote that their property should be returned to them. The treaty merely promised that Congress would "recommend" to the states to restore their property. Everybody took it for granted, however, that neither the nation nor the states, both burdened with a nearly worthless currency and heavy war debts, would do much about the Loyalists. Eventually Britain helped many of them with money and land in Canada.

French foreign minister Vergennes was astounded at England's generosity! "The English buy the peace rather than make it; their concessions as to boundaries, the fisheries, the Loyalists, exceed everything I had thought possible."

Why the British lost. At the end of the war, George Washington wrote that people in future years would hardly believe that the Americans could have won. "It will not be believed that such a force as Great Britain has employed for eight years in this country could be baffled in their plan of subjugating it by numbers infinitely less—composed of men sometimes halfstarved, always in rags, without pay, and experiencing at times every species of distress which human nature is capable of undergoing." Even today it is not easy to understand how the Americans managed to win.

It is easier to explain why the British lost. The British were separated from their headquarters by a vast ocean. Their lines of communication were long. The British government was badly informed. They thought the Americans were much weaker than they really were. And they expected help from uprisings of thousands of Loyalists. But these uprisings never happened.

The most important explanation was that the British had set themselves an impossible task. Though they had an army that was large for that day, how could it ever be large enough to occupy and subjugate a continent? The British knew so little of America that they thought their capture of New York City would end the war. After the Battle of Long Island in August 1776, General Howe actually asked the Americans to send him a peace commission, and cheerfully expected to receive the American surrender. But he was badly disappointed. For the colonies had no single capital that the British could capture to win the war.

American success was largely due to perseverance in keeping an army in the field throughout the long, hard years. George Washington was a man of great courage and good judgment. And Americans had the strengths of a New World—with a new kind of army fighting in new ways. Still, it is doubtful the Americans could have won without the aid of France.

Although many Americans opposed the Revolution, and some were lukewarm, it was a people's war. As many as half of all men of military age were in the army at one time or another. Each had the special power and the special courage that came from fighting for himself, for his family, and for his home.

See "Section 3 Review answers," p. 76E.

Section 3 Review

1. Identify or explain: mercenaries, Hessians, *The Crisis,* Cornwallis, Burgoyne, Lafayette von Steuben, Morgan, de Grasse, Rochambeau.

2. Locate: Long Island, Trenton, Delaware River, Princeton, Saratoga, Valley Forge, Monmouth, Vincennes, King's Mountain, Yorktown.

3. How was war in America unlike war in Europe?

4. Point out how each of the following groups took part in the war or were affected by it: (a) farmers, (b) women, (c) blacks, (d) Loyalists.

5. How did the Treaty of Paris affect America?

6. **Critical Thinking: Testing Conclusions.** Some historians have said that the British were responsible for defeating themselves in the Revolutionary War. What evidence, if any, supports this conclusion?

Chapter 4 Review

See "Chapter Review answers," p. 76E.

Focusing on Ideas

1. What were the results of the Treaty of Paris?

2. How did the attitudes of the colonists change between the time that the First Continental Congress met and the meeting of the Second Continental Congress?

3. Why did Thomas Paine write *Common Sense*?

4. What problems and difficulties did George Washington face when he set about creating the Continental Army?

5. Today, in many parts of the world, people who share a common language, history, or culture seek to set up independent nations. Were the American colonists motivated by a common language, history, or culture? Explain your answer.

Taking a Critical Look

1. **Testing Conclusions.** "The American Revolution took place because the British government, even with the best of intentions, did not understand what America and Americans had become." Challenge or defend this statement using evidence in the text.

2. **Distinguishing False from Accurate Images.** It has been said that the American Revolution was a people's war for the Americans and a "soldier's war" for the British. How does the evidence presented in this chapter support or contradict this conclusion?

Your Region in History

1. **Geography.** What battles, if any, were fought in your region during the Revolutionary War?

2. **Culture.** What Revolutionary War heroes are honored by place names in your state?

3. **Economics.** Did Britain profit from your region before the Revolutionary War? Explain your answer.

Historical Facts and Figures

Testing Hypotheses. Historians often make hypotheses, or educated guesses, about the reasons past events occurred. Historians then test the hypothesis by examining the data and determining if it supports or contradicts the hypothesis. (a) Use the data on the chart below to test the hypothesis: "Colonial boycotts seriously affected trade with Great Britain." (Keep in mind that the colonists boycotted British goods in 1765, 1766, 1768, 1769, 1775, and 1776.) (b) Write a brief paragraph summarizing the data to see if it supports the results of your test.

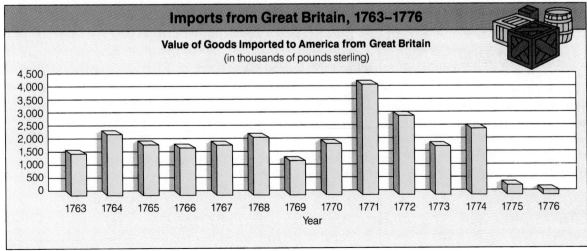

Imports from Great Britain, 1763–1776

Value of Goods Imported to America from Great Britain
(in thousands of pounds sterling)

Source: *Historical Statistics of the United States*

101

Chapter 5
From Confederation to Nation

Identifying Chapter Materials

Objectives	Basic Instructional Materials	Extension Materials
1 New State Governments • List the basic principles reflected in the first state constitution and explain the importance of written constitutions to Americans. • Explain why legislatures were strong and governors weak in the early state governments.	**Annotated Teacher's Edition** • Lesson Plans, p. 102C **Instructional Support File** • Pre-Reading Activities, Unit 2, p. 15	**Documents of American History** • The Concord Town Meeting Demands a Constitutional Convention, Vol. 1, p. 104 • The Quock Walker Case, Vol. 1, p. 110
2 The Continental Congress • Identify and evaluate the successes and failures of the Second Continental Congress. • Identify a least six members of the Congress.	**Annotated Teacher's Edition** • Lesson Plans, pp. 102C–102D	**Extension Activity** • The Continental Congress
3 A Weak Confederation • List the accomplishments and failures of the Articles of Confederation.	**Annotated Teacher's Edition** • Lesson Plans, pp. 102D–102E	**Enrichment Support File** • No Neighbors for miles: the Northwest Territory **American History Transparencies** • Our Multicultural Heritage, p. C51
4 Writing a Nation's Constitution • Explain how the Constitutional Convention came about and describe the major compromise in the writing of the Constitution.	**Annotated Teacher's Edition** • Lesson Plans, pp. 102E–102F **Instructional Support File** • Skill Application Activity, Unit 2, p. 19 • Critical Thinking Activity, Unit 2, p. 20	**Enrichment Support File** • The Philadelphia Convention (See "In-Depth Coverage" at right.) **Suggested Secondary Sources** • See chart at right. **American History Transparencies** • Time Lines, p. E11
5 The States Ratify • List arguments presented for and against the new Constitution and explain why the Bill of Rights was added to the Constitution. • Trace the order of Constitutional ratification from state to state. • Compare the Federalists and the Anti-Federalists.	**Annotated Teacher's Edition** • Lesson Plans, p. 102F **Instructional Support File** • Reading Activities, Unit 2, pp. 16–17 • Skill Review Activity, Unit 2, p. 18 • Chapter Test, Unit 2, pp. 21–24 • Additional Test Questions, Unit 2, pp. 25–28	**American History Transparencies** • Critical Thinking, p. F7

Providing In-Depth Coverage

Perspectives on the Philadelphia Convention

From 1776 to 1789 the United States was a confederation of thirteen sovereign states. The Articles of Confederation governed relations between these states and any common actions. Chapter 5 explains how the Philadelphia Convention replaced the Articles of Confederation with a federal government based on the United States Constitution, as well as examining the compromises that went into the making of that Constitution.

The end result of the framing of the Constitution was a federal government with much more power than the government under the Articles of Confederation.

For this chapter, *A History of the United States* as an instructional program provides two types of resources you can use to offer in-depth coverage of the Philadelphia Convention: the *student text* and the *Enrichment Support File*. A list of *Suggested Secondary Sources* is also provided. The chart below shows the topics that are covered in each.

THE STUDENT TEXT. In Boorstin and Kelley's *A History of the United States* the chronology of events unfolds as the key players at the Philadelphia Convention struggle to create the first written constitution.

AMERICAN HISTORY ENRICHMENT SUPPORT FILE. This collection of primary source readings and classroom activities reveals the atmosphere and events that took place during the Philadelphia Convention.

SUGGESTED SECONDARY SOURCES. This reference list of readings by well-known historians and other commentators provides an array of perspectives on the events that took place during the Philadelphia Convention. (See chart below.)

Locating Instructional Materials

Detailed lesson plans for teaching the Philadelphia Convention as a mini-course or to study one or more elements of the Convention in depth are offered in the following areas: in the *student text*, see individual lesson plans at the beginning of each chapter; in the *Enrichment Support File,* see page 3; for readings beyond the student text, see *Suggested Secondary Sources.*

IN-DEPTH COVERAGE OF THE PHILADELPHIA CONVENTION

Student Text	Enrichment Support File	Suggested Secondary Sources
• The Philadelphia Convention, p. 116 • Compromises, pp. 116–120 • Ratification of the Constitution, pp. 121–124 • Separation of Powers, pp. 120–121 • James Madison, pp. 117, 118, 122 • Virginia Plan, p. 118 • Edmund Randolph and the New Jersey Plan, p. 118	• Lesson Suggestions • Multimedia Resources • Overview Essay/The Birth of the Constitution: The Philadelphia Convention • Songs in American History/Celebrating the Constitution • Primary Sources in American History/ Opposing Views from the Philadelphia Convention • Biography in American History/James Madison • Great Debates in American History/The Great Compromise • Making Connections	• *1787: The Grand Convention* by Clinton Rossiter, pp. 79–137. • *The Ordeal of the Constitution: The Antifederalists and the Ratification Struggle of 1787–1788* by Robert A. Rutland, pp. 3–16, 36–48. • *The Great Rehearsal: The Story of the Making and Ratifying of the Constitution* by Carl Van Doren, pp. 36–109.

New State Governments

FOCUS

To introduce the lesson, ask: Why did Americans want their states to have written constitutions? Then discuss with the class the historical reasons for what they sought.

Developing Vocabulary

The words listed in this chapter are essential terms for reading and understanding particular sections of this chapter. The page number after each term indicates the page of its first or most important appearance in the chapter. These terms are defined in the text Glossary (text pages 1000–1011).

Constitution (page 104); **import** (page 106).

INSTRUCT

Explain

Ask students to write, define, or describe the following: Concord constitutional plan, rights retained by people, two-house legislature, Pennsylvania legislature, power of governor, Pennsylvania attitude toward governor, posts changed from appointive to elective, voting qualifications, representation in legislatures, early attitudes toward slavery.

☑ Writing Process Activity

Identifying Central Issues Ask students to play the role of a citizen at the Concord town meeting. In preparation for delivering a speech challenging the procedure in which the provisional assembly draws up the new government, have them outline their objections. Students should begin their speech with a strong statement in which they summarize their position, and they should organize their ideas in order of importance. Have students revise for logical argument and persuasive language. After proofreading, they can deliver their speeches at a mock town meeting.

Section Review Answers

Section 1, page 106

1. The people elected assembly representatives who then set about deciding on a form of government. 2. They feared that the legislature would become too powerful. If the legislature drew up the constitution, the legislature could also change the constitution. 3. A written constitution would be less ambiguous and more accessible than an unwritten one. 4. The British constitution includes the Magna Carta and a Bill of Rights as well as a combination of tradition, habit,

and belief. 5. Loyalist estates broken up and sold to other Americans; farm prosperity enabled some people to buy farms and others to increase the size of their farms. 6. The new state constitutions reduced the powers of the governors because Americans were wary of giving any one person too much authority; they had had enough of kings. 7. A Massachusetts court abolished slavery; the legislatures of Pennsylvania, Connecticut, and Rhode Island passed laws that provided for the gradual abolition of slavery; Virginia and North Carolina allowed owners to set their slaves free. 8. The new state constitutions promoted social equality by reducing the amount of property a person had to own in order to vote or hold office; the result was that most white males qualified as voters.

CLOSE

To conclude the lesson, ask students to discuss the differences between state constitutions, and have the class attempt to reach a consensus about which differences a truly national agreement would have to resolve.

The Continental Congress

FOCUS

To introduce the lesson, have students draw a vertical time line for the period 1777–1789 in their notebooks. Use the time line to record the events in this chapter dealing with the development of our national government. Start with "Congress Approves the Articles of Confederation." Be sure to include treaties and ordinances.

INSTRUCT

Explain

The Second Continental Congress maintained the government of the thirteen colonies during the Revolution. Despite its considerable successes, including the adoption of the Articles of Confederation, the Congress was hampered by its inability to raise taxes.

★ Independent Activity

Recognizing Bias Ask each student to list the names, states of origin, and occupations of at least six members of the Continental Congress. Then ask students to answer the following questions: What was the approximate age of most of the members? What were their occupations? What economic class or classes did they represent? Do you think this group adequately represented the needs and interests of all the colonists? Why or why not?

Section Review Answers

Section 2, page 108

1. Most members of the Continental Congress were young, prosperous, and educated leaders. Most were just over 40 years old; almost half of them were lawyers; and they were all men. 2. The quality of the Congress declined during the war because many of the most talented men went home to work in the state governments, which had become more powerful. 3. The Continental Congress had many successes. It issued the Declaration of Independence, organized a military force and appointed George Washington to command it, supplied the army with ammunition, maintained resistance to Great Britain, created a diplomatic corps, persuaded France to recognize the United States as an independent nation, created a postal service, and drew up the Articles of Confederation. But the Congress had trouble obtaining needed revenues; its greatest failure was in financing war.

CLOSE

To conclude the lesson, remind the students that the First Continental Congress met only briefly (for about seven weeks) in 1774. The Second Continental Congress convened in May of 1775. Ask: Based on the evidence you have compiled today, how would you evaluate the Congress?

Extension Activity

To extend the lesson, have students write a one-page biographical sketch of one member of the Continental Congress. Students should include any specific contributions which their subject made to the Congress.

Section 3 (pages 108–115)

A Weak Confederation

FOCUS

To introduce the lesson, have students make a three-column list for the Articles of Confederation. As they read, in one column ask them to list the weaknesses of the Articles, in the second the accomplishments, and in the third the failures. Then ask them to explain how each of the failures was a result of one or more of the weaknesses they have identified.

Developing Vocabulary

currency (page 108); **admiralty** (page 109); **ordinance** (page 111); **territory** (page 111).

INSTRUCT

Explain

Under the Articles of Confederation, the government was able to plan for the settlement of the western lands, sign a peace treaty with England, and bring the war to an end. However, the government was unable to solve severe economic and diplomatic problems. The rebellion of Massachusetts farmers led by Daniel Shays convinced many people that the government needed more power.

☑ Writing Process Activity

Formulating Questions Ask students to imagine that as members of the Ohio Company of Associates, they are being interviewed for a magazine article about their experiences. Have them prepare by brainstorming possible *who, what, where, when, why,* and *how* questions they might be asked. In writing their responses in interview format, they should consider why they decided to leave Massachusetts, what it was like traveling to Ohio, and how they went about establishing Marietta. Students should revise for completeness and specific detail. After proofreading, they can choose a partner to help them act out the interview.

Section Review Answers

Section 3, page 115

1. Congress could deal with foreign countries, declare war and negotiate peace, run the postal service, print and borrow money, ask for revenue from the states, and negotiate conflicts between states. But it could not require the states to pay taxes or abide by decisions of Congress. 2. Land-poor states feared that states with western lands would be able to sell land to pay off their war debts and reduce state taxes. 3. First, when there were very few people in the region, Congress would appoint the territory's governor and other administrators. Then, as soon as 5000 adult free men settled in a region, they could establish a legislature. When the free population reached 60,000, they could apply for statehood. New states would be on an equal footing with the original states. 4. The Northwest Ordinance, the victory over Britain, and the Treaty of Paris with England in 1783. 5. Shays insisted that the Massachusetts legislature supply more paper money, reduce taxes, and end the practice of imprisoning those who could not pay their debts. Shays's Rebellion aroused many fears. People of property feared that the debtors' demands would be met, a change that would cost creditors dearly; many Americans worried that there would be more unrest. As a result, Shays's Rebellion persuaded many people that changes were needed in the Articles of Confederation.

5

CLOSE

To conclude the lesson, ask students to consider the financial position of the farmers who joined Daniel Shays as "shotgun reformers." Have students prepare a statement explaining what these men hoped to gain by preventing debt collection and threatening violence; whether they were justified in their actions; how effective these actions were; what alternatives they might have chosen.

Section 4 (pages 115–121)

Writing a Nation's Constitution

FOCUS

To introduce the lesson, ask students what a *value* is. (Something that a person believes is good, or thinks is worthwhile or important. Usually a value can be summed up in one word.) Ask: What are some examples of things people value? (Friendship, success, power, equality, etc.) Point out that values affect the things people do and the ways they think and write, and that they affected what the framers wrote in the Constitution.

Developing Vocabulary

anarchy (page 116); **federal** (page 116); **federalism** (page 116); **amendment** (page 120); **separation of powers** (page 120); **executive branch** (page 120); **legislative branch** (page 120); **judicial branch** (page 120); **President** (page 120); **Congress** (page 121); **House of Representatives** (page 121); **Senate** (page 121); **Supreme Court** (page 121).

INSTRUCT

Explain

Help students define the terms *sovereign, national,* and *federal,* and using information from their reading, discuss how these three types of government differ.

✿ Cooperative Learning Activity

Testing Conclusions Break the class into small groups and explain that each will write a summary of part of the United States Constitution. Appoint a discussion leader, recorder, and reporter for each group. Then assign each group an Article or sections of the Constitution (pages 965–999). Have all group members read the assigned sections and the Origins of each found in the Appendix of their texts. While the group recorder takes notes, have group members discuss the meaning of each section and compose a summary of it. Have the recorder write the final summary drafted by the group. Have group reporters read their summaries to the class. Allow time for questions and discussion.

Section Review Answers

Section 4, page 121

1. a) 1786 gathering of representatives of several states called to discuss the regulation of commerce. b) insisted that the delegates at Annapolis call for another, larger meeting to revise the Confederation. c) a representative of Virginia at the Constitutional Convention and author of the Virginia Plan. d) presented the Virginia Plan to the Constitutional Convention. e) proposed that the new Congress have two houses, with representation in each based on population. f) author of the New Jersey plan. g) proposed that Congress consist of one house with each state having one vote. 2. The Great Compromise provided for two houses of Congress—one in which all states would have an equal number of votes and another in which representation would vary with population. It resolved the deadlock between the small and large states at the Constitutional Convention. 3. The three-fifths compromise resolved the debate about how slaves would affect taxation and representation in Congress; each slave was to be counted as three-fifths of a person. 4. The Constitution granted the new government the power to tax, to regulate commerce, to raise and maintain an army and navy, and to put down rebellions. And by creating a strong President and a government with direct power over all the states and their people, the Constitution created a government strong enough to exercise its powers and enforce its decisions. 5. In the 1700s "federal" referred to some action or relationship among sovereign countries. A federal union would be a weak association of basically independent states. A national union would bring the states together under the authority of a larger government.

CLOSE

To conclude the lesson, ask students to list for homework two values held by each of the following: themselves; the authors of their textbook; their U.S. history teacher.

Section 5 (pages 121–124)

The States Ratify

FOCUS

To introduce the lesson, ask students to imagine that they were alive between 1787 and 1790. Tell them to use text pages 121–124 to answer this question: In what order would you have to travel to the states to see each one ratify the Constitution? (Delaware, Pennsylvania, New Jersey, Georgia, Connecticut, Massachusetts, Maryland, South Carolina, New Hampshire, Virginia, New York, North Carolina, Rhode Island.) You can make the students' task easier by telling them that the date of ratification is also the date of admission to the Union.

Developing Vocabulary
ratify (page 121); **Federalists** (page 121); **Bill of Rights** (page 123).

INSTRUCT

Explain
Review with students the following points: At the time of ratification there were many persons who still supported the idea of state autonomy; the Federalists won because of their respected leaders and their willingness to compromise.

☑ Writing Process Activity
Identifying Alternatives To prepare for a debate about the ratification of the Constitution, ask students to choose the Federalist or the Anti-Federalist role. After outlining the arguments for the side they have chosen, they should write a summary of their position. Ask them to consider the arguments of the opposing side and to refute them as they defend their stand. Students should revise their arguments for clarity and logic, then proofread to eliminate errors. Students can then deliver their arguments for or against constitutional ratification in a mock debate.

Section Review Answers
Section 5, page 124
1. The fact that special conventions of the people of the states, not their legislatures, ratified the Constitution indicated that the national government came from the people, not from the states, and the Constitution was superior to state laws. 2. Anti-Federalists feared that the Constitution gave too much power to the President and national government. The proposed national Constitution had no bill of rights to safeguard liberties won by the Revolution. 3. Massachusetts showed the other states a way of overcoming some of the major objections to the Constitution. It ratified the Constitution but proposed amendments to safeguard the rights of citizens. Several other states followed this example. 4. The example set by Massachusetts helped the cause of ratification in New York and Virginia. Both states proposed amendments when they ratified the Constitution. In addition,

George Washington's strong support of the Constitution helped persuade Virginians to ratify it. In New York ratification was aided by news of Virginia's acceptance, by Hamilton's efforts, and by the *Federalist Papers*, a series of essays written by Hamilton, Madison, and Jay that brilliantly explained and defended the Constitution. 5. The brevity of the Constitution has contributed to its long life by increasing its flexibility. Since many details of the government's operations were not spelled out in the Constitution, the government can adapt more easily to changing times.

CLOSE

To conclude the lesson, ask: What were the characteristics of Federalists and Anti-Federalists? List students' answers on the board. For ideas, tell them to refer to the text on pages 121–122. For homework, ask students to write a paragraph describing Federalists and a paragraph describing Anti-Federalists.

Chapter Review Answers

Focusing on Ideas
1. Elected delegates to convention wrote a new constitution subject to citizens' approval. 2. A strong but not domineering government giving states final word on important matters. But this restricted firm federal action in times of need. 3. They included instructions within it for change. 4. Separatism: differing pasts; state officials sought power; economic interests collided; rival western claims; primitive transportation, communication. Unity: wanting British defeat; needing interstate commerce, uniform money system; surrender of western lands to Congress.

Taking a Critical Look
1. States: many responsibilities—education, welfare, etc.; Congress: narrower powers. Short Constitution has fewer details needing change; decisions left to legislatures. 2. Convinced many that Articles needed change. 3. Abuses cited in Declaration addressed in Bill of Rights. Declaration cites King as centralized authority; Constitution provides separation of powers. Declaration states no changes for light and transient reasons; Constitution allows complicated amending process. Both honor popular sovereignty.

Your Region in History
1–3. Answers will vary depending on your region. Consult your local library or historical society.

Historical Facts and Figures
(a) National government—foreign policy is a delegated power. (b) The national government regulates interstate and foreign commerce. (c) Taxes—levying taxes is a concurrent power.

Chapter 5

Focusing the Chapter: Have students identify the chapter logo. Discuss what unit theme the logo might symbolize. Then ask students to skim the chapter to identify other illustrations or titles that relate to this theme.

From Confederation to Nation

When the assembled American colonies declared their independence on July 4, 1776, thirteen nations were created, not just one. The resolution that announced independence on July 2, 1776, had proclaimed "That these United Colonies are, and of right ought to be, free and independent *States*." The first heading at the top of the Declaration of Independence called it "The Unanimous Declaration of the thirteen united States of America." They used a small "u" for united because it was only a hope.

Each state called itself "sovereign," which meant that now it had all the highest powers of government. Each state had all the powers to levy taxes, to raise an army and build a navy, to enter into treaties, and to make war and peace. When Franklin was in Paris as a representative for the Continental Congress, trying to persuade the French to give war aid, he found "ambassadors" from three separate American states.

The very same reasons that had made the colonists willing to revolt made them unwilling to unite. The people of Virginia were fighting to be free from a government in far-off London. Why should they submit to a government in far-off New York? The very same feelings that gave Americans strength, that explained why their scattered-everywhere army could not be defeated by a regular army of empire, also explained why it would be hard for them to become a nation. The task of making a nation had only begun.

In 1799 when William Russell Birch made this engraving of Second Street, Philadelphia was the largest and most prosperous city in the United States and still the nation's capital.
See "Lesson Plan," p. 102C.

1. New state governments

Even before the Second Continental Congress had worked out a frame of government for the united States, the individual states began to deal with the problem themselves. Of this process James Madison wrote:

> Nothing has excited more admiration in the world than the manner in which free governments have been established in America; for it was the first instance, from the creation of the world . . . that free inhabitants have

been seen deliberating on a form of government, and selecting such of their citizens as possessed their confidence, to determine upon and give effect to it.

Following old patterns. What the new states did, of course, was strongly influenced by their pasts. They did not return to the "state of nature" (when there were supposed to be no governments) that John Locke and other political writers had imagined once existed. In fact, the new states already had governments operating,

More from Boorstin: "The Revolution, as John Adams later explained, had expressed 'principles as various as the 13 states that went through it, and in some sense almost as diversified as the individuals who acted in it.' So local were the sentiments that in Virginia, for example, the Revolution was sometimes called (1780–81) the 'Tobacco War.'" (From *The Americans: The National Experience*)

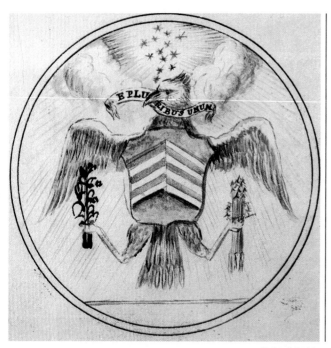

Charles Thomson sketched this design for the Great Seal of the United States in 1789.

since the provincial assemblies continued to meet after the Revolution broke out and the royal governors fled.

The colonists really had no desire or intention to form brand-new governments. They had been practicing a form of self-government for 150 years. They had nothing in particular against their colonial governments. Their main desire now was to change certain features so that government could never again become tyrannical.

How were they to go about forming—or "reforming"—these colonial governments? The Declaration of Independence said, and English and American experience agreed, that governments derive "their just powers from the consent of the governed." Plainly, "the consent of the governed" had to be secured in each colony and in the whole new nation.

Ways of constitution making. Beginning in 1776 the thirteen states (formerly the colonies) began creating new governments. In most states the existing assemblies drew up the new

constitutions. In some, special elections were held for the assembly that was to draw up the constitution. But whether a special election was held or not, the legislators assumed that, because they had been elected, they had the "consent" of the people. So they drew up new constitutions and put them into operation.

In Massachusetts, the provisional assembly asked the local town meetings to consent to its drawing up a new government. Most towns agreed, and the assembly went to work. But then Concord objected. The Concord town meeting, in a series of resolutions that were circulated throughout the colony, challenged this procedure. The people of Concord pointed out that if the regular legislature wrote the constitution, it would be able to change it just as easily later on. To the people of Concord, that did not seem much protection for their liberties. Instead, Concord suggested that a special assembly should be elected that would have no other purpose than to draw up a new constitution. When it had finished its job, it would go out of existence.

The Massachusetts assembly paid no attention to Concord. But the independent-thinking townspeople of the state were listening. The assembly's new constitution was quickly rejected by the voters of the state when it was presented for their approval in 1778. The main reason was that they disapproved of the way it was drawn up.

The Massachusetts assembly finally followed the procedure demanded by the citizens of Concord. In 1779 a constitutional convention was called. The elected members drew up a new constitution, which was submitted to the people in March 1780 and approved by them in June.

A similar procedure was followed by other states when they revised their constitutions and, a few years later, when the whole new nation made a new frame of government.

Americans had found a way to make government by the consent of the governed into a living reality.

Written constitutions. These new frames of government, no matter who drew them up, were all *written constitutions*. Like the consti-

See "Lesson Plan," p. 102C for **Writing Process Activity: Identifying Central Issues** relating to drawing up a new state constitution for Massachusetts.

tutional convention, the written frame of government was an American institution that would be admired and imitated all over the world for centuries to come. Colonial charters themselves provided a handy framework for new written constitutions. In Connecticut and Rhode Island, for example, the colonial charters had been so liberal that all that was needed was to strike out mention of the king. Then these charters could become the new constitutions.

The British constitution was a plan of government that could not be picked up and read. It consisted of some basic documents like the Magna Carta and the English Bill of Rights. But much of it was a concoction of tradition, habit, and belief. Many Americans thought their rights to govern themselves would be safer if these were stated in plain language so that government officials could see them and citizens would never forget them.

✖ The new state constitutions.

The new state constitutions followed a pattern. Generally they began with a brief declaration of independence. Then came a section declaring the rights that the citizens reserved for themselves against any government. These included freedom of the press, the right to petition the government against abuses, freedom from unreasonable search of their homes, freedom from the burden of standing armies, and the right to trial by jury and other proper legal procedures.

Most state constitutions provided a framework similar to that of the old colonial governments. All but one state had a governor, an upper house, and a lower house of the legislature. But now all were elected directly by the people or by their elected representatives. Only in Pennsylvania did the constitution create a one-house legislature.

In all colonies there was an attempt to weaken the powers of the governor. He had represented the king in colonial days and had become a symbol of government from afar. Now most states deprived the governor of his power to veto legislation or to dismiss the legislature or suspend its meetings. In many states the governor was now elected by the legislature for a short term. The legislature could impeach the

governor. The people of Pennsylvania were so fearful of the governor's powers that they abolished that position entirely.

Other posts that had been appointive in colonial times were made elective. Members of the upper houses and the judges—all formerly appointed by the crown—were selected by the voters.

Equality in the states. Although Jefferson, in the Declaration of Independence, asserted that "all men are created equal," there were many ways in which the colonial governments treated people as if they were unequal. Most Americans probably thought Jefferson's phrase meant that Americans were the equals of the English. But the statement itself, and the Revolution, led people to think more about the meaning of equality. In every colony in order to vote, a man had to own property or have a certain income. In no colony were women allowed to vote or hold public office. And then, of course, there were the slaves, who did not even have civil rights, much less political rights like the right to vote or hold office.

In most colonies from Pennsylvania south, settlers in the West had not been as well represented in their assemblies as were settlers in the East. The new state constitutions did give Westerners in those states somewhat better representation in the legislatures, but Easterners still continued to hold more than their share of the power. The amount of property needed to vote or to hold office was generally reduced. Most white American males did hold property and could vote.

The war helped to redistribute wealth. Loyalist estates were broken up and sold to other Americans. Wartime prosperity, especially on the farms, assisted more people to buy farms or enlarge their existing acreage.

First moves against slavery. As early as 1774, Rhode Island passed a law providing that "those who are desirous of enjoying all the advantages of liberty themselves should be willing to extend personal liberty to others." Any slave brought into the colony from that time on would be free.

✖ **Critical Thinking Activity: Making Comparisons** How were the constitutions written for the new state governments? Ask students to describe what it feels like to learn a new sport—for example, swimming or riding a bicycle. What "old" skills are they able to use? What "new" skills did they have to develop? Have students compare these experiences with the newly created states that had to write their own constitution for the first time. What past experiences would have helped them? What new skills did they have to call upon?

Abigail Adams wrote to her husband, John, who was away attending the Congress, "It always appeared a most evil scheme to me to fight ourselves for what we are daily robbing and plundering from those who have as good a right to freedom as we have." That same year the Continental Congress passed a law that no slaves were to be imported after December 1, 1775.

When Jefferson tried to include the slave trade in the Declaration of Independence as one of the king's abuses, the southern colonies objected. Still, the War of Independence did lead to freedom for many blacks. Some, as we have seen, received their liberty for fighting in the American cause. When a slave in Massachusetts sued for his freedom because the new state constitution declared, "all men are created free and equal," the court agreed with him. With that decision in 1783, slavery ended in Massachusetts.

Pennsylvania began the gradual abolition of slavery in 1780. Connecticut and Rhode Island followed with their own gradual abolition plans in 1784. Virginia and North Carolina, which had long prohibited the practice, now passed laws that allowed owners to free their slaves.

See "Section 1 Review answers," p. 102C.

Section 1 Review

1. What was unique about the way in which American governments were formed?

2. Why did the townspeople of Concord object to having the state legislature draw up a new constitution for Massachusetts?

3. Why did Americans want *written* constitutions?

4. Describe some of the elements of the British constitution.

5. Name one way in which the American economy was altered by the Revolutionary War.

6. Why did the new state constitutions reduce the power of the governor's office?

7. How did some states try to end slavery?

8. **Critical Thinking: Identifying Central Issues.** How did some state constitutions promote social equality?

See "Lesson Plan," p. 102C.

2. The Continental Congress

When, on June 7, 1776, Congress declared war on Great Britain, it also called for a plan of confederation to help the states cooperate in the war effort. A committee of thirteen, with John Dickinson of Pennsylvania as chairman, prepared Articles of Confederation. These Articles, adopted by Congress in November 1777, were not ratified by the last of the thirteen states until March 1, 1781.

An illegal assembly. Because the Articles of Confederation were not ratified for so long, the

Multicultural Connection: The 6th clause of the Northwest Ordinance stated that there should be no slavery or involuntary servitude, except as punishment for criminal behavior, in the Northwest Territory. However, the Ordinance did include a provision for returning fugitive slaves who had escaped into the territory. (See page 111.)

John Trumbull painted the Continental Congress signing the Declaration of Independence.

Second Continental Congress, though still an "illegal" assembly, assumed the powers of government. The central governing was done for six years by the Continental Congress, which took the place of the British government. This Congress issued the Declaration of Independence, advised the states to form governments, and conducted the war against Great Britain nearly to its successful conclusion at Yorktown.

Young congressmen. At the beginning of the war, the Continental Congress was an assembly of talented men which included almost every leader of the Revolution. Jefferson, his teacher George Wythe, and Richard Henry Lee were there from Virginia. So was Washington, until he was sent off to lead the army. Sam and John Adams, Elbridge Gerry, and John Hancock came from Massachusetts. Ben Franklin and Robert Morris were delegates from Pennsylvania. Roger Sherman and Oliver Wolcott were there from Connecticut.

The members of Congress were young—most ✂ were just over 40, and Jefferson was only 33 in 1776. They generally stood to lose a good deal of property—and possibly their heads as well—if the Revolution was lost. Of the 56 men who signed the Declaration of Independence, 25

✂ **Critical Thinking Activity: Determining Relevance** Who were the delegates to the Continental Congress? Have students list the qualities they feel a delegate to the Continental Congress should have possessed. Explain why each of these qualities would have been important. Ask students to compare their fictitious delegate to the actual participants. How are they similar and how are they different? If the qualities they possessed were different, ask why those qualities might have been viewed as important in the 1700s.

were lawyers, 8 were merchants, 6 were physicians, and 5 were farmers. The rest came from a variety of occupations. They were clearly not a rabble in arms.

During the war, the quality of the members of Congress declined. Many of the most talented men went back to their states as the state governments became more powerful. For the states kept their independence. They had their own armies and navies, competed with Congress for supplies, and some sent out their own "ambassadors." At the same time, Congress had to face the difficulties of wartime. It had to avoid being captured by the British army. Sometimes it had too few members present to pass laws. Often its members were late arriving for meetings of Congress. Sometimes members went home when they were tired, when they did not like the weather, or just when they had something else to do. In these ways Congress was not unlike the militia.

Congress's successes and failures. Despite the difficulties of wartime, the lack of any legal grant of power, and the jealousy of the states, the achievements of the Second Continental Congress were substantial. It established the army, navy, and marines. It had the wisdom to appoint George Washington to lead the army—and to keep him there through bad times. It kept the army supplied with ammunition. No battle after Bunker Hill was ever lost because of lack of gunpowder. Congress had more of a problem keeping Washington's troops fed, clothed, and paid.

Congress's greatest failure was in financing the war, and that was largely due to the states. They would not give Congress the right to tax, and when Congress asked for money, the states often failed to contribute. As a result, to obtain money Congress simply used the printing press. By the time the government under the Continental Congress was replaced by the new government under the Articles of Confederation, it was costing more to print the paper bills than they were worth as money.

The Continental Congress created a diplomatic corps, and won a great diplomatic victory when France recognized the United States as an independent nation and entered the war. In addition, it created a postal service and drew up the Articles of Confederation. For any assembly—legal or illegal—this was an impressive record.

See "Section 2 Review answers," p. 102D.

Section 2 Review

1. Characterize Continental Congress members.
2. Why did the quality of the members of Congress decline during the war?
3. **Critical Thinking: Drawing Conclusions.** Evaluate the successes and failures of the Continental Congress.

See "Lesson Plan," p. 102D.

3. A weak confederation

When the Continental Congress turned to the problem of setting up an effective central government, they found it was easier to get rid of a government than to create a new and better one. Their new government would have to handle all the problems the empire had dealt with—regulating trade, making war and peace, and imposing taxes—yet none of the members of Congress had any experience in imperial administration.

The states and Congress. Congress also had to cope with the jealousy of the states. The states, having disposed of one tyranny, were wary not to put themselves under another. They had rid themselves of royal officials—governors, judges, and hated customs collectors. They had no desire to create a whole new set of officials to interfere in their affairs. They were happy to be able to levy their own taxes, to set up their own courts, and to regulate their own commerce, currency, and the right to vote.

The states wanted a new government strong enough to serve them but not so potent that it might dominate them. They feared the powers of a central government so far away that it would be beyond the people's control. Therefore the Articles of Confederation, which the Continental Congress now drew up, announced a "perpetual union" of the states and "firm league of friendship." But it preserved for each state "its sovereignty, freedom and independence, and every power and jurisdiction and right" that was not expressly delegated to the new Congress under the Articles of Confederation.

There was an argument over how the states were to vote in the Congress of the Confederation. It was finally decided—though the more populous states did not like it—to give each state just one vote. That would show that this was only a confederation of the thirteen sovereign states, and not a new government representing the people themselves. The agreement of nine states was required for important matters, and any change in the Articles had to receive the vote of every state. There was no provision for a President or other executive officers or for judges or courts.

The powers of Congress.

Congress was given the sole power to deal with foreign countries, to settle disputes between the states, to decide admiralty cases (those involving ships at sea), to declare war, and to make peace. It could coin money, run the postal service, establish weights and measures, and trade with the Indians outside the states. It could borrow money, and it could request each state to contribute money in proportion to the value of the property in the state. Under this arrangement a large state, which had only one vote, was still supposed to donate more money than its less wealthy neighbors. Congress could only request financial support from the states. But if a state refused to help, there was nothing the Congress could do.

In fact, the Articles only outlined what the Continental Congress was already doing. But many people feared the powers of the new Congress and imagined that it might "swallow up the states." Despite these fears the Congress actually had no way to enforce its decisions. The Articles of Confederation provided, in the words of Gouverneur Morris of Pennsylvania, nothing but a "government by supplication"—a government by begging and pleading.

When the Articles of Confederation were sent to the states, the same questions that the Continental Congress had debated were now

American Antiquarian Society

This 1770s woodcut shows a mail carrier on the Boston Post Road bringing news.

discussed all over again in town meetings and in the state legislatures. Most of the amendments suggested by the states would further limit the powers of Congress. Americans did not want to rush into a new government.

Western lands.

Some of the smaller states were especially worried about the large areas of land that other states claimed in the West. Massachusetts, Connecticut, Virginia, North and South Carolina, and Georgia had claims from "sea to sea" based on their colonial charters. Virginia's claim was strengthened by George Rogers Clark's conquest of the Northwest, which had been carried out in the service of Virginia. New York claimed western lands, on the basis of treaties made with the Indians, but in 1780 voted to cede them to Congress.

The small states that had no western land claims were led by Maryland. They refused to agree to a general government until the other states gave up their claims to the land west of the Appalachians. The land-poor states thought that the land-rich states like Virginia and Massachusetts would be able to pay their war debts and the day-to-day costs of state government with the income from the sale of their western lands. This would let those states keep their taxes low compared to the land-poor states. The

Enrichment Support File Topic

Continuity and Change: The Constitution Explain to students that Presidents have, in the past, sent troops to various parts of the world without the consent of Congress. In fact, when President Johnson wanted to send troops to Vietnam under the Tonkin Gulf Resolution, he felt there had been precedents set by Truman in Korea, Eisenhower in Lebanon, and Kennedy in Cuba. The Tonkin Gulf Resolution passed, but not without some debate about its constitutionality. (See pages 809.)

Western Land Claims Ceded, 1784-1802

☐ States in 1792

☐ Lands Ceded to Congress

0 _____ 500 Miles

0 _____ 500 Kilometers

small states feared their citizens would leave to go to the big land-rich states where taxes were lower.

Here an interesting, enterprising, and especially American kind of businessman came on the stage of history—the speculator. He would play a lively and leading role in developing the American continent. Land speculators had formed their companies and bought land from the Indians out west. The officials of Virginia had refused to recognize their claims. But the speculators thought the Congress might support their interests.

The small states and the speculators, both protecting their own self-interests, worked to have the Articles revised to give Congress

⊕ Geography and History: Regions Refer students to the map above and ask the following questions: Which states claimed western land that was not contiguous to (touching) their borders? (Massachusetts and Connecticut) What state made the smallest western land claim? (South Carolina) Which state made the largest land claim? (Virginia)

control over the western lands. Most states, under wartime pressure, were willing to sign the Articles simply to get some kind of government going to conduct a successful struggle for independence. They planned to amend the Articles later. But land-poor Maryland refused to take the risk. The Articles could not go into effect until all the states—including Maryland—accepted them.

Virginia gives in. Finally the stalemate was broken when Virginia gave in. It was the largest state and the one with the best claim to the western lands. When the British army under Lord Cornwallis headed their way, Virginians needed little persuading that a strong, well-supported union of the states was required to help them win independence. On January 2, 1781, the state offered to cede its land to the central government. At the same time, Virginia insisted that as the land filled with people new states should be admitted with the same "rights of sovereignty, freedom, and independence as other States."

But Maryland—continuing to cooperate with the speculators—still refused to sign the Articles. As Marylanders felt British troops breathing down their necks, they asked the French naval forces to protect them. Then the French again aided the American cause. They refused to do anything to help Maryland until the state agreed to the Articles. In February 1781, Maryland finally signed, and on March 1 the Articles of Confederation became the law of the land.

The treasury of the nation. This new government had no power to enforce its will on the states, yet it had to finish the war and guide the country into peace. Despite its weakness, the new government would accomplish a great deal.

(p. 110) The western lands became the treasury of the new government. Since the Confederation had no power to tax and could only beg the states to donate money, lands took the place of taxes. These unsettled tracts (called the "public domain") were larger than all the settled states put together. By selling the land, the weak new government obtained the money that it could find in no other way.

The vast unsettled West would give the new government an important peacetime job. No nation, new or old, had been blessed with such a land-treasure in its own backyard. What should be done with it? This public domain, which belonged to all the states together, was far larger than France or England or Spain.

Unlike the sparsely settled lands controlled by those European nations, these lands would not become colonies. They would not be used by the thirteen original states to make themselves rich and strong.

Instead they would become (in Jefferson's phrase) an "Empire for Liberty." This Empire would be built by adding new states. Each new state would be the equal of all the older states. Nowadays this seems an obvious and sensible way for a nation to grow. But in those days it was quite a new idea.

Congress took the first step by passing the Land Ordinance of 1785. It provided that the land be carefully surveyed into townships—areas of land 6 miles square made up of 36 sections, each containing 640 acres. One section in each township was reserved for the support of public schools; four more were reserved for the central government. The rest were to be sold.

The Northwest Ordinance of 1787: an Add-a-State Plan. For many years Thomas Jefferson, with his usual uncanny foresight, had been working on a plan for settlements in the western wilderness. The Northwest Ordinance of 1787 put his scheme into law. This American way of growing gave instructions for what we can call an Add-a-State Plan.

The plan was simple. Every part of the public domain would in time become a full-fledged state of the Union "on an equal footing with the original states in all respects whatsoever." This goal was reached by three simple stages described in the Northwest Ordinance. First, when there were still almost no people in a territory, it would have a governor, a secretary, and three judges named by Congress. Then, as soon as there were 5000 adult free men, there would be a legislature where the people of the territory could make laws for themselves. And finally,

(p. 112)

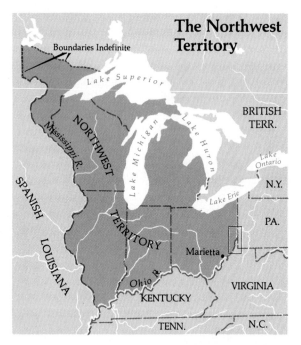

The Northwest Territory

Boundaries Indefinite

Lake Superior

NORTHWEST

Mississippi R.

Lake Michigan

Lake Huron

BRITISH TERR.

Lake Ontario

SPANISH

TERRITORY

N.Y.

Lake Erie

LOUISIANA

PA.

Marietta

Ohio R.

VIRGINIA

KENTUCKY

TENN.

N.C.

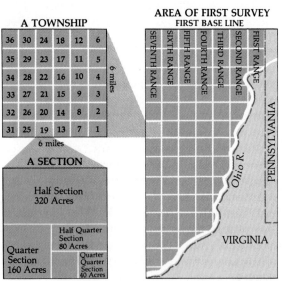

A TOWNSHIP

36	30	24	18	12	6
35	29	23	17	11	5
34	28	22	16	10	4
33	27	21	15	9	3
32	26	20	14	8	2
31	25	19	13	7	1

6 miles

6 miles

A SECTION

Half Section
320 Acres

Half Quarter
Section
80 Acres

Quarter
Section
160 Acres

Quarter
Quarter
Section
40 Acres

AREA OF FIRST SURVEY
FIRST BASE LINE

SEVENTH RANGE · SIXTH RANGE · FIFTH RANGE · FOURTH RANGE · THIRD RANGE · SECOND RANGE · FIRST RANGE

Ohio R.

PENNSYLVANIA

VIRGINIA

Members of Congress did not realize that the treeless plains were some of the richest farmland in the world—and were all the better for farming because they were not cluttered by trees. Since the rumors made western land seem so poor, it was decided that the new states would have to be big. The Northwest Ordinance of 1787 therefore said that in the whole area northwest of the Ohio River there should eventually be "not less than three nor more than five states."

The Ordinance also provided for religious freedom. And in a section probably inserted to attract New Englanders to the Northwest Territory, slavery was prohibited there.

New Englanders settle along the Ohio. The year after the Congress of the Confederation passed the Land Ordinance of 1785, a group of New Englanders formed the Ohio Company of Associates to promote the settlement of land (p. 113) along the north bank of the Ohio River. The first Ohio Company had been founded by Virginians in 1748 to explore the Ohio territory. But it was the company formed in 1786 that made the first organized settlements in Ohio—indeed in the Northwest Territory.

One of the leaders was General Rufus Putnam who, like his cousin General Israel Putnam, served with distinction in the Revolution. Another leader was the Reverend Manassah Cutler of Ipswich, Massachusetts. Cutler was a talented man with wide interests. He had practiced law and medicine, measured the distances of the stars, surveyed the altitude of Mt. Washington in New Hampshire, and made the first systematic account of the plant life of New England.

As soon as the Ohio Company was organized, Cutler went to New York City to persuade the Congress to give the company the right to buy up to 1.5 million Ohio acres at about 8 cents an acre. A government contract was signed on October 27, 1787. While in New York Cutler helped to draft the Northwest Ordinance.

Before the year's end, General Putnam was on his way west with an advance party. The 48 pioneers had set out in two units—one from Danvers, Massachusetts, and the other from

when the free population numbered 60,000, the people could apply for admission to the Union as a state.

How many new states should there be? It was anybody's guess. Congress had heard that the land out there was not good for much. It was said, for example, that there were vast areas that did not have even a single bush on them.

Geography and History: Regions Ask: How is the "Area of First Survey" shown on the map of the Northwest Territory? (As a rectangle northeast of Marietta) How is "A Township" shown on the map of the First Survey? (As a gray square in the seventh range) How is "A Section" represented on the Township map? (As gray square number 19) How many acres are in a section? (640) In a township? (83,040) Are there more miles to the inch on the First Survey map or on the map of the Northwest Territory? (Northwest Territory) Why were different scales used? (To give desired degree of detail in a limited amount of space)

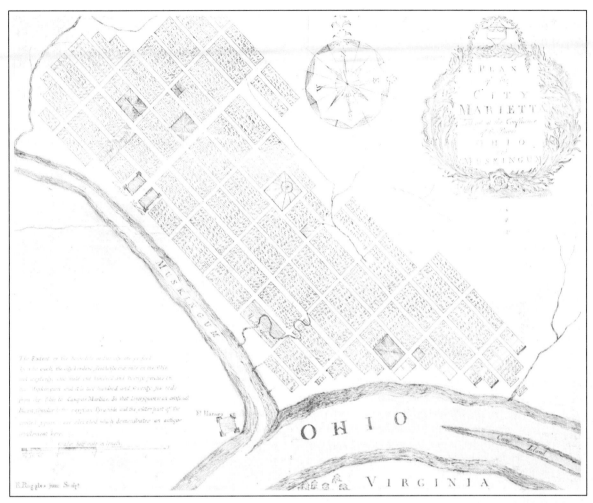

Town-building in the Northwest Territory began at Marietta and spread westward along the Ohio.

Hartford, Connecticut. On April 2, 1788, they all embarked together from Sumrill's Ferry in western Pennsylvania for the trip down the Monongahela and then down the Ohio River. On April 7 the party landed on the east bank of the Muskingum where it joined the Ohio, just opposite Fort Harmar.

Under Putnam's direction the men quickly laid out their town on the compact New England model. Each settler was given a small "in-lot" within the town for a residence and an "out-lot" of eight acres for crops. On July 2, 1788, the agents and directors of the Ohio Company held their first meeting on the spot and named the town Marietta. Again following the New

England example, they promptly provided a church and a school, both of which were operating before the end of July. Within a few months fifteen more families and many single men joined the town.

The Indians raided small parties that were tempted to go off and settle by themselves. This soon taught the Ohio pioneers to build garrison settlements of fifty or more people. One such raid in 1791 induced some settlers to build Fort Frye. It was a triangular palisade enclosing twenty families, ten single men, and eight or ten soldiers from Fort Harmar. Soon there was a string of such groups along the Ohio—at Farmers Castle, Belpre, Columbia, Losantiville,

See "Lesson Plan," p. 102D for **Writing Process Activity: Formulating Questions** relating to the Ohio Company of Associates.

Geography and History: Place Point out that the map above was made in the late 1700s about the time that the city of Marietta was founded. Ask students to study the map and find two reasons the location of Marietta might have been considered strategic. (River junction; across from a fort)

Fort Washington (later called Cincinnati), North Bend, Gallipolis, Manchester, and many other places.

The heroic individual—like Daniel Boone, Meriwether Lewis and William Clark, Zebulon Pike—has held the spotlight of history. But in the settlement of the American continent the lone adventurer was rare. Early settlers, those who took one-way passage and became the backbone of new western communities, generally went together. People moving these great distances into an unknown landscape, threatened by numerous nameless dangers, banded together. They did so not because they especially loved their neighbors or had any ties to them, but because they needed one another.

Successes and failures of the Confederation. Planning an Empire for Liberty—charting the settlement of the vast western public domain—was the greatest single achievement in domestic policy for the Confederation. In military matters, the Confederation brought the War of Independence to a successful end.

In foreign policy the Confederation's greatest achievement—really its only one—was the peace treaty with England. In other foreign affairs the Confederation was a failure. England did not even bother to send a minister to the United States until 1792. Though King George III graciously received John Adams as our first minister to England in 1785, Adams could not get the commercial treaty we badly needed. Even France did not take the United States seriously. Jefferson, our minister to France from 1785 to 1789, wrote home, "We are the lowest and most obscure of the whole diplomatic tribe."

Out beyond the mountains there were diplomatic problems, too. Great Britain held onto its fur trading posts on United States territory in the Northwest. Spain hoped to coop up the United States behind the Appalachians and even to make the settlers in Kentucky and Tennessee become part of the Spanish Empire. To encourage this move, Spain closed the mouth of the Mississippi to citizens of the young nation. Since that was the easiest way for western settlers to ship goods out, Spain hoped the settlers there would join the Spanish Empire in order to use the Mississippi.

When Spain closed the mouth of the Mississippi, it was bad enough for the Westerners. Then Congress was about to make a treaty with Spain giving up the right to use the Mississippi for 25 years in return for the right to use Spanish ports to sell American goods. This would have favored eastern merchants and hurt western settlers. Such an agreement would have permanently alienated the Westerners, but luckily the treaty was defeated in Congress.

Each state could keep out the farm produce and manufactured goods of its neighbors, much as the British Empire had kept out the products of the French. Instead of facing one large power across the ocean, each of the new states now found itself surrounded here in America by a lot of other annoying little states.

The great depression. These problems were all bad enough, but with the end of the war there soon came a financial depression. As long as the war lasted there had been a business boom. When goods were scarce, anybody with something to sell found lots of buyers. After the peace in 1783, Americans were still hungry for the things they could not buy during the war. Once again they began importing from Great Britain. But they bought a good deal more than they could pay for.

Each state issued its own paper money. Nobody knew just how much a New York dollar was worth compared to one from Pennsylvania or Rhode Island. The more money there was in circulation, the less a dollar bought. Then came the financial collapse. Paper money was refused as worthless. Gold and silver were hoarded by people who feared the future. For five long years after 1784 there was the worst business depression the colonies had ever suffered.

Shays's Rebellion. The depression hit people in debt especially hard. Their paper dollars were refused as payment. They had no gold or silver.

In the prosperous days of the war and its aftermath, many farmers had gone into debt to improve their farms, buy more land, or just to purchase luxuries they wanted. But the

Multicultural Connection: Jean Baptiste Pointe du Sable (1745–1818), the founder of Chicago, was the Haitian-born son of a French mariner and an enslaved African woman, and was educated in France. He worked in his father's import-export business until he was shipwrecked off the coast of New Orleans in 1765. Fearing capture into slavery, he went up the Mississippi to explore and traveled throughout much of the Midwest. In 1772 he opened a trading post on Lake Michigan. The settlement that grew up around the trading post eventually became the city of Chicago.

depression meant they could sell their crops only at very low prices. Thus it took many more bushels of corn or wheat than it once had to pay their debts and the taxes on their land. Farmers and debtors wanted their states to issue paper money with which they could pay their bills. Rhode Island passed a law that made it illegal for a person to refuse to accept that state's worthless dollars. Other states also tried to help the debtors by issuing paper money. But some states, including Massachusetts, refused to injure those who had loaned money just to help those who had borrowed it.

Debtors were often hauled into court where they had to pay high fees to lawyers and judges. And if they still failed to pay their bills, they could go to jail and be kept there until they finally did pay. The farmers of western Massachusetts were particularly upset about all this. In one year alone, 1784, there were more than 2000 suits for debt in Worcester County. Farmers there—and elsewhere—rioted to protest against the failure of the states to help them.

In western Massachusetts the popular Daniel Shays, a former captain in the Continental Army, led a rebellion. He demanded more paper money, tax relief, relief for debtors, and an end to imprisonment for debt. During the summer of 1786, these Shaysites traveled around the state preventing the collection of debts or the sale of property for debt. In January 1787, when Shays and his mob of farmers went to the Springfield armory to get more guns and ammunition, they were met by the state militia, which had been paid by wealthy merchants. Shays and his men were driven off, then pursued and captured in February 1787.

The effect of this rebellion was to swing many people over to demanding a change in the national government. In fact, things were not nearly as bad as they seemed. The depression was now coming to an end. The country was growing stronger.

Still, the central government lacked the power to deal with the states. As James Wilson pointed out in the summer of 1787, the states by their "jealousy and ambition" had reduced the Confederation to an "impotent condition." Men of property saw Shays's Rebellion as

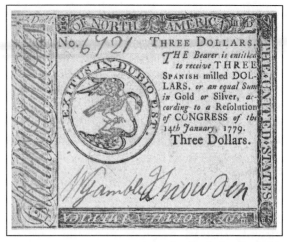

Congress could not keep its promise to redeem "continental currency" in gold or silver.

an attack on them. They considered cheap paper money as bad as taxation without representation.

See "Section 3 Review answers," p. 102D.

Section 3 Review

1. Name some powers of Congress under the Articles of Confederation. What important power did it lack?

2. Why did the land-poor states want western lands ceded to the central government?

3. Describe the provisions of the Northwest Ordinance of 1787.

4. What were the major achievements under the Articles of Confederation?

5. **Critical Thinking: Recognizing Cause and Effect.** How did Shays's demands lead to change in the national government?

See "Lesson Plan," p. 102E.

4. Writing a nation's constitution

The thirteen new American governments had found it impossible to live with a strong London government. They now found it impossible to live without it. Yet nobody wanted to risk replacing the old British tyranny by a new American tyranny.

✂ Critical Thinking Activity: Formulating Questions How did Shays's Rebellion exemplify the drawbacks of a loose confederation of states? Have student volunteers imagine that they are people who have just witnessed Shays's capture at the Springfield armory. Ask the class to develop a list of interview questions for these eyewitnesses. (For example: What really happened? How will this affect other malcontents? Are the reforms needed?) Offer students an opportunity to act out the situation, taking the part of eyewitnesses and reporters.

This was a decisive moment in history. Would America become another Europe? Would the New World become only a new battlefield for thirteen new little nations? Had they risked their "lives, their fortunes, and their sacred honor" only to turn the continent into a sea of anarchy?

Wise Americans dared not let this happen. Their children and their grandchildren, they said, would curse them if they threw away this opportunity to explore together and in peace the vast, mysterious, rich New World.

The Annapolis meeting. In January 1786, Virginia sent an invitation to all the states to meet and discuss one of their major problems— the regulation of commerce. Nine states accepted the invitation, but only twelve men (representing five states) actually came to the meeting at Annapolis, Maryland, that September. By then farm workers could barely support themselves on their declining wages. Money lenders were seizing farms, and the Shaysites were rampaging through Massachusetts.

With fewer than half the states represented at Annapolis, there was not much they could do. Luckily, one of the twelve men there was the bold young Alexander Hamilton. Born in the Virgin Islands of a family that had fallen on hard times, he had attended King's College (later Columbia University) in New York City. During the war General George Washington, recognizing Hamilton's brilliance, made him his close adviser and gave him the job of organizing military headquarters.

In 1786 when Hamilton was only 29 years of age, he saw that the thirteen states would never prosper until they formed a strong union. He demanded that the states send delegates at once to a larger meeting to see what could be done. The Congress of the Confederation issued the invitations. If Hamilton had never lived another day, his courage and vision at the Annapolis convention would entitle him to a place in American history.

The Philadelphia Convention. The states responded to the call. Within a year 55 delegates from twelve states met in Independence Hall in Philadelphia in the hot summer of 1787. They were only a block from Carpenters' Hall, where the First Continental Congress had met in 1774. The thirteenth state, little Rhode Island ("Rogue Island," a Boston newspaper called it), simply ignored the convention.

The invitation to this meeting was vague. It was not at all clear what the convention was supposed to do. The object was somehow to remodel the Articles of Confederation and "to take into consideration the situation of the United States."

The first of many questions that bewildered the delegates was this: What power did they really have? The wiser men did not worry about whether they had the right to do more than suggest amendments to the Articles of Confederation. Instead they thought about the job they had to do—to redesign the government to make life better in all the colonies.

Nothing was newer about the New World than the Constitutional Convention in Philadelphia. Never before had there been a meeting quite like this one. History gave the delegates very little to go on.

A federal or a national union? Despite the confusion, there was one fact on which nearly all the delegates agreed. Each of the states they represented was somehow "sovereign." That is, the people in each state believed they had *all* the powers to run *all* their own affairs. The American Revolution had been fought to prove it. This was not a mere technicality. It was everybody's starting point. And it was what made the job of the convention so hard.

What the delegates really had on their hands, then, was a kind of problem in international relations. This was precisely what they meant when they said they wanted to make a new plan for the "federal" union.

In those days "federal" meant something different from what it means today. It was still commonly spelled "foederal," because it came from the Latin word *foedus*, which means "treaty." A treaty was, of course, an agreement made by a sovereign state (or nation). And a "federal" union, then, would be a kind of international association held together by fully

Enrichment Support File Topic

Continuity and Change: The Constitution Explain to students that the unresolved issues of states' rights and slavery would remain central in national politics during the first half of the nineteenth century. Legislation, such as the Missouri Compromise and the Compromise of 1850 would be created in the effort to resolve these constitutional issues. Unfortunately, these were only temporary solutions. The conflict over these issues would have to be resolved by the Civil War. (See pages 216 and 308.)

Historical Society of Pennsylvania

The Constitutional Convention met in Philadelphia at the State House, later renamed Independence Hall. This 1790 engraving by William Birch shows a rear view of the hall.

sovereign states that had made treaties with one another. Of course, that would be a very different kind of thing, and would have much less power, than something like the government of England or of France. Could such a weak, loose international association of the thirteen new states do the job for America?

"No!" was the answer of many delegates to the Philadelphia Convention. Some of the most energetic men—like Alexander Hamilton of New York, James Madison of Virginia, and Gouverneur Morris of Pennsylvania—were sure that would not be good enough. To do the job, the government would have to be "national." That was the word they used, and by it they meant something more or less like the government of France or of England.

A "national" union would not be merely a collection of different states, each with its own government. It would be something much stronger. It would actually make laws, would have its own courts, would levy its own taxes, would control commerce, and exercise supreme power over all the people and all the states under it. To make that possible each of the "sovereign" states would have to give up some of its "sovereign" powers.

The need to compromise. It would not be easy to persuade people to do this. You would have to ask the people in each state to take powers away from their own Massachusetts, or New Jersey, or Maryland, which the people in that state loved and still called their "country." And you would have to give those powers to some imaginary new nation that did not even exist. There

More from Boorstin: "Their [the Framers'] product significantly omitted both the words federal and 'national,' which had figured prominently and acrimoniously in the theoretical discussions. Instead, the Constitution simply referred at every point to 'the United States.' By the end of their deliberations the delegates seem to have recognized their creation as an important new hybrid among political species." (From *The Americans: The National Experience*)

were good reasons to fear a powerful new government with its headquarters far outside your state. The best reason of all was the recent bitter experience with King George III and with the British Parliament. But there were other reasons.

The thirteen states—some large, some small—were very different from one another in other ways, too. What was good for seafaring New England might be bad for tobacco-raising Virginia. Even after giving up their western land claims, Virginia and New York were still large states, owning unmeasured stretches of wilderness. But Maryland and New Jersey and tiny Rhode Island felt themselves pushed up against the sea by these powerful neighbors.

If under the new plan for a government the states were all to be equal, then the small poor states, with very little to lose, could lord it over the large rich states and make them share their wealth. Or, if the states were all to be unequal, and each state had power in the central government proportioned to its own size or wealth, then what would happen to the little ones?

If any large number of delegates had stuck by their guns and demanded that everything go their way, there would never have been a Constitution. Luckily that did not happen. Although the convention was held in Philadelphia, which was the headquarters of the uncompromising Quakers, what prevailed in 1787 was the practical spirit of compromise.

Before the convention had any meetings it was plain that, if there was to be a new government at all, everybody would have to be satisfied with half a loaf. George Washington, the chairman of the convention, was used to bringing people together. With the glory of victory behind him, he had enough prestige to keep the delegates on the track. The good-humored Benjamin Franklin, already 81 years old, was able to keep them talking instead of fighting. Most of the convention members were wise enough to distrust their own wisdom.

The delegates in Philadelphia debated for the whole hot summer of 1787. We do not know exactly what they said. They had decided in advance to keep everything they said a secret. No complete record was made. We have to depend on the private notes taken by a few members, especially those of James Madison. But we do know what came out of their meetings. It was the same Constitution of the United States of America that (with only a few amendments) we live under today. (See pp. 965, for the text of the Constitution.)

They were able to make a Constitution only because they were ruled by the spirit of compromise. Everybody got something he wanted. Nobody got everything he wanted.

The Great Compromise. The first question of major importance was the matter of representation. The large populous states naturally wanted the number of representatives in the new Congress to be based on population. Edmund Randolph of Virginia presented a plan to the convention that had been drawn up by James Madison. The Virginia Plan provided that there would be two houses of Congress and that in each one representation would be based on population. Then William Paterson of New Jersey replied with a plan more to the liking of the small states that had few people. The New Jersey Plan proposed that there would be only one house in which each state would have just one vote. At times the argument became heated.

Finally Roger Sherman, William Samuel Johnson, and Oliver Ellsworth of Connecticut suggested the Connecticut Compromise. Like many other ideas that have made history, it was remarkably simple. Why not divide the Congress into two houses? In one house (the Senate) each state, regardless of its population, would have the same number of representatives. In the other house (the House of Representatives) each member would represent nearly the same number of people. Quite appropriately this came to be called the Great Compromise. For it broke the deadlock and made it possible for the large states and the small states ✖ to work together.

The three-fifths compromise and the commercial compromise. Other major compromises came on slavery and on the control of commerce. The southern states, where the

✖ Critical Thinking Activity: Identifying Central Issues What does *compromise* mean? Have students suggest their own definitions. Then guide students toward a shared definition to be used by the class. Divide the class into four groups. Assign groups to research Sections 1–4 of Chapter 5 to find examples of compromises. Combine the group lists into a master list for the entire class. You may wish to extend the activity by asking students to write a brief paragraph explaining how critical compromise was during the early years of the United States.

Oliver Ellsworth, who helped to work out the Great Compromise, and Abigail Wolcott Ellsworth are seen in their library. Painter Ralph Earl cleverly showed their house and yard in the window.

slaves were really treated as property, still wanted the slaves counted as people for the purposes of representation in the new House of Representatives. Some delegates argued that if one kind of property was counted for representation, other kinds should be, too.

The issue was resolved when slavery and taxation were linked. It was assumed that Congress would need to raise some money by levying direct taxes on the basis of population. That would mean that if *all* slaves were counted for the purposes of representation, then *all* slaves would be counted for taxation. In that case, Southerners decided they were willing to lower their demands. By the three-fifths compromise it was agreed that three-fifths of the number of slaves would be counted *both* for representation and for levying direct taxes.

In other ways, too, there were forebodings that slavery, a great moral issue, would threaten the very existence of the nation. The northern states wanted to prohibit the slave trade. They also wanted to give the central government power to regulate commerce. The South feared that export duties might be placed on its tobacco, rice, and other crops. These two questions were compromised by stating that the slave trade could not be prohibited for twenty years and that Congress could regulate commerce but could never levy duties on exports.

A government "partly national and partly federal." To satisfy those who wanted a union truly "national," the new government was given the power to tax, to control commerce, to make war, to raise an army and a navy, and to conduct foreign relations. To satisfy those who wanted a union merely "federal," the Constitu-

David Martin painted a bewigged and well-dressed Benjamin Franklin in England in 1767.

White House Historical Association

tion gave each state the power to make the laws controlling its daily life and all the powers not expressly given to the new central government.

This new government, as one member put it, was "partly national, partly federal." In the Constitution you will not find either the word "federal" or the word "national." The members of the convention knew that each of these words would be a red flag to some members. They purposely left everybody to guess to what extent the new government was either federal or national. That way each side could think it had won a little more than the other.

If they did not call the new arrangement either "federal" or "national," what would they call it? Their answer was very wise and very simple. Every time they themselves mentioned the new government in the Constitution, they just called it "the United States."

The members of the convention were also wise enough to include in the Constitution itself instructions for changing it. Then, if the people in the future found they needed changes, they would not have to junk the whole Constitution and start all over again. They could keep the Constitution as a whole, while following the rules for making the few amendments they needed. This was a masterstroke, and was as new as anything else the convention did.

The final document repaired many of the weaknesses of the Articles of Confederation. The government under the Articles had no President and lacked the power to tax or to raise and maintain an army and a navy. The new government had three separate branches—executive, legislative, and judicial—each with its own special powers and duties. Spreading the powers and duties among the branches enabled them to check and balance each other. Then no one branch could become a danger to the freedom of the people.

The President was made Commander-in-Chief of all the nation's armed forces. He had the power to negotiate treaties, but the Senate had to approve them by a two-thirds majority of all senators present. The President was also given wide powers to appoint officials. But some of his choices, such as justices of the

❖ See "Lesson Plan," p. 102E for Cooperative Learning Activity: Testing Conclusions relating to the Constitution.

Supreme Court and ambassadors to foreign lands, had to be approved by the Senate.

Each house of Congress was given special powers. The House of Representatives, whose members represented the people rather than the states, had the sole power to initiate all bills for raising revenue. And only the Senate could approve treaties and certain appointments. Many specific powers were also granted to Congress. These included enacting taxes, providing for defense, declaring war, fixing tariffs, coining money, and setting up post offices. Surprisingly important in the long run was the power given to Congress to pass all laws "necessary and proper" to carry out its specifically assigned functions. This came to be called the "elastic clause," because it would be stretched in so many ways.

The Supreme Court was created to hear all cases raised under the Constitution and the laws of the United States, and certain others. Since the Constitution and the laws of the United States were "the supreme Law of the Land," the Supreme Court would wield great ❧ power to shape the new government. (The text (p. 120) of the Constitution and its amendments will be found in the Appendix on pp. 965. A detailed analysis also appears there, including information on why its major parts were included— "origins"—and what changes have occurred over time—"afterlife.")

See "Section 4 Review answers," p. 102E.

Section 4 Review

1. Identify or explain: Annapolis meeting, Alexander Hamilton, James Madison, Edmund Randolph, Virginia Plan, William Paterson, New Jersey Plan.
2. Describe the Great Compromise. Why was it important?
3. What was the three-fifths compromise?
4. What powers that the Confederation lacked did the new government have under the Constitution?
5. **Critical Thinking: Making Comparisons.** Explain the difference between a federal union (as interpreted in 1700) and a national union.

See "Lesson Plan," p. 102F.

5. The states ratify

It was not enough for the delegates to the Constitutional Convention to draft the document. It had to be ratified too. Here again the convention showed its wisdom—and its ability to go beyond the letter of the law.

Bypassing the states. The convention submitted the Constitution to Congress and asked that it be sent to state constitutional conventions for approval. This procedure would assure that it was ratified by the people themselves and not only by the state governments. Many believed that this would make it clear that the Constitution was superior to state laws. The state legislatures might not have made an impartial decision, because they were destined to lose powers under the new government. To go into effect the Constitution required the approval not of all thirteen but of only nine states. This would keep an obstinate few from sabotaging the work of the cooperative many.

The fight for approval. Since the convention had done its work in secret, there was great public interest both in what the new Constitution said—and in what it really meant. Those who supported the new Constitution were called *Federalists*, and their opponents were called *Anti-Federalists*. The Anti-Federalists feared that the new Constitution would create a super-government that might destroy the very liberty that the Revolution was fought to win. The Constitution contained no bill of rights like that found in the state constitutions. And what would prevent the President from becoming a king?

The bitter struggle for ratification had intelligent, well-meaning people on both sides. The outcome was not certain until the very end. Only hard work and a number of political tricks by the Federalists brought about ratification of the document by the required number of states.

The process began easily enough. On December 7, 1787, Delaware by unanimous vote became the first state to give the new Constitution its approval. The Pennsylvania Federalists planned to rush through approval before the

⊡ See "Lesson Plan," p. 102F for **Writing Process Activity: Identifying Alternatives** relating to ratification of the Constitution.

Anti-Federalists could muster their forces and reach the voters. They bought up newspapers to keep Anti-Federalist speeches from being printed. And their undemocratic strategy succeeded on December 12, when the Constitution won Pennsylvania's approval 46–23. New Jersey, Georgia, and Connecticut followed within a month.

Massachusetts, a key state. When the Massachusetts state convention met, the Anti-Federalists seemed to be in a majority. Luckily for the Federalists, the cleverest politicians were on their side. At first the ambitious John Hancock, the influential presiding officer of the convention, was opposed. But the Federalists persuaded him to change his mind. They promised to elect him governor of Massachusetts and hinted that he was the obvious choice for Vice-President of the new nation. When Hancock went before the convention to urge that it ratify the Constitution, he also proposed a series of amendments to the Constitution to guard citizens' rights. The convention accepted both of Hancock's suggestions. On February 6, 1788, Massachusetts ratified the Constitution by the close vote of 187–168.

What Massachusetts did suggested to other states that they too might approve the Constitution as it was and at the same time propose amendments to remove the objections and allay the fears of some of their citizens. Maryland ratified without conditions on April 26, 1788. South Carolina approved in May, but proposed amendments. New Hampshire ratified with amendments after a bitter struggle and a close vote on June 21.

Virginia and New York seal the victory. Now nine states had approved, and technically the government could go into operation. But, in fact, no central government could be effective without including Virginia and New York. Virginia was the largest state in the Union and had some of its best-known and ablest leaders— Washington, Jefferson, Madison, and many others. In Virginia there was a tough fight because Patrick Henry, George Mason, and so

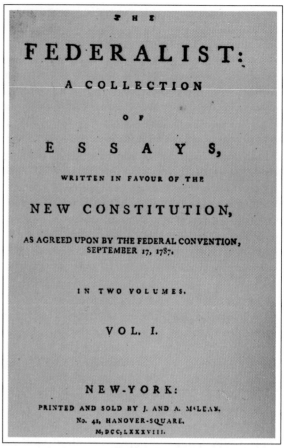

THE

FEDERALIST:

A COLLECTION

OF

E S S A Y S,

WRITTEN IN FAVOUR OF THE

NEW CONSTITUTION,

AS AGREED UPON BY THE FEDERAL CONVENTION, SEPTEMBER 17, 1787.

IN TWO VOLUMES.

VOL. I.

NEW-YORK:

PRINTED AND SOLD BY J. AND A. M'LEAN, No. 41, HANOVER-SQUARE. M,DCC,LXXXVIII.

The *Federalist Papers*, written by Madison, Hamilton, and Jay, helped to persuade New York to vote for the Constitution.

many who had been active in the Revolution feared the powers of the new government and became outspoken Anti-Federalists. But Washington's strong support for the Constitution was decisive. In a close vote Virginia finally approved, while suggesting amendments.

Still the crucial state of New York had not announced its decision. Luckily many voters there would be persuaded by a series of brilliant propaganda essays, called the *Federalist Papers*. Written by James Madison, Alexander Hamilton, and John Jay, these essays not only helped turn the tide in New York, but became (and remain) the classic statement of why freedom-loving people need a strong central government.

The news of Virginia's ratification, rushed north by an express rider, also helped New York to decide. On July 26, 1788, the delegates to the New York convention approved (though with many amendments) by a scary narrow margin (30 to 27). A change of only two votes would have meant the rejection of the Constitution by New York. Then perhaps the whole effort to frame an effective government for the new nation might have collapsed. Hamilton led the fight in New York and deserves much of the credit for ratification by that state.

✖ Now the new government could go into action, despite the strong Anti-Federalists in two states. North Carolina did not ratify until November 21, 1789, after the Constitution was operating. When Rhode Island (which always went its own way) finally ratified on May 29, 1790, it had the distinction of being the last of the original colonies to approve the Constitution.

The Federalists promised that they would add to the Constitution a bill of rights—a series of amendments guaranteeing certain rights and liberties to the people. Without this promise the Constitution might never have been ratified. Had the Constitutional Convention included a bill of rights at the beginning, the struggle for adoption might have been far easier.

After the long and bitter arguments in the state conventions, there was widespread rejoicing when the Constitution was adopted.

An express rider took eight days to carry the news to the New York ratifying convention in Poughkeepsie that Virginia had ratified the Constitution. This news helped sway the delegates at the New York State convention to ratify. Virginia's resolution, as we see, expressed hope for early amendments to correct the Constitution's imperfections.

New York Public Library, Rare Book Division, Astor, Lenox and Tilden Foundations

POGHKEEPSIE,
July 2d, 1788.

JUST ARRIVED

BY EXPRESS,

The Ratification of the New Constitution by the Convention of the State of Virginia, on Wednesday the 25th June, by a majority of 10 ; 88 agreeing, and 78 dissenting to its adoption.

"WE the Delegates of the People of Virginia, duly elected in Pursuance of a Recommendation of the General Assembly, and now met in Convention, having fully and fairly investigated and discussed the Proceedings of the Federal Convention, and being

With these Impressions, with a solemn Appeal to the Searcher of Hearts for the Purity of our Intentions, and under the Conviction, that whatsoever Imperfections may exist in the Constitution, ought rather to be examined in the Mode prescribed therein, than to bring the Uni-

✖ **Critical Thinking Activity: Making Inferences** How did the thirteen states stand on the ratification of the Constitution? Ask students to offer their own interpretation of the political cartoon on the following page. This can be achieved by asking students to identify and assign a meaning to each symbol in the cartoon. What can be inferred from the writing on the cartoon? Direct students' attention to North Carolina and Rhode Island. Why might these states have hesitated to ratify the Constitution? What effect would this cartoon have had on these two states?

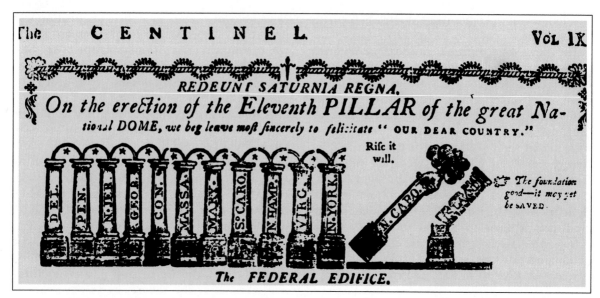

The CENTINEL   VOL IX

REDEUNT SATURNIA REGNA.

On the erection of the Eleventh PILLAR of the great Na-
tional DOME, we beg leave most sincerely to felicitate "OUR DEAR COUNTRY."

Rise it
will.

The foundation
good—it may yet
be SAVED.

The FEDERAL EDIFICE.

The New-York Historical Society

In 1788 the Massachusetts *Centinel* urged North Carolina and Rhode Island to complete the federal edifice by ratifying the Constitution. North Carolina did so the next year. Rhode Island, shown with a broken pillar but a firm foundation, followed in 1790.

Dinners, processions, and fireworks signaled the nation's new beginning.

A government in skeleton. Still, the Constitution provided only the skeleton for a government. The first President, the Congress, and the Supreme Court would have to put flesh on the skeleton. Why has this federal Constitution had such a long and successful life? How has a short document written over two centuries ago for thirteen struggling seaboard colonies been able to give strength and liberty to a vast, two-ocean nation of more than 250 million people?

Oddly enough, the shortness of the document itself is one explanation. The Constitution did not go into details. It left to future generations the right and the opportunity to apply the scheme, and so to grow in unpredictable ways. It is not surprising then that one of the shortest constitutions ever adopted by a nation was to become in time the oldest living written constitution.

See "Section 5 Review answers," p. 102F.

Section 5 Review

1. Why was it significant that voters rather than state legislatures ratified the Constitution?
2. Why did some people oppose passage of the Constitution?
3. What did Massachusetts do that assisted in getting other states to ratify the Constitution?
4. What factors helped to win ratification in Virginia and New York?
5. **Critical Thinking: Testing Conclusions.** Is it true that the short length of the Constitution has contributed to its long life? Explain your answer.

More from Boorstin: "The virtue of the Federal Constitution seemed its flexibility, rather than any novel principle of federalism or republicanism. Its real immortality would consist in its capacity, by amendment, to 'keep pace with the advance of the age in science and experience' [Jefferson]." (From *The Lost World of Thomas Jefferson*)

Chapter 5 Review

See "Chapter Review answers," p. 102F.

Focusing on Ideas

1. Describe the process that authors of the state constitutions followed to make "consent of the governed" a living reality.

2. What type of new government had the states wanted to see created? Were their expectations realistic? Explain.

3. How did the framers of the Constitution plan for necessary future "repairs"?

4. Certain situations in the 1780s promoted separatism among the states, while others promoted greater unity. Give examples of these situations (or forces) and explain them.

Taking a Critical Look

1. **Demonstrating Reasoned Judgment.** The state constitutions were (and still are) longer and more detailed than the United States Constitution. Why might you expect this? What advantage, if any, do you see in a relatively short constitution?

2. **Determining Relevance.** What is the relationship between Shays's Rebellion and the Constitution?

3. **Making Comparisons.** How does the Constitution reflect the ideas contained in the Declaration of Independence?

Your Region in History

1. **Geography.** How was your state affected by the Northwest Ordinance?

2. **Government.** When was your state's constitution adopted? How was it drafted? If you live in one of the original thirteen states, investigate and report on the struggle for ratification of the federal Constitution in your state. When did your state ratify the Constitution?

3. **Economics.** How did the three-fifths compromise and the commercial compromise affect your state?

Historical Facts and Figures

Drawing Conclusions. Use information on the chart below to help answer the following questions. In each case explain how the information on the chart helped you draw your conclusion. (a) Did the writers of the Constitution feel that the national government or the state governments should deal with the governments of other countries? (b) Under what conditions or circumstances did the writers of the Constitution think that the federal government should become involved in business or private enterprise? (c) Is it more likely that there will be conflicting state and federal laws concerning copyrights and patents, taxes, or marriages?

System of Federalism

Examples of Delegated Powers	Examples of Concurrent Powers	Examples of Reserved Powers
Regulate immigration naturalization	Borrow money	Create corporation laws
Regulate interstate foreign commerce	Provide for health, safety, and welfare	Regulate intrastate commerce
Set standard weights and measures	Administer criminal justice	Establish and maintain schools
Create and maintain armed forces	Set minimum wage	Establish and maintain local governments
Make copyright and patent laws	Charter banks	Determine eligibility requirements for elected state officials
Establish postal system	Levy taxes	Determine and regulate laws of marriage, divorce, and professional licenses
Establish foreign policy		
Create lower courts		
Print money		
Declare war		

Review Chapter
Beginnings to 1789

Identifying Chapter Materials

Objectives	Basic Instructional Materials	Extension Materials
1 The American Discovery • Identify the Mayas, Aztecs, and Incas. • Describe some cultural features of North American Indians. • Cite several reasons for European exploration in the 1400s and 1500s.	**Instructional Support File** • Skill Review Activity, Unit 1, p. 4	**Enrichment Support File** • The First Americans **Documents of American History** • Privileges and Prerogatives Granted to Columbus, Vol. 1, p. 1 **American History Transparencies** • Time Lines, p. E3 • Critical Thinking, p. F3
2 The Making of America • Describe the population of the early colonial period. • Trace the steps leading to colonial self-government.	**Instructional Support File** • Skill Application Activity, Unit 1, p. 33	**Enrichment Support File** • Settling the New World **Documents of American History** • Mayflower Compact, Vol. 1, p. 15 • First Charter of Massachusetts, Vol. 1, p. 16 **American History Transparencies** • Time Lines, p. E7
3 Forming a New Nation, 1763–1789 • Describe the major events leading to the American Revolution. • Characterize the government under the Articles of Confederation, and compare it to the government provided by the Constitution. • Compare the Federalists and Anti-Federalists. • Describe the "Add-a-State plan."	**Instructional Support File** • Skill Review Activity, Unit 2, p. 5 • Critical Thinking Activity, Unit 2, p. 20 • Review Chapter Test, Unit 2, pp. 47–50	**Enrichment Support File** • To Arms! The Revolution Begins • Writing the Declaration of Independence • No Neighbors for Miles: The Northwest Territory • The Birth of the Constitution: The Philadelphia Convention **Documents of American History** • Stamp Act, Vol. 1, p. 53 • Declaration of Causes and Necessity of Taking Up Arms, Vol. 1, p. 92 **American History Transparencies** • Geography and History, pp. B3, B5, B7, B9 • Critical Thinking, p. F9

Review: Beginnings to 1789

TEACHING STRATEGIES

The two review chapters in this book may be adapted to suit the knowledge level of your students and the particular needs of your curriculum. Below are three suggested strategies for this review chapter:

★ Assign the chapter and chapter review as a regular lesson to students who may be unfamiliar with the material in the first five chapters of the text before the class begins Chapter 6. You can administer the Review Chapter Test from the Instructional Support File to check students' competency when they have completed the chapter.

★ Assign the review chapter to students as a quick review of material they have learned previously. Then work through the questions in the chapter review together before beginning Chapter 6.

★ As a useful tool for assessment, give students the Review Chapter Test from the Instructional Support File. Then assign specific readings from this chapter or from earlier chapters in the text to supplement student knowledge where the test indicates any weaknesses.

Chapter Review Answers

Focusing on Key Facts and Ideas

1. a) a pre-Columbian Indian civilization in what is now Mexico. b) a pre-Columbian Indian civilization in Central America. c) a pre-Columbian Indian civilization in what is now Peru. 2. The mass printing of books, the development of astronomy and Copernicus's theory of Earth's movement around the sun, advances in navigation prompted by Prince Henry of Portugal, and the growth of modern nation states helped to shape the Age of Discovery. 3. The competition among nations brought extra pressure to discovery and exploration in the New World. 4. a) Spanish explorer, conquered the Aztecs in 1519. b) conquered the Incas in 1531. c) French explorer of the east coast of North America. d) French explorer of the St. Lawrence River. e) founded New France; established the first permanent French settlement in America at Quebec. f) strong governor of the Massachusetts Bay Colony. g) English soldier and reformer, founded Georgia. h) replaced James II as ruler of Great Britain in 1689. 5. Good planning: Organization helped the Puritans of Massachusetts Bay and the Quakers in Pennsylvania. Bad planning: The Georgia colony, Locke's elaborate scheme of government for the Carolinas, etc. Good luck: The arrival of Squanto; help from Indians; Rolfe's finding of tobacco as a "money crop"; outstanding leaders; etc. Bad luck: Fight with Spain delaying help for Roanoke colony; swampy ground at Jamestown; outbreak of infectious diseases; hostility of Indians in some places; etc. 6. A system of salutary neglect in which England did not enforce its regulations (particularly the Navigation Acts) and the colonies prospered. It ended in the 1760s. 7. England gained Canada and all French lands between the Appalachian Mountains and the Mississippi. 8. Non-English colonists adopted English laws, culture; became American; they all wanted independence for political and economic reasons. 9. The colonies were very different, founded at different times for different reasons. Bringing the diverse colonies together to work toward a common goal seemed nearly impossible. 10. Federal: Constitution gave each state power to make laws controlling its daily life and all other powers not specifically given to central government. National: gave central government the power to tax, to control commerce, to make war, to raise an army and a navy, and to conduct foreign relations. 11. They included instructions within it for change.

Taking a Critical Look

1. Many early sea explorations were to find a Northwest Passage, yet new landforms and waterways were discovered instead. Rumors of wealth tempted other explorers who went on to make more "accidental" discoveries. 2. While the British government was occupied with problems at home, the American colonies were governing themselves. The population of the colonies grew and their wealth accumulated. 3. Not enforcing the Navigation Acts and other aspects of the mercantile system permitted the colonies to thrive economically; England reaped the benefits. 4. The colonies had economic and political independence by resisting the Navigation Acts, coining their own money, etc. Socially, American culture emerged. 5. Abuses cited in Declaration addressed in Bill of Rights. Declaration cites King as centralized authority; Constitution provides separation of powers. Declaration states no changes for light and transient reasons; Constitution allows complicated amending process. Both honor popular sovereignty. 6. Defend: British leader never visited colonies; expected gratitude for military protection and acceptance of "justified" taxes. Challenge: Franklin warned Parliament about tax opposition; merchants noticed trade decline, leaders couldn't accept colonial spirit of self-government.

Your Region in History

1–5. Answers will vary depending on your region. Consult your local library or historical society.

REVIEW: Beginnings to 1789

Focusing the Chapter: Have students identify the chapter logo. Discuss what unit theme the logo might symbolize. Then ask students to skim the chapter to identify other illustrations or titles that relate to this theme.

For teaching suggestions, see "Lesson Plan," p. 126B.

The history of the United States begins in Europe before an America was known there, and in America before Europeans came. In the Age of Columbus the peoples of Europe were discovering the world anew, reaching out to far and fabulous places. Columbus's wonderful, puzzling find enticed other adventurers to risk their lives for riches and empire.

The America they found already held many millions of people. These Native Americans had neither the ships nor the science to reach out. What for Europe spelled empire and success, for most Native Americans spelled a losing fight to keep their lands and ways of life. The hopes that people brought from the Old World to the New were as varied as their nations. Some came for gold or glory or adventure, some to worship in their own way, others to escape poverty, prison, or oppression. Some came without hope—to serve as slaves on plantations, and in mines and mills. Gradually life in America made them all Americans.

In the late 1500s Theodore De Bry's engravings showed Europeans the strange wonders of America.

John Carter Brown Library at Brown University.

1. The American discovery

The discovery of America was the world's greatest surprise. When the first Europeans came, their maps of the world left no place for America. They knew only three continents—Europe, Asia, and Africa.

Columbus was not looking for a new continent. He thought he was on the way to China and India. Europeans were disappointed to find unexpected lands in the way. Still they insisted on calling the natives here "Indians." So America was discovered by accident.

As more Europeans came and explored the unknown lands, their disappointment became surprise. They had found a world for new beginnings.

Before discovery. It was only for the people of Europe that America had to be "discovered." Millions of Native Americans were already here! For them, Columbus and all the sailors, explorers, and settlers who came later provided their "discovery" of Europe!

For Europeans the "discovery" of America offered vast lands, treasures of gold and silver and timber, places to build cities and places of refuge. For them this was a happy discovery. In the long run it would be a great discovery for the world. But for the millions of Native Americans already here their "discovery" of Europeans was not quite so happy. For some it meant the end of their Native American civilization. For some it meant slavery. For nearly all, the Europeans brought shock, disease, and change.

The Native Americans whom Columbus mistakenly called Indians were the descendants of people who came to America from Asia thousands of years ago, perhaps during the last great ice age. They spread across two continents and created widely different societies.

The grandest of these Native American cultures astonished the Europeans. South of the present United States—from Central Mexico to Peru—they found the Aztecs, the Mayas, and the Incas. These people had created great civilizations, but they were not prepared for the guns and the even more deadly diseases of the Europeans.

Northern Native Americans. In America north of Mexico, there were perhaps some 4 million Native Americans. They were as varied as the peoples of Europe. There were countless tribes and hundreds of languages. Some tribes made elegant gold jewelry and elaborate pottery, while others were still in the Stone Age. Some wove handsome rugs and wore textiles of beautiful design. Others knew only skins and furs. Their meat depended on the place. Deer were nearly everywhere, and on the plains were herds of buffalo. The seashore and streams abounded in fish and shell food. The Indians planted corn, which made their bread, and beans, squashes, and many other crops. They knew where to find, and how to enjoy, the nuts and berries and mushrooms and other delights of the woods. They raised and smoked tobacco, which was not known in Europe.

Because the Indians lived close to nature, most of them had religions in which natural things played a major role. The Indians saw and worshiped Nature. They had learned to know the stones, the animals, and the plants. They were adept at using what they found for food, shelter, and clothing.

More from Boorstin: "Columbus reported to his surprise and somewhat to his disappointment, that 'in these islands I have so far found no human monstrosities, as many expected, on the contrary, among all these peoples good looks are esteemed. . . . Thus I have neither found monsters nor any report of any, except . . . a people . . . who eat human flesh . . . they are no more malformed than the others.' These Indians, he reassured the Spanish sovereigns, were 'very well built, of very handsome bodies and very fine faces.'" (From *The Discoverers*)

The great pyramid at Chichén Itzá, Mexico, was part of a Mayan religious center.

Why Europeans went exploring. For centuries all these people and their cultures lay hidden from Europe. What happened to stir Europeans to reach out to this vast unknown?

The Renaissance, beginning about 1300, marked the end of the Middle Ages. It revived the questioning spirit of the ancient Greeks. Scholars translated books of poetry, adventure, and science from Greek, Arabic, Hebrew, Persian, and other eastern languages. Ambitious princes led new city-states in Italy. They built palaces and churches in the style of Greece and Rome. Artists discovered perspective. Leonardo da Vinci and Michelangelo kept notebooks of all the wonders of the world and painted masterpieces. Gutenberg invented printing with movable type. He printed his first Bible in 1456 and opened a new world for books, which before had to be copied by hand. Modern astronomy was born. Copernicus showed that the earth revolved around the sun, and the word went everywhere in books.

At the same time, the modern nation state took shape. Strong kings conquered weak feudal lords. The nation's laws, taxes, armies, and courts replaced those of the local nobles. The wealth of the nation commanded by the new monarchs would outfit the ships to explore the world.

The Portuguese, inspired by Henry the Navigator, pushed their voyages of discovery down the coast of Africa seeking a water route to the "Indies." They invented the "caravel" with lateen sails that could be set to catch the wind so if they sailed somewhere with the wind they could still sail back, even with the wind against them.

All the forces at work in western Europe came together in Columbus's great adventure—the most important seafaring voyage in history. Columbus opened a half-century of Spanish exploration and conquest. For Europe the 1500s be- ✕ came the Age of Discovery and a time of grand adventure.

For more than 50 years after Columbus, the Spaniards had the New World mostly to themselves. Who dared challenge Spain—the richest and most powerful nation in Europe? One Spanish adventurer after another went out seeking conquest and treasure. Cortez conquered Mexico, Pizarro looted Peru, Coronado sought the rumored Seven Cities of Cibola, and de Soto, too, hunted for those wondrous places with their emerald-studded walls.

French and English exploration.   For many years the Spanish dominated the New World, but they did not have it all to themselves. John Cabot (who, like Columbus, was born in Genoa in Italy) sailed for Henry VII of England in 1497. He first reached land in Newfoundland (and so "discovered" North America), probably not far from where a Norseman, Leif Eriksson, had made his settlement 500 years before. Cabot sailed again the following year. This expedition disappeared without a trace. But for the next two centuries his first voyage remained the basis of England's claim to the whole mainland of North America.

The French sent out Verrazzano, but his discoveries led nowhere. It was really Jacques Cartier who was to turn French interest into reality. On his first voyage in 1534, he discovered and explored the Gulf of St. Lawrence. So he began to open the great passage to the continent's interior. Later, he sailed as far as what is now the site of Montreal and even spent a winter near present-day Quebec. Though Cartier never succeeded in establishing a permanent settlement, hardy French adventurers kept coming back to Canada to fish and trade for fur. They also tried to establish colonies in South Carolina and Florida, but there would not be a "New France" until Samuel de Champlain planted a permanent settlement at Quebec in 1608, just one year after the English established Jamestown and one year before the Spanish founded Santa Fe.

Three centuries ago the kings and queens of Europe regarded as their own private property any lands that ships flying their flags discovered. They granted these lands as they pleased to settlers or trading companies. Vast tracts of land in America were sold for cash or given away to their favorites. In what is now the continental United States there were settlements granted by the States General (parliament) of the Netherlands and by the English, French, Spanish, and Swedish kings.

2. The making of America

The American colonies were an assortment of dreams and hopes and fears. They offered samples of nearly every kind of feeling. The first settlers, who thought anything was possible here, were not far wrong. Some came with definite plans, others with troubled consciences. Some came as charity cases, owing everything to a few rich men in London. Others came desperately seeking refuge. Some came as indentured servants, semi-slaves for a term. Later, others

✕ Critical Thinking Activity: Making Comparisons How do the motivations of modern space explorers and Renaissance explorers compare? Have students construct a chart on the chalkboard. Across the top write "Motivations," "Renaissance Explorers," and "Modern-day Explorers." Under "Motivations," list possible reasons for exploration, such as religion, money, conquest, nationalism, and knowledge. Have students check off the motivations as they apply to each group. Then instruct them to write a paragraph comparing the motivations of Renaissance and modern-day explorers.

would be brought here as slaves. They came without hope. All would become Americans.

The first plantations. From the beginning America was a place of testing and trying. They called the settlements along the Atlantic fringe in the earliest days "plantations." It was a good word. "Plant" originally meant a cutting from a growing thing set out to grow in another place. The plantations—later called colonies—were European cuttings set out to grow three thousand miles away across the Atlantic.

The English became experts at planting people in faraway places. They were never more successful than when they planted in America. For the people here were really *planted.* They did not come, as did so many of the Spanish, only as explorers or as gold seekers. Instead, they took root, found new nourishment in American soil, grew in new ways in the varied American climates, and in less than two centuries would outgrow Mother England.

But the settlers were not always successful. Whether a plantation died or lived and how it grew depended on many things. Much depended on the climate and the soil and the animals and the Indians. Much depended on whether the settlers had planned, and what they had planned, and how quickly they could learn what the continent had to teach. And much depended on luck.

The Puritans come to New England. In the mysterious New World, you would surely be lost unless you had some plans of your own. If you had goals, they would encourage you while you were discovering what America was really like. Your plans had to be definite, but not too definite. You had to be willing to change your plans when you ran into trouble, or when the New World did not offer what you expected. You had to be prepared for disappointment. Yet you had to have unending self-confidence, faith in your mission and in yourself.

In England, one group of people happened to be equipped with precisely this odd combination of hopes and fears, optimism and pessimism, self-confidence and humility. They were called "Puritans." Their appearance at just this time was one of the most remarkable coincidences in history.

The Puritans wanted to cleanse and purify the established church of fancy ceremonies and rituals. Some Puritans remained inside the Church of England and worked for reform there. Others were known as "Independents" or "Separatists." They, illegally, went out of the church—separated from it.

The first Puritan settlement in New England was established by a group of Separatists who were given permission to settle in Virginia. Instead, after a long voyage on the little ship *Mayflower,* the Pilgrims arrived in the wrong place. The pilot had brought them by mistake to Cape Cod, where they landed on November 21, 1620. They had no right to own land in this area, for that required a *patent,* or land grant. They had no power either to establish a government, for that required a charter.

But they had something far better. They had a plan to build a purified society, and they had a guide in the Bible, to encourage them while they were discovering what America was really like.

In place of the government they lacked, the Pilgrims drew up their Mayflower Compact. In it the men pledged allegiance to the king, combined themselves "into a civil body politic," and bound themselves to obey all the laws enacted by the majority. They created an instant government. It worked surprisingly well for the infant colony, and later became the foundation for the state of Massachusetts. The Mayflower Compact was similar to the covenants, or agreements, made among Separatists when they created new churches. Almighty God was seen as the source of everything.

All the Puritans had a grand purpose. John Winthrop, who was governor of the Massachusetts Bay Colony for many years, spoke to another group of settlers on the boat coming over:

> We shall be as a City upon a hill, the eyes of all people are upon us; so that if we shall deal falsely with our god in this work we have undertaken and so cause him to withdraw his present help from us, we shall be made a story and a by-word through the world.

Winthrop was saying what many Americans then and since have felt. The American example could help shape the lives of people everywhere.

With their beliefs, it would have been difficult for the Puritans to fail. Even the Devil, who was alive for them, could not really defeat them. Sooner or later, they knew, God always won. And as Winthrop said, as long as they did not deal "falsely" with their God, He would be on their side. The Puritans were ready for what wilderness America demanded.

The woes of a charity colony. If New England benefited from the beliefs of its settlers, Georgia suffered because of its English founders' ignorance and

This 1734 engraving by Pierre Fourdrinier was designed to attract settlers to Savannah, Georgia.

Methodist Collection of Drew University, Madison, New Jersey

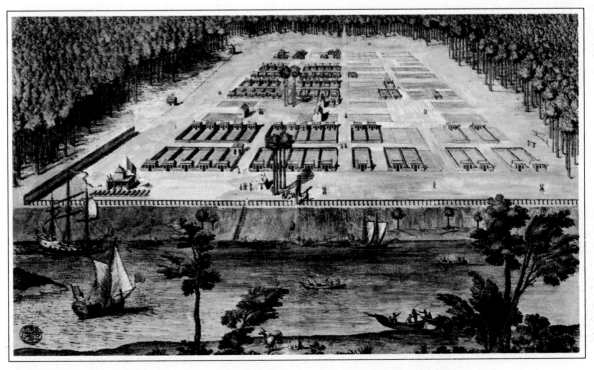

📖 **More from Boorstin:** "The failure of New England Puritans to develop a theory of toleration, or even freely to examine the question, was not in all ways a weakness. It made their literature less rich and gave much of their writing a quaint and crabbed sound, but for a time at least, it was a source of strength. Theirs was not a philosophic enterprise; they were, first and foremost, community-builders." (From *The Americans: The Colonial Experience*)

idealism. The 21 men who secured a charter for Georgia in 1732 thought they were very practical. The best known of them was James Oglethorpe, a tough-minded soldier who combined a passion for building the British Empire with a passion for reform. Oglethorpe and his friends had their eyes not so much on the Bible or on their own consciences as on the practical problems of their day. In London they worried over the growing unemployment and the increasing crime.

The land south of the Carolinas was rumored to be a paradise. Here they would settle some of London's criminals and the drunken, idle poor. That also happened to be right where the British needed to block the Spaniards, who were trying to push their settlements northward. In Georgia, named after King George II, these unlucky people could serve as a human barricade. At the same time, in that tropical climate they could grow exotic products wanted at home in England.

The founders even knew what the colony ought to produce—silk. At that time Britain was spending a fortune in gold and silver to buy silk. If the English could make silk themselves, they would save their gold and silver and also provide work for the unemployed. The London promoters therefore ordered every settler in Georgia to grow mulberry trees so the leaves would be food for silkworms. Unfortunately, the black mulberry trees that grew in Georgia were not the kind the silkworms liked. This was a little fact that the London promoters had not bothered to notice.

Plans bred more plans. The ill-informed trustees of Georgia, sitting in their easy chairs in London, went on drawing their plans. Because the people who were sent out were charity cases, they were not allowed to govern themselves. The inhabitants of Georgia had everything decided for them.

It is not surprising that colonial Georgia did not flourish. An empire builder's dream turned out to be a nightmare. The settlers rebelled, and the trustees who had founded the colony gave up. By the time of the American Revolution, Georgia—the spoiled child of charitable London—was the least prosperous and least populous of all the English colonies.

A land of many peoples.   During the seventeenth century the English settlements in America grew slowly. One hundred years after the landing at Jamestown, the colonies still held only 250,000 people. Then the 1700s saw immigration and a high birthrate create the first American population explosion. The number of people more than doubled every 25 years. By 1765 they counted 2.25 million. These were no longer just European emigrants, but a new breed of people, shaped by a New World.

The people who lived in the thirteen colonies at the end of the French and Indian War in 1763 came from many lands. But the population was more English than it would ever be again. Since about 60 percent of all white settlers had come from England, it was natural that the English language, English customs, English law, and English ways of government dominated the land.

What transformed Britons into Americans was that here they had the challenges of living with Africans, Indians, Scots, Scotch-Irish, Irish, Germans, Portuguese Jews, Swedes, Finns, French, Swiss, and even a few Austrians and Italians. This made life here much more interesting than life back home. Of course it made some new problems, but it also created new opportunities.

More from Boorstin: "[The Trustees] investigated the moral character of applicants and the circumstances which accounted for their distress. They even advertised the names of prospective emigrants in London newspapers a fortnight before departure so that creditors and deserted wives might have ample warning. Very few, perhaps not over a dozen, imprisoned debtors were brought to Georgia. Even these were chosen because they showed promise of becoming sturdy colonists." (From *The Americans: The Colonial Experience*)

The colonists govern themselves. For 150 years after the founding of the first English colony, new colonies were settled, and the English empire grew, with little attention from England. In the seventeenth century the English people had problems enough at home. They were moving from the medieval world of monarchy into a modern world of representative government. During these years they suffered through wars between Parliament and the king, the execution of the king, rule by Oliver Cromwell, who had led Parliament's armies against the king, the return of the royal Stuarts, and finally the dethroning of the Stuarts by Parliament in 1688 in the "Glorious Revolution." Parliament replaced them with William and Mary and opened a new era of representative government. Parliament had shown that it was supreme. The monarch owed power to the people's representatives in the House of Commons. Never again would there be an absolute ruler in England.

Prince William of Orange, who came to the throne with his wife, Mary (the eldest daughter of James II), was also the leader of the Dutch. They had been fighting against France for their independence. The French under Louis XIV had replaced Spain as the dominant power on the continent. So in 1689, William brought England into the battle against the French on battlefields that stretched across the world—from Europe to Egypt to the West Indies to Canada to England's American colonies. Meanwhile—when the government in London was too busy to notice—the American colonies were prospering.

This handsome manuscript (from the Latin word for "written by hand") is the charter given by James II for the Dominion of New England. The king's likeness is in the upper left-hand corner.

Massachusetts State Archives

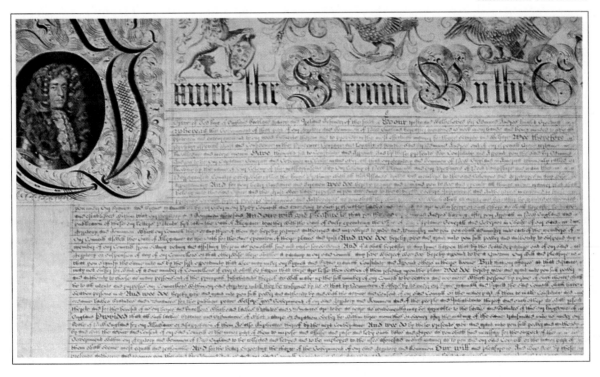

Salutary neglect.   During these years of salutary (or healthful) neglect by the mother country, the colonies developed their own ways of governing themselves. These ways would make it difficult for England ever again to rule them. Even if the American colonists had not already been independent minded and determined to govern themselves, the vast ocean would have made them so. In the days before the steamship or the transatlantic cable, when it took at least three weeks to cross the ocean, the colonial office could not govern from three thousand miles away. The ocean fostered self-government.

Although each colony had its own representative assembly, the person who had the greatest power and the highest social prestige was the governor. In most colonies he came from England, and he received his orders from London. The Lords of Trade, who managed colonial affairs, depended on him for information about his colony. But it was hard and slow to send messages across the ocean. If no ship was sailing or when harbors were iced over in winter, no letters could pass. Even after mail actually reached an English port, it might take weeks for it to be carried overland to London. Papers were sometimes lost in the customshouse, or might lie there a year before anyone bothered to deliver them.

The Navigation Acts were supposed to control such things as where the colonists traded and what they manufactured. But the colonies generally ignored these laws and the British did not always enforce them. They were too busy fighting France. And it is not surprising that the adventurous colonists, who were just beginning to explore the resources of a vast new world, would not let themselves be fenced in. They wanted to ship everywhere and buy everywhere.

This painting from the 1750s shows British privateers and captured French ships in New York Harbor.

The "Old Colonial System," as the years of salutary neglect were called, turned out to be a "system" for not enforcing the Navigation Acts. It seemed to work as long as everybody agreed to leave well enough alone. And so, during the many years while England's wars kept the government busy, the population of the colonies grew and their wealth accumulated. Between 1700 and 1760, the foreign trade of the thirteen mainland colonies increased fivefold.

Britain against France. The growth of the English colonies made a clash with France inevitable. From Louisbourg on Cape Breton Island through Quebec, Montreal, Detroit, Sault Ste. Marie, Vincennes, and Natchez to New Orleans and Mobile, a string of French forts tied together an immense, thinly settled empire. These forts stretched down the North American continent to the west of the English colonies.

America was a battlefield for European rivalries. For some time the French and English in America stayed far enough apart so that they did not bother each other. But the English were ever pushing westward encroaching on French colonies. It was not long before the two leading colonial powers of North America were at war.

A series of conflicts began as attacks by French soldiers and their Indian allies upon outlying English settlements. The English, with their own Indian allies, fought back. King William's War (1689–1697), Queen Anne's War (1702–1713), and King George's War (1744–1748) climaxed in the French and Indian War proper (1754–1763). Under the brilliant and self-confident William Pitt, who came to power as prime minister of England in 1757, new life poured into the nation's armies and its fleets spread over the globe. In the Peace of Paris signed by Britain and France in 1763, France ceded to England all of Canada and all French lands between the Mississippi and the Appalachian Mountains. Now Britain was supreme in North America. Yet just thirteen years later the thirteen American colonies that had helped England triumph would declare their independence.

3. Forming a new nation, 1763–1789

Winning the American Revolution, John Adams once said, was like trying to make thirteen clocks strike at once. The colonies were so different that it would have been an astonishing coincidence if they had come to the same idea at the same time. Starting as colonies at different times and with different goals, they moved to independence in thirteen different ways. To bring the people of one colony—Massachusetts or Pennsylvania or New York—to agree was difficult enough. To lead thirteen different colonies to take common action seemed next to impossible. This was the main American problem in the War of Independence.

The British take a collision course. After their victory over the French in 1763, the British Empire was bigger than ever, which made the thirteen American colonies only a small part of the empire. To the north of the thirteen colonies the British had added all of Canada and, to the west and south, all the regions east of the Mississippi River, including Florida. Now the British felt they must bring order to their vast empire and especially to the American colonies.

George Grenville as "Chancellor of the Exchequer" was in charge of the British treasury. He was desperate for ways to pay the bills left over from a century of wars. The colonists had eventually benefited from the successful wars against the enemies of the empire. Why should not Americans now at last pay a fair share of the bills for keeping peace and defending the empire?

Grenville therefore persuaded Parliament to pass a number of new taxes: a Sugar Act, which contained a realistic, collectible duty on molasses, as well as higher duties on several other commodities, and worst of all a Stamp Act. If these new policies continued, Americans thought, they would no longer be American members of the British Empire with all the rights of freeborn Englishmen. They would simply be slaves of Parliament, where they were not represented. Even in England, some people warned against the new policies.

The Americans quickly organized against the new taxes. They held protest meetings and refused to buy British goods. They terrorized the agents who tried to sell the hated tax stamps. British sales to America quickly fell off, and London merchants themselves began to worry. Then they, too, demanded that Parliament repeal the Stamp Tax.

The rulers of Britain might have saved the situation. If they had known the colonists better, they would have realized that these Americans would not let their lives be run by others. A wiser British government might have worked out a co-operative empire. Then there might never have been a War of Independence. But the rulers of Britain were shortsighted. They thought that government by Parliament had to be all-powerful or it would have no power at all. They repealed the Stamp Act on March 18, 1766, but then passed a Declaratory Act stating that Parliament still had power to make laws for Americans "in all cases whatsoever." They did not realize that a new age had arrived. Over two million people—one-fourth as many as in England—were now living in the thirteen colonies. And now they were beginning to be a new people—Americans.

The British government continued on its collision course. In 1767 the Townshend Acts, named after Charles Townshend who was now Chancellor of the Exchequer, imposed new duties and reorganized the customs service to be more effective in collecting them. In response, American merchants again decided not to buy British goods.

In the face of American opposition and the boycott, which was again severely injuring British trade, the British government retreated. They repealed all the Townshend duties, except for a small tax on tea, which King George III insisted should be kept in order to prove that Parliament had the right to tax the colonies.

When England backed down, the colonial scheme of non-importation collapsed. And many Americans, though it went against their principles, paid the tea tax and the Sugar Act's tax on molasses. They had won most of their points and the threat of interference was much less. So the colonists traded and prospered.

At this point the government in England made a grave mistake. To help the British East India Company, which was in financial trouble, it allowed the company to sell its tea in America without paying any customs in England. Colonial merchants stood to lose their profitable trade in smuggled tea. They cried "monopoly" against the East India Company and predicted that the company would raise the price of tea as soon as American merchants went out of busi-

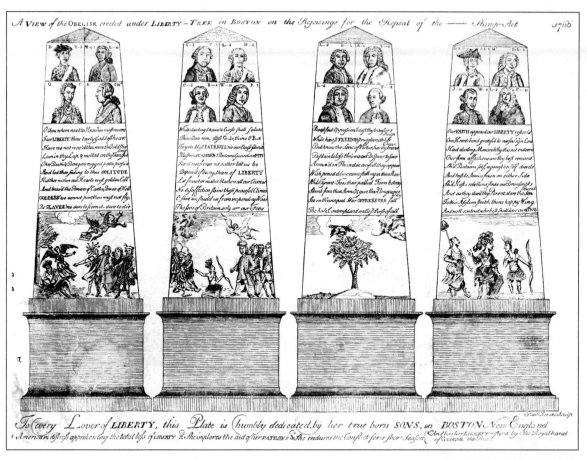

This engraving by Paul Revere shows a monument that Bostonians put up on their Common to celebrate the repeal of the Stamp Act.

ness. Most of the colonists refused to buy any of the tea, which quickly became a symbol of British tyranny.

Boston became a center of agitation. On the night of December 16, 1773, a group of townspeople enjoyed the most famous tea party in history. It was also a costume party because they put on the disguise of Mohawk Indians before they boarded the tea ships in Boston Harbor and threw overboard 342 chests of tea.

The "Boston Tea Party" made the British government decide to use force. In a series of acts in 1774, called the "Coercive Acts" in Britain and the "Intolerable Acts" in America, the British rulers tried to punish Boston. They closed its port. They undermined the independence of the colonial government by taking from the Assembly (the lower house of the legislature) the power to appoint the Governor's Council (the upper house) and giving that power to the king. They interfered with local governments by forbidding the town meetings in which New England towns normally conducted their affairs. They declared that government officials and soldiers accused of crimes punishable by death could be tried in England or Nova Scotia. They gave British troops in America the power to take over taverns, and even to live free in private homes.

137

The colonists rebel. Until the conflicts with the British government, the colonies had gone their separate ways. Now within only a few years, the bungling politicians in London did more to push the colonies together than colonial statesmen had accomplished in over a century.

After the passage of the Intolerable Acts, Massachusetts called for an end to all trade with Great Britain. In response, twelve colonies—all except Georgia—sent delegates to Carpenters' Hall in Philadelphia on September 5, 1774. The meeting called itself the Continental Congress. It was not really the congress of any government, for there was no *American* government. It could be nothing more than a *continental* congress—a collection of delegates from the colonies that happened to be neighbors on the same continent.

The Congress agreed to form a Non-Importation Association and to cease all trade with Great Britain. Committees chosen in every county and town were to see that the boycott was obeyed.

The delegates also dealt with the difficult problem of the relationship of the colonies to Parliament. The colonists, they told the British government, could only be taxed by their own assemblies. To show that they were not unreason-

This engraving by Amos Doolittle shows how British soldiers fought out in the open in neat rows and bright uniforms. From the Indians Americans had learned a different way of fighting. Here minutemen hiding behind a stone wall harass the British retreating from Concord in 1775.

able, however, they agreed to *allow* Parliament to regulate trade as it had been doing by the Navigations Acts before 1763.

The hopes of some Americans of finding their way back into the empire soon came to an abrupt end. At Lexington, British troops on their way to seize a supply of arms at Concord clashed with a small number of Massachusetts minutemen—militia who had agreed to be ready at a minute's notice. The British killed eight and wounded ten Americans before hastening to Concord. As if by magic, the countryside sprang to arms. From nowhere appeared thousands of American militiamen. They harassed the British troops, who, before returning to their ships in Charlestown Harbor, suffered nearly 300 dead and wounded while the American losses were fewer than 100.

Now talk was at an end. War had begun. There was no turning back.

Declaring independence. When delegates from twelve colonies (all but Georgia's, who arrived late) met again in their Second Continental Congress in the Philadelphia State House in May 1775, they were no longer American children pleading for their better treatment from the British parent country. Instead they were armed colonists demanding their rights. Though Congress said that it did not want to separate from Great Britain, the breach between the two sides was widening.

In April 1776 the Continental Congress abolished a century's worth of Navigation Acts, and in May it advised all the colonies to form their own governments. Still, it was not until July 2, 1776, that the Continental Congress adopted a short resolution "that these United Colonies are, and of right ought to be, free and independent states," and that all political connection with Great Britain was now broken.

With the resolution on July 2, Americans *announced* their independence. They gave out the news that a new nation was born, but they had not yet given out the reasons. Strictly speaking, American independence was not yet *declared.* ("Declare" comes from the Latin word meaning *to make clear.*) It was not the mere announcement, but the "declaration"—the explanation—of independence that Americans would always celebrate. For Americans were proud of the reasons for the birth of their nation. These reasons gave the new nation a purpose that it would not forget.

Thomas Jefferson, who wrote the Declaration, did not try to be original. He only tried to state clearly what everybody already believed. The opening part of the Declaration, usually called the "preamble," was cribbed from various books and declarations that Englishmen had written a hundred years before when, at the time of the Glorious Revolution, they removed James II and replaced him with William and Mary. The British could not possibly deny Jefferson's words in his Declaration—that governments derive "their just powers from the consent of the governed." Nor "that whenever any form of government shall become destructive of these ends"—life, liberty, and the pursuit of happiness—"it is the right of the people to alter or to abolish it, and to institute new government . . . in such form as to them shall seem most likely to effect their safety and happiness." Their own British government, as they were repeatedly saying after 1688, was made by precisely that formula. You could hardly call an idea radical if it 𝕄 was the basis of the very respectable government in England.

After the common sense in the preamble there came a long list—"a long train

𝕄 **More from Boorstin:** "One explanation, given by Thomas McKean, a member of Congress from Pennsylvania who had been present on July 4, was that the purpose of the Declaration as finally signed was to provide a kind of public loyalty-oath, a pledge of allegiance to the course already taken. Or (as he put it), 'to prevent traitors or spies from worming themselves among us.' It seems to have been decided for security's sake that 'no person should have a seat in Congress during that year until he should have signed the declaration of independence.'" (From *The Americans: The National Experience*)

The Second Continental Congress approves the Declaration of Independence. Benjamin Franklin is seated in the center.

of abuses and usurpations." Every item showed how the British king, George III, had disobeyed his own laws. Jefferson's Declaration simply ignored the British Parliament. For, according to Jefferson, Parliament had no rights over the colonies. It was the king's duty to hold the empire together and to protect all his subjects. The Americans demanded nothing but their simple rights as British subjects. The king had denied those rights. The law was on the side of the Americans. If Americans wondered why they were fighting, here was their simple answer.

Jefferson had written an eloquent birth certificate of the new United States. It would inspire people all over the world. A few years after the American Revolution was won, when the French people decided to defend their own rights against their king, they found inspiration in Jefferson's words. In the 1820s, when colonists in South America separated from Spain, they turned to the same source. Jefferson's Declaration of Independence, like other documents that live and shape history, has had the magical power to evoke new ideas. In the twentieth century, when colonists in Asia and Africa tried to explain to the world why they were fighting for their independence, they still recalled the Declaration of Independence of the thirteen American colonies.

A weak confederation.   When the assembled American colonies declared their independence on July 4, 1776, thirteen nations were created, not just one. The resolution that announced independence had proclaimed the colonies "free and independent *States.*" The first heading at the top of the Declaration of Independence called it "The Unanimous Declaration of the thirteen united States of America." They used a small "u" for united because it was only a hope.

The very same reasons that made the colonies willing to revolt made them unwilling to unite. The people of Virginia were fighting to be free of the government in far-off London. Why should they submit to a government in far-off New York? The task of making a nation had only begun.

In June 1776, the Continental Congress appointed a committee of thirteen, one representative from each colony, to prepare Articles of Confederation for the states. These Articles, after lengthy and sometimes bitter debate, were finally adopted by Congress in November 1777, but they were not ratified by the last of the thirteen states until March 1, 1781. Because of this long delay the Continental Congress, an "illegal" assembly, assumed the powers of government for six years. It issued the Declaration of Independence, advised the states to form governments, and conducted the war to its successful conclusion.

"The United States in Congress Assembled," which after 1781 carried on the war, was not a congress of one nation. It was simply a meeting of ambassadors, like the Assembly of the United Nations. Each state had one vote. Nine of the states had to agree on the most important issues and all thirteen had to approve any amendments to the Articles. Such an assembly of ambassadors could not force any state to support it with money and, of course, it had no power at all over individual citizens. It was a miracle that this loose arrangement was able to run a war and force the British Empire to give up.

Then came the bad years. As long as the war lasted there had been a business boom. Goods were scarce. Anybody with something to sell found lots of buyers. After the Treaty of Paris in 1783, Americans were still hungry for the things they could not buy during the war. Once again they began importing from Great Britain. But they bought a great deal more than they could pay for.

Each state issued its own paper money. Nobody knew precisely how much a New York dollar was worth compared to one from Pennsylvania or Rhode Island. The more money there was in circulation, the less a dollar bought. Then came the financial collapse. Gold and silver were hoarded by people who feared the future. For five long years after 1784 there was the worst business depression the colonies had ever suffered.

The thirteen new American governments had found it impossible to live with a strong London government. They now found it impossible to live without it. Yet nobody wanted to risk replacing the old British tyranny with a new American tyranny.

This was a decisive moment in history. Would America become another Europe? Would the New World become only a new battlefield for thirteen new little nations? Had they risked their "lives, their fortunes, and their sacred honor" only to turn the continent into a sea of anarchy?

Writing a nation's constitution. Just five states came to a meeting in Annapolis, Maryland, in 1786 to discuss the difficult problem of how to regulate the commerce of the country. Since so few were present, the delegates could do little. But one person there was the brilliant 29-year-old Alexander Hamilton. He saw the thirteen states would never prosper until they formed a strong union. He demanded that the states send delegates at once to a larger meeting to see what could be done. The Congress of the Confederation issued the invitations. If Hamilton had never lived another day, his courage and vision at the Annapolis convention would entitle him to a place in American history.

More from Boorstin: "Perhaps the dominant fact about the relationship of the colonies to each other was this reluctance of any one colony to send its militia to join in the defense of its neighbor . . . For a long time Virginia regularly sent a messenger to New York and New England to bring back word on the movements of the hostile French and the northern Indians—never to see whether help was needed in the North, but simply to be forewarned against a possible attack on themselves." (From *The Americans: The Colonial Experience*)

The Constitutional Convention met in Philadelphia at the State House, later renamed Independence Hall. This 1790 engraving by William Birch shows a rear view of the hall.

The states responded to the call. Within a year, 55 delegates from twelve states ✄ (all but Rhode Island) met in Independence Hall in Philadelphia in the hot summer of 1787.

Nothing was newer about the New World than the Constitutional Convention in Philadelphia. Never before had there been a meeting quite like this one. History gave the delegates very little to go on.

To accomplish their end of forming a more perfect union and yet protecting the rights of the states, the delegates had to make a number of compromises. In the end what emerged was a document creating a government that was partly federal and partly national.

To satisfy those who wanted a union truly "national," the new government was given the power to tax, to control commerce, to make war, to raise an army and a navy, and to conduct foreign relations. To satisfy those who wanted a union merely "federal" (that is, more like a treaty between sovereign states), the Constitution gave each state the power to make the laws controlling its daily life and all the powers not expressly given to the central government.

In the Constitution you will not find either the word "federal" or the word "national." The members of the convention knew that each of these words would be a red flag to some members. They purposely left everybody to guess to what extent the new government was either federal or national. That way each side could think it had won a little more than the other.

✄ **Critical Thinking Activity: Determining Relevance** Who were the delegates to the Continental Congress? Have students list the qualities they feel would have been important. Ask students to compare their fictitious delegate to the actual participants. How are they similar and how are they different? If the qualities they possessed were different, ask why those qualities might have been viewed as important in the 1700s.

If they did not call the new arrangement either "federal" or "national," what would they call it? Their answer was very simple and very wise. Every time they themselves mentioned the new government in the Constitution, they just called it "the United States."

The new government. The members of the convention were also wise enough to include in the Constitution itself instructions for changing it. Then, if the people in the future found they needed changes, they would not have to junk the whole Constitution and start all over again. They could keep the Constitution as a whole, while following the rules for making the few amendments they needed. This was a masterstroke, and was as new as anything else in the Constitution.

The final document repaired many of the weaknesses of the Articles of Confederation. The government under the Articles had no President and lacked the power to tax or to raise and maintain an army and a navy. The new government had three separate branches—executive, legislative, and judicial—each with its own special powers and duties. Spreading the powers and duties among the branches enabled them to check and balance each other. Then no one branch could become a danger to the freedom of the people.

The President was made Commander-in-Chief of all the nation's armed forces. He had the power to negotiate treaties, but the Senate had to approve them by a two-thirds majority of all senators present. The President was also given wide powers to appoint officials. But some of his choices, such as justices of the Supreme Court and ambassadors to foreign lands, had to be approved by the Senate.

Each house of Congress was given special powers. The House of Representatives, whose members represented the people rather than the states, had the sole power to initiate all bills for raising revenue. But only the Senate could approve treaties and certain appointments. Many specific powers were also granted to Congress. These included enacting taxes, providing for defense, declaring war, fixing tariffs, coining money, and setting up post offices. Surprisingly important in the long run was the power given to Congress to pass all laws "necessary and proper" to carry out its specifically assigned functions. This came to be called the "elastic clause," because it would be stretched in so many ways.

The Supreme Court was created to hear all cases raised under the Constitution and the laws of the United States, and certain others. Since the Constitution and the laws of the United States were "the supreme Law of the Land," the Supreme Court would wield great power to shape the new government.

Ratifying the Constitution. Like the state constitutions, the new Constitution of the United States was a *written constitution*. Like the constitutional convention, which was also used by the states, the written frame of government was an American institution that would be admired and imitated all over the world for centuries to come.

The British constitution was a plan of government that could not be picked up and read. It consisted of some basic documents like the Magna Carta and the English Bill of Rights. But much of it was tradition, habit, and belief. Many Americans thought their rights to govern themselves would be safer if these were stated in plain language so that government officials could see them and citizens would never forget them.

Since the convention had done its work in secret, there was great public interest both in what the new Constitution said—and in what it really meant. Those who supported the new Constitution were called Federalists and their opponents were called Anti-Federalists. The Anti-Federalists feared that the new Constitution would create a super-government that might destroy the very liberty that the Revolution was fought to win. The Constitution contained no bill of rights like those found in some of the state constitutions. Federalists argued that the Constitution did not need one, since the government under it had only limited powers, all the rest being reserved for the states. Anti-Federalists were not convinced, and the fight over ratification became extremely close.

When the Massachusetts state convention met, the Anti-Federalists seemed to be in a majority. Luckily for the Federalists, the cleverest politicians were on their side. At first the ambitious John Hancock, the influential presiding officer of the convention, was opposed. But the Federalists persuaded him to change his mind. They promised to elect him governor of Massachusetts and hinted that he was the obvious choice for Vice-President of the new nation. When Hancock went before the convention to urge that it ratify the Constitution, he also proposed a series of amendments to the Constitution to guard citizens' rights. The convention accepted both of Hancock's suggestions.

What Massachusetts did suggested to other states that they too might approve the Constitution as it was and at the same time propose amendments to remove the objections and allay the fears of some of their citizens.

A short document. One of the first things the new Congress did after it convened in 1789 was to draw up a series of amendments to the Constitution to limit the power of the federal government and guarantee certain rights and liberties to the people. These amendments were submitted to the states soon afterward. The first ten amendments, known as the Bill of Rights, became part of the Constitution in December 1791 when Virginia became the eleventh state to ratify them.

The Constitution provided only the skeleton for a government. The first President, the Congress, and the Supreme Court would have to put flesh on the skeleton. Why has this federal Constitution had such a long life? How has a short document written over two centuries ago for thirteen struggling seaboard colonies been able to give strength and liberty to a vast, two-ocean nation of more than 250 million people?

Oddly enough, the shortness of the document itself is one explanation. The Constitution did not go into details. It left to future generations the right and the opportunity to apply the scheme, and so to grow in unpredictable ways. It is not surprising then that one of the shortest constitutions ever adopted by a nation was to become in time the oldest living written constitution.

An Empire for Liberty. It turned out to be lucky for the new nation that there had been two kinds of colonies—"haves" and "have nots." There were seven "have" colonies: Massachusetts, Connecticut, New York, Virginia, the two Carolinas, and Georgia. Each had claims for land stretching from "sea to sea" based on their colonial charters.

Critical Thinking Activity: Making Inferences How did the thirteen states stand on the ratification of the Constitution? Ask students to offer their own interpretation of the political cartoon on page 145. This can be achieved by asking students to identify and assign a meaning to each symbol in the cartoon. What can be inferred from the writing on the cartoon? Direct students' attention to North Carolina and Rhode Island. Why might these states have hesitated to ratify the Constitution? What effect would this cartoon have had on these two states?

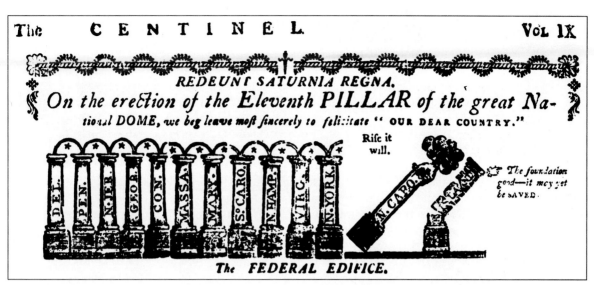

In 1788 the Massachusetts *Centinel* urged North Carolina and Rhode Island to complete the federal edifice by ratifying the Constitution. North Carolina did so the next year. Rhode Island, shown with a broken pillar but a firm foundation, followed in 1790.

The small states that had no western land claims refused to accept the Articles of Confederation until the other states had given up their claims to the land west of the Appalachians. These small states were led by Maryland. They said they would only accept the Articles if the seven "have" states gave up all their unsettled western lands. These would go into a treasury belonging to all thirteen states. Virginia began giving up its lands on January 2, 1781. When New York gave up its lands two months later, Maryland signed the Articles of Confederation. It was another twenty years before Georgia, the last of the "have" states, fulfilled its promise and put its lands in the common treasury.

These western lands helped pay for the Revolutionary War. By selling the land, the weak government under the Articles of Confederation could get money it could find no other way. It could even pay the Revolutionary soldiers in land instead of money.

No nation, new or old, had been blessed with such land-treasure in its own backyard. What should be done with it? This "public domain" was already settled by Native Americans, but they were viewed by the European-Americans as merely an annoying barrier to be cleared away. These lands belonged to all the states together and were then far larger than France or England or Spain or any other western European nation.

Unlike the sparsely settled lands controlled by those European nations, these lands would not become colonies. They would not be used by the thirteen original states to make themselves rich and strong.

Instead they would become (in Thomas Jefferson's phrase) an "Empire for Liberty." This empire would be built by adding new states. Each new state would be equal to all the older states. Nowadays this seems an obvious and sensible way to grow. But in those days it was quite a new idea.

The Northwest Territory

Boundaries Indefinite

Lake Superior

NORTHWEST

Mississippi R.

BRITISH TERR.

Lake Michigan

Lake Huron

Lake Ontario

Lake Erie

N.Y.

PA.

TERRITORY

Marietta

SPANISH LOUISIANA

Ohio R.

KENTUCKY

VIRGINIA

TENN.

N.C.

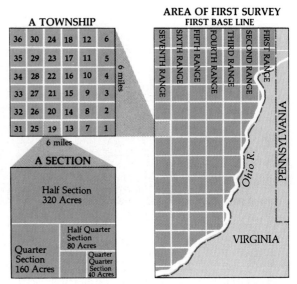

A TOWNSHIP

36	30	24	18	12	6
35	29	23	17	11	5
34	28	22	16	10	4
33	27	21	15	9	3
32	26	20	14	8	2
31	25	19	13	7	1

6 miles

6 miles

A SECTION

Half Section
320 Acres

Quarter Section
160 Acres

Half Quarter Section
80 Acres

Quarter Quarter Section
40 Acres

AREA OF FIRST SURVEY
FIRST BASE LINE

SEVENTH RANGE | SIXTH RANGE | FIFTH RANGE | FOURTH RANGE | THIRD RANGE | SECOND RANGE | FIRST RANGE

Ohio R.

PENNSYLVANIA

VIRGINIA

The Add-a-State plan. For many years Thomas Jefferson, with his usual uncanny foresight, had been working on a plan for settlements in the western wilderness. The Northwest Ordinance of 1787 put his scheme into law. The American way of growing gave instructions for what we can call an "Add-a-State plan."

The plan was simple. Every part of the public domain would in time become a full-fledged state of the Union "on an equal footing with the original states in all respects whatsoever." This goal was reached by three simple stages described in the Northwest Ordinance. First, when there were still almost no people in a territory, it would have a governor, a secretary, and three judges named by Congress. Then, as soon as there were 5000 adult free men, there would be a legislature where the people of the territory could make laws for themselves. And finally, when the entire free population numbered 60,000, the people could apply for admission to the Union as a state.

At the Constitutional Convention, some delegates were fearful and some distrusted the future. They wanted to write into the Constitution some kind of guarantee that the thirteen old Atlantic states would always be more powerful than all the new states put together. Fortunately, the men who looked for and hoped for change, and wanted to encourage new states, prevailed. In the Constitution they included another promise: "The United States shall guarantee to every State in this Union a republican form of government." In this way they made it plain that the new Union would not be merely a mother country for new colonies.

In America, change would be normal. The power to grow gave the nation the power to live.

Geography and History: Location Ask: How is the "Area of First Survey" shown on the map of the Northwest Territory? (As a rectagle northeast of Marietta.) How is "A Township" shown on the map of the First Survey? (As a gray square in the seventh range.) How is "A Section" represented on the Township map? (As gray square number 19.) How many acres are in a section? (640) In a township? (83,040) Are there more miles to the inch on the First Survey map or on the map of the Northwest Territory? (Northwest Territory.) Why were different scales used? (To give desired degree of detail in a limited amount of space.)

Chapter Review

See "Chapter Review answers," p. 126B

Focusing on Key Facts and Ideas

1. Who were the Aztecs, Mayas, and Incas?

2. What political and cultural developments in Europe contributed to interest in and support for exploration?

3. What role did rivalries among European nations play in the discovery and exploration of the New World?

4. Identify or explain: Hernando Cortez, Francisco Pizarro, Giovanni da Verrazzano, Jacques Cartier, Samuel de Champlain, John Winthrop, James Oglethorpe, William of Orange.

5. Both planning and good luck were crucial to the success of the European settlements in America. Find an example of good or bad planning and luck in the chapter.

6. Describe the "Old Colonial System."

7. What was the outcome of the French and Indian War?

8. Today, in many parts of the world, people who share a common language, history, or culture seek to set up independent nations. Were American colonists motivated by a common language, history, or culture? Explain your answer.

9. John Adams said that winning the American Revolution was like trying to make thirteen clocks strike at once. What did he mean by this? Explain.

10. How was the Constitution both "federal" and "national"?

11. How did the framers of the Constitution plan for necessary future "repairs"?

Taking a Critical Look

1. **Recognizing Cause and Effect.** The story of the first European explorations of the Western Hemisphere is full of "accidents" and rumors. How did accidents and rumors affect where exploration took place?

2. **Determining Relevance.** What impact did the Glorious Revolution have on the development of the colonies as a nation?

3. **Identifying Assumptions.** Britain's "Old Colonial System" worked best when it worked least. Why might this have been the case?

4. **Testing Conclusions.** It has been said that there was an "American Revolution under way long before fighting broke out." Do you agree or disagree? State your reasons.

5. **Making Comparisons.** How does the Constitution reflect the ideas contained in the Declaration of Independence?

6. **Testing Conclusions.** "The American Revolution took place because the British government, even with the best of intentions, did not understand what America or the Americans had become." Challenge or defend this statement using evidence in the text.

Your Region in History

1. **Culture.** What Indian groups lived in your region about the year 1500? What sort of culture did they have? What, if any, artifacts did they leave behind?

2. **Geography.** What Indian or European settlements existed within 50 miles of your home by 1763? Describe how people lived in these settlements.

3. **Economics.** How did the early settlers of your area earn a living? What environmental factors influenced their choices? What impact did the first settlers have on the environment?

4. **Geography.** What battles, if any, were fought in your region during the Revolutionary War?

5. **Government.** When was your state's constitution adopted and how was it drafted? If you live in one of the original thirteen states, investigate and report on the struggle for ratification of the federal Constitution in your state. When did your state ratify the Constitution?

Identifying Chapter Materials

Objectives	Basic Instructional Materials	Extension Materials
1 The Nation in the 1790s ■ Describe the geography of the United States in the 1790s and compare European and American social classes and social mobility at that time. ■ Discuss changes that did and did not occur in the United States after 1776. ■ List occupations surviving from 1790 to today.	**Annotated Teacher's Edition** ■ Lesson Plans, p. 148C **Instructional Support File** ■ Pre-Reading Activities, Unit 2, p. 29 ■ Critical Thinking Activity, Unit 2, p. 34	**Extension Activity** ■ Benefits of a Good Road System **American History Transparencies** ■ Geography and History, p. B13 ■ Our Multicultural Heritage, p. C55
2 George Washington Sets the Course ■ Describe the presidency of George Washington and compare the ideas of the nation's first two political parties. ■ Explain the contribution Alexander Hamilton made to national development as first Secretary of the Treasury and summarize his economic views.	**Annotated Teacher's Edition** ■ Lesson Plans, pp. 148C–148D	**Enrichment Support File** ■ Taking Sides: the Creation of American Political Parties (See "In-Depth Coverage" at right.) **Suggested Secondary Sources** ■ See chart at right.
3 Foreign Affairs for a New Nation ■ Identify the major developments in foreign afffairs during Washington's second term as President, and explain how those developments affected domestic events. ■ Appreciate the differences between the French and American Revolutions. ■ State the causes and outcome of the Whiskey Rebellion.	**Annotated Teacher's Edition** ■ Lesson Plans, pp. 148D–148E	**Documents of American History** ■ The Jay Treaty, Vol. 1, p. 165 ■ The Pinckney Treaty, Vol. 1, p. 160 ■ Washington's Proclamation of Neutrality, Vol. 1, p. 162 ■ Washington's Farewell Address, Vol. 1, p. 169 **American History Transparencies** ■ Geography and History, p. B31, B33
4 John Adams and the Rise of Parties ■ List the accomplishments and the problems of the presidency of John Adams. ■ Explain the motives for passage of the Alien and Sedition Acts. ■ Discuss provocations of the French government that led America to the brink of war with France.	**Annotated Teacher's Edition** ■ Lesson Plans, p. 148E **Instructional Support File** ■ Reading Activities, Unit 2, pp. 30–31 ■ Skill Review Activity, Unit 2, p. 32 ■ Skill Application Activity, Unit 2, p. 33 ■ Chapter Test, Unit 2, pp. 35–38 ■ Additional Test Questions, Unit 2, pp. 39–42 ■ Unit Test, Unit 2, pp. 43–46	**Documents of American History** ■ The Alien and Sedition Acts, Vol. 1, p. 175 ■ The Kentucky and Virginia Resolutions of 1798, Vol. 1, p. 178

Providing In-Depth Coverage

Perspectives on the Creation of American Political Parties

As the new government began to take shape, differing ideas forced a split in the ranks of men running the government. The United States government, which began as a cooperative effort by all, became a two-party system, with all the infighting and compromises which politics entail.

The chapter traces the development of the two-party system, including strong versus weak central government, and broad versus strict interpretation of the Constitution.

For this chapter, *A History of the United States* as an instructional program provides two types of resources you can use to offer in-depth coverage of the creation of American political parties: the *student text* and the *Enrichment Support File.* A list of *Suggested Secondary Sources* is also provided. The chart below shows the topics that are covered in each.

THE STUDENT TEXT. Boorstin and Kelley's *A History of the United States* unfolds the chronology of events and the key players in the creation of American political parties.

AMERICAN HISTORY ENRICHMENT SUPPORT FILE. This collection of primary source readings and classroom activities reveals the origins of the two-party system.

SUGGESTED SECONDARY SOURCES.
This reference list of readings by well-known historians and other commentators provides an array of perspectives on the origins of the two-party system. (See the chart below.)

Locating Instructional Materials

Detailed lesson plans for teaching the two-party system as a mini-course or to study one or more elements of the creation of American political parties in depth are offered in the following areas: in the *student text,* see individual lesson plans at the beginning of each chapter; in the *Enrichment Support File,* see page 3; for readings beyond the student text, see *Suggested Secondary Sources.*

IN-DEPTH COVERAGE ON THE CREATION OF AMERICAN POLITICAL PARTIES		
Student Text	**Enrichment Support File**	**Suggested Secondary Sources**
<ul><li>"Broad" versus "strict" construction, pp. 135</li><li>Attitudes toward France, pp. 138–139</li><li>Election of 1796, pp. 142–143</li><li>Alien and Sedition Acts, pp. 145–146</li><li>Election of 1800, pp. 147–148</li></ul>	<ul><li>Lesson Suggestions</li><li>Multimedia Resources</li><li>Overview Essay/Taking Sides: The Creation of American Political Parties</li><li>Songs in American History/Party Songs</li><li>Primary Sources in American History/Parties Emerge in the Young Political System</li><li>Art in American History/Taking Sides Through Political Cartoons</li><li>Biography in American History/Alexander Hamilton</li><li>Great Debates in American History/Should There Be Political Parties in the United States?</li><li>Making Connections</li></ul>	<ul><li>*Parties and Politics in the Early Republic, 1789–1815* by Morton Borden, pp. 1–56.</li><li>*Political Parties in a New Nation: The American Experience, 1776–1809* by William Nesbit Chambers, pp. 34–52.</li><li>*The Jeffersonian Republicans: The Formation of Party Organization, 1789–1801* by Noble Cunningham, pp. 67–87.</li><li>*Federalists in Dissent: Imagery and Ideology in Jeffersonian America* by Linda Kerber, pp. 173–215.</li></ul>

The Nation in the 1790s

FOCUS

To introduce the lesson, write on the board these words: Occupations Surviving from 1790 to Today. Have students prepare a list of such occupations. Then discuss their responses as a class.

Developing Vocabulary

The words listed in this chapter are essential terms for understanding the chapter. The page number after each term indicates the page of its first or most important appearance. These terms are defined in the text Glossary (text pages 1000–1011).

aristocracy (page 151)

INSTRUCT

Explain

In Europe, birth, family names, titles, wealth, and education affected status. In the United States, wealth, talent, and education affected status.

✿ Cooperative Learning Activity

Drawing Conclusions Explain that students will work in pairs to write a diary entry describing a hypothetical trip along the Post Road in 1790. Assign to each group one of the following routes: 1) from Portland, Maine to New York City; 2) from New York City to Philadelphia; 3) from Philadelphia to Savannah, Georgia. Explain that descriptions should be based upon all that students have learned thus far about the settling of America, particularly from Chapter 3, *Many Kinds of Americans*, and Chapter 6, *The Nation in the 1790s*. Each pair should first determine who this traveler is and where he or she is travelling to and why. Have partners decide who will write the final copy and who will illustrate it. Have students read and compare entries.

Section Review Answers

Section 1, page 152

1. Take the Boston Post Road south to Philadelphia and then take the Forbes Road to the Ohio or sail to Philadelphia and then take the Forbes Road. 2. In 1789 the person who received the largest number of votes from the electors became President; the person receiving the second highest number of votes became Vice-President. 3. In 1789 the largest stretches of cleared land were in southern New England and the Middle States. Philadephia and New York were the chief cities. 4. The roads were unpaved and bumpy. Mail service was irregular and slow. As a re-

sult, news took a long time to travel from the nation's capital to the states. People tended to think of their state, not the nation as a whole, as their "country." 5. In Europe there was little movement between social classes. In America "aristocrats" gained their status mostly from their wealth or the land they owned; people could move from one social class to another.

CLOSE

To conclude the lesson, ask students: How was the United States different from Europe in the 1790s? By now the students should be able to point out many differences: greater opportunity, relative unimportance of family name and titles, existence of slavery, republican form of government, a vast frontier.

Extension Activity

To extend the lesson, have students write a 200-word essay answering the following question: What are the benefits of a good system of roads?

George Washington Sets the Course

FOCUS

To introduce the lesson, ask: Should we put a protective tariff on Japanese cars to give American cars an advantage? As students respond, you might want to write their answers on the chalkboard under the headings: Advantages and Disadvantages.

Developing Vocabulary

advice and consent (page 154); **Cabinet** (page 154); **strict construction** (page 157); **broad construction** (page 157); **tariff** (page 157).

INSTRUCT

Explain

George Washington was a strong executive. Under the leadership of Alexander Hamilton and Thomas Jefferson, the political parties of the Federalists and Republicans began.

☑ Writing Process Activity

Drawing Conclusions Explain to students that they will write an evaluative essay about the first term of Washington's presidency. In preparation, ask them to consider his political beliefs, personality, Cabinet choices, and domestic and diplomatic policies. Have them begin their essays with a thesis statement summarizing their view of Washington's first term. They can organize their support chronologically or by order of importance. Students should revise for completeness and objectivity. After proofreading, they can compare evaluations with those of their classmates.

Section Review Answers

Section 2, page 159

1. a) appointed the first Secretary of War. b) the decision of the federal government to take responsibility for debts that the states had run up during the Revolution and not yet paid. c) In a strict construction, the federal government has only those powers spelled out in the Constitution. According to a broad construction, the federal government has the right to do all those things that are necessary and proper to carry out the powers specified in the Constitution. 2. The Cabinet is made up of the heads of major departments of the federal government and advises the President. This tradition originated when President Washington began to ask various department heads for advice. 3. Hamilton's Report on Public Credit laid out a plan that he hoped would restore the nation's credit while strengthening the national government and stimulating the economy. Through his Report for a National Bank he hoped to provide the currency needed for economic growth. His Report on Manufactures presented a plan that he hoped would lead to the development of American manufacturing. 4. Washington, D.C., became the nation's capital when Hamilton suggested that his supporters would vote to move the capital to a site on the Potomac River if Madison and his allies would endorse the federal government's assumption of the states' war debts. 5. Strong v. weak central government; government by "the people" v. aristocrats; farms v. manufacturing.

CLOSE

To conclude the lesson, ask students to summarize Hamilton's reasons for wanting a protective tariff. Then ask: Was a protective tariff needed in Hamilton's day (the 1790s)? Is it needed today? What, if anything, has changed?

Section 3 (pages 159–165)

Foreign Affairs for a New Nation

FOCUS

To introduce the lesson, some background might be useful on the excesses that occurred during the French Revolution in the name of equality and freedom, and the horror with which the Revolution was viewed by the rest of Europe. An excellent source for

dramatic reading to the class is Charles Dickens's *A Tale of Two Cities.*

Developing Vocabulary

republic (page 164); **sectionalism** (page 164).

INSTRUCT

Explain

It is essential that students understand how different the French Revolution was from the American Revolution and why Americans were so divided over whether to applaud it or condemn it.

★ Independent Activity

Recognizing Cause and Effect The severity with which the Whiskey Rebellion was treated by Washington can best be understood when it is related to the economic conditions of the United States at the time. Tell the students that today 4 percent of the federal tax revenue comes from excise taxes. In 1793 it was 8 percent. The Whiskey Rebellion can be called the first large-scale protest demonstration after the federal government was organized under the Constitution. Ask students to discuss, in a short essay, the relationship between the Federalists' reaction to the Whiskey Rebellion and to the events going on in France.

Section Review Answers

Section 3, page 165

1. a) French ambassador to the United States who created controversy by interfering in American politics and by seeking help for France in its wars against other European nations. b) left many problems unresolved but did state that England would abandon fur posts in American territory. This treaty established a precedent for settling disputes through joint commissions. c) established free navigation of the Mississippi, agreement on the southern boundary of the United States, and the right of Americans to transfer cargo at New Orleans without paying a duty. d) an agreement with the Indians of the Northwest Territory that brought peace and opened most of the Ohio territory to settlers. 2. (a) The British were refusing to follow the peace treaty of 1783; they still held fur posts in the Northwest Territory; and their agents were helping Indians who were resisting settlers. (b) The Spanish were refusing to let American ships pass freely through New Orleans and were supporting the Indians who were attacking the settlers. (c) Washington faced the problem of living up to treaty obligations with France without being drawn into France's wars. 3. The Revolution appalled many Americans because of its brutality. 4. Washington warned against sectionalism, secession, partisanship, and alliances with other nations. 5. The Whiskey

Rebellion was significant because Washington showed that the federal government had the strength to enforce its laws; his action attracted supporters to the Federalist cause.

CLOSE

To conclude the lesson, have the students construct a time line of the important events covered in this chapter, and underline the items that would have pleased the Federalists more than the Republicans. (The Federalists were more pleased by the Proclamation of Neutrality, Jay's Treaty, the use of federal power to end the Whiskey Rebellion, and the election of Federalist, John Adams, as President.)

Section 4 (pages 165–170)

John Adams and the Rise of Parties

FOCUS

To introduce the lesson, divide the class into small groups. Ask each group to make a list of the qualities and experience they would want in a President. Then have students review the first three paragraphs of this section (p. 143). How does Adams match their criteria? Ask each group if it would vote for Adams.

Developing Vocabulary
administration (page 166); **alien** (page 167); **sedition** (page 167); **frigate** (page 168); **states' rights** (page 169).

INSTRUCT

Explain
Explain that modern war and diplomacy are both the same and different from war and diplomacy in the 1800s. Most modern leaders agree that the destructiveness of modern weapons makes war over "national honor" unreasonable. However, irrational rulers do appear in modern times—Hitler, Khomeini, Saddam Hussein. Finally, instruments for the resolution of tensions between nations do exist today, the United Nations in particular.

☑ Writing Process Activity
Expressing Problems Clearly Ask students to imagine that as Republicans, their right to free speech is being suppressed by the Alien and Sedition Acts. Ask them to write a letter to someone in England explaining how these two laws influence their lives. As they outline the ideas they want to include, ask them also to explain how these acts led to the

downfall of the Federalist party. Students should begin their letter with a sentence summarizing their fears. Have them revise for clear organization and concise word choice. After proofreading, students can evaluate one another's perspectives.

Section Review Answers
Section 4, page 170
1. Jefferson received the second highest number of votes from electors because Hamilton's tactics for preventing Adams from gaining the Presidency failed. 2. The XYZ affair was an incident in which agents of the French government tried to bribe envoys of the United States. In the United States the affair stirred resentment of France and support for President Adams. 3. The Alien and Sedition Acts were passed to suppress the Republicans and protect the power of the Federalists. 4. The Twelfth Amendment provided that each elector would vote separately for the President and Vice-President. The amendment was passed in response to the election of 1800, when the election had to be decided in the House of Representatives. 5. Adams followed in the footsteps of George Washington with his attitude toward political parties. He put great stock in his own opinion, which overshadowed the reality of active, influential political parties.

CLOSE

To conclude the lesson, write the following headings on the board: Chief Executive, Head of State, Chief Diplomat, Commander in Chief, Chief Legislator, Head of a Political Party. Explain that these are some of the roles of the President. Ask students to offer examples of how Washington and Adams filled each of those roles. (Washington, of course, was not the head of a political party.)

Chapter Review Answers
Focusing on Ideas
1. Washington was determined to present strong and forceful leadership and to establish the dignity of the office of President. He staffed a fine New York home with uniformed servants and dressed formally for state parties. He created a body of advisors to discuss state matters, which later evolved into the Cabinet. 2. The government borrowed money to fight the war. Paying the debt established U.S. credit. 3. Both expected less white settlement if Indian lands remained under British or Spanish control. 4. Although Adams felt strong war sentiment in the nation, he readily accepted Talleyrand's offer to send a new American Commission to France.

Taking a Critical Look
1. Answers will vary. 2. See especially page 157 for

contrasting views of Hamilton and Jefferson. 3. A tax revolt aimed at changing tax laws or amending state and federal constitutions to limit taxing power. Such a movement does exist. Citizens might also stage protest demonstrations.

Your Region in History

1–3. Answers will vary depending on your region. Consult your local library or historical society.

Historical Facts and Figures

Possible questions: What do the two columns have in common? Who contributed the most money to the bank? How can one be both a borrower and a lender of the bank?

Answers to "Making Connections"

(See "Using Making Connections" on p. 172.)
Answers will vary, but may include one or more of the following examples. Answers based on the time line callouts are in italics.

1. The colonies seemed to lack a critical center. As a result, winning battles did not win the war for the British. For example, despite *Paul Revere's 1775 warning that the British were planning an attack*, the colonists lost the Battle of Lexington. They also lost the Battle of Bunker Hill. Yet Washington did not surrender. He simply moved west and continued fighting. *In 1776 the British* poured 2,000 troops into New York City. Their *strategy was to take control of the Hudson River in 1777, cutting off New England from the other colonies.* Once again the military victory fell to the British. However, *the colonists* continued fighting until they *won*—as they did *in a 1780 surprise militia attack that captured 1200 troops in South Carolina.* Thus the independent spirit of the colonies eventually caused the British to lose the war despite their many successful battles and campaigns. 2. There was no way a weak confederacy could deal with the grave diplomatic problems it faced with Britain to the northwest and Spain west of the Mississippi. There were domestic problems as well. There was a lot of petty bickering along state borders. Then, *in 1784, an economic depression began, burdening the young nation for the next five years.* This exacerbated the situation to the point that *Daniel Shays led a rebellion in western Massachusetts in 1787.* The effect of the rebellion was that many people demanded a national government with the power to deal with the states. 3. The persuasive arguments in the *"Federalist Papers," published in 1787*, pointed out the advantages of a strong, united country. The following year, the Constitution with its strong federal system was ratified. That Americans now saw themselves as a truly united nation can be seen clearly in their actions over the following years. It can be seen in *Alexander Hamilton's 1790 proposal for a National Bank.* And it can be seen in their reaction—calling out the militia—to the Whiskey Rebellion in 1794.

6

Chapter 6

Focusing the Chapter: Have students identify the chapter logo. Discuss what unit theme the logo might symbolize. Then ask students to skim the chapter to identify other illustrations or titles that relate to this theme.

The United States Begins

The new Constitution stated that the President should be elected by "electors" from the states. Each state was to have as many electors as it had senators and representatives in Congress. These electors were to be chosen as the state legislatures saw fit. They were then to meet in their own states, and each elector was to cast one ballot on which he had written the names of his two choices for President. When all the votes were counted, the person with the highest number of electoral votes was to be President and the second highest was to be Vice-President.

Every elector wrote George Washington's name on his ballot. John Adams of Massachusetts received the next largest number of votes and became Vice-President. So to them would fall the difficult job of starting the new government on its way when they took office in April 1789.

This engraving by Amos Doolittle is the only contemporary view of George Washington's first inauguration in 1789. Another scene of Federal Hall and the street where it stood is on page 153.

I.N. Phelps Stokes Collection, Miriam & Ira D. Wallach Division of Art, Prints and Photographs, The New York Public Library, Astor, Lenox and Tilden Foundations.

See "Lesson Plan," p. 148C.

✿ 1. The nation in the 1790s

The country George Washington was to lead as first President had changed only slightly from the land he had known as a boy. Of course, the population was larger. The first federal census in 1790 would reveal that there were nearly 4 million people in the country's 865,000 square miles. The nation occupied less than one-quarter the territory it was destined to fill by the late 1900s.

A rural land. The land was covered by a virgin forest of oak, chestnut, beech, sycamore, poplar, pine, and hemlock trees, which had been growing for centuries. Only in a few areas, such as southern New England and the Middle States, were there large stretches of cleared land.

Some sections of the country contained stands of dead trees. People starting farms in the great forest killed the trees by girdling (cutting all around the bark) and only removing them after they had fallen. In the meantime, they planted their crops in between.

Most people were farmers. Only a few Americans lived in cities. In 1789, there were just six cities with over 8000 people. Philadelphia with 42,000 people was by far the largest, cleanest, and most attractive. New York was second with 33,000, but was dirty and smelly, though busy and rapidly growing. Much smaller were Boston, Charleston, Baltimore, and Salem. Only New York and Philadelphia had begun to install such modern conveniences as water pipes, curbs, and sidewalks. Philadelphia had many paved streets, but the rest had streets chiefly of dirt or cobblestone which were never cleaned. Not surprisingly, these cities were often plagued by disease.

Difficulties of travel and communication. Transportation was little better than in the days of the French and Indian War. There had been few improvements in the road Washington had followed when he marched with General Braddock on the way to western Pennsylvania in 1755. "Road" was not quite the right word for the peculiar kind of obstacle course filled with rocks, stumps, and holes that extended from Maine to Georgia. In many sections it was just a wide track through the dense forest. In 1801 Abigail Adams took this road from the new capital city of Washington to her home in Massachusetts. By the time she arrived in Baltimore she reported to President Adams that she was beaten and bruised.

Even on the best roads travel was slow and expensive. It took two days for the stagecoach to go from New York City to Philadelphia. A ticket cost six dollars—not including the price of a night in an inn. In wet weather many sections of the road were impassable.

We cannot be surprised, then, that about two-thirds of the American people lived within fifty miles of the tidewater, where waterways provided a cheaper, more trouble-free passage. It was easier to travel several hundred miles by water than a much shorter distance by land, even though ships were still propelled only by oar, wind, and current.

⊕

In 1788 and again in 1790 the clever inventor (p. 150) John Fitch operated his steamboats on the river at Philadelphia. But he found most Americans uninterested and even suspicious of boats that belched smoke and carried fire that threatened to consume the boat's cargo and its passengers.

In general, farmers who had crops to take to market waited until winter when the ground was hard and there was less to do on the farm. Then Southerners who did not live on the water's edge rolled their hogsheads (large barrels) of tobacco to the closest boat landing. But the rough roads made it hard work. One observer reported that he saw two slaves struggling with a team of horses that was having a hard time moving a single hogshead.

Out west, some farmers floated their crops all the way down the Mississippi to New Orleans, and then walked the dangerous way back home. Or they sailed on to Philadelphia and then returned to their homes by walking over the mountains. Others converted their grain into whiskey, a more compact and portable form in which to deliver it across the mountains. Still others fed the grain to their hogs and then drove the hogs to market.

✿ **Multicultural Connection:** According to the census of 1790, a total of 757,363 African Americans lived in the United States. Of this number, 59,466 were free and 697,897 were enslaved. Only one state, Massachusetts (and its territory of Maine), had no slave population at all.

Lake Superior

BRITISH
NORTH
AMERICA

Montreal

Norwich
Portland
Portsmouth
Salem
Boston

Lake Michigan

Lake Huron

Lake Ontario

Mohawk Trail
Albany
Hartford
Boston Post Rd.
Providence
New Haven
New York

Ft. Niagara

Lake Erie

Ft. Detroit

Ft. Sandusky

Great Trail

Ft. Duquesne
(Pittsburgh)
Forbes
Rd.
Trenton
Philadelphia
Wilmington

NORTHWEST

TERRITORY

Scioto Trail

Zane's Trace

Lancaster
Cumberland Fort Cumberland Rd.
Braddock's
Rd.
Baltimore

Chillicothe

Ohio R.

Sonioto

Great Valley Rd.
Alexandria
Fredericksburg

St. Louis

Ohio R.

Harrod's
Town

Warrior's Path

Williamsburg
Richmond
Norfolk

SPANISH

LOUISIANA

Wilderness
Rd.

Cumberland Gap

Trading Path

Western Rd.

Avery's Trace

Nashville

Cumberland R.

Great Trace

Nickajack
Trace

Raleigh
Charlotte
Virginia Rd.
Cape Fear Rd.

Mississippi R.

Tennessee R.

Trader's

Charleston
Path

Wilmington

Arkansas Post

Chickasaw (Natchez) Trail

Path

Augusta
Post Rd.

Savannah R.

Main

Charleston

Natchez

Savannah

WEST FLORIDA

Surveyed

Pensacola

Trail

St. Augustine

SPANISH
FLORIDA

New Orleans

GULF   OF   MEXICO

APPALACHIAN MTS

Major Roads in 1800

—— Roads

– – – Paths

0 |————————————————| 300 Miles

0 |————————————————| 300 Kilometers

⊕ **Geography and History: Movement** Have the students look
at the map above. Tell them that it took two full days for a
stagecoach to travel from New York to Philadelphia. Based on
that fact, have them estimate how long it would take to travel
from Boston to Savannah by land in 1790. Note that water
travel was much faster than land travel and that large cargoes
could be moved by ship. What effect did this have on cities
and their location? (It made rivers that connected to the sea
important, and encouraged the growth of cities on those rivers.)

Mail service was slow and uncertain. Twenty-nine days passed before news of the Declaration of Independence reached Charleston from Philadelphia. There was no regular mail service from Maine to Georgia until 1800, and even then a letter took three weeks to arrive.

All in all, the states remained as separate from each other as they were in colonial days. People still tended to think of their state as their country. Even worse—from the point of view of uniting the separate states—settlements had now grown up beyond the Appalachian Mountains. The nation was stretching west.

Daniel Boone and other bold frontier men and women began settling in Kentucky and Tennessee shortly before the Revolution. The (p. 152) path to those settlements across the mountains from the seaboard states was slow and hard. Even so, by 1790 there were 36,000 people in Tennessee and 74,000 in Kentucky. On June 1, 1792, Kentucky became a new state of the Union. But to trade and communicate with the world, the people who lived over the mountains depended on the broad Mississippi water-highway and its tributaries. These rivers provided a convenient network along the borders of Kentucky and the western territories and through their heartlands. Whether or not these lands could remain part of the Union would depend on who controlled the Mississippi River.

The American "aristocracy." In 1789 England, the old mother country, was a land of rigid social classes. Here in America there were no

The painting below depicts the front door of George Washington's beloved home, Mt. Vernon. On the other side of the house is the large, columned porch, which overlooks the Potomac River. Washington said that no other estate in America was "as pleasantly situated."

National Gallery of Art, Washington, Gift of Edgar William and Bernice Chrysler Garbisch 1955

See "Lesson Plan," p. 148C for **Cooperative Learning Activity: Drawing Conclusions** relating to travel in the late eighteenth century.

kings and nobles. But there was an American kind of aristocracy marked off less by ancestry than by land and money. Of course, nobody could change his ancestors. But in so vast and so empty a continent there were many new opportunities for new businesses. An enterprising person—provided he was not a slave—had a good chance to move up the social ladder. Social classes were much more fluid than in the Old World. The American "aristocracy" of land and cash consisted of the rich merchants of New England, New York, and Pennsylvania, and the great planters of the South. Some of them went about wearing powdered hair, knee breeches, ruffles, and silver buckles on their shoes. They aped the fancy manners of English lords and ladies. But the frills of an aristocracy of birth really had no place in the new-world nation. As the careers of American Presidents would soon show, here a person might rise by hard work, intelligence, skill, and perhaps a little luck, from the lowest position to the highest.

By the early 1800s it had become difficult to acquire the large tract of land needed for a successful tobacco plantation. So it was harder to move into the aristocracy in the South than it was in New England. Still, the demand for cotton by the rapidly growing English cotton industry and the invention of the cotton gin in 1793 by Eli Whitney of Connecticut soon opened up chances to enter the American aristocracy even in the South.

See "Section 1 Review answers," p. 148C.

Section 1 Review

1. Use the map on page 150 to show two ways for New Englanders to reach the Ohio River.
2. Explain how the President was chosen in 1789.
3. In 1789 where were the largest stretches of cleared land? Which were the chief cities?
4. What problems did the government confront in the 1790s in trying to deal with transportation and communication difficulties?
5. **Critical Thinking: Making Comparisons.** In what ways were American "aristocrats" different from European aristocrats?

See "Lesson Plan," p. 148C.

2. George Washington sets the course

George Washington took office with a firm faith. The "sacred fire of liberty" as well as "the destiny of the republican model of government" depended on the outcome of the "experiment" the Americans had undertaken. No country in the world had ever tried this form of government. Washington knew that it was up to the first President and the first Congress to see that the experiment did not fail.

A strong executive. Washington believed that if the young nation was to survive in an envious, hostile world, the Chief Executive of the new government must lead. By showing the courage to be strong at a time when people accused him of trying to become a king, he earned a place too as an American peacetime hero. He had done more than anyone else to help the nation win independence. He now led the nation along the path to survival.

Washington's personal prestige gave the Presidency the dignity it needed. His physique and his stature helped. He was six feet, two inches tall, and his face appeared chiseled from granite. He looked every inch the national leader. But his commanding manner and his elegant way of life seemed to justify the suspicions of those who feared he wanted to seduce the nation to monarchy. He rented one of the finest houses in New York City, the nation's first capital, and staffed it with servants in uniform. He traveled in a canary-colored coach (drawn by six horses) on which was painted the Washington coat-of-arms. He held formal parties where he appeared in black velvet and silk stockings.

Washington wanted his office to seem dignified and important to all the world. He well knew, as he wrote, that "there is scarcely any part of my conduct that may not hereafter be drawn into precedent."

Creating a new government. The federal government, with no money, inherited numerous war debts to the French government, to Dutch bankers, and to its own citizens. To make the new nation respectable and trusted, Congress

📖 More from Boorstin: "After the admission of the two new states of Vermont and Kentucky, Congress in 1794 enacted that the flag should have fifteen stripes and fifteen stars, but defeated a proposal 'to fix forever the Flag of the United States.' Even after the number of states had further increased, this fifteen-star, fifteen-stripe flag flew over American ships in the War of 1812; such was the flag which Francis Scott Key saw." (From *The Americans: The National Experience*)

Federal Hall, in the center of this engraving, was located in New York City on Wall Street at the head of Broad Street. Here George Washington took the oath of office as the first President.

would have to raise money and begin to pay off those debts. Congress also had to provide for the national defense and deal with the Indian tribes. To fix the number of seats for each state in the House of Representatives, the Constitution said the federal government must take a national census each ten years. Congress also needed to organize territories, establish federal courts, and regulate trade. Then there were diplomatic and commercial problems with England, France, and Spain. There were the executive departments to be set up—and a host of other tasks to accomplish.

The new House of Representatives, advised by Representative James Madison of Virginia, at once turned its attention to the first ten amendments—the Bill of Rights. These were drawn up by Madison based on the objections to the Constitution that had been raised by some of the states. The House also quickly passed a modest tariff bill to bring in some badly needed money.

Meanwhile, the Senate turned to creating the federal courts. The Judiciary Act of 1789 set up the Supreme Court, three circuit courts, and thirteen district courts (one in each state). To each district court it attached a United States Attorney to serve as a federal prosecutor and a United States Marshal to serve as the federal police. The act also set procedures for the federal courts. Disputes over the meaning of federal laws and treaties would, in the end, be settled by the United States Supreme Court as would conflicts between state and federal law.

The Congress also set up the departments of Treasury, State, and War. These, with the Attorney General and the Postmaster General, were the only executive departments at the start.

For the important post of Secretary of the Treasury, Washington chose his brilliant young friend and onetime aide, Alexander Hamilton. Edmund Randolph of Virginia became Attorney General. The War Department was entrusted to

Continuity and Change: Government and Politics Point out to students that the federal government may manipulate money in order to produce a desired economic effect within the American economy. In the 1790s the government sought to pay off war debts from the Revolution completely, and to assume the debt of the states in order to restore national credit, create wealth, and promote new business. During the Great Depression, the government purposely ran up large deficits to get money into circulation, promote private spending, and hasten the return of prosperity. (See page 626.)

General Henry Knox of Massachusetts. Thomas Jefferson was called home from Paris, where he had been minister since 1785, to become the first Secretary of State.

Roles are clarified. The relationship of the new departments and their Secretaries to the Congress or even to the President was not at all clear. Some people thought that the new departments should just carry out the laws and keep out of politics. The Secretaries, then, would stay in office under successive Presidents. Hamilton saw the department heads as having a share in making policy. He thought that Secretaries, like English cabinet members, would go to Congress to speak in favor of bills that they wanted passed. But Congress refused to hear Hamilton when he tried to report, so the executive departments did not form close ties with Congress.

Some thought that the Senate, because it was to "advise and consent" on treaties, might become like the English Privy Council, which advised the king. One day Washington arrived at the Senate, sat down in the Vice-President's chair, and told the Senate that he and the Secretary of War had come to get their advice on an Indian treaty. But the Senate refused to debate the question in his presence. The Senate wanted to discuss the treaty without being overawed by the President. So Washington left without any advice and soon gave up trying to get the counsel of the Senate.

In domestic affairs, Washington believed it was the President's job to enforce the laws Congress made, not to lead the Congress in making laws. He allowed Hamilton to go his own way in handling the financial affairs of the country. But diplomatic problems were different. Washington often consulted with Jefferson, and he soon began to call in the Attorney General, and the Secretaries of State, War, and the Treasury for advice on complex problems in foreign affairs. Acting as an advisory group, the department heads slowly became the President's ⬚ Cabinet.

Alexander Hamilton prepares financial plans. During Washington's first term the great questions concerned finances. The disputes that arose produced the first significant arguments over the nature of the Constitution and drew the issues for our first political parties. Alexander Hamilton put the issues into focus. Though not tall (he was 5′6″), he was handsome and debonair. Intelligent and hard

The bank note below is similar to those issued by the first Bank of the United States.

⬚ See "Lesson Plan," p. 148C for **Writing Process Activity: Drawing Conclusions** relating to Washington's presidency.

working, he had earned the full confidence of President Washington. But Hamilton's personal ambition and his lack of faith in the people sometimes tempted him to grand and clever schemes.

The House of Representatives, under Madison's leadership, directed the Secretary of the Treasury to prepare proposals for collecting the revenue and dealing with the public credit. Hamilton was told to present these plans to the House of Representatives—where, according to the Constitution, money bills had to originate.

In response to these directions Hamilton put together a design of breathtaking scope. He presented that program in three major reports: on the Public Credit (January 1790), on a National Bank (December 1790), and on Manufactures (December 1791). These reports were to help shape the future history of the United States.

The Report on the Public Credit.

Upon taking office, Hamilton found that the United States had debts amounting to $54 million. Of this sum, $10 million was owed to our wartime ally, France, and to Dutch bankers. The remainder was owed to United States citizens. In addition, many of the states had unpaid war debts amounting to $20 million.

Hamilton saw an ingenious way to use this heavy debt to strengthen the central government. His plan would provide capital for a national bank and even create wealth that could be invested in new private enterprises. He proposed that the United States should pay all these debts in full. But they would be paid in a way that would both stimulate business and give the wealthy classes good reason to support the new government.

Now everyone agreed that the United States must repay the French and the Dutch if the credit of the United States was to be any good in the outside world. Who would lend us money in the future if we failed to pay these debts?

There was opposition, however, to paying back American holders of the nation's debt. The reason for this dispute had to do with the history of the debt.

During the war Congress had issued paper certificates, or bonds, which promised to pay the holder at some point in the future the amount printed on the face of the paper plus interest at a certain rate. These bonds had been sold to people at their face value or given to soldiers to induce them to enlist. During the years of war and depression many of these original holders had been forced to sell their bonds for whatever they could. Speculators willing to gamble on the future bought up the bonds for as little as 15 or 20 cents on the dollar. Even as Secretary of the Treasury Hamilton made his proposal, some members of Congress, joining the other speculators, bought all the bonds they could find.

Madison tried to persuade Congress to accept a complicated proposal to pay bondholders differing amounts based upon when they had bought their bonds. Congress rejected this plan and followed Hamilton. And Congress was right—even if some of its members stood to make money by their votes. The whole point of Hamilton's bill was to restore national credit. That could only be done if all those who had bought the bonds, at any time and for whatever reason, were paid in full.

Before the vote was taken on the payment of the debt of the United States, the question of having the national government pay the debts of the states had to be settled. This was even more difficult than the problem of the national debt. Some states, such as Virginia and Maryland, had already paid a large part of their debts. Why should they have to help pay the debts of states like Massachusetts and South Carolina? Hamilton replied that since the war had been fought for the benefit of *all* the states, the government which now represented all the states should pay the whole debt.

Madison had enough votes to defeat Hamilton's proposal to assume the state debts. But Madison believed that the United States should pay its own debts. The speculators warned him, however, that if he defeated assumption of the state debts by the national government, they would defeat the payment of the national debt.

At this point there was struck the most famous "deal" in American political history. The permanent site of the nation's capital had not yet been decided. Hamilton had a suggestion for

American Antiquarian Society

The cartoonist here accuses Robert Morris, a prominent Federalist from Philadelphia, of some trickery in the moving of the capital from New York City to Philadelphia. Morris carries the Capitol (Federal Hall) on his shoulder, while the devil leads him on.

Thomas Jefferson, who had just arrived from France to become Secretary of State. Hamilton would have his supporters in Congress vote to locate the capital at Philadelphia for the years 1790–1800, and then move it to a spot on the Potomac River favored by Virginia. In return, Madison and his friends should allow the federal government to assume the state debt. Madison and Jefferson accepted Hamilton's bargain, so the bill dealing with the debt was passed in July 1790.

The total debt of $75 million was then "funded." This meant exchanging the old bonds for new ones bearing interest, some at 6 percent, some at 3 percent. The new bonds went mainly to bankers, merchants, and wealthy speculators who owned most of the old bonds.

As Hamilton had predicted, these influential people then became firm supporters of the national government. It had to survive in order to preserve the value of the new bonds. When the federal government assumed the state debts, it undercut the importance of the state governments to those who had once held the state bonds. And the national credit was now secure.

Hamilton's opponents accused him of creating a new wealthy class—those people who had bought the national and state bonds at low prices. But that was just what Hamilton intended. If the nation was to develop from a land of farms into a dynamic country of mines, factories, ships, and shops, it needed persons of wealth who were willing and able to invest large sums of money in new projects.

Hamilton's plan was both farsighted and daring. The opposition to it, however, disclosed a sectional split between the agrarian South and the mercantile North. That split, reinforced by the great moral issue of slavery, would endanger the future of the nation.

The Report on a National Bank.
Hamilton revealed the next phase of his plan in December 1790. He proposed that the United States create a new bank. The federal government would put in $2 million (one-fifth ownership) of the bank's $10 million capital and appoint one-fifth of the bank's directors. Private investors would supply the rest of the capital and elect the other directors. And they were even to be allowed to use their government bonds for part of their share.

What would the United States get for its money? Far more than just another commercial bank. This bank would serve as the government's financial agent—collecting taxes, providing a safe place to deposit the government's cash, and lending the government money when needed.

The bank could also provide a much-needed paper currency. Based on its capital, the bank would issue bank notes to supplement specie (gold and silver coin), which was in short supply. These bank notes could be used to pay taxes and import duties. They would keep the currents of commerce flowing.

The Bank of the United States, by lending its funds, would also help develop new businesses. This goal, too, was very much in Hamilton's view. For at that time, when the nation had only three banks, business leaders were in desperate need of capital.

"Broad" versus "strict" construction of the new Constitution.
The bank proposal at once ran into heated opposition. Thomas Jefferson voiced the belief of many Americans that farmers were "the chosen people of God." They did not want to see America become a land of cities, mills, mines, and factories. Instead they wanted a pastoral land where people tilled the soil and put their faith in the rewards of hard work and the produce of sun and rainfall. Only reluctantly had they gone along with Hamilton on

paying the national and state debts. The new bank proposal was too much.

Jefferson, joined by Madison, told President Washington that since the Constitution did not give Congress the power to establish a bank, the bank should not be allowed. This kind of argument became known as a "strict construction" of the Constitution. They argued that the Congress or the President had no power to do anything unless the Constitution gave the federal government that power in so many words.

On the other side, Hamilton defended his bank by arguing that the government had the right to do everything necessary and proper to carry out any of the powers granted in the Constitution. The bank, he argued, was a necessary and proper way to borrow money and to regulate the currency, both of which powers the Constitution had plainly assigned to the Congress. This became known as a "broad" construction of the Constitution. Washington was never entirely convinced by Hamilton's theory. But seeing the nation's need for banks, he ✄ signed the bill into law on February 25, 1791.

The dispute that began over the first Bank of the United States between the "strict" and the "broad" interpretation of the Constitution still continues. But who takes which side never stays the same. In general, strict interpretation has been used by those out of power against those who hold the Presidency. As political parties began to emerge behind Jefferson and Madison opposing the followers of Hamilton, strict construction was advocated by the Jeffersonians. But when Jefferson came to power himself, he soon found he needed to follow the path of broad construction.

The Report on Manufactures.
The capstone to Hamilton's economic policy was his Report on Manufactures of December 1791. Having provided capital and credit through the first two parts of his program, he now called for the development of American manufactures. The key feature of this report was a request for Congress to pass a protective tariff. This was a tariff high enough to keep out goods made in Europe even if they were cheaper. Then people would

✄ **Critical Thinking Activity: Demonstrating Reasoned Judgment** How should the Constitution be interpreted? Ask students to describe the concept of a "strict interpretation" of the Constitution and that of a "broad interpretation." Have students discuss to which point of view they believe George Washington and John Adams subscribed.

Independence National Historical Park Collection

Independence National Historical Park Collection

Thomas Jefferson (above left) and Alexander Hamilton (above right) strongly disagreed over the question of establishing a national bank. But both recognized the talents of Charles Willson Peale and commissioned him to paint their portraits.

make them here, and the nation's factories would grow.

Planters and farmers opposed Hamilton's tariff plan because it meant they would have to pay higher prices for their manufactured goods. They were joined by northern merchants who made their living by importing tools, glassware, furniture, and other items that the farmers and planters purchased, and who saw that the protective tariffs would keep out their merchandise. So this part of his grand design did not pass Congress. For many years the tariff would be used only to raise money to pay the costs of government, not to promote manufacturing at home as Hamilton had wished.

 **The rise of political parties.** Hamilton's program built a national economy. At the same time, it strengthened the central government over the states. But it divided the country into

two camps—the new "political parties"—each shaping its politics according to a varying mix  of economic interest, social position, and philosophical belief.

The followers of Hamilton, called Federalists, favored his economic program. Generally they supported a strong central government and had little faith in the mass of the people. They saw themselves as "the wise, the good, and the rich," or "the rich, the well-born, and the able." What they wanted was a government "of gentlemen, by gentlemen, for gentlemen." Some Federalists were even said to regret the separation from the empire. In the wars of that time between France and England they tended to support England. The French Revolution of 1789 frightened them, and they did not want it to happen here.

On the other side were the followers of Jefferson and Madison. Jefferson disliked cities and

 **More from Boorstin:** "Early voting laws, like those in Pennsylvania, which as late as 1796, when no printed ballots were supplied by the government, required names to be *handwritten*. One enterprising Republican party candidate covered the states with printed tickets from which voters could conveniently copy the names; and he also asked his Republican friends and their families to write out copies of the party ticket, which voters could then take to the polls and hand in as their ballots." (From *The Americans: The National Experience*)

factories which, according to him, were sure to produce slums. His ideal was a nation of small farmers all of whom owned property and so had a stake in society. The Republicans (as the followers of Jefferson and Madison were called) opposed Hamilton's economic policies. They feared a strong central government here and did all they could to help the common people of France to overthrow the French nobility.

President Washington's support of Hamilton's economic policy seemed to make him a Federalist in the eyes of some Republicans. But actually Washington hated the whole idea of political parties. The infighting and compromises of politics did not appeal to him. He preferred the clear and simple principles of patriotism. What he really wanted was to go home to Virginia when his first term ended. But Madison, Jefferson, and Hamilton all told him that the nation needed him. Again obeying the call of duty, Washington reluctantly agreed to serve another term.

See "Section 2 Review answers," p. 148D.

Section 2 Review

1. Identify or explain: Henry Knox, debt assumption, "strict" and "broad" construction.
2. What is the Cabinet? How did it evolve?
3. Name Hamilton's famous reports. Tell what he hoped to achieve in each plan.
4. How did Washington, D.C., become our capital?
5. **Critical Thinking: Making Comparisons.** On what issues did Federalists and Republicans differ?

See "Lesson Plan," p. 148D.

3. Foreign affairs for a new nation

The key to understanding George Washington's second term, which began on March 4, 1793, is found in foreign affairs, and especially in the turbulent events of the French Revolution. It was not, in fact, domestic divisions alone that had persuaded Washington to serve again. It was also, as he put it, "the delicate posture of our foreign affairs." The United States had difficult problems with the three largest nations of western Europe: Great Britain, France, and Spain.

Great Britain and the Indians in the Northwest. The British refused to carry out the peace treaty of 1783. They still held fur-trading posts inside the United States. Their agents from Canada were giving arms and gunpowder to Indians who welcomed this support for their resistance to the invasion of their lands by the European settlers.

Full-scale combat with the Indians of the Northwest started in 1790 when General Josiah Harmar led a force from Fort Washington (Cincinnati) against Indian towns near what is now Fort Wayne. Harmar's troops failed and had to retreat. The following year a new force of 1400 men was sent out under General Arthur St. Clair. Badly trained and poorly equipped, it met disaster. It was ambushed while camped near the Wabash River, and 900 men—two-thirds of the army—were killed. This terrible defeat exposed the whole Northwest to the vengeance of the Indians.

Relations with Spain. To the south, Spain also menaced United States interests. The Spanish still refused to allow our shipping to pass freely through New Orleans. In addition, they supported the Creeks and Cherokees against the settlers moving onto their lands. For Spain still wanted to hold the Southwest and perhaps even to detach Kentucky and Tennessee from the United States.

The United States dared not go to war over these differences with England and Spain. To have done so would have exhausted the strength of the new Republic and crippled the commerce that was now reviving. The weak new nation had to try to negotiate its differences.

Troubles with France. France was the greatest problem of all. Having done so much to help the United States win its revolution, France had become our strongest ally. But when the French undertook their own very different kind of revolution, that nation's leadership and its direction changed from year to year, even from month to month. How, then, could the young

United States fulfill its treaty obligations to satisfy the whims of the Paris mobs?

Only five days after Washington first took office in 1789, the revolutionary French Estates General (national assembly) met at Versailles. In the next two years it swept away age-old oppressive privileges of the king, the nobility, and the higher clergy.

The French revolutionaries first went to war against Austria and Prussia. Soon the French government fell into the hands of the extreme radicals, the Jacobins of Paris. Aristocrats and priests were massacred. The monarchy was overthrown for a republic. King Louis XVI and Queen Marie Antoinette were beheaded. When Washington was inaugurated for his second term, the Jacobins were preparing to crush the other factions. Their "reign of terror" was government by the guillotine. But the French people could not be silenced by terror. The opposition to the Jacobins simply multiplied and went underground.

Declaring a "world revolution," the French radicals announced their intention to assist any people who wished to overthrow their government. The menace of anarchy and rebellion thus led the governments of Britain, Spain, and Holland to join Austria and Prussia in war against the aggressive French Republic.

"Citizen" Genêt's mission. Shortly after his second term began, Washington had to face the serious question of our relations with the slippery government of France. On April 8, 1793, the new French minister to the United States, "Citizen" Edmond Genêt, whose ship had been blown off course, landed at Charleston. He was greeted warmly everywhere on his four-week journey from Charleston to Philadelphia.

All this attention misled Genêt into thinking that the sympathies of the whole American people were on the side of the French radicals. But opinions here were, in fact, deeply divided. Hamilton, who was appalled by the bloodshed in France, was opposed to receiving Genêt at all. On the other hand, Jefferson had developed a deep affection for the French when he was American minister in Paris. He believed that Genêt should be received and that the new government should be recognized.

There was no denying that at a crucial moment France had furnished us with men and money to help us win our independence. By the treaty of alliance in 1778 we had promised to help France defend its West Indian islands if they were attacked, as now seemed likely. We had also agreed to allow France to bring into our ports any ships it might capture in wartime.

Washington, despite his horror at the atrocities committed in Paris, sided with Secretary of State Jefferson. He agreed that the United States must recognize the new government. At the same time, however, he was determined that our weak young nation should stay out of war. That war was a by-product of the French

Federalists and Republicans clashed over the issue of the French Revolution. The beheading of the French king, Louis Capet (Louis XVI), shocked the Federalists and prompted this broadside.

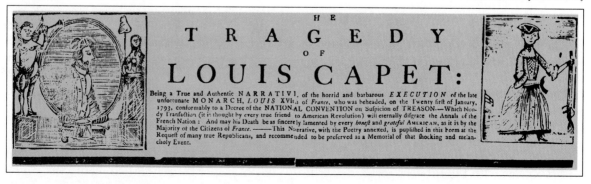

Critical Thinking Activity: Expressing Problems Clearly How did the turmoil in France affect the political parties of the United States? Have students discuss the reasons for public reaction to the French Revolution. Why were some people sympathetic while others were not? How was this revolution similar to and different from the American Revolution? Ask students to take the view of a Federalist or a Republican and to write an editorial advising the United States as to its role in the French Revolution.

Americans were horrified that 20,000 people were beheaded on the guillotine or killed by mobs during the French Revolution.

Revolution and now was spreading all over Europe—and even to America and other continents. On April 22, 1793, the President issued a Proclamation of Neutrality, which declared that we would not take sides in the struggle.

Jefferson had opposed this decision. He had wanted first to extract some concessions from Britain. He wanted Washington to declare that we might become neutral if Great Britain would remove its troops from the Northwest and give the United States trading privileges throughout the British Empire. But the Proclamation gave away that bargaining position. Soon afterward, Jefferson announced that he would resign.

"Citizen" Genêt ignored the Proclamation of Neutrality and defied the rule of diplomacy that forbade interference in the politics of the host country. He appealed to the "true" republicans here to support their "sister republic" across the Atlantic. He enlisted sailors and fitted out privateers in United States ports to prey on British commerce in the West Indies. He tried to stir up the Canadians to revolt. He even prepared an expedition against Spanish New Orleans. His conduct was so outrageous that even Jefferson, despite his sympathy for the French, agreed that Genêt must go home.

Genêt's mission and the war between Great Britain and France brought a new bitterness into American party politics. Federalists and Republicans shrieked at each other with a new rudeness. Federalists were shocked by the bloodshed and violence of the French Revolution. In addition, they wished to preserve our valuable trade with the British Isles. They despised the Republican supporters of France as "filthy Jacobins" and "frog-eating, man-eating, blood-drinking cannibals." The Republicans replied by singing the "Marseillaise" (the battle hymn of the French Revolution) and by sneering at the Federalists as "aristocratic snobs," "Anglo-men," and "British boot-lickers."

Jay's Treaty. In spite of Washington's Proclamation of Neutrality, the United States barely escaped war with Great Britain. In December 1793, Britain began to seize American ships trading with the French West Indies. Great Britain also stopped our ships, took off the sailors whom they claimed to be British citizens, and "impressed" them to serve in the British navy. War fever swept the country. People heard about a speech by the British governor-general of Canada to the Indians telling them to do their worst on the frontier. A bill cutting off all trade with England passed the House of Representatives. It was defeated in the Senate only by the tie-breaking vote of Vice-President Adams.

The Federalists, who liked England, still wanted to avoid war. Hamilton saw his whole financial plan on the edge of ruin, since the country's revenue depended on the duties received from British imports. Hamilton urged Washington to try to make peace.

In May 1794, the President sent Chief Justice John Jay to London to try to make a treaty. Unfortunately for Jay, Hamilton had let the British know that the United States would not join Denmark and Sweden in an alliance against the

British seizure of neutral shipping. Knowing that, the British had no reason to give in to Jay.

After a year's labor Jay returned home with the best terms he could get. But when the treaty was seen in America it was greeted with cries of outrage. Nothing had been accomplished in the area of maritime rights—one of the main reasons for seeking a treaty. Britain would not stop searching our vessels at sea nor cease "impressing" sailors considered to be British subjects. Great Britain did open India and the West Indies to American trading vessels, but only under tight restrictions. Shippers remained dissatisfied. Not a word was said about compensation for the slaves England had carried off during the Revolution.

The one really positive point Jay had won was England's agreement to leave the frontier fur posts in American territory by June 1, 1796. Nothing at all was done about the disputed boundary between Canada and the United States, the damages for ships seized by the English, or the debts Americans still owed British merchants. These items were left to a joint commission in the future. Though no one knew it at the time, joint commissions would become the chief means to settle British and American differences. At this point, the mention of such a future commission seemed just one more failure of Jay's Treaty.

Washington hesitated to send the treaty to the Senate. But he finally concluded that the treaty with all its faults was the only way to keep peace with Great Britain. In the Senate it was barely approved by the necessary two-thirds vote—and probably would not have been ratified at all without the prestige of the President behind it.

Pinckney's Treaty with Spain. Jay's Treaty had one important, if unexpected, result. It made Spain fear that an alliance between England and the United States might follow. Europe's problems now became America's opportunity. Spain had made a separate peace with France, while England remained at war. Now Spain feared that England might work with the United States to seize the Spanish possessions in North America—Florida and Louisiana. Our special envoy Thomas Pinckney went to Madrid to seek the freedom of American citizens to navigate the Mississippi. He found the Spanish minister, Godoy, surprisingly eager to please.

By a treaty concluded in October 1795, Spain granted every point that Americans had been demanding for a dozen years: (1) free navigation of the Mississippi, (2) acceptance of 31° north latitude as the southern boundary of the United States, and (3) "right of deposit." This was the right to transfer cargoes at New Orleans from riverboats to ocean-going vessels without paying duty.

The Treaty of Greenville. Also in 1795, following the total victory of General "Mad Anthony" Wayne at the Battle of Fallen Timbers in northwestern Ohio the previous year, the United States made a treaty with the Indians of the Northwest. The chiefs of the Delaware, Shawnee, Wyandot, Miami Confederacy, and other tribes agreed to open up most of the Ohio territory to settlement.

These three treaties of 1795 were important in establishing the security of the new American Republic. They reduced, for a time, the fear that Kentucky and Tennessee would join Spain. They brought peace, if only temporarily, to the Northwest. They gained recognition of the borders won from England in the Revolution. They enabled the United States for a few more years (p. 163) to stay out of the war that was raging in Europe. They allowed Washington to end his term with the nation at peace with the world.

The Whiskey Rebellion. This busy—and successful—diplomacy strengthened the struggling young nation, and especially increased the influence of the Federalist party. So, too, had an event that occurred the previous year. In 1794 the farmers of western Pennsylvania protested against the whiskey tax. This was an "excise" tax—an internal tax—passed a few years before to raise additional funds for the national government.

The whiskey tax angered farmers in the West because it was usual there to make grain (corn or wheat) into whiskey in order to carry it more

More from Boorstin: "When the terms of . . . [Jay's] treaty were published in March, 1795, furor shook the country. . . . Attacks on Washington, who was held responsible for the treaty, were collected by Benjamin Bache, Franklin's grandson, who printed many of them in his *Aurora* in Philadelphia . . . 'If ever a nation was debauched by a man, it added in December, 1796, the American nation has been by Washington.'" (From *The Americans: The National Experience*)

Indian Land Cessions and Other Treaties, 1784-1810

Boundaries as of 1810

- ▨ Indian Lands Ceded before 1784
- ▨ Indian Lands Ceded, 1784-1800
- ▨ Indian Lands Ceded, 1800-1810
- ◇ British Forts Given Up in Jay's Treaty, 1796
- ✕ Battle Sites

easily across the mountains to market. Also, where specie and bank notes were in short supply, whiskey was used as a form of money. To the farmers Hamilton's excise tax on whiskey seemed to be a tax directed against them and their crops. They refused to pay the tax when the United States marshal tried to collect it, and in 1794 they staged a "rebellion." The governor of Pennsylvania thought the courts could handle the matter. But Washington, urged on by Hamilton, saw the "rebellion" as a direct attack

on the authority of the government. Just as in the days of Daniel Shays, it seemed the state had become a victim of mob rule.

Fulfilling his duty under the Constitution to maintain a "republican form of government," Washington called out the militia. Fifteen thousand strong, it marched west to put down the farmers. In no mood to fight the militia, they returned to their homes. But the ringleaders were seized. Two of them were convicted of treason but were pardoned by the President, who

⊕ **Geography and History: Regions** Refer students to the map above and ask the following questions: Which battle was fought closest to Lake Erie? (Fallen Timbers) When was the last battle fought? (1794—Fallen Timbers) Which fort is the farthest west? (Fort Dearborn) What future state gained the most territory in the Treaty of Greenville? (Ohio) How many forts did the British give up in Jay's Treaty? (Eight)

wanted only to prove the strength of the new government. His decisive handling of this affair attracted supporters to the Federalist cause.

The Farewell Address. In September 1796, in his "Farewell Address," Washington announced that he would not serve again. One of the most important statements ever made by an American President, it was largely written by Alexander Hamilton. Although Washington never delivered it as a speech, it was published in the newspapers. Washington still called the United States an experiment. He urged his fellow citizens to remain loyal to the Union and to a republican form of government. He warned against sectionalism, foresaw the danger of secession, and cautioned against political partisanship. His most memorable warning was against "entangling alliances"—playing favorites in the community of nations.

The election of 1796. The Federalist candidate for President in the election of 1796 was John Adams. His services to his country had put him far ahead of any other member of his party. The Republicans nominated Thomas Jefferson. In the electoral college, Adams won by a narrow margin—71 to 68.

Since he had the second largest number of votes, according to the Constitution Jefferson became Vice-President. Hamilton, who did not like the independent-minded Adams, had wanted someone in office who shared his belief in the virtues of the rich. That was not Adams. So Hamilton had tried to persuade the Federalist electors to leave Adams's name off their

After the Battle of Fallen Timbers, General Anthony Wayne negotiated the Treaty of Greenville, by which Indian tribes of the Northwest Territory ceded their lands to the United States. A member of Wayne's staff painted this picture, showing Wayne meeting with a group of Indians.

Chicago Historical Society

ballots and instead elect Adams's vice-presidential running mate, Thomas Pinckney, to the Presidency. But Adams's New England friends also knew how to use the electoral college. They simply left Pinckney's name off their ballots. The result was that the votes for Pinckney were fewer than those for Jefferson, so Jefferson became Vice-President.

Washington goes home. George Washington had led his country through its first difficult years. He had led the nation to victory in its battle for independence. A major influence in shaping the new Constitution, he had been the chief force in starting the new government. Now he had given the country time to grow by avoiding a needless war with England. Cold, practical, lacking the brilliance of Jefferson or Hamilton, he made up for his shortcomings by his unswerving devotion to his country. He deserved the country's gratitude. Still, some envious partisans accused him of kingly ambitions and rejoiced when he left public life.

See "Section 3 Review answers," p. 148D.

Section 3 Review

1. Identify or explain: Edmond Genêt, Jay's Treaty, Pinckney's Treaty, Treaty of Greenville.
2. As Washington's second term opened, what problems did he face: (a) with England, (b) with Spain, (c) with France?
3. Why were some Americans upset by the French Revolution?
4. What dangers did Washington warn against in his Farewell Address?
5. **Critical Thinking: Identifying Central Issues.** What was the significance of the Whiskey Rebellion?

See "Lesson Plan," p. 148E.

4. John Adams and the rise of parties

To John Adams now fell the difficult task of guiding a young nation divided by party strife at home and endangered by war in Europe. But Adams was no military hero. Short of stature, with an acid personality, he lacked Washington's enormous prestige.

Sixty years of age when he became President, Adams was the descendant of a line of solid Massachusetts small farmers. He trusted neither the rich nor the poor, but only the wise and the able. And he had served his country well in the trying years of revolution. He had been in both the First and the Second Continental Congress. There he had helped write the petition to the king and the Declaration of Rights and Grievances, and had recommended Washington for commander of the army. Having served on the committee that wrote the Declaration of Independence, he then defended that document vigorously. His 80 committee assignments during the war (he chaired 25 of these committees!) included the crucial Board of War and Ordnance. Then he represented the new nation abroad—in England, France, and Holland. In his home state of Massachusetts, he was principal author of its new constitution of 1780. Working with Franklin and John Jay, he negotiated the peace treaty with Great Britain in 1783. Most recently he had filled the thankless position of Vice-President for eight years. There was no doubt of his patriotism, honesty, and courage.

Adams was, in fact, a great man. But he was also vain, willful, stubborn, prickly, and lacking in tact. Benjamin Franklin described him as "always an honest man, often a wise one, but sometimes and in some things, absolutely out of his senses." Confident of the rightness of his opinions, he made little attempt to harmonize conflicting views in his Cabinet, in the Congress, or in his party. He followed Washington in refusing to take account of political parties. But by his time party politics had already become fierce, and party demands could not be ignored.

The Cabinet. Adams made his first, and one of his worst, mistakes when he retained the chief Cabinet officers of Washington's second term. These men, Secretary of State Timothy Pickering, Secretary of the Treasury Oliver Wolcott (Hamilton had resigned in 1795), Secretary of War James McHenry, and Attorney General

Adams National Historic Site: photo by George Dow

John Adams was born in the house on the right. He and his wife, Abigail, later lived in the house on the left, and there John Quincy Adams was born. The two houses still stand in Quincy, Massachusetts, where the much larger family home may also be visited.

Charles Lee were second-raters. Even worse, they were devoted friends of Adams's personal enemy, Alexander Hamilton, from whom they continued to take their orders. In Adams's defense, it might be said that, of course, there was still no tradition for Cabinet members to be replaced at the end of a President's term. This was the first time the Presidency had changed. But even after he learned that these men were not really working for him, Adams waited too long to change his top command.

Renewed troubles with France. Adams's administration was dominated by the problem of France. A new government of five men, called the Directory, had come into power in France in 1795. They had been angered by Jay's Treaty and by the recall of our minister, James Monroe. As a Republican, Monroe had been too friendly to the French for Federalist tastes. The French Directory began seizing our ships

in their harbors, refused to receive C. C. Pinckney, Thomas Pinckney's brother, whom President Washington had sent to replace Monroe, and actually ordered Pinckney to leave France.

Angered by the treatment of our minister, Adams declared in a speech to Congress that we must convince France and the world that we were "not a degraded people, humiliated under a colonial spirit of fear." But since he was still determined to keep the nation at peace, he sent John Marshall and Elbridge Gerry to join Pinckney as a commission to deal with the French.

The XYZ Affair. These envoys immediately ran into problems. The French foreign minister, Talleyrand, would not see them personally, but instead sent secret agents to meet them. The French agents told them that there could be no talks unless the United States apologized for

President Adams's speech, promised to loan France $10 million, and paid a bribe of $250,000 to Talleyrand.

When they heard these insulting demands, the envoys answered, "No! no, not a sixpence." Marshall and Pinckney returned home at once. There they stirred the nation's patriotism and fervor against France by the story of their treatment. The whole incident was known as the "XYZ Affair," because the Secretary of State had substituted the letters X, Y, and Z for the names of the agents whom Talleyrand had sent to ask our commissioners for bribes.

Naval war with France. Republicans and Federalists alike rallied to support Adams in his measures to compel respect for our envoys as "representatives of a great, free, powerful, and independent nation." For a rare moment in his life, the peppery John Adams was popular everywhere. Fellow citizens applauded his language of defiance. They bellowed the new national song, "Hail, Columbia." They adopted as a slogan (to serve again and again later in our history) the toast proposed at a banquet for the returning hero John Marshall: "Millions for defense, but not one cent for tribute!" Preparations for war were begun. Again Washington was called to lead the army, though it was agreed that he would not be expected to leave his home at Mt. Vernon unless there was open battle. Hamilton was to be second in command. A new Navy Department was created by Congress.

War was not formally declared, but Congress renounced the treaty with France that had been signed in 1778 and authorized our ships to prey upon French commerce. Actually, during the two years 1798–1800 a state of war at sea existed with France. More than 80 French ships were captured.

Talleyrand now saw that he could not threaten or bribe the United States. Not wanting war, he hastened to assure our minister to Holland that a new American commission would be received with due respect. At that moment President Adams, to his everlasting credit, resisted the demands of Hamilton and many other Americans (including his own Cabinet) that the nation should fight. That might have been a popular decision, but it would not have served the weak new nation. To the surprise of Federalist Hamiltonians, Adams sent a message to Congress simply nominating a new minister to France. He would send envoys to deal with this sly Talleyrand. Four days after the new envoys sailed, the upstart Napoleon Bonaparte overthrew the corrupt Directory.

Napoleon, intent on establishing his power in France and Europe, wanted no trouble with the United States. In September 1800, therefore, he signed an agreement that ended the treaty of alliance of 1778, thus freeing the United States from any obligation to help France in war. In return the United States gave up all claims against France for damages done to our shipping by French cruisers since 1793. This fair bargain enabled the United States to enter the 1800s at peace.

The Alien and Sedition Acts, 1798. In 1798 ≒ when anger against the French had become the most violent, the Federalists took advantage of the situation. They passed a series of laws to suppress Republican opposition and insure power for their own party. But, in fact, they misjudged the temper of the nation. Their oppressive measures outraged many Americans and helped lead to the downfall of the Federalist party.

Leading Federalists believed—or pretended to believe—that most foreigners who came to the United States joined the Republicans. In the Naturalization Act, then, they extended the time it took to become a citizen from 5 to 14 years. In the Alien Act they gave the President at once the power to deport any alien he thought dangerous to the nation's security and then, in time of war, the power to deport or arrest all aliens who came from an enemy nation.

The Sedition Act was especially harsh. It provided a heavy fine and a jail term for any person found guilty of "combining and conspiring to oppose the execution of the laws, or publishing false, scandalous, or malicious writings against the President, Congress, or the government of

≒ **Continuity and Change: Government and Politics** Point out to students that the motivations behind the Federalists' Sedition Act of 1798, passed to control public criticism of the government, were similar to the motivations of the Democrats during Woodrow Wilson's administration, who passed their own Sedition Act of 1918 to control criticism of the United States' involvement in World War I. (See page 566.)

the United States." These words were so vague and general that the Federalists could use the law to stop public criticism of the government by their opponents. This would spell the end of free representative government.

Some Federalist leaders, including Hamilton, actually disapproved of these laws that were pushed through Congress by extremist members of their party. John Adams had not promoted the measures, but on the other hand he did not veto them or prevent their use against 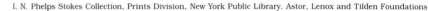 the Republicans.

The Virginia and Kentucky Resolutions. The Sedition Act was used to silence Republican writers and newspaper editors who criticized President Adams. For example, Thomas Cooper, who later became president of South Carolina College, wrote a pamphlet in which he said Adams "was hardly in the infancy of politi-

"Preparations for a War to Defend Commerce," William Birch entitled his 1800 engraving. It shows work on the frigate *Philadelphia*, which was not completed in time for the undeclared naval war with France.

I. N. Phelps Stokes Collection, Prints Division, New York Public Library. Astor, Lenox and Tilden Foundations

See "Lesson Plan," p. 148E for **Writing Process Activity: Expressing Problems Clearly** relating to the Alien and Sedition Acts.

cal mistake" when he took office. Cooper admitted Adams had not yet interfered with a court of justice, though he implied Adams might still do so. For his writings, Cooper was fined $400 and spent six months in jail.

Only ten Republicans were convicted under the Sedition Act. Many other members of that party—but no Federalists—were tried. This attack on freedom of speech and the press outraged Republicans. Even some Federalists, most notably John Marshall, who was later to become Chief Justice, spoke out against it.

If the courts would not defend the people against the Alien and Sedition Acts or other tyrannical measures, who could do so? Madison and Jefferson believed that in this situation the only power able to oppose the federal government was the states. Resolutions passed by the Virginia legislature (and drafted by Madison) declared that each state had the right to judge the constitutionality of measures passed by Congress. The Kentucky Resolutions, which Jefferson wrote, went even further. He said that a state could declare acts of Congress "null and void" and that the rightful response to an unconstitutional act of Congress was *"nullification"* by the states.

The Constitution did not say who was to judge if Congress went beyond the powers granted in the Constitution. Madison and Jefferson believed the states had that right. The states' rights doctrine they championed would at last be carried so far that it would lead to civil war. Then it would be clear that the federal government, through its courts, had to be the judge of its own powers.

The election of 1800. John Adams was proud of what he had accomplished as President. He had a right to be, even though his main achievement was to keep the nation out of war. He hoped, however, that in a second term he could make a more positive record.

But Adams was not reelected, in part because of the Alien and Sedition Acts, but mostly due to the enmity of Alexander Hamilton, who was a member of his own party. Republicans stumbled across Hamilton's bitter criticism of

Adams and published it in their newspapers. At the same time Hamilton worked to defeat Adams in the electoral college in order to elect Adams's running mate, C. C. Pinckney. Hamilton's opposition took its toll. Meanwhile, of course, the Republicans had taken their own more careful steps to defeat Adams.

When all the electoral votes were counted, Adams had 65 votes, and Pinckney had 64. Then came the surprise. The Republicans had won a very close election, but their two candidates for President and Vice-President, Jefferson and Aaron Burr, each had 73 votes. The Republicans had made a serious mistake. Since the electors in the electoral college had to vote for two persons on their ballots without distinguishing between President and Vice-President, one Republican elector was supposed not to vote for Burr. That would have made Jefferson President and Burr Vice-President. Instead, they all voted for Burr. Since there was then a tie, according to the Constitution the election had to be decided in the House of Representatives.

As the country eagerly awaited the name of its next President, Congress gathered on Wednesday, February 11, 1801, in a partly completed Capitol in the raw new capital city of Washington. The House then voted on and off for several days. Some Federalists hoped to make Aaron Burr President. But Hamilton, despite his personal dislike for Jefferson, showed his patriotism and good judgment by opposing Burr. "Jefferson is to be preferred," he wrote his friends. "He is by far not so dangerous a man; and he has pretensions to character." Finally, on Monday, February 16, after receiving assurances that the public credit and the navy would be maintained, and that there would be no mass eviction of their fellow party members from office, the Federalists allowed Jefferson to be elected President.

After this election, the Twelfth Amendment to the Constitution was enacted in 1804. It provided for the naming of the President and the Vice-President separately on each elector's ballot.

The election of 1800 was the last time the Federalists came close to winning an election. (p. 170)

✖ Critical Thinking Activity: Formulating Questions How did John Adams feel about the important issues of his day? Ask students to speculate about how well John Adams would perform in a modern presidential press conference. Have them write interview questions for President Adams. Then hold a mock press conference with a student volunteer or the teacher playing the part of John Adams. The teacher may wish to extend the lesson by having the class write a news article for the local paper summarizing the press conference.

Harvard University Portrait Collection,
Bequest-Ward Nicholas Boylston

John Singleton Copley, one of America's most skilled artists, was in London in 1783 when he painted this portrait of John Adams as a peace commissioner.

But their Presidents—Washington and Adams—had served their country well. They put the nation on its way and set many useful precedents. They laid the foundation for a government based on broad construction of its powers. True enough, they failed to resolve the hard questions of the links between the executive and the legislature or between the central government and the states. That would take time—and in the end would cost the bloodshed of a civil war. Meanwhile they helped the nation grow strong by keeping the nation at peace during its critical early years.

John Adams, the last Federalist President, was a better man than history has often credited him with being. He sadly left the city of Washington early on the morning of Jefferson's inauguration and returned to Massachusetts. During the years that followed, he made up his differences with his former friend, Thomas Jefferson. They began a lively correspondence full of wit and wisdom that lasted the many years till their death. By an uncanny coincidence John Adams, then 90 years old, died in Massachusetts on the very same day that Jefferson, who was 83, died at Monticello in Virginia. That day was July 4, 1826, the fiftieth anniversary of the Declaration of Independence.

See "Section 4 Review answers," p. 148E.

Section 4 Review

1. How did it happen that Jefferson became Adams's Vice-President?
2. What was the XYZ Affair and why was it significant?
3. Why were the Alien and Sedition Acts passed?
4. What did the Twelfth Amendment provide for and why was it passed?
5. **Critical Thinking: Testing Conclusions.** Many people feel that President Adams's refusal to bow to any political party proved to be a foolish decision. Explain why you agree or disagree with this statement.

More from Boorstin: "Even after the defeat of the Federalists, Jefferson never expected that the rightness of Republican views would conquer all opposition. 'An association of men who will not quarrel with one another is a thing which never yet existed, from the greatest confederacy of nations down to a town meeting or a vestry.'" (From *The Lost World of Thomas Jefferson*)

Chapter 6 Review

See "Chapter Review answers," p. 148E.

Focusing on Ideas

1. What lasting precedents did George Washington establish as President of the United States?

2. Why did the new government start out with a big national debt? How did paying the debt in full benefit the country?

3. Why did the Indians of the Northwest and Southeast form an alliance with the British and Spanish against the United States?

4. How did President John Adams avoid going to war with France between 1798 and 1800?

Taking a Critical Look

1. **Demonstrating Reasoned Judgment.** List in order of importance some of the Washington administration's major accomplishments. Justify your rankings.

2. **Making Comparisons.** How did Hamilton and Jefferson differ in their views of the ideal America? In which sections of the country were Hamilton's views most popular? Jefferson's? Why?

3. **Predicting Consequences.** The Whiskey Rebellion was a tax revolt. How do you think contemporary Americans would respond to what they considered unfair taxation?

Your Region in History

1. **Geography.** How large was the population of your state or region in 1790? What was its largest city?

2. **Culture.** The 1700s saw the rise of an American "aristocracy." Who would have fallen into this category in your region? Explain.

Historical Facts and Figures

Formulating Questions. Asking good questions is often the key to understanding a chart. Draw up a list of questions that will help people looking at the chart below understand Hamilton's grand plan for the Bank of the United States. Questions should draw forth information on the complex relationships that exist between the bank, the federal government, and private citizens in the United States.

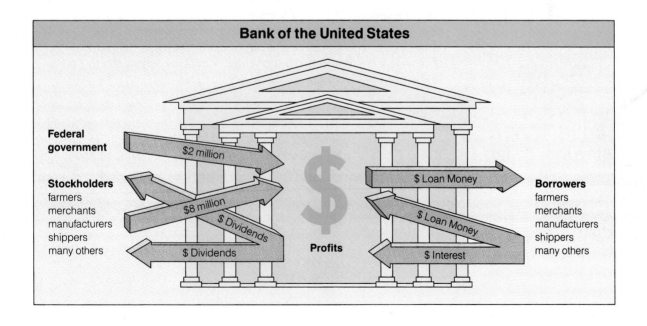

Bank of the United States

Federal government — $2 million
Stockholders: farmers, merchants, manufacturers, shippers, many others — $8 million — $ Dividends — $ Dividends
Profits
$ Loan Money — $ Loan Money — $ Interest
Borrowers: farmers, merchants, manufacturers, shippers, many others

MAKING CONNECTIONS
Unit 2

This unit began on page 75 with the observation that winning the American Revolution and establishing a new nation was very much like trying to make thirteen clocks strike all at once:

> *To lead thirteen different colonies [or states] to take common action seemed next to impossible.*

This conclusion was supported by the three unit themes that are reprinted in **dark type** below. Use the time line and the information in Unit 2 to answer the questions that follow the unit themes.

THEMES IN HISTORY

1. **The British have trouble subduing the colonies because of the colonies' variety and lack of a critical center.** CONFLICT
   Why might the British have viewed the American colonies as "a monster with many heads" during the American Revolution? (Distinguishing False from Accurate Images)

2. **The states' desire for self-rule and their fear of tyranny result in a weak central government under the Articles of Confederation.** GOVERNMENT AND POLITICS
   Why did Americans eventually decide that a strong central government was necessary? (Recognizing Cause and Effect)

3. **The drafting and the ratification of a new constitution begin the process of binding Americans together into one nation.** THE CONSTITUTION
   How did the writing and ratification of the Constitution bring about not only a new government, but a change in the way Americans looked at themselves? (Drawing Conclusions)

Events in American History

1765
Britain's Parliament passes the Stamp Act, a tax on goods the colonists used.

1775
Paul Revere warns Massachusetts residents that the British are planning to attack arms stored in Concord.

| 1760 | 1765 | 1770 | 1775 |

Events in World History

1776
The Second Continental Congress issues the Declaration of Independence.

172

1776
The British pour 32,000 troops into New York City, where 25,000 colonists live.

1777
The British plan to take control of the Hudson River, cutting off New England from the other colonies.

1780
An American militia captures 1200 British troops in a surprise attack in South Carolina.

1784
An economic depression begins, burdening the young nation for the next five years.

1787
Daniel Shays leads a farmers' rebellion in western Massachusetts.

1787
The *Federalist Papers* argue for ratification of the United States Constitution.

1787
The Constitutional Convention begins in Philadelphia, Pennsylvania.

1788
Following New York's ratification, the Constitution is officially in effect.

1790
Alexander Hamilton proposes a plan for a National Bank.

1780	1785	1790	1795	1800

1778
France enters the Revolutionary War on the side of the American colonists.

1789
The French Revolution begins, taking inspiration from the American Revolution.

Unit 3

E pluribus unum: One Made from Many 1800–1840

The Americans had won their independence and established a government. But they had not yet created a strong nation. The number of people was small and scattered over hundreds of square miles of wilderness. They had few roads and even fewer cities. The very vastness of the land—a source of pride and future power—was also a weakness. For the people tended to be more closely tied to their states and their regions than to the weak central government in its swampy forest clearing on the banks of the Potomac.

But the nation discovered new ways to grow. It fought a "second war of independence" with England. Its politics and political parties became ever more democratic. This created new traditions and fed national pride, which would begin to tie all the states and all the regions together. Americans were shaping a new kind of government.

 THEMES IN HISTORY

- The nation discovers new ways to grow.   ECONOMICS
- The nation's growth is marked by the rise of two opposing forces: nationalism and sectionalism.   SOCIAL CHANGE
- The nation's political process becomes more democratic.
  GOVERNMENT AND POLITICS

⊡ This detail from Thomas Cole's "Sunny Morning on the Hudson River" captures the wild grandeur of America the painter loved.
Museum of Fine Arts, Boston, M. and M. Karolik Collection

Chapter 7
Jefferson in Power

Objectives	Basic Instructional Materials	Extension Materials
1 The Man and His Policies • Summarize the life and accomplishments of Thomas Jefferson. • Compare the political philosophies of Jefferson and Hamilton.	**Annotated Teacher's Edition** • Lesson Plans, p. 176C **Instructional Support File** • Pre-Reading Activities, Unit 3, p. 1 • Skill Review Activity, Unit 3, p. 4	**Documents of American History** • Jefferson's First Inaugural Address, Vol. 1, p. 186
2 Buying Lousiana • Explain the controversy surrounding the Louisiana Purchase and describe its importance to the United States. • Discuss the reasons Jefferson decided to buy Louisiana despite his philosophical opposition to the purchase. • State Napoleon's interest in Haiti, and link his military troubles in Europe to the sale of Louisiana.	**Annotated Teacher's Edition** • Lesson Plans, pp. 176C–176D **Instructional Support File** • Skill Application Activity, Unit 3, p. 5	**Documents of American History** • Jefferson on the Importance of New Orleans, Vol. 1, p. 189 • The Cession of Louisiana, Vol. 1, p. 190 • Jefferson's Message on the Burr Conspiracy, Vol. 1, p. 195 **American History Transparencies** • Geography and History, pp. B13, B15
3 Jefferson, Marshall, and the Courts • State the principle of judicial review derived from *Marbury v. Madison,* and discuss John Marshall's role in establishing it. • Describe the importance of Supreme Court decisions.	**Annotated Teacher's Edition** • Lesson Plans, pp. 176D–176E	**Enrichment Support File** • The Rise of the American Judiciary (See "In-Depth Coverage" at right.) **Suggested Secondary Sources** • See chart at right.
4 Trouble on the Seas • Identify the factors that influenced the foreign trade of the United States from 1800 to 1820. • Explain the history of United States exports and imports from 1790 to 1820. • State Jefferson's purpose in calling for the Embargo Act.	**Annotated Teacher's Edition** • Lesson Plans, p. 176E **Instructional Support File** • Reading Activities, Unit 3, pp. 2–3 • Critical Thinking Activity, Unit 3, p. 6 • Chapter Test, Unit 3, pp. 7–10 • Additional Test Questions, Unit 3, pp. 11–14	**Documents of American History** • British Orders in Council, Vol. 1, p. 200 • The Milan Decree, Vol. 1, p. 201 • Embargo Act, Vol. 1, p. 202 • The Non-Intercourse Act, Vol. 1, p. 203 **American History Transparencies** • Our Multicultural Heritage, p. C59

Providing In-Depth Coverage

Perspectives on the American Judiciary

Created to uphold the Constitution and the laws of the United States, the court system held great power which could affect the shaping of the new national government. Up until the time of John Marshall's appointment as Chief Justice it appeared as though the Court's impact would be minimal.

However, in the landmark case, *Marbury* v. *Madison*, the Supreme Court established its power of judicial review. This chapter concentrates in part on this power of the Supreme Court to overrule the decisions of Congress and the President on matters of Constitutional interpretation and the establishment of the Supreme Court as a great power in the building of a strong central government.

For this chapter, *A History of the United States* as an instructional program provides two types of resources you can use to offer in-depth coverage of the rise of the American judiciary: the *student text* and the *Enrichment Support File.* A list of *Suggested Secondary Sources* is also provided. The chart below shows the topics that are covered in each.

THE STUDENT TEXT. Boorstin and Kelley's *A History of the United States* unfolds the chronology of events and the key players in the rise of the American judiciary.

AMERICAN HISTORY ENRICHMENT SUPPORT FILE. This collection of primary source readings and classroom activities reveals details of the growth of the power of the courts.

SUGGESTED SECONDARY SOURCES. This reference list of readings by well-known historians and other commentators provides an array of perspectives on the growth of the power of the courts. (See the chart below.)

Locating Instructional Materials

Detailed lesson plans for teaching the rise of the American judiciary as a mini-course or to study one or more elements of the judiciary in depth are offered in the following areas: in the *student text,* see individual lesson plans at the beginning of each chapter; in the *Enrichment Support File,* see page 3; for reading beyond the student text, see *Suggested Secondary Sources.*

IN-DEPTH COVERAGE OF THE RISE OF THE AMERICAN JUDICIARY		
Student Text	**Enrichment Support File**	**Suggested Secondary Sources**
▪ Establishment of federal courts, p. 119 ▪ Judiciary Act of 1789, p. 119 ▪ "midnight judges," p. 153 ▪ Judiciary Act of 1801, pp. 153–154 ▪ *Marbury* v. *Madison*, p. 154 ▪ judicial review, p. 154 ▪ Samuel Chase, pp. 154–155	▪ Lesson Suggestions ▪ Multimedia Resources ▪ Overview Essay/Checks and Balances: The Rise of the American Judiciary ▪ Primary Sources in American History/ Jefferson's View of the Judiciary and the Separation of Powers ▪ Biography in American History/ John Marshall ▪ Great Debates in American History/Can the Supreme Court Decide Constitutionality? ▪ Simulation/Samuel Chase's Day in Court ▪ Making Connections	▪ *Marbury v. Madison and Judicial Review* by Robert L. Clinton, pp. 4–30. ▪ *The Jeffersonian Crisis: Courts and Politics in the Young Republic* by Richard Ellis, pp. 36–68. ▪ *The Supreme Court under Marshall and Taney* by R. Kent Newmeyer, pp. 1–55. ▪ *John Marshall: Defender of the Constitution* by Francis N. Stites.

Section 1 (pages 177–182)

The Man and His Policies

FOCUS

To introduce the lesson, tell students that when a number of winners of the Nobel Prize were invited to the White House in 1961, President Kennedy described them as "the most extraordinary collection of talent, of human knowledge, that has been gathered at the White House, with the possible exception of when Thomas Jefferson dined alone." With the text as a guide, have the students find information to support Kennedy's statement about Jefferson's talent and knowledge.

Developing Vocabulary

The words listed in this chapter are essential terms for reading and understanding particular sections of the chapter. The page number after each term indicates the page of its first or most important appearance in the chapter. These terms are defined in the text Glossary (text pages 1000–1011).

naturalization (page 181)

INSTRUCT

Explain

Jefferson's first term as President was quite successful. A remarkably talented, complex person, Jefferson was able to work with the Federalists.

★ Independent Activity

Making Comparisons Historians consider Jefferson and Hamilton great men. Yet they were rivals with contrasting political philosophies. Have students compile a profile of the personality and values of each man, and write an essay entitled, "Jefferson or Hamilton—Which had the More Lasting Influence on American Life?" Donald B. Chidsey's *Mr. Hamilton and Mr. Jefferson* provides interesting background information.

Section Review Answers

Section 1, page 182

1. a) a free black mathematician who helped lay out and survey Washington, D.C. b) the architect for Washington, D.C. c) Jefferson's house in Virginia. d) the phrase Jefferson used to describe his election to the presidency. e) Jefferson's Secretary of the Treasury. f) Morocco, Algiers, Tunis, and Tripoli extracted payments from other nations for protection from pirates. g) hero in the war against Tripoli in 1804 and leader of the naval forces sent against the pirates in 1815. 2. Presidents Washington, Jefferson, Madi-

son, and Monroe made up the "Virginia dynasty." In Virginia at the time only owners of substantial property could vote or hold high office. As a result, a few wealthy families dominated the state. 3. Jefferson demonstrated many talents as well as some contradictions. He was a plantation owner, architect, surveyor, philosopher, scientist, inventor, writer, and politician, and he spoke several languages. He thought slavery was wrong, but he owned slaves. Leader of the Republicans, he wanted to reduce the size of the federal government and hoped the nation would remain a community of small farmers; but the policies he followed as President did not differ much from those of the Federalists. 4. In his first term Jefferson adopted a conciliatory tone toward his opponents and selected an able Cabinet. He greatly reduced the national debt and the army and navy. He maintained peace with European nations but took action against the Barbary pirates.

CLOSE

To conclude this lesson, tell the class that Jefferson wrote his own epitaph: "Here lies Thomas Jefferson, Author of the American Declaration of Independence, of the Statute of Virginia for Religious Freedom, and Father of the University of Virginia." Ask the class to write another 25 to 50 words to add to this epitaph.

Section 2 (pages 182–189)

Buying Louisiana

FOCUS

To introduce the lesson, ask students to open their texts to the map on page 219 and locate Haiti. Briefly discuss Napoleon's interest there. Then direct students to the map on page 195 and discuss the Napoleonic Wars raging in Europe at the time. How did these events influence Napoleon's decision to sell the Louisiana territory?

Developing Vocabulary

ambassador (page 184); **precedent** (page 189); **treason** (page 189).

INSTRUCT

Explain

The Louisiana Purchase was a bold and controversial move that strengthened the United States and doubled its size.

☑ Writing Process Activity

Predicting Consequences Have students imagine that they are members of the Lewis and Clark expedition. In preparation for writing about their experiences, have them freewrite about one day of sights, sounds, feelings, and reactions to vast new territory. Ask students to begin their story with a topic sentence that captures reader interest and to recreate their experiences with vivid details. Students should revise for chronological order and colorful word choice. After proofreading, students might display stories with an expedition map on a classroom bulletin board.

Section Review Answers

Section 2, page 189

1. a) American ambassadors who accepted Napoleon's offer to sell the Louisiana Territory. b) leader of the blacks of Haiti who destroyed a French army. c) Indian woman who helped guide the Lewis and Clark expedition. d) explored the heart of the North American continent. e) served as Vice-President in Jefferson's second term; he was tried for treason but acquitted. f) Massachusetts senator who tried to form a northern confederacy apart from the Union. 2. Napoleon dreamed of making the Louisiana Territory part of a new French empire. When the Haitians repelled a French army, Napoleon concluded that he would be unable to control Louisiana and he offered to sell the entire territory to the United States. 3. Congress had approved the purchase of just a small piece of land; the Louisiana Purchase went far beyond what Congress had authorized. The Constitution said nothing about giving the government power to buy land from foreign countries. In the past, Jefferson had argued for a strict interpretation of the Constitution; he had to reverse himself and argue for a broad interpretation. 4. The Louisiana Purchase doubled the area of the United States, secured the Mississippi, and opened the way for the push to the Pacific Ocean. 5. The Lewis and Clark expedition provided information about the vast Louisiana Territory, and strengthened the United States claim to the Oregon region. 6. Some Federalists opposed the Louisiana Purchase because they feared that settlers there would favor the Republicans. Federalists also feared that new states formed there would dominate the Union. 7. Burr's trial set a precedent that protected political liberties. As a result, after the trial it was difficult to use charges of treason to silence political opponents.

CLOSE

To conclude the lesson, ask students to use the map of the United States on pages 956–957 in the text to list the thirteen states partly or wholly created out of land acquired in the Louisiana Purchase (shown on map on page 187). The answers can be found by checking the map on page 301.

Jefferson, Marshall, and the Courts

FOCUS

To introduce the lesson, ask: Why are Supreme Court decisions so important? (They set precedents; they can strike down laws; they are the final court of appeal; they interpret the Constitution.)

Developing Vocabulary
patronage (page 190); judicial review (page 191); unconstitutional (page 191).

INSTRUCT

Explain
Make sure students understand that the Supreme Court does not review acts of Congress or of executive officials on its own initiative. Someone must bring a case into a lower federal court and argue that the law—or some part of it—is contrary to the Constitution. Most laws are not challenged on constitutional grounds. The Supreme Court rarely overturns a federal law, but it often declares state laws—or parts of them—to be unconstitutional.

❉ Cooperative Learning Activity
Expressing Problems Clearly Break the class into small groups and explain that each will compile a list of ten major events during Jefferson's presidency that helped shape America's government. Have each group choose one member to act as recorder. Then assign each of the four sections of Chapter 7 to one or two students in every group. Have students review their assigned section and list major events and the consequences of those events for the nation's government. Have group members come together to discuss lists and reach agreement on the ten most important events and their consequences. Have the group recorder prepare the final list to be submitted.

Section Review Answers
Section 3, page 193

1. a) appointed on the last night of President Adams's term as part of the Federalists' attempt to maintain control of the federal courts. b) the first act of Congress to be declared unconstitutional by the Supreme Court. c) Chief Justice of the Supreme Court who asserted the right of the Supreme Court to review the constitutionality of laws and transformed the Court into a powerful institution. 2. The Federalists hoped to retain power by seeing that Federalists continued to hold government positions such as judgeships. As

7

part of this strategy, they created new judgeships and some minor judicial offices, and appointed people to fill these positions, just before Adams's term ended.
3. Chief Justice Marshall used the case of *Marbury* v. *Madison* to assert the Supreme Court's power of judicial review—that is, its power to rule on the constitutionality of acts of Congress. The Court has acted as guardian of the Constitution ever since, judging the actions of both the President and the Congress.
4. Samuel Chase's impeachment trial was important because it set a precedent that limited the offenses that could be considered grounds for impeachment. If Chase had been convicted, those in power might have been able to impeach political opponents for minor offenses.

CLOSE

To conclude the lesson, ask the class what view their text presents of the outcome of the impeachment trial of Samuel Chase. (Favorable—"Fortunately, the Senate decided that Chase's behavior did not amount to an impeachable offense . . . Every party in power would have tempted to use the tool of impeachment to destroy its political enemies," p. 192.) How might the trial's outcome have affected future court decisions?

Section 4 (pages 193–196)

Trouble on the Seas

FOCUS

To introduce the lesson, ask: How do you think the United States would react if some other nation cut off the flow of oil from, say, Saudi Arabia to the United States? Then point out the similarities to and differences from the situation in 1806–1807 with the British Orders in Council and the French imperial decrees.

Developing Vocabulary

merchant marine (page 194); **impressment** (page 194); **embargo** (page 195); **nonintercourse** (page 196)

INSTRUCT

Explain

Two issues of contemporary significance stand out in this section. First is the embargo as a weapon in international relations. Cite examples of recent embargoes. Another issue is the right of persons to leave their native land to seek a better life elsewhere. Cite current day examples.

☑ Writing Process Activity

Recognizing Ideologies Have students imagine that they are American sailors who fear impressment by the British navy. Ask them to compose a song or a poem about some aspect of the situation and their reactions to it. As they brainstorm ideas, students might consider a protest song, a sad lament of an American torn from his shipmates, or a narrative of a particular incident. As they revise, ask students to concentrate on arousing strong feelings of support or anger in their listeners. After they proofread, have students recite their song or poem to the class.

Section Review Answers

Section 4, page 196

1. a) British decrees that forbade ships of neutral countries to trade with ports controlled by France. b) French declarations that authorized the French navy to seize any ships that traded with Britain or that allowed themselves to be searched by the British. c) a confrontation between a British warship and the American warship, the *Chesapeake*. d) British practice of searching American ships, seizing sailors, and forcing them to serve in the British navy. e) British foreign secretary who responded to Jefferson's demand that Britain end impressment and apologize for the *Chesapeake* affair. f) a cutoff of trade. 2. Britain's Orders in Council, its policy of stopping and searching American ships and impressing sailors, and, more specifically, its behavior in the *Chesapeake* affair all angered Americans. 3. The Embargo Act prohibited American ships from sailing to foreign ports. It failed to force France and England to change their behavior, but it did have consequences in the United States. Although shipowners disobeyed the embargo, American trade was still devastated, and people were thrown out of work. The Republicans lost support in the northern states, and talk of secession rose again in New England. In 1809 the Embargo Act was replaced with the Nonintercourse Act, which forbade trade only with England and France. 4. The Republicans lost some of their widespread popularity by losing support in the New England states. 5. Both England and France tried to prevent neutral countries like the United States from trading with the other.

CLOSE

To conclude the lesson, discuss this question: What factors affected the foreign trade of the United States from 1800 to 1820? Ask students what general observations they might draw from this question about the following: Restrictions on exports (very unpopular; quickly repealed); the effect of sea war on trade (reduces volume); and the effect of a protective tariff on imports (reduces volume).

Chapter Review Answers

Focusing on Ideas

1. Depended on it to transport goods to earn their living; secured their access to the river. 2. Answers will vary. Jefferson took personal and party risks in purchasing Louisiana Territory. 3. 1804 landslide showed overwhelming approval of his reducing the national debt, increasing foreign trade, and purchasing Louisiana. 4. Shifted views on strict Constitutional interpretation when purchased Louisiana; on opposing Adams's "midnight judges" patronage by creating his own patronage; by allowing Bank of America to continue.

Taking a Critical Look

1. Conflicts over trade and customs rights would have caused tension, possibly leading to war. 2. Probably not. 3. Achievements: spokesman of democracy; opposition to Federalists, party of economic privilege; acquisition of Louisiana; standing up to Barbary pirates, giving U.S. a respectable international image. Failures: unsuccessful Embargo Act; economizing in national defense, perhaps leading to War of 1812; failure to encourage industry and manufacturing.

Your Region in History

1–3. Answers will vary depending on your region. Consult your local library or historical society.

Historical Facts and Figures

1806—Orders in Council, 1807—Embargo Act: By 1808, U.S. imports and exports had declined by two-thirds; U.S. commerce faced ruin. 1809—Embargo Act repealed. U.S. trade began to increase slowly.

7

Focusing the Chapter: Have students identify the chapter logo. Discuss what unit theme the logo might symbolize. Then ask students to skim the chapter to identify other illustrations or titles that relate to this theme.

Jefferson in Power

Four of the first five Presidents of the United States were Virginia men. These were Washington, Jefferson, Madison, and Monroe. We usually call them the "Virginia dynasty." They had faith in the people.

Why did so many of our nation's first leaders come from a single state? An explanation lies in the special features of colonial Virginia. Young aristocrats like Washington and Jefferson and Madison and Monroe led a cozy life. A few families owned the largest tobacco plantations and most of the slaves. They not only ran the government, but members of these lucky families might hold more than one office. George Washington, for example, was at the same time a church vestryman, a justice of the peace, a commander of the militia, and a delegate to the House of Burgesses. This was aristocracy American-style.

For Virginia's representative government there had to be elections. But these were very different from today's rough-and-tumble contests. In our day, anybody can run for office and nearly every adult can vote. But not in colonial Virginia! There only property owners could vote, and only the well-to-do were eligible for high office. Virginia had no cities where unruly immigrants or discontented working people could secure a share in government. Is it any wonder that Virginia's aristocrats had faith in what *they* called representative government? The only kind of representative government they knew was safe and sane. Even the ownership of slaves helped to reinforce their belief in "representative" government. It meant that their poor workers had no hope of voting or sharing in the government.

When these Virginia aristocrats talked of "the people," they meant substantial property owners like themselves and other smaller property owners who respected their "betters." We can understand why they had a great deal less fear of "the people" and a great deal more confidence that "the people" would choose good representatives than did other thoughtful Americans of that age. But northern leaders like John Adams and Alexander Hamilton knew the fickle big city mobs. They put their faith elsewhere.

Architect Benjamin Latrobe showed in this painting how he expected the Capitol to look.

See "Lesson Plan," p. 176C

1. The man and his policies

Thomas Jefferson became the President of a sharply divided country. The Federalists called him "godless" because he was no orthodox churchman, because he was so tolerant, and especially because he had supported the bloody French Revolution. They feared that this country too might soon be swept by a "reign of terror." But Thomas Jefferson's first term was to be one of the most successful presidencies in American history. A surprising number of Americans in all sections of the country were drawn into a united nation.

The new capital city. Jefferson was the first President of the United States to be inaugurated in the new capital, which his deal with Hamilton in 1790 had located on the Potomac River. The city had been laid out and surveyed in the following years. One of those who did this important job was Benjamin Banneker, a free black mathematician and scientist. Banneker was probably the first black civilian to work for the federal government.

The architect for the city had been a Frenchman, Major Pierre-Charles L'Enfant, who had served with the American army during the Revolutionary War. In 1801 the long vistas, grand avenues, and noble buildings he had envisioned for the wilderness were far from complete. Washington was only in its first stages of construction. The two wings of the new Capitol building, on a height overlooking the future city, were nearly finished, but the rotunda in the middle was still open to the skies. Since there were no hotels, the members of Congress stayed in nearby boardinghouses.

Between the Capitol and the President's house, one and a half miles away, lay swamp

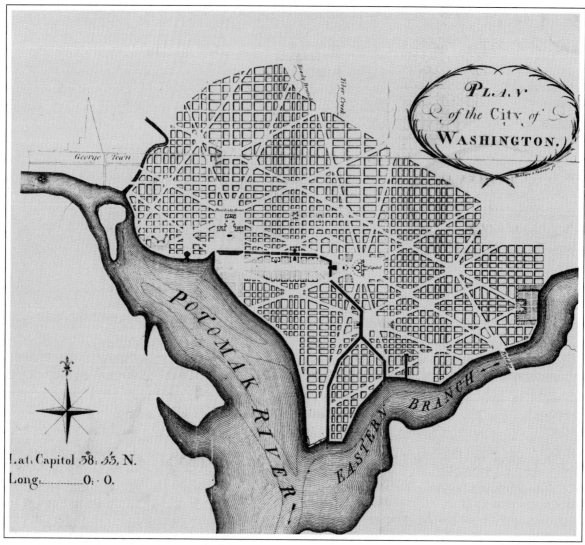

L'Enfant's 1792 plan of Washington showed broad avenues crisscrossing the capital.

and woodland crossed only by a muddy track which was grandly named Pennsylvania Avenue.

The President's "palace" was not yet known as the White House. It only got that name after it was burned by the British in the War of 1812. Then the Acquia Creek sandstone of which it was built was painted white to cover the scorch marks from the fire. The house was still unfinished in March 1801, but it had been lived in during the previous fall and winter by President Adams and his family. When the sharp-tongued

Abigail Adams saw the new capital city for the first time, she described it as having "houses scattered over a space of ten miles, and trees and stumps in plenty." Mrs. Adams estimated it would take 30 servants to run the "castle of a house" when it would be completed. Meanwhile, she dried the family wash in the unplastered East Room during stormy weather.

"We need nothing here," one senator reported, "but men, women, and other little trifles of the kind to make our city perfect." In sober fact this new federal city had no shops, no

Multicultural Connection: Washington, D.C. might not have been the admirably designed city it is if it had not been for Benjamin Banneker (1731–1806). This brilliant African American mathematician and astronomer was appointed by George Washington to the commission to survey and plan the new capital in the District of Columbia. When L'Enfant, the architect, left the commission because of a dispute with Washington, the plans for the city disappeared. Banneker was instrumental in reproducing the plans.

theaters, no libraries—and few people. The legislators suffered the discomforts of monks living in a monastery, but they had taken no monastic vows.

Thomas Jefferson. On March 4, 1801, the day of his inauguration, Thomas Jefferson stepped out the door of the boardinghouse where he was staying and walked the short distance to the Capitol. He was escorted by a crowd of congressmen and other citizens.

Looking like a "tall, raw-boned farmer," he avoided the pomp that Washington and Adams had thought necessary for the President. Six feet tall, thin and angular, with light-colored hair tinged with red, Jefferson, unlike his predecessors, did not wear a wig. His clothing was—depending upon your point of view—either casual or just plain sloppy.

In place of the formal weekly receptions begun by Washington there were now informal gatherings. Citizens, with or without invitations, thronged to shake the President's hand. But life in the White House was far from simple, for Jefferson was still a southern aristocrat. He liked to live well, and during his years in Paris he had developed a taste for elegant French cooking. At his gracious dinner parties in the President's mansion, his lucky guests enjoyed a French chef's masterpieces. These were washed down by French wines of choice vintages. In a single year Jefferson's wine bill came to $2800.

Relaxed and easygoing in a small company, Jefferson was a charming conversationalist. But he disliked crowds. He was a halting public speaker, and he generally avoided formal public speeches. He did not follow the practice—begun by Washington and Adams—of addressing Congress in person. Jefferson said that he did not want to act like a king speaking to Parliament from a throne. But perhaps this was just an excuse to save himself from the public appearances which he never enjoyed.

Jefferson believed that slavery was a great moral evil. Still, he saw no easy way to abolish the institution that supported the southern plantation system. "We have the wolf by the ears," he once wrote, "and we can neither hold him, nor safely let him go. Justice is in one

Kirby Collection of Historical Paintings, Lafayette College, Easton, PA

This portrait of Thomas Jefferson shows the Natural Bridge in Virginia, a spectacle which he much admired. His *Notes on Virginia* describes these natural wonders.

scale, and self-preservation in the other." He was himself the owner of large plantations and about 150 slaves. But unlike George Washington, he did not free his slaves upon his death.

A remarkably versatile man, Jefferson was also one of the best American architects of his

More from Boorstin: "[In line with his belief that America was destined to be an agricultural country,] Jefferson designed an American order of architecture—a column fashioned like a bundle of cornstalks, and a capital in the shape of leaves and flowers of tobacco." (From *The Lost World of Thomas Jefferson*)

David M. Doody/Tom Stack & Associates

Thomas Jefferson designed his home Monticello after an ancient Roman building that he saw in the south of France. It can be seen near Charlottesville, Virginia.

age. He designed his own home in Virginia, and throughout his life he worked to improve it. We can still visit the delightful Monticello and can enjoy the gardens he planned and planted. We can admire his ingenious contraptions including a clock two stories high, designed to alert the household to the hours of their duties. To this house he brought his beloved wife, Martha Wayles Skelton, in 1772. She bore six children—four of whom died in childhood. When she herself died only ten years after her marriage, Jefferson was plunged in grief. Partly to recover from this tragedy, he threw himself into an active public life.

Jefferson was also a surveyor, a philosopher, a scientist, and an inventor. At ease in French, Italian, and Spanish, as well as Latin and Greek, he corresponded with the eminent thinkers of his day wherever they were. He declared that they were all citizens of a worldwide ✂ "Republic of Letters."

The inaugural address. In his inaugural address Jefferson tried to play down the differences between himself and his opponents. He said they were "all Republicans, all Federalists"

in their devotion to the Union. He promised (1) "equal and exact justice to all men" of every shade of political and religious opinion; (2) friendship with all nations but no alliances; (3) respect for the rights of the states while still preserving the "constitutional vigor" of the national government; (4) encouragement of agriculture and commerce; (5) freedom of speech, press, and elections; (6) economy and honesty in the management of the country's finances.

This was hardly a program to frighten the Federalists. Jefferson saw that many Federalists were unhappy with their leaders and were ready to become Republicans if he followed a moderate course. Elected by only a narrow margin, he had to widen the base of his public support if he was to govern successfully.

In later years Jefferson called his election "the revolution of 1800." He believed that election had turned the country away from militarism and monarchy. But he probably exaggerated those dangers. John Adams had already saved the nation from militarism by avoiding war with France, and there was never a real threat of monarchy.

Jefferson, unlike Hamilton, did not want to

✂ Critical Thinking Activity: Demonstrating Reasoned Judgment What qualities made Jefferson an effective President? Explain that Thomas Jefferson was a writer, a politician, an inventor, an architect, a large landowner, and farmer. Ask if these interests and accomplishments made him a better President. Have students explain their opinions.

see an industrialized nation of cities. He hoped the country could remain a community of farmers who governed themselves in local assemblies. The government in Washington should confine itself, he thought, to managing the nation's dealings with foreign powers. Such a task could be performed by only a few public servants. Pursuing this policy, Jefferson aimed to reduce the army and navy and to apply the public revenue to paying off the public debt. No longer, Jefferson said, would the government "waste the labors of the people under the pretense of taking care of them."

For his Cabinet Jefferson selected the ablest men, including the architect of the Constitution, James Madison of Virginia, to be Secretary of State and Albert Gallatin, a brilliant Swiss-born financier from Pennsylvania, to be Secretary of the Treasury.

Following Jefferson's ideas Gallatin insisted on strict economy in government. He introduced a modern budget with specific sums for each item of national expense. The amount of money spent on the army and navy was reduced by half, and about 70 percent of the nation's revenue, more than $7 million a year, was used to pay off the national debt.

The Alien and Sedition Acts, which had expired at the end of the Adams administration, were not renewed. A new naturalization act was passed, restoring the short five-year waiting period for those who wanted to become citizens. The Bank of the United States was allowed to continue, as was the tariff. But the excise tax that had started the Whiskey Rebellion was repealed. There was not a great deal to distinguish Jefferson's policies from those of the Federalists.

The Barbary pirates. We remained at peace with the nations of Europe during Jefferson's first term. Our commerce and wealth increased rapidly. But one foreign problem grew more serious as our commerce expanded. For many years the Arab rulers of the Barbary States on the north coast of Africa (Morocco, Algiers,

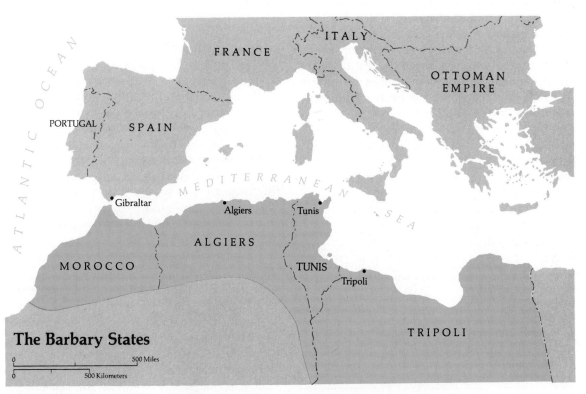

The Barbary States

0   500 Miles

0   500 Kilometers

⊕ **Geography and History: Regions** Using the map above, have students locate the North African countries that harassed American ships in the early 1800s. Discuss: Under what circumstances, if any, are appeasement and bribery acceptable as an alternative to war? In effect, we paid bribes for the release of the Bay of Pigs invasion survivors, the Pueblo sailors, and the embassy hostages in Iran. The United States has paid ransoms because of the high value we place on human life, although some say that the captives should have been sacrificed to avoid setting a precedent of paying ransoms.

Tunis, and Tripoli) had sent out pirates to seize ships on the ocean, especially in the Mediterranean Sea, and hold their crews for ransom. The European nations paid tribute to these pirates and kidnappers as a cheap substitute for war. And we had done the same. In the decade 1790–1800 we gave them "presents" amounting to $2 million.

(p. 181) Jefferson was determined to put an end to the payments to these racketeers. So in spite of his devotion to peace and economy, he sent naval squadrons to punish the pirates. This was a costly business, and Congress had to impose an extra 2.5 percent tax on imports as a "Mediterranean Fund." But the results justified the sacrifice. The peace concluded with Tripoli in January 1805 discouraged the piratical raids.

The other Barbary States continued to ask for payments, though at a lower rate, and after the War of 1812 this problem had to be faced again. In 1815 Stephen Decatur, who had been a hero in the earlier war with Tripoli, was sent with a fleet to the Mediterranean. He promptly seized two Algerian frigates. He then forced the Algerian ruler to sign a treaty renouncing both raids and tribute. Decatur also received similar guarantees from Tunis and Tripoli. Although in 1804 and in 1815 our navy had performed an international service, leading the world toward freedom of the seas, the problem of the pirates was not entirely solved until France conquered Algiers in 1830.

See "Section 1 Review answers," p. 176C.

Section 1 Review

1. Identify or explain: Benjamin Banneker, Pierre-Charles L'Enfant, Monticello, "revolution of 1800," Albert Gallatin, Barbary States, Stephen Decatur.
2. Who were the "Virginia dynasty"? How did they gain experience in public affairs and faith in representative government?
3. Characterize Thomas Jefferson.
4. **Critical Thinking: Identifying Central Issues.** Name several accomplishments in Jefferson's first term.

See "Lesson Plan," p. 176C.

2. Buying Louisiana

Jefferson's two basic political doctrines were strict adherence to the letter of the Constitution and severe economy in spending public money. He was a great leader because he could adapt his old beliefs to new needs without endangering the liberties of the people. Suddenly events in Europe caused him to stretch the Constitution as he had never thought would be necessary, and at one stroke to spend more money than any Federalist had ever dared.

The Mississippi River: artery for a continental nation. As more and more Americans settled between the Appalachian Mountains and the Mississippi River they floated their crops down many rivers—the Wisconsin, the Illinois, the Kaskaskia, the Wabash, the Miami, the Ohio, the Cumberland, the Yazoo, and still others. All these ran into what Americans called the "Father of Waters," the great Mississippi—down to the Gulf of Mexico, into the ocean, and out to the world. An enemy holding the mouth of the Mississippi could shut the Westerners off, destroy their trade, and make their crops useless.

President Jefferson understood this very well. His own state of Virginia was a land of many rivers. Jefferson wanted Americans to move out west over the mountains and start new farms, for he believed in the farmers' virtues. And the Mississippi River was the highway that made possible the life of the western farmer. When Jefferson became President, he began to worry over how to keep open the western Americans' highway to the world. It looked at first as though he would have to deal with Spain, which possessed the land on both sides of the mouth of the river.

Napoleon's dream. But suddenly everything changed. Napoleon, now dictator of France, had some grand and complex plans. He had a scheme to create a new French Empire in America. The former French lands west of the Mississippi had been named "Louisiana" after the French King Louis XIV. These lands had been ceded to Spain as a result of the wars of the

The Mississippi River Basin

☐ Drainage Area of the Mississippi River

0   500 Miles

0   500 Kilometers

GULF OF MEXICO

eighteenth century. Napoleon, who had won-derful powers of persuasion (reinforced by his large French armies), actually got the Spanish to give him back all of "Louisiana." For reasons of his own, this had been accomplished in secret.

When word leaked out that the Mississippi River was no longer controlled by weak and dec-adent Spain, but by the clever, powerful, and ambitious Napoleon, Americans were more wor-ried than ever. And they had good reason be-cause the French soon showed that they knew how to use New Orleans. They shrewdly made this gateway to the Mississippi into a kind of tollgate. The French understood that they could

extract whatever price they pleased for allowing Americans to pass through. To people who lived along the Mississippi River and its tributaries, the freedom to carry their produce out to the world was a matter of life and death.

When President Jefferson heard that France (p. 184) was taking control of the mouth of the Missis-sippi, he was upset. He wrote to Robert Living-ston, the American minister at Paris, that though the United States had always looked upon France as her "natural friend" there was

on the globe one single spot, the possessor of which is our natural and habitual enemy. It is New Orleans, through which the produce

🌐 **Geography and History: Regions** Have students look at the maps on this page to familiarize themselves with the Louisiana Territory. Into what body of water does the Mississippi River empty? (The Gulf of Mexico) Name three major rivers that empty into the Mississippi River? (The Missouri, the Ohio, the Arkansas) How much of the Mississippi River Basin was included in the Louisiana Purchase? (The portion west of the Mississippi)

In 1803 when this view was painted, New Orleans was small but bustling. The artist thought that as part of the United States the town would thrive.

of three-eighths of our territory must pass to market. . . . France, placing herself in that door, assumes to us the attitude of defiance. . . . The day that France takes possession of New Orleans . . . [we will be forced to] marry ourselves to the British fleet and nation.

Then Jefferson sent his friend James Monroe of Virginia as his special ambassador to France. Jefferson told Monroe and Livingston to buy from France the land at the mouth of the Mississippi or to find some other way to guarantee that western Americans could come in and out of their river. If there was no other way, they were to buy New Orleans and all the lands on the east bank of the river (then called West Florida). For this little piece Congress provided $2 million. But Congress told them they could pay up to $10 million if they had to.

Haiti upsets Napoleon's plans. Meanwhile, France was having trouble in the Caribbean. Before Napoleon could recapture the glories of the French Empire, he would have to retake the island of Haiti, then called Saint Dominique. Only the small western end of the island had been in the hands of the French before the French Revolution, yet it produced far more wealth for the empire than any other part.

Of the 600,000 people living on Haiti, 500,000 were slaves. They revolted during the French Revolution and slaughtered the whites. At that point, the French National Assembly abolished slavery and appointed the black genius Pierre Dominique Toussaint L'Ouverture as commander in chief of the armies on the island. Soon Toussaint ruled all of Haiti. But the French government got more than it bargained for. Toussaint had a mind of his own and would not be a lackey of the French. Napoleon, always

Continuity and Change: Economics Point out to students that American expansion has often been motivated by the need to protect trade. In 1803 Jefferson agreed to the purchase of the Louisiana Territory to protect American access to the Mississippi River and the port of New Orleans. A century later, in search of a faster way to move goods from ocean to ocean, Theodore Roosevelt secured the isthmus of Panama, across which the canal was dug to link the two oceans. (See page 541.)

mindful of military strategy, believed that he had to command the island if he was to build his grand new French Empire. Late in 1801 Napoleon sent out from France 25,000 crack troops under the command of his brother-in-law, General LeClerc, to conquer Toussaint and reduce the people of Haiti to slavery once again. At that point, the future of Louisiana, and perhaps of the United States, hinged on the actions of Toussaint L'Ouverture and his black followers.

As the second step in the revival of the French Empire, a great expedition was formed to sail for Louisiana in September 1802. But it never sailed because Haiti had not yet been reconquered. Toussaint was captured by treachery, but still the war went on. By January 1803 the French General LeClerc was dead of fever, Haiti was a ruin, and the French army had been destroyed by its black opponents and by yellow fever. Tons of expensive supplies had been lost. General Rochambeau, who succeeded LeClerc, wrote home that he must have 35,000 new troops to put down the blacks.

Napoleon decides to sell Louisiana. Napoleon was a man who could make up his mind quickly. He could change his mind just as quickly. Since he could not control Haiti, he wondered how he could hold huge Louisiana. Without telling anyone, he suddenly decided to get what he could for his American empire. When the Americans in Paris offered to buy the small piece of land around the entrance to the Mississippi River, there was an amazing reply. Napoleon would *not* sell or even rent them that little piece. But he *would* sell them the whole of Louisiana!

Napoleon's offer to sell all of Louisiana was the last answer Monroe and Livingston had expected. They were not prepared for it. What should they do? Should they simply tell Napoleon they could give no answer till they had word from the President and Congress back in Washington? That would take weeks—or maybe even months—and by then the changeable Napoleon might very well say the deal was all off. Or should they, for the sake of their country, do what they really had no power to

do? Should they snatch up this unexpected bargain and then pray that the people back home would support them?

This was one of the fateful moments of American history. It was not surprising that the French dictator had made a bold decision. But the young United States was a representative government under a Constitution that carefully described and limited the powers of the Congress. Could this self-governing nation match Napoleon's boldness? Or were the people of the Republic doomed to be slow and timid?

The American ministers in Paris, Livingston and Monroe, took the bold and dangerous way. They decided to take up Napoleon's offer. On their own judgment they offered $15 million for all Louisiana. And Napoleon accepted. As soon as the deal was closed, they began wondering whether what they would have to share was praise or blame. It was some years before either of them dared claim any credit for this move.

Jefferson makes a hard decision. When the news finally reached the United States, it was greeted by shock, delight, and dismay. These two Americans, some complained, had been sent to Paris simply to buy a small piece of land in order to keep the riverways open in the West. Instead, they had allowed a whimsical dictator to trap them into buying half a billion acres of worthless wilderness!

This was perhaps the greatest test of statesmanship that Jefferson ever had to face. He was on the spot. The Constitution said nothing at all about whether or how Congress could buy land from a foreign country. Again and again, in many other cases, Jefferson had argued that Congress had only those powers that the Constitution had assigned in so many words. Maybe the power to buy land from foreign countries had been left out of the Constitution *on purpose*—to prevent the United States from playing the dangerous, old-fashioned game of empire. The people of the new United States had tried to escape from the ways of the Old World, where the rulers were in the habit of buying and selling, bartering and gambling faraway lands and unknown peoples.

Now would Jefferson go against everything he

had been saying for years? If he had been weak, he would have been afraid to change his mind. But he decided to show the same courage that Livingston and Monroe had shown in Paris. It was harder for him, because he had to stand up and change his mind in public. All his enemies were there to hoot at him. Still, Jefferson decided to ask the members of Congress to vote the money to buy Louisiana. He asked them to forget technicalities—"metaphysical subtleties" is what he called them—and instead to think of the future of the nation. He asked the Congress to approve afterwards what it had not been foresighted enough to authorize in advance.

After long and bitter debate, the Congress agreed. In October 1803, when the Senate ratified the treaty with Napoleon, Louisiana became the property of the United States. Within a year, an American governor was sitting in New Orleans, where he could see that the Mississippi River would stay open. Western Americans would have their highway to the world.

A new world. The Louisiana Purchase was a triumph in more ways than we can count. It was one of the first modern proofs that in a battle of wits between a dictator and a government of the people the popular government does not need to lose. It showed that a people could have a Constitution to protect them against tyrants, and still make speedy decisions. If courageous leaders did what the nation needed, the people's representatives would approve.

And the Louisiana Purchase provided far more than a mere pathway from western America to the world. It helped make the new nation itself into a new world. The Louisiana Purchase *doubled* the area of the United States. It made it possible for Americans to keep going west— far across the Mississippi River. It made it possible to carry the Add-a-State Plan westward to the Pacific. It made it possible to build a continent-wide Empire for Liberty. Some people from eastern states had opposed Jefferson's purchase of Louisiana because they feared that too many new states might be carved out of the West. Then the United States would no longer be an Atlantic-seacoast nation. The original thirteen would no longer run the Union.

In time, thirteen new states and parts of states, some of the richest land in the nation, would be formed from the Louisiana Purchase. The timid Easterners were wrong in imagining what the United States ought to be. The first thirteen states were nothing but a beginning: a starting line for the race across North America to the Pacific. There had been other one-ocean nations. Ours was to be a two-ocean nation.

The exact outlines of what we had bought in the Louisiana Purchase were uncertain. No one, not Jefferson or even Napoleon himself, knew exactly how far Louisiana reached up north or out west. But these vague boundaries would be gateways for new states of the great new American Union. Napoleon had provided Americans with expandable boundaries for their Empire for Liberty. The Louisiana Purchase freed Americans from the sharp, confining western boundary of the Mississippi River. The nation would no longer be imprisoned by the borders of the old British Empire.

The Lewis and Clark expedition. The Louisiana Territory roused widespread interest, for it occupied about half of the vast expanse stretching 1700 miles from the Mississippi to the Pacific coast. Jefferson was curious about the area. Indeed, even before the purchase, he had made secret plans to explore the lands beyond the Mississippi. Now Congress appropriated $2500 "to send intelligent officers with ten or twelve men, to explore even to the western ocean." They were to look for a water route to the Pacific, to study the Indian tribes, the rocks, the plants, and animals of the region. The expedition, after passing the Rockies, would be moving into territory beyond the western boundary of the United States. But this did not appear to trouble the President. He chose (p. 187) his private secretary, a captain in the army named Meriwether Lewis, to lead the expedition. William Clark, the younger brother of George Rogers Clark, was his lieutenant.

Lewis and Clark, with about 40 men, including Clark's black servant York, started westward from the mouth of the Missouri River in the spring of 1804. They spent the winter of 1804–1805 at Fort Mandan, a trading post in

Multicultural Connection: Another, but less well-known, Native American woman guide was Marie Dorion (1781–1841), a member of the Iowa tribe. In 1811–1812 Marie Dorion helped guide a party that traveled 3,500 miles overland from St. Louis to Astoria, Oregon. While acting as a guide and interpreter, Dorion also had the added responsibility of her two children and, in fact, gave birth to a third on the trail. Unfortunately, the child died eight days later.

Lewis and Clark and Pike
Explore the West

← Route of Lewis and Clark

← Route of Pike

0 ————————— 500 Miles

0 ————————— 500 Kilometers

present-day North Dakota. There they hired Toussaint Charbonneau, a French-Canadian fur trapper, and his wife Sacajawea, a Sho-shone Indian, as interpreters. Sacajawea, carrying her infant child, guided the expedition and persuaded the Shoshones to help them. Without her, it is doubtful the expedition could have been successful.

During the summer of 1805, the explorers crossed the "Great Divide" in the Rocky Mountains, and by November they had reached the Columbia River, where they began a turbulent descent. On December 3, 1805, in a fierce, cold rainstorm they reached the Pacific Ocean.

There Clark carved on a tall yellow pine tree, "William Clark December 3rd 1805. By land from the U. States in 1804 and 1805."

This historic moment confirmed the claim of the United States to the whole Oregon region. The claim had been based on the discovery of the mouth of the Columbia River in 1792 by Robert Gray, captain of a fur-trading ship out of Boston. But the Lewis and Clark expedition did even more. It began to sketch in details of the vast heartland that the nation had purchased. The samples of rocks and plants and animals the explorers brought back revealed unsuspected natural treasures.

(p. 186)

(p. 188)

🌐 Geography and History: Movement Ask: Lewis and Clark followed what two rivers going west on their expedition? (The Missouri and Columbia rivers) What other river did they follow part of the way on their return trip? (The Yellowstone River) What major settlements did Pike pass through on his expedition of 1806–1808? (St. Louis, Santa Fe, Chihuahua, San Antonio, and Natchitoches)

In order to report on all they had seen, Lewis and Clark kept journals illustrated with drawings, such as this one of a wild fowl.

About the same time (1805–1807) the daring Captain Zebulon Pike, after exploring the upper Mississippi, ventured as far west as the Rockies. There he saw and described one of the continent's grandest mountains, which came to be called Pikes Peak. Then Pike turned southward. After he crossed into Spanish territory he was picked up by Spanish soldiers. They took him first to their settlement at Santa Fe and then on to Chihuahua. There they questioned him, took all his papers, and let him go. When Pike returned home, he gave the government valuable information on the number and types of troops that Spain had in the area.

Pike also wrote a description of the lands that he had crossed. From his report of wide sandy deserts came the misleading idea that these lands were not worth much—that the heart of the continent was "the Great American Desert."

The Federalist protest. The Louisiana Purchase relieved the economic fears of the western settlers and made Jefferson popular with them. But the Federalists saw the Purchase as a threat to their party and all they believed in. They feared that the settlers of the new lands would support the Jeffersonian Republicans. If those settlers were brought into the Union with all the rights of the earlier citizens of the United States, they would soon control Congress. Then the Federalist party would represent only a few states on the Atlantic fringe. The new states, they thought, would surely pass laws unfairly favoring farmers and debtors and damaging to the commercial and banking interests of the East.

In the spring of 1804 some New England Federalists, under the lead of Senator Timothy Pickering of Massachusetts, became desperate. They actually considered breaking up the Union and setting up a northern confederacy. When Hamilton opposed the idea, they turned to Aaron Burr and promised him the presidency of the new confederacy if he could bring in his state of New York.

Burr, who had not been renominated by his party for a second term as Vice-President, now ran as a Federalist for governor of New York. From this position, it was hoped, he could make the state part of the proposed confederacy. But Hamilton put his patriotism above his party loyalty. Distrusting Burr, he joined with the Republicans to keep the ambitious Vice-President out of a position where he might disrupt the Union.

Burr was badly beaten in the election. He blamed his loss on Hamilton, who had also helped to keep him from the Presidency in 1800. During the campaign, Burr claimed that Hamilton had expressed "a despicable opinion of him," and he used this as an excuse to challenge Hamilton to a duel. So it was that the two men faced one another with pistols on the banks of the Hudson River at Weehawken, New Jersey, early in the morning of July 11, 1804. After each had fired a shot, Hamilton fell mortally wounded. Washington's brilliant Secretary of the Treasury, the leader of the Federalist party, died the following day. Burr was forced to

See "Lesson Plan," p. 176C for **Writing Process Activity: Predicting Consequences** relating to the Lewis and Clark expedition.

flee murder charges in both New Jersey and New York. The secessionist plans of the New England Federalists soon collapsed.

The Burr conspiracy. After this, the public career of the charming and talented, but erratic and ambitious, Aaron Burr went steadily downward. Since his duel with Hamilton had destroyed his political position in New York, he sought a new career out west.

What Burr really intended to do has never been clear. He may have hoped to seize New Orleans and then set up an independent country there. Perhaps he planned to conquer northern Mexico and carve an empire out of Spanish territory. Maybe his aim was quite innocent— simply to plant a colony of the United States west of the Mississippi. It is possible that he did not know what he was going to do but hoped to grasp the main chance. For some of his schemes he actually tried to secure aid from both the British and the Spanish.

Burr's trips to the West finally aroused suspicion in Washington. Then Burr was betrayed by the governor of Louisiana, General James Wilkinson, who had been involved with Burr's plots. To save himself, Wilkinson reported a part of Burr's plans to Jefferson, who ordered Burr to be arrested.

Burr was charged with treason and tried in Richmond, Virginia, in August 1807. Although Jefferson was eager to have Burr convicted, Chief Justice John Marshall defined treason in such a way that Burr was acquitted. Later, Burr returned to his prosperous law practice in New York, where he lived to a ripe age.

The trial of Aaron Burr is a landmark in the history of American liberties. President Jefferson disliked Burr and probably would have been glad to see him jailed for any reason. But, under the constitutional definition of treason, it had to be proved that Burr was guilty of "levying war on the United States." Chief Justice Marshall, insisting on the letter of the Constitution, instructed the jury that Burr must have made open war on the country and that there had to be two witnesses to his act. Respecting these requirements, the jury failed to convict Burr. Marshall's strict definition was at least

partly due to his dislike of Jefferson. But, whatever his motives, the result was good for the nation. After the Burr precedent it would be difficult for the party in power to muzzle political opponents with a charge of treason. Ever since, trials for treason have been rare in the United States.

See "Section 2 Review answers," p. 176D.

Section 2 Review

1. Identify: Robert Livingston, James Monroe, Toussaint L'Ouverture, Sacajawea, Zebulon Pike, Aaron Burr, Timothy Pickering.
2. What was Napoleon's dream for Louisiana? How did events in Haiti upset his plans?
3. What were some of the major problems that Jefferson faced in asking Congress to approve the Louisiana Purchase?
4. How did the Louisiana Purchase change the United States?
5. What were the results of the Lewis and Clark expedition?
6. Why did some Federalists oppose the Louisiana Purchase?
7. **Critical Thinking: Drawing Conclusions.** What did Aaron Burr's trial accomplish?

See "Lesson Plan," p. 176D.

3. Jefferson, Marshall, and the courts

During his first term Jefferson had tried to keep the Federalists happy. He had been moderate in his approach to most problems. He had even managed to help New England merchants (mainstay of the Federalist party) by his attack on the Barbary pirates who were menacing their commerce. New England fishermen were pleased that he supported a bounty on codfish.

The "midnight judges" and the patronage. At one point, however, Jefferson directly attacked the Federalists. After their loss of the Presidency and of Congress in the 1800 elections, the Federalists tried to keep control of the federal courts and of as many other offices as possible. In the Judiciary Act of 1801, passed

National Portrait Gallery, Smithsonian Institution

Keen-witted and persuasive, John Marshall was Chief Justice of the United States for 34 years.

commissions on his final night in office. The last-minute appointees were sneeringly called "the midnight judges."

Adams had spent his last days seizing every chance to maintain Federalist influence by appointing many lesser officers: collectors of customs, consuls, postmasters, and clerks.

Jefferson was angered by this attempt of the defeated Federalists to keep "a dead clutch on the patronage." Once in office, he sent word to all those whose commissions had not yet been delivered to consider the appointments as never having been made. His first Congress then quickly repealed the Judiciary Act of 1801.

In this way began the first struggle between the political parties over the right to fill the offices of government with members of their own party. The struggle would never cease. The party going out of power always wanted to keep its supporters in office. Yet the victors in the election assumed that they had a right to appoint officials who supported their party. Jefferson naturally believed that he should have Republicans helping him in government offices if he was to do his best. Also this would help build a strong political party. After refusing to honor the commissions that Adams had signed at the end of his term, Jefferson picked Republicans for these posts. Whenever a job opened up due to a death or retirement, a Republican was appointed. In this way, by the end of his first term, Jefferson had named members of his own party to about half the highest positions in the government.

There was one position, however, that he had not been able to do anything about. The high office of Chief Justice of the Supreme Court was held by his cousin and fellow Virginian, John Marshall. In his personality and his manners Marshall was much like Jefferson. He was sloppy in his dress and easygoing. Like Jefferson he had a brilliant and vigorous mind. And like Jefferson he insisted on seeing things his own way. But there were hardly any issues on which the two great men agreed. Before Marshall's appointment, it did not seem that the Supreme Court would play a major role in shaping the new nation. But under Marshall's leadership the Court became an active force

just before they went out of power, they had actually increased the number of judges and added some minor judicial offices. They intended, of course, to fill these places with appointees from their own party before Jefferson and his Republicans took office on March 4. President Adams hastily nominated Federalists for the new positions, and they were quickly confirmed by the Senate. In order to put a small army of Federalists into these important permanent jobs, Adams signed some of their

protecting private property from state interference and building a strong central government.

Marbury *v.* Madison.   When Jefferson refused to deliver the commissions signed by Adams, he gave Chief Justice Marshall the chance he had been looking for. One of Adams's "midnight" appointees, William Marbury, applied to the Supreme Court for a writ (a written court order) commanding Secretary of State James Madison to deliver his commission (already signed and sealed by President Adams) as justice of the peace. Marshall used the case to assert—even to create—crucial powers for the Supreme Court. The case of *Marbury* v. *Madison*, heard by the Supreme Court in February 1803, would become a landmark in American history.

Chief Justice Marshall said that Marbury had a right to his commission as a justice of the peace. But he did not let the matter rest there. If he had, Marbury's name would be unknown in American history. Instead, Marshall went on to declare that the section of the Judiciary Act of 1789 that gave the Supreme Court the right to issue writs in cases like Marbury's was unconstitutional, since no such right was granted in the Constitution. As a result, Marshall concluded there was no way for Marbury to get his commission from Madison.

The important question, of course, was not whether the unknown William Marbury should hold the lowly office of justice of the peace. Of the greatest significance to the nation was whether the Supreme Court had the power to declare a law of the land unconstitutional. In his brilliant, if devious, decision the strong-willed Chief Justice answered that question with a resounding, epoch-making Yes!

The Founding Fathers had, in fact, assumed that the Supreme Court would have the power to declare acts of Congress unconstitutional. But they had not put that power in so many words in the Constitution. So by a strict reading of the Constitution the Court had no such right. Nor had it ever used the right since the Supreme Court was created in 1789. Now in 1803 the Court suddenly assumed the right of *judicial review* in its role as guardian of the Constitution. The leading role ever since of the Supreme Court in American history has followed from this bold decision of Chief Justice Marshall.

Enrichment Support File Topic

This small ornate room in the Capitol is where the Supreme Court met until 1860.

Office of the Supreme Court

The Supreme Court makes its decisions by a majority vote. In Marshall's day, when there were only six justices on the Supreme Court, any four of the justices had the power to over-rule the President and the Congress on the meaning of the Constitution. Today, when there are nine justices on the Court, this power rests in the hands of five justices. In few other nations have the courts held such powers.

An attempt to change the courts by impeachment. Jefferson and the Republicans feared the power of judges. They were appointed for life, and there was no way for the Jeffersonians—or anybody else—to remove them except by the long impeachment process. What guarantee was there that these judges (who did not owe their positions to the voters) would show a proper respect for the will of the majority? Of course the Republicans feared the judges more because so many happened to be Federalists.

The Republicans started impeachment pro-ceedings against several judges. Most impor-tant was their trial of Samuel Chase of the Supreme Court. Though a signer of the Decla-ration of Independence, Chase was open to at-tack. In his charges to juries in cases brought under the Sedition Act, he had gone out of his way to denounce Republicans. He called them "Jacobins" and "revolutionaries." The trial of Justice Chase before the Senate in January 1805 was especially dramatic. It was presided over by the flamboyant Vice-President Aaron Burr, who had only recently killed the famous patriot Alexander Hamilton. Burr took his role as judge seriously and conducted the trial with an even hand. All the while Jefferson, who felt his political prestige and power were at stake, was putting pressure on members of the Senate to convict Chase. Though the Republicans held a majority of seats in the Senate, Chase was acquitted.

The problem faced by the Senate was that the Constitution said (Art. III, sec. 1) that judges "shall hold their office during good behavior." But what did "good behavior" mean? Another section of the Constitution (Art. II, sec. 4) gave a clue. It declared that civil officers, meaning all government officers except those in the military, might not be impeached except for "treason, bribery, or other high crimes and mis-demeanors." Fortunately, the Senate decided that Chase's behavior did not amount to an impeachable offense.

If Chase had been convicted, the next candi-date for impeachment would probably have been Chief Justice John Marshall. And if Mar-shall had been impeached—simply because of an honest difference between him and the Pres-ident over the meaning of the Constitution—the government of the United States might have been very unlike what it has become. Again and again, every party in power would have been tempted to use the tool of impeachment to de-stroy its political enemies. A system of two strong and freely disagreeing political parties might never have survived.

The election of 1804. Few administrations in our history have been as successful as Jeffer-son's first term. Our foreign trade had doubled. The customs' receipts far outran Gallatin's esti-mates. In fact, the national debt was reduced by $25 million, even after paying for the Louisiana Territory. The country between the Alleghenies and the Mississippi was filling rapidly. Missis-sippi had become a territory in 1798. Indiana had followed in 1800. Ohio had enough people to become a state in February 1803.

Except for what Jefferson called "bickerings" with Spain over West Florida, an area Jefferson still wanted to make part of the United States, our relations with European nations were friendly. Our commissioners under Jay's Treaty had satisfied the British merchants by award-ing them more than $2.5 million in payment of long-standing debts from American citizens. We had compelled respect for the American flag by the Barbary pirates. We had acquired a vast domain west of the Mississippi.

The quarrelsome opposition of a few Federal-ists was drowned in the general chorus of ap-proval. It was no wonder that in the next elec-tion Jefferson carried all but one state. Of the 176 electoral votes cast, Jefferson received 162. He won in a landslide over South Carolina's C. C. Pinckney, the Federalist candidate.

Here was a President whose election four

📖 More from Boorstin: "The contempt for the judiciary which Jefferson expressed freely and re-peatedly had been occasioned by immediate political imitations, but it did betray his inability to feel respect for law. When judges crossed Jefferson's political aims, they became 'the corps of sappers and miners' working to undermine the independence of the states and to consolidate political power . . ." (From *The Lost World of Thomas Jefferson*)

❀ years before had brought predictions of the ruin of our commerce, the end of efficient government, and the destruction of the social order. The happy result of Jefferson's first term had been quite the opposite. When Jefferson took the oath of office a second time, on March 4, 1805, he congratulated his fellow countrymen that "not a cloud appeared on the horizon."

See "Section 3 Review answers," p. 176D.

Section 3 Review

1. Identify or explain: "midnight judges," Judiciary Act of 1789, John Marshall.
2. How did the Federalists seek to retain influence in the government after their defeat in 1800?
3. Why is *Marbury* v. *Madison* a landmark case?
4. **Critical Thinking: Determining Relevance.** Why was Samuel Chase's impeachment trial important to the future of the Supreme Court?

See "Lesson Plan," p. 176E.

4. Trouble on the seas

In the spring of 1803 war between England and France was renewed. In October 1805 Lord Nelson destroyed the combined French and Spanish fleets off Cape Trafalgar near the Strait of Gibraltar. A few weeks later Napoleon defeated the Russian and Austrian armies at Austerlitz. So, like the tiger and the shark, Napoleon was master of the continent of Europe, and England ruled the seas. What would this division of empires mean for the young United States?

British Orders and French decrees. Each of the two great powers now tried to damage the other by shutting off its commerce. The British issued *Orders in Council*, forbidding neutral ships to trade with ports under Napoleon's control on the continent. Napoleon replied with *imperial decrees* that authorized French seizure of all ships that traded with the British Isles or that allowed themselves to be searched by a British cruiser. Naturally, the British Orders

⊕ (p. 195)

Beginning in 1785, ships from the United States began to trade with China. Here the American flag flies with other flags over Canton, the only Chinese city open for foreign trade until 1842.

The Peabody Museum, Salem: photo by Mark Sexton

❀ See "Lesson Plan," p. 176D for **Cooperative Learning Activity: Expressing Problems Clearly** relating to Jefferson's presidency.

were more damaging to America since Britain controlled the seas, but both orders and decrees cost Americans ships and cargoes.

The commerce of the United States was threatened with ruin. As a neutral nation willing to trade with all nations, we had profited from the wars in Europe by building up a prosperous foreign trade throughout the world. The sturdy American sailing ships were the favorite carriers for the merchandise of South America, the West Indies, and the Far East to all the ports of Europe. Our own exports too—the fish and lumber of New England, the cotton and rice of the South, the wheat and livestock of the trans-Allegheny country—had increased threefold since Washington took office.

Our merchant marine was growing at a rapid rate. So many new ships were added in 1805 that 4200 more sailors had to be hired. Sailors' wages rose from $8 to $24 a month. To share this prosperity, hundreds of foreign seamen, mostly British, became naturalized citizens of the United States. They wanted to escape the brutal discipline of the British navy. They wished to enjoy the higher pay, better food, and more humane treatment found on American vessels. But this brought some unexpected new problems.

The Chesapeake *affair.* The United States frigate *Chesapeake*, Captain Barron commanding, weighed anchor from Norfolk, Virginia, on June 22, 1807. She was bound on the long voyage to the Mediterranean, so her guns were still unmounted and her decks littered with tackle. Shortly after the *Chesapeake* reached the sea, the British warship *Leopard* overtook her. *Leopard* tricked *Chesapeake* into stopping by saying that they had dispatches for her. After the *Chesapeake* had heaved to, the *Leopard* demanded to be able to search the American ship for deserters from the British navy. Captain Barron refused and the British vessel thereupon poured three full broadsides into the *Chesapeake*, killing three men and wounding eighteen, before Captain Barron could reply. Unprepared to resist, Captain Barron struck his colors after firing a single gun.

Then the British officers took four alleged deserters from the American frigate. They left her to limp back into Norfolk with her dead and wounded.

The impressment of American seamen. Napoleon showed no more respect than England had shown for American rights on the sea. But he did not have the cruisers to capture our ships on the high seas, to force them to France to pay duties, or to search them for departing sailors. All he could do was to seize our ships in his continental ports and sell their cargoes for the benefit of his treasury. Compared to the British, the French could do the American merchant marine very little damage.

In its desperate struggle with Napoleon, Great Britain needed every man who could be found to serve in the navy. It mattered little that the sailor had American naturalization papers. British law did not allow a British subject to switch his loyalty to another country. Furthermore, many of the naturalization papers were forged.

No one knows just how many legitimate American citizens were taken off United States ships by the British impressment officers. Shortly before the United States went to war with Great Britain in 1812, President Madison told Congress that more than 6000 American seamen had been "impressed and held in bondage" during the preceding years. And this was probably a good estimate.

Jefferson's difficulty. The British firing on the *Chesapeake* in June 1807 caused a storm of fury in the United States. Had he wished it, Jefferson could have had war in a minute. But Jefferson did not want war. Instead, he at once ordered British warships to stay out of our waters. He also sent orders to James Monroe, our minister in London, to demand an apology for the attack on the *Chesapeake* and an end to impressment.

The British were in no mood for the complete surrender that Jefferson demanded. Their government was determined to let nothing stand in the way of crushing Napoleon. "An insignificant

See "Lesson Plan," p. 176E for **Writing Process Activity: Recognizing Ideologies** relating to the impressment of American sailors by the British.

Napoleonic Europe

- French Empire
- Dependent on Napoleon
- Allied with Napoleon
- ✕ Battle Sites

0   500 Miles

0   500 Kilometers

and puny power," as one newspaper called the United States, certainly could not be allowed to interfere with Britain's control of the seas.

The reply of the British foreign secretary, George Canning, came in December 1807. Canning wished to avoid war and was eager to right the wrong done by the attack on the *Chesapeake.* Indeed, the admiral whose orders led to that attack had already been dismissed from his command. But on the crucial question of the right of search and impressment, the British ministry would not yield.

The embargo. Cutbacks in the army and navy under Jefferson left them too weak to fight a war. Jefferson figured that our trade was so important to the nations of Europe that we would not need to fight for what we wanted. If

we cut off our trade, they would be sure to do as we wished. Now he decided to try this form of "peaceful coercion" to bring both Britain and Napoleon to terms.

On December 17, 1807, Jefferson asked Congress for a law prohibiting any American vessel from sailing for any foreign port. Congress quickly passed the Embargo Act by large majorities.

The Embargo Act failed to scare Britain and France into a change of policy. It would take time for the British and the French merchants and workers to be hurt by the loss of our trade. But by that time, the embargo might then have destroyed the very American commerce it was designed to protect.

Soon there were signs that the merchants' worst fears were well founded. Ships were tied

🌐 **Geography and History: Interaction** Refer students to the map above. Have them list the countries dependent on Napoleon. Ask: In which country was the Battle of Austerlitz fought? (Austria) Battle of Moscow? (Russia) Where was the only sea battle fought? (Trafalgar) Why do you think it was fought there? (close to the strategic Strait of Gibralter)

THE IMPRESSMENT OF AN
American Sailor Boy,

The New-York Historical Society

Americans sang songs like this protesting British impressment of American seamen.

up at the wharves. Merchandise spoiled in warehouses. Thousands of people in the shipping ports were thrown out of work. Planters and farmers saw their exports of cotton, tobacco, rice, wheat, corn, and livestock fall off sharply. Our foreign trade during the "embargo year" of 1808 shrank to one-third of its value in 1807.

The farmers and the laborers, who had formed the chief support of the Republicans in the northern states, now began to desert the party. Shipowners disobeyed the embargo. Town meetings in New England passed resolutions of protest. Once again there was serious talk of New England leaving the Union.

But the increasing numbers of people on the frontier across the Appalachians had a different point of view. They thought the British were arming the Indians against them. Frightened and angry, they had little use for such soft measures as an embargo. They wanted war. They even talked of capturing Canada.

The embargo repealed. The year 1808 was an election year. Jefferson wanted his Secretary of State, James Madison, to succeed him. He per-

suaded the Republican members of Congress to pick Madison as the party's candidate. A congressional caucus (party meeting) was the usual nominating method at that time. But the election looked very doubtful. "The Federalists will turn us out by the 4th of March next," Albert Gallatin wrote in June. Yet these fears proved unfounded. True enough, as expected, Madison lost every New England state except Vermont. But the South and the West stood by him, and Madison defeated his Federalist opponent, again General C. C. Pinckney, by 122 electoral votes to 47.

In spite of their impressive victory, the Republicans could see that the embargo was destroying their broad support in the nation and was wrecking their party. On March 1, 1809, three days before Jefferson left office, the Republican Congress repealed the embargo. In its place they passed a Nonintercourse Act that forbade trade only with Great Britain and France. Furthermore, Congress authorized the President to reopen trade with either country should it cease to violate our neutral rights.

Jefferson continued to believe that, if the embargo had been kept in force, Great Britain and France would have come to respect American rights. He thought that the embargo had not been given a fair test. He hated war, for he thought that commerce was the proper weapon of civilized people.

See "Section 4 Review answers," p. 176E.

Section 4 Review

1. Identify or explain: Orders in Council, imperial decrees, *Chesapeake* affair, impressment, George Canning, embargo.

2. What British actions at sea angered a great number of Americans?

3. What was the Embargo Act? Describe its results. What law replaced it?

4. What effect did the Embargo Act have on the 1808 election?

5. **Critical Thinking: Recognizing Cause and Effect.** How did war in Europe affect American commerce?

Continuity and Change: Economics Explain to students that there has been a tradition of protest against restrictions of American trade. People protested and disobeyed Jefferson's Embargo Act, much as they had the Navigation Acts and Stamp Act before the Revolutionary War. The laws and protests of both periods resulted in a sharp decline in foreign trade, unemployment, and spoiled goods. In both cases, the people's intolerance of economic sanctions led the nation into war with Great Britain. (See page 79.)

Chapter 7 Review

See "Chapter Review answers," p. 176F.

Focusing on Ideas

1. Why was control of the Mississippi vital to the western settlers? How did the Louisiana Purchase affect this situation?

2. Find examples in this chapter in which political leaders put their personal or party interests ahead of what seems to have been the national interest. Can you find an example in which someone put the national interest above personal or party advantage?

3. How did Jefferson's presidential victory in 1804 compare to his first election in 1800? What factors contributed to the change?

4. American Presidents have often shifted from the views they expressed before taking office. What turnabouts did Jefferson make and why?

Taking a Critical Look

1. **Predicting Consequences.** If the United States had not bought the Louisiana Territory, would it have been difficult for the United States to maintain good relations with a French neighbor on the western side of the Mississippi? Explain.

2. **Drawing Conclusions.** Would the United States have an effective system of checks and balances if the Supreme Court had never asserted its right to declare acts of Congress unconstitutional?

3. **Determining Relevance.** In 1962, a panel of 75 historians ranked Thomas Jefferson as one of five "great" Presidents of the United States. What achievements, in order of their importance, would merit such a rating? What failures or mistakes did Jefferson make that you would expect such a panel to consider in arriving at a fair judgment?

Your Region in History

1. **Geography.** If your state became part of the United States as a result of the Louisiana Purchase, what were some noteworthy features of the land and native population?

2. **Culture.** How was your state influenced by English culture? By French culture? By Spanish culture?

3. **Economics.** If your state is east of the Mississippi, how and to what extent was it probably affected by Jefferson's embargo?

Historical Facts and Figures

Determining Relevance. Using information in Chapter 7 and data from the graph, determine which of the events listed below seem to have had an impact on the volume of American exports and imports. Explain how this impact is reflected on the graph.

1803 The Louisiana Purchase
1806 Imperial Decrees and Orders in Council
1807 The Embargo Act
1808 James Madison elected President
1809 Embargo Act repealed
1811 Battle of Tippecanoe
1812 War of 1812

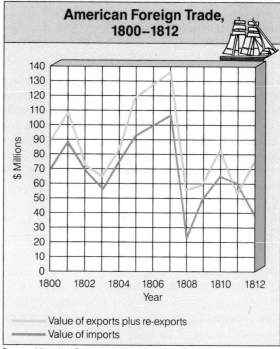

Source: *Historical Statistics of the United States*

Chapter 8
Struggles of a Young Nation

Identifying Chapter Materials

Objectives	Basic Instructional Materials	Extension Materials
1 The War of 1812 ▪ Identify the causes of, objections to, and course of, the War of 1812. ▪ Point out differing views among historians on the main causes of the war.	**Annotated Teacher's Edition** ▪ Lesson Plans, p. 198C **Instructional Support File** ▪ Pre-Reading Activities, Unit 3, p. 15 ▪ Skill Application Activity, Unit 3, p. 19	**Documents of American History** ▪ Macon's Bill, No. 2, Vol. 1, p. 204 ▪ Madison's War Message, Vol. 1, p. 207 ▪ Report and Resolutions of the Hartford Convention, Vol. 1, p. 209 **American History Transparencies** ▪ Geography and History, pp. B31, B33
2 Madison and Monroe ▪ Cite reasons for the growth of nationalism and sectionalism under Presidents Madison and Monroe. ▪ Explain significant decisions reached by Chief Justice John Marshall during his tenure on the Supreme Court. ▪ Discuss the implications of these decisions.	**Annotated Teacher's Edition** ▪ Lesson Plans, pp. 198C–198D **Instructional Support File** ▪ Skill Review Activity, Unit 3, p. 18	**Documents of American History** ▪ Madison's Veto of Bonus Bill, Vol. 1, p. 211 ▪ The Rush-Bagot Agreement, Vol. 1, p. 213 ▪ *McCulloch* v. *Maryland*, Vol. 1, p. 213 **American History Transparencies** ▪ Geography and History, pp. B13, B15, B17
3 The Missouri Compromise ▪ Explain why the Missouri Compromise was only a temporary solution to the issue of balance between slave and free states. ▪ Describe the effects of the Compromise on the territories of Kansas, Nebraska, and Oregon.	**Annotated Teacher's Edition** ▪ Lesson Plans, pp. 198D–198E	**Documents of American History** ▪ The Missouri Compromise, Vol. 1, p. 224
4 The Monroe Doctrine ▪ State the four principles that make up the Monroe Doctrine and explain its significance. ▪ Explain the historical situations in Europe and Latin America at the time of the Monroe Doctrine.	**Annotated Teacher's Edition** ▪ Lesson Plans, p. 198E	**Documents of American History** ▪ The English Background of the Monroe Doctrine, Vol. 1, p. 234 ▪ The Monroe Doctrine, Vol. 1, p. 235
5 A National Spirit ▪ Describe the national spirit that flourished in the 1820s, and give examples of its manifestations. ▪ Explain the meaning of nationalism.	**Annotated Teacher's Edition** ▪ Lesson Plans, pp. 198E–198F **Instructional Support File** ▪ Reading Activities, Unit 3, pp. 16–17 ▪ Critical Thinking Activity, Unit 3, p. 20 ▪ Chapter Test, Unit 3, pp. 21–24 ▪ Additional Test Questions, Unit 3, pp. 25–28	**Enrichment Support File** ▪ Proud to Be American: A New Spirit of Nationalism (See "In-Depth Coverage" at right.) **Suggested Secondary Sources** ▪ See chart at right.

Providing In-Depth Coverage

8

Perspectives on American Nationalism

In the wake of the American Revolutionary War and the War of 1812, Americans, despite sectional differences, found themselves more united than ever before by a sense of pride in themselves and their country.

Chapter 8 focuses on this spirit of nationalism in the early nineteenth century and its expression through slogans, symbols, and national heroes.

For this chapter, *A History of the United States* as an instructional program provides two types of resources you can use to offer in-depth coverage of nationalsim in America: the *student text* and the *Enrichment Support File.* A list of *Suggested Secondary Sources* is also provided. The chart below shows the topics that are covered in each.

THE STUDENT TEXT. Boorstin and Kelley's *A History of the United States* discusses the spirit of nationalism found in early-nineteenth century America.

AMERICAN HISTORY ENRICHMENT SUPPORT FILE. This collection of primary source readings and classroom activities reveals the spirit of nationalism in America.

SUGGESTED SECONDARY SOURCES. This reference list of readings by well-known historians and other commentators provides an array of perspectives on the spirit of nationalism in America. (See the chart below.)

Locating Instructional Materials

Detailed lesson plans for teaching American nationalism as a mini-course or to study one or more elements of nationalist spirit in depth are offered in the following areas: in the *student text*, see individual lesson plans at the beginning of each chapter; in the *Enrichment Support File*, see page 3; for readings beyond the student text, see *Suggested Secondary Sources.*

IN-DEPTH COVERAGE OF AMERICAN NATIONALISM		
Student Text	**Enrichment Support File**	**Suggested Secondary Sources**
▪ Nationalism, p. 161 ▪ National words, slogans, and symbols, p. 180 ▪ Revolutionary war heroes, p. 180 ▪ Nationalism and education, pp. 180–181 ▪ Noah Webster, pp. 180–181 ▪ Jedidiah Morse, p. 181	▪ Lesson Suggestions ▪ Multimedia Resources ▪ Overview Essay/Proud to be American: A New Spirit of Nationalism ▪ Literature in American History/ "The Prairies" ▪ Songs in American History/"Hail America" ▪ Primary Sources in American History/ "The Prospect Before Us" ▪ Art in American History/ The Hudson River School ▪ Simulation/Creating an American Symbol ▪ Making Connections	▪ *The Awakening of American Nationalism, 1815–1828* by George Dangerfield, pp. 1–35. ▪ *The Era of Good Feelings* by George Dangerfield, pp. 105–121. ▪ *Mr. Madison's War: Politics, Diplomacy, and Warfare in the Early American Republic, 1793–1830* by J.C.A. Stagg, pp. 3–47, 501–518. ▪ *The Republic Reborn: War and the Making of Liberal America, 1790–1820* by Steven Watts, pp. 3–108.

The War of 1812

FOCUS

To introduce the lesson, ask students what the main idea is of the first paragraph under the heading "The War of 1812" on page 199. (The War of 1812 was peculiar, but the United States emerged from it stronger.)

Developing Vocabulary

The words listed are essential terms for understanding this section. The page number after each term indicates the page of its first or most important appearance. These terms are defined in the text Glossary (text pages 1000–1011).

status quo (page 207)

INSTRUCT

Explain

The War of 1812 was favored by the West and South and opposed by New England. Reasons given for the war included blockades, incitement of the Indians, and impressment.

★ Independent Activity

Recognizing Cause and Effect Tell students that as the nation moved toward war, many of its people were moving westward. As they did so, Indians were pushed further west. Have students write a 500-word research report on the Tecumseh Confederation. The report should include details about who formed the Confederation and why, the area it covered, what it accomplished, and what happened to it.

Section Review Answers

Section 1, page 209

1. a) reopened trade with Britain and France and authorized the President to reimpose an embargo on either nation if the other lifted its restrictions on American commerce. b) helped lead the War Hawks. c) another leader of the War Hawks. d) a politician and warrior of the Shawnee Indians who formed a confederation to preserve Indian lands. e) Tenskwata, Tecumseh's brother and a religious visionary. He helped form the Indian confederation. f) captured the British ship *Macedonia*. g) defeated in the presidential election of 1812. h) uttered the famous words "Don't give up the ship." i) defeated the British on Lake Erie and reported "We have met the enemy and they are ours." 2. The following places are shown on the map on page 203: Tippecanoe, Fort Dearborn, the Thames River, Put-in-Bay, Fort McHenry. York is

now called Toronto, which is shown on the map on page 949. 3. The War Hawks championed nationalism and westward expansion, and they argued that the British and Spanish were inciting the Indians to attack western settlers. They wanted the United States to capture Canada. 4. Fort Dearborn and Detroit (which were British victories); the *Constitution* and the *Guerriere* and the *United States* and the *Macedonia* (American); the *Chesapeake* and the *Shannon* (a British victory); at Put-in-Bay on Lake Erie (American); at the Thames River (American); at Washington, D.C., (British); at Baltimore and Fort McHenry (American); on Lake Champlain (American victory); and at New Orleans (American). 5. The treaty provided for a return to the conditions that existed before the war and included an agreement that certain issues would be settled later. 6. Federalists and New Englanders led the opposition. Every coastal state north of Maryland voted against Madison in 1812—which meant voting against the war. New England gave little money to finance the war. In 1814 delegates from New England states met at the Hartford Convention where they denounced the war. 7. It began after the official reason for it had ceased to exist; because the main victory of the United States occurred after the peace treaty had been negotiated; and because the treaty changed little, if anything.

CLOSE

To conclude this lesson, ask students which argument seems stronger on the main cause of the War of 1812. This discussion should be wide open, and should probably reach no conclusions.

Madison and Monroe

FOCUS

To introduce the lesson, ask the students: Who was John Marshall? In this section several cases decided by Marshall's Court are explained.

Developing Vocabulary

specie (page 210); **dividend** (page 211); **diplomacy** (page 212); **ultimatum** (page 213).

INSTRUCT

Explain

Remind students of how the ocean tied the southern plantation economy to England (pp. 53–54). Planters opposed tariffs because they did not want to pay higher prices for imported goods.

Writing Process Activity

Drawing Conclusions Ask students to imagine that they are Southerners who have changed their mind about supporting the Bank of the United States. Before they write an editorial explaining this change, ask them to list their ideas about why the second Bank is important. Students should begin their editorials with a strong topic sentence summarizing their reasons. Ask them to revise for unity and coherence and to proofread carefully. Students can share and discuss their editorials in small groups.

Section Review Answers

Section 2, page 214

1. a) name given to Madison's program for national development. b) new industries. c) a plan to pay for new roads and canals. d) the phrase used to describe the period of nationalism that began with Monroe's inauguration. e) an 1817 pact between Great Britain and the United States banning warships on the Great Lakes. f) settled territorial disputes between the United States and Spain. 2. It proposed measures that would strengthen national institutions and included something for every section. 3. (a) The North supported a protective tariff because it would help new industries. The South opposed a tariff because the South imported finished goods. The West was neutral on the tariff. (b) The North opposed federal funding of internal improvements because northern states could pay for their own improvements. The South and especially the West supported federal funding of internal improvements because they needed help to pay for them. (c) The North opposed the national bank because it had become a Republican idea. Southerners supported the national bank. Some Westerners preferred state banks because they were providing cheap money. 4. Madison vetoed the Bonus Bill because the Constitution does not specifically grant the federal government the power to finance internal improvements. 5. In 1817 Great Britain and the United States agreed not to fortify the Great Lakes. In 1818 they agreed that the 49th parallel would mark the boundary between the United States and Canada as far west as the Rockies and that the two countries together would occupy the Oregon territory jointly for ten years. 6. General Jackson took over Florida. The Adams-Onís Treaty resulted. The United States acquired Florida; the boundary dispute concerning the Louisiana Territory was settled; the United States gave up its claim to Texas; and Spain abandoned its claim to the Pacific Northwest. 7. Marshall's decisions established the supremacy of the national government and provided a means for the Constitution to grow and change with the needs of the nation.

CLOSE

To conclude the lesson, ask the students: What view does the text present of President Madison? (Unfavorable.) What view does the text present of John Quincy Adams as Secretary of State? (Favorable.)

Section 3 (pages 214–216)

The Missouri Compromise

FOCUS

To introduce the lesson, write the following terms on the chalkboard: *compromise, truce, stalemate*. As they read, ask students to decide if the Missouri Compromise a true compromise, a truce, or a stalemate.

INSTRUCT

Explain

Tell students that two territories formed out of the Unorganized Territory were Kansas and Nebraska, both of which would leave the decision of whether to be a slave or a free state up to the citizens. Show students how this would violate the terms of the Missouri Compromise.

❧ Cooperative Learning Activity

Identifying Alternatives Post the following statements: 1) Western farmers needed new lands where they could grow crops without careful cultivation. 2) Slavery was necessary for Southern prosperity. Pair students and assign one statement to each pair. Explain that partners will work together to write a reaction to the assigned statement. The reaction may support or oppose the statement, but must explain student's thinking. When all pairs have prepared their reactions, have students read and discuss them. In the discussion, ask students to suggest alternative courses of action to those presented in the statements.

Section Review Answers

Section 3, page 216

1. The Missouri Compromise was designed to maintain a balance of power between proslavery and antislavery forces in the Senate. Missouri was admitted to the Union as a slave state while Maine was admitted as a free state; in the rest of the lands of the Louisiana Purchase, slavery was prohibited north of the southern boundary of Missouri (parallel 36°30″), except in Missouri itself. 2. (a) Eli Whitney's cotton gin allowed plantations to produce cotton very profitably so long as they had the necessary labor supply.

Slaves provided that supply. (b) As the cotton industry grew, planters sought more land; they moved west, bringing slaves with them.

CLOSE

To conclude the lesson, discuss in what cases compromise is appropriate and in what cases, if any, it is not. (Nuclear war? Death penalty? Proposed legislation? Murder cases? Sharing the last piece of cake?) Ask: Is it ever better not to compromise?

Section 4 (page 217)

The Monroe Doctrine

FOCUS

To introduce the lesson, ask students to describe the reaction of the United States if the Soviet Union tried to overthrow the government of Mexico. Explain that the cornerstone of United States policy in reaction to European interference in the Americas is the Monroe Doctrine.

INSTRUCT

Explain

The newly independent nations of Latin America sought security against attack by European powers. Spain was too weak to reconquer its former colonies, but in the early 1820s the Holy Alliance (Austria, Russia, Prussia, and France) authorized France to intervene on Spain's behalf. Fortunately for the United States, Great Britain's desire (backed up, of course, by its great naval power) to keep the Latin American nations independent so it could exploit them commercially prevented France from attacking Spain's former American possessions.

☑ Writing Process Activity

Identifying Central Issues Ask students to imagine that they live in a European country in 1823 and have just learned about the Monroe Doctrine. In preparation for writing a letter to an American business associate, have students brainstorm the benefits and drawbacks of the doctrine to both sides. Students should begin their letters with a sentence summarizing their reactions. After they have proofread, have students read their letter to the class.

Section Review Answers

Section 4, page 217

1. Monroe believed that the President should define the nation's role in foreign affairs and carry out the laws made by Congress. 2. The Monroe Doctrine said that the United States would guarantee the independence of the new republics of Latin America and would not interfere with European concerns. 3. The United States did not have the power to enforce the Monroe Doctrine. It coincided with British foreign policy at the time and therefore would be supported by the British fleet. 4. Yes; the United States did not want other European countries helping Spain to reclaim its Latin American possessions once those colonies had broken away from Spain.

CLOSE

To conclude the lesson, ask: Does the Monroe Doctrine give the United States the right to interfere in the affairs of Latin American nations? Did the Monroe Doctrine prevent Europeans from intervening in Latin America?

Section 5 (pages 218–220)

A National Spirit

FOCUS

To introduce the lesson, find recordings of "America the Beautiful," "The Star-Spangled Banner," "This Land is Your Land," and "America." Play them as the students come into class. After they are seated and have listened to all the patriotic music, begin the lesson by announcing that the topic for the day is nationalism. Have the class develop a definition of nationalism in a discussion. (Nationalism is pride in and devotion to one's country before all others.)

Developing Vocabulary

citizen (page 218)

INSTRUCT

Explain

A strong national spirit flourished in the United States in the 1820s. It found expression in slogans, songs, and symbols, and in reverent attitudes toward the Constitution.

★ Independent Activity

Making Comparisons Have students fold a sheet of paper in half lengthwise to make two columns. Tell students that in the first column they will list 5 ways in which people expressed their nationalism in the 1820s. In the second column they will list 5 ways in which people express their nationalism today.

Section Review Answers

Section 5, page 220

1. The flag, the bald eagle, and the sharpshooting rifleman in buckskin became symbols of the nation;

"liberty," "freedom," and "union" became national slogans. 2. All these men reflected and promoted nationalism by creating works that encouraged Americans to learn about and take pride in distinctively American topics.

CLOSE

To conclude the lesson, select details from the section and have students tell how each provides information to support the hypothesis that a national spirit was alive in the years after the War of 1812.

Chapter Review Answers

Focusing on Ideas

1. 1817—Rush-Bagot Agreement on unfortified borders with Canada; 1818—Agreement with British on U.S. northern boundaries and joint occupation of Oregon; 1819—Adams-Onís Treaty with Spain. Compromises with Britain benefited both parties. Spain was in no position for war; areas difficult to govern; and U.S. willing to buy rather than fight. 2. Madison: Embargo—lifted against France but enforced against Britian; Bonus bill—vetoed. Monroe: Supported Jackson acts in Florida, sent Spain an ultimatum; declared "hands off" doctrine for Latin America. 3. To form a confederation to block advance of whites into Indian territory.

Taking a Critical Look

1. The Compromise at least limited the spread of slavery. 2. Symbols and slogans inspire national feeling. 3. "Flag waving"—use of patriotic slogans, anthems, hero worship—less pronounced today. Nationalism aroused now by international sports, insults of foreigners (hostage-taking), national elections.

Your Region in History

1–3. Answers will vary depending on your region. Consult your local library or historical society.

Historical Facts and Figures

(a) All increased, the West most dramatically. (b) U.S. continued to expand; Western region grew very rapidly. (c) Population will continue to increase in West followed by North. (d) Americans continued to move west; North's need for industrial labor increased.

8

Struggles of a Young Nation

The presidencies of Madison and Monroe were marked by the growth in American minds of two opposite sentiments. The first was *nationalism*, the sentiment that binds people to their country and makes them feel that from it all their blessings flow. But growing along with nationalism was the spirit of *sectionalism*. This was the belief that your section of the country, be it the North, the South, or the West, was where you actually owed your loyalty and your love. During the last years of the Virginia dynasty of Presidents, national enthusiasm—fed by war, foreign affairs, and visions of a great future for the United States—was growing rapidly. But lurking in the background, ready to leap out at any moment over everyday issues like roads and canals and banks and tariffs, were the forces of sectional interest.

The United State's greatest success in the first year of the War of 1812 came when the U.S.S. *Constitution* forced H.M.S. *Guerrière* to surrender. After this victory, the ship was called "Old Ironsides" because British shot bounced right off it. The historic frigate can still be seen in Boston.

U.S. Naval Academy Museum

See "Lesson Plan," p. 198C.

1. The War of 1812

The War of 1812 was the most peculiar conflict in our history. It began after the cause for it had ceased to exist. It was not fought for the reason declared. The nation's main military victory came after the peace treaty had been signed. The peace itself gave Americans none of the things they had fought for. But despite all these failings, the United States emerged from the war a prouder, stronger, and more unified nation. It was ready at last to turn its back on the affairs of Europe and to build an American Empire for Liberty.

James Madison. The man who succeeded Thomas Jefferson came from a wealthy Virginia family and lived on a grand 2500-acre estate called Montpelier. James Madison was admirably trained to be a President. A leader in the Constitutional Convention, he kept the most complete records of what everybody said. His skillful arguments helped secure ratification. Then he served President Washington as adviser, and he did as much as anyone else to shape the new government. A disciple of Jefferson, he helped found the old Republican party and served loyally as Jefferson's Secretary of State.

The wrinkled little Madison was 58 years old when he became President. With friends he could be charming, brilliant, and entertaining, but he lacked the great leader's power to dominate. He was a man of ideas.

Macon's Bill No. 2. When Jefferson's embargo was lifted, it was replaced by a Nonintercourse Act that forbade trade only with Great Britain and France. This act was due to expire in 1810. As the deadline approached, Madison was hesitant and indecisive. The Congress, without guidance from the President, had to grope for its own policy. The result was a law that would cause trouble, Macon's Bill No. 2. Named for the chairman of the Senate foreign relations committee, it threw our commerce open to all the world. But it authorized the President, in case either Great Britain or France should withdraw its restrictions on our commerce, to cut off trade with the other power.

National Gallery of Art, Washington.
Ailsa Mellon Bruce Fund

This painting of James Madison by Gilbert Stuart was one of hundreds from his studio.

Now the wily Napoleon saw his chance. The French dictator quickly promised to lift his decrees if we would then stop trading with Great Britain. Madison fell into the trap. Though France in fact continued to seize our ships—and in spite of warnings from our ambassadors abroad that it was a trick—Madison agreed to Napoleon's terms. The President really wanted to believe that our diplomacy was working—that at last the French decrees would be repealed and that a renewed threat of nonintercourse with Britain would bring about a change in the British Orders. So he accepted Napoleon's word and in February 1811 issued orders that forbade all trade with Great Britain and its colonies.

✂ *The rise of the War Hawks.* When Congress met in November 1811, there were many new faces. These representatives championed a new spirit of expansive nationalism that had swept through the South and West. Tired of cautious diplomacy, they demanded a firm defense of our national rights. The leaders of this movement had little or no experience in public affairs, but they were bright, energetic, and young. Among them were men like Henry Clay of Kentucky and John C. Calhoun of the South Carolina hill country. They soon became known as the "War Hawks." Though not in a majority, they were so shrewd politically that they were able to elect Clay as Speaker of the House. Then these few young men pushed the nation into war.

Clay and his friends were not merchants or shippers. The frontier they cared about was not on the sea but in the American West. They wanted more land. In our day it seems strange that in a nation with millions of empty acres some people still called for more. The reason lay in the very abundance of the land and in the scarcity of people. The virgin western lands produced well enough for the first men, women, and children who farmed them. But after a few years the land could produce plentifully only with fertilizer, crop rotation, and careful cultivation. This meant lots of labor, which America had very little of. Here land was cheap, but labor was scarce. Instead of nursing the land, it was easier on the frontier to abandon old farms and make new farms in the wilderness.

But the way west was now blocked by Indians who would not let themselves be pushed around. The frontier people imagined that the Indians opposed their advancing settlements only because they were stirred up by outsiders—

"First Harvest in the Wilderness," painted by Asher Durand in 1855, suggests the grueling effort needed to carve a farm out of forested highland. Durand belonged to the Hudson River School, a group of painters who painted the wild and wonderful beauties of the American landscape.

The Brooklyn Museum

✂ Critical Thinking Activity: Making Predictions Who were the "War Hawks"? Before the class actually studies the rise of "War Hawks" around 1811, have students suggest definitions for the term "War Hawk." Based on the information available to them, who would have been a "War Hawk" in the early 1800s? Who would be labeled a "War Hawk" today? Through a class discussion have students share and elaborate on their answers.

the British in Canada and the Spanish in Florida. Therefore, they argued, Great Britain and Spain must be driven out of America.

The Battle of Tippecanoe. Over the years, the most common way for the advancing settlers to acquire land from the Indians was for the government to purchase it. In this way, between 1795 and 1809, the Indians of the old Northwest gave up 48 million acres of land, and in general they obeyed their treaties. But white settlers squatted on the Indian lands, and then attacked the people they had dispossessed.

Finally some Indians, led by two able and intelligent Shawnee brothers, said they had had enough. Tecumseh, the politician and warrior, and Tenskwatawa, the religious leader known as the Prophet, decided to form all the Indian tribes from Canada to Florida into one large confederacy. They would sell no more land and would fight to keep the white people out. Settlers on the frontier were frightened.

Governor William Henry Harrison of Indiana Territory took action. He persuaded some other Indians to make a treaty that took away from Tecumseh and his people 3 million acres of their hunting grounds. This brought the frontier of settlement to within 50 miles of Tecumseh's village. Tecumseh went to the capital at Vincennes. There in a moving speech before armed white men and Indians and the governor himself, he demanded the lands back. He told the governor that if the United States agreed and also promised not to buy any more land except with the consent of all the Indian tribes, he would join them against the British.

Harrison did not accept this offer. Instead he waited until Tecumseh had gone south to persuade the Creeks, Cherokees, and Choctaws to join his confederacy. Then Harrison gathered a force of 900 men and marched to the Tippecanoe River, close to Tecumseh's village. Tecumseh had left strict orders to avoid war, but the Indians feared they were about to be attacked, so they struck first. In a brief encounter on November 7, 1811, Harrison's men defeated the Indians and then burned their village.

Most frontier people believed that British officials had been inciting the Indians. Harrison

Area of the Tecumseh Confederation

lent substance to their fears when he reported the capture at Tippecanoe of new guns and "ample supplies of the best British glazed powder." The British had, in fact, helped the Indians resist the invasion of their lands and had encouraged the formation of an Indian confederacy. But they had also opposed war. The Indians were happy to accept British help, though they needed no encouragement to defend their homelands.

After Harrison's attack, the Indians of the old Northwest went on the warpath. They killed settlers or drove them back to the few scattered towns and forts. The Battle of Tippecanoe became the first battle of the War of 1812, for it inflamed the West and stirred the War Hawks to cry for war. They could easily take Canada, they said, and that would end the Indian menace for good. John Randolph of Virginia complained that all he heard in Congress was "one eternal monotonous tone—Canada, Canada, Canada."

Geography and History: Place Have students look at the map above and ask: What fort is closest to the site of the Battle of Tippecanoe? (Dearborn) What city is shown on the map? (Cincinnati) What was the strategic importance of the placement of British forts within Tecumseh's Confederation? (They controlled access to the Great Lakes.)

The declaration of war. During the winter of 1811–1812, the war spirit rose steadily in the West and South. Only those occupied with commerce in the East resisted it as a threat to their trade and prosperity. They also feared that an American victory in the war would strengthen the political power of the South and the West.

The War Hawks made fiery speeches. They predicted that a thousand Kentucky riflemen could easily take Canada. So they swept the nation toward a war for which it was unprepared. In April 1812, Congress imposed a 60-day embargo on American shipping in order to give our ships time to reach home before war was declared. In May, news arrived from England that the British ministry refused to change its Orders in Council until it was convinced that Napoleon had really repealed his decrees. This dispatch, Madison wrote many years later, was "the more immediate impulse to war." We had to choose, he said, between war and submission to shameful treatment.

On June 1, 1812, President Madison sent a message to Congress in which he reviewed "the injuries and indignities which had been heaped upon our country" by Great Britain: impressment, blockades, incitement of the Indians. A divided Congress, representing a divided country, responded to Madison's message by voting 79 to 49 in the House and 19 to 13 in the Senate to go to war. The states of the South and West, joined by Pennsylvania and Vermont, favored war. New York, New Jersey, and the seaside New England states were for peace.

This was expected to be a short war. Canada would fall quickly and then it would all be over. After declaring war, therefore, Congress adjourned without even voting the higher taxes needed to arm the nation.

The avoidable war. As the United States moved toward a declaration of war, its ban on trade with England was at last beginning to work. At the same time Napoleon, who was at the height of his power, prevented Great Britain from trading with western Europe. British factories closed, and British workers were thrown out of work because the warehouses were already full of goods that could not be sold. On top of that, a crop failure in 1811 led to a food shortage and high food prices in the following winter.

The British Prime Minister Spencer Perceval was seriously considering the repeal of the Orders in Council when he was assassinated by a madman on May 1, 1812. By the time his successor, Lord Castlereagh, acted and lifted the Orders, the United States had declared war. Jefferson's policy of peaceful persuasion had succeeded—but too late. A President who could not lead and a foolhardy Congress had already shoved the nation into a war it did not need and for which it was not ready.

False hopes of readiness to fight. The United States thought it could win easily. In the first place, we were now the unwitting ally of Napoleon, who invaded Russia just six days after our declaration of war. Our population was now more than 7 million. Canada had only 500,000 people, many of them French-Canadians who were less than eager to help the British.

The fighting forces of the two nations, however, were not so lopsided. Canada had 8500 regular troops—four British and four Canadian regiments. These would be helped by some 4000 militia and more than 3000 of Tecumseh's warriors. Against them the United States had fewer than 7000 men in its regular army. Congress had voted to increase this number to 15,000, but enlistments came in slowly. More than 400,000 militia, the home guard of all men who bore arms, were called up during the war. The militia still showed all the weaknesses they had revealed during the Revolution.

The United States Navy had only 16 sea-going vessels to face Britain's 97 vessels on this side of the ocean. The fast new American frigates were superior to the British ships, but they were greatly outnumbered.

The war in 1812–1813. The first summer of action saw a series of defeats on land. The grandiose plans to invade Canada ended in the loss of Fort Dearborn (Chicago) on August 15, 1812, and Detroit the following day. This left the British in control of a large part of the old Northwest. (p. 203)

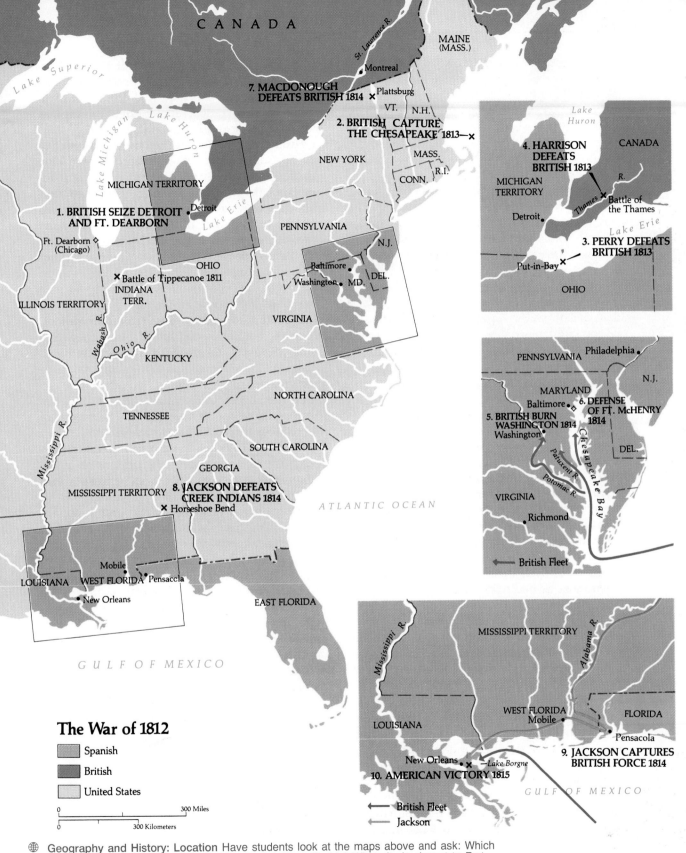

The War of 1812

CANADA

Lake Superior

Lake Michigan

Lake Huron

St. Lawrence R.

Montreal

MAINE (MASS.)

7. MACDONOUGH DEFEATS BRITISH 1814 ✕ Plattsburg

VT. N.H.

2. BRITISH CAPTURE THE CHESAPEAKE 1813 ✕

NEW YORK

MASS.

CONN. R.I.

MICHIGAN TERRITORY

1. BRITISH SEIZE DETROIT AND FT. DEARBORN   ● Detroit

Ft. Dearborn ◇
(Chicago)

Lake Erie

PENNSYLVANIA

N.J.

● Baltimore

Washington ● MD. DEL.

OHIO

✕ Battle of Tippecanoe 1811

INDIANA TERR.

ILLINOIS TERRITORY

Wabash R.

Ohio R.

VIRGINIA

KENTUCKY

NORTH CAROLINA

TENNESSEE

Mississippi R.

SOUTH CAROLINA

GEORGIA

8. JACKSON DEFEATS CREEK INDIANS 1814

✕ Horseshoe Bend

MISSISSIPPI TERRITORY

ATLANTIC OCEAN

LOUISIANA   **WEST FLORIDA** ● Pensacola

Mobile ●

● New Orleans

EAST FLORIDA

GULF OF MEXICO

Lake Huron

CANADA

4. HARRISON DEFEATS BRITISH 1813

MICHIGAN TERRITORY

Thames R.

✕ Battle of the Thames

Detroit ●

Lake Erie

3. PERRY DEFEATS BRITISH 1813

Put-in-Bay ✕

OHIO

PENNSYLVANIA   Philadelphia ●

N.J.

MARYLAND

Baltimore ● ◇ **6. DEFENSE OF FT. McHENRY 1814**

5. BRITISH BURN WASHINGTON 1814
Washington ●

DEL.

Patuxent R.

Potomac R.

Chesapeake Bay

VIRGINIA

Richmond ●

← **British Fleet**

MISSISSIPPI TERRITORY

Mississippi R.

Alabama R.

LOUISIANA

WEST FLORIDA
Mobile ●

FLORIDA

Pensacola ●

9. JACKSON CAPTURES BRITISH FORCE 1814

New Orleans ● ✕ ← *Lake Borgne*

10. AMERICAN VICTORY 1815

GULF OF MEXICO

← **British Fleet**
← **Jackson**

The War of 1812

▨ Spanish

▨ British

☐ United States

0 ————— 300 Miles

0 ————— 300 Kilometers

🌐 **Geography and History: Location** Have students look at the maps above and ask: Which part of the land shown is controlled by Spain? (East Florida) What city is closest to Fort McHenry? (Baltimore) The Battle of the Thames was fought in an area under the control of what country? (Britain) Roughly how many miles is it in a straight line from Jackson's victory in the Mississippi Territory to the site of his most famous military victory? (About 300 miles to New Orleans)

New York Historical Association

The fierce battle at Put-in-Bay on Lake Erie in 1813 was shown in this early painting.

The navy, however, helped relieve the gloomy picture. The *Constitution* ("Old Ironsides") defeated the *Guerrière* and the *Java* in 1812, while the *Wasp* was whipping the *Frolic*. The frigate *United States*, commanded by Stephen Decatur, even seized the British frigate *Macedonia* and brought her home as a prize. The British were stunned—just as the Americans were elated—by these naval victories. But their main result was to lift American morale. For soon most United States warships were blockaded in home ports.

Madison won a second term in the fall of 1812. Yet DeWitt Clinton of New York, supported by Federalists and Republicans who wanted peace, carried every eastern state north of the Potomac except Pennsylvania and Vermont.

The war might have ended in 1812 if the British had been willing to stop taking British sailors from American ships and impressing them into their navy. They would not concede this point, so the war went on.

In 1813, United States military actions did not fare much better. In June the unlucky frigate *Chesapeake* accepted a challenge for a fight from Britain's *Shannon*. Outside Boston Harbor, Captain James Lawrence was killed and the *Chesapeake* was captured. Before he died, however, Lawrence spoke his memorable words, "Don't give up the ship."

Hundreds of miles away, those words were to fly on Commodore Oliver Hazard Perry's blue battle flag when he fought the British at Put-in-Bay on Lake Erie in September. Perry had built his fleet of small vessels during the winter of 1812—1813. Overcoming many difficulties, he was able to get his ships into Lake Erie and face the British fleet in September. There was a hot battle, during which the fleets fired away at each other at point blank range. Perry was able to report, "We have met the enemy and they are ours." He had worried about his new sailors, "blacks, soldiers, and boys," but they had fought bravely. Of the 50 blacks in his crew, he said, "they seemed absolutely insensible to danger."

Perry's success meant that the British at Detroit could be cut off from Canada. So they were forced to retreat. William Henry Harrison, now a general, led 10,000 Kentucky volunteers in pursuit. The Americans overtook the British at the Thames River on the Ontario peninsula and routed them. The British commander was almost captured, and the brave and visionary warrior Tecumseh—now a brigadier general in the British army—was killed.

Other American generals had less success in 1813. So, as winter closed in, the conquest of Canada was little nearer than it had been the year before. In the meantime, the British blockade grew tighter. Few ships were able to enter or leave our ports. Trade dropped to almost nothing.

Our swift-sailing privateers stayed abroad and successfully attacked the British merchant marine on all its worldwide lines of commerce. Even in the English Channel they were not safe from our raiders which, during the course of the war, captured some 1300 British ships and cargoes valued at $40 million.

Great Britain takes the offensive. During 1812 and 1813 the British were more concerned about fighting Napoleon in Europe than the United States in America. But the Russian winter would bring Napoleon's downfall. With his exile to Elba in April 1814, England was free to turn its full attention to the war with the United States. Some 14,000 of the Duke of Wellington's battle-seasoned regulars were now sent to America to bring about a quick British victory.

Offensive operations by the British began in August 1814 when a large fleet sailed into Chesapeake Bay and 4000 regulars landed on the banks of the Patuxent River. They brushed aside a militia force outside Washington and entered the capital on August 24. President Madison and his intelligent and attractive wife, Dolley, gathered a few valuables and fled to Virginia. Since an American force had burned York (Toronto) in 1813, the British now retaliated. After capturing the city, they set fire to the Capitol (with the Library of Congress), the White House, and some other public buildings.

The triumphant redcoats then sailed to Baltimore, where the citizens had been strengthening their defenses during the attack on Washington. There the British troops were repulsed, and their commanding general was killed. But before they gave up and headed out of Chesapeake Bay, their fleet undertook an all-night bombardment of Fort McHenry, the American stronghold.

It was during that "perilous night" of shelling that a young Washington lawyer, Francis Scott Key, watched from an American ship "until dawn's early light" revealed to his relief that "our flag was still there." "The Star-Spangled Banner" was written under these painful circumstances.

In early September 1814 another large, well-trained British army containing some of Wellington's tough regulars was following Burgoyne's route along the shore of Lake Champlain. They were opposed by a much smaller force of American militia stationed behind strong fortifications at Plattsburg in upstate New York. The British put a strong fleet on the lake to support their attack. An American

This painting shows "The President's House" after British troops burned it in 1814. When the building was repaired, the white-gray limestone was painted white and people started calling it the White House.

The White House Historical Association

naval force on the lake was commanded by Commodore Thomas Macdonough. Although only 30 years old, he was already an experienced naval officer. His fleet was outgunned by the British vessels, but he handled his weaker force so skillfully that he gained a decisive victory. With the Americans in control of the lake, the British army turned back on September 12, 1814.

Macdonough's victory and the British departure from Baltimore at last lifted American spirits. Until then the nation's future had seemed dark. Our war vessels had been driven from the ocean, our coasts blockaded, and our commerce ruined. The Treasury was empty. The Capitol and the President's house lay in scorched ruins.

Andrew Jackson wins fame. There were other heartening events in 1814 that brightened the nation's future and created a new national hero. These were the deeds of the tall, rough-hewn Tennessean, General Andrew Jackson. Westerners were delighted when he invaded the lands of the Creek Indians and defeated them in the Battle of Horseshoe Bend. Then by the Treaty of Fort Jackson he forced them to give up two-thirds of their Alabama lands.

For his successes Jackson was promoted from the position of general of volunteers to the post of major general in the regular army. He invaded Spanish East Florida in November

"The Battle of New Orleans" was painted from sketches that the artist, an engineer with the American army, had made on the battlefield. The final battle was fought on plantations four miles south of the city. Note the strong American defensive positions.

New Orleans Museum of Art. Gift of Colonel and Mrs. Edgar Garbisch

1814 and captured a British force at Pensacola. Hastening to New Orleans in case the British should arrive there, he reached the city just in time.

Jackson quickly rounded up anyone who would fight to defend the city. Despite his preparations, before he knew it a British force of 2000 men landed and came within eight miles of New Orleans. He did not hesitate. On the night of December 23, Jackson's men struck in full force and stopped the British advance. If the British had been able to regroup and attack Jackson's forces right then, they probably would have defeated him. But they delayed to await reinforcements and gave his motley band of militia, blacks, and pirates time to throw up earthworks and bring in their artillery.

(p. 208)

Twice the British—now 7500 strong—attacked and twice they were thrown back. The all-out charge, which came at dawn on January 8, 1815, was a disaster for the British. They suffered some 2000 killed and wounded and lost their commanding general. Incredibly, only 13 Americans died.

The redcoats then boarded their ships and sailed away. Jackson became "the hero of New Orleans." A future President—one of the nation's strongest leaders—had been created. Among the many oddities of the War of 1812 none was odder than the fact that its greatest victory, the Battle of New Orleans, was won after peace had already been negotiated in a distant European town.

The Treaty of Ghent. Peace discussions between American and British envoys had begun in Ghent, Belgium, in August 1814. The British demanded large tracts of land in their first proposals, but then Macdonough's victory on Lake Champlain made them realize that Britain could not win the war. The depletion of their treasury by the long Napoleonic Wars, together with many new problems in Europe, forced the English envoys to lower their demands. On December 24, 1814, a peace treaty was signed. If telegraph, telephone, or radio had existed, the Battle of New Orleans would probably not have been fought two weeks later. But, in fact, America did not learn of the treaty until the middle of February 1815.

The terms of the treaty made at Ghent simply provided for a return to the conditions that existed before the war. Lawyers called that the *status quo ante bellum.* It was agreed that certain issues would be settled later. Since neither side gained or lost anything, the treaty became the basis for a reconciliation between the parent country and its former thirteen colonies. Unlike most peace treaties, this one did not bear the seeds of future war. The peace was ratified unanimously by the Senate on February 14, 1815.

There is good reason to call the War of 1812 the Second War of Independence, for now at last the new American nation had stood up with its own army and navy in full-scale war against a major European power. And this was in spite of some dangerous quarrels at home.

Opposition in New England to the war. As the war was drawing to a close, opposition in the North was rising rapidly. Every seaside state north of Maryland had voted against Madison (which meant against the war) in the election of 1812. New England, the richest section of the country, subscribed for less than

The American and British flags both appear on this Cambridge, Massachusetts, invitation to a dance celebrating the end of the war.

The Huntington Library, San Marino, California

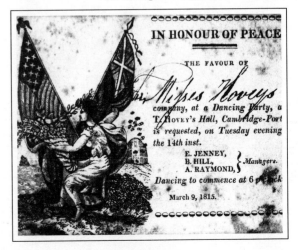

Multicultural Connection: Two hundred and eighty African-American soldiers from New Orleans and 150 from Santo Domingo were part of a force of over 600 African-American soldiers who, led by their own officers, helped in army engineering and fought for Andrew Jackson at the Battle of New Orleans.

$1 million of an $11 million loan authorized by Congress in 1812. "Organize a peace party," the Massachusetts legislature recommended a week after the war was declared. "Express your sentiments without fear and let the sound of your disapproval of this war be loud and deep. . . . Let there be no volunteering except for a defensive war." Some New Englanders were so disgusted with the war that they sold beef to the British army in Canada. The New England states and New York were unwilling to let their militias serve outside their home states.

The British blockade closed off the seaborne commerce of the United States. Exports and imports in 1814 were a mere 10 percent of what they had been in the peak year of 1807. One observer later reported, "Our ships were rotting in every creek and cove where they could find a place of security; our immense annual products were mouldering in our warehouses."

Impoverished towns petitioned the Massachusetts legislature to take steps toward amending the Constitution of the United States to "secure them from further evils." Pessimists began to fear that the Union itself was in danger.

The Hartford Convention. At the suggestion of the Massachusetts legislature, delegates from the five New England states met in a convention at Hartford, Connecticut, on December 15, 1814. These delegates, remnants of the old Federalist party, denounced the "ruinous war." They adopted resolutions, like those of Virginia and Kentucky in 1798, in which they proclaimed that when the Constitution was violated it was the duty of the states to "interpose their authority for the preservation of their liberties." They also proposed a number of amendments to the Constitution that were designed to lessen the power of the South and West, to

The cartoonist accuses four of the New England states present at the Hartford Convention of planning to rejoin England. George III seems eager to welcome back his "Yankey boys."

More from Boorstin: "[Some Federalists opposed expansion of the United States,] . . . fearing that the original partners would be overwhelmed and that before long there would be a new nation with a new constitution . . . No wonder, then, that during the War of 1812, when British troops approached New Orleans, loyal New Englander Timothy Pickering hoped that city would fall to the British. Then the trans-Appalachian West might join the British victors, leaving a smaller but tidier United States." (From *The Americans: The National Experience*)

secure the interests of commerce, and to check the seemingly endless succession of Presidents from Virginia.

By a lucky coincidence the messengers carrying these disruptive demands arrived in Washington just at the moment when events made their demands seem absurd. For the city was rejoicing over the news of Jackson's victory at New Orleans and the tidings of the peace from Ghent, which reached Washington on the same day. The Republican triumph was complete, and the Federalist party was doomed.

There was nothing "treasonable" in the propositions of the Federalists at Hartford, for they were trying to amend the Constitution. But they made a bad mistake in their timing. As a party measure they were opposing a war at a time when it had become a struggle for the nation's very existence. Therefore there was reason enough for many Americans to call the Hartford Convention unpatriotic. The Federalists as a party put partisan or sectional interests above those of the whole country. For the last time, in the presidential election of 1816, the Federalists named a candidate. Rufus King of New York was easily defeated by the Republican James Monroe, Madison's Secretary of State. The Virginia dynasty would govern the nation for another eight years.

See "Section 1 Review answers," p. 198C.

Section 1 Review

1. Identify or explain: Macon's Bill No. 2, Henry Clay, John C. Calhoun, Tecumseh, the Prophet, Stephen Decatur, DeWitt Clinton, James Lawrence, Oliver Hazard Perry.
2. Locate: Tippecanoe, Fort Dearborn, Thames River, Put-in-Bay, York, Fort McHenry.
3. Why did the War Hawks argue for war?
4. List some major land and sea battles in the War of 1812 and give their results.
5. Summarize the terms of the Treaty of Ghent.
6. Describe the opposition to the War of 1812.
7. **Critical Thinking: Distinguishing False from Accurate Images.** Was the War of 1812 the "most peculiar conflict in our history"? Explain your answer.

See "Lesson Plan," p. 198C.

2. Madison and Monroe

The War of 1812 had hardly been a great American success story. It had revealed grave weaknesses in our government—especially in the nation's finances and in defense. At times during the conflict, the fate of the nation had hung in the balance.

Yet the war finally produced solid benefits. Never again would Great Britain believe that the United States could easily be defeated on the battlefield. Americans would no longer assume that Canada could be conquered by a thousand Kentucky riflemen. Both nations—the former homeland and the nation of former colonies—would be more willing to settle their differences at a conference table.

The other result was stranger. Out of a war in which the nation had attained none of its declared goals, the people emerged more united, more patriotic, and more filled with national pride than ever before.

"We have met the enemy and they are ours," "Don't give up the ship," and other fighting slogans became popular. "The Star-Spangled Banner" would become our national anthem. An energetic Jackson and his frontiersmen, blacks, and pirates were remembered trouncing the British at New Orleans. The near loss of much of the Northwest and the burning of Washington were almost forgotten.

The annual message of 1815. The new national spirit was revealed in President Madison's annual message to Congress in December 1815. This Republican President's program included: (1) funds for national defense, (2) frigates for the navy, (3) a standing army and federal control of the militia, (4) federal aid for building roads and canals, (5) a protective tariff to encourage manufactures, (6) re-establishing the national bank, and (7) federal assumption of some state debts. It seemed that Hamilton had replaced Jefferson as the idol of the old Republican party.

Henry Clay later referred to this program as the "American System," which would benefit every section of the country. The protective tariff would aid the manufacturers of the

Northeast and create a large market for their products in the South and West. Internal improvements—roads and canals—would tie the country together and make it easier for Westerners and Southerners to get their crops to eastern markets. The national bank would provide the currency and the capital for the entire nation's economic growth. But each section found something in the package that it did not like.

The Tariff of 1816.

American manufacturers wanted a protective tariff. After the British blockade had cut off our foreign commerce, large sums of capital were switched to manufacturing, in New England especially, so that we might make the items we had once imported. By the end of 1815 the cotton mills in New England had multiplied. Iron manufacturing was booming in Pennsylvania. Pioneer industries—in iron, wool, and cotton—had even appeared in the Ohio Valley between Pittsburgh and Cincinnati.

The British manufacturers who had supplied the rapidly growing American demand ever since colonial days did not wish to lose their market. Even before the Senate ratified the Treaty of Ghent, British ships were waiting off New York Harbor, loaded with goods that had been dammed up in English warehouses during the wars in Europe and America. These goods were to be sold even below cost in order to bankrupt America's new manufacturing plants.

To protect America's "infant industries" Congress enacted a tariff (April 1816) that continued the high duties that had been imposed as a war measure in 1812. South Carolina—later to lead the opposition—now strongly favored the tariff. Representative John C. Calhoun of South Carolina supported the measure because he believed the United States needed to build up its army, pay its national debt, and develop its new industries. Only in that way, he argued, could the United States be truly independent. The South as a whole, however, was not convinced. Southern members of Congress voted heavily against the tariff.

The second Bank of the United States.

The Bank of the United States, which had not been rechartered in 1811, had closed its doors. Without a national bank it was doubly difficult for the nation to pay for the war. Instead of being able to borrow from one central bank, the government had to deal with many. Without any Bank of the United States, state banks (private banks chartered by the states) had multiplied rapidly, each issuing its own paper money. There was no one national currency. In the dark days of the war, after the British burned Washington, many holders of these state bank notes tried to convert them to gold and silver (specie) as the banks had promised. But, lacking specie, the banks refused. As a result the value of the state bank notes declined. The bonds of the federal government sold below their face value, and the national debt soared.

To deal with these hard economic problems, the federal government decided to charter a bank similar to Hamilton's bank of 1791, but with a larger capital. Again the government would hold one-fifth of the stock and would name one-fifth of the directors. Southern statesmen who had argued against the consti-

The tariff of 1816 was designed to protect small industries like this one in West Point, New York.

The New-York Historical Society

Critical Thinking Activity: Demonstrating Reasoned Judgment What special concerns did the separate regions of the United States have? Ask the class to construct a chart on the chalkboard to describe regional interests. Divide the chart into North, South, and West. Next to each region have students list special interests. Then ask students which interests were shared by more than one region. Have students summarize the information on the chart by completing this sentence: "The growth of regional interests affected the rising spirit of nationalism by . . ."

tutionality of the old bank now suddenly changed their tune. They favored the second Bank of the United States. Madison, who had called Hamilton's bank unconstitutional, signed the new bank bill on April 10, 1816.

Calhoun's Bonus Bill. One of the lessons of the war was the need for better means of transporting goods and troops. All the sails, cannon, and cordage (ropes and lines) for Perry's fleet on Lake Erie and for Macdonough's on Lake Champlain had been laboriously carried overland. Supplies for the army were dragged over rough trails in the wilderness. Western farmers found it difficult and expensive to bring their crops and livestock to market.

John C. Calhoun, eloquent spokesman for the South, warned Congress that unless it found ways to tie the rapidly growing nation together there was a strong chance of "disunion." In December 1816, Calhoun introduced a bill to pay for roads and canals—what were called "internal improvements." The $1.5 million that the new Bank of the United States would pay for its charter (the so-called bonus) would support these new projects. In addition, the dividends that the United States would receive on its fifth of the bank's stock would help build roads and canals. The bill passed Congress in February 1817.

President Madison now suddenly returned to his old Republican beliefs. He had called for building roads and canals in his 1815 message. But now he decided that Congress had no such powers because they were not expressly given in the Constitution. So Madison vetoed the Bonus Bill.

It was unfortunate for his place in history that Madison chose to show constitutional scruples so near the close of his presidency. The "American System" of the tariff, bank, and internal improvements was a package. Few liked all three items. Some Westerners were against the bank because they liked the easy money of the state banks. The South opposed the tariff. And New England disliked both the bank (now that it was a Republican measure) and internal improvements at government expense. Only the Middle States—New York, New Jersey, and Pennsylvania—voted for all three. When Madison vetoed the Bonus Bill, the "system" ceased to exist. Now the West, which most wanted roads and canals, felt left out.

A further problem with the veto was that the northern states had the money to spend for internal improvements while the South did not. When the North built roads and canals and, later, railroads to the West, the trade of the West naturally was drawn to the northern states. As a result the South remained agricultural, raising the staple crops of rice, tobacco, cotton, and sugar. With internal improvements at national expense, the economy of all the sections might have been different. And the South might have developed a mixed economy of farm and factory instead of becoming enslaved to slavery.

The "Era of Good Feelings." Madison's veto of the Bonus Bill was his last official act. The next day he saw his hand-picked successor, James Monroe, the last of the Virginia dynasty, take the oath of office.

The inauguration of President James Monroe began a curious period in American party politics. When the new President toured the North and the West, he was so well received that even a staunchly Federalist Boston newspaper called him the herald of an "era of good feelings."

President Monroe's term in office proved to be an era without political parties. The Federalist party died in 1816. The Jeffersonian Republicans had taken over their issues—banks, tariffs, and an active central government. When only New Englanders were found in the Federalist party, it had ceased to be national.

As the Federalists disappeared, so too did the Republicans. Without opposition there was no reason for them to stay together, and they fell apart into squabbling factions. With astonishing swiftness, the Era of Good Feelings became an era of bad feelings marked by the hot pursuit of the Presidency by several self-seeking so-called Republicans. Sectional bitterness boiled up, and a coherent national policy disappeared. Meanwhile, James Monroe avoided making domestic policy and drifted with the times.

(p. 212)

See "Lesson Plan," p. 198D for **Writing Process Activity: Drawing Conclusions** relating to the Bank of the United States.

Economic sectionalism. In Monroe's day the United States was divided into geographic sections each as large as a European nation, each with its own economic interests. The East depended on commerce and industry. The South lived on an economy of large plantations. The West was a land of small farms. The differing economic interests of the sections produced conflicting ideas about the tariff, banks, internal improvements, slavery, the right to vote, and almost everything else.

For a time after the War of 1812 these sectional differences remained hidden. While the whole country prospered, national feelings overshadowed all others. But with the onset of a severe depression in 1819, people in each section looked for someone—elsewhere in the nation—to blame. Each section demanded new laws in its own special interest.

This striking portrait of James Monroe shows him as he looked in 1816 at the age of 58.

Smithsonian Institution

Adjustments with Great Britain. Monroe's term of office began well, however, and a national spirit filled the air—a pride promoted by American diplomatic successes.

John Quincy Adams, Monroe's Secretary of State and the son of former President John Adams, was one of the ablest and most farsighted statesmen in our country's history. The agreement with Great Britain that he negotiated in 1817 (and which survives to this day) pledged each country not to keep warships on the Great Lakes. This policy was later expanded to a pledge not to arm the land borders between the United States and Canada. As a result, the northern border of the United States remains the longest unfortified international border in the world. The pact came to be known as the Rush-Bagot Agreement because it was contained in an exchange of notes between the acting Secretary of State, Richard Rush, and the British minister to the United States, Charles Bagot.

In the following year it was agreed that the 49th parallel would mark the boundary between Canada and the United States from Lake of the Woods in Minnesota to the Rocky Mountains. Also, for ten years Britain and the United States would jointly occupy the Oregon territory between the Rockies and the Pacific.

Spain cedes Florida. The United States had long wanted all of Florida. Then in 1818, the federal government ordered General Jackson to protect southern and western settlers against Indian attacks from eastern Florida. He was told that he could follow Indian raiding parties back into Spanish Florida. Jackson—who was no Indian lover—responded to this assignment with enthusiasm. Supposedly chasing Indians, he swept across East Florida, capturing the Spanish strongholds of Pensacola and St. Marks on the way. During this campaign he executed two Englishmen who were suspected of supplying arms to the Indians. When Jackson went back to Tennessee in May 1818, he had turned Florida into a conquered province.

Jackson's deeds made him a hero in the West but seriously embarrassed the government. He

Continuity and Change: Social Change Explain to students that there has been a relationship between sectional interests and the breakdown of political parties. The different economic interests of the regions of the United States contributed to the death of the Federalist party and breakdown of the Republican party during the Monroe administration, just as the polarization over the slavery issue caused the breakdown of the national political parties into northern and southern factions in the years prior to the Civil War. (See page 322.)

might easily have caused a war with both Spain and England. The President's Cabinet was divided. Secretary of State John Quincy Adams supported the rash Jackson. But all the other Cabinet members wanted him to be censured and his acts disavowed. Adams and Jackson prevailed, and the President sent Spain an ultimatum: either control the Indians or sell Florida to the United States.

The weak Spanish government, plagued by revolts in its other American colonies, had no way to control the Indians. So rather than have the United States take Florida for nothing, Spain decided to sell the land for what it could get. In the Adams-Onís Treaty of 1819, the United States received Florida. In return the United States government agreed to pay to its own citizens about $5 million—the damages American shippers claimed against Spain for Spanish interference with American commerce during the Napoleonic Wars.

The same treaty finally fixed the boundary between the Louisiana Territory and Spanish holdings to the west. This line had been in dispute ever since 1803. The United States gave up its claim to part of Texas, but in return Spain gave up its claim to the Pacific Northwest. The border of the United States now was drawn all the way to the Pacific!

John Marshall's decisions. The rise of nationalism during these years was encouraged by a series of decisions of the Supreme Court under its strong Federalist Chief Justice John Marshall. When the Supreme Court decides a case, the justices write opinions giving the reasons for their decisions. Usually one justice will write an opinion for the majority. Marshall was noted both for the masterful opinions that he wrote and for his skill in winning other members of the Court to his views.

In *Martin* v. *Hunter's Lessee* (1816) and *Cohens* v. *Virginia* (1821) the Supreme Court insisted on its right to review decisions of state courts that dealt with matters arising under the federal Constitution.

In 1819 in the *Dartmouth College Case*, the Court protected private property from state in-

terference. It annulled an act of the New Hampshire legislature that would have altered the college charter. States were forbidden by the Constitution to "pass any law impairing the obligation of contracts" (Art. I, sec. 10). A charter passed by a state legislature, Marshall said, was a "contract." Marshall was always willing to interpret the Constitution broadly when it increased the powers of the national government— or the Supreme Court. The decision in this case also encouraged business firms to invest their capital and to rely on the charters of their corporations without fearing the whimsies of state legislatures.

Marshall's most famous opinion came in *McCulloch* v. *Maryland* (1819). That decision became a bulwark of a strong central government in the United States. The state of Maryland had tried to force the Bank of the United States out of the state by taxing it. Marshall asserted that no state had the right to hinder or control any national institution established within its borders. "The power to tax," he said, "is the power to destroy."

Marshall seized the occasion to deal once again with the question whether the Constitution gave Congress the power to set up a national bank. Before signing the bill that had created the first Bank of the United States, President Washington had received conflicting advice on the issue from Thomas Jefferson and Alexander Hamilton (p. 158). But the power of Congress to create the bank had not been tested in the courts. Now Marshall had a chance to deal with the clause that gave Congress the right "to make all laws necessary and proper" for carrying out the powers granted it under the Constitution (Art. I, sec. 8).

Did these words mean "absolutely necessary and therefore proper"? Marshall said No! To carry out any of its direct powers, Congress could choose the appropriate means. Congress could create a bank as a convenient or useful means to carry out its direct powers to collect taxes and borrow money. It was only necessary that the means be within "the letter and spirit of the Constitution" and not prohibited by it. The decision therefore had the effect of

Multicultural Connection: Almost fifty Hispanics have served in the United States Congress in the nation's history. The first was Joseph M. Hernández, who played a prominent role in the early affairs of Florida. Shortly after Spain ceded Florida to the United States in 1821, Hernández was appointed the first Territorial delegate to Congress. In 1824 Hernández was elected president of the Legislative Council of the Territory which met in the newly built capital of Tallahassee. He also served as city council and mayor of St. Augustine.

broadening the powers of Congress and thereby the national government. The laws of the United States were "the supreme law of the land," and the states had no power to prevent the growth of a national government.

In *Gibbons* v. *Ogden* (1824), the famous "Steamboat Case," the Marshall Court drew some powerful conclusions from the clause in the Constitution that gives to Congress the power to regulate commerce with foreign nations, between the states, and with the Indian tribes (Art. I, sec. 8). A monopoly of steamboat passenger service on the Hudson River that New York had granted to Robert Livingston and Robert Fulton could not be allowed to stand. Marshall now defined "commerce" so broadly that the champions of "states' rights" accused him of trying to abolish the state governments altogether. Ultimately, Congress, by overseeing "interstate commerce," would regulate telephones, telegraphs, and oil pipelines. Even manufacturing *within* a state would be regulated when the workers, the raw materials, or the products came from or went to other states.

After Fulton and Livingston's steamboat monopoly was broken, competition flourished.

New York State Historical Association, Cooperstown

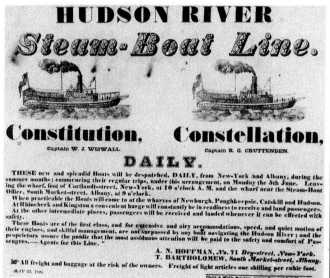

Henry Clay and other promoters of the "American System," advocates of a strong, unified nation, welcomed Marshall's words.

See "Section 2 Review answers," p. 198D.

Section 2 Review

1. Identify or explain: "American System," "infant industries," Bonus Bill, "Era of Good Feelings," Rush-Bagot Agreement, Adams-Onís Treaty.
2. How did Madison's annual message to Congress in 1815 express a spirit of nationalism?
3. What did the North, South, and West each like or dislike about (a) a protective tariff, (b) internal improvements, (c) the national bank?
4. Why did Madison veto the Bonus Bill?
5. What important agreements were made with Great Britain in 1817–1818?
6. What events led to the treaty with Spain in 1819? What were its chief provisions?
7. **Critical Thinking: Determining Relevance.** Why were the cases decided by the Supreme Court under John Marshall important to the growing power of the national government?

See "Lesson Plan," p. 198D.

3. The Missouri Compromise

One sectional interest in America was more sensitive and more explosive than all others—slavery. Unlike other economic issues, slavery was a great moral problem. In the early days of the Republic, it had appeared that slavery might die out. The price of tobacco was so low that many plantation owners were finding the use and care of slaves unprofitable. But then a single invention suddenly changed the picture.

Eli Whitney was a recent Yale College graduate who had gone south to be a tutor to the children of a plantation family. In those days there were few public schools in the South. The children of slaves were not sent to school, and the children of plantation owners were usually taught by a private tutor who came and lived in the mansion. The position of tutor was no longer vacant when Whitney reached Savannah

This scene of the steamboat *Yellowstone* on its way down the Mississippi was painted by George Catlin, the Pennsylvania painter who portrayed the American West. Besides being a bustling river port, St. Louis in the background was a stagecoach center for those heading east or west.

in the fall of 1792, but he was invited to remain in Georgia for a time as the guest of Catherine Littlefield Greene, the widow of the Revolutionary War General Nathanael Greene.

While on Mrs. Greene's plantation, Whitney saw how well short-staple cotton grew in the southern uplands. He also saw that a slave had to labor a whole day to pick the seeds out of a pound of cotton in order to make the cotton usable for thread or for cloth. Whitney, who was handy with tools, was urged by Catherine Greene to try to find a better way to remove the seeds. He was a clever young man. Within ten days he built a device that pushed the cotton through slots so narrow the seeds were left behind. By April 1793 he had a working machine that made it possible for one slave to clean 50 pounds of cotton of its seeds in a single day.

Whitney's cotton "gin" (for "engine") suddenly made the production of short-staple cotton highly profitable. Plantations would prosper if only they could find the workers to plant, to cultivate, to pick, and to "gin" the cotton. Black slaves seemed the obvious labor supply, and slavery began to seem "necessary" for southern prosperity. At the same time planters wanting more land to grow more cotton were moving rapidly westward.

The slavery question rises in the West. By 1818 some 60,000 settlers had crossed the Mississippi and were pushing up the valley of the Missouri River. St. Louis was a bustling city and the center of the western fur trade. Although most of the settlers in Missouri were from the states north of the Ohio, where the Northwest Ordinance prohibited slavery, there were some from slaveholding states like Kentucky and Tennessee. They had brought with them about 10,000 slaves.

Missouri's request for admission to the Union opened up a heated argument over the

Geography and History: Regions Have students look at the map on page 216. Ask: What slave state was bordered on three sides by free states or territories? (Missouri) Name the two slave territories. (Arkansas and Florida) Name one state that would eventually be added to the Union from the Spanish possessions. (Texas or California) Tell what the 36° (degree) 30′ (minute) line is. (A line of latitude)

expansion of slavery. The question began as a matter of power. Up to this time when new states entered the Union, there had been an effort to keep an even balance between free and slave states. Slaveholding Alabama was about to come into the Union and then there would be 11 free states and 11 slave. That would mean that there would be an even vote between the two groups in the Senate. But there seemed to be no free state at that time that could be paired with Missouri to keep the balance even. And if Missouri was brought in alone, the slave states would have a two-vote majority in the Senate.

In 1819, the year when the issue came to a head, a deep economic depression split the country. The Bank of the United States was under attack as the villain that had created the depression to enrich a few greedy Northerners. Manufacturers in the Northeast called for higher protective tariffs, which would have raised the price of nearly everything Southerners bought. Whoever controlled the Senate, it was argued, would then be able to control government policy on the Bank, on tariffs, on federal outlays for roads and canals, and especially on slavery. Slave-owning Southerners began to see a life-and-death struggle. How long could it be before Northerners would insist on abolishing slavery? And how could the South survive without the labor force that produced its cotton? A new bitterness entered the halls of Congress.

Achieving a compromise. The "Missouri Compromise," which Congress passed in 1820 after a whole year of debate, was not so much a compromise as a stalemate. Following the rules of the North-South tug-of-war, which had already been going on for at least twenty years, each side added one new state to its team. Missouri was added as a slave state, while Maine came in as a free state. At the same time the law drew a line through all the rest of the lands of the Louisiana Purchase excluding slavery "forever" from north of the parallel of 36°30′ (the southern boundary of Missouri) except for the state of Missouri itself.

Although people at the time called it a compromise, it was not really like the compromises

Missouri Compromise 1820

▢ Free States and Territories

▢ Slave States and Territories

▤ Maine. Admitted as a Free State, 1820

▨ Missouri. Admitted as a Slave State, 1821

made by the framers of the Constitution in 1787. Those earlier compromises—for example, the one between the large and small states—were designed to give each side on every question part of what it wanted. Then everybody could consider the question settled and move on to other things. But slavery was a different kind of question. Both sides saw it as all-or-nothing. Both sides were simply biding their time.

Farsighted leaders realized that the Missouri Compromise was nothing more than a truce that announced the opening of a fight to the finish. The aged Thomas Jefferson, retired at Monticello on his Virginia mountaintop, was saddened. This was, he said, "a fire-bell in the night . . . the [death] knell of the Union." John Quincy Adams saw it as "a title page to a great tragic volume."

See "Section 3 Review answers," p. 198D.

Section 3 Review

1. What was the Missouri Compromise designed to settle? How was it supposed to do so?

2. **Critical Thinking: Recognizing Cause and Effect.** How did Eli Whitney influence (a) the growth of slavery and (b) its westward expansion?

❖ See "Lesson Plan," p. 198D for Cooperative Learning Activity: Identifying Alternatives relating to farming and slavery.

See "Lesson Plan," p. 198E.

4. The Monroe Doctrine

President Monroe played only a minor role in the crisis that finally produced the Missouri Compromise. In domestic affairs, he believed, it was the job of Congress to make the laws, and the President should only carry them out. But in foreign affairs, it was plainly the President's duty to lead the way in defining the nation's role. Monroe was assisted by his strong-minded Secretary of State, John Quincy Adams. Behind their determination to make the United States a leader in world affairs they had the support of the American people. Despite growing sectional differences, Americans of all regions shared a new national pride. The young nation's Second War of Independence, the War of 1812, had given them all a lift. The nation's growing self-confidence was revealed in the Monroe Doctrine.

(p. 219)

Europe and America. During the Napoleonic Wars the Spanish-American colonies had begun to break away from Spain and to follow the example of the United States by declaring their independence. For those colonies it was a time of struggle—and an hour of decision. The United States feared that the continental European powers—Austria, Russia, Prussia, and France—would help Spain to reconquer its colonies.

At this point the British foreign secretary, George Canning, proposed that the United States and Great Britain make a public declaration against the attempt of European nations to use force to keep their former colonies in subjection. Monroe thought that we should accept Canning's offer. Madison and Jefferson agreed. But Secretary of State John Quincy Adams had misgivings. He knew the ins and outs of European diplomacy from his fourteen years as minister to the Netherlands, Prussia, Russia, and Great Britain, and he had helped negotiate the treaty with Britain that ended the War of 1812. Adams distrusted the British government and thought the United States should make its own foreign policy. The United States, he told the Cabinet, should not "come in as a cockboat in the wake of the British man-of-war."

Monroe's message to Congress. Following Adams's advice, President Monroe announced a new policy to the world in his annual message to Congress on December 2, 1823. Though containing the ideas of John Quincy Adams, it came to be called the Monroe Doctrine: (1) The Western Hemisphere was no longer open to further colonization by European powers. (2) Any attempt of those powers to extend their political system (government by kings and not by elected representatives) to any portion of the American continents would be taken as a sign of unfriendliness toward the United States. (3) The United States would not meddle with European politics. (4) In return, Europe must not disturb the political status of the republics on this side of the ocean. In 1822 the United States had already recognized the independence of the new republics created from the old Spanish Empire. Now we proceeded to guarantee their independence against European interference.

The Monroe Doctrine was a defiant warning to strong and belligerent European powers. But like some later ringing American declarations it was a warning that the United States did not have the power to enforce. Then, as later, there were dangers in making threats if there was no strong army or navy behind them. At that time the only hope for enforcing the Monroe Doctrine was that it coincided with British foreign policy and that therefore it would be supported by the large British fleet. Whether European governments would pay attention to it in the future if it did not coincide with British policy would depend on the power of the young nation itself.

See "Section 4 Review answers," p. 198E.

Section 4 Review

1. What did Monroe believe about the role of the President?

2. What did the Monroe Doctrine proclaim?

3. What was the central weakness of the Monroe Doctrine? How was this weakness overcome?

4. **Critical Thinking: Testing Conclusions.** Is it true that the Monroe Doctrine was an outcome of revolutions in Latin America? Explain.

See "Lesson Plan," p. 198E for **Writing Process Activity: Identifying Central Issues** relating to the Monroe Doctrine.

See "Lesson Plan," p. 198E.

5. A national spirit

Enrich-
ment
Support
File Topic

In 1824 President Monroe invited the French hero of the American Revolution, the aged Marquis de Lafayette, then nearing 70, to visit the United States again. He arrived in August, and his triumphal tour through all parts of the country lasted a full year. The wild enthusiasm that greeted Lafayette everywhere showed that despite sectional differences a national spirit flourished.

Words, slogans, and symbols. Perhaps the chief symbol of the new American nationalism was the flag. On June 14, 1777, Congress had adopted the first flag, which had 13 alternate stripes of white and red, and a circle of 13 white stars on a blue field in the upper left-hand corner. Later the small stars were arranged in the form of a large star, but finally they were set in horizontal lines on the field of blue. An act of Congress of April 4, 1818, provided that a new star should be added for each new state.

Another symbol was the American bald eagle. Benjamin Franklin had jokingly suggested that the turkey should be our symbol. But instead the fierce eagle was chosen. It appeared on the official seal of the United States and on coins. It was a popular decorative device on walls, in pictures, on signs—wherever people could think to use it.

The Constitution itself, the nation's instrument of government, also became a revered symbol. After the Constitution was ratified, it was the custom to refer to the Constitution as if it had always existed. The Constitution became the nation's sacred document, the final arbiter of any discussion. Of course, people might differ over what the Constitution *meant*, but who dared question its authority?

"Liberty," "freedom," and "union" became national slogans. Although the nation was still young, it already had a history, with heroes and stirring mottoes. At the Battle of Bunker Hill, General Putnam ordered: "Don't fire until you see the whites of their eyes." When the British commanded John Paul Jones to surrender his ship, he retorted, "I have not yet begun to fight." With the War of 1812, "Don't give up the ship" entered the vocabulary of American patriotism. The sharpshooting Kentucky rifleman in his buckskins—who had fought at the Thames and New Orleans—now was hailed as a new, and peculiarly western, national hero.

Heroes of the Revolution. The American people were long reminded of their fight for independence by the inspiring presence of men who had actually fought in the Revolution. No Fourth of July parade was complete without a veteran of the war. Some of the best American artists like Gilbert Stuart and Charles Willson Peale made their reputations (in those days before photography) painting portraits of heroes of the Revolution. John Trumbull told the whole history of the Revolution in a series of panoramic paintings. The nation's leading museum, in Philadelphia, featured Peale's portraits of the leaders in the fight for freedom.

The grand hero of the Revolution, of course, was George Washington. Painting his portrait became an industry in itself. Gilbert Stuart copied his own first portrait of Washington 39 times. He painted the President twice thereafter and made more copies. Washington's birthday began to be celebrated by the nation even before his death. His Farewell Address became a classic of schoolroom oratory. It is still read in the Congress every February 22.

The cult of George Washington was further promoted by solemn biographies like that by John Marshall (in five large volumes!) and popular lives like that by Parson Weems, who invented the famous story about Washington cutting down the cherry tree.

A national education. After the Revolution numerous plans were proposed for a national system of education. Democracy surely could not succeed without an educated citizenry. This meant, of course, that everyone should go to school and learn to read. Elementary schools and high schools were left to the local communities. But there were many proposals for a national university. Every President from Washington through John Quincy Adams favored some kind of national university that would instill patriotism and prepare citizens to govern.

Continuity and Change: Social Change Point out to students the intense spirit of nationalism which ensued in the wake of the American Revolution and the War of 1812. People were inspired by the heroes and stirring phrases of the wars. Nationalism bound the country together despite sectional differences. This unifying nationalist spirit, which has resurfaced again and again during times of conflict, was conspicuously absent during the Vietnam conflict. Rather than feeling proud and inspired by the actions of their country, citizens protested openly against the war on a grand scale, refusing to join the armed forces, and harassing and condemning those who did. (See page 812.)

The Americas in 1823

- British Territory
- United Provinces of Central America
- Spanish Territory
- Territory Claimed by England and United States

Protected by Monroe Doctrine

0 ——————————— 1500 Miles
0 ——————————— 1500 Kilometers

CANADA

OREGON

NEWFOUNDLAND

42°

UNITED STATES

EMPIRE OF MEXICO

CUBA
JAMAICA
REPUBLIC OF HAITI
PUERTO RICO

BRITISH HONDURAS
GUATEMALA
HONDURAS
EL SALVADOR
NICARAGUA
COSTA RICA

VENEZUELA
GREATER COLOMBIA
BRITISH GUIANA
DUTCH GUIANA
FRENCH GUIANA

ECUADOR

PERU

EMPIRE OF BRAZIL

UPPER PERU (BOLIVIA Independent, 1825)

PARAGUAY

CHILE

UNITED PROVINCES OF RIO DE LA PLATA

URUGUAY (Independent, 1828)

🌐 **Geography and History: Interaction** Have students trace the borders of Brazil and of the United States in 1823 on separate sheets of paper, using the map above as a base. Place the map of Brazil over the map of the United States. Ask: Which country was larger in 1823, Brazil or the United States? (Brazil) How many countries were independent in the Western Hemisphere in 1823? (Ten—Brazil, United Provinces of Rio de la Plata, Paraguay, Chile, Peru, Greater Colombia, United Provinces of Central America, Haiti, Mexico, and the United States)

In the United States, unlike most other countries of the world, the public schools would not be run by the national government. But a national spirit would still stir the American schools through textbooks—like those of Noah Webster and Jedidiah Morse. Webster, beginning in 1782, wrote spelling and other books which he hoped would create a uniform and pure *American* (as opposed to English) language. With the same hope in 1828 he produced the first important *American* dictionary. It was so respected that in the United States the name "Webster" has become a synonym for our dictionary. Just as Webster bred pride in our language, Jedidiah Morse helped spread knowledge of our land and pride in our land by his popular American geographies.

Some enthusiastic patriots went off the deep end. "The United States was larger than all the universe beside," recalled a New Hampshire student of the 1820s. "We were taught every day and in every way that ours was the freest, the happiest, and soon to be the greatest and most powerful country in the world."

See "Section 5 Review answers," p. 198E.

Section 5 Review

1. Name some symbols and slogans that reflected the emerging national spirit of this period.

2. **Critical Thinking: Recognizing Ideologies.** How did the works of Gilbert Stuart, Charles Willson Peale, John Trumbull, and Noah Webster reflect and promote nationalism?

The Reverend Jedidiah Morse, author of the first textbook on American geography, uses a globe for a family geography lesson. Samuel F. B. Morse, inventor of the telegraph, painted this watercolor of his parents' household in 1811 when he was only 20 years old.

National Museum of History and Technology, Smithsonian Institution

Chapter 8 Review

See "Chapter Review answers," p. 198F.

Focusing on Ideas

1. Following the War of 1812, the United States was able to settle international disputes in 1817, 1818, and 1819 without going to war. Identify these three disputes. Why was each settled peaceably rather than by war?

2. One way to remember Presidents is to link them with the decisions they made on one or two major issues. What were two major issues facing Madison? Monroe? What important decisions did each make on these issues?

3. Tecumseh and the Prophet tried to organize Indian groups in defense of their rights. What was their strategy?

Taking a Critical Look

1. **Drawing Conclusions.** How could a member of Congress opposed to slavery on moral grounds have voted for the Missouri Compromise? Explain.

2. **Recognizing Cause and Effect.** How do symbols and slogans help people in every state feel they are all Americans?

3. **Making Comparisons.** Compare the way Americans express their nationalism today with the ways they expressed it in the 1820s.

Your Region in History

1. **Geography.** Mexico won independence from Spain in 1821. If your state was once a part of Mexico, what Mexican settlements did it have in the early 1820s?

2. **Culture.** If your region was once a part of Mexico, how were feelings of pride in Mexican nationhood expressed? Are there still cultural ties to Mexico? If so, what are they?

3. **Economics.** How was your region affected by the Missouri Compromise? Identify economic activities that were affected because slavery was permitted or prohibited in your state after 1820.

Historical Facts and Figures

Predicting Consequences. Use the data, or information, from the graph below to answer the following questions: (a) How did each region's population change between 1800 and 1830? (b) Describe two trends in the United States's population growth between 1800 and 1830. (c) Based on data in the graph, what predictions can be made about future population changes in each of the regions? (d) What other information about the United States during this period supports your prediction?

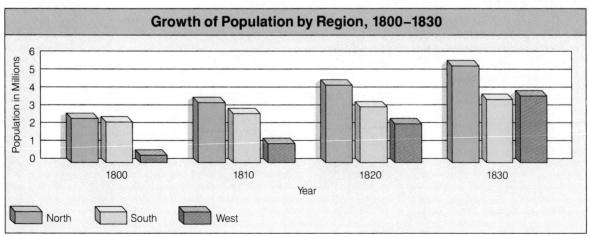

Source: *Historical Statistics of the United States*

Chapter 9
The Jacksonian Era

Identifying Chapter Materials

Objectives	Basic Instructional Materials	Extension Materials
1 A Second Adams in the White House • Describe the election of 1824 and evaluate the presidency of John Quincy Adams. • Show how the presidential candidates of 1824 reflected sectional interests.	**Annotated Teacher's Edition** • Lesson Plans, p. 222C **Instructional Support File** • Pre-Reading Activities, Unit 3, p. 29	**Documents of American History** • The Nationalism of President J.Q. Adams, Vol. 1, p. 242
2 The New Politics • Describe how voting and national politics changed during the 1820s. • Describe the new politician, using Jackson as an example. • Discuss the origins, advantages, and disadvantages of the spoils system.	**Annotated Teacher's Edition** • Lesson Plans, pp. 222C–222D **Instructional Support File** • Skill Review Activity, Unit 3, p. 32 • Critical Thinking Activity, Unit 3, p. 34	**Extension Activity** • Voter Qualifications
3 Jackson Takes Command • Cite the major issues and conflicts of Jackson's first administration. • Demonstrate how tariffs provide advantages to some and disadvantages to others.	**Annotated Teacher's Edition** • Lesson Plans, pp. 222D–222E	**Enrichment Support File** • The Trail of Tears: Native Americans During the Jackson Presidency (See "In-Depth Coverage" at right.) **Suggested Secondary Sources** • See chart at right. **American History Transparencies** • Geography and History, pp. B31, B33
4 Banks and Money • Explain why Jackson attacked the Bank of the United States and describe the results of his economic policies. • Discuss economic conditions in the United States in 1830.	**Annotated Teacher's Edition** • Lesson Plans, pp. 222E–222F **Instructional Support File** • Reading Activities, Unit 3, pp. 30–31 • Skill Application Activity, Unit 3, p. 33 • Chapter Test, Unit 3, pp. 35–38 • Additional Test Questions, Unit 3, pp. 39–42 • Unit Test, Unit 3, pp. 43–46	**Documents of American History** • Jackson's Veto of the Bank Bill, Vol. 1, p. 270 • The Removal of the Public Deposits, Vol. 1, p. 274 • The Specie Circular, Vol. 1, p. 283 • Jackson's Message on the Specie Circular, Vol. 1, p. 284

Providing In-Depth Coverage

Perspectives on the Trail of Tears

The Indian removal policies of the early- to mid-nineteenth century operated on the premise that the best place for the Indians was somewhere else. Indians were forced off their lands in one way or another whenever Americans needed space to spread out.

Chapter 9 highlights the trials endured by the Indian nations during the Jackson administration and the federal government's general lack of concern for the welfare of Indian people.

For this chapter, *A History of the United States* as an instructional program provides two types of resources you can use to offer in-depth coverage of Indian removal: the *student text* and the *Enrichment Support File*. A list of *Suggested Secondary Sources* is also provided. The chart below shows the topics that are covered in each.

THE STUDENT TEXT. Boorstin and Kelley's *A History of the United States* unfolds the chronology of events, the key players, and, as an interpretive history, the controversy of Indian removal.

AMERICAN HISTORY ENRICHMENT SUPPORT FILE. This collection of primary source readings and classroom activities reveals the circumstances leading up to the Trail of Tears.

SUGGESTED SECONDARY SOURCES. This reference list of readings by well-known historians and other commentators provides an array of perspectives on the circumstances leading up to the Trail of Tears. (See the chart below.)

Locating Instructional Materials

Detailed lesson plans for teaching the Trail of Tears as a mini-course or to study one or more elements of Indian removal in depth are offered in the following areas: in the *student text*, see individual lesson plans at the beginning of each chapter; in the *Enrichment Support File*, see page 3; for readings beyond the student text, see *Suggested Secondary Sources*.

IN-DEPTH COVERAGE OF THE TRAIL OF TEARS		
Student Text	**Enrichment Support File**	**Suggested Secondary Sources**
▪ Jackson's Indian policy, p. 234 ▪ Cherokees, pp. 235–236 ▪ *Worcester* v. *Georgia*, pp. 235–236 ▪ Trail of Tears, p. 236 ▪ Indian removals (map), p. 237	▪ Lesson Suggestions ▪ Multimedia Resources ▪ Overview Essay/The Trail of Tears: Native Americans During the Jackson Presidency ▪ Literature in American History/Tsali of the Cherokee ▪ Primary Sources in American History/The President and a Cherokee Speak ▪ Biography in American History/John Ross ▪ Geography in American History/Where They Cried ▪ Making Connections	▪ *Cherokee Sunset: A Nation Betrayed* by Samuel Carter III, pp. 253–266. ▪ *Trail of Tears: The Rise and Fall of the Cherokee Nation* by John Ehle, pp. 1–54. ▪ *Fathers and Children: Andrew Jackson and the Subjugation of the American Indian* by Michael Paul Rogin, pp. 206–250. ▪ *Cherokee Tragedy: The Story of the Ridge Family and the Decimation of a People* by Thurman Wilkins.

A Second Adams in the White House

FOCUS

To introduce the lesson, have the students open their texts to the list of Presidents on page 958, and list the names of five very successful Presidents. After they have completed this list, ask them to name five very unsuccessful Presidents. Compile a list on the board from volunteered information, and discuss the criteria students relied on to make their judgments. How many of the most successful Presidents were elected by large popular majorities? How many were not? Ask the same questions about the most unsuccessful Presidents. Encourage the class to hypothesize about the meaning of this connection. Why is winning a large popular majority often so important in determining how successful a President is?

Developing Vocabulary

The words listed below are essential terms for understanding particular sections of the chapter. The page number after each term indicates the page of its first or most important appearance. These terms are defined in the text Glossary (text pages 1000–1011).

caucus (page 223); **Democratic party** (page 225).

INSTRUCT

Explain

Historians evaluate Presidents by asking how many of their goals were good for the nation, and by determining how many of those worthwhile goals they were able to achieve—by, for example, getting Congress to enact new laws. As students read, discuss John Quincy Adams's goals and his inability to achieve them.

☑ Writing Process Activity

Demonstrating Reasoned Judgment Ask students to play the role of John Quincy Adams or Andrew Jackson during the election of 1828. Before they write their political autobiography, ask them to do any necessary research about their previous government experience. They should begin their autobiography with a statement of why they should be elected, and they should organize their details chronologically or in order of importance. Students should revise for completeness and coherence, then proofread carefully. Ask them to deliver their autobiography as a campaign speech.

Section Review Answers

Section 1, page 225

1. a) a meeting of members or leaders of a political party. b) supported Adams and favored an active federal government with programs for national development. c) supported Jackson. 2. The election of 1824 was decided by the House of Representatives because no candidate received a majority of the electoral votes. Henry Clay, a losing candidate, controlled the votes that could decide the election. He supported Adams, and Adams won. Then Adams made Clay Secretary of State. Adams's opponents charged that Clay had made a "corrupt bargain" with Adams. 3. Adams asked Congress to pass an extensive program for national development. None of his major proposals were passed in part because feelings of sectionalism and distrust of the federal government were on the rise, and also in part because Adams refused to compromise and lost touch with his supporters. 4. In 1824 there was no organized opposition party, so the Republicans were under no pressure to unite behind one candidate. As a result, many members of Congress did not attend the party caucus, and Republican candidates were nominated not only by the party caucus but also by mass meetings and state legislatures.

CLOSE

To conclude the lesson, discuss this question: Why do television newscasters spend so much time analyzing the credibility and voter appeal of third-party candidates in presidential elections? How can the presence of more than two major candidates affect an election?

The New Politics

FOCUS

To introduce the lesson, ask the class to imagine that the next presidential election will be held under the rules and procedures that prevailed in the mid-1820s. Ask them how the election will differ from what they are accustomed to. As students respond, write their statements on the board.

Developing Vocabulary

suffrage (page 226); **frontier** (page 227); **convention** (page 228); **democracy** (page 229); **spoils sytem** (page 230).

INSTRUCT

Explain

Throughout much of the history of the United States, the frontier provided a strong influence for increased democracy and equality. Ask students to speculate about the qualities of life on the frontier that led to a democratic sense of equality.

❧ Cooperative Learning Activity

Recognizing Cause and Effect Break the class into groups of three and explain that each group will prepare a chart showing the changes that have occurred in the election process from the early 1800s to the present day. The charts will have 3 column headings: Voter Qualifications, The Voting Process, The Nomination Process. The rows should be labeled "Then" and "Now." Each student will be responsible for researching and summarizing information for one column of the chart. After all group members have reviewed the completed chart, select one of the students to present the group's chart to the rest of the class.

Section Review Answers

Section 2, page 230

1. Between 1800 and the mid-1820s many states eliminated property requirements for voting, so white adult males without property could vote. 2. The private party caucuses of leaders that had picked the nominees were replaced by county and state conventions and then, in 1832, by national conventions. Hotels made the national conventions possible because they provided spacious enough lodgings and meeting space for all these delegates. 3. Jackson's special appeal rested on his reputation as a self-made, ordinary man with whom the average voter could identify. 4. The "spoils system" is the practice of rewarding supporters with jobs in the government. 5. Printed paper ballots made it easier for people to vote. But these printed ballots also simplified the work of corrupt politicians, because each party printed its ballot on paper of a different color, making it easy to see who was voting for whom.

CLOSE

To conclude the lesson, have the students respond to the following assumption: "Democracy assumes that one person's vote is as good as another's." Compare this statement with the view of historian Will Durant that the fatal flaw in democracy is that ignorance reproduces much faster than, and is less tolerant than, intelligence. Do these statements apply to our system?

Extension Activity

To extend the lesson, have students investigate the voting qualifications in your state and write one or two paragraphs reporting their findings.

Section 3 (pages 231–238)

Jackson Takes Command

FOCUS

To introduce the lesson, ask students to study the reproduction on page 233 of Healy's famous painting of Webster's reply to Hayne. Tell students that Webster's speech was hours long and filled 73 printed pages. Ask a student to read the closing paragraphs of Webster's oration to the class. Then, using the text as a guide, discuss the arguments of both speakers.

Developing Vocabulary

nullification (page 232); **secession** (page 237).

INSTRUCT

Explain

Students will be able to see dramatic examples of how personal relationships sometimes affect public decisions in this section.

☑ Writing Process Activity

Recognizing Ideologies Ask students to imagine that they are a member of the Seminole or Cherokee people. Before writing a personal essay about their reaction to Jackson's policies for relocating the Indians, have them freewrite about the facts of the situation as well as their feelings. They might focus on battles with U.S. troops, interruptions in their daily lives, or the events of the "Trail of Tears." Students should revise their essays for specific detail and logical order. After proofreading, students can share their essays with a partner.

Section Review Answers

Section 3, page 238

1. a) wife of Jackson's Secretary of War. She was the source of a split between Jackson and his Cabinet. b) name of the group of friends Jackson turned to for advice. c) organized a plan for a slave rebellion in 1822. d) South Carolina senator who demanded the cheap sale of public lands and who said that states could nullify acts of Congress. e) led Fox and Sauk Indians who tried to return to their homelands in Illinois and Wisconsin. f) Seminole leader who waged a long but unsuccessful battle to keep lands in Florida. g) invented the Cherokee alphabet. h) case in which the Supreme Court ruled that Georgia had no juris-

diction over Cherokee lands in the state and therefore no right to force the Cherokee off their lands. i) general who captured the last Cherokees in the East and drove them west. j) name given to the route taken by the Cherokees to Oklahoma. k) Indian Territory is now Oklahoma. l) led a slave revolt in Virginia in 1831. m) authorized the President to use federal forces to collect duties in South Carolina. 2. Van Buren won Jackson's favor by engineering the resignations of all but one of Jackson's Cabinet members, ending the Eaton controversy. Calhoun lost favor because his wife led the opposition to Peggy Eaton, and because Jackson learned that earlier Calhoun had favored punishing Jackson for his Florida campaign. 3. Calhoun argued that the Union was a compact of states and that any state therefore could nullify a law that it considered unconstitutional. 4. The chief issue in the Webster-Hayne debate was nullification, state's rights, and the nature of the Union. Jackson took his stand at a Jefferson Day dinner when he gave a toast declaring support for a strong Union. 5. The Indians were forced to give up their lands and move west of the Mississippi. 6. South Carolina called a state convention, which declared the tariff null and void, forbade its citizens to pay the duties, and stated that any attempt to enforce tariff laws would be cause for the state to secede.

CLOSE

To conclude the lesson, have students write a paragraph on the Peggy Eaton affair. Suggest an appropriate topic sentence, such as the following: "Soon after Andrew Jackson became President, a minor problem arose that divided his administration."

Section 4 (pages 238–244)

Banks and Money

FOCUS

To introduce the lesson, have students reread text pages 238–241, under the headings "The war on the Bank" and "The removal of the deposits." Ask: What point of view does your text present on the bank war? (anti-Jackson and pro-Bank.)

Developing Vocabulary
charter (page 238); **Whigs** (page 242).

INSTRUCT

Explain

In the 1830s, Americans had only gold or silver coins or bank notes for currency. There were no paper bills,

bank checks, or credit cards. Specie, or coin, was scarce. Thus much business was carried on with bank notes. A $100 bank note was the bank's promise to pay the bearer $100 in gold or silver coins. The bank notes circulated with little or no government regulation, and the value of the notes fluctuated from bank to bank. The notes of the Bank of the United States circulated at their face value. The existence of such acceptable notes helped to keep state banks in line. In addition, the national bank redeemed the state bank notes it received in day-to-day transactions. However, the Bank of the United States also tended to drain specie away from the South and West to the North.

★ Independent Activity

Recognizing Cause and Effect Have students reread the material under the headings "The Specie Circular" and "The Presidency of Martin Van Buren" on pages 241–243 of their text. Students will then write a one-page essay on the causes of the panic of 1837 and the ensuing depression. Their essays should include Jackson's role in causing the panic and depression.

Section Review Answers

Section 4, page 244

1. a) president of the Bank of the United States. b) would have extended the life of the Bank of the United States past 1836, when its charter expired. Jackson vetoed the bill. c) carried out Jackson's plan to deposit government funds in small "pet banks" instead of the National Bank. d) Jackson's declaration forbidding the Treasury to accept anything but gold and silver in payment for public lands. e) name the National Republicans gave themselves in 1840, implying that Jackson was a tyrant. f) slogan used by the Whigs in the election of 1840 for Harrison's campaign. 2. Clay forced Jackson to act on the question of rechartering the Bank of the United States because he thought Jackson's opposition to the Bank would lead to his defeat. 3. Van Buren issued an order that no one could work more than ten hours a day on a federal project. 4. The campaign of 1840 was the first modern presidential campaign. It was filled with slogans and name calling. 5. By depositing government money around the country in "pet banks," which loaned and issued money wildly, Jackson helped set off a spending spree that fueled an economic boom. Then when he said public land could be paid for only in gold and silver, land sales plummeted, and banks cut back on their loans and stopped redeeming their bank notes in gold and silver. These events, along with changes in the international economy and bad crops, helped bring on the panic of 1837.

CLOSE

To conclude the lesson, ask: What other information would you like to see before deciding whether you agree with your text's negative assessment of Jackson's economic policies? Have students write a 100-word essay specifying some of the questions they would need answered before making this decision.

Chapter Review Answers

Focusing on Ideas

1. From "A National program": would not retreat; preferred ideals to party compromises; ignored followers, etc. 2. The rising political strength of the West; decline of property requirements for voting; and rise of party nominating conventions. 3. (a) In the West, everyone owned property and was thus qualified. (b) It was about opening Western public land. (c) Indian removal was designed to promote unrestricted white settlement. (d) The Bank was a restraining force on Western land speculation.

Taking a Critical Look

1. **(a)** Strong prejudice against aristocrats led to a duel; to preferring Kitchen Cabinet; to soured relationship with Calhoun. **(b)** Prejudice against Indians led to Indian removal policy; financial prejudices to reject Bank rechartering, use of state banks, Specie Circular; favoritism for common people led to spoils system. 2. Democratic experience of Western frontier: new states saw vote as everyone's right. Candidates appealed to new voters by supporting popular causes.

Your Region in History

1–3. Answers will vary depending on your region. Consult your local library or historical society.

Historical Facts and Figures

(a) Yes—Jackson. (b) No—Crawford in popular, Clay in electoral votes. (c) While Jackson's popularity was obvious, he could not win presidency. (d) Clay. (e) John Q. Adams. (f) Answers will vary.

Answers to "Making Connections"

(See "Using Making Connections" on p. 246)
Answers will vary, but may include the following examples. Answers based on the time line callouts are in italics.

1. Between 1800 and 1840 the nation doubled in size as a result of the 1803 Louisiana Purchase. It also acquired Florida in 1819. The nation grew in maturity as well. This was marked by a variety of events including: the *War of 1812;* the *Rush-Bagot Agreement in 1817;* and the *declaration of the Monroe Doctrine in 1823.* 2. Events that encouraged nationalism included: the acquisition of Louisiana and Florida; building a national capital in Washington; writing a national anthem; *Supreme Court decisions such as McCollough v. Maryland.* The War of 1812 reflected sectionalism *in 1814 easterners called the Hartford Convention to denounce the war.* Most divisive was the sectional division over slavery. The Missouri Compromise reflected this sectionalism. *Nullification, an issue raised in the Webster-Hayne debate in 1820,* was an extreme solution to sectionalism. The challenge of nullification was met by President Jackson when he *threatened to use troops to enforce tariffs in 1832.* 3. The political process became more responsive to the people between 1800 and 1840. This can be seen in the *1828 election of Jackson* who was seen to represent the "common man." *The introduction in 1820 of the printed paper ballot made it easier for everyone to vote* and the establishment of conventions by political parties meant more people had a say in the nominating process.

9

Chapter 9

Focusing the Chapter: Have students identify the chapter logo. Discuss what unit theme the logo might symbolize. Then ask students to skim the chapter to identify other illustrations or titles that relate to this theme.

The Jacksonian Era

> Gen. J.[ackson] will be here abt. 15 Feb.—Nobody knows what he will do when he does come. . . . My opinion is That when he comes he will bring a breeze with him. Which way it will blow, I cannot tell. . . . My *fear* is stronger than my *hope*.

So wrote Senator Daniel Webster of Massachusetts as the nation waited for the beginning of the Presidency of Andrew Jackson. For now the people—the common folk of America—were to have their first President. He was an unknown, rawboned old man from Tennessee about whom little more was known than that he was the hero of the Battle of New Orleans. Wealthy merchants and bankers—the friends of Daniel Webster—were worried. They would not like Andrew Jackson much better when his Presidency was over. But by then there would be no doubt that a fresh breeze had blown and that American political parties and elections had been completely transformed since the dignified days of the Virginia dynasty.

This portrait of Andrew Jackson with his Tennessee estate behind him was painted about 1832.

National Portrait Gallery

See "Lesson Plan," p. 222C.

1. A second Adams in the White House

In 1824 as the second term of President Monroe was coming to an end, candidates appeared on all sides to try to succeed him. Each section of the country had its favorite, but there was no opposition political party. As a result, the Republicans were under no pressure to unite behind a single candidate.

There was not yet anything like a national party convention. Each party brought together its members of Congress in a "caucus," and they agreed on their party's candidate for President. Now with so many hoping to be candidates and with the lack of an opposition party, this caucus system broke down. Only about one-third of the Republican congressmen attended their party caucus. They nominated William H. Crawford of Georgia. Additional candidates were nominated in other ways—by mass meetings and state legislatures, which added John Quincy Adams of Massachusetts, Andrew Jackson of Tennessee, and Henry Clay of Kentucky to the list.

Secretary of the Treasury Crawford, the favorite of the old South, was supported by Madison, Monroe, and Jefferson. But he had been stricken by paralysis from which he had not yet recovered in 1824.

New England's candidate, the experienced Secretary of State John Quincy Adams, was the son of former President John Adams. He was well equipped for the Presidency, but his frigid manner made him a poor vote-getter. Speaker of the House Henry Clay, warm and charming "Harry of the West," was an all-around good fellow who constantly promoted the "American System" of tariffs, internal improvements, and a national bank. No one had a more passionate desire to be President. His support came not only from his home state of Kentucky but also from Missouri, Illinois, Ohio, and Louisiana.

Tennessee nominated Andrew Jackson, "Old Hickory," the popular hero of the Battle of New Orleans. Since no one knew where he stood on the important issues, he had few enemies. His center of support was in the old Southwest.

South Carolina put forward its native son John C. Calhoun, Monroe's Secretary of War. He was an able administrator, a patriot, a gentleman with fine manners, "fascinating in conversation, kind and generous in his feelings, and a personality to look up to with reverence, admiration and confidence." When Calhoun withdrew from the race in order to run unopposed for Vice-President, he was only 42 years of age. There was still plenty of time, he thought, to become President. (p. 224)

The election. The bitter campaign became a contest of prejudice and name-calling. When the votes were counted, Jackson had the greatest number of popular votes, with strong support over all the Union except in New England. He led also in the electoral college with 99 votes. Adams, who carried New England and New York, followed with 84. Crawford received 41 from the Southeast, and Clay had 37 from the old Northwest. Since no candidate had a majority of the electoral votes, for the second time a presidential election was thrown into the House of Representatives.

According to the Twelfth Amendment, the House had to choose between the three highest candidates. That put Clay out of the race. The paralyzed Crawford was no longer a serious contender. The competition then was between Jackson and Adams. The outcome lay in the hands of Henry Clay, who controlled the three states that he himself had carried. Clay, who felt threatened by Jackson as his political rival in the West, threw his support to John Quincy Adams. Only 7 states voted for Jackson and 4 for Crawford, while Adams received the votes of 13 states and so won on the first ballot. President Adams had been elected by the House of Representatives just as the Constitution prescribed, but there were grave disadvantages to not being a popularly elected President.

The "Corrupt Bargain." John Quincy Adams, like his father, was cold, tactless, and devoted to public service. He believed that the best men should hold office, and he did not suffer from excessive modesty. He had not the slightest doubt that he was more fit than Andrew Jackson to be President of the United States. Before

Critical Thinking Activity: Recognizing Bias Do biases influence behavior? Political campaigns are often structured to influence behavior. Have students read the descriptions of the candidates in the 1824 election on pages 183–184. Ask students to find passages that express opinions about the candidates. Ask students to vote for one candidate and to explain how their choice was made. Did the descriptions influence their decision? Ask students what else they would need to know about the candidate before making an informed decision.

JOHN QUINCY ADAMS.

The Citizens of Cincinnati, friendly to the elevation of this Gentleman to the Presidency of the United States, are requested to meet at the Presbyterian Church, on Walnut street, at 4 o'clock this afternoon, to adopt such measures as shall be deemed most advisable for the attainment of that object.

CINCINNATI, APRIL 24, 1824.

THE PEOPLE.

Supporters of John Quincy Adams in Cincinnati are called to a meeting to organize and win Ohio's electoral votes for Adams in the election of 1824. But the Ohio legislature was among those that nominated Henry Clay, who then carried the state in the election that fall.

his election by the House, Adams had met with Henry Clay to agree on their political futures. All the details of their discussion were never known. But when John Quincy Adams named Henry Clay to be his Secretary of State, their enemies shouted "Corrupt Bargain." Adams, they said, was now paying off Clay for his support in the recent contest for the Presidency.

The two men were natural allies. They both distrusted and disliked Jackson. Also, to be a successful President and have his policies adopted by Congress, Adams needed the support of the West, which he hoped Clay could deliver. But Adams and Clay both misjudged human nature. The "Corrupt Bargain" charge disrupted Adams's Presidency from the start. It also sank Clay's chances to be President himself. The "Corrupt Bargain" kept coming back to haunt Clay. When it was known that he would be Secretary of State, one western newspaper that despised Adams called Clay "morally and politically a gambler, a blackleg and a traitor." Many voters would always believe so.

Jackson, thinking that he deserved to be President, attacked Clay as "the *Judas* of the West" for blocking his election. He resigned his seat in the Senate and began a four-year campaign to oust Adams and Clay and restore the government to "the people."

A national program. In his first annual message to Congress, John Quincy Adams called for a strongly national program. The laws he proposed might have passed in the era of national solidarity that followed the War of 1812. But now sectional feeling was on the rise. The realistic Henry Clay wanted Adams to tone down his demands. Adams would not retreat. He called for huge federal outlays—for roads and canals, for an enlarged navy, for new national institutions of learning. His proposals would touch every American. Yet most citizens still distrusted the federal government and were not ready for such a program.

Adams was a visionary. He preferred ideals and principles to the compromises of political parties. And he did not mend his political fences by keeping in touch with his supporters around the country. He ignored his followers—who were now called the *National* Republicans

See "Lesson Plan," p. 222C for **Writing Process Activity: Demonstrating Reasoned Judgment** relating to the election of 1828.

because of their nationalistic program. Thurlow Weed, a savvy New York politician who had delivered New York's vote to Adams in 1824, observed, "Mr. Adams during his administration failed to cherish, strengthen, or even recognize the party to which he owed his election; nor, so far as I am informed, with the great powers he possessed did he make a single influential friend."

The "Tariff of Abominations." Adams's tragic Presidency was a list of failures. The only major bill to pass was a tariff created by his opponents. The supporters of Andrew Jackson, who called themselves the *Democratic* Republican party (soon shortened to Democratic), controlled Congress. They posed as friends of industry and of the working class by favoring a higher tariff. At the same time they wanted to keep the friendship of the South by not actually passing any new bill that would increase the cost of living there. With these two contradictory purposes in mind, they created a bill with so many new duties and higher rates—so many "abominations"—that they expected even friends of the tariff to defeat it. Sarcastic John Randolph of Virginia remarked of the new tariff bill that it "had nothing to do with manufactures except the manufacture of a President."

The trick did not work. Supporters of the tariff accepted the new bill, bad as it was, and the "Tariff of Abominations" became law in 1828, much to the surprise of the Jackson men. But the shrewd Andrew Jackson himself had said little about the tariff.

The election of 1828. The presidential campaign of 1828 turned out to be a contest of personalities. Of course Adams and Jackson differed over banks, the tariff, internal improvements, and other important matters. But the politicians tried to fuzzy up these issues.

For four years Jackson and his supporters had been working toward this moment. They received all the electoral votes of every state west of the Appalachians and south of the Potomac. In addition, they took Pennsylvania and won 20 of 36 votes in New York. Adams carried only

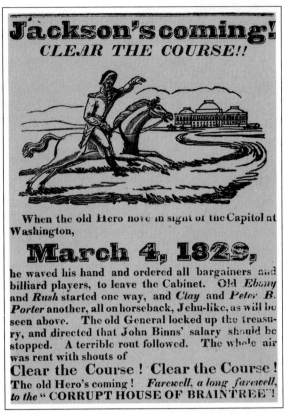

When the old Hero now in sight of the Capitol at Washington, **March 4, 1829,** he waved his hand and ordered all bargainers and billiard players, to leave the Cabinet. Old *Ebony* and *Rush* started one way, and *Clay* and *Peter B. Porter* another, all on horseback, Jehu-like, as will be seen above. The old General locked up the treasury, and directed that John Binns' salary should be stopped. A terrible rout followed. The whole air was rent with shouts of **Clear the Course! Clear the Course!** The old Hero's coming! *Farewell, a long farewell,* to the "CORRUPT HOUSE OF BRAINTREE"!

This gleeful Jacksonian broadside calls the defeated Adams and his Cabinet the "House of Braintree," after Adams's home town.

New England, Delaware, and Maryland. The total electoral vote was 178 for Jackson to 83 for Adams. In popular votes, Jackson was given 647,286 to Adams's 508,064.

See "Section 1 Review answers," p. 222C.

Section 1 Review

1. Identify or explain: party caucus, National Republicans, Democratic Republicans.

2. How was the election of 1824 decided? What was the "Corrupt Bargain"?

3. What measures did John Quincy Adams ask Congress to pass? What was the outcome?

4. **Critical Thinking: Identifying Central Issues.** Why did the system for nominating presidential candidates break down in 1824?

Continuity and Change: Government and Politics Explain that at times the issues in an election take second place to the personalities of the candidates. Andrew Jackson defeated John Quincy Adams in 1828 because of his greater popular appeal. The voters felt that Jackson, unlike Adams, would represent the "common people." In the election of 1960, John F. Kennedy's more obvious warmth, charm, and wit gained him more votes than Richard Nixon. To a great extent, Jackson's and Kennedy's victories were the result of the personal reactions of the voters to the men themselves, not their policies. (See p. 776.)

See "Lesson Plan," p. 222C.

2. The new politics

On Inauguration Day, March 4, 1829, the tall and distinguished-looking Andrew Jackson walked from his boardinghouse to the Capitol. After taking the oath of office, he rode on horseback down the still-unpaved Pennsylvania Avenue to the White House. A motley crowd pursued him right into the building hoping to shake the hand of "their" President—and drink his orange punch. "One hundred and fifty dollar official chairs," one observer noted, were "profaned by the feet of clod-hoppers" in that hilarious, pushy mob. Exhausted, Jackson finally escaped back to his boardinghouse leaving the White House staff to get rid of the noisy guests by putting the punch bowl out on the lawn. The common people who had felt annoyed by an aristocrat—from Virginia or from New England—presiding from the "President's Palace" at last had their own President. He seemed to like them, to be one of them, and to have been elected by them.

Widening the suffrage. To understand how the suffrage (the right to vote) was widened so people felt the President represented them, we must remember that the Constitution allowed each state to decide for itself which of its citizens could vote. Early in the 1800s you might be a respectable farmer or a hardworking businessman, but you still could not vote unless the laws of your state included you among the voters. The chief qualification (other than being a male) was to own property—usually a certain amount of land. For it was believed that only by owning property would you have a "stake" in good government. That was necessary, it was felt, to make you a solid citizen with sound judgment about the candidates. If you were a woman, you could not vote. If you were black, you were probably a slave. But even if you were free, you could vote only in a few states.

In 1776 in most of the states, these laws did not keep many white men from being able to vote, since most Americans were farmers and owned land. But as the country grew, and with

When this watercolor was painted about 1826, Washington, D.C., was still a village. On the left is the White House. On the right in the background is the Capitol dome, which was completed in 1825.

it the cities, there was always a body of men who could not vote. More and more people felt this was unfair. As the author James Fenimore Cooper wrote, "Every man who has wants, feelings, affections, and character has a stake in society." Therefore every man should vote whether he had property or not.

Early in the 1800s one state after another began to give the vote to adult white males even if they did not own property. Some of the first states to open up voting were in the newly occupied lands across the Appalachian Mountains. On that frontier there were no "old families," no long-established plantation or commercial aristocracy. For example, in Ohio, which in those days was still "West," the state constitution of 1802 gave the vote to almost all adult white men. And so did the constitutions in other new western states—Indiana (1816), Illinois (1818), and Alabama (1819)—and the new eastern state of Maine (1820).

The democratic influence of the frontier was echoed in the East by politicians looking for voters, by middle-class reformers, and by spokesmen for the propertyless worker. Many of the original thirteen states revised their constitutions. Connecticut (1818), Massachusetts (1821), and New York (1821) gave up their property requirement for voting. In some older states there was a bitter struggle. Former President John Adams—who had helped write the Declaration of Independence and had been a leader in the Revolution—was the chairman of the Massachusetts Constitutional Convention in 1820. He distrusted the common people, and he warned of anarchy and mob rule if Massachusetts gave the vote to men who had no property.

In aristocratic Virginia change was slow. Madison, Monroe, and Chief Justice Marshall—all members of the Virginia dynasty—wanted to keep the property qualification. Even after the new Virginia constitution of 1831, about one-third of the adult white men (some 80,000 people) and all the blacks still were not allowed to vote. It was 1851 before Virginia finally abolished the property requirement. But Virginia was an exception.

At the same time that the right to vote was widened, written ballots made it easier to vote, as we shall see. In addition, more people began to read about, hear about, and take part in politics through party newspapers, political conventions, and rallies. Candidates became (or were advertised as) just common men, not aristocrats like the Virginia dynasty. As a result more people began to go to the polls than ever before. Twice as many of the nation's adult white males voted in the election of 1828 as had voted in 1824. John Quincy Adams, the loser, actually received a larger popular vote in 1828 than *all* the candidates combined in 1824.

The process of voting. In early colonial times, voting was a kind of community ritual where a voter announced his choice aloud to the cheers (or jeers) of his neighbors. When the candidate received a vote, he would rise, bow, and personally thank the voter. "Mr. Buchanan, I shall treasure that vote in my memory. It will be regarded as a feather in my cap forever."

This vocal way of voting had been brought over from England. By the time the Constitution was ratified, it was still used in three states. Some of the new western states followed this procedure for voting when they entered the Union, so it continued long into the 1800s. It was 1890 before Kentucky, the last state, finally gave up voice voting in presidential elections.

Gradually voice voting gave way to paper ballots. At first there were no printed ballots, and people had to write down their own votes. In the Pennsylvania election of 1796, for example, even if you had the right to vote, the only way you could vote for President of the United States was to write the names of fifteen different electors on your ballot. This was a great nuisance and increased the chance of making mistakes—especially for the people who were not used to writing at all.

The political parties soon recognized that they could help the voters—and win their votes—by printing ballots with the names of their party's candidates on them. Usually each party printed its ballot in a different color so they could be sure who was voting their party ticket.

The printed paper ballot made it easy to vote for all the electors and other candidates for

More from Boorstin: "[After New York broadened its suffrage] . . . the Irish played a newly conspicuous part in elections. . . . [They] passionately admired General Jackson, the son of poor Irish immigrants, who had trounced the English at New Orleans. . . . Two hundred Irishmen in New York City's Eighth Ward, according to a witness, 'were marched to the polls by one of the Jackson candidates who walked at the head with a cocked pistol in each hand and then without leaving the polls, they voted three times apiece for the Jackson ticket.'" (From *The Americans: The Democratic Experience*)

Library Company of Philadelphia

This unfinished etching and engraving of an exciting election day was done about 1815.

became a popular pastime. But who would make up the official party "ticket"? The old "caucus" where a few leaders got together and privately chose the candidates would no longer do. Everybody now wanted his say—not only about who was elected, but even about who was nominated.

To do this new job of ticket-making, the parties began to hold conventions. Members of the party in each county met to choose delegates to a state convention. There the delegates would meet to make up their party ticket. They listed their candidate for governor and for all the other state offices.

The state conventions were great fun. In the days before movies or radio or television, and when other public entertainment was scarce, farmers and villagers were delighted to have an excuse to visit the big city. A state convention was less like a solemn committee meeting than like a church picnic or a state fair. People exchanged jokes and gossip, and enjoyed plenty of refreshments. And, of course, delegates made speeches about their candidates, talked about party politics, and gave three cheers for the party. By the late 1820s and the 1830s state party conventions were being held all over the country. American politics was beginning to be a popular hobby. But it was not yet everybody's game. It would still be many years before blacks or women would be allowed to vote.

The next step, of course, was the national party convention. In the presidential election of 1832, for the first time, national nominating conventions were held by all the major parties.

Hotels serve convention delegates. National conventions were now possible because of a new American institution—the hotel. Nearly everything about the American hotel was new. Even the word was new to the English language. "Hotel" was borrowed from the French language, where it meant a noble house or a city hall. The old English "inn" was a modest building with a few rooms where tired travelers could sleep. In England "tavern" was the name for the place where you could get food or drink. The American "hotel" combined the services of the inn and the tavern.

office, but it was not so good for the timid voter whose landlord or boss might be watching. These ballots simplified the task of corrupt politicians. The color of the ballot showed whether a man voted the way he had been paid to vote. American elections became increasingly influenced by bribery, violence, and other forms of intimidation. It would not be until after the Civil War that voting became truly secret.

Nominating the candidates. A "party ticket" was the new name for the list of candidates supported by a political party. "Ticket-making"

The architecture was new. The American hotel was often the biggest and most imposing building in a city. It looked more like a great church or a palace than like a modest English inn. The St. Charles Hotel in New Orleans struck English visitors in 1846 by its "large and elegant Corinthian portico and the lofty swelling dome." American hotels were impressive public buildings. They came to be called "Palaces of the Public" or "People's Palaces." And they deserved the name. For they were the social centers where a democratic people could meet, just as European nobles had met in the lobbies and courtyards of their ruling princes.

The spacious new American-style hotel was an ideal convention headquarters for candidates and for the party. One reason why so many early national conventions were held in Baltimore was that city boosters there had built one of the grandest hotels in the country. Barnum's City Hotel was an elegant six-story building with 200 apartments. These national party conventions were even livelier and more festive than the smaller state conventions. Delegates could come from all over, enjoy their stay in a grand hotel, and go to the meeting hall to hear speeches by famous men. These large audiences whipped up enthusiasm for the party platform and for the party's candidates.

The new candidates. The candidates changed, too. Now that nearly every adult white male could vote, almost everybody had an opinion about who should be President. As more and more people could vote, American politics became more and more democratic, and the personal appeal of the politician became more important.

The frosty, standoffish manner of an aristocrat from Virginia or Massachusetts could no longer attract votes. It was not enough to be a statesman. The successful candidate would have to be a popular politician. That meant shaking hands and kissing babies—and liking it!

Andrew Jackson, who was elected in 1828, was the first President of this new brand. He was a self-made man. His father was a poor immigrant from Ireland, and both his parents died before he was fifteen. He never went to high school or college, but he studied law and became a lawyer. Even before Tennessee was a state, Jackson had settled in the fast-growing (p. 230) western town of Nashville, and then he grew up with the place. Aggressive and outspoken, he helped write the first constitution of the state in 1796. He represented Tennessee as congressman and as senator, and became a judge of the state supreme court. In 1804, with an impressive public career behind him, he "retired" to private life at age 37.

Jackson was the owner of a plantation with many slaves. He was a gambler, a duelist, a cockfighter, and a horse racer. He bore a sabre scar on his head from being struck by a British officer whose boots he refused to polish. He had successfully led American troops against the Indians and the British. And, as we have seen, he was hailed as a hero when he defeated the British at New Orleans in 1815.

It was not quite clear how the talents of a military hero would make a successful President. Jackson did not have the learning or the eloquence or the experience of an Adams or a Jefferson. But in the new era of popular politics, that was not what the voters were looking for. To the voters he seemed one of the common people, although in fact he was a wealthy member of the Tennessee frontier upper class.

Still, Jackson transformed American politics. Unlike Jefferson, who was a man of learning and who liked to speak of the international Republic of Letters, Jackson was proud of not being literary. He was not good at spelling, and once even said that he had no respect for a man who could think of only *one* way to spell a word!

Democracy in office-holding. Although he was a wealthy plantation owner and slaveholder when he became President, Andrew Jackson thought of himself as one of the common people. After all, he had not inherited his wealth but had earned it by his own efforts. And couldn't other industrious Americans do the same? Although the people thought they had been robbed of their choice by the "Corrupt Bargain" between Adams and Clay in the election of 1824, now in 1828 they finally had their man.

See "Lesson Plan," p. 222D for **Cooperative Learning Activity: Recognizing Cause and Effect** relating to changes in the election process.

This wooden figure of Andrew Jackson was carved for the ship *Constitution* in 1834.
Museum of the City of New York

It was not enough, Jackson argued, for the common people to have their own President. They had the right to hold all the offices in their government. According to Jackson this meant that anybody would be about as well qualified as anybody else—provided, of course, that they had supported Jackson.

"The duties of all public officers are so . . . plain and simple," he said, "that men of intelligence may readily qualify themselves for their performance." Instead of there being an office-holding class, the government offices should be "passed around." President Jackson was happy to use this persuasive democratic argument to throw out of office the followers of the hated Adams and Clay and make way for his own henchmen.

This "spoils system" of rewarding political supporters with jobs was an old story in many states, especially in New York. Jackson's bark was worse than his bite, however, for in the eight years of his Presidency only about one government employee in six was removed from office. That was not much different from what earlier Presidents had done. But Jackson and his political friends actually boasted of these removals as if they were a new kind of public service. The Jacksonian motto (borrowed from the battlefield)—"to the victors belong the spoils"—became the guiding principle of the national political parties.

See "Section 2 Review answers," p. 222D.

Section 2 Review

1. How did voter qualifications change between 1800 and the mid-1820s?
2. How did the method of nominating candidates change? How did hotels help to promote this?
3. What was Jackson's special voter appeal?
4. What was the "spoils system"?
5. **Critical Thinking: Recognizing Cause and Effect.** How did the early printed paper ballots affect voter turnout and corruption?

✕ Critical Thinking Activity: Making Comparisons Who would Andrew Jackson's "common man" be today? Remind students that Jackson was elected in part because he represented the "common man." Have students define who the "common man" was in 1828. Ask students to write a brief description of who the "common man" would be today. Have the class list qualities in a presidential candidate that would appeal to their modern "common man." Ask students to compare their candidate to Andrew Jackson.

See "Lesson Plan," p. 222D.

3. Jackson takes command

Andrew Jackson believed in the southern code of honor, which required a gentleman to fight a duel against another gentleman who insulted him or his family. In 1806 Jackson faced a man who had insulted Mrs. Jackson. His opponent, Charles Dickinson, was a successful young lawyer who had learned his profession from Chief Justice John Marshall. He was a fine young southern gentleman—and a crack shot, too. When the two men aimed pistols at each other on the dueling grounds, Dickinson fired first, swiftly and surely. His shot hit Jackson near his heart but missed the fatal spot because Jackson's coat hung so loosely on his tall, thin frame. For a moment, Jackson believed he had been killed. But by force of his powerful will he held himself upright, waited for his eyes to clear, and then shot the man opposite him. His rival died the following day.

The incident clearly revealed several traits that marked Jackson as President—his fierce pride, his deep sense of honor, his unbending will.

The problem of Peggy Eaton. Andrew Jackson, at age 61 when he took office, felt sick and tired. His beloved wife, Rachel, had died only two months before. But, despite his grief, the gaunt, grayhaired old general radiated power.

It was his good luck, however, that in those days, although the President took office on March 4, the Congress did not assemble until the first Monday in December. So Jackson was able to spend his first nine months in office regaining his health, coping with the hordes of office seekers, and surveying the tasks of a President. One item that took much of his energy was nowhere listed in the laws or the Constitution. It was the troublesome problem of pretty Peggy O'Neale.

The daughter of a Washington tavernkeeper, Peggy was married to John Eaton, whom Jackson appointed Secretary of War. But she was not thought to be socially acceptable by Vice-President John C. Calhoun's wife, Floride, or by the wives of the other Cabinet members. This minor social problem would not be worth a line in a history book except that Andrew Jackson sided with the Eatons. He stopped meeting with his Cabinet and started taking advice from a group of friends, whom his enemies referred to as the "Kitchen Cabinet." Even more important, Secretary of State Martin Van Buren of New York used the problem to win the special favor of Andrew Jackson.

A blond, dapper little man, Van Buren liked to wear white trousers, a tan coat, a lace tie, and yellow gloves. He was a member of the new class of professional politicians, and he knew how to deal with people. He was always friendly, never angry, and never bothered to justify his actions with elaborate explanations. As an experienced New York politician he knew the spoils system and how to use it.

Van Buren, like Jackson, was a widower. So he could join Jackson without creating problems at home. His kindness to Peggy Eaton made Jackson grateful to him.

At last, the clever Martin Van Buren found a way to solve the problem of Peggy Eaton. He resigned as Secretary of State and engineered the resignations of Eaton and all but one of the other Cabinet members. For ridding him of the Eatons and the Cabinet members he could not work with, Jackson thought so highly of Martin Van Buren that Van Buren became his candidate for the next President of the United States. ✂

At the same time, Calhoun had lost the President's confidence because his wife had been a leader in snubbing Peggy Eaton. This trivial incident checked, at least temporarily, Calhoun's march to the Presidency. Instead of Calhoun's rising as he had hoped from Vice-President to President with Jackson's support, Jackson now favored someone else. The South's most able spokesman would not be President during the coming struggle between the sections for national power.

South Carolina and the tariff. Southerners opposed the protective tariff because it raised the prices of the manufactured goods they purchased. Since the higher prices went to northern manufacturers, they felt that they were being impoverished to enrich the businessmen in another section of the country. In South

✂ **Critical Thinking Activity: Drawing Conclusions** How would you have advised President Jackson to have handled the Peggy Eaton situation? Review with the class the facts involving the Peggy Eaton dilemma. Ask the class to act as an advice columnist, such as "Dear Abby." Write a letter to Andrew Jackson advising him how to handle the political situation. Have the class share their letters. Ask students to contrast their suggestions with the solution the President actually used, and to speculate why Jackson handled the situation that way.

Carolina, a state that had been especially hard hit by the depression of 1819, the opposition was violent. Overproduction had made cotton prices plummet. The price of cotton fell from almost 31 cents a pound in 1818 to less than 10 cents in 1828. This caused great distress in South Carolina. There the worn-out fields produced fewer pounds per acre than did the new fields west of the mountains.

The slaveholding South Carolinians had other reasons, too, to be worried. In 1822 they had discovered what appeared to be a widespread slave conspiracy. It was headed by Denmark Vesey, a free black who lived in Charleston. Thirty-six blacks were executed, and many others were exiled. But since none of the plotters would talk, their exact plans were never discovered. Still, South Carolinians were terrified. They put the blame for the Vesey rebellion on the northern critics of slavery who had spoken out during the debates over the Missouri Compromise. They began to feel that slavery—the South's "peculiar institution"—must be treated as if it were a sacred institution. They would not consider any change, and they dreaded to discuss the issue. They also began to imagine that enemies of the South lurked everywhere.

So they became strong opponents of tariffs and internal improvements by the federal government. If a strong federal government could take money away from the South with a protective tariff to benefit the businessmen of another section (the North), if it could enter a state to build a road or canal, what would prevent it from entering a state to meddle with, or even abolish, slavery?

When the Tariff of Abominations was passed in 1828, flags were flown at half-mast in Charleston. South Carolina orators urged a boycott against the states that profited from the tariff. One excited journalist even announced that it was high time "to prepare for a secession from the Union."

The most influential protest came from the pen of Vice-President Calhoun. He continued to think of himself as a nationalist, but he felt the Union could not be preserved if the rights of the states could be so infringed. In an unsigned essay, "The Exposition and Protest of South Carolina," he argued that a protective tariff was unconstitutional because it unfairly taxed one section of the country for the benefit of another. He reviewed the ideas of the Virginia and Kentucky Resolutions of 1798 that the Union was a compact of states. Each state, then, had the right to judge whether Congress was exceeding its powers. Within its borders, Calhoun argued, any state could nullify an act of Congress that it considered unconstitutional. For Congress to override that "nullification," it would then be necessary to use the long and clumsy amending process described in the Constitution. For that purpose the power asserted by the Congress, even if questioned by only one state, would have to be approved by three-fourths of the states.

The Webster-Hayne debate. Soon this very question (and Calhoun's theory of "nullification") would be debated in Congress. The issue arose over the public lands. Many Easterners believed that the price of western land still owned by the government should be kept high. In that way the settlement of the West would proceed only slowly. Money and workers would not be drained away from the industrial East. But naturally enough, Westerners wanted all the land they could get. They wanted it fast, and they wanted it cheap!

At this point, southern planters saw their chance to create an alliance with the West. If they could join forces in Congress, the Westerners could get cheap land in return for their promise to help block any laws that touched slavery. On January 21, 1830, Senator Robert Y. Hayne of South Carolina moved in that direction. In his long speech that demanded the opening up of the public lands, he preached Calhoun's doctrine of nullification.

The reply to Hayne was delivered on January 26–27 by Senator Daniel Webster of Massachusetts. Someone said that no one could really be as great a man as Webster seemed to be. He was not only one of the nation's most skillful lawyers, but in the style of his time he was a tireless orator. He had a rich, deep voice and held his

Multicultural Connection: Denmark Vesey was an African-American ship's carpenter who had purchased his freedom with money he had won in a lottery. Vesey was widely traveled and spoke several languages. Through the skilled application of his trade, he had acquired money and property, but had never forgotten what it was like to be enslaved. The uprising he eventually attempted took six months of planning. Only the leaders knew the full extent of the plan, which included capturing arsenals, guardhouses, and naval stores.

City of Boston Art Commission, painting located at Faneuil Hall, Boston

Webster replies to Robert Hayne (front, hands folded) in the chamber used by the Senate until 1860. Visitors crowd the galleries and pages sit at the front in this painting by G. P. A. Healy.

audience spellbound. His high forehead, thick eyebrows, burning eyes, and powerful form made him overwhelming and impressive in debate—a "great cannon loaded to the lips," Ralph Waldo Emerson called him. This particular speech, according to some listeners, was the most powerful ever given in the United States Congress.

Over the course of some six hours of oratory in two days, Webster made his case. He rejected the idea that the Union was only a league of sovereign states. According to Webster, not the states but the people had made the Union. "It is, sir, the people's Constitution, the people's government made for the people, made by the people, answerable to the people." Only the Supreme Court had the power to declare a law void. If Pennsylvania could annul one law, Alabama another, and Virginia a third, then Congress would soon become a mockery. The Constitution would be a mere "rope of sand." The Union would fall apart, and the states would return to anarchy. In his emotional ending, Webster prayed to God that he would never live to see the Union destroyed. He rejected the idea of "Liberty first and Union afterwards." Instead he called for "Liberty *and* Union, now and forever, one and inseparable."

Webster's speech swept the nation. For generations schoolchildren memorized its famous passages. He had caught the spirit of the United States in 1830 as Hayne and Calhoun had not. Few Americans were fearful any longer that a strong federal government would follow the example of King George III. The colonial experience was two generations in the past. Since the War of 1812 they had come to realize that their liberties could be preserved only by a strong

Union. But John C. Calhoun, Robert Y. Hayne, and other Southerners believed that slavery was a sacred institution on which the prosperity of their region depended. They were not compromisers, and they had already set out on a collision course that could only lead to bloody civil war.

The Jefferson Day dinner.

President Jackson had not, of course, played any part in the great debate in the Senate. Some of Calhoun's supporters, however, hoped that the President from Tennessee could be enlisted on the southern side. In that same year of 1830 they arranged a banquet at Brown's Indian Queen Hotel in Washington to celebrate Jefferson's birthday (April 13). In that way they could call attention to the late Thomas Jefferson's Kentucky Resolutions, which they thought supported Calhoun's theory of "nullification."

When Jackson was invited to the celebration he realized that if the evening went off as Calhoun and his friends had planned, it might menace the stability of the Union. So he carefully prepared a toast to deliver at the dinner. When he was called on, he lifted his glass, looked at Calhoun, and proposed, "Our Union, it must be preserved." The Vice-President rose with the rest of the audience and drank the toast, but his hand trembled visibly.

Everybody knew that the President's words were a direct challenge to the Vice-President. "An order to arrest Calhoun where he sat," wrote one of the diners, "could not have come with more staggering, blinding force." After the shock had passed, it was the Vice-President's turn to toast. "The Union—next to our liberties, most dear!" he said. Then he added, "May we always remember that it can only be preserved by respecting the rights of the states and by distributing equally the benefits and burdens of the Union."

The issue was clear. In brevity as well as sentiment, Jackson had won the day. The news of the dinner and of Jackson's toast was soon out, and a wave of nationalism swept the country. Calhoun was observed in the Senate looking "crinkled and careworn."

A month later Calhoun was struck by another blow. He received a letter from the President asking if it was true that Calhoun had favored punishing Jackson for his Florida campaign back in 1818 (p. 212). The report was, in fact, correct. But Calhoun had been able to conceal his old attitude until now. When Calhoun was unable to explain himself, Jackson ceased speaking to him. At that point, Calhoun realized that his chance to become President was gone. Calhoun and his loyal southern followers knew as never before that their interests within the Union were in danger.

Indian policy.

Like most frontiersmen and Indian fighters, Andrew Jackson felt that the best place for the Indians was somewhere else. He believed that the only way to handle the Indians who lived on the eastern side of the Mississippi was to move them all to the other side of the river. Settled on lands forbidden to the whites, they could be forever separated from the people of the United States. In that way, according to Jackson, there would be no more battles with the Indians. Presidents Monroe and Adams had proposed the same "solution" to the Indian problem. But it took President Jackson, who was no aristocrat from Virginia or Massachusetts but a rough man of the frontier, to carry out the brutal program to uproot the Indians from the land of their ancestors.

During his two terms in office, by fair means and foul, 94 Indian treaties were signed. Tribes agreed for varying amounts of compensation to give up their lands and go west. Some tribes went peaceably, though all went unhappily, to the lands west of the Mississippi. Other tribes dared to fight against superior forces of United States troops. In 1832 a few hundred Sauk and Fox Indians under Chief Black Hawk bravely tried to return to their homelands in Illinois and Wisconsin. Pursued by a United States force of regulars and militia, they were disastrously defeated on August 2, 1832, in the Battle of Bad Axe.

The courageous Seminole Chief Osceola in Florida led his people in the most successful Indian opposition the United States regulars

More from Boorstin: "Before the Civil War, the western lands became pawns in the North-South conflict over slavery. Many on each side hoped that the Indians would be a permanent dam against westward expansion by the other. . . . During the debate in 1837 over an Indian territory bill, Southerners proposed to block Northern expansion by giving the Indians all the land north of Missouri and west of the Missouri River up to the Rockies. Comparable Northern plans to settle the Indians in the southwest seemed to have a similar objective." (From The Americans: The National Experience)

ever had to face. The Seminoles hid their wives and children deep in the swamps. Helped by runaway slaves, but with meager supplies, they showed a surprising power to resist. Osceola was finally captured when the United States violated a flag of truce, and he died in Fort Moultrie at Charleston, South Carolina, in 1838. The Seminoles continued to defy the regulars into the 1840s. During these years many were captured and forcibly transported west of the Mississippi.

The Cherokees, more than any other Indian tribe, had adopted the ways of the white man. They were mostly settled in Georgia, where their farms, factories, and schools were not much different from any others. But they had no alphabet for their language until the brilliant Sequoya actually invented one. With this new alphabet the tribe printed its first newspaper. It was fitting that this Cherokee hero would later be commemorated in the great California redwoods, which are called "Sequoias."

The Cherokees went to court to retain their lands. In the case of *Worcester* v. *Georgia* (1832) the Supreme Court led by John Marshall ruled that the state of Georgia had no jurisdiction

(p. 237)

Private Collection

George Catlin painted this scene of Winnebago Indians gathering wild rice in Wisconsin. During Jackson's Presidency, the Winnebagos and other Wisconsin tribes were forced to give up their lands and move west.

Multicultural Connection: Second Seminole War (1835–1843) was the longest and most costly Indian war in the nation's history. More than 11,500 soldiers were killed and approximately $40,000,000 was spent in this war. Joseph Hernández, a Floridian of Hispanic ancestry, raised a militia of volunteers that fought Native Americans near St. Augustine. Later in the war Hernández was involved in the capture of the great Seminole chief Osceola.

National Portrait Gallery, Smithsonian Institution,
on loan from the National Museum of American Art

Self-trained George Catlin painted 600 portraits from life of Indian leaders like this one of the Seminole chief, Osceola.

over Cherokee lands. But Georgia ignored the Court, and Jackson refused to intervene. "John Marshall has made his decision," Jackson was reputed to have said, "now let him enforce it." Jackson really hoped that the Indians would quietly leave Georgia as soon as possible. He feared that Georgia's clear resistance to the law of the land would encourage South Carolina's efforts to nullify the acts of Congress.

The Cherokees did not give in. Finally, in 1838, the army under General Winfield Scott rounded up those remaining in the East. During that October and November the soldiers drove 15,000 Indian men, women, and children westward. Through cold and rain the troops forced these innocent and bewildered Cherokees away from their homeland to the new "Indian Territory." This would later be called

Oklahoma. The Cherokees called this path their "trail of tears." And it was the right name, for 1500 of their tribe died on the way.

Enrichment Support File Topic

The nullification controversy. In 1832 Congress enacted a new tariff to replace the Tariff of Abominations. Though the rates were lower than those of 1828, this was still a high protective tariff. The planters of South Carolina were outraged. They were especially frightened because this tariff had passed by big majorities, which meant that the government's tariff policy would not soon change.

Meanwhile in Virginia in August 1831 a black preacher named Nat Turner led a slave rebellion during which 60 white men, women, and children were killed. The terrified whites put down the rebellion by killing at least 100 blacks, many of whom had no part in the revolt. The situation was so serious that the Virginia Assembly in 1832 lengthily debated the issue of abolishing slavery (p. 286). South Carolinians too were in a mood to review the threatening past—the Missouri Compromise, the uprisings of Denmark Vesey and Nat Turner, the radical debates in the Virginia Assembly. In several southern states where the blacks outnumbered the whites, the whites saw no way to handle this situation except by keeping the blacks in slavery. Now this peculiar institution seemed especially vulnerable to hostile federal laws. The new tariff offered no hope that the federal government would cease tampering with property within the states. Would the next step be to free the slaves?

South Carolinian planters decided that they must protect their property—which to them meant their institution of slavery. They imagined that Calhoun's procedure for "nullifying" federal laws might be their salvation. That way not only could they get rid of the burdensome tariffs, but they would be prepared to void any federal laws that might interfere with slavery. A state convention was called to meet in November 1832, and delegates were elected. The nullifiers swept all before them.

The South Carolina convention voted by a margin of five to one that the tariff acts of 1828 and 1832 were unconstitutional and therefore

See "Lesson Plan," p. 222D for **Writing Process Activity: Recognizing Ideologies** relating to Indian removal policy.

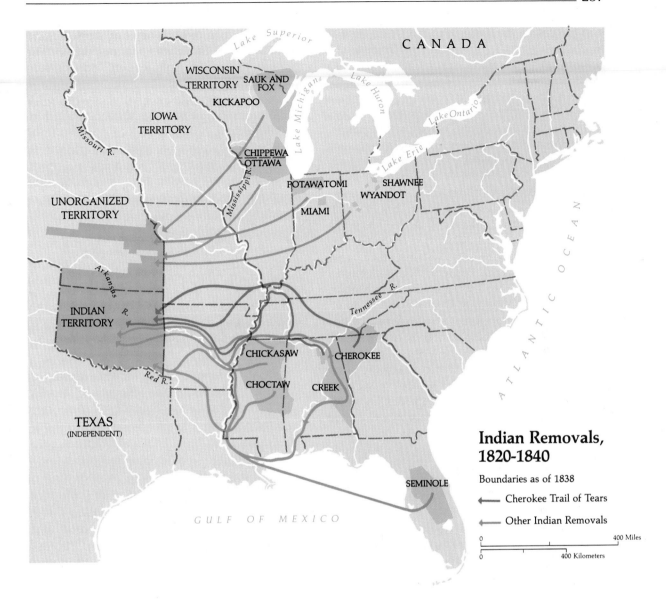

Indian Removals, 1820-1840

Boundaries as of 1838

← Cherokee Trail of Tears

← Other Indian Removals

0   400 Miles

0   400 Kilometers

null and void. They forbade South Carolinians to pay the duties required by these laws. The convention went even further and stated that any attempt by federal authorities to enforce tariff laws in South Carolina would be "a just cause for the secession of the state from the Union." Still the convention did leave one opportunity for compromise, for nullification was not to go into effect until February 1, 1833.

Jackson's response to nullification. Meanwhile, at the very time of that convention, the national presidential campaign was under way. On December 5, 1832, Andrew Jackson was reelected by an overwhelming majority. Jackson, always a nationalist, reacted immediately to the challenge from South Carolina. Within days of his reelection his words to the nation posed the issue loud and clear. "I consider the power to annul a law of the United States, assumed by one state, incompatible with the existence of the Union." Since the nation was supreme over the states, no state could refuse to obey any federal law. And, of course, no state

🌐 **Geography and History: Movement** Have students look at the map above. Ask: What major rivers did the Cherokees have to cross to arrive in their assigned Indian Territory? (The Tennessee and the Mississippi rivers) How many different paths are shown for the Cherokee "Trail of Tears"? (Three) What group had the farthest to travel to the new territory? (The Seminoles) What Indian group had land bordering the Mississippi River before the removal? (The Chippewa, the Ottawa, and the Chickasaw)

had the power to secede from the Union. "I will meet treason at the threshold," he wrote to the customs collector of the port of Charleston. "In forty days I will have 50,000 men in South Carolina to enforce the law."

The people of the nation rallied around Jackson, who was now at the height of his power. His unhesitating leadership had given new courage to all who loved the Union. Even Georgia, which was ignoring the Supreme Court's order concerning the Cherokees, supported the President. The uncompromising John C. Calhoun, who had resigned the Vice-Presidency in December in order to be elected to the Senate by South Carolina, now saw that his state must retreat. So he turned to Henry Clay—the man most responsible for the hated tariffs. Calhoun and Clay were united by their dislike of Jackson, and they shared a desire to avoid bloodshed. But Clay was also moved by his devotion to the Union.

Clay drew up a new bill that reduced the tariff rates but still preserved the protective system. Calhoun reluctantly went along with Clay's bill. Since it was offered as a compromise under pressure from South Carolina, it seemed to give Calhoun a way to save face, to stay in the Union, yet not give up his principles. The new bill reduced tariffs over a nine-year period until they finally were brought back down to the levels of 1816. It was signed into law by Jackson on March 2, 1833.

When the South Carolina convention met again a few days later, the domineering Calhoun advised the delegates to accept the new compromise tariff and rescind the nullification. This they did by an overwhelming vote. But then in a proud, if empty, gesture they turned around and nullified the "Force Bill" by which Congress had authorized the President "to employ the army and navy of the United States to collect duties in South Carolina."

Both sides now claimed victory. South Carolina planters felt they had compelled Congress to lower the tariff. Union supporters believed that Congress had forced South Carolina to back down and repeal nullification. Unfortunately this compromise bought time but offered no long-term solution. Since neither side had

changed its principles, they had settled nothing. The day of battle was only postponed. The fighting language of nullification and secession would not be forgotten.

See "Section 3 Review answers," p. 222D.

Section 3 Review

1. Identify or explain: Peggy Eaton, "Kitchen Cabinet," Denmark Vesey, Robert Y. Hayne, Black Hawk, Osceola, Sequoya, *Worcester* v. *Georgia,* Winfield Scott, "trail of tears," Indian Territory, Nat Turner, Force Bill.
2. How did Martin Van Buren win Jackson's favor? Why did Calhoun fall out of favor?
3. Explain Calhoun's theory of nullification.
4. What was the *chief* issue in the Webster-Hayne debate? Where and how did Jackson take a stand on this issue?
5. Describe the treatment of the Indians under Jackson.
6. **Critical Thinking: Determining Relevance.** How did South Carolina's response to the 1832 tariff foreshadow secessionist sentiments?

See "Lesson Plan," p. 222E.

4. Banks and money

A successful plantation owner and land speculator, Andrew Jackson was a practical, self-made man with strong prejudices. He distrusted banks. He disliked the cheap and sometimes worthless paper money they printed. The only money he trusted was hard money—gold and silver. He was especially bitter against the Bank of the United States, which with its monopoly of the government's business was a symbol of all hated special privilege. He thought it was evil as well as unconstitutional, and he loathed it.

The war on the Bank. The charter of the Bank of the United States was not due to expire until 1836. Its president, Nicholas Biddle, was aware of Jackson's feelings. So he felt that the Bank should lie low and try to arrange a truce with the President. The ambitious Henry Clay

Continuity and Change: Government and Politics Explain to students that Jackson's threat to send troops to South Carolina to enforce the tariff acts during the "nullification" controversy is similar to Eisenhower's 1957 order to send troops to Little Rock, Arkansas to prevent state interference in the school integration process, mandated by *Brown* v. *Board of Education.* Both conflicts tested the sovereignty of the federal government over that of individual states; one taking place before, and one after, the supreme test of states' rights—the Civil War. (See page 739.)

thought he saw in the Bank an issue that might defeat Jackson in the 1832 election. Clay was the unanimous choice of the National Republicans to oppose Jackson and the Democratic Republicans.

To bring the issue to a head, and reap the political benefit, Clay induced Biddle to apply for a new charter for the Bank early in 1832. He believed that if Jackson dared to veto the recharter bill, as he hoped he would, the President would lose enough votes in the East to cost him the election.

The recharter bill went to President Jackson on July 4, 1832. Jackson was sick in bed at the time, and he said to his running mate, "The Bank, Mr. Van Buren, is trying to kill me, but *I will kill it.*" Six days later he returned the bill to Congress with a veto which, in Nicholas Biddle's words, "had all the fury of a chained panther biting the bars of his cage."

Jackson, armed with his veto, attacks the many-headed monster, the second Bank of the United States and its branch banks. Bank president Nicholas Biddle is the large, top-hatted head in the center. Helping Jackson is Major Jack Downing (right), the legendary backwoodsman in many Jacksonian cartoons. Martin Van Buren, piously declaiming that he dislikes dissension, eagerly congratulates those on both sides.

New York Historical Society

Jackson could have sent Congress a brief message stating his objections to the bill. Instead he sent a long message that was shrewdly designed to garner votes. Jackson stressed that the Bank and its stockholders were claiming special privileges and wanted a democratic government to treat them like aristocrats. Of course in any human society there were some natural distinctions which God himself had made—"of talents, of education, or of wealth." But the government must not make laws that added to the "natural and just advantages artificial distinctions." When laws made "the rich richer, and the potent more powerful," the people had to protest.

Henry Clay and Nicholas Biddle thought that Jackson's demagogic appeal would have the opposite effect from that he intended. Jackson's words revealed how little he understood the Bank. Still he proved that he did understand what the people wanted. To the mass of voters it seemed that "Old Hickory" was the champion of all the little people against the money-kings. On election day Clay carried only six states with 49 electoral votes, while Jackson carried sixteen for a whopping 219.

The removal of the deposits. After this decisive victory over "the Monster," Jackson was impatient to kill the Bank at once. But its charter ran till 1836. He was determined not to wait four years until the charter expired. He decided to deposit no new funds in the Bank and to pay the nation's bills with the funds already on deposit there. These actions would rapidly remove all the government's money from the clutches of the hated Bank. It was not easy to find a Secretary of the Treasury who would help him mur-

The building of the second Bank of the United States, which may still be seen in Philadelphia in Independence National Park, was modeled after the Parthenon in Greece. This painting was made in 1836, the year the bank lost its charter.

der the bank. After two unsuccessful tries he finally appointed his Attorney General, Roger B. Taney (pronounced Tawney), who agreed to do Jackson's bidding. On October 1, 1833, Taney began depositing government funds in certain "pet banks" around the country. The whole nation would soon suffer from this vindictive act.

The Bank of the United States had been a wholesome influence on the nation's economy. Its officers had made sound loans that aided business. Now, using the vast government deposits, the imprudent "pet banks" lent their funds wildly and without counting the consequences. Reckless spending and uncontrolled economic growth followed. The government debt was paid off, and the surplus money that piled up in the "pet banks" spurred more and more growth. Sales of public land, which had been less than $2 million in 1830, rose to $24 million in 1836. The numerous new banks that sprang up throughout the West fed the spending mania. They issued more money, which was used by land speculators to buy more land. Senator Thomas Hart Benton of Missouri had hated the Bank of the United States. But now he complained, "I did not join in putting down the Bank of the United States to put up a wilderness of local banks. I did not join in putting down the paper currency of a national bank to put up a paper currency of a thousand local banks."

The Specie Circular and the distribution of the Treasury surplus. Jackson, who shared Benton's distrust of paper money, was in a position to do something about it. On July 11, 1836, he issued his "Specie Circular," which forbade the Treasury to receive anything but gold or silver in payment for public lands. At once the land boom stopped. In that same year Congress voted to distribute to the states the surplus funds in the Treasury. Again the nation was to suffer from Jackson's ill-considered and ✂ hasty financial policies. But this time the results would not appear until his unfortunate successor had taken office.

Jackson's Presidency proved that the Chief Executive had the power to do more than sim-

Library of Congress

Jackson, dressed as "King Andrew the First," tramples with dainty shoes on bills passed by Congress and on the Constitution. The cartoonist makes clever use of the eagle as a leg for the table next to the throne.

ply execute the policies prescribed by Congress. He actually could make government policy and change that policy as he pleased. If the people supported him, there was little the opposition could do. His enemies were free, of course, to call him names, and they labeled him King Andrew I. To make it plain that he was a tyrant, the National Republicans renamed themselves

✂ Critical Thinking Activity: Identifying Central Issues How are analogies used to express an idea? An analogy explains an idea by comparing it to something similar. Have students study the political cartoons and campaign literature for this section. Ask the class to list all of the analogies that are made by each of the graphics. Have the class evaluate the usefulness of expressing a thought in the form of an analogy. Ask the students to create their own analogies for this section.

AN UGLY *MUG* OF
LOG-CABIN HARD CIDER

A BEAUTIFUL GOBLET OF
WHITE-HOUSE CHAMPAGNE.

the "Whigs," after the British party that had struggled against the king back in the 1700s.

The popular and energetic Jackson was still unshaken. One opponent confessed, "General Jackson may be President for life, if he wishes." When Jackson had enough of presidential power, he decided to retire to his beloved home, "The Hermitage," in Tennessee. As his successor he handpicked his favorite adviser, the dapper Martin Van Buren. In the election of 1836 the Whigs did not select a single candidate, but let each section choose its own in the hope of throwing the election into the House of Representatives. Still Martin Van Buren won easily over Senator Daniel Webster of Massachusetts, Senator Hugh L. White of Tennessee, and the military hero William Henry Harrison of Ohio.

The Presidency of Martin Van Buren. Martin Van Buren had been an adroit political manager. For some reason he proved unable to exercise that skill when he became President. To make matters worse, Jackson's reckless financial policies were coming home to roost. When Jackson had removed specie from the banks through the Specie Circular and the distribution of the surplus in the Treasury to the states, the banks began to restrict their loans and to stop redeeming their bank notes in gold and silver. At the same time a financial crisis in Britain caused the Bank of England to reduce the flow of specie out of that country. It was this British gold and silver coming to the United States that had helped finance the boom during Jackson's second term. So, still another support to the American economy was lost. On top of that, farmers suffered a year of bad crops.

All these influences together brought on a financial panic in 1837. By 1839 the nation was suffering a severe depression. Land sales became a mere trickle. Banks failed and factories closed their doors. The surplus in the Treasury soon disappeared. States that counted on these

By pulling a tab on the bottom of this Van Buren campaign curiosity, you could turn the bitter cup of William Henry Harrison into the sweet goblet of Martin Van Buren.

funds to pay for the construction of elaborate systems of roads, canals, and railroads had to stop the projects. Thousands were thrown out of work. Van Buren's whole administration was blighted by this business depression.

Van Buren achieved only one lasting change during his Presidency. On March 31, 1840, he issued an executive order that no person could work more than ten hours a day on a federal project. For the first time government workers found that they no longer had to labor from dawn to dusk. Years later Michael Shiner, a free black who worked in the Washington Navy Yard, wrote in his diary that for establishing the ten-hour day Van Buren's name should be recorded in every workingman's heart.

The election of 1840. The Whigs spent these unhappy years of Van Buren's administration preparing to put their own candidate in the White House. Just as Andrew Jackson was the first new-style President, so the first rip-snorting modern presidential campaign took place in 1840. When the Whig party held its national nominating convention in Harrisburg, Pennsylvania, on December 4, 1839, it passed over the able Senator Henry Clay. He was too well known and had made too many enemies in his years in office. Instead the Whigs chose the old soldier William Henry Harrison, about whom most people knew little except that he had defeated the Indians at the Battle of Tippecanoe.

In order to pick up southern votes, the Whigs nominated John Tyler of Virginia for Vice-President. His only reason for being a Whig was that he shared their hatred for Andrew Jackson. The party drew up no platform (a list of what it stood for) because it could not agree on anything except the desire to defeat Van Buren, whom the Democratic party renominated.

This presidential campaign, like many to follow, did not center on key national issues, but resounded with empty slogans and name calling. When a Democratic newspaperman sneered that Harrison really did not care to be President but simply wanted a barrel of hard (alcoholic) cider to get drunk on and a log cabin to live in, the Whigs had their clue. They eagerly took up the cry: Hurrah for the log cabin and hard cider! Being an ordinary man who lived in a log cabin and liked to drink cider, they said, was no disgrace! On the contrary, that proved Harrison was a man of the people.

The log cabin idea had great appeal. General Harrison had really been born of an old, well-to-do Virginia family, and he lived in a mansion. But his supporters soon invented a log cabin that he was supposed to have been born in. The "aristocrat" Van Buren was pictured living in the White House enjoying fine foods and costly

The Whigs used log cabins and hard cider to elect Harrison in 1840. Here a desperate Van Buren, encouraged by his mentor Andrew Jackson, tries to shut off the cider.

Boston Athenaeum

More from Boorstin: "In the 'Log Cabin and Hard Cider' campaign of 1840, the Whigs boasted that their candidate, William Henry Harrison, lived on wholesome 'raw beef without salt,' while his aristocratic opponent, President Martin Van Buren, was alleged to luxuriate in strawberries, raspberries, celery, and cauliflower. 'Democratic' enthusiasm at first made a virtue of crude and tasteless food, and obsession with the delights of the palate was considered a symptom of Old World decadence." (From *The Americans: The Democratic Experience*)

William Henry Harrison's inauguration as President took place, as was already traditional, at the East Front of the Capitol in Washington, D.C. The many spectators enjoyed the festive occasion with all its pomp and ceremony. Unfortunately, old "Tippecanoe," worn out by the election and office seekers, took sick and died just one month later.

wines, indifferent to the suffering of the starving unemployed.

"Tippecanoe and Tyler too!" became the battle hymn of Harrison's supporters. At the Whig rallies, hard cider flowed freely from barrels on a stage-set of log cabins. The Whigs floated to victory on a sea of alcohol! "We were sung down, lied down, drunk down," a Democratic paper complained. Harrison and Tyler carried all but seven states, and against Van Buren's 60 electoral votes they won 234.

Harrison had proved himself the perfect new-style candidate. But it was one thing to be an appealing vote-getting candidate, and something else to be an effective President. As the Jacksonian era drew to a close, the nation was beginning to come apart at the seams. The country needed strong, farsighted leadership. The issues could not be washed away in hard cider. It would take more than songs and slogans to hold the young nation together.

See "Section 4 Review answers," p. 222E.

Section 4 Review

1. Identify or explain: Nicholas Biddle, bank re-charter bill, Roger B. Taney, "pet banks," Specie Circular, Whigs, "Tippecanoe and Tyler too."

2. How did Henry Clay use the Bank issue to influence the election of 1832?

3. How did Van Buren make labor history?

4. Describe the election campaign of 1840.

5. **Critical Thinking: Determining Relevance.** What role did Jackson's financial policies play in the economic boom and financial panic?

Chapter 9 Review

See "Chapter Review answers," p. 222F.

Focusing on Ideas

1. John Quincy Adams was said to have made a bargain to become President, but his general unwillingness to bargain hurt his Presidency. Explain using evidence from the text.

2. What political factors contributed to the "choice of the common man" for President rather than the Virginia or New England aristocrat?

3. How was western land beyond the Appalachians involved in changes in suffrage qualifications? the Webster-Hayne debate? Jackson's Indian policy? Jackson's war on the Bank?

Taking a Critical Look

1. **Recognizing Ideologies.** Andrew Jackson was a man of "strong prejudices." What were some of his prejudices? How did they affect his personal relationships? his policies?

2. **Drawing Conclusions.** How did extending the right to vote reflect the growing influence of the "common man"?

Your Region in History

1. **Geography.** What percentage of the land in your state was taken from the Indians under the terms of Andrew Jackson's Indian removal policy? Where were the Indian groups in your state relocated?

2. **Culture.** When did your state grant voting rights to nearly all adult male citizens? To adult female citizens? What steps must you take to qualify to vote in your state?

3. **Economics.** How, if at all, did the Tariff of Abominations affect the economy of your state? Why did the tariff affect some industries more than others? Why were some industries not affected at all? How did people involved in industries especially hard-hit by the tariff respond? Cite specific examples to support your answer.

Historical Facts and Figures

Comparing graphs. Use the information in Chapter 9 and the two graphs below to answer the following questions: (a) Did the same candidate win the largest percentage of both the popular vote and the electoral vote? (b) Did the same candidate rank last in both the popular and the electoral votes? (c) How can you explain these results? (d) Which candidate had the largest difference between his percentage of the popular vote and his percentage of the electoral vote? (e) Which candidate won the election of 1824? (f) Do you think this was a fair election? Explain your answer.

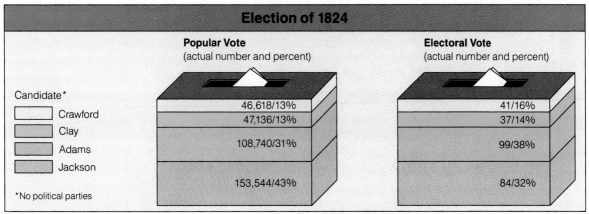

Election of 1824

	Popular Vote (actual number and percent)	Electoral Vote (actual number and percent)
Crawford	46,618/13%	41/16%
Clay	47,136/13%	37/14%
Adams	108,740/31%	99/38%
Jackson	153,544/43%	84/32%

Candidate*

*No political parties

Source: *Historical Statistics of the United States*

MAKING CONNECTIONS

Unit 3

This unit began on page 175 with the observation that the years 1800 to 1840 presented a great challenge to the people of the United States:

> *The Americans had won their independence and established a government. But they had not yet created a strong nation.*

This conclusion was supported by the three unit themes that are reprinted in **dark type** below. Use the time line and the information in Unit 3 to answer the questions that follow the unit themes.

THEMES IN HISTORY

Using "Making Connections": Have students look at the unit themes printed in dark type. Explain that each event on the time line relates to one of these themes. Ask students to decide which events are related to which theme. Students should use events from the time line in their answers and explain how events are related. You may also wish to have students go back through the text of Unit 3 to find other events related to the unit themes.

1. **The nation discovers new ways to grow.** ECONOMICS
How did the nation develop both in terms of size and maturity during the years 1800–1840? (Identifying Central Issues)

2. **The nation's growth is marked by the rise of two opposing forces: nationalism and sectionalism.** SOCIAL CHANGE
Do you agree that events and attitudes during this period acted like two large magnets on the nation, sometimes pulling it together, sometimes pulling it apart? Explain your answer. (Recognizing Cause and Effect)

3. **The nation's political process becomes more democratic.** GOVERNMENT AND
What evidence would support the idea that the political process grew POLITICS more responsive to the people between 1800 and 1840?
(Drawing Conclusions)

Events in American History

1803
Chief Justice John Marshall decides the case of *Marbury* v. *Madison.*

1800
Thomas Jefferson is elected President of the United States.

1804
Lewis and Clark begin to explore the area of the Louisiana Purchase.

| 1795 | 1800 | 1805 | 1810 |

Events in World History

1803
France sells Louisiana to the United States.

1830
The issue of nullification is raised in the Webster-Hayne debate.

1832
President Jackson threatens to use federal troops to enforce tariffs in South Carolina.

1819
Chief Justice Marshall hands down a decision in *McCulloch* v. *Maryland*.

1828
Andrew Jackson is elected President of the United States.

1832
President Jackson opposes rechartering the National Bank.

1814
Representatives from the New England states meet at the Hartford Convention.

1820s
The printed paper ballot is introduced, making voting easier.

| 0 | 1815 | 1820 | 1825 | 1830 | 1835 |

1812
The United States goes to war against Britain.

1817
The Rush-Bagot Agreement leads to the establishment of the U.S.-Canadian border.

1823
President Monroe outlines U.S. policy concerning European intervention in the Western Hemisphere.

Unit 4

Writing About History and Art: Direct students' attention to the unit introduction, illustration, and list of themes on pages 248–249. Have the introduction and unit themes read aloud. After a brief discussion of the subject matter of the unit, instruct students to write a brief paragraph, explaining how the art:

—relates to the unit themes;
—exemplifies the unit title and illustrates the introduction; and
—is an appropriate choice for the unit.

A Nation Growing and Dividing 1800–1860

In 1831, Alexis de Tocqueville, a 26-year-old French aristocrat, arrived here to study the new nation. By steamer, stagecoach, and horseback, he traveled for eight months over 7000 miles—as far west as Green Bay and Sault Ste. Marie and as far south as New Orleans. He saw a great deal of the United States and talked to many Americans. Back in France, Tocqueville wrote *Democracy in America*, one of the best books about our country.

"An attentive examination of what is going on in the United States," Tocqueville wrote, "will easily convince us that two opposite tendencies exist in that country, like two distinct currents flowing in contrary directions in the same channel." These two opposite forces were nationalism and sectionalism. As the nation grew, both forces would continue to grow. In these next decades national leaders and sectional leaders worked hard to hold the country together. They debated and passed laws of compromise. We will see how strenuously they tried and how sadly they failed. A divided nation was coasting down the road to civil war.

THEMES IN HISTORY

- The development of new transportation and communication systems draws Americans closer together.
  SCIENCE, TECHNOLOGY AND SOCIETY
- The growth of reform movements and a surge of western expansion forces the nation to face the slavery issue.
  RELIGION/ETHICS AND VALUES

◉ This painting, "Geese in Flight," was done about 1850. It reflects the interest of Americans in transportation.
Leila T. Bauman; National Gallery of Art, Washington; Gift of Edgar William and Bernice Chrysler Garbisch (detail)

Chapter 10
The Flourishing Land

Identifying Chapter Materials

Objectives	Basic Instructional Materials	Extension Materials
1 Drawing the People Together • Demonstrate how transportation and communication improved during the first half of the nineteenth century in the United States.	**Annotated Teacher's Edition** • Lesson Plans, p. 250C **Instructional Support File** • Pre-Reading Activities, Unit 4, p. 1 • Skill Application Activity, Unit 4, p. 5	**American History Transparencies** • Critical Thinking, p. F11
2 The Industrial Revolution • Define "Industrial Revolution," identify its dates in the United States, and describe its impact on the nation.	**Annotated Teacher's Edition** • Lesson Plans, pp. 250C–250D **Instructional Support File** • Critical Thinking Activity, Unit 4, p. 6	**Enrichment Support File** • On the Job: Industrialism in America (See "In-Depth Coverage" at right.) **Suggested Secondary Sources** • See chart at right.
3 America's Leading Import: People • Explain the chief reasons for pre-Civil War immigration, and identify some contributions of Irish and German immigrants.	**Annotated Teacher's Edition** • Lesson Plans, p. 250D **Instructional Support File** • Skill Review Activity, Unit 4, p. 4	**Extension Activity** • Irish and German Cultures **American History Transparencies** • Our Multicultural Heritage, pp. C9, C87
4 The Rise of the West • Describe the cities built west of the Appalachian Mountains between 1815 and 1850. • Illustrate how Americans improved home construction techniques.	**Annotated Teacher's Edition** • Lesson Plans, pp. 250D–250E	**Extension Activity** • American Scouts and Explorers
5 The Cotton Kingdom • Describe the life and treatment of slaves in the South and compare the northern and southern viewpoints on slavery.	**Annotated Teacher's Edition** • Lesson Plans, pp. 250E–250F **Instructional Support File** • Reading Activities, Unit 4, pp. 2–3 • Chapter Test, Unit 4, pp. 7–10 • Additional Test Questions, Unit 4, pp. 11–14	**Extension Activity** • The "Middle Passage"

Providing In-Depth Coverage

Perspectives on Industrialism in America

The Industrial Revolution began in Britain, but Samuel Slater started a textile mill in the United States in 1792. By 1850, manufacturing in the United States was done largely in factories.

The Industrial Revolution, as discussed in the chapter, provides a backdrop for the emergence of a national economy and the ensuing transportation revolution as well as negative aspects, including the implementation of child labor and the crowding of industrial areas.

For this chapter, *A History of the United States* as an instructional program provides two types of resources you can use to offer in-depth coverage of work in the Industrial Age: the *student text* and the *Enrichment Support File*. A list of *Suggested Secondary Sources* is also provided. The chart below shows the topics that are covered in each.

THE STUDENT TEXT. Boorstin and Kelley's *A History of the United States* unfolds the chronology of events and the key players, and, as an interpretive history, the controversy of working in the Industrial Age.

AMERICAN HISTORY ENRICHMENT SUPPORT FILE. This collection of primary source readings and classroom activities reveals the positive and negative aspects of working in the nation's new factories during the Industrial Age.

SUGGESTED SECONDARY SOURCES. This referencelist of readings by well-known historians and other commentators provides an array of perspectives on working in the nation's new factories during the Industrial Age. (See the chart below.)

Locating Instructional Materials

Detailed lesson plans for teaching working during the Industrial Age as a mini-course or to study one or more elements of the Industrial Age in depth are offered in the following areas: in the *student text*, see individual lesson plans at the beginning of each chapter; in the *Enrichment Support File*, see page 3; for readings beyond the student text, see *Suggested Secondary Sources*.

IN-DEPTH COVERAGE OF INDUSTRIALISM IN AMERICA		
Student Text	**Enrichment Support File**	**Suggested Secondary Sources**
• The factory system, pp. 260–262 • "Waltham" or "Lowell" labor system, pp. 262–263 • Eli Whitney and interchangeable parts, pp. 263–264 • "Wage slavery," p. 263 • Mass production, pp. 264–265 • Samuel Slater, pp. 259–260, 263	• Lesson Suggestions • Multimedia Resources • Overview Essay/On the Job: Industrialism in America • Literature in American History/Voices of the Industrial Age • Songs in American History/Challenge and Opportunity in the Industrial Revolution • Primary Sources in American History/Two Views on Life in the Mills • Biography in American History/Thomas Alva Edison • Geography in American History/The New England Cotton Mills: Location Pays • Great Debates in American History/Wealth of Progress *vs* Poverty of Spirit • Simulation • Art in American History/America's First Skyscrapers	• *Women at Work: The Transformation of Work and Community in Lowell, Massachusetts, 1826–1860* by Thomas Dublin, pp. 86–107. • *Workingmen's Democracy: The Knights of Labor and American Politics* by Leon Fink, pp. 219–233. • *Rockdale: The Growth of an American Village in the Early Industrial Revolution* by Anthony F. C. Wallace, pp. 124–185.

Drawing the People Together

FOCUS

To introduce the lesson, have students study the painting on page 248 and ask: From this painting, what do you think this unit is about? (Possible answers: transportation, life-styles, westward movement, changes in life.)

INSTRUCT

Explain

The Erie Canal made enormous amounts of money even though the movement of freight on it was relatively slow. There was a high volume of freight because there was no better way, at that time, to move goods to and from the West.

☑ Writing Process Activity

Determining Relevance Ask students to imagine they are among the first passengers on a new canal, steamboat, or railroad. In preparation for writing a description of this experience, ask them to make a chart of the various sense impressions they might have gathered. They should begin with a topic sentence that captures reader interest, and they should organize their ideas in chronological order. After revising for vivid word choice and realistic detail, they should proofread. Students can display their writing with route maps on a bulletin board.

Section Review Answers

Section 1, page 259

1. a) road on which users must pay a fee (toll). b) reformer and New York governor who, in 1816, proposed the idea of building the Erie Canal. c) developed the first successful steamboat (1807). d) steamboats with high-pressure engines that raced with each other on western rivers and often exploded. 2. Lancaster Turnpike is the road between Lancaster and Philadelphia shown on page 128. The National Road appears on the map on page 252 labeled Cumberland Road and National Pike. The Mohawk Valley parallels the Mohawk River in upstate New York; it and the Erie Canal are on the map on page 254. 3. State and local governments helped finance roads and canals because these projects improved and increased trade and because they hoped the tolls charged to users would cover the costs or even bring in revenue. 4. The Erie Canal was the first great canal in America. It allowed goods from upstate New York and the Great Lakes to reach the Atlantic by way of New York City. 5. American railroads were laid haphazardly, often with only one set of tracks for travel in both directions. In Europe there were two sets of tracks, and they were carefully planned. European engines were designed for safety. Engines in the United States were created for speed. 6. In the 1840s Congress reformed the postal system; the Post Office Department issued the first national stamps; Samuel F. B. Morse developed the first working telegraph system that covered the nation. 7. Steamboat travel was luxurious, comfortable, and fast. Unfortunately, the engines of these boats often exploded under pressure, especially when racing another boat.

CLOSE

To conclude the lesson, ask students to answer the following questions in an essay titled "The Importance of New Methods of Transportation to the Growing United States": Could the United States safely expand its boundaries without a strong transportation system? Why is a transportation system necessary for settlement?

The Industrial Revolution

FOCUS

To introduce the lesson, ask: What does the term *industrialization* mean? Through discussion help students to develop a useful definition.

Developing Vocabulary

The words listed are essential terms for understanding particular sections of the chapter. The page number after each term indicates the page of its first or most important appearance. These terms are defined in the text Glossary (text pages 1000–1011).

Industrial Revolution (page 259); **lithograph** (page 260); **corporation** (page 261); **interchangeable parts** (page 264).

INSTRUCT

Explain

Use Lego blocks or Tinkertoys to illustrate the concept of interchangeable parts.

★ Independent Activity

Recognizing Cause and Effect Have students make a list of the ways in which industrialization affected Americans to include in a short story about a family during the Industrial Revolution. Students should include ideas such as industrialization made the machine (or tool) more dominant than the worker, replaced crafts with unskilled jobs, and took some control of the work environment away from the worker, but also led to more leisure time and a higher standard of living.

Section Review Answers

Section 2, page 265

1. The Industrial Revolution provided the know-how and machines that made the Transportation Revolution possible. The Transportation Revolution helped the Industrial Revolution because it expanded the factories' markets by allowing people far away from the factories to buy the factories' products. 2. The Lowell factories set a precedent by establishing a successful, well-run, attractive industrial center in the United States. They employed large numbers of workers—especially women—who were no longer needed on the farms. 3. Eli Whitney came up with the idea of using interchangeable parts to mass-produce manufactured goods. 4. The Industrial Revolution improved trade between regions and encouraged each region to specialize in producing certain goods, making the various regions of the country more dependent on each other.

CLOSE

To conclude the lesson, ask students: Was the advent of the factory system in America ultimately beneficial or harmful? Allow students to express their opinions, and encourage class debate.

Section 3 (pages 265–269)

America's Leading Import: People

FOCUS

To introduce the lesson, ask: Why did northern Europeans immigrate to the United States in such large numbers from 1820 to 1860? List students' answers on the board. Then group the responses into social, political, religious, and economic factors.

INSTRUCT

Explain

Define *emigration* and *immigration*. *Emigration* is the leaving of one's homeland, while *immigration* is the entry into a new homeland.

☑ Writing Process Activity

Recognizing Ideologies Ask students to imagine that they are immigrants from Ireland or Germany.

Before they write a diary entry about their experiences in the United States, ask them to brainstorm their reasons for coming. As they compose their entries, have them include an evaluation of whether their lives fulfill their expectations. Students should revise for vivid language and realistic detail, then proofread carefully. They can share their entries with classmates, comparing and contrasting reactions.

Section Review Answers

Section 3, page 269

1. A famine in Ireland, crop failures in Germany, lack of farmland, dictatorships, and political upheavals. 2. Irish immigrants made up a big part of the labor force that completed the Erie Canal; many helped build the canals that followed and then the railroads. 3. Between the Revolution and Civil War, there were revolutions and dictatorships in France, Spain, Germany, Greece, Italy, and Belgium. Many Europeans sought to escape from this unrest by emigrating to the United States.

CLOSE

To conclude the lesson, tell students that between 1820 and 1850, 5 million immigrants entered the United States, mostly from northern Europe. Ask students if any of their ancestors came to America during this period and invite students to share information about their roots with the class.

Extension Activity

To extend the lesson, have students investigate Irish or German culture, and compile a list of five to ten cultural contributions of that particular ethnic group still found in contemporary American society.

Section 4 (pages 269–271)

The Rise of the West

FOCUS

To introduce the lesson, ask for a show of hands to the question: How many of you plan to move more than 25 miles from your present home after you graduate from high school? (Most usually raise their hands.) Ask: Why do you want to leave your hometown? (Common answers are boredom, jobs, and adventure.) Tell the class that the average American moves a number of times in a lifetime. Have the class compile a list of reasons people move in a lifetime. Have the class compile a list of probable reasons people moved in the 1800s. What has changed since then? What has not?

INSTRUCT

Explain

Have students turn to the map of the United States on page 949 and locate the cities mentioned on page 269. Tell students where those cities ranked in terms of population according to the 1980 census: Chicago 2; Detroit 6; Memphis 15; Cleveland 19; Denver 25; St. Louis 27; Kansas City 28; Pittsburgh 31; Cincinnati 33; Minneapolis 35; Buffalo 39; Toledo 40; Omaha 48; Louisville 49; St. Paul 54; Rochester 57; Des Moines 74.

❖ Cooperative Learning Activity

Formulating Questions Break the class into small groups. Tell students that each group will use outside resources to prepare a report on one of the western cities listed in Chapter 10, *Instant cities*. Explain that each report must include one section describing how the city was established and its early history, and another section summarizing the city's growth and development to the present day. Have group members begin by using one of the maps in Chapter 10 to reach consensus on a city on which to report. Then have students decide who will prepare each section of the report. When all reports have been submitted, make them available for students to read.

Section Review Answers

Section 4, page 271

1. A few people might first publish a newspaper and build a hotel where they hoped a city might grow. Then those people would advertise to attract settlers to build the city. Cities were built on the rivers and at the places where rivers joined. 2, 3. The balloon-frame house could be built without the help of skilled carpenters, did not require heavy timbers, could be built quickly.

CLOSE

To conclude the lesson, write the following two quotations on the board: "With us (in Europe) railways run to the towns; but in the States the towns run to the railways." "A man builds a house in which to spend his old age, and he sells it before the roof is on." Discuss the significance of the quotations with students. Is "community" an American value?

Extension Activity

To extend the lesson, tell students that they will pretend they are famous scouts or explorers such as Daniel Boone, Jim Bowie, or Zebulon Pike. In a one-page essay, have students write their impression of the various things they have seen during their explorations.

Section 5 (pages 271–276)

The Cotton Kingdom

FOCUS

To introduce the lesson, draw a three-column table on the board with the title, Effects of Slavery. Label the columns with these headings: Political, Economic, and Social. Then, with text pages 271–275 as a guide, have students list the effects under each column. Discuss these. Ask students to indicate which if any effects they consider positive and which negative.

Developing Vocabulary

middle passage (page 272); **peculiar institution** (page 273).

INSTRUCT

Explain

To help students see why craftspeople and farmers received less for their labor in a system that allowed slaves, cite the following example. Suppose carpenters around the country normally charge $20.00 per hour for their work. You want to get one of the three available carpentry jobs building garages in town. Three other carpenters in town normally charge only $15.00 for their work. In order to get one of the three available jobs, you too will have to charge only $15.00. Slaves were like the carpenters charging the lower fee. Except, of course, that slaves did not receive the benefits of their own work.

☑ Writing Process Activity

Recognizing Ideologies Ask students to imagine that they have overheard an argument between a Northern abolitionist and a Southern slave owner. To recreate a heated dialogue, students should brainstorm the political, economic, and social positions of each side. As they recreate the actual conversation, students should capture realistic speech and emotional issues. Have students revise their dialogues for unity and coherence. After proofreading, they can choose partners and act out the argument.

Section Review Answers

Section 5, page 276

1. The horrible journey of captive blacks from Africa to the Americas. 2. Some owners were kind, others brutal. Some slaves had decent living conditions and work schedules; others did not. But all were considered the property of others and denied their freedom. To resist the slaveowners, some slaves organized or joined revolts, faked illness or worked carelessly, sabotaged the owner's property or tried to escape.

3. Slavery blocked the path to economic development in the South and helped divide the South from the rest of the nation. 4. As Northern abolitionists began denouncing both slavery and the South, the South began to feel that it was under attack. As a way of defending themselves, Southerners began to argue that slavery was not just necessary but also good.

CLOSE

To conclude the lesson, review with students how to evaluate cause-and-effect reasoning: (1) find the cause and effect, and (2) decide how well the author connects the two. In the material under "A world of their own" (page 275), slave religion is identified as a prime cause of the sense of unity that arose among black slaves. Read this section over and evaluate the cause-and-effect reasoning.

Extension Activity

To extend the lesson, tell students to imagine that they are Africans being brought to the New World to be sold into slavery. Have them freewrite their sense impressions of the experience known as the "middle passage."

Chapter Review Answers

Focusing on Ideas

1. (a) Local roads were built by states and localities. The national government funded the National Road.

Turnpikes were generally built by private companies with state investment. (b) Canals were financed by state bonds. (c) Railroads were chiefly private with local, state, and federal land grants, loans, and stock purchase. These were highly speculative enterprises and benefited the general public. 2. Slater, Lowell, and Whitney contributed to the factory system; or pioneers in transportation. 3. Abundant farm land; job opportunities in factories, and in construction of cities and roads; peace. 4. Abolitionists: moral, religious, and humanitarian arguments; Southerners: slavery was a "positive good."

Taking a Critical Look

1. (a) Lower cost of shipping to the East and improved marketing; (b) more potential buyers and lower freight costs; (c) speedier and lower-cost travel; (d) more travellers through Albany. 2. See text pages 223–225 for comparison. 3. Western cities were often built before people came.

Knowing Your Region

1–3. Answers will vary depending on your region. Consult your local library or historical society.

Historical Facts and Figures

(a) Growing numbers of immigrants. (b) Declines in immigration. (c) Economic and political conditions in Europe led many people to seek jobs and freedom in America.

Chapter 10

The Flourishing Land

By the time of the Civil War there were distinct American ways of life. There were new ways of making houses, muskets, locks, and clocks—and nearly everything else. There were new ways of growing. The United States was the world's largest importer of people. And cities sprouted from raw western villages with a speed that startled Europeans.

But the sections did not grow all in the same way or at the same pace. Some regions were as different from others as, a century before, life in Great Britain had been different from life in the far-off American colonies. Thoughtful observers wondered if the Constitution that had been made to hold thirteen seaboard states together could really bind a continent.

In 1816 Thomas Birch painted this peaceful scene of a Conestoga wagon on the Pennsylvania Turnpike.

The Shelbourne Museum

250

See "Lesson Plan," p. 250C.

1. Drawing the people together

At the time of the War of 1812 it took 75 days for a fully loaded wagon pulled by four horses to travel the 1000 miles from Worcester, Massachusetts, to Charleston, South Carolina. Letters and news traveled little faster. Could any union last if its people and their produce were so hard to bring together?

The age of roads and turnpikes. During the early years of the Republic, the land was gradually covered by a network of trails and roads. One of the most popular kinds of roads was the "turnpike." This was a road where the user had to pay a toll. It was named after a kind of revolving barrier with spikes on it that had been used on paths in England to prevent horses from passing through. The first turnpike in the United States was built during George Washington's second term to cover the 62 miles between Lancaster and Philadelphia in Pennsylvania.

The success of this Lancaster Turnpike began a wave of turnpike building in New England and the Middle States that lasted until about 1825. Most of the turnpikes were built by private companies. States and local governments (p. 252) sometimes helped. But the high toll-fees charged per ton discouraged their use for the farmers' bulky products.

Funds from the federal government would change the picture. In 1802 and 1803 Congress voted to use money received from the sale of the public lands for a National Road through the mountains and across Ohio. In 1806 Cumberland, Maryland, was selected as the road's starting point. This, the most important federal transportation project of the time, took a half-century. Work began in 1811. The road reached Wheeling, West Virginia, on the Ohio River in 1818 and did not reach Vandalia, Illinois, until 1852. It became a vital wagon highway to the West.

Even after the turnpikes were built, the majority of roads were just bumpy trails, many with stumps a foot high in the middle. Most Americans lived on farms, and without a good cross-country road the farm family was isolated.

The canal-building boom. The roads and turnpikes usually went to villages near the water where goods could be floated to their destination. In the West, streams and rivers led down to the broad Mississippi, which carried produce all the way to New Orleans, then out to the Gulf of Mexico and the world.

New Orleans flourished from the trade of the West which was drained into her harbors. Eastern cities wanted a larger share. New York's Governor DeWitt Clinton in 1816 came up with a daring scheme. Before becoming governor, Clinton had been five times elected mayor of New York City. Madison had defeated him for President in 1812.

Clinton was a battler for reforms. He was an abolitionist, he defended poor debtors, and he wanted Roman Catholics to have the right to vote. Now, to promote commerce he aimed to dig the longest canal ever seen in America. It would run 363 miles through the level Mohawk Valley from Buffalo on Lake Erie to Albany on the Hudson River. Western crops, instead of floating down the Mississippi to enrich the merchants of New Orleans, would go through the Great Lakes into the canal and down the Hudson River to New York City. This was a grand and startling idea. At the time there were only 100 miles of canals in the whole United States. And none was more than 2 miles long!

There was a fight in the state legislature. Some said it would be too expensive. Farmers along the Hudson River and on Long Island feared the competition of produce from western farmers. But Clinton won. In 1817 the lawmakers voted $7 million for the project. They took it for granted that clever men would find a way to dig the long ditch. And they were right. In 1825 when the canal finally opened, the whole state celebrated. Clinton proudly took national leaders down the canal and the Hudson River from Buffalo to New York City and dumped a barrel of water from Lake Erie into the Atlantic Ocean.

At once the canal was a success. Its whole cost was repaid in nine years from the tolls charged the users. The cost per ton for sending shipments from Buffalo to New York dropped from 20 cents to less than 1 cent a mile. Farm products in western New York and the Ohio

Continuity and Change: Science, Technology and Society Point out to students that by 1800, although the colonies had united to form a nation, the lack of good roads kept them as separate as they ever were before the Revolution. At that time most "roads" were no more than tracks through wooded areas. After the War of 1812, the building of turnpikes and the National Road and the invention of the railroad helped tie the United States together. Improvements in roads and the development of trains meant faster communication, which brought the states closer to being truly "united." (See page 149.)

CANADA

Lake Superior

Lake Michigan

Lake Huron

Mississippi R.

Lake Ontario

Portland

Boston

Albany

Providence

Buffalo · Mohawk Road

Catskill Turnpike

Seneca Road

Detroit

Chicago Turnpike

Lake Erie

New York

Chicago

Cleveland

Harrisburg

Pittsburgh

Philadelphia

Pennsylvania Road

(Cumberland Road)

Columbus

Baltimore

Michigan Road

Maysville Turnpike

Northwestern Turnpike

Washington, D.C.

National Road

Indianapolis

Maysville

Traffic

Boone's Lick Road

Vandalia

Valley Turnpike

Richmond

Norfolk

St. Louis

Louisville

Wilderness Road

APPALACHIAN MOUNTAINS

Great Valley Road

Harrodsburg

Cumberland Gap

Raleigh

Mississippi R.

Nashville Road

Wilmington

Nashville

Coastal

Chattanooga

Unicoy Road

Memphis

Augusta

Charleston

Natchez Trace

General Jackson's Military Road

Savannah

Major Roads about 1851

Natchez

St. Augustine

New Orleans

GULF OF MEXICO

ATLANTIC OCEAN

Valley doubled in value now that they could so easily reach the eastern market. Cities on the Great Lakes—Buffalo, Cleveland, Detroit, and Chicago, and many more—soon rivaled the older river cities of Pittsburgh, Cincinnati and St. Louis. New York City became the nation's commercial metropolis.

The success of the Erie Canal sparked a canal-building boom. By 1840 more than $125 million had been spent all over the North and the West on a vast canal system of 3326 miles.

(p. 254)

Most canal projects were halted by the Panic of 1837 and the depression that followed. Some states, like Pennsylvania and Indiana, which built canals in haste without figuring how to cover their cost, were near bankruptcy. Many states now amended their constitutions to forbid use of the state's credit for canals or other internal improvements. One result was that, when railroads were built in the 1840s and 1850s, though aided by state funds, they were built by private companies.

The age of the steamboat. For all human history, boats had been driven either by manpower or by windpower. There seemed to be no other way. Then, in 1807, Robert Fulton imported a steam engine from England, put it in his boat the *Clermont*, and astonished Americans. Fulton was clever and versatile. He was an expert gunsmith during the American Revolution, and then he became a painter. He had even designed underwater torpedoes and made a kind of submarine. Now he steamed upstream from New York to Albany in 32 hours. He proved to Americans that the steamboat could be used in commerce. Only four years later the first steamboat was launched west of the mountains on the Ohio River.

For Westerners the steamboat solved many problems. They could still float their crops on rafts downriver to New Orleans. But now they could ride back upriver in comfort in a fast-traveling, luxurious side-wheeler. Soon western rivers were alive with the tall, colorful stacks of the crowded vessels.

The steamship on western waters was unlike anything seen before. It was driven by a new type of engine—the high-pressure engine, which was light. The pioneer maker of these engines was Oliver Evans, from the neighborhood of Philadelphia, who was a genius at labor-saving devices. He had made a flour mill that used chutes and moving belts in place of manpower. And he actually had a plan for a steam-driven carriage that might have been a pioneer automobile. At first, people said he was crazy. When the gadgets worked, people stopped laughing and began stealing his ideas.

The high-pressure engines were faster than anything known before. They burned lots of wood to keep up the steam pressure, but that was not serious in the virgin forests of the West. With a full head of steam their boilers sometimes exploded. But American pioneers were willing to risk anything to get there first. Their motto was "Go ahead anyhow."

Since these steamboats had to operate on shallow western rivers filled with snags, rocks, and sandbars, they were built with a shallow draft. The engine was set on deck inside a high superstructure. In 1838 there were twenty steamboats that could operate in only 30 inches of water. Some captains joked that their ships could run on a heavy dew! Not only were these ships light and fast, but they were inexpensive to build. That was a good thing because with the American passion for speed the boats did not last very long.

On these western steamboats the accidents were shocking. Without safety valves on the crude boilers or with the valves tied down, unlimited speed meant unlimited disaster. Europeans were appalled.

"The democrats have never liked to remain behind one another," a traveling German nobleman reported from the West about 1840. "On the contrary each wants to get ahead of the rest. When two steamboats happen to get alongside each other, the passengers will encourage the captains to run a race. . . . The races are the cause of most of the explosions, and yet they are still constantly taking place. The life of an American is, indeed, only a constant *racing*, and why should he fear it so much on board the steamboats?"

These western racers, called "brag" boats, lived a short, exciting life. Of all the steamboats

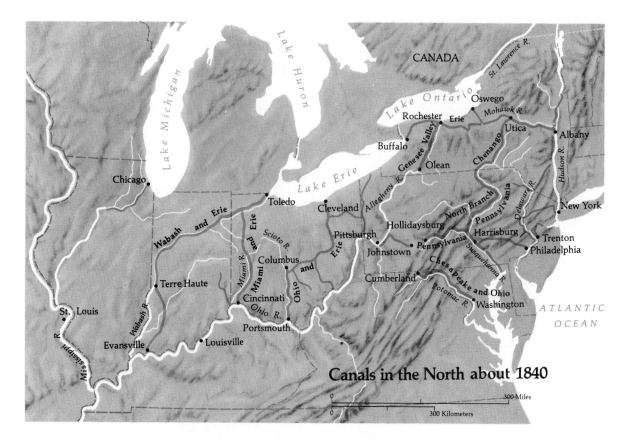

Canals in the North about 1840

built before the mid-1800s, nearly a third were lost in accidents. The main cause was explosions, which killed scores of passengers by bursts of flying wreckage and floods of scalding steam. Some steamboat owners sent the passengers who had not yet paid their fares to the back part of the vessel. Then, in case of explosion, they were less likely to be killed, and the owner could still collect his fares from them.

The triumph of the railroads. The United States did not invent the railroad. But this country luckily was free from the artificial barriers of national boundaries that had grown up over the centuries in Europe. Here vast expanses of wilderness were filling up with people. Hordes of eager settlers wanted a speedy path to their new homes. Thousands of empty acres were suddenly populated by farmers and merchants who needed supplies brought in and who had to ship out their produce. Boston, Baltimore, and Charleston met the challenge of the

Erie Canal. They built railroads to capture the commerce of the West.

It took time before everybody saw that the railroads would be the arteries that united the nation. Pennsylvania ignored the first successful railroads built in 1830. It chose instead to reach westward with a canal. But by 1840, in the country as a whole, there were as many miles of track as there were of canals.

The great wave of railroad building came in the vast American West in the 1850s. In a single decade the nation's tracks increased from 8879 miles to 30,626 miles—more than enough to circle the globe. Ohio and Illinois, then still called the "West," led the nation in their miles of track. Chicago, which did not become an incorporated city until 1833, within 30 years had grown to be the greatest railroad center in the world.

Railroad building in the United States. Cautious European railroad builders came over

Travel by steamboat could be quite luxurious. The interiors were often full of carved wood panels and elegant velvet draperies. The exterior, as shown in this 1850s photograph of steamboats crowded at a small dock, was trimmed with carved wood.

here in the 1840s and 1850s to see how Americans had managed to lay their tracks so fast over such vast distances. They were horrified. Just as the reckless Americans had pushed ahead on the rivers with high-pressure engines on their steamboats, so now it seemed that railroading Americans were taking terrible risks. Instead of laying two sets of tracks—one for each direction—they saved time and money by laying only a single set of tracks. Of course, this increased the danger of collision. They did not trouble to level hills, to cut tunnels, or to lay their tracks in long, gentle curves. Sometimes they actually laid tracks on top of the snow—with disastrous results when the spring thaw came. No wonder the American trains so often went off the rails as they came rocketing down the steep hills or failed to maneuver the sharp curves.

By 1850 railroad wrecks were as common as steamboat explosions. Experienced travelers rode in the middle cars, rather than at front or back. Fast American trains of the middle 1800s gave all the excitement of a roller coaster, but they were much less safe.

In their headlong pursuit of speed, Americans made some discoveries. Perhaps the most important was how to design light engines that put less strain on the track and still could hold the track around sharp curves. The heavy early engines were built with large wheels mounted rigidly on axles like those of the old horse

Railroads, 1850-1860

— Railroads in 1850

— Railroads Completed, 1850-1860

0 — 400 Miles

0 — 400 Kilometers

carriage. John Bloomfield Jervis, a self-taught engineer from New York, saw another way. He made a separate little truck (called a "bogie") with four low wheels and put it under the front end of the locomotive. Since the bogie wheels were low, small, and could swivel, they were not so apt to derail, even on sharply curving track.

American railroads were built by private companies with both state and private funds. The ⊕ companies were aided by the federal govern-

ment with free surveys and lower tariffs on iron rails. After 1850 they were given thousands of acres of public land. In England, where railroads were also being built, they usually went from one big city to another. But in the United States, where people were only beginning to fill up the continent, things were different. Here, as an amused foreign editor remarked, the railroads often went "from nowhere in particular to nowhere at all."

⊕ **Geography and History: Place** Have students look at the map above. Ask: What is the distance in a straight line between Cincinnati, Ohio, and Richmond, Virginia? (400 miles) According to the map, what two methods of transportation would be important in New York, Boston, Cleveland, and Detroit? (Railroads and ships. All these cities have railroad terminals, and they all lie either on the Atlantic coast or on the Great Lakes.)

Laying a railroad across the vast, empty stretches of the American West was a costly business. The tracks were expensive. Whole communities of laborers had to be moved out and provided for on the prairie, on a mountainside, or in the deep forests. There the teams surveyed the track, constructed roadbeds, laid rails, cut tunnels, and built bridges. Enormous capital was required, which private firms did not yet have. The states and the federal government provided large grants of land that could be sold to make up the difference.

By 1860 steam had transformed transportation over the land and on the lakes and rivers of the United States. The railroad had opened whole new areas to settlement, spurred the growth of factories, and turned the trade of the West from the South toward the East. Instead of floating most of their produce down to New Orleans or to the southern states, Westerners now shipped their goods by rail and canal to eastern cities. These same railroads and canals brought back to them the products of the East. The economic interests of western farmers and eastern factory workers were newly united. All this would have political consequences.

(p. 259)

Letters in every mailbox. A workable national mail system was slow in coming to the nation. The framers of the federal Constitution in 1787 had given Congress the power "to establish Post Offices and Post Roads." A post road was a main road with special stations ("posts") to provide fresh horses for the riders who carried the mail. For some years, almost all postal service was on one main post road along the Atlantic coast. People used the mail very little. When George Washington was President, the letters in the mail averaged less than one for every twelve Americans each year.

In those early years the postage on a letter was usually paid by the person who received it. If you did not want to pay the postage, you never got your letter. There was no home delivery. To get your mail you had to go to the post office.

Then in 1825 came the dim beginning of modern mail delivery. The postmaster in each town was allowed to give letters to mail carriers to deliver to people's homes. The carriers still

WANTED!
3,000 LABORERS
On the 12th Division of the
ILLINOIS CENTRAL RAILROAD
Wages, $1.25 per Day.

Fare, from New-York, only - - $4⅛

By Railroad and Steamboat, to the work in the State of Illinois.

Constant employment for two years or more given. Good board can be obtained at two dollars per week.

This is a rare chance for persons to go West, being sure of permanent employment in a healthy climate, where land can be bought cheap, and for fertility is not surpassed in any part of the Union.

Men with families preferred.

For further information in regard to it, call at the Central Railroad Office,

173 BROADWAY,
CORNER OF COURTLANDT ST.
NEW-YORK.
R. B. MASON, Chief Engineer.
H. PHELPS, Agent,

July, 1853.

State Historical Society of Wisconsin

To get the tracks laid and the trains moving quickly, the railroads needed thousands of construction workers from the East Coast.

were paid no government salary. They lived by collecting a small fee from the person to whom they delivered a letter. If you were not at home to pay, they would not leave your letters in your mailbox.

In the 1840s the growing country desperately needed a cheap and efficient postal system. The service was still so haphazard and expensive that there was widespread demand to abolish

More from Boorstin: "The railroad builders, who had to name every station along the way faced an exhausting task. Since they came in from the outside, they knew little or nothing of local traditions. But often there was really nothing to know since the places they were naming did not yet exist . . . A vice president of the Milwaukee railroad actually named thirty-two stations in the state of Washington, including Warden ('after a heavy stockholder'), Othello ('after the play'), and Horlick ('after the malted milk')." (From *The Americans: The National Experience*)

The illustration above shows the cover for sheets of original music dedicated to Cyrus W. Field in honor of the transatlantic telegraph cable.

✕ **Critical Thinking Activity: Making Comparisons** How did new and improved forms of communication bring Americans closer together? (For the purposes of this exercise, define the term *communication* as anything that brings people's thoughts and ideas closer together.) Have students list some forms of communication they use in a typical day. Ask students to designate which of these forms would have been available in 1860. How would these limited forms of communication shape their present lives?

the Post Office. People called it an "odious monopoly" and said that private businesses could do better.

As a result, in 1845 Congress passed a law establishing cheap postage and tried to reform the whole system. At first each postmaster printed his own stamps, and there was chaos. Then, in 1847, the reformed Post Office Department issued the first national postage stamps— a 5-cent stamp showing the head of Benjamin Franklin and a 10-cent stamp with the head of George Washington

Still, for most of the century, people outside of big cities had to go to the post office to pick up their mail. It was not until 1896 that Congress adopted "Rural Free Delivery"—RFD, for short. Then every family could have the mail brought to their own mailbox.

Morse and the telegraph. Some people dreamed of faster methods of communicating. But it was hard to imagine a system that did not depend on seeing signals or on sending written messages. Samuel F. B. Morse, an artist and a man of many talents, found a way to make an electric current do the job. The idea came to him on the sailing ship *Sully* coming back from a trip to Europe. After talking to a fellow passenger about electricity, he asked why it could not be used to send messages. Others before him had asked the same question—and got nowhere with their answer. But Morse did not know enough about the subject to be discouraged. He suddenly decided to make an electric "telegraph" (from the Greek words for "far writer").

It took Morse five years to make a telegraph instrument that would work and six more years to convince Congress to build the first line. During that time he supported himself by giving painting lessons. Finally, in 1843, Congress appropriated $30,000. With this money Morse stretched a telegraph line from Baltimore to Washington. On May 24, 1844, he sent his famous message, "What hath God wrought?" from Washington to Baltimore.

By 1848, Morse and two partners had built a telegraphic network that stretched from Maine to South Carolina and westward to St. Louis, Chicago, and Milwaukee. Regular newspaper columns offered the latest bulletins under the heading, "By Magnetic Telegraph." Newspapermen boasted of the "mystic band" that now held the nation together.

Cyrus W. Field, a visionary New York businessman, thought there ought to be a telegraph line all the way to Europe. He formed a company to undertake the difficult task. After several years and many failures, the long line on the bottom of the ocean was finished in 1858, and telegraph messages began to pass between America and England. Within weeks the line failed, and then the Civil War prevented the laying of a new cable until 1866.

See "Section 1 Review answers," p. 250C.

Section 1 Review

1. Identify or explain: turnpike, DeWitt Clinton, Robert Fulton, "brag" boats.
2. Locate: Lancaster Turnpike, National Road, Mohawk Valley, Erie Canal.
3. Why were state and local governments willing to finance roads and canals?
4. What was the importance of the Erie Canal?
5. How did American railroads and engines differ from those built in Europe?
6. Name some significant developments in American communications in the 1840s.
7. **Critical Thinking: Expressing Problems Clearly.** Discuss the advantages and drawbacks of steamboat travel.

See "Lesson Plan," p. 250C.

2. The Industrial Revolution

The Industrial Revolution is a name for the great changes brought by the modern factory system. It came first to Britain. The British government, hoping to keep its leadership, made it a crime to take out of the country the designs of its new factory machinery. It was a crime even for workmen from one of these advanced factories to go to work in another country. But people and ideas were on the move—and America was the place for an ambitious workman.

Samuel Slater, on his own, defeated Britain's

See "Lesson Plan," p. 250C for **Writing Process Activity: Determining Relevance** relating to means of transportation.

Smoke from the factories of Lazell, Perkins & Company was a daily reminder to Bridgewater, Massachusetts, that the Industrial Revolution had arrived. This late 1850s hand-colored lithograph advertised the firm's "Forgings . . . Casting and all Kinds of Machinery."

shortsighted scheme of industrial secrecy. While he worked in one of the up-to-date English cotton textile mills, he memorized the design for the machinery. Then he came to the United States—with some of the most prized industrial secrets. Helped by two American businessmen in Pawtucket, Rhode Island, he set up the first American textile factory just like the most advanced factories in England. It opened in 1792 with 72 spindles and a work force of nine children.

The rise of the factory system.

In 1850 the 7th Census of the United States reported a great change in American ways of making things that soon reshaped American ways of living. Eventually this would create an American Standard of Living. The Census noted that in earlier times "the bulk of general manufacturing done in the United States was carried on in the shop and the household by the labor of the family or individual proprietors who apprenticed assistants." But now most manufacturing was being done by a "system of factory labor, compensated by wages and assisted by power." This new factory system had begun to displace the old system of household manufacturing. Before, Americans had made the things they needed in their own homes and for their own use. Now goods were produced in factories and by machines for sale to anybody willing to pay for them.

This Industrial Revolution helped bring about a Transportation Revolution. The same steam power and new techniques that made factories possible also brought the steamboats and the railroads to carry products of farm and factory out to the wider world. The Transportation Revolution reached the thousands of new customers needed to buy the masses of goods now produced in the factories. Wherever canals, railroads, or steamboats went, they provided new customers for farmers, too.

The rise of a new economy. Now farmers began to buy factory-made clothing, furniture, kitchen utensils, and all the other output of industrial America. The pioneer family was no longer so isolated. A national economy began to emerge. Each region would specialize in what it could do best. The Northeast and the Middle States produced finished goods in their factories, the West grew wheat and corn, while the South specialized in cotton, tobacco, rice, and sugar. The produce of the South and West flowed to the Northeast, and from that region finished goods moved back to the South and West.

The United States, which only a century before was mostly an unsettled wilderness, surprised the world. Suddenly this nation became a strong competitor in the industrial marketplace. The country was lucky in its virgin forests, fertile fields, and untapped minerals. A stable government favored industry. The growing population was becoming ever more varied. People from everywhere who were persecuted, restless, or dissatisfied made the United States their mecca. They were enterprising and industrious, and they made the country stronger.

This was becoming a nation of nations. In Europe, national borders and jealous governments stopped the free flow of goods and of people over the land. But not here. The Founding Fathers had designed a great federal nation. They foresaw the need to let people and goods flow from state to state, back and forth across the whole country. "Everything new is quickly introduced here," one foreign observer re-

marked. "There is no clinging to old ways; the moment an American hears the word 'invention' he pricks up his ears."

The corporation. The cost of these new factories was usually beyond the means of any one person, or even a partnership of a few people. Vast sums had to be collected. For this purpose a new social invention was at hand. The "joint stock company" had not been invented here, but had already been used in England for just this purpose. "Joint stock" ventures had brought some of the first English settlers to America. Now, when a "joint stock" company was chartered by a state, it became a "corporation." This meant that it had a life of its own and would survive in legal theory even if the shareholders died. The corporation could sue in court and in other ways was like a real person.

Shares of stock were sold to numerous investors. Each then owned a "share" in the company. Of course they might lose whatever they had invested. But a clever legal arrangement provided that they could not be held responsible for the company's debts. This was called "limited liability." Hundreds of small investors put in a few dollars each. They could share the profits but still not risk losing large sums if the company was badly managed. In this way, funds were gathered to build a great industrial nation. And not only rich people but small investors, too, could have a share of the profits.

Waltham and the factory system. In 1813 Francis Cabot Lowell and his associates in the Boston Manufacturing Company in Waltham, Massachusetts, brought together under one roof, for the first time ever, all the processes for making cotton cloth. This required a large capital investment and a new kind of factory. It was risky business. Only bold organizers dared to take the lead—just as none but bold men would have built the Erie Canal.

Lowell came upon the idea for his factory on a trip to England during 1810–1812 when he visited the cotton textile factories. Soon after his return to the United States, the War of 1812 stopped his importing and exporting business. This gave him time to make plans for his

Waltham factory. The factory was such a success that the Boston Associates decided to expand. They found a site on the Merrimack River, where its 30-foot falls provided power to drive the machines. There in 1822 they built a new and bigger factory. They named the town "Lowell." Soon textile factories sprouted in Massachusetts, New Hampshire, and Maine. In hilly New England they could use the waterpower of the many streams that tumbled toward the ocean.

Foreign visitors noticed that the air of American factory towns was clear. The air of European cities was filling with smoke from the fuel that fired the steam engines. But New England factories used the streams. They were built in the pleasant countryside. An Englishwoman, 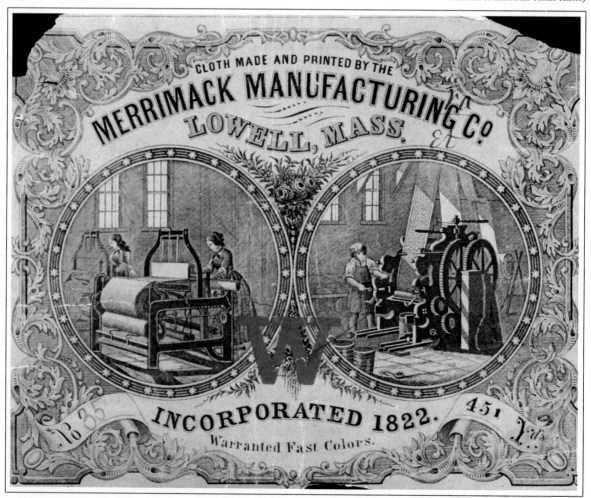 Harriet Martineau, in 1836 saw the fortunate American workers in Lowell. There they "might catch as beautiful glimpses of Nature's face as western settlers."

The "Waltham" or "Lowell" labor system. What impressed European visitors even more than the landscape was the work force. They were mostly young women! Francis Cabot

The Boston Associates named their Lowell works the Merrimack Manufacturing Company after the river that powered the machines. The women in this label are weaving cloth. The worker on the right is printing calico—a light cotton cloth once imported from Calcutta in India.

Museum of American Textile History

CLOTH MADE AND PRINTED BY THE
MERRIMACK MANUFACTURING CO.
LOWELL, MASS.
INCORPORATED 1822.
Warranted Fast Colors.

More from Boorstin: "When Harriet Martineau, herself the daughter of a Norwich manufacturer, visited [Waltham and Lowell] in 1835, she feared that any accurate description would tempt most of England's workers to the New World." (From *The Americans: The National Experience*)

The Metropolitan Museum of Art, Harris Brisbane Dick Fund, 1941

Many Irish immigrants helped to build the Erie Canal. This lithograph shows the excavation process at Lockport, New York. A horse drives the treadmill that powers the primitive crane.

somehow gained. Over there, 1816 was the terrible "year without a summer." The Rhine River flooded, floating away barns and livestock. Autumn storms uprooted fruit trees. Hunger and misery cursed the farmer. We cannot be surprised then that during the following year about 8000 Germans arrived in American ports. Again in 1829–1830, the winter was one of the worst in the history of Europe. People froze because there was not enough wood to burn in fireplaces. Food was scarcer than ever, and prices went up.

By 1832, more than 10,000 Germans were coming to America in a single year. As suffering in the German countryside deepened, it became plain that their government was not going to help. Then Germans started coming to America by the tens of thousands. They continued to arrive in vast numbers till nearly the end of the

1800s. In 1854 alone (when Germans were half of all immigrants to the United States) they numbered nearly a quarter-million. The move to America became a craze. Overnight, people would decide to leave Germany, and they would depart the next morning. A 13-year-old boy with a pack on his back walked 300 miles to the French port of Le Havre in order to find passage to America.

The Germans revolt. Throughout these years, revolutions were brewing in Germany. In 1815 at the end of the Napoleonic Wars the rulers of Europe met at the Congress of Vienna to shuffle boundary lines and restore the old monarchies. Nearly 40 German states were organized into a loose German Confederation dominated by Austria. Wanting democratic rule and freedom from Austria, students formed secret

See "Lesson Plan," p. 250D for **Writing Process Activity: Recognizing Ideologies** relating to German and Irish immigrants in the United States.

societies and studied new constitutions. Peasants refused to pay taxes and roughed up tax officials.

In central Europe, Prince Metternich, the clever and calculating Austrian foreign minister, was in charge. He had seen the terror of the French Revolution of 1789, and he hated democracy, which he imagined was always government by a mob. He organized tyranny in Germany. But even Metternich could not prevent protests like that in May 1832 when 25,000 people gathered in a small German town to drink the health of Lafayette (the hero of the American Revolution) and to demand a republic.

Metternich's policies created a rising flood of refugees. By 1848 there was civil war and a full-fledged revolution in Germany. The land was in turmoil, and many had to flee when the rebellion collapsed.

The political refugees. These political refugees from Germany were not many—perhaps only a few thousand. But they included some, like the daring Carl Schurz, who became eminent here and helped to build in the United States the democracy they could not build in Germany. Back in Germany he had joined the rebel forces against the government. When the leader of his movement was put in prison, at the risk of his own life he helped his friend escape. When the German Revolution failed, Schurz came to the United States. His career covered the whole country. After becoming a lawyer in Milwaukee, he campaigned for Lincoln in 1860 and fought as a general on the northern side at Gettysburg. He was minister to Spain, senator from Missouri, and then served in the Cabinet as Secretary of the Interior.

As the career of Carl Schurz and many other liberty-loving Germans showed, Germany's loss was America's gain. New Americans from Germany built whole cities like Milwaukee, and helped make Milwaukee a brewing center for American beer. They spread all over the country, becoming farmers, teachers, professors, lawyers, doctors, and journalists. They built prosperous businesses. Many others besides

The Huntington Library, San Marino, California

The flags of the United States and Germany decorate the menu cover for a party on March 2, 1899, honoring Carl Schurz.

Carl Schurz fought on the Union side in the Civil War.

The Germans brought with them some new ideas for schools. They believed in physical education, and many early physical education teachers were German. They persuaded Americans to build gymnasiums attached to schools. Until the Germans came, it was not usual to send children to school before they were old enough to read. The Germans brought over the *Kindergarten* (a German word meaning "garden for children") where children as young as four years old could learn by playing. The idea ✂ caught on, and soon there were American kindergartens everywhere.

The great migration. In the half-century before the Civil War, although the largest num-

✂ Critical Thinking Activity: Recognizing Cause and Effect What contributions did immigrants make to the growth and development of the United States? Ask students to list some of the ethnic groups represented in their school and in the community. Have students think of specific contributions these ethnic groups have made to the community, such as architecture, art, music, festivals, foods, education, and working skills. Then discuss the contributions that early immigrants made to the developing United States.

bers came from Germany and Ireland, immigrants were coming from other places, too. Thousands came from the Scandinavian countries, from the Netherlands, Belgium, Switzerland, France, Italy, and elsewhere.

The nation was growing by a great migration. And these other new Americans, like the Irish and the Germans, worked in factories and on farms. They, too, helped dig the canals and build the railroads which transformed the United States from a land of farmers into an industrial giant, a leader of the world.

See "Section 3 Review answers," p. 250D.

Section 3 Review

1. Name some factors that led 5 million immigrants to enter the United States between 1820 and 1860.
2. What part did the Irish play in the Transportation Revolution?
3. **Critical Thinking: Recognizing Cause and Effect.** How was civil unrest in Europe related to immigration to the United States?

See "Lesson Plan," p. 250D.

4. The rise of the West

Between 1815 and 1850 the lands west of the Appalachian Mountains became the nation's breadbasket. American workers would eat better than ever before. The farmers of the American West also fed the factory laborers of Europe. Though the South did not realize it, wheat—not cotton—was king.

The moving American. "In the United States," the young French traveler Alexis de Tocqueville noted during his visit in the 1830s, "a man builds a house in which to spend his old age, and he sells it before the roof is on." The people of the United States had become Americans by moving from other lands. They continued to move after they reached the New World. Over the next hill, round the next bend, in the next state, there they hoped to find the will-o-the-wisp "success."

In their constant movement these migratory people transformed half a continent. They cleared the forest and broke the thick turf of the prairies with the improved steel plows of the Industrial Revolution. They cut the grain with new mechanical harvesters.

In 1810 only one American in seven lived west of the Appalachians. By 1840 more than one in every three lived there. Most of these Westerners still lived on farms in the forest or on the prairies, where they grew corn and wheat and raised meat for home and market. To serve them and handle their crops, new cities sprang up and began to dot the land.

Instant cities. In places where people still alive could remember the sound of the Indian war whoop and the shadow of the virgin forest, there sprouted cities. On riverways and the joining of rivers appeared Pittsburgh, Cincinnati, St. Louis, Louisville, Memphis, Minneapolis and St. Paul, Davenport, Des Moines, ✄ Omaha, and hundreds of others. On the Great Lakes and at the river entrances to the Lakes, men and women created Rochester, Buffalo, Cleveland, Toledo, Detroit, and Chicago. An astonishing crop of cities sprang up quickly in the lands west of the Appalachians.

When before had so many cities grown so fast? In the years between the Revolution and the Civil War, Americans went west to start new cities. Many hoped to make their living out of city-building. Some hoped to make money out of selling the land. The wilderness was worth very little, but once a city was there, land became valuable. Then some people would want to buy land for houses, others for farms to raise vegetables and chickens and eggs for the people of the nearby city.

The great cities of the Old World had been built on their rich past. People had come first, and then there followed newspapers to give them news, inns to house the travelers, theaters and opera houses to entertain the crowds, colleges and universities where learned men could gather and the young could be educated.

But that was much too slow and haphazard for impatient, purposeful Americans. Western city-builders wanted their city first. They wanted to see it even *before* the people were

✄ Critical Thinking Activity: Drawing Conclusions What sparked the growth of cities in the West? Have students look at the maps of the United States on pages 948 and 949, and ask them to locate the following cities: Pittsburgh, Cincinnati, St. Louis, Louisville, Memphis, Minneapolis, St. Paul, Davenport, Des Moines, and Omaha. Ask students to carefully examine the locale for each city, noting geographic features, roadways, etc. How did these factors influence the development of each city? Ask students to summarize their findings in a written paragraph.

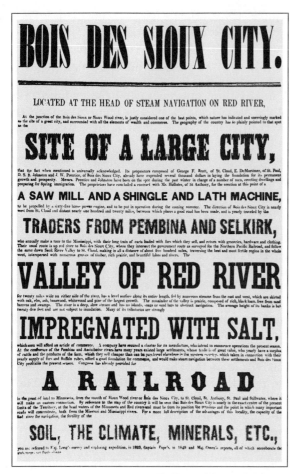

The Historical Society of Wisconsin

Breckenridge, Minnesota, and Wahpeton, North Dakota, are at the river junction cited in this ad. Bois des Sioux remained only a dream.

there. If they already had a newspaper, hotel, theater, and college, then surely people would come. But if they waited, then some other city might provide all those attractions first. People would then go on to Cleveland instead of staying in Pittsburgh, or they would move on from Kansas City to Omaha, or from Omaha to Denver.

The optimistic Americans were not always careful to distinguish between what had already happened and what they hoped (or felt sure) would happen. Foreigners complained that the cheery Americans did not always tell the truth. But the self-confident Americans replied that they were simply boosters. Why should they fail to report "facts" simply because they "had not yet gone through the formality of taking place"?

The families who went west in the early 1800s were often going to cities that did not yet really exist. To them a city was not just any place where lots of people happened to live. It was where people were building a community together. They built not only for their needs but also for their hopes.

For example, in Europe a city did not have a newspaper until it already had a large reading community. But in the American West, the city's own newspaper was actually founded *before* the city. Your place might never even become a city unless you *started* with a newspaper.

Hotels were constructed in the middle of nowhere. The large and elegant "Gayoso House" was built in the remote forest on the site of the future Memphis, Tennessee. It was three years before the city was even incorporated and ten years before there would be a railroad. Where were the guests? In the future, of course. When the English novelist Anthony Trollope traveled across America in the 1800s, he noted:

> When the new hotel rises up in the wilderness it is presumed that people will come there with the express object of inhabiting it. The hotel itself will create a population—as the railways do. With us [in Europe] railways run to the towns; but in the States the towns run to the railways. It is the same thing with the hotels.

(p. 271)

Every man his own carpenter. In their instant cities Americans needed houses. And they needed them quickly. There were no grandparents or other relatives to live with until you had a home of your own. There were no old houses to rent or to buy. And out in the West carpenters were scarce or nonexistent. If you wanted shelter, you had to provide it yourself. So Americans invented a new way of building.

In England, builders of houses had got into a rut. They believed there was only one right way to build a wooden house. You built it around a frame of heavy timbers. Each long timber was a

More from Boorstin: "[It was not by churches or government building but by hotels that cities were judged. They were] . . . public information centers, where new arrivals brought the latest word from distant places. In Presidential election years, the citizens who recorded their preferences in the hotel register made it one of the first opinion polls . . . The hotel became the headquarters of the first local telegraph office . . . After a fire, the hotel was usually the first building reconstructed." (From *The Americans: The National Experience*)

foot square, and the timbers had to be carefully fitted together by a complicated technique called "mortise and tenon." You rested your floors on these heavy supports, and closed in the sides with mud, plaster, or wood. All this produced a sturdy building, but to make it required skilled carpenters clever with the crude tools of the day. In new western towns like Cincinnati, Chicago, and Omaha, carpenters were not to be found, and people themselves did not have the skill—much less the time—to build their own houses in the old style.

All these needs produced the "balloon frame." Probably the first was built in Chicago in 1833, but we do not know who invented this new American building. Old-fashioned builders ridiculed the light "balloon-frame house" and said it would blow away in a high wind.

What was the balloon frame? The idea is so simple that it is hard to believe it ever had to be invented. The first notion was to forget that you ever needed a frame of heavy timbers with their ends neatly carved for a mortise and tenon to fit into one another. Instead make the lightest possible frame! Get a supply of long pieces of lumber about two inches thick and four inches wide. Then buy some long heavy nails. Stand up some of the light two-by-fours—say, eighteen inches or two feet apart—and nail other boards across them to hold them together.

Once you have your frame up, cover it outside and in with thin wide clapboards or any other material you wish. Nothing could be simpler. About three-quarters of the wooden houses in the United States are now built this way.

Of course, to build a balloon frame you need plenty of nails. In the old days nails had been extremely expensive because each one was fashioned by hand. But here again the Industrial Revolution helped the West. By 1830 New England nail-making machines were turning out nails by the thousands, better and cheaper than ever before.

The new way of building was speedy. It took less than half the time to build a balloon-frame house than one of the same size built in the old style. In Chicago, within one week in April 1834, seven new buildings of this kind appeared. By mid-June there were 75 more. By October an additional 500 were in use.

The balloon frame proved to have other advantages that nobody had counted on. It turned out to be even stronger and more durable than the old heavy-timbered construction. On top of that it helped Americans on the move because it was easily taken apart and then could be quickly put together again in some other place. St. Mary's Church in Chicago, said to be the first balloon-frame building built anywhere, within ten years of its construction was taken down, moved away, and re-erected three times. Now finally Americans on the move had the kind of house they could knock down and take along.

See "Section 4 Review answers," p. 250E.

Section 4 Review

1. How were cities constructed in the West?
2. What were the benefits of the "balloon-frame house" to the settlers?
3. **Critical Thinking: Drawing Conclusions.** How did the "balloon-frame house" help western cities to grow?

See "Lesson Plan," p. 250E.

5. The cotton kingdom

The South was a vast land of many different areas with different climates, different soils, different societies. It included tidewater Virginia with its dignified old families, the jungles and everglades of Florida where Seminole Indians still lived (along with many escaped slaves), and states west of the Appalachian Mountains that were more western than southern.

One thing drew all these states together. It was not so much that they were southern states, but that they were *slave* states.

The South on the defensive. Southerners opposed internal improvements because they feared that such federal projects would provide a precedent for "interfering" within a state in other ways, too. The federal government might start tampering with slavery.

❋ See "Lesson Plan," p. 250E for **Cooperative Learning Activity: Formulating Questions** relating to the growth of cities.

Beginning in the 1830s their fears increased as the voices of northern reformers who demanded that this ancient evil be abolished sounded louder and louder. Before long, abolitionist literature covered the country. It awakened Northerners to the horrors of slavery. It made them despise slavery. It also made them lump together all people in the South as if all Southerners wanted slavery. More and more Northerners began to hate the South and to hate Southerners.

As the northern propagandists against slavery became more passionate, Southerners too became more unreasonable. Instead of worrying over how to get rid of slavery, Southerners began to worry over how to defend slavery, and the South and themselves, against all outside attack.

Leaders in the South stopped saying that slavery was only a "necessary evil." "Slavery is not an evil," declared the governor of South Carolina in 1829. "On the contrary, it is a national benefit." Soon no voice could be raised in the South to suggest that slavery might someday, somehow, end.

One of the strongest supporters of slavery was Senator John C. Calhoun of South Carolina. The former Secretary of War and Vice-President of the United States was now the leading southern thinker. "Many in the South," he said, "once believed that it [slavery] was a moral and political evil; that folly and delusion are gone; we see it now in its true light, and regard it as the most safe and stable basis for free institutions in the world."

Calhoun was supported by many others when he called slavery "a positive good." Southern ministers said the Bible required that the blacks be slaves. Southern "scientists" said the blacks were an inferior race—the product of a "separate creation" that God made in the beginning on the African continent. George Fitzhugh, a Virginia thinker and writer, even changed the defense into an attack. He claimed that the so-called equal rights of the North merely allowed the strong to oppress the weak. The strong in the North were masters without responsibilities. In the South, on the other hand, a master had to take care of the slaves for life. In this way the weak were protected. It was through slavery, Fitzhugh claimed, that Greece and Rome had achieved "their great prosperity and high civilization." Astonishing nonsense was written by otherwise sane people—all to show that slavery was the greatest thing that ⌑ had ever happened to the human race.

The "middle passage."   Most people had come to America because they had wanted to come. But not the slaves. They had been brought in chains to America from Africa. In Africa, they had come from many different societies. Some were great empires, like Songhai and Melle. Some were complex cultures, like Benin and Yoruba. The Bantu and Bushmen came from societies that were more primitive. All these societies practiced slavery, as had all of Europe at one time. Some African chiefs captured members of other tribes and sold these slaves to black or white slave traders, who then marched them to the slave stations on the Atlantic coast. There the white men put them on ships to send to America. Of course, some of these terrified Africans tried to get away. And some preferred death to slavery. One slave trader reported, they were "so wilful and loth to leave their own country that they have often leap't out of the canoes, boat and ship, into the sea and kept under water till they were drowned."

The "middle passage," as the voyage to America was called, was a horrendous experience. Packed tightly below decks and chained together, frightened men, women, and children died in great numbers. Those who survived the torture of this long journey to the West Indian islands, Brazil, the United States, or wherever in America, were then sold at auction to the highest bidder.

The slave trade to the United States was legally abolished in 1807. But in later years slaves still were smuggled into the country and a flourishing domestic slave trade continued. Though many Southerners tried to avoid seeing the inhumanity of slavery—the purchase and sale of people as if they were things—the proof was often before their eyes.

⌑ See "Lesson Plan," p. 250E for **Writing Process Activity: Recognizing Ideologies** relating to debate over the slavery issue.

New York Historical Society

This rare early photograph shows slaves in South Carolina bringing cotton in from the fields. At least one woman has her baby in her arms. The man at the head of the line is probably the foreman.

From dawn to dusk. To the slave owner, slavery was first and foremost a system of labor control. Just as cash wages were the system of control in the North, so slavery was the method in the South. Slavery was a way to use man-, woman-, and child-power to raise crops for sale. The largest of these crops was cotton, which the Southerners thought was "King" of all crops, but also important were tobacco, rice, hemp, and sugar.

It was the black slave, working from dawn to dusk, who planted, tended, and harvested these crops, as well as built fences, cut wood, and fed farm animals. Particularly at harvest time the work could be grueling. Under the eyes of the owner, an overseer, or a black "driver," the slaves would sometimes be pushed to exhaustion. And failure to perform up to expectations could lead to a whipping.

But the "peculiar institution," as Southerners came to call it, like all human institutions should not be oversimplified. While there were cruel masters who maimed or even killed their slaves (although killing and maiming were against the law in every state), there were also kind and generous owners. The institution was as complex as the people involved. Though most slaves were whipped at some point in their lives, a few never felt the lash. Nor did all slaves work in the fields. Some were house servants or skilled artisans. Many may not have even been terribly unhappy with their lot, for they knew no other. But certainly others were, as the Nat Turner revolt revealed. And there were many

More from Boorstin: "It took time for [blacks] to forget their African language and to learn the language of the master; African languages were so numerous and slaves came from so many different language groups that at first it was difficult for them to communicate even with their fellow slaves . . . What a Babel it must have been! Masters did not condescend to learn the language of slaves; and slaves, often unable to use their mother tongue to communicate with one another, had to learn or invent a pidgin if they were to communicate at all." (From *The Americans: The National Experience*)

This lively watercolor of slaves dancing on a festive occasion was found in Columbia, South Carolina. The artist is unknown, but the painting was made about 1800.

planned or rumored uprisings that were cut off before they happened. Though white Southerners claimed their slaves were happy, they lived in constant fear of slave revolts.

There were other ways to resist owners than by armed revolt. Slaves might just work slowly and carelessly. Sickness could be faked. When all else failed, some tried to run away—despite the certainty of severe punishment if they were caught. A number actually made it to freedom. And a few even risked being enslaved again by returning to help others escape. In the North they faced the trials of living in a society made for whites. Still many thought that was better than slavery.

In the earlier days of slavery, some slaves were freed by their owners, or allowed to earn money to buy their own freedom and that of their wives and children. Under the attack of abolitionists, Southerners grew ever more defensive. Southern states passed laws making it harder and

harder to free slaves. For this reason, there were a small number of black slaveholders in the South. They held slaves as a way to "free" friends or family.

Slaves and their families lived closely with owners and their families. They usually dwelt on isolated plantations where white and black depended on each other. About one-half of all slaves were owned in groups of 20 (about four families) or less. Sometimes a single slave worked on a family farm and managed to live much the same life as a white hired hand. There were only a few large plantations—where the other half of all slaves lived. No more than 10,000 Southerners had plantations with more than 50 slaves.

Not surprisingly in such a close-knit society, there were white Southerners who loved their slaves and who were loved by them in return. Usually the wives of plantation owners took care of slaves who were sick, saw that they had the

Multicultural Connection: In 1737 Spanish governor Mañuel de Montiano established the first free African-American town in present-day United States. It was called Gracia Real de Santa Teresa de Mose, known as Fort Mose, and was located two miles north of St. Augustine. Thirty-eight families of Africans formerly enslaved by the British lived outside the walls of Fort Mose where they planted crops. Currently, Florida archaeologists are excavating the site and soon a permanent exhibit will be established to tell the world about America's first free African-American settlement.

Texas and Oregon

FOCUS

To introduce the lesson, ask how many students have seen movies that portray the seige of the Alamo. How were the defenders portrayed? How was William Travis portrayed? How were the Mexicans portrayed? Point out that before the siege Travis had received orders from Sam Houston to abandon the Alamo at once. Ask: What do you suppose would have happened to Colonel Travis if he had not been killed at the Alamo along with his men? (He would have been brought before a court martial for disobeying direct orders to abandon an undefendable position.)

Developing Vocabulary

gag rule (page 295); **annex** (page 297); **Manifest Destiny** (page 298).

INSTRUCT

Explain

President Tyler had opened negotiations with the British in 1844. He proposed the 49th parallel as the border between the United States and Canada—just as John Quincy Adams had earlier—but the British turned him down. They wanted the Columbia River as the border. Fort Vancouver was on the north bank of the Columbia, and the British wished to keep control of that trading post. By 1844 there were around 700 British subjects north of the Columbia compared to a handful of Americans. One might wonder if Polk's demand for all of Oregon was intended to give the United States negotiators some bargaining power.

☑ Writing Process Activity

Demonstrating Reasoned Judgment Ask students to play the role of historians who must explain to elementary school children the significance of two catch phrases of western expansion: "Remember the Alamo!" and "Fifty-four forty or fight!" Have them begin by outlining the events leading to coining the phrases, including the people and places involved. As they write, ask students to concentrate on presenting the facts simply. They should revise for clarity and conciseness. After proofreading, they might present their explanations to a class of elementary school students.

Section Review Answers

Section 4, page 298

1. a) Mexican dictator who unsuccessfully tried to crush the Texas rebellion. b) leader of the Texan army that defeated Santa Anna. He became the first president of the Lone Star Republic. c) the decision by the House of Representatives not to hear any more petitions against slavery. d) Harrison's Vice-President and became President when Harrison died after only a few weeks in office. e) a relatively unknown figure who is seeking a political office. f) dark horse in the presidential election of 1844. g) antislavery Whigs in New York who refused to vote for Henry Clay because he advocated the admission of Texas to the Union. h) small antislavery party in New York that tipped the scales to Polk by preventing Clay from carrying the state. 2. Coahuila-Texas, the Alamo, Goliad, and San Jacinto are all on the map on page 295. The "fifty-four forty" line is shown on the map on page 298. 3. Admitting Texas to the Union would disrupt the delicate balance between free and slave states in the United States Senate. 4. The Oregon issue was settled when the United States and Great Britain agreed that the 49th parallel would be the boundary line separating the United States and British North America. 5. John Winthrop had preached to his followers that North America offered them the opportunity to create a fortress of godliness for the world to look upon and learn from. The belief in "manifest destiny" opened up the possibility of creating an empire of democracy for the world to learn from.

CLOSE

To conclude the lesson, ask: What is it about the Battle of the Alamo that has made it so memorable in the history of Texas and the United States? (People have always been fascinated by anyone who chooses to die nobly for a cause when escape is possible. A similar famous incident is the death of Leonidas and 300 Spartans at Thermopylae, in their struggle against the invading Persians in 480 B.C.) Even though more men died at Goliad, they are not remembered as heroic but rather as victims—because they had already surrendered.

War with Mexico

FOCUS

To introduce the lesson, ask students what they know about the Vietnam War. What was the reaction to that war at home? (The war was very controversial.) Point out that for many Americans of the 1840s the Mexican War was just as unpopular. Abraham Lincoln, then a Whig member of Congress, said, "the war was unnecessarily and unconstitutionally commenced by the President." Ask: Was it?

☑ Writing Process Activity

Recognizing Bias Ask students to imagine they are either Northern or Southern critics who must review Theodore Dwight Weld's book, *Slavery As It Is: Testimony of a Thousand Witnesses*. In preparation for writing, have them brainstorm the position they might take. As they write, ask them to consider Weld's method of gathering data, his point of view on the issue, and his purpose in publishing the book. Students should revise their reviews for clarity. After proofreading, they can analyze the differences between Northern and Southern perspectives.

Section Review Answers

Section 2, page 288

1. a), b) abolitionists who had been born and brought up in the South. Their outspoken views eventually forced them to move to the North. c) compiled newspaper stories on slavery into a best-selling horror book *Slavery As It Is: Testimony of a Thousand Witnesses*. d) outspoken militant abolitionist, agitator, and editor of an abolitionist newspaper. e) newspaper owner and editor who became a martyr for the abolitionist cause when a proslavery mob tried to silence him. f) raised money to send black Americans to Africa. g) abolitionist newspaper edited by William Lloyd Garrison. 2. Growing pressure from Northern abolitionists made many Southerners feel that they had to insulate themselves from the rest of the nation.

CLOSE

To conclude the lesson, discuss with students what this section's information on the role of abolitionism adds to their understanding of the causes of the Civil War.

Section 3 (pages 288–294)

Westward Ho!

FOCUS

To introduce the lesson, have students locate the Santa Fe Trail, the Oregon Trail, and the California Trail on the map on page 292. Ask the students: What was so difficult about traveling west in the mid-1800s?

INSTRUCT

Explain

This section explains how the American settlements in the West paved the way for our acquisition of much of the territory comprising the western states of today.

Underscore the importance of the first sentence of the section: "The national differences over slavery might not have come to a head so soon if the nation had not been growing and moving so fast." Point out that getting more land in the West would raise the critical issue of whether slavery would be permitted there.

❀ Cooperative Learning Activity

Drawing Conclusions Explain that students will work in pairs to make one or more graphs showing the population statistics from *Westward Ho!* Have pairs decide how to divide up this section of the text so that partners share responsibility for finding and listing population information. Tell students to be sure to include dates and locations and to identify specific groups of people as they compile their lists. Then have partners work together to plan a graph or graphs to represent all the statistics listed. Display completed graphs and ask members of the class to interpret and explain the information presented.

Section Review Answers

Section 3, page 294

1. a) obtained a grant from the Mexican government to settle Texas in 1821. He founded Austin, Texas, and attracted 8,000 immigrants. b) led a group of settlers to Santa Fe and established the Santa Fe Trail. c) American trader who settled in New Mexico and attracted other American settlers to the area. d) made a fortune in the fur trade and was the first to attempt to create a permanent American settlement in Oregon. e) led a group of Methodists to settle in Oregon. f) husband-and-wife missionary team. She was one of the first two American women to cross the Rockies. g) New Englander who vividly described his journey on the Oregon Trail. h) Jesuit priest known to the Indians as "Blackrobe." He set up a number of Catholic missions in Oregon. 2. The Mormons had to move west to escape persecution from their fellow Americans, and their migration was more organized than most. 3. Specific members of their group were given authority to keep the established order and to divide the workload among the members of the group.

CLOSE

To conclude the lesson, tell students that Americans began to settle in Texas in 1821. Trappers and fur traders formed an "American faction" in New Mexico. Missionaries sparked interest in the Oregon Country, traders and ranchers settled in California, and the Mormons settled in Utah. Ask: Which of these groups of settlers do you think were the most successful in their endeavors and why? The least successful?

An Age of Reform

FOCUS

To introduce the lesson, ask students: Do women have equal opportunities in our society today? Are they denied any rights?

Developing Vocabulary

The words listed are essential terms for understanding particular sections of the chapter. The page number after each term indicates the page of its first or most important appearance. These terms are defined in the text Glossary (text pages 1000–1011).

temperance (page 279)

INSTRUCT

Explain

Historians disagree about the effects of industrialization on the status of women. Some scholars believe that because women earned their own income they were more independent, had more leisure time, and more control over their lives. Some historians believe that women's economic role on the farm was more valued and that they had less control over their work in the mills.

★ Independent Activity

Drawing Conclusions Ask students to list at least five of the reformers mentioned in section 1 of the chapter. Tell students they will select one name from their lists and, based on their independent research, write a two-page biography about that person. They should include the person's area of reform, his or her accomplishments, and the importance of those accomplishments in paving the way for further advances in that area.

Section Review Answers

Section 1, page 285

1. a) eloquent spokesperson for the Transcendentalists. b) wrote *Essay on the Duty of Civil Disobedience.* c) Transcendentalist preacher who attacked slavery. d) devised popular utopian schemes that failed. e) wrote *Little Women.* f) editor, literary critic, and author of *Women in the Nineteenth Century.* g) crusaded for educational reform. h) crusaded for better treatment of the mentally ill. i) one of the organizers of the Women's Rights Convention in Seneca Falls, New York, in 1848. j) other organizer of the Convention. k) born a slave, worked for the rights of women and blacks. l) leader in the fight for women's rights. m) both became medical doctors. n) an astronomer. o) edited an influential magazine, *Godey's Lady's Book.* 2. (a) By 1860 many states were providing free elementary education, and there were some public high schools. (b) By 1860 some progress was being made in the education of women. At least in New England nearly all women could read and write; a few boys' academies admitted a small number of women; and the first college for women (Wesleyan College in Georgia) and the first coeducational college (Oberlin College) had opened. 3. Dorothea Dix sought better facilities for the mentally handicapped and urged that they be treated with compassion and medical care instead of being treated as criminals or worse. 4. Women could not vote, and in some states women had no legal rights because they had no legal existence apart from their husbands. Between 1828 and 1860 some states liberalized divorce laws and gave women control over their own property, the right to sue, and a share in the guardianship of their children. 5. By the middle of the nineteenth century, Protestant churches in the United States were stressing that individuals could improve the world.

CLOSE

To conclude the lesson, ask students: Are women better off today than they were in 1848? In what ways has progress been made? In what ways has it not? Discuss, accepting all reasonable responses.

The Abolition Movement

FOCUS

To introduce the lesson, ask: In what ways was slavery a more difficult reform issue than education, treatment of the mentally ill, women's rights? (Abolition, like the issue of women's rights, threatened the existing social order, but it was easier to make gradual adjustments in the case of women's rights.)

Developing Vocabulary

abolitionist (page 286)

INSTRUCT

Explain

You may want to point out that the American Colonization Society represented a mixture of good will and deep racial prejudice. Point out that leaders among the free blacks—living in the North, of course—vigorously opposed colonization.

Providing In-Depth Coverage

Perspectives on the Oregon Trail

During the first half of the nineteenth century, the westward expansion that led settlers from the United States as far as Texas, California, and Oregon ultimately led to a war with Mexico and the acquisition of all the territory now in the continental United States.

The chapter provides a view of the various groups of settlers who made their way west, the hardships they faced, and the relative successes and failures of their attempts to settle the untamed land of the western half of the continent.

For this chapter, *A History of the United States* as an instructional program provides two types of resources you can use to offer in-depth coverage of the Oregon Trail: the *student text* and the *Enrichment Support File*. A list of *Suggested Secondary Sources* is also provided. The chart below shows the topics that are covered in each.

THE STUDENT TEXT. Boorstin and Kelley's *A History of the United States* unfolds the chronology of events and the key players in the settlement of the Oregon Territory.

AMERICAN HISTORY ENRICHMENT SUPPORT FILE. This collection of primary source readings and classroom activities reveals the experiences of those who traveled the Oregon Trail.

SUGGESTED SECONDARY SOURCES. This reference list of readings by well-known historians and other commentators provides an array of perspectives on the experiences of those who traveled the Oregon Trail. (See the chart below.)

Locating Instructional Materials

Detailed lesson plans for teaching the experiences of the travelers of the Oregon Trail as a mini-course or to study one or more elements of the Oregon Trail in depth are offered in the following areas: in the *Student text*, see individual lesson plans at the beginning of each chapter; in the *Enrichment Support File*, see page 3; for readings beyond the student text, see *Suggested Secondary Sources*.

IN-DEPTH COVERAGE ON THE OREGON TRAIL		
Student Text	**Enrichment Support File**	**Suggested Secondary Sources**
▪ Oregon settlement, pp. 288, 290–291 ▪ Oregon Trail, p. 290 ▪ Missionaries, pp. 290–291 ▪ Narcissa Whitman and Elizabeth Spaulding, p. 290 ▪ Nathaniel J. Wyeth, p. 290 ▪ Father Pierre de Smet, pp. 290–291	▪ Lesson Suggestions ▪ Multimedia Resources ▪ Overview Essay/Along the Oregon Trail ▪ Literature in American History/ *The Way West* ▪ Songs in American History/ The Sioux Indians ▪ Primary Sources in American History/ Diaries of Travelers West ▪ Biography in American History/ Narcissa Prentiss Whitman ▪ Simulation/Packing to Go West ▪ Making Connections	▪ *Women and Men on the Overland Trail* by John Mack Faragher, pp. 66–87. ▪ *Frontier Women: The Trans-Mississippi West, 1840–1880* by Julie Roy Jeffrey, pp. 25–50. ▪ *Women's Diaries of the Westward Journey* by Lillian Schlissel, pp. 165–185, 187–198. ▪ *The Plains Across: Emigrants and the Trans-Mississippi West, 1840–1860*, by John D. Unruh, Jr., Chapter 3, "Motivations and Beginnings."

Chapter 11
Reforming and Expanding

Identifying Chapter Materials

Objectives	Basic Instructional Materials	Extension Materials
1 An Age of Reform • Describe religious trends before the Civil War and identify the characteristics and leaders of pre-Civil War reform movements.	**Annotated Teacher's Edition** • Lesson Plans, p. 278C **Instructional Support File** • Pre-Reading Activities, Unit 4, p. 15 • Skill Review Activity, Unit 4, p. 18 • Critical Thinking Activity, Unit 4, p. 20	**Documents of American History** • Dorothea Dix's Memorial to the Legislature of Massachusetts, Vol. 1, p. 301
2 The Abolition Movement • Trace the development of the abolition movement in the North and describe the reaction to abolition in the South.	**Annotated Teacher's Edition** • Lesson Plans, pp. 278C–278D	**Documents of American History** • The Liberator, Volume I., No. 1, Vol. 1, p. 277
3 Westward Ho! • Describe how Americans settled in Texas, New Mexico, Oregon, and California and locate the routes to the various Western settlements.	**Annotated Teacher's Edition** • Lesson Plans, p. 278D	**Enrichment Support File** • Along the Oregon Trail (See "In-Depth Coverage" at right.) **Suggested Secondary Sources** **American History Transparencies** • Our Multicultural Heritage, pp. C67, C71 • Fine Art, pp. D29, D37
4 Texas and Oregon • Trace the course of Texas's progress from Mexican state to one of the United States. • Explain the significance of the seige of the Alamo and the massacre at Goliad in Texas's struggle for independence.	**Annotated Teacher's Edition** • Lesson Plans, p. 278E **Instructional Support File** • Skill Application Activity, Unit 4, p. 19	**Documents of American History** • Texas Declaration of Independence, Vol. 1, p. 281 • The Webster-Ashburton Treaty, Vol. 1, p. 298 • The Annexation of Texas, Vol. 1, p. 306 **American History Transparencies** • Critical Thinking, p. F15
5 War with Mexico • State the immediate reasons for war with Mexico in 1846, describe the course of the war, and state the terms of the Treaty of Guadalupe Hidalgo and the Gadsden Purchase.	**Annotated Teacher's Edition** • Lesson Plans, pp. 278E–278F **Instructional Support File** • Reading Activities, Unit 4, pp. 16–17 • Chapter Test, Unit 4, pp. 21–24 • Additional Test Questions, Unit 4, pp. 25–28	**Documents of American History** • Polk's Message on War with Mexico, Vol. 1, p. 310 • Treaty of Guadalupe Hidalgo, Vol. 1, p. 313 **American History Transparencies** • Geography and History, pp. B13, B15, B17

Chapter 10 Review

See "Chapter Review answers," p. 250F.

Focusing on Ideas

1. Describe the role of federal, state, and local governments in the development of roads, canals, and railroads. Why did people seek such help from the government?

2. Identify at least three people who played major roles in the early stages of the American Industrial Revolution. Show how each contributed to the growth of industry.

3. What "favorable conditions" awaited immigrants to the United States?

4. What arguments would you expect an abolitionist to use in condemning slavery? What arguments did some white Southerners use to defend the institution of slavery?

Taking a Critical Look

1. **Identifying Central Issues.** Explain how the completion of the Erie Canal might have benefited each of the following: a wheat farmer in northern Ohio; a merchant in Buffalo; a Dutch immigrant family headed for Michigan Territory; an Albany hotel owner.

2. **Making Comparisons.** Compare pre-Civil War Irish and German immigration with regard to: motives for coming; dates; numbers; settlements; and contributions.

3. **Demonstrating Reasoned Judgment.** How was the birth of western cities a testament to American optimism?

Your Region in History

1. **Geography.** Identify major roads, canals, and railroads built in your state or region between 1820 and 1860. How did these transportation developments affect where people in your state or region chose to settle?

2. **Culture.** What immigrant groups settled in your state or region between 1820 and 1860? When and where did they settle? What contributions did they make?

3. **Economics.** What kinds of manufacturing, if any, developed in your area in the period 1820–1860? Why did they develop there?

Historical Facts and Figures

Synthesizing Information. Look at the table below to help you complete the following exercises: (a) Summarize the overall immigration trend between 1820 and 1855. (b) Summarize the changes in the overall immigration trend that occurred between 1856 and 1860. (c) Using information from this chapter, write a hypothesis that explains the immigration trends between 1820 and 1860.

	Ireland	Scotland, England, Wales	Germany	All Other	TOTAL
1821–25	16,540	11,300	2,362	18,686	48,888
1826–30	37,798	16,189	5,367	43,582	102,936
1831–35	72,257	32,182	45,593	102,462	252,494
1836–40	135,124	43,628	106,862	62,107	347,721
1841–45	187,095	80,186	105,188	57,867	430,336
1846–50	593,624	186,858	327,438	174,995	1,282,915
1851–55	645,056	235,981	647,273	220,114	1,748,424
1856–60	219,436	187,993	304,394	137,967	849,790

Origins of Immigrants to the United States, 1820–1860

Source: *U.S. Immigration and Naturalization Service*

Robert Brammer and Augustus A. Von Smith

"Oakland House and Race Course, Louisville, [Kentucky]," painted in 1840, gives a sense of the pleasant life of many white Southerners and suggests why they resisted all talk of change.

"In northern vessels [the Southerner's] products are carried to market, his cotton is ginned in northern gins, his sugar is crushed and preserved by northern machinery; his rivers are navigated by northern steamboats, . . . his land is cleared with a northern axe, and a Yankee clock sits upon his mantle-piece; his floor is swept by a northern broom, and is covered with a northern carpet; and his wife dresses herself in a northern looking-glass." This was only a slight exaggeration.

How had this come about? How had the home of Jefferson's small farmer become a backwater? No wonder that many Southerners, looking for someone to blame, decided to make Northerners the enemy. They began to think the backwardness of the South had been a product of a northern conspiracy. It seemed that somehow northern businessmen had been able to use the federal government for their own selfish purposes. The government subsidized northern shipbuilding. The tariff protected northern manufacturers so they could charge higher prices to southern planters.

Had not the southern states been pioneers in colonial days? They gave the nation its Washington, Jefferson, Madison, Monroe, and Jackson—its leaders in war and in peace. Now that the United States was prospering, must the South remain a colony within a nation?

See "Section 5 Review answers," p. 250E.

Section 5 Review

1. What was the "middle passage"? How did it come to be called that?
2. Show how the treatment of slaves differed. How did some slaves resist the will of their owners?
3. What were some effects of slavery on the South?
4. **Critical Thinking: Drawing Conclusions.** Why did Southerners turn from calling slavery a "necessary evil" to calling it a "positive good"?

proper clothes and food, and attended their weddings, funerals, and church services. Some even (against the law) taught a favored black child to read. While there were owners who killed their slaves, there were others like Rachel O'Connor of Louisiana, who wrote of a sick young black slave: "The poor little fellow is laying at my feet asleep. I wish I did not love him as I do, but it is so, and I cannot help it."

A world of their own. Whether an owner was kind or brutal, the slave was still considered by the law to be a chattel, just a piece of property to be bought and sold. Slaves were always at the mercy of their owners. It was in the interest of the owner to keep the slaves healthy and content enough to tend the crops that made the plantation thrive. But slaves could be whipped, beaten, confined, chained and even sold away from family and friends at the whim of the owner. So whether happy or sad, well cared for or ill, the slaves could never feel the joy or the dignity of freedom.

Despite what laws may say, people remain human. Even under the most dreadful oppression they create a life for themselves. The churches and most owners recognized that blacks were human, with souls that could be saved by God. The slaves seized upon this awareness of their humanity to influence their owners to treat them better. Most masters seemed to believe that happy slaves did better work than unhappy ones. So the slaves used their owners' profit motive to get small benefits— the right to farm their own kitchen gardens or to sell a few products in town.

In their simple log huts in the slave quarters— huts often not much different from those occupied by poor Southern whites—they built their private world. There they married (though sometimes owners conducted these ceremonies), worshiped, celebrated the birth of a child, mourned the death of a friend, in their own way. In their new American homeland, as their owners wanted, the blacks became Christians. But they also combined this Christianity with some elements from Africa and made it special. They often went to the master's church on Sun-

day morning, where they sat in a separate section. But it was at their own service later in the day that they could freely practice their religion. There they heard the sermons of eloquent black preachers.

It was their own religious experience—their special mix of song, dance, prayer, call and response—that set them apart from the whites. Out of this experience blacks, even while they were slaves, were able to proclaim their moral worth. It was from their religion, perhaps more than in any other way, that black slaves who were separated from each other on scattered plantations were able to form a sense of their human unity. From their religious beliefs and practices and their past as slaves, black Americans formed the basis for their own culture—a culture which was to mix with and enrich the culture of the United States.

The effect of slavery on white Southerners. Most white Southerners were not slaveholders. In 1860 one-fourth of the white people in the South owned all the slaves. Still, even the nonslaveholders were generally convinced that slavery must continue. Some supported it because they saw no other way to control this "different" group in their midst. Even the poorest white people in the South liked to think of themselves as somehow superior to blacks. As one poor white farmer explained, "Now suppose they was free, you see they'd all think themselves as good as we."

The South paid a high price for slavery. All craftsmen and farmers received less for their labor because of the competition of slaves. Immigrants, unwilling to compete with slave labor, avoided the South. The money that might have gone into commerce or industry was tied up in slaves. As a result the South remained an agricultural community which exported crops and imported manufactured goods.

This made the whole South—white and black—a kind of colony of the North. "With us every branch and pursuit of life, every trade, profession, and occupation, is dependent upon the North," an Alabama newspaper complained.

Critical Thinking Activity: Recognizing Bias Was the institution of slavery defensible? Divide the class into two groups. Have one group list all of the arguments against the institution of slavery in the South; the other group should list arguments in favor of slavery in the South. Ask each group to present their reasons to the entire class. Assign students to write an opinion paragraph on the institution of slavery: "Was slavery just or unjust?" Direct students to incorporate points from the group work.

INSTRUCT

Explain

The territory acquired between 1845 and 1853 increased the size of the United States by more than one half again its previous size.

★ Independent Activity

Recognizing Cause and Effect Write the following column headings on the chalkboard: Territory Name, Date Acquired, From Whom Acquired, How Acquired (purchase, treaty, war, or a combination of all three), and Present-Day States Included. Ask students to copy the chart and provide the needed information for each column for each of the following acquisitions: Florida, West Florida, Louisiana Purchase, Texas Annexation, Oregon Country, The Mexican Cession, Gadsden Purchase.

Section Review Answers

Section 5, page 302

1. a) American general in the Mexican War who captured Monterrey in northern Mexico. b) American general who captured Mexico City in September 1847. c) explored the West and helped Americans set up a republic in California in order to speed the American conquest of the area and prevent any other nation from seizing it. d) name given to the flag that briefly flew over California when it was an independent republic. 2. The Nueces River, the Rio Grande, Monterrey, Buena Vista, and Mexico City are shown on the map on page 299. The Gadsden Purchase can be found on the map on page 301. 3. The Treaty of Guadalupe Hidalgo provided that Mexico give up all claims to Texas and hand over all the lands between Texas and the Pacific to the United States.

CLOSE

To conclude the lesson, have students prepare a time line for the years 1821–1853 and list all the events in sections 3, 4, and 5 of this chapter that relate to American expansion, beginning with Austin's Texas settlement and concluding with the Gadsden Purchase.

Chapter Review Answers

Focusing on Ideas

1. Include Baptists, Congregationalists, Quakers, etc. as well as Amish, Shakers, etc. Later, mainline churches divided into northern and southern bodies. 2. (a) Slavery, inequality for women, poor schools, mistreatment of mentally handicapped. (b) Abolition, schools for females, improved teacher training and schools, mental hospitals. 3. Cooperation was more effective in preventing and warding off Indian attacks and making daily progress. 4. Treaty of Guadalupe Hidalgo gave U.S. territory in present-day Texas, New Mexico, Colorado, Utah, Nevada, Arizona, and California. 5. Adventurers: settler families; fur trappers and trail guides; and Mormons seeking religious freedom.

Taking a Critical Look

1. Educational reform concerned Americanization of immigrants, literacy for rising number of voters, common language and training for increasing variety of jobs in industrialized urban society. 2. Social reformers' religious and humanitarian sentiments led to condemnation of slavery. 3. Many who would have eagerly supported it feared the extension of slavery into new territories.

Your Region in History

1–3. Answers will vary depending on your region. Consult your local library or historical society.

Historical Facts and Figures

(a) It nearly quadrupled. (b) Approximately 6%. (c) Approximately 100%. (d) Efforts were made to reform the American educational system. (e) See pages 280–282.

11

Chapter 11

Focusing the Chapter: Have students identify the chapter logo. Discuss what unit theme the logo might symbolize. Then ask students to skim the chapter to ident-ify other illustrations or titles that relate to the theme.

Reforming and Expanding

The half-century before the Civil War was a time of ferment in the United States. Factories were built, instant cities were created, immigrants poured in. From Missouri, long lines of wagons headed west to their promised lands—Texas, California, and Oregon. The Americans who stayed home looked for a more perfect society where they lived. These two movements of expansion and reform forced the nation to face an issue many Americans wished to avoid: What was the future of slavery in the United States?

Lake Michigan forced much northern land traffic past Chicago. The city had no railroad tracks at all in 1850, but by 1857 when this advertisement was printed it was a major railway center.

Chicago Historical Society

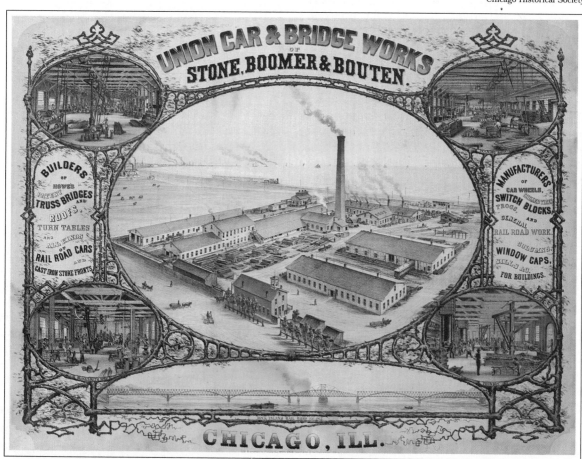

See "Lesson Plan," p. 278C.

1. An age of reform

In a land where even cities could appear overnight it was easy to believe that a perfect world could be created. Many Americans, like the first settlers, continued to feel that they were a "City upon a hill." For the whole world to see, they wanted to create a nation where there was no injustice, where all had an equal chance to succeed, and where citizens ruled themselves. They wanted to help the insane, the orphans, the prisoners, and the blind. Americans organized themselves into groups working for peace, for temperance in the use of alcohol, for improved education, for women's rights—and for the abolition of slavery.

A religious age. There was a Christian church to suit every taste and every temperament. Unitarians tried to bring together all men and women of goodwill without any dogma or sharp theology. Millerites proclaimed that the world would come to an end in the year 1843 and urged their fellow Americans to repent while there was still time. Shakers and Rappites and others each believed they had the one and only formula for an ideal community. Visitors from abroad came to think that there were as many denominations as there were Americans. A perceptive English lady, Mrs. Trollope, saw religious Americans "insisting upon having each a little separate banner, embroidered with a device of their own imagining."

The Protestant churches moved away from the old Puritan belief in a stern God who had decreed in advance the fate of each person for all time. Instead churches now emphasized how close each individual was to God and how much freedom each possessed to improve the world and make his or her own future. The world of Christians seemed more democratic, more self-governing than ever before.

These ideas were stressed between the 1820s and the 1850s in the religious revivals which constantly swept the land. Perhaps the greatest single force in this movement was Charles Grandison Finney. He used every means to excite his listeners to a sense of their sinfulness and to save their souls. His revival meetings and those of other preachers brought many Americans to support a wide variety of reforms.

The Transcendentalists. One small group of intellectuals had an influence all out of proportion to their numbers. They called themselves "Transcendentalists." They believed that the most important truths of life could not be summed up in a clear and simple theology but actually "transcended" (went beyond) human understanding and brought together all people—high or low, rich or poor, educated or ignorant. For them God was an "oversoul" who was present showing everybody what was good or evil. It is not surprising then that Ralph Waldo Emerson, their most eloquent voice, declared:

> What is man born for but to be a Reformer, a Reformer of what man has made; a renouncer of lies; a restorer of truth and good. . . .

Since man was good, in time the whole world would become perfect. Then, of course, there would be no need for government.

Each person had to find his or her own path to heaven. Henry David Thoreau found his lonely way to the good life in a solitary cabin on the shores of Walden Pond near Concord, Massachusetts. While he stayed there by himself for two years, he earned his living making pencils and only went to town for groceries. He found his own way to protest against the policies of his government that he believed to be evil. When the nation waged war against Mexico—to add new slave states, he thought—he simply refused to pay his taxes. For this he spent only one night in jail, since to his irritation his aunt paid the tax for him. But his explanation for his protest—in his *Essay on the Duty of Civil Disobedience* (1849)—rang down the years and reached across the world. A century later when Mahatma Gandhi led the people of India in their struggle for independence, he declared himself a follower of Henry David Thoreau.

Theodore Parker, another member of the group, was a born reformer who joined movements and attacked slavery from pulpits and lecture platforms. Bronson Alcott was a mystic

More from Boorstin: "[Others worked] to relieve all kinds of misfortune . . . Dr. Samuel Gridley Howe set out to improve the education of the blind . . . His most spectacular achievement was educating the deaf-blind child, Laura Dewey Bridgman. She entered his school just before she was eight; within a year he had put her in communication with the world and soon he proved for the first time that the deaf-blind were not necessarily defective in intelligence. Later Laura herself occasionally taught other deaf-blind students . . ." (From *The Americans: The National Experience*)

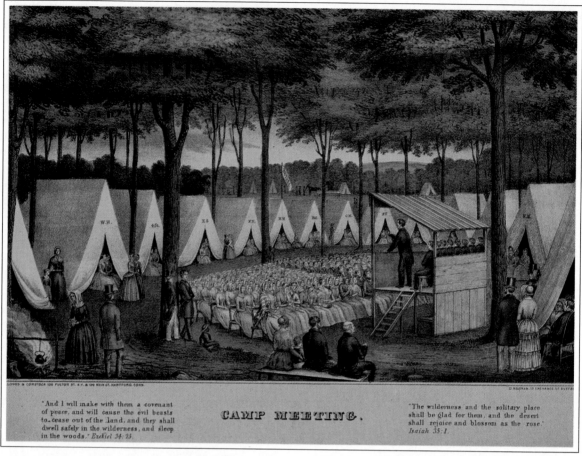

"And I will make with them a covenant of peace, and will cause the evil beasts to cease out of the land, and they shall dwell safely in the wilderness, and sleep in the woods." *Ezekiel 34: 25.*

CAMP MEETING.

"The wilderness and the solitary place shall be glad for them, and the desert shall rejoice and blossom as the rose." *Isaiah 35:1.*

Old Dartmouth Historical Society Whaling Museum

Religion was a mighty force for reform. All over America, but especially on the frontier, camp meetings allowed people to come together for several days to pray, to sing, and to listen to visiting preachers give impassioned sermons.

and a dreamer who worked for perfection but failed at everything. His educational ideas—which included physical exercises for students, attractive classrooms, and the pleasures of learning—seemed shocking to people of those times when schools were grim and discipline harsh. Alcott's school failed as did his attempt to build a new Eden at "Fruitlands." Alcott was never able to earn enough to live comfortably until his practical and courageous daughter Louisa May made a great success with her book *Little Women* (1868).

The Transcendentalists loved to tell what they thought. While Thoreau wrote and Parker and others preached, Emerson both wrote and lectured. Bronson Alcott talked. In his pop-

ular "conversations"—wandering monologues—Alcott entertained large audiences in the East and Northwest.

The "conversation" was also used by brilliant Margaret Fuller. She gathered a group of young Boston women around her and instructed them. From this experience came her influential book, *Women in the Nineteenth Century* (1845), which spurred on the women's rights movement. Fuller also edited the *Dial*, the Transcendentalist magazine, and worked as a literary critic for Horace Greeley on the *New York Tribune.*

Reform in education. America—a new nation, full of open land and business challenges—

Continuity and Change: Religion Point out to students that although the United States experienced periods of increased religious fervor in the mid-1800s and again in the 1950s, the basis for each revival was different. The religious revival of the nineteenth century centered around a variety of reforms aimed to improve life and to make the world as some people believed God intended. Americans in the mid-twentieth century turned to religion to help them cope with the fears and complexities of modern life and the global environment, such as the Cold War and the increased proliferation of nuclear weapons. (See page 764.)

was a wonderful laboratory for reformers. It is not surprising that the reformers focused on education. The ability to read and write, they argued, was the foundation of a democratic life.

The modern public school movement began in the 1830s in Massachusetts. This was quite natural because the Puritan founders of New England in the 1630s had believed in education. Now, 200 years later, the determined Horace Mann worked to fulfill the Puritan dream of an educated citizenry. He had hated the dull teaching he received as a boy, so he gave up a successful legal career to work for educational reform. Mann was appointed the first secretary of the new state board of education in 1837, and for the next twelve years he tried hard to better the training and pay of teachers, to erect new school buildings, to enlarge school libraries, and to improve textbooks. In other states crusaders followed Mann's example.

By 1860 the fruits of these efforts were impressive. The states were generally committed to providing free elementary education. Many pupils were still poorly taught, and laws did not yet require all children to attend school, but the nation had begun to realize that education was the foundation of a republic.

For students who wished more than a grammar school education, there were only 300 public high schools in the whole country and almost 100 of these were in Massachusetts. There were, however, an additional 6000 private academies, many of which charged only a small tuition to poor children. By 1860 many states were thinking of providing high schools open to all, but even by 1890 it was unusual to go to school beyond eighth grade.

Higher education. Colleges and universities were still small—few had over 100 students—and ill equipped, but their numbers had increased since colonial times. In fact, there had been a college-founding mania. Just as every instant city needed a newspaper and hotel even before it contained any people, so it needed what was loosely called a college. Usually the college was started by one of the many religious denominations, but the hopeful cities-of-the-future quickly joined in. Julian Sturtevant,

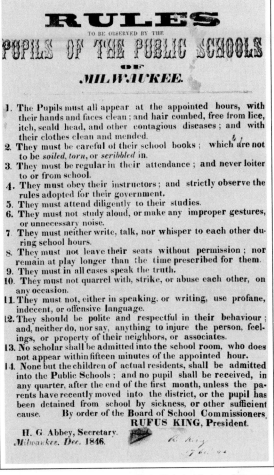

State Historical Society of Wisconsin

Students in Milwaukee in 1846 did not have to wonder about how they should behave.

founder in 1830 of Illinois College, said, "It was generally believed that one of the surest ways to promote the growth of a young city was to make it the seat of a college." So before the Civil War 516 colleges were founded—many little better than the private academies—but only 104 survived to the 1900s. These "colleges" were still chiefly concerned with educating young men for the professions and public life.

In many American cities, so-called mechanics' institutes were started for those who wished to learn the mechanical arts. And in 1824 a new kind of institution of higher learning, Rensselaer Polytechnic Institute, opened at

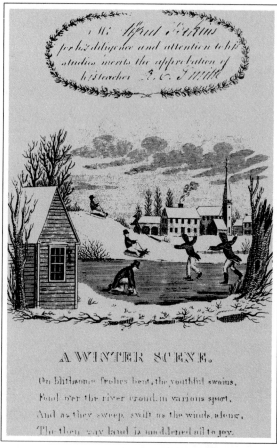

A WINTER SCENE.

On blithsome frolics bent, the youthful swains,
Feul o'er the river crowd in various sport,
And as they sweep, swift as the winds, along,
The then gay land is maddened all to joy.

In some schools, students who behaved well could earn certificates of merit like this one for consistently good conduct.

Troy, New York, to instruct men "in the application of science to the common purposes of life."

Education for girls and women. In colonial days girls were taught the household arts but were not expected to learn to read and write. People thought that "book learning" would put an undue stress on their delicate minds and bodies! It was a long while before women were allowed to show their full vigor. Progress came slowly and step by step. In Massachusetts girls began to attend summer sessions of the public grammar schools in the late 1700s. Still, in Revolutionary times only about half the women of New England could sign their names. By 1840 the efforts of reformers were showing results, and nearly all New England women could read and write.

But it was a while before women were given their chance at a college education. At first, small numbers of them were allowed to attend the boys' academies until secondary schools were set up especially for women. Finally in 1836 (200 years after Harvard College was founded for men) Wesleyan College in Georgia was chartered as the first college for women. Then the very next year Oberlin College in Ohio started the new era of coeducation. At last it was possible for at least some men and women to hear the same lectures and treat each other as intellectual equals.

The mentally ill and retarded. For centuries people who were mentally ill or retarded had been treated like criminals and stigmatized as "insane." They were feared, imprisoned, and tortured. But the American reformers felt pity for them and took up their cause. Their heroic champion was Dorothea Dix, a young Boston schoolteacher who taught a Sunday School class in the women's department of a local prison. There she found people, whose only "crime" was their mental illness, being confined and punished.

In 1843, after two years spent investigating the jails and poorhouses in Massachusetts, she submitted her epoch-making report to the state legislature. She had seen the innocent insane confined "in cages, closets, cellars, stalls, pens! Chained, naked, beaten with rods, and lashed into obedience." She asked the legislature and all her fellow citizens to share her outrage. But old ways of thought and old fears were strong. Many would not believe the shocking truth, and others accused her of being softhearted. She stood her ground.

Finally Dorothea Dix succeeded in persuading the Massachusetts legislature to enlarge the state mental hospital. She began a new crusade—which lasts into our own time—to treat the mentally ill with compassion and medical aid. She traveled in America and in Europe pleading her humane cause. Seldom has a reform owed so much to one person.

This watercolor, probably painted in the first half of the 19th century, shows an evening school for girls. They are working by candlelight as their bonneted teachers watch.

Women's rights. Dorothea Dix always found it best to let men present her findings to legislatures. It was widely believed that there was something unladylike about a woman speaking in public. It was difficult for women to secure permission even to attend reform meetings.

The Industrial Revolution had freed many women—married and unmarried alike—from having to make many of the things necessary for the home and family. While in the early days thread had to be spun and cloth woven in each household, now cloth was mass-produced in factories. Crude, ready-made clothing could be bought in stores. At the same time, the role of the homemaker became more specialized. Now, as factory processes made the price of manufactured goods cheaper, more women could afford to buy many of the things they had once made for themselves. No longer did they have so many of the varied tasks of the frontier wife. Women found new work outside the home. The factories of Lowell and other New England towns were largely staffed by women. And the new public schools created jobs for women teachers.

By the rules of English law, brought here in colonial days, married women had no rights to property—in fact their only legal existence came through their husbands. All of a woman's property became her husband's when she married, including her wages if she worked. She could not even make a will without his approval!

The lowly position of women had long been obvious to some women. The strong-minded Abigail Adams, for example, had made the point again and again to her husband, President

Culver Pictures

Culver Pictures

The women's rights movement included strong-minded leaders like Elizabeth Cady Stanton (left) and Susan B. Anthony (right).

John Adams. But now in an era of reform, when women were eager to lead movements to improve education, to treat the insane more humanely, and to free the slaves, the rights of women seemed essential to a better America. A new status for women—their opportunity for an adequate education and the right to speak out in public—would mean a richer life for all.

Leaders of the women's rights movement. Two energetic and outspoken reformers, Lucretia Mott and Elizabeth Cady Stanton, organized a Women's Rights Convention that met at Seneca Falls, New York, on July 19, 1848. The convention finally issued a clever statement based on the Declaration of Independence. The preamble stated that "all men and women are created equal." Their list of grievances was not against King George but against men, who had deprived women of their rights. They demanded that women "have immediate admission to all the rights and privileges which belong to them as citizens of the United States." They even went so far as to demand the right to vote, although many of the women delegates feared this was asking too much.

Similar conventions were held in other states. But there were plenty of people foolish enough to think that they could stop the movement by breaking up the meetings. In 1851, when the Ohio convention in Akron was disrupted, a careworn black woman of commanding stature rose and, to the surprise of all, began her eloquent appeal. The unexpected speaker, named Sojourner Truth, had been

Critical Thinking Activity: Predicting Consequences How have reform movements shaped our American character? List the following nineteenth-century reformers on the chalkboard: Charles Grandison Finney, Henry David Thoreau, Horace Mann, Dorothea Dix, and Elizabeth Cady Stanton. Ask students to pair these names with their area of reform. Divide class into groups, and assign each group one of the reformers listed. Have students speculate about what reforms this person would call for today in his or her field. Each group should be able to offer an explanation for their conclusions.

Sophia Smith Collection (Women's History Archive),
Smith College, Northhampton, Massachusetts

Sojourner Truth, a former slave, was an eloquent leader in the cause of women's rights.

born a slave in New York. She replied to a minister's charge that women needed special assistance from men by pointing out that she had never received any help from men.

> I have ploughed and planted and gathered into barns. . . . And ain't I a woman? I could work as much and eat as much as a man—when I could get it—and bear de lash as well! And ain't I a woman? I have borne thirteen children and seen 'em mos' all sold off to slavery, and when I cried out with my mother's grief, none but Jesus heard me! And ain't I a woman?

It took a while, but within a generation Sojourner Truth's message about the equality of women began to spread across the land.

The reforming women, led by Susan B. Anthony and Elizabeth Cady Stanton, were, of course, widely ridiculed and accused of acting more like men than women. But they did make progress. New York led other states in giving women control over their own property, a share in the guardianship of their own children, and the right to sue. Divorce laws were liberalized.

But the right to vote still seemed far in the future. In 1853 a leading national journal, *Harper's New Monthly Magazine*, proclaimed that the very idea of women voting was "infidel . . . avowedly anti-Biblical . . . opposed to nature and the established order of society."

Elizabeth and Emily Blackwell braved male opposition and actually became qualified medical doctors. Maria Mitchell became an astronomer, a member of the American Academy of Arts and Sciences, and the first professor of astronomy at the new Vassar College for women when it opened in 1865. Sarah Josepha Hale edited the influential magazine *Godey's Lady's Book* for nearly 50 years, and in its interesting pages she recounted the progress of women and argued their rights to be free, fulfilled Americans.

See "Section 1 Review answers," p. 278C.

Section 1 Review

1. Identify: Ralph Waldo Emerson, Henry David Thoreau, Theodore Parker, Bronson Alcott, Louisa May Alcott, Margaret Fuller, Horace Mann, Dorothea Dix, Lucretia Mott, Elizabeth Cady Stanton, Sojourner Truth, Susan B. Anthony, the Blackwells, Maria Mitchell, Sarah Josepha Hale.

2. By 1860 what advances had been made in (a) public education? (b) the education of women?

3. What changes did Dorothea Dix seek in the treatment of the mentally handicapped?

4. How were women's rights restricted? What gains were made between 1828 and 1860?

5. **Critical Thinking: Identifying Central Issues.** What developments in religion were linked to the movements for social reform?

See "Lesson Plan," p. 278C.

2. The abolition movement

The first moves to end slavery had come in the North at the time of the American Revolution (p. 105). But even in the South men like Washington and Jefferson were unhappy about slavery. Jefferson had actually inserted in the Declaration of Independence an item attacking George III for promoting the slave trade to America. It was finally taken out in deference to southern prejudices. Many other Southerners of goodwill who opposed slavery comforted themselves with the thought that it was a dying institution. Then the cotton gin led to a new demand for slaves to raise cotton. More than ever before, Southerners came to believe that slavery was the very foundation of the South.

The southern antislavery movement. Still, some Southerners continued to look for a way to get rid of slavery. In 1816–1817 the South became the center of an antislavery movement built around the American Colonization Society. Since its members believed that the blacks could never be assimilated into American life, they raised money to send all the blacks back to Africa. The Society established a colony in Africa in what is now the nation of Liberia.

In its first twenty years the Society was able to send only 4000 blacks back to Africa—and many of those were not slaves. By 1830 there were 2 million slaves in the United States, and their number was increasing through new births at the rate of 500,000 every ten years.

Most blacks did not want to go back to Africa. In 1817 a group of free blacks in Philadelphia stated positively, "We have no wish to separate from our present homes for any purpose whatever."

As the attacks of northern abolitionists became more bitter, talk of freeing the slaves became more and more dangerous in the South. Southerners like James G. Birney of Kentucky and Sarah and Angelina Grimké of South Carolina who opposed slavery felt obliged to go north. The last debates over slavery in the South were those in Virginia. By 1831 many people in Virginia were worried about slavery. The new governor, who himself owned twelve slaves, tried to persuade the state legislature to make a plan for gradually abolishing slavery. The Virginia legislature held a great debate on slavery which lasted most of the month of January 1832. Then they voted 73 to 58 to keep slavery. The vote was a tragic mistake. It made it almost inevitable that if slavery was to be abolished in Virginia, it would have to be by force from the outside.

By 1833 no reform was welcome in the South. If one reforming "ism" (even pacifism) entered their section, Southerners feared that it might soon be followed by that worst "ism" of all— abolitionism. So the South turned inward and cut itself off from the outside world, keeping out northern books, checking the mails for abolitionist literature, and even preventing the discussion of slavery in Congress (p. 316).

The movement heats up. The problem for Southerners was that the abolitionist attacks had become so strong. Many abolitionists were devout Christians. They believed that Jesus hated slavery. "Do unto others as you would have others do unto you." You do not want to be a slave yourself. What right, then, have you to enslave others? Christianity, they said, was the religion of love—love for everyone. The abolitionists wanted to preach love. But before very long they were also preaching hate.

It was easy enough to go from hating slavery to hating slaveholders. And easy enough, too, to go from hating slaveholding Southerners to hating all white Southerners. Since abolitionists were more interested in horror stories than in statistics, they did not advertise the fact that most white Southerners were not slaveholders. In their hatred of slavery they painted a picture of the South that had no bright spot in it. If there was any virtue in the South, why had not Southerners already abolished this monstrous evil for themselves?

The abolitionists were printing all the worst facts about slavery. Of course there were plenty of horrifying facts to be told about the mistreatment of individual slaves and the separation of black families.

Theodore Dwight Weld, a New England minister, started his career on a crusade against

📖 **More from Boorstin:** "[Southern writer] George Fitzhugh gave a whole chapter of his *Cannibals All!* (1857) to 'The Philosophy of Isms—showing why they abound at the North, and are unknown at the South.' The disarmingly simple reason he offered was that in the North reforms were more needed, while the South, blessed by slavery, lacked the very evils against which reforms might be directed." (From *The Americans: The National Experience*)

alcohol. Then, inspired by English abolitionists, he began to fight slavery. In 1839 he published *Slavery As It Is: Testimony of a Thousand Witnesses*, put together from items he had sifted from 20,000 copies of newspapers.

The book was a chamber of horrors. His purpose, Weld wrote, was to "see the inside of that horrible system. . . . In the advertisements for runaways we detect the cruel whippings and shootings and brandings, practiced on the helpless slaves. Heartsickening as the details are, I am thankful that God in his providence has put into our hands these weapons [these facts] prepared by the South herself, to destroy the fell monster."

Nearly everybody likes to read horror stories. The book spread through the North. Within the first four months it sold 22,000 copies, within a year more than 100,000. Northerners now began to get their picture of the South from Weld's lurid book and from others like it.

The abolition movement grew larger and more outspoken. William Lloyd Garrison, editor of the abolitionist newspaper *The Liberator* and one of the most angry of the abolitionists, actually burned a copy of the Constitution of the United States. He called the Constitution a covenant with death and an agreement with Hell—because it allowed slavery. Garrison's extreme attacks angered even his fellow Northerners. They mobbed and nearly killed him several times.

Elijah Parish Lovejoy was a convinced reformer like many others. He was against lots of things—including alcoholic drinks, the Catholic church, and slavery—all of which he attacked in his newspaper in Missouri. But Missouri was a slave state. So Lovejoy moved to Illinois, where slavery was not allowed, to find a safer place for his newspaper. Even there the aggressive proslavery forces reached across the border.

Abolitionist editor Elijah Lovejoy was killed when a proslavery mob attacked his Alton, Illinois, printing plant in 1837. A magazine of the day featured this illustration of the attack.

Culver Pictures

☑ See "Lesson Plan," p. 278D for **Writing Process Activity: Recognizing Bias** relating to Theodore Dwight Weld's book, *Slavery As It Is: Testimony of a Thousand Witnesses*.

His printing presses were destroyed by pro-slavery ruffians again and again. Each time that he set up a new press the armed proslavery mob came back to destroy it. Lovejoy's press was protected by 60 young abolitionists who begged him to leave town for his own safety. But instead of fleeing he preferred to die for a just cause. One night during an attack on the warehouse where Lovejoy was guarding his new press, the proslavery men set the warehouse on fire. When Lovejoy leaped out, he was shot dead.

Elijah Parish Lovejoy thus became a martyr for abolitionists everywhere.

Both sides were collecting their heroes and martyrs. It was becoming harder and harder to imagine that the people of the North and the South could be kept within a single nation.

See "Section 2 Review answers," p. 278D.

Section 2 Review

1. Identify or explain: James G. Birney, Grimké sisters, Theodore Dwight Weld, William Lloyd Garrison, Elijah Parish Lovejoy, American Colonization Society, *The Liberator*.

2. **Critical Thinking: Expressing Problems Clearly.** As of 1833 the South tried to isolate itself from the rest of the nation. Explain.

See "Lesson Plan," p. 278D.

3. Westward ho!

The national differences over slavery might not have come to a head so soon if the nation had not been growing and moving so fast. But Americans were pushing into Texas, into New Mexico, into California, and into the vast Oregon country north of California. The transplanted Americans out there naturally wanted their new homes to become part of the United States. In the East, stay-at-home Americans dreamed of a grand Empire for Liberty stretching from the Atlantic to the Pacific Ocean.

The push into Texas. In the Mexican province of Texas, Stephen F. Austin started an American settlement in 1821. A Virginia-born man only 27 years old, he had attended Transylvania University in Lexington, Kentucky, and did not look or act like a frontiersman. Seeking his fortune, he had lived for a while in Missouri before moving on to Arkansas and then to Louisiana. He had run a store, directed a bank, edited a newspaper, and served as an officer in a militia unit. Though only five feet, six inches tall, Stephen F. Austin had strong features and was a natural leader.

Austin's original grant from the government of Mexico allowed him to bring 300 families into Texas. Each family was to receive free of charge one *labor* of land (177 acres) for farming and one league (4428 acres) for stock grazing. In return the settlers were expected to become Roman Catholics and to pay 12 1/2 cents per acre to Austin for his services. At this time the government of the United States was charging $1.25 per acre in cash, and the nation was still suffering the effects of the depression of 1819. No wonder that Texas was greeted as a land of opportunity!

It seemed not too hard to reach Texas from the eastern states. If you had enough money, you could travel comfortably on a boat around the Gulf of Mexico and up one of the broad rivers. Or if you lacked money and were hardy, once you had crossed the Mississippi River you could ride your horse or bring your wagon over the rolling open prairie.

Austin had no trouble finding people to join his new colony. He was a good-natured dictator and his people prospered. The number of immigrants to Texas from the United States grew rapidly until by 1830 there were nearly 8000. More than half of them lived on Stephen F. Austin's grants.

Traders and trappers in New Mexico. At the same time, other daring men were pushing into a more populated part of Mexico. In New Mexico an isolated Spanish-Mexican frontier community included some 35,000 people. They lived in large towns, like Santa Fe and Albuquerque, and in scores of remote villages. They made their living by raising sheep and growing corn. From the 1600s to 1865 these Spanish and mestizo settlers were constantly at war with neighboring Indian tribes—Apache, Ute, Navaho, and Comanche. Like the Indians they

Critical Thinking Activity: Identifying Central Issues How did abolitionists protest slavery in the South? On the chalkboard make three columns labeled "Objectives," "Methods," and "Degree of Success." Under "Objectives," have students write the objectives of the abolitionist movement. Under "Methods," have students list methods that were used by nineteenth-century abolitionists. Under "Degree of Success," have students write whether or not each method was successful. Discuss why some methods worked better than others.

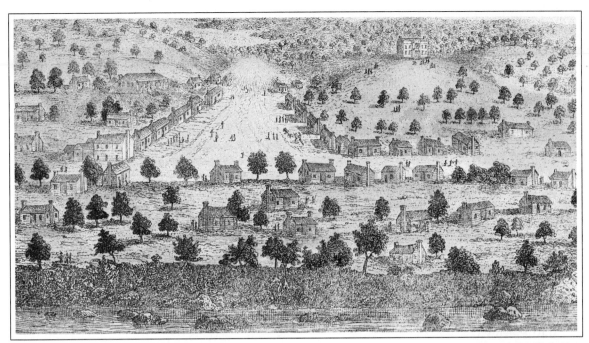

This handcolored lithograph of Austin, Texas, in 1840 shows the capital only four years after Texans declared their independence (p. 294). The grand house on the hill belonged to Texan President Mirabeau Lamar.

fought, they came to think of their captives as prizes of war to be kept as slaves or exchanged in commerce.

In their midst the Pueblo Indians were living and farming in their own way. Often the Pueblos and New Mexicans fought side by side against the other Indians.

Under Spain this separate society had been barred from contact with the United States. Traders who made their way to Taos or Santa Fe were most likely to end in jail and lose their trading goods.

All of this changed, however, with the Mexican declaration of independence in 1821. Suddenly contact with New Mexico was allowed. That same year Captain William Becknell of Missouri, who had gone west to trade with the Indians, happened into New Mexico. There, much to his surprise, he was given a friendly reception. The next year Becknell put together a large expedition of wagons loaded with goods for trade in Santa Fe. On this trip Becknell established the famous Santa Fe Trail. For decades to come, it would be a frontier highway for wagon trains headed west.

American influence in New Mexico grew through an influx of traders like Charles Bent and fur trappers like Kit Carson. They settled in Taos, Santa Fe, and other New Mexican towns. These men often married Spanish-Mexican women and soon formed a growing "American" faction.

The mountain men. The trappers who traveled through the West seeking furs discovered the hidden valleys and the easy passes across the mountains. They learned the language and the customs of the Indians, who often became their friends. The fur trade had drawn explorers to the West from early colonial times, but their great days were in the years after 1825. By 1840, however, the Rocky Mountains were nearly trapped out. As one mountain man remarked, so little was left that "lizards grow

Multicultural Connection: One of the great mountain men was James P. Beckwourth (1789–1867). Beckwourth was born in Virginia to a white Revolutionary army officer and an enslaved African-American woman. He went west to become a leading mountain man, friend of Jim Bridger and Kit Carson, and a member of the Blackfeet and Crow tribes. In 1844 he discovered the lowest pass through the Sierra Nevada to California. It was named Beckwourth Pass in his honor. This trail was later used by the first railroad in the territory.

poor, and wolves lean against the sand banks to howl." Meanwhile the fur-trapping mountain men, who marked off and explored the cross-country trails, became the pathfinders for later generations of westward-moving pioneers.

On to Oregon.

On the Pacific Coast in the far Northwest, the pioneers were American sailors. Soon after the Revolution they had visited the Oregon ports to pick up furs with which they sailed to China to trade for tea and other exotic goods. The first attempt by an American to set up a permanent settlement in the Oregon country was made by John Jacob Astor, a hard-driving German immigrant. He had already made a small fortune in the fur trade and was to become the richest man in America before his death in 1848. The men of his Pacific Fur Company built Astoria on the Columbia River in 1811, but during the War of 1812 they sold the fort to the British.

In 1832 Nathaniel J. Wyeth of Massachusetts, a successful 30-year-old businessman and inventor, led a small group overland to trade in the Oregon country. His route became famous as the Oregon Trail—another grand pioneer-way to the promised lands of the West. The adventures of that trail were later vividly described by another young New Englander, Francis Parkman. His book, *The Oregon Trail* (1849), soon became an American classic.

Wyeth's attempts to make money in Oregon were failures, but he blazed the way for others. On his second trip, in 1834, he escorted a party of Methodist missionaries headed by mild, easy-going Jason Lee. When Lee arrived in Oregon at the fort of the Hudson's Bay Company, he and his party were welcomed by a huge, bearded Canadian, Dr. John McLoughlin, the director of the company's fur-trading operations in Oregon. McLoughlin helped Lee, as he was to assist many American settlers, and persuaded him to settle in the Willamette Valley.

The news of the success of the Methodists in establishing a mission encouraged other denominations to follow. In 1836 the Presbyterians sent out Dr. Marcus Whitman and Henry H. Spaulding, who founded a mission at Walla Walla. The missionaries' wives, Narcissa Prentice Whitman and Elizabeth Hart Spaulding, accompanied them. Their feat as the first white women to cross the Rockies inspired other families to make the long trip to Oregon.

Father Pierre de Smet, the friendly and

St. Ignatius Mission, founded by the Jesuits in Montana Territory in 1845, was painted in this watercolor by Peter Peterson Tofft, a Danish immigrant who also portrayed the Oregon country.

Museum of Fine Arts, Boston, M. and M. Karolik Collection

learned Jesuit whom the Indians called "Black-robe," went to Oregon in 1844. During the next few years he assisted in setting up a number of Catholic missions in the Oregon country.

By 1843 there were about 1000 American settlers in Oregon. They had come to this promised land because of the financial depression that had begun in 1837 (p. 242) and because they had heard tall tales that Oregon was a fertile country where it was always springtime.

Since Congress paid little attention to the small settlement, they followed the example of earlier pioneer communities and made their own government. In an old barn belonging to one of the missions, on July 5, 1843, they adopted a constitution "for the purposes of mutual protection and to secure peace and prosperity among ourselves . . . until such time as the United States of America extend their jurisdiction over us."

Nearly 1000 settlers came to Oregon during the course of 1843 in the first successful mass migration. The next year brought 1500 more settlers. And the following year an additional 3000 arrived. The government back in Washington could neglect the distant "republic" of Oregon no longer.

(p. 292)

California in the 1830s.

The first Americans to reach the Mexican province of California came by boat. They traded to the missions and the ranches all kinds of goods in exchange for the products of the cattle ranches—tallow for their candles and hides for shoes and saddle bags. This trade and the beauties of California, as well as the life of common sailors of those days, were described by Richard Henry Dana in *Two Years Before the Mast* (1840).

The Mexican government broke up the Christian missions in 1834. The lands were supposed to go to the Indian converts but instead were carved into huge ranches. American traders, who lost some of their most reliable customers, the Franciscan fathers of the missions, now appointed trading agents in California towns. These agents, who supervised dealings with the ranchers, later became important in the drive to make California part of the United States.

In the 1830s there were only about 4000 Mexicans scattered along the California coast between the two deep-water ports of San Francisco and San Diego. Americans from the crowded eastern seaboard thronged westward in long wagon trains to the magical country that sailors and traders had extolled. Most of these found their way to the West Coast by following the Oregon Trail to Great Salt Lake and then heading southwest to California. A thriving center sprang up in the Sacramento Valley. A focus of community life was the fort built by John Sutter. A wandering Swiss citizen who had arrived in California in 1839 from Hawaii, he received an enormous grant of land from the Mexican government.

Wagon towns moving west.

From the very beginning of American history, the people who came here came in groups. And when Americans decided to move farther west in the years after the Revolution, they seldom went alone. Americans traveling to Oregon and California also moved in groups. You might start out alone with a few friends and family from the settled states. But you were not likely to reach very far into the unknown West unless you soon joined with 50 or 100 others.

Most of the West was still unknown except to the mountain men and the explorers. The few wagon ways that had been marked by the explorers were the only paths through the wilderness. The most important trails started from a little Missouri town called Independence 200 miles west of St. Louis.

At Elm Grove, just outside Independence, people from all over collected because they wanted to go west. Some had never seen one another before. Just as people in Chicago, Cincinnati, St. Louis, and a hundred other places were quickly coming together and forming their instant cities, so these people with wagons were forming their own kind of instant towns. These were wagon towns, towns made to move.

It was not safe to travel alone. Indians were apt to attack a small party, but a large group might frighten them off. And with enough wagons in your party, you could make a kind of fort every night. The wagons would be formed into a

More from Boorstin: "Behind them, transients left their past, with most of its accumulated inequalities . . . In settled communities, inherited possessions distinguish a person by advantages he had not himself earned . . . [But on the trail West,] items that elsewhere marked off the rich from the poor—elegant clothes, heavily carved furniture, or silver service—had to be left behind." (From *The Americans: The National Experience*)

Trails to the Far West, 1835-1850

—— Santa Fe Trail   —— Mormon Trail

—— Gila Route   —— Oregon Trail

—— Old Spanish Trail   - - - California Trail

Boundaries as of 1835

0   500 Miles

0   500 Kilometers

hollow circle or square, which was like a small walled town. People were protected while they cooked their meals. They could sing and dance, or hold meetings to talk about the problems of the trip. If the Indians attacked, women and children could be safe in the hollow center while the men and boys shot back at the Indians from behind the wall of wagons.

The covered wagon used for crossing the continent was about 10 feet long and 8 1/2 feet to the top of the canvas. It was usually drawn, not by horses, but by three pairs of oxen. Even if two oxen were lost, the four that remained could still pull the wagon. When fully loaded, it could carry a ton.

Getting this heavy wagon up a hill, across rivers, and down steep inclines was never easy. But it was much easier if you were in a large party. Then the whole party could help push or pull with their teams or their muscles.

The trip across the continent was long and slow. From Independence on the lower Missouri River to Sutter's Fort in California, it was about 2000 miles on the wagon trail. The normal speed for a wagon was only two miles an hour. Even with good luck, the wagon ride from Independence to the Pacific might take five months.

When so many people lived together for so long, they had to be organized. They had to make rules for health and safety. They had to

🌐 **Geography and History: Place** On the map above, have students locate the Santa Fe Trail, Santa Fe, Albuquerque, the Oregon Trail, Astoria, Whitman Mission, the California Trail, Sutter's Fort, San Francisco, San Diego, Independence, and Great Salt Lake. Which forts can be found along the Oregon Trail? (Fort Boise, Fort Hall, Fort Bridger, Fort Laramie, and Fort Kearney) Where do the Gila Route and the Old Spanish Trail begin? (Santa Fe) What trail ends as Salt Lake City? (The Mormon Trail)

appoint commanders and judges, select juries, and punish criminals. They had to keep order, arrange marriages, and perform funerals. They felt all the needs of people in Cincinnati or Chicago or St. Louis, and had additional problems, too. If the trip was not to take forever, the group had to see that everybody did a share of the work and risked a share of the danger.

What they did was very much like what the Pilgrims on the *Mayflower* had needed to do 200 years before. They made a government for themselves. Like the first pilgrims, each wagon train made its Mayflower Compact. Each had its own do-it-yourself government. They wrote out their own laws, which everybody signed. They elected a captain, who was like the captain of a ship. He had the difficult job of assigning tasks and settling quarrels. The fate of the whole wagon train might depend on his good humor and good judgment.

The Mormons move to Utah. The best organizers were the best captains of wagon trains. The Mormons were remarkably successful. With their new American religion they looked to the West for their promised land. They set up instant cities of their own in Missouri and Illinois. When the Mormons prospered, however, their envious neighbors believed all kinds of strange stories about them and persecuted them. In late June 1844 the founder of their religion and their leader Joseph Smith as well as his brother Hyrum were killed by an Illinois mob that feared and hated these distinctive people. The Mormons had to move on.

In February 1846 their new leader, the able Brigham Young, began taking them across Iowa toward the faraway land near Great Salt Lake. There they would be hundreds of miles from the nearest settlement. They traveled in carefully organized groups, building their own roads and

A pioneer headed for California made this sketch of his wagon train crossing the Platte River on July 20, 1849. The broad, empty plains stretch out endlessly before them.

≋ Continuity and Change: Religion Explain to students that as religious faith motivated the Mormons to venture into the wilderness of Utah and found Salt Lake City, so did it motivate another persecuted group, the Puritans of the Massachusetts Bay Colony, to found their "City upon a hill" in seventeenth century New England. The strong belief in the protection of God, hard work, cooperation, and discipline helped both groups to overcome the trials of settling in uncharted lands. (See page 41.)

bridges as they went. They even planted seeds along the trail so Mormon wagon trains the next season could harvest the crops for food as they came by. One wagon train that reached Utah in October 1847 brought 1540 Mormons in 540 wagons, together with 124 horses, 9 mules, 2213 oxen, 887 cows, 358 sheep, 24 hogs, and 716 chickens.

≋ By cooperation, discipline, and hard work, the Mormons made the dry land bloom. They
(p. 293) dug elaborate irrigation systems and laid out a city with broad avenues. In time they were to create many towns and cities in their distant, difficult land.

The Mormons were not the only ones who expected to find a promised land in the unknown West. Hundreds of other wagon towns were held together by their own vague hopes of ❀ a prosperous future.

See "Section 3 Review answers," p. 278D.

Section 3 Review

1. Identify: Stephen F. Austin, William Becknell, Charles Bent, John Jacob Astor, Jason Lee, the Whitmans, Francis Parkman, Pierre de Smet.

2. How did the Mormon migration differ from most of the other migrations?

3. **Critical Thinking: Making Comparisons.** How were wagon train parties similar to the earlier voyage of the Pilgrims across the Atlantic Ocean?

See "Lesson Plan," p. 278E.
4. Texas and Oregon

The first opportunity for the flag to follow the American people into the new lands of the West came in Texas. But this question soon divided the nation. And it also led to war with Mexico.

The Lone Star Republic. By 1835 there were nearly 30,000 settlers from the United States living in the huge Mexican state of Coahuila-Texas. They had become Mexican citizens, but they had complaints about Mexican rule. Saltillo, the state capital, was 700 miles away from their settlements on the Brazos and Colorado rivers. These settlers from the eastern United States were in a majority in Texas proper. But they were only a small minority in the vast state of Coahuila-Texas. They had only a few representatives in the state legislature. They missed the Bill of Rights and all the guarantees of the United States Constitution, including especially the right to trial by jury.

These new Texans had come mostly from the southern United States. Since they had brought their slaves with them, they were outraged that the Mexican government tried to outlaw slavery. When that government imposed heavy customs taxes and stationed troops among the settlers, their thoughts naturally went back to the American Revolution. In 1835 they revolted and drove out the Mexican troops. Like the colonists who had revolted against George III 60 years before, the Texans declared their independence on March 2, 1836.

The convention that issued the declaration also elected a temporary government. David G. Burnet, an emigrant from Ohio who in his youth had fought for Venezuelan freedom from Spain, was elected president for the time being. Lorenzo de Zavala was made vice-president. He was an ardent republican who had been exiled from Spain. He had fought for Mexican independence and served that new nation as a state governor, cabinet minister, and ambassador to France. In 1834 when General Santa Anna took over the government and began to rule as dictator, de Zavala fled to Texas.

General Santa Anna led an army to crush the Texas rebellion. The first battle took place at San Antonio. The Texas defenders were led by William B. Travis, a 27-year-old lawyer, and James Bowie, reputed inventor of the bowie knife. The force included Davy Crockett, the famous frontiersman, two black slaves, and many Mexican Texans. Greatly outnumbered, ▽ they fortified themselves in an abandoned mis- (p. 296) sion, the Alamo. In the end, 183 died in the siege, but they killed or wounded 600 of the 2400 Mexican soldiers. This bloody battle, ⊕ which ended on March 6, 1836, was a military (p. 295) defeat. But it was also a kind of spiritual victory, for it provided the battle cry "Remember the Alamo," which Texans would never forget.

❀ See "Lesson Plan," p. 278D for **Cooperative Learning Activity: Drawing Conclusions** relating the populations of western settlements.

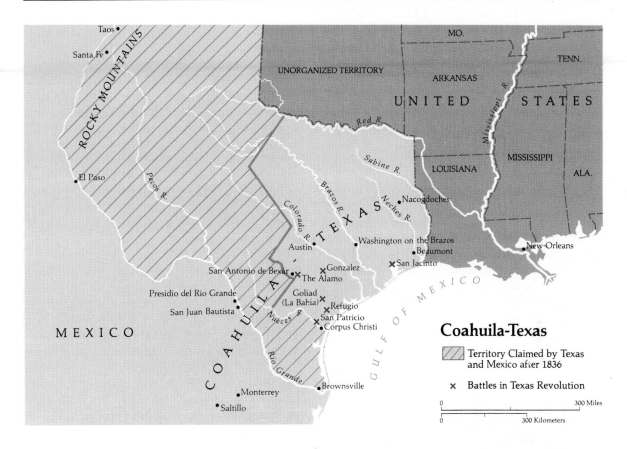

Coahuila-Texas

▨ Territory Claimed by Texas and Mexico after 1836

✕ Battles in Texas Revolution

0 ——————— 300 Miles

0 ——————— 300 Kilometers

The fury of the Texans was kept hot when three weeks later all the defenders at Goliad were massacred after they had surrendered.

The Texan army was led by tall and magnetic Sam Houston, a veteran of the War of 1812, onetime governor of Tennessee, Indian trader, and adopted son of the Cherokees. Houston retreated with his small army until he felt the right moment had come to fight. Then he turned and attacked. In the Battle of San Jacinto on April 21, Houston's army routed the Mexican army, captured Santa Anna, and forced him to sign a treaty recognizing Texas independence. A republic was set up with Houston as the first president. A constitution modeled on those of the states of the Union was adopted. To reassure the settlers from the southern United States, the constitution of Texas forbade the Texas Congress from interfering with slavery. The new Republic of Texas offered the curious spectacle of people who had fought for their right to govern themselves—and for the right to keep thousands of their fellow Texans in slavery.

Texas at once asked for admission to the Union. But Texas was so big that there was no telling how many new states might be carved from its territory. Since all Texas was slave country, the northern states saw that the balance of North and South might be upset forever simply by creating numerous small slave states there. Some Northerners said that Texas was nothing but a slave owners' plot to smuggle a lot of new slave states into the Union.

The gag rule. Northerners were especially sensitive about slavery at this time because of the so-called gag rule in Congress. Faced with a flood of abolitionist petitions in 1836, the House of Representatives refused to discuss any further petitions against slavery. Northern opponents of slavery called this the "gag rule." Former President John Quincy Adams, now a representative from Massachusetts, protested

⊕ **Geography and History: Regions** Have students look at the map above. Point out that Austin's colony stretched from San Jacinto on the Gulf of Mexico westward to about the "o" on Refugio and northward to a little beyond Washington on the Brazos. Ask: What are the natural western boundaries of the territory claimed by Texas and Mexico after 1836? (The Rio Grande and the Rocky Mountains) What river flows into the Rio Grande? (The Pecos River)

that such a restriction of free speech in the Congress was "a direct violation of the Constitution of the United States, of the rules of the House, and of the rights of my constituents." "Old Man Eloquence," as Adams came to be called, angered members of the House with his lengthy orations against the gag resolution. He finally managed to secure its repeal in 1844 by convincing members that limiting free speech endangered the Union.

Southerners tried every measure—legal and illegal—to prevent the delivery of abolitionist literature into their states. When extremists in Charleston, South Carolina, seized and burned a sack full of abolitionist pamphlets, the Congress agreed with the Postmaster General that southern postmasters did not have to deliver such mail.

This early daguerreotype was taken of John Quincy Adams in 1843 when he was 76.

The Metropolitan Museum of Art, Gift of I. N. Phelps Stokes, Edward S. Hawes, Alice Mary Hawes, Marion Augusta Hawes, 1937

The passions of the slavery issue blazed high over Texas. It seemed that to placate the slavery forces by bringing Texas into the Union would incite war with Mexico and so cost American lives. Texas was kept out of the Union. The government of the United States recognized the Republic of Texas as a separate nation in 1837 and opened diplomatic relations with the new country. First Andrew Jackson and then Martin Van Buren refused to propose bringing Texas into the Union. The question played no part in the rowdy "log-cabin" campaign of 1840 when the Whig candidates, Harrison and Tyler, were elected.

The Texas question reopened. A surprising turn of events prevented the election of the Whig President William Henry Harrison from producing the results that voters intended. The aged Harrison caught a cold during his inauguration and died a few weeks later. Vice-President John Tyler, a states-rights Virginia Democrat, had been put on the Whig ticket with Harrison simply to attract votes. The Whig leaders expected that he, like Vice-Presidents before him, would be inactive. They never dreamed that he would do more than preside over the Senate. Now, to their shock and dismay, they had actually put him in the White House!

President Tyler left not a moment's doubt that he was a full-fledged President and would follow his own policies whether or not the Whigs liked it. He vetoed Whig bills to create a new Bank of the United States, and he opposed a higher tariff. The desperate Whig leaders could do nothing but read him out of the Whig party (to which he had never really belonged). They labeled him a "traitor" and a "President by accident." All of President Harrison's Cabinet resigned, except Secretary of State Daniel Webster. He waited until 1842 in order to complete negotiations for the Webster-Ashburton Treaty (p. 301).

Tyler as a Virginia Democrat naturally wanted to annex Texas. And of course he could expect no support from the Whigs, who by accident had put him in the White House. He was forced to look to the South. At first, he hoped to avoid a violent showdown over the slavery question.

Multicultural Connection: Juan Seguín fought bravely for Texan independence. After the war Lt. Colonel Seguín was placed in charge of San Antonio. He was in the difficult position of defending the Hispanic citizens from both Mexican attacks and Anglo abuses. Eventually, he was charged with treason and had to seek safety in Mexico. Santa Anna arrested Seguín, releasing him only when he agreed to join the Mexican army. However, after the war he went back to Texas, living there until his death.

So he simply evaded the problem of Texas. But Great Britain soon made him face the issue.

Tyler learned that Texas was negotiating with Great Britain for aid and protection. The adept British diplomats saw that if they could make a firm alliance with Texas, they might block the south-westward expansion of the United States. At the same time they would secure a new source of cotton and a promising new market for manufacturers. The French government, too, supported an independent Republic of Texas.

Alarmed by this unexpected willingness of Texas to enlist the great powers of Europe, Tyler saw a new urgency in the issue. He quickly began negotiating with the government of Texas. In April 1844 John C. Calhoun, who was now Secretary of State, concluded a treaty that provided for the independent Republic of Texas to enter the United States as another state of the Union.

Unfortunately for the treaty's chances in the Senate, Calhoun used it as one more time to defend slavery. This merely confirmed Northerners in their belief that the annexation of Texas was a slave owners' plot. Over all brooded a fear that annexation would bring on war with Mexico. The treaty was rejected by the decisive vote of 16 to 35.

The election of 1844. While Calhoun's treaty was being discussed in the Senate, the national conventions met to choose their candidates for President. To no one's surprise, at Baltimore on May 1 the Whigs ignored Tyler and named Henry Clay. At Clay's request, the Whig platform was silent on the subject of Texas. The Democrats also met at Baltimore, where it was expected that they would nominate their best-known leader, Martin Van Buren, who had already been President once. But Van Buren had committed himself against annexing Texas in order to gain the votes of the North. So he was passed over.

Then for the first time in American history a party nominated a "dark horse," a man who was not nationally known and who had not been thought of as a candidate. If there were few arguments in his favor, there was little to be said against him. Such a candidate, they thought, might have wider appeal than some famous man who had won loyal friends but also had made bitter enemies. The "dark horse" was James K. Polk, once governor of Tennessee and a loyal Democrat. The Whigs ridiculed the Democratic choice. Earlier that year the polka had become the most popular dance in Washington. "The *Polk*-a dance," they said, "will now be the order of the day. It means two steps *backward* for one step forward."

There was a surprise in store for the Whigs. The unknown Polk soon proved to be an adept politician. His formula for compromise was a single watchword: *Expansion!* To annex Texas all by itself expanded the slave area and seemed a menace to the North. But if at the same time you annexed the vast Oregon Territory, you had something to give the North in return. That was Polk's platform. Expand everywhere at once, and then there would be something for everybody. The very thought of stretching the nation all the way to the Pacific was exhilarating. Perhaps the nation could be united simply by marching westward together. In a divided nation, growth itself was a kind of compromise, something that everybody could agree on.

Henry Clay saw that Polk had found a popular issue. Clay had published a letter on April 27 (when he thought that Van Buren would be the Democratic candidate) opposing annexation. When he saw himself running against the expansionist Polk, he changed his tune. Clay was so anxious to be President that there were few things he would not do to smooth his path to the White House. Now he wrote that he "would be glad to see Texas admitted on fair terms" and that "slavery ought not to affect the question one way or another." But Clay misjudged the voters. His shifty behavior caused Conscience (antislavery) Whigs in New York to switch their votes to James G. Birney, the candidate of the small antislavery Liberty party. As a result Polk carried New York by a slim margin, which made it possible for him to win a close election. Henry Clay had outsmarted himself.

Ignoring the narrowness of Polk's victory, President Tyler, who had always wanted to annex Texas, called the election a "mandate"

☑ See "Lesson Plan," p. 278E for **Writing Process Activity: Demonstrating Reasoned Judgment** relating to catch phrases of western expansion.

Oregon Boundary Settlement

///// Disputed Area

0 ——————— 600 Miles
0 ——————— 600 Kilometers

The catch phrase for this whole expansive movement was provided by a New York newspaperman, John L. O'Sullivan, who wrote that it was "our manifest destiny to overspread and to possess the whole continent which Providence has given us for the development of the great experiment of liberty and federated self-government entrusted to us." *Manifest destiny!* The idea that the American destiny was clear (or manifest) challenged, elated, and exhilarated. It was an up-to-date, expanded 1800s-version of an old American refrain. The Puritan City of God, their "City upon a hill," was transformed into a continental Empire for Liberty. Both would be beacons for the world.

Fifty-four forty or fight! Polk at first demanded a stretch of Oregon that reached all the way up to the borders of Alaska (then owned by Russia). "All Oregon or none!" shouted American champions of manifest destiny. "Fifty-four forty or fight!"—a reference to the latitude of the territory's northern border—became their slogan. But when the annexation of Texas brought on war with Mexico, Polk prudently decided not to risk war also with Great Britain. The two countries agreed in June 1846 to extend the 49th parallel as the border between the United States and Canada all the way to the Pacific. Western expansionists were outraged. They felt that Polk had broken his campaign promise and put the whole nation into the hands of the dreaded Slave Power.

(p. 297)

from the people. Not even waiting for Polk to come into office, in February 1845 he secured the passage of a resolution in both houses of Congress admitting Texas to the Union. The measure also provided that with the consent of Texas not more than four additional states might some time be carved from its territory, and that the Missouri Compromise line would extend westward above Texas. That was something for the South. Later that year, living up to his campaign promise, Polk claimed for the United States the whole vast Oregon Territory, which we had been sharing with Great Britain. That was something for the North.

Manifest destiny. Americans were thrilled by the vision of their Empire for Liberty reaching to the Pacific. "Why not extend the 'area of freedom' by the annexation of California?" asked the usually conservative *American Whig Review.* "Why not plant the banner of liberty there?" Then there would be no question of Old World monarchies existing in America.

See "Section 4 Review answers," p. 278E.

Section 4 Review

1. Identify or explain: Santa Anna, Sam Houston, gag rule, John Tyler, "dark horse," James K. Polk, Conscience Whigs, Liberty party.

2. Locate: Coahuila-Texas, the Alamo, Goliad, San Jacinto, the "fifty-four forty" line.

3. How was the annexation of Texas linked to the slavery issue?

4. How was the Oregon issue settled?

5. **Critical Thinking: Recognizing Ideologies.** How did the idea of "manifest destiny" echo the Puritans' belief in a "City upon a hill"?

⊕ **Geography and History: Regions** Ask students to look at the map above and locate the 54°W 40°N latitude. Ask: Why did American champions of manifest destiny use the slogan "Fifty-four forty or fight!"? (They demanded the stretch of Oregon that reached up to that latitude—all the way to the borders of Alaska.) Ask: What major rivers were included in the Oregon Territory? (The Fraser, Columbia, and Snake rivers)

See "Lesson Plan," p. 278E.

5. War with Mexico

The nation's troubles with Mexico were far from settled. Mexico considered the annexation of Texas (which it said was still a part of Mexico) to be an act of war by the United States. It also disputed the boundary of Texas. Meanwhile, the American settlers in California were a new trouble spot. Following the example of Texas, they too wanted to join the United States. Polk was also eager to bring California into the Union. But he hoped to find a way that would avoid war.

The declaration of war. Polk sent an agent to Mexico to offer as much as $30 million for New Mexico and California. In addition the United States would assume all claims of its citizens against Mexico if Mexico would accept the Rio Grande instead of the Nueces River as the border of Texas. But Mexico was on the brink of a revolution. Feelings against the United States ran high. Both claimants for the presidency of Mexico played upon these feelings, even refusing to meet Polk's agent.

President Polk then decided on "aggressive measures." He sent General Zachary Taylor with 2000 regular troops to the Rio Grande. The Mexicans ordered Taylor to withdraw from the disputed territory. When he refused, a Mexican unit crossed the Rio Grande and ambushed a scouting party of Americans, killing or wounding sixteen men (April 25, 1846).

Polk had already drafted a message asking

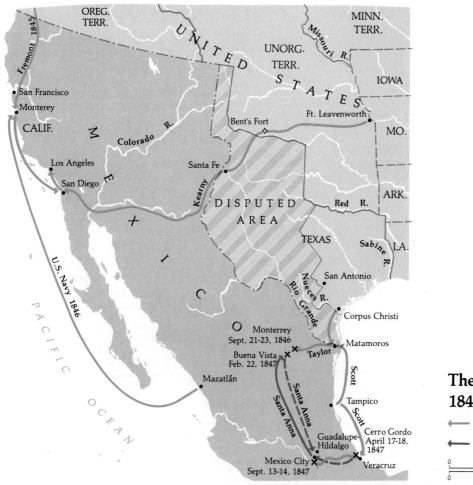

The Mexican War, 1846-1848

⟵ U.S. Forces

◀— Mexican Forces

0 ——— 500 Miles

0 ——— 500 Kilometers

⊕ **Geography and History: Location** Have students look at the map on this page. What general led the United States forces to Monterrey? (Taylor) What general led the United States forces to Mexico City? (Scott) To San Diego? (Kearny) Name four United States cities on the Pacific coast that were once considered part of Mexico. (San Francisco, Monterey, Los Angeles, San Diego)

Congress for a declaration of war against Mexico. Upon receiving news of the attack upon Taylor's troops, he tore up his first draft and wrote a new one. Now he declared that, in spite of his efforts to keep the peace, the war had already begun "by the act of Mexico." He asked Congress to recognize that a state of war existed and then to provide funds and troops to fight it.

Northerners feared that victory over Mexico might add still more territory and lead to even more slave states in the Southwest. But once the fighting had begun, patriotic passions prevailed. The opposition proved weak, and Congress voted for war.

Northern fears proved to be well founded. After United States victories by General Taylor's army at Monterrey in northern Mexico (September 21–23, 1846) and at Buena Vista (February 22, 1847), Mexico City was captured by an army commanded by General Winfield Scott (September 14, 1847). The helpless Mexican government then gave up.

(p. 299)

Winfield Scott was the triumphal commander of the United States forces that captured Mexico City. This scene, painted about 1847, shows the general in his broad-brimmed hat reviewing his troops.

National Trust for Historic Preservation.

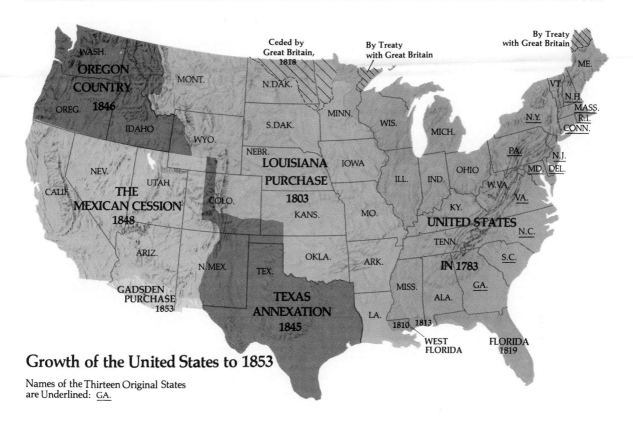

Growth of the United States to 1853

Names of the Thirteen Original States
are Underlined: <u>GA.</u>

The conquest of New Mexico and California.
In June 1846, upon hearing of the war with
Mexico, the explorer John C. Frémont and his
band of frontiersmen helped American settlers
in California to set up a republic under the famous "Bear Flag." But soon the navy arrived
and the flag of the United States replaced the
Bear Flag. Meanwhile, soldiers under General
Stephen Kearny marched from Fort Leavenworth to Santa Fe and raised the United States
flag over New Mexico. Then, with a small unit of
cavalry, Kearny continued on his 1800-mile
journey to California. When they came out of
the mountains in December 1846, Kearny and
his little force met brief but stiff resistance from
Mexican Californians. With the aid of the navy,
Kearny was able to put down this opposition
and give the United States complete control of
California.

The peace treaty and the Gadsden Purchase.
In the Treaty of Guadalupe Hidalgo (1848)

Mexico dropped all its claims to Texas and
agreed that Texas belonged to the United
States. But that was only the beginning of Mexican losses. In addition it handed over all the
lands between Texas and the Pacific. That included California, New Mexico, and most of the
present states of Utah, Nevada, Arizona, and
Colorado. In return, the United States paid
Mexico $15 million and assumed claims of our
citizens against Mexico of some $3 million.

After the Webster-Ashburton Treaty (1842)
had finally resolved the long-disputed border
between Maine and Canada, the Treaty of Guadalupe Hidalgo (1848) nearly filled in the outlines
of the present United States except for Alaska
and Hawaii. The final piece, a small strip of land
south of the Gila River in Arizona and New
Mexico, was bought from Mexico in 1853 for
$10 million in the Gadsden Purchase (p. 312).
This piece of land was believed to offer the best
rail route across the southern Rockies to the
Pacific.

Geography and History: Regions Have students look at the map above. Ask: Why are the
names of certain states on the east coast underlined? (They are the original thirteen states.
This is shown on map key.) During what ten-year period did the United States seem to be
the most active in acquiring territory? (Between 1845 and 1853) Florida was acquired in how
many stages? (Three) What were the dates of these stages? (West Florida became part of
the United States in 1810 and 1813. The rest of Florida was added in 1819.)

By A. J. Fountain Jr. Courtesy of Gadsden Museum, Mesilla, N. M., A. D. & Mary V. Alexander

By the Gadsden Purchase, the United States added 30,000 square miles of desert lands south of the Gila River to the southern borders of Arizona and New Mexico. This contemporary painting shows Americans and Mexicans celebrating the purchase in Mesilla, New Mexico Territory, on July 4, 1854.

The lands (including Texas) taken from Mexico after the war were larger than all the Louisiana Purchase or all the United States when the Constitution was adopted. This should have satisfied any American's yen for expansion. Yet (p. 301) when President Polk asked the Senate to approve the Treaty of Guadalupe Hidalgo, a dozen senators voted against it because they wanted to annex the *whole* of Mexico. "We believe it is a part of our destiny to civilize that beautiful country," the *New York Herald* proclaimed. Antislavery men also opposed the treaty, as did Whigs who envied Polk and the Democrats their success. So the treaty only squeaked through the Senate by 38 to 14, just 3 more votes than the necessary two-thirds.

It took no prophet to predict that more western lands spelled more trouble. Every new acre was a subject for debate, for a quarrel—or even for a battle. Southerners and Northerners alike thought of nothing but whether the new lands would spread the Slave Power.

In the bitterly divided nation, every stroke of national good luck struck a note of discontent. Each section somehow was afraid that the other would gain more. Ralph Waldo Emerson wrote in his journal as the United States invaded Mexico, "The United States will conquer Mexico, but it will be as the man swallows the arsenic, which brings him down in turn. Mexico will poison us."

See "Section 5 Review answers," p. 278F.

Section 5 Review

1. Identify or explain: Zachary Taylor, Winfield Scott, John C. Frémont, "Bear Flag."
2. Locate: Nueces River, Rio Grande, Monterrey, Buena Vista, Mexico City, Gadsden Purchase.
3. **Critical Thinking: Recognizing Cause and Effect.** How did the Treaty of Guadalupe Hidalgo change the geography of the United States?

Chapter 11 Review

See "Chapter Review answers," p. 278F.

Focusing on Ideas

1. A chief feature of American Protestantism was its division into many denominations and sects. Identify some of these divisions.

2. Humanitarianism—concern for human welfare and human dignity—was at the heart of many reform movements. What were some of the most common violations of human welfare and dignity? What reforms were proposed to deal with these violations of people's most basic rights?

3. Individualism has long been regarded as an American trait, but it had to be limited on the western wagon trains. Why?

4. How did the Mexican War increase the land holdings of the United States?

5. Describe the kinds of people who helped to open the American West for settlement.

Taking a Critical Look

1. **Recognizing Cause and Effect.** Name some changes in American life between 1790 and the 1840s that led reformers to demand better schools. How were improvements in education linked to these changes in American society?

2. **Identifying Central Issues.** Why were people who defended slavery wary of social reformers?

3. **Drawing Conclusions.** How did the slavery issue complicate the idea of manifest destiny?

Your Region in History

1. **Geography.** From your locality, trace the route a family might have traveled in the 1830s or 1840s to reach Texas, California, or the Oregon country. If you live in Texas, California, Oregon, or Washington, pick a city on the east coast and trace the route a new settler might have followed in those years to reach your present home town.

2. **Culture.** Find out if the reform movements discussed in this chapter had any particular impact on your state. For example, what changes—if any—did your state make in public education, care of the mentally ill and retarded, women's rights?

3. **Economics.** How did the opening of the West affect business opportunities in your region?

Historical Facts and Figures

Developing Hypotheses. Study the chart below to help answer the following questions: (a) What happened to the total number of students between 1840 and 1870? (b) By what percentage did the school-age population increase from 1850 to 1870? (c) By what percentage did the number of students increase during the same period? (d) Write a hypothesis explaining why the number of students increased at a faster rate than the number of Americans age 5–19. (e) What facts can you find in this chapter to support your hypothesis?

School Enrollment Rates, 1840–1870				
	1840	**1850**	**1860**	**1870**
Total number of students: primary, secondary, and higher	2,025,636	3,642,694	5,477,037	7,209,938
Total population, 5 to 19 years of age	(not available)	8,661,689	11,253,475	13,641,490
White population, 5 to 19 years of age	5,275,479	7,234,973	9,494,432	11,799,212

Chapter 12
The Failure of the Politicians

Identifying Chapter Materials

Objectives	Basic Instructional Materials	Extension Materials
1 The Compromise of 1850 ▪ Explain how the Compromise of 1850 settled the slavery issue only temporarily. ▪ Identify three positions on the issue of the extension of slavery.	**Annotated Teacher's Edition** ▪ Lesson Plans, p. 304C **Instructional Support File** ▪ Pre-Reading Activities, Unit 4, p. 29 ▪ Skill Application Activity, Unit 4, p. 33	**Enrichment Support File** ▪ "Come Along to Freedom": The Underground Railroad (See "In-Depth Coverage" at right.) **Suggested Secondary Sources** ▪ American History Transparencies ▪ Critical Thinking, p. F15
2 How the Compromise Collapsed ▪ Identify the major events of the 1850s that increased tensions between the North and the South. ▪ Explain the similarities and differences among the elections of 1848, 1852, and 1856.	**Annotated Teacher's Edition** ▪ Lesson Plans, pp. 304C–304D	**Documents of American History** ▪ The Ostend Manifesto, Vol. 1, p. 333 ▪ The Kansas-Nebraska Act, Vol. 1, p. 331 **American History Transparencies** ▪ Geography and History, pp. B21, B23
3 The Nation Comes Apart ▪ Cite four events that occurred between 1856–1861 that increased hostility between North and South. ▪ Explain the importance of the Republican Party in the election of 1856.	**Annotated Teacher's Edition** ▪ Lesson Plans, pp. 304D–304E **Instructional Support File** ▪ Skill Review Activity, Unit 4, p. 32	**Documents of American History** ▪ Dred Scott v. Sandford, Vol. 1, p. 339 ▪ Lincoln's House Divided Speech, Vol. 1, p. 345 ▪ The Lincoln-Douglas Debates, Vol. 1, p. 347 ▪ John Brown's Last Speech, Vol. 1, p. 361 **American History Transparencies** ▪ Time Lines, p. E15
4 The Election of 1860 ▪ Explain the importance of the election of 1860. ▪ Describe in detail the factors which contributed to Lincoln's victory in the election.	**Annotated Teacher's Edition** ▪ Lesson Plans, pp. 304E–304F **Instructional Support File** ▪ Reading Activities, Unit 4, pp. 30–31 ▪ Critical Thinking Activity, Unit 4, p. 34 ▪ Chapter Test, Unit 4, pp. 35–38 ▪ Additional Test Questions, Unit 4, pp. 39–42 ▪ Unit Test, Unit 4, pp. 43–46	**Documents of American History** ▪ South Carolina Ordinance of Secession, Vol. 1, p. 372 ▪ South Carolina Declaration of Causes of Secession, Vol. 1, p. 372 ▪ The Constitution of the Confederate States of America, Vol. 1, p. 376 ▪ Lincoln's First Inaugural Address, p. 385 **American History Transparencies** ▪ Geography and History, pp. B21, B23, B25, B27 ▪ Critical Thinking, p. F19

Providing In Depth Coverage

Perspectives on the Underground Railroad

As sectional debate over the issue of slavery heated up, efforts to compromise only angered Northern abolitionists more. The Underground Railroad, an organization which worked to "conduct" slaves through the Northern states to freedom in Canada, was in direct defiance of laws aimed at preserving the Union by keeping slavery legal in the Southern states and requiring the return of any slaves who had managed to escape to states in which slavery was illegal.

The chapter provides a brief overview of the establishment of the Underground Railroad and its efforts to aid runaway slaves.

For this chapter, *A History of the United States* as an instructional program provides two types of resources you can use to offer in-depth coverage of the Underground Railroad: the *student text* and the *Enrichment Support File*. A list of *Suggested Secondary Sources* is also provided. The chart below shows the topics that are covered in each.

THE STUDENT TEXT.

Boorstin and Kelley's *A History of the United States* unfolds the chronology of events, the key players, and, as an interpretive history, the controversy of the Underground Railroad.

AMERICAN HISTORY ENRICHMENT SUPPORT FILE.

This collection of primary source readings and classroom activities reveals the workings of the Underground Railroad.

SUGGESTED SECONDARY SOURCES.

This reference list of readings by well-known historians and other commentators provides an array of perspectives on the workings of the Underground Railroad. (See the chart below.)

Locating Instructional Materials

Detailed lesson plans for teaching the Underground Railroad as a mini-course or to study one or more elements of the Underground Railroad in depth are offered in the following areas: in the *student text*, see individual lesson plans at the beginning of each chapter; in the *Enrichment Support File*, see page 3; for readings beyond the student text, see *Suggested Secondary Sources*.

IN-DEPTH COVERAGE ON THE UNDERGROUND RAILROAD		
Student Text	**Enrichment Support File**	**Suggested Secondary Sources**
▪ Fugitive Slave Act, pp. 307–310 ▪ Underground Railroad, p. 310 ▪ Harriet Tubman, p. 310 ▪ *Uncle Tom's Cabin*, pp. 311–312 ▪ Harriet Beecher Stowe, pp. 311–312	▪ Lesson Suggestions ▪ Multimedia Resources ▪ Overview Essay/"Come Along to Freedom": The Underground Railroad ▪ Literature in American History/"Harriet Tubman" ▪ Songs in American History/African-Americans Sing of Flight and Freedom ▪ Primary Sources in American History/Reminiscences of Levi Coffin ▪ Biography in American History/Harriet Tubman ▪ Geography in American History/The Lines of the Underground Railroad ▪ Making Connections	▪ *The Underground Railroad* by Charles Blockson, pp. 31–44, 100–124. ▪ *The Slave Catchers: Enforcement of the Fugitive Slave Law, 1850–1860* by Stanley W. Campbell, pp. 96–147. ▪ *The Liberty Line: The Legend of the Underground Railroad* by Larry Gara. ▪ *The Underground Railroad: From Slavery to Freedom* by Wilbert Siebert, pp. 17–46.

The Compromise of 1850

FOCUS

To introduce the lesson, have students turn to the map on page 301. Review the tremendous growth of the U.S. from 1846 to 1849. Ask the class to suggest some problems that came with this dramatic expansion. (One answer: The problem of deciding whether or not the new lands should permit slavery.)

Developing Vocabulary

The words listed in this chapter are essential terms for reading and understanding particular sections of the chapter. The page number after each term indicates the page of its first or most important appearance in the chapter. These terms are defined in the text Glossary (text pages 1000–1011).

popular sovereignty (page 308); **daguerreotype** (page 309); **Underground Railroad** (page 310).

INSTRUCT

Explain

Review the provisions of the Missouri Compromise (page 214).

☑ Writing Process Activity

Drawing Conclusions Ask students to do some research about Harriet Tubman or Harriet Beecher Stowe. After taking notes about the woman's life, career, and actions during the 1850s, students should organize their ideas chronologically or by order of importance. In their topic sentence, they should summarize the woman's contributions to the antislavery movement, and then support this main idea with specific examples. Ask them to revise for unity and coherence. After proofreading, students can publish a collection of biographies.

Section Review Answers

Section 1, page 312

1. a) designer of clipper ships. b) never passed, proposed that Congress prohibit slavery in the territory newly acquired from Mexico. c) Democratic candidate for President in 1848. d) antislavery Whig senator from New York. e) proposed policy of letting the people in a new territory decide whether slavery would be allowed in the territory. f) the concept of self determination. g) became President in 1850 when Taylor died. h) wrote *Uncle Tom's Cabin*. 2. The gold rush of 1849 brought thousands of people to California—enough to qualify that territory for statehood.

They asked to be admitted to the Union as a free state. The problem was that the admission of California to the Union would upset the balance between slave and free states. 3. The Free-Soil party took enough votes away from the Democrats in the election of 1848 to allow the Whigs to win New York, and thus the presidency. The Free-Soil party also managed to win some seats in Congress. 4. (a) The Compromise of 1850 was supposed to settle the question of whether slavery would be allowed in territories acquired from Mexico. (b) According to the Compromise, California was admitted as a free state; the slave trade was stopped in Washington, D.C., but slavery itself was maintained there; and a strong Fugitive Slave Act was passed. (c) Clay proposed the Compromise of 1850; Webster, who had long opposed the extension of slavery, supported the compromise; Douglas provided needed political skill and pushed the elements of the compromise through Congress. 5. The Fugitive Slave Act demanded that state and local governments and citizens help capture and return runaway slaves. In response, northern states passed laws that prohibited officials and citizens from helping to enforce the Fugitive Slave Act and that tried to protect runaway slaves. Northerners also expanded efforts to help slaves escape. 6. *Uncle Tom's Cabin* roused the nation's awareness of slavery and heightened emotions, inspiring many Northerners to support the abolitionist movement and making harmony between North and South less likely.

CLOSE

To conclude the lesson, ask the students: Was the Compromise of 1850 a success or failure? Encourage class discussion and debate; be sure students use facts to support their opinions.

How the Compromise Collapsed

FOCUS

To introduce the lesson, ask students to write a brief description of one of the dumbest things they ever did because they were angry. Tell them not to put their names on it, but let them know that you will be collecting them and randomly reading some aloud. After they have had a few minutes to complete their accounts, collect them. Read a few until you find one or two that are suitable to read aloud. Be sensitive to potential hurt feelings—keep the mood of the class light with some examples of your own. After everyone has had a chance to volunteer examples of anger causing foolish behavior, ask students: Why is it so difficult to think rationally when you are angry? How can anger be redirected so that it does not prevent a leader from acting rationally?

Developing Vocabulary
Republican party (page 314); **Know-Nothing party** (page 315).

INSTRUCT

Explain
While Sumner slowly recovered from Brooks's brutal beating, Brooks was fined $300 in a Washington court and Southern admirers sent him scores of whips and canes to use on other abolitionists.

★ Independent Activity
Identifying Central Issues Ask students to make a time line for the years 1850–1856. The following items should be placed on the time line: Compromise of 1850, *Uncle Tom's Cabin* published, Kansas-Nebraska Act, formation of the Republican party, creation of the Know-Nothing party, the Ostend Manifesto, attack on Charles Sumner.

Section Review Answers
Section 2, page 317
1. a) negotiated the purchase of a small section of Mexican land, known as the Gadsden Purchase. b) tried to negotiate the purchase of Cuba. c) Secretary of State, organized the meeting of American foreign ministers who issued the Ostend Manifesto. d) urged the United States to acquire Cuba by whatever means necessary. e) official name for the Know-Nothing party, which opposed immigrants, Catholics, and other "foreigners." f) rifles supplied to Free-Soil immigrants in Kansas. g) fanatical abolitionist who led bloody raids against supporters of slavery in the Kansas Territory. h, i) abolitionist senator who was savagely caned in the Senate chamber by a South Carolina representative, Preston S. Brooks. 2. Lower California can be seen on the map on page 948. Santo Domingo, now called the Dominican Republic, is shown on the map on page 949. The Gila River is shown on the map on page 299. The Kansas and Nebraska territories can be seen on the map on page 314. 3. Pierce and Marcy tried to buy northern Mexico and Lower California from Mexico, and Cuba from Spain; Pierce was also interested in acquiring Hawaii, a base on Santo Domingo, and Alaska. Southerners hoped, and Northerners feared, that new territories would lead to the spread of slavery. 4. The Kansas-Nebraska Act organized the Kansas and Nebraska Territories and repealed the Missouri Compromise,

thus reopening the possibility that slavery might be allowed in these new territories. The act declared that popular sovereignty would determine whether slavery would be permitted in these territories. Douglas proposed the act to win support from southern senators for organizing the territories and building a railroad through them. Then, he hoped, his home city of Chicago would become the eastern terminal of a transcontinental railroad. 5. In May 1856 Senator Charles Sumner of Massachusetts was beaten unconscious by South Carolina Representative Preston Brooks after Sumner gave a speech attacking the South and some southern senators; a proslavery mob sacked and burned the anti-slavery town of Lawrence, Kansas; and John Brown led an antislavery raid that killed five men in the proslavery settlement of Pottawatomie Creek, Kansas. 6. The Republican party was organized to oppose the spread of slavery; the Know-Nothing party grew out of a secret organization formed to combat the political influence of immigrants. After the 1854 election the Know-Nothings and Republicans together controlled Congress.

CLOSE

To conclude the lesson, note that a resolution to expel Representative Brooks from the House of Representatives for his savage attack on Senator Sumner failed by a few votes. Discuss why so many representatives would vote against condemning Brooks for his behavior. Ask: Can you think of any issues today that arouse great passion among proponents and opponents? (Abortion, gay rights, busing, etc.)

Section 3 (pages 317–321)

The Nation Comes Apart
FOCUS

To introduce the lesson, discuss three items with students: the Dred Scott case and its implications for slavery in the territories; Lincoln's position on slavery and its expansion; Stephen Douglas's position on slavery and the matter of popular sovereignty.

INSTRUCT

Explain
The march towards the Civil War can be traced in the events that preceded it.

☑ Writing Process Activity
Identifying Central Issues Ask students to imagine they were members of John Brown's raid in 1859. In preparation for writing a letter of explanation to their

families before they are hanged, ask them to brainstorm their motives for joining Brown, the events of the raid and its results, and their personal reactions to what happened. Remind students that in saying goodbye to their loved ones, they want to create a clear understanding that they are not dying in vain. Students should revise for specific detail and logical organization. After proofreading, they can read their letters to the class.

Section Review Answers

Section 3, page 321

1. a) slave who sued for his freedom on the grounds that he had lived in a free state for several years. b) Chief Justice of the Supreme Court who wrote an influential opinion arguing the majority position in the Dred Scott case. In his decision Taney declared that blacks could not be citizens and that the Constitution protected slavery in the territories. c) proslavery constitution proposed for the new state of Kansas that was adopted when antislavery Kansans boycotted the vote. It was later rejected in another vote. d) name given to Douglas's effort to satisfy both proslavery and antislavery forces during his Senate campaign of 1858 against Lincoln. In it, Douglas claimed that territories could stop slavery by refusing to enforce the laws protecting it, even though they could not outlaw slavery directly. e) location of the United States arsenal where John Brown conducted his last raid against slavery. 2. The Dred Scott decision pleased the South and outraged the North because in that decision the Supreme Court ruled that Congress could not restrict slavery in the territories. The decision reopened questions that had been settled by past compromises and heightened emotions, thus widening the split between North and South. 3. Douglas broke with Buchanan because Buchanan supported the Lecompton Constitution, which called for the admission of Kansas as a slave state. Since the votes on the constitution had been boycotted first by antislavery forces and then by proslavery forces, Douglas considered the constitution a "travesty" of popular sovereignty. Buchanan's position therefore endangered the survival of Douglas's doctrine of popular sovereignty. 4. Lincoln opposed the extension of slavery into the territories. Douglas had taken a neutral position and had argued that the issue should be settled by popular sovereignty, but the Dred Scott decision made that impossible in the territories. Therefore Douglas tried to evade the issue by offering his Freeport Doctrine. This doctrine hurt Douglas because it made Southerners suspicious and lost him much of their support. 5. To abolitionists, John Brown became a martyr after his Harpers Ferry raid. To Southerners, he represented all that they had come

to hate about the abolitionists. The raid aroused their fear that there was a conspiracy to incite a rebellion by slaves throughout the South.

CLOSE

To conclude the lesson, ask students how the showing made by the Republican party in 1856, the Dred Scott decision, and John Brown's raid all contributed to the growing hostility between North and South.

Section 4 (pages 321–326)

The Election of 1860

FOCUS

To introduce the lesson, ask: Why do you think that a whole section of this textbook was devoted to an election? Discuss students' answers. Have students turn to the maps on the 1860 Election on page 324 of their text. Have them answer the following questions in their notebooks: Why are there no votes in the gray areas? (They are not states.) What do you notice about where the candidates won their electoral votes? (They are almost completely sectional—Lincoln in the North, Douglas and Bell in the border states, and Breckinridge in the South.) Based on what you read in the previous section, why did Lincoln have no popular appeal in the South? (In the debates with Douglas he took a stand against the expansion of slavery into the territories.) Did Lincoln have a majority of the electoral votes? (Yes.) Popular votes? (no.) How do you explain this? (Lincoln carried the big electoral vote states, such as New York, Pennsylvania, and Ohio.) What evidence is there from the map that Lincoln might have lost had the Democrats (Douglas and Breckinridge) not split? (The combined popular vote for Douglas and Breckinridge was greater than the vote for Lincoln.) What evidence is there against this idea? (Their combined electoral vote total is not as great as Lincoln's, and on the popular vote map they do not seem to have enough combined strength to take any one state away from Lincoln.)

Developing Vocabulary
confederacy (page 324)

INSTRUCT

Explain
At this time, political parties actually helped to break apart the Union. The parties represented sectional interests.

❖ Cooperative Learning Activity

Demonstrating Reasoned Judgment Divide the class into teams of four. Explain that students will prepare to debate the issue of the South's secession from the Union. Have each team choose a leader two debators, and a recorder. As team recorders take notes, have half the teams list arguments supporting Lincoln's decision not to accept secession and the other teams list arguments against this decision. Then have pairs of teams volunteer to debate the issue in front of the class. After the debate is completed, have students evaluate the arguments of each volunteer team.

Section Review Answers

Section 4, page 326

1. a) Vice-President of the United States and the presidential candidate of the proslavery southern Democrats who had walked out of the Democratic convention of 1860. b) nominated as the presidential candidate of the Constitutional-Union party in 1860. c) leader of an 1832 Indian rebellion. Lincoln served as a captain of the Illinois militia in the battles to suppress this rebellion. d) proposed a series of "unamendable amendments" to the Constitution to bring the South back into the Union without war. These amendments would have extended the Missouri Compromise line west to California and forever forbidden the federal government to interfere with slavery south of this line. e) off Charleston, South Carolina, was the site of the first battle of the Civil War. 2. Lincoln won the election by combining victories in just the right states to pick up a sufficient number of electoral votes. 3. The election of Lincoln was too much for the South. First South Carolina seceded. Then six other southern states declared their independence. Representatives of these seven states met in Montgomery, Alabama, in February 1861 to write a new Constitution and form a new nation, the Confederate States of America. 4. Some politicians tried to avoid war by proposing constitutional amendments that would extend the Missouri Compromise line west to California and forever prohibit the federal government from interfering in slavery. Lincoln and the Republicans opposed the proposal, and it was defeated in Congress. 5. The Union had let Confederate forces take over all but a few strong federal posts in the South without resistance. Fort Sumter, a federal post in Charleston harbor, was running out of supplies. Lincoln decided to make the South fire the first shots of the war by attempting to resupply Fort Sumter—an act he knew would provoke the South to attack. 6. Lincoln's ancestors came from England, and various descendants had gradually worked their way west. He symbolized what people thought the typical American was—a product of humble immigrant ancestors, born poor, but able to become prosperous through hard work.

CLOSE

To conclude the lesson, tell students for homework to convert the results of the 1860 Election into two pie graphs, one for the electoral vote and one for the popular vote. Tell students to round off the popular vote to the nearest thousand (1,866,352 becomes 1,866,000), and not to forget to add up the total vote first in order to figure percentages. Remind them also that all graphs need titles.

Chapter Review Answers
Focusing on Ideas

1. Slaves would be a threat to northern jobs and wage rates; slavery clashed with the democratic social system; racial prejudices. 2. Divide students into committees to do reports. 3. Mexican Cession and Wilmot Proviso: Opened question of extending slavery to former Mexican lands; Fugitive Slave Act further aroused northern abolitionists who aided escaped slave; *Uncle Tom's Cabin*: Won the uncommitted to the abolitionist position, Ostend Manifesto: Firmly identified slavery with expansion; Kansas raids: Violence superseded discussion on slavery extension; Sumner's attack: Violence; Dred Scott decision: Enraged antislavery movement by suggesting legal remedies were not available; Lecompton Constitution Fraud may have alienated people; doubts cast on effectiveness of popular sovereignty; Brown's raid: Convinced southerners that abolitionists would stop at nothing to end slavery.

Taking a Critical Look

1. The Fugitive Slave Act was unacceptable to abolitionists; popular sovereignty on slavery in Utah and New Mexico territories roused further conflict. 2. No etablished party could clearly reflect the views of all its members. As issues became more clearly defined, party members broke away to form their own party.

Your Region in History

1–3. Answers will vary depending on your region. Consult your local library or historical society.

Historical Facts and Figures

(a) 3800%. (b) 200% (c) No; invention of cotton gin.

Answers to "Making Connections"

(See "Using Making Connections" on p. 328.)
Answers will vary, but may include one or more of the following examples. Answers based on the time line callouts are in italics.

12

1. New forms of transportation and communication systems revealed the uniqueness and accentuated the differences among the regions of the United States. In fact, new methods of transportation drove the South further apart from the West and the North, even while joining all three regions in a closer way than ever before. In the nation's first years, transportation was poor, and the regions were very independent of one another. A far-sighted Congress saw the need to bind the nation together. *In 1803 it set aside funds to build a road linking the East and the West.* Ultimately, that National Road linked Cumberland, Maryland, to Vandalia, Illinois. Despite the National Road and other new routes, most farms in the United States were still very isolated and the regions had little contact. Then the country entered a canal-building era that began *in 1817 with the beginning of construction on the Erie Canal*. The Erie Canal formed a strong link between the North and the West. Growing ties between those regions left the South feeling outnumbered and unprotected. The South, of course, was the only region in the country to maintain the slave system. Few immigrants settled in the South because they did not wish to compete with forced labor. The South did not build cities with the vigor of the North and West. There were some economic ties between the South and the West because many Western farmers sent their crops down the Mississippi to New Orleans. That changed with the speedy development of the railroads, which again strengthened the ties between the North and the West. *By 1860 there were 30,626 miles of railroad track crisscrossing the United States*. But there were far more routes linking North and West than either North and South or West and South. The South, defensive about slavery and worried about the spread of abolitionist doctrine, kept its money tied into slave capital. Thus, while new roads, canals, and railroads did link the entire nation, they actually highlighted the uniqueness of the South. 2. The American political tradition of compromise prolonged slavery for many years until the issue finally erupted in the Civil War. The framers of the Constitution compromised on slavery. Then came the *Missouri Compromise of 1820*. When Missouri asked for admission to the Union, it opened up a heated argument about the spread of slavery. Part of the issue was representation in Congress. Until that time there had always been an equal number of slave and free states, so each section had the same number of votes in the Senate. However, there seemed to be no free state to match with Missouri. The Missouri Compromise, produced after a year of debate, was more of a stalemate than a compromise, but it solved the immediate problem. Missouri was added to the Union as a slave state; Maine entered as a free state. The law also drew a line through all the lands of the Louisiana Purchase, excluding slavery "forever" from north of the parallel 36°30″ except for the state of Missouri itself. However, the abolitionist movement continued to grow, demanding that slavery be ended in all of the United States. *The abolition of slavery in Great Britain in 1833* made the American anti-slavery movement press harder. But their efforts were delayed when *Congress adopted the "gag rule" in 1838* and refused to debate any petitions against slavery. Former President John Quincy Adams finally secured the repeal of the "gag rule" by convincing enough representatives that it hurt the Union to limit free speech. However, Congress continued to compromise on the slavery issue with the Compromise of 1850 and the Kansas-Nebraska Act. As abolitionists grew more demanding and southerners more defensive, compromise finally became impossible. *In 1852 Harriet Beecher Stowe produced her famous book, Uncle Tom's Cabin*. It made many previously uncommited Northerners into abolitionists. It helped turn voters to Lincoln, and with his election, all compromises were off and war was on.

Chapter 12

Focusing the Chapter: Have students identify the chapter logo. Discuss what unit the logo might symbolize. Then ask students to skim the chapter to identify other illustrations or titles that relate to this theme.

The Failure of the Politicians

The poison pill of the western lands soon began to do its work. The organization of every inch was disputed between the North and South. And the problem always was whether—and where—slavery should be allowed in the vast new West. Over this question Americans would kill each other in Kansas, political parties would collapse or split, and finally the nation itself would divide.

This hand-colored engraving by George Caleb Bingham shows an election day in Missouri in 1854. Voting was then a public event. It is clear that not every citizen took his duty seriously.

Collection of Mr. and Mrs. Wilson Pile

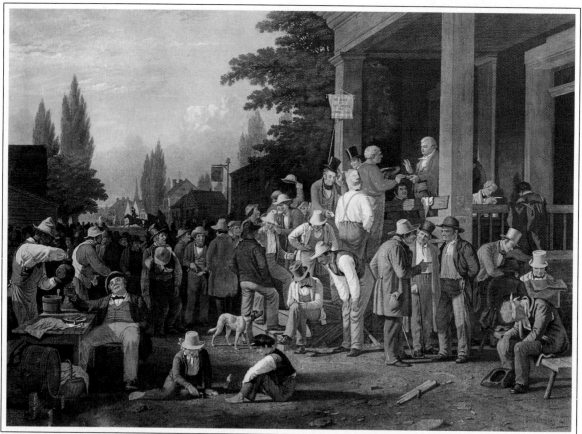

Multicultural Connection: During the gold rush, newspapers such as Horace Greeley's *New York Tribune* campaigned against Chinese immigration, calling the Chinese, "uncivilized, unclean and filthy." In 1850, as part of the anti-Chinese movement, California passed an exorbitant Foreign Miners License Tax requiring non-native-born citizens of the United States to pay $20 per month to mine. This tax was designed to prevent Chinese and Mexicans from working in the gold mines.

Workers at Sutter's Mill were the first to discover gold in California.

See "Lesson Plan," p. 304C.

1. The Compromise of 1850

Emerson spoke for many Americans when he foresaw that the millions of acres acquired from Mexico—all raw material for new states—would produce strife and tragedy for the nation as a whole. The first act of this drama would end in a great "compromise." Many optimistic Americans, north and south, mistakenly believed this might settle the slavery question for good. But the moral issue of slavery was not a subject for compromise. The only question for a nation "conceived in liberty" was when and how slavery would be abolished.

The gold rush. By an astonishing coincidence, gold was discovered near Sutter's Mill in California in the very same year when Mexico handed over California to the United States. Gold rushers flocked to California. *(p. 304)*

Thousands went west by wagon train across the plains, through mountains and desert. Their trail was marked by broken wagons, dead animals, and human skeletons—relics of pioneers who had the spirit but lacked the strength or the equipment to carry them through. Others sailed to Panama and walked across the malaria-ridden isthmus to battle for a place on a steamer going up the California coast. Some came all the way by sea, surviving an eight-month journey around Cape Horn. Often they formed companies to purchase old vessels. Then, like the members of the westward-going wagon towns, they drew up rules, elected officers, and sailed for the gold fields.

The clipper ships. Among the ships that sailed for California were some of the most splendid sailing vessels ever built. The swift clipper ships (so called because they could "clip"

More from Boorstin: "From Independence, Missouri, to Sutter's Fort (near the present Sacramento, California) about 2,000 miles on the wagon trail, a reasonable time was five months." (From *The Americans: The National Experience*)

State Street Bank and Trust Co, Boston

The advertisement for *Neptune's Car* boasts of the speedy 97-day sail to California.

time off a passage) were built in New England, spurred by the need to speed to California. Huge profits rewarded the fastest ships. The grandest of the clippers were made by the master shipbuilder Donald McKay. As a young man he had emigrated from Nova Scotia. With a rare sense of design and a fine eye for detail, working in East Boston he turned out the speediest, most beautiful ships of the age. He became a hero for his generation, like the great designers of automobiles or airplanes for a later age. In April 1851 the *Flying Cloud*, the finest of McKay's many vessels, set a record of 89 days from New York to San Francisco.

Many clipper captains brought their wives. Mary Brown Patten took command of *Neptune's Car* when her husband became ill. At the age of 19, while caring for her sick husband, she

navigated an 1800-ton clipper for the remaining 52 days on the way to California.

In the 1850s, after a railway was built across Panama, the day of the clipper ships was on the wane. British steamships, larger and more dependable than the clippers, brought the great age of sail to an end.

California asks for admission to the Union. People rushed to California from everywhere. Nantucket lost a quarter of its voting population in nine months. French soldiers and government officials deserted the Marquesas islands in the Pacific. Thousands came from the Mississippi Valley. Americans—north and south—sang

> Oh Susannah, don't you cry for me.
> I've gone to California with my wash-bowl on
>   my knee.

During 1849 more than 80,000 people arrived in California. It was no surprise that these Americans wanted to join the Union as a new state. But in 1849 there were 30 states altogether, and the national score showed 15 slave and 15 free states. To admit California as a free state, as its people requested in 1849, would break the precarious tie.

The Wilmot Proviso. And what was to be done with all the rest of the newly acquired lands? How was slavery to be dealt with out there? That question had been raised early in the Mexican War when President Polk asked Congress for money to negotiate a Mexican boundary settlement. Antislavery congressmen knew that this would lead to demands for more territory from Mexico. So David Wilmot, a Democrat from Pennsylvania, offered an amendment to Polk's bill. Wilmot proposed that "neither slavery nor involuntary servitude shall ever exist in any part of the territory" acquired from Mexico. Antislavery men and Westerners who were bitter over the failure to take all of Oregon joined to support this amendment. It passed several times in the House in 1846–1847, but the Senate always voted it down. Americans were now divided by the problems of expansion.

The South through its leaders, John C.

Calhoun of South Carolina and Jefferson Davis of Mississippi, opposed the Wilmot Proviso. Congress, they said, had no right to interfere with slavery in the territories. More than that, they insisted that Congress had a positive duty, under the Constitution, to protect the property of Southerners in the territories. This meant their right to own slaves. Slavery might be forbidden only when a territory achieved statehood, and then only by act of the state itself.

Between the extremes—those who would bar slavery altogether and those who would protect slavery—many compromises were proposed. For example, some suggested that the Missouri Compromise line of 36°30′ be extended all the way to the Pacific, dividing California and New Mexico into free and slave sections (map, p. 216). Others urged "popular sovereignty," which meant leaving the slavery question up to the settlers of each territory.

The election of 1848. As the election of 1848 approached, both political parties wanted to avoid all divisive questions. Since President Polk decided not to seek reelection, the Democrats nominated Governor Lewis Cass of Michigan. He was a strong expansionist, sympathetic to the South, and cared little about slavery one way or the other.

The Whigs, though they had opposed the war, nominated the hero of the Battle of Buena Vista, General Zachary Taylor. A professional soldier and a Louisiana sugar planter, he was the owner of 300 slaves. He had no experience in politics. This easygoing southern gentleman had not even voted for some years. The Whigs counted on his war record to sweep their "Old Rough and Ready" into office. To be doubly safe against the accusation that they really did stand for something, the Whigs had no party platform.

Voters who had strong feelings on the slavery issue were angered that the major parties offered them no real choice. As a result the "Free-Soil" Democrats combined with Conscience Whigs and abolitionists to form the new Free-Soil party. They nominated Martin Van Buren for President and Charles Francis Adams, the son of John Quincy Adams, for Vice-President.

The Bancroft Library, University of California, Berkeley

This hopeful young prospector was one of those who traveled by land to California in 1849 to mine gold.

Their party supported the Wilmot Proviso and called for "Free Soil, Free Speech, Free Labor, and Free Men."

The Free-Soilers took away enough votes from Cass to give New York's 36 electoral votes to Taylor, who won a close election with 163 electoral votes to Cass's 127. The Free-Soilers won no state, but 291,263 people voted for them, and they elected 13 members to the House of Representatives.

Clay has a plan. When the Senate met in December 1849 to decide the future of California and of the other lands taken from Mexico, the air was charged with fear and hate. For everyone at the time it was a moment of high drama. The nation's elder statesmen were still trying to resolve by words and by debate what would be settled only in blood and on the battlefield.

This was the last appearance in the congressional arena of three men who had played leading political roles ever since the War of 1812. All

Critical Thinking Activity: Recognizing Ideologies What were the issues of the 1848 election? Divide the class into three groups and assign each group one of the political parties running a candidate in the 1848 election (Democratic party, Whig party, Free-Soil party). Have each group review the issues that concerned their party and then create an appropriate campaign slogan. Have each group share their slogan with the class. Discuss the significance of each slogan.

Free-Soilers organize in Massachusetts in 1848.

were giants on the national stage. Each was a hero to his part of the country. Henry Clay of the western state of Kentucky was there, 73 years old and in failing health. John C. Calhoun, relentless champion of the South, was at the end of his long senatorial career. Daniel Webster, shrewd New Englander at the height of his powers, never thundered more eloquently.

Senator Calhoun, sick and near death, had to have his speech read for him as he sat nearby and listened. He made impossible demands. He insisted that in order to "do justice" by giving the South "an equal right" in the new lands, the North must admit slavery to California and New Mexico. Calhoun went even further and seriously proposed a fantastic constitutional amendment that provided for the election of two Presidents—one from the slave states and one from the free states.

On the other side, William H. Seward, a new antislavery Whig senator from New York, was just as uncompromising. Any concession to the slave cause, he declared, was "essentially vicious." On the issue of slavery he refused even to appeal to the Constitution. He preferred a "higher law."

Leading the forces of conciliation was Senator Clay, who had a plan. By nature a compromiser, he had the half-hearted support of many but the enthusiasm of very few. This legislative mix-master whom the nation had three times defeated for its President now offered the bundle of laws that was to become the "Compromise" of 1850. California was to be admitted as a free state (something for the North). A strong Fugitive Slave Act would protect the right of owners to recapture slaves who had escaped to the North (something for the South). The slave trade would be abolished in the District of Columbia (something for the North), but slavery would still be protected there (something for the South). He had offered something for everybody. But he had still left the main question unanswered.

What would become of all the rest of the vast new area taken from Mexico? Would it be free or slave? Clay's compromise simply postponed the answer. The people of those areas, he proposed, should in the future decide that for themselves. This arrangement was called "popular sovereignty" by those who admired it and "squatter sovereignty" by others.

Daniel Webster favors compromise. Finally, on March 7, 1850, Daniel Webster, the nation's most famous orator, rose to his feet to bring the lengthy debate to its climax. He was still an impressive and powerful figure. The galleries were crowded and the people listened patiently. For several hours the great Webster delivered one of his most carefully prepared orations. The audience did not hear what it expected.

Webster had put himself on record as being opposed to any extension of slavery. But now, sensing that the Union was truly in danger, he supported Clay's compromise at every point. He declared that slavery would never actually invade the deserts and plateaus of New Mexico. Why then insist on the Wilmot Proviso, which the South looked on as a "taunt and reproach"? He maintained there was a constitutional duty to return fugitive slaves. As to the abolitionists, he said they "had produced nothing good or valuable in their operations for twenty years."

Webster was bitterly denounced in the North

Henry Clay posed for this daguerreotype in 1849. The photographer was Mathew Brady.

Library of Congress

the sudden death of President Taylor that saved Clay's compromise in 1850. After attending the Fourth of July ceremonies held at the base of the unfinished Washington Monument on one of the hottest days on record, President Taylor was stricken with a severe stomach ailment. Within five days he was dead, and in his place a professional politician, the compromising Vice-President Millard Fillmore, came to the White House.

As a result of the skilled political maneuvering of Senator Stephen A. Douglas of Illinois, who took over from an exhausted Clay, the several parts of Clay's compromise were passed separately. President Fillmore signed them into law in September 1850. Among them was the Fugitive Slave Act, which would become the special target of antislavery passion.

Shortsighted optimists hailed the Compromise of 1850 as a "final" settlement. But a second look showed that it only put off the day of ⊕ reckoning. There had been no true compromise. Northerners had voted for particular bills that favored their section, while Southerners supported measures that helped their area. Only the fact that a few persons actually compromised their interests made passage of all the bills possible.

The great issue of slavery was far from settled. But the compromises of 1850 did give the North time to grow stronger—in manpower, railroads,

for this speech. Longtime admirers deserted him. But northern businessmen who feared the loss of their valuable southern trade approved his stand and circulated 200,000 copies of his speech. To many, especially the abolitionists, it seemed the issue was more clearly posed than ever—between money and humanity. Webster was accused of being the heartless mouthpiece of people who valued their bank accounts more than the freedom of their fellow Americans.

Congress accepts the compromise. Still the debate went on. President Taylor wanted Congress at once to admit as free states both California and New Mexico. Taylor was so insistent that it was feared he would veto Clay's compromise. But once again the course of history was shaped by a quite unexpected event. It was no eloquent oration nor any rational argument but

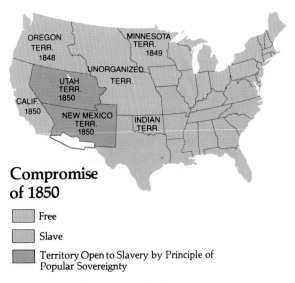

Compromise of 1850

☐ Free

☐ Slave

☐ Territory Open to Slavery by Principle of Popular Sovereignty

⊕ Geography and History: Regions Ask students to look at the map above. Have the students volunteer the names of the slave states and the free states in 1849. List the names on the chalkboard. Ask: What problem did the acquisition of so much new land create for the nation in 1849? How did it affect the U.S. Senate?

and factories. For those who loved the Union, Clay and Douglas had performed a valuable service. They had bought time. When the evil day of armed conflict would come, that strength would help decide the issue for the North and for Union.

The revolt against the Fugitive Slave Act.

The Fugitive Slave Act of 1850 kept tempers hot in the North. It provided that state and city authorities and even plain citizens should assist in the capture and return of runaway slaves.

State after state passed Personal Liberty laws. These forbade state officials or private citizens to assist federal courts in enforcing the Fugitive Slave Act. The laws also tried to guarantee protection and a fair trial to runaways.

Northerners showed their defiance of the Fugitive Slave Act dramatically and effectively by expanding their efforts to help slaves escape. The "Underground Railroad" was a well-organized series of routes and stopovers (stations) leading north to Canada for runaway slaves. By 1861 this scheme had helped some 75,000 slaves escape to freedom.

Enrichment Support File Topic

The most famous of all the "conductors" on the Underground Railroad was Harriet Tubman, herself an escaped slave. From 1849 to the Civil War she risked her life many times on trips into the South. During her long courageous career she helped spirit away to freedom her own elderly parents and some 300 other slaves.

The election of 1852.

There was no chance of preventing the two great national political parties from splitting into northern and southern factions unless the Compromise of 1850 was really "final" and somehow the discussion of slavery was itself abolished. But could so great an issue be simply wished away?

The Democrats, in their convention of 1852, pledged themselves to abide by the compromise measures. They nominated Franklin Pierce of New Hampshire. He was a pleasant man lacking force or decisiveness. But he had a good record as a politician and as a general in the Mexican War.

The Whigs were in a worse condition than the Democrats. President Fillmore had the backing

Library of Congress

Harriet Tubman was called "Moses" by fugitives whom she led from slavery to freedom.

of the southern wing of the party but was opposed by northern Whigs because he had supported the compromise. At the Whig convention it was not until the fifty-third ballot that they settled on a military hero, Virginia-born General Winfield Scott, who had captured Mexico City. The Whig platform also accepted the "finality" of the compromise measures.

But the Whigs failed to repeat the triumphs of General Harrison in 1840 and General Taylor in 1848 with this their third military hero. The Democrat Franklin Pierce won in a landslide carrying all but four states and receiving 254 electoral votes to Scott's 42. The bitter divisions in the nation were revealed in the fact that Pierce was the only President to win a popular majority between 1840 and 1864. With this defeat the Whig party began to fall apart.

Multicultural Connection: The real person behind the Uncle Tom story may have been Josiah Henson (1789–1883), an escapee from slavery. Henson was born in Maryland and became a preacher in 1828. At this time he tried to buy his freedom, but when he was sent to New Orleans to be sold, he escaped. On October 28, 1830 he crossed into Canada, where he later established a community for enslaved escapees in Dresden, Ontario. Henson met Harriet Beecher Stowe during his travels in Massachusetts, and Stowe wrote an introduction to Henson's autobiography.

Harmony was the key word of Franklin Pierce's inaugural address on March 4, 1853. The compromise measures of 1850, he said, were "strictly constitutional and to be unhesitatingly carried into effect." He sincerely hoped that no sectional ambition or radical excitement might again "threaten the durability of our institutions or obscure the light of our prosperity."

A book forces the issue. But an event had already occurred during 1852 that made Pierce's hope unlikely. It was the publication of a book, *Uncle Tom's Cabin*, by Harriet Beecher Stowe.

(p. 310)

Mrs. Stowe found much of the ammunition for her antislavery novel in Theodore Dwight Weld's *Slavery As It Is*. In her book she tried to portray the entire range of experiences a slave could have, from good owners to bad, from being bought and sold to attempts to escape to freedom. In the end, the hero of the story—the Christ-like black, Uncle Tom—is flogged to death by the brutal plantation owner, Simon Legree, because he will not give away the hiding place of two escaped slaves.

The book quickly sold more than 100,000 sets of an expensive two-volume edition. Then it was put out in a single cheap volume for 37 1/2 cents. Within a year it had sold a total of 300,000 copies. It was made into plays and musical comedies. Uncle Tom skits at fairs and circuses showed the escaping slave "Eliza Crossing the Ice" with her baby in her arms, and then Little Eva was yanked up to heaven by pulleys. "Uncle Tom's Cabin played here last night," said one newspaper. "The bloodhounds

This advertisement for *Uncle Tom's Cabin* indicates some of the many different editions that were available as well as the wide variety of prices. Harriet Beecher Stowe posed for this Mathew Brady daguerreotype in the 1840s. Brady, who learned the process from Samuel F. B. Morse, became the great photographer of the Civil War.

The Bettmann Archive   Brown Brothers

See "Lesson Plan," p. 304C for **Writing Process Activity: Drawing Conclusions** relating to Harriet Tubman and Harriet Beecher Stowe.

were good." The book sold enormously in England. It was quickly published in translation all over Europe. *Uncle Tom's Cabin* became America's all-time worldwide best-seller.

Mrs. Stowe gave one of the first copies to her congressman one day as he was about to board the train for Washington. He started reading the book on the train. The story was so sad that he began to cry. He attracted the attention of the other passengers as he wiped the tears from his face and blew his nose. To avoid embarrassment, he got off the train at the next stop, where he rented a hotel room and sat up all night finishing the book. There, in the privacy of his room, he could weep to his heart's content. Many other people, too, reported that the book had upset them. There must have been thousands of tear-stained copies of *Uncle Tom's Cabin*.

It is possible that, without this book, Lincoln never could have been elected President. During the Civil War, Mrs. Stowe went to see President Lincoln. "Is this the little woman," Lincoln asked her, "whose book made such a great war?"

See "Section 1 Review answers," p. 304C.

Section 1 Review

1. Identify or explain: Donald McKay, Wilmot Proviso, Lewis Cass, Zachary Taylor, William H. Seward, popular sovereignty, Millard Fillmore, Harriet Beecher Stowe.
2. How was the gold rush of 1849 linked to the slavery controversy?
3. How did the Free-Soil party affect the election of 1848?
4. Explain the Compromise of 1850 by (a) naming the chief issue it was supposed to settle, (b) giving its main provisions, and (c) describing the roles of Clay, Webster, and Douglas.
5. What was the Fugitive Slave Act and how did Northerners defy it?
6. **Critical Thinking: Drawing Conclusions.** What was the social and political significance of *Uncle Tom's Cabin*?

See "Lesson Plan," p. 304C.

2. How the compromise collapsed

In his inaugural address President Pierce had boldly declared that his administration would not be controlled "by any timid forebodings of evil from expansion." This proved to be the understatement of the age. He went full speed ahead searching for new territories. He sent James Gadsden to buy the northern part of Mexico and all of Lower California. He sent Pierre Soulé as minister to Spain with orders to buy Cuba. He then reached out for Hawaii, sought a naval base in Santo Domingo, and explored the purchase of Alaska from the Russians.

Mexico had no interest in selling any large stretch of land. But Gadsden did succeed in arranging the purchase of a small tract south of the Gila River. Even then northern congressmen, wary of adding new territory for the slave power, were opposed. The Gadsden Purchase was approved only after 9000 extra acres Mexico was willing to sell were removed from the treaty. Expansion was no longer a means of compromise.

The Ostend Manifesto. The climax of aggressive nationalism came over Cuba. Southerners and their friends, including President Pierce, believed the island would add a large and profitable slave territory to the United States. But Spain did not want to sell.

In response to instructions from Secretary of State William L. Marcy, during the summer of 1854 the American ministers to Spain, England, and France met at Ostend in Belgium to shape the United States policy on Cuba.

The "Ostend Manifesto" which the ministers drew up was supposed to be a confidential dispatch to Marcy. But it soon reached the press and created an uproar. The possession of Cuba, the American ministers asserted, was essential to the welfare of the United States. And if Spain would not sell the island, they advised the United States to take Cuba by force. Pierce and Marcy said at once they had not had anything to do with the Manifesto. But that was no help. President Pierce was now branded as a proslavery man and a warlike expansionist. The

---

Continuity and Change: Ethics and Values Point out to students that to bring about reform, the public must be made aware of existing injustice or wrongdoing. Harriet Beecher Stowe's *Uncle Tom's Cabin* (1852) dramatically publicized the cruel realities of slave life, just as Ida Tarbell's 1904 *History of the Standard Oil Company* exposed to a wide audience the harm caused by large trusts. These books did alert the public to specific injustices—readers in turn put pressure on government—and, thus, greatly influenced the movement toward reform. (See page 529.)

Ostend Manifesto had now firmly identified slavery with expansion.

The Kansas-Nebraska Act.   The only hope for the success of the Compromise of 1850 was to keep the question of slavery out of Congress. The advance of technology and the growth of industry and commerce soon made that impossible. By an ironic twist of fate the man who was destined to revive the slavery issue in Congress and so disturb the delicate balance was a main architect of the Compromise of 1850, Senator Stephen A. Douglas.

In the 1850s, of course, Americans had not yet begun to dream of reaching the moon. They had their own grand dream—to build a railroad all the way across the continent to unite East and West. No American city could want a greater prize than to be chosen as the eastern terminus of the nation's transcontinental railway. New Orleans, Memphis, St. Louis, Chicago, and many smaller towns all hoped they would be selected and so become the bustling headquarters for reaching the wealth and commerce of the West.

Douglas wanted his home city of Chicago to receive the prize. But a railroad through the empty land of the West could only be built with the aid of government land grants. And these land grants could be made only if the region the railroad passed through was already organized politically and surveyed. With this in mind, Senator Douglas introduced a bill to organize the lands west of Iowa and Missouri. In its final form the bill provided for a Kansas Territory and a Nebraska Territory. But Southerners would never vote for a railroad through land that was forever closed to slavery. And Douglas could not pass his bill without southern votes.

In order to win southern support, Senator Douglas, the wizard of compromise, concocted two special provisions. The Missouri Compromise of 1820 would be repealed and replaced by the Compromise of 1850. The decision whether Kansas and Nebraska should be free or slave would be made by popular sovereignty—the vote of the people living there. Douglas knew, as he said, that there would be "a hell of a storm" over the repeal of the 34-year-old Missouri Com-

American Antiquarian Society

Stephen A. Douglas, the "Little Giant," is shown carrying off the White House.

promise. But he had to have the southern votes and that was the only way. He believed also that he could survive the storm and finally pass his bill with the help of the pro-South Pierce administration. Then, he imagined, the whole problem would quickly go away.

Douglas, an experienced politico who knew the ins and outs of Congress, actually managed to get his controversial Kansas-Nebraska bill passed in 1854, after nine months of debate. This was a great victory for Douglas, but it was an even greater victory for the South. For the whole Kansas-Nebraska territory was north of the old freedom-line of the Missouri Compromise. "Popular sovereignty" now might open those lands to slavery.

✕ Critical Thinking Activity: Identifying Central Issues How does the concept of "popular sovereignty" hold up today? Have students define the term "popular sovereignty" (the vote of the people living in a specific area) and explain how it was used by Stephen Douglas in the 1850s. Then, ask students to make a list of today's issues that they believe should be left up to popular sovereignty. Have students explain their choices and discuss the practicality of such an approach.

Kansas-Nebraska Act 1854

■ Free States and Territories

■ Slave States and Territories

■ Open to Slavery under Compromise of 1850

■ Open to Slavery under Kansas-Nebraska Act

Angry rallies were held across the North in protest over the Kansas-Nebraska Act. The question of slavery in the United States had now been transformed into a battle over whether slavery should be allowed to spread into the territories.

Expansion and slavery. There was one odd but significant truth about the bitter congres- (p. 316) sional battle over the spread of slavery into the territories. It was a battle over slavery where it did not exist and might never go. This did not make the struggle any less heated. Yet it did conceal an important fact. Many Northerners, of course, were against the expansion of slavery because they hated the "peculiar institution." But many others opposed its spread into the territories not so much because they disliked slavery as because they did not want to live near or compete with blacks. Several midwestern states such as Illinois and Indiana had even put in their constitutions a ban against blacks moving into their states. These restrictions were seldom enforced. Many Northerners would have been willing to guarantee slavery where it already existed in order to be sure they would never run into blacks—slave or free—in the western territories.

Southerners failed to recognize the extent to which the opposition to the spread of slavery was actually opposition to blacks. They saw it as an attempt to bar them and their property (slaves) from the territories. To them it appeared to be just one more way the power of the North was being used to injure the South and prevent it from growing.

The new Republican party. The Kansas-Nebraska bill was greeted by anger in the North. Public meetings were held in many states. At one such meeting at Ripon, Wisconsin, the members decided to organize a new party to resist the *extension* of slavery. To show their connection to Jefferson's Democratic-Republican party, they now chose the name "Republicans," which had been dropped by the Democrats.

On July 6, 1854, the party was launched at a meeting in Jackson, Michigan. Its platform (1) declared that slavery was "a great moral, social, and political evil," (2) demanded the repeal of the Kansas-Nebraska Act and the Fugitive Slave Act, and (3) resolved to sink all political differences and unite in the battle against the extension of slavery until the fight was won. During the summer and fall of 1854, conventions in Maine, Vermont, Massachusetts, Ohio, and New York organized units of this new Republican or "Anti-Nebraska" party.

The congressional elections in November 1854 produced a revolution in American politics. The old Whig party—which in recent years had been held together by nothing but the desire for office—was shattered. Its northern members deserted and moved into the ranks of other parties. The Democratic party staggered but did not collapse. Of the 42 northern Democrats who had voted for the Kansas-Nebraska Act, only 7 were reelected to Congress in 1854. The Democrats had held a substantial majority in the 1852 Congress, but in 1854 there were only 83 Democrats to face 108 of these new Republicans and 43 representatives of another new party—the Know-Nothings.

The Know-Nothing party. Numerous parties quickly appeared and as quickly disappeared during the active year of 1854. Only two of these new parties proved significant—the

Republicans and the Know-Nothing party. The Know-Nothings were a reaction to the ever-increasing flood of immigrants into the country. The party grew out of the Order of the Star-Spangled Banner. This was a secret association formed in 1849 to combat the political influence of "foreigners," especially Roman Catholics. Its real name was the American party, but everyone called it the Know-Nothing party because its members evasively replied, "I don't know," when asked about the party's activities. Ever since then, "Know-Nothing" has been a name for people who refuse to face the real issues of their day and instead seek refuge in hate and prejudice.

In the election of 1854 the Republicans and the Know-Nothings together won enough seats to control Congress. It was not always clear, in fact, who was a Republican and who a Know-Nothing, since the Know-Nothings were still partly secret. It appears that nearly a majority of the members of the House were *both* Republican and Know-Nothing.

Bleeding Kansas. When the Kansas-Nebraska bill became law, Douglas boasted that "the struggle over slavery was forever banished from the halls of Congress to the western plains." He was wrong about the halls of Congress but right about the western plains. For the Kansas-Nebraska Act would bring bloodshed to Kansas.

The major problem with the doctrine of "popular sovereignty" was that it did not say *when* a territory could decide about slavery. As a result, there was a race for Kansas from South and North. The first to gain control, the first to create a majority—of Northerners or Southerners—would decide the fate of slavery in the territory.

Antislavery New Englanders organized and raised money to rush Free-Soil emigrants to

During the 1850s Kansas was known as "Bleeding Kansas." In this lithograph, the Battle of Hickory Point, a village about 25 miles north of Lawrence, is shown. A band of proslavery men, armed with a cannon, are attacking the settlement of Free-Soilers.

Anne S. K. Brown Military Collection, Providence, RI (detail)

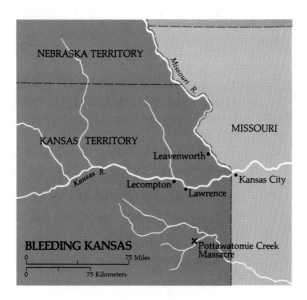

NEBRASKA TERRITORY

Missouri R.

KANSAS TERRITORY

MISSOURI

Kansas R.

Leavenworth

Lecompton

Kansas City

Lawrence

BLEEDING KANSAS

Pottawatomie Creek
Massacre

0   75 Miles
0   75 Kilometers

Kansas." He attacked the South and several of its senators with every insulting word he could command. Representative Preston S. Brooks of South Carolina was the nephew of a senator from that state who had been insulted. In the southern tradition he avenged the "honor" of his uncle and the South—not with words but with a cane. On May 22, 1856, Brooks walked up to Senator Sumner, who was seated at his desk in the Senate Chamber, and beat him senseless. When Brooks was censured by the House, he resigned. He was then reelected by the people of his congressional district with only six dissenting votes. Brooks became a southern hero. Senator Sumner never completely regained his health and became a northern martyr. For several years before his return

Kansas. On the suggestion of the eminent minister Henry Ward Beecher, Mrs. Stowe's brother, these emigrants were supplied with rifles—"Beecher's Bibles." Armed proslavery men from neighboring Missouri and elsewhere in the South also flocked to the territory. "Popular sovereignty," it seemed, would be decided not by votes but by guns.

Acts of violence were inevitable in Kansas, but only twice did the situation become critical. In May 1856 a proslavery sheriff led a mob into antislavery Lawrence, sacking and burning the town. In revenge the self-proclaimed antislavery messiah John Brown led a party including his four sons to a proslavery settlement on Pottawatomie Creek. They dragged five men from their beds in the dead of night and murdered them by splitting their skulls with broadswords. Somehow Kansas avoided becoming a territory of total anarchy and civil war. Still, bands of armed men were killing each other over slavery.

Charles Sumner is attacked. The mounting violence reached even into Congress. Charles Sumner of Massachusetts—intelligent, vain, outspoken, and tactless—delivered a speech in the Senate that he called "The Crime Against

John Brown led the vengeful abolitionist attack party that massacred five men in the proslavery town of Pottawatomie Creek, Kansas, in 1856.

Boston Athenaeum

Geography and History: Regions Have students look at the map above and the map on page 314. Ask them to locate: Kansas Territory, Lawrence, and Pottawatomie Creek. Ask: What territories were open to slavery under the Compromise of 1850? (The Utah and New Mexico territories) What were the free territories? (The Washington, Oregon, and Minnesota territories) Ask students to name five free states and five slave states.

his empty seat in the Senate proclaimed that northern and southern leaders were no longer on speaking terms.

See "Section 2 Review answers," p. 304D.

Section 2 Review

1. Identify or explain: James Gadsden, Pierre Soulé, William L. Marcy, Ostend Manifesto, American party, "Beecher's Bibles," John Brown, Charles Sumner, Preston S. Brooks.

2. Locate: Lower California, Santo Domingo, Gila River, Kansas Territory, Nebraska Territory.

3. What moves did President Pierce and Secretary Marcy make to expand United States territory? How was the slavery issue involved?

4. What was the Kansas-Nebraska Act? Why did Douglas want it?

5. Name the events in May 1856 that further inflamed the slavery issue.

6. **Critical Thinking: Identifying Central Issues.** Why were the Republican and Know-Nothing parties formed? Were they successful? Explain.

See "Lesson Plan," p. 304D.

3. The nation comes apart

The word of God could no longer hold Americans together. Even churches were dividing. In 1844 the Methodists had split into northern and southern wings, and the Baptists followed in 1845. One of the great national parties, the Whigs, had now nearly disappeared. In its place there stood a purely sectional party—the Republicans. They were looked upon with fear and loathing in the South.

The election of 1856. In the week following Brooks's attack on Sumner in the Senate, as violence convulsed Kansas, the Democratic national convention met at Cincinnati. The delegates were careful not to nominate any candidate who could be held responsible for what was happening in Kansas. They passed over both Pierce and Douglas. Instead, they chose James Buchanan, a dignified and conservative Pennsylvanian. He had had the good fortune to be out of the country during the past four years as the American minister in Great Britain. His "availability" consisted chiefly of two negative facts: He had no connection with Kansas and no abolitionist leanings that would offend the South.

The Republicans chose as their candidate John C. Frémont, the romantic "Pathfinder of the West" and "Conqueror of California." Their slogan was "Free speech, Free press, Free soil, Free men, Frémont." The Know-Nothing party split over the issue of slavery. Its southern wing nominated Millard Fillmore. But its northern wing, the "North Americans," joined the Republican party in nominating John C. Frémont to keep from dividing the anti-Democratic vote.

The campaign then became not national but sectional. Buchanan ran against Fillmore in the South and against Frémont in the North. Buchanan's greatest strength was in the South where he carried every slave state except Maryland, which went for Fillmore. In the North and West he carried five free states to Frémont's eleven. Buchanan's electoral vote was 174 to 114 for Frémont.

Still the Republicans in this their first national campaign had made a remarkable fight and shown astonishing strength. They polled 1,339,932 votes to 1,832,955 for Buchanan. Fillmore had received 871,731. So Frémont could have been elected had he won some of the votes in the North that went to Fillmore. Frémont had received no electoral votes in the South, where the Republican party seemed the instrument of the devil. As one southern newspaper said, "If they should succeed in this contest . . . they would repeal the fugitive slave law . . . they could create insurrection and servile war in the South . . . they would put the torch to our dwellings and the knife to our throats." Some Southerners had counseled the South to secede from the Union if Frémont was elected.

Dred Scott v. Sanford, 1857. In his inaugural address President Buchanan expressed the ill-founded belief that the long agitation over

United States Supreme Court

Chief Justice Roger Taney created a storm of controversy with his decision in the Dred Scott case.

slavery was now "approaching its end." And he expressed his hope that the Supreme Court would use its authority to settle the slavery issue for good. Two days later (March 6, 1857) the Supreme Court handed down one of the most momentous and most controversial decisions in its history. It dealt with the case of the slave Dred Scott. Some years before he had been taken by his master to Illinois, where the Northwest Ordinance of 1787 had forbidden slavery, and then to Minnesota, where slavery had been prohibited by the Missouri Compromise. Afterwards he had returned to Missouri. Now he sued for his freedom.

The case finally came up to the United States Supreme Court, which had to review the decision of the federal circuit court for Missouri. That court had declared that Scott remained a slave despite his travels and that, as he was not a citizen of Missouri, he did not even have the right to bring suit. To review this decision, the justices had to decide whether Scott was a citizen. That, of course, meant deciding whether he was free—which was what the case was all about. So the court decided to answer these two questions—was Scott a citizen and was he free?

The decision against Scott was 7 to 2. Its clarity was confused by the fact that each judge wrote his own opinion to support his vote. But the opinion of Roger B. Taney (pronounced Tawney) as the Chief Justice was the most important. Blacks, according to Taney, could not be citizens. The Constitution had been made by and for white men only. So Scott could not bring suit in court. And Scott was not free either. The Missouri Compromise (and by inference the Northwest Ordinance of 1787 and the Kansas-Nebraska Act as well) was unconstitutional. Why? (1) A slave was the property of his owner. (2) The Constitution nowhere gave Congress the right to deprive a citizen of the United States of his slaves in the territories, lands which were the common property of all the states.

What the Dred Scott decision meant was that Congress could do nothing about slavery in the territories. The people there had no power to ✕ restrict or abolish slavery until they applied for admission as a state.

The South rejoiced that at last the highest court in the land had endorsed the proslavery doctrine of John C. Calhoun and Jefferson Davis. It now seemed that slavery would be able to spread into all the territories. The North was outraged. Some Northerners vowed to overturn the decision. Stephen A. Douglas and others who had hoped to bury the slavery issue through popular sovereignty were embarrassed. The Supreme Court, which was supposed to settle constitutional issues, had now deepened the nation's divisions and moved the nation's politics to the brink of war.

The Lecompton Constitution. To make matters worse, the trouble in Kansas boiled up

✕ **Critical Thinking: Demonstrating Reasoned Judgment** How was the Dred Scott case decided? Have students describe and explain the ruling issued by Chief Justice Taney in the controversial Dred Scott case. Ask students to list the pros and cons of the decision. From this information, have students write their own decision for the Dred Scott case. Ask students to share their work with the class. The teacher may wish to extend the activity by having student volunteers choose sides and debate the issues.

again. In November 1857 a convention met at the small town of Lecompton to draw up a constitution under which Kansas might come into the Union as a state. Most of the delegates favored slavery, since the Free-Soilers had refused to take part in the election of delegates. They had feared that pro-slavery men from Missouri would cross the border and vote illegally. The proslavery convention, realizing that the constitution they framed might be rejected in a popular vote, allowed a popular vote only on the question of whether the constitution would be adopted "with slavery" or "without slavery." If it was adopted with slavery, slaves might be brought into Kansas without limit. If without slavery, then no more slaves could be brought in. In either case the 200 slaves already in Kansas would remain slaves.

The Free-Soilers refused to go to the polls to vote on this tricky proposition. The result was that the Lecompton Constitution was adopted with slavery. It was clear, however, that the great majority of the people of Kansas did not want slavery. When a newly elected legislature submitted the Lecompton Constitution *as a whole* to the people, the Kansas voters (this time with the proslavery forces not voting) rejected it on January 4, 1858. The Free-Soil vote was much greater than the slavery vote had been.

Douglas breaks with Buchanan. President Buchanan had pledged himself in his inaugural address "to secure to every resident inhabitant of Kansas the free and independent expression of his opinion" on the subject of slavery. But now, in spite of the fact that the voters had just rejected the Lecompton Constitution, he sent it to Congress. He asked that Kansas be admitted as a slave state. Despite the advice of the governor whom he had appointed for the Kansas Territory that the constitution was a "fraud," Buchanan called on party loyalists to support its adoption.

This was simply too much for Douglas, who had staked his political future on the doctrine of popular sovereignty. He immediately protested the Lecompton Constitution as a "travesty and mockery" of popular sovereignty. Douglas wanted a new constitution to be framed in Kansas and then submitted to an honest vote of the people there. The government had no right to force either slavery or freedom upon them. That was a question they should decide for themselves.

Buchanan used all the force of the Presidency to induce Congress to admit Kansas as a state with the Lecompton Constitution. He even withdrew all official patronage from Douglas. But the plucky Illinois senator fought back. He joined forces with the Free-Soil Republicans to defeat the admission of Kansas under the Lecompton Constitution. Kansas remained a territory until the withdrawal of the southern members of Congress on the eve of the Civil War. On January 29, 1861, Kansas was finally admitted as a free state.

Lincoln against Douglas. Douglas's second term as senator was now about to expire. So he returned to Illinois in the summer of 1858 to seek reelection. His Republican rival was a self-educated lawyer from Springfield who had served four terms in the Illinois legislature, one term in the Congress, and had already been defeated once before in his try for the United States Senate. His name was Abraham Lincoln. A former Whig, Lincoln had joined the new Republican party on the Kansas-Nebraska issue and had risen to be their leading politician in Illinois. But he was still unknown to the nation. When Lincoln announced against the famous Douglas, who had caught the national spotlight during his fifteen continual years in the Congress, there was little doubt who would win. No one could predict that this campaign would set Lincoln on the path to his great career as hero and symbol of what was most American.

Douglas believed that the free and slave states could continue to live together in peace. He cared not at all whether slavery was "voted up or voted down." Lincoln was certain that slavery was a moral wrong. In his acceptance speech in June 1858, at the Illinois convention that nominated him as the Republican candidate for senator, Lincoln said:

National Portrait Gallery, Smithsonian Institution

This miniature was painted of Abraham Lincoln in 1860. Lincoln said that the portrait was "an excellent one. To my unpracticed eye, it is without fault."

'A house divided against itself cannot stand.' I believe this government cannot endure permanently half slave and half free. I do not expect the Union to be dissolved—I do not expect the house to fall—but I do expect it will cease to be divided. It will become all one thing, or all the other.

📖 **The Lincoln-Douglas debates, 1858.** On Lincoln's challenge, Douglas agreed to a series of debates. The difference between the candidates was striking. Douglas was scarcely five feet in height, thickset, quick, volcanic in speech and in gesture. Lincoln, six feet four, lank and awkward, was a superb stump speaker. Slow, hesitant, and thoughtful at first, he captured his audience and carried it with him to share his beliefs.

Douglas kept referring to Lincoln's "house divided" speech as an incitement to civil strife. He contrasted the fairness, the democracy, and the "Americanism" of his own policy of "popular sovereignty." Lincoln, on the other hand, insisted that the territories be kept free from slavery. He denounced the Dred Scott decision as a southern conspiracy. At the same time he made it clear that he did not want to interfere with slavery in those states where it was established.

The high point of the debates was reached at Freeport, Illinois, on August 27. There Lincoln asked Douglas whether the people of a territory could lawfully exclude slavery before they had become a state. Douglas was caught on the horns of a dilemma. If he answered "Yes," he would seem to defy the Dred Scott decision. If he answered "No," he would oppose his own doctrine of "popular sovereignty."

Douglas tried to find a way to support both. Even though the Supreme Court had decided that slavery was lawful in a territory, the institution "could not exist anywhere for a day or an hour," he said, without the support of "local police regulations."

This was Douglas's famous "Freeport Doctrine." It was his way of evading the central, moral issue of slavery. By failing to pass laws for the protection of slavery, he said, the legislature of any territory could in fact exclude it. Lincoln challenged: "Then a thing may be lawfully driven away from a place where it has a lawful right to be."

In those days senators were not elected by popular ballot. Douglas won by eight votes in the Illinois legislature. But his Freeport Doctrine had made him many enemies in the South. Southerners would oppose his nomination for President on the Democratic ticket. At the same time he had helped make a national reputation for Abraham Lincoln.

John Brown's raid, 1859. At this time a man made of the stuff of saints and martyrs produced a drama that underlined all the worst fears of the South. John Brown, who had led

📖 More from Boorstin: "The brevity of the American tradition and the scarcity of sacred political texts gave the Great Debates (Webster–Hayne, Lincoln–Douglas, etc.) a peculiar role in helping the nation publicly discover itself. [A contemporary writer] boasted that from the thirteenth century B.C. to the third century B.C. 'Athens did not produce more than fifty-four distinguished orators and rhetoricians. We have had many more than that number within half a century.'" (From *The Americans: The National Experience*)

the Pottawatomie massacre in Kansas, now decided that he would invade the South, arm the slaves, and let them fight for their own freedom. The most famous of black abolitionists, the eloquent Frederick Douglass, gave Brown some advice but refused to join him. And when Brown talked to a colony of fugitive slaves in Chatham, Ontario, he could not persuade them to join him either.

But Brown pursued his wild plan. In October 1859 with his little band of 18 followers (13 white and 5 black) he seized the United States arsenal at Harpers Ferry, Virginia. Then, raiding the estates of a few nearby planters, the party forcibly "freed" about 30 slaves. Taking these reluctant people with them, Brown and his men retreated to the arsenal. Ironically, the first person to die in the affair—killed by John Brown and his men—was an already-free black gunned down by these "liberators."

The countryside immediately rose against the invasion. Five of Brown's followers escaped, but the rest were trapped in the arsenal, surrounded as it was by rivers and mountains. A detachment of United States Marines commanded by Colonel Robert E. Lee arrived on the scene. After battering down the doors, they easily made captives of the surviving members of Brown's band. The remaining ten had been killed or mortally wounded in the raid. The survivors, including two blacks, were all hanged by the state of Virginia for their part in the raid.

Brown, who had been only slightly wounded, was promptly tried in a state court for treason to Virginia. That was his finest hour. After being sentenced to be hanged, he said, "Now if it is deemed necessary that I should forfeit my life for the furtherance of the ends of justice and mingle my blood . . . with the blood of millions in the slave country whose rights are disregarded by wicked, cruel, and unjust enactments, I say let it be done." One month later, John Brown was a corpse on the gallows. But his spirit marched on. Celebrated in song and legend, the impractical John Brown, who had not the force to hold a single arsenal, became a spirit leading thousands to risk their lives

against slavery. Emerson compared him to Christ on the cross.

No other single event alarmed white Southerners more than Brown's deed. In their eyes ☑ his rash exploit at Harpers Ferry seemed part of a widespread abolitionist plot, supported by the "black" Republican party, to incite slave rebellion throughout the South.

See "Section 3 Review answers," p. 304E.

Section 3 Review

1. Identify or explain: Dred Scott, Roger B. Taney, Lecompton Constitution, Freeport Doctrine, Harpers Ferry.
2. How did the Dred Scott decision widen the split between North and South?
3. Why did Douglas break with Buchanan?
4. How did Lincoln and Douglas differ on the issue of the extension of slavery? How did his "Freeport Doctrine" hurt Douglas?
5. **Critical Thinking: Recognizing Cause and Effect.** What were the effects of John Brown's raid?

See "Lesson Plan," p. 304E.

4. The election of 1860

As late as 1860, some people still thought the nation might avoid a civil war. Even if Americans could not agree on the issues, maybe they still could agree on a man. Perhaps the right American President—a man elected by all the people—could hold the Union together.

When the presidential election year of 1860 approached, the Democrats were still a national party. A tug-of-war was going on inside their party, but they still had support all over the country. If only the political battle could be fought out *inside* the party! Then perhaps there would be no more need for John Browns, no more Bleeding Kansas! Perhaps free debate—a battle of words—and friendly compromises at the party convention could settle matters. Perhaps the politicians from the North and South would stick together (as politicians often do) in order to be able eventually to share the rewards

☑ See "Lesson Plan," p. 304D for **Writing Process Activity: Identifying Central Issues** relating to John Brown's raid.

of a political victory. Could the good-natured game of politics take the place of the bloody game of war?

The Democrats divide. When the political parties met in their national conventions during the spring and summer of 1860, it quickly appeared that politics was not the road to reunion. By an evil fate the convention of the Democratic party was scheduled to meet at a traditional capital of the slaveholding South, Charleston, South Carolina. There the southern delegates demanded that the party declare its support for slavery in the territories. Douglas and other Northerners rejected this proposal. Bitter arguments followed. When Northerners finally refused to adopt the southern program, the delegates from eight southern states left the convention.

The great Democratic party was coming apart. The convention adjourned, and after a month it met again (without the delegates of the eight southern states). Then yet another group of Southerners withdrew. What was still left of the Democratic party, of course, was not a national party at all. As its candidate for President of the United States this northern remnant nominated Senator Stephen A. Douglas of Illinois.

The southern Democrats who had left the convention gathered at Richmond, Virginia. There they named their own candidate, John C. Breckinridge of Kentucky, who was then Vice-President of the United States. He believed in protecting slavery, and he thought states had a right to secede. The damage was done! Even the "national" political parties were no longer national.

Constitutional-Unionists and Republicans. The Constitutional-Union party also appeared. It was made up chiefly of former Whigs and Know-Nothings, conservatives who feared the breakup of the Union if the Republican candidate was elected. This party sought to avoid the slavery issue entirely and ran on a single-plank platform for "the Constitution of the country, the Union of the states, and the enforcement of the laws." John Bell of Tennessee and Edward Everett of Massachusetts carried its standard.

The main opposition to the Democrats, however, was the six-year-old Republican party. The antislavery party of the West and the North, it had been founded for the very purpose of opposing the spread of slavery. Still vainly hoping for some national appeal, the Republicans named one of the most conservative men they could find in their party. He had not made any radical statements, and he sounded like the soul of easygoing common sense. Abraham Lincoln, nicknamed "The Rail-Splitter," came from Illinois.

"Honest Abe." At the moment when the nation was coming apart, it was a stroke of rare

This oil painting showing a beardless Lincoln splitting rails was done about 1858.

Chicago Historical Society

More from Boorstin: "Although [Lincoln] is one of the giants of an 'American' literature, virtually his whole literary fame rests on his spoken utterances. He drew together the two divergent and complementary streams of American declamatory literature. Purifying the public oration of its pomposities, its circumlocutions, and its affectations, at the same time he purified the anecdotal, horse-sense saying of its vulgarity . . ." (From *The Americans: The National Experience*)

good luck that Lincoln happened to be here. For there never was a better symbol of all America. Lincoln's own life was a capsule history of the whole nation. His restless family had come from England to New England and then to Pennsylvania. Lincoln's great-grandfather had lived in Virginia, where he had five sons. Four of them moved west. In 1786 Lincoln's grandfather, who had gone to Kentucky, was killed by Indians while clearing his farmland in the forest. There in Kentucky Abraham's father was raised, and there the future President was born in 1809.

Unlike other "log-cabin" candidates before him, Lincoln really was born in a log cabin. When he was only seven, his family moved again—on to Indiana. And when he was twenty-one, he moved with them once more, still farther west to Illinois. Working his way up in the world, he did a little of everything. He built a flatboat and navigated it down the Mississippi to New Orleans. For a while he worked as a surveyor, managed a mill, ran a country store, and served as a village postmaster. He was elected captain of the militia that chased Chief Black Hawk and his Indians back into the Wisconsin wilderness.

Lincoln educated himself, and made himself into a lawyer. He was especially successful before juries. His political career had been brief and not impressive. After serving in the Illinois legislature, he had one term in Congress (1847–1849), where he opposed the Mexican War. Then in 1858 he was defeated for the United States Senate by the much better known Stephen A. Douglas.

Lincoln had magic in his speech. With his slow backwoods drawl, using the simple words of the Bible, he uttered the wisdom of a cracker-barrel philosopher. He sometimes told slightly vulgar jokes, and yet he had the uplift power of a first-class preacher. He spoke the way the average man could imagine himself speaking.

(p. 322)

On the slavery issue Lincoln was firm, but he was no fire-eater. He was no abolitionist. In his debates against Douglas in 1858 he showed that he was about as conservative as an antislavery man could be. He tried to narrow down the whole slavery question into how to prevent slavery from spreading westward into the territories.

Himself of southern ancestry, and married to a Southerner, he did not hate the South. He believed in making every possible concession—short of allowing the spread of slavery. If anyone could have held the Union together, it would have been Lincoln. If an Abraham Lincoln—with Lincoln's shrewdness, with his charity, with his generous understanding of the South and its problems, with his feeling for compromise—could not do it, the Union was surely beyond the help of politics.

Lincoln is elected. The fateful presidential election of November 1860 confirmed fears that there were no longer any *national* parties. It convinced the South that their hope was not in words but in weapons. From ten southern states, Lincoln received not a single electoral vote. In the electoral college, Lincoln carried all eighteen free states, and Breckinridge carried eleven slave states. Douglas received many popular votes in the North, but carried only Missouri and a minority of New Jersey's split electoral vote. John Bell, the Constitutional-Union candidate from Tennessee, carried three border slave states.

Although Lincoln easily won in the electoral college (with 180 votes to 123 for all the others), he received only 39 percent of the popular vote. (p. 324) This was the smallest proportion ever for a successful candidate and far less even than many unsuccessful candidates had won. His opponents all together had received nearly a million votes more than Lincoln. But strangely, Lincoln would have won even if the votes for the other candidates had been combined, for he received his votes in just the right states.

When word of Lincoln's election reached South Carolina, that state seceded from the Union. It was quickly joined by five other states from the lower South: Mississippi, Florida, Alabama, Georgia, and Louisiana. Then their delegates met in Montgomery, Alabama, in February 1861, even before Lincoln was inaugurated. Soon they were joined by Texas. They wrote a ❀

❀ See "Lesson Plan," p. 304F for **Cooperative Learning Activity: Demonstrating Reasoned Judgment** relating to the South's secession.

new constitution and announced that a new nation, the Confederate States of America, was born.

Attempts to prevent war. Meanwhile confusion reigned in Washington. President Buchanan did not know what to do. He hoped that his term might come to an end before the storm broke. He believed secession was illegal. But he also thought the government had no right to compel a state to remain in the Union. Northern abolitionists such as William Lloyd Garrison were glad to see the "sinful" South separate itself from the Union. Pacifists like Horace Greeley, editor of the influential *New York Tribune*, would let the cotton states "go in peace" rather than engage in a war to "pin" them to the rest of the states "by bayonets."

In Congress even after the election, during December of 1860, desperate last-minute attempts were made to work out another compromise between the sections. Senator John J.

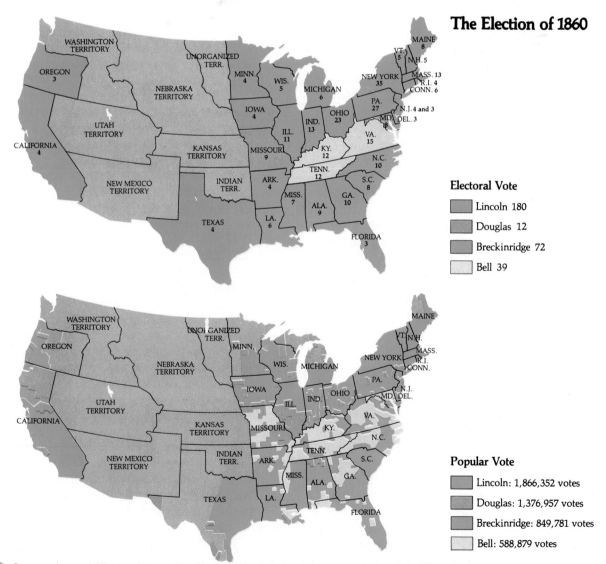

The Election of 1860

Electoral Vote

- Lincoln 180
- Douglas 12
- Breckinridge 72
- Bell 39

Popular Vote

- Lincoln: 1,866,352 votes
- Douglas: 1,376,957 votes
- Breckinridge: 849,781 votes
- Bell: 588,879 votes

🌐 **Geography and History: Interaction** Have students look at the maps above. Ask: What do the small numbers in each state in the top map stand for? (The number of electoral votes that each state has) Lincoln defeated Douglas in this election by how many *popular* votes? (489, 395) Which candidate received the second highest number of *electoral* votes? (Breckinridge)

Lincoln's inauguration in 1861 was perhaps the first to be recorded by a photographer. Scaffolding and equipment for building the Capitol's large new dome can be seen in the upper right corner.

Crittenden of Kentucky proposed a set of "unamendable amendments" to the Constitution. The most important of these would extend the Missouri Compromise line of 36°30′ to California as the dividing line between slavery and free soil. It would forbid the federal government ever to interfere with slavery in the states.

But the Republicans, on orders from President-elect Lincoln, held firmly to their refusal to allow slavery to go into any territories, even below 36°30′. Lincoln was convinced this would only lead to attempts to seize more territory south of the line in order to make more slave states. So the compromise—a compromise the South probably would have accepted—was defeated by the votes of the Republicans. They had heard the threats of the southern hotheads for so many years. They believed a confession of northern weakness would simply encourage the Southerners to make even bolder demands. The North must stand firm. If it did, they believed, many southern Unionists would flock to the Union banner and form common cause against the secessionists.

Lincoln faces a crisis. The Confederate States of America viewed the United States as a foreign nation. The seceded states therefore could no longer allow the United States to keep its arsenals and forts inside their borders. Using their own state troops, they at once began seizing federal posts. To avoid bloodshed, United States troops gave up all but a few strong positions. One of the strongest was a place right in Charleston Harbor called Fort Sumter.

As soon as Lincoln was inaugurated, on March 4, 1861, he had to make one of the great decisions in American history. He discovered that if Fort Sumter did not receive food soon, it would have to surrender. What should he do? Should he let the South have Fort Sumter and go its own way? That would mean no civil war. But it would also mean the end of the Union. Or

Continuity and Change: Ethics and Values Lincoln's decision to fight a civil war rather than give up Fort Sumter and, thus, the Union, parallels the decision made a century later by John F. Kennedy, when he enforced a blockade around Cuba until the Soviets removed the nuclear missiles they had installed on the island. By standing his ground, Lincoln made clear to the South his determination to preserve the Union, as Kennedy indicated to the Soviet Union his willingness to do what was necessary to preserve the security of the United States. (See page 785.)

should he send the needed supplies and risk a fight that might go on for years to keep all the states inside one great nation?

Lincoln decided to stand firm for the Union. He would not give up Fort Sumter. He would fight if necessary. But he would let the South fire the first shot. He notified South Carolina that he was sending supplies to Fort Sumter. South Carolina then decided to take the fort. At 4:20 A.M. on April 12, 1861, Confederate General P. G. T. Beauregard, a West Point graduate who had once fought for the Union in the Mexican War, began bombarding Fort Sumter from the Charleston shore batteries. At 2:30 the next afternoon Major Robert Anderson, also a West Point graduate who had fought alongside Beauregard in the Mexican War, surrendered the fort. No one had been wounded, but war had begun. The first, the quickest, and the most bloodless battle of the war was over. It was not a fair sample of what was to come.

See "Section 4 Review answers," p. 304F.

Section 4 Review

1. Identify: John C. Breckinridge, John Bell, Black Hawk, John J. Crittenden, Fort Sumter.
2. How did Lincoln manage to win in 1860 with only 39 percent of the popular vote?
3. Describe the founding of the Confederacy.
4. What attempts were made to prevent war?
5. How did Lincoln deal with Fort Sumter?
6. **Critical Thinking: Determining Relevance.** How did Lincoln and his family typify the nation's history?

A Currier and Ives lithograph showed the shelling of Fort Sumter in 1861. Nathaniel Currier and James M. Ives became partners in 1857. Their lithographs were popular when photographs were rare and in black and white.

Art Resource, NY

✂ Critical Thinking Activity: Identifying Alternatives Should Lincoln have allowed Fort Sumter to fall to the South? Ask students to describe the effect of Lincoln standing firm on the issue of Fort Sumter. Have students list the possible consequences of President Lincoln's actions if he had allowed the South to take over Fort Sumter. Then ask students to imagine that they are Lincoln's advisers. Using the ideas they have just generated, have them prepare 30-second speeches to the President advising him what he should do about Fort Sumter.

Chapter 12 Review

See "Chapter Review answers," p. 304F.

Focusing on Ideas

1. Why did some Northerners who were not opposed to slavery in the South want to keep it out of northern states and territories?

2. Show the influence of the slavery issue on presidential elections from 1848 to 1860. Consider the choice of candidates, party platforms and slogans, and the rise of splinter parties.

3. How did each of the following further enflame the slavery issue: Mexican Cession, Wilmot Proviso, Ostend Manifesto, raids in Kansas, attack on Charles Sumner, Dred Scott decision, Lecompton Constitution, and John Brown's raid on Harpers Ferry?

Taking a Critical Look

1. **Expressing Problems Clearly.** Some optimists saw the Compromise of 1850 as a "final solution" to the slavery issue. Name at least two features of the Compromise that would prevent it from being a solution.

2. **Determining Relevance.** How did the growth of political parties between the 1820s and 1860s reflect divisiveness of the country?

Your Region in History

1. **Geography.** What route would a person from your locality probably have traveled in order to reach California in 1849 to prospect for gold or other minerals?

2. **Culture.** What was the reaction to *Uncle Tom's Cabin* in your region? Consult local newspapers from the era for this information. Why do you think people responded as they did?

3. **Economics.** What were the principal businesses and/or industries in your region in the mid-nineteenth century? How might the abolition of slavery have affected the operation of those enterprises?

Historical Facts and Figures

Comparing Graphs. Use the information in the graphs below to derive answers to the following questions: (a) By what percentage did cotton production increase between 1800 and 1860? (b) By what percentage did the slave population increase during the same period? (c) Was the increase in cotton production a direct result of the increase in the slave population? Explain.

Cotton Production and Slave Population, 1800–1860

Cotton	Year	Slaves
▯	1800	🧍🧍🧍🧍🧍
▯	1810	🧍🧍🧍🧍🧍🧍
▯▯	1820	🧍🧍🧍🧍🧍🧍🧍🧍
▯▯▯▯	1830	🧍🧍🧍🧍🧍🧍🧍🧍🧍🧍🧍
▯▯▯▯▯▯▯	1840	🧍🧍🧍🧍🧍🧍🧍🧍🧍🧍🧍🧍🧍🧍
▯▯▯▯▯▯▯▯▯▯	1850	🧍🧍🧍🧍🧍🧍🧍🧍🧍🧍🧍🧍🧍🧍🧍🧍🧍
▯▯▯▯▯▯▯▯▯▯▯▯▯▯▯▯▯▯	1860	🧍🧍🧍🧍🧍🧍🧍🧍🧍🧍🧍🧍🧍🧍🧍🧍🧍🧍🧍🧍

▯ = 200,000 Bales of Cotton   🧍 = 200,000 Slaves

MAKING CONNECTIONS
Unit 4

This unit began on page 249 with Alexis de Tocqueville's observation that two distinct trends, nationalism and sectionalism, were developing in the United States:

> "An attentive examination of what is going on in the United States will easily convince us that two opposite tendencies exist in that country, like two distinct currents flowing in contrary directions in the same channel."

This conclusion was supported by the two unit themes that are reprinted in **dark type** below. Use the time line and the information in Unit 4 to answer the questions that follow the unit themes.

THEMES IN HISTORY

Using "Making Connections": Have students look at the unit themes printed in dark type. Explain that each event on the time line relates to one of these themes. Ask students to decide which events are related to which theme. Students should use events from the time line in their answers and explain how events are related. You may also wish to have students go back through the text of Unit 4 to find other events related to the unit themes.

1. **The development of new transportation and communication systems draws Americans closer together.**   SCIENCE, TECHNOLOGY, AND SOCIETY
   How did new forms of communication reveal the uniqueness and accent the differences between the regions of the United States?
   (Expressing Problems Clearly)

2. **The growth of reform movements and a surge of western expansion forces the nation to face the slavery issue.**   RELIGION/ETHICS AND VALUES
   How did the American political tradition of compromise prolong slavery?   *(Recognizing Cause and Effect)*

Events in American History

1813 ─
The first full-fledged textile mill is opened in Waltham, Massachusetts.

┌ 1803
Congress sets aside funds for building a road linking East and West.

┌ 1817
Construction begins on the Erie Canal, which will connect the Great Lakes and the Hudson River.

┌ 1820
Congress passes the Missouri Compromise, declaring some states free and others open to slavery.

| 1800 | 1810 | 1820 | 1830 |

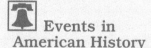
Events in World History

1816 ─
The Rhine River floods, destroying farmland in Germany and France.

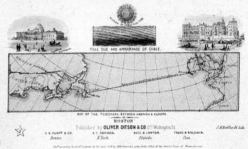

1838
Congress adopts the "gag rule," refusing to discuss abolition of slavery.

1834
Cyrus McCormick receives a patent for his reaper, a labor-saving farm implement.

1844
Samuel Morse sends first message over telegraph lines from Washington, D.C., to Baltimore.

1852
Harriet Beecher Stowe's *Uncle Tom's Cabin* is published.

1860
There are 30,626 miles of railroad track crisscrossing the United States.

| 1830 | 1840 | 1850 | 1860 |

1833
Slavery is abolished in Great Britain, fueling the American abolitionist movement.

1840
A total of 599,125 people have emigrated to the United States since 1830.

1845
Ireland's potato crop is hit by blight, leaving thousands of Irish hungry.

Unit 5

Writing about History and Art: Direct students' attention to the unit introduction, illustration, and list of themes on pages 330–331. Have the introduction and unit themes read aloud. After a brief discussion of the subject matter of the unit, instruct students to write a brief paragraph, explaining how the art:

—relates to the unit themes;
—exemplifies the unit title and illustrates the introduction; and
—is an appropriate choice for the unit.

The Rocky Road to Union 1860–1890

The Civil War began over the simple question of whether this was one nation, or whether any state or group of states could leave the Union and create a new nation. But soon, the North and the South were fighting over whether the institution of slavery should be allowed to exist. The North's triumph on the battlefield gave a decisive answer to both questions.

What was not decided with guns, however, was how the Southern states were to be treated after the war and the status of the newly freed blacks. In his second inaugural address, Abraham Lincoln expressed his hope that these problems could be solved "with malice toward none" and "with charity for all." But this was not to be.

To some Americans, the Civil War and Reconstruction were only far-off conflicts. During these years Northerners and Southerners alike were moving into the great American West. Pursuing the American dream, they hoped to conquer the wild West and open a new land of opportunity.

THEMES IN HISTORY

- The Civil War becomes a fight over the legitimacy of the institution of slavery. CONFLICT
- Lincoln's assassination dashes whatever chance the nation has of solving post–Civil War problems "with charity for all." SOCIAL CHANGE
- Increasing numbers of Americans seek new opportunities in the American West during and after the Civil War.
  GEOGRAPHY

▣ Winslow Homer's "A Rainy Day in Camp" shows Yankee soldiers cooking over a campfire while their horses are tethered nearby (detail).
Metropolitan Museum of Art, Gift of Mrs. William F. Milton (23.77.1)

Chapter 13
The Civil War

Identifying Chapter Materials

Objectives	Basic Instructional Materials	Extension Materials
1 A New Kind of War ▪ List the military and economic advantages and disadvantages of the Union and the Confederacy and describe several changes in warfare that developed during the Civil War. ▪ Explain why many in the North thought that the war would be short. ▪ Examine Lincoln's motives in delaying the emancipation of the slaves in the border states.	**Annotated Teacher's Edition** ▪ Lesson Plans, p. 332C **Instructional Support File** ▪ Pre-Reading Activities, Unit 5, p. 1 ▪ Skill Application Activity, Unit 5, p. 5	**Enrichment Support File** ▪ Experiences of the Civil War Soldier (See "In-Depth Coverage" at right.) **Suggested Secondary Sources** ▪ See chart at right. **American History Transparencies** ▪ Geography and History, pp. B21, B23, B25, B27 ▪ Fine Art, p. D41
2 The First Year: 1861–1862 ▪ Identify and describe the major events of the first year of the Civil War. ▪ Characterize Robert E. Lee as the South's foremost military leader.	**Annotated Teacher's Edition** ▪ Lesson Plans, pp. 332C–332D	**Documents of American History** ▪ McClellan Outlines a Policy for President Lincoln, Vol. 1, p. 413 **American History Transparencies** ▪ Fine Art, p. D45
3 The Widening Conflict ▪ Explain the impact of the Emancipation Proclamation on the North, the South, and Europe; and describe the contributions of African Americans to the war. ▪ Analyze Lincoln's position and actions on emancipation.	**Annotated Teacher's Edition** ▪ Lesson Plans, pp. 332D–332E	**Documents of American History** ▪ The Emancipation Proclamation, Vol. 1, p. 420 ▪ Opposition to the Emancipation Proclamation, Vol. 1, p. 421
4 Gettysburg to Appomattox, 1863–1865 ▪ Describe the major events of the last years of the Civil War and explain the terms given by Grant to Lee. ▪ Explain the ideas and values contained in the Gettysburg Address. ▪ Discuss the geography at the Battle of Gettysburg and explain the role it played in the Union victory.	**Annotated Teacher's Edition** ▪ Lesson Plans, p. 332E **Instructional Support File** ▪ Reading Activities, Unit 5, pp. 2–3 ▪ Skill Review Activity, Unit 5, p. 4 ▪ Critical Thinking Activity, Unit 5, p. 6 ▪ Chapter Test, pp. 7–10 ▪ Additional Test Questions, pp. 11–14	**Documents of American History** ▪ The Gettysburg Address, Vol. 1, p. 428 ▪ The Burning of Columbia, S.C., Vol. 1, p. 446 ▪ Lee's Farewell to His Army, Vol. 1, p. 447 **American History Transparencies** ▪ Critical Thinking, p. F19

Providing In-Depth Coverage

Perspectives on the Civil War Soldier

The Civil War was a new kind of war. Chapter 13 provides background concerning the technological and tactical changes that made this war everybody's war. Soldiers faced death on a daily basis and it was necessary to lie for long periods in muddy trenches. When attacking, soldiers had to keep moving or risk being easy targets for sharp-shooters. The "Indian" tactics of hiding and attacking became a more common method of warfare.

More than just North against South, the Civil War pitted friend against friend and brother against brother. Casualty rates were high, and meant that the war touched nearly every American family.

A History of the United States as an instructional program provides two types of resources you can use to offer in-depth coverage of the experiences of Civil War soldiers: the *student text* and the *Enrichment Support File*. A list of *Suggested Secondary Sources* is also provided. The chart below shows the topics that are covered in each.

THE STUDENT TEXT. Boorstin and Kelley's *A History of the United States* depicts the technology and events affecting the day-to-day experiences of Civil War soldiers.

AMERICAN HISTORY ENRICHMENT SUPPORT FILE. This collection of primary source readings and classroom activities reveals the day-to-day realities of being a soldier in the Civil War.

SUGGESTED SECONDARY SOURCES. This reference list of readings by well-known historians and other commentators provides an array of perspectives on the life of a soldier in the Civil War.

Locating Instructional Materials

Detailed lesson plans for teaching the experiences of the Civil War soldier as a mini-course or to study one or more elements of the Civil War in depth are offered in the following areas: in the *student text*, see individual lesson plans at the beginning of each chapter; in the *Enrichment Support File*, see page 3; for readings beyond the student text, see *Suggested Secondary Sources.*

IN-DEPTH COVERAGE OF SOLDIERS IN THE CIVIL WAR		
Student Text	**Enrichment Support File**	**Suggested Secondary Sources**
• New weapons, pp. 334–335 • Trench warfare, p. 335 • Women and the war effort, pp. 337–339 • Blacks in arms, p. 352	• Lesson Suggestions • Multimedia Resources • Overview Essay/Experiences of the Civil War Soldier • Literature in American History/ *The Red Badge of Courage* • Songs in American History/The Sadness of War • Primary Sources in American History/ Those Who Survived • Art in American History/Photographing War • Making Connections	• *Embattled Courage: The Experience of Combat in the American Civil War* by Gerald Linderman, pp. 7–79. • *Civil War Soldiers: Their Expectations and Their Experiences* by Reid Mitchell, pp. 24–54. • *Rank and File: Civil War Essays in Honor of Bell Irvin Wiley*, James I. Robertson, Jr. and Richard M. McMurray, eds., pp. 113–136. • *Toward a Social History of the American Civil War: Exploratory Essays*, Maris A. Vinovskis, ed., pp. 78–92. • *The Common Soldier of the Civil War* by Bell Irvin Wiley.

Section 1 (pages 333–341)

A New Kind of War

FOCUS

To introduce the lesson, ask students to list the reasons that Northerners thought they would win the war quickly.

Developing Vocabulary

The words listed in this chapter are essential terms for reading and understanding particular sections of the chapter. The page number after each term indicates the page of its first or most important appearance in the chapter. These terms are defined in the text Glossary (text pages 1000 – 1011).

Union (page 333); **habeas corpus; writ of** (page 340); **emancipation** (page 340).

INSTRUCT

Explain

As the population figures in the text indicate, most persons in the North and South remained at home despite four bitter years of war. Yet almost every home was touched by the tragedy of war since the casualty rate was high compared to other wars involving Americans.

☑ Writing Process Activity

Recognizing Bias Ask students to imagine they are journalists during the Civil War. Before they write an informative news article, have them cluster possible topics, such as the role of women, new warfare techniques, and so forth. Students should choose a single topic to cover thoroughly, and they should decide whether they are writing for a Northern or Southern paper. As they revise, they should check to see that they have covered the important facts in the first several paragraphs. After proofreading, students can contrast Northern and Southern presentations of the same material.

Section Review Answers

Section 1, page 341

1. a) the new type of warfare in which one destroys an enemy's resources until the enemy has lost the will to resist. b) pioneer photographer who recorded events of the Civil War with his camera. c) the first Superintendent of Women Nurses during the Civil War. d) was a nurse in a Union military hospital. e) founded the American Red Cross. f) a voluntary organization that assisted the Union by creating hospitals, promoting sanitation in military camps, and distributing sup-

plies. g) a court order calling for the release of a person who is being held in jail illegally or without just cause. h) states that decided to stay in the Union. i) refers to the freeing of slaves. 2. The rifle allowed the defender to fire many times with accuracy at attackers before the attackers could get close enough to have a chance to hit the defenders. Rifles were so deadly that soldiers had to dig trenches to protect themselves, which made the spade an important military tool. 3. The Union strategy was to attack and destroy Southern railroads and blockade Southern seaports in order to deny the Confederacy the resources it needed. 4. Women on both sides worked in munitions factories and hospitals and made uniforms and tents and other war goods. They ran farms, businesses, and plantations when the men left to fight. Some women also disguised themselves as men so they could fight. 5. The Civil War called for new ways of thinking about the craft of war. Soldiers benefited from the use of the rifle which had a longer and more accurate range, and the "caplock" which was more reliable than the earlier flintlock. Trench warfare replaced the European tactic of armed engagement in open areas. The railroad became the lifeline for troops, carrying supplies, ammunition, food, and bandages.

CLOSE

To conclude the lesson, ask students to identify the importance of the following factors in prolonging the war: the rifle, the "Conda," the decision of the border states to remain in the Union.

Section 2 (pages 341–349)

The First Year: 1861–1862

FOCUS

To introduce the lesson, ask the class to help you compile a list on the board of some of the common reasons wars are often won or lost. (The list will include size of opponents' population, element of surprise, degree of military preparedness of each side, tactics, strategy, civilian and military leadership, industrial base, allies, etc.)

INSTRUCT

Explain

Both the North and the South could have crippled their opponent, possibly winning the war in the years 1861–1862—yet neither side did so.

❀ Cooperative Learning Activity

Identifying Central Issues Assign students to work in groups of four to write headlines which summarize significant events of the first year of the Civil War. Assign half the groups to write headlines as they might have appeared in Southern newspapers and the other groups to write headlines as they might have appeared in Northern papers. Have group members begin by reaching agreement on a list of twelve important events of the year 1861–1862. Then have group members divide the list and each member compose the headlines for his or her three assigned events. When all groups have finished, bring the class together to compare Northern and Southern headlines for the same events.

Section Review Answers

Section 2, page 349

1. a) Union general defeated at the first Battle of Bull Run. b) commander of the United States army who advocated the anaconda policy. c) a plan to defeat the South by seizing control of its major rivers, encircling the Confederate states, and cutting off all their shipping. d) the Southern general who defeated McDowell's army at the first Battle of Bull Run. e) Southern general whose men's firm stand at Bull Run earned him the name "Stonewall." f) became the Union commander in the East after McDowell's defeat at Bull Run. 2. Manassas Junction is on the map on page 342. Fort Henry and Fort Donelson are on the map on page 345. Shiloh is on the map on page 345. Vicksburg is on the map on page 345. Hampton Roads is on the map on page 347, between Norfolk harbor and open sea. 3. First Bull Run (Confederate victory), Fort Henry (Union victory), Fort Donelson (Union victory), Shiloh (Union victory), New Orleans (Union victory), the *Monitor* and the *Merrimac* at Hampton Roads (a draw), the peninsular campaign and the Seven Days' Battles (Confederate victory), second Bull Run (Confederate victory), and Antietam (draw). 4. Grant's ability to create new rules for fighting the Civil War allowed him to plan an offensive strategy. Only by "consuming" the resources necessary for fighting the war would the South be exhausted and forced to surrender.

CLOSE

To conclude the lesson, list the following battles on the chalkboard: First Battle of Bull Run, Shiloh, *Monitor* vs. *Merrimac*, Peninsular Campaign, Second Battle of Bull Run, Antietam. For each battle, ask students to list the date, place, victor, and significance of the battle.

The Widening Conflict

FOCUS

To introduce the lesson, ask students to write answers to the following three questions about the Emancipation Proclamation: Whom did it free? When did it free them? Whom did it not free? Then write this heading on the chalkboard: Impact of the Emancipation Proclamation. Ask students to describe the impact of the document on the North, the South, and Europe.

INSTRUCT

Explain

Federal expenditures in 1861–1865 exceeded total federal spending from 1789 to 1860. A Treasury official in 1869 estimated direct Union war costs to be about $4.2 billion—and total costs including veteran pensions and property destruction (North and South) at $9 billion, or "three times as much as the slave property of the country was ever worth." While these costs seem insignificant in terms of today's federal budget, they were enormous at that time.

☑ Writing Process Activity

Recognizing Ideologies Ask students to imagine they are slaves living in the South in 1862–1863. Before they write a diary entry about their reactions to Lincoln's Emancipation Proclamation, ask them to freewrite about what it will mean to their lives. They can also include the reactions of Southern slave owners. Have them begin their entries with a topic sentence that summarizes the changes they expect, and ask them to support this main idea with specific examples. Students should revise for logical organization and clear word choice. After proofreading, students can read their entries to the class.

Section Review Answers

Section 3, page 353

1. Issuing the Emancipation Proclamation gave Northerners a worthy cause to fight for. 2. The South said that it was a "fiend's" act that "destroyed $4 billion worth of property." Confederate President Jefferson Davis said it made reunion impossible. The North was divided over the Proclamation. Abolitionists were delighted—although they regretted that Lincoln had not freed the slaves everywhere. Many Northerners were displeased because they wanted to fight only for the Union. 3. Blacks—some 185,000 of them—fought in the Union army. Some served as spies or

13

worked as laborers for the Union cause. 4. The North financed the Civil War by borrowing, by placing direct taxes on the states, by raising tariffs, by levying sales and other internal taxes, and by taxing incomes. 5. The westward migration of Americans continued throughout the Civil War. New farm land and the lure of California gold mines were the enticements.

CLOSE

To conclude the lesson, have students suggest a list of the factors that may have influenced President Lincoln's decision to issue the Emancipation Proclamation. (Some possible answers: Domestic effects, international effects, effects on border states, effects on Northern and Southern morale.)

Section 4 (pages 353–358)

Gettysburg to Appomattox, 1863–1865

FOCUS

To introduce the lesson, ask students to list at least four values that Abraham Lincoln believed in, basing their answers on information found in the Gettysburg Address. Discuss their answers. (Possible answers: freedom, democracy, equality, the power of God, national unity, that some causes are worth fighting and dying for, bravery, the special place of the United States in world history.)

INSTRUCT

Explain

The Union secured the Mississippi River in July 1863, broke the Southern advance at the Battle of Gettysburg, and then slowly weakened the South.

★ Independent Activity

Determining Relevance Ask students to write a letter from one of Lee's soldiers describing the scene at the surrender at Appomattox Court House and the terms of the surrender as Lee defined them to his men.

Section Review Answers

Section 4, page 358

1. a) Union general defeated by Lee at Chancellorsville. b) Union general who defeated Lee at Gettysburg. c) Confederate general who surrendered Vicksburg to Grant. d) Northern general who followed Sherman's new style of total warfare, having his troops destroy or seize whatever they encountered in

their march through Virginia's Shenandoah Valley. 2. Gettysburg is on the map on page 354. Port Hudson and Chattanooga are on the map on page 345. Petersburg is on the map on page 357. The Shenandoah Valley is on the map on page 345, along the Shenandoah River on the left. Appomattox is on the map on page 357. 3. General Grant and General Lee dealt with each other calmly, courteously, and respectfully. Grant did not seek to impose vengeful terms on the surrendering Southerners. 4. General Sherman expected to seize or destroy the South's resources and break the South's spirit.

CLOSE

To conclude the lesson, ask students to prepare a time line of the Civil War from the fall of Fort Sumter to the Confederate surrender at Appomattox Court House.

Chapter Review Answers

Focusing on Ideas

1. Rifle; instant forts; fighting from trenches; railroads for supply; destroying railroads for defense; destruction of enemy's resources, not merely armies; etc. 2. See pages 337–339. 3. See page 353. 4. Anaconda plan: Naval blockade of South plus seizure of New Orleans and control of Mississippi River. Engagements: Fort Henry, Fort Donelson, Nashville, and Pittsburgh Landing (Shiloh). Farragut's seizure of New Orleans; defense of the blockade by the *Monitor*.

Taking a Critical Look

1. This item might be used for a student's report. 2. To keep the support of the border states; believed the North needed this moral issue to shore up its support of war and his own antislavery feelings; limited to any state or part of a state still in rebellion on January 1, 1863; answers will vary. 3. Warfare became totally unlike the old tactics generals had learned at West Point. The winning generals, like Grant and Sherman, were those who disregarded the old rules.

Your Region in History

1–3. Answers will vary depending on your region. Consult your local library or historical society.

Historical Facts and Figures

(a) The brown side. (b) Brown could rely on its own resources to fuel its war effort; Tan had to rely upon imports and exports. (c) Population—soldiers, production; manufactured goods—to supply the troops; railroads—for transporting troops, supplies, etc. (d) Brown represents the Union, tan the Confederacy—the largely agricultural South did not have the resources of the industrialized North.

Chapter 13

The Civil War

Focusing the Chapter: Have students identify the chapter logo. Discuss what unit theme the logo might symbolize. Then ask students to skim the chapter to identify other illustrations or titles that relate to this theme.

The American Civil War was not quite like any war that had ever happened before. Half a nation fought against the other half over the freedom of a small minority. This itself was something new. It was as new, as strenuous, and as unpredictable as everything else in America. Leaving more than 600,000 dead, the Civil War would be the bloodiest in all American history—and the bloodiest war in the whole western world during the nineteenth century. Of every ten men who fought, four became casualties (killed or wounded). No other modern nation paid so high a price to hold itself together.

Southerners did not see themselves simply as slave owners fighting to preserve their property, or as rebels trying to tear the Union apart. Instead they imagined they were fighting the American Revolution all over again. White Southerners, they said, were oppressed by Yankee tyrants. The people of the South were now playing the role of the gallant American colonists. Northerners were the oppressive British, and Abraham Lincoln was another George III. If the British had no right to force American colonists to stay inside their empire, why did the United States government have any right to force Southern states to stay inside the Union?

Abraham Lincoln, in his first inaugural address, had tried to persuade Southerners that they had nothing to fear from his administration. But he told them there was no right under the Constitution for a state to leave the Union. And he declared, "In *your* hands, my dissatisfied fellow countrymen, and not in *mine,* is the momentous issue of civil war."

Southerners said they were fighting for self-government. One flaw in this argument was that it left out the whole question of slavery. Self-government—for *whom* and by *whom?* White Southerners who said they were fighting for their own right to govern themselves were also fighting *against* the right of millions of blacks to have any control over their own lives. Of course, Calhoun and other defenders of slavery had not seen it quite that way. Self-government, they said, was for white people only.

Continuity and Change: Conflict Point out to students that during the Civil War, advanced weapons technology and the lack of progress in medicine combined to cause the high number of fatalities. Medical advances such as blood banks and wonder drugs used by highly-skilled physicians kept the casualty rates down in later wars. Also, because later conflicts involving the United States were fought primarily on foreign soil, civilian deaths have not greatly contributed to the total American casualty counts since the Civil War. (See pp. 699, 731, and 827.)

General Grant (on horseback to the right of the flag) watches as his troops move on Fort Donelson.

See "Lesson Plan," p. 332C.

1. A new kind of war

Shocked by the fall of Fort Sumter, Northerners sprang into action. President Lincoln at once called for 75,000 militia to help put down what he termed an insurrection. With Lincoln's call for troops the states of the upper South seceded. They had hesitated to leave the Union, but they felt they could not fight against the other Southern states. The North and the South now hastened to prepare for war.

The sides compared. The two sides were vastly different from each other. If we ignore Maryland, Kentucky, and Missouri, which were still in doubt, the Union (the Northern states) had 20 million people. The Confederacy had 9 million, which included 3.6 million slaves. In other resources the North was way ahead, too. It had 22,000 miles of railroad tracks to the South's 9000. It had far more factories and factory workers, more money, more bank credit, more ships, more locomotives, more steel and iron, more farm machinery, more firearms. The North grew many kinds of crops, while the South was glutted with a few staples—tobacco, cotton, and rice—which it had to export in order to obtain all the things it lacked.

The North also had lots of labor-saving devices like the reaper to free men for the army, while the South depended for labor on its slaves. These slaves might at any moment turn out to be a "fifth column"—an enemy force behind the lines—because they had very good reasons for helping the North. Every third Southerner was black. White Southerners therefore lived in fear of a civil war all their own—if the blacks ever decided to take up arms.

Because Southerners did not see slaves as people they also failed to use them well in the war. Even if it seemed too dangerous to give slaves arms, they might have helped in the army as a labor force and so have released whites to fight. The North, on the other hand, decided in December 1862 to use blacks in its armed forces. It was strengthened by more than 185,000 who fought on its side.

Worst of all for the South, it suffered from delusions which prevented it from seeing the facts. Southerners believed that the North was so divided that it would not be able to put up a strong fight. In fact, Southerners were astonished that any power on earth dared make war on the world's greatest producer of cotton. They had long told themselves "Cotton is King," and they believed Great Britain and France would break the Northern blockade and come to the South's aid just to get the cotton needed to keep their textile factories going. The South imagined too that only Southerners were civilized and that one Southerner "could whip a half-dozen Yankees and not half try." The South's grandiose dreams turned into nightmares.

In the end the substantial advantages of the North would produce victory. The South, unable to replace its losses of equipment, would finally die of economic strangulation. But it was a very near thing. The South came close to victory too many times for anyone to say that the leaders of the Confederacy should have foreseen the result.

The "short war."   When Southerners said that they merely wanted to secede from the Union, they also gave themselves a military advantage. To win their point all they had to do was to declare their independence and go their own way. On the other hand, the North would have to *force* the Southern states to stay in the Union. The North would have to invade the South, occupy it, and subjugate it. The North had to attack.

At the beginning, many Northerners optimis-

tically called it "the six months' war." They expected it to be over in short order. For the North seemed stronger in every way. Also the military men had been taught that the attacking army always had a great advantage. The textbooks used at West Point explained that the way to succeed was to mass your forces, invade the enemy's land, and win the war by a decisive battle or the decisive capture of the enemy's capital.

The rifle.   The old-fashioned weapons had given almost no advantage to the defenders. For the old smoothbore flintlock musket (which was standard equipment in the British army during the Revolution and in European armies even later) was inaccurate. It had a short range, and it was slow to reload. That meant that the attacking forces could come very close before the defenders could shoot them down, and most of them would get through before they could be hit. If, as the Union generals at first imagined, the North could only keep the advantage of the attack, they could win a few decisive battles, capture the enemy capital at Richmond, Virginia, and then the war would be over.

These generals were wrong, though some never realized it. The war lasted four blood-soaked years. This new warfare would be as different from earlier American wars as an elephant is different from a mosquito.

A number of great changes made the difference. While the standard British weapon in the American Revolution was the flintlock musket, many American backwoodsmen had begun using the rifle. But it was not until the Civil War that the rifle became the standard American army weapon. All the textbooks that the Civil War generals had read at West Point came from the earlier age of the smoothbore flintlock.

The rifle was so called because the inside of its barrel was "rifled"—cut with spiral grooves. Then when the bullet was pushed out, it was set spinning. This gave it a longer range (500 yards instead of 50 yards) and a much more accurate aim. Another improvement was the "caplock," which used a new chemical (fulminate of mercury) enclosed in a cap to make the explosion

Enrichment Support File Topic

that sent the bullet. The caplock was reliable even when the old flintlock—which struck a piece of flint against steel to make a spark—would not have worked because of wet weather. Also the old muskets had been "muzzle loaders," but some of the new rifles were "breechloaders." This meant they loaded more quickly from the back near the trigger.

Soldiers learn to dig in. Now, with their accurate long-range rifles, the defenders sat protected behind battlements in well-supplied positions. They could pick off the attackers before they even came close. They could fire again and again because of the range of their weapons. The attacking force then had to keep moving. If they stopped to reload, they were sitting ducks.

In time the generals would learn that armies could no longer confront each other in solid ranks. Everyone had to take cover. Attackers had to spread out into small parties of skirmishers to make more dispersed targets. Now the "Indian" tactics, which Americans had used with success in the Revolution, would become common. Attacking soldiers had to make instant forts—of logs, bales of hay, rocks, anything in sight—so that they could get some of the advantages of defenders.

Most important, soldiers learned to make the earth itself into a fort by using the spade. This was the start of trench warfare. In the old days, generals thought it made soldiers cowardly to hide in a hole in the ground. Now the soldiers had no choice. When General Robert E. Lee ordered his men in the Army of Northern Virginia to work hard at digging trenches, at first they laughed at him as the "King of Spades." But they soon thanked him for giving them protection against enemy rifles. The spade was now as important as the gun.

The importance of railroads. The attacking army had to carry enormous supplies of ammunition, food, and bandages. It had to build its own fortifications as it advanced. The railroad, which had never been used much in wars before, was now a great help. But once the supplies left the rails, they still had to be carried by

Virginia State Travel Service

The accurate long-range rifle made defensive positions all-important. Confederate troops defended this wall near Fredericksburg in some of the bloodiest fighting of the war in 1862.

horse or mule over bumpy roads, through mud, and across streams.

In this kind of warfare, railroads were lifelines. They were slow and hard to build, but quick and easy to cut. If you could cut the rails, the enemy would eventually have to stop fighting. The Civil War therefore became more and more a war aimed at the enemy's communication lines. The first Battle of Bull Run (July 1861) was still very much like the old-fashioned warfare, with solid lines of soldiers standing up against each other to fight a "decisive" battle. By the time of the Battle of Petersburg three years later, the Union army was aiming at the Confederate railroads.

The war of exhaustion. This new kind of warfare was a war of exhaustion. It was not enough to cut off the enemy's supplies by railroad. You also had to stop supplies from coming in by water. The ocean and the Gulf of Mexico surrounded the Southern states. They had few deep-water ports, but there were many places

Library of Congress

These elaborate fortifications were erected near Atlanta in 1864.

on the 3500-mile coast where supplies could be landed. The South still had many highways to the world. The North therefore had to capture or blockade the Southern ports and coast if the South was to be strangled.

The South did wonders with small fast ships which constantly pierced the blockade at many points. Still the scores of Union ships offshore made it difficult for the South to export cotton and kept large merchant ships or Confederate naval vessels from reaching Southern ports.

The war of exhaustion hit everybody in the South, civilians as well as the military. The same ships that would have brought arms and ammunition to the armies also would have brought locomotives for the railroads, machinery for the factories, food and clothing and medical supplies for all. The Northern blockade against the South worked slowly but it worked surely. People called it the "Conda" after the

anaconda, a huge snake that kills its prey by squeezing.

The war of exhaustion was slow. It was not won by a few knockout blows like the Battle of Waterloo, where Napoleon was defeated, but by slowly taking away everything the South needed. In this war all the enemy's resources had to be destroyed until the will to resist was gone. European experts, who had never seen this kind of war before, began to think it was not a war at all. One Prussian general in 1864 sneered that he would not even study the battles of the war because they were nothing but "the combats of two armed mobs." Another Old World critic compared the North and South to two lunatics playing chess—both knew a few moves, yet neither understood the game.

But this kind of war was no longer a game. The old rules of war which the generals had learned at West Point were not of much use.

✄ Critical Thinking Activity: Testing Conclusions How did the Civil War force soldiers to use new battle tactics? Write this statement on the chalkboard: *The Civil War proved to be a war of broken rules on the battlefield.* Have students cite evidence in the chapter that would prove this statement. (The digging of trenches; the cutting off of supplies by ship and railroad.) Ask students to suggest reasons for the rules of war changing.

The Union man-o-war (left) is shown overtaking a Confederate blockade runner in this oil painting. Rather than surrender, blockade runners sometimes ran their ships aground in the hope that part of the cargo might be carried ashore.

This was all-out war, with no holds barred. The winning generals turned out to be those, like U. S. Grant, who had never believed the old rules, or those, like William T. Sherman, who were good at forgetting them.

Everybody's war. The Civil War was everybody's war. In both the North and the South nearly every family lost a soldier. And in quite new ways the gore was brought into every home. For the first time in history, the battles were thoroughly covered by newspaper correspondents. They telegraphed back eyewitness accounts so that civilians could read the horrors next morning at breakfast.

The *New York Herald* alone once had forty men in the field, and spent a half-million dollars on them. Northern reporters, who would have been shot as spies if discovered, smuggled themselves behind Southern lines disguised as women or as Confederate soldiers. When some generals objected that the newspapers were giving away valuable information to the enemy, the *New York World* protested that this was a "people's war."

The pioneer photographer Mathew Brady and his large crew took photographs at the risk of their lives and sent them back home to show everyone the battle action. Soldiers sometimes ran away from Brady's camera because they had never seen a camera before and imagined it to be a new kind of gun. Brady's photographic buggy, which soldiers called the "What-is-it?", was a conspicuous target. On several occasions, Brady barely escaped being killed.

Women at war. In the "people's war" women played a new and important part. Dorothea Dix,

More from Boorstin: "But photography was still cumbersome and complicated. Traveling across the battlefields, Brady needed a special wagon to carry his equipment . . . The equipment for even a single day commonly weighed more than a hundred pounds . . ." (From *The Americans: The Democratic Experience*)

Library of Congress

Women played an important role in nursing the wounded on both sides. Clara Barton helped the injured on the battlefield and later founded the American Red Cross.

Alcott went more confidently on to her next patient.

Clara Barton, one of the first female clerks in Washington, left her job to help the injured troops. So began a career of caring for the sick and the wounded that lasted throughout the war. Clara Barton was never an official in the war effort. As a volunteer this brave woman brought food, bandages, and supplies to the wounded out on the battlefield. Then, for four years after the war, she was in charge of the search for missing Union soldiers. She identified thousands of graves at the Confederate prisoner-of-war camp at Andersonville, Georgia. In 1877 Clara Barton founded and became president of the American Red Cross. It would serve the nation and the world in later wars.

Women helped set up the voluntary United ☬ States Sanitary Commission. It assisted the

The Civil War pitted friend against friend and neighbor against neighbor. In this photograph, Union Lieutenant George A. Custer is shown with his friend, West Point classmate, and prisoner, Confederate Major James Washington.

Library of Congress

the courageous New Englander who had braved public opinion before (p. 283), arrived in Washington right behind the first troops. On June 10, 1861, she was appointed the first Superintendent of Women Nurses with the job of selecting and assigning women to hospitals. It took gumption to find any place for women in the army, and she was the pioneer.

Louisa May Alcott, later to make her name as the author of *Little Women*, came to Washington and worked in a hospital for Miss Dix until illness forced her to leave. She was appalled when the first group of dirty, injured soldiers appeared. But, she wrote, "I drowned my scruples in my washbowl, clutched my soap manfully, and, assuming a business-like air, made a dab at the first dirty specimen I saw." Luckily, he was a cheery Irishman, and with a good deal of laughter the job was done. Louisa May

☬ **Multicultural Connection:** Many African-American and Hispanic women played important roles in the Civil War. These included Sojourner Truth, Harriet Jacobs, and Josephine Ruffin, who assisted and cared for the refugees, and Mary Ann Shad Cary, who was the only officially commissioned woman recruiter. Cuban-born Loretta Janet Velásquez enlisted in the Confederate army disguised as a man in 1860. She fought in the battles of Bull Run, Ball's Bluff, and Fort Donelson. In 1862 she was discovered to be a woman and was discharged.

military by creating hospitals, caring for the injured, promoting sanitation in military camps, and distributing all kinds of supplies "from currant wine to canton flannel underwear" to the troops. Supplies and money for this ambitious program were raised by women's groups throughout the Union.

Female clerks were rare in 1860, but that too changed with wartime. Soon there were large numbers of women in the Treasury Department, while others worked at the government printing plants or made cartridges in the arsenal and the navy yard. Women were usually paid less for this work than men, and several times groups of women went on strike for higher pay.

In the South, as well, women did many jobs in the government. They too made cartridges in munitions factories. They nursed the wounded in hospitals, and sewed soldiers' clothes or rolled bandages at home. "Ladies who never worked before," one Southern woman observed, "are hard at work making uniforms and tents."

In North and South, as the men went off to war, women had to take over businesses, farms, and plantations. Some women were so anxious to do their part in the war that several hundred of them pretended to be men and served in the ranks as soldiers wearing men's uniforms until they were discovered.

The border states. Like the generals, the political leaders of the opposing sides had to be able to forget peacetime rules. And here Lincoln was wiser than the Confederate president, Jefferson Davis. When the war began, Lincoln was not even sure who was on his side or whether Washington could be held. The city was surrounded on three sides by Maryland, a slave state. If Maryland seceded, Washington would be lost. When the first Union troops, the 6th Massachusetts militia regiment, passed through on their way to protect the capital, they were mobbed. Four soldiers were killed.

Lincoln now showed his instinctive grasp of the deeper meaning of the conflict for this nation. He felt that the Constitution could not contain the seeds of its own destruction. If he had to bend the Constitution in order to save the Constitution and the Union, he would do so. If he hesitated or retreated from the harsh words of Southern sympathizers in the North, the Union might be lost before a battle was fought.

So Lincoln moved swiftly. He imposed martial law in Maryland, suppressed newspapers, arrested civilians, and even refused to let them

Sallie Tompkins received a commission as a captain in the Confederate army for her work.

Valentine Museum, Richmond, Virginia

See "Lesson Plan," p. 332C for **Writing Process Activity: Recognizing Bias** relating to journalism during the Civil War.

The Confederacy

— Boundary of the Confederacy

Original Confederate States

States that Seceded Later

Border States that Stayed in the Union

West Virginia Separated from Virginia in 1861; Statehood 1863

Jan. 9, 1861 Date of Secession

appear before civilian judges to hear why they were being held. This is called suspending the *writ of habeas corpus*. This writ, or court order, gives a judge the power to free a person who is being held illegally or without just cause. It serves to keep people from being held in jail without a fair trial. When Chief Justice Taney issued a writ of habeas corpus for a secessionist named Merryman, the military commander of the area refused to free the man. Taney then issued an opinion that the President had no right to suspend the writ of habeas corpus, only Congress could do that. Lincoln believed that he must act to save the Union—even if he had to break the law to do so. So he ignored Taney's decision.

It was by actions such as these that Maryland was held in the Union and Washington was saved. Union sentiment within the state had time to grow. By June 1861, Maryland was filling its quota of enlistments in the United States Army.

Missouri and Kentucky were crucial too. If they seceded, the Confederate border would be pushed to the Ohio River, and then even southern Illinois might be lost. Lincoln handled each state differently. In Missouri, he moved swiftly to seize control. In Kentucky, he moved slowly in order to allow Union sentiment to develop. The result was the same in both states—they were saved for the Union.

The question of emancipation. Lincoln was a strong leader. As a politician, he knew how important it was, in everybody's war, to keep everybody's support. At the beginning of the war, in order to keep in the Union the border slave states—Delaware, Maryland, Kentucky, and Missouri—he refused to emancipate the slaves. When General Frémont, commander of the Western Department, on August 30, 1861, freed the slaves of rebels in Missouri, Lincoln stepped in firmly and overruled him.

Lincoln's priorities were always clear. Much

Geography and History: Regions Have students look at the map above, and at the text on page 333. Write the headings "North" and "South" on the board. Under each heading list: number of states; population; railroad miles; types of crops; types of labor; economic assets (factories, etc.); role of blacks; and motives for war. Discuss the advantages that one side might have over the other in a war. Ask: Why did the South think it could win against the North? (The South thought that the North was divided, and would not be able to put up a strong fight.)

as he might have liked to free the slaves, his first job was to save the Union. When told that freeing the slaves would put God on the Union side, Lincoln replied, "We would like to have God on our side, but we must have Kentucky."

See "Section 1 Review answers," p. 332C.

Section 1 Review

1. Identify or explain: "war of exhaustion," Mathew Brady, Dorothea Dix, Louisa May Alcott, Clara Barton, Sanitary Commission, writ of habeas corpus, border states, emancipation.

2. How did the rifle give defenders an advantage? How did it make the spade a tool of war?

3. What was the Union strategy with regard to Confederate railroads and seaports?

4. Describe the role of women in the war.

5. **Critical Thinking: Demonstrating Reasoned Judgment.** Why did Civil War soldiers view the war between the North and South as a new kind of conflict?

See "Lesson Plan," p. 332C.

2. The first year: 1861–1862

The Civil War was fought mainly in three areas: (1) between Richmond and Washington, (2) in the valley of the Ohio, Cumberland, and Tennessee rivers, and (3) in the Mississippi River valley. The eyes of much of the world were on the classic battle in the East where two great armies maneuvered and fought in the small area between the Potomac and the James rivers and from the Atlantic to the Blue Ridge Mountains. Here the able Southern generals Robert E. Lee and "Stonewall" Jackson, though always outnumbered, faced and usually defeated the poorly led Northern Army of the Potomac in a series of titanic battles. The decisive war, however, took place beyond the Appalachians in the West.

The first Battle of Bull Run (Manassas). Northerners thought the war would be short and easy. They urged General Irvin McDowell to move with the main army of 30,000 men against the rebels, to seize Richmond, and so (they hoped) to end the war quickly. Since McDowell's volunteer troops and militia were not yet properly organized or drilled, and their three months' term of enlistment was about to expire, they had to be strengthened by some units of the regular army. But the Confederates were also untrained. So McDowell, thinking his forces stronger, asked to be allowed to attack.

General Winfield Scott, commander of the United States Army, protested. He outlined to the Cabinet another more long-term plan. He doubted that this war could be won in the lightning stroke of a single battle. Scott offered a plan to blockade the South, to seize New Orleans and the Mississippi River, and so "envelop the insurgent states." In this way, Scott thought, the South could be brought to terms with little bloodshed. He was wrong on the last point, and the strategy would take much longer than he expected. But at age 75, and having served in the army since Jefferson's time, "Old Fuss and Feathers" knew the realities of war. It was his plan, later called the "anaconda," reinforced by some bloody and brutal years of fighting, that would finally bring victory to the North.

The North was not yet ready to face the realities of the military situation. So Scott withdrew his opposition to McDowell's plan for a quick knockout blow to the Southern capital. Lincoln and the Cabinet then agreed to allow McDowell to move forward—"On to Richmond!"

McDowell's "grand army" met General Joseph E. Johnston's force of 22,000 on July 21, 1861, at Manassas Junction, a little town near Bull Run, a creek 35 miles from Washington. The untrained federal troops had the more difficult job of attacking, but they did well until mid-afternoon. Then fresh Confederate troops arrived by train and turned the tide of battle. Shouting loud "rebel yells," the Confederates broke the attack and sent the Federals fleeing in terror back toward Washington. Upon hearing the news of the retreat, hard-driving Southern General Thomas J. Jackson, who earned the name "Stonewall" for the firm stand of his men in the battle, shouted, "Give me 5000 fresh men

See "Lesson Plan," p. 332D for **Cooperative Learning Activity: Identifying Central Issues** relating to the events during the first year of the Civil War.

The Civil War, 1861-1865

	United States
	Border States (Slaveholding Union States)
	Confederate States
×	Union Victory
×	Confederate Victory

0   200 Miles

0   200 Kilometers

Labels on map:

WIS. — Lake Michigan — MICH. — Lake Erie — PENNSYLVANIA — N.J.

IOWA — OHIO — 5. GETTYSBURG 1863 — MD. — DEL.

Mississippi R. — INDIANA — 1. BATTLES OF BULL RUN 1861 AND 1862 — Washington — Manassas Junction

ILLINOIS — Ohio R. — WEST VIRGINIA 1863 — Chancellorsville — 4. FREDERICKSBURG 1862

VIRGINIA — 9. FALL OF RICHMOND 1865

MO. — KENTUCKY — 10. LEE SURRENDERS AT APPOMATTOX 1865 — Norfolk

Cairo — Cumberland R. — Raleigh

Ft. Henry — Ft. Donelson — Tennessee R. — NORTH CAROLINA

Nashville — TENNESSEE

Pittsburg Landing — 7. CHATTANOOGA 1863

Memphis — 2. SHILOH 1862 — Chickamauga — Columbia — SOUTH CAROLINA

ARK. — Atlanta — Charleston — Ft. Sumter — Union Blockade

MISSISSIPPI — ALABAMA — 8. ATLANTA, SAVANNAH 1864 — ATLANTIC OCEAN

6. VICKSBURG 1863 — GEORGIA — Savannah

LA. — Mississippi R.

Mobile

Port Hudson

3. NEW ORLEANS 1862 — FLORIDA

Union Blockade

GULF OF MEXICO

and I will be in Washington tomorrow." But the disorganized Confederate forces were in no position to seize the strategic moment. Their President Jefferson Davis did not order an advance.

In the long run the South was actually hurt by this first victory. Now the Southerners made the mistake of believing that it would be easy to defeat the North. For the North, on the other hand, the defeat at Bull Run made people

🌐 **Geography and History: Location** Have students use the scale on the map above to determine the distance from Washington to the site of the Confederate victory at Bull Run (35 miles). Make an analogy to places just 35 miles away from the high school. Then break the class up into small groups and have them search their texts for answers to the following question: Why did the North attack at Bull Run before the Union army was ready?

realize that the war could not be won in a few days. And they steeled themselves for the hard years ahead.

Command in the East was now turned over to red-haired General George B. McClellan, who was not yet 35 years old. Like most of the generals—North and South—he had gone to West Point and had fought in the Mexican War. He had then used his talents for discipline and organization to help survey the difficult route for the Northern Pacific Railroad through the Cascade Mountains. He had also been a railroad president in the Middle West. Returning to the army at the outbreak of the Civil War, his able command of Union troops in western Virginia had saved for the Union the area that two years later became the state of West Virginia. McClellan insisted on precision in drill and demanded ample supplies for his troops, who trusted and loved him for it. He spent the remainder of 1861 training the Army of the Potomac to meet his high standards of readiness for battle.

⊕
(p. 342)

The Trent affair. In November 1861 a Union warship stopped the British steamer *Trent* bound for London. Two Confederate diplomats, James M. Mason and John Slidell who had boarded the ship in Cuba, were removed from the vessel. They were on their way to England and France to seek recognition of the Confederacy.

The British people were outraged at this violation by the United States of the freedom of the seas for neutral vessels. Many called for war, and 8000 British troops were rushed to Canada. It was a dangerous moment for the United States, since war with Britain would have made it impossible to conquer the South. Fortunately, President Lincoln and Secretary of State Seward recognized the danger. Mason and Slidell were freed and allowed to continue on their way, and the United States admitted it had acted wrongly. This ended the crisis.

The war in the West. The Tennessee and the Cumberland rivers pointed like pistols at the heart of the Confederacy, while the Mississippi River cut it in two. On these rivers the fate of the Confederate States of America would be decided.

The operations in the West brought to prominence the greatest Union general, Ulysses S. Grant. Also a West Point graduate who had served with credit in the Mexican War, he had resigned from the army in 1854 when he was accused of being a drunk. The outbreak of the Civil War had found him, at the age of 39, working as a clerk in his father's hardware and leather store in Galena, Illinois. Military success was to make him the hero of the Union and later President of the United States.

Grant soon revealed that he had the special talents needed to succeed as a general. He had a genius for seeing the whole scene—and then quickly deciding what needed to be done. He possessed a silent, grim, cool courage and persistence. General Sherman later wrote to Grant, "My only points of doubt [about you as a general] were as to your knowledge of grand strategy, and of books of science and history; but I confess your common sense seems to have supplied this." Perhaps because he was not a "book" soldier, but a man of supreme common sense, Grant recognized early that this was a new kind of war. "The art of war is simple enough," he said. "Find out where your enemy is. Get at him as soon as you can. Strike him as hard as you can, and keep moving on."

Henry, Donelson, and Shiloh. Grant's first successes came in Tennessee. There he showed that by a clever combination with naval forces he could make the riverways of the South serve as highways for Northern victory. Confederate forts guarded the lower Tennessee and Cumberland rivers. On February 6, 1862, with the vital aid of a fleet of ironclad gunboats under Flag Officer A. H. Foote, Grant captured Fort Henry and so opened the Tennessee River all the way to Alabama. Within ten days Foote had taken his gunboats back to the Ohio and up the Cumberland. In another joint military and naval operation, Grant compelled the surrender of Fort Donelson with all its 14,000 defenders. Then defenseless Nashville fell without a blow to another Union army under General D. C. Buell.

Next Grant moved an army of 40,000 men up the Tennessee River to Pittsburg Landing near the Mississippi state border. They kept on moving inland as far as a country meeting-house called Shiloh Church. Here his men, who had not yet learned to dig defensive positions, were surprised on April 6, 1862, by a Confederate army under the able and experienced General Albert Sidney Johnston, (not a relation of Joseph E. Johnston of Bull Run fame). The Union troops were driven back to the edge of the river, where they dug in and held. The Confederates had won the day, but at a heavy cost. When General Johnston was killed in that battle, they lost one of their boldest and most seasoned military leaders.

Grant was not so easily stopped. The very next day, strengthened by reinforcements, he attacked and drove the Confederate troops from the field. There were appalling losses on both sides—13,000 dead and wounded for the North and 11,000 for the South.

(p. 345) At Shiloh, Grant learned that he was in a war far different from what he had counted on in the beginning. He had thought at first that the rebellion would collapse "suddenly and soon, if a decisive victory could be gained over any of its

armies." But he had actually won such victories at Fort Henry and Fort Donelson. Then instead of collapsing, the Southern forces turned around, took the offensive, and nearly defeated him. Now he knew that this would be a war to exhaustion. There would be no Northern victory unless his forces were allowed to "consume everything [in the South] that could be used to support or supply armies."

New Orleans. Meanwhile Foote and General John Pope were working down the Mississippi River, opening it as far as the Confederate bastion at Vicksburg. At the other end of the river a bold move by the amazing David Glasgow Farragut captured New Orleans for the Union.

Farragut, the son of a naval officer, had been commissioned a midshipman at the age of nine. He had seen action in the War of 1812 when he was only eleven. His orders commanded him as he entered the river from the Gulf of Mexico first to capture the two forts at the mouth of the Mississippi that protected New Orleans. But disregarding orders he raced

This vivid lithograph of the Union charge at Shiloh appeared on the title page of a song.

American Antiquarian Society

Multicultural Connection: Approximately 10,000 Hispanics fought in the Civil War, on both sides. The most famous Hispanic was David Farragut who became the nation's first admiral. Farragut's successful blockade of the South and his fleet's control of the Mississippi River greatly assisted the North victory over the South.

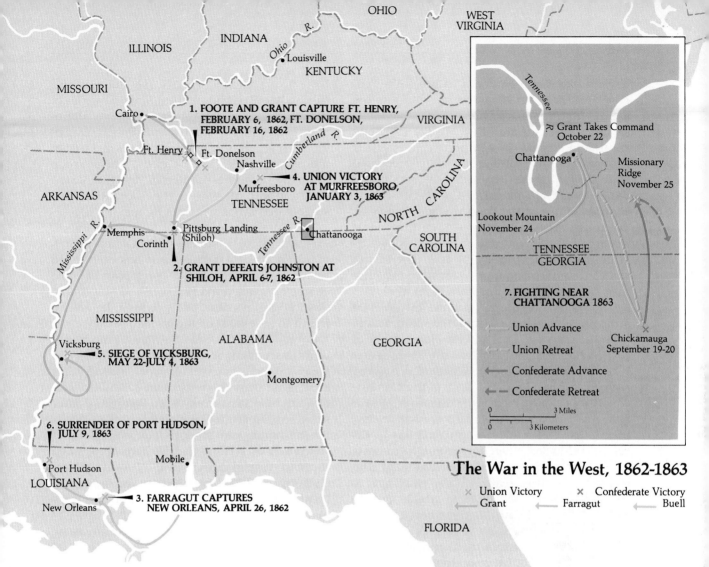

The map shows:

1. FOOTE AND GRANT CAPTURE FT. HENRY, FEBRUARY 6, 1862, FT. DONELSON, FEBRUARY 16, 1862

4. UNION VICTORY AT MURFREESBORO, JANUARY 3, 1863

2. GRANT DEFEATS JOHNSTON AT SHILOH, APRIL 6-7, 1862

5. SIEGE OF VICKSBURG, MAY 22-JULY 4, 1863

6. SURRENDER OF PORT HUDSON, JULY 9, 1863

3. FARRAGUT CAPTURES NEW ORLEANS, APRIL 26, 1862

Inset map (Chattanooga area):

Grant Takes Command October 22

Missionary Ridge November 25

Lookout Mountain November 24

7. FIGHTING NEAR CHATTANOOGA 1863

Chickamauga September 19-20

Union Advance
Union Retreat
Confederate Advance
Confederate Retreat

0 ——— 3 Miles
0 ——— 3 Kilometers

The War in the West, 1862-1863

× Union Victory   × Confederate Victory
← Grant   ← Farragut   ← Buell

past the two forts (losing only three of his seventeen ships). He defeated an astounded Confederate fleet, sinking eleven of its ships. Then at one blow he seized the coveted prize—New Orleans, queen city of the South. Farragut took the city on April 26, 1862, almost before anyone knew he was in the neighborhood. Now the South could no longer support its troops in the West with supplies brought in from the Gulf of Mexico.

The war in the East. In the East, however, the prospects of the Federal forces were not nearly so rosy. Northern operations were paralyzed by the caution and indecision of General McClellan. He did not move forward. Although

he actually commanded an army grown to 180,000 men, which was twice the size of the forces under General Joseph E. Johnston, he still believed he was outnumbered. And he blamed the "imbecile" administration at Washington for not sending him more reinforcements. General Johnston had his men well entrenched on the old Bull Run battlefield.

The Monitor and the Merrimac. While McClellan was hesitating, a historic sea battle was taking place. A new chapter in naval warfare was being opened. On March 8, 1862, a strange-looking ironclad vessel with sloping sides covered by four-inch iron plates and with a powerful iron ram on its bow came steaming out of

⊕ **Geography and History: Interaction** Refer students to the map above. Ask: What does the brown map at the right-hand side of the larger map represent? (An enlarged area surrounding Chattanooga, Tennessee.) What is the only Confederate victory shown on these maps? (The victory at Chickamauga on the detail map.) What important objective was the North trying to achieve in its battles at Fort Henry, Pittsburgh Landing, and Chattanooga? (Those battles show that the North was trying to open up the Tennessee River.)

Norfolk into Hampton Roads to attack the Federal blockading squadron there. This was the C.S.S. *Virginia*, usually known by its old name as the U.S. frigate *Merrimac*. To the astonishment and dismay of Northern sailors, their shots just bounced off her sides. She proceeded to destroy with ease the wooden sailing ships of the Federal fleet—including the 50-gun frigate *Cumberland* and the 30-gun sloop *Congress*. When the *Merrimac* returned to Norfolk, it seemed that the next day she would easily destroy the rest of the Federal fleet. Then what would prevent her from going right up the Potomac and shelling the Northern capital?

Before dawn on March 9, however, an even stranger craft steamed into Hampton Roads from the open sea. This was the *Monitor*, one of the small Union ironclads that the clever Secretary of the Navy, Gideon Welles, had ordered early in the war. From the deck of the *Monitor*, which was almost flush with the water, rose a revolving turret within which were two eleven-inch guns. This made the ship look like "a tin can on a shingle." When the seemingly "unbeatable" *Merrimac* appeared later that day, the *Monitor* was there ready for the challenge. A spectacular duel took place in which neither ironclad did much harm to the other. Then the *Merrimac* withdrew again to Norfolk.

The Union blockade of the South was not to be broken. The Confederacy's one day as ruler of the seas was over. And this first fight in history between ironclads marked the end of navies of wooden ships.

The peninsular campaign. After continual prodding by Lincoln, McClellan finally made up his mind to move. Following the West Point textbooks, he decided to try to take Richmond by a classic maneuver. He transported his large and well-equipped army by water to the peninsula between the James and the York rivers. Proceeding slowly, he worked his way to within a few miles of Richmond. The church towers of the town were visible from the Union front lines.

Then McClellan's weakness showed again. Instead of advancing swiftly to fulfill his plan before the enemy could get their bearings, he halted long enough to give the Confederates time to figure out how to beat him. In a series of battles, during which General Joseph E. Johnston was injured and General Robert E. Lee took command, McClellan saved his army from a near defeat. He finally ended up in a strong defensive position—protected by the Union navy and with his back to the James River, but surrounded by Confederate troops. (p. 347)

The Confederate Army of Northern Virginia was now in the command of the tactical genius of the Civil War—the man who has been called the greatest general of the age. A man of noble character, Lee felt his first love and first loyalty was for Virginia. But, oddly enough, he was no friend to secession or to slavery.

Robert E. Lee, a true Southern blue blood, was a descendant of one of Virginia's finest families and had married Martha Washington's great grand-daughter. He had graduated second in his class from West Point and later served as superintendent there. In his character the honor and the loyalty of a soldier prevailed over everything else. He had commanded the Marines who captured John Brown at Harpers Ferry in 1859. When the Civil War broke out, Lieutenant Colonel Lee had been offered command of all the Union forces by his fellow Virginian, General Winfield Scott, under whom he had served brilliantly in the Mexican War. Lee felt that he could not fight against Virginia. When that state asked him in April 1861 to command its armies, he agreed. Then in June President Jefferson Davis called him into Confederate service to be his personal military adviser.

As commanding general of the Army of Northern Virginia, Lee knew that he must act promptly and with daring if the South was to win its independence. Since General Lee's talents were well known in the North, his name there inspired respect and fear.

The second Battle of Bull Run (Manassas). General McClellan was now replaced. John Pope, who took over the command, had led an army that successfully cleared important points on the Mississippi. Lincoln hoped that this new brash and boastful leader would live up to his

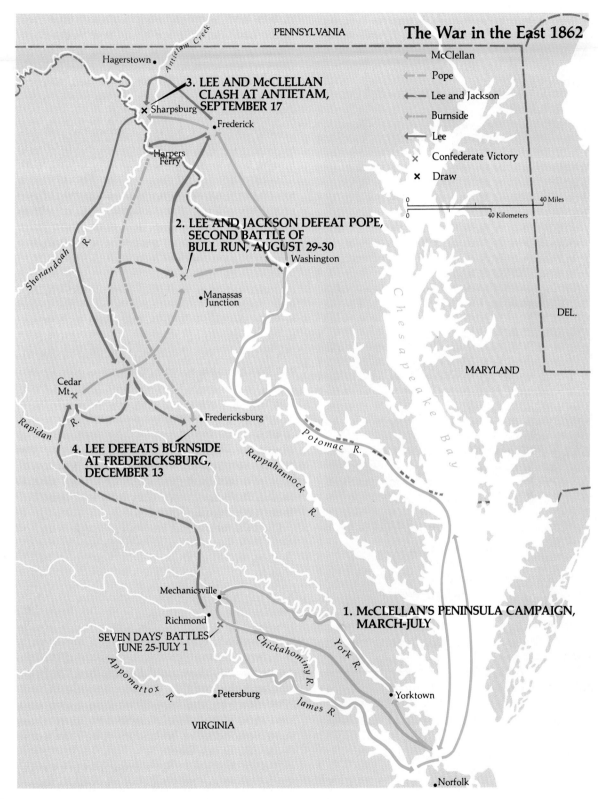

The War in the East 1862

McClellan
Pope
Lee and Jackson
Burnside
Lee
× Confederate Victory
× Draw

0   40 Miles
0   40 Kilometers

PENNSYLVANIA

Hagerstown

3. LEE AND McCLELLAN CLASH AT ANTIETAM, SEPTEMBER 17

× Sharpsburg

Frederick

Harpers Ferry

Antietam Creek

Shenandoah R.

2. LEE AND JACKSON DEFEAT POPE, SECOND BATTLE OF BULL RUN, AUGUST 29-30

× Washington

Manassas Junction

Chesapeake Bay

MARYLAND

DEL.

Cedar Mt. ×

Rapidan R.

Fredericksburg ×

4. LEE DEFEATS BURNSIDE AT FREDERICKSBURG, DECEMBER 13

Rappahannock R.

Potomac R.

Mechanicsville

Richmond ×

SEVEN DAYS' BATTLES JUNE 25-JULY 1

1. McCLELLAN'S PENINSULA CAMPAIGN, MARCH-JULY

Chickahominy R.

York R.

James R.

Yorktown

Appomattox R.

Petersburg

VIRGINIA

Norfolk

⊕ **Geography and History: Movement** Have students look at the map above. Ask: What time frame is covered by the map? (From March to December, 1862.) What device does the map-maker use to distinguish between the routes of the various campaigns? (Different colors, and broken lines.) What do three of the four battles highlighted have in common? (Lee fought at three of the battles.)

Valentine Museum, Cook Collection

Handsome General Robert E. Lee posed for his picture in 1864 in full-dress uniform. When the war ended, Grant generously let the Confederate officers keep their swords.

boasts and show a boldness that McClellan never had. Before Pope could march on Richmond and "end the war," he was attacked by Lee and Jackson at Bull Run (August 29–30, 1862). There his army was defeated. General Pope was speedily removed and his troops again placed under McClellan.

These reverses stirred resentment against Lincoln and his administration. Enlistments fell off and desertions increased. People hesitated to buy Union war bonds. The congressional elections were in doubt. England considered recognizing the Confederacy. Southern hopes were high. The tide seemed to have turned for the South. Now perhaps Washington could be captured.

Antietam.   After Bull Run, Lee moved quickly. His army of 55,000 battle-hardened men crossed the Potomac into Maryland on September 4, 1862. Singing "Maryland, My Maryland," his troops expected soon to be joined by Southern friends. But somehow no one came to join them. When a Federal force at Harpers Ferry was not evacuated as expected, Lee divided his army and sent a unit to drive out the Union troops. Then a copy of Lee's orders, showing where his soldiers were located, fell into the hands of McClellan. If McClellan had moved rapidly, he might have destroyed Lee's army. But as usual, McClellan took his time and gave the enemy the chance to organize.

The two forces met at Sharpsburg, near Antietam Creek. Lee was heavily outnumbered, and the Potomac River was at his back.

All day long on September 17, in the bloodiest battle of an appallingly bloody war, the battle lines moved back and forth. At nightfall, Lee still held his position. The next day, although badly weakened, Lee's men faced McClellan's and dared them to attack. Once again, McClellan hesitated. That night Lee crossed the Potomac and returned to Virginia, leaving behind 2700 dead on the battlefield. The Union had lost 2100 killed. Each army had more than 9000 wounded. For both sides it was the worst single day of the war.

The battle, so far, was a draw, but Lee's invasion of the North had reached its farthest point.

✕ **Critical Thinking Activity: Recognizing Bias** How did the Civil War engagements appear to the news reporters who covered them? Remind students that the Civil War was the first armed conflict in the United States to be covered by newspapers on a daily basis. Have students select a battle to write an article on as a news reporter. Remind students to consider point of view—would the North and South report each battle in the same way? Have students share their work.

This was the high tide of the Confederacy. When news of Antietam reached England, the British decided to await further developments before taking any action. Never again would the Confederate States of America be so close to receiving the recognition from abroad that it desperately needed.

See "Section 2 Review answers," p. 332D.

Section 2 Review

1. Identify or explain: Irvin McDowell, Winfield Scott, anaconda policy, J. E. Johnston, Thomas J. Jackson, George B. McClellan.

2. Locate: Manassas Junction, Fort Henry, Fort Donelson, Shiloh, Vicksburg, Hampton Roads.

3. List six key military engagements in 1861–1862 and tell the outcome and significance of each.

4. **Critical Thinking: Explaining Problems Clearly.** General Grant realized that the Civil War would be a war of exhaustion if the North were to win. Explain.

See "Lesson Plan," p. 332D.

3. The widening conflict

Abraham Lincoln had long been under pressure to make the war into a crusade against slavery. But he had resisted. To Horace Greeley, whose newspaper strongly criticized him for not freeing the slaves, Lincoln had written in August 1862:

> My paramount object in this struggle *is* to save the Union, and is *not* either to save or destroy Slavery. If I could save the Union without freeing *any* slave, I would do it; and if I could save it by freeing *all* the slaves, I would do it; and if I could do it by freeing some and leaving others alone, I would also do that. What I do about Slavery and the colored race, I do because I believe it helps to save this Union; and what I forbear, I forbear because I do *not* believe it would help to save the Union.

Abraham Lincoln and slavery. For putting the Union ahead of everything else, Lincoln has sometimes been criticized. But there is no doubt that Lincoln felt deeply that slavery was "a moral, social, and political wrong." He said:

> Let us discard all this quibbling about this man and the other man—this race and that race and the other race being inferior and therefore they must be placed in an inferior position. . . . Let us discard all these things and unite as one people throughout this land, until we shall once more stand up and declare that all men are created equal.

Abraham Lincoln was every inch a politician. He was not a crusader. The passionate reformers—the John Browns and William Lloyd Garrisons—also had their role. The nation needed them, too, if it was to fulfill its mission as "the last best hope of earth." Lincoln realized that his job was not to express his feelings but to shape the real world. The people of the North had entered the war mainly because of their love of the Union. Lincoln knew that if the South were allowed to secede and become a nation based on slavery, all would be lost. In the long run only if the Union was saved would the reformers in the North be able to abolish slavery in the South. While the result of the Civil War was still in doubt, Lincoln realized that people cared more deeply for morals than for politics. As the casualties increased, he saw that the North would have to pay a high price in blood and tears. To pay that price they would have to be persuaded that this was a war against slavery.

The Emancipation Proclamation. Lincoln had, in fact, already drafted his *Preliminary* Emancipation Proclamation when he wrote to Horace Greeley in August 1862. But he was persuaded to wait for some kind of victory on the battlefield. Otherwise it might look, he later said, like "our last *shriek* on the retreat."

Antietam now gave him his chance. On September 23, 1862, Lincoln issued his Preliminary Emancipation Proclamation. He warned that on January 1, 1863, anyone held as a slave in any state or part of a state where the people were "in rebellion against the United States, shall be then, thenceforward, and forever free."

A. A. Lamb; National Gallery of Art, Washington, Gift of Edgar William and Bernice Chrysler Garbisch

"The Emancipation Proclamation," an allegorical painting made about 1863, shows Lincoln holding his proclamation and following the goddess of liberty.

Neither in this early warning nor even in the Emancipation Proclamation itself, which was issued on January 1, 1863, did Lincoln free a single slave. That would only come with the success of the Union armies. The South viewed Lincoln's proclamation as a "fiend's" act that "destroyed $4 billion worth of property and bid the slaves rise in insurrection." Jefferson Davis said it made reunion "forever impossible."

The North was divided over the proclamation. Abolitionists were delighted—though they regretted that Lincoln had not freed the slaves everywhere. Many Northerners were displeased because they wanted to fight only for the Union. In Europe antislavery feeling was so strong that the Emancipation Proclamation helped to kill any chance of recognition of the Confederacy. Now this was not merely a war for a political Union, but a war against slavery, an evil that had afflicted the world.

Ending slavery. Early in the war Lincoln had attempted to persuade the Union states of Missouri, Kentucky, Maryland, and Delaware to free their slaves and be compensated for it by the federal government. To his great disappointment, he had failed. Congress had approved his plans, and in April 1862 it had abolished slavery in the District of Columbia and provided payments to the owners for the loss of their property. Two months later it had ended slavery in the territories without giving any compensation. But Congress could not do anything about slavery in the states.

West Virginia entered the Union in 1863 with a constitution that provided for gradual

See "Lesson Plan," p. 332D for **Writing Process Activity: Recognizing Ideologies** relating to reactions to the Emancipation Proclamation.

emancipation. Maryland ended slavery in 1864, and a state convention in Missouri abolished it within that state in January 1865. But Delaware and Kentucky refused to act. The peculiar institution lingered in those states until the ratification of the Thirteenth Amendment was completed in December 1865.

Gloom in the North. For a while after Antietam the war did not go well for the North. A new general in the East, Ambrose Burnside (whose name supplied the word "sideburns"!), showed that he had learned nothing about the new warfare. He attacked Lee's fortified position at Fredericksburg (December 13, 1862). The North suffered 10,000 dead and wounded to fewer than 5000 for the South. Out west, Grant and Sherman also suffered reverses. They had not yet found a way to take Vicksburg. Only in the middle theater, in central Tennessee, did a Union success at Murfreesboro lighten the gloom.

This was a bad time for Lincoln. There were demands that he reorganize his Cabinet. In the fall elections, the Democrats (who were no enthusiasts for the war) gained 32 seats in the House. Defeatism was widespread. Carloads of civilian clothing were being smuggled into the Union lines to aid deserters to escape. Voluntary enlistments fell so low that, in March 1863, the government was forced to pass its first draft law. It made all men between 20 and 45 liable for service in the national forces for a term of three years. But service could be avoided by payment of $300 or by finding a substitute to enlist for three years. The first drawing of names provoked four days of rioting in New York City in July.

The draft provided only a small proportion of total Union troops. More important were the (p. 352) bounties (as high as $1000) paid by federal, state, and local governments for voluntary enlistment. But this system suffered from "bounty jumping," enlisting and deserting again and

John Gaddis of the 12th Wisconsin painted this watercolor of his regiment in 1862. He showed the troops cheering as a train crossed a bridge they had built.

State Historical Society of Wisconsin

Continuity and Change: Conflict Point out to students that the draft was first used as a recruitment method during the Civil War, when the level of voluntary enlistment fell. To avoid going to war, draftees could pay a fee of $300.00, or find a replacement to serve their three year term. Felt to be unfair by those who could not afford the fee, the draft touched off a series of riots. The draft instituted during World War I did not allow the hiring of substitutes. Thus resistance to this draft was not so violent. (See p. 561.)

This chromolithograph was part of an advertisement published to urge blacks to volunteer for the Union army.

again. The South had turned to conscription in 1862. But a clause that exempted one slaveholder or overseer for every twenty slaves outraged many Southerners and brought desertions from their army.

Blacks in arms. The Emancipation Proclamation had provided another source of manpower for the Union army. It approved taking blacks into the armed services. They had, in fact, already fought in the war, and Congress had authorized the recruiting of blacks. But only with the Emancipation Proclamation were the gates really opened.

In time, more than 185,000 blacks were enlisted in the Northern armed forces. And some 38,000 were to die from sickness or wounds. During the Civil War black soldiers, for the first time in United States history, could join the militia and the regular army. The United States Colored Volunteers were pleased to be able to sing

We look like men a'marching on
We look like men o'war

They did all sorts of things—a small number were officers of black units, some were spies in the South, many were laborers or garrison troops. They showed their bravery in battle, for example in July 1863, when the 54th Massachusetts charged Fort Wagner outside Charleston, South Carolina. Black troops had the satisfaction of being present when the war came to an end at Appomattox Court House.

Banks, bonds, and currency. The needs of the war in 1863 brought about the creation of a new banking system. Up to now the United States had tried to pay the costs of the conflict by borrowing, by placing direct taxes on the states, by raising tariffs, by levying sales and other internal taxes, and by taxing incomes. The first income tax in our history had been passed in August 1861. All income over $800 a year was taxed at a rate of 3 percent.

In addition to these steps, beginning in 1862 a new type of currency, called United States notes, or greenbacks, was issued. This money was not based on gold or silver in the Treasury. It fluctuated widely in value depending upon the confidence of the people in the successful outcome of the war. By the end of the struggle $432 million of these notes had been issued.

Still it was clear as 1862 came to a close that even more needed to be done. So in February 1863, at the request of Secretary of the Treasury Salmon P. Chase, Congress passed a law that provided for national banks and national bank notes. The new banks were chartered by the national government. They were required to purchase at least $30,000 worth of national bonds (which would help pay for the war). Then they were allowed to issue national bank notes up to the value of 90 percent of the bonds. This would provide a more uniform and stable currency than the existing state bank notes or greenbacks. With only minor changes, the national bank system continued until it was replaced by the Federal Reserve Act of 1913 (p.538).

The trans-Mississippi West, 1861–1865. During the Civil War, the westward movement of Americans continued. Some 300,000 men, women, and children made the long trek to California and Oregon, or moved into other western territories. Some went to farm. Others hoped to find gold or silver. And many wished to escape the draft.

The Far West kept up with news of events in the East by the telegraph. The first message from the East Coast to San Francisco was transmitted on October 24, 1861. All at once communication between the East and the West was instantaneous. Until then the fastest way to send word was by the Pony Express (which only lasted from April 1860 to October 1861). Spry young riders on relays of fast horses

carried letters for $10 an ounce in ten days from St. Joseph, Missouri, to San Francisco.

When the Civil War broke out, the army units in the West were called east to fight the Confederates. Soon after they were gone, Indian war broke out in Minnesota, Colorado, and Montana. Untrained militia units were to try to put down some of the uprisings. But better fighting forces were the 1st through 6th Infantry Regiments, United States Volunteers, whose membership was made up of Confederate veterans enlisted from prisoner-of-war camps to fight the Indians. At one point fighting was so severe in Colorado that Denver was cut off from communication with the outside world.

Still the farmers and miners went west. By 1863 enough people had moved into Idaho for it to become a territory. There were 25,000 people in the Boise area alone. That same year Arizona was also made a territory. The next year Nevada came into the Union as a state, and Montana became a territory. The growth of the West seemed scarcely checked by the Civil War.

See "Section 3 Review answers," p. 332D.

Section 3 Review

1. What was Lincoln's chief reason for issuing the Emancipation Proclamation?
2. Describe the reaction to the Emancipation Proclamation in the South and the North.
3. What roles did blacks play in the war?
4. How did the North finance the war?
5. **Critical Thinking: Recognizing Cause and Effect.** What was the Civil War's effect on westward migration?

See "Lesson Plan," p. 332E.

4. Gettysburg to Appomattox, 1863–1865

The war was now reaching its climax.

In the western theater, Grant led one of the most brilliant campaigns of the war. At the beginning of May 1863 he cut his army loose from its supply lines. While living off the land, the troops fought five battles in three weeks, isolated Vicksburg, and on May 22 began the siege

More from Boorstin: ". . . Secretary of the Treasury Salmon P. Chase, complaining that the lack of statistics made it impossible to estimate what the tax might yield, never collected the [1861] tax. In 1862, an income tax was again enacted, to become the first income tax actually collected by the federal government . . . . The Confederacy, too, imposed an income tax, with rates exceeding 15 percent for certain classes of income over $10,000." (From *The Americans: The Democratic Experience*)

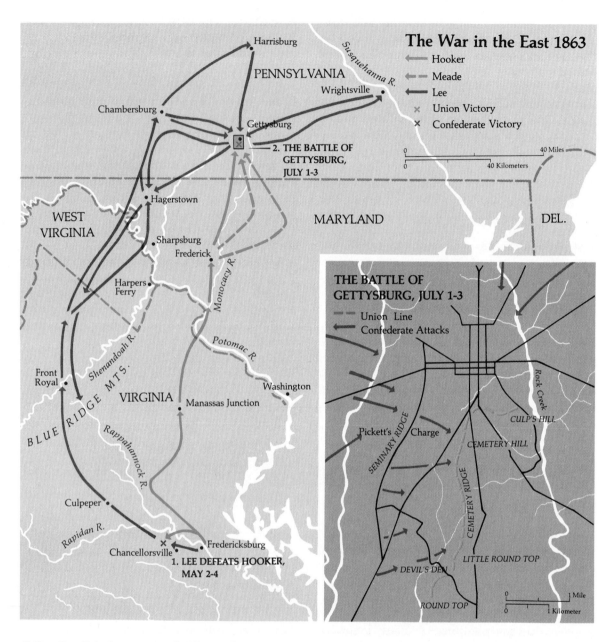

The War in the East 1863

→ Hooker
⇢ Meade
→ Lee
× Union Victory
× Confederate Victory

2. THE BATTLE OF GETTYSBURG, JULY 1-3

1. LEE DEFEATS HOOKER, MAY 2-4

PENNSYLVANIA

Harrisburg

Wrightsville

Chambersburg

Gettysburg

Susquehanna R.

Hagerstown

WEST VIRGINIA

Sharpsburg

Frederick

MARYLAND

DEL.

Harpers Ferry

Monocacy R.

Shenandoah R.

BLUE RIDGE MTS.

Front Royal

VIRGINIA

Potomac R.

Washington

Manassas Junction

Rappahannock R.

Culpeper

Rapidan R.

Chancellorsville

Fredericksburg

0   40 Miles
0   40 Kilometers

THE BATTLE OF GETTYSBURG, JULY 1-3

‑ ‑ Union Line
→ Confederate Attacks

Rock Creek

SEMINARY RIDGE

Pickett's Charge

CULP'S HILL

CEMETERY HILL

CEMETERY RIDGE

DEVIL'S DEN

LITTLE ROUND TOP

ROUND TOP

0   1 Mile
0   1 Kilometer

of the South's last stronghold on the Mississippi River.

In the East, Lee defeated another Union general, "Fighting Joe" Hooker, in the Battle of Chancellorsville (May 2–4) in northeastern Virginia. But that victory could not balance Lee's loss of his most valued general, the powerhouse "Stonewall" Jackson, not yet 40 years old, by mistake shot and killed by his own men.

President Davis and General Lee now decided to move north. Lee hoped that by invading Pennsylvania he might demoralize the North and bring foreign recognition of the Confederacy.

The Battle of Gettysburg. Lee crossed the Potomac on June 15, 1863, leading an army of 70,000 men. The Union army under sound, steady George Gordon Meade followed the Confederates. Units of the two armies stumbled into each other at the sleepy little town of

⊕ **Geography and History: Movement** Have students refer to the map above and answer the following questions: What Southern victory is shown on the map? (Chancellorsville.) How many kilometers is it from Harrisburg to Gettysburg? (About 40.) Why do you think Lee went so far to the west and then back to the east in his invasion of the North? (To keep the Blue Ridge Mountains between the Union army and his army. That way the Northern general would be uncertain about his location and his intentions.)

Gettysburg, Pennsylvania. Both armies then hastened to the spot. Here 165,000 men were to fight the greatest single battle ever to take place in the Western Hemisphere. Nearly twice as many Americans were to die at Gettysburg as were lost in the entire American Revolution.

Lee had the advantage on the first day, before Meade had securely established his forces on high ground. Southern hesitation enabled the North to hold key points—Culp's Hill and Little Round Top—the loss of which might have led to a Northern defeat. If the bold "Stonewall" Jackson had been there, the result might have been quite different.

The South needed a victory, not another inconclusive battle. So on the third day, Lee made a desperate bid. He sent 15,000 infantry, including General George Pickett and his brave Virginians, against the middle of the Union line. But the artillery and the fire of Northerners protected by defensive works was too much. A hundred men reached the Union line, but they were all captured or killed. The Battle of Gettysburg was over.

On the afternoon of the next day, July 4, 1863, Lee began his retreat. He had lost 28,000 killed, wounded, or missing.

The South divided. On that same day, though Lee did not know it, there was another critical defeat of the South. General Pemberton surrendered to Grant the great stronghold of Vicksburg—the key to control of the Mississippi. With the loss of that city went 170 cannon, 50,000 small arms, and 30,000 Southern soldiers as prisoners of war.

Five days later Port Hudson, the last Confederate post on the river, gave up. As Lincoln said, "The Father of Waters again goes unvexed to the sea." The Confederacy was cut in two between East and West. The supply line over which had come meat and munitions from Texas and Mexico was closed.

After Gettysburg and Vicksburg the death of the Confederacy was only a matter of time. But still the war went on. In fact, it would last for nearly two more years. Many thousands more would die so that (as Lincoln said at Gettys-

burg) "this nation under God shall have a new birth of freedom and that government of the people, by the people, for the people, shall not perish from the earth."

The North's victories at Gettysburg and Vicksburg were followed by Southern success at Chickamauga Creek near Chattanooga, Tennessee, in September 1863. The defeated Union troops then retreated into Chattanooga where they were trapped. At last, Grant's skill was recognized when he was made commander of all the Union forces in the West. At the end of November, assisted by reinforcements rushed 1200 miles by rail from the East, Grant defeated and pushed back the Southern troops surrounding Chattanooga, in the battles of Lookout Mountain and Missionary Ridge. Now the North was in a position to strike for Atlanta and then to split off another large section of the South by driving for the sea.

(p. 354)

The drives for Petersburg and Atlanta. On March 9, 1864, Lincoln promoted Grant to Lieutenant General—a rank last held by George Washington—and then gave him command of all the armies of the United States. Grant had finally figured out how this war had to be fought. Only if everybody attacked the South at the same time could its ability to fight be destroyed. Lincoln immediately understood: "Those not skinning can hold a leg."

In May 1864 began the final, brutal, bloody battles of exhaustion. Grant's forces suffered enormous losses, but he knew that he could afford them while Lee could not. In 40 days Grant, constantly fighting, moved around Richmond until he reached the important railway junction of Petersburg. The carnage of these days was beyond belief. Grant lost 55,000 dead and wounded to Lee's 30,000. But these losses weakened the Confederacy far more than the Union. Now Lee was pinned down. He could not leave Petersburg without giving up Richmond.

For Northerners the months of July and August 1864 were to be the darkest days of the war. The lists of Northern dead grew ever longer, but they seemed to bring no great victories. Would this war never end? Lincoln feared that he would be defeated in the fall elections by

More from Boorstin: "To many of the cattlemen and cowboys who gathered in the West in the late 1860's and '70's. the Civil War had given a new familiarity with all kinds of fire-arms . . . [as] illustrated in the remarkable career of Wild Bill Hickok . . . . His service as scout and spy for the Union in the Civil War . . . kept his shooting arm well practiced. In the public square in Springfield, Missouri, he killed a former friend of his, a fellow Union scout who had joined the Confederates." (From *The Americans: The Democratic Experience*)

Soldiers in trenches outside Fredericksburg wait for the battle to begin.

the Democratic candidate, General George McClellan.

Just then the tide miraculously turned. The general responsible was the profound but unbending William Tecumseh Sherman, now in command of Union forces in the West. He understood that this really was everybody's war. When Sherman entered Atlanta on September 2, he told the mayor, "War is cruelty and you cannot refine it." Believing that the age of total war had come, he aimed to break the spirit of the civilian South.

In the Shenandoah Valley in Virginia the young and ruthless Philip Sheridan, whose victories had made him a Union general when he was barely 30, was following Sherman's theory of the new warfare to its logical conclusion. He burned mills and barns and whatever his men could not carry. He told his men to leave the people "nothing but their eyes to weep with."

These advances helped bring Lincoln a heavy soldiers' vote from the field, and he decisively won reelection. He carried every state but New Jersey, Delaware, and Kentucky for 212 electoral votes to 21 for McClellan.

Sherman's march to the sea. On November 14, while Grant still held Lee in Petersburg, Sherman abandoned his supply and communication lines (as Grant had done before striking Vicksburg). After he set fire to Atlanta and burnt down most of the city, he led his 60,000 men on a free-wheeling, march of devastation "from Atlanta to the sea." His army traveled light. He told his men to carry only their arms, for he expected them to loot food, blankets, and whatever else they needed along the way. This would help exhaust the enemy at the same time that it solved his own problem of supply. He ordered them to move fast, without waiting to protect their rear.

For three weeks wild rumors spread through the North concerning Sherman's "lost army." In the meantime it was cutting a swath some 60 miles wide and 300 miles long through the breadbasket of the Confederacy. The newly gathered harvests were devoured or destroyed.

Railroads were torn up. Barns, buildings, depots, machine shops, bridges, cotton gins, and stores of cotton were destroyed. Tens of thousands of horses and mules needed to pull the plows and wagons were taken. The civilian and military resources of the state were damaged beyond repair.

On December 10, after the 25-day march, Sherman reached Savannah. Two weeks later Lincoln received a telegram from him announcing "as a Christmas gift the city of Savannah,

with 150 heavy guns, plenty of ammunition, and about 25,000 bales of cotton."

Sherman turns north. On January 16 Sherman and his men began to head north through South Carolina, the state that more than any other they blamed for starting the war. The state capital, Columbia, and other towns were left in ashes. It did not seem possible, but this march was even more cruel and devastating than the one through Georgia. Late in March, Grant renewed his attack on Petersburg. That stronghold fell on Sunday, April 2. Quickly, Jefferson Davis and other government officers left Richmond. Union troops entered the city the next day.

Lee tried to escape with his dwindling army to North Carolina, where he hoped to join forces with General Joseph E. Johnston, who was opposing Sherman. But Sheridan's cavalry headed him off. On April 7 Grant wrote to

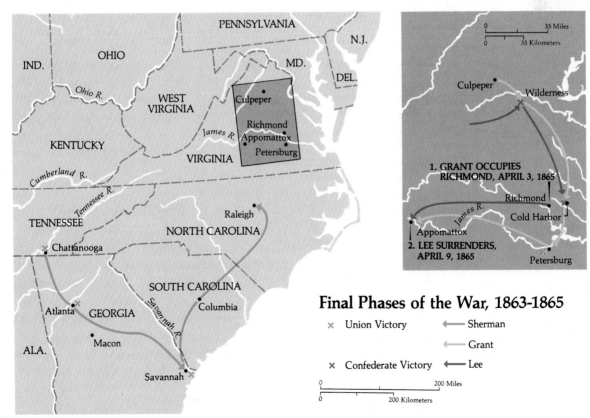

Final Phases of the War, 1863-1865

× Union Victory   ← Sherman

← Grant

× Confederate Victory   ← Lee

0   200 Miles

0   200 Kilometers

Geography and History: Location Have students look at the maps above. Ask them to name the states through which Sherman passed in the final stages of the war. (Tennessee, Georgia, South Carolina, and North Carolina.) What were the locations of the Union victories? (Chattanooga, Atlanta, Savannah, and Petersburg.) Of the Confederate victories? (Wilderness and Cold Harbor.) Where did Lee surrender? (Appomattox, April 9, 1865.)

A Richmond flour mill in ruins was photographed by Mathew Brady at the end of the Civil War.

Lee, "General, the result of the last week must convince you of the hopelessness of further resistance."

The end—Appomattox Court House.
(p. 359) On the afternoon of April 9, 1865, General Lee, accompanied only by his military secretary, rode his horse to a little white house in the town of Appomattox Court House in central Virginia. He went to arrange his surrender. There occurred one of the most remarkable and one of the most encouraging episodes in American history. It would show that, despite the monstrous indecencies of war, the respect of one American for another had not been destroyed.

Grant, who had just come in from the field, was dusty and even more unkempt than usual. Confronting him in the living room of the house that he had taken for his headquarters was General Lee—handsome, erect, in a spotless uniform, and wearing his dress sword. The men sat down and then exchanged recollections of their fighting together twenty years before in the Mexican War. The two great generals talked to each other calmly, with courtesy and respect.

Now that the fighting was over, it seemed that humanity had suddenly returned. Lee heard Grant's terms of surrender. Grant was more generous than he needed to be. He allowed the Southern officers to keep their swords—the symbols of their honor—and he let the officers and men keep their horses so that they could go home and plant their crops. Lee was touched. "This," he said, "will have a very happy effect upon my army."

A renewed nation, fused in the fires of war, would now seek its destiny in peace.

See "Section 4 Review answers," p. 332E.

Section 4 Review

1. Identify: Joseph Hooker, George G. Meade, John Pemberton, Philip Sheridan.
2. Locate: Gettysburg, Port Hudson, Chattanooga, Petersburg, Shenandoah Valley, Appomattox.
3. What hopeful note for the future was struck in the surrender at Appomattox?
4. **Critical Thinking: Drawing Conclusions.** What did General Sherman expect to accomplish by his marches through Georgia and South Carolina?

Critical Thinking Activity: Recognizing Cause and Effect How did the surrender at Appomattox Court House offer hope for the nation? Have students review the text on page 303 headed *The end—Appomattox Court House.* Ask students to identify and discuss: the choice of meeting location, the attire of Lee and Grant, the tone of the meeting, and terms of surrender. Have students write a brief paragraph analyzing the symbolism of the meeting between the two generals and summarizing what it might have meant for the future of the war-torn nation.

Chapter 13 Review

See "Chapter Review answers," p. 332E.

Focusing on Ideas

1. List some aspects of the Civil War that would seem strange to an observer who was familiar with old-fashioned warfare.

2. Identify two women who played prominent roles in the Civil War and describe their contributions to the war effort.

3. Describe two developments that affected the lives of Americans west of the Mississippi during the Civil War.

4. What was the "anaconda" plan? Name some military and naval engagements that were designed to carry out the plan.

Taking a Critical Look

1. **Making Comparisons.** How did the North's General Grant and the South's General Lee compare as military leaders?

2. **Identifying Central Issues.** Why did Lincoln delay in issuing the Emancipation Proclamation? Why did he finally issue the proclamation freeing slaves? What limits were put on emancipation? Does Lincoln deserve to be called "the Great Emancipator"?

3. **Recognizing Cause and Effect.** How did industrial and technological developments such as the railroad and the rifle affect the course and outcome of the Civil War?

Your Region in History

1. **Geography.** Locate on a map and describe any Civil War battles or other military engagements that took place in your state or locality. What were the results?

2. **Culture.** What Civil War monuments, plaques, or other memorials can be seen in your area?

Historical Facts and Figures

Predicting Consequences. Study the chart below to help answer the following questions: (a) Which side—the Blue or the Green—had the advantage in each resource category? (b) How would having a greater supply of each resource have been an advantage during the Civil War? (c) Which resources do you think were most important in determining the outcome of the conflict? (d) Which color do you think represents the Union? The Confederacy? Explain your answer.

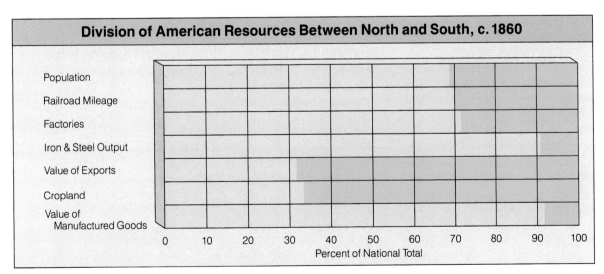

Division of American Resources Between North and South, c. 1860

Population
Railroad Mileage
Factories
Iron & Steel Output
Value of Exports
Cropland
Value of Manufactured Goods

0 10 20 30 40 50 60 70 80 90 100
Percent of National Total

Multicultural Connection: Among the officers present at Appomattox was Colonel Ely Parker, a Seneca Indian who served as an aide to General Grant. As Grant's military secretary, Colonel Parker wrote out the final terms of the Confederate surrender. In 1867, Parker became a brigadier general, but resigned from the army in 1869 to accept President Grant's appointment as the first Native American Commissioner of Indian Affairs.

Chapter 14
To Punish or to Forgive?

Identifying Chapter Materials

Objectives	Basic Instructional Materials	Extension Materials
1 "With Malice Toward None" • Compare Lincoln's plan for reuniting the nation after the Civil War to the Wade-Davis plan. • Tell the circumstances of Lincoln's assassination.	**Annotated Teacher's Edition** • Lesson Plans, p. 360C **Instructional Support File** • PreReading Activities, Unit 5, p. 15 • Skill Application, Unit 5, p. 19	**Documents of American History** • Lincoln's Plan of Reconstruction, Vol. 1, p. 429 • The Wade-Davis Bill, Vol. 1, p. 436 • Lincoln's Proclamation on the Wade-Davis Bill, Vol. 1, p. 436
2 Andrew Johnson and the Radicals • Explain why President Andrew Johnson was unsuccessful in dealing with Congress. • State the provisions of the Fourteenth Amendment and tell how the South reacted to it. • Describe the activities of the Freedmen's Bureau.	**Annotated Teacher's Edition** • Lesson Plans, pp. 360C–360D	**Documents of American History** • The Freedmen's Bureau, Vol. 1, p. 451 • Black Code of Mississippi, Vol. 1, p. 452 • The Civil Rights Act, Vol. 1, p. 464 • Veto of the Civil Rights Act, Vol. 1, p. 465
3 "Black Reconstruction" • Analyze the myth and reality of Black Reconstruction. • Explain why impeachment proceedings against President Johnson took place and what their result was.	**Annotated Teacher's Edition** • Lesson Plans, pp. 360D–360E **Instructional Support File** • Critical Thinking Activity, Unit 5, p. 20	**Enrichment Support File** • The Realities of Reconstruction (See "In-Depth Coverage" at right.) **Suggested Secondary Sources** • See chart at right.
4 The North Withdraws • Describe the scandals and economic crises of the post-Civil War period.	**Annotated Teacher's Edition** • Lesson Plans, p. 360E	**Extension Activity** • Election of 1876, Lesson Plans p. 360E
5 The Divided South • Define racism and explain its persistence despite the freeing of the slaves and the passage of new civil rights laws, and summarize the principles of *Plessy* v. *Ferguson*.	**Annotated Teacher's Edition** • Lesson Plans, p. 360F **Instructional Support File** • Reading Activities, Unit 5, pp. 16–17 • Skill Review Activity, Unit 5, p. 18 • Chapter Test, pp. 21–24 • Additional Test Questions, pp. 25–28	**Documents of American History** • *Plessy* v. *Ferguson*, Vol. 1, p. 628

Providing In-Depth Coverage

Perspectives on Reconstruction

The dozen years following the Civil War—the period called Reconstruction—were among the most important in American history. For the first time, a President was murdered in office. Another President was impeached. Federal troops occupied and governed an entire region of the country. Black people became citizens, and black men gained the vote. The Republican Party established itself, and the South emerged as a solidly Democratic region.

Chapter 14 notes that the era of Reconstruction was marked by great animosity between the executive and legislative branches of the federal government resulting from disagreement over treatment of the South.

A History of the United States as an instructional program provides two types of resources you can use to offer in-depth coverage of Reconstruction: the *student text* and the *Enrichment Support File*. A list of *Suggested Secondary Sources* is also provided. The chart below shows the topics that are covered in each.

THE STUDENT TEXT. Boorstin and Kelley's *A History of the United States* clarifies the chronology of events, the key players, and, as an interpretive history, the controversy of Reconstruction.

AMERICAN HISTORY ENRICHMENT SUPPORT FILE. This collection of primary source readings and classroom activities reveals the misconceptions and truths surrounding the Reconstruction government.

SUGGESTED SECONDARY SOURCES. This reference list of readings by well-known historians and other commentators provides an array of perspectives on the myths and realities of Reconstruction.

Locating Instructional Materials

Detailed lesson plans for teaching Reconstruction government as a mini-course or to study one or more elements of Reconstruction in depth are offered in the following areas: in the *student text*, see individual lesson plans at the beginning of each chapter; in the *Enrichment Support File*, see page 3; for readings beyond the student text, see *Suggested Secondary Sources*.

IN-DEPTH COVERAGE OF RECONSTRUCTION		
Student Text	**Enrichment Support File**	**Suggested Secondary Sources**
▪ Lincoln's Plan, p. 362 ▪ Wade-Davis bill, pp. 362–363 ▪ Military reconstruction, pp. 369–370 ▪ New state constitutions, p. 372 ▪ Black reconstruction, pp. 372–373 ▪ Southern opposition, pp. 373–375 ▪ Assessment, pp. 381–382	▪ Lesson Suggestions ▪ Multimedia Resources ▪ Overview Essay/The Realities of Reconstruction ▪ Songs in American History/Music of Reconstruction ▪ Primary Sources in American History/Reconstruction Governments Draw Praise and Criticism ▪ Art in American History/The Political Cartoon and Reconstruction ▪ Great Debates in American History/Governing the Conquered South ▪ Making Connections	▪ *Those Terrible Carpetbaggers* by Richard Current, pp. 68–90. ▪ *Reconstruction: America's Unfinished Revolution, 1863–1877* by Eric Foner, pp. 228–280. ▪ *Reconstruction: After the Civil War* by John Hope Franklin, pp. 69–84. ▪ *Retreat from Reconstruction, 1869–1879* by William Gillette, pp. 1–24. ▪ *The Era of Reconstruction, 1865–1877* by Kenneth Stampp, pp. 3–25.

"With Malice Toward None"

FOCUS

To introduce the lesson, ask students to imagine how they might view the Reconstruction era as residents of the South. Of the North? Why is Reconstruction a critical period in our nation's history?

INSTRUCT

Explain

In dealing with the defeated South, Lincoln wished for "malice toward none," while Congress took the "eye for an eye" approach.

☑ Writing Process Activity

Demonstrating Reasoned Judgment Have students imagine they are Radical Republicans who must write a position paper on what to do about the South following the Civil War. Ask them to outline their plan and their reasons, contrasting it with Lincoln's. Students should begin with a topic sentence that summarizes their political point of view on this issue. After proofreading, students can discuss the merits and drawbacks of both positions.

Section Review Answers

Section 1, page 364

1. a) members of Congress who wanted to punish the South after the Civil War. b) a Radical Republican especially hostile to the South. c) the Radical Republican leader in the Senate. d) Lincoln's plan to reunite the Union and Confederacy. e) a promise of future loyalty to the Constitution and the sworn statement that one had not held office or fought in the Confederate Army. f) assassinated Abraham Lincoln on April 14, 1865. 2. Lincoln believed that states did not have the power to secede from the Union, so the Southern states had not seceded and were therefore still states of the Union. The Radical Republicans argued that the Southern states had ended their statehood when they seceded; they could be treated as conquered provinces. 3. Lincoln's plan was lenient. He would pardon Southerners who took an oath to support the Constitution in the future and recognize the government of a state as soon as (a) the state abolished slavery and (b) 10 percent of the voters in the state took an oath of loyalty to the Constitution. 4. Each Southern state had to hold a convention to make a new state constitution, but could do so only after a majority of white men in the state took an oath of loyalty to the Constitution. Only people who took an oath swearing that they had not served in the Confed-

erate government or army could vote for delegates to the state constitutional conventions. Most white men in the South could not have taken such an oath. 5. Lincoln was a great political leader who might have been able to overcome the problems of Reconstruction, heal the nation's wounds, and rebuild the Union in a charitable way.

CLOSE

To conclude the lesson, ask: Why is Lincoln considered one of our greatest Presidents? Discuss as a class the qualities students feel all "great" Presidents must have, and determine the five "greatest" Presidents.

Andrew Johnson and the Radicals

FOCUS

To introduce the lesson, have students work in small groups to answer the following questions using the Fourteenth Amendment, other parts of the Constitution, and the text: What factors determine citizenship in the United States? What penalty is to be imposed on a state that denies the right to vote to any citizen who should have that right? What disability was imposed on some of the people who had fought for the Confederacy? How could this disability be removed? Payment of what debt was guaranteed? What debt was rejected?

Developing Vocabulary

The words listed below are essential for understanding particular sections of the chapter. The page number after each term indicates the page of its first or most important appearance. These terms are defined in the Glossary (text pages 1000–1011).

Black Codes (page 365); **Reconstruction** (page 367); **veto** (page 368).

INSTRUCT

Explain

Post-war hatred made it difficult to fashion an agreeable, workable reconstruction plan.

❀ Cooperative Learning Activity

Determining Relevance Break the class into groups of five. Explain that students will demonstrate their understanding of the Fourteenth Amendment by identifying situations that would constitute violations of it. To begin, assign each group member one section of the amendment. Have students study the assigned sections and explain their meaning to the other members of the group. Then for each section, have group members brainstorm situations that would be in violation of the Fourteenth Amendment. Each student is responsible for reporting to the class the group's ideas for his or her assigned sections.

Section Review Answers

Section 2, page 369

1. From April to December 1865 (a) the Southern states wrote new state constitutions under the lenient conditions set by Johnson. (b) Some Southern states even ignored the few suggestions Johnson made regarding the new constitutions. (c) The new Southern legislatures severely limited the rights of African Americans by adopting Black Codes. These laws made it difficult for African Americans to find new jobs; they were not allowed to vote; and their freedom and civil rights were restricted in other ways. 2. The Freedmen's Bureau bill was intended to extend the life and expand the activities of the Freedmen's Bureau, which helped refugees of the war, white and black. The Civil Rights bill was intended to protect blacks in the South by allowing the federal government to intervene in a state to protect the civil rights of citizens. 3. The Fourteenth Amendment was proposed in order to meet constitutional objections against the Civil Rights bill. The amendment (a) defined United States citizenship; (b) forbade any state to deprive its citizens of their rights; (c) reduced the Congressional representation of any state that didn't allow its adult male citizens to vote; (d) prohibited states from repaying their Confederate debt; and (e) said that no one who had supported the Confederacy after holding state or federal office could take office again without being pardoned by a vote of two-thirds of Congress. 4. Johnson clashed with the Republican majority in Congress when he announced conditions for readmitting the Southern states to the Union and when he vetoed the Freedmen's Bureau bill and the Civil Rights Act. These clashes drove moderate Republicans to abandon Johnson and join with the Radicals.

CLOSE

To conclude the lesson, have students help you compile a list on the board of the actions of Andrew Johnson that were likely to anger Northerners—and especially the Radical Republicans. Ask: Why did President Johnson choose to do each of these things? What did he hope to accomplish in each situation? Why did he fail? How might he have done these things differently?

Section 3 (pages 369–375)

"Black Reconstruction"

FOCUS

To introduce the lesson, write a five-column chart on the board with the following headings: Lincoln's and Johnson's Approach, Stevens's Approach, Former Confederate Leaders' Approach, Wade-Davis Bill Approach, and Military Reconstruction Approach. Below and to the left, write side headings such as the following: Readmission to the Union, Treatment of Former Confederate Officers, Treatment of Former Slaves. Break the class up into five groups and have each group fill in the column for one of the plans. After the groups have finished their work, discuss their answers.

Developing Vocabulary

impeach (page 370); **bloody shirt** (page 372); **scalawags** (page 372); **carpetbaggers** (page 372); **Ku Klux Klan** (page 374); **welfare** (page 372).

INSTRUCT

Explain

By 1870 the civil rights of Southern blacks were in jeopardy. Over the next 25 years they would practically disappear.

☑ Writing Process Activity

Identifying Central Issues Ask students to imagine they are Radical Republicans insistent upon removing Andrew Johnson from the presidency. In preparation for writing a speech to be delivered to the Senate, ask them to brainstorm reasons for impeachment. Students should begin their speeches with a topic sentence that summarizes their position, and they should organize their reasons in order of importance. Have students revise for unity, coherence, and persuasive logic. After proofreading, students can deliver their speeches to the class.

Section Review Answers

Section 3, page 375

1. a) established by Congress to draw up a plan for Reconstruction. b) passed by Congress in an attempt to take away the President's constitutional right to act as Commander in Chief. c) said that the President could not dismiss any federal official without the consent of the Senate. d) procedure established by the Constitution for removing a high government official from office. e) elected President in 1868. f) Democratic nominee in 1868. g) name given to white

Southerners who worked in the Reconstruction governments of their states. h) name given to Northerners who came South to work in the Reconstruction government. i) secret army of Old Confederates who terrorized and sometimes killed blacks to prevent them from voting or exercising other civil rights. j) Thirteenth, Fourteenth, and Fifteenth Amendments to the Constitution. 2. They had to abolish slavery, ratify the Fourteenth Amendment, allow all adult males except former Confederates to vote, and write new state constitutions. 3. Johnson was impeached for firing Secretary of War Stanton in violation of the Tenure of Office Act. In his trial in the Senate, the vote fell one short of the two-thirds majority needed to convict Johnson and remove him from office. 4. Grant won many more electoral votes than the Democratic nominee, Horatio Seymour, but Grant's victory in the popular vote was small. If Grant had not had the votes of Southern blacks, he would not have won the popular vote. 5. The Republicans raised taxes and states' debts increased, and they refused to accept blacks as equals.

CLOSE

To conclude the lesson, write the words Military Reconstruction on the top of the chalkboard. Below it write two column headings: Advantages and Disadvantages. Have the students volunteer answers to fill in the columns. Then discuss the following: Why was the South divided into military districts? Why did Johnson veto the Military Reconstruction Act? Who could and who could not vote in the South?

Section 4 (pages 375–379)

The North Withdraws

FOCUS

To introduce the lesson, list the following scandals or grafters on the chalkboard: Crédit Mobilier scandal, the "whiskey fraud," the "salary grab," the Indian supplies scandal, and the Tweed Ring. For each item listed, have students provide information to answer the following questions: Who? What? Where? and When?

INSTRUCT

Explain
To what extent do students think that a President is responsible for the actions of people he appoints to office? Use current examples.

★ Independent Activity
Demonstrating Reasoned Judgment Ask students to prepare a short essay answering the following question: Should we expect our politicians to be more honest than we, the people, are?

Section Review Answers
Section 4, page 379

1. a) the Democratic candidate for President in 1872. b) Grant's Secretary of War impeached for accepting bribes but resigned before the Senate could convict him. c) a Maine Republican suspected of giving illegal help to the railroads, passed over for the presidential nomination in 1876. d) an Ohio Republican who won the controversial election of 1876. e) the Democratic nominee in 1876. f) a group of powerful Democrats who ran New York City's government and stole more than $45 million through corruption. g) a cartoonist who stirred public resentment against the Tweed Ring. h) set up by Congress to decide which of the disputed electoral votes in the 1876 election would be counted. 2. The Grant administration endured the exposure of the Crédit Mobilier scandal in the building of the transcontinental railroad, the "salary grab" attempted by Congress and signed into law by Grant, a conspiracy between distillers and Treasury officials to avoid the tax on whiskey, a scandal involving the Secretary of the Navy, as well as impeachment of the Secretary of War for bribery. 3. The strain on the nation's financial resources that resulted from the rapid growth of railroads and factories, the losses that insurance companies suffered as a result of major fires in Chicago and Boston, and the collapse of Jay Cooke's investment firm. As a result, the Republicans were badly beaten in the election of 1874.

CLOSE

To conclude the lesson, ask: Are there any situations in the lives of politicians that encourage them to be less than totally honest or impartial? (The need to raise campaign funds; the need to reward loyal campaign workers; constituent pressure to get public improvements in a district; the need to trade votes for votes when considering legislative issues; etc.) Are politicians necessarily corrupt when they respond to the pressures of these situations? What distinguishes political corruption from mere politics as usual?

Extension Activity
To extend the lesson, have students develop an alternative plan for settling the disputed election of 1876. Students will outline their plans in a one-page essay, making sure to include who would win the election based on their plans.

Section 5 (pages 379–382)

The Divided South

FOCUS

To introduce the lesson, write on the top of the board the words Reconstruction Scorecard. Below that, write two column headings: Achievements and Failures. Have students supply responses to fill in the columns. Have them use the information under the heading "Black Reconstruction—myth and reality" on pages 372–373 as well as the information under the last heading in this section.

Developing Vocabulary

racism (page 379); **Jim Crow laws** (page 379); **segregation** (page 379); **separate but equal** (page 380).

INSTRUCT

Explain

Racism, the belief that one race is naturally better than another, persisted after slavery ended. Eventually, informal segregation appeared and was institutionalized with *Plessy* v. *Ferguson.*

☑ Writing Process Activity

Making Comparisons Have students write a diary entry in which they compare and contrast what they expected from emancipation with what they actually experienced after the Civil War. (You may have them look at the diary entry they wrote from the point of view of a slave—Chapter 13, Section 3.) They should begin by making a chart of the similarities and the differences. Have students write a topic sentence that captures the differences, and ask them to organize their ideas so that they logically present the contrasts. Students should revise for clarity and coherence. After proofreading, have them share both entries with partners.

Section Review Answers

Section 5, page 382

1. Racism is the belief that one race is naturally superior to another. The belief that blacks were inferior spurred efforts by Southern whites to prevent blacks from exercising their rights and to keep blacks and whites separate; it justified segregation and discrimination. Thus the racism of Southern whites helped motivate and justify efforts to keep the South split into two "nations." 2. In it the Supreme Court approved segregated facilities that were "separate but equal." The decision showed that blacks could not turn to the federal courts for protection from the Jim Crow laws. 3. Jim Crow laws required the segregation of blacks and whites. These laws undermined early attempts to treat blacks fairly because they provided Southern officials with an excuse for keeping blacks in separate, inferior facilities.

CLOSE

To conclude the lesson, ask students to write a letter from an American living in the early 1950s (before the *Brown* decision which reversed the doctrine of "separate but equal") to a member of the 1896 Supreme Court, respectfully explaining why the *Plessy* decision was incorrect.

Chapter Review Answers

Focusing on Ideas

1. Radical referred to punishment of the South as it was being rebuilt (reconstructed) under Republican control. Harm: delayed readmittance; alienated white moderates; long-term animosity toward North. Help: Black Southerners got some political experience; some laws beneficial. 2. (a) Revenge for loss of property (Stevens), bodily injury (Sumner); severe limits on former leaders. (b) Freedmen's Bureau, Civil Rights Act of 1866, efforts to enfranchise Blacks. (c) Republican control. 3. (a) Almost none—Lincoln wanted to forgive, restore Union. (b) State constitutional conventions.

Taking a Critical Look

1. A natural reaction but not practical. They were experienced; planters might have been more magnanimous in helping blacks than poor whites who gained power. 2. Similar: Blacks in inferior social and economic position. Difference: Blacks could escape peonage more easily; could marry, raise families; some educational opportunity; lack of economic security of slavery.

Your Region in History

1–3. Answers will vary depending on your region. Consult your local library or historical society.

Historical Facts and Figures

(a) South Carolina, Louisiana, and Florida. (b) Virginia, North Carolina. (c) and (d) Answers will vary.

Focusing the Chapter: Have students identify the chapter logo. Discuss what unit theme the logo might symbolize. Then ask students to skim the chapter to identify other illustrations or titles that relate to the theme.

Chapter 14

To Punish or to Forgive?

The Civil War had cemented the Union that it was fought to preserve. Lee's surrender to Grant at Appomattox brought peace. But peace brought new problems. How to find jobs for the million men who left the Union and the Confederate armies? How to change factories from making cannons and rifles and bullets to making harvesters and sewing machines? How to rebuild the war-torn South?

When the South agreed to unconditional surrender, they put themselves at the mercy of the North. This gave the North a troublesome new problem—what to do with the conquered South. Now that the blacks were at last free, what was to be the relationship of the races to each other?

Winslow Homer painted this scene of "A Visit from the Old Mistress" in Virginia. It is one of several he painted in 1876 of life among the recently freed slaves. Another may be seen on p. 381.

National Museum of American Art

See "Lesson Plan," p. 360C.

1. "With malice toward none"

There were wide differences of opinion in the North. Was it more important to punish the former rebels, to teach them a lesson they would never forget, so they would never again try to break up the Union? Or was it better to forgive, to welcome the rebels back into the Union, so they would feel at home and never again want to leave?

Of course the South had already been punished. A quarter of a million Southerners had died in the war. The Confederacy was a land of cinders and desolation—of charred plantation houses, broken bridges, twisted railways, and desecrated churches. An Englishman who traveled halfway across the South said he did not see a single smiling face. But the North also had suffered with its own one-third of a million dead. And for the Northerners who had lost fathers, sons, or husbands, no punishment of the South would be enough.

Yet this was not just a question of feelings. Unless the North wanted to feed and house millions of Southerners, it was important to get the South back into working order. This meant getting crops planted, factories built, railroads running, and pupils and teachers into schools. It also meant getting the Southern states organized to govern themselves, to collect their own taxes, to keep the peace, and to protect life and property.

It was not easy to bring people to agree on how to revive the Southern states. There was wide disagreement over what the war had really meant. What the North called "The War of the Rebellion" in the South was called "The War between the States." The Southerners argued that their state governments had never been destroyed. Once a state always a state!

Lincoln against the Radicals. Lincoln himself almost agreed with the Southerners on this point. He also believed, once a state always a state! But for Lincoln this meant that the Southern states had no power to secede. And if these states had never legally seceded, then after the Civil War they were still within the Union.

Culver Pictures

Mathew Brady made this touching photograph of Lincoln and his son Tad in 1864.

Of course, once the war was over, Southerners wanted to agree with Lincoln. As Lincoln said, they still had their states and therefore could still run their own affairs. The most, then, that the North could properly ask was that some Confederate leaders be barred from office.

Some Republicans and most Democrats agreed with Lincoln. But on the other side were Northern avengers and reformers. The most powerful of them were some Republican members in Congress called "Radicals." They were bitter against the Southern rebels. They wanted to punish white Southerners, and they also wanted to see that the newly freed slaves

✂ Critical Thinking Activity: Identifying Alternatives How could the Union be restored most productively? Divide the class into small groups with the task of devising their own plan for reconstruction. Student plans should address the issue of unemployment, the Southern economy, the relationship between the North and South, and race relations throughout the United States. Have students submit formal proposals that could be voted on by the class. Each group should be prepared to explain their plan.

received fair treatment. To accomplish these ends, the Radical Republicans claimed that the Southern states had actually "committed suicide." By trying to rebel, they had actually destroyed their own states.

People who thought like this believed that after the war the Southern "states" could claim *no* rights under the Constitution. They had no right to govern themselves or to be represented in the Congress. They were nothing but so much territory—like parts of the sparsely settled West. And like those western territories, they could be governed in any way Congress decided.

Congress could treat them as "conquered provinces." They could be ruled by military governors—generals of the Union army. When, if ever, would they be allowed to govern themselves and take part in the national government? This would depend on how they behaved themselves and what the victorious Congress wanted. Such a view offered anything but a cheerful prospect for white Southerners.

Thaddeus Stevens and Charles Sumner.

Two leaders of the Radical Republicans were Thaddeus Stevens and Charles Sumner. Thaddeus Stevens of Pennsylvania, a power in the House of Representatives, was one of the strangest men in American history. He was sometimes called "a humanitarian without humanity." He seemed to use up all his good feelings on large and noble causes, so that he had very little left for individuals. Born with a clubfoot, Stevens seemed to have a grudge against the world. Some said he had been raised on sour milk. He never showed charity to opponents in his speeches. Just as Lincoln inspired love and respect, Stevens inspired fear.

Very early in life Stevens took up the great cause of abolishing slavery. He never abandoned that cause. Nor did he ever forgive men who had held slaves or who had been entangled in the web of slavery. When the Confederate army invaded southern Pennsylvania in 1863, they destroyed Stevens's ironworks and burned the nearby city of Chambersburg. After Appomattox, Stevens made it his purpose in life to punish all "traitors." Old age never mellowed him. At the age of 75 he boasted that he would spend his remaining years inventing new ways to make the hated Southern rebels suffer.

In the Senate the leader of the Radicals was grim Charles Sumner of Massachusetts. Three and a half years after being brutally beaten by Brooks (p. 316), and still not fully recovered, Sumner had returned to his Senate seat. As early as 1862 he had begun to fight for equal rights for blacks. He was a proud, vain man, bitter against white Southerners and intolerant of all opposition. But in the Senate he was the conscience of the North. And he was just as bitter against the white South and just as concerned about black Southerners as Thaddeus Stevens. They formed an odd and awesome alliance.

Lincoln's plan for reunion.

During the Civil War, Lincoln had shown his greatness—and his forgiving spirit—by his plan for bringing Southerners back to the Union. He was less interested in the past than in the future. Back on December 8, 1863, in his Proclamation of Amnesty and Reconstruction, he had explained his plan. He would pardon almost all Southerners, even if they had fought against the Union.

All that Lincoln asked was that Southerners take a solemn oath to support the Constitution of the United States in the future. As soon as enough citizens of a Southern state took the oath, Lincoln would recognize the government of that state and let the people rule themselves. Of course they must agree to abolish slavery. It would be enough, Lincoln said, if a number equal to only one-tenth of the voters in the 1860 presidential election took the oath of loyalty.

The Wade-Davis plan.

Lincoln's plan did not satisfy the Radical Republicans. During the war they were busy in Congress concocting a plan of their own. Their Wade-Davis bill breathed quite another spirit. They could not take their eyes off the past. Under their plan each Southern state was to make a list of all its white men. The state could not be recognized until a *majority* of the people on that list took a new oath to support

See "Lesson Plan," p. 360C for **Writing Process Activity: Demonstrating Reasoned Judgment** relating to Reconstruction and the Radical Republicans.

the Constitution. Then (since the Radicals believed that the old Southern states had committed suicide) there would have to be an election to call a convention to make a new constitution for each Southern state.

No one could even vote in that election, much less be a delegate to help make the new constitution, unless he took the "ironclad oath." This oath was not merely a promise of future loyalty but also an oath of past purity. You had to swear that you had never held office under the Confederacy or fought in the Confederate army. By the end of the war, most white men in the South could not honestly have taken such an oath.

Under the Radicals' scheme it would have been years before any Southern state could set up a majority government. It would have had to wait until the whole Civil War generation was dead. But that did not bother the Radical Republicans. They were quite willing to keep the Southern states under rule by Northern generals. The Radical Republicans said that they were in favor of liberty. But they were not willing to give it to hated white Southerners.

The Wade-Davis bill passed Congress on July 2, 1864. To become law it had to be signed by President Lincoln. What would Lincoln do?

Lincoln refused to sign. But he was shrewd. Instead of simply attacking the bill as a message of hate, he issued a new proclamation. He would not sign the Wade-Davis bill into law, he said, because he did not think it should be the only way a Southern state could get back into working order. Any "seceded" state that wanted to follow the Wade-Davis plan should feel free to do so.

But now, Lincoln said, there ought to be two possible paths. Any state ought to be allowed to choose between Lincoln's one-tenth plan and the Radicals' majority ironclad-oath plan. Lincoln was doing his best to avoid a head-on clash with Congress.

The assassination of Lincoln. Lincoln, cheerful and happy now that the long agony of war was over, called his Cabinet together on April 14, 1865, to discuss how to deal with Re-

construction. He urged them to use charity. He had already declared his generous spirit of "malice toward none." Now he begged them to put an end to the bitterness and hatred of war. His words helped calm the passions of four years of bloodshed. Still, it was hard to translate words of charity into acts of charity. Could

Four persons implicated in Booth's plot were hanged, and four more went to prison. John Surratt was arrested but not convicted. His mother, Mary E. Surratt, who harbored the gang, went to the gallows.

Library of Congress

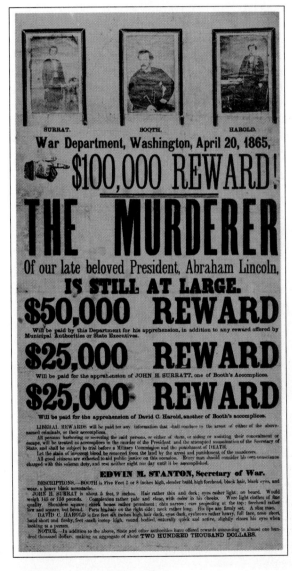

More from Boorstin: "The greatest and most durable monument to the power of the spoken word in that age is Abraham Lincoln. . . . No one better combined the virtues of . . . [public oration and the anecdotal saying] to create classics of declamatory literature which would long speak to a federal nation." (From *The Americans: The National Experience*)

President Lincoln have succeeded in that nearly impossible task?

We shall never know. For at this point there occurred one of those unexpected events that change the course of history. Now quite suddenly the South's hatred of Lincoln was focused in a single violent deed by a mad actor.

That very night President and Mrs. Lincoln went to Ford's Theater in Washington to attend a play. A far greater tragedy than had ever been performed on that stage was suddenly acted out in the President's box. It was one of the great tragedies of all American history. And it fulfilled an elaborate conspiracy which had been cooking for at least six months.

John Wilkes Booth, who planned it all, had a twisted feeling for drama. His father had made a great reputation on the London stage. Then he had come to settle in Maryland, where he had three sons. They all succeeded in the thea-

ter. Edwin, the oldest, became the most famous American actor of the age and was especially noted for portraying Shakespeare's tragic heroes. John Wilkes, though less successful, had also grown to be a well-known actor. A handsome, charming, and colossally conceited man, he was a passionate Confederate patriot. Having persuaded himself that slavery was the greatest thing that ever happened to humankind, he used his talents to enlist conspirators in a fantastic plot. His first idea was to kidnap Lincoln and so persuade the North to surrender or at least to give up its Southern prisoners.

When this plan failed, he organized a team to kill the President, Vice-President Johnson, and Secretary of State Seward in one fell swoop. It was less than a week after Appomattox. That night at the theater, Booth quietly entered the President's box, shot Lincoln, then leaped to the stage. *"Sic semper tyrannis!"* ("Thus ever to tyrants!") he screamed. Seward was seriously wounded, but the man assigned to kill Johnson lost his nerve.

Booth and his fellow conspirators were caught. He was killed, but legend said he still stalked the land. Now Lincoln, the martyr-President, was even larger in death than in life. He became a symbolic and heroic figure for all Americans and freedom-loving people everywhere.

Abraham Lincoln's funeral train took twelve days to carry him back to Springfield, Illinois. As it wended its way to his old home, the train stopped in several cities so people could mourn their dead President. The funeral procession pictured below was in New York City on April 25, 1865, and shows the casket about to pass Union Square.

Anne S. K. Brown Military Collection, Brown University Library

See "Section 1 Review answers," p. 360C.

Section 1 Review

1. Identify or explain: Radical Republicans, Thaddeus Stevens, Charles Sumner, Proclamation of Amnesty and Reconstruction, "ironclad oath," John Wilkes Booth.

2. How did Lincoln and the Radical Republicans differ in their views on the legal status of the "seceded" states?

3. Describe Lincoln's plan for reunion.

4. What were the provisions of the Wade-Davis bill? How would this plan delay reunion?

5. **Critical Thinking: Drawing Conclusions.** Why was Lincoln's assassination "one of the greatest tragedies of all American history"?

See "Lesson Plan," p. 360C.

2. Andrew Johnson and the Radicals

Andrew Johnson, the new President, was in some ways like Lincoln. Both had been born in the South to poor parents. Both had served in the state legislature and in Congress. With no schooling Johnson began life as a poor tailor. His wife, Eliza, taught him to write. Though he came from Tennessee, he had stood against secession. As Democratic senator from Tennessee, he was the only Southern senator to support the Union after the Confederates fired on Fort Sumter.

Still, Johnson was no Lincoln. He lacked Lincoln's tact and warmth and wit. He did not know how to use a joke to make a serious point. Just as Lincoln was gentle, generous, and compromising, so Johnson was crude, stubborn, and argumentative. His weaknesses would not have been serious in an ordinary citizen. But in a President they were disastrous.

When Johnson became President in April 1865, Congress was not in session and was not due to meet again until December. Many Republicans distrusted Johnson because he had been a Democrat. In 1864 they had picked him for Vice-President on their "Union party" ticket, hoping that he would draw Democratic votes.

The Republicans wanted President Johnson to call Congress into special session to make new rules for the South, but he refused. Johnson declared his intention to follow the rules already announced by Lincoln. He alone—not the Congress!—would decide when the Southern states had satisfied Lincoln's requirements and so could govern themselves.

The Southern state conventions. Northerners were impatient to hear the South say "Uncle" and admit their defeat. The Southerners needed to be told what they had to do.

President Johnson now suggested that the Southern conventions gathered under his plan ought to repudiate (refuse to pay) their war debts, nullify their ordinances of secession, and adopt the Thirteenth Amendment freeing the slaves. These conditions were the least the

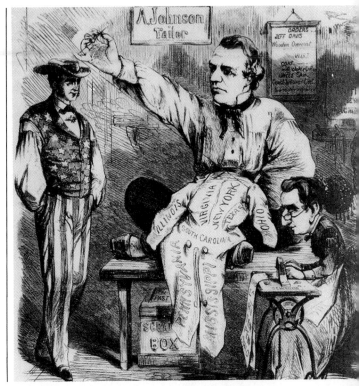

American Antiquarian Society

Andrew Johnson, once a tailor, sews up the Union in this cartoon from about 1865.

North would accept as a signal that the South knew it was beaten.

But Johnson did not actually demand these terms. So South Carolina repealed rather than nullified its ordinance of secession. This implied that secession had been legal all along. Mississippi refused to adopt the Thirteenth Amendment. Instead, it announced that the slaves were free by the force of Northern arms. South Carolina and Mississippi refused to repudiate their wartime debts. Lacking firm direction from Andrew Johnson, those Southerners who were willing to give in and start life anew felt abandoned. Meanwhile the Southern fire-eaters—the extremists—were gaining strength.

The "Black Codes." Northerners were disturbed by the action of these Southern state conventions. They were even more shocked when the legislatures of the new state governments, at their first meetings, adopted "Black Codes." These were based on old slave codes, Northern vagrancy laws, and laws passed in the British West Indies after emancipation was enacted there. These laws were supposed to provide for the new situation of the blacks now that they were no longer slaves. The laws strictly limited the freedom of the blacks. They could not vote. They were not allowed to marry whites. In some states they could be witnesses only in trials involving other blacks.

Many former slaves were using their new-found freedom to travel about and see something of the nation. This did not suit white planters who wanted to grow cotton again. So the Black Codes restricted the newly freed people to agricultural jobs or domestic service. And to keep them hard at work, harsh vagrancy laws were passed. Then they could not look for a new kind of job. In Mississippi, for example, if a black man was convicted of being a "vagrant"—a wandering person without a job—he could be fined $50. If he could not pay the fine, he could be hired out against his will to anybody who would pay the fine in return for his labor.

Northerners began to wonder if their young men had died in a Civil War merely to preserve slavery under a new name.

This store in Richmond, Virginia, was decorated to celebrate "Liberation Day," the anniversary of the Emancipation Proclamation.

Valentine Museum, Richmond, Virginia

Confederates elected to office. On top of all this, the Southern states proceeded to elect important former Confederates to Congress. Instead of opposing this and warning the South of Northern reactions, President Johnson pardoned these men of the crime of rebellion after they had been elected to Congress.

By the time Congress met in December 1865, Andrew Johnson, a Democrat and a former slave owner, had been President for seven months. All the old Confederate states except Texas had formed new governments. In Washington, waiting to take their seats in Congress, were former leaders of the Confederacy. Among them were the Vice-President, six Cabinet members, 58 members of the Confederate Congress, and a number of high-ranking army officers. In no Southern state had steps been taken to give blacks the vote. Instead a new form for slavery—the Black Codes—had been instituted. To many Republicans it seemed that the South had learned nothing from the war.

To make matters worse, the Southern states would return to Congress with more members than when they had left the Union. For representation was now based on all the people in the South instead of counting the whites and only three-fifths of the slaves. If Southerners joined with Northern Democrats, the Republicans would lose control of Congress. The Republican programs for industrial growth, for railroads, and for protection of the blacks would soon be voted down.

When the congressmen from Johnson's "restored" states tried to take their seats in Congress, they were abruptly shut out. Moderate Republicans joined Radical Republicans to tell the Southerners that they were not really members of Congress at all—because the Southern states were not really states at all. Even if the Confederate states had followed the President's rules, the Republicans said, the President had no power to make the rules. Only Congress (by which, of course, they meant the Republican majority) had that power.

Congress set up a Committee of Reconstruction made up of members of both houses—the Joint Committee of Fifteen—to draw up its own plan. It was led by the Radical avenger Thad-

Library of Congress

Republican Thaddeus Stevens of Pennsylvania chaired the Joint Committee of Fifteen, which was set up by Congress to create a plan for re-admitting the Confederate states.

deus Stevens, but the Joint Committee was not yet an entirely Radical group. It began by trying to produce some bills that would take care of several matters of real concern to the North.

The Freedmen's Bureau. The first bill extended the life of the Freedmen's Bureau and enlarged its activities. The Bureau had been set up six weeks before Lincoln's death to help war refugees get Southern farms back in working order. It was also formed to help the recently freed blacks (who were called "freedmen," no matter what their sex) to start a new life.

The Freedmen's Bureau did a great deal of good work that nobody else could do. It handed out millions of free meals to black and white refugees. It built hospitals. It treated half a million cases of illness. And it brought thousands of white Southerners back onto farms where they could make a living again. The Bureau also helped freedmen to find jobs, and, in the new bill, it tried to protect them against the new slavery of the Black Codes.

The Bureau's most important work was in building schools and in providing teachers to give blacks the education they had been denied under slavery. The Bureau helped Howard University, Hampton Institute, Atlanta University, and Fisk University, which were set up for black students of college age. A quarter of a million black children were sent to school for the first time.

The moderate Republicans who drew up the new Freedmen's Bureau Bill thought President Johnson had told them he would sign it. But in February 1866 he vetoed it because it gave the

Students of many ages attended the primary schools for freedmen in Richmond, Virginia.

The Granger Collection

Bureau the power, through military courts, to deal with any question concerning discrimination or infringement of civil rights. The local courts were open, Johnson said, and they were perfectly capable of dealing with such questions. Johnson even declared that Congress should pass no legislation at all before the Southern members had returned to their seats in Congress.

Johnson's sabotage of their program angered many Republican members of Congress. But they did not yet have the votes to override his veto. Instead they passed a resolution saying that no congressman from a Southern state would be admitted until Congress had decided that the state was entitled to representation.

The Civil Rights bill. Congress followed the Freedmen's Bureau bill with a Civil Rights bill. The idea behind this bill was to protect blacks in the South. It allowed the federal government to intervene in a state's affairs to protect the rights of all United States citizens. Moderates urged Johnson to accept this law, which had passed with large majorities. But his background as an old-fashioned states' rights Democrat kept him from doing so. He vetoed the bill and insisted that the federal government had no constitutional right to interfere within a state to protect civil rights.

With this veto—and with his angry personal attacks on the Radical leaders—Johnson drove away the moderates and strengthened the Radicals. It is difficult to imagine Lincoln in this same situation failing to find a middle road. (p. 369)

Republican members of Congress who had tried to work with the President now gave up. They joined the Radicals and passed the Civil Rights Act over the President's veto. Then they passed a new Freedmen's Bureau bill, and when Johnson vetoed it, they again overrode his veto.

The Fourteenth Amendment. Then Congress drew up a new amendment to the Constitution— the Fourteenth. It attempted to answer all Johnson's constitutional objections to the Civil Rights Act. It defined United States citizenship and forbade any state from depriving citizens of their rights and privileges. It reduced the

Critical Thinking Activity: Expressing Problems Clearly How did the Freedmen's Bureau assist Black Americans after the Civil War? Have students select some aspect of the Freedmen's Bureau to promote with an advertisement in the form of a poster. Remind the class that the literacy rate among Freedmen was low, so their posters will need to allow for this factor. Ask students to share their work, and to explain why they designed their posters as they did.

representation of any state that did not allow its adult male citizens to vote. It ruled that no state could choose to pay its Confederate debt. And it said that no one who had held state or federal office under the Union, and then supported the Confederacy, could hold office without being ❧ pardoned by a vote of two-thirds of Congress.

(p. 370)

Here at last were the North's clear terms to the South. If they accepted this amendment, they could enter the Union. No one knew what might happen if they rejected it.

Tennessee promptly ratified the Fourteenth Amendment and had its senators and representatives admitted to Congress. For Tennessee, Reconstruction was largely over. But the other states followed Andrew Johnson's lead and refused to adopt the amendment.

Now the Republicans and the President were totally at odds. Johnson even decided to try to form a new party of Democrats and moderate Republicans to oppose the Republicans in the autumn 1866 congressional elections. He became the first President to travel the country and give aggressive speeches in order to bring people to his side. But since no President had ever done this before, voters were shocked at such undignified, "Un-Presidential" behavior. The result in the elections was a landslide for the Republicans and an increase in the power of the Radicals.

See "Section 2 Review answers," p. 360D.

Section 2 Review

1. Describe Southern action from April to December 1865 with respect to (a) writing new constitutions, (b) meeting Johnson's "suggestions" for reunion, (c) limiting the rights of African Americans.

2. What were the purposes of the Freedmen's Bureau and Civil Rights bills?

3. Why did Congress propose the Fourteenth Amendment? What were its provisions?

4. **Critical Thinking: Identifying Central Issues.** Cite examples of President Johnson's clashes with the Republican majority in Congress. Why were these clashes significant?

See "Lesson Plan," p. 360D.

3. "Black Reconstruction"

When Congress met in December after the 1866 elections, it was ready to carry out its own Reconstruction of the South. Congressional Reconstruction would combine revenge, idealism, and political opportunism. Now the Joint Committee of Fifteen said the South was a "conquered province," and nobody would be allowed to forget it. Northern troops would be sent to occupy the South.

Enrichment Support File Topic

Military Reconstruction. Congress passed a law that divided the old Confederacy, excluding Tennessee, into five military districts. Each of the five districts would be ruled by a Northern general. The Radical Republicans in Congress laid down rules for building new Southern states. They wished to see the new states designed to keep political control in Republican hands. Some of the Radical demands, such as abolishing slavery and giving civil rights to blacks by ratifying the Fourteenth Amendment, were of course just and necessary. But others were not.

Worst of all was the Radical refusal to forgive or forget. They denied leading citizens of the Old South the right to vote or to hold any office in state or local government. Hungry for power, the Radicals wanted to rule the South through their own friends. Anxious to hold their Republican majority in Congress, they believed that freely elected Southern members might be against them. They said that they loved liberty, but really they were afraid of it. They were afraid to give political liberty to their old enemies.

Yet even now, Congress did not go as far as Thaddeus Stevens and the most ardent Radicals wanted. Stevens insisted that economic power was more important than political power. He wanted to seize rebel property and give every onetime slave 40 acres and a hut. But at this Congress balked. Unfortunately, few former slaves ever received any property after the war. Most remained dependent on white property owners for jobs and pay.

Although Johnson vetoed the vindictive act that turned the states into conquered provinces, it was passed over his veto. The South

⚏ **Continuity and Change: Social Change** Point out to students that Andrew Johnson's assertion that the federal government had no right to protect civil rights in the states slowed the assimilation of blacks into society after the Civil War. Similarly, during the election of 1948, a Democratic platform for civil rights legislation alienated southern Democrats, who asserted the doctrine of states' rights and insisted on the continued segregation of blacks. The resulting party chasm prevented the passage of any civil rights legislation initiated during the Truman administration. (See p. 719.)

American Antiquarian Society

Neither Johnson (left) nor Stevens will give way on his plans for Reconstruction.

The impeachment of Andrew Johnson. At the same time that the Radicals dealt with the troublesome South, they turned against the President. Under the Constitution he was supposed to enforce the laws of Congress. Though Johnson believed many of these laws were unwise, he still tried to enforce them. But now the Radicals were out to "get" Johnson. They could not bear the idea of a President who was not in their pocket. They passed laws taking away powers that the Constitution had given to the President. Even though the Constitution had made the President the Commander in Chief, the Radicals passed a Command of the Army Act taking away his power to command.

They were spoiling for a fight. They hoped to lure the President into violating even one law. Then they would have an excuse to oust him and seize his powers for themselves. Johnson watched his step. He was careful to obey the letter of the law and follow all the instructions of Congress.

Still, there was a limit to his patience. When the Radicals passed the Tenure of Office Act, which said the President could not dismiss any federal official without the consent of the Senate, that was too much. Secretary of War Stanton, whom Johnson had inherited in the Cabinet from Lincoln, had become Johnson's enemy and was actually plotting against him. So the President fired Stanton to test the Tenure of Office Act, which he believed to be against the Constitution. This was a small thing but enough to give the Radicals their chance. They took it.

The framers of the Constitution, being wise men, had provided a way to remove a criminal President. They had not made it too easy. The Constitution said (Article II, sec. 4) that the President could not be removed except "on impeachment for, and conviction of, treason, bribery, or other high crimes and misdemeanors." First the House of Representatives would have to "impeach" the President. This meant that a majority would have to vote to support a list of accusations. Then the President would actually be tried by the Senate. The Chief Justice of the United States would preside. But to remove a President a mere majority of the Senate was not

was stunned. Suddenly, two years after the war had ended, they were right back where they had started in April of 1865. Johnson had never warned them that this might happen. The Southerners' old fears of a slave rebellion seemed now to be coming true. They believed that they would be ruled by a mass of illiterate blacks.

The new military districts were quickly set up. They were to oversee elections for delegates to new constitutional conventions. The voters were to include all adult males regardless of color except those who were banned. And the banned persons included all the former leaders of the community—anybody who had once held any office in the state or the nation and who had then supported the Confederacy.

❈ See "Lesson Plan," p. 360C for **Cooperative Learning Activity: Determining Relevance** relating to the Fourteenth Amendment.

☑ See "Lesson Plan," p. 360D for **Writing Process Activity: Identifying Central Issues** relating to the impeachment of Andrew Johnson.

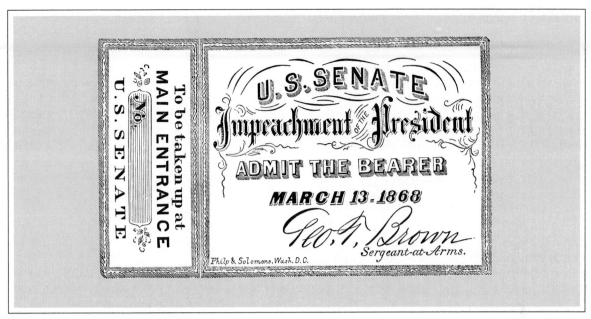

Johnson's impeachment trial drew large crowds to the gallery of the Senate. Visitors had to show tickets to be admitted.

enough. The framers showed their special wisdom when for such a drastic act they required the support of *two-thirds* of the members present.

When the Senate met on March 30, 1868, to try President Andrew Johnson on the impeachment brought by the House, the nation was in breathless suspense. Few really believed that Andrew Johnson had been guilty of "treason, bribery, or other high crimes and misdemeanors."

Johnson, like Lincoln, was a man of rock-ribbed honesty. No one could prove otherwise. Earnestly he had followed his oath "to preserve, protect, and defend the Constitution of the United States, against all enemies foreign and domestic." Perhaps he had sometimes lost his temper, or had shown bad judgment, or had used language that a President should not use. But these were not crimes. His only "crime" had been that he believed it his duty to obey the Constitution as he saw it.

On May 16, 1868, when the vote of the Senate was finally taken, 35 senators voted "guilty" and 19 voted "not guilty." This was a big majority against the President. But, luckily, it was *one* vote less than the two-thirds which the Founding Fathers required. The strength of the Constitution and the American system was upheld when even the President's bitter enemies accepted the result. Andrew Johnson remained President.

This was the first time American politicians came near to removing a President during his term of office. If they had succeeded, they would have opened the way for a new kind of dictatorship—a dictatorship of Congress.

The election of 1868. During the impeachment trial of Andrew Johnson, the Republican party met in Chicago and nominated General Ulysses S. Grant for President. Tough, silent, inscrutable Grant was the North's war hero. He knew nothing at all about politics, but many Northerners loved him.

To oppose Grant, the Democrats nominated the dignified and honest wartime governor of New York, Horatio Seymour. He had a reputation for being against both abolitionists and Southern extremists. Although he had opposed fighting to keep the South in the Union, he had raised troops to meet New York's quota in the army. He was a man of decency and moderation.

In the savage postwar campaign the Republicans "waved the bloody shirt" to remind people of how they had freed the slaves and saved the Union. Grant received 214 electoral votes to Seymour's 80, but Grant's popular majority was only 300,000 in a total of 5,700,000. Without 650,000 votes from blacks in the South, Grant would have lost the popular vote.

These figures made the Republicans more eager than ever to control the Southern governments and hold the black vote. With these political ambitions in mind they proposed the Fifteenth Amendment to the Constitution. It forbade the United States or any state to deny the right of voting to any citizen on account of

General Grant's lack of concern with military neatness—a rumpled, unbuttoned uniform—was captured by photographer Mathew Brady.

Culver Pictures

"race, color, or previous condition of servitude." It became a part of the Constitution on March 30, 1870.

The new state constitutions. Meanwhile in the South new constitutions had been written and new governments set up. The constitutional conventions had white majorities in every state except South Carolina and Louisiana. Many of the black delegates were illiterate, but some were well educated and had experience in politics. Surprisingly, the blacks in the conventions showed no hatred toward their old masters. In many cases they even asked that the political rights of former Confederates be restored.

Naturally, the conventions did what Congress had commanded. They barred Confederates from state office and granted black suffrage. Beyond that, they provided a wide range of social welfare programs new to the Southern states. For the first time they called for free public schools. They made new provision for orphans and the handicapped.

The new state constitutions were bitterly criticized by white Southerners. It was difficult to get them approved, largely because blacks had played a role in framing them. But even after the Reconstruction governments were gone, these constitutions, largely unchanged, continued in use.

Black Reconstruction—myth and reality. The "myth" of Black, or Carpetbag, Reconstruction is that these governments were dominated by foolish blacks who were manipulated by a few evil whites, that the governments were corrupt and extravagant, and that the South suffered under them for a decade. The reality is quite different.

The governments that took office under the new constitutions were made up of what Southerners called "scalawags" (white Southerners), "carpet-baggers" (Northerners who had come South with no more belongings, it was said, than they could carry in a carpetbag), and blacks. The blacks dominated none of these governments. In South Carolina blacks controlled the lower house until 1874, but they never had a majority in the senate or held the post of governor.

It has been charged, with some truth, that these governments were extravagant. They had to rebuild the damaged South. They were also eager to repair and expand the railroads. They set up schools and offered other public services that had never been provided before. Of course, all this cost money, and as a result taxes rose. Naturally enough, planters complained. Many refused to pay the higher taxes. The result was that the tax receipts were less than expected. Southern states had to borrow, and their debts rose ever higher.

Another myth of Reconstruction is that these governments were always corrupt. Again, there is some truth to the charge. But in those days corruption was not peculiar to the South. The whole nation, including the governments of cities and states, was plagued by bribery, fraud, and outright theft. The stealing by Southern politicians was minor when compared with the activities of William M. Tweed, political boss of New York City, and his henchmen. Nor did corruption in the South cease when the Reconstruction governments were replaced by "conservative" governments. Good Confederates, it turned out, were just as apt to misuse the people's money as carpetbaggers, scalawags, and blacks.

For better or worse, in most of the old Confederacy the Reconstruction governments did not last long. In Tennessee, Virginia, and North Carolina they survived only until 1870. When Georgia moved out from Radical rule in 1871, the governor announced that the "long cheerless night of misrule" was over. That "long night" had lasted less than two years. Texas went Democratic in 1873, Alabama and Arkansas in 1874, and Mississippi (which had an excellent Radical government) went Democratic in 1875. Only in Louisiana, Florida, and South Carolina did Republican rule last until 1877.

The South fights back. The Radical Republican governments were able to remain in power in the South only so long as blacks voted for

Library of Congress

Four of the men shown in this 1870 poster with Frederick Douglass (center) served in Congress: Hiram Revels in the Senate and Benjamin Turner, Josiah T. Walls, and Joseph Rainey in the House. Also pictured are writer William Wells Brown and Bishop Richard Allen, founder of the African Methodist Episcopal Church.

them. Some Southern whites decided to make sure that blacks did *not* vote. The South was now at war with itself. Southerners said that they were only fighting against "outsiders." But they were really fighting against their fellow Southern blacks who wanted to be free and equal.

Before long, certain Old Confederates in the South had organized a secret army. Its purpose was to carry on the Civil War under another

Multicultural Connection: In 1870, Hiram Revels (1822–1901) became the first African American to serve in the United States Congress. Ordained in 1845, Revels acted as chaplain to African-American troops during the Civil War and organized the formation of African-American regiments. In 1870 he was elected to the U.S. Senate to finish out the term left to Confederate President Jefferson Davis. After completing the term, Revels became president of Alcorn College and editor of the *Southwestern Christian Advocate*.

name. Although slavery was abolished by law, many Southerners still hoped to preserve as much as possible of their former way of life.

This secret army called itself the Ku Klux Klan—perhaps from the Greek word *kyklos*, meaning circle. Soon many branches, or circles, appeared all over the South. Klan members traveled the countryside flogging, maiming, and sometimes killing blacks who tried to vote or who in other ways presumed to be the white man's equal. The Klan uniform was a pointed hat with a white hood to conceal the face, and a long white or black robe.

Scores of other organizations joined in the bloody work—the Tennessee Pale Faces, the Louisiana Knights of the White Camelia, the North Carolina White Brotherhood, the Mississippi Society of the White Rose, the Texas Knights of the Rising Sun, the Red Jackets, and the Knights of the Black Cross. In 1871 alone, in a single county in Florida, 163 blacks were murdered, and around New Orleans the murders came to over 300. These organizations kept the lists of their members secret to save them from punishment for their crimes. Thousands of blacks were driven from their homes, maimed, or tortured. Whole communities were terrorized by masked thugs on parade, by burning crosses, by kidnapping and tar-and-feathering.

Under pressure from Northern Radical Republicans, some Southern states passed laws against these outrages. On December 5, 1870, President U. S. Grant delivered a special message to Congress. "The free exercise of franchise," he warned, "has by violence and intimidation been denied to citizens of several of the States lately in rebellion." Congress then passed the Ku Klux Klan Acts to outlaw these organizations and to protect all citizens. But these laws had little effect. The state governments set up in the South by the Radical Republican Congress were replaced by old-fashioned Southern state governments. Confederate heroes were back in charge. Despite all the bloodshed of the Civil War, land and factories were still owned by white Southerners.

The work that first had been done by terrorists was now done "legally" by the state governments. Although the Southern states had approved the Civil War amendments (Thirteenth, Fourteenth, and Fifteenth) to the Constitution, although they had abolished slavery and their laws "guaranteed" the blacks their rights in the South, all these guarantees proved to be mere technicalities. Before long it was plain that slavery itself was just about the only thing the Civil War had abolished.

Thaddeus Stevens died in 1868, and soon enough his avenging spirit—along with his special concern for the rights of black people—was dead. Now more and more Northerners were anxious to "leave the South alone." In practice this meant putting the South back in the hands of white Southerners. And the South then remained divided into the same two nations—a "superior" race and an "inferior" race.

The viper Ku Klux Klan, about to devour the messenger dove sent by the goddess of Peace, destroys chances for reconciliation.

American Antiquarian Society

More from Boorstin: "Even after emancipation, . . . the American Negro's experience did not cease to be distinctive. However oppressed the Negro was under slavery, that was a status plainly recognized by law, which was openly attacked by some and which many respectable Southerners openly defended. But when the Negro had become, in law, a free American, his status as an indelible immigrant became an anachronism as well as an injustice." (From *The Americans: The Democratic Experience*)

The South would not really become united with the rest of the United States until the South itself had become one. And this would take time.

See "Section 3 Review answers," p. 360D.

Section 3 Review

1. Identify or explain: Joint Committee of Fifteen, Command of the Army Act, Tenure of Office Act, impeachment process, Grant, Seymour, scalawags, carpetbaggers, Ku Klux Klan, Civil War amendments.

2. What did the Southern states under military rule have to do to rejoin the Union?

3. What "illegal" act led to Johnson's impeachment? How did the trial turn out?

4. Describe the election of 1868.

5. **Critical Thinking: Recognizing Ideologies.** Why did some white Southerners fight back against Radical Republican rule in their states?

See "Lesson Plan," p. 360E.

4. The North withdraws

In the election of 1872, Grant ran for a second term against Horace Greeley, the candidate of the Democrats and of a new Liberal Republican party. Greeley was the editor of the *New York Tribune.* He was best known for his advice, "Go West, young man, go West!" Right there in New York City, Greeley himself had found it possible to be a pioneer. He had organized the printers on his newspaper into a union. He had stood against slavery and championed women's rights.

But the nation was in no mood for reform. President Grant was easily reelected. Then his troubles began. Although Grant could pick the best lieutenants on the battlefield, in the world of politics he was as gullible as a child. He was an honest man himself, but he could not recognize crooks even when they appeared in his own Cabinet.

The Crédit Mobilier scandal. Soon after Grant's reelection, the first of a string of major government scandals broke. The transcontinental railroad had been authorized by Congress in 1862. The Union Pacific Railroad was to build westward from Omaha while the Central Pacific worked eastward from Sacramento. To build its part, the Union Pacific founded another company named the Crédit Mobilier of America. Using federal funds, the Union Pacific paid the Crédit Mobilier Company huge fees for work done—or not done. The Union Pacific officers, who were also the owners of Crédit Mobilier, made enormous sums from this swindle.

To persuade Congress not to look into the situation too closely, Vice-President Schuyler Colfax, Representative James A. Garfield (later to be President), and several other members of Congress were bribed with Crédit Mobilier stock. All this had taken place, in fact, before Grant became President. But Grant's administration was blackened by the exposures.

Other scandals. The same year of the Crédit Mobilier exposures, 1873, there occurred the notorious "salary grab." Greedy congressmen voted themselves a 50 percent increase in salary. On top of that they made it apply to the two preceding years. They also raised the pay of Supreme Court justices. The President, who signed the bill into law, had his salary doubled from $25,000 to $50,000. Under the Constitution a President's salary may not be increased during the term for which he has been elected. Grant avoided this provision by signing the bill the day before his second term began. The public outcry against the salary grab brought about its repeal—except for the increases for the President and the Supreme Court.

The following year brought the whiskey frauds. A large number of distillers conspired with Treasury officers to avoid the tax on whiskey. They cheated the government out of millions of dollars.

Scandal even reached into Grant's Cabinet. The Secretary of the Navy was shown to have received favors from men who stood to win government contracts. The Secretary of War, W. W. Belknap, was impeached by the House in 1876. He was accused of accepting bribes from a War

More from Boorstin: "Horace Greeley, a leading Whig opponent of the [Mexican] war, noted bitterly that while the United States government somehow had the power to send troops to dash out the brains of Mexican children, . . . it lacked the power to feed the starving." (From *The Americans: The Democratic Experience*)

Department agent charged with providing supplies to the Indians. He was saved from conviction in his trial by the Senate only because Grant was tricked into allowing him to resign.

The panic of 1873. Along with scandal and corruption, the country suffered a severe financial panic. After the war, the rapid growth of railroads and factories had strained the nation's financial resources. Two major fires—in Chicago in 1871 and in Boston the next year—cost insurance companies $273 million, and laid a colossal burden on these pillars of the financial community. The collapse of Jay Cooke's investment firm, which had put too much of its money in railroad construction, began the panic in 1873.

Soon a full-scale depression, one of the worst in the nation's history, was under way. It lasted for five years, shutting down mills and factories, bankrupting railroads, closing banks, bringing unemployment and starvation to thousands of workers, and spreading despair across the country.

The disputed election of 1876. Under this cloud of depression and scandal the Republicans were badly beaten in the congressional elections of 1874. A large majority of Democrats won seats in the House, giving them control for the first time since the Civil War. No longer could the Republicans win elections by "waving the bloody shirt" of war.

In their convention of 1876, the Republicans passed over their "Plumed Knight," the eloquent Speaker of the House James G. Blaine of Maine. He was suspected of granting illegal favors to a railroad, and in the climate of the times this made him an impossible choice. Instead, they picked a little-known Union general, Rutherford B. Hayes, who had built a solid reputation as a reform governor of Ohio. He was an honest man with moderate views on the Southern issue.

The Democrats named Governor Samuel J. Tilden of New York. He had an even more impressive reform record than Hayes, for it was his political courage and cleverness as a lawyer

that had exposed the Tweed Ring. "Boss Tweed," a self-made, warmhearted man, had used Tammany Hall, a clique inside the Democratic party, to become the most powerful politician in New York City. He and his friends stole more than $45 million by having contractors on city jobs charge double what the work actually cost and then having the extra amount paid

Critical Thinking Activity: Distinguishing False from Accurate Images Was President Grant responsible for the scandals of his administration? Have students list the scandals of Grant's administration. Ask students to discuss how responsible they feel Grant was for these scandals. Remind them that Grant was elected largely because of his military heroics and he was not much of a politician. Have students create a political cartoon expressing their viewpoint on Grant's connection to the misdeeds of his administration.

The Boston Fire of 1872 was stopped near the State House, atop Beacon Hill, on the right of this Currier and Ives lithograph.

over to them. Tilden was helped to destroy the Tweed Ring by Thomas Nast, a clever German-born cartoonist. Nast stirred up outrage against Tweed by his drawings in *Harper's Weekly* showing Tweed as a vulture or a fat, rich thief. Nast kept up his attacks even after Tweed offered him $500,000 to stop.

The 1876 election campaign was one of the most bitter in United States history. The Democrats saw a good chance to gain the Presidency for the first time since 1860, and the Republicans fought to retain power. The finale was even more exciting because the electoral votes were so close. Late in the evening of election day it appeared that Tilden had been chosen. He had carried states with 184 votes—only one less

shall, in the presence of the Senate and the House of Representatives, open all the certificates, and the votes shall then be counted." The president of the Senate was a Republican. If he had the right to choose which set of votes he would *count*, as well as "open," he would naturally take the Hayes votes and declare him elected by a vote of 185 to 184. If however, the disputed votes were thrown out, or even one of them counted for Tilden, he would be elected President.

The electoral commission. A few weeks before the date for inaugurating a new President, Congress created a commission of fifteen members—five representatives, five senators, and five members of the Supreme Court—to determine which of the disputed returns should be accepted. The commission included seven Republicans, seven Democrats, and one independent, Justice David Davis of Illinois. But then Davis was elected to the Senate, and a new justice had to be chosen. As there were only Republican members left on the Supreme Court to choose from, the commission was finally made up of eight Republicans and seven Democrats. It was no surprise, when the commission counted the disputed electoral votes, that it split along party lines and announced that Hayes had 185 to Tilden's 184.

The compromise of 1877. The crisis was not yet over. The nation seemed once again on the verge of civil war. Both houses of Congress had to approve the commission's report before a President could take office. Since the Democrats controlled the House of Representatives, they could prevent a Hayes victory. But a group of conservative Southern Democrats there, seeing the chance to use the crisis for their political advantage, had meanwhile been talking with spokesmen for Hayes. For the first time in many years, the politicians were trying the art of compromise.

The upshot was an agreement that these Southerners would break with their party and vote to accept the commission's report. In return, Hayes would grant four favors. (1) The last

October 21, 1871

Harpers Weekly

Boss Tweed's head is a moneybag in this Nast cartoon. Thomas Nast made Tweed's diamond tiepin famous.

than a majority. Hayes had 165. Then came confusion. The three Southern states (South Carolina, Louisiana, and Florida) that were still ruled by Republicans sent in two sets of returns. The Republican set certified that Hayes electors had been chosen. The Democratic set said that a majority of the state votes had been cast for Tilden. Also Oregon had one disputed vote. In all, 20 electoral votes were in question.

There was no provision in the Constitution or any law of Congress for deciding which set of returns was legal. The Constitution simply says (Amendment XII), "The president of the Senate

federal troops would leave the South. This would mean the end of the Radical Republican state governments in Florida, Louisiana, and South Carolina. (2) At least one Southerner would get a post in the Cabinet. (3) Hayes would give conservative Southern Democrats control of part of the local patronage. (4) He would support generous spending for internal improvements in the South.

On March 2, only two days before Inauguration Day, the conservative Southern Democrats voted with the Republicans to approve the commission's report. The Republican Senate of course at once agreed, and the crisis at last was over.

In April 1877, after only a month in office, President Hayes withdrew the last of the federal troops from the South. In May he decorated the graves of the Confederate dead at Chattanooga. But "reconciliation" between the whites of the North and of the South—the end of Reconstruction—only occurred because the North no longer cared to protect the rights of black Southerners.

Tilden had actually won a large majority of the popular votes, and he knew that he had been cheated out of the nation's highest office. But he proved a good patriot and a good sport. He treated the whole matter as settled and retired from politics. When he died in 1886, he left his fortune to found the great New York Public Library.

See "Section 4 Review answers," p. 360E.

Section 4 Review

1. Identify or explain: Horace Greeley, W. W. Belknap, James G. Blaine, Rutherford B. Hayes, Samuel Tilden, Tweed Ring, Thomas Nast, electoral commission.

2. Describe the scandals of the Grant administration.

3. **Critical Thinking: Recognizing Cause and Effect.** What factors led to the panic of 1873? How did it and the scandals affect the 1874 elections?

See "Lesson Plan," p. 360F.

5. The divided South

Peace and reunion had brought an end to slavery. But the roots of slavery ran deep. They reached into every nook and cranny of Southern life.

One of its roots was racism—the belief that one race was naturally better than another. This belief had helped keep slavery alive. At the same time slavery had kept racism alive. Under slavery, nearly all blacks in the South did lowly tasks. Therefore, it was easy for white people to believe that God had meant it that way.

Slavery could be abolished simply by changing laws. But it was much harder to abolish the belief that one race was better than another. Many generations of white Southerners had taught that to their children. After the war, it was still rooted in their minds and hearts.

And after the war it became clearer and clearer that the South was still split into two "nations." Much of the time these two "nations" lived at peace. Some of the time they lived in a nervous truce. Occasionally they were actually at war. Obviously the United States could not be truly united until the races ceased to be divided. And while this was a national problem, at first it belonged largely to the South because most blacks lived there.

Black voting. When Hayes withdrew the federal troops from South Carolina and Louisiana, the last of the Reconstruction governments finally collapsed. (Florida's had already fallen.) This did not mean that throughout the South blacks no longer voted or held office, or that segregation ("Jim Crow") laws suddenly appeared. It took time for the white South to come to a fixed conclusion about the place of blacks in Southern society.

Most white Southerners assumed that blacks were inferior. At the same time, many Old Confederates believed that they had a responsibility to the blacks. They believed that the "superior" white and the "inferior" black could work together to the advantage of both. So there were attempts by conservatives to bring blacks into the Democratic party. Blacks continued to hold

More from Boorstin: "While historians disagree over the extent of residential segregation and Jim Crowism in the South just after the Civil War, the evidence suggests that the most rigid and humiliating forms of Jim Crow segregation did not come to the South until the end of the nineteenth century, and then they were actually imported from the North." (From *The Americans: The Democratic Experience*)

Museum of American Political Life/Photo by Steven Laschever

The political drawing above appeared in *Judge* magazine on July 30, 1892. It shows members of the Ku Klux Klan barring the polls to black voters even though, as the sign behind them says, "The Constitution gives the Negro the right to vote." More devious ways of keeping blacks from voting came later.

political office in both state and nation. There were black members in every Congress but one from 1877 to 1900.

The rise of "Jim Crow" laws. Segregation was practiced in the new public schools of every Southern state except Mississippi and South Carolina from the beginning. But blacks and whites shared trains, hotels, and other public places. Then more and more in the 1880s informal segregation began to appear. At last, with the drive to remove blacks as a political force during the Populist period (p. 646), there also came new segregation laws.

The expression "Jim Crow" to describe the forced segregation of the races originated in a (p. 379) popular old minstrel song. Some white Southerners were shocked by the Jim Crow laws. One

sensible South Carolina editor showed how absurd the whole idea was:

> If there must be Jim Crow cars on the railroads, there should be Jim Crow cars on the street railroads, also on passenger boats. . . . If there are to be Jim Crow cars, moreover, there should be Jim Crow waiting saloons at all stations, and Jim Crow eating houses. . . . There should be Jim Crow sections of the jury box, and a separate Jim Crow dock and witness stand in every court— and a separate Bible for every colored witness to kiss.

The Supreme Court approves "Jim Crow." What this editor ridiculed soon came to pass. And when "Jim Crow" became a reality, surprisingly few in the North or in the federal gov-

✂ Critical Thinking Activity: Distinguishing Fact from Opinion Is forced segregation of races ever appropriate? Have students list arguments used for and against racial segregation in the late 1800s. Ask students to evaluate these arguments and to determine which are based on fact and which are merely opinions. Have students write a "letter to the editor" on the subject of *Jim Crow* laws. Share students' letters and discuss their ideas.

ernment spoke out against it. The Supreme Court, in 1896, in the case of *Plessy* v. *Ferguson* actually approved segregated facilities that were "separate but equal." The majority even argued that if blacks saw this as "a badge of inferiority" it was "solely because the colored race chooses to put that construction upon it." Justice John Marshall Harlan, a Kentuckian, spoke out in a bold dissent. He "regretted that this high tribunal . . . has reached the conclusion that it is competent for a state to regulate the enjoyment by citizens of their rights solely upon the basis of race."

(p. 383)

The problem, of course, was that there really could never be such a thing as "separate but equal" facilities for the two races. When any race was kept apart from another, it was deprived of its equality—which meant its right to be treated like all other citizens. And the slogan became an excuse for providing inferior schools and washrooms and everything else for the race regarded as inferior.

Few blacks received any land after they were freed. Most had no choice but to go to work for whites. Since few whites had any cash after the war—or wanted to spend it if they had any—the system known as sharecropping soon appeared. A black or white family would be given a section of land to cultivate and then allowed to keep a share of whatever they grew while they paid the rest as rent. Ideally, this would have meant that in a good year the sharecropper would have received a share of the extra profits.

In fact, after the Civil War there were few good years. The price of cotton stayed low until 1900. Sharecroppers earned barely enough to stay alive. In bad years they could not even buy groceries. So to feed their families they borrowed from their landlord or from the local storekeeper. The landlord and the storekeeper, in

"The Cotton Pickers," painted in oil by Winslow Homer in 1876, shows an endless field ready for harvesting. Homer tried to capture the true look of outdoor light.

Continuity and Change: Social Change Explain that in 1896, in the case *Plessy* v. *Ferguson*, the Supreme Court ruled that separate facilities for blacks and whites were legal as long as they were "equal." This decision in favor of segregation was used to justify keeping African Americans in inferior schools and other such facilities. In 1954, the Supreme Court unanimously voted in *Brown* v. *Board of Education* to overturn *Plessy* v. *Ferguson*. The Court declared that all American public schools must be integrated, because separate facilities are by definition unequal. (See p. 738.)

Library of Congress

When the Fifteenth Amendment extending the right to vote was ratified, black Americans celebrated.

turn, often had to borrow at high rates of interest. To repay their own debts, they made the sharecropper stop growing food and instead plant a crop that could be sold for cash. In practice this meant cotton. As a result landowner, storekeeper, and sharecropper were all kept in bondage to that piece of land and to that single crop.

The Reconstruction scorecard. Radical Reconstruction had increased white Southerners' fears of blacks. It had also helped to make the Two-Nation South into a One-Party South. When the Old Confederates once again took charge of the Southern states, they had no love for the Republican party. That was the party of Yankees, the party that had made war on the South and had then ruled the South with an army. By controlling the state governments, the Confederate heroes gave new strength to their old Democratic party.

The Radical Republicans had seen the evil of slavery. But they had not seen that the roots of slavery could not be pulled up in a year or two—nor perhaps even in a generation. Still, they

had attempted to deal with the question of the place of blacks in the Southern states. The new, more liberal constitutions that Radical Reconstruction brought to the Southern states actually benefited the poor of both races. They laid the foundation of free public education for whites as well as blacks. Reconstruction gave the blacks a new role in political life—and valuable political experience. It was under Reconstruction that the Fourteenth and Fifteenth amendments were passed. And these would become the bulwark of equal rights.

See "Section 5 Review answers," p. 360F.

Section 5 Review

1. What is racism? How did it continue to split the South into two "nations"?

2. Why was the *Plessy* v. *Ferguson* case important?

3. **Critical Thinking: Recognizing Cause and Effect.** What were "Jim Crow" laws? What effect did they have on Reconstruction-era attempts to protect blacks' rights?

See "Lesson Plan," p. 360F for **Writing Process Activity: Making Comparisons** relating to the lives of African Americans after the Civil War.

Chapter 14 Review

See "Chapter Review answers," p. 360F.

Focusing on Ideas

1. Explain the term "Radical Reconstruction." How did Radical Reconstruction both harm and help Southerners?

2. How were the Reconstruction policies of Congress motivated by a desire for vengeance? How were they motivated by concerns for the rights and welfare of black Southerners? Which policies were motivated by political party ambitions?

3. What elements of Military Reconstruction resembled Lincoln's plan for reconstruction and the Wade-Davis bill?

Taking a Critical Look

1. **Drawing Conclusions.** Was it reasonable for northern leaders to try to exclude the Old Confederate leaders from leadership positions during Reconstruction? Why? How might the exclusion of these former leaders have affected the South?

2. **Making Comparisons.** How was the treatment of black Southerners in 1890 similar to and different from their treatment in 1850?

Your Region in History

1. **Geography.** If you live in a former Confederate state, use an outline map to locate and identify the military district to which your state was assigned.

2. **Culture.** If you live in a former Confederate state, make a time line of important events in Reconstruction history (1865–1877) in your state.

3. **Economics.** How did the panic of 1873 affect businesses in your region? What industries or businesses were especially hard-hit by the depression from 1873 to 1877? What industries or businesses, if any, prospered during these years? Check with your local, regional, or state's Chamber of Commerce.

Historical Facts and Figures

Formulating Hypotheses. Study the map below to help answer the following questions: (a) In which states did it take the white Democrats the longest amount of time to regain control? (b) the shortest? (c) Develop a hypothesis to explain this difference. (d) Does the information in the chapter support your hypothesis?

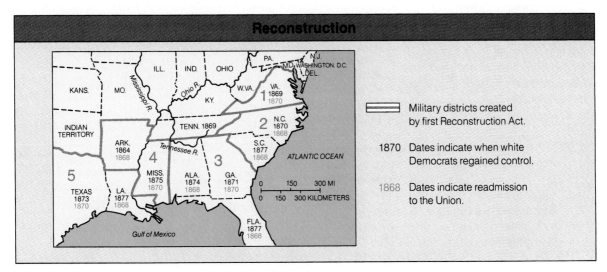

Reconstruction

Military districts created by first Reconstruction Act.

1870 Dates indicate when white Democrats regained control.

1868 Dates indicate readmission to the Union.

Multicultural Connection: Even before *Plessy* v. *Ferguson*, the Supreme Court had already handed down decisions that eroded progress made by African Americans during Reconstruction. In 1876 *U.S.* v. *Cruikshank* and *U.S.* v. *Reese* together implied that voting rights were not necessarily a right of citizenship, that rights to suffrage could come only from the states, and that the Fourteenth Amendment guaranteed civil rights but did not confer additional rights, such as the right to vote.

Chapter 15
The Passing of the Frontier

Identifying Chapter Materials

Objectives	Basic Instructional Materials	Extension Materials
1 Indian Wars and Resettlement • Trace changes in national policy toward the Indians as white settlers moved westward.	**Annotated Teacher's Edition** • Lesson Plans, p. 384C **Instructional Support File** • Pre-Reading Activities, Unit 5, p. 29 • Skill Review Activity, Unit 5, p. 32 • Critical Thinking Activity, Unit 5, p. 34	**Documents of American History** • The Indian Problem, Vol. 1, p. 556 • The Dawes Act, Vol. 1, p. 574 **American History Transparencies** • Geography and History, pp. B31, B33, B35 • Fine Art, p. D33
2 Seeking Gold and Silver • Describe the laws and lawmaking in western mining communities and summarize the significance of mining in our national development. • Identify the sources of supply for minerals to his or her own state.	**Annotated Teacher's Edition** • Lesson Plans, pp. 384C–384D	**Extension Activity** • Mining Songs, Lesson Plans, p. 384D
3 The Cattle Kingdom • Identify the reasons for the long drive of the cowboy era and explain why the open range ended. • Discuss the daily life of the cowboy and contrast this with the romantic images of the cowboy era. • Locate the early cattle trails.	**Annotated Teacher's Edition** • Lesson Plans, pp. 384D–384E **Instructional Support File** • Skill Application Activity, Unit 5, p. 33	**Enrichment Support File** • Life on the Great Plains: The Cattle Kingdom (See "In-Depth Coverage" at right.) **Suggested Secondary Sources** • See chart at right. **American History Transparencies** • Fine Art, p. D49
4 The Farmers' Frontier • Describe the positive and negative aspects of homesteading on the Great Plains and explain population growth on the Plains between 1870 and 1890. • Summarize the consequences of the Homestead Act.	**Annotated Teacher's Edition** • Lesson Plans, p. 384E **Instructional Support File** • Reading Activities, Unit 5, pp. 30–31 • Chapter Test, pp. 35–38 • Additional Test Questions, Unit 5, pp. 39–42 • Unit 5 Test, pp. 43–46	**Documents of American History** • Homestead Act, Vol. 1, p. 410 **American History Transparencies** • Fine Art, p. D53 • Time Lines, p. E19

Providing In-Depth Coverage

Perspectives on the Cattle Kingdom

Chapter 15 provides the basic material about the life of the cowboy, both on the ranches of the Great Plains and on the "long drive." The demand for beef and the extension of the railroads led to the long drive of cattle from Texas to the Mid-West.

Often a former Confederate soldier or a former slave, a cowboy earned about eighty cents for a 15-hour workday. Owning little more than boots, a saddle, and a hat, cowboys signed on with cattlemen for the long drive, and some would eventually work as cowhands on the ranches. They lived off the resources of the West, a land which rewarded people who had vision, self-confidence, courage, and perseverence.

A History of the United States as an instructional program provides two types of resources you can use to offer in-depth coverage of the life of cowboys on the Great Plains: the *student text* and the *Enrichment Support File*. A list of *Suggested Secondary Sources* is also provided. The chart below shows the topics that are covered in each.

THE STUDENT TEXT. Boorstin and Kelley's *A History of the United States* unfolds the chronology of events leading to the rise of the cattle kingdom on the Great Plains.

AMERICAN HISTORY ENRICHMENT SUPPORT FILE. This collection of primary source readings and classroom activities focuses on the lives of those working on ranches and during "the long drive."

SUGGESTED SECONDARY SOURCES. This reference list of readings by well-known historians and other commentators provides an array of perspectives on the cattle kingdom of the nineteenth century.

Locating Instructional Materials

Detailed lesson plans for teaching about life on the Great Plains as a mini-course or to study one or more elements of the cattle kingdom in depth are offered in the following areas: in the *student text*, see individual lesson plans at the beginning of each chapter; in the *Enrichment Support File*, see page 3; for readings beyond the students text, see *Suggested Secondary Sources*.

IN-DEPTH COVERAGE ON THE CATTLE KINGDOM		
Student Text	**Enrichment Support File**	**Suggested Secondary Sources**
• Cattle raising on the Great Plains, pp. 397–398 • Cattle drives, pp. 398–399 • Cow towns, pp. 399–401 • Cattle trails and cow towns, *map*, p. 400 • Cattle ranches, p. 401	• Lesson Suggestions • Multimedia Resources • Overview Essay/Life on the Great Plains: The Cattle Kingdom • Songs in American History/Cowboys Sing of the Lonely Trail • Primary Sources in American History/ Journal of James Bell, Cattle Driver • Art in American History/The Old West and Frederic Remington • Biography in American History/Jesse Chisholm • Geography in American History/The End of the Open Range • Making Connections	• *The Cattle Towns* by Robert Dykstra, pp. 3–73. • *The Chisholm Trail* by Wayne Gard, pp. 125–139. • *The Far West and the Great Plains in Transition, 1859–1900* by Rodman W. Paul, pp.183–219. • *The Great Plains* by Walter Prescott Webb.

Indian Wars and Resettlement

FOCUS

To introduce the lesson, tell the class that when the first Europeans came to the New World, Indians were the only occupants of the land. Today Indians live on a few reservations, and almost all the nation's land is occupied by non-Indians. Ask how this situation came about.

Developing Vocabulary

The words listed in this chapter are essential terms for reading and understanding particular sections of the chapter. The page number after each term indicates the page of its first or most important appearance in the chapter. These terms are defined in the text Glossary (text pages 1000–1011).

frontier (page 385); **reservations** (page 386).

INSTRUCT

Explain

Tell the class that the introduction of the horse by the Spanish explorers and settlers revolutionized Indian culture on the Plains.

★ Independent Activity

Identifying Central Issues Ask students to work independently to make lists identifying the highlights of the Indian policy of the federal government, using these dates as benchmarks: 1820–1850, 1850–1867, 1867–1886, 1887–1934. In one or two paragraphs, ask students to tell how the Indians reacted to these policies.

Section Review Answers

Section 1, page 391

1. a) an American general who had fought in the Civil War and then went west to fight the Indians. b) a general of the 7th U.S. Cavalry who was killed, along with all his men, at the Battle of Little Big Horn. c) invented the six-shooter. d) was one of the Sioux chiefs who led the attack on Custer at Little Big Horn. e) the other Sioux chief who defeated Custer at Little Big Horn. f) the chief of the Nez Percés who led his people on a 1300-mile trek to escape the United States army and reach safety in Canada. g) "Buffalo Bill"—hunted buffalo to provide meat for the railroad crews. h) wrote *A Century of Dishonor* and *Ramona* to dramatize the crimes against the Indians. i) daughter of a Paiute chief, argued the cause of the Indians in her books and lectures. j) attempted to Americanize Indians by dividing tribal land into plots of private property. 2. The Great Plains are shown on the whole of both maps on page 386. The Little Big Horn River is located by the site of the Battle of Little Big Horn on the map on page 388. 3. In 1860 the two western frontiers were, roughly, a line running from Minnesota through Texas and a line running along the edge of the mountains, through western California, Oregon, and Washington. 4. They were very mobile because of their skill on horseback and could fire their weapons (bows and arrows) faster than whites could fire theirs (single-shot rifles). 5. The government's policy in the 1820s was to push the Indians westward across the Mississippi River. Around 1870 the Indians were being confined to smaller reservations, and the government soon stopped dealing with the Indian tribes as independent nations and began considering them wards of the government. In 1887 the Dawes Act attempted to Americanize Indians on reservations by introducing private ownership of land. 6. The buffalo were slaughtered by hunters to provide food for railroad workers and then by sportsmen for fun and by hunters for the profit that could be made selling buffalo hides as robes. The disappearance of the buffalo deprived the Plains Indians of food, shelter, and clothing.

CLOSE

To conclude the lesson, ask: Why did the United States government allow whites to take the Indians' land? How strong were the land claims of Indians and of whites?

Seeking Gold and Silver

FOCUS

To introduce the lesson, ask students to open their texts to page 394. Ask how many students have visited any of the mining towns shown on the map or heard their names. If you are near one of the towns shown, recast the question by asking how many have visited or heard of the towns in another state. Ask how many students have seen movies depicting life in a mining town? Make a list on the chalkboard of the films and another of the images from them that students can recall. Filth, greed, lawlessness, and violence are usually the images that viewers retain from these films. Have students look at the pictures on pages 392–395 and ask: Do the people and towns look like the ones portrayed in the movies? In what ways does the reality differ from the films?

INSTRUCT

Explain

Tell students that frontier towns attracted gamblers, thieves, and murderers, as well as eager miners. At times the usual law enforcement agencies—the U. S. marshal and his deputies—were located many days' ride from the mining community. According to legend, two desperadoes were arrested for murdering a shopkeeper in one of the mining communities. When a mob started to gather the mayor urged calm and patience, but a local merchant named William T. Coleman argued that the people should not leave the matter to the courts. The people had no confidence in the execution of the law by police officers. Instead they organized a court and had the prisoners brought before them. The verdict was to hang them. Thus the first vigilantes on the western frontier began executing swift justice. Other communities quickly accepted Coleman's advice. Many towns even had a favorite hanging tree.

☑ Writing Process Activity

Predicting Consequences Ask students to imagine they are gold or silver prospectors who have headed West in search of their fortune. In preparation for writing a letter home to their families, ask them to freewrite about attempting to find riches and living in the newly formed mining towns. Students should begin with a topic sentence that captures the essence of their experiences, and they should use vivid details to make their activities come alive for those back home. Ask students to revise for logical organization and specific word choice. After proofreading, students can read their letters to the class.

Section Review Answers

Section 2, page 396

1. a) laid out Denver City in the hopes of getting rich by selling land and supplies to miners and other settlers. b) claimed the property on which the Comstock Lode was discovered, but sold it for only $11,000. 2. Pikes Peak is near Leadville and Denver on the map on page 394; its exact location can be seen on the map on page 187. The Black Hills are in the north central region of the map on page 394. Cherry Creek is on the map on page 394. Virginia City is on the map on page 394, in western Nevada. Last Chance Gulch is on the map on page 394. Deadwood is on the map on page 394. 3. It taught Americans about the great mineral wealth of their land, expanded settlement to the last reaches of the West, and provided an impetus for railroads, farmers, and cattle ranchers to follow the miners west. 4. They were made by large companies that had the capital to invest to dig deeper than the earlier miners.

CLOSE

To conclude the lesson, ask: In light of what you have learned about the dangers of vigilante justice, why do you suppose movies about it are so popular? (Provides an easy answer to complicated problems, provides swift and satisfying revenge, lots of action, good and bad sides clearly labeled, etc.)

Extension Activity

To extend the lesson, ask students to write a mining song. Each song should be not less than ten lines long and express the experiences of the miners at that time. Songs such as "Oh Susannah" and "My Darling Clementine" are good examples of mining songs of the period.

Section 3 (pages 396–401)

The Cattle Kingdom

FOCUS

To introduce the lesson, read the following quotation about the cowboy or write it on the chalkboard: "He emerged as a man of functional style, a style that told the world that he was a horseman of the Plains." Ask students to study the painting on page 399 and list what elements made up the cowboy's equipment.

INSTRUCT

Explain

About a third of the cowboys were former slaves and most of the others were former Confederate soldiers.

❧ Cooperative Learning Activity

Making Comparisons Call students' attention to the maps *The Mining Frontier* and *Cattle Trails and Cow Towns* in Chapter 15. Explain that students will combine the information from these two maps to make one map that shows how both mining and cattle changed the frontier. Divide students into pairs and have partners decide how to represent mining and cow towns on their map. Then have partners decide how they will share these tasks: 1) reproducing a map of the United States in the late 1800s 2) preparing the legend and scale of miles 3) showing the settlements. Display completed maps, then allow partners time to evaluate how they worked together.

Section Review Answers

Section 3, page 401

1. a) a Norwegian immigrant professor who described the life of farmers on the Great Plains in his book *Giants in the Earth*. b) made a fortune by selling cattle to miners, travelers, railroad workers, and United

States army troops. c) took the risk of driving cattle from Texas to Wyoming for the chance of selling them at a handsome profit. d) started the cow town of Abilene, Kansas and made a fortune shipping cattle from there to Chicago. e) the movement of a herd of cattle from Texas north to one of the cow towns on the railroads. f) land no one owned where ranchers put their cattle out to graze. 2. Abilene, Dodge City, and Cheyenne appear on the map on page 400. 3. The cattle and mining frontiers mainly attracted men on the move, not men who wanted to settle down with a family. Women who did settle on the farms in the West played the roles of farmer, rancher, parent, teacher, and Indian fighter. 4. Mexicans introduced the practice of raising long-horned cattle on the Plains and developed many of the tools and much of the clothing and vocabulary used by the cowboys. 5. The open range ended because of overgrazing followed by two consecutive bad winters. Farmers also broke up the open range by acquiring and cultivating land that had once been open for grazing. When the open range ended, cattle owners bought land, fenced in their pastures, grew feed for winter, supplied water by well and windmill, and carefully bred and fattened cattle for market.

CLOSE

To conclude the lesson, discuss with students some of the films and television programs they have seen about cowboys. Ask: Considering what the cowboy's life was really like, how did he come to be thought of as such a romantic figure?

Section 4 (pages 401–406)

The Farmers' Frontier

FOCUS

To introduce the lesson, ask: What motivated settlers to apply for a homestead on the Great Plains? If you had been alive in 1862, would you have been likely to take advantage of the free land offered in the Homestead Act? Why or why not?

Developing Vocabulary

territory (page 406)

INSTRUCT

Explain

Life on the Great Plains was hard for settlers. At first the land provided by the Homestead Act was not enough for successful farming, but eventually people learned how to conserve water and soil.

☑ Writing Process Activity

Drawing Conclusions Ask students to imagine they are Eastern farmers who have moved to the Great Plains. In preparation for writing a story about what life was like, ask them to list details about the terrain, weather, living conditions, and so forth. They should decide on a particular conflict to portray. Have students begin their story with a topic sentence that will draw readers into the action. Ask them to revise their story for vivid detail and logical order. After proofreading, students can publish a collection of Great Plains stories.

Section Review Answers

Section 4, page 406

1. a) designed an easy-to-make, easy-to-use type of barbed wire. b) stated that the government would give a settler 160 acres of land if that settler cultivated a part of it and lived on it for at least five years. c) land owned by the public or government. d) a method designed to keep and use the scant moisture in the soil of the Great Plains. e) settlers who claimed land in Oklahoma illegally before the shot was fired at noon on April 22, 1889, to indicate that settlement could begin. 2. Farm families on the Great Plains were faced with a lack of wood for housing and fuel, extremes of weather, little rain during the growing season, prairie fires, plagues of grasshoppers, hard work, and loneliness. 3. The railroads and the Homestead Act attracted settlers to the West. Barbed wire (to keep cattle in or out), windmills (to draw water from deep wells), and mechanized farm equipment (to let one farmer handle enough land to make a farm profitable) helped farmers convert the West from the Great American Desert to one of the most productive agricultural areas in the world.

CLOSE

To conclude the lesson, discuss why, even considering the hardships, the Homestead Act was such a great success. (It motivated hundreds of thousands of immigrants to settle in the West.) Students might be interested to know that homesteading is still possible on government-owned land in Alaska. Ask how many students hope to homestead in Alaska after they finish school. Discuss why students do or (more likely) do not want to. (Life and opportunities are generally too good to risk for such a difficult and dangerous undertaking.)

Chapter Review Answers

Focusing on Ideas

1. In eastern markets the supply of cattle was relatively low presumably because farmers could get the

best return from their land and labor by raising other things besides cattle; demand for beef was relatively high because owners had little money tied up in investment. Demand for beef in Texas was low because the population was sparse; the people there could raise or hunt their own meat supply. 2. (a) By increasing greatly the value of their investment and by freeing capital for use in laying track and buying rolling stock; (b) By making transportation available and agriculture products more marketable; land became more valuable; (c) Contributed to economic growth; transportation, trade; rate discounts for the federal government. 3. It provided food, clothing, shelter, and fuel. 4. On the size, staking, and defense of mining claims; on deciding what was a crime and how it was to be punished; procedures for settling disputes over claims; on town operation.

Taking a Critical Look

1. (a) Easier in the 1830s when western lands were considered unsuitable for settlement. (b) Slower economic development of the West; where development occured on reservations, the tribes could have shared in the rewards. (c) Indian pride enhanced; Indian-white conflict reduced. 2. See map on page 394. Differences: Absence of paved streets, sidewalks, parks, etc.; relative lack of variety of stores, cultural attractions, and service establishments.

Your Region in History

1–3. Answers will vary depending on your region. Consult your local library or historical society.

Historical Facts and Figures

(a) Greatly declined. (b) 1870–1880; (c) 1850–1860; (d) See pages 385–391 for Indian-white conflicts of the late 1800s.

Answers to "Making Connections"

(See "Using Making Connections" on p. 408.)
Answers will vary, but may include one or more of the following examples. Answers based on the time line callouts are in italics.
1. States' rights was an issue that could raise its head without a link to slavery. It had been present at the writing of the Articles of Confederation and the Constitution. It appeared again in the Kentucky and Virginia Resolutions. However, in the mid-1800s, every time the states' rights issue appeared, the question of slavery stood by its side. The Kansas-Nebraska Act in 1854 granted popular sovereignty on the slave question, throwing a bone both to slavery and states' rights supporters. *In late 1860, South Carolina seceded from the Union on the grounds that a state has a right to divorce itself from that union.* However, it was very clear that what had moved South Carolina to secede was Lincoln's firm stand against slavery in

the territories. Lincoln made preservation of the Union his reason for war, but in the minds of many, North and South, slavery was the rub. *With Lincoln's announcement of the Emancipation Proclamation in 1863* it became clear that states' rights was an issue primarily because of what some states claimed to be their right to preserve—slavery. 2. Andrew Johnson had several strikes against him even before he assumed the Presidency. First, he was a Southerner from Tennessee, and an ex-slaveholder at that. Second, Johnson was a Democrat whom Republicans had paired with Lincoln in 1864 to attract votes. Third, Johnson had a personal style that was abrupt and uncompromising, a style not suited for dealing with a Republican Congress that was out for ex-Confederate blood. Once in the Presidency, Johnson quickly made some enemies by refusing Republicans who wanted him to call Congress into immediate session. In 1866 he vetoed the Freedmen's Bureau bill and the Civil Rights bill on the grounds that Congress should leave these matters to local and state authorities. *Congress retaliated in 1867 by overriding Johnson's vetoes of several severe Reconstruction measures.* Had Lincoln survived his second term there is reason to believe that his easy homespun manner would have produced more compromise with Congress and less hostility. However, it was Lincoln's strong intention to make peace with the South as his mild 10% Plan indicated. This would not have pleased Stevens, Sumner, and fellow Radicals in Congress. 3. *When the firing of a gun signaled the opening of Oklahoma Indian Territory to white settlement in 1889,* it also marked the closing of an era. For 40 years, *lured by gold in* California (1849) *and Colorado (1858),* land for the taking, and a vast assortment of other riches, settlers had been pouring west, causing, for example, *the population of Kansas to grow from 364,000 in 1870 to 1.4 million by 1890.* Among the values that fueled this mass migration was a land ownership ethic that collided with the Indian belief that Mother Earth was not ownable. There was also a belief by many settlers that western resources were limitless. This, coupled with the American Dream of making one's fortune, led many Easterners and immigrants to bulldoze their way through Indian reservations, buffalo herds, mining fields, and timber stands. But the newcomers brought with them more than the ethics of Grab. They imported a genius for home-made government, and enough grit to brave the loneliness, the cold, and the dry. They displayed an ingenuity that could turn Nebraska sod into homes, buffalo chips into heat, and *barbed wire into cattle-proof fencing.* Add to this, "dry farming" techniques and creative homesteading laws, and the Great American Desert became the new home for millions of Americans.

Chapter 15

Focusing the Chapter: Have students identify the chapter logo. Discuss what unit theme the logo might symbolize. Then ask students to skim the chapter to identify other illustrations or titles that relate to this theme.

The Passing of the Frontier

By the time of the Civil War, more than two centuries after the first colonist arrived in New England, half the nation's land was still nearly empty. The frontier—a ragged line of settlements from the East—ran through part of Minnesota, along the border of Iowa, Missouri, and Arkansas and then swung westward into Texas. Reaching in from the West Coast there was also a thin line of settlement in California, Oregon, and Washington. Between these two frontiers there were only a few islands of settlers, such as the Mormons in Utah, the miners in Colorado, and the Mexican Americans in New Mexico. Even in the "settled" areas on the edge of the open land, it was often a long way between neighbors.

In that vast open space between the two frontiers there lay an empire. A land as large as all the rest of the occupied United States. A half-known land as large as all of western Europe. It had often been passed through by trappers hunting furs, miners seeking gold, and settlers hurrying on to California, Washington, and Oregon. But the highest mountains were still unclimbed, the swiftest rivers still unmapped.

During and after the Civil War, the American people pushed into the unknown. They settled the land even before it was discovered by the explorers, geographers, painters, and naturalists. And the fact of settlement before discovery allowed Americans to dream big dreams. It fostered an optimistic, competitive, booster spirit. It produced a new kind of American. The Go-Getter out there helped find and develop the riches of the new American empire. New American ways of life were invented by a wide assortment of Go-Getters—cattle ranchers and cowboys, miners, farmers and their families.

Critical Thinking Activity: Drawing Conclusions What did it mean to be a "Go-Getter" on the American frontier? Have students develop a list of criteria to describe the "Go-Getter." Have students match these elements to cattle ranchers, cowhands, miners, and farmers. Divide the class into four groups; ask each group to evaluate their "Go-Getters" based on the criteria established. Have groups present their results by writing a descriptive paragraph on their topic.

Worthington Whittredge was traveling in the West with two friends in 1866 when he painted this scene of "A Wagon Train on the Plains" by the Platte River in Colorado. Whittredge was a member of the Hudson River School—painters who tried to capture the beauty of the American wilderness.

See "Lesson Plan," p. 384C.

1. Indian wars and resettlement

Today the Old West is a place of romance—the scene for an exciting book, or movie, or TV program. But for a long time the West between California and the Missouri River was a place to avoid. Until just before the Civil War the area between the line of settlement in the East and the Rocky Mountains was marked on maps as the "Great American Desert." In 1856 the *North American Review* described the area of plains and mountains between California and Iowa as (p. 386) "a country destined to remain forever an uninhabited waste." Yet this area included some of the richest grasslands in the world. And it was not deserted. Thousands of Indians made their living off the land which was still the home of millions of buffalo.

In time, cattle ranchers, cowboys, miners, farm families, soldiers, and railroad construction crews would all begin to move into or through the Great Plains and the mountains. Then they would come face to face again with the land's first occupants—the Indians.

The Indians of the Great Plains. Spread over the whole inland empire between the frontiers were some 225,000 American Indians. Of these, perhaps half were the fierce occupants of the Great Plains. Seldom have people adapted more perfectly to their environment. The buffalo was the basis of the Indians' way of life. This was the American name for a shaggy kind of ox technically called the bison, which had also once roamed Europe but was no longer common there. It gave them food, clothing, shelter, and fuel.

When Europeans first reached the Great Plains, they had only single-shot long rifles. They were no match for the Plains Indians. Wonderfully at home on horseback, an Indian

Natural Vegetation of the Prairies and the Great Plains

Tall Grass   Forests

Short Grass   Highlands

0   300 Miles

0   300 Kilometers

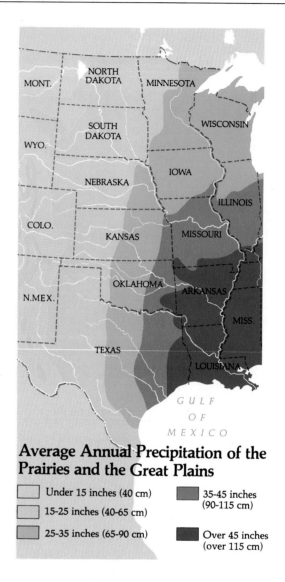

Average Annual Precipitation of the Prairies and the Great Plains

Under 15 inches (40 cm)   35-45 inches (90-115 cm)

15-25 inches (40-65 cm)

25-35 inches (65-90 cm)   Over 45 inches (over 115 cm)

warrior could hold on by his heel and use the horse's body as a shield while he fired a barrage of arrows under his horse's neck. Carrying a short bow, he could shoot twenty arrows while galloping a distance equal to three football fields. His shield of buffalo hide was so hard that a bullet could pass through only if it hit straight on.

Not until Samuel Colt invented the six-shooter—a revolver designed to hold six bullets at a single loading—did the white invader have a weapon equal to the Indians'. Even then, according to General William Tecumseh Sherman,

3000 United States soldiers could be halted by 50 Indians.

The old Indian policy. Beginning in the 1820s the government's policy was to push the eastern Indians westward across the Mississippi River. Let the Indians live on the "Great American Desert"! That would be their "one big reservation." If the land was not good enough for white settlers—or if white settlers did not have the skills to make their living there—leave it to the Indians!

In the 1850s (although they never planned it

⊕ **Geography and History: Regions** Have students look at the maps above to locate the states of the prairies and Great Plains. Point out that experts consider 40 to 45 inches to be an ideal annual rainfall for growing purposes in a temperate climate. These maps can be used again with Section 4, "The Farmers' Frontier," but in this lesson focus on how the Indian culture was adapted to the Great Plains habitat, and why "Great American Desert" was a misnomer.

that way) white men, women, and children began to move into these areas once reserved for Indians. Some settled in Kansas and Nebraska, others moved on to Oregon, and still others went from place to place searching for gold. At first, the army in the West tried only to keep the trails open so that settlers, traders, trappers, and miners could travel across the land. Forts were built across the plains and treaties arranged with Indian tribes. Still the Indians, desperate to stop the invasion of their lands, organized deadly raids on the settlers and their wagon trains.

At the same time, numerous tribes who had lived for centuries on the edge of the plains were persuaded to give up their lands and move west. This stirred discontent among the tribes already there. Times were ripe for war.

Indian wars and a new policy. Although there were some good government agents who wanted to help the Indians, many were inept and some were corrupt. Supplies promised the Indians were often slow to reach them. The Sioux went on the warpath in 1862 because they had not received the regular payments they expected and so were unable to buy food.

The many conflicts of the following years led the government to rethink its Indian policy. In 1865, when there were 25,000 soldiers armed against the Indians, a congressional investigation concluded that a new approach must be found. A Peace Commission sent out west held two large meetings and then signed treaties with the Indians in 1867 and 1868. There the Indians were told that they would be gathered together in large areas that would belong to them and where they were not to be bothered by the whites. Although the Indians did not realize it at the time, these treaties really announced the beginning of the end of the old Indian way of life.

New battles and smaller reservations. The Indians naturally resisted. So for twenty years after the Civil War the American West was plagued by a quite different kind of war. In one sense it was another kind of civil war—between two groups of Americans both trying to make their living off the North American continent, the earliest settlers against the latest settlers.

White Americans did not understand what the Indians had achieved. With their spears and bows and arrows and different manner of

Jules Tavernier, a French immigrant who was for many years an illustrator for *Harper's Weekly*, painted "Indian Camp at Dawn" while on a cross-country trip in the 1870s.

The Thomas Gilcrease Institute of American History and Art, Tulsa

More from Boorstin: "[The Texas settlers'] encounters with the Indians were commonly on horseback. But the skillful Comanche could ride three hundred yards and shoot twenty arrows in the time it took the Texan to reload his firearm once. Even if a Texan went the limit and actually carried two heavy single-shot pistols in addition to his rifle, he still had no more than three shots before he was forced to stop and reload. Anyway, the rifle could not be used effectively from horseback." (From *The Americans: The Democratic Experience*)

living, they had mastered the ways of the American wilderness. The Indians had learned to get along with nature by following in the footsteps of their forefathers. Most of them lived a wandering way of life because they needed large areas to support even a few people. Against them were the latecomers who had brought with them all the modern equipment of European civilization. In this unequal war it was not hard to predict who would win in the long run.

Before the issue was decided, thousands died and more thousands lived in fear while blood and tears were shed on both sides. The wild American West had become a battlefield. In 1864 a militia force under Colonel John M. Chivington slaughtered about 450 Cheyenne and Arapaho men, women, and children who had thought they were under the protection of the United States. Only a few years later, soldiers under Captain W. J. Fetterman were ambushed by a group of Sioux, and all 92 troopers were killed. It was all-out war.

These battles and many others led to a new policy of even smaller "reservations." Here the Indians were too confined and the lands too unfamiliar for them to carry on their hunting and foraging way of life. No longer could they roam the plains in pursuit of the buffalo or other wild game. Deprived of their ancient ways of making a living, the Indians were forced to look to the United States government. In 1871 the government even ceased � dealing with the tribes as independent nations. No more treaties would be made. Now they were considered wards of the state, and they would be dealt with by acts of Congress.

Strangely, the same Congress that was trying to bring equality and integration to the blacks of the South approved the destruction of the Indians. General William T. Sherman, who had done much to free the slaves, now set about either killing the Indians or making them "beg for mercy."

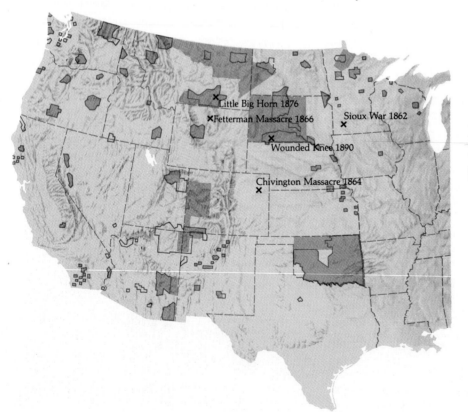

Indian Reservations, 1875 and 1890

▮ Reservations in 1875

▱ Reservations in 1890

⇒ Continuity and Change: Geography Explain to students that in the pre-Columbian era most Plains tribes had lived in nomadic hunter-gatherer societies, taking only what they needed to survive from the plant and animal populations. By the end of the nineteenth century, Europeans had pushed most of the Indians off the Plains, and made it increasingly difficult for these people to continue pursuing their traditional ways of life. For example, the severe depletion of the buffalo population and the confinement of Native Americans to reservations contributed to the destruction of the Plains culture. (See p. 8.)

The defeat of the Indians. The next years were marked by many battles until, in 1874, peace finally seemed to have arrived. Then unexpectedly in the Black Hills (an area which had been given to the Indians "forever") gold was discovered. Hordes of settlers rushed in from East and West. Once again the Indians were crowded out. The fearless Sioux under the leadership of Chief Crazy Horse and Chief Sitting Bull made another desperate effort to hold back the flood. This battle in June 1876 came to be called "Custer's Last Stand," because when General George A. Custer got himself trapped near the Little Big Horn River in Montana he and his 264 troopers from the 7th Cavalry were killed to the last man. But it might more accurately have been called the Sioux's Last Stand, for in other battles Crazy Horse was captured, Sitting Bull fled to Canada, and the desolate Sioux were left conquered and leaderless.

The reservation policy produced a saga of Indian courage in the face of overwhelming odds and certain defeat. As the Nez Percés in Oregon were about to go to a new reservation, some whites stole their horses. This provoked a group of young braves to go on the warpath. Chief Joseph, who had wished all along to avoid a fight, now tried to lead his people to safety in Canada.

There followed one of the great stories of the West. Chief Joseph led his tribe, defended only by their 300 warriors against a well-equipped United States army, on a spectacular 1300-mile trek. On their way across Oregon, Idaho, and Montana the warriors fought a series of amazing battles, regularly defeating much larger army forces. Finally, after several months of marching and fighting, Chief Joseph and his depleted tribe reached a point only 30 miles from the Canadian border. Thinking they were already safe, they paused to rest. Then suddenly a United States army group galloped in from an unexpected direction. After suffering a five-day siege, it was plain to Chief Joseph and his courageous people that they had to surrender. Chief Joseph said,

I am tired of fighting. Our chiefs are killed. Looking-Glass is dead. Too-hul-hut-sote is dead. The old men are all dead. It is the young men now who say "yes" or "no." He who led the young men is dead. It is cold and we have no blankets. The little children are freezing to death. My people, some of them, have run away to the hills and have no blankets, no food. No one knows where they are, perhaps freezing to death. I want to have time to look for my children and see how many of them I can find. Maybe I can find them among the dead. Hear me, my chiefs. My heart is sick and sad. From where the sun now stands I will fight no more, forever.

The final act in the tragedy of the Indian wars came on December 29, 1890, at Wounded Knee (p. 390) in South Dakota. There, shortly after the killing of their famous leader Chief Sitting Bull, a band of men, women, and children was arrested by the 7th Cavalry. Somehow a fight broke out. The soldiers opened fire upon the unarmed Indians and left more than 200 dead.

The sadness of a lost cause creases Chief Joseph's face in this old photograph.

Smithsonian Institution

⊕ Geography and History: Regions Have students locate Oklahoma on the map on page 388. Explain that although Oklahoma was virtually surrounded by populated lands in 1890, only one small portion of Oklahoma itself had been settled. Ask students to explain why most of Oklahoma was still unsettled in 1890. (The map shows that most of Oklahoma was an Indian reservation. This meant that most of the land was only open to settlement by Indians.)

The buffalo slaughter. Whether the Plains Indians won or lost battles did not, in the long run, matter. They were doomed to defeat, not only by the guns of the army and the ever-increasing number of settlers who occupied their land, but most of all by the destruction of their food supply—the buffalo.

At the close of the Civil War the buffalo roaming the Great Plains numbered about 15 million. Sometimes a single herd would spread over 50 miles. The first force to endanger these clumsy, slow-moving beasts was the railroad. It split the herd into a northern and a southern group and at the same time brought hunters into their midst. The most famous of the buffalo hunters was William Cody, better known as "Buffalo Bill." At first he and the other hunters shot the buffalo for meat to feed the large crews of railroad workers. Later, city slickers who went west for adventure and for sport shot thousands from the safety of railroad cars. In 1871 a commercial method was found of treating the skins to make them usable as robes. The slaughter was on. Hunters roamed the range killing every buffalo in sight. The kill finally reached three million a year. The southern herd was gone by 1878, and the northern herd had disappeared by 1884. In 1889 all that was left of the millions of these noble animals was about one thousand.

Indians hunt buffalo on horseback in this 1832 painting of "The Buffalo Chase, Mouth of the Yellowstone" by George Catlin.

National Museum of American Art, Smithsonian Institution, gift of Mrs. Joseph Harrison, Jr.

Multicultural Connection: At this time a new cult developed among several Native American tribes based on a ceremonial dance called the "Ghost Dance." This cult was an attempt by the Native Americans to retain their cultural identity. It was based on the revelations of the prophet-dreamers that soon their dead ancestors would return, all whites would be destroyed, leading to the restoration of Indian lands and traditional ways of life. In 1890 a confrontation between Ghost Dance worshippers and soldiers ended in the deaths of over 200 Sioux at Wounded Knee Creek.

With the animal that supplied their food, clothing, fuel, and shelter gone, the Plains Indians had to give up. These people who knew the plants and animals of the West better than any who came after them were condemned to reservations. Though wonderfully skillful and knowledgeable at wresting their living from the land, they now depended on the charity of the invaders.

Indian policy reform. In the West most settlers saw the Indians only as a menace. But many Americans, especially those raised back east away from the battles, were troubled by the sad plight of the Indians and wondered what they could do to help. Just as 30 years earlier Harriet Beecher Stowe had stirred the nation's conscience for the slave in her book *Uncle Tom's Cabin* (1852), now another eloquent woman awakened white Americans to the sufferings of the Native Americans. Helen Hunt Jackson, who came from Massachusetts before she moved to Colorado Springs, wrote *A Century of Dishonor* (1881) and *Ramona* (1884) to dramatize the crimes against the Indians. Another voice for decency was Sarah Winnemucca, daughter of a Paiute Indian chief. She had shown wonderful courage as "guide, messenger, and interpreter" to General O. O. Howard in the Bannock War of 1878. Now she pled the Indian cause in her popular *Life among the Paiutes, Their Wrongs and Claims* (1883), and drew large crowds to her lectures around the country.

These two women—and other champions of the underdog—demanded that the nation adopt a more humane policy toward the Indians. The Dawes Act of 1887 seemed to have this purpose. In an attempt to "Americanize" the Indians it divided up the reservation land and assigned each family a 160-acre farm. After 25 years these Indians were to receive title to this land and also become United States citizens. The act aimed to break up the tribes and make the Indians behave like all other Americans. Its very purpose was to destroy the Indians' culture. It was not surprising that somehow or other the best reservation lands ended up in the hands of whites. Between 1887 and 1934 the unlucky Indians lost more than half of all their lands.

Not until 1934 and the "Indian New Deal" did the United States government policy change. An attempt was made to rebuild the tribes and their tribal culture. The Native American population then grew rapidly. By 1980 the Indians numbered over 1.3 million—probably more than when Columbus came to America.

See "Section 1 Review answers," p. 384C.

Section 1 Review

1. Identify or explain: W. T. Sherman, George A. Custer, Samuel Colt, Crazy Horse, Sitting Bull, Chief Joseph, William Cody, Helen Hunt Jackson, Sarah Winnemucca, Dawes Act.
2. Locate: the Great Plains, Little Big Horn River.
3. Where were the two western frontiers in 1860?
4. What were the advantages of the Plains Indians as fighters?
5. What was the government's Indian policy in the 1820s? Around 1870? After 1887?
6. **Critical Thinking: Identifying Central Issues.** Why and how were the buffalo slaughtered? How did their disappearance affect the Plains Indians?

See "Lesson Plan," p. 384C.

2. Seeking gold and silver

All the problems of Indian-white relations were complicated by the sudden appearance in the West of thousands of miners seeking their fortune from gold or silver. In much of the West the impatient, foot-loose miner arrived before the cattle rancher or the pioneer farmer.

The mining frontier was one of the most action-packed in our history. The very names of mining towns stir visions of adventure and violence: Tombstone, Deadwood (with Wild Bill Hickok and Calamity Jane), Last Chance Gulch, and Virginia City.

Today the West is covered with the sad remnants of once-booming communities. We call them ghost towns. First came the news that gold had been found. Then came the rush to the spot and the quick appearance of an entire city.

An unknown artist painted this watercolor about 1858 of Pundt & Koenig's general store in Omaha City, Nebraska. Two wagons heading west have stopped for provisions as the would-be prospectors stock up for the next leg of their journey across the Great Plains.

Next, with the gradual petering out of the gold the people departed. They left behind a ghost town or one with only a few occupants. This cycle was often repeated.

From 1858 until about 1880 mining created new communities—all the way from the Sierra Nevada to the Rockies and into the Black Hills of South Dakota. It was mining that attracted the people who created the territories of Colorado (1861), Arizona (1863), Idaho (1863), Montana (1864), and Wyoming (1868). Mining focused the nation's attention—its hopes and its imagination—on the West.

"Pikes Peak or Bust." In 1858, news began to reach the East that gold had been found near what is now Denver. With careless enthusiasm, many workers threw down their tools, painted "Pikes Peak or Bust" on the sides of their wagons (though Pikes Peak was 80 miles south of the find), and headed west. General Sherman reported from Kansas that 25,000 people had

left to go to the new mine fields even before there was any reliable news that there really was gold in Colorado. Many would return "Busted." But a few would make their fortune, though not always from gold.

William Larimer, born and raised in Pennsylvania, had tried his hand at various businesses before he heard that gold had been found at Cherry Creek, Colorado. Without hesitating he set out for the West. Larimer did not intend to make his own fortune by digging or panning for gold. He hoped instead to get rich by laying out a city near the mine fields. Then he would be prepared to sell the land—or anything else—to the thousands who swarmed in from the East. He found the perfect site and claimed it. In February 1859 he was able to write, "I am Denver City."

Very few got rich in the Cherry Creek gold fields, for the gold soon ran out. At first the small miner might make good money—$50 or even a $100 a day—in those early diggings. There were many later gold discoveries in Colorado, but generally the Colorado gold was hard to get at. In the long run, there, as in most other mine sites in the West, only a big company with large capital and elaborate machinery could extract the gold with much profit.

Virginia City. Rumors that there was gold around Virginia City in what is now Nevada began to be heard in 1859 during the "Pikes Peak" gold rush. Miners whose dreams had not come true in Colorado headed for Nevada. Arriving there, they were disappointed to find that the gold was hard to extract because it was mixed with "blue stuff." When someone took the trouble to analyze the blue stuff, each ton was found to contain $1595 in gold—and $4791 in silver! Now, to rival the Cherry Creek gold rush, Virginia City sprouted and prospered with its silver rush. Soon, where nothing had

"Mountainjack and a Wandering Miner," painted in oil by E. Hall Martin in 1850, evokes the majestic grandeur of the Rocky Mountains.

The Oakland Museum. Gift of Concours d'Antiques, Art Guild of the Oakland Museum Association

California State Library

Miners working the California rivers for gold hoped to get rich, but most were lucky if they found a little gold dust.

lot about mining. He used his earnings to buy an old mine on the Comstock Lode. By ingenuity and new equipment he extracted more silver than anyone had thought possible. With these profits he bought other mines that were thought to be worked out. In 1873, using these new methods, he began to mine the amazing "Big Bonanza" from which he would take more than $100 million.

Mackay made his millions from mines that others had given up. He was willing to invest more capital and dig deeper than others. Not many people were as lucky—or as enterprising—as John W. Mackay. Still, in the years after the Civil War thousands of impatient, ambitious, hopeful Americans on the move rushed out to new mines. Mackay's example lured them on. Behind them they left Last Chance Gulch and its Crab City (later Helena, Montana), Boise, Silver City, Centerville, Leadville, and finally, as the dead end of the miner's frontier, Deadwood, South Dakota.

Law in mining fields and towns. The mining towns were wild, but they were not without law. For the miners, like all the people who were on the front edge of America, made their own laws.

We have seen how the people on the *Mayflower* formed a community. And in the same

stood, according to Mark Twain, "Money was as plenty as dust." Newly rich citizens built showy houses where everything seemed to be silver plated. One man even had silver shoes made for his horses.

This rich silver find was called the Comstock Lode. Henry Comstock had not himself made the great discovery, but somehow he managed to claim the property. When he sold the mines, in bits and pieces, he received a total of only $11,000.

To extract great wealth from the mines required the energy and organizing ability that Comstock lacked. The person who had those talents, and was lucky enough to be on the spot, was John W. Mackay. He was a poor Irish boy whose parents had brought him to this country when he was nine. Eleven years later, in 1851, he decided to seek his fortune in the California gold fields. Mackay worked in various gold and silver fields, making little money but learning a

The Mining Frontier

- Gold-mining
- Silver-mining

Geography and History: Place Refer students to the map above. How did the discovery of valuable minerals affect the Indians? Have students locate each mining site on the map. Ask students to draw conclusions about concerns miners and Indians might have had when mining sites overlapped Indian territories or reservations (e.g., the Black Hills were mined although they were sacred lands to the Sioux).

Life in a western mining town was not easy, as this photograph of Helena, Montana, clearly shows. When it rained or snowed, the dirt of the streets turned to mud. Long skirts were not helpful.

way each wave of men and women who moved west into places that had no organized government had to make their own rules. In the mine fields and mining towns laws had to be made about the size, staking, and defense of mining claims. Where there was still no government, the first comers had to decide what was a crime and how it was to be punished.

These laws seemed so natural, following the traditions and customs of the mines, that many miners thought they actually did not have any law. When Congress passed its first major Mining Act in 1866, it enacted the rules that had been adopted by the miners themselves.

The significance of the mining frontier. The mining frontier, the first of the last frontiers, opened up the country from the Rocky Mountains to the Sierra Nevada. It taught Americans something of the natural wealth of this continental heartland. The finding and the getting of copper, iron ore, lead, zinc, coal, molybdenum, uranium, and oil were all still to come. The mines and the miners out there created new needs for railways. And by quickening the invasions of Indian lands they brought the Indian problem to a head. In some areas, especially in Idaho and Montana, the mining frontier opened up a new farming frontier because, when the gold ran out, miners remained to work the land. And, of course, mining towns demanded meat and so stimulated the cattle business.

Between 1860 and 1900 the mining frontier produced more than $2 billion in gold and silver. Much of this went into the pockets of people who had never before seen so much money. (p. 396)

See "Lesson Plan," p. 384D for **Writing Process Activity: Predicting Consequences** relating to the experiences of prospectors living in the new mining towns.

The quick-paced life of the mining West, so full of surprises, left a wonderful legacy of folklore—and the stories of Mark Twain and Bret Harte.

See "Section 2 Review answers," p. 384D.

Section 2 Review

1. Identify: William Larimer, Henry Comstock.
2. Locate: Pikes Peak, Black Hills, Cherry Creek, Virginia City, Last Chance Gulch, Deadwood.
3. How was the mining frontier significant?
4. **Critical Thinking: Making Comparisons.** How did later mining ventures differ from the earlier ones?

See "Lesson Plan," p. 384D.

3. The cattle kingdom

While the miners were opening up the mountains and the land of the Great Basin between the Rockies and the Sierra Nevada, cattle ranchers were opening up the Great Plains. At the same time, the Indians were forced onto smaller and ever less desirable reservations and the buffalo were killed off.

The cattle frontier and the mining frontier mainly attracted men. Cowboys driving herds or riding the range, miners chasing from one spot to another after gold, soldiers pursuing Indians—all these were men on the move who had not the time or the opportunity to settle down to family life. A few hardy women did live on the lonely ranches, in the mining towns, or at the army forts, but they were far outnumbered by the migratory men.

Only as families began to settle the plains and cultivate farms did this situation change. The farming West, too, was a difficult and often frightening place for man, woman, and child. We can still share their troubles and their delights in the great novel *Giants in the Earth* by the Norwegian immigrant Ole Rölvaag, who helped build the Scandinavian community as a professor at St. Olaf College in Minnesota. Rölvaag described a new settler viewing the treeless plains where she must make her home: "How will human beings be able to endure this place, she thought. Why, there isn't even a thing that one can *hide behind*."

To survive and build a family on the Great Plains, a woman had to be many things. She

"One Sunday in July, Forbestown, California" was painted by an amateur artist about 1850.

The Oakland Museum

More from Boorstin: "Nevada silver was not the hard-won reward of penniless prospectors but the loot which wealthy bankers and businessmen, mostly from San Francisco, systematically drained from Nevada mines. In the twenty years after 1859, about $500 million in silver and gold was extracted. From the time of its discovery until the mid-1800's, the Lode was producing annually about half the silver being mined in the United States." (From *The Americans: The Democratic Experience*)

By the 1890s, when this picture of women branding was taken on the Fritz Becker ranch in southeast Colorado, cattle ranching had become a family enterprise.

had to be a soldier holding off Indians, a farmer and a rancher, a parent and a teacher. Without women's courage and their efforts the vast open West might never have grown its permanent settlements. It is not surprising, then, that in 1869 Wyoming Territory became the first place in the nation to give women the vote and that western states were among the first to elect women governors.

Cattle and cowboys. About the time of the Civil War, the western cattle trade became big business. The men who made money from it were as different as possible from the European peasant who kept his few cattle at night in the room where he slept. The peasant could keep only a few because his house was small and he had to feed his animals by hand in winter.

The western cattleman numbered his stock by the thousands. He did not have to give them a roof, for western cattle were tough enough to look after themselves on the range. And on the great western plains there grew "buffalo grass" which survived drought and provided free food right on the ground throughout the winter.

Raising cattle on the northern plains. Western cattlemen were bold and adventurous, willing to take big risks in a wild country. One of the first and most energetic of these Go-Getters on horseback was John Wesley Iliff. Though his parents offered to set him up on a farm in Ohio, Iliff wanted to go west to seek his fortune. He did not find gold in the Colorado mountain streams. But he did find it in the cattle that came there with Americans pushing westward.

Iliff bought oxen from the people seeking gold who wanted to lighten their load before they headed up into the mountains. In Colorado he fed these cattle free on the open range that belonged to nobody and to everybody. He also bred more cattle. When his animals were fattened, Iliff sold them to butchers in the mining camps, to travelers returning east who needed oxen to pull their wagons, or to the government to feed the army and the Indians on the reservations.

Critical Thinking Activity: Synthesizing Information What was life like on the long drive? Remind students that cowhands often sang to their herd to prevent a stampede. From these songs we are given a glimpse of the cowhand's life. Have students write their own song describing life on the long drive. Suggest to the students that they can use a tune from a familiar song and supply their own words. Have students share their work.

When railroads—promoted by eastern Go-Getters—pushed west, they opened another new market. Now western beef could be shipped to the growing eastern cities. At the same time, hard-working crews building the railroads had to be well fed, and what they most wanted was meat. Iliff agreed to deliver cattle by the thousands to the Union Pacific Railroad construction gangs and to the United States troops guarding them against the Indians.

This was easier said than done. He had to find more beef than anyone had ever yet seen in one place. And he had to bring it to the middle of nowhere, where railroads were still to be built.

Iliff was helped by still another brand of Go-Getter, the western trailblazer. In 1868 a remarkable man with the unlikely name of Charles Goodnight agreed to deliver to Iliff's camp near Cheyenne, Wyoming, $40,000 worth of cattle from Texas.

To get the cattle from Texas to Wyoming, Goodnight had to find his own way over some of the driest and most unfriendly land in the whole continent—what maps before the Civil War called the "Great American Desert." It was a risky business, but it seemed worth trying when a steer, bought for $4 in Texas, sold for $40 in Wyoming. Multiply that by 3000 (the number of cattle Goodnight hoped to take on each trip), and it added up to a handsome profit. Goodnight succeeded because of the skills of Texas cowboys and the nature of long-horned cattle.

Texas longhorns. When Americans had come to Texas in the 1820s, thousands of long-horned cattle were running wild. These were the descendants of a few animals brought over by Spanish explorers. The first cattle raising on the plains was started by Mexicans whose herds flourished on the rich grass. When later Americans arrived, they learned many things and borrowed much of their way of life from the Mexicans already there. These included the Mexican saddle, the lariat, along with the chaps, boots, spurs, and big hat, all suited for the rough life of the range. Many of the new words they used—"sombrero," "rodeo," "lariat," and "chaps"

(*chaparajos*)—were borrowed from Mexico, too. The six-gun was also part of their outfit. All these things which made the cowboy picturesque to others were only his working weapons, clothes, and tools.

The cowboys' work was risky. The long-horned cattle of Texas, it was said, were "fifty times more dangerous than the fiercest buffalo." Armed with sharp horns which sometimes spread as much as eight feet from tip to tip, these bold beasts could not be managed by workers on foot. The longhorns made the Texas cowboy get on his horse, and they kept him there.

The long drive. The Texas longhorns were well equipped for long trips. Their sense of smell, the cowboys said, was as much superior to that of an ordinary eastern cow as the blood-hound's was to that of a parlor poodle. Where water was hard to find, the longhorn's nose for water could make the difference between life and death.

The real problem was how to keep all those 3000 cattle together and moving at just the right speed. If they were allowed to stop or dawdle, they might never reach their goal. But if they were allowed to trot, they might get out of control or exercise off the weight that was worth money in Wyoming. Even with no problems and the cattle moving smoothly it would take from two to four months to reach their destination.

The crews who drove the cattle usually were made up of sixteen or eighteen cowboys for a herd of 3000. They were led by a trail captain. There was also a cook driving a chuck wagon and a boy to take care of the eight or ten horses needed for each man. Often a few of the cowboys were freed slaves.

Stationed at the front, or "point," of the herd were two of the most experienced men, called "pointers." They navigated for the whole herd, following the course set ahead by the foreman. Bringing up the rear were three steady cowboys whose job it was to look out for the weaker cattle—the "drags." To prevent the herd from straggling out for miles, the whole party moved no faster than the weakest "drags" at the rear. The rest of the cowboys were stationed along

Enrichment Support File Topic

More from Boorstin: "The Longhorn's skill at finding food became a legend. . . . He had a remarkable ability to graze *up*. There was the apocryphal story of the dry cowhide (with bones inside) seen hanging high up in a tree. 'Great browsers, those cattle of mine,' the owner is supposed to have explained. 'Spring of the year, and that old Longhorn clumb the elm like a squirrel to eat the buds, and jest accidentally hung himself.'" (From *The Americans: The Democratic Experience*)

the sides to keep the herd compact and all the same width.

Communication between the front and rear of the herd was difficult. The rumbling of hoofs smothered words. The cowboys, then, borrowed a clever system of hand signals from the Plains Indians.

Apart from Indian raids, the greatest peril was a stampede. The cowboys sang to the herd at night to try to keep it calm. But suddenly a quietly dozing herd might rouse into a thundering mass. To stop a stampede, experienced cowboys on their horses drove the cattle in a circle, always round to the right. Then by tightening their circle they squeezed the stampeding cattle tighter and tighter together till they had no place to run. The milling herd was forced to halt.

If the encircling tactic failed, all was lost. The stampede would get out of control. Then the cattle would fly out like sparks into the night, and they might never be seen again.

The cow town. At the end of the long drive came the "cow town," which was as American as the cowboy. It was simply another smaller kind of "instant city" like those already dotted over the West. The cow town was where cowboys delivered their herd to the cattle dealers and the railroads. There, after long lonely weeks on the trail, cowboys enjoyed the company of strangers, bought liquor, and gambled away their money.

Go-Getting cattlemen made these instant towns prosper. One cattleman, Joseph G. McCoy, picked a place along the Kansas Pacific

Frederic Remington won fame for his paintings, illustrations, and sculptures of the "Wild West." He painted "The Stampede" in 1908.

The Thomas Gilcrease Institute of American History and Art, Tulsa

Multicultural Connection: Between 3,000 and 5,000 African-American cowboys worked in Texas during this period. Among these cowboys were Henry Beckwith, one of the best cow handlers of the time; Bill Williams, who developed a bronco-busting technique admired and copied by Teddy Roosevelt; Bose Ikard, who helped blaze the Goodnight-Loving cattle trail; and Bill Pickett and Henry Clay, who won fame as part of the 101 Ranch Wild West Show, performing their steer-wrestling feats and rope tricks around the world.

Cattle Trails and Cow Towns

▨ Original Home Range of Texas Longhorn

▢ Range and Ranch Cattle Area

500 Miles

500 Kilometers

GULF OF MEXICO

⊕ Railroad. In 1867, when he first made his plans for Abilene, it was a village of about a dozen log huts with sod roofs.

It was not much of a town, but there was open land around it and plenty of good grass and water for the cattle. So McCoy bought the whole town for $2400 and quickly built a shipping yard, a big barn, and a three-story hotel. It was all finished in 60 days, and by September 1867 the first shipment (twenty carloads of cattle) left Abilene for Chicago. Soon Abilene was sending thousands of cattle east, and the town was booming. McCoy was offered more for a single city lot than he had paid for the whole town. And before the end of the second year the Kansas Pacific owed him $250,000 in commissions for the cattle shipped.

Other prosperous cow towns followed Abilene. There were Schuyler, Fort Kearney, North Platte, Ogallala, and Sidney in Nebraska. In

(p. 399)

⊕ **Geography and History: Movement** Have students answer the following questions, using the map above and the text on pages 398–399. About how many miles was the drive along the Western Trail from Bandera to Ogallala? (Between 1300 and 1400 miles.) From San Antonio to Ellsworth along the Chisholm Trail? (Around 1000 miles.) If a herd averaged 10 miles a day along the Chisholm Trail, how long did the trip from Austin to Abilene take? (About 100 days.) About how many horses were needed for this trip? (Between 128 and 180—eight to ten for each of sixteen or eighteen cowhands.)

Wyoming there were Pine Bluffs, Rock River, Rock Creek, Laramie, Hillsdale, and Cheyenne. Montana had Miles City, Glendive, and Helena.

The cow towns did not suffer from modesty. More than one boasted she was the "Queen of Cow Towns." Dodge City, in Kansas, and others competed for the title of the "Wickedest Little City in America."

Western cattlemen and cowboys were among the first and bravest of the Go-Getters. They tried the impossible and succeeded in making something from nothing. They captured wild cattle which belonged to nobody. Then they fed the cattle on the free open range on buffalo grass which nobody had even imagined could be food. And finally they transported the cattle on their very own feet for thousands of miles to places where they could become beef.

Who could have imagined that the "Great American Desert" would become the greatest beef factory in the world?

The end of the open range. The success of the ranchers was also their ruin. Everyone wanted to invest in cattle. As more and more ranches were started, more and more cattle were put out to feed on the range. In 1885, there came a hard winter, followed by a dry summer. This destroyed some of the grass and weakened the cattle. Then another bad winter in 1886 wiped out whole herds.

At the same time that cattle ranches were multiplying, farm families were pushing in, trying another way to make their living on the Great Plains. To protect their cattle the ranchers had been stretching miles of fence—even around land that they did not own. The newly arrived farmers had gone to great trouble to secure legal ownership of the lands they settled. Naturally enough they demanded government help against the high-handed ranchers.

All these forces—too many cattle, bad weather, farmers, and government intervention—would bring an end to the cattle kingdom of the open range. As farmers moved in, the ranchers could no longer graze their cattle free on the public lands. Now ranchers had to develop new methods. They actually had to buy their grazing land. Pastures were divided up

and fenced. Better cattle were bred. Food was grown for winter feed. Water was supplied by well and windmill so that cattle would not have to walk far and lose weight. The cowboy became a cowhand working year-round and round the clock. No longer could he, as one recalled, "sit around the fire the winter through" doing no work "except to chop a little wood to build a fire to keep warm by."

Some people specialized in breeding cattle, others in fattening them for market. Cattle raising became a scientific business. It was no longer the wild, romantic adventure it once had seemed. The day of the cattle kingdom was gone. The new era belonged to the ranch hand and the farmer.

See "Section 3 Review answers," p. 384D.

Section 3 Review

1. Identify or explain: Ole Rölvaag, John W. Iliff, Charles Goodnight, Joseph G. McCoy, long drive, open range.
2. Locate: Abilene, Dodge City, Cheyenne.
3. Why were women a small minority on the cattle and mining frontiers? What roles did women play in the development of the West?
4. How did Mexicans influence the cattle frontier?
5. **Critical Thinking: Drawing Conclusions.** What forces brought an end to cattle raising on the open range? How did cattle raising change thereafter?

See "Lesson Plan," p. 384E.

4. The farmers' frontier

The American farmer and his family had avoided the Great Plains. It was a strange place, and at first they did not like it. They were accustomed to the wooded lands of the East. Some had become acquainted with the flat prairies that stretched from Illinois to Iowa and from Canada to Texas—land known for its rich soil, regular rainfall, and tall grass. But the Great Plains were different. Out there, trees were rare. The grass was short. Worst of all, there was very little rain. It is not surprising, then, that for

See "Lesson Plan," p. 384D for **Cooperative Learning Activity: Making Comparisons** relating to how mining and cattle affected the frontier.

The Jerns family posed on their farm in Dry Valley, Nebraska, in 1886. By that time they had all the necessities for living on the plains. They had built several sod houses, erected a windmill, and strung barbed wire to keep their cattle from wandering away.

a while the farmer had gladly left the West to others.

Problem on the farmers' frontier. When finally farmers decided to move onto the plains, they faced new problems. Since there was no wood for houses, they had to learn to make houses of sod. To their astonishment they found that sod houses could be warm and cozy in winter, cool in summer. These did not blow down in high winds. And they were wonderfully fireproof, which was welcome protection against the prairie fires that threatened the Great Plains. But these sod houses were dark, and the ceilings dripped with rain. The old

familiar wooden buildings had a lot to be said for them. Nearly every pioneer family looked forward to the day when it could build a frame house.

Whether in sod houses or frame houses, every farm family needed fuel for their fireplaces to cook food and to keep warm in the bitter winters. At first buffalo chips (dry manure) could be used, but soon the buffalo were gone. Then, at one time or another they tried everything in sight—cow manure, sunflower stalks, and hay. Until the railroads came carrying coal, nothing was quite satisfactory.

Then the weather offered new problems, for it ⚑ brought only extremes. In the spring there were

⚑ **Continuity and Change: Geography** The nature of the Great Plains has often made life there tenuous and unpredictable. During initial settlement of the Great Plains in the late 1800s, farmers managed to survive and raise crops despite freezing winters, blazing summers, fires, floods, and plagues of insects. In the 1920s, rain was abundant, and farmers plowed more of the land. Unfortunately, this threatened farm life once more during the Great Depression. With few living roots left to hold the soil in place, wind swirled clouds of dust into the sky, creating one large "Dust Bowl" in the heart of the United States. (See page 643.)

floods, in the summer searing heat, in the winter raging blizzards and sub-zero cold. And there were occasional prairie fires, started by lightning, which destroyed everything. Sometimes grasshoppers blackened the sky in countless numbers and in a few hours ate a whole year's crops. One very hot summer 30,000 people abandoned the Great Plains for places where life was easier. One refugee wrote on the side of his wagon that he was returning "From Kansas, where it rains grasshoppers, fire, and destruction."

Getting a farm. It has been said that civilization approached the Great Plains on three legs—water, wood, and land. But on the Great Plains only land could be found in abundance.

The railroads helped to make life easier by bringing in coal and other supplies and taking crops out to market. In addition, they encouraged settlers to come to the West. For the railroads had land to sell. To persuade the railroad companies to lay their tracks across the empty lands of the West, the state and federal governments gave them wide strips of land along the tracks. So every time these companies sold a piece of land and brought out a new family of settlers, they created customers for their railroads.

At the same time, there was free land for the asking all over the West. In 1862 President Lincoln had signed the Homestead Act, which offered everybody who could get there the chance to be a landowner. To the European peasant it must have seemed a dream. The whole American West was begging for people. All you had to do was come. You only needed to be 21 years of age and to say that you intended to become a

It took lots of wood to build the balloon-frame houses of the nation's fast-growing cities. This photograph was taken in 1892 of a special train loaded with lumber for Omaha, Nebraska.

State Historical Society of Wisconsin

Critical Thinking Activity: Distinguishing False from Accurate Images What was farm life like in the West? Have students examine the photograph opposite and make a list of the picture's details. Discuss the picture, asking students to evaluate how representative this photo is of all farms in the West. Tell students to use this information to write a descriptive paragraph about farm life out West, in the late 1800s. Have students share their work in class.

citizen. Then you picked a 160-acre plot of "homestead" land somewhere on the vast public domain which belonged to the United States government. If you simply lived on it and cultivated a part, then the whole 160 acres would be yours at the end of five years. You paid nothing but a small registration fee.

This was an Old World dream come true. Everyone a landowner!

But the "free" land was not really as free as it seemed. In the western plains, where most of the best homesteads were found, it cost labor and money to make wild land into a farm. Before anything could be planted, the ground had to be broken. The prairie grass had roots that grew in thick mats, unlike anything known in Europe. The familiar Old World plow would not cut through but was quickly twisted by the heavy sod. It was slow work to plow up enough land to support a family, and it was expensive to hire a worker with the right tools to do the job.

Then you needed to find water. Where streams and springs were rare, the only answer was to dig a well. And to pump up the water, you had to build a windmill. On the treeless plains you had to buy the lumber for your house. Posts and barbed wire for fencing had to be brought from great distances. All this added up. You needed about $1000 to make your homestead livable. That was a big fortune for a landless peasant.

Still, if you were healthy, and willing to work year-round, and not afraid to spend a few winters in a crude sod house, you might manage. The Homestead Act allowed you to be away from your land for six months each year without losing your claim. Some energetic homesteaders used this time to earn money by working as lumberjacks in the pine forests of Minnesota, Wisconsin, and Michigan. Others helped to build the short "feeder" railroads that branched off through the countryside. Or they worked as farm laborers.

The railroads, of course, tried to persuade people to come. They sent agents to Europe to tell them about the wonderful lands along their tracks. Their agents helped with information and loans. Sometimes the railroads actually provided newcomers with a house while they were getting settled.

Often the railroad builders were granted the best lands in the West. And, anyway, once the railroads were built, the land nearest the tracks—since there were no automobiles and few roads—would be the most valuable. While railroad lands sold at higher prices, they were usually much more attractive than the more remote lands left over for distribution under the Homestead Act. In addition, in the arid West 160 acres could not support a family, so more land had to be bought somehow.

Fencing the Great Plains. Neither the railroad nor the Homestead Act was enough to bring settlement. Pioneer farming could not really come to the Great Plains until the land could be fenced to keep out the cattle. There was no wood for fences, so various methods, such as the thorny, fast-growing "Osage orange" hedges, were tried to provide an inexpensive natural fence. But you had to wait some seasons till the hedges grew, and they were never quite tight enough. Then in the early 1870s, the answer was found in barbed wire. People tried all kinds of outlandish designs. There are still examples of at least 100 different kinds of barbed wire which show us how hard the inventors tried. As was true with other important discoveries, several people seem to have come up with the right idea at the same time. The most successful of these was an Illinois farmer, Joseph G. Glidden. He designed a wire that could be easily manufactured, was durable, and not too hard to string on posts. By 1875 he was making his fortune selling this new product. And by 1883 one company alone was turning out 600 miles of barbed wire a day!

Water and "dry farming." Of course fences did not solve all the farmers' problems. They still needed water. Even today the lack of water plagues farmers on the Great Plains.

The water under the plains could be reached only by deep wells. When drilling for oil, people learned to dig deep for water, too. To bring up the water that their steam engines needed, the railroad companies used windmills. The

More from Boorstin: "[O]ne day in 1835 [Jonathan] Turner heard from an itinerant preacher about a thorny plant, the Osage Orange, that grew on the banks of the Osage River in Arkansas. He secured a few plants and seeds, and so found the solution to the Illinois farmers' fencing problem. . . . Some called the professor's fantastic fence 'Turner's Folly,' but his business prospered. . . . Turner's success with the Osage Orange persuaded him that future generations of farmers needed a new kind of 'higher learning.'" (From *The Americans: The Democratic Experience*)

ranchers, and soon after them the farmers, followed their example.

The first windmills could supply only enough water for family use or for the stock. Irrigation of the fields was not possible. New methods of farming that preserved the scanty rainwater had to be developed to raise crops on the Great Plains.

"Dry farming," this was called. Developed by the Mormons in Utah, it was a way of keeping and using the moisture already in the soil. First the land was plowed deep to increase its ability to hold water. Then the topsoil was firmed so the moisture below could not escape. After every rain the farmer stirred the surface to keep a blanket of soil over the moisture in the ground.

This system needed a large area and big machines. It required the tractors, harrows, disks, and cultivators turned out in large numbers by factories after the Industrial Revolution. Now farming, like mining and ranching, had become big business.

(p. 406)

The growth of the West. Spurred by the discovery of gold, the open land, the Homestead Act, the railroads, and the flood of immigrants from Europe, the settlers in the West multiplied. Kansas had a population of 364,000 in 1870; it reached 1,428,000 by 1890. In those twenty years Nebraska grew from 123,000 to 1,063,000; Dakota Territory from 2000 to 540,000.

Senator Peffer of Kansas noted in the *Forum* of December 1889 that "a territory greater than the original area of the United States was peopled in half a dozen years." Kansas became a state in 1861, Nevada in 1864, and Nebraska in 1867. These were followed by Colorado in 1876, North and South Dakota, Montana, and Washington all in 1889, and Idaho and Wyoming in 1890. And new territories were established: Arizona in 1863 and Oklahoma in 1890. Each of these would become a new state before many decades had passed.

Oklahoma had been set aside for the Five Civilized Tribes. In 1834 these unfortunate Indians—the Cherokees, Chickasaws, Choctaws, Creeks, and Seminoles—had been forced to move there from their ancestral lands in the

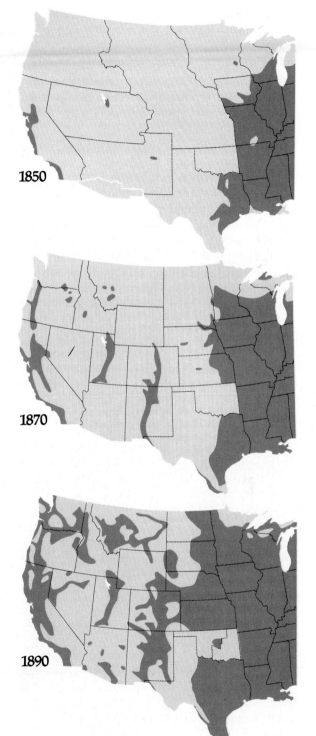

1850

1870

1890

The Vanishing Western Frontier

Settled Area (2 or more people per square mile)

Geography and History: Interaction Have students look at the maps. Ask: In 1850, which five states marked the eastern edge of the frontier—the line where civilization ended and unsettled land began? (The frontier line ran through Wisconsin, Iowa, the western border of Missouri, the western border of Arkansas, and eastern Texas.) Point out that on both the 1850 map and the 1870 map, areas of the North and West were still unsettled. Ask why settlers would be slow to move to the far northern United States. (Because of climate extremes, and inaccessibility to railroads before the 1880s.)

Southeast. At first when white "Boomers," as they were called, illegally entered Oklahoma Indian Territory, the army sent them away. When the pressure of new white settlers became too great, the government purchased some Indian lands and announced that on April 22, 1889, this land would be opened to homesteaders.

At noon a shot was fired, and thousands of hopeful homesteaders who had been held back by troopers rushed across the border for the new land. When they arrived, they were astonished and disappointed to find that the lands were already occupied by illegal settlers who were "Sooner." These had eluded the army guards and staked their claims ahead of time, leaving the law-abiding land seekers behind. Ever since then the people of Oklahoma have jokingly called themselves "Sooners." The sooner and later comers by the evening of that first day numbered 10,000 in Oklahoma City and 15,000 in Guthrie.

The next frontiers would be in cities, in factories, and in shops all over America.

See "Section 4 Review answers," p. 384E.

Section 4 Review

1. Identify or explain: Joseph Glidden, Homestead Act, public domain, dry farming, "Sooners."

2. Describe the hardships facing pioneer farm families on the Great Plains.

3. **Critical Thinking: Recognizing Cause and Effect.** How did each of the following influence the development of the farming frontier: railroads, the Homestead Act, barbed wire, windmills, mechanized farm equipment?

These campers are awaiting the signal to join the Oklahoma land rush in 1889.

Western History Collections, University of Oklahoma Library, Norman

See "Lesson Plan," p. 384E for **Writing Process Activity: Drawing Conclusions** relating to settlers on the Great Plains.

Chapter 15 Review

See "Chapter Review answers," p. 384E.

Focusing on Ideas

1. Why was the price of cattle in the 1860s ten times higher in eastern markets than in Texas? List the factors that influenced supply and demand in both markets.

2. How did railroad land grants benefit railroad stockholders? pioneer farmers and ranchers? the nation?

3. In what specific ways were the buffalo important to the Plains Indians?

4. Describe the laws necessary to maintain order in a mining town.

Taking a Critical Look

1. **Predicting Consequences.** Look at the map of Indian reservations on page 388. Suppose that five or ten times as much land had been set aside for Indians. In which decade—the 1830s or 1870s—would such a policy have been easier to adopt? Why? How might such an Indian-land policy have affected our national economic development? Social development?

2. **Making Comparisons.** Identify three mining boom towns in the 1870s and 1880s. As a traveler at that time, what differences would you see from towns of a similar size on the East Coast?

Your Region in History

1. **Geography.** Using an outline map of your region mark the cattle trails and/or wagon train trails that passed through your area. What cities do these trails pass through? Label them.

2. **Culture.** During what period of history was your locality a part of the American or Spanish frontier? How was frontier life in your locality similar to and different from life on one of the frontiers described in this chapter?

3. **Economics.** To what extent, if at all, has mining influenced the development of your state? What industries now use or have used the resources of these mines?

Historical Facts and Figures

Recognizing Cause and Effect. Study the chart below to help answer the following questions: (a) What was the overall trend of the Indian population between 1850 and 1900? (b) Which decade saw the smallest decline in the Indian population? (c) Which decade saw the largest decline in population? (d) What events and policies discussed in the chapter might have influenced these population shifts?

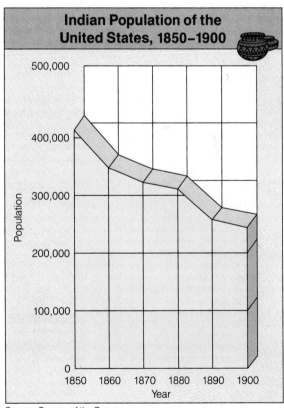

Indian Population of the United States, 1850–1900

Source: *Bureau of the Census*

MAKING CONNECTIONS
Unit 5

This unit began on page 331 with the observation that the mid-nineteenth century was an era of varied interests and conflict for the nation:

> *The Civil War began over the simple question of whether this was one nation, or whether any state or group of states could leave the Union and create a new nation. . . . To some Americans, the Civil War and Reconstruction were only far-off conflicts.*

These conclusions were supported by the three unit themes that are reprinted in **dark type** below. Use the time line and the information in Unit 5 to answer the questions that follow the unit themes.

THEMES IN HISTORY

Using "Making Connections": Have students look at the unit themes printed in dark type. Explain that each event on the time line relates to one of these themes. Ask students to decide which events are related to which theme. Students should use events from the time line in their answers and explain how events are related. You may also wish to have students go back through the text of Unit 5 to find other events related to the unit themes.

1. **The Civil War becomes a fight over the legitimacy of the institution of slavery.** CONFLICT
   If the institution of slavery had not existed, would the issue of states' rights have emerged as a point of national debate in the mid-1800s? (Predicting Consequences)

2. **Lincoln's assassination dashes whatever chance the nation has of solving post–Civil War problems "with charity for all."** SOCIAL CHANGE
   What factors contributed to the hostile relationship between President Andrew Johnson and Congress? Would these conflicts have developed had Lincoln not been assassinated? (Identifying Central Issues)

3. **Increasing numbers of Americans seek new opportunities in the American West during and after the Civil War.** GEOGRAPHY
   What skills and values prepared easterners and new immigrants for the opportunities and problems they faced in the West? (Drawing Conclusions)

Events in American History

1858 — News that gold had been discovered in Colorado reaches the East.

1860 — South Carolina secedes from the Union, claiming states' rights.

1860

Events in World History

1861 — Czar Alexander II abolishes serfdom in Russia.

1863
Lincoln announces the Emancipation Proclamation.

1865
The Thirteenth Amendment, abolishing slavery, is ratified by the states.

1867
Congress passes the Reconstruction amendments against President Johnson's wishes.

1875
Joseph Glidden makes a fortune selling barbed wire to farmers.

1890
The population of Kansas reaches 1.4 million, up from 364,000 in 1870.

1889
The firing of a gun signals the opening of the Oklahoma Indian territory to white settlement.

| 1865 | 1870 | 1875 | 1880 | 1885 | 1890 |

1867
Russia sells Alaska to the United States for $7.2 million.

1873
Financial panic strikes Vienna in May, and New York in September.

1891
The Triple Alliance among Germany, Austria, and Italy is renewed for 12 years.

Unit 6

Writing About History and Art: Direct students' attention to the unit introduction, illustration, and list of themes on pages 410–411. Have the introduction and unit themes read aloud. After a brief discussion of the subject matter of the unit, instruct students to write a brief paragraph, explaining how the art:

—relates to the unit themes;
—exemplifies the unit title and illustrates the introduction; and
—is an appropriate choice for the unit.

The New Industrial Age 1865–1900

After the Civil War the United States was as large and varied as all western Europe. Immigrants from everywhere would find someplace to feel at home here—on lands not so different from where they had lived in the "Old Country." The English could settle on the rolling landscape of "New" England, the Swedes could farm the flat, snowy stretches of Minnesota and the Dakotas, and Italians could plant orchards and vineyards in sunny California. Imported people spread across the land. But how could these scattered people become a nation? They would have to invent ways to bring everybody closer together. The world was startled to see how Americans used railroads, telegraph wires, and bridges to bind a vast nation.

The continent did not yet seem overcrowded when Americans sent skyscrapers high in the air. For the first time in history, thousands came to live and work in a single towering building. In American cities, people would be close packed and piled up together as never before. Could so many varied city people still find national leaders to speak for them? And would the farm families who fed the nation also find champions? Could a nation where everything was becoming bigger still care for the little people?

THEMES IN HISTORY

- Immigrants from across Europe pour into the United States.   ECONOMICS

- The rise of new cities and the growth of older cities give the nation an increasingly urban character.   SOCIAL CHANGE

- Urban industrialization and falling farm prices lead farmers and factory workers to protest the politics and big business of the Gilded Age.   GOVERNMENT AND POLITICS

◉ New materials and new methods for using them transformed the nation during the Industrial Age. This detail from John Ferguson Weir's painting called "The Gun Foundry" shows molten metal being poured.
Bethlehem Steel Corporation

411

Chapter 16
The Nation Transformed

Identifying Chapter Materials

Objectives	Basic Instructional Materials	Extension Materials
1 Railroads and Big Business • Describe the growth of the railroads from 1865 to 1900.	**Annotated Teacher's Edition** • Lesson Plans, p. 412C **Instructional Support File** • Pre-Reading Activities, Unit 6, p. 1 • Skill Application Activity, Unit 6, p. 5	**Enrichment Support File** • Linking a Nation: The Railroads (See "In-Depth Coverage" at right.) **Suggested Secondary Sources** • See chart at right.
2 Rock Oil Lights up the World • Explain the significance of rock oil and describe how Standard Oil became the largest oil company in the country. • Describe the history of petroleum imports and oil consumption in the United States.	**Annotated Teacher's Edition** • Lesson Plans, pp. 412C–412D	**Extension Activity** • Drilling for Oil, Lesson Plans, p. 412D
3 City Goods for Country Customers • Explain the origins and business practices of the large mail-order companies and describe the impact of the large department store on customer buying.	**Annotated Teacher's Edition** • Lesson Plans, p. 412D	**Extension Activity** • Mail-Order Catalogs, Lesson Plans, p. 412D
4 Buyers' Palaces • Describe the merchandising changes that occurred in American cities.	**Annotated Teacher's Edition** • Lesson Plans, pp. 412D–412E	**American History Transparencies** • Critical Thinking, p. F11
5 Things by the Millions • Describe how improvements in industrial production and efficiency changed the way factory work was organized.	**Annotated Teacher's Edition** • Lesson Plans, p. 412E **Instructional Support File** • Skill Review Activity, Unit 6, p. 4	**Extension Activity** • Important Inventions, Lesson Plans, p. 412E
6 Labor Begins to Organize • Describe the slow growth of early labor unions and identify the role of Samuel Gompers in the labor movement. • Analyze the working conditions common to the 1890s and compare these with contemporary working conditions.	**Annotated Teacher's Edition** • Lesson Plans, p. 412F **Instructional Support File** • Reading Activities, Unit 6, pp. 2–3 • Critical Thinking Activity, Unit 6, p. 6 • Chapter Test, pp. 7–10 • Additional Test Questions, Unit 6, pp. 11–14	**Documents of American History** • *Commonwealth* v. *Hunt*, Vol. 1, p. 296 • Preamble of Constitution of the Knights of Labor, Vol. 1, p. 546 **American History Transparencies** • Critical Thinking, p. F23

Providing In-Depth Coverage

Perspectives on Building the Railroads

The growth of the railroads in the late nineteenth century reflected a changing America, a country which was constantly moving, building, and expanding.

Expansion and growth of the railroads led to the rapid growth of cities and towns. As cities and towns grew, more people moved westward, resulting in the closing of the frontier. Railroads also contributed to the growth of big business, ushering in the age of "Go-Getters," as well as robber barons. The chapter focuses on the railroad as a means of linking the vast area of land which Americans now occupied.

A History of the United States as an instructional program provides two types of resources you can use to offer in-depth coverage of the growth of the railroad: the *student text* and the *Enrichment Support File*. A list of *Suggested Secondary Sources* is also provided. The chart below shows the topics that are covered in each.

THE STUDENT TEXT. Boorstin and Kelley's

A History of the United States unfolds the chronology of events and the key players in the building of the railroads.

AMERICAN HISTORY ENRICHMENT SUPPORT FILE. This collection of primary

source readings and classroom activities reveals the importance of railroads in the early development of the nation.

SUGGESTED SECONDARY SOURCES.

This reference list of readings by well-known historians and other commentators provides an array of perspectives on the importance of railroads to the nation.

Locating Instructional Materials

Detailed lesson plans for teaching the building of the railroads as a mini-course or to study one or more elements of the railroad in depth are offered in the following areas: in the *student text*, see individual lesson plans at the beginning of each chapter; in the *Enrichment Support File*, see page 3; for readings beyond the student text, see *Suggested Secondary Sources*.

IN-DEPTH COVERAGE OF THE RAILROADS		
Student Text	**Enrichment Support File**	**Suggested Secondary Sources**
▪ Railroads and the growth of the west, pp. 398, 403–406 ▪ Railroad expansion, pp. 413–415, *map*, p. 414 ▪ Standard time and standard gauge, pp. 415–416 ▪ Railroads and big business, pp. 418–419, 421 ▪ Railroads and growth of cities and towns, pp. 437, 455, 456	▪ Lesson Suggestions ▪ Multimedia Resources ▪ Overview Essay/Linking the Nation: The Railroads ▪ Literature in American History/The Impact of the Iron Horse ▪ Songs in American History/Railroads Change the Face of the Nation ▪ Primary Sources in American History/ Controversial and Exciting Times ▪ Biography in American History/Making Dream Into Reality: The Chinese and Irish Workers on the Transcontinental Railroad ▪ Geography in American History/Geography and Movement: The First Transcontinental Link ▪ Great Debates in American History/A Clash Between Management and Labor ▪ Making Connections	▪ *Men of the Steel Rails: Workers on the Atchison, Topeka, and Santa Fe Railroad, 1869–1900* by James H. Ducker, pp. 24–52. ▪ *The Life and Decline of the American Railroad* by John Stover, pp. 62–99. ▪ *Railroads and the Character of America, 1820–1887* by James Arthur Ward, pp. 151–170. ▪ *A Great and Shining Road: The Epic Story of the Transcontinental Railroad* by John Hoyt Williams, pp. 69–92.

Railroads and Big Business

FOCUS

To introduce the lesson, ask students: What methods of transportation were available to American businesses in 1870?

Developing Vocabulary

The words listed in this chapter are essential terms for reading and understanding particular sections of the chapter. The page number after each term indicates the page of its first or most important appearance in the chapter. These terms are defined in the text Glossary (text pages 1000–1011).

trust (page 417); **holding company** (page 417); **stockholder** (page 417); **antitrust** (page 418); **financier** (page 418).

INSTRUCT

Explain

Remind the class that, as their textbook points out, as many miles of railroad track were laid in the 1880s alone as in all the years from 1828 to 1870.

✿ Cooperative Learning Activity

Formulating Questions Divide the class into groups of three. The members of one group will portray John D. Rockefeller, Andrew Carnegie, and J.P. Morgan at a press conference. This group should work together in preparation for answering any questions which may be asked by reporters. Assign one of the three moguls to each of the remaining groups. The group will do research in order to make up three questions to ask Rockefeller, Carnegie, and Morgan. One member of each group will act as recorder and write down the group's questions. Hold a mock press conference with the businessmen responding to the questions asked by the reporters.

Section Review Answers

Section 1, page 419

1. a) four belts of the United States in each of which it is exactly the same time. The time in each zone is an hour ahead of the time in the next zone to the west. b) the width between railroad tracks, and thus the width between the wheels of any car that will run on those tracks. c) made a fortune in the oil business by devising ways to eliminate his competition. d) a group of companies in an industry that agreed to adopt the same prices and avoid competing against each other in order to maximize profits. e) a "paper company" set up to buy stock in a variety of companies within an industry to gain control of them and thus of the industry. f) a financier who specialized in reorganizing companies to ensure maximum profit. g) a poor immigrant boy who became a multimillionaire by building the Carnegie Steel Company. 2. (a) Once the railroads were built, the surrounding lands rose in value, and the companies were able to earn handsome sums by selling these lands. The public benefited because the land grants encouraged the railroad companies to build more railroads. (b) Standard time permitted more accurate scheduling. (c) Standard gauge meant that all tracks were the same width, so one train could travel across the whole country. 3. They would hand over stock in their firms to a board of "trustees" and receive trust certificates in return. The point was to gain control of an industry and maximize profits while avoiding laws against conspiracy. 4. The owners were thousands of stockholders scattered around the country who rarely saw the business in operation.

CLOSE

To conclude the lesson, ask: How did the railroads help to transform the United States into an industrial giant? Use examples from the text to support your answer.

Rock Oil Lights up the World

FOCUS

To introduce the lesson, have the students work on the graph on oil production and related questions under "Historical Facts and Figures" in the Chapter Review (p. 435 of the text).

INSTRUCT

Explain

The descendant of the original Standard Oil of New Jersey is Exxon Corporation. There are other descendants such as Standard Oil of California and Standard Oil of Indiana.

☑ Writing Process Activity

Demonstrating Reasoned Judgment Ask students to imagine they are George H. Bissell who is trying to persuade businessmen to invest in the Pennsylvania Rock Oil Company. In preparation for making a persuasive business presentation, ask them to brainstorm the varied uses of rock oil as well as the procedure by which it can be removed from the earth. Students should begin their speech with a strong topic sentence, and they should organize their points by order of importance. Ask students to revise for persuasive, logical evidence. After proofreading, students can deliver their presentations to the class.

Section Review Answers

Section 2, page 422

1. a) petroleum. b) formed the Pennsylvania Rock Oil Company to drill for oil underground. c) a Yale professor who determined that rock oil was useful for fueling lamps and for lubrication. d) the town in Pennsylvania closest to the sites of the biggest finds of surface oil. e) refunds from the official price offered by railroads to special customers. 2. Because he dominated the oil business of Cleveland, the railroads there needed his business. He was able to force them to give him special rates, which gave him an advantage over the competition.

CLOSE

To conclude the lesson, divide the class into small groups. Ask each group to make a list of the positive and negative effects of Standard Oil upon the United States in the nineteenth century. Ask groups to compare lists and as a class make an overall judgment about the most important ways the company affected the United States.

Extension Activity

To extend the lesson, tell students to imagine themselves as time travelers going back to Titusville, Pennsylvania in the year 1859. Upon arrival they spot Edwin Drake at his first oil well. Have students write a short skit depicting the encounter in which they tell Drake about the effect which oil has on the future of the country.

Section 3 (pages 422–425)

City Goods for Country Customers

FOCUS

To introduce the lesson, ask students to bring a contemporary mail-order catalog to class. Obtain a few copies of old Sears or Montgomery Ward catalogs for use in class. Divide the class into small groups and distribute one copy of an old mail-order catalog to each group. Allow them to peruse the old catalog and compare it to a new one.

INSTRUCT

Explain

Other retail businesses became well-known in the late 1800s. From a small upstate New York variety store, F. W. Woolworth expanded his idea of a "Five-and Ten-Cent Store" to a nationwide "poor man's department store" chain.

★ Independent Activity

Expressing Problems Clearly Have each student choose an item from one of the old catalogs you brought to class. Have students assume that they have ordered and received this merchandise and find it unsatisfactory in some specific respect(s). Students are to write a cover letter to send back with the merchandise. Require students to use the standard business letter format.

Section Review Answers

Section 3, page 425

1. a) created the mail-order catalog—a new way of selling products to people far from cities and their shops. b) created or improved advertising methods such as the use of color in catalogs. 2. Mail-order buying offered a wider selection of goods and lower prices than the rural store.

CLOSE

To conclude the lesson, ask: What factors were (and are) necessary for a mail-order business to be successful? (Adequate mail service; confidence of customers; quality and variety of merchandise; presses able to print large catalogs; sufficient income among customers, in the beginning particularly farmers.) What previously unsatisfied needs were met by shopping through mail-order catalogs? (home delivery for those not near stores; information about new products; broadening of cultural horizons, etc.)

Extension Activity

To extend the lesson, students may select a nineteenth-century product and create a catalog advertisement for it. Students should keep in mind their target customers, mainly farm families, and represent their products in a way which would appeal to these people.

Section 4 (pages 425–427)

Buyers' Palaces

FOCUS

To introduce the lesson, have students read the first four paragraphs of the "Buyers' Palaces" section, on page 425 of the text. Then ask: In what way did American hotels of the late nineteenth century resemble the department stores that appeared in the cities during the same period?

INSTRUCT

Explain

Mention to the class that new types of stores and merchandising techniques have also been developed in this century. Encourage them to name these changes. (Shopping malls, credit cards, supermarkets, super stores, TV shopping channels, etc.)

☑ Writing Process Activity

Identifying Central Issues Ask students to imagine they are people from a small town visiting New York City for the first time in 1860. In preparation for writing a letter to friends back home, tell them to make a chart of the sense impressions they might have gathered during their visit. Students should revise for vivid detail and spatial organization. After proofreading, they can share their letter with a partner.

Section Review Answers

Section 4, page 427

1. a) had the first cast-iron department store built. b) designed Stewart's cast-iron, eight-story department store. 2. It offered long views of appealing merchandise and it was an exciting place to visit. 3. Unlike small shops in Europe, they were open to anyone who wanted to come in. The same goods were available to everyone.

CLOSE

To conclude the lesson, point out that before department stores became popular, customers went to small shops to buy goods. What advantages came with the department store? (It brought democracy to shopping—everybody was welcome; prices were often lower; there was a wider selection of goods.)

Section 5 (pages 427–430)

Things by the Millions

FOCUS

To introduce the lesson, reinforce understanding and appreciation of the effects of standardization and other aspects of scientific management by having each student write the steps involved in some repetitive job.

INSTRUCT

Explain

Thomas Edison considered himself a good inventor but a poor manufacturer. For a product to reach the marketplace, the skills of both inventor and manufacturer are needed.

❀ Cooperative Learning Activity

Formulating Questions Tell students that they will work in pairs to write a "Biography of a Product." Explain that students are to describe how the product was created, its component parts, and how the parts function within the whole. To begin, have partners decide on a product that they themselves use and that they would like to learn more about. Then have partners find and share sources of information on the product. Assign one partner to take notes as the pair composes the biography and to write the final copy. Have the other partner prepare an illustration or diagram and present the biography to the class.

Section Review Answers

Section 5, page 430

1. a) held in 1876 in Philadelphia, a celebration of the nation's hundredth anniversary that showcased new American products. b) a Connecticut manufacturer known for his inexpensive clocks. c) the pioneer in the study of "Scientific Management." 2. The systematic analysis of manufacturing to increase efficiency. Workers feared that when scientific management was put into practice, they would lose their jobs or control over how they worked or would be forced to work harder. 3. Edison's work was of benefit to all Americans. His electric light bulb brightened homes and work places. His creativity sparked the imagination of millions of Americans, encouraging them to think in new ways about old ideas.

CLOSE

To conclude the lesson, ask students how they think the functions performed in some of the repetitive tasks described in the focus activity might have been performed before they were standardized—before some of the other machinery that makes standardization possible was invented.

Extension Activity

To extend the lesson, have each student choose what he or she considers to be the three most important inventions of the nineteenth century. Students should write a brief paragraph about each item to justify their choices.

Labor Begins to Organize

FOCUS

To introduce the lesson, ask students to describe some jobs they are familiar with and to compare current working conditions and benefits with those of the 1890s.

Developing Vocabulary

labor union (page 430)

INSTRUCT

Explain

At one time, strikes made many people angry. Today, many people become angry when public service workers such as teachers or police strike.

☑ Writing Process Activity

Recognizing Cause and Effect Explain to students that they will write an essay discussing the causes and effects of labor organization. Ask them to begin by making a chart of the causes and effects. As they revise, ask students to be sure they have used transition words such as *reason, because*, and *consequently* to distinguish cause and effect. After they proofread, ask students to compare their essays with those of other group members.

Section Review Answers

Section 6, page 434

1. a) In this case, the Supreme Court opened the path for unions by declaring that they were just as legal as any other clubs organized to help members for a legitimate purpose. b) was the federation formed by several trade unions in the early 1800s. c) a secret society organized by coal miners in eastern Pennsylvania in the 1870s. d) the name given to the unexplained explosion at a labor demonstration in Chicago in 1866. e) occurred at a steel plant in Homestead, Pennsylvania, in 1892. f) occurred in the Midwest in 1892 and brought the trains to a halt. g) reorganized the Cigarmakers' Union, helped form the American Federation of Labor, and became its president. h) the first successful federation of unions in America. 2. Workers in a few skilled trades such as printing and stonecutting had organized national unions to improve their wages and working conditions. 3. After 1870 labor-management conflict became more frequent and violent. 4. The Knights of Labor hoped to bring all workers into one big union. They opposed child labor, advocated an eight-hour day, and were against strikes. The decline in public support for all labor activists after the Haymarket Massacre destroyed the Knights. 5. American unions would concentrate on goals that directly affected the workers' material well-being such as better wages, shorter hours, and safer working conditions.

CLOSE

To conclude the lesson, ask: Why did the early labor movement grow so slowly? (Hampered by state laws against strikes, labor violence, and comparatively high wages.)

Chapter Review Answers

Focusing on Ideas

1. Railroads: connected U.S., made land more valuable, standard time system; Trusts: moved the nation from individual proprietorships into highly competitive organizations; New merchandising: gave consumer more choice; Standardization: encouraged production, moving the U.S. into forefront of industrialized nations; Unions: narrowed the gap between business and labor, created by large factories and expanding forms of business organization. 2. Early captains of industry: aggressive, imaginative, daring, dedicated (workaholics), persuasive, well-organized, etc. Today: similar, but aggressiveness and ruthlessness have to be suppressed to conform to laws and accepted business practices. 3. The middle-class could attain goods and services previously only available to the wealthy.

Taking a Critical Look

1. Hamilton would have celebrated. He envisioned the U.S. as a powerful commercial/industrial nation, with agriculture important but not necessarily predominant. Jefferson would have wept because he envisioned a nation of independent farmers, artisans, and shopkeepers. 2. Standardization drove down unit costs. Examples: steel production; telephone usage nationwide.

Your Region in History

1–3. Answers will vary depending on your region. Consult your local library or historical society.

Historical Facts and Figures

(a) 1870: 5 million barrels; 1900: 65 million barels. (b) The 1870s. (c) 125%. (d) 220,035,000,000 barrels of oil in 1990. (e) Students should do research.

16

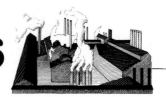

Chapter 16

The Nation Transformed

The everyday life of the American people was transformed in the generation after the Civil War. This nation would be not merely a democracy of people but also a democracy of things. It became easier for more and more Americans to share the good things of life. Farmers and ranchers found ways to make the American land yield more and better food. And many others played their parts in creating the American standard of living. A peculiarly American breed were the Go-Getters. These were men and women of all races and from all nations. The Go-Getters found new opportunities here, saw new ways to make a living for themselves, and at the same time helped build a better life for others. Without even intending it, they were bringing the whole nation together.

William Henry Jackson, who took this picture, has been called the greatest of all photographers of the West. He hand-colored this powerful scene of a Denver & Rio Grande Railway double-headed train.

Colorado Historical Society

See "Lesson Plan," p. 412C.

1. Railroads and big business

To make a profit from their land, farmers had to send their crops to market. To work their land, they needed tools from city factories. As factories grew to supply the nation's wants, the factories consumed more and more raw materials—iron, wood, and cotton. To keep the whole process going, the vast nation, spread across a continent, needed transportation. The nation was already served by its broad rivers, its many canals, and roadways. But there had to be easier, speedier ways.

Enrich-
ment
Support
File Topic

Railroads gird the nation. To meet the demand, Go-Getters pushed railroads into every nook and cranny of the United States. As many miles of track were laid in the 1880s alone as in all the years from 1828 to 1870. By 1900 the nation had more miles of railroad track than all of Europe, including Russia.

When the first transcontinental railroad was completed in 1869, the time required to cross from ocean to ocean dropped from one month to one week. Within another 25 years four more transcontinental railroads were built. All but one of these railroads received generous land grants from the federal government to encourage them to build across the vacant West. Altogether, American railroads received 131 million acres from Congress and 49 million acres from the states. At the time they were given to the (p. 414)

In their hurry to lay track, transcontinental railroads often built temporary wooden bridges. The permanent bridge over the Green River in Wyoming is already under construction (left) in this 1868 photograph. Citadel Rock is in the background.

The Oakland Museum

Multicultural Connection: Chinese immigrants were hired by the Central Pacific Railroad to build the western portion of the national rail system. The Central Pacific owners hired over 12,000 Chinese workers form 1863 until the joining of the two railroads at Promontory Point, Utah on May 10, 1869. Today, it is generally acknowledged that the railroad could not have been built without Chinese labor.

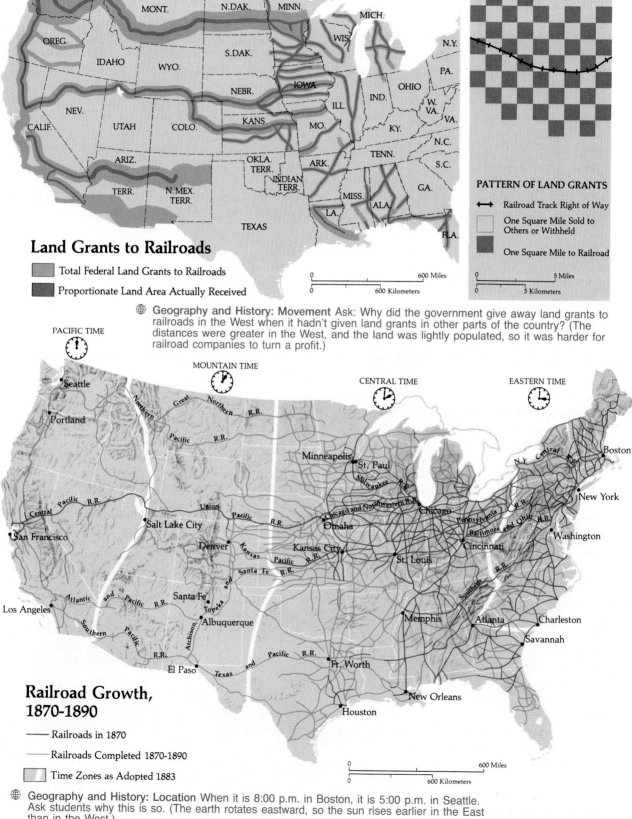

Land Grants to Railroads

Total Federal Land Grants to Railroads

Proportionate Land Area Actually Received

PATTERN OF LAND GRANTS

├──┤ Railroad Track Right of Way

☐ One Square Mile Sold to Others or Withheld

■ One Square Mile to Railroad

0 ——————— 600 Miles
0 ——————— 600 Kilometers

0 ——————— 5 Miles
0 ——————— 5 Kilometers

🌐 **Geography and History: Movement** Ask: Why did the government give away land grants to railroads in the West when it hadn't given land grants in other parts of the country? (The distances were greater in the West, and the land was lightly populated, so it was harder for railroad companies to turn a profit.)

PACIFIC TIME

MOUNTAIN TIME

CENTRAL TIME

EASTERN TIME

Railroad Growth, 1870-1890

——— Railroads in 1870

——— Railroads Completed 1870-1890

Time Zones as Adopted 1883

0 ——————— 600 Miles
0 ——————— 600 Kilometers

🌐 **Geography and History: Location** When it is 8:00 p.m. in Boston, it is 5:00 p.m. in Seattle. Ask students why this is so. (The earth rotates eastward, so the sun rises earlier in the East than in the West.)

companies, the lands were worth little or nothing. They only became valuable after the railways were built. Then these lands would become prosperous farms and profitable sources for the nation's iron, copper, and oil.

Standard time. Americans loved speed. And railroads made it possible for them to race across the continent faster than ever before. The trains that sped from city to city brought strange new problems. One trouble which had not been noticed till then was that every town had its own clocks set to its own particular time. The astronomers said that it was "noon" when you saw the sun reach its zenith—the highest point in the heavens. Since the earth was constantly in motion, and since the sun rose sooner when you were more to the east, then whether it was yet noon obviously depended on *where* you were.

Imagine what this meant for a railroad! The Pennsylvania Railroad tried to use Philadelphia time on its eastern lines. But that was 5 minutes earlier than New York time and 5 minutes later than Baltimore time. In Indiana there were 23 different local times. In Illinois there were 27, and in Wisconsin 38.

Most railroads used the local time for their arrival in each station. In between cities there was the greatest confusion. Yet for speeding trains a few minutes could make the difference between a clear track and a fatal collision.

Finally it was suggested that instead of using "sun time" they should use a new kind of "railroad time"—which would be "standard time."

For the United States as a whole, you could mark off on a map a few conspicuous time belts—up and down the whole country. You would only need four—eastern time, central time, mountain time, and Pacific time—each several hundred miles wide. Standard time would be exactly the same for all the places within each zone. At the edge of each belt the time would change by a whole hour. These time zones would be marked on maps, and then everybody could know exactly what time it was everywhere.

This was a sensible plan, but it took a long time to convince everybody that they ought to

The Thomas Gilcrease Institute of
American History and Art, Tulsa

In the oil painting above, Chinese workers cheer as a Central Pacific train heads into a snowshed built to protect it from heavy snow in the Sierras.

tamper with "God's time." Finally, at noon on November 18, 1883, the plan for standard time was adopted, and people everywhere set their watches to the new time.

Standard gauge. Standard time helped to draw all the nation's railroads together. But other steps were needed too. In 1860 there were about 350 different railroad companies and about 30,000 miles of railroad tracks in the United States. Yet there was not really a national railroad network. The main reason was that the many railroad lines were not on the same "gauge." The gauge is the distance between the two rails measured from the inside of one rail to the inside of the other. There were many different gauges. Some railroad builders put their tracks six feet apart, but some put them closer together. There were at least eleven gauges in general use. A railroad car that would just fit one gauge would not run on narrower or wider gauges.

If you wanted to send a package any distance by railroad, it had to be taken out of the car that fitted one gauge and moved into a car to fit the gauge of the next railroad. In 1861 a package

✖ Critical Thinking Activity: Making Comparisons How have our daily lives benefited from standardization? A standard time and a standard gauge are only two of the many uniformities that industrialization has demanded. Have students make a list of everyday items that have been standardized (e.g., telephone lines, highway signs/symbols, computer systems, etc.). Tell students to write a paragraph about one of these items, explaining its function and why the item has been standardized.

The Huntington Library, San Marino, California

The poster shows how new railroad lines sprang up as demand grew.

During the Civil War, in order to ship arms and troops quickly from place to place, many railroads changed to standard gauge. And then when the transcontinental railroad was completed with the standard gauge in 1869, that settled the question. Now if a railroad wanted to join the traffic across the continent, its rails had to be set 4 feet, 8 1/2 inches apart.

By 1880 about four-fifths of the tracks in the United States had been converted to standard gauge. Most of the other gauges were in the old Confederate South. Finally, in 1886, the southern railroads decided to change all their 13,000 miles of track to the national standard. A month in advance, crews went along loosening the old track. They measured the distance for the new standard gauge and put spikes along the wooden ties. On May 31 and June 1, the men worked frantically. One record-breaking crew on the Louisville and Nashville Railroad changed eleven miles of track in 4 1/2 hours. June 1, 1886, was a holiday along the southern tracks. By 4 P.M. the southern railroads had joined the Union.

Businesses compete. As the railroads crisscrossed the land, the nation's businesses grew in number and size because they could reach more people. These were challenging times for businessmen. Competition in certain fields—like oil, steel, and the railroads—was fierce. On top of that, thirteen of the years from 1873 to 1897 were years of recession or depression. John D. Rockefeller, who made a fortune in the oil business, once looked back on those years and marveled that he had managed to survive them.

> How often I had not an unbroken night's sleep, worrying about how it was all coming out. . . . Work by day and worry by night, week in and week out, month after month. If I had foreseen the future, I doubt whether I would have had the courage to go on.

Rockefeller did go on, and he prospered by devising ways to limit competition. He orga-

sent by railroad from Charleston, South Carolina, to Philadelphia had to change railroad cars eight times.

From the beginning, quite a few lines happened to have the same gauge. George Stephenson, the English railroad inventor, had designed his locomotive to measure 4 feet, 8 1/2 inches between the wheels—the usual distance between wheels on a wagon. When Stephenson locomotives were imported to the United States, they had this "standard gauge." And of course many early railroad lines built their tracks to fit the imported trains.

Continuity and Change: Economics Explain to students that the Boston Tea Party (1773) is an early and dramatic example of public reaction to a monopoly. Later, the Supreme Court attacked monopolies in the decision *Gibbons v. Ogden* (1824). By the late 1800s, in reaction to the oppression of farmer and small businessmen by railroad conglomerates, Congress began to pass legislation, such as the Interstate Commerce Act, to control large corporations by making it illegal for the railroads to charge inconsistent rates. (See pp. 82 and 214.)

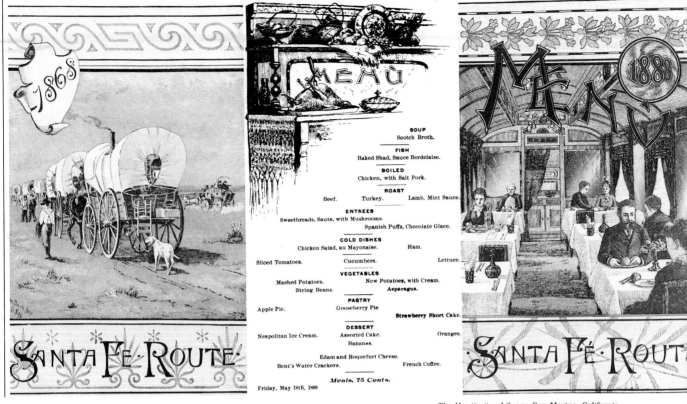

The front and back covers of this menu from the Santa Fe railroad reveal the change in transportation across the continent that took place between 1868 and 1888. The comfortable passengers in the dining car had a gourmet menu to choose from.

The Huntington Library, San Marino, California

nized "pools" in which a group of companies agreed not really to compete but instead to keep their prices the same. The law often treated these agreements as a kind of conspiracy. Since there was no legal means to enforce the pools, they usually collapsed.

(p. 416) Then Rockefeller and some other big businessmen tried another device. They figured out a clever new way to use an old English institution. This was the "trust." In early times in England the "trust" was invented for charities. Money would be given to "trustees" who invested it and gave the profits to the poor and the needy. The trustees controlled the money for the benefit of others. Now business firms set up "trusts"—not for charity, but to get around the

laws against conspiracy. A group of companies would hand over all their stock to a board of "trustees" and receive trust certificates in return. The new trustees would then control all the companies, but the original owners—the holders of the trust certificates—would still get the profits. Still another ploy they used was the holding company. Its only purpose was to "hold" the stock, and so the control, of other companies.

For some years the trust proved to be an effective way to get around the law, to combine companies, limit competition, and increase profits. The first and most famous was Rockefeller's Standard Oil Trust, but there were also trusts in cottonseed oil, linseed oil, lead, whiskey,

More from Boorstin: "[P]otent new legal devices made it possible to conduct the largest transactions in the deepest secrecy . . . . For years John D. Rockefeller had been adept at hiding his consolidating activities. The men who were negotiating with the Standard Oil Company had been writing their letters under assumed names, and Rockefeller had cautioned them 'not to tell their wives.'" (From *The Americans: The Democratic Experience*)

sugar, and other products. By 1890 Congress began to pass antitrust laws, and the courts decided that business combinations formed to limit competition were illegal. But many trusts continued to operate, and their powers lingered on.

J. Pierpont Morgan and Andrew Carnegie. In the railroads, as well, combination became the answer to overexpansion and cutthroat competition. Here the main actor was the giant of finance J. Pierpont Morgan. Born to wealth, he was trained in the London office of his father's bank. His swashbuckling in the money world led people to call him a pirate. Actually he did not mind that. He had the look of a pirate, with his great frame, piercing eyes, and bulbous red nose. He named his luxury yacht (302

Sturdy J. P. Morgan, with his hawklike stare, was known as the financier extraordinary.

Culver Pictures

feet long!) the *Corsair*, which was the old French name for a pirate ship. Once, when Morgan was asked by a would-be yacht owner what it cost to run the *Corsair*, he replied, "If you have to ask, you can't afford it." But Morgan was also a man of culture. He built a great collection of rare books and works of art from all over the world, which he gave to the public.

Morgan was an amazing organizer. When hard times bankrupted many railroads during the late 1800s, Morgan put them back on their feet by reorganizing them. He often combined several weak companies to make a single strong one. In time he controlled eleven railway systems with 19,000 miles of track. He also organized the biggest steel company of all. But to do so he had to take over Carnegie Steel.

Andrew Carnegie, controlling partner in Carnegie Steel, was a talkative, intelligent steel industrialist who had been born of a poor family in Scotland. His family came to the United States in 1848, and Andrew at age 13 went to work as a bobbin boy in a cotton factory for $1.25 a week. But instead of settling for that, he educated himself by reading books and rose rapidly to better jobs. By his energy and his power to enlist the talents of others, he built the Carnegie Steel Company and became one of the richest men in America. In 1900 alone he made $25 million. And since there was no income tax in those days, he kept it all! Meanwhile, he never forgot the power of books. He devoted much of his fortune to founding libraries all over the United States in order to give others the chance to educate themselves and rise in the world. More than any one person, Andrew Carnegie was responsible for the spread of the free public library. Along with the public school, it became a keystone of American democracy.

Now Morgan wanted to buy Carnegie's company and bring his own "system" to the steel industry. Carnegie asked almost half a billion dollars for his share—and Morgan paid. Carnegie Steel and several other steel companies then were merged to form the United States Steel

Brown Brothers

Astute Andrew Carnegie created the nation's largest steel company.

Corporation. It soon produced 60 percent of the nation's steel. Morgan's banking house made money, too, by selling the stock and bonds of the company to the public for a billion and a half dollars.

The new mighty corporations alarmed many people. They were richer and more powerful than any state government. These huge impersonal concerns were run by managers who were quite separate from the thousands of stockholders who really owned the business. The stockholders, each of whom owned "shares" in the company, were spread across the land. Most never even saw the factories of which they were part owners. The factory workers, instead of working for a single human boss who owned the company, now felt that they were employed by an inhuman giant. It was these companies and many smaller ones that made the United States, by 1890, the greatest industrial nation

❀ See "Lesson Plan," p. 412C for **Cooperative Learning Activity: Identifying Alternatives** relating to the career of J. Pierpont Morgan.

in the world. Their products, as well as the wealth they created and the salaries they paid, transformed American life.

See "Section 1 Review answers," p. 412C.

Section 1 Review

1. Identify or explain: time zones, narrow gauge, John D. Rockefeller, pool, holding company, J. P. Morgan, Andrew Carnegie.
2. How did both the railroads and the public benefit from (a) the railroad land grants? (b) the switch to standard time? (c) the change to standard-gauge track?
3. Explain how a dozen big sugar companies might have formed a trust. Why would they want to do so?
4. **Critical Thinking: Expressing Problems Clearly.** In what sense did the giant corporations become more impersonal and inhuman?

See "Lesson Plan," p. 412C.

2. Rock oil lights up the world

Americans before the Civil War, before anyone heard of an electric light, had to light their houses and their factories with oil lamps. People tried all sorts of mixtures hoping to find an oil that was cheap and safe, that burned well, and did not smell. They tried oils from the sap of trees, from vegetables, from fish, whales, or other animals. One oil called "camphene" was a mixture of turpentine (from pine trees) and alcohol. Another, invented in 1850 and made from coal, was called kerosene (from *keros*, the Greek word for wax). Camphene gave off good light but emitted an explosive gas. All except kerosene were smelly. Kerosene worked best, but it was expensive. So most homes were not lit at night. And people went to bed when the sun set.

Drilling for oil. In the mid-1850s George H. Bissell formed the Pennsylvania Rock Oil Company to buy lands in western Pennsylvania where oil was found floating in ponds. At that time rock oil (what we call "oil") was used

American Antiquarian Society

This sheet music cover celebrates the Tarr Farm Oil Creek in Pennsylvania.

mostly for medicine. Bissell found that he could not make enough money selling the oil for medicine to pay the expenses of collecting it. So he hired a famous Yale professor of chemistry, Benjamin Silliman, Jr., and agreed to pay him $500 to find out what else rock oil might be good for.

Professor Silliman's report opened a new age for rock oil. He found that rock oil—by now also called "petroleum" from *petrus*, Latin for rock, and *oleum* for oil—would make an excellent oil for lamps. His process was cheap. He simply distilled the rock oil—that is, heated it and collected the gas that came off. When the gas cooled down into a liquid, it formed a lamp oil that was just as good as kerosene made from coal. Kerosene made from rock oil gave a bright, white light, with almost no smoke, and would not explode.

The rock oil itself also had wonderful lubricating powers. It would keep the wheels and gears of machines from wearing out and would make them run quietly and smoothly.

Rock oil, with these valuable uses, could surely be sold in large quantities. But until then the only known way to collect it was to find it on the surface or by accident in a salt well. Sometimes people would dig a shallow ditch to increase the flow where it was already bubbling up.

Then one day, the story goes, Bissell saw an advertisement for rock oil from an old salt well. It was a sheet printed to look like paper money that featured the numeral 400. "A.D. 1848," it read. "Discovered in *boring* for salt water . . . about FOUR HUNDRED FEET below the Earth's surface." Boring! If oil could be obtained when you bored for salt water, why not simply bore for the oil?

"Oil coming out of the ground!" exclaimed a friend. "Pumping oil out of the earth the way you pump water? Nonsense! You're crazy."

But Bissell and other Go-Getting businessmen in the Pennsylvania Rock Oil Company decided to try. From New Haven, Connecticut, they sent Edwin L. Drake out to the oil fields. One reason they picked him was that since he had been a railroad conductor, he still had a free pass on the railroads. He could go out to western Pennsylvania without it costing anybody anything.

When Drake reached Titusville, the town closest to the biggest finds of surface oil, he decided to drill for oil. At first he could not find a driller willing to do the job. The drillers all thought that boring for oil was silly.

Then, luckily, he found an old salt driller, "Uncle Billy" Smith, who was also a skilled blacksmith and knew how to make drilling (p. 421) tools. Uncle Billy began drilling in June 1859, and on August 29 the hole still reached down less than 70 feet. When Drake and Smith came back two days later, the hole was full of oily black stuff.

"What's that?" Drake asked.

Uncle Billy replied, "That's your fortune!"

Soon there was an oil mania. Everybody wanted to get rich from oil. The map of northwestern Pennsylvania was dotted with such new names as Oil City, Oleopolis, and Petroleum Center.

John D. Rockefeller sets up the Standard Oil Company.

One of the most spectacular of all American Go-Getters was John D. Rockefeller. He was not an inventor or an explorer. Like J. P. Morgan and Andrew Carnegie, he was an organizer.

Young Rockefeller went to school in Cleveland, but he never went to college. His father, who traveled through the West selling patent medicines, left young John in charge of the family long before he was grown. John D. Rockefeller was ambitious. "I did not guess what it would be," he recalled. "But I was after something big."

Even as a boy in Cleveland, young Rockefeller was systematic and well organized. While still struggling to make his way, he gave one-tenth of his income to the Baptist church and to charities. But when it came to organizing his oil business, he did not always use Sunday school methods.

Cleveland was a good place to organize "something big" in the oil business. At the receiving end of two railroads that came from the western Pennsylvania oil fields, Cleveland was on a lake big enough for large ships as well as on two major east-west railroads. Rockefeller determined to make Cleveland the center of the oil business and from there to command the biggest oil company in the world. Beginning with a small sum he had made in a grain-trading business, in 1865 he bought a Cleveland oil refinery. There crude oil from the fields was made into kerosene for lighting and oil for lubricating. Then he bought up other refineries in Cleveland and many oil wells in Pennsylvania.

As other oilmen went out of business, the railroads that carried the oil needed Rockefeller's freight more than ever. He was clever at making the two big railroads passing through Cleveland compete for his business. He bargained with one railroad by threatening to give all his business to the other. And he finally forced them to charge him lower prices than they charged anybody else. By secret arrangements he pretended to pay the regular rates. Then the railroads gave him back a "rebate"—a refund on each barrel of his oil that they had hauled. Soon they even gave him rebates on what opposing oil companies shipped.

After he perfected these tactics, he went to the small refiners in other parts of the country and asked them to sell their companies to him. "If you don't sell your property," he would say, "it will be valueless, because we have advantages with the railroads." He would then offer a price far below what the owners thought their refineries were worth. But they usually sold because they knew that Rockefeller could drive them out of business.

When it became cheaper to pump oil through pipelines instead of carrying it in barrels, Rockefeller organized his own pipeline. Then, when a different kind of oil was found in Ohio, Rockefeller hired chemical engineers to invent new kinds of refineries.

Rockefeller's Go-Getting business reached around the world. To the Chinese, his Standard Oil Company sold inexpensive lamps by the

Alarmed by the growth of large corporations, this 1881 cartoonist compares Standard Oil with an octopus.

Historical Pictures Service, Chicago

✂ millions—and then sold the oil to fill them. Before long, people on all continents were using lamp oil from American wells. Between the Civil War and 1900 over half the American output went abroad. In those years Rockefeller, the Giant Go-Getter, helped light up the world. Now Americans could afford a lamp in every room, and they did not have to go to bed at sunset.

In the 1900s, Rockefeller's business would grow in ways even he had never imagined. After the automobile was invented, petroleum was refined into gasoline—and rock oil made it possible for a whole nation to move on wheels.

See "Section 2 Review answers," p. 412D.

Section 2 Review

1. Identify or explain: rock oil, George H. Bissell, Benjamin Silliman, Jr., Titusville, rebates.

2. **Critical Thinking: Determining Relevance.** How did Rockefeller use the railroad to organize and build the giant Standard Oil Company?

See "Lesson Plan," p. 412D.

3. City goods for country customers

During the colonial years, an American farm family made for themselves almost everything they needed. They built their own house (with the help of a few neighbors), and they made their own furniture. The wife and daughters spun the thread, wove the cloth, and then sewed the family's clothes. The pots and pans and metal tools which they could not make for themselves they would buy from a peddler. But they bought very few things. There were not many ready-made things for them to buy.

Then, in the years before the Civil War, American know-how drew upon ideas from Europe's Industrial Revolution to develop a new kind of manufacturing. Lots of new things were produced in vast new quantities. The new American System of Manufacture, which Eli Whitney and Samuel Colt had organized to make guns and revolvers, also turned out clocks and locks,

and countless other items—both better and cheaper. Now farmers could afford to buy them.

But when farm families wanted any of these things, they had to go to the nearest village and visit the general store. Children loved the place because there you could buy candy and toys. Since the storekeeper kept a good fire in the stove, the store was where you could stay warm in winter. There you could meet friends and exchange ideas year-round.

But it was no place for bargains. The country storekeeper, who bought only a little bit of everything, could not command the best wholesale prices from the big-city manufacturers. Things would get dusty and out of date before they could be sold. And on top of that there were costly freight charges. Each item had to be hauled by wagon over bumpy backwoods roads.

Montgomery Ward. Soon after the Civil War an inventive young salesman, who had covered the West selling goods to the owners of general stores, began to think of a new plan. His name was A. Montgomery Ward. He had done all sorts of things, from working in a barrel factory and in a brickyard to selling dry goods. Often in his travels he had heard farmers complain about the small choice of goods and the high prices.

Young Ward's idea was to sell goods in an entirely new way. Instead of the old general store which had stocked only a few of each item, Ward imagined a mail-order store. The storekeeper would stay in the big city where it was easier to collect a large stock of all sorts of goods. He would send out to farmers lists of his goods with descriptions and pictures. The farmer would not need to come to the store because the store—in the form of a catalog—would go to the farmer. And the farm family would order by mail, picking out whatever they wanted from the catalog. Then the storekeeper would mail ✂ the family the goods they had ordered.

(p. 423)

If this new scheme worked, the storekeeper would be selling not only to the few customers in one village. He could sell all over America—to anyone within reach of a mailbox.

The possible customers of this new kind of store would not be just a few hundred, they might be millions! And then Ward could buy his

✂ Critical Thinking Activity: Recognizing Cause and Effect What are the common traits of "Go-Getters" like John D. Rockefeller, Andrew Carnegie, and J. P. Morgan? To answer this question have students construct a chart. Across the top of the blackboard write "Business Field," "Business Achievements," and "Contribution to Society." Down the side of the chart write "Rockefeller," "Carnegie," and "Morgan." Have students fill in the chart. Ask students to decide whether the common traits are coincidence or whether the traits determined the future of these entrepreneurs. Have them explain their decision in a brief paragraph.

goods from the manufacturer by the hundreds and thousands. The manufacturer could afford to give him a lower price.

For the customers, too, there were advantages. They had a much wider selection of goods. And they paid a lower price because the mail-order storekeeper, with so many more customers, could take a smaller profit on each item and yet would make more money in the long run.

Young Montgomery Ward had lost nearly all his savings in the Chicago fire of 1871, but in the very next year he managed to scrape together enough to make a start with his new idea. He put in $1600 and a partner added $800. They rented a small room over a stable, and started modestly. Their single price-sheet listed the items for sale and told how to order. Within two years Ward was issuing a 72-page catalog with illustrations. By 1884 the catalog numbered 240 pages and listed nearly 10,000 items. Within another 30 years it was over 1000 pages and included just about anything a person could imagine for animals or people.

Trust was the most important thing for a mail-order store. If you bought in a general store, you were buying from a storekeeper you knew. You could see the goods and handle them to satisfy yourself. But when you bought from a mail-order store, you had to trust somebody you had never seen. You had to believe that the storekeeper would really send you the exact thing described in the catalog.

Ward was a spectacular success. The first secret of his success was not a secret at all. It was simply to be honest, give good value, and always let the customer be the judge. On everything Ward's gave an ironclad guarantee. "Satisfaction or your money back!" If you did not like the goods when they arrived, you could always return them. If something arrived damaged, you could send it back to Ward's to be replaced. The company paid the postage both ways.

Of course there had to be trust on the company's side, too. The company had to be willing to cash the customers' checks, to believe their complaints, and to replace damaged goods without a lot of investigating. Ward was willing to do this, and to take the risks.

"NOW I GUESS I'VE GOT THE BULGE ON THE MIDDLEMAN."

G.H.BUEK & CO. LITH. N.Y.   OVER.

Ward's boasted that buying from them would save the customers money.

The spread of mail delivery to the rural countryside enabled farm families to buy goods from mail-order firms in the cities.

The catalog showed pictures of Ward himself and of the men in charge of the different departments. This was to convince the customers that they were dealing with real people. Some customers wrote in to say how pleased they were to deal with such "fine looking men." Some even named babies after Ward, and said he would be an inspiration to their children.

Ward saw that their letters were promptly answered—even if they were not ordering goods but only asking advice. One customer asked how to find a baby to adopt. Parents asked how to handle disobedient children. Some wrote him simply because they were lonely and had nobody else to write to.

Just as the tobacco planter in colonial times had asked his London agent to send him whatever he needed, now the lonely farmer asked Ward's. One customer wrote asking them to send him "a good wife." Ward's answered that it was not a good idea to select a wife by mail. "After you get the wife and you find that she needs some wearing apparel or household goods," Ward's added, "we feel sure we could serve both you and her to good advantage."

Sears and his catalog. It is not surprising that the mail-order store was a roaring success. Of course, in an age of Go-Getters, Ward was not the only man who tried his hand at building

More from Boorstin: "[Sears'] business was built around a catalogue which combined scrupulously honest guarantees ('Satisfaction or Your Money Back') with flamboyant unprovable claims (goods were 'The Best in the World' and would 'Last Forever') . . . . Sears' clever advertising became proverbial. There was the story, for example, of a Sears advertisement which offered a 'sewing machine' for $1—for which the customer duly received a needle and thread." (From *The Americans: The Democratic Experience*)

a mail-order store. One of the most creative of these others was a young man named Richard Sears. He began selling jewelry by mail. He found a partner in Alvah Curtis Roebuck, a watchmaker who ran a print shop where they could turn out their catalogs.

Sears was a clever man, and a near-genius at selling by mail. He was always improving his catalog. He developed a new quick-drying ink, new systems of color printing, and thinner paper that would take color but was cheaper to mail. He found, for example, that four pages of advertisements in color would sell as much of the same goods as twelve pages in black and white. His improvements were widely copied by other advertisers and by publishers of newspapers and magazines.

(p. 424)

As the mail-order catalog reached more and more people on remote farms and in small villages, it became more and more important in their daily lives. While the family kept the Bible in the living room, they kept the Sears or Ward catalog in the kitchen. That was where they really lived.

There were all sorts of stories about how much faith people put in this big book. When one little boy was asked by his Sunday school teacher where the Ten Commandments came from, he said he supposed they came from Sears.

Just as Puritan boys and girls in colonial times had studied the *New England Primer* with its stories about God and the Devil, now Americans on farms studied the Sears catalog. In country schoolhouses, where there were few textbooks, teachers made good use of the catalog. They used it to teach reading and spelling. For arithmetic, pupils filled out orders and added up items. And they learned geography from the catalog's postal-zone maps.

Nothing did more than the new mail-order stores to make rural life in America something new. Before the 1900s most Americans still lived on the farm. Now that the American farm family could order from Ward or Sears, their lives became even more different from that of European peasants. Their view of the good things in the world was no longer confined to the shelves of the little village store. The up-to-

date catalogs brought news of all kinds of new machines, new gadgets, and new fashions. Now American farm families could buy big-city goods at prices they could afford and from someone they could trust.

See "Section 3 Review answers," p. 412D.

Section 3 Review

1. Identify: Montgomery Ward, Richard Sears.
2. **Critical Thinking: Making Comparisons.** What advantages did mail-order buying have over shopping at the rural general store?

See "Lesson Plan," p. 412D.

4. Buyers' Palaces

Meanwhile other Go-Getters were inventing ways to attract the new millions of city customers. The big stores that now grew up in American cities were as different from the little London shops as the grand new American hotels were different from the modest Old World inns.

The new American hotels were People's Palaces. Anybody could meet friends in the elegant lobby or, if you had the money, entertain them in a dining room with a crystal chandelier. The new department stores were Buyers' Palaces. And they, too, were democratic.

In London, only people who looked like "gentlemen" or "ladies" were admitted to the elegant shops. Unless the shopkeepers knew who you were, they would not let you in. You had to be a "person of quality" (as the upper classes were called) to see "goods of quality."

Department stores changed all this. Suddenly there were vast Buyers' Palaces, some large enough to fill a whole city block—specially designed to display goods of every shape, price, and description. Anybody could walk in. Now everybody could look at stylish jewelry, clothing, and furniture of the kind once reserved for the eyes of the rich.

Stewart's new store. This department-store revolution, which began shortly before the Civil War, changed the lives of American customers within a few decades. Stewart's Cast Iron

Stewart's department store in New York was one of the first of the new buyers' palaces. This 1876 engraving shows the Broadway front of the block-large cast-iron building.

Palace, completed in 1862 in New York City, was one of the first big department stores. It was the product of two different kinds of Go-Getters—a businessman and an inventor.

A. T. Stewart, the merchant who built up the business, came to the United States from Ireland at age 17. He started by selling the Irish laces he had brought with him. But he soon branched out into all kinds of goods. He was a bold, ambitious businessman. And he decided to spend a fortune on an enormous building in an entirely new style. To help him plan his grand new store, he picked an inventing genius who was sure to try something new.

James Bogardus, the man Stewart chose, had started as a watchmaker's apprentice in upstate New York. He first became famous by his design for an eight-day clock. Then he invented all kinds of new machines—for making cotton thread, for mixing lead paint, for grinding sugar, for metering gas, and for engraving postage stamps. He patented a metal-cased pencil with a lead that was "forever pointed."

His most important new idea was to construct buildings of cast iron. Bogardus's own five-story factory, built in 1850, was probably the first cast-iron building in America. The store he built for Stewart overwhelmed every-

✄ Critical Thinking Activity: Making Comparisons How was the modern department store a product of growing technology? Have students make a list of technological advances that aided the development of the first department stores. Next to each item, describe its contribution. Have students make a second list—this time of technological advances that have contributed to the department store of today. Ask students to observe the similarities and differences between the two lists.

body at the time by its height— eight stories. It quickly became famous as the biggest store in the world.

Bogardus used cast iron to make an impressive Buyers' Palace. On the ground floor the outside walls no longer needed to be thick—as they had to be when a tall building was made of stone. Now there could be larger windows on every floor. Slender iron columns held up the high ceiling of display rooms a city-block wide. The ground floor was made even more palatial by a grand central staircase and a great rotunda reaching up the full height of the building, topped by a glass roof through which the sunlight streamed. You could enjoy long indoor vistas of appealing merchandise—gloves, umbrellas, suitcases, coats, furniture, all kinds of things in all shapes and sizes and colors. All the people busy looking, buying, and admiring helped make a splendid spectacle.

Naturally the Go-Getting department store-keepers wanted to display their goods to everybody who walked down the street. The thin cast-iron building frames made this easier, but it would not have been possible without a new kind of window. Before the age of the department store, glass was expensive. Windows had to be small. They were made to admit a little daylight or to look out of.

Then, not long before the Civil War, an Englishman invented an inexpensive way of rolling out glass in large sheets. These large sheets of glass now at last made possible the "show window." Americans invented this expression for the new kind of window that was made to look into. Now the goods could advertise themselves. The department store was a new, very American, and very democratic kind of entertainment where the admission was always free.

See "Section 4 Review answers," p. 412E.

Section 4 Review

1. Identify: A. T. Stewart, James Bogardus.
2. Why was Stewart's store so successful?
3. **Critical Thinking: Identifying Central Issues.** In what way were the new department stores "democratic"?

See "Lesson Plan," p. 412E.

5. Things by the millions

On July 4, 1876, the nation celebrated its hundredth birthday with a Centennial Exposition held at Philadelphia. On the fairgrounds there were no rifle ranges or roller coasters or freak shows. There was no need for any. American products of all shapes and sizes—from shiny new bicycles to Alexander Graham Bell's strange machine that sent your voice over a wire—were themselves quite enough to entertain and amaze.

Visitors from Europe were astonished at how fast the United States had moved ahead. It was now threatening to take England's place as the leading manufacturing nation in the world. Machinery Hall, which drew the biggest crowds at the fair, was dominated by the gigantic Corliss steam engine. The largest ever, it was 40 feet high, weighed 700 tons, and produced over 2000 horsepower.

But it was not only size and quality that impressed visitors from the Old World. They were astonished by how cheaply Americans could make so many different things. Early in the 1800s one ingenious Connecticut manufacturer, Eli Terry, had already managed to turn out clocks that sold for so little it was not worth having an old one repaired. By the time of the Civil War good American clocks sold for less than 50 cents each, and New England factories were producing a half-million clocks each year.

Now in 1876, Europeans who saw the Philadelphia exhibits were convinced that Americans would change the world. The American machines, one Swiss engineer predicted, would "overwhelm all mankind with a quantity of products which, we hope, will bring them blessing."

Machine tools. To make things by the millions, Americans first had to create whole new industries and whole new ways of thinking. Newest and most essential was the industry for making machine tools. Machine tools were the parent machines—the machines for making the sewing machines, the gun-making machines, the clock-making machines, and all the rest. Since all these machines themselves were

See "Lesson Plan," p. 412E for **Writing Process Activity: Identifying Central Issues** relating to the sights and sounds of a city in the late nineteenth century.

made of metal, machine tools were mostly metal-cutting tools.

One of the most remarkable of the American machine-tool makers was William Sellers of Philadelphia. By the time of the Centennial Exposition his work was already famous. He had invented machines that could measure and cut metal at the same time. These were essential for turning out standard-size screws and bolts.

And now these fasteners were more important than anyone could imagine before. They held together the millions of metal parts of the new machines. In the old days each bolt had been specially made for use at one place in one particular machine. If you took a piece of machinery apart, you had to label each bolt so you could put it back in the same place.

Now that would not do. What good was it to make guns or clocks with standard-size parts unless you could hold them together with standard-size fasteners?

In his *System of Screw Threads and Nuts* (1864), William Sellers offered his own standard designs for the tiny grooves. After that, if you said your machine used a "Sellers Number 6," then everybody knew exactly what you meant. The United States government adopted Sellers's system in 1868. Before the end of the century an international congress in Switzerland made it the standard for Europe, too.

Efficiency experts. While Sellers was pioneering in standard design, other Americans were inventing a whole new way of thinking about factories. In the old days, the individual craftsman in his shop would simply do things the way they had always been done before. This was called the "rule-of-thumb." You did the job in a rough, practical way, using your thumb instead of a precise measure.

But the new American factory could not be run that way. If the old gunsmith's handiwork was crude or inefficient, it meant simply that he made less money or that people stopped buying guns from him. But in a factory where hundreds of people labored elbow to elbow, everybody suffered if one worker blundered. If your work was not precise, your mistakes were carried all over the country in the thousands of misshapen parts that came off your machine.

Now there was need for a new science—a science of avoiding waste. "Efficiency" was another name for it. The Go-Getting engineer ✘ who invented it called it the "Science" of Management.

The efficiency pioneer, Frederick W. Taylor, was born in 1856 in Philadelphia. His mother, a fervent abolitionist, wanted to liberate men and women from slavery. Taylor hoped to liberate men and women from waste. He was astonished that people who worried about conserving forests and waterpower and soil and minerals paid so little attention to conserving human effort.

He believed that there was one best way to do anything. But the one way that was least wasteful was not necessarily the way it had always been done.

Early in life he experimented to find the most efficient way to walk. He counted his steps and measured his stride. Then he figured out the best way to walk at different times and to different places. Taylor, who loved sports, even designed his own tennis racket, with a curved handle that made it look like a spoon. People laughed at him—until 1881 when Taylor and his partner (with Taylor using his spoon-handle racket) won the United States doubles championship.

The Bethlehem Iron Company hired Taylor to help make their huge plant more efficient. Every year millions of tons of coal and iron ore were shoveled into furnaces. Paying the men to shovel was one of the largest expenses of making iron. Each man brought his own shovel and shoveled any way he wanted. But wasn't it possible, Taylor asked, that there was actually only one best way to shovel?

Taylor and his crew went into the factory and wrote down exactly what the men were already doing. Each worker was using his one favorite shovel no matter what he was shoveling. A shovelful of "rice coal" weighed only 3 1/2 pounds, but a shovelful of iron ore weighed 38 pounds.

"Now," Taylor asked, "is 3½ pounds the

✘ Critical Thinking Activity: Predicting Consequences How did the "Science" of Management affect manufacturing? Observing our own inefficiency helps us to understand the work of Frederick Taylor. Ask students to define *efficiency* and to cite examples. Now ask for suggestions of some areas in which school could be run more efficiently. Divide the class into planning groups to develop proposals for the most efficient way to operate these areas. Groups should create a detailed outline of their approach and describe the anticipated outcome(s).

proper shovel load or is 38 pounds the proper shovel load? They cannot both be right. Under scientific management, the answer to the question is not a matter of anyone's opinion; it is a question for accurate, careful, scientific investigation."

Taylor experimented until he found the right-sized shovel for each job. Taylor had discovered a Science of Shoveling! He designed different shapes and sizes of shovels and then tested each one to see that it was best suited to the stuff it had to carry. His small flat shovel was for the heavy ore, and his immense scoop was for light rice coal. Soon there were fifteen kinds of shovels in the Bethlehem toolroom, and the number of men needed to do the work dropped from 600 to 140. Taylor had abolished the waste.

This system, said Taylor, made it possible to pay each shoveler 60 percent more in wages. The wages of workers did rise somewhat. But, naturally enough, many workers were afraid they would lose their jobs. Others were afraid that, even if they kept their jobs, they would have to work harder. Many were afraid they would be regimented. They liked their own shovels. They did not like anybody telling them how to do their simple job.

Still, all over the country, "Scientific Management" became more and more popular with employers. They discovered that by making a science of the simplest jobs, they usually could find a better way.

☙ *Edison and his invention factory.*
Thomas A. Edison invented a new kind of factory—an "invention factory." Its purpose was to invent new kinds of things to make. In the 1870s Edison set up his first "invention factory" with $40,000 he received from his own early inventions.

Edison and the clever people he brought to his "invention factory" were tireless testers and imaginative mechanics. One of their first feats was to help make electric lighting possible. The hardest problem had been to find the right thread, or "filament," to put inside the bulb: It had to be one that would give light when elec-

tricity was sent through it and yet would not quickly burn out. They tried all sorts of materials—carbon, bamboo, hair, platinum, copper, and scores of other substances. They finally discovered that a filament of carbonized thread served well if it was in a vacuum. This made possible in 1879 the commercial production of light bulbs, which soon replaced Rockefeller's oil lamps.

Edison and his fellow inventors, looking for a way to record the human voice, invented the phonograph. They worked on a way to use the new art of photography to show "moving" pictures. In 1891 Edison patented a

This 1895 painting of "The Bessemer Converter" by S. B. Shiley shows foundry workers making steel at the Bethlehem Pennsylvania plant.

Bethlehem Steel Corporation

❧ See "Lesson Plan," p. 412E for **Cooperative Learning Activity:** Formulating Questions relating to inventions of the late nineteenth century.

☙ **Multicultural Connection:** African-American inventor and draftsman Lewis Latimer patented the first incandescent electric lamp with a carbon filament and wrote the first textbook used by the Edison company on its lighting system. Latimer also created drawings of the first telephone for Alexander Graham Bell and was the chief draftsman for General Electric and Westinghouse.

❧ "kinetoscope"—a kind of peep show which (p. 429) showed moving pictures inside a box.

Edison fired the imagination of the American people. He was nicknamed the "Wizard." When Congress awarded him a special gold medal in 1928, it was announced that his inventions had been worth $15,599,000,000 to humanity! But this was only to say that there really was no way of measuring his enormous contribution to American life. By the time of his death at the ripe age of 85, in 1931, he had become an American hero—a truly democratic hero because his work benefited every living American.

This photo of bustling Herald Square in New York City was taken about 1910. Note the large advertisement for Edison's phonograph.

The Museum of the City of New York

See "Section 5 Review answers," p. 412E.

Section 5 Review

1. Identify or explain: Centennial Exposition, Eli Terry, Frederick Taylor.
2. What is "Scientific Management"? What fears did it arouse in workers?
3. **Critical Thinking: Identifying Assumptions.** What assumption underlies the opinion that Thomas Edison was a "democratic" hero?

See "Lesson Plan," p. 412F.

6. Labor begins to organize

The growth of American business—the development of "scientific" ways of shoveling, of new kinds of stores, of bigger factories, of assembly lines, of huge corporations—transformed the lives of workers. They became cogs in a great machine. No longer were they skilled artisans, controllers of their tools. Instead they were becoming servants of the expensive tools of their employers. Workers no longer labored at home or in small groups alongside a boss who was both the owner of the business and their friend. Of course, even in those days they had worked from dawn to dark. But now they started and ended work when the factory whistle blew, and they worked twelve to sixteen hours a day in badly lighted and poorly ventilated buildings. Women and children made up more than half the work force. And the pleasant conditions of the early factories located in the countryside—in places like Waltham and Lowell—had disappeared under pressure of competition.

The rise of trade unions. Trade unions had existed for a long time. In the 1790s in New York, Philadelphia, and other cities, certain skilled workers such as shoemakers, printers,

Leslie's Illustrated Weekly, March 17, 1860

Strikes were still an uncommon event when the shoemakers in Lynn and Natick, Massachusetts, left their jobs in 1860 to demand higher wages. Soon other workers throughout New England also struck for more pay. Some 800 women shoemakers are shown parading in Lynn during a March snowstorm. They were led by the Lynn City Guards and their band. Ultimately, they won many of their demands.

and carpenters organized to protect their interests. But the prospects for organizing more of the nation's workers were not good. At first the courts held that unions were illegal because they were conspiracies. Then the Massachusetts Supreme Court in *Commonwealth* v. *Hunt* (1842) opened the path for unions when it declared that they were just as legal as any other club organized to help members for a legitimate purpose. Some states followed, but many still treated strikes, the unions' weapon for survival, as illegal.

In a few cities the trade unions joined to-gether in federations. But the largest of these, the National Trades Union, collapsed with the Panic of 1837.

By the time of the Civil War a small number of skilled trades—printers, iron molders, hat finishers, stonecutters, and cigarmakers, among others—had organized national unions to improve their wages and working conditions. But most American workers were not members of unions. It was harder here than in Great Britain, France, and other European countries to persuade workers to take the trouble and the risks of joining a union. For generally speaking,

More from Boorstin: "The case of *Commonwealth* v. *Hunt* had arisen in 1840 out of the . . . indictment against the Boston Journeymen Bookmakers' Society for conspiracy . . . . [They] were defended by Robert Rantoul, Jr., a versatile reformer who had been an energetic member of the Commonwealth's first Board of Education, a temperance leader and an opponent of capital punishment . . . . [He argued] that the English common law of conspiracies was not in force in Massachusetts. It was part, he said, 'of the English tyranny from which we fled.'" (From *The Americans: The National Experience*)

American workers were already better off than those abroad and had more hopes of rising in the world. Even with the arrival of large numbers of immigrants during the 1840s and 1850s and the increased competition for jobs, wages in the United States remained above those in other industrial nations.

The Molly Maguires tried to help members by harassing the mine bosses.

Brown Brothers

MOLLY MAGUIRE WARNING, No. 1

MOLLY MAGUIRE WARNING, No. 2

MOLLY MAGUIRE WARNING, No. 3

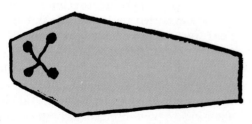

MOLLY MAGUIRE WARNING, No. 4

Labor strife. As the size of factories increased and more and more businesses became large corporations, the gap between worker and employer grew wider. Especially in large cities, it became easier to think of labor as merely a commodity to be bought at the lowest possible cost. A big company with lots of money could afford to close its factory when times were bad and wait for conditions to improve. But a worker still had to eat every day—in good times or bad. If workers complained, or went off the job on strike, the company could bring in new workers—strikebreakers.

Of course, workers resented this treatment. The nation that had recently been a military battleground between North and South now became a scene of industrial battles between workers and their employers. Large numbers of workers (even many not organized into unions) were willing to go on strike. They were risking their jobs to improve their lives. Their aim was shorter hours and better wages. Workers also wanted more of a feeling of independence, of control over their own lives and working conditions. To win this, peaceful means were sometimes not enough.

Beginning in the 1870s labor battles became more frequent. In 1872 nearly 100,000 builders and mechanics in New York City went on strike. They refused to work longer than eight hours in one day. After several months, they won their point.

Miners in the eastern Pennsylvania coalfields organized a secret society called the "Molly Maguires." In 1875, on flimsy and possibly false evidence that private detectives had gathered for the employers, ten Molly Maguires were hanged for murder. Then in 1877 a railroad strike that began on the Baltimore and Ohio Railroad spread across the country bringing death and destruction in its wake (p. 459). The industrial battleground was becoming a place of bloodshed.

In 1886 came the so-called Haymarket Massacre in Chicago. A bomb killed 7 policemen and wounded 70 more after they tried to break up a meeting of workers called by anarchists and Communists. In a fight at the steelworks at Homestead, Pennsylvania, in 1892, seven men

See "Lesson Plan," p. 412F for **Writing Process Activity: Recognizing Cause and Effect** relating to the causes and effects of labor organization.

were killed. The Pullman Strike in 1894 again tied up the railroads. In the Middle West, American troops, trying to keep the trains moving, were actually fighting American workers.

The Knights of Labor. Laborers tried a variety of ways of getting together to solve their problems. In 1869 the garment cutters of Philadelphia organized the Knights of Labor. Its idealistic aim was to bring all workers, skilled and unskilled, black and white, into one big union. They hoped that this union would give workers "a proper share of the wealth they create," more leisure time, more of all the benefits of society. They tried to set up companies owned by the workers themselves. They opposed child labor and demanded the eight-hour day.

The Knights were against strikes. But some of their radical members went on strike anyway when the railroads cut wages in 1884. After they won this fight for better wages, membership in the Knights boomed to 700,000. But then the Knights of Labor were involved in the Chicago strikes at the time of the Haymarket Massacre. Although they were not radical at all, a fearful public opinion lumped them together with anarchists and Communists. Their membership then rapidly declined.

Samuel Gompers and the AF of L. Labor leaders learned a good deal from the collapse of the Knights of Labor with its idealistic program and its attempt to combine all workers in one big union. One of them was a Go-Getter organizer named Samuel Gompers.

Born in London, Gompers left school at age 10 to begin work as a cigarmaker. He was 13 when his family came to the United States. Finding work in New York City, he became a member of the cigarmakers' union that took part in a strike that failed in 1877. Then he set about reorganizing the union on a nationwide basis. He charged high dues to build up cash reserves for strikes, and he strengthened discipline within the national union. Strikes were only allowed when the union had the money to support the workers so they could hold out long enough to succeed.

Gompers had developed a special American

AF of L-CIO

Practical and businesslike Samuel Gompers was the founder of the American Federation of Labor. This photograph was taken by a company detective as Gompers prepared to visit miners at a West Virginia coal mine.

approach to the problems of labor. In those years many workers in Europe were organizing to make revolutions. Over there desperate workers were trying to abolish capitalism and take over the factories themselves. But Gompers was no revolutionary. A hardheaded, practical man, he believed that in the long run American workers would be better off if they organized swiftly for a larger share of the profits. They should be as businesslike as the employers themselves. This was "bread and butter" unionism—aimed at higher wages, shorter hours, and safer working conditions.

✗ Critical Thinking Activity: Demonstrating Reasoned Judgment What benefits did labor unions offer American workers? Have students generate a list of problems facing labor in the late nineteenth century. Next to each item, ask students to suggest ways that a labor union could alleviate the problem. Based on this work, ask students to decide whether they would have joined a labor union and to explain their decision.

Library of Congress

The colorful poster from the Locomotive Firemen's union honors English inventor George Stephenson, who is known as the "father" of the locomotive.

Library of Congress

The Longshoremen's membership card bears several patriotic emblems and inspiring mottoes.

This approach was so successful that other trades followed the example. Gompers became the father of national unions in the United States. In 1881 he brought many unions together in the Federation of Organized Trades and Labor Unions. In 1886 this was reorganized as the American Federation of Labor. With Gompers as president, the AF of L grew steadily in size and power. By 1904 it had 1.75 million members.

Still, most workers remained unorganized. As late as 1923, steelworkers were laboring twelve hours a day, seven days a week. Labor had a long way to go. Unions would not come into their own until the days of the New Deal and World War II.

(p. 432)

See "Section 6 Review answers," p. 412F.

Section 6 Review

1. Identify or explain: *Commonwealth* v. *Hunt*, National Trades Union, Molly Maguires, Haymarket Massacre, Homestead Strike, Pullman Strike, Samuel Gompers, AF of L.

2. What progress had labor unions made by the time of the Civil War?

3. Describe labor-management conflict after 1870.

4. What were the aims of the Knights of Labor? Why did their membership decline?

5. **Critical Thinking: Identifying Central Issues.** Explain Samuel Gompers's "bread and butter" unionism.

Continuity and Change: Economics Point out to students that the organization of labor under Samuel Gompers was aimed at attaining better working conditions. However, despite the union's goals of higher pay and shorter hours, the AF of L catered to skilled workers only, excluding the majority of workers who were unskilled (i.e., miners, factory workers), along with African Americans, and women. Not until the creation of the Committee for Industrial Organization (CIO) would these groups, as well as immigrants from Eastern and Southern Europe, become part of organized labor. (See p. 654.)

Chapter 16 Review

See "Chapter Review answers," p. 412F.

Focusing on Ideas

1. How did each of the following developments help transform the United States between 1865 and 1900: railroad growth; trusts and other business combinations; new methods of merchandising; standardization in manufacturing; scientific management; labor unionism?

2. List some personal traits of the captains of industry and finance such as Rockefeller, Carnegie, and Morgan. Do you think the same traits characterize leaders of industry and finance today? Explain.

3. How did the technological developments of the late nineteenth century serve to democratize American life?

Taking a Critical Look

1. **Predicting Consequences.** Had Alexander Hamilton and Thomas Jefferson been able to see the United States in 1900, one of them probably would have celebrated and the other probably would have wept. Who would have celebrated? Who would have wept? Why?

2. **Identifying Central Issues.** The key to rapid industrialization of the United States was not so much the invention of machines and gadgets as it was standardization of parts. Discuss, giving examples.

Your Region in History

1. **Geography.** Using the maps on page 414 describe the growth of railroads in your region between 1870 and 1890. How was your area affected by standard time?

2. **Culture.** Use the newspaper archives at your local library to research the first department stores in your community. What types of goods and services did they offer? What impact did they have on the community at large? What happened to smaller stores that offered similar goods and services?

3. **Economics.** Identify and describe the achievements of some business or labor leaders in your state between 1870 and 1900. How were these people linked to developments described in this chapter?

Historical Facts and Figures

Predicting Consequences. Use the chart below to help answer the following questions: (a) How many barrels of oil were produced in 1870? In 1900? (b) Which decade saw the largest percentage increase in oil production? (c) What was the average percentage increase per decade between 1870 and 1900? (d) If oil production continued to increase at the same rate after 1900, how many barrels of oil would be produced today? (e) How do you think your estimate compares with the amount of oil actually produced in the United States today? Find out from the United States Department of Energy how much oil was produced last year. If this figure differs from your estimate, explain what factors might account for the difference.

Production and Value of Crude Petroleum, 1870–1900		
Year	**Production (in barrels)**	**Value/ Barrel**
1870		$3.86
1874		$1.17
1880		$.94
1886		$.71
1890		$.77
1892		$.51
1900		$1.19

= 5 Million Barrels of Petroleum (210 Million Gallons)

Source: *Historical Statistics of the United States*

Chapter 17
The Challenge of the Cities

Identifying Chapter Materials

Objectives	Basic Instructional Materials	Extension Materials
1 The Growth of an Urban Nation • Explain the growth of American cities during the second half of the nineteenth century. • Discuss the typical problems and benefits posed by immigration.	**Annotated Teacher's Edition** • Lesson Plans, p. 436C **Instructional Support File** • Pre-Reading Activities, Unit 6, p. 15 • Skill Review Activity, Unit 6, p. 18 • Skill Application Activity, Unit 6, p. 19	**Enrichment Support File** • Ellis Island: Gateway to America (See "In-Depth Coverage" at right.) **Suggested Secondary Sources** • See chart at right. **American History Tranparencies** • Geography and History, p. B39 • Our Multicultural Heritage, pp. C9, C11, C13, C27, C91, C95
2 Reformers and Self-Helpers • Identify reformers prominent between 1880 and 1900 and identify the issues they sought to resolve. • Discuss the concept of Social Darwinism. • Identify liberal and conservative viewpoints on pressing social issues and their solutions.	**Annotated Teacher's Edition** • Lesson Plans, p. 436D	**Documents of American History** • W.C.T.U. Declaration of Principles, Vol. 2, p. 22 **American History Transparencies** • Fine Art, p. D57
3 The Spread of Learning • Describe how educational opportunities for Americans expanded in the late 1800s.	**Annotated Teacher's Edition** • Lesson Plans, pp. 436D–436E	**Documents of American History** • The Morrill Act, Vol. 1, p. 412
4 Bridge-Building Heroes • Point out the significance of bridges and skyscrapers and identify James B. Eads and the Roeblings.	**Annotated Teacher's Edition** • Lesson Plans, p. 436E	**Extension Activity** • Bridge Statistics, Lesson Plans, p. 436E
5 Going Up! Elevators and Skyscrapers • Identify reasons for building skyscrapers in the late 1800s.	**Annotated Teacher's Edition** • Lesson Plans, p. 436F	**Extension Activity** • Skyscrapers, Lesson Plans, p. 436F
6 New Towns in the Country • Explain the purposes and characteristics of company towns and garden cities. • Discuss the differing historical assessments of life in one particular company town, and evaluate the evidence offered on each side.	**Annotated Teacher's Edition** • Lesson Plans, pp. 436F–436G **Instructional Support File** • Reading Activities, Unit 6, pp. 16–17 • Critical Thinking Activity, Unit 6, p. 20 • Chapter Test, pp. 21–24 • Additional Test Questions, Unit 6, pp. 25–28	**Extension Activity** • Company Towns and Garden Cities, Lesson Plans, p. 436G

17

Providing In-Depth Coverage

Perspectives on Immigration

The immigrants who arrived at Ellis Island in the late 1800s saw the United States as a land of opportunity, where even the poorest of souls could amass a fortune.

Between 1860 and 1915, America's urban population grew by more than 700 percent, largely as a result of immigrants pouring in from overseas. This massive influx of immigrants had an immeasurable effect on American culture and society. Education was improved to accommodate the swelling population, though at the same time thousands were living in slums and becoming involved with the political machines in the cities.

The chapter focuses on the changes brought on by this wave of immigrants, including attempts on the part of some to restrict immigration.

A History of the United States as an instructional program provides two types of resources you can use to offer in-depth coverage of the arrival of immigrants at Ellis Island: the *student text* and the *Enrichment Support File*. A list of *Suggested Secondary Sources* also provided. The chart below shows the topics that are covered in each.

THE STUDENT TEXT.

Boorstin and Kelley's *A History of the United States* unfolds the chronology of events leading to the wave of immigrants in the late-nineteenth century.

AMERICAN HISTORY ENRICHMENT SUPPORT FILE.

This collection of primary source readings and classroom activities reveals what it was like for the immigrants who arrived at Ellis Island in the late 1800s.

SUGGESTED SECONDARY SOURCES.

This reference list of readings by well-known historians and other commentators provides an array of perspectives on the arrival of immigrants in the late 1800s.

Locating Instructional Materials

Detailed lesson plans for teaching immigration as a mini-course or to study one or more elements of immigration in depth are offered in the following areas: in the *student text*, see individual lesson plans at the beginning of each chapter; in the *Enrichment Support File*, see page 3; for readings beyond the student text, see *Suggested Secondary Sources*.

IN-DEPTH COVERAGE ON IMMIGRATION		
Student Text	**Enrichment Support File**	**Suggested Secondary Sources**
• Urbanization, pp. 437–438 • Slums, pp. 438–440 • Political machines, pp. 441–442 • Attempts to restrict, pp. 443–444 • Immigration Restriction League, pp. 443–444 • Immigrants and Education, p. 447	• Lesson Suggestions • Multimedia Resources • Overview Essay/Ellis Island: Gateway to America • Literature in American History/"Ellis Island" • Primary Sources in American History/ Voices from the Island of Liberty • Art in American History/Lewis Hine at Ellis Island • Geography in American History/Immigrants in Chicago, 1892: A Geographic Profile • Great Debates in American History/ Should Immigration Be Restricted? • Making Connections	• *The Transplanted: A History of Immigrants in Urban America* by John Bodnar, pp. 57–84. • *The Uprooted* by Oscar Handlin, pp. 34–57. • *The Huddled Masses: The Immigrant in American Society, 1880–1921* by Alan M. Kraut, pp. 42–73. • *The Golden Door: Italian and Jewish Immigrant Mobility in New York City, 1880–1915* by Thomas Kessner, pp. 3–23. • *The Distant Magnet: European Emigration to the U.S.A.* by Philip A. M. Taylor, pp. 167–209.

The Growth of an Urban Nation

FOCUS

To introduce the lesson, read the following statements, write them on the chalkboard, or copy and hand them out. Have students write *agree* or *disagree* after each statement. Discuss the students' answers as a class.

Immigrants cause increased unemployment among American workers.

Immigrants help our country by bringing new skills with them.

Immigrants cause slums to grow.

Immigrants cause a drain on our country's resources because they depend on welfare and social services.

Immigration to the United States helps immigrants improve their life situation.

Immigrants fit in easily with the American way of life.

Most immigrants come to the United States to improve their economic circumstances.

Developing Vocabulary

The words listed in this chapter are essential terms for reading and understanding particular sections of the chapter. The page number after each term indicates the page of its first or most important appearance in the chapter. These terms are defined in the text Glossary (text pages 1000–1011).

political machine (page 441); **immigrant** (page 441); **immigration** (page 443); **literacy test** (page 443); **Anglo-Saxons** (page 443).

INSTRUCT

Explain

The immigrants generally endured horrible conditions on crowded ships before they even reached the United States. Before the steamship, trips took at least one month; on a steamship, ten days.

★ Independent Activity

Identifying Central Issues Assign each student one of the following topics: Why Cities Grew, City Slums, Politics in the Cities, and Anti-Immigrant Attitudes. Students will work independently to compile a list of five statements relating to their topic from the chapter text.

Section Review Answers

Section 1, page 444

1. a) metaphor used to describe cities because they brought immigrants from all over the world together and made them Americans. b) a large apartment building constructed for the poor according to a new design. c) the group of New York political operators under Boss Tweed who swindled New York City out of some $100 million between 1866 and 1871. d) neighborhood organizations in cities that offered jobs, money, and social services to the poor in return for political loyalty and votes. e) elected members of a city's governing body, such as a city council. f) Turner's thesis was that for decades the ability to move west had provided a safety valve for Americans who wanted or needed a new start. When the frontier lands became fully settled, social unrest increased because people who wanted to flee civilization had nowhere to go. g) founded to pressure Congress to pass legislation restricting immigration. h) restricted Chinese immigration to the United States. i) said that the Japanese would prevent their people from emigrating to the United States. 2. Farmers moved to the cities for new jobs and foreign immigrants arrived in search of political freedom and economic opportunity. 3. Tenement houses were usually six or seven stories high and were designed to hold the largest possible number of families. There were solid blocks of buildings whose inside rooms had no windows or ventilation. 4. Americans feared the new immigrants, blamed them for the country's problems, and believed they represented inferior races. The Immigration Restriction League pressed for a law that would require people to pass a literacy test before they could be admitted to the United States. President after President vetoed the bill, but in 1917 it was passed over President Wilson's veto. In 1882, the Chinese Exclusion Act became law, and the Gentlemen's Agreement of 1907 limited Japanese immigration. 5. Many immigrants did not have enough money to go farther west. Once in the cities, they wanted to live with people from their homelands. These colonies lost their separateness because the people in them became more and more alike as the children mixed with children from other backgrounds, learned English, feared being thought "foreign," and married people from other backgrounds.

CLOSE

To conclude the lesson, ask students: How did immigration affect life in the United States in the late 1800s? Why did some people want to restrict immigration? Should immigration have been restricted? Discuss students' answers as a class.

Section 2 (pages 444–446)

Reformers and Self-Helpers

FOCUS

To introduce the lesson, ask students to list the names of three reformers mentioned in this section. Have them provide words or phrases for each reformer to fill columns titled Goals, Methods, and Achievements.

Developing Vocabulary
settlement house (page 445)

INSTRUCT

Explain

Settlement houses were among the few resources for people needing help with problems relating to disease, poverty, crime, unemployment. Today there are many more government-funded agencies that provide such services.

☑ Writing Process Activity

Drawing Conclusions Ask students to imagine they are among the first social workers fighting for reforms. In preparation for writing an article on their experiences for their local newspaper, ask them to brainstorm possible topics. They might consider an interview with Jane Addams or Frances Willard, or they might describe the various reforms these women instituted. Students should write a topic sentence that will capture reader interest. Ask them to revise for logical order and specific detail. After proofreading, students can collect their articles in a magazine about the reform movement.

Section Review Answers

Section 2, page 446

1. Settlement houses offered immigrants in the cities a refuge and a club—a place to gather for social and educational purposes. All sorts of projects were begun there for young and old alike. The settlement houses also trained the first social workers and helped spark a movement for such reforms as laws limiting child labor. 2. Willard was a president of the Women's Christian Temperance Union in the 1870s. She worked both to secure women's right to vote and to promote abstinence from alcoholic beverages. Wells-Barnett, who was born a slave, became a newspaper writer in Tennessee but was driven out of the state after she exposed the facts about a lynching. In New York City she set up clubs that became

the foundation of the National Association of Colored Women. She also helped to organize the NAACP in 1909 and started a settlement house for black migrants to Chicago in 1913.

CLOSE

To conclude the lesson, remind the class that the issue of government responsibility for social services has not been clearly resolved in the United States. The government slowly became more involved in meeting different needs until the Great Depression of the 1930s, when FDR's New Deal greatly expanded government's role. Today necessary social services are provided by a variety of government programs and agencies as well as by private charitable organizations. Some people feel this works well. Others feel it does not. Who are the leading proponents of each view in our public life today? How do those leaders explain their views?

Section 3 (pages 446–450)

The Spread of Learning

FOCUS

To introduce the lesson, ask students to list those groups of Americans for whom new educational opportunities opened in the late 1800s. Ask students to list two benefits to the nation as a whole from increased education for each group listed. (Example: Education for immigrants helped them to get good jobs and to understand and participate in the American system.)

Developing Vocabulary
land-grant colleges (page 448)

INSTRUCT

Explain

Progress in education for Southern blacks was slow. "Separate but equal" schools remained the rule until the 1950s.

✿ Cooperative Learning Activity

Recognizing Ideologies Divide the class into teams of four and explain that students will prepare to debate Booker T. Washington's approach to black education versus that of W.E.B. DuBois. Within each group assign a team leader and a recorder. Have half the teams prepare a list of arguments supporting Washington's approach and the other teams a list of arguments supporting DuBois's approach. Randomly select teams from each side to debate the issue. Collect argument lists from all groups.

Section Review Answers

Section 3, page 450

1. a) a Congressman from Vermont who sponsored a law that turned federal land over to establish public colleges. b) founded Vassar a college for women. c) founded by Booker T. Washington in 1881 to train blacks in farming and mechanics. d) a group led by W.E.B. DuBois that demanded in 1905 that blacks be allowed to exercise their civil rights. 2. The schools brought together children from many different cultures and taught them the English language and American customs. 3. The Morrill Act opened the doors to a college education to Americans of many backgrounds and incomes because it led to the establishment of many new public colleges. 4. Vassar was established in 1861. Wellesley, Smith, Bryn Mawr, and many other women's colleges opened over the next twenty years. For blacks, Booker T. Washington founded the Tuskegee Institute in 1881 to help blacks learn skilled trades. 5. Washington believed that blacks should be patient, work hard, and hope to win their rights step by step by demonstrating their competence. DuBois believed that blacks should demand immediate equality and full civil rights.

CLOSE

To conclude the lesson, ask: Did the reformers of the late 1800s succeed in creating a universal education system? What, if anything, remains to be done?

Section 4 (pages 450–453)

Bridge-Building Heroes

FOCUS

To introduce the lesson, ask students to identify long or high bridges in or around a nearby or familiar large city. Ask how the disappearance of one of these bridges would affect the city. What adjustments would have to be made in the region?

INSTRUCT

Explain

A famous New York bridge is the Verrazano-Narrows Bridge which stretches from Staten Island to Brooklyn. It is 60 feet longer than San Francisco's Golden Gate Bridge. The Verrazano-Narrows Bridge was completed in 1964.

☑ Writing Process Activity

Expressing Problems Clearly Ask students to imagine they are present at the dedication of the Mississippi or the Brooklyn bridge. Before they write a historical account of the experience, ask them to make a chart of the sense impressions evoked by the scene. They can also include an explanation of the problems of building the bridge. Students should begin with a topic sentence summarizing the significance of the dedication. As they revise, they should check that their details are organized in spatial or chronological order. After proofreading, students can compare their accounts.

Section Review Answers

Section 4, page 453

1. Eads developed a diving bell that could be used to explore a river's bottom and—using a new type of steel—built the bridge that crossed the Mississippi at St. Louis. John Roebling became famous when he designed a wire-supported suspension bridge over the Niagara River in 1855. Then he designed the Brooklyn Bridge, which was built under the supervision of his son, Washington Roebling. 2. Many big cities were on the banks of rivers. As city populations grew, ways had to be found to cross those rivers easily, so people could get to and from outlying areas. Bridges made that possible.

CLOSE

To conclude the lesson, note that much of the surviving architecture of ancient civilizations is religious, memorial, or symbolic. Ask students: If you were an archeologist in A.D. 5000, scouring the area once called America for clues to its civilization, what surviving structures would you be likely to find? (Underground missile bunkers, great canal locks, remnants of skyscrapers, rocket launcher platforms, etc.) What would those structures tell you about the people who lived here? (They were concerned with military security; they built many large buildings very close to each other in a few places and did not build them at all in other places.)

Extension Activity

To extend the lesson, have students research five different types of bridges and create a table of the longest bridges of those types located in the United States. Their tables should include the type of bridge, its name, length, and location.

Section 5 (pages 453–455)

Going Up! Elevators and Skyscrapers

FOCUS

To introduce the lesson, ask the class: What advantages do skyscrapers bring to an urban area? (Many people can work and live in a tiny area; dramatic skylines can be achieved through their outlines against the sky.) What disadvantages can you think of? (Increased urban density may rapidly deplete the resources of the city—air, water, and electric power—and worsen congestion; immensity of the buildings may overwhelm their sites, and create wind-tunnel effects for pedestrians at street level.)

Developing Vocabulary
Bessemer process (page 454)

INSTRUCT

Explain

The Japanese have had to adapt to severe space limitations. The Japanese ambassador to the United States once remarked that the most amazing thing about American houses was their size. There was a separate room for each function, many of which were not used all day. His entire house in Japan was smaller than the garage of the home he occupied outside Washington. Ask students to research the ways the Japanese use their space to accomodate many more people and functions in a smaller area than Americans.

★ Independent Activity

Drawing Conclusions Have students write one paragraph in response to each of the following questions on recent developments in city expansion: Why are both new and bigger downtown skyscrapers and two- to ten-story buildings on the city fringes being built? Why has most recent expansion of shopping facilities occurred at the edge of cities and in the suburbs rather than downtown?

Section Review Answers

Section 5, page 455
1. After the Civil War, the cities of the United States grew quickly. Skyscrapers made it possible to put more living and working space on the same parcel of land by building up. The expense of land in the cities made it attractive to developers and builders to add many stories to a new building thereby increasing its value. 2. Otis invented a brake that would automatically clamp an elevator cage to the sides of the shaft if the cable broke. This invention made elevators safer and encouraged the trend toward higher buildings, which in turn allowed American cities to grow. Bessemer invented a furnace that made possible the mass production of good, cheap steel.

CLOSE

To conclude the lesson, conduct a class debate on the following question: Are huge cities contrary to basic American values? Students should be prepared to support their positions with solid reasoning.

Extension Activity

To extend the lesson, have students do a profile of a particular skyscraper. Encourage students to explore a diversity of buildings, not necessarily the most famous ones such as the Sears Tower or the Empire State Building. (You may want to refer them to the February, 1989 issue of National Geographic (Vol. 175, No. 2) which contains the article "Skyscrapers: Above the Crowd," by William S. Ellis.) Students' one-page reports should include such things as the architect's name, the building's dimensions, and its function.

Section 6 (pages 455–456)

New Towns in the Country

FOCUS

To introduce the lesson, divide the class into four small groups. Have the groups debate in pairs the proposition that Pullman was a good place to live. Give each team an opportunity to speak and an opportunity to make a rebuttal. Each part of the debate should be timed. (You may want to refer to the Critical Thinking Worksheet.)

Developing Vocabulary
company town (page 455); **utopia** (page 456)

INSTRUCT

Explain

The quality of life in Pullman is still under debate. Historians are still sifting the evidence, a task made difficult by the fact that much of the evidence seems to have been biased or distorted by one side or the other.

☑ Writing Process Activity

Demonstrating Reasoned Judgment Ask students to imagine they are new residents of a company town or a garden city. In preparation for writing a letter to friends, ask to list details about their new home and lifestyle. Students should begin their letter with a topic sentence that persuasively states the advantages of moving. As they revise, ask them to be sure that they have included the disadvantages as well. Details and reasons should be arranged in order of importance. After proofreading, students can read letters to the class.

Section Review Answers

Section 6, page 456

1. Early suburbs included the "garden cities" of Llewellyn, New Jersey; Riverside, Illinois; Old Greenwich, Connecticut; Lake Forest, Illinois; Shaker Heights, Ohio; and Radburn, New Jersey. 2. Company towns gave workers a place to live near their places of work and out of the city slums. But in these towns workers were completely dependent on the company.

CLOSE

To conclude the lesson, ask students: Does having a lot of evidence necessarily make a historical argument strong? (No. The evidence has to be evaluated, and the historian has to use good reasoning, also.) Based on the information given here, there is no "right" answer to the lesson focus question. There is conflicting evidence about Pullman, and your students, as historians, should be ready to evaluate that evidence.

Extension Activity

To extend the lesson, have students design their own company town or garden city. Students should also write a brief description to accompany their "blue-prints." The descriptions should include the purposes and features of their design as well as the town or city's location.

Chapter Review Answers

Focusing on Ideas

1. Villages: a church school(s), a blacksmith, doctor, perhaps a bank, store(s), a lawyer, etc. Cities: these services and newspaper(s), mills, factories, offices. 2. Water supply, sewerage, gas lines (and later telephone and electric lines), street building and maintenance, public transportation, hospitals, police and fire protection, schools. Corruption occurred in awarding building permits and contracts, land acquisition, payroll padding, protection of vice, awarding of franchises for natural monopolies. 3. Cities with new skyscrapers, bridges, department stores, etc., revealed slums, corrupt politics, and discrimination in schools, jobs, and housing.

Taking a Critical Look

1. Changes easy to blame on Newcomers: rising crime rates, strikes involving alien workers, higher taxes for public services, rise of slums, low wages (foreigners willing to work for less), crowding, disease, noise. 2. Cities offered numerous jobs requiring formal education and provided educational institutions.

Your Region in History

1–3. Answers will vary depending on your region. Consult your local library or historical society.

Historical Facts and Figures

(a) 15% in 1850; 28% in 1880; and 40% in 1900. (b) 52,803,000 people. (c) Nearly 17,000,000. (d) Most immigrants chose to live in urban areas. (e) Yes, refer to text p. 437.

Chapter 17

The Challenge of the Cities

In 1873, two years after the fire that had destroyed Chicago, architect Louis Sullivan visited the center of the city. He found it

> magnificent and wild; a crude extravaganza, an intoxicating rawness, a sense of big things to be done. For "big" was the word . . . and "biggest in the world" was the braggart phrase on every tongue. . . . [The men of Chicago] were the crudest, rawest, most savagely ambitious dreamers and would-be doers in the world . . . but these men had vision. What they saw was real.

✖ This, too, was the spirit of the years between the end of the Civil War and the turn of the century. It was called the "Gilded Age" to describe its vulgar, cheap, and gaudy aspects. But though it was sometimes ruthless, corrupt, and destructive, for the most part it was moving, building, expanding, reforming, and dreaming.

In 1837 Chicago had just 4200 people. This "Bird's-Eye View" shows the busy city in 1898.

Chicago Historical Society

✖ Critical Thinking Activity: Formulating Questions What challenges did American cities face between 1865 and 1900? Have students carefully observe the photographs, illustrations, and graphics in the chapter. Have students use their observations to suggest topics that would concern American cities in the late nineteenth century. Tell students to write these topics in the form of questions for posting in the classroom while they study Chapter 17.

See "Lesson Plan," p. 436C.

1. The growth of an urban nation

During the years after the Civil War there was not only a movement westward to settle the Great Plains, but also another great movement of people from the country to the cities. When the Civil War began, only one American in five was living in a city. By 1915, cities held half of all Americans. Between 1860 and 1915 the nation's rural population just about doubled, but the urban population grew more than 700 percent.

Farmers move to the city. The new cities grew mainly in the East, the Middle West, and the Far West, but they could be found wherever industry was developing. The new city-people came from everywhere.

Railroad builders sent salesmen overseas to boast the wonders of the American farms and persuade immigrants from European cities and farms to come settle along their tracks in the West. At the same time, many American farmers in the East and Midwest were moving away from the land to the city. Behind them in the countryside they left ghost villages. One such village in New England had a population of two inhabitants, one living on each side of the broad street. The abandoned church and the dilapidated schoolhouse were being taken apart for lumber and for kindling wood. Some of the farmers had gone west, but most had gone to the cities. By 1910 more than a third of the people living in American cities had moved in from American farms.

Immigrants come to the cities. Of the 25 million immigrants who came to the United States between the Civil War and World War I, most settled in the cities. Outside of cities many of them would have felt lonely and lost. They loved the friendly bustle and wanted to be close to people like themselves. And some of them had no choice. They had spent everything to cross the ocean and had no money left for a trip west.

Within the big American cities there sprouted little immigrant cities. By 1890 New York City held as many Germans as Hamburg, twice as many Irish as Dublin, half as many Italians as

State Historical Society of Wisconsin

Immigrant women gather in the market square of a middlewestern town in the 1890s. One (far left) has adopted an American-style hat.

Naples. And besides, there were large numbers of Poles, Russians, Hungarians, Austrians, Norwegians, Swedes, and Chinese. Four out of five New Yorkers either were born abroad or were the children of foreign parents. The Germans and Irish who had come before 1880 were found nearly everywhere in the United States. There were also lots of Canadians in Boston and Detroit, Poles in Buffalo and Milwaukee, Austrians in Cleveland, and Italians in New Orleans.

The urban mixture. Cities were sometimes called the nation's "melting pots." Perhaps they should have been called "mixing bowls." The adult immigrant sometimes became Americanized only slowly. But very quickly a whole colony found its special place in American life. Just as the new United States had first been made from thirteen different colonies, now a great nation was being made from countless colonies of immigrants.

Wherever you came from, you could find a neighborhood in New York or in the other big cities where you could feel at home. Whether you were from Germany, Italy, Hungary, or Poland, you could shop in your own old-country

Continuity and Change: Social Change Point out to students that most of the immigrants arriving in the United States between the Civil War and World War I were drawn to the cities. This was unlike the immigrants arriving from 1820 to 1850, who went out into the countryside to work on the new roads and canals and to buy the inexpensive land. This flocking of new immigrants to cities contributed to the United States' shift from a rural to an urban society. (See p. 265.)

On tenement back porches, like those shown in this photograph by Jacob Riis about 1900, clotheslines stretched from post to post and from porch to backyard alley. Notice the flowerpots and plant boxes on the railings.

language, buy familiar old-country foods, and attend a church offering your old-country services. By 1892 nearly a hundred newspapers in German were published in American cities. And there were dailies in French, Italian, Japanese, Polish, Yiddish, and a dozen other languages.

Although these immigrant colonies tried to keep separate, they could not stay separate forever. The people from different colonies became more and more alike. Children went to school and learned English. They stopped speaking their parents' language and sometimes stopped going to their parents' church. They were afraid to seem foreign. Then, too, a young man from the Italian colony might marry a young woman whose parents spoke German. In the city, people could not help feeling closer to one another.

City slums. If the crowds were the joy of the city, crowding was the curse. New York—the nation's biggest city and busiest seaport and the magnet for the world's immigrants—was where the problem was worst. And in New York, American know-how, which at the same time was building grand cast-iron palaces for department stores, produced another, but unlucky, American invention. This was the "tenement house."

New Yorkers, of course, did not invent the slum. European cities had their streets of ancient rickety buildings and evil-smelling hovels where the poor were tumbled together. But in the years after the Civil War, New York City produced a new kind of slum—the tenement-house slum.

Most newcomers to the city could not afford to pay much rent. Back in the early years of the 1800s the poorer people of New York had lived in shacks on the swamps at the edge of Manhattan Island. But as the island filled with people, specially designed buildings went up for the city's new poor. Tenement houses were buildings six or seven stories high designed to hold the largest possible number of families. They were solid blocks of deep buildings whose inside rooms had no windows or ventilation. There were also helter-skelter buildings of many other kinds.

The dumbbell building. Then in 1878, to help find something better, *The Plumber and Sanitary Engineer*, a builders' magazine, announced a contest for architects. The editors offered a $500 prize for the best plan for tenement apartments for the poor.

The winning plan was the "dumbbell" tenement. It was called that because the whole building, looked at from above, was thin in the middle and bulged at both ends like the dumbbells used in gymnasiums. This plan had a good deal to be said for it compared with the plan of the flimsy firetraps that were common before. The dumbbell tenement, usually built of brick, was supposed to be fireproof.

It was designed to fit on a narrow lot. On each of the seven floors there were four sets of apartments—two in front and two in back. Since the

Enrichment Support File Topic

⊕ **Geography and History: Location** Have students compare the maps to the right. Ask: How many cities of 100,000 inhabitants or over were there on the Great Lakes in 1870? (Two.) In 1900? (Seven.) In what direction(s) did the population seem to be spreading by 1900? (West and South.) According to the text on pages 437 and 438, what are some of the reasons for rapid city growth? (Cities grew wherever industry was developing; farmers were moving from the land to the cities; and of the 25 million immigrants who arrived in the United States between the Civil War and World War I, most settled in cities.)

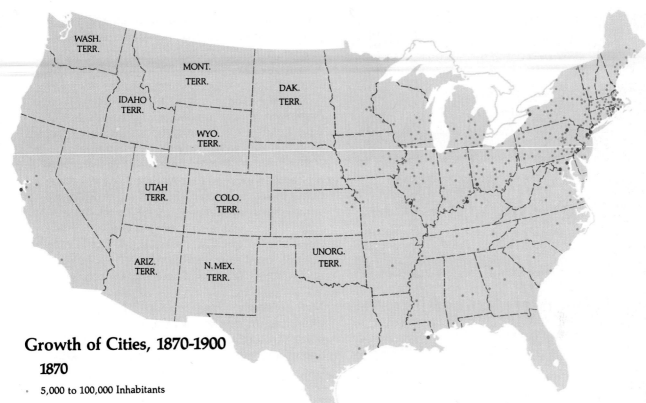

Growth of Cities, 1870-1900

1870

· 5,000 to 100,000 Inhabitants

• 100,000 Inhabitants and Over

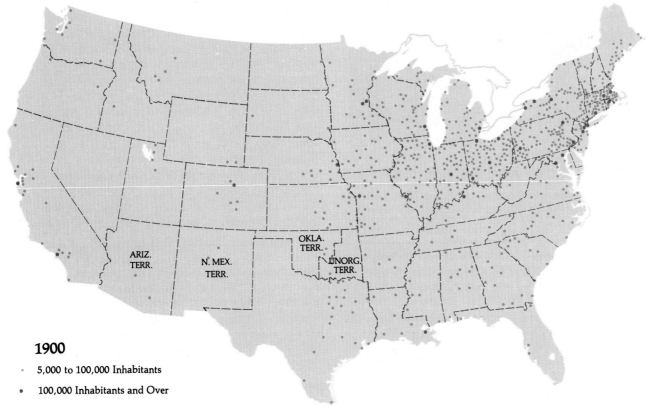

1900

· 5,000 to 100,000 Inhabitants

• 100,000 Inhabitants and Over

DATA: CARNEGIE INSTITUTION OF WASHINGTON.

The Museum of the City of New York

The Museum of the City of New York

The tenement kitchen was a multipurpose room. It was a second bedroom (top) for many poor families. It also provided a workshop (bottom) for others. The sewing machine provided a livelihood for thousands of immigrant families. Both photographs are by Riis.

stairway ran up the middle, the front and back rooms got some light and air from their windows on the street. Many people could be crammed into a small space.

What was new about the plan was that the inside rooms were also supposed to get some

light and air. When another tenement like it was built alongside, between them there was a narrow air shaft on which each inside room had a window. This became the standard plan for tenements.

By 1900 on the island of Manhattan alone there were more than 40,000 buildings of this type, holding 1,500,000 people. A prizewinning plan had produced the world's prize slum! (p. 438)

The air shaft between the buildings was only 56 inches wide—so narrow that it did not really bring in light. Instead the foul air brought up smells from the garbage piling up at the bottom. If there was a fire, the air shafts became flues which quickly inflamed all the rooms around. Up the air shaft resounded the noise of quarreling neighbors. There was no privacy.

Dirt, disease, and crime. The primitive plumbing in the hallway on each floor was shared by four families. It bred flies and germs. Sometimes the toilets became so disgusting that the tenants would not use them but depended on the plumbing at work or at school. There were no bathtubs with running water. Nearly every one of these tenement houses had at least one sufferer from tuberculosis, and sometimes there were many more.

When Theodore Roosevelt was governor of New York, he appointed a commission in 1900 to report on the tenement-house slums. They were not at all surprised that these buildings festered with poverty, disease, and crime. But they were surprised that, in spite of it all, so many of the people raised there managed to become decent and self-respecting. And the commission reported that the slums were even worse than they had been 50 years before.

Slum neighborhoods were given names like "Misery Lane" and "Murderers' Alley." This was hardly the America that the thousands of hopeful immigrants were looking for.

Boss rule. Under the influx of people and the pressures of rapid growth, the governments of big cities broke down. Streets were unrepaired, sewers nonexistent, garbage uncollected. Big cities were described as the worst-governed units in this democratic nation. In New York City during the days of Boss Tweed between 1866 and 1871, the city was looted of some $100 million by the boss and his underlings. Other political groups, "rings" as they were called at the time, robbed Philadelphia, Pittsburgh, and other cities.

Many reformers blamed this state of affairs on the immigrant who, they said, was "a European peasant whose horizon has been narrow, whose moral and religious training has been meager and false, and whose ideas of life are low." But Philadelphia, where 47 percent of the population was native born of native-born parents, was as corrupt as New York, where 80 percent of the residents were of foreign birth or foreign parentage.

The immigrant and the politician.

Immigrants did tend to vote for the boss and the followers of his political "machine." But this was because the machine members—often aldermen, or city councillors—provided friendly help. They supplied government jobs and money and advice. A new arrival who was arrested for a petty crime could turn to the alderman of his ward to find him a lawyer or to persuade the judge to let him off. The alderman

Everett Shinn, who began his career as a newspaper artist, painted "Cross Streets of New York" in 1899. He was one of the group of painters known as the "ashcan school" because they chose scenes from everyday city life as subjects for their canvases.

The collection of the Corcoran Gallery of Art. Gift of Margaret M. Hitchcock

organized benefit dances. The money paid for dance tickets would go to some worker who had been crippled at his work or to a widow who had no way of supporting her children. The alderman found doctors for the sick and brought groceries to the poor. He reached into his pocket to give a few dollars to needy orphans or to men wanting a new start in business. He was a one-man United Fund. No wonder immigrants voted for him and for the machine again and again.

The disappearing frontier. The problems of the Gilded Age—corruption in government and business, strikes, and labor violence—worried Americans. Why was it all happening? One bright young historian, Frederick Jackson Turner, who had been raised in the backwoods of Wisconsin, thought he knew the reason. The Census of 1890 had announced that the United States no longer had an unbroken line of wilderness frontier. Turner proposed the theory that this disappearance of the frontier explained many of the country's troubles.

According to Turner, what had made America the Land of Promise was not cities but the frontier. The free land out west, he said, had also been a safety valve. In earlier times if a family in an eastern city wanted a second chance, they could move out west. But now that the country

Austrian-born J. Keppler's lithograph cartoon from the magazine *Puck* shows a group of well-to-do Americans barring the entry of a new immigrant. The Newcomer sees what the Oldcomers cannot— the shadows looming behind them of their own immigrant fathers.

Culver Pictures

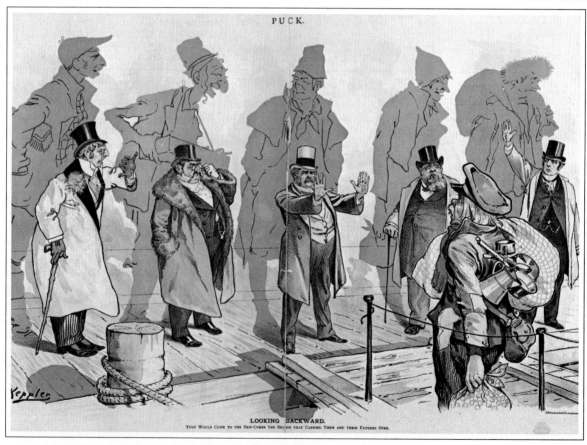

LOOKING BACKWARD.
THEY WOULD CLOSE TO THE NEW-COMER THE BRIDGE THAT CARRIED THEM AND THEIR FATHERS OVER.

More from Boorstin: "Machine politics was a natural product of the emigrant frame of mind. What is the main difference between a political machine and a political party? A party is organized for a purpose larger than its own survival. A political machine exists for its own sake; its primary, in a sense its only, purpose is survival. A political party may succeed and make itself obsolete by attaining the purpose for which it was organized . . . . [A] political machine succeeds only by surviving." (From *The Americans: The Democratic Experience*)

was being filled up, it was no longer possible to find a second chance by going out to the edge of civilization. Now if you were an unlucky newcomer in a slum, there appeared to be no escape.

Oldcomers versus Newcomers.   For a while it seemed that the country might be divided between Oldcomers and Newcomers. Oldcomers themselves, of course, had come from immigrant families, but their families had been here for a long time. Among them were the rich and famous. Few of them were crowded into slums.

In the older eastern states that still controlled Congress, the Oldcomers were in charge. They were most of those who had money and education and power. But the Oldcomers did not agree on how to cure the country's ills. Some tried to help the immigrant learn new ways, but some were simply frightened. They wanted to keep the country the way it was. They blamed the troubles on the Newcomers. Their answer was to slam the door. Simply because *their* families had been here longer, they felt that the whole nation belonged to them.

At Harvard College a group of New England blue bloods thought that their world was coming to an end. Three young men in the class of 1889, Charles Warren, Robert DeCourcy Ward, and Prescott Farnsworth Hall, had been taught by their professors that there was an "Anglo-Saxon" race superior to all others. The race was supposed to be separated from other races not by color but by their homeland. The "superior" people were supposed to be from England and Germany. And that just happened to be where the families of Warren and Ward and Hall had come from!

These young men had been raised near Boston. Their parents were horrified by the hordes of "vulgar" immigrants and especially by those with unfamiliar ways from Ireland and from southern and eastern Europe. These New England aristocrats said that the nation's problems could be solved by keeping out all people who were not like themselves.

Five years after their graduation, Warren and Ward and Hall formed the Immigration

Louis Stein Collection/California Historical Society

Chinese immigrants, dressed in traditional clothes and with their hair in long pigtails, walk down a street in San Francisco's crowded Chinatown about 1880.

Restriction League to persuade Congress to pass laws to keep out all "undesirable" immigrants. In their League they enlisted famous professors and writers. Their real object was to keep out the "new" immigrants—the Newcomers. These new immigrants, they argued, were the main cause of the increasing crime, the strikes, and most of the troubles of the country.

The literacy test.   To keep out "undesirables" they proposed a "literacy test." According to their proposed law persons over fourteen years of age who wanted to come into the United States would have to prove that they could read

Multicultural Connection: The first national immigration legislation was passed on May 6, 1882, barring persons ineligible for citizenship from immigration to the United States. The law was specifically directed at Chinese immigrants, and became known as the Chinese Exclusion Act. It was the first immigration act to bar a particular national group from entering the United States.

and write. They did not have to know English, provided they could read and write their own native language.

At first sight the test seemed harmless enough. Actually it was aimed against people from certain countries, such as Italy and Greece, where poor peasants had no chance to go to school. The Boston blue bloods believed that because Newcomers from such countries were not "Anglo-Saxons" they must be "inferior."

But in their proposed law they did not dare list particular countries. There already were many people in the United States from those countries. They would be insulted—and they, too, elected members of Congress.

Year after year the Immigration Restriction League tried to persuade Congress to pass a literacy test. But even when they finally pushed their bill through Congress, they did not manage to make it into a law. One President after another vetoed the bill. President Grover Cleveland called the law "underhanded," because it did not say what it really meant. President William Howard Taft said the United States needed the labor of all immigrants and should teach them to read. President Woodrow Wilson agreed.

All three Presidents said the law was un-American. The United States had always been "a nation of nations." It made no sense to keep out people simply because they had been oppressed. America was a haven for the oppressed. Here the starving could find bread, and the illiterate could learn to read.

In 1917, however, when the war in Europe was frightening Americans, the literacy test finally had enough votes in Congress to pass over President Wilson's veto.

Out on the West Coast, Oldcomers feared Newcomers from Asia. They worried about imaginary hordes that might come across the Pacific. And they had persuaded Congress to pass a Chinese Exclusion Act in 1882. Then, in 1907, President Theodore Roosevelt without the use of any law against the Japanese persuaded the Japanese government to stop their people from emigrating. This un-American

agreement came to be called the "Gentlemen's Agreement." And this became the slang expression for any agreement to discriminate against people when you were ashamed to admit what you were really doing.

See "Section 1 Review answers," p. 436C.

Section 1 Review

1. Identify or explain: "melting pots" and "mixing bowls," dumbbell building, Tweed Ring, political machines, aldermen, Turner's frontier thesis, Immigration Restriction League, Chinese Exclusion Act, Gentlemen's Agreement.
2. What movements accounted for the growth of cities after the Civil War?
3. Describe a typical tenement house.
4. Why and how was a start made on limiting immigration?
5. **Critical Thinking: Recognizing Cause and Effect.** Why did immigrant colonies form in the cities? Why did they lose their separateness?

See "Lesson Plan," p. 436D

2. Reformers and self-helpers

Not all the Oldcomers were frightened. Some became reformers. If the country had too many strikes and too much crime, they said, that could not be blamed on those who had just arrived.

It was mainly the fault, they said, of the Americans who had been here longest and who had had the most chance to make the country better. Who had built the cities and the slums where the poor were condemned to live? Who were the members of Congress and the leaders of business and the police officers? It was not the immigrants' fault if the nation was not prepared to receive them.

Jane Addams. One of the most remarkable of the reformers and one of the most original Americans of the age was Jane Addams. She was born with a deformity of the spine which made her so sickly that after graduating from college in 1882 she had to spend two years in

More from Boorstin: "[Robert Hunter's] *Poverty* (1904) which H. G. Wells called 'compulsory reading for every prosperous adult in the United States,' was an instant success. He described the extent and the consequences of poverty in the United States by drawing on the statistics of pauperism, of charitable society caseloads, of pauper burials, and of wage rates. His shocking conclusion was that in a total population of some 80 million, there were no fewer than 10 million persons living 'in poverty.'" (From *The Americans: The Democratic Experience*)

bed. When she was well enough to travel, her wealthy family sent her abroad to study art and architecture. What she really learned in Europe was something quite different.

In June 1888, when she happened to visit the famous Toynbee Hall in London, she discovered her life's purpose. There in the poorest section of the city lived a group of Oxford and Cambridge graduates helping the people of the neighborhood. Why not try something like that in the United States?

Jane Addams's plan was simple. In the poorest, most miserable city slum she would settle a group of educated young men and women from well-to-do families. Like Toynbee Hall, the place would be called a "settlement house." The well-bred young men and women newly "settled" in the midst of a slum reminded her of the early colonial "settlers" who had left the comforts of English life to live in an American wilderness.

The young men and women who came to live in the slum, seeing the struggles of the poor, would learn things they could never learn from books. At the same time, the people of the slum would use the settlement house as a school, a club, and a refuge.

Hull House. Since she knew Chicago, she decided to do her work there. In the neediest neighborhood she persuaded the owner of a large old house to let her have it free. That became her settlement house—between an undertaker's parlor and a saloon. She called it "Hull House" after the man who had built it for his home years before.

In the neighborhood of Hull House there were Newcomers from all over Europe—Italians, Germans, Polish and Russian Jews, Bohemians, French Canadians, and others. For the young, Jane Addams set up a kindergarten and a boys' club. And she paid special attention to the very old people whom nobody else seemed to care about.

Jane Addams's work became famous. All sorts of unexpected projects started at Hull House. The Little Theater movement, of amateur actors putting on plays to entertain themselves and their friends, developed there and

Culver Pictures

Jane Addams was a kind and gentle woman whose concern for needy newcomers led her to open Hull House settlement in Chicago. Many others were later to follow her example.

spread all over the country. She started a book bindery and a music school.

Settlement houses on the Hull House model appeared in big cities everywhere. Future playwrights, actors, composers, and musicians who had happened to be born into poor slum families now found their chance.

Thousands of lonely immigrants discovered that somebody else cared about them. Jane Addams—without the aid of governments or politicians—had helped make America the promised land.

Critical Thinking Activity: Predicting Consequences What community services were "settlement houses" able to provide? Divide the class into groups of six. Tell each group to imagine they are a six-member staff running a settlement house in 1900. Have them draw up a list of weekly activities that will be provided for immigrant families in the neighborhood. Ask each group to present their plans to the rest of the class.

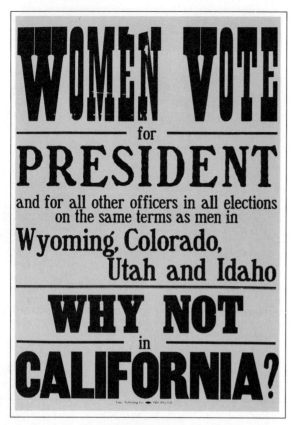

WOMEN VOTE
for
PRESIDENT
and for all other officers in all elections
on the same terms as men in
**Wyoming, Colorado,
Utah and Idaho**
WHY NOT
in
CALIFORNIA?

Tma. Publishing Co. Palo Alto, Cal.

The Bancroft Library, University of California, Berkeley

A women's suffrage amendment was sent to a narrow defeat by California's voters in 1896 after a strenuous campaign.

Other reformers. In Hull House and other settlement houses the first social workers—many of them women—were trained, and they became a growing force for change. They moved beyond private charity to use the power of the state to improve conditions. Their first activities produced laws limiting child labor and governing the hours and conditions of labor for women.

Frances Willard was an Oldcomer who fought for reform in another way. In the Wisconsin wilderness, where she grew up, she became a good hunter. The only schooling she received came from her mother, but she learned enough to attend a college in Illinois and become a teacher. Then she was caught up by the temperance movement. Abstinence in the use of alcoholic beverages, she felt, would protect the home and

Christian life. With her talent for organization and for oratory, in 1874 she was made president of the Women's Christian Temperance Union in Chicago and five years later was elected national president.

From that position Frances Willard worked also for women's right to vote. It was not surprising that the first progress came on the western frontier. There it was plain that new communities depended on pioneer women. Why shouldn't they be allowed to vote? Wyoming came into the Union in 1890 with women's suffrage. Then other western states gave women the right to vote—Colorado (1893), Utah (1896), and Idaho (1896). But the movement stalled, and little progress was made for over a decade.

Out of the South, too, there came other women reformers. Ida B. Wells-Barnett, who had been born a slave in Mississippi, became a newspaper writer in Tennessee. But when she wrote fearless stories exposing the facts about a lynching, she was driven out of the state. Then she went to New York City where she helped set up black women's clubs which became the foundation of the National Association of Colored Women in 1896. In 1909 she helped to organize the National Association for the Advancement of Colored People. And in 1913 she established a settlement house in Chicago to help black newcomers from the South find jobs and homes in the big city.

See "Section 2 Review answers," p. 436D.

Section 2 Review

1. How did settlement houses help immigrants?
2. **Critical Thinking: Making Comparisons.** Compare the reform work of Frances Willard and Ida Wells-Barnett.

See "Lesson Plan," p. 436D.

3. The spread of learning

In the city and on the countryside the public schools helped make Americans. They were free, and the states passed laws requiring all children to attend. There the children of Irish, German, Italian, and all sorts of other families

See "Lesson Plan," p. 436D for **Writing Process Activity: Drawing Conclusions** relating to late nineteenth-century reformers.

learned and played—and sometimes fought—together. They came to know one another better than their parents knew people from other countries. And some of these young people went on to study at new colleges and learned to become leaders.

The schools make Americans. At home many families spoke Polish or Italian or some other language, but in school everybody spoke English. Even if the parents spoke English with a foreign accent, soon the children sounded like other Americans. At home the children taught their parents English and all kinds of American customs. One little girl in New York City who had learned to use a toothbrush brought it home from school. She showed it to her mother, who had been born in a peasant hut in Poland and had never seen such a thing. Her mother, too, was soon brushing her teeth in the American manner.

Now many children could go on to the free public high school, which was an American invention. After 1870 these new public high schools spread across the country. By 1900 there were 6000 high schools attended by nearly 520,000 students, more than two and a half times the number attending only ten years before.

The flourishing schools made the United States one of the world's first literate nations. Thousands of the peasants and poor city workers who arrived from Europe had never learned to read. But in the United States the proportion of people who could read and write steadily increased after the Civil War. Unfortunately in the South the promising start made during Reconstruction was not followed by the Old Confederates when they took office.

Growth of the colleges. America had always been a land of help-yourself. But it was not easy for Newcomers to become leaders. So many respectable institutions remained in the hands of the Oldcomers whose families had been here for a century or more. For example, Harvard College—our oldest college, where young blue bloods had learned their ideas of Anglo-Saxon superiority—was run by Oldcomers. It was

State Historical Society of Wisconsin

This photograph taken at the end of the 19th century shows pupils from a school near Black River Falls, Wisconsin, assembled with their teacher for their annual school picture.

The Museum of the City of New York

Jacob Riis, a Danish immigrant, helped to improve the lot of New York City's poor with his books and striking photographs. This one showed Christmas Eve at a settlement house.

hard even to become a student there if you were not one of them.

New institutions offered the best chance for Newcomers who wanted to become leaders. Among the most remarkable and most American were the scores of new colleges and universities.

More from Boorstin: "The report on American secondary education which [Charles W.] Eliot prepared . . . (1892), urged higher standards and greater uniformity in the high schools: more 'modern' subjects should be taught to all, and all subjects should be taught in the same way to all students. This was a wide departure from the established American practice which still took for granted that all girls, and the boys who did not intend to go on to college, needed no more than an 'elementary' education." (From *The Americans: The Democratic Experience*)

At the outbreak of the Civil War there were only seventeen state universities. Then, in 1862 an energetic Republican congressman, Justin S. Morrill from rural Vermont, secured the passage of the Morrill Act. This act granted lands to the states from the public domain—30,000 acres for each of the states' senators and representatives in Congress—to support new state colleges. In these "land-grant" colleges students would be taught to be better farmers. The land-grant colleges also often offered solid courses in engineering, science, and literature. So here Newcomers, too, found an opportunity to learn.

After the Civil War, hundreds of other colleges and universities were founded. In the later years of the 1880s, some of the wealthiest Go-Getters gave millions of dollars to found and endow still more institutions of higher learning. In 1876 Johns Hopkins University was established from the fortune left by a Baltimore merchant. In 1885 a railroad builder, Leland Stanford, in memory of his son, set up Leland Stanford, Jr., University. In 1891 John D. Rockefeller, the Go-Getting oil millionaire, created the University of Chicago. And there were scores of others.

Many of these college founders had themselves never gone to college. But they shared the American faith in education. Even before the end of the 1800s, the United States had more colleges and universities than there were in all western Europe. And a larger proportion of the citizens could afford to go to college here than in any other country. The children of poor immigrants, along with millions of other Americans, now had a better chance to rise in the world.

Frances Benjamin Johnston, a prominent turn-of-the-century photographer, caught this senior American history class at Booker T. Washington's Tuskegee Institute.

Library of Congress

Continuity and Change: Social Change Explain to students that an increasing number of colleges and universities built after the Civil War created a need for students. This need was fulfilled by the invention of the free public high school. Once the idea caught on, change in American education was rapid. By 1970, 90 percent of Americans between the ages of 14 and 17 attended high school, and enrollment in colleges and universities included 50 percent of college-aged Americans. (See p. 764.)

Jacob Riis took this picture of immigrant children saluting the flag at the Moss Street Industrial School in New York City in the early 1900s. In rural areas the one-room schoolhouse was usual.

Women's colleges multiplied rapidly in the years after the Civil War. In 1861 Matthew Vassar, who had been born in England and had made his fortune as a brewer and in whaling, founded Vassar College. When Vassar advertised to attract students to his college, he also publicized the importance of higher education for women. Before long there were more women's colleges, including Wellesley (1870), Smith (1875), and Bryn Mawr (1880). Many other new colleges, especially in the Middle West, were open to women as well as men. And the number of women in college grew from 9000 in 1869 to more than 20,000 in 1894.

Education for black Americans. Wealthy men and women, mostly from the North, also gave millions of dollars to help educate black people. By 1900 there were already about 30,000 black teachers. John D. Rockefeller, for example, had contributed over $50 million, most of it to train more teachers for black schools. The South spent less money than other parts of the country on education of all kinds. And blacks there had to attend separate, and inferior, schools. How then were they to get ahead? Black leaders could not agree.

One way was proposed by Booker T. Washington. Born a slave, Washington worked his own way upward until he was famous throughout the world. His own story of his life, *Up from Slavery* (1901), was read by millions.

In 1881 Washington founded Tuskegee Institute in Alabama. There he trained thousands of blacks to be better farmers and mechanics, to make a good living, and to help build their communities.

He believed in a step-by-step way "up from

Multicultural Connection: In 1870 only 3.07% of southern African Americans had attended school. By 1890 this percentage had risen to 18.7%. Literacy rose from 30% in 1880 to 42.9% in 1890. Several colleges and universities were established including Fisk, Trinity, Gregory (all 1866), and Howard (1867).

slavery." He did not want blacks to spend their efforts learning history and literature and foreign languages and science and mathematics. Instead, he said, they should train quickly for jobs—and mostly for jobs they could do with their hands. The vote, which had been taken away from them in the 1890s (p. 646), could wait. Self-respect, self-education, and self-help, he said, would bring blacks the opportunities they desired.

Many who admired Booker T. Washington still did not agree with him. Why should blacks have to wait for their rights? Twenty-five years after Booker T. Washington started his Tuskegee Institute in Alabama, a group met at Niagara Falls.

Their black leader was W. E. B. Du Bois. His life had been very different from that of Booker T. Washington. Born in Massachusetts after the Civil War, he studied at the University of Berlin in Germany and then received a Ph.D. degree from Harvard in 1895. Du Bois was a poet and a man of brilliant mind and vast learning. Why should anyone try to tell Du Bois and others like him to be satisfied to work with their hands?

In 1905 the declaration by Du Bois's Niagara Movement expressed outrage. It demanded for blacks *all* their human rights, all their rights as Americans, and *at once.* It opposed all laws and all customs that treated blacks as if they were ❀ different from other people. And of course, it demanded the right to vote.

See "Section 3 Review answers," p. 436E.

Section 3 Review

1. Identify or explain: Justin Morrill, Matthew Vassar, Tuskegee Institute, Niagara Movement.
2. How did public schools help to Americanize the immigrants?
3. What was the importance of the Morrill Act?
4. Trace the growth of colleges for women and for blacks.
5. **Critical Thinking: Recognizing Ideologies.** Contrast the views of Booker T. Washington and W.E.B. Du Bois.

❀ See "Lesson Plan," p. 436D for **Cooperative Learning Activity: Recognizing Ideologies** relating to Booker T. Washington and W.E.B. DuBois.

See "Lesson Plan," p. 436E.

4. Bridge-building heroes

Many of the fast-growing American cities were on the banks of rivers—the highways of the pioneers. As immigrant families and farm families pressed in, the cities had to expand. They had to find ways of carrying thousands of daily passengers out beyond the old city limits. This meant that in order to hold their citizens together they had to span the neighboring waterways. Go-Getting engineers transformed the ancient art of bridge building to reach out to 📷 the new city frontiers.

(p. 451)

Bridging the Mississippi. Something about bridge building attracted and inspired the American inventive genius. James Buchanan Eads, the man who would build the bridge for St. Louis, had proven himself during the Civil War. In 1861, as an adviser to the Union navy, he proposed a fleet of ironclad gunboats to control the Mississippi River. Then, when the government took up his suggestions, he built the needed ships in 65 days.

After the war the people of St. Louis, which was on the west bank of the Mississippi, saw that they had to bring the railroad across the wide river and into their city if St. Louis was to grow. Many schemes were offered. But all were rejected until Eads appeared. As a boy he had worked on a river steamboat. When only 22 years old, he had invented a diving bell to salvage ships that had sunk in the river. And then he had done a lot of walking underwater on the very bottom of the Mississippi. He knew that river bottom almost as well as other men knew the city streets.

What Eads had learned was important. Building a bridge across the Mississippi depended first on finding solid support under the sandy river bottom. As Eads had moved along 65 feet below the surface of the water, he had seen the currents churning up the sands. He knew that the supports for his bridge would have to go far below those river sands all the way down to bedrock.

In 1867, when Eads began construction, his first problem was to lay the foundations of the two stone towers that would hold up the arches of the bridge in midstream. The towers would rise 50 feet above water level. The foundation of one would have to go down 86 feet below water level, and the other, where bedrock was deeper, would have to go down 123 feet. But was this possible?

Working underwater. Eads's plan was to use his own diving bell together with some new caissons—watertight working chambers—that had recently been perfected in England. The 75-foot-wide caissons would keep out the water while the men dug beneath the river sands to reach solid rock.

When Eads's men finally reached bedrock, they were working ten stories below the surface of the water! Because of the great pressures at that depth, the men could stay down only 45 minutes at a time. They had to come up slowly, and they rested long periods between shifts. Despite all precautions thirteen men died of "caisson disease" (sometimes called "the bends") from too rapid change in air pressure.

The bridge completed. Steel had never been used in such a large structure, but Eads decided to use it for the three vast arches of the bridge. When the standard carbon steel did not meet his tests, he ordered large quantities of the new chromium steel, and then supervised its production. While chromium steel was more costly, it was rustproof and needed no covering.

It took Eads seven years to bridge the Mississippi. Finally in 1874 in a grand ceremony the former Union general, William T. Sherman, pounded the last spike of the double-track railroad crossing the bridge. Then fourteen locomotives, two by two, chugged triumphantly across the river. President Grant came to St. Louis to proclaim Eads an American hero.

A bridge to Brooklyn. And there were other heroic bridge builders who helped open ways to the suburban frontiers. Few cities were quite so hemmed in by water as New York. Manhattan Island, heart of the city, was surrounded by the East River, the Hudson River, and the Atlantic

Smithsonian Institution

Bridge-builder John A. Roebling's vision and drive seem to come through in this photograph. He suffered an accident and died not long after this picture was taken.

Ocean. For a half-century there had been proposals for a bridge across the East River, connecting lower Manhattan Island to Brooklyn. When the fierce winter of 1866–1867 stopped all ferry service and isolated Brooklyn from Manhattan for days, it was plain that something had to be done.

John Roebling was ready with a plan. When he came to the United States from Germany as a young man, he opened the first factory for making wire rope out of many strands of wire twisted together. This new material was wonderfully suited for reaching over wide rivers where it was difficult or impossible to build masonry towers in midstream. From high towers on both ends you could suspend the strong wire rope to hold up the bridge.

If the Niagara River, for example, was to be spanned near the Falls, it would have to be by

📖 **More from Boorstin:** "One of the most brilliant . . . [lawyer-organizers] was James Frederick Joy . . . . He founded canal companies to connect with his rail lines. And he became a pioneer bridge builder. The crucial weakness of his Burlington line between Chicago and Kansas City was the lack of a bridge across the Mississippi. He formed a company in 1868 to build the bridge at Quincy and defied critics by spending $1.5 million on the project. The Burlington's business in that area doubled the following year." (From *The Americans: The Democratic Experience*)

THE GRAND DISPLAY OF FIREWORKS AND ILLUMINATIONS

AT THE OPENING OF THE GREAT SUSPENSION BRIDGE BETWEEN NEW YORK AND BROOKLYN

ON THE EVENING OF MAY 24th, 1883.

VIEW FROM NEW YORK, LOOKING TOWARDS BROOKLYN.

The Bridge crosses the river by a single span of 1,595 ft. suspended by four cables 15½ inches in diameter, each composed of 5,434 parallel steel wires. Strength of each cable, 12,000 tons. Length of each land span, 930 ft. New York approach, 1,562 ft. Brooklyn approach, 971 ft. Total length of Bridge and approaches, 5,988 ft. 6 ins. Height of Towers, 278 ft.

Height of Roadway above high water, at tower, 119 ft. 3 ins., at centre of span, 135 ft. Width, 85 ft., with tracks for cars, roadway for carriages, and walks for passengers. The Bridge is lighted by the United States Illuminating Co. with 70 Electric lights, of 2,000 candle power each. Construction commenced, January, 1870. Completed May, 1883. Estimated total cost, $15,000,000.

The grand opening of the Brooklyn Bridge on May 24, 1883, was celebrated with gun salutes and fireworks as this colorful Currier and Ives lithograph reveals.

such a "suspension" bridge. In 1855 Roebling completed a wire-supported bridge over the Niagara—strong enough to carry fully loaded trains. This feat made John Roebling famous. In 1860 he completed another suspension bridge, just outside Pittsburgh, reaching 1000 feet across the Allegheny River. And by 1867 he had completed still another outside Cincinnati across the Ohio River.

A bridge from Manhattan to Brooklyn would have to stay high above water level in order to allow the sails and smokestacks of large ocean-going vessels to pass underneath. Could a sus-

pension bridge, Roebling-style, solve New York's problem? Roebling's ambitious plan in 1867 proposed towers at both ends 271 feet above water level, holding up a main suspension span of 1595 feet. That was far longer than any suspension bridge ever built before.

Washington Roebling carries on. During the very beginning of construction in 1869, a ferry crushed John Roebling's foot against the dock, and he died from tetanus infection in two weeks. John Roebling's son, Washington Roebling, was ready to carry on. He too was a man

Critical Thinking Activity: Making Comparisons What events prior to 1865 were equal in stature to engineering feats such as the Brooklyn Bridge? Ask students to list events in American history before 1865 that had the same effect on American lives as the building of bridges across the Mississippi River or the East River. Encourage students to explain why these events were significant. Teachers may wish to extend the lesson by having students make analogies. (Brooklyn Bridge: Manhattan. Transcontinental Railroad: the East.)

of courage and had proved himself on the Gettysburg battlefield.

On his father's death, Washington Roebling at once took over the building of the bridge. In 1872, when fire in the Brooklyn caisson threatened the whole project, Roebling stayed below for seven hours in the compressed-air chamber. As a result he acquired "caisson disease."

Washington Roebling never fully recovered. Too weak to supervise the bridge on the spot, he would sit in a wheelchair in his apartment and watch the work through field glasses. Then he would give instructions to his wife, Emily, who carried them down to the bridge. All his communications with the world were through her. Efforts were made to remove him from the job, but his mind remained active, and he would not give up the command.

The dedication of the bridge. At 1:30 on the afternoon of May 24, 1883, fourteen years after John Roebling had begun the job, President Chester A. Arthur and his Cabinet joined with Governor Grover Cleveland of New York for the formal opening of the Brooklyn Bridge. Six warships anchored below the bridge fired a resounding salute, and from the center of the bridge came a dazzling display of fireworks. The orator of the occasion declared that this, the world's greatest bridge, was a triumph of "the faith of the saint and the courage of the hero."

The "saint," Emily Warren Roebling, attended the celebrations. But Washington Roebling, the heroic bridge-building son of a heroic father, was too ill to leave the room from which he had overseen the work. The President of the United States went to Roebling's simple apartment at No. 110 Columbia Heights to give his congratulations.

See "Section 4 Review answers," p. 436E.

Section 4 Review

1. What contributions did Eads and the Roeblings make to bridge construction?
2. **Critical Thinking: Identifying Central Issues.** How did bridge building contribute to the growth of cities?

See "Lesson Plan," p. 436F.

5. Going up! elevators and skyscrapers

After the Civil War, Americans were not only stretching *out.* They began using their own know-how—together with materials and know-how from all over the world—to stretch their cities *up.*

Although some Americans were moving to the suburbs, more people than ever before wanted to live and work right in the center of the city. Businessmen wanted to be where the action was. And many people who could afford to live in the suburbs still preferred to live downtown.

Solving problems. With old kinds of construction the tallest buildings had seldom been over five or six stories high. There were two problems that had to be solved before buildings could go higher.

The first problem—how to get the people up and down—was beginning to be solved even before the Civil War. In a few luxury hotels, elevators already carried guests up to the fifth and sixth floors. And in some early department stores the elevator was an attractive curiosity. Still, people were afraid to use them. Elisha Graves Otis invented a brake that would automatically clamp the elevator cage to the sides if the rope broke. To calm people's fears, Otis staged a sensational demonstration. He rode the elevator to the top. Then while an attendant cut the rope, Otis waved nonchalantly to the astonished spectators. Otis's early steam-driven elevators were slow, but before 1880 the improved "hydraulic" elevators (pushed up by water pressure in a long vertical cylinder) were climbing at 600 feet a minute. By 1892 an electric motor was carrying passengers up so fast that it "stopped" their ears.

The second problem—how to hold up the building—began to be solved when James Bogardus and others used cast iron for their Buyers' Palaces. No longer was it necessary to build a tall building like a pyramid, with thick supporting walls on the lower floors.

From dreams to reality. The time was ripe for the "skyscraper." Of course Bogardus was only

See "Lesson Plan," p. 436E for **Writing Process Activity: Expressing Problems Clearly** relating to the building of the Mississippi and Brooklyn bridges.

By the 1890s the new steel-framed skyscrapers were going up everywhere. Here is the Syndicate Building in New York City.

Library of Congress

buildings of true skyscraper design. Its frame was a tall iron cage. If the cage was strong and rigid, and solidly anchored at the bottom, then the building could go up high without needing thick walls at the bottom. This was "skeleton" construction. The building was held up, not by wide foundations but by its own rigid skeleton.

The first time Bogardus actually tried this, in 1855, he built a skeleton-framed tower eight stories high for a factory.

It was one thing to build a tower but quite another to trust the lives of hundreds to such a newfangled way of building. The first real try was in Chicago, where the pioneer was William Le Baron Jenney. An adventurous man of wide experience, he had helped build a railroad across Panama before there was any canal. In the Civil War he served on General Sherman's staff as an engineer.

In 1884 when the Home Insurance Company decided to construct a new office building in Chicago, they gave him the job. Jenney, who had probably heard of Bogardus's tower built 29 years before, decided himself to use an iron skeleton. In the next year his building was completed.

Steel and the age of the skyscraper. Even before Jenney's first skyscraper was completed, a better new material had been perfected. This new material, steel, like wrought iron, was made from iron ore, but was far superior. While wrought iron was easily shaped into beams, it bent too readily to be suitable for a skyscraper frame. Steel was the answer. And it was the material that made higher and higher American skyscrapers possible.

Though people had known how to make steel for centuries, the process had been difficult and time consuming. Steel was so expensive that it was used only for small objects. The swords used by knights in the Middle Ages were made by endlessly hammering and reheating and then again hammering the blades. Until the mid-1800s this was the usual way to harden iron to make it into steel.

Then an Englishman, Henry Bessemer, invented his new mass-production steel furnace.

dreaming when he forecast buildings "ten miles high." But he was not far wrong when he told American builders that only the sky would be the limit.

Bogardus himself constructed one of the first

By blowing air through the molten iron mass, the carbon in it was burnt out much more quickly. Now it was possible to produce 100 tons of steel from a single furnace in twelve hours. Before the end of the nineteenth century, the United States—borrowing English methods, improved by American know-how—was producing about twice as much steel as Great Britain, and now led the world. Better, cheaper steel meant more tall buildings. The age of the skyscraper had arrived.

See "Section 5 Review answers," p. 436F.

Section 5 Review

1. Why did Americans build "up" as well as "out"?

2. **Critical Thinking: Determining Relevance.** How did the work of Otis and Bessemer affect cities?

See "Lesson Plan," p. 436F.

6. New towns in the country

As the whole country became more citified, there grew up new kinds of instant cities. At first their aim was not to grow big, but to stay small—and so escape the troubles of the crowded metropolis.

Business firms were looking for new places to put their factories. Workers were anxious to escape the tenements and the darkened, crowded cities. Prosperous merchants and lawyers and doctors were eager to raise their families out in the open air.

Company towns. With the new railroad network there was less reason than ever for factories to stay in big cities. Almost any spot along a railroad line would do. Raw materials could be brought in from anywhere and finished products could be transported to any place.

If an industrialist built a factory away from a big city, the workers would not have to live in slums. Then why not build a "company town"? Out where land was less expensive, each worker could have a neat little house with a garden. The employer could provide parks and play-grounds, and workers might be more content. After the Civil War many energetic businessmen had this idea.

In 1881 Andrew Carnegie built a steel plant and a whole new town called Homestead seven miles up the Monongahela River from Pittsburgh. Besides small houses for the workers and their families, Carnegie provided a library and even bowling alleys. Homestead was not beautiful, but at least it lacked the crowds and the filth of the slums in the big cities.

George M. Pullman, inventor of the Pullman sleeping car for railroads, also decided to build a new town ten miles outside Chicago. In 1884 he bought a tract of land on the shores of Lake Calumet. He named it after himself and hoped it would be a model for other company towns. Pullman's architect designed the whole town, including a central square with town hall, churches, a library, and parks. All the buildings, including the small houses for the workers, were of dark-red brick.

In the company towns that sprang up all over the country, workers could escape the worst horrors of the big city. But they found some new horrors. Living in a company town was something like being a feudal serf in the Middle Ages. The company not only controlled your job but also decided where you would live and where (and at what price) you could buy your food. The company controlled your schools and even hired your police.

Some of the most violent strikes were in these company towns. When the Carnegie Steel Company cut wages at its Homestead plant in 1892, the angry workers went on strike. In the resulting violence a dozen men were killed.

Garden cities. But the company town was not the only new-style city that grew up at the end of the 1800s. On the "suburban frontier" there appeared the garden city. The first of these had been started even before the Civil War when, in the 1850s, Llewellyn Park in New Jersey was created. It was followed in the 1860s by Riverside, Illinois, outside Chicago. There Frederick Law Olmsted and his partner Calvert Vaux laid out a planned, garden-like community along

✕ **Critical Thinking Activity: Recognizing Cause and Effect** What is the perfect recipe for a city? Tell students that they are all great chefs and have been given the difficult task of creating an original recipe. Their dish will be the perfect American city. Have students name their recipe, write out the ingredients (buildings, parks, roads, honest officials, programs for the underpriveleged, etc.) Ask students to present their recipes to the class.

The Carnegie Steel Company's enormous plant at Homestead, Pennsylvania, in the 1890s.

the winding Des Plaines River. Olmsted and Vaux had also helped bring the country to the city when they designed and created Central Park in New York during the 1850s.

Soon other towns followed the pioneer garden cities. Some rich families who owned summer houses in the country near cities began living out in the suburbs year-round. For example, some businessmen who worked in New York City preferred living in Old Greenwich, Connecticut, forty-five minutes away on the railroad. These rich suburban pioneers set up their own country clubs and tried to keep their communities "exclusive"—for Oldcomers only and not for any of the Newcomer immigrants.

The push for new garden cities was encouraged by an English reformer. Ebenezer Howard had come to America as a young man and had spent five years around crowded Chicago. Then in his book, *Garden Cities of Tomorrow* (1898), he offered his blueprint for a suburban utopia. He urged people to group together to build garden cities—new small towns out in the country. These towns, he said, should be planned with a garden belt all around. Then, if the garden city was connected to the big city by a railroad, it gave its residents the best of both worlds.

Other Americans followed Howard's advice and built garden cities. These were no longer only for the very rich, but they were not yet for people of modest means. Lake Forest outside Chicago and Shaker Heights outside Cleveland tried to make the garden city more romantic than the big city. Instead of the monotonous parallel streets of checkerboard city blocks, the garden city streets wound across the countryside. Wide lawns separated the houses from the roads and from one another. Before long, garden cities like Radburn, New Jersey, were being specially planned for people of modest income. In 1910 a New York architect made a new design for space-saving "garden apartments" with "kitchenettes" (a new American word for a compact kitchen and pantry). Now you no longer needed to be rich to live out in a garden suburb.

(p. 455)

See "Section 6 Review answers," p. 436G.

Section 6 Review

1. Identify some early suburbs.
2. **Critical Thinking: Identifying Central Issues.** What were good and bad aspects of company towns?

See "Lesson Plan," p. 436G for **Writing Process Activity: Demonstrating Reasoned Judgment** relating to company towns and garden cities.

Chapter 17 Review

See "Chapter Review answers," p. 436G.

Focusing on Ideas

1. While some rural villages almost vanished in the farm-to-city movement, the number of rural towns and villages (places with fewer than 2500 residents) increased decade after decade until about 1930. How did the rural village serve the farm population? What additional services were provided in American towns and cities?

2. Rapid city growth required expansion of public services. What were some of these services? How was the expansion of such services linked to political corruption?

3. The "Gilded Age" of American history was a time when things appeared shiny and new from the outside, but a closer look at the under layers revealed decay and corruption. What are some examples of this paradoxical image?

Taking a Critical Look

1. **Expressing Problems Clearly.** Suppose that you were an Oldcomer in a big city in the 1890s. What changes taking place might upset you? Which of these changes might be easy to blame on the Newcomers?

2. **Recognizing Cause and Effect.** Between 1870 and 1910, total U.S. population increased about 230 percent, high school graduates per year rose 950 percent, and college enrollment jumped about 700 percent. How did the growth of cities help to bring about this rapid rise in educational attainment?

Your Region in History

1. **Geography.** To what big city or cities does your community have close ties? When did those cities grow most rapidly?

2. **Culture.** Identify a college or university in your area and research its origin. Who or what was it named after? Was it a product of the Morrill Act? What type of students would have attended this institution in 1900?

3. **Economics.** What economic developments after the Civil War led to the rapid growth of cities in your state?

Historical Facts and Figures

Testing Hypotheses. Use the graph below to answer the following questions: (a) Approximately what percentage of the population lived in cities in 1850? in 1880? in 1900? (b) How much did the total population grow between 1850 and 1900? (c) About how many immigrants came to the United States during this same period? (d) What hypothesis, or educated guess, can you make about where most immigrants chose to live during this period? (e) Does the information in this chapter support your hypothesis? Explain your answer.

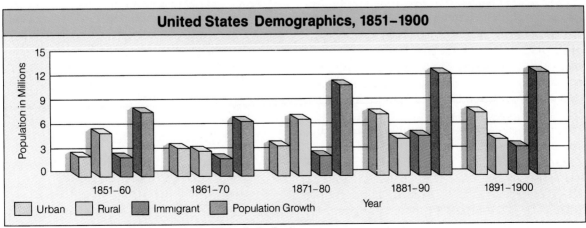

Sources: *Bureau of the Census; U.S. Immigration and Naturalization Service*

Chapter 18
Politics in the Gilded Age

Identifying Chapter Materials

Objectives	Basic Instructional Materials	Extension Materials
1 Parties in Balance ▪ Describe the close party balance between 1876 and 1892 and identify some of its effects on the Presidents of the time. ▪ Explain historical rankings of one-term presidents.	**Annotated Teacher's Edition** ▪ Lesson Plans, p. 458C **Instructional Support File** ▪ Pre-Reading Activities, Unit 6, p. 29 ▪ Skill Review Activity, Unit 6, p. 32	**Documents of American History** ▪ The Bland-Allison Act, Vol. 1, p. 547 ▪ President Hayes's Veto of Bland-Allison Act, Vol. 1, p. 548
2 The Democrats Come and Go ▪ Identify tariffs and trusts as important political issues of the late 1800s. ▪ Discuss the similarities and differences of the elections of 1884 and 1888.	**Annotated Teacher's Edition** ▪ Lesson Plans, pp. 458C–458D **Instructional Support File** ▪ Skill Application Activity, Unit 6, p. 33	**Documents of American History** ▪ Cleveland's Tariff Message of 1887, Vol. 1, p. 576 ▪ The Interstate Commerce Act, Vol. 1, p. 579 ▪ The Sherman Anti-Trust Act, Vol. 1, p. 58
3 The Farmers' Revolt ▪ Identify problems facing farmers, the Granger laws, and the Populist party. ▪ Explain the thinking behind the Omaha Platform.	**Annotated Teacher's Edition** ▪ Lesson Plans, pp. 458D–458E	**Enrichment Support File** ▪ Farmers Unite: The Populist Party (See "In-Depth Coverage" at right.) **Suggested Secondary Sources** ▪ See chart at right.
4 Our Money: Gold versus Silver ▪ Name the candidates, issues, and results of the election of 1896. ▪ Discuss the political, economic, and social forces at work in the United States in the 1890s. ▪ Analyze the effects of William Jennings Bryan's "Cross of Gold" speech at the Democratic convention in 1896.	**Annotated Teacher's Edition** ▪ Lesson Plans, p. 458E **Instructional Support File** ▪ Reading Activities, Unit 6, pp. 30–31 ▪ Critical Thinking Activity, Unit 6, p. 34 ▪ Chapter Test, pp. 35–38 ▪ Additional Test Questions, Unit 6, pp. 39–42 ▪ Unit 6 Test, pp. 47–50	**Documents of American History** ▪ The Republican Platform of 1896, Vol. 1, p. 623 ▪ Bryan's "Cross of Gold" Speech, Vol. 1, p. 624

18

Providing In-Depth Coverage

Perspectives on the Populist Party

The Populist party called for sweeping reforms in a variety of areas. Their party platform called for government control of railroads, telegraph, and telephone, direct election of senators, shorter working days, free silver, and an income tax.

Beginning as a group of farmers, radicals, and reformers, the Populist party was an indication of the failure of the leaders of the time to fulfill their responsibilities to the electorate.

The chapter focuses on the Populist party's attempts to bring about reform in order to aid groups such as farmers and laborers.

A History of the United States as an instructional program provides two types of resources you can use to offer in-depth coverage of the Populist party: the *student text* and the *Enrichment Support File*. A list of *Suggested Secondary Sources* is also provided. The chart below shows the topics that are covered in each.

THE STUDENT TEXT. Boorstin and Kelley's *A History of the United States* unfolds the chronology of events and the key players involved in the development of the Populist party.

AMERICAN HISTORY ENRICHMENT SUPPORT FILE. This collection of primary source readings and classroom activities reveals the origins and ideals of the Populist party.

SUGGESTED SECONDARY SOURCES. This reference list of readings by well-known historians and other commentators provides an array of perspectives on the beginnings of the Populist party and the issues that its members supported.

Locating Instructional Materials

Detailed lesson plans for teaching the Populist party as a mini-course or to study one or more elements of the party in depth are offered in the following areas: in the *student text*, see individual lesson plans at the beginning of each chapter; in the *Enrichment Support File*, see page 3; for readings beyond the student text, see *Suggested Secondary Sources.*

IN-DEPTH COVERAGE ON THE POPULIST PARTY		
Student Text	**Enrichment Support File**	**Suggested Secondary Sources**
▪ Formation of Populist party, pp. 471–472 ▪ Election of 1892, p. 472 ▪ Jacob Coxey, p. 474 ▪ William Jennings Bryan, pp. 475–476 ▪ Election of 1896, p. 476	▪ Lesson Suggestions ▪ Multimedia Resources ▪ Overview Essay/Farmers Unite: The Populist Party ▪ Songs in American History/"The Farmer Is the Man" ▪ Primary Sources in American History/Farmers Reach for Political Power ▪ Biography in American History/Mary E. Lease ▪ Geography in American History/Where, When, and Why: Geography and the Populists ▪ Great Debates in American History/Is the American Way of Life in Danger? ▪ Making Connections	▪ *People and Politics: William Alfred Peffer and the People's Party* by Peter H. Argensinger, pp. 22–57. ▪ *Democratic Promise: The Populist Moment in America* by Lawrence Goodwyn. ▪ *Populist Vanguard: A History of the Southern Farmers Alliance* by Robert C. McMath, pp. 110–131. ▪ *The Populist Context: Rural Versus Urban Power on a Great Plains Frontier* by Stanley B. Parsons, pp. 22–34. ▪ *The Populist Response to Industrial America* by Norman Pollack, pp. 25–42.

Parties in Balance

FOCUS

To introduce the lesson, have the students turn to page 961 and read the names of the Presidents and the Vice-Presidents of the United States. Ask: Which Presidents served only one term? Of the one-term Presidents, which do you think are rated above-average or great by historians? (A panel of 75 historians gave only John Adams and James Polk above-average ratings—Adams for avoiding war with France, Polk for doubling the size of the nation.) Why?

Developing Vocabulary

The words listed below are essential terms for understanding particular sections of the chapter. The page number after each term indicates the page of its first or most important appearance. These terms are defined in the Glossary (text pages 1000–1011).

deflation (page 459); **greenbacks** (page 459); **inflation** (page 459); **civil service** (page 460); **Stalwarts** (page 460); **plurality** (page 461); **free silver** (page 459); **electoral college** (page 461).

INSTRUCT

Explain

Several Presidents are discussed in this section. Garfield's term in office was too brief for judging his administration. Both Hayes and Arthur have been rated "average" by a panel of historians.

❀ Cooperative Learning Activity

Distinguishing False from Accurate Images Divide the class into pairs. Tell students that they will write their own definitions for the terms used to describe politics in the "Gilded Age." Have students work together to define the following: *party boss, political machine, professional politician, party faithful, party regulars, party politics, patronage,* and *favoritism.* Then bring the class together to discuss the significance for the nation of the kind of political activity these terms describe.

Section Review Answers

Section 1, page 463

1. a) the period from 1865 to 1900, a time of great extremes of wealth and poverty. b) a general decrease in prices that occurs when the amount of money in circulation increases less than the production of goods and services. c) a general increase in prices because the amount of money in circulation has increased more than the production of goods and services. d) money of lowered value, which buys fewer goods, but makes debts less burdensome. e) the proposal that the government mint as much silver as possible in order to increase the money supply and thus provide cheap money. f) the old-fashioned Republican bosses who opposed civil service reform and supported Radical Reconstruction. g) a Republican senator from New York and leader of the Stalwarts. h) one of Conkling's aides in New York. President Hayes asked him to resign as part of his attempt to end the spoils system. i) Republicans who supported civil service reform and a hands-off attitude toward the South. j) the leader of the Half-Breeds. 2. Hayes sent federal troops to five states to break the railway strike. He felt that he had to honor the requests of the governors of these states. 3. The depression that began in 1873; Congress passed the Bland-Allison Act of 1878, which called for limited coinage of silver. President Hayes vetoed the bill, but Congress overrode his veto. 4. "Half-breed" Republicans favored civil service reform. Hayes managed to end the spoils system in the New York customshouse and ordered government employees not to work in political campaigns. Arthur called for civil service reform and signed the Pendleton Act. 5. Garfield was killed by a job-seeker who felt he had been denied his rightful "spoils" for his party work. Arthur, who succeeded Garfield, saw what terrible effects the spoils system could have so he proposed and signed civil service reform legislation.

CLOSE

To conclude the lesson, ask: What information does the text provide to show that the two major parties were in balance between 1876 and 1892? (The close votes in presidential elections and the lack of one-party control of Congress.)

The Democrats Come and Go

FOCUS

To introduce the lesson, have the students look at the cartoon on page 465 of their texts. Help them see why tariffs and trusts were twin political issues in the late 1800s—and to focus on the effects of both in restraining competition. Have students identify the trusts represented by the heads of the hydra.

Chapter 18

Politics in the Gilded Age

Focusing the Chapter: Have students identify the chapter logo. Discuss what unit theme the logo might symbolize. Then ask students to skim the chapter to identify other illustrations or titles that relate to this theme.

In American history the years between 1865 and 1900 are known as the Gilded Age. And for a good reason. Anything "gilded" is covered with a thin layer of gold. It glitters on the surface. But what is underneath is seldom so attractive. In this Gilded Age the surface of American life shone with many kinds of new wealth, made by adventurous and enterprising Go-Getters. That glitter covered a multitude of sins. It was a world of crowded cities, mammoth businesses, and extremes of wealth and poverty.

Despite the gloomy future predicted if the Democrats were elected, Cleveland defeated Blaine.

Museum of American Political Life

The effects of a Tariff exclusively for Revenue as laid down in the Democratic Platform and which the Democratic Congressmen tried to enact last winter at Washington.

The effects of Protection to American Industries as guaranteed by the Republican Party and Platform.

Democratic Free-Trade Means low wages, children in rags and ignorance

If you are satisfied with this picture vote for Cleveland and Hendricks.
And G. M. WOODWARD, the Free Trader.

Republican Protection Means good wages, happy homes and education for your children.

If you prefer this picture vote for Blaine and Logan.
And O. B. THOMAS.

Multicultural Connection: The census of 1890 reported 7,488,676 African Americans living in the United States representing 11.9% of the population. Also at this time 241,855 African Americans who had been born in the South now lived in the North and West, while only 23,268 born in the North or West lived in the South.

458

ment. (c) Either—cheap money increases wages, raises cost of living. (d) Cheap money; depends on farm prosperity. (e) Sound money; bank wants loans fully repaid. 2. Civil Service reform: Pendleton Civil Service Act limited spoils system. Railroad monopolies: Interstate Commerce Act established fair shipping rates and standards. Trade reform: Sherman Antitrust Act, an attempt to limit monopolies. 3. Some Presidents worry about their place in history and become "statesmen" instead of "partisans."

Taking a Critical Look

1. Republican presidents: 12 years; Democratic, 8 years; divided control of Congress. Presidents lacked strong stands fearing loss of support and opposition of Congress. Populists had reasonable chance of winning, particularly seats in Congress. 2. Failed to guide Congress on I.C.C. Act; vetoed pensions to save money; opposed higher tariff; allowed Wilson Gorman to become law without signature; but did take stands on "sound money" issues. Ideally, both.

Your Region in History

1–3. Answers will vary depending on your region. Consult your local library or historical society.

Historical Facts and Figures

(a) Highest: 1867; lowest: 1890. (b) As output increased, price declines. (c) If prices low, profits would not make up for investments. Possible solutions: farm cooperatives, diversify crops, organize politically, limit production to increase demand.

Answers to "Making Connections"

(See "Using Making Connections" on p. 478.)

Answers will vary, but may include one or more of the following examples. Answers based on the time line callouts are in italics.

1. *A new wave of immigrants began to arrive in the United States from Southern and Eastern Europe in 1885.* The adult immigrants became Americanized very slowly. But very quickly a whole colony found its special place in American life and made that place as much like home as possible. *By 1892, for instance, nearly a hundred newspapers in German were published in American cities.* There were forces at work, however, that would not allow immigrant colonies to stay separate forever. Schools exerted a strong influence on the children. *In 1870 public high schools were established across the United States to educate and Americanize immigrants. In 1889 Jane Addams founded Hull House in Chicago in part to aid urban immigrants.* Settlement houses helped immigrants to learn English and American customs. 2. After the Civil War, railroad and trolley lines allowed the development of "garden cities," suburbs where people could live in country-like areas and commute to jobs in the city. Technology also made it possible to build up as well as out. City land was expensive, so buildings of many stories were very practical. Otis's improved elevator brakes made skyscrapers safe and eventually Bessemer steel made them reasonable in cost. *In 1855, Bogardus built the first skeleton frame skyscraper eight stories high.* Science and technology produced the tools needed for building bridges so that river cities could welcome the railroads and carry on commerce. *In 1868 construction began on the Brooklyn Bridge designed by John Roebling.* At the time, science and technology were seen as the key to many of the problems of the world. Did poor people live in squalor in city slums? Design better housing for them. The result of such thinking was the infamous dumbbell tenement. *In 1900 in Manhattan more than 40,000 tenements housed 1,500,000 people.* Science and technology added to the "livability" and beauty of the nation's cities—and also to their horrors. 3. Farmers and factory workers believed that the riches of North America belonged to all its citizens, not just the wealthy. Americans have also always believed in the efficacy of working together to solve their problems and fight for their rights. Factory workers found strength in numbers to make changes in the laws and systems that affected their lives. With the advent of huge factories such as *the big steel factory built by Andrew Carnegie at Homestead, Pennsylvania, in 1881,* workers became ever more like cogs in a giant machine. They worked long hours for little pay in unhealthful conditions. Slowly workers began to form unions. But unions were not accepted at first, and their first strikes were often bloody. *In 1877, there was a great railroad strike prompted by wage reductions following the 1873 depression.* The President called out federal troops to break the strike. Workers and unions persisted, however, until unions were a part of the American tradition. Farmers, too, sought strength in numbers. *In 1892, discouraged by overproduction and falling crop prices, disenchanted farmers formed the national Populist Party.* Many of the reforms they sought eventually became law.

18

group and have members choose a manager and a recorder. To begin, have the group manager lead members in a discussion of the policies and positions of the assigned party. Then have the recorder take down notes as members agree on which policies to feature and how to represent them. Next have the manager gather the materials the group needs and assign the tasks of lettering and illustrating the poster. Display students' completed work.

Section Review Answers

Section 3, page 475

1. a) founded in 1867, the first national farm organization. b) Supreme Court decision upholding an Illinois law that set maximum rates for grain storage. c) organizations of farmers in the South and the West who became politically active during the 1880s and 1890s. d) a Populist leader from Kansas who said that farmers should "raise less corn and more hell." e) a colorful Populist leader and speaker from Kansas. f) Populist representative from Georgia who fought for farmers' interests in Congress. g) Populist candidate for President in 1892. h) self-made business success, reformer, and Populist who led a group of five hundred protesters to Washington in 1894. i) Democratic senator from South Carolina. 2. Declining prices, high rates from the railroads and grain elevator companies, difficulty in paying mortgages, and foreign competition. 3. (a) Populists supported the cause of Southern blacks and conservative southern Democrats tried to fight reform. (b) Harrison sent federal troops to suppress riots in Coeur d'Alene, thus alienating many voters. 4. (a) Cleveland tried to get Congress to repeal the Sherman Silver Purchase Act. (b) He tried to win tariff reform, but Congress passed the Wilson-Gorman tariff, a slightly modified tariff but definitely not a reform. (c) He sent federal troops to put down the Pullman strikers in Illinois in 1894. 5. The federal courts used the Sherman Antitrust Act against unions, declaring that unions were illegal conspiracies and issuing injunctions that ordered unions to end strikes. 6. The Populists' platform demanded (a) government ownership of railroads; (b) a shorter working day; and (c) an increase in the money supply, free coinage of silver, an income tax, and government ownership of the telegraph and telephone lines.

CLOSE

To conclude the lesson, ask students to list as many planks of the Populist platform as they can. Which of these planks were later adopted by our government? Tell students to keep this in mind as they read later chapters. Which remain alive today?

Section 4 (pages 475–476)

Our Money: Gold versus Silver

FOCUS

To introduce the lesson, ask: Did you know that *The Wonderful Wizard of Oz*, is an *allegory*? Ask students if they know from their English class what an allegory is. Then point out that *The Wonderful Wizard of Oz* was written to represent symbolically the political, economic, and social situation in the 1890s.

INSTRUCT

Explain

William Jennings Bryan was the Populist and Democratic candidate for President in 1896. He supported free silver. He was defeated by Republican William McKinley, who supported the gold standard.

☑ Writing Process Activity

Drawing Conclusions Ask students to imagine they hear William Jennings Bryan speak at the 1896 Democratic convention. In preparation for writing a journal entry, ask them to freewrite about audience reactions and perceptions about his suitability as a presidential candidate. Students should begin their entry with a topic sentence that focuses on one aspect of their experience. Have students revise for logical organization and specific support. After proofreading, they can share their journal entry with a classmate.

Section Review Answers

Section 4, page 476

1. He captured the imagination of the delegates to the Democratic convention with his magnificent speech attacking the gold standard. 2. Mark Hanna used various tricks to persuade factory workers that they would lose their jobs if Bryan was elected, and he was careful to have McKinley keep quiet and stay home.

CLOSE

To conclude the lesson, have students read the end of William Jennings Bryan's "Cross of Gold" speech on page 476 of the text. Ask: How does Bryan use language to electrify his audience? What do the words "crown of thorns" and "cross of gold" call to mind? (Jesus' death on the cross.)

Chapter Review Answers

Focusing on Ideas

1. (a) Sound money; inflation erodes savings. (b) Cheap money; boost farm prices, ease debt pay-

Developing Vocabulary

Mugwumps (page 463); **commerce** (page 464); **regulation** (page 464); **filibuster** (page 466); **tariff** (page 466); **monopoly** (page 467).

INSTRUCT

Explain

Westerners had no strong sectional interest in the tariff, but some members of Congress from western states supported the McKinley tariff in exchange for Republican support on the silver issue.

☑ Writing Process Activity

Identifying Central Issues Ask students to play the role of Mugwumps during the election of 1884. In preparation for writing an attack against presidential candidate James Blaine, students should brainstorm possible criticisms. Have students begin their articles with a strong statement about Blaine's shortcomings, and have them support their main premise with specific examples. Students should revise for logical order and strong word choice. After proofreading, they can publish their criticisms in a class newspaper.

Section Review Answers

Section 2, page 468

1. a) Republicans who left their party to support Grover Cleveland in the presidential election of 1884. b) Illinois senator who oversaw the passage of the Interstate Commerce Act of 1887. c) a campaign in which the candidate mostly stayed home, met a few selected people, and made short speeches. d) Speaker of the House during Benjamin Harrison's Presidency. e) Republican representative from Massachusetts who wrote a bill that would have allowed the federal government to guarantee blacks' voting rights. f) Republican-controlled Congress during the first two years of Harrison's Presidency. 2. It outlawed rebates to favorite customers, required railroads to publish rates, and required that those rates be proportional to the distance traveled. Each of these provisions ended a common unfair practice of the railroads. 3. Cleveland vetoed pension bills and tried to lower tariffs in order to decrease the surplus in the Treasury. 4. They wanted to secure equal voting rights for blacks in the South, who were overwhelmingly Republican. It did not pass because Southern senators filibustered and western senators from silver-producing states made a deal to support the Southerners in exchange for their support of a new silver coinage bill. 5. In July 1890 the Sherman Antitrust Act was passed in an attempt to punish firms that tried to restrict free competition. It was not very effective because Presidents were reluctant to en-

force it and, when they did, the Supreme Court usually overturned lower court decisions against the trusts. 6. The major issues were falling farm prices, rising interest rates, silver and the money supply, the spoils system, congressional spending, and tariffs. The election was a landslide victory for the Democrats. 7. Northern industrialists and business people benefited most from a high tariff. Farmers, miners, and mine owners benefited most from increased silver coinage.

CLOSE

To conclude the lesson, write on the chalkboard the words Elections of 1884 and 1888. Have the class list at least four items under each of two column headings: Similarities and Differences.

Section 3 (pages 468–475)

The Farmers' Revolt

FOCUS

To introduce the lesson, ask students: What is a party platform? (A statement of party positions on a number of issues important in an upcoming presidential election.) Discuss their answers. Use examples from recent campaigns if possible.

Developing Vocabulary

foreclosure (page 469); **Grangers** (page 469); **platform** (page 471); **injunction** (page 474); **gold standard** (page 474).

INSTRUCT

Explain

Historians swing back and forth on the Populist movement. In the 1950s, Richard Hofstadter argued that while the Populists did some good, they did even more harm by trying to move back the clock and striking out at scapegoats such as African Americans, Jews, and new immigrants. In the 1960s, historians disputed Hofstadter's negative view of the Populists. Norman Pollack praised the Populists concern that modern technology be used with respect for human dignity.

❀ Cooperative Learning Activity

Recognizing Bias Break the class into groups of four and explain that each will create a campaign poster for the election of 1892. Assign one of the political parties—Republican, Democrat, Populist—to each

See "Lesson Plan," p. 458C.

1. Parties in balance

The two main political parties were nearly even in strength between 1876 and 1892. In three of the five presidential elections during those years the difference in the popular vote between the Republican and the Democratic candidates was less than 1 percent. In 1876 the Democrats had a popular majority of 3 percent but lost the election. And again, in 1888, the Democrat Cleveland had 100,000 more votes than the Republican Harrison, but Harrison won. Garfield in 1880 defeated Winfield Scott Hancock by only 7000 votes in over 9 million cast. Victory seemed almost an accident.

During these years Presidents seldom had their own party in control of both houses of Congress. This inability to win both houses, combined with the closeness of the presidential vote, made an age of timid Presidents. Any new step might lose the few votes that meant a lost election and lost power.

Rutherford B. Hayes. Rutherford B. Hayes was a cold, honest, and straightforward man whose position as President was weakened by the way he came to office. His enemies referred to him as "His Fraudulency" or "Rutherfraud" B. Hayes. But Hayes himself never doubted that by a fair count he deserved to be President. Hayes further weakened his position, however, by announcing that he would serve only one term. This meant that his enemies within the party were willing to oppose him, since they knew that he would not be the party's candidate in 1880.

The great railway strike. Hayes took office in March 1877 during the deep depression that (p. 460) had begun in 1873. Labor strife erupted almost at once. The trouble began on the Baltimore and Ohio Railroad where the workers had suffered a series of pay cuts. In July the trainmen of the B & O went on strike. They were soon followed by railway workers in other states. Strikes, rioting, and looting shook Baltimore, Pittsburgh, Chicago, St. Louis, and many other cities. At the request of the state governors, Hayes sent federal troops to Martinsburg, West

Virginia, and to Pittsburgh to protect property. He did not like using troops as strike breakers, but he felt that he had no choice but to agree to the governors' requests.

The money question. The depression that brought the "year of violence" of 1877 brought demands for an increase in the amount of money in circulation. This demand would come time and time again in the Gilded Age. Between 1865 and 1896 prices were falling. It was a time of *deflation*, which meant that a dollar would buy more every year. So farmers and people in business who had borrowed money had to pay back their loans in dollars that were worth more than the dollars they had borrowed. For example, a debt that could have been paid off in 1890 with the sale of 1000 bushels of corn took 2320 bushels in 1896. As a result, farmers and others who borrowed money pushed for "cheaper money." Money became cheaper when there was more of it. So the "borrowing classes" demanded that the government either issue more "greenbacks"—paper money that had no backing in silver or gold—or coin silver in large quantities.

Increasing the supply of silver dollars was the favored approach. If the government was required to mint all the large supplies of silver then being mined in the West, the quantity of money would be much increased. A rise in the supply of money tends to lift the general level of prices. This is called *inflation*. If the price of wheat and cotton and corn went up, the farmers' problems might be solved. This proposal for minting silver was called "free silver" because it meant the "free"—that is, unlimited—coining of silver dollars.

The farmers were unable to persuade Congress to go that far. The most they could get was a bill for a limited coining of silver. In 1878 the Bland-Allison Act, named for its sponsors, Representative Richard "Silver Dick" Bland of Missouri and Senator William Allison of Iowa, passed both houses of Congress. It required the government to buy and coin at least $2 million worth of silver a month. Hayes vetoed the bill because he thought that coining silver dollars that were worth less than 90 cents in gold was

See "Lesson Plan," p. 458C for **Cooperative Learning Activity: Distinguishing False from Accurate Images** relating to politics in the Gilded Age.

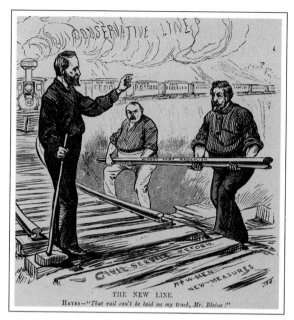

THE NEW LINE.
HAYES—"*That rail can't be laid on my track, Mr. Blaine!*"

This 1878 political cartoon shows upright and honest President Hayes pursuing a conservative course and building a solid new railroad line with civil service reform. He rejects James G. Blaine's rail of bloody-shirt radicalism.

dishonest. The bill passed over his veto. But it only partially satisfied the demand for a larger money supply. The question would return to haunt other Presidents.

The spoils system. Since Andrew Jackson's day, government jobs had been given to people who had worked hard to help the party win the election. "To the victors belong the spoils" was the motto of both parties. Every change of administration was marked by a wild scramble for government jobs. These were simply rewards for party loyalty. Thousands of offices were filled by people who had no other qualification. After they were on the government payroll, they were still expected to work for the party in election campaigns. They even had to hand over a part of their pay to support the party.

Some people believed that the problems of government might be solved if this system was changed. Their slogan was "Out with the party hacks." Only qualified people should hold government jobs. This program was called civil

service reform. After the Civil War, influential citizens like Carl Schurz and George W. Curtis, the editor of *Harper's Weekly*, worked hard to abolish the "spoils system." Finally in 1871 Congress passed a law authorizing the President to make rules to reform the civil service. President Grant appointed a commission. But the "Stalwarts"—the old-fashioned Republican bosses—managed to prevent the commission from getting anything done. Their leader was the clever and knowledgeable Senator Roscoe Conkling, the New York State boss whose power was based on the spoils system.

The vain, handsome Conkling walked with "a turkey-gobbler strut" and was a master of ridicule. He called it "snivel" service reform. He sneered that the reformers "forget that parties are not built up by deportment or by ladies' magazines or by gush!" (p. 461)

Hayes and civil service reform. President Hayes did not agree. Wanting to abolish the spoils system, he revived the Civil Service Commission. He ordered that government employees must not work in political campaigns and must not be assessed for party "contributions."

In the opening battle of his war against the spoils system, President Hayes aimed to control the hiring in the New York customshouse. The 1000 people employed there collected two-thirds of all the nation's tariff revenue. First he asked Conkling's aides in New York, Collector of Customs Chester A. Arthur and Naval Officer Alonzo B. Cornell, to resign. But Conkling needed to control those jobs to keep himself and his party in power. So Conkling fought back.

Hayes won this battle of the customshouse, but he did not win the war for civil service reform. Cornell went on to become governor of New York, and Arthur, only a year later, was nominated for the Vice-Presidency. Now the professional politicians in his own party were Hayes's enemies, and Democrats controlled the House of Representatives. It is not surprising, then, that Hayes accomplished little during his last two years in office.

The Republicans name Garfield and Arthur. Hayes had been an honest, hardworking Presi-

More from Boorstin: "When Bell's telephone was displayed at the Philadelphia Centennial Exposition in 1876, in the very year that Alexander Graham Bell had received his first telephone patent, it was still a great curiosity. Only two years later the first telephone appeared in the White House, under President Rutherford B. Hayes." (From *The Americans: The Democratic Experience*)

dent who deserved the people's respect by his firm stands for what he believed was right. Although he had improved the Republican party's tarnished image from the days of Grant, he had made too many enemies among the leaders of his own party. They looked for a different kind of candidate to run in 1880.

The battle was between the Stalwarts led by Roscoe Conkling, who wanted a return to the "good old days" of President Grant when the bosses had their own way, and those whom the Stalwarts called the "Half-breeds." The party regulars sneered at these so-called "Half-breeds." Those people were only half loyal to the old-time Republican policies. They did firmly support the business interests, but they also were for civil service reform and took a hands-off policy toward the South. Their leader was the most magnetic politician of the age, James G. Blaine. He had the knack of making any cause seem a noble crusade, and so was called the "Plumed Knight."

The convention deadlocked between the Stalwart candidate U. S. Grant and the Half-breed Blaine. In the end it chose a "dark horse"—the popular James A. Garfield of Ohio. He had served gallantly in the Union army during the Civil War. Since then he had been a loyal Republican party leader in the Congress, but he had no particular program. In an attempt to please Roscoe Conkling and the disappointed Stalwarts, the convention named Chester A. Arthur for Vice-President. The angry Conkling tried to persuade Arthur to refuse the second-place nomination. Arthur accepted because, as he explained, "The office of the vice-presidency is a greater honor than I ever dreamed of attaining."

The party platform did plump for civil service reform but clearly avoided other issues. "What are we up here for?" a Texas delegate complained. "I mean that members of the Republican party are entitled to office, and if we are victorious we will have office."

Also aiming to win votes by avoiding the troublesome issues, the Democrats decided simply to prove their loyalty to the Union. They nominated General Winfield Scott Hancock, a professional army officer who had graduated from West Point. He was famous for fending off an

Culver Pictures

THE NEW OFFICIAL DOOR-KEEPER.
CONKLING—" Well, just at this moment, I feel as though I was a bigger man than old Hayes!"

Senator Roscoe Conkling appears still triumphant in 1878 during his fight with Hayes over the customs-house. But Conkling was soon to lose.

attack by General Lee at Gettysburg but had no experience in politics.

Garfield is elected. The politicians fought a hard campaign without facing the nation's problems. By waving the "bloody shirt," Garfield managed to squeak into office—with a bare 7000-vote plurality out of more than 9 million votes cast. His electoral college vote was 214 to 155.

The southern states, now free of all federal interference for the first presidential election since 1860, cast a solid vote for the Democrat Hancock. The "solid South" became a new expression and a new institution in American politics. For the next years in every local, state, and national election the South was found solid in the Democratic column. Not until 1920 would a Republican candidate for President win a state of the former Confederacy.

Garfield was an intelligent, adaptable man. During his long career in the House of Representatives he had shown skill in party politics and parliamentary maneuver. But he had not

X Critical Thinking Activity: Synthesizing Information What would be the advantages of civil service reform? The political cartoon has often been used as a persuasive tool in heavily contested issues. Civil service reform in the late 1800s was just such a topic, as is reflected by the cartoons on pages 460 and 461. Have students draw their own political cartoon that represents a specific point of view on civil service reform. Allow students to share and discuss their work.

This campaign ribbon for Garfield and Arthur in 1880 was fittingly the color of the "bloody shirt" they waved during the campaign.

escaped the taint of the Crédit Mobilier scandals. Many people did not believe him when he denied that he had been bribed with stock in the company.

His brief Presidency is remembered mainly for its violent end. The big issue right from the start was who would get what jobs. Garfield began by naming a Conkling rival to head the New York customshouse, and this move led to his death. On July 2, 1881, as the President entered the Washington railroad station for a trip to New England, Charles Guiteau, a crazed Chicago lawyer, shot him in the back. Guiteau was one of the thousands of party loyalists who had failed to get the government jobs they thought that they deserved. "I am a Stalwart," he shouted, "and Arthur is President now." For eleven weeks, Garfield lingered in pain before dying on September 19.

Arthur as President. Many people were shocked at the thought of Conkling's henchman, the Stalwart Arthur, in the White House. The dapper, wealthy Arthur was, in fact, an able organizer who had brought improved systems to the huge New York customshouse. But he also managed to take care of the party faithful. Even after his accidental rise to the White House, many voters continued to think of him as just another Stalwart, a high-class party hack.

The party regulars had a surprise in store for them. When President Arthur sent his first annual message to Congress, in an astonishing turnabout he called for civil service reform! The assassination of a President by a partisan office seeker outraged public opinion. Even Stalwart Republicans now had to go along. They feared defeat in the election of 1884 and saw "reform" as the only way to keep their own followers in office.

As a result, the Civil Service bill sponsored by Democrat George H. Pendleton of Ohio passed both houses of Congress in January 1883. Certain government jobs were "classified." This meant that they would be filled by the winners in competitive examinations to test "the fitness of applicants for the public service." A nonpartisan Civil Service Commission would do the examining and grade the candidates. The Pendleton Act forbade appointments to office for political reasons and made it illegal to assess jobholders to support the party.

Arthur named a strong head for the new Civil Service Commission and made strict rules to prevent evasion of the law. Fifteen thousand government employees (15 percent of the total) were put into the "classified" service.

President Arthur's whole administration showed that the office of President could actually lift a man above sordid party politics. He fought against wasteful "pork barrel" bills that would have spent the nation's money on unneeded river and harbor projects. He worked for tariff reform. He began the much-needed modernization of the navy. Before his term of office was over, he had surprised both his supporters and his opponents. But the people in both camps never stopped wondering how reliable he would be. They asked, "Can a leopard change his spots?" The eloquent perennial candidate, James G. Blaine, opposed Arthur for the Republican nomination in 1884 and was nominated on the fourth ballot.

See "Section 1 Review answers," p. 458C.

Section 1 Review

1. Identify or explain: Gilded Age, deflation, inflation, "cheap money," "free silver," "Stalwarts," Roscoe Conkling, Alonzo B. Cornell, "Halfbreeds," James G. Blaine.
2. How did Hayes respond to the railway strike of 1877? Why?
3. Why did demands for "cheaper money" arise in the 1870s? What was Congress's response?
4. Who favored civil service reform? What steps toward it were made under Hayes? under Arthur?
5. **Critical Thinking: Recognizing Cause and Effect.** How did a tragedy hasten civil service reform?

See "Lesson Plan," p. 458C.

2. The Democrats come and go

Blaine had been around for a long time, and he had made many enemies. So to oppose him the Democrats shrewdly chose a political newcomer, Governor Grover Cleveland of New York.

Grover Cleveland, the "reformer." Cleveland was the son of a poor Presbyterian minister, and his early life was spent in a small-town parsonage. There he learned the virtues of honesty, hard work, devotion to duty, and obedience to law. At the same time he was a jovial man. He weighed 250 pounds, which showed how much he loved good food and drink. He never went to college but became a self-trained lawyer. After serving as assistant district attorney and sheriff, in 1881 he was elected as a "reform" mayor of Buffalo. There he became known as the "veto mayor," for he opposed any measures that smacked of favoritism or waste.

In an age of shady political bosses, he stayed independent. He was just what honest Democrats wanted in their candidate for governor of New York. So they nominated Cleveland for governor in 1882, and he was elected in a landslide. He did not disappoint the reformers who supported him. For he lived up to his reputation as the sworn enemy of Tammany Hall—the organized bosses in his very own party. And he annoyed the bosses more than ever by his nonpartisan courage in the statehouse. There he supported the laws to clean up the government of New York City which were proposed by a bumptious 24-year-old Republican legislator named Theodore Roosevelt.

Blaine versus Cleveland. Grover Cleveland's political career was one of the speediest in American history. Only three years after being elected mayor of Buffalo, he was nominated for the Presidency. Suddenly this reforming upstart from New York was plunged into a mudslinging national election campaign.

When the "Plumed Knight" Blaine was nominated by the Republicans, the Democrats advertised the bribe he had once received in Congress to favor an Arkansas railroad. This charge had kept him from being nominated in 1876 and 1880. The Republican machine bosses were against him, too. Some nasty remarks he once made against Boss Conkling had turned Conkling into his enemy. Although Blaine had helped make his party modern and responsible, many Republicans still considered Blaine himself to be little better than a Stalwart. He had a talent for inspiring intense personal dislike. Carl Schurz, George W. Curtis, and other reformers left the party and filled the newspapers with their onslaughts.

Now the Republican regulars answered with their own name-calling. They ridiculed the reformers for being pompous and self-important. So they cleverly picked up an old Algonquin Indian word for chief or high-muck-a-muck and called them "Mugwumps." This name was so appealing that no one could forget it. And they went on with personal attacks on Cleveland for being immoral and a drunkard.

The election on November 4, 1884, was another close one. Cleveland received 29,000 more votes than Blaine. A swing of only 600 votes in

See "Lesson Plan," p. 458D for **Writing Process Activity: Identifying Central Issues** relating to the Mugwumps and the election of 1884.

New York would have carried that state for Blaine and made him President.

Two trivial events during the campaign may have cost Blaine the election. In his presence a New York minister said that the Democrats were the party of "rum, Romanism, and rebellion." Blaine may not even have heard the remark, or perhaps he was just not paying attention. Anyway the unlucky Blaine did not disagree on the spot. The alert Democrats quickly advertised this insult to the religion and the drinking customs of thousands of Irish Catholic voters. Many of these were recent immigrants still struggling to make ends meet. On that same day, some of the city's richest men gave a dinner in Blaine's honor. The *New York World* portrayed Blaine feasting while "thousands of children in this great city whose fathers labor twelve hours a day, went to bed hungry and many supperless."

The Interstate Commerce Act of 1887.

Grover Cleveland accomplished little during his first two years in office—partly because the Senate remained Republican, but also because he did not believe a President should be very active. Without guidance from the President, Congress tried to get fair treatment from the railroads for the small customers. Senator Shelby M. Cullom had helped his home state of Illinois to pass legislation regulating the railroads. As governor he had strictly enforced those laws. But Cullom was convinced that only the national government could control the railroads. Individual states were not strong enough to deal with the rich and powerful interstate railroads. So in 1887 Cullom oversaw the passage of the Interstate Commerce Act.

The railroads had given special low rates and also offered rebates to large companies like Standard Oil. They did not set their rates according to the distance the freight had to be carried. Where there was no competition, their rates were exorbitant. Since the railroads kept their rates secret, the small farmers could not know what it would cost to take their produce to market. And they could not count on the rates being fair. The new law banned rebates and the other favors given to powerful shippers. New rates would be proportional to distance. Rate schedules would be public and open to inspection by the new Interstate Commerce Commission.

This was the first of many attempts of Congress to solve the problems of the new industrial age by regulating "big business."

Pension vetoes.

President Cleveland, determined to reduce government spending, was at his best when he could oppose something. In 1886 he vetoed many Civil War pension bills for people who really did not deserve pensions. Then, in January 1887 Congress passed a bill awarding a pension to any needy veteran who had served in the ranks for more than 90 days. Refusing to let the pension list become an excuse for fraud, Cleveland vetoed the bill.

The issue of the tariff.

Finding that the United States Treasury was taking in $100 million a year more than it spent, President Cleveland aimed to stop the "unnecessary taxation" that produced this surplus money. In December 1887 he devoted his entire annual message to the need to reduce the tariffs—the customs duties that raised the price of goods that were imported. Both business and labor leaders had favored the high tariffs as a way to protect Americans against foreign competition.

With this message Cleveland threw down the gauntlet to the Republican party. Now, for the first time in many years, a presidential campaign would have a real issue. Many Republicans welcomed the challenge. James G. Blaine had long wanted his party to take a bold stand in favor of a high tariff.

The presidential campaign of 1888.

The tariff was debated in Congress for months. It became the "burning issue" of the day. The Democrats nominated Cleveland for another term and declared in their platform that "all unnecessary taxation is unjust taxation." When Blaine's poor health convinced him not to run again, the Republicans settled on Benjamin Harrison of Indiana. Their platform stressed

PUCK.

A HYDRA THAT MUST BE CRUSHED — AND THE SOONER THE BETTER.

Joseph Keppler sided with Grover Cleveland on the tariff issue. In this imaginative cartoon of March 1888 Keppler showed the tariff as a "hydra"—a many-headed monster from Greek mythology. The heads were the trusts that supported the tariffs that made them thrive.

the need for a high tariff to protect "the general business, the labor, the farming interests of the country."

The Republican candidate was the great-grandson of a signer of the Declaration of Independence and a grandson of President William Henry Harrison. He entered the Civil War as commander of a volunteer regiment from Indiana, then rose to become a general. He was an aloof, unfriendly man, unwilling to take the courageous positions that might have made outspoken enemies or firm allies. After a career as lawyer for corporations, he had served one term as senator from Indiana.

The campaign was waged almost entirely over the tariff issue. Harrison wanted to avoid making mistakes that Blaine had made in New York by going out and mingling with the crowds. He stayed home and conducted a traditional "front porch" campaign. Delegations would come to see him, and he would make harmless short speeches promising to help them if they helped send him to the White House. Now at last the Republicans abandoned the old hatreds of the Civil War and stopped waving the "bloody shirt." Instead they tried appealing to everybody's pocketbook. This brought the Knights of Labor to their side. Wealthy businessmen, too, now gave millions of dollars to put the party back in power.

In one of the most corrupt campaigns in American history, the Republicans spent a fortune buying votes in the big doubtful states like New York and Indiana. Those states had gone for Cleveland in 1884. The Republicans did not succeed in buying a popular national majority, for Cleveland received almost 100,000 more votes than Harrison. But with the crucial support of those two states Harrison won the electoral vote by 233 to 168. The Republicans also carried both houses of Congress. Cleveland's strength was largely in the farm states. In the key industrial states, the Republicans convinced business people and laborers that the tariff really did work in their favor.

"Czar" Reed and Congress. Harrison, unbending and abrupt, made enemies even when he tried to do the right thing. Senator Cullom said, "I suppose he treated me about as well in the patronage as he did any other senator, but whenever he did anything for me it was done so ungraciously that the concession tended to anger rather than please."

Oddly enough, the first session of Congress under Harrison produced more important legislation than any session since Reconstruction. This was due not so much to the man in the White House as to a powerful leader in the House of Representatives. The Republicans had only a thin margin of votes in the House, and

Thomas Nast captured portly House Speaker "Czar" Reed making a ruling in this sketch.

THOMAS BRACKETT REED, Member of Congress and Speaker of the House. Author of "Reed's Rules" and Editor of "Modern Eloquence"

This drawing by Thomas Nast was presented to the Authors Club by Frederic Rowland Marvin

this slight edge made the leader's role more important than ever. Representative Thomas B. Reed from Maine was an overpowering man in more ways than one. Standing six feet, three inches tall, he actually weighed 300 pounds. He ruled the House so firmly that he was nicknamed the "Czar." He forced the House to adopt the "Reed Rules." These prevented the minority from blocking bills and gave the Speaker and the majority the power to push through their program.

Electoral reform. One of the first measures that the House considered was the electoral reform bill that Harrison had called for in his inaugural address. It was a pioneer civil rights bill. President Harrison was disturbed over the way Southerners often prevented blacks from voting. Since the blacks were usually Republicans, Republican Representative Henry Cabot Lodge of Massachusetts drew up a bill that allowed the federal government to see that there were fair elections.

The House passed the Lodge bill. But the rules of the Senate (unlike the House) allowed a senator to stop the regular business and prevent a vote by talking endlessly and refusing to "yield the floor." "Filibuster," the name for this practice, came from a Spanish word for the troublemakers who stirred up revolution in Latin America. Southern senators used the filibuster to block action on the tariff bill that many Republicans wanted to pass. So in order to get their tariff, the Republicans had to put aside the Lodge bill. When it was brought up later, Republican senators from the silver-producing states themselves helped to defeat it in return for southern support for a new silver coinage bill. The time for equal voting rights had not yet come.

A new tariff. The McKinley tariff bill, named for Representative William McKinley of Ohio, raised the duty on almost every article produced outside the country that competed with American production. The list included food, clothing, furniture, carpets, fuel, tools, kitchenware, thread, and countless other items. Articles such as tea, coffee, spices, and drugs that were not produced in the United States were admitted free. Sugar also was put on the free list. But a bounty or subsidy of 2 cents a pound was to be paid to domestic producers of raw sugar. McKinley boasted that his bill, which passed the House in May 1890, was "protective in every paragraph and American in every line and word."

The senators from silver states were willing to help pass the tariff only if something was also done for silver. They said that under the Bland-Allison Act of 1878 the government still was not buying enough silver to inflate the currency or to keep the price of silver from falling. These Westerners wanted "free and unlimited" coinage of silver at the old ratio of 16 to 1 (that is, 16 ounces of silver was to be equal in value to 1 ounce of gold). Many Republicans wanted to avoid free silver, but at the same time they were determined to pass the McKinley tariff. So on July 4, 1890, the Sherman Silver Purchase Act (named after its author, Senator John Sherman of Ohio) provided that the government would purchase 4 1/2 million ounces of silver every month. This was more than double the amount required by the Bland-Allison Act. It equaled the whole current production of silver at the time. In addition, the bill provided for the issue of paper money (Treasury notes) to the full amount of the silver purchased. This would inflate the currency. And it would help farmers who wanted to pay off their mortgages in cheap money.

The bargain over silver won western votes for the McKinley tariff bill, which now finally passed the Senate. President Harrison signed the bill into law on October 1, 1890, only 35 days before the midterm elections.

The Sherman Antitrust Act. Congress also faced the growing demand that they do something to help farmers and small businesses against trusts like the Standard Oil Company. Everywhere big companies seemed to be taking over. Bigness meant monopoly. And monopoly meant that a few people had the power to dictate to everybody else.

By 1880 the Standard Oil Company, by fair means and foul, had captured control of 90 percent of the lamp-oil refining in the United States. In the 1890s, if you wanted sugar for your table, you had to buy it from the E. C. Knight Company. Your tobacco was controlled by the American Tobacco Company.

How could small businesses and buyers in general be protected against these tyrants of "unlawful restraint and monopoly"? Many states passed laws outlawing trusts. Still the most powerful monopolies were organized in nationwide networks. This was a national problem.

In 1888 both major parties wrote antitrust planks into their platforms. President Harrison called for legislation in his annual message to Congress in 1889.

The result in July 1890 was the Sherman Antitrust Act (also named after John Sherman). This epoch-making law aimed to punish "restraint of trade or commerce." Now it was a crime for business firms to combine to prevent competition. But the language of the law was vague. And the law would not be effective at all unless the government worked hard to enforce it.

Yet any President who wanted to be reelected had to be careful not to offend powerful business leaders. It is not surprising that Presidents usually pretended that the law did not exist. If a President dared prosecute a trust, the Supreme Court often came to the rescue by technicalities. In 1895, for example, the Attorney General prosecuted the E. C. Knight Company, which controlled 98 percent of the nation's sugar refining. But the Supreme Court held the company *not* guilty under the Sherman Antitrust Act—because it was in "manufacturing" and not in "commerce." Only a fearless President like Theodore Roosevelt would be willing to use the act to smash monopolies (p. 523).

The billion-dollar Congress. This busy Republican Congress also passed many bills that were costly for the Treasury. They voted funds for river and harbor improvements, for steamship subsidies, and even to return the federal taxes paid by the northern states during the Civil War. Tight-fisted President Cleveland had vetoed the Dependent Pension Act, which old soldier Harrison now willingly signed into law.

More from Boorstin: "When consumers and politicians become alarmed at the growth of monopolies, they passed the Sherman Antitrust Act in 1890 against 'every contract, combination . . . or conspiracy in restraint of trade or commerce among the several states.' But the Go-Getting builders of big enterprise, aided by their legal metaphysicians, were not to be stopped. Legislating against them was like passing a law against the wind." (From *The Americans: The Democratic Experience*)

THE VULTURES' ROOST

Cartoonist Edward Kemble saw the trusts as evil vultures feeding off the Senate. Seats were advertised for sale because senators were still chosen by the state legislatures.

Pension outlays rose from $81 million in 1889 to $135 million in 1893. The "billion-dollar" Congress, as it came to be called, rapidly depleted the Treasury surplus which had worried President Cleveland. The surplus was gone by 1894, and there has never been one since.

In the congressional election campaign after this session the Republicans told the voters that they had accomplished a great deal. Many Americans did not agree. Once again farmers faced falling prices and rising mortgage payments. The Silver Purchase Act angered bankers and bondholders. At the same time, it did not go far enough to satisfy the silver interests and the farmers. Reformers felt that President Harrison had not lived up to his promise to abolish the spoils system, while party bosses felt that he had not given them enough patron-

age. Voters were troubled by Congress's spending spree. And now it seemed that the McKinley tariff might raise prices all over the land.

The election of 1890 was a landslide for the Democrats. They elected 235 members to the House, and the new Populist party surprised everybody by electing 9. The Republicans returned only 88—their smallest House delegation in 30 years. Even McKinley himself, after serving seven terms, was defeated. During the last two years of Harrison's term—with a President of one party and a House of Representatives of the other—no important laws were passed.

See "Section 2 Review answers," p. 458D.

Section 2 Review

1. Identify or explain: Mugwumps, Shelby M. Cullom, "front porch" campaign, "Czar" Reed, Henry Cabot Lodge, "billion-dollar" Congress.

2. What were the provisions of the Interstate Commerce Act? What abuses were they designed to stop?

3. How did Cleveland show his determination to keep a tight rein on government spending?

4. Why did the Republicans want a civil rights bill? Why did it fail to pass?

5. What effort was made to end business monopolies? Was it effective? Why?

6. What were the issues in the 1890 election campaign? What was the outcome?

7. **Critical Thinking: Recognizing Bias.** Whose interests did the tariff issue serve? Whose interests did the silver issue serve?

See "Lesson Plan," p. 458D.

3. The farmers' revolt

During the Civil War, farmers—in both North and South—had prospered. While food was needed for the armies, there were fewer people working on the farms, and the prices of farm products went up.

Then, a few years after Appomattox, the farmers' troubles began. A bushel of wheat, which in 1873 still sold for $1.21, twelve years later went for 49 cents. A pound of cotton, in 1873 priced

Critical Thinking Activity: Expressing Problems Clearly How does our use of language add color and expression to the issues of the day? Tell students that a "lexicon" is a dictionary that contains a specialized vocabulary. Have students identify words in this section that would fit in a lexicon for the Gilded Age. Suggestions might be words such as "Mugwump" or "cheap money." Ask students to invent their own word and its definition, to describe some aspect of the Gilded Age. Compile these terms in a class lexicon for the era.

at 21 cents, in twenty years sank to 5 cents. Other prices that made up the farmers' income also fell. But western railroad rates remained high along with some items controlled by monopolies. Farmers constantly had to borrow to meet their mortgage payments, to buy the new machinery they needed, or to pay their help until they sold the next harvest. The heartless sheriff with a long mustache who threatened to "foreclose" the mortgage was no joke between 1870 and 1900. Thousands of poor families lost their farms.

The farmers organize. Farmers, like city workers, did not take their troubles lying down. In fact, the first national farm organization, the Patrons of Husbandry, entered the scene in 1867 at almost the same moment that the Knights of Labor was organized. The farmers' league was started by Oliver H. Kelley, a clerk in the Department of Agriculture at Washington. He had seen the loneliness and poverty of farm life, and he organized the Patrons as a social and educational society. Within ten years there were members all over the country in twenty thousand local lodges called "Granges."

Naturally enough, when the farmers gathered they began to discuss their troubles. More and more land was being owned by absentee landlords while more and more farmers became tenants. The burden of interest on their farm mortgages seemed to become heavier every year. The companies that owned the railroads and the grain elevators were always raising their rates. So, farmers in the Granges and later in Farmers' Alliances organized cooperatives to save money by buying seed and fertilizer in large quantities. They bought their own grain elevators and even set up factories to make farm machinery that members could buy for less.

The farmland under cultivation in the United States had increased enormously after the Civil War. At the same time new mechanical devices—reapers, binders, threshers—were invented and spread across the land. Production soared. Now the farmers fed the growing population with ease and still had large amounts of surplus crops to sell abroad. There they had to compete

Haymaking in 1895 on the Fred Judas farm near Medford, Wisconsin, required the work of the entire family. This photograph was made for a handbook promoting farm opportunities in the state.

State Historical Society of Wisconsin

Improved farm machinery of the sort advertised here helped farmers boost production.

with produce from the newly opened lands of Argentina, Australia, and Canada. As the quantity of food produced went up, the prices the farmer received went down.

The "Granger laws." Farmers did not understand the complex reasons for their plight. They blamed it on the greedy banks, railroads, and grain elevators. In about a dozen midwestern and southern states, new farmers' political parties appeared. They called for state control of corporations, particularly of railroads, for "cheap money," for economy in government,

and for other reforms. Many Grangers joined the farmers' parties, and in the 1870s they managed to pass state laws regulating railroad and grain elevator rates. Unfortunately for the farmers, these "Granger laws" were not effective. The powerful railroads sometimes simply ignored the laws. Or they "persuaded" the legislatures to repeal them. In other cases the overawed courts nullified the laws by their decisions.

One important exception was the case of *Munn v. Illinois* (1876). Here the Supreme Court upheld the Illinois law that set maximum rates for grain storage. The "police power" of

✄ **Critical Thinking Activity: Determining Relevance** How are the Granger laws of the 1870s still a part of our lives today? Have students discuss the court decision of *Munn* v. *Illinois* (1876). Ask: What did the court find?

the state under the Constitution, they said, gave the state the right to regulate private property "affected with a public interest." This became a precedent for the right of the public to regulate large corporations in other ways.

The Farmers' Alliances. When prosperity returned to the farms for a few years in the late 1870s and early '80s, farmers felt less need for the Grange and their own farmers' political parties. But when prices fell once again, the farmers suffered.

New organizations of farmers, called "Alliances," were formed in the 1880s and 1890s. They went actively into politics. In the western states they formed their own parties. In the South they worked among the Democrats who, for all practical purposes, were the only political party. The farmers' successes in the 1890 elections persuaded the western farm leaders to try to form a separate national party. They hoped that the southern farmers would join them in their effort to give a single loud voice to all the forces of discontent in the land.

Southern farmers of all races were ready for a change. So ready even that old racial prejudices began to soften. Some white farmers now were willing to work with blacks to gain the reforms that would bring all a better life.

The Populist party is formed. Western and southern farmers along with an odd assortment of radicals and reformers met at Omaha, Nebraska, in early July 1892. They called themselves "Populists"—from the Latin word *populus*, meaning "the people." Their platform declared that they were meeting "in the midst of a nation brought to the verge of moral, political, and material ruin." Everywhere they saw corruption. They also saw "business prostrated, homes covered with mortgages, labor impoverished, and the land concentrated in the hands of capitalists." The major parties seemed interested only in "power and plunder."

The Populists called for sweeping reform. They demanded the free coinage of silver and an increase in the money supply to $50 per person. They wanted an income tax to put a larger share of the burden on the wealthy. The government,

Enrich-
ment
Support
File Topic

they said, should take over ownership of railroads, telegraph, and telephone. The platform also called for a shorter working day for industrial laborers and the direct election of senators.

The farmers' leaders were not afraid to shock the rich and comfortable people. One of their best was the handsome, outspoken Mary Elizabeth Lease of Kansas, the mother of four. "What you farmers need," she urged, "is to raise less corn and more Hell!" She also went on:

> Wall Street owns the country. It is no longer a government of the people, by the people, and for the people, but a government of Wall Street, by Wall Street, and for Wall Street. The

Fiery orator Mary Elizabeth Lease won many Kansas farmers over to the Populist cause.

Kansas State Historical Society

Continuity and Change: Government and Politics Explain to students that farmers' alliances, such as the Populist party, created to gain political power were not new in the nineteenth century. By pulling together farmers had attempted to change the policy and practice of the past to ensure the survival of their farms and families. In 1787, with the country in the midst of a business depression, many farmers could not repay debts and the state governments failed to help them. The revolt of a group of farmers under the leadership of Daniel Shays contributed toward major change in the structure of the national government. (See page 114.)

great common people of this country are slaves, and monopoly is the master.

Then, also from Kansas, there was "Sockless Jerry" Simpson. Once when he ran for Congress, he accused his well-dressed opponent of wearing silk stockings. A reporter then sneered that Simpson was so crude that he wore no socks at all. Simpson made this into a boast. Always after that he was known as "Sockless Jerry."

Crusaders like the rabble-rousing Tom Watson of Georgia spoke for them in Congress and spoke loud and clear. "Before I will give up this fight," Watson warned, "I will stay here till the ants tote me out of the keyhole."

The election of 1892. The two major parties had held their conventions in June. The Republicans had picked Harrison again. The Democrats had chosen their strongest candidate, Grover Cleveland. He had the support of many business leaders because he opposed free silver

"Sockless Jerry" Simpson's looks hid the fact that he was extremely witty.

The Kansas State Historical Society

and inflation and therefore was "sound" on the money question.

The Populists, with the eloquent and honest General James B. Weaver as their candidate, conducted a vigorous campaign. In the South they made common cause with all the poor, both white and black. Conservative southern Democrats, desperate to defend themselves against reform, raised the cry for white supremacy. They denounced all Populists as the enemies of law and order. (p. 473)

General Weaver, an outspoken man of courage, declared:

> There is but one issue in the South. That is competition to see who can most hate the Negro. The man that wins gets the nomination. The whole thing is a dead-drag on the country. . . . Slavery must be the greatest of crimes. Here we are, all these years after it has been abolished, and we are still paying the penalty for it.

During the campaign summer of 1892 the nation was torn by labor strife. First came the bloody Homestead Strike (p. 432). When striking miners rioted in Coeur d'Alene, Idaho, President Harrison sent in federal troops at the governor's request. In these stormy times, people put their faith in Grover Cleveland. He had already proved once that he could be a competent, pacifying President. Cleveland received 373,000 more votes than Harrison and won with an electoral vote of 277 to Harrison's 145. The Democrats also won both houses of Congress. The Populist General Weaver actually received over a million popular votes, but he carried only four states—Colorado, Kansas, Nevada, and Idaho. The Populists elected three United States Senators and eleven members of the House.

Cleveland's second term. Grover Cleveland's second term was as much a disaster as his first had been a success. It began with one of the nation's worst depressions, one that lasted his entire four years in office. Negative policies were no longer enough.

One major problem was that the Treasury was rapidly losing gold. Under the Sherman Silver Purchase Act, the Treasury notes issued to buy

≶ **Continuity and Change: Government and Politics** Point out to students that Cleveland's attempts to combat economic depression in the late nineteenth century, by reducing tariffs and stopping the drain on gold, failed. President Hoover's early attempts to cope with the problems of the Great Depression in the 1930s, like Cleveland's, produced few results. Hoover's policies to aid farmers and provide jobs were ineffective because, like Cleveland, he refused to provide direct and immediate relief to individuals. (See p. 608.)

Museum of American Political Life/photo by Sally Anderson-Bruce

In the days before radio and television numerous items were produced to advertise political candidates. This colorful handkerchief bearing Grover Cleveland's image was one of many articles manufactured for the election campaign of 1892.

silver could be redeemed for gold. Since gold dollars were more valuable than silver dollars, people naturally turned in their silver Treasury notes for gold dollars. But the Treasury had to reissue the Treasury notes—which were then turned back in for gold again. It is not surprising that the Treasury was about to run out of gold.

Cleveland called a special session of Congress in August 1893 to demand repeal of the Sherman Silver Purchase Act. He wanted the government to stop spending $50 million a year taking in "cheap" silver for valuable gold. After some hard fighting that split both parties, his measure passed.

A new tariff and an income tax. President Cleveland now turned to the tariff, which the party platform had promised to revise. But the Wilson-Gorman tariff (named for Representative William Wilson in the House and Senator Albert Gorman in the Senate) was little different from the McKinley tariff. Cleveland was so disgusted by the bill that he refused to sign it. But since it did contain some reductions, he did not veto it. As long as Congress is in session, bills become laws after ten days even if the President neither vetoes nor signs them (Art. 1, sec. 7). The President allowed this act to become law without his signature.

The Wilson-Gorman tariff did include one interesting feature. It provided for a tax of 2 percent on incomes above $4000. But before the tax was ever collected, the Supreme Court, in *Pollock* v. *Farmers' Loan and Trust Co.* (1895), declared the law unconstitutional. By a 5 to 4 vote they found an income tax to be a "direct tax." This settled the matter because the

❖ See "Lesson Plan," p. 458D for **Cooperative Learning Activity: Recognizing Bias** relating to the election of 1892.

Constitution declared that any direct tax had to be levied in proportion to the population (Art. I, sec. 2, par. 3). The Sixteenth Amendment to the Constitution (1913) would have to be passed before Congress could levy an income tax.

Labor discontent. Meanwhile the depression was causing havoc. Millions were out of work. The winter of 1894 brought widespread suffering. In April a successful self-made businessman, reformer, and Populist, Jacob Coxey, led an "army" of 500 workers on a march from Ohio to Washington to publicize the plight of the poor. In May federal troops were fighting the Pullman strikers outside Chicago (p. 433). For the first time, and to many people's surprise, the Sherman Antitrust Act was turned against

In 1894 Jacob Coxey, shown here on horseback, led a small "army" of protesters to Washington to make known the problems of the poor.

Library of Congress

the workers. The act had been passed to control large corporations. But now a federal court declared that the striking union was a "conspiracy in restraint of trade," forbidden by the act. The court enforced its decision by issuing an order, called an "injunction," that told the union to stop the strike. This was a powerful new weapon. It made the strikers criminals if they refused to obey the court order and go back to work. The companies could now turn to the courts to stop a strike.

President Cleveland still seemed powerless against the depression. He had refused to give people "cheap money." He had used federal troops against starving workers. It is no wonder that he lost the voters' support. In the fall elections of 1894, the Populists' vote increased by 42 percent. And the Republicans, from being a minority in the House, jumped to a 141-seat majority. This was the largest congressional gain ever recorded. They also won control of the Senate.

Plugging the drain on gold. Grover Cleveland believed that a big part of the nation's economic trouble was public fear about the value of the American dollar. "Sound money"—not one dropping in value—would restore confidence and get the wheels of industry turning again. And sound money, it was widely believed, depended on the *gold standard.* A chief feature of the gold standard is that the government will, on demand, exchange its paper money for gold.

The repeal of the Sherman Silver Purchase Act in 1893 failed to stem the fall of the Treasury's gold reserves. Existing greenbacks and silver certificates could still be turned in for gold. How could the government stop the drain of gold? For a time, the sale of government bonds helped. But not for long. Cleveland was desperate to find a way to save the nation's credit by keeping a gold reserve in the Treasury. He turned to J. P. Morgan, the "organizer extraordinary"—the nation's most powerful banker. By organizing a group of bankers to sell United States bonds in Europe, Morgan brought in more than $65 million in gold. Of course Morgan reaped an enormous profit, though he never revealed how much.

Multicultural Connection: One goal of the Populists in the South was to politically unite poor African Americans and poor whites as evidenced in this quotation by Tom Watson, who ran for governor of Georgia in 1892. "Now the People's Party says . . . you are kept apart that you may be separately fleeced of your earnings . . . . You are deceived and blinded so that you may not see how this antagonism perpetuates a monetary system which beggars you both."

Populists and Silverites were angered by President Cleveland's deals with the men of Wall Street. Within his own Democratic party his name became "a hissing and a byword." Ben Tillman, a Democrat, earned his nickname, "Pitchfork," when he told the people of South Carolina who had elected him senator, "[Cleveland] is an old bag of beef and I am going to Washington with a pitchfork and prod him in his old fat ribs."

See "Section 3 Review answers," p. 458E.

Section 3 Review

1. Identify or explain: Patrons of Husbandry, *Munn* v. *Illinois*, farmers' alliances, Mary Elizabeth Lease, Jerry Simpson, Tom Watson, James B. Weaver, Jacob Coxey, Ben Tillman.

2. Identify problems faced by farmers in the years after 1870.

3. How was the election of 1892 affected by (a) the race issue? (b) labor strife?

4. In Cleveland's second term what action did the President and/or Congress take on (a) the money problem? (b) the tariff? (c) strikes?

5. How did the federal courts assist business managers during their struggles with labor?

6. **Critical Thinking: Determining Relevance.** Which planks in the 1892 Populist platform represented the demands of (a) farmers? (b) industrial workers? (c) both?

See "Lesson Plan," p. 458E.

4. Our money: gold versus silver

In these times of troubles, the nation, and especially the farmers, wanted a cure-all. Many people came to believe that the cure-all might be free silver. There was something magical and mysterious about money. The amounts of money seemed to change the value of everything else. Money seemed a medicine for everybody's
✂ ills. So money became the key to the election of 1896.

William Jennings Bryan. Inside the regular parties the most successful of the farm crusaders was William Jennings Bryan. Some called

Library of Congress

Silver-tongued William Jennings Bryan was a three-time Democratic candidate for President.

him the "Great Commoner" because he championed the common people. Others called him the "Prairie Avenger," or the "Boy Orator of the Platte"—after the river near his Nebraska home. Born in Salem, Illinois, he studied law in Chicago and then practiced law in small towns. He distrusted rich people and people of "good family."

A tall, handsome man of great energy, Bryan loved a political battle. And he had a talent for making issues seem very simple. After he had explained it, every political battle seemed to be between Bryan and God on one side, and his opponents and Satan on the other. His enemies said that Bryan did not really understand how complicated the problems were. Even his friends had to admit that what made him famous was not his sharp mind but his loud musical voice.

The "silver-tongued" William Jennings Bryan had decided that "free silver" would cure the

✂ Critical Thinking Activity: Expressing Problems Clearly What issues did free silver symbolize? On the chalkboard list all the issues that free silver had come to symbolize by the election of 1896. Ask students to determine which items they would support. Conclude this activity by having students write a paragraph on their stand for or against free silver.

nation's ills. When Bryan arrived at the Democratic convention in Chicago on July 7, 1896, he was 36 years old—one year over the minimum age for a President. He had served only four years in Congress and was barely known outside of Nebraska. Unlike the other leading candidates, he did not have rich supporters.

As the convention met, it was still not decided whether the Democratic party would stay with the gold standard or whether they would join the farmers for free silver. Until Bryan came to the rostrum, the speakers at the Chicago convention had been dull and long-winded. Since there was no public-address system, most of the speakers could hardly be heard. Bryan was the final speaker for free silver.

This was young Bryan's great chance. The first sound of his ringing voice awakened the perspiring audience. They responded to his words with laughter and applause "like a trained choir," as he said, down to his last syllable. He spoke without hesitating, for he had given much the same speech many times before—to farm audiences all over Nebraska. "We will answer their demand for a Gold Standard," he ended, "by saying to them: You shall not press down upon the brow of labor this crown of thorns. You shall not crucify mankind upon a cross of gold."

The crowd went wild. Their yelling and cheering lasted for an hour. This one speech had transformed a Nebraska small-town lawyer into a front runner for President!

On the next day, the Democratic convention named him to lead their ticket. Then the Populists at their national convention also nominated him for President.

The campaign and election of 1896. The campaign offered one of the most spectacular contrasts in American history. The "Boy Orator of the Platte" hurried about the country by train, making speeches far into the night at every little town and often in between. On some days he made 36 speeches. Meanwhile, his conservative Republican opponent, William McKinley, remained calmly seated on his front porch in Canton, Ohio. McKinley made almost no speeches. When he did, he was careful to say

nothing in particular—except that he was in favor of "sound money" (the gold standard) and "restoring confidence."

Mark Hanna, a clever Cleveland businessman and political boss who had secured the Republican nomination for McKinley, managed McKinley's campaign. Hanna counted on letting Bryan talk himself to defeat. And he used every trick to convince voters that Bryan was a dangerous radical. For example, he persuaded some factory owners, as a stunt, to pay their workers in Mexican dollars (worth only 50 United States cents). This was supposed to show the workers what their wages would really be worth if Bryan won. Employees in some factories were actually told that the businesses would shut down if Bryan won.

Hanna's tactics succeeded. McKinley overwhelmed Bryan by 600,000 votes, the greatest margin since 1872. The Republicans retained their control of both houses of Congress. Despite all this, Bryan's performance had really been spectacular. With little money or organization, deserted by the "gold wing" of his party, Bryan had polled some 6.5 million votes, more than had ever before been cast even for a winning candidate. The change of about 19,000 votes, distributed in six states, would have won him the election in the electoral college.

Bryan's fatal weakness was his inability to carry a single one of the urban-industrial states. He was a one-issue candidate, and his one issue—free silver—did not appeal to factory workers or city people. Still, he had attracted so many votes that the Democratic leaders could not ignore him. Twice again—in 1900 and 1908—he would be named the Democratic candidate for President. Bryan never won.

See "Section 4 Review answers," p. 458E.

Section 4 Review

1. Why did the Democrats and Populists choose Bryan as their candidate for President in 1896?

2. **Critical Thinking: Drawing Conclusions.** What tactics enabled McKinley to win the 1896 election?

See "Lesson Plan," p. 458E for **Writing Process Activity: Drawing Conclusions** relating to William Jennings Bryan and the cause of free silver.

Chapter 18 Review

See "Chapter Review answers," p. 458E.

Focusing on Ideas

1. In the 1880s and 1890s, what stand on the "cheap money" vs. "sound money" issue would you expect each of the following persons to take and why: An elderly city couple living on their savings? A Kansas wheat farmer? A factory worker? A merchant selling chiefly to farmers? A banker?

2. The Gilded Age was a period of governmental reforms. Describe three important reforms.

3. How did President Arthur's administration prove that the office of President can lift a person above narrow party politics?

Taking a Critical Look

1. **Expressing Problems Clearly.** Show that control of the national government was closely divided between the two major parties from 1876 to 1896. How did this situation make for "an age of timid Presidents"? How did it stimulate the rise of the Populist Party?

2. **Distinguishing Fact from Opinion.** Grover Cleveland has been criticized for being more concerned with managing the government and controlling spending than with facing the issues of the day. What evidence can you find for or against this criticism? Which is more important for a President—to be a good manager or to be a political leader?

Your Region in History

1. **Geography.** Which party's candidate received your state's electoral votes in the presidential elections of 1876, 1880, 1884, and 1888? Compare your state's election results to the returns in other states in your region. Did your region vote as a bloc?

2. **Culture.** What leaders from your state or region were active in national politics and the struggles of the Gilded Age? What were some of their accomplishments?

3. **Economics.** Can you identify a great-grandparent or other relative who lived during America's Gilded Age? How did he or she earn a living? What economic reforms would he or she have supported or opposed? Give reasons for your answer.

Historical Facts and Figures

Drawing Conclusions. Study the chart below to help answer the following questions: (a) In what year were the profits from the sale of wheat the highest? the lowest? (b) What was the relationship between the amount of wheat produced and the price farmers could obtain for their crop after 1870? (c) If you were a wheat farmer facing a wheat market in which that relationship between price and production existed, what would be your economic concerns? How would you protect your investment in farmland, livestock, crops, and equipment?

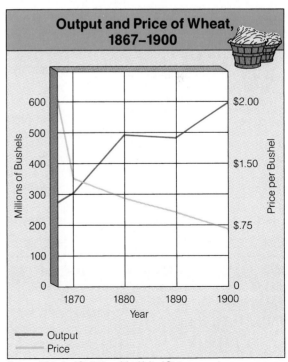

Source: *Historical Statistics of the United States*

MAKING CONNECTIONS
Unit 6

This unit began on page 411 with the observation that after the Civil War the United States was as large and diverse as western Europe. This raised the question:

Could a nation where everything was becoming bigger still care for the little people?

This question was explored by the three unit themes that are reprinted in **dark type** below. Use the time line and the information in Unit 6 to answer the questions that follow the unit themes.

THEMES IN HISTORY

Using "Making Connections": Have students look at the unit themes printed in dark type. Explain that each event on the time line relates to one of these themes. Ask students to decide which events are related to which theme. Students should use events from the time line in their answers and explain our events are related. You may also wish to have students go back through the text of Unit 6 to find other events related to the unit themes.

1. **Immigrants from across Europe pour into the United States.** ECONOMICS
   In what ways were American cities of the late nineteenth century "melting pots" and in what ways were they "mixing bowls"?
   (Distinguishing False from Accurate Images)

2. **The rise of new cities and the growth of older cities give the nation an increasingly urban character.** SOCIAL CHANGE
   How did technology and science affect the character and growth of American cities? (Recognizing Cause and Effect)

3. **Urban industrialization and falling farm prices lead farmers and factory workers to protest the politics and big business of the Gilded Age.** GOVERNMENT AND POLITICS
   How was the American spirit reflected in the political activism of its farmers and factory workers? (Recognizing Ideologies)

 **Events in American History**

1870 —
Public high schools are established across the U.S., helping to educate and "Americanize" many immigrants.

1877
Wage reductions following the 187: depression promp the great railway strike.

1855	1860	1865	1870	1875	1880

Events in World History

1855
Bogardus builds the first skeleton-framed skyscraper, eight stories high.

1864
First International Workingmen's Association formed in London by Karl Marx.

1868
Construction begins on the Brooklyn Bridge, designed by John Roebling.

1892
Nearly 100 German-language newspapers are published in American cities.

1881
Andrew Carnegie opens his steel plant in Homestead, Pennsylvania.

1889
Jane Addams founds Hull House in Chicago, in part to aid urban immigrants.

1892
Overproduction and falling crop prices lead disenchanted farmers to form the national Populist party.

1894
The Immigration Restriction League is formed by Americans opposed to immigration.

1900
In Manhattan, there are more than 40,000 tenements housing 1,500,000 people.

1880	1885	1890	1895	1900

1883
The World Exhibition opens in Amsterdam, highlighting new inventions.

1885
Due to political and economic instability, a new wave of immigrants begins to arrive in the U.S. from southern and eastern Europe.

1893
The Independent Labour party is founded in England.

Review Chapter
The United States, 1789–1898

Identifying Chapter Materials

Objectives	Basic Instructional Materials	Extension Materials
1 A New Nation ▪ State the principle of judicial review and discuss John Marshall's role in establishing it. ▪ Describe the controversy surrounding the Louisiana Purchase and describe its importance to the United States.	**Instructional Support File** ▪ Skill Application Activity, Unit 3, p. 5	**Enrichment Support File** ▪ Checks and Balances: The Rise of the American Judiciary ▪ Proud to Be American: A New Spirit of Nationalism **Documents of American History** ▪ The Cession of Louisiana, Vol. 1, p. 190 ▪ *Marbury* v. *Madison,* Vol. 1, p. 191 **American History Transparencies** ▪ Geography and History, pp. B13, B15 ▪ Time Lines, p. E11
2 A Nation Expanding, Reforming, and Dividing ▪ Explain the reasons for war with Mexico and state the terms of the Treaty of Guadalupe Hidalgo. ▪ Cite the events from 1850–1860 that led to the Civil War. ▪ Describe Reconstruction under the Radical Republicans.	**Instructional Support File** ▪ Skill Review Activity, Unit 5, p. 18 ▪ Critical Thinking Activity, Unit 4, p. 34	**Enrichment Support File** ▪ "Come Along to Freedom": The Underground Railroad ▪ Experiences of the Civil War Soldier ▪ The Realities of Reconstruction **Documents of American History** ▪ Compromise of 1850, Vol. 1, p. 319 **American History Transparencies** ▪ Geography and History, pp. B13, B15, B17, B21, B23, B25, B27 ▪ Time Lines, p. E15
3 The Nation Transformed ▪ Describe the impact of the Industrial Revolution on the United States. ▪ Demonstrate how transportation and communication improved in the United States during the nineteenth century.	**Instructional Support File** ▪ Skill Review Activity, Unit 6, p. 32 ▪ Skill Application Activity, Unit 6, p. 19 ▪ Review Chapter Test, Unit 6, pp. 43–46	**Enrichment Support File** ▪ On the Job: Industrialism in America ▪ Linking the Nation: The Railroads ▪ Ellis Island: Gateway to America **American History Transparencies** ▪ Critical Thinking, p. F11

Review: The United States, 1789–1898

TEACHING STRATEGIES

The two review chapters in this book may be adapted to suit the knowledge level of your students and the particular needs of your curriculum. Below are three suggested strategies for this review chapter:

★ Assign the chapter and chapter review as a regular lesson to students who may be unfamiliar with the material in the first eighteen chapters of the text before the class begins Unit 7. You can administer the Review Chapter Test from the Instructional Support File to check students' competency when they have completed the chapter.

★ Assign the review chapter to students as a quick review of material they have learned previously. Then work through the questions in the chapter review together as a class before beginning Unit 7.

★ As a useful tool for assessment, give students the Review Chapter Test from the Instructional Support File. Then assign specific readings from this chapter or from earlier chapters in the text to supplement student knowledge where the test indicates any weaknesses.

Chapter Review Answers

Focusing on Key Facts and Ideas

1. a) Washington's Secretary of the Treasury. b) Chief Justice of the Supreme Court who asserted the right of the Supreme Court to review the constitutionality of laws and transformed the Court into a powerful institution. c) the power of the Supreme Court to declare acts of Congress unconstitutional. d) A compromise intended to settle the question of whether slavery would be allowed in territories acquired from Mexico. e) slave who sued for his freedom on the grounds that he had lived in a free state for several years. f) fanatical abolitionist who led bloody raids against supporters of slavery in the Kansas Territory. g) located off Charleston, South Carolina; site of the first battle of the Civil War. h) producing large quantities of items of exactly the same kind. i) monopoly formed by combining the ownership of several formerly separate corporations under a board of trustees. 2. Strict: the government had only those powers that the Constitution had given in so many words. Broad: the govern-ment had the right to do everything necessary and proper to carry out the powers expressly granted in the Constitution. 3. Depended on it to transport goods to earn their living. Secured their access to the river. 4. Treaty of Guadalupe-Hidalgo gave U.S. territory in present-day Texas, New Mexico, Colorado, Utah, Nevada, Arizona, and California. There would be a great deal of conflict over the existence of slavery in the newly acquired land. 5. Abolitionists: moral, religious, and humanitarian arguments; Southerners: slavery was a "positive good," the foundation of their economy and their culture. 6. Continued expansion heated up the controversy; continued efforts for compromise failed, causing party sectionalism; Antislavery Republicans gained strength when Democrats divided resulting in Lincoln's election in 1860. 7. (a) Revenge for loss of property (Stevens), bodily injury (Sumner); severe limits on former leaders. (b) Freedmen's Bureau, Civil Rights Act of 1966, efforts to enfranchise blacks. 8. Interchangeable System provided jobs for unskilled immigrants; great quantities of items could be produced and cost less for consumers than those made individually by skilled craftsmen. 9. Abundant farm land; job opportunities in factories and in construction of cities and roads; peace. 10. (a) By increasing greatly the value of their investment and by freeing capital for use in laying track and buying rolling stock; (b) by making transportation available and agriculture products more marketable; land became more valuable; (c) contributed to economic growth; transportation, trade; rate discounts for the federal government.

Taking a Critical Look

1. Probably not; there would be no effective way to "check" Congress's lawmaking. 2. The Compromise at least *limited* the *spread* of slavery. 3. Western cities were often built before people came. 4. Social reformers' religious and humanitarian sentiments led to condemnation of slavery. 5. The Fugitive Slave Act was unacceptable to abolitionists; popular sovereignty on slavery in Utah and New Mexico roused further conflict. 6. Similar: Blacks inferior social and economic position. Difference: Blacks could escape peonage more easily; could marry, raise families; some educational opportunity; lack of economic security of slavery.

Your Region in History

1–5. Answers will vary depending on your region. Consult your local library or historical society.

REVIEW: The United States, 1789–1898

Focusing the Chapter: Have students identify the chapter logo. Discuss what unit theme the logo might symbolize. Then ask students to skim the chapter to identify other illustrations or titles that relate to this theme.

For teaching suggestions, see "Lesson Plan," p. 480B.

The years between the adoption of the Constitution and the war with Spain in 1898 were to see the United States transformed. The country that George Washington was to lead had changed only slightly from the land he had known as a boy, although the population had grown. The first federal census in 1790 reported nearly 4 million people in the country's 865,000 square miles. The nation occupied less than one-quarter the territory it would fill by the late 1900s. Within its boundaries were areas still contested by the British. During the nineteenth century the United States increased to some 92 million people spread from sea to sea. American per capita income was the highest in the world. The once-rural nation had become an industrial giant, producing more coal, iron, and steel than any other nation.

Smoke from the factories of Lazell, Perkins & Company was a daily reminder to Bridgewater, Massachusetts, that the Industrial Revolution had arrived. This late 1850s hand-colored lithograph advertised the firm's "Forgings . . . Casting and all Kinds of Machinery."

The Corcoran Gallery of Art, Museum Purchase, Mary E. Maxwell, Washington

1. A new nation

When the members of the new government gathered in New York City in April 1789, many questions needed to be answered. The federal government, with no money, inherited war debts to the French government, to Dutch bankers, and to its own citizens. Besides raising money to pay off those debts, Congress had to provide for the national defense and deal with the Indian tribes. The Constitution required the federal government to take a census each ten years to fix the number of congressmen for each state in the House of Representatives. The territories had to be organized and federal courts established. All the executive departments had to be set up, to provide the nation an army and navy, customs officers, ambassadors abroad, and a postal service at home.

Defining the Constitution. Many of the new government tasks could be accomplished by laws. But sometimes there were questions of what was allowed by the Constitution. For example, when Secretary of the Treasury Alexander Hamilton in 1790 suggested that the United States create a bank jointly with private investors to be the government's financial agent, Thomas Jefferson and James Madison objected that the Constitution did not expressly give Congress the power to establish a bank. This kind of argument became known as a "strict construction" of the Constitution. They argued that the new government had only those powers that the Constitution had given in so many � words.

On the other side, Hamilton asserted that the government had the right to do everything necessary and proper to carry out the powers expressly granted in the Constitution. The bank, he declared, was a necessary and proper way to borrow money and to regulate the currency, both of which powers the Constitution had plainly assigned to the Congress. This became known as a "broad" construction of the Constitution.

The dispute that began over the first Bank of the United States between the "strict" and the "broad" interpretation of the Constitution still continues. But who takes which side never stays the same.

Did the Constitution allow the federal government to set up a national bank? This question was not settled until 1819 when Chief Justice John Marshall made one of his most famous decisions in *McCulloch* v. *Maryland*. That decision would become a bulwark of a strong central government in the United States. The state of Maryland had tried to force the bank out of the state by taxing it. Marshall asserted that no state had the right to hinder or control any national institution established within its borders. "The power to tax," he said, "is the power to destroy."

Marshall seized the occasion to ask whether the Constitution gave Congress the power to set up a national bank. Now he dealt with the clause that gave Congress the right "to make all laws necessary and proper" for carrying out the powers granted it under the Constitution (Art. I, sec. 8).

Did these words mean "absolutely necessary and therefore proper"? Marshall said No! To carry out any of its direct powers, Congress could choose the appropriate means. Congress could create a bank as a convenient or useful means to carry out its direct powers to collect taxes and borrow money. It was only necessary that the means be "within the letter and spirit of the Constitution" and not

✕ **Critical Thinking Activity: Demonstrating Reasoned Judgment** How should the Constitution be interpreted? Ask students to describe the concept of a "strict interpretation" of the Constitution and that of a "broad interpretation." Have students discuss to which point of view they believe George Washington and John Adams subscribed.

This small ornate room in the Capitol is where the Supreme Court met until 1860.

prohibited. The decision therefore had the effect of broadening the powers of Congress and thereby the national government.

John Marshall served as Chief Justice from 1801 until his death in 1835. Among his many important decisions that strengthened the national government, one of the earliest and most significant was in the case of *Marbury* v. *Madison* in 1803. In this case Marshall declared a section of the Judiciary Act of 1789 unconstitutional. The Founding Fathers had assumed that the Supreme Court would declare acts of Congress unconstitutional. But they had not put that power in so many words in the Constitution. So by a strict reading of the Constitution the Court had no such right. Nor had it ever used the right since the Supreme Court was created in 1789. Now in 1803 the Court boldly assumed this right of *judicial review* as guardian of the Constitution. Since John Marshall's time this has remained the leading role of the Supreme Court in American history.

John Marshall was noted for his masterful opinions and his skill in winning other members of the Court to his views. In *Martin* v. *Hunter's Lessee* (1816) and *Cohens* v. *Virginia* (1821) the Supreme Court insisted on its right to review decisions of state courts in matters arising under the federal Constitution. In the *Dartmouth College Case* (1819) the Court protected private property from state interference when it ruled that a charter passed by a state legislature was a "contract." States were forbidden by the Constitution to "pass any law impairing the obligation of contracts" (Art. I, sec. 10). The decision in this case broadened the national power. It also encouraged business by allowing firms to invest their capital and rely on their charters without fearing the whimsies of state legislatures.

In *Gibbons* v. *Ogden* (1824), the famous "Steamboat Case," the Marshall Court drew some powerful conclusions from the clause in the Constitution that gives to Congress the power to regulate commerce (Art. I, sec. 8). Marshall defined "commerce" so broadly that champions of "states' rights" accused him of trying to abolish the state governments. In later years Congress, overseeing "interstate commerce," would regulate telephones, telegraphs, and oil pipelines. Even manufacturing *within* a state would be regulated when the workers, the raw materials, or the products crossed state lines.

Who shall judge? The Constitution did not say who was to judge if Congress went beyond the powers granted in the Constitution. The question came to a head over the Alien and Sedition Acts of 1798. The Alien Act let the President deport any alien he found dangerous. The Sedition Act provided a heavy fine and a jail term for any person found guilty of "combining and conspiring to oppose the execution of the laws, or publishing false, scandalous, or malicious writings against the President, Congress, or the government of the United States." These vague and general words could be used to stop public criticism of the government and spell the end of free government.

Still, the courts did not strike down the Alien and Sedition Acts. If they would not, who could? James Madison and Thomas Jefferson believed that in this situation the only power able to oppose the federal government was the states. Resolutions drafted by Madison and passed by the Virginia legislature declared that each state had the right to judge whether measures passed by Congress were constitutional. The Kentucky Resolutions that Jefferson wrote went even further. Since any state could declare acts of Congress "null and void," the rightful response to an unconstitutional act of Congress was simply "*nullification*" by the states.

This states' rights doctrine first championed by Madison and Jefferson would later be carried so far that it led to civil war. During the War of 1812, delegates from the five New England states met in a convention at Hartford, Connecticut, on December 15, 1814. These delegates, remnants of the old Federalist party, denounced the "ruinous war." They adopted resolutions like those of Virginia and Kentucky declaring that when the Constitution was violated it was the duty of the states to "interpose their authority for the preservation of their liberties."

Again, in 1828 after the Tariff of Abominations was passed, Vice-President John C. Calhoun argued that each state had the right to judge when Congress was exceeding its powers. Within its borders, he argued, any state could nullify an act of Congress that it considered unconstitutional. For Congress to override that "nullification," it would be necessary to use the long and clumsy amending process provided in the Constitution. Then the power asserted by Congress, even if questioned by only one state, would have to be approved by three-fourths of the states.

In 1832 a South Carolina convention voted to nullify the tariff acts of 1828 and 1832. They forbade South Carolinians to pay the duties required by these laws. And they further stated that any attempt by federal authorities to enforce tariff laws in South Carolina would be "a just cause for the secession of the state from the Union." President Andrew Jackson reacted swiftly. He threatened to use troops to enforce the law.

After Jackson's threat, and a compromise tariff passed by Congress, South Carolina rescinded its nullification. Then in a proud, but empty, gesture they turned around and nullified the "Force Bill" by which Congress had authorized the President "to employ the army and navy of the United States to collect duties in South Carolina." The day of battle was only postponed. The fighting language of nullification and secession would not be forgotten.

The Louisiana Purchase. The Add-a-State plan of Thomas Jefferson provided an easy way of growing. And soon a procession of new states entered the Union— Vermont (1791), Kentucky (1792), Tennessee (1796), and Ohio (1803). All were carved out of lands that had belonged to the American colonies. All were east of the Mississippi River. But could the United States remain fenced in forever by its old colonial boundaries? Would the new nation be only a new way of organizing those territories between the Mississippi River and the Atlantic Ocean long ago claimed by the British? Or would the new nation reach out on its own, to enlarge its new-style Empire for Liberty?

The answer came quickly enough—and in a surprising way. It all began as more and more Americans were settling between the Appalachian Mountains and the Mississippi River. They needed transportation. It was very hard to carry produce back east overland. It was easier to float their crops down the many rivers to what Americans called the "Father of Waters," the great Mississippi— down to the Gulf of Mexico, into the ocean, and out to the world. An enemy holding the mouth of the Mississippi could shut the Westerners off, destroy their trade, and make their crops useless. When Jefferson became

In 1803 when this view was painted, New Orleans was small but bustling. The artist thought that as part of the United States the town would thrive.

President, he began to worry over how to keep open the western Americans' highway to the world.

Jefferson was especially troubled when the French under Napoleon got Louisiana back from Spain and began to charge tolls for the use of the river. To people who lived along the Mississippi River and its tributaries, the freedom to carry the produce to the world was a matter of life and death. So Jefferson tried to buy from France the land at the mouth of the Mississippi. But suddenly Napoleon, who had just found it difficult even to hold on to Haiti, offered to sell *all* of Louisiana to the United States. And our envoys abroad, Robert Livingston and James Monroe, boldly agreed to buy it all.

Now Jefferson was on the spot. The Constitution said nothing about whether or how Congress could buy land from a foreign country. In many other cases, Jefferson had argued that Congress had only the powers the Constitution had assigned it in so many words. Now would Jefferson dare go against everything he had been saying for years?

If Jefferson had been weak, he would have been afraid to change his mind. But he showed the same courage that Livingston and Monroe had shown in Paris. He decided to ask the members of Congress to vote the money to buy Louisiana. And after a bitter debate, Congress agreed.

The Louisiana Purchase provided far more than a pathway from western America to the world. It helped make the new nation itself into a new world by *doubling* the area of the United States. In time, thirteen new states and parts of states, some of the richest lands in the nation, would be carved out of the Loui- 🏛 siana Purchase.

2. A nation expanding, reforming, and dividing

The half-century before the Civil War was a time of ferment. Instant cities were created, factories were built, immigrants poured in. Long lines of wagons headed west to their promised land—Texas, California, and Oregon. The Americans who stayed home worked to make a more perfect society where they lived. These two movements of expansion and reform forced the nation to face an issue many Americans wished to avoid. What was the future of slavery in the United States?

The problem of slavery. In a land where towns could appear overnight, many Americans, like the first settlers, still believed they were building a "City upon a hill" for the whole world to see. They wanted a nation where there was no injustice, where all had an equal chance to succeed, and where citizens ruled themselves. They wanted to help the sick, the insane, the orphans, the prisoners, and the blind. Americans organized themselves into groups working for peace, for temperance in the use of alcohol, for improved education, for women's rights—and for the abolition of slavery.

The religious revivals that swept the land between the 1820s and 1850s made these ideas popular. By the 1850s one reform was increasingly becoming more important than any other—the move to abolish, or at least limit, slavery. The first attempts to end slavery had come in the North at the time of the American Revolution. But even in the South, people of goodwill who opposed slavery

🏛 **More from Boorstin:** "[Uncertainty about the boundaries of the Louisiana Purchase] . . . left open many possibilities. Robert R. Livingston [who negotiated the treaty with France] happily discovered (in Henry Adams' phrase) 'that France had actually bought West Florida without knowing it, and had sold it to the United States without being paid for it.' And so arose the American claim to West Florida." (From *The Americans: The National Experience*)

comforted themselves with the thought that it was a dying institution. Then the invention of the cotton gin in 1793 led to a new demand for slaves.

Southerners came to believe that slavery was the foundation of their economy and their culture. Northern attacks on slavery seemed to threaten their very lives. By 1833 Southerners feared all reforms. If one reforming "ism" came South, they expected it soon to be followed by that worst "ism" of all—abolitionism. So the South turned inward and cut itself off from the outside world. Southerners kept out Northern books, checked the mails for abolitionist literature, and tried to prevent the discussion of slavery in Congress.

The national differences over slavery might not have come to a head so soon if the nation had not been growing and moving so fast. Beginning in the 1820s, settlers from the United States were pushing into Texas, New Mexico, and California. In the 1830s, they moved into the vast Oregon country north of California.

Texas enters the Union.   The first opportunity for the flag to follow the American people into the new lands of the West came in Texas. Would Texas become a new stronghold for slavery? The question of annexing Texas soon divided the nation. It also would lead to war with Mexico.

By 1835 there were nearly 30,000 settlers from the United States living in the huge Mexican state of Coahuila-Texas. They had become Mexican citizens, but they had complaints about Mexican rule. Saltillo, the state capital, was 700 miles away and these settlers had few representatives in the legislature there. They missed the Bill of Rights and all the guarantees of the United States Constitution, including especially the right to trial by jury.

These new Texans had come mostly from the Southern United States. Since they had brought their slaves with them, they were outraged that the Mexican government tried to outlaw slavery. When that government imposed heavy customs taxes and stationed troops among the settlers, their thoughts naturally went back to the American Revolution. In 1835 they drove out the Mexican troops. Like the colonists who had rebelled against King George III 60 years before, the Texans declared their independence on March 2, 1836.

When the Mexican government tried to crush the Texas rebellion, they failed. A republic was set up with a constitution modeled on those of the states of the Union. But to reassure the settlers from the Southern United States, the Texas constitution forbade the legislature to interfere with slavery.

Texas at once asked for admission to the Union. Yet how many new states might be carved from its vast territory? The Northern states feared that the balance of North and South, which had continued since the Missouri Compromise in 1820, might be upset forever simply by creating numerous slave states out of Texas. Some Northerners said that Texas was only a slave owners' plot to smuggle more slaves into the Union.

A formula for admitting Texas was offered by James K. Polk when he ran for President in 1844. His slogan was a single watchword: *Expansion!* To annex only Texas would expand slave territory and menace the North. But if at the same time free territory was expanded by annexing the vast Oregon Territory, the North would have something in return. This compromise was Polk's winning platform. Expand North and South at the same time. There would be

More from Boorstin: "The same John Quincy Adams who, 25 years earlier, had insisted 'that the United States and North America are identical' in 1843 led the fight against annexing Texas. [He and other] prominent Americans warned that annexation was a Southern imperialist conspiracy; it would destroy the Union. . . . With equal enthusiasm, others promoted an 'All Mexico' movement. [Poet] Walt Whitman wrote in an editorial titled 'More Stars for the Spangled Banner,' that Yucatàn 'won't need a long coaxing before joining the United States.'" (From *The Americans: The National Experience*)

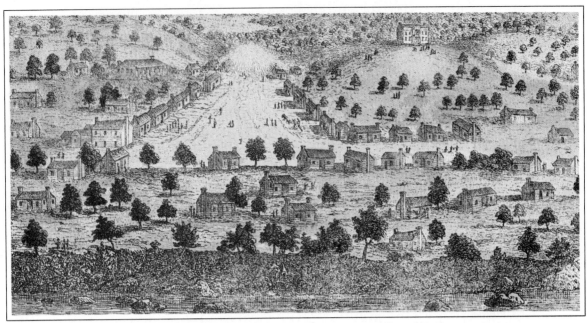

This handcolored lithograph of Austin, Texas, in 1840 shows the capital only four years after Texans declared their independence (p. 294). The grand house on the hill belonged to Texan President Mirabeau Lamar.

something for everybody. The very thought of stretching the nation all the way to the Pacific was exhilarating.

War with Mexico. Mexico considered the annexation of Texas to be an act of war by the United States. Texas, they said, was still a part of Mexico. There was also disagreement over the location of the boundary between Texas and Mexico. Polk sent American troops into the disputed area and refused a Mexican demand to withdraw. A Mexican unit crossed the Rio Grande and, on April 25, 1846, ambushed an American scouting party.

After a year and a half, Mexican troops were defeated in battle by the United States forces. In the Treaty of Guadalupe Hidalgo (1848), Mexico gave up all claims to Texas and agreed that Texas belonged to the United States. This was only the beginning of Mexican losses. In the course of the fighting, the Mexican government had also lost New Mexico and California. So in the peace treaty Mexico handed over to the United States all the lands between Texas and the Pacific. That included California, New Mexico, and most of the present states of Utah, Nevada, Arizona, and Colorado. In return, the United States paid Mexico $15 million and assumed claims of American citizens against Mexico for some $3 million.

The lands (including Texas) taken from Mexico after the war were larger than the entire Louisiana Purchase or all the United States when the Constitution was adopted.

It took no prophet to predict that more western land spelled trouble. Every

new acre was a subject for debate, and a prologue to battle. Southerners and Northerners alike thought of nothing but whether the new lands would spread the Slave Power.

The Compromise of 1850. The millions of acres acquired from Mexico—all raw material for new states—were to produce strife and tragedy for the nation as a whole. The first act of this drama ended in a great "compromise." Many optimistic Americans, North and South, mistakenly believed this might settle the slavery question. But the moral issue of slavery was not a subject for compromise. The only question for a nation "conceived in liberty" was when and how slavery would be abolished.

The Compromise of 1850, introduced by Henry Clay of Kentucky and pushed through Congress by the clever Stephen A. Douglas of Illinois, tried to give something to everyone. California, where gold had been discovered in 1848, was to be admitted as a free state (something for the North). A strong Fugitive Slave Act would protect the right of owners to recapture slaves who had escaped to the North (something for the South). The slave trade would be abolished in the District of Columbia (something for the North), but slavery would still be protected there (something for the South).

Clay had still left the main question unanswered. What would become of all the rest of the vast new area taken from Mexico? Would it be free or slave? Clay's compromise simply postponed the answer. The people of those areas, he proposed, should in the future decide for themselves. This arrangement was called "popular sovereignty" by those who admired it and "squatter sovereignty" by others.

The Compromise of 1850 only put off the day of reckoning. There had been no true compromise. The great issue of slavery was far from settled. But the Compromise of 1850 did give the North time to grow stronger—in manpower, railroads, and factories. For those who loved the Union, Clay and Douglas had performed a valuable service. They had bought time. When the evil day of armed conflict came, that strength would help decide the issue for the North and for Union.

The Kansas-Nebraska Act. The only hope for the success of the Compromise of 1850 was to keep the question of slavery out of Congress. The advance of technology and the growth of industry and commerce soon made that impossible. By an ironic twist of fate, the main architect of the Compromise of 1850, Senator Stephen A. Douglas, was destined to revive the slavery issue in Congress and so disturb the delicate balance.

In the 1850s Americans had a grand dream—to build a railroad across the continent uniting East and West. No American city could want a greater prize than to be the eastern terminus of the nation's transcontinental railroad.

Douglas wanted his home city of Chicago to receive the prize. But a railroad through the empty land of the West could only be built with the aid of government land grants. And these land grants could be given only if the region the railroad passed through was already organized politically and surveyed. With this in mind, Senator Douglas introduced a bill to organize the lands west of Iowa and Missouri. In its final form his bill provided for a Kansas Territory and a Nebraska Territory. But Southerners would never vote a railroad through land

During the 1850s Kansas was known as "Bleeding Kansas." In this lithograph, the Battle of Hickory Point, a village about 25 miles north of Lawrence, is shown. A band of proslavery men, armed with a cannon, are attacking the settlement of Free-Soilers.

that was forever closed to slavery, as the Missouri Compromise of 1820 had provided. Yet Douglas could not pass his bill without Southern votes.

In order to win Southern support, Senator Douglas, the wizard of compromise, concocted two special provisions. The Missouri Compromise of 1820 would be repealed and replaced by the Compromise of 1850. The decision whether Kansas and Nebraska should be free or slave would be made by "popu- ✂ lar sovereignty"—the vote of the people living there.

Douglas got his Kansas-Nebraska Act passed in 1854 after nine months of bitter debate. This was a great victory for Douglas. But it was an even greater victory for the South because the whole Kansas-Nebraska territory was north of the old freedom line of the Missouri Compromise. "Popular sovereignty" now might open those lands to slavery.

Angry rallies were held across the North to protest the Kansas-Nebraska Act. The question of slavery in the United States had now been transformed into a battle over whether slavery should be allowed to spread into the territories. A new political party came into existence to resist the *extension* of slavery. To show their connection with Jefferson's Democratic-Republican party, the members chose the name "Republicans," which had been dropped by the Democrats many years before.

When the Kansas-Nebraska Act became law, Douglas boasted that "the struggle over slavery was forever banished from the halls of Congress to the western plains." He was wrong about the halls of Congress but right about the western plains. For the Kansas-Nebraska Act brought bloodshed to Kansas, as both

✂ Critical Thinking Activity: Identifying Central Issues How does the concept of "popular sovereignty" hold up today? Have students define the term "popular sovereignty" (the vote of the people living in a specific area) and explain how it was used by Stephen Douglas in the 1850s. Then, ask students to make a list of today's issues that they believe should be left up to popular sovereignty. Have students explain their choices and discuss the practicality of such an approach.

Northern and Southern settlers tried to form governments that promoted their different views.

In the election of 1856, the Democratic candidate James Buchanan won. But, most important for the American future, the antislavery Republicans, in this their first national campaign, showed astonishing strength. Their candidate, John C. Frémont, running on a slogan of "Free speech, Free press, Free soil, Free men, Frémont," actually received 114 electoral votes to Buchanan's 174. It was an omen for the future that Frémont had received no electoral votes in the South. There the Republican party seemed the instrument of the devil.

The Dred Scott case. In his inaugural address, President Buchanan expressed the ill-founded belief that the long agitation over slavery was now "approaching its end." And he voiced his hope that the Supreme Court would use its authority to settle the slavery issue once and for all. Two days later (March 6, 1857) the Supreme Court handed down one of the most momentous and most controversial decisions in its history. In the Dred Scott case the Court decided that Congress could do nothing about slavery in the territories and that the
✕ people there had no power to restrict or abolish slavery until they had achieved statehood.

When Lincoln and Douglas met in their famous debates during the 1858 Illinois contest for the United States Senate, the Dred Scott decision caused Douglas grave problems. He favored popular sovereignty, but he also wanted to uphold the Court to please Southerners. So he tried to find a way to support both. Even though the Supreme Court had decided that slavery was lawful in a territory, the institution "cannot exist a day or an hour anywhere," he said, without the support of "local police regulations."

This was Douglas's famous "Freeport Doctrine" (because he stated it at Freeport, Illinois). It was his way of evading the central, moral issue of slavery. Lincoln thought it absurd that "a thing may be lawfully driven away from a place where it has a lawful right to be."

Douglas narrowly won reelection by the Illinois legislature, which then had the power to name the senators. But his Freeport Doctrine had made him many enemies in the South. Southerners would oppose his nomination for President on the Democratic ticket. At the same time he had helped make a national reputation for Abraham Lincoln.

John Brown. In 1859 a real-life drama at Harpers Ferry, Virginia, underlined the great moral issue of slavery and reinforced all the worst fears of the South. John Brown was a passionate idealist not troubled by the hard facts of life. On his own he decided that he would invade the South, arm the slaves, and let them fight for their own freedom. In October 1859, with a little band of 18 followers (13 white and 5 black), he seized the United States arsenal at Harpers Ferry, freed a small number of slaves from nearby plantations, and then retreated into the arsenal. There Brown and most of his followers were captured or killed. In a public execution John Brown was hanged, as were the other survivors, by the state of Virginia. But John Brown lived on in American folklore and music as a martyr to the cause of freedom and a symbol of courage to die for what was right.

No other single event alarmed white Southerners more than John Brown's

✕ Critical Thinking: Demonstrating Reasoned Judgment How was the Dred Scott case decided? Have students describe and explain the ruling issued by Chief Justice Taney in the controversial Dred Scott case. Ask students to list the pros and cons of the decision. From this information, have students write their own decision for the Dred Scott case. Ask students to share their work with the class. The teacher may wish to extend the activity by having student volunteers choose sides and debate the issues.

attack at Harpers Ferry. In their eyes he seemed part of a widespread abolition-ist plot, supported by the "black" Republican party, to incite slave rebellion throughout the South.

The election of 1860. The fateful presidential election of November 1860 con-vinced the South that their hope was not in words but in weapons.

When news of the election of the Republican candidate, Abraham Lincoln, reached South Carolina, that state seceded from the Union. It was quickly joined by five other states from the lower South: Mississippi, Florida, Alabama, Georgia, and Louisiana. Each state declared its own independence. Then their delegates met in Montgomery, Alabama, in February 1861, even before Lincoln was inaugurated. Soon they were joined by Texas. They wrote a new consti-tution and announced the birth of a new nation, the Confederate States of America.

The Confederate States of America viewed the United States as a foreign na-tion. The seceded states therefore could no longer allow the United States to

A Currier and Ives lithograph showed the shelling of Fort Sumter in 1861. Nathaniel Currier and James M. Ives became partners in 1857. Their lithographs were popular when photographs were rare and in black and white.

Art Resource, NY

keep its arsenals and forts inside their borders. Using their own state troops, they at once began seizing federal army posts. To avoid bloodshed, United States troops gave up all but a few strong positions. One of the stronger was in South Carolina—a place right in Charleston Harbor called Fort Sumter. Soon after his inauguration, Lincoln made the fateful decision to try to resupply the fort to prevent its surrender. In response, the South opened fire. Fort Sumter soon fell. No one had been wounded, but war had begun. The first, the quickest, and the most bloodless battle of the war was over. It was not a fair sample of what was to come.

Civil War. The Civil War began over the simple question of whether this was one nation, or whether any state or group of states could, under the Constitution, legally secede from the Union and create a new nation. Southerners did not see themselves simply as slave owners fighting to preserve their property, or as rebels trying to tear the Union apart. Instead they imagined they were fighting the American Revolution all over again. White Southerners, they said, were oppressed by Yankee tyrants. The people of the South were now playing the role of the gallant American colonists. Northerners were the oppressive British, and Abraham Lincoln was another King George III. If the British had no right to force American colonists to stay inside their empire, why did the United States government have any right to force Southern states to stay inside the Union?

Abraham Lincoln, in his first inaugural address, had tried to persuade Southerners that they had nothing to fear from his administration. But he told them there was no right under the Constitution for a state to leave the Union. And he declared, "In *your* hands, my dissatisfied fellow countrymen, and not in *mine*, is the momentous issue of civil war."

Southerners said they were fighting for self-government. One flaw in this argument was that it left out the whole question of slavery. Self-government—for *whom* and by *whom?* White Southerners who said they were fighting for their own right to govern themselves were also fighting *against* the right of millions of blacks to have any control over their own lives. Of course, John C. Calhoun and other defenders of slavery had not seen it quite that way. Self-government, they said, was for white people only.

As the fighting went on, the war turned from being about whether states could leave the Union to being over whether the institution of slavery would be allowed to exist. The American Civil War was not quite like any war that had ever happened before. Half a nation fought against the other half over the freedom of a small minority. This itself was something new. It was as new, as strenuous, and as unpredictable as anything else in America. Leaving more than 600,000 dead, the Civil War would be the bloodiest in all American history—and the bloodiest war in the whole western world during the nineteenth century. Over the course of the four long years of war, of every ten men who fought, four became casualties (killed or wounded). No other modern nation paid so high a price to hold itself together.

Reconstruction. When the South agreed to unconditional surrender, they put themselves at the mercy of the North. This gave the North a troublesome new problem—what to do with the conquered South. Now that the blacks were at last free, what was to be the relationship of the races to each other?

There were wide differences of opinion in the North. Was it more important to punish the former rebels, to teach them a lesson they would never forget, so they would never again try to break up the Union? Or was it better to forgive, to welcome the rebels back into the Union so they would feel at home and never again want to leave? Lincoln, in his famous second inaugural address, spoke the language of forgiveness:

> With malice toward none; with charity for all; with firmness in the right, as God gives us to see the right, let us strive on to finish the work we are in; to bind up the nation's wounds; to care for him who shall have borne the battle, and for his widow, and his orphan—to do all which may achieve and cherish a just, and a lasting peace, among ourselves, and with all nations.

But Lincoln would not live to put his forgiving spirit into law. He was assassinated just as the war ended and was succeeded by Andrew Johnson, a man without Lincoln's prestige for guiding the North to victory. Johnson, a former Democrat, was also a man with little influence within the Republican party. And he lacked Lincoln's political skill.

"The Emancipation Proclamation," an allegorical painting made about 1863, shows Lincoln holding his proclamation and following the goddess of liberty.

A. A. Lamb; National Gallery of Art, Washington, Gift of Edgar William and Bernice Chrysler Garbisch

More from Boorstin: "The greatest and most durable monument to the power of the spoken word in that age is Abraham Lincoln. . . . No one better combined the virtues of . . . [public oration and the anecdotal saying] to create classics of declamatory literature which would long speak to a federal nation." (From *The Americans: The National Experience*)

The death of Lincoln and the ineptitude of Johnson allowed those Northerners who wanted revenge and radical reform to take control. These Republican members of Congress, led by Senator Charles Sumner of Massachusetts and Representative Thaddeus Stevens of Pennsylvania, came to be called "Radicals." Bitter against the Southern rebels, they wanted to punish all white Southerners. They also wanted to see that the newly freed slaves received fair treatment.

In the beginning, it was not clear who would win this postwar congressional battle over how the South would be reconstructed. President Andrew Johnson from Tennessee had his own ideas. He vetoed a bill extending the life of the Freedmen's Bureau and also a Civil Rights law that allowed the federal government to intervene in a state's affairs to protect the rights of all citizens. So he alienated even many moderates.

Then Congress drafted the Fourteenth Amendment to the Constitution. (The Thirteenth, abolishing slavery, had been submitted to the states and ratified during 1865.) This new amendment attempted to answer all Johnson's constitutional objections to the Civil Rights Act. In its most important provision, it defined United States citizenship and forbade any state from depriving citizens of their rights and privileges. Other clauses reduced the representation of any state that did not allow all its adult male citizens to vote, and prevented the payment of Confederate debt. Persons who had held state or federal office under the Union, and then supported the Confederacy, could only hold office after being pardoned by a vote of two-thirds of Congress.

Here were the North's clear terms to the South. If they accepted this amendment, they could enter the Union. No one knew what might happen if they rejected it.

Tennessee promptly ratified the Fourteenth Amendment and had its senators and representatives admitted to Congress. For Tennessee, Reconstruction was largely over. But the other states followed Andrew Johnson's lead and refused to adopt the amendment. Now the Republicans and the President were in a tug-of-war.

Congress takes charge. When Congress met in December 1866 it passed a law that divided the old Confederacy, excluding Tennessee, into five military districts, each to be ruled by a Northern general. The Radical Republicans in Congress laid down rules for building new Southern states. They wished to see the new states designed to keep political control in Republican hands. Some of the Radical demands, such as abolishing slavery and giving civil rights to blacks by ratifying the Fourteenth Amendment, were of course just and necessary. But others were not.

Worst of all was the Radical refusal to forgive or forget. They denied leading citizens of the Old South the right to vote or to hold any office in state or local government. Hungry for power, the Radicals wanted to rule the South through their own friends. Yet even now, Congress did not go as far as Thaddeus Stevens and the most ardent Radicals wanted. Stevens insisted that economic power was more important than political power. He wanted to seize rebel property and give every onetime slave 40 acres and a hut. But at this Congress balked. Unfortunately, few former slaves ever received any property after the war. Most remained dependent on white property owners for their living.

The new military districts were quickly set up. They oversaw elections for

✂ Critical Thinking Activity: Expressing Problems Clearly How did the Freedmen's Bureau assist Black Americans after the Civil War? Have students select some aspect of the Freedmen's Bureau to promote with an advertisement in the form of a poster. Remind the class that the literacy rate among Freedmen was low, so their posters will need to allow for this factor. Ask students to share their work, and to explain why they designed their posters as they did.

delegates to new constitutional conventions. The voters included all adult males regardless of color, except anybody who had ever held any office in the state or the nation and then supported the Confederacy. These former leaders were banned.

The constitutional conventions had white majorities in every state except South Carolina and Louisiana. They drew up new state constitutions and, not surprisingly, they did what Congress had commanded. They barred Confederates from state office and granted black suffrage. Beyond that, they provided a wide range of social welfare programs new to the Southern states. For the first time they called for free public schools. They made new provisions for orphans and the handicapped. And though these constitutions were bitterly criticized by whites because blacks had played a role in framing them, they survived even after the Reconstruction governments were gone.

The new Reconstruction governments elected under these constitutions began the hard job of rebuilding the ruined South. They began to repair and expand railroads. They set up schools and offered other public services that had never been provided before. For this they were accused by whites of being ex-

This store in Richmond, Virginia, was decorated to celebrate "Liberation Day," the anniversary of the Emancipation Proclamation.

Valentine Museum, Richmond, Virginia

travagant. They were also charged with being corrupt. While there was some corruption, that was not peculiar to the South and it did not cease when the Reconstruction governments were replaced by "conservative" governments. Good Confederates, it turned out, were just as apt to misuse the people's money as were carpetbaggers, scalawags, and blacks.

The Radical Republicans had attempted to deal with the place of blacks in the Southern states. Their new, more liberal constitutions benefited the poor of both races. They laid the foundation of free public education for whites as well as blacks. Reconstruction gave the blacks a new role in political life—and valuable political experience. It was under Reconstruction that the Fourteenth and Fifteenth amendments were passed. And these would become the bulwark of equal rights.

When Democrats had recaptured the government in all the old Confederate states, this did not mean that throughout the South blacks no longer voted or held office, or that segregation ("Jim Crow") laws suddenly appeared. It took time for the white South to come to a fixed conclusion about the place of blacks in Southern society. But as the nineteenth century progressed, more and more "Jim Crow" laws were passed and devious ways were thought up to keep blacks from voting.

Finally in 1896 the Supreme Court, in the case of *Plessy* v. *Ferguson*, actually approved segregated facilities that were "separate but equal." The problem, of course, was that the facilities were almost never equal. And, as the Supreme Court would later rule, there really could never be such a thing as "separate but equal" facilities for the two races. The separation of the races created its own kind of inequalities.

3. The nation transformed

The decades from the end of the Civil War to the close of the nineteenth century were to see a new nation emerge. The Industrial Revolution and the Transportation Revolution worked their wonders. They enabled the United States to become a democracy of things as well as a democracy of people. They made it possible for the cities to grow upward and outward. They allowed the conquest of the Great Plains and brought about the final disappearance of the frontier. This was a period that was sometimes ruthless, corrupt, and destructive, but for the most part it was moving, building, expanding, reforming, and dreaming.

The Industrial Revolution. The "Industrial Revolution" which transformed America during the nineteenth century was beginning in America soon after Washington became President. It is a name for the great changes brought by the modern factory system, which came first to Britain. There laws tried to prevent competition by making it a crime to take new machines or their designs out of the country. But still a few bold workers brought the plans to the United States in their heads. The first American textile factory opened in Rhode Island in 1792 with 72 spindles and a work force of nine children.

By 1850 the Census of the United States reported a great change. Where once "the bulk of general manufacturing . . . was carried on in the shop and the

X Critical Thinking Activity: Distinguishing Fact from Opinion Is forced segregation of races ever appropriate? Have students list arguments used for and against racial segregation in the late 1800s. Ask students to evaluate these arguments and to determine which are based on fact and which are merely opinions. Have students write a "letter to the editor" on the subject of *Jim Crow* laws. Share students' letters and discuss their ideas.

household," now it was being done by "a system of factory labor, compensated by wages and assisted by power."

These new large factories, where all the processes were brought together under one roof, were usually beyond the means of any one person, or even a partnership. To build and own these factories a recently rediscovered social invention was at hand, the "joint stock company." It brought together the funds of many small investors.

Also speeding the Industrial Revolution was the "Interchangeable System" which manufactured thousands of the same product by standardizing the parts. In the United States Eli Whitney first applied it to muskets, but it was soon in use in making all sorts of things. Even before the Civil War, locks and watches made by this system were cheaper in the United States than in European countries with many skilled locksmiths and watchmakers. This was "mass production"—making at the same time masses of the same product. As Whitney explained, it used the skill of the machine instead of the skill of the worker.

Whitney's system came at just the right place and at the right moment. The growing United States was drawing an energetic, eager-to-learn population from all over. But there was a scarcity of immigrants who had been highly trained in the ancient skills for making watches or guns. To everyone's surprise, this proved to be an advantage. If the United States had attracted thousands of skilled gunsmiths, Whitney might never have developed his Interchangeable System.

The Transportation Revolution. The Industrial Revolution helped bring about a Transportation Revolution. The same steam power and new techniques that made factories possible also brought the steamboats and the railroads. These carried farm and factory products out to the world. This Transportation Revolution reached the thousands of customers needed to buy the masses of

The Carnegie Steel Company's enormous plant at Homestead, Pennsylvania, in the 1890s.

Library of Congress

497

In their hurry to lay track, transcontinental railroads often built temporary wooden bridges. The permanent bridge over the Green River in Wyoming is already under construction (left) in this 1868 photograph. Citadel Rock is in the background.

goods from the new factories. Wherever canals, railroads, or steamboats went, they provided customers for farmers, too.

The first great wave of railroad building came in the American West in the 1850s. In only ten years the nation's tracks increased from 8879 miles to 30,626 miles—more than enough to circle the globe. Ohio and Illinois, then still called the "West," led the nation in miles of track. Chicago, which did not become an incorporated city until 1833, only 30 years later was the greatest railroad center in the world.

To make a profit, farmers had to send their crops to market. To work their land, they needed tools from city factories. As factories grew to supply the nation's wants, the factories consumed more and more raw materials—iron ore, wood, and cotton. The vast new nation, spread across a continent, needed transportation. Aggressive businessmen pushed railroads into every nook and cranny of the United States. The first transcontinental railroad was completed in 1869 and that was just the beginning. As many miles of track were laid in the

1880s as in all the years from 1828 to 1870. By 1900 the nation had more miles of railroad track than all of Europe, including Russia.

The rise of trusts. As the railroads crisscrossed the land, the nation's businesses and factories grew in number and size because they could reach more people. These were challenging times for businessmen. Competition for raw materials and customers was fierce. And the years from 1873 to 1897 were often troubled by depression.

To survive and prosper, businessmen tried to limit competition. To build monopolies they used an old English institution originally invented for charities. The "trust" was a way for individuals known as "trustees" to hold money and property for the benefit of others. Now business firms set up "trusts"—not for charity but to get around the laws against conspiracy. A group of companies would hand over all their stock to a board of "trustees" and receive trust certificates in return. The new trustees would then control all the companies. But the original owners, the holders of the trust certificates, would still get the profits.

For some years the trust proved to be an effective way to get around the law, to combine companies, limit competition, and increase profits. The first and most famous was John D. Rockefeller's Standard Oil Trust, but there were also trusts in cottonseed oil, linseed oil, lead, whiskey, sugar, and other products. By 1890 Congress began to pass "antitrust" laws, and the courts decided that business combinations to limit competition were illegal. Still, many of these monopolies held on.

Immigration and the cities. After the Civil War the United States was as large and varied as all western Europe. Immigrants from everywhere would find someplace to feel at home here—on lands not so different from where they had lived in the "Old Country." The English could settle on the rolling landscape of "New" England, the Swede could farm the flat, snowy stretches of Minnesota and the Dakotas, and Italians could plant orchards and vineyards in sunny California. Imported people spread across the land.

But of the 25 million immigrants who came to the United States between the Civil War and World War I, most settled in the cities. Within the big, fast-growing American cities there sprouted little immigrant cities. By 1890 New York City held as many Germans as Hamburg, twice as many Irish as Dublin, half as many Italians as Naples. And besides there were large numbers of Poles, Russians, Hungarians, Austrians, Norwegians, Swedes, and Chinese. Four out of five New Yorkers either were born abroad or were the children of foreign parents. The Germans and Irish who had come before 1880 were found nearly everywhere in the United States. There were also lots of Canadians in Boston and Detroit, Poles in Buffalo and Milwaukee, Austrians in Cleveland, Italians in New Orleans, and African Americans in all the large cities.

Cities were sometimes called the nation's "melting pots." Perhaps they should have been called "mixing bowls," for instead of melting together the groups tended to stay separate in their own neighborhoods. Just as the new United States had been made from thirteen different colonies, now a great nation was being made from countless colonies of immigrants.

Although these immigrant colonies tried to keep separate, they could not stay

 More from Boorstin: "[P]otent new legal devices made it possible to conduct the largest transactions in the deepest secrecy. . . . For years John D. Rockefeller had been adept at hiding his consolidating activities. The men who were negotiating with the Standard Oil Company had been writing their letters under assumed names, and Rockefeller had cautioned them 'not to tell their wives.'" (From *The Americans: The Democratic Experience*)

separate forever. The people from different colonies became more and more alike. Children went to school and learned English. They stopped speaking their parents' language and sometimes stopped going to their parents' church. They were afraid to seem foreign. Then, too, a young man from the Italian colony might marry a young woman whose parents spoke German. In the city, people could not help feeling closer to one another.

A new nation. In the hundred years since George Washington was inaugurated, the United States had become a completely different land. When he took his oath of office, most Americans were farmers and only a few lived in cities. Philadelphia with 42,000 people was the largest city. By 1890 one of every three Americans lived in an urban area (considered then to be any place of 2500 inhabitants or more) and nearly 4 million Americans lived in one of the three largest cities—New York, Philadelphia, and Chicago. The West had been occupied. The frontier had disappeared. From a rural land of farmers, the United States had become a citified, industrial giant tied together by a web of railroads. And the growing nation looked outward to the world.

Everett Shinn, who began his career as a newspaper artist, painted "Cross Streets of New York" in 1899. He was one of the group of painters known as the "ashcan school" because they chose scenes from everyday city life as subjects for their canvases.

The collection of the Corcoran Gallery of Art. Gift of Margaret M. Hitchcock

✖ Critical Thinking Activity: Distinguishing False from Accurate Images What words describe the growing American city of 1900? Tell students to write down five descriptive words that could stand alone as an advertisement for the American city of 1900. Have students design appropriate ads to display their copy. Ask students to share their work. Use a class discussion to evaluate the group's choice of words.

comic strip. c) another press lord and Pulitzer's competitor. d) Spanish ambassador whose criticisms of McKinley strained relations between the United States and Spain. e) the naval commander who captured the Philippines. f) people eager for a war. g) the name of Theodore Roosevelt's cavalry regiment. 2. Havana, the Philippines, and Santiago are on the map on page 511. Guam and Puerto Rico are on the map on page 515. Beijing, China, is on the map on page 955. 3. Anti-Imperialists believed expansion violated the fundamental principles of American democracy, that the United States would go to war with Japan, and that the United States could not be a democracy and an empire. 4. Cuba could not make any treaty that would limit its sovereignty or allow any foreign power to acquire any of its territory; it had to lease areas for naval bases to the United States; it could not acquire debts with interest payments greater than current revenues could meet; and it had to allow the United States to intervene in its internal affairs in order to protect life, property, or liberty. 5. The "Open Door" policy proclaimed that no one nation could claim exclusive rights over any area in China; instead, all nations had the right to exploit China equally. Hay implemented this policy suggesting it to England, France, Germany, Japan, and Russia and then claiming that they had accepted the policy. 6. It was an unsuccessful attempt by nationalists in China to drive all foreigners out. The Chinese government was impressed by United States actions after the rebellion was suppressed. The United States insisted on the preservation of Chinese independence and would not accept reparations that exceeded the actual damages suffered in the rebellion. 7. (a) Weyler was the Spanish general whose brutality in suppressing the Cuban rebels helped rouse support in the United States for the war. (b) Cuban rebels declared independence from Spain in 1895. Americans were sympathetic to their cause. (c) The United States blamed Spain for the disaster. (d) He ordered Dewey to attack the Spanish. (e) President McKinley declared war on Spain even though he knew the Spanish would meet American demands. (f) The Yellow Press called for war and generally inflamed the emotions of the public.

CLOSE

To conclude the lesson, have students debate the following question: Was President McKinley pushed into the Spanish-American War by the yellow press and jingoes? Have them answer this question in a 100-word essay for homework.

Chapter Review Answers

Focusing on Ideas

1. Republicans and Democrats of all economic classes and social groups opposed American imperialism; believed the U.S. was contradicting the Declaration of Independence; feared entanglement in foreign conflicts; were bothered by Philippine resistance movement. 2. (a) Politically: establishing itself as equal to other empire-building nations. (b) Socially: raised morale, Americans felt they could benefit the rest of the world. (c) Economically: opened hundreds of new markets. 3. U.S. gained Alaska, Hawaii, Philippines, Wake, Midway, and Guam; made Puerto Rico a protectorate. 4. Americans wanted broader markets and cheaper raw materials.

Taking a Critical Look

1. (a) France interfered with the independence of an American nation; (b) Cleveland interpreted British pressure on Venezuela as interference; (c) Cuba had to promise not to forfeit independence to any foreign power, except U.S. 2. American West—large amounts of available, open land; Overseas—land already highly populated. (b) American West—no preexisting government, set up territorial governments; Overseas—attempts to overthrow existing governments.

Your Region in History

1–3. Answers will vary depending on your region. Consult your local library or historical society.

Historical Facts and Figures

Foreign trade steadily increased, most dramatically in early 1900s. Evidence: territory in the South Pacific, Hawaii, Alaska provided new markets as Puerto Rico and Cuba did after the Spanish-American War.

☑ Writing Process Activity

Identifying Central Issues Ask students to play the role of Henry Cabot Lodge and write a letter to Theodore Roosevelt about his reactions to Captain Mahan's book *The Influence of Sea Power Upon History*. Students should begin by listing the points Mahan makes as well as Lodge's and Roosevelt's own beliefs about the navy and about annexing territory. Ask them to begin their letter by recommending the book to Roosevelt. Students should revise for clear organization and effective support. After proofreading, students can read their letter to the class.

Section Review Answers

Section 2, page 510

1. a) naval officer who helped set up the Naval War College and persuaded many American leaders that both expansion overseas and a strong navy were essential to the nation's future. b) Assistant Secretary of the Navy under President McKinley. c) Massachusetts senator who was a believer in Mahan's message and called for a larger navy. d) the ruler of Hawaii overthrown by American settlers in 1893. 2. An American empire would be good for Americans and good for the world. The United States needed overseas markets for its surplus products, it needed a strong navy and foreign outposts to secure these markets, and that the people in foreign lands would be lucky to come under our influence. 3. Cleveland believed that the Monroe Doctrine was at stake. During the dispute Cleveland and his Secretary of State asserted an expanded version of that doctrine, claiming the right to intervene in Latin American affairs. The incident demonstrated both the usefulness of arbitration (which finally settled the dispute) and a new assertiveness in American foreign policy. 4. In 1893 Americans living in Hawaii, with some help from United States Marines, overthrew the Hawaiian queen and asked the United States to annex Hawaii. A treaty of annexation was submitted to the Senate, but President Cleveland withdrew the treaty when he learned how the queen had been overthrown. Then, in 1898 Hawaii was annexed by the United States. 5. The United States needed to expand. The nation needed overseas markets, and it must have a strong navy to secure and protect those markets. Lodge and Roosevelt were persuaded by Mahan's arguments, and they worked for a bigger navy, annexation of Hawaii, and a canal in Panama.

CLOSE

To conclude the lesson, ask the class to what extent, if any, air power and the development of nuclear weapons have reduced the importance of sea power for a strong nation today. Use students' answers to move the class toward an understanding of Mahan's thesis. The following additional questions should help: What tasks performed by navies one hundred years ago are still naval tasks today? (Projecting power, transporting troops and supplies, convoying ships in dangerous areas, serving as our first line of defense in remote areas.) What new tasks do navies perform? (Carrying aircraft, serving as mobile missile-launching platforms above and below the surface of the oceans.)

Section 3 (pages 510–518)

War with Spain

FOCUS

To introduce the lesson, ask students to make a list of all the reasons the United States declared war on Spain. Then try to reach a consensus ranking of the causes in order of their importance.

Developing Vocabulary

yellow press (page 511); **jingoism** (page 512); **imperialism** (page 514); **sphere of influence** (page 517).

INSTRUCT

Explain

Theodore Roosevelt's impetuous actions during the Spanish-American War paved the way for the rest of his career as Vice-President and President.

❀ Cooperative Learning Activity

Distinguishing Fact from Opinion Break the class into groups of six and give each a copy of the Debate page of a current issue of *USA TODAY*. Have students look over the page. Then explain that they will use it as a model to create their own debate page. Provide the class with a strongly worded editorial written about the new American imperialism following the Spanish-American War. Assign each member of the group to complete one of the following components of the page: a guest column in support of the editorial viewpoint, an opposing viewpoint, an editorial cartoon, quotelines, and the "man on the Street" opinions. Remind students to imagine they are living and writing in 1900. Have group members mount the completed sections of their page on poster board or butcher paper.

Section Review Answers

Section 3, page 518

1. a) owner of a New York paper that started the Yellow Press. b) cartoonist who created the "Yellow Kid"

Looking Outward

FOCUS

To introduce the lesson, ask students to list places mentioned in this section where the United States expanded geographically, diplomatically, militarily, and commercially.

Developing Vocabulary

The words listed in this chapter are essential terms for reading and understanding particular sections of the chapter. The page number after each term indicates the page of its first or most important appearance in the chapter. These terms are defined in the text Glossary (text pages 1000–1011).

arbitration (page 507)

INSTRUCT

Explain

The expanding economy of the United States after the Civil War required expanding markets.

★ Independent Activity

Demonstrating Reasoned Judgment Ask students to write an essay with the following title: "The United States Became a World Power in 18___." Students will select and defend their choice of a date.

Section Review Answers

Section 1, page 508

1. a) negotiated a treaty with the Chinese in 1844 that secured "most favored nation" status for the United States. b) naval officer who persuaded Japan to allow some trade with the United States. c) agreement in 1854 secured by Perry. d) Lincoln's Secretary of State who strongly supported the purchase of Alaska. e) Thinking the area a frozen wasteland, opponents to the Alaskan purchase dubbed it "Seward's Folly." 2. Canton and Nagasaki are on the map on page 955. Siam is on the map on page 517. The Yukon Valley is along the Yukon River on the map on page 948. The Virgin Islands are on the map on page 543. Pago Pago is in American Samoa on the map on page 515. Valparaiso, a city on the coast of Chile, is on the map on page 950. 3. Before the Civil War the United States expanded into the Far East through trade and diplomacy, obtaining a commercial treaty with Siam, most favored nation status from China, and a treaty opening trade with Japan. American traders, whalers, and missionaries had established presence in Hawaii, and the United States had declared that it would not allow the islands to be controlled by another na-

tion. 4. It settled disputes that had arisen between the United States and Britain during the Civil War. Ships made in England for the Confederacy had destroyed or damaged many Union ships, and the United States was seeking reparations for the damage. 5. In the Samoan islands the United States almost went to war over the harbor of Pago Pago. Instead, in 1899 the United States, Germany, and Great Britain agreed to rule the islands jointly, although Britain later withdrew. France had taken control of Mexico during the American Civil War. After the war, the United States warned France that it would not tolerate French control of Mexico, and the French withdrew. Chile refused to apologize and pay damages for an attack on American sailors in Valparaiso. When the United States seemed ready to go to war over it, Chile offered an apology and reparations. 6. Many members of Congress and other Americans doubted that Alaska, a "frozen wasteland," was worth its price. Since Seward had jumped at the chance to buy Alaska, it was called "Seward's Folly."

CLOSE

To conclude the lesson, ask: Considering the way Europeans and Americans acted when they had superior power and wanted something from weaker nations, what lesson might the Western nations have learned by watching each other? (The same thing the Japanese learned: The only hope a nation had of maintaining its independence was to be sure that none of its adversaries gained a military or economic advantage over it.)

Expanding on the Seas

FOCUS

To introduce the lesson, ask how many students have ever seen a warship. What type was it? What impressed you the most about it? Then draw the students' attention to the pictures of warships on pages 504 and 514 of the text. Ask: What is it about these warships that is so impressive?

INSTRUCT

Explain

The farthest a coal-burning warship could sail without refueling was only a few thousand miles. By occupying strategic islands in the Pacific Ocean and making sure there were no refueling stations near or in the Americas, the United States could prevent attack by sea.

Providing In-Depth Coverage

Perspectives on the Spanish-American War and American Imperialism

By the end of the Spanish-American War, the United States had acquired an overseas colonial empire, consisting mainly of islands such as Hawaii, the Philippines, Guam, and Puerto Rico, in addition to Alaska, which was purchased before the war.

The chapter notes that though these acquired territories provided vast new markets for American products, many anti-imperialists felt that this quest for empire was contrary to the fundamental values upon which the country was founded.

A History of the United States as an instructional program provides two types of resources you can use to offer in-depth coverage of the Spanish-American War: the *student text* and the *Enrichment Support File*. A list of *Suggested Secondary Sources* is also provided. The chart below shows the topics that are covered in each.

THE STUDENT TEXT. Boorstin and Kelley's *A History of the United States* unfolds the chronology of events, the key players, and, as an interpretive history, the controversy of imperialism and the Spanish-American War.

AMERICAN HISTORY ENRICHMENT SUPPORT FILE. This collection of primary source readings and classroom activities reveals the war as manifestation of America's imperialistic character.

SUGGESTED SECONDARY SOURCES. This reference list of readings by well-known historians and other commentators provides an array of perspectives on the Spanish-American War and the onset of American imperialism.

Locating Instructional Materials

Detailed lesson plans for teaching the Spanish-American War as a mini-course or to study one or more elements of American imperialism in depth are offered in the following areas: in the *student text*, see individual lesson plans at the beginning of each chapter; in the *Enrichment Support File*, see page 3; for readings beyond the student text, see *Suggested Secondary Sources*.

IN-DEPTH COVERAGE ON AMERICAN IMPERIALISM		
Student Text	**Enrichment Support File**	**Suggested Secondary Sources**
• Imperialism, pp. 505–518 • Cuba, p. 511 • Spanish-American War, pp. 512–514 • Philippines, pp. 513–516 • Guam, p. 513 • Puerto Rico, pp. 513, 517 • Anti-imperialists, pp. 514–516	• Lesson Suggestions • Multimedia Resources • Overview Essay/The Spanish American War: Door to Imperialism • Songs in American History/"On American Island Wars" • Art in American History/Yellow Journalism and the Political Cartoon • Biography in American History/The Tenth United States Cavalry • Geography in American History/Persuasive Geography: Why America Became an Empire • Literature in American History/"On American Island Wars" • Great Debates in American History/Isolationism vs. Interventionism • Making Connections	• *Twelve Against Empire: The Anti-Imperialists, 1898–1900* by Robert L. Beisner, pp. 215–239. • *The Splendid Little War* by Frank Freidel, pp. 3–12, 59–80, 143–174. • *The Mirror of War: American Society and the Spanish-American War* by Gerald F. Linderman, pp. 114–173. • *American's Road to Empire: The War with Spain and Overseas Expansion* by H. Wayne Morgan, pp. 37–84. • *The War with Spain in 1898* by David F. Trask, pp. 145–177.

Chapter 19
The United States and the World

Identifying Chapter Materials

Objectives	Basic Instructional Materials	Extension Materials
1 Looking Outward • Describe how and why the United States expanded internationally from the early 1800s to 1892. • Discuss the response of Japan to Commodore Perry's arrival and the opening of trade with the United States.	**Annotated Teacher's Edition** • Lesson Plans, p. 504C **Instructional Support File** • Pre-Reading Activities, Unit 7, p. 1	**Documents of American History** • The Purchase of Alaska, Vol. 1, p. 492 **American History Transparencies** • Our Multicultural Heritage, p. C75
2 Expanding on the Seas • Evaluate the belief that sea power determines a nation's strength. • Tell how and why the United States annexed Hawaii.	**Annotated Teacher's Edition** • Lesson Plans, pp. 504C–504D	**Documents of American History** • The Annexation of Hawaii, Vol. 1, p. 602 • Cleveland's Withdrawal of Treaty for Annexation, Vol. 1, p. 603 • Cleveland's Message on the Venezuela Boundary Controversy, Vol. 1, p. 620 **American History Transparencies** • Geography and History, pp. B13, B15, B17
3 War with Spain • Analyze the reasons for and results of the Spanish-American War.	**Annotated Teacher's Edition** • Lesson Plans, pp. 504D–504E **Instructional Support File** • Reading Activities, Unit 7, pp. 2–3 • Skill Review Activity, Unit 7, p. 4 • Skill Application Activity, Unit 7, p. 5 • Critical Thinking Activity, Unit 7, p. 6 • Chapter Test, pp. 7–10 • Additional Test Questions, Unit 7, pp. 11–14	**Enrichment Support File** • The Spanish-American War: Door to Imperialism (See "In-Depth Coverage" at right.) **Suggested Secondary Sources** • See chart at right. **American History Transparencies** • Fine Art, p. D61 • Critical Thinking, p. F27

Unit 7

Writing About History and Art: Direct students' attention to the unit introduction, illustration, and list of themes on pages 502–503. Have the introduction and unit themes read aloud. After a brief discussion of the subject matter of the unit, instruct students to write a brief paragraph, explaining how the art:

—relates to the unit themes;
—exemplifies the unit title and illustrates the introduction; and
—is an appropriate choice for the unit.

Democratic Reforms and World Power 1890–1920

Until the Civil War the United States had seemed a world of its own. Almost every needed crop or animal or mineral was found somewhere within the nation and its territories. But after the war, the nation began to reach outward. There was still room to import people by the millions. American farmers and factory workers and business owners sought faraway customers. At the same time, American factories and homes wanted silk from Italy and China, rubber from Ceylon and Sumatra, coffee from Brazil, tin from the Malay peninsula, chrome from Rhodesia—and a thousand other items from across the oceans.

The years from 1890 to 1920 would test anew the belief of Americans in democracy. At home they worked to make government and business answer to the needs of the people. Abroad, how could the United States assist other nations to become democratic without choosing their governments for them?

Europe suffered from intrigue, tyranny, and old-fashioned monarchs. War was that continent's disease. Would our newly powerful nation be tempted to enter wars and try to run the affairs of people everywhere? How could Americans keep their ideals in this different kind of world? These years would offer many new challenges, and a few new answers.

THEMES IN HISTORY

- The United States begins to reach outward as a result of rapid industrialization. GEOGRAPHY
- The United States becomes a world leader. ETHICS AND VALUES
- The Progressive Era produces significant reforms in American business and government. GOVERNMENT AND POLITICS

◉ Childe Hassam's "Allies Day" captures the beauty of American, French, and English flags fluttering over 5th Avenue in New York City in May 1917.
National Gallery of Art, Washington, gift of Ethelyn McKinney in memory of her brother, Glenn Ford McKinney

Chapter Review

See "Chapter Review answers," p. 480B.

Focusing on Key Facts and Ideas

1. Identify or explain: Alexander Hamilton, John Marshall, judicial review, Compromise of 1850, Dred Scott, John Brown, Fort Sumter, mass production, trust.

2. Explain the difference between "strict construction" and "broad construction" of the Constitution.

3. Why was control of the Mississippi vital to the western settlers? How did the Louisiana Purchase affect this situation?

4. How did the Mexican War increase the land holdings of the United States? How did it contribute to the problems surrounding slavery?

5. What arguments would you expect an abolitionist to use in condemning slavery? What arguments did some white Southerners use to defend the institution of slavery?

6. Explain the influence of the slavery issue on presidential politics from 1848 to 1860.

7. How were the Reconstruction policies of Congress motivated by a desire for vengeance? How were they motivated by concerns for the rights and welfare of black Southerners?

8. Explain the significance of Eli Whitney's contribution to the Industrial Revolution.

9. What favorable conditions awaited immigrants to the United States?

10. How did railroad land grants benefit railroad stockholders? Pioneer farmers and ranchers? The nation?

Taking a Critical Look

1. **Drawing Conclusions.** Would the United States have an effective system of checks-and-balances if the Supreme Court had never asserted its right to declare acts of Congress unconstitutional? Explain.

2. **Checking Consistency.** How could a member of Congress opposed to slavery on moral grounds have voted for the Missouri Compromise?

3. **Demonstrating Reasoned Judgment.** How was the birth of western cities a testament to American optimism?

4. **Identifying Central Issues.** Why were people who defended slavery wary of all social reformers?

5. **Expressing Problems Clearly.** Some optimists saw the Compromise of 1850 as a "final solution" to the slavery issue. Name at least two features of the Compromise that would prevent it from being a solution.

6. **Making Comparisons.** How was the treatment of black Southerners in 1890 similar to and different from their treatment in 1850?

Your Region in History

1. **Geography.** How large was the population of your state or region in 1790? What was its largest city?

2. **Culture.** How was your state influenced by English culture? By French culture? By Spanish culture?

3. **Geography.** Identify major roads, canals, and railroads built in your state or region between 1820 and 1860. How did these transportation developments affect where people in your state or region chose to settle?

4. **Culture.** Find out if the reform movements discussed in this chapter had any particular impact in your state or region. For example, what changes, if any, did your state make in public education, care of the mentally ill, women's rights?

5. **Economics.** Can you identify a great-grandparent or other relative who lived during America's Gilded Age? How did he or she earn a living? What economic reforms would he or she have supported or opposed? Give reasons for your answer.

Chapter 19

The United States and the World

During the Gilded Age, the United States filled its land with farms, factories, and cities. Busy in their vast nation, most Americans felt no need to go abroad. Protected by broad oceans, they paid little attention to events elsewhere. Then, in 1898, war with Spain suddenly thrust the United States upon the world stage. "The guns of Dewey at Manila have changed the destiny of the United States," the *Washington Post* observed. "We are face to face with a strange destiny and must accept its responsibilities. An imperial policy!"

Because of the urging of Captain Alfred Thayer Mahan, supported by Theodore Roosevelt and Henry Cabot Lodge, the United States had a modern navy of steel ships when war broke out in 1898. Commodore George Dewey commanded the American Asiatic squadron based in Hong Kong. His small armada of four cruisers and two gunboats destroyed the larger Spanish fleet at Manila on May 1, 1898. Spain lost 381 sailors while the United States suffered only 8 wounded. This painting celebrated the triumph and its title proclaimed "Dewey? We do!"

Art Resource, NY

See "Lesson Plan," p. 504C.

1. Looking outward

From time to time, earlier in the 1800s, a few traders, whalers, missionaries, and diplomats did look outward. The expansion of other nations gave the United States the chance— and the excuse—to seek American advantages overseas.

Early expansion to the distant East.
American merchants had been visiting Canton to trade with China since 1785. After the Opium War of 1839–1842, Great Britain secured special privileges in China. Then President Tyler sent out Caleb Cushing, the able champion of expansion, to secure the same privileges for Americans. In the Treaty of Wanghia (1844), Cushing won for the United States "most favored nation" status. This meant that in China the United States was to receive the best treatment offered any country. Four new Chinese ports in addition to Canton were opened to American merchants for the first time. Magnificent American clipper ships and other grand trading vessels also went venturing out to the Philippines, Java, India, and other distant lands. In 1833 a commercial treaty was signed with faraway Siam.

The rulers of Japan, fearing corruption by foreign ways, kept out the foreigners. They allowed only a small colony of merchants of the Dutch East India Company to live on an island at Nagasaki. United States merchants wanted to trade with Japan, but this was not easy to arrange. It required a man of adventurous spirit and imagination. Luckily, in 1852, President Millard Fillmore found that man. He was Commodore Matthew C. Perry, a bold naval officer. He had an interest in ideas and the courage to risk danger. Perry tried to improve the education of midshipmen. He had fought pirates in the West Indies and had helped suppress the slave traffic from Africa. Now he would try to open trade with Japan. He awed the Japanese with his great "Black Ships"—bigger than any ever seen there before. When his ships arrived off the coast of Japan, he was firm and skillful in his diplomacy. He refused to deal with minor officials. He demanded that the Japanese

Courtesy U.S. Naval Academy Museum

This 1853 painting shows Commodore Perry on his first visit to Japan. Do you think an American or a Japanese created it?

respect the Americans. And he secured the Treaty of Kanagawa (1854), opening two ports to ships from the United States. (p. 506)

Meanwhile, American traders had already arrived in Hawaii in the 1790s. They were followed in the 1820s by whalers and missionaries. As early as 1849, the United States declared that it could never allow the Hawaiian Islands to pass under the dominion of any other power.

When President Pierce had tried to annex Hawaii in 1854 (p. 312), the treaty was not even sent to the Senate. Every question was bedeviled by the issue of slavery. The same problem defeated his efforts to buy Cuba, Alaska, and all of Lower California. Now the slavery issue was out of the way. Expansion was no longer stopped by sectional rivalry. The whole nation's factories and farms hungered for new markets.

More from Boorstin: "[Two of the first people to take advantage of the opening of trade to China and Japan] . . . were George F. Gilman and George Huntington Hartford, two merchants from Maine. In 1859 they opened a small store on Vesey Street in New York City under the name The Great American Tea Company. By cutting out middlemen, by buying tea in quantity, and by importing it themselves from China and Japan, they offered tea at the spectacularly low price of 30 cents a pound when others were charging $1. This was the beginning of the A&P grocery store chain." (From *The Americans: The Democratic Experience*)

This scene from a Japanese scroll shows the ceremonies upon Commodore Perry's arrival in Japan in 1854. The artist omitted the stripes and stars on most of the American flags flying from the longboats that had brought the delegation ashore.

Steamships and telegraph cables were drawing Americans out toward the world.

Seward pursues expansion. After the Civil War, Secretary of State William H. Seward became the champion of these expansionist hopes. When the Russians asked whether the United States might want to buy Alaska, he jumped at the chance. He could expel one more monarchy from the American continent. Seward also believed that a strong United States outpost on the other side of Canada would help to force the British out of Canada. Then Canada, too, could be added to the American Empire for Liberty!

But many sensible congressmen had their doubts. Was Alaska anything but a frozen wasteland? The eloquent Senator Charles Sumner of Massachusetts shared Seward's hope to include Canada within the United States. He finally persuaded the Senate to approve the Alaska treaty (April 19, 1867). Opponents never ceased to call it "Seward's Folly." In order to secure approval by the House of Representatives of the $7.2 million purchase price, the Russian minister to the United States had to bribe some members of Congress.

When the federal government was still burdened by a Civil War debt of $3 billion, it did seem a wild extravagance to spend millions for "Seward's icebox." Few then imagined what a bargain they had made. The gold taken from the Yukon Valley since 1897 has paid for Alaska many times over. Besides, there would be North Slope oil. Best of all, this vast, untamed wilderness was a new frontier for all Americans.

The Caribbean, too, would offer its own kind of tropical frontier. Seward negotiated a treaty

✂ Critical Thinking Activity: Identifying Assumptions What made Commodore Matthew C. Perry successful at opening trade with Japan? Using the information on page 414, ask students to list the assumptions that Matthew Perry made about the Japanese and their government when he arrived in 1854. Have students decide if Perry's assumptions were useful to his mission or harmful.

in 1867 to pay $7.5 million for the Danish West Indies (now the Virgin Islands). Since the Senate was slow to approve, the islands did not become part of the United States until they were purchased for $25 million in 1917.

The Alabama claims.

Secretary of State Seward could not give all his efforts to the future. The Civil War had left him problems from the past. One of the knottiest concerned the so-called *Alabama* claims. These were claims for damages to Union shipping by a number of Confederate vessels that had been built in Great Britain. British law forbade anyone in the realm from arming a ship to be used by a foreign state against any nation at peace with Great Britain. The Confederate navy had evaded this law by having ships built in Great Britain and then taking them elsewhere to be armed.

By 1863 many of these commerce raiders were on the high seas menacing the Union. Our minister to Great Britain, Charles Francis Adams, objected in vain. Then the British government changed its policy, to favor the Union cause. Two powerful ironclad vessels, the "Laird Rams" (built for the South by the Laird shipyard in Liverpool), were not allowed to go to sea.

During the war the British-built ships already at sea destroyed 257 Union vessels. Union shipowners tried to escape this threat by a technicality. They "registered" their ships under foreign flags. More than 700 vessels were shifted to foreign registry. By 1865 only 26 percent of our foreign trade was carried in ships of United States registry.

The British-built *Alabama* alone destroyed more than 60 merchant ships. Finally in June 1864 the United States ship *Kearsarge* caught up with and sank the *Alabama* off the coast of France.

The United States demanded that Britain pay for the damages done by the *Alabama* and the other ships that had been made in Britain for the South. Seward claimed only $19 million. Charles Sumner, head of the Senate Foreign Relations Committee, had other ideas. He presented a much larger bill of damages against Great Britain. In an hour-long Senate speech he demanded $15 million for vessels destroyed and $110 million for driving our commerce from the ocean. This was only a beginning. Sumner asked $2 billion more for "indirect damages." That was half the Union's cost for the Civil War! The British owed so much, said Sumner, because the British-built vessels had made the war last twice as long. They could pay this enormous bill easily enough just by handing over Canada to the United States.

The Treaty of Washington.

Of course, the British refused to take Senator Sumner's claim seriously. But many Americans approved. Finally in 1871, American and British commissioners signed a treaty at Washington. The *Alabama* claims would be submitted to an arbitration court at Geneva, Switzerland. In 1872 this panel of eminent judges from Switzerland, Italy, and Brazil found that during the Civil War Great Britain had violated the international laws of neutrality. They awarded $15.5 million in damages to the United States.

This peaceful way to settle differences was a happy precedent for later years.

Napoleon III's Mexican "empire."

Another troublesome legacy of the Civil War was the many French troops in Mexico. Napoleon III, like his uncle Napoleon I, had dreamed of a French empire in North America. In 1863, when the United States was fighting the Civil War, Napoleon III sent an army to Mexico. He overthrew the Mexican government. On the Mexican throne he seated his puppet "emperor," the young Austrian archduke Maximilian.

The United States objected. But during the war it was in no position to use troops to put down this flimsy Mexican emperor. After Appomattox, the 50,000 federal troops in Texas could easily move into Mexico. They were President Johnson's and Secretary Seward's message that the French had better go home. In the summer of 1866 Napoleon III removed the French troops. But the foolish and romantic emperor actually thought he could hold onto his throne alone. Maximilian was the only one surprised when, in the summer of 1867, he was executed by a Mexican firing squad.

The United States and Samoa. A wide variety of reasons led the nation to reach across the world. When steamships were powered by coal, coaling stations were needed everywhere. On the remote Samoan island of Tutuila, American sailors had long been interested in the fine harbor of Pago Pago. In the South Pacific Pago Pago had a strategic importance like that of Pearl Harbor in Hawaii in the North Pacific. The United States Navy tried, and failed, to set up a protectorate over the Samoan Islands. Germany also tried to seize control.

After narrowly evading war over Samoa, delegates from Germany, Great Britain, and the United States met in Berlin in 1889. They agreed to establish a joint protectorate. Ten years later Great Britain withdrew. The islands were divided between Germany and the United States. The tiny Samoan Islands enticed the United States onto the stage of world diplomacy.

The joint protectorate, our Secretary of State observed in 1894, was "the first departure from our . . . policy of avoiding entangling alliances with foreign powers in relation to objects remote from this hemisphere."

Problems with Chile. But Latin America was in this hemisphere. And Secretary of State Blaine aimed to capture trade with our neighbors to the south. In 1889 at the 1st International American Conference in Washington the nations founded the International Bureau of American Republics—now called the Organization of American States. The idea was to encourage more cordial and more equal relations among these unequal countries.

The United States was an overpowering neighbor. It was not easy to enforce a neighborly spirit. In Chile, in October 1891, American sailors on shore leave from the cruiser *Baltimore* were attacked by a mob on the streets of Valparaiso. Two sailors were killed and eighteen injured. The Chilean government refused to apologize and put the blame on the Americans.

On January 25, 1892, President Harrison sent a special message to Congress that seemed to invite a declaration of war on Chile. When a

squadron of eight United States cruisers was readied in the Pacific, the Chilean government yielded. They apologized and agreed to pay damages to the families of the killed and wounded sailors.

See "Section 1 Review answers," p. 504C.

Section 1 Review

1. Identify or explain: Caleb Cushing, Matthew Perry, Treaty of Kanagawa, William H. Seward, Seward's Folly.
2. Locate: Canton, Siam, Nagasaki, Yukon Valley, Virgin Islands, Pago Pago, Valparaiso.
3. What kind of United States "expansion" to the Far East took place in the period before the Civil War?
4. Explain the dispute that was settled by the Treaty of Washington.
5. What kinds of diplomatic problems arose in Samoa, Mexico, and Chile? How was each resolved?
6. **Critical Thinking: Recognizing Bias.** Why did some people continually refer to the purchase of Alaska as "Seward's Folly"?

See "Lesson Plan," p. 504C.

2. Expanding on the seas

By 1900, without thinking of the consequences, the United States had become the third-ranking naval power in the world. This large navy was no solution to the problems of depression, farm revolt, labor unrest, free silver, and Populism. If the nation continued to build its costly navy, there must be some grand purpose. What was it?

Mahan and sea power. Captain Alfred Thayer Mahan, a scholarly naval officer who helped set up the Naval War College in Newport, Rhode Island, had an answer. To be strong in the modern world, he said, the United States must sell its products on all continents. To secure and protect these foreign markets, the nation needed a powerful navy. Drawing on his study of ancient and modern times, he wrote *The Influence of Sea Power upon History* (1890). It

(p. 509)

Continuity and Change: Geography Explain to students that the United States' involvement in the Samoan Islands controversy marked a change in policy from certain aspects of the Monroe Doctrine (1823). Although the United States government continued to be fairly successful in keeping foreign powers out of the Western Hemisphere, the United States would no longer be able to stand completely outside the arena of international politics, even when isolationism was the goal. (See p. 217.)

was sea power "that made, and kept a nation great." Captain Mahan called for a strong navy, a canal across the Isthmus of Panama, United States dominance in the Caribbean, and control of Samoa and Hawaii.

Among the many who read and believed Mahan's message was Senator Henry Cabot Lodge of Massachusetts. He came from one of the oldest New England families and had inherited wealth. His upper-class background did not keep him from being a skillful politician. With a Harvard Ph.D. degree in history and a talent for writing history, he knew the American past and was fascinated by the struggle for power. During the 1890s again and again Lodge called for a bigger navy, annexation of Hawaii, a canal across the Isthmus of Panama, and the purchase of the Danish West Indies to protect the approaches to the canal. He also wanted to bring Greenland and Cuba under United States control and to dominate the Caribbean.

Lodge's colorful friend, Theodore Roosevelt of New York, was another follower of Mahan. He believed a nation should grow strong and be ready to fight. He shared Mahan's hopes and Lodge's plans for American expansion. As Assistant Secretary of the Navy under President McKinley, he worked for these goals.

☑ (p. 510)

Lodge and Roosevelt believed that a great nation must be strong. The world was full of weak nations. The American empire builders said that American power was only a force for good. Other nations should be glad to be ruled by us. And the American people would profit by reaching abroad. According to Senator Albert J. Beveridge of Indiana:

> American factories are making more than the American people can use; American soil is producing more than they can consume. Fate has written our policy for us; the trade of the world must and shall be ours. We will establish trading posts throughout the world as distributing points for American products. We will cover the ocean with our merchant marine. We will build a navy to the measure of our greatness. Great colonies

Culver Pictures

Captain Alfred Thayer Mahan, naval officer and eloquent historian, persuaded Theodore Roosevelt and others that the United States must become a great power.

governing themselves, flying our flag and trading with us, will grow about our posts of trade.

Renewed attempts to annex Hawaii. The people who lived in those potential "great colonies" did not all agree with Senator Beveridge. When Queen Liliuokalani came to the throne of Hawaii in 1891, she tried to shake off the control by American settlers. She wanted to restore the royal rights that her brother had given up. But she was frustrated in her struggle for freedom. In January 1893 the settlers, encouraged by the Harrison administration and assisted by United States Marines from the cruiser *Boston*, overthrew the queen. The new pro-America government drew up a treaty of annexation which President Harrison sent to the Senate for approval. The Democrats prevented Senate approval before Harrison left office.

Grover Cleveland, back in the White House again, was against expansion. Upon coming to office in 1893, he sent an agent to Hawaii to find out what had happened. The agent

✄ Critical Thinking Activity: Synthesizing Information How would the United States benefit from a strong navy? Alfred Mahan believed that a strong nation existed because of its sea power. Ask students to list specific uses for a large navy. How many of these were being used by the United States in 1890? In what ways is the United States Navy being used today?

reported that the American minister to Hawaii had fomented the revolution. Cleveland withdrew the treaty to annex Hawaii. Instead he tried to restore "Queen Lil" to her throne. Not until after the Spanish-American War was Hawaii finally annexed by joint resolution of Congress (July 1898). Would the United States follow the European example and build an empire by conquest? Or could the Empire for Liberty in North America add states in the far Pacific?

The Venezuelan boundary dispute. It was not easy for the growing United States to find its proper role. The new Latin American nations had only recently been colonies of European empires. The Venezuela-British Guiana boundary question was a test. President Cleveland thought the Monroe Doctrine (p. 217) was at stake. Great Britain claimed that 23,000 square miles of disputed borderland belonged to its colony of British Guiana (now the nation of Guyana). Venezuelans relied on the United States guarantees under the Monroe Doctrine. They begged the United States to defend them and save their land.

The United States urged arbitration of the dispute. But Britain refused. Then Cleveland's Secretary of State, Richard Olney, saw his chance to establish the right of the United States to intervene in Latin America. In a new version of the Monroe Doctrine he warned Great Britain. He said that the United States, "practically sovereign on this continent," would "resent and resist" any attempt by the British to take Venezuelan soil. The vast ocean between England and America, he said, made "political union between a European and American state unnatural and inexpedient." Again he called for arbitration. The British Prime Minister, Lord Salisbury, replied that the Monroe Doctrine was no part of international law. This boundary dispute was no business of the United States.

President Cleveland responded with threats. He asked Congress to vote $100,000 for a boundary commission, which was only a start. He would defend his extension of the Monroe Doctrine—even if it meant war. Congress agreed.

But many Americans feared the conse-

quences and rose in protest. The bellicose Theodore Roosevelt was disgusted. "The clamor of the peace faction," he wrote to his friend Senator Lodge, "has convinced me that this country needs a war."

Fortunately, calmer heads prevailed. The British already had enough troubles of their own, fighting for control of South Africa. Why turn the United States into an enemy over a petty border dispute? The British agreed to submit to arbitration. In October 1899 a tribunal in Paris (generally favoring Great Britain's claim) peacefully settled the boundary that had been debated for more than half a century.

The Venezuelan affair had expressed a more aggressive American spirit. "It indicates," Captain Mahan wrote, "the awakening of our countrymen to the fact that we must come out of our isolation . . . and take our share in the turmoil of the world."

See "Section 2 Review answers," p. 504D.

Section 2 Review

1. Identify: Alfred T. Mahan, Theodore Roosevelt, Henry Cabot Lodge, Queen Liliuokalani.
2. What was Senator Beveridge's message?
3. What was the importance of the Venezuelan boundary dispute to the United States?
4. How did the United States obtain control of Hawaii?
5. **Critical Thinking: Recognizing Bias.** What was Captain Mahan's "message"? How did it influence Lodge and Roosevelt?

See "Lesson Plan," p. 504D.

3. War with Spain

Many Americans who never read Captain Mahan's history books had their own reasons to reach out across the world. Some were crusaders who wanted to spread Christianity. Others wanted to teach the lessons of American democracy to faraway peoples. Still others thought that the nation would not be secure without bases in every ocean. And some wanted adventure—escape from economic hard times and the humdrum life at home.

See "Lesson Plan," p. 504D for **Writing Process Activity: Identifying Central Issues** relating to Mahan's *The Influence of Sea Power Upon History*.

The Spanish-American War

← U.S. Forces

← Spanish Forces

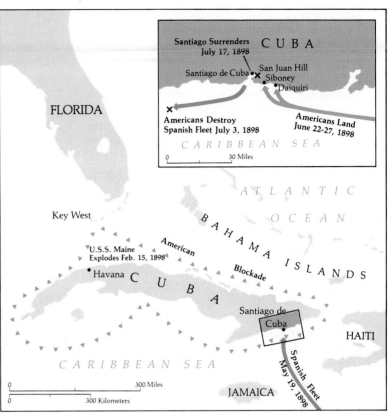

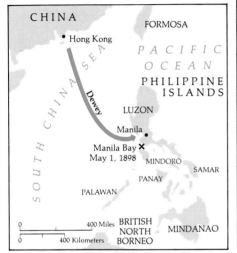

Problems in Cuba. The United States had long been interested in Cuba. As early as 1823 John Quincy Adams called Cuba a natural appendage of the North American continent. Later Presidents, too, tried to acquire the island from Spain. In 1868, just after the Civil War, rebels in Cuba began agitating for independence.

In the United States many people felt sympathy for this latest American revolution. In February 1895 when Cuban rebels declared their independence, the Spanish government sent in troops. Their ruthless general was Valeriano "Butcher" Weyler. He ordered "all inhabitants of the country" to "concentrate themselves in the towns." Anyone found outside a town after February 10, 1896, would be shot. Cuban towns were made into "concentration camps." Cuban rebels were tortured. Innocent men, women, and children—including some United States citizens—were herded together, to die of disease and starvation.

The "Yellow Press." American newspapers splashed "Butcher" Weyler's atrocities on their front pages. The new speed presses flooded the cities with six editions each day. By 1896 rural free delivery of mail brought one of these editions daily even to remote farms. The larger a paper's "circulation"—the more copies it sold—the more it could charge for advertising.

Joseph Pulitzer, an adventurous Hungarian immigrant, had secured passage to America by enlisting in the Union army. His energy and enterprise made him a fortune in the newspaper business. He built circulation by championing the interests of his "American aristocracy"—the aristocracy of labor—and by printing sensational stories. If there was no startling news, he would invent some. He once sent Nelly Bly traveling around the world to beat the legendary record of 80 days.

To make his *New York World* interesting for readers of all ages, he invented the comic strip.

⊕ **Geography and History: Movement** Have students look at the map above. Ask: In which direction was the Spanish fleet going when it sailed out of Santiago Harbor? (West.) About how far is Manila from Hong Kong? (About 700 miles or 1200 kilometers.) Which island was blockaded by American naval forces? (Cuba.) Based on the map, do you think Spain owned Jamaica? Haiti? (No—the United States would have blockaded these islands, too, if Spain owned them.)

He hired a clever cartoonist, Richard F. Outcault, to draw the adventures of a bad boy called the "Yellow Kid." Then when these comics appeared regularly in the Sunday *World*, Pulitzer's leading competitor, William Randolph Hearst, hired Outcault to do another Yellow Kid series for his own *New York Journal.* Because both of these sensational newspapers featured the Yellow Kid, they were soon called the "Yellow ✄ Press." And the Yellow Press was more inter-(p. 513) ested in selling papers than in keeping peace.

✿ ***The United States readies for war.*** American business firms had invested more than $50 million in Cuban sugar. Hoping to prod the United States to intervene, in 1895 the rebels destroyed these sugar plantations and their mills. Then, in 1896, William McKinley was elected

On the day after the formal United States declaration of war on Spain, Hearst's *San Francisco Examiner* called "to arms" and ran the navy signal flags for "Remember the Maine" and "Commence Firing."

The Oakland Museum

President with his twin promises: Protect American business! Free the Cuban people!

When Spain began to negotiate with the United States about the freedom of the Cubans, it seemed that there would be no need to fight. But the Yellow Press now cleared the path to war. On February 9, 1898, the *New York Journal* printed a stolen letter. The Spanish ambassador, Dupuy de Lôme, had written that President McKinley was "weak and a bidder for the admiration of the crowd, besides being a would-be politician who tries to leave a door open behind himself while keeping on good terms with the jingoes of his party." Though de Lôme quickly resigned, Americans were angered by his insults. Before they could calm down, a more serious incident occurred.

To protect American lives and property, the United States battleship *Maine* had been sent to Havana Harbor. At 9:40 on the night of February 15, 1898, the *Maine* was shattered by an explosion, and 260 officers and men were killed. The Navy's court of inquiry reported that the cause was an underwater mine. (Later investigations seem to indicate it was an internal explosion.) Still they could not say for sure whether or not the Spanish were to blame. Anyway the Yellow Press called for war against Spain, and headlined the slogan, "Remember the *Maine*!"

When the excitable Assistant Secretary of the Navy, Theodore Roosevelt, heard that McKinley was hesitating, he said the President "had no more backbone than a chocolate éclair." On February 25 the Secretary of the Navy made the mistake of taking the afternoon off. That left impatient Teddy as Acting Secretary—in charge of the whole United States Navy. Without consulting anyone, he cabled his friend Commodore George Dewey, who commanded the United States fleet in Asian waters. Make sure, he ordered, to have your ships ready for sea. In case of war attack the Spanish fleet in the Philippines.

When the Secretary of the Navy returned to his office next day, he was astonished. "Roosevelt," he wrote in his diary, "has come very near causing more of an explosion than happened to

✿ Multicultural Connection: Cuba's greatest hero was José Martí, who lived as an exile in the United States from 1881 to 1895. He worked as a journalist, poet, writer, and teacher in New York City. He also organized the struggle for Cuban independence and frequently traveled to Key West, Tampa, and other cities in the U.S. to raise funds for the Cuban Revolution. He became the President of the Partido Revolucionario Cubano (Cuban Revolutionary Party) and was among the first to die during the war of 1895 which ultimately brought freedom to Cuba.

the *Maine*." But it was too late to change the order. So even *before* war had begun in nearby Cuba, Teddy had arrayed the United States fleet for war on the other side of the world.

The United States goes to war. If McKinley had been a stronger man, he would not have been afraid to keep the peace. The government of Spain now told him they would give Cuba its independence. But the Yellow Press was still demanding Spanish blood. The "jingoes"—the people who loved to see a fight—wanted war. Their name came from a line of British song of the 1870s, "We don't want to fight, yet by Jingo! if we do, We've got the ships, we've got the men, and got the money too." The jingoes had their way.

On April 11, the day *after* President McKinley learned that Spain would agree to do everything Americans said they wanted, he asked Congress to declare war.

The war lasted only a few months—but that was long enough to create the greatest confusion. At the training camp in Tampa, Florida, commanding officers could not find uniforms. Yet for weeks fifteen railroad cars full of uniforms remained on a siding 25 miles away. The commander of United States troops in Cuba, Major General W. R. Shafter, weighed 300 pounds and was therefore "too unwieldy to get to the front." Unprepared for combat, the Army committed every kind of foolishness.

The Navy was in better shape. On May 1, when Commodore George Dewey, following Roosevelt's impulsive orders, attacked the Spanish warships in the Philippines, he finished off the Spaniards in seven hours. The rest of the Spanish fleet, which was in North American waters, was bottled up in Santiago Harbor on the southeastern tip of Cuba.

(p. 511)

Roosevelt and the Rough Riders. Meanwhile Teddy Roosevelt had himself named lieutenant colonel of a new regiment of cavalry. At a training camp in San Antonio, Texas, he gathered cowboys, sheriffs, and desperadoes from the West, and a sprinkling of playboy polo players and steeplechase riders from the East.

On June 22, Roosevelt's Rough Riders arrived in Cuba. In the battle to capture Santiago, they stormed both Kettle and San Juan hills. Without their horses, which had been left in Florida, the Rough Riders had to charge on foot. "I waved my hat and went up the hill with a rush," Roosevelt recalled. After bloody fighting they reached their goals.

Theodore Roosevelt never suffered from modesty. When Roosevelt published his book *The Rough Riders*, the humorist "Mr. Dooley"—Finley Peter Dunne—said Teddy should have called it "Alone in Cuba."

The decisive naval battle occurred even before the Americans could place their big guns on San Juan Hill overlooking Santiago to bombard the enemy navy below. When the Spanish fleet tried to run for the open sea, the United States Navy sank every one of their warships. All over the United States, cheering Americans celebrated their victory.

The "splendid little war." By the standards of American history, this had not been a full-sized war. There were 385 battle deaths—less than one-tenth the deaths in the American Revolution, and only one-twentieth the deaths at the Battle of Gettysburg alone. While the American Revolution had lasted nearly eight years and the Civil War had lasted four years, the Spanish-American War lasted only four *months*. Future Secretary of State John Hay called it "a splendid little war." Even this "little" war cost a quarter-billion dollars and several thousand deaths from disease.

The little war marked a big change in the relationship of the United States to the world. The tides of history were turned.

The defeated Spain gave up to the United States an empire of islands. And this nation, born in a colonial revolution, would now have its own colonies. All were outside the continent; some were thousands of miles away. The United States acquired Puerto Rico at the gateway to the Caribbean along with Guam, important as a refueling station in the mid-Pacific. The Philippine Islands (all 7000 of them, of which more than 1000 were inhabitable!) off the coast of

Enrichment Support File Topic

Critical Thinking Activity: Formulating Questions What is "Yellow Press" journalism? "Yellow press"—sensational journalism—became popular in the 1890s and remains popular to this day. Have students list newspapers and magazines that specialize in sensational articles. Ask students to decide if these are examples of "yellow press." Finally, ask the class to devise a set of 4–6 questions that could be asked of any piece of journalism to determine if it is "yellow press."

CELEBRATING JULY 4th, 1898 — "THE TRIUMPH OF THE AMERICAN BATTLE-SHIP."

The naval victories over Spain in 1898 showed that the United States was now a world power on the seas. Keppler's cartoon portrays all European powers but England as distressed by this development.

China were sold to the United States for a bargain price of $20 million.

These new American colonies added up to 100,000 square miles, holding nearly 10 million people. That was not much, compared to the vast empires of England, France, or Germany. But for the United States it was something quite new.

The meaning of this Spanish-American War in American history, then, was actually less in what it accomplished than in what it proclaimed. The American Revolution had been our War of Independence. Now the Spanish-American War at the threshold of the 1900s was our first War of Intervention. We had joined the old-fashioned race for empire.

Americans opposed to empire. Many Americans were worried. Some were saddened, and even angry. They called themselves "Anti-Impe-

rialists," for they hated to see the United States become an empire. To be an empire, they said, meant lording it over people in faraway places. They also feared that seizing land in the Pacific might someday lead to war with Japan. Some felt Asians could never be part of a democracy. And most wondered how the United States could uphold the Declaration of Independence if it became an empire. Anti-Imperialists included Democrats and Republicans, of all sections and classes—labor leader Samuel Gompers, industrialist Andrew Carnegie, President Charles W. Eliot of Harvard and President David Starr Jordan of Stanford, philosopher William James, social worker Jane Addams, and popular writer Mark Twain. William Jennings Bryan was also opposed to America's new imperialism. (p. 515)

The Anti-Imperialists were especially disturbed by the situation in the Philippines. The Filipinos did not want to be ruled by the United

Multicultural Connection: Many others saw the United States as the haven for democracy in the world. Syngman Rhee (1875–1965), born in Hwanghae Province, Korea, initially came to the United States in 1904 to protest Japanese imperialism in Korea. Although unsuccessful, Rhee stayed in the U.S., finished his post-graduate work, and continued to fight against Japanese domination in Korea. After Korea's liberation in 1945, Rhee returned home in 1948 to become the first President of the Republic of Korea.

States any more than by Spain. Led by Emilio Aguinaldo they fought against the Americans. Guerrilla warfare went on for three years. The United States used more troops and spent more money than in the entire war against Spain. Many Americans were shocked by the brutal methods we used to put down the Filipinos.

It was not until April 1902 that the last rebel surrendered and the Philippines were officially declared "pacified." Even before then, however, in 1900 under the direction of William Howard Taft, first as head of the Philippine Commission and then as civil governor, the large land holdings of the Catholic friars were distributed to the people. Under Taft's wise direction roads were built, harbors and sanitation improved, and the Philippines started on the path to self-government.

McKinley was renominated by the Republicans at Philadelphia in 1900 with a unanimous shout. Theodore Roosevelt, governor of New York and "Rough Rider" hero, was the vice-presidential candidate. Once nominated, Roosevelt threw himself into the campaign with his usual boyish vigor. Up and down the country he denounced the "mollycoddles" who would have us "scuttle" out of the Philippines.

The Democrats met at Kansas City on Independence Day and nominated William Jennings Bryan. Although Bryan insisted on a free-silver plank in the platform, the campaign was not fought on that dead issue. The Republican Congress had already passed an act making gold the only standard of currency. The issue was imperialism. A huge American flag hanging from the rafters of the Democratic convention hall proclaimed, "The flag of the Republic forever, of an Empire never."

In 1900 that slogan was already too late. People did not like what they heard about the

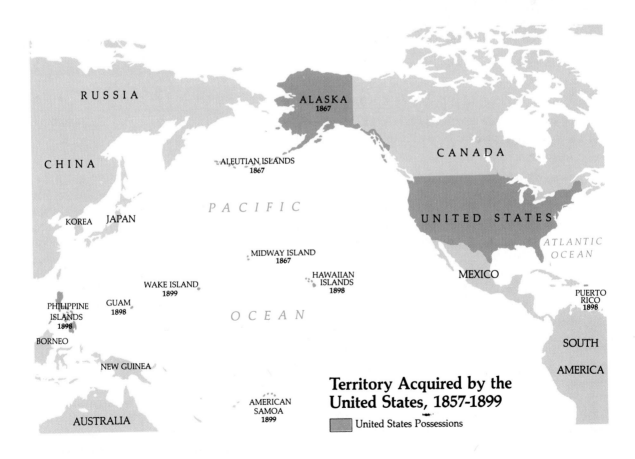

Territory Acquired by the United States, 1857-1899

United States Possessions

⊕ Geography and History: Location Have students look at the map above. Ask: Which islands were acquired first? (Aleutians and Midway.) Which United States possession is farthest from the continental United States? (Philippines.) The United States in 1900 had a significant navy and interests in both the Atlantic and Pacific Oceans. Where might the United States want to build a canal to increase the usefulness and mobility of its navy? (Latin America, south of Mexico.)

PUCK

DECLINED WITH THANKS.

THE ANTIS.— Here, take a dose of this anti-fat and get thin again!
UNCLE SAM.— No, Sonny! I never did take any of that stuff, and I 'm too old to begin!

An expanding Uncle Sam turns down reducing medicine as McKinley fits him with larger clothes.

Filipinos fighting against American control, even though censorship kept them from hearing the worst. Still, the war had helped to return prosperity to the United States. McKinley, "the advance agent of prosperity," was easily reelected by 292 electoral votes to Bryan's 155.

The reorganization of Cuba. For better or worse—and without much thought of what it all meant for the future—the United States was now running a colonial empire.

The administration had already begun setting up governments for the former Spanish islands. The Teller Amendment was attached to Congress's war resolution of April 20, 1898. It pledged that the United States would not exercise sovereignty over Cuba. We would leave government of the island to its people.

Still, United States troops did not leave. Under the military governor General Leonard Wood (1899–1902) the ruins wrought by the revolution were repaired. A school system was organized. The finances of the island were set in order. Peace lasted while the Cubans drew up a new constitution. But what use was a new constitution to people weakened and dying of the tropical disease of yellow fever? A commission headed by Major Walter Reed of the Army Medical Corps proved that yellow fever was carried by a mosquito (the female *Aëdes aegypti*) which bred in stagnant waters. Reed helped to stamp out the disease so Cuba could prosper.

The United States wanted certain assurances before it withdrew its army from Cuba. Cuba must make no treaties with foreign powers that would limit its independence. It should not

Continuity and Change: Geography Explain to students that the Platt Amendment, which Cuba was compelled to accept after the Spanish-American War, would enforce American influence there until 1934. At that time, under the auspices of FDR's "Good Neighbor" Policy, the Platt Amendment was replaced by a new treaty, in which the United States gave up its formal rights of intervention. (See p. 659.)

permit any foreign power to acquire Cuban territory. Cuba should sell or lease to the United States land for coaling or naval stations. Cuba should not contract debts whose interest could not be met out of current revenues. And, finally, Cuba should allow the United States to step in whenever necessary "for the protection of life, property, and individual liberty."

The Platt Amendment, named for Senator Orville H. Platt of Connecticut, attached all these provisions to an army money bill. The provisions would have to appear in any constitution of the Cubans. And they would also be included in a treaty with the United States. Otherwise the United States would not withdraw its troops.

The Cubans protested these terms but finally wrote them into their constitution. American troops were then withdrawn. The Platt Amendment became a "permanent" treaty with Cuba in 1903.

A new status for Puerto Rico. The island of Puerto Rico, with a population of almost a million, willingly came under the rule of the United States. The Foraker Act of April 1900 organized Puerto Rico as a compromise between a colony

and a territory. The President would appoint a governor and a council of 11, including 5 Puerto Ricans. Puerto Ricans would elect a legislature of 35 members. The Spanish courts were swept away and replaced by a court system like that of the United States. Works of sanitation, education, road building, and agricultural development were begun. In 1901 Congress abolished customs duties between the island and the United States.

(p. 516)

The "Open Door" in China. On the other side of the world were more lands waiting to be occupied by the new imperial powers. After China had been defeated in a war with Japan, in 1894–1895, the country lay at the mercy of the great powers. China was cut up into "spheres of influence." France, Germany, Japan, and Russia forced the Chinese government to grant them "leases" of great areas. Within each of these the lucky foreigners seized valuable railroad and mining rights and even abolished China's political rule.

The United States took Hawaii and the Philippines at the very moment when this piecemeal division of China was under way. The China trade was appealing to American merchants.

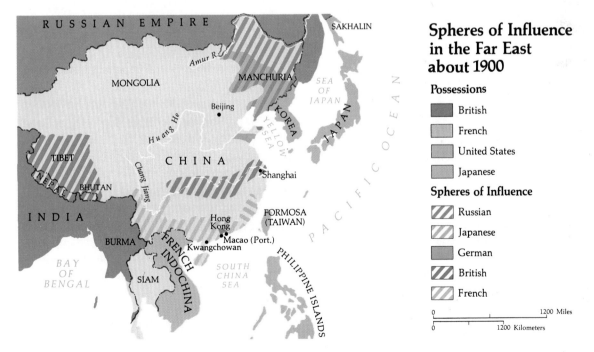

🌐 Geography and History: Regions Have students look at the map above. Ask: What western country possessed the greatest amount of land in the Far East around 1900? (Great Britian.) What eastern Chinese cities were possessed by or were under the sphere of influence of Great Britain? (Shanghai and Hong Kong.) What countries had spheres of influence or land possessions bordering the Yellow Sea? (Great Britain, Germany, Russia, and Japan.)

Knowing that Great Britain wanted the same opportunities, McKinley's Secretary of State, John Hay, sent identical notes to enlist England, France, Germany, Japan, and Russia. They were not to interfere with the rights of any of the 22 ports in China, nor to disturb the regular collection of the Chinese duties. They were not to increase railroad rates or harbor dues or in any way to close their own "spheres of influence" to other nations. Every nation was to have equal commercial treatment throughout China.

When Hay addressed the Great Powers, they avoided giving a direct answer. Hay went ahead anyway. On March 20, 1900, he announced that their consent had been "final and definitive." In this very casual way, without realizing what the "Open Door" in China might mean, the United States plunged deeper into world affairs.

The Boxer Rebellion. Meanwhile many Chinese would not let their country and themselves be treated like foreign property. They rushed to join a patriotic society called the "righteous Fists of Harmony" (shortened to "Boxers"). In May 1900 they rose up against the "foreign devils" hoping to drive them out of China. The Boxers killed missionaries and their families. They besieged the foreigners' neighborhood in Beijing. It took seven weeks for a makeshift army of American, British, French, German, Russian, and Japanese troops to reach Beijing and drive off the mob.

The foreign powers doing business in China wished to take their revenge and prevent this happening again. They wished to overthrow the government and divide China among themselves. Still, Secretary Hay stuck by his policy of the Open Door. He insisted that Chinese independence be preserved. Hay urged that, instead of overthrowing the shaky government of China, they only force the government to punish the ringleaders of the Boxer Rebellion and pay damages. The whole sum was finally fixed at a stiff $334 million. When it was found that

less than half the $24 million allotted to the United States was enough to pay our military expenses, Congress returned the balance to China.

The Chinese government said that it was "profoundly impressed with the justice and great friendliness of the United States." It put (p. 517) the American money in a trust fund to send hundreds of young Chinese to colleges and universities in the United States.

The United States had not only acquired colonial outposts in the Far North, in the Caribbean, and the North and South Pacific. This nation had even committed itself to preserve the independence and the territorial integrity of China—a vast, half-understood country on the other side of the globe. These varied commitments, so casually undertaken, held a dangerous destiny. The New World was no longer simply a place of refuge for oppressed peoples from everywhere. Our nation had become one of the world's great powers.

See "Section 3 Review answers," p. 504D.

Section 3 Review

1. Identify or explain: Joseph Pulitzer, Richard Outcault, W. R. Hearst, Dupuy de Lôme, George Dewey, "jingoes," Rough Riders.

2. Locate: Havana, Philippines, Santiago, Guam, Puerto Rico, Beijing.

3. Why did American Anti-Imperialists oppose expansion?

4. List the provisions of the Platt Amendment.

5. How did Secretary of State John Hay achieve the "Open Door" policy?

6. What was the Boxer Rebellion? How did it influence our relations with China?

7. **Critical Thinking: Determining Relevance.** What part did each of the following play in bringing on the Spanish-American War: (a) "Butcher" Weyler? (b) Cuban rebels? (c) the sinking of the *Maine*? (d) Theodore Roosevelt? (e) William McKinley? (f) the Yellow Press?

See "Lesson Plan," p. 504D for Cooperative Learning Activity: Distinguishing Fact from Opinion relating to American imperialism.

Theodore Roosevelt's Square Deal

FOCUS

To introduce the lesson, present the following situation to the class: The coal miners union declares a strike against the mine owners, but the owners refuse to talk with the union, calling the union leaders agitators. Winter is coming on and many people are afraid that they will freeze without coal to heat their homes if the strike continues. Should the government get involved in this situation? Discuss students' answers.

Developing Vocabulary

The words listed in this chapter are essential terms for reading and understanding particular sections of the chapter. The page number after each term indicates the page of its first or most important appearance in the chapter. These terms are defined in the text Glossary (text pages 1000–1011).

interstate (page 524)

INSTRUCT

Explain

Remind students that the Progressive Era, a time of reform, followed the Gilded Age. Historical eras do not have clear-cut starting and ending points.

☑ Writing Process Activity

Demonstrating Reasoned Judgment Ask students to imagine they are historians who must evaluate Theodore Roosevelt's two terms as President. Before they begin their essay, ask them to brainstorm about his political beliefs, his mastery of public relations, his reforms, and so forth. Students should begin their essay with a thesis statement summarizing their viewpoint about his effectiveness, and they should support their position with specific examples. As they revise, have them check for logical organization and coherence. After proofreading, students can compare their evaluations.

Section Review Answers

Section 1, page 527

1. a) a corporation organized to hold the stock of and thus control other companies. b) the Democratic presidential candidate in 1904. c) (1906), allowed the Interstate Commerce Commission to regulate railroads. d) wrote *The Jungle* to expose problems in stockyards and packing plants. 2. Roosevelt met with mine owners and threatened to send the army to seize the mines if the owners did not deal with the strikers. They gave in and submitted the dispute to arbitration. 3. (a) The Hepburn Bill; (b) the Pure Food and Drug Act; (c) the Employers' Liability Act; and (d) the Newlands Reclamation Act. 4. Roosevelt practiced his belief that a president should lead. Examples include the coal miners' strike of 1902, trust busting, and conservation.

CLOSE

To conclude the lesson, ask students to compile a list of areas which were subject to government intervention during the Progressive era? (Possible responses include: big business, conservation, labor disputes.)

Middle-Class Reformers

FOCUS

To introduce the lesson, have students turn to the Lewis Hine photograph on page 530 and ask: How much skill did it take for this girl to operate this machine? (Probably not much.) Did the girl or the machine control the pace of the work? (The machine.) Compare this picture with the picture on page 262 of earlier industrialization. How does industrialization seem to have changed the way the work gets done?

Developing Vocabulary

nonpartisan (page 527); **lobby** (page 528); **initiative** (page 529); **referendum** (page 529); **recall** (page 529); **muckraking** (page 529); **media** (page 530); **ashcan school** (page 530)

INSTRUCT

Explain

A number of the reforms sought by the Progressives had been previously sought by the Populists. Review Chapter 18, Section 3 if needed.

❧ Cooperative Learning Activity

Recognizing Ideologies Explain that students will work in five small groups to design symbols of the Progressive movement. Assign each group one of the following areas of reform: 1) city government, 2) regulation of business, 3) help for the poor and needy, 4) aid to the workers, and 5) the election process. To begin, have group members brainstorm ways to illustrate Progressive ideas in the reform area assigned to their group. Have the group decide who will prepare the final illustration and lettering and who will explain the symbol to the class.

Providing In-Depth Coverage

Perspectives on Women's Suffrage

The struggle for women's suffrage in America dates at least as far back as the mid-seventeenth century and a woman named Margaret Brent. She owned and ran her own plantation in colonial Maryland, and led a group of men in stopping a rebellion against the governor. As the governor's estate manager and an attorney for Lord Baltimore, she felt that she was entitled to a vote in the colonial assembly. Denied that right she moved to Virginia and continued to run successfully a large estate until her death.

Throughout American history women have been treated as second-class citizens despite their proven success in a "man's world." Finally, through increased efforts on the part of reformers around the turn of the century, women won the right to vote in the 1920s. This was a giant step for women's rights.

A History of the United States as an instructional program provides three types of resources you can use to offer in-depth coverage of the struggle for women's suffrage: the *student text*, the *Enrichment Support File,* and *Perspectives.* The chart below shows the topics that are covered in each.

THE STUDENT TEXT. Boorstin and Kelley's *A History of the United States* unfolds the chronology of events, the key players, and, as an interpretive history, the controversy of the women's rights movement.

AMERICAN HISTORY ENRICHMENT SUPPORT FILE. This collection of primary source readings and classroom activities reveals the means by which women gained the vote.

PERSPECTIVES: READINGS ON AMERICAN HISTORY IN THE 20TH CENTURY. In this edited collection of secondary source readings, well-known historians and political commentators (including Boorstin) provide an array of perspectives on the women's rights movement.

Locating Instructional Materials

Detailed lesson plans for teaching women's suffrage as a mini-course or to study one or more elements of the women's rights movement in depth are offered in the following areas: in the *student text,* see individual lesson plans at the beginning of each chapter; in the *Enrichment Support File,* see page 3; in *Perspectives,* see the Teacher's Guide for this topic.

IN-DEPTH COVERAGE OF THE WOMEN'S RIGHTS MOVEMENT		
Student Text	**Enrichment Support File**	**Perspectives**
▪ Women's Rights Convention, pp. 238–239 ▪ Lucretia Mott and Elizabeth Cady Stanton, pp. 238–239 ▪ Frances Willard, pp. 382–383 ▪ Progressives and Women's Suffrage, p. 529 ▪ Nineteenth Amendment, p. 485	▪ Lesson Suggestions ▪ Multimedia Resources ▪ Overview Essay/The Reformers: A Struggle for Women's Rights ▪ Songs in American History/Women's Suffrage Picks Up Steam ▪ Great Debates in American History/ Should Women Have the Right to Vote? ▪ Biography in American History/ Anna Howard Shaw ▪ Art in American History/The Struggle of Women Artists ▪ Geography in American History/Geography's Tale: The Women's Suffrage Movement ▪ Making Connections	▪ "The Mixed Legacy of Women's Liberation" by Alvin P. Sanoff ▪ "'You've Come a Long Way, Baby'" by Winifred D. Wandersee ▪ "The Legacy of Mary Richards" by Joyce Purnick ▪ "Looking Ahead" by Gina Allen ▪ "Marriage Can Make Women Secure" by Phyllis Schlafly ▪ "The Second Stage" by Betty Friedan

Chapter 20
The Progressive Era

Identifying Chapter Materials

Objectives	Basic Instructional Materials	Extension Materials
1 Theodore Roosevelt's Square Deal • Describe the background, philosophy, and reform legislation of Theodore Roosevelt.	**Annotated Teacher's Edition** • Lesson Plans, p. 520C **Instructional Support File** • Pre-Reading Activities, Unit 7, p. 15 • Skill Application Activity, Unit 7, p. 19	**Documents of American History** • President Roosevelt and the Trusts, Vol. 2, p. 20 • The Conservation of Natural Resources, Vol. 2, p. 48
2 Middle-Class Reformers • Define the Progressives as a group and identify some reform movements of the time. • Discuss the working conditions of child laborers in the United States in the early 1900s.	**Annotated Teacher's Edition** • Lesson Plans, pp. 520C–520D **Instructional Support File** • Skill Review Activity, Unit 7, p. 18 • Critical Thinking Activity, Unit 7, p. 20	**Enrichment Support File** • The Reformers: A Struggle for Women's Rights (See "In-Depth Coverage" at right.) **Perspectives** • Feminism (see "In-Depth Coverage" at right.)
3 Taft in the White House • Summarize the main events of the Taft administration. • Analyze the relations between Taft and Roosevelt and explain the political effect of their split on the 1912 election.	**Annotated Teacher's Edition** • Lesson Plans, pp. 520D–520E	**Documents of American History** • Taft's Defence of the Payne-Aldrich Tariff, Vol. 2, p. 54 • Roosevelt's Candidacy in 1912, Vol. 2, p. 65 • Roosevelt and the New Nationalism, Vol. 2, p. 66
4 Woodrow Wilson and the New Freedom • Identify the Federal Reserve Act and other reforms made under Woodrow Wilson's administration. • Discuss the personal characteristics of Wilson and compare these with Teddy Roosevelt's.	**Annotated Teacher's Edition** • Lesson Plans, p. 520E	**Documents of American History** • Wilson's First Inaugural Address, Vol. 2, p. 82
5 Seeking a World Role • Describe the continuing involvement of the United States in world affairs. • Explain and give examples of the Roosevelt Corollary, Taft's "dollar diplomacy," and Wilson's moral foreign policy. • Discuss the importance of the Panama Canal to the United States.	**Annotated Teacher's Edition** • Lesson Plans, pp. 520E–520F **Instructional Support File** • Reading Activities, Unit 7, pp. 16–17 • Chapter Test, pp. 21–24 • Additional Test Questions, Unit 7, pp. 25–28	**Enrichment Support File** • Through Mud and Disease: Building the Panama Canal **American History Transparencies** • Critical Thinking, p. F27

Chapter 19 Review

See "Chapter Review answers," p. 504E.

Focusing on Ideas

1. What groups of Americans opposed American overseas expansion? Why were they against imperialism?

2. How did the United States benefit politically, socially, and economically from expansion in the late nineteenth century?

3. Describe the territorial changes of the United States that occurred as a result of the Spanish-American War.

4. The value of the goods and services produced by Americans nearly doubled between 1870 and 1900. How was this economic growth linked to demands for overseas expansion?

Taking a Critical Look

1. **Determining Relevance.** What was the relevance of the Monroe Doctrine to the Maximilian affair? the Venezuelan boundary dispute? the Platt Amendment?

2. **Making Comparisons.** How did the overseas expansion of the United States differ from American westward expansion with regard to (a) settlement and (b) the way in which the new territories were governed?

Your Region in History

1. **Geography.** Was your state or locality involved in any special way in the overseas events described in this chapter? Investigate any events you discover and report to the class on the involvement.

2. **Culture.** Did any newspaper serving your community take a stand on the Spanish-American War? (Your public library or newspaper office may have a file or microfilm of back issues.) What stand did it take? What reasons did it give?

3. **Economics.** How did the vast increase in the value of goods and services produced in the United States affect the standard of living of residents in your region during the period 1870–1890?

Historical Facts and Figures

Summarizing Information. Study the graph below to help answer the following questions: (a) What was the value of foreign trade in 1865? In 1885? In 1915? (b) What caused the temporary decline between 1880 and 1890? (c) Write a hypothesis describing the trend in American foreign trade for the period 1865 to 1915. (d) What events in this chapter would support your hypothesis?

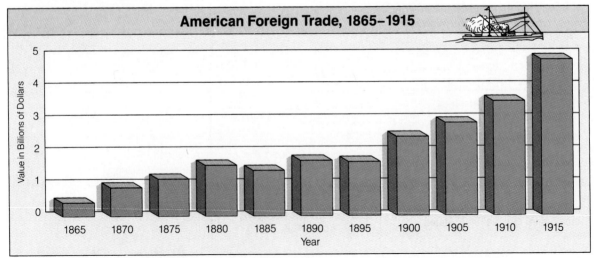

American Foreign Trade, 1865–1915

Value in Billions of Dollars / Year

Source: *Historical Statistics of the United States*

Section Review Answers

Section 2, page 531

1. a) replaced the mayor and city council with an elected, nonpartisan commission. b) Wisconsin governor who called for many Progressive reforms. c) an election in which the voters, rather than party bosses, choose the candidates for public office. d) a procedure that allows citizens to propose a bill. e) a vote in which the voters themselves can accept or reject a law. f) a petition by citizens that forces an official to stand for reelection even though the official's term of office has not expired. g) a muckraker who depicted misgovernment in American cities. h) wrote an exposé of the Standard Oil Company. i) wrote about the power of railroad companies in California and about the wheat exchange in Chicago. j) a group of artists who depicted slums. k) a photographer best known for his pictures of slum children. 2. Reformers tried to change the form of government so that corrupt politicians could not easily gain control. 3. (a) the direct primary, secret ballot, direct election of United States senators, initiative, referendum, recall, women's suffrage, and restrictions on lobbying; (b) commissions to regulate railroad companies and public utilities, and supervision of state banks; (c) laws restricting child labor and minimum-wage and worker's compensation laws; (d) tax laws that put a heavier burden on the rich and compulsory insurance for the sick, disabled, and aged; 4. The "muckrakers" were writers who exposed injustice and corruption in government and business. Their work resulted in reform movements in Philadelphia, Chicago, Kansas City, Minneapolis, Los Angeles, and San Francisco.

CLOSE

To conclude the lesson, have students evaluate the photograph by Jacob Riis on 531, either in class or for homework. (Answer: It has basically the same characteristics as the other photograph, except that it is not a posed shot.) You can carry this analysis further by getting a collection of Riis's or Hine's photographs—both are available in paperback.

Section 3 (pages 532–536)

Taft in the White House

FOCUS

To introduce the lesson, ask students to list Taft's major actions as President, Roosevelt's criticisms of Taft, Roosevelt's platform in 1912, and Wilson's platform in 1912. Then ask students to label the elements in the platforms that were Progressive with a "P."

INSTRUCT

Explain

President Taft disappointed Progressive reformers by signing the Payne-Aldrich tariff and firing Pinchot from the Forest Service.

☑ Writing Process Activity

Making Comparisons Explain to students that they will write an essay in which they contrast the presidencies of William Howard Taft and Theodore Roosevelt. Students should write a thesis statement that summarizes the contrast. Ask them to organize by treating a point about Roosevelt with a corresponding point about Taft. Students should revise for unity and completeness. After proofreading, they can exchange essays with a partner.

Section Review Answers

Section 3, page 536

1. a) failed to lower tariffs significantly, representing a failure by Taft and the Republicans to honor their campaign promises. b) Chief of the Forest Service under Roosevelt. Taft fired him, which angered Roosevelt and the Progressives. c) Taft's Secretary of the Interior, accused of favoritism when he sold public coal lands in Alaska. d) Progressives who acted apart from and even against the Republican leadership. e) the Speaker of the House whose dictatorial tactics angered the insurgents. f) (1910) gave the Interstate Commerce Commission jurisdiction over the telephone, telegraph, cable, and wireless companies. g) (1913) authorized Congress to collect income taxes. h) the symbol of the Progressive Party in 1912. i) the presidential candidate of the Socialist party in 1912. 2. Taft disappointed reformers by (a) failing to revise the existing tariff significantly and instead signing and praising the Payne-Aldrich tariff, and (b) by supporting Secretary of Interior Ballinger, who was accused of favoritism in his sale of public lands, and firing Pinchot. Taft's successes included many indictments against trusts; the Mann-Elkins Act; the extension of civil service to cover more jobs; the addition of more than a million acres to the national forest; ensuring that the government retained the mineral resources beneath public lands sold to private buyers; establishing a new parcel post service and postal savings bank for people in small towns; and sponsorship of the income-tax amendment, which would be ratified in 1913. 3. (a) Taft's failure to satisfy Progressives; (b) Roosevelt's public criticism of Taft and support for the insurgents; (c) Taft's nomination at the Republican convention; (d) Roosevelt's willingness to be the candidate of a new party. The Progressive party split the ranks of the Republicans and thus helped the Democratic candidate, Woodrow Wilson.

4. Wilson's "New Freedom" was more conservative than Roosevelt's "New Nationalism." Wilson's program called for the government to be an umpire and emphasized individual initiative. Roosevelt's gave a stronger role to the government in regulating business and insuring the welfare of the people.

CLOSE

To conclude the lesson, ask: Would Wilson have won the election of 1912 if the Republican party had not split? Why or why not? (Probably not. He received only 42 percent of the popular vote.)

Section 4 (pages 536–540)

Woodrow Wilson and the New Freedom

FOCUS

To introduce the lesson, ask students to make a list of the personal characteristics of Woodrow Wilson. (They can find some stated and infer something about others by looking at text pages 536–537.) Then ask: Which of these characteristics would help someone as President? Which would hurt?

Developing Vocabulary
Federal Reserve System (page 539); **interlocking directorates** (page 539).

INSTRUCT

Explain
Draw a diagram of the banking system before the Federal Reserve Act.

★ Independent Activity
Identifying Central Issues Write on the board the words *Wilson's Reforms.* Below this, write two column headings: *Purpose* and *Provisions.* Then write the following side headings: *Underwood-Simmons Tariff Act, Federal Reserve Act, Clayton Antitrust Act, Federal Trade Commission Act, Seamen's Act, Federal Farm Loan Act,* and *Labor Reforms.* Using the text as a guide, have students complete the chart independently.

Section Review Answers
Section 4, page 540

1. a) a system of twelve regional banks overseen by a central board in Washington, D.C. b) exist when the same people sit on the boards of directors of several corporations. c) demand that an unlawful practice be halted. d) improved the living conditions and wages of the merchant marine. e) provided long-term loans to farmers at low interest rates. 2. The Underwood-Simmons bill made major cuts in tariff rates. 3. The Federal Reserve Act was created to help a bank stop a "run" on its deposits and created a flexible national currency—Federal Reserve notes—so that the money supply could be adjusted as needed. 4. The Clayton Antitrust Act prohibited stock takeovers and interlocking directorates that lessened competition. 5. The Federal Trade Commission was supposed to draw up rules of fair trade and enforce them. It could issue "cease and desist" orders against companies that engaged in unfair or anticompetitive practices and could punish companies that disobeyed those orders. 6. La Follette's Seamen's Act, the Federal Farm Loan Act, and laws that restricted an eight-hour day for railroad workers. 7. Wilson and Roosevelt both wrote many books; both had been governors; and both supported many reforms. Roosevelt was an exuberant outdoorsman, while Wilson was scholarly, moralistic, and bookish.

CLOSE

To conclude the lesson, ask: What additional improvements might have protected the money of bank customers and prevented the run on banks that occurred during the Great Depression? (Federal Deposit Insurance Corporation.) Ask: Why do you suppose it was not added in 1913? (Not deemed necessary.)

Section 5 (pages 540–544)

Seeking a World Role

FOCUS

To introduce the lesson, have students turn to the map of the Far East on page 517 and compile a list of the world powers in 1900. (United States, France, England, Germany, and Russia.) Distribute outline maps of the world, or have students trace them. Then have students locate the areas of conflict in the Far East over which Russia and Japan fought, including Manchuria and Korea, and fill them in on their maps. Ask: What is the goal of a foreign policy based on the concept of the balance of power? (To ensure that no world power succeeds in becoming more powerful than any other world power.)

Developing Vocabulary
balance of power (page 540); **isthmus** (page 541); **corollary** (page 542); **de facto** (page 543)

INSTRUCT

Explain

Some historians have questioned the wisdom of the Treaty of Portsmouth, partly because it made Japan the dominant sea power in the Pacific, for which we would pay a heavy price in 1941.

☑ Writing Process Activity

Demonstrating Reasoned Judgment Using Roosevelt's "Speak softly and carry a big stick" and Taft's "dollar diplomacy" as examples, explain to students that they will invent a slogan that captures President Wilson's foreign affairs policy. Have them begin by freewriting about Wilson's dealings with foreign nations. Students should then create their slogan and explain how and why they chose it. Have them revise their writings for logic and coherence. After proofreading, students can share their work, comparing and contrasting their approaches.

Section Review Answers

Section 5, page 544

1. a) (1908) allowed Japan to annex Korea and pursue its interests in Manchuria, but otherwise leave the Pacific alone. b) included 16 United States warships that sailed around the world. c) directed the effort that controlled yellow fever in Panama. d) stated that the United States would intervene in badly governed Latin American nations. e) was a meeting that produced a settlement of the dispute between France and Germany over Morocco. f) Taft's Secretary of State who believed in "dollar diplomacy." g) accepts a government's authority without judging whether that government is legal. h) a Mexican general who overthrew the Mexican government and was opposed by Wilson. i) Huerta's chief rival. j) led a new revolt in which his raiders killed people on both sides of the border. 2. Manchuria is on the map on page 517. The Isthmus of Panama, Columbia, and the Dominican Republic are on the map on page 543. Morocco is on page 951. Veracruz is on the map on page 299. The ABC powers—Argentina, Brazil, and Chile—are on page 950. 3. Roosevelt attempted to maintain the independence of China, the existing balance of power between Russia and Japan, and good relations with Japan. 4. The United States bought the rights to build a canal across the Isthmus of Panama, then a part of Colombia, from a French company that had been working on a canal for years. Colombia would not accept the terms of a treaty leasing the land for the canal to the United States. A treaty negotiated to pay Colombia for the loss of Panama was not ratified by the Senate until 1921. 5. Taft pushed American bankers to invest in China and he sent marines to Nicaragua in 1912 to protect United States

business interests. 6. The United States Marines landed in Veracruz, Mexico, and took control of the city to prevent a shipment of German arms from reaching Huerta's forces. In 1916 an American expedition pursued Pancho Villa into Mexico in order to stop his raids against Americans near the Mexican border. 7. The United States would not only stop other countries from intervening in Latin America but would itself intervene.

CLOSE

To conclude the lesson, break the class up into small groups and assign the groups research projects on the Panama Canal. Topics might include: difficulties met by the engineers, its historical and military significance, the engineering feats, the conquest of malaria and yellow fever, the significance of the canal to the United States, and the physical details of the canal.

Chapter Review Answers

Focusing on Ideas

1. Interest in nature, many interests, persistence, forcefulness, pride (keeping blind eye a secret), self-assertiveness, energy. 2. Workers: Long hours, low wages, strikebreaking, unsafe conditions, dishonest count of worker output, payment in scrip, lack of insurance, child labor. Consumers: High prices due to monopolies, impure food and drugs, false labeling, poor services by public utilities. Business competitors: Killing off/forcing small businesses to join a trust, railroad rebates, price discrimination. Other victims: taxpayers: high government costs. 3. He carried a big stick in the coal strike, Northern Securities case, Hepburn Bill, Panama Canal, Dominican Republic, and the navy in the Pacific. He was often outspoken. 4. Because reformers' efforts were so successful.

Taking a Critical Look

1. Intolerable conditions aroused public opinion, and politicians to action, only when widely publicized. 2. "Big Brotherism" is often found demeaning and is highly resented, so its long-term effect may be harmful. 3. It would help reduce abuses relating to "jacked-up" prices and poor quality resulting from monopoly.

Your Region in History

1–3. Answers will vary depending on your region. Consult your local library or historical society.

Historical Facts and Figures

(a) Western. (b) Midwest; other states west of Mississippi. (c) Eastern. (d) Include women pioneers role in settling the West leading to suffrage. (e) See pages 528–529.

20

Chapter 20

Focusing the Chapter: Have students identify the chapter logo. Discuss what unit theme the logo might symbolize. Then ask students to skim the chapter to identify other illustrations or titles that relate to this theme.

The Progressive Era

In the opening years of the 1900s, the reformers were so successful that the period came to be called the *Progressive Era.* American voters would have more to say than ever before in selecting their candidates. New laws would control big business. This was accomplished by no one leader or party but by a wonderfully varied crew—the aggressive Theodore Roosevelt, the genial William Howard Taft, and the ascetic Woodrow Wilson. Reformers appeared in Congress, statehouses, and city halls. Journalists and other social critics stirred public opinion and prodded officials to move forward. Within twenty years these forces of reform pushed the nation further into the world scene. There the United States would play a reluctant but decisive role.

These suffragettes marched in New York City in 1917 to demand their right to vote.

Image Finders, Inc.

See "Lesson Plan," p. 520C.

1. Theodore Roosevelt's Square Deal

Fortune seemed to smile on President McKinley as he took the oath for his second term on March 4, 1901. The nation had sent him back to the White House with a solid vote of confidence. His early months in office were uneventful. In the spring he made a grand tour of the country. Then he spent a two-month summer vacation at his home in Canton, Ohio. In September he went to Buffalo, New York, to speak at the Pan-American Exposition. There at a brief public reception a man suddenly walked up to him and, without warning, shot the President twice. Just over a week later McKinley was dead.

The 28-year-old assassin, Leon Czolgosz, called himself an anarchist, which meant that he was against all government. But in a stroke of irony, Czolgosz unintentionally put the government of the United States under a strong and inspiring leader. "It's a dreadful thing to come into the Presidency this way," Roosevelt wrote a friend, "but it would be a far worse thing to be morbid about it." To the delight of the nation, "TR" would enjoy being President just as he seemed to enjoy everything else.

Library of Congress

The ever-ebullient TR gives a rousing speech in New Castle, Wyoming, in 1903.

The Republican Roosevelt. No one who had visited Theodore Roosevelt as a child could have guessed that he would become a champion of the ordinary American. His father was a well-to-do New York banker who owned country houses and took his family to Europe for vacations. Among Teddy Roosevelt's early memories were seeing the Pope during a walk in Rome and visiting the tomb of Napoleon in Paris.

Young Teddy had no worries about money. But he had other worries. He suffered from asthma, which made it hard for him to exercise, and his eyesight was poor. He became interested in nature and began collecting specimens of plants and animals. When he was 12, his mother told a maid to throw away some dead mice that the boy had stored in a dresser drawer. "The Loss to Science," Teddy cried. "The Loss to Science!"

His father built a gym for the boy at home.

There Teddy worked with a punching bag and did pull-ups on the horizontal bars. He also took boxing lessons. By age 17 he was expert in such track events as running, pole vaulting, and high jumping. On his grandfather's country estate at Oyster Bay on Long Island, he became an enthusiastic horseman and a crack shot. All his life Teddy Roosevelt felt that he had to make up for the childhood weakness of his body.

Roosevelt never lost his boyish excitement. He kept up his boxing. After he was hit in the eye while boxing with a young army officer, his left eye became blind. He managed to keep this a secret, and he devised ways to prevent people from knowing that he could see in only one eye. In spite of it, he became world famous as an explorer and big-game hunter in Africa and South America.

From the White House he preached "The Strenuous Life." Some genteel European diplomats dreaded being assigned to Washington when TR was in the White House. They could not do their diplomatic duty by sipping tea and making polite conversation. TR expected them—along with panting Cabinet members and generals—to join his exhausting tramps in the country. "You must always remember," a British ambassador explained, "that the President is about six years old."

Dynamic energy was the key to Roosevelt's character. The variety of his interests and curiosities was enormous. His published works on history, politics, ethics, travel, and sport fill twenty volumes. Though born to wealth and an old family, he was no snob. Cowboys, ambassadors, social workers, labor leaders, senators, clergymen, writers, and prizefighters were his friends. They met one another in the reception room of the White House and sat down at his table together. He loved power. And he used it with confidence that his policies were right. He was certain that they would benefit the American people. He believed the President had all the powers not forbidden in the Constitution. He also saw the Presidency as a "bully pulpit" from which in his high-pitched, squeaky voice he spread his ideas. He was the first President since Lincoln to use fully the powers of the office.

TR believed the President should lead. And he liked a good fight—not only in the boxing ring, but also in politics. He had been shocked that earlier Presidents and the Supreme Court had not enforced the laws against monopolies. Their growing power worried him. "Of all forms of tyranny," he complained, "the least attractive and the most vulgar is the tyranny of mere wealth."

The coal strike. Hardly had TR moved into the White House when he had his first chance to show how a President should lead. The owners of the nation's anthracite (hard coal) mines were reckless of the safety of their men. Workers were dying needlessly each year. In 1901 alone, 441 men were killed in mining accidents in the anthracite fields of Illinois, Ohio, Pennsylvania, and West Virginia.

The men had received no raise in wages in twenty years. They were paid by the weight of the coal they dug, but the companies were not weighing honestly. A man might have to dig 4000 pounds before getting credit for a ton. Miners were sometimes paid in scrip that could only be used in "company stores" which charged high prices.

By 1902 the miners could endure no more. The union leaders decided to take action. John Mitchell, then the energetic young president of the United Mine Workers, was the son of a miner who had lost his life in the mines. Mitchell himself had begun mining at age 12. His union—150,000 strong—included thousands of immigrant newcomers who spoke over a dozen languages.

The coal miners went on strike in May 1902. But the mine owners refused to deal with the union. They tried to force the miners back to work. George F. Baer, the president of the Philadelphia and Reading Coal and Iron Company, was the chief spokesman for the owners. "The rights and interests of the laboring man," he declared, "will be protected and cared for not by the labor agitators, but by the Christian men to whom God in his wisdom has given the control of the property interests of the country."

By October with winter coming on, people feared that the railroads would have to stop running and that they would freeze without coal to heat their homes. Then the President came to the rescue. No matter who owned the mines, Roosevelt insisted that nobody owned the miners. He called the mine operators and John Mitchell to the White House. When the owners refused to arbitrate, he let them know he might send the army into the mines. At last on October 13 the owners gave in and agreed to deal with the union. The miners went back to work and later won most of their demands. When the strike ended, TR had shown how, in the new age of big business, it was possible for the federal government to help. He had proven himself a champion of the ordinary American. He had seen that the miners received a "square deal." That was what he wanted for all Americans.

The Northern Securities case. The coal strike was only the beginning of TR's flamboyant defense of the public interest against the trusts. His most famous target was the Northern Securities Company. It was a holding company, a corporation set up to hold a controlling part of the stock of other companies. It had been formed by railroad builder James J. Hill of the Great Northern, the Rockefellers, J. P. Morgan, and E. H. Harriman of the Union Pacific to control the four big railroads of the Northwest.

After a fierce battle over the control of the stock of one of the railroads, this holding company had brought peace between the competitors. But the people in the Northwest were now at the mercy of one big railroad combine. They depended on the railroad to bring in supplies and to take their produce to market. Now they would have to pay whatever rates the railroads wanted to charge.

The Northern Securities Company gave TR his perfect issue—and his chance to prove that he was a master of public relations. He used it skillfully to revive the Sherman Antitrust Act and to show the power of the federal government. These men of great wealth had plagued a whole region and disrupted the nation's stock market by their fight for monopoly. So the President had the company sued under the Sherman Act.

J. P. Morgan was shocked. He went to the White House and told TR, "If we have done anything wrong, send your man [meaning the Attorney General] to my man [one of Morgan's lawyers] and they can fix it up." The President later remarked of this incident, "That is a most illuminating illustration of the Wall Street point of view. Mr. Morgan could not help regarding me as a big rival operator, who either intended to ruin all his interests or else could be induced to come to an agreement to ruin none."

But Roosevelt pushed the case, and in 1904 the Supreme Court, by a vote of 5 to 4, held that the Northern Securities Company did

This 1903 cartoon called for new legislation to expose the activities of the trusts.

violate the Sherman Antitrust Act. The Court ordered the company to dissolve. After this first victory, TR moved against other unpopular trusts—the beef trust, the oil trust, and the tobacco trust.

In his own mind Roosevelt always made a distinction between "good" trusts and "bad" trusts. The law should be used to break up the bad trusts, those that were formed to gouge the public by trying to end competition. Good trusts should only be regulated. A good trust might simply beat its rivals because its prices were lower, its products better, or its management more efficient. By getting Congress to add a new Department of Commerce and Labor to the Cabinet, TR showed that he meant what he said. A Bureau of Corporations within the Department was formed to help judge which trusts were good and which were bad. The government, the President declared, must be "the senior partner in every business."

President in his own right. Roosevelt's battles for labor and against the trusts made his first term a smashing success. He easily won the election of 1904 against the Democrats' dull and conservative candidate, Judge Alton B. Parker of New York. Roosevelt carried the entire North and West with 336 electoral votes. Parker was left with only 140 votes from the "solid South." For every two popular votes for Parker, Roosevelt collected three.

Now that Roosevelt was President in his own right, he moved swiftly for major reforms. His first goal was to strengthen the Interstate Commerce Commission so it could really regulate the railroads. But he had to be both inventive and persistent to overcome the opposition of the railroads and the big businesses that benefited from their rebates. Finally, in 1906, after a sixteen-month battle in the Senate during which he used all his skills as a leader, the Hepburn bill became law. It gave the ICC power over pipelines, express and sleeping car companies, bridges, ferries, and terminals. Railroad rebates and free passes were forbidden. If a shipper complained about any unfair rate, the Commission could reduce the rate until a federal court ruled on its fairness. To Roosevelt the Hepburn

Act marked a major step on the path to effective federal regulation of business.

Other reform legislation. Roosevelt went on to prove that a free society was not powerless against large corporations. The Meat Inspection Act gave federal officials the right to inspect all meat shipped in interstate commerce to see whether it came from healthy animals and was packed under sanitary conditions. Upton Sinclair had written a popular novel, *The Jungle*, showing the miseries of workers in the stockyards—and describing the rotten meat packed for sale. When the law passed in 1906, Sinclair said his book had tried to hit people in their heart, and instead had hit them in their stomach.

The year 1906 was a banner one for reform. A Pure Food and Drug Act was passed. The manufacture and sale of impure foods, drugs, and liquors was forbidden. Labels on patent medicines had to list the contents. The Employers' Liability Act provided accident insurance for workers in the District of Columbia and on interstate railroads.

Conservation of natural resources. President Roosevelt gave a new meaning to "conservation"—the movement to conserve the nation's resources for future Americans. His own experience had shown him the need. As a young man out west he had enjoyed the open spaces. On his ranch in Dakota Territory he had ridden the range and explored the wilderness. He loved everything about the West—the cowboys, the life of the trail, fishing, and hunting. When he became President, he was shocked to see lumber companies wasting forests that had taken centuries to grow. He knew that the untouched wilderness could never be put back.

He saw some parts of the country troubled by floods while others lacked water. Saving rivers and streams and using their water wisely were just as important as protecting the land or the forests. In June 1902 his strong support helped to secure the passage of the Newlands Reclamation Act. Money from the sale of public lands in sixteen western states and territories was to be used to build large dams and canal systems to

Continuity and Change: Ethics and Values Explain to students that antitrust legislation used against corporations such as the Northern Securities Company continue to be effective in breaking monopolies. In 1974 the Department of Justice, in a successful suit against American Telephone and Telegraph (AT&T) under the antitrust laws, declared that the company's control of telephone service across the country constituted the kind of monopoly that had to be broken up. In 1983 AT&T lost its monopoly on long-distance service. (See p. 902.)

Photographer Carleton Watkins made an extensive record of life and development on the Pacific Coast. He was probably the first person to take pictures of Yosemite Valley. This one was made in the 1860s.

The works of painters and photographers sparked tourist interest in the Far West. In the 1880s the Denver & Rio Grande advertised the beauty of its route across the continent.

conserve water for irrigation. Vast stretches of arid lands in the West were once worth just a cent or two an acre because they were good only for cattle grazing. Now they were worth hundreds of dollars an acre for growing crops.

In 1891 Congress had given the President power over "public lands wholly or in part covered with timber." He could set them apart as forest reserves. Presidents Harrison, Cleveland, and McKinley had set aside 50 million acres. Now Roosevelt increased the number of national forests to 149 totaling over 190 million acres, an area equal to Great Britain and France combined.

TR also withdrew from sale millions of acres of public land having waterpower sites and deposits of coal, oil, and phosphates. He took steps to prevent illegal use of the public lands by lumber companies and cattle raisers. He transferred forests from the Public Land Office to the United States Forest Service, headed by his enthusiastic supporter, Gifford Pinchot. For Pinchot, "conservation" meant scientific land management. So he planned "reforesting"—the planting of trees—to go along with the cutting of trees. He saw the nation's forests as a living resource that always had to be renewed.

The panic of 1907. In the summer of 1907, when prices fell sharply on Wall Street, a number of banks and businesses failed. Some newspapers blamed Roosevelt. Even many of his supporters urged him to "go slow" against the large corporations. Roosevelt did not relax his efforts for reform.

But he was willing to compromise. He agreed

Critical Thinking Activity: Determining Relevance How did Roosevelt implement his "square deal"? Ask students to list on the chalkboard some of TR's reforms that would ensure a "square deal" for all Americans (resolution of the coal miners' strike, the dissolution of the Northern Securities Company, the passing of the Pure Food and Drug Act, and so on). Then have students list some social reforms that have taken place within their lifetimes that have helped to ensure a "square deal" for all Americans today.

German-born Albert Bierstadt, who went west as early as 1858, was renowned for his heroic canvases of natural subjects. Here he painted the giant redwoods and the native Indians.

Author-naturalist John Muir was a leader in the drive to make Yosemite a national park. He also helped to persuade Theodore Roosevelt of the importance of conserving forest land.

when J. P. Morgan explained the need for United States Steel to purchase its largest competitor. The Tennessee Coal and Iron Company was near collapse. Without making "any binding promise" not to prosecute under the antitrust laws, TR told Morgan to go ahead.

Further efforts for reform. Prosperity soon returned. Then Roosevelt's messages to Congress in December 1907 and January 1908 called for still more reforms. On his list were income and inheritance taxes, federal rules for the stock market, limits on the use of labor in-

junctions, and more effective control of business. The panic, he insisted, had been caused not by enforcement of the law but by the corporations' refusal to obey the law.

Roosevelt's interest in social reform and his outspoken attacks on "predatory wealth" led conservatives to call him a socialist. But he really had no sympathy with socialist doctrine. He did not believe in public ownership of the means of production and distribution. His large purpose, he said, was to "avoid the extremes of swollen fortunes and grinding poverty." He believed in capitalism, but he wanted to make it

See "Lesson Plan," p. 520C for **Writing Process Activity: Demonstrating Reasoned Judgment** relating to the presidency of Theodore Roosevelt.

benefit all the people. Always the reformer, he hoped to save the United States he knew by making capitalism work.

See "Section 1 Review answers," p. 520C.

Section 1 Review

1. Identify or explain: holding company, Alton B. Parker, Hepburn Act, Upton Sinclair.
2. What role did Theodore Roosevelt play in the coal strike of 1902?
3. What measures were passed to provide (a) improved transportation regulation, (b) consumer protection, (c) accident insurance, (d) conservation of resources?
4. **Critical Thinking: Checking Consistency.** Theodore Roosevelt believed that a President should lead. Were his actions consistent with his beliefs? Explain.

See "Lesson Plan," p. 520C.

2. Middle-class reformers

The movement Theodore Roosevelt led was broad and deep. It reached out to states and cities across the nation.

The main centers were medium-sized cities and small towns. Support came from doctors, lawyers, ministers, small-business owners, merchants, white-collar workers, social critics, and intellectuals. Mostly Americans of old families, they had been disturbed by the strife and violence of the 1890s. They disliked the city political bosses and distrusted the great business corporations. They wanted to help the poor and the needy.

The Progressives no longer believed it was good enough for the government to be only an ✻ umpire. Even in a democracy, the powers of a citizen and a corporation were not equal. In the 1900s more and more Americans expected their government to be their guardian.

Reform in the cities. Beginning in 1889, reform mayors were elected in many cities. But bosses soon took over again. Still, some reformers managed to stay in office. Among them were some wealthy business leaders. For example, Hazen S. Pingree brought good government to Detroit. And there was Toledo's colorful Samuel M. "Golden Rule" Jones. He said, "I don't want to rule anybody, each individual must rule himself." Jones had already given his factory workers unusual benefits when he entered politics. Angered by his early reforms, the Republican machine dropped him as their candidate for mayor. But he easily won reelection as an independent.

In some cities the reform movements petered out. And then the old political machines would return to power. To prevent this, some reformers changed the form of city government. Under one plan, first used in 1900 in Galveston, Texas, the mayor and city council were replaced by a small commission usually elected on a nonpartisan ballot. Each of its members ran a city department. The commission passed laws and decided policies for the city. By 1912 more than 200 cities were using the commission plan.

Many more cities turned to a city manager. On the model of other large businesses, a ✂ trained manager was hired to run the city. A (p. 529) small council set the policies, and the manager carried them out. The manager was not a politician. The city manager system was most successful in small cities. It was harder to find skilled managers for big cities as well as more difficult to keep politics out. So, though city managers still run some large cities, among them the old mayor-council form of government is most common today.

State government reform. Reformers in the cities soon found that to reach their goals they had to reform the state governments, too. The earliest and ablest of the reform governors was Robert M. La Follette. In 1900 the people of Wisconsin elected "Battling Bob." After fierce fights he brought the state legislature under his control. And in his three terms it enacted a wide range of "Progressive" measures. The direct primary gave the voters the right to choose the candidates for public office. A commission was formed to control railroad rates. A competitive civil service was set up. Restrictions were put

✻ See "Lesson Plan," p. 520C for **Cooperative Learning Activity: Recognizing Ideologies** relating to the Progressive movement.

on lobbying. Laws were passed for conservation, for supervision of state banks, and for higher taxes on corporations. TR later called Wisconsin "a laboratory for democracy," and other states followed its lead.

By 1912 three-fourths of the states had passed child-labor laws barring the employment of young children and regulating the working hours of all young people. Workmen's compensation laws made the employer pay for injuries caused by defective machinery or dangerous tasks. In many states compulsory insurance systems created funds for the sick, the disabled, and the aged. In 1912 Massachusetts passed the first minimum-wage law for women. Other states regulated women's hours and conditions of work. State after state outlawed intoxicating liquors. By the beginning of World War I, 26 states were "dry."

The reformers changed the tax laws to put a heavier burden on the rich. New charges were laid upon the profits of corporations, on the inheritance of fortunes, and on large incomes. At the same time most states formed railroad and public utility commissions to keep down rates and keep up the quality of services.

Direct democracy and women's suffrage.

Enrichment Support File Topic

Time after time the efforts of the reformers were blocked by political bosses and "the special interests." So the Progressives looked for ways to break their power. If the people's representatives would not respond to the calls for reform, let the voters themselves play a more direct role.

The reformers started with the ballot. In most states voters were still using colored ballots printed by the parties (p. 227). Reformers felt that if voting was made truly secret, elections would be more honest, and better representatives would be elected. Political bosses would no longer be able to tell by the color of a ballot which way a person voted. In 1888 Massachusetts became the first state to print and distribute ballots containing the names of all those running for office. The secret ballot was soon adopted by most of the states.

But the secret, or Australian, ballot (named for its place of origin) did not break the power of the political bosses. The Progressive reformers then tried to give the voters the right to choose the party candidates for public office. The *direct primary* might break the power of party bosses to dictate who would run. Mississippi in 1902

"Battling Bob" La Follette and his wife, Belle Case La Follette, were vigorous battlers for reform. She influenced many as a magazine editor, speaker, and organizer. He served as the Progressive governor of Wisconsin, as a U. S. Senator, and ran for President in 1924.

State Historical Society of Wisconsin

State Historical Society of Wisconsin

More from Boorstin: "'Reform school,' an American expression which implied a special attitude toward young offenders, had come into the language by 1859; and there developed a new branch of criminology, new institutions, and a new literature of 'juvenile delinquency.' In 1899 Illinois enacted the first 'juvenile court' law (incidentally introducing another Americanism), and by 1912 twenty-two states had established juvenile courts." (From *The Americans: The Democratic Experience*)

and Wisconsin the next year led the way. In some southern states, however, the Democrats said their party was a private club open only to white voters (p. 646). It would be many years before the Supreme Court outlawed this barrier to black voters.

A second reform was direct election of United States Senators. But the "rich man's club," as the Senate was called, blocked the proposal time after time. Oregon in 1904 began to allow voters to name their choice. Then the legislature "elected" the person so chosen. By 1910 more than enough states to ratify an amendment were electing their senators this way. So at last the Senate gave in. The Seventeenth Amendment, ratified in 1913, took the election of senators away from the state legislatures and gave it to the voters.

The reformers found two other ways to deal with balky lawmakers. The *initiative* allowed 5 to 8 percent of the voters to "initiate" or start a bill by petition. In some states the bill was then put on the ballot for the voters to pass or defeat in a *referendum*. In other states there would be a referendum only if the legislature failed to pass the bill by a certain time. South Dakota in 1898 was the first of about 20 states to adopt these two measures.

A dozen states and many cities and counties adopted the *recall*. By petition, voters could force an official to stand for reelection at any time.

Perspectives Topic Some Progressives took up the cause of women's suffrage. They thought women would be more inclined than men to support reform legislation. By 1896 four western states had granted women full voting rights (p. 446). Between 1910 and 1914 seven more states—all west of the Mississippi—granted women the ballot.

The muckrakers. With reform politicians came reform journalists and novelists. Roosevelt called them "muckrakers," and the name stuck. He compared them to the man in John Bunyan's *Pilgrim's Progress* who was so busy raking the filth on the ground that he never lifted his eyes to heaven.

The muckrakers looked everywhere—in government, in Wall Street, in labor unions, in the trusts—for crime and corruption. Where they couldn't find a crime they might invent one. The new speed presses and cheap paper carried their message in the new daily newspapers and mass magazines to millions in the cities. Rural free delivery of mail took the word to remote farms.

The great wave of muckraking began in October 1902 when *McClure's Magazine* carried "Tweed Days in St. Louis." The author of this exposé was the young Lincoln Steffens, one of the most fearless journalists of modern times. He was the pioneer investigating reporter. He wrote articles on misgovernment in the cities. Later he brought them together in his book *The Shame of the Cities* (1904).

The clever Ida Tarbell published her angry attack on the Standard Oil Company. Her father believed that Rockefeller had ruined him and had driven his partner to suicide. Since she had

This photograph of Ida Tarbell was taken in 1904, when her *History of the Standard Oil Company* caused a sensation. Her exposé had first appeared in nineteen installments in the popular *McClure's Magazine*.

Culver Pictures

✂ Critical Thinking Activity: Expressing Problems Clearly How were the cities reformed? Have students construct a list of reforms that changed the face of the cities. Ask students to examine their own town or city today and recommend some reforms. Divide the class into small groups. Assign each group a reform. The students are to describe the reform, who and what it would address, and the anticipated outcomes of the reform. Have groups present their proposals to the class. How closely related are their reforms to those from the Progressive Era?

Lewis Hine was hired in 1908 by the National Child Labor Committee to travel the country to record the plight of child laborers. In 1911 he photographed this young cotton mill spinner in Virginia.

spent five years collecting materials for her articles, she was well armed with facts. Then she wrote about the Standard Oil Company not as a business enterprise but as Public Enemy Number One.

A new force—media power—had entered American politics. To read the shocking stories, true, half-true, and sometimes false, readers flocked to *McClure's*. Other mass magazines, like *Munsey's*, *Cosmopolitan*, and *Everybody's* went into this profitable business of exposing evil. Finley Peter Dunne's witty and philosophical newspaper character "Mr. Dooley" complained that whatever magazine he picked up he always got this one message: "Ivrything has gone wrong."

But the muckrakers' message got through. Within six years after Steffens's *The Shame of*

the Cities, reform movements appeared in Philadelphia, Chicago, Kansas City, Minneapolis, Los Angeles, and San Francisco.

The muckrakers wrote some sensational and persuasive novels, which we can still enjoy. Frank Norris wrote about the powerful railroads in California (*The Octopus*, 1901) and the wheat exchange in Chicago (*The Pit*, 1903). Theodore Dreiser used muckraking themes for novels which outlived the Progressive Era. His books were epics of wealth, power, success— and poverty. *The Financier* (1912), *The Titan* (1914), and *An American Tragedy* (1925) became classics.

Painters, too, found a way to join the muckrakers. A new "ashcan school" of artists chose some unusual subjects. John Sloan, George Luks, Robert Henri, and others filled the re-

Multicultural Connection: Narciso General Gonzales was a famous reporter. In 1891, Gonzales founded *The State,* an outstanding newspaper. In his editorials, Gonzales denounced the lynching of African Americans, child labor, and governmental corruption. When South Carolina Lieutenant Governor Jim Tillman ran for governor in 1902, Gonzales exposed his corruption and Tillman lost the election. Six months later, in front of many witnesses, Tillman shot Gonzales. He died four days later. The jury found Tillman innocent, finding the shooting justifiable since Gonzales had hurt his reputation.

The Museum of the City of New York

 Jacob Riis made this shot of New York waifs between 1880 and 1910.

(p. 530)

spectable galleries with high-priced canvases showing alleys and tenements. The bold Danish immigrant photographer, Jacob Riis, published shocking pictures of starving children in garbage-ridden slums.

Social workers, sociologists, and historians also did their bit for reform. John Spargo described the horrors of child labor in *The Bitter Cry of the Children* (1906). Gustavus Myers made his *History of the Great American Fortunes* (1909) a rogues' gallery of crooks. Ray Stannard Baker told the story of racial discrimination in *Following the Color Line* (1908). Burton J. Hendrick's disclosures in *Story of Life Insurance* (1907) led to laws regulating New York's large insurance companies.

See "Section 2 Review answers," p. 520D.

Section 2 Review

1. Identify or explain: commission plan, Robert La Follette, direct primary, initiative, referendum, recall, Lincoln Steffens, Ida Tarbell, Frank Norris, "ashcan school," Jacob Riis.

2. How did reformers try to improve city government?

3. Name some state reforms designed (a) to improve government, (b) to regulate business, (c) to aid workers, (d) to help the needy.

4. **Critical Thinking: Identifying Assumptions.** How did the "muckrakers'" attitudes about government affect their reform efforts?

Continuity and Change: Ethics and Values Point out to students that "muckrakers," through their books, continued to heighten public awareness and, in that way, brought about reform. For example, Rachel Carson's *Silent Spring* (1962) resulted in legislation to curb pollution and help protect the environment. Ralph Nader's *Unsafe at Any Speed* (1965) spurred Congress to pass the Highway Safety Act in 1966, which set safety standards for new cars and tires. (See p. 802.)

See "Lesson Plan," p. 520D.

3. Taft in the White House

Theodore Roosevelt had said that he would not run for a third term. His hand-picked successor was his Secretary of War—the jovial 300-pound William Howard Taft. The Republicans in Chicago in June 1908 chose Taft on the first ballot. The Democrats, meeting at Denver, decided to try again with William Jennings Bryan.

Taft won by over a million votes and an electoral vote of 321 to 162. But the election was more an endorsement for Roosevelt's candidate and policies than it was for the Republican party. The Democrats gained new strength from farmers and from workers organized in unions. Several states that voted for Taft elected Democratic governors. The Republicans also lost seats in the House, but they still retained control.

The new President. William Howard Taft took office on March 4, 1909. He was a comforting and comfortable man. But he was no cowboy and no crusader. He had served as United States Solicitor General and as a federal judge. As governor of the Philippines he had brought reforms without stirring up resentment. TR had appointed him Secretary of War, but he had never before been elected to office. Besides being a proven administrator, he was a learned and successful lawyer. By temperament and training he was deliberate and cautious. He was a huge man. And the movement of his mind was as sedate as his walk. He faced public issues like a judge weighing arguments. And he always preferred to postpone a decision rather than risk error or haste.

Naturally enough, Taft was troubled by the new schemes of "direct democracy" that were being pushed by the reformers. Wise legislation, he thought, should always be preceded by careful, time-consuming study. He favored the slow, dignified methods of courtrooms. He feared demagogues—lawmakers who would gratify popular prejudice to stay in office.

Taft disappoints the reformers. The tariff was a troublesome issue. A high tariff, which protected some American industries and their

The Huntington Library, San Marino, California

Theodore Roosevelt scores by getting rotund Taft the nomination in 1908. Notice that basketball was played with a closed basket.

workers, raised prices for all consumers. The tariff issue had plagued many Presidents. Somehow it had been avoided by TR. In the Republican party platform of 1908 Taft and Roosevelt had inserted an ambiguous plank. It promised "substantial revision" of the existing Dingley tariff, which had stood unchanged for a dozen years.

Soon after taking the oath of office, Taft boldly called a special session of Congress to revise the tariff. People expected something dramatic. A bill that began in the House added items to the free list and lowered many duties. But the Senate, led by Nelson W. Aldrich of Rhode Island, revised the bill out of all recognition. What finally emerged hardly lowered duties below the level of the Dingley tariff.

This Payne-Aldrich tariff was a plain betrayal of party pledges. Yet Taft signed the bill without protest. To make matters worse, he soon called it the "best tariff ever passed by the Republican party." The press was filled with fiery editorials on the "hoax" of tariff revision. Progressives everywhere were beginning to wonder what kind of a President they had elected.

Taft lost what was left of Progressive support by a scandal in the sale of public land. During the summer of 1909 an argument arose between Gifford Pinchot, Chief of the Forest Service, and Richard A. Ballinger, Taft's Secretary of the Interior. In a sale of government coal lands in Alaska to a group controlled by J. P. Morgan and Daniel Guggenheim, Ballinger was accused of favoritism. Taft stood by Ballinger. When Pinchot kept on fighting, Taft fired him—even though Taft knew this would anger conservationists and especially Theodore Roosevelt.

The "insurgent" revolt. The Progressives sympathized with Pinchot. The Ballinger-Pinchot affair and the Payne-Aldrich tariff persuaded them that Taft was a "tool of the interests." They decided to become "insurgents" and strike out on their own. First they attacked the "stand pat" Speaker of the House, Joseph G. Cannon of Illinois. He appointed the Rules Committee where he was chairman. The committee decided whether a bill would be considered and even had the power to put bills "on the shelf." This made Cannon dictator of the House. Now the angry insurgents managed to strip him of his power. In the future, members of the Rules Committee would be elected by the House, and the Speaker would not be allowed to serve on the committee.

When Taft asked for a new act to increase the power of the Interstate Commerce Commission over railroads, the insurgents moved to make the act even stronger. By the Mann-Elkins Act (1910) they extended the ICC's powers to cover telephone, telegraph, cable, and wireless companies.

The royal progress of Theodore Roosevelt. As soon as Taft took the oath of office, Roosevelt sailed for a long hunting trip in East Africa. He was now a private citizen for the first time in twenty years. He wanted to avoid any sign of his wishing to control Taft.

When Roosevelt "emerged from the jungle" in the spring of 1910, he held the spotlight of the

Library of Congress

New York's docks were booming about 1900. Dockworkers and shipowners hoped lower tariffs would make ports even busier.

whole Western world. His progress from Egypt through Italy, Austria, Germany, France, Holland, and England was a triumphal procession. When he landed at New York in June, he was welcomed by a huge cheering crowd.

Still only 51 years old, the vigorous TR was just not able to sit on the sidelines. And he did not like what was happening during Taft's Presidency. Pinchot had persuaded him that Taft ✄ was wrong in the Ballinger affair. Restless Roosevelt soon embarked on a nationwide speaking tour. He criticized Taft and praised the insurgents. In August, at the Kansas home of John Brown, he called upon the memory of the old fanatic who had given his life for freedom.

He announced his own reform program, which he called the "New Nationalism." Listing the Progressive reforms (and adding some), he called for strict regulation of large corporations and a real tariff revision. He wanted federal income and inheritance taxes, nationwide workmen's compensation laws, and publicity for gifts to political campaigns. He asked for more protection of women and children in industry,

✄ Critical Thinking Activity: Identifying Assumptions Did Roosevelt expect Taft to follow in his footsteps? Remind students that Roosevelt hand-picked Taft to be his Republican successor, and although Taft had been a part of Roosevelt's administration they proved to be very different leaders. Have students write a letter to William Howard Taft from Theodore Roosevelt, offering advice to the newly elected President on the duties of his office. What recommendations would Roosevelt offer Taft? What expectations would Roosevelt have of Taft?

for direct primaries, and for the initiative, referendum, and recall. It was a long list which included every one of Taft's hates.

The elections of 1910.

In the congressional elections of 1910, the splits within the Republican party produced an overwhelming Democratic victory. For the first time in eighteen years the Democrats were in control of the House. The Republican majority in the Senate was much reduced. With a dozen Progressive Republican insurgents in the Senate, Taft lacked effective support in either house of Congress. In the states, the Republicans lost eight governorships to the Democrats. In New Jersey the Democratic party elected the former president of Princeton University, Woodrow Wilson, as governor.

The Progressive Republican insurgents felt the time had come for them to take over the party. "Battling Bob" La Follette emerged as their strongest candidate for President in 1912. Some of TR's followers said they wanted him back in the White House again. Roosevelt said that he really did not want to run. But he loved a good fight. And Taft's policies had angered him—all the more because Taft had begun as TR's protégé. Taft had brought 45 indictments (criminal charges) against trusts. One was against U.S. Steel, during which Roosevelt's role in the company's takeover of Tennessee Coal and Iron came out. TR saw this as an attack on him. He still believed that the federal government should distinguish between bad and good trusts and should indict only the bad ones. Taft preferred to indict one and all, and then allow the courts to decide. Roosevelt was a man of strong dislikes, and for his own reasons, perhaps tinged with jealousy, he could not stand La Follette.

At first TR seemed to waver. But few people doubted that he really wanted to be President again. In February he announced that he would accept the nomination: "My hat is in the ring."

Taft versus Roosevelt.

Taft's administration had its varied successes. More jobs came under the civil service. Over a million acres of forest in the Appalachian Mountains became part of the national reserves. In addition, Taft saw to it that the federal government would keep the coal, oil, and other minerals beneath the surface of public lands sold to private buyers. The new parcel post service and postal savings bank would help people in small towns. The Department of Commerce and Labor became two separate departments. New Mexico and Arizona were admitted as states in 1912. Taft also sponsored the income-tax amendment, which would become the Sixteenth Amendment in 1913.

President Taft controlled the 1912 Republican convention in Chicago, and he wanted to be nominated. From some states the badly divided party sent opposing conservative and Progressive delegations. But nearly all disputes were decided in favor of the Taft loyalists. TR was counted out, and the convention nominated Taft.

TR and Hiram Johnson ran together in 1912.

University of Hartford: Museum of American Political Life

Many Progressives then walked out. Gathered in another hall, they condemned the convention as a "fraud." They urged TR to lead a new party. He did not need much persuading. The unreluctant TR plunged in with the slogan: "We stand at Armageddon, and we battle for the Lord."

A few weeks later the new Progressive party met again and nominated Roosevelt. With a crusading spirit, the delegates sang "The Battle Hymn of the Republic" and "Onward Christian Soldiers." TR was in his element. He loved the smell of battle. The platform declared that "the first task of the statesmanship of the day" was to destroy the "invisible government" of special privilege. Then they repeated the long list of Progressive demands. They favored more direct democracy, conservation, minimum wages for women, and an end to child labor. They demanded tariff revision and closer regulation of interstate commerce by expert commissions. When someone asked Roosevelt about his health, he said he was "strong as a Bull Moose." The Progressive party chose the Bull Moose for its symbol and set forth to "build a new and nobler commonwealth."

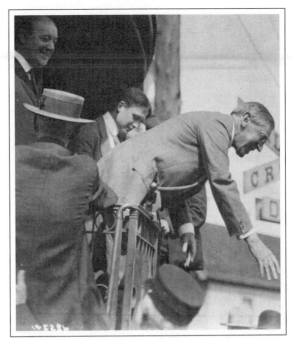

Culver Pictures

Campaigning by train in the days before air travel and television, Woodrow Wilson greeted the voters of Marion, Indiana, in 1912.

The election of 1912. The Democrats met at Baltimore. The split in the Republican ranks raised their hopes. But they faced a hard three-cornered fight for the nomination. Representative Oscar Underwood of Alabama had the support of the South. Champ Clark, the strong Speaker of the House, was backed by newspaper publisher William Randolph Hearst and other rich party members.

The third contender was a new face and an unlikely figure on the political scene. Scholarly Woodrow Wilson only two years before had been elected to his first political office, governor of New Jersey. His reform record there and his inspiring call for a moral revival of the nation had brought many delegates to his side. Clark had the most delegates when the convention began. Finally, with the support of William Jennings Bryan, Wilson won on the 46th ballot.

Like the Republicans, the Democrats called for conservation and banking and currency reform. The Republicans asked for mild revision of the tariff while the Democrats wanted much lower duties. The Republicans would only regulate the trusts. The Democrats wanted to break up all monopolies.

The campaign was really a battle between Roosevelt and Wilson. Taft had little popular support. Also on the fringe, with no chance to win, was the self-educated Eugene V. Debs, the colorful (and perpetual) Socialist candidate. He had organized railroad workers into unions. He called for public ownership of natural resources and the major industries.

Roosevelt and Wilson were both Progressives, but there was a distinct difference between them. Roosevelt called on the American people to realize that the country had entered a new age. Individualism and old-fashioned democracy, he said, would no longer work. An urban, industrial society needed a "New Nationalism." This meant a strong national government to

See "Lesson Plan," p. 520D for **Writing Process Activity: Making Comparisons** relating to the presidencies of Taft and Theodore Roosevelt.

regulate business and insure the well-being of the people. He offered a full program of social legislation—all the items in the Bull Moose platform.

Wilson had no such well-constructed program when he was nominated. During the campaign he worked out his own approach, which he called the "New Freedom." His program was more conservative and more traditional. He wanted the government to be only an umpire. He demanded that both business and labor be freed from control by monopolies. According to Wilson, Roosevelt's New Nationalism would put big business in control of the government. This would then enslave the ordinary worker. Wilson wanted to restore competition. He was for putting teeth into the Sherman Antitrust Act. He knew American history. With his preacherly eloquence, Wilson begged the nation to return to its traditions of individualism and open opportunity. The New Freedom, he hoped, would look after "the men on the make rather than the men who are already made."

When the votes were counted, it appeared that TR had split the Republican party. But he failed to divide the Democrats. Though Wilson received only 42 percent of the popular vote, he carried 40 of the 48 states. And he won four-fifths of the votes in the electoral college.

The election showed that an overwhelming majority of Americans really were Progressives in spirit. More than 10 million voted for Roosevelt and Wilson (who both favored Progressive reforms) while only 3.5 million voted for Taft. Debs received almost 1 million votes. Could Wilson now unite all Progressives behind his program?

Along with the Presidency, the Democrats won control of both houses of Congress. In all the decades since the election of James Buchanan, the Democrats had achieved such success only once before. They also elected governors in 21 of the 35 states where elections were held that year.

Taft cheerfully retired from the White House. A man of judicial temperament, he was more at home in a courtroom. What he really wanted was a seat on the Supreme Court. He finally reaped the reward for his troubled years in the White House. In 1921 President Harding appointed him Chief Justice. He presided over the Court until his death in 1930. He is still the only man to have been both President and Chief Justice.

See "Section 3 Review answers," p. 520D.

Section 3 Review

1. Identify or explain: Payne-Aldrich tariff, Gifford Pinchot, Richard Ballinger, "insurgents," Joseph Cannon, Mann-Elkins Act, Sixteenth Amendment, "Bull Moose" symbol, Eugene Debs.

2. How did Taft disappoint the reformers (a) on the tariff? (b) on conservation? What were some of his successes?

3. What steps led to the formation of the Progressive party? How did this party affect the election of 1912?

4. **Critical Thinking: Making Comparisons.** How did Wilson's "New Freedom" differ from Roosevelt's "New Nationalism"?

See "Lesson Plan," P. 520E.

4. Woodrow Wilson and the New Freedom

Woodrow Wilson's father was a Presbyterian minister. Born in Staunton, Virginia, Woodrow absorbed from his parents a devout, unbending spirit. He decided against becoming a minister himself, but in some ways he always thought and talked like one.

Like Theodore Roosevelt, Wilson was a literary President, the author of many books. In almost every other way he was TR's opposite. While TR's first book was on sea power, young Wilson wrote about moral questions for the North Carolina *Presbyterian*. While TR adored "The Strenuous Life," Wilson lived in the world of ideas, "longing to do immortal work." At the age when TR was out west learning to ride broncos and was hunting with cowboys, Wilson was sitting in political science classes at Johns Hopkins University in Baltimore. Though Wilson wrote a book called *Congressional Government*, he had never even bothered to make the short trip to Washington to see Congress in session.

Wilson was an indoor sort of man. After a brief career as a professor, he was chosen president of Princeton University. His educational reforms there won him national fame. They also angered the alumni and some of the faculty, so he was glad to be asked to run for governor of New Jersey in 1910. It was his success as governor—his only political experience—that brought him the nomination for President in 1912. He could inspire people in large groups or from the printed page. But face to face he was stiff and standoffish. He had trouble making close friends.

While Wilson had some of William Jennings Bryan's religious appeal, his tone was very different. Bryan sounded like a preacher at a country tent meeting. Wilson could have been the minister of the richest church in town. Both could persuade voters that they were joining the Army of the Lord. Wilson, like Bryan, championed the struggling farmers and underpaid workers. As a more moderate kind of Bryan, Wilson had a wider appeal.

A new dedication.

Woodrow Wilson set the tone for his Presidency on the day he took office. In his inaugural address he announced that he had come to Washington "to cleanse, to reconsider, to restore." Certain new laws were needed—tariff revision, currency and banking reform, breaking up the trusts. Beyond that, however, he had come "to lift everything that concerns our life as a Nation to the light that shines from the hearthfire of every man's conscience and vision of the right." Arriving at the White House was his moment of high dedication. He allowed no inaugural ball.

Wilson's kind of leadership was useful at this moment in the nation's history. He could both describe what needed to be done and then had the eloquence to rally people to the job. While he was riding the wave of Progressive reform, he could also enlist the enthusiasm of loyal Democrats. Their party had been out of office so long that now the Democrats in Congress were glad to follow Wilson. He would help them build a stronger party.

Library of Congress

Wilson and Taft rode together to Wilson's Inauguration in 1913.

Tariff reform.

Wilson immediately called a special session of Congress to enact his urgent program. Laws must be passed to break down the barriers to individual enterprise. In the recent past, Presidents had sent a written message to open each session of Congress. The message was then droned out by a clerk. Instead, Wilson made a ceremony of this occasion. He went to the Capitol and became the 📖 first President since Washington and Adams to deliver his address in person.

In a brief and forceful speech Wilson dramatized his personal leadership. At the same time he focused the nation's attention on Congress. He made it clear that it was the duty of Congress to take action. Instead of scattering his shots, in this address he spoke only of the reform of the tariff. It was not "free trade" that he desired, but free opportunity for American business. The proposed duties would provide some revenue for the Treasury but would not enrich industries that no longer needed tariff protection.

Representative Oscar W. Underwood, who had spent his life studying the tariff, worked closely with Wilson. The new tariff bill reduced duties about 11 percent from the Payne-Aldrich

📖 **More from Boorstin:** "Under President Wilson, something like the present formal and regular White House press conferences came into being. Although interrupted by the First World War, the institution was continued in one form or another by all presidents after him." (From *Hidden History*)

Act. To make up for the lost revenue, an income tax with low rates was included. As usual, there was a bitter fight in the Senate. Then Wilson stepped in to denounce the "insidious lobby" at work in Washington. The Senate began its own inquiry that revealed how the business interests of some senators affected their attitude toward the tariff. An aroused public opinion now helped clear the road for major cuts in the tariff rates. After months of wrangling, the Underwood-Simmons bill was signed into law on October 3, 1913. It was the first real tariff reform since the Civil War.

Currency and banking reform. Even before the tariff bill was passed, Wilson called for currency and banking reforms. There was wide agreement on the need to create a currency that would expand and contract as the economy

In 1909, when Scott Joplin, a leading composer of ragtime, wrote this dance music, Wall Street was already the financial heart of the nation. Ragtime, a precursor of jazz, was popular until about 1915.

Museum of the City of New York. The J. Clarence Davies Collection

required. Ever since the 1870s the money supply had failed to keep pace with the rising output of goods and services. And this had led to the calls for "cheap money."

The nation still had no banking system that could help a bank stop a "run" on its deposits. At the start of a business panic, most of the depositors might run to their bank to take out their money. But a bank keeps only a small cash reserve. For the bank to earn a profit, it must lend out most of its deposits. A "run" could force a bank to shut down in a few hours.

Bank "runs" in a number of places at the same time could start or worsen a panic. In addition to its small cash reserve, a bank would keep part of its required (legal) reserves in a big-city bank. And the big-city banks, in turn, kept part of their reserves in New York City banks. Thus much of the nation's deposit reserves tended to move to Wall Street, New York's financial district. The New York banks would lend large amounts "on call." This meant that the borrower had to repay the loan as soon as the bank called for its money. Many of the "on call" loans went to stock-market speculators. When small-city banks demanded their reserves, the big banks called in their loans. Then a wave of selling in the stock market—by the speculators to get money to repay their loans—caused further panic and "runs" on more banks.

The Progressive-Bryan faction wanted a system of reserve banks under federal control—that is, central banks that would hold part of the deposits (legal reserves) of the private banks. Conservative Democrats feared Bryan. To them Bryan always seemed radical. They also wanted a federal reserve system free from Wall Street control, but they wanted it to be owned and controlled by private interests. Wilson steered a middle course. Under his skillful prodding a compromise emerged. ✕

The Federal Reserve Act. The Federal Reserve Act was signed into law in December 1913. It divided the country into twelve districts, each with a Federal Reserve bank owned by the member banks. All were supervised by a Federal Reserve Board, whose members were appointed by the President. Every national bank had to

✕ Critical Thinking Activity: Making Comparisons How would today's President compare to Woodrow Wilson? This section begins by contrasting Wilson and Roosevelt—but how would our President today compare with Wilson? Have students identify categories useful to such as comparison, such as education, political career, hobbies, statesmanship, and so on. Using these categories, list the traits of Wilson and the current President. Have students summarize their comparison by formulating a hypothesis on common traits among Presidents.

become a member of the Federal Reserve System. Each subscribed some of its capital and surplus to form the capital of the reserve bank in its district.

These Federal Reserve banks were the central banks for their regions. They were the "bankers' banks." They held the member banks' reserves, lent money to a member bank when it was needed, and performed other services for the member banks. In case of a "run" on a bank, the member bank could pay its depositors by borrowing from the Federal Reserve bank. The "run" might not even start if the depositors believed that the bank could surely meet its obligations.

The Federal Reserve Act also created a flexible new national currency, *Federal Reserve notes.* These could be issued according to the needs of the business community.

This act provided a way to mobilize the banking reserves in time of panic. When bank withdrawals caused loans to be called in, threatening the closing of businesses and even of the banks themselves, the Federal Reserve banks could rush to the rescue. The Federal Reserve Act was a perfect example of the New Freedom. Private interests did the job, but the public supervised.

Regulating business. After the Federal Reserve Act became law in December, Wilson at last let the weary lawmakers go home for a month's recess. When they returned in January, he offered his program to regulate business. The Sherman Antitrust Act had been aimed at certain business practices that tended to limit competition. Wilson said that was not enough. He asked Congress for a law to break up monopolies.

"To supplement existing laws against unlawful restraints and monopolies," Congress passed the Clayton Antitrust Act of 1914. It prohibited one company from taking over the stock of another if it created a monopoly. It forbade anyone to serve as a director of two or more corporations when the effect was to lessen competition. This was to prevent "interlocking" directorates, like those used by J. P. Morgan & Co. The law exempted labor and farm groups

from prosecution as combinations in restraint of trade. But later court decisions undercut this exemption.

No law could spell out in advance all the unfair practices that wily businessmen might dream up. Then what should the government do? A Boston lawyer, Louis D. Brandeis, had made a reputation for fighting what he called "the curse of bigness." He helped Wilson with an answer. The law should not just outlaw unfair trade practices in general. It should set up a Federal Trade Commission with powers to stop any unfair practices whenever they occurred. This was more like TR's "New Nationalism" than the "New Freedom," but Wilson now decided he had no other choice. After a hard fight the Federal Trade Commission Act was passed in September 1914, and the federal government was committed to regulate business.

The Federal Trade Commission (FTC) had five members. Advised by experts from different industries, they drew up fair trade rules. When the FTC found a company engaging in a practice that was unfair or in restraint of trade, it could issue a "cease and desist" order. And if the company disobeyed, it was punished. The main purpose of the commission was to help individual businesses obey the law.

More Progressive legislation. With these measures, Wilson's reforms were complete. For a moment, he turned against further reforms and even blocked a bill that forbade child labor. The mid-term elections of 1914 brought some gains for the Republicans. But the Democrats kept control of Congress. Wilson saw that he must continue Progressive reforms if he was to be reelected in 1916. So he offered a new program. Much of what he asked for came from Roosevelt's "New Nationalism." In 1915 the La Follette Seamen's Act improved the quarters, food, and wages in the merchant marine. The following year several important laws were passed. A Federal Farm Loan Act provided farmers long-term loans at low interest rates. A child-labor law finally limited employment of young children in factories, mines, and quarries. And an eight-hour day was enacted for workers on the railroads.

President Wilson's first term showed the most far-reaching legislative program ever passed in a single administration. The Democrats, he boasted, had not only carried out their own platform. They had "come very near to carrying out the platform of the Progressive party."

See "Section 4 Review answers," p. 520E.

Section 4 Review

1. Identify or explain: Federal Reserve System, interlocking directorates, "cease and desist" orders, La Follette Seamen's Act, Federal Farm Loan Act.
2. How did the Underwood-Simmons bill reform the tariff?
3. What chief weakness of the banking system was the Federal Reserve Act designed to correct? How did the new law help solve the currency problem?
4. What kinds of business practices did the Clayton Act declare illegal?
5. How was the Federal Trade Commission supposed to promote fair business competition?
6. What other Progressive legislation did Congress enact in Wilson's first term?
7. **Critical Thinking: Making Comparisons.** How were Woodrow Wilson and Theodore Roosevelt alike? How were they different? Consider their backgrounds, experiences, and personal traits.

See "Lesson Plan," p. 520E.

5. Seeking a world role

Progressive leaders, who showed concern for the poor at home, sent the nation in search of power abroad. The United States played a new commanding part in Latin America.

TR and foreign affairs. Theodore Roosevelt had a clear view of the new role he wanted for the United States. Although he distrusted the power of large corporations, he loved power for the nation and for himself. He wanted the United States to hold the center of the world stage. For practical purposes he was his own Secretary of State. Though he never shrank from a good fight, he saw himself as a champion of peace. His motto was "Speak softly and carry a big stick." Still, he seemed to enjoy bellowing while waving his big stick at home and abroad.

He wanted this two-ocean nation to become a power on the sea. An enthusiastic disciple of Admiral Mahan, he wanted the United States to have a great navy. In the Spanish-American War we had only 5 battleships and 2 armored cruisers. Before Roosevelt left the White House in 1909, we had 25 battleships and 10 heavy cruisers. We had become, next to the British, the strongest naval power in the world.

The United States and the Far East. Events in the Far East offered TR a welcome chance to play the delicate game of power politics. Soon after he took office, the Russians began to move to control Manchuria. This was against our Open Door policy. But Roosevelt saw that there was little we could do to stop them.

In that part of the world Russia's great rival was Japan. When these two powers began to fight, Roosevelt drew the United States to the side of Japan. But Roosevelt did not want to see Russia driven out of the Far East, for Russia could keep the lid on Japan. Roosevelt aimed to insure a balance of power there. Only in that way, he thought, could China stay independent. So Roosevelt helped bring the Russo-Japanese War to a close before Japan could crush Russia. At Portsmouth, New Hampshire, the envoys of Russia and Japan met with him, and in August 1905 they announced the terms of peace. For this he was awarded the Nobel Peace Prize.

The peace had been won only by a bargain in which the United States, too, played a part. It was agreed that Japan would be allowed to annex Korea and to pursue its own interests in Manchuria. In return, Japan assured the United States that otherwise things would remain the same in the Pacific. Japan would not meddle with our colonies. The Root-Takahira Agreement of 1908 outlined these understandings.

Most Americans believed that all people should be allowed to govern themselves. They objected that in this pact we were bartering the

Multicultural Connection: On October 11, 1906, the San Francisco School Board segregated ninety-three Japanese children as a political ploy engineered by Mayor Schmitz to focus attention away from a possible investigation of graft within his administration. The resulting furor entangled President Theodore Roosevelt and the nation of Japan in the 1907–1908 Gentlemen's Agreement by which Japan agreed to stop emigration of laborers to the United States. (See also page 444.)

independence of others. They recalled George Washington's warnings against "entangling alliances." In fact, the agreement only recognized the existing situation.

Theodore Roosevelt was a realist. He was in favor of the Open Door policy as long as it could be maintained by diplomacy. But in Manchuria the Japanese were willing to risk war to get their way. He believed that the United States should take a firm stand only when it was in our national interest to fight for our position.

Roosevelt thought the United States should stay on good terms with Japan. But we should not let the Japanese think we were weak. In 1907 he sent around the world our navy's "great white fleet" of 16 battleships—chiefly to impress Japan.

Enrichment
Support
File Topic

The Panama Canal. In the Caribbean, TR would be more aggressive. For here he saw the vital interests of the United States. He thought that the United States should dominate the Caribbean. And he favored building an isthmian canal.

As a world power, the United States had to be able to move its navy speedily from one ocean to another. Besides the old reasons of commerce, this was an urgent new reason to cut a waterway through Central America.

For years Americans going westward had tried to find ways to shorten the voyage to California. When TR came to the White House, a French company had already been working on a canal for twenty years. They were plagued by tropical disease. And early in 1902 they agreed to sell their canal rights for $40 million. The United States still had to get a lease on the land for the canal route. It was in Colombia's province of Panama.

TR would let nothing stop him. First, Secretary of State John Hay drew up a treaty with an envoy from Colombia. We agreed to pay Colombia $10 million at once—and later, $250,000 a year. In 1903 the senate of Colombia balked. They wanted $20 million—and another $10 million from the French company.

Then suddenly a revolution broke out in Panama. A lucky coincidence for the United States! But there was evidence that the United States

Culver Pictures

Teddy Roosevelt, portrayed here wearing his Rough Rider uniform with his Nobel Prize in his pocket and his big stick handy, had grand ideas about his place among Presidents.

had helped start the revolt. And the United States Navy had prevented Colombian troops from landing to put it down. Quickly the new "independent" Republic of Panama made a treaty leasing the Canal Zone to the United States.

Work began in 1904 but halted the next year because the workers in the swamps came down with yellow fever. To build the canal, Americans first had to stop the sickness. Under the direction of Dr. William Gorgas, who had worked with Dr. Walter Reed in Cuba to prevent yellow fever, the breeding places of the mosquitoes that carried the disease were destroyed. Once the mosquitoes were gone, the battle against the disease was won. Gorgas made the canal possible—and helped conquer yellow fever around the world.

Work resumed in 1906, and within eight years ships were passing through the canal. The Panama Canal had cost more than a half-billion dollars, but its benefits were beyond measure.

"I took the Canal Zone and let Congress debate," TR later declared, "and while the debate goes on the canal does also." Wilson's Secretary of State, William Jennings Bryan, negotiated a new treaty with Colombia. The United States agreed to pay $25 million for the loss of Panama, with "sincere regret that anything should have occurred to mar the candid friendship" between the two nations. Roosevelt denounced the treaty as "a crime against the United States and an attack on its honor." The Senate rejected the treaty twice. In April 1921, after Roosevelt's death, the treaty was ratified by a Republican Senate with the expression of sincere regret left out!

The Roosevelt Corollary.

After the Panama Canal was opened, the United States worried about the governments in that neighborhood. When the Dominican Republic (formerly Santo Domingo) went bankrupt, European creditors threatened to use force to collect their money. Roosevelt then declared a new American policy. In his message to Congress in December 1904, he explained what the United States would do in case of the "chronic wrongdoing or impotence" of a Latin American state. He said that we were bound to intervene, "however reluctantly," and to "exercise our international police power."

With the consent of the president of the Dominican Republic, the United States took over the financial affairs of that country. Soon the debts were paid, and the creditors in Europe were then satisfied.

In the past the United States had told European powers not to interfere in the Americas.

Now TR declared that the United States would police a whole continent. Though nobody else was allowed to, forces of the United States might intervene in Latin America. The nation that had inspired the world by its Declaration of Independence now shook the world with a new declaration of intervention! This was the "Roosevelt Corollary" to the Monroe Doctrine. TR meant what he said, and later Presidents agreed. Under this policy, the United States would intervene—sometimes more than once—in the Dominican Republic, Cuba, Panama, Haiti, and Nicaragua.

The Algeciras Conference.

It seemed unlikely that the restless, aggressive TR could stay out of the international politics of Europe. France and Germany were on the point of war over control of Morocco. At first TR hesitated to do anything. Then "to keep matters on an even keel in Europe" he stepped in. He persuaded the two nations to attend a conference in 1906 at Algeciras, Spain. There United States delegates helped France and Germany come to a peaceful settlement. Could it be said anymore that America had a set of interests separate from those of Europe?

Foreign affairs under Taft.

TR never cared much about the economics of foreign affairs. Commerce was not nearly as dramatic as clashing navies or expanding boundaries. But for his successor, President Taft, money was the measure of diplomacy. "Dollar diplomacy"—the nickname for his foreign policies—meant using United States ambassadors (and armed forces) to promote business. Taft and his Secretary of State, Philander C. Knox, urged Americans to invest abroad to build American influence. Then our government would protect United States investors.

Taft pushed American bankers to invest in China. And there, as a response to Taft's dollar diplomacy, Japan and Russia enlarged their own spheres of interest.

"Dollar diplomacy" explained Taft's actions in Latin America, too. When civil war broke out in Nicaragua in 1912, United States Marines were sent in to protect American business interests.

Geography and History: Location Have students look at the map at the right. Ask: What islands belonged to the United States in 1933? (Puerto Rico and the Virgin Islands.) In which countries did the United States have financial supervision? (Nicaragua, Haiti, and the Dominican Republic.) What does the map inset show? (An enlargement of the Panama Canal Zone.) Why was the Canal Zone so important to the United States? (As a world power, the United States felt it should be able to move easily from one ocean to another.)

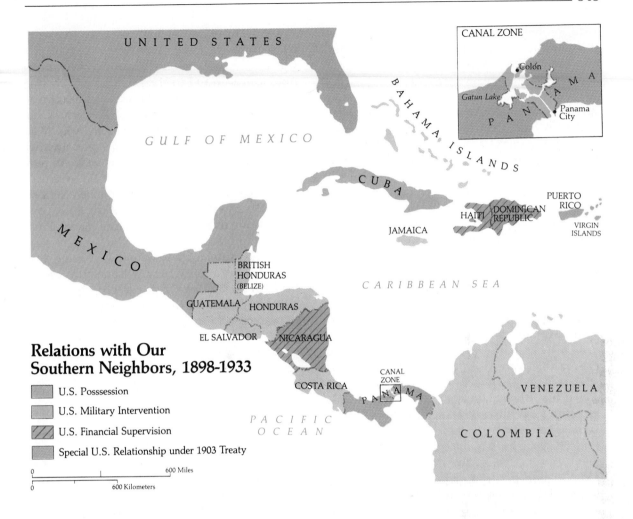

Relations with Our Southern Neighbors, 1898-1933

- U.S. Possession
- U.S. Military Intervention
- U.S. Financial Supervision
- Special U.S. Relationship under 1903 Treaty

0   600 Miles

0   600 Kilometers

While there, the marines supervised the national elections. A small detachment stayed until 1925. Latin Americans began to wonder whether the people of the United States had forgotten their own Declaration of Independence.

A "moral" foreign policy. President Wilson's first foreign policy test came in Mexico. Then and there he would set the moral tone that was to dominate his foreign policy.

Just before Wilson took office, a liberal government in Mexico, headed by Francisco Madero, had been overthrown by a cruel general, Victoriano Huerta. Madero was murdered while being taken to jail—probably on Huerta's orders.

Other Mexican revolutionaries opposed Huerta. But he controlled four-fifths of his country. Twenty foreign governments recognized Huerta as Mexico's president *de facto*. This meant that they did not judge whether Huerta's government was really legal. They only recognized that *in fact* he was in control.

Woodrow Wilson—the preacherly President—had other ideas. Formerly the United States had recognized *de facto* governments whenever they came to power. Now Wilson declared that he would not "extend the hand of welcome to anyone who obtains power in a sister republic by treachery and violence." He called upon Huerta to step down, and Huerta refused. Then Wilson ☑ turned to a policy of "watchful waiting."

Problems at Tampico and Veracruz. After a time Wilson plotted to force Huerta from power. He allowed arms to be sent to Huerta's chief

☑ See "Lesson Plan," p. 520F for **Writing Process Activity: Demonstrating Reasoned Judgment** relating to the foreign policies of Taft and TR.

rival, Venustiano Carranza. Soon a crisis arose. A shore party of American marines collecting supplies in Tampico, Mexico, was arrested and sent to jail. The marines were soon released and Huerta apologized, but he refused to fire a salute to the United States flag as we demanded.

On April 20, 1914, Wilson asked Congress to approve the use of armed force "to obtain from General Huerta the fullest recognition of the rights and dignity of the United States." The next day a wireless message came from the navy. It reported that a German steamer loaded with arms for Huerta was expected to dock at Veracruz in a few hours. So before Congress had even acted, the President ordered the seizure of the city to prevent their delivery. A detachment of marines was landed, and 19 Americans and 126 Mexicans were killed before the marines controlled the city. Mexicans—including Huerta's chief rival, Carranza—united against the United States, and it appeared that war was near.

The large republics of South America—Argentina, Brazil, and Chile, known as the ABC powers—now offered to mediate between the United States and Mexico. They recommended that Huerta give way to a provisional government. Huerta refused, but they had so undercut his position that he could no longer keep control. He stepped down in July, Carranza entered Mexico City in triumph, and in November Wilson withdrew American troops from Veracruz.

Chasing Pancho Villa. Still Wilson's Mexican troubles were not over. Carranza's most successful general was Pancho Villa, a former bandit and a brilliant cavalry leader. When Villa began a new revolt, civil war raged again. Villa's raiders killed people on both sides of the border. Finally, when he burned Columbus, New Mexico, in March 1916, many United States citizens were killed.

Wilson, with Carranza's reluctant permission, sent out General John J. Pershing and an expedition of 15,000 men to get Villa "dead or alive." The National Guard, 150,000 strong, was ordered to the border. A West Point graduate, Pershing had commanded cavalry against Chief Geronimo and had fought in the Spanish-American War and in the Philippines.

The pursuit of Villa and the mobilization of the National Guard soon showed how ill-prepared the United States was for war. Villa struck again in the United States, and another force of 8000 men was sent into Mexico in pursuit, only to end up in a clash with Carranza's forces. Once again war with Mexico seemed near. But by now the thunder of the great powers fighting in Europe put a bandit general in a new perspective. The United States might soon be drawn into a global conflict. Seeing this prospect, in January 1917 Wilson withdrew the forces from Mexico. With the entrance of the United States into World War I in April 1917, the Progressive Era would end.

See "Section 5 Review answers," p. 520F.

Section 5 Review

1. Identify or explain: Root-Takahira Agreement, "great white fleet," William Gorgas, Roosevelt Corollary, Algeciras Conference, Philander C. Knox, *de facto* recognition, Victoriano Huerta, Venustiano Carranza, Pancho Villa.

2. Locate: Manchuria, Panama Canal, Colombia, Dominican Republic, Morocco, Veracruz, ABC powers.

3. How did President Theodore Roosevelt try to advance the interests of the United States in the Far East?

4. Trace the steps leading to the construction of the Panama Canal and the political and economic settlement with Colombia.

5. Cite instances of Taft's "dollar diplomacy."

6. Why and how did the United States intervene in Mexican affairs in 1914 and 1916?

7. **Critical Thinking: Identifying Assumptions.** Why did President Roosevelt stretch the meaning of the Monroe Doctrine?

✂ Critical Thinking Activity: Recognizing Bias How would the Presidents of the Progressive Era have responded to today's foreign events? Bring a newspaper to class and read the headlines aloud. Have students identify those dealing with foreign affairs and list them on the chalkboard. Then ask students to describe how each President of the Progressive Era would have reacted to these events. Extend the activity by having students write a policy statement for Roosevelt, Taft, or Wilson on one of these items.

A Spark Ignites Europe

FOCUS

To introduce the lesson, ask students "What were the causes of World War I?" List their answers on the board. Then ask: What factors caused the United States to enter World War I? List the answers. Emphasize that these are two different historical events, and that students should keep the causes of them separate in their minds. For example, submarine warfare is not a cause of World War I, but is a cause of the American entry into the war.

Developing Vocabulary

The words listed in this chapter are essential terms for reading and understanding particular sections of the chapter. The page number after each term indicates the page of its first or most important appearance in the chapter. These terms are defined in the text Glossary (text pages 1000–1011).

neutrality (page 548); **mediation** (page 549); **international law** (page 550); **contraband** (page 550); **pacifism** (page 553).

INSTRUCT

Explain

Discuss with students why the United States did not get involved in World War I at the beginning of the hostilities.

❧ Cooperative Learning Activity

Recognizing Cause and Effect Divide the class into pairs and tell students that they will devise a diagram to show how one event led to another until the United States was drawn into World War I. Explain that partners are to use some design element, for example arrows, to show the cause-effect relationships described in Section 1 of Chapter 21. Have partners work together to plan the layout of the diagram, with one partner doing the drawing and recording the events. Have the other partner explain the completed diagram to the class.

Section Review Answers

Section 1, page 556

1. a) heir to the Austro-Hungarian throne, assassinated in Sarajevo on June 28, 1914, sparking World War I. b) the German ruler. c) small German submarines. d) British luxury liner torpedoed without warning by a German submarine on May 7, 1915. e) promises made by Germany in 1915 and 1916 after Americans had been killed by Germany's sinking of the *Arabic* and the *Sussex*. f) lost to Wilson in the election of 1916. g) Wilson's plan for ending World War I and ensuring future peace. 2. The Balkans, Sarajevo, Serbia, Belgrade, and Belgium are on the map on page 548. 3. After the Archduke's assassination, Austria-Hungary declared war on Serbia. Russia, Serbia's ally, began to mobilize for war. Fearing an attack from Russia and its ally France, Germany declared war on both and quickly struck France through neutral Belgium. Then England, which had a treaty with France, joined the war against Germany. 4. (a) Overseas trade made the United States vulnerable because both sides interfered with American overseas trade. Because trade with Britain grew while trade with Germany lessened, trade became a factor pushing the United States to side with Britain. (b) The preparedness program represented a move away from a resolve to avoid military involvement. (c) Submarine warfare produced violations of neutral rights and incidents in which the Germans looked like barbarians, pushing American sympathies further toward Britain and away from neutrality. (d) The Zimmerman note pushed Wilson to take the step of arming American merchant ships, and infuriated Americans. (e) Wilson cast the war as not just a fight for neutral rights but as a crusade for freedom and democracy. 5. Neutral ships were guaranteed "freedom of the seas," the right to continue trading with both of the warring sides. If one of the warring nations stopped a neutral ship, it was to do nothing but seize war materials. 6. Wilson wanted the United States to be a moral force in the world, not a military one. When Wilson finally decided that the United States had to enter the war, it was for a moral reason—to "make the world safe for democracy."

CLOSE

To conclude the lesson, ask: What do you think is the main reason the United States entered World War I? Be sure to justify your response. (Possibilities include: ties to Britain, atrocity stories about Germany, German submarine warfare, the Zimmerman note.)

Helping to Win the War

FOCUS

To introduce the lesson, ask students: Do you think technological advances in weaponry make it more difficult or easier to kill one's enemies? Why?

Developing Vocabulary

armistice (page 464)

Providing In-Depth Coverage

Perspectives on the War Effort at Home

In order to win a war, not only do the armed forces have to be organized and prepared, but so do the people at home. The chapter focuses on the supportive efforts on the home front which contributed to the war effort.

When the United States entered World War I, government intervention in public life was greatly increased, allowing the impressment of private boats, control over private businesses, and the draft. Though some felt that this greater government power was an attack on civil liberties, the majority of the population was infused with a strong sense of nationalism and war fever to such a degree that Americans were united behind a single purpose like never before.

For this chapter, *A History of the United States* as an instructional program provides two types of resources you can use to offer in-depth coverage of the war effort: the *student text* and the *Enrichment Support File*. A list of *Suggested Secondary Sources* is also provided. The chart below shows the topics that are covered in each.

THE STUDENT TEXT. Boorstin and Kelley's *A History of the United States* unfolds the chronology of events and the key players involved in the war effort on the home front.

AMERICAN HISTORY ENRICHMENT SUPPORT FILE. This collection of primary source readings and classroom activities reveals the ways in which Americans at home supported the war effort.

SUGGESTED SECONDARY SOURCES. This reference list of readings by well-known historians and other commentators provide an array of perspectives on the efforts at home to support the soldiers in the war overseas.

Locating Instructional Materials

Detailed lesson plans for teaching the home front as a mini-course or to study one or more elements of the war effort in depth are offered in the following areas: in the *student text*, see individual lesson plans at the beginning of each chapter; in the *Enrichment Support File*, see page 3. For readings beyond the student text, see *Suggested Secondary Sources* below.

IN-DEPTH COVERAGE ON THE WAR EFFORT AT HOME		
Student Text	**Enrichment Support File**	**Suggested Secondary Sources**
▪ Homefront, pp. 560–567 ▪ Financing the war, p. 563 ▪ Government control of business, p. 563–564 ▪ War Industries Board, pp. 564–565 ▪ Women and blacks in the work force, pp. 565–566 ▪ Nationalism and war fever, p. 566 ▪ Attack on civil liberties, pp. 566–567	▪ Lesson Suggestions ▪ Multimedia Resources ▪ Overview Essay/Liberty Bread and War Bonds: Supporting Our Soldiers in World War I ▪ Songs in American History/"Over There" ▪ Primary Sources in American History/Americans on the Home Front ▪ Art in American History/Posters of World War I ▪ Biography in American History/Bernard Baruch ▪ Simulation/Decision-Making: Taking Over the Railroads ▪ Making Connections	▪ *Historians on the Homefront: American Propagandists for the Great War* by George T. Blakely, pp. 34–56. ▪ *American Financing of World War I* by Charles Gilbert. ▪ *Over Here: The First World War and American Society* by David M. Kennedy, pp. 93–143.

Chapter 21
The United States and World War I

Identifying Chapter Materials

Objectives	Basic Instructional Materials	Extension Materials
1 A Spark Ignites Europe • Identify the reasons why the United States entered World War I.	**Annotated Teacher's Edition** • Lesson Plans, p. 546C **Instructional Support File** • Pre-Reading Activities, Unit 7, p. 29 • Skill Review Activity, Unit 7, p. 32 • Skill Application Activity, Unit 7, p. 33	**Documents of American History** • The First *Lusitania* Note, Vol. 2, p. 102 • The *Sussex* Affair, Vol. 2, p. 111 • Peace Without Victory, Vol. 2, p. 125 • The Zimmerman Note, Vol. 2, p. 128 • Wilson's Speech for Declaration of War Against Germany, Vol. 2, p. 128 • The Fourteen Points, Vol. 2, p. 137 **American History Transparencies** • Critical Thinking, p. F31
2 Helping to Win the War • Describe trench warfare and explain how United States forces were decisive in ending the war. • Explain the differences in battlefield tactics between World War I and World War II. • Describe the consequences of the Industrial Revolution on World War I.	**Annotated Teacher's Edition** • Lesson Plans, pp. 546C–546D	**Extension Activity** • War Poetry, Lesson Plans, p. 546D
3 The Home Front • Identify the measures that put the United States on a wartime footing in 1917. • Discuss Oliver Wendell Holmes's belief that certain constitutional rights may be suspended during the crisis of wartime.	**Annotated Teacher's Edition** • Lesson Plans, pp. 546D–546E	**Enrichment Support File** • Liberty Bread and War Bonds: Supporting Our Soldiers In World War I (See "In-Depth Coverage" at right.) **Suggested Secondary Sources** • See chart at right.
4 Losing the Peace • Understand why the United States Senate refused to approve the Treaty of Versailles. • Compare Woodrow Wilson's performance as President with that of Theodore Roosevelt.	**Annotated Teacher's Edition** • Lesson Plans, pp. 546E–546F **Instructional Support File** • Reading Activities, Unit 7, pp. 30–31 • Critical Thinking Activity, Unit 7, p. 34 • Chapter Test, pp. 35–38 • Additional Test Questions, Unit 7, pp. 39–42 • Unit 7 Test, pp. 43–46	**Documents of American History** • President Wilson's Exposition of the League of Nations to the Senate Committee on Foreign Relations, Vol. 2, p. 158 • The Defeat of the League of Nations, Vol. 2, p. 161 **American History Transparencies** • Time Lines, p. E23

Chapter 20 Review

See "Chapter Review answers," p. 520F.

Focusing on Ideas

1. What traits in the young TR showed up in President Theodore Roosevelt? Explain.

2. The text names or implies many business abuses. Which chiefly affected workers? Consumers? Business competitors? Were there other victims? Explain.

3. How did Roosevelt "carry a big stick" in both domestic and foreign affairs? Did he observe the first part of his motto "Speak softly"?

4. Why do many historians refer to the early 1900s as "the Progressive Era"?

Taking a Critical Look

1. **Recognizing Cause and Effect.** Why would reforms have been less likely to occur without the "muckrakers"?

2. **Demonstrating Reasoned Judgment.** Assume that United States intervention in the Dominican Republic in 1904 and in Nicaragua in 1912 helped those countries straighten out their economic and/or political affairs. Would the "good result" justify the action taken? Explain.

3. **Predicting Consequences.** Would a business climate of more vigorous competition have led to less severe or extensive abuses? Explain.

Your Region in History

1. **Geography.** Did any big city in your state or region experience major reform in the early 1900s? What were the results?

2. **Culture.** Examine the literary and journalistic writings of the "muckrakers." How do they describe your locality in the Progressive Era?

3. **Economics.** List some Progressive measures aimed at reforming business that the legislature of your state passed between 1900 and 1914.

Historical Facts and Figures

Formulating Hypotheses. Use the map below to help answer the following questions: (a) In which region did women have equal suffrage in 1919? (b) In which region did they have partial suffrage? (c) In which region did women have no statewide suffrage? (d) Develop a hypothesis that explains this regional difference. (e) Does the information in this chapter support your hypothesis?

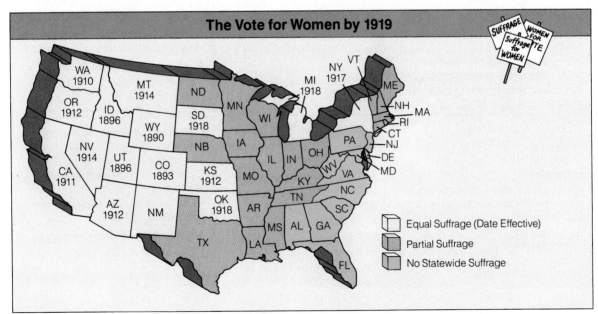

The Vote for Women by 1919

INSTRUCT

Explain

Review the situation of the war in 1917, before the arrival of United States troops. Refer to the map on page 557. Discuss why the entry of the United States was so pivotal.

☑ Writing Process Activity

Making Comparisons Ask students to imagine they are American soldiers in Europe during World War I. In preparation for writing a letter home about their experiences, ask them to cluster ideas about how warfare has changed them. They should begin their letters with a sentence summarizing their reactions, and they should support this main idea with vivid details about life in the trenches. Ask students to revise for logical organization and specific word choice. After proofreading, students can read their letters to the class.

Section Review Answers

Section 2, page 560

1. a) commanded the American army in Europe during World War I. b) the name given to the American forces fighting in Europe in World War I. c) a suspension of hostilities by mutual consent. 2. World War I involved more nations than earlier wars, and more people were killed in it than in any previous war. The use of submarines, chemical warfare, and trench warfare also made WW I especially brutal. 3. The AEF turned the tide by stopping the Germans from taking Paris and then advancing against the Germans. Thus they crushed German hopes of taking Paris and forced the Germans to surrender before American troops could make a difference.

CLOSE

To conclude the lesson, ask: How did the Industrial Revolution affect World War I? (It helped produce new, more efficient weapons.) Did the new weapons seem to help the soldiers fighting on the offensive or the defensive side more? (Defensive. Remind students that the efforts of technology in the Civil War were pointed out in Chapter 13, on pages 333–335. The effects of the rifle were devastating on ranks of men in the open, so soldiers learned to dig in.)

Extension Activity

To extend the lesson, conduct a class poetry reading using poems written about and during World War I. Have each student select a poem by one of the following authors: Rupert Brooke, Wilfred Owen, Joyce Kilmer, Alan Seeger, Siegfried Sassoon, John McCrae. Students will read the poems they have selected to the class.

Section 3 (pages 560–567)

The Home Front

FOCUS

To introduce the lesson, read aloud to the class the following statement of Justice Oliver Wendell Holmes on the need to curtail civil liberties in wartime: "When a nation is at war, many things that might be said in time of peace are such a hindrance to its effort that their utterance will not be endured . . . and no court could regard them as protected by any constitutional right." Have students give their opinions about this statement; encourage debate.

Developing Vocabulary

convoy (page 562); **civil liberties** (page 566).

INSTRUCT

Explain

Explain the constitutional basis for government's increased power during wartime.

✿ Cooperative Learning Activity

Checking Consistency Explain that students will work in groups of four to create a bulletin that might have been published by the Creel Committee in 1917. Have all group members decide what war news to include in their bulletin. Then have half of the members in each group write the news in a way that would enlist support for the United States war effort. Have the remaining members prepare the illustrations for the bulletin. Have groups exchange and read completed bulletins.

Section Review Answers

Section 3, page 567

1. a) (1917) put a military draft into effect. b) government bonds sold to raise money to finance the war. c) decided what goods to produce and to set the prices for goods purchased by the government. d) headed the War Industries Board. e) ran the Belgian War Relief program and the Food Administration office during World War I. f) created to arbitrate labor disputes and to prevent wartime strikes. g) a government organization created to "sell the war to America." h) chairman of the Committee on Public Information. i) imposed heavy penalties against anyone who gave information about any place connected with national defense and made it a crime to urge resistance to laws, refuse military duty, or hinder the draft. It gave the President powers of censorship. j) required American newspapers that were printed in a foreign language to give the Postmaster General an English translation of everything published about the

21

war. k) imposed penalties on anyone who used "disloyal, profane, scurrilous, or abusive" language about the United States government, flag, or uniform and allowed the Postmaster General to refuse to deliver mail to certain persons. l) Industrial Workers of the World. 2. Draft, National Guard brought into federal service, voluntary enlistment, mammoth ship-building program, impressing ships into service. Industry was mobilized through new government offices that were given dictatorial powers over the economy. 3. (a) rationing, shortages, price increases, and the desire to avoid anything associated with Germany; (b) higher prices and incentives to produce more enabled them to pay off their mortgages and improve their equipment. (c) Women workers were able to obtain jobs formerly held only by men. (d) Organized labor obtained government support of an eight-hour workday, protection against discharge of workers for union activities, and arbitration of disputes in return for promising not to strike. 4. The Espionage Act, Trading with the Enemy Act, and Sedition Act suppressed dissent and abridged freedom of press, speech, and assembly. 5. The government encouraged patriotism through propaganda and censorship. It created spy scares, hunts for traitors, and anti-German prejudice that outlasted the war.

CLOSE

To conclude the lesson, tell students that to raise money for World War I, the Treasury enlisted the help of famous personalities of the day, such as film stars, to sell "Liberty Bonds." These were known as "four-minute speakers." Have students write a brief, informal "speech" convincing listeners to buy bonds. After they have finished, ask some students to read their speeches aloud. (A very successful technique is to videotape the speeches for class presentation.)

Section 4 (pages 567–570)

Losing the Peace

FOCUS

To introduce the lesson, tell the class that historians rate Wilson among the great Presidents. Yet historians who point out Wilson's superior record as a reformer and wartime leader are also quick to list his weaknesses: too narrow an approach to right and wrong and a stubbornness that made compromise impossible. Have students list the accomplishments and failures of the Wilson administration and then compare his performance as President with that of Theodore Roosevelt. Who do they feel was more successful? Why?

Developing Vocabulary

treaty (page 567); reparations (page 568).

INSTRUCT

Explain

The Senate refused to approve the Treaty of Versailles because of opposition to Article 10 and because Wilson lacked influence in the Senate.

☑ Writing Process Activity

Identifying Central Issues Ask students to imagine they are members of the Senate in 1919. In preparation for delivering a speech opposing the League of Nations, students should brainstorm the reasons why the United States should not join. Have students begin their speech with a sentence summarizing their chief objections, and ask them to organize their support in order of importance. Students should revise for completeness and persuasive language. After proofreading to eliminate errors, students can deliver their speeches in a mock Senate hearing.

Section Review Answers

Section 4, page 570

1. a), b), c), d) At the Peace Conference in Paris, Woodrow Wilson, David Lloyd George, Prime Minister of Great Britain, Georges Clemenceau, Premier of France, and Vittorio Orlando, Premier of Italy, collectively known as the "Big Four," represented their countries. e) payments that the loser of a war is forced to make to the victor to repair the damage caused by a war. f) Republican senator from Kansas and a leader of the opposition to United States membership in the League of Nations. g) Republican senator from Massachusetts, another leader of the fight against American membership in the League. h) Republican candidate for President in 1920. 2. Wilson had snubbed the Republican party and the Senate when he chose the members of the Peace Commission to Paris, then refused to work out a compromise with Lodge. 3. Article 10; it pledged each nation in the League to respect and help preserve all the other members of the League against external aggressors. 4. The Allies in Europe; it was an opportunity for them to "punish" Germany for its aggression, and a chance to acquire land, power, and wealth.

CLOSE

To conclude the lesson, tell students that Wilson's physical breakdown was no surprise. During September 3–25, 1919 he delivered 40 speeches. Unable to sleep, the President experienced great fatigue and painful headaches. Finally ordered by his doctor to return to Washington, Wilson collapsed on the train, and suffered a stroke from which he never recovered. Wilson's Cabinet and his wife conducted the day-to-day business of the Presidency for the next year and a half. Ask: What would happen if a President became unable to fulfill the requirements of his office today?

Chapter Review Answers

Focusing on Ideas

1. "Soft" protests on British seizure of cargo; Wilson's insistence that Americans could travel on British ships and into the war zone; enormous trade with and loans to Allies. Norris pointed out that U.S. had kept its vessels out of the German zone, and could have embargoed both nations but did not. 2. Winners: organized labor; farmers (higher prices); women and blacks (job opportunities). 3. Speech, press, assembly; right to strike, rationing; loss of owner-control of certain businesses (railroads).

Taking a Critical Look

1. Some said German submarine warfare was necessary for defense. The moral issue appealed to Congress (to declare war) and to the nation. 2. Get bipartisan support during policy-making; attend to sensitive powerful leaders; consult with, not preach at, people whose support is needed; compromise negotiable points to achieve broad objective.

Your Region in History

1–3. Answers will vary depending on your region. Consult your local library or historical society.

Historical Facts and Figures

(a) Britain. (b) Russia. (c) U.S. spent the least and had the fewest casualties. (d) Nations with the heaviest losses in money/casualties would want comparable reparations. Yet given the key role played by the U.S. (without losses comparable to other nations), we must assume that other factors influenced the treaty-making process.

Answers to "Making Connections"

(See "Using Making Connections" on p. 572)

Answers will vary, but may include one or more of the following examples. Answers based on the time line callouts are in italics.

1. United States foreign policy was, in part, due to its business and economic interests. One book published in *1890—Alfred Mahan's* The Influence of Sea *Power Upon History*—makes this link. Many of the things Mahan called for came to pass due, in part, to the fact that Theodore Roosevelt and Assistant Secretary of State Lodge were Mahan followers. *In 1898, the Yellow Press called for war against Spain running the headline "Remember the Maine."* This was a clear linking of business and military as American firms had invested more than $50 million in Cuban sugar. Then *in 1900, Secretary of State John Hay announced the Open Door Policy in China.* This was an obvious attempt to position the United States as a major trading nation and to eliminate economic competitors who had set up exclusive "spheres of influence." Another example was the *1904 Roosevelt corollary to the Monroe Doctrine.* It declared that the United States would intervene in the Western Hemisphere in cases of wrong doing or impotence of a Latin American state. This corollary was invoked on a number of occasions such as *in 1912 when United States Marines were sent to Nicaragua to protect American business interests.* It could even be said that the United States was drawn toward the British side of World War I because trade with England and its allies was so extensive. 2. Many of the political and social forces that made the United States a world leader were the very same forces that linked the economic interests and foreign policy. For example, *Mahanism* and the *Yellow Press* led to *the Roosevelt Corollary, the Spanish-American War,* and *the sending of the marines to Nicaragua*—all events signaling the expanding power of the United States. 3. Theodore Roosevelt's position gave him a unique opportunity to affect legislation. *In 1897, he revived the Sherman Anti-Trust Act and pushed the Supreme Court to apply it to railroad monopolies.* He also used his position to get *other reform legislation passed*—the Meat Inspection Act, and *the Pure Food and Drug Act,* and the Newlands Reclamation Act. Reformers in less exalted positions did what they could to bring about reform. Painters known as the "ashcan school" and writers known as muckrakers wrote about the problems they saw. *One such muckraker, Ida Tarbell, published an exposé of Standard oil in McClure's Magazine.* Other reformers worked on making the government more responsive to the will of the people. Initiative, referendum, and recall all became tools of reform. The success of these reformers was reflected in *the passage of the Seventeenth Amendment in 1913 which provided for the direct election of senators.*

Chapter 21

The United States and World War I

The First World War began as an Old World war. Everything about it expressed the world that Americans hoped they had left behind. That Old World was a battlefield of national ambitions, religious persecutions, and language barriers. European armies had fought over whether a nation's boundary should be on one side or the other of a narrow river. Old World monarchs had

✖ transferred land from one flag to another, bartering people as if they were mere real estate.

In the 1800s the empires of Great Britain, France, and Germany had expanded over the whole world to the deserts and jungles of Africa, the high mountains of Asia, and the islands of the Pacific. Each empire sent out its own merchants and colonial settlers. Each built its strong navy to protect and police the ocean highways. Each built a vast army to guard the homeland and to suppress colonial uprisings anywhere on the globe.

At the same time in Europe national hopes had been growing and stirring up new conflicts. Ordinary citizens who had learned to read became proud of their own languages and their own national heroes. Daily newspapers now alerted citizens to their "national honor," awakened political hopes and ambitions, and nourished pride in the nation's exploits in faraway places. Kings and queens, princes and princesses, czars and czarinas—who were cousins and uncles and aunts—added their own family loves and hates to all the other reasons for peace or war.

Harvey Dunn, Army Center of Military History

In the trench warfare of World War I hundreds of thousands of men died fighting over small amounts of land. Harvey Dunn caught a sense of the bleak desperation of the soldiers in this painting.

See "Lesson Plan," p. 546C.

1. A spark ignites Europe

By 1914, a world war might have begun almost anywhere. It happened to be sparked in the most confused part of Europe. In the mountainous Balkans of southeastern Europe, small nations jostled and offended one another with their ancient feuds and jealous princes. For centuries these mini-nations had been dominated by Turkey, Russia, Austria, and other major powers. The word "Balkan," in fact, came to describe any community that was broken up into small warring groups.

We cannot be surprised that this was where World War I began. It started in Sarajevo, the capital of Bosnia, a small province of the old patchwork empire of Austria-Hungary. On June 28, 1914, Archduke Francis Ferdinand, heir to (p. 548) the Austro-Hungarian throne, and his wife were paying a state visit there. Suddenly they were shot down by a young Slavic nationalist from the little neighboring kingdom of Serbia. The Austro-Hungarian government blamed Serbia for not preventing the crime, and refused Serbia's offer to arbitrate the dispute. On July 28 Austria-Hungary declared war and bombarded Belgrade, the Serbian capital.

The powderkeg had exploded. Instantly Europe erupted into war. The elaborate system of alliances came into play. Russia, leader of the Slavic world, felt it must aid Serbia, so it began to mobilize. This brought Germany, allied with Austria-Hungary, onto the scene. Russia was allied with France. Germany had long feared that it might be squeezed by an attack from both Russia and France at the same time. So Germany decided to strike them first. On August 1, Germany declared war on Russia and two days later on France. Then Germany moved swiftly to destroy France before the slow-moving giant, Russia, could get into action. Germany, ignoring its treaty that "guaranteed" Belgian

Europe in 1914

- Allied Powers
- Central Powers
- Neutral

0 |———|———| 500 Miles
0 |———|———| 500 Kilometers

ATLANTIC OCEAN

NORWAY

SWEDEN

St. Petersburg

Moscow

NORTH SEA

BALTIC SEA

DENMARK

RUSSIAN EMPIRE

IRELAND

GREAT BRITAIN

London

NETH.

Berlin

GERMAN EMPIRE

BELG.

LUX.

Paris

FRANCE

SWITZERLAND

Vienna

AUSTRIA-HUNGARY

Belgrade

ROMANIA

BLACK SEA

PORTUGAL

Sarajevo

SERBIA

BULGARIA

MONTENEGRO

ALBANIA

Constantinople (Istanbul)

SPAIN

CORSICA

Rome

ITALY

ADRIATIC SEA

Ankara

MEDITERRANEAN SEA

SARDINIA

GREECE

TURKISH EMPIRE

SICILY

AEGEAN SEA

AFRICA

CRETE

CYPRUS (Br.)

---

neutrality, struck through Belgium into France. Now England, which had a defense agreement with France, plunged in against Germany. Then Bulgaria and Turkey joined the Central Powers—Germany and Austria-Hungary. Later, Japan and Italy came to the side of the Allies. By the time the war ended, in all of Europe only Norway, Sweden, Denmark, Holland, Spain, and Switzerland had remained neutral.

The United States struggles for neutrality. It is not surprising that Americans did not foresee the vast and tragic battle that would massacre millions, topple kings, and spark a half-dozen revolutions. They took it for granted that the bloody Civil War, fifty years in the past, was the last time many Americans would be called to battle. Americans of the Progressive Era tended to be optimistic and with good reason. The Spanish-American War had been only a mini-

🌐 **Geography and History: Location** Have students identify the neutral countries on the map above. (Spain, the Netherlands, Denmark, Norway, Sweden, and Switzerland.) Which neutral countries were bordered by both Allied and Central Powers? (Switzerland, and the Netherlands.) Which of the Powers had the largest land mass? (The Allied Powers—mainly because of Russia.) Why were the German Empire and Austria-Hungary called the Central Powers? (Because of their location between the Allied Powers—Great Britain, France, and Italy on the west, and the Russian Empire on the east.)

war. It made Theodore Roosevelt a hero but did not awaken the nation to the miseries of battle. The competition for markets waged by captains of industry seemed so much more sensible than shooting and killing. American leaders hoped that the United States would be a model for a world at peace.

At first Americans withdrew in shock when war broke out in the distant Balkans. What reason could there be for Americans to become involved? On August 4, 1914, President Wilson proclaimed the neutrality of the United States. Automaker Henry Ford chartered a Peace Ship. He sent it to the Scandinavian countries in a vain attempt to persuade them to mediate between the warring powers. Many Americans poked fun at what they thought was a foolish errand. The President called on all Americans to be impartial in thought as well as deed. That was not possible, even for Wilson.

Ties that bind. Most Americans, including the President, were drawn by powerful unseen forces toward the British cause. We spoke the English language and read the English classics. Our laws and customs were built on English foundations. We had fought an American Revolution to preserve our rights as Englishmen. Early in the war the British cut the transatlantic cable that brought news to the United States direct from Germany. After that, all news from Europe was channeled through England. This gave the British a great advantage that few Americans noticed.

There were millions of people in the United States who favored the Central Powers because

In 1915 automobile manufacturer Henry Ford sent a "Peace Ship" to Scandinavia in the hope of ending the war by Christmas. Women made up a large part of the delegation. Here Jane Addams of Hull House (second from left) and others hold up a large peace banner. Despite their good intentions, the venture failed.

Culver Pictures

they or their parents had been born in Germany, Austria, or Hungary. And there were more millions like the Irish who were glad to see anyone fight the British, because their own ancestors had suffered under British rule. But even some German Americans did not approve of Germany's actions. Kaiser Wilhelm had made so many warlike statements that many Americans saw Germany as a militaristic nation. Their feelings were confirmed when the kaiser's forces invaded Belgium and his prime minister called the German neutrality treaty with Belgium nothing but "a scrap of paper." The British circulated atrocity stories (some of them true) about how the invading German soldiers mistreated women and children in Belgium. Yet, until 1917 neither propaganda nor sentiment was strong enough to draw Americans to the battlefields of Europe.

The problem of neutral rights. There were great commercial advantages to staying out of the war. Over the years the nations of the world had agreed on a set of rules for the use of the seas. By these rules when a war broke out the neutral nations were still allowed to trade with both sides.

For more than a century the United States, far from Old World rivalries, had profited from being the great neutral commerce carrier of the world. In 1812 the nation had gone to war against Britain to protect its neutral rights on the sea. Again, in the 1900s, the United States would have to fight for the right to trade with the world.

Warring nations, by international law, were allowed to stop and inspect neutral vessels at sea. This was to make sure they were not ships of the enemy hiding under neutral flags. The warring nations were allowed to seize certain war materials ("contraband"—explosives, guns, and ammunition) even from a neutral ship. They were not supposed to seize other goods carried by neutrals. Before sinking a commercial ship, the attacker had to give warning, to see that the passengers were safe, and do everything else reasonable to save civilian lives.

Such rules as these were what people meant by *international law*. There was no court or police force to make nations obey. But the rules were still called "law" because so many people believed they ought to be obeyed. These special rights of neutrals were called the "freedom of the seas."

In 1914, when World War I broke out in Europe, these rules were still much the same as they had been for about 200 years. But the navies had changed. Most important was a new kind of ship—the submarine. Its great strength was the power to surprise. At the same time, however, it was thin-skinned and easy to sink. If it surfaced to warn a vessel, one shot from even a small "defensive" gun might send the submarine swiftly to the bottom.

To insist that all warring nations still had to follow the old rules would make the submarine useless. This would not have bothered Great Britain, who had the greatest navy in the world. But for Germany, with its smaller navy, submarines might make all the difference.

Great Britain intended to use its control of the seas to starve Germany into submission. The British government changed or interpreted the rules of war to suit its own needs. It enlarged the list of contraband to include all sorts of goods—even food!—that neutral ships had always been allowed to carry. The British insisted that all neutral ships go into British ports to be searched. They seized vessels bound for neutral countries, such as Holland or Denmark. This was to prevent the cargoes being resold to Germany. They declared the North Sea a military area and filled it with mines—underwater bombs that would explode when any ship came near. None of this was according to international law.

The United States protested. But since Wilson did not want war, he avoided making his language too strong. And when the language of the United States did become harsh, it was softened by our pro-British ambassador to London. Ambassador Walter Hines Page was convinced that the Allies must win to save Europe and the world from German domination. The British also wisely agreed to pay for all goods seized, so American merchants were not too concerned.

More from Boorstin: "[The growing sympathy for the Allied cause fostered support for Prohibition.] Among explanations for passage of national prohibition, we must include the wartime concern for conserving grain for food and chauvinistic feeling against the German-Americans who were prominent in brewing and distilling." (From *The Americans: The Democratic Experience*)

Germany unleashes its submarines. Germany could hardly sit still and allow itself to be strangled. Its submarines, however, could only do their deadly work if they, too, disobeyed international law. Germany therefore decided in 1915 to use its still-small fleet of 27 submarines for all they were worth and to let others worry about the rules.

On February 4, 1915, the Germans declared the waters around the British Isles a war zone. They warned neutral vessels against the danger of entering this zone in which their *Unterseeboote* (U-boats) would operate freely. The Germans advertised in American newspapers urging Americans not to travel on British ships.

Secretary of State Bryan wanted to keep Americans from doing so. But Wilson insisted that under international law Americans had the right to sail on any ships—even those of Great Britain. He warned Germany that it would be held strictly accountable for any loss of American ships or lives.

Great Britain took this moment to announce another violation of international law, which they said was necessary for British victory. Blockades were supposed to be carried out only by vessels stationed near the enemy's ports. Now Britain said it would seize vessels carrying goods for Germany wherever they were found. "Germany is like a man throttled with a gag,"

World War I brought a new horror—submarine warfare. In 1915, when a German submarine like this torpedoed the British liner *Lusitania*, 1198 passengers died.

Culver Pictures

First Lord of the Admiralty Winston Churchill declared. "You know the effect of such a gag. . . . The effort wears out the heart, and Germany knows it. This pressure shall not be relaxed until she gives in unconditionally."

Germany went ahead with its campaign of terror. On the afternoon of May 7, 1915, the British luxury liner *Lusitania* was torpedoed without warning off the coast of Ireland by the German submarine U-20. The ship went down in just 18 minutes taking with it 1198 men, women, and children including 128 Americans. The *Lusitania* tried to appear to be neutral by flying the American flag. Actually it was carrying 4200 cases of small-arms ammunition and 1250 shrapnel cases. Even so, according to international law that did not give Germany the right to sink the *Lusitania* without warning.

The Arabic and Sussex *pledges*. President Wilson sent a strong protest to Germany. He insisted on neutral rights. And he said this meant the right of Americans to travel wherever they pleased—even on the ships of fighting nations and right into the war zone. Wilson said this was a matter of national honor.

Many Americans, including an increasingly belligerent Theodore Roosevelt, now called for war. But Wilson resisted. "There is such a thing," he declared, "as a nation being so right it does not need to convince others by force that it is right." Secretary of State Bryan feared that Wilson's insistence on the right of Americans to travel into the war zone would draw the nation into war. He resigned in protest and was replaced by Robert Lansing.

The sinking of another British liner, the *Arabic*, brought the loss of two more American lives. Now Germany was faced with the danger that the United States might join the war on the side of the Allies. Since the Germans did not yet have enough U-boats to defeat Great Britain, they backed down. On September 1, 1915, the German ambassador in Washington made the so-called *Arabic* pledge by which Germany promised not to sink unarmed liners.

Then in March 1916 a German submarine sank the French channel steamer *Sussex*. Now there was another crisis between the United States and Germany. Once more, fearing American intervention, the German government gave a pledge—the *Sussex* pledge of May 31, 1916. Again they agreed to abide by the rules of visit and search. Germany insisted that the United States should compel Great Britain also to observe international law.

The Germans were right, of course, to demand that both sides play by the same rules. But the Germans were at a disadvantage. Submarine warfare, their trump card, was spectacular and openly took neutral lives. Britain's blockade, on the other hand, quietly starved the civilians of Germany and Austria. It took only the property of neutrals, not their lives.

Trade with the Allies. More and more the United States was drawn to the British side. Our trade with England and the Allies was enormous. We had become their storehouse—for munitions, food, and raw materials. And when the Allies could no longer pay for all the supplies, American bankers loaned them $2 billion. Secretary of State Bryan had protested that money was "the worst of all contrabands because it commands everything else." But if Bryan's policy of refusing loans to the Allies had been followed, the United States trade abroad would have ceased. This would have plunged the nation into a depression. President Wilson, who understood economics better than Bryan did, insisted on continuing our loans to the Allies.

During the early years of the war, in 1914–1916, American trade with Britain and its allies rocketed from $800 million to over $3 billion. At the same time, as a result of the British blockade, trade with Germany and its allies plummeted from nearly $170 million to about $1 million. It was plain where the nation's commercial interest lay.

Preparedness. At first Wilson opposed "preparedness"—which meant arming and organizing for war. He intended that the United States be not a military but a moral force. But the Republicans, led by Theodore Roosevelt, demanded that the nation be prepared to fight. To

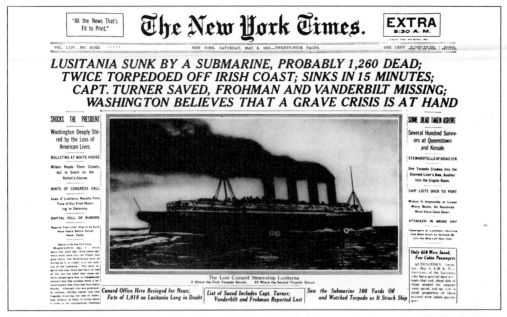

Of the 188 Americans aboard the *Lusitania*, 114 were lost. Among those drowned were the famous theatrical manager Charles Frohman and wealthy Alfred Gwynne Vanderbilt, a great grandson of Cornelius Vanderbilt.

avoid handing them a campaign issue in 1916, and to win votes himself, Wilson made preparedness his own cause.

In November 1915 the President called for a larger army and navy. Pacifists and farm-state Progressives like Bryan thought preparedness would only benefit big business and Wall Street. Wilson was forced to go to the people. Finally in the summer of 1916 part of his program was passed by Congress, and the United States was on the road to war.

Wilson knew that he could not win the coming election by the votes of Democrats alone. He needed support from at least some of the former Progressives. So in 1916 he garnered their votes by passing more reform legislation— much of it Roosevelt's New Nationalism (p. 535). "We are all Progressives," he now declared.

The campaign of 1916. When the Democrats met in St. Louis, they nominated Wilson by acclamation. Wilson was able to go to the country as a peace candidate. With a Progressive program enacted and "preparedness" under way,

he offered something for nearly everybody. The party slogan was, "He kept us out of war."

The tireless TR made still another try for the Republican nomination. But the Republicans had had enough of the old Bull Moose. In a world at war his aggressive, boyish spirit seemed risky in a President. Instead the Republicans chose the safe and sane Charles Evans Hughes. As governor of New York he had sponsored far-reaching labor and welfare laws. Since 1910 he had served on the United States Supreme Court.

Wilson conducted his own kind of front-porch campaign from his New Jersey summer home. He pointed to all the reforms passed during his first term and to his firm defense of American rights at sea. Hughes toured the country. He denounced the administration for its Mexican policy, its bungling diplomacy abroad, and its lack of a program. But the Republican candidate provided no clearcut alternatives.

Before midnight of election day, it looked as though Hughes had been elected. He went to bed confident that he would move into the White House. He had carried almost all the

A campaign truck in 1916 urges the reelection of Woodrow Wilson and Thomas R. Marshall. A vote for Wilson was a vote for "Peace with Honor."

northern states east of the Mississippi. The next day as the returns came in from the western states, the tide began to turn. When Wilson finally carried California by a slim margin, he was reelected by a small plurality and an electoral vote of 277 to 254. This was the closest race since the Hayes-Tilden campaign of 1876. This time the losing Republican candidate accepted the result without protest.

Still, the Republicans had increased their power in the Congress. They reduced the Democratic majorities in the Senate and in the House. Wilson's narrow victory had been made possible by the votes from the West of former Progressives. Except for Wilson's win, it was very much a Republican victory.

Wilson's efforts for peace. Taking his reelection as approval of his efforts for peace, Wilson again tried to stop the war. Twice before, in 1915 and 1916, he had sent his friend and adviser Colonel Edward House to Europe to try to arrange a peace. House became a mystery figure because no one knew how much power he really had. Anyway, he failed to persuade the warring nations to a compromise peace. And when Wilson tried once again in the winter of 1916–1917, he still found both sides bent on total victory. Wilson saw that the only hope for peace was for both sides to give up their dreams of conquest. On January 12, 1917, he called for "a peace without victory."

Nine days later Germany announced that it

was starting unlimited submarine warfare. The kaiser had now decided that he had enough submarines to starve England into submission. He was confident that even if the United States finally came into the war, it would be too late to save the Allies.

Wilson broke off diplomatic relations with Germany. He still hoped that by some miracle he could avoid sending American soldiers to Europe.

The Zimmermann note. One thing after another now carried the United States down the road to war. The German foreign minister, Arthur Zimmermann, sent a foolish message to the German ambassador in Mexico. Zimmermann asked Mexico to join the German side. In return Germany promised to help the Mexicans recapture from the United States all of Texas, Arizona, and New Mexico. The message was intercepted and decoded by the British. Then they eagerly relayed it to Woodrow Wilson.

On February 26, Wilson asked Congress for the power to arm American merchant ships to protect them against the German submarines. He also asked for authority to take other measures to protect American commerce. Few people objected to his proposal to arm merchant ships in self-defense. But it was quite another matter to grant the President power to wage an undeclared naval war.

To persuade Congress to give him these wider powers, Wilson published the Zimmermann note. A wave of anger swept the country, and the Armed Ship bill passed the House by 403 to 13. Still, a small group of farm-state Progressives in the Senate, led by Robert La Follette of Wisconsin, refused to be stampeded. This "little group of willful men," as Wilson called them, ✤ talked the bill to death in the closing days of the session.

The United States goes to war. Wilson did not wait for a new law to be passed. Instead he interpreted an old law so as to give him authority to arm American merchant ships. In his second inaugural address on March 4, 1917, he insisted that he was only preserving an "armed neutrality." The pace of events was now quickening. On March 15 a revolution in Russia drove Czar Nicholas from the throne. The very next day three American merchant vessels were sunk by German submarines with the loss of six lives.

Woodrow Wilson had won a second term with the slogan, "He kept us out of war." Now it seemed that, in spite of his hopes and promises, he could not insulate the nation from Old World rivalries. European conflicts had made the whole planet a single battlefield. On April 2, 1917, before a special session of Congress, he asked for a declaration of war against Germany. He no longer spoke merely about neutral rights. "The world," Wilson said, "must be made safe for democracy." Americans must fight "for the rights and liberties of small nations" and to "bring peace and safety to make the world itself at last free."

As usual, Wilson spoke eloquently of rights and liberties. He asked Americans to be soldiers of righteousness. But there was a good practical reason why the United States did not want to see the British lose. Americans had felt free to invest their nation's wealth in schools and factories and railroads, in a better life for all citizens. They had little need for large armies and navies like those that consumed the treasure of the warring nations of Europe. This had been possible because our two-ocean nation had the good luck to be protected by the great British navy.

As long as the friendly British ruled the waves, we could carry our cargoes and our people safely all over the world. The British, like the Americans, did not want to see other European nations build new empires in North and South America. The Monroe Doctrine had actually been enforced by the British navy. This arrangement was effective and economical. What would happen if imperial Germany drove the British from the sea? The United States would have to replace British sea power with a strong and costly navy of its own.

Wilson's dream. In January 1918, President Wilson went before Congress again—to explain the American program for the future of the world. He listed Fourteen Points. They were a

✤ See "Lesson Plan," p. 546C for **Cooperative Learning Activity: Recognizing Cause and Effect** relating to the causes of American involvement in World War I.

noble list that applied to the 1900s the ideals of the nation's founders. Secret diplomacy was to be abolished. All treaties would be "open covenants openly arrived at." The bright light of publicity would make rulers ashamed to trade away other people's lives and liberties. Freedom of the seas would be restored. National borders would be adjusted to allow all people to govern themselves. And there would be a League of Nations to preserve peace and insure justice.

The Fourteen Points impressed the world. They were a kind of Declaration of Democracy for the planet. They stirred the world more than any other American statement since the Emancipation Proclamation or the Declaration of Independence. They reminded Americans of the principles that gave life to their New World nation. But could they reshape the whole world?

President Wilson proved himself one of the greatest preachers in modern history. He lifted the spirits of Europe's battle worn, and he expressed the hopes of millions everywhere. But to make his dreams come true the eloquence of a preacher was not enough.

See "Section 1 Review answers," p. 546C.

Section 1 Review

1. Identify or explain: Archduke Francis Ferdinand, Kaiser Wilhelm, U-boats, *Lusitania, Arabic* and *Sussex* pledges, Charles Evans Hughes, Fourteen Points.

2. Locate: Balkans, Sarajevo, Serbia, Belgrade, Belgium.

3. Trace the development of World War I from Sarajevo to the entrance of Great Britain into the war.

4. How did each of the following draw the United States into the war: (a) overseas trade, (b) the preparedness program, (c) submarine warfare, (d) the Zimmermann note, (e) Wilson's idealism?

5. What were the rights of neutral ships under international law?

6. **Critical Thinking: Recognizing Bias.** How did Woodrow Wilson's religious upbringing influence his thinking about the war?

See "Lesson Plan," p. 546C.

2. Helping to win the war

When the United States entered the war, few Americans realized that the Allies were desperate. Germany's submarine warfare had been so successful that the Allies needed everything. They suffered shortages of food, munitions, money, and men. The war was almost lost.

War on the western front. Trench warfare in Europe was like nothing ever seen before. When the war broke out in 1914, both German generals and French generals had their own plans for a knockout blow to end the war in a hurry. But the new machine guns and automatic rifles were deadly accurate against attack. Very soon *both* armies had to go on the defensive.

This was stationary warfare. Both armies dug their trenches, lived underground, and fired at each other from fixed positions. For three and a half years, the trenches stretched from the Swiss border to the North Sea. Month after month the battle lines hardly moved.

On both sides the trenches became elaborate systems. There was usually a line of front

There were many ways to help the war effort.

Art Resource, NY

Continuity and Change: Government and Politics Point out to students that Wilson's development of the League of Nations demonstrated how the United States had become the world's moral, as well as military, policeman. With his plan, Wilson led and encouraged the war-weary people of Europe much as John F. Kennedy's 1963 speech at the Berlin Wall gave hope to the free world during the Cold War. Both Wilson and Kennedy reinforced the position of the United States as world leader by asserting that the U.S. would not, on moral grounds, stand idly by and let war or oppression spread unchecked. (See p. 782.)

World War I, 1914-1917

Central Powers
Allied Powers
Neutral Nations
German Submarine Zone

Trench Warfare, 1915-1917
Farthest Advances of Central Powers
Eastern Front Armistice Line, December 1917
Boundaries as of 1914

1. ARCHDUKE FERDINAND ASSASSINATED, JUNE 28, 1914
2. GERMAN ATTACK AUG. 1914
3. RUSSIANS DEFEATED, AUG. 1914
4. ITALY ENTERS THE WAR, MAY 1915
5. RUSSIAN REVOLUTION, MARCH 1917; RUSSIANS SIGN ARMISTICE, DEC. 1917

trenches, held as outposts. Behind were networks of supply and command trenches, some reaching back as far as five miles. These were connected by complicated tunnels and even by narrow railways. Soldiers became human moles, hiding by day and burrowing by night. As soon as darkness fell, they went to work, digging new trenches, stringing barbed wire, and connecting telephone lines.

Men in the front trenches had a terrible feeling of isolation. They were threatened not only by enemy gunfire, but by darkness, cold, and mud. Out of the filth and fatigue arose new ailments which came to be called "trench fever," "trench foot," and "trench mouth." Poison gas blistered the skin, burned the eyes, and corroded the lungs. Soldiers wore gas masks which gave them the look of robots. The heavy, ceaseless artillery fire created a new mental disorder known as "shell shock."

In this kind of warfare, a "battle" meant that large numbers of men from one set of trenches

Multicultural Connection: African-American inventor Garrett Morgan (1877–1963) received a patent in 1912 for the Safety Hood and Smoke Protector. During World War I American soldiers wore an improved model of this gas mask to protect them from poisonous chlorine gas. Morgan's invention was also used by firefighters and has been responsible for saving many lives. Morgan was also the inventor of the first three-way automated traffic signal.

rushed out and tried to break through the enemy's trenches. The hope was always to force a gap so that your troops could pour through and attack the whole enemy line from the rear. But advancing soldiers were tangled and torn apart in barbed wire, then mowed down by deadly machine-gun fire.

Early losses in the war. In the opening battles in 1914, even before the trenches were dug, each side lost a half-million men—more than there had been in the entire German army 50 years before. Then, during 1915, the British and French did not advance more than three miles at any point. Still the French lost a million and a half men in 1915 and a million in 1916. At the Battle of the Somme—which lasted for five months in 1916—the Germans lost more men than had been killed during the whole four years of the American Civil War. On one bloody day nearly 20,000 British soldiers were killed.

Never before had so many men been slaughtered so rapidly or so senselessly. Before the war was over, the soldiers killed on both sides would number 10 million, and another 10 million civilians would die from disease, starvation, and the revolutions that grew out of the war.

When the United States finally plunged in, both sides were weary and sick of the bloodshed. The Germans were near victory. They had made peace with the Russians and now could concentrate all their forces on the western front. In May 1918 the German trenches were within 50 miles of Paris. The Germans hoped that when they reached Paris they would be able to force the Allies to surrender before the arrival of American troops could make a difference.

Men of the 18th Infantry march through the ruins of a small French town near St. Mihiel.

Wide World Photos

Geography and History: Interaction Tell students to look at the map on page 557 and have them list the Central Powers, the Allied Powers, neutral nations, and five battles. Ask: In which battle were Russian forces defeated? (Tannenberg.) In which country was there a revolution? (Russia.)

World War I, The Western Front 1918

— Farthest German Advance, Sept. 1914

— Stabilized Front, 1917-1918 (Spring 1918)

— Farthest German Advance, June-July 1918

-·- Armistice Line, November 11, 1918

× Battles Involving American Troops

Boundaries of 1914

0 ——— 80 Miles
0 ——— 80 Kilometers

1. FIRST VICTORY FOR AMERICAN TROOPS, MAY 28

2. ALLIES REPULSE MARNE OFFENSIVE: TURNING POINT OF WAR, JULY-AUGUST

3. AMERICANS AT SEDAN CUT GERMAN SUPPLY LINE, OCTOBER-NOVEMBER

The American Expeditionary Force. But the Americans came in time. At the end of May, the Second and Third divisions of the American Expeditionary Force (AEF) were sent into action. They fought bravely at Belleau Wood and Vaux near Château-Thierry. In July, 85,000 Americans were there to help save Paris. By August an American army of a half-million under General John J. Pershing advanced against the Germans on the southern front. Before the end of September a million and a quarter Americans were fighting in France.

After a bloody battle in October, the Americans advanced to Sedan, 50 miles behind the trenches that the Germans had held for three years. The Americans then cut the railroad that had supplied the German army in their sector. The German defense opposite them began to ⊕

⊕ Geography and History: Movement Have students identify the battles involving American troops on the map above. According to the map, where was the first victory of the American troops? (Cantigny.) What was the final action of the American troops that immobilized the German army before the November 11 armistice? (The American troops cut off the railroad that had supplied the German army.) How long was the United States' military involvement in World War I? (A little over five months—from the end of May to the beginning of November 1918.)

National Archives

Wide World Photos

Troops from the United States played a key role in the battles of 1918. Members of the all-black 369th Regiment fight from a trench in France. (top) Another group of Americans charges. (bottom)

See "Lesson Plan," p. 546D for **Writing Process Activity: Making Comparisons** relating to experiences of American soldiers in World War I.

fall apart. At the same time, the French and the British were advancing all along the line.

The German generals and their emperor had made a bad mistake. They had not imagined that American help at the last moment could turn the tide. Though the Americans arrived late in the battle, they actually did make the difference that decided the war. The United States lost 50,280 men in action. But this was nothing compared to the 4 million lost by Russia, France, and Great Britain and the millions lost by the lesser powers. They had done the real dirty work.

The bloodiest war yet in history—a first "World War"—ended with the armistice on November 11, 1918. In New York, San Francisco, Dallas, Chicago, and Atlanta, Americans danced in the streets.

See "Section 2 Review answers," p. 546D.

Section 2 Review

1. Identify or explain: John J. Pershing, American Expeditionary Force, armistice.

2. In what ways was World War I different from earlier wars?

3. **Critical Thinking: Recognizing Cause and Effect.** How did the arrival of the AEF affect the Allies' war effort?

See "Lesson Plan," p. 546D.
3. The home front

American troops had tipped the scale for the Allies. But it had been a near thing. The United States preparedness program had been inadequate. With the outbreak of the war the nation suddenly found that it had to mobilize men, money, machines, and minds to aid its struggling friends. To get this task done, the President was given new and sweeping powers. The government, acting through scores of boards, commissions, and committees, regulated daily life. It dictated what (and how much) people should eat. It rationed their sugar and their fuel, and discouraged their travel. It even tried to tell them what to think. The free enterprise system that business was accustomed to came

Enrichment Support File Topic

to a halt. The government told industry what it could buy, what it could produce, even where it could build factories. This was the first experiment in total war. Never before had the nation been so organized for a single purpose.

🔯 *Mobilization of men and women.* First of all the nation needed an army. The American tradition, expressed in the Constitution, distrusted a large standing army in peacetime. Experience since ancient times showed that ambitious rulers could use the army against the people. Congress passed a Selective Service Act on May 28, 1917, by a nearly unanimous vote in both houses. The law required all men between the ages of 21 and 31 to register for military service. During the Civil War, a person who was drafted could hire a substitute—if he could afford it. But not now.

Despite fears of draft riots like those during the Civil War, draftees were registered peaceably on June 5. Nearly 10 million men were listed. It was decided that a lottery would be the fairest way to choose whom to draft. Each man who had registered was given a number between 1 and 10,500. On July 20, 1917, these numbers were placed in a bowl, and blindfolded officials withdrew enough numbers to call 687,000 men into the army. Before the war was over 24 million men between the ages of 18 and 45 entered the Selective Service rolls. Almost 3 million of these were called into service. The militia, now called the National Guard, was also brought into federal service. By the time of the armistice in 1918 nearly 4.8 million people—enlistees, draftees, and National Guard—were serving in the armed forces. Among them were women in the Nurses Corps of the army and navy. About 11,000 female yeomen enlisted for office jobs when the Navy Department decided that its right to enlist "persons" included women.

This vast army had to be fed, clothed, equipped, and armed. In the beginning, of course, there were shortages. Before many

A YWCA poster, top right, reminded Americans that women were "over there," too. Some women, like the Broadway chorus girls shown lower right, signed up for military training to serve in the Home Guard.

The Oakland Museum

Brown Brothers

🔯 **Multicultural Connection:** Among the millions of Americans serving in World War I, there were 371,000 African Americans, many of whom were decorated. For example, for courage in battle, Henry Johnson and Needham Roberts became the first Americans to be awarded the Croix de Guerre, France's highest military honor.

months American factories were supplying the needed pistols, rifles, machine guns, shells, and bullets. The heavy equipment—the artillery, the tanks, and the airplanes—was still provided by the French and the English.

The war at sea. To move American troops and supplies to Europe there had to be "a bridge of ships." German submarines were sinking ships faster than they could be replaced. "They will win," the British admiral Sir John Jellicoe warned, "unless we can stop these losses—and stop them soon."

Luckily, at the start the United States Navy was in better shape than the army. Fast destroyers were thrown into the battle against the U-boats. Rear Admiral William S. Sims insisted that all ships headed across the Atlantic should travel in convoys. A convoy was an organized group of merchant and passenger ships surrounded and protected by naval vessels armed to ward off submarine attacks. This system worked so well that the German submarines did not kill a single member of the huge AEF on its way to France.

To provide the bridge of ships, the United States began a mammoth shipbuilding program. The government contracted for 10 million tons of ships and built shipyards to construct them. In fact, few of these vessels would be delivered in time to help the war effort. But by seizing the German vessels that happened to

In new shipyards like the one in the poster, the United States began an all-out shipbuilding program during World War I. Few ships were finished during the war, but by 1921 the United States had the world's largest merchant fleet.

ON THE JOB FOR VICTORY

·UNITED STATES SHIPPING BOARD·   EMERGENCY FLEET CORPORATION·

THEY KEPT THE
SEA LANES
OPEN

L.A. SHAFER

INVEST IN THE
VICTORY LIBERTY LOAN

This poster asks support for the last, or Victory, Loan.

be in American waters in April 1917 and by impressing into service almost everything that could float, the government partly filled the gap. Meanwhile more than 1 million American soldiers and millions of tons of equipment were carried to France by the British merchant marine.

Mobilizing money. The expenses of the army and navy, and credit and materials for the Allies, ran into billions of dollars. Money, too, had to be mobilized for war. At least $23 billion was spent for the American war effort, and more than $10 billion went in war loans to the Allies.

The government used both taxes and loans to pay these huge expenses. Increased taxes brought in $10.5 billion. The rest was borrowed

from the people through the sale of government bonds. Four Liberty Loans and a Victory Loan, "to finish the job," brought in $23 billion.

The government takes control. Of course, a nation geared to peace could not all at once meet the demands of war. Under the pressure of war, the government took over some private businesses. In December 1917, when the overburdened railroads were near collapse, the government took them over. Secretary of the Treasury William McAdoo became director-general of the railroads. He ran them as a single system but left day-to-day operations in the hands of the private managers. Half a billion dollars was invested in improvements and equipment. Soon the railway express companies and the

Brown Brothers

The nation's effort in World War I was spurred on and supported by war bonds. Women sold them on the street.

inland waterway systems also came under McAdoo's control. Before the end of the war, government control was extended to telephone, telegraph, and cable companies.

To mobilize industry and agriculture, the preparedness legislation of 1916 had provided for a Council of Defense. In May 1917 this Council set up a national food-control program. It was headed by a hard-driving mining engineer who had run the Belgian War Relief program. His name was Herbert Hoover. Born a Quaker, he combined engineering efficiency and Quaker charity to bring help to the starving Belgians without offending their self-respect.

Hoover's board had no legal power to do its task. Wilson therefore asked Congress for broad powers over the production and distribution of food, fuel, fertilizer, and farm machinery. Hoover was named head of the new Food Administration. All sorts of measures were tried. There were voluntary "wheatless, meatless, heatless days." Hoover urged men and women to plant "war gardens." Prices on farm crops were set high enough to encourage farmers to raise more food and fiber. The use of grain to make beverage alcohol was banned. Coal was rationed

for home use. Fuel and food output rose as home consumption went down.

While American "doughboys" were mired in trenches overseas, not all Americans were suffering equally from the war. The big rise in demand for food—for our soldiers and for the armies and the civilian population of the Allies—sent food prices skyrocketing. Farmers could pay off their mortgages, paint their barns, and buy new farm machinery. The price of land rose, too. But higher crop prices enabled farmers to extend their acreage. They began to plant marginal land that would not have paid off under ordinary conditions. When the war was over, and American farmers were no longer expected to feed European armies, food prices would plummet. Farmers would have to pay a peacetime price for their wartime prosperity.

The War Industries Board. The Council of National Defense set up in July 1917 to mobilize industry actually lacked the authority to do its job. As a result, by January 1918 the industrial war effort was on the verge of collapse. As heavy snows fell it seemed even the weather would not cooperate. The chairman of the Senate committee investigating the war effort saw "inefficiency in every bureau of the

A parade in New York City helped raise support for the fourth of the Liberty Loans.

Brown Brothers

government." Republican senators called for a War Cabinet of three men. This would make President Wilson a mere figurehead.

Wilson fought to keep control and put the mobilization on track. He submitted a bill that gave him wide powers to reorganize the government and expend funds as he wished. Even before the Overman Act giving him these powers was passed in May 1918, Wilson created the War Industries Board. Bernard M. Baruch, a Wall Street financier of great energy and vision, was put in charge. He showed how a statesman of the business world could bring his wisdom to the national service.

The job of the War Industries Board was to decide what goods should be produced. It could also set prices for government purchases of supplies. For two years Bernard Baruch was the economic dictator of the country. But he seldom had to use force. He had other means of "persuasion." One day Baruch was having trouble getting the automakers to cut down on the output of automobiles. He had them listen in while he phoned the railroad office to stop train service to their plants. Next he called on the army to seize the auto firms' stockpiles of steel. The automakers promptly gave in. Under Baruch's direction the WIB soon gained control of the industrial war effort. Production went up, waste went down, and criticism lessened.

The labor force. The 4 million men enlisted in the armed forces were withdrawn from the nation's labor supply. A million women helped to fill the gap, doing jobs that they had never been allowed to do (nor known that they could do). The war helped them discover themselves as they streamed into mills and factories. They became furnace stokers, managed assembly lines, and wore the uniforms of railroad and streetcar conductors.

Some reformers announced that economic freedom for women had at last arrived. They were wrong. After the war, women were asked to leave their jobs as an act of "patriotism" so the men could return. By 1920 the proportion of women in the labor force had dropped below the level of 1910.

Blacks by the thousands moved north to take

The Food Administration, run by Herbert Hoover, urged Americans to waste no food.

advantage of the new chances for jobs. After suffering in the South from wages that dropped to as low as 75 cents a day in 1914–1915, they saw the North as a promised land. Within a few years there were more than 75,000 blacks in the coal mines and 150,000 on the railroads.

The shortage of labor sent wages up as the government and private firms bid against each other. To fill essential jobs in vital industries, there was a United States Employment Service.

"This is labor's war," said AF of L president Samuel Gompers, and he pledged labor's support. In return for a promise not to strike, unions would get some direct support from the government. Early in April 1918, a National War Labor Board was created to arbitrate labor disputes. Some 1500 cases were submitted to this board. In the few instances in which labor refused to accept the decisions, the President used the pressure of public opinion to compel

More from Boorstin: "During World War I, when labor was scarce, the large grocery merchants had turned to self-service, and the customer was provided a basket to carry the purchases he selected off the shelves." (From *The Americans: The Democratic Experience*)

✄ workers to return to their jobs. In extreme cases, he took over the plant.

Employers, on their part, were forbidden to discharge workers for union activities. Wherever possible, the government insisted on reducing the workday to eight hours. As a result of government support, the membership of labor unions doubled. In spite of a 50 percent rise in prices between 1914 and 1918, labor's *real* income rose 20 percent above the prewar level.

Mobilizing minds. The government also wanted to enlist the minds of the people in the war effort. Millions of Americans had opposed our entry into the war. Some German Americans, naturally enough, did not want to fight against the land of their ancestors. Some Irish Americans felt themselves traditional enemies of the English. Socialists declared that the war was only a capitalist dogfight. Midwest Progressives said the nation should devote itself to reform rather than war. And then there were the pacifists who said that war—only murder under another name—could never be justified.

How could the government convert these reluctant citizens? How could it whip up enthusiasm for our friends and hatred for our enemies? How could it sell war bonds and keep people hard at work? For these tasks President Wilson created the Committee on Public Information. George Creel, a journalist, was appointed chairman, assigned to "sell the war to America." In May 1917 the Creel Committee began publishing a daily *Official Bulletin* of the war news that the administration wished to make public. The committee hired professors, writers, artists, and lecturers by the thousands. Their job was to convince and to reassure Americans that the war was a crusade for freedom and democracy. The Germans were portrayed as hateful beasts, barbarous "Huns" out to dominate the Western world.

This effort helped create a war fever with sad aftereffects which long outlasted the war. It stirred up spy scares and a frantic hunt for traitors. Otherwise sensible Americans now refused to play Beethoven or Wagner. They dropped German courses from the schools.

They turned "sauerkraut" into "liberty cabbage" and converted "hamburger" into "Salisbury steak." But this anti-German madness was really anti-American. For without the hundreds of thousands of immigrants from Germany the nation would have been much poorer. The United States—"a nation of nations"—had been created by people from everywhere and was enriched by all their languages and cultures. ✿

(p. 567)

The attack on civil liberties. The Espionage Act of 1917 gave the President powers of censorship. It enacted heavy penalties against anyone who handed out information about any place connected with the national defense. To urge resistance to the laws of the United States, to refuse to do military duty, or to hinder the draft now became crimes punishable by prison terms. The Trading with the Enemy Act of 1917 obliged any newspaper printed here in a foreign language to furnish the Postmaster General with English translations of everything it published about the war.

The Sedition Act of 1918 went even further than the infamous Sedition Act of 1798 against which Jefferson and Madison had protested. For the 1918 law imposed penalties on anyone who used "disloyal, profane, scurrilous, or abusive" language about the United States government, flag, or uniform. It empowered the Postmaster General to refuse to deliver mail to anyone who, in his opinion, was using the postal service in violation of the act.

With this barrage of propaganda and new laws, Americans who disagreed in any way with the activities of the government were hounded and harried. In 1917 more than 1100 striking copper miners who were members of the radical Industrial Workers of the World were taken forcibly from Arizona to New Mexico, where they were interned. IWW leaders were thrown into jail. Eugene V. Debs, the many-time Socialist candidate for President, was sentenced to jail for ten years for denouncing the war in 1918. While still in jail he ran for President in 1920. His sentence was finally commuted in 1921.

This was a strange way to fight a war for freedom and democracy. How could the nation im-

✄ **Critical Thinking Activity: Drawing Conclusions** How did the mobilization of the war effort at home change Americans' daily lives? Tell students that women, black Americans, and American labor were each affected by the United States' entry into the war. Ask students to select one of these groups and write a diary entry using this group's point of view. Remind students to focus on the changes that their lives have undergone as a result of the war. Have students share their work. This activity could be extended to diary entries covering different aspects of the war and treaty ratification.

Historical Pictures Service, Chicago

This cartoon pokes fun at the government by suggesting that it *might* let Socialist Eugene V. Debs out of jail if only he would apologize.

prove its war effort if citizens were not allowed to criticize the government or the armed forces? In fact, opposition to the war was slight and scarcely hampered the war effort. But the mania of these times would last even after the war. The virus of witch-hunting and super-patriotism was not easy to cure.

See "Section 3 Review answers," p. 546D.

Section 3 Review

1. Identify or explain: Selective Service Act, Liberty Loans, War Industries Board, Bernard Baruch, Herbert Hoover, National War Labor Board, Committee on Public Information, George Creel, Espionage Act, Trading with the Enemy Act, Sedition Act, IWW.

2. How was industry mobilized for war?

3. How did the war affect consumers? Farmers? Women workers? Organized labor?

4. Describe wartime attacks on civil liberties.

5. **Critical Thinking: Recognizing Cause and Effect.** How did the government encourage patriotism? What were some results?

See "Lesson Plan," p. 546E.

4. Losing the peace

When the Germans agreed to the armistice in November 1918, they believed that the peace would be generous—and based on Wilson's high-minded Fourteen Points. They were in for a brutal shock.

The Versailles Treaty. President Wilson, announcing that he would go to the Peace Conference in Paris, gave ammunition to his critics. He said his only purpose was to help achieve the goals of his Fourteen Points. They said he was more anxious to be the Preacher to the World than to be the Protector of the United States. No President while in office had ever before gone to Europe.

In Paris the three Allied leaders whom Wilson had to bargain with were clever and tough. They were Prime Minister David Lloyd George of Great Britain, Premier Georges Clemenceau of France, and Premier Vittorio Orlando of Italy. Each of them remembered the enormous cost of the war to his country. Each wanted to get as much as possible in lands and wealth and (p. 568) power for his own country. Each hoped to punish the enemies so that they would never rise again.

Wilson irritated the other members of the "Big Four." They saw him as a self-righteous leader who always said he was worrying about "all mankind." They compared the Points that Wilson had announced from Washington with the Commandments given to Moses on Mount Sinai. "Mr. Wilson bores me with his *Fourteen Points*," Clemenceau sneered. "Why, God Almighty has only ten!"

The Versailles Treaty that came out of the Paris Peace Conference, was not as selfish or as vengeful as the European leaders would have wished. Nor was it nearly as just and noble as President Wilson might have hoped. Each victor got land it had been promised in secret treaties. The German colonies were parceled out among the Allies. Yet, at the same time, some new smaller republics—like Czechoslovakia and Poland—were created so that at last these people could govern themselves.

The provisions most poisonous for the future

❀ See "Lesson Plan," p. 546D for **Cooperative Learning Activity: Checking Consistency** relating to the American war effort during WW I.

ICELAND

ATLANTIC
OCEAN

NORTH
SEA

NORWAY

SWEDEN

FINLAND

Leningrad

ESTONIA

LATVIA

LITHU-
ANIA

SOVIET
UNION

IRISH
FREE
STATE

GREAT
BRITAIN

DENMARK

BALTIC SEA

London

NETH.

Danzig

EAST
PRUSSIA

Versailles
Paris

BELG.

LUX.

Berlin

Warsaw

Brest-
Litovsk

GERMANY

POLAND

Rhine

FRANCE

CZECHOSLOVAKIA

AUSTRIA

HUNGARY

BESSARABIA

ROMANIA

CASPIAN SEA

SPAIN

ITALY

YUGOSLAVIA

BLACK SEA

Rome

ALBANIA

BULGARIA

GREECE

Constantinople
(Istanbul)

TURKEY

PERSIA

Europe and the Near East
after the Treaty of Versailles
and Other Peace Settlements

MEDITERRANEAN
SEA

CYPRUS
(Br.)

SYRIA
(Fr. Mandate)

Baghdad

LEBANON
(Fr. Mandate)

IRAQ
(Br. Mandate)

PALESTINE
(Br. Mandate)

Territory Lost by

Russia

Germany

Austria-Hungary

Turkish Empire

Boundaries as of 1926

TRANS-JORDAN
(Br. Mandate)

LIBYA
(Ital.)

EGYPT

HEJAZ AND NEJD

RED SEA

Riyadh

Medina

0   600 Miles

0   600 Kilometers

NETHERLANDS

Rhine

BELGIUM

RHINELAND

GERMANY

LUX.

SAAR

FRANCE

ALSACE-LORRAINE

SWITZ.

of Europe had to do with "reparations." These were payments the Allies demanded from Germany to "repair" all the war damage. When the Germans signed the armistice, they knew they might have to pay for the damage to civilians.

The British and the French raised the damages to include the *total* cost of the whole war to all the Allies. This meant not only the homes and farms and factories destroyed, but also the cost of guns and ammunition, the uniforms and pay for soldiers, and even the pensions to wounded Allied soldiers and to their relatives. This sum was so vast and so hard to estimate that the Allies refused to name a figure—or even to name a time in the future when the Germans would be allowed to stop paying.

⊕ **Geography and History: Regions** Have the students study the map above and the terms of the Treaty of Versailles on pages 567–569. Ask: Did the terms of the Treaty of Versailles sow the seeds of World War II? Why? How would you have redrawn the map of Europe and settled the peace treaty differently? Would history have been different if the United States had joined the League of Nations? Why? Assign an essay: How the United States Won the War, but Lost the Peace.

President Wilson did manage to put his own scheme for permanent peace—the League of Nations—in the very same package with all those things the other Allied powers really wanted. He believed that, even if the treaty was not perfect, his new League of Nations could correct the mistakes later.

The fight over the treaty begins. When President Wilson returned to the United States, he was greeted like a hero. An escort of festive warships led him into New York Harbor. Ten thousand people welcomed Wilson at Union Station in Washington.

His triumph was short. Now his political mistakes came home to roost. When Wilson had chosen the American Peace Commissioners to go to Paris, he had snubbed both the Republican party and the Senate. Yet the Republicans held the majority in the Senate. And before any treaty became law, the Senate would have to approve it by a two-thirds majority.

President Wilson simply could not believe that there were reasons why sensible Americans might not want to approve his treaty. What frightened Americans most was the plan for a League of Nations—especially Article 10. Wilson, with typical obstinacy, said that Article 10 was the heart of the League, and that the League was the heart of the whole treaty.

In Article 10 each League member promised to respect and preserve all the other members of the League against "external aggression." At first sight that looked harmless enough. But the real purpose of the Article was to make each member of the League regard an attack on any other member as an attack on itself. In that case, each League member would be expected to prepare for war and then presumably fight to protect all the other members.

To agree to this would overturn one of the oldest American traditions. Should the United States let itself be *required* to plunge into some future European war?

Borah and Lodge lead the opposition. Two able, contrasting Republicans led a relentless battle against allowing the United States to join Wilson's League. One was Senator William E.

Culver Pictures

Crowds cheered President Wilson on July 8, 1919, when he returned from the Paris Peace Conference. Watchful Secret Service men in white straw hats accompanied him.

Borah of Idaho. Borah, like Wilson himself, was the son of a Presbyterian minister who had wanted him also to go into the ministry. A graduate of the University of Kansas, he was as eloquent as Wilson but had more experience in politics. Although a Republican, he supported many Democratic measures when he happened to agree with them. He had worked for the income tax and had fought against the trusts.

Senator Borah's own rule in politics was to stay independent, and then support whatever measures seemed best. In the same way, he believed that the United States should not be de-

See "Lesson Plan," p. 546E for **Writing Process Activity: Identifying Central Issues** relating to the League of Nations.

The National Portrait Gallery, Smithsonian Institution

Renowned portraitist John Singer Sargent showed a pensive Henry Cabot Lodge in 1890.

pendent on other countries. He bitterly opposed our joining the League of Nations for fear it would take away our independence.

The other leader of the anti-League forces was the learned Senator Henry Cabot Lodge of Massachusetts. He, too, had had a long career as a politician. At the time of the World War he was chairman of the Senate Committee on Foreign Relations. That committee had the power to recommend to the Senate whether or not they should adopt the treaty. Unlike Senator Borah, Lodge was a man of strong personal hates. He distrusted Woodrow Wilson, and so he feared Wilson's League.

The failure to enter the League. Then President Wilson made his fatal decision to appeal directly to the American people. In early September 1919, though already in ill health, he traveled 8000 miles, visited 29 cities, and gave 40 speeches in 22 days. At Pueblo, Colorado, he collapsed and had to be taken back to the White

House. There he suffered a stroke. For nearly eight months he could not even meet his Cabinet. Edith Wilson, his wife, carried messages back and forth from everybody else to the President. It was never quite clear which messages actually reached him.

Before the election of 1920 Wilson made another grave blunder. If he had been willing to work with Senator Lodge, he still might have found some compromise. Then he might have succeeded in steering the treaty and the League through the Senate. Instead Wilson once again became the preacher. "Shall we," he asked "or shall we not, redeem the great moral obligation of the United States?" He declared that the election of 1920 would be a "solemn national referendum" on the League of Nations.

The Democratic candidate for President, Governor James M. Cox of Ohio, stood up for the League. The weak, but likable Republican candidate, Senator Warren G. Harding of Ohio, opposed the League. He said vaguely that he favored some sort of "association of nations." Americans chose the Republican Harding by a resounding majority of 7 million votes.

The United States never joined President Wilson's League of Nations. Wilson was saddened that the American people chose a "barren independence." But he did not give up his hope that what a union of states had accomplished in North America, a union of nations might someday accomplish for the whole world.

See "Section 4 Review answers," p. 546E.

Section 4 Review

1. Identify or explain: David Lloyd George, Georges Clemenceau, Vittorio Orlando, "Big Four," reparations, William E. Borah, Henry Cabot Lodge, Warren Harding.

2. What mistake made it hard for Wilson to secure Republican support for the treaty?

3. What feature of the League of Nations was most opposed by Americans?

4. **Critical Thinking: Demonstrating Reasoned Judgment.** Which nations' interests were being served by the Treaty of Versailles? Explain.

Continuity and Change: Government and Politics Explain to students that United States' resistance to the League of Nations contrasts sharply with the leading role taken by the United States later in the organization of the United Nations. Though the Senate rejected the League of Nations following World War I, after World War II the Senate voted decisively to ratify the United Nations charter. (See p. 707.)

Chapter 21 Review

See "Chapter Review answers," p. 546F.

Focusing on Ideas

1. Senator Norris of Nebraska was one of 56 members of Congress to vote against the declaration of war. He explained that the United States had violated its status as a neutral nation. What were some partisan actions of the United States prior to 1917? How did the government justify them?

2. Critics of the war pointed to huge gains made out of the war by Wall Street and big business. Who were other "winners" on the home front?

3. What kinds of freedoms were curtailed during the war? Explain.

Taking a Critical Look

1. **Identifying Assumptions.** In his War Message, President Wilson said that the German government's January 31, 1917, announcement of unrestricted submarine warfare was "in fact nothing less than war against the government and people of the United States." Then he spoke about a moral crusade to make the world "safe for democracy." Do you think he needed to make our entrance into the war a moral issue? Explain.

2. **Drawing Conclusions.** What are some important lessons that other Presidents might have learned from President Wilson's efforts to persuade the United States to take a leading role in world affairs?

Your Region in History

1. **Geography.** Was your area strategically located to support the war effort? Explain your answer, identifying military installations and/or factories involved in war production. If factories served the war effort, what products did they make?

2. **Culture.** What World War I memorials exist in or near your community? What contributions to the war effort do they commemorate?

3. **Economics.** How was the standard of living in your community affected by the war?

Historical Facts and Figures

Drawing Inferences. Study the graph below to help answer the following questions: (a) Which Allied power spent the most money during World War I? (b) Which nation suffered the most casualties? (c) How did the costs of war for the United States compare to those of its allies? (d) How were these costs reflected in the terms of the Treaty of Versailles?

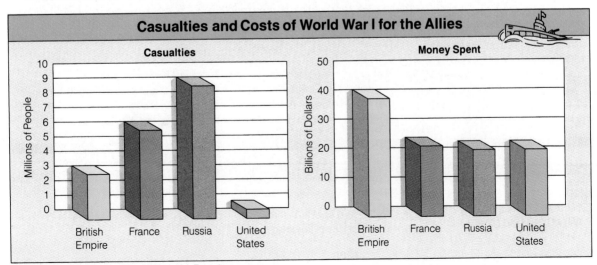

Source: *A Concise History of World War I*, V.J. Esposito

MAKING CONNECTIONS
Unit 7

At the beginning of this unit, on page 503, several questions were raised concerning the United States role in the world:

> *Would our newly powerful nation be tempted to enter wars and try to run the affairs of people everywhere? How could Americans keep their ideals in this different kind of world?*

These questions were explored by the three unit themes that are reprinted in **dark type** below. Use the time line and the information in Unit 7 to answer the questions that follow the unit themes.

THEMES IN HISTORY

Using "Making Connections": Have students look at the unit themes printed in dark type. Explain that each event on the time line relates to one of these themes. Ask students to decide which events are related to which theme. Students should use events from the time line in their answers and explain how events are related. You may also wish to have students go back through the text of Unit 7 to find other events related to the unit themes.

1. **The United States begins to reach outward as a result of rapid industrializatlon.** GEOGRAPHY
   How was the United States's foreign policy in part a result of its economic and business interests? (Recognizing Cause and Effect)

2. **The United States becomes a world leader.** ETHICS AND VALUES
   What political and social forces were at work in the country to bring the United States into the forefront of world leadership? (Identifying Central Issues)

3. **The Progressive Era produces significant reforms in American business and government.** GOVERNMENT AND POLITICS
   How did reformers attempt to make American business and government fairer and more democratic? (Drawing Conclusions)

Events in American History

1897
The Supreme Court applies Sherman Antitrust Act to railroad monopolies.

1898
The Yellow Press calls for war against Spain, with the headline "Remember the Maine."

1890   1895

Events in World History

1890
A. Mahan's *The Influence of Sea Power upon History* is published.

572

1921
Shipbuilding during World War I gives the United States the world's largest merchant fleet.

1902
The muckraker Ida Tarbell's exposé of Standard Oil is published.

1906
Congress passes the Pure Food and Drug Act, responding to consumers' fears.

1918
Woodrow Wilson outlines his Fourteen Points in a message to Congress.

1900
Secretary of State John Hay announces the Open Door Policy for China.

1912
The U.S. Marines are sent to Nicaragua to protect American business interests during an uprising.

1913
Congress enacts the Underwood-Simmons tariff reform bill.

1913
The Seventeenth Amendment provides for direct election of senators.

1900	1905	1910	1915	1920

1900
The Boxers seize Beijing, China, and attack foreigners.

1904
T. Roosevelt establishes his corollary to the Monroe Doctrine.

1914
Archduke Francis Ferdinand is assassinated in Sarajevo, leading to World War I.

1919
The Treaty of Versailles is signed, ending World War I.

Unit 8

Writing About History and Art: Direct students' attention to the unit introduction, illustration, and list of themes on pages 574–575. Have the introduction and unit themes read aloud. After a brief discussion of the subject matter of the unit, instruct students to write a brief paragraph, explaining how the art:

—relates to the unit themes;
—exemplifies the unit title and illustrates the introduction; and
—is an appropriate choice for the unit.

From Boom to Bust 1918–1932

President Calvin Coolidge told Congress in December 1928 that the nation had never faced "a more pleasing prospect." At home, he declared, "there is tranquility and contentment . . . and the highest record of years of prosperity. In the foreign field there is peace. . . ." The twenties, most Americans agreed, had been a wonderful decade.

Before the next year was out the stock market had crashed, and the ranks of the unemployed had begun to swell. The following years would see banks and factories close and find millions out of work. Most distressing of all to Americans, the government of the able engineer Herbert Hoover seemed unable to solve the nation's pressing problems. "In Hoover we trusted," placards read, "now we are busted." The President constantly made encouraging statements. He said that the crisis would soon pass. But it did not pass. From the euphoria of the booming "Jazz Age," Americans were plunged into the Great Depression. They no longer would wonder how high up women's skirts and the price of stocks on the market would go. Instead it seemed that the entire American system might collapse.

THEMES IN HISTORY

- The "Roaring Twenties" are characterized by experimentation, great changes in daily life, and booming economic growth.   SOCIAL CHANGE

- The stock market crash of 1929 signals the end of the "Roaring Twenties" and leads many Americans to grow disillusioned with the American economic system. ECONOMICS

▣ Thomas Hart Benton's painting "Boomtown" with its oil wells evokes the spirit of the 1920s.
Memorial Art Gallery of the University of Rochester, New York; Marion Stratton Gould Fund (detail)

575

Chapter 22
Return to Normalcy, 1918–1929

Identifying Chapter Materials

Objectives	Basic Instructional Materials	Extension Materials
1 The Postwar Reaction • Describe and account for the fear of radicalism in the postwar United States. • Explain the historical background for the Immigration Act of 1924.	**Annotated Teacher's Edition** • Lesson Plans, p. 576C **Instructional Support File** • Pre-Reading Activities, Unit 8, p. 1	**Documents of American History** • The Immigration Act of 1924, Vol. 2, p. 192 • Bartolomo Vanzetti's Last Statement in Court, Vol. 2, p. 218
2 Searching for the Good Old Days • Describe the election and the administration of Warren G. Harding. • Analyze the qualifications of Harding for the office of the presidency, and contrast these with those of Lincoln.	**Annotated Teacher's Edition** • Lesson Plans, pp. 576C–576D	**Documents of American History** • Treaty of Peace with Germany, Vol. 2, p. 172 • The Four-Power Treaty, Vol. 2, p. 183 • The Nine-Power Treaty, Vol. 2, p. 184 • Teapot Dome, Vol. 2, p. 191
3 "Keeping Cool with Coolidge" • Name the candidates, issues, and outcomes of the elections of 1924 and 1928 and show how the Coolidge administration helped business and failed to help farmers. • Analyze the role of religion in the election of 1928 and other American campaigns of both the 19th and 20th centuries. • Discuss the influence of the Ku Klux Klan on the election of 1924.	**Annotated Teacher's Edition** • Lesson Plans, pp. 576D–576E **Instructional Support File** • Skill Application Activity, Unit 8, p. 5	**Documents of American History** • The LaFollette Platform of 1924, Vol. 2, p. 194 • The McNary-Haugen Bill, Vol. 2, p. 210 • Coolidge's Veto of the McNary-Haugen Bill, Vol. 2, p. 213
4 Life in the Jazz Age • Examine the changes in American society during the 1920s. • Analyze, in particular, the effects of the automobile on American society in the same period.	**Annotated Teacher's Edition** • Lesson Plans, pp. 576E–576F **Instructional Support File** • Reading Activities, Unit 8, pp. 2–3 • Skill Review Activity, Unit 8, p. 4 • Critical Thinking Activity, Unit 8, p. 6 • Chapter Test, Unit 8, pp. 7–10 • Additional Test Questions, Unit 8, pp. 11–14	**Enrichment Support File** • The Harlem Renaissance During the Jazz Age (See "In-Depth Coverage" at right.) **Perspectives** • American Music in the Jazz Age (See "In-Depth Coverage" at right.) **American History Transparencies** • Our Multicultural Heritage, p. C83 • Fine Art, p. D77

Providing In-Depth Coverage

Perspectives on the Jazz Age

The Roaring Twenties or the Jazz Age, one of the most colorful periods in our history, was a period of seemingly great and lasting prosperity. Republicans dominated the nation's politics and let business rule; the Democrats were in hopeless disarray, divided between Eastern city-dwellers, often immigrant and Catholic, and rural Southerners and Westerners who favored Prohibition and restriction of "foreign" elements. All the while, factories cranked out more and more things for consumers to buy, and stock prices soared. No one dreamed it would all come crashing down before the decade was out.

A History of the United States as an instructional program provides three types of resources you can use to offer in-depth coverage of the Jazz Age: the *student text*, the *Enrichment Support File*, and *Perspectives*. The chart below shows the topics that are covered in each.

THE STUDENT TEXT. Boorstin and Kelly's *A History of the United States* unfolds the chronology of events and the key players involved in the advent of the Jazz Age.

AMERICAN HISTORY ENRICHMENT SUPPORT FILE. This collection of primary source readings and classroom activities focuses on the works of black Americans connected to the "New Negro Movement" in Harlem.

PERSPECTIVES: READINGS ON AMERICAN HISTORY IN THE 20TH CENTURY. In this edited collection of secondary source readings, well-known historians and political commentators (including Boorstin) provide an array of perspectives on American music in the Jazz Age.

Locating Instructional Materials

Detailed lesson plans for teaching the Harlem Renaissance as a mini-course or to study one or more elements of the Jazz Age in depth are offered in the following areas: in the *student text*, see individual lesson plans at the beginning of each chapter; in the *Enrichment Support File*, see page 3; in *Perspectives*, see the Teacher's Guide pages for this topic.

IN-DEPTH COVERAGE ON THE JAZZ AGE		
Student Text	**Enrichment Support File**	**Perspectives**
▪ Jazz music, p. 592 ▪ "The Roaring Twenties," p. 593 ▪ W.E.B. DuBois, p. 649 ▪ "New Negro Movement," p. 649	▪ Lesson Suggestions ▪ Multimedia Resources ▪ Overview Essay/The Harlem Renaissance During the Jazz Age ▪ Literature in American History/The Flowering of Literature ▪ Songs in American History/Voices of the Harlem Renaissance ▪ Art in American History/An Artistic Renaissance ▪ Biography in American History/Bessie Smith ▪ Making Connections	▪ "Tunes of the Twenties" by Mark Sullivan ▪ "Blues, Boogie-woogie, Swing" by Russell Lynes ▪ "The Radio Invades the American Home" by David Ewen ▪ "Symbols of Liberation" by Paula S. Fass ▪ "The Jazz Age" by Ben Sidran

The Postwar Reaction

FOCUS

To introduce the lesson, tell the class that Congress severely restricted immigration into the United States in 1924. Ask: Why do you think some Americans wanted to restrict immigration? List students' answers on the board.

Developing Vocabulary

The words listed in this chapter are essential terms for reading and understanding particular sections of the chapter. The page number after each term indicates the page of its first or most important appearance in the chapter. These terms are defined in the text Glossary (text pages 1000–1011).

Bolshevik (page 577); **lynch** (page 578); **anarchy** (page 579); **alien** (page 579); **Red** (page 579); **Prohibition** (page 582).

INSTRUCT

Explain

You may wish to emphasize the legacy of the war as a factor in the "Red Scare." Remind students that the work of the Creel Committee had made Americans suspicious of anything un-American.

★ Independent Activity

Expressing Problems Clearly Have each student compile a list of the problems that troubled the postwar United States. Then ask students to look for connections among the problems and summarize their findings in one or two paragraphs.

Section Review Answers

Section 1, page 582

1. a) Communists led by Lenin who took control of Russia in November 1917. b) Republican vice-presidential nominee in 1920. c) set the number of people from specific countries who could enter the United States each year. d) two Italian immigrants in Massachusetts who were tried and executed for a robbery in which two men were killed. e) worked to discourage the use of alcoholic beverages. f) created Prohibition. g) granted women the right to vote. h) American poet who described the postwar world as *The Waste Land.* i) novelist who criticized his own age in his work. 2. In 1918 the United States joined Britain, France, and Japan in sending troops into Russia against the Bolsheviks, an act that brought Russian distrust of the Western powers. 3. Violence marked both labor and race relations after World War I. Workers who were anxious about rising prices and eager to maintain the benefits gained in wartime went on strike. But the public, the government, and the courts had turned against unions, and strikes often brought violence. Union membership fell. Meanwhile, antiblack feeling rose. In the year after the armistice 70 blacks, including some black soldiers, were lynched, and in the summer of 1919 there were more than 25 race riots. 4. Labor strife, urban riots, and bomb scares; Palmer decided that these were the work of Bolsheviks, anarchists, and aliens and that these groups threatened the survival of the nation. He raided Communist meetings and arrested or deported many innocent people. 5. The KKK sought to protect the privileged position of white Protestants. It used violence to harass and terrorize blacks, Jews, Roman Catholics, and all "foreigners." 6. Felt it would lead to decreases in gambling, organized crime, and political corruption; insure sober workers. Many average citizens were now lawbreakers; bootlegging became a source of wealth and power for gangsters. 7. Prohibition was approved during World War I because of the wartime need to conserve grain, the desire to strike at German Americans who brewed beer, and the need for sober workers and soldiers. Results included disrespect for laws and the rise of organized crime.

CLOSE

To conclude the lesson, have students prepare a written explanation of the National Origins Act of 1924, a description of its supporters, and an explanation of their reasons for supporting it.

Searching for the Good Old Days

FOCUS

To introduce the lesson, use the picture of Harding on page 583 along with the paragraph on his background to initiate a discussion of the qualifications we look for in a President.

Developing Vocabulary
disarmament (page 584)

INSTRUCT

Explain

Harding promised to lead the country back to "normalcy," and proposed higher tariffs, lower taxes, less government spending, and aid to farmers. His administration was crippled by scandal.

☑ Writing Process Activity

Drawing Conclusions Ask students to imagine they are journalists reporting on the Washington Conference in 1921. Before they write an article, ask them to outline the provisions of the *Four*, *Five*, and *Nine Power* treaties. Students should begin with a sentence summarizing the historical significance of the conference. While revising their work, have students check to be sure that their first paragraph answers all of the *who, what, where, when, why* and *how* questions employed in journalism and that they have organized their material logically. After proofreading their articles, students can publish a class newspaper about the Washington Conference.

Section Review Answers

Section 2, page 587

1. a) Budget and Accounting Act; for the first time all proposed government expenditures would be listed in a single budget. b) New tariffs raising duties on many products, disrupting foreign trade and leading European nations to raise their tariffs against American goods. c) Cut taxes, especially for industry and the wealthy. 2. Colonel Charles R. Forbes stole money from the Veterans Bureau; Jesse Smith, an aide in the Justice Department, sold his influence; Thomas W. Miller, Alien Property Custodian, sold for profit valuable property taken from Germans during the war; and Secretary of the Interior Albert Fall leased public oil fields to private interests in return for a bribe. Harding did not take direct part in these scandals, but his poor judgment in appointing cronies and his blind trust in them allowed the corruption to occur. 3. The Washington Conference (1921) produced three treaties: the *Five Power Treaty*, the *Nine Power Treaty*, and the *Four Power Treaty*. This was the first successful disarmament conference in modern history, even though no way of enforcing the treaties was established.

CLOSE

To conclude the lesson, ask: What qualifications for the Presidency did the President have before taking office? Was he more or less qualified than Harding? Than Lincoln? Why? Did looks play a large part in his election? Point out that many of our greatest Presidents would find it extremely difficult to be elected in the age of television. Lincoln was ugly and, we are told, had an unpleasant voice. Franklin Roosevelt was handicapped. Thomas Jefferson had a high, soft voice and was so shy that when he spoke to a large group his voice could barely be heard even in the front rows. Discuss the implications of this for future presidential elections in the United States.

Section 3 (pages 588–592)

"Keeping Cool with Coolidge"

FOCUS

To introduce the lesson, make two columns on the board. Label one, "The Good Things Big Government Can Do," and the other, "The Dangers of Big Government." Break the class up into small groups and have the students list as many items as they can think of under each column.

INSTRUCT

Explain

The government was dominated by the Republican party in the 1920s. President Coolidge, elected in 1924, favored business. In 1928, another Republican, Herbert Hoover, easily defeated Al Smith.

❧ Cooperative Learning Activity

Making Comparisons Tell students that they will write an essay comparing the policies of Wilson's administration prior to World War I with those of Harding and Coolidge following the war. Pair students and assign one partner to write a summary of the information in the text on Wilson's administration, while the other partner summarizes the Harding/Coolidge years. Have partners share their completed summaries, but have each student write his or her own essay comparing the policies of the two times. Have volunteers read their work to the class.

Section Review Answers

Section 3, page 592

1. a) Director of the Budget under Harding and then Vice-President under Coolidge. b) deadlocked with Al Smith in the race for the Democratic presidential nomination in 1924. c) sought the Democratic presidential nomination unsuccessfully in 1924 and then won the nomination, but lost the election, in 1928. d) Democratic presidential candidate in 1924. e) governor of Nebraska and William Jennings Bryan's brother, was the Democratic vice-presidential candidate in 1924. f) a new party in 1924. Its presidential candidate was "Battling Bob" La Follette of Wisconsin, who was labeled a radical by both Republicans and Democrats. g) elected governor of Texas in 1924. h) elected governor of Wyoming in 1924. 2. The Democratic convention of 1924 deadlocked and after more than a hundred ballots picked a compromise candidate, Davis. La Follette left the Republican Party and ran as candidate of a third party, the new

Progressive party. For a third-party candidate he received a surprisingly high number of votes. More than a hundred women were elected to state legislatures, and in two states the new governors were women. 3. a) He believed that "the business of America is business" and that the federal government should not set rules for business, and he appointed people who shared that belief to head government regulatory agencies. b) They encouraged mergers, monopolies, and price-fixing. c) The Supreme Court defined "restraint of trade" so strictly that it would allow one corporation to gain control of a huge share of a market and would permit industrial trade groups to set prices. This encouraged mergers and monopolistic practices and made the antitrust laws ineffective against business. 4. The more they produced, the less they received for their products. While the prices they received for their crops fell, their costs and taxes were rising. Congress tried to help farmers by passing the McNary-Haugen bill, but Coolidge successfully vetoed it twice. 5. Al Smith, the colorful governor of New York, was the Democratic candidate for President in 1928; Herbert Hoover, the bland but popular Secretary of Commerce, was the Republican choice. Smith was Catholic and represented urban interests and opposed Prohibition. Hoover stood for big business and small-town, Protestant America and supported Prohibition.

CLOSE

To conclude the lesson, ask: What (if anything) could or should the United States government have done in the 1920s to ensure competition in agriculture?

Section 4 (pages 592–596)

Life in the Jazz Age

FOCUS

To introduce the lesson, write the word *auto* with a circle around it in the center of the blackboard, and have students do the same in the center of a page in their notebooks. Tell the class to draw two lines out from their circle and at the end of each line write an effect of the automobile on American society. Take several of their answers and write them on the board. Have students continue to write down effects on their sheets. After a few minutes stop the students and ask for more effects. List five or six on the board. Draw a circle around each of these and tell the students to do the same to each of their effects.

Have the class focus on one of the effects on the board, by asking: What are the effects of this effect? For example, "more travel" might lead to such effects

as more gas stations, more oil production, more restaurants, more auto accidents, and so forth. More restaurants could then lead to such effects as change in diet, more service jobs, large restaurant chains, and so forth.

Developing Vocabulary

speakeasy (page 593); **assembly line** (page 594); **productivity** (page 596).

INSTRUCT

Explain

The presence of a new technology can have a ripple effect on a people's whole way of life. During the 1920s, new inventions and developments such as the automobile changed life dramatically.

☑ Writing Process Activity

Determining Relevance Ask students to imagine they are teenagers during the 1920s. In preparation for writing a brief story about the changes they are experiencing in their lives, have them brainstorm possible topics, such as cars, movies, sports, and so forth. Once they have selected a topic, have them continue to brainstorm for specific details. Students should begin with a sentence that captures readers' interest, and they should develop their narrative with specific details. Ask students to revise for word choice and organization. After proofreading, they can read their story to the class.

Section Review Answers

Section 4, page 596

1. Automobiles, movies, radios, and refrigerators; new highways and the first shopping centers were developed; new music, jazz and blues, was available on records. Opportunities for education expanded, and the most threatening childhood diseases—typhoid, diphtheria, and measles—were being brought under control. 2. Factory production was made more efficient by the spread of "scientific management," by increased use of the assembly line and electricity, and by improvements in the operation of assembly lines. 3. "Roaring" captures the excitement of the times—the excitement of a business boom and buying new products on time, of speakeasies and flappers, jazz and the blues, and huge crowds watching sporting events.

CLOSE

To conclude the lesson, tell students that they should get in the habit of projecting the consequences that might arise as a result of new inventions or other changes. For homework, have them pick any invention in the recent or distant past and make a cause-

and-effect diagram for it, similar to the one they did for the automobile. Some possible choices are: radio, computer, airplane, light bulb, steamboat, photocopier machine, and television.

Chapter Review Answers

Focusing on Ideas

1. Aliens and recent immigrants; Catholics; Jews; blacks; Union members, non-conformists. Sufferings: expulsion, beatings, threats, lack/loss of jobs, housing restrictions; ridicule, contempt, ethnic slurs. Prejudice stereotypes. 2. Anarchists: extreme personal freedom; government replaced by voluntary cooperation; often revolutionary. Socialists: public ownership of production (attained and sustained democratically.) Communists: public ownership (through revolution, "dictatorship of the proletariat" [party leaders]). Anarchists—poorly organized, but sometimes violent; socialists—peaceful change; communists—highly organized, revolutionary. 3. Disturbing: Strikes, race riots, sudden inflation, Klan, women and blacks resisting a return to former roles, etc. Agreeable: Radio, phonographs, new mobility from machines. Technological progress easier to accept than changing roles.

Taking a Critical Look

1. Regulatory agencies aided business; agreements to share information; court injunctions broke strikes. 2. Focus on election because of image; naive attitudes toward own administrations.

Your Region in History

1–3. Answers will vary depending on your region. Consult your local library or historical society.

Historical Facts and Figures

(a) 1 million cars. (b) 1929. (c) 1921. (d) 110%. (e) "Buy Now, Pay Later." (f) Answers will vary.

22

Chapter 22

Return to Normalcy 1918–1929

In the 1920s the sound of radios and phonographs began to fill the air. For the first time motion pictures opened fantastic vistas for the millions. Americans started their love affair with the automobile. Women's skirts—which had once been thought dangerously high when they revealed a glimpse of the ankle—now suddenly shot up to the knee. Long hair had been called a woman's "crowning glory." Now respectable women cut their hair short in a "boyish bob"—and actually wore lipstick. Some even smoked cigarettes in public!

At the same time there were still many old-fashioned Americans. They were shocked by what they saw. Women, they said, ought to be put on a pedestal, where they had neither the freedom nor the temptations of the rest of the human race. In this and other ways the twenties was an age of conflict, confusion, excitement, and experiment. Never was the nation more American. This was still a New World where people might try anything—at least once.

In this 1928 painting John Sloan presented the feeling of New York City nightlife.

The Metropolitan Museum of Art, Gift of friends of John Sloan

See "Lesson Plan," p. 576C.

1. The postwar reaction

The cease-fire in Europe did not bring a quick end to the problems of war. The war itself had created new problems. It had left a trail of starvation and death and opened the floodgates of revolution. Peace on the battlefield brought another sort of warfare—in parliaments and factories. All over Europe, dissatisfied people seized the chance to turn their nations upside down. In the United States there was worry that the virus of revolt would infect Americans.

Allied intervention in Russia. In March 1917 a revolution in Russia toppled the government of Czar Nicholas II. Then the new liberal Provisional Government led by Alexander Kerensky had in turn fallen in November before radical Bolsheviks (Communists) led by V. I. Lenin. They promptly took Russia out of the war. Hoping to keep German troops from moving to the western front, the Allies stepped in. They said their purpose was to help Russia form a stable government. Some Western leaders, however, no doubt hoped that they could "strangle Bolshevism at its birth," as Winston Churchill later put it. Japan, for its part, hoped to secure control over eastern Siberia.

As a result, when the armistice came in 1918, many American troops stayed in Europe. They were fighting a new kind of war—a war against communism. Earlier that year the United States had joined Britain, France, and Japan in sending troops into northern and eastern Russia. The Allies lifted the hopes of the enemies of the Bolsheviks within Russia and so prolonged the "Great Russian Civil War" of 1918–1920. In the new Russia—now called the Union of Soviet Socialist Republics—the distrust of the Western powers would fester for many years.

During World War I, the Creel Committee had made the people of the United States suspicious of anything un-American. Now the mysterious Communists seemed to threaten to overturn the governments of Europe. They had even formed a party in the United States. It was small and harmless, but many Americans were still jittery, and other events in the country increased their fears.

The Granger Collection

This cover of a 1926 issue of the original *Life* magazine was done by John Held, Jr., whose drawings captured the flavor of the 1920s.

Labor strife. Within the United States the truce between employers and workers came to an end as soon as the war was won. Workers were anxious to keep the wartime benefits they had gained and felt threatened by soaring prices. In 1919 some 4 million workers went out on strikes costing $2 billion in lost sales and wages. Union violence at home frightened the public.

In the autumn of that year, after the Boston police walked out in a labor dispute, looting and violence spread across the city. When the mayor asked for help, Governor Calvin Coolidge called out the National Guard to keep order. He declared that there was "no right to strike against the public safety by anybody, anywhere, anytime." This statement—and his prompt action against the striking policemen—brought him the Republican vice-presidential nomination in 1920.

A strike against United States Steel, during which eighteen workers were killed, failed. A coal strike, which President Wilson called "not only unjustifiable but unlawful," was broken by a court injunction. These defeats forecast the decline of the unions during the 1920s. Opposed by business, government, the courts, and popular opinion, union membership fell from 5 million in 1921 to 4.3 million in 1929. In these same years total nonfarm employment rose by nearly 7 million.

Urban riots. The end of the war was also marked by an increase in racial friction. Though blacks had served bravely on the battlefield and skillfully in the factories, anti-black feeling had increased. During the year after the armistice 70 blacks, including at least 10 soldiers in uniform, were lynched. "Lynching" was named after a Colonel Charles Lynch of Virginia. It was the barbarous act of a mob that hanged a person without a legal right to do so.

In the summer of 1919 there were more than 25 race riots. The worst occurred in Chicago, where a dispute at the beach set off six days and nights of rioting. Hundreds were injured, and 15 whites and 23 blacks were killed. The trigger-happy Attorney General A. Mitchell Palmer was haunted by Bolshevik ghosts whom he imagined to be everywhere. During that "Red Summer," without reason he accused the Chicago rioters—along with anybody else he disliked—of being Communist agitators.

(p. 579)

Bomb scares. At the same time there really was an epidemic of terrorism that made many citizens nervous. In Seattle early in 1919 Mayor Ole Hanson had taken measures to break a general strike. Then on April 28, he received a bomb in the mail. It was discovered before anyone was hurt. The next day Senator Hardwick of Georgia received a package that was opened by his maid, who had both her hands blown off. Later, 36 similar packages were found that had not been delivered because they lacked sufficient postage. These were addressed to such people as Attorney General Palmer, the

Postmaster General, the Secretary of Labor, J. P. Morgan, and John D. Rockefeller.

Only a month later other parts of the country were shaken by a series of explosions. One of these damaged the front of Attorney General Palmer's house and killed the person carrying the bomb. The bombings came to a climax at noon on September 16, 1920. On the corner of Broad and Wall streets in the heart of New York's financial district, the busy lunchtime crowds were blasted without warning. Thirty-eight people were killed and hundreds injured.

A. Mitchell Palmer pursues the Bolsheviks. Attorney General Palmer lacked a sense of perspective. Instead of seeing the bombings as scattered acts by a few misguided terrorists, he imagined that the very existence of the nation was in peril. The strikes, race riots, and bombings seemed to him "the blaze of revolution." The whole country, he said, was infested by

A 1920 cartoon of an angry Uncle Sam reflects the hysterical fear of "Reds" and anarchists then sweeping the country.

Culver Pictures

WHOSE COUNTRY IS THIS, ANYHOW?

Continuity and Change: Social Change Point out to students that the race riots during the summer of 1919 (the "Red Summer") were brought on by increased racial tension following World War I. Nearly five decades later, during the summers of 1965, '66, and '67, racial tension again hit the breaking point, resulting in the worst race riots in United States history. (See p. 807.)

This dramatic photograph shows the powerful effect of the bomb that exploded at lunchtime on Wall Street on September 16, 1920. The 38 dead and the hundreds of victims needing medical care had been removed by the time the picture was taken.

Bolsheviks and anarchists. Any alien, he screamed, might prove to be a bomb thrower. And if Palmer could make himself the nation's savior, he might eventually move into the White House.

In November 1919 he had 250 members of the Union of Russian Workers arrested. Most were guilty of no wrongdoing and later had to be released. In December 249 aliens, whose only crime in a majority of cases was that they were anarchists, were herded aboard the transport *Buford*, called the "Soviet Ark," and shipped to the Soviet Union. Palmer declared that there were thousands of "Reds" all over

the country sworn and trained to tear the nation apart.

On January 2, 1920, he ordered raids on Communist meetings all over the country. Everyone who was present, Communist or not, was rounded up and more than 4000 people were thrown into jail. In all, 556 aliens were deported.

By now, however, criticism of Palmer was surfacing. His illegal arrests were doing more harm to American institutions than were the small groups of real "Reds" in the country. The ambitious and jittery Palmer was brewing trouble for millions of innocent and patriotic Americans.

✂ Critical Thinking Activity: Checking Consistency How did Attorney General Palmer threaten democracy? Ask students to read pages 578–580, and describe Palmer's reaction to "terrorist" groups in the United States after World War I. In a class discussion have students determine if these actions were in keeping with the democratic principles that Palmer would have subscribed to. To conclude, assign students this sentence to complete: "The real paradox in Attorney General Palmer's behavior was . . ."

Following his example, excitable citizens were roused to vent their fears and their hates against any Americans who seemed "different." These included blacks, Jews, and Catholics, along with all reformers. Somehow, forgetting that the nation had been built by immigrants, Palmer and his followers aimed their blasts against all "foreigners."

The fear of foreigners.

During the war the Immigration Restriction League had finally obtained passage of the law that every immigrant must be able to read to be admitted to the United States (p. 443). But they were not interested just in literacy. They had strong racial, religious, and ethnic prejudices. In fact, they wanted to cut down immigration from Russia, Poland, Italy, and the other countries of eastern and southern Europe. The nation had been enriched by the thousands who had come here from those countries between 1890 and 1910. But the restrictionists had an odd theory of their own about "superior" and "inferior" races. They pretended that it was a science. Really it was only a way of dressing up their prejudices. Their own ancestors happened to come from northern and western Europe. They liked to think, therefore, that all the best people came from there. The restrictionists included university presidents and were led by eminent New Englanders. It would take many years to remove the stain they left on our immigration laws.

The nation seemed to have forgotten its own origins! Free immigration had made the United States a free nation. Then in 1921 national quotas for immigrants were introduced. The National Origins Act of 1924 reduced quotas until, in 1929, only 150,000 immigrants were allowed to enter the United States each year. The quota from each country was based on the "national origins" of the people of the United States in 1920. This favored northern and western Europe, since the large immigration from other parts had come more recently.

The National Origins Act barred all Chinese, Japanese, and other Asians. It is not surprising that in Japan there were "hate America" meetings held on "Humiliation Day," July 1, 1924.

On the other hand, Canadians and Latin Americans were exempt from the law's provisions. The 1920s saw the first large immigration to the United States of Mexican Americans.

The "new" Klan.

While the Immigration Restriction League used the laws, another group was using terror and violence to enforce their prejudices. A new Ku Klux Klan appeared in the South and the West. It pretended to be in the old southern tradition to defend the rights of the "best" people. But in fact it was led by a collection of roughnecks and human dregs, with some respectable followers, who made a career of harassing blacks, Jews, Roman Catholics, and all "foreigners." Somehow they were able to enroll about 4.5 million "native born, white, gentile Americans." These included many who wanted someone to blame for lack of jobs and many who were worried by the turmoil of postwar Europe. Somehow the Klan came to dominate the politics of several states.

To enlist and keep its members, the Klan shrewdly used all sorts of hocus-pocus. They had passwords, marched about in white sheets, and held secret meetings. But they were no laughing matter. They whipped and killed innocent citizens. They burned buildings and brought terror to whole communities. Yet they seldom went to jail for their crimes, because they bullied sheriffs and judges into joining them.

The conviction in 1925 of the Indiana Grand Dragon for murdering his secretary marked the beginning of the end of the "new" Klan. The newspapers then began to expose the crimes of the Klan, and respectable Americans avoided it like the plague.

Sacco and Vanzetti.

Every epoch of American history has had its martyrs. Their names enter the folklore. John Brown was a willing martyr of the fight against slavery. In this later age Nicola Sacco and Bartolomeo Vanzetti, two Italian-born immigrants, became unwilling martyrs in the struggle for equal justice for all.

In 1920 a holdup took place at a South Braintree, Massachusetts, shoe factory. A paymaster

More from Boorstin: "When famine struck Russia in 1921, . . . soon after Attorney General Palmer's reckless arrests and deportations of communists and alleged communists, the efforts to keep charity separate from policy were strained. Herbert Hoover took the lead. . . . In 1922, his organizing talent brought medicine, food, and clothing to some 10 million destitute Russians. . . . At an official banquet in Moscow, the President of the Council of People's Commissars, whose government was still not recognized by the United States, honored Hoover." (From *The Americans: The Democratic Experience*)

Ben Shahn's grim 1930s painting of Nicola Sacco and Bartolomeo Vanzetti shows them handcuffed together as they stoically await their fate.

and guard were killed. Shortly afterward Sacco and Vanzetti were arrested. They were both gentle men with no criminal record. But they believed the philosophy of anarchy. They were tried, found guilty, and sentenced to die. There was no solid evidence against them. It was widely thought that they were really victims of the frenzied fear of radicals and aliens.

The belief in the innocence of Sacco and Vanzetti was so widespread that in 1927 the governor of Massachusetts finally had to appoint a committee to review the fairness of their trial. But the committee itself was loaded with prejudice. The author of its report was Harvard President A. Lawrence Lowell, long an officer of the Immigration Restriction League, who was well

known for his belief in the "superiority" of the Anglo-Saxon peoples. It is not surprising that this committee reported that the trial had been fair.

When Sacco and Vanzetti were executed, millions of Americans mourned. They believed that the two gentle Italian immigrants were victims of fear and prejudice.

The disillusioned writers. Some of the brightest American writers did not like what they saw. The brilliant H. L. Mencken, a Baltimore journalist, used his acid pen to ridicule American follies in phrases that would not be forgotten. He laughed at democracy and called the American people the "Booboisie." The

Multicultural Connection: For example, on November 13, 1922, the Supreme Court ruled that Takao Ozawa, born in Japan, raised in Hawaii, and educated at the University of California at Berkeley, was unqualified for naturalization since he was neither a white nor an African American. Denied the right of naturalization because of his race, Ozawa's predicament foreshadowed the treatment of Chinese, Japanese and Korean immigrants who would be declared "aliens ineligible for citizenship." This situation remained in effect until 1943 for Chinese emigrants and until 1952 for Japanese and Korean emigrants.

American-born poet T. S. Eliot, who had moved to England, described the postwar world as *The Waste Land.*

Yet the age produced the greatest crop of writers ever to light up an American generation. Novelists Sinclair Lewis, Sherwood Anderson, F. Scott Fitzgerald, William Faulkner, and Ernest Hemingway, along with playwright Eugene O'Neill, made their criticism of their own age into enduring literature.

The nation goes dry. The temperance movement—to discourage the use of intoxicating liquors—was as old as the Republic. Ever since the 1830s it had won the support of some reformers and industrial leaders. As early as 1851, the state of Maine passed a model temperance law. More and more citizens believed that control of liquor was necessary to decrease gambling, organized crime, and political corruption. They were troubled to see workmen wasting their paychecks at saloons while their families went hungry. In the new industrial age, too, a drunk at a machine could injure himself and many others.

By World War I, half the states of the Union had passed laws banning the sale of alcoholic beverages. Then came the war, and all at once "Prohibition" became a national concern. It would conserve grain. It would strike at the German Americans who brewed beer. And it would insure sober, clearheaded workers and soldiers. The wartime Congress passed a Prohibition amendment to the Constitution and sent it to the states. It became the Eighteenth Amendment when it was ratified by three-fourths of the states by January 1919. The sale of beer, wine, and distilled liquors was to stop in January 1920.

In theory, the whole nation was now "dry." All but two states ratified the amendment, yet many Americans had no intention of giving up drinking. Millions of Americans who could see nothing "criminal" about enjoying a glass of beer or wine suddenly became lawbreakers. Only 1520 federal agents were hired to try to stop the flow of liquor. Prohibition could not be enforced. So it bred a disrespect for all law.

Since law-abiding citizens could no longer deal in liquor, the trade became a source of wealth and power for gangsters. "Booze" became the plague of the nation.

Women's suffrage. A more successful by-product of World War I was women's suffrage. Like the temperance campaign, the move to give women the vote had long been a goal of reformers. The war finally brought them success. "The services of women during the supreme crisis have been of the most signal usefulness and distinction," Woodrow Wilson wrote. What good reason could there be for depriving half the nation's adults of the right to vote? President Wilson's support, in 1919, helped the suffrage amendment pass Congress with little opposition. Only fourteen months later, the thirty-sixth state ratified the Nineteenth Amendment. At last women became first-class citizens.

See "Section Review answers," p. 576C.

Section 1 Review

1. Identify or explain: Bolsheviks, Calvin Coolidge, immigration quotas, Sacco and Vanzetti case, temperance movement, Eighteenth Amendment, Nineteenth Amendment, T. S. Eliot, F. Scott Fitzgerald.

2. What action in 1918 brought Russian distrust of the Western powers?

3. Describe the main developments in labor relations and race relations in the period after World War I.

4. What events were troubling Americans in 1919–1920? How did Attorney General Palmer react?

5. Describe the goals and methods of the new Ku Klux Klan.

6. Describe some of the benefits reformers felt would come about as a result of the passage of the Eighteenth Amendment. What were some drawbacks?

7. **Critical Thinking: Demonstrating Reasoned Judgment.** How and why was the Prohibition amendment approved? What were some of its results?

See "Lesson Plan," p. 576C.

2. Searching for the good old days

The rash of postwar fears and headaches—bombs, Bolsheviks, riots, and strikes—made many Americans yearn for the "good old days." The nation was tired of their preacher-President. They wondered whether the United States should try to settle the problems of turbulent old Europe and the world. Their election of the Republicans' Warren G. Harding and Calvin Coolidge showed the desire of Americans to turn inward. "America's present need," Harding explained, "is not heroics, but healing, not nostrums but normalcy, not revolution but restoration, not surgery but serenity."

Warren G. Harding. President Harding had started as the owner of a weekly paper in the small town of Marion, Ohio. His newspaper grew and prospered with the town, and he became a power in state politics. He had served in Ohio's senate and as lieutenant governor and had just completed a term as a United States Senator. When he was nominated for the nation's highest office, he had little training and even less capacity to be President of the United States. But he was friendly and likable. Silver haired and dignified, he looked so much like a President that voters easily imagined he had other qualifications, too. The Republicans picked him because the party was badly divided between its abler men—General Leonard Wood, Governor Frank Lowden of Illinois, and Herbert Hoover. The little-known Harding had few enemies.

Harding got off to a promising start. He seemed to know his own limitations and said he would choose some of the "best minds" to help him. And that he did. Charles Evans Hughes, one of the wisest Republicans in the country, was named Secretary of State. Herbert Hoover became Secretary of Commerce. Andrew W. Mellon, one of the nation's richest men and a wizard of finance, headed the Treasury. He would remain there for twelve years under three Presidents. Henry C. Wallace, widely known as the editor of a farm journal and a champion of conservation, became Secretary of Agriculture.

Brown Brothers

In 1923 Harding became the first President to address the American people over the radio.

Some of Harding's other appointments were less wise, and a few were disastrous. Albert B. Fall of New Mexico, an old friend from Harding's Senate days, was named Secretary of the Interior. But he was opposed to conservation. That seemed an odd qualification for the head of a department founded to conserve the nation's resources. For Attorney General the President chose Harry Daugherty of Ohio. His only recommendation for the job was that he had "groomed" Harding for the Presidency and managed his campaign. It soon appeared that this would be a government by "cronies." The least able and more self-seeking officials seemed to be in charge. Harding's old friends, who ✂ spent more time playing cards together than planning the national welfare, came to be called

✂ Critical Thinking Activity: Testing Conclusions What personal traits should a President possess? American voters assumed because Harding looked like a President he would make a good Chief Executive. Ask students to list the traits they feel are essential to have in a President. When the list is complete, ask students to decide which of these traits were possessed by Harding. Then ask students to evaluate the current President as well.

the "Ohio Gang." They were not ashamed to use their offices to enrich themselves. Their crimes would make the weak Harding a synonym for incompetence, and their activities would help bring about his death.

Foreign affairs. As President, Harding was out of his depth. The affairs of the larger world were really too much for him, but he tried to seem decisive. In his inaugural address he declared that he wanted nothing to do with the League of Nations. "We seek no part in directing the destinies of the Old World," he said. "We asked the sons of this republic to defend our national rights, not to purge the Old World of the accumulated ills of rivalry and greed." As a result the Versailles Treaty was ignored, and the United States made a separate peace with Germany. It was signed by Harding on July 2, 1921.

The First World War had shown that when the world was at war no one could feel at peace. The great island-nations, Great Britain and Japan, needed strong navies—both for commerce and to protect their shores. And the United States was a two-ocean nation. After the war, each of these nations built up its navy. The world was supposed to be at peace, but these countries seemed to be preparing for war at sea. Where would it end?

Few Americans wanted to pay the cost of an arms race. At the call of President Harding, delegates from nine great powers with interests in the Far East met in Washington in the fall of 1921.

From their meetings three treaties emerged in 1922. In the *Five Power Treaty,* Great Britain, Japan, the United States, France, and Italy agreed to limit the number of their capital ships (vessels over 10,000 tons displacement). They would scrap 2 million tons of ships. The two biggest powers—Great Britain and the United States—each were allowed to keep 500,000 tons, Japan 300,000 tons, and France and Italy 175,000. In addition the powers agreed not to build any more forts or naval bases on their possessions in the Pacific—except for Hawaii.

Once the treaty was concluded, the Western powers feared that they had given Japan a free hand in the Pacific. They then managed to obtain the so-called *Nine Power Treaty.* This protected Western interests by binding all to observe the Open Door in China. They promised to respect China's integrity and not seek land or special privileges there.

To free Great Britain from its military alliance with Japan, a *Four Power Treaty* was signed between the United States, Great Britain, Japan, and France. They agreed to respect one another's possessions in the Pacific. Any issue that seemed likely to disturb the peace of the Far East would be sent to a joint conference. The Senate, though still fearing entangling alliances, accepted this treaty. But the senators did so with the reservation that the United States assumed "no commitment to armed force, no alliance, no obligation to join in any joint defense."

The Washington Conference was the first successful disarmament conference in modern history. But there was no way to enforce the agreements. Japan, with expanding industry and a growing population crowded onto its islands, was determined to become a great power. These treaties provided a decade of peace. They also gave Japan the time to organize and to become a great Asian power without interference. Still, our nation's relations with Japan could not be happy so long as the Immigration Act of 1924 was in effect as an insult to the Japanese people.

Harding's domestic program. The way back to "normalcy," as Harding found, was a rocky road. A sharp decline in business began in 1920. To deal with the problems of depression and conversion to peacetime, the President called Congress into special session in April 1921. He asked for higher tariffs, lower taxes, less government spending, and aid to disabled soldiers and to farmers.

One of his proposals would open a new era in planning federal spending. He asked Congress to create a bureau to sift the money demands of each department. All requests would go into a single budget to be sent to Congress for its review and approval. For the first time, Congress and the people would be able to see all at one

See "Lesson Plan," p. 576D for **Writing Process Activity: Drawing Conclusions** relating to the Washington Conference.

time and in one document how the government intended to spend the people's money. In response, Congress passed the Budget and Accounting Act. This set up the Bureau of the Budget. At the same time a General Accounting Office headed by a Comptroller General would check to see that the money was spent for the legal purposes and would recommend economies.

The President proposed new high tariffs to protect farmers from Canadian competition. An emergency tariff raised duties on 28 farm products. The next year the Fordney-McCumber tariff gave industrialists, too, the protection they wanted.

The effects of these trade barriers were not good. The Fordney-McCumber Act clogged the flow of foreign trade. Europeans needed to sell their goods here in order to get dollars to buy our products. To no one's surprise, then, European nations retaliated by raising their tariffs against goods from the United States. American business firms had trouble selling their products abroad. The tariff race, like the arms race, would be costly to everybody.

Secretary of the Treasury Mellon asked that the high wartime taxes (to support the armed forces) at once be reduced. Industry would not grow without more capital investment, which he believed the wartime taxes were preventing. In 1921 Congress repealed the wartime excess profits tax on industry. It also reduced the top level of taxes on the wealthy from 65 percent to 50 percent. (Mellon had wanted it to be 25 percent.) Congress also lowered taxes for middle- and lower-income people, which Mellon had not

The dignitaries who posed for their pictures at the opening of the Washington Conference in November 1921 were soon thereafter stunned by Secretary of State Hughes's call for disarmament.

UPI/Bettmann Archives

asked for. Mellon finally had his way in 1924 when a new tax bill reduced the top tax to 25 percent. In the next few years it was cut even more. During one tax debate someone observed that Mellon would receive a larger personal reduction than all the taxpayers in the state of Nebraska put together.

The bonus bill. When a war veteran was discharged, he received a "bonus" of $60. Disabled veterans could get hospital care and other special benefits. Veterans' organizations were demanding that those who had served in the armed forces in wartime deserved special treatment when the nation enjoyed the peace they had helped to bring. They asked for another and larger "bonus." Harding argued that the soldiers had never expected a bonus. He said that serving in the army was only their patriotic duty. He vetoed the "bonus" bill, and Congress failed to override his veto.

The veterans' groups kept up their pressure. In the spring of 1924, after Calvin Coolidge had become President, a new bonus bill (the Adjusted Compensation Act) was passed. This gave a veteran an insurance policy totaling in value $1.25 for every day spent overseas and $1 a day for service in the United States. Veterans could borrow up to 25 percent of the value of their policies. Coolidge vetoed the bill, but Congress easily passed it over his veto.

📖 ***The war debts.*** The $9 billion in war debts owed to the United States by its former allies—Great Britain, France, and Italy—created a baffling problem. This money had been mostly spent in the United States to finance the war against Germany. The Allied powers argued that the United States should cancel the war debts because the money had been spent also in defense of the United States.

The Harding administration insisted that the war debts should not be canceled. So they were paid back in installments. The money came from the huge reparations the Versailles Treaty forced Germany to give the victorious European nations to repair the damage caused by the war. And the only way Germany could pay was by borrowing from the United States. With the depression of the 1930s, this whole merry-go-round stopped. Only Finland ever paid its entire debt.

The death of Harding. While the whole world was trying to find a way out of these vast and puzzling problems, Americans were plagued by corruption and by the bad judgment of their President. In 1923 Harding began to hear stories about what some of his "Ohio Gang" had been up to. He had made the mistake of appointing a chance acquaintance, Colonel Charles R. Forbes, head of the Veterans Bureau. This was a huge enterprise that had charge of the hospitals and all other forms of veterans' relief. In two years $250 million was wasted or stolen from these programs. Even after Attorney General Daugherty told Harding of the rumors about Forbes, the President, ever loyal to his friends, let Forbes leave the country. From Europe, Forbes resigned. When the Senate began a probe of the Forbes case, the Veterans Bureau's legal adviser, Charles F. Cramer, committed suicide.

Soon after hearing about Forbes, Harding learned that Jesse Smith, Daugherty's close friend and aide in the Justice Department, had been selling his influence. Smith himself committed suicide in May 1923.

The stories about Harding's "friends" revealed a scale of corruption not known since the days of President Grant. The pleasant, easygoing President was shocked. "I have no trouble with my enemies," Harding said. It was his friends who kept him "walking the floors at night."

The saddened President left Washington for a trip to the West Coast and Alaska in June 1923. During the trip he asked Secretary Hoover and others again and again what a man should do when he had been betrayed by his friends. During his travels Harding was taken ill. He died suddenly in the evening of August 2, 1923.

The Harding scandals. The nation mourned Harding's death. Soon the truth about his administration began to come out. At first the probes were called mere efforts at "character assassination" of Harding. But not for long.

📖 **More from Boorstin:** "President Coolidge's succinct and often quoted 'They hired the money, didn't they?' summed up the official American position [on war debts]." (From *The Americans: The Democratic Experience*)

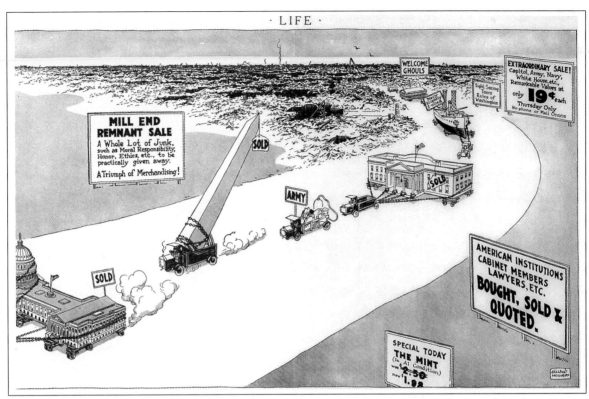

Jones, Brakeley & Rockwell, Inc. © *Life—The Humor Magazine*

The attempt of Harding's associates to enrich themselves by selling and leasing public property for their own profit brought this reaction from a cartoonist. Everything—from Cabinet members to the Mint—could be bought at bargain prices. Honor and ethics were "practically given away."

Forbes was sent to Leavenworth prison for two years. Thomas W. Miller, Alien Property Custodian, was also sent to jail for selling for the profit of the Ohio Gang valuable property taken from the Germans during wartime. Attorney General Daugherty was tried, but he was not convicted.

The most sensational of the scandals was the attempted theft of the national oil reserves. Oil had taken the place of coal to power the ships of the navy. It had become a prime need for commerce and national defense. The government in 1912–1915 had set aside three promising oil fields as reserves for the nation's future. But Harding's Secretary of the Interior, Albert Fall, leased two of these—Teapot Dome in Wyoming, and Elk Hills in California—to private interests

in return for $325,000 in gifts and "loans." Fall ended up with a year in prison, and the leases were later canceled by the Supreme Court.

See "Section 2 Review answers," p. 576D.

Section 2 Review

1. What did the Harding administration accomplish in (a) control of spending? (b) tariff revision? (c) tax cutting?

2. What scandals took place during Harding's administration? Was Harding to blame?

3. **Critical Thinking: Identifying Central Issues.** Why was the Washington Conference historically significant even though the terms of the agreement were unenforceable?

Brown Brothers

When photographers began to follow Presidents everywhere, they took pictures of them in all sorts of situations. "Silent Cal," who never appeared comfortable in front of a camera, can be seen here posed stiffly in a hayfield. It seems doubtful that he intended to do any real work.

See "Lesson Plan," p. 576D.

3. "Keeping cool with Coolidge"

Vice-President Calvin Coolidge was spending his vacation at his father's home in the little village of Plymouth Notch, Vermont, when he was awakened with the news of Harding's death. By the light of a kerosene lamp his father, John Coolidge, a justice of the peace, administered the oath of office.

Coolidge had never even seen Washington, D.C., before he became Vice-President. He had hardly ventured beyond the borders of his native state of Vermont or neighboring Massachusetts, where he had built his political career. He had been mayor of Northampton, lieutenant governor, and then governor of Massachusetts.

Home for Coolidge, his wife, Grace, and their two sons was half a double house in Northampton. This he rented for $27 a month.

President Coolidge. If a playwright had invented a character to contrast with Harding, he could not have done better. Harding was a genial, unbuttoned good fellow who liked to sit around the White House smoking cigars and playing cards with his cronies. This new President was reticent, plain, and thrifty. A man of few words, "Silent Cal" was not one to warm the cockles of your heart. He naturally tempted comedians to make jokes about his quiet manner and his immobile face. Once when a rumor

See "Lesson Plan," p. 576D for **Cooperative Learning Activity: Making Comparisons** relating to the Wilson, Harding, and Coolidge administrations.

started that he had died, a wit remarked, "How would you know?"

But Coolidge was like Harding in one way. He too was an admirer of American business. His best-known utterance was: "The business of America is business." Like Harding, he was anxious not to trouble business with government rules. In the 1900s Calvin Coolidge still shared Thomas Jefferson's belief that the government is best which governs least.

The election of 1924.   This let-alone policy fit the temper of the times. Most Americans were tired of the rules and rationing of the war years. Coolidge followed the Harding policies. Only a year after Coolidge had been thrust into the White House, the Republicans meeting in Cleveland chose him to run for President in the next election. Charles G. Dawes, a banker who had served ably as Director of the Budget, was named for Vice-President.

When the democrats met in their convention, the party was deeply divided. The split in the party mirrored a split in the nation. The Americans who still made their living on farms were troubled by the new ways of life in the growing cities. City dwellers believed they were the vanguard of progress. By a one-vote margin the convention actually refused to denounce the Ku Klux Klan (p. 580) by name. There were dozens of candidates who took advantage of the confusion.

Finally the main battle was between William G. McAdoo of California and Al Smith of New York. McAdoo, Woodrow Wilson's son-in-law, had served as Wilson's energetic and able Secretary of the Treasury and wartime director of the railroads. He was the candidate favored by the rural South and West. The colorful city politician Alfred E. Smith had left school at eleven. He had received his education on the sidewalks of New York, which was easy to tell because he spoke with a resounding New York accent. He was opposed to Prohibition, and he was a devout Roman Catholic.

Between Smith and McAdoo the convention deadlocked. After 102 ballots, the weary delegates settled on the safe and colorless John W. Davis. He was a conservative New York corporation lawyer. For Vice-President the Democrats chose William Jennings Bryan's brother, Governor Charles W. Bryan of Nebraska. At last the delegates could go home after sixteen days spent in the hot Madison Square Garden in New York City.

The Republicans, like the Democrats, would also suffer from the division between the city and the country. When the Republican convention adjourned, "Battling Bob" La Follette of Wisconsin broke with his party. Coolidge, he said, "had literally turned his back on the farmers." Senator La Follette himself then ran for President as the candidate of a new Progressive party. Both Republicans and Democrats attacked La Follette as a dangerous radical.

When the votes were counted, it was plain that most Americans preferred to "keep cool with Coolidge." He received 15 million votes to Davis's 8.5 million and La Follette's surpris-

The Democratic convention of 1924 took 103 ballots to nominate a presidential candidate. Among the delegates and alternates were many women, including this group from Missouri.

ingly large 4.8 million. During that election 123 women won seats in state legislatures. And two women, Miriam A. "Ma" Ferguson of Texas and Nellie T. Ross of Wyoming, wives of former governors, were elected governors of their states.

Government helps business. "If the federal government should go out of existence," President Coolidge once said, "the common run of the people would not detect the difference for a considerable length of time." That was the way he thought it ought to be. For him "free enterprise" simply meant the freedom of business from government rules. Regulation, he believed, would make business less profitable. And, according to Coolidge, it was profitable businesses that made the whole nation happy and prosperous. "The man who builds a factory builds a temple," he declared. "The man who works there worships there." Some people said the President was making business into a religion.

Regulatory agencies, like the Federal Trade Commission and the Federal Reserve Board, were put in the charge of men who would help the businesses they were supposed to regulate. The FTC urged whole industries to agree on trade policies. Some of these agreements tended to create monopolies. Secretary of Commerce Hoover also promoted these "fair practice" agreements so that industries could share information on products and markets. Hoover believed that the day of cutthroat competition was over. Now, he thought, the Department of Commerce should help them cooperate for better products and higher output.

The Supreme Court helped this process along. In 1920 the Court ruled that United States Steel was not a monopoly even though the company controlled 40 percent of the steel industry. This still did not, the Court said, "unreasonably restrain trade." With this green light—and with the help of Hoover and the regulatory agencies—companies all across the land merged to create larger units. By 1929, only 1289 firms produced three-fourths of all goods turned out by corporations. In many industries a few big firms were setting prices through trade associations. The Supreme Court still said that these industrial trade groups were not restraining trade.

And the country prospered. Most Americans were doing better. The price of shares on the stock market was going up rapidly. The economic picture looked promising.

The farm problem. There were a few areas that were slow to recover after the war. The textile, leather, and soft coal industries were weak. Blacks, Indians, and Mexican Americans still had little share in American prosperity. The obvious big problem was the distress on the farms. Now no one could ignore this problem, because the farmers had learned to speak up.

Farmers were growing poorer while much of the rest of the country was growing richer. It seemed that the more they produced, the less they were paid for their crops. At the same time their clothes, their farm implements, their fuel, and the other products they had to buy were going up. Their taxes were rising. When the farmers demanded help, they did get higher tariff protection. But this did little good. High tariffs on farm products could not keep prices up when there were surplus crops.

Now the farmers demanded more direct aid. Senator McNary of Oregon and Representative Haugen of Iowa devised a scheme to use government money to save the farmer from the free market. The idea behind their complex plan was to keep up the price of staple crops regardless of what happened to other prices. The federal government would buy the surpluses that would have driven down farm prices if they went on the open market. The government then would either hold the produce until the market for it improved or it would sell the produce abroad. The McNary-Haugen bill failed to pass Congress in 1924 and 1926. In the next two years it did pass, but Coolidge vetoed it each time. "Farmers have never made money," he said. "I don't believe we can do much about it."

The election of 1928. Near the end of his fourth year in office, Calvin Coolidge announced (in one of his *longer* speeches), "I do not choose to run for President in 1928." In his place the Republicans named the able and (p. 591)

✂ Critical Thinking Activity: Drawing Conclusions What was the effect of Coolidge's pro-business policy? Calvin Coolidge said, "The business of America is business." Write this Coolidge quote across the chalkboard. Beneath it write "Who benefits" and "Who doesn't benefit." Ask students to list, in the appropriate column, groups that would be observed by a pro-business President and groups that would suffer under the same. Have students use this information to evaluate the success of Coolidge's business stance.

ambitious Secretary of Commerce, Herbert Hoover.

The Democrats nominated the "Happy Warrior," Alfred E. Smith. Smith had made a superb record as governor of New York. He had been opposed by many bigoted Democrats from the small towns and from the South who feared that a Catholic President would be only an agent of the Pope. But this time they were not strong enough to deny him the nomination he deserved.

Party platforms were not important in this election. Instead it was what the candidates seemed to stand for. Al Smith, with his New York East Side accent, his brown derby and cigar, and his Roman Catholic religion, was the image of the big city. City people liked his call for the repeal of Prohibition and the return of liquor control laws to the states. Hoover, on the other hand, seemed to stand for big business,

The Bettmann Archive, Inc.

Herbert and Lou Hoover greet the crowd from their train at a "whistlestop" during the 1928 campaign.

Ever the "happy warrior," Al Smith waves to his enthusiastic supporters who line the streets of New York City in the midst of his race with Hoover.

Culver Pictures

for small town and rural America, and for Protestantism and Prohibition.

Prohibition and Smith's Catholic religion were the chief issues of the campaign. Smith met the religious issue squarely. He said that his devotion to his church meant as well devotion to the Constitution and the principle of separation of church and state. But his nomination stirred up much prejudice and fear, especially in the rural South and Middle West where the new Ku Klux Klan had been strongest.

Even without the Catholic issue Hoover could scarcely have failed to win in 1928. Although he lacked personality, his humanitarian record in the war and his policies in the Department of Commerce had made him popular. The country was prosperous, and most Americans were still Republicans. Few observers were surprised when Hoover trounced Smith. He received 21

More from Boorstin: "Ironically, Calvin Coolidge was the first president to become a radio personality. On December 4, 1923, four months after he succeeded to the presidency, his opening message to Congress (the first of these to be broadcast by radio) established the new style of public utterance, and incidentally made President Coolidge a distinctive human figure. His flat conversational delivery in his characteristic nasal twang was punctuated by the turning of his manuscript pages, clearly audible through the microphone." (From *The Americans: The Democratic Experience*)

million votes to Smith's 15 million and captured all but eight states. He even carried five states in the formerly solid South—the first Republican to do so since the days of Reconstruction.

Hoover's easy victory hid some trends that were important for the Democrats. Smith had attracted many new votes in the twelve largest cities, which had formerly been strongly Republican. For the first time since the Civil War, these population centers showed a net plurality for the Democrats. The key to future elections would be in these cities that could carry the big states with their large electoral votes. But for now this crucial fact was hidden by the rosy glow of Republican prosperity.

See "Section 3 Review answers," p. 576D.

Section 3 Review

1. Identify or explain: Charles G. Dawes, William G. McAdoo, Al Smith, John W. Davis, Charles Bryan, Progressive party, Miriam Ferguson and Nellie T. Ross.
2. What were some unusual features of the campaign and the election of 1924?
3. In the 1920s how was business "helped" by (a) Coolidge's attitude toward business? (b) the regulatory agencies? (c) the Supreme Court?
4. Why were farmers in trouble in the 1920s? How did Congress propose to help them? What was Coolidge's response?
5. **Critical Thinking: Making Comparisons.** Who were the presidential candidates in 1928? How did they differ?

See "Lesson Plan," p. 576E.

4. Life in the Jazz Age

During the 1920s the United States seemed a land of miracles. Never before were factories making so many new things. Never before had the daily life of a nation been so quickly transformed.

New products for living. At the opening of the 1900s the automobile was still such an oddity

that in Vermont the law required a driver to send someone an eighth of a mile ahead with a red flag. By 1918 there were nearly 7 million cars on the road. Auto and truck production topped the 2 million mark in 1922 and climbed to more than 5 million in 1929. With the spread of automobiles came the building of new highways and the paving of the roads. Now Americans no longer had to live close together and near their jobs and shops. They could work and shop in places too far to walk to, and out of reach of a streetcar. The first "shopping center" for the newly mobile American was built in Kansas City in 1922.

Back in 1900 the closest thing to a movie was the crude "nickelodeon." In return for your nickel you looked into a box to see pictures move for a few minutes. In 1929 one hundred million tickets were being sold to the movies every week, and the movies could actually talk!

Until World War I most Americans had not even heard of the radio. The first broadcasting station—KDKA in Pittsburgh—did not open until 1920. Its first broadcast carried the Harding-Cox election returns. By 1929 the annual turnout of radio sets numbered 4 million. Television was still in the future. It seemed amazing enough that voices could be sent without wires.

The phonograph was a commercial success by 1905, and within ten years half a million phonograph records were being sold annually. By 1921 production had reached 100 million a year, and a music new to many Americans was sweeping the land. Blacks moving north during World War I brought with them their jazz and blues, and soon recording companies began making records of these surprising sounds. Blacks were now giving the United States a fresh kind of original American music. New heroes and heroines appeared on the scene—Louis Armstrong, "Duke" Ellington, "King" Oliver, Earl "Fatha" Hines, Ferdinand Joseph La-Menthe Morton, known as "Jelly Roll," Bessie Smith, and many others.

During the 1920s everyone began to want a refrigerator to replace the inconvenient old ice box. At the beginning of the decade only about 5000 mechanical refrigerators were made each

Enrichment Support File Topic

Perspectives Topic

Continuity and Change: Social Change Remind students that in addition to being a great technological advance, the automobile, like the railroad, brought many changes to American society. The automobile contributed to the growth of the suburbs just as the railroad contributed to the growth of western cities a half a century ago by allowing people on the fringes of population centers to receive goods and remain in contact with those cities. (See p. 403.)

year. By 1931 over a million a year were being produced by the nation's factories. Now even city people could easily keep milk and fresh fruit and vegetables in all seasons.

Health and education. With advancing medical knowledge now at last the diseases that most threatened children—typhoid, diphtheria, and measles—were coming under control. Americans were healthier and were living longer than ever before. They were also making the highest wages in history—and working shorter hours.

Education in the United States was better and reached a larger proportion of the people than in any other country. By 1928 the money that Americans spent each year for education was more than that spent by all the rest of the world put together. In most European countries only a grade school education was free. But in the United States a free high school education was normal, and millions could hope to go to college.

"The Roaring Twenties." The 1920s have been called "the Roaring Twenties." And with good reason. There were the speakeasies (the illegal bars) and the flappers (young women with short hair and short skirts). There was the new music—jazz, ragtime, and blues suddenly blaring out of millions of phonographs and radios. For the first time in our history huge crowds gathered to watch sporting events. In a single ball park on many afternoons 50,000 fans cheered Babe Ruth as he was breaking all records with his home runs. One hundred forty-five thousand people paid $2.6 million to watch the second fight between Gene Tunney and Jack Dempsey. And a charming young southern gentleman from Georgia named Bobby Jones delighted the nation by defeating the world's best at golf.

The climax of national pride and excitement came May 21, 1927. That night the handsome Charles A. Lindbergh, "Lucky Lindy," landed in Paris. He had made the first solo nonstop flight from New York to Paris in 33 1/2 hours. The nation was inspired to see how courage and the airplane could shrink the Atlantic Ocean.

Culver Pictures

John Held, Jr., helped to create the image of "flappers" and "flaming youth" in the 1920s.

Millions of New Yorkers roared their admiring welcome when he returned. As he was paraded through the streets, 1800 tons of shredded paper rained down from the surrounding skyscrapers. Americans admired Lindbergh's modesty as much as his bravery. He called his book *We* and always shared credit for his feat with his airplane, with those who built it, and with all the Americans who had made his adventure possible. The nation had a new hero—and a new kind of hero. He toured the nation to encourage the rise of air mail and to promote air travel. (p. 594)

The roar of the factory. More than the roar of music or crowds, the sounds that marked the twenties were the hum of the electric dynamo, the clatter of machines, the rhythm of the

Multicultural Connection: At this time, with the rise of blues and jazz and the great flowering of African-American culture, several African-American women singers and songwriters came to prominence. Bessie Smith and Billie Holiday were among the greatest writers and performers of this era. Josephine Baker became a tremendous success on the stage in Paris and achieved great fame throughout Europe.

Charles Lindbergh was the first person to fly nonstop between New York and Paris and the first to fly across the Atlantic alone. He is shown here with his plane in which he made the flight. "The Spirit of St. Louis" can be seen at the National Air and Space Museum, Washington, D.C.

factory assembly line. The nation was finding and making new ways to manufacture radios, refrigerators, airplanes, automobiles, and all sorts of gadgets by the millions. Now a great new force—electric power—was added to the steam power that drove the first modern factories.

The ideas of Frederick W. Taylor on "scientific management" (p. 428) became more and more popular with employers. By making a science of the simplest jobs, they could find a better way to do them.

In an astonishingly short time the American factory took on a different look. Scientific management engineers invented a whole new way of organizing a factory. Instead of having you walk around to pick up parts and bring them to your workbench, the management engineers designed a workbench that moved. Then you could stay in one place and keep your mind on your proper job. The bench (now a moving belt driven by electricity) would carry along the heavy parts from one worker to another.

This new kind of moving workbench was called an "assembly line" because on it the whole machine was put together or "assembled."

In April 1913 a bold mechanic named Henry Ford decided to try an assembly line for making automobiles. He wanted to make cars so cheaply that he could sell them by the millions. He made some improvements of his own in the assembly line. For example, he arranged the moving belt so that it would always be "man-high." Nobody had to waste energy bending down or reaching up.

Ford also varied the speed of the belt. He explained:

The idea is that a man must not be hurried in his work—he must have every second necessary but not a single unnecessary

More from Boorstin: "Lindbergh was an authentic hero. Yet this was not enough. Or perhaps it was too much. . . . [His] newspaper success was unprecedented. . . . A large proportion of the news soon consisted of stories of how Lindbergh reacted to the 'news' and to the publicity about himself. Lindbergh became the biggest pseudo-event of modern times. . . . His achievement, actually because it had been accomplished so neatly and with such spectacular simplicity, offered little spontaneous news. The biggest news about Lindbergh was that he was such big news." (From *Hidden History*)

A Prosperous Nation

FOCUS

To introduce the lesson, write these terms on the chalkboard: corporation, stocks (or shares), stock market, dividend, speculation, buying on margin. Elicit explanations of each term.

Developing Vocabulary

The words listed in this chapter are essential terms for reading and understanding particular sections of the chapter. The page number after each term indicates the page of its first or most important appearance in the chapter. These terms are defined in the text Glossary (text pages 1000–1011).

stock (page 600); **speculator** (page 600).

INSTRUCT

Explain

The total price of outstanding shares in a corporation should reflect the actual value of the company. Margin buying increased demand and bid prices up on fixed stock shares.

✣ Cooperative Learning Activity

Formulating Questions Break the class into small groups. Explain that students will use the library, newspapers, magazines, and any other resources they can think of to find out about the stock market. Have group members divide the following list and describe in writing what each item is: 1) NYSE 2) AMEX 3) NASDAQ 4) Wall Street 5) mutual fund 6) money market fund 7) Standard & Poors 500 8) Wall Street Journal 9) Dow Jones Industrial Average 10) prospectus 11) tax-free money fund 12) stock broker 13) investment 14) Bear market 15) Bull market. Bring the class together and call on students to read their descriptions.

Section Review Answers

Section 1, page 600

1. Hoover had a wealth of experience as an able administrator and some experience of other countries. He headed the Commission for Relief that aided Belgium during World War I and then the Food Administration in the United States. After the war he was in charge of economic relief for Europe and then served as Secretary of Commerce under Harding and Coolidge. 2. People can either receive dividends or sell the stock at a higher price than they paid for it. 3. Margin loans enabled people to buy large numbers of stock with only a small amount of cash, dramati-

cally increasing the number of people buying stock and driving prices up. Gambling on the stock market became a nationwide mania.

CLOSE

To conclude the lesson, ask: How did speculation and margin buying affect the stock market? Discuss students' answers to the question. (Both speculation and margin buying led to a great increase in stock prices, called a bull market. Margin buying also led to a steeper decline in stock prices—a crash—when they began to drop. The price of RCA stock fell to $28 per share on November 13, 1929, for example.) Review with the students the economic concepts they have learned: stock market, share of stock, speculation, margin loan, bull market, stock market crash.

The Big Crash

FOCUS

To introduce the lesson, ask: What is a depression? List student answers on the board: decline in gross national product (GNP), high unemployment, lower prices, increased bankruptcies. Discuss these characteristics.

Developing Vocabulary
depression (page 603)

INSTRUCT

Explain

Use the illustrations on pages 604–607 to point out that the Depression's impact varied considerably from family to family. While millions of families weathered the depression with only minor hardships, thousands of people who remained employed took substantial wage cuts or worked reduced hours. Many families supported relatives who lost their jobs.

☑ Writing Process Activity

Recognizing Cause and Effect Explain to students they will write an essay discussing the causes and effects of the Great Crash or the Great Depression. They should begin by making a chart of the causes and effects. Students can organize their ideas by explaining the effects followed by the causes to answer the question *Why?*, or they can present the causes and then describe the effects to answer the question *How?* As they revise, ask students to be sure they have used transitions such as *reason, because*, and *consequently* to distinguish cause and

Providing In-Depth Coverage

Perspectives on the Great Depression

The collapse of the economic prosperity of the 1920s and Hoover's inability to grasp the need for dramatic and bold government leadership in dealing with the economic trauma of the Great Depression brought Democrat Franklin Roosevelt to the presidency in 1933. Although the era of the New Deal had begun, millions of citizens wondered what this cheerful, confident man could possibly do to restore the spirit of the American people.

A History of the United States as an instructional program provides two types of resources you can use to offer in-depth coverage of the Great Depression and its effect on the average American: the *student text* and the *Enrichment Support File*. A list of *Suggested Secondary Sources* is also provided. The chart below shows the topics that are covered in each.

THE STUDENT TEXT. Boorstin and Kelley's *A History of the United States* unfolds the chronology of events affecting the average American during the Great Depression.

AMERICAN HISTORY ENRICHMENT SUPPORT FILE. This collection of primary source readings and classroom activities reveals the day-to-day struggles of those who lived during the Depression.

SUGGESTED SECONDARY SOURCES. This reference list of readings by well-known historians and other commentators provides an array of perspectives on the Great Depression and its effect on the average American.

Locating Instructional Materials

Detailed lesson plans for teaching the day-to-day effects of the Great Depression as a mini-course or to study one or more elements of the Depression in depth are offered in the following areas: in the *student text*, see individual lesson plans at the beginning of each chapter; in the *Enrichment Support File*, see page 3; for readings beyond the student text, see *Suggested Secondary Sources*.

IN-DEPTH COVERAGE OF THE GREAT DEPRESSION

Student Text	Enrichment Support File	Suggested Secondary Sources
• Distribution of Wealth, p. 603 • Farmers, pp. 604, 608, 626–627, 638, 643–646 • Hoovervilles, p. 606 • Unemployment, pp. 606–607, 628–630 • African Americans, p. 646 • Women, p. 651	• Lesson Suggestions • Multimedia Resources • Overview Essay/The Great Depression: A Struggle to Survive • Literature in American History/*Bound for Glory* • Songs in American History/"1928–1934" • Primary Sources in American History/"There Were Many Beggars" • Biography in American History/Gordon Parks • Geography in American History/The Great Depression Shakeup: Population Change in the 1930s • Making Connections	• *Let Us Now Praise Famous Men* by James Agee, pp. 115–197. • *The Invisible Scar* by Caroline Bird, pp. 2–40. • *A Nation in Torment: The Great Depression, 1929–1939* by Edward Robb Ellis, pp. 116–131. • *Down and Out in the Great Depression: Letters from the Forgotten Man*, Robert S. McElvaine, ed., pp. 95–112. • *Hard Times: An Oral History of the Great Depression* by Studs Terkel, pp. 129–155, 247–271.

Chapter 23
The Coming of the Great Depression

Identifying Chapter Materials

Objectives	Basic Instructional Materials	Extension Materials
1 A Prosperous Nation • Explain how speculation and margin buying affected the Stock Market. • Describe the stock market boom during the last half of the 1920s.	**Annotated Teacher's Edition** • Lesson Plans, p. 598C **Instructional Support File** • Pre-Reading Activities, Unit 8, p. 15	**Documents of American History** • The Philosophy of Rugged Individualism, Vol. 2, p. 222
2 The Big Crash • Explain factors that caused the collapse of the stock market and the nation's economy. • Analyze the problems of income distribution in the United States between 1928 and 1977.	**Annotated Teacher's Edition** • Lesson Plans, pp. 598C–598D **Instructional Support File** • Skill Review Activity, Unit 8, p. 18 • Skill Application Activity, Unit 8, p. 19 • Critical Thinking Activity, Unit 8, p. 20	**Enrichment Support File** • The Great Depression: What it Meant to the Average American (See "In-Depth Coverage" at right.) **Suggested Secondary Sources** • See chart at right.
3 Foreign Affairs in a Gloomy World • Describe the events in the 1920s and early 1930s that foreshadowed the outbreak of World War II.	**Annotated Teacher's Edition** • Lesson Plans, pp. 598D–598E	**Documents of American History** • The Kellogg Peace Pact, Vol. 2, p. 221 • American Intervention in Nicaragua, Vol. 2, p. 208 • The Stimson Doctrine, Vol. 2, p. 225
4 The Election of 1932 • Describe the candidates, issues, and outcome of the presidential election of 1932. • Analyze the charge that Herbert Hoover was to blame for the Great Depression.	**Annotated Teacher's Edition** • Lesson Plans, p. 598E **Instructional Support File** • Reading Activities, Unit 8, pp. 16–17 • Chapter Test, Unit 8, pp. 21–24 • Additional Test Questions, Unit 8, pp. 25–28 • Unit 8 Test, pp. 29–32	**Documents of American History** • The Democratic Platform of 1932, Vol. 2, p. 237

Chapter 22 Review

See "Chapter Review answers," p. 576F.

Focusing on Ideas

1. Identify some groups who suffered from the fears and hysteria of the early 1920s. How did they suffer? Why were they the targets of fear and government investigation?

2. The radicals in the 1920s included anarchists, socialists, and communists. What were the beliefs of each of these groups? Why were they considered dangerous by some Americans? Should all these radical groups have been regarded as equally dangerous? Explain.

3. Many Americans in the early 1920s yearned for a return to the calmer prewar era. What postwar changes might they have found disturbing? What changes occurring later in the 1920s might most Americans have found agreeable? From your lists of the two kinds of changes, what conclusion can you draw about the kinds of social and cultural changes that Americans will be likely to resist and the kinds they will welcome in the future?

Taking a Critical Look

1. **Recognizing Cause and Effect.** How did governmental support help business to prosper?

2. **Making Comparisons.** Compare postwar corruption under Grant and under Harding. Consider the nature and extent of the fraud, the parties involved, and the President's role in it.

Your Region in History

1. **Culture.** Trace the migration of black Americans from or to your region, state, or locality during and after World War I. If substantial numbers of blacks moved to your region, what kinds of jobs did they find? How were they treated?

2. **Economics.** Trace the history of a local business in your area. How was it affected by government controls? What role did labor unions play in its development? How, if at all, did it use "scientific management"?

Historical Facts and Figures

Recognizing Cause and Effect. Study the graph below to help answer the following questions: (a) How many cars does each figure in the pictogram stand for? (b) In what year were the most cars sold? (c) In what year were the least sold? (d) By approximately what percentage did car sales increase during the decade of the 1920s? (e) What information in this chapter helps explain why more Americans were able to buy cars in 1929 than in 1920? (f) What other businesses or industries would have expanded as a consequence of increased car sales?

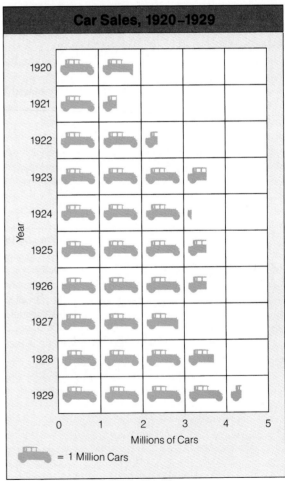

Car Sales, 1920–1929

= 1 Million Cars

Source: *Historical Statistics of the United States*

ments for consumer goods promised comfort, health, beauty, status.

Even more important in selling goods was buying on credit. Now you did not have to wait to buy what you wanted until you had saved enough money. "Buy Now, Pay Later," the ads screamed. By 1928 Americans owed more than $1 billion for the automobiles they had bought on the installment plan.

Buying "on time" can help keep business booming so long as people can afford to buy all that the factories produce. But in the 1920s wages did not rise as fast as output. The real wages of American workers rose 26 percent between 1918 and 1929 while their productivity was going up 40 percent. Without more money, workers could not buy—even "on time"—all the automobiles, refrigerators, radios, washing machines, vacuum cleaners, and other expensive items that fueled the economy.

Most Americans were unaware of any problems. They agreed with Herbert Hoover who caught the spirit of the time in his inaugural address in March 1929:

> Ours is a land rich in resources, stimulating in its glorious beauty, filled with millions of happy homes, blessed with comfort and opportunity. In no nation are the institutions of progress more advanced. In no nation are the fruits of accomplishment more secure. In no nation is the Government more worthy of respect. No country is more loved by its people. I have an abiding faith in their capacity, integrity, and high purpose. I have no fears for the future. . . . It is bright with hope.

See "Section 4 Review answers," p. 576E.

Some automakers emphasized color and style. Henry Ford said his customers could have *any* color—so long as it was black!

Culver Pictures

Color. Nature abounds in beautiful and harmonious color combinations. The birds, the flowers, the sunset skies, set perfect examples—and point the way to brilliant color schemes all in perfect taste.

Yet what artistry is required in the selection of shades and tones to satisfy the modern vogue for color in motor cars! Packard has a special Board of Color made up of men of long experience and artistic judgment. These men create the standard color combinations which charm the eye in such wide variety on today's Packard Six. And they advise on the special requirements of those who buy the Packard Eight.

Whether Six or Eight is your choice you may be as sure of the charm and good taste of the Packard's color scheme as you are of its lasting beauty. For Packard lavishes as much care and effort on the unusual processes which preserve the car's color and finish as upon the selection of the shades which will appeal to Packard's discriminating clientele.

Nothing finer is offered anywhere in the world than the enduring brilliance of Packard cars —long in life and long in beauty of lines and finish.

P A C K A R D
ASK THE MAN WHO OWNS ONE

Section 4 Review

1. What kinds of new consumer goods and services became widespread in the 1920s?
2. What changes were making factory production more efficient?
3. **Critical Thinking: Drawing Conclusions.** Why was "roaring" an appropriate description of the decade of the 1920s?

See "Lesson Plan," p. 576E for **Writing Process Activity: Determining Relevance** relating to teenagers in the 1920s.

second. . . . The man who puts in a bolt does not put on the nut; the man who puts on the nut does not tighten it. On operation number 34 the budding motor gets its gasoline. . . . On operation number 44 the radiator is filled with water, and on operation number 45 the car drives out.

Henry Ford opened his new plant with its electric-powered conveyor belt in 1914, and the time it took to put together a Model T dropped from 14 hours to 93 minutes. By 1925 the process was so perfect that one car rolled off the assembly line every 10 seconds. Machines that had not been imagined 50 years before now cost so little that they changed the lives of ordinary Americans.

Selling the products of the factories. There grew up a powerful American business to sell ✖ this outpouring of new products. Advertising had been around for a long time, but only about $1 billion a year was spent on it before World War I. By 1929 more than $3 billion a year was spent for advertising through newspapers, magazines, billboards, direct mail, and—fastest growing of all—the radio. Advertise-

Henry Ford's assembly line introduced a new standard for efficiency in mass production. Instead of going from task to task, workers stayed in place and a moving belt brought their work to them.

Brown Brothers

✖ Critical Thinking Activity: Making Comparisons How do the new products of the 1920s compare with today's new items? Have students make a list of new products and technology available to Americans in the 1920s. Next to each item tell students to write a sentence describing its impact on the daily lives of Americans. Now have students describe two or three new products that have changed their lives. Ask students to compare the effect of these changes with those in the 1920s.

effect. After proofreading, they can read their essay to a partner.

Section Review Answers
Section 2, page 609

1. a) October 29, 1929, when stock prices fell so sharply that it was the worst day in history for the New York Stock Exchange. b) created in 1929 and given the power to lend money to farm cooperatives to help them market their products. It was also supposed to keep crop prices steady, but failed in this task. c) increased duties on more than a thousand items and weakened international trade. d) created the Federal Farm Board. e) shantytown built of cartons and scrap wood. f) designed to save large corporations, banks, and insurance companies from bankruptcy by lending money. 2. New York's most powerful bankers agreed to invest $30 million to support stock prices. Prices did rise and then held steady for two days, but then they resumed their steep fall. 3. The crash was very visible and was taken as a sign of the state of the economy. When the stock market crash frightened the wealthy out of spending and investing, the rest of the country did not have enough money to spend to keep the economy going. Inventories piled up; workers were laid off; the economy spiraled downward. 4. Lowered the income tax, created the Agricultural Marketing Act, passed the Hawley-Smoot Tariff Act, and created the Reconstruction Finance Corporation, Federal Home Loan Bank, and public works. All were useful, but they were too little too late. 5. Needy people could not obtain jobs or enough money for housing, clothes, or even food. People put off getting married; they went hungry; they moved in with relatives or into shacks made of cartons; many took to the road in search of jobs.

CLOSE

To conclude the lesson, ask students to list and briefly explain the measures taken by the Hoover administration to deal with the depression. In discussing their lists, remind students that present-day techniques for dealing with a serious downturn in business were simply not thought of in the 1930s.

Section 3 (pages 609–613)

Foreign Affairs in a Gloomy World

FOCUS

To introduce the lesson, write on the board the words World Events in the 1920s and 1930s. Below them write these three column headings: Event, Date, and Effect. Break the class up into small groups and have the students use this section of their texts to fill in the columns. Ask them to list the events in chronological order. (Rise of Mussolini in Italy; Mexico Expropriates Oil Fields; Kellogg-Briand Pact; London Naval Conference; Japanese seize Manchuria; Japanese bomb Shanghai; U.S. Withdraws Marines from Nicaragua; Hitler Rises to Power in Germany.)

Developing Vocabulary
default (page 609); **belligerent** (page 610).

INSTRUCT

Explain

When groups have finished, compile a master list of events on the board and ask: How were foreign affairs in the late 1920s and early 1930s linked to the Great Depression? (European nations had difficulty paying war debts during the Depression; high tariffs around the world drove prices up, limited world trade; democracies, wanting to reduce military expenditures, signed disarmament pacts; and the U.S. and other nations refused to implement trade sanctions against aggressor nations like Japan.) How did U.S. relations with Latin America improve during this time? (We negotiated with Mexico on the issue of ownership of the oil fields, abandoned the Roosevelt Corollary to the Monroe Doctrine, recognized *de facto* governments in Latin America, and withdrew Marines from Nicaragua.) Ask students to explain how each of these steps taken by the Coolidge and Hoover administrations improved relations with Latin America by appearing to renounce our role as "big brother."

✿ Cooperative Learning Activity

Testing Conclusions Divide students into pairs and explain that each pair will prepare a report on a treaty between the United States and a Latin American country. Have partners choose a country in Latin America and use outside resources to gather information about any treaty that country signed with the United States prior to 1940. Have partners work cooperatively to compose a brief report summarizing the treaty. Assign one partner to take notes as the report is drafted and to prepare the final copy. Have the other partner present the report to the class.

Section Review Answers
Section 3, page 613

1. a) postponement of the payment of a debt. b) signed in August 1928, an agreement by more than 60 nations that renounced war as an instrument of national policy. c) meeting at which the United States, Great Britain, and Japan agreed to continue

limits on the numbers of ships they could have, but an "escalator" clause allowed a country to build ships beyond the agreed limits if its national security was threatened. d) Secretary of State under Hoover. e) takeover of private property by a government. f) chosen by Coolidge to be ambassador to Mexico and find a peaceful settlement to the dispute over Mexican oil fields owned by American companies. 2. Dominican Republic and Nicaragua are on the map on page 543. Manchuria and Shanghai are shown on the map on page 517. 3. He said that the United States would postpone for one year the payment of war debts owed to it and urged the Allies to do the same for German reparations and for the money they owed each other. 4. United States policy toward Latin America showed respect and good will. American Marines were pulled out of the Dominican Republic in 1924. In 1927 Mexico and the United States settled their dispute over the confiscation of American-owned oil fields. Hoover made a goodwill tour of Latin America before taking office and declared that the United States would no longer interfere in the domestic affairs of Latin American countries. The Roosevelt Corollary was renounced, and the United States said it would recognize *de facto* governments, whether we liked them or not.

CLOSE

To conclude the lesson, draw students' attention to the importance of the failure to apply economic sanctions against Japan for its aggression in China in 1931–1932. Ask: What sanctions might the United States have taken? (Cut off some or all trade, withdrawn ambassadors.) Why did it not do so? (According to the text, Hoover feared it might start a larger war.) According to the text, what was the result of this failure to take action? (Gave green light to other potential aggressor nations.)

Section 4 (pages 613–614)

The Election of 1932

FOCUS

To introduce the lesson, ask students to turn to page 600 in the text and read Hoover's credo (under the heading "Hoover's beliefs"). Study the paragraph sentence by sentence, and identify its underlying values. (Freedom, competition, and limited government involvement.) Ask: Does Hoover's credo overlook any important factors that influence a person's chances for success? (Arguably, parents, connections, environment, and timing all have considerable influence.)

INSTRUCT
Explain

For years the Democrats have invoked the name of Herbert Hoover to show how little Republicans care about the average person and how shortsighted they can be. However, in recent years, Hoover is being treated a little more kindly. (President Reagan hung a picture of Hoover in his office.)

☑Writing Process Activity

Testing Conclusions Ask students to imagine they are Herbert Hoover during the election of 1932. In preparation for writing a campaign speech, students should brainstorm the reasons Hoover might cite to convince people to reelect him. Have students begin their speech with a persuasive sentence summarizing his strengths as President, and have them support this main idea with specific examples. Students should revise for logical organization and persuasive language. After proofreading, students can analyze why Hoover's speech did not obtain the results he hoped for.

Section Review Answers

Section 4, page 614

1. Who was responsible for the Great Depression; what the government could do to end it. Hoover condemned Roosevelt's experimental ideas and said that they would destroy both the American government and free enterprise. Roosevelt blamed the Republicans for causing the depression by encouraging reckless speculation in the stock market. He called for a more equitable distribution of the nation's goods and promised a rapid economic recovery. Also, the Republicans supported the continuation of Prohibition; Roosevelt called for its repeal. 2. The Democrats won because the Republicans were blamed for the depression.

CLOSE

To conclude the lesson, compile on the board a list of Hoover's successes and failures in office and discuss whether Hoover's Presidency overall was a success or a failure.

Chapter Review Answers

Focusing on Ideas

1. Amounts involved and a forced sale to cover the margin may leave the investor with nothing; paying cash allows one to sell by choice. 2. Details of modest background, working his way through college, his success with the Commission for Relief in World War I. Hoover felt people can accomplish anything they desire. 3. The stock market crash signaled producers

to cut back. Layoffs cut consumer buying, bringing more layoffs in affected industries. More layoffs led to others (such as suppliers) to reduce production, adding to unemployment.

Taking a Critical Look

1. European banks could not repay large loans to American banks. Nations couldn't pay off war debts; abandoned gold standard; became unreliable market for American goods. 2. Treaties had made no provision for cooperative action to stop aggression. False security engendered by the pacts told potential aggressors there was little to fear by going to war to achieve national ambitions.

Your Region in History

1–3. Answers will vary depending on your region. Consult your local library or historical society for relevant information.

Historical Facts and Figures

(a) 1926 (b) In 1929 only 3% of the workforce was unemployed. Given the business cycle we can assume that high employment accompanied solid wages, consumer spending, rise in goods and services, and profits on business investments. (c) Minimal consumer spending and an overall cutback in production of goods and services, and 25% of the workforce was unemployed. Students' ideas about how they would handle the economic crisis will vary.

Answers to "Making Connections"

(See "Using Making Connections" on p. 616)

Answers will vary, but may include one or more of the following examples. Answers based on the time line callouts are in italics.

1. The image of a candle burning at both ends is reminiscent of a person concerned only with the pleasures of the present, not with the possible problems of tomorrow. This is an apt description of the mood of the twenties. Technology and science had brought new inventions to the United States. Two that had a large impact in the twenties were radio and the car. The first radio broadcast in the United States—by KDKA in Pittsburgh—was heard in 1920. For the first time a musical performance could be heard by people more than a block or so away, at the very time it was taking place. Listening to the radio became a national pasttime and *people from coast to coast were introduced by musicians to jazz, blues, and ragtime. A dance craze swept the nation.* Not content with cutting the rug at home, people flocked to the dance halls in nearby communities. This would not have been feasible before the advent of the automobile. But *by 1925 one automobile rolled off the assembly-line every ten seconds.* More and more Americans were driving. Despite the fact that the *Eighteenth Amendment prohibited the sale of alcoholic beverages,* speakeasies across the country served illegal liquor to their patrons in addition to providing musical entertainment and the opportunity to dance. In many ways *Charles Lindbergh, the first pilot to fly alone across the Atlantic from New York to Paris,* was symbolic of his age. In fact a dance named after him—the Lindy—became the rage after his successful flight. The "Roaring Twenties" did give off a "lovely light" for a while. Like the candle in the poem, however, the frenzied search for pleasure came to a dark end.

2. Americans reacted to the Depression in a number of ways. The pleasure-loving "Roaring Twenties" came to an abrupt end in *1929 when the stock market crashed on October 24—Black Thursday.* There was little time between the stock market crash and a full-scale depression. By *1931, 2,298 banks had closed as Americans demanded their savings.* Some Americans cut back on spending, put off marriages, and did not go to college. For the hardest hit such measures were not enough. They went hungry and had no place to live. Some Americans did not take their losses lying down. *In the spring of 1932, thousands of unemployed veterans formed a "Bonus Army" and marched on Washington.* Hoover tried to help. *In 1932 he asked Congress to create the Reconstruction Finance Corporation to provide jobs for the unemployed.* But despite all efforts, the Depression dragged on and spread throughout the world. *In 1931 Austria suffered economic collapse, signaling financial failures across Europe.* Wanting a change, Americans defeated Hoover when he ran again and elected Franklin Delano Roosevelt.

The Coming of the Great Depression

When Herbert Hoover took the oath of office in March 1929, trade was booming, industry was flourishing. Unemployment was low, wages were up, prices were steady, and corporations were making big profits and paying fat dividends. Some people had not felt this tide of prosperity, but even they seemed to take it for granted that their time would come.

Yet before the end of Hoover's first year in office, the stock market had collapsed. The nation was beginning to slide into the worst depression in its history. And by the time Hoover left office in 1933, many citizens had lost faith in their business leaders. Some had begun to question the American economic system and even democracy itself.

Russian-born Isaac Soyer realistically portrayed the despair of life during the depression.

Whitney Museum of American Art, New York

See "Lesson Plan," p. 598C.

1. A prosperous nation

Most Americans were confident that with Hoover, the Great Engineer, at the helm, their country's growth and prosperity would never end. Progress, it seemed, must go on forever. Then, in late October 1929, came terrifying signs that the success story might have an unhappy ending.

Herbert Hoover, engineer. Herbert Hoover was a perfect symbol of the ideals and hopes of the American business community in the 1920s. He showed that to succeed in the United States and to be elected President you did not have to come from a rich, upper-class family. His life proved that in America character, intelligence, and hard work could make a national leader. Born of Quaker parents on a small farm in Iowa in 1874, he had been orphaned at the age of ten. He worked his way through Stanford University, where he studied engineering. Then he made his fortune as a mining engineer in Australia, Africa, China, Latin America, and Russia. He was a millionaire by the time he was 40.

When World War I broke out, Hoover was living in London. His Quaker heritage and his desire to soften the miseries of war drew him quickly into relief work. He did a speedy and spectacular job as head of the Commission for Relief, which fed 10 million starving people in Belgium and northeastern France. When we entered the war, he came home to lead the Food Administration. And at the war's end, Wilson put him in charge of economic relief for all Europe. Hoover and his team, as English economist John Maynard Keynes observed, "not only saved an immense amount of human suffering, but averted a widespread breakdown of the European system."

"The ungrateful governments of Europe," Keynes added, "owe much more to the statesmanship and insight of Mr. Hoover and his band of American workers than they have yet appreciated or will ever acknowledge."

In September 1919 when Hoover returned to the United States, he was a national figure—though it was not clear to what political party

United Press International Photo

The future of the country looked bright on March 4, 1929, as Calvin Coolidge (left) and Herbert Hoover posed for this picture just before going to Hoover's inauguration.

he belonged. "He is certainly a wonder," Assistant Secretary of the Navy Franklin D. Roosevelt then wrote, "and I wish we could make him President of the United States. There could not be a better one."

Had Hoover played his cards right, he might have been nominated—and elected—in 1920. Instead, he declared that he was a Republican, without lining up the support of that party. Now the Democrats could not nominate him. The Republican bosses could hold him in reserve, meanwhile naming a man they could control—Warren G. Harding.

If Hoover had become President in 1920, he

might have established a reputation in the next eight years as one of our most successful Presidents in times of prosperity. Instead he became Secretary of Commerce under Harding and Coolidge. He made the young Department of Commerce an important new force in government. With the focus of an engineer, he formed an Office of Simplified Practice. The more efficient ways devised by this office saved business and government more money than the entire budget of the Department of Commerce.

Hoover's beliefs. Hoover believed in the American capitalist system. He had shared its success. And he had seen it become more responsible. He did not believe in big government, but he saw the federal government playing a larger role than imagined by Harding or Coolidge. He declared for the nation the credo of his own life:

> It is as if we set a race. We through free and universal education provide the training of the runners; we give to them an equal start; we provide in the government the umpire of fairness in the race. The winner is he who shows the most conscientious training, the greatest ability, and the greatest character.

The stock market boom. When Hoover took office, the country was in the grip of a speculative fever. The New York stock market was where people bought and sold stocks—"shares"—in the largest corporations. The owner of a share really owned part of the company. If the company grew and made a large profit, then the owner of the share would be paid a dividend as part of the profit. And if the dividends grew, the value of the share would go up. Naturally, everybody wanted to own shares in the most profitable companies.

Stock prices began to increase from 1921 on. But the stock market mania did not begin until 1927. Then many people started to buy shares hoping to make their profits not from the earnings of the company, but from the higher price that other stock market gamblers would pay them for their shares. More and more people began risking their money in the stock market.

They expected to get rich when the price of their shares would suddenly go up. And with the money they made, they would buy other shares that they hoped would also go up.

(p. 601)

Margin loans. People borrowed on "margin" to buy stocks. When buying on margin, all you had to do was put down a small amount of cash to buy each share of stock. Then you could borrow the rest of the purchase price on the value of the stock itself. When the stock went up in price, you could make a great deal of money on a small investment. But if the price went down, you could lose all you had put in. For a time, stock prices appeared only to go up. Everyone seemed to know someone who had grown rich overnight.

Stock market gambling became a mania, a contagious disease. Americans who never would have thought of borrowing money to bet on the horse races now were borrowing to bet on stocks. The more the stock mania grew, the less connection there was between the real value of a company and the price people were paying for that company's shares on the stock market. Businesses found they could make more money with their cash by giving it to brokers to use for margin loans than by investing in new machines and factories.

Some people voiced concern over what was happening on the stock market, and especially over the size of brokers' margin loans. President Coolidge said it was only due to the "natural expansion of business." But later he told a reporter that "any loan made for gambling in stocks [is] 'excessive.'"

See "Section 1 Review answers," p. 598C.

Section 1 Review

1. What experiences qualified Herbert Hoover for the Presidency?

2. What are the two ways in which a person can make a gain by owning corporation stock?

3. **Critical Thinking: Recognizing Cause and Effect.** What was the effect of margin loans on the stock market boom?

✂ Critical Thinking Activity: Recognizing Ideologies Could Hoover's personal credo apply today? Ask students to discuss how President Hoover's personal credo could work in today's world. Have students revise his credo or construct an original credo that would be more appropriate for modern times. Let students share their credo and its message.

The Bettmann Archive, Inc.

Brokers at the Curb Market in New York buy and sell stock for their clients. During the 1920s speculating in stocks became a nationwide mania.

See "Lesson Plan," p. 598C.

2. The big crash

On September 3, 1929, the booming rise in the market came quietly to a halt. Even though a few stocks later reached new highs, the market began a slow decline. Soon the decline would become a collapse. It would wipe out the speculators, stop the economy, and lead to the greatest depression in United States history.

Black Thursday. During October the stock market had some bad days. Then, suddenly, on October 24 ("Black Thursday" it would be called) prices began to fall, and buyers on margin had to sell their stocks. The rush to sell made prices fall even faster.

On Black Thursday, New York's most powerful bankers met at the offices of J. P. Morgan & Co. They decided to pool their resources to the amount of $30 million to support the stock market. The action of the bankers was confirmed when Richard Whitney, the acting president of the Stock Exchange and a known agent of the Morgan firm, began placing orders above current prices. Prices at once began to move upward. At the end of the day the market had recovered much of its earlier losses. Some speculators had been wiped out during the course of the wild day, but the panic seemed over. On Friday and Saturday, prices remained steady. From Washington, President Hoover, who had never approved of the speculation, reassured the nation. "The fundamental business of the country," he said, "that is, the production and distribution of goods and services—is on a sound and prosperous basis."

See "Lesson Plan," p. 598C for **Cooperative Learning Activity: Formulating Questions** relating to the stock market.

The Great Crash. But on Monday prices again dropped rapidly. The bankers, who were overcommitted in the market themselves, now decided that they could do nothing. Black Tuesday, October 29, 1929, was the worst day of all. Some 16.5 million shares changed hands (a record-high volume for 39 years). Prices fell steeply. The next day prices recovered somewhat, only to fall again the following day. And that became the pattern.

(p. 603)

In the weeks that followed, the prices of stocks sank lower and lower. A share in U. S.

This was the *New York Times* headline on the morning of October 29, 1929. Worse was still to come.

STOCK PRICES SLUMP $14,000,000,000 IN NATION-WIDE STAMPEDE TO UNLOAD; BANKERS TO SUPPORT MARKET TODAY

Sixteen Leading Issues Down $2,893,520,108; Tel. & Tel. and Steel Among Heaviest Losers

A shrinkage of $2,893,520,108 in the open market value of the shares of sixteen representative companies resulted from yesterday's sweeping decline on the New York Stock Exchange.

American Telephone and Telegraph was the heaviest loser, $448,905,162 having been lopped off of its total value. United States Steel common, traditional bellwether of the stock market, made its greatest nose-dive in recent years by falling from a high of 202½ to a low of 185. In a feeble last-minute rally it snapped back to 186, at which it closed, showing a net loss of 17½ points. This represented for the 8,131,055 shares of common stock outstanding a total loss in value of $142,293,446.

In the following table are shown the day's net depreciation in the outstanding shares of the sixteen companies referred to:

Issues.	Shares Listed.	Losses in Points.	Depreciation.
American Radiator	10,096,289	10⅜	$104,748,997
American Tel. & Tel.	13,203,09[illegible]	34	448,905,162
Commonwealth & Southern	30,764,468	3⅛	96,138,962
Columbia Gas & Electric	8,477,307	22	186,500,754
Consolidated Gas	11,451,188	20	229,023,760
DuPont E. I.	10,322,481	16⅝	103,030,625
Eastman Kodak	2,229,703	41⅞	93,368,813
General Electric	7,211,484	47½	342,545,490
General Motors	43,500,000	6¾	293,625,000
International Nickel	13,777,408	7⅞	108,497,088
New York Central	4,637,086	22⅝	104,914,071
Standard Oil of New Jersey	24,843,643	8	198,749,144
Union Carbide & Carbon	8,730,173	20	174,615,460
United States Steel	8,131,055	17½	142,293,446
United Gas Improvement	18,646,835	6	111,881,010
Westinghouse Elec. & Mfg.	2,589,265	34½	88,682,326

PREMIER ISSUES HARD HIT

Unexpected Torrent of Liquidation Again Rocks Markets.

DAY'S SALES 9,212,800

Nearly 3,000,000 Shares Are Traded In Final Hour—The Tickers Lag 167 Minutes.

NEW RALLY SOON BROKEN

Selling by Europeans and "Mob Psychology" Big Factors in Second Big Break.

The second hurricane of liquidation within four days hit the stock market yesterday. It came suddenly,

Continuity and Change: Economics Point out to students that in October, 1929, stock prices dropped further and more rapidly than ever before, bringing on the Great Depression. In 1987, again there was a drastic drop in stock prices, the worst in American history. However, the reforms made later, during the 1930s, helped to prevent another economic collapse like the Great Depression, such as federal insurance on bank accounts, the Securities and Exchange commission, and the Federal Reserve System. (See p. 926.)

Steel, which on September 3 had sold for $262, by November 13 had fallen to $150. A share in Montgomery Ward, which had hit $138, dropped to $49. The average price of 50 leading stocks sank by half. In the last four months of 1929 the overall value of stocks plummeted by $40 billion. And their fall would continue. U. S. Steel would drop to $22. Montgomery Ward would reach $4. General Motors, once at $73, would fall to $8.

The unequal distribution of wealth. Why should it matter, in 1929, if gamblers on the stock market lost their money? The automobile factories and the people with the know-how were still there, just as good as ever. The wealth of the land and the energy of the people were still there. America was still a good investment. Wasn't Hoover right that "the fundamental business" of America was sound?

President Hoover was not quite right. There were serious weaknesses in the economy that had hardly been noticed up to then. As we have seen, while the output of American workers increased steadily during the twenties, their wages had not kept pace (p. 596). At the same time, business profits and the incomes of the wealthy had shot up. In 1929 the 36,000 wealthiest families in America had a combined income equal to that of the nearly 12 million families with incomes of less than $1500 per year. Yet the cost of necessities for a family was $2000 per year.

This meant that "prosperity"—the whole economy—depended on the spending and reinvestment of their money by the wealthy and by business firms. When the stock market panic frightened them, they stopped spending and investing. And the mass of the people could not pick up the slack. They had bought all they could on time, and they had no spare cash. Most consumers could no longer afford to buy the new cars and radios and refrigerators. Inventories piled up. Factories laid off more and more workers.

Other flaws in the economy. Another weakness in the economy lay in our relations with the rest of the world. As a result of the war,

many nations owed the United States money. Yet our tariff walls kept them from trading with us. So we had to make loans and investments abroad if the foreign nations were to pay us. Once the flow of American money slowed down, these nations could not pay their debts. And they could no longer afford to buy American goods. This was another cause for factories to shut down, throwing still more Americans out of work.

The rise of "holding companies" had created some special problems that did not quickly meet the eye. During the 1920s more and more of these companies had been formed to hold the stock of other companies. Business power was being concentrated in fewer hands. Also, investment trusts were set up to sell their own stock and then invest the proceeds in the stock market. Naturally, the investment trusts and holding companies depended on the earnings of the companies they held. If anything happened to those, the holding companies and investment trusts would collapse. Then confidence in business throughout the nation would drop even more.

But the worst flaw in the economy of the late 1920s was the stock market itself. It provided a gambling arena where whims, unfounded fears, and unjustified hopes could trigger disaster. The stock market provided a stage where the whole nation could watch the price of Wall Street's stocks go *boom* and then *bust!* That made it hard for citizens to realize that what was roller-coastering was only the price and not the value of the nation's product. Doubt and fear spread across the nation.

Hoover takes action. It took a little time for the stock market crash to bring on a full-scale depression. Secretary of the Treasury Andrew Mellon adopted the traditional approach that the government should do nothing to end the depression or ease its effects. "Let the slump liquidate itself," he advised. "Liquidate labor, liquidate stocks, liquidate the farmers, liquidate real estate. . . . It will purge the rottenness out of the system."

When the collapse came, President Hoover did not sit still. He used all the familiar ways to

See "Lesson Plan," p. 598C for **Writing Process Activity: Recognizing Cause and Effect** relating to the Great Depression.

The aimlessness and despair of life during the 1930s were caught by talented photographers employed by the Farm Security Administration. Dorothea Lange, one of the best, took the picture directly above and on page 605.

relieve suffering. He called upon cities, states, and all private charities to help feed the hungry. He brought business and labor leaders to the White House, where they promised to keep up wages and keep the factories going. He actually cut his own presidential salary by one-fifth.

In November 1929 Hoover even took the daring step for those days of persuading Congress to cut income taxes. He hoped this would leave people some money to buy goods to keep the factories going. But for most people income taxes were still so low that the tax cut made little difference. A family with a $4000 income saw its tax decline from $5.63 to $1.88. The wealthy, of course, saved much more. But they were frightened of the future, and so did not dare to increase their spending.

Aid for the farmers and for business. The farmers, who had not shared in the prosperity of the twenties, had just received some federal aid. During a special session of Congress in the spring of 1929, an Agricultural Marketing bill passed by large majorities. This created a Federal Farm Board with $500 million to lend to farm cooperatives to help them market their crops. The board was also told to use its funds to keep farm prices steady.

But the Farm Board had no control over production. Though its agencies bought huge amounts of wheat and cotton, it could not keep prices up. By the close of 1931 wheat had sunk from $1 to 61 cents a bushel and cotton from 16 cents to 6 cents a pound. On the purchases of wheat and cotton alone the government's loss was $185 million.

Hoover had also asked for a "limited revision" upward of the tariff to help the textile factories and a few other depressed industries. Instead, Congress gave him just what the country did not need. In 1930 the Hawley-Smoot Tariff Act actually boosted duties on a thousand items. Within seventeen months after President Hoover signed the law, United States exports and imports were cut almost in half.

The run on banks. Hoover's "engineering statesmanship" was widely praised. The *Boston Globe* was pleased that the nation had "at

Multicultural Connection: The Depression hit hardest the Southern African Americans who worked in agriculture. Two-thirds of Southern African Americans were sharecroppers or wage laborers. In 1930, 1,112,510 African Americans were employed as agricultural laborers. By 1940 this figure had dropped to 780,312.

the White House a man who believed not in the philosophy of drift, but in the dynamics of mastery."

Still the country plunged deeper into depression. If stocks could fall so fast, maybe nothing was worth as much as people thought.

People lost their faith in banks. In the Federal Reserve Act of 1913, Congress had tried to reduce public fears over bank failures (p. 538). Depositors would not be tempted to run to their bank to draw out their money when they heard about a bank failure here and there. If a run did start, the banks could get prompt help from their district's Federal Reserve bank. But this system could not stand up under the severe strains that came with the stock market crash.

Foreign banks had large deposits in banks over here in order to carry on trade. These foreign bank deposits dropped sharply after 1930. Next, the whole rural credit system collapsed. Low prices for farm crops meant that farmers could not pay back their loans. Then rural banks could not pay their depositors.

So bank failures began to rise sharply. People everywhere seemed to want to draw out their money at the same time. When they could not produce the cash their depositors wanted, banks failed by the hundreds. The number reached 642 in 1929 and more than doubled the next year. In 1931 the 2298 banks that closed held deposits of $1.6 billion. People who had spent years saving to buy a house or to send their children to college had their hopes blasted. People who had scrimped for a lifetime to feel secure in their old age all at once were penniless.

The beginning of the Great Depression.

The Great Crash became the Great Depression. The factory owners who could not sell their products slowed down their factories and laid off workers. Jobless workers who had lost their savings could not afford to buy anything. Still more factories closed down. The collapse of the stock market had signaled the collapse of industry and helped to bring on a severe economic depression not just in the United States, but in developed nations around the world.

Before the end of 1932 there were 12 million able-bodied Americans (about one in every four workers) who were unemployed. Many who had jobs were working only part-time. When they could not afford to pay their rent, they had to squeeze in with friends or relatives. Thousands took to the roads, drifting from place to place, desperately hoping that somehow in the next town they would find a job. Respectable Americans who only a few months before had lived in decent houses now had to seek shelter in shantytowns of cartons and wood scraps on vacant lots. These were called Hoovervilles. The young people with no money, no job, and no prospects did not dare marry. Within three years, the number of marriages dropped by one-quarter. College enrollments sank.

Millions went hungry. Children cried for the food their parents could not give them. Two-thirds of the children in New York City suffered from malnutrition. Some parents went wandering through alleys, rooting in garbage pails for scraps to keep their families alive.

The unemployed strike back.

Where were the bright hopes of the New World? It is not surprising that energetic Americans, whose lifeblood was optimism, would not take all this lying down.

Desperate unemployed people went on hunger marches. In Henryetta, Oklahoma, 300 men broke into food stores. In Iowa and Nebraska, farmers who could no longer pay their mortgages used their pitchforks to drive off the sheriffs who came to seize their land. Between 1930 and 1934 one million families lost their farms.

In the spring of 1932 thousands of unemployed veterans formed a "Bonus Army." They demanded that the full cash value of their insurance policies should be paid them by the government at once. They marched on Washington. When they arrived in the capital, of course, they could not afford to stay in hotels. So they camped in empty government buildings and on government land waiting for their

Desperate for a little income, some of the unemployed sold apples at a nickel each as the man in this photo is doing in sight of the nation's Capitol.

United Press International Photo

✂ **Critical Thinking Activity: Expressing Problems Clearly** What group of factors brought on the Great Depression? Ask to students to list, on a sheet of paper, the elements that contributed to the Great Depression. Next to each item, tell students to describe a solution that might have eliminated or addressed the trouble. As a class, compile this work in a master summary of problems and possible solutions. Have students save their work for comparison with Hoover and Roosevelt's approaches to the same issues.

United Press International Photo

When unemployment struck, a person's automobile was one of the first things that had to go for whatever price it would bring—even if the price was low.

bonus. President Hoover called out the army to drive them away. "What a pitiful spectacle," the *Washington News* observed, "is that of the great American Government, mightiest in the world, chasing unarmed men, women, and children with Army tanks. If the Army must be called out to make war on unarmed citizens, this is no longer America."

Where would it end?

Who had killed prosperity? In the panic many Americans lost their heads. Everybody wanted someone to blame. Crackpots offered fantastic cure-alls. Abolish banks! Print more money! Some even said that the end of the world was near.

Hoover tries to help. Never was there a more honest or more hard-working President. But Herbert Hoover was no politician. He did not like to persuade people. He did not enjoy the arts of compromise. As an engineer he felt that he saw problems clearly. After he had carefully prepared his solution, he thought people ought to follow his plan without arguing.

Wearing a high stiff collar, he was a stiff man who inspired respect but not love. He had none of William Jennings Bryan's eloquence, nor any of Theodore Roosevelt's pep. In ordinary times he might have been a good President to keep America on the familiar road to success. But these were not ordinary times. The skills of an engineer were not enough. The nation also needed in great measure the traditional American talents—for imagination and experiment.

Hoover used the Agricultural Marketing Act to try to keep up the prices of tobacco, cotton, corn, and wheat and help the farmers. In December 1930 he started a large program for the construction of public works. By the end of his term of office he would spend more than $2 billion on roads, buildings, and other public construction.

Alexander Hogue's painting "The Dust Bowl," made in 1933, captured the bleakness of the land when drought came to the Great Plains and nothing would grow.

To save large corporations, banks, and insurance companies from bankruptcy, he asked Congress to create the Reconstruction Finance Corporation. The bill, to provide jobs by saving companies and to help "start the country forward all along the line," was enacted early in 1932. The RFC had $2 billion to lend to needy banks, railroads, insurance companies, and farm credit associations. Congress also passed at Hoover's request the Federal Home Loan Bank Act to help people with mortgages from losing their homes. As Hoover said, that was "one of the tragedies of this depression."

Hoover's limitations. Hoover did more than any other President before him had ever done to check a depression. But he refused to provide direct relief for individuals. He said it was dan-(p. 609) gerous to get people in the habit of receiving charity from the national government.

What Hoover did helped, but it was not enough. The disaster was more far-reaching than he realized. And it required remedies more novel than he could imagine.

Then to complicate his problem, one of the worst droughts in recent history hit the nation in 1930. On half a million farms in eighteen states from Virginia to Oklahoma crops withered and cattle died of thirst. Hoover went along when Congress voted $45 million to help farmers feed their livestock, but he opposed giving $25 million to feed the farmers and their families. Finally he allowed Congress to vote $20 million for loans. To give the money, the President said, "would have injured the spiritual response of the American people." But the times

Continuity and Change: Economics Remind students that the Reconstruction Finance Corporation operated on the premise that saving companies from financial ruin would provide jobs and stimulate the economy. Like political leaders of the 1980s, Hoover was hesitant just to give people government funds. The "supply-side" economics of the 1980s was based on the belief that if the government cut taxes for businesses and individuals with sizeable incomes, then the money would be reinvested in more businesses, which in turn would employ more people and produce more goods and services, thereby helping the economy grow. (See p. 898.)

called for new measures. The American spirit would have to be lifted by a more adventurous American willing to try new ways.

See "Section 2 Review answers," p. 598D.

Section 2 Review

1. Identify or explain: Black Tuesday, Federal Farm Board, Hawley-Smoot Tariff Act, Agricultural Marketing Act, Hooverville, Reconstruction Finance Corporation.

2. Who tried to stop the collapse of the stock market? How was this attempt made? What happened?

3. Why did it matter that the stock market crashed?

4. What steps did President Hoover and Congress take to stop the business decline? Why did these steps fail?

5. **Critical Thinking: Drawing Conclusions.** How did the Great Depression affect people's daily lives? How did some people react to hard times?

See "Lesson Plan," p. 598D.

3. Foreign affairs in a gloomy world

The depression also left its mark on foreign affairs. American banks had made large loans to banks in Europe. As panic and depression spread, European banks also came under pressure from their depositors. In June 1931 Germany and Austria were on the verge of financial collapse. Hoover said that we would postpone for one year any payments on the war debts owed to us by our former allies. And he asked them to do the same on their debts to one another and on the German reparations.

Even this *debt moratorium* did not save the situation. Nation after nation was forced to give up the gold standard. They refused any longer to tie the value of their money to gold. Still, the President, supported by American business opinion, refused to allow the war debts to be canceled. Nations should follow the same rules as private individuals! President Coolidge had said, "They hired the money, didn't they?" Anyway, all the debtor nations except Finland ended up defaulting, or not paying. Many Europeans felt that their own depression and unemployment were caused by these war debts and by the high American tariffs against their goods. They expected the United States to be more charitable than other nations.

The Kellogg-Briand Pact. Not only the war debts but the memory of battlefield horrors haunted Americans. During the Coolidge years the United States along with Great Britain, France, Italy, Germany, Japan, and some 60 other nations had signed a peace pact. They had promised to "renounce war as an instrument of national policy in their relations with one another." They agreed to seek the solution of all disputes or conflicts, "of whatever nature," by peaceful means. This Kellogg-Briand Pact—named for Secretary of State Frank Kellogg and French Foreign Minister Aristide Briand—was signed in Paris in August 1928.

After World War I, according to this cartoon, the Kellogg Pact remarried Peace to the wicked world.

Library of Congress

The Bettmann Archive

Noted lawyer Frank B. Kellogg became Coolidge's Secretary of State in 1924.

Some hardheaded Americans said that the Kellogg-Briand Pact did no more than express a pious hope. They warned that Americans should not feel secure simply because they hated war. Others had more confidence in the peace pact. They even thought it would now be safe to agree to reduce the size of the costly American navy.

In January 1930 a new naval conference of the United States, Great Britain, Japan, Italy, and France met in London. The United States, Great Britain, and Japan agreed to continue the limits on the number of large capital ships (p. 584). They also accepted fixed ratios for cruisers, destroyers, and submarines.

But new forces were rising in Europe. A few farsighted writers saw another world conflict brewing. The belligerent Mussolini had brought fascism to Italy in 1922. And it was the old tragedy—only with new villains—all over again. Fearing Italy, France refused to limit its naval power. Italy, openly warlike, refused to sign any agreement. Finally the whole purpose of the

London naval treaty was frustrated by an "escalator" clause. This allowed any country to build ✂ more ships if another power threatened its "national security." Still, Secretary of State Henry L. Stimson said he looked forward to further conferences "confident that we shall obtain ever increasing security with ever decreasing armaments."

Coolidge and Latin America. United States relations with Latin America during the Coolidge years had been a strange mixture. At times we seemed interested only in "dollar diplomacy." Then again, we would seem to be a sincere "good neighbor." In 1916 the United States Marines were sent into the Dominican Republic to protect the sugar and fruit holdings of United States businesses. Then in 1924 these troops were pulled out. A treaty was agreed upon that ended our military rule there, and the troops were brought home.

The United States had long shown a special interest in Nicaragua. It was a possible site for a canal between the oceans. And American business had invested there in coffee, banana, and sugar plantations. But Nicaragua's main crop seemed to be revolutions. In 1912, marines were sent there to protect American interests. Hardly had they been withdrawn in 1925 when another revolution broke out. The United States sent back the marines, who put a friendly party in power. But the Nicaraguan guerrillas had their own ideas. The drama of civil war followed. The United States finally gave up armed intervention and withdrew the marines in 1933.

In Mexico it was oil that attracted special United States interests. The Mexican constitution of 1917 had declared that all oil deposits now belonged to the state. This was true even if they had been granted earlier to private companies. The name for this takeover was *expropriation*. Oil companies were supposed to apply for oil leases on land they thought they had already purchased. The United States protested, and it was not until 1925 that Mexico began to enforce its control over the oil. President Coolidge objected that Mexico was "confiscating property legally owned by American citizens."

✂ Critical Thinking Activity: Demonstrating Reasoned Judgment What were the inherent flaws of the Kellogg-Briand Pact? Have students use the information in this section to build a list of evidence demonstrating the weakness of the Kellogg-Briand Pact. Ask students to discuss ways that the pact could have been written to avoid these pitfalls.

Charles A. Lindbergh was welcomed with great enthusiasm after his nonstop flight from Washington, D.C., to Mexico City. Here he is shown being greeted by General Alvarez upon his arrival.

In January 1927 Congress called for the peaceful settlement of the issues. Coolidge sent a former Amherst College classmate, the shrewd and able Dwight W. Morrow, as ambassador to Mexico. Morrow, a partner in J. P. Morgan's firm, showed what could be done by tact and sympathy. With his understanding of Mexico's problems he won the confidence of the government and the people.

When America's hero Charles A. Lindbergh made a nonstop goodwill flight of 2200 miles from Washington to Mexico City in December 1927, he too became an "ambassador of goodwill." There Lindbergh met Ambassador Morrow's brilliant and attractive daughter Anne. They married in 1929. Sharing a love of the airplane, they flew around the nation and the world exploring new air routes. They awakened enthusiasm for the Air Age. The Lindberghs also wrote popular books about their experiences and cheered the country by their romantic collaboration.

Hoover and Latin America. President Hoover and his Secretary of State Stimson were determined somehow to improve our relations with the countries of Latin America. For 30 years the United States had been intervening in their affairs, and now it was no easy matter to remove their suspicions. Before taking office, Hoover had shown that he meant business when he spent ten weeks on a goodwill trip. In Argentina he announced that the United States would no longer interfere in the domestic affairs of those nations.

By the Roosevelt Corollary to the Monroe Doctrine (p. 542), the domineering TR had declared the right of the United States to intervene in Latin America when United States interests were threatened. Now, it was announced, the Roosevelt Corollary was no longer our policy. "The Monroe Doctrine," Secretary Stimson said, "was a declaration of the United States versus Europe—not of the United States versus Latin America."

More from Boorstin: "A second event which kept Lindbergh alive as a celebrity was the kidnapping of the couple's infant son in 1932. The case was never fully solved, and despite the execution of the supposed kidnapper, no one can know whether the child would have been returned unharmed if the press had behaved differently. But the press unwittingly destroyed real clues and garnered and publicized innumerable false clues. They exploited Lindbergh's personal catastrophe." (From *Hidden History*)

The Hoover administration declared that it would respect the facts of South American political life—whether we liked them or not. Any "de facto" government, that is, one that in fact controlled a country, would be recognized by the United States.

Japan ends the peace. On the other side of the world in 1931, the Japanese army seized Manchuria and the next year turned it into the puppet state of Manchukuo. Americans were shocked but could not be surprised. The firm agreements in the Nine Power Treaty and the high hopes of the Kellogg-Briand Pact were shattered. What could Americans do?

Secretary of State Stimson sent a note of protest. The United States, he said, would not recognize such changes made by force. The Council of the League of Nations, with an American "observer" present for the first time, invoked the Kellogg-Briand Pact to outlaw Japan. In January 1932, Japanese forces attacked Shanghai and bombed the city, killing thousands of civilians. But neither the League of Nations nor the people of the United States would risk war to restrain this aggression. Americans were more troubled by their depression than by the sufferings of the distant Chinese.

Stimson urged economic sanctions—a trade boycott—against Japan. Hoover refused, for he feared that sanctions would be the first step to war.

Meanwhile, war-loving leaders were rising to power in Italy and Germany. Later, Mussolini and Hitler would remember the timidity of the United States and other peaceful nations. If the high-sounding agreements had no power

The port city of Hankou on the Yangtze River fell to Japanese troops in October 1938. This photograph of triumphant soldiers with the Rising Sun flag was taken for *Life* magazine by Paul Dorsey.

Paul Dorsey

❖ See "Lesson Plan," p. 598D for **Cooperative Learning Activity: Testing Conclusions** relating to treaties between the United States and Latin American countries.

against an aggressive Japan, why should other aggressive powers hold back? Fascist Italy and Nazi Germany—the forces of tyranny and barbarism—saw their green light.

See "Section 3 Review answers," p. 598D.

Section 3 Review

1. Identify or explain: debt moratorium, Kellogg-Briand Pact, London Naval Conference, Henry Stimson, expropriation, Dwight Morrow.
2. Locate: Dominican Republic, Nicaragua, Manchuria, Shanghai.
3. How did Hoover try to ease financial stress in Europe?
4. **Critical Thinking: Checking Consistency.** Was the United States's Latin American policy consistent during the period 1920–1932?

See "Lesson Plan," p. 598E.

4. The election of 1932

By 1932 industrial production in the United States was only half what it had been in 1929. Countless Americans were working only part-time, and 12 million more were out of work. President Hoover was the handiest person to blame, even though the depression had actually begun almost before he had moved into the White House. One folk song of the unemployed declared, "Hoover made a soup hound out of me." A man's empty pocket turned inside out was called a "Hoover flag." People looked forward to a change in the White House.

The Conventions. Still, the Republicans felt they could not reject Hoover or his policies. When they met in the Coliseum at Chicago in June 1932, they renominated Hoover and Vice-President Curtis on the first ballot. The platform stood firmly on the merits of the Hoover administration. It warned against the dangers to business if the Democrats came to power. It supported Prohibition. In a word, it stood "pat"—hoping that natural forces would solve the nation's problems.

When the Democrats met in the same building a few days later, the leading candidate was Governor Franklin D. Roosevelt of New York. He had been Assistant Secretary of the Navy under Wilson and had run for Vice-President in 1920. His main rival was Al Smith, former governor of New York, who had the support of Tammany Hall. After a hard fight, the Roosevelt forces won the delegates of California and Texas, who had favored Speaker of the House John Nance Garner of Texas. Roosevelt won the nomination on the fifth ballot, and Garner was named for Vice-President.

FDR was no radical, but he loved to try new things. He was not afraid to break precedent, by flying from Albany to Chicago to deliver his speech of acceptance. "Let it be from now on," he declared, "the task of our party to break foolish traditions."

The campaign. FDR loved campaigning. And his campaign delighted him with cheering crowds everywhere. The unlucky Hoover was often booed and heckled. "I've been traveling with Presidents since Theodore Roosevelt," one Secret Service agent remarked, "and never before have I seen one actually booed, with men running out into the streets to thumb their 📖 noses at him. It's not a pretty sight."

During the campaign Hoover argued that the real causes of the depression were world conditions that the United States could not control. He condemned Roosevelt's experimental ideas. He said they would destroy American free enterprise and the American system of government. If the Democrats were elected, he predicted, grass would grow in the streets of a hundred 🗐 cities.

(p. 614)

Roosevelt attacked the Republicans for encouraging the reckless stock market speculation that had brought on the panic. He was eloquent, persuasive, and smilingly confident. He promised a "New Deal" and a rapid recovery of prosperity for business and agriculture. But he did not produce a blueprint for recovery. He offered proposals that seemed to appeal to all the nation's varied groups. He supported many Progressive policies. He called for repeal of Prohibition, and he declared that everyone had a right to a comfortable living. The products of industry, he said, should be distributed more fairly.

📖 **More from Boorstin:** "When President Herbert Hoover appeared at the 1931 World Series, he was booed, but a Cardinal rookie named Pepper Martin was cheered for his .500 Series batting average." (From *The Americans: The Democratic Experience*)

The urbane Franklin D. Roosevelt, here reaching to shake hands, and his running mate the homespun "Cactus Jack" Garner of Texas (right) were greeted with cheers and applause as they toured the nation during the 1932 campaign. Baltimore's mayor is in the middle.

Except on a few issues, Roosevelt's speeches were so general that it was hard to disagree with them. Hoover thought FDR kept shifting his positions and called him "a chameleon on plaid." The usually wise commentator Walter Lippmann criticized FDR as "a pleasant man who, without any important qualifications for the office, would very much like to be President."

(p. 615) But it did not matter much what Roosevelt said. Almost anybody could have beaten Hoover. Who wanted to vote *for* the depression? To no one's surprise, the Democrats won a mighty victory. FDR received some 23 million votes and carried 42 states. Hoover, with fewer than 16 million votes, carried only 6 states. In the electoral college the count was 472 to 59. The Democrats won a majority of 191 in the House and 22 in the Senate. The American people had given their mandate to change the policies of government. Could FDR meet the challenge?

See "Section 4 Review answers," p. 598E.

Section 4 Review

1. What were the issues in the election campaign?

2. **Critical Thinking: Identifying Assumptions.** Why did people vote overwhelmingly for Franklin D. Roosevelt in the 1932 election?

See "Lesson Plan," p. 598E for **Writing Process Activity: Testing Conclusions** relating to the election of 1932.

Chapter 23 Review

See "Chapter Review answers," p. 598E.

Focusing on Ideas

1. Buying stock in corporations always involves some risk. How does "buying on margin" increase the risk?

2. What were two experiences in Hoover's early life that helped shape his personal creed? Explain how each experience contributed to Hoover's world view.

3. A business recession has a "snowball effect"—growing in size and picking up speed as it rolls downhill. Show how the 1929 crash sent the economy spinning downhill. How did a collapse in one part of the economy lead to other business failures?

Taking a Critical Look

1. **Recognizing Cause and Effect.** How did the sagging economies of post-war Europe contribute to the depression?

2. **Identifying Alternatives.** Although peace was their goal, many post-World War I treaties and pacts carried the seeds of future violence. How might the agreements have been shaped to avoid future resentment and conflict?

Your Region in History

1. **Geography.** If your region was part of the dust bowl during the depression, prepare a map showing where the dust bowl struck. How did the dust bowl affect the population of your region? What is the condition of the land today?

2. **Culture.** Interview two or more persons who lived in your community or nearby between 1930 and 1932. How were their families affected by the depression? Find out as many details as you can about lay-offs, bank failures, mortgage foreclosures, and so on.

3. **Economics.** Find out how a particular business in your area fared in the early years of the Great Depression.

Historical Facts and Figures

Making Hypotheses. Use the information in the graph below to help answer the following questions: (a) When was unemployment at its lowest point? (b) This chapter began with the statement that when Herbert Hoover took office in 1929, "Unemployment was low, wages were up, prices were steady, and corporations were making big profits and paying fat dividends." Do the data on the graph support this point of view? Explain. (c) Formulate a hypothesis about the state of the nation's economy in 1933, when Franklin D. Roosevelt took office. Identify factors that contributed to those economic circumstances. Predict how President-elect Roosevelt would attempt to address the nation's economic difficulties. How would you have handled the situation FDR faced?

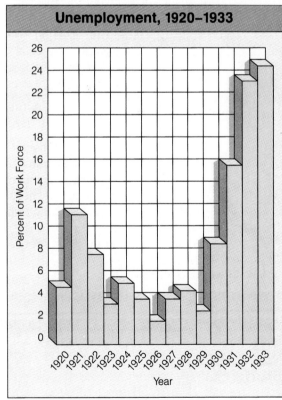

Source: *Historical Statistics of the United States*

Multicultural Connection: FDR did not receive much support from African Americans in the election of 1932, as many were still loyal to the Republican Party. Also, African American James W. Ford was the vice-presidential candidate for the Communist Party, and many African Americans voted for him. In each subsequent presidential election, however, FDR accumulated more and more of the African-American vote. For example, in Chicago he received only 23% of the vote in 1932, but 49% in 1936, and 52% in 1940.

Using Making Connections: Have students look at the unit themes printed in dark type. Explain that each event on the time line relates to one of these themes. Ask students to decide which events are related to which theme. Students should use events from the time line in their answers and explain how events are related. Have students go back through the text of Unit 8 to find other events related to the unit themes.

MAKING CONNECTIONS
Unit 8

This unit began on page 575 with a description of a nation experiencing extremes during the years 1918 to 1932:

> *President Calvin Coolidge told Congress in 1928 that the nation had never faced "a more pleasing prospect," [declaring] "there is tranquility and contentment . . . and the highest record of years of prosperity . . ." Before the next year was out . . . [placards proclaimed] "In Hoover we trusted, now we are busted."*

This description was supported by the two unit themes that are reprinted in **dark type** below. Use the time line and the information in Unit 8 to answer the questions that follow the themes.

THEMES IN HISTORY

1. **The "Roaring Twenties" are characterized by experimentation, great changes in daily life, and booming economic growth.** SOCIAL CHANGE
   How does the following poem, "First Fig," by Edna St. Vincent Millay, symbolize the extreme character of the 1920s? (Determining Relevance)

   My candle burns at both ends; / It will not last the night; / But ah, my foes, and oh, my friends— / It gives a lovely light.

2. **The stock market crash of 1929 signals the end of the "Roaring Twenties" and leads many Americans to grow disillusioned with the American economic system.** ECONOMICS
   How did Americans react to the "Black Thursday" stock market crash and the Great Depression that followed? (Recognizing Cause and Effect)

Events in
American History

1919
The Eighteenth Amendment prohibits the sale of alcoholic beverages.

1919

Events in
World History

1918
The Armistice is signed on November 11th, ending World War I.

616

1920s
Musicians introduce the world to jazz, blues, and ragtime, and people dance.

1920
Attorney General Palmer orders the arrests of thousands of suspected Communists.

1920
The Nineteenth Amendment gives American women the right to vote.

1925
One automobile rolls off the assembly line every ten seconds.

1929
October 24—Black Thursday—the stock market crash begins.

1931
2298 banks close as Americans demand their savings from the banks.

1931
Japan breaks the Kellogg-Briand Pact by seizing Manchuria.

1931
Austria and Germany suffer economic collapse, signaling financial failures across Europe.

1932
Congress creates the Reconstruction Finance Corporation to provide jobs for the unemployed.

1932
The veterans' "Bonus Army" marches on Washington and is dispersed by federal troops.

| 1925 | 1927 | 1929 | 1931 | 1933 |

1920
The Nazi party is established in Germany.

1927
Charles Lindbergh flies alone across the Atlantic from New York to Paris.

1930
Congress enacts the Hawley-Smoot Tariff Act to restrict foreign imports.

Unit 9

Writing About History and Art: Direct students' attention to the unit introduction, illustration, and list of themes on pages 618–619. Have the introduction and unit themes read aloud. After a brief discussion of the subject matter of the unit, instruct students to write a brief paragraph, explaining how the art:

—relates to the unit themes;
—exemplifies the unit title and illustrates the introduction; and
—is an appropriate choice for that unit.

Depression at Home and Aggression Abroad 1933–1945

On March 4, 1933, when Franklin Delano Roosevelt became the thirty-second President of the United States, the nation was in the deepest depression in its history. Poverty stalked the land. Some observers believed a revolution was at hand. But FDR was not discouraged. In his inaugural address he asserted his faith in democracy. He declared, "The people of the United States have not failed, . . . they want direct, vigorous action."

Roosevelt gave the nation action aplenty during the next twelve years. He did not always find solutions to problems, but he kept trying. The majority of voters never lost their faith in him or in their democracy.

In war, too, FDR would lead the nation with zest and confidence. Roosevelt had not expected war, but he organized the nation for its greatest defensive effort in history. His eloquent, strong leadership inspired his fellow Americans. He enlisted farmers and factory workers to overwhelm the forces of barbarism with American arms and supplies. As Commander in Chief he would send the armed forces to far corners of the earth. And he enlisted other world leaders in a grand strategy for victory.

 THEMES IN HISTORY

- Franklin Roosevelt's strong leadership and New Deal programs ease the impact of the Great Depression on poverty-stricken Americans. GOVERNMENT AND POLITICS

- The rise of the dictators and fascism in Europe threatens the peace of the entire world. ETHICS AND VALUES

- The allied nations triumph in a world war on two fronts, but with victory comes a host of new fears and problems. CONFLICT

▣ Max Weber's 1930s painting "Wayfarers" is a timeless rendering of the plight of those forced from their homes by poverty, prejudice, or war.
Photo Research International (detail)

Chapter 24
"Nothing to Fear but Fear Itself"

Identifying Chapter Materials

Objectives	Basic Instructional Materials	Extension Materials
1 Franklin Roosevelt's New Deal • Explain the proposals that were made during the New Deal to cure the Depression.	**Annotated Teacher's Edition** • Lesson Plans, p. 620C **Instructional Support File** • Pre-Reading Activities, Unit 9, p. 1 • Critical Thinking Activity, Unit 9, p. 6	**Enrichment Support File** • Alphabet Soup: New Deal Legislation (See "In-Depth Coverage" at right.) **Perspectives** • FDR and the Legacy of the New Deal (See "In-Depth Coverage" at right.) **American History Transparencies** • Critical Thinking, p. F35
2 From Recovery to Reform • Describe how Roosevelt's administration shifted in emphasis from recovery to reform after the 1934 Congressional elections. • Explain the long-term effects of programs initiated during Roosevelt's second term. • Discuss the history of the Social Security program in detail.	**Annotated Teacher's Edition** • Lesson Plans, pp. 620C–620D **Instructional Support File** • Skill Review Activity, Unit 9, p. 4	**Documents of American History** • *Schechter Poultry Corp.* v. *United States*, Vol. 2, p. 278 • The National Labor Relations Act, Vol. 2, p. 311 • The Social Security Act, Vol. 2, p. 325 • The Republican Platform of 1936, Vol. 2, p. 353 • The Democratic Platform of 1936, Vol. 2, p. 358
3 The End of the New Deal • Evaluate the effects of the New Deal on American life. • Analyze differing historians' viewpoints on the era.	**Annotated Teacher's Edition** • Lesson Plans, pp. 620D–620E **Instructional Support File** • Reading Activities, Unit 9, pp. 2–3 • Skill Application Activity, Unit 9, p. 5 • Chapter Test, Unit 9, pp. 7–10 • Additional Test Questions, Unit 9, pp. 11–14	**Documents of American History** • Reform of the Federal Judiciary, Vol. 2, p. 382 **American History Transparencies** • Fine Art, p. D73

24

Providing In-Depth Coverage

Perspectives on New Deal Legislation

During this period, known as the New Deal, Franklin Roosevelt pushed Congress to create numerous new government agencies. Often, these agencies were known only by their initials; for example the NRA, or National Recovery Administration. This "alphabet soup" of social programs helped to lessen the effects of the depression, but they were also surrounded by controversy. Some believed that the nature of such new and sweeping legislation eroded America's values and independent spirit, and made the federal government much too powerful.

A History of the United States as an instructional program provides three types of resources you can use to offer in-depth coverage of the New Deal: the *student text*, the *Enrichment Support File*, and *Perspectives*. The chart below shows the topics that are covered in each.

THE STUDENT TEXT. Boorstin and Kelley's *A History of the United States* unfolds the chronology of events, the key players, and, as an interpretive history, the controversy of New Deal legislation.

AMERICAN HISTORY ENRICHMENT SUPPORT FILE. This collection of primary source readings and classroom activities focuses on FDR's New Deal programs.

PERSPECTIVES: READINGS ON AMERICAN HISTORY IN THE 20TH CENTURY. In this edited collection of secondary source readings, well-known historians and political commentators (including Boorstin) provide an array of perspectives on FDR's New Deal.

Locating Instructional Materials

Detailed lesson plans for teaching New Deal legislation as a mini-course or to study one or more elements of the New Deal in depth are offered in the following areas: in the *student text*, see individual lesson plans at the beginning of each chapter; in the *Enrichment Support File*, see page 3; in *Perspectives*, see the Teacher's Guide pages for this topic.

IN-DEPTH COVERAGE OF THE NEW DEAL

Student Text	Enrichment Support File	Perspectives
• SEC, pp. 625, 634 • CCC, p. 626 • TVA, pp. 626–627 • FHA, pp. 627–628 • AAA, pp. 628, 634, 638 • NRA, pp. 628–629, 632 • PWA and CWA, pp. 629–630 • WPA, pp. 631, 638 • NLRB, pp. 633–634	• Lesson Suggestions • Multimedia Resources • Overview Essay/Alphabet Soup: New Deal Legislation • Songs in American History/New Deal Programs Strike a Chord • Primary Sources in American History/A Mixed Response to the New Deal • Art in American History/Art of the WPA • Biography in American History/Mary McLeod Bethune • Geography in American History/The Taming of the Tennessee River • Great Debates in American History/Is the New Deal a Threat to American Freedom? • Simulation/The New Deal in Your Community • Making Connections	• "Roosevelt Through European Eyes" by Sir Isaiah Berlin • "Roosevelt's Leadership" by Edgar Eugene Robinson • "A Nationally Advertised President" by Daniel J. Boorstin • "Franklin Roosevelt" by John Morton Blum • "The New Deal: The Conservative Achievements of Liberal Reform" by Barton J. Bernstein • "In the Shadow of FDR" by William E. Leuchtenberg

Franklin D. Roosevelt's New Deal

FOCUS

To introduce the lesson, review with the class what a depression is (decline in GNP, high unemployment, increase in bankruptcies and business failures) and what the situation was in March 1933. (You can use the first paragraph under the heading Franklin D. Roosevelt's "New Deal" on page 621.)

Developing Vocabulary

The words listed in this chapter are essential terms for reading and understanding particular sections of the chapter. The page number after each term indicates the page of its first or most important appearance in the chapter. These terms are defined in the text Glossary (text pages 1000–1011).

bank holiday (page 621); **lame duck** (page 622); **legal tender** (page 624); **Keynesian** (page 626); **parity** (page 628).

INSTRUCT

Explain

FDR decided to change American tradition and deeply involve the federal government in the economy in order to deal with the economic collapse.

❧ Cooperative Learning Activity

Determining Relevance Explain that students will work in pairs to prepare an outline of FDR's New Deal. Assign one partner to outline the First New Deal program as described in Section 1 of Chapter 24. Have the other partner outline the Second New Deal, explained in Sections 2 and 3 of the chapter. Partners can then share their outlines for use in completing the Review for these sections.

Section Review Answers

Section 1, page 631

1. a) first hundred days after Roosevelt's inauguration. b) changed the day for the gathering of Congress to January 3 and the swearing in of the President to January 20. c) temporary closing of a bank. d) Roosevelt's radio talks to the American public. e) changes the relationship between a currency and gold, although the currency is still secured by gold. f) created in 1934 to regulate the stock market to prevent false advertising, fraud, and other abuses. g) repealed Prohibition. h) headed FDR's National Recovery Administration. i) headed FDR's Public Works

Administration. j) one of FDR's closest advisors and director of programs created by the Federal Emergency Relief Act. He also headed the Civil Works Administration. 2. Cheerful optimism, friendliness, determination, courage, imagination, and willingness to experiment. 3. It created the Federal Deposit Insurance Corporation. Since depositors now knew that their money was guaranteed, the psychology of "runs" on banks was broken. 4. The CCC planted trees, stocked fish, and built fire lanes and trails. The TVA prevented floods and helped farmers improve their land. 5. The TVA helped farmers by providing cheap electricity, fertilizer, flood control, and other benefits. The AAA helped by paying them to take land out of production to raise prices. The Farm Credit Act enabled farmers to keep and expand their farms. 6. The NRA suspended antitrust laws and allowed leaders of each industry to write codes that specified what would be produced and at what price. Labor was helped because labor leaders helped write these codes and the codes included maximum hours and minimum wages. In addition, the NRA upheld the right of workers to join unions. 7. Putting people to work; the PWA worked on large-scale public projects and a high percentage of its funds went to nonlabor costs; the CWA was intended to be a temporary program, to put people to work more quickly than the PWA, and to spend a higher percentage of its funds on wages. It took on smaller projects than the PWA. 8. This informal group of highly educated, intelligent people advised FDR and helped devise New Deal legislation. Their varied viewpoints provided FDR with broad choices that could be used to revamp the economy.

CLOSE

To conclude the lesson, tell the class that there were many possible ways FDR could have tried to cure the depression. FDR and his advisers chose the path that the New Deal actually followed. FDR had some important decisions to make when he was inaugurated in March 1933. For homework, ask students to prepare a program of no more than three proposals to cure the depression. In the next class you may want to discuss the New Deal program in comparisons with student programs.

From Recovery to Reform

FOCUS

To introduce the lesson, ask students to turn to pages 633–635 and list the new laws passed during Roosevelt's "second hundred days" in the summer of 1935. (Social Security Act, Revenue Act, Public Utility Holding Company Act, and National Labor Relations Act.) Ask: How were these programs different from the ones passed in the "first one hundred days"? (These were long-term reform programs that involved a fundamental redistribution of the nation's wealth rather than short-term relief measures.)

Developing Vocabulary

anti-Semitism (page 632); **social security** (page 633); **organized labor** (page 633); **collective bargaining** (page 634).

INSTRUCT

Explain

The New Deal won support from the unemployed, laborers, the aged, and the poor.

☑ Writing Process Activity

Identifying Central Issues Ask students to imagine they are conservative opponents of FDR's programs. In preparation for writing a negative evaluation of the second New Deal, ask them to brainstorm their objections and their reasons for them. Students should begin with a topic sentence that summarizes their position, and they should organize their criticism in order of importance. When they revise, ask them to be sure that each of their main points supports their main idea. After proofreading, students can compare their evaluations in small groups.

Section Review Answers

Section 2, page 637

1. a) provided work for the able-bodied unemployed. b) branch of the WPA for people between 16 and 25 years old. c) formed by conservative opponents of the New Deal from Louisiana. d) Louisiana Senator opposed to FDR and his programs. e) the "radio priest," a fascist, anti-Semitic critic of FDR. f) New Deal critic who proposed a pension plan for the elderly. g) head of the AFL who threatened that labor would oppose FDR in the 1936 election. h) Supreme Court ruled that the NRA was unconstitutional. i) program that became part of the Social Security system. j) created by the NRL Act to oversee elections in which workers would decide which union would bargain for them and to stop unfair practices against unions. k) gave the Secretary of Labor the power to set minimum wages and maximum hours and to prohibit child labor in firms doing business with the federal government. l) liberal Republican candidate who ran against FDR in 1936. m) new party formed by a coalition of FDR's opponents. 2. The WPA reduced unemployment by providing work to the able-bodied unemployed, and

produced needed public works as well as works of art. 3. a) Social insurance, which provided retirement income; b) public assistance, which provided aid for the aged, blind, and dependent children; and c) unemployment insurance, which provided temporary income for laid-off workers. 4. a) It made rich corporations and rich individuals pay more; b) broke up many large utility holding companies and gave federal agencies the power to regulate companies that sold natural gas or electric power across state lines; c) spelled out the rights of labor unions and restrictions on employers but said nothing about the obligations of labor unions. 5. The plan to help farmers by limiting overproduction was written as a soil conservation act. To help workers while avoiding the Supreme Court's objections, the New Dealers came up with a law that allowed the Secretary of Labor to set minimum wages and maximum hours for workers in firms doing business with the government. 6. Conservatives who had found the NRA beneficial but thought other New Deal programs amounted to socialism; union leaders who were disappointed with the results of the New Deal; and individuals like Huey Long, Father Coughlin, and Dr. Townsend.

CLOSE

To conclude the lesson, tell students that no presidential candidate who has advocated reducing Social Security benefits has ever been elected. Ask: Why is this so? (The millions who benefit from Social Security or who expect to after they retire demand that the cuts come from somewhere other than their benefit programs. No elected official can afford to incur the wrath of such a large voting bloc.) Are there any dangers inherent in implementing social welfare legislation in a democracy? (To win votes, politicians might be tempted to spend money without raising the necessary taxes to cover the costs. The long-term effects of this might be disastrous to the nation's economy.)

Section 3 (pages 637–640)

The End of the New Deal

FOCUS

To introduce the lesson, ask students to list as many New Deal agencies and laws still in operation today as they can.

INSTRUCT

Explain

FDR, the master politician, badly misjudged the respect of most Americans for the Supreme Court.

★ Independent Activity

Demonstrating Reasoned Judgment Have students select one piece of New Deal legislation and draw a political cartoon which either supports or criticizes it.

Section Review Answers

Section 3, page 640

1. a) the economic slump of 1937–1938. b) program of farm relief. c) a stable supply of farm products. d) provided that the second AAA insure wheat crops against natural disaster. e) applied to all industries involved in interstate commerce, gradually reduced the work week and gradually raised the minimum wage. 2. The recession was brought on by a tightening of credit by the Federal Reserve, the cutting of 1.5 million people from the WPA, and by the first collection of Social Security taxes. 3. The second AAA provided a new way of keeping surpluses down in order to keep prices up, continued the benefits of the Soil Conservation Act, allowed growers to set marketing quotas under certain conditions, and set up the Federal Crop Insurance Corporation. The Fair Labor Standards Act limited the work week and child labor, raised the minimum wage, and required employers to pay time and a half for overtime. This encouraged employers to hire more workers and helped boost worker's wages. 4. It would have given the President the power to increase the number of justices on the Supreme Court from nine to fifteen if the justices refused to retire at the age of 70. It was dubbed "court packing" because it was an obvious attempt to add pro-New Deal justices.

CLOSE

To conclude the lesson, ask: Overall, how does your text evaluate the New Deal? Have students refer to the material under the heading "The New Deal—an appraisal" on pages 639–640. Discuss: How did the New Deal change the United States? Ask students to venture opinions—and back them up—on whether the change was for the better or the worse.

Chapter Review Answers

Focusing on Ideas

1. Nearly all were experimental or more extensive except tax legislation. Those with roots in earlier laws; bank reform; gold standard, SEC, aid to agriculture. 2. Workers: CCC, PWA, CWA, WPA; Social Security Act; National Labor Relations Act, Government Contracts Act; Fair Labor Standards Act. Consumers: FDIC; Owners of business: NRA, Guffey-Snyder Coal Act; legislation protecting farm owners and construction industry. 3. Fears that federal government was getting too powerful; shift from recovery to reform disturbed those opposed to reform; once the country was recovering, Republicans and conservative Democrats felt no pressure to cooperate. 4. NRA, farm mortgage relief, AAA, etc.; decisions against federal and state wage and hour laws.

Taking a Critical Look

1. Keynes advocated budget deficits. FDR favored a balanced budget. 2. First: directed mainly toward recovery—of banks, business (NRA), employment through public works, home mortgage business, construction industry, etc. Second: directed chiefly toward reform—social security, labor-management; tax laws to redistribute income, breaking up the powerful public utilities.

Your Region in History

1–3. Answers will vary depending on your region. Consult your local library or historical society.

Historical Facts and Figures

(a) Amount of money taken in is less than amount spent. (b) Amount of money taken in exceeds that spent. (c) 1928. (d) 1930. (e) 1936. (f) The devaluation of the dollar under the Gold Reserve Act of 1934; Relief programs (CCC, PWA, and TVA); Recovery programs (AAA).

Chapter 24

"Nothing to fear but fear itself"

Herbert Hoover had tried harder than any other President to save the nation from a depression. But it had been too little and too late. The crisis was too severe to be solved by the old ways—even under the leadership of the "Great Engineer." The American people wanted new directions from their new President. Franklin D. Roosevelt with his wonderful feeling for words had been precise when he promised a "New Deal." In most ways he was a conservative. He did not want to change all the rules of the American game. Instead he would try to use the government to deal out the cards so that everybody would have a better chance to win a good life.

A genial Franklin D. Roosevelt chats with reporters in Warm Springs, Georgia. This jaunty FDR pose was used in hundreds of cartoons.

United Press International Photo

See "Lesson Plan," p. 620C.

1. Franklin D. Roosevelt's New Deal

Millions were out of work. Factories stood idle. Banks were tottering. In many states to keep the banks from collapsing the governors had ordered the banks to close for a "holiday." Farmers and homeowners, unable to make the regular payments on their mortgages, were losing the property they had bought with their life savings. Cities and states ran out of funds to feed the unemployed. While people in the cities were starving, farmers were burning their unsold corn simply to keep their families warm.

The homespun humorist and critic of American life Will Rogers observed:

> We got more wheat, more corn, more food, more cotton, more money in the banks, more everything in the world than any nation that ever lived ever had, yet we are starving to death. We are the first nation in the history of the world to go to the poorhouse in an automobile.

Franklin Delano Roosevelt. The Democrats had happened to pick one of the most winning men in American history. Franklin Delano Roosevelt was a distant cousin of Theodore Roosevelt's. And, like his cousin, he had a confident smile and a wonderfully winsome, cheerful personality.

Although few people in the country realized it at the time, FDR was a man of heroic character. The only child of wealthy, upper-class parents, he was brought up by tutors, governesses, and a doting mother. From his youth he had enjoyed sports. He had always loved politics and had been the Democratic candidate for Vice-President in 1920. One August day in 1921, while on vacation with his family in Canada, he was stricken with polio and was left paralyzed. This single, sudden thunderclap of bad luck reduced him from a bouncy, athletic, runabout politician to a bedridden invalid. A man of weaker character might have given up.

Instead, after his bad luck, he became more determined than ever to be active in politics. An old friend who came on a sympathy visit to the hospital was surprised when FDR gave him a strong, good-natured wallop. "You thought you were coming to see an invalid," FDR laughed from his bed. "But I can knock you out in any bout."

People who went to cheer him up found that FDR gave them a lift instead. Sometimes he joked about his affliction. FDR wrote a friend that he had "renewed his youth" by "what was fortunately a rather mild case of *infantile paralysis*."

His case really was far from mild. He was never able to walk again. Only after long and painful exercises and by wearing heavy braces did he learn to use his hips so he could get around on crutches. He told his friends that he had an advantage. While they were running around, he could sit still and think. He used his long period of recovery in bed to write hundreds of letters to politicians all over the country. He wrote not about his own problems, but about politics and how to build a stronger Democratic party. All over the country the party's leaders valued his advice.

FDR made a fantastic comeback. When the Democratic convention in Chicago in 1932 chose him to head their ticket, it was not only because of his heroic personal qualities. For he had already proven himself a highly successful politician in New York. In 1928, only seven years after he had been stricken with polio, he managed to be elected governor of his state. He did so well as governor that when he ran again in 1930 he won by the biggest majority ever.

With his broad, contagious smile, Roosevelt was a wonderful persuader. He loved people, and he could make them love him. People cheered up when they saw his jaunty cigarette holder and felt his warm, firm handshake. He had all the human qualities that Herbert Hoover lacked. And these were what the nation wanted in that dangerous year of 1932.

FDR was no radical. In fact, during the campaign he was careful not to offend anybody. When he made speeches, he sounded more like William McKinley than like William Jennings Bryan. Some people who thought the nation needed stronger medicine criticized FDR. They said he was too eager to please everybody and had no real ideas about how to end the depression.

Those critics were wrong. FDR had courage in politics just as much as in his private life. And as soon as he took office on March 4, 1933, he showed both his courage and his imagination.

"A New Deal for the American people!" This was what FDR had announced in Chicago when he accepted the nomination. He promised to *experiment.* The nation and all its wealth were still there, he reminded people in his inaugural address. "We are stricken by no plague of locusts. Compared with the perils which our forefathers conquered because they believed and were not afraid, we have still much to be thankful for. Nature still offers her bounty and human efforts have multiplied it. Plenty is at our doorstep." Franklin Roosevelt had faith that there really were lots of new ways that could be tried.

"The only thing we have to fear," he said, "is fear itself." His courage and his optimism, like his smile, were contagious. Americans were encouraged most of all because they believed that their new President really would experiment. He would try one thing, and then another—until ways would be found to put the country back on the track and to put people back to work.

The Brain Trust. To plan the measures that would bring *relief* to those in need, *recovery* to the economy, and *reform* so it would never happen again, Roosevelt assembled a varied group of advisers. That they were divided among themselves over what to do bothered the President not at all. He enjoyed the chance to be able to choose a course of action from a number of options.

In his Cabinet he had the calm, conservative Cordell Hull as Secretary of State. Harold L. Ickes was Secretary of the Interior. A onetime Republican and Bull Moose, Ickes firmly believed in Progressive reform. Henry A. Wallace, another former Republican, became Secretary of Agriculture—the post his father had held under Harding and Coolidge. James A. Farley,

a canny political manager who had directed Roosevelt's campaign, took over as Postmaster General. He could hand out hundreds of jobs to loyal party members. From 1934 to 1945 the Secretary of the Treasury was Henry Morgenthau, Jr., a close friend and New York neighbor of FDR's.

In one of FDR's striking departures from tradition, he chose capable and experienced Frances Perkins to be Secretary of Labor. She was the first woman Cabinet member. She had worked with Jane Addams at Hull House in Chicago. When she returned east, she became New York State Industrial Commissioner. Secretary Perkins would be important in shaping the New Deal legislation.

The Cabinet members were not Roosevelt's only advisers. When he found or heard of people anywhere in the country who he thought could help, he invited them to the White House and charmed them into the nation's service. He did not care whether they had government experience. What mattered was their imagination, their energy, and their ability to devise new experiments to save the nation. He consulted lawyer Samuel Rosenman, social worker Harry Hopkins, and many professors. Among these were Raymond Moley, Rexford Tugwell, Adolph A. Berle, Jr., and Felix Frankfurter. Each of these professors helped the President find and enlist their ablest graduates. Never had a President been so successful in seeking out and using the nation's best minds. This informal group of advisers made up what was called President Roosevelt's "Brain Trust." Scores of New Deal laws would bear the imprint of their thinking.

(p. 623)

The "hundred days" begin. Roosevelt had to wait four months before he became President. The election was held in early November, but the President was not sworn in until early March. During these intervening months when the people's choice was waiting in the wings, the "lame duck" President in the White House could accomplish very little. The Twentieth Amendment, ratified on January 23, 1933, changed this. Now January 3 is the date for the

Multicultural Connection: Among the African Americans appointed to high positions by FDR was Robert Weaver (1907–). Weaver eventually became the first African American in the Cabinet, but he started his career as an aide to the Secretary of the Interior in 1933. In 1934, Weaver became an adviser to the PWA Housing Division and in 1938 Special Assistant to the Administrator of the U.S. Housing Authority. Later, in 1961, Weaver became head of the Federal Housing and Finance Agency, and in 1966 was appointed to the Cabinet as the first director of the Department of Housing and Urban Development.

Frances Perkins, Secretary of Labor, was the first woman Cabinet member. Here she stands with Representative Peyser (left) and Senator Wagner of New York as FDR signs a bill to combat the effects of unemployment in June 1933.

gathering of Congress, and the President takes the oath on January 20.

After he was elected and before he took office, FDR was asked by President Hoover to support his measures for dealing with the depression. But FDR wanted to make a fresh start. He did not want to be stuck with Hoover's policies.

On March 4, 1933, Roosevelt made his grand entrance. The need for leadership and experiment was so desperate that, for a time, he might have persuaded Congress to pass almost any law he asked for. "The whole country is with him, just so he does something," Will

Rogers said. "If he burned down the capital we would cheer and say, 'Well, we at least got a fire started anyhow.'"

For the first time in history the whole nation was listening—to the radio. The voice they heard was warm, informal, and beautifully modulated. They felt closer to their President than ever before. And when FDR received half a million pieces of fan mail, he knew the people's response to his message of hope.

As soon as he arrived in the White House, there was a flurry of activity. He called a special session of Congress and declared a nationwide

❖ See "Lesson Plan," p. 620C for **Cooperative Learning Activity: Determining Relevance** relating to FDR's New Deal programs.

"bank holiday." Congress gathered on March 9 and received a hastily prepared emergency banking bill. Since there had not even been time to make enough copies to hand out, it had to be read aloud. "The house is burning down," the Republican floor leader announced, "and the President of the United States says this is the way to put out the fire." Within 40 minutes the House passed the bill. The Senate soon followed, and by 8:30 that night the President had signed it into law. So began the exciting first one hundred days of Franklin D. Roosevelt's first term.

Banking laws. The Emergency Banking Act approved the President's closing of the banks. The law gave the Secretary of the Treasury the power to investigate all banks and then open them as he saw fit. On March 12, FDR went on the radio in the first of his many "fireside chats." In calm and friendly tones and in words that anyone could understand, the President explained the whole banking problem to the listening people. They were reassured.

The examination of the banks showed that four-fifths of them were in much better condition than the public had imagined. They were soon reopened, and confidence in them was restored. The run on the banks stopped. Within a month a billion dollars of deposits flowed back. By midsummer three-fourths of the nation's banks (holding 94 percent of all deposits) were in business again.

Within three months Congress passed a banking reform bill to help the people keep their confidence in their banks. The Glass-Steagall Act created the Federal Deposit Insurance Corporation, which protected depositors in insured banks up to $5000. All members of the Federal Reserve System had to belong to the FDIC, and others could join. The banking act added savings banks to the Federal Reserve System and widened the powers of the Federal Reserve Board. These new powers would enable the board to prevent the kind of wild speculation that had brought on the Great Crash.

There was a good deal of feeling in Congress in favor of government ownership of the whole banking system. But the President said that improved government supervision would be enough. "The policies which vanquished the bank crisis were thoroughly conservative policies," Brain Truster Raymond Moley later remarked. "The sole departure from convention lay in the swiftness and boldness with which they were carried out."

The currency crisis. The country was troubled too, by *deflation*. Since there was so little demand for goods and so many people were looking for jobs, prices and wages sank (that is, were "deflated"). If the government printed more money and put it into circulation, it was argued, wages and prices would rise. Then it would be easier for wage earners and farmers to buy. It would be easier to pay debts, too. But how much inflation was needed? Some economists feared runaway price increases.

Again, as he had in the banking crisis, the President took a fairly conservative course. He put the country on a modified gold standard. There would still be a limit to how much money could be printed. Every dollar would still have to be secured by some gold in government vaults. People were ordered to deliver all their gold coins and gold certificates to the Federal Reserve banks and to accept Federal Reserve notes in exchange. From then on, anyone owing money could pay it back dollar for dollar in any coin or currency (legal tender) that the government declared was lawful at the time.

In the Gold Reserve Act of 1934, Congress gave the President power to reduce the gold backing of the dollar by as much as 50 percent. He then issued a proclamation fixing the gold value of the dollar at 59.06 cents. The main purposes of this "devaluation" of the dollar were to (1) provide more dollars for people to spend, (2) raise the prices of goods here at home, (3) boost exports, and (4) decrease the burden of debt. The move was especially popular among the nation's troubled debtors. Now they could pay back their debts with a cheaper dollar.

On the other hand, bondholders and other creditors called this devaluation "legalized

More from Boorstin: "Commentators praised FDR's radio technique and called him 'a real pro'—much as Americans a century earlier might have called Daniel Webster a great orator. . . . While radio created the friendly national politician, it could also become a tool for demagogues. But it was significant that both Hitler and Mussolini (even in the Age of Radio) built their movements with huge face-to-face rallies where the hysteria of the whole crowd and storm-troop discipline could enforce the dictated enthusiasm." (From *The Americans: The Democratic Experience*)

robbery." They had loaned dollars worth 100 cents in gold but would be forced to accept repayment in dollars worth only 59.06 cents in gold. When they took their case to the courts in 1935, the Supreme Court upheld the law.

Securities regulation. One of the lessons of the stock market crash was the danger of dishonest and overblown advertising by people who sold securities—stocks and bonds. Men and women were being tempted to gamble what they thought they were only investing. In June 1934 Congress set up a Securities and Exchange Commission (SEC) to regulate the stock market and prevent these and other abuses. The SEC was given the power to (1) license and regulate stock exchanges, (2) require basic data on stocks and bonds offered for sale, (3) regulate activities of investment advisers, and (4) prosecute persons engaged in fraud. To reduce the temptation to gamble on the stock market, the Federal Reserve Board was given the power to fix margin requirements. Similar regulations were later applied to the commodity (wheat, sugar, cotton) exchanges.

Economy and beer. Balancing the budget was the traditional way for the government to cope with a depression. It was thought that the government must bring its income and spending into line and be conservative in its financial affairs. Then whatever had produced the

The caption for this cartoon read "Nonsense! If it gets too deep, you can always pull me out." Some critics looked on New Deal spending as carefree and unconcerned about the taxpayer who they felt would drown in government debts and deficits.

Library of Congress

downturn in the economy would disappear. Business leaders would regain their confidence in the system. They would resume spending on plants and equipment, and in time prosperity would return.

During the 1930s, however, a new solution was proposed. It was known as the Keynesian approach after its developer, the English economist John Maynard Keynes. He suggested that instead of cutting back on spending, the government should do just the reverse. It should lower taxes, spend money, and purposely run up large deficits. Public spending would put people to work and get money into circulation. This would promote private spending, and prosperity would return.

In between the extremes of balancing the budget and running large deficits as Keynes suggested, there were those who argued for letting the budget be unbalanced for a short time to "prime the pump." But then the government should step aside, cut expenses, and let private business take over.

During his campaign Roosevelt had promised to balance the budget. So one of the first measures he asked Congress to pass was an Economy Act. Within a week the bill was passed allowing FDR to cut government salaries and veterans' pensions and take other steps to reduce the deficit.

Roosevelt did not give up his hope of balancing the budget. But he found it impossible. The needs of the hour were too great. He was not willing to let citizens suffer simply to fulfill a campaign promise.

FDR showed what a clever politician he was as he worked for the passage of his Economy Bill. After the November election and the victory of the "wet" Democrats, Prohibition was on its way out. Even before FDR took office, Congress had passed and sent to the states a proposed Twenty-first Amendment to the Constitution repealing the Eighteenth (Prohibition) Amendment. Since it was clear that this amendment soon would be ratified, Roosevelt did not wait. Following his Economy Bill, he at once submitted a bill to legalize the sale of beer and light wines. Now, if the divided Congress paused too long to debate the Economy Bill, they would be keeping thirsty Americans from their beer. So both bills passed quickly, and the unhappy "noble experiment" of Prohibition finally came to an end.

Conserving the land and the people. One of Roosevelt's most ingenious pet projects was a Civilian Conservation Corps. The idea was to provide 250,000 unemployed young men between the ages of 18 and 25 with useful work in the healthful outdoors. They would help conserve the nation's natural resources in the national parks and forests by planting trees, stocking fish in lakes and rivers, and building fire lanes and wilderness trails. The CCC would also restore the historic sites of Revolutionary and Civil War battles.

On an even larger scale he devised a plan to lift people's hopes, to improve the life and conserve the land of whole regions. Many of the 3.5 million people who lived in the mountains of western Kentucky, Tennessee, and Alabama, and in the valley of the Tennessee River were poorly off. Their land was exhausted. They could not afford to pay for electricity to light their houses or to operate their farms. Of course, factories would not move in without the electric power to run them.

FDR proposed building dams on the Tennessee and other rivers of the region. These dams would have a double purpose. They would protect against floods. And the water flowing through the dams would turn generators to make cheap electricity. With this power two old munitions plants left over from World War I could be converted into government factories to make fertilizer to improve the farms. All these purposes actually were accomplished by the Tennessee Valley Authority (TVA).

The Tennessee Valley was brightened in more ways than one! Doctors used this chance to rid the countryside of malaria. Librarians sent "bookmobiles" out to the farms. With better homes came better hospitals and better schools.

Of course, some people objected. They accused FDR of trying to be a dictator. Some owners of private electric and fertilizer companies

Continuity and Change: Government and Politics Point out to students that the TVA, in addition to building dams and opening government-run fertilizer factories to improve the exhausted land for farming, also spurred outreach programs for the people of the region, improving hospitals and schools, ridding the countryside of malaria, and sending bookmobiles out to the farms. Volunteers in Service to America (VISTA), a type of domestic Peace Corps, was a provision of LBJ's Economic Opportunity Act of 1964. Like the TVA, the program was designed to help the poor, using government resources and creativity to help people earn their own living and improve their lives. (See p. 799.)

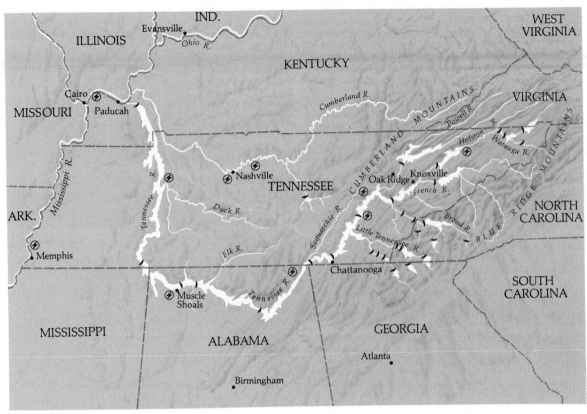

The Tennessee Valley Authority

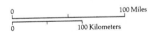
Drainage Basin of the Tennessee River

❯ Major Dams

⚡ Major Steam-Electric Plants

0   100 Miles

0   100 Kilometers

complained that the government was competing unfairly.

The TVA naturally did not solve all the problems of the poor farmers in the Tennessee Valley. Yet the experiment was a success. It was an inspiring example of how imagination and government resources could improve people's lives and help them earn their own living.

Help for housing. Owners of homes needed government help, too. Many were out of work or had lower earnings and could not meet their mortgage payments. This meant they might lose their homes and be forced out on the street. In June 1933, the Home Owners Loan Corporation was set up with the right to issue $2 billion in bonds to refinance mortgages. This was followed in 1934 by the National Housing Act, which established the Federal Housing Administration (FHA). It insured loans by banks, building and loan associations, and other private groups to homeowners for repair and to finance mortgages for new houses.

Under the Resettlement Administration, started in 1935, three entirely new towns, "greenbelt communities," were built. These were based on the ideas of Ebenezer Howard and the experiment at Radburn, New Jersey (p. 456). But not until 1937 was anything done about housing for the urban poor. Then the Wagner-Steagall Act was passed. It set up the United States Housing Authority to make loans to cities and states to clear away slums and to

⊕ **Geography and History: Regions** Have students use the TVA map above to answer the following questions: Which seven states are served by TVA? (Tennessee, Kentucky, Virginia, North Carolina, Georgia, Alabama, and Mississippi.) Where does the Tennessee River begin and end? (From the junction of the Holston and French rivers in Tennessee it flows to the Ohio River at Paducah, Kentucky.) In which direction is the Tennessee River flowing as it nears the Ohio River? (North.)

build low-cost housing. Under this law, some 350 projects were built or under way by 1940.

The Agricultural Adjustment Act.

Farmers all over the nation had their problems, too. They had never shared in the prosperity of the twenties. To help them now, the Agricultural Adjustment Act (AAA) was passed in May 1933. Its purpose was to raise the real income of farmers to "parity." That was a name for the higher price level that farmers had enjoyed before World War I (1910–1914). The act aimed to remove the chief cause of low prices by reducing the surplus of farm products. This would be accomplished by limiting the production of wheat, corn, cotton, hogs, tobacco, and milk. To pay the farmers for taking land out of production, the Treasury would issue cash bonuses. The money would come from a "processing tax" on the industries that made the raw products into finished goods. These were the industries that milled wheat into flour, that converted cotton into cloth, and made tobacco into cigarettes. The processor could pass the tax along to the consumer in the form of higher prices.

To deal with looming surpluses from crops already planted and young animals already born, the act provided that the cotton growers should "plow under" about 30 percent of their growing crop. Six million little pigs were slaughtered to keep them from growing into rotund, salable hogs.

At a time when people were hungry, it seemed foolish to hold down the production of food and to kill piglets that might have fed many families. But these were strange times. And the life of a great industrial nation was not simple. Secretary of Agriculture Wallace explained that farming was not a charitable enterprise. The farmers had to earn enough to live, and he said that this was a way to make sure that they did.

The AAA succeeded where Hoover's farm program had failed. For it managed to prevent the surpluses either before they were grown or before they could reach the market. The prices of farm products rose rapidly. Net farm income went up 240 percent between 1932 and 1935.

Farm mortgages, many refinanced on better terms by another New Deal measure, the Farm Credit Act, dropped by $1.5 million. After the AAA, American farming would never again be the same. In exchange for the security of price supports, American farmers—Thomas Jefferson's ideal independent people—had bartered away their independence.

The fight for industrial recovery.

Industrial workers were not much better off than the farmers. Millions were out of work. Industry alone seemed unable to absorb these jobless men and women, but perhaps the government could help. During World War I the government had mobilized factories for the war effort and then in the 1920s worked closely with trade associations. These were examples of a new kind of partnership between business and government. On this pattern FDR planned the National Industrial Recovery Act of June 16, 1933.

This act represented the thinking of business groups like the Chamber of Commerce, the National Association of Manufacturers, and the leading trade groups. It created a new National Recovery Administration (NRA), under which codes of fair dealing for each industry would be made by leaders of business and labor. These codes aimed to keep up prices and wages. They set maximum hours of work and minimum wages. They spelled out what goods should be made, how many of each thing, and at what price. These were the very same kinds of deals that up to now big business had been punished for making. When business firms agreed on output and prices in this way, it had been called monopoly.

This new law said that the antitrust laws did not apply. To win support of the labor unions, section 7a was written into the NRA act giving workers the right to organize into unions.

The NRA came under the command of a profane and colorful general. Hugh Johnson was his name. In World War I he had shown his talents on the War Industries Board. Now he threw himself with the fury of a wildcat into the task of drawing up codes for all the nation's businesses. Industries large and small rapidly organized. These included steel and textiles—but also dog food and hair curlers! The energetic Johnson seemed to be everywhere. But he kept the spotlight on himself, constantly made statements to the press, and offended many people. Though his job was to get people to work together, he was a hard man to work with.

Soon the NRA was being criticized from all angles. Owners of small firms said that it was helping the monopolies to swallow them up and that anyway it cost too much. Labor unions said that businesses were ignoring section 7a. Business leaders said that the codes gave unions an unfair advantage. Everybody seemed to consider the codes a means of self-protection.

Work relief. As another way to put people to work, a Public Works Administration (PWA) was set up by Congress with $3 billion to build roads, new government buildings, and other public projects. General Hugh Johnson had moved like a tornado, but Interior Secretary Ickes, the "old curmudgeon," pushed ahead with PWA projects only slowly and after careful planning. Some observers thought that Johnson and Ickes should have switched jobs. Still the PWA did manage, with very little waste, to build sewers, schools, post offices, hospitals, tunnels, housing projects, and even the aircraft carriers *Yorktown* and *Enterprise.*

The weakness of the PWA under Ickes was that it did not move fast enough. Roosevelt wanted as quickly as possible to put people to work. The Federal Emergency Relief Act of May 12, 1933, did exactly what President Hoover had refused to do—what he had said would destroy the American character. It provided $500 million for aid to the unemployed. Most of this was in the form of direct relief. Enemies of the program called it a "dole"—which meant that everyone who received it was a charity case. The New Dealers said this was unfair because really every citizen in need was entitled to help from the government. This program was directed by Harry Hopkins, a former social worker who became one of the President's closest advisers. The thin and sickly Hopkins

The New-York Historical Society

Government, labor, and business are shown united in the fight against the depression.

proved fiercely energetic and surprised everybody by his effective leadership.

Roosevelt and Hopkins supported the dole only because it was the quickest way to help people in need. What they really wanted was to give people jobs. They believed people who could work should be paid only for working. Handouts to people who wanted to work would undercut their self-respect and self-reliance.

To avoid mere charity and really put people to work, the Civil Works Administration (CWA) was started in the fall of 1933. Again Hopkins was in charge, and he had $400 million to spend. This was not meant to be a permanent program, but only to help people until other jobs came along. The PWA had been set up to construct buildings and other large-scale public projects. In contrast the CWA was supposed to lay out as little as possible for bricks and mortar

Enrichment Support File Topic

and to spend most of its money for wages.

In the one winter of 1934 "General" Hopkins managed to "mobilize" as many people as had served in the American armed forces in World War I. The CWA speedily put to work 4 million people in 180,000 programs improving and building roads, parks, playgrounds, and airports. It employed teachers in cities and rural areas. A billion dollars was pumped into the economy. But then the President and others began to fear that the CWA was creating a permanent class dependent on government grants. They were shocked at the huge cost. So Roosevelt ended the CWA that spring.

The election of 1934. Most of the New Deal programs alienated American business leaders. They asked if the great free enterprise nation could look forward only to "economic chaos with no end in sight." By June 1934 the New Deal spending—for relief, public works, home mortgages, benefit payments to farmers, and loans to business—had reached a staggering $5 billion. The national debt had nearly doubled since 1929. But the President insisted that the "human budget" must be balanced before the government's budget could be. He compared the war for economic survival to a war against invasion.

The immediate benefits of the New Deal programs were substantial. By the fall of 1934, two million people had been put to work, and national income was up 25 percent. Yet there was a long way to go to get the country back to

New Deal opponents thought that Roosevelt's programs tied up too many government resources.

The Condé Nast Publications, Inc.

normal. When the 1934 congressional elections came around, the unemployed still numbered 11 million. Full of their usual optimism, American voters were more impressed with what had been accomplished than with what remained to be done. The Democrats won three-fourths of the seats in the House. In the Senate they gained ten seats, which gave them more than a two-thirds majority. When FDR made a campaign tour that fall, he said that he could see a remarkable change in the temper of the people from the time of his campaign two years before. "Now," he said, "they are a hopeful people." Much of the credit for that change was due to the vigorous and ebullient FDR himself.

Perspec-
tives
Topic

See "Section 1 Review answers," p. 620C.

Section 1 Review

1. Identify or explain: "hundred days," Twentieth Amendment, "bank holiday," "fireside chats," modified gold standard, Securities and Exchange Commission, Twenty-first Amendment, Hugh Johnson, Harold Ickes, Harry Hopkins.
2. What personal traits helped Franklin Roosevelt succeed in politics?
3. Since 1933 we have had very few "runs" on banks. How did the Glass-Steagall Act help prevent such bank "runs"?
4. How did the CCC and TVA each promote conservation?
5. Describe measures passed to aid farmers.
6. How did the NRA seek to help industry? Labor unions?
7. What was the chief aim of both the PWA and CWA? How did the two programs differ?
8. **Critical Thinking: Determining Relevance.** How did FDR's "Brain Trust" illustrate his policy of bold experimentation?

See "Lesson Plan," p. 620C.

2. From recovery to reform

Roosevelt won a resounding victory in the congressional elections of 1934. But now the great mass of New Deal laws provided a handy target for both conservatives and radicals. Before long, a conservative Supreme Court would strike down some of the New Deal laws that FDR believed to be the mainstays of his attack on the depression. As a result he would have to do much of his work all over again. He would need a Second New Deal.

Reorganizing relief. These problems lay in the future when Congress met in January 1935. In response to the President's request, Congress created still more enormous relief programs. The new $5 billion Works Progress Administration (WPA) would provide work for the able-bodied unemployed. Those who could not work were to be taken care of by cities and states.

The WPA, under Harry Hopkins, tried to enlist as many people as possible in building roads, bridges, public buildings, and other public works. Before it ended in 1943, the WPA would spend $11 billion and employ 8.5 million people. The National Youth Administration (NYA), a branch of the WPA, offered work to young people between 16 and 25. In one school year, for example, it aided 750,000 students in thousands of colleges and high schools. The WPA surprised and delighted many by helping people whom the government had never directly helped before. Writers, artists, actors, and musicians were put to work. They prepared guidebooks, decorated government buildings, wrote plays, and performed concerts to lift the nation's spirit. But some people worried that artists might be less free in the long run if the government ever became their main patron.

Thunder from the Right and Left. Conservatives were more and more troubled by FDR's programs. When the government helped business with the NRA, it seemed not too bad. The rest of the New Deal—especially the TVA—they called socialism. In 1934 some of these right-wing opponents of the New Deal—including even Democrats like John W. Davis and Al Smith, as well as some wealthy Republicans—formed the American Liberty League. Their purpose was "to combat radicalism, preserve property rights, and uphold and preserve the Constitution." In April 1935 the leaders of the Chamber of Commerce—which had earlier

More from Boorstin: "[The artists] celebrated the American landscape and everything else they found characteristically American. Forced home from the Paris Left Bank by the Depression, they were inspired by the New Deal and supported by the Works Progress Administration (W.P.A.). And their regional painting, unlike much of the earlier American genre and landscape painting, was not bland and genteel. It was a vigorous search for roots . . ." (From *The Americans: The Democratic Experience*)

This cartoon was drawn after Harry Hopkins said that the needy numbered "one person out of every ten."

supported Roosevelt—joined their fight against FDR and the New Deal.

At the same time, FDR was being attacked from the Left. Senator Huey Long was a fast-talking, long-talking vote getter. He used the radio to sell himself to the people of Louisiana. As governor he had brought many reforms to his state. But he had also brought corruption and many wild hopes. Under his "Share the Wealth" program, he said, every man would be a king! There would be no more enormous fortunes and every family would have a guaranteed income. Of course, Ol' Huey would be "The Kingfish."

There were others who joined Long's attack on FDR. One of the most vicious and successful was the rabble-rousing Father Charles E. Coughlin. He called himself the radio priest, but he spread hate instead of love. He built a huge national following from his church in Royal Oak, Michigan. Money poured in from millions of listeners. At first he had supported the New Deal and called it "Christ's Deal." But when FDR did not follow Father Coughlin's own peculiar program—which increasingly turned toward fascism and anti-Semitism—he spoke out against the President. And he made himself a prophet of confusion and discord.

Another rabid critic of the New Deal was elderly Dr. Francis Townsend from Long Beach, California. He saw the extreme poverty of the aged and proposed a plan for old-age pensions that he said would solve the nation's problems. He wanted the government to give every man and woman 60 years old or older $200 a month—with the condition that they had to spend it each month. This would take care of old people and provide jobs for everyone else. Of course it would also have taken half the national income and turned it over to only 9 percent of the people. It is not surprising that many older people—but few others—became "Townsendites."

The early labor union support for FDR soon turned to opposition. Since section 7a had not fulfilled their hopes, union leaders were calling the NRA the "national run around." William Green, head of the AF of L, threatened that labor would oppose Roosevelt in the 1936 election.

Then a stroke of lightning hit the New Deal from an unexpected but most respectable source. The Supreme Court, in a series of shattering decisions, struck at the heart of FDR's program. In *Schechter* v. *United States* (May 1935), the Court declared the NRA unconstitutional. It also struck down laws passed to prevent foreclosures on farm mortgages and to provide pensions for railroad workers. Roosevelt was stunned. How could the nation solve its modern problems if Congress could not experiment with modern remedies? He declared that the justices of the Supreme Court were trying to push the country back to the days of the "horse and buggy."

The second one hundred days. When the NRA was declared unconstitutional, Congress was preparing to go home. They had done little

See "Lesson Plan," p. 620D for **Writing Process Activity: Identifying Central Issues** relating to conservative opposition to the New Deal.

since January. Now the President sprang into action. He kept Congress in session for another one hundred days, during the hot Washington summer. He insisted that they pass a law that would provide income for the elderly and for laid-off workers. He wanted a law that would boost labor's bargaining power. He called for a "soak the rich" tax and the breakup of certain holding companies. The First New Deal had been directed mainly toward recovery from the depression. This Second New Deal aimed at reform.

Social Security. The United States was far behind the industrial nations of Europe in protecting citizens against the risks of unemployment and old age. Under prodding from Dr. Townsend and his followers, from the AF of L, as well as some members of Congress, Roosevelt in January 1935 asked for an insurance plan. But until the *Schechter* decision, Congress had failed to act. Now the President pushed hard for his new idea of social insurance. While people were working, each of them would pay a small amount every month, with their employers paying the same amount, into a national Social Security fund in the Treasury. Then when a worker was too old to work, he or she would receive a monthly payment. The payouts would not start until 1940, since workers would have to build up some credits in their Social Security account. And only workers in trade and industry were covered at first. So the law also had a plan to take care of those in need.

This second part of the Social Security Act came to be known as *public assistance.* It was not social insurance, since the persons getting the monthly welfare checks did not pay into an insurance fund. Public assistance was a federal-state program. Any state that accepted the plan would get federal funds covering about half of the costs. The money would come from general state and federal revenues. The aged, the blind, and the dependent children covered by public assistance would have to prove their need for aid.

Unemployment insurance was a third part of the new law. It was also a joint federal-state program. The plan was to give laid-off workers some income for a number of weeks while they were hunting for a new job or waiting to be re-hired. The money would come from a payroll tax paid by employers of eight or more persons. Each state would set up its own system under standards set by federal law.

The Social Security Act meant that millions of people would not have to live in fear of starving. And since persons getting old-age insurance would have put some of their own hard-earned money into the fund, they would not have to feel like charity cases. "Social Security" was a good name for the plan. It made millions feel more secure.

Moving against concentrated wealth and power. The Social Security Act took the wind out of the sails of Dr. Townsend. The President's series of "soak the rich" taxes helped him win away followers of "Kingfish" Long. FDR asked for higher estate and gift taxes, higher income taxes on the largest incomes, and a corporate income tax graduated to the size of the profits of businesses. The President said the bill would help "to prevent an unjust concentration of wealth and economic power" and reduce "social unrest and a deepening sense of unfairness." These measures were passed in a Revenue Act in August 1935.

Roosevelt also moved against the powerful utility companies that provided the nation's gas and electricity. Just thirteen holding companies controlled 75 percent of all the country's electric power. The Public Utility Holding Company Act was designed to restrict each company to operating a single system in a single area. A "death sentence" clause—enacted only after a bitter fight—empowered the SEC after January 1, 1940, to dissolve any utility holding company that could not prove that it was saving the consumers money. Under this law most of these great holding companies were broken up within the next three years. The law also gave federal agencies the power to regulate companies that sold natural gas or electric power across state lines.

Helping labor. FDR was the greatest friend of organized labor who had ever lived in the White

✕ Critical Thinking Activity: Formulating Questions What factors did FDR have to consider before proposing reforms for the nation? FDR's second hundred days were aimed at long-term reforms in the government. Tell the class to review the causes of the Depression. Taking these into consideration, have students develop 3 to 5 questions that a President would have to ask before suggesting broad reforms in the national government. Ask students to explain their choices. Are the causes of the depression reflected in FDR's reforms?

"Come along. We're going to the Trans-Lux to hiss Roosevelt."

Drawing by Peter Arno. Copyright © 1936,
1964 The New Yorker Magazine, Inc.

These wealthy opponents of FDR were headed for the Trans-Lux, a theater which showed newsreels and short features.

House. His Second New Deal included the National Labor Relations Act. Senator Robert Wagner of New York had first proposed this act as early as 1934, but then FDR thought that section 7a of the NRA would give labor all the help it needed. After the Supreme Court killed the NRA, the President threw his support to Wagner's labor bill.

The new Wagner Act guaranteed the right of workers to join unions and to bargain collectively. It set up the National Labor Relations Board (NLRB) to oversee elections by which workers would decide which union, if any, would bargain for them. The Board could also stop unfair practices by employers against unions. Since the law put no obligations at all on the unions, it is not surprising that many employers thought the act was unfair and one-sided. Passed in July 1935, the law was upheld by the Supreme Court in 1937. The unions called it "Labor's Magna Carta."

By the time the second hundred days of the New Deal came to an end, in August 1935, the President found that most business leaders and wealthy people were against him. But he saw his reform program as nearly complete. Now, he said, there would be a "breathing spell."

More trouble with the Supreme Court. During 1936 the Supreme Court struck down the AAA. The judges declared that the so-called "processing tax" could not be collected because it was not really a tax at all. Instead, they said, it was an unconstitutional way to limit farm output. Did this mean that the federal government could do nothing at all to solve the problem of farm surpluses? To get around the Court's objections, Roosevelt had Congress pass a Soil Conservation and Adjustment Act (February 1936) that restricted production under the name of conservation. The government paid farmers to plant soil-conserving crops on part of their land.

In April the Supreme Court limited the powers of the SEC. It also struck down the Guffey-Snyder Coal Act of 1935, which had tried to set up a "little NRA" by enacting the NRA coal code into law.

The President was concerned to find a constitutional way to protect workers by setting minimum wages. But the conservative Court ruled (5–4) against a New York state law that had set minimum wages for women. The majority argued that the Fourteenth Amendment left the state "without power by any form of legislation to prohibit, change, or nullify contracts between employers and women workers as to the amount of wages to be paid." In 1923 the Court had already struck down a federal wage law for women in the District of Columbia. Now the Court seemed to be saying that neither the states nor the federal government could set minimum wages. Still, FDR did not give up. He asked Congress for a law that he hoped the Court might accept. In the Government Contracts Act of June 1936, Congress gave the Secretary of Labor power to set minimum wages and maximum hours for workers in firms doing business with the federal government. It also prohibited them from employing boys under 16 or girls under 18. Since thousands of firms wanted to sell part of their output to the government, the new law improved the lot of many workers.

☸ ***The election of 1936.*** In early 1936, of course, FDR focused his attention on the coming presidential election. He believed that his New Deal had already proven itself a substantial success and that he deserved to be reelected. By June industrial production had returned to the level of 1923–1925. Factory employment was up. Farm income and weekly wages for workers had risen. The unemployed, who numbered more than 10 million in the winter of 1934–1935, had now dropped to 7 million. National income had increased 60 percent over 1933. Although the depression was far from over, Franklin D. Roosevelt was the most popular President since his cousin Teddy.

When the Republicans met at Cleveland in June, they had the impossible task of naming someone who could defeat the attractive "miracle worker" in the White House. To be named the Republican candidate that year was like being handed a lottery ticket that was sure to lose. On the first ballot they chose Governor "Alf" Landon of Kansas, a liberal Republican and onetime Bull Moose progressive. Despite the opposition of conservative Republicans to the New Deal, he ran on a surprisingly liberal platform. The Republicans seemed to have little choice but to endorse most of the New Deal programs. It was difficult to attack old-age and unemployment benefits, the right of labor to organize and bargain collectively, minimum-wage and maximum-hour laws for women and children, and soil conservation. The depression, FDR, and the New Deal had somehow changed the point of view of a whole nation. And despite lingering suspicions of "big government," the Republican party, too, came right along.

It was no surprise when the Democrats nominated Roosevelt and Garner again. FDR used

Shoppers on Main Street in 1936 saw campaign banners like these.

Library of Congress

☸ Multicultural Connection: The second Hispanic to serve in Congress was Dennis Chávez. He was born into a poor Mexican family in New Mexico in 1888 and had to drop out of school at the age of 13. However, he continued to learn on his own, and later graduated from Georgetown University. Chávez was elected to the House of Representatives in 1930. Five years later, upon the death of the incumbent, Chávez was appointed to the Senate. In 1936, he was elected to the Senate in his own right and remained until his death in 1962.

his acceptance speech to set the tone of the campaign. He considered much of the criticism of business leaders to be mindless. And he directed all his considerable talents of wit and irony against them. He called them "economic royalists." He said they were anxious to build their personal dynasties, to control the government, and to exploit the workers—rather than to serve the nation's interests. "They denied the Government could do anything to protect the citizen in his right to work and his right to live." It was time, he said, to destroy their antidemocratic power. "This generation," he proclaimed, "has a rendezvous with destiny."

The Democratic platform spelled out the far-reaching duties it believed the government should fulfill. Among these were to protect the family and the home, establish a democracy of opportunity for all, and aid those overtaken by disaster.

To the left of Roosevelt there were other candidates. The mild-mannered intellectual Norman Thomas, who had led the Socialists in 1928 and 1932, was again their candidate. The Communist party also entered the race. A new "Union party" drew together several unhappy groups—the followers of Father Coughlin, of Dr. Townsend, and of Huey Long. (Senator

FDR was our first President to use the radio effectively. His friendly, mellifluous voice was able to reach right into the homes of the three out of four families who owned radio receivers in 1936.

United Press International Photo

Long had been assassinated on the steps of the Louisiana state capitol in September 1935.) Their candidate was Representative William Lemke of North Dakota.

But it was Roosevelt all the way. His margin of 11 million votes over "Alf" Landon was the largest in history until that time. He carried every state but Maine and Vermont. "I knew I should have gone to Maine and Vermont," he joked. "But Jim Farley wouldn't let me." All together the Socialists, Communists, and Unionists polled only about 1 million votes.

The new majority party. The election of 1936 revealed that, for the first time since the Civil War, Roosevelt had succeeded in making the Democrats the party of the majority. The party's enlarged support came mostly from those whom the New Deal had been able to help. FDR would be spokesman for "the Forgotten Man." This meant the immigrants and their children, the farmers and the laborers—Americans who somehow had not won the race for money and success. Teachers, social workers, and reformers of many sorts felt that FDR was their leader. Blacks were swinging to the Democrats in ever larger numbers.

Many of these "forgotten people" lived in the big cities, and they provided him a solid following. Their votes could carry the largest states, which themselves had nearly enough electoral votes to win the election for President.

A new kind of Presidency. Roosevelt's success was not all due to his programs. Now his personal charm and his warm resonant voice could reach the whole nation. FDR was our first radio President. In his fireside chats over the radio, he came right into everybody's living room. He explained what he was doing in simple language that anybody could understand. Even his paralysis somehow became an advantage. He had to sit down while he talked. This meant that when he spoke to the nation he did not sound like a politician making a speech but like a member of the family in friendly conversation. When he began a radio talk, he did not say "Fellow citizens," but "My friends."

He also held many press conferences, which pleased the newspaper reporters. In all his four years President Hoover had offered only 66 press conferences. FDR met the press 337 times during his first term. He made the reporters his friends. This was plain in the stories they wrote about their President.

See "Section 2 Review answers," p. 620D.

Section 2 Review

1. Identify or explain: WPA, NYA, American Liberty League, Huey Long, Father Coughlin, Francis Townsend, William Green, *Schechter* v. *United States,* social insurance, NLRB, Government Contracts Act, "Alf" Landon, Union party.

2. Explain the importance of the Works Progress Administration.

3. Describe the three main programs set up by the Social Security Act.

4. Why would the tax law, the holding company law, and the labor law in 1935 displease business leaders?

5. How were laws to aid farmers and wage earners written to avoid Supreme Court objections?

6. **Critical Thinking: Recognizing Bias.** Who were some of the critics of the New Deal? How did their complaints reflect their own prejudices?

See "Lesson Plan," p. 620D.

3. The end of the New Deal

When FDR began his second term, everything pointed to more success in his effort to give the nation a New Deal. His inaugural address on January 20, 1937, admitted that much still remained to be done: "I see one-third of a nation ill-housed, ill-clad, ill-nourished." He promised to do something to help them. But soon he was (p. 638) involved in a struggle that wasted his energies and undercut his influence with Congress.

The attack on the Supreme Court. On February 5, 1937, without consulting his Cabinet or

≢ **Continuity and Change: Government and Politics** Point out to students that the development of new communications media changed politics in the twentieth century. Franklin D. Roosevelt's "fireside chats" were delivered in simple, clear language which was easy to understand, making his political speeches seem like a conversation with friends. This sense of intimacy gained voter support for FDR. In the same way, John F. Kennedy was the first politician to benefit from television. JFK's charm, poise, and good looks were communicated clearly to millions of voters, who found him more likeable than his opponent, Richard Nixon. (See p. 776.)

the Democratic party leaders, Roosevelt sent to Congress a plan to reorganize the federal courts. Although he did not say so, nobody doubted that his target was the Supreme Court. FDR proposed that the President should have the power to increase the number of justices on the Supreme Court from nine to fifteen if the justices refused to retire at the age of 70.

What he offered as a plan to "reform" the Court really was a way to make the Supreme Court approve the New Deal laws. If he had come out and declared his purpose, he would have lost much support. So he pretended that the nation needed his "reforms" because the courts were behind in their work. His plan came to be called a scheme for "court packing." And the name was not unfair.

Roosevelt's "court packing" message split the Democratic party and the nation. He had grown overconfident because of his great victory at the polls. He made the mistake of thinking that the nation would follow wherever he pointed.

Chief Justice Charles Evans Hughes was adroit in his opposition. He pointed out that the Court was up to date in its work and that a larger Court would be inefficient. He even timed a Court decision to help his cause. The Court upheld a Washington state minimum-wage law, reversing its decision of just ten months before, and showing that the Court did not always strike down reform legislation. One headline proclaimed, "A Switch in Time Saves Nine." Then the Court upheld the Wagner Act and the Social Security Act.

The Senate rejected Roosevelt's plan to pack the Court. In its place, Congress passed a law that allowed federal judges to retire at age 70 with full pay. One conservative justice retired while the debate was going on. Another retired the next year. FDR claimed that he had really gained what he wanted. It was more accurate to say that he won his battle but he lost the war. To win that battle he had lost much of the goodwill of Congress.

The Roosevelt recession. During 1937 the President learned a harsh lesson in economics. Business was booming. There were still 7 million unemployed, but some of his advisers feared a runaway inflation. In his first election campaign Roosevelt had promised to balance the budget. He now took the necessary steps. The Federal Reserve Board began to put the brakes on credit. Then the government cut the WPA by 1.5 million people. Now, when Social Security taxes were collected for the first time, still more money was drained out of the economy. At the end of 1937, business had slumped, and the number of unemployed had risen to 10 million. To stimulate the economy the President saw that he would have to resume his large-scale spending.

In April 1938 Roosevelt sent to Congress a message asking for an increase of the WPA work force—this time by 1.5 million, the same number who were cut in 1937. He said he would need $3 billion more for recovery and relief. The act was passed in June. Only by these means did the Roosevelt recession come to an end.

New farm and labor reforms. In 1938 the President also asked Congress for new measures to help the farmer and to control wages and hours in industry. The second Agricultural Adjustment Act (which Secretary of Agriculture Wallace called the best program of farm relief ever enacted) provided an "ever-normal granary." This meant putting farm products in storage in years of surplus and then releasing them in years of scarcity. Prices could then be stabilized around the "parity" level of 1910–1914. The second AAA continued giving to farmers the benefits of the Soil Conservation Act. And it allowed growers of certain crops to set marketing quotas if two-thirds of them agreed. A new Federal Crop Insurance Corporation insured wheat crops against natural disasters like drought, flood, and plant disease. Wheat itself could be used to pay the insurance premium.

Congress also passed a Fair Labor Standards Act. In all industries involved in interstate commerce, the length of the work week would gradually be reduced to 40 hours. The minimum wages (first set at 25 cents an hour) would increase over eight years to 40 cents an hour. Time and a half was to be paid for overtime. The law also forbade labor by children under 16.

More from Boorstin: "Only a century before, the passionate crusader Dorothea Dix had had trouble awakening a few state legislators to the predicament of 'paupers' who, along with the insane, were confined in almshouses and jails. In 1937, when President Franklin D. Roosevelt in his second inaugural address described 'one-third of a nation ill-housed, ill-clad, ill-nourished,' he sounded a national alarm; and the nation listened." (From *The Americans: The Democratic Experience*)

The purpose of this Fair Labor Standards Act was to boost the buying power of wage earners. Also, the cut in the work week, along with the overtime pay rule, would induce employers to hire more workers. People were astonished when they learned that 750,000 workers had to receive raises to bring their wages up to 25 cents an hour.

The attempted "purge." FDR's fight over the Court had soured his relations with Congress. At the same time, the demands of the unions (p. 634) and the new government-spending policy upset the conservatives in both parties. Roosevelt's pet measures—such as his proposal for six regional projects similar to the TVA—were defeated by an alliance of Republicans and conservative Democrats.

Then the angry President decided to try to "purge" his party of his conservative opponents. Most of these were from the South. In 1938 he made the mistake of intervening in primary elections by writing letters, attending conferences, and making speeches. This effort boomeranged. In nearly every case where he interfered, the conservative candidate won.

Republicans saw their chance to take advantage of the splits in the Democratic party. And they profited from the rising tide of conservatism. They gained 75 seats in the House and 7 seats in the Senate. They elected 11 governors and polled 51.5 percent of the vote outside the "solid South."

The election of 1938 really marked the end of the New Deal. Republicans and conservative Democrats now had enough votes in Congress to block any more New Deal laws. And the President turned to problems abroad. Fascist Italy, Nazi Germany, and Imperialist Japan were on the march.

The New Deal—an appraisal. So the New Deal came quietly to a close. What had it accomplished? Many Americans were not sure. Millions were still out of work. Prosperity would not return until the nation was forced to try the Keynesian approach in a big way by World War II. Then massive government spending would put all the factories back to work.

Library of Congress

The "ever-normal granary" program helped to fill huge grain elevators like these shown in 1941 by FSA photographer John Vachon.

✂ Critical Thinking Activity: Identifying Central Issues How was the average person helped by the New Deal? As a class have students list adjectives that describe the New Deal. Each students is to select one of the adjectives to illustrate as a symbol. Have the class arrange their symbols as an emblem of the New Deal's achievements. Ask the class to write one sentence to summarize their emblem's message. Display the emblem in class.

Library of Congress

Because of the effects of polio, President Franklin D. Roosevelt is often seen in photographs sitting in a car. Still, his cheerfulness and optimistic outlook lifted the spirits of the nation. While his handicap meant that he had to speak to workers like this coal miner aboveground, his wife, Eleanor, could go into the mines and report back to him the conditions she found there.

Still the experimental Franklin D. Roosevelt had magically lifted the nation's spirit. "It was this administration," he said, "which saved the system of private profit and free enterprise after it had been dragged to the brink of ruin." The President had avoided the extremes. He had taken a middle course. Rejecting the dogmas of socialism, he yet increased government control over the economy—over banking, agriculture, and public utilities. The federal government played a new role in setting standards for wages and hours of work and in providing some income support for farmers, the aged, and the unemployed.

Americans discovered new strength. On the whole, the federal Constitution proved remarkably adaptable to the needs of a new age. Americans had survived their worst peacetime disaster—without spreading hate, without inciting civil war or abridging liberties. And they had not been seduced by a dictator. Freedom had proved the best atmosphere in which to keep freedom alive.

See "Section 3 Review answers," p. 620E.

Section 3 Review

1. Identify or explain: Roosevelt recession, second AAA, ever-normal granary, crop insurance, Fair Labor Standards Act.

2. Name some government actions that helped to bring about a recession in 1937–1938.

3. Describe measures that were enacted by Congress in 1938 to help farmers and workers.

4. **Critical Thinking: Making Comparisons.** What was Roosevelt's plan to "reform" the Supreme Court? How did it compare with his other New Deal reforms?

Chapter 24 Review

See "Chapter Review answers," p. 620E.

Focusing on Ideas

1. Compile a list of New Deal laws and programs described in this chapter. Which of these laws and programs were "experimental," or represented new or greatly broadened areas of federal activity?

2. Identify and describe New Deal measures designed to help workers, consumers, and owners of businesses.

3. Why was there increasing congressional opposition to President Roosevelt's proposals during his second term?

4. What United States Supreme Court decisions disrupted President Roosevelt's New Deal program? Explain.

Taking a Critical Look

1. **Checking Consistency.** What did John Maynard Keynes believe a nation should do to lift itself out of a depression? How did Roosevelt respond to this idea?

2. **Making Comparisons.** How did the first "hundred days" of the New Deal compare to the second "hundred days"?

Your Region in History

1. **Culture.** Identify buildings, roads, parks, or other projects in your locality that were built or improved under the Public Works Administration, Works Progress Administration, or other work-relief programs of the New Deal. Are the works of any artists or writers employed by the WPA on display in your community or in your local archives?

2. **Economics.** Name some New Deal measures that you think would have received wide support in your community in the 1930s and explain why. Which measures would probably have had little support? Why do you think many people would have opposed these programs?

Historical Facts and Figures

Using Evidence. Using the information provided in the graph, define (a) a budget deficit, (b) a budget surplus. (c) In what year was the budget surplus the greatest? (d) In what year did deficit-spending begin? (e) In what year was the deficit largest? (f) What information in this chapter helps explain the origins and growth of the budget deficit between 1930 and 1940?

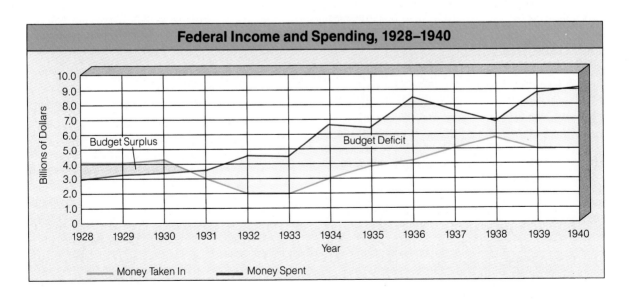

Federal Income and Spending, 1928–1940

Chapter 25
Reshaping American Life

Identifying Chapter Materials

Objectives	Basic Instructional Materials	Extension Materials
1 Problems on the Farm • Describe some of the problems faced by farmers in the 1930s and describe some New Deal efforts to solve those problems. • Discuss the distribution of tenant farms in the United States in 1930.	**Annotated Teacher's Edition** • Lesson Plans, p. 642C **Instructional Support File** • Pre-Reading Activities, Unit 9, p.15 • Critical Thinking Activity, Unit 9, p. 20	**Enrichment Support File** • The Dust Bowl (See "In-Depth Coverage" at right.) **Suggested Secondary Sources** • See chart at right.
2 The Problems of Black Americans • Describe the situation of black Americans in the 1930s. • Evaluate the relationship between the federal government and black Americans during the New Deal. • Tell why blacks abandoned the Republican party and joined the Democratic party at this time.	**Annotated Teacher's Edition** • Lesson Plans, pp. 642C–642D	**Extension Activity** • W.E.B. DuBois, Lesson Plans, p. 642D
3 The New Deal and Women • Describe the status of women in the 1930s and give examples of the increased role of women in Franklin D. Roosevelt's administration.	**Annotated Teacher's Edition** • Lesson Plans, pp. 642D–642E	**Extension Activity** • Influential Women in the '30s, Lesson Plans, 642E
4 The Struggles of Labor • Give reasons for the growth of labor unions in the 1930s and compare the AFL to the CIO. • Analyze accounts of the 1937 Memorial Day Massacre for accuracy.	**Annotated Teacher's Edition** • Lesson Plans, pp. 642E–642F **Instructional Support File** • Reading Activities, Unit 9, pp. 16–17 • Skill Review Activity, Unit 9, p. 18 • Skill Application Activity, Unit 9, p. 19 • Chapter Test, Unit 9, pp. 21–24 • Additional Test Questions, Unit 9, pp. 25–28	**Documents of American History** • Constitution of the Congress of Industrial Organizations, Vol. 2, p. 512 **American History Transparencies** • Our Multicultural Heritage, pp. C9, C11, C13, C15

Providing In-Depth Coverage

Perspectives on the Dust Bowl

In the early 1950s, along with plummeting food prices, farmers on the Great Plains also suffered from a period of drought. Without life-giving rain, crops died, and the topsoil was blown away into the sky by powerful winds. Great dust storms raged on the prairies of Kansas, Oklahoma, and Texas for days at a time. This dry, desolate area became known as the "Dust Bowl." In response to this disaster, thousands of farm families packed up their belongings and abandoned their farms to move West in search of new prosperity.

A History of the United States as an instructional program provides two types of resources you can use to offer in-depth coverage of the Dust Bowl: the *student text* and the *Enrichment Support File*. A list of *Suggested Secondary Sources* is also provided. The chart below shows the topics that are covered in each.

THE STUDENT TEXT. Boorstin and Kelley's *A History of the United States* unfolds the chronology of events resulting in the Dust Bowl of the early 1900s.

AMERICAN HISTORY ENRICHMENT SUPPORT FILE. This collection of primary source readings and classroom activities focuses on the water distribution, settlement, farming techniques, and dust storms of the Dust Bowl.

SUGGESTED SECONDARY SOURCES. This reference list of readings by well-known historians and other commentators provides an array of perspectives on the Dust Bowl.

Locating Instructional Materials

Detailed lesson plans for teaching the Dust Bowl as a mini-course or to study one or more elements of the Dust Bowl in depth are offered in the following areas: in the *student text*, see individual lesson plans at the beginning of each chapter; in the *Enrichment Support File*, see page 3; for readings beyond the student text, see *Suggested Secondary Sources*.

IN-DEPTH COVERAGE ON THE DUST BOWL		
Student Text	**Enrichment Support File**	**Suggested Secondary Sources**
• Precipitation and Vegetation on the Plains, *maps*, p. 386 • Dust Storms, p. 643 • Conservation of Farm Land, pp. 643–644 • Farm Tenants and Sharecroppers, pp. 644–645	• Lesson Suggestions • Multimedia Resources • Overview Essay/Nature's Fury: The Dust Bowl • Literature in American History/*The Grapes of Wrath* • Songs in American History/"So Long, It's Been Good to Know Yuh" • Primary Sources in American History/"The Dust-Covered Desolation" • Geography in American History/Geography and the Black Blizzards • Making Connections	• *A Nation in Torment: The Great Depression, 1929–1939* by Daniel Robb Ellis, pp. 451–488. • *The Great Depression: The United States in the Thirties* by Robert Goldston, pp. 193–207. • *California and the Dust Bowl Migration* by Walter J. Stein, pp. 3–31. • *Dust Bowl: The Southern Plains in the 1930s* by Donald Worster, pp. 9–64.

Problems on the Farm

FOCUS

To introduce the lesson, have students turn to the vegetation map of the Great Plains on page 386. Tell students that the Dust Bowl area was roughly the "short grass" land from just below the southern edge of the Texas panhandle stretching to Nebraska (some Dust Bowl maps include southwest South Dakota.) Add to this area a bulge into central Kansas (generally the land in Oklahoma with 15–25 inches of annual precipitation on the precipitation map on the same page). Students should note that the Dust Bowl was centered in a region of light rainfall that was formerly grassland. High prices for wheat in World War I had encouraged farmers to plow under the grass to make wheat fields on land that normally received barely enough rain for tough rooted grass to grow. When two or three very dry years followed in succession, there was nothing to hold the topsoil when the winds blew.

Developing Vocabulary

The words listed are essential terms for understanding particular sections of the chapter. The page number after each term indicates the page of its first or most important appearance. These terms are defined in the Glossary (text pages 1000–1011).

Dust Bowl (page 643); **sharecroppers** (page 644); **tenant farmers** (page 645).

INSTRUCT

Explain

Dust storms acerbated farmers' problems in the 1930s. Tenant farmers and sharecroppers were helped by the Bankhead-Jones Farm Tenant Act, and the Farm Security Administration provided clean camps for migrants. Conservation efforts tried to preserve the soil.

☑ Writing Process Activity

Expressing Problems Clearly Have students imagine they are sharecroppers in the 1930s. Before they write a letter to FDR explaining the problems they face and asking him for help, have them freewrite about what their lives are like as tenant farmers. Students should begin their letters with a clear statement of what they need, and they should support their plea with specific examples. As they revise, remind students to check for clarity, specificity, and a respectful tone. After proofreading, students can read their letters to the class.

Section Review Answers

Section 1, page 646

1. a) the wife of FDR. She became well known for her efforts on behalf of the unemployed, the aged, blacks, and others facing hard times. b) name given to the Great Plains in the 1930s when the topsoil blew away because of a drought. c) wrote *The Grapes of Wrath*, a novel that described the people who moved from the Dust Bowl to California in a desperate search for a new life. d) farmers who do not own the land they farm and are not paid wages; instead, they receive a share of the crops they produce. e) head of the Resettlement Administration, which moved sharecroppers and other tenants from land too poor to support them to better land. f) provided long-term loans to help tenants buy the farms they worked. g) replaced the Resettlement Administration and had the added responsibility of providing clean camps for migratory farm workers. 2. By giving them seeds, equipment, and loans; by trying to resettle some on better land; and by providing long-term loans so they could buy the land they farmed. 3. The REA provided loans at low interest rates to companies or farmers' cooperatives that would build their own generators and install power lines, therefore helping most farm families by bringing electricity to their farms. 4. They killed crops and livestock and blew away the topsoil, forcing many farmers on the Great Plains to abandon their land and move west in search of a new start in life.

CLOSE

To conclude the lesson, ask: What efforts did government make to alleviate the suffering of the people in the Dust Bowl and to try and correct the factors that had caused it? (Relief funds, low interest loans, irrigation projects, sources of low-cost electricity, soil conservation incentives, education programs, etc.)

The Problems of Black Americans

FOCUS

To introduce the lesson, ask: Based on the text, why was the Great Depression even more difficult for blacks than for whites? List answers on the board: greater unemployment; lower incomes; denial of rights; poor education; poor housing; inadequate health care, etc. Tell students that blacks and members of other minority groups were often the last to be hired and the first to be fired during hard times. In farm areas, blacks often had cash incomes averaging less than $200 a year. In cities, conditions for blacks were usually not much better—especially when food was scarce.

Developing Vocabulary

grandfather clause (page 646); **literacy test** (page 647); **poll tax** (page 647).

INSTRUCT

Explain

Discrimination and the Great Depression made it difficult for blacks to have rights and prosper under either Washington's or Du Bois' approach.

❖ Cooperative Learning Activity

Identifying Central Issues Break the class into groups of four and divide chalkboards in the classroom so that each group has its own space. Allow students to use chalk to create graffiti boards illustrating their feelings and attitudes about the life and struggles of black Americans in the early 1900s. Encourage groups to compare and discuss boards.

Section Review Answers

Section 2, page 649

1. a) leader of the Niagara Movement, a founder of the NAACP, and editor of the NAACP's magazine, *The Crisis*. b) National Association for the Advancement of Colored People, founded in 1909 to help blacks fight for their rights through the courts, to awaken all Americans to the rights of blacks, and to avoid racial violence. c) black adviser to FDR. She headed the Division of Negro Affairs of the National Youth Administration and helped thousands of black youngsters to stay in school or learn trades. d) also known as the "New Negro Movement," occurred in the 1920s. It began in Harlem, where black poets, writers, scholars, painters, and musicians gathered, but its influence spread to other cities. 2. "Grandfather clauses" required that people pass various tests before they could vote, but exempted from those tests people who had the right to vote on January 1, 1867, and their descendants; the effect, and the intent, was that blacks but not whites had to pass various tests before voting. Another device was to require voters to pass a literacy test and to ask blacks who took the test difficult, if not impossible, constitutional questions. The poll tax prevented the poor and, therefore, most blacks from voting. 3. It failed to prevent discrimination in jobs, education, and housing; by allowing the TVA and the NRA to discriminate against blacks; and by failing to end the poll tax. Moreover, FDR refused to support an anti-lynching bill. However, FDR did speak out against lynchings,

and he gave blacks some positions of leadership in his government.

CLOSE

To conclude the lesson, ask: Why did blacks abandon the Republican party and join the Democratic party, considering the limited real improvement that the New Deal offered them? (Roosevelt's support, limited as it was, was more substantial than any national political leader had offered them in half a century. Blacks who moved North became city-dwellers. Along with other working-class urbanites, they benefited from the activities of the mostly Democratic urban political machines and so increasingly identified with the Democratic Party.)

Extension Activity

To extend the lesson, have students research and write a short biography of African American activist W.E.B. DuBois, highlighting what they believe were his most important contributions to American society.

Section 3 (pages 649–651)

The New Deal and Women

FOCUS

To introduce the lesson, ask: What do you think the situation of women in the labor force was in the 1930s? Discuss their answers. Some students may infer that since times were tough in the 1930s, people probably argued that women should be laid off to allow male breadwinners to keep their jobs. Have students reread the material under the heading "The economic inequality of women" on page 651 to verify this.

INSTRUCT

Explain

Women for the first time gained substantial political influence during the Roosevelt administration, but women were not often given supervisory jobs and were criticized for taking jobs from men.

☑ Writing Process Activity

Drawing Conclusions In preparation for writing a report, ask students to do research about one of the influential women in government during FDR's presidency, such as Eleanor Roosevelt, Frances Perkins, or Mary McLeod Bethune. They should take notes on the role she played and the significance of her accomplishments. Students should begin their report with a thesis statement summarizing the woman's role in politics, and they should organize their information chronologically. Ask students to revise for completeness and objectivity. After proofreading, students can publish a class collection of women's biographies.

Section Review Answers

Section 3, page 651

1. a) directed the work of women in the Democratic party and tried to increase the number and influence of women in government. b) Secretary of Labor in FDR's administration. 2. She exerted influence herself, advised her husband, attracted women reformers to Washington, and pushed to increase the number and influence of women working in the government. 3. It decreased the number of jobs generally, and many Americans thought that men should be hired first so that they could support their families. They did not want women competing with men for jobs when jobs were so scarce.

CLOSE

To conclude the lesson, ask students these follow-up questions about the argument that women should not compete with men: Why had the prosperity phase of the business cycle often been the best time for an equality movement for women, blacks, Indians, Hispanics, or other groups? (Deprived groups are seen as less threatening if unemployment is relatively low; there is a bigger "pie" for everyone to have a "slice" of.) In a recession today, would you expect any politician to call on women to sacrifice their job ambitions to save the jobs of "family breadwinners"? (Probably not, because more women than ever are family breadwinners; there are more voting-age females than males, and voter turnout percentages are about equal for males and females; women have made gains that they are not willing to give up; and the fallacies in the argument are more widely recognized than in the 1930s. Nevertheless, the position is still advanced by some.)

Extension Activity

To extend the lesson, have students create a list of the ten most influential women of the 1930s. (Encourage the class to research figures not mentioned in the text book.) Then through class discussions use individual lists to create a class list.

Section 4 (pages 652–654)

The Struggles of Labor

FOCUS

To introduce the lesson, ask: Are labor strikes ever violent? (Some students may recall the violence they read about earlier in the text, such as in the Pullman and Homestead strikes.) What causes this violence?

Developing Vocabulary

sit-down strike (page 653)

INSTRUCT

Explain

Students should note that one provision of the National Labor Relations Act guaranteed workers the right to organize and bargain collectively for improvements in wages, hours of work, and working conditions. Have students review two chief functions of the National Labor Relations Board (p. 634): to oversee company elections for union representation, and to act on union charges of unfair labor practices by employers. Even with the help of the Wagner Act, labor's effectiveness in organizing seems remarkable in light of the continuing massive unemployment during the 1930s. Part of the reason for the unions' successes lies in the development of the CIO industrial unions. The mass production industries—steel, auto, rubber, etc.—had made a strong comeback from the depths of the Depression and wanted to continue operations. To do so, they were forced to accept unionization by the new CIO unions. The large number of new union members helped to swell the ranks of organized labor.

★ Independent Activity

Identifying Central Issues Have students set up an outline with the roman numeral headings of American Federation of Labor and Congress of Industrial Organizations. List as subheads for each part: Founding, Organization, Qualifications for Membership, and Industries Organized. Ask students to work independently to complete their outlines, using the information in the text.

Section Review Answers

Section 4, page 654

1. a) head of the United Mine Workers and the leading force in the formation of the CIO. b) helped found the AFL and became its president. c) succeeded Gompers as president of the AFL. d) Congress of Industrial Organizations, a labor organization that became independent from the AFL in 1935 and worked to organize unions for particular industries (such as steel, auto, and so on) and to include unskilled workers in these unions. 2. They hired private police to intimidate or attack strikers. 3. American labor unions organized in mass-production industries; membership in unions rose from 4 million to 6 million; the unions gained support of their rights from the federal government; and the power of factory

owners over workers was reduced. 4. Workers in mass-production industries, especially the unskilled workers, immigrants from southern and eastern Europe, Puerto Ricans, women, and blacks. 5. A craft union is made up of workers who have a particular skill, such as plumbers or carpenters. An industrial union is made up of all those who work in a particular industry, such as autos or steel. The industrial union therefore includes both skilled and unskilled workers.

CLOSE

To conclude the lesson, have students write a one-page essay on how the violence started at the Memorial Day massacre. Have students rewrite the essay into polished form for homework.

Chapter Review Answers

Focusing on Ideas

1. Sharecroppers faced debt bondage to landowners, loss of tenancy when land was taken out of production, and low prices. New Deal hurt when owners took land out of production but helped with production loans, mortgage loans, or resettlement on better land. 2. FDR spoke out against lynching and brought more blacks into government. Business recovery and tem-porary public jobs benefited blacks. Sometimes more benefits went to blacks because of their higher unemployment rate. 3. Strikes; industrial unions; political action (lobbying). All were fairly effective. 4. "She adopted all the nation's unhappy and neglected people as her foster children."

Taking a Critical Look

1. Applaud: female Cabinet member and other officials; influence of Eleanor Roosevelt; equality of representation on Democratic Platform Committee. Setback: layoffs of women to preserve jobs for men. 2. Blacks, women, immigrants, the poor. Today: many poor, unemployed, homeless, and perhaps illegal aliens.

Your Region in History

1–3. Answers will vary depending on your region. Consult your local library or historical society.

Historical Facts and Figures

(a) 1900: 500,000; 1920: 5,000,000, and 1940: 8,500,000. (b) 1600%. (c) Approximately 55 million. (d) The government supported workers organizing; CIO recruitment of women and all ethnic groups; efforts of AF of L to compete by increasing its membership.

Focusing the Chapter: Have students identify the chapter logo. Discuss what unit theme the logo might symbolize. Then ask students to skim the chapter to identify other illustrations or titles that relate to this theme.

Chapter 25

Reshaping American Life

In 1933 another Bonus Army descended on Washington. This time, instead of being driven away, they were housed and fed by the government. Their leaders talked to the President. Then one day these veterans were startled to meet a tall, gawky woman with appealing eyes and a wide, toothy smile trudging through the mud to the old army barracks where they were housed. The visitor was Eleanor Roosevelt, wife of the President of the United States. She sat and talked with them, listened to their troubles, and joined in their singing. And she carried her sympathy back to the White House.

Eleanor Roosevelt personified the change in the government. Her humane spirit represented to many groups—blacks, immigrants, migrant workers, the aged, and the unemployed—the hope that through the New Deal they, too, might somehow someday enjoy the plenty of American life.

✕ William C. Palmer's 1934 painting "Dust, Drought, and Destruction" shows the ravages wrought by the great dust storms of the 1930s. The farm has been abandoned, the windmill has fallen, the tree has died, and the wind swirls the soil away through the air.

Whitney Museum of American Art, New York

✕ Critical Thinking Activity: Identifying Central Issues How did artists express the plight of farmers in the New Deal? Have students list the issues that had to be addressed for farmers by the New Deal. Ask students to identify which of these issues Palmer looks at in his painting "Dust, Drought, and Destruction." Have students write one sentence that summarizes the painting's message. Let students take turns reading their sentences. As a follow-up activity students might want to create their own artwork on the topic.

See "Lesson Plan," p. 642C.

1. Problems on the farm

But it was far easier for Eleanor Roosevelt to sing with the Bonus Army or for FDR to speak warmly to "my friends" over the radio than for the government to change the daily lives of people in trouble. The problems of the farmers, for example, were varied and complicated. No single law could give all they needed. Some farmers needed electricity. Some were fighting dust storms. Others, working as tenants, were not getting a square deal from their landlords and had no way to share in the government's bounty. Many could not afford to buy the tractors or combines to make their land profitable. Still others, who lived on worn-out land, had no money to buy fertilizer. Nor did they know how to renew their land by planting diverse crops.

Their problems seemed as overwhelming and unmanageable as nature itself.

Enrichment Support File Topic

The dust storms. In the 1930s the Great Plains began to blow away. Bountiful rains in the 1920s had encouraged farmers to plow the fragile grasslands without worrying about the future. Then the rains ceased. Drought cursed the whole mid-continent from Canada to Mexico.

The sun baked the land into a brittle, powdery crust. Nineteen states in the heart of the nation became one enormous "Dust Bowl." Crops shriveled. Cattle died. When the wind blew, the topsoil—with no living roots to hold it in place—swirled into the air. Great, dark, yellowish clouds filled the sky, choking the nose and throat, blotting out the sun and causing street lights to be turned on at midday. The precious soil of the Great Plains blew all the way to the East Coast—even sifting into the White House—and on out into the Atlantic Ocean.

Many families whose fields grew only dust gave up. They loaded their old cars with what they could carry and left the land where they had been raised. The "flivver" that Henry Ford had invented no longer carried them to a holiday in town. Now instead it took them on their desperate quest for a better life—anywhere. They moved in all directions, without a clear destination and with no real plan. The "Okies" from Oklahoma and the "Arkies" from Arkansas

headed west. A third of a million people from those states and from Texas, the Dakotas, Kansas, and Nebraska hit the road. Thousands ended up in California as migrant laborers picking fruit and vegetables and living in squalid camps. Their hard journeys and their frustrated lives can never be forgotten, for they became the long-suffering heroes of John Steinbeck's powerful novel, *The Grapes of Wrath.*

The mild climate and the legend of its golden land made California the number one goal of the migrants. In 1939 that state tried to stem the tide by passing a law forbidding poor migrants to enter. But two years later the Supreme Court declared the law unconstitutional.

A quarter-million Mexicans seeking work went to California during the 1930s. Other Mexicans, along with Filipinos, Okies, Arkies, and other migrants—at least another 100,000—moved north into Colorado, Wyoming, and Montana to work in the sugar beet fields. But, unlike the Okies, they had no Steinbeck to tell their story.

Conserving the land. FDR's own experience had shown him the need for soil conservation. The land on his ancestral estate at Hyde Park, New York, had been worn out by centuries of unscientific farming. He renewed that land by planting thousands of trees "in the hope that my great grandchildren will be able to try raising corn again—just one century from now." Trees would help stop the dust storms on the Great Plains. Farmers across the nation followed their President's example. With seedlings from the government they planted 200 million trees across the expanse extending from the Dakotas to Texas. For years experts had said no trees would grow on the western plains. But these trees took root. Their growth surprised the experts and helped other farmers, too, by making new "shelter-belts," conserving water and holding in place the precious topsoil.

The New Deal, from its start, tried new ways to help the farmer. As early as 1933 a Soil Erosion Service was set up to preserve the farmer's most valuable resource. Farmers and CCC boys were taught terracing and contour farming. Then the Soil Conservation Act of 1936 aimed

The depression forced many families to go on the road in search of work. A large number headed for the West Coast, where they hoped to find jobs in the orchards and vineyards. In this photograph by Dorothea Lange in November 1936 a family in California uses their car for a home.

(p. 645) to reduce surpluses and also to promote soil conservation (p. 634). Today we still profit from the New Deal experiments—the TVA, the great dams in the West, reforestation, and grazing control—all ways to preserve and renew the American land.

The lot of farm tenants. After the Civil War, there were no longer slaves to till the soil in the South. Their place was taken by a new class, the *sharecroppers* (p. 381). These farmers— white and black—did not own the land they lived on, and they were not paid wages for their work. Instead they received a share of the crops, and the owner of the land got the rest.

Sharecroppers were not legally slaves, but they were tied to their plot of land by the bonds of debt and despair. Since they had no capital,

the only way they could secure the seed for the next year—and the food and clothing for their family—was to pledge their share in advance. One year of bad crops was enough to drown them in debt. They could not survive on their land, yet they dared not leave.

Although it was not planned that way, the condition of the sharecroppers was made even worse by the first AAA. The law paid landowners to take some acres out of production, and this was often the marginal land the sharecroppers farmed.

To help the poor sharecroppers and other tenants who still could work their land, Harry Hopkins under the Federal Emergency Relief Act loaned them money and gave them seeds and equipment. When their land was too poor to support them, he tried to resettle them on

See "Lesson Plan," p. 642C for **Writing Process Activity: Expressing Problems Clearly** relating to the problems faced by sharecroppers in the 1930s.

better lands. In 1935 FDR moved these activities to the Resettlement Administration under Rexford Tugwell.

But all these efforts hardly made a dent in the problem. Senator John Bankhead of Alabama proposed a new approach. The Bankhead-Jones Farm Tenant Act of 1937 provided long-term loans to help tenants buy the farms they worked. Blacks and whites were treated alike. And the unfortunate Okies and the Arkies who became migratory farm laborers, following the ripening crops, were at least provided with clean camps. The Farm Security Administration replaced Tugwell's agency to carry out these programs.

The problems of American farmers—of the poor tenants, sharecroppers, and migrants—were as broad and as varied as the continent. These were not to be solved in a few years, nor by a single farm program in Washington. Still, the New Deal efforts could give them hope and cheer them with the news that they were not forgotten.

Rural electrification. By the mid-1930s electricity had reshaped the daily lives of Americans in cities. It was lighting their homes at night, running their radios, cooling their refrigerators. But not for farmers. They fed an electrified nation, but they themselves had not yet entered the electric age. Only one farm family in ten had electricity.

On May 11, 1935, President Roosevelt set up the Rural Electrification Administration to help

"Roasting Ears" was painted by Thomas Hart Benton of Missouri in the 1930s.

Continuity and Change: Government and Politics Point out to students that cousins Franklin Roosevelt and Theodore Roosevelt were both concerned with conservation of natural resources. TR implemented a plan of reforestation, and withdrew from sale millions of acres of public land having waterpower sites and deposits of coal, oil, and phosphates. FDR supported projects to plant trees on the Great Plains to conserve water and hold the topsoil in place, to help stop dust storms. (See p. 525.)

bring electric power to the farms of America. The REA could loan money at low interest to help private companies or farmers' cooperatives build their own generators and install power lines. This produced an electrical revolution. By 1941, four out of five American farms were enjoying the comforts that only electricity could bring. More than any other transformation, this showed that their government, which now remembered them, could draw them into the mainstream of modern America.

See "Section 1 Review answers," p. 642C.

Section 1 Review

1. Identify or explain: Eleanor Roosevelt, "Dust Bowl," John Steinbeck, sharecroppers, Rexford Tugwell, Bankhead-Jones Farm Tenant Act, Farm Security Administration.

2. How did the New Deal try to help poor tenant farmers?

3. How did the REA help most farm families?

4. **Critical Thinking: Recognizing Cause and Effect.** What was the effect of dust storms on farmers in the Great Plains?

See "Lesson Plan," p. 642C.

2. The problems of black Americans

In 1930 around 80 percent of all black Americans were still living within the borders of the old Confederacy. There they were not allowed to vote. Little money was spent on their education, and they went to separate and inferior schools. They found it hard to borrow money to buy houses or farms. In some southern states the blacks made up more than half the population. Yet the paths to wealth and political power were closed to these black citizens.

It was no wonder then that, in 1938, President Roosevelt called the South "the nation's No. 1 economic problem." By almost any measure—health, housing, schools, auto ownership, farm equipment, or family income—the South was the worst-off section of the whole United States. And in the impoverished South, the blacks were the poorest of all.

Yet new forces were at work in America. Among them were black leaders themselves. Even under slavery there had been brave rebels like Nat Turner and Denmark Vesey. The persuasive Frederick Douglass had been a leader in the abolition movement. During the Civil War he had helped recruit blacks for two regiments in the Union army. After the war he became marshal of the District of Columbia and United States consul general in Haiti. In the early 1900s, too, there were many kinds of black leaders who offered different views of American life and the doors to opportunity. Booker T. Washington and W. E. B. Du Bois, each in his own way, pointed in new directions for black Americans (p. 449).

Black Southerners lose the right to vote. When the Populists had tried to unite all the poor—black and white—behind economic reforms in the South (p. 471), they provoked an extreme reaction. White Democrats defeated the Populists by pointing with alarm to the fact that they worked with blacks. And soon white Populists admitted they could never win elections if the race question was used against them. Southern whites combined their energy and ingenuity to find ways to keep blacks out of the polling booths. This was no easy task. The Fifteenth Amendment, adopted during Reconstruction, had plainly declared that the right of citizens to vote should not be denied "by the United States or by any state on account of race, color, or previous condition of servitude."

Southerners tried using the "grandfather clause." A state would simply pass a law giving the right to vote to those persons who did have the right to vote on January 1, 1867 (before the Fifteenth Amendment) and to those persons' descendants. Anyone else who wanted to vote had to pass all sorts of impossible tests. Of course that included blacks. They would not be allowed to vote simply because their grandfathers did not have the right to vote! Beginning in 1895 seven southern states passed "grandfather" laws. Not until 1915 did the United States Supreme Court declare that these laws violated the Constitution.

Another trick was the so-called literacy test. It

✕ Critical Thinking Activity: Making Comparisons How did the condition of Southern blacks in 1930 compare with their condition during Reconstruction? Write the following categories on the chalkboard: "Suffrage," "Education," and "Economic Opportunities." Divide the class into three groups, assigning each one a topic. Ask the groups to use their topic to compare the condition of Southern blacks in 1930 to their condition during the Reconstruction. Have each group report back to the class. Ask students to write a summary statement that synthesizes their findings.

In spite of the high unemployment in the nation's cities in the 1930s, black families from the rural South continued their farm-to-city migration. In Chicago they had no choice but to live in the black belt on the South Side—often in houses like the one in this 1930s' photograph.

pretended to limit the vote to people who could read. But when blacks came to vote, the white election judges gave tests that they themselves probably could not have passed. They would ask a black to explain the most difficult part of the Constitution. A white person only had to read out a simple sentence.

Some southern states also used the poll tax. That was a tax that everybody had to pay before going to the polls to vote. Most blacks in the South were so poor that they really could not afford the few dollars for the tax. And even if a black person paid the tax, the election judge could always find some mistake in the tax receipt, and so keep the black person from voting.

The craftiness of some white Southerners seemed endless. They even went so far as to

National Portrait Gallery, Smithsonian Institution;
Gift of Walter Waring in memory of his wife,
Laura Wheeler Waring through the Harmon Foundation.

W. E. B. Du Bois was an ardent fighter for civil rights and a distinguished scholar.

pretend that the great political parties in the South were not political parties at all, but only private clubs. Therefore, they said, nobody except white "members" had a right to vote in the primary election when their "club" picked its candidates for public office.

Since the Democratic party was in complete control in most of the South, winners in that party's primary would win the offices. By keeping black people from voting in the primary, then you would take away their votes.

Working for rights for blacks. Thoughtful citizens all over the country became ashamed that the nation had been so slow to give all Americans their simple rights. The Niagara Movement, sparked by W. E. B. Du Bois, grew stronger (p. 450). The National Association for the Advancement of Colored People (NAACP) was founded in 1909 on Lincoln's birthday. It was formed in response to shocking race riots like the one in 1908 in Springfield, Illinois,

Lincoln's burial place. Du Bois became the impassioned editor of the NAACP magazine, *The Crisis.*

Americans of all races and religions, from all parts of the country, joined hands. People, like Jane Addams, who already were working for the poor of all races in the northern city slums, gave money to pay for lawyers to help blacks secure their rights in the South. The president of the NAACP, Boston lawyer Moorfield Storey, argued the case when the Supreme Court in 1915 set aside the "grandfather" laws. The NAACP also won other important cases. One of these declared that no trial of a black could be a fair trial (as the Constitution required) if blacks were kept off the jury. During the next years the NAACP was the most important group trying to awaken all Americans to the rights of blacks.

Things were getting better for blacks. But the progress was painfully slow—and there was a long way to go.

Failures of the New Deal. For millions of black Americans—especially in the South and in the big city slums in the North—there still seemed almost no change. Black workers were the last hired and the first fired. Black children still had less money spent on their education. Blacks were not allowed to live wherever they could afford, but had to live in special neighborhoods. Even under the New Deal, blacks were not always given their fair share. For example, they were not allowed to live in the model towns built with government money in the Tennessee Valley.

Most of those blacks whom Du Bois called the "Talented Tenth" still had to take lowly jobs. When then NRA codes allowed blacks to be paid less than whites, blacks began to say that NRA just meant "Negroes Ruined Again." *The Crisis* said in 1935 that blacks "ought to realize by now that the powers-that-be in the Roosevelt administration have nothing for them."

Yet more and more blacks voted for FDR and the New Deal. In Chicago, for example, where in 1932 only 23 percent had voted for Roosevelt, 49 percent favored him in 1936, and 56 percent in 1940. But the New Deal had done nothing to remove the poll tax. In most of its programs,

Multicultural Connection: One of the greatest poets of the Harlem Renaissance was Langston Hughes (1901–1967). Born in Missouri, Hughes was educated at Columbia and Lincoln universities. He was poet-in-residence at the University of Chicago from 1949–1950, and the recipient of Guggenheim and Rosenwald fellowships. Hughes' work dealt with the African-American experience in America. One of his most famous poems, "A Dream Deferred," deals with the effects of the frustration and anger many African Americans felt at white injustice and at the inaccessability of the American Dream.

blacks were still treated unequally. And when an anti-lynching bill was introduced to Congress, FDR refused to support it. "If I come out for the anti-lynching bill now," Roosevelt told Walter White of the NAACP, "they [southern senators] will block every bill I ask Congress to pass to keep America from collapsing. I just can't take that risk."

Blacks in government.   Despite the failings of the New Deal, Roosevelt did convince most blacks that he sided with them in their fight for equal treatment. He spoke out against lynching as "collective murder." Under Woodrow Wilson and his Republican successors, blacks in government jobs were segregated. Now those who were brought into the growing bureaucracy were given their rightful place with other Americans. A "Black Cabinet" or "Black Brain Trust" became close advisers of the President. Among the persons in the large and ever-shifting group were William H. Hastie, Assistant Solicitor in the Department of the Interior, and Mary McLeod Bethune, the forceful director of the Division of Negro Affairs of the National Youth Administration. Mrs. Bethune channeled large amounts of aid to thousands of black youngsters, helping them stay in school or learn new trades.

As usual, Eleanor Roosevelt helped blacks to feel that the administration cared about them. She was known to be a good friend of Mary McLeod Bethune's. She invited the National Council of Negro Women to tea at the White House. She was seen, and photographed, visiting black schools and other projects useful to black citizens.

A "Black Renaissance."   After World War I a movement called the "Black Renaissance" or the "New Negro Movement" began in Harlem. This neighborhood in New York City became a gathering place for black poets, writers, scholars, painters, and musicians. Poets like Langston Hughes and Countee Cullen revealed whole new vistas of American experience. Also in Harlem then was Du Bois, who told the exciting story of the renaissance in *Black Manhattan* and *Along This Way.*

The Harlem Renaissance ended about 1930, but its influence spread outward. In cities across the nation there were small but active groups of poets, writers, painters, and actors. The movement was helped along by the New Deal's Federal Writers' Project. (p. 648)

The rights for black Americans would come gradually—but not fast enough for W. E. B. Du Bois. He lost faith in America and in democracy. He joined the Communist party and then renounced his United States citizenship. In 1961, at the age of 93, he moved to the new African country of Ghana. But, as we shall see, others of stronger faith—the Rev. Martin Luther King, Jr., for example—continued their struggle in and for America. They would bring historic victories of justice and equality, not only for blacks, but for all Americans.

See "Section 2 Review answers," p. 642D.

Section 2 Review

1. Identify: W. E. B. Du Bois, NAACP, Mary M. Bethune, "Black Renaissance."

2. Name and explain devices used in southern states to keep blacks from voting.

3. **Critical Thinking: Expressing Problems Clearly.** How did the New Deal fail to help black Americans? In what ways did it help them?

See "Lesson Plan," p. 642D.

3. The New Deal and women

Many Americans had thought that winning the right to vote would allow women to become an independent force in politics. This had not happened. Many women failed to go to the polls. And because they did not vote, politicians had little reason to respect their special demands. It would take more than the Nineteenth Amendment to bring women into the mainstream of American political life. It would take a long program of education and the slow discovery that women were not shaped by nature only for roles as wives and mothers. They were just as qualified as men for leadership and service in government, business, and the arts. In the

✿ See "Lesson Plan," p. 642D for **Cooperative Learning Activity: Identifying Central Issues** relating to the struggles of African Americans in the early 1900s.

experimental spirit of the New Deal era millions of Americans—women and men—were awakened to these opportunities.

Eleanor Roosevelt. The person best placed to help them was the President's wife. Eleanor Roosevelt's mother had died when she was eight, and her father, just before her tenth birthday. Raised by her grandmother, she had lived a lonely life. Perhaps her own unhappiness as a girl had made her sympathetic to the needs of others who felt alone and abandoned. She adopted all the nation's unhappy and neglected people as her foster children. And she dared to speak up for them in her regular press conferences. She wrote a newspaper column and gave radio talks. She traveled everywhere. In 1933

alone she covered 40,000 miles. One newspaper headlined on its society page, "Mrs. Roosevelt Spends Night at White House." FDR, in his wheelchair, could not move about as she did. She became the conscience of the New Deal and the eyes of the President. It was not unusual for him to tell the Cabinet that something needed to be done because "My Missus told me so and so."

Women in government and politics. With Eleanor Roosevelt in the White House, women for the first time gained substantial political influence and positions of power on the national scene. Women reformers came to Washington in large numbers to work for the government. Mary (Molly) Dewson, a friend of the

Because FDR was unable to walk, Mrs. Roosevelt traveled everywhere, becoming his eyes and ears outside the White House.

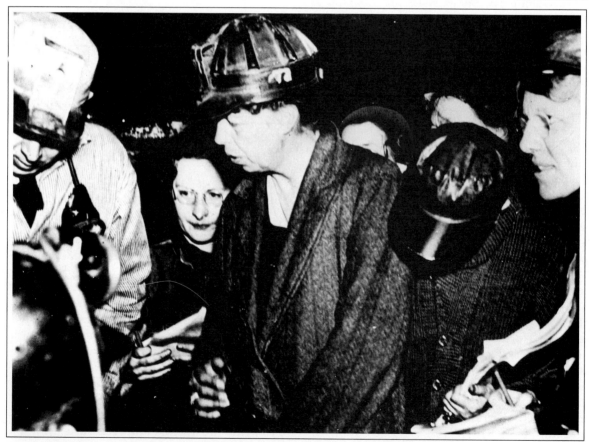

Continuity and Change: Government and Politics Remind students that during FDR's administration there was a growth in opportunities for women in the political arena. The 1936 Democratic Convention ruled that each member of the Platform Committee had to have an alternate of the opposite sex and Frances Perkins became the first woman cabinet member. Women would continue to gain substantial political influence and positions of power on the national scene. But it was not until the 1984 Democratic Convention that the nation would see the first major party nomination of a woman; Geraldine Ferraro, for the Vice-Presidency. (See p. 914.)

Roosevelts', took over the direction of women's work in the Democratic party. In 1936 the Democratic convention ruled that each member of the Platform Committee had to have an alternate of the opposite sex. The *New York Times* called this "the biggest coup for women in years."

Eleanor Roosevelt and Mary Dewson fought hard to get women into the government and to see that New Deal programs helped women. In 1930, women held only 17.6 percent of the postmaster positions, but six years later their share had gone up to 26 percent. The Civil Works Administration employed 100,000 women by the end of 1933.

Some of the most important positions in FDR's administration were given to women. Frances Perkins was Secretary of Labor. Florence Allen became a judge of the Circuit Court of Appeals. Other women became ambassadors and top officers of the WPA and other agencies. Formerly all the women executives in the federal government could meet for dinner in a small clubroom. Now they needed a large hall.

Eleanor Roosevelt thought that women could help humanize government. The aim of the New Deal, as she saw it, was to promote "the general happiness of the working man and woman and their families." Women had something special to offer.

The economic inequality of women. Still, during these years women were usually given jobs that were considered "women's work"—as teachers, typists, clerks, nurses, and textile workers. They were seldom put in supervisory positions. Though 80 percent of the schoolteachers of the nation were women, in superintendent positions they were only 1.5 percent. One-third of all graduate degrees were awarded to women, yet they made up only 4 percent of the college professors. Even when they did the very same work, women often were paid less than men.

In those depression days of widespread unemployment, many Americans—including leading women—feared that women would take jobs from men. This would increase the unem-

United Press International Photo

Among the most active supporters of a larger role for women in the government and the Democratic party during the New Deal were Eleanor Roosevelt and Mary Dewson (above).

ployment of the traditional family "breadwinners." Florence Kahn, congresswoman from California, declared, "Women's place is not out in the business world competing with men who have families to support." Secretary of Labor Frances Perkins agreed.

While women were heartened by the examples of Eleanor Roosevelt, Frances Perkins, Mary McLeod Bethune, Mary Dewson, and others like them on the national scene, they still had a long road to travel toward economic equality.

See "Section 3 Review answers," p. 642E.

Section 3 Review

1. Identify: Mary Dewson, Frances Perkins.
2. How did Eleanor Roosevelt help women achieve political influence?
3. **Critical Thinking: Drawing Conclusions.** How did the depression affect women's job prospects?

See "Lesson Plan," p. 642D for **Writing Process Activity: Drawing Conclusions** relating to women in government in the 1930s.

See "Lesson Plan," p. 642E.

4. The struggles of labor

The New Deal hoped to enlist the help of organized labor to improve the lot of "forgotten Americans"—blacks, women, immigrants, the poor. Through section 7a of the NRA, and then by the Wagner Act and its National Labor Relations Board, the government lent its support to the attempts of workers to organize.

The growth of the AF of L. Loss of jobs had cut union membership after the Great Crash. Then the unions began to recover in 1934. But they were still unable to organize the great mass-production industries—steel, autos, rubber, textiles. The AF of L was a federation of craft unions and so was better suited to the

John L. Lewis, shown here after a trip down into a mine, was the tough and charismatic leader of the CIO in the 1930s.

Wide World Photos

past than to the future. Its ways of thinking were not adapted to a world of vast factories, of power-driven machinery, and mass production.

The Carpenters' Union, for example, had grown by moving from the construction trades into any industry that dealt with things made of wood and finally anything "that ever was made of wood." In this way—and by expanding into many new and smaller fields—the AF of L had reached a membership of 3.5 million by 1936.

The birth of the CIO. Some union leaders were not happy with the craft approach. They felt that the age of crafts had gone out with the horse and buggy. John L. Lewis, the massive, shaggy-browed leader of the United Mine Workers, believed that the industrial world of the 1900s required a new kind of labor organization. The American Federation of Labor, led by Samuel Gompers and William Green, had organized the aristocracy of American labor. They believed that the skilled workers in the old crafts—carpenters, plumbers, and bricklayers—could only lose if they threw in their lot with the millions of unskilled workers in factories and mines.

Lewis had begun working in the mines when he was 16. Even after he became a high union official he never forgot that he was a miner. And he was confident that if labor was to become a great power and defend its interests it would have to organize in a new way. Unions would never get into the steel mills or auto plants if the company had to deal with a dozen craft unions. Each union would want what was best for its own members. Lewis said that a single union should bargain for all the workers—skilled and unskilled—in a giant industry. There should be one industrial union for steel, not a dozen or more craft unions.

The AF of L had never organized the steel industry. For it did not fit into the old craft pattern. Now Lewis wanted to unionize the steelworkers because steel mills were the largest single users of coal. Their owners also owned coal mines.

In 1935 the Committee for Industrial Organization (later the Congress of Industrial Organi-

---

Multicultural Connection: Although from the beginning, the AFL had a long history of discrimination and segregation, race was largely unimportant to the CIO leadership and members. The CIO created interracial unions in steel, automobile, rubber, and packinghouse plants and factories. The generally integrated United Mine Workers was particularly instrumental in the maintenance of equal unionization.

zations) was formed by Lewis. He was joined by other labor leaders who agreed that American labor needed a new approach—Sidney Hillman of the Amalgamated Clothing Workers, Charles Howard of the Typographical Union, and Thomas McMahon of the Textile Workers. This "CIO" quickly changed the direction of American labor organization. At first the founders said they only wanted to advise the AF of L on how to organize the giant industries. But the conservative leaders of the AF of L resisted these efforts. In 1937 when the CIO leaders and their members were expelled from the AF of L, the CIO declared its independence and became an important new force in American life.

The CIO quickly stepped up its efforts. In 1937 alone production was halted by 4740 strikes. That winter the workers themselves invented an ingenious new weapon that worked

for a short while. When they went on strike, instead of leaving the factory they simply stayed there and sat down at their machines. They refused to work or let others work. They had food brought in and slept on the factory floor. They said that since it was their work that made the factory valuable, the factory really partly belonged to them. But the Supreme Court disagreed, and in 1939 "sit-down strikes" were ✄ banned.

Of course, the strikers did not always simply sit down. And employers sometimes hired private police who were reckless of the rights and the lives of workers. Outside the Republic Steel plant in Chicago ten striking workers were killed. From these struggles came a new era for labor unions in the United States. During 1937, General Motors, Chrysler, U.S. Steel, and many smaller steel companies as well as

Employees at a General Motors Corporation plant in Flint, Michigan, sat down by their machines in 1937 in the nation's first sit-down strike. They were seeking recognition of their new CIO union, the United Automobile Workers, and their tactic prevented the company from running the plant with strikebreakers. They won their demands, but the sit-down strike was soon declared illegal.

United Press International Photo

✄ **Critical Thinking Activity: Expressing Problems Clearly** What limitations should be placed on labor's right to strike? Remind students that the Supreme Court ruled in 1939 against the use of "sit-down strikes" by labor unions. Ask students to discuss some possible reasons for this decision. Have students write a paragraph defining what limits should be placed on the right to strike. Allow students to share their work.

University of South Carolina at Aiken

During the 1930s the number of women working increased from 10.6 to 13 million. Many worked in factories and were able to join the CIO.

Firestone Rubber, General Electric, and some major textile firms signed CIO contracts. Unions would play a strong new role in American industrial life. As never before, workers would look to them to hear their grievances and protect their rights. The power of factory owners over their workers was much reduced. Through the NLRB, the federal government supported the unions.

Challenged by the success of the CIO, the AF of L swung into action to expand its membership. Between 1936 and 1938 membership in all unions increased from 4 million to 6 million. Soon big labor would face big business.

New union members. The membership of the old-line craft unions of the AF of L had been mostly Americans of the older immigration—English, Scots, Germans, Irish, and Scandinavians. Out of fear and from prejudice these unions commonly excluded the later comers from southern and eastern Europe in addition to blacks and women. The new CIO unions welcomed all these groups with their theme song, "Solidarity Forever."

Women found new openings in the factory because the CIO began to recruit workers without regard to sex. Within a few years nearly a million women joined the unions. But even in the unions women were not yet quite equal. For example, the liberal Amalgamated Clothing Workers still allowed women to be paid less than men for the same work.

The unions themselves showed dramatic changes. The International Ladies Garment Workers Union, whose members had been largely Jewish at the end of World War I, now in the mid-1930s was nearly half Italian. Before 1940 many of its members were Puerto Ricans. By opening their doors the unions had the power to open opportunity for new immigrants and the children of immigrants.

The labor movement continued to harbor large pockets of prejudice. Despite the example of the CIO, certain unions—especially in building trades—continued to exclude blacks, Puerto Ricans, Mexicans, and others whom they considered "different." Farm laborers, migratory workers, and domestic servants remained outside the ranks of organized labor.

Neither the unions nor the New Deal could bring an end to unemployment. Even after the mobilization for war in 1940 had provided thousands of new jobs, there were still 6 million out of work in 1941. Not until 1943 would the nation reach full employment.

See "Section 4 Review answers," p. 642E.

Section 4 Review

1. Identify: John L. Lewis, Samuel Gompers, William Green, CIO.

2. How did some employers try to break strikes?

3. What gains did American labor unions make in the years 1936–1938?

4. What groups formerly left out of unions made big gains through the efforts of the CIO?

5. **Critical Thinking: Making Comparisons.** How did an industrial union differ from a craft union?

📖 **More from Boorstin:** "The first market for typewriters was among authors, editors, and ministers, and it was assumed that the machine would be mainly a tool for the world of letters. Mark Twain boasted of his willingness to use this curious new machine, and The Adventures of Tom Sawyer is reputed to be the first typewritten manuscript to be set into a book. (By 1930, union printers were refusing to set books from any other kind of manuscript.)" (From *The Americans: The Democratic Experience*)

Chapter 25 Review

See "Chapter Review answers," p. 642F.

Focusing on Ideas

1. What economic problems were sharecroppers facing in the 1930s? Did the New Deal benefit these farmers?

2. What New Deal laws or other actions of the Roosevelt administration helped black Americans of the 1930s? Explain how these laws and actions improved black people's lives.

3. What tactics did labor use to improve its position in the 1930s? Which tactics were the most successful? Why?

4. How did Eleanor Roosevelt represent the "spirit" of the New Deal?

Taking a Critical Look

1. **Recognizing Bias.** How would you expect a leader for women's rights in 1940 to assess the decade of the 1930s—the progress and setbacks for women?

2. **Making Comparisons.** Who were the "forgotten Americans" of the 1930s? What groups, if any, would you call "forgotten Americans" today? What are the similarities and differences between the two groups?

Your Region in History

1. **Geography.** Using a state map, locate the areas of your state that benefited from the Rural Electrification Administration during the New Deal. How did electricity change the way people in your state lived?

2. **Culture.** The 1930s were rich with musical diversions for those suffering from the depression. Interview people in your community to learn the titles and lyrics of songs made popular during the period. Ask them whether the music of the period made it easier to bear the difficult conditions of the depression.

3. **Economics.** Some older women in your community probably obtained their first jobs in the 1930s. Find out from them—and from other sources—what kinds of jobs were available for women in the 1930s. Ask women who did find their first job during these years how employment outside the home changed their lives. Report your findings to the class.

Historical Facts and Figures

Synthesizing Information. Study the graph below to help answer the following questions: (a) How many American workers were members of labor unions in 1900? In 1920? In 1940? (b) By what percentage did the number of union members increase during the period 1900–1940? (c) If the 8,500,000 union members in 1940 represented 15.5% of all workers, what was the approximate size of the total labor force? (d) What information in the chapter helps explain why the number of union members increased so dramatically during this period?

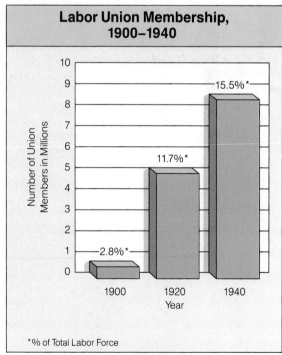

Labor Union Membership, 1900–1940

*% of Total Labor Force

Sources: *Historical Statistics of the United States*
Statistical Abstract of the United States

Chapter 26
Clouds of War

Identifying Chapter Materials

Objectives	Basic Instructional Materials	Extension Materials
1 Foreign Affairs, 1933–1939 • List the causes of World War II. • Explain the sentiment for neutrality on the part of the United States. • Define the problem of anti-Semitism in Germany, and tell how the Jews were used as scapegoats.	**Annotated Teacher's Edition** • Lesson Plans, pp. 656C–656D **Instructional Support File** • Pre-Reading Activities, Unit 9, p. 29 • Skill Review Activity, Unit 9, p. 32 • Skill Application Activity, Unit 9, p. 33 • Critical Thinking Activity, Unit 9, p. 34	**Documents of American History** • Neutrality Act of 1937, Vol. 2, p. 378 • The New Order in the Far East, Vol. 2, p. 411 • F.D. Roosevelt's Appeals for Peace in Europe, Vol. 2, p. 415 • The Neutrality Act of 1939, Vol. 2, p. 420
2 The Battlefield is Everywhere • Trace the spread of the war in Europe and cite FDR's efforts to aid the Allies. • Analyze FDR's "Four Freedoms" speech.	**Annotated Teacher's Edition** • Lesson Plans, p. 656D	**Documents of American History** • Exchange of Destroyers for Air and Naval Bases, Vol. 2, p. 444 • F.D. Roosevelt's "Four Freedoms" Speech, Vol. 2, p. 446 • The Lend Lease Act, Vol. 2, p. 449 • The Atlantic Charter, Vol. 2, p. 451
3 War Comes to the United States • Trace the circumstances that led to an alliance between the United States and the Soviet Union and describe the attack on Pearl Harbor. • Summarize the German military campaign to subdue the Soviet Union and tell why it failed.	**Annotated Teacher's Edition** • Lesson Plans, pp. 656D–656E **Instructional Support File** • Reading Activities, Unit 9, pp. 30–31 • Chapter Test, Unit 9, pp. 35–38 • Additional Test Questions, Unit 9, pp. 39–42	**Enrichment Support File** • Air Raid! Pearl Harbor and the U.S. Declaration of War (See "In-Depth Coverage" at right.) **Suggested Secondary Sources** • See chart at right.

Providing In-Depth Coverage

Perspectives on December 8, 1941

At 7:55 A.M. Honolulu time, December 7, 1941, waves of Japanese aircraft streaked low over the unsuspecting naval base at Pearl Harbor. As the enemy bombs struck in giant explosions, the nucleus of America's Pacific fleet was destroyed. The next day, President Roosevelt asked Congress for a declaration of war against Japan. The declaration was quickly passed by the House and Senate, with only one opposing vote. America was at war.

A History of the United States as an instructional program provides two types of resources you can use to offer in-depth coverage of December 8, 1941, the day the U.S. declared war: the *student text* and the *Enrichment Support File.* A list of *Suggested Secondary Sources* is also provided. The chart below shows the topics that are covered in each.

THE STUDENT TEXT. Boorstin and Kelley's *A History of the United States* unfolds the chronology of events, the key players, and, as an interpretive history, the controversy of the U.S. declaration of war on December 8, 1941.

AMERICAN HISTORY ENRICHMENT SUPPORT FILE. This collection of primary source readings and classroom activities reveals the details of that day in history and what Americans were doing when they heard that the U.S. had declared war.

SUGGESTED SECONDARY SOURCES. This reference list of readings by well-known historians and other commentators provides an array of perspectives on the U.S. declaration of war on December 8, 1941.

Locating Instructional Materials

Detailed lesson plans for teaching the declaration of war as a mini-course or to study one or more aspects of December 8, 1941 in depth are offered in the following areas: in the *student text,* see individual lesson plans at the beginning of each chapter; in the *Enrichment Support File,* see page 3; for readings beyond the student text, see *Suggested Secondary Sources.*

IN-DEPTH COVERAGE ON DECEMBER 8, 1941		
Student Text	**Enrichment Support File**	**Suggested Secondary Sources**
• U.S. Neutrality, pp. 659–661 • Japanese-American Relations, pp. 659, 663, 670–671 • U.S. War Preparations, p. 667 • "Magic," p. 671 • Pearl Harbor Attack, pp. 671–672	• Lesson Suggestions • Multimedia Resources • Overview Essay/Air Raid! Pearl Harbor and the United States Declaration of War • Primary Sources in American History/December 8, 1941 • Biography in American History/Clare Booth Luce • Great Debates in American History/Isolationism vs Interventionism • Simulation/An American Play: The Effect of Pearl Harbor • Making Connections	• *December 7, 1941: The Day the Japanese Attacked Pearl Harbor* by Gordon W. Prange, pp. 3–54. • *Pearl Harbor: The Verdict of History* by Gordon W. Prange, pp. 141–332. • *Infamy: Pearl Harbor and Its Aftermath* by John Toland, pp. 3–56. • *Pearl Harbor: Warning and Decision* by Roberta Wohlstetter, pp. 279–338.

Foreign Affairs, 1933–1939

FOCUS

To introduce the lesson, write the heading "Causes of War" on the board. Label four columns beneath it as follows: Name of War, Underlying Causes, Secondary Causes, Spark. Explain to students that it helps to analyze the causes of war by considering the three levels of causation on the chart.

Developing Vocabulary

The words listed in the chapter are essential terms for reading and understanding particular sections of the chapter. The page number after each term indicates the page of its first or most important appearance in the chapter. These terms are defined in the text Glossary (text pages 1000–1011).

dictatorship (page 657); **Master Race** (page 657); **concentration camps** (page 658); **quarantine** (page 660); **isolationism** (page 660); **appeasement** (page 662).

INSTRUCT

Explain

The seeds of war can often be found in economics and prejudice.

☑ Writing Process Activity

Recognizing Cause and Effect Ask students to imagine they are German citizens who have just learned about Adolph Hitler. Before writing a journal entry about his philosophy, political approach, and appeal, students should freewrite about their reactions to the new leader. In their topic sentence they should make clear whether they take him seriously. As they revise, students should check for clear organization and specific examples of his behavior. After proofreading, students can discuss how and why Hitler won support from the German people.

Section Review Answers

Section 1, page 663

1. a) leader of the Nazi party who became dictator in Germany in the 1930s. b) book in which Hitler laid out his ideas. c) the Nazi party, blamed the Treaty of Versailles and the Jews for Germany's problems and advocated militaristic policies to solve its problems. d) places where the Germans held, tortured, and exterminated millions of Jews, anti-Nazi Protestants, and Catholics. e) dictator of the Soviet Union. f) leader of the Fascist party and dictator of Italy. g) Fascist general who led his troops against the republican government in the Spanish Civil War. h) President of Mexico who in 1938 announced the expropriation of foreign oil properties in Mexico. i) American gunboat sunk in the Yangtze River in China by the Japanese. j) provided that the Philippines would be granted independence twelve years after the act was passed. k) series of laws passed in the 1930s to keep the United States neutral in the European conflict by preventing or regulating arms shipments from the United States to the warring nations. l) British prime minister who tried to maintain peace by negotiating the Munich Pact. m) policy of granting concessions to an aggressor in the hope that the aggressor will be satisfied and stop the aggression. 2. Ethiopia, the Rhineland, the Sudetenland, Albania, Estonia, Latvia, and Lithuania are all shown on the map on page 661. Montevideo is shown on the map on page 950. Manchuria is found on the map on page 684. The Yangtze River is on the map on page 517. 3. Widespread unemployment, runaway inflation, resentment of the Versailles Treaty and the reparations it required, factionalism, and weak democratic institutions. 4. The government removed American troops from Haiti, declared that no nation had the right to interfere in the affairs of another, negotiated a new treaty in which the United States gave up the right to intervene in Cuba, and negotiated a settlement of the claims of American oil companies in Mexico. 5. The Munich Pact was unsuccessful. Hitler made a mockery of it by annexing all of Czechoslovakia and then, six months after that, invading Poland. 6. Hitler and Stalin made a nonaggression pact, which freed Germany from the fear of war on two fronts. Secret terms of the agreement allowed Germany to take western Poland and Russia to take eastern Poland and the Baltic states. On September 1 Hitler invaded Poland, and England and France then declared war on Germany. 7. They believed that any involvement in European affairs would draw us into war and that the United States could fence itself off from the rest of the world. Specifically, they pushed laws in 1935 and 1936 that prevented the United States from sending arms to warring nations; they pushed another law in 1937 that permitted sales to warring countries (excluding munitions) but only if the country paid for the goods in advance and transported them on their own ships; and they pushed, unsuccessfully, for a constitutional amendment that would have required a popular vote before Congress could declare war.

CLOSE

To conclude the lesson, point out that the infamous Munich Pact is better understood in light of American neutrality and Hitler's promise that the Sudetenland was "the last territorial demand that I have to make in Europe." Britain and France, who had barely won World War I *with* American aid, were not about to start another war without it. The Munich Pact made Chamberlain "the hero of the hour" in Great Britian and America. He deserved, said the *New York Herald Tribune*, "heartfelt applause." Winston Churchill, however, warned that "Britain and France . . . chose dishonor. They will have a war." He was right. Hitler's seizure of the rest of Czechoslovakia less than six months later finally shattered all hopes that Nazi Germany could be contained without a war.

Section 2 (pages 664–670)

The Battlefield Is Everywhere

FOCUS

To introduce the lesson, ask students the following questions: What did the isolationists want the United States to do about involvement in the affairs of the rest of the world? (Keep out.) What are some examples of isolationist statements or actions in American history? (Washington's Farewell Address, Monroe Doctrine, rejection of the League of Nations, Neutrality Acts.) If you were Roosevelt in 1940, would you have pushed to help the Allies, even if it meant war, or would you have tried to stay neutral? Discuss student answers as a class.

Developing Vocabulary

blitzkrieg (page 664); **Lend-Lease** (page 669); **Atlantic Charter** (page 670).

INSTRUCT

Explain

The gravity of German and Italian aggression was heightened by new elements of warfare—air power, *blitzkrieg* tactics, and the use of submarines.

★ Independent Activity

Identifying Central Issues Tell students that against the realities of air power, submarine warfare, and *blitzkrieg* tactics, FDR had to prepare the nation for war. Ask students to find and write down five examples of speeches or actions which show that FDR was trying to move the United States away from isolationism in 1940 and 1941.

Section Review Answers

Section 2, page 670

1. a) elaborate defense that France constructed on its border with Germany. b) describes the six months

between Germany's invasion of Poland and the next attack. c) prime minister of Britain during World War II. d) competed unsuccessfully for the Republican nomination in 1940. e) ran against FDR in 1940. f) exchange devised by FDR in which the United States gave Britain 50 destroyers and Britain gave the United States the use of 8 naval bases. g) up-to-date version of Wilson's Fourteen Points. 2. *Blitzkrieg* means "lightning war," and the Nazi advance was just that. It was an attack that came, like lightning, from the sky, because it included airplanes. And it was an extremely rapid strike in which airplanes, tanks, and trucks rushed into the enemy's territory. 3. He felt that air power could be used against cities, industrial centers, and supply centers rather than troops to bring victory to whichever side had superiority in the air. 4. Roosevelt warned Congress and his radio audience that the nation needed to rearm, planned to turn out 50,000 planes a year until the Nazis were defeated, and asked for the funds to build a two-ocean navy. 5. "Ultra" told the British when and where German bombers were coming so they could intercept them. 6. Roosevelt's "Lend-Lease" proposal and "Destroyer for Bases" Deal provided war materials for the British without directly involving the United States in their war.

CLOSE

To conclude the lesson, discuss the following question with the class: What was President Roosevelt's policy on the war in Europe in 1940 and 1941? From the Four Freedoms Speech, students should be able to see that President Roosevelt was not an isolationist. Rather, he was pushing for all means of helping the democracies short of declaring war.

Section 3 (pages 670–672)

War Comes to the United States

FOCUS

To introduce the lesson, have students turn to the map on page 661 and locate the western boundaries of the Soviet Union after the division of Poland in 1939. Then use the map on page 671 to find Leningrad, Moscow, Stalingrad, and Berlin. Estimate the distances separating these cities. (Approximately 400 miles from Leningrad to Moscow, and 550 miles from Moscow to Stalingrad. From Berlin to Russian cities: Leningrad, 800; Moscow, 1,000; and Stalingrad, 1,300 miles.) Have the students use the map of North America on page 949 to find comparable distances in the United States. (For example, Berlin to Moscow is approximately the same distance as from Denver to San Francisco.)

Developing Vocabulary
militarism (page 671)

INSTRUCT

Explain
There are a number of myths about the attack on Pearl Harbor, including one that FDR knew about the impending bombing and allowed it to happen so the United States would declare war. However, there is no evidence to support this myth.

☑ Writing Process Activity
Determining Relevance Have students imagine they are Navy commanders stationed at Pearl Harbor. In preparation for writing a letter to their family about the events of December 7, 1941, ask them to outline the events, including their reactions, and to list the reasons why the United States should enter the war. Tell students to begin their letters with a topic sentence that captures the feelings they experienced on the day of the bombing. During revising, students should concentrate on choosing effective words and on checking for logical organization. After proofreading, students can read their letters to a partner.

Section Review Answers
Section 3, page 672

1. a) the name that the Japanese gave to the islands they conquered. b) led the Chinese fight against Japan. c) general who took control in Japan in October 1941. d) name used for information obtained by the United States after breaking Japanese codes. 2. All of these places are shown on the map on page 684. 3. The Japanese wished to seal off the Burma Road, seize all French, Dutch, and British colonies, and conquer China. 4. It is likely that the United States would have entered World War II even if Japan had not attacked. The extreme aggression of the Axis, our ties to Britain, our attempts to aid the Allies— at some point these causes would have escalated to give reason for war.

CLOSE
To conclude the lesson, ask students to make a time line of all the events in this chapter. Ask them to put a star next to the events that *cannot* be considered causes of World War II or of the United States entry into the war.

Chapter Review Answers
Focusing on Ideas
1. FDR: good neighbor, offering help when asked; TR: U. S. as police officer. 2. Inadequate pressure to halt invasion of Ethiopia, remilitarization of the Rhineland, outside aid in the Spanish civil war, Japanese aggression in China; U. S. absence from League of Nations and enactment of neutrality laws; Munich Pact, weak response to Hitler's treatment of Jews. 3. Should include acts to help British, to "punish" aggressor nations, to build up U. S. defenses; to occupy Greenland and Iceland; "Lend-Lease," "Destroyers for Bases" deal. 4. Hilter saw he could avoid a two-front war. Stalin got more Communist territory and a western buffer zone with Germany. Surprises: Hitler gained power partly by his anti-Communist views; the Rome-Berlin-Tokyo Axis was in fact an anti-Communist pact.

Taking a Critical Look
1. All basic freedoms; protection of private property; respect for property, women, human life; respect for minorities' cultural diversity. 2. The blitzkrieg suddenly made air power of primary importance and trench warfare futile. Radar made battle plans harder to keep secret. As in the past, new technology changes strategies.

Your Region in History
1–3. Answers will vary depending on your region. Consult your local library or historical society.

Historical Facts and Figures
(a) Britain (b) Germany (c) France (d) Germany (e) Britain is an island nation; France and Germany share a border as well as long-held disputes. (f) Germany was best prepared.

Focusing the Chapter: Have students identify the chapter logo. Discuss what unit theme the logo might symbolize. Then ask students to identify other illustrations or titles that relate to this theme.

Clouds of War

While Americans were trying the New Deal experiments in democracy, desperate and hungry people in Europe were handing over their lives and liberties to ruthless dictators. Some of the most civilized peoples of Europe had returned to an age of barbarism. In Italy, only ten years before FDR entered the White House, Benito Mussolini and his Fascists (as his party was called) marched on Rome. They seized the government, abolished democracy, destroyed the liberties of the Italian people—all on the promise of jobs and glory. In Germany, too, in the very month when FDR took his oath of office, Adolf Hitler, with his gang of Nazis, was made dictator.

Adolph Hitler knew how to use mass rallies and theatrical settings to excite the Germans and make them feel proud. One million people were present to cheer *der Führer* (the leader), as Hitler was often called, at the 1937 Harvest Day Festival. In this photograph, just left of center, he is shown shaking hands with some of his rapturous followers.

Hugo Jaeger, LIFE Magazine © Time Warner Inc.

See "Lesson Plan," p. 656C.

1. Foreign affairs, 1933–1939

When Franklin D. Roosevelt moved into the White House in March 1933, the world prospects were grim. The outlook for civilization was darker than at any earlier time in American history. Two decades before, when President Wilson was elected, European nations were battling for empire and for the world's treasure. Now the threats to peace came from national leaders who screamed their hatred of democracy and modern civilization. They declared war on the ideals of equality and representative government on which the United States was founded.

The rise of Hitler. During the next years, European diplomacy would be dominated by Adolf Hitler, the most destructive dictator of modern times. He was not really a German, because he was born in Austria. A high school dropout, he wanted to be an artist, but twice failed the admission examination for the art academy in Vienna. He lived on charity and by selling copies that he made of picture postcards. In World War I he joined the German army. He was gassed and wounded, and never reached a higher rank than corporal. After the war he began to organize his own political party, aiming to seize the government and lead Germany to world power. Driven by a passionate, senseless anti-Semitism, he was determined to exterminate the Jews—whom he blamed for Germany's defeat.

In 1923, after his Nazi thugs failed to take over in the southern German state of Bavaria, where they surrounded the leading officials in a beer hall, he was sent to prison. There he wrote his 800-page *Mein Kampf* (My Struggle), which became the bible of the Nazis, and then of all Germany. He declared that the Germans were the "Master Race," entitled to rule the world. Democracy, he said, was a fraud, and the only good government was a dictatorship. The dictator should rule not by truth but by the "Big Lie." Christianity, according to him, was also a fraud, invented by the Jews to make cowards of the Master Race. Hitler's plans for a "Third Reich" to last a thousand years were so simple-minded and so immoral that few people outside Germany took them seriously.

But inside Germany, thousands, and then millions were joining his National Socialist (Nazi) party. They resented the Versailles Peace Treaty after World War I and the reparations that had been imposed on the German people. Partly as a result of these heavy payments, the economy fell apart and inflation ran wild. A loaf of bread that cost ten marks one week would be priced at one thousand marks the next week, and then would quickly skyrocket to a billion marks. Money lost its value so fast that salaries and wages had to be paid every 24 hours. Life savings became worthless.

Hitler comes to power. The democratic government within Germany after the war was weak. The German parliament, split into a dozen political parties, was unable to organize the nation's economy. Millions were unemployed, and goods were scarce. The world depression that in the United States had led Americans to try their New Deal left the Germans leaderless, hungry, and hopeless. Who could help them? Whom should they blame?

At this moment Hitler, with his mad vision of world power, came on the scene. He gave them their scapegoat—the Jews—upon whom they could blame everything. But he was not so mad that he could not organize spectacular meetings with swastika flags flying for thousands to hear his hour-long orations of hate and glory. And he was a master of the radio. He appealed to the unemployed and the rabble made up of both the ambitious and the disappointed.

Reasonable leaders in other countries found his schemes so outrageous that they would not believe they were real. Yet respectable Germans sat by watching while his thugs beat up opponents, assassinated enemies, sent innocent millions to concentration camps, and filled the newspapers with their Big Lies. Hitler showed that people were more timid than was ever before imagined.

The Germans made Hitler their God. When they greeted each other, they no longer said "Grüss Gott" (God be with you!) but "Heil Hitler!" And anyone who used the old greeting was

More from Boorstin: "Hitler and the millions of German Nazis had enriched the rest of the world's community of scientists by driving out of Germany and German-occupied Europe those brilliant physicists who, according to the Nazis, were not 'racially pure.' These were to be the very same men and women who played a crucial role in conceiving and planning the atomic bomb." (From *The Americans: The Democratic Experience*)

The photograph above shows guards rounding up women and children to be sent to concentration camps where Adolf Hitler and his followers tortured and murdered millions.

suspected of treason. They set up their German Christian church to make Christianity serve the Master Race.

The main new institution they invented was the concentration camp. To these places of torture they sent millions of Jews and countless other anti-Nazi Protestants and Catholics. There they used gas chambers to kill children, women, and men whom they considered their enemies. They extracted the gold from the teeth of the corpses to buy armaments and used human ashes to fertilize their fields. And one of the most difficult tasks facing FDR and his supporters was to persuade Americans that this was not just a nightmare.

Communist Russia, at the same time, was in the grip of the wily and vicious Josef Stalin. There, too, people who spoke up were tortured and sent to labor camps in remote Siberia. In Japan the expansion-minded army leaders were shaping the nation's policies. And the Italians under Mussolini were planning to create a new Roman Empire.

The looming threat of war. Italy, Russia, and Japan had all been American allies in the First World War. President Wilson had called that a war "to make the world safe for democracy." (p. 659) Now these same countries had become threats both to democracy and to peace. Germany, risen from defeat, was building an enormous new army, making weapons at frightening speed, and menacing its neighbors. Any one of the new military powers had a better-equipped army than the old democracies had.

In 1935, pursuing its dreams of empire, Italy invaded Ethiopia and bombed innocent villages from the air. In 1936 Germany moved its army

See "Lesson Plan," p. 656C for **Writing Process Activity: Recognizing Cause and Effect** relating to German reactions to Hitler.

back into the Rhineland, which had been demilitarized after World War I. Seeking a base for their aggressions in western Europe, Hitler and Mussolini slipped arms and men into Spain to support the Fascist General Francisco Franco. Spain became the world's battlefield in a bloody civil war. Fascist forces from everywhere fought against the republican government, which was aided by Communist Russia and supporters from France, England, and the United States.

Except to the cheeriest optimists, it was plain that another world war was brewing. Should the United States sit by and see the forces of savagery dominate the world?

The Good Neighbor policy. Roosevelt came into office in 1933 pledging that the United States would be "the good neighbor" in world affairs. We would be "the neighbor who resolutely respects himself and, because he does so, respects the rights of others." He meant his statement to apply to all the world, but the "Good Neighbor policy" became a label for his Latin American policy.

Roosevelt intended to continue the policies of Herbert Hoover toward our southern neighbors. We would not try to run their governments. To prove his point, FDR withdrew our marines from Haiti. But when Cuba was torn by another revolution, our pressure brought the conservatives to power. Some Latin Americans wondered then whether the United States had really changed. FDR tried to reassure them. At a Pan-American conference at Montevideo, Uruguay, in 1933, Secretary of State Cordell Hull joined in a declaration that "no state has the right to intervene in the internal or external affairs of another."

The United States gave solid evidence of the new policy. Back in 1901 our Congress had forced the Cubans to add the Platt Amendment (p. 517) to their constitution as a condition for the withdrawal of American troops from the island. Cuba promised to provide the United States with naval and coaling stations. They also gave the United States the right to intervene to preserve order and maintain Cuban independence. It amounted to a Cuban declaration of dependence on the United States. Now, in May 1934, by a new treaty the United States gave up its right to intervene. At last Cuba would be treated like a sovereign nation.

The real test of the Good Neighbor policy came in Mexico. In 1938 President Lázaro Cárdenas suddenly announced that the Mexican government was taking over all foreign oil properties. The holdings of the seventeen British and American companies were valued at nearly half a billion dollars. The British broke off diplomatic relations with Mexico. Some Americans urged us to send in our troops, but Secretary Hull was patient. He preferred to negotiate and reached a settlement in 1941. Mexico agreed to pay the oil companies for their properties and also settled other claims of United States citizens. The Roosevelt administration began to persuade our Latin American neighbors that the United States was ready to treat them as equals.

Japanese-American relations. On the other side of the world, a military clique in control of Japan reached across the narrow Sea of Japan to conquer an empire. When the Japanese seized Manchuria in 1931, the League of Nations condemned Japan as an aggressor. The Japanese withdrew from the League and in 1937 attacked weak China. The democracies of western Europe uttered bold, brave words against the Japanese, but they were afraid to act. They preferred to let Japan enslave Asian millions rather than risk war themselves.

On December 12, 1937, the United States gunboat *Panay* on the Yangtze River in China was sunk by Japanese bombs. Two American sailors died. The United States protested. A prompt apology from Japan, with an indemnity of $2 million, closed the incident, but left Americans worried.

FDR and neutrality. President Roosevelt warned that if aggression continued in Asia, Africa, and Europe, the whole world would be engulfed in war. The United States could not remain a mere spectator. If the democracies of

Continuity and Change: Ethics and Values Point out to students that despite efforts to remain neutral, the United States was drawn into World Wars I and II. The difficulty of maintaining neutrality during World War II was swiftly and easily disposed of with the attack on Pearl Harbor. In World War I, the struggle to remain neutral was more difficult; there was no turning point to make the decision easier. Finally, German aggression against civilians in addition to American cultural ties to England led to America joining the Allies. (See p. 555.)

WAKE UP! WAKE UP, UNCLE!

Daniel Bishop, *St. Louis Star-Times*

As world war approaches, Uncle Sam sleeps and is tied down by opponents of involvement.

asked, if the United States had remained at peace? The seeds of the world's problems, they said, were planted in World War I. Perhaps a neutral United States might have prevented the follies of the Treaty of Versailles. Some sensational hearings presided over by Senator Gerald P. Nye of North Dakota seemed to show that arms manufacturers and bankers had led us into the war for their own profit.

The obvious answer seemed to be to pass a law. If Congress had the power to declare war—why could not Congress simply declare peace? Why could not strong, clear "Neutrality Acts" keep us neutral? Some thought that the United States occupation of the Philippines might involve us with Japan in the Pacific. In 1934 the Tydings-McDuffie Act provided for the independence of the Philippines in twelve years. Early the next year, Roosevelt recommended to the Senate that we join the World Court, which had been set up by the League of Nations. But isolationists feared that even the "advisory opinions" given by the Court might draw us onto the battlefields of Europe.

As war clouds gathered, Americans' fond hopes for neutrality grew ever stronger—and more futile. Acts were passed in 1935 and again in 1936 to prevent Americans from sending arms to the nations at war. Americans were warned that they traveled at their own risk on the ships of nations at war. When the Spanish civil war broke out in 1936, the neutrality laws were extended to bar shipments of arms to either side. But this hurt only the Spanish republicans. Franco was already receiving all the arms he needed from Hitler and Mussolini.

The isolationists came up with still another "neutrality" law in 1937. This permitted sales to belligerents, but only "cash-and-carry." A country at war had to pay cash for its goods before the goods left our shores. And the country at war had to carry the goods in its own ships. The law embargoed munitions and also allowed the President to extend the embargo to other exports. The isolationists believed that at last ✕ they had passed a law that would keep the United States out of war.

Still, some isolationists sought an amendment to the Constitution that would prevent

Europe were conquered by the Nazis and their allies, the United States would be next on their list. He called for a "quarantine" of the aggressor nations. But for the moment he could do little more to help the free nations of Europe. Americans had not forgotten the senseless slaughter in the First World War. More and more Americans said, "Never Again!" Some were becoming pacifists, saying they would never go to war for any reason. Still others became "isolationists," hoping to fence off the New World. Naturally enough, Americans who had come from Italy or Germany did not like the idea of fighting against their old homeland. Americans of Irish descent remembered the English tyranny over their island. A few people even became American Nazis.

Some historians argued that if the United States had really been neutral during World War I, our nation would not have had to go to war at all. Might the world have been better, they

German and Italian Aggression, 1935-1939

- Germany and German Possessions
- Italy and Italian Possessions
- Areas of German Expansion
- Areas of Italian Expansion

Boundaries as of 1935

Congress from declaring war without first submitting the question to a popular vote. A poll of the American people in 1937 showed that 75 percent favored such an amendment. President Roosevelt was strongly opposed. He warned that "it would encourage other nations to believe that they could violate American rights with impunity." And the House refused to submit the amendment to the states.

Neither President Roosevelt nor a dozen acts of Congress could block the world's drift toward war. In January 1938, FDR suggested a world conference to reduce armaments and promote national economic security, but the British Prime Minister Neville Chamberlain said no.

Hitler on the march. One of Hitler's goals was 🌐 to bring into the "Third Reich" all the millions of people of "German blood" in Austria, Czechoslovakia, and Poland. Of course, there was no

🌐 **Geography and History: Location** Have the students look at the map above and locate Ethiopia, the Rhineland, and Spain. Ask: What part did each of these areas play in the steps leading to World War II? (Italy's easy triumph over Ethiopia led Mussolini to be overly confident in joining Hitler's aggression later; the seizure of the Rhineland by the Nazis was a test of French will to resist, leading the Nazis to believe that the French did not want to fight; and Spain's civil war provided a testing ground for equipment and tactics that Hitler would use successfully later against the Allies.)

A German motorized detachment rides through a Polish town already destroyed by bombs.

such thing as "German blood," but some German professors supported him, and the millions of German people went along.

In March 1938 Germany invaded and annexed Austria. Hitler's next target was the strategic Sudetenland on the Czech border with Germany. It contained 3 million people of German ancestry. The Czechs mobilized, expecting aid from Great Britain, France, and Russia. But those countries would not risk war to save the Czechoslovak republic.

Prime Minister Chamberlain of Britain and Premier Daladier of France met Hitler and Mussolini at Munich, Germany, on September 28, 1938. There, in an attempt to appease Hitler, they agreed to dismember Czechoslovakia—the one democracy in Europe that survived east of the Rhine—and give a piece to Germany. As Hitler occupied the Sudetenland, Chamberlain reported to Parliament that the Munich Pact guaranteed "peace in our time."

We know today that if Britain and France had resisted at this moment, German generals were planning to remove Hitler. But Hitler was riding high. He and his German people began to think he was unbeatable. Could anything prevent a world war?

"There can be no peace," Roosevelt warned, "if national policy adopts as a deliberate instrument the threat of war." In November 1938 when Hitler increased his brutal persecution of the Jews, Americans were more horrified than ever. Now FDR demanded that the arms embargo be removed from the neutrality law so the United States could help the victims of aggression. Still, most Americans were optimists. And many others were isolationists hoping that we could remain an island of peace and prosperity in a world of war and misery.

On March 15, 1939, Hitler seized the rest of Czechoslovakia. The policy of appeasement was now exposed as a failure. Great Britain pledged aid to Poland in case its independence was threatened. When Mussolini invaded little Albania on April 7, Britain gave a similar guarantee to neighboring Greece and Romania.

In a desperate effort to keep all Europe from catching fire, President Roosevelt asked Mussolini and Hitler to promise to refrain for ten years from attacking a list of 31 nations. In return these nations would promise not to attack Italy or Germany. But Hitler replied with sarcasm. In his shrieking, abusive speech before the German Reichstag (legislature) he ridiculed FDR. He knew that the democracies were not prepared for war. He was determined to have his own way and dominate the world before the democracies dared stand against him.

President Roosevelt asked Congress to repeal or modify the arms embargo because it was helping the aggressor nations, who were well supplied with arms from their own factories. By a vote of 12–11, the isolationists in the Senate

Foreign Relations Committee put off any changes in the law until the next session of Congress, which was to meet in January 1940.

Continuing problems with Japan. Meanwhile, on July 26, 1939, the State Department moved against the Japanese war machine. Japan was told that in six months we would end the Japanese-American Commercial Treaty of 1911. This freed Congress to stop the sale of war materials to Japan. The Japanese had been invading China with arms bought in the United States. And the Japanese were disturbed by news that their new ally Nazi Germany had made a sudden alliance with Japan's old enemy Russia. For a time Japanese expansion in Asia was slowed.

War comes to Europe. In Europe the attempts to appease Hitler seemed only to whet his appetite for more conquests. He had risen to power by telling the German people that Communist Russia was their prime enemy. Now he shocked the whole world when he announced a nonaggression pact with Stalin in 1939. The secret terms gave Germany western Poland, while the Soviet Union was free to take Finland, Estonia, Latvia, eastern Poland, Bessarabia (in Romania), and Lithuania. The Nazis believed that in this way they would protect themselves against war on two fronts. In return Russia would gain a buffer zone against Germany— and a temporary assurance against attack.

Throughout the summer of 1939 Hitler demanded that Poland return to Germany certain districts containing people of "German blood." Poland, bolstered by Britain and France, stood its ground. Then on September 1, without warning, Hitler invaded Poland. Two days later England and France declared war on Germany. Then Stalin's armies marched into Poland from the east on September 17. Within two weeks, on September 29, brave, long-suffering Poland was divided between the two tyrants.

The United States reacts. Unlike President Wilson 25 years before, Roosevelt did not ask the American people to be neutral in thought as well as deed. He invoked the Neutrality Act of 1937 when war broke out. But in a fireside chat, he reminded the American people, "Even a neutral cannot be asked to close his mind or his conscience."

President Roosevelt called Congress into special session on September 21, 1939. He asked them to change the "cash and carry" Neutrality Act of 1937 and repeal the embargo on selling or shipping arms to the belligerents. He believed it was urgent for the United States to find ways at once to help the Allies against Hitler. If the United States waited, the barbaric forces might win, and then it would be too late. Many voices were raised against his attempt to break out of our isolation. Among them were Senator William E. Borah of Idaho and the nation's hero, Colonel Charles Lindbergh. "Preparedness" Republicans like Henry Stimson and Frank Knox supported the President. After a bitter debate Congress voted the Neutrality Act of 1939. It helped the forces of democracy by repealing the arms embargo.

See "Section 1 Review answers," p. 656C.

Section 1 Review

1. Identify or explain: Adolf Hitler, *Mein Kampf*, National Socialist party, concentration camps, Josef Stalin, Benito Mussolini, Francisco Franco, Lázaro Cárdenas, *Panay*, Tydings-McDuffie Act, neutrality laws, Neville Chamberlain, appeasement.

2. Locate: Ethiopia, Rhineland, Montevideo, Manchuria, Yangtze River, Sudetenland, Albania, Estonia, Latvia, Lithuania.

3. What conditions in Germany led the people to accept a dictator?

4. Cite instances where the government followed Roosevelt's Good Neighbor policy.

5. What was the outcome of the Munich Pact?

6. What events in the summer of 1939 led to the outbreak of World War II?

7. **Critical Thinking: Recognizing Cause and Effect.** What factors contributed to the isolationism of many Americans? How did these Americans try to isolate the United States?

United Press International Photo

Hoping to start life anew, a family returns to its farm near Bromberg, Poland, in November 1939 after Nazi bombings have left it in ruins.

See "Lesson Plan," p. 656D.

2. The battlefield is everywhere

For six months, while Germany was moving its armies back from Poland, there was no fighting in western Europe. The British were busy moving their forces to France. The French sat smugly behind their Maginot line along the border of Germany. They thought that no enemy could pierce this 350-mile line of tunnels, concrete forts, and antitank fields. The headlines spoke of a "phony war." In November the giant Soviet Union attacked its tiny neighbor, Finland. The bravery of the Finns against hopeless odds stirred the admiration of the free world. But part of Finland came under the Communist heel. Then, in April 1940, Hitler launched a stunning new kind of war.

The new warfare. Blitzkrieg (lightning war) was Adolf Hitler's surprising strategy. This depended on air power. And it was nothing like the battles that generals had read about in their textbooks. The idea was to strike with lightning speed. Using the fastest new vehicles (airplanes, tanks, trucks, and even motorcycles), the Nazis would thrust rapidly into the very heart of enemy territory. Their sluggish enemies would be overwhelmed.

Blitzkrieg also meant war that struck like lightning—from the sky. Air power made it possible. Leaping over "standing" armies, over water barriers and coastal fortifications, the Nazi air force would strike at the heart of the defenseless nations.

On April 9, 1940, Hitler ended the "phony

war" and shocked the world by invading Denmark and Norway. One month later he rushed into the Netherlands, Belgium, and Luxembourg. From there he quickly bypassed the "impregnable" Maginot line and lunged deep into France. On June 14 his Nazis marched into Paris. Thousands of weeping men and women lined the streets, helpless against this lightning invasion. France surrendered by the end of June. Meanwhile in England pugnacious Winston Churchill had replaced the ineffective Neville Chamberlain as Prime Minister.

The battlefront was now everywhere. The airplane had transformed warfare. What the submarine had done to the freedom of the seas, the airplane was doing to almost all the other rules of warfare.

Billy Mitchell advertises air power. Just as Admiral Mahan had alerted Americans to the influence of sea power on history, so during World War I the bold and outspoken Billy Mitchell had begun to advertise air power.

Air power was then so new that few took it seriously. In the Civil War and the Spanish-American War, light observation balloons had been used. But "military ballooning," as it was called, was still thought of mostly as a sport or a hobby. In 1913 when Mitchell was a young officer in the Signal Corps, he began to be intrigued by the airplane's military uses. Then, during World War I, as General Pershing's Chief of Air Services, he was impressed by what warplanes could do.

At the end of the war, American generals and admirals still considered the airplane as merely another weapon. Like a new machine gun, it was to be used by either the army or the navy in their own regular operations.

Billy Mitchell had other ideas. He was

The German "Stuka" dive bombers, shown here flying in formation in 1941, served the Nazi "blitzkrieg." Swooping out of the sky, they devastated all below.

Wide World Photos

Continuity and Change: Ethics and Values Point out to students that like subs in WWI, airplanes in WWII added literally another dimension to the horrors of war. In WWII airplanes were used to make sudden attacks on civilian populations from the air as submarines in WWI were used to hit civilian merchant vessels in the sea. Both machines brought the consequences of war directly to the people at home, adding a new degree of terror to twentieth-century warfare. (See p. 551.)

convinced that airplanes really ought to be put into an entirely new military unit, under a command all their own. So long as Americans thought of airplanes only as helpers for the army and navy, he argued, we were sure to be left behind. We would lose the next war to nations who saw that air power was something new and world-shaking.

Air power, Mitchell said, had shifted the main targets. No longer were they the enemy *armies*. Now the targets would be the "vital centers"— the centers of industry, the centers of supply, and the centers of the enemy's will to resist. "Armies themselves can be disregarded by air power," he explained, "if a rapid strike is made against the opposing centers."

Americans could not bear the thought of a new warfare that was so horrible. They hated to believe that whole cities might have to be destroyed.

Mitchell was an expert at getting publicity. He made speeches and wrote magazine articles and books to alert all citizens to the importance of air power. Many of his fellow officers disliked

The charm of Billy Mitchell, champion of U. S. air power, shows in this early picture.

Wide World Photos

him for it. Some called him "General of the 'Hot Air' Force."

Mitchell gives a demonstration. But Mitchell was not to be put off. Battleships were supposed to be "unsinkable." To prove that airplanes were effective against battleships, he planned a spectacular show. He arranged to have the German battleship *Ostfriesland*, which had been surrendered at the end of World War I, hauled to a position 60 miles off the Virginia coast. It was a ghost ship, with not a soul on board.

Just before noon on July 21, 1921, a flight of Mitchell's army bombers left Langley Field 85 miles away. As they arrived over the battleship, they dropped six 2000-pound bombs. Within twenty minutes the "unsinkable" battleship was at the bottom of the ocean. It was the first time a battleship had ever been sunk by planes.

When admirals and generals still refused to grasp the full meaning of air power, Mitchell tried other tactics. He publicly denounced the conduct of our defense by the War and Navy departments as incompetent, criminally negligent, and "almost treasonable." This was the sure road to court martial—and that seemed to be his purpose. On December 17, 1925, a panel of generals found General Billy Mitchell guilty of "conduct, which brought discredit upon the military service." They sentenced him to a five-year suspension from active duty.

Building air power. Mitchell's campaign had already forced President Calvin Coolidge to take some action. The committee he appointed did not support all Mitchell's demands, but they did urge the buildup of an American air force.

Then, on May 21, 1927, Charles Lindbergh made his famous nonstop flight from New York to Paris. As the military meaning of Lindbergh's feat sank in, Americans began to realize that some of Billy Mitchell's "wild" ideas were not so wild. Now it seemed quite possible that some day the United States might be attacked by airplanes that came nonstop across the ocean. The nation began to take Mitchell, and air power, seriously.

In 1935 the new American long-range B-17

bomber (soon called the "Flying Fortress" and equipped with the super-accurate Norden bombsight) first went into the air. Now it was hard to doubt that air power would change the meaning of war. Air war against "vital centers" would be as different as possible from the old trench warfare. The United States Navy also had its champion of air power. He was as different from Billy Mitchell as night from day. Admiral William A. Moffett, a pilot and aviation enthusiast, was quiet and diplomatic, just as Mitchell was noisy and brash. Each in his own way served the cause of air power.

Moffett became head of the navy's newly created Bureau of Aeronautics in 1921. He worked steadily for the development of aircraft carriers and for catapult-launched airplanes on battleships and cruisers. His farsighted work would help to make possible the United States victory over Japan in World War II.

♛ *The United States prepares for war.* President Roosevelt had long recognized the Nazi menace. Even before the Germans had overrun France, he had sent a special message to Congress warning the nation to rearm. He announced a bold plan to turn out 50,000 planes in the next year, 1941, and every year until the Nazis were beaten. And he asked for billions of dollars to create a two-ocean navy. In one of his most effective fireside chats over the radio, he alerted the nation:

> The Nazi masters have made it clear that they intend not only to dominate all life and thought in their own country, but also to enslave the rest of the world. . . . We cannot escape danger, or the fear of danger, by crawling into a bed and pulling the covers over our heads. . . . No nation can appease the Nazis. No man can tame a tiger into a kitten by stroking it. . . . Let not the defeatists tell us that it is too late. It will never be earlier.

Still there were those who believed they could ward off the Nazi menace by the old-fashioned magic word "Neutrality!"

The isolationists hoped the Neutrality Act of 1939 would keep us out of war. But Roosevelt saw during 1940 that if Great Britain was not to fall, it would have to receive more help from the United States. Could he convince the country in time?

The Battle of Britain. Great Britain now stood alone against Hitler and Mussolini. "The battle of France is over," the eloquent Prime Minister Winston Churchill told the House of Commons. "I expect that the Battle of Britain is about to begin." He warned that on its outcome depended the future of the world. "Let us therefore brace ourselves to our duties, and so bear ourselves that, if the British Empire and its Commonwealth last for a thousand years, men will say 'This was their finest hour.'"

Hitler sent hundreds of bombers to rain devastation and death upon London and other British cities during the summer and fall of 1940. He was determined to force the British to surrender before a rearmed America could come to their aid.

A key factor in the Battle of Britain—and in the entire war against Germany—was that the British had figured out how to read Germany's most secret coded messages. These intercepted messages were referred to by the British as "Ultra," from Ultra Secret. Through Ultra and helped by "radar"—a word made up of *ra*(dio) *d*(etecting) *a*(nd) *r*(anging)—the British often knew when the German bombers were coming and where they were headed. In this way they were able to move the small fleet of Royal Air Force (RAF) fighter planes from place to place to intercept the incoming bombers.

But even Ultra was not enough to save Great Britain from terrible losses. About 3:00 P.M. on November 14, 1940, the Ultra signals revealed that the city of Coventry was to be attacked that evening. It was too late to evacuate the city, but its officials were alerted and enabled to prepare for the attack. The warning from Ultra also gave time for the RAF to station fighter planes over the city. But many German bombers got through. Hundreds of people died as thousands of houses and Coventry's grand old cathedral were destroyed in the raid.

With the help of Ultra the British defense against German bombers was increasingly

♛ **Multicultural Connection:** The Selective Service Act passed in September 1940 in preparation for the war contained an amendment introduced by Representative Hamilton Fish of New York. This Act provided that in the selection and training of men under the Act, there would be no discrimination because of race or color. This was the first legislation to make this stipulation.

United Press International Photo

The cheerful fortitude of the English during the Battle of Britain became legendary. Here Londoners sleep between the rails or on the platform of a subway station to escape German bombs.

successful. That fall Hitler decided that he had to postpone "Sea Lion," his plan to invade England across the channel. But throughout the winter the Germans continued the bombing of British cities.

World affairs and the presidential campaign of 1940. As the Battle of Britain raged, the United States held an election campaign. The Republican convention at Philadelphia in June surprised nearly everybody. Thomas E. Dewey, the racket-busting young district attorney of New York, had been the leading candidate. But an eleventh-hour drive brought to the front a man who was no politician and had never run for office.

Wendell L. Willkie was the bright, dynamic president of Commonwealth and Southern, a large public utilities corporation. Born in Indiana, where he attended the state university, he practiced law in Ohio before becoming a man of wealth and a powerful corporation lawyer in New York City. He had a warm, boyish appeal, and his trademark was a floppy lock of hair which marked his informal approach to life. He was persuasive in a very different way from FDR. Instead of FDR's cultivated Harvard accent, he spoke with the voice of the Middle West and for the values of self-made America. He so much disliked the New Deal emphasis on government aid that, though he had been a Democrat all his life, he finally became an outspoken Republican in 1940. He had made a name for himself fighting against the TVA, which he said unfairly competed with his company. Willkie was nominated on the sixth ballot. The conven-

📖 **More from Boorstin:** "By the time that World War II broke out in Europe, the federal government had been given the statutory duty to supervise and scrutinize all forms of American aid to countries at war. . . . As late as the Lend-Lease Act of March 11, 1941, Americans were trying to preserve the traditional distinction between the voluntary gifts of citizens for charitable or ideological motives and the acts of government which were matters of international finance and foreign policy." (From *The Americans: The Democratic Experience*)

tion chose Senator McNary of Oregon, known as a friend of farmers, to run for Vice-President.

In mid-July 1940 in Chicago, the Democrats did not surprise many when they chose FDR. But no one in American history had ever run for a third term as President. Secretary of Agriculture Henry A. Wallace of Iowa was picked as his running mate.

Although Willkie opposed FDR's New Deal policies, he shared the President's determination to aid Great Britain and to arm the United States against the aggressor. Foreign policy was not as much an issue in the election as the isolationists had hoped. Willkie also favored conscription, which Roosevelt had asked for in June. His support helped the measure to pass in September. This draft law provided for the registration of men between the ages of 21 and 35. No more than 900,000 were to be called into the service at any one time during peace, and the act was to expire on May 15, 1945.

The destroyer deal.

Roosevelt tried every legal device to help the Allies secure supplies. To get around the law, he approved selling American military equipment to private companies that were buying for the British. But offering the goods on American shores was not enough. Italian and German submarines were sending these supplies to the bottom of the sea before they reached Britain. Winston Churchill asked for American destroyers to convoy these essential supplies, to hunt down and ward off the enemy submarines. "I must tell you," the British prime minister cabled to FDR in July 1940, "that in the long history of the world this is a thing to do now."

If he did as Churchill asked, Roosevelt feared that the isolationists would accuse him of bringing the United States into the war without the approval of Congress. Candidate Willkie assured him that he would not make the transfer of destroyers an issue in the campaign. Still, to protect himself against isolationist attacks, the President shrewdly devised a "Destroyers for Bases" deal. In September the President, as Commander in Chief of the Navy, transferred 50 old, but still useful destroyers to Great Britain. In exchange, we received the use of eight British naval bases all along the Atlantic coast from Newfoundland to British Guiana (Guyana). Great Britain promised that, if conquered, it would not surrender its fleet to Hitler.

The end of the campaign.

As the election campaign wore on, Willkie, desperate for a winning issue, accused FDR of leading the nation into war. When Willkie became reckless in his attacks, Roosevelt became reckless in his responses. "I have said this before," he told American parents, "but I shall say it again and again and again: Your boys are not going to be sent into any foreign wars."

FDR won handily—though not as easily as in 1936. Willkie polled 45 percent of the popular vote, but he carried only ten states with 82 electoral votes to Roosevelt's 449. The precedent-breaking FDR had broken another precedent. He was the first person to be elected President for a third term.

Helping the British.

Soon after the election, Roosevelt was faced with a dilemma. The British had run out of cash and were running out of ships. If the neutrality law was not quickly changed, the United States might not be able to get help to the British before they were defeated by the Nazis.

FDR showed his usual genius for compromise and for persuasion. He offered a clever plan called "Lend-Lease." We would "lend" or "lease" to the British—or any other country whose defense the President considered vital to the defense of the United States—whatever war supplies we could make. In that way the British would not need cash, and the hesitating members of Congress might be persuaded that we were getting value in return. (p. 668)

At the same time, in January 1941, in his annual message to Congress, President Roosevelt proclaimed the Four Freedoms. After the war he hoped for "a world founded upon four essential human freedoms"—freedom of speech, freedom of religion, freedom from want, and freedom from fear. Later that year, after a secret meeting with Churchill on a warship off the coast of Newfoundland, the two men issued

✂ **Critical Thinking Activity: Determining Relevance** How does the idea of "four freedoms" fit into our world today? Review with students the Four Freedoms that became the basis of the Atlantic Charter in 1941 and their application at that point in history. Ask students to write an essay describing the "four freedoms" that they feel are most necessary in today's world. Have students share their writing with the class.

the Atlantic Charter. This was an up-to-date version of Woodrow Wilson's Fourteen Points (p. 555).

See "Section 2 Review answers," p. 656D.

Section 2 Review

1. Identify or explain: Maginot line, "phony war," Winston Churchill, Thomas E. Dewey, Wendell Willkie, "Destroyers for Bases" deal, Atlantic Charter.
2. Why was the Nazi advance called a blitzkrieg?
3. Discuss Billy Mitchell's ideas on air power.
4. What steps did FDR take to rearm the nation?
5. How did "Ultra" help defeat Hitler?
6. **Critical Thinking: Demonstrating Reasoned Judgment.** How was Roosevelt able to supply the Allies while remaining an isolationist?

See "Lesson Plan," p. 656D.

3. War comes to the United States

Step by step the United States moved closer to war. Of course Americans did not want to send our troops into battle. But how could that be avoided? The aggressor nations were everywhere triumphant. Could we let them succeed?

The war spreads. President Roosevelt extended the zone "necessary to the defense of the United States" far out into the North Atlantic. Our troops occupied the island of Greenland in April 1941 and Iceland in July. On May 7 Congress authorized our government to seize 92 ships in our ports. These ships belonged to Germany and Italy and to countries like France, Holland, and Norway, which Hitler had conquered. German and Italian property in the country was "frozen" on June 14.

Eight days later Hitler made his great blunder. In his crazy belief that all battlefields were alike, and that blitzkrieg could conquer all, on June 22, 1941, only a year after conquering France, he suddenly invaded Russia. If he had studied history, he might have learned that more than a hundred years before, Napoleon had lost his empire in the same desperate gamble. Vast, frigid Russia embraced and paralyzed

(p. 671)

invaders. At first it seemed that Hitler might conquer Russia as quickly as France. But when the Germans were deep into Russia—only fifteen miles from Moscow—the Russian winter arrived. The fingers of Nazi soldiers became numb. Frozen oil crippled the motors of tanks. The Nazis had to stop to await the return of warm weather.

Meanwhile the German navy stepped up its submarine warfare in the Atlantic. The United States was already convoying American merchant ships. On September 1, 1940, we began to convoy British ships, too. Then on September 4, 1941, the United States destroyer *Greer* was attacked by a submarine. The President issued new orders for our ships to shoot German subs on sight. He did not tell the American people that the *Greer* had been following the Nazi sub and reporting its position to the British. FDR now ordered our merchant ships to be armed. He let them sail to the ports of the countries at war.

On October 17 the destroyer *Kearny* was hit and badly damaged with the loss of eleven lives. Then on October 31 the destroyer *Reuben James* was sunk by a German submarine with the loss of half its crew. In the Atlantic Ocean the United States had entered an undeclared war.

Trouble in the Pacific. Still, it was not Germany but Japan that plunged the United States into World War II. In 1940 Japan had become a partner of Nazi Germany and Fascist Italy. Japanese aggression was building what they called the Greater East Asia Co-Prosperity Sphere. This was a fancy name for Japanese domination of the Far East. German victories in Europe had encouraged the Japanese to try to seize all the poorly protected French and Dutch lands in Asia. Perhaps they could also take the British colonies. And China, too, was on their list.

To prepare for all this, the Japanese planned to seal off the Burma Road—the Allied supply route for China. Then China could not receive aid when the Japanese attacked. The Japanese managed to occupy bases in the north of French Indochina. And in July 1941 they took the

Multicultural Connection: In 1940, African-American surgeon Charles Drew was in Great Britain to direct that country's blood plasma project and served briefly as director of collection of blood plasma for the American military. His blood blank system became the model for blood banks operated by the Red Cross in World War II and was responsible for saving many wounded soldiers' lives. Drew was recognized internationally as one of the world's great hematologists.

Europe at the Peak of the Axis Power 1942

Axis Nations

Farthest German Advance, December 1941

Axis-Controlled Territory, November 1942

Vichy-Controlled Territory

Maginot Line

Boundaries of 1937

bases in the south. The United States responded with an embargo on all trade with Japan.

In the discussions that followed between Japan and the United States, the one sticking point was China. The Japanese demanded that the United States cut off aid to the Chinese Generalissimo Chiang Kai-shek. Secretary Hull not only refused to abandon the Chinese but demanded that the Japanese withdraw from China at once. Faced with the choice of giving up their dreams of empire or go to war, the Japanese militarists chose war. In mid-October a more warlike government under General Hideki Tojo came to power in Japan.

The United States had broken Japan's diplomatic and naval codes. We called the intelligence we received this way "Magic." Having read their dispatches, we knew that the Japanese would attack, but not where. It appeared that they were aiming at Thailand, the Malay peninsula, and the Dutch East Indies (Indonesia)—perhaps even the Philippines. United States forces there were alerted to expect attack. But the navy did not know that on November 26 a Japanese aircraft carrier force had left Japan headed for Pearl Harbor in Hawaii.

The attack on Pearl Harbor. Just before 8 o'clock on Sunday morning, December 7, 1941,

🌐 Geography and History: Location Have students use the map above to find Leningrad, Moscow, Stalingrad, and Berlin. Estimate the distances separating these cities. (Approximately 400 miles from Leningrad to Moscow, and 550 miles from Moscow to Stalingrad. From Berlin to the Russian cities: Leningrad, 800; Moscow, 1000; and Stalingrad, 1300 miles.) The Maginot Line separated what two large countries? (France and Germany.) What country borders France, Vichy France, Germany, Austria, and Italy? (Switzerland.)

On December 7, 1941, the majority of the United States Navy's Pacific fleet was caught unaware by the Japanese attack on Pearl Harbor. This photograph was taken when the destroyer *Shaw* exploded.

while Japanese diplomats were pretending to discuss peace at the White House, a fleet of 191 Japanese warplanes attacked American airfields at Pearl Harbor. Then they dropped bombs on the ships of the United States Navy anchored in the harbor. An hour later came a second fleet of 170 Japanese warplanes.

The attack was a perfect surprise—and the greatest military disaster in American history. One hundred and fifty American warplanes—the bulk of our air force in the Pacific—were destroyed on the ground. It was a better demonstration than Billy Mitchell could have imagined, and the fulfillment of his most dire prophecies. Of the 94 American ships in Pearl Harbor at the time, all the most powerful—the 8 battleships—were put out of action, together with 3 cruisers and 3 destroyers. More than 70 civilians and 2300 servicemen were killed.

The next day President Roosevelt appeared before Congress to announce that Japan's "Day of Infamy" had plunged us into war. Three days (p. 673) later Germany and Italy declared war on the United States.

See "Section 3 Review answers," p. 656E.

Section 3 Review

1. Identify or explain: Greater East Asia Co-Prosperity Sphere, Chiang Kai-shek, Hideki Tojo, "Magic."

2. Locate: Burma Road, French Indochina, Thailand, Dutch East Indies, Pearl Harbor.

3. What were the Japanese war goals in the Far East in 1941?

4. **Critical Thinking: Predicting Consequences.** If Japan had not attacked Pearl Harbor, would the United States have ever entered World War II? Explain.

Enrichment Support File Topic

See "Lesson Plan," p. 656E for **Writing Process Activity: Determining Relevance** relating to the attack on Pearl Harbor.

Chapter 26 Review

See "Chapter Review answers," p. 656E.

Focusing on Ideas

1. How did Franklin D. Roosevelt's policies toward Latin America differ from those of Theodore Roosevelt?

2. Cite actions by the world democracies in 1933–1938 that tended to encourage aggressive acts by Germany, Italy, and Japan.

3. How did the United States shift from a position of strict neutrality in 1935 to one of active help for the Allies by October 1941? Cite specific actions by FDR and Congress.

4. Why did Adolph Hitler and Josef Stalin sign a nonaggression pact in 1939? Why did it surprise the world?

Taking a Critical Look

1. **Recognizing Ideologies.** Some Americans praised the European dictators for putting the jobless back to work and getting the "trains to run on time." What values were they overlooking in their praise of the dictators?

2. **Making Comparisons.** How did new technology affect the way World War II was fought? Compare this to what you have learned about the effects of new technology in earlier wars, such as the Civil War.

Your Region in History

1. **Geography.** What was the ethnic composition of your area at the outbreak of World War II? On a world map, plot the countries that were represented in your community. How would this ethnic distribution have affected attitudes about our involvement in World War II?

2. **Culture.** Through interviews with older residents and research of local papers published in the 1930s, try to determine the extent of isolationist sentiment in your community in the late 1930s.

3. **Economics.** How did your region benefit from the sale of arms during World War II?

Historical Facts and Figures

Drawing Inferences. Study the graph below to help answer the following questions: (a) In 1939 which nation had the most naval vessels? (b) Which nation had the most airplanes? (c) Which had the most tanks? (d) Which nation had the largest number of armed forces? (e) What geographic facts help explain why Britain had a large navy? Why France had a large number of troops? (f) What does the information in the graph suggest about the relative military preparation of these nations prior to World War II?

Comparative Military Strengths of Allies, 1939			
United States	🧍🧍	✈✈	🗄	🚢🚢🚢🚢
Britain	🧍	✈✈	Data not available	🚢🚢🚢🚢🚢
France	🧍🧍🧍🧍	✈✈✈	🗄🗄🗄🗄🗄🗄🗄🗄🗄🗄🗄🗄	🚢🚢
Germany	🧍🧍🧍🧍🧍🧍🧍🧍🧍	✈✈✈✈	🗄🗄🗄🗄🗄🗄🗄🗄🗄🗄🗄	🚢🚢

🧍 = 200,000 Soldiers   ✈ = 1,000 Planes   🗄 = 200 Tanks   🚢 = 100 Ships

Source: *The Crucial Years*, Hanson W. Baldwin

✖ **Critical Thinking Activity: Recognizing Cause and Effect** How did the attack on Pearl Harbor affect the average American? Ask the class to think of ways that the average American's life was changed by the Japanese attack on Pearl Harbor. Write student suggestions on the chalkboard. Have class prioritize items, with number 1 being the most immediate change. Use this activity as a spring-board for the class to write a sentence (as a group) that describes the effect of Pearl Harbor on the average American.

Chapter 27
A World Conflict

Identifying Chapter Materials

Objectives	Basic Instructional Materials	Extension Materials
1 Mobilizing for Defense • Examine the effects of mobilization for war on American society. • Analyze the wartime increase in federal taxes.	**Annotated Teacher's Edition** • Lesson Plans, p. 674C **Instructional Support File** • Pre-Reading Activities, Unit 9, p. 43 • Skill Application Activity, Unit 9, p. 47	**Enrichment Support File** • World War II: Japanese Americans (See "In-Depth Coverage" at right.)
2 "The End of the Beginning"—1942 • Show how the fortunes of war began to favor the Allies in 1942.	**Annotated Teacher's Edition** • Lesson Plans, pp. 674C–674D	**Documents of American History** • The Declaration of Panama, Vol. 2, p. 419 • Casablanca Conference, Vol. 2, p. 474
3 Victory in Europe • Describe the course of the war in Europe. • Analyze the conference at Yalta and discuss possible alternatives to the settlement reached.	**Annotated Teacher's Edition** • Lesson Plans, pp. 674D–674E	**Documents of American History** • Yalta Conference, Vol. 2, p. 487 • The Surrender of Germany, Vol. 2, p. 500
4 The War in the Pacific • Describe the end of World War II and describe the cost, impact, and significance of the war. • Summarize the arguments for and against dropping the atomic bomb on Japan.	**Annotated Teacher's Edition** • Lesson Plans, p. 674E **Instructional Support File** • Reading Activities, Unit 9, pp. 44–45 • Skill Review Activity, Unit 9, p. 46 • Critical Thinking Activity, Unit 9, p. 48 • Chapter Test, Unit 9, pp. 49–52 • Additional Test Questions, Unit 9, pp. 53–56 • Unit 9 Test, pp. 57–60	**American History Transparencies** • Time Lines, p. E27 **Perspectives** • The Decision to Drop the Atomic Bomb (See "In-Depth Coverage" at right.)

Providing In-Depth Coverage

27

Perspectives on World War II

Two of the most controversial events of World War II were the internment of Japanese Americans and the dropping of the atomic bomb. The controversy over the legality and justice of the relocation of the Japanese Americans continues even today. Some Americans view it as one of the greatest violations of civil liberties in American history. Others maintain that a wartime emergency places hardships on all Americans. However, the U.S. government has acknowledged some wrong-doing. In 1990 President Bush signed a national apology, which also provided the first reparations to Japanese interred during the war.

Historians also continue to debate the reasons why the U.S. utilized the atomic bomb. Some believe Truman only wanted to shorten the war and prevent additional American casualties. Others think the weapon was used simply because it existed or that the U.S. dropped the atomic bomb in order to keep the Soviet Union from becoming involved in the Pacific theater.

A History of the United States as an instructional program provides three types of resources you can use to offer in-depth coverage of events during World War II: the *student text*, the *Enrichment Support File*, and *Perspectives on the 20th Century*. The chart below shows the topics that are covered in each.

THE STUDENT TEXT. Boorstin and Kelley's *A History of the United States* unfolds the chronology of events and the key players affecting life and politics in the United States during WWII.

AMERICAN HISTORY ENRICHMENT SUPPORT FILE. This collection of primary source readings and classroom activities focuses on the internment of Japanese Americans during World War II.

PERSPECTIVES: READINGS ON AMERICAN HISTORY IN THE 20TH CENTURY. In this edited collection of secondary source readings, well-known historians and political commentators provide an array of perspectives on the important decision to use the atomic bomb.

Locating Instructional Materials

Detailed lesson plans for teaching about the internment of Japanese Americans as a minicourse or to study one or more elements of WWII in depth are offered in the following areas: in the *student text*, see individual lesson plans at the beginning of each chapter; in the *Enrichment Support File*, see page 3; in *Perspectives*, see the Teacher's Guide for this unit.

IN-DEPTH COVERAGE OF THE HOME FRONT DURING WWII		
Student Text	**Enrichment Support File**	**Perspectives**
• Internment of Japanese Americans, p. 677 • Black Americans on the Home Front, p. 677 • Women and the War Effort, pp. 677–678 • Financing the War, p. 679 • The Atomic Bomb, p. 698	• Lesson Suggestions • Multimedia Resources • Overview Essay/The Internment of Japanese Americans During World War II • Literature in American History/*Farewell to Manzanar* • Primary Sources in American History/Executive Order 9066 • Geography in American History/Selective Discrimination: The Geographical Background • Great Debates in American History/How Should the United States React to Foreign-Born Citizens During Wartime? • Making Connections	• "The Decision to Drop the Bomb" by Clark Clifford • "The Bomb" by Dwight Macdonald • "The Atomic Bomb—the Penalty of Expediency" by Hanson W. Baldwin • "Why the Bomb Was Used" by Barton J. Berstein • "The War in Asia" by Stephen E. Ambrose

Mobilizing for Defense

FOCUS

To introduce the lesson, break the class up into small groups and have the groups list at least ten significant effects of the war on American society, based on information found in their texts. As soon as they have finished, bring the class back together and have each group list its answers on the board. Then review and discuss the lists with the class.

Developing Vocabulary

The words listed in this chapter are essential terms for reading and understanding particular sections of the chapter. The page number after each term indicates the page of its first or most important appearance in the chapter. These terms are defined in the text Glossary (text pages 1000–1011).

arsenal (page 675); **ration** (page 675); **internment** (page 677).

INSTRUCT

Explain

War cannot only stimulate an economy. It can accelerate social change.

❋ Cooperative Learning Activity

Demonstrating Reasoned Judgment Remind students that after World War I the number of women in the labor force dropped to prewar levels, while a much greater proportion of women were offered peacetime work after World War II. Ask students to work in small groups using outside resources to prepare a report on how and why the role of women changed following the second World War. Have group members decide what tasks need to be done and who will complete each task. When reports are finished, call on volunteers to summarize their group's findings.

Section Review Answers

Section 1, page 679

1. a) way of dividing scarce resources. To buy rationed goods, a person must present not only money but also a government-issued coupon (or something similar). b) branch of the Army for women. c) women in the Navy. d) women in the Coast Guard. e) black messman who shot down four Japanese planes during the attack on Pearl Harbor. f) black doctor who developed the blood bank. 2. a) expanded overall production of war materials. b) filled the places of men who had become soldiers and volunteered for the armed forces. c) worked at industrial jobs previously closed to them and served in the military. 3. They were forced to sell their homes and businesses on extremely short notice and were then confined in internment camps. 4. a) raised taxes and borrowed money. b) sold war bonds and froze wages and prices. 5. Women found jobs outside the home in both world wars. They were able to maintain these jobs after World War II, unlike the previous war. Blacks also found more job opportunities due to both wars. Inroads were made to ease racial segregation during the latter war.

CLOSE

To conclude the lesson, tell students that all men between the ages of 18 and 65 had to register for the draft during World War II, and all physically fit men between the ages of 18 and 45 (later 36) were liable for military service. Many colleges graduated their students six months early so as to speed up their eligibility for military service. By the end of 1942, three-quarters of the undergraduates at Yale had enlisted. Conscientious objectors were few, and usually restricted to religious rather than political grounds. Many of these served in noncombat units, particularly in the Medical Corps. About 5000 pacifists were jailed between 1940 and 1945 for refusing to serve in the war effort in any capacity.

"The End of the Beginning"—1942

FOCUS

To introduce the lesson, have students list the dates and significance of these key World War II engagements: Guadalcanal, Midway, Pearl Harbor, El Alamein, Coral Sea, Stalingrad, Battle of France (1939), conquest of Poland (1939), Bataan, Okinawa, D-Day, Fall of Rome, Battle of the Bulge, Iwo Jima, Hiroshima, Fall of Berlin. (Note: This exercise extends into the next section.)

Developing Vocabulary

Allies (page 679); **puppet government** (page 681).

INSTRUCT

Explain

By analyzing battle victories it is possible to chart the ebb and flow of a war. In 1942 success in North Africa, the invention of radar and sonar, the Battle of the Coral Sea, the Battle of Midway, and the Battle for

Guadalcanal marked "the end of the beginning" and a turning point in the war.

☑ Writing Process Activity

Drawing Conclusions Ask students to imagine that as reporters, they must report on the raid on Tokyo, the battle of the Coral Sea, the Battle of Midway, or the battle for Guadalcanal. Have them begin by listing the facts surrounding the battle, the results, and the significance. Students should begin their news article with a topic sentence that clearly summarizes the basic facts, and they should organize their information in a logical fashion. Students should revise for clarity and completeness. After proofreading, they can publish a newspaper about some of the major battles of World War II.

Section Review Answers

Section 2, page 685

1. a) leader of Germany's Afrika Korps. b) elite German force in North Africa. c) British general who led the Eighth Army to defeat the Afrika Korps. d) puppet government that ruled the unoccupied part of France and cooperated with the Nazis. e) led the 1942 raid of B-25s on Tokyo. f) leader of the Japanese fleet who decided to force a major sea battle with the Allies in 1942 at Midway. g) leader of the American fleet at Midway. 2. El Alamein, Tunisia, and Casablanca are on the map on page 680. Stalingrad is on page 671. Midway, Wake, and the Marshall Islands, Port Moseby, the Solomon Islands, the Coral Sea, and Guadalcanal are shown on page 684. Savo Island is near Guadalcanal. Samoa is on the map on page 515. 3. Victory at El Alamein; success in taking Morocco, Algeria, and Libya, and in breaking the siege of Stalingrad; victory at Midway. 4. a) Tactical success for the Americans because the Japanese had to recall an invasion force that was part of their drive toward Australia. b) Japan's first great naval defeat; it turned the balance of power in favor of the United States. c) A victory for the Americans that stopped the Japanese advance, protecting Australia and the Solomon Islands. 5. The Allies were helped in their battle of the Atlantic by the inventions of radar and sonar.

CLOSE

To conclude the lesson, have students use the map on page 684 to locate Japan's "defensive perimeter" (described on page 683) and draw it on an outline map. Ask: Why was it so important to prevent the Japanese from conquering Port Moresby? (Security of Australia.) Why was the battle of Midway important? (Security of Hawaiian islands, Alaska, western United States.)

Section 3 (pages 685–695)

Victory in Europe

FOCUS

To introduce the lesson, have students read the material under the heading "Conferring at Yalta" on pages 691–692 and answer the following question: What point of view does the text present on the question of how well Roosevelt negotiated at Yalta? (It says that Roosevelt and Churchill negotiated an agreement that was not worth much because Stalin had no intention of sticking to it. However, it also points out the difficulties for Roosevelt and Churchill in, for example, having Soviet troops in control in Eastern Europe. Overall, the text gives the impression that Stalin was in control of the conference.)

Developing Vocabulary

unconditional surrender (page 685)

INSTRUCT

Explain

In early 1945, and the war nearly won, FDR met with Stalin and Churchill in Yalta, USSR to discuss the terms of German surrender and the fate of Eastern Europe.

★ Independent Activity

Checking Consistency Explain to students that two historic conferences of the twentieth century occurred in Munich in 1938 and Yalta in 1945. Have students work independently to compile lists of the specific promises made by Hitler at Munich and Stalin at Yalta and which of these promises were kept.

Section Review Answers

Section 3, page 695

1. a) American B-17 bombers that were heavily armed with machine guns for defense. b) German flying bombs and rockets. c) Supreme Commander of the Allied Forces in Western Europe and director of the D-Day invasion. d) American general who led the Third army in the initial breakthrough across France. e) French Forces of the Interior, the Resistance—French people who fought the Nazis. f) American general who led the Seventh Army. g) led the troops of the First Army. h) line of German fortifications along the western border of Germany. i) became President in 1945 upon FDR's death. j) Republican defeated by FDR in the 1944 election. k) commanding general of the 101st Airborne Division who refused to surrender at Bastogne. l) May 8, 1945, when the Germans surrendered unconditionally. 2. Sicily is

27

shown on the map on page 680. All other locations shown on map on page 693. 3. a) The Allies could launch an invasion of Sicily and Italy from Tunis; tens of thousands of Axis troops were captured; Italian morale was destroyed; and the Mediterranean was open to British shipping. b) The Allied invasion of France was delayed, Italy signed an armistice, Rome was liberated, and many German troops were tied up in the campaign, weakening German forces elsewhere. 4. British planes carried out saturation bombing of German cities at night. The American planes made "pinpoint" attacks on factories during the day. 5. The Germans lost France, the Ukraine, most of Poland, Romania, Bulgaria, and Yugoslavia. 6. It was Germany's last bid to break the Allies. It was an Allied victory in which the depleted German forces lost yet more men. 7. Elbe River; meant that Allied forces were still west of Berlin and that Soviet forces had extended and consolidated their control of Eastern Europe, including Berlin and Prague. 8. At Yalta the division of Germany was agreed upon; the Allies agreed to give the Soviet Union half of all German reparations and to allow the Soviet Union to conquer Outer Mongolia and take some strategic Japanese islands; and the Soviet Union agreed to allow the countries of Eastern Europe to choose their own governments, to declare war against Japan once Germany was defeated, and to join the United Nations after the war. The Western powers believed it was necessary to make these agreements because Soviet forces already controlled Eastern Europe and the Western powers thought they needed Soviet help in completing the defeat of Germany and Japan.

CLOSE

To conclude the lesson, point out that disagreements first began to arise among the Big Three (Roosevelt, Churchill, and Stalin) at Yalta. This marked an important starting point for the Cold War (described in Chapter 28). Yet all through World War II the conferences had gone well. Ask: How do you explain why this conference went so poorly? (Hitler was largely defeated when this conference was held. Thus the leaders had little to unite them.)

Section 4 (pages 695–700)

The War in the Pacific

FOCUS

To introduce the lesson, ask students to list as many costs of World War II as they can. Include secondary costs such as geniuses who died before making their contribution.

INSTRUCT

Explain

For nearly half a century the world has debated the justification of dropping atomic bombs on Hiroshima and Nagasaki.

☑ Writing Process Activity

Demonstrating Reasoned Judgment Ask students to play the role of historians who must explain how the atomic bomb finally ended World War II. Have them begin by outlining the events that led to the bombing of Hiroshima and Nagasaki. Students should begin their essay with a topic sentence summarizing the historical significance of the atomic bomb, and they should organize their ideas logically. As they revise, ask students to check for clear explanation and an objective tone. After they proofread, students can compare their evaluations.

Section Review Answers

Section 4, page 700

1. a) American general who was defeated in the Philippines but recaptured the islands. b) famous German physicist. c) helped to create the atom bomb. d) name given to the atomic bomb project. e) German attempt to kill all European Jews. 2. All items are shown on the map on page 700. 3. The Allies planned to advance toward the Philippines from the southwestern Pacific islands and from the central Pacific—taking Japanese-held islands along the way and then recapturing the Philippines—and to prepare for a final attack on Japan itself. Major battles occurred at Tarawa, Kwajalein, Saipan, and Leyte Gulf. 4. The existence of atomic weapons made the cost of any major war too high to contemplate. The containment of small wars became a new goal—if any war grows too large or involves nuclear powers, disaster may occur for the entire world.

CLOSE

To conclude the lesson, have students write a one-page essay showing that the United States was or was not justified in dropping the atomic bombs. Tell them to include two pieces of evidence in their argument and to designate each piece of evidence with an *E* in the margin.

Chapter Review Answers

Focusing on Ideas

1. Many unemployed not reabsorbed in work force during recovery; women entering the labor force. Also, elderly; jobs for those under 18 (baby boomers reach 18); workers holding two jobs may have been counted twice. 2. Warfare became highly mobile in

contrast to combat from fixed positions in World War I: tanks, trucks, armored personnel carriers; air power became decisive; property destruction was far more widespread. 3. Victory in North Africa; halting the Germans at Stalingrad; the end of Japanese efforts to take Australia, Japanese withdrawal from Guadalcanal. 4. All Latin American countries broke diplomatic relations with Axis; most eventually entered war, were valuable sources of supply.

Taking a Critical Look
1. Civilian hardships were more emotional than economic; despite rationing, standard of living rose. 2. Germany: land war with air support required reoccupation of vast territories. Japan: naval and air war heavily using marines; battle for strategic bases.

Your Region in History
1–3. Answers will vary depending on your region. Consult your local library or historical society.

Historical Facts and Figures
(a) Soviet Union: 58%; Britain: 3% (b) German: 31%; American: 3% (c) The Soviet Union (d) The war was not fought in the U. S. (e) Produced a feeling of bitterness toward other nations on both sides whose losses were less; determination to prevent such a tragedy from happening again.

Answers to "Making Connections"
(See "Using Making Connections" on p. 702.)
Answers will vary, but may include one or more of the following examples. Answers based on the time line callouts are in italics.
1. Roosevelt did indeed break many precedents in his New Deal, as he had promised in his acceptance speech at the nominating convention in Chicago. During the first "hundred days" Roosevelt was able to persuade Congress to pass many innovative bills because the members of Congress felt a desperate need for leadership and experimentation. Some of the first bills—*such as the 1934 bill that set up the Security and Exchange Commission*—were aimed at shoring up the banking system and preventing a repetition of the Crash of '29. Other innovative bills reached into every nook and cranny of American life— a radical departure from the traditional hands-off ap-

proach. They also made the federal government the employer of a rapidly growing segment of the American population. *By 1943, for example, the Works Progress Administration alone had spent $11 billion to employ 8.5 million people. 2. The 1930s depression and the reparations required by the Versailles Treaty* were partially responsible for creating an atmosphere in which it was possible for fascism to take root and spread throughout Europe. These two factors contributed to the *instability of the German economic and political systems*. In their desperation, the German people turned to Hitler with his promises to regain lost territory and restore the former glory of their country. Italy also hoped to gain glory. *In attempting to create an empire, Italian troops invaded Ethiopia in 1935*. The reluctance of democratic countries to get involved in another war also aided the rise of dictators. *In 1936, for example, Congress passed neutrality laws preventing the United States from arming either side in the Spanish Civil War between the Fascists and the Republicans*. And in Europe, England and France allowed so many countries to fall without protest that *Stalin and Hitler felt free to sign a non-aggression pact in 1939*. 3. There are many lessons to be learned from World War II. A few are listed below. The events from which the lessons could be learned follow in parentheses. The seeds of future wars are often buried in the peace treaties of past wars. (*In the 1930s, the Depression and reparations required by the Versailles Treaty left the German economic and political system unstable.*) War is so devastating it pays to explore every peaceful means to prevent it. (*In 1938, Neville Chamberlain rejected FDR's proposed international conference on armaments and economic security.*) Even an ocean as wide as the Pacific is not enough to prevent a sneak attack in the age of the airplane. (*In 1941, the Japanese attacked Pearl Harbor and the United States entered the war.*) Peace should be pursued harder than ever now that people have the potential to render the earth totally uninhabitable. (*In 1945, the United States revealed a devastating new weapon when it dropped the atomic bomb on Hiroshima and Nagasaki.*) Agreements are only as good as the word of the people that make the agreements. (*In 1945, Churchill, Roosevelt, and Stalin met at Yalta to plan for the Nazi surrender.*)

27

Chapter 27

Focusing the Chapter: Have students identify the chapter logo. Discuss what unit theme the logo might symbolize. Then ask students to skim the chapter to identify other illustrations or titles that relate to this theme.

A World Conflict

The United States now faced war on two fronts. For the first time in our history, this two-ocean nation was threatened by enemies on both oceans. And the enemies were winning everywhere. In the Pacific, Japan followed the Pearl Harbor surprise with attacks on the Philippines, Wake Island, Guam, the Dutch East Indies, Malaya, and Hong Kong. In the Atlantic, German submarines were disrupting our vital supply lines. The Nazis controlled western Europe from the Norwegian Sea to the Aegean. They had overrun the Balkans and stood at the gates of Moscow. Russia seemed ready to fall. The Italians had taken Libya. In southern Russia German forces were poised to cut through the Caucasus to Iran and Iraq, hoping to meet the Japanese army in India. For the Allies it would be a long road back.

A U. S. soldier stands in the ruins of Cologne, Germany. Beyond him rise the spires of the city's ancient cathedral. Although damaged in the heavy wartime bombing, the magnificent building was saved.

Wide World Photos

Continuity and Change: Conflict Remind students that during World War II for the first time in its history, the United States faced a war on two fronts, threatened by powerful enemies on both oceans. During the American Revolution and the War of 1812, Americans lived almost exclusively in the Eastern part of the continent and were buffered on the West by the "Great American Desert." The Civil War was a war that involved only Americans, and during World War I, the threat was from Europeans only. World War II was indeed a global conflict, forcing the split of American resources between two distant theaters of war. (See pp. 93, 203, 342, and 557.)

674

See "Lesson Plan," p. 674C.

1. Mobilizing for defense

The United States was not prepared for World War II, but it was in much better shape than in 1917. The draft had been started in 1940, and by the time of the attack on Pearl Harbor the army had grown to 1.6 million. A mammoth defense program had been launched to produce a torrent of guns, planes, tanks, and ships.

Converting to wartime. Before Pearl Harbor many industries, just emerging from the depression, were not eager to convert to wartime production. Labor expected a larger share of the new prosperity. In 1941 strikes multiplied fivefold.

With the United States entry into the war, the nation turned to the urgent task of becoming the "arsenal of democracy." Again, as in World War I, government agencies were created to focus the nation's life—the work of factories, farms, and mines, the research of industries and universities—on this great purpose.

Rationing was needed to be sure that everyone had a fair share, enough but not too much, of scarce items like heating oil, shoes, meat, sugar, and coffee. Every man, woman, and child received coupons for a share of rationed items. Gasoline, too, was rationed, not because it was in short supply, but to conserve rubber in tires, which was dangerously scarce. Americans were not used to this sort of regulation. Still, daily life in the United States was less regulated than in most other countries at war. Our own armed forces and those of our allies suddenly demanded all that the country could produce. Full employment replaced unemployment. Prosperity returned on the home front.

By 1942 American production equaled that of Germany, Italy, and Japan combined. And by 1944 it was *double* theirs. Even in ships, where the United States had failed badly in World War I, production was enormous. From July 1940 to August 1945, United States shipyards produced a tonnage equal to two-thirds the merchant marines of all the Allied nations combined. Before the war was over, American factories turned out 250,000 planes, 100,000 armored cars, 75,000 tanks, 650,000 pieces of

Brown Brothers

Library of Congress

Stunned by Pearl Harbor, the most crushing disaster in our history, Americans vowed not to forget. They saved rubber, metal, and paper to be made into armaments and war supplies.

More from Boorstin: "Department stores and supermarkets brought together many kinds of merchandise under one roof. During World War II the scarcity of certain goods had increased this tendency toward 'scrambled' merchandising. When drugstores could not get some of their usual items, they stocked small appliances, food, luggage, and toys, while supermarkets carried clothing, kitchenware, hardware, drugs, and cosmetics, and department stores branched out into food, liquor, and a variety of new services." (From *The Americans: The Democratic Experience*)

artillery, and millions of tons of bombs, shells, and bullets.

Women in the armed forces. To fight the war it was necessary to build a huge army. Ultimately 15 million men and women served—10 million through the draft and 5 million as volunteers. Now all the services began to enlist women to perform all sorts of duties except those of combatants. In 1945 there were 258,000 women serving as Army WACS, Navy WAVES, Coast Guard SPARS, and women marines. Over 1000 women flew as civilians in the Women's Air Forces Service. They performed the hazardous job of ferrying military planes to Great Britain and other theaters of war. In 1979 the air force belatedly recognized these women pilots as war veterans who were entitled to all veterans' benefits.

Racial segregation and the war. Of the 15  million in the armed forces, about 1 million were blacks. They suffered less discrimination than in World War I. During World War II, the Marine Corps no longer kept them out, and before the war was over there were 17,000 black "Leathernecks." It became easier for qualified blacks to become officers. The air force trained black officers and pilots, and more than 80 won the Distinguished Flying Cross. Even the navy, which before had taken blacks only for kitchen work and as waiters, began to open up. The example of Dorie Miller at Pearl Harbor may have helped. Even though only an untrained messman, he grabbed a machine gun during the attack and shot down four Japanese planes. For his heroism Dorie Miller received the Navy Cross.

Blacks served in every theater of the war. After the Japanese captured the Burma Road lifeline to China, black engineering battalions helped perform the incredible feat of building the Ledo Road. They pushed this new supply line through the steaming jungles and mountainous terrain of northern Burma.

One black doctor made a major contribution to the war effort that helped save countless lives of soldiers of all colors. Charles Drew developed the blood bank for collecting and storing the blood plasma which injured fighting men so badly needed. Ironically, over the strong objection of Dr. Drew, the blood plasma of whites and blacks—for no scientific reason—was kept segregated.

The long shadow of the divided South remained. At first, most blacks, once more fighting for democracy, were still segregated in the services. Some progress was made during the course of the war in breaking down segregation. All shared equally the risks of battle. Death was no racist. Newspaper correspondents noted that there was no color line in the foxholes. After the war, President Harry S Truman appointed a national committee to recom-

During World War II, blue stars were hung in windows to indicate that family members were away in the armed forces. Gold stars were shown for those who died in the war. This woman had three sons in the service.

Library of Congress

Multicultural Connection: More than 400,000 Hispanics served in the armed forces during World War II. In fact, Hispanics fought in a higher percentage than any other ethnic group in the nation. Twelve Hispanics were given the Congressional Medal of Honor, the highest military award.

mend action to bring racial equality into the armed services. By 1949 the army, navy, and air force had abolished racial quotas. They finally realized, as *The Crisis* had said during World War II, "A jim crow army cannot fight for a free world." In the Korean War of 1950–1953 Americans of all races fought side by side.

Black Americans and the home front.

One of the most effective fighters for racial equality at home was the black labor leader, A. Philip Randolph. Born in Florida, he attended the City College of New York, founded a magazine, and became active in the Socialist party. He created the Brotherhood of Sleeping Car Porters in 1925 and after a bitter fight won recognition from the Pullman Company, which manufactured and ran the sleeping cars on American railroads. The march on Washington that Randolph organized in 1941 threatened to bring 100,000 blacks to the capital to protest against racial discrimination in wartime hiring.

Under this pressure, even before the march could take place, President Roosevelt issued his historic Executive Order 8802. This outlawed any discrimination on the basis of race, creed, color, or national origin in the federal government or in defense factories. A Fair Employment Practices Committee (FEPC) was appointed to enforce this policy. Roosevelt's order did not end discrimination. But substantial progress was made in both industry and government.

As in World War I the flood of blacks from the South to northern cities for jobs in the booming war factories increased racial tensions. In 1943 there were race riots in a number of cities. The worst of them, in Detroit, left 25 blacks and 9 whites dead.

After World War I about 80 percent of all blacks in the United States still lived in the South. But by 1950 nearly half of them lived in other parts of the country. During the war, black Americans, like other Americans, were becoming more and more citified. Outside the South nearly all of them were living in cities. And in the South they too were moving off the farm. Along with other Americans, they were churning quickly and easily around the country. It was harder than ever for the old South to keep its old ways.

Japanese Americans are interned.

Japanese and Americans of Japanese ancestry had long faced discrimination on the West Coast. After Pearl Harbor their situation became much worse. For no good reason, other citizens blamed them for what the Japanese militarists had done and even began to suspect that they might be helping the enemy across the Pacific. Western politicians and frightened military men pressured FDR to remove them from the coastal states. President Roosevelt gave in. Early in 1942, under the excuse of national security, 110,000 Japanese Americans were rounded up. There was no evidence that these Americans were disloyal. They were forced to sell their homes and businesses on short notice and at sacrifice prices. They then were confined in camps, watched by armed guards, and treated as if they were dangerous. Not until after the presidential election of 1944 did the government change its policy and begin to release these innocent citizens.

Despite this humiliating treatment, 1200 men volunteered from the camps to serve in the United States armed forces. In a segregated unit these soldiers in the 442nd Regimental Combat Team fought heroically in Italy. Another Japanese American battalion was recruited from Hawaii, where there was no internment because there were so many Japanese.

In time of war it is harder than ever for a free nation to preserve its freedoms. Defending the country becomes a matter of life and death. Dissenters are open to the charge of being traitors. ✕ This is a true testing time of democracy. In World War II, except for the disgraceful treatment of Japanese Americans, the nation's record was far better than it had been in World War I.

Women and the war effort.

The need for workers opened economic opportunities for women. Now, instead of being dissuaded from

Enrichment
Support
File Topic

✕ Critical Thinking Activity: Demonstrating Reasoned Judgment Can the internment of Japanese Americans during World War II be justified? The text states, "In time of war it is harder than ever for a free nation to preserve its freedoms." Ask students to decide if this statement justifies the internment of Japanese Americans during World War II. What evidence would support or dispute this idea? Have students offer their viewpoint in an essay.

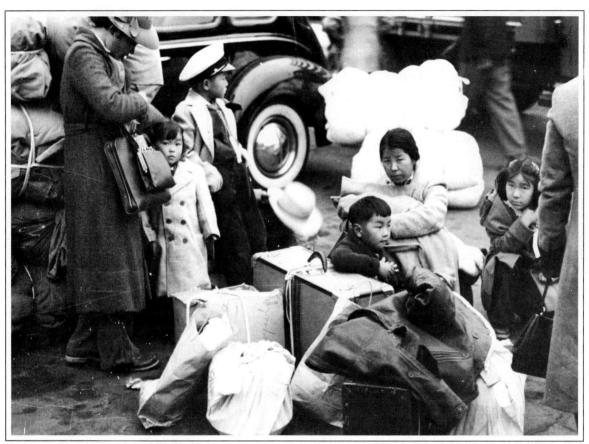

Ordered to leave their homes and businesses on short notice by the United States government, anxious Japanese Americans wait in Los Angeles for a train to take them to an internment camp.

taking jobs as they had been during the depression, they were urged to go to work. Six million women joined the 12 million already in the labor force. They took on a wide variety of jobs and surprised the men who had said they were too weak and delicate to be lumberjacks, blast furnace operators, stevedores, or blacksmiths. They proved that they could handle all these jobs. And they also operated complex machines in shipyards and airplane factories. Many for the first time could show their talents as doctors, dentists, chemists, and lawyers. "Rosie the Riveter" became an inspiration for all Americans.

Black women benefited, too. Before the war a greater percentage of black women worked than white. But they were generally restricted to low-paying jobs as domestic servants or farm laborers. When war came, they found more interesting and better-paying jobs. Nearly half a million black women who had worked as domestics left that work during the war to take positions in factories.

When World War II ended, it seemed that once again women might be forced to leave their jobs to make places for returning servicemen. But this time a much larger proportion was offered work in peacetime production. Prodded by war, the nation discovered its women and helped ❀ women discover themselves.

❀ See "Lesson Plan," p. 674C for **Cooperative Learning Activity: Demonstrating Reasoned Judgment** relating to the role of women in World War II.

Library of Congress

For some, the war opened new opportunities. These two women welders worked in a Connecticut factory in 1943.

Raising money. War was expensive. From 1941 to 1945 the federal government spent $321 billion—twice as much as was spent during all the years from 1789 to 1941! Even during the depression, when people were alarmed by the size of the federal budget, the government had paid out only $8 billion each year.

Americans were paying the highest taxes in the nation's history. To prevent great fortunes from being made from the war, the federal income tax reached 94 percent for the highest incomes. Still, taxes brought in only 41 percent of the cost of the war. The rest was borrowed from banks, corporations, and individuals.

When everyone was employed, when wages were high but there were few goods to buy, prices went up rapidly. This was wartime inflation. But if people loaned their money to the government for war bonds, they would have less to spend on goods. So prices might be kept down. The government therefore ran a massive campaign and sold $100 billion in war bonds.

To prevent prices going sky-high, wages and prices were frozen by the government in 1942. In spite of these efforts, in the course of the war the cost of living went up 29 percent. Manufacturing wages went up more than 50 percent. Farmers earned more than ever before. The depression now seemed ancient history. The needs of a world at war had brought prosperity to Americans at home.

See "Section 1 Review answers," p. 674C.

Section 1 Review

1. Identify or explain: rationing, WACS, WAVES, SPARS, Dorie Miller, Charles Drew.

2. In what ways did each of the following contribute to the war effort: (a) industry, (b) women, (c) blacks?

3. How were West Coast Japanese Americans treated during the war? Why?

4. How did the federal government (a) raise money to pay for the war? (b) try to control inflation?

5. **Critical Thinking: Making Comparisons.** How did the gains of women and black Americans during World War II compare with gains made during World War I?

See "Lesson Plan," p. 674C.

2. "The end of the beginning"—1942

Soon after the United States entered the war, the Allies agreed that the first goal was to defeat the Germans. It was clear that if the Germans won in Europe, the United States would be left to face the aggressor nations all alone. So the United States postponed the offensive in the Pacific. There we would have to be satisfied ✘

✘ Critical Thinking Activity: Formulating Questions What was the strategy of the United States for fighting the war? Divide the class into groups. Assign each group a geographic area in which the war was fought, such as Europe, the Pacific, or North Africa. Ask each group to develop three questions that the Allies might have had to consider before they could plan their strategy for defeating the Axis powers on that front. Have groups share their work. How were the considerations similar and different for the regions?

World War II, The Mediterranean, 1942-1944

←── Allied Forces

× Allied Victories

▢ Axis Nations

▢ Axis-Controlled Territory, 1942

▢ Vichy-Controlled Territory, 1942

▢ Allied Nations

```
0                    500 Miles
0        500 Kilometers
```

with "active defense" until we had disposed of Mussolini and Hitler.

The battle of the Atlantic. The battle of the Atlantic was being lost to the "wolf packs" of German submarines. Month after month they were sending thousands of tons of Allied supplies to the bottom of the ocean. In May 1942, for example, 120 ships were sunk. Unless the submarines were beaten soon, Allied forces would be left without food or weapons, and the war would be lost. These critical months of the battle of the Atlantic were between mid-1942

and mid-1943. By good research (and good luck) the Allies invented radar and sonar in the nick of time. Airplanes using radar could locate and destroy submarines or direct armed ships to the attack. Navy ships using sonar—*so*(und) *na*(vigation) *r*(anging)—could hear distant propeller noises from subs. They could also locate their targets by echo-ranging. Sharp-sounding "pings" were sent out from a submarine destroyer, which found the enemy when these sounds rebounded off the submarine hulls.

Success in North Africa. ⊕ While the battle of the Atlantic was being fought, the Allies began their first offensive moves in North Africa. German and Italian forces there were commanded by the "Desert Fox," General Erwin Rommel, one of the most shrewd, daring, and resourceful commanders of the century. His forces had reached El Alamein, only 70 miles west of Alexandria, Egypt. They now threatened the Suez Canal and the oil fields of the Middle East. At

⊕ **Geography and History: Movement** Have students review the information under the heading "Success in North Africa" (pp. 680–682) and then look at the map above. Ask: How does this map help to explain why the first two weeks of November 1942 were so significant for the Allies? Why was stopping the Germans in north-central Egypt so important? (Kept Suez Canal and oil fields of the Middle East in Allied hands.) Why were Allied landings made on the North African coast opposite Spain? (It was easy for the Allies to win the support of the French in Vichy-controlled territory, and Spain was neutral.)

this moment of danger the British were again aided by Ultra, their secret decoding machine. It revealed Rommel's plans for his crack *Afrika Korps*. With great sacrifices of men and weapons, the British managed to hold their lines and then began to build up for a counteroffensive.

Meanwhile the Russians were pressing the Allies to open a "Second Front" in Europe with a new invasion of the continent into lands held by the Axis powers. This would divert the enemy from their attack on the Russians. Instead the Allies decided in July 1942 to use their forces to clear Africa of the Germans and Italians. They would try to divert Rommel by invading and attacking North Africa from the west.

To strengthen Allied forces in Africa, British troops were withdrawn from other fronts and sent to Egypt. Using Ultra, the British were able to destroy German supply vessels. On October 23, General Bernard Montgomery led the British Eighth Army in the attack. At first Rommel's lines held. Then, on November 4, Montgomery's army broke through. They began chasing Rommel's Afrika Korps, which had a reputation for being unbeatable. Within a week Hitler had the news that his precious Afrika Korps was in disarray. Rommel's failure to take Egypt had cost him 500 tanks, 400 guns, and 60,000 men.

At this strategic moment, United States and British forces struck their stunning surprise blow. On November 8, 1942, a huge Allied force, guarded by 350 warships, landed from 500 transports onto the west and north coasts of Africa. Most of these had come from Great Britain, but 101 ships carrying 35,000 soldiers had crossed the ocean from the United States. This gigantic operation had been planned and launched in only four months.

The Allied landing was an immediate success. At the time, that area was ruled by the "Vichy" French, who had been conquered and were helping the Nazis. They had that name because the town of Vichy in central France was the new capital of their puppet government. But now the Vichy French in North Africa quickly sided with the Allies. Within three days all of North Africa to the borders of Tunisia was in Allied hands. The Germans fleeing from the west had

managed ahead of the Allies to reach Tunisia, where they met the remnants of Rommel's Afrika Korps. There the Nazis gathered and regrouped their forces hoping to counterattack.

When Montgomery's army arrived at the borders of Tunisia, the two Allied forces united to surround the Germans. So 1942 ended with Tunisia firmly held by a still-dangerous Axis force and the land around them held by the Allies.

In November 1942 the Russians had gone on the counteroffensive. After some of the

Robert Capa, one of the top photographers of World War II, caught this picture of a United States paratrooper in full battle dress preparing for a jump into Germany.

Robert Capa/Magnum

More from Boorstin: "The new techniques which the British Coastal Command had required in World War II for the training records they made to illustrate the difference between the sounds of German and of British submarines eventually produced 'full frequency range reproduction' (ffrr), and set a new standard of fidelity for reproduced music." (From *The Americans: The Democratic Experience*)

bloodiest fighting of the war, they broke the siege of Stalingrad and surrounded an entire German army. After that army was captured in February 1943, the Russians swept rapidly westward. Meanwhile in January the siege of Leningrad had ended. The tide was beginning to turn.

World War II and Latin America. The "Good Neighbor policy" paid dividends in World War II. In 1939, by the Declaration of Panama, an Inter-American Conference drew a 300-mile off-shore defense zone around the whole hemisphere south of Canada. The warring nations were warned to avoid combat within this zone. At a conference of foreign ministers of the Latin American countries in January 1942, twenty-one of them agreed to break off diplomatic relations with Nazi Germany and its Fascist allies.

Some of them went further. Nine Caribbean republics declared war on the German-Italian-Japanese Axis in December 1941. Mexico and Brazil joined them in 1942. All the New World nations finally declared war on the Axis. Pro-Fascist Argentina did not join the Allies until almost the end of the war.

The Latin American nations provided vital war materials—rubber, quinine, tin—along with naval and air bases. Brazil sent troops to Europe, and Mexico had an air squadron in the Pacific. The Mexican and Cuban navies patrolled the Caribbean for German subs. In return, the United States gave military equipment and loans.

Japanese tanks cross a makeshift bridge over a stream during their campaign against Burma early in 1942.

UPI/Bettmann Newsphotos

Active defense in the Pacific. In the Pacific for months after Pearl Harbor the Japanese knew nothing but success. By March 1942 they controlled all the waters from the Gilbert and Solomon islands to the mainland of Asia, a distance of 4500 miles. They held every island within that area except for the southern part of New Guinea and the Bataan peninsula of Luzon in the Philippines, where a doomed American force bravely fought on until May 1942. The Japanese were masters of the Malay peninsula, the British bastion of Singapore, and Thailand. They had invaded Burma. During all this fighting, the Japanese destroyed their enemies' navies while they themselves lost no ship larger than a destroyer.

The Allies had to take steps at once to prevent their being knocked out of the Pacific before they could finish off the Nazis. They decided on a policy of more active defense. They had to hold what little remained to them in the Pacific. Otherwise they would not have bases to start from when they finally went on the offensive. They had to be sure to keep Hawaii and Samoa, and of course they needed to protect the sea lanes from the United States to the great stronghold of Australia. Fortunately, the Japanese had fewer submarines than the Germans and tended to use them against warships, so Allied supply convoys were seldom attacked.

The raid on Tokyo. By great good luck the United States aircraft carriers had happened to be at sea when the Japanese hit Pearl Harbor. During this period of active defense the navy used them for nuisance raids on Wake and other Japanese-held islands. Then, on April 18, 1942, General James B. Doolittle led B-25s launched from a carrier to attack Tokyo. This first raid on the Japanese capital did little real damage to the city. But it gave the Japanese people a hint of what was to come. And it lifted American morale.

After Doolittle's raid, the Japanese decided to establish a new line—a "defensive perimeter"—running from the Aleutian Islands in the north, through Midway, Wake, the Marshalls, the Gilberts, Fiji, and Samoa to Port Moresby in New Guinea and to Tulagi in the Solomons. At this line they hoped to stop air raids like the one on Tokyo. They also planned to disrupt the sea transport between the United States and Australia. Planes would patrol the waters between the scattered islands. The Japanese navy would be stationed near the center, ready to be rushed wherever needed. This would help them "save face." It was also a symptom of what a Japanese admiral later called the "victory disease."

The Battle of the Coral Sea. The skilled Japanese Admiral Yamamoto hoped to bring on a major sea battle with the Allied Pacific Fleet in 1942. Unless that fleet was destroyed, he feared that by the next year the Allies would be strong enough to launch an offensive against Japan.

(p. 684)

The first collision between the two fleets occurred in the Battle of the Coral Sea, May 7 and 8, 1942. This historic naval battle showed how modern science had changed war. For the first time in history in a great naval encounter, no ship on either side was within sight of an opposing ship. Now it was aircraft carrier against aircraft carrier.

During the battle both sides made mistakes, and both suffered heavy losses. The Japanese sank the United States carrier *Lexington*. For them this made it a "tactical" victory. "Tactics" had to do with winning the box score in a particular battle. But it was a "strategic" success for the United States. "Strategy" (from the Greek word for "general") had to do with the big picture and the war as a whole. To gain their advantage in the Coral Sea, the Japanese had to recall their invasion force headed for Port Moresby. So they were forced to stop their drive toward Australia.

The Battle of Midway. From the Japanese point of view the island of Midway was the key to the whole perimeter scheme. From there they could bomb Pearl Harbor and make it useless as an offensive base for our Pacific Fleet.

Admiral Yamamoto intended to force a showdown at Midway with the American Pacific Fleet of Admiral Nimitz, which was still suffering from the disaster inflicted by the Japanese on December 7. But the United States had the advantage of the "Magic" decoder. Our forces knew where the Japanese were going. So they were ready and waiting when the Japanese struck at Midway on June 4, 1942. During the battle that followed, United States carrier planes sank four of Japan's best carriers and destroyed some of their most skilled air groups. The United States lost one carrier, but handed Japan its first great naval defeat.

For the first time in World War II, the balance of naval power in the Pacific had now shifted to the United States. In this one decisive battle the whole strategic situation in the Pacific was transformed. The Japanese had to abandon their plans for taking Midway, Fiji, and Samoa.

The battle for Guadalcanal. The Japanese decided to risk one more try to take Port Moresby in New Guinea. To protect that gamble they seized Guadalcanal, one of the nearby Solomon Islands, and established an air base there. Under the Allied policy of active defense, this could not be allowed. Guadalcanal was the

Japanese Conquests in Far East to August 1942

Japanese-Controlled Territory

× Allied Victories

1. PEARL HARBOR BOMBING, DECEMBER 7, 1941

2. BATTLE OF CORAL SEA, MAY 7-8, 1942

3. JAPANESE DEFEATED AT MIDWAY, JUNE 4, 1942

stepping stone that the Allies needed for returning to the Philippines and finally for invading Japan itself.

The Allied attack on the position the Japanese were building on Guadalcanal was nicknamed "Shoestring." It had to be undertaken with very little in the way of men or equipment because at that same moment forces and supplies were being gathered for the invasion of North Africa. On August 7, 1942, some 20,000 marines were landed on Guadalcanal and the neighboring island of Tulagi. These landings were followed, in the early morning hours of August 9, by the Battle of Savo Island. There a Japanese cruiser force sank four out of the five United States and Australian heavy cruisers that were protecting our transports unloading on Guadalcanal. This terrible defeat forced the withdrawal of the transports, which left the marines short of supplies.

War in the steaming jungles of Guadalcanal was old-fashioned hand-to-hand fighting. There the alert dodging of an enemy's knife could mean life instead of death. The marines had been trained for this sort of combat. They never were put to a harder test. The Allied marines lived up to their reputation for heroism. On land, this may have been the only time the Japanese were ever outfought by an enemy they met on equal terms. Finally the beaten Japanese evacuated the island on February 9, 1943. At heavy cost of pain and life, it was there at Guadalcanal that the Japanese advance was finally stopped.

The end of the beginning. Early in January 1943 President Roosevelt and Prime Minister Churchill met at Casablanca in Morocco to plan future operations. There had been a striking improvement in the military outlook since their

Geography and History: Place The map above can serve to illustrate the vastness of Japan's post-Pearl Harbor conquests. Remind students that some of the Pacific islands were Japanese mandates from World War I peace settlements. But others were quickly occupied after Pearl Harbor. The Japanese met little resistance and could hold many places with just a handful of troops. Have students use the map to locate Japan's "defensive perimeter" (described on page 683) and draw it on an outline map. Ask: Why was it so important to prevent the Japanese from conquering Port Moresby? (Security of Australia.)

last meeting a year before. The Soviets had won the Battle of Stalingrad and were beginning to turn the tide in Russia. Egypt had been saved and Morocco, Libya, and Algeria taken for the Allies. Guadalcanal would soon be taken from Japan. The RAF and the United States Eighth Air Force were bombing Germany with deadly accuracy and increasing frequency.

"Now, this is not the end," Churchill said. "It is not even the beginning of the end. But it is, perhaps, the end of the beginning."

See "Section 2 Review answers," p. 674D.

Section 2 Review

1. Identify: Erwin Rommel, Afrika Korps, Bernard Montgomery, Vichy French, James Doolittle, Admiral Yamamoto, Admiral Nimitz.

2. Locate: El Alamein, Tunisia, Stalingrad, Midway, Wake, Marshall Islands, Samoa, Port Moresby, Solomon Islands, Coral Sea, Guadalcanal, Savo Island, Casablanca.

3. What successes in 1942 gave the Allies hope of winning the war?

4. What was the chief result of the battle (a) of the Coral Sea? (b) of Midway? (c) for Guadalcanal?

5. **Critical Thinking: Recognizing Cause and Effect.** How did recent inventions affect the outcome of the "battle of the Atlantic"?

See "Lesson Plan," p. 674D.

3. Victory in Europe

The Allies were divided on where they should go after they seized Tunisia, as they confidently expected to do. At Casablanca the Americans argued for an invasion of France in 1943, but again the British resisted. They wanted first to free the Mediterranean completely by taking Sicily and then knocking Italy out of the war. The British view finally prevailed. The Allies also agreed that they could now begin to take the offensive in the Pacific. Most important, the Allies announced that they would not stop fighting until they had won "unconditional surrender" from all their enemies. Some people thought this was a strategic error and might prolong the war.

The fall of Tunisia. The Axis army in Tunisia was now trapped. They tried to fly out their best troops, and some did escape that way. But then the Allied bombers caught their transport planes on the ground and destroyed them. On March 7, 1943, Rommel was recalled to Germany, where Hitler confessed that Africa was lost. When Rommel asked him if he still believed that total victory was possible, Hitler replied, "I know it is necessary to make peace with one side or the other [Russia or the Western powers], but no one will make peace with me."

On May 7, 1943, General von Arnim surrendered the Axis forces in Tunisia. He and sixteen other generals were taken prisoner along with a quarter-million Axis troops, including some of Germany's best-trained and best-armed soldiers. This victory was as dramatic and as decisive as Stalingrad. Italian morale was destroyed, and Great Britain's Mediterranean lifeline was opened again. Now the way was prepared to act on the Allies' secret decision to invade Italy from the south.

The battle in Italy. On the morning of July 10, 1943, swiftly and suddenly 250,000 American and British troops landed along 150 miles of Sicilian coastline. It was the greatest amphibious operation of all time. Never before had so many troops been landed at once for a single attack. Unfortunately, because the plan was faulty, the German and Italian forces were allowed to escape from the island of Sicily to the mainland of Italy.

But the Italians had now had enough of war. Mussolini was forced to resign, and a new government was installed. At the end of July the Italians began to put out peace feelers to the Allies. After much bargaining, an armistice was signed on September 3 with Italian forces. But during those long negotiations the Nazis rushed reinforcements to Italy to hold the country till the bitter end.

When British and American troops landed on the toe of Italy, they ran into fierce German resistance. Not until June 4, 1944, did the Allies

See "Lesson Plan," p. 674D for **Writing Process Activity: Drawing Conclusions** relating to the raid on Tokyo, the Battle of the Coral Sea, the Battle of Midway, and the battle for Guadalcanal.

✂ Robert Capa took this picture of the jubilant citizens of a small Sicilian town in 1943 welcoming the
(p. 687) American troops who have liberated them. Capa was killed covering the Vietnam War.

finally enter Rome. Still the Germans held on. For the United States this invasion of Italy was one of the deadliest campaigns in the war. Seventy thousand Americans were killed. By their courage and that of the British, Poles, and other Allied troops, they tied up 23 German divisions and weakened the Nazis everywhere else.

The air war. While the Allies were making their slow way toward the invasion of France

in 1944, Germany was already being invaded by air.

The lightning strike of air power at Pearl Harbor had shocked Americans into seeing that the world faced a new kind of war. Now the battlefield was everywhere. There was no place where civilians could hide from the airborne terror. Warplanes sometimes flew so high they could not be seen and could barely be heard, to strike at homes and factories.

卐 **Multicultural Connection:** Many Japanese Americans fought bravely in WWII. For example, PFC Sadao S. Munemori was awarded the Medal of Honor (posthumously) for his combat heroism in Italy. Munemori was a member of the 442nd Regimental Combat Unit, a segregated Army unit of Japanese Americans fighting in Europe. This unit became one of the most highly decorated units of WW II. Another group of Japanese-American soldiers graduated from the Military Intelligence Service Language School and saw action in the Pacific, working in intelligence and as translators.

The British began bombing Germany in 1941 when the RAF dropped 46,000 tons of bombs on enemy targets. British bombers flew over Germany at night and "saturation" bombed whole areas. Incendiary bombs set fire to entire cities. Since these attacking bombers could not be seen from the ground, British losses were not heavy. They hoped that by destroying cities, disorganizing labor, and shattering civilian morale, they could force the Nazis to surrender even before the Nazi armies were conquered.

The United States Army Air Force made its first raid on Germany in August 1942. It pursued another plan—"pinpoint" attacks in daylight. When bombers could see their targets, they could focus their bombs on the crucial factories and could report whether they had hit their targets. At the same time the Germans could see the approaching planes. The Americans thought their B-17 bombers—called "Flying Fortresses" because they bristled with so many machine guns—were so heavily defended

This American B-17 "Flying Fortress" bomber has just made a direct hit on a huge aircraft plant in East Prussia where the Germans had thought they were outside the Allied bombing range.

United Press International Photo

✖ Critical Thinking Activity: Predicting Consequences How did photojournalists in World War II portray the war? The extensive work of photojournalists during World War II provided Americans with their closest look at armed conflict. Ask students to study the photographs in this chapter. Have students write a detailed description of one of the photographs. As a class, discuss the impressions that these pictures would offer about the war. Would these pictures support the war effort, or call it into question?

that the Germans could not deal with them. But soon German fighters were downing American bombers in disastrous numbers. In response, the United States developed new long-range fighter planes to protect the bombers and so continued their precision bombing. Soon the skies of Germany were raining bombs day and night.

The Germans responded with their V-1 flying bombs and their even more terrifying V-2 rockets, which dropped suddenly and silently from the sky carrying death-dealing one-ton bombs. Never before in the history of warfare was there so much suffering by civilians. But bombing did not end the war. German factories continued to produce airplanes and other war machines in large numbers. The military effect of Allied bombing was to force the Nazis to use up their energies on fighter planes and antiaircraft weapons for their own defense. And this drained away the Nazi power to attack.

Allied planes killed nearly a third of a million Germans and destroyed 5 million homes. Still, bombing did not have a substantial effect on the German war effort until 1944. Then the bombs were concentrated on specific war industries—airplane, tank, truck, and ball-bearing factories, oil and gas production. Since Germany had dispersed its factories to defend against air attack, the Allied attack on railroads and highways helped paralyze Nazi war production.

D-Day in France. The United States and Great Britain secretly agreed that in June 1944 they would invade France by landings across the English Channel. This was the most important—and the best-kept—secret of the war. The invasion would be directed by the American General Dwight D. Eisenhower, who became Supreme Commander of the Allied Forces in Western Europe. The Allies intended at the same time to keep maximum pressure on Italy and to invade the south of France.

The cross-channel invasion was a dangerous maneuver, for the Germans had been building up their forces to meet an expected attack. They had had four years to construct their coastal fortifications. They had brought 58 divisions to France. But the Allies could pick the time and place to attack. Allied bombings had already brought chaos to the Nazi transportation system. And the Allied invaders could count on aid from the French Resistance, men and women who at great risk gave secret help to the Allies.

To mislead the Nazis, the Allies skillfully led the Germans to believe that the attack would come in the area of Calais at the narrowest part of the English Channel. By radio broadcasts, arranged so that the Nazis would get the message, they gave the Germans the impression that a great invasion force was prepared to land there.

During the night of June 5 on the orders of General Eisenhower, a mighty force of 600 warships and 4000 supporting craft carrying 176,000 men moved toward the coast of Normandy. They were protected by an air cover of 11,000 planes. At 5:30 A.M. the navy began its bombardment of the coast of Normandy. At 6:30 A.M. the first troops hit the beach between the mouth of the Seine River and Cherbourg. The Allies had achieved tactical surprise, and despite some trouble spots the initial landings were a success.

The German generals now wanted to throw all their armored forces—the German name was "Panzer," meaning armor—against the invaders in one great counter stroke. But Hitler, who thought that he was wiser than his generals, overruled them. He still was sure that the main invasion would come at Calais. So Rommel, the army group commander on the spot, was forced to hold back the Panzer divisions. The Allied men, armor, and supplies managed to reach shore and establish a secure beachhead. After the first few days the invading force was out of danger. It was one of the greatest Allied achievements of the war. In a single week the Allies had landed 326,000 men, 50,000 vehicles, and 100,000 tons of supplies.

The Allies on the move. The battle of the Normandy invasion lasted from June 6 to July 24, 1944. At the end of that time, the Allies had landed more than a million men and controlled 1500 square miles of Normandy and Brittany. The breakthrough and the beginning of the

General "Ike" Eisenhower gives a pep talk to a group of paratroopers about to be dropped into France on D-Day. The men's faces are darkened to lessen their chances of being seen.

battle for France came on July 25 when General George Patton's Third Army struck hard at the Germans. Soon thousands of Patton's tanks were pouring through. The FFI (French Forces of the Interior—the Resistance) now came out into the open to aid the Allies. Up from the Mediterranean came the United States Seventh Army under General A. M. Patch to join the eastward-moving Allied troops. Paris was liberated on August 25, Brussels and Antwerp a few days later. Within six weeks after the breakthrough all France had been cleared of Germans. And the Germans had lost nearly half a million men and untold amounts of machinery and material.

Units of General Courtney Hodges's First Army moved onto the "sacred soil" of Hitler's "unbeatable" Thousand Year Reich on September 12, 1944. Soon six Allied armies with 3 million men were facing the powerful Siegfried line of fortifications that extended the whole length of Germany's western border.

Meanwhile from the east, huge Soviet armies were hastening toward the German border. A great Russian offensive had speedily swept 460 miles across the Ukraine and Poland to the

Trucks, guns, tons of equipment and thousands of men are unloaded on the beachhead at Normandy as barrage balloons float overhead.

gates of Warsaw. There, unfortunately, the Russians stopped. This gave the Germans time to crush a heroic revolt of the Polish underground in the city.

When the Russians moved toward the south, Romania and Bulgaria surrendered quickly. On October 20 the Russians reached Belgrade. In December at Budapest the Germans dug in and put up stubborn resistance.

On the western front, meanwhile, the Allies were once again divided over their strategy. Should they strike straight for Berlin, or instead advance on a broad front? One try at the sudden-thrust strategy was an attempt to jump the river-barriers of the Meuse, the Waal, and the lower Rhine with three airborne divisions. One British officer called it "a bridge too far." And so it proved. When this failed, the Allies settled for the slower strategy.

The election of 1944. In the United States, despite the war-to-the-death against totalitarian powers, politics continued as usual. During the summer that saw the liberation of France,

Franklin D. Roosevelt was unanimously nominated for his fourth term as President. He said he only wanted to go home to Hyde Park, "But as a good soldier . . . I will accept and serve." The strains of the Presidency in wartime had taken their toll on FDR. How long could he bear up?

The Vice-Presidency was more important than ever before. At the Democratic convention the real battle was over FDR's running mate. In the end the convention named Senator Harry S Truman of Missouri. He had begun his career as a machine-politician in Kansas City. But he made a name for himself in the Senate as the head of a committee looking into defense contracts.

Wendell Willkie hoped once again to win the nomination of the Republican party. Now his liberal international views troubled many of the party leaders. Governor Thomas E. Dewey of New York soundly defeated him in the Wisconsin primary. Then Willkie withdrew from the race, and Dewey was nominated as the Republican candidate. Willkie was to die in October after a series of heart attacks.

On November 7 the nation gave President Roosevelt a decisive victory. He won by 3.6 million votes and by 432 to 99 in the electoral college. The Democrats also won substantial majorities in both houses of Congress. Just as during the Civil War, when Abraham Lincoln was reelected, the nation had decided "not to change horses in the middle of the stream."

The Battle of the Bulge.

On December 16, 1944, the Germans made a final desperate bid to break the Allies. With two armies they struck a weakly held front in the Ardennes district of France intending to sweep through and seize Antwerp, the main Allied base. This would have cut the Allied army in two and left the northern half without access to its supply harbor. The German attack was favored by foul weather, which grounded Allied planes. Heavily wooded terrain screened the Nazi movements and gave them the advantage of surprise over the unwary Allies.

The German attack got off to a good start. Spearheaded by Panzer divisions of heavily armored vehicles, they penetrated 60 miles, almost to the Meuse River, creating a large "bulge" in the Allied lines. Finally they were stopped by the armies of Patton and Montgomery. There at the vital rail junction and road center of Bastogne, the 101st Airborne Division under General McAuliffe made its heroic stand. When he was surrounded by the Germans and asked to surrender, McAuliffe made his historic one-word reply—"Nuts!" McAuliffe's 101st disrupted the German timetable, halted the attack, and held out until relieved by the Third Army. By the end of January the Bulge was "pinched off" and the Germans were forced back to their Siegfried line. United States losses were heavy, but the "Battle of the Bulge" had cost the dwindling Nazis 120,000 of their best remaining men.

Conferring at Yalta.

In February 1945, when the defeat of the Nazis appeared to be in sight, President Roosevelt met with the other Allied leaders, British Prime Minister Churchill and Russian dictator Josef Stalin. At Yalta, a Russian summer resort on the Black Sea, they would agree on their plans for the Nazi surrender. Germany was to be taken apart. Once again, the Germans would have to pay enormous "reparations."

Stalin was a tough and clever bargainer. At first he demanded that Poland be put under a Communist puppet government. When Roosevelt and Churchill objected, Stalin promised to let the Polish people choose their government by free elections. Then, arguing that the Soviet Union had been the most devastated of the Allies, he made them agree to give Russia half of all the German reparations.

Stalin promised to declare war against Japan soon after the defeat of Germany and said that when the new United Nations was organized, the Soviets would join. In return the Soviets gained some strategic Japanese islands. Stalin would also be allowed to conquer Outer Mongolia—a vast area twice the size of Texas—on the Russian border in central Asia. At the same time, Stalin solemnly promised not to interfere in the countries along the Russian border in Eastern Europe. He said he would let the people

Churchill, Roosevelt, and Stalin, the leaders of "the Big Three," pose for photographers in a courtyard during their important meetings at the Russian summer resort of Yalta. FDR, tired and haggard, was to die only two months later.

of Poland, Czechoslovakia, Hungary, Romania, and Bulgaria elect their own governments.

Too soon the democratic leaders would discover what Stalin's promises were worth. Looking back, some historians say that Roosevelt and Churchill should have known better than to believe anything Stalin said. Again and again the Communist leaders had called democracy a fraud. But at the time, the British and American leaders did not have much choice. The Soviet armies still had unrivaled power in Eastern Europe. The Western powers thought they desperately needed the help of those armies to finish off the Nazis and Japanese. All they were able to demand from their Russian ally was promises. They felt lucky even to get those! For the next twenty years the free world would pay the price for Stalin's lies.

The failure to take Berlin. Now the Allies closed in for the kill. On March 7, 1945, the First Army crossed the Rhine bridge at Remagen. Crossings were also soon made at other locations, and by the first week of April all the Allied armies were across the river. Caught between the Russian Communist armies speeding westward and the Anglo-Americans speeding eastward, German resistance was now rapidly collapsing.

General Dwight D. "Ike" Eisenhower, who had successfully directed the invasion of Europe, now faced a decision that would shape the future of Europe. If he wanted, he could quickly move his forces into Berlin, the capital of Germany, and also into Prague, the capital of Czechoslovakia. In Anglo-American hands, these capitals would be strongholds to help the ⊕

⊕ Geography and History: Movement Have students look at the map on page 693 and answer the following questions: Which happened last—the liberation of Paris, the Battle of the Bulge, or D-Day? (Battle of the Bulge.) Which two Allied victories in the Soviet Union are shown? (Kursk and Stalingrad.) At war's end, was Munich under American-British control or under Soviet control? (American-British.) Who controlled Berlin? (The Soviets. The clue to both these questions is that the blue arrows moving from west to east are the Americans and the British, while the blue arrows moving east to west are the Soviets.)

World War II, European Theater, 1944-1945

Axis-Controlled Territory 1942

Allied Forces

Allied Victories

4. RUSSIAN AND AMERICAN TROOPS MEET AT THE ELBE, APRIL 25, 1945

5. GERMANS SIGN SURRENDER AT REIMS, MAY 7, 1945

1. D-DAY, JUNE 6, 1944

2. PARIS LIBERATED, AUG. 25, 1944

3. BATTLE OF THE BULGE, DEC 16-26, 1944

democracies enforce Stalin's promise to let the people of Eastern Europe choose their own governments.

Or, General Eisenhower could wait to mop up the German troops behind his own lines—meanwhile letting the Russians overrun more of Eastern Europe and consolidate their positions in Berlin and Prague. But in Communist hands, those capitals would help the Russians to foist their dictatorship on all the surrounding peoples. The Russians could then make the border countries—Poland, Czechoslovakia, Hungary, Romania, and Bulgaria—into a group of "satellites" revolving around Moscow.

The farsighted Winston Churchill saw this threat. "I deem it highly important," he warned General Eisenhower, "that we should shake hands with the Russians as far to the east as possible." But Eisenhower was anxious to avoid the loss of more American soldiers, and FDR did not interfere. Instead of rushing the democratic forces eastward, Ike decided to stop 50 miles west of Berlin at the River Elbe. Stalin applauded this fateful decision, for now both Berlin and Prague were left to the Russians.

Until the last minute, Churchill kept trying to persuade President Roosevelt to push speedily on to Berlin and Prague. The new "mortal danger to the free world," he said, was our so-called "ally," Russia. How tragic, after the long struggle against the Nazi tyranny, to hand over half of Europe to a Communist tyranny!

The death of Roosevelt. Before Churchill's wisdom could prevail in Washington, President Roosevelt was dead. Worn down by wartime burdens, he had gone for a rest to Warm Springs, Georgia, where he often went for treatment of his paralyzed legs. On April 12, 1945,

he complained of a headache, and within minutes a blood vessel had burst in his brain. The valiant, cheerful leader, who had helped raise his fellow Americans from the depth of the Great Depression and who had organized their battle against Nazi barbarism, did not live to have the satisfaction of receiving the Nazi surrender.

The nation grieved as it had grieved for few Americans since Lincoln. Men and women wept in their offices, at home, and in the streets. They felt that they had lost not only a national leader but a personal friend.

Germany surrenders. Russian and American troops met at the Elbe on April 25. Other Russian troops were fighting their way from house

Elie Wiesel, winner of the 1986 Nobel Peace Prize, was among the slave laborers liberated by American troops at Buchenwald. Wiesel is second to the right of the man with the bandaged head.

Wide World Photos

to house through the heaps of rubble of Berlin. Hitler committed suicide in Berlin. Meanwhile his old henchman Mussolini had been captured by Italian partisans and executed. To show their contempt for the strutting dictator who had brought their beautiful land to ruins, they hung up Mussolini's body by the heels for all to see. On May 8, 1945, the Germans signed terms of unconditional surrender at General Eisenhower's headquarters in the French city of Reims. The day was celebrated joyously in the victorious countries as V-E (Victory in Europe) Day.

See "Section 3 Review answers," p. 674D.

Section 3 Review

1. Identify: Flying Fortresses, V-1 and V-2 missiles, Dwight Eisenhower, George Patton, FFI, A. M. Patch, Courtney Hodges, Siegfried line, Harry Truman, Thomas Dewey, A. C. McAuliffe, V-E Day.

2. Locate: Sicily, Calais, Normandy, Cherbourg, Brittany, Ardennes, Bastogne, Yalta, Berlin.

3. What were the chief results of (a) the Allied victory in North Africa? (b) the Italian campaign?

4. How did the British air attacks on Germany differ from those by the American planes?

5. How did Germany's situation change between June and November 1944?

6. Why was the Battle of the Bulge important?

7. Where did the Anglo-American and Russian armies meet? Why was this meeting line significant?

8. **Critical Thinking: Drawing Conclusions.** What agreements were made at Yalta? Do you agree or disagree that it was necessary at the time to make them?

See "Lesson Plan," p. 674E.

4. The war in the Pacific

"The victory is but half won," President Truman warned. "The West is free but the East is still in bondage. When the last Japanese division has surrendered unconditionally, only then will our fighting job be done."

The struggle for the islands. After the fall of Guadalcanal in February 1943, a two-year struggle began to regain other islands and to prepare for the final attack on the Japanese homeland. General Douglas MacArthur and his troops would advance through the islands of the western Pacific from New Guinea to Mindanao in the Philippines. At the same time the navy and marines would have to cross the central Pacific in a series of amphibious operations by way of the Gilbert, Marshall, and Mariana islands. So long as the Japanese held these central Pacific islands, their airplanes could attack anything that moved along the New Guinea-

General MacArthur, brilliant leader of the army in the Pacific, was generous in victory.

United Press International Photo

Mindanao path of General MacArthur. Both advances had to succeed together.

Japan fiercely resisted every landing and stubbornly contested every inch of ground. Our losses were high in the capture of Tarawa in the Gilberts in November 1943, and of Kwajalein and other islands in the Marshalls and of Saipan in the Marianas in February 1944. The tiny island of Iwo Jima was the scene of some of our heaviest losses and some of the most memorable American heroism. After a month of desperate fighting (February-March 1945), at the frightful cost of 5000 dead, the marines planted the American flag there on Mount Suribachi. With the capture of Iwo Jima and Okinawa (April-June 1945), where 11,000 more troops died, we were within striking distance of the Japanese homeland. Victory was in sight.

The return to the Philippines. Meanwhile in the southwest Pacific in a series of brilliant campaigns, General MacArthur's forces were leap-frogging toward the Philippines. Two years before, when MacArthur had left the Philippines and Allied prospects were dim, he had promised, "I shall return!" Now, on October 20, 1944, he fulfilled his promise when the Americans swarmed ashore at Leyte Island on the southeast tip of the archipelago. Again and again the Japanese vainly tried to land reinforcements on Leyte.

Before the Allies could clinch their victory in the Pacific, they would have to fight the greatest sea battle of all time. They would have to end, once and for all, the Japanese navy's ability to keep the Allies off their home islands. In the Battle of Leyte Gulf on October 23–25, the Japanese were so badly defeated that their navy was knocked out of the war.

American troops were now free to land on the main Philippine island of Luzon. The first troops went ashore on January 9, 1945, and were followed by later waves. They fought toward Manila from the north and the south. When they reached the city, the Japanese stood firm. Each house became a fortress for a few Japanese soldiers who gave their lives to delay the American advance. Finally on March 9, after fierce street fighting the last Japanese soldier

in the city gave up. During the battle for Manila, MacArthur declared the Commonwealth of the Philippines to be reestablished. "My country has kept the faith," he said; "your capital city, cruelly punished though it be, has regained its rightful place—citadel of democracy in the East."

On July 4, 1946, (fulfilling the promise made by the McDuffie Act back in 1934) the Republic of the Philippines was proclaimed independent. In the following March, a 99-year agreement was signed, giving the United States military and naval bases in the islands.

Splitting the atom. Upon the death of President Roosevelt in April 1945, the tremendous task of finishing the war and planning the peace suddenly fell to the courageous, peppery new President Harry S Truman. He was a man of decision destined to make some of the most fateful decisions in modern history. And he was prepared for great decisions. Ever since he was a young man, he had been reading books of history. He especially admired President Jackson and President Lincoln. He knew how earlier American Presidents had shaped the future. When he took his oath of office, he felt overwhelmed, and he asked the nation to pray for him.

His first great decision was on a subject so secret that even as Vice-President he had not heard of it. It concerned the colossal American project that had already nearly succeeded—to build an atomic bomb. "Atom" was a word of Greek origin that meant something unbreakable. It was believed to be the smallest possible unit of matter. To create a bomb by the splitting of tiny atoms would be the most gigantic, most costly single scientific effort of the war. This startling achievement would change the relations between all nations, possibly for the rest of human history.

Those who made the American bomb possible were (in addition to many American scientists) a "Who's Who" of world science. From Germany came the greatest physicist of the age, Albert Einstein. Because he was a Jew, the Nazis had taken away his German citizenship and seized his property. From Italy, as a refugee from

American infantry wade ashore from amphibious landing craft onto Leyte Island in the Philippines. The jungle still smolders from the pre-attack naval and air bombardment.

Mussolini, came the brilliant Enrico Fermi, who was one of the first to propose an atomic bomb as a practical possibility. Scientists, engineers, and mathematicians came also from Hungary, Austria, Denmark, and Czechoslovakia—refugees from all the enslaved parts of Europe. The barbarism of the enemies had brought together in the United States the greatest scientific minds of the age.

To build an atomic bomb certain theoretical questions first had to be answered. Was it really possible to achieve "the controlled release of atomic energy"? If it was possible to break the atom, and create a "chain reaction," then an enormous amount of energy would be released even from one atom. If a chain reaction could be started, then when one atom was split it would split the other atoms touching it, and a fantastic blast of energy would suddenly explode. But could it be done? And if a chain reaction was started, could it be controlled so that one exploding atom would not destroy the world? These were the two great practical questions.

The answer came at 3:25 on the afternoon of December 2, 1942, in a secret laboratory that had been a squash court on the campus of the University of Chicago. Professor Enrico Fermi supervised the experiment. When everything was prepared, he gave the signal to pull out the control rod. Suddenly the Geiger counters resounded with telltale clicks from the radiation made by the successful breaking up of uranium atoms. The dignified scientists let out a cheer. They had produced a chain reaction that transformed matter into energy. And they had been able to prevent it from blowing them up! The Atomic Age had begun.

One of the physicists hurried to the telephone and gave the code message to be relayed to the President of the United States.

"You'll be interested to know," he reported with mock casualness, "that the Italian navigator has just landed in the New World. The earth was not as large as he had estimated, and he arrived in the New World sooner than he had expected."

After the victory over Germany, this dramatic poster, with a map of the world as background, symbolically showed the full force of the Allies being directed at Japan.

"Is that so?" he was asked. "Were the natives friendly?"

"Everyone landed safe and happy." This meant that Professor Fermi (the "Italian navigator") had succeeded even ahead of schedule. The "New World" was, of course, the uncharted world of atomic power.

■ **The atomic bomb.** In May 1942, only seven
Perspec- months before the Fermi experiment suc-
tives ceeded, President Roosevelt had set up the
Topic super-secret Manhattan Project to prepare to build a bomb. But it took another three years and a cost of $2 billion for the Manhattan Project to do the job.

At 5:30 on the morning of July 16, 1945, on a remote desert near Alamogordo, New Mexico, the moment came to prove that the bold thinking of the scientists could be matched by the practical know-how of engineers. The answer required no delicate Geiger counter to detect it. The world's first atomic bomb exploded—with a blinding flash and a towering mushroom cloud ⋹ such as had never been seen before.

By the time the bomb was perfected, the Germans and Italians had already surrendered. Of the enemies now only Japan remained. On July 26 the Allied leaders gave the Japanese a solemn warning that "the alternative to surrender is prompt and utter destruction." Still they did not surrender.

Should the United States use the atomic

⋹ **Continuity and Change: Conflict** Point out to students that the multi-billion dollar development and use of the first atomic bomb on July 16, 1945 would lead the United States into an arms race with the Soviet Union. Forty years later, on December 7, 1987, Soviet General Secretary Gorbachev and President Reagan signed the Intermediate Nuclear Force (INF) Treaty, which called for the removal and destruction of all missiles with ranges of 300 to 3400 miles from Eastern and Western Europe. This was the first time in history when politicians aimed to reduce the size of weapons forces rather than to build them up. (See p.927.)

bomb? No one knew how long Japan would hold out. Despite the terrifying fire raid of March 10, 1945, when more than 100,000 people died and much of Tokyo was destroyed, the Japanese militarists appeared determined to resist. If the war dragged on and Americans had to invade Japan, it might cost a million lives. The atomic bomb, President Truman knew, might kill many thousands of innocent Japanese. But life for life, the odds were that it would cost less.

On August 6, 1945, three weeks after that first blinding blast on the New Mexico desert, a single American B-29 dropped an atomic bomb on Hiroshima. About 75,000 people were killed outright. Tens of thousands more perished later from wounds or radiation. The Japanese still held on. A few days later another plane dropped an atomic bomb on Nagasaki. Then the Japanese finally caved in. They announced ☑ their surrender on August 14, 1945.

The cost of World War II. The human cost of World War II can never be finally known. The United States lost 292,000 lives in combat, over five times the toll of World War I. Without the brilliant medical advances of the war—the blood banks and wonder drugs, the skilled

In 1945 Nagasaki, Japan, like Hiroshima, was obliterated by an atomic bomb. Only reinforced concrete buildings remained standing after the blast. Everything else was blown away.

United Press International Photo

☑ See "Lesson Plan," p. 674E for **Writing Process Activity: Demonstrating Reasoned Judgment** relating to the atomic bomb and the end of World War II.

World War II, Pacific Theater, 1942-1945

← MacArthur
← Nimitz
✕ Allied Victory
▨ Japanese-Controlled Territory 1942

0 — 1200 Miles
0 — 1200 Kilometers

5. UNITED STATES DROPS ATOMIC BOMBS ON HIROSHIMA AND NAGASAKI, AUGUST 6 AND 9, 1945

4. ALLIES TAKE IWO JIMA AND OKINAWA, FEBRUARY-JUNE, 1945

3. BATTLE OF LEYTE GULF, OCTOBER 23-25, 1944

2. ALLIED FORCES CAPTURE TARAWA, 1943

1. BATTLE FOR GUADALCANAL, AUGUST 7, 1942 - FEBRUARY 3, 1943

---

doctors and nurses—the number of combat deaths would have been far higher. Still, the cost for the United States was small compared to the rest of the world, where perhaps 60 million died— 27 million Russians, 4 million Germans, 2 million Japanese, possibly 22 million Chinese, and millions of others. Most horrible of all was the Nazis' gigantic crime, the Holocaust (from the Greek *holo*, "whole," and *kaustos*, "burnt"). This was their attempt to kill all European Jews. Six million Jews were exterminated in gas chambers and concentration camps.

(p. 701)

At last World War II was over. The menace from Germany and Japan was destroyed. But the world was haunted by a host of new fears. These had been created by the war itself.

See "Section 4 Review answers," p. 674E.

Section 4 Review

1. Identify or explain: Douglas MacArthur, Albert Einstein, Enrico Fermi, Manhattan Project, Holocaust.

2. Locate: New Guinea, Mindanao, Tarawa, Kwajalein, Saipan, Iwo Jima, Okinawa, Leyte Gulf, Luzon, Hiroshima, Nagasaki.

3. What was the Allied strategy in the Pacific in 1943–1944? Name the major battles.

4. **Critical Thinking: Predicting Consequences.** How did Truman's decision to use the atomic bomb forever change the nature of international relations?

⊕ **Geography and History: Location** Have students look at the map above and answer the following questions: Which Japanese-controlled territory on the map is farthest North? (Manchuria.) What battle did MacArthur's forces fight after leaving Manila? (Okinawa.) According to the map, what were the last two islands captured by the Americans? (Okinawa and Iwo Jima.)

Chapter 27 Review

See "Chapter Review answers," p. 674E.

Focusing on Ideas

1. From 1939 to 1943 the number of workers in nonfarm jobs jumped from 30 million to 42 million. How was the rapid expansion of the labor force achieved at a time when the armed forces were growing by more than 8 million people?

2. How did technological advances change warfare in World War II from what it had been in World War I? Give examples.

3. How did "the tide turn" in late 1942 and early 1943?

4. How did the "Good Neighbor policy" pay dividends in World War II?

Taking a Critical Look

1. **Making Comparisons.** For the civilian population, how did wartime hardships compare with the depression hardships a few years earlier?

2. **Checking Consistency.** What were some major differences between the war against Germany and the war against Japan?

Your Region in History

1. **Geography.** Identify any military camps or other armed forces facilities in your state that served the war effort between 1940 and 1945.

2. **Culture.** Find out how high school students in your area helped on the home front.

3. **Economics.** What kinds of goods were produced in your community or state to aid the war effort in World War II?

Historical Facts and Figures

Predicting Consequences. Study the graph below to help answer the following questions: (a) What percentage of all the soldiers who died in World War II were citizens of the Soviet Union? Of Britain? (b) What percentage of wounded soldiers were German citizens? Americans? (c) What nation suffered the most civilian deaths during World War II? (d) Why were there so few American civilian deaths? (e) How might the overall number of casualties experienced by the Soviets have affected Soviet society and its attitudes toward war?

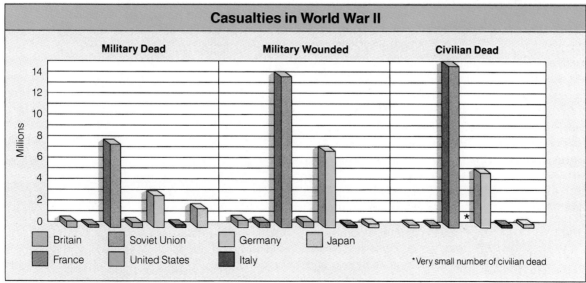

Source: *The Second World War*, Henri Michel

✄ **Critical Thinking Activity: Recognizing Cause and Effect** What did the war cost? Have students work in small groups to prepare a sales receipt for the war, including lives lost, lives altered, land destroyed, and so on. Have each group present their total bill as a poster. Use these posters as a basis for the class to write a thesis statement about the "cost" of World War II.

MAKING CONNECTIONS
Unit 9

This unit began on page 619 with Franklin D. Roosevelt's observation that strong leadership and decisive action would guide America's future:

"The people of the United States have not failed, . . . they want direct, vigorous action."

This conclusion was supported by the three unit themes that are reprinted in **dark type** below. Use the time line and the information in Unit 9 to answer the questions that follow the themes.

THEMES IN HISTORY

Using "Making Connections": Have students look at the unit themes printed in dark type. Explain that each event on the time line relates to one of these themes. Ask students to decide which events are related to which theme. Students should use events from the time line in their answers and explain how events are related. Have students go back through the text of Unit 9 to find other events related to the unit themes.

1. **Franklin Roosevelt's strong leadership and New Deal programs ease the impact of the Great Depression on poverty-stricken Americans.** GOVERNMENT AND POLITICS
   What elements of Franklin Roosevelt's New Deal were a radical departure from earlier government programs? (Making Comparisons)

2. **The rise of the dictators and fascism in Europe threatens the peace of the entire world.** ETHICS AND VALUES
   What conditions in the world made it possible for Nazism and fascism to take root and spread throughout Europe? (Recognizing Cause and Effect)

3. **The allied nations triumph in a world war on two fronts, but with victory comes a host of new fears and problems.** CONFLICT
   What lessons for the future might world leaders have learned from World War II? (Predicting Consequences)

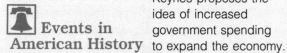 **Events in American History**

1930s
Keynes proposes the idea of increased government spending to expand the economy.

1934
The Securities and Exchange Commission is set up to regulate the stock market.

1936
Congress passes neutrality laws preventing the United States from arming either side in the Spanish Civil War.

1930	1932	1934	1936

Events in World History

1930s
Depression and reparations required by Versailles Treaty leave German economic and political system unstable.

1935
Attempting to create an empire, Italian troops invade Ethiopia.

1936
The Spanish Civil War begins as the Fascists and republicans fight for control.

1943
The Works Progress Administration has spent $11 billion to employ 8.5 million people.

1945
Churchill, Roosevelt, and Stalin meet in Yalta and plan for the Nazi surrender.

1945
The United States reveals a devastating new weapon in dropping the atomic bomb on Hiroshima and Nagasaki.

1941
The Japanese attack Pearl Harbor, and the United States enters World War II.

| 1938 | 1940 | 1942 | 1944 | 1946 | 1948 |

1939
Stalin and Hitler sign a nonaggression pact and agree to divide Poland.

1938
Neville Chamberlain rejects FDR's proposed international conference on armaments and economic security.

Unit 10

Postwar Problems 1945–1960

With the explosion of the first atomic bomb in New Mexico on July 16, 1945, a new era in the history of the world had begun. Under the menacing shadow of the atomic bomb, war between great powers could never again be the same. Isolation was no longer possible. Could the United States shape a foreign policy for survival in this frightening world?

In the postwar age, the American ways of living, thinking, and doing would be transformed. Magic machines would change the meaning of space and time. Faraway events would be seen in everybody's living room. Now millions, in their two-week vacations, could jet to Paris or Rome or Tokyo and see the world for themselves. Computers took over old jobs and created new jobs. Suburbs and highways changed the places where people lived and worked, went to school and shopped. The nation was ruled by machines that no one had imagined a few years before. Could Americans still preserve the self-government of the simpler days of the Republic? Could a machine-America keep alive the spirit of adventure that had conquered a continent?

THEMES IN HISTORY

- Tensions between the United States and the Soviet Union, and the shadow of atomic weapons produce an era of "cold war." GOVERNMENT AND POLITICS

- Growing demands for racial equality produce new leadership and new government policies. SOCIAL CHANGE

- Technological advances transform American ways of living, thinking, and doing during the Truman and Eisenhower years. SCIENCE, TECHNOLOGY AND SOCIETY

◉ The smallest air current moves the parts of Alexander Calder's hanging sculptures, creating ever-changing patterns. Mobile and technically refined, they reflect qualities of the United States in the post-World War II era.
Whitney Museum Exhibit. Photo Researchers, Inc. © Farrel Grehen 1976

Chapter 28
Truman: Neither War nor Peace

Identifying Chapter Materials

Objectives	Basic Instructional Materials	Extension Materials
1 Beginnings of the Cold War ▪ Cite causes of tension between the United States and the Soviet Union after World War II. ▪ Analyze the origins of the Cold War and discuss which nation was more to blame for its early life.	**Annotated Teacher's Edition** ▪ Lesson Plans, p. 706C **Instructional Support File** ▪ Pre-Reading Activities, Unit 10, p. 1 ▪ Skill Review Activity, Unit 10, p. 4	**Documents of American History** ▪ Truman's Statement on Fundamentals of American Foreign Policy, Vol. 2, p. 503 ▪ Constitution of UNESCO, Vol. 2, p. 506 ▪ The Truman Doctrine, Vol. 2, p. 525 ▪ American Aid to Greece and Turkey, Vol. 2, p. 528 ▪ The Marshall Plan, Vol. 2, p. 532 **American History Transparencies** ▪ Time Lines, p. E31
2 Dealing with a New World ▪ Identify ways in which the United States converted to peacetime. ▪ Examine the value and legality of the Nuremberg trials.	**Annotated Teacher's Edition** ▪ Lesson Plans, pp. 706C–706D **Instructional Support File** ▪ Skill Application Activity, Unit 10, p. 5	**Documents of American History** ▪ The Atomic Energy Commission, Vol. 2, p. 518 ▪ Taft-Hartley Act, Vol. 2, p. 537 ▪ National Security Act, Vol. 2, p. 541 ▪ The North Atlantic Treaty, Vol. 2, p. 548
3 President in His Own Right ▪ Identify the causes of the second "red scare" in the United States. ▪ Discuss how the Korean War affected American opinion. ▪ Explain arguments for and against General MacArthur's threatened incursion into China.	**Annotated Teacher's Edition** ▪ Lesson Plans, pp. 706D–706E **Instructional Support File** ▪ Reading Activities, Unit 10, pp. 2–3 ▪ Critical Thinking Activity, Unit 10, p. 6 ▪ Chapter Test, Unit 10, pp. 7–10 ▪ Additional Test Questions, Unit 10, pp. 11–14	**Enrichment Support File** ▪ Korea: The Unknown War (See "In-Depth Coverage" at right.) **Suggested Secondary Sources** ▪ See chart at right. **American History Transparencies** ▪ Our Multicultural Heritage, p. C99

Providing In-Depth Coverage

Perspectives on the Korean War

In 1950 the Communist government of North Korea, backed by both the Soviet Union and the People's Republic of China, sent troops into South Korea. The United Nations called for the defense of South Korea, and they feared the spread of communism. The United States answered the call.   Led by General Douglas MacArthur, combined United States and United Nations forces finally stopped the North Koreans in South Korea and pushed them back within their own borders. MacArthur then pushed on into North Korea. The Chinese Communists rushed to the defense of their ally. The American troops fought on for two years, until July 1953, when a truce was called.

A History of the United States as an instructional program provides two types of resources you can use to offer in-depth coverage of the Korean War: the *student text* and the *Enrichment Support File*. A list of *Suggested Secondary Sources* is also provided. The chart below shows the topics that are covered in each.

THE STUDENT TEXT. Boorstin and Kelley's

A History of the United States unfolds the chronology of events, the key players, and, as an interpretive history, the controversy of the Korean War.

AMERICAN HISTORY ENRICHMENT SUPPORT FILE. This collection of primary

source readings and classroom activities provides a comprehensive explanation of the "whys" of the Korean War.

SUGGESTED SECONDARY SOURCES.

This reference list of readings by well-known historians and other commentators provides an array of perspectives on the Korean War.

Locating Instructional Materials

Detailed lesson plans for teaching Presidential imperialism as a mini-course or to study one or more elements of the Korean War in depth are offered in the following areas: in the *student text*, see individual lesson plans at the beginning of each chapter; in the *Enrichment Support File*, see page 3; for readings beyond the student text, see *Suggested Secondary Sources*.

IN-DEPTH COVERAGE OF THE KOREAN WAR		
Student Text	**Enrichment Support File**	**Suggested Secondary Sources**
▪ The Korean War, pp. 723–726, 731 ▪ Korean Civil War, pp. 723–724 ▪ United Nations Intervention, p. 724 ▪ U.S. Aid to South Korea, p. 724 ▪ Armistice, p. 731	▪ Lesson Suggestions ▪ Multimedia Resources ▪ Overview Essay/Korea: The Unknown War ▪ Literature in American History/*Your Own Beloved Sons* ▪ Biography in American History/Dwight D. Eisenhower ▪ Geography in American History/The Geographic Limitations of the War in Korea ▪ Great Debates in American History/Containment vs Expansion ▪ Making Connections	▪ *The Forgotten War: America in Korea* by Clay Blair, pp. 3–115. ▪ *The Origins of the Korean War: Liberation and the Emergence of Separate Regimes, 1945–1947* by Bruce Cummings, pp. 179–213. ▪ *The Wrong War: American Foreign Policy and the Dimensions of the Korean Conflict, 1950–1953* by Rosemary Foot, pp. 83–130. ▪ *A Short History of the Korean War* by James Stokesbury, pp. 79–96.

Beginnings of the Cold War

FOCUS

To introduce the lesson, ask: What is the cold war? Give students examples of extreme tensions in the cold war, such as the Berlin blockade, the Korean war, the Soviet invasion of Hungary, the Cuban revolution, the Bay of Pigs invasion, the Cuban missile crisis, the Vietnam War, the Soviet invasion of Czechoslovakia, the Sino-Soviet conflict, the normalization of U.S. relations with China, the Soviet invasion of Afghanistan, the U.S. embargo on grain shipments to the Soviets, the Olympic boycotts, the rise of Solidarity and the imposition of martial law in Poland, and so forth.

Developing Vocabulary

The words listed in the chapter are essential terms for reading and understanding particular sections of the chapter. The page number after each term indicates the page of its first or most important appearance in the chapter. These terms are defined in the text Glossary (text pages 1000–1011).

iron curtain (page 708); **satellite nations** (page 711); **coup d'etat** (page 711); **containment** (page 711).

INSTRUCT

Explain

How did the UN differ from the League of Nations?

★ Independent Activity

Identifying Central Issues Ask students to work independently to construct a chart outlining the differences between the Truman Doctrine, the Marshall Plan, and the Four Point Program.

Section Review Answers

Section 1, page 711

1. a) division of U.N. which has the power to look into disputes and act against any nation threatening the peace. b) how Churchill described the Soviet's hold on Eastern Europe. c) diplomat who advocated the containment policy. d) Under Secretary of State who thought that the Soviets wished to conquer the world. e) leader of Yugoslavia who broke with Moscow in 1948. f) Secretary of State who proposed the aid program known as the Marshall Plan. g) holds that the United States must prevent the Soviet Union from expanding its power and influence. h) countries domi-

nated by the Soviet Union. 2. Dumbarton Oaks is an estate in Washington, D.C. Latvia, Lithuania, Estonia, and the Black Sea are shown on page 716. Trieste is on the map on page 680. Iran is on page 746. 3. The General Assembly includes delegates from every member nation. It prepares the UN budget, admits new members, and elects members to UN agencies; in addition, it can debate any issue within the scope of its character and make recommendations. The Security Council investigates disputes and can take action to preserve peace. It includes five permanent members plus ten member nations elected for two-year terms. The Secretariat manages the daily affairs of the United Nations. The International Court of Justice deals with legal questions that arise between members of the UN. 4. The Baruch plan proposed a world agency to control atomic energy and inspect all atomic-energy plants. The plan was not put into effect because the Soviet Union insisted on having a veto over the agency and demanded that the United States destroy its atomic weapons before the plan's controls were set up. 5. Churchill and Kennan both warned that the Soviets would seek to expand their power. 6. The Marshall Plan was proposed to prevent the spread of communism in Europe by providing needed aid. Supporters argued that containing communism was essential for our own security and for our economy. Billions of dollars were sent to Europe. The plan was a great success; communism did not spread to Western Europe and that area experienced a remarkable economic recovery. 7. Britain was stopping its aid to the Greek government, which was engaged in a civil war, and Truman feared that Communists would take over there.

CLOSE

To conclude the lesson, assign a one-page essay for homework on the question, "Who primarily caused the Cold War?" Have students find three pieces of evidence to support their arguments and cite them in footnotes.

Dealing with a New World

FOCUS

To introduce the lesson, ask students to compare the postwar United States in 1946–1948 to the postwar nation in 1919–1920.

Developing Vocabulary

G.I. (page 712); **G.I. Bill of Rights** (page 712); **closed shop** (page 714); **union shop** (page 714);

right-to-work laws (page 714); **lockout** (page 714); **desegregation** (page 715); **war criminals** (page 716); **cold war** (page 717); **NATO** (page 717); **bipartisan** (page 719).

INSTRUCT

Explain

The postwar United States faced problems of providing veterans' aid, unemployment, labor unrest, and the Soviet blockade of Berlin.

☑ Writing Process Activity

Identifying Central Issues Ask students to imagine they are union workers after World War II. In preparation for writing a speech they will deliver to their fellow workers, ask them to brainstorm details about working conditions and about their reactions to the Taft–Hartley Act. Have students begin their speech with a topic sentence that makes their position clear, and ask them to support their main idea with specific examples. As they revise, students should check for clear organization and persuasive language. After they proofread, ask students to deliver their speeches to the class.

Section Review Answers

Section 2, page 720

1. a) provided numerous benefits to veterans. b) created to control the use of atomic energy and encourage its peaceful use. c) passed to help provide jobs. d) prohibited any President after Truman from serving more than two full terms. e) changed the line of succession in the event of a President's death. f) Truman's plan for the nation. g) set up a new structure for the nation's defense establishment. h) The Central Intelligence Agency was the first permanent, worldwide intelligence service in United States history. i) placed Nazi leaders on trial for war crimes. j) set up by the Soviet Union in 1948 to stop the Western powers from forming one West German government. k) created NATO. 2. Demobilization in 1946 was very rapid after riots among the troops. The veterans received extensive help from the GI Bill of Rights. 3. Truman asked Congress to declare a state of emergency whenever a strike endangered national safety, to deny employment benefits to workers who continued to strike, and to draft them. The strikers returned to work before the Senate voted on the bill. Truman wanted to continue wartime price controls in response to the inflation of 1946. Congress refused, and wholesale prices soared. 4. It was passed to curb the power of unions and to control corruption and Communist influence. The law outlawed the closed shop, allowed states to pass "right-to-work" laws, and gave the President the power in some strikes to

call for a "cooling off period." 5. The Marshall Plan, the Truman Doctrine, and the National Security Act; opposed Truman when it passed a tax cut that favored the wealthy over Truman's veto and when it rejected his requests to help public housing, expand Social Security, and aid education. 6. Truman was a long-time, strong supporter of civil rights. 7. In 1948 the United States and Western European nations formed the German Federated Republic (West Germany) in 1949. The Soviet Union then responded by establishing the German Democratic Republic in East Germany. 8. Republican Thomas Dewey—a rather reserved, dignified, formal man—opposed the homey and feisty Democrat Harry Truman. In addition, two groups split from the Democrats and ran their own candidates. The Republicans said it was "Time for a change." The Democrats called for a repeal of the Taft-Hartley Act, recognition of Israel, and laws to protect civil rights. With the help of the farm vote, Truman won an upset victory, and the Democrats took control of Congress. 9. NATO was the first alliance that the United States ever entered in peacetime.

CLOSE

To conclude the lesson, ask students to make a chart showing the presidential succession before and after enactment of the Twenty-second Amendment.

Section 3 (pages 721–726)

President in His Own Right

FOCUS

To introduce the lesson, break the class up into small groups and have them discuss the following questions: Against whom was the "second red scare" directed? What situations and events sparked it? What actions were taken to meet the real and assumed threats? Who were some of the leading "red hunters"? How were the two "red scares" alike, and how were they different? (Students will have to review pages 577–580 to answer this question. Note the factor of political ambition in both "scares"—Palmer, Nixon, and McCarthy.)

Developing Vocabulary

totalitarianism (page 723); **parallel** (page 723).

INSTRUCT

Explain

Communist expansionism and McCarthyism led to the second "red scare."

❧ Cooperative Learning Activity

Distinguishing False from Accurate Images Explain that students will judge whether or not Harry S Truman was in fact as the text describes him, "equal to all his great decisions," "courageous," and "decisive." Break the class into small groups and have each group choose a discussion leader and a recorder. Assign half of the groups to list facts from the text supporting the image of Truman as a great president. Have the remaining groups list facts contradicting this image. When all groups have completed their lists, bring the class together to discuss Truman's strengths and weaknesses, successes and failures.

Section Review Answers

Section 3, page 726

1. a) held public hearings during the "second red scare." b) accused of being a spy by Chambers. c) led the anti-Communist forces that fled China. d) led the Chinese Communists. e) led an investigation of "communists" in government. f), g) passed to restrict the operation and immigration of Communists. h) convicted of spying and executed in 1953. i) the elected President of South Korea in 1950. j) Chairman of the Joint Chiefs of Staff during the Korean War. k) commanded the Eighth Army in Korea. l) security treaty signed by Australia, New Zealand, and the United States in 1951. 2. Taiwan is shown on the map on page 746. All other locations are on the map on page 725. 3. Congress raised the minimum wage, extended Social Security, funded housing programs, and increased funds for the TVA, rural electricity, and water projects. On the other hand, it did not repeal the Taft-Hartley law, and rejected the plans for civil rights laws, national health insurance, and aid to education. 4. The Truman administration ordered loyalty checks on all federal employees and declared 90 organizations "disloyal." HUAC held hearings that ruined reputations and spurred the creation of black lists. 5. When South Korea mobilized its army and announced that it would liberate North Korea, North Korea invaded the South. Truman asked the UN to take action and send arms and naval and air support to South Korea. Truman sent American troops into battle when the UN called on member nations to aid South Korea. 6. At first North Korean forces pushed back South Korean and UN troops. But by fall, 1950, UN forces had recaptured Seoul. In October, UN forces crossed the 38th parallel. Truman dismissed MacArthur for publicly denouncing the decision of Truman and the Joint Chiefs to keep the war inside Korea. 7. Many Americans could not understand the victory of Communists in China. The charge that there were Communists in the United States government provided an explanation and led to the "second red scare."

CLOSE

To conclude the lesson, have students turn to the map on page 725 and discuss the Korean War. Ask: How did the war affect American popular opinion? (It provided an ideal background for Senator McCarthy's claims that Communists in the United States government seriously impeded America's ability to halt the spread of communism.)

Chapter Review Answers
Focusing on Ideas

1. Soviet Union intent on expansion; UN charter demanded presence of the U.S., the strongest military and economic power whose resources required economic reconstruction. 2. Insistence on veto power in UN; rejection of atomic-energy plan; violation of Yalta; Greek support of rebels; pressure on Turkey; spy rings; reluctance to withdraw troops from Iran; unwillingness to share European reconstruction; obstruction of peace plan for Germany. 3. Counteract promises of economic progress and exploitation of unrest. Expanded markets for U.S. goods; loans used to buy U.S. products; gifts of products to remove surpluses which depress prices. 4. Truman's loyalty check; McCarran Act, McCarran-Walter immigration act; House UnAmerican Activities Committee; weak responses to McCarthyism.

Taking a Critical Look

1. Employers: all provisions. Union leaders: most opposed to banning closed shops; "right-to-work" laws. Also, "cooling off" period and ban on political contributions. 2. Accomplishments: Many foreign policy decisions; maintaining and extending New Deal reforms; support of civil rights. Failures: timidity on opposing "second red scare;" ignoring China's warnings about North Korea; abrasive behavior.

Your Region in History

1–3. Answers will vary depending on your region. Consult your local library or historical society.

Historical Facts and Figures

(a) Southwest—France; southeast—U.S.; northwest—Britain; northeast—Soviet Union; (b) the northeast; (c) Western: the Benelux countries; northern Denmark; eastern: Poland, Czecholslovakia, southern: Switzerland, Austria. (d) Allies couldn't agree.

Chapter 28

Truman: Neither War nor Peace

At the end of World War II, the United States faced a world in ashes. The old order was burnt out, and nothing had arisen to take its place. Some Americans yearned to return to the former isolation of the Western Hemisphere. But world trade was more important than ever before. To prosper, the United States had to exchange goods with the nations of Europe, Asia, and Africa. Now, with airplanes and atomic weapons, the battlefield was everywhere. On this new-fashioned planet, Americans could not withdraw. The end of the war did not break our ties with Europe. And before long we would be drawn into the battles of Asia.

French artist Marc Chagall made this stained-glass window at the United Nations in New York City as a memorial for UN Secretary-General Dag Hammarskjöld and 15 who died with him in a plane crash in 1961.

Courtesy, United Nations

See "Lesson Plan," p. 706C.

1. Beginnings of the cold war

The United States and Great Britain had been the allies of Soviet Russia for only one reason—to defeat Adolf Hitler. Since the two Western powers had never trusted Stalin, they had not even told him about the atomic bomb. The Communist leaders feared the capitalist nations but expected the whole world to become Communist. They hoped for the collapse of the democracies.

Still, American leaders thought that these differences would not have to bring on another war. Perhaps the Soviets could be persuaded to join a new and stronger League of Nations, where capitalists and Communists might talk to each other instead of shoot at each other. Before long, Americans would discover that the Soviet leaders had a very different view of the future.

Harry S Truman. The day after taking the oath of office, President Truman held a press conference. "Last night," he told the reporters in his midwestern twang, "the moon, the stars, and all the planets fell on me." To the surprise of many (including, perhaps, the new President himself), Harry S Truman proved equal to all his great decisions.

Harry Truman was born in Lamar, Missouri, in 1884. After high school, he worked as a bank clerk and then ran the family farm. In World War I, he served in the field artillery and rose to the rank of major. When the war was over, he started a clothing business, which failed during the postwar recession. Between 1922 and 1934 he was the elected County Judge (county commissioner) in Jackson County, Missouri. He studied law in night school.

In 1934, with the help of the political machine run by Kansas City's boss, Tom Pendergast, Truman was elected to the United States Senate. At that point he was considered only a routine machine politician. But Truman soon became known for his hard work, his intelligence, and his fairness. As head of the Senate Committee Investigating the National Defense Program during World War II, he held the national spotlight.

Building a new world organization. In 1943 Britain, the United States, and Russia had agreed to set up a new organization to replace the League of Nations. At the beautiful Dumbarton Oaks estate in Washington in 1944, China joined these three to make detailed plans. Then, on April 12 the next year, 200 delegates from 50 nations met in San Francisco to form the United Nations (UN). This was not a peace conference, for the war was still being fought on all fronts.

The Soviet Union and the United States disagreed over the use of the veto in the Security Council. They both thought there should be a veto so the great powers could protect themselves from unfavorable United Nations decisions. But on matters not concerning themselves directly, Russia and the United States parted company. The Soviets thought that any action should be able to be vetoed. The United States disagreed, fearing that this would paralyze the new organization. Despite these differences, a charter emerged for the United Nations. After World War I the Senate had rejected the League of Nations. But now, on July 28, 1945, the Senate ratified the United Nations charter by the decisive vote of 82–2.

The UN aimed to preserve the peace and provide a better life for all. The General Assembly included delegates from every member nation. There each nation had one vote, except for the USSR, which had three votes—one for itself and one each for the Ukraine and Byelorussia. This concession to Russia had been offered at Yalta to persuade the Soviets to join the UN. The General Assembly could discuss any subject within the scope of the charter. And it made recommendations to the small and powerful Security Council. The Assembly fixed the UN budget, admitted new members approved by the Security Council, and elected member nations to the many UN agencies.

The Security Council had eleven (later fifteen) members. Of these the Big Five (United States, Britain, the Soviet Union, France, and China) had permanent seats and the right to a veto. The six other members were elected for two-year terms but had no veto. This Security Council had the power to look into disputes and to

Department of Energy

Postwar leaders faced the task of controlling the fearsome power of the atom bomb.

act against any nation that threatened the peace.

The Secretariat, headed by a Secretary-General, would handle the UN's day-to-day affairs. Trygve Lie of Norway was the first person to head this office. An American, Dr. Ralph Bunche, the grandson of a former slave, served for many years as Under Secretary.

The International Court of Justice was the court for the UN. It could deal with legal questions that arose between members. Many other agencies were set up under the Economic and Social Council (UNESCO) to build the world community. The United Nations Relief and Rehabilitation Administration (UNRRA) was financed mainly by the United States. It supplied food and clothing to nations devastated by the war.

Controlling the atom. What could the UN do to control the menacing new power of the atom? In June 1946 Bernard Baruch, for the United States, proposed a world agency with control over atomic energy and the right to inspect atomic-energy plants anywhere. If the inspection system was set up, the United States said it would destroy its atomic bombs. Under Baruch's scheme no vetoes would be allowed. But Russia once again sabotaged the plan by insisting on its right to veto. The Soviets demanded that the United States destroy its weapons even before the new controls were created. As a result, there was no progress.

Problems with the Russians. The dispute over the atom was only one signal of the widening gulf between the United States and Russia. Time after time the Soviets refused to live up to their promises. At Yalta Stalin had pledged to hold free elections in Poland for the formation of a new government. Instead he forced a Communist government on the Poles. The Soviets also retained their hold on the former Baltic republics (Latvia, Lithuania, and Estonia). And they supported Communist forces in Hungary, Bulgaria, and Romania. Russia's goal was to keep "friendly" states all along its borders. If those people would not vote for a Communist government, Stalin was ready to fasten it on them with guns and tanks. And if communism was crammed down the throats of the people of Eastern Europe, what about the lands that bordered those nations? Now a Communist tyranny threatened Europe.

To broadcast the new danger, Truman sponsored a speech by Winston Churchill at Westminster College in Fulton, Missouri. There on March 5, 1946, the eloquent Churchill sounded the alarm. "From Stettin in the Baltic to Trieste in the Adriatic an iron curtain has descended across the Continent," he warned. "I do not believe that Soviet Russia desires war. What they desire is the fruits of war and the indefinite expansion of their power and doctrines."

Continuity and Change: Government and Politics Point out to students that the Truman Doctrine represents a change in the United States' attitude toward its own role in foreign affairs. The Monroe Doctrine and the Roosevelt Corollary were essentially isolationist. Now the United States declared itself an active participant in world affairs. (See pp. 217 and 542.)

Churchill's words were reinforced by Russia's failure to keep its promise to remove its troops from Iran. The Soviets were also squeezing Turkey to give them military bases and control of the straits leading from the Black Sea bordering southern Russia to the Mediterranean. Then the Russian navy could move freely back and forth.

In Greece, civil war erupted in the fall of 1946. The right-wing government was under attack by Communist insurgents supported from the neighboring Communist countries. Would the Soviets try to force their ways on the world? A Soviet spy ring in Canada (including a member of the Canadian parliament) was exposed. Atomic secrets, it was learned, had been sent to Russia.

Warnings about Russia.

Meanwhile some thoughtful American leaders were alarmed by the Soviet threat to the free world. One was the learned George F. Kennan, our minister-counselor in Moscow. Another was our Under Secretary of State, the suave and cultivated Dean Acheson. They believed that the Russian Communists intended to conquer the world. As Kennan warned in a long telegram to the State Department from Moscow in February 1946, Russia must be "contained" within its present limits. Soviet communism would then either collapse from within or the Russian people would force a change in policy.

Kennan and Acheson—and President Truman himself—believed that if Hitler had been stopped at Munich instead of being "appeased," World War II might never have happened. Now, to prevent a third world war, the United States must stand up to Russia. And they were encouraged in this belief by events in Iran. After a strong warning from Britain and the United States (and the threat of force), Russia withdrew its troops from Iran in May 1946.

The Greek civil war.

By the beginning of 1947 the situation in Greece was serious. Great Britain had been sending troops and money to the Greek government. Still the British had problems enough of their own at home. They could no longer afford to support the anti-Communist cause in Greece. Without that support the right-wing government would probably fall and the Communists would take over. Americans feared that this would put the USSR in control. "A highly possible Soviet breakthrough might open three continents to Soviet penetration," Acheson warned. "Like apples in a barrel infected by one rotten one, the corruption of Greece would infect" Asia, Africa, and Europe.

The Truman Doctrine.

Acheson's appraisal of the situation was probably overdrawn. In 1948 Yugoslavia's ruling Communists, under Marshal Tito, would break with Moscow. Like the Yugoslavs, the Greek leftists were not just another wing of Soviet Russia. But Acheson did not know that. From his view the withdrawal of British support meant the Communists would take command and Stalin would be in charge.

To prevent this, Secretary of State George Marshall, working with Acheson, quickly devised a program of military and economic aid for Greece. Marshall had been Chief of Staff of the Army during World War II. Truman sent the program to a special session of Congress in March 1947. He asked $300 million for military and economic aid to Greece and $100 million for aid to Turkey. He also asked Congress to allow him to send civilian and military personnel to Greece and Turkey to oversee the use of our aid and to train their people. "It must be the policy of the United States," Truman declared, "to support free peoples who are resisting attempted subjugation by armed minorities or by outside pressure. . . . We must assist free people to work out their own destinies in their own way." This was called "the Truman Doctrine." ⩶

The Greek-Turkish Aid bill became law in May (p. 708) 1947. Congress and the President declared that the United States was threatened wherever Communists challenged. To oppose Communist expansion, peacetime military aid to other countries would be a regular tool of our diplomacy. The Truman Doctrine would guide the foreign policy of the United States for a ✄ generation.

The Russians denounced the aid bill as an invitation to war. Critics at home (led by former Vice-President and now Secretary of Commerce

✄ Critical Thinking Activity: Identifying Central Issues How have presidential doctrines reflected the mood of the era? Remind students that since 1823 the United States had been given three significant doctrines describing our relationship to the rest of the world. As a class build a chart listing each policy (the Monroe Doctrine, Roosevelt Corollary, Truman Doctrine); its description; factors influencing the doctrine; and ways that each policy reflected the mood of the nation. Ask students to determine what common threads exist between these policies.

Shown next to President Truman in 1950 are Dean Acheson (left) and George Marshall (right), the main architects and managers of foreign policy in the Truman years.

Henry Wallace) did not share President Truman's distrust of the Soviets. For opposing his "get tough" policy, Truman fired Wallace. Meanwhile United States aid—especially military advisers and equipment—helped defeat Communist and other guerrilla forces in Greece and Turkey. This weakened Soviet influence there.

Marshall proposes a plan. In May 1947, while Congress was debating the Truman Doctrine, Winston Churchill described Europe as "a rubble heap, a charnel house, a breeding ground of pestilence and hate." The home-grown Communist parties of France and Italy (supported by the Soviets) became ever stronger. It seemed that nothing could prevent the Communist conquest of Europe.

The Policy Planning Staff of the State Department set itself a difficult task. Was there some way, short of war, to stop the Communist advance and "contain" the Russians? Could a new

plan of economic aid somehow preserve free governments? Poverty and unemployment made people desperate and brought dictators to power. Prosperity and jobs could save democracy. But how could war-torn Europe be healed? The Truman Doctrine was a way to stop the advance of communism. But how could we advance freedom?

In his memorable speech at Harvard University on June 5, 1947, Secretary of State Marshall proposed a plan. During the next three or four years the United States ought to help Europe with substantial gifts to prevent "economic, social, and political deterioration of a very serious character." This would not be military aid but would be directed "against hunger, poverty, desperation, and chaos."

Russia was invited to join, but the Soviets refused to take part. And they kept Poland and Czechoslovakia (which was still attempting to keep free of Soviet domination) along with the

More from Boorstin: "The Marshall Plan after World War II was, of course, a dramatic departure from earlier American policy: a leap from the war-debt psychology of foreign aid, from the vocabulary of the banker to that of the missionary, the humanitarian, and the social scientist. After World War I, politicians had talked of reparation and 'honest debtors,' of interest rates and the capacity of countries to pay back what they had borrowed. Now, after World War II, they were talking about standards of living." (From *The Americans: The Democratic Experience*)

other East European "satellite" nations from accepting American aid. By staying out, the Russians made it easier to persuade Congress to pass the plan.

The European Recovery Program. For ten months Congress debated the pros and cons. Supporters of Marshall's European Recovery Program (ERP) explained that it was necessary for our own defense and economic survival. Opponents, led by Senator Robert Taft of Ohio, charged that it would cost far too much. It would also expose us to new dangers abroad, which might lead to another world war. On the left, Henry Wallace denounced the plan as an attack on Russia—a "Martial Plan."

A bloodless Communist coup d'etat in Czechoslovakia in February 1948 helped the supporters of ERP. Senator Taft himself voted for the bill, and the measure was passed by large majorities in both houses of Congress. The Marshall Plan, signed into law by President Truman on April 3, 1948, provided $5.3 billion for European recovery over the following year. The United States was now committed to save Western Europe. "Containing" Soviet Russia, as Ambassador Kennan had urged, would not only strengthen American defense. It would also create new markets for our goods.

As it turned out, ERP was a brilliant success. Of the $12 billion spent in Marshall aid, more than half went to Britain, France, and West Germany. By 1950 these nations of Europe had increased their output by 25 percent over prewar levels. As European nations became more prosperous, they could buy more of our goods. This in turn would help keep our economy booming.

The Point Four program. The Marshall Plan was later followed by another generous program of aid, also intended to fight communism by promoting economic growth. This, too, would create new markets for American farms and factories. "Point Four," it was called, because it was the fourth point in President Truman's 1949 inaugural address. This program would give economic and technical aid to the poor free

nations of Asia, Africa, and Latin America. For these purposes billions of dollars were—and still are—being spent abroad.

See "Section 1 Review answers," p. 706C.

Section 1 Review

1. Identify or explain: Security Council, "iron curtain," George Kennan, Dean Acheson, President Tito, George C. Marshall, containment policy, "satellite" nations.
2. Locate: Dumbarton Oaks, Baltic republics, Trieste, Iran, Black Sea.
3. Name the chief United Nations agencies and describe their functions.
4. What was the Baruch plan for atomic energy? Why was it not put into effect?
5. What warnings about the Soviet Union were sounded by (a) Churchill and (b) Kennan?
6. Describe the Marshall Plan by giving the reason for it, its provisions, and its results.
7. **Critical Thinking: Recognizing Cause and Effect.** Why was the Truman Doctrine proclaimed in 1947?

See "Lesson Plan," p. 706C.

2. Dealing with a new world

The nation had to shift somehow to a peacetime way of life when World War II ended. How could we combat the threats of inflation and unemployment? How could we meet the pent-up demands of business and labor? How could we help men and women change over from the armed forces to civilian life? All this and more had to be accomplished under a new and untried President.

Bringing the boys home. As soon as the war ended, Truman faced extreme pressure to "bring the boys home." At first the plan was to decrease the size of the armed forces only slowly and stay alert to any new threats abroad. But when there were riots by troops who wanted to go home, the President gave in and suddenly reduced the army. By midsummer 1946 the armed forces had been cut back from 12 million to 3 million. Truman warned that this was

David Seymour/Magnum

After the Second World War the people of Europe carried on with their lives among the ruins. This woman created a flourishing garden within bombed-out walls.

"disintegration" rather than demobilization. Still the United States—the sole possessor of the atomic bomb—remained the most powerful nation on earth.

Fortunately, Congress had prepared for the return of the veterans. In June 1944 it had passed a Servicemen's Readjustment Act— usually called the "GI Bill of Rights." This provided hospitals for the sick and wounded and clinics to help the disabled. It offered payments to veterans without jobs. It gave them preference for jobs in the federal civil service. Money was earmarked to help them buy homes, farms, and businesses. Free tuition, books, and expenses for job training, college, or other advanced education were given to those who wanted them. Eight million veterans of World

War II used this educational program at a cost of $14.5 billion.

The Atomic Energy Act. How could a nation at peace use the newfound power in the atom? Both political parties agreed that the federal government had to keep control of the raw materials of atomic power. These rare metals— uranium and plutonium—were called "fissionable materials" because their atoms could be split. But the two parties disagreed on whether control should be put in the hands of civilians or of the army.

A compromise, the Atomic Energy Act, was signed by President Truman on August 1, 1946. It preserved the government monopoly of fissionable materials. A five-member civilian 📖

📖 **More from Boorstin:** "The next stage in atomic weapons research, the quest for a 'super' (or hydrogen) atomic bomb, was prodded by the revelation in 1949 that the Soviets possessed the bomb, and further dramatized the overwhelming force of this New Momentum. The moral uncertainty which briefly delayed the decision to proceed with the bigger bomb was dissolved as soon as the uncertainty over the possibility of building the new bomb was dissipated." (From *The Americans: The Democratic Experience*)

Atomic Energy Commission (AEC) was put in control. It was to encourage private and government research and development in both military and peaceful uses of atomic energy. In less than a decade the commission would employ 7000 workers and spend $2.5 billion a year.

Converting to peacetime. To help provide peacetime jobs, Congress passed the Employment Act in February 1946. A new Council of Economic Advisers would advise the President and Congress on how to create jobs and national prosperity. In fact, the nation adjusted swiftly to peace. There was no lack of jobs.

Instead, the nation was troubled by shortages of materials, by strikes, and by inflation. With the end of the war, labor, whose wages had been held down by government controls, was keen on seeking wage increases. A nationwide railroad strike threatened to tie up transportation, and the coal miners also went on strike. On President Truman's order the government seized both the railroads and the coal mines. The coal strike was soon settled, but the Engineers and Trainmen refused the compromise accepted by eighteen other railroad unions.

The angry President then asked Congress for power to declare a state of national emergency whenever a strike in a vital industry endangered the national safety. Workers who continued to strike would lose all benefits of employment and seniority and be drafted into the army. The House passed this extreme measure. But the Senate had not yet acted when the strikers returned to work.

Consumer goods—refrigerators, stoves, and cars, for example—were scarce until factories could shift to peacetime production. The new prosperity gave money to people who had waited years to buy these products. Truman wanted to continue price controls to prevent runaway inflation. But Congress refused to

War veterans picket a mine in 1946 claiming that they should have back the jobs filled by "outsiders" who were hired during the war.

Wide World Photos

extend wartime controls. Between 1946 and 1947, the wholesale prices of food, clothing, and fuel went up 25 percent.

The attitude of the 80th Congress. In the midst of the strikes and shortages, inflation at home and challenges from abroad, elections for Congress took place in the fall of 1946. The Republicans campaigned on the slogan, "Had Enough?" They won control of both houses of Congress for the first time since 1928.

The 80th Congress, elected in 1946, expressed the desire of many Americans to turn back the clock to the simpler days before World War II. They hoped to cut government spending and to undo much of the New Deal. The leading speaker for this yearning was Senator Robert A. Taft of Ohio, the son of President William Howard Taft. He was a man of sharp intelligence,

Ohio Senator Robert A. Taft was known to Americans in the 1950s as "Mr. Republican."

See "Lesson Plan," p. 706D for Writing Process Activity: Identifying Central Issues relating to union workers after World War II.

high principles, and utter honesty, although he lacked a sense of humor and was not a good mixer. Senator Taft wanted to limit United States commitments abroad and to free the individual at home. He wanted, as he said, "to break with the idea that we can legislate prosperity, legislate equality, legislate opportunity. All of these good things came in the past from free Americans working out their destiny."

The Taft-Hartley Act. The most important single piece of domestic legislation passed by this Congress was the Taft-Hartley Act of 1947. Fed up with strikes and disturbed by corruption and communism in some unions, Congress hoped to curb union power. The bill did not go as far as either Senator Taft or Congressman Hartley had wanted. But it aimed to achieve a better balance between labor and management. It outlawed the "closed shop," which had allowed only dues-paying members of a union to be hired. It did not ban the "union shop," which required workers to join a union after they had been hired. Instead the law permitted a state to enact what came to be called a "right-to-work" law. This would forbid the union shop in that state.

An interesting clause of the Taft-Hartley Act was the "cooling off" period. If the President saw that a strike might endanger the public safety, he could require the parties to "cool off" for 60 days. During this period there could be no strike or lockout, while labor and management tried to agree. The law forbade unions to make political contributions. Union officers had to sign statements that they were not Communists if they wished to bring cases before the NLRB. The law was passed over Truman's veto.

The unions bitterly attacked the Taft-Hartley Act. They called it a "slave labor" law meant to destroy their unions. But in fact the law worked quite well. In spite of the fears of union leaders, the unions continued to grow. Between 1945 and 1952 their members increased from 14.6 million to 17 million. Big labor now began to oppose big business.

An active Congress. Republican members of Congress believed that the income tax was unfair to people with higher incomes. They argued that the "soak-the-rich" taxes would destroy the profit motive. So in 1948 Congress lowered taxes all along the line, but most of all for the wealthy. When Truman vetoed the bill, it was passed over his veto. To economize, Congress cut aid to farmers and refused the President's requests to help public housing, to expand Social Security, and to aid education.

The 80th Congress was fighting an old battle. It was really attacking the New Deal and the four-term President, FDR. Congress passed the Twenty-second Amendment to limit any President after Harry Truman to two terms. This amendment was ratified by the required three-fourths of the states by February 1951.

In 1947 Congress also passed the Presidential Succession Act. Seven times in our history until then, American Presidents had died in office. In each case the Vice-President had been sworn in as Chief Executive. The next officer in line for the Presidency after the Vice-President was the Secretary of State and then on through the Cabinet in the order in which their positions were created. Cabinet members, of course, are appointed by the President. But Truman believed that the President should always be someone who had run for office and been elected by the people. The 1947 act made the succession pass from the Vice-President to the Speaker of the House and then to the presiding officer of the Senate. Cabinet members were to follow these three officials in the same order as before.

Truman tries to extend the New Deal. In the anti-New Deal 80th Congress Harry Truman found a perfect foil for his own election campaign. During 1947 and 1948 he sent to Congress bill after bill for his "Fair Deal." Most were extensions of the New Deal, but in 1948 he also asked for far-reaching civil rights laws.

Truman had long been worried by discrimination against blacks. In 1924 he had been defeated in an election because he opposed the Ku Klux Klan. In 1946 he had set up a Committee on Civil Rights to find better ways to protect the civil rights of all the people. Their report showed the evil effects of segregation, and in February 1948 Truman called upon Congress to act to end racial injustice. He asked for anti-lynching and anti-poll tax laws and a permanent Fair Employment Practices Committee, along with stronger and better-enforced laws for civil rights.

When southern senators threatened to filibuster, Congress refused to act on his proposals. Still the President did what he could on his own. In 1948 he began the desegregation of the armed forces (p. 676). He appointed the first black governor of the Virgin Islands and the first black judge in the federal courts. He strengthened the Civil Rights Section of the Justice Department. And he ordered the Department to assist blacks in their own civil rights cases.

The decisive Congress. Because Congress had failed to enact much of his Fair Deal, during the election of 1948 Truman called the 80th Congress the "Do-Nothing" Congress.

Yet this was actually one of the most effective Congresses in United States history. It put the Truman Doctrine and the Marshall Plan into effect. It passed the National Security Act, which placed all the armed forces under a new Cabinet department with a civilian Secretary of Defense. The Secretaries of the Army, Navy, and Air Force now served under him and were without Cabinet rank. The act also placed military leadership in the Joint Chiefs of Staff. It created the National Security Council, a super-Cabinet to plan and coordinate defense. This Council included the President and Vice-President, the Secretaries of State and of Defense, and the Director of the Office of Emergency Planning. The act also set up the Central Intelligence Agency (CIA)—the first permanent, worldwide intelligence agency in United States history.

The problem of Germany. After Germany surrendered, it was split up into zones of occupation among France, Great Britain, Russia, and the United States. Berlin also had been divided among all four victorious powers, but it was surrounded by Soviet-controlled territory. The leaders of the Big Three wartime powers—Stalin, Truman, and Churchill—met at the

Multicultural Connection: President Truman appointed the first African-American ambassador, Edward R. Dudley. Dudley was appointed ambassador to Liberia in 1948. William H. Hastie was appointed by President Truman in 1946 as Governor of the Virgin Islands. Hastie had been appointed to the U.S. District Court for the Virgin Islands by Roosevelt in 1937. He later became a judge on the Third U.S. Circuit Court of Appeals.

Europe after World War II

- U.S. Zone
- British Zone
- French Zone
- Russian Zone
- Annexed by U.S.S.R.
- Annexed by Poland

0 ___ 600 Miles
0 ___ 600 Kilometers

NORWAY
FINLAND
SWEDEN
Stockholm
ESTONIA
LATVIA
Moscow
LITHUANIA
U S S R
NORTHERN
IRELAND
GREAT
BRITAIN
IRELAND
DENMARK
Gdansk
EAST
PRUSSIA
NORTH
SEA
BALTIC SEA
London
NETH.
Berlin
Warsaw
POLAND
Kiev
BELG.
GERMANY
LUX.
CZECHOSLOVAKIA
Paris
Rhine
Nuremberg
Prague
ATLANTIC
OCEAN
FRANCE
SWITZ.
AUSTRIA
Budapest
HUNGARY
ROMANIA
Belgrade
YUGOSLAVIA
Danube R.
BLACK
SEA
PORTUGAL
SPAIN
CORSICA
ITALY
BULGARIA
Lisbon
Madrid
Rome
ALBANIA
Istanbul
SARDINIA
GREECE
TURKEY
MEDITERRANEAN
SICILY
SEA
SPANISH
MOROCCO
MOROCCO
(FRENCH)
ALGERIA
(FRENCH)
TUNISIA
(FRENCH)

BERLIN
Wall Built 1961
0 ___ 15 Miles
0 ___ 15 Kilometers
WEST
BERLIN
EAST
BERLIN

Berlin suburb of Potsdam in July 1945 to discuss ending the war against Japan and solving postwar problems in Europe. They decided that the future of Germany should be worked out by the foreign ministers of the United States, Great Britain, Russia, and France.

At Potsdam the Big Three leaders confirmed that "war criminals" would be brought to justice swiftly. In October a four-power tribunal meeting at Nuremberg, Germany, began to try Nazi leaders for crimes committed during the war. Ten of these Nazis were executed. Hundreds of German soldiers were also sentenced to death by the Allies' military courts, and 500,000 other Germans were punished for

their Nazi activities. Later, Japanese leaders were also tried in Japan, and Premier Tojo and six others were executed. Four thousand Japanese were sent to jail, and 400 Japanese officers were sentenced to death for committing atrocities.

The Allies could not agree on what to do with Germany. So in March 1948, the United States, England, France, and the Benelux nations (Belgium, the Netherlands, and Luxembourg) announced plans to make the Western Zone of Germany a single unit. A federal government would be set up there. And West Germany would come into the European Recovery Program.

⊕ **Geography and History: Regions** Have the students look at the map above and list the countries that were behind the iron curtain. Tell them where the two cities mentioned by Churchill in his reference to the iron curtain (page 708) are located: Stellin is on the border between East Germany and West Germany on the Baltic Sea, and Trieste is on the border of Yugoslavia and Italy on the Adriatic Sea. Students should recall that Greece and Turkey were not under Soviet control. They should also see from the map that the Soviets only controlled a portion of Austria.

The Berlin blockade. Hoping to prevent the Western powers from setting up a separate West German government and to keep Germany from helping European recovery, the Russians put pressure on West Berlin. On June 24, 1948, they banned all traffic between the Western Zone and Berlin by railroad, highway, or canal. This combat without open fighting came to be called the "cold war."

Harry Truman never considered giving in. "We are going to stay, period," the feisty President said. There would be no backing down to the Russians as long as Truman was in the White House. The United States, England, and France began to supply the city by air. Food, coal, clothing—all kinds of things the people of the city needed—were flown in. Four thousand tons of supplies reached Berlin each day.

On May 12, 1949, the Western powers approved the Basic Law for the German Federated Republic (West Germany). On the same day Stalin recognized his defeat and ended the blockade. Then in September the West Germans began to rule themselves. In military and foreign affairs they were still controlled by the occupying powers. One month later the Russians responded by setting up their German Democratic Republic in East Germany. West Germany formally was given full sovereignty in 1955. East Germany remained a Russian satellite. Hitler's "Thousand Year Reich" had become a divided nation. Could Germany ever be reunited without threatening the peace of Europe?

The creation of NATO. Out of the Berlin blockade came the North Atlantic Treaty Organization (NATO). The Atlantic Pact that established NATO allied the United States and Canada with ten Western European nations extending from Norway to Portugal. Later,

When the Russians blockaded West Berlin in 1948–1949, the Western powers responded with a gigantic airlift which brought thousands of tons of supplies to Berlin each day.

Fenno Jacobs/Black Star

Continuity and Change: Government and Politics Remind students that the divided Germany of 1949 would not be reunited for forty years, until November 9, 1989, when the border was reopened. Soon thereafter, the Berlin Wall erected in 1961 was taken down. (See p. 933.)

NATO

North Atlantic Treaty Organization Nations 1949

Soviet Union and Satellite Countries

0   1500 Miles

0   1500 Kilometers

when Greece, Turkey, and West Germany joined, the membership numbered fifteen. The Atlantic Pact was signed by the foreign ministers on April 4, 1949.

Under Article 5 of this pact an attack on any one of the parties would be treated as an attack on them all. Some senators argued that this committed the United States to go to war without a declaration by Congress. This same fear had defeated the League of Nations in the Senate in 1919. But now the senators approved the Atlantic Pact in July 1949 by a vote of 82 to 13. The Senate followed our long tradition by avoiding calling this an "alliance." And Congress actually did retain the right to declare war. Yet there was no doubt in anyone's mind that whatever NATO was called, the United States had made a major shift. We had joined the first peacetime alliance in our history. General Eisenhower was named commander of the NATO forces. He set up Supreme Headquarters, Allied Powers in Europe (SHAPE) at Paris early in 1951.

The Republicans scent victory in 1948. In the midst of the Berlin blockade, the United States held a presidential election. The Republicans, after taking control of Congress in 1946, thought they would easily win. Now shortages and strikes, though less worrisome than they had been, remained a nuisance. The world still seemed on the brink of war. No wonder plain little Harry Truman seemed an easy man to bring down.

Many Republicans wanted the chance to run against Truman. Among the hopefuls were Senator Robert A. Taft, called "Mr. Republican," Governor Harold Stassen of Minnesota, Governor Earl Warren of California, and the 1944 candidate Governor Thomas E. Dewey of New York. Some leaders in both parties hoped to

Geography and History: Regions Have students look at the map above. Ask: What do you notice about the NATO countries on this map? (They control most of the northern hemisphere's usable seacoasts—the Arctic Ocean, of course, is usually frozen.) What effect would this have? (NATO countries will enjoy a great advantage in oceangoing shipping.) How would this help the NATO countries? (Militarily, it will enable them to keep supply lines open; economically, it will enable them to trade freely and quickly with each other.) Have students list the names of the countries in NATO.

draft the war hero General Dwight Eisenhower. But he refused to be a candidate.

The Republicans, meeting at Philadelphia, feared that an outspoken anti-New Dealer like Taft could not win. They turned again to the moderate Tom Dewey and chose Earl Warren as his running mate. New York and California! That seemed an unbeatable team. The Republican platform approved many popular New Deal reforms. It also accepted the "bipartisan" foreign policy—the policy agreed on by both parties—that had been followed ever since Pearl Harbor. There were, in fact, real questions about the policy of containment that deserved public discussion. Yet these important issues were not debated by the candidates because foreign policy was supposed to be bipartisan. In the campaign the Republicans simply insisted that they could run the country better. Their slogan said, "Time for a change."

The Democrats divide. The Democrats also met in Philadelphia. And many party leaders wanted to dump Truman. They were sure he would lose. But he was self-confident—and he loved a fight. Using his powerful position in the White House, he was able to win on the first ballot. His friend, Alben W. Barkley of Kentucky, the Democratic leader in the Senate for eleven years, took the second spot on the ticket.

The Democratic platform favored repeal of the Taft-Hartley Act. It pledged recognition of the new state of Israel, which was struggling to be born in Palestine. It came out for strong civil rights legislation—abolition of poll taxes in federal elections, a national anti-lynching law, fair employment legislation, and the end of segregation in the armed forces. The Democrats were bidding for the continued support of the black voters who now held the balance of power in the big northern cities. Their votes might well swing their states into the Democratic column.

The adoption of the civil rights plank split the party wide open. Thirty-five members of the Mississippi and Alabama delegations walked out of the building. Only two days after the Democratic convention adjourned, delegates from thirteen southern states held their own convention in Birmingham, Alabama. In a hall flanked with Confederate flags and resounding with rebel yells, they nominated Governor J. Strom Thurmond of South Carolina for President. Governor Fielding Wright of Mississippi was named his running mate.

They called themselves States Rights Democrats or "Dixiecrats." Their platform asserted the doctrine of states' rights. It condemned the civil rights plank of the Democratic convention and insisted on the segregation of blacks.

It appeared even more certain that Truman would lose when Henry A. Wallace and his followers also left the party to create a party of their own. Calling themselves "Progressives," his supporters chanted, "One, two, three, four— we don't want another war." Wallace was convinced that both at home and abroad Communists and liberals should work together. The Communist party endorsed his candidacy. The Progressive platform called for the repeal of the draft, strong civil rights laws, cooperation with Russia, banning atomic bombs (and destroying all American bombs), and freedom of speech and political action for Communists. Senator Glenn H. Taylor of Idaho, the self-styled "Singing Cowboy," was the Progressive nominee for Vice-President.

The election of 1948. People remembered that the election of 1946 had already shown a swing to the Republicans. Now the Progressives and the Dixiecrats split the Democratic vote. Public opinion polls showed strong support for Dewey. The Republicans considered their victory certain. Many Democrats privately agreed with them, and most big-city newspapers predicted that Truman was a sure loser.

Meanwhile, Truman was not sitting still. He called the 80th Congress back into special session and challenged them to enact the platform the Republicans had issued at their convention. When they failed, the President scorned them as the "Do-Nothing" Congress throughout the election.

Truman now shrewdly could run against the Republican 80th Congress instead of against Governor Dewey. He convinced people that the Congress had done nothing but serve the powerful corporations. Through the Taft-Hartley

✖ Critical Thinking Activity: Identifying Alternatives What issues were addressed by political parties in the 1948 election? Tell students that the 1948 election promised many things to many different people, which might be why both Republicans and Democrats found themselves split over the issues. Have students divide into small groups to form their own political party and party platform for the 1948 election. Allow time for each party to present their platform to the class. Have the class decide which party they would want to vote for.

law, he said, Congress had tried to enslave the workers. By keeping America's doors closed against the displaced persons of Europe, Congress had struck a blow against all immigrants. He continued to appeal to blacks by calling for civil rights laws.

Truman conducted a rough-and-tumble, whirlwind campaign. He traveled on a special train that made countless quick whistle-stops— just long enough for his speech and some friendly greetings from the townspeople. He gave 356 speeches, covered 30,000 miles by train, and met 12 million people. On the other hand Dewey, a reserved and dignified man, acted coolly and quietly as he thought befit the next President of the United States. One reporter quipped, "How long is Dewey going to tolerate Truman's interference in the government?"

In the 1948 campaign, for the first time, television was important. On TV and on the road,

Truman gleefully displays the headline that too hastily announced his defeat in 1948.

Wide World Photos

President Truman seemed relaxed and homey. Critics said that Governor Dewey appeared stiff and formal like the bridegroom on a wedding cake. Television offered a vivid new chance for American voters to size up their candidates.

On the morning after election day, based on the early returns the *Chicago Tribune* headlined that Dewey had won. In fact, the spunky Harry Truman—who never gave up—had turned defeat into victory. President Truman's favorite picture of himself showed him holding up a copy of that *Chicago Tribune*. When the later returns from the farm belt turned the tide, Truman's popular vote was 24 million to nearly 22 million for Dewey and over 1 million each for Thurmond and Wallace. In the electoral college Truman had 303, Dewey 189, Thurmond 39, and Wallace 0. In addition the Democrats won a majority of 93 seats in the House and 12 in the Senate. Nearly everybody was surprised— except Harry Truman.

See "Section 2 Review answers," p. 706D.

Section 2 Review

1. Identify or explain: GI Bill of Rights, Atomic Energy Commission, Employment Act of 1946, Twenty-second Amendment, Presidential Succession Act, "Fair Deal," National Security Act, CIA, Nuremberg trials, Berlin blockade, Atlantic Pact.

2. Describe demobilization in 1946. How were the war veterans helped?

3. How did Truman respond to the strikes and inflation in 1946? What was the result?

4. List some purposes and provisions of the Taft-Hartley Act.

5. On what measures did the 80th Congress support Truman? Oppose him?

6. Describe Truman's stand on civil rights.

7. Why was Germany divided in 1948–1949?

8. Describe the candidates, the issues, and the outcome of the 1948 presidential election.

9. **Critical Thinking: Checking Consistency.** How did the creation of NATO depart from American tradition?

See "Lesson Plan," p. 706D.

3. President in his own right

Harry Truman's second four years in office were momentous. They would be marked by hysterical spy hunts, by the "loss" of China, by Russia's explosion of an atomic bomb, by defensive alliances, and by an undeclared war in Korea. Through it all Harry Truman was courageous and decisive. But many Americans did not agree with his decisions.

Truman asks for a Fair Deal for all. President Truman interpreted his victory in 1948 as a signal that the nation approved his "Fair Deal." Instead when he tried to persuade Congress to pass his Fair Deal laws, he ran into strong opposition from both Republicans and Democrats. Still, during the next four years he did manage to persuade Congress to raise the minimum hourly wage from 40 to 75 cents and to extend Social Security to an additional 10 million Americans. He signed laws to clear slums, to renew cities, and to provide low-income housing. Congress voted more funds for the TVA, for bringing in electricity to rural areas, and for the expansion of hydroelectric, water-control, and irrigation projects. But Truman suffered defeats on civil rights, on national health insurance, on the repeal of the Taft-Hartley Act, on federal aid to education, and on his plan to keep up farm incomes.

The second red scare. The stresses of the cold war with Russia, along with the 1946 reports of spying in Canada, frightened Americans. On very little evidence, they began to suspect that there was a strong Communist conspiracy to take over the United States. Truman, who had some reasons of his own to distrust the Russians, joined the crowd. On March 22, 1947, the President issued an Executive Order for the FBI and the Civil Service Commission to check on the loyalty of all federal employees. The honest, hardworking government workers were made miserable. The order made it seem that they were guilty of disloyalty until they proved they were innocent.

Within the next four years 3 million employees were cleared, 2900 resigned, and 300 were dismissed as being of doubtful loyalty. The criteria for suspicion were so broad that it may well be that none of these people was ever a Communist or else had only been a Communist before the war. In December 1947 Attorney General Tom Clark listed 90 organizations said to be disloyal to the United States. The listed groups were not allowed to prove that they were not disloyal. Membership in one of these groups at once became cause for suspicion that the person was a Communist.

Meanwhile, the 80th Congress breathed new life into the House Un-American Activities Committee (HUAC). One of its most active members was a young congressman from California, Richard M. Nixon. The committee held numerous public hearings and treated those who refused to answer its questions as guilty. Its free-swinging actions led to many ruined reputations and produced blacklists in the movies, radio, and TV.

The most famous case to come out of the HUAC was that of the charming and successful Alger Hiss. He had served in the government since 1933, had been an adviser to the President at Yalta, and then temporary secretary at the San Francisco conference to set up the United Nations. In 1946 he was elected president of the Carnegie Endowment for International Peace. In 1948 Alger Hiss was accused by Whittaker Chambers, a confessed former Soviet courier. Chambers said that Hiss had provided him with classified documents, which then had been photographed by Communist agents and returned to government files.

Hiss sued Chambers for libel. He denied Chambers's charges before a New York grand jury. In one trial the jury could not agree. After a second trial Hiss was convicted of perjury in January 1950. High-ranking Democrats were among the character witnesses for Hiss. And President Truman made the mistake of saying that the Hiss case was a "red herring" put out by the 80th Congress to prove that it was actually doing something. Many Americans, already upset by the crisis with Russia, now believed that the Democrats were "soft on communism."

See "Lesson Plan," p. 706E for **Cooperative Learning Activity: Distinguishing False from Accurate Images** relating to the presidency of Harry S Truman.

Chinese Communist troops had just taken Nanjing from the forces of Chiang Kai-shek in 1949 when famed French photographer Henri Cartier-Bresson took this picture.

The world situation worsens. In September 1949, several years earlier than expected, the Soviet Union exploded an atomic bomb. No longer did the United States have its monopoly. Then in February 1950, Klaus Fuchs, a scientist who had helped to make the first atomic bomb, was arrested by the British as a spy. He confessed that from 1943 to 1947 he had given the Russians important secrets about the bomb.

Our former ally Chiang Kai-shek was driven from the vast mainland of China to the small island of Taiwan (Formosa). By October 1949 the Chinese Communists, led by Mao Zedong, were in control of the Chinese mainland. At first the United States had given Chiang large amounts of aid. We had tried to mediate between him and Mao to form a single government. But neither of them had been willing to compromise. When fighting broke out between them, the United States had backed Chiang. Many Americans who did not want to see communism come to China still were only lukewarm supporters of Chiang. They saw him as another dictator and disliked the corruption in his government. But his fall and the loss of mainland China to the Communists seemed one more defeat for the United States.

More from Boorstin: "In 1945–48 the Nationalist Chinese received $2 billion in aid (in addition to war matériel), but mainland China became Communist and the American ally on Formosa, Chiang Kai-shek, was hardly democratic. A by-product of the Communist Revolution in China was the Korean War. Korea, too, for some years the recipient of the largest quantity of foreign aid, remained far from the democratic ideal. And [another] recipient of major foreign aid in Asia . . . was South Vietnam." (From *The Americans: The Democratic Experience*)

The rise of McCarthy. At this moment a clever and unscrupulous politician began to play upon the fear and helplessness felt by Americans. It was hard to explain how the strongest nation in the world had reached such a pass. Was this the fault of traitors inside the United States? Joseph R. McCarthy, Republican senator from Wisconsin, gave them the answer they wanted to hear. On February 9, 1950, in a speech in West Virginia he charged that the State Department was infested with Communist agents. He waved a piece of paper on which he said were listed their names. His charge, repeated over and over, increased the alarm. Even after McCarthy was unable to find a single Communist in the State Department, many troubled Americans still listened to him. McCarthy became the strongest political power in the country outside of the major party leaders. Even Presidents feared to cross him.

Protecting the United States. Members of Congress, too, seemed panicked by the internal threat for which there was so little proof. But most of all they wanted to prove that they were not soft on communism. In 1950 Congress passed the McCarran Internal Security Act. It required Communist or "Communist-front" organizations to register with the Attorney General. These included groups that were not Communist at all but which, it was suspected, might harbor some Communists. Of course, it was impossible in practice for any large organization to prove that it had no Communists. The suspect groups had to provide membership lists and financial statements. Membership in the Communist party itself was not made a crime, but employment of Communists in defense plants was forbidden. In case of an internal security emergency, the act gave the President sweeping powers to round up and detain anyone who might even possibly commit espionage or sabotage. President Truman vetoed the McCarran Act. He said that it was worse than the Sedition Act of 1798 (p. 167) and that it took a "long step toward totalitarianism." But the law was passed over his veto.

Using the excuse of "internal security," in 1952 Congress passed a new immigration law,

the McCarran-Walter Act. Again Truman vetoed the bill, but again it was passed over his veto. The law kept the quota system, which favored immigrants from northern and western Europe. It provided a complicated and insulting system of loyalty checks for foreigners who wished to visit the United States. It also gave the Attorney General the power to deport immigrants for being members of Communist and Communist-front groups even after they had become citizens. The law did include one small victory for the American tradition. It finally allowed Asians living in the United States to become citizens and set a quota permitting about 2000 to enter the country each year.

The fears of Communist subversion were heightened by the arrest of Julius and Ethel Rosenberg and Morton Sobell, on the report of Klaus Fuchs that they had passed key secrets about the atomic bomb to the Russians. In March 1951 the Rosenbergs, after a lengthy trial, were sentenced to death for a crime "worse than murder." Sobell was sentenced to 30 years. The Rosenbergs were executed in 1953. As with Sacco and Vanzetti back in the 1920s, many citizens doubted that the Rosenbergs were guilty. Or they believed that even if they were guilty, the nation was not well served by inflicting this drastic penalty in peacetime.

Civil war in Korea. Troubled by these problems at home, Americans soon discovered that from the other side of the globe the Soviets could find ways to threaten the American peace of mind. Civil war exploded in Korea in June 1950. Korea was an ancient country (the size of Mississippi and Indiana together) on a peninsula in East Asia, opposite Japan. Its borders touched Communist China and the Soviet Union. It had been annexed by Japan in 1910 and was surrendered to the Allies in 1945. At the end of the war Russian troops had moved into the country as far as the 38th parallel. American troops had freed the country south of that line.

Korea was supposed to be united under a government chosen by free elections ordered by the UN in 1947. But the Soviet Union prevented the vote from taking place. Instead the Soviets set

Enrichment
Support
File Topic

up a separate puppet government in the North. Elections were held in the South for a national assembly, which adopted a constitution and chose Syngman Rhee as the president. Rhee had been struggling for Korean freedom for 50 years. The Japanese had imprisoned him. He had then come to the United States where he studied at Harvard and Princeton.

After the United States removed its troops from Korea in June 1949, both sides of the divided country threatened war. Skirmishes took place along the 38th parallel. Early in 1950 South Korea mobilized its army. In March Syngman Rhee boldly announced that his troops would liberate North Korea. Suddenly on June 25 from•North Korea a strong force of 60,000, armed and organized by the Soviets, plunged south into the Republic of Korea. They came without warning and seemed headed for quick victory.

The United States helps South Korea. When news of the invasion reached President Truman, he reacted speedily and with vigor. He asked Secretary of State Dean Acheson, who had succeeded Marshall in 1949, to bring the issue before an emergency meeting of the Security Council of the UN. Six months before, the Soviet Union had stalked out of the Council when the UN refused to seat a Chinese Communist delegate. Now, free from the Russian veto, (p. 725) the Council lost no time in adopting (9–0) a resolution that condemned the invasion as "a breach of the peace." The UN called for an end to the fighting. The invaders were ordered to withdraw to north of the 38th parallel. All UN members were asked to help see that its resolution was obeyed.

That evening and the next, Truman met with his advisers in Washington. He ordered the Seventh Fleet to protect Taiwan, where Chiang Kai-shek and the remnants of a non-Communist China were in charge. General MacArthur, who was in command of our occupation forces in Japan, was now told to furnish arms and naval and air support to the South Koreans. This seemed to go beyond the UN resolution. But both Democrats and Republicans praised Truman for his strong decision. Members of the House stood and cheered the news of his actions.

The United Nations enters the war. On June 27, 1950, the Security Council called on member nations to aid the Republic of Korea. The UN had no ready military forces of its own. Russian vetoes had prevented that. But now the UN established a United Nations Command and invited the United States to name the general to lead it. In time, nineteen member nations contributed arms or troops. Still, Americans made up four-fifths of the UN forces. MacArthur was put in command.

Truman thought that as Commander in Chief under the Constitution he could order United States troops into battle in Korea. So he did not ask for congressional approval. Congress might well have supported his decision at the time. Still there was, in fact, little discussion of the legality of Truman's action.

The early days of the war in Korea were nip-and-tuck. South Korean and United Nations forces were driven into an ever-smaller area around Pusan at the southern end of the Korean peninsula. Then General MacArthur, who had carefully built up his forces, went on the offensive. On September 15, 1950, in a daring flank movement, MacArthur landed his forces from the sea at Inchon. His brilliant gamble worked. The South Korean capital of Seoul was soon retaken, and half the invaders south of the 38th parallel were killed or captured.

China attacks. Now the question became whether the UN forces should stop at the 38th parallel or move on to attempt to conquer the North and then unify Korea. On October 7 the UN General Assembly created a committee on unification and declared that the UN aimed to create "a unified, independent and democratic government." The next day UN forces passed beyond the 38th parallel. The Chinese Communists now warned that "if the U.S. or UN forces crossed the 38th parallel, China would send troops to the Korean frontier to defend North Korea." This threat was not taken seriously.

Soon UN forces were above the 38th parallel driving the North Koreans toward the Yalu River boundary of Manchuria.

Here the Chinese had massed a million "volunteers." For weeks MacArthur seemed to ignore the appearance of more and more "volunteers" in the battle. Then on Thanksgiving Day, 1950, he launched a great attack designed to drive the enemy beyond the Yalu and end the war before Christmas. The Chinese Communists lived up to their threat. They crossed the river and swept down upon the UN troops. World War III seemed at hand. The retreating UN forces lost Seoul to the Chinese. It required several weeks of desperate fighting before the UN troops were finally able to stabilize a defense line 60 miles below the 38th parallel.

The brand new war. General MacArthur now declared that this was "an entirely new war." He urged that the United States blockade the Chinese coast, bomb the mainland, and help Chiang Kai-shek invade China from Taiwan. The Joint Chiefs of Staff refused to give him the order he requested. Their chairman, General Omar Bradley, stated flatly that a war with China would be "the wrong war, at the wrong place, at the wrong time, and with the wrong enemy."

In January 1951 the Joint Chiefs of Staff ordered General MacArthur and General Matthew B. Ridgway, in command of the Eighth Army in Korea, to restrict their activities to the Republic of Korea. They warned the American generals not to provoke a general war with China. Slowly the UN forces worked their way back up toward the 38th parallel, at the same time taking a heavy toll of enemy lives.

The President fires MacArthur. MacArthur spoke out angrily against the strategy of a limited war. Merely to free South Korea, he said,

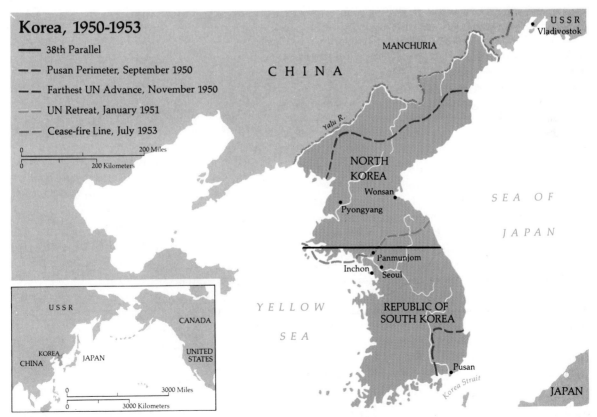

⊕ **Geography and History: Location** Have students look at the map above and answer the following questions: The Yalu River forms the border between what two countries? (China and North Korea; also, the very small border between North Korea and the USSR.) Which Korean city shown on the map is closest to Japan? (Pusan.) If you started at Pusan, what route would you follow to make a seaborne attack on Inchon? (West-southwest through Korea Strait, north through Yellow Sea.)

would leave the Koreans at the mercy of their Communist neighbors. But Truman had not forgotten his powers as President. The Constitution said that the President was Commander in Chief of all the United States armed forces. Now MacArthur was openly challenging Truman's orders to keep the war inside Korea. President Truman called a surprise press conference at one o'clock in the morning on April 11, 1951. He announced that General MacArthur had been removed.

MacArthur was a true American hero. His generalship in the Pacific during World War II had been brilliant, and as Supreme Commander in Japan after the war his economic and political reforms had transformed that nation into a modern democracy. Huge crowds greeted him on his return to the United States. On April 19, he gave an oration to Congress. "In war," he urged in his deep baritone voice, "there can be no substitute for victory."

But even as the sound of the general's voice died away, more and more Americans saw that Truman was talking sense. You could no longer talk about "victory" as the general did. Communist Russia now had its own atomic bomb. If there was another world war, both "winners" ✘ and "losers" would go up in atomic blasts. The only hope for mankind, said President Truman, was to keep the fighting limited. Now even "little" wars carried big risks.

The United States builds its defense. While the United States was fighting in Korea, it was also building up defenses in Europe. Military supplies in ever-growing amounts were shipped to our allies there. Four American divisions were sent to General Eisenhower's new NATO command. A vast system of air bases was set up in England, France, Italy, North Africa, and Turkey within easy striking distance of key Soviet centers. Russia had been targeted as the main enemy.

At the same time, the United States was working to create a system of security pacts in the Pacific. A mutual defense treaty with the Philippines was concluded on August 30, 1951.

Two days later Australia, New Zealand, and the United States signed the Tripartite Security Treaty, which came to be known as the ANZUS pact.

Then at San Francisco on September 8, 1951, a "peace of reconciliation" was signed between Japan and 48 other nations, not including Russia. It was largely the work of John Foster Dulles, adviser to the State Department, who wanted to make Japan a bastion against communism. Japan was made to give up its overseas empire, but there were no punishing reparations. Full sovereignty was restored to the Japanese people. On the same day, the United States concluded a security treaty with Japan that granted the United States land, sea, and air bases on Japanese soil. Japan—which only recently had been the leading Asian enemy—had now become the cornerstone of the United States security in the Far East. Across the world, an armed United States and its allies faced a hostile Soviet Russia and its satellites.

See "Section 3 Review answers," p. 706E.

Section 3 Review

1. Identify or explain: HUAC, Alger Hiss, Chiang Kai-shek, Mao Zedong, Joseph McCarthy, McCarran Act, McCarran-Walter Act, the Rosenbergs, Syngman Rhee, Omar Bradley, Matthew Ridgway, ANZUS pact.

2. Locate: Taiwan, Korea, Pusan, Inchon, Yalu River, Seoul, 38th parallel.

3. In 1949–1952 what parts of Truman's Fair Deal program were passed, and which parts were defeated, by Congress?

4. How did Congress respond to the alarms sounded by Joseph McCarthy?

5. What were the causes of the Korean War? Evaluate Truman's response.

6. Describe the course of the Korean War in 1950–1951. Why did President Truman dismiss General MacArthur?

7. **Critical Thinking: Recognizing Cause and Effect.** How did the fall of China lead to the "second red scare"?

✘ Critical Thinking Activity: Predicting Consequences How does new technology change the nature of war? Remind students of Truman's view that the atomic bomb limited the type of conflicts between nations. Have students construct a chart that reflects the future of defense technology and the limitations it will place on international conflicts: Write across the top of the chalkboard "Technological Advances," "Effect," "Limitations Of." Fill in the columns with both present and future defense technology, such as biological warfare.

Chapter 28 Review

See "Chapter Review answers," p. 706E.

Focusing on Ideas

1. Why could the United States not return to an isolationist foreign policy after World War II?

2. Identify actions that increased Western distrust of the Soviet Union.

3. How did American leaders expect our economic aid to foreign countries to halt the spread of communism? Promote prosperity in the United States?

4. Fear of Communist influence in the United States pervaded the Truman years. How did government officials respond to this fear? Cite as many examples as possible.

Taking a Critical Look

1. **Recognizing Bias.** As an employer, what provisions of the Taft-Hartley Act would you most favor? Why? As a union leader, what provisions would you most oppose? Why?

2. **Distinguishing Fact from Opinion.** In 1962 a panel of historians ranked Harry Truman as one of our "near great" Presidents. What accomplishments—and failures—would you expect historians to consider in arriving at this judgment of President Truman?

Your Region in History

1. **Geography.** What products from your region might have been sold to buyers in countries receiving American economic aid in the Truman years?

2. **Culture.** Interview older people in your community about their experiences and/or impressions of the "red scare." Ask them to describe the political climate during the McCarthy hearings.

3. **Economics.** Interview World War II or Korean War veterans to find out how they benefited from the "GI Bill." Share your findings with the class.

Historical Facts and Figures

Understanding Geography. Following World War II, the territory of Germany was divided among the victorious Allies. (a) What nation controlled the southwestern part of the country? The southeast? The northwest? The northeast? (b) In what part of Germany was divided Berlin situated? (c) What were the boundaries of East and West Germany? (d) What information in the chapter helps explain why Germany was divided into two nations?

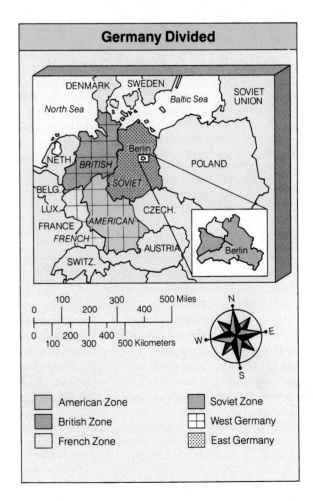

Germany Divided

Chapter 29
Eisenhower, Moderate Republican

Identifying Chapter Materials

Objectives	Basic Instructional Materials	Extension Materials
1 The Republicans Return • Describe the election of 1952 and trace the United States-Soviet relations in the early 1950s. • Discuss the history of campaign appeals in presidential elections from 1796 through 1952.	**Annotated Teacher's Edition** • Lesson Plans, p. 728C **Instructional Support File** • Pre-Reading Activities, Unit 10, p. 15	**Documents of American History** • Southeast Asia Treaty Organization, Vol. 2, p. 598 • Secretary Dulles' Strategy of Massive Retaliation, Vol. 2, p. 590
2 Everybody's New Deal • List and describe the policies of the Eisenhower administration, including its response to Senator Joseph McCarthy's accusations about Communists in government. • Examine Eisenhower's position in the political spectrum, with attention to the stances he took on specific issues.	**Annotated Teacher's Edition** • Lesson Plans, pp. 728C–728D	**Documents of American History** • Eisenhower's Security Program—Executive Order 10450, Vol. 2, p. 582 • Senate Censure of Senator McCarthy, Vol. 2, p. 601
3 The Fight for Equality • Trace the achievements of the civil rights movement through the 1950s. • Explain the relatively slow progress achieved by blacks in fighting oppression since becoming citizens in 1868.	**Annotated Teacher's Edition** • Lesson Plans, pp. 728D–728E	**Enrichment Support File** • Martin Luther King's Nonviolent Way to Civil Rights (See "In-Depth Coverage" at right.) **Perspectives** • The Impact of the Civil Rights Movement (See "In-Depth Coverage" at right.) **American History Transparencies** • Time Lines, p. E31
4 Difficulties Abroad • Cite some of the international events that made 1956 a difficult year. • Analyze actions taken by Eisenhower in each of these crises during his second term.	**Annotated Teacher's Edition** • Lesson Plans, pp. 728E–728F **Instructional Support File** • Reading Activities, Unit 10, pp. 16–17 • Skill Review Activity, Unit 10, p. 18 • Skill Application Activity, Unit 10, p. 19 • Critical Thinking Activity, Unit 10, p. 20 • Chapter Test, Unit 10, pp. 21–24 • Additional Test Questions, Unit 10, pp. 25–28	**Documents of American History** • Eisenhower Address on American Foreign Policy in the Middle East, Vol. 2, p. 620 • The Eisenhower Doctrine, Vol. 2, p. 622 • The U-2 Affair, Vol. 2, p. 647 • Eisenhower's Farewell Address, Vol. 2, p. 652 **American History Transparencies** • Critical Thinking, p. F79

Providing In-Depth Coverage

Perspectives on Civil Rights

King believed that the principles of Christian love could be a tool of social progress through nonviolent direct action. He called for actions that would protest segregation and, by setting an example of nonviolence, persuade opponents of equality of the error of their ways. King led the boycott to victory and segregation was declared illegal on Montgomery's buses. Shortly thereafter King formed the Southern Christian Leadership Conference, which became one of the most important organizations in the fight for civil rights.

A History of the United States as an instructional program provides three types of resources you can use to offer in-depth coverage of Martin Luther King, Jr. and civil rights: the *student text*, the *Enrichment Support File*, and *Perspectives*. The chart below shows the topics that are covered in each.

THE STUDENT TEXT. Boorstin and Kelley's *A History of the United States* unfolds the chronology of events, the key players, and, as an interpretive history, the controversy of the civil rights movement.

AMERICAN HISTORY ENRICHMENT SUPPORT FILE. This collection of primary source readings and classroom activities focuses on Martin Luther King, Jr. and the nonviolent civil rights movement.

PERSPECTIVES READINGS ON AMERICAN HISTORY IN THE 20TH CENTURY. In this edited collection of secondary source readings, well-known historians and political commentators (including Boorstin) provide an array of perspectives on the impact of the civil rights movement.

Locating Instructional Materials

Detailed lesson plans for teaching Martin Luther King, Jr. as a mini-course or to study one or more elements of the civil rights movement in depth are offered in the following areas: in the *student text*, see individual lesson plans at the beginning of each chapter; in the *Enrichment Support File*, see page 3; in *Perspectives*, see the Teacher's Guide for this unit.

IN-DEPTH COVERAGE OF THE CIVIL RIGHTS MOVEMENT		
Student Text	**Enrichment Support File**	**Perspectives**
▪ *Brown* v. *Board of Education*, pp. 738–739 ▪ Martin Luther King, Jr., pp. 740–741, 790–791, 805–806 ▪ Rosa Parks, p. 740 ▪ Montgomery Bus Boycott, p. 741 ▪ Civil Rights Acts of 1957 and 1960, p. 741	▪ Lesson Suggestions ▪ Multimedia Resources ▪ Overview Essay/Martin Luther King, Jr.'s Nonviolent Way to Civil Rights ▪ Literature in American History/"For Andy Goodman, Michael Schwerner, and James Chaney" ▪ Songs in American History/Songs of the Difficult Path of Nonviolent Resistance ▪ Primary Sources in American History/"I Have a Dream" ▪ Biography in American History/Martin Luther King, Jr. ▪ Geography in American History/The Freedom Rides: Movement, Place, and Region ▪ Great Debates in American History/Civil Disobedience vs Violence ▪ Making Connections	▪ "What Happened to the Civil Rights Movement" by C. Vann Woodward ▪ "A Record of Change" by Robert Weisbrot ▪ "Affirmative Action" by Archibald Cox ▪ "The Negative Effects of Affirmative Action" by Thomas Sowell ▪ "Black and White in America" by David Gelman with Karen Springen, Karen Brailsford, and Mark Miller

The Republicans Return

FOCUS

To introduce the lesson, divide the class into two groups. Ask one group to prepare an Eisenhower campaign speech, focusing on the "failures" of the Democrats. Ask the other group to prepare a Stevenson speech, rebutting the Republican claims. Read the campaign speeches to the class.

Developing Vocabulary

The words listed are essential terms for understanding particular sections of the chapter. The page number after each term indicates the page of its first or most important appearance. These terms are defined in the Glossary (text pages 1000–1011).

GOP (page 730); **demilitarized zone** (page 731); **massive retaliation** (page 731); **nationalize** (page 733); **summit conference** (page 733).

INSTRUCT

Explain

The 1952 campaign was the first in which television played a significant part. Eisenhower won as much on the strength of his personality and military record as on the issues.

☑ Writing Process Activity

Demonstrating Reasoned Judgment Ask students to play the role of political analysts during the election of 1952. Before they write an essay about what conditions made it ripe for the Republicans to take office, ask them to brainstorm the characteristics of Eisenhower that made him a perfect candidate. Students should begin with a topic sentence that summarizes how the time and the man made the outcome of the election predictable. Ask students to revise for logical organization and an objective tone. After proofreading, students can exchange essays with a partner.

Section Review Answers

Section 1, page 734

1. a) Democratic candidate in 1952. b) Eisenhower's Secretary of State. c) hydrogen bombs, far more destructive than atom bombs. d) Vietnamese Communist who led the fight first against the Japanese and then the French in Viet Nam. e) Southeast Asia Treaty Organization, formed in 1954. f) signed by the Middle East Treaty Organization. g) treaty in which Western powers gave full sovereignty to West Germany. h) king of Egypt, deposed in 1952. i) premier of Iran, overthrown in 1953. j) headed the Soviet gov-

ernment shortly after Stalin's death. k) high-flying spy plane. 2. The Korean demilitarized zone is the area around the cease-fire line shown on the map on page 725. Indochina, which includes Vietnam, Laos, and Cambodia, is shown on the map on page 810, as is Dienbienphu. Iran is shown on the map on page 746. 3. In 1952 Republican Eisenhower, known for his grin as well as his war record, ran against the eloquent, intellectual Stevenson. The main foreign policy issues concerned the spread of communism, the "fall" of China, and the war in Korea. Domestic issues included the Republican calls for a balanced budget, decreased national debt, and honesty in government. Eisenhower won a large victory over Stevenson and the Republicans won a slight majority in Congress. 4. Negotiations reopened in 1953 after the United States threatened to bomb China and use the atomic bomb on Korea. Then an armistice was signed in 1953 that gave neither side much of anything. It put the border between North and South Korea near the 38th parallel and established a demilitarized zone around it. 5. Containing communism and overthrowing Communist governments. He practiced "brinksmanship," threatening retaliation against the USSR and China if they attacked any country. Later, he softened his policy. He set up a series of treaties to prevent the spread of communism and isolate the Soviet Union. 6. The United States sent money and arms to help the French fight Communist-led resistance. 7. By 1955 a new Soviet govenment had replaced Stalin and officials were eager to reduce world tension. They proposed a summit, and Eisenhower accepted. 8. Eisenhower was a career soldier. He had commanded the Allies in their victory over Germany and then held the posts of Chief of Staff of the Army, president of Columbia University, and Supreme Commander of NATO forces in Europe. He had shown that he was a competent and honest leader, able to persuade others to cooperate.

CLOSE

To conclude the lesson, divide the class into groups. Assign each group one of these treaty organizations: NATO, SEATO, METO. Have groups prepare a map showing the location of the organization's member nations.

Everybody's New Deal

FOCUS

To introduce the lesson, have students speculate on the meaning of "moderate Republican" in the chapter title. Ask students to consider Eisenhower's stand on off-shore oil deposits. What stand would a conservative Republican have taken? a liberal Republican?

INSTRUCT

Explain

Senator Joseph McCarthy received a standing ovation at the Republican convention in 1952. Soon afterwards, McCarthy advised Eisenhower to delete a favorable reference to General Marshall from a speech. McCarthy had villified the author of the Marshall Plan as being part of a Communist conspiracy. Eisenhower complied.

✿ Cooperative Learning Activity

Identifying Assumptions Tell students that they will work in small groups to create a one-minute television ad for Eisenhower's 1956 election campaign. Have each group begin by choosing a manager and a recorder. Then have the manager lead the group in discussing what people will see and hear in the ad and how it will be presented to the class. Have the group recorder take notes and prepare any written material. Other group members can be assigned by the manager to prepare visual displays. After each ad is presented, have the class identify assumptions about the American public upon which the ad is based.

Section Review Answers

Section 2, page 738

1. a) claimed by both the federal government and the states. b), c) first Secretary of the Department of Health, Education, and Welfare—HEW. 2. Flexible price supports allowed the Secretary of Agriculture to lower the price supports for farmers, in hopes of discouraging them from overproducing. The "Soil Bank" paid farmers to take land out of production. These measures were not successful. Production continued to rise. 3. Increase in Social Security benefits and extension of its coverage to additional workers, slum clearance, public housing, government support of medical research and hospitals, and the creation of HEW. 4. Eisenhower avoided contact with McCarthy and began his own program to hunt for "security risks" in government. 5. McCarthy charged that Brigadier General Zwicker was shielding Communists, and the Army struck back with charges of its own against McCarthy. During televised hearings to air the charges, McCarthy showed himself as an unscrupulous bully, and his influence fell. A few months later the Senate condemned his conduct. 6. Eisenhower followed the viewpoint of the Republican party that business ran most successfully without government interference.

CLOSE

To conclude the lesson, tell the class: Assume that President Eisenhower held a strongly conservative point of view. Why do you think that after 1954 he took the liberal position on many issues? (One possible answer is on pages 737–738—the Democrats gained control over both houses of Congress in the 1954 congressional elections.) Discuss with students the influence of practical politics on personal beliefs. President Eisenhower had to become more liberal if he was to get along with Congress.

Section 3 (pages 738–742)

The Fight for Equality

FOCUS

To introduce the lesson, ask students to read the first two paragraphs under the heading "The nonviolent way" (pp. 740–741). Then ask: When did blacks come to America? (Almost all before 1809.) When did they officially become citizens with the same rights as whites? (1868, with the ratification of the Fourteenth Amendment to the U.S. Constitution.) Make a list on the board of the problems blacks faced in 1868. (Prejudice; racist violence; poor housing; lack of educational opportunities, etc.) Then ask: What problems did blacks face in 1955? (Same ones.)

INSTRUCT

Explain

In the 1930s the NAACP had begun a sustained effort to prove inequality in the schools. They started suing for equal access to higher education because southern states had almost no graduate or professional schools for blacks.

✎ Writing Process Activity

Recognizing Ideologies Ask students to imagine they are white residents of Little Rock, Arkansas, in 1957–1958. After deciding whether they support or oppose integration, students should freewrite about their reactions to having their children attend school with blacks, to mob violence, and to the closing of the schools. As they write a letter to a friend living in the north, ask them to capture the emotionality of the issue. During revision, students should check for realistic detail and logical explanation. After proofreading, students can read their letter to the class.

Section Review Answers

Section 3, page 742

1. a) case in which the Supreme Court upheld the doctrine of "separate but equal" treatment. b) denun-

ciation of the Supreme Court's call for school integration signed by more than 100 members of Congress. c), d) two southern senators who did not sign the manifesto. e) governor of Arkansas who sent the National Guard to help prevent the integration of schools in Little Rock. f) black woman whose arrest for not yielding her seat on a bus sparked the Montgomery, Alabama, bus boycott. 2. Ghana is shown on the map on page 951. Topeka, Little Rock, and Montgomery are shown on the map on page 758. 3. Black Americans, who had done their full share as citizens, increased their resistance to second-class treatment. 4. The Supreme Court ruled that segregated schools were unconstitutional and that public schools must be desegregated. 5. Southern members of Congress denounced the *Brown* decision in their "Southern Manifesto," and many Southerners resisted integration. Eisenhower ordered federal troops to enforce the Court's decision when violence flared in Little Rock. 6. They gave help to blacks who tried to exercise their right to vote. In addition, both political parties had worked for these laws making civil rights an American, not a partisan, goal. 7. Martin Luther King, Jr., was an inspirational leader of the struggle for racial equality. He preached that equality would be won by persuading Americans that discrimination was unjust, and that the struggle for equality must be nonviolent.

CLOSE

To conclude the lesson, ask: Why was the civil rights movement more successful in eliminating segregation laws in the South than actually achieving equal treatment for blacks? (Equality is a much more ambiguous and difficult thing to achieve. Unfair laws are clear targets, and different groups can unite to attack them. Confronting the many complex facets of discrimination requires much more complicated strategies. Coalitions are splintered rather than united by complexity and diversity.)

Section 4 (pages 742–748)

Difficulties Abroad

FOCUS

To introduce the lesson, ask: To what extent should the United States be involved in world affairs? Students should see that many situations arise around the world, and that these situations call for a range of possible responses by the United States. There are no easy solutions to these situations. They call for clear thinking by American leaders. Discuss some recent U.S. responses to world events, such as Panama and the Gulf War.

Developing Vocabulary

military-industrial complex (page 748)

INSTRUCT

Explain

Historians rate President Eisenhower as "average." More than any other President of modern times, however, he received the trust and affection of the American people.

★ Independent Activity

Formulating Questions Ask students to imagine themselves as reporters. Ask each student to select one of the crises discussed in this section and to prepare a list of five questions that he or she would like to ask President Eisenhower about the crisis. What responses would students expect?

Section Review Answers

Section 4, page 748

1. a) built for Egypt by the Soviet Union. b) sent to Gaza in 1957 to maintain peace. c) first artificial earth satellite; launched by the USSR in 1957. d) first successful American satellite. e) provided federal funds for the improvement of science education. f) National Aeronautics and Space Administration, established in 1958 to coordinate research and development of space-related technology. g) leader of Jordan, aided by Britain when violence threatened his government in 1958. h) veteran Soviet leader who visited the United States while Vice-President Nixon visited the Soviet Union. i) presidential retreat in Maryland where Eisenhower and Khrushchev held talks in 1959. j) overthrew the longtime dictator of Cuba and then turned his country over to communism and the Soviet Union. k) British territory, located west of the Jordan River, from 1923 until the establishment of the state of Israel in 1948. 2. All of these places are shown on the map on page 746. 3. a) developed a liquid-fuel rocket engine; b) developed the V-2 rockets during World War II; c) American undercover mission that brought German rocket scientists to the United States after the war to develop American rockets; d) German scientist who became the head of rocket research for the United States Army; e) developed the first earth satellite. 4. Americans reacted to *Sputnik* with both fear and a determination to compete with Soviets in space. 5. The Eisenhower Doctrine stated that the United States would help any country in the Middle East to resist Communist military aggression. It was applied when the United States sent troops into Lebanon in 1958, even though there was no real Communist threat there. The government that the United States supported was replaced. 6. In 1958 the Chinese Communist govern-

ment bombed the islands of Quemoy and Matsu, which were held by the Nationalist government on Taiwan. The Soviet Union warned the Western powers in 1958 that if they did not leave West Berlin, Western access to the city might be cut off. In Cuba Castro led the overthrow of Batista in 1958 and then set up a repressive regime of his own, outlawing other political parties and imprisoning opponents. He formed very close ties with the Soviet Union. 7. In 1959 Vice-President Nixon visited the Soviet Union while a Soviet leader visited the United States. Then Soviet Premier Khrushchev visited the United States and held productive talks with Eisenhower at Camp David. The "spirit of Camp David" was shattered in 1960, when an American spy plane was shot down over the Soviet Union, and a scheduled summit meeting was canceled as a result. 8. Eisenhower's military background made the warning a surprise.

CLOSE

To conclude the lesson, ask students to make a time line of the events discussed in the section.

Chapter Review Answers

Focusing on Ideas

1. Policymaker in military, NATO; administrator in army, NATO, president of Columbia; diplomat—heading Allied forces, NATO commander; leader—whole career. 2. Forceful: aid to French in Vietnam; troops to Lebanon; Quemoy-Matsu affair; not withdrawing from Berlin; defense treaties, threat of "massive retaliation." Diplomatic: Geneva Conference; UN resolution on Suez; summit conferences, other meetings with Soviets. 3. Desegregation—preserved order but no tremendous moral influence; civil rights laws—no great leadership; Hungarian affair—UN protest and refugee program.

Taking a Critical Look

1. Democratic majority reminded him that public opinion would not undo New Deal. Conservative approach would have alienated those whose support was necessary to get things done. 2. Yes, when compared with preceding and succeeding events, especially in domestic affairs (with the exception of civil rights). 1950s saw many crises in foreign affairs. Judgments will vary on need for "breather."

Your Region in History

1–3. Answers will vary depending on your region. Consult your local library or historical society.

Historical Facts and Figures

(a) White: approximately $3,500; non-white, $2,000. (b) For both, steadily upward. (c) Income disparity grew markedly in last 10 years. (d) How did government policy affect this economic growth? What other factors? What was inflation rate?

Chapter 29

Focusing the Chapter: Have students identify the chapter logo. Discuss what unit theme the logo might symbolize. Then ask students to skim the chapter to identify other illustrations or titles that relate to this theme.

Eisenhower, Moderate Republican

The end of the Truman years found the United States locked in a hot war in Asia and a cold war in the rest of the world. The declared American purpose was to "contain" international communism. "Containing" meant to box in communism where it already was and keep it from expanding. Fear of Communists within the United States was running rampant, fanned most of all by Senator Joseph R. McCarthy.

In fact, the threats at home and abroad were nowhere near as serious as many Americans feared. Communism was not a single, solid force. It was found in many nations, and everywhere was the declared enemy of the democracies. But each country had its own history. People had their patriotism as well as their communism. Where the Soviets ruled nations from the outside, they had trouble keeping their forced allies under control.

The secretive, insecure Soviets were at least as afraid of the United States as Americans were of them. Communists were taught that in the long run, out of war and confusion, the capitalist democracies were sure to lose. But they were impressed by the power of the United States, by our technology and our comfortable way of life. Many of them realized that all peoples of the world would be losers in a third world war. Somehow in the years ahead the United States and the Soviet Union had to exist together.

Eisenhower fought a hard battle for the Republican nomination in 1952. But in 1956, after four years as President, he was renominated by the wildly cheering crowd.

See "Lesson Plan," p. 728C.

1. The Republicans return

For twenty years our Presidents had been Democrats. They had led the United States through a depression, hot war and cold, and now into a "police action" in Korea. What would happen to the domestic and foreign policies forged during these years when a Republican again became President?

Ike and Adlai. The Republican National Convention met at Chicago on July 7, 1952. The party's chances of winning the election in the fall looked good. The war in Korea was at a stalemate. The country was plagued by inflation.

China was lost to communism. And some petty corruption had surfaced in Washington—even touching friends of the President. The main competition for the nomination was between Senator Taft of Ohio with his conservative followers, and the liberal international wing of the party, which had persuaded General Dwight D. Eisenhower to enter the race.

Eisenhower won on the first ballot after skillful early convention moves by his supporters. His running mate was the eager anti-Communist Senator Richard M. Nixon of California. He had been elected to the Senate in 1950 in a mud-slinging campaign when he recklessly accused his opponent of links to the

Communists. The Republican platform attacked Democrats for their foreign policy, blaming them for the loss of China and the war in Korea. The Republicans were not satisfied merely to "contain" communism. Instead they intended to free the captive peoples behind the iron curtain. At home, they wanted to balance the budget, lower the national debt, and "return honesty to government."

When the Democrats arrived in Chicago for their convention, they had no leading candidate. President Truman had declined to run again but had urged the urbane Adlai E. Stevenson, governor of Illinois, to be the nominee. The wellborn Stevenson was as different as possible from the rough-hewn, self-made Truman. The grandson of a former Vice-President, he was a graduate of Princeton, a prosperous lawyer, and a full-fledged intellectual. Stevenson refused Truman's suggestion. The chance of beating the nation's war hero looked slim. But Stevenson roused the interest of the delegates with his wise and witty speech that opened the convention. When no candidate received a majority on the first two ballots, the delegates drafted Stevenson.

The election of 1952. Governor Stevenson declared that it was time to "talk sense to the American people." They were faced with "a long, patient, costly struggle which alone can assure triumph over the great enemies of man—war, poverty, and tyranny—and the assaults upon human dignity which are the most grievous consequences of each."

Stevenson waged one of the most eloquent campaigns in United States history. Still it was hard to beat the friendly and attractive war hero everyone knew as "Ike." "I like Ike," the buttons read. With earnest charm, Ike promised to go to Korea to end the war. He pounded at Communists and corruption in government. Eisenhower had found the formula for victory.

Sixty-one million Americans went to the polls. On the evening of November 4, millions watched the returns on television as Eisenhower swept to victory. He carried thirty-nine states, including the usually Democratic south-ern states of Virginia, Tennessee, Florida, and Texas, piling up a total of 442 electoral votes. Stevenson's 89 votes came from the other nine southern states. The popular vote was 33.6 million to 26.6 million.

The victory was more a nationwide approval of the famous war hero than an endorsement of the program of the "GOP"—the Grand Old Party, as the Republicans liked to call themselves. In sharp contrast to the Eisenhower landslide, the Republicans won Congress by only the slim margin of one vote in the Senate and eight in the House. The popular "Ike" had ended twenty years of Democratic Presidents. ☑

Dwight David Eisenhower. "He has the power of drawing the hearts of men toward him as a magnet attracts the bits of metal," British General Montgomery said of Eisenhower. "He merely has to smile at you, and you trust him at once." This was what attracted people to Ike—even more than his successful leadership of the Allied invasion of Europe.

Ike was a career soldier. Born in Texas in 1890, he moved with his family to Abilene, Kansas. After high school, he went to the United States Military Academy at West Point. When he graduated in 1915, he began his army career. He served under MacArthur in the Philippines (1935–1940), then speedily rose in rank to command the huge Allied Expeditionary Force that was to win victory over Germany.

Ike's great skill as a general was not in leading armies in the field but in persuading other generals to cooperate. He had a quick temper, but he kept it under control. He was good at smoothing over the differences between the talented but touchy commanders from many nations. All these men had to work together if Hitler was to be defeated.

After the war he remained in the army as Chief of Staff. In 1948 he became president of Columbia University. Three years later he was called back to serve as the first Supreme Commander of NATO forces in Europe. That was his job when he resigned in June 1952 to return home and campaign for the GOP nomination for President.

☑ See "Lesson Plan," p. 728C for **Writing Process Activity: Demonstrating Reasoned Judg-ment** relating to the election of 1952.

Achieving peace in Korea. Ike had promised that if elected he would go to Korea to end the war. He kept his promise and went to Korea one month after his election. There was no simple way to end the conflict. Talks had collapsed in October 1952. Now, in 1953 when the United States threatened to bomb China and use atomic bombs in Korea itself, the negotiations were reopened at Panmunjom. Neither side gained much in the armistice signed between North Korea and the United Nations on July 27, 1953. The border, protected by a demilitarized zone, was put back near the 38th parallel.

The Korean peace was no "victory" for the United States. The American dead had numbered 35,000. But at least the immediate threat of an atomic war was removed. This was a kind of victory for humanity.

A new foreign policy. For his Secretary of State Ike chose John Foster Dulles, a leading Washington lawyer. The chief Republican spokesman on foreign policy, Dulles had negotiated the United States-Japanese peace treaty. Now, with the end of the Korean War, Eisenhower and Dulles could turn to reshaping the nation's foreign policy. Ike believed in balancing the budget, and this meant spending less money on defense. The result was a "New Look" for the armed forces, which reduced their size. Many units were brought back to the United States to serve as a "mobile strategic reserve."

Because of these cutbacks, the national defense depended more on the atomic bomb. In 1952 the United States had successfully tested a new kind of atomic bomb—the hydrogen bomb (H-bomb). This was 500 times more powerful than the bomb exploded over Hiroshima. Russia followed with its own H-bomb in 1953. Secretary of State Dulles now threatened "massive retaliation" against the Soviet Union or Communist China if they attacked any country. It was necessary, he warned, to go "to the brink of war" to preserve the peace of the world. "Brinkmanship," his critics called this policy.

At first Dulles wanted not only to "contain" communism but also to turn back the tide. He said we were going to remove the Seventh Fleet

Wayne Miller/Magnum

Ike's broad grin and impressive military record had wide appeal.

from the Formosa Strait. This would "unleash" Chiang to attack the Communist Chinese mainland from Taiwan. We would also free all the "captive peoples" still under Soviet rule. In time, when Dulles saw the facts of life, he would give up these grandiose visions.

War in Indochina. But before that time there would be some dangerous moments. The first came on another, larger peninsula that, like Korea, also bordered on Communist China. This peninsula, in Southeast Asia, was known as Indochina. In the part called Vietnam, there was a fierce struggle. At the fall of Japan in 1945, Vietnam had been liberated from the Japanese empire by forces led by a Vietnamese Communist named Ho Chi Minh. Even France had recognized him as head of an independent state—the Democratic Republic of Vietnam. To win that recognition, Ho had allowed the French to send in 15,000 soldiers. Then the French began to become difficult. Like other old imperial powers after World War II, France, even including its Communists, wanted to hold onto its former colonies. Now the French moved to bring down Ho and replace him with their own puppet. In 1947 Ho and his Viet Minh troops took to the hills.

After the fall of China to the Communists, the United States began to view Vietnam as a bulwark needed to "contain" the Communists. The French resistance to Communist forces in Vietnam, it seemed, was part of the large battle against Communist advances that we were then fighting in Korea. In 1950 the United States began helping the French with money and arms. In 1953 Eisenhower asked $60 million for such aid. And by 1954 the United States was bearing 80 percent of the cost of the war between the French and the Communists in Vietnam.

But the struggle was going badly. As the end of the Korean War approached, the Chinese Communists increased their help to the Communist Viet Minh troops. In a great push to defeat the French, these troops trapped a large French force at Dienbienphu.

Many in the United States government wanted to assist the French by an air strike around Dienbienphu. Ike disagreed. He wanted some sort of joint move with other nations so that the United States would not seem to be fighting to put back the old colonial system. The British government warned that it would not support such an action because it might lead to general war in the Far East. Leaders in Congress, also fearing a larger war, were cool to the idea. For the moment, plans to use American forces in Indochina were abandoned.

On May 8, 1954, the day after the fall of Dienbienphu, a conference opened in Geneva, Switzerland, to settle the Indochina question. The great powers—France, Great Britain, the Soviet Union, China, and the United States—attended along with delegates from Vietnam, Cambodia, and Laos. There it was decided to temporarily divide Vietnam in two. The northern half would become a Communist state, and the southern half would be a "free" government under the former emperor of Vietnam, Bao-Dai.

"Pactomania." With the division of Vietnam, Secretary of State Dulles feared that all Asia might fall to the Communists. He pushed for a treaty organization similar to NATO to protect the Pacific area. At a meeting held in Manila, there were delegates from Australia, Britain, France, New Zealand, Pakistan, the Philippines, Thailand, and the United States. On September 8, 1954, they signed a pact creating the Southeast Asia Treaty Organization (SEATO). They pledged joint action in case of aggression against any member. Cambodia, Laos, and South Vietnam—the non-Communist nations that had once been part of French Indochina—were to get special protection.

This was the beginning of what critics called Dulles's "pactomania"—the attempt to encircle the Communists by treaties. In December 1954 Dulles took his next step when he signed a mutual defense treaty with the Chinese Nationalists on Taiwan. This committed the United States to the defense of that island. A similar treaty with South Korea in October 1953 had committed us also to their defense.

These pacts were capped by the Baghdad Pact of 1955, which was also promoted by Dulles. This group, known as METO (the Middle East Treaty Organization), included Great Britain, Turkey, Iraq, Iran, and Pakistan. To the Western powers—especially Britain—the oil of the Middle East was vital. In the struggle against the Soviets it seemed important to cut them out of that area. But to avoid provoking the Communists, the United States did not join this pact.

The European Defense Community. A further step to isolate the Soviets was the Paris Pact of October 1954. In this treaty the Western powers agreed to full sovereignty for the Federal Republic of Germany. This was the part of Germany that the Russians had not taken over and forced to become Communist. West Germany was admitted to NATO and was allowed an army of 500,000 men to serve under NATO command. The United States and Great Britain promised to keep large forces on the European continent so long as they were wanted by the Western European nations—another bulwark against the spread of the Communists.

Undercover operations. Meanwhile, the United States was also working under cover,

Secretary of State John Foster Dulles signs the SEATO pact in Manila on September 8, 1954.

through the Central Intelligence Agency. In 1952 it may have helped Gamal Abdel Nasser and other young army officers to depose the decadent and corrupt playboy King Farouk of Egypt. In 1953 in Iran the CIA also helped topple the government of Premier Mossadegh, who had tried to nationalize the British-controlled oil industry. The Shah of Iran was returned to his throne. This new, friendly government gave the United States valuable oil concessions. On our side of the world, in the following year, the CIA helped an opposition group in Guatemala to overturn a government there that seemed too sympathetic to the Communists.

Meeting at the summit. Stalin, the cruel Soviet dictator, had filled Siberian prison camps with his opponents. He would stop at nothing to stay in power. Yet he could not live forever. When he died in 1953, a new clique headed finally by Nikita Khrushchev came to power. Inside Russia there was a struggle to control the government. The insecure leaders sought to

ease world tensions. They called for "peaceful coexistence." On his side Eisenhower, ever since he came to office in 1953, had offered to negotiate all issues. To show that they were now serious, the Soviet Union at last agreed to make peace with Austria and remove its troops from the zone they occupied. On May 15, 1955, a peace treaty was signed between Austria, the United States, France, Great Britain, and the Soviet Union. The occupying troops of all four countries were withdrawn. Austria now became a neutral country—free of the fear of becoming a Soviet satellite. Then the Soviets proposed a "summit" conference. Each country would send its chief of state to discuss the issues between Russia and the West. Dulles opposed this, but the President overrode him.

The heads of government of the United States, the USSR, Britain, and France met in Geneva, Switzerland, in July 1955. President Eisenhower proposed that there should be "open skies" so that each nation could inspect the other by aerial photography. This was to protect each nation from the chance—and the fear—of massive surprise attack. But the Russians turned down any kind of inspection. In fact, the conference brought no solid results. Still, the optimistic Ike hoped that it might be a beginning of a better understanding between East and West. Anyway, even without Soviet permission, the United States soon began spy flights over Russia by the new model U-2, which could fly 13 1/2 miles in the air, higher than any plane before.

See "Section 1 Review answers," p. 728C.

Section 1 Review

1. Identify or explain: Adlai Stevenson, John Foster Dulles, H-bombs, Ho Chi Minh, SEATO, Baghdad Pact, Paris Pact of 1954, King Farouk, Premier Mossadegh, Nikita Khrushchev, U-2.

2. Locate: Korean demilitarized zone, Vietnam, Dienbienphu, Cambodia, Laos, Iran.

3. Describe the candidates, issues, and results of the presidential election of 1952.

4. How did the Korean War end?

5. What kind of foreign policy did Dulles first call for? What strategy did he later adopt?

6. How was the United States involved in the French-Vietnamese war?

7. Why was a summit conference held in 1955?

8. **Critical Thinking: Identifying Assumptions.** Trace the career of Dwight David Eisenhower. Why did this record make many Americans think Eisenhower would be a good President?

See "Lesson Plan," p. 728C.

2. Everybody's New Deal

Many Democrats feared that the return of Republican rule would mean the end of New Deal and Fair Deal measures and a retreat to the 1920s. In some ways the Republicans gave them cause for alarm. Douglas McKay, Eisenhower's Secretary of the Interior, proclaimed, "We're here in the saddle as an administration representing business and industry." But before very long, the New Deal was safe. The Republican President even began to expand some of these measures, describing his program as "dynamic conservatism."

Reducing government activities. At first Ike sounded as if he intended to undo the New Deal. He aimed to cut back on government—on the size of the budget, on taxes, and on regulation of the nation's business. As one step to lessen government control of business, Ike ended the price and wage controls imposed during the Korean War. Congress gave him the authority to sell to private industry government-owned factories for making synthetic rubber. The Atomic Energy Act was amended to give private companies a larger role in atomic research and the making of atomic power.

The President had to face the question whether the federal government or the states owned the vast oil deposits thought to exist under the seas lapping the nation's shores. Twice, in 1946 and 1952, Congress passed bills giving title to the states. On both occasions President Truman blocked the action. With stern vetoes, he said that the offshore oil belonged to all the people. But Eisenhower wanted to reduce the activities of the federal government. He denied such sweeping national claims. He gladly signed a compromise in May 1953. Title to submerged coastal lands went to the states, but only within their historic boundaries. The Supreme Court in May 1960 set these boundaries at the usual three-mile limit except for Texas and Florida. Their historic boundaries were said to extend 10 1/2 miles out into the sea.

Public vs. private power. The President also had to face another issue between private industry and government ownership. In 1953 there began a bitter battle over whether dams on the Snake River in Idaho should be built by a private power company or the federal government. No one was surprised when the President supported private ownership.

Eisenhower had another chance to oppose government ownership of public power in dealing with the TVA. In 1953 he referred to the

Authority as "creeping socialism." But when asked if he would sell the TVA, the President admitted that it probably was not possible without wrecking the whole enterprise. Still, he attempted to keep it from growing any larger and favored private power companies instead.

The farm problem. While people in many other countries were starving, in the United States the basic farm problem was overproduction. The number of Americans on farms continued to decline. Still, food output went on climbing. New machinery, better seeds, more powerful fertilizers and pesticides, and more efficient marketing made the difference. Farmers were alarmed at their declining numbers. They feared that they would lose their political influence. They wanted the federal government to continue to guarantee the prices of their produce. They wanted at least the 90 percent parity payments which they were receiving under the Agricultural Act of 1949. ("Parity" was defined as the relation of farm to nonfarm prices during the period 1910 to 1914.) The surpluses, they said, could be used to fight hunger throughout the world. But Secretary Benson called for lower and more flexible price supports. He said that the government could never solve the problem of mounting surpluses until it stopped paying farmers to overproduce.

In 1954 Congress passed Benson's Agricultural Act. This replaced rigid supports with flexible supports. Now Benson could lower the parity payments in order to discourage overproduction. Farmers were outraged. Since Ike did not want to lose the votes of farmers, Benson did not make much use of his power.

In the election year of 1956, to make farmers happy the administration asked Congress for a "Soil Bank" plan. This was a way of paying farmers for not planting their land. The theory was that this saved the nation's soil for the future. Congress provided a billion dollars for farmers who took land out of production and

American farmers were so productive that sometimes they had to store their output in the streets.

Kenneth Jarecke, Contact Press Images/Woodfin Camp

📖 **More from Boorstin:** "Haunted by his military background, the President was determined to keep American life civilian-oriented and peace-minded. In December 1960, only a few weeks before his farewell address to the nation, President Eisenhower refused to approve funds to continue the space program toward a moon landing. In the farewell address on January 17, 1961, he warned the nation to 'guard against the acquisition of unwarranted influence, whether sought or unsought by the military-industrial complex.'" (From *The Americans: The Democratic Experience*)

used it instead as pasturage or forest. Still farm surpluses mounted, and farm income continued to decline.

The Republicans become more moderate.

Although Eisenhower had come to office wanting to turn back the clock, he was always a practical man. He soon saw that the New Deal measures were popular. Most Americans had come to believe that a more active government served the general welfare. In 1954 Ike stated his new view. The administration had to be "liberal when it was talking about the relationship between government and the individual, and conservative when talking about the national economy and the individual's pocket book." As one White House aide noted, "The President's changed, we've all changed since we came here."

(p. 735)

As a result, in 1954 and 1956 Social Security benefits were increased. The system was broadened to make eligible 10 million more workers. In 1955 Congress and the President compromised on a law lifting the minimum wage from 75 cents to one dollar an hour.

New programs were voted for urban slum clearance and public housing. Congress also was asked to provide federal support for private health insurance plans—but refused. Instead money was voted for medical research and hospitals. On April 1, 1953, President Eisenhower signed a bill (first proposed by President Truman) creating a Cabinet Department of Health, Education, and Welfare. HEW was to oversee Social Security, health programs, food and drug acts, welfare legislation, and educational programs. Mrs. Oveta Culp Hobby of Texas, who had been the successful commander of the WACs in World War II, became the first Secretary of the department.

The search for Communists.

Senator Joseph McCarthy of Wisconsin, now the chairman of the Government Operations Committee, was in full cry against Communists in government. He accused the Democrats of "twenty years of treason" and claimed that they had let Communists take many government positions. Ike, the brave military leader, did not show his usual courage in dealing with the senator. And McCarthy would soon discredit the President's party. Ike's approach was to avoid a head-on collision with McCarthy. As one of his aides said, he did not want "to offend anyone in Congress."

To beat McCarthy to the punch, Ike issued his own security order on April 27, 1953. This widened the area of behavior that might make anyone a "security risk." If any charge—no matter how foolish or unsupported by facts—was brought against a government employee, he or she would be suspended until proved innocent. This reversed the American tradition that in a free country a person is presumed to be innocent until proved guilty. Government officials were no longer treated with the respect shown to other citizens. The morale in the government service sank to the lowest point in our history. The administration actually boasted that a thousand "security risks" had been fired. In time it appeared that only a small number of individuals had been removed under the security procedures. But the damage was done.

The fall of McCarthy.

Still none of this satisfied McCarthy. He admitted that the Eisenhower administration was doing well in some areas by ridding the government of Communists. But he said that they were batting zero in other areas. And he broadened his wild attacks. He forced the removal of "Communist" books (books that he did not agree with) from United States libraries overseas. In 1954 he accused the Secretary of the Army of concealing evidence of espionage activities at Fort Monmouth, New Jersey. In February he accused Brigadier General Ralph Zwicker of shielding Communists and called him a disgrace to his uniform. At long last the White House supported the army when it struck back. The army charged that McCarthy had sought privileged treatment for an aide who had been drafted.

Televised hearings were held over the charges and countercharges. Hardly had the first session opened than McCarthy interrupted the chairman. "A point of order, Mr. Chairman. May I raise a point of order?" And over the following months as 20 million watched, McCarthy interrupted constantly with his made-up

✖ Critical Thinking Activity: Demonstrating Reasoned Judgment How could President Eisenhower have successfully censured Senator McCarthy's activities? Although Eisenhower privately disliked McCarthy's Communist witch-hunt, he preferred to remain silent and avoid any head-on collision with the Senator. Have students write a letter to President Eisenhower advising him how to handle Senator McCarthy's committee hearings and anti-Communist forays. Allow students to share their letters with the class.

Senator Joe McCarthy, during the Army-McCarthy hearings, uses a map for the locations of Communists. Joseph Welch, the chief counsel for the army, listens in dismay. The day before, June 9, 1954, Welch had called McCarthy a "cruelly reckless character assassin."

points of order. He treated witnesses rudely and showed himself an unscrupulous bully. Television exposed and defeated McCarthy, though his fellow senators could not and the President would not. His influence rapidly declined. Only a few months later, in December 1954 he was condemned by the Senate for conduct "contrary to senatorial traditions." McCarthy's reign of terror was over.

The election of 1956. President Eisenhower was renominated along with his Vice-President Richard M. Nixon at the Republican convention in San Francisco in August. His fellow party members were not troubled by Ike's health problems—which included a serious heart attack. Adlai Stevenson had conducted a spirited and successful fight in the presidential primaries. He was renominated when the Democrats had met in Chicago a week before the Republicans. Senator Estes Kefauver of Tennessee, Stevenson's chief rival in the pre-convention campaign, was named for the Vice-Presidency.

Both parties ran short campaigns, and both relied heavily on television. The Republicans had the advantage of the nation's prosperity and Ike's continuing popularity. Stevenson ❀ somehow lacked the verve he had shown in his first campaign. Eisenhower swept the country, winning 35.5 million votes and carrying 41 states to Stevenson's 26 million votes and 7 states. But while they "liked Ike," the voters still favored Democratic domestic policies. In both houses of Congress the Democrats increased

❀ See "Lesson Plan," p. 728D for **Cooperative Learning Activity: Identifying Assumptions** relating to Eisenhower's 1956 election campaign.

the majorities they had won in 1954. Not since 1848 had the party that won the Presidency lost both houses of Congress.

See "Section 2 Review answers," p. 728D.

Section 2 Review

1. Identify or explain: offshore oil rights, Oveta Culp Hobby, HEW.
2. How did flexible price supports and the "Soil Bank" seek to reduce farm surpluses? Were these measures successful?
3. Cite some New Deal-type programs adopted between 1953 and 1956.
4. How did the Eisenhower administration react to Joseph McCarthy's anti-Communist campaign of the early 1950s?
5. Trace the events leading to McCarthy's fall.
6. **Critical Thinking: Recognizing Ideologies.** Why was President Dwight Eisenhower in favor of "less government" in business?

See "Lesson Plan," p. 728D.

3. The fight for equality

After World War II, all around the globe there was a new struggle by poor people and colonial peoples for freedom and a better life. As old empires fell, former colonies everywhere suddenly became independent nations. A new republic appeared in Africa in 1957 when Ghana became independent from Britain. By 1965 there were 30 new African member-states in the United Nations.

In the United States, too, black people struggled to be equal. Soldiers who had fought for democracy, and workers who had helped bring victory, refused to be second-class citizens. They objected to segregation and every other kind of inequality.

The Supreme Court rules for equality. Back in 1896 in *Plessy* v. *Ferguson* (p. 380) the Supreme Court had declared that laws requiring blacks to use separate washrooms, schools, and railroad cars did not violate the Fourteenth Amendment. It was all right, the Court had said, for services to be separate so long as they were "equal."

Who had the power to complain if the schools were not really equal? Most blacks were kept from voting in the South, so they had no way of forcing government officials to listen. The Supreme Court had okayed the two-nation South.

In the South, blacks continued to have the worst of everything. In any case, people who are forced to use washrooms and water fountains and schools not used by other Americans are not being allowed to be equal. Simply because they were separate, the schools for blacks could not possibly be equal.

Finally in a series of decisions the United States Supreme Court began to outlaw southern practices and laws that had taken from blacks their full rights as Americans. In three separate decisions—in 1944, 1947, and 1953—the Court declared that the laws that kept blacks from voting in Democratic primaries violated the Fourteenth Amendment. Beginning in 1938 the Court had started to narrow the "separate but equal" doctrine. It began to insist that what was separate had to be really equal. It outlawed segregation in interstate commerce. And in 1950, after hearing a case argued by persuasive Thurgood Marshall for the NAACP, the Court declared that the black law school in Texas could not possibly be made equal to the prestigious University of Texas Law School.

In 1953, President Eisenhower appointed former Governor Earl Warren of California as the Supreme Court's new Chief Justice. Warren, more politician than lawyer, was to preside over the Court until 1969. He was to be deeply influenced by two of the Court's most forceful justices, Hugo Black and William O. Douglas. During the Warren years the Supreme Court would make many far-reaching decisions on segregation, the rights of criminals, and legislative apportionment within the states (pp. 819–820).

Perhaps no decision of the Warren Court was more significant than *Brown* v. *Board of Education of Topeka, Kansas* in 1954. This case too had been argued by Thurgood Marshall, who would become the first black to sit on the

Multicultural Connection: Thurgood Marshall (1908–) was the first African American to be appointed to the United States Supreme Court. Previous to the appointment, Marshall had a distinguished legal career with the NAACP as director of its Legal Defense and Education Fund from 1936 to 1961. One of Marshall's greatest triumphs was as the head of the legal team that argued the case of *Brown* v. *Board of Education* before the Supreme Court, which culminated in a decision from the Court against legalized segregation based on race. Marshall stepped down from the Supreme Court in 1991.

Supreme Court when he was appointed by President Johnson. A unanimous Court ordered that, under the Constitution, public schools could not be separated by race. Americans had a right to go to school with all other Americans of their age and grade. This was a part of their education. No American should be deprived of that right. The opposite of separation was "integration"—bringing together into one. And the Supreme Court now seemed to say that all public schools in the United States had to be "integrated."

The South resists. The South, however, resisted integration. In 1955 the Supreme Court ordered that the integration of schools was to go forward "with all deliberate speed." While progress was made in Washington, D.C., and in many border states, the lower South held out. And they were encouraged to resist when, in March 1956, more than 100 southern members of Congress signed the "Southern Manifesto." They bitterly attacked the Supreme Court decision and promised "to use all lawful means to bring about the reversal of this decision which is contrary to the Constitution." In the Senate only three southern senators—Lyndon Baines Johnson of Texas and the two senators from Tennessee, Estes Kefauver and Albert Gore— did not sign the manifesto. The South was now launched on its policy of "massive resistance" to the order of the Supreme Court.

The first serious incident occurred in the fall of 1957 when the Little Rock, Arkansas, school board moved to integrate its high schools. Governor Orval Faubus suddenly declared that there was a danger of violence in Little Rock and sent in the National Guard. The National Guard prevented the black children from attending school. Then a federal judge forced the National Guard to be removed. On September 23, when the black children again tried to attend school, a white mob forced them to leave.

The government intervenes. President Eisenhower hesitated to involve himself in the integration of the schools. He later said he believed that the Supreme Court decision in *Brown* was

Don Uhrbrock/Life Magazine © Time, Inc.

Georgia students picket a southern lunch counter where they were not allowed to sit down.

correct, but at the time he was silent. He thought that a President should not approve or disapprove of court decisions. Southerners, he said, should be given a chance to adjust to this great change. The process would have to go ahead slowly, Eisenhower said, because "we have got to have reason and sense and education, and a lot of other developments that go hand in hand in this process—if this process is going to have any real acceptance in the United States."

But the mob violence was too much. The President finally acted. He ordered the Arkansas National Guard into the federal service so that Governor Faubus could not use them to stop integration. Then he sent in 1000 paratroopers and opened the schools. Still the story

Continuity and Change: Social Change Point out to students that as late as 1987, thirty years after the attempted integration of Little Rock schools, entire neighborhoods in Little Rock were segregated as a result of whites moving to the suburbs. The government then tried to reintegrate the schools through busing and the merging of school districts, the end result being that many whites moved away to avoid the busing, and schools were again segregated. (See p. 850.)

One thousand paratroopers insured that the integration of Little Rock High School would be peaceful.

had only begun. The paratroopers stayed, but in the fall of 1958 Governor Faubus ordered the high schools closed to prevent integration. They were closed the entire school year. Virginia also closed some schools that same year to prevent them from being integrated. The battle for integration would be long and hard.

Martin Luther King and Mrs. Rosa Parks. In the 1950s the nation was ready for the work of Martin Luther King, Jr. He began in a small way and in one place. Within a few years his message had carried out to the world.

Born in Atlanta in 1929, the son of a minister, he attended Morehouse College and received a doctor's degree in theology from Boston University. He was a natural leader, American to the core. He combined the common sense of a Booker T. Washington with the impatient visions of a Du Bois.

On December 1, 1955, Rosa Parks, a tired black seamstress returning from work, boarded a crowded bus in Montgomery, Alabama. She took a seat in the front row of the section of the bus reserved for black passengers. When she was told to give up her seat to a white man and move farther back in the bus, she refused. The police arrested her for violating the law.

Martin Luther King, who was then a Baptist minister in Montgomery, agreed with Mrs. Parks that it was time for action. It was time to stop any Americans from being degraded.

The nonviolent way. Although King was indignant and saddened, he was not angry. He was a thoughtful man, and a Christian, and he decided to try another way. He called it the only true Christian way. It was the way of Thoreau and Mahatma Gandhi. It was the way of massive and nonviolent opposition to unjust laws.

Enrichment Support File Topic

See "Lesson Plan," p. 728D for **Writing Process Activity: Recognizing Ideologies** relating to the desegregation of schools in Little Rock, Arkansas.

He did not tell people to burn the buses or fight the police. No, he said. All people need to be educated in the ways of peace and decency. If you fight your enemies with violence, you will be using their weapons and brutalizing yourself. But if you are peaceful and simply do not go along with them, you will eventually prevail. And if you win this way, your victory will not merely be the truce in a running battle. It will actually be peace. Your enemies will understand, and they will begin to be decent, too.

So he preached to the blacks in Montgomery. He told them to stop using the buses until the buses gave them their place as Americans. Of course many blacks were angry. But Martin Luther King begged and pleaded with them to keep their heads, and to keep love in their hearts, even while they joined the bus boycott.

For 381 days the blacks of Montgomery refused to ride the buses. It was difficult. Some formed car pools. Some were given rides by friendly white neighbors. Many walked miles to work. Others simply did not get to their jobs and had to lose their wages. And the bus company was about to go bankrupt.

In the end the Supreme Court ruled that segregation on buses was illegal. The blacks and all the decent people of Montgomery had won. They had brought an end to another form of injustice. When the buses ran again, every passenger was treated like all the others. Martin Luther King, Jr., called this a "Stride Toward Freedom."

It was a step along a new path. Many Americans were encouraged to walk along that path in the years that followed. By 1960 many blacks in the South were using this new way to fight segregation. They sat down at lunch counters where they had not been allowed to sit. They swam in swimming pools that had been denied to blacks. And they worshiped in churches that had kept out blacks. They did not fight the police or strike out at anyone. Quietly and peacefully, they simply acted like decent Americans who knew their rights.

Civil rights laws. Now the federal government moved, too. In August 1957 the Eisenhower administration finally won the first Civil Rights

Bob Fitch/Black Star

Martin Luther King stands beneath a picture of Mahatma Gandhi, the Indian leader who taught the way of nonviolence.

Act since the days of Reconstruction. It was not an earthshaking law. The main thing that it did was to give the Justice Department the right to bring suits on behalf of blacks who were denied the right to vote. The real significance of the measure was that it passed and that it was a truly bipartisan measure. Republicans and Democrats working together overcame the resistance and the filibusters of the southern members to pass this bill. One of the leaders in its passage was a Texas senator named Lyndon B. Johnson, the Democratic leader of the Senate.

This was followed in 1960 by another Civil Rights Act, again passed with bipartisan support. It gave even more aid to blacks who wanted to vote. When the Republicans and the Democrats met in their conventions to draw up platforms and select candidates for the Presidency in 1960, both parties supported desegregation. At last the nation was turning back to

Perspectives Topic

Continuity and Change: Social Change Point out to students that in a truly bipartisan effort, Republicans and Democrats worked together in 1957 to pass the first civil rights bill since Reconstruction. A step forward for civil rights, the bill allowed the Justice Department to bring suits on behalf of African Americans who were denied the right to vote. The last civil rights measure to become law, passed in 1866, allowed the federal government to intervene in a state's affairs to protect the rights of all U.S. citizens. (See p. 368.)

the unsolved problems of the Civil War. And blacks themselves were in the vanguard bringing about that change.

See "Section 3 Review answers," p. 728D.

Section 3 Review

1. Identify or explain: *Plessy* v. *Ferguson*, "Southern Manifesto," Lyndon Johnson, Estes Kefauver, Orval Faubus, Rosa Parks.
2. Locate: Ghana, Topeka, Little Rock, Montgomery.
3. How did World War II influence the struggle for racial equality?
4. What did the Supreme Court decide in *Brown* v. *Board of Education*?
5. Describe southern resistance to the *Brown* desegregation decision. How did President Eisenhower respond?
6. How did enactment of the Civil Rights Acts of 1957 and 1960 help in the movement for racial equality?
7. **Critical Thinking: Drawing Conclusions.** What role did Martin Luther King, Jr., play in the struggle for racial equality? What was his strategy?

Eric Lessing/Magnum

Hungarians burn Stalin's picture in 1956.

See "Lesson Plan," p. 728E.

4. Difficulties abroad

Eisenhower could claim no great diplomatic victories during his first years. He had, in fact, slowly retreated from aggressive anti-communism. Now Chiang Kai-shek was discouraged from starting a new war to drive communism from mainland China. The United States talked less of "massive retaliation." The policy was simply to contain communism and "coexist."

A difficult year. The year 1956 made clear that the world's problems were fearfully complex. Secretary of State Dulles's hope to liberate the people behind the iron curtain had been dealt a blow in 1953. A workers' revolt in East Berlin and other East German cities was harshly put down by the Communists. There was little protest from the West. At the end of October 1956 a people's uprising against Communist rule in Hungary was ruthlessly crushed by Soviet tanks and troops. Without going to war, the United States could do little to aid these enslaved neighbors of Russia in their fight for freedom against the great invader. But afterwards the American people (as they had done again and again) could and did offer refuge to those who fled from tyranny.

In that same year, the Middle East also blew up. Egypt had long been a colonial puppet of the Western powers—especially of the British and the French. Gamal Abdel Nasser, the able young officer who had led the army coup to dethrone King Farouk, was the new leader of Egypt. With the other Arab leaders, Nasser refused to recognize Israel.

Israel had emerged after World War II in the land of Palestine. The British ruled Palestine between the World Wars and during these years many Jews were allowed to emigrate to their ancient homeland. Great Britain tried to

Multicultural Connection: Undersecretary to the UN at this time was African-American diplomat Ralph Bunche, appointed in 1955. Bunche was a self-made man who grew up in the slums of Detroit and eventually earned a Ph.D. from Harvard University. In 1941 Bunche entered government service with the State Department. In 1955 he was appointed an Undersecretary of the UN and in 1958 was promoted to Undersecretary of Special Political Affairs. Among his distinguished accomplishments was the Nobel Peace Prize awarded in 1950 for his work as UN moderator for Palestine in 1948–1949.

establish a Jewish-Arab state, but the Arabs would have none of it. After World War II, the United Nations tried to solve the problem by dividing the country between the Palestinian Arabs and the Jews. Following the UN decision, the Jews announced their new state of Israel on May 14, 1948, and were immediately recognized by the U.S. and the USSR. The next day Israel was invaded by armed forces from a number of Arab states—Transjordan (Jordan), Egypt, Syria, Lebanon, and Iraq. But the poorly trained and ill-equipped Arabs were no match for the Israelis. Israel quickly seized most of Palestine. Transjordan took the area of Palestine called the West Bank (because it was on the west bank of the Jordan River). Hundreds of thousands of Palestinians fled. These refugees were to create problems for decades to come.

As leader of Egypt, Nasser armed and assisted raiding parties of Palestinians to attack Israel from the Egyptian-occupied Gaza Strip. Israel's powerful raids in response showed how militarily weak Egypt was. So Nasser made an arms deal with the Soviet Union (by way of Czechoslovakia) and began importing large quantities of new weapons. Nasser also wanted to build a vast and costly dam at Aswan to control the flooding of the Nile River and use the water for irrigation. At first the United States had offered to help. But Nasser's new friendliness with the Soviet Union led the United States to withdraw in July 1956. Nasser then seized and nationalized the Suez Canal, which was run by an Anglo-French company. He said he would use the revenue from its operation to pay for the dam.

Goaded by the border raids and fearful that Egypt's new arms would be used to destroy them, the Israelis attacked Egypt on October 29, 1956. Two days later Britain and France amazed the world by joining the attack. The British feared their loss of control of the Suez Canal, while the French were angered by Egyptian aid to the rebellion against their rule in Algeria. British and French forces seized the northern third of the canal while Israel struck across Egypt's Sinai peninsula. The Egyptian air force was quickly destroyed.

All this was convenient for the Soviets. It helped the Russians turn world attention from their slaughter of the rebels against their rule in Hungary. Premier Khrushchev screamed that England, France, and Israel were aggressors in Egypt. Posing as a friend of the Arabs, he threatened to send air and naval forces to Egypt and then even launch missiles against London and Paris. Once again a third world war seemed at hand.

The United States did not rush to the defense of its allies. Eisenhower and Dulles had not been consulted before the British and the French took military action. They were angry. And they feared another world conflict. Ike joined Khrushchev to support a UN resolution demanding a cease-fire and quick withdrawals from Egyptian territory. Britain, France, and Israel had no choice but to comply, since they were threatened by the Soviet Union and opposed by the United States. In March 1957 a UN Emergency Force made up of troops from Colombia, Denmark, India, Norway, and Sweden arrived in Gaza to patrol the shaky peace. Meanwhile, the Soviets ignored a UN resolution calling upon them to withdraw their troops from Hungary.

Developing missiles. During this crisis in the Middle East, there was the threat of a menacing new weapon—the long-distance rocket. This weapon was designed to rise high into the air, even beyond the earth's atmosphere. Such a weapon could go farther than any other, and it was hard to detect. But it was extremely difficult to design. Out beyond the atmosphere, of course, airplanes would not work. Every airplane engine then known was driven either by an internal combustion engine (like that in an automobile) that used gasoline to turn a propeller, or by a jet engine that pushed ahead by burning gases. Both required oxygen. Up over 250 miles, beyond the atmosphere, there is no oxygen. A very special kind of engine was required.

To solve these and other problems of space travel, we needed a twentieth-century Columbus. The exploring spirit that had inspired the first settlers was still alive. A young American physicist, Robert H. Goddard, dreamt of traveling in space. When people first heard him, they laughed, just as they had laughed at Columbus. His idea was to use rockets to push through outer space. A rocket carries its own fuel and also carries its own "air." This is usually in the form of liquid oxygen to keep the fuel exploding. The rockets exploding behind push the spacecraft forward.

In 1914 the 32-year-old Goddard received a patent for his liquid-fuel rocket engine. In his technical report for the Smithsonian Institution in Washington, he explained his rocket engine. He said this engine would make it possible someday to reach the moon. The *New York Times* and other respectable newspapers wrote editorials ridiculing his idea. For the rest of his life Goddard distrusted newspapers. Unlike Billy Mitchell, who had used the newspapers to promote the new airplane, Goddard hated publicity and kept his work secret. He went ahead perfecting his rocket engine and finally secured 214 patents on the improvements that made space travel possible.

When Goddard died in 1945, few Americans yet believed that human beings would ever travel through space.

The V-2 rocket.   The people of England, however, already had reasons enough to know that rockets could work. Raining down from the skies in 1944 came more than a thousand German V-2 rockets. Aimed from launching pads 200 miles away in Holland, they did not carry pilots but still reached their English targets. Traveling far faster than the speed of sound, they fell silently from a height of 60 or 70 miles. Each held a ton of explosives.

The V-2 rockets were the work of German scientists who had been experimenting since 1932. When the Nazis came to power and plunged the world into war, the Nazis had provided these scientists with a secret new laboratory in Peenemünde, a little German fishing village on the Baltic Sea.

By 1944 some 12,000 Germans were making V-2 rockets. These were pouring death and destruction on English cities every day. The name "V-2" came from German words meaning "Vengeance Weapon, No. 2." It was, next to the atom bomb, the most terrifying weapon of the war because it struck without warning and no defense against it could be found.

The race for rockets.   At that very moment the Russians were speeding westward across Europe in their final triumphal march. They hastened to Peenemünde to capture the German rocket factory—for their own future use. When they arrived they found, to their dismay, that the most valuable resource, the rocket scientists themselves, had already fled to the West.

"This is absolutely intolerable," Dictator Stalin raged. "We defeated the Nazi armies; we occupied Berlin and Peenemünde; but the Americans got the rocket engineers!" Stalin was especially angered because the Russian Communists lacked big bombing planes. Their only weapons, then, for a future long-distance attack on the United States would be long-distance rockets.

Some farsighted American generals had organized the project to rescue the German rocket engineers, the V-2 equipment, and 14 tons of documents for the West under the code name "Operation Paperclip." They collected 127 of the best German rocket scientists (including their chief, Wernher Von Braun) and signed them up to work on rockets and space travel for the United States. The brilliant Von Braun later became head of the United States Army rocket research. In time, the Russians also captured German rocket scientists who went to work on rocket research for them.

The United States and Communist Russia began a terrifying new arms competition. This time it was rockets. By 1956 the chief of the Russian Communist party, Nikita Khrushchev, boasted that Soviet military rockets soon would be able to hit any target on earth.

Then, on October 4, 1957, the Russians sent up the first man-made earth satellite. It was a package of instruments weighing 184 pounds. They called it *Sputnik*, which in Russian meant "fellow traveler" (of the earth). One month later they launched a much heavier satellite, *Sputnik II*, which weighed 1120 pounds. This satellite carried a dog, called Laika, to see how a living creature would react to life in outer space.

More from Boorstin: "The world press outdid itself in headlining snide epithets like 'Kaputnik' (London *Daily Express*) or 'A Pearl Harbor for American Science' (Tokyo *Yomiuri*). . . . These accumulating evidences of Soviet superiority in space technology triggered a concern bordering on hysteria, for the quality of American education, especially in mathematics and the sciences. And the Soviet challenge did influence the curriculum of some schools." (From *The Americans: The Democratic Experience*)

Could an animal from earth live out there where everything floated and nothing had any weight? Laika survived.

The space race was on! The Soviets had exploded a hydrogen bomb in 1953. If they had rockets powerful enough to launch satellites, what would prevent them from bombarding the United States with nuclear weapons? Now it seemed that Khrushchev's boasts were true.

The early American efforts to make rockets were not always successful. The White House announced that on December 6, 1957, the United States would launch its own satellite with a Vanguard rocket. While the whole nation watched on television, this much-advertised rocket collapsed on the wet sand. The next try (p. 744) did succeed. Two months later *Explorer I*, the first American satellite, went into orbit.

The United States reacts to Sputnik. Americans were still frightened to see the Russians so far ahead in the space race. According to Senator Henry Jackson of Washington, *Sputnik* was a "devastating blow to the prestige of the United States." Americans now began to fear that the Soviet educational system which had trained the scientists who produced the satellites was better than ours. In a series of articles, *Life* magazine proclaimed a "Crisis in Education." Congress voted the National Defense Education Act in 1958. Its $1 billion program was intended to produce more scientists and teachers of science. It made available money for loans to high school and college graduates to enable them to continue their scientific education. Funds were also provided for laboratories and scientific equipment for schools and colleges.

Shortly after *Sputnik* the President appointed James R. Killian, Jr., the president of the Massachusetts Institute of Technology, as his Special Assistant for Science and Technology. He was, Ike said, "to have the active responsibility for helping me to follow through on the scientific improvement of our defense."

In 1958 Ike's already large defense budget was increased by another $4 billion for rocket and missile research and development and for the conquest of outer space. The new National

Wide World Photos

Muscovites gaze at a model of *Sputnik I*, the satellite that opened the Space Age.

Aeronautics and Space Administration (NASA) would coordinate these space efforts.

Problems in the Middle East. Meanwhile, during 1957, the United States was losing influence in the Middle East as Egypt's Nasser fanned anti-Western feelings and promoted Arab nationalism. Nasser's ties to the Soviets made his actions especially worrisome. The oil from this region was vital to the economies of the Western nations. They could not just watch the area fall to the Communists.

To combat this new threat, the President announced the Eisenhower Doctrine, which was adopted by Congress in a joint resolution in March 1957. The United States would help any Middle East country that requested aid to resist military aggression from any Communist-controlled country. Still, the main threat to American influence in the Middle East came from the weakness of the existing governments. So the policy was soon modified to include American help for pro-Western governments

Critical Thinking Activity: Expressing Problems Clearly How could the nation promote science education? The race for space made the United States examine science education in the nation's schools. The result was an intense campaign to emphasize science courses throughout a child's education. Have students develop a campaign slogan and companion poster to promote science education in the late 1950s. Have students share their work.

against Communist-supported attempts to overthrow them.

Still, the situation worsened. Syria and Egypt joined hands in the United Arab Republic. Violence threatened the friendly government of King Hussein in Jordan. In May 1958 civil war broke out between Christians, who favored keeping Lebanon independent and pro-Western, and Muslims, who supported an alliance with Egypt and Syria. Finally in July the king and the prime minister of Iraq were murdered by pro-Nasser army officers and another friendly government seemed lost to the West.

After this change of the government in Iraq, Jordan and Lebanon asked for help under the Eisenhower Doctrine. Britain supported King Hussein of Jordan with paratroopers, and the United States landed 14,000 marines in Lebanon. The large United States force also served as a warning to the new Iraqi government not to nationalize its oil fields. British and American forces were soon withdrawn. They had, at least for a time, helped to stabilize the situation in the Middle East and proved to Nasser that there were limits on what he could do to promote Arab nationalism and anti-Western feeling. They also showed him that there were limits to the support he could expect from the USSR. That nation had voiced disapproval of the troop movements, but had taken no other action.

More crises. Even as the United States struggled to preserve its position in the Middle East, war threatened on the other side of the globe. In August 1958 the Chinese Communists began to shell the Nationalist Chinese islands of Quemoy and Matsu off the mainland. President Eisenhower declared that the United States would join the fighting if the Communists seized the offshore islands as part of a campaign against (p. 747) Taiwan, seat of the Republican Chinese government of Chiang Kai-shek. Ike sent the powerful Seventh Fleet into the Formosa Strait off Taiwan to back up his warning.

Reeling from crises in Suez, Lebanon, and the Formosa Strait, the United States suddenly faced a stern new test from Russia. On November 27, 1958, the Soviet government called on the Western powers to leave West Berlin and make Berlin a "free" city. The Russians threatened that if the Western powers did not pull out of Berlin within six months, Russia would withdraw from East Berlin and sign a peace treaty with the East German regime, which then

Trouble Spots of the Cold War, 1950s

Communist Bloc

might cut off Western access to West Berlin. The Western powers rejected the Soviet proposal, but neither side forced a showdown.

Relaxing the cold war. To ease tensions, in the summer of 1959 Vice-President Nixon went on a goodwill tour of the Soviet Union and Poland, while the veteran Soviet leader Anastas Mikoyan came to the United States. Nixon and Khrushchev, in front of television cameras, debated the merits of the two nations' economic systems while inspecting a kitchen display at an American exhibit in Moscow. A war of words was better than any other kind! Vice-President Nixon thought that Khrushchev really ought to see the United States.

In August President Eisenhower announced that he and Khrushchev would exchange visits. Then in mid-September the President received the Russian leader. While traveling to the West Coast, Khrushchev said he wanted to visit Disneyland. He was infuriated when, for security reasons, his request was refused. The spirit was better when he conferred with the President at Camp David in the Catoctin Mountains of Maryland. That good feeling came to be called the "spirit of Camp David." The two leaders agreed to settle the Berlin issue by negotiation, and the Soviets withdrew their six-month time limit. They also agreed to continue their talks at a later summit meeting.

"At this wondrous moment," British Prime Minister Macmillan said, "we seem on the threshold of genuine practical steps toward peace." The next meeting was set for May 16, 1960, at Paris.

Collapse of the conference. The spirit of Camp David was shattered on May 5, 1960. Khrushchev announced that Soviet forces had shot down an American U-2 plane engaged in aerial reconnaissance over the Soviet Union. Thinking the pilot had died in the crash or committed suicide as ordered, the United States flatly denied the charge of spying. Then Khrushchev revealed that the pilot had been captured and had confessed.

Americans were surprised when the President in a television address accepted personal

Rene Burri/Magnum

Tempers rose during Khrushchev and Nixon's famous "debate" that took place at a model American kitchen display in Moscow in 1959.

responsibility for the aerial spying and defended it. Since Khrushchev was already facing opposition within the Soviet Union and was being criticized by the Chinese for not being tough enough on the imperialist Americans, he angrily demanded an apology. Eisenhower refused.

The heads of state gathered in Paris, but they never conferred. Khrushchev bitterly attacked Eisenhower and the United States. He withdrew his invitation to the President to visit the Soviet Union. He said he would have no more meetings with Eisenhower until he apologized. The President again refused. The thaw between the superpowers ended and relations iced over again.

Troubles in Latin America. The United States faced critical new problems even with our neighbors in the Western Hemisphere. Since the days of the Good Neighbor policy and World War II, the nation's attention had been directed mainly to the large challenges farther away.

⊕ Geography and History: Location Use the map on page 746 to locate trouble spots around the world in Eisenhower's second term. You might deal with all the crises at once: Hungary, Egypt, Lebanon, Formosa Strait, Berlin, the U-2 incident, and Cuba. Ask: Did the Eisenhower Doctrine provide a new direction for American foreign policy? (It was simply a restatement of the Truman Doctrine with emphasis on the Middle East; it was really the news media that elevated the pronouncement to the status of "doctrine.")

The United States had tried to prevent the spread of communism by supporting governments that proclaimed their anti-communism. But this policy sometimes backfired. We often ended up helping repressive governments. We found ourselves bolstering dictatorships—merely because they were anti-Communist. This lost us friends among freedom-loving people. In many parts of the world, where free institutions were weak, we had no easy choice.

United States weakness in Latin America was exposed by the rapid movement of events in Cuba. In 1958 the longtime dictator of that country, the corrupt Fulgencio Batista, was overthrown by a young lawyer, Fidel Castro. For three years Castro had led guerrilla forces operating from the Cuban hills. Castro seized the large foreign (mainly United States) holdings in Cuba. He collectivized the farms. He freed the country from its dependence on the United States. But he tied himself to the Soviets and set up a new police state. "Cuba, sí, Yanqui no!" was Castro's popular rallying cry. An eloquent and long-winded speaker, he soon became a folk hero. He was famous for his big Havana cigars and his friendly manner with Cuban peasants. He outlawed all parties except the Communists and set up prison camps for his enemies. With Soviet aid, Castro built up one of the strongest military forces in Latin America. This loaded pistol was only 90 miles off the coast of the United States.

Eisenhower steps down. If it had not been for the Twenty-second Amendment, Ike could probably have run for and won a third term. Unlike TR or FDR, he had not been a strong President. But his calm and friendly way and his good-humored honesty helped ease the bad temper and quiet the jumpy nerves that troubled the nation when he took office. In addition, he had consolidated the New Deal economic and social programs. He made them all-American institutions when he adopted them for the Republicans. And most important of all, the nation was no longer involved in any foreign wars.

Before leaving office, Eisenhower followed the example of another General-President, George Washington, more than a century and a half earlier. Like Washington, Eisenhower turned his farewell address into a warning against the dangers hidden in the future. He cautioned against the "military-industrial complex" that was making its influence "felt in every city, every state house, every office of the federal government." In the future, he admitted, our nation would certainly need vast military forces and enormous factories. What troubled him was "the potential for the disastrous rise of misplaced power. . . . We must never let the weight of this combination endanger our liberties or democratic processes." Still beloved by the mass of Americans, Ike retired to his farm in Gettysburg, Pennsylvania. He left the many unsolved problems of the nation and the world to a promising young President, John F. Kennedy.

See "Section 4 Review answers," p. 728E.

Section 4 Review

1. Identify or explain: Aswan Dam, UN Emergency Force, *Sputnik, Explorer I*, National Defense Education Act, NASA, King Hussein, Anastas Mikoyan, Camp David, Fidel Castro, Palestine.

2. Locate: Suez Canal, Sinai peninsula, Gaza, Syria, Jordan, Lebanon, Iraq, Quemoy, Matsu.

3. What part did each of the following play in the development of rockets, missiles, and earth satellites: (a) Robert Goddard, (b) German scientists, (c) "Operation Paperclip," (d) Werner Von Braun, (e) Russian scientists?

4. How did the United States react to *Sputnik*?

5. What was the Eisenhower Doctrine? Where was it applied? What were the results?

6. Describe the crises centering at Taiwan, Berlin, and Cuba.

7. What efforts were made in 1959–1960 to relax the cold war? How did they turn out?

8. **Critical Thinking: Recognizing Bias.** Why was it surprising that Eisenhower warned Americans about the dangers of a "military-industrial complex" in his farewell address?

Chapter 29 Review

See "Chapter Review answers," p. 728F.

Focusing on Ideas

1. The President needs to be a policymaker, administrator, diplomat, and leader. How did Eisenhower's career up to 1952 provide experience in these roles?

2. Cite instances when the Eisenhower administration made a *forceful response* (use of military force or threat of force) to troublesome events in foreign affairs. On what occasions did the United States use diplomacy or make other non-threatening responses to tension-filled overseas events?

3. What events in the 1950s gave Eisenhower chances to exert leadership for human rights? How did he respond?

Taking a Critical Look

1. **Recognizing Cause and Effect.** During six years of his eight-year Presidency, Eisenhower had to work with a Democratic majority in Congress. How might this have influenced his move to "moderate Republicanism"?

2. **Distinguishing False from Accurate Images.** Some observers see the Eisenhower years as a period of relaxation for the United States—after the turbulent years of depression, world war, and postwar adjustment. Is this an accurate image of the postwar period? Explain.

Your Region in History

1. **Geography.** Describe your locality along racial and ethnic lines in the 1950s. Develop a demographic map of the population of your area for this time period. How has this population distribution changed over time?

2. **Culture.** How were schools in your state affected by the Supreme Court's 1954 school desegregation decision? If change had to take place, how was the matter handled?

3. **Economic.** Identify changes that took place in your city or county during the Eisenhower years focusing on such areas as housing, other construction, industry, and population. Were any of these changes stimulated by federal laws enacted in these years?

Historical Facts and Figures

Formulating Questions. Study the graph below to help answer the following questions: (a) What was the median income for white families in 1940? For non-whites? (b) What was the trend in family income for white families from 1940 to 1980? For non-white families? (c) Was there a clear difference in the economic conditions of the two groups during this period? Explain. (d) What questions would a historian need to ask to determine the reasons for the differences you noted? Make a list of the questions you have identified.

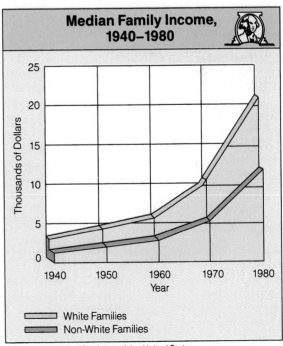

Sources: *Historical Statistics of the United States*
Statistical Abstract of the United States

Chapter 30
Mobile People and Magic Machines

Identifying Chapter Materials

Objectives	Basic Instructional Materials	Extension Materials
1 A Changing People • Cite the demographic changes that changed American society after World War II.	**Annotated Teacher's Edition** • Lesson Plans, p. 750C **Instructional Support File** • Pre-Reading Activities, Unit 10, p. 29 • Skill Review Activity, Unit 10, p. 32	**Documents of American History** • *Baker* v. *Carr*, Vol. 2, p. 671 • *Reynolds* v. *Sims*, Vol. 2, p. 681 **American History Transparencies** • Geography and History, pp. B39, B41, B43 • Our Multicultural Heritage, p. C19 • Fine Art, p. D65
2 Everyday Life Transformed • Describe the growth and characteristics of the American economy between 1945 and 1970. • Summarize the impact of TV on American life. • Discuss the significance of SMSAs and the national plan of interstate highways.	**Annotated Teacher's Edition** • Lesson Plans, pp. 750C–750D **Instructional Support File** • Skill Application Activity, Unit 10, p. 33 • Critical Thinking Activity, Unit 10, p. 34	**Enrichment Support File** • The Age of Affluence (See "In-Depth Coverage" at right.) **Perspectives** • Advertising and Mass Consumption (See "In-Depth Coverage" at right.)
3 Education and Religion • Trace the growth of higher education in the United States through the 1970s and describe changes in religious expression and organized religion in the postwar period.	**Annotated Teacher's Edition** • Lesson Plans, pp. 750D–750E	**Extension Activity** • Religious Denominations, Lesson Plans, p. 750E
4 Art and the Machine • Identify some contemporary American authors and their works and describe the impact of books and other cultural forces in our society. • Describe the importance of reading materials to the process of historical investigation.	**Annotated Teacher's Edition** • Lesson Plans, p. 750E **Instructional Support File** • Reading Activities, Unit 10, pp. 30–31 • Chapter Test, Unit 10, pp. 35–38 • Additional Test Questions, Unit 10, pp. 39–42 • Unit Test, Unit 10, pp. 43–46	**Documents of American History** • William Faulkner's Nobel Prize Speech, Vol. 2, p. 688

Providing In-Depth Coverage

30

Perspectives on the Age of Affluence

By the middle of the Eisenhower years the United States was enjoying an extraordinary economic boom which changed the face of the nation. With Europe and Japan still recovering from the war, the United States, with only 6% of the world's population, produced half of the world's manufactured goods.

A History of the United States as an instructional program provides three types of resources you can use to offer in-depth coverage of prosperity in the late 1940s and early 1950s: the *student text*, the *Enrichment Support File*, and *Perspectives*. The chart below shows the topics that are covered in each.

THE STUDENT TEXT. Boorstin and Kelley's *A History of the United States* unfolds the chronology of events leading to the prosperity of the late 1940s and early 1950s.

AMERICAN HISTORY ENRICHMENT SUPPORT FILE. This collection of primary source readings and classroom activities focuses on the surge of consumerism in the late 1940s and early 1950s.

PERSPECTIVES: READINGS ON AMERICAN HISTORY IN THE 20TH CENTURY. In this edited collection of secondary source readings, well-known historians and political commentators (including Boorstin) provide an array of perspectives on advertising and mass consumption in the mid-twentieth century.

Locating Instructional Materials

Detailed lesson plans for teaching consumerism in the late '40s and early '50s as a mini-course or to study one or more elements of the age of affluence in depth are offered in the following areas: in the *student text*, see individual lesson plans at the beginning of each chapter; in the *Enrichment Support File*, see page 3; in *Perspectives*, see the Teacher's Guide for this topic.

IN-DEPTH COVERAGE ON THE AGE OF AFFLUENCE

Student Text	Enrichment Support File	Perspectives
▪ Postwar Prosperity, pp. 756–757 ▪ Reasons for Prosperity, p. 757 ▪ Technology and Prosperity, pp. 757–763 ▪ Automobile, pp. 757–758 ▪ Television, pp. 760–761 ▪ Arts and Literature in the Age of Affluence, pp. 766–768	▪ Lesson Suggestions ▪ Multimedia Resources ▪ Overview Essay/The Age of Affluence ▪ Literature in American History/"To an American Poet Just Dead" ▪ Songs in American History/"Little Boxes" ▪ Biography in American History/William Bernbach ▪ Geography in American History/The Age of the Suburb ▪ Great Debates in American History/Television—Positive or Negative? ▪ Making Connections	▪ "An Age of Innovation and Growth" by Robert Sobel ▪ "The Educator of New Technology" by Charles Goodrum and Helen Dalrymple ▪ "The Assault on Childhood" by Ron Goulart ▪ "The Wilderness of Commodities" by Max Lerner ▪ "The Good News of Advertising" by Daniel J. Boorstin

A Changing People

FOCUS

To introduce the lesson, ask: If *demos* is the Greek word for "the people," what do you think demography means? (The study of populations.) What do you think demographers study about populations? (Changes in size and composition, and the causes and effects of those changes.) Why would we be interested in demographic changes in American history? (Demographic changes are caused by historical events that influence later historical events.)

Developing Vocabulary

The words listed are essential terms for understanding particular sections of the chapter. The page number after each term indicates the page of its first or most important appearance. These terms are defined in the Glossary (text pages 1000–1011).

demography (page 751); **census** (page 751); **reapportionment** (page 751); **baby boom** (page 751); **suburbs** (page 753); **SMSA (Standard Metropolitan Statistical Area)** (page 754); **metropolitan** (page 754); **megalopolis** (page 755).

INSTRUCT

Explain

Much of this section is a description of our American society during the last quarter century, and you might encourage students to examine your school and community as a microcosm of the country as a whole. Illustrations in pictorial histories, such as Time-Life's *This Fabulous Century—1950–1960* and *1960–1970* will be helpful.

☑ Writing Process Activity

Recognizing Cause and Effect Ask students to play the role of the head of the Bureau of Census. Before they write the governmental report that will accompany a statistical breakdown, ask them to list the demographic trends of the 1950s and explain the reasons behind them. Students should begin their report with an introductory paragraph that summarizes the trends, and they should organize chronologically or by order of importance. As they revise, students should check for clarity, unity, and coherence. After they proofread, ask them to discuss their findings.

Section Review Answers

Section 1, page 756

1. a) study of populations—how they grow, move, and otherwise change. b) population cluster made up of a densely populated area with a central city that has at least 50,000 people. c) a giant urban area consisting of contiguous SMSAs. 2. Between 1945 and 1960 the rate of population growth in the United States increased steadily, mainly because of an increased birthrate, and then slowed during the 1960s. People were living longer, and the number of elderly people grew. Also between 1945 and 1970 large numbers of Americans moved from cities to suburbs and from east to west. At the same time black Americans were moving out of the South, often to northern cities. After 1960 whites moved from the North to the South. 3. Black Americans gained political clout as their population became concentrated in cities. Also, the needs of a growing, moving population stimulated building and other industries, creating jobs.

CLOSE

To conclude the lesson, divide the class into eight groups and assign each group one of the following topics: birthrate, population, immigration, internal migration, farm population, suburban population, mobility, and longer life span. Ask each group to summarize the material in the section about the assigned topic. Ask students to speculate about some of the possible results of the demographic changes described.

Everyday Life Transformed

FOCUS

To introduce the lesson, discuss the impact television has had on the lives of Americans. Some questions to guide the discussion include: How is TV watching related to academic success? What is your opinion of television programming? Why is television a successful advertising medium?

Developing Vocabulary

standard of living (page 757); **gross national product—GNP** (page 757); **per capita** (page 757); **automation** (page 761).

INSTRUCT

Explain

Point out to the class a few additional details about TV and American life: 99.9 percent of American homes have at least one television set. The average American watches more than 35 hours of television per week. Some 100 million Americans watch television nightly. Nielson figures reveal that close to a million two- to eleven-year-olds are up watching TV at midnight. Educational programs such as *Sesame Street,* used in conjunction with teaching and supplementary materials, can improve children's test scores. The average teenager will spend more time watching television than in class.

✿ Cooperative Learning Activity

Making Comparisons Break the class into groups of four. Explain that students will use outside resources to prepare a report on the standard of living of Western Europeans during the same postwar period in which Americans prospered. Assign one country—Britain, France, or West Germany—to each group. Then appoint members of each group to identify and gather resources, to use those resources to write the report, and to prepare a presentation to the class. Following the presentations, lead the class in a discussion comparing the American and Western European standards of living in the postwar period.

Section Review Answers

Section 2, page 763

1. Demand for goods—such as houses and appliances and automobiles—that had been pent up by the war, wartime savings, continued government spending, flourishing exports, and new products. 2. Research and development created new tools, new products, and new jobs. 3. Political candidates would not have to worry so much about their "image," and; would have to work harder to meet the people; no televised debates. Radio would be far more important as a source of news and entertainment. Advertising would not be as big an industry as it is today. Newspapers, books, and magazines would have higher sales. Newspaper reporters and columnists would have national reputations such as those held by the anchors on television news programs. Events would not have a certain immediacy we are used to.

CLOSE

To conclude the lesson, ask students to compare the impact of the automobile on the post-World War II period with its impact in the 1920s (discussed in Chapter 22, Section 4, pp. 592–596).

Section 3 (pages 763–765)

Education and Religion

FOCUS

To introduce the lesson, gather memorabilia of high school education on the 1950s: yearbooks, school newspapers, lists of course offerings, lists of rules, dress codes. Invite a current or retired teacher who taught during the 1950s to provide the class with some recollections of the period. Then have students make two lists, one for differences between their school experience and what they have learned about the 1950s, the other for similarities. Ask: How has high school changed significantly since the 1950s?

INSTRUCT

Explain

A number of studies critical of American education appeared in the 1980s. One of the most influential was *A Nation at Risk* issued by the U.S. Special Commission on Excellence in Education. It proposed better teacher preparation, a longer school year, more homework, and tougher graduation requirements.

☑ Writing Process Activity

Drawing Conclusions Ask students to do research about how the Russo-American space race influenced education in the United States. Students might concentrate on James Bryant Conant and his book, suggested revisions in math and science curricula, or some other aspect that interests them. Have students begin their report with a thesis statement that summarizes their particular focus on the topic. As they revise, students should check for clarity, completeness, and logical organization. After they proofread, have them share their report with group members.

Section Review Answers

Section 3, page 765

1. a) educational philosopher who believed that children learn by doing. His writings stimulated the "Progressive Education" movement that shaped American schools. b) wrote *The American High School Today* in which he proposed a minimum size for high schools, higher standards, and greater emphasis on traditional academic courses. c) Catholic priest who had a weekly television show during the 1950s. d) attracted thousands to his religious meetings and reached millions more by radio and television. e) wrote *The Power of Positive Thinking*. 2. The Soviets' successful launching of the first satellite led some Americans to question whether American schools were inferior to Soviet schools and sparked calls for educational reform. 3. Some clergymen found gimmicks to attract people into their churches while others were able to reach millions in their homes by radio and public television.

CLOSE

To conclude the lesson, ask students to write an essay evaluating one of the changes suggested in *A*

Nation at Risk. In their essays, ask them to be sure to answer the following questions: How might this change be accomplished? Is this change realistic— *i.e.,* can it be done? What effects would this change have on education today? What effects would this change have on my school experience?

Extension Activity

Have students select a religious denomination in existence during the years 1945–1960. Students will research their choice and write a short essay reporting on its progress or lack of progress during this time period.

Section 4 (pages 766–768)

Art and the Machine

FOCUS

To introduce the lesson, ask: What are the books on the current best-seller list? Write the titles on the chalkboard. If the newspaper provides capsule summaries of the books, read them to the students. (If yours does not, *The New York Times Book Review*, available at many newsstands and libraries, does.) Then ask: What do these book titles and subjects tell us about our society? (Some obvious points can be brought out, such as what the number of health and diet books show about our society.) Repeat the process with the books mentioned under the heading "Writers in a complex world" in the text. Ask: What do these books tell us about American society in the post-World War II years? Ask the class: Based on what we have said about the best-seller list today and the popular books in the 1950s and 1960s, how is our society different today from what it was then?

Developing Vocabulary

Abstract Expressionism (page 766)

INSTRUCT

Explain

The new technology of the postwar period had an effect on the arts. Painting, music, and writing changed through new forms and styles.

★ Independent Activity

Identifying Alternatives Ask students to imagine that they are historians who come to the United States fifty years from now to find out about society today. Have students make a list of the sorts of things they would look at to get an idea of what society was like in the late twentieth century. (Some possibilities include: news magazines, newspapers, tabloids, art, movies, TV programs, concerts, sporting events.)

Section Review Answers

Section 4, page 768

1. Many stopped representing the world outside and instead painted abstract designs or private visions.
2. Americans bought and read more books than ever before. Television and movies brought new revenue to authors and to the book industry, because best-selling novels were often made into movies or television shows. Sometimes, too, movies were turned into novels.

CLOSE

To conclude the lesson, point out to the class that the aspects of society they have been discussing (art, movies, TV, concerts, sports), together with many others, are called a society's culture. Have students write a 200-word essay about American culture for homework.

Chapter Review Answers
Focusing on Ideas

1. The study of population. Population explosion due to a soaring birthrate and many refugee immigrants. 2. See pages 752–753 for changes in farming (*e.g.,* declining farm populations). Note some occurred before 1950. 3. Answers will vary, but should include declining demand for untrained office and factory workers. 4. Include continued vigor of churches and synagogues; religious programs on radio and TV; flourishing religious cults; testimony of religious influence of prominent Americans; legal battle over prayer in the schools, abortion, and so on.

Taking a Critical Look

1. Rising political conservatism; attempts of younger workers to limit Social Security and welfare programs for elderly; more public housing for the elderly; sharing of big homes by elderly groups; adult education programs; possible decline in crime since many are committed by youthful offenders; conversion of surplus school houses for programs for the elderly. 2. Answers will vary; may include historical novels, movies, and TV; stories told by elders; taped oral history; visits to historical sites.

Your Region in History

1–3. Answers will vary depending on your region. Consult your local library or historical society.

Historical Facts and Figures

(a) Approximately 1 million in 1948; 46 million in 1960. (b) 1948; .05%: 1960, 25% (c) Advertising-supported broadcasting encouraged consumer spending; world events on TV as they happened; smaller world.

Answers to "Making Connections"

(See "Using Making Connections," p. 770.)

Answers will vary, but may include one or more of the following examples. Answers based on the time line callouts are in italics.

1. *George Kennan's warning in 1946 that the Soviets must be contained to prevent a third world war was well founded.* After the war, it quickly became clear that the Soviets could not be trusted to live up to their promises. They forced a Communist government on Poland and retained hold of Latvia, Lithuania, and Estonia. They supported Communist forces in Hungary, Bulgaria, Romania, and Greece. It also became clear that the Soviets had recruited spies in democratic countries, such as Klaus Fuchs, who was accused of sending atomic secrets to Russia from Canada. Despite such preventative measures as the *1947 Truman Doctrine, which granted military aid to governments opposed to Communism,* Communism continued to spread. *In 1948 the Soviets blockaded West Berlin, necessitating an airlift of food by the United States. McCarthy's warning about suspected Communists in the United States in 1953,* on the other hand, turned out to be greatly exaggerated.
2. *In 1954 the Supreme Court decision in* Brown v. Board of Education *that "separate but equal" facilities were unconstitutional* changed the way in which civil rights were viewed. This case (ably argued by Thurgood Marshall, who later himself became a Supreme Court Justice) outlawed segregation, the method by which blacks had been held back for generations. Once the law of the land supported integration, it was possible for leaders such as *Martin Luther King, Jr., to organize protests such as the 1955 Montgomery, Alabama, bus boycott* in which Rosa Parks was arrested for riding in the front of a bus. It also made it easier for *Congress to pass new laws such as the Civil Rights Act of 1957, the first civil rights legislation since Reconstruction.* 3. Developing technologies were a factor in demographic changes. For example, the improvement of farm equipment, fertilizers, seeds, and pest control made it possible for American farmers to feed more and more people per farmer. Fewer farmers were needed, which led to a population movement from the country to the city. The increased use of the automobile was largely responsible for another population shift. *In 1960 more Americans lived in the suburbs than cities largely as a result of the automobile.* Technology also increased industrial production across the board. Consumer products were offered in larger quantities and at more reasonable prices than ever before. As a result, the standard of living rose. People bought more new appliances and machines than ever before for the home, the factory, and the office. *By 1970, 95% of American homes had at least one television set.*

30

Focusing the Chapter: Have students identify the chapter logo. Discuss what unit theme the logo might symbolize. Then ask students to skim the chapter to identify other illustrations or titles that relate to this theme.

Chapter 30

Mobile People and Magic Machines

In every war, besides the killing and the misery, large changes are at work. Wars set people on the move. There are not only the men and women serving in the armed forces. Thousands move to the factories in distant cities making arms and tanks and planes. Wars change the way the nation grows. Families are separated. Young people cannot settle down and raise new families.

Wars also produce new machines. The nation's scientists and engineers must invent new devices to defeat the enemy. They have to find new ways to send information across great distances, to move troops, to feed and shelter people at home and at the front. Out of the machines of war eventually come machines of peace. The radio and the airplane, which were tried and proven in World War I, changed American life in the years that followed. And so from World War II came new medicines like penicillin and electronic machines like television.

The forces of mobile people and magic machines have a "momentum"—a power to keep themselves going. In this chapter we will see how the forces that gathered strength during World War II (and had started even before) gained momentum. They transformed the country during the eras of Truman and Eisenhower. And these forces still continue to shape the nation today.

Courtesy, Motorola Museum Archives

This advertisement exaggerates only slightly how Americans felt about their first TV sets.

☑ See "Lesson Plan," p. 750C for **Writing Process Activity: Recognizing Cause and Effect** relating to demographic trends of the 1950s.

See "Lesson Plan," p. 750C.

1. A changing people

After World War II dramatic changes took place in the population—in the rate of growth and length of life—as well as in the occupations people held and the places where they lived. All this had far-reaching effects on the lives of every American.

Studying the population. The study of population is called "demography." This comes from the Greek words *demos* (people) and *graphein* (to write or record). Demographers point out that, at different times and places, the population grows in different ways. For example, during wartime when young men and women are away from home in the armed forces, families have fewer children. The "birthrate" normally goes down. After wars, husbands and wives are reunited, more young people marry, and the birthrate goes up. So it was after World War II.

Demographers analyze statistics about population. Such statistics are important for planning by government and business. The framers of the Constitution back in 1787 knew that the growing nation would need up-to-date facts about the moving population. So they established the federal census (Art. I, sec. 2), requiring the national government to count the population every ten years. Then the members of the House of Representatives could be reapportioned according to the changes.

As the census became more detailed, the public could use this information to plan the water supply and roads and schools. Businesses could build factories where workers would be living. They could predict the size of the market for their product. The Bureau of the Census (now in the Department of Commerce) became an American institution. It has gathered all sorts of facts about our people. And demographers even invented ways to estimate the changes occurring between the regular decennial (every ten years) census.

(p. 750)

The nation grows. After World War II the United States experienced a "population explosion." When the Great Depression finally ended, people had more money to support a family.

And then when veterans returned home at the war's end, the birthrate increased. But this was not just the normal increase after any war. The population soared so fast that even expert demographers were astonished.

In 1940 there were 132 million people in the United States. During the decade of the 1930s our population had increased just 7.2 percent—the smallest proportionate increase in the nation's history. By 1950 there were 151 million, an increase of 14.5 percent over 1940. Between 1950 and 1960 the number of people went up even faster—by 18.5 percent—to a total of over 179 million. This was mainly due to the high birthrate. At the same time, refugees from war and Nazism and communism swelled the number of immigrants coming to the United States from 1 million during the decade of the 1940s to 2.5 million in the 1950s.

By the end of 1950 one person was being added to the nation every twelve seconds. This explosive growth was equal then to another Richmond, Virginia, every month and a whole Maryland every year. It put strains on cities and states, which were forced to build bigger hospitals, to hire more police and firefighters, and especially to add new schools to cope with the large numbers of children.

Slowing the boom. During the 1960s the population boom began to slow down. Still the nation grew by 13.5 percent, which meant adding nearly 24 million people to make a population of 203 million by 1970. The nation now had twice the number of people it had only 50 years before.

By the end of 1972 the baby boom was over. The Census Bureau reported then that American women were not having quite enough babies to keep the population steady. But the many male and female babies born during those years of population explosion would grow up and in time have their own children.

Moving west, north, and south. Even while the rate of growth of the American population changed, the people never ceased to move. After World War II, the lure of the West drew millions all the way to the shores of the Pacific. By 1964

Critical Thinking Activity: Predicting Consequences How do demographic changes affect individuals? Tell students they are responsible for zoning an undeveloped part of their community. To determine the most appropriate use of the land they must do some demographic research. Have students list demographic considerations such as the size of the community, rate of growth, percentage of people in various age groups, economic means of the residents, and so on. Ask students to discuss the ways their research would give direction to the zoning process.

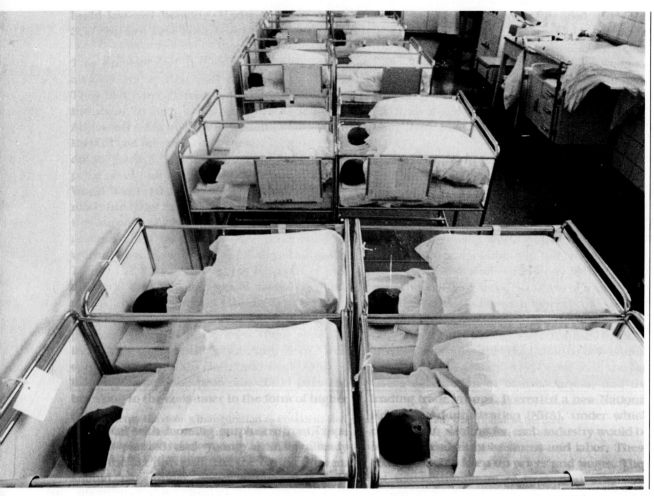

During the 1950s, our population increased so rapidly that experts said we were in the midst of a "baby boom."

California, with 10 percent of the nation's people, had become the most populous state in the Union.

At the same time there were new north-south movements. Between 1920 and 1960 many blacks left the South heading north, hoping for better jobs, more equality, more opportunity. In 1940 three-quarters of all blacks still lived in the South. But by 1970 half of all black Americans lived in the North. After 1960 a new migration of whites from North to South more than made up in numbers for the departing blacks. The "Sunbelt," as the states in the South and Southwest were called, was now growing faster than any other section.

Moving off the farms. All across the nation there was another great and speedy migration—from the countryside to the city. In 1920 the nation's rural and urban populations were equal in size. At the same time, one of every three Americans lived on a farm. In 1970 only one American in every 22 still lived on a farm. Each year farms held a smaller and smaller proportion of the people. The number of farms had fallen from a peak of 6.8 million in 1935 to

More from Boorstin: "Just as new states and counties and upstart cities had offered new arenas for political democracy in the nineteenth century, so thousands of new suburbs with myriad local problems awakened the interests and political energies of mid-twentieth-century Americans. . . . [Suburbs] revived the spirit of an earlier age. Despite the rising divorce rate and other widely advertised forces which loosed the marriage bond, the suburbs . . . strengthened home and family." (From *The Americans: The Democratic Experience*)

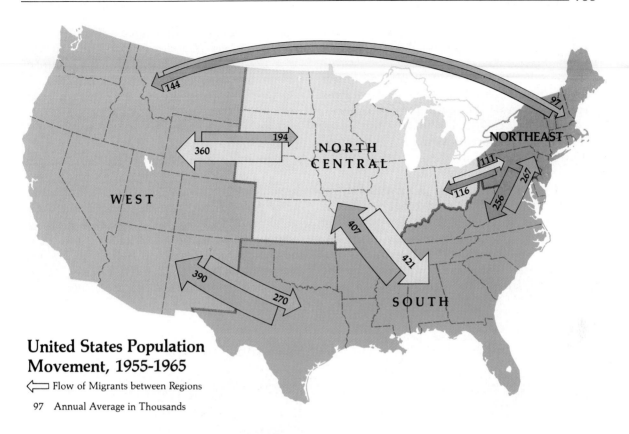

United States Population Movement, 1955-1965

Flow of Migrants between Regions

97   Annual Average in Thousands

under 3 million in 1970, and it was continuing to fall rapidly. Of course, at the same time, the farms that remained grew much larger in size. Farmers still spoke with a powerful voice in national politics. The 4.5 million American farm workers in 1970 were more numerous than all the workers in the steel, automobile, and transportation industries combined.

Back in 1820 the average farm worker could produce only enough to feed four people. Now, modern farm machinery, improved seeds, better fertilizers, and scientific methods had enormously increased what each farmer could produce. By 1950 one farm worker could feed 15, and by 1970 each one could produce enough for 45! American farmers helped feed people in Russia, India, and all over the world.

For those who remained on the farm, life became less isolated during the postwar years. The spread of telephones and automobiles meant that farm families could see or talk to their neighbors more easily. Television brought to the farmhouse the same news broadcasts, sports programs, and other entertainment seen by apartment dwellers in the big cities. Some American farmers drove large tractors equipped with air conditioning, citizens' band (CB) radios, TV sets, and high fidelity sound systems. The experiences of all Americans were becoming more and more alike.

The move to the suburbs.   Meanwhile, the city people did not sit still in the centers of their growing metropolises. After 1950 they moved in large numbers out of the central cities to the nearby suburbs. In 1950, 35 percent of the nation's people lived in the central cities and almost as many—27 percent—in the suburbs. By 1970 the suburbs were winning, for 31 percent lived in the central cities and 37 percent in the suburbs. This gave many Americans a new opportunity to enjoy fresh air, to mow their lawns, to watch birds, and plant gardens of flowers and vegetables. But it also produced "suburban

(p. 752)

Geography and History: Movement Use the map above for discussion of population mobility. One of the chief purposes of this map is to remind students that migration is a two-way street after an area has once been settled. Ask: Which region had the largest net loss of population resulting from interregional migration? Why? (The North Central, losing 150,000 annually. The drop in farm population was a big factor, with many retired farm people moving South and West and many young people choosing other careers.)

sprawl" and new traffic jams! Homes and factories and shopping centers were jumbled together in ugly mixes.

To describe this America, it was no longer possible to talk simply of "cities." Americans were spread across the country in new clusters. The Office of Management and Budget called these clusters Standard Metropolitan Statistical Areas (SMSAs). Until the 1980s each SMSA was supposed to be a dense population (including suburbs) surrounding a central city of 50,000. But then it was found that population often flowed to smaller towns or groups of towns and that these too were becoming metropolitan areas—though without any major central city. To describe these new areas better the government dropped its requirement of a large central city and created three different classes of Metropolitan Statistical Areas. Now all that was needed was a central town or group of towns and a dense metropolitan area. Benton Harbor, Michigan, for example—with a population in 1980 of 14,707—was defined as metropolitan because it was the heart of an area with over 170,000 people.

The most striking population change of the 1970s, however, was the discovery that "rural" areas were growing faster than metropolitan areas for the first time since the decade from 1810 to 1820. These were not farms, but new communities in the countryside. Many businesses, factories, workers and their families were moving into the remote fringes of the big metropolitan areas. Still, by the 1980s three-

After World War II, suburban tract housing like Levittown, Pennsylvania, shown here, was rapidly built to hold the growing population.

Standard Metropolitan Statistical Areas

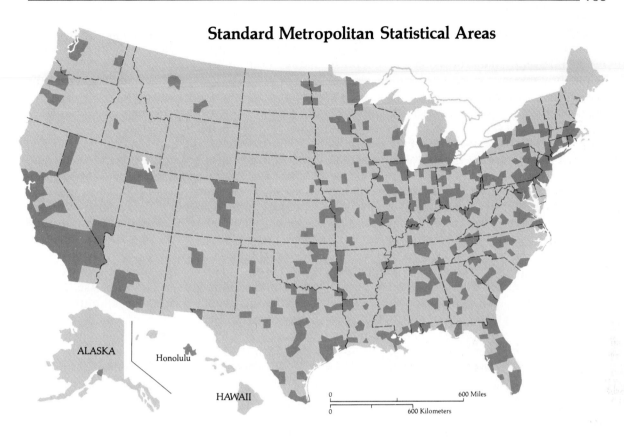

ALASKA

Honolulu

HAWAII

0 — 600 Miles

0 — 600 Kilometers

fourths of the American people lived in cities or their surrounding suburbs—with the larger part in the suburbs.

The metropolitan areas were often so close together that it was hard to know where one ended and another began. Looking down from an airplane flying northward from Norfolk, Virginia, to Bangor, Maine, what you saw looked like one big super-city. This needed a new name, and people began calling it a "megalopolis" (from the Greek words for "giant" and for "city"). Sprawling giant-cities grew also in Texas, Florida, California, and on the edge of the Great Lakes.

One surprising fact was that—although the heart of the continent had been filling up for two centuries—more than half of all Americans now lived within 50 miles of the oceans, the Gulf of Mexico, or the Great Lakes.

A mobile people. Even when they reached California or Florida or arrived in their chosen city, Americans did not settle down. Every year after 1948 one American in five moved to a new place—down the street, to a nearby town, or on to another state. The census found that in a single year in the 1970s more than 36 million people had changed houses. Of course, most of them had just moved within the same city or county. Still, they had to get used to a new neighborhood with different stores and schools. In 1970 a quarter of all the people in the United States were living in a different state from where they had been born.

This moving around made problems—and opportunities—for all Americans. For example, most black Americans were transformed from rural to urban citizens. In 1940 one-third of all employed blacks worked on farms. By 1970 fewer than 4 percent were farm workers, and four-fifths of the black population lived in urban areas. Most were still prevented from moving to the suburbs by their own poverty or by white prejudice. In the half-century after the

Geography and History: Interaction Have students look at the map above. Ask: What areas of the United States have the lowest population density? (The northern midwest, Alaska, northern New England, and the island of Hawaii.) What do the denser population areas tend to have in common? (They are often found bordering a body of water.)

Civil War the proportion of blacks in the whole population of the United States declined from 13 to 11 percent. That proportion has remained about the same ever since.

In a fast-moving America—of Americans living close together—it was easier for blacks to demand their rights. The first successes of Martin Luther King, Jr., and Rosa Parks were in crowded Montgomery and on the buses that carried people to work (p. 740).

The concentration of this 11 percent in the cities also gave blacks an increased political power. They were a voting bloc that could be easily identified and (because of segregation) easily found. Now at last, even in the South, they were allowed to vote. Their support for Kennedy in 1960 and for Carter in 1976 helped provide the narrow margins for victory. In the cities, where they lived closer together, it was easier for them to support their candidate. Their votes brought Atlanta, Georgia, its first black mayor in 1973. By then there were black mayors in Los Angeles and Detroit and in 90 other cities.

In 1964 there were only four blacks in Congress, but by 1972 there were fifteen, including Edward Brooke, Republican senator from Massachusetts. Black influence at the polls would have been even greater if more blacks had voted. In the late 1970s only one-third of the 15 million blacks eligible to vote had registered, and only one-third of those registered bothered to cast their ballots.

As the barriers were slowly broken down, during the 1960s an increasing number of blacks began to join fellow Americans in the suburbs. There they rose from 2.5 percent to 4.2 percent, still far below their 11 percent in the total population. Political power now lay with the suburbs because more voters lived there than in either the cities or the rural areas.

An aging population. The nation was reshaped—not only by how the population moved but by how the population grew. After World War II, there was a striking increase in the number of Americans over 65. People were living longer because of better diet, advances in medicine and surgery, and the invention of "miracle drugs" (like sulfa and penicillin), which cured diseases that had often been fatal. In 1900 the average life expectancy of all Americans at birth was only 47, and people over 65 represented only 4 percent of the population. By the 1940s the average life expectancy reached 65. By 1970 it had climbed to 71.

The census showed that men generally did not live as long as women. In the 1970s men at birth had a life expectancy of 67 while for women it was nearly 75. By 1970 the number of people over 65 had grown to 20 million—10 percent of the whole population. They outnumbered the people in all the twenty smallest states combined. And they had their own special hopes. They were another new group whom the successful politician had to please. American youth usually looked for adventure and opportunity. "Senior citizens" cared more for security and leisure. In the 1960s and 1970s, could these different hopes be matched?

See "Section 1 Review answers," p. 750C.

Section 1 Review

1. Explain: demography, SMSA, megalopolis.
2. Point out major trends in population growth and movement from 1945 to 1970.
3. **Critical Thinking: Drawing Conclusions.** How was population mobility beneficial?

See "Lesson Plan," p. 750C.

2. Everyday life transformed

The new world of adventure was the world of science and of machines. Ever since the colonists had "invented" their nation, and devised a new kind of written constitution, Americans had loved to experiment. They also liked to buy new things. Visitors from abroad noticed that Americans were machine minded.

The famous cartoonist Rube Goldberg said the American motto ought to be, "Do it the hard way!" Americans loved complicated ways of simplifying everyday life. Why walk if you could ride? Why use a wooden pencil if you could use a metal pencil with retractable lead—including many colors that you really did not need? Why

❖ See "Lesson Plan," p. 750D for **Cooperative Learning Activity: Making Comparisons** relating to the standard of living of Western Europeans after World War II.

write with a pencil or pen if you could use a typewriter? Or why use a simple hand-operated typewriter when there was a much more complex electric machine? Why write it yourself at all if you could first dictate it into a machine that recorded your voice on a tape, which would be put into another machine to be played back to someone who would transcribe the words on an electric typewriter? In the machine-rich United States, everyday life was full of fantastic surprises.

A growing economy. All these machines helped create the American standard of living. They helped make life more interesting, as well as more complicated. They opened opportunities for investors to put their money into new ventures in hopes of profit, for business leaders to build factories, for skilled workers to make the machines—and for salespeople and advertising experts to sell these machines by the millions. After the war the economy expanded and prospered.

Enrich-
ment
Support
File Topic The quarter-century from the end of World War II until about 1970 brought the nation its longest period of prosperity. There were brief recessions, but the statistics of economic growth were astonishing. The Gross National Product (GNP)—the total value of all goods and services produced in the nation—measured in 1958 dollars rose from $355.2 billion in 1945 to $722.5 billion in 1970. In the same period, per capita income before taxes increased (in 1958 dollars) from $1870 to $3050. Most Americans prospered as they shared one of the highest per capita incomes in the world.

Reasons for prosperity. Immediately after World War II, there was a large, pent-up demand for housing and for all peacetime products, such as automobiles and kitchen appliances, that were hard to get during the war. This demand, backed by wartime savings, gave a big boost to sales. Government spending did not decline and kept the economy booming. American export trade, supported by the billions of dollars the United States government paid out for foreign aid, flourished.

(p. 756) All sorts of new machines—radios, high fi's,

Christopher Springmann/Black Star

Stores encouraged their customers to "Charge it!" and the nation's economy boomed.

television sets, washing and drying machines, deep freezes, power lawnmowers, and countless others—kept factories busy and customers eager to buy. None was more important than the automobile. Fewer than 1 million new automobiles were produced during World War II. By 1970, 8 million a year were being turned out. These consumed one-fifth of the nation's new steel, half its malleable iron, and two-thirds of its rubber and lead.

All these cars needed highways. In 1956, then, the nation began the largest road construction program in its history. Under President Eisenhower, Congress voted $33 billion (later increased) for a ten-year program to build a whole 42,500-mile network of interstate superhighways. By 1975, because of inflation, it would cost $39 billion just to finish the last 5500 miles of the system. In 1978 President Carter signed a highway bill that provided $9.3 billion a year for three years. Many more billions were spent by states and localities.

The automobile and the suburbs. In earlier days cities had grown up near waterways. Then

Continuity and Change: Science, Technology, and Society Point out to students that just as the age of the automobile led to the development of highways in the twentieth century, the turnpikes of the early 1800s allowed for more efficient wagon travel. Like the wave of highway building due to the popularity of automobiles, there was a similar wave of turnpike and road building in the early years of the nation. As highways tied the suburbs to the cities, so did turnpikes tie the farmers to their markets. (See p. 251.)

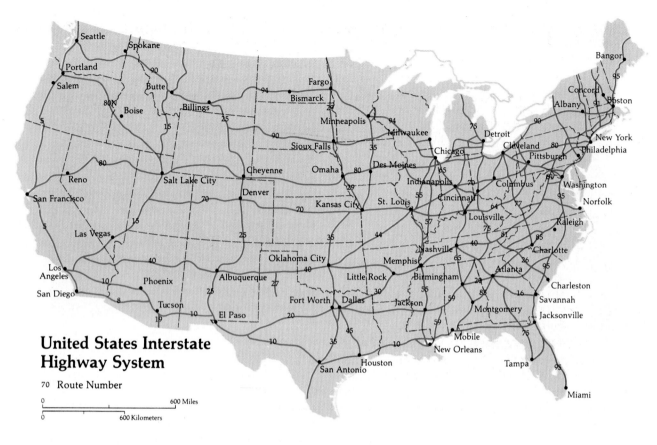

United States Interstate Highway System

70 Route Number

0   600 Miles

0   600 Kilometers

railroads went to the cities, and new cities grew along the railroads. Even before the automobile, streetcars took people out to the suburbs to live and back into the center of the city to work and to shop. The automobile gave its owner a new freedom. Of course, railroads and streetcars had to stay on their special tracks. But the car would take Americans of the twentieth century anywhere there were roads. Factories, stores, and movie theaters moved out to shopping centers in the suburbs. The "downtown" of a big city was no longer the center of people's lives.

Americans had fallen in love with their automobiles. In 1971 alone, they spent the staggering sum of $180 billion to buy new and used cars. This was more than four times what they spent for their public elementary and high schools. From their homes in the suburbs Americans could drive to work every day. Life in the suburbs—shopping, going to school, visiting friends—required a car.

Living with the automobile. The automobile brought strange by-products. One of these was the "credit card." The first credit cards were offered by the large gasoline companies to attract customers. They gave out these identifying cards so that people could charge gasoline purchases anywhere on the road at one of their hundreds of stations. After 1950, other businesses picked up the credit card idea.

The parking problem was also new. To attract customers to the central city, huge parking garages were built in choice locations. So automobile traffic increased. Then the poor pedestrians had to risk their lives when they crossed the street. Cars ruled the surface of the earth. Millions of automobiles polluted the atmosphere with carbon monoxide and hydrocarbons. It was hard to live *without* automobiles, but could Americans learn to live *with* them?

Machines to do everything. Of course, the automobiles needed accessories—windshield

⊕ **Geography and History: Movement** Have students look at the map above. Ask: What interstate route stretches all the way from San Francisco to New York City? (Route 80.) What routes would you take to travel by car from Tampa, Florida, to Tucson, Arizona? (Routes 75, 10, and 8.) What route would best take you from Bangor, Maine, to Miami? (Route 95.)

John Launois/Black Star

Even the large-scale construction of superhighways like this could not prevent traffic jams when the nation's automobiles multiplied after World War II.

wipers, turn signals, car radios. This created new industries by the hundreds. Also Americans wanted, made, and bought new electric appliances for the home, for the factory, and for the office. These included air conditioners, dehumidifiers, electric blankets, electric knives and toothbrushes, automatic washing machines and dryers, dishwashers, garbage disposals, pencil sharpeners, typewriters, cash registers, and countless other items. The factories to make these products, and the factories to make the machines that went into the factories, created new jobs by the thousands.

To produce the electricity to run these homes and factories, the nation burned the old reliable coal, which had driven the factories in the preceding century. The factories also were powered by oil and natural gas brought in by giant

pipelines from the West and Southwest to the cities of the South, Midwest, and East.

Light metals like aluminum, magnesium, and titanium were combined with chromium into sparkling, rust-free new alloys. Aluminum production leaped from 287,000 tons in 1940 to 2 million tons in 1960 and over 4 million in 1970. Industrial chemists invented "plastics"—which were cheaper than wood or metal, easier to shape into the new tools and toys and gadgets. There were man-made wash-and-wear textiles like nylon and Dacron, which never lost their press. And countless other "synthetics" were used for detergents, drugs, insecticides, and fertilizers.

All these products had to be put in packages. The packaging was as new as the product. In the 1800s, people had taken their own containers to the general store to carry home their milk or coffee or crackers. Then, after World War I, the rise of advertising, national brands, and supermarkets created a whole new "packaging" industry. As customers walked through the aisles of supermarkets to serve themselves, they bought their groceries in familiar packages. Sometimes even when they didn't really need something, they bought it simply because they were attracted by the colorful, much-advertised package.

Perspectives Topic

The spread of television. Advertising these packaged products became still another big industry. This advertising supported broadcasting on radio and television, and filled American living rooms with "commercials."

Television, one of the most magical of American machines, conquered the nation with astounding speed. In 1948 there were only 200,000 television sets in all the United States, and of every hundred families only one owned a set. But by 1970 nearly every American home (95.5 percent) had at least one television set. After the first commercial communications satellite, *Early Bird*, was put into space in 1965, live broadcasts could be sent from Europe to the United States. In the 1970s satellites brought events from all over the world—even President Nixon's visit to far-off China—into the nation's homes.

Now Americans could see and hear events as they happened. The war in Vietnam, civil rights marches, riots in the streets—along with entertaining series, cartoons, old movies, and sports events—all appeared on the TV screen. The magic of television brought a new kind of confusion. The wonderful box in everybody's living room created the Instant Everywhere. You could stay wherever you were and see what was happening at that instant all over the United States—and all over the world. Americans felt magically close to events in Vietnam, on the civil rights battlegrounds of Alabama and Mississippi, even on the moon! They sometimes forgot how far away those fearful and exciting events really were.

"Network" programs, which cost a fortune to produce, made celebrities out of the newscasters. Citizens all over the nation could see and hear their President and watch events in Washington. There was a new danger that they would pay less attention to their mayor or their governor or the real neighbors in their own town.

Americans, for the first time, could see events "replayed." They forgot that this, too, was a modern miracle. Before photography or radio or television, an event happened only once. Then it was gone forever unless an artist painted it in a picture or a writer told the story. In the age of television, by the 1960s when you watched a sporting event, you could not only see the game played once. You could see the most thrilling moments played again and again on instant replay. With your tape recorder, also developed after World War II, you could reproduce music from radios, records, and live groups to be played again whenever you wanted. You could

Here the distant Statue of Liberty is bracketed by a new feature of the American landscape.

Bruce Davidson/Magnum

Critical Thinking Activity: Identifying Central Issues How did the growth of suburbs lead to technological change? List the following items on the chalkboard: "Suburb," "Automobile," "Credit Card," "Pollution," "Industry," "Appliances," "New Materials," "Television." Remind students that advancements of the 1950s and 1960s could be expressed as a chain reaction. Using this idea, ask students to write eight sentences demonstrating the relationship of each item on the board to the next. Have students share their work. Synthesize these ideas into a class set of sentences.

record your family gatherings at Christmas or Thanksgiving. Members of the family could send each other greetings in their own voices.

New-style pioneers. There were many American pioneers on these new machine-frontiers. The age of the Go-Getter was not over. Instead of clearing the land and building cities in the wilderness, the modern pioneer built machines no one else had imagined, to satisfy needs never before felt. One clever inventor, Edwin H. Land, devised an instant camera and film that not only took pictures, but developed them on the spot. Imaginative Chester F. Carlson, who had worked his way through the California Institute of Technology, invented a new copying system. Bold businessmen in Rochester, New York, supported his research and invested in his machine to make an image on paper. They renamed his process "xerography" (from the Greek words *xeros*, "dry," and *graphein*, "to write"). Soon Xerox machines were everywhere. Offices and libraries all over the country were reproducing letters and books. It was easier than ever before to make a copy of anything.

More machines, and more machines to make machines! All these required energy, which meant more electricity. Between 1940 and 1970 the production of electricity in the United States increased over sevenfold. We used far more energy than any other nation. As a result of improved machines and better working methods, between 1947 and 1970 the output of factories per working hour more than doubled!

Machines to run machines. There seemed no end to the powers of machine magic. The next step was to invent machines to run the machines. In the years after World War II, that actually happened. About 1946, Americans began to use another new word, "automation." The fantastic new machine was the "computer." Its main inventor was a brilliant Hungarian immigrant, John von Neumann, who had helped plan the atomic bomb and now was a professor at Princeton. In a few seconds the electronic computer would count and calculate what once had busied a hundred workers for days. High-speed computers could count, sort, remember,

and select information—then use it to run factories or oil refineries.

In the 1960s and 1970s computers found thousands of new uses—to monitor patients in hospitals, to process checks in banks, to handle credit-card bills, and to keep track of library books. They solved problems for scientists, mathematicians, educators, engineers, and business leaders. The computer even moved into supermarkets and provided a machine that could read the lines on packages, then add up the price. The take-it-for-granted customer in-

An athlete working to improve his tennis stroke uses a computer to analyze his movements and help him do better.

Dan McCoy/Black Star

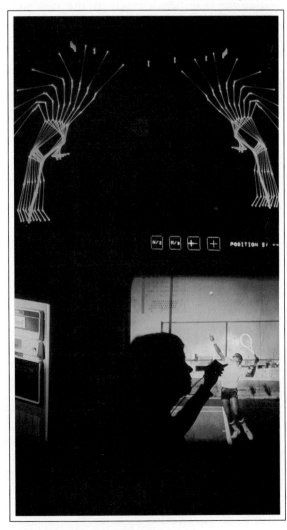

More from Boorstin: "As broadcasting techniques improved, they tended to make the viewer's experience more indirect, more controlled by unseen producers and technicians. Before, the spectator attending a national political convention would, simply by turning his head, decide for himself *where* he would look, but the TV watcher in the living room lacked the power to decide. Cameramen, directors, and commentators decided for him, focusing on this view of a brutal policeman or that view of a pretty delegate." (From *The Americans: The Democratic Experience*)

stantly had a neat shopping list with the name and price of each item.

In all sorts of factories, the work was transformed. In automobile factories, for example, welding machines with electronic memories made some of the decisions live workers once had to make. After a "live" welder guided the computers once through their jobs, the machines were then "programmed" to remember what to weld and then they would repeat it over and over again as each car came by.

The advantages of these miraculous machines were obvious. They took the place of a great deal of drudgery. But, like all other machines, they had their price. They put people out of work. And until those people could be trained for new jobs created by the new machines, they might feel lost and useless. This was the kind of price that other new machines had always extracted. Here was another challenge to American enterprise, education, and government.

Planning for the new. Whenever someone invented something, most Americans asked, "Why not try it?" And they did. They were anx-ious to have a new gadget or a new model even if they weren't sure that it was better. Wasn't it better just *because* it was new?

But this made problems, too. New machines made old machines obsolete. The changes in assembly-line factories had to be carefully planned. On the assembly line one piece after another was added to the car's chassis as it moved along. Each piece had to be fitted into all the others. To make a new model car was complicated and required long-range planning.

Henry Ford thought his Model T was the best car that could be made. For many years he refused to change the design. Then General Motors and other manufacturers invented the idea of an "annual model"—changing the design every year. Customers now had a reason to sell their old car—even if it still worked—so they could buy another car of this year's stylish design.

Customers liked the idea. But car manufacturers had to plan the new models years in advance so the factory machinery would be ready. Every fall Americans waited for that year's models to appear. In Europe the car manufacturers changed their designs only slowly and over

Americans always waited eagerly for each year's new cars. In this 1950 advertisement Oldsmobile trumpeted that its latest model had "rocket" performance.

many years. Some American car makers in the 1960s even began to change their models twice a year. Change was becoming ever more rapid. Was the new model really new?

The hidden frontiers: research and development. The many new products—from the life-changing computer to the electric toothbrush—did not appear just by accident. Electronics had developed rapidly because of the World War II research to make more accurate weapons and better ways to track enemy aircraft, ships, and submarines. In peacetime, too, scientists, engineers, and technicians worked together on hidden frontiers in laboratories all over the country. Supported by universities, by businesses, by government, or by their own hopes and savings, they went in search of answers to all sorts of questions. Could they make a camera that would photograph under water, an inexpensive highway cement that would dry quickly and not crack in summer or winter? In 1970, $27 billion was spent on research and development (R&D)—more even than the nation's total expenditure of $23 billion on higher education. Two-thirds of this came from federal funds and the rest from private industry.

The industrial research laboratory had not been invented in the United States, but in Germany. Americans followed the lead. Ever since Thomas A. Edison built his invention factory in Menlo Park, New Jersey, in 1876, research and development had shaped American life. Large corporations like General Electric (GE), American Telephone & Telegraph (AT&T), and International Business Machines (IBM) would invest millions asking a new question or finding new answers to old questions. By the 1950s the nation had over 200 large laboratories and 2000 smaller ones. Out of them came the tiny transistor for pocket radios and portable TV sets, photovoltaic cells that change sunlight into electricity, the new form of light known as the laser (which can cut through steel and reach to the moon), microprocessors (tiny chips of silicon that hold thousands of pieces of information), and hosts of other inventions that made dreams come true.

A changing work force. Machines created by experts and technicians needed a world of experts and technicians to keep them alive and in good working order. Automation made jobs in new industries and changed the jobs that people did. A strong arm, a sturdy back, the power to handle a shovel and lift heavy weights—these were no longer so useful.

Fewer jobs could be done by those who had no skills. At the end of World War II, one-third of all jobs could still be handled by untrained people. By 1970 only half as many jobs could be performed by the unskilled. As a result, in the late 1970s untrained teenagers suffered twice the rate of unemployment of the older, skilled workers.

Section 2 Review

See "Section 2 Review answers," p. 750D.

1. Why did the nation prosper during the period 1945–1970?
2. What part did "research and development" play in the postwar prosperity?
3. **Critical Thinking: Predicting Consequences.** What would American life be like if the television had never been invented?

See "Lesson Plan," p. 750D.

3. Education and religion

These were difficult times. To find jobs, young Americans needed skills. To enjoy their life, to understand the complex world, to explore history and science—they needed a "liberal" education. This meant an education to "liberate" them—to lift them out of their hometown and open the wide world of books. And to find peace and try to cope with the stresses of the postwar world, most Americans turned to their houses of worship and their religious leaders.

The spread of high school education. The free public high school was an American invention—a foundation of democracy and opportunity. It was needed to provide students for the multiplying American colleges and universities.

☑ See "Lesson Plan," p. 750D for **Writing Process Activity: Drawing Conclusions** relating to the American-Russian space race and its effect on education.

In 1900 only about 10 percent of young people between 14 and 17 years of age were in high schools or private secondary schools. Among young people of college age, only 1 person in 25 went on to college. Then the change was rapid and spectacular. By 1930 half of all Americans aged 14 to 17 were in high school. By 1950 high school enrollment had reached three-quarters of that age group, and by 1970 it was 90 percent. In that same year college enrollment, which was only 10 percent in 1930, had reached 50 percent of all college-age Americans.

Veterans of World War II, Korea, and Vietnam were rewarded by the "G.I. bills." These laws paid the veterans' way to college or technical training. Millions were qualified because they had graduated from high school.

Were schools mainly to prepare those who were going on to a "higher" learning in college? Or should they be designed for everyone? One answer came from John Dewey, whose writings on education during his long life (1859–1952) shaped the philosophy of thousands of teachers. Brought up on a Vermont farm, he knew from his own experience raising chickens and planting vegetables how children learned by actually doing. Dewey noticed that as more families moved into the city, fewer children had his experience. He believed that schools could take its place. "Education," Dewey said, "is a process of living and not a preparation for future living." He planned schools where children would learn by doing. They made things as they worked together.

Other educators, like President Robert Maynard Hutchins of the University of Chicago, disagreed. They believed it was more important for schools to teach people to learn by reading. Students should read and discuss the great books of the past. In school, Hutchins said, students should be taught about science and history and geography, because later on they would have plenty of time to learn by doing.

When *Sputnik* suddenly appeared in the sky in 1957 (p. 745), many Americans began to fear that the Russian achievement was produced by better schools. James Bryant Conant, who had recently retired as president of Harvard University, in his influential book *The American High*

(p. 763)

School Today (1959) called for changes in the high schools. He proposed a minimum size for high schools, higher standards, and greater emphasis on courses in English, foreign languages, mathematics, science, and social studies. Still, the philosophy of Dewey and his followers in the "Progressive Education" movement permeated the schools. Grammar schools and high schools would continue to accommodate "all the youth of a community."

Religion in postwar America. Just as education took new forms, so did religion. In America religion always seems to be either in the doldrums or booming. After World War II, the Catholic, Jewish, and Protestant religions in the United States all experienced revivals. Millions of dollars were spent to build new churches and synagogues, and Americans in ever larger numbers flocked to religious services.

The years from 1945 to 1960 were an "Age of Affluence" as goods poured from American factories, unemployment and inflation remained low, and wages rose. But they were also an "Age of Anxiety" as communism spread, war came to Korea, and the United States and the Soviet Union built and tested more and more nuclear weapons. Perhaps their anxiety was one reason many Americans returned to their churches.

They also read books by religious leaders and listened to them on radio and TV. One of the first to publish a best-seller was Rabbi Joshua Loth Lieberman, who in 1946 showed how the discoveries of the great Austrian psychoanalyst Sigmund Freud could lead to *Peace of Mind*, as his book was titled. In the 1940s and 1950s, through radio and television and in his book *Peace of Soul*, Monsignor Fulton J. Sheen reached millions of people and brought many converts into the Catholic church.

The Protestant minister Norman Vincent Peale's *Guide to Confident Living* (1948) and *The Power of Positive Thinking* (1952) were read by millions who found in them a road to inner peace. Millions more listened to Peale on radio and records, read his articles, and watched him on TV. One of the most persuasive preachers of the 1950s and after was Billy Graham. Graham was in the grand old American

✕ Critical Thinking Activity: Supporting Opinions What label applies to today's society? Social scientists have called the period from 1945 to 1960 an "Age of Affluence" and an "Age of Anxiety." Write these two labels on the board and ask students to cite evidence to support these headings. Have students suggest an appropriate label for today's society and cite evidence to demonstrate its accuracy.

tradition of the evangelical revival. (Evangelical comes from the word *evangel*, which comes from a Greek word meaning "bringer of good news.") His revival meetings drew hundreds of thousands to make "decisions for Christ" while vast audiences listened on radio and watched on television.

Still, by the end of the 1950s, the American revival was losing force and attendance at churches was dropping off. Some theologians began to say that religion had lost its power in the United States. "God is dead," they mourned.

The 1960s were a troublesome time for churches as they were for all Americans. The civil rights movement and the war in Vietnam revealed the gap between American ideals and American reality. They sharpened the great moral issues that would haunt the nation in the years to come.

Some ministers began to fear that somehow the churches were not really speaking to the problems that most worried Americans. They tried new ways to attract people to their churches with rock music, guitars, and new seating arrangements. Many ministers marched for civil rights and in protest against the Vietnam War. Black ministers, and most especially Martin Luther King, Jr., were in the forefront of the fight for civil rights. And King early raised his eloquent voice against the war in Vietnam.

In the confusion and chaos of the 1960s some people turned away from traditional Western religions and sought their answers in Hinduism and Zen Buddhism. Among the young, some turned to nihilism ("nothing"-ism, the total rejection of law and institutions) and violence, while others withdrew into communes where they could invent their own customs and traditions.

These troubles of the 1960s stirred the Fundamentalist Protestants. While some people were turning away from old values, Fundamentalists spoke out for them. About a third of all Protestants in the 1980s were Fundamentalists. They believed in the literal truth of the Bible and the need to be "born again" in Christ. Organized in groups like the Moral Majority

Elliot Erwitt/Magnum

Baptist minister Billy Graham, shown here with Richard Nixon, was a friend of many Presidents, both Republican and Democratic.

they could bring strong political support to candidates who shared their beliefs.

Despite the vigor of the Fundamentalists, some historians noted a turning point in American history. The Protestant values that had dominated American life from the beginning no longer seemed supreme. American religion had entered a new age.

See "Section 3 Review answers," p. 750D.

Section 3 Review

1. Identify: John Dewey, James B. Conant, Fulton J. Sheen, Billy Graham, Norman Vincent Peale.
2. Explain some events occurring outside the United States that affected American education.
3. **Critical Thinking: Recognizing Cause and Effect.** How did technology affect religion in the United States?

Continuity and Change: Science, Technology, and Society Remind students that a series of religious revivals in the 1820s to 1850s led to thousands attending the camp meetings of traveling preachers such as Charles Grandison Finney. In the 1950s, with many people again turning to religion, the development of television and radio enabled the messages to evangelists such as Norman Vincent Peale and Billy Graham to reach millions. (See p. 279.)

See "Lesson Plan," p. 750E.

4. Art and the machine

Meanwhile the machines and new ways of life left their mark on the arts. After the camera was invented, anybody with a camera could make a picture exactly like what he saw. It was no trick anymore to make a "likeness" of a person or a landscape. So the artists, too, tried to make something different. They experimented with new ways to paint and new kinds of statues. These were no longer pretty figures of men and women, trees or flowers. Instead they were abstract patterns showing the artist's private vision.

Adventurous artists. The most famous of these was Jackson Pollock (1912–1956), who had been born in Cody, Wyoming, and was trained to paint in the traditional style. He invented his own kind of Abstract Expressionism called "action painting." He would put his large canvas on the floor and then (he explained) paint with "sticks, trowels, knives, and dripping fluid paint or a heavy impasto with sand,

broken glass and other foreign matter added." Along with Pollock came Willem de Kooning, Helen Frankenthaler, Franz Kline, Adolph Gottlieb, Mark Rothko, Barnett Newman, and Robert Motherwell, each with another new vision of how to paint. Some people wondered whether what they produced was really "art." But many more enjoyed what they saw. They believed Americans should experiment with art, just as they did with everything else.

Collectors, museums, and galleries began snatching up "minimal art" at high prices. This art did little or nothing to change an object, and simply considered the object as art. Andy Warhol's "pop art" offered larger-than-life paintings of Campbell soup cans and Brillo boxes. Claes Oldenburg's pop art produced a huge statue of a lipstick or a canvas of a *Hamburger with Pickle and Tomato Attached.*

Rock 'n' Roll. Popular music, too, was transformed during the 1950s and 1960s and would never be the same again. The new music, growing out of black rhythm and blues, was given a

Jackson Pollock's "Autumn Rhythm" was one of the artist's "action paintings."

The Metropolitan Museum of Art, George A. Hearn Fund, 1957

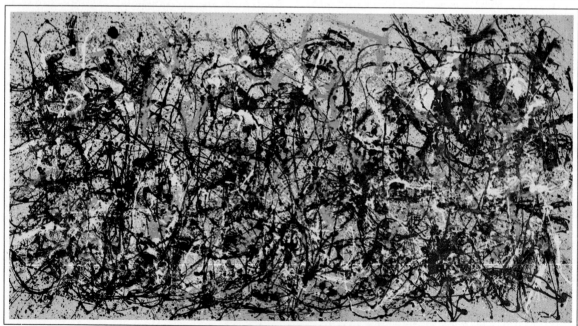

More from Boorstin: "In the democratic booster-enthusiasm for life enrichment through art and hobby-fun, the wider meaning of these techniques was easily overlooked. It was easy to see that the camera and the phonograph instantly increased knowledge or widened experience. But it was hard to foresee that in the longer run, these and other machines that made experience repeatable could actually dilute experience, dull consciousness, and flatten sensations." (From *The Americans: The Democratic Experience*)

different form by country and western singers. Finally it emerged as "Rock 'n' Roll." Rock was deeply influenced by modern machines—electric guitars, loudspeaker systems, and the magic created in recording studios by audio tapes, mixers, and other complex devices.

The first great popular star of Rock 'n' Roll was Elvis Presley. From the small town of Tupelo, Mississippi, Presley burst upon the music scene in the 1950s and swept all before him. Across the Atlantic, four young singer-musicians in the English port city of Liverpool picked up this new sound. During the 1960s the music of the Beatles, as they called themselves, would conquer the world.

The Beatles were far more original and more talented than Presley. They created their own distinctive sounds. And the Beatles' influence on the young went beyond music. Their long hair, their casual clothes and manners, their irreverent humor, and their flirtations with drugs excited and captivated young people around the world. Rock 'n' Roll groups both reflected and shaped the outlook of young people in the turbulent 1960s (pp. 808–809).

Writers in a complex world. Writers also had trouble casting the new world of speedy change and all-powerful machines in the old patterns. Herman Wouk's *The Caine Mutiny* (1952) told about the problems, of command in the modern navy. James Jones's World War II novel, *From Here to Eternity* (1951), showed characters who were lonely and lost. J. D. Salinger's *Catcher in the Rye* (1951) was a story of an adolescent trying to escape hypocrisy. In *Invisible Man* (1952), Ralph Ellison's black hero gradually saw that he was powerless and that the world was out of his reach. Ellison made the black man in a white world a symbol of everyone's puzzling experience in the industrial age. Joseph Heller's *Catch-22* (1969), a hilarious tale of wartime red tape, became a name for all the no-win situations in modern America. Carson McCullers portrayed the silent world of two mutes in *The Heart is a Lonely Hunter* (1940) and the loneliness of a young girl in *The Member of the Wedding* (1946). Eudora Welty in *Delta Wedding*

Helen Frankenthaler. Blue Territory. 1955. Oil on canvas. 113 × 58 inches. Collection of Whitney Museum of American Art. Purchase, with funds from the Friends of the Whitney Museum of American Art. 57.8

Helen Frankenthaler painted "Blue Territory."

(1948) and *Losing Battles* (1970) described the intimate ties that bind families together. Katherine Anne Porter described us all in *Ship of Fools* (1962).

William Faulkner wrote about how the South (and America) lost the simple ideals of the farming past. In a mythical county in Mississippi in *The Hamlet* (1940), *The Town* (1957), and *The Mansion* (1959) he told the long story of the

Multicultural Connection: Carlos Bulosan (1913–1956), born in the Pangasinan province in the Philippines, came to the U.S. in 1930. After spending years working in the fish canneries and as a migrant worker along the Pacific coast, he sought to improve the lives of Filipino workers and helped to form a labor union. Later, he developed his literary talents and produced and important Filipino-American autobiography, *America Is in the Heart,* in 1946.

UPI/Bettmann

Ralph Ellison's extraordinary novel *Invisible Man* grew out of his own experiences.

greedy and unpleasant Snopes clan. Faulkner won the Nobel Prize for literature in 1950.

Still other writers, like Saul Bellow, who also won the Nobel Prize, described the problems that thoughtful men and women faced inside themselves. Norman Mailer, after writing *The Naked and the Dead* (1948), his action-novel about World War II, turned to writing about himself. His new "journalism" report on the anti-Vietnam march on Washington in 1967 was called *The Armies of the Night*.

In spite of all the hi-fi's and television sets and the other entertainment machines, Americans bought and read more books than ever before. Each year's new titles numbered more than 40,000. Inexpensive paperback books, hardly known in this country before the war, flooded the market. Readers could find them everywhere—not only in bookstores, but now also in drugstores, supermarkets, and airports. Millions joined book clubs. Best-selling books often went on to become movies or television shows. And sometimes movies were turned into novels.

To help it use all sources of knowledge, back in 1800 the Congress had set up its own library.

By the late twentieth century the Library of Congress was the largest in the world—with about 20 million books (in 468 languages!) and about 80 million other items. Besides books, magazines, and newspapers, there were photographs, motion picture films, musical recordings, art prints, maps and globes, the manuscripts of famous men and women, and braille books and "talking books" for the blind. It served all other libraries, along with writers, scholars, and all the people. Like the Congress itself, it was a symbol of democratic America that everybody could visit on Capitol Hill in Washington. And it, too, was using the magic of the computer to control its millions of items and offer them to Congress and the nation.

Americans were delighted and bewildered, frustrated and challenged by the kaleidoscope-world of new machines. Books, the movie ✖ screen and the TV tube, the works of painters and sculptors helped make sense of their world. Political leaders, the men and women whom Americans elected to represent them and to manage their government, were still the most conspicuous shapers of American life. In the next generation, could these elected leaders offer the uplift and the direction the nation needed?

The forces of mobile people and magic machines, unlike the terms of Presidents, did not end on a particular day. These forces came to a climax under Presidents Truman and Eisenhower. But the forces were rooted in World War II, and even earlier, and did not end with any President's term. The forces we have described would become stronger with the passing years. They help explain the new problems and new opportunities that the nation would face in the turbulent 1960s and after.

See "Section 4 Review answers," p. 750E.

Section 4 Review

1. How did painters break with tradition in the postwar era?

2. **Critical Thinking: Recognizing Cause and Effect.** What effect did television and movies have on the book publishing industry?

✖ Critical Thinking Activity: Expressing Problems Clearly What forms did artistic expression take between 1950 and 1960? As a class write a description of the art scene in the 1950s and 1960s. Have each student in the class contribute one sentence. Ask students to relate their description of the art scene to trends in music and literature of the period (e.g., traditional styles of expression were challenged, new definitions were applied, and so on).

Chapter 30 Review

See "Chapter Review answers." p. 750E.

Focusing on Ideas

1. What is "demography"? What general trends have demographers noticed concerning the population of the post–World War II United States?

2. How have farming and farm life in the United States changed since 1950?

3. Identify ways in which computers and other forms of automation affect you and your family.

4. What evidence do you see that religion continues to have a significant influence on American life?

Taking a Critical Look

1. **Predicting Consequences.** What social changes would you expect to see in the United States as the proportion of young people declines and the proportion of elderly people rises?

2. **Identifying Central Issues.** What are some "learning by doing" school experiences that you have had in the past ten years? How else do you learn history besides reading history books?

Your Region in History

1. **Geography.** Study the "Flow of Migrants" map on page 753. Did your region have an overall gain or loss of population from the migration? Which other region, if any, received the heaviest flow of migrants from your region? What particular attractions might have brought people to relocate to your region during the period 1955 to 1965?

2. **Culture.** Interview leaders of a local church or synagogue about changes that have occurred in their local or national institutions since 1950. Ask them what changes in American life have contributed to changes in their religious institutions.

3. **Economics.** To what extent have blacks or Hispanics gained political office and government jobs in your locality in recent years? Other minorities? To what factors do you attribute these social and political changes?

Historical Facts and Figures

Determining Relevance. Study the graphs below to help answer the following questions: (a) How many Americans owned television sets in 1948? In 1960? (b) What percentage of Americans owned televisions in 1948? In 1960? (c) What economic or cultural changes occurred in the United States as a result of the invention and widespread sale of the television? Find evidence in the chapter to support your conclusions.

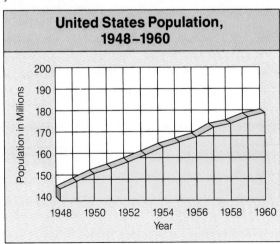

Homes with Television Sets, 1948–1960

= 5 Million Homes with Television Sets

Source: *Statistical Abstract of the United States*

United States Population, 1948–1960

Source: *Statistical Abstract of the United States*

MAKING CONNECTIONS
Unit 10

This unit began on page 705 with the observation that a new era of history had begun in the years between 1945 and 1960:

Under the menacing shadow of the atomic bomb, war between great powers could never again be the same. Isolation was no longer possible, . . . [and] in the postwar age, the American ways of living, thinking, and doing would be transformed.

This conclusion was supported by the three unit themes that are reprinted in **dark type** below. Use the time line and the information in Unit 10 to answer the questions that follow the unit themes.

THEMES IN HISTORY

Using "Making Connections": Have students look at the unit themes printed in dark type. Explain that each event on the time line relates to one of these themes. Ask students to decide which events are related to which theme. Students should also use events from the time line in their answers and explain how events are related. Have students go back through the text of Unit 10 to find other events related to the unit themes.

Events in American History

GOVERNMENT AND POLITICS

1. **Tensions between the United States and the Soviet Union and the shadow of atomic weapons produce an era of "cold war."**
   How did the Soviet Union's actions after World War II fuel America's fear of communism? Was this fear well-founded? (Distinguishing False from Accurate Images)

2. **Growing demands for racial equality produce new leadership and new government policies.** SOCIAL CHANGE
   How did the Supreme Court's decision in *Brown* v. *Board of Education* change the way in which civil rights issues were confronted? (Determining Relevance)

3. **Technological advances transform American ways of living, thinking, and doing during the Truman and Eisenhower years.** SCIENCE, TECHNOLOGY, AND SOCIETY
   How did technological advances realized between 1945 and 1960 change American life? (Recognizing Cause and Effect)

┌ 1947
The Truman Doctrine—granting military aid to governments opposed to communism—is introduced.

1946 ─────────
George Kennan warns that the Soviets must be contained to prevent a third world war.

| 1935 | 1940 | 1945 | 1950 |

Events in World History

1945 ─────────
The United Nations is formed, with its headquarters in New York City.

└ 1948
The United States air-lifts food to West Berlin, following the Soviet blockade.

1952
General Eisenhower is elected
President of the United States.

1953
McCarthy launches his campaign to rid
the country of suspected Communists.

1954
The Supreme Court declares "separate
but equal" doctrine unconstitutional in
Brown v. *Board of Education*.

1955
Martin Luther King, Jr., leads
Montgomery, Alabama, bus
boycott.

1957
Congress passes first
civil rights legislation since
Reconstruction.

1970
95% of American homes have at
least one television set.

1960
More Americans live in suburbs
than in cities as a result of the
automobile.

1955   **1960**   **1965**   **1970**

1955
The countries of eastern Europe
form the Warsaw Pact as a
NATO equivalent.

1953
Nikita Khrushchev replaces
Stalin as leader of the
Soviet Union.

Unit 11

Writing About History and Art: Direct students' attention to the unit introduction, illustration, and list of themes on pages 772–773. Have the introduction and unit themes read aloud. After a brief discussion of the subject matter of the unit, instruct students to write a brief paragraph, explaining how the art:

—relates to the unit themes;
—exemplifies the unit title and illustrates the introduction; and
—is an appropriate choice for the unit.

Turbulent Times 1961–1974

"Let the word go forth from this time and place, to friend and foe alike, that the torch has been passed to a new generation of Americans, born in this century, tempered by war, disciplined by a hard and bitter peace, proud of our ancient heritage. . . ."

So John F. Kennedy introduced his Presidency, and so began a turbulent era for the United States. During the following thirteen years one President would be assassinated. Another would decline to run again because of opposition to his foreign policy. And a third, facing impeachment, would resign. During these years, which had begun with so much hope, Americans would be distressed and divided by the actions of their government and their Presidents.

The United States not only survived. The Republic drew new strength by discovering that the people could control their government. They would not wage war without understanding the reasons. They could even replace their President. Never before had Americans seen so clearly how the Constitution had given power to the people.

THEMES IN HISTORY

- John F. Kennedy's 1000 days in office bring optimism to the nation. GOVERNMENT AND POLITICS
- Lyndon Johnson's strong leadership expands opportunities for all Americans while deeply dividing the country over the war in Vietnam. SOCIAL CHANGE
- The Watergate scandal tests the nation's constitutional system of government and leads to President Nixon's resignation. THE CONSTITUTION

◉ "Blues" by Adolph Gottlieb seethes with energy contained and released. It foreshadows the turbulence of the new era.
National Museum of American Art, Smithsonian Institution, Gift of the Woodward Foundation

Chapter 31
Years of Hope and Promise

Identifying Chapter Materials

Objectives	Basic Instructional Materials	Extension Materials
1 John F. Kennedy Wins ▪ Describe the election of 1960 and trace the background and experience of John F. Kennedy. ▪ Explain the importance of religion in presidential campaigns in this century.	**Annotated Teacher's Edition** ▪ Lesson Plans, p. 774C. **Instructional Support File** ▪ Pre-Reading Activities, Unit 11, p. 1 ▪ Skill Review Activity, Unit 11, p. 4 ▪ Critical Thinking Activity, Unit 11, p. 6	**Documents of American History** ▪ John F. Kennedy's Inaugural Address, Vol. 2, p. 654
2 Learning Hard Lessons ▪ Identify the hard lessons in foreign policy learned by President Kennedy.	**Annotated Teacher's Edition** ▪ Lesson Plans, pp. 774C–774D **Instructional Support File** ▪ Skill Application Activity, Unit 11, p. 5	**Enrichment Support File** ▪ The Berlin Wall: Past and Present (See "In-Depth Coverage" at right.) **Suggested Secondary Sources** ▪ See chart at right. **American History Transparencies** ▪ Time Lines, p. E35
3 Facing Communist Challenges ▪ Describe President Kennedy's actions during the Cuban missile crisis and trace the growing United States involvement in Vietnam.	**Annotated Teacher's Edition** ▪ Lesson Plans, pp. 774D–774E	**Documents of American History** ▪ The Cuban Missile Crisis, Vol. 2, p. 674 ▪ The Nuclear Test Ban Treaty, Vol. 2, p. 680
4 A New Frontier ▪ Identify Kennedy's economic and "New Frontier" policies and describe the "black revolt" of the 1960s. ▪ Discuss the limits on free expression in a democracy.	**Annotated Teacher's Edition** ▪ Lesson Plans, pp. 774E–774F	**Documents of American History** ▪ Kennedy's Message on Federal Aid to Education, Vol. 2, p. 656
5 The Tragic End ▪ Recount the details of President Kennedy's assassination and public reaction to his death. ▪ Evaluate the Kennedy years.	**Annotated Teacher's Edition** ▪ Lesson Plans, p. 774F **Instructional Support File** ▪ Reading Activities, Unit 11, pp. 2–3 ▪ Chapter Test, Unit 11, pp. 7–10 ▪ Additional Test Questions, Unit 11, pp. 11–14	**Documents of American History** ▪ The Warren Report, Vol. 2, p. 694

Providing In-Depth Coverage

Perspectives on the Berlin Wall

In the late 1940s Russian expansion abroad and communist subversion at home became the preoccupation of both official Washington and millions of Americans. The Cold War began—a continuing rivalry between the two nations that threatened to turn into World War III.

The Berlin Wall, a grim, gray barrier cutting through the heart of the city, built to prevent East Germans from escaping to freedom through West Berlin, stood as a reminder of the increased tension between the two superpowers. This tension lasted for nearly thirty years, until 1989, when the wall was dismantled.

A History of the United States as an instructional program provides two types of resources you can use to offer in-depth coverage of the Berlin Wall: the *student text* and the *Enrichment Support File*. A list of *Suggested Secondary Sources* is also provided. The chart below shows the topics that are covered in each.

THE STUDENT TEXT. Boorstin and Kelley's *A History of the United States* unfolds the chronology of events leading to the erection of the Berlin Wall.

AMERICAN HISTORY ENRICHMENT SUPPORT FILE. This collection of primary source readings and classroom activities reveals the role of the United States in opposing the building of the wall originally and its reaction to the dismantling of the wall.

SUGGESTED SECONDARY SOURCES. This reference list of readings by well-known historians and other commentators provides an array of perspectives on the Berlin Wall, past and present.

Locating Instructional Materials

Detailed lesson plans for teaching the Berlin Wall as a mini-course or to study one or more elements of the construction of the Berlin Wall in depth are offered in the following areas: in the *student text*, see individual lesson plans at the beginning of each chapter; in the *Enrichment Support File*, see page 3; for readings beyond the student text, see *Suggested Secondary Sources*.

IN-DEPTH COVERAGE ON THE BERLIN WALL

Student Text	Enrichment Support File	Suggested Secondary Sources
• Beginnings of the Cold War, pp. 707–711 • A Divided Germany, p. 717 • Building the Wall, pp. 781–782 • Kennedy Speaks in Berlin, p. 782 • The Wall Comes Down, p. 933 • Reunification of Germany, pp. 934–935	• Lesson Suggestions • Multimedia Resources • Overview Essay/The Berlin Wall: Past and Present • Primary Sources in American History/ The Wall Rises, the Wall Falls • Geography in American History/The Geopolitical Significance of the Berlin Wall • Great Debates in American History/ How Real is the Soviet Threat? • Simulation/A "Berlin Wall" in Your Community • Making Connections	• *The Wall Came Tumbling Down: The Berlin Wall and the Fall of Communism* by Jerry Bornstein. • *The Ides of August: The Berlin Wall Crisis—1961* by Curtis Cate, pp. 91–204. • *Berlin: The Wall is Not Forever* by Eleanor Lansing Dulles, pp. 47–78. • *The Berlin Crisis, 1958–1962* by Jack M. Schick, pp. 29–69.

John F. Kennedy Wins

FOCUS

To introduce the lesson, play a recording of Kennedy's inaugural address or ask a student with an interest in oratory or dramatics to read the speech. Ask: How would the line "we shall pay any price" be received by youth today? Would you be inspired today by Kennedy saying, "Ask not what your country can do for you, ask what you can do for your country"? Explain.

Developing Vocabulary

The words listed in this chapter are essential terms for reading and understanding particular sections of the chapter. The page number after each term indicates the page of its first or most important appearance in the chapter. These terms are defined in the text Glossary (text pages 1000–1011).

inauguration (page 777)

INSTRUCT

Explain

After the 1960 debates, Lyndon Baines Johnson refused to participate in a televised debate during the campaign in 1964. The unfortunate Nixon refused to debate in 1968 and again in 1972.

☑ Writing Process Activity

Testing Conclusions Provide students with Kennedy's inaugural address, and ask them to imagine they were in the audience when he delivered it. In preparation for writing an evaluation of what President Kennedy stood for, ask them to outline the main ideas in the speech. Students should begin with a sentence summarizing what they expect him to accomplish as President, and they should support their main idea with examples from the address. Ask them to revise for logical organization and coherence. After proofreading, students can compare their evaluation with that of the textbook authors.

Section Review Answers

Section 1, page 778

1. The debates were four one-hour sessions televised nationwide. For most of the time the candidates were answering the reporters' questions. Debates like these risk giving too great an advantage to a candidate who is merely a good performer. The ability to do well answering questions on television may have little to do with the ability to be an effective President, yet televised debates can have a decisive effect on an election. 2. He served in the House of Representatives and in the Senate. 3. During the "great debates," Kennedy claimed that the nation was stagnating and not moving forward; he warned of a recession. He said that the government neglected those who needed special help—the old, the young, the poor, and minorities. He criticized the conditions in cities and in public schools. He also pointed out that the nation lagged behind the Soviet Union in weaponry and that we needed better weapons for small wars. In his inaugural address, Kennedy did not say very much about domestic affairs. He feared that his slim margin of victory might make it difficult to get many bills through Congress. Instead, he concentrated on foreign policy, saying that the citizens of the United States would do what was necessary to "assure the survival and success of liberty."

CLOSE

To conclude the lesson, have students write an essay of 100–200 words entitled "The Effects of TV on American Presidential Elections." Remind them to explain the connection between the cause (television) and the effects they list. Have them include several examples to support their argument, and label the effects with an "E" in the margin.

Learning Hard Lessons

FOCUS

To introduce the lesson, have students locate Laos on the map on page 810. Ask: What countries border it? (China, Vietnam, Cambodia, Thailand, and Burma) Point out that it is about twice the size of Pennsylvania, and mountainous with dense forests. Then discuss the following questions: Why was the United States involved in Laos? (As part of its global commitment to contain the spread of communism) How did Kennedy avoid the use of American troops in Laos? (By participating in a British-sponsored conference that set up a neutral government, and then signing a multinational treaty agreeing to respect Laos's neutrality) Point out that despite the settlement, the American CIA, the North Vietnamese, and the Chinese remained active in Laos before and during our subsequent involvement in the Vietnam War. As recently as 1979, 30,000 Vietnamese troops remained in Laos. Many Laotians could be found in the stream of refugees that entered the United States after the end of the Vietnam War.

INSTRUCT

Explain

JFK learned of the planned invasion of Cuba shortly after his inauguration. There wasn't much time to stop the operation because Castro was about to receive warplanes from Russia, and the rainy season would soon begin. Under much pressure from Allen Dulles, who argued that for Kennedy to reject the invasion would be "refusing to allow freedom-loving exiles to deliver their homeland from a Communist dictatorship," Kennedy gave in.

★ Independent Activity

Demonstrating Reasoned Judgment Ask students to select one of the following topics and write an essay on the lesson that the Kennedy administration learned from it: Laos, Bay of Pigs, Berlin Wall.

Section Review Answers

Section 2, page 783

1. a) Communist faction in Laos. b) director of the CIA who proposed a plan for an invasion of Cuba by Cuban refugees armed and trained by the United States. c) Secretary of Defense in the Kennedy administration. d) erected by the Soviet Union in August 1961 to seal East Berlin off from West Berlin. e) Khrushchev's description of various civil wars or wars against colonial powers. f) leader of Guinea, befriended by President Kennedy. 2. The government that the United States had helped to install in Laos faced armed opposition from both a Communist faction and a faction that wanted to be neutral in the American-Soviet conflict. Kennedy faced the problem of how to prevent a Communist takeover without sending American troops into battle. 3. The landing was expected to trigger a popular uprising that would overthrow Castro. No uprising occurred, and the invasion force was defeated. Eventually, American companies and individuals paid Castro to release hundreds of anti-Castro troops who had been captured. 4. East Germans continued to try to escape to the West through West Berlin. West Berlin amounted to a living advertisement for the West in the heart of East Germany. 5. It called for the United States to develop forces that would provide an alternative between doing nothing and using the "massive retaliation" against the Soviet Union and China that Dulles had threatened. 6. The goal of the Alliance for Progress was to reduce the possibility of Communist inroads in Latin America. A secondary goal, of course, was the improvement of life in the countries that were to make reforms in order to receive aid. The goal of the Peace Corps was to prove that the United States was interested in promoting freedom around the world—rather than just wishing to stop communism.

CLOSE

To conclude the lesson, remind students that containment has been the cornerstone of United States foreign policy since the 1950s. Write on the chalkboard: Laos, Bay of Pigs, "flexible response," Alliance for Progress, and Peace Corps. Ask students which items are examples of attempts to contain communism.

Section 3 (pages 783–788)

Facing Communist Challenges

FOCUS

To introduce the lesson, ask students to use the text index to find material on the Monroe Doctrine, the Roosevelt Corollary, and FDR's Good Neighbor Policy. Then ask: Which of these policies supports Kennedy's actions in Cuba during the missile crisis?

Developing Vocabulary

ballistic missile (page 784); **superpower** (page 786); **junta** (page 788).

INSTRUCT

Explain

The question raised in the three sections on the missile gap, disarmament, and the test-ban treaty can be consolidated in a class discussion. Help students see one of the basic issues—a very persistent one: How important is equality or superiority in long-range nuclear weaponry when each side presumably has the capability to destroy the other?

⊘ Writing Process Activity

Predicting Consequences Ask students to imagine that President Kennedy has announced the naval blockade of military equipment to Cuba. In preparation for writing a diary entry about the situation, ask students to freewrite about their fears about the Russians and about the possibility of war. They should begin their entry with a sentence that captures their reactions, and they should use factual information to support their fears. Have students revise for specific detail and logical order. After proofreading, students can exchange their entry with a partner.

Section Review Answers

Section 3, page 788

1. a) referred to the belief that the United States trailed the Soviet Union in nuclear missiles. b) mis-

siles that can carry nuclear warheads from silos in the American heartland to the Soviet Union. c) type of missile carried by American submarines. d) first nuclear-powered submarine. e) sent in an orbiting satellite by the Soviets in 1961. He was the first person to be sent into outer space. f) American sent on a flight more than a hundred miles above the earth in 1961. g) President of France who vetoed Britain's application to join the Common Market and in 1966 pulled France out of NATO. h) permitted the President to reduce tariffs by 50 percent and, if Britain were admitted to the European Common Market, to remove tariffs on articles heavily traded by the United States and Western Europe. i) President of South Vietnam who refused to hold the election called for by the Geneva accords of 1954. j) National Liberation Front, created by opponents of Diem in 1960. k) the name Diem gave to the Vietnamese Communists. 2. Increased spending on intercontinental bombers, ICBMs, and submarine-launched ballistic missiles. The buildup fulfilled Kennedy's campaign pledges and was intended to satisfy Congress and to ensure that the Soviet Union would not be tempted to launch a surprise attack. 3. He promised that the United States would land a man on the moon before 1970. 4. In 1963 Great Britain, the United States, and the Soviet Union agreed to ban nuclear tests in the atmosphere, in outer space, and underwater, but allowed underground testing to continue. 5. The Soviet Union promised to withdraw its missiles from Cuba, and the United States promised not to invade the island. 6. Yugoslavia had split from Moscow, and now several Eastern European countries began to diverge from strict adherence to Soviet policies. A break occurred between China and the Soviet Union in 1960. 7. He sent supplies and advisers to the South Vietnamese forces. 8. Took France out of NATO, and ordered American troops to leave the country. France began building its own nuclear weapons.

CLOSE

To conclude the lesson, discuss the following question: Did President Kennedy make a wise decision in the confrontation with the Soviets over the Cuban missile crisis? Have students write a 200-word essay answering that question for homework.

Section 4 (pages 788–792)

A New Frontier

FOCUS

To introduce the lesson, play a recording of Martin Luther King, Jr., delivering his "I Have a Dream"

speech or have a student read the speech aloud to the class. Ask students: Has King's dream become a reality? What did the March on Washington achieve?

Developing Vocabulary

civil rights (page 790); **freedom riders** (page 790); **sit-in** (page 790).

INSTRUCT

Explain

In a speech to the nation, Kennedy said: "Our nation is founded on the principle that observance of the law is the eternal safeguard of liberty . . . Americans are free to disagree with the law, but not to disobey it."

❀ Cooperative Learning Activity

Expressing Problems Clearly Break the class into groups of three and tell students that they will prepare a 45-second news item for television news. Explain that each group will choose one of the events described under *The black revolt* and will use outside resources to write and present a news item about that event. Have the members of each group decide who will gather resources, who will write the news, and who will act as newscaster in presenting the item to the class. After the presentations, have each group evaluate how well its members completed their tasks.

Section Review Answers

Section 4, page 792

1. a) provided billions of dollars for urban renewal. b) provided money to create new industries and retain workers in "distressed areas." c) used by Kennedy to control inflation. d) Baptist hymn which became the anthem of the civil rights movement. e) people who took buses south to protest racial segregation in southern bus stations. f) black veteran who tried to enroll in the all-white University of Mississippi and was opposed by the governor of the state and by rioting whites. g) head of the Mississippi NAACP, murdered in 1963. 2. Congress rejected or delayed action on Kennedy's proposals for federal aid to education, medical care for the aged, and a tax cut. It did pass his proposals for investment tax credits, urban renewal, an increase in the minimum wage, an extension of Social Security to cover more workers, and aid for economic development in distressed areas. 3. By an investment tax credit and by a tax cut. Congress did not approve the tax cut while Kennedy was alive. 4. JFK appointed blacks to some influential government posts, signed an order to desegregate public housing, proposed a civil rights bill stronger than any bill previously proposed, supported the efforts of southern blacks to vote, and used the powers

of the federal government to enforce the rights of blacks seeking admission to public colleges. In addition, Congress passed the Twenty-fourth Amendment, outlawing the poll tax. On the other hand, JFK appointed several prosegregation judges to federal district courts. 5. Television brought the civil rights movement to the attention of people around the country and showed the violence of those who were trying to maintain segregation.

CLOSE

To conclude the lesson, ask: Which of Kennedy's proposed plans or measures were later adopted? (General aid to education, Medicare, the war on poverty, and a strong civil rights law)

Section 5 (pages 792–794)

The Tragic End

FOCUS

To introduce the lesson, ask: Why is President Kennedy viewed so favorably as a President? List the words used to describe the Kennedy presidency on the chalkboard. Ask the class: Based on this list, how would you say most people feel about the Kennedy presidency? (The list will probably show that most people have a very favorable view.) Why do they have such a favorable view?

INSTRUCT

Explain

The days of Kennedy's assassination and burial were ones of deep shock and grief for the entire nation. Many Americans can remember exactly where they were and what they were doing when the news came that the President had been shot.

☑Writing Process Activity

Making Comparisons Explain to students that they will write an evaluation of Kennedy's presidency. Ask them to begin by brainstorming the ways in which he created Camelot and the ways in which he failed. Have them consider his appointments and his foreign and domestic policies. Students should write a thesis statement summarizing their point of view, and they should organize their details in order of importance or in chronological order. As they revise, they should check for specific detail and clear explanation. After proofreading, ask students to contrast their conclusions with their expectations (Chapter 31, Section 1).

Section Review Answers

Section 5, page 794

1. a) Democratic governor of Texas who was wounded during the assassination of President Kennedy. b) arrested for the assassination of JFK but was himself murdered two days later. c) shot and killed Lee Harvey Oswald. d) investigated the assassination of Kennedy and concluded that no conspiracy was involved. 2. When Kennedy was assassinated the nation's optimism was temporarily suspended. Struggles of the 1960s would still have occurred, but there may have been a different attitude about change.

CLOSE

To conclude the lesson, ask students to make a list of the JFK's achievements during the 1,000 days of his presidency.

Chapter Review Answers

Focusing on Ideas

1. Youth, charm, poise, good looks; having held other elected offices; conservative Congressional record. 2. Tax cuts, wage-price controls or guidelines; size of budget deficits, efforts to balance budget, etc. 3. Foreign: Cuban missile crisis, nuclear test-ban treaty, Trade Expansion Act, firmness on Berlin, Peace Corps. Domestic: Stepped-up defense program, moon-race decision, Area Redevelopment Act, proposals on civil rights, poverty.

Taking a Critical Look

1. Charm may help to recruit people to administration, "sell" proposals to decision makers, foster public enthusiasm. Charm is harmful if it prevents clear analysis. 2. Vietnam: more clearly a civil war; involved disregard of agreements; began as guerrilla warfare, not clash of armies; had no UN support; US began by providing only "advisers" and weapons, not armed forces.

Your Region in History

1–3. Answers will vary depending on your region. Consult your local library or historical society.

Historical Facts and Figures

(a) 8.9 million in 1965; 7.5 million in 1975; 8.9 million in 1980. (b) 225.5 million in 1965; 17.8 million in 1975; 19 million in 1980. (c) 1960: 34.3%; 1980: 32.2%. (d) 1960: 17.8%; 1980: 10.1%. (e) Based on population figures, more whites than blacks below the poverty level. Percentages show poverty more likely for blacks than whites. (f) Include information from (e).

Focusing the Chapter: Have students identify the chapter logo. Discuss what unit theme the logo might symbolize. Then ask students to identify other illustrations or titles that relate to this theme.

Chapter 31

Years of Hope and Promise

The White House took on a new tone when John F. Kennedy, his beautiful wife, Jacqueline, and their vigorous little children moved in. To many people the Kennedys, with their youth, good looks, charm, and culture, created in Washington something like a fairy tale with all its magic. Camelot, they called it, after King Arthur's palace and the idyllic happiness of the time. This Camelot was to last only a brief 1000 days. Then Americans would awaken again to the real, hard world.

John F. Kennedy, his wife, children, and numerous dogs are seen here a few months before his death.

John F. Kennedy Library

See "Lesson Plan," p. 774C.

1. John F. Kennedy wins

The 1960 campaign would be the first fought mainly on television. Both candidates were carefully "packaged" for sale to the American public. For the first time, all who wished to watch could see them face each other on TV in "great debates."

Nominating the candidates. Before the national convention there were two serious Republican contenders. The energetic Nelson A. Rockefeller who had been elected governor of New York in 1958, represented the liberal wing. But in December 1959, finding that the party leaders would not support him, he withdrew from the race. When the Republicans met in Chicago in July 1960, the road was cleared for Vice-President Richard M. Nixon of California. He was nominated for President. Then Henry Cabot Lodge, Jr., a former senator from Massachusetts and now ambassador to the UN, was chosen for second place because of his experience in foreign affairs.

The Democrats faced a heated contest. The main candidates were all senators—John F. Kennedy of Massachusetts, Hubert H. Humphrey of Minnesota, Lyndon B. Johnson of Texas, and Stuart Symington of Missouri. Adlai Stevenson, although not active in the race, waited in the wings hoping that the nod would come his way once more. The most important early fight was between Humphrey and Kennedy. Hubert Humphrey hoped to rally all the old Roosevelt and Truman liberals. The 42-year-old Kennedy was a proven vote-getter and had a conservative record in the House and Senate. His chief handicap was that he was a Roman Catholic. Many party leaders wondered whether a Catholic could be elected President.

The first test of this question came in the primary in West Virginia, where the voters were 95 percent Protestant. The Democrats there would choose whether their delegates to the Democratic convention would support Kennedy or Humphrey. Kennedy won a smashing victory. This knocked Humphrey out of the race and did much to quiet the religious issue. Then Kennedy went on to other victories. When the delegates gathered at the convention in Los Angeles, a last-minute push by Lyndon Johnson failed, and Kennedy was nominated on the first ballot.

Kennedy, wanting to make peace with his strong rival and to unify the party, chose Johnson for his running mate. The powerful majority leader of the Senate surprised everyone by accepting. Since LBJ came from Texas, he would help "balance" the ticket and attract votes in the South and Southwest.

The "great debates." Kennedy argued that, under the Republicans, the nation was stagnating and not moving ahead. During the 1950s, he said, the Gross National Product (the total of all the goods and services produced) had not been growing as it should. He warned of a recession. According to him, the government had neglected all those who needed special help— the young and old, the poor and minorities. Our cities were plagued by slums. Our schools were not doing their job. The general in the White House, he said, had not improved our defense. The nation was behind Soviet Russia in nuclear missiles, and our other arms could not deal with the small "brushfire wars." His slogan was, "Let's get the country moving again." He pointed the way toward a "New Frontier." "Mr. Nixon says, 'We never had it so good.' I say we can do better."

The two candidates appeared together on television in a series of four one-hour programs. People called these the "great debates." But they were not like the old-fashioned Lincoln-Douglas debates a century earlier. In those debates one man spoke for an hour, his opponent replied for an hour and a half. Then the first speaker had another half hour to reply. Now the candidates would only speak for 8 minutes in the first and last debates. All the rest of the time reporters would ask them questions. Each candidate had only 2 1/2 minutes to give his answer.

These "great debates" reached the largest audience that had ever watched a political discussion. Seventy million citizens saw each program. In earlier times the only people who could hear a candidate were those he could reach with his own voice—outdoors or in a meeting hall. 📖

📖 **More from Boorstin:** "The application of the quiz show format to the so-called 'Great Debates' between Presidential candidates in the election of 1960 . . . might have been called the $400,000 Question (Prize: a $100,000-a-year job for four years)." (From *The Image: A Guide to Pseudo-Events in America*)

John Kennedy's performance on television in the "great debates" swung many voters to his side.

Now a whole nation could see and hear both candidates at once. Kennedy seemed to gain more from the debates than Nixon. Though he was less well known, now his charm, poise, and good looks came into everybody's home. His adept handling of questions undercut criticism of his youth and inexperience. The United States had become a television democracy. And there were new dangers. The man who showed up best on TV was bound to be the best "performer." He could give the cleverest response in 2 1/2 minutes to questions that he had just heard—and look the best doing it. But was that a good test for a President?

The election of 1960 was a cliffhanger. The final count showed the narrowest popular edge (3/10th of a percent of all votes cast) since 1880. Alaska had entered the Union in January 1959 and Hawaii followed in August, so there were now 50 states. In the electoral college,

Kennedy carried, sometimes by razor-thin margins, enough states to give him 303 votes to Nixon's 219.

There were enough disputed ballots in key states so that Nixon might have challenged the result. But like most other losers of close presidential races, Nixon decided for the good of the nation not to contest the numbers.

John F. Kennedy.   Kennedy was the youngest man ever elected President, although not the youngest ever to hold the office. That distinction belonged to Theodore Roosevelt. Kennedy, who had been born in Brookline, Massachusetts, on May 29, 1917, was still only 43 when he took office. He came from a large Irish Catholic family. His grandfathers on both sides had been leaders in Democratic politics in Boston. His father, Joseph P. Kennedy, made a fortune in business and finance, and supported FDR

Multicultural Connection: Hawaiian statehood changed the ethnic composition of the Congress. Hiram Fong (1907–), a Hawaiian-born Chinese American was elected to the Senate in 1959 and subsequently re-elected twice (1964 and 1970). Born in 1907 of parents who came to work on Hawaii's sugar cane plantations, Fong attended the University of Hawaii and Harvard Law School. Returning to Hawaii, he worked as an attorney, ran and won various local and territorial elections, and worked for statehood.

for election. FDR appointed him to the Securities and Exchange Commission and then sent him as ambassador to Great Britain. The young Jack Kennedy inherited a love of politics and of the Democratic party.

The year when Jack graduated from Harvard, 1940, was a time of crisis for the free world. The young Kennedy felt the crisis. He revised his student thesis and made it into a book called *Why England Slept.* He told how English statesmen had appeased the Nazis and let them become the menace to the peace of Europe. Then during World War II Jack Kennedy served as a naval officer for four years and won Navy and Marine Corps medals for heroism. He had risked his life to rescue the crew of his PT boat when it was cut in two by a Japanese destroyer. After the war no one was surprised to see another Kennedy enter Massachusetts politics. Of course he was a Democrat. He was elected to the United States House of Representatives in 1946 and then was elected to the Senate in 1952 and 1958. But Jack Kennedy did not leave an impressive record as a lawmaker.

Like FDR he turned bad luck into an opportunity. He had injured his back in college playing football, and the crash of his PT boat made it worse. After a back operation in 1954 he could not leave his bed for six months. During his slow and painful recovery he wrote another book, *Profiles in Courage.* This story of brave choices by American statesmen won the Pulitzer Prize for biography in 1957.

While Kennedy was writing his book about courage, the Senate was deciding whether to censure Senator Joseph R. McCarthy for his reckless attacks on government servants. Kennedy now kept silent. He did not cast his vote on the McCarthy condemnation because he was recovering from his operation. And he never revealed how he might have voted had he been present on the Senate floor. His critics wondered whether he really understood the meaning of courage.

When Kennedy became President, he brought to the White House youth, vigor, broad culture, and a quick mind. His ability as a speed reader became a legend. He loved to sail, and people were pleased to see that their President was energetic enough to enjoy touch football.

But before he became President, Jack Kennedy had run nothing larger than his Senate office. The nation had not shown great enthusiasm for him. He had won election by the smallest of margins. Could this attractive but inexperienced young man really lead the country to a "New Frontier"?

The inaugural address. On January 20, 1961, a bright sunny day in snow-covered Washington, John F. Kennedy was inaugurated. After the New England poet Robert Frost recited a poem, JFK took the oath of office. His inaugural address was short and eloquent. Since his slim victory might make it difficult for him to get major bills through Congress, Kennedy spoke chiefly on foreign affairs. The first President born in this century, he announced that a "new generation of Americans" had taken control. "Defending freedom in its hour of maximum danger," his generation, too, would hold the line against communism. "Let every nation know, whether it wishes us well or ill, that we shall pay any price, bear any burden, meet any hardship, support any friend, oppose any foe to assure the survival and success of liberty." He called on his fellow citizens to "ask not what your country can do for you—ask what you can do for your country."

Many Americans were ready for Kennedy's call after the quiet, steady General Eisenhower. But some remembered the ringing, world-resounding words of Woodrow Wilson. And some feared that Kennedy's brave words, too, might lead us into a world conflict.

The new administration. Kennedy brought into office a whole new team. The President himself clearly planned to play a leading role in foreign affairs. For his Secretary of State he appointed a calm, quiet Georgian, Dean Rusk, who was president of the Rockefeller Foundation. For Secretary of Defense he chose Robert S. McNamara, who was only a year older than Kennedy. As president of the Ford Motor Company, McNamara had earned a national

See "Lesson Plan," p. 774C for **Writing Process Activity: Testing Conclusions** relating to Kennedy's inaugural address.

Black Star

John and Jacqueline Kennedy brought youth and glamor to the White House. Beside them at the Inaugural Ball are John's parents, Joseph and Rose Kennedy, and Lyndon and Lady Bird Johnson.

reputation for finding new ways of running a vast organization. McNamara's slick hair showed his concern for neatness and precise control. Kennedy asked C. Douglas Dillon, a Republican and a wealthy New York investment banker, to become Secretary of the Treasury. This appointment, the new President hoped, would quiet fears that he might be "unsound" in economic matters.

Family feeling was strong among the Kennedys. Now President Jack appointed his brother Robert as Attorney General. Robert Kennedy had only served a brief stint as a lawyer in the Justice Department and then as counsel for Senator Joe McCarthy, before the senator was condemned, and for other congressional committees. He had managed his brother's campaign with skill and ruthlessness. "I see nothing wrong," JFK joked, "with giving Bobby some legal experience before he goes out to practice law." Robert Kennedy remained his brother's closest adviser and turned out to be a forceful Attorney General.

See "Section 1 Review answers," p. 774C.

Section 1 Review

1. Describe the Kennedy-Nixon television debates. What were the dangers in such debates?
2. What qualifications did Kennedy have for the Presidency?
3. **Critical Thinking: Checking Consistency.** How did Kennedy's inaugural address deal with issues of which he had been critical during the "great debates"?

See "Lesson Plan," p. 774C.

2. Learning hard lessons

The new Kennedy team came to power believing that they could solve all problems. They would soon discover that both at home and abroad some issues were too complex for their hopeful, youthful energies. The first blows to their self-confidence came in foreign affairs.

Trouble in Laos. One of the nations created from French Indochina was Laos. A pro-Western faction was put into power there with the secret help of the CIA. The Communists, and those who wished to remain neutral between Russia and the United States, tried to overturn this regime. "You might have to go in there and fight it out," Ike told JFK. On March 23, 1961, Kennedy publicly warned that the United States would use armed force to prevent a Communist takeover of Laos.

Kennedy was urged by some of his advisers to send in American troops. But to avoid war he agreed to compromise. The British helped persuade the Soviets to come to a conference to set up a new government that would be neutral.

A truce was then arranged. Finally, in June 1962, the three warring factions in Laos came together. They formed a "coalition" government—in which each had a part. Then at Geneva in July, the United States, Russia, Great Britain, and eleven other countries signed a treaty promising to keep the country neutral. Without the use of American forces, it did prevent—or at least postpone—a Communist takeover. Two years later, to nobody's surprise, the Communist faction (the "Pathet Lao") backed

At a March 1961 conference President Kennedy makes a point about the Laotian situation.

out of the coalition. Laos was still a battle-ground.

The Bay of Pigs.

President Kennedy had good reason to be cautious in Laos. For meanwhile close to home—only 90 miles off the Florida coast—the United States suffered a shocking setback. In September 1960 President Eisenhower had approved a plan proposed by Allen Dulles (brother of Secretary of State Dulles), director of the CIA. The United States would supply money and arms in Guatemala for a force of anti-Castro Cubans. This force was trained and ready to go by April 1961. Kennedy and his advisers expected that when the small invasion force landed, the Cuban people would seize the

JFK consulted Ike a number of times during his Presidency. This photograph was made after the Bay of Pigs fiasco in 1961.

Wide World Photos

chance to overthrow Castro. So the President gave the signal for the invasion to proceed.

Some 1500 Cuban refugee fighters landed at the Bay of Pigs (Bahía de Cochinos) on the south coast of Cuba on April 17. They were not greeted by the popular uprising they expected. Instead, within hours their attack had bogged down, and they were in trouble. On April 18 Khrushchev threatened that the Soviet Union would go to Cuba's assistance if the United States did not "call a halt to the aggression against the Republic of Cuba." Soon the fighting was over, and 1200 of the anti-Castro troops were captured. In December 1962 after American companies and individuals paid Castro a ransom of $50 million in food and drugs and $3 million in cash, the unlucky refugee troops were freed.

Conference at Vienna.

The Bay of Pigs disaster shook President Kennedy and his advisers. It dismayed our European allies and made further problems with the Soviets. At the peace settlement in Potsdam after World War II, the democracies had made the mistake of dividing the great capital city of Berlin and allowing the Soviets to surround it with their troops. Now once again Khrushchev called for the evacuation of West Berlin before the end of 1961 by France, Britain, and the United States and the creation there of a "free city."

Prosperous West Berlin was an outpost of democracy and free enterprise in the very heart of Communist East Germany. It was a living advertisement for freedom, which Russia and the Communist dictators of East Germany feared. The East German leaders would not allow their people to escape to the free world. Still some of their desperate and courageous citizens risked their lives to slip through to West Berlin. The democratic powers were supplying West Berlin by highways controlled by the Communists. Khrushchev again threatened to sign a peace treaty with East Germany. This would allow the East German Communists to starve West Berlin by cutting off all the food that came by land.

At the same time, the unpredictable Khrushchev also made some friendly gestures. He

Multicultural Connection: Upon their return from prison in Cuba, 211 Bay of Pigs veterans entered the United States Army, Marine Corps, Navy, and Air Force. All were commissioned as officers. Many of these participated in the Vietnam War, where some were wounded or killed in action. Most of the officers have now retired from the armed services after reaching the rank of colonel.

M. Scheler/Black Star

The Brandenburg gate is seen here from the West Berlin side of the wall built by the Soviets. The sign warns: "Attention! You are now leaving West Berlin."

released some American airmen whose RB-47 plane had recently been shot down over Russia. And he told the American ambassador in Moscow that he would like to meet Kennedy. So in June 1961 JFK flew to Vienna, Austria. It was not expected that this would be a full-fledged "summit" meeting, where important treaties would be signed. Instead this was supposed to be merely a chance for discussion.

The talks did not go well. Made even bolder by the Bay of Pigs fiasco, Khrushchev stormed and threatened. But Kennedy was not adept at handling the Russian leader. Still, he did get a Soviet promise to work for peace in Laos, and he stood fast on Berlin. At the end he said to the Soviet premier, "I see it's going to be a very cold winter."

The Berlin Wall. In a somber speech to the American people soon after his return, President Kennedy made it clear that, if necessary, the United States would stand and fight for Berlin. Now he increased the draft quotas. He called up reserve and National Guard units. And he asked Congress for $3.2 billion to enlarge our armed forces. At the same time Kennedy made it clear that the United States was ready "to search for peace."

In August 1961 the Russians suddenly sealed off East Berlin from West Berlin, first by erecting a fence and then by building a grim, high wall. No longer could Easterners escape to freedom through West Berlin. Kennedy responded by sending a force of 1500 men to the city as a signal that the United States would act.

Continuity and Change: Government and Politics Remind students that the Berlin Wall, erected in August, 1961 to keep Easterners from escaping through West Berlin, was not taken down until almost thirty years later on November 9, 1989, at which time the border was reopened and thousands flooded across the border into West Berlin. (See p. 933.)

The firm refusal of the Western powers to give in led Khrushchev to back down. In October he withdrew his year-end deadline. In 1963 Kennedy encouraged the free world when he went to Berlin and stated "I am a Berliner." This was an American President declaring that the United States would not allow free people to be strangled.

"Flexible response." During these crises spread across three continents—in Laos, Cuba, and Berlin—President Kennedy was trying to make over American foreign policy. He had been impressed by a speech of Khrushchev's in January 1961 that promised Soviet aid for "wars of national liberation." Khrushchev would use these wars by people to throw off the yoke of colonial rule as a way to spread communism. Kennedy wanted to oppose this threat. But as McNamara put it, the United States ought to be able to use "a flyswatter where a flyswatter is a proper weapon, instead of using a sledgehammer." The President did not want to choose only between doing nothing or threatening "massive retaliation." He thought we should have armed forces capable of a "flexible response" based on the size and the danger of the challenges.

The large purpose of our foreign policy would remain the same—to stop the growth of communism. Still, as JFK showed in Laos, when United States interests were not directly threatened, we would not use force against governments that were neutral. Kennedy believed that we should support progressive governments. Removing poverty and injustice would discourage Communist revolutions. He was friendly to the new nations of Africa. Sékou Touré, Guinea's leader, once called him "my only true friend in the outside world."

The Alliance for Progress. Kennedy proposed that we join the nations of Latin America in an Alliance for Progress. Similar to the Marshall Plan for Europe, this promised to Latin American nations $20 billion in economic aid over ten years. In August 1961 an Inter-American Conference in Uruguay accepted the plan. To receive economic aid the Latin American nations would improve their farms, reduce poverty, and promote industry.

They promised to invest $80 billion. In fact, few of these reforms were ever undertaken. Wherever possible, they avoided spending their own money. And the Kennedy administration did not insist that they live up to their promises. The United States tended to aid any government that was anti-Communist, that worked with the Alliance, and that had some popular support.

The Alliance made some friends—but it also made enemies. Critics in Latin America saw us using the Alliance to keep dictators in power. They said that the United States was more interested in stopping communism than in promoting freedom.

The Peace Corps. A favorite new program of JFK's—the Peace Corps—was designed to answer those arguments. This would show that the United States wanted to help all the poverty-stricken people in the world. (p. 783)

The plan was to train thousands of young Americans to work in underdeveloped countries. They would have all their expenses paid and receive some "severance pay" at the end of their two-year term. But they would not get a salary. They would be "volunteers"—like volunteers for the army in wartime—but their job would be peace. They would serve as teachers, nurses, doctors, engineers, and carpenters. Wherever they were sent, they would help the needy people raise better crops or build roads and bridges or improve their water supply. The President began the program even before Congress provided funds. By 1965 the project was costing $115 million a year.

Unfortunately, the Peace Corps was not the complete success all hoped it would be. Curing the ills of needy people was not so simple. Every country had its own large problems. To solve these you had to understand its language, its religion, and its history. Intelligent young Americans with high ideals seldom had enough of the knowledge or the skills required. Most of them had never before lived outside the United States. Some were lonely. It was hard to learn

✕ **Critical Thinking Activity: Formulating Questions** How should the United States respond to crises around the world? Remind students that President Kennedy developed the idea of "flexible response" for our armed forces—the armed forces would be capable of reacting to each world challenge appropriately. Have the class develop five or six questions that a President would need to ask when determining the most suitable response to a "challenge" or "threat" from another nation.

Courtesy of the Peace Corps

Peace Corps volunteers of all ages served in many lands. This woman offered help in Sri Lanka.
See "Lesson Plan," p. 774D.

the customs of a remote country. Some countries even asked the Americans to leave. Yet many members of the Peace Corps helped people in ways they could not help themselves. And nearly all the volunteers learned more about the world. When it began, the program lifted the nation's spirit and helped bring a new patriotism in peacetime.

See "Section 2 Review answers," p. 774D.

Section 2 Review

1. Identify or explain: Pathet Lao, Allen Dulles, Robert McNamara, Berlin Wall, wars of national liberation, Sékou Touré.
2. What problems did Kennedy face in Laos?
3. Explain the purpose and the outcome of the landing at the Bay of Pigs.
4. Why did the Communists want the Western powers to leave Berlin?
5. What was the policy of "flexible response"?
6. **Critical Thinking: Making Comparisons.** How did the goals of the Alliance for Progress differ from those of the Peace Corps?

3. Facing Communist challenges

Wherever they looked around the world, JFK and his advisers saw tests of America's determination to stand for peace and freedom. Responding to these challenges would call upon all the young President's will and resourcefulness.

The "missile gap." During the election campaign the candidates had disagreed over the nation's power to wage war. Were we trailing the Soviet Union in nuclear missiles? Kennedy declared that we were. Nixon, who knew because of secret information from the U-2 flights, said we were not. But the Vice-President could not reveal how he knew, so the argument continued. Upon entering office JFK found that there was no gap. Anyway, the Kennedy team decided to build more missiles. This was partly to satisfy Congress. And it was partly to have extra strength. Then we could survive a "first-strike" attack by the Soviet Union and still be able to hit back. If we had that strength, perhaps the USSR would never dare launch a surprise attack.

This policy was called "assured destruction" or "*m*utual *a*ssured *d*estruction" (MAD). The

More from Boorstin: "The roots of foreign aid, of the Peace Corps, and of numerous other American institutions of diplomacy and foreign relations lay deep in the American missionary tradition which thrived in the nineteenth century." (From *The Americans: The Democratic Experience*)

aim was to deter the Soviet Union from attacking the United States or any of our allies by having enough nuclear weapons—in silos, airplanes, or submarines—to assure the destruction of the USSR even if they mounted a nuclear attack first. Deterrence through "assured destruction" has been the U.S. defense policy ever since.

With this purpose Congress voted new funds for the ICBMs (*intercontinental ballistic missiles*). Known as Minutemen, they were stored in concrete silos buried deep in the ground.

In addition there was the Polaris SLBM (*submarine-launched ballistic missile*), carried by nuclear submarines. Unlike earlier subs, those driven by atomic power could circle the globe without ever surfacing for fuel, supplies, or air. They carried missiles underwater. The first nuclear-powered sub, the *Nautilus*, had been launched in 1954. Then in July 1960 the first Polaris missile—weighing 14 tons with its deadly nuclear warhead—had been tested. It landed 1150 miles away right on target.

By 1964 the stepped-up Kennedy defense program had provided the United States with 1100 intercontinental bombers, 800 land-based ICBMs, and 250 Polaris missiles under the sea. In every class the Soviets were far outnumbered.

Putting a man on the moon. But we were still behind the Russians in outer space. On April 12, 1961, they had sent up the first man in space. Yuri Gagarin went whirling around the earth in a satellite and made nearly a full orbit—in 89 minutes. The best the United States could do was a flight 115 miles into the sky by Alan B. Shepard on May 5. Some Americans feared that the Russians might use their lead in outer space to launch weapons against the United States. President Kennedy took up the challenge.

Sending a man into outer space was much more risky than exploring the arctic or another continent on earth. Could a human being survive out beyond the earth's atmosphere? Since humans needed oxygen to live and there was none in outer space, they would have to carry their oxygen with them. Could they carry

enough? Also the President remembered that when we had first tried to put an object in space the missile had collapsed on the sand. The United States should not risk another fiasco.

Some Americans said that the $40 billion needed to reach the moon might be better spent. But the persuasive Vice-President Lyndon B. Johnson was a space enthusiast. And President Kennedy decided to take the grand risk. After the Russians sent Yuri Gagarin into [IMAGE] orbit and after Shepard had made his successful flight, JFK promised that the United States would land a man on the moon before 1970. This spectacular success would make America the pioneer once more—this time out to another New World. Although Kennedy would not live to see it, his promise would be kept.

Working for disarmament and a test-ban. If the United States led the way to outer space, what would the Russians do? Wouldn't they be tempted to build up their arsenal? President Kennedy still hoped somehow to stop the costly arms race. To halt the testing of nuclear weapons would be a first step. Beginning in the 1950s, people began to learn more about radiation. This was the deadly cancer-causing side effect of testing nuclear weapons.

In November 1958, Russia, Great Britain, and the United States—the only nations that at that time had nuclear bombs—had met in Geneva to discuss the problem. The United States promised that it would do no more testing so long as the Soviets did none. During the next two years the talks dragged on. Meanwhile Khrushchev was pushed by his own scientists and by Chinese criticism that he was "soft" toward the United States. In September 1961 he allowed testing in the atmosphere to begin again. Khrushchev boasted to a Communist party congress that Russia had exploded a 50-megaton bomb. This meant a bomb equal to 50 million tons of TNT, a bomb 2500 times bigger than the one that had killed instantly 75,000 people at Hiroshima!

JFK answered by ordering the United States to begin testing underground. The dangers of radiation there were much less. Then at the United Nations he called for complete

More from Boorstin: "Phoning Gagarin his congratulations, Khrushchev crowed, 'Let the capitalist countries catch up with our country!'" (From *The Americans: The Democratic Experience*)

disarmament. "Mankind must put an end to war," he told the delegates, "or war will put an end to mankind."

When Kennedy received no reply from Russia, in March 1962 he ordered new tests in the atmosphere. In fact, JFK did not believe these tests were really necessary. But he did not want the Russians to think the United States was weak or afraid.

The Cuban missile crisis. During the summer of 1962, the Soviets stepped up the cold war. They began to move ballistic missiles and nuclear warheads into nearby Cuba. On October 14, 1962, clear pictures of Soviet missile sites under construction were obtained by one of our U-2 spy planes. How should President Kennedy act against this threat of enemy weapons right on our doorstep? The policy of deterrence seemed to depend on making the Soviet Union really believe the United States would fight if it was pushed too far.

The Joint Chiefs of Staff recommended an invasion to seize the missiles and bring down Castro. At the very least, they wanted a general air strike—at targets all over the island. Kennedy wisely rejected this advice. Still, he did risk a showdown. In a dramatic television address on Monday, October 22, he denounced this "secret, swift, and extraordinary build-up of Communist missiles." He stated that he had ordered the navy to begin "a strict quarantine [blockade] on all offensive military equipment under shipment to Cuba."

War now seemed to hang in the balance. Would the Soviet ships that were on their way to Cuba turn back? What would Khrushchev do? Of course, the Soviets denied there were any missiles on the island. Then at an emergency meeting of the UN Security Council, our

This sharp photograph from a high-flying U-2 shows one of the medium-range missile sites under construction by the Soviets in Cuba. It was released by the Defense Department on October 28, 1962, the same day that Khrushchev announced that the missile sites would be dismantled.

Wide World Photos

See "Lesson Plan," p. 774D for **Writing Process Activity: Predicting Consequences** relating to the naval blockade of military equipment to Cuba.

Ambassador Adlai Stevenson proved with photographs that the missiles were there. On Wednesday, five Soviet ships stopped short of the quarantine zone. On Friday, the Russians began to signal that maybe the question could be negotiated. Then Kennedy received two letters from Khrushchev. He decided, on the advice of his brother Robert, to answer the one that held out some hope of peace.

On Sunday Khrushchev broadcast that he had ordered the missiles to be dismantled and removed from Cuba in return for an American pledge not to invade the island. "We should like to continue the exchange of views," he added, "on the prohibition of atomic and thermonuclear weapons, general disarmament, and other problems relating to the relaxation of international tension." To the relief of the world, the superpowers had drawn back from the brink of nuclear war.

The weakening alliances. Still, the world could see that the war of words could easily become a war of missiles. The allies of the United States in NATO feared someone's bad guess or a miscalculation. The proud president of France, Charles de Gaulle, had disliked following the lead of the United States. Now, he said, the missile crisis showed how a single member of the NATO alliance could drag the other countries into war against them all.

To draw all the NATO nations closer together, President Kennedy had proposed his *Grand Design* for Western Europe in 1962 before the missile crisis. The United States would join the European Common Market in lowering tariffs. Congress approved this plan by the Trade Expansion Act of 1962. The President was permitted to reduce tariffs 50 percent and remove the tariffs entirely on articles heavily traded by the United States and Western Europe. But Congress said Kennedy could not remove the tariffs entirely unless Great Britain was admitted to the Common Market.

De Gaulle said that Kennedy's Grand Design was simply a plan for control of Western Europe by Great Britain and the United States. In January 1963 France vetoed Britain's application to join the Common Market. De Gaulle hoped to create a new power bloc—a Third Force—led by France, which was building its own nuclear weapons. In 1966 de Gaulle took France out of NATO and ordered American forces to leave his country. In 1967 NATO headquarters was moved from Paris to Brussels, Belgium.

The Communist alliance had its own problems. Satellites like Poland and Romania struggled to show at least a little independence. The great split in the Communist world was between China and the Soviet Union. In 1960, after a series of quarrels, the Russians withdrew their technical experts from Communist China. Then when China attacked India in a border dispute in 1962, the Soviets supported India. After Khrushchev's retreat in the Cuban missile crisis, Mao's Chinese Communists sneered at the Soviets. They said that the USSR was only a "paper tiger." And the Soviet leaders answered that war would not turn the world to communism.

A test-ban treaty. Once again in June 1963 President Kennedy called for an end to the arms race. Nearly fifty years earlier, Woodrow Wilson had wanted "to make the world safe for democracy." Now Kennedy expressed a more modest hope. "If we cannot end now all our differences, at least we can help make the world safe for diversity." He revived the test-ban talks. In July, Great Britain, the United States, and the Soviet Union agreed to outlaw nuclear tests in the atmosphere, in outer space, and underwater. The treaty did not touch the vast arsenal of nuclear weapons still held by the Big Three. And it allowed underground testing to continue. The treaty was signed and approved by the Senate ✄ 80 to 19 on September 4, 1963.

More than 100 nations agreed to the test-ban treaty. No one was much surprised when the French, who had recently exploded their own atomic bomb, and the Communist Chinese, who soon would have a bomb of their own, refused to sign.

Problems in Vietnam. His success with the missile crisis and the test-ban treaty encouraged JFK to think that bold diplomacy might save the world from atomic war. The civil war in

On October 7, 1963, as members of the administration and of Congress looked on, John F. Kennedy signed the test-ban treaty. It barred testing nuclear weapons anywhere but underground.

South Vietnam proved a tougher problem. The Geneva peace conference of 1954 had decided that elections to unify all Vietnam would be held by July 1956. But Ngo Dinh Diem, who was now leading South Vietnam, refused to go along. He was sure that he would lose to the Communist North. The United States agreed with Diem. Neither South Vietnam nor the United States had signed the Geneva accords.

After South Vietnam refused to take part in elections, guerrilla warfare against Diem's government broke out. The war was led by former members of the Communist Viet Minh. Enormous amounts of money and supplies were already pouring into the country from the United States. Now we began to send in "advisers" to train the South Vietnamese army. In 1960, opponents to Diem—including Communists and others—created the National Liberation Front (NLF). Their goal was to overthrow Diem and reunify the country. Diem named them the "Viet Cong," meaning Vietnamese Communists.

President Kennedy continued the support of Diem begun by Eisenhower. As NLF victories increased, he resisted advice from Vice-President Johnson and others to send in many more troops. Still, the number of American "advisers" slowly grew.

These advisers urged Diem to carry out reforms to strengthen his support in the country. Instead of making reforms, Diem brutally put down all opposition. When Buddhists staged demonstrations against him, his troops opened fire on them. Several Buddhist monks—in desperate protest—burned themselves to death in public. Kennedy now began to see that outsiders could not solve the problems of the South Vietnamese. "It is their war," he declared. "They are the only ones who have to win it or lose it."

At that time the American military advisers in South Vietnam came to 16,000. The United States military leaders wanted to send more. On November 2, 1963, Diem was overthrown, with American knowledge and approval, by a military junta. Diem was murdered. The military outlook for the anti-Communists became worse and worse. But President Kennedy would not live to make the next move.

See "Section 3 Review," p. 774D.

Section 3 Review

1. Identify or explain: missile gap, ICBM, Polaris missile, *Nautilus*, Yuri Gagarin, Alan B. Shepard, Charles de Gaulle, Trade Expansion Act of 1962, Ngo Dinh Diem, NLF, Viet Cong.
2. How and why did the Kennedy administration step up the defense program?
3. How did Kennedy challenge the Russians in the space race?
4. How were problems concerning the testing of nuclear weapons resolved in 1963?
5. How did the Cuban missile crisis turn out?
6. What splits appeared in the Communist bloc?
7. How did Kennedy respond to the problem in Vietnam?
8. **Critical Thinking: Expressing Problems Clearly.** How did France disrupt efforts to strengthen NATO?

See "Lesson Plan," p. 774E.

4. A New Frontier

President Kennedy found that domestic affairs were just as tricky as foreign affairs. Since he had been elected by only a hair's breadth, he had no clear "mandate" for any policy. In Congress he faced an unfriendly coalition of Republicans and conservative southern Democrats.

The domestic program that JFK outlined in 1961 was mostly an extension of the New Deal. He aimed to stop the business recession, to spur the nation's growth rate, and to "get the country moving again." There were few bold new proposals in what Kennedy called the "New Frontier."

Congress refuses to act. The hardest blow was when Congress refused to pass Kennedy's ambitious bill for federal aid to education. He hoped to help make education more equal in the different states. Of the $5.6 billion he requested, the states would receive $2.3 billion for public school construction and teachers' salaries. The rest would go to needy college students. The bill passed the Senate easily enough. Then Roman Catholic leaders insisted that it be amended to provide aid to parochial schools. Though President Kennedy was himself a Catholic, he would not yield. Enough Roman Catholic Democrats joined the Republicans to defeat the bill in the House of Representatives. A similar bill failed again in 1962.

Kennedy offered an equally ambitious plan to use the Social Security system to provide medical care for the aged. But his proposal did not receive serious consideration from Congress. The powerful American Medical Association called it "socialized medicine." JFK did not push the measure, since he knew he could not win.

Some successes. All was not disappointment and defeat. The Housing Act of 1961 provided $4.9 billion for urban renewal. The minimum wage went up from $1 to $1.25 an hour. In order to get the increase, JFK agreed to exclude 700,000 workers in laundries and small intrastate businesses. An Area Redevelopment Act offered $300 million to create new industries and retrain workers in "distressed areas" suffering from unemployment. Federal insurance under Social Security (p. 633) was extended to more of the unemployed, and federal funds were provided.

Congress also approved the Twenty-fourth Amendment to outlaw the poll tax. This tax was still being used in five southern states to discourage poor people—chiefly blacks—from voting. This amendment became part of the Constitution in January 1964.

Controlling the economy. These measures, together with the large sums spent for defense and for space programs, helped end the recession that had started in 1960. But unemployment remained high. Kennedy also worried about inflation caused by rising government spending.

To control inflation, JFK proposed "wage-price guideposts." These tied any increase in wages to an increase in output. If a firm making

1000 items for $10,000 could boost output to 1100 for the same $10,000 cost, the productivity increase would be 10 percent. Wages could then rise by that amount while the company could still sell the items to its customers for the same price. There would be no price inflation.

A conflict with the steelmakers. At the large United States Steel company, the employers and the workers signed a new labor contract on March 31, 1962. To avoid inflation, the union accepted a modest wage increase well within the President's guidelines. The workers took it for granted that the company would not raise prices. Then on April 10, the president of United States Steel announced a large increase in the price of steel. Other steel companies followed.

Since steel was used in so many products, the rise in its price would push other prices up. An enraged President Kennedy denounced the company and demanded that they roll back their prices. They soon gave in. The whole business community, which had been unsure of the President's attitude toward business from the start, was shaken by his anger. In May 1962, partly as a result, the stock market suffered its sharpest decline since the Great Crash of 1929.

As it turned out, the President's quarrel with business was not deep or lasting. His first friendly gesture was a Revenue Act in September 1962. It granted $1 billion a year in special investment tax credits for business firms making new outlays for machines and equipment. He did not object when some steel companies announced price increases early in 1963. Wall Street was encouraged, and prosperity seemed on its way.

Getting the economy moving. President Kennedy still thought that the gross national product was not growing fast enough. Russia's GNP was growing more rapidly, and he feared that in time we might lose our lead.

From the start of Kennedy's term, his Council of Economic Advisers had urged a big cut in taxes. The government was already running into debt, spending more on arms and services than it brought in through taxes. Still they argued that cutting taxes would be a good idea. If people had to spend less on their taxes, they would have more to spend on other things. Business would prosper, and in the long run more taxes would come in to help balance the budget. JFK did not manage to convince Congress to make the cut.

The problem of poverty. The economy was growing during most of the postwar years. Yet certain areas of poverty seemed never to be touched by private business or government programs. There had always been some poverty in 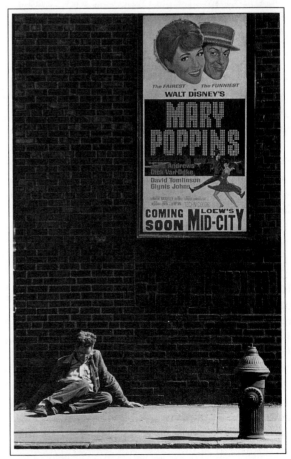 the United States. But as the nation became ever richer, some people hoped that ours might be the first country where nobody was poor.

The poor and homeless were not as carefree as Mary Poppins in the popular 1964 movie.

Bob Adelman/Magnum Photos

More from Boorstin: "According to the Department of Commerce in 1968, an American was living in poverty if he had an annual income of less than $1,748 ($1,487 on farms) for a single person, less than $2,774 for a family of three members ($2,352 on farms), less than $4,706 for a family of six ($4,021 on farms)." (From *The Americans: The Democratic Experience*)

In his popular book, the author Michael Harrington called the nation's poor *The Other America* (1962). These were "the unskilled workers, the migrant farm workers, the aged, the minorities, and all the others who live in the economic underworld of American life." Even in the United States, he wrote, there were millions "maimed in body and spirit, existing at levels beneath those necessary for human decency. If these people are not starving, they are hungry. . . . They are without adequate housing and education and medical care." President Kennedy began to worry as much about these people as about the nation's business. He began to plan a war on poverty.

The problem of civil rights. "Civil rights" described the rights of all Americans to vote and to have a fair trial. It also meant the right to have an equal chance at any job they could handle and to live and play wherever they could afford. President Kennedy believed that the federal government should pass laws to guarantee these rights to all Americans everywhere in the country.

During the election campaign of 1960, he had criticized Eisenhower for not doing enough. Now he himself moved only slowly. He was afraid that if he demanded these reforms, he would lose the support of southern members of Congress for his "New Frontier" bills. Finally, in 1962, he signed his name to an order to desegregate public housing projects supported with federal funds.

Just as Ike had done, he appointed a Committee on Equal Employment Opportunity. It was to see that companies that worked for the government gave everybody an equal opportunity. He directed his brother Robert at the Department of Justice to support the efforts of blacks to vote in the Deep South.

JFK encouraged blacks by his appointments. He named Carl Rowan ambassador to Finland and Andrew Hacker as associate press secretary. He appointed a number of blacks as United States district judges and Thurgood Marshall as judge of a United States Court of Appeals. He tried to set up a Cabinet Department of Urban Affairs and put Robert Weaver at its head. But conservative Democrats and Republicans defeated the bill. On the other hand, to keep on the right side of southern Democrats, he named several segregationist judges to federal district courts.

The black revolt. The pressures to do more were building rapidly. In 1961 "freedom riders," blacks and whites from North and South, took buses south to protest segregation of the races in bus stations. They were greeted by riots and beatings. Their buses were burned. On May 29, 1961, Attorney General Robert Kennedy called on the Interstate Commerce Commission to ban segregation in interstate bus terminals. That was finally done in September.

In the fall of 1962, a black air force veteran, James Meredith, tried to enroll in the all-white University of Mississippi. A court ordered that he be admitted. Still, Governor Ross Barnett personally prevented him from registering. When Meredith finally did enroll, riots followed that caused two deaths and injuries to hundreds. President Kennedy ordered 5000 federal troops to the scene to restore quiet. Meredith remained at the University of Mississippi—protected by federal troops.

All this violence to prevent one young black man from going to college! It was seen by millions on TV across the country. Now the civil rights struggle came into everybody's living room. Television was bringing the nation together. Civil rights was the whole nation's problem.

The pressure for an end to segregation—in schools, colleges, hotels, restaurants, employment, and all American life—grew enormously in 1963. Sit-ins and demonstrations forced the desegregation of lunch counters, hotels, and theaters in 300 cities in the South. Slowly the hated signs telling people what could be used by "white" and what by "colored" were coming down.

In April 1963 Martin Luther King, Jr., and his Southern Christian Leadership Conference (SCLC) began a drive to end segregation in Birmingham, Alabama. There segregation was

Continuity and Change: Government and Politics Point out to students that if a President attempts to push certain controversial bills through Congress, he may risk losing support for other measures. Often he is forced to prioritize, with difficulty, the items on his personal agenda. If Kennedy had tried to force a civil rights bill through Congress, he would have lost support for his other "New Frontier" bills. In the 1930s, Franklin Roosevelt refused to support an anti-lynching bill, realizing that if he did so, Congress would attempt to block other important legislation needed to save America from economic collapse. (See p. 649.)

enforced by local laws. King insisted that the struggle should be peaceful. He and his demonstrators were opposed by Chief "Bull" Connor's police with electric cattle prods, snarling dogs, and fire hoses. Birmingham exploded with rioting and fire bombing. And all this, too, was seen on television.

In June Governor George Wallace prevented two blacks from enrolling in the University of Alabama. He promised segregation in the state of Alabama "today, tomorrow, and forever." But strong pressure from JFK finally made Wallace give in, and he allowed the blacks to register.

A new civil rights law. By now, one hundred years after the Emancipation Proclamation, it was clear that if blacks were to be treated equally with whites, new federal laws were needed. On June 11, 1963, Kennedy addressed the nation on television. "Are we," he asked, "to say to the world and, much more importantly, to each other that this is a land of the free except for Negroes; that we have no second-class citizens except Negroes; that we have no class or caste system, no ghettos, no master race except with respect to Negroes?" Later that same night Medgar Evers, head of the Mississippi NAACP, was murdered outside his home.

A week later Kennedy sent a new civil rights bill to Congress. It was not nearly as strong as many people wanted. Still, it went far beyond any civil rights law ever requested before.

The march on Washington. To put pressure on Congress to pass Kennedy's bill, supporters staged a mammoth march on Washington. It was organized by Bayard Rustin, who had helped A. Philip Randolph organize an earlier march on Washington, back in 1941. Kennedy tried to discourage the march because he feared a backlash in Congress. But on August 28, 1963, there was one of the largest demonstrations in American history. More than 200,000 black and white "Freedom Marchers" gathered in Washington before the Lincoln Memorial. The eloquent Reverend Martin Luther King, Jr., stirred the audience—and the nation watching on television—with his dream of a United

Wide World Photos

Thousands gathered at the Lincoln Memorial to listen to Martin Luther King, Jr., during the 1963 March on Washington.

States where all people are equal. A place "where all of God's children, black men and white men, Jews and Gentiles, Protestants and Catholics, will be able to join hands and sing in the words of the old Negro spiritual, 'Free at last! free at last! thank God almighty, we are free at last!' " And, led by Mahalia Jackson, they all sang the old Baptist hymn that had become the anthem of the civil rights movement, "We Shall Overcome." (p. 792)

But the nation was large, and prejudice had deep roots in history. In September Americans received another lesson of how far away lay the

See "Lesson Plan," p. 774E for **Cooperative Learning Activity: Expressing Problems Clearly** relating to black revolt in the early 1960s.

fulfillment of the Reverend King's dream. A bomb exploded at a Birmingham church, and four little black girls were killed.

See "Section 4 Review answers," p. 774E.

Section 4 Review

1. Identify or explain: Housing Act of 1961, Area Redevelopment Act, "wage-price guideposts," "We Shall Overcome," "freedom riders," James Meredith, Medgar Evers.

2. What major Kennedy proposals did the House of Representatives and the Senate reject? What were his successes?

3. How did President Kennedy propose to hasten economic growth? How did both houses of Congress respond?

4. List successes and failures in JFK's civil rights record.

5. **Critical Thinking: Recognizing Cause and Effect.** What was the effect of television on the American civil rights movement?

See 'Lesson Plan," p. 774F.

5. The tragic end

In November 1963 President Kennedy took time out to mend his political fences. He thought of the presidential election coming in 1964. And he wanted to arouse support for himself and "New Frontier" bills that still had not been passed. Like many Presidents before him, he went out on the road. He traveled to the two southern states he hoped to carry in 1964, to Florida and then to Texas. The crowds were large and enthusiastic.

Death in Dallas. JFK had been warned that there was bitter feeling against him in Dallas. Only a month before, an angry crowd had pushed and spat upon Adlai Stevenson when he went there to speak on United Nations day. Yet if the President visited Texas, he could not skip the state's second largest city. So he scheduled a three-hour visit for November 22, 1963.

The presidential party included Jacqueline Kennedy, Vice-President and Mrs. Lyndon B. Johnson, and Governor and Mrs. John B. Connally of Texas. Their motorcade passed through cheering crowds on its way to the Trade Mart, where the President was to deliver a luncheon address. As the President's car passed through Dealey Plaza, rifle shots were heard. One bullet ripped through Kennedy's neck and another through his brain. Governor Connally was wounded. The President was dead by the time his car reached a hospital. The dream of Camelot had ended in nightmare.

Lee Harvey Oswald, a solitary, neurotic young man, was seized for the crime. Only two days later the nation watching television saw Oswald, escorted by police, being taken to the Dallas county jail. Before the nation's eyes Oswald was gunned down by a nightclub owner named Jack Ruby.

The first reaction to all of this was disbelief. Had the youngest elected President really been murdered at the height of his powers? America was stunned and could find no ready explanation. Who had killed the President, and why? One of the great tragedies of American history would also remain one of the mysteries.

The Warren Commission. A commission headed by Chief Justice Earl Warren would spend nine months trying to get to the bottom of the matter. They called scores of witnesses, took the advice of ballistic experts, and interviewed hundreds. They concluded that Lee Harvey Oswald had acted alone and so had Jack Ruby. Still the commission failed to pursue many leads and left many questions unanswered.

In 1979 a committee of the House of Representatives reported the results of their own year-long study. They used a new kind of sound analysis to tell how many shots had been fired and from where. And they concluded that more than one rifle had been fired at JFK. They also suggested that when he killed Oswald, Ruby might have been acting for others. But who held the second rifle, if there was one, and why had Oswald and Ruby fired their deadly shots? These questions were never fully answered.

The people's reaction. The shocked American people watched the tragedy played again and

✖ Critical Thinking Activity: Drawing Conclusions What were John F. Kennedy's achievements in the area of civil rights? "We Shall Overcome" became the anthem of the civil rights movement. Ask students to identify obstacles to civil rights that were "overcome" during JFK's presidency. Have students construct a time line of civil rights progress beginning with President Kennedy's administration and continuing on through the current presidential administration. Given these achievements, can the civil rights movement be termed a success?

UPI/Bettmann

Ninety minutes after John F. Kennedy died, Lyndon Johnson was sworn in as President aboard Air Force One. His wife is on the left in the picture and a stunned Jacqueline Kennedy is on the right.

again on television. On their screens, in their living rooms, they mourned at the President's funeral.

John F. Kennedy was the fourth President in 100 years to die at the hands of an assassin. Was it no longer safe for an American President to move among the people?

Even JFK's political opponents were overwhelmed by the tragedy. Everyone was reminded how unpredictable was history. People who had not voted for JFK still wept at the wasted talents of a brilliant leader. After his death, his friends naturally inflated what he had accomplished in his 1000 days. "Robbed of his years," one journalist wrote, "he is being rewarded and honored in death as he never was in life. Deprived of the place he sought in history, he has been given . . . a place in legend."

The Kennedy years: An appraisal. JFK's months in office are less important for the laws that were passed than for a new uplifting spirit. The young President was still growing and learning his job. No one could say whether he would have done better in a second term. There was always the chance. His untimely death left him a President noted more for his promise than for his achievement.

In foreign affairs, he led the cold war. He believed that the United States had to remain stronger than the Russians. He was also worried that we should not even seem to be weak. But the force of events, the power of the Russians, and the creeping spread of communism gradually changed his hopes. Whether we liked it or not, Kennedy concluded, we must accept a world that was not all free. "No one can doubt," he said, "that the wave of the future is not the conquest of the world by a single dogmatic creed but the liberation of the diverse energies of free nations and free men."

JFK always disliked "experts." He felt that they had led him into the Bay of Pigs disaster. Yet when he moved away from "massive retaliation" to "flexible response," he created new experts. The RAND (*Research and Development*) Corporation was set up by the air force to plan for air and space needs. And there were other new "think tanks." More than ever before, universities were drawn into research for the Defense Department and the CIA.

✂ Critical Thinking Activity: Making Comparisons How should John F. Kennedy's presidency be evaluated? Have students reread the section's appraisal of the Kennedy years. Remind them that this is one historical analysis of the period. Ask students to write their own brief evaluation of President Kennedy's years in office. Tell students that they must be able to defend their viewpoint with facts. Have students compare their analysis with that of the text in a class discussion.

Dan McCoy/Black Star

As millions watched on television, the funeral cortege of John F. Kennedy moved grimly toward Arlington Cemetery. The riderless horse symbolized the loss of a leader.

What remained from John F. Kennedy's brief Presidency was a lively and cheerful, but not substantial, inheritance. Humor, charm, vigor, and excitement were his trademarks. After his administration it was hard for people anywhere to think that the United States was a tired old nation. And the New World nation would not lack new young leaders.

☑ See "Lesson Plan," p. 774F for **Writing Process Activity: Making Comparisons** relating to an evaluation of the Kennedy presidency.

See "Section 5 Review answers," p. 774F.

Section 5 Review

1. Identify or explain: John Connally, Lee Harvey Oswald, Jack Ruby, Warren Commission.

2. **Critical Thinking: Predicting Consequences.** How might society be different had JFK not been assassinated?

Chapter 31 Review

See "Chapter Review answers," p. 774F.

Focusing on Ideas

1. What factors contributed to the nomination and election of John Kennedy in 1960?

2. How did Kennedy attempt to stimulate the economy while at the same time controlling inflation?

3. What were Kennedy's most significant achievements in foreign affairs? In domestic affairs?

Taking a Critical Look

1. **Testing Conclusions.** Evaluate the following opinion: "It is critically important to elect a President who has great personal charm and the ability to attract supporters." What information in the chapter supports or contradicts this viewpoint?

2. **Making Comparisons.** How did the Vietnam conflict differ from the earlier war in Korea? Consider both the nature of the problems and the responses of the United States government.

Your Region in History

1. **Geography.** Freedom marches punctuated the civil rights movement during the Kennedy years. Trace the routes followed by civil rights marchers in your region.

2. **Culture.** Interview people who participated in or observed the civil rights movement in your area during the Kennedy years. Find out how these people reacted to the civil rights movement and/or the effect that their "participation" had on the community.

3. **Economics.** How, if at all, has the economic position of black people in your state or locality changed since 1960? What factors have contributed to this change?

Historical Facts and Figures

Distinguishing False from Accurate Images. Study the graphs below to help answer the following questions: (a) How many blacks lived below the poverty level in 1965? in 1975? in 1980? (b) How many whites lived below the poverty level in those same years? (c) What percentage of blacks lived in poverty in 1960? In 1980? (d) What percentage of whites lived in poverty in 1960? In 1980? (e) How does the presentation of the information in the two graphs affect the conclusions you draw about people living in poverty? Would either graph shown by itself present a biased picture? (f) Write a paragraph that combines your conclusions into one statement about poverty in the United States.

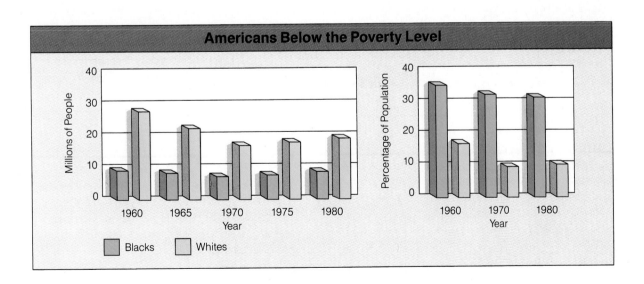

Americans Below the Poverty Level

Chapter 32
LBJ: From the Great Society to Vietnam

Identifying Chapter Materials

Objectives	Basic Instructional Materials	Extension Materials
1 Taking the Reins • Give reasons for calling Lyndon Baines Johnson a "master politician." • Discuss the issues and outcome of the presidential election of 1964.	**Annotated Teacher's Edition** • Lesson Plans, p. 796C **Instructional Support File** • Pre-Reading Activities, Unit 11, p. 15	**Documents of American History** • Civil Rights Act of 1964, Vol. 2, p. 687 • Economic Opportunity Act of 1964, Vol. 2, p. 691
2 The Great Society • Define the "Great Society," give examples of its programs, and show how its programs contributed to inflation.	**Annotated Teacher's Edition** • Lesson Plans, pp. 796C–796D	**Documents of American History** • Social Security Amendments of 1965, Vol. 2, p. 703
3 Black Revolt and Youth Rebellion • Describe the nature of the black revolt and youth rebellion of the late 1960s. • Summarize the recommendations of the National Advisory Commission on Civil Disorders.	**Annotated Teacher's Edition** • Lesson Plans, pp. 796D–796E **Instructional Support File** • Skill Review Activity, Unit 11, p. 18 • Skill Application Activity, Unit 11, p. 19 • Critical Thinking Activity, Unit 11, p. 20	**Documents of American History** • Voting Rights Act of 1965, Vol. 2, p. 709 • Civil Rights Act of 1968, Vol. 2, p. 725 **American History Transparencies** • Fine Art, p. D69
4 Vietnam: "The Most Unpopular War" • Explain why the Vietnam War became our "most unpopular war."	**Annotated Teacher's Edition** • Lesson Plans, pp. 796E–796F **Instructional Support File** • Reading Activities, Unit 11, pp. 16–17 • Chapter Test, Unit 11, pp. 21–24 • Additional Test Questions, Unit 11, pp. 25–28	**Enrichment Support File** • Vietnam: The War at Home (See "In-Depth Coverage" at right.) **Perspectives** • Why Were We in Vietnam? (See "In-Depth Coverage" at right.) **American History Transparencies** • Our Multicultural Heritage, p. C111

Providing In-Depth Coverage

Perspectives on the Vietnam War
The Johnson administration's story, which is the basis for Chapter 32, provides a dramatic backdrop for an in-depth focus on America's role in the Vietnam War. Johnson's presidency is characterized by its rise to success and its plunge to failure. Between 1963 and 1966 he achieved many goals in Congress, seeing to the passage of social legislation that was in many ways more dramatic than FDR's New Deal.

In 1964 he won the election with what is still the highest percentage of the popular vote any President has ever captured. Yet he ended his presidency in despair and controversy after massive civil rights disturbances tore America's cities apart and the American military intervention in Vietnam turned sour.

A History of the United States as an instructional program provides three types of resources you can use to offer in-depth coverage of America's role in the Vietnam War: the *student text*, the *Enrichment Support File*, and *Perspectives*. The chart below shows the topics that are covered in each.

THE STUDENT TEXT. Boorstin and Kelley's *A History of the United States* unfolds the chronology of events, the key players, and, as an interpretive history, the controversy of Vietnam.

AMERICAN HISTORY ENRICHMENT SUPPORT FILE. This collection of primary source readings and classroom activities reveals the social impact that the Vietnam War had on the American "home front."

PERSPECTIVES: READINGS ON AMERICAN HISTORY IN THE 20TH CENTURY. In this edited collection of secondary source readings, well-known historians and political commentators (including Boorstin) provide an array of perspectives on the reasons for the conflict and the rationale behind the United States presence in Vietnam.

Locating Instructional Materials
Detailed lesson plans for teaching the Vietnam War as a mini-course or to study one or more elements of the war in depth are offered in the following areas: in the *student text*, see individual lesson plans at the beginning of each chapter; in the *Enrichment Support File*, see page 3; in *Perspectives*, see the Teacher's Guide for this topic.

IN-DEPTH COVERAGE ON VIETNAM		
Student Text	**Enrichment Support File**	**Perspectives**
• Beginnings, pp. 731–732 • J.F. Kennedy, pp. 786–788 • L.B. Johnson, pp. 809–814 • R. Nixon, pp. 822, 824 • End of the War, pp. 824–825 • Pentagon Papers, p. 831 • Fall of South Vietnam, p. 865 • Memories of the war, pp. 912–913	• Lesson Suggestions • Multimedia Resources • Overview Essay/Vietnam: The War at Home • Literature in American History/The American Soldier Comes Home • Songs in American History/Music of the War • Primary Sources in American History/Opposing Viewpoints on the War • Art in American History/The Vietnam Veterans Memorial • Biography in American History/J. William Fullbright • Geography in American History/Vietnamese Immigration to the United States • Great Debates in American History/Volunteerism vs. the Draft • Simulation/Creating a New Memorial • Making Connections	• "The Second Indochina War: The Reasons Why," by Bernard Fall • "Giap Remembers," by Stanley Karnow • "America in Vietnam," by Richard Barnet • "Why We Were in Vietnam," by Norman Podhoretz • "Setting the Vietnam Record Straight," by Arthur Kobler, W. Gage McAfee, and Warren Williams • "The Americans Leave" by Arnold R. Isaacs

Taking the Reins

FOCUS

To introduce the lesson, ask: What were Johnson's qualifications for the Presidency? Write on the chalkboard two headings: Training and Personal Characteristics. Have students use the section to fill in the appropriate data (years in Congress, Senate Majority Leader, perseverance, compassion, ambition, intelligence). Then remind students of a President's many hats: Party Chief, Commander in Chief, Chief Legislator, Chief Diplomat, and Chief Executive. Ask: In what areas was Johnson strongest? (Chief Legislator, Chief Executive) In what areas was he weakest? (Chief Diplomat)

Developing Vocabulary

The words listed in this chapter are essential terms for reading and understanding particular sections of the chapter. The page number after each term indicates the page of its first or most important appearance in the chapter. These terms are defined in the text Glossary (text pages 1000–1011).

filibuster (page 798); **cloture** (page 798); **tactical atomic weapons** (page 800).

INSTRUCT

Explain

It has been difficult for historians to get a handle on the LBJ personality. One of his appointees once said, "Everything about him, from his ears to his ego, was just too big." Johnson moved at a run, was continually on the telephone, and was brutal to work for. After exploding in wrath at a member of his staff, something he did often, LBJ never apologized. Instead, he tried to make amends with some act of kindness.

✿ Cooperative Learning Activity

Identifying Alternatives Divide students into pairs and explain that they will design t-shirts illustrating a message about wilderness conservation. Distribute a copy of a blank t-shirt form drawn on paper to each pair. Then have students begin by learning more about the wilderness areas of the United States and about efforts to preserve these areas. Appoint one member of each pair to locate sources of information on this topic. Then have partners discuss the information and reach agreement on a message they would like to convey. Have partners decide who will illustrate the shirt. Display completed work and have the class judge which is the most effective message.

Section Review Answers

Section 1, page 800

1. a) Minnesota senator, Johnson's running mate in 1964. b) rule that restricts debate in the United States Senate. c) LBJ's campaign to end poverty in America. d) agency established by LBJ to enlist volunteers to help the poor in the United States. e) expanded aid to schools and colleges. f) set aside nine million acres of public land to be left untouched, in its natural state as wilderness. g) won the Republican nomination for President in 1964 and then lost to LBJ in a landslide. 2. It was passed in part as a memorial to Kennedy. It tried to promote the right of blacks to vote and their right to employment, but it also went beyond past measures by forbidding racial discrimination in places of public resort. 3. By giving people the tools to help themselves. 4. Johnson served in Congress for many years, first in the House of Representatives, then in the Senate where he became the Senate Majority Leader. He also served as Kennedy's Vice-President.

CLOSE

To conclude the lesson, ask: Why would Johnson get practically all the votes of black Americans? (Goldwater had voted against the Civil Rights Act; his stands on the issues held out little hope of progress for blacks.)

The Great Society

FOCUS

To introduce the lesson, tell students that LBJ said "The Great Society is one that provides abundance and liberty for all." Ask students to write a brief paragraph describing the changes necessary to make our current society fit the definition of "Great."

Developing Vocabulary

Appalachia (page 802); **urban renewal** (page 802); **ecology** (page 803).

INSTRUCT

Explain

The Meat Inspection Act of 1906 was probably the first example of a consumer protection law.

☑ Writing Process Activity

Identifying Central Issues Ask students to imagine they are members of Congress who must write a letter to their constituency explaining the legislation passed to put LBJ's "Great Society" into practice. Students should begin by brainstorming details about bills for medical insurance, aid to education, clean air, and so forth. Ask students to write a topic sentence clarifying their position on the legislation. As they revise, ask them to be sure to explain each bill and how it will benefit the community. After proofreading, students can read their letter to the class.

Section Review Answers

Section 2, page 804

1. a) Johnson's term for both his program and his aim. He proposed a series of federal programs that he hoped would advance the quality of American life. b) government program added to the Social Security system that provides low-cost hospital insurance and supplemental medical insurance for older Americans. c) provides federal money to states that establish programs to help poor people obtain medical care. d) provided federal aid to the nation's elementary and high schools. e) providing factual and accurate information about products. f) poverty-stricken mountainous region that stretches down through Pennsylvania to Alabama and Georgia. 2. a) Medicaid and Medicare; b) the Elementary and Secondary Education Act; c) the Water Quality Act and the Clean Water Restoration Act; d) a Truth-in-Packaging law and the Highway Safety Act; e) the Appalachian Regional Development Act; f) the Housing and Urban Development Act. 3. There was additional money in the economy from spending for Vietnam and from the 1965 tax cut. To hold down inflation, Johnson asked Congress for a tax surcharge, and he cut spending on some programs. 4. Rachel Carson's *Silent Spring* alerted Americans to the dangers that pesticides can create, and more generally, awakened concern for the environment. This concern was reflected in Great Society legislation that tried to control pollution and regulate the use of pesticides. Similarly, in *Unsafe at Any Speed,* Ralph Nader aroused alarm about the safety of American automobiles. His campaign helped push Congress to pass the Highway Safety Act of 1966.

CLOSE

To conclude the lesson, ask students to refer to their notes on FDR and the New Deal (Chapter 24 and Chapter 25). Ask: Which program went further, Johnson's Great Society or FDR's New Deal? (Students should agree that Johnson's did.) Which was a greater change from the status quo at the time? (FDR's) Then discuss whether each program was a success or a failure, and which has had a more lasting impact on American life. If students conclude that

FDR has had a more lasting impact (as they probably will), ask them to speculate on reasons why and keep the question in mind as they read the rest of this chapter.

Section 3 (pages 804–809)

Black Revolt and Youth Rebellion

FOCUS

To introduce the lesson, direct student attention to a key explanation of the black revolt and youth rebellion in the section introduction: hopes aroused + lack of quick results = frustration, anger, violence. Discuss the role of rising expectations in rebellions and revolutions.

Developing Vocabulary
Black Power (page 807)

INSTRUCT

Explain
Closely associated with "Black Power" was the movement to instill "Black Pride." A favorite slogan was "Black is beautiful," and much emphasis was given to instilling pride in the African heritage.

★ Independent Activity
Making Comparisons Have students select one of the following black leaders who rejected Dr. King's philosophy: Malcolm X, Elijah Muhammad, Stokely Carmichael, Eldridge Cleaver, Huey Newton. Have students research their chosen subject and prepare a two-page biographical report, making sure to include how that particular leader's philosophy differed from that of Dr. King.

Section Review Answers

Section 3, page 809

1. a) governor of Alabama, major leader of the fight to resist integration. b) black neighborhood in Los Angeles. In 1965 riots in Watts shocked the nation. c) radical black leader who broke with the Black Muslims to form his own group. d) members of a religious group, the Nation of Islam. They rejected integration. e) young black leader of SNCC who began urging "Black Power." f) goal and motto of some blacks in the 1960s who needed to exercise power themselves. g) black judge who headed the NAACP and argued the *Brown* case in 1954, appointed to the Supreme Court by LBJ. h) a radical group founded in 1962 to organize protest among college students

against injustice. 2. It tried to register blacks in Mississippi to vote. Three workers on the project were murdered. These murders shocked the country and helped build support for passage of the Civil Rights Act of 1964. 3. The Voting Rights Act stopped whites from intimidating or turning away any blacks who tried to vote. It sent federal registrars to polling places where blacks had not been voting in normal numbers and gave these registrars the power to enroll new voters. 4. The frustration at lack of results from new programs; the seemingly endless poverty of some urban blacks; the years of discrimination and violence directed at blacks, specifically the shooting of James Meredith; the disarray of the civil rights movement; the anger of some champions of "Black Power."

CLOSE

To conclude the lesson, ask students to summarize in their notebooks the recommendations of the National Advisory Commission on riots. Then ask: Have we taken action to cure the underlying problems that the commission felt led to riots? (Some action has been taken, but unemployment among blacks, especially black youths, is extremely high. Poverty and hopelessness continue to be problems.)

Section 4 (pages 809–814)

Vietnam: "The Most Unpopular War"

FOCUS

To introduce the lesson, have students review the material under the heading "The Tonkin Gulf Resolution" on pages 809–810 of the text, and locate the Gulf of Tonkin on the map on page 810. Point out that the gulf is several hundred miles north of the demilitarized zone of the 17th parallel. Have students write a brief news story headlined "LBJ Urges Passage of Tonkin Gulf Resolution." They should include (a) what powers LBJ sought; (b) why he sought them; and (c) who opposed LBJ in the Senate and why. Have several students read their stories aloud, and have the class discuss them.

Developing Vocabulary

Viet Cong (page 810); **domino theory** (page 810); **hawks** (page 813).

INSTRUCT

Explain

Students will better visualize LBJ's escalation of the Vietnam War if you write on the chalkboard the words

American Troops in Vietnam, and below it write the following list:

1963—16,500	1966—400,000
1965—161,000	1967—475,000

☑ Writing Process Activity

Recognizing Bias Ask students to imagine they are college males of draft age in 1965. In preparation for writing a letter to their parents explaining why they are or are not going to Washington, D.C., to protest the war in Vietnam, ask them to freewrite about their reactions to the war and to the protest marches against it. Students should begin their letter with a sentence summarizing their viewpoint, and they should organize their reasons by order of importance. Have students revise for clear explanation and realistic detail. After proofreading, students can discuss their letters and reactions in small groups.

Section Review Answers

Section 4, page 814

1. a) Secretary of State under Presidents Kennedy and Johnson. b) senator from Oregon, one of only two senators who voted against the Tonkin Gulf Resolution. c) if one country becomes a Communist nation, then its neighbors will follow, one by one. d) term used to describe LBJ's inability to maintain the public's confidence that he was telling the truth. e) Chairman of the Senate Foreign Relations Committee who began to criticize American policy in Vietnam in the mid-1960s. f) Secretary of Defense who commissioned the Pentagon Papers. g) government study of the role of the United States in Vietnam since World War II. The report was leaked to the press in 1971. h) attack by Viet Cong and North Vietnamese troops at the beginning of 1968 that demonstrated that the Communist forces were still strong enough to take the military initiative. i) challenged LBJ for the Democratic presidential nomination in 1968. 2. He feared (unnecessarily, it later appeared) that Communists would come to power. 3. As Johnson increased the American commitment in Vietnam, casualties rose, there was little if any sign of progress, and public opposition to the war grew. In 1965 he had begun building up American forces, and students began the first organized opposition to the war. In 1966 and 1967 American casualties grew, and the bombing of North Vietnam seemed to have no effect. By 1967 there were large public protests in New York and Washington. In January 1968 the Tet offensive demonstrated that the Viet Cong and North Vietnamese forces were not on the verge of defeat. According to public opinion polls, less than a third of Americans thought Johnson was handling the war well. Opponents of the war organized around the presidential campaign of Eu-

gene McCarthy in the New Hampshire primary in surprisingly small numbers. 4. It marked the beginning of an escalation of American involvement in the war. After the incident, Johnson sent American planes to attack targets in North Vietnam and asked Congress to approve a vaguely worded resolution stating that the President was empowered to "take all necessary measures . . . to prevent further aggression."

CLOSE

To conclude the lesson, ask: What was the purpose of the U.S. actions in Vietnam, and were those actions justified? The lesson will likely raise more questions than it answers. These issues could be topics for further student research. For homework, have students write a 200-word essay answering the above question.

Chapter Review Answers

Focusing on Ideas

1. Aid to education, Civil Rights Act of 1964, tax cut, war on poverty, medical insurance for aged, changes in immigration law. LBJ's success: sympathy for JFK's effort, economic prosperity, support of southern conservatives, civil rights fervor. 2. Right to be served in public places; desegregation (including schools); voting; more jobs. 3. Equality: Civil Rights

Act of 1964, Equal Opportunity Act, schools in poverty areas, Appalachian development, immigrant quotas. Environment: antipollution laws, Wilderness Act, highway beautification. Consumer: safety standards, pesticide control, Truth-in-Packaging Act. 4. King: stir conscience of nation; nonviolence. Malcolm X: power to run own affairs. Carmichael: political power from running movement and own institutions. King: broadest appeal, least antagonistic.

Taking a Critical Look

1. Include: stopping aggression, domino theory; honor. 2. South Vietnam undemocratic; civil war; U.S. didn't sign Geneva Conference agreements; Communist Vietnam not real menace to U.S.; victory would require heavier commitment; alienating allies.

Your Region in History

1–3. Answers will vary depending on your region. Consult your local library or historical society.

Historical Facts and Figures

(a) white—70.7%; black—58.5%; Hispanic—not available; (b) approximately 10%; approx. 3%; approx. 5%; (c) decrease in percentage of population voting; (d) Civil Rights Act of 1964, Voting Rights Act increased black voting by 50% from 1965 to 1966; (e) small or even decreasing number of black and Hispanic voters.

32

Focusing the Chapter: Have students identify the chapter logo. Discuss what unit theme the logo might symbolize. Then ask students to skim the chapter to identify other illustrations or titles that relate to this theme.

Chapter 32

LBJ: From the Great Society to Vietnam

This would be a time of triumphs and troubles. Led by a strong President, Lyndon B. Johnson, the Congress found new ways to protect the rights of some citizens and to widen the opportunities for all. At home it was an age of fulfillment. The injustices of centuries would begin to be righted. Yet this would take time. Impatient Americans turned to violence. Meanwhile, an undeclared war on the other side of the world, in a place most Americans had never heard of, would cost thousands of American lives. There, too, the President said, Americans were defending freedom. But the nation was unconvinced. He did not persuade Americans that they needed to be fighting there—nor did he tell them all they wanted to know. One of the best-qualified, strongest Presidents became the leading figure in an American tragedy. People would forget his successes at home because of his failures abroad.

The helicopter was first widely used in warfare during the conflict in Vietnam. But despite the ease of movement this gave to American troops, they were unable to defeat the enemy, who were at home in the jungles of Southeast Asia. This photograph of U. S. troops and fleeing Vietnamese boarding helicopters reveals some of the chaos of war.

Hiroji Kubota

See "Lesson Plan," p. 796C.

1. Taking the reins

The nation, stunned by the loss of its young President, wanted to hear a clear, commanding voice. Lyndon B. Johnson, the new man in the White House, saw what the times needed. As he later explained:

> Everything was in chaos. We were all spinning around and around trying to come to grips with what had happened, but the more we tried to understand it, the more confused we got. We were like a bunch of cattle caught in the swamp, unable to move in either direction, simply circling 'round and 'round. I understood that; I knew what had to be done. There is but one way to get the cattle out of the swamp. And that is for the man on the horse to take the lead, to assume command, to provide direction. In the period of confusion after the assassination, I was that man.

Lyndon Baines Johnson. Johnson was perfectly trained to take charge. He was not as young or as witty as JFK. But he stood a commanding six feet three—as tall as Texans are supposed to be. And he spoke with a Texas drawl that carried a charm all his own. He had spent most of his life in the House of Representatives and the Senate. He knew the members of Congress by their first names. He respected them and they respected him. Better than any other man alive, he knew how to put laws through Congress.

LBJ's life had centered upon politics. His father had been a state legislator in Texas, and the young Lyndon loved to go to the statehouse to watch and listen. Even more, he enjoyed traveling around with his father, visiting the voters of their district during election campaigns. "Sometimes," he recalled, "I wished it would go on forever."

While still a student at Southwest Texas State College, Johnson worked as campaign manager in the successful reelection of a state senator. After graduating from college in 1930, Johnson taught for a year in a high school in Houston. His political skills were already recognized, and he was asked to be the aide of a Texas congress-

Fred Ward/Black Star

LBJ here exerts his famous powers of persuasion in the Oval Office in 1964.

man. In 1932, at the age of 24, he arrived in Washington, where he would spend most of the remaining 41 years of his life.

One brief break came from 1935 to 1937 when he returned to Texas as state director of the National Youth Administration. Even then his sympathy for the downtrodden was clear. Years later an aged black leader recalled how "we began to get word up here that there was one NYA director who wasn't like the others. He was looking after Negroes and poor folks, and most NYA people weren't doing that."

Johnson was elected as a Democrat to the House of Representatives in 1939. In 1941 he was the first member of Congress to enlist in the armed forces. His navy career was cut short a year later when FDR ordered all senators and representatives back to Washington. He remained in the House until 1948, when he was elected to the Senate.

The Senate was the perfect stage for a man of LBJ's character and talent. Since there were only 96 senators, and each served for six years, it was a kind of club. All the members of the House of Representatives were elected every two years, and there were more than 400 of them. The Senate was a more intimate place. LBJ was a careful student of both people and issues. And he was always doing favors for others.

He earned a reputation as a superb "horse trader." Johnson used to roam the halls seeking senators whose help he needed on some bill. When he "accidentally" met one of them, he would give him "The Treatment." In his colorful Texas slang, the overpowering LBJ would plead, threaten, accuse, cry, laugh, complain—until his fellow senator agreed. "The Treatment" might last minutes or hours. A senator who knew called it "an almost hypnotic experience that rendered the target stunned and helpless." But Johnson was not just acting. "What convinces is conviction," he said. "You simply *have* to believe in the argument you are advancing. If you don't, you are as good as dead."

When he was majority leader of the Senate from 1955 to 1961, LBJ ran the place as if he owned it. Then when John F. Kennedy asked him to join his ticket as candidate for Vice-President, LBJ accepted. The tall Texan wanted to use the office to become a national figure.

He hoped it might be a stepping-stone to the White House. Since the inauguration of Lincoln a century earlier, five Vice-Presidents had become President. Still, for an energetic and ambitious politician, being Vice-President was frustrating. The Vice-President had to support the President's policies, yet he had no executive powers of his own. And Presidents had seldom consulted their Vice-Presidents.

Suddenly fate thrust LBJ into the post he wanted most of all. It was the perfect moment for the man who knew how to manage Congress. Goals had been set by President Kennedy. But the laws had not been passed. Now LBJ—the great wheeler-dealer—could work his magic.

A new civil rights law. Five days after the assassination, Johnson addressed the Congress. He called for national unity. He asked Congress to complete the programs begun by JFK, and he stressed civil rights. "No memorial oration or eulogy," he told Congress, "could more eloquently honor President Kennedy's memory than the earliest possible passage of the civil rights bill for which he fought so long. We have talked long enough in this country about equal rights. We have talked for one hundred years or more. It is time now to write the next chapter—and to write it in the books of law."

Johnson was determined to be more than just a southern President. He wanted to be President of all the people. For him, civil rights was the nation's problem. To swing the liberals of his party to his side, he would try to pass Kennedy's bill without any of the weakening changes that are usual in the process of enacting laws.

Ordinarily Johnson tried to reach his ends by compromise. This time there was to be no compromise. The bill ran into a record filibuster by southern senators who tried to talk the civil rights bill to death. They talked for 83 days. Meanwhile, Johnson, the adroit veteran of the Senate, worked ceaselessly to put together a winning alliance of Republicans and Democrats. Finally the Senate, under the floor leadership of Senator Hubert Humphrey, adopted *cloture.* This rule, then requiring a two-thirds majority vote by those present and voting, restricted further debate to one hour per person. In this way the Senate in a few days would be forced to vote on the issue. The Senate passed the bill on June 20, and the House accepted the Senate version on July 2, 1964. President Johnson signed the bill that same day.

The Civil Rights Act of 1964 forbade racial discrimination in the use of federal funds and in places of public resort, such as hotels, amusement parks, and other public facilities. It tried to protect the right of blacks to vote. It

Continuity and Change: Social Change Remind students that the Civil Rights Act of 1957 gave the Justice Department the right to bring suits on behalf of blacks who were denied the right to vote; not a radical piece of legislation, but a start. The Civil Rights Act of 1964, passed just seven years later was a measure of greater import. This law threatened to deny federal funding to places and programs where discrimination existed. (See p. 741.)

sought to protect their right to jobs by setting up an Equal Employment Opportunity Commission. It empowered the Attorney General to start court cases to speed the desegregation of schools. And it created a Community Relations Service to assist individuals and officials with racial problems at the local level.

(p. 798)

LBJ pushes Congress onward: A blizzard of laws. Congress also passed the tax cut asked by Kennedy. This lowered taxes by $11.5 billion, left more money in people's pockets, and so began to stimulate the economy.

At the President's urging, Congress passed a billion-dollar Economic Opportunity Act for a war on poverty. It contained a Community Action Program to let the people of an area decide what they thought needed to be done. It set up job- and work-training programs. Funds were provided for loans to college students and for small businesses to hire the unemployed. It also established VISTA (Volunteers in Service to America), a domestic Peace Corps to provide a chance for people to help the poor.

LBJ also encouraged Congress to pass the National Defense Education Act for expanded aid to schools and colleges. And Congress increased the food stamp program for people on welfare and granted $1.4 billion to the states for hospitals and health centers. A $375 million program helped cities with their mass-transit systems.

Expanding cities and extending highways meant there were more people who wanted and needed to get close to nature. But where would they go? The very businesses that gave Americans a better life had transformed wilderness into farm and factory. For years Congress had debated laws to protect millions of acres of public land as wilderness forever. This meant keeping out dams, buildings, roads, automobiles, and other motorized vehicles. The lands could be used only for camping, hiking, or horseback riding. Naturally enough, ranchers who grazed cattle and sheep on the public lands and the companies that cut and sold timber, that mined coal or oil or copper—under federal permits and leases—objected. They said that the nation needed to use these resources now. Conserving wilderness, they said, was simply a way of "locking up" the rich American lands.

The nature lovers replied that conserving the wilderness was "now or never." You could mine or cut timber elsewhere, they said, but you could never "put back" the wilderness. They wanted to keep intact 60 million acres. The Wilderness Act of 1964 set aside 9 million acres of national forest and national park land as "wilderness." There Americans could continue to use and enjoy the wilderness that once was all America.

Seldom has Congress passed so many important laws in such a brief time. It was a stunning performance. In a few months LBJ showed that he really deserved his reputation as a wizard at handling Congress. JFK had outlined the program, and his death set the stage. But LBJ's congressional magic had made the hopes into laws. Since it seemed certain that LBJ would be the Democratic candidate in the coming election, many Democratic members of Congress

President Johnson so "played upon" Congress that it produced any tune he wished.

Karl Hubenthal

voted with him to earn his support for their own reelection.

Choosing the candidates. The Republicans were caught up in a bitter fight for control of their party. Conservatives, led by the earnest Senator Barry Goldwater of Arizona, were resolved to oust the liberal eastern wing of the party, which had named the candidate at every convention since 1940. They wanted to get away from what they called "me-too" Republicans. They would offer the nation "a choice, not an echo."

The liberal Republicans did not realize what was happening until it was too late. At the Republican convention in San Francisco, Goldwater was nominated easily on the first ballot. He did nothing to make himself more palatable to the liberals. In his acceptance speech he proclaimed, "Extremism in the defense of liberty is no vice." This seemed to seek support from the most right-wing elements in the party. And he made no effort to "balance" the ticket. Instead, his choice for Vice-President was Congressman William Miller, a little-known conservative from New York State. This did not help to heal the breach in the party ranks. Seasoned observers were surprised. They expected that Senator Goldwater, once he became a candidate for President, would try to appeal to all the voters. Instead he stuck by his guns and ran on the principles of Barry Goldwater. Many Americans admired his personal honesty, but not so many shared his dogmas of American life. He lost the votes of millions of Republicans.

President Johnson was in full control when the Democrats met at Atlantic City, New Jersey, in August. The only drama LBJ could create was over who would be his running mate. He kept the delegates guessing until nearly the last moment, when he named ebullient, talkative Senator Hubert H. Humphrey of Minnesota. Humphrey had a record that would appeal to the more liberal wing of the Democratic party.

LBJ triumphant. Not since 1936 had there been a presidential campaign where the candidates were so unevenly matched. Johnson was masterful. He tried to please nearly everyone.

On foreign affairs, he showed wise restraint— even while he was secretly discussing plans for deeper moves into Vietnam. On domestic policy he stood for the Civil Rights Act of 1964, the war against poverty, and federal aid to education. Johnson dominated the middle-of-the-road.

Goldwater, on the other hand, promised voters a clear-cut choice. He had voted against the Civil Rights Act, the Test Ban Treaty, and most of the Kennedy-Johnson welfare measures. During the campaign he opposed the government programs that had already become popular. He suggested the sale of the TVA, and he questioned the Social Security system. He gave the impression that he believed violent conflict with the Soviet Union was inevitable. For that reason he proposed giving control of tactical atomic weapons to NATO commanders in the ✖ field. Sometimes he said things he did not really mean and then he tried to take them back. "Don't print what he *says*," one of his aides told reporters, "print what he *means*."

Goldwater's campaign went steadily downhill. On election day Lyndon B. Johnson received 61 percent of the vote, the largest majority in history until that time. His popular vote was 43 million to Goldwater's 27 million. He captured 486 electoral votes to Goldwater's 52.

The message seemed clear. Most Americans really wanted the federal government to do something for them. They expected new programs to help them meet new problems.

See "Section 1 Review answers," p. 796C.

Section 1 Review

1. Identify or explain: Hubert Humphrey, cloture, "war on poverty," VISTA, National Defense Education Act, Wilderness Act, Barry Goldwater.

2. Explain the significance of the Civil Rights Act of 1964.

3. How was the Economic Opportunity Act supposed to conquer poverty?

4. **Critical Thinking: Demonstrating Reasoned Judgment.** What experiences in Johnson's political career qualified him to be President?

✖ Critical Thinking Activity: Recognizing Ideologies How were the two candidates in the 1964 election in sharp contrast to each other? Have students discuss the qualities unique to Johnson and Goldwater. Record their ideas on the chalkboard. Tell students to express these ideas in a political cartoon that contrasts the two presidential candidates. Have students share their work. Ask the class to suggest what themes political cartoons might have addressed during the 1964 campaign. How does their work resemble the cartoons from that period?

See "Lesson Plan," p. 796C.

2. The Great Society

In a speech at the University of Michigan in May 1964, LBJ had put a name on the program he wanted for America. This was to be the "Great Society." During the past century, he said, Americans had been settling and subduing a continent. "The challenge of the next half century," he declared, "is whether we have the wisdom to use that wealth to enrich and elevate our national life, and to advance the quality of our American civilization." Nearly all Americans shared his dreams. But, he would find, many doubted that LBJ had staked out the path to make them real.

The fruits of victory. LBJ's great election victory gave the President for the first time since 1938 a firm working majority in both houses of Congress. Now his party's majority was so large that to enact his program he would not really need the votes of conservative southern Democrats.

Nobody understood this better than LBJ. And he moved quickly. As a seasoned politician he knew that he must act while his support was still strong. All during 1964 he had put task forces to work on bills to send to Congress. The two at the top of his list were medical care for the aged and federal aid to elementary and high school education. He put them there because he knew it would be hard to get them passed. Perhaps he could push them through in the afterglow of his triumph at the polls. And he did!

Medical insurance and aid to education. The Medicare bill, which he signed into law in July 1965, had been changed by Congress. It provided even wider protection than LBJ had asked. Citizens over 65 received low-cost hospital insurance financed by an increase in the Social Security payroll tax. If they wished, they could have medical insurance for doctors' bills and other out-of-hospital expenses with the government paying half the cost of the insurance premium. Another part of the law, called *Medicaid*, offered federal grants to states that wanted to set up their own plans to help needy people below the age of 65. The first limited program of medical aid for the needy aged had been enacted in 1950. It helped only those who were not receiving Social Security payments. It had been greatly expanded in 1960 to cover all older people who were not able to meet their medical expenses. These earlier medical aid plans were now superseded by Medicare and Medicaid.

The President's next message to Congress asked $1.3 billion for aid to education, "the key which can unlock the door to the Great Society." Past attempts to give federal aid to education had been stopped by the religious issue. The Constitution (First Amendment) forbade Congress to make any law "respecting an establishment of religion." If Congress gave federal funds to "parochial schools"—those supported by a particular church—did this violate the Constitution? President Johnson sidestepped the issue. He offered aid to a school chiefly according to the number of its students whose families had annual incomes below poverty level. No school could receive aid unless it obeyed the laws against segregation.

Harry Truman was unable to pass a national health law, so LBJ made sure he received the pens used to sign the 1965 Medicare Act.

Lyndon Baines Johnson Library

More from Boorstin: "Certain developments . . . have tended to encourage or enforce a greater uniformity in American educational institutions . . . [such as the] interpretation of the federal Constitution . . . to insure the constitutional right of students to nondiscrimination in educational opportunities. One consequence has been a general reduction in the differences between institutions, even where their differences showed a variety of interest rather than an intention to discriminate. . . ." (From *The Republic of Technology: Reflections on Our Future Community*)

To sign the Elementary and Secondary Education Act, LBJ went back to the one-room schoolhouse in Stonewall, a mile from his birthplace in Texas, where he had gone as a boy. He knew how to make the ceremony into a warm human drama. Present there were his first teacher and also seven Mexican Americans who had attended the school in Cotulla, Texas, where he had taught before graduating from college.

A flood of bills. President Johnson had chosen the right strategy. After these two controversial bills passed so easily, his others found clear sailing. The list of important laws passed by the 89th Congress was eye-popping. It covered the nation. There were laws to beautify the highways (supported by his wife, Lady Bird)

Appalachia was a main target of the War on Poverty. Amid great natural beauty, millions lived there in extreme poverty.

and laws for clean air. There was a law to insure truth in packaging. The Appalachian Regional Development Act gave to the poverty-stricken mountainous region stretching from Pennsylvania to Alabama and Georgia $1.1 billion for highways, health centers, and industrial development.

The cities, too, received their share. The Housing and Urban Development Act of 1965 aided construction of a quarter-million units of low-rent public housing. "Urban Renewal"—the clearing of slums and rebuilding of cities—received $2.9 billion. The rents of low- and moderate-income families were subsidized. Congress created a Department of Housing and Urban Development. To head the department Johnson named Robert C. Weaver, the first black in the Cabinet. The following year, Congress established the Department of Transportation.

The Immigration Act of 1965 abolished the quota system. Each year 120,000 persons could come from Western Hemisphere lands. Another 170,000 could be admitted from all other nations, but not more than 20,000 of these could come from any one country. Families of people already in the country, skilled workers, and refugees had priority. Congress voted billions for the war on poverty—and for exploring outer space. LBJ's program offered something for nearly everybody.

The power of books. Presidents had great power. But so did authors. Rachel Carson, a slight, modest woman, graduated from Johns Hopkins University and became a famous marine biologist. Her poetic books about the oceans and the seashore introduced Americans to the wonders of life in the unpolluted sea. Then in 1962 she published *Silent Spring*—a blockbusting book on a most unlikely subject. She showed that pesticides—especially DDT—were damaging the environment more than anyone suspected. The poisonous new chemicals used to wipe out destructive insects were passing through the food chain—from the insects to the birds who ate the insects. Birds were dying from the poisons meant for insects. One day, she warned, we might awaken to a

See "Lesson Plan," p. 796C for **Writing Process Activity: Identifying Central Issues** relating of LBJ's "Great Society."

Elliot Erwitt/Magnum

Bruce Roberts/Rapho/Photo Researchers

Here we see a price for the nation's spectacular industry and high standard of living. Highways crisscross the landscape and smog darkens the sky.

"silent spring." No birds would be left to sing.

Rachel Carson alerted Americans to "ecology." This was the science of the relation between organisms and their environment. President Kennedy had set up a commission to study the questions raised by Rachel Carson.

Just as the pesticides aimed at insects were killing birds, so the exhaust fumes of automobiles could pollute the air that everybody breathed. Now President Johnson persuaded Congress to pass laws to reduce pollution from the exhaust pipes of cars and trucks and from factory chimneys.

The waters of our lakes and rivers were polluted by chemicals dumped from mines and factories. Junkyards and cemeteries for dead automobiles made a mess of the wild and beautiful American countryside. People called this "visual pollution." New laws were passed requiring fences around these eyesores. The number of billboards was limited. Pesticides were controlled.

The wonderful power of books was proved again in 1965 when Ralph Nader, a bright 31-year-old lawyer, stirred the nation with his *Unsafe at Any Speed*. In that year alone, he wrote, nearly 50,000 Americans would die in automobile accidents and more than 4 million would be injured. He argued that many of these deaths and injuries would be the fault of the automakers. He accused them of being more interested in selling cars than in saving lives. They cared too much, he said, about car styling and sales gimmicks and too little about safety features.

Bumpers were not even strong enough to resist an impact of over three miles an hour, and car bodies were not much stronger. Nader's campaign helped spur Congress to pass the Highway Safety Act of 1966. It set safety standards for new cars and for tires.

LBJ and administration. Never before in American history had Congress produced so many social programs so speedily. Between 1965 and 1968 the reform laws came to 500. It was much easier to pass a law than to change the way people behaved. LBJ was a wizard in the Congress. But making all the new laws work was quite another matter. The restless President Johnson had a way of asking for more new laws even before old laws on the same subject had been tried out. For example, the standards for the Water Quality Act of 1965 had not yet been set when the Clean Water Restoration Act was passed calling for the setting of still more standards.

✘ Administering all these new programs, finding the good people to run them, was itself a colossal job. Meanwhile the President was being distracted by some other colossal problems, thousands of miles away, in Vietnam.

"Wartime" inflation in peacetime. Just like earlier wars, the undeclared war in Vietnam suddenly increased the demand for goods. After the tax cut of 1965, citizens had more money, and the government was now spending billions on defense. Though the nation had not actually declared war, wartime inflation was here again! Prices began to shoot up. The Consumer Price Index had risen by an average of only 1 percent a year during the Kennedy years. Then it went up 3 percent in 1967 and 5 percent in 1968. The government's wage and price guidelines collapsed.

To slow down inflation and pay the ever-higher costs of the Vietnam War, LBJ asked Congress for a temporary 10 percent surcharge on income taxes in 1967. (Taxpayers would figure their regular tax and then add 10 percent to it.) But by that time Congress was becoming less cooperative. They asked whether a tax increase was really necessary. To pay for the war,

President Johnson was forced to cut back on nondefense spending. "Great Society" programs suffered. Still, every year the federal government went deeper into debt. From $3.8 billion in 1966, the deficit rose to $8.7 billion in 1967, and $25.2 billion in 1968. In June 1968, when the tax surcharge finally became law, inflation was on the rise.

See "Section 2 Review answers," p. 796D.

Section 2 Review

1. Identify or explain: "Great Society," Medicare, Medicaid, Elementary and Secondary Education Act, Truth-in-Packaging, Appalachia.
2. What important laws were passed under President Johnson on (a) health care, (b) education, (c) pollution, (d) consumer protection, (e) regional development, (f) housing and rents?
3. Why did inflation speed up in the late 1960s? How did Johnson try to deal with it?
4. **Critical Thinking: Recognizing Cause and Effect.** How did Rachel Carson and Ralph Nader influence "Great Society" legislation?

See "Lesson Plan," p. 796D.

3. Black revolt and youth rebellion

President Kennedy and President Johnson had raised high the hopes of many Americans that injustice, inequality, and poverty could be erased. The failure to achieve quickly the difficult goals they proclaimed may have been inevitable. But among certain groups—blacks and the middle-class young especially—the result was frustration and anger and ultimately violence.

The beginnings of black revolt. Centuries of discrimination could not be wiped out in a few years. Black Americans were disappointed that the eloquent speeches and beautiful promises were not all fulfilled overnight. Disappointment became frustration. And frustration led to revolt. In the northern states that had fought to free the slaves, the discontent was most acute. There segregation continued not by law, as it did in the South, but in everyday fact.

✘ Critical Thinking Activity: Drawing Conclusions Is Lyndon Johnson's "Great Society" around today? Ask the class to describe the characteristics of Johnson's "Great Society." Then have students list some characteristics of our society today. Ask: How would President Johnson feel if he could see what life is like in present-day America? Close this activity by asking students to name three things that would make him unhappy.

Civil rights laws could do little for the 50 percent of the black Americans in the North. They had to live by themselves in special neighborhoods. They were not admitted to some of the best schools and clubs. Even if they were bright and well trained, they could not get jobs in the building trades, or as executives in businesses or banks, or in the best law firms. Since laws had helped so little, they flailed about trying to find ways to awaken their fellow Americans. They staged a "stall-in" of autos to disrupt the opening of the New York World's Fair in 1964. And riots erupted in Rochester and New York City.

The Summer Freedom Project in Mississippi in 1964 aimed to register blacks so they could vote. Civil rights workers (white and black) came down from the North. Three of them were murdered and became martyrs to the cause of equality. Many of the civil rights missionaries were beaten or wounded. Black homes and churches were burned. Because of these violent tactics, blacks feared to demand their rights, and only 1200 new voters were registered.

The murders in Mississippi had their effect.

But it was not what the plotters expected. The national outrage helped to push the stronger Civil Rights Act of 1964 through Congress in July. Then, even in Mississippi, public places—such as restaurants—began to serve both races. When schools opened there in September, a few white and black children of Mississippi began going to school together. The last strongholds of segregation started to fall.

The Voting Rights Act. In 1964 the Reverend Martin Luther King, Jr., received the Nobel Peace Prize. The Nobel Prizes had a strange history. They were founded by Alfred Nobel, a Swedish manufacturer of arms who invented dynamite (both the chemical and the name). He was worried that his products were used mainly by people at war to kill one another. His guilty conscience led him to leave his huge fortune to create a foundation that would give prizes in science, literature, and peacemaking. All people in the world were eligible, and there was no greater honor awarded anywhere.

Upon his return from Sweden, early in 1965, King announced his drive to register 3 million

Both black and white leaders joined Martin Luther King, Jr., and Coretta Scott King in the march from Selma to Montgomery in March 1965.

United Press International Photo

voters in the South. He began his push in Selma, Alabama, a city with 15,000 blacks, but almost no black voters. Once again black Americans were clubbed, shocked with electric cattle prods, and arrested—only for trying to exercise their rights. The horrified nation saw it all on TV screens in their living rooms.

Then King announced that he would lead a march for freedom from Selma to the Alabama capitol in Montgomery. On March 7 the freedom marchers were attacked by the police and turned back. Two days later they tried again, and again they were turned back. Governor George Wallace did everything he could to stop the march. He went to court. He told President Johnson that Alabama could not afford to protect the marchers. On March 15, LBJ called units of the Alabama National Guard into federal service and ordered federal marshals and the FBI to Alabama.

That same day President Johnson went before Congress—while the nation watched on television. He denounced the denial of constitutional rights to the black citizens of Mississippi. He demanded a law to provide federal registrars at the polls wherever blacks were not already voting in normal numbers. These registrars would have the power to enroll new voters so that no person could be denied the right to vote on account of race. LBJ compared the battle of Selma to the battles of Lexington and Concord in the American Revolution. He repeated the slogan of the civil rights forces—"We *Shall* Overcome."

On March 21 the great march from Selma to Montgomery began under the protection of federal marshals, the FBI, and the Alabama National Guard. Ministers, priests, and rabbis from all over the country went to Selma to join Martin Luther King in the march. Four days later the demonstrators peacefully entered Montgomery. But that night a white woman civil rights worker was shot and killed.

For the first time in history all American citizens at the same time could see their fellow citizens in another part of the country demanding their rights. It was before their eyes on television. No wonder, then, that Congress now passed the Voting Rights Act.

President Johnson signed it into law on August 6, 1965. Only one year later the number of blacks registered to vote had gone up 50 percent, from 870,000 to 1,289,000. Soon black officials began to be elected in communities throughout the South. At last it appeared that the dreams of Radical Republicans after the Civil War might finally be achieved.

Burn, baby, burn. Hardly had the Voting Rights Act of 1965 passed than Watts, a black ghetto in Los Angeles, exploded in violence. This was only the first of more than 100 riots that would rage in many cities across the nation during the long, hot summers of the next three years.

LBJ was stunned by Watts. He had just signed his great Voting Rights Act into law— and now this. "How is it possible," he asked, "after all we've accomplished?" Johnson was understandably bitter. For the riots hurt his Great Society programs. They seemed so aimless and only served to destroy, when what was needed was to build. They created a backlash among many whites who already felt blacks were receiving too much from the government. This was less a revolution than an explosion. The President tried to understand. "God knows how little we've really moved on this issue," he said, "despite all the fanfare. As I see it I've moved the Negro from D+ to C−. He's still nowhere. He knows it. And that's why he's out in the streets."

The riots drew attention to the more radical black leaders. The handsome Malcolm X was an ex-convict who had become a member of Elijah Muhammad's Nation of Islam—usually called the Black Muslims. Muhammad rejected integration. He called all whites "devils." He thought whites and blacks should be separate and that blacks should have a nation of their own. Malcolm's eloquent voice carried a message of hate. "When I speak," he said, "I speak as a *victim* of America's so-called democracy."

Malcolm X split off from Elijah Muhammad's Black Muslims and formed his own group. He did not follow Martin Luther King's Christian gospel of nonviolence. But after a pilgrimage to Mecca, where all true Muslims were supposed to go once in their lives, he began to change his view that all whites were born evil. For true Muslims believed that all races were equal. Malcolm X's career ended in a blaze of gunfire from several of his many black opponents in February 1965. His powerful *Autobiography*, which came out after his death in 1965, fanned both black anger and black pride.

Black Power. The summer of 1966 was a season of riots in northern cities. In the South, James Meredith, the first black to attend the University of Mississippi, tried to walk from Memphis, Tennessee, to Jackson, Mississippi, to encourage black people not to be afraid. He was shot and wounded. This provoked some black leaders to think that maybe Malcolm X was right. Stokely Carmichael, a young black radical, began to preach "Black Power." Martin Luther King had preached love and human brotherhood. Now the angry champions of

"Black Power" mainly wanted to be able to "get even." They wanted their chance to lord it over others.

By the fall of 1966 the civil rights movement was divided and in disarray. White backlash grew stronger. For the first time in recent years, a civil rights measure failed to pass Congress. The summer of 1967 saw the worst rioting in United States history. Blacks went on the rampage, destroying their own neighborhoods and leaving smoking rubble in Newark and Detroit. In Detroit alone 43 died and 5000 were left homeless. The Soviet newspaper *Pravda* gleefully printed a picture of army tanks on the streets of Detroit.

Again during 1967, LBJ asked for new civil rights laws, but Congress was no longer sympathetic. About all that LBJ could do that year was to appoint Thurgood Marshall to the Supreme Court. A graduate of the Howard University Law School, he had headed the legal staff of the

Massive rioting in Detroit in 1967 brought death and destruction. Federal troops and the Michigan National Guard were sent into the city to restore order.

Bob Clark/Black Star

Multicultural Connection: In 1967 President Johnson announced, in response to the civil unrest in the country, the formation of a Special Advisory Commission on Civil Disorders (also known as the Kerner Commission) to investigate racial disorders and to recommend remedial action. In its report, the Commission placed the blame for civil unrest on white racism and recommended that all levels of governments work to provide more employment opportunities, better housing and schools, and additional police protection to African Americans.

National Association for the Advancement of Colored People, and he had successfully argued the case against segregation in 1954. Now he was the first black ever to serve on the highest court in the land.

A new generation. This was a time of troubles and struggles. The nation's young people had been the source of hope and optimism. But now, in the 1960s, many acted as if they had been raised on sour milk. They were the product of the "baby boom"—born during and soon after World War II. Between 1960 and 1970 the number of Americans aged 15 to 24 grew by 50 percent—from 24 million to 36 million. This was more than they had increased in all the last seven decades.

This new generation was different. They were

Hippies tried to show that they rejected the values of most Americans.

Charles Moore/Black Star

the first generation to have lived all their lives under the shadow of nuclear weapons. They were the first TV generation. Their parents were sobered by knowledge of the Great Depression. But the society that these young people knew had enjoyed almost continuous prosperity since their childhood.

They had been surrounded with countless new things—TV, high-fidelity records, stereo, FM radio, wide-screen movies with wrap-around sound, large cars dappled with chrome, ✄ superhighways and supermarkets. At the same time they heard the dire warnings of Rachel Carson, Ralph Nader, and other prophets of doom. They could see that all the many wonderful things in American life still did not solve the ancient problems of justice and equality. And on TV they would see their young President assassinated, their cities smoldering in riots, their generation dying on the distant battlefield of Vietnam—and people of scores of new nations starving in Africa and Asia. The world seemed confusing and frustrating as never before. Where was the new frontier?

Hippies and the New Left. Different young people reacted in different ways. Most went about their business. They attended classes, read their textbooks, and prepared themselves to make a living. But some joined in the so-called "counterculture," which was opposed to the culture accepted by most Americans. They used drugs, they let their hair grow long, they wore beads, fringe jackets, army and navy surplus clothes, and long dresses. They wanted to look as different as possible from other Americans. They called themselves "hippies" (from the slang expression "hip," meaning knowledgeable, worldly-wise, "with it").

Hippies often reacted to American life by "dropping out"—by refusing to be a part of it. Other students organized in a New Left to transform America. The first active New Left group was the Student Nonviolent Coordinating Committee (SNCC). This was a small group mainly of southern black students. It was founded in 1960 to coordinate student activities, especially sit-ins (p. 741), for civil rights. SNCC was soon joined in its efforts by members

✄ Critical Thinking Activity: Predicting Consequences What "firsts" have underscored the ideals of this generation? Remind students that the young people of the '60s were the first generation to grow up with TV, nuclear weapons, stereo, FM radio, and so on, and that these things had an impact on the decisions they made. Ask the class to list things that their generation is the first to grow up with. Have students discuss the effect this will have on the decisions their generation will make.

of Students for a Democratic Society. SDS was an arm of an old social-democratic organization named the League for Industrial Democracy. Early in the 1960s SDS broke away from its parent to present a more radical reform program for America. Both SNCC and SDS were born as reform movements, but both soon were to reject reform and turn to anarchism and disruption.

For SDS the center of opposition became the university. Its members thought that by attacking the universities—their rules and regulations, their research contracts to help with the war in Vietnam, and their support of a supposedly unjust American society—they could make students radical and turn them into revolutionaries. But their revolutionary aims were vague and negative. Soon colleges and universities from Berkeley in California to Harvard in Massachusetts were in disarray. Daily the TV screen showed students picketing, occupying buildings, shouting obscenities, and stopping all classes. They demanded "Student Power." Across the country, people outside universities wondered what had happened to the American love of learning and the Jeffersonian tradition of free debate.

Still, most students seemed less concerned with "revolution" than with the war in Vietnam. The New Left became more and more frustrated as the 1960s wore on. SNCC turned to a racial movement for "Black Power" and so lost funds and members. SDS collapsed and a few of the most embittered activists went off to make bombs against the society they despised.

See "Section 3 Review answers," p. 796D.

Section 3 Review

1. Identify: George Wallace, Watts, Malcolm X, Black Muslims, Stokely Carmichael, "Black Power," Thurgood Marshall, SDS.

2. What was the Summer Freedom Project of 1964? What was its unexpected effect?

3. How did the Voting Rights Act help to assure the voting rights of southern blacks?

4. **Critical Thinking: Recognizing Cause and Effect.** What were some causes of the riots between 1965 and 1967?

See "Lesson Plan," p. 796E.

4. Vietnam: "The most unpopular war"

During 1964 the United States sank deeper and deeper into the war in Vietnam. In the course of the campaign for President, Senator Barry Goldwater had asked LBJ to send more American troops. But the President resisted. He had promised during the campaign, "We are not about to send American boys nine or ten thousand miles from home to do what Asian boys ought to be doing for themselves." Still, Johnson would not negotiate with North Vietnam. "We do not believe in conferences to ratify terror," he declared. Secretary of State Dean Rusk said that just as our duties to the free world required us to stay in Berlin—so now we must defend freedom in Vietnam.

(p. 810)

The Tonkin Gulf Resolution. Off North Vietnam in the Tonkin Gulf on August 2 and 4, 1964, two United States destroyers were attacked by North Vietnamese gunboats. This brought matters to a head. President Johnson said they were attacked without cause. (Later it appeared that they had been protecting South Vietnamese gunboats making raids on the North.) He went on television to announce "that repeated acts of violence against the United States" must be answered. At that moment, he revealed, United States planes were attacking targets in the North.

The next day, August 5, he asked Congress for a joint resolution to empower "the President, as Commander in Chief, to take all necessary measures to repel any armed attack against the forces of the United States and to prevent further aggression." It passed without a single negative vote in the House. In the Senate there was debate only because the independent Senator Wayne Morse of Oregon threatened a filibuster if there was no discussion. Morse said the resolution violated the Constitution by giving the President powers that belonged to Congress. Senator Ernest Gruening of Alaska called it "a predated declaration of war." But only these two voted No.

In fact, President Johnson did not believe that he really needed the resolution. He believed that as Commander in Chief he had the right to

Continuity and Change: Social Change Point out to students that in the late 1800s, American faith in education led to the founding of large numbers of colleges and universities. Increased opportunities to attend college gave Americans a better chance to rise in the world, and the institutions themselves became centers of learning where people went to become leaders. In the turbulent decade of the 1960s, learning sometimes became secondary as colleges and universities became centers of agitation for political change. College-centered protests were influential in helping to bring about an end to the Vietnam War. (See p. 447.)

Villiam
— Demarcation Line of 1954

0 ————————— 300 Miles
0 ————————— 300 Kilometers

SOUTHEAST ASIA 1945

send armed forces wherever necessary. He said that this meant even sending troops to Vietnam. He followed the example of Truman in Korea, Eisenhower in Lebanon, and Kennedy in the Cuban missile crisis, who had not asked Congress for permission to use armed force. But LBJ wanted a resolution to protect himself from later congressional criticism. Americans agreed that the President must use troops to defend the United States. It was not so clear that he should send Americans into a civil war on the other side of the globe.

The widening Asian commitment: Vietnamese Communists. In January 1965 Johnson's advisers warned him that the United States would have to increase its aid if South Vietnam was to be saved from the Communists. In February there was a Communist attack on a United States military unit, and 7 Americans were killed and 100 wounded. To retaliate, LBJ ordered the bombing of North Vietnam. Still, he hesitated to order all-out bombing or to commit more troops. "If there is one thing that the American people will not take," he said, "it is another shooting war in Asia." Despite his worst fears, that was exactly what Americans were in.

Could the United States now afford to "lose" South Vietnam? That was the unwelcome question. To avoid defeat more and more American power was needed. In March American planes were bombing regularly. On April 1, 1965, against his own promises, LBJ sent American troops against the Viet Cong. A few days later, with no public announcement, he added another 20,000 men to help the 27,000 already in Vietnam. American troops were sinking into the quicksand and disappearing into the jungles of Southeast Asia.

Why we were in Vietnam. It was not easy to make clear to the American people why we were in Vietnam at all. The simplest explanation was offered by President Eisenhower (who, in fact, carefully stayed out of Vietnam). This was the "domino theory." Vietnam, he said, was like the first in a row of standing dominoes. If you toppled it over, the other dominoes (the neighboring countries) would fall, too. All Southeast Asia would quickly be taken over by the Communists.

Another reason was to stop aggression. Early in 1965 there were still only a small number of North Vietnamese soldiers in South Vietnam. But American military leaders remembered how Europe had fallen to the Nazis because Britain and France had not acted soon enough.

Perspectives Topic

⊕ **Geography and History: Location** Have students refer to the map above and note or locate the following: the 1945 boundaries of French Indochina; Dienbienphu; and the demarcation line of 1954. Using text pages 731–732 as a guide, have students answer these questions: Why did the United States become involved in France's Vietnam War? (It seemed a part of the global struggle against communism.) How did the United States help at first? (Money and arms.)

A third reason for going into Vietnam was to protect our reputation. We wanted other free countries to believe that we would stand by them if they were attacked by Communists. This was called our "credibility." If we did not protect South Vietnam, we feared other nations would not believe we would help them. Then our whole worldwide system of defense and deterrence against the Communists might collapse.

For all these reasons in July 1965 President Johnson committed the United States to victory in Vietnam. By the year's end the American troops there numbered 185,000. Were we in so deep that it no longer mattered why we were there? The urgent task now, a State Department spokesman explained, was "to avoid humiliation." While this was seen as a patriotic duty, it was not inspiring.

The Dominican Republic. The Communist issue was still very much alive in the Caribbean—on our own doorstep. In the Dominican Republic a revolution had overthrown the government on April 24, 1965. No one could tell who would take power. When civil war broke out, the American ambassador in Santo Domingo panicked. He feared that Juan Bosch, the last popularly elected president, was winning and that he supported the Communists. The ambassador asked Washington for troops to protect American lives and "prevent another Cuba." LBJ sent in American forces. By May 5, when a truce was arranged, the United States had 22,000 men in the Dominican Republic.

Johnson defended this intervention. "The American nation," he said, "cannot, must not, will not, permit the establishment of another Communist government in the Western Hemisphere." Later, it became plain that the situation in the Dominican Republic had not been as bad as we had thought. The Communists had not been about to take over after all.

Widening the "credibility gap." Even after LBJ decided to commit troops to the fighting in Vietnam, he refused to admit that there had been any shift in United States policy. In July 1965, when he decided to build up our forces in

Vietnam, he chose not to reveal to Congress or the people what he intended to do. He announced that he was sending 50,000 men right away, and he asked for more money to pay for that commitment. But he did not let Congress know what the full cost would be.

President Johnson later explained that he feared if he told the whole truth he would not be able to pass his Great Society legislation. He was on the verge of achieving his dream "of improving life for more people than any other political leader, including FDR." If Congress began to debate foreign policy, that might be the end of the Great Society. "I was determined to be a leader of war *and* a leader of peace."

LBJ had not fully shared his intentions or fears about Vietnam or the Dominican Republic with the American people. And in domestic affairs, when news leaked out of what he was going to do, he would sometimes change his plans and do something else. Soon there developed a "credibility gap." This was a gap between what the President wanted people to believe and what was credible (really believable). As the months of the Vietnam War went on, that gap widened. The American people began to doubt what Johnson told them about Vietnam—or anything else.

A "peace offensive." During 1965 all across the nation there appeared signs of growing opposition to the war in Vietnam. The influential Senator J. William Fulbright of Arkansas, chairman of the Senate Foreign Relations Committee, had voted for the Tonkin Gulf Resolution. Now he argued that we were in too deep and should withdraw. At the University of Michigan students and professors staged a new kind of demonstration. Part study group, part political rally, this was the first antiwar "teach-in." In October a few young men burned their draft cards. The climax came in November 1965 (p. 812) when 30,000 antiwar protesters marched on Washington.

Ever since July, Secretary McNamara had been urging a halt in the bombing of North Vietnam. He said this would be a goodwill gesture to encourage the Communists to negotiate. As opposition to the war grew, Secretary of State

See "Lesson Plan," p. 796E for **Writing Process Activity: Recognizing Bias** relating to reaction to the Vietnam War.

Rusk moved to that position, too. So on December 23, 1965, LBJ announced a halt in the bombing and a "peace offensive." The President explored many diplomatic avenues. Still there was no reply from North Vietnam. Early in 1966, after a 37-day pause, the B-52s resumed bombing North Vietnam.

Johnson loses support. Even while public opposition to the war increased, the United States commitment in Vietnam was also growing. By the end of 1966 there were 400,000 American men and women there. The casualties (killed, wounded, missing) were rising rapidly. There were 2500 in 1965 and 33,000 in 1966. Yet the war seemed to make no progress, and no end was in sight. All this provided opponents of the war with new arguments. Students, led by a small but loud group who called themselves the New Left, sabotaged public meetings and refused to allow debate. Many others who opposed the war were disgusted by their violence and bad manners. By late 1966 President Johnson had to restrict his public appearances.

Still a considerable number of Americans believed that, even though the war might never be "won," the United States dared not walk away from Vietnam. They feared that if the Communists from the North occupied South Vietnam they would kill thousands of innocent Vietnamese who had opposed the Communists.

As 1966 drew to a close, Secretary of Defense McNamara was becoming more and more gloomy about the war. Since the continued heavy bombing of the North did not seem to be forcing the enemy to give in, he advised that the bombing be stopped. He urged LBJ to make stronger efforts for a negotiated peace. He even suggested that we offer "a role for the Viet Cong in negotiations, postwar life, and government of the nation." But no such plans were made, and the war dragged on.

In November 1965 the opinion polls showed that 66 percent of the American people approved of the way Johnson was running the country. By October 1966 only 44 percent thought he was doing well. In elections that fall the Republicans gained in both the House and the Senate. The main reason was the voters' unhappiness over the war in distant Vietnam. The nation, puzzled over why we were there at all, was still more puzzled over why we stayed.

Mounting opposition to the war. In May 1967 Secretary McNamara expressed the rising discontent. "The picture of the world's greatest superpower," he wrote to LBJ , "killing or seriously injuring 1000 noncombatants a week, while trying to pound a tiny backward nation into submission on an issue whose merits are hotly disputed, is not a pretty one." The United States was dropping more bombs each month on little Vietnam, which is the size of New Mexico, than had been dropped in total on Nazi Germany during all the months of heaviest bombing in World War II.

In June 1967 McNamara commissioned a study of the role of the United States in Vietnam since World War II. The study showed that the American people had been deceived about the real situation. That fall McNamara resigned. In 1971 this report, called the Pentagon Papers, was finally leaked to the press (p. 831).

Throughout 1967 the number of United States troops in Vietnam continued to increase. They reached 475,000, and casualties that year climbed to 80,000. Opposition to the war became ever more shrill. In New York 300,000 marched in protest, and a crowd of 100,000 tried to close the Pentagon in the nation's capital. The bitter cry, "Hey, hey, hey, LBJ, How many kids did you kill today!" was heard at demonstrations in colleges across the land.

The Tet offensive. All this was just a prelude to 1968. In January, General William Westmoreland, the American commander in Vietnam, issued another optimistic report telling how the war was being won. Four days later, on the Vietnamese New Year's holiday called "Tet," the Viet Cong and North Vietnamese suddenly launched their strongest offensive. They struck at cities throughout South Vietnam, even penetrating the heavily guarded grounds of the United States embassy in Saigon. Within a few days, most of the fierce fighting was over. Only in the city of Hué, which had fallen to the Viet

⧉ Enrichment Support File Topic

📖 **More from Boorstin:** "During the Viet Nam War an unwilling American draftee, . . . responded to his draft notice by informing the President that, in a great American tradition, instead of going into the United States Army, he would secede and become a nation all by himself." (From *Hidden History: Exploring Our Secret Past*)

Cong, and a few other spots did fighting continue. General Westmoreland claimed correctly that the Tet episode was actually a victory for the United States and South Vietnam. The Communists had suffered enormous losses. It would take them years to rebuild their strength. But the Communists had seized the offensive and in this, the first war shown on TV, the American public had witnessed the horrors. When General Westmoreland called for 206,000 more troops and more fighter squadrons, it seemed that we had not won, but lost, during the Tet offensive.

Shortly after Tet, the American public was shocked to hear that United States troops had killed some 300 civilians, mostly women and children, in the little village of My Lai. The fact that the Viet Cong had murdered many hundreds of civilians during their month-long occupation of Hué was lost in the American distress over the atrocity committed by U.S. troops in My Lai.

Clark Clifford, a trusted personal adviser of LBJ, now replaced McNamara as Secretary of Defense. He was a "hard-liner" (a "hawk") on the war. This meant that he believed we should continue fighting in Vietnam even at great cost. But when he studied the detailed military reports, Clifford himself began to have doubts. Soon he, too, began to work for "winding down"—removing our troops and moving out.

The fall of LBJ. After Tet, at the very moment when the fighting in Vietnam was heaviest, the presidential campaign in the United States was getting under way. Senator Eugene McCarthy of Minnesota, a gentle man of poetic temperament who had enlisted some college students and other opponents of the war, challenged Johnson for the party's nomination. He called for a negotiated settlement and a prompt withdrawal of all American forces.

The first primary contest was held in New Hampshire in mid-March 1968. As the unknown McCarthy toured New Hampshire, LBJ's rating in the opinion polls continued to fall. By March the polls reported that only 36 percent of the people approved of his Presidency, and a mere 26 percent thought he was handling the

Wide World Photos

These Americans marched in the streets proclaiming opposition to the war in Vietnam.

war well. McCarthy made a surprisingly strong finish in the New Hampshire race against LBJ— with 42 percent of the votes. This was not a victory, but it was as good as one. A President in office was supposed to win easily.

The vote for McCarthy was, in fact, a protest against LBJ. Many who voted for McCarthy actually favored the war—but they thought it was being badly handled. When McCarthy's success showed that Johnson might be beaten, on March 16 Senator Robert F. Kennedy, a younger brother of President Kennedy's, entered the race.

Secretary of Defense Clifford, LBJ's old friend, reported that he had consulted leaders around the country. Once they had been for the war. Now they thought we ought to get out. When Johnson himself consulted his advisory group of former and present government officials, they agreed with Clifford.

Philip Jones Griffiths/Magnum

A desperate refugee in Vietnam carrying household goods trudges past United States troops.

On March 31, 1968, LBJ announced on television that he had ordered sharp restrictions in the bombing. He called for peace talks. Then he stunned his listeners. He declared at the end that in order to keep his actions on Vietnam from being thought of as just playing politics, "I shall not seek, and I will not accept the nomination of my party for another term as your President."

Three days later, the North Vietnamese agreed to begin talks to end the war. The next day in Memphis, Tennessee, Martin Luther King, Jr., was assassinated. Blacks in cities across the nation exploded. They burned, looted, and rioted in 100 cities. In Washington, the flames of smoldering buildings in black neighborhoods, fired by blacks themselves, could be seen from the White House. The problems of the United States on the battlefields of Vietnam, halfway around the world, seemed on the way to solution. But in the nation's own front yard the challenges remained.

Peace talks began in Paris in May and dragged on throughout the months of the presidential campaign. On June 23, 1968—with the count starting from December 22, 1961, when the first American serviceman had died in Vietnam—the war became the longest in United States history.

See "Section 4 Review answers," p. 796E.

Section 4 Review

1. Identify or explain: Dean Rusk, Wayne Morse, "domino theory," "credibility gap," J. William Fulbright, Robert McNamara, Pentagon Papers, Tet offensive, Eugene McCarthy.

2. Why did President Johnson intervene in the Dominican Republic?

3. Trace the decline of support for the war in Vietnam and for President Johnson.

4. **Critical Thinking: Drawing Conclusions.** How did the Tonkin Gulf incident lead to our increased involvement in Vietnam?

✖ Critical Thinking Activity: Identifying Alternatives What factors contribute to making the Vietnam War the longest in United States history? Have students work in small groups to construct a list of elements that contributed to making the Vietnam War the longest war in U.S. history. Ask each group to order their list and to explain their choices. Have each group present their work. Construct a class list with the results. Conclude by asking students to recommend policy changes that might have shortened the war.

Chapter 32 Review

See "Chapter Review answers," p. 796F.

Focusing on Ideas

1. What legislation was John Kennedy unable to convince Congress to pass? Why was President Johnson able to gain congressional approval for the same legislation?

2. How did the Civil Rights Act of 1964 change the lives of blacks living in the Deep South?

3. How did legislation enacted between 1964 and 1966 seek to promote greater equality? A better environment? Consumer protection?

4. Summarize the philosophies of Martin Luther King, Malcolm X, and Stokely Carmichael—the three principal black leaders of the 1960s. Which leader had the most lasting influence on the civil rights movement?

Taking a Critical Look

1. **Demonstrating Reasoned Judgment.** Which of the reasons cited for the United States's involvement in Vietnam do you consider the most compelling? The least compelling? Why?

2. **Recognizing Bias.** What reasons would you expect an antiwar activist in the 1960s to give when explaining why the United States should withdraw from Vietnam?

Your Region in History

1. **Geography.** Locate wilderness areas in your region that were preserved by the Wilderness Act of 1964.

2. **Culture.** Did any political demonstrations or urban riots in the 1960s take place near where you live? What brought them on? What happened? If your locality remained calm, how do you account for this?

3. **Economics.** How was your region directly affected by "Great Society" programs?

Historical Facts and Figures

Predicting Consequences. Study the graph below to help answer the following questions: (a) What percentage of whites voted in 1964? Blacks? Hispanics? (b) By approximately what percentage did white voter turnout decrease from 1964 to 1984? Black voter turnout? Hispanic voter turnout from 1972 to 1984? (c) Summarize the trends in voter turnout depicted by the graph. (d) What information in this chapter helps explain these trends? (e) How might these figures have differed had the civil rights legislation proposed by the Johnson administration not been enacted?

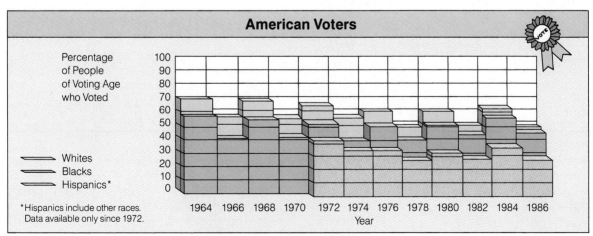

American Voters

Percentage of People of Voting Age who Voted

Whites
Blacks
Hispanics*

*Hispanics include other races. Data available only since 1972.

Year: 1964 1966 1968 1970 1972 1974 1976 1978 1980 1982 1984 1986

Source: U.S. Bureau of the Census, Department of Commerce, *Current Population Reports*

Chapter 33
The Rise and Fall of Richard Nixon

Identifying Chapter Materials

Objectives	Basic Instructional Materials	Extension Materials
1 Electing the President, 1968 • Summarize the major events of the 1968 presidential election and identify some of the controversial decisions of the Warren Court.	**Annotated Teacher's Edition** • Lesson Plans, p. 816C **Instructional Support File** • Pre-Reading Activities, Unit 11, p. 29 • Skill Review Activity, Unit 11, p. 32 • Skill Application Activity, Unit 11, p. 33 • Critical Thinking Activity, Unit 11, p. 34	**Documents of American History** • *Miranda* v. *Arizona*, Vol. 2, p. 713 • *Escobedo* v. *Illinois*, Vol. 2, p. 684
2 Nixon's First Term • Describe how the Vietnam War ended and the impact of the Vietnam War on the nation. • Explain the importance of Nixon's trip to China.	**Annotated Teacher's Edition** • Lesson Plans, pp. 816C–816D	**Documents of American History** • Nixon's Address on Vietnamizing the War, Vol. 2, p. 738 • Nixon's Statement on the Invasion of Cambodia, Vol. 2, p. 744 • The SALT Negotiations: ABM Limitation Agreement, Vol. 2, p. 750 • President Nixon and China, Vol. 2, p. 752 • Strategic Arms Limitation Agreements, Vol. 2, p. 772
3 The Fall • Trace the course of the Watergate affair. • Discuss the justifiable limits which may be placed on civil rights and liberties in times of national crisis. • Explain some historical consequences of landslide presidential elections.	**Annotated Teacher's Edition** • Lesson Plans, pp. 816D–816E **Instructional Support File** • Reading Activities, Unit 11, pp. 30–31 • Chapter Test, Unit 11, pp. 35–38 • Additional Test Questions, Unit 11, pp. 39–42 • Unit Test, Unit 11, pp. 43–46	**Enrichment Support File** • Presidential Power: Changes in the Twentieth Century (See "In-Depth Coverage" at right.) **Perspectives** • Is the President Imperial? (See "In-Depth Coverage" at right.)

Providing In-Depth Coverage

Perspectives on the Imperial Presidency

When President Nixon was reelected, he made clear his intention to exert his power to the fullest extent possible. He asked for the resignation of all his cabinet members. Although he did not intend to replace these officials, he wanted to show that they served completely at his pleasure. He also wanted it understood that he demanded strict personal loyalty from his subordinates.

The actions of Nixon as described in Chapter 33 provide a backdrop for an in-depth study of the move toward an imperial Presidency and the theory that American Presidents were becoming too powerful for the good of the country.

A History of the United States as an instructional program provides three types of resources you can use to offer in-depth coverage of the imperial Presidency: the *student text*, the *Enrichment Support File*, and *Perspectives*. The chart below shows the topics that are covered in each.

THE STUDENT TEXT. Boorstin and Kelley's *A History of the United States* unfolds the chronology of events, the key players, and, as an interpretive history, the controversy of the rise of the imperial presidency.

AMERICAN HISTORY ENRICHMENT SUPPORT FILE. This collection of primary source readings and classroom activities focuses on the rise of the imperial presidency.

PERSPECTIVES: READINGS ON AMERICAN HISTORY IN THE 20TH CENTURY. In this edited collection of secondary source readings, well-known historians and political commentators (including Boorstin) provide an array of perspectives on the President as an imperial leader.

Locating Instructional Materials

Detailed lesson plans for teaching the rise of the imperial presidency as a mini-course or to study one or more elements of the presidency in the twentieth century in depth are offered in the following areas: in the *student text*, see individual lesson plans at the beginning of each chapter; in the *Enrichment Support File*, see page 3; in *Perspectives*, see the Teacher's Guide for this topic.

IN-DEPTH COVERAGE OF THE IMPERIAL PRESIDENCY		
Student Text	**Enrichment Support File**	**Perspectives**
▪ Constitutional Powers of the President, p. 120 ▪ FDR, pp. 622–640, 657–672 ▪ Harry S Truman, pp. 707–726 ▪ LBJ, pp. 798–814 ▪ Richard Nixon, pp. 820–838	▪ Lesson Suggestions ▪ Multimedia Resources ▪ Overview Essay/Presidential Power: Changes in the Twentieth Century ▪ Literature in American History/"To Theodore Roosevelt" ▪ Primary Sources in American History/President Truman Addresses Congress and the *New York Times* Responds ▪ Great Debates in American History/Who Has the Power to Declare War? ▪ Art in American History/The Cartoonist Views the Imperial Presidency ▪ Making Connections	▪ "The Presidency Ascendant: Korea" by Arthur M. Schlesinger, Jr. ▪ "The Facade of Unlimited Presidential Power" by Theodore C. Sorensen ▪ "The Stewardship of Jimmy Carter" by Theodore H. White ▪ "Ronald Reagan" by George F. Will ▪ "Presidential Power" by Anthony Lewis

Electing the President, 1968

FOCUS

To introduce the lesson, divide the class into two groups. Ask students in one group to make a time line showing the major events for the Democratic party in 1968. Ask students in the second group to make a time line for the Republican party in 1968. Then ask students to list factors that aided Nixon's campaign.

INSTRUCT

Explain

Before the Supreme Court decision requiring reapportionment in legislative districts, 13 percent of the voters in Florida could elect a controlling majority in the legislature.

★ Independent Activity

Expressing Problems Clearly Ask students to select a Supreme Court case. In a brief essay, have students summarize the ruling and describe the controversy that surrounded it. Some possible cases include *Gideon* v. *Wainwright*, *Escobedo* v. *Illinois*, *Miranda* v. *Arizona*.

Section Review Answers

Section 1, page 820

1. a) campaigned unsuccessfully for the Democratic nomination in 1968. b) assassinated Robert Kennedy. c) nickname for the members of the irreverent Youth International Party. d) ran unsuccessfully for the Republican presidential nomination in 1968. e) Nixon's running mate in 1968. f) Nixon's term for Americans who did not take part in the protests of the 1960s. g) formed to help Wallace in the 1968 election. h) Chief Justice of the Supreme Court during the 1950s and 1960s. i) case in which the Supreme Court ruled that states must provide lawyers for poor clients in all criminal cases. j) produced rulings in which the Supreme Court outlined rights of those accused of crime. 2. Robert Kennedy, a leading contender for the nomination, was assassinated. The widely televised violence at the Democratic convention hurt Humphrey, and Nixon's promises to fight violence and crime helped his campaign. 3. a) The Warren Court ruled that the federal courts could step in to ensure equality of representation. b) The Warren Court also ruled that organized religious exercises in public schools violated the separation of church and state. c) It asserted that people accused of crimes had the right to an attorney and the right to be told just what their

rights were. These decisions aroused much controversy because they dealt with practices that were considered state and local matters. 4. Wallace received more votes than the difference between Nixon's and Humphrey's totals. But if Wallace had not run in 1968, Nixon might simply have won by a larger majority, since Wallace's politics were closer to Nixon's than to Humphrey's.

CLOSE

To conclude the lesson, ask: How did Wallace's candidacy affect the election of 1968? Would the outcome have been different had he not run? (Had Wallace not run, Humphrey may have won or Nixon may have won by a landslide instead of such a narrow margin.)

Nixon's First Term

FOCUS

To introduce the lesson, ask: How is Richard Nixon's background on the House Un-American Activities Committee (page 821) related to his trips to Beijing and Moscow (pages 828–829)? Point out the controversial nature of Nixon's actions, and especially of his visit to Beijing. Nixon could take these steps because he had been such a strong anti-Communist that no one could accuse him of being soft on communism. Ask: What was President Nixon's policy toward the two Communist powers called? (Détente)

Developing Vocabulary

The words listed in this chapter are essential terms for reading and understanding particular sections of the chapter. The page number after each term indicates the page of its first or most important appearance in the chapter. These terms are defined in the text Glossary (text pages 1000–1011).

bureaucracy (page 821); **SALT** (page 828); **antiballistic missiles** (page 828); **détente** (page 828).

INSTRUCT

Explain

Only in the 1980s did the full impact of the Vietnam War begin to hit the nation. We are still just beginning to explore the war experience in novels, plays, and movies.

☑ Writing Process Activity

Drawing Conclusions Ask students to imagine they are astronauts who have just completed the first successful landing on the moon. In preparation for writing a diary entry about the experience, ask students to brainstorm what happened, how they felt about it, and why this event was so important. Students should begin their entry with a topic sentence summarizing the significance of the moon landing, and they should organize their details logically. Ask them to revise for specific detail and effective word choice. After proofreading, students can discuss the range of reactions.

Section Review Answers

Section 2, page 830

1. a), b) important members of Nixon's staff. c) Nixon's chief adviser on foreign affairs. d), e), f), g) astronauts who took the Apollo 11 spacecraft to the moon. h) invasion of Cambodia in April 1970 by American troops. i) National Guardsmen killed four students at the university. j) leader of the USSR during the SALT negotiations. k) Strategic Arms Limitation Treaty, an arms control treaty between the United States and the Soviet Union that limited nuclear weapons and missile sites. l) Nixon's choice for Chief Justice of the Supreme Court. 2. He was elected to the House of Representatives in 1946. The Hiss case helped him win election to the Senate in 1950. He was Vice-President under Ike, from 1952–1960. He lost the presidential election of 1960 and the election for governor of California in 1962. 3. Events to be placed on the time line include: 1969—March, secret bombing of Cambodia; June, Nixon announces troop withdrawal; "Sense of the Senate" resolution tells President not to commit troops or funds to any foreign country without Congressional approval; September, another announced troop withdrawal; October, November, antiwar rallies. 1970—April, U.S. troops enter Cambodia; May, Kent State incident; June, Senate repeals Gulf of Tonkin resolution. 1971—February, South Vietnamese troops invade Laos; March, North Vietnamese invade South Vietnam. 1972—spring, U.S. mines Haiphong Harbor; October, North Vietnam announces agreement to end the war; December, intense bombing by American planes; U.S. halts bombing; January, Nixon announces end of U.S. offensive action; cease-fire accord reached. 4. a) Nixon hoped to appoint conservative judges to the Supreme Court. Although Congress did not approve two of Nixon's nominees to the Court, its decisions did move into line with his philosophy. b) Nixon's main goal for the economy was to control inflation. When inflation rose in 1969–1971, Nixon imposed wage-price controls, took the dollar off the gold standard, and devalued it. Inflation was reduced, at least in 1972. c) Nixon's foreign policy goals included a resolution of the Vietnam War and an easing of tensions with Communist powers. He did conclude

an agreement for the withdrawal of American forces from Vietnam, took the first steps toward normalizing relations with China, and reached numerous agreements with the Soviets. 5. Unlike previous explorations, the moon landing was watched by hundreds of millions of people.

CLOSE

To conclude the lesson, ask: What did President Nixon achieve by his visits to the People's Republic of China and the Soviet Union? (Easing of tensions, reduced the risk of war) Point out that Nixon wanted history to remember him for this, his greatest achievement. Ask: Is this what President Nixon is remembered for? (No—for Watergate.)

Section 3 (pages 830–838)

The Fall

FOCUS

To introduce the lesson, ask students to review the steps in the impeachment process and review the impeachment of Andrew Johnson (pages 370–371).

Developing Vocabulary

amnesty (page 832); **clemency** (page 834); **subpoena** (page 836); **partisan** (page 837).

INSTRUCT

Explain

Discuss the justification for secrecy in matters of national security and the need for limits on civil rights and liberty when national security is at stake.

❁ Cooperative Learning Activity

Formulating Questions Explain that students will work in groups of three to create crossword puzzles using terms from Chapter 33, *The fall*. Have each group choose a recorder. Then have group members divide the following list of terms: 1) hush money 2) extortion 3) harass 4) cover-up 5) conspiracy 6) kickback 7) money drop 8) bribery 9) bugging 10) unethical 11) petty 12) scheming 13) espionage 14) counterespionage 15) backbiting. Have each member develop clues for his or her terms, using a dictionary as needed. Have students work cooperatively to arrange the terms into a puzzle, with the recorder preparing the final copy. Duplicate puzzles and have groups exchange and solve.

Section Review Answers

Section 3, page 838

1. a) devices placed on telephones to record conversations without the speakers' knowledge. b) leaked

the "Pentagon papers." c) group Nixon set up to stop leaks of information to the press. d) Democratic presidential candidate in 1972. e) McGovern's running mate. f) chairman of the Democratic National Committee whose office in Watergate was bugged by the Plumbers. g) reported on Watergate for the *Washington Post*. h) investigated the 1972 election. i), j) Attorney General who resigned rather than carry out the order to fire Cox, the Special Prosecutor investigating Watergate. k) tells how a vacancy in the office of Vice-President shall be filled. l) appointed Vice-President after Agnew resigned. m) established in 1973 by Arab states. n) October 21, 1973, when the Attorney General and Deputy Attorney General resigned rather than carry out Nixon's order to fire Cox. o) became Special Prosecutor after Cox resigned. 2. Nixon won easily in 1972 in part because of division within the Democratic party, McGovern's poor handling of the vice-presidential nomination, McGovern's welfare plan and stands on other issues, the benefits of being an incumbent President, an improved economy, and the claim that peace was "at hand" in Vietnam. 3. June 6—Watergate burglars caught; Nixon begins the cover-up. Early 1973—Ervin committee set up; burglars go on trial. April 1973—Nixon fires his chief aides; names new Attorney General to appoint a special prosecutor. May—Ervin Committee and Special Prosecutor Cox demand the tapes. October—Nixon receives court order to surrender tapes; Nixon replies with the "Saturday Night Massacre"; House Judiciary Committee begins impeachment hearings; Nixon appoints new Special Prosecutor. March 1974—chief aides to Nixon indicted; Nixon releases edited transcripts of some of the tapes. July—House Judiciary Committee votes to impeach Nixon. July 24—Supreme Court orders Nixon to surrender the tapes; he complies; cover-up is revealed. August 8—Nixon resigns. 4. Nixon believed that his "enemies"—those who opposed his policies—threatened national security and therefore he could fight them in any way possible, legal or illegal.

CLOSE

To conclude the lesson, compare Nixon's threatened impeachment with Andrew Johnson's impeachment (pp. 370–371). Discuss the accusations made against the President, the motives of the accusers, and the results of the whole process. Ask students to speculate on the likelihood of a President ever being removed by impeachment. Ask: How does the impeachment process protect the national interest even when it is not carried through to its conclusion? (The resignation of a President or other high official who is sure to be removed from office accomplishes the

same end, since the only punishment that can go with impeachment is removal from office. The likelihood is strong that Congress would not attempt to take on an elected President in this way unless it was very sure of its charges. In that case, a resignation is no less effective than a conviction.)

Chapter Review Answers
Focusing on Ideas

1. Growth of federal programs and proliferation of agencies; far-reaching involvement in world affairs; President's great mobility, complicated schedule. Problems: too much authority in hands of one or two assistants; shielding of President; manager instead of leader. 2. To prevent open conflict with Communist powers; had excellent anti-Communist credentials. 3. One-sided withdrawal; disguised American defeat. This is in fact what occurred. 4. Agnew's resignation permitted Ford's appointment as V.P.; Nixon's resignation left Ford President.

Taking a Critical Look

1. If the war had been popular, there would not have been this concern over President's power to wage it. 2. Ford's pardon of Nixon perhaps a factor in his 1976 defeat; campaign financing laws; CIA shake-up; respect for investigative reporting; new set of "heroes."

Your Region in History

1–3. Answers will vary depending on your region. Consult your local library or historical society.

Historical Facts and Figures

(a) 1968—534,700; 1970—414,000; 1973—fewer than 250; (b) Nixon kept his promise to reduce number of troops in Vietnam. Graph is misleading; reduction in troops did not mean reduction in fighting. Chapter: While Nixon publicly withdrew to stem anti-war protests, he secretly expanded military actions.

Answers to "Making Connections"

(See "Using Making Connections" on p. 840.)

Answers will vary, but may include one or more of the following examples. Answers based on the time line callouts are in italics.

1. John F. Kennedy's 1000 days as President breathed new life into the federal government. To some extent this was due to innovative programs such as *the Alliance for Progress and the Peace Corps*. To a large extent, however, it was Kennedy's firm leadership that inspired the American people. Kennedy did not turn away from unpleasant situations. When the *Soviet Union built the Berlin Wall in 1961*, President Kennedy sent 1500 soldiers to the city, as a signal that the United States would act. Moral courage and firmness were apparent in his

treatment of civil rights as well. When people refused to obey civil rights laws Kennedy did not ignore the situation. He backed up his words with troops. Americans responded to Kennedy's stand. *To put pressure on Congress to pass his new civil rights bill, supporters staged a mammoth march on Washington in August, 1963.* 2. Both Johnson's domestic and foreign policies raised questions. While many Americans supported the "Great Society," others questioned whether government was taking too great a role. Should not individuals, or perhaps local communities, be taking on many of the responsibilities now being assumed by the federal government? Conservatives wondered whether people would simply ask for more and more. This question became sharper after the *1967 race riots in Detroit, Cleveland, Boston, Newark, and other cities.* Why were blacks rioting when they were in fact being aided more now by government than ever before? Had not Johnson supported *the 1965 Voting Rights Act* and other civil rights legislation? It was Johnson's foreign policy—particularly his policy regarding Vietnam—however, that raised the most questions. Initially Vietnam was not considered controversial. Only two senators voted against the *1964 Tonkin Gulf Resolution, which expanded U.S. involvement in Vietnam.* As the fighting expanded, however, more and more people questioned the war. The *1968 Tet Offensive of the North Vietnamese, which surrounded American troops* in southern cities including Saigon, raised these questions to a fevered pitch. Ultimately it was Johnson's inability to answer these questions satisfactorily which led to his decision to withdraw from the 1968 presidential race. 3. It was Nixon's belief in a strong presidency that in the end led to Watergate and his downfall. As his first term drew to a close, opinion polls showed him riding a crest of popularity. Domestically he was praised for the strength with which he responded to the recession in *1971 by announcing a 90 day wage and price freeze.* And *the establishment of relations with the People's Republic of China in 1972 was nothing less than a diplomatic coup.* Yet that same strength and determination led to an atmosphere in which he believed that as President he was above the law. *The 1973 Congressional hearings into the Watergate affair* made it clear that this was not the case. And in 1974 Richard Nixon became the first United States President to resign.

33

Chapter 33

The Rise and Fall of Richard Nixon

The Presidency of Richard M. Nixon produced a crisis in the life of the nation. In 1972 he and Vice-President Agnew won a second term with a popular majority of 18 million votes, the greatest number in history. Yet within two years, Agnew had resigned to avoid trial for bribery and income-tax evasion, and Nixon himself had left office to avoid impeachment. The ordeal of the nation was without precedent. But it also offered a unique opportunity for the representatives of a free people to show that the President was not above the law.

An unhappy Richard Nixon said goodbye to the White House staff after his resignation.

Mark Godfrey

See "Lesson Plan," p. 816C.

1. Electing the President, 1968

The election campaign of 1968 brought into the open many of the hopes and fears of the American people. In its course the short, blazing political career of Robert F. Kennedy would be snuffed out. It would see armed guards, barbed wire, and rioting in the streets of Chicago during the Democratic National Convention. And its end would find Richard M. Nixon, who had barely lost in 1960, now narrowly achieving his consuming ambition to be the President of the United States.

The race for the Democratic nomination.
The Vietnam War ended the long political career of Lyndon B. Johnson. It also pushed Robert F. Kennedy into the presidential race. He campaigned across the country in the primaries against Senator Eugene McCarthy of Minnesota. Campaigning in the critical race for California's 174 convention delegates, Kennedy drove himself to exhaustion. And he won that state's support in the coming Democratic convention. On the same day, June 5, he also won in South Dakota.

RFK went to the ballroom of the Ambassador Hotel in Los Angeles to thank the workers who had made his California victory possible. After his brief speech, he suddenly decided to leave the hall by the kitchen to avoid the crush of his well-wishers. There Sirhan Sirhan, a Jordanian who disliked Kennedy's support of Israel, was waiting. He fired three shots at the senator, who died the next day.

The nation had not yet recovered from the shock of the assassination in April of Martin Luther King. Now, only two months later, another prominent leader was murdered. The people who mourned their loss were also lamenting the rise of violence in American life.

When Lyndon Johnson stepped aside in March 1968, his buoyant, voluble Vice-President, Hubert Horatio Humphrey, decided to enter the race. Humphrey ran in no primaries, but he had the support of the leaders of the Democratic party. When he arrived in Chicago for the party convention, he had enough votes to win the nomination on the first ballot.

Chaos in Chicago. The events that occurred in Chicago during the Democratic convention of 1968 were played out on television. What people saw damaged Hubert Humphrey's chances to win the Presidency.

Inside the convention hall, protected by guards and barbed wire, there was a nasty name-calling fight over the platform plank on the Vietnam War. One side, the followers of Eugene McCarthy and the late Robert Kennedy, demanded an immediate end to the bombing and the quick withdrawal of United States and North Vietnamese troops. They called for a

The 1968 Democratic nomination was won by Hubert Humphrey after a bitter contest inside the convention hall in Chicago.

Fred Ward/Black Star

coalition government of all South Vietnamese parties. The other side, followers of Johnson and Humphrey, supported peace talks. But they opposed withdrawing unless North Vietnam also withdrew. They wanted to stop the bombing of North Vietnam only when it "would not endanger the lives of our troops." Finally the Johnson-Humphrey resolution won. New York State's antiwar delegates pinned on black armbands of mourning.

In most cases, national party conventions in the United States had been good-humored. Festive delegates wore colorful hats, sang, joked, and cheered. At those times the nation could see each convention end in happy unity. Now the dark shadow of the Vietnam War had turned a circus into a funeral. The bitterness and violence of European and Latin American politics had somehow infected American life.

Outside, on the streets and in the parks of downtown Chicago, thousands of opponents of the war swarmed. Most conspicuous were the "Yippies"—the Youth International Party—who made fun of the whole affair. They nominated a pig, Pigasus, for President. But the fun soon ceased as fierce fighting broke out between the police and those who hated the war. The hot weather did not help. The result was an unpleasant spectacle, seen by millions on television just as Hubert Humphrey was nominated for President.

Humphrey would never escape the scenes of Chicago. They seemed to reflect the worst side of the United States of recent years—the war, the angry young people, the rioting in cities and on college campuses. The divided, wrangling Democrats did not look like a party that was prepared to solve the nation's problems.

During the Democratic convention in Chicago, streets teemed with youthful demonstrators: Yippies, members of SDS, and McCarthy supporters. Police, demonstrators, and bystanders finally met in a bloody clash which thousands of Americans watched on television.

Dennis Brack/Black Star

The Republicans choose Nixon. The Republican fight for the nomination was, as usual, a far more gentlemanly affair. Richard Nixon had led the race all the way. Though challenges were made by Governor Rockefeller of New York and Governor Ronald Reagan of California, Nixon won easily at Miami, Florida. For his vice-presidential nominee, he chose Governor Spiro T. Agnew of Maryland. Agnew had begun as a liberal Republican, but after a riot in Baltimore following the death of Martin Luther King, he had emerged as a strong spokesman for law and order.

In his acceptance speech, Nixon called for the support of the "silent majority." These Americans were "the non-shouters, the non-demonstrators, that are not racist or sick, that are not guilty of the crime that plagues our land." And on the war he made it clear that he would bring peace. "Those who have had a chance for four years and could not produce peace," he declared, "should not be given another chance."

The American Independent party. A third candidate, former Governor George C. Wallace of Alabama, opposed the federal push to integrate the schools, and he spoke out against the courts that "coddled criminals." He protested the attempts of the government to halt segregation in the sale or rental of all housing. He wanted to "win" in Vietnam. "I think we've got to pour it on there," he said. Wallace hoped to appeal to enough discontented voters to keep either of the major candidates from winning. Then the election would be thrown into the House of Representatives. There his supporters could use their votes for trading purposes to achieve Wallace's goals.

The issue of the courts. The main issue of the campaign was clearly the war in Vietnam. Nearly as important was the question of law and order. This issue touched everyone—especially people living in the slums of the cities, where the crime rate had soared. In the country as a whole during the 1960s, while the population went up only 13 percent, violent crimes climbed 148 percent.

Some people blamed this on the Supreme Court. Under Chief Justice Earl Warren, who had been appointed by President Eisenhower, the Court seemed to be overturning old standards and interfering everywhere.

It was constantly intruding within the states. In the *Brown* case it had decided for school integration. Then it began to lay down new rules for elections. In 1962 the Court declared that federal courts could step in to guarantee equal representation to all citizens in all states. For some years Americans had swarmed from farms into cities and their suburbs. Still many states had not changed their laws that apportioned representatives in the state legislatures. City voters did not have enough representatives, while farmers were overrepresented. In 1964 the Court required all state legislatures to reapportion both their houses and their congressional districts on the principle of "one man, one vote." The people who lost their overrepresentation naturally did not like it.

The Supreme Court also decided some hard cases involving the separation of church and state. In 1962 the use of a prayer composed by the New York Board of Regents in public school classrooms was found to violate the First Amendment, which prohibited the establishment of religion. The next year the Court outlawed Bible readings in public school classrooms for the same reason. These decisions provoked outcries from some citizens. They denounced the Court for undermining the religious faith of American young people. They recalled that in the 1950s "under God" had been added to the Pledge of Allegiance and "In God We Trust" printed on all our currency. But others applauded the Supreme Court's defense of the First Amendment and said that religion was strong in the United States because it was not enforced by the government.

Many more Americans were troubled by the decisions of the Supreme Court which, they said, showed too much sympathy for persons accused of crime. They did not like the Court's rule in *Gideon* v. *Wainwright* (1963) that the state had to furnish legal counsel to poor defendants even in minor criminal cases. They objected when the Court decided in *Escobedo* v. *Illinois* (1964) and *Miranda* v. *Arizona* (1966)

More from Boorstin: "Legislators represent people,' Chief Justice Warren declared in 1964, 'not trees or acres. Legislators are elected by voters, not farms or cities or economic interests.'" (From *The Decline of Radicalism: Reflections on America Today*)

that a conviction would not stand unless the police had informed the accused of the right to remain silent and to have an attorney present when questioned. Suspects also had to be warned that any statement they made could be used against them in court. And in 1968 the Court ruled that in capital crimes (punishable by death) a person who opposed the death penalty could not for that reason be kept off the jury. This meant that many of the 435 persons awaiting execution on death row would have to be retried.

To many Americans these attempts of the Court to safeguard the constitutional rights of the individual against the power of the state just seemed another way of "pampering" criminals. In July 1968 a Gallup poll revealed that three Americans out of every five were unhappy over the Supreme Court's decisions. Candidate Nixon promised that when there were openings on the Court, he would appoint "strict constructionists"—judges who would interpret the Constitution strictly.

Nixon wins. The election turned out to be closer than anyone had expected. Humphrey's

campaign, which started slowly, began to pick up steam toward the end. And Wallace's drive, though weaker than he had hoped, won 10 million voters. Thirteen percent of the total cast their ballots for George Wallace and gave him five southern states. Nixon defeated Humphrey by only 510,000 votes out of the 73 million cast, and he received only 43.4 percent of the total vote. This gave him the lowest winning majority since Woodrow Wilson in 1912. The Democrats retained their control of both houses of Congress.

See "Section 1 Review answers," p. 816C.

Section 1 Review

1. Identify or explain: Eugene McCarthy, Sirhan Sirhan, "Yippies," Ronald Reagan, Spiro Agnew, "silent majority," American Independent party, Earl Warren, *Gideon* v. *Wainwright*, *Escobedo* and *Miranda* cases.

2. How did violence affect the 1968 election campaign? Give examples.

3. What stand did the Warren Court take on (a) equality of representation? (b) school religious exercises? (c) criminal rights? Why did the Court's decisions arouse criticism?

4. **Critical Thinking: Predicting Consequences.** Would the outcome of the 1968 election have been different if George Wallace had not run? Explain your answer.

After taking the oath of office, President Nixon received the congratulations of LBJ. Vice-President Agnew looks on (right).

Elliot Erwitt/Magnum

See "Lesson Plan," p. 816C.

2. Nixon's first term

On election night Nixon declared that the theme of his Presidency would be to bring the American people together again. He said that he would try to calm the conflicts that were tearing the nation apart. But by nature he was a fighter and not a conciliator. He had battled his way— to the Congress, to the Vice-Presidency, and now to the White House—by attacking Communists and others whom he called enemies of the people. He was at home in the rough and tumble of politics. He was not well qualified to unite a troubled and divided nation.

Continuity and Change: The Constitution Point out to students that many Americans saw the Supreme Court decisions in the cases of *Gideon v. Wainwright, Escobedo v. Illinois,* and *Miranda v. Arizona* as showing excessive sympathy for criminals. These decisions could also be viewed as reaffirmations of the Bill of Rights, a series of amendments guaranteeing certain rights to individuals, without which the Constitution might never have been ratified. (See p. 123.)

Richard M. Nixon. Richard Nixon had been born in California to Quaker parents. As a boy he had worked hard in their grocery store. After attending Whittier College in his hometown, he went to Duke University Law School in North Carolina. He practiced law in Whittier. Then during World War II he worked for the Office of Price Administration in Washington before going into the navy. After he was discharged in 1946, he ran for Congress as a Republican and was elected to the House of Representatives.

Nixon made his reputation as the relentless pursuer of Communists on the House Un-American Activities Committee. There he won national attention in the Alger Hiss case (p. 721). With the personality of a prosecuting attorney, he made many bitter enemies and many lukewarm friends. The Hiss case helped elect him to the Senate from California in 1950. Two years later he was nominated to run for Vice-President with General Eisenhower.

When he ran for President against John F. Kennedy in 1960, he lost by the smallest of margins. Then in 1962 he ran for governor of California, and again he lost. When Nixon's political career seemed over, he moved to New York City to join an important law firm. But he never really gave up politics. And he stayed in the public eye by his travels to foreign countries and his speeches for Republican candidates. In 1968 he ran again for President, and this time he won.

Although Richard Nixon had spent many years in the national political spotlight, few people felt that they knew the "real" Nixon. He was the most private of men. Even his supporters wondered whether they knew the sort of man he really was.

The Nixon White House. President Nixon proclaimed that he was going to keep the most open White House in history. He would appoint only the ablest people to his Cabinet, and they would help him make policy. The President's staff, he said, would merely collect information. The decisions would be made by others. But soon Nixon's White House staff became the governing force in the country.

He organized his staff with the military neatness and chain of command that General Eisenhower had brought to the Presidency. As chief of staff to guard the President's time and arrange his calendar, Nixon enlisted H. R. Haldeman, an efficient advertising man who had been a leader in Nixon's election campaign. As his assistant on foreign affairs he named Henry Kissinger, a witty and scholarly Harvard professor. John D. Ehrlichman, a 44-year-old Seattle lawyer and campaign aide, became assistant to the President for domestic affairs.

Soon President Nixon had set up a presidential staff of 48 personal assistants and hundreds of secretaries and other employees—the largest in history. In firm command and with these many assistants, he hoped to secure effective control of the huge and sprawling federal government. The people working in the nation's bureaucracy now numbered over 3 million—more than the country's whole population at the signing of the Declaration of Independence. Was it possible for any President to direct so enormous an enterprise?

President Nixon was never satisfied with his plan. Again and again he reorganized his staff and rearranged his Cabinet. Oddly enough, the result always seemed to be that power flowed into fewer and fewer hands. The President seemed to become isolated from the vast army of government workers—and the people who directed them.

The adventures in space. Nixon had been in the White House only six months when the great adventure of the century climaxed in success. The moon-landing project had been started by President Kennedy and pushed by President Johnson.

The enormous and costly project needed all the support it could find from the Presidents, the Congress, and the people. For there were great risks to life, and the costs ran to billions of dollars. When a fire exploded in 1967 during tests of a spaceship, three of the most experienced astronauts were killed. The final price tag on the moon shot came to $25 to $35 billion. Still, there were incalculable benefits—new industries, new products, and employment in new jobs for a third of a million people all over the country. And, most important, it gave a boost to the nation's courage and confidence along with new breath for the exploring spirit.

"We work in a place," boasted someone at the Manned Spacecraft Center in Houston, Texas, "where 13,000 men can feel like Columbus."

Finally, after nine years of preparing and two trial voyages around the moon and back, on July 16, 1969, Americans set out to land on the moon. Neil Armstrong headed the mission, Michael Collins piloted the command ship *Apollo 11*, and Edwin E. Aldrin, Jr., was to work with Armstrong during the landing.

None of these astronauts was a great scientist. None came from a family that was rich or famous. But they shared a passion for flying. All three were athletes in top physical condition. They were modest men who had practiced working together.

The dangerous voyage.

The moon trip was unlike earlier explorations of unknown lands. For this voyage was watched on television by the whole world—including the explorers' own families. Hundreds of millions of people could share the adventure and the suspense.

The three astronauts shot up in the command ship *Apollo 11*, which took them orbiting around the earth. Then, after 2 1/2 orbits, they steered *Apollo 11* off toward the moon, more than 200,000 miles away. After the three-day journey through interplanetary space, they arrived in their moon orbit. Armstrong and Aldrin climbed into a small "lunar module" attached at the nose of *Apollo 11*. They called this little ship *Eagle*.

They separated *Eagle* from the command ship. After orbiting the moon to the agreed position, they landed *Eagle* on the moon at 4:17 P.M. eastern daylight time on July 20, 1969.

There were risks till the last instant of the landing. As the computer guided them down, Armstrong noticed that they were about to settle in a deep crater about the size of a football field, filled with large boulders. He seized the controls and guided *Eagle* to a safe, smoother site.

Footsteps on the moon.

Six and a half hours after landing, the first man, an American, stepped out on a heavenly body. For that moment the whole world, except those whose dictators forbade them to know, watched proudly together.

Surrounded by the footprints of the first earthlings on the moon, there remains to this day the launching stand from which Armstrong and Aldrin took off from the moon in their lunar module. And on it is a plaque that may last forever. For on the moon there is no atmosphere, there is no wind to blow, no oxygen to rust, and no water to erode. The message on the plaque does not boast an American achievement but proclaims the hope of the world. "Here men from the planet earth first set foot upon the moon, July 1969, A.D. We came in peace for all mankind."

(p. 823)

Winding down the war.

The nation had been reunited in these exhilarating moments. Watching together, people knew that this was another triumph of Americans working together—sharing resources with the whole world of science.

But when the day of success in outer space was past, Americans still remained divided by the miseries of the no-win war in Vietnam. President Nixon had promised to end that war. He told the nation again in May 1969 that he intended to keep that pledge. But he "ruled out either a one-sided withdrawal . . . or the acceptance of terms that would amount to a disguised American defeat." To make his message doubly clear to North Vietnam, in March he had actually taken the risk of widening the war. He then began secret large-scale bombing of suspected North Vietnamese and Viet Cong bases in Cambodia. To avoid antiwar protests, Nixon did not tell Congress or the American public. In fact, this operation was so hush-hush that even the Secretary of the Air Force was kept from knowing about it.

While Nixon secretly enlarged the war, he began publicly to withdraw from it. When he took office, there were half a million American troops in Vietnam. In June he announced that 25,000 American soldiers would be coming

See "Lesson Plan," p. 816C for **Writing Process Activity: Drawing Conclusions** relating to the first human being on the moon.

The first human beings to step on the desolate surface of the moon were two United States astronauts. Neil Armstrong took this dramatic photograph of Edwin E. Aldrin, Jr.

More from Boorstin: "At the launching of Apollo II, a member of President Kennedy's family, R. Sargeant Shriver, poignantly recalled that in 1961 at the time of announcing the national commitment to go to the moon, President Kennedy had remarked, 'I firmly expect this commitment to be kept. And if I die before it is, all you here now just remember when it happens I will be sitting up there in heaven in a rocking chair just like this one, and I'll have a better view of it than anybody.'" (From *The Americans: The Democratic Experience*)

home. And in September he announced that another 35,000 would be withdrawn during the following months.

Opposition to the war. Still the President's actions did not satisfy those who wanted the United States out of the war. In October and November 1969 they held antiwar rallies in Washington and elsewhere. Opposition to the war now included large numbers from all parts of American society. The Senate, too, was making it clear that it intended to play a more active role in foreign affairs. In June a "Sense of the Senate" resolution, passed by the overwhelming majority of 70–16, told the President not to commit men or funds to any country without the express approval of Congress.

Nixon's policy, as he explained to the nation during 1969, was to decrease American involvement while at the same time letting the South Vietnamese take over the struggle. On April 20, 1970, he informed the country that over the next year he would remove 150,000 more United States troops from Vietnam. This decision, he said, "means that we finally have in sight the just peace we are seeking."

Ten days later the nation was staggered to learn that United States troops had entered Cambodia, a small country that shared a long border with Vietnam. This was called an "incursion," to make clear that it was just a brief raid—to strike at supplies and the "headquarters for the entire Communist military operation in South Vietnam."

The Cambodian "incursion" was greeted by a storm of opposition, especially in colleges and universities across the United States. At Kent State University in Ohio students became so violent that the governor called out the National Guard. And then, on May 4, a frightened Guard unit opened fire on the students, killing four. Soon more than 80 colleges and universities suspended classes, seething with opposition to the war. Thousands of demonstrators, including college presidents, professors, and students, gathered in Washington.

All this impressed and persuaded the Congress. On June 24, 1970, the Senate voted 81–10 to repeal the Tonkin Gulf Resolution (p. 809).

Peace at last. Even as the United States wound down American involvement and brought fighting men home, the conflict in Indochina continued to spread. This war seemed to have its own terrible momentum. In February 1971 South Vietnamese troops, aided by American helicopters and bombers, invaded Laos. Later the State Department explained that this was only an attempt to protect the withdrawal of United States forces. That November, Congress was still disturbed by Nixon's failure to end the war. An amendment was tacked on a military procurement bill calling for the withdrawal of the United States by a "date certain" after the release of United States prisoners of war. The President signed the bill but said he would ignore the amendment.

In March 1972, thousands of North Vietnamese troops openly invaded South Vietnam. The United States replied by unleashing the largest and most powerful air force in history in bombing raids all across Indochina. Two months later there was still no word from North Vietnam. The President increased the pressure by allowing mines to be dropped into Haiphong Harbor, even though Russian ships there might be endangered. Still, in late August he announced that by December 1972 there would be only 27,000 American fighting men left in Vietnam.

Within months after Nixon took office, secret peace talks between the United States and North Vietnam had begun. Finally, in the fall of 1972, terms for a cease-fire were reached. But the South Vietnamese had not been informed of the talks and they refused to agree. Still, the United States presented the South Vietnamese demands to the North Vietnamese. With that, the agreement collapsed. Then, on December 18, United States planes began the fiercest bombing attacks of the war on North Vietnam. They were meant to force the North to accept the agreement with the United States. They were also intended to persuade the South Vietnamese to go along by showing that the United

States would support them if North Vietnam ever violated the cease-fire. The United States, without any public explanation, halted the attacks on December 30.

On January 15, 1973, Nixon announced that so much progress had been made in the peace talks that he was calling a halt to all United States offensive action in Vietnam. Then on January 27 a cease-fire accord was finally reached in Paris. All fighting was to stop in Vietnam, and the North Vietnamese were to release the American prisoners of war. The United States was to withdraw completely from Vietnam.

After losing 46,104 men in combat and with 1200 missing, the United States was doing exactly what President Nixon had said we never would do. This was both "a one-sided withdrawal" and "the acceptance of terms that would amount to a one-sided defeat." American troops withdrew while North Vietnamese troops remained. When the United States had entered the war in a big way in 1965 there were, according to the State Department, 20,000 North Vietnamese in South Vietnam. When we left there were 145,000. But American soldiers were no longer fighting in South Asia.

The United States and Indochina. The United States was involved in Vietnam for so

At its peak strength in 1968 the United States had over 500,000 troops in Vietnam. But despite their superior equipment, the U.S. and the South Vietnamese could not defeat the North Vietnamese and the Viet Cong. This was a strange war where there was no front line. The Communist enemy could be anywhere and everywhere in South Vietnam.

Bruno Barbey/Magnum Photos

Multicultural Connection: Among the thousands of Hispanics who participated in the Vietnam War were navy pilot Everett Alvarez, the first prisoner captured by North Vietnam, and Captain Felix Sosa Camejo, who was killed while trying to rescue a group of his soldiers in Huey and was given the Silver Star medal posthumously.

long that it is useful to pause and review the complicated story. It all began in 1950 when Harry Truman was President. The United States was fighting in Korea against the Communist North Koreans. At home, Senator Joseph McCarthy was recklessly playing up the fear of Communists and communism. The French were struggling in their fight against Communists in Indochina. Following the belief that communism had to be stopped in every corner of the world, Truman aided the French with a small amount of money and military supplies.

Support for the French increased under President Eisenhower. He was also advised by the chairman of the joint chiefs of staff to use United States bombers against the Vietnamese Communists, the Viet Minh, to prevent them from overrunning the French strongpoint at Dienbienphu. But Eisenhower was cautious. He had just extricated his country from the unpopular war in Korea and he would not commit U.S. armed forces anew without the approval of Congress and the support of our Western allies, especially Britain. Ike tried to persuade the British to join the United States in battle against the Viet Minh, but the British refused to be "hurtled into injudicious military decisions," as their experienced Foreign Secretary Anthony Eden put it.

The first Indochina War came to an end in 1954. After a peace conference in Geneva, Switzerland, a cease-fire was declared in Cambodia, Laos, and Vietnam. The Cambodian Communists (the Khmer Rouge) and the Laotian Communists (the Pathet Lao) gained only a cease-fire, but the more successful Viet Minh were granted the northern part of Vietnam. They were to move all their troops there, while the French would put all their forces in the South. This division of the nation was to continue only until a nationwide election could be held in 1956. The United States did not sign these agreements, but said it would respect them as

Ho Chi Minh, left, devoted most of his life to fighting for a free Communist Vietnam.

Marc Riboud/Magnum Photos

long as there was no aggression by the Communists.

When the time for the election came, the South Vietnam government, backed by the United States, refused to participate because it feared the Communists would win. Then Communists living in the South, supplied by the North, began to use force to overthrow the South Vietnamese government. The second Indochina war was under way. American aid and the number of U.S. military advisers were increased.

After President Kennedy came to office in 1961, he gradually increased the number of military advisers from about 700 to more than 16,000. Some of them even began to take part in combat operations, although Kennedy denied it.

Johnson commits combat troops. President Kennedy was assassinated in 1963. The new President, Lyndon Baines Johnson, followed the path laid out by his predecessors. But now North Vietnam began to support the Viet Cong, as the South Vietnamese Communists were called, by sending more and more of its own battle-hardened troops down the Ho Chi Minh trail which traced its way through the jungles of Laos and Cambodia into South Vietnam.

On August 4, 1964, President Johnson announced to the American people on television that two United States destroyers had been fired upon by North Vietnamese gunboats in the Tonkin Gulf off North Vietnam. The United States, he said, was now sending American planes to attack North Vietnam in response. He also asked Congress for a joint resolution to empower "the President, as Commander-in-Chief, to take all necessary measures to repulse any further armed attack against the forces of the United States and to prevent further aggression." Congress quickly gave Johnson the power he wanted. Only later did it turn out that our destroyers might never have been fired upon at all. On a stormy night, they had probably been confused by false images on their radar screens.

President Johnson pledged during the 1964 election campaign not to send "American boys" to do what "Asian boys ought to be doing for themselves." But then he was advised, early in January 1965, that United States aid would have to increase or South Vietnam would be lost to the Communists. LBJ did not want anyone to be able to say that as President he had allowed the Communists to advance. After a Viet Cong attack on an American base holding military advisers early in February, Johnson ordered heavy air attacks on North Vietnam. Soon B-52s were dropping tons of bombs and napalm on the north.

At the same time, the United States began to commit more and more troops to the war effort. On March 8, 1965, the first U.S. combat troops went ashore at Danang. In April, there were 27,000 American soldiers and marines in Vietnam. By year's end, there were 185,000. But as the American commitment in Vietnam grew, opposition at home also increased. People of all ranks, from senators like J. William Fulbright, chairman of the Foreign Relations Committee, to students in colleges across the country, began to speak and demonstrate against the war. The number who marched at one time grew from a few thousand in 1965 to hundreds of thousands in 1967 as United States casualties (killed, wounded, and missing) in Vietnam soared from 2500 in 1965 to 33,000 in 1966, to 80,000 in 1967.

Then in January 1968 during a temporary cease-fire for the Vietnamese New Year holiday called "Tet," the North Vietnamese and Viet Cong struck at cities throughout South Vietnam. The Communists suffered heavy losses in their "Tet" offensive, but television pictures of their troops in the American embassy and press reports of the destruction they caused, along with the American commander's subsequent call for 206,000 more troops, made it seem more like a defeat for the United States than the victory it actually was. The Communists had been severely weakened by their casualties.

Leaving Vietnam. By now, Johnson was listening to more and more advice that we should get out of Vietnam. This was coming even from people who had previously supported the war. On March 31, 1968, LBJ announced that he had ordered sharp restrictions on the bombing raids on North Vietnam. He called for peace talks. Then he surprised his listeners by saying that he would not run for reelection so that he could pursue peace without being accused of playing politics. Peace talks did begin in May, but they failed to bring a rapid end to the war.

The election campaign of 1968 was dominated by the Vietnam War. Its shadow disrupted the Democratic nominating convention. There was bitter name-calling within the convention hall and fighting between police and antiwar demonstrators outside on the streets of Chicago. The spectacle—shown on television in living color in homes across the nation—may have cost the Democratic candidate, Vice-President Hubert Humphrey, the election. He was defeated by former Vice-President Richard Nixon, who said that the Democrats had not been able to bring peace and "should not be given another chance."

But Nixon, although he soon opened secret talks with the North Vietnamese, said he would not end the war in a way that amounted to a "disguised American defeat." He turned to extremely heavy bombing of Laos and Cambodia to try to stop the flow of North Vietnamese supplies down the Ho Chi Minh trail. Attempting to avoid even more antiwar protests, Nixon concealed these operations. At the same time, he publicly began to bring American troops home. Still, opposition at home to the war increased, reaching a peak of violence at Kent State University in Ohio in May 1970, when frightened and inadequately trained National Guard soldiers fired on demonstrating students, killing four.

The war raged on even as the secret talks continued. But the number of American troops in Vietnam fell rapidly from 500,000 when Nixon took office to just 27,000 in 1972. As the troops came home and draft calls declined, public marches against the war diminished. At last, a cease-fire was achieved in January of 1973. This brought to an end American participation in a conflict that one author described as "the war nobody won," because all sides paid such a high price.

Although the United States was no longer in-volved, the war was still not over. Fighting continued throughout Indochina into 1975. In that year, the Communist forces took control in Vietnam, Cambodia, and Laos (p. 865). But then, to the world's surprise, Communist turned against Communist. People wondered if there would ever be peace in Indochina.

Moscow and Beijing. The world had become smaller than most Americans imagined. The jet airplane had brought the continents close together. In the middle of July 1971 Nixon startled the American people when he announced that he intended to fly to Communist China. The People's Republic of China, with its 800 million people, had become a leading power in the world. Still, after 22 years, the United States had not recognized the government or exchanged ambassadors. Early in August, the President declared that the United States would reverse its position and support Red China's membership in the UN. Nixon was able to make these moves because no one could challenge his credentials as a fighter against communism.

On February 21, 1972, President Nixon landed in Beijing. There, aided by Secretary of State Kissinger, he began to bring the relations of the two countries back to normal. This was the boldest diplomatic move by an American President since Jefferson bought Louisiana.

The Chinese and the Russians, though both had Communist governments, were bitter rivals. A clever American diplomacy required that the United States balance its new friendliness to China with a new gesture to the Soviets. A few months later, therefore, President Nixon went to Russia for a summit meeting with Soviet leader Leonid Brezhnev. The two men were to sign a series of agreements on the environment, space, health, and science. But the main document was the Strategic Arms Limitation Treaty (SALT). The two countries had been working on it since 1969. That treaty, signed on May 26, 1972, aimed to slow down the dangerous and expensive nuclear arms race. Each country agreed to set up only two antiballistic missile (ABM) defense sites. Both agreed to build no more ICBMs or SLBMs.

The Beijing and Moscow trips were successful

Magnum

One of the highlights of President and Mrs. Nixon's visit to the People's Republic of China was a formal Chinese banquet hosted by Zhou Enlai, the Chinese premier (second from left). Under the flags of both nations, Nixon and Zhou toasted the newly opened communications between their two countries.

steps in Nixon's plan to ease tensions and reduce risks of war with the Communist powers. The new expression for this was détente (from the French word meaning to ease or relax). Truman had aimed at "containment"—to keep the Communists boxed in. But Nixon's main hope was to prevent open conflict.

Nixon and domestic affairs. At home, too, the President said he wanted to reduce conflict. He criticized the Supreme Court for giving the "green light" to criminals and for failing to slow down the integration of the schools. During his election campaign he had promised to appoint more conservative justices to the Court. In May 1969 he nominated, and the Senate confirmed, Judge Warren Burger of Minnesota as the Chief Justice in place of Earl Warren, who was retiring. But in its first decision the Burger Court unanimously ruled that segregation in Mississippi schools—and also, this meant, throughout the nation—must end "at once." The Nixon administration had joined the state of Mississippi in asking for a delay.

President Nixon had the opportunity to name three more members of the Supreme Court. But

Critical Thinking Activity: Formulating Questions What did President Nixon hope to achieve by traveling to Beijing and Moscow? Ask for volunteers to play Richard Nixon, Zhou Enlai, and Leonid Brezhnev. The rest of the class will play news reporters. The setting is a fictitious joint-press conference called by the leaders of the United States, China, and the Soviet Union at the end of 1972. Have the student-reporters prepare questions and interview the student-world leaders.

the Senate was suspicious of his nominees. They refused to confirm two of them, saying they were not qualified. With the new appointees whom the Senate did approve, the Supreme Court changed. It did continue to press for school integration. But it was less active than the Warren Court (p. 819), and it tended to interpret the Constitution so as to narrow somewhat the rights of those accused of crimes.

Richard Nixon was mainly interested in foreign affairs. He had no grand dream for a new domestic policy to remake the face of the nation. Like President Eisenhower, he wanted to cut the cost of government and turn over more activities to the states. He wanted to balance the budget and bring inflation under control. But since the Democrats controlled Congress throughout his time in office, he had trouble reaching his goals.

A troubled economy. Inflation was becoming familiar. It had begun under LBJ and was Nixon's gravest domestic problem. During the election he had promised to end inflation. He hoped to do this by balancing the budget (then about $200 billion) and, if possible, by producing a surplus. Still, inflation kept rising. Congress continued to pass expensive programs. And a tax reform act in 1969 ended President Johnson's income-tax surcharge. Meanwhile, the unhappy war in Vietnam increased the demand for everything and kept the spiral of prices going up. Even so, the country went into its first business recession since 1961.

During 1969 and 1970, Nixon avoided setting wage-price guidelines. He hoped that the mild business recession of 1969–1970 and his economic policies would slow the upward rise of prices. Instead, between January 1969 and August 1971, prices went up 14.5 percent. This rapid rise forced Nixon to change his policies. On August 15, 1971, he announced a 90-day wage-price freeze. He was the first President ever to use mandatory wage-price controls in peacetime.

At the same time, he cut the dollar loose from gold. This meant that the United States would no longer let foreign governments turn in their dollars for our gold. He also asked foreign nations to let their own money become more valuable in dollars. And he put a 10 percent surcharge on foreign imports. President Nixon hoped in this way to promote the sale of American goods abroad and also discourage Americans from buying foreign products.

After these policies were adopted, inflation fell in 1972 to 3.5 percent. With a budget that in 1971 showed a $22.3 billion deficit and with an even larger deficit projected for 1972, the economy began to thrive and unemployment dropped from 5.9 percent of the work force in 1971 to 5.6 percent in 1972. For President Nixon—and the nation—these were welcome facts as he planned for reelection.

See "Section 2 Review answers," p. 816D.

Section 2 Review

1. Identify or explain: H. R. Haldeman, John Ehrlichman, Henry Kissinger, Neil Armstrong, Michael Collins, Edwin E. Aldrin, Jr., *Apollo 11*, Cambodian incursion, Kent State incident, Leonid Brezhnev, SALT, Warren Burger.
2. Summarize Nixon's career up until 1968.
3. Make a time line showing key events in the Vietnam War, including responses to the war at home, from 1969 to 1973.
4. What were Nixon's goals for (a) the Supreme Court, (b) the economy, (c) foreign policy? To what extent was he successful in achieving those goals?
5. **Critical Thinking: Making Comparisons.** In what ways was the moon-landing project different from previous explorations of the unknown?

See "Lesson Plan," p. 816D.

3. The fall

The election of 1972 was to see Richard Nixon win the greatest popular majority in the history of the United States. Yet less than two years after his great victory he would become the first President ever to resign from office.

The Nixon outlook. The destruction of Richard Nixon began long before the campaign. Perhaps it began as far back as 1960 when he lost to Kennedy by such a narrow margin. For that convinced Nixon that he must never again leave anything undone in an election campaign—no matter how certain victory might appear.

His trouble was rooted in his view of himself and his opponents. Nixon the fighter never failed to see politics as a battleground—where you used whatever tactics were needed to win. "His use of football analogies was so revealing," Cabinet member Elliot Richardson explained. "Anything was OK except what the referee sees and blows the whistle on."

Perspec-
tives
Topic

◖ *Pursuing enemies.* It was not surprising that Nixon had a passion for secrecy. Those who opposed him he called his enemies. His special targets were people in the antiwar movement and his newspaper and TV critics. Against them he believed that he had the right to wield all the powers of the President. To spy on them and harass them he used government agencies such as the CIA, FBI, IRS, and FCC. Even when these activities were not technically illegal, they were an abuse of his presidential powers.

Nixon was determined to find out how the news of the secret bombing of Cambodia had reached the newspapers. In 1969, then, he ordered the FBI to place wiretaps (without the court orders required by law) on certain government employees and reporters. Believing that the antiwar protesters were actually tied to the Communists, in 1970 he tried to create his own super-secret intelligence group. This group would open mail, tap telephones, and even break into private homes and offices to get evidence to prove that his political opponents—his "enemies" —were really traitors. If his personal spies were caught, the answer would be that it was all for "national security"—to protect the nation. This plan was dropped, however, because J. Edgar Hoover, the man who had built up the FBI and was the nation's chief spy-catcher, refused to go along. "The risks are too great," he warned.

In June 1971 the *New York Times* began to publish the "Pentagon Papers." This was the secret study of United States involvement in Vietnam that Secretary McNamara had ordered in 1967 (p. 812). The document had been given to the *Times* by Daniel Ellsberg, who had worked on the report. The government said the report would reveal secret information damaging to the national security and therefore sued to stop the *Times.* When the case went to the Supreme Court, the Court refused to intervene and allowed the papers to be printed.

The Department of Justice then indicted Daniel Ellsberg for theft, conspiracy, and espionage. President Nixon remained deeply disturbed. He was determined to track down his enemies—even if he had to set up his own system of counterespionage!

Within the White House, Nixon now formed a secret special unit. Since the job of this unit was to "stop leaks" of information, it was called the "Plumbers." Their first assignment was to find some way to ruin the reputation of Daniel Ellsberg. But the Plumbers were inept. Hoping to uncover some embarrassing information, they broke into the Los Angeles office of Ellsberg's psychiatrist. They found nothing. This was only one in a series of illegal acts that would destroy Nixon and his closest aides. For

Elliot Richardson held several posts under Nixon. He became Attorney General in 1973.

Dennis Brack/Black Star

the Plumbers would soon turn from "national security" to party politics. And they would finally bring down the President, whom they were supposed to protect.

McGovern wins the Democratic nomination.
One part of the Nixon campaign strategy for re-election in 1972 was to divide the Democrats against themselves. Then the Nixon group would promote the candidate who was the easiest to defeat. This scheme included giving financial support to George Wallace of Alabama, opposing middle-of-the-road Edmund Muskie of Maine, and favoring the candidacy of George McGovern of South Dakota. It also included a variety of "dirty tricks." False letters were sent out attacking one candidate under the name of another. "The idea," one of the Nixon managers explained, "was to get the candidates backbiting each other."

Despite some enthusiastic support, George McGovern was badly defeated in 1972.

Lawrence Fried/Magnum

George Wallace's push for the Democratic nomination was cut short by a shocking act of violence. While delivering a campaign speech in Laurel, Maryland, he was shot by an angry listener. Three bystanders were also shot. At first it seemed that Wallace might not survive. He lived but became paralyzed from the waist down and was no longer a serious contender.

Muskie's campaign faltered early, and George McGovern took the lead. He had helped to reform the party rules after 1968. More women, blacks, and young people would be delegates at the convention in 1972. He made a special effort to appeal to each of these groups.

When the party met in Miami Beach early in July, Senator McGovern won the nomination easily on the first ballot. As his running mate he chose Senator Thomas F. Eagleton of Missouri. But soon it came out that Eagleton had been hospitalized for psychiatric problems. McGovern asked Eagleton to step down. As a replacement the Democratic National Committee named Sargent Shriver, a brother-in-law of John and Robert Kennedy's. McGovern's judgment and his stability were called into question by his handling of this problem. At first he had said that he was behind Eagleton "1000 percent." Then suddenly he turned around and dropped him.

The 1972 campaign. The Republicans also met in Miami Beach and quickly renominated Nixon and Agnew. They had an easy campaign. President Nixon seldom left the White House. He took a strong stand against busing and for the local control of schools. He also opposed abortion. He was against legalizing the smoking of marijuana and against welfare payments for those who would not work. He kept the bitter Vietnam issue alive by opposing amnesty for those who had avoided fighting in the war by deserting from the armed forces or by dodging the draft. At the same time the news in late October that peace seemed to be at hand in Vietnam was a boost for Richard Nixon's campaign.

McGovern was openly against the war in Vietnam. He favored allowing the states to permit abortions, and making the smoking of marijuana a noncriminal offense. He was for cutting defense spending and changing the welfare system. Some of his proposals were not well thought out and were easy to attack. The Republicans called him a far-left candidate with far-out ideas.

On election day Nixon won a resounding victory. With 60.2 percent of the vote, he carried 49 of the 50 states. McGovern had hoped for strong support from the new young voters. In 1971 the Twenty-sixth Amendment had been passed allowing any citizen 18 or over to vote. But many of these 11.5 million new voters failed to vote at all, and of those who did, many voted for Nixon. Only 55.7 percent of all Americans old enough to vote went to the polls—the lowest number since 1948.

Spying on the Democrats. The result showed that the Republicans had such an easy win that they really could have played by all the rules and still gained a large majority. Yet, for some reason they would not leave well enough alone. The nervous Nixon team, to make their victory doubly sure, had turned to underhanded tactics. As early as January 1972 Attorney General John Mitchell, who was soon to resign to devote full time to heading Nixon's campaign, heard one of the Plumbers present a program of secret, illegal campaign activities. A $1 million program of kidnapping, wiretapping, and "dirty tricks" to hurt the Democrats was suggested. Mitchell rejected the plan as too expensive. Though he was the nation's chief law-enforcement official, the Attorney General said nothing about the idea being wrong.

Finally, the campaign managers agreed to spend $250,000 on a new kind of political intelligence-gathering plan. None of them really liked it. In fact, one later said, "We feared that it might be a waste of money and also that it might be dangerous." But the White House wanted to know what its political opponents were up to. John Mitchell and the others approved an elaborate criminal plan, which included "bugging" the office of Lawrence O'Brien, head of the Democratic National Committee.

The first wiretap on O'Brien's phones did not work. Then, on the night of June 16, the Plumbers once again broke into the Democratic National Committee offices in the Watergate office building. And this time they were caught! They carried evidence that might link them to the White House and so open the President to ❀ the charge of being a criminal conspirator.

Nixon orders a cover-up. President Nixon did not know about the Watergate break-in until after it happened. But then easily, almost carelessly, he moved to cover up the crime. As soon as he and his aides did that, they were committing a crime themselves.

First the President ordered his staff to tell the CIA to stop the FBI from investigating the case. They were to say that "national security" was at stake. Richard Helms, Director of Central Intelligence, refused to have the CIA involved. So Nixon saw that money was paid to the Plumbers to keep them quiet about their connection to the White House. By September 1972 these men had received $220,000 in hush money.

Somehow the Watergate affair did not really catch the public's attention when it took place. Still, newspaper reporters Robert Woodward and Carl Bernstein kept probing the strange events surrounding Watergate. Their reports, published in the *Washington Post*, kept the time bomb of Watergate ticking. It would go off, however, only after Nixon was safely reelected. Watergate would prove to be one of the oddest— and most unnecessary—crimes in American history.

Investigating the campaign. Soon after the Senate convened in 1973, it voted 77–0 to set up a committee to look into any "illegal, improper, or unethical activities" in the 1972 election. Senator Sam Ervin of North Carolina was to head the committee.

When the Ervin Committee began its hearings, President Nixon and his aides felt pressure from three sides. If anyone involved in the burglary told the truth to a judge or to the Department of Justice or to the Ervin Committee, the White House link to the Plumbers would be revealed. So the President and his aides tried to devise still more ways to cover up their connection to the crime.

❀ See "Lesson Plan," p. 816D for **Cooperative Learning Activity: Formulating Questions** relating to the Watergate scandal.

Nixon sank deeper and deeper into a new crime—the crime of the cover-up. The American people might have excused a President for making mistakes. But they would not tolerate a President who did not take seriously his sworn duty to obey and enforce the law.

Nixon under pressure. Hoping to lift some of the pressure, on April 17, 1973, the President issued a statement that because of "major developments in the case" he had ordered "intensive new inquiries." He said that he had not learned until March 21, 1973, that there were attempts to cover up the scandal. This was a lie, for he had known ever since late June 1972. Nixon now heard that some of the people involved in the cover-up were beginning to talk. He was desperately trying to save himself. He had been informed by Attorney General Richard Kleindienst that the Department of Justice had enough information to indict Haldeman, Ehrlichman, and John Mitchell. He knew, too, that

he could be impeached. So he began to thrash about, talking of using "a million dollars" and "clemency" to end this disaster.

On April 29, Nixon told his chief aides, Ehrlichman and Haldeman, who were in deep trouble, that they were fired. The following day, he told the nation on TV that he was naming a new Attorney General, Elliot Richardson, who was empowered to appoint a special prosecutor to investigate the Watergate case.

The discovery of the tapes. "The Greatest Show on Earth," as the Ervin Committee hearings soon were called, opened its televised proceedings on May 17, 1973. They went on for three months. Millions watched fascinated by all the strange doings of the Nixon men— "enemies lists," money drops, dirty tricks, millions raised illegally from corporations, and attempts to use the IRS to harass enemies.

Then, late in the hearings, the news came out that since February 1971 there had been tape

During the Watergate hearings, a cartoonist showed the White House as a giant tape recorder.

Tony Auth © 1973 *Philadelphia Inquirer*, reprinted with permission from Universal Press Syndicate, all rights reserved.

More from Boorstin: "The Vietnam War was the first American war which was a television experience. Watergate was the first national political scandal which was a television experience. The college-student protests of the sixties were the first nonsporting college events to become television experiences." (From *Hidden History: Exploring Our Secret Past*)

recording machines in the White House and Executive Office Building. Unknown to all but a few, these machines had been taping everything said there by the President and his aides. Nixon had been anxious that the events of his Presidency should be amply recorded for future historians. The tapes would make history in a way he never imagined. They would finally destroy Richard Nixon.

As soon as the existence of the tapes was known, both the Ervin Committee and the new special prosecutor, Harvard professor Archibald Cox, wanted to hear certain key conversations. Nixon refused to hand over the tapes. He insisted that the President could not do his job if his records were not kept confidential. So the matter went to the courts. On October 12, the Court of Appeals ruled, 5–2, against the President. "Though the President is elected by nationwide ballot," the court declared, "and is often said to represent all the people, he . . . is not above the law's commands." Nixon had a week to decide whether to appeal the decision, to turn over the tapes, or to take some other action.

Agnew resigns. At this moment when the net was closing ever more tightly around the struggling President, Vice-President Agnew—who had risen to power by preaching law and order—was accused of serious crimes. On August 1, 1973, he was told by the Department of Justice that he was being investigated for income-tax evasion, conspiracy, bribery, and extortion. There was evidence that he had accepted kickbacks from Maryland state contractors as governor and even as Vice-President.

At first Agnew protested his innocence. Then, after bargaining with the prosecution, he decided to resign as Vice-President and to plead "no contest" to tax evasion. This meant that he would not try to prove his innocence in court and that he would accept the penalties of being guilty. In return, the government was willing to drop the other charges against him. The prosecution also asked the court for leniency "out of compassion for the man, out of respect for the office he has held, and out of appreciation for

the fact that by his resignation he has spared the nation the prolonged agony that would have attended upon his trial." The court fined him $10,000 and placed him on probation for three years. The government then released in detail the evidence against him.

Fortunately, in 1967 the Twenty-fifth Amendment to the Constitution had been adopted. It came from the time of President Eisenhower's illness and was mainly intended for a situation when the President was not physically able to carry on the duties of his office. In case of a vacancy in the office of the Vice-President, the President would nominate someone who was to be confirmed by both houses of Congress. President Nixon now made the first use of the amendment. For the new Vice-President he chose Gerald R. Ford of Grand Rapids, Michigan, the Republican floor leader in the House of Representatives. Well known and respected in Congress, he was quickly confirmed.

War in the Middle East. To add to Nixon's troubles, on October 6, 1973, war broke out anew in the Middle East. Egypt and Syria attacked Israel on Yom Kippur, the holiest day of the Jewish year. Then, on October 12, the President decided to go all out to aid the Israelis and offset the supplies the Arabs were receiving from Russia. He ordered a massive airlift from the United States all the 6450 miles to Israel—including helicopters, howitzers, and even 50-ton tanks. In response, the Arabs embargoed oil shipments to the United States. The winter of 1973–1974 found the United States faced with its first gasoline shortage.

The Saturday Night Massacre. President Nixon now made a move that was to lose him much of whatever support he had left in the country. First, he announced on Friday, October 20, that Watergate was sapping the strength of the nation. To resolve the crisis, he said he would compromise on the issue of the tapes. He would offer summaries of their contents. He also revealed that he had ordered Special Prosecutor Cox to stop trying to get the tapes.

The following day Cox refused to accept the President's order. He demanded the actual tapes. Nixon then told Attorney General Richardson to fire Cox. But Richardson had promised both Cox and the Senate that he would not interfere with the Special Prosecutor, so he resigned. Then Nixon asked the Deputy Attorney General to fire Cox. But he, too, resigned rather than carry out the order. Finally, Robert Bork, the Solicitor General, who believed that the President had the right to fire Cox, whatever might be the wisdom of the act, discharged the Special Prosecutor.

This was called "the Saturday Night Massacre." Elliot Richardson later said that by firing Cox, President Nixon wanted to show the world that he was still in charge of the government. "It was like the 1970 action in Cambodia," he said. "He wanted to show Moscow and Peking his determination, and to do that he would pay the necessary domestic price."

But Nixon had misjudged the American people. To them his actions seemed an admission of guilt. *Time* magazine, which had never before run an editorial in all its 50 years, now said, "The President Should Resign."

The President's troubles mount. At this point the House Judiciary Committee began hearings to decide whether the President should be impeached. Nixon finally gave in. He agreed to give up to the court the tapes that had been subpoenaed and to appoint a new Special Prosecutor.

As if Nixon did not have enough problems at this point, his personal finances were also being investigated. A House committee revealed that he had paid less than $1000 in taxes in both 1971 and 1972 even though he had earned $200,000 each year. His low taxes were based on a questionable gift of his vice-presidential papers (which he valued at $570,000) to the National Archives in 1969. This had saved him $235,000 in taxes. It also came out that $10 million in federal funds had been spent on his properties at Key Biscayne in Florida and San Clemente in California and on his daughters' houses. Even though the money was said to be for security for the President and his family, the amounts seemed to be way out of line.

By early 1974 President Nixon was under such pressure that he was no longer able to govern effectively. But still he held on, although he spent as little time as possible in Washington.

On March 1, 1974, Mitchell, Haldeman, Ehrlichman, and five others were indicted by a grand jury for conspiring to cover up the Watergate break-in, for obstructing justice, and for perjury. In a secret report the grand jury also named Nixon as a co-conspirator. He was not indicted because the new Special Prosecutor, Leon Jaworski, argued that a President could not be indicted until he had been impeached and removed from office.

Nixon made one last desperate attempt to escape his problems. On April 29, 1974, he went on television. He was seated before a tall stack of blue notebooks, which he described as the transcripts of more tapes that he had recently been asked for—and which he had refused to hand over. These, he said, contained everything about Watergate "and what I did about it."

Committee chairman Sam Ervin swears in H. R. Haldeman during the Senate probe of the Watergate break-in.

James H. Pickerell

The transcripts astounded the country. They revealed the President and his aides as petty men, speaking in vulgar expletives. They were constantly scheming about how to "get" their enemies. Senator Hugh Scott of Pennsylvania, leader of the Republicans in the Senate, called the tapes "a shabby, disgusting, immoral performance."

Still the Judiciary Committee and Jaworski continued to press Nixon for the actual tapes themselves. When he refused, the question went on its way to the Supreme Court.

The House committee favors impeachment. Under the Constitution, the House of Representatives has to vote the articles of impeachment against a President. Then the President is tried by the whole Senate, with the Chief Justice presiding.

On July 24, after nearly three months of private hearings, the House Judiciary Committee began its public televised debate over the articles of impeachment. On July 27 the committee voted 27 to 11 in favor of Article 1—that the President had followed a "course of conduct or plan" to obstruct justice in the cover-up of the Watergate break-in. Six Republicans had joined the 21 Democrats to vote against their President. Two days later, the committee voted a second article of impeachment—that the President had abused his power when he used the Plumbers, the IRS, FBI, CIA, and other government agencies in violation of the constitutional rights of citizens. Finally, on July 30, it voted 21 to 17 to impeach the President also for failing to abide by legal House subpoenas. The committee voted against attempting to impeach the President for the secret bombing of Cambodia or for evading taxes or for using government funds on his homes.

The whole nation watched in sadness—but also in awe and admiration—as they saw the men and women of the committee show such judicial fairness. The committee as a whole seemed to rise above the bitterness of partisan politics. The nation was inspired to see its representatives take such pains to cleanse the White House. As it became plain that the committee would have to vote to impeach the

President Nixon sits before a stack of notebooks containing what he claimed to be the full transcripts of the Watergate tapes.

President, some committee members of both parties were in tears. They, too, were saddened at what they had to do.

The President resigns. Even at this point, it seemed possible that the House of Representatives might vote not to approve the committee's report. Or, even if they did approve the three articles of impeachment, perhaps the President would not be convicted by the Senate. Some members of Congress still felt that the committee had not found the "smoking gun"—the clear, unmistakable evidence of a presidential act to cover up the break-in. Without such evidence, should a few hundred representatives in Congress vote to remove from office a Chief Executive who had been voted into office by a majority of millions of Americans? Some of the

⇉ Continuity and Change: The Constitution Remind students that many were concerned that Nixon's impeachment would set a precedent enabling Congress to remove a President from office simply over personality conflict or policy differences. However, the Constitution makes it very difficult to remove a President from office. In 1868, at the impeachment trial of Andrew Johnson, accusers had to prove him guilty of (as outlined in the Constitution) "treason, bribery, or other high crimes and misdemeanors." Since they were unable to do this because Johnson had not committed a crime, he remained in office. (See p. 370.)

```
            THE WHITE HOUSE
              WASHINGTON

            August 9, 1974


Dear Mr. Secretary:

I hereby resign the Office of President of the
United States.

              Sincerely,

              Richard Nixon

                              11.35 AM

The Honorable Henry A. Kissinger           HK
The Secretary of State
Washington, D.C.  20520
```

Nixon's Materials Project, National Archives

Richard Nixon's brief letter of resignation was delivered to Secretary of State Henry Kissinger. The time and Kissinger's initials are in the lower right-hand corner.

That night, as the fall of the President seemed certain, Secretary of Defense James R. Schlesinger took the unheard-of action of ordering all United States military commanders to refuse to accept orders from the White House unless they were countersigned by him. The President could no longer be trusted. The following day Nixon informed the Cabinet that he still would not resign. Congress would have to impeach him. But on August 7 three of the most respected Republican leaders—Senator Hugh Scott, Senator Barry Goldwater, and Representative John Rhodes—called on President Nixon and made it clear that he had no support. If he tried to stand and fight, they said, he would be impeached by the House, and then he would be convicted by the Senate.

The next day Nixon, on television to the nation, announced his decision to resign. On August 9, 1974, he signed the official letter of resignation. He was the first President ever forced to leave office before the end of his term.

While the tearful former President was flying across the nation to his home in San Clemente, California, back in Washington Gerald Ford was being sworn in as the thirty-eighth President of the United States.

(p. 837) members of Congress still feared that they would set a precedent. Would some future Congress remove a President simply because they did not like him or disagreed with his policy?

The tapes (which the President himself had ordered to insure his place in history!) proved Richard Nixon's final undoing. The Supreme Court decided on July 24 that he had to hand them over. Then the President could hide no longer. On August 5, 1974, he confessed that portions of the tape for June 23, 1972, were "at variance with certain of my previous statements." That tape clearly recorded the President in his own voice ordering Haldeman to get the CIA to stop the FBI investigation of the break-in. This showed that Nixon had lied all along about when he knew of the cover-up and that he had, in fact, personally ordered the cover-up.

See "Section 3 Review answers," p. 816D.

Section 3 Review

1. Identify or explain: wiretaps, Daniel Ellsberg, "Plumbers," George McGovern, Sargent Shriver, Lawrence O'Brien, Woodward and Bernstein, Ervin Committee, Elliot Richardson, Archibald Cox, 25th Amendment, Gerald Ford, oil embargo, "Saturday Night Massacre," Leon Jaworski.

2. Account for President Nixon's easy victory in the 1972 election.

3. Recount the highlights of the Watergate affair from the break-ins to Nixon's resignation.

4. **Critical Thinking: Recognizing Ideologies.** How was Nixon's preoccupation with "national security" reflected in his pursuit of his "enemies"?

Critical Thinking Activity: Determining Relevance How did Richard Nixon's resignation affect the nation? Construct a chart on the chalkboard with the heading "Richard Nixon's resignation." Then form two columns labeled "Pluses" and "Minuses." Have the class complete the chart by suggesting appropriate evidence for both columns. Using the information from the chart have students discuss the effect of Nixon's resignation on the nation. Encourage students to support their opinions with items in the chart.

Chapter 33 Review

See "Chapter Review answers," p. 816E.

Focusing on Ideas

1. Why have modern Presidents required a large White House staff? What problems arise from this arrangement?

2. Why did President Nixon undertake to establish relations with the People's Republic of China? Why was Nixon well suited to bring about this change of policy?

3. In May 1969 what conditions did Nixon rule out in the Vietnam peace negotiations? Were those conditions met? Explain.

4. How did two resignations bring Gerald Ford to the Presidency?

Taking a Critical Look

1. **Drawing Conclusions.** How did the "Sense of the Senate" resolution in 1969 reflect popular opposition to the Vietnam War?

2. **Recognizing Cause and Effect.** Opinion polls taken in 1973 and 1976 showed a sharp drop in people's "trust in government." What may have been some other side effects of Watergate?

Your Region in History

1. **Geography.** Was your state legislature reapportioned as a result of the 1984 Supreme Court decision in *Reynolds* v. *Sims*? If so, how has your county or other election district been affected by reapportionment?

2. **Culture.** Was your school district affected by the 1962 and 1963 Supreme Court decisions on religious exercises? Explain. How do those decisions affect your school today?

3. **Economics.** Collect data on the cost of living, rate of unemployment, and average salary earned for your region during the Nixon era. How does this information relate to major Nixon Administration economic policies? Did Nixon win a majority of votes in your region in his bid for reelection?

Historical Facts and Figures

Synthesizing Information. Study the graph below to help answer the following questions: (a) Approximately how many American soldiers were in Vietnam in 1968? In 1970? In 1973? (b) Contrast the following list of events with the information presented in the graph:

1970 American troops sent into Cambodia to attack enemy bases. Secret bombings of Cambodia begin.

1971 American helicopters and bombers help South Vietnamese invade Laos.

1972 United States resumes bombings over North Vietnam.

1973 Peace agreement and cease-fire begin.

What information in the chapter helps explain why the United States was reducing troop strength at the time that our involvement in the Indochina war was expanding?

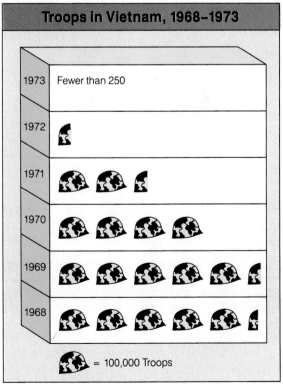

Source: Department of Defense

MAKING CONNECTIONS
Unit 11

This unit began on page 773 with the observation that the 1960s would herald the beginning of a turbulent era for the United States, punctuated by the convictions of a new generation:

"Let the word go forth from this time and place, to friend and foe alike, that the torch has been passed to a new generation of Americans. . . ."

This declaration was supported by the three unit themes that are reprinted in **dark type** below. Use the time line and the information in Unit 11 to answer the questions that follow the unit themes.

THEMES IN HISTORY

Using "Making Connections": Have students look at the unit themes printed in dark type. Explain that each event on the time line relates to one of these themes. Ask students to decide which events are related to which theme. Students should use events from the time line in their answers and explain how events are related. Have students go back through the text of Unit 11 to find other events related to the unit themes.

Events in American History

GOVERNMENT AND POLITICS

1. **John F. Kennedy's 1000 days in office bring optimism to the nation.**
   How did John F. Kennedy lift American spirits? What did he accomplish?   (Drawing Conclusions)

2. **Lyndon Johnson's strong leadership expands opportunities for all Americans while deeply dividing the country over the war in Vietnam.**   SOCIAL CHANGE
   What questions did President Johnson's domestic and foreign policies raise concerning American values?   (Formulating Questions)

3. **The Watergate scandal tests the nation's constitutional system of government and leads to President Nixon's resignation.**   THE CONSTITUTION
   How did President Nixon's beliefs about the powers of the Presidency create an atmosphere in which the Watergate affair occurred?   (Recognizing Ideologies)

┌1961
President Kennedy proposes the Peace Corps and the Alliance for Progress.

┌1963
200,000 black and white freedom marchers gather at the Lincoln Memorial to demand civil rights reform.

1961   **1963**

Events in World History

└1961
The Soviet Union builds the Berlin Wall, sealing off East Berlin.

└1963
Ngo Dinh Diem, South Vietnam's president, is overthrown in a military coup.

1964
Congress passes the Tonkin Gulf Resolution, expanding U.S. involvement in Vietnam.

1965
The Voting Rights Act aids black voter registration.

1971
President Nixon announces a 90-day wage-price freeze.

1967
Race riots erupt in Cleveland, Detroit, Boston, Newark, and other cities.

1972
The United States establishes relations with the People's Republic of China.

1973
Congress begins hearings into the Watergate affair.

1974
Richard Nixon becomes the first United States President to resign.

| 1965 | 1967 | 1969 | 1971 | 1973 | 1975 | 1977 |

1968
North Vietnam launches the Tet offensive, surrounding American troops.

1971
The United Nations votes to admit the People's Republic of China and to expel Taiwan.

Unit 12

Writing about History and Art: Direct students' attention to the unit introduction, illustration, and list of themes on pages 842–843. Have the introduction and unit themes read aloud. After a brief discussion of the subject matter of the unit, instruct students to write a brief paragraph, explaining how the art:

—relates to the unit themes;
—exemplifies the unit title and illustrates the introduction; and
—is an appropriate choice for the unit.

The United States Looks Ahead

When the United States had its two-hundredth birthday in 1976, it was already the oldest of the new nations. And when in 1987 Americans celebrated the two-hundredth anniversary of the framing of the Constitution, the nation was living by the world's oldest written constitution still in use.

Since the Civil War, Americans had been seeking ways to keep their country young in spirit. The nation had been kept young by always asking what it meant to be an American.

In these next years the nation, more anxiously than ever before, would seek equality of opportunity for all Americans. Congress passed laws, and citizens organized, to bring women, as well as black, brown, and red Americans, and handicapped Americans into the mainstream of national life.

Competition—within the nation and between nations—was still strenuous and demanding. The unusual American opportunities and needs to compete had made the nation strong and would keep the nation strong.

The millions of immigrants, their children and their children's children, would still seek new opportunities for themselves and all other Americans to show what they could do. "We can no longer say there is nothing new under the sun," Thomas Jefferson had written back in 1801. As the twentieth century neared its close, the United States remained a nation of experiments.

 THEMES IN HISTORY

- Congress passes legislation intended to extend equality of opportunity to all Americans.   SOCIAL CHANGE
- Conflicts with other nations create new problems for the United States.   CONFLICT
- The end of the cold war brought new opportunities and new challenges for the United States.   GOVERNMENT AND POLITICS

▣ Modern computers, developed after World War II, excel not only at mathematical calculation but can be used for a wide variety of other applications—even art. This picture, created on a computer by artist David Em, was entitled "Escher" after Dutch artist M. C. Escher whose strange pictures often, like this one, contained odd optical illusions that baffled the eye.
"Escher, 1979" © David Em/Represented by Spieckerman Associates, San Francisco

Chapter 34
In Pursuit of Civil Rights for All

Identifying Chapter Materials

Objectives	Basic Instructional Materials	Extension Materials
1 The Two Ideals • Explain how the struggle to ensure equal opportunity in America comes into conflict with the ideal of individual freedom.	**Annotated Teacher's Edition** • Lesson Plans, p. 844C **Instructional Support File** • Pre-Reading Activities, Unit 12, p. 1	**American History Transparencies** • Our Multicultural Heritage, p. C31
2 Dealing with Racism • Understand the progress toward equality for blacks since 1954.	**Annotated Teacher's Edition** • Lesson Plans, pp. 844C–844D	**Documents of American History** • *Regents of the University of California* v. *Bakke*, Vol. 2, p. 830
3 Women Seek Equality • Identify the barriers overcome since the 1950s and the barriers remaining to equality for women.	**Annotated Teacher's Edition** • Lesson Plans, pp. 844D–844E **Instructional Support File** • Skill Application Activity, Unit 12, p. 5 • Critical Thinking Activity, Unit 12, p. 6	**Documents of American History** • *Roe et al.* v. *Wade*, Vol. 2, p. 798 **American History Transparencies** • Fine Art, p. D81
4 The American Indians • Describe the policy of the United States government toward Native Americans since the New Deal.	**Annotated Teacher's Edition** • Lesson Plans, pp. 844E–844F	**Extension Activity** • Native American Tribes Today, Lesson Plans, p. 844F
5 Spanish-Speaking Peoples • Explain the diversity among Hispanics in the United States.	**Annotated Teacher's Edition** • Lesson Plans, pp. 844F	**American History Transparencies** • Our Multicultural Heritage, p. C107
6 New Waves of Immigration • Identify recent changes in immigration patterns and legislation.	**Annotated Teacher's Edition** • Lesson Plans, pp. 844F–844G	**Enrichment Support File** • Building a Nation (See "In-Depth Coverage" at right.) **Perspectives** • The New Immigrants (See "In-Depth Coverage" at right.)
7 New Vistas of Equality • Identify the demands for equality of special groups in our society.	**Annotated Teacher's Edition** • Lesson Plans, pp. 844G–844H **Instructional Support File** • Reading Activities, Unit 12, pp. 2–3 • Skill Review Activity, Unit 12, p. 4 • Chapter Test, Unit 12, pp. 7–10 • Additional Test Questions, Unit 12, pp. 11–14	**Extension Activity** • Theme Link, Lesson Plans, p. 844H.

Providing In-Depth Coverage

34

Perspectives on the New Immigrants

In 1986 the United States celebrated the centennial of the Statue of Liberty. The statue represented the hopes of the millions of immigrants who entered New York Harbor. Today, immigrants are more likely to arrive at airports in Florida, New York, and Los Angeles, or to cross the border from Mexico. The new Americans of today are most likely to come from Asia, Latin America, the Caribbean, or the Middle East, rather than from Europe.

Most of these new immigrants—old and young—eventually adapt to the American way of life. The traditions they keep, however, contribute to a unique American culture.

A History of the United States as an instructional program provides three types of resources you can use to offer in-depth coverage of immigration to the United States in the late twentieth century: the *student text*, the *Enrichment Support File*, and *Perspectives*. The chart below shows the topics that are covered in each.

THE STUDENT TEXT. Boorstin and Kelley's *A History of the United States* unfolds the chronology of events and the controversy of new waves of immigration in the late twentieth century.

AMERICAN HISTORY ENRICHMENT SUPPORT FILE. This collection of primary source readings and classroom activities focuses on Asian immigrants in the late twentieth century.

PERSPECTIVES: READINGS ON AMERICAN HISTORY IN THE 20TH CENTURY. In this edited collection of secondary source readings, well-known historians and political commentators (including Boorstin) provide an array of perspectives on the immigrants of the late twentieth century.

Locating Instructional Materials

Detailed lesson plans for teaching Asian immigrants as a mini-course or to study one or more elements of the new wave of immigration in depth are offered in the following areas: in the *student text*, see individual lesson plans at the beginning of each chapter; in the *Enrichment Support File*, see page 3; in *Perspectives*, see the Teacher's Guide for this topic.

IN-DEPTH COVERAGE OF THE NEW IMMIGRANTS

Student Text	Enrichment Support File	Perspectives
▪ Asians from many nations, p. 868 ▪ Spanish-speaking peoples, pp. 864–867 ▪ Latin America and the Caribbean, pp. 868–869 ▪ Immigration Reform, p. 869	▪ Lesson Suggestions ▪ Multimedia Resources ▪ Overview Essay/Building a Nation: Immigration in the 1980s ▪ Literature in American History/Lost and Found ▪ Art in American History/Enriching American Art ▪ Biography in American History/Haing Ngor ▪ Great Debates in American History/ Should the Classroom Be Bilingual? ▪ Making Connections	▪ "Young Immigrant Wave Lifts New York Economy," by Richard Levine ▪ "La Frontera" by Bill Barich ▪ "Give Us Your Brainpower" by Mortimer B. Zuckerman ▪ "The Splintered Society" by Richard D. Lamm and Gary Imhoff ▪ "America's Changing Face" by Tim Mathews with Anne Underwood and Clara Bingham

The Two Ideals

FOCUS

To introduce the lesson, write on the board the words "Complete Freedom the Goal," and have students list examples of what life might be like in a country where no restraints are placed on individuals. (The strongest and most forceful would soon manage to take charge. The weakest would be left with little or nothing. The strong, of course, would try to maintain their position, and thus even freedom would be lost.) In another column write "Complete Equality the Goal," and have students list what life might be like in a country in which no one is allowed to lag behind or get ahead of anyone else—in schooling, in jobs, in income, in housing, even in clothing. (Dull, unmotivated, likely to lose its creativity and excellence, less than free, etc.) Looking at the absolutes in this way will help students see that "freedom" does not mean the complete absence of rules and restraints, and that "equality" does not mean an enforced sameness for everybody.

Developing Vocabulary

The words listed in this chapter are essential terms for reading and understanding particular sections of the chapter. The page number after each term indicates the page of its first or most important appearance in the chapter. These terms are defined in the text Glossary (text pages 1000–1011).

natural aristocracy (page 846); **discrimination** (page 848).

INSTRUCT

Explain

Discuss whether the scenarios in the Focus activity could coexist. Introduce the notion of equal opportunity.

☑ Writing Process Activity

Expressing Problems Clearly Ask students to imagine they are immigrants who have experienced discrimination. In preparation for writing an article for a neighborhood newspaper, ask students to brainstorm details about how civil rights laws can guarantee them the freedom and equality promised by the Constitution. Students should begin their article by explaining what happened and what needs to be changed. As they revise, students should check that they have used facts and examples to clarify their position. After proofreading, students can publish a newspaper of immigrant concerns.

Section Review Answers

Section 1, page 850

1. The Old World aristocracy was made up of people who were born into the ranks of the nobility and therefore had wealth, status, and the power to rule. Jefferson's "natural aristocracy" was to include those who were most able, most industrious, most educated. They would be elected to rule because of their talents and knowledge. 2. Discrimination is a "social disease" because it harms society in several ways. First, discrimination obviously harms the group or groups that suffer inequalities. They are not given their fair chance for success. They may become angry and lash out in violence and riots, which hurts everyone. Society is deprived of the contributions of all its members if some groups are not allowed to achieve their full potential. 3. Free education theoretically gives everyone a chance to start the "race" of life equally; it theoretically gives everyone an equal chance to "win" in life. 4. Equality means that each person in American society should have education, health, and decent housing. Each person should be eligible for schools, jobs, housing, clubs. No one should be kept out because of race, sex, religion, or where their family came from. Freedom means that each person is free to achieve and do as much as he or she can or desires. A person's income and status depend to a great extent on his or her actions. Everyone cannot be an equal winner if there is true freedom. Some people will always be richer, smarter, and stronger than others.

CLOSE

To conclude the lesson, tell the class that by 1980 the nation and Supreme Court had failed to reach a consensus on affirmative action. (Note the 5–4 vote and the number of different opinions expressed by the justices on both the *Bakke* case and the *Weber* case.) The distinctions drawn in the *Bakke* and *Weber* decisions leave the legality of other quota programs up in the air. The issue is likely to remain ambiguous in the United States for some time.

Dealing with Racism

FOCUS

To introduce the lesson, have students scan the section entitled "Deep-seated problems" and locate the evidence suggesting substantial gains for blacks in recent years. Ask the class to explain those gains in historical terms.

Developing Vocabulary

affirmative action (page 850); **reverse discrimination** (page 851); **quota** (page 851).

INSTRUCT

Explain

Review school desegregation and affirmative action as attempts to end discrimination. Discuss the objective of each policy, how it affected individual freedom, and the gains and problems that resulted.

★ Independent Activity

Demonstrating Reasoned Judgment Have each student write a brief speech arguing for or against busing or affirmative action. Should the student choose to argue against the policy, he or she should propose an alternate method of eliminating discrimination. After proofreading for logic and coherence, students may read their arguments to the class.

Section Review Answers

Section 2, page 855

1. a) idea that a person's race determines his or her character or ability, and that one race is superior to others; prejudice against or preference for the members of a race. b) separation of people according to some standard, usually race—in schools, housing, industry, and public facilities. c) an end to segregation. 2. School segregation continued in part because of housing segregation, partly because whites wanted it to continue. If blacks and whites live in separate neighborhoods and children are assigned to schools based on where they live, then schools will also tend to be segregated. Often, whites made sure this was the case by building new schools and drawing school district lines in ways that guaranteed segregated schools. In addition, whites kept schools segregated by taking their children out of public schools and establishing new, all-white private schools. 3. It pressured the country into passing laws that decreased racial discrimination and gave blacks some tools that would allow them to protect their rights. As a result, blacks broke barriers that had kept them out of colleges and high-status jobs. 4. Affirmative action means taking positive, active steps to undo the damage of decades or even centuries of discrimination. For example, it means not just allowing blacks into medical schools or women into executive positions but making special efforts to recruit blacks and women. Sometimes affirmative action programs have set goals for hiring a certain number of minorities and women; as a result, minorities or women might be hired instead of equally qualified or even more qualified white males. In these cases white males are in the position that minorities and women usually hold:

they are put at a disadvantage just because of their race or sex. Hence affirmative action programs have been called "reverse discrimination."

CLOSE

To conclude the lesson, ask students to prepare short talks on the issues of homelessness and drug use among urban minorities. Ask students to explain in their talks how these problems are related to urban poverty in the United States.

Section 3 (pages 855–860)

Women Seek Equality

FOCUS

To introduce the lesson, ask students: What are the effects of increasing employment among women? (Some possible answers: increasing divorce rate, lower birth rate, more people living alone.) Students may recognize that some of the factors they listed as causes they are now listing as effects. Thus they may have committed the post hoc fallacy—they may have listed something as a cause that may actually be an effect.

INSTRUCT

Explain

Explain the difference between formal and informal barriers to equality. Using the issue of hiring, have students contribute examples of both.

☑ Writing Process Activity

Recognizing Ideologies Ask students to imagine they are magazine reporters with the task of explaining the women's equal rights movement. Students should first consider whether they are pro- or anti-feminist. In their article, they might contrast the movements of the 19th and 20th centuries, or they might write an interview with Betty Friedan or Phyllis Schlafly. Students should begin with an introductory paragraph that clarifies their position and the particular aspect they have chosen. During revising, students should check for logical organization and completeness. After proofreading, they can publish a women's rights magazine.

Section Review Answers

Section 3, page 860

1. a) founder of the National Organization for Women. b) National Organization for Women. c) proposed amendment which would have barred discrimination on the basis of sex; it was never adopted. d) case in which the Supreme Court ruled that the states could

34

not make it illegal for women to have abortions. 2. Attitudes and customs kept women from achieving equality. For example, women were expected to take care of the home and children, a fact that discouraged employers from giving women top jobs. 3. a) Increased presence of women in positions of political power and in jobs once held only by men. There were 1168 women in 1987 state legislatures and holding statewide office, compared to just 301 in 1969. In the 1980s, 50 percent of the Bachelors degrees given by colleges and universities went to women. By 1986, 20 percent of all lawyers were women and 18 percent of all doctors. In some other professions, women held half of the jobs as compared to one-third as recently as 1983. b) In the workplace, a female college graduate can expect to earn only slightly more than a male high school dropout. Daycare centers are scarce, making it difficult for women with children to work outside the home.

CLOSE

To conclude the lesson, ask: How have women's roles in the workplace changed dramatically in the United States and why? (Students should recognize that changes have been the result of other changes in our society, and have contributed to further changes.)

Section 4 (pages 860–863)

The American Indians

FOCUS

To introduce the lesson, tell the students that members of the American Indian Movement occupied the offices of the BIA in Washington in 1972, and in 1973 they took over the village of Wounded Knee, where they fought with government agents and destroyed property. Other Indians worked to win their rights by taking their case to the courts and by gaining influence in government agencies responsible for Indian affairs. Then ask: What course would you be likely to follow if you were an American Indian and faced the conditions and treatment that Indians endure in the current era?

Developing Vocabulary
reservations (page 860)

INSTRUCT

Explain
Tell students that in the 1980s, the Bureau of Indian Affairs counted about 650,000 Indians residing on or

near reservations. The largest group is the Navaho (parts of Arizona, New Mexico, and Utah). Other large reservations include the Creek, Cherokee, and Choctaw in Oklahoma; the Southern Pueblos in New Mexico; and the Pine Ridge and Rosebud (Sioux) in South Dakota.

★ Independent Activity
Identifying Central Issues Have students construct a chart with the following three column headings: Policy, Rationale, and Results. Using pages 234–236, 385–391, and 867–870 in their texts, students will fill in the columns with the different approaches the United States has adopted for dealing with Native Americans.

Section Review Answers
Section 4, page 863

1. a) granted full citizenship to American Indians. b) village on the Oglala Sioux Pine Ridge Reservation in South Dakota. In 1890 Indians were slaughtered there by United States soldiers; in 1973 armed members of the American Indian Movement took over the village. c) member of the Blackfoot tribe, appointed Assistant Secretary of the Interior for Indian Affairs in 1977. 2. The "termination" policy tried to end federal involvement in Indian affairs and shift all responsibility for the Indians to the states. The states failed to provide adequate health, education, and welfare services. The "relocation" policy tried to induce Indians to move to cities. But many Indians who did relocate felt displaced. 3. President Johnson persuaded Congress to enact federal aid programs for Indians to raise their standard of living, a reversal of the termination policy initiated under President Eisenhower. President Nixon called explicitly for an end to the termination policy and proposed that Indians themselves run the federal programs on Indian reservations. The relocation program also ended during the Nixon administration, in 1972. 4. Indians regained millions of acres of land and more control over their resources by winning suits in the courts. In addition, passage of the Indian Self-Determination and Education Assistance Act of 1975 promised Indians greater control over their reservations and educational programs. 5. Members occupied the offices of the BIA in Washington in 1972, and in 1973 they took over the village of Wounded Knee. Other Indians worked to win their rights by taking their cases to the courts and by gaining influence in government agencies responsible for Indian affairs.

CLOSE

To conclude the lesson, ask students whether they would recommend that the government adopt an approach that is different from the one it is currently following under the Indian Self-Determination and Education Assistance Act. Ask: Why doesn't the government close the reservations and treat Indians just like any other citizens? (The legacy of taking their lands for settlement, and the experience of the disastrous effects for the Indians of Eisenhower's termination and relocation programs.)

Extension Activity

Ask students to choose an Indian tribe which is still in existence today. Tell students that they are to research the tribe and write a short report detailing its present-day activities.

Section 5 (pages 864–867)

Spanish-Speaking Peoples

FOCUS

To introduce the lesson, ask: How many of you have ancestors who were immigrants? (Point out that all Americans—probably even American Indians—are descended from people who were immigrants.) Did your ancestors help the country? Should the country have kept them out? What is the difference between your ancestors' immigration and the new immigration of Spanish-speaking peoples, Southeast Asian refugees, and Haitians?

Developing Vocabulary

Chicano (page 864); **boycott** (page 865); **commonwealth** (page 866).

INSTRUCT

Explain

Remind students that the Immigration Act of 1924, in setting up the quota system, had put no quota on immigration from independent nations of the western hemisphere (p. 580). This policy had been continued in the McCarran-Walter Act of 1952. Then the Immigration Act of 1965 provided an annual limit of 120,000 persons from Canada and Latin America. (Refugees were an exception to this limit.) A 1976 amendment to the 1965 law kept the overall limit of 120,000 for the western hemisphere but put a limit of 20,000 on immigration from any one country. And instead of admitting these western hemisphere immigrants on a first-come, first-serve basis, the 1976 law gave preference to close relatives of U.S. residents and to persons with needed talents and skills. The effect of the 1965 law and the 1976 amendments was to put restraint on Latin American immigration.

✿ Cooperative Learning Activity

Making Comparisons Break the class into groups of three. Explain that students will collect data to make a graph showing population statistics for the different groups of Spanish-speaking peoples in the United States in 1990. Have group members decide whether to make a pictograph or a bar or a pie graph. Then have group members decide who will prepare the graph and who will explain it to the class. Display completed graphs following the presentations.

Section Review Answers

Section 5, page 867

1. a) "the people." Mexican Americans sometimes call themselves *La Raza.* b) city neighborhoods populated by Mexican Americans. c) senator from New Mexico, opposed Tijerina's "Brown Power" movement. d) Chicano leader who founded the Crusade for Justice in Denver in 1965. e) first elected governor of the Commonwealth of Puerto Rico. He helped develop both Operation Bootstrap and the plan that made Puerto Rico a commonwealth of the United States. f) plan for improving Puerto Rican agriculture and attracting industry to the island. 2. Mexican Americans, Puerto Ricans, and Cubans. A large percentage of Mexican Americans live in California, Colorado, Texas, Arizona, and New Mexico. About half of the Puerto Ricans who have settled on the mainland live in New York. A very high proportion of Cuban Americans have settled in Florida, especially Miami. 3. Unlike Hispanics who have come to this country from other nations, Puerto Ricans who come to the United States mainland are already United States citizens. However, they cannot vote in national elections and do not pay federal income taxes on money earned in Puerto Rico. 4. By organizing a union of farm laborers Cesar Chavez gained better wages and working conditions, as well as greater freedom and dignity, for farm workers in California, many of whom were Mexican Americans.

CLOSE

To conclude the lesson, tell students to write an immigration law as homework. Tell them to recall the issues discussed in class as they complete the assignment.

Section 6 (pages 868–869)

New Waves of Immigration

FOCUS

To introduce the lesson, have students imagine that they are living in one of the countries mentioned in this section. Ask each student to write a letter to the

Immigration Service explaining why he or she would like to emigrate to the United States. Each letter should contain at least two reasons.

INSTRUCT

Explain

Write these words on the blackboard:

> Give me your tired, your poor,Your huddled masses yearning to breathe free,The wretched refuse of your teeming shore, Send these, the homeless, tempest-tossed, to me: I lift my lamp beside the golden door.

Ask: Where are these words inscribed? (The base of the Statue of Liberty. They are from the poem "The New Colossus" by Emma Lazarus.) What immigration policy do they show? (On the basis of whether the immigrant wants to enter.) Should this policy be continued today? What are the arguments for restricting immigration? (Fear of increased urban poverty and overcrowding, fear of competition for jobs, etc.)

☑ Writing Process Activity

Identifying Central Issues Ask students to imagine that as President during the 1970s or 1980s, they must have a clear policy regarding illegal aliens. In preparation for writing a speech about this issue, have students outline the reasons why they do or do not want to pass a law against illegal aliens. Students should begin their speech with a strong topic sentence that summarizes their position, and they should support it with facts and examples. Ask students to revise for logical organization and persuasive language. After proofreading, students can deliver their speeches to the class.

Section Review Answers

Section 6, page 869

1. In the 1970s and 1980s, many refugees from South Vietnam, Laos, and Cambodia fled to the United States when Communists took over their countries. Immigrants from Asia came in large numbers seeking a better life. Another major group of immigrants came from Haiti. They were fleeing repression and violence. Refugees from war and strife in Central America also made their way to the United States. 2. The old laws were not consistently enforced. Many illegal immigrants worked hard for many years in the United States, and their children were United States citizens. It did not seem right to deport them. However, the enormous number of illegal aliens crossing our borders had to be reduced. 3. In the Sanctuary movement of the 1980s, religious groups such as churches and synagogues offered safety, homes, and jobs to people fleeing from Central America who were in the United States illegally. The oper-

ators of the Underground Railroad moved runaway slaves through the country into freedom in Canada. The Sanctuary movement violated immigration laws. The Underground Railroad violated laws against helping runaway slaves. One major difference between the two is that the Sanctuary movement attempted to hide refugees permanently, whereas the Underground Railroad moved the slaves out of the United States to Canada.

CLOSE

To conclude the lesson, ask students to think about the various ethnic groups represented in their own neighborhoods. What are the benefits of a mixed neighborhood? Are there any drawbacks? If students live in primarily homogeneous neighborhoods do they feel positively or negatively about this? Discuss these issues as a class, allowing for all points of view. Be sure students provide facts to support their opinions.

Section 7 (pages 869–874)

New Vistas of Equality

FOCUS

To introduce the lesson, write on the board names of other minority groups who face discrimination (the physically or mentally handicapped, homosexuals, language minorities). Have students list changes in our society or laws that each group has worked for.

Developing Vocabulary

mainstreaming (page 872); **bilingual** (page 873).

INSTRUCT

Explain

Point out to students that voters in some states are attempting to prevent legislation that provides civil rights protections for homosexuals. The courts are in the process of determining if this is legal.

☑ Writing Process Activity

Identifying Alternatives Ask students to imagine they are teachers in a school that has a large number of immigrants. In preparation for debating the issue of bilingual education in front of the school board, ask them to take a stand on this issue and to list their reasons. Students should begin their essay with a statement expressing their position, and they should defend it with specific facts and examples. As they revise, students should be sure they have considered the arguments of the other side. After proofreading, pairs of students representing different positions can debate the issue in a mock school board meeting.

Section Review Answers

Section 7, page 874

1. The Rehabilitation Act of 1973 forbade discrimination against the physically disabled in programs and facilities supported by federal funds; numerous federal regulations made everyday life easier for the handicapped, giving them better access to public facilities; and laws and court decisions brought handicapped children out of special institutions and into the nation's public schools and colleges. 2. Taking the handicapped out of special institutions and bringing them into the mainstream of American education. 3. Primarily to make children proud of their cultural heritage.

CLOSE

To conclude the lesson, point out that by 1980 thirteen states had mandated bilingual education programs, and some federal judges had ordered its use in certain school districts or even over entire states. There is no question that it will remain a controversial topic. Why does the prediction of demographers that by the year 2000 Hispanics will be the largest minority in the United States make this such an important issue? (Ramifications for national unity, political effects.) Ask: Do you think that the United States should follow the example of Canada (where French is required as well as English) and have every American, regardless of ethnic background, learn Spanish as well as English? Why or why not?

Extension Activity

Have students look at the Unit themes listed on page 843 of their texts and select the one which they believe best relates to this section of the chapter. Students will then write a paragraph or two defending their choice by providing information from the section.

Chapter Review Answers

Focusing on Ideas

1. Competition leads to the largest amount of goods and services—a bigger "pie" for all to share. Costs may include inequalities and use of unfair tactics. 2. Easy acquisition of land and few rules inhibited the development of an aristocracy. However, slavery allowed a landed aristocracy to develop in the South. 3. Equality: Any law that removes political disabilities or provides benefits to the poorer classes. A discussion should elicit that those at the top try to keep their advantages and that unrestricted competition could limit equality.

Taking a Critical Look

1. Answers may vary. Example might include deregulation laws which promote competition or minimum income laws to get rid of worst cases of inequality. 2. Political equality helps bring about and maintain other equalities—religious, economic, and so on. 3. The relocation program ended during the Nixon administration in 1972. In the 1970s Indians regained land and control by winning suits in court. The Indian Self-Determination and Education Assistance Act passed in 1975.

Your Region in History

1–3. Answers will vary depending on your region. Consult your local library or historical society.

Historical Facts and Figures

(a) 1955—35.7%; 1965—39.3%; 1990—57.5%; (b) affirmative action; the 1972 Equal Employment Opportunity Act; the rising level of education for women; inflation; the rising American standard of living. (c) 1995, 60%; 2000, 63% (d) Answers should point out that the number of working women depends on several factors.

Chapter 34

Focusing the Chapter: Have students identify the chapter logo. Discuss what unit theme the logo might symbolize. Then ask students to skim the chapter to identify illustrations or titles that relate to this theme.

In Pursuit of Civil Rights for All

The late twentieth century was a time of climax. Never before had Americans cared so much for the ideal of equality. Never before had they worked so hard to keep Americans free—to choose their President, to decide on their laws, to know their government. It was not surprising, then, that this was a difficult time.

It was difficult, too, because the nation was built not only on the ideal of equality, but also on the ideal of freedom. Equality and freedom were twin ideals. Equality meant the right to be equal at the ballot box and in the courts. Freedom meant the right to have your say, to believe and worship as you pleased, to grow and be educated according to your talents, to choose your job, and to compete for the best things in life. In the two centuries of the nation's life both these ideals had grown. And it had combined the two quests—for equality and for freedom—more successfully than any other nation.

Equality meant opportunity, freedom meant competition. Although the twin ideals—equality and freedom—both came from the American Revolution, as the years went on the two ideals had not always worked together.

After the famous physicist Albert Einstein came to the United States in 1933 to escape Nazi anti-Semitism, Ben Shahn made this painting of him arriving carrying his violin. Among the other immigrants portrayed is the Lithuanian-born Shahn himself. He is the man wearing number 76.

See "Lesson Plan," p. 844C.

1. The two ideals

We can understand why equality and freedom sometimes conflicted if we think of life in America as a kind of game. Of course everyone wanted to be a winner. But to keep the factories and the farms going, and to keep life pleasant, the game had to be played by certain rules. That meant, of course, that there would be winners and losers. The nation would be strong and keep its place in the world only if the rules made it possible for everybody to have a chance to play—and then let the best person win. This meant that there could be no rules to keep anyone out because of race, sex, religion, or where their family came from. This meant, too, that to keep the chances fair, everybody was entitled to education, health, and decent housing. This was the American idea of equality.

Still, everybody knows that some people are stronger than others, some are brighter, some work harder. Freedom meant the opportunity for everyone to show the ability to try to win in the competition. In Communist countries and other tyrannies people are assigned their jobs by the government, which also tells them where they have to work, and what they can earn. The winners are named by the government. But freedom is a chancy world. It means keeping the market open for ideas to compete against one another. It means keeping the nation open for everybody to try to become a winner. Extra rewards then ought to go to anyone who is especially able.

Naturally everyone wants a fair chance, and the ideal of equality aims to guarantee that chance. Still, everybody cannot be an equal winner. The ideal of freedom aims to guarantee everybody's right to be as successful as that person can be—even more successful than somebody else.

This tradition of the two ideals goes back to the nation's very beginning. Every age must find new ways to live these ideals. The great drama of American life in our time has been the struggle to make the two ideals work happily together.

The Declaration of Independence. Back in 1776 the Declaration of Independence declared the right of Americans "to assume among the powers of the earth, the separate and equal station to which the Laws of Nature and of Nature's God entitle them." The British government had not allowed Americans their equal rights to govern themselves and vote on their own taxes. It had not given them the freedom to trade where they wanted and to produce what they wished. The American Revolution, then, was fought to give this new nation both equality and freedom in the world of nations.

Within the nation, too, these ideals of equality and freedom would rule. "We hold these truths to be self-evident, that all men are created equal, that they are endowed by their Creator with certain unalienable Rights, that among these are Life, Liberty, and the pursuit of Happiness." According to Jefferson, the bulwark of rights was education. He preached a "crusade against ignorance." "Diffusion of knowledge among the people" was the only "sure foundation . . . for the preservation of freedom and happiness."

The "natural aristocracy." Every generation, Jefferson believed, had enough of its own bright and able people to run the government and preserve freedom. While all men were "created equal," with equal rights before the law, Jefferson did not believe that every individual person was just as clever and as talented as everybody else. He said there was a "natural aristocracy." This was nothing like the Old World aristocracy. Over there certain lucky people had high-sounding titles and power in the government only because their parents and grandparents were rich, owned lots of land, or were friends of the king or queen. No one had elected them, and they had not earned their wealth or their high position.

The "natural aristocracy"—a democratic aristocracy—in this country would be a different breed. They would be the ablest, most industrious, and best educated. And they would be elected to government positions because of their very own talents and knowledge.

Jefferson outlined a system of education to train these people and prepare them to lead. All would compete, and then the people who did best in the examinations would move up to the next level of schools. In this way, he hoped, the nation would be well supplied with the kind of "aristocrats" needed in a free republic.

This was a grand idea. If it was perfected to include everyone, it would save this new nation from the prejudices and the unfair advantages that had ruled the older nations of Europe. On (p. 847) the whole, in the long run the United States did not do too badly in working toward the ideal. But there were some serious problems that plainly got in the way of the system, even in Jefferson's day.

Thomas Jefferson wrote the Declaration of Independence in Philadelphia on this lap desk. Jefferson's proclamation of human equality and unalienable rights would guide Americans through many challenging years.

Smithsonian Institution

More from Boorstin: ". . . the proper role of the citizen and the statesman here is one of conservation and reform rather than of invention. He is free to occupy himself with the means of improving his society; for there is relatively little disagreement on ends. [Frederick Jackson] Turner summed it up when he said: 'The problem of the United States is not to create democracy, but to conserve democratic institutions and ideals.'" (From *The Genius of American Politics*)

National Gallery of Art, Washington

A neat one-room schoolhouse about 1900 as caught in this watercolor made by Perkins Harnly. The month was February, when Valentine's Day sentiments mingled with patriotic feelings on the birthdays of Washington and Lincoln. Students of the different grades sat together.

The difficult dream. Thomas Jefferson himself was a wealthy Virginia aristocrat in the Old World sense of the word. From his father he had inherited a plantation of several thousand acres and slaves to work the land. His mother came from a family with high social position. He had the advantage of an excellent education at the College of William and Mary. He became a lawyer, and then was easily elected to the Virginia House of Burgesses. If he had been born in the slave quarters, we might never have heard of him. He might never have had the opportunity to use his great abilities. Jefferson himself believed that slavery was a curse that violated the will of God. But he lived on a plantation in Virginia where nearly all the blacks were slaves.

To make Jefferson's dream of a full-fledged "natural aristocracy" come true, many changes would have to be made in the life of that Virginia. In his time, no person would even have a chance to take the examinations for higher education without the good luck to be a son born into a white family that could send him to school to learn to read and write. Jefferson did not believe that women should be taught the same subjects that were taught to men.

In this book we have traced the progress, over the centuries of American history, of efforts to widen opportunity. We have seen the rise of the American public school, the free public high school, the wonderful growth of American private schools, private colleges, and state and land-grant public universities.

Critical Thinking Activity: Distinguishing False from Accurate Images Who would belong to Jefferson's "aristocracy" today? Ask students to volunteer their own definitions of the "natural aristocracy" of Thomas Jefferson's invention. In a class discussion have students describe who would be part of the "natural aristocracy's" membership today, and what opportunities are available to this group of people. Ask if they would want to be a part of this select group of individuals.

It would take a long time to make opportunity equal for all Americans. There would never be perfectly equal opportunity, even with a whole system of free education for all. There would always be differences between families. Naturally, some parents would be more anxious than others for their children to go on with their education. And, of course, better-educated parents in homes where there were lots of books would be able to give their children a head start in the competition.

Still, a great deal could be done to make opportunities more equal. In the southern states where slavery had flourished and where blacks continued to be treated as second-class citizens, the public schools were not equal at all. And in big cities in the North, segregated black neighborhoods tended to leave their children at a real disadvantage.

When the Supreme Court of the United States in 1954 outlawed segregation in the public schools, it took a big step to insure that educational opportunities would be more equal. The 1962 law against segregation in federally funded public housing helped. After the anti-poll tax amendment to the Constitution (Twenty-fourth Amendment) was finally adopted in 1964 and the Voting Rights Act was passed in 1965, blacks in the South were able to use their votes to elect officials who would protect their rights and improve their opportunities. The years after World War II saw these and other strenuous efforts to fulfill the American dream of equal opportunity.

Immigrant problems and immigrant inequality. The blacks were not the only Americans whose opportunities had not been equal. Every immigrant group except the English had their painful problems. They had been kept out of the best schools, the best colleges, the best neighborhoods, and the best jobs. With only a few exceptions, there had been no civil rights laws or constitutional amendments to protect them. In fact, as we have seen (p. 443), some of the most respectable, richest, and best-educated Americans actually formed organizations purposely to discriminate against new immigrants.

When the Irish came here in the 1840s as refugees from the potato famine and from religious persecution, they were treated as intruders by some of New England's oldest residents. Factories and offices needing employees displayed the sign saying, "No Irish Need Apply." The Know-Nothing party, beginning as a secret society in New York City in 1849, organized discrimination against Catholics and immigrants. Its special targets were the new Irish Americans and the many German Americans who had been moving into the Middle West. Hatred against Catholics was again organized in 1887 in a group that called itself the American Protective Association. Its members poured slanders on the thousands of recent Italian and Polish immigrants. In 1894, when the flood of immigrants came from central, eastern, and southern Europe, many leading Bostonians (whose parents had immigrated some time before) joined with professors and university presidents from Harvard, Wisconsin, and California to form the powerful Immigration Restriction League.

Among the groups most discriminated against were the Jews. Seeking refuge from ghettos and persecution in Germany, Poland, and Russia, Jews brought with them a tradition of learning and a reverence for books and education. Many were eager to pursue their studies in the best universities and medical schools. But the best universities, like Harvard and Yale, set up shameful restrictive quotas, which deprived Jews of their equal chances.

Chinese, Japanese, and Korean immigrants, too, suffered discrimination—simply because they also wanted their full opportunities as Americans. The school board in San Francisco even tried to force their segregation in the public schools until President Theodore Roosevelt made them stop.

At the dawning of the twentieth century there were 76 million people in the United States. Of these, more than 10 million had been born outside the country, and more than one-third of all Americans—26 million—had at least one foreign-born parent. Although people boasted that this was a nation of immigrants, nearly

A. Ramey/Woodfin Camp

Nearly two thirds of all Spanish-speaking people in the United States are of Mexican origin. These people at a Mexican Independence Day parade in Los Angeles, California, are celebrating their cultural heritage.

every kind of immigrant at some time had suffered some sort of discrimination!

The social disease of discrimination lasted violently into the modern century. In the 1920s the Ku Klux Klan, along with its hocus-pocus and its costume of white sheets, terrorized Catholics, Jews, and blacks in the South and the Midwest. When the able Al Smith ran for President in 1928, he lost votes merely because he was a Catholic. During World War II, FDR gave in to panic and put thousands of innocent Japanese and Japanese Americans into concentration camps. And when John F. Kennedy was nominated for President in 1960, political leaders wondered whether the time had yet come when a Catholic could be elected.

Prejudice and discrimination, then, were not the monopoly of any one part of the country or of any one period in our history. Perhaps they would never be entirely cured. But the United States had made a good start. The traditional American open door policy at home gave refuge to oppressed people from the whole world. The Emancipation Proclamation and the Thirteenth, Fourteenth, and Fifteenth amendments to the United States Constitution were long-overdue steps. In World War II the United States had fought the discrimination, barbarism, and racial superstitions of the German Nazis. Now Americans were ready again to move ahead. Civil rights laws, supported by Presidents of both parties beginning with Truman, signaled that the American conscience had been reawakened. In our land the twentieth century would be another century of progress for human equality.

☑ See "Lesson Plan," p. 844C for **Writing Process Activity: Expressing Problems Clearly** relating to discrimination against immigrants.

See "Section 1 Review answers," p. 844C.

Section 1 Review

1. How did Jefferson's "natural aristocracy" differ from the Old World aristocracy?
2. What makes discrimination a "social disease"?
3. How is a system of free education, open to all, related to the ideal of equality?
4. **Critical Thinking: Expressing Problems Clearly.** Why do the twin American ideals of freedom and equality sometimes lead to social conflict?

See "Lesson Plan," p. 844C.

2. Dealing with racism

Righting past wrongs was not easy. Americans loved speed. They expected to accomplish in a few years what elsewhere had required centuries—or had never been tried. And Americans, too, had a faith that laws could cure almost anything. By the Eighteenth Amendment and the laws against alcoholic beverages, Americans showed that they believed laws could cure the social ills of drunkenness. In that they were disappointed. But could laws speedily cure discrimination?

Congress and the states passed new laws and set up new commissions. Still, the problem was more complicated and deeper rooted than it seemed at first. Programs to cure past ills also created new problems.

Trying to integrate the schools. The Supreme Court decision in 1954 outlawed racial segregation. Southerners fought a long, losing battle against the law of the land, but by the late 1970s legal segregation in the South had ceased. The age-old system of separate public schools and colleges for the races came to an end. But racism survived in the form of private schools that white parents set up to avoid integration. Increasing numbers of white students went to these private schools or moved to other school districts where there were fewer blacks. In some areas, schools which had been integrated after the Supreme Court decision came to be attended largely by blacks, which defeated the purpose of integration.

In northern cities, neighborhoods were often racially segregated. Sometimes, too, school boards tried to prevent integration. They built new schools and drew the lines of school districts to keep the races separate. The courts held this kind of segregation just as unconstitutional as that of the separate schools in the South.

To prevent segregation the courts took control in some cities. But the courts had no experience in running public schools. They ordered that students be bused to schools in other neighborhoods to provide a racial balance. Violence erupted in communities where white parents tried to stop the buses. Boston was scarred by the struggle. A judge there ran the school system for over ten years. School officials in Buffalo, New York, by contrast, aided by federal money and patient parents, peacefully integrated the schools. Buffalo showed how "magnet" schools with special programs could bring white students back to the public schools.

In 1987 a judge found segregation again in Little Rock, Arkansas, just 30 years after federal troops had overseen the admission of black students to Central High. During those years, whites had moved to the suburbs and whole neighborhoods had become segregated. So the city and nearby school districts continued to battle in the courts over the best ways to integrate the city's schools.

Busing was one method of counteracting segregation. But it brought many new problems. Some children had to waste long hours riding on buses. It was hard for parents to stay in touch with teachers who were no longer in their neighborhood. To avoid busing, many whites moved away and soon the schools were segregated again. All across the country parents disagreed. Some felt that the benefits of mixed schools outweighed all the problems. Others—white and black—missed their neighborhood schools.

"Affirmative action" and "reverse discrimination." Another new kind of problem was created by what were called "affirmative action" programs. Affirmative action grew out of the

The purpose of affirmative action, which many Americans approved, was to better the chances of people who, for centuries, had been forced to play the game with the rules stacked against them, people whose difficulties in the present could be traced to discrimination in the past. But people who were not in the "minority" groups now felt they were being discriminated against. They thought it was not their fault that women, blacks, Latinos, Native Americans, or Asians had suffered in the past. "Backlash" described a new kind of prejudice created by the efforts to remove old prejudices. Some white male workers and students could not understand why others were receiving special preference. They called this "reverse discrimination," and brought lawsuits to secure their equal rights.

The Supreme Court and affirmative action. The Supreme Court was unsure how to deal with affirmative action. In the *Bakke* case in 1978, it ruled that setting a specific quota for minority students in each class at a medical school that received federal funds was unconstitutional. But the Court said that some more flexible program might be legal. And the very next year, in the *Weber* case, the Court approved a job-training program designed to reflect the racial characteristics of the area surrounding a private company's factory.

Under President Reagan, the Justice Department tried to stop affirmative action plans. Justice Department officials said that they wanted a "color-blind, gender-neutral society" where all paths were open and no special help was given to anyone. They were heartened when the Supreme Court ruled that the Memphis Fire Department could not ignore its seniority system to keep newly hired blacks while it laid off longer-serving whites. The Court said that the Memphis blacks could not show that they personally were victims of discrimination.

In 1987, however, the Supreme Court upheld a lower court decision that allowed officials in Santa Clara County, California, to promote a woman over a man who had received a higher score in the job interview. The Court called the county's affirmative action plan "moderate and

Alex Webb/Magnum

To bring about racial balance in northern schools, students were sometimes bused from one neighborhood to another.

civil rights movement of the 1960s. It was designed first for blacks, and then for other minority groups and for women, to combat the continuing effects of past discrimination. It gave preference to women, blacks, and other minority persons for particular jobs or for college and professional school admissions, even though they were not better qualified than other applicants. This tended to produce "quota" systems. The programs meant, of course, that all equally qualified persons did not have an equal chance for these jobs or schools.

✕ **Critical Thinking Activity: Expressing Problems Clearly** How have the nation's courts legislated equality? Ask students to develop a list of examples of when the nation's courts have attempted to eliminate inequality on the basis of race. Ask students to discuss the success of this approach to eliminating racism. How is this approach dependent on the mood of the courts? How would the courts deal with the subject today?

flexible." This was the Court's first ruling on a plan intended to help women.

The Supreme Court remained uneasy about affirmative action, and the Justice Department continued to push for a "color-blind, gender-neutral" approach to discrimination. As the Court's membership became more conservative under President Reagan and then, after 1988, under President Bush, the justices began to be more sympathetic to the Justice Department's view.

In January 1989, in the case of *Richmond* v. *Croson,* a 5–4 majority came out firmly against most affirmative action programs. They struck down a law of the city of Richmond, Virginia, which ordered that 30 percent of all public works funds should go to minority-owned construction companies. The Court said that the law violated the rights of white contractors to "the equal protection of the laws" (sec. 1, XIVth Amendment). And the majority made it clear that they would view any law favoring blacks with as much suspicion as they would a law favoring whites. Justice Sandra Day O'Connor, for the majority, wrote that any other approach would mean that "the ultimate goal of eliminating entirely from government decision making such irrelevant factors as a human being's race will never be achieved."

The majority said that it would allow such laws only if they served the "compelling" purpose of correcting "identified discrimination." But they made it clear that any law of that type would be subject to "strict scrutiny"—that is, it would be looked at closely to see that it remedied only a specific problem and did no more. Few laws, followers of the Supreme Court noted, ever survived strict scrutiny.

The minority objected strongly to the decision of the majority. Justice Harry A. Blackmun wrote, "I never thought that I would live to see the day when the city of Richmond, Virginia, the cradle of the Old Confederacy," wanting to limit "persistent discrimination," would be prevented from doing so by the Supreme Court, "the supposed bastion of equality."

Later that same year the Court interpreted Title VII of the Civil Rights Act of 1964 in such a way that critics felt it had been nullified. While saying that they still agreed with their 1971 decision in *Griggs* v. *Duke Power Co.* the justices, in fact, turned it around. In *Griggs* the Court had ruled that an employer had to prove it was not discriminating. The Court ruled that Duke Power Co. had not proved that the high school diploma it required for employment was necessary. "Good intent or absence of discriminatory intent does not redeem employment procedures or testing mechanisms," it had said, "that operate as 'built-in headwinds' for minority groups and are unrelated to measuring job capability." But now in their 1989 decision in *Ward's Cove Packing Co.* v. *Antonio,* the Court said employers no longer had to prove that a requirement was necessary. Instead, the Court ruled that it was now up to applicants and employees to prove that a requirement was unnecessary and discriminatory. This made it extremely difficult to prove discrimination, civil rights lawyers complained.

A few days later the Supreme Court ruled that even affirmative action settlements reached with the approval of lower courts could be challenged. The Court said, in *Martin* v. *Wilks,* that an eight-year-old agreement in Birmingham, Alabama, that had tried to open up senior positions in the fire department to blacks could be legally challenged by white firemen. Chief Justice Rehnquist wrote, "A voluntary settlement in the form of a consent decree between one group of employees and their employer cannot possibly 'settle,' voluntarily or otherwise, the conflicting claims of . . . employees who do not join in the agreement." This ruling, which also applied to agreements involving sex discrimination, seemed to open up again many agreements long thought settled.

Civil rights activists were deeply disturbed by these decisions. The Court had now brought to an end, they feared, what some called the Second Reconstruction—the progress on civil rights that began with the 1954 school desegregation case, *Brown* v. *Board of Education of Topeka, Kansas.*

The Supreme Court further restricted civil rights laws when, in a 1989 decision upholding the Civil Rights Act of 1866, they limited its reach. They ruled 5–4 that while the act did

Williams Photography Studio

These two construction company owners in Richmond, Virginia, had a better chance of getting work before the Supreme Court struck down the city's affirmative action law.

prevent discrimination in hiring practices, it did not, as some lower courts had assumed, prohibit discrimination at work.

Still, even now, not every Court decision went against extensions of civil rights. In a case involving Kansas City, Missouri, the Court ruled 5–4 in April 1990 that a judge had the power to order a local government to raise taxes in order to carry out programs to reduce school segregation. And that June it upheld two federal affirmative action programs aimed at increasing the number of minority-owned television and radio stations. The Court said that the federal government had greater leeway in creating affirmative action programs than did state and local governments.

In response to the Court's limitations on affirmative action programs, Congress in 1990 passed a bill that, while explicitly denying any attempt to prescribe quotas, tried to allow such programs. But George Bush, who had become President in 1989, vetoed the bill, saying that it would still lead to quotas. Congress failed by one vote to override his veto.

Deep-seated problems. In education, and in the better jobs opened up by education, there was real progress for black Americans. By the 1980s blacks spent almost as many years in school as whites. Far more blacks were finishing high school and going on to college. But there was a troubling sign. The percentage of blacks, Hispanics, and Native Americans enrolled in colleges and universities peaked in the 1970s and then began to decline. Enrollments for blacks rose again in the late 1980s, only to fall in the early 1990s. Graduation rates for blacks remained much lower than for whites.

The percentage of blacks in skilled jobs rose 📖 in the 1960s by about 50 percent. Between 1960 and 1980, the number holding professional, technical, and managerial jobs skyrocketed. Law schools and medical schools vigorously searched for qualified students. Special scholarships were offered and colleges scrambled to find black professors for their faculties. Now there were many more blacks in the courts, in banks, and businesses. In the early 1980s, blacks gained places on the highest courts of ten states.

Back in 1967 President Johnson had appointed the first black, Thurgood Marshall, to the Supreme Court. He also brought the first black into the Cabinet, when he named Robert C. Weaver as Secretary of the new Department of Housing and Urban Development. President Carter named a black woman, Patricia Roberts Harris, to that position in his Cabinet. Later Harris became head of the huge Department of Health, Education, and Welfare. When Thurgood Marshall retired from the Court in 1991, President Bush appointed another black man, Clarence Thomas, to take his place. In 1993, President Clinton named Ronald Brown as his Secretary of Commerce, Michael Espy as Secretary of Agriculture, Hazel O'Leary as Secretary of Energy, and Joycelyn Elders as the United States Surgeon General. They were the first black Americans ever to hold those posts.

📖 **More from Boorstin:** "The voting power of the Negro had become so considerable . . . that in 1960 for the first time in American history, Negro voters were widely assumed to have played a decisive role in a presidential election. Some knowledgeable observers credited Negro voters for the narrow popular margin of 120,000 which elected President John F. Kennedy." (From *The Americans: The Democratic Experience*)

Eli Reed/Magnum Photos

New opportunities for education and jobs, which became increasingly available from the 1960s on, allowed some blacks to advance economically.

In politics, the Civil Rights Act of 1964 and the Voting Act of 1965 had far-reaching consequences. By 1992 some 8000 blacks were holding public office. In the fall of 1990 Virginia elected Lieutenant Governor L. Douglas Wilder, a successful trial lawyer and the grandson of slaves, the first black governor in American history, and New York City elected its first black mayor. Many other large cities already had black mayors. In 1992, Illinois voters sent the first black woman, Carol Moseley Braun, to the U.S. Senate. When President Johnson was working to pass the Civil Rights Act of 1964, he was warned by his old friend, politically powerful Senator Richard Russell of Georgia, that if he pushed the act through "it's going to cost you the South and cost you the [1964] election." Johnson replied, "If that's the price I've got to pay, I'll gladly pay it."

In fact, in 1964 Johnson handily defeated Senator Barry Goldwater. But he did lose five southern states and no Democratic candidate since, including Jimmy Carter, has been able to win the votes of a majority of the southern white voters. And this helps to explain why, from 1968 through 1992, the Democrats have won the Presidency only twice.

At first, whites outside the South were not disturbed by the Civil Rights and Voting acts. Those laws seemed to be aimed at correcting wrongs in the South. But affirmative action and continuing moves for school desegregation in the North distressed many whites. They disliked the Democratic party's continuing strong stand for Civil Rights and its solid support by black voters. So in presidential elections they, too, often voted for the Republicans. In congressional elections, however, Democrats continued to receive enough votes to win. The result was divided government, with the Democrats in the majority in the Senate and always in control of the House of Representatives.

During these years, the difference between the wages paid to black and to white workers narrowed significantly. But the gap among blacks themselves widened. Successful blacks tended to move to the suburbs, leaving the poor and uneducated behind in the crowded cities. There they faced a host of problems. By 1993 over two-thirds of all black children were born to unwed mothers. Many of these mothers were teenagers. The black families who had no father at home rose from 21 percent in 1960 to over 50 percent in the 1990s. Blacks suffered more than twice the rate of unemployment of whites.

While much has changed for the better over the past 30 years, it has remained harder for blacks than for whites to fulfill their American dreams. Black Americans disagreed about what needed to be done. Some agreed with moderate and conservative whites that "welfare"—government aid designed to help the poor, the unemployed, and others in dire straits—created dependency and stifled initiative. These black leaders urged their followers to put their hope not in the government but in themselves, in their churches, and in education. Other black leaders thought government ought to do much more to fight poverty and unemployment. But black and white, conservative and liberal, agreed that the problems of black Americans belonged to the country at large, for the nation had grown and prospered on the ideal of equal opportunity.

See "Section 2 Review answers," p. 844D.

Section 2 Review

1. Identify or explain: racism, segregation, desegregation.
2. How and why did school segregation continue after legal segregation ended?
3. Did the civil rights movement bring the nation closer to the ideal of equality? Explain.
4. **Critical Thinking: Recognizing Bias.** What is "affirmative action"? Why do some people call affirmative action "reverse discrimination"?

See "Lesson Plan," p. 844D.

3. Women seek equality

Since women were more than half the American population, technically they were not a minority. During these years of awakening conscience, new voices called women the forgotten majority.

Women were among the earliest champions for all the suffering and disadvantaged. Dorothea Dix, as we have seen, took the side of the mentally ill who had been treated as criminals and prisoners. The pioneer American abolitionists Elizabeth Cady Stanton and Lucretia Mott had been refused seats in the antislavery convention in London because they were women. Then, in 1848, they assembled their own convention in Seneca Falls, New York. If it was unjust to discriminate against people because of the color of their skin, was it any better to discriminate against them because of their sex? They demanded the right to vote and equal rights for women to education and to jobs. In 1869 the National Woman Suffrage Association was founded, and in that year Wyoming Territory was the first to grant women the right to vote. Utah, Colorado, and Idaho—other western states that pioneer women had helped to build—gave women the vote by 1896.

The women's rights movement in the new century was based on the hope that if women only had the right to vote, they could then remove their other inequalities. This was the belief of Progressive leaders, too. Still, even after the Nineteenth Amendment was ratified in 1920 insuring women the right to vote, they stayed unequal in countless other ways. Then, along with the civil rights movement for blacks, a new women's movement gained momentum in the 1960s.

The women's rights movement reawakens. The new feminist movement, too, showed the power of a book. Betty Friedan, who had been born in Peoria, Illinois, and had graduated from Smith College, wrote *The Feminine Mystique,* which was published in 1963. She denied the popular notion that women could be fulfilled only by bearing children and doing housework. Women, she said, were just as able as men

Western states granted women the right to vote much earlier than did eastern states or the Constitution. These women were photographed at the polls in Colorado.

(maybe more able) to do every kind of job. They, too, should be allowed to lead the world in science, politics, and business. Modern advertising, in newspapers and magazines and on television, had reinforced the old-fashioned idea that women were the "weaker sex." This mistaken notion she called "the Feminine Mystique." It had kept women frustrated and unfulfilled, confined at home in their "comfortable concentration camp." In that same year, a report issued by a Commission on the Status of Women—originally appointed by President Kennedy and headed by Eleanor Roosevelt—had found discrimination against women in every part of life. In 1966 eloquent Betty Friedan founded the National Organization for Women (NOW) and in 1970 she organized a nationwide Women's Strike for Equality. She urged women to speak up for their rights.

Many conservative Americans—men and women—were irritated by these demands and by the ideas in The Feminine Mystique. They found the new feminists to be raucous, unladylike, and "unfeminine." In a way their objections proved the point that the new feminists were trying to make. Why, the feminists asked, shouldn't women have the same right as men to speak up? It was considered manly for men to stand up for their rights—so why shouldn't that also be womanly?

Others were puzzled because it seemed that in the United States women already had more freedom to go where they pleased and do what they pleased than women anywhere else. In fact, there were few formal or legal barriers. Instead, the style of American life stood in the way. Women (unlike men) were always expected to put home and family first. This kept them from reaching the top in business and the professions. It also discouraged employers from giving women the high positions for which they were qualified. If a woman had another child, or if her husband's job was moved to another city, then she was expected to give up her own job—in order to care for her child or go with her husband. Even if a woman was single, employers feared she might marry and then they would lose her. As famed anthropologist Margaret Mead observed, "The very fact that the formal barriers are down reduces women to battling with feather-soft barriers that never really yield but instead smother the attacker."

The status of women. Statistics confirmed the arguments of the new feminists. In 1971, for example, full-time working women were paid only 59 percent as much as men were paid. Women with college degrees earned only half as much as men with similar educations. Because of increasing educational opportunities, because of the rising American standard of living, and because of inflation, more and more women were entering the labor force. Women made up 38 percent of the labor force in 1970 and 45 percent in 1990, which meant that 56 million women were working, many of them wives and mothers. Many women wanted jobs that would challenge and reward them, but few were in positions that their talents deserved. One-third of all female workers were employed in clerical tasks—as secretaries, file clerks, and telephone operators. Few were executives or managers. In the early 1970s women accounted for only 7 percent of physicians and only 3 percent of lawyers.

Women now demanded equal opportunity, and the American tradition of free speech and the right to organize ensured that they would be heard. The pioneer and the immigrant traditions also played a part. When a family first came to America or moved into the unfamiliar West, women had to make important decisions. They had to find new ways to keep the family well fed, well schooled, and happy together. Ever since colonial times, foreign visitors to this country had noticed the power of American women and sometimes made fun of it. But the opportunities for women had not yet been brought into an urban age of technology and large industry.

The drive for equal rights. The new feminist movement took many forms. Betty Friedan's National Organization for Women demanded changes to bring women into "the mainstream of American society . . . in fully equal partnership with men." Small militant groups even called for female separation, the end of the family, and the end of separate masculine and feminine roles.

The first national success of the women's rights movement came by accident. When the House of Representatives was debating the Civil Rights Act of 1964, Congressman Howard Smith of Virginia offered an amendment to Title VII to bar job discrimination on the basis of sex as well as race. He did this not to assist women, but because he thought this would help defeat the entire measure. Instead the bill, with his amendment, became law. This ban against sexual discrimination would be used in businesses, schools, and colleges.

As the movement gained momentum, Congress added its support. In 1972, two-thirds of the members of both houses of Congress approved an "Equal Rights" Amendment and sent it to the states. A similar amendment had been proposed in 1923 but had repeatedly failed to get approval by Congress. The proposed amendment now read: "Equality of rights under the law shall not be denied or abridged by the United States or any state on account of sex." It was quickly ratified by 22 states. Then it ran into strong opposition.

The feminist movement and the Equal Rights Amendment were opposed by critics such as

---

📖 **More from Boorstin:** "The most potent of the myths that had prevented coeducation was that woman, 'the weaker vessel,' could not survive the rigors of academic discipline. It was expected that women might faint from the strain, and that while losing 'the delicate bloom of womanhood,' they would inevitably lower the academic standards for men. . . . But it was found that the female physique could survive, and even thrive, in a college atmosphere."
(From *The Americans: The Democratic Experience*)

American women in 1977 joined in International Women's Day to demonstrate for their equal rights.

forceful, articulate Phyllis Schlafly and others. They valued the privileges more than the rights of women. They believed in the old tradition. There was no more important work, they insisted, than bearing and raising children. They thought that nature intended women for different roles from men. Reformers in the Progressive Era had demanded special laws to protect women in factories. "Equal rights" might mean the end of such special protection for women. It might also mean the end of "alimony," the money awarded by courts to divorced women.

To adopt the Equal Rights Amendment, the Constitution required ratification by three-quarters of the states. In 1979, when the amendment was still three states short of the needed number, Congress extended the deadline for ratification to June 30, 1982. Even that

was not enough. The amendment failed to receive enough votes and died. Many believed that because of Supreme Court decisions and new laws the amendment was unnecessary. Still, a number of states included its principles in their own constitutions.

Aid from the government and the courts. Meanwhile the federal government found new ways to use its power to end discrimination. In 1972, President Nixon's Secretary of Labor ordered companies that contracted with the government to set goals and timetables for hiring women and minorities. The Justice Department started suits under Title VII of the 1964 Civil Rights Act to force large business firms to end job discrimination. Colleges and universities that received federal aid were investigated

≋ Continuity and Change: Social Change Point out to students that one of the long-standing arguments against civil rights for women has been that it is unnatural for women to be equal to men. When the women's movement began in the mid-1800s with women seeking voting rights, *Harper's New Monthly Magazine* proclaimed that giving women the right to vote was "opposed to nature and the established order of society." Today as women seek economic equality in equal pay for equal work and an end to discrimination in hiring practices, some of these same attitudes exist as they did during the struggle for women's suffrage. (See p. 285.)

to see if they discriminated against women. The Equal Employment Opportunity Act, passed in 1972, required employers to pay equal wages for equal work. Other laws barred discrimination against women when they applied for credit.

And again the Supreme Court played a role. In 1971 the Court ruled that unequal treatment based only on sex violated the Fourteenth Amendment. In 1973, in one of its most controversial decisions, *Roe* v. *Wade,* the Court held that, except in the later stages of pregnancy, states could not make it illegal for women to have abortions. The new feminists hailed this decision as a victory. They said that a woman's most important right was to control her own body. But their passionate "Right-to-Life" opponents said that the unborn child had rights of its own and that abortion was murder. Efforts of the "right-to-lifers" bore fruit as a number of states began to limit the right to abortion—by prohibiting poor people from using government medical aid to pay for abortions, by requiring waiting periods, by requiring all women to notify their husbands before obtaining abortions, and by requiring all minors to obtain parental consent. The Supreme Court upheld many of these limits, and abortion opponents hoped that it would overturn *Roe* itself. But in June 1992, in *Webster* v. *Reproductive Health Services,* the Court, while upholding a Pennsylvania law that imposed strict limits, reaffirmed a woman's basic right to choose an abortion, calling it "a rule of law and a component of liberty we cannot renounce."

Women move ahead. In 1960, only 35 percent of American college students were women, but by 1978 that figure had risen to 48 percent; by 1990, to 55 percent. By the 1990s, 40 percent of American law and medical students were women. The avenues of choice were widening; women were moving into nearly every occupation. Women now worked as truck drivers, car mechanics, business leaders, architects, computer scientists, and even as astronauts.

In the early 1990s, 20 percent of all lawyers and doctors were women. In the other profes-

Ralf-Finn Hestoft/SABA

During the 1980s and early 1990s, women became more successful in seeking political office. In 1992 Carol Moseley Braun, from Illinois, became the first black woman to be elected to the United States Senate.

sions counted by the Department of Labor—including scientists, teachers, librarians, engineers, psychiatrists, and social workers—women held half of all the jobs compared to only one-third as recently as 1983. Now women ✖ were also governors, mayors, Cabinet officers, members of the Senate and the House of Representatives, and justices of the U.S. Supreme Court.

Yet problems remained. The median working income of working women was just 71 percent of that of working men. If a woman wanted to work after having a baby, she needed a good child care center. Many unions made child care an issue, because one-third of all union members were women. Some large companies, like Ford and General Motors, now agreed to help with child care.

Although they had come a long way, women still had a long way to go. In 1979, for the first time an American silver dollar had appeared with the likeness of a real woman—Susan B. Anthony (p. 285), the courageous leader who fought all her long life for women's rights. Her

✖ **Critical Thinking Activity: Checking Consistency** How has the image of women's work changed over the past thirty years? Have students find magazine and newspaper advertisements that depict women in a variety of roles. Ask students to share their findings and to keep a list of the roles portrayed. Have students describe how the same advertisements would be different if they had appeared thirty years earlier. Ask: Why do these differences exist? Ask students to evaluate the impact of the women's movement on the way women and their work are portrayed.

Rob Nelson/Picture Group

In the years after World War II women entered new and exciting fields that once would have been closed to them.

face on the coin bore an important new message. "For the first time in modern history," a woman journalist observed, "a woman is born into a society which has acknowledged her right to the freedom to choose the role she wants."

See "Section 3 Review answers," p. 844D.

Section 3 Review

1. Identify or explain: Betty Friedan, NOW, Equal Rights Amendment, *Roe* v. *Wade*.

2. If there were few legal barriers to the advancement of women by the 1960s, what factors held back their efforts to achieve equality?

3. **Critical Thinking: Distinguishing Fact from Opinion.** Cite evidence showing (a) gains by women by the 1970s and 1980s and (b) continued male-female inequality.

☑ See "Lesson Plan," p. 844D for Writing Process Activity: Recognizing Ideologies relating to the women's equal rights movement.

See "Lesson Plan," p. 844E.

4. The American Indians

After World War II, when Americans tried once again to make opportunities equal, injustices of the American past came home to roost. It was one thing to give all Americans an equal chance for education and for jobs. That was difficult, but not impossible. It was quite another thing to try to undo history.

This problem arose in regard to the very first Americans. They were here, of course, centuries before the first Europeans or Africans. As the United States grew, their own cultures had not prospered. American Indians were not immigrants, were not settled in big cities, and for many years could not vote. They had little appeal for politicians. In colonial times, and for much of the 1800s, newer Americans considered them simply part of the wilderness to be cleared away. Later they were treated as "wards" of the government and put on reserva-

⊕
(p. 862)
tions (p. 387). These reservations were usually on land that nobody else wanted. Then, during the twentieth century, their numbers grew. Though in 1900 they totaled less than a quarter-million, by the 1990 census they numbered over 2 million. Not until the Snyder Act of 1924 were all Indians born in the United States admitted to full citizenship.

The Native Americans had been the victims of varying whims of United States officials. Under FDR there was an Indian "New Deal," which aimed to halt the sale of their land, to restore tribal landholding, to rebuild the tribes, and to promote tribal culture. In a bold move, FDR appointed outspoken and combative John Collier, the executive director of the American Indian Defense Association, as head of the Bureau of Indian Affairs. Between 1933 and 1945, Collier fought to enable the Indians both to preserve their old ways and to participate fully in American life.

During World War II, 25,000 American Indians served in the armed forces. They felt that they had earned their right to be full-fledged American citizens, with fully equal opportunities. But after World War II, the Native Americans still had the least education, the lowest incomes, the highest unemployment, the worst health, the shortest life expectancy, and the highest suicide rate of any large group in the country.

Termination and relocation. In the 1950s, under President Eisenhower, the federal government's policy toward the Indians changed once again. Congress enacted laws for a new program called "termination." The idea was to end all federal involvement with the Indians and leave the states to deal with them. But most states would not provide the health, education, and welfare services that the Indians needed.

Another new program called "relocation" offered jobs to induce Indians to relocate in cities. There, it was hoped, they would earn a better living and fit into the larger society. This program, too, was a disaster, precisely because many were persuaded to relocate. The proportion of Native Americans living in urban areas increased from 10 percent in 1930 to 45 percent in 1970. But the effects were not what was planned. Indians in cities generally had higher incomes and were better educated than those on reservations. Still, in the cities many of them felt displaced and unhappy. They created new urban Indian ghettos. In 1972 the program was finally dropped.

New help for Indians. President Lyndon Johnson, in a special message to Congress in 1968, called the Indian "The Forgotten American." He pointed to their poor housing, their alarming 40 percent unemployment, and the fact that only half of the young Indians completed high school. He asked Congress to enact a program to give Native Americans a standard of living equal to that of other Americans. Congress replied by voting $510 million for Indian aid programs—the highest amount ever.

President Nixon, too, tried to find new ways to help the Indians. He called for the end of the "termination" program. He also proposed that federal programs on the old Indian reservations be run by the Indians themselves. Native Americans were appointed to twenty top positions in the Bureau of Indian Affairs (BIA). And the Office of Education, after a two-year study, recommended that tribal history, culture, and languages be stressed in Indian education and that Indians be given a larger role in running their schools.

Indian Power. Some Native Americans began to take violent action to call attention to their wants. During 1969 an angry group of 78 Indians seized Alcatraz Island with its deserted prison in San Francisco Bay. They demanded that it be made an Indian cultural center. Finally, in 1971, they were evicted by United States marshals.

In 1972 the militant American Indian Movement (AIM) occupied the offices of the BIA in Washington. They demanded all the rights and the property that they said had been guaranteed to the Indians in the past by their treaties with the United States government. After a week of talks—and damage estimated at a half-million dollars—the Indians left the building.

The following year, more than 200 armed members of AIM took over the village of Wounded Knee on the Oglala Sioux Pine Ridge Reservation in South Dakota. They opposed the local tribal government and demanded other reforms. This town near the site of the last battle of the Indian wars—the massacre at Wounded Knee Creek in 1890 (p. 389)—was a symbol of Indian suffering. The occupation continued for two months. The Roman Catholic church, the trading post, and other buildings were destroyed. Two Indians were killed in the shooting between Indians and government agents.

The Indians themselves were sharply divided. The militants at the BIA and at Wounded Knee wanted to oust from authority all Indians who did not follow their orders. Many other Indians rejected violence. They preferred to seek their rights through the courts.

The Indian Self-Determination and Education Act of 1975 assured the Indians of more say on their own reservations. To advance Indian interests, in 1977 President Carter created a new post of Assistant Secretary of the Interior for Indian Affairs. He named knowledgeable Forrest J. Gerrard, a Blackfoot, to the position.

Secretary of the Interior James Watt made the position of the Reagan administration clear. He called Indian reservations examples of "the failures of socialism." Government interference, Watt said, was the cause of all the Indians' problems. As with other government programs, funds for Indians were cut back under Reagan.

Still, in 1987, Interior Secretary Donald P. Hodel estimated that $3 billion a year was spent on Indian programs. With his Assistant Secretary for Indian Affairs, Ross Swimmer, a

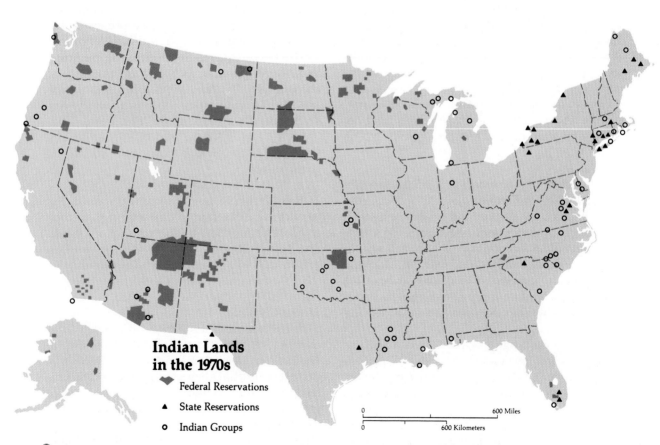

Indian Lands in the 1970s

◆ Federal Reservations

▲ State Reservations

○ Indian Groups

0 ——— 600 Miles

0 ——— 600 Kilometers

🌐 **Geography and History: Location** Have students look at the map above and locate federal and state Indian reservations. Tell students that by 1980 the Bureau of Indian Affairs counted 650,000 Indians residing on or near reservations. The largest group is the Navaho (parts of Arizona, New Mexico, and Utah), totaling around 155,000. Other large reservations include the Creek, Cherokee, and Choctaw in Oklahoma; the Southern Pueblos in New Mexico; and the Pine Ridge and Rosebud (Sioux) in South Dakota. Ask: How were the locations for these reservations probably chosen? (These were probably the pieces of land that seemed least desirable for whites.)

former chief of the Cherokee Nation of Oklahoma, Hodel recommended that the tribes be allowed to decide how to spend government funds.

Indians turn to the courts. Native Americans from Maine to California went to court during the 1970s and 1980s to win the return of lands taken from their ancestors centuries or decades before. They also demanded the right to raise their children on reservations, to hunt and fish when they wished, and to control valuable mineral, water, and grazing rights on the reservations.

In the mid-1970s, the Department of the Interior, which the Indians had long regarded as their enemy, began to side with them. Time after time the Indians won in the courts. The state of Rhode Island returned 1800 acres taken illegally from the Narragansets many years before. The Penobscot and Passamaquoddy Indians of Maine were granted thousands of acres and millions of dollars to settle their claims. The Sioux of the Black Hills won a ruling that 7 million acres of their land had been taken from them illegally and the Federal Indian Claims Commission awarded them $105 million. But the Indians rejected the offer. They wanted the land. A bill in Congress which proposed to give them 1.3 million acres never came to a vote. Members of Congress believed that it was impossible for the government to right all the wrongs of history.

The White Earth Indian Reservation in Minnesota illustrated the problems. Scattered across northern Minnesota, it contained 844,000 acres when it was set aside for the Chippewa in 1867. Over the years, the Indians were robbed and cheated of much of their land. By 1975, when they had only 58,000 acres left, they filed claims with the government for the return of 100,000 acres. But this situation made trouble for the innocent farmers now living on the land that unscrupulous whites had taken from the Indians many years before. Because of the Indian claims, the banks would not lend them money to work the land and buy machinery. But nobody else would purchase their land. Bad feelings grew between the

T. Campion/Sygma

Wilma Mankiller is the highly respected Principal Chief of the Cherokees.

whites and the Indians. Here was just another example of how efforts to right old wrongs could make new ones.

When Native Americans won greater control of their land and resources, they had new power. Some Indian groups used this power to seek new opportunities to raise money. One of the ways they did this was by opening gambling casinos which drew many visitors. They also gained power from their inherited wealth, for their reservations contained about 16 percent of the nation's valuable coal, uranium, and oil.

See "Section 4 Review answers," p. 844E.

Section 4 Review

1. Identify or explain: Snyder Act of 1924, Wounded Knee, Forrest Gerrard.

2. What were the "termination" and "relocation" policies? What were their results?

3. How did federal policy toward the Indians change under Presidents Johnson and Nixon?

4. Describe gains made by Indians in the 1970s.

5. **Critical Thinking: Identifying Alternatives.** What action did members of the American Indian Movement take to win Indian rights? What other strategy did Indians use?

✗ **Critical Thinking Activity: Drawing Conclusions** What has been the policy of recent Presidents towards American Indians? Divide the class into small groups. Assign each group one of the following Presidents: Johnson, Nixon, Carter, and Reagan. Tell each group to summarize their President's American Indian policy and to present it to the class. Have students decide which policy American Indians might prefer. Ask them to explain their choice in a written paragraph.

See "Lesson Plan," p. 844F.

5. Spanish-speaking peoples

After women and blacks, the largest group to organize for equal rights in the 1960s and 1970s was the Spanish-speaking people, whom the census bureau called Hispanics. They had come from many places and at many times. Some of their ancestors came to America with the Spanish conquerors in the century after Columbus, and their families had lived here for more than 400 years. Others emigrated to the mainland United States from Spain, Cuba, Puerto Rico, and other Caribbean islands, as well as from Latin American countries.

The Mexican Americans. Nearly two-thirds of all Spanish-speaking people in the United States are Mexican Americans. They are both the newest of the new immigrants and the oldest of the old. The ancestors of many of them settled in the Southwest and California in the 1600s and 1700s (p. 29). Those early settlers were followed by millions of others. By 1990 there were over 13 million Mexican Americans in the United States and thousands more were entering the country every year. By far the largest number of them have continued to settle where their first settlements lay—in California, Arizona, New Mexico, Colorado, and Texas. Their language and their culture give a special rich flavor to the food and shape the music, the architecture, and the literature in the whole region.

Many Mexican Americans are descended from the intermarriage of Spanish and Indian peoples. They proudly trace their heritage back to the great Aztec and Mayan civilizations. They generally call themselves by a variety of names: Mexican or Mexicano, Mexican American, Chicano (a form of Mexicano), Hispano, Latino, mestizo, and sometimes just La Raza (meaning "the people"). Mexican Americans are largely Roman Catholic, with strong family ties, and they cling to the Spanish language.

Cesar Chavez organized migrant workers in California into a union and led them in a long and finally successful strike against vineyard owners. He then tried to help other farm workers.

Bob Fitch/Black Star

❀ See "Lesson Plan," p. 844F for Cooperative Learning Activity: Making Comparisons relating to the population of Spanish-speaking peoples in the United States in 1990.

Although originally a rural people, now, like the whole nation, they are mainly urban. Fully 80 percent have settled together in city neighborhoods, which they call barrios.

From the very beginning the differences of religion, language, skin color, and culture between the Mexican Americans and white Americans (whom they call "Anglos" or "gringos") created conflicts. Each group tended to think its own way of doing things was better. But in most areas Anglos were the majority, in control of government, courts, and schools. Mexican Americans were often discriminated against. Great numbers of them ended up in low-paying jobs where no training was needed.

The rise of a "Brown Power" movement.

The Mexican Americans organized to voice their needs. Their first civil rights group, founded in 1929, was the League of United Latin American Citizens. The thousands of veterans who had fought in World War II formed the Mexican G.I. Forum. Then, in the tumultuous 1960s, Mexicans began to speak out more loudly.

During the 1960s there developed a Chicano or "Brown Power" movement. Among its most outspoken leaders was the feisty Reies Lopez Tijerina, or El Tigre. Born in Texas, he led a fight in New Mexico for the return of the lands he said the Anglos had stolen from the first Spanish-speaking settlers. But many of the conservative Mexican Americans, like Senator Joseph Montoya of New Mexico, disapproved of Tijerina's radical program. And instead of "Chicano," which some of the young had begun to use as a symbol of pride, they preferred to be simply Americans.

Another high-spirited leader was Rodolfo "Corky" Gonzales of Colorado. He was a former prizefighter and once director of a war-on-poverty youth program. In 1965 his Crusade for Justice in Denver began to build Chicano pride by providing jobs and social services in Chicano communities.

Organizing farm laborers.

Many Mexicans and Mexican Americans worked as poorly paid farm laborers. Some of these *braceros* (a Spanish word meaning laborers) came north under contracts to work in the fields. Others entered the country illegally by slipping across the long and difficult-to-patrol border between Mexico and the United States. They were called "wetbacks" because some of them swam or waded across the Rio Grande.

Farm workers had always been the most difficult laborers to organize into a union. Since they came to work only for a season, and were spread across the countryside, it was hard to bring them together for meetings. But the shrewd and eloquent Caesar Chavez decided to try. He had worked as a farm laborer himself. In 1962 he began to organize the migrant laborers—brown, white, and black—into a union. In 1965, when 900 Filipino grape pickers in another union went out on strike, Chavez's union decided to go out, too. The following year, the two unions merged to form the United Farm Workers Organizing Committee.

Chavez, like Martin Luther King, Jr., believed in nonviolence. He stuck to his principles through the long, painful years of the strike against the owners of the vineyards in Delano, California. This dedication won him public support from church groups, from other unions, and from political leaders like Robert F. Kennedy.

A brilliant publicist, Chavez organized an effective nationwide boycott of California grapes. (p. 866) When some of his followers resorted to violence, he protested by fasting for 25 days—and badly injured his health. But nonviolence prevailed. Finally, the opposition of the vineyard owners started to crumble. In 1970, after five years, many of them signed with Chavez's union. He had actually organized farm laborers into a union and won better pay and working conditions for them. Chavez had done what seemed impossible.

Chavez himself stayed out of politics, but other Mexican Americans won high office. Both New Mexico and Arizona have elected Mexican American governors. Other Mexican Americans have been chosen for the Senate and the House, or to be mayors of large cities, like Henry Cisneros of San Antonio, Texas, and Federico Peña in Denver, Colorado. A Mexican American woman, Romana A. Bañuelos, was

Critical Thinking Activity: Identifying Central Issues What forces shaped the "Brown Power" movement? Ask students to list factors that organizers of the "Brown Power" movement had to consider if they were to reach all members of the Mexican American community. Have students explain each of these elements as they relate to the background(s), economic classes, and degree of assimilation in the Mexican American community. Ask students to draw parallels between this movement's organization and the "Black Power" movement.

Wide World Photos

Puerto Rican Day is a time for parades and celebration in New York City.

named by President Nixon to be Treasurer of the United States. President Reagan appointed Lauro F. Cavazos as his Secretary of Education. President George Bush retained Cavazos and also appointed Manuel Lujan, Jr., Secretary of the Interior, and Antonia C. Novello, Surgeon General. After Bill Clinton was elected President in 1992, he appointed Federico Peña as his Secretary of Transportation and Henry Cisneros as his Secretary of Housing and Urban Development.

Puerto Rico and the Puerto Ricans. The Puerto Ricans were different from most other Hispanics because all of them were citizens of the United States before they arrived on the mainland. The special relationship between Puerto Rico and the rest of the United States allowed them to go back and forth to their home island at will.

The island of Puerto Rico had been visited by Columbus in 1493, even before any Spaniards

had come to mainland America. When Columbus arrived, the Arawak Indians were already there. During the colonial period the island was settled by Spaniards and by black slaves imported from Africa. The land and the climate were ideal for raising sugar cane. And from the sugar was made the famous Puerto Rican rum. In 1898, after the Spanish-American War, the United States took over the island.

One of FDR's braintrusters, Rexford G. Tugwell, was sent to Puerto Rico as governor in 1941. There he and Luis Muñoz Marín, a poetic and inspiring Puerto Rican political leader, produced "Operation Bootstrap." It was a program to improve agriculture and attract industry to the island. In 1948 Muñoz Marín became the island's first popularly elected governor. He led the way toward a special "Commonwealth" status for Puerto Rico within the United States. The Commonwealth of Puerto Rico was proclaimed on July 25, 1952. The following years showed how the resourcefulness and intelligence of people might make up for the lack of other natural resources.

Under the ingenious "Commonwealth" plan, Puerto Rico became an independent, self-governing state in voluntary association with the United States. Puerto Rico is represented in Congress by a resident commissioner who can speak but has no vote, except in committees. Puerto Ricans do not pay federal income tax on money earned in Puerto Rico, and they do not vote in national elections. By 1970, with the aid of "Operation Bootstrap," Puerto Rico had the highest per capita income and the best standard of living in Latin America. Still, Puerto Rican incomes were low compared to those in the mainland United States.

After World War II when the population grew rapidly, producing widespread unemployment, thousands of Puerto Ricans moved to the mainland. The emigration slowed in the 1970s, but by the late 1980s more than 2 million Puerto Ricans were living in the continental United States. About one-half lived in New York City, where many worked in the garment trades. The city now held more than twice as many Puerto Ricans as the island capital of San Juan. They were citizens, but in other ways they suffered

Multicultural Connection: Filipino Americans have a long history in the labor movement, dating from the 1920s. In the 1960s, when the AFL-CIO created the Agricultural Workers Organizing Committee, Larry Dulay Itliong (1914–1977) was chosen to organize field workers. In 1965, the Committee led the California Filipino agricultural workers in a strike against the Delano grape growers. (During the strike, Cesar Chavez's organization merged with them to form the United Farm Workers Organizing Committee.)

many of the problems of earlier immigrants. Since they spoke another language, they felt strange and they formed their own neighborhoods where the signs were in Spanish. Strangers, without the advantages of money or education, they, too, joined the American quest for equal opportunity.

Many Puerto Ricans were not satisfied. Some resorted to violence to try to win independence so that Puerto Rico could be a separate nation. Others wanted Puerto Rico to become a state in the Union. Still, in election after election the majority of Puerto Ricans voted to keep the unusual Commonwealth status. Meanwhile, Puerto Rico, with its delightful tropical beaches and its Spanish-American flavor, became a favorite vacation spot for thousands from the mainland. And Puerto Ricans, such as opera singers Martina Arroyo and Justino Diaz, guitarist José Feliciano, violinist José Figueroa, and actors José Ferrer, Rita Moreno, Chita Rivera, Raul Julia, and Hector Elizondo, were enriching the culture of the United States.

The flight from Cuba. Throughout its history
ॐ the United States has been a refuge for people fleeing turmoil and repression. After Fidel Castro seized power in Cuba in 1959 and began to create a Communist state, over half a million islanders fled to the United States. Some went on to settle in other lands, but nearly 400,000 chose to remain here. Many stayed in Florida, especially around Miami.

Some of these newcomers dreamed and planned only for the day when they could return to their Cuban homeland. But others became Americans and began a new life.

The Cubans who came to the United States in the first years after Castro's takeover were generally well educated, and over two-thirds were trained for white-collar jobs. Hardworking and ambitious, some of them soon rose to head banks and businesses. Large sections of Miami became almost as Cuban as Havana itself.

This first wave of refugees was joined in 1980 by more than 100,000 Cubans who fled when Castro suddenly allowed dissatisfied citizens to leave. These new migrants were called "Marielitos" because they had come to the

Olivier Rebbot/Woodfin Camp & Associates

In 1980 Fidel Castro suddenly allowed dissatisfied Cubans to sail from the port of Mariel for Florida. In a brief period 100,000 went by small boats across the dangerous waters to Key West.

United States in a massive flotilla of boats that shuttled between the Cuban harbor of Mariel and Key West in Florida. These migrants, too, worked hard, built businesses, and often prospered. Once again the United States was a haven and a land of new opportunity.

See "Section 5 Review answers," p. 844F.

Section 5 Review

1. Identify or explain: La Raza, barrios, Joseph Montoya, Rodolfo Gonzales, Luis Muñoz Marín, Operation Bootstrap.

2. What are the chief groups that make up the Spanish-speaking peoples of the United States? Locate at least three major areas of settlement.

3. How does the legal status of Puerto Ricans differ from that of other Hispanic immigrants to the United States?

4. **Critical Thinking: Drawing Conclusions.** How did the work of Caesar Chavez help bring about greater equality for all Mexican Americans?

ॐ Multicultural Connection: Cuban-American Armando Valladares spent 22 years in a Communist prison in Cuba where he was tortured and beaten frequently. Upon his release he published an account of his long years in prison. His book, *Against All Hope,* was published in 1986 in several languages. President Reagan appointed Valladares to the U.S. Delegation of the United Nations Human Rights Commission in 1987.

See "Lesson Plan," p. 844F.

6. New waves of immigration

In the 1970s and 1980s, immigration continued. Refugees from war, revolution, persecution, poverty, and tens of thousands simply seeking a better life—all flocked to what they considered the New-World promised land. They, too, sought equality and freedom. They enriched the nation with their hopes and their efforts, but they added problems. In the 1990s, the United States sometimes decided to reduce the flow.

Asians from many nations. The fall of South Vietnam, Laos, and Cambodia to the Communists in 1975 set off a massive emigration by land, sea, and air. Refugees fled to Thailand, Malaysia, Hong Kong, the Philippines, and China. Many hoped to come to the United States. To help those who had aided the United States during the Vietnam War, 125,000 Vietnamese were allowed to enter the country right away. It seemed that this was enough relief at the time.

With the rapid rise in the number of Asians in the United States, new Asian shops and restaurants catered to the tastes not only of the new immigrants but also of native-born Americans.

Bart Bartholomew/Black Star

But thousands more continued to flee. They filled the refugee camps in Southeast Asia and overflowed to the United States and other nations. By 1985, 728,000 of them had come to the United States. These new immigrants from distant lands did well. They were eager to become Americans. They worked hard and added a delightful new Asian spice to the life (and food) of the United States. Many Asian young people overcame the language handicap and did exceedingly well in school. President Reagan, in his State of the Union message to Congress in 1985, pointed to Jean Nguyen, who was seated in the balcony beside Mrs. Reagan. Just ten years before she had fled Vietnam with her family, and now she was about to graduate from the United States Military Academy at West Point. In 1988, in New York City, eleven of the fourteen finalists in a nationwide science competition were Asians.

From other parts of Asia—from India, Taiwan, Korea, and the Philippines—they came by the tens of thousands. In the 1980s Asian Americans were the nation's fastest-growing minority, and the visible success of so many Asian Americans led some observers to call them "the model minority." In fact, many Asian Americans, particularly South East Asian Americans, experienced severe economic hardship in America, with low incomes and high rates of dependence on welfare for survival.

Refugees from Latin America and the Caribbean. Another wave of unhappy people arrived from troubled Central America, and from strife-torn Guatemala, Nicaragua, and El Salvador. Many came in haste and terror without passports or visas. A third wave came from the poverty-stricken and turbulent islands of the Caribbean. From Haiti, they were fleeing the brutal dictatorship of the Duvaliers, "Papa Doc" and his son "Baby Doc." Half the people had no jobs on that island of hunger. Even after the long Duvalier rule (1957–1986) ended, they still came. To check the flow, the government began to send back those who came without permits. Other refugees were detained in prisons and camps while courts decided whether they should be granted political asylum.

See "Lesson Plan," p. 844G for Writing Process Activity: Identifying Central Issues relating to government policy regarding illegal aliens.

After the Haitian military overthrew President Jean-Bertrand Aristide in 1991, the exodus increased so dramatically that President Bush ordered the immediate return of thousands of people fleeing by boat. In 1993 and 1994, President Clinton continued that policy, while working with the United Nations to impose a trade embargo that he hoped would force the military to reinstate President Aristide. The military responded to international pressure with repression, and more Haitians, with no sure destination, left that troubled country's shores.

In 1994, a new flood of refugees left Cuba for Florida. Cuba's economy was in tatters, and since the breakup of the Soviet Union (p. 930), Cuban President Castro had no strong ally. By creating a refugee crisis, Castro hoped to pressure the United States to end the trade embargo on Cuba. But President Clinton refused to end the embargo, or allow Cuban refugees to enter the United States, until Castro reformed his Communist dictatorship.

🔖 *Immigration reform.* Immigrants came from trouble-spots on all continents—from Afghanistan, South Africa, the Soviet Union, Ethiopia, and Ireland. They came for a job and for a better life. Even if they had entered illegally they often found work. They were willing to take jobs that other Americans shunned, and they worked hard. Their children who were born here were citizens of the United States, according to the Constitution. And if they became legal residents, their relatives would be admitted to join them.

President Carter proposed a law in 1977 to make legal all the illegal aliens who had been here since 1970. After that, employers would be fined for hiring illegal aliens. President Reagan asked for a similar law. But Congress refused to act. By 1986 the whole nation was troubled. The United States had been built by those seeking asylum from poverty and tyranny. How were we to adjust this tradition to the circumstances and problems of the late twentieth century?

In 1986 there were millions of illegal aliens in the United States. Unemployment and inflation

Perspectives Topic

in neighboring Mexico drove more across our southern border every day. In late 1986, the Immigration and Naturalization Service reported that in just one year it had caught a record 1.8 million people, most from Mexico, who were trying to slip in. Thousands of others never became statistics.

Finally Congress passed the Immigration Reform and Control Act in 1986. Illegal aliens who could prove that they had been in the United States since January 1, 1982, were allowed to become legal residents. For the first time, anyone hiring illegal immigrants would be fined. And our borders were to be more closely patrolled.

Not everyone was happy with the law, but it ✂ was generally welcome. Until then there really was no clear policy. Laws on the books were sometimes enforced, sometimes ignored. For the moment, our doors were not open wide to all comers. But neither were they closed all the way.

Enrichment Support File Topic

See "Section 6 Review answers," p. 844G.

Section 6 Review

1. What major immigrant groups sought refuge in the United States in the 1970s and 1980s? Why did they leave their homes?

2. Why were many Americans in favor of reforming immigration laws in the 1970s and 1980s?

3. **Critical Thinking: Making Comparisons.** In what ways is the "sanctuary movement" of the 1980s like the "underground railroad" of the mid-1800s? In what ways does it differ?

See "Lesson Plan," p. 844G.

7. New vistas of equality

As other groups of people sought equal rights, Americans were forced to reexamine the meaning of the word *equality*. They discovered new opportunities and new problems.

Gay and lesbian rights. This "minority" was not an immigrant group. It included Americans of all races, all religions, and both sexes. It was

✂ **Critical Thinking Activity: Recognizing Cause and Effect** How has immigration reform impacted the local community? Review the Immigration Reform Act with the class. Ask students to discuss ways that this legislation would affect their community. List the positive and negative effects on the chalkboard. Ask students to write a letter to the editor of the local paper on the subject of immigration reform.

While thousands of Americans demonstrated for equal rights for gays and lesbians each year, many critics argued that special legislation is not needed to prevent discrimination against homosexuals.

found in every state and every city of the nation. With the increased concern for the civil rights first of blacks and then of other groups, it became easier for homosexuals to demand equal treatment.

Many Americans were shocked by the calls for homosexual rights. They believed that the Bible clearly condemned homosexuality, and that it was unnatural and even evil. But homosexuals of both sexes, and many heterosexuals, argued that they, too, should have the right to live their lives without facing discrimination. Instead of the familiar word *homosexual,* men preferred to call themselves "gay." Women homosexuals called themselves "lesbians."

While certain cities, like San Francisco and New York, passed antidiscrimination laws, they were bitterly opposed in others. In 1977 the Miami, Florida, Metro Commission barred discrimination against homosexuals in em-

ployment, housing, public places, and transportation. A citizens' group strongly protested and the ordinance was then put to a public referendum, where it was defeated by a large vote. Many of the critics of gay rights' legislation in Miami and elsewhere argued that even without new laws homosexuals could find ample housing, jobs, and education. In Massachusetts, Cardinal Law of the Roman Catholic church, while saying it was "unjust" to discriminate against homosexuals, said that no additional laws were needed to protect them.

In the fall of 1987, 200,000 homosexuals and their supporters gathered in Washington, D.C. They called for an amendment to the Civil Rights Act of 1964 to bar discrimination on the basis of 'affectional and sexual orientation." Their fight with those Americans seeking to prevent special protection raged into the 1990s. Despite setbacks the movement grew and showed its strength in the summer of 1994, when hundreds of thousands of homosexuals marched, demonstrated, held "gay Olympics," and celebrated to mark the 25th anniversary of the "Stonewall Rebellion," the 1969 Greenwich Village, New York, riot out of which the homosexual rights movement was born.

Equal rights for the physically disabled. Then there were the disabled—people whose physical disability made it difficult for them to compete on an equal basis with other Americans. They included the blind and the deaf, and persons who lacked the use of one or more of their limbs, or who suffered from an illness like epilepsy. Some were veterans. Their numbers were large. In 1990 it was estimated that 43 million Americans—more than all the blacks, Latinos, and Indians taken together—were physically or mentally handicapped.

The Rehabilitation Act of 1973 forbade discrimination against the physically disabled in any of the programs, activities, and facilities that were supported by federal funds. Other laws aimed to prevent job discrimination against disabled persons. The new federal regulations for equal opportunity eased the everyday lives of the disabled in some conspicuous ways. In 1977 federal regulations required that public sidewalks must not have a slope greater than 5 percent and could not be interrupted by steps. Every public building had to have at least one main entrance designed for wheelchairs. In public places, too, some telephone booths and toilets had to be provided for use by the disabled. In 1978 federal specifications required that new buses have a facility for boarding passengers in wheelchairs.

To help the blind, the signs in public buildings had to be made with raised letters or numbers. Doorknobs leading to rooms not intended for public use had to have special ridges to make them identifiable to the touch. Wherever warning signals were given by sounds, there also had to be visual signals to warn the deaf. On TV, many programs were "closed-captioned" for the deaf. This meant that a special

New laws to prevent discrimination against the handicapped have assisted many skilled individuals like this receptionist to find productive jobs and take their rightful place in the work force.

Jim Pickerell/Click/Chicago

decoder would let the hearing impaired see the program accompanied by printed captions.

Even in 1978, when Congress was cutting other costs, it authorized $5.2 billion to be spent over the next four years to provide equal opportunities and legal protection for the disabled.

Mainstreaming. Mentally ill and mentally retarded people also gained. In 1965, community health centers were virtually unknown. Only ten years later they numbered more than a thousand. During these years, too, education of the mentally retarded was improved. By 1979 ten states had declared that their disabled students had a right to receive an equal education.

Everywhere there were signs of concern. By a series of laws and court decisions during the 1970s the federal government insisted that education in the nation's schools and colleges should be opened to all qualified mentally and physically disabled. This was called "mainstreaming"—taking the disabled out of special institutions and bringing them into the mainstream of American life.

Homelessness is rapidly becoming a national problem. An increasing number of the homeless today are young children.

Will Dent McIntyre/Photo Researchers

But not all programs were successful. One approach had some unhappy results. This was the effort to take mentally ill persons out of state mental hospitals and return them to their communities. In the late 1960s and 1970s many people who were not dangerous were being locked away for years and yet received little treatment. The tragedy of their lives was dramatically presented by Ken Kesey in his novel and the engrossing movie *One Flew Over the Cuckoo's Nest.* But when they were sent out without help they created new problems for themselves and the community.

The change was hastened when the Supreme Court ruled in 1975 that the mentally ill who were not dangerous to themselves or others could not be confined against their will. Meanwhile, new medicines and federal aid through Medicare and Medicaid seemed to provide support for the mentally ill if they were released from state hospitals.

But often it did not work that way. Few local communities had planned for this new responsibility. Many of those released became homeless. They lacked skills and could not find jobs. Who would look after them? The result, as the American Psychiatric Institute noted in 1984, was a major tragedy for society.

The mentally ill really needed "halfway ≋ houses." There—just halfway back into the community—they could be trained for jobs while they had medical help. Then when they were ready they would try to return to a normal life. Halfway houses were already helping convicts, alcoholics, and drug addicts. But few communities would pay for the urgently needed services. By the late 1980s the homeless, on the streets of the nation's cities, were attracting wide attention.

In 1990 Congress passed and the President signed into law the Americans with Disabilities Act. It was the most sweeping civil rights legislation since the Civil Rights Act of 1964 (p. 798). It gave federal protection against discrimination to 43 million mentally and physically impaired Americans. Most businesses, restaurants, and public places were required by the new law to make employment and access available to all those who were severely

≋ **Continuity and Change: Social Change** Remind students that in the early 1800s the mentally ill were often treated like criminals. Dorothea Dix became the champion of the cause of the mentally ill, treating them with compassion and medical aid. Today, others carry on her life's work, helping to ease the mentally ill back into the community. At halfway houses, the mentally ill are trained for jobs while receiving medical help until they are ready to return to a normal life. (See p. 282.)

Bob Daemmrich Photography, Inc.

These Native American students are receiving instruction both in English and their tribal language.

limited in "a major life activity," like walking or seeing, or by a physical or mental impairment.

The United or disunited States of America?
Never before had a nation tried so strenuously to give all of its people equality and pride in themselves. But by the 1990s, with so many groups of people going out of their way to distinguish themselves and to seek power by virtue of their racial and ethnic differences, many people worried that the United States of America was becoming disunited; that we were losing sight of what we have in common—the ideals and the heritage that we shared.

✂ Consider, for example, the debate about bilingual education. In Europe, Asia, and Africa, people had fought wars and killed each other to determine what language they would use in school. But the United States had always tried to be a nation of nations. Here people from everywhere found that they could all learn to speak the same language. Immigrant parents who knew only German or Polish or Italian learned English from their children who went to American public schools.

Gradually one language helped to make one nation. The languages from the old country lived on at home, in churches, in clubs, and in special newspapers and magazines. But English was the language of the public schools. The English language took on a wonderful new life here.

In the 1970s and 1980s, in the new quest for equality and pride, some groups began to demand that their children should use their own home language as well as English in the public schools. Bilingual education, they said, would make the Spanish-speaking, the Indians, and other Americans proud of their heritage. Of course, it was important that Americans of all groups should know their heritage and not forget the language of their parents. This approach would enrich the whole nation. Still, there was a danger. If all Americans were not required also to learn and speak the English language well, they might lose their opportunity to compete for the best jobs. The one nation might be broken into small groups that could not speak to one another, could not read the same books, or understand the same TV programs.

And there were other problems, too. In the crusade for equality some people objected to all examinations. They argued that it was unfair to

✂ **Critical Thinking Activity: Determining Relevance** Is our English language adequate for expressing the diversity of the American fabric? Remind students that as a nation of immigrants our ancestors arrived speaking a variety of languages. Ask students to list the different languages represented in their community. How have these languages contributed to the development of a truly "American" English language? Ask students to decide if this language can meet the needs of all Americans. Have students explain their answers and recommend changes if necessary.

give tests for entrance to colleges or to find the most qualified people for jobs. They wanted "open-admissions"—which meant admission for all whether or not they could pass a test. Others, who followed the tradition of Thomas Jefferson, continued to believe in a "natural aristocracy." They argued that all Americans must be given the opportunity to become prepared. Then the examinations would find those who could benefit most from the education or could do the job best. Equal opportunity had to begin with equal kindergartens and elementary schools and high schools for all. In the long run everybody would profit if all Americans could show their true abilities, could be tested impartially, and compete fairly.

Equality among nations. Abroad, too, in the community of nations, Americans faced the challenge of equality. President Kennedy noted "a worldwide declaration of independence," which within 30 years had broken up a few old empires into 90 new nations. Each became a member of the United Nations. There in the General Assembly they would have an equal vote and an equal voice. This group had become a strange community of unequals. A few of these nations had populations of more than 200 million people spread across continents. Many others were tiny islands with populations of less than 100,000. Half the nations who are members of the United Nations have a smaller population than the single state of North Carolina. And four out of every five states in the United States have a larger territory than 30 of these newly independent countries.

By 1994, there were 184 member nations in the United Nations, and new nations were being created with dizzying speed. This situation would make new problems for the community of nations. International law declared that all nations of the earth were entitled to equal treatment. That meant one thing when the community of nations was dominated by a few big nations. These nations usually had languages of their own, and long and separate histories. In those times the voices of the smallest nations were hardly heard.

Now a small nation with an atomic bomb was the equal in terror to any other. Large nations would have to show a new self-restraint. Small nations, too, would have to learn the ways of the world and show new respect for others.

See "Section 7 Review answers," p. 844H.

Section 7 Review

1. Describe efforts in the 1970s to provide equality for the disabled.
2. What is "mainstreaming"?
3. **Critical Thinking: Identifying Assumptions.** Why do some groups want bilingual education in the public schools?

See "Lesson Plan,"p. 844G for Writing Process Activity: Identifying Alternatives relating to bilingual education.

See "Chapter Review answers," p. 844H.

Focusing on Ideas

1. How does a society benefit when its people engage in lively competition for income and social status? What are the "costs" of such competition?

2. Why did the Old World aristocracy not become firmly established in most of colonial America? In which region here did a landed aristocracy thrive? Why?

3. List kinds of United States laws and government programs that are designed to promote the ideal of equality. List laws and programs designed to promote competition. Are these efforts too much, too little, or about right? Explain.

Taking a Critical Look

1. **Recognizing Cause and Effect.** Analyze several recent federal laws or major bills now in Congress and show how they will promote or restrain competition; and advance or retard equality.

2. **Drawing Conclusions.** How is political equality linked to social and economic equality?

3. **Making Comparisons.** How has United States government policy regarding American Indians changed, if at all, since President Lyndon Johnson referred to the American Indian as the "Forgotten American"? Why has this change taken place?

Your Region in History

1. **Economics.** Does your school district have an affirmative action program? What changes has it produced? How have people in the community responded to these programs?

2. **Government.** Have any Indian groups in your state or region taken legal action to obtain land, special fishing or hunting rights, or other compensation? What settlements or proposed settlements have been reached?

3. **Culture.** How has the drive for equality affected your community? Consider both costs and benefits.

Historical Facts and Figures

Predicting Consequences. Study the graph below to help answer the following questions: (a) What percentage of women worked outside the home in 1955? In 1965? In 1990? (b) What events or trends discussed in this chapter are related to this increasing percentage? (c) If the rate of increase remains constant, estimate the percentage of women who will be working outside the home in 1995. In 2000. (d) Do you think this trend will continue over the next 25 years? Explain your answer.

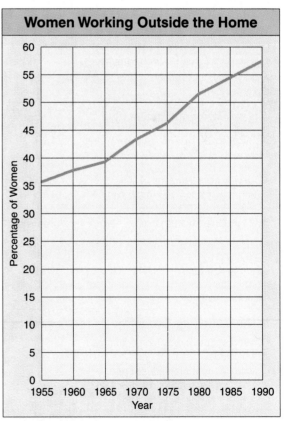

Women Working Outside the Home

Source: *Statistical Abstract of the United States*

Chapter 35
Changing Leaders in Washington

Identifying Chapter Materials

Objectives	Basic Instructional Materials	Extension Materials
1 Gerald Ford Becomes President • Cite the major events of the administration of Gerald Ford and describe the election of 1976.	**Annotated Teacher's Edition** • Lesson Plans, pp. 876C–876D **Instructional Support File** • Pre-Reading Activities, Unit 12, p. 15 • Critical Thinking Activity, Unit 12, p. 20	**Documents of American History** • Ford's Testimony on His Pardon of Nixon, Vol. 2, p. 814 • Report on Foreign and Military Intelligence Activities of the United States, Vol. 2, p. 823 • Pardon for Vietnam Draft Evaders, Vol. 2, p. 825
2 Carter: A Campaigner as President • Describe Carter's difficulties as President. • Discuss issues related to the energy crisis of the late 1970s in detail.	**Annotated Teacher's Edition** • Lesson Plans, p. 876D **Instructional Support File** • Skill Application Activity, Unit 12, p. 19	**Enrichment Support File** • Fueling a Nation: Energy and the Environment (See "In-Depth Coverage" at right.) **Suggested Secondary Sources** • See chart at right.
3 The United States and the World • Explain what happened after United States forces withdrew from Vietnam and identify some successes of shuttle diplomacy.	**Annotated Teacher's Edition** • Lesson Plans, pp. 876D–876E	**Documents of American History** • Agreement on Ending the War and Restoring Peace in Vietnam, Vol. 2, p. 793
4 New Foreign Initiatives by Carter • Describe Carter's foreign policy decisions. • Discuss the factors influencing governmental stances on human rights.	**Annotated Teacher's Edition** • Lesson Plans, pp. 876E–876F **Instructional Support File** • Skill Review Activity, Unit 12, p. 18	**Documents of American History** • Panama Canal Treaties, Vol. 2, p. 828 • Strategic Arms Limitation Treaty II (SALT II), Vol. 2, p. 839 **American History Transparencies** • Time Lines, p. E39
5 New Directions • Explain Reagan's position on the economy. • Summarize governmental involvement in the economy by means of its fiscal and monetary policy.	**Annotated Teacher's Edition** • Lesson Plans, pp. 876F–876G	**Documents of American History** • Reagan's State of the Union Address, Vol. 2, p. 847
6 The Changing Economy • Describe how the economy changed in the 1980s. • Evaluate the arguments for and against the adoption of an industrial policy for the nation in the 1980s.	**Annotated Teacher's Edition** • Lesson Plans, p. 876G **Instructional Support File** • Reading Activities, Unit 12, pp. 16–17 • Chapter Test, Unit 12, pp. 21–24 • Additional Test Questions, Unit 12, pp. 25–28	**Documents of American History** • *Garcia* v. *San Antonio Metropolitan Transit Authority* and *Donovan* v. *San Antonio Metropolitan Transit Authority*, Vol. 2, p. 862 **Enrichment Support File** • The Decline of the Family Farm

Providing In-Depth Coverage

Perspectives on Energy and the Environment

Energy is vital to modern civilization and to the continued growth of the American economy. Until the 1970s it was so plentiful it was almost taken for granted. Throughout the first half of the twentieth century, the United States relied on large domestic oil reserves to satisfy growing energy needs. Few noticed the growing dependence on imported foreign oil.

The energy shock of the 1970s alerted Americans to the dangers of this growing dependence. At the same time, many Americans became more aware of the limited supplies of oil and other key natural resources. Such limits challenge American industry and consumers to use resources more efficiently and to find substitutes for resources that are in short supply.

A History of the United States as an instructional program provides two types of resources you can use to offer in-depth coverage of energy needs and the environment: the *student text* and the *Enrichment Support File.* A list of *Suggested Secondary Sources* is also provided. The chart below shows the topics that are covered in each.

THE STUDENT TEXT. Boorstin and Kelley's *A History of the United States* unfolds the chronology of events resulting in conflict over energy needs vs. environmental protection.

AMERICAN HISTORY ENRICHMENT SUPPORT FILE. This collection of primary source readings and classroom activities focuses on the environmental movement vs. the need for vast natural resources.

SUGGESTED SECONDARY SOURCES. This reference list of readings by well-known historians and other commentators provides an array of perspectives on energy needs and the environment.

Locating Instructional Materials

Detailed lesson plans for teaching energy vs. environment as a mini-course or to study one or more elements of energy needs and environmental protection in depth are offered in the following areas: in the *student text*, see individual lesson plans at the beginning of each chapter; in the *Enrichment Support File,* see page 3; for readings beyond the student text, see *Suggested Secondary Sources.*

IN-DEPTH COVERAGE OF ENERGY AND THE ENVIRONMENT

Student Text	Enrichment Support File	Suggested Secondary Sources
• The energy problem, p. 885 • Action for the environment, pp. 885–886 • Nuclear Power, pp. 886–887 • A weak energy program, p. 887 • Energy crisis, pp. 887–888	• Lesson Suggestions • Multimedia Resources • Overview Essay/Fueling a Nation: Energy and the Environment • Literature in American History/*Artic Dreams* • Songs in American History/"What Have They Done to the Rain?" • Art in American History/Ecology and the Artist • Biography in American History/L. Hunter Lovins • Geography in American History/Hazardous Waste • Great Debates in American History/Offshore Drilling: Energy Necessity or Environmental Tragedy? • Simulation/Special Town Meeting: Nuclear Waste Treatment Center. • Making Connections	• *Energy and the Environment: A Risk-Benefit Approach,* Holt Ashley et. al., eds. • *Energy and American Values* by Ian Barber et. al., pp. 199–210. • *U.S. Energy Policy: Crisis and Complacency* by Don Kask and Robert Rycroft, pp. 257–280. • *The Oil Follies of 1970–1980* by Robert Sherrill, pp. 470–505.

Gerald Ford Becomes President

FOCUS

To introduce the lesson, ask students to write one sentence explaining why Ford acted in the best interests of the nation in pardoning Richard Nixon and one sentence explaining why the pardon was unfair to those Nixon appointees who served time in jail for their crimes. Then discuss the pros and cons of the pardon.

Developing Vocabulary

The words listed in this chapter are essential terms for reading and understanding particular sections of the chapter. The page number after each term indicates the page of its first or most important appearance in the chapter. These terms are defined in the text Glossary (text pages 1000–1011).

pardon (page 877); **impound** (page 879); **OPEC** (page 880).

INSTRUCT

Explain

Carter did not wear formal attire at his "people's inaugural." After the swearing-in ceremony, Carter, his wife, and their daughter walked from the Capitol to the White House.

✤ Cooperative Learning Activity

Testing Conclusions Break the class into groups of three and tell students that they will use outside resources to judge the conclusion, stated in their texts, that Gerald Ford "had served his nation well." Explain that students are to work together to prepare an essay on why they agree or disagree with this conclusion. Make every group member responsible for locating at least one source of information to share with the group, and have each group prepare a bibliography of the resources used. Explain that the grade each group receives will be based on both the essay and the bibliography.

Section Review Answers

Section 1, page 882

1. a) promised those who had deserted the armed forces or evaded the draft during the Vietnam War that they would not be punished if they took an oath of allegiance and did public service work for two years. b) required government agencies to provide, with a few exceptions, documents in their files to any-

one who asked for them. c) gave citizens the right to see information collected about them and to correct it. d) restricted the size of contributions to candidates and provided federal funds for presidential candidates. e) required a President to inform the House and Senate within 48 hours after putting American troops where they might be involved in combat. Unless both houses of Congress vote to allow the troops to stay, they must be withdrawn within 90 days. f) first director of the Congressional Budget Office. g) head of Libya who demanded a higher price for Libyan oil in 1971. h) Organization of Petroleum Exporting Countries, organized in 1960. i) oil tanker that ran aground in Prince William Sound, spilling 11 million gallons of oil into the water. 2. In accordance with the Twenty-fifth Amendment Ford named Rockefeller as his choice for Vice-President. After a three-month investigation, Congress approved the selection. 3. To put the Watergate scandal behind the nation so he could govern effectively. 4. The House and Senate appointed new Intelligence Committees to oversee the CIA, and President Ford appointed an Intelligence Oversight Board to monitor the agency. At the FBI the new director promised to keep the agency under tight control. At the same time, the Privacy Act and amendments to the Freedom of Information Act helped put the FBI and CIA under control by making it easier for the press and other citizens to find out what these agencies were doing. These efforts to control the CIA and FBI were necessary because they had abused their power and violated laws in the past. 5. The United States had become dependent on imported oil; the Arab states had begun demanding higher prices for their oil; the Arab states placed an embargo on oil shipments to the U.S. after the United States helped Israel in the Yom Kippur War of 1973. 6. Nixon proposed an increase in taxes on oil and a reduction in speed limits in order to reduce the demand for fuel as well as greater use of coal and nuclear energy so that the country would be less dependent on petroleum products.

CLOSE

To conclude the lesson, ask the class: How did changes in oil supply and demand in the United States and the rest of the world affect the production of oil? (Students will have to refer to Critical Thinking Worksheet. The changes should have increased the number of significant producers of oil, led people to substitute other energy sources, and decreased somewhat the barrier to explore for more oil by increasing the profits on any oil found. In other words, the changes would make oil production less susceptible to the control of a cartel.) As a result, what might have happened to OPEC later in the 1970s, or in the

1980s? (It should have broken down, depending on how much more oil was found, and what energy alternatives substituted.)

Section 2 (pages 882–888)

Carter: A Campaigner as President

FOCUS

To introduce the lesson, ask: Was the conclusion reached at the end of the previous section about the decline of OPEC shown to be valid in the late 1970s? (No.) Why not? (Two possible answers: The conclusion was wrong, or the long-term effects would take longer to appear.)

Developing Vocabulary
seniority (page 884); **special interest groups** (page 884); **political action committee—PAC** (page 884); **inflation** (page 884); **nuclear power** (page 886).

INSTRUCT

Explain
In the 1980s the price of oil did not rise, but declined somewhat.

☑ Writing Process Activity
Predicting Consequences Ask students to imagine that a nuclear reactor is about to be constructed near their home. In preparation for writing a letter to the editor, students should take a stand on the issue and list the reasons they support or reject the idea. Have students begin their letter with a topic sentence that makes their position clear, and have them organize their support by order of importance. As they revise, students should check for logic and clarity. After proofreading, they can read their letters to the class.

Section Review Answers
Section 2, page 888
1. a) Carter's description of the program that he sent to Congress in 1977 to deal with the energy crisis. b) when the amount of goods sold abroad is less than the amount bought abroad. c) Environmental Protection Agency, established in 1970 to set and enforce standards for air and water quality, the use of pesticides, and the disposal of wastes. d) form of pollution that kills fish and damages forests. It is produced by the burning of coal and the exhaust from cars. e) one of the least expensive ways of mining coal, involves cutting away large strips of the earth's surface. f) ele-

ment used to run a nuclear reactor. g) nuclear power plant in Pennsylvania. A major accident at the plant in 1979 raised questions about the safety of the entire nuclear power industry. h) ruled Iran for many years and was friendly toward the United States. 2. The Watergate scandal had spurred suspicion of any President and increased the assertiveness of members of Congress; the influence of party ties had decreased while the influence of interest groups had increased; Carter lacked experience in dealing with Congress, made tactical mistakes by sending too much to Congress at once, and failed to establish good personal relations with members of Congress. 3. The rising price of oil, a higher minimum wage, increased Social Security taxes, increases in wages to keep pace with inflation, as well as costly environmental and safety regulations. Carter tried to control inflation with wage-price guidelines. 4. Specific collisions between energy and environmental concerns occurred when Carter and Congress had to decide whether to force strip miners to reclaim strip-mined land after the coal had been extracted—a policy that would make coal more expensive—and when they had to choose whether to set aside millions of acres in Alaska as wilderness or allow oil and other resources to be extracted from these lands.

CLOSE

To conclude the lesson, tell the class that in the 1980s the OPEC cartel had a difficult time keeping member countries from breaking agreements on prices. Much of this problem for OPEC was caused by a significant decrease in the demand for imported oil by Americans. Is there anything in this section that indicates why Americans later cut their demand for oil? (The deregulation of natural gas prices and tax deductions for home energy conservation are probably important. The OPEC price hike to $41 per barrel probably did as much itself as our own government's policies. The exhorbitant price of oil drove more and more people to substitute other energy sources and to reduce oil use. That is, OPEC may have brought about its own demise.)

Section 3 (pages 888–891)

The United States and the World

FOCUS

To introduce the lesson, ask students to tell you what they know about the Soviet Union. List their answers on the board. Then ask: How was the Soviet Union

35

different from the United States? How was it similar? Write on the board two column headings, Similarities and Differences, and list students' responses in the appropriate columns. (Some similarities: large land areas, large populations, many different ethnic and cultural groups, military superpowers, very influential in other countries around the world. Some differences: totalitarian vs. democratic government; communist vs. capitalist economic system; censorship, oppression, and government control of everyday life vs. freedom and emphasis on individual rights.)

Developing Vocabulary
shuttle diplomacy (page 889)

INSTRUCT

Explain
Amerasian children (those born of an American father and Vietnamese mother) have suffered greatly in Vietnam. In 1983, Secretary of State George Schultz announced that the United States would accept all Amerasian children and their families who wanted to emigrate to the United States.

★ Independent Activity
Identifying Central Issues Have students do independent research in preparation for writing a two-page report on the current status of U.S.-Russian relations. Their reports should include any recent developments affecting the relations between the two countries.

Section Review Answers
Section 3, page 891

1. a) diplomacy involving frequent air travel between nations. b) signed in 1975 by 35 nations, including the United States and the Soviet Union, to settle issues that had lingered since World War II. c) Cambodian Communists who seized control of the country in 1975. d) Communist faction in Laos, took control of the country in 1975. e) people who fled Cambodia, often in flimsy boats. 2. Yes; Cambodia Laos, and South Vietnam fell to the Communists, much as the domino theory had suggested.

CLOSE

To conclude the lesson, tell students that each year the United Nations Commission on Human Rights and other human rights advocacy organizations issue reports of violations of human rights around the world. Contact the UN, or Amnesty International, or some other such group to get a copy of their latest report. Ask students: How many of you have ever heard of these reports? How many of you have ever read any? Ask them to speculate on which countries' governments were cited as most abusive of human rights in the most recent reports. Then ask: Which of those governments does the United States support? Why? (Strategic, political, and economic reasons.) Were you aware of our support for these governments? List on the board, in no particular order, all of the criteria for making foreign policy decisions that have been mentioned in the course of this discussion. (Human rights, struggle against communism, other political interests, economic interests, military and strategic interest.) Ask students to rank these criteria in order of importance and then write a paragraph explaining why they chose the order they did, or why they put their first item first and their last item last.

Section 4 (pages 891–895)

New Foreign Initiatives by Carter

FOCUS

To introduce the lesson, ask: Is it ever necessary for governments to deny people basic human rights? Have students explain circumstances that might merit such a response. (Some instances that might come up: war, national disaster, revolution, attempts to capture terrorists.)

Developing Vocabulary
Third World (page 893); **embassy** (page 894).

INSTRUCT

Explain
Obtain recent information from Amnesty International or the United Nations about human rights violations around the world and share the material with students.

☑ Writing Process Activity
Demonstrating Reasoned Judgment Tell students that as political analysts during the Carter administration, they must choose one area of the world, such as Russia or the Middle East, to analyze. Before writing an essay about the effect of Carter's human rights position on foreign policy in the area they have chosen, students should brainstorm the causes and effects of U.S. diplomacy. Students should begin their essay with a thesis statement that summarizes the conflict and Carter's efforts to resolve it. Have students revise their essays for logical development and organization. After proofreading, students can discuss their analyses in small groups.

Section Review Answers

Section 4, page 895

1. a) second Strategic Arms Limitation Treaty between the United States and the Soviet Union, signed in 1979 but never ratified by the United States Senate. b) includes nations that had no strong attachment to the United States or the Soviet Union. c) president of Egypt who became the first leader of an Arab country to visit Israel. He signed a peace treaty with Israel in 1979. d) prime minister of Israel who negotiated the peace treaty with Sadat. e) fanatical Muslim religious leader who replaced the Shah as ruler of Iran. f) leftists who led the fight to overthrow Somoza and took control of Nicaragua in 1979. 2. The United States was dismayed to see its ally the Shah of Iran overthrown. Despite warnings of reprisals against embassy personnel, President Carter allowed the shah to enter the United States for medical treatment. When rebels toppled the Somoza government of Nicaragua, the United States recognized the new government. 3. Carter brought Sadat and Begin together at Camp David and worked with them for thirteen days to negotiate the framework for a peace treaty. Then in 1979 he traveled to Egypt and Israel to settle the last differences that were blocking the signing of a peace treaty between the two countries. 4. His stand was intended to force totalitarian governments to stop abusing their citizens. It set back relations with the Soviet Union, and critics charged that it would anger our allies without influencing our enemies. Victims of tyranny praised Carter's stand.

CLOSE

To conclude the lesson, ask: Was the U.S. involvement in the Vietnam War consistent or inconsistent with American foreign policy goals as expressed by Carter and Vance? The involvement in the peacekeeping forces in Lebanon in 1982 and 1983? The invasion of Grenada in 1983? Ask the same question of any U.S. overseas involvement that has been in the news recently.

Section 5 (pages 896–899)

New Directions

FOCUS

To introduce the lesson, ask: What is fiscal policy? What is monetary policy? (Answers: Fiscal policy concerns governmental spending and tax revenues. Monetary policy is the control of the supply of money.)

Developing Vocabulary

budget (page 897); **supply-side economics** (page 897); **deficit** (page 898); **recession** (page 898); **entitlements** (page 898).

INSTRUCT

Explain

After being shot, as Reagan was being wheeled into the operating room, he grinned at the doctors and said he hoped they were all Republicans. Later he complained that he had worn a new suit and now it was ruined. Such charm and bravery was hard to resist.

❈ Cooperative Learning Activity

Identifying Central Issues Divide the class into groups of three. Explain that the grade each student receives will be based on the work of his or her entire group. Have each group member prepare written responses to the questions in the Section 5 Review of Chapter 35. Then have group members critique each other's written work, passing around papers until all group members have read every member's work. Explain that students may revise their answers based on the feedback from other group members before turning in their final drafts.

Section Review Answers

Section 5, page 899

1. a) Chairman of the Federal Reserve Board when the Federal Reserve's decision to restrict the money supply and let interest rates go where they wanted caused a recession. b) legal ways of reducing one's tax bill. c) nation's central bank. It controls such things as the amount of money in circulation, the financing of the federal debt, and the amount of reserves a bank must hold. d) economic theory favored by President Reagan. e) British economist who said that government should spur the economy by programs to provide money for citizens to purchase goods and services. 2. Supply-side economics says that the engine of economic growth is the supply of goods and services provided by business, and that to stimulate growth the government should therefore stimulate investment in business by cutting taxes, especially for those with large incomes. According to supply-side theory, if taxes are cut, these people will save and invest more; then, because of increased investment, businesses will supply more goods and services and hire more people in order to do so; thus the economy will grow. In contrast, Keynesian theory emphasizes the importance of the demand for goods and services. According to Keynesian theory, the primary way to stimulate economic growth is to put money into consumers' hands so they will demand

more goods and services; then businesses will increase the supply of goods and services to meet this demand; thus the economy will grow. 3. Beginning in 1979 the Federal Reserve Board slowed the growth of the money supply in order to bring inflation under control. This "tight money" policy pushed interest rates up, which slowed business activity, bringing on the recession of 1981–1982. 4. Unlike other Presidents since FDR, Reagan wanted to reverse the direction of the government in accordance with a conservative ideology. Reagan viewed government as the source of the nation's basic problems, not as a tool for solving them.

CLOSE

To conclude the lesson, ask: How do fiscal and monetary policy affect the American economy? Then ask students to write a paragraph arguing that increased interest rates do or do not cause increases in unemployment, based on information found in the text and any other information they may have at hand.

Section 6 (pages 899–904)

The Changing Economy

FOCUS

To introduce the lesson, ask: What roles does the United States government play in the economy? (Some of the many roles: levies and collects taxes; spends billions of dollars each year; regulates some industries; controls the money supply; and subsidizes some businesses.) Then ask: Are there other roles government could play?

Developing Vocabulary
deregulation (page 902)

INSTRUCT

Explain
Ask students to find the cause and effect relationships outlined in the subsection "Decline of the smokestack industries" (p. 899).

☑ Writing Process Activity
Recognizing Cause and Effect Ask students to imagine that they are the owners of a major airline. Using standard letter format, each student will write a letter to the Interstate Commerce Commission, either praising or criticizing deregulation. Explain to students that their letters should include an opening statement expressing their pro or con position concerning deregulation, at least three pieces of evidence to support their position, and a closing sentence summing up their argument. After proofreading, students may share their letters with the rest of the class.

Section Review Answers
Section 6, page 904

1. a) steel, textile, and automobile industries. b) area in California noted for its many companies that create goods and services related to computers. c) controlled telephone service across the United States until 1983. d) monitor air traffic. e) fertilizers, better seeds, and modern-farming techniques which helped countries such as India and the Philippines to produce enough rice and wheat to feed themselves. f) reduction of government control over business and other activities. 2. Inflation, government regulations, and increased competition from foreign countries, especially from plants built to replace those destroyed in World War II. 3. They went on strike despite the fact that their contract barred them from striking. 4. The Department of Justice sued the company under the antitrust laws. According to the settlement of the government's suit, AT&T sold its local phone companies, continued its long-distance service, and was allowed to enter the computer industry. As a result of this action, there was new competition in both the telephone and the computer industries.

CLOSE

To conclude the lesson, ask: Should the United States adopt an industrial policy? Ask: What are the advantages and disadvantages of industrial policy? (Advantages: It could promote economic growth and an intelligent approach to economic change. Disadvantages: It would put government policymakers in the place of business decisionmakers; it could lead to big mistakes that would be paid for by the taxpayers; it would expand the size of government.)

Chapter Review Answers
Focusing on Ideas

1. Carter could not keep all his promises, which led to low public approval ratings. 2. Hard to compromise issues include abortion, gun control, religious exercises in public schools, neighborhood schools vs. busing. 3. Support: an unsafe world as long as human rights are violated; active concern for fellow humans is a moral imperative; and so on. Attack: self interest should be the keystone of foreign policy; pushing for human rights threatens our relationships with nations we have to deal with; and so on. 4. Inflation control: helps people with fixed incomes, businesses, consumers. Dollar gains value: helps Ameri-

cans abroad, foreign companies selling in U.S.; hurts U.S. companies selling abroad. Unemployment rises: hurts workers. Interest rates rise: hurts people making large purchases; start-up or expanding companies; helps lenders who can find borrowers.

Taking a Critical Look

1. Arguments for clemency: forgiveness as a cherished value resting on religious principles; the illegality of the war in that it was not declared; and so on. Arguments against: sets a bad example for dealing with future cases of draft evasion and desertion; unfair to those who served honorably. 2. Make this a brainstorming session, since so many points of comparison and contrast are possible. 3. Cause: Fall in demand for products of unionized companies. Effects: Unions settle for smaller wage increases and look for ways to be more productive to keep their companies in business.

Your Region in History

1–2. Answers will vary depending on your region. Consult your local library or historical society.

Historical Facts and Figures

(a) from about 1950 to 1952, from 1965 to 1968, and from 1980 to 1985. (b) 1950: the Korean War, the Cold War; 1965: the Vietnam War; 1980: the Cold War, Reagan's policy on defense. (c) rising national debt, new leadership and policies, the end of the Cold War.

35

Chapter 35

Changing Leaders in Washington

The American people had proven their power to remove their President. But it was much easier to change the nation's President than to solve the nation's long-term problems. How could the United States profit from the lessons of Vietnam and Watergate and still give the President the power to lead? Inflation, the energy crisis, and difficulties with Communist and other nations were not the fault either of any one political party or of any one President. Now new leaders would have to face these hard problems.

Former Presidents can often offer solid advice to their successors. In this photograph Gerald Ford (right) talks to President Carter in the Oval Office of the White House.

Black Star

More from Boorstin: "We have nearly lost interest in those real examples from the human past which alone can help us shape standards of the humanly possible. So we compare ours with a mythical Trouble-Free World, where all mankind was at peace. We talk about the war in Vietnam as if it were the first war in American history to which many Americans were opposed. We condemn our nation for not yet having attained perfect justice, and we forget that ours is the most motley and miscellaneous great nation in history." (From *Democracy and Its Discontents: Reflections on Everyday America*)

See "Lesson Plan," p. 876C.

1. Gerald Ford becomes President

Gerald Ford, the first man to become President without being elected President or Vice-President, faced an awesome task. The people's faith in the honesty and integrity of their political leaders had been shaken. Congress and the executive branch were at odds. The economy was in tatters as the nation sank into the worst recession since World War II, and inflation soared.

The new President. Ford was neither a dashing man nor an eloquent speaker, but at this moment in the nation's history he was something more important. There was nothing devious about him. He was honest and open. And his long experience in the Congress gave him much knowledge and some wisdom about how Washington functioned.

When he became President in August 1974, Ford wanted to put an end to the Watergate problems, restore the people's faith in their government, and cure the nation's economic ills—especially inflation. He promised to run an open administration and to work with Congress. As he took the oath of office on television, Ford reminded the nation's voters that, since they had not chosen him, he had a special duty to earn their confidence.

Selecting a Vice-President. Now that the Vice-Presidency was vacant, under the Twenty-fifth Amendment Ford had to name a new Vice-President, who would take office if confirmed by both houses of Congress. Ford chose and Congress confirmed Nelson A. Rockefeller, the cheerful, dynamic, and experienced grandson of John D. Rockefeller. A leading liberal Republican, Rockefeller had sought the Presidency himself in 1964 and 1968. He had served Presidents of both parties, from FDR to Eisenhower, and between 1958 and 1973 he was the highly effective governor of New York.

Pardon and clemency. Soon after taking office, Ford revealed that he was thinking of moderating any punishment for former President Nixon. At first he said that he would not do any-

thing until the courts had acted. Then, less than two weeks later, he went on television to announce that he was granting Nixon a full pardon for *any* crimes he might have committed during his time as President. Ford said he feared that unless the people and the government put Nixon and Watergate behind them, it would be impossible for him to govern effectively. The nation would continue to be torn apart by the troubles of the past.

Nixon accepted the pardon. Although he admitted that he had handled the Watergate question badly, he still failed to say that he had done anything wrong. Pardoning Nixon lost Ford much public support. Some people felt that the former President should have been tried in the courts for his acts.

As another way to bury the past, Ford announced a program of clemency for those who

Energetic Nelson Rockefeller (left) was Ford's choice for Vice-President.

Fred Ward/Black Star

had deserted from the armed forces or evaded the draft during the Vietnam War. They would not be punished if they took the oath of allegiance to the United States and then did up to two years of alternative service in jobs that would "promote the national health, safety, or interest." Since this plan was not an outright pardon, most of the 124,000 draft evaders and deserters refused Ford's offer. Some Americans felt that these men had shirked their duty and deserved to be punished. President Carter later pardoned nearly all the draft evaders. But this action provoked less comment because by then the passions of war had begun to cool.

Controlling the CIA and the FBI.
The Watergate and impeachment hearings had led to serious charges against the Central Intelligence Agency and the Federal Bureau of Investigation. Soon President Ford appointed a commission under Vice-President Rockefeller to study the CIA. Committees in the House and Senate began their own probes of the CIA and FBI.

These studies showed that under six Presidents, from Franklin D. Roosevelt to Richard Nixon, the FBI had abused its powers. Without legal permits its agents had tapped telephones, read private mail, broken into buildings, placed

Ford's pardon of Nixon upset many Americans.

Ford Presidential Library

listening devices in homes and offices, and kept records on thousands of innocent citizens.

The CIA had also been spying on Americans and opening their mail. It had even experimented on unsuspecting people with dangerous mind-control drugs. Abroad, the CIA had worked secretly to bring down a democratically elected, Marxist regime in Chile and then had denied doing so to Congress. It was also accused of having plotted to assassinate unfriendly foreign leaders.

Clearly the nation needed the CIA to gather information from every part of the world, and the FBI to enforce federal laws. But, Congress wanted to oversee both agencies. In Communist countries and in dictatorships, citizens were at the mercy of the police. But in a free country innocent citizens had to be protected from harassment and from snoopers.

Was it possible to devise a system of oversight that would neither give away our secrets nor hamstring our intelligence operations at home and abroad? President Ford set up an Intelligence Oversight Board made up of three private citizens to monitor the CIA. Both the House and Senate appointed their own committees. At the FBI, a new director promised to take firm control of the bureau's agents and activities. Congress worked on laws to define more strictly the activities of the two agencies.

Opening up government and protecting elections.
Watergate also created a strong feeling in Congress that the activities of all the hundreds of government agencies had to be opened up so people could know what their government was doing. A little-used Freedom of Information Act, passed in 1966, was strengthened by a series of amendments in 1974 and 1976. Government departments and agencies now had to give copies of documents in their files to anyone—even Soviet officials—who asked for them. Only a few exceptions for national defense, foreign policy, and law enforcement were allowed. A Privacy Act, also passed in 1974, gave citizens the right to see the information collected about them and to correct it. With these laws, the United States government became the most open in the world.

The Watergate hearings had also revealed large-scale illegal gifts to the Nixon reelection campaign. To limit the size of political contributions—and reduce temptations—a Federal Election Campaign-funding Reform Act was passed in 1974. It also provided federal funds for candidates in presidential primaries and elections.

Congress strengthens its hand. Congress moved on other fronts as well to assert its power. While Nixon was still President, Congress had tried to reclaim its right under the Constitution to declare war. Senators and representatives felt that since World War II, Presidents had bypassed the Constitution, especially during the fighting in Korea and Vietnam. In November 1973, over Nixon's veto, Congress had passed the War Powers Act. This act declared that the President must inform the House and Senate within 48 hours of putting American troops where they might be involved in fighting. The President had to bring the troops home within 90 days unless both houses voted to let them stay.

On the domestic front, Congress also acted to hold its powers. In the Budget and Impoundment Act of 1974, it declared that a President could not "impound" funds—that is, refuse to spend money Congress had voted. Nixon had done this late in his Presidency. This law also created a new Congressional Budget Office (CBO) to provide Congress with its own income and expense figures. Previously, legislators had received the budget figures from the President and had no way to check their accuracy. A bright, professional economist, Alice Mitchell Rivlin, was appointed the first director of this important new office.

Problems with the economy. While President Nixon was distracted by Watergate, he had not managed to bring inflation under control. By 1973 inflation was running annually at 8.5 percent. In 1974 it had increased to 12 percent, and a recession had begun. By raising prices, and so decreasing the amount a dollar could buy, inflation hurt every American.

When Gerald Ford came to the White House, he viewed inflation as the nation's number-one problem. He believed that government spending kept prices going up, and he used his veto 66 times to try to check it. But the largest factor in the inflation of the 1970s was the price of oil.

Oil and inflation. Until 1953, the United States produced more oil than it could use, and regularly exported petroleum and petroleum products. But as the economy expanded and everybody used machines for everything, we came to use more oil and gasoline than we produced. Homes and automobiles, farms and factories, needed the energy made from oil. The nation needed more and more imported oil.

As the 1970s began, there were substantial reserves of oil throughout the world. These large reserves, combined with government support of the major American oil companies, should have been enough to keep the price of oil from rising. In fact, it appeared that the price of oil might drop to below one dollar a barrel (it cost only 25 cents a barrel to produce). But then in 1971, the revolutionary government of Colonel Muammar el-Qaddafi of Libya demanded higher prices for Libyan oil. The United States government failed to help the oil companies resist the demand—and even suggested that Libya's request was fair. So Libya raised the price of its oil. Other oil-producing countries quickly followed Libya's example. Now prices began to rise rapidly. By the fall of 1973 they had quintupled.

Then came the 1973 Yom Kippur War (p. 835). In anger at Nixon's very public aid to Israel, the Arab nations of the Middle East cut off their oil shipments to the United States. The Netherlands, another supporter of Israel, was refused oil, too. By purchasing oil from other nations, especially Canada, Iran, and Indonesia, the United States kept its shortage down to 7 percent. But American drivers panicked. For the first time in American history they waited in long lines to fill their tanks. Gas stations became a scene of bad-tempered scuffling for a few more gallons.

As the demand increased worldwide, governments and dealers bid up the price for some oil to what was then an astonishing $17.40 per barrel in December 1973.

✂ Critical Thinking Activity: Identifying Alternatives Did the United States government take adequate steps to restore the public's faith in its political leaders and system of government? Have students list reforms in the government during the Ford administration. Ask students to explain the rationale behind each reform, and have them add to the list their own suggestions for additional reforms. Conclude by asking students to discuss the advantages and disadvantages of having the public know everything that the government is doing.

OPEC. Some of the oil-producing countries, led by Venezuela, had begun to organize back in 1960. But their Organization of Petroleum Exporting Countries (OPEC) had never been strong. Each oil-producing country wanted all it could get for its oil and feared that higher prices would decrease its sales and income. But the price rises that had begun in 1971 had made the OPEC nations rich. Now they could afford to ask for even more, and the high prices received for some oil in December 1973 revealed that the world could be made to pay. Meeting in Teheran, Iran, at the end of the month, they set the price for all of their oil at nearly $12 per barrel. Then they limited production to force customers to pay this high price. The Western world, Japan, and the developing nations were hit hard.

Despite warnings of our growing dependence on imported oil, the Nixon administration had made no provision for dealing with an oil cutoff or high prices. Now Nixon proposed a number of short-term measures, such as increased

Filling-station managers found amusing ways to say "No Gas Today" during the Arab oil embargo of 1973–1974.
Dennis Brack/Black Star

taxes on oil and a 55-mile-per-hour speed limit. For long-term measures he proposed more nuclear power plants (despite growing concerns about their safety) and greater use of coal (despite great concern about air pollution). And we would push ahead with a pipeline across Alaska to the vast oil deposits on the edge of the Arctic Ocean. This oil had been discovered early in 1968. Had the pipeline been completed in 1973, the United States would easily have replaced the lost Arab oil from its own sources. But construction had been held up by fears of the damage it might do to the fragile northern environment. Years later, in 1989, these fears would be realized when the oil tanker *Exxon Valdez* went aground in Alaska's Prince William Sound. It spilled 11 million gallons of oil in the water and killed countless fish, birds, and other wildlife.

When Gerald Ford became President, the worst of the oil shortage brought on by the Arab nations had passed. But because of high energy prices, the United States was still in the worst recession since World War II. Ford now tried urgent measures to get the economy moving again. Taxes were cut and large government deficits, running over $50 billion, pumped new money into the economy. The economy did recover and, due to the lingering effects of the recession, inflation in 1976 fell to below 5 percent.

⊕ (p. 881)

Running for President. The presidential campaign of 1976 was one of the longest in our history. Gerald Ford announced in July 1975 that he wanted to be President in his own right. His main opponent for the Republican nomination was Ronald Reagan, a former movie star and a persuasive public speaker who had served two terms as governor of California. He represented the conservative wing of his party. An outspoken anti-Communist, he criticized the policy of détente with Russia. Reagan wanted the Republican party to take a strong, conservative position on every issue. Ford favored more moderate positions to broaden the party's appeal. After a series of primaries early in 1976, the two candidates were neck and neck. When the party gathered in Kansas City, Mis-

OPEC, 1975

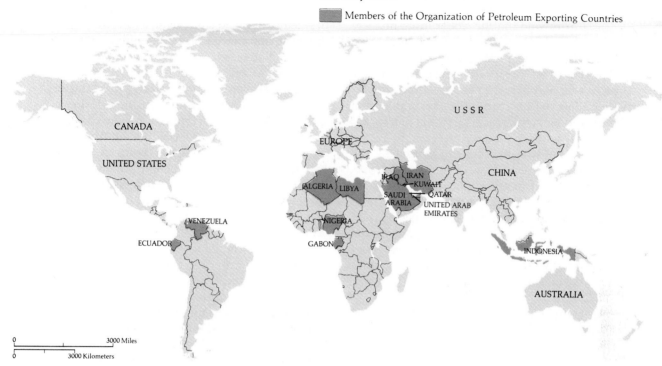

Members of the Organization of Petroleum Exporting Countries

souri, for its convention, Ford narrowly won the nomination.

The first Democrat to declare his candidacy was Georgia governor James Earl Carter. Carter, who called himself and signed his name Jimmy Carter, had been born and raised in the small towns of Plains and Archery, Georgia. After high school, Carter was appointed to the United States Naval Academy. He graduated from Annapolis in 1946, and that same year he married Rosalynn Smith of Plains.

Carter spent the next seven years in the navy, first on battleships and then on the early nuclear submarines. In 1953 when his father died, Carter returned to Plains to run the family peanut farm and warehouse. From there he went on to become a state senator in 1964 and governor of Georgia in 1970. He was outspoken in his opposition to racial discrimination. And his supporters applauded his reorganization of the state government.

Carter's term as governor ended in January 1975. Since state law barred him from succeeding himself, he began to spend all his time

campaigning for the Democratic nomination for President. He was little known outside Georgia, however, and as late as October of that year, few people considered him a serious contender.

But this was soon to change. He showed a single-minded devotion to his purpose. A "born again" Christian and a member of the Baptist church, he impressed people with his simple manner, his honesty, and his sincerity. He was also helped by the fact that he had had nothing to do with Vietnam or Watergate. In 1976 he began to win primary after primary over the many other Democratic hopefuls. When the party met in New York City for its convention, Carter was clearly in the lead. He was chosen on the first ballot and named Walter F. Mondale, an attractive liberal senator from Minnesota, to run for Vice-President.

The election of 1976. In the campaign, President Ford pushed hard to sell the country on his achievements. He pointed out how he had cut federal spending, lowered the rate of inflation, and decreased unemployment. For the

⊕ **Geography and History: Location** Have students look at the map above to locate the members of OPEC in 1975. Ask: How many OPEC countries are shown on the map? (Thirteen) What African OPEC countries share a border? (Algeria and Libya) What geographical characteristic is common to all OPEC countries? (They all have access to a body of water.) Why is this important? (For ease of oil shipment.) In what circumstances could military conflict among OPEC nations adversely affect the nation's economy? (If an OPEC nation loses control of water access, oil shipment, and therefore the nation's entire economy, can be affected.)

first time in years, Ford stressed, no United States soldiers were in combat anywhere in the world. Carter said that he would bring honesty and integrity back to the government and bring government back to the people.

The result of the election was very close. Carter won just over 50 percent of the popular vote to Ford's 48 percent. The electoral margin was the narrowest since 1916, as Carter received 297 votes to Ford's 240. Again the number of people who bothered to vote at all declined; only 53 percent went to the polls.

In his inaugural address Jimmy Carter declared, "For myself and for our nation I want to �֎ thank my predecessor for all he has done to heal our land." An unelected President, Gerald Ford had served his nation well.

See "Section 1 Review answers," p. 876C.

Section 1 Review

1. Identify or explain: clemency program, Freedom of Information Act, Privacy Act, Federal Election Campaign-funding Reform Act, War Powers Act, Alice M. Rivlin, Muammar el-Qaddafi, OPEC, *Exxon Valdez.*

2. How did Nelson Rockefeller become Vice-President?

3. According to Ford, why did he pardon Nixon?

4. What new controls were placed on the CIA and the FBI? Why?

5. Why was there an energy crisis in 1973 and 1974?

6. **Critical Thinking: Identifying Alternatives.** What were some proposed solutions to the energy problem?

See "Lesson Plan," p. 876D.

2. Carter: a campaigner as President

In his bid for office, Jimmy Carter had run against the government in Washington. He profited from the disrespect for government and for politicians that spread after Vietnam and Watergate. Now he had to prove that an "outsider"—a "peanut farmer," his supporters reminded voters—actually could make the government efficient and responsive to the needs of the people. But he came into office at a time when the country faced a number of staggering problems, and the same cynicism toward government that got him the job made it difficult for him to succeed.

Carter's proposals and their fate. Carter came to Washington with a burning desire to get things done. In his first year in office he sent Congress proposals for legislation on the economy, welfare, social security, health care, election laws, and energy. Yet his proposals ran into immediate difficulty in Congress, and even three years into his Presidency he had little to show for them. Instead of a major economic stimulus package, he settled for a modest jobs program. He never delivered proposals for major tax reform, and Congress blocked his proposals for election reform and welfare reform. When Congress finally passed an energy bill in 1978, it was a much weaker bill than the one that Carter had initially proposed.

Carter did succeed in raising money for the social security system, which was paying out much more money than it was taking in. Experts predicted that in a few years the whole system would be bankrupt. Unless the federal government voted funds, the disabled and the elderly would no longer receive their pensions. The law that President Carter signed in December 1977 raising social security taxes was the largest peacetime tax increase in American history.

When a President is of one party and Congress is dominated by the other, it is not hard to explain his domestic policy difficulties. But Carter was a Democrat and his party controlled both houses of Congress. To understand Carter's difficulties, we have to look at his experience and leadership, his relations with Congress, the economy he inherited, and the nature of the problems he tried to solve.

Experience and leadership. Carter picked a capable Cabinet, but as his closest staff aides he kept the young and inexperienced Georgians who had helped in his campaign. His most trusted adviser was the bright Rosalynn Carter who, more than most previous Presi-

✖ See "Lesson Plan," p. 876C for Cooperative Learning Activity: Testing Conclusions relating to the presidency of Gerald Ford.

Jimmy and Rosalynn Carter brought a relaxed air and informal clothes to the White House. During the four years of Carter's Presidency, his wife was his most trusted adviser.

dents' wives, shared in his highest decisions on people and policies. To keep up with what was being planned, she sometimes sat in on Cabinet meetings—the first "First Lady" to do so. Unfortunately neither the President, his closest advisers, nor Rosalynn Carter knew the leaders of Congress or the way things worked in Washington. Their inexperience, when combined with an honorable if naive refusal to play the game by the old rules, made for strained relations with Congress.

Carter got off to a clumsy start. Seeking to make good on his campaign promise to cleanse government of waste and corruption, Carter immediately announced the elimination of a number of expensive dam and water projects— critics called them "pork barrel" projects— from the federal budget. Those projects, however wasteful, made many Congressmen popular at home. Carter's efforts cost him im-

portant friends on Capitol Hill. Angry Congressmen complained that Carter should at least have consulted them before announcing his decision.

In the early months of 1977, Congress also complained that the administration was trying to do too many things too quickly, without proper deliberation and care. Carter announced his energy program with great fanfare, calling it "the moral equivalent of war." He then proceeded to ask for legislation on many other matters. Congress and the nation wondered what his priorities were. When Carter sent the energy bill to Congress in April, experts found it full of technical flaws. By October 1977, the leaders of Congress were pleading with the President to stop sending his proposals. Congress was swamped. Carter's own aides complained that he had set deadlines that were impossible to meet.

More than once in Carter's first year in office he submitted an important proposal but then, in the face of opposition, suddenly surrendered. His forceful pushing of projects and then his hasty retreats left his supporters on Capitol Hill feeling bewildered and angry. Part of Carter's clumsiness with Congress lay in inexperience, part in his own character. He did not make friends easily. He had been a warm and friendly campaigner, but once in office he became remote and hard to reach. He failed to seek the advice of more experienced politicians who might have steered him through the thickets of Washington. He immersed himself in the details of important projects. And while he studied new proposals, the government lacked a strong leader.

The changing nature of Congress and the rise of the special-interest state. Carter's relations with Congress were made more difficult by changes in Congress brought on by Watergate. The new members elected in 1974 and 1976 tended to view every presidential act with suspicion. Members of Congress themselves now had larger staffs to give them information, which made them more independent of the President and the House and Senate leaders. The seniority power of long-term members was reduced and dispersed to many committee and subcommittee heads. All these developments made it much harder to pass the laws that a President wanted.

Party loyalty had also declined. The major political parties had been forces for moderation, compromise, and discipline in a large and diverse nation. To elect a President or a member of Congress or to pass a law, people with different goals had to come together. And the parties had helped.

A great change was in the making. In late twentieth-century America citizens were organizing less around their political parties than around their own particular interests. Big businesses, small businesses, labor unions, farmers, environmentalists, pro- and anti-gun forces, blacks, Hispanics, doctors, lawyers, mayors, governors, consumers, pro- and anti-abortion groups, and others pushed for their own special programs. Many of these groups had their own Political Action Committees (PACs), which contributed large sums to elect their favorite candidates. These special interests wielded great influence in Congress.

With the power of these groups growing greater all the time, the broad issues of national concern were lost. The rise of television, opinion polls, and public relations helped the groups attract attention. Politicians were attacked or supported, not for their general political outlook, but for their stand on a single issue. In Congress, under such pressures, party loyalty declined. Members of Congress were less apt to follow the President's lead or pass measures for the good of the party.

The problem of inflation. Inflation was Carter's greatest domestic problem, as it had been Nixon's and Ford's before him. While Carter urged voluntary restraints and set government wage-price guidelines, the rate of inflation soared, reaching 1 percent a month during the first half of 1979. The problem of inflation was deep-seated and complex. It was produced by the rising cost of oil, a higher minimum wage enacted in 1977, the increased social security taxes, costly environmental and safety regulations, and ever-higher wages as workers sought to keep their standard of living in the face of ever-rising inflation. The many welfare programs to aid the sick, the poor, the aged, and the unemployed played their part, too. The government's constant attempts to stimulate the economy to provide more jobs also made the problem worse. The nation saw a baffling new phenomenon: stagnation of the economy and inflation of prices. People called this "stagflation."

Carter came into office promising to fight inflation and stimulate the economy; to combat unemployment and bring the budget deficit under control; to reform welfare and cut government spending; to lessen our dependence on foreign oil and save the environment. Those were all worthy goals, but they were complex and interrelated. Measures that stimulated the economy often increased inflation; measures that cut inflation tended to slow the economy.

Carter cared deeply about the plight of the unemployed and the unemployable in America's inner cities; he imagined a public works project that would provide skills and jobs. But he also cared about bringing government spending under control, and when he realized how expensive public works would be, at least in the short run, he scaled back his plans, leaving many of his liberal supporters feeling betrayed.

Carter found his own staff's plans for welfare reform prohibitively expensive. These plans would have increased the minimum wage, provided job training and jobs for welfare recipients who could work, and a decent income for those who could not work. Perhaps none of the problems Carter confronted were as tangled as the energy shortage, the economy, and the environment.

The energy problem. The United States was the most profligate energy user in the world. With only 6 percent of the world's population, the United States used 33 percent of all the world's energy! Even with our own rich oil fields, we imported more than 30 percent of our oil. As OPEC raised prices, our annual oil bill soared; during the 1970s, it went from $1.5 billion to $60 billion. Of course this increase
✂ pushed up the price of electricity, of gas for cars and trucks and buses, heating oil for homes, and fuel to run factories.

As these prices rose, so did the price of everything produced on the farms and in the factories. As American dollars poured out of the country to pay for oil, our "trade deficit" mounted. This deficit was the amount of goods we sold abroad compared to what we bought abroad. So the purchasing power of the dollar overseas declined.

Action for the environment. In the 1970s, at the same time Americans experienced gas shortages, skyrocketing oil prices, and inflation, they became aware of the damage they were doing to their environment. They initiated new efforts to curtail pollution and conserve the wilderness. But every attempt to solve one problem complicated another. On January 1,

Kindra Clineff/The Picture Cube

As dumps filled, Americans realized they could save space and energy by recycling.

1970, President Nixon had signed the National Environmental Policy Act, initiating a "now-or-never" fight on pollution by a new Council on Environmental Quality. Almost unnoticed, the law also stated that all projects involving federal funds, property, or permits would have to be accompanied by environmental impact statements on how the project would affect the environment. This clause helped to protect wildlife and our land and water, but also brought costly delays and expensive lawsuits.

Nixon signed other laws to clean up our air and water and to protect federal lands in the West. In December 1970 the new Environmental Protection Agency (EPA) brought together the agencies dealing with water quality, air pollution, and the disposal of the millions of tons of bottles, paper, and other solid waste that Americans throw away every week. It also set standards for the disposal of nuclear waste and regulated the use of pesticides.

✂ Critical Thinking Activity: Identifying Problems What energy concerns face your local community? Have students list energy concerns in their community and how they are evidenced. In a class discussion ask students to determine what effect the energy crisis of the late 1970s has had on their current concerns. Have students express their conclusions in a political cartoon contrasting events of the late 1970s with energy issues today.

Harald Sund

The Alaska National Interest Lands Conservation Act of 1980 preserved millions of acres of unspoiled wilderness.

Another cause of air pollution was the automobile. The exhaust pipes of cars emit carbon monoxide and other pollutants that can irritate the eyes and lungs. In big cities like Los Angeles, New York, and Chicago, thousands of cars fill the air with pollutants, which leave a blue-gray pall hovering in the heavens. "Smog" (smoke and fog) was the new word for it. Devices added to car engines reduced these dangerous emissions. But the devices themselves added to inflation by increasing the cost of the car.

When President Carter took office, he announced his strong support for environmental protection. But his efforts, like Nixon's and Ford's, quickly collided with the need to conserve oil. When environmentalists proposed preserving millions of acres of land for national parks and wilderness, some members of Congress bitterly opposed the plan. Instead of leav-

ing millions of acres in Alaska untouched, they said, the government ought to encourage efforts to explore Alaska for oil and use its resources by mining and timbering. President Carter sided with the environmentalists, and in December 1980, the Alaska National Interest Lands Conservation Act set aside 103 million acres in Alaska—an area larger than all of California.

The problem with coal. Some people thought the United States should turn to coal as the solution to our energy problem. We had more coal than any other nation in the world—enough to supply our needs for hundreds of years. But burning coal fouled the air with sulfur dioxide, which helped to create still another problem. When mixed with moisture high in the sky, the oxides of sulfur and nitrogen that came from burning coal and from car exhausts produced "acid rain." Containing sulfuric and nitric acid, this rain killed fish in lakes and threatened forests. To keep the air clean, factories and power plants had been urged to switch from coal to oil. Then, with the oil shortage, President Nixon urged the electric power companies to switch back again to coal. But the equipment needed to reduce the pollution from burning coal was expensive.

Strip mining was the cheapest way to get coal. Sod and trees were stripped away to get at the seams of coal below. President Carter supported strict laws to put the land back. These efforts to save the environment added still more to inflation.

Nuclear power. Other Americans hoped that nuclear power, produced by splitting atoms of uranium, would provide clean energy long into the future. But no one had found a safe way to dispose of the used-up uranium, and even after the uranium no longer had the energy to run a nuclear reactor, it remained dangerously radioactive and could cause cancer. The government stored it in temporary holding places until a solution could be found.

There were other fears about nuclear reactors. If something went awry in the plant, radioactive material might be released in the air,

Enrichment Support File Topic

≋ Continuity and Change: Conflict Point out to students that the Alaskan issue was not the first time that the need for energy came into conflict with the need to preserve the environment. Theodore Roosevelt, in an effort to prevent the illegal use of public lands by lumber companies and cattle raisers, increased the number of national forests and withdrew from sale millions of acres of public land having waterpower sites, and deposits of coal, oil, and phosphates. (See page 524.)

Robin Moyer/Black Star

An accident at the Three Mile Island nuclear plant in 1979 sparked fears about the safety of such plants.

A weak energy program. In 1977, his first year in office, President Carter succeeded in creating a new Department of Energy, which took over most federal energy agencies. The following year, eighteen months after Carter had asked for it, Congress finally passed an energy bill. It was far different from what he had wanted. It began to free newfound natural gas from government price regulation, but failed to remove price controls on old gas and all domestic oil. It required most electric power plants to burn coal. New taxes and tax credits encouraged conservation, as did government laws that demanded improved gasoline mileage for new cars.

Energy crisis. In 1979, a revolution in Iran toppled the friendly government of Shah Mohammad Reza Pahlavi. This crisis stopped the flow of oil from Iran, which had provided 10 percent of the oil for the non-Communist world. The government of the fanatic Ayatollah Khomeini (p. 894) produced chaos. Then OPEC, reckless of the world economy and the well-being of the developing countries, again increased its oil prices. During this "second oil shock" some prices reached a staggering $41 a barrel.

Despite all the warnings, the United States and other Western nations had failed to prepare for another oil crisis. Delegates of the seven leading industrial nations, including President Carter, met in June 1979 in Tokyo, Japan. All the nations agreed to cut their use of oil. Carter hastened home to find that lines at gas stations had been growing, and American tempers were rising.

Carter scheduled a national television address on energy, then suddenly canceled it. His advisers had told him something more substantial was needed. To Camp David he called more than 100 of America's leading business people, clergy, and professionals. They discussed the energy crisis, the state of the nation, and Carter's popularity and "image." Ten days later, Carter addressed the nation. He attacked the growing cynicism, selfishness, and present-mindedness of the American people. He was critical of his own leadership. He said there was

endangering lives for miles around. This threat appeared remote during the first twenty years of nuclear power. Then suddenly, in the spring of 1979, something went wrong at the Three Mile Island nuclear plant near Harrisburg, Pennsylvania. For several days there seemed to be a danger of a massive escape of radiation. Though the immediate problem was brought under control by the end of a week, the full cleanup would take decades. This incident advertised the problems of the whole nuclear power industry—which already supplied 12 percent of the nation's electricity.

By the 1980s, problems of safety, pollution, and soaring costs resulted in the cancellation of all new nuclear plants ordered after 1973. To many observers, it appeared that energy from coal, small plants producing electricity from streams and rivers, windmills, and such new alternative sources as solar power might be the wave of the future.

☑ See "Lesson Plan," p. 876D for Writing Process Activity: Predicting Consequences relating to nuclear reactors.

a "crisis of confidence." Then he briefly outlined his energy plan. Reporters were reminded of the campaigning Jimmy Carter, who often sounded as if he were delivering sermons.

The following day he announced the details of his program—"the most massive peacetime commitment of funds and resources in the nation's history." He aimed to cut oil imports in half by 1990. He proposed ways for the nation to produce synthetic fuels in large amounts, to develop solar and nuclear power, and to conserve energy.

Hardly had Carter announced these sweeping proposals when he ordered a major shake-up of his Cabinet. Altogether, five Cabinet members resigned or were fired. The Cabinet changes were part of Carter's attempt to prepare for the 1980 presidential campaign. But they diverted attention from the energy problem and his energy program at a critical time. Carter's Presidency was in serious trouble. Public opinion polls showed that only 25 percent of the people approved of his performance in office. That rating was lower than Richard Nixon's during Watergate.

See "Section 2 Review answers," p. 876D.

Section 2 Review

1. Identify or explain: "the moral equivalent of war," trade deficit, EPA, acid rain, strip mining, uranium, Three Mile Island, Shah Mohammad Reza Pahlavi.

2. What were some of the causes of Jimmy Carter's inability to get his programs passed by Congress?

3. What caused the steep inflation of the late 1970s? How did Carter try to halt it?

4. **Critical Thinking: Recognizing Ideologies.** Show how environmental and energy concerns collided.

See "Lesson Plan," p. 876D.

3. The United States and the world

Despite the sudden turns of domestic politics and the rapid changes in the outside world, the foreign policy of the United States remained surprisingly consistent. The war in Vietnam still left its mark. But the nation continued to pursue the goals of national security and détente. The aim was to keep old friends and try to avoid making new enemies. If we could help relax world tensions and reduce the dangers of war anywhere, our nation, with others, might hope for a generation of peace.

Henry Kissinger and foreign affairs. During the long months while the nation struggled over Watergate and the possible impeachment of President Nixon, our foreign policy did not 🕮 falter. Nor was it inactive. This was largely due to the talents of Henry Kissinger. In 1969 Nixon had chosen Kissinger, then a professor of government at Harvard, to be his special assistant for national security affairs. In 1973 Nixon had named him Secretary of State.

Kissinger had been 15 years old when his family fled to the United States from Germany to escape Hitler's persecution of the Jews. He served in the United States Army and attended Harvard. He never entirely lost his German accent, and he joked about that as he did about much else. Unlike the solemn diplomats, he was witty and outspoken, yet he was good at keeping diplomatic secrets.

Kissinger's personal brand of diplomacy produced results. He finally negotiated an end to American involvement in the war in Vietnam, and he helped open United States relations with Communist China. He promoted détente with the Soviet Union. And he led the way toward peace between Egypt and Israel. When President Ford came to office, he kept Kissinger as Secretary of State and so preserved the continuity of American foreign policy.

During the early 1970s some old problems were resolved. The struggle between the "two Germanys"—a Communist east and a democratic west—had threatened European peace ever since the end of World War II. In 1972 East Germany and West Germany finally signed a treaty of mutual recognition. Both nations joined the UN in 1973.

In 1975, the European Security Conference, made up of 35 nations, including the United States, met in Helsinki, Finland. It settled more

🕮 **More from Boorstin:** ". . . [I]nternational relations could be viewed as the counterpart in *space* for what history is in *time*: history shows things that can be otherwise in a society because they *have been* otherwise; international relations shows that they can be otherwise because they *are* otherwise in other societies." (From *The Americans: The Democratic Experience*)

of the remaining issues of World War II. Among the many terms of the Helsinki Agreements were recognition of the new national borders drawn after the war, and an agreement by all the nations—including the Soviet Union and its East European satellites—to respect human rights. As usual, it turned out that the Communist dictatorships did not share the democratic nations' belief in human rights. When some Soviet citizens tried to monitor Soviet compliance with the treaties, they were harassed, imprisoned, or forced into exile.

A pause in the Middle East. After the Yom Kippur War between the Arabs and Israel in 1973 (p. 835), the United States and the Soviet Union pushed a cease-fire resolution through the UN Security Council. Troops representing the United Nations were sent in to separate the opposing forces. Then Kissinger's personal brand of "shuttle diplomacy" served a very practical purpose. Since the two sides would not speak to each other, Kissinger shuttled between them. He made it possible for them to communicate and finally reach some sort of agreement. The result was a pullback of the troops of both sides. Buffer zones between Egypt and Israel and between Israel and Syria were patrolled by UN forces.

By another exercise in shuttle diplomacy in 1975, Kissinger persuaded Egypt and Israel to renounce the use of force to settle their differences. They both agreed to move farther back and create a much larger buffer zone. The 1975 agreement was made possible because the United States agreed to station 200 American civilian technicians at two main passes on the Sinai peninsula. They would monitor the cease-fire to give an early warning in case either side moved to attack.

The fall of Cambodia. The long United States presence in the former lands of French Indochina came to an end in 1975. Even after the signing of a cease-fire for Vietnam early in 1973 and the withdrawal of United States armed forces, the fighting had never stopped. As Communist troops in South Vietnam, Cambodia, and Laos advanced, President Ford asked Con-

Marvin Newman/Woodfin Camp & Associates

Henry Kissinger arrives in Israel on one of his "shuttle diplomacy" missions.

gress to increase military aid to the non-Communist governments. But Congress had had enough. It refused to act.

Nixon had widened the war in Vietnam by attacking North Vietnamese troops that were illegally using Cambodia as a refuge from American and South Vietnamese forces. The Cambodians, who hated the Vietnamese, had allowed them to use these sanctuaries because they were not strong enough to push them out. In March 1970, Prince Norodom Sihanouk, the wily neutralist leader who had carefully kept Cambodia out of the war, was toppled by General Lon Nol, a right-wing nationalist. He believed it would be easy to drive out Cambodia's ancient enemy. With the American bombings and the "incursion" by U.S. troops (p. 824), the Cambodians thought they saw their chance and attacked the North Vietnamese. The North Vietnamese quickly overran half the country and worked hard to arm and train the Khmer Rouge (Red, or Communist, Cambodians).

The Khmer Rouge in Cambodia were a violent, deadly force that had no desire for peace or compromise. They moved forward steadily against the nationalist forces. The United States, whose interest remained centered on Vietnam, did little to stop them. On April 12, 1975, Phnom Penh, the capital of Cambodia, fell to the Khmer Rouge. Then, as the movie *The Killing Fields* later showed, the Khmer Rouge were ruthless. They emptied the city of its people—even driving the sick and wounded from the hospitals—and forced them back to the countryside. Phnom Penh and other Cambodian cities became as silent as tombs. Millions died. In 1978, even so strong an opponent of the Vietnam War as George McGovern, called for an international force to invade Cambodia to save the people from their own government.

The victory of North Vietnam. The end in South Vietnam also came with stunning swiftness. In the face of ever-stronger attacks by North Vietnamese and Viet Cong forces, the South Vietnamese army collapsed. North Viet-namese soldiers, escorted by tanks, entered Saigon on April 30, 1975.

As the war came to its rapid close, the bitterness and divisions it had produced in the United States were still much in evidence. When President Ford asked Congress for $722 million in military assistance to help evacuate South Vietnamese who had aided the United States during the war, Congress refused. These were the people most in danger from the Communists, but many members of Congress feared that the request was an excuse for more American involvement. In the end, Congress did approve $300 million for the evacuation of Americans and for "humanitarian" purposes, and some 100,000 did escape one way or another before the Communist takeover. However, thousands of South Vietnamese who had thought we would help them were left behind—as others had been in Cambodia.

The end in Indochina. The government of Laos, the country north of Cambodia and west of North Vietnam, had slowly become weaker

As the North Vietnamese swept toward Saigon, thousands of South Vietnamese fled in terror.

Aventurier/Gamma-Liaison

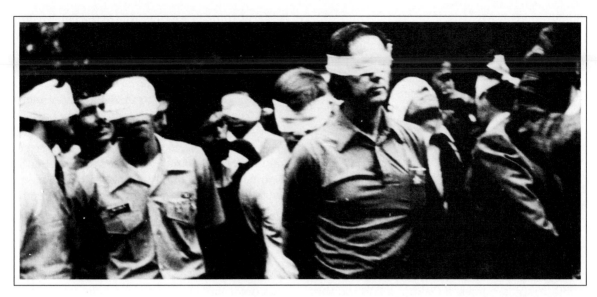

A mob seized the United States embassy in Teheran and held 52 Americans hostage in Iran for more than a year.

Nicaragua, the largest country in Central America. Somoza's father had been helped to power in 1933 by United States Marines (p. 610), and his family had run the country as if it were their private property. The United States quickly recognized the rebel government and hoped by working with it to keep Nicaragua from becoming another base for Communist expansion. But soon the leftists were in full control. They were called Sandinistas after César Augusto Sandino, one of the leaders of the rebellion against the United States Marines from 1927 to 1933.

The Soviets invade Afghanistan. On Christmas Day 1979, the Soviet Union had given the world another shock. It poured invading troops into Afghanistan, which borders the Soviet Union, Iran, and Pakistan. The Soviets aimed to prop up a friendly puppet government there. The Afghan people, at home in their rugged mountains, fought back bravely, first with primitive weapons, and then with stinger missiles supplied by the United States.

The United Nations General Assembly called for the Soviet Union to withdraw. To protest the Soviet move, the United States placed an embargo on the sale of grain to the Soviets, and with 61 other nations boycotted the 1980 summer Olympic games in Moscow. Still, the Soviet invaders stayed on. They were unable to pacify the Afghans. But now Soviet troops and airfields stretched along a large part of the Iranian border, and Soviet planes were several hundred miles closer to the vital oil sources on the Persian Gulf.

See "Section 4 Review answers," p. 876F.

Section 4 Review

1. Identify or explain: SALT II, Third World, Anwar el-Sadat, Menachem Begin, Ayatollah Khomeini, Sandinistas.

2. How did the United States government respond to revolutions in Iran and Nicaragua?

3. What contribution did Jimmy Carter make to the peace treaty between Egypt and Israel?

4. **Critical Thinking: Recognizing Cause and Effect.** What was the purpose of President Carter's bold stand for human rights? What was its effect on U.S. foreign policy?

See "Lesson Plan," p. 876F.

5. New directions

As the nation entered the presidential election campaign in the fall of 1980, it was plagued by problems at home and abroad. Inflation seemed to be soaring. The economy had stopped growing. Fifty-two of our citizens were held hostage in Iran. No longer did critics complain of "the Imperial Presidency." Many Americans were afraid that it might not be possible for any President to control Congress and the huge executive department or assert our dignity in the world.

Carter vs. Reagan. Jimmy Carter's inability to solve the hostage problem, the energy crisis, and inflation haunted him in the election of 1980. In midsummer, a Gallup poll found that only 21 percent of the people approved of his handling of the Presidency—the lowest rating in the 45-year history of the poll. Senator Edward M. Kennedy of Massachusetts, the youngest brother of President John F. Kennedy, challenged the President for the Democratic party's nomination, arguing that Carter had failed as a leader and had abandoned the Party's traditional concern for the poor and powerless. But with the great powers of the Presidency at his disposal, Carter was able to win the nomination.

Carter's opponent in the general election was the personable Ronald Reagan. At 69, Ronald Reagan would be the oldest man ever elected President. But his lively manner, ruddy complexion, and full head of brown hair made him seem much younger. His years in the movies, on radio and television, as governor of California, and on the lecture circuit had made him easy to listen to, polished and persuasive. He had developed a firm and clear-cut conservative philosophy that was opposed to many of the ideas that had influenced government since the days of Franklin D. Roosevelt.

Reagan's conservative message remained much the same as it had been in 1976, when the Republicans nearly nominated him over President Ford. (p. 881). He wanted to get tough with the Soviet Union, end inflation, stimulate economic growth, and reduce the size, cost, and regulatory role of the federal government. Only for defense did he want to see increased government expenses. This time Reagan's party and the American people were ready to listen.

When Reagan and Carter debated on television, Reagan was in his element. He charmed the vast audience with his easy manner and good humor. "There you go again," Reagan responded with a smile to Carter's tense debating points. On election day, Ronald Reagan swept to victory with 8 million more votes than Jimmy Carter. He took all but seven states and, for the first time since 1952, the Republican party carried the Senate.

Reagan takes charge. Reagan's inauguration was held, for the first time, at the West Front 𝕞 instead of the East Front of the Capitol. The new location, facing the Washington Monument and the Lincoln Memorial, seemed to symbolize his intention to reverse the direction of the government. His message of change was clear: America's first problem was inflation. A major cause, he said, was the enormous government spending that produced massive deficits. "In the present crisis," he said, "government is not the solution to our problem; government is the problem."

Only moments after Reagan had taken the oath of office, and after months of negotiation by President Carter and his aides, the Iranians released the 52 hostages. They had been held 444 days. President Reagan tactfully sent Jimmy Carter to meet them.

The new President moved quickly. He sent to Congress a package of cuts in domestic programs, reductions in personal and corporate taxes, and large increases in spending for defense. He spoke of his hope to stir private citizens and businesses toward active competition and new initiative.

After Jimmy Carter's troubles in trying to put his programs through Congress, it seemed unlikely that Ronald Reagan could get his way. But Reagan telephoned many members of Congress and brought them to the White House to ask their support. He went on television and was dazzlingly persuasive.

𝕞 **More from Boorstin:** "In the United States, . . . we see very few monuments to the uncertainties, the motley possibilities, of history, or for that matter, to the rise and fall of grand theories of society. Our main public buildings were erected for much the same purpose for which they are now being used. The Congress of the United States is still housed in the first building expressly constructed for that purpose." (From *Hidden History: Exploring Our Secret Past*)

Ronald Reagan's friendly and relaxed manner on the campaign trail helped to persuade the American people to vote for him. He easily defeated Jimmy Carter in 1980.

He was also lucky. In gaining popular support for his program, President Reagan was actually assisted by an attempt on his life. On March 30, 1981, a 25-year-old man, whom a jury later found insane, shot and severely wounded the President as he left a Washington hotel. The bullet came within an inch of his heart. Reagan's jaunty good humor and courage in the hospital charmed the nation and kept people behind him. Within a month he was standing before a cheering Congress and asking support for his economic program. In July, Congress passed the President's tax cuts and the new budget, which shrank social programs and slowed the growth of the budget even as it began large increases in defense spending.

Supply-side economics. The Reagan program was based on a new economic theory called "supply-side economics." This idea differed from the ideas of the brilliant British economist

John Maynard Keynes (p. 626), which had been followed by the government since the late 1930s. Keynesians thought that government policies could smooth out the booms and busts of a free enterprise economy. In a time of recession or depression, for example, the Keynesians thought that the government should run large deficits and start programs that would put money in the hands of the people. With this money people would buy what they wanted and the economy would revive. This was called influencing "demand," because people would be able to buy (or demand) more goods and services. Then industry would work to supply them.

The "supply-siders" reversed the equation. They said that the ideas of Keynes were not working to end "stagflation." They wanted to try a new way. They said government ought to influence not "demand," but "supply." If the government cut taxes on businesses and individuals—especially those with large incomes—

this money, they thought, would be reinvested in more businesses. These new and improved businesses would employ more people, produce more goods and services, and help the economy grow. As business boomed, more people would work and pay taxes, and government income would go up. Even with lower tax rates, the "supply-siders" said, more money would come to the government from the new workers and businesses. They boldly predicted that the deficit would disappear.

A troubled economy. The Republicans controlled the Senate, but the Democrats enjoyed a majority in the House. To achieve his program Reagan, like all successful Presidents, had to compromise. But as the Reagan tax proposals went through Congress, many additional tax cuts and "loopholes" (ways to avoid or decrease taxes) were added. As a result, the final bill reduced tax revenue far more than Reagan had wanted.

The Reagan program was also hard hit when the economy went into a recession even deeper than the one inherited by Gerald Ford in 1974. By 1982, when the unemployment rate hit 10 percent, it turned out to be the worst since the Great Depression of the 1930s. This recession was largely a result of the policies of the Federal Reserve System, the nation's central bank.

The "Fed" controls the amount of money in our economy, the financing of the national debt, the amount of reserves banks must hold, and the interest on money it loans to banks. In 1979, the Federal Reserve Board, led by the newly appointed chairman—tall, cigar-smoking Paul Volcker—had concluded that a major cause of inflation was Federal Reserve policy. The board decided to restrict the money supply and let interest rates find their own level. "Tight money" caused interest rates to soar. Since borrowing for home building, automobiles, and other things became increasingly expensive, the country went into a recession. The recession helped control inflation, but it caused new problems for the budget.

In a recession, government revenues fall because people out of work pay less in taxes. But government expenses increase, because more money has to be spent in unemployment payments, food stamps, and other welfare programs. As inflation fell and the recession worsened, the projected deficits (the amount by which expenses exceeded revenue) grew. By fall 1981, the estimate for 1984 predicted an enormous deficit of $162 billion.

Reducing the government. Ronald Reagan wanted to reduce the size and role of the federal government, and he succeeded in many areas. He cut the budget of the Environmental Protection Agency, and the agency became less active in preserving pure air and water. He cut back government spending on social programs, like job training and aide to poor families with dependent children. And although he said he supported those welfare programs that served as a "safety net" for the poor, the old, the unemployed, and the handicapped, he cut many of those programs, too. Government statistics soon revealed that more people were then living in poverty than at any time since the days before Lyndon Johnson's Great Society programs (pp. 801–802).

Reagan slowed the growth of the welfare system and cut many other government programs, but he had trouble with the budget deficit—the amount the government was spending over what it was receiving in taxes. That was partly because he was unable to cut the cost of entitlement programs including Social Security, Medicare, and veterans' benefits to which many people were legally "entitled" because of age, unemployment, illness, or having served in the armed forces. These benefits went to a wide variety of Americans who firmly opposed any tampering with their claims.

But the largest cause of rising budget deficits was President Reagan's insistence that the United States increase its defense spending. In 1981 he proposed that the United States spend $1.64 trillion (1640 billion) over the next five years for defense. Reagan and his Secretary of Defense, Caspar Weinberger, argued that the safety of the nation depended on a strong defense. They fought every effort to cut defense spending. So government spending soared and the deficit grew. (p. 899)

✖ Critical Thinking Activity: Testing Conclusions How has decreased federal support made the private sector more accountable for social service programs? Have students make a list of social services available in their community. Next to each item have students identify who provides the service. Ask students to determine which of the services are provided by the private sector and which by the public sector. Ask: Does this information reflect a reduction in government spending?

In the recession of 1981, unemployment rose dramatically and many jobs disappeared for good. Here unemployed carpenters in New York City sign up for a retraining program at their union's headquarters.

See "Section 5 Review answers," p. 876F.

Section 5 Review

1. Identify or explain: Paul Volcker, tax loopholes, Federal Reserve, "supply-side economics," John Maynard Keynes.

2. How does "supply-side economics" work in theory? How does it differ from the economic theories of Keynes?

3. How did the actions of the Federal Reserve Board contribute to the recession of 1981–1982?

4. **Critical Thinking: Recognizing Ideologies.** How was Ronald Reagan's view of government different from Jimmy Carter's? From FDR'S?

See "Lesson Plan," p. 876G.

6. The changing economy

At the peak of the recession more than 11 million Americans were unemployed. But by the end of 1982, the economy began to improve. The nation was learning that the economy was changing in fundamental ways.

The decline of the smokestack industries. American industry had been one of the wonders of the world. But in the late 1960s the productivity of American workers was no longer increasing. Industry had been hit by inflation, ever-changing government regulations, and increased foreign competition from new factories built in the countries devastated in World War II. Now the "smokestack industries"—the old factories with tall smokestacks that made steel, textiles, and automobiles—were closing whole plants and laying off millions of workers. This threatened industries and communities like Detroit and Pittsburgh that depended on them.

As Americans bought more and more of their clothes, cars, radios, and TVs from other

❖ See "Lesson Plan," p. 876F for Cooperative Learning Activity: Identifying Central Issues relating to the Section 5 Review.

Billy Barnes/Click/Chicago

Many schools used computers to teach their students new skills.

nations, and as American companies bought more raw materials and machine tools from other nations, the United States balance of trade—the amount in dollars that all its companies sold abroad balanced against the amount that Americans bought from abroad—grew steadily worse. Even the surprising fall in the price of oil, brought about by the huge surpluses created when the world quickly turned to conservation after the oil shocks of the 1970s (pp. 879–880), was not able to solve the problem of the trade deficit. In 1986 the United States bought $170 billion more from abroad than it sold. Millions of American jobs were being lost to other nations.

The unfavorable balance of trade fueled the already enormous federal deficit. The government was deeply in debt and had to borrow to keep going. It did this by issuing bonds and notes that paid interest to the holders. Large quantities of these issues were bought by foreigners who liked their safety and high interest rates.

These foreigners bought dollars in order to buy United States bonds. And this forced up the price they paid for dollars in other currencies. The American dollar became more expensive abroad, which made American products more expensive for foreigners. Naturally they bought less, and our trade deficit increased.

In only a few years the United States went from being the world's richest creditor nation to being the world's greatest debtor. Economists thought that if the American dollar could be made cheaper for foreigners the situation would improve. Our government and other industrial nations allowed the value of the dollar to fall steeply in 1986 and 1987, which did help to reduce the trade deficit. But it also brought down the American standard of living. Now that the dollar was worth less abroad, Americans could afford to buy fewer imported products, and foreign travel was more expensive.

The world of the future. During these years, the computer was changing American ways of working, learning, and playing with dizzying speed. Computers were becoming steadily smaller, smarter, and quicker. They appeared everywhere—in schools, libraries, hospitals, banks, factories, stores, and homes. There seemed to be no end to the new uses for these clever machines.

Computers started a new "information" industry. Information in huge amounts could be stored in computers, analyzed with lightning speed, and instantly sent over thousands of miles to other computers. By 1994 people were talking about an "information superhighway." 📖

The computer also opened opportunities for daring and enterprise. In northern California, the area called "Silicon Valley" (after the wafer-thin silicon chips that make computers work) became a boom town for young go-getters of the

📖 **More from Boorstin:** "American history, more perhaps than that of any other modern nation, has been marked by changes in the human condition—by novel political arrangements, novel products, novel forms of manufacturing distribution, and consumption, novel ways of transporting and communicating. To understand ourselves and our nation, then, we must grasp these processes of change and reflect on our peculiarly American ways of viewing these processes." (From *The Republic of Technology: Reflections on Our Future Community*)

Advances in computer technology have introduced a whole new array of multimedia products, including interactive video games and virtual reality simulations.

age of computers. There they created new hardware and software to make computers "friendlier" (easier to use). Whole regions of the country were transformed. After New England lost its textile and shoe factories, computer companies moved in and provided jobs.

The new Computer Revolution, like the earlier Industrial Revolution, brought its own problems. In the automobile industry, for example, computer-run robots could now be programmed to do several different, complicated operations. And since computer-run robots worked more cheaply than human workers, they took people's jobs.

On other frontiers, biologists were plumbing the mysteries of the gene. In the heart of each plant or animal cell, genes carry the blueprint of heredity. Understanding the gene could help grow new and better crops, improve animals, and even control some diseases, perhaps even cancer.

Doctors were using new techniques to implant organs such as livers, kidneys, and hearts. Since the first human heart transplant in 1967, the operation had been done many times. Twenty years later it was estimated that 4000 Americans were alive with replaced hearts. Wonderful vaccines had been found against polio, mumps, and measles. On the new frontiers, scientists were creating whole new industries—making jobs and saving lives.

One of the most exciting scientific breakthroughs of the 1980s was the discovery in 1987 of new materials that made it possible to achieve superconductivity at higher temperatures than ever before. Superconductivity (the transmission of electricity with almost no resistance) could be used to increase the speed of computers, to improve telephone cables, and even to develop high-speed trains. The Japanese had already built an experimental train that used superconductivity in magnets to allow it to float on air and shoot smoothly along at over 300 miles an hour. With the newly discovered materials, such trains might no longer be just expensive experiments but an everyday convenience for high-speed travel.

Across the country in the 1980s new businesses, most of them small businesses in service industries, appeared by the thousands. With them came many new jobs. Women were in the forefront of this boom, starting new companies at an even faster rate than men.

The spirit of the times—the search for adventure and the attempt to solve old problems in new ways—did not always seem practical. One dreamer was Paul MacCready, Jr., who in his forties founded a company to study energy and environmental problems. He built an airplane, powered like a bicycle by the passenger, which flew across the English Channel. He made another plane that ran by solar energy.

Deregulation. Ever since the Interstate Commerce Commission had been created in 1887 to oversee the railroads (p. 524), the government had been adding more regulatory agencies. Airlines, banks, telephone companies, and interstate trucks, buses, and moving companies were told where they could operate and what they could charge. They often were protected from the competition of new companies and new techniques.

Deregulation had begun in the late 1960s, but the big shift came under Jimmy Carter. He brought about the deregulation of the trucking industry, the railroads, some of the banking industry, and the airlines.

New, low-cost airlines appeared and fare wars broke out. Passengers profited from lower fares. But when the government no longer told air lines where they should fly, people in smaller cities lost their airplane service. The result was not always what was predicted. The purpose was to increase competition, but after a decade of deregulation, only eight major airlines existed where there had been twelve before deregulation. It was feared that they might not compete as much as they had before and that fares might rise again.

In 1974, the Department of Justice brought suit under the antitrust laws against the American Telephone & Telegraph Company (AT&T), which owned and ran the Bell telephone sys-

Deregulation allowed airlines to fly where and when they wanted. The new competition helped passengers by lowering fares, but sometimes it led to crowded conditions and long delays on the ground.

Ian Berry/Magnum

See "Lesson Plan," p. 876G for Writing Process Activity: Identifying Central Issues relating to the deregulation of the airlines.

tem. They charged that the company, which controlled telephone service across the country, was the kind of monopoly that had to be broken up. Finally, in 1983 AT&T and the government reached a settlement. AT&T sold all of its local telephone companies. But it continued to compete against smaller companies with long-distance calls. Competition did lead to lower long-distance prices. But many Americans were confused and unhappy when they lost their old reliable "Ma Bell."

Labor in difficult times. During the years after World War II the number of workers in unions went from 35 percent of the work force to less than half that. The unions were hurt by the decline of the smokestack industries, deregulation, and foreign imports. Some companies went bankrupt. Others found that they had to lower prices to compete with new companies. Often this meant that they had to reduce their labor costs. Naturally, workers did not want to see their pay go down or to lose their jobs to machines. The results were strikes and changes in the relations of business and labor.

President Reagan thought that big unions were as troublesome as big government. In August 1981 the air traffic controllers went on strike for higher pay and shorter hours. The controllers were employed by the Federal Aviation Administration to see that planes flew in and out of airports safely and did not run into each other in the skies. They were working under a contract that barred them from striking. Reagan ordered them to return to work or be fired. When they continued their strike, he fired all 11,500 strikers. By a variety of means, most airline flights continued while new controllers were trained to replace the members of the union.

For many years, businesses had given labor unions much of what they had asked for. The increased costs were passed along to the consumer in higher prices. But when competition from abroad increased, the high costs of labor could no longer be passed along.

As a result, there were some new features in labor contracts. In "give-backs," the workers gave up some of the benefits they had won in better times. To keep their firms out of bankruptcy and their jobs alive, workers accepted temporary wage freezes, or fewer vacations, and allowed companies to hire new workers at lower wages. In return, workers received job security and sometimes bonuses from the company's profits.

The farmers. American farmers were the most productive in the world. In 1953, one farmer could feed 17.2 people. Today that same farmer can produce enough food to feed 75! For many years they had little world competition. But with the worldwide recession of the early 1980s the boom ended. Food prices fell, and soon farmers could not make enough money to meet their expenses and pay off the loans they had taken out to buy land and equipment. The banks that loaned money to the farmers and the businesses that sold to them also suffered. Farm foreclosures, rare since the Great Depression, were now in the news again. Some farmers even went hungry. The recession in agriculture was longer and deeper than that in the rest of the economy.

Farmers, too, were now in a new world of competition. The "green revolution" of fertilizers, better seeds, and modern-farming techniques helped India, the Philippines, and other countries to produce enough wheat and rice to feed themselves. Even more surprising, in 1986 the United States began to import more food than it exported. Fruit and vegetables came from Mexico, oranges from Brazil, beef from Costa Rica, and even wheat from Canada. Suddenly it seemed that every nation had a crop to sell here. Now the world was feeding Americans. This nation, once the world's largest food exporter, suddenly became the world's second-largest food importer.

The first Reagan farm program, Payment-In-Kind (PIK), paid farmers in surplus crops from government storage bins for not planting their land. So many farmers took part that it cost far more than Reagan had expected. A new law, the Food Security Act of 1985, reduced the amount the government would loan farmers on their crops and allowed farmers to sell certain

Roy Roper/Gamma-Liaison

Economic conditions for farmers in the 1980s were the worst since the Great Depression. Many farmers, like the couple above, were forced to sell everything to pay off their debts.

crops, like rice and cotton, for whatever they could. It was hoped this would lower the price of American farm products so exports would increase and food costs for American consumers would go down. Farmers who participated in the program by limiting production and not planting part of their land were guaranteed direct payments from the government to protect them from loss. The program seemed to help ✂ farmers, but it, too, was more expensive than the program's supporters expected. By 1987, the farm crisis seemed to be ending. Farmers were doing much better, as were the businesses and banks that dealt with them.

See "Section 6 Review answers," p. 876G.

Section 6 Review

1. Identify or explain: "smokestack industries," Silicon Valley, AT&T, air traffic controllers, "green revolution," deregulation.

2. What were some of the causes of the decline of America's "smokestack industries"?

3. Why did Reagan fire the striking air traffic controllers?

4. **Critical Thinking: Recognizing Cause and Effect.** Why was AT&T's monopoly broken up? What were some of the effects of this breakup?

✂ Critical Thinking Activity: Making Comparisons What is the effect of our changing economy? List the following words on the chalkboard: "Computer," "Farmers," "Deregulation." Divide the class into three groups, and assign one of the words to each group. Have the groups write a paragraph describing the effect of our changing economy on their particular topic. Ask each group to present their work. As a class, have students list points that are common to all three groups. Turn this information into a statement that could describe the nation's economy.

Chapter 35 Review

See "Chapter Review answers," p. 876G.

Focusing on Ideas

1. In the 1976 election campaign Jimmy Carter made many promises—far more than candidates customarily had made. How did this strategy hurt him after he became President?

2. Like slavery in the 1850s, some of today's issues that concern special-interest groups do not lend themselves to compromise. What are some hard-to-compromise issues? How did the major political parties approach them in the 1970s?

3. Support or attack the idea that the advancement of human rights around the world should be a cornerstone of American foreign policy.

4. During Reagan's first term, inflation was brought under control and the dollar gained value in foreign markets. Unemployment and interest rates rose also. Identify groups who would benefit from each of these economic trends, and groups who would be hurt by them.

Taking a Critical Look

1. **Recognizing Bias.** What arguments would you expect people to give for or against President Ford's plan for Vietnam War deserters and draft evaders?

2. **Making Comparisons.** John F. Kennedy served as President for 34 months and Gerald Ford for 29 months. Compare their problems and successes.

3. **Recognizing Cause and Effect.** In recent years the role of unions has begun to change from challenger of management to occasional partner of management. What caused this change?

Your Region in History

1. **Geography.** How have antipollution regulations of the Environmental Protection Agency affected industries in your area? What have been the effects on your family or neighborhood?

2. **Economics.** What measures were taken by your state to deal with the energy crisis?

Historical Facts and Figures

Synthesizing Information. Study the graph below to help answer the following questions: (a) During which three periods did the defense budget increase markedly? (b) Based on what you have read, how do you explain each of these periods of increased defense spending? (c) What do you think are some of the factors leading to the relative decrease in defense spending after 1985?

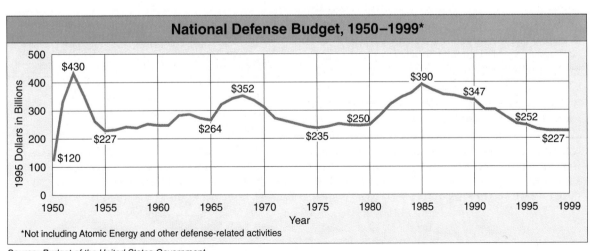

National Defense Budget, 1950–1999*

*Not including Atomic Energy and other defense-related activities

Source: *Budget of the United States Government*

Identifying Chapter Materials

Objectives	Basic Instructional Materials	Extension Materials
1 Troubles Abroad ▪ Understand the United States role in the world during Reagan's first term.	**Annotated Teacher's Edition** ▪ Lesson Plans, p. 906C **Instructional Support File** ▪ Pre-Reading Activities, Unit 12, p. 29	**Extension Activity** ▪ Central America, Lesson Plans, p. 906C
2 Successes and Failures ▪ Describe the challenges of Reagan's second term.	**Annotated Teacher's Edition** ▪ Lesson Plans, pp. 906C–906D **Instructional Support File** ▪ Critical Thinking Activity, Unit 12, p. 34	**Documents of American History** ▪ The Challenge of Peace: God's Promise and Our Response, A Pastoral Letter on War and Peace, Vol. 2, p. 855
3 New Problems for the "Teflon President" ▪ Identify the causes for the decline in Reagan's popularity that began in 1986.	**Annotated Teacher's Edition** ▪ Lesson Plans, pp. 906D–906E **Instructional Support File** ▪ Skill Review Activity, Unit 12, p. 32	**Documents of American History** ▪ The Iran-contra Affair, Vol. 2, p. 872
4 The End of the Reagan Years ▪ Describe the issues facing the country during the last two years of Reagan's presidency.	**Annotated Teacher's Edition** ▪ Lesson Plans, p. 906E	**Extension Activity** ▪ South African Activists, Lesson Plans, p. 906E
5 The End of the Cold War ▪ Describe the chain of events that occurred in Eastern Europe in 1989 leading to the end of the cold war. ▪ Explain the significance of the Charter of Paris.	**Annotated Teacher's Edition** ▪ Lesson Plans, pp. 906E–906F	**Enrichment Support File** ▪ The End of the Cold War (See "In-Depth Coverage" at right.) **Perspectives** ▪ Is the Cold War Over? (See "In-Depth Coverage" at right.)
6 A Dangerous World ▪ Identify three world conflicts that occurred during the Bush administration and U.S. response to each.	**Annotated Teacher's Edition** ▪ Lesson Plans, pp. 906F–906G	**American History Transparencies** ▪ Time Lines, p. E39
7 The State of the Nation ▪ Describe the major events and issues during Bush's last two years in office and during the 1992 presidential campaign.	**Annotated Teacher's Edition** ▪ Lesson Plans, p. 906G	**American History Transparencies** ▪ Critical Thinking, p. F43
8 The Clinton Presidency ▪ Describe the major issues during Clinton's first two years in office.	**Annotated Teacher's Edition** ▪ Lesson Plans, pp. 906G–906H **Instructional Support File** ▪ Reading Activities, Unit 12, pp. 30–31 ▪ Skill Application Activity, Unit 12, p. 33 ▪ Chapter Test, Unit 12, pp. 35–38 ▪ Additional Test Questions, Unit 12, pp. 39–42 ▪ Unit Test, Unit 12, pp. 43–46	**American History Transparencies** ▪ Critical Thinking, p. F47

Providing In-Depth Coverage

Perspectives on the End of the Cold War

The cold war, a period of tension between two major world factions, shaped world politics for almost 45 years. Then, in 1989, a whirlwind of events sparked change in Eastern Europe. Nations such as Hungary, Poland, Romania, and Czechoslovakia turned away from communism, some through peaceful demonstration, others through violence and bloodshed. The culmination of these changes occurred on November 9, 1989, when the gates of the Berlin Wall were opened, leading to the imminent reunification of Germany. When the dust settled a new post–cold war world emerged along with the hope for future international cooperation and mutual respect among nations.

A History of the United States as an instructional program provides three types of resources you can use to offer in-depth coverage of the end of the cold war: the *student text*, the *Enrichment Support File*, and *Perspectives*. The chart below shows the topics that are covered in each.

THE STUDENT TEXT. Boorstin and Kelley's *A History of the United States* unfolds the chronology of events and the key players involved in bringing the cold war to an end.

AMERICAN HISTORY ENRICHMENT SUPPORT FILE. This collection of primary source readings and classroom activities reveals what the end of the cold war has meant to the United States.

PERSPECTIVES: READINGS ON AMERICAN HISTORY IN THE 20TH CENTURY. In this edited collection of secondary source readings, well-known historians and political commentators (including Boorstin) provide an array of perspectives on the end of the cold war.

Locating Instructional Materials

Detailed lesson plans for teaching the end of the cold war as a mini-course or to study one or more elements of the ending of the cold war in depth are offered in the following areas: in the *student text*, see individual lesson plans at the beginning of each chapter; in the *Enrichment Support File*, see page 3; in *Perspectives*, see the Teacher's Guide for this topic.

IN-DEPTH COVERAGE OF THE END OF THE COLD WAR		
Student Text	**Enrichment Support File**	**Perspectives**
▪ Beginnings of the Cold War, pp. 707–711, 715–718 ▪ Trouble Spots in the 1950s, *map*, p. 746 ▪ Efforts to Relax, p. 747 ▪ The End of the Cold War, pp. 924–930	▪ Lesson Suggestions ▪ Multimedia Resources ▪ Overview Essay/The End of the Cold War ▪ Songs in American History/"Merry Minuet" ▪ Primary Sources in American History/America Without the Cold War ▪ Biography in American History/Mikhail Gorbachev ▪ Great Debates in American History/The Future of American Defense Spending ▪ Making Connections	▪ "The Rise of the European Superpower" by Ronald Steel ▪ "Eastern Europe and the Soviet Union" by Robert G. Kaiser ▪ "Separation Anxiety" by the editors of the New Republic ▪ "Soviet-American Relations: The Cold War Ends" by Lawrence T. Caldwell ▪ "Sweeping Change" by John Newhouse ▪ "All Over? Not Quite" by Brian Crozier

Section 1 (pages 907–912)

Troubles Abroad

FOCUS

To introduce the lesson, divide students into groups. Have each group list the action the United States took in one of these countries: Nicaragua, El Salvador, Lebanon, Argentina (Falklands), Grenada, USSR, Vietnam.

Developing Vocabulary

The words listed in this chapter are essential terms for reading and understanding particular sections of the chapter. The page number after each term indicates the page of its first or most important appearance in the chapter. These terms are defined in the text Glossary (text pages 1000–1011).

terrorism (page 909); **nuclear freeze** (page 911).

INSTRUCT

Explain

Review the roles of the President and Congress in making foreign policy.

★ Independent Activity

Identifying Central Issues Ask students to make a list of places in the world which the United States considers to be strategically important. Ask students to write two or three sentences about each area on their lists explaining why it is considered important.

Section Review Answers

Section 1, page 912

1. a) small, densely populated nation in Central America. b) Palestine Liberation Organization. c) small island nation in the Caribbean. d) an unofficial labor union formed in Poland in 1980. e) president of France who urged NATO to reject Soviet demands that NATO call off its plan to deploy new American missiles in Europe. f) became the head of the Soviet Union after Brezhnev died in 1982. g) became head of the Soviet Union in 1984, after Andropov's death. 2. In 1970 the PLO moved into Lebanon. From Lebanon it launched attacks on Israel. In 1975 civil war erupted between Christian and Muslim groups in Lebanon. An Arab peacekeeping force soon managed to keep the conflicts from erupting again into full-scale civil war. In 1982 Israel invaded Lebanon to stop the PLO from using it as a base for attacks against Israel. An international peacekeeping force was withdrawn. The peacekeeping force was sent back to Beirut, and in October 1983 more than 240 American marines were killed in one of these at-

tacks. Reagan withdrew the marines a few months later. 3. Third World countries needed funds to finance economic development and the high inflation of the 1970s made borrowing look cheap and their debts reasonable. During the 1980s many of the Third World nations could not pay even the interest they owed. Their debts created disputes between them and the industrial nations and threatened the banking systems and economies of all nations. 4. President Reagan believed in taking a tough stance, and early in his term stopped many discussions with the Soviet Union. Eventually, he entered into negotiations with the Soviet Union. But when he failed to reach an agreement for controlling intermediate-range nuclear weapons, he successfully urged the NATO allies to go ahead with the deployment of new American missiles in Europe. In response, the Soviets broke off arms control talks, matching Reagan's tough stance with tough policies of their own. 5. Reagan and his advisers believed that if the rebels of El Salvador gained power and the government of Nicaragua remained in power, then allies of the Soviet Union would soon be at the borders of the United States.

CLOSE

To conclude the lesson, discuss the following questions: Is the United States powerful enough to hold its allies and potential allies to a strong standard of human rights for their citizens? If so, is such a use of U.S. power appropriate? Is protecting human rights an important enough goal? Or should we just stick to attempts to check the spread of communism and human rights violations by Communist countries?

Extension Activity

To extend the lesson, ask students to choose one of the Central American countries mentioned in this section. Then have students research their country and write a two- to three-page report on the history of that country. Students should include in their reports the relationship of that country to the United States.

Section 2 (pages 912–917)

Successes and Failures

FOCUS

To introduce the lesson, have students design a report card for Reagan's second term, based on the program he outlined in his State of the Union address. Then ask: Where did you give the President high marks? Where low marks? Students should back their evaluations with specific evidence of programs that were either implemented successfully or else failed to succeed.

Developing Vocabulary

glasnost (page 916); *perestroika* (page 916); **Strategic Defense Initiative (SDI)** (page 917).

INSTRUCT

Explain

Discuss what a President must do in order to implement a program successfully. On the chalkboard, list the factors that may affect the implementation.

☑ Writing Process Activity

Recognizing Ideologies Explain to students that they will write an evaluative essay about whether a woman could be elected Vice-President of the United States. In preparation, ask students to research the Mondale–Ferraro campaign, considering whether Reagan's landslide victory over them was a factor of his appeal or whether it was a reaction against the first female nominee. Ask students to begin their essay with a sentence summarizing their point of view on this issue. Students should revise for logical organization and complete evidence.

Section Review Answers

Section 2, page 917

1. a) proposed balanced budget amendment to the Constitution that would require a reduction of the national debt over several years until it would be possible to write budgets that called for spending only as much as the government took in. b) new leader of the USSR after Chernenko. c) Russian word used for Gorbachev's plan to restructure the Communist party and the government. d) word for Gorbachev's plans for a more open society in the USSR. e) Strategic Defense Initiative, proposed defensive shield to help keep the United States safe from a nuclear attack. 2. Reagan opposed abortions, the Equal Rights Amendment, affirmative action, busing to achieve racial integration, and a nuclear freeze. He favored constitutional amendments to permit organized prayer in the public schools and to require balanced federal budgets. 3. Robert Bork was rejected because he was perceived as being insensitive to the rights of minorities. Ginsburg withdrew his name from consideration when it was revealed that he had smoked marijuana. Kennedy was a moderate conservative whose views did not offend most senators. 4. The SDI was the issue on which the Reykjavik talks foundered. The Soviets demanded that the United States promise to test the SDI only in the laboratory for the next ten years. Reagan refused. 5. Inconsistent: He did not attempt to cut such things as defense

spending sufficiently to reduce the deficit or propose raising taxes. However, although the deficit rose tremendously during his administration, part of that rise was due to inflation. Congress has the final say on budget cuts.

CLOSE

To conclude the lesson, tell students that some critics say American politics is dominated by personalities and television rather than by issues. Ask students to write an essay entitled "Issues or Personality: Which Was More Important in the Election of 1984?" They should research newspapers and magazines of November 1984 to find evidence of reasons people voted for Reagan.

Section 3 (pages 917–920)

New Problems for the "Teflon President"

FOCUS

To introduce the lesson, have students draw a political cartoon focusing on how one of the events discussed in this section reflects on Reagan's leadership.

INSTRUCT

Explain

In 1986, Reagan suffered a series of setbacks, including revelations about administration activities regarding Qaddafi, the Iran-contra Affair; the rejected nomination of Bork to the Supreme Court; the withdrawal of Ginsburg as a nominee to the High Court; and troubles in the Persian Gulf.

❈ Cooperative Learning Activity

Expressing Problems Clearly Begin this activity by discussing the meaning of the quotation by Justice Louis Brandeis under "Iranscam"—The Iran-contra Affair." Then pair students and have each pair compose their own "quotable quote" expressing a point of view or sentiment on one of the topics discussed in Section 3 of this chapter. Have pairs read their quotations to the class and invite discussion.

Section Review Answers

Section 3, page 920

1. a) nickname for Reagan because failures or criticisms never seemed to stick to him. b) name given to the Iran-contra Affair, in which money from secret arms sales to Iran were diverted to the Nicaraguan rebels. c) staff member at the National Security

Council who directed the activities of a mysterious organization dedicated to aiding the contras. 2. If officials of the government disobey the law—even for the highest motives—the ordinary citizen cannot be expected to obey the law. When there is no rule of law, there is complete chaos.

CLOSE

To conclude the lesson, tell students that one of Reagan's nicknames was the "Great Communicator," for his ability to reach the American public, foreign heads of state, Congress, and others. How do such nicknames originate? Can they do any harm? Ask students to name other Presidents who have earned nicknames, and explain their origins.

Section 4 (pages 921–924)

The End of the Reagan Years

FOCUS

To introduce the lesson, list the world changes discussed in this section—in China, Latin America, South Africa, and Afghanistan—on the blackboard. Have students suggest more recent material to update the class on each country's current political situation.

INSTRUCT

Explain

Many international and domestic problems faced the nation during the last years of Reagan's presidency, including a stock market crash. "Hot spots" in the world included the Middle East, and South Africa. International attention was focused on the United States election of 1988.

☑ Writing Process Activity

Identifying Central Issues Ask students to imagine they are stockholders in a company that invests heavily in South Africa. In preparation for writing a letter to the board of directors, ask them to take a stand on *apartheid* and brainstorm its consequences. Students should begin their letter with a topic sentence supporting or protesting the company's involvement in South Africa, and they should recommend a future course of action. Ask students to revise for persuasive language and logic. After proofreading, students can compare their letters.

Section Review Answers

Section 4, page 931

1. a) succeeded Mao Zedong as leader of China. b) name for the South African system of separating people of color from the white minority. Apartheid also serves to exploit people of color economically. c) leader in the struggle against apartheid. d) had the second highest number of delegates at the 1988 Democratic convention. 2. New laws and increased government insurance allowed savings banks to make risky loans. When the market crashed in 1987, less money came in and many who had borrowed could not repay. When these banks failed, the deficit increased when the government had to pay to cover insured deposits. 3. Similarities: in both cases a great power found itself fighting an unpopular war in difficult terrain against a small, but dedicated guerrilla force. Differences: the role of China in Vietnam, the openness of antiwar activities in the United States, the gradual involvement of the United States in Vietnam compared to the sudden invasion of Afghanistan.

CLOSE

To conclude the lesson, help students identify the unresolved issues mentioned in this section. Ask students to select an unresolved issue and write three questions about it for the current President to answer.

Extension Activity

To extend the lesson, ask students to select one of the crusaders for the rights of black South Africans, such as Nelson Mandela or Archbishop Desmond Tutu. Then have students research that person's life and compile a one-page biographical sketch of him or her.

Section 5 (pages 924–930)

The End of the Cold War

FOCUS

To introduce the lesson, on the chalkboard create a time line of the events occurring in Eastern Europe in 1989 which led to the end of the cold war. (You may wish to use the time line as a guide when teaching this section of the chapter.)

INSTRUCT

Explain

Since the end of World War II the political structure of the world consisted of two major powers centered in NATO and the Warsaw Pact countries. For nearly 45 years the two major powers representing these groups, the United States and the Soviet Union, were engaged in a cold war. The end of communism in Eastern Europe brought about a new world order under which it was hoped there would be an atmosphere of international cooperation.

❀ Cooperative Learning Activity

Formulating Questions Break the class into groups of eight and explain that students will write a review quiz for another group. Assign each of the eight sections of Chapter 36 to one student in every group. Have each student list five important terms—names of people, events, organizations, treaties, etc.—discussed in the section assigned. For each term have students write a brief description to be used in a "matching" type of quiz. Have a group recorder prepare the final quiz, listing all the group's terms and their descriptions in random order. Bring group members together to prepare an answer key. Duplicate quizzes and have groups exchange and complete the matching.

Section Review Answers

Section 5, page 930

1. a) leader of Solidarity, elected president of Poland in 1990. b) Communist leader of East Germany, replaced in October, 1989. c) describes the peaceful revolution resulting in the collapse of the Communist government in Czechoslovakia. d) dissident playwright, leader of the opposition in Czechoslovakia. e) Chancellor of West Germany. f) leader of Moscow Communist party, elected president of the Russian Republic in 1990. g) Lithuania, Latvia, and Estonia; pushed for independence from Soviet Union. 2. In 1989 the fence separating Hungary and Austria came down, and in September 1989, the Austro-Hungarian border was opened. East Germans could now escape to the West via Hungary and Austria. Those who wanted to remain in East Germany began clamoring for reform; late 1989 brought on a whirlwind of events culminating in the opening of the East German-West German border and the fall of the Berlin Wall in November. 3. When Germany surrendered, it was split up into zones of occupation among France, Great Britain, Russia, and the United States. The Allies could not agree on a plan for Germany. In 1948 the western powers set up a federal government in West Germany. The Russians responded by setting up a communist Republic in East Germany that remained a satellite of the Soviet Union until the reunification of Germany. 4. If Russia and the other former republics do not succeed in their reforms, political and economic chaos could threaten democracy and lead to dictatorship. The United States is also concerned with the control of nuclear weapons in the former republics.

CLOSE

To conclude the lesson, either as a class discussion or a written exercise, ask: How might the end of communism in Eastern Europe affect the future of the United States?

Section 6 (pages 930–933)

A Dangerous World

FOCUS

To introduce the lesson, ask students how world events affected the midterm elections in the United States. Discuss the various issues and their impact.

INSTRUCT

Explain

In the post-cold war era, the United States has maintained its position as a world power. During the Bush administration, there were several conflicts around the world in which the United States became involved.

☑ Writing Process Activity

Drawing Conclusions Ask students to imagine they are political commentators who must explain the U.S. invasion of Panama or the build-up of U.S. military forces in the Middle East during Iraq's invasion of Kuwait. In preparation for writing a news article, ask them to outline the events of one of the situations and to brainstorm the reasons and outcomes involved. Students should begin their article with a sentence justifying or criticizing this country for intervening in the affairs of another country. Ask students to revise for clear explanation and organization. After proofreading, students can deliver their commentaries to the class.

Section Review Answers

Section 6, page 933

1. a) location of pro-democracy demonstration in Beijing where the army was unleashed on the demonstrators, killing hundreds. b) commander of Panamanian military and police forces, overthrown in December, 1989. c) War between Iraq and coalition forces led by the United States to liberate Kuwait from Iraq. Iraq was beaten and agreed to withdraw from Kuwait and abide by UN resolutions. d) Iraqi leader who ordered Iraq's armies to seize Kuwait in August 1990. e) anti-missile missiles used by the U.S. against Iraqi missiles. f) Iraqi missiles launched against targets in Israel and Saudi Arabia during the Gulf War. 2. Its purpose was to topple Noriega's re-

gime. Critics claimed that these actions were in violation of the Charter of the Organization of American States, which the U.S. had signed. 3. Hitler had been allowed to conquer neighboring countries, resulting in a world war. 4. Answers will vary. Students should justify their opinions with evidence from the text.

CLOSE

To conclude the lesson, point out to students that for the first time since World War II, Western countries directly intervened in events in the Middle East. Then ask: What do you think will be the long-term significance of this intervention? Will it have a positive or negative effect on world politics?

Section 7 (pages 933–939)

The State of the Nation

FOCUS

To introduce the lesson, ask students to brainstorm a list of domestic problems that faced the country in the early 1990s.

INSTRUCT

Explain
Domestic problems and events, including a recession, unemployment, poverty, the Los Angeles riots, AIDS, and crime hurt Bush's chances of reelection.

☑ Writing Process Activity
Identifying Central Issues After doing additional research, ask students to write a letter to the editor expressing their views about either the Anita Hill hearings or the Los Angeles riots. Ask students to revise for persuasive language and logic. After proofreading, students can compare their letters.

Section Review Answers
Section 7, page 939

1. a) moderate conservative member of the Supreme Court from New Hampshire appointed by Bush. b) member of the Supreme Court appointed by Bush. Accused by Anita Hill of sexual harassment during his confirmation hearings. c) third-party candidate in the 1992 election. 2. the Savings and Loan bail out, decreased defense spending, increased oil prices, and the federal deficit. 3. issues of race, poverty, and violence, and whether the government was giving too much or too little aid. 4. He was an outsider who was not beholden to special-interest groups and he was not a politician at a time when many people were frustrated with government.

CLOSE

To conclude the lesson as a class discussion ask: What lessons do you think the country can learn from the Los Angeles riots? What actions should the government and communities be taking to avoid such events in the future?

Section 8 (pages 939–944)

The Clinton Presidency

FOCUS

To introduce the lesson, ask students to compare what they have read about Clinton's domestic agenda and his relationship with Congress to President Jimmy Carter's agenda and relationship with Congress (pages 882–884). How were the two Presidents similar and different?

INSTRUCT

Explain
In his first two years in office, Clinton faced many setbacks with Congress over issues such as his economic stimulus package and health care reform. Clinton also eked out a few victories with Congress, including NAFTA, a national service program, the Family Leave Act, and a crime bill.

★ Independent Activity
Predicting Consequences Ask each student to research the status or results of one of the following initiatives or policies enacted during Clinton's first two years in office: Deficit reduction, the crime bill, the national service program, NAFTA. Ask each student to report back to the class in a brief presentation.

Section Review Answers
Section 8, page 944

1. a) required employers to allow workers to take up to 12 weeks of unpaid leave after the birth or adoption of a child or in the event of a family emergency. b) first woman attorney general. c) second woman to be appointed to the U.S. Supreme Court. d) Supreme Court justice appointed by Clinton. 2. Clinton proposed a uniform package of government-enforced health benefits for all Americans, based on employer mandates and consumer alliances to reduce costs. 3. Answers will vary. In part because Somalia and Haiti presented relatively small-scale problems that could be solved in a short time. Problems in Bosnia were much more complex, and involvement would cost more lives and would last much longer.

CLOSE

To conclude the lesson, ask small groups of students to update the class on the status of events in one of the following countries or regions: Bosnia, North Korea, Somalia, Haiti, South Africa, or the Middle East.

Chapter Review Answers

Focusing on Ideas

1. Lesson 1: Avoid internal disputes of distant nations. Learners of this lesson oppose involvement in Central America, Bosnia, and so on. Lesson 2: Do not get involved unless you intend to win. Learners of this lesson applaud Grenada, Haiti, and are prepared for involvement in Central America. 2. (a) Soviet Union's economy in ruin, had to worry about its own needs, letting the Warsaw Pact countries go their own way; poor economic conditions and desire for freedom produced dissatisfaction with Communist governments. (b) The opening of the Austro-Hungarian border contributed to the fall of the Berlin Wall and German reunification. (c) Soviet *glasnost* policy; Gorbachev's promise to leave other countries free from outside interference in their development; reduced tension between the superpowers; winding down of the cold war. 3. a) The United States government had traded arms in exchange for the release of hostages. This set a dangerous precedent and may have encouraged future acts of terrorism. b) Military aid was given to the contras by an organization directed by White House staff despite congressional bans on such aid. c) the President had failed in his constitutional duty to see that the laws be faithfully executed. 4. Gorbachev's coming to power; glasnost; Soviet withdrawal from Afghanistan; efforts to reduce nuclear weapons (INF Treaty); end of the cold war; working cooperatively to stop Hussein.

Taking a Critical Look

1. The United States invaded Grenada because it feared the island would become a base for exporting communism to nearby countries. Also, there was concern about 1000 Americans being taken as hostages. The United States did not invade Haiti but rather intervened peacefully to restore a democratically elected president. Both were relatively small-scale military operations. 2. Domestic problems including a recession, unemployment, poverty, the Los Angeles riots, AIDS, and crime. Also Perot's candidacy may have helped Clinton.

Your Region in History

1–2. Answers will vary depending on your region. Consult your local library or historical society.

Historical Facts and Figures

(a) 1970—41%; 1980—24%; 1990—26% (b) the Vietnam War (c) government spending on interest more than doubled, rising from 6% to 15% (d) a growing national debt (e) federal spending on grants to states and localities dropped from 16% to 11% between 1980 and 1990 (f) this drop in federal grants forced many states and localities to increase their taxes in order to provide essential services and fund needed programs.

36

Answers to "Making Connections"

(See "Using Making Connections" on p. 942)

Answers will vary, but may include one or more of the following examples. Answers based on the time line callouts are in italics.

1. Laws passed by Congress since 1950 have contradicted Thomas Jefferson's belief in a "natural aristocracy." Instead Congress and the nation, more anxiously than ever, sought equality of opportunity for all Americans. Jefferson thought that those who did the best at certain examinations would continue their education and eventually be the "aristocrats" needed to run the government. Jefferson did not expect that black and female Americans would win places in the competition, but of course they did. However, they did not receive a chance to compete fairly. To rectify that situation *Congress passed the Equal Employment Opportunity Act in 1972, which guarantees equal pay for equal work.* Physically handicapped Americans were also prevented—sometimes by architectural barriers such as staircases—from competing equally. *In 1973 Congress made a start at rectifying that by passing the Rehabilitation Act that forbids discrimination against the physically handicapped* in programs, activities, and facilities supported by federal funds. 2. New conflicts include: *hostages in Iran, Nicaragua, Iraq,* Lebanon, Afghanistan, *Bosnia,* Haiti, Panama; old conflicts resolved or partially resolved include: *Israel and Egypt, Israel and the PLO,* Israel and Jordan, *Soviet Union/Russia, East Germany,* South Africa, and Vietnam. 3. The sweeping changes in the governments of Eastern Europe and the *fall of the Berlin Wall* led to the reduction of Communist power in that part of world, and signaled the end of the Cold War. The U.S. now had opportunities to improve relations with Eastern bloc countries, including Russia. But the U.S. also faced the challenge of maintaining peace under the new world order. This could be dangerous, as when a U.S.-led coalition *forced Saddam Hussein's troops to retreat from Kuwait.*

Focusing the Chapter: Have students identify the chapter logo. Discuss what unit theme the logo might symbolize. Then ask students to skim the chapter to identify other illustrations or titles that relate to this theme.

Chapter 36

The Emergence of a New World

Ronald Reagan came to the Presidency proclaiming the Soviet Union an "evil empire." But he was to see surprising changes there during his eight years in office. And his successors, George Bush and Bill Clinton, would see even more.

In 1993 President Bill Clinton presided over a ceremony at which Israel's Yitzhak Rabin and the PLO's Yasir Arafat signed a historic peace agreement. As a result of the agreement, the Palestinians established self-rule in Gaza and the West Bank town of Jericho.

Lee Stone/Sygma

The Nations of Central America

See "Lesson Plan," p. 906C.

1. Troubles abroad

Few of President Reagan's associates came into the government with experience in foreign affairs. They would find world problems harder to solve than those of a changing economy.

Nicaragua and El Salvador. In Nicaragua, in Central America, the Marxist Sandinistas had taken control in 1979 (p. 895) and were forging close ties with Cuba and the Soviet Union. That same year, in El Salvador—a tiny country about the size of Massachusetts and the most densely populated in Central America—guerrillas, some of them Marxists, began to try to topple the government. They said the government helped only the interests of the few very rich, who owned most of the nation's land. The Reagan administration feared Marxist governments in Central America. As allies of the Soviet Union, they might threaten our borders. To prevent this, the United States aided the government in El Salvador and pressured Nicaragua to become democratic.

The United States, through the Central Intelligence Agency (CIA), armed rebels to oppose the Sandinistas. The "contras" (a shortened form of the Spanish for *counter-revolutionaries*) attacked Nicaragua from bases in Honduras and Costa Rica. Some of these were former followers of the deposed dictator Somoza. President Reagan hoped that helping the contras would stop the Soviet Union and Cuba from shipping arms through Nicaragua to the guerrillas in El Salvador. But Congress thought he also wanted to topple the Sandinistas. To an appropriations bill in 1982, Congress attached the Boland amendment, named for Congressman Edward P. Boland of Massachusetts. It forbade using government funds to overthrow the Sandinistas.

In April 1984, it was learned that the CIA had helped the contras to plant mines in the harbors of Nicaragua. The CIA had also given the contras a war manual which told them how to carry out blackmail and assassinations. Congress was troubled by what seemed a violation

⊕ **Geography and History: Regions** Ask students to look at the map above and to read the section headed "Nicaragua and El Salvador." Ask: Why was the Reagan administration concerned about El Salvador becoming Marxist? (Because of El Salvador's close proximity to the United States and to other Central American countries.) What countries share a border with El Salvador? (Guatemala and Honduras.) Why were many Americans concerned about United States involvement in El Salvador? (Because they feared that this involvement would lead to an undeclared war that the United States could never win.)

of the law. They voted the contras only nonmilitary aid—food, clothing, and medicine. Military aid was barred for two years. In another Boland amendment, in October 1984, Congress barred the CIA and any other government agency involved in intelligence from giving military aid to the contras, "directly or indirectly."

Israel, Lebanon, and the Middle East. Meanwhile, the Middle East festered with religious hatred and political chaos. The assassination in 1981 of peace-loving Anwar el-Sadat of Egypt by Muslim fundamentalists kept the pot boiling. And Israel took new steps to defend itself against those Arabs who said it had no right to exist. Israel bombed a nuclear reactor in Iraq and annexed the Golan Heights, which it had seized from Syria in 1967. This too, Israel argued, was in self-defense.

To complicate matters even more, Iraq and Iran were locked in a bloody war. It had begun in September 1980 when Iraq invaded Iran hoping to seize a contested piece of land, but the Iraqis soon bogged down and tried to with-

Palestinian youth attacked Israeli troops in the occupied territories early in 1988.

M. Milner/Sygma

draw. Iran refused to make peace and the war dragged on.

Still, the worst problem in the Middle East was Lebanon. For a time it was a haven of peace and prosperity. But it had begun to slide toward chaos in 1970 after the Palestine Liberation Organization (PLO), driven out of Jordan by King Hussein, moved in. Soon one-tenth of the population was Palestinian. They would set off the explosion that would blow the country into anarchy.

Lebanon was a mix of ethnic groups and warring sects of Christians and Muslims. It could remain a nation only as long as they were willing to work together. But the PLO had seized control and was using Lebanese territory as a military base against Israel. The PLO was not interested in building a unified, independent Lebanon.

In June 1982, Israeli troops invaded Lebanon in an attempt to end its use as a base for attacks on Israel. Thousands died as Israeli tanks and troops, under cover of their strong air force, swept halfway up the country. They entered West Beirut in August, trapping the PLO.

Philip Habib, President Reagan's patient envoy, shuttled between Lebanon, Israel, and Syria. He worked out an agreement for the PLO guerrillas to leave Beirut for other countries. Under the protection of a peacekeeping force from the United States, Italy, and France, the PLO departed. After they had left, the peacekeeping force, which had promised to protect the Palestinian refugees still in Beirut, went home.

With the guerrillas gone, it seemed that peace might return. But then the newly elected Christian president of Lebanon, Bashir Gemayel, was assassinated even before he could be inaugurated. In revenge, his Christian Lebanese followers entered the Palestinian refugee camps in Israeli-occupied West Beirut. There they massacred over a thousand men, women, and children.

Trying to bring peace to Lebanon. In desperation, the international peacekeeping force of United States, French, and Italian troops returned to Lebanon. They were later joined by British troops. This force hoped to prop up the government of new President Amin Gemayel, Bashir's brother, and stop the fighting between the warring Christian and Muslim groups. But the deep religious hatreds in Lebanon seemed incurable. The peacekeepers themselves became a target. On September 1, 1983, after the 800 American marines in Lebanon came under attack, Reagan sent in 2000 more to help protect them.

In April 1983, the people of the United States had been sickened when a truck full of explosives was used to blow up the American embassy in Beirut. Forty-seven people in our embassy died. Iranian radicals took credit for the crime. The unseen force of fanatical terrorists was more frightening than the bullets from soldiers in uniform.

Then on Sunday morning, October 23, another truck packed with explosives raced past marine guards and hit the main marine building near the Beirut airport. The explosion killed the driver of the truck and 241 marines asleep in their barracks. This act marked the beginning of the end of American involvement in Lebanon. Though President Reagan had said he would not withdraw our troops in response to terrorism, he had to face the fact that the peacekeeping force was a failure. Finally, at the end of February 1984, all the marines were pulled out.

Grenada. In October 1983, just two days after the marine headquarters in Lebanon was blown up, 1900 United States Marines and airborne troops invaded the small Caribbean island nation of Grenada. The leftist government

President and Mrs. Reagan greeted wounded marines at a memorial service for the 241 marines who were killed when terrorists attacked the peacekeeping forces in Beirut.

of Grenada had been overthrown and its leaders murdered by an even more radical group. The United States and several of Grenada's neighbors said they feared that the island would become a base for exporting communism to nearby countries. There was also concern that the 1000 Americans on Grenada, many of them young medical students, might be held hostage by the unpredictable new government. Reagan did not want to face another Iran. The military occupation of Grenada took several days longer than expected, and finally 6000 U.S. soldiers and marines landed on the island.

The Reagan administration hoped the Grenada attack would show that the United States would stand by its friends. It also wanted to prove to friend and foe—and especially to Nicaragua—that our nation had not been paralyzed by Vietnam. We still could and would use force, if needed.

Opinion polls showed that a majority of the American people applauded the invasion of Grenada. But some Americans doubted that any government in Grenada posed a real threat to the United States. Other Americans argued that in any case the United States should set the example of not invading another country.

They asked how the United States could condemn the Soviet use of force in Afghanistan, and still use force in the Caribbean.

The problem of Third World debts. Argentina, Mexico, Brazil, and other Third World countries faced severe economic problems. During the prosperous years after World War II they had financed their development by borrowing large sums from banks in the industrial nations. Especially during the years of high inflation in the 1970s, it had seemed cheap to borrow. The debt could be paid back with money worth much less than when it was borrowed.

By 1983 Third World countries and others had run up debts totaling $700 billion. They could not even pay the interest. Their problems had been created by high oil prices and by the worldwide recession of the early 1980s, which made it difficult to sell their products abroad. This debt crisis fueled the disputes between the industrial nations and the developing countries. It continued on into the 1990s, threatening the banking systems and the economies of the whole world.

The United States and the USSR. Relations between the United States and the Soviet

The United States brought troops and supplies to Grenada in mammoth transport planes.

Abbas/Magnum

Union worsened during Reagan's first years in office. The President and his aides viewed the problems of the world chiefly as the results of the aggressive and expansionist policies of the Soviet Union.

Events in Poland brought further strains. A new unofficial labor union called "Solidarity" had appeared there in 1980. For a time it seemed to force the Polish government to be more open. But the Soviet Union would not allow it. Military maneuvers on the Polish border helped to put new Soviet puppets in power. In December 1981, they imposed martial law and the movement for freedom was crushed.

Discussions between the United States and the USSR on arms control stopped. Still, both countries continued to abide by the SALT agreements. SALT II had been condemned by Reagan during the presidential campaign, and because of the Soviet invasion of Afghanistan the Senate had never acted on it. But when President Reagan found that the United States actually did benefit by the treaty, we continued to observe it.

To defend against the new Soviet missiles stationed in Eastern Europe, the United States and its NATO allies decided to place intermediate-range Pershing II missiles and cruise missiles in Western Europe. The cruise missiles were so called because they flew (cruised) to their targets at low altitudes instead of arching high into the sky like other missiles. These weapons could not only hit Eastern Europe, but could reach the Soviet Union.

Reagan offered not to put these new missiles in place if the Soviet Union would remove its own new rockets from Eastern Europe. The Soviet Union refused because, they said, both Britain and France had missiles aimed at them.

The Soviets threatened to break off all arms talks if the new missiles were deployed. The president of France, François Mitterrand, called the crisis the most dangerous since the Berlin blockade of 1948 and the Cuban missile crisis of 1962. An official of the English government stated that the Soviet missiles had created "an imbalance of terror." Mitterrand and other European leaders argued that in response, the NATO alliance must show strength and unity.

In Europe and the United States, hundreds of thousands of people marched and demonstrated. Some called for a "freeze" on the building of nuclear weapons, or even one-sided disarmament by the West.

Even before the new missiles arrived in Europe in December 1983, relations between the Soviet Union and the West had worsened. On September 1, a Soviet fighter plane shot down a South Korean airliner, killing all 269 people aboard. The civilian plane, on its regularly scheduled flight, had wandered over Soviet territory and close to missile and naval bases. The free world was outraged by what appeared to be the cold-blooded slaughter of innocent civilians. The Soviets had, it was later revealed, mistaken the airliner for a United States Air Force reconnaissance plane that had been in the area keeping tabs on the Soviet bases.

Sudden and unpredictable changes of Soviet leaders made other problems for the West. Soviet leaders were not elected by the people. They were chosen by a few insiders. Their choice was mysterious to the outside world. Leonid Brezhnev, who had led the nation since 1964, died in November 1982. In his place they named Yuri K. Andropov, a former head of the KGB, the infamous Soviet security police. But Andropov, a sick man, died in February 1984. He was replaced by 72-year-old Konstantin U. Chernenko, a run-of-the-mill Communist official and the oldest man to run the country since the Russian Revolution. Americans could not expect friendly new proposals from him.

Memories of Vietnam. Despite the passage of years, the war in Vietnam remained a burning memory. In November 1982, a monument to the 58,132 Americans who died in Vietnam during the war was dedicated in Washington, D.C. The name of every one of them was inscribed on a black marble wall. Americans finally were honoring the many Americans who had died fighting for their country.

The United States continued to demand a report from the Vietnamese on what had happened to the nearly 2500 American servicemen and civilians who were still missing in Vietnam. It was not until 1993 that the United States,

More from Boorstin: "We have, of course, our modern abolitionists, those who believe that the abolition of slavery in Russia is the sole issue in the world. . . . Soviet communism provides them the sense of 'givenness,' of obviousness in their objective. For them, Communists embody the spirit of Satan . . . Some of them would seem almost willing . . . to burn the Constitution in order to attain their admirable objective." (From *The Genius of American Politics*)

prompted by business leaders and encouraged by Vietnam's seemingly honest efforts to account for all the missing soldiers, lifted its decades-old trade embargo on its former enemy.

See "Section 1 Review answers," p. 906C.

Section 1 Review

1. Identify or explain: El Salvador, PLO, Grenada, Solidarity, François Mitterand, Yuri K. Andropov, Konstantin U. Chernenko.

2. What events in Lebanon since 1970 led to the stationing of an international peacekeeping force there in 1982 and 1983? What happened to the peacekeeping force?

3. Why did Third World countries go heavily into debt to foreign banks in the developed nations? What effects did this have on the economies of both?

4. How did Reagan approach relations with the Soviet Union? How did the Soviets respond?

5. **Critical Thinking: Identifying Assumptions.** Why did Reagan and his advisers want to stop the rebels in El Salvador and help the rebels in Nicaragua?

See "Lesson Plan," p. 906C.

2. Successes and failures

Despite all the trouble-spots abroad, Americans who watched on television as Ronald Reagan delivered his annual State of the Union message to Congress on January 25, 1984, saw only optimism and pride. With this speech he opened his campaign for reelection. "America is back," he said, "standing tall, looking to the eighties with courage, confidence, and hope."

Reagan's program. The President pointed to the success of his economic program and called for measures to insure steady economic growth, including a constitutional amendment to require a balanced budget. He gave special attention to the social issues that his administration had put on the back burner while it dealt with the economy. He emphasized his support for prayer in the public schools and his opposition to abortion. He offered to work to improve relations with the Soviet Union and to seek peace in Central America and the Middle East.

To aid the nation's effort to conquer "our next frontier," he called for a costly new program to

A stark new memorial in Washington, D.C., listed all members of the U.S. armed forces who died in Vietnam during the war, or were still missing.

Joel Stettenheim/SABA

✄ **Critical Thinking Activity: Expressing Problems Clearly** What is the United States' foreign policy today? Create a chart on the chalkboard using the following columns: "Country," "U.S. Interest," and "Strategy." In the first column have students describe United States' interests in each country, and the methods we have used to realize our goals and objectives with each country. Ask students to write their own statement summarizing United States foreign policy, using the chart as a basis.

establish a manned space station. There scientists could live weightless in space and do research on metals, medicines, and communications that would be impossible on earth.

A basis for this plan was the space shuttle begun by his predecessors, which had now achieved success. The shuttle was the first space vehicle designed to rocket into space and then return to land like an airplane. It could serve the space station. The long-planned first flight by the space shuttle *Columbia* had gone into space in 1981 and then returned to land gently on earth. *Columbia* became the first reusable space vehicle when it went back into space a few months later.

The fight for the Democratic nomination. A large field of candidates for the Democratic party's presidential nomination narrowed rapidly to three: Walter Mondale of Minnesota, a former U.S. senator and Vice-President under Jimmy Carter; Senator Gary Hart of Colorado; and the Reverend Jesse Jackson, a black minister who had worked with Martin Luther King, Jr.

After a bitter struggle, Mondale gathered just enough delegates to claim a majority and the nomination. For Vice-President, Mondale selected Geraldine Ferraro, the daughter of Roman Catholic, Italian immigrants and a third-term member of Congress from Queens in New York City. She became the first woman to be nominated for the vice-presidency by a major party. Quick and intelligent, Representative Ferraro was to add zest to the campaign of the more reserved Walter Mondale.

The race for the election. The team of Ronald Reagan and George Bush was renominated by acclamation in Dallas, Texas. They hitched their wagon to the spectacular economic recovery, promising more of the same. Mondale and Ferraro insisted that not all Americans were benefiting from the recovery. They proposed higher taxes for the wealthy, an increase in government spending for jobs, housing, and education, vigorous protection of the environment, and aggressive promotion of equal rights for women and for blacks.

Phil Huber/Black Star

Walter Mondale chose Geraldine Ferraro as his running mate—the first woman to run on a major party's national ticket.

On election day, some 92 million people— only 53 percent of the voting-age population— went to the polls. In a landslide, Reagan took 59 percent of the popular vote and swept the electoral vote with the highest number in history—525 to 13. Mondale carried only his home state of Minnesota and the District of Columbia. Still, there was some solace for the Democrats. They continued to control the House, and the Republican margin in the Senate declined. Many people who voted for Reagan disagreed with him on particular issues. But they liked Reagan personally and admired his ability to lead the nation. No President had served two full terms since Dwight D. Eisenhower in the 1950s. They hoped he could solve the hard problems he faced as he began his final four years.

The growing federal debt. The federal deficit was hurtling out of control. The national debt

See "Lesson Plan," p. 906D for **Writing Process Activity: Recognizing Ideologies** relating to the possibility of a woman Vice-President.

was expected to go over $2 trillion in 1986. This was more than double what it had been when Reagan took office. Just paying interest on this enormous debt would use up almost 25 percent of the entire federal budget.

At last, in December 1985, Congress took drastic action. The new Balanced Budget and Emergency Deficit Control Act set budget goals that would reduce the deficit each year until a balanced budget was achieved in 1991. But every time the year for a balanced budget approached, the date was postponed by members of Congress who feared the impact of the cuts.

Some people called this the "meat axe" approach to the budget problem. Instead of selecting unnecessary projects to be cut, the law was entirely automatic. If Congress appropriated more than the goals allowed, "across-the-board" cuts came into action and all federal programs were slashed by the same proportion. Only a few exceptions (like Social Security and pensions) were allowed. The act showed that Congress was unwilling to take political risks to save important programs. Programs were measured only in dollars and not by the nation's need.

A new tax law. President Reagan had argued that tax reform was needed to keep the free-enterprise system prosperous. He had used his charm and persuasive powers on television in May 1985 to call for sweeping tax reform. The old tax laws had become so complicated that filling out the forms had become a puzzle and a headache for all citizens. And the rates were so high for people with large incomes that Reagan said they were being discouraged from starting new enterprises. The Tax Reform Act of 1986 did not make the laws any simpler, but it did make a big cut in the tax rates. Two basic rates replaced the 14 earlier brackets, and many tax deductions, often called "loopholes" because of the tax revenue that fell through them, were reduced or eliminated. The new law was not supposed to increase or decrease the government's total revenue. But it was expected that 60 percent of individual taxpayers would pay less. Some corporations complained that businesses would pay more.

The Supreme Court. Since justices of the Supreme Court serve until they retire or die, their influence on the nation reaches far beyond the term of any one President. Therefore President Reagan was especially concerned to appoint conservative justices. His first appointment was Sandra Day O'Connor. A conservative Republican, she had earned respect on the Arizona Supreme Court as a skilled, forthright, and hard-working judge. Easily approved by the Senate, in 1981 she became the first woman to sit on the United States Supreme Court.

Not until 1986 was Reagan given the opportunity for another appointment. Chief Justice Warren E. Burger stepped down in June and the President nominated the brilliant William H. Rehnquist, a conservative Associate Justice, to take his place. After a hard fight, he was approved by the Senate. To fill Rehnquist's seat on the Court, the President named Antonin Scalia, an intelligent, scholarly, and witty appeals court judge, who was also conservative. The son of an Italian immigrant, he was speedily and unanimously approved by the Senate. He symbolized American opportunity as he became the first American of Italian descent to sit on the Supreme Court.

The President's future choices for the Court would not have such smooth sailing. The next opening came when Justice Lewis F. Powell, Jr., decided to step down in 1987. Now it was not just a question of another justice. Justice Powell had been an important "swing" vote, providing the crucial fifth vote on important issues. He had been nominated by President Nixon, and was himself a conservative. But he was conspicuously open minded, and his vote was often unpredictable.

To replace Powell, President Reagan nominated Judge Robert Bork of the United States Court of Appeals for the District of Columbia. Bork was a bearded, learned, and especially outspoken conservative. He had been a professor at Yale Law School. For 30 years he had taught, written, and spoken against Supreme Court decisions on abortion, privacy, and civil rights. As Solicitor General of the United States under Nixon, Bork had carried out Nixon's

≢ **Continuity and Change: Government and Politics** Point out to students that the United States did not always have such an immense national debt. In 1887, during the Cleveland administration, the United States Treasury was actually taking in $100 million a year more than it spent. By 1894, the "billion dollar" Congress during Benjamin Harrison's term had erased the surplus and the nation has been in debt ever since. (See p. 467.)

Presidents can never be sure how their appointees to the Supreme Court will vote. But Reagan hoped the justices he selected would be more conservative than their immediate predecessors.

order to fire special prosecutor Archibald Cox (p. 836).

The Constitution requires that the Senate confirm the President's nominations for the Supreme Court before they can be sworn into office. The fight over the Bork nomination was one of the most bitter in American history. Bork's champions defended him as a wise and courageous conservative. His opponents, led by Senator Edward Kennedy of Massachusetts, attacked him for being insensitive to the rights of minorities and standing outside the mainstream of American social progress. After three weeks of televised public hearings, during which Bork expounded his views on many subjects, the Senate Judiciary Committee voted 9 to 5 against the nomination. It was defeated in the full Senate 58 to 42, the largest margin by which a Court nominee had ever been rejected.

In haste and anger, President Reagan then nominated the young and little-known Douglas H. Ginsburg, who had only recently been named to the United States Court of Appeals.

Then, to everyone's surprise, it was revealed that Ginsburg had smoked marijuana while he was a professor at Harvard Law School. This embarrassed an administration that was so strongly for "law and order" and on an antidrug crusade.

Judge Ginsburg speedily withdrew his name from consideration. President Reagan, retreating from his fight with the Senate, finally made a choice that was not controversial. He named Judge Anthony M. Kennedy of the United States Court of Appeals. A moderate and pragmatic conservative, Kennedy was confirmed without a dissenting vote early in 1988.

Relations with the Soviet Union. In March 1985, after only 13 months in office, the ailing, aged Soviet leader Chernenko died. Succeeding him as General Secretary was the dynamic, tough, and intelligent Mikhail S. Gorbachev. At 54 he was the youngest leader of the USSR since Josef Stalin. The world wondered where he would lead the Communist world.

At first Gorbachev seemed as hard-line as his predecessors. But he soon agreed to meet President Reagan. A "summit" meeting in Geneva, Switzerland, in November 1985 was the first between the leaders of the Soviet Union and the United States since 1979 (p. 892). At least, it was hoped, Reagan and Gorbachev would get to know each other. And when the talks ended, both men expressed high hopes for better relations between their two countries.

Nuclear disaster. Mikhail Gorbachev swiftly showed a new style of Soviet leadership. He went out and talked to the people on the streets and in the factories. Two Russian words became his slogan. *Glasnost* meant a more open society. *Perestroika* meant restructuring of the economy, the party, and the government. They were supposed to carry a message of "new thinking" about old problems.

Gorbachev was only beginning to entrench himself in power when he was shaken by a catastrophe inside the Soviet Union. A nuclear reactor at Chernobyl, near Kiev, exploded and burned in April 1986. Radioactive waste spewed into the air and spread terror across Europe. The radiation released was equal to all the radiation that had ever been released from the explosions and tests of nuclear bombs throughout the world. At Chernobyl 31 people were killed and several hundred injured. Experts estimated that anywhere from 17,000 to 475,000 might die from radiation exposure over the next 70 years.

Reykjavik. Reagan had great faith in the personal approach. He met again with Gorbachev on October 11 and 12, 1986, this time at Reykjavik, Iceland. Some hoped that by frank discussion the two leaders might make progress on nuclear arms reduction. They even talked of abolishing all strategic (long-range) nuclear weapons. But our allies in Western Europe were afraid of this proposal. They thought these weapons were needed to keep the Soviets from conquering westward.

President Reagan and General Secretary Gorbachev held a summit meeting in Washington, D.C., in 1987, during which they signed a treaty removing their intermediate-range missiles from Europe.

The short talks ended suddenly with no decisions. Gorbachev objected to Reagan's Strategic Defense Initiative (SDI). This was a system of advanced defensive weapons often called "Star Wars." The Soviets demanded that for the next ten years Americans should test it only in the laboratory. But many Americans believed—as the Soviets later confessed—that the Soviets were already working on their own SDI. Why should they let Americans match it?

The Strategic Defense Initiative. Reagan had first proposed the Strategic Defense Initiative in a speech in 1983. He hoped to build a defensive shield of advanced weapons, some operating in outer space, to make the United States safe from nuclear attack. To reassure the Soviets, Reagan even said that we would share the technology with them. Critics, including some scientists, objected that the system would cost billions of dollars and might not even work.

Still, everyone knew that Gorbachev wanted to improve the standard of living of the Soviet people. This meant spending less on weapons. So he had an interest in slowing down the arms race. If he could only stop American progress on SDI, the Soviets might be able to cut back on their own arms budget. As it turned out, Reagan's unbuilt SDI proved to be a powerful bargaining chip against the Soviets.

Reducing nuclear arms. Despite the impasse at Reykjavik, talks went on in Vienna, Austria. In February 1987, Gorbachev suddenly offered to sign an agreement for eliminating both Soviet and United States medium-range missiles. These were missiles that could not cross the ocean, but with them the Soviet Union and Western Europe could hit each other. Tough verifying procedures would allow each country to station representatives outside the other country's plants that had manufactured these weapons. This would actually place Americans at a plant in Sverdlovsk, the very city where the U-2 had been shot down in 1960 (p. 747).

On December 7, 1987, a smiling, handshaking Gorbachev arrived in the United States. He had schooled himself in American techniques of public relations. On the following day General Secretary Gorbachev and President Reagan signed the new Intermediate-Range Nuclear Forces (INF) Treaty. This would remove all missiles with ranges of 300 to 3400 miles from Eastern and Western Europe. All 2611 missiles of this type would be destroyed—859 by the United States and 1752 by the Soviet Union.

For the first time in history, the INF Treaty 📖 aimed to reduce the size of nuclear forces. It did not really insure peace, because both nations still had enough long-range missiles and nuclear warheads to destroy each other. Some Americans and American allies actually believed it would make the world less safe, for the treaty would leave Western Europe exposed to the much stronger, regular armed forces of the Soviet Union. Still, it was a way of testing the willingness of the world's greatest adversaries to come together. And it might be a first step away from the world's atomic self-destruction.

See "Section 2 Review answers," p. 906D.

Section 2 Review

1. Identify or explain: Balanced Budget Act, Mikhail S. Gorbachev, *perestroika, glasnost,* SDI.
2. What controversial stands did President Reagan take during his 1984 reelection campaign?
3. Why were Robert Bork and Douglas Ginsburg rejected as nominees to the Supreme Court? Why was Anthony Kennedy then confirmed?
4. What was the significance of the Strategic Defense Initiative (SDI) during the Reykjavik superpower summit?
5. **Critical Thinking: Checking Consistency.** Was the tripling of the national debt during Ronald Reagan's Presidency consistent with his strong stand for a balanced budget? Why or why not? List factors to support your answer.

See "Lesson Plan," p. 906D.

3. New problems for "the Teflon President"

A witty critic once called Ronald Reagan "the Teflon President." Teflon was a patented new material for pans which never let anything

📖 **More from Boorstin:** "In each successive world war, the competition in technology has become more fierce—and more effective. The splitting of the atom and the exploring of space bear witness to the stimulus of competition, the convergence of efforts, the involuntary collaboration of wartime enemies. Technology is the natural foe of nationalism." (From *Hidden History: Exploring Our Secret Past*)

stick to it, so it always looked clean. President Reagan was not only lucky. Somehow failures or criticisms never seemed to stick to him. But by the fall of 1986, the Teflon stopped working. The last two years of Ronald Reagan's terms were marked by national tragedy, foreign policy scandal, and economic shock.

Challenger.

In 1986, on January 28, a day much colder than normal in Florida, the space shuttle *Challenger* lifted off from Cape Canaveral. One member of its crew of seven was a sprightly young schoolteacher, Christa McAuliffe, who had been selected from many competitors to be the first "citizen observer" to go into space. A senator and a congressman had gone on earlier missions. Only 74 seconds into the flight, the millions watching on television were horrified to see the *Challenger* disappear in an enormous explosion. Americans were reminded that the space adventure carried mortal risks. Astronauts were soldiers staking their lives for the nation's progress.

The *Challenger* tragedy led to the grounding of the shuttle fleet. But it was hoped that the nation's space program could continue with unmanned rockets. This hope, too, was suddenly shattered by a series of mishaps. In April 1986 a Titan 34D rocket, which was probably carrying a secret spy satellite, exploded on lift-off. All Titan rockets were grounded. Then in May, a Delta rocket carrying a weather satellite went out of control and had to be destroyed. The United States space program was at a standstill until October 1987, when it successfully launched another Titan 34D.

(p. 919)

Arms and hostages.

In October 1986, a cargo plane carrying supplies to the contra rebels in Nicaragua was shot down. Two American crew members were killed and an American cargo handler, Eugene Hasenfus, was captured. Hasenfus told the Nicaraguans that he was working for the CIA. The United States vehemently denied this confession. The Boland amendment had banned military aid to the contras. Many people did not believe the administration's denial. They wondered where else the contras could be getting their arms.

NASA

The crew of the *Challenger* makes its way to the shuttle shortly before lift-off.

On November 3, a Lebanese magazine reported that Robert MacFarlane, President Reagan's former National Security Adviser, had visited Iran in order to arrange arms shipments. The President's supporters could not believe the story. The United States had been trying to stop other countries from supplying arms to Iran. And the President was known for his attacks on all who dealt with terrorists. But to the dismay and astonishment of friends and critics alike, the President admitted that for 18 months the United States had been dealing with Iran. He listed four reasons: to renew friendly relations with Iran; to try to end the long war between Iran and Iraq; to end terrorism by Iran; and to bring the American hostages held in Lebanon safely home. He puzzled the nation when he said, "We did not, repeat, *did not* trade weapons or anything else for hostages—nor will we."

Two weeks later, the President confessed that he had "not been fully informed" about the Iran

Multicultural Connection: Lieutenant Colonel Ellison S. Onizuka (1946–1986), born in Hawaii, was the first Japanese American astronaut. As a member of the *Challenger* space shuttle crew, he and his comrades lost their lives in the ill-fated mission of 1986.

policy. An investigation by Attorney General Edwin Meese, he said, now disclosed that millions of dollars from the Iranian arms deals had been diverted to the Nicaraguan contras. He also said that his National Security Adviser, Admiral John Poindexter, and an aide, Lieutenant Colonel Oliver North, would be dismissed from the White House.

"Iranscam"—The Iran-contra affair. The President appointed a commission headed by former Senator John Tower of Texas to untangle the story. Their report criticized the President for not being fully informed. Their analysis made it clear that despite President Reagan's denials, the United States had traded arms for hostages. Antitank and antiaircraft missiles had been sold to Iran in 1985 and 1986, with the understanding that the American hostages held by Iranian-backed groups in Lebanon would be released. Three hostages were freed, but three more Americans were seized to take their place.

The whole story was bizarre, bordering on the unbelievable. The money received from Iran was hidden in secret bank accounts and then used by a mysterious organization called "the enterprise" to aid the contras and support other covert activities. This shady outfit owned a ship, a warehouse, airplanes, and a whole airfield. And this organization, it appeared, had run the supply operation to Nicaragua and employed Eugene Hasenfus.

"The enterprise" was outside the law—funded and managed by private citizens who did not have to report to the United States government. Instead, they were personally directed by the swashbuckling Lieutenant Colonel Oliver North, merely a staff member of the National Security Council. North's activities were so secret that not even the Secretary of State or the Secretary of Defense knew about them. Admiral Poindexter and William Casey, director of the CIA, had known about and approved this secret organization. Since Casey died in May 1987, he never revealed the full story.

The nation was treated to a new version of an old American institution. Congressional hearings, now on television, gave the whole nation a chance to see the posturing of the handsome Colonel North. Millions heard his self-righteous preachments on how he was saving the continent from communism by conducting his personal foreign policy with a private army. The hearings added the appeal of a TV soap opera when North's attractive and devoted secretary, who had made him her hero, testified. Other countries had been entangled in the web of intrigue. Israel had acted as middleman between the United States and Iran. Saudi Arabia and the Sultan of Brunei had contributed millions for the contras at the request of government officials.

The committees were never able to find out exactly what the President knew or how the money was spent. Reagan admitted authorizing the sale of arms to Iran, but he said he did not know of the diversion of funds to the contras. Poindexter shocked the nation when he said that he kept the President in the dark in order to give him "deniability," in case the project turned sour.

The majority report of the committees, signed by both Republicans and Democrats, was disastrous for the President. They said that if he did not know what was happening it was just as bad, for it was his duty to know. "The ultimate responsibility for the events in the Iran-contra affair," the majority wrote, "must rest with the President." The President, they said, had failed in his constitutional duty to "take care that the laws be faithfully executed." The committees' report ended with a 50-year-old quotation from Supreme Court Justice Louis Brandeis: "If the government becomes a lawbreaker, it breeds contempt for law, it invites every man to become a law unto himself, it invites anarchy." (p. 920)

The crash of 1987. One of the most unpleasant domestic surprises of the decade came in October 1987. It surfaced where the nation least expected it—in the stock market. Encouraged by an improving economy, the price of stocks had begun climbing in August 1982. Five years later, the Dow Jones stock average, which was a barometer of the financial weather, had gone up 230 percent. The rising market was called a "bull market," for the buyers were charging ahead. This was the third-best bull market in American history.

Then in August 1987, the stock market began slowly to go down. After the government reported a trade deficit $1.5 billion higher than expected on October 14, the Dow Jones average suddenly fell a record 95 points.

Modern communications, speeded by the computer, had linked the world. This startling decline in New York was registered far away during the night in Tokyo and London. The next day the New York market fell another 57 points and on Friday it was down still another 108 points. On Monday the collapse came—an astonishing drop of 508 points! In just one day stocks had lost over 20 percent of their market value. This drop, even deeper than that of the Great Crash of 1929 (p. 601), now became the worst in American history. President Reagan appointed a committee to find the causes. They reported that the main reason was the huge, new computer trading programs. The computers could instantly generate large sell orders even as the market was only beginning to fall. This meant that the tendency of prices to fall

was self-accelerating. The more prices fell, the faster they fell.

Would the crash of 1987 trigger another great depression (pp. 606–607)? Economists thought it was doubtful. During the 1930s, as a result of the crash of 1929, many laws had been passed to protect the nation's savers and investors. These included federal insurance on bank accounts and the Securities and Exchange Commission to police the stock market and protect and inform the small investor. The revised Federal Reserve System was unlikely to repeat the mistakes that had helped bring on the Great Depression.

See "Section 3 Review answers," p. 906D.

Section 3 Review

1. Identify or explain: "Teflon President," "Iranscam," Oliver North.

2. **Critical Thinking: Expressing Problems Clearly.** Explain this quotation of Justice Louis Brandeis: "If the government becomes a law-breaker, it breeds contempt for law, it invites every man to become a law unto himself, it invites anarchy."

In 1987, United States Navy ships began escorting Kuwaiti tankers, flying the American flag, through the dangerous waters of the Persian Gulf.

D. Hudson/Sygma

❀ See "Lesson Plan," p. 906D for **Cooperative Learning Activity: Expressing Problems Clearly** relating to "quotable quotes" on contemporary topics.

See "Lesson Plan," p. 906E.

4. The end of the Reagan years

As Ronald Reagan approached the end of his Presidency, he no longer dominated the scene as he had for much of his two terms. Events abroad created problems that the next President would have to face.

Troubles in the Persian Gulf. The long war between Iran and Iraq dragged on. In 1987, attacks increased on the tankers that carried much-needed oil from the area to Europe, Japan, and the United States. As the ships came through the Persian Gulf they were subject to attack by either side. On May 17, an Iraqi plane mistook a U.S. Navy frigate for an enemy ship. Since the officers of the *Stark* considered the Iraqis to be friendly, they did not prepare for defense. The Iraqis hit the ship with two missiles that killed 37 crew members.

In July 1988 the USS *Vincennes,* on patrol in the Persian Gulf, mistook an Iranian civilian airliner for an attacking Iranian F-14 fighter and shot it down. Two hundred and ninety people died. Iran declared it would "avenge the blood of our martyrs." That December Pan American Airlines flight 103, on its way to the United States, exploded high over Scotland and 259 people aboard and 11 on the ground were killed. There were many indications that the Iranians had ordered the bombing.

Palestinian Revolt. The Iran-Iraq war and the events in the Persian Gulf drew world attention away from Israel and the problem of the Palestinians. But protesting Palestinian youth captured the news when they took to the streets in Gaza and the Israeli-occupied West Bank. They repeatedly attacked Israeli soldiers with stones. Israeli troops responded with rifle fire and almost daily young Palestinians died. The Palestinian problem apparently was not going to go away until the Palestinians, too, had their own homeland.

Afghanistan. The war in Afghanistan had no end. It had begun in 1979 when the Soviet Union sent in troops to support a Communist government which was facing growing guerrilla opposition (p. 895). But the Soviets found themselves mired in their own Vietnam. The rebels, with weapons supplied mainly by the United States, Saudi Arabia, and China, were able to control most of the country outside the main cities. On April 14, 1988, the Soviets seemed to admit that the cost of the conflict was too great when they agreed to remove their troops. The last Soviet soldier left in February 1989. Afghanistan, where some 1 million people had died in the fighting, was to be allowed to settle its own affairs. But still the Communist government held onto power, and the war went on.

Nicaragua. To help the people of Nicaragua and other Central American countries solve their own problems, in February 1987 President Oscar Arias Sanchez of Costa Rica proposed a peace plan. The presidents of Costa Rica, Guatemala, El Salvador, Honduras, and Nicaragua signed an accord in August. The plan called for an end to all outside aid to guerrilla groups, for restoration of freedom of the press and political activity, and for free elections. Arias's plan was given a boost when he was awarded the Nobel Peace Prize.

Finally, after several years of continuing pressure from President Arias and the other Central American leaders, the Sandinistas allowed free elections in Nicaragua in February 1990. To their great surprise, the opposition swept to an overwhelming victory. It was led by the courageous Violeta Barrios de Chamorro, whose husband's assassination by followers of Somoza had helped ignite the Sandinista revolt. She was inaugurated president in April in the first democratic change of government in the history of her country.

The new president faced a land battered by civil war and on the verge of economic collapse. The angry and still powerful Sandinistas, who controlled most of the government workers, made it difficult for her to rule. Still, Nicaragua was better off than neighboring El Salvador, where the bitter civil war continued.

The military dictatorship in Argentina, which had maintained its rule by kidnapping, torturing, and often murdering its opponents, collapsed after the junta lost the war it had started

✖ **Critical Thinking Activity: Determining Relevance** How is history continuing to be made? Remind students that history is being made daily and that the picture of events painted in this section has already been altered. List the following items on the chalkboard: "Persian Gulf," "Palestinians," "Afghanistan," "Apartheid," "Central America." Have students divide into small groups to write a brief update about one of these topics. Tell students their job is to create a bridge between where the text left off and what is happening today.

with Great Britain over the Falkland Islands. And there were some signs of a swing from dictatorship to democracy elsewhere in Latin America, including Brazil. But as in Nicaragua, the new democracies faced daunting problems. Their populations were exploding. Their economies were troubled. And their troubles became headaches for the whole world when their large foreign debts, which they could not pay, began to endanger the world's banking system.

China.   In China too, there were some encouraging signs. Mao Zedong, who had been almost worshipped as a god, had died in 1976. A new leader, clever and resilient Deng Xiaoping, had emerged. He seemed more concerned about achievement than about ideology. To stimulate China's economic life, he moved away from strict Marxist-Leninism and even tried small experiments in free enterprise. Trade between the United States and China increased.

South Africa.   Americans were increasingly distressed by South Africa's system of apartheid. This was a scheme devised by the white

New leaders appeared around the world in the 1980s. Archbishop Desmond Tutu spoke out for black South Africans.

Neil Victor/Sygma

minority after World War II to control and exploit the black majority. The word in Afrikaans meant, literally, "apart-hood," but it really was racism at its worst. After 1984, violence was increasing there and the world was isolating and ostracizing South Africa. Bishop Desmond Tutu, a brave, black Anglican priest and a leader there of the peaceful struggle against apartheid, was awarded the Nobel Peace Prize.

Economic sanctions by the United States and the departure of American companies from South Africa, along with pressure from much of the rest of the world, persuaded the South African government to begin to abandon apartheid. And in 1990 it freed black leader Nelson Mandela, who had been sentenced to life in prison in 1964 for founding a group committed to armed violence against apartheid. This gave his followers new hope. But opposition from many whites, along with bloody fighting between black factions, made progress toward equality and democracy slow.

The election of 1988.   As Ronald Reagan entered the last year of his Presidency, he could at least be pleased with his efforts for peace. But he was plagued by the suspect behavior of his aides, including Michael Deaver—Reagan's former deputy chief of staff and longtime associate from California—and Attorney General Edwin Meese, both of whom tried to use their connections with the Reagan administration for profit for themselves or their friends. Critics said there had been a distressing number of cases of questionable or illegal activities by officials or nominees of President Reagan's administration.

These problems were not helpful to the President's loyal Vice-President, George Bush, who hoped to succeed Ronald Reagan in the White House. But the question that caused candidate Bush the most trouble was what he knew about the Iran-contra affair and what he had said to the President about it. Bush insisted his advice was confidential. Still, the Democrats mocked him with calls of "Where was George?"

George Bush's choice of a vice-presidential running mate was also controversial. He astonished voters when he named a young (41),

See "Lesson Plan," p. 906E for **Writing Process Activity: Identifying Central Issues** relating to U.S. company holdings in South Africa.

Vice-President George Bush and his running mate Senator Dan Quayle, helped by the continuing popularity of Ronald Reagan, were elected after a long campaign.

wealthy, good-looking, and little-known right-wing Republican senator from Indiana, Dan Quayle. The press accused Quayle of having used family influence to avoid military service in Vietnam. Many people wondered about Bush's judgment in selecting such a person to stand only a heartbeat away from the White House.

In the race for the Democratic nomination, Massachusetts governor Michael Dukakis got out to an early lead and never faltered. But the articulate and compassionate minister and activist Jesse Jackson surprised friends and foes alike by winning the second highest number of delegates in the primaries, where he gained the solid support of fellow blacks and an unexpectedly large number of discontented whites.

Both presidential candidates had long political experience, but of different sorts. Bush knew the national and international scenes—as Vice-President for eight years, as congressman, as envoy to the United Nations and to China, and as head of the Republican National Committee and of the Central Intelligence Agency. Dukakis, son of Greek immigrants, had been an energetic, three-term governor. On the campaign trail, the tall and athletic Bush of an old New England family had a relaxed, preppy look, while Dukakis, slight of build, was stiff and intense.

Bush could hold on to President Reagan's coattails, and promise more years of Reagan peace and prosperity. But Dukakis had to make it on his own. Could he convince voters of the need for a change? The campaign became a slugfest of personal attacks. Both candidates shrouded the great issues in a fog of slogans. Bush was criticized for his "negative ads" which, instead of saying what he would do, accused Dukakis of releasing on parole dangerous black criminals and failing to clean up Boston Harbor. It was not an inspiring contest.

In the end, on November 8, 1988, the voters chose to stay with the policies of Ronald Reagan. George Bush was elected President with nearly 54 percent of the votes to Dukakis's 46 percent. But he set a record by carrying fewer members of his party into Congress than had any of his predecessors. He would need the support of the Democrats, who were now in firm control of both the House and the Senate.

George Bush in the White House. George Herbert Walker Bush, unlike Jimmy Carter and Ronald Reagan, had not run against Washington in his pursuit of the Presidency. As the son of a senator, and as a man who had spent many years in the capital, he came to Washington as an insider. He moved quickly to put the nastiness of the election campaign behind him. He met old opponents and the Democratic leaders of Congress. He stressed his desire to bury the hatchet and be President of all the people.

The bicentennial inauguration. The new President repeated his call for bipartisanship in his inaugural address. He did not proclaim sweeping new domestic programs because, he said, we lacked the money. But he appealed for private volunteer organizations, which he called "a thousand points of light," to make "kinder the face of the nation."

Bush took the oath of office with his hand on the Bible that George Washington had used for his oath as first President two hundred years before. Despite the heavy budget deficit, his inaugural address breathed optimism. And he named a capable and experienced Cabinet.

Troubles with Savings and Loans and nuclear weapons. President Bush faced a large budget deficit and a total national debt that had nearly tripled during the Reagan years. Still, saying "Read my lips," he had repeatedly promised "no new taxes" throughout his campaign. A staggering new burden came from the collapse of Savings and Loan Associations insured by the federal government. It was also costly but urgent to clean up pollution at nuclear weapons plants.

The problem at the Savings and Loans was due to carelessly drawn laws passed by Congress and inadequate and negligent oversight. It was worsened by the undue influence of a few senators protecting from the regulators certain bankers who had contributed to their political campaigns.

Government insurance on deposits had been increased and new laws now allowed the savings banks to make loans that were risky. These risky loans at high interest rates were profitable to the banks and enabled them to attract more large, federally insured deposits from savers. While depositors felt secure because of the insurance, the bankers were lending their money to people who later could not pay it back. And with lots of money coming in, Savings and Loans attracted both dishonest and inept bankers. Then, with the stock market

crash of 1987 (p. 919), it became difficult for the Savings and Loan banks to continue their high-flying ways. Soon it appeared that some 800 of these banks, holding about one-third of all the Savings and Loan assets, would fail. In 1990 it was estimated that for the government to pay off all the losses would cost American taxpayers $500 billion.

The extensive pollution from careless handling and disposal of nuclear materials at weapons plants across the country created another costly problem. The Energy Department thought the cost of the cleanup over 30 years might be $200 billion.

See "Section 4 Review answers," p. 906E.

Section 4 Review

1. Identify or explain: Deng Xiaoping, apartheid, Desmond Tutu, Jesse Jackson.

2. Describe how the Savings and Loan crisis occurred. Why did it affect the national deficit?

3. **Critical Thinking: Making Comparisons.** What are the similarities and differences between the Soviet invasion of Afghanistan and the United States involvement in Vietnam?

See "Lesson Plan," p. 906E.

5. The end of the cold war

The year 1989 would go down in history as an epoch of dramatic, stunning changes. The drama, with its first act in the Soviet Union and Eastern Europe, would have a whole new cast of actors playing out unpredicted plots. The "cold war" that shaped world politics in the postwar years had been a conflict of two superpowers. Europe had been divided between the Western democratic powers and the Eastern Communist powers. But now, suddenly, this lineup began to fall apart. Many lesser powers began to play new roles.

Enrichment Support File Topic

The return of Solidarity. The process began quietly in Poland. There the economy was in such bad shape that the Communist government had to turn to the outlawed Solidarity union for help. On April 5, 1989, after a long series of talks, the government agreed to make

✿ See "Lesson Plan," p. 906F for Cooperative Learning Activity: Formulating Questions relating to key people, events, organizations, and treaties in the chapter.

the union legal and to call new, "free" elections. But in voting for the powerful lower house of the legislature, 40 percent of the seats would still be reserved for the Communists. The government also agreed to cut down on censorship and allow the union to publish in the state-run press. Fears were widespread that the Soviets would clamp down as they had before. But the Soviet Union declared it would not interfere.

When the votes were counted early in June 1989, Solidarity had swept to victory in Poland. The Communists were shocked when all but one of their candidates failed to be elected in the first round.

In the face of Solidarity's triumph, the Communist Polish leader General Wojciech Jaruzelski hesitated to run for the powerful new post of president, fearing he might be defeated. But in this strange new world, the shrewd Lech Walesa, the leader of Solidarity, urged him to run. Jaruzelski was elected president and then named one of Walesa's aides as prime minister. Later, overwhelmed by Poland's severe economic problems, Jaruzelski stepped aside, and in December 1990 Walesa himself was elected president.

The Soviet Union lived up to its promise not to intercede in Poland. As early as February 1986 Gorbachev, in his new era of *glasnost,* had said that the Soviet Union had "unconditional respect" for the right of every country "to choose the paths and forms of its development." Then in July 1989, the Warsaw Pact countries of Eastern Europe, led by Gorbachev, and over the opposition of Czechoslovakia and East Germany, affirmed that each country should be allowed to "develop independently . . . without outside interference."

Change comes to Hungary and East Germany. Peaceful changes were also coming to ✄ Hungary. Early in 1989, the Communist leaders there agreed to allow other political parties. Negotiations began with these parties over how to make the transition from communism to democracy. In February, the government admitted that the rebellion of 1956, which had been crushed by Soviet tanks, had been a popular revolution. And in June, Imre Nagy, the leader of that revolution whose body had been placed in an unmarked grave, was reburied with honor on the thirty-first anniversary of his

Solidarity leader and Polish President Lech Walesa supported radical measures to lead Poland into the world's free-market economy.

Georges Merillon/Gamma Liaison

✄ **Critical Thinking Activity: Recognizing Cause and Effect** Evaluate the events on the political scene shortly before and during 1989 that may have contributed to the end of the Cold War. As a class, make a list of these causal events. Then for each event discuss and list any possible effects.

execution. As the year continued, the nation moved ever farther from Communist control.

The changes in Hungary hastened the collapse of the unbending Communist government in East Germany. The Berlin Wall was just one part of the iron curtain across Eastern Europe that prevented people from escaping to the West. In May 1989, the Hungarian government began to take down the fence that separated Hungary from Austria. This action had unexpected results. East Germans, who could vacation in Hungary without visas, now began to slip across the border into Austria. To avoid angering their East German allies, the Hungarians increased their border patrols. Soon thousands of Germans were camped in Hungary, waiting to cross into Austria. Then on September 10, Hungary broke its long-term pact with East Germany, opened its border, and let the Germans go. Then, even more rushed to Hungary from East Germany. Others fled to Poland and Czechoslovakia, also hoping to escape.

By October 7, 1989, when East Germany celebrated its founding 40 years before, some 50,000 had left. Thousands of others marked that anniversary by taking to the streets to demonstrate for reform. They marched under banners that said, "We are staying." After 5000 demonstrators clashed with the police, more demonstrations finally forced the Communist party to dump their old hard-line leader, Erich Honecker, who had headed East Germany for 18 years. His successor, Egon Krenz, head of the secret police, tried to introduce reforms but could not stem the torrent. In late October, 300,000 marched in Leipzig. When, on November 5, a crowd of a million people rallied in East Berlin, the Communist government surrendered. Gates in the Berlin Wall were opened on November 9. Thousands of East Germans streamed into West Berlin to gawk at the well-stocked shops and buy what they could afford. Soon the grim wall, symbol of Communist tyranny, was being torn down.

When East Berlin opened the gates in the grim wall that had divided the city since 1961, it was a cause for joyful celebration. Here Berliners can be seen standing on the wall with the Brandenburg Gate, Berlin's triumphal arch on the Unter den Linden, in the background.

Anthony Swan/Black Star

The dizzying pace of change in Eastern Europe accelerated. On November 10, 1989, the longest-ruling Communist leader in Eastern Europe, Todor I. Zhikov of Bulgaria, stepped down. His successor, also a Communist, confessed that the nation had to be transformed. "We have to turn Bulgaria into a modern, democratic and lawful country," he said.

"The velvet revolution." And now change came to Czechoslovakia. The General Secretary of the Communist party, Milos Jakes, told a conference on November 12 that the party would not tolerate demonstrations or relax its control of the country. When, five days later, a small demonstration by students was violently broken up by riot police, ever-larger demonstrations took place. On November 24 when Jakes resigned, 350,000 Czechs and Slovaks wildly cheered their popular, liberal Communist leader Alexander Dubcek. He had led the country briefly until he was overthrown by armies of the Warsaw Pact in 1968. Now the pressures on the Communist party increased, and millions of Czechoslovaks went out on a general strike. At a brewery, one worker addressed his fellows in the memorable words of Thomas Jefferson: "We hold these truths to be self-evident, that all men are endowed by their creator with certain unalienable rights, that among these are life, liberty and the pursuit of happiness. Americans," he continued, "understood these rights more than 200 years ago. We are only now learning to believe that we are entitled to the same rights." All this occurred peacefully and the Communist government collapsed. The opposition leader Vaclav Havel, a dissident playwright, called this "the velvet revolution."

On December 28, 1989, Dubcek was elected chairman of the still-Communist parliament, and the following day Havel, who had been jailed many times by the Communist government, and had last been arrested just two months earlier, was elected interim president. To the world's astonishment, on February 21, 1990, he was speaking to a joint session of the United States Congress and asking the United States to help the Soviet Union!

Patrick Piel/Gamma-Liaison

President Bush met Chancellor Kohl, now leader of a united Germany, in November 1990.

As 1990 began, the nations of Eastern Europe had started the painful move from Communist dictatorships to democracy and free markets. The economies of Eastern Europe were a wreck. Even for those nations that had once experienced democracy, freedom was only a memory dimmed by a half-century of oppression.

The reunification of Germany. By the end of 1989, some 340,000 East Germans had moved ✄ to West Germany. East Germans joked that the last one to leave the country should turn off the lights. But the lights of communism were being extinguished by a disillusioned people. Some West Germans feared that their nation might be overrun. "Stay home," West German Chancellor Helmut Kohl begged the East Germans. "Together, we will get the country going again." The only way to stop the flood seemed to be to reunify the nation—to incorporate East Germany into West. But would the Soviet Union allow it? The Soviets had lost 27 million people to German invaders in The Great Patriotic War, as they called World War II. The vision of a strong, united Germany, with 80 million people and West Germany's economic might in the heart of Europe, frightened them.

✄ **Critical Thinking Activity: Predicting Consequences** How might the reunification of Germany affect the political structure of Europe? How might these changes in Europe affect NATO? Have students share their ideas through class discussion.

There were many other problems. The division of Europe and of Germany between the democratic powers and the Soviets was the basis of the peace agreements after World War II. What would happen now to the Warsaw Pact and NATO? Would a reunited Germany be a member of NATO, as the NATO allies wanted, or neutral, as the Soviet Union wished? The Soviet Union feared being left out of the new order in Europe. The democratic countries of Western Europe worried that the United States might now withdraw the troops who helped defend them against Soviet aggression. Could there be peace and security in Europe if the United States did not continue to play an active role?

But now the reunification of Germany seemed inevitable. So on February 13, 1990, the four major World War II allies—the United States, USSR, France, and Great Britain—agreed upon the ways for reunification. At the same time, the United States and the Soviet Union would each cut their troops to 195,000 in Central Europe. The details of reunification would be worked out by the two Germanys after a new government was chosen in free elections in East Germany on March 18. Then the two parts of Germany would negotiate with the four wartime allies over future European security arrangements. These were called the "two-plus-four" talks.

When East German voters elected conservatives to parliament, it became clear that Germany was hurtling toward reunification. In July, the currencies of the two countries became one. That same month Gorbachev gave his blessing to a united Germany. He even agreed to its being in NATO, which he thought less dangerous than a neutral Germany, not linked to any regional security group. The Soviet Union was to have four years to withdraw its forces from East Germany. Meanwhile the new Germany would help pay part of the cost of the troops and would help to finance housing for the troops when they went home. All this, costing $7.5 billion, was called the "price of unity" by West Germany's foreign minister.

Two months later the four wartime allies finally changed the arrangements which had ended World War II. They signed a treaty giving up their occupation rights and leaving the two Germanys free to unite. Chancellor Kohl called it the "first reunification of a country in modern history without war, pain, or strife." The two Germanys became one on October 3, 1990.

On November 21 in Paris, the end of the division of Europe between the East and the West was officially marked by 34 European and North American nations. In the Charter of Paris for a New Europe, they committed themselves to fundamental freedoms and human rights, to "prosperity through economic liberty and social justice," and to "equal security for all countries." As President Bush said, "The cold war is over. In signing the Charter of Paris we have closed a chapter of history."

But for Eastern Europe the birth pangs of a new world had just begun. Free elections in Czechoslovakia were a triumph for the eloquent Havel who, like the splintering Solidarity in Poland, faced the tasks of a bankrupt economy. And how would they deal with the staggering pollution of air and water, the legacy of reckless Communist regimes? Even without these problems the transition to strange new democratic institutions would have been hard enough.

Change in the Soviet Union. The dramatic collapse of the Communist regimes in Eastern Europe was the result of conditions in the USSR. When Mikhail Gorbachev became General Secretary in 1985, he saw that the Soviet economy was in ruin. Food was scarce and people had to stand in long lines even to buy children's clothing. He hoped his program of *perestroika*—restructuring—would be a remedy. But even his cautious first attempts stirred up opposition from hard-liners. Still Gorbachev persisted.

When the Soviet Union could not even supply its own needs, Gorbachev saw it would be impossible any longer to prop up the Warsaw Pact countries. He had to let them go their own way. He did not expect them to leave the socialist camp, but when they did, he still did not order Soviet troops to intervene.

And Gorbachev moved the Soviet Union itself toward a freer and more democratic nation. On February 7, 1990, he called on the Communist party to give up its monopoly of political power

Vladimir Vyatkin/SABA

In 1990 Lithuanians demonstrated for independence from the Soviet Union.

and to allow rival parties. It could remain the ruling party, he said, but only strictly "within the framework of the democratic process." And two days later the Communist party voted to do just as Gorbachev said. March elections in the republics of Russia, Byelorussia, and Ukraine put dissident Communists and independents in control of local governments in Moscow, Leningrad, and Kiev.

When the Soviet Parliament met, it voted to change the constitution to deprive the Communist party of its monopoly and also to create, as Gorbachev requested, a powerful new post of president of the Soviet Union. The president could declare martial law and take other actions in emergencies, but he would be restricted to two, five-year terms. Parliament elected Gorbachev to this new post. He continued to hold the office of General Secretary of the Communist party. It seemed that Gorbachev was trying to rid himself of the problems of governing through the party and its many hard-line members.

But others in the Communist party were even more liberal than Gorbachev. That spring of 1990 Boris Yeltsin, leader of the Moscow Communist party whom Gorbachev helped to power, and then fired in 1987, was elected president of the Russian Republic. Now Yeltsin criticized Gorbachev for not being more aggressive in his political and economic reforms. In July, Yeltsin shocked the full Communist party congress by abruptly resigning from the party. He was soon followed by others.

The Soviet Union in distress. While Gorbachev struggled to increase his power and reshape the Soviet Union, the country seemed to be falling apart. Soap, meat, and even bread disappeared from the shelves of Moscow stores. One observer called it "chaos on a grand scale." The central planning system that had brought the Soviet Union into the modern industrial age was not fulfilling its promise. Gorbachev and others recognized that the Soviet Union must convert to a market economy. But this turned out to be difficult—like trying to put Humpty Dumpty together again. And the "solution" itself would create new problems.

Could the Soviet Union now hold together? It was a country of 104 nationalities, peoples speaking different languages, of different races, religions, and traditions. Might it soon break up into separate countries? Gorbachev seemed more popular in the West than at home. He and the other leaders of the Kremlin were booed during the May Day celebration in Moscow in 1990.

Perspectives Topic

The Baltic states of Lithuania, Latvia, and Estonia had been incorporated into the Soviet Union during World War II by a treaty with Hitler. When the Kremlin now confessed that the treaty was illegal, these states, too, pushed for independence. The Lithuanian Parliament, still dominated by Communists, voted unanimously that Lithuania was a separate, sovereign state. But Soviet threats and pressure, including the threat to cut off their oil, persuaded them to suspend their vote.

Ethnic unrest was contagious and spread across the vast Soviet territories. The pent-up hates of centuries brought bloody fighting between the Azerbaijanis and Armenians and between the Kirghiz and Uzbeks. The different national groups within the Soviet Union argued over the dozens of borders that marked off their states.

In August 1991, just as the republics of the Soviet Union were about to sign a new agreement that would have transferred power from the central government to them, hard-line Communists attempted to overthrow Gorbachev. Hundreds of thousands of people, led by Russian president Boris Yeltsin, rallied against the coup, surrounding the Parliament and holding rebellious soldiers at bay. The coup collapsed, and within days Gorbachev stripped the 74-year-old Communist party of most of its power. By the end of the month, 10 of the 15 republics had declared independence. In December, the Soviet Union officially disbanded and most of the former republics joined a Commonwealth of Independent States. Gorbachev, who had done so much to set the revolution in motion, was out of a job. The republics faced huge problems, not all of them economic. Who could prevent their ambitious military leaders from menacing their neighbors? Deadly nuclear weapons were located in many remote places far from Moscow. Who would be in charge of them? But the empire that had awed and inspired the world since 1917 with its size and rapid economic development, and since World War II with its military might, was dead.

See "Section 5 Review answers," p. 906F.

Section 5 Review

1. Identify or explain: Lech Walesa, Erich Honecker, "velvet revolution," Vaclav Havel, Helmut Kohl, Boris Yeltsin, Baltic states.

2. How did change in Hungary contribute to revolution in East Germany?

3. Discuss some of the ways that the reunification of Germany was related to the resolution of World War II.

4. **Critical Thinking: Testing Conclusions.** Why is it important that the United States government take an active interest in the success or failure of the economic reforms of Russia and the other republics of the former Soviet Union? Explain your answer.

See "Lesson Plan," p. 906F.

6. A dangerous world

After the heady experience of watching the Soviet Union and the nations of Eastern Europe struggle in their separate ways toward democracy and free markets, it was hard for the people of the United States to realize that there were still dangers in the world that could bring on fighting and bloodshed.

Repression in China. The rebels against communism and central planning were not everywhere successful. China began to move toward a market economy under Deng Xiaoping in the late 1970s. Here the second act of the drama of the year 1989 took place. Inspired by hopes for a new freedom, in May and June students and workers staged huge demonstrations for democracy in Beijing and Shanghai. But Deng reacted with brutal violence. Using the army against the unarmed demonstrators in Tiananmen Square in Beijing, he massacred them by countless hundreds. The world was outraged,

Students with their statue of the Goddess of Democracy demonstrated in Tiananmen Square.

Erica Lansner/Black Star

and the democratic movement was suppressed—at least for a time. But, like Solidarity in Poland, when might it rise again?

The invasion of Panama. Panama was a trouble spot of special concern to the United States. That small country in Central America contained the canal between the oceans that was vital to United States commerce and defense. Corrupt and ruthless Manuel Noriega, commander of the Panamanian military and police forces, was in control there. In 1988 federal grand juries indicted Noriega on drug-trafficking charges. Then President Reagan imposed economic sanctions on Panama, hoping to force Noriega to resign. But when an election for president was held in May 1989, Noriega's hand-picked candidate won by stuffing ballot boxes. Outside observers there, including former President Jimmy Carter, declared that Noriega had stolen the election. In October, a military coup against Noriega failed. President Bush simply watched and waited.

Finally, on December 20, 1989, the President sent in United States forces for what was called "Operation Just Cause" to topple Noriega for good. During the invasion several hundred Panamanians and 23 United States soldiers were killed. Noriega took refuge in the Vatican embassy in Panama City. After 10 days he emerged from the embassy and surrendered to United States forces. Taken to Miami, he was jailed to await trial on the drug charges.

Iraq seizes Kuwait. The greatest setback to the worldwide movement toward freedom and decency came in the long-troubled Middle East. Suddenly on August 2, 1990, the ruthless dictator of Iraq, Saddam Hussein, sent his armies crashing into neighboring Kuwait. Within days he had incorporated all of Kuwait into Iraq. President Bush at once sent United States forces to Saudi Arabia to defend that country, neighboring Kuwait, from becoming the next victim of Saddam. Moving swiftly, the United Nations Security Council also acted. With the United States, the Soviet Union, and China all agreeing, it imposed a trade and financial boycott on Iraq.

Vienna Report/Sygma

Saddam Hussein, the dictator of Iraq, invaded Kuwait in 1990 and his armed forces were defeated in the Persian Gulf War.

The United States forces in Saudi Arabia were soon joined by troops from many other nations. Saddam Hussein said he was fighting for all the Arab world, but Egypt, Syria, Saudi Arabia, and several other Arab lands joined the forces against him.

The midterm elections. Even as the crisis over Kuwait was building, the nation faced midterm elections. Because of the pressures of the budget deficit and his promise of "no new taxes," President Bush had not called for major new domestic legislation. Apparently this satisfied most Americans, because public opinion polls consistently had found him to be even more popular than Ronald Reagan—until late in 1990.

That fall President Bush stumbled badly in the complicated negotiations with Congress

During the Persian Gulf War, an international coalition of armed forces, led by the United States and supported by the United Nations, attacked the Iraqi military and liberated Kuwait from Iraqi occupation in 1991.

over the budget. His popularity was damaged by what appeared to be his constantly changing positions, especially when he went back on his promise of no new taxes. Everyone, from members of Congress to the voters, was confused. Some critics complained that he lacked the strong beliefs of his predecessor and that he was failing to lead.

Many Republicans feared that the President's actions would hurt them in the fall elections. But this did not happen. Still, numerous Americans voiced their general disillusionment with politicians. Citizens in both Colorado and the most populous state, California, showed their discontent by voting to limit the number of terms a person could stay in office.

The allies attack. The buildup of American military might in the Middle East was the most rapid commitment of a large force in United States history. There were already more than 200,000 men and women of the United States armed forces in Saudi Arabia in November, when President Bush decided to increase their number. Ultimately, the United States would have well over 500,000 men and women stationed in Saudi Arabia.

President Bush feared that if Saddam was allowed to get away with seizing his neighbor, it would endanger all the world's hope for peace and encourage other nations to threaten their neighbors. In addition, with Kuwait in his pocket, Saddam held 20 percent of the world's oil. If he seized Saudi Arabia he could control nearly 50 percent. And oil is the lifeblood of the world's industry and trade.

Despite the forces arrayed against him, the brutal dictator of Iraq would not budge. In a new spirit of unity, the Soviet Union and the United States worked together to thwart President Hussein. The Soviets did not send troops, but they joined the United States and ten other nations in the UN Security Council in a vote to authorize the United States and its allies to use force if Iraq did not leave Kuwait by January 15, 1991.

On January 12, after an earnest three-day debate, the United States Congress gave its approval of President Bush's use of United States armed forces to carry out the UN resolution. The President received a majority of 67 in the House, but in the Senate his margin was only a narrow 5 votes. Still, it was enough.

When President Saddam Hussein did not withdraw Iraqi troops from Kuwait by the deadline, the United States and the 28 other nations in the coalition decided to attack. What had been called "Operation Desert Shield" now became "Operation Desert Storm." In the early morning hours of January 17, 1991, the allied forces, led by the United States, struck from the air with bombs, rockets, and cruise missiles at communication and military targets all over Iraq. Peace would only return, President Bush insisted, when Iraq acceded to the UN resolution and withdrew completely from Kuwait. The only response from the dug-in Iraqis was to fire SCUD rockets toward cities in Saudi Arabia, Israel, and Bahrain. Many SCUDS were intercepted and destroyed in the air by United States Patriot missiles, but civilians and soldiers were killed in the attacks.

For 38 days the allies pounded the Iraqis with rockets, with "smart" bombs that were so precisely guided they could go down chimneys, and with a variety of regular, or "dumb," bombs. It was the most massive air attack in history. Then the allies unleashed their ground attack. Sweeping into Iraq in tanks, armored vehicles, and helicopters they swiftly bypassed the entrenched Iraqi troops in Kuwait and cut their lines of supply and retreat. Then they turned to destroy them.

Before the land battle had even begun, the Iraqis allowed millions of barrels of oil to flow into the Persian Gulf, creating ecological havoc and endangering the Saudi water supply drawn from the Gulf through desalination plants. Then, in the face of defeat, vicious Saddam or-

dered Kuwait's oil wells destroyed and set afire. The allied forces entered Kuwait by the eerie light of hundreds of burning oil wells, and the sky was darkened by the black smoke of the fires. Experts predicted that it would take at least two years to put out all the fires. What the damage to the world's environment would be was still to be discovered.

After exactly 100 hours of ground fighting, with heavy Iraqi losses and extremely light casualties for the allies, the allies suspended hostilities. And soon a beaten Saddam agreed to withdraw from Kuwait and abide by all the UN resolutions concerning that country. Kuwait, ✖ devastated and looted by the Iraqis, was free once more. Now the United States had to struggle to bring lasting peace to that troubled part of the world.

See "Section 6 Review answers," p. 906F.

Section 6 Review

1. Identify or explain: Tiananmen Square, Manuel Noriega, Gulf War, Saddam Hussein, Patriot missiles, SCUDs.

2. Explain the purpose of "Operation Just Cause." What were some criticisms of this operation?

3. Why did the Gulf War remind many Americans of events leading to WWII?

4. **Critical Thinking: Identifying Alternatives.** Evaluate President Bush's response to the invasion of Kuwait. Do you think his response was adequate? Why or why not?

See "Lesson Plan," p. 906G.

7. The State of the Nation

In the winter of 1991, in the wake of the Gulf War, George Bush's popularity was astounding. Ninety percent of the American people approved of his performance. Political pundits considered him unbeatable in the 1992 presidential election, and none of the leading Democrats seemed willing to challenge him. But there was trouble on the horizon. With the end of the cold war, the break-up of the Soviet Union, and the victory over Saddam Hussein,

✖ **Critical Thinking Activity: Drawing Conclusions** Four years after the end of the Persian Gulf War, Iraq still had not abided by all of the United Nations resolutions drawn up at the end of the war. In addition, Iraq once again amassed its troops along the Kuwaiti border in October, 1994. A speedy deployment of U.S. troops to the region caused Hussein to withdraw his troops. Ask students to consider whether or not strict international sanctions against Iraq should have been dropped or maintained.

the United States was without a menacing enemy for the first time in fifty years. Americans began looking inwards, at the state of the nation. Many did not like what they saw.

The economy. President Reagan had had the good fortune to oversee the largest peacetime economic boom in American history. President Bush had the misfortune of being President when the bills for the excesses of that period came due. The economy, sluggish for Bush's first two years in office, went into a recession in the middle of 1990. Large increases in defense spending had fueled the boom. Now, with the end of the cold war, cuts in defense spending contributed to the slump. Rising oil prices also hurt, as did the ever increasing cost to taxpayers of bailing out the failed Savings and Loans (p. 924). And despite the budget compromise of 1990, in which Bush had reluctantly agreed to raise taxes, the budget deficit exceeded 300 billion dollars.

(p. 935) Economists reported that the number of people living in poverty had risen by 2.1 million in 1991. In June 1992, five months before the presidential election, unemployment reached 7.8 percent, an eight-year high.

Supreme Court appointments. President Bush made two appointments to the high Court. In 1990, liberal justice William Brennan retired after 33 years on the Court. Bush nominated David Souter, a moderate and highly qualified federal judge from New Hampshire. Souter breezed through hearings before the Senate Judiciary Committee and was easily confirmed by the full Senate. The following year, eighty-three-year-old Thurgood Marshall retired. Marshall was the first and only black man to serve on the Court. To replace him, George Bush nominated another black man, Clarence Thomas, a forty-three-year-old federal judge. Thomas's ideas could not have been more different from Marshall's. As head of the Equal Employment Opportunity Commission (EEOC) under Ronald Reagan, he had been an outspoken opponent of affirmative action and other government efforts to eliminate inequality.

Liberal groups, including the NAACP, insisted that Thomas, with neither experience nor proven judicial talent, was a poor choice to replace the judicial giant who, years before, had led the legal battle against segregation. Women's groups were further angered when Thomas, in hearings before the Judiciary Committee, was evasive about his position on the constitutionality of abortion. Despite that opposition, Thomas seemed headed for confirmation when word leaked out that Anita Hill, a black professor of law who had worked for Thomas at the EEOC, charged that Thomas had sexually harassed her on the job ten years before. The Judiciary Committee reopened its hearings, and millions of Americans were held spellbound by three days of dramatic, televised testimony by Hill and Thomas and supporting witnesses for both sides.

The Senate confirmed Thomas by a vote of 52–48. Women's groups, though appalled at the way Professor Hill was treated by the Judiciary Committee, were pleased that the hearings triggered a nationwide debate about the complicated problem of sexual harassment.

In October 1991, Anita Hill testified before a Senate panel that she had been sexually harassed by Supreme Court nominee Clarence Thomas.

UPI/Bettmann

Critical Thinking Activity: Identifying Central Issues What is our relationship with Russia? Have students write three sentences describing what they believe to be our relationship with Russia. Have students find information to support their point of view. Then have students rewrite their description, incorporating the evidence. Ask students to share their work. Have students suggest other sources they might consult for further evidence to support their conclusions.

The L.A. riots. A tragic series of events in Los Angeles sparked an equally widespread debate about race, poverty, and violence. In March 1991 when, after a car chase, four policemen stopped Rodney King, a black motorist, for speeding, they pinned him to the pavement, kicked him, and struck him more than fifty times with their nightsticks. The incident might have ended there had not a bystander with a video camera captured the incident on film.

The Los Angeles police department defended the officers by saying that King was high on drugs and was resisting arrest. But to the millions of Americans who watched the videotape on local and national news, it did not seem that the police were in any danger. King was treated for multiple skull fractures, a broken leg, and an injured eye.

A grand jury indicted the four officers on charges that included assault with a deadly weapon. But in May 1992, a jury, without a black man or woman on it, found them not guilty. News of the verdict sparked rioting, looting, and arson in black and Hispanic South Central Los Angeles. Before the army and the National Guard were able to restore order, 600 buildings had been set ablaze and 52 people had died. Damage exceeded one billion dollars. There were less serious disturbances in other cities and widespread debate about the deeper causes of the violence. Was it caused by not enough government aid, or by too much?

The four officers were retried in federal court and this time two were found guilty and sentenced to prison. But with the incidence of hate crimes against blacks, women, homosexuals, and Jews on the rise nationwide, many Americans began to ask the question that Rodney King himself had asked in the midst of the riots: "Why can't we just get along?"

In May 1992, a jury found the four officers accused of assaulting black motorist Rodney King not guilty. The verdict sparked rioting, looting, and arson in South Central Los Angeles.

Barr/Gamma-Liaison

✴ **Critical Thinking Activity: Predicting Consequences** How would another depression affect our daily lives? Have students reread the section on the Great Depression (p. 606). Divide students into groups representing different sectors of today's economy (business, labor, agriculture, and so on). Ask each group to generate a list of economic or social changes that could result from a stock market crash and subsequent depression. Have students compare and contrast the effect of a depression on different sectors of the economy.

Matt Herron

The AIDS quilt is a personal memorial to Americans who have died of the disease. In 1992, the quilt was displayed before the Capitol. It contained 26,000 panels—only one sixth of the total number of Americans who had succumbed to AIDS by that time.

The AIDS crisis. The spread of Acquired Immune Deficiency Syndrome (AIDS) added to America's sense of despair. AIDS is a disease for which no cure has been found. It is caused by a virus that destroys the body's immune system which protects us against disease. People who get AIDS die from other diseases, infections, and cancers which their bodies can no longer resist.

AIDS is most often transmitted through physical sexual relations and through the shared needles of drug users. Those most at risk from the disease were homosexuals and certain drug addicts. Scientists feared that it might spread through the whole population. Suddenly, sexual license, a popular idea in the 1960s, was found to be dangerous to the health of all. Since there was no known cure, education and sexual abstinence became the only ways to slow the spread of AIDS. Dr. C. Everett Koop, Surgeon General under Ronald Reagan,

set a wise example by urging that grade school students be taught about the disease. AIDS, the shocking discovery of the early 1980s, threatened to become a worldwide catastrophe. It is estimated that by 2000, only twenty years later, nearly 10 million people will have died of it.

The anxious middle class. Unemployment, poverty, racial tensions, and AIDS were not new to the 1990s. They had all been problems in the 1980s, despite the economic boom. What was new was that in the early 1990s a great many middle-class Americans began to feel the pinch. They worried about losing their jobs and that the economy was not producing the kinds of jobs that would make their children's lives as comfortable as their own. Americans also worried about their schools, and about drugs, guns, gangs, and crime. Some went so far as to say that America's best days were in the past. The nation's mood had changed dramatically since the end of the Gulf War.

The election of 1992. Arkansas Governor Bill Clinton entered the race for the Democratic party's presidential nomination when George Bush still looked unbeatable. Clinton was to be rewarded for his boldness. Born in 1946 and inspired by President Kennedy when he was in his teens, Clinton went into politics after attending Georgetown University, two years at Oxford as a Rhodes Scholar, and Yale Law School. In 1978, at thirty-two, he was elected governor of Arkansas, the youngest in the state's history. Clinton was intelligent, articulate, and well informed about a wide range of issues. He promised that his equally intelligent and hardworking wife Hillary Rodham Clinton, a successful lawyer and social activist, would play an important role in his administration.

Clinton had rivals for the nomination, including former Massachusetts senator Paul Tsongas, and former California governor Jerry Brown. But in the primaries Clinton's toughest opponent turned out to be his own past. Reports that he had been unfaithful to his wife, that he had dodged the draft during the Vietnam War, and had smoked marijuana threatened repeatedly to knock him out of the race. He survived so many brushes with disaster that the press began to call him the "comeback kid."

The primary season was enlivened by the folksy, fast-talking Texas billionaire H. Ross Perot. Perot charged that the Democrats and Republicans were like two peas in a pod. What was needed to break the gridlock in Washington was an independent and successful businessman who was not beholden to special interests and lobbyists. Although Perot had more to say about what was wrong with America than about how he would make it right, in the late spring some polls showed him running even with or ahead of Bush and Clinton. Then to everyone's surprise, in the middle of the Democratic national convention he suddenly dropped out of the race.

The Democrats held their convention in New York City in July, more united than at any convention since 1964, when they had nominated Lyndon Johnson. As his running mate, Clinton chose Tennessee Senator Albert Gore, an expert on the environment and foreign policy. Clinton and Gore called themselves New Democrats. They said they would demand as much from the American people as they offered in social programs. They promised a break with the trickle-down economics of Reagan and Bush. They kicked off their campaign with a cross-country bus tour that capitalized on their skill in face-to-face meetings with voters and emphasized their concern with ordinary Americans.

George Bush's renomination was never in doubt. But he was challenged in the primaries by Patrick Buchanan, who represented the Republican party's right wing. Buchanan criticized Bush for breaking his "no new taxes" pledge and for paying too much attention to foreign affairs. Then, at the national convention in Houston, Buchanan delivered a divisive, prime-time speech in which he strongly suggested that Democrats and even moderate Republicans who did not agree with him about

Democratic nominees Bill Clinton and Al Gore went on a bus tour of the country to win voters' support in 1992.

Cynthia Johnson/Gamma Liaison

school prayer and abortion were godless and un-American. The speech set the tone for the entire convention and hurt the President's cause.

A three-way race. Bush and Quayle tried to focus people's attention on Clinton's character and lack of national experience. Clinton and Gore wanted voters to think about the economy. With just thirty days to go before the election, Ross Perot reentered the race. Spending 60 million dollars, most of it to buy television time, he decried the damage that the deficit was doing to the economy and the cloud it cast over America's future. He appeared with Clinton and Bush in all three of the lively, televised presidential debates. Perot never regained the support he had had in the early summer. Many former supporters considered him a quitter.

Still, he seemed to be drawing votes away from the President and was therefore an important factor in the race.

Election day. Ten million more people voted in 1992 than in 1988. When the votes were counted, Clinton had won the election with only 43 percent of the popular vote, but 370 electoral votes. Bush received 37 percent of the popular vote and 168 electoral votes. Perot did not win any electoral votes, but his 19 percent of the popular vote was more than any independent candidate had received since Theodore ⩛ Roosevelt in 1912. Democrats maintained control over the House and Senate, but hostility toward Congress resulted in many incumbents losing their seats. Women, blacks, and Hispanics were elected to Congress in record numbers.

After twelve years of Republican rule, the American public cast a vote for change in 1992. Democrat Bill Clinton promised to address the federal deficit, revive the economy, and push for health care reform.

Ira Wyman/Sygma

⩛ **Continuity and Change: Politics** Ross Perot won 19 percent of the popular vote in the 1992 presidential election. This was more than any independent candidate had received since Theodore Roosevelt in 1912. Ask students to review pages 534–536 in their text and to draw comparisons between the election of 1912 and the election of 1992. Ask students to consider what the role of third party candidates has been in American politics.

See "Section 7 Review answers," p. 906G.

Section 7 Review

1. Identify or explain: David Souter, Clarence Thomas, H. Ross Perot.
2. What factors contributed to the economic recession in 1990?
3. What issues did the Rodney King incident raise for national debate?
4. **Critical Thinking: Drawing Conclusions.** Why did H. Ross Perot's candidacy appeal to so many Americans?

See "Lesson Plan," p. 906G.

8. The Clinton Presidency

On January 20, 1993, William Jefferson Clinton was inaugurated as the 42nd President of the United States. He promised "an end to the era of deadlock and drift and a new season of American renewal." He asked the American people to join him in meeting the challenges of a rapidly changing world. But he was to find that it was one thing to talk about change, another to put the old habits behind.

Clinton in office. Clinton quickly demonstrated that he meant business and announced an array of policy initiatives, including proposals intended to stimulate the economy, cut the deficit, reform the welfare system, fight crime, and establish a national service program for young Americans. He signed executive orders reversing Reagan and Bush administration restrictions on abortion. And he signed the Family Leave Act—twice vetoed by George Bush—that required employers to allow workers to take up to 12 weeks of unpaid leave after the birth or adoption of a child or in the event of a family emergency. He announced that Hillary Clinton would head his task force on health care reform—the most important official position ever held by a first lady.

Clinton and Congress. Clinton's relations with Congress were expected to be difficult. The Democrats controlled Congress, but only by a narrow margin, and many southern Democrats were much more conservative than their Presi-

Larry Downing/Sygma

Hillary Rodham Clinton directed the work of the President's task force on health care reform.

dent. Republicans were quick to remind the President that he had been elected with only a minority of the popular vote. They insisted he could not lead without them.

Republicans quickly demonstrated their clout by killing the President's economic stimulus package—16 billion dollars for jobs, public works, schools, and social welfare programs. Then they attacked his deficit reduction plan, saying it would raise taxes too much and cut spending too little. Ross Perot joined the attack. But the President fought back, and after months of painstaking negotiations in which he had to give up a broad-based energy tax and some increases in social spending, in August 1993 Congress passed a bill that reduced the deficit by 500 billion dollars. Clinton won another narrow victory at the end of his first year in office, this time with Republican support, when he persuaded Congress to approve the North American Free Trade Agreement (NAFTA). Negotiated by the Bush administration, NAFTA eliminated tariffs and other barriers to trade with Canada and Mexico. Labor

✂ **Critical Thinking Activity: Determining Relevance** Ask students to consider the following question. Did Bill Clinton receive a clear mandate from voters in the 1992 election? How might the election results have affected his ability to pass his legislation in Congress?

President Clinton appointed Florida's chief prosecutor Janet Reno to be the nation's first woman attorney general.

leaders and many Democrats in Congress argued that NAFTA would mean a loss of jobs in the United States to lower-paid workers in Mexico. Clinton argued that it would create new jobs and economic growth.

Three popular appointments. Three of Bill Clinton's most important appointments met widespread approval. As attorney general, he named Janet Reno, Florida's chief prosecutor, known to be both tough on crime and deeply concerned with crime prevention. Reno was the first woman to hold that job. Then Clinton nominated federal district court judge Ruth Bader Ginsburg to replace retiring Supreme Court justice Byron White. Ginsburg was a pioneer in the struggle for the legal rights of women. After quick confirmation by the Senate, she became the second woman justice in history and the first Jewish justice in 24 years. The following year, when Justice Harry Blackmun retired, Clinton nominated Stephen Breyer, another federal judge, to replace him. Known for both his intelligence and his ability

to reconcile judges with different points of view, Breyer won the support of conservatives and liberals alike and was confirmed without notable opposition.

Health Care. Republicans and conservative Democrats in Congress made Clinton fight tooth and nail for every victory in his second year in office. They even tried to defeat his crime bill, which provided billions of dollars for police and prisons and harsher sentences for repeat offenders, although they had been calling for similar legislation for years. They objected to the bill's ban on 17 kinds of assault weapons and to the large sums for crime prevention. Congress eventually passed the crime bill, but when it came to health care reform, the centerpiece of Clinton's domestic program, his opponents dealt him a stunning defeat.

For those with good health insurance, America had the best health care system in the world. But nearly 40 million Americans were uninsured, and the cost of health care was soaring. Universal health care had been the dream of every Democratic party President since Harry Truman, as well as of some Republicans. Richard Nixon had thought that every employer ought to provide health insurance for every employee.

In September 1993, Clinton announced the recommendations of his health care reform task force to a joint session of Congress. He proposed a uniform package of government-enforced health benefits for all Americans, based on employer mandates and consumer alliances to reduce costs.

The plan came under immediate attack from a number of powerful interests. Insurance companies opposed government regulation of their business, and small business owners were worried that the cost of providing health insurance for their employees would make it harder for them to compete. These and other interest groups spent millions of dollars on public relations campaigns against Clinton's plan. They argued that it was too costly, too bureaucratic, and that it would reduce freedom of choice and impair the quality of our health care. The administration was slow to realize

Bob Daemmrich/Sygma

George Bush, Jr., the former President's son, was one of many Republican candidates celebrating a huge victory for their party in the 1994 midterm elections. While Bush won the governorship of Texas, other Republicans managed to win a majority of seats in the United States House and Senate for the first time since 1954. Not a single Republican incumbent failed to be reelected.

that the millions of Americans who had expressed support for major health care reform in 1992 and 1993 might be convinced by these groups that reform was too risky. In the summer of 1994, the President's allies in Congress rushed to produce a plan that would provide universal care while addressing the concerns of the critics of the President's proposals. But by the end of August, the public and many members of Congress were confused by all the different plans under consideration. It was clear that there was neither enough time nor votes in Congress to enact major health care reform in 1994.

Clinton at midterm. Although Clinton had had some notable victories, his defeats loomed larger. While the economy was on the mend, voters were as worried about America as they had been when they elected him—and as frustrated with Washington. As a result, Democrats suffered huge losses in the November 1994 midterm congressional elections and Republicans gained a majority of seats in the United States House and Senate for the first time since 1954.

Observers disagreed about what had gone wrong. Some blamed Clinton himself, and had lingering doubts about his character. Had the very optimism he had bred in 1992 raised expectations so high, and set so ambitious an agenda, that he was destined to disappoint people? Some said he had been too slow to realize that he could enact major legislation only by working with Republicans. Others said just the opposite—that he had been so ready to compromise that it was not clear what he stood for. Some, including Clinton himself, criticized the media for focusing on conflict instead of fostering reasonable discussion.

Americans had elected Clinton because they did not think Bush was doing enough. But they still feared that under Clinton, government might try to do too much. They had voted for change, but once Clinton was in office they were troubled by Republican warnings of high taxes and big government. American politics still seemed stuck between those who thought government could help us solve our problems and those who thought government was the problem. Halfway through Clinton's term it was not clear how that deadlock would be broken.

Continuity and Change: Government and Politics In the November 1994 midterm elections, Republicans gained control of both the United States House and Senate. Ask students to review pages 714–715 in their text and to read about relations between Harry Truman and the 80th Congress. Ask students to discuss the difficulties of governing with a divided government in which one party controls the White House and the other party controls the Congress.

Clinton and the world. Clinton wanted to be a domestic policy president, but he quickly found that the world would not stand still while he put America in order. No large country threatened us, but many small countries created painful dilemmas. While there were problems on the international scene, there were historic breakthroughs as well.

Foreign policy in the post-cold war world. In the drought- and famine-ridden East African nation of Somalia, where thousands of people were dying of starvation every day, warring tribal leaders hijacked food and medical supplies sent into the country for the sick and hungry. Yugoslavia had broken into a half-dozen independent republics after the breakup of the Soviet Union. There, Serbian nationalists

waged merciless civil war against Muslims and Croats in Bosnia in order to increase the size of their country. They shelled homes, hospitals and schools, killed thousands of civilians, and drove others into camps that reminded some observers of Nazi concentration camps in World War II. In North Korea, the government was suspected of making nuclear weapons out of plutonium intended for power plants, in violation of international law. In Haiti the military dictatorship terrorized its opponents and reneged on its agreement to reinstate the elected leader, Father Jean-Bertrand Aristide.

What were we to do? In President Bush's last months in office, television images of starving Somalis had generated public support for sending thousands of American troops to insure that international aid reached the people

The United States military entered Haiti peacefully in September 1994 after military dictator Raoul Cédras agreed to step down and allow the return of ousted President Jean-Bertrand Aristide.

Steve Lehman/SABA

who needed it. A year later, images of American soldiers killed or captured by Somali warlords generated the pressure that forced President Clinton to bring the troops home. Serbian aggression seemed to cry out for intervention, but opponents of intervention said that we had no national interests at stake and that by aiding the Muslim's we would only increase the carnage. Opponents of intervention in Haiti made similar arguments. They opposed use of American troops to tell people how to govern themselves. And they observed that Haiti had no tradition of democratic institutions. But supporters of intervention in Haiti, including the Black Caucus in Congress, said we had an interest in democracy everywhere, especially so close to our shores.

Breakthrough in the Middle East.   In September 1993, after months of secret negotiations, leaders of Israel and the PLO signed an agreement that would lead to Palestinian self-rule in the West Bank town of Jericho and the Gaza Strip, occupied by Israel since the 1967 Six Day War. The PLO renounced terrorism and finally recognized Israel's right to live in peace and security. Israel finally recognized the PLO as the official representative of the Palestinian people.

In a dramatic ceremony on the lawn of the White House, Israeli Prime Minister Yitzhak Rabin and PLO Chairman Yasir Arafat gave moving, conciliatory speeches. "Enough of blood and tears. Enough," Rabin said. Then, encouraged by President Clinton, the two arch-enemies shook hands. Among those in the audience, or watching on television, there were not many dry eyes. Few had thought that they would live to see the day that these two warriors would take the first steps towards peace.

Jordan quickly signaled its willingness to negotiate with Israel and these two countries also signed a peace agreement in October 1994. Even Syria, the sponsor of radical terrorists in Lebanon and Iran, seemed ready to talk about peace. There were still huge problems to overcome, especially the economic devastation and demoralization of the Palestinian people. But, many people thought, if Rabin and Arafat could

AFP photo

In October 1994, President Clinton attended the signing of a historic peace treaty between Israel and Jordan.

shake hands, any two people could, and perhaps the most intractable problems and conflicts could eventually be resolved.

Democracy in South Africa.   Events in South Africa also gave hope. After the government released Nelson Mandela from prison in 1990, the transition from apartheid to interracial democracy was swift. In July 1993, Mandela and South African President F. W. de Klerk announced that the country's first all-race elections would be held in April 1994. Despite attempts by white extremists to terrorize blacks and to foment violence between black groups and between blacks and whites, the country's first truly democratic elections were held in

Louise Grubb/JB Pictures

Nelson Mandela emerged victorious as president following South Africa's first all-race, democratic elections in April 1994.

relative peace. The world watched in awe and wonder as black South Africans patiently waited in long lines to vote for the first time in their lives. Nelson Mandela was elected president. Now came the awesome task of rebuilding a nation handicapped for decades by apartheid, inequality, poverty, and economic sanctions.

Crises in Haiti and Cuba. At the very same time that President Clinton struggled with Congress over crime and health care, he seemed overwhelmed by his effort to enforce democracy in Haiti and to deal with Fidel Castro in Cuba. During the summer of 1994, thousands of refugees began fleeing political violence and economic crises in Haiti and a deteriorating economy in Cuba. The President negotiated an end to the Cuban refugee problem by agreeing to increase the number of Cubans allowed to enter the United States each year. But neither negotiations nor sanctions moved the brutal

dictators in Haiti. There, at the end of September 1994, it took the threat of force. Only after President Clinton announced the imminent invasion of the island, and United States troops were on their way, did the junta agree to transfer power peacefully back to President Aristide. Many Americans feared that our troops would be mired in Haiti and were troubled by the President's priorities.

See "Section 8 Review answers," p. 906G.

Section 8 Review

1. Identify or explain: Family Leave Act, Janet Reno, Ruth Bader Ginsburg, Stephen Bryer.
2. Describe Clinton's plan for health care reform.
3. **Critical Thinking: Making Comparisons.** Why do you think the United States intervened direclty in Somalia and Haiti but not in Bosnia-Herzegovina?

Chapter 36 Review

See "Chapter Review answers," p. 906H.

Focusing on Ideas

1. How did the memory of the Vietnam War continue to influence American policy into the 1980s and 1990s?

2. What conditions may have combined to cause the changes that swept through Eastern Europe in 1989?

3. What were the major issues in the Iran-contra affair?

4. Why did relations between the United States and the Soviet Union improve in the later 1980s?

Taking a Critical Look

1. **Making Comparisons.** Compare the United States invasion of Grenada in 1983 to the United States intervention in Haiti in 1994.

2. **Drawing Conclusions.** What factors led to Bill Clinton's defeat of George Bush in the 1992 election?

Your Region in History

1. **Government.** What were the 1992 and 1994 election results in your state?

2. **Economics.** Which industries in your area were most affected by the recession that began in 1990? How did the recession affect the unemployment rate in your state?

Historical Facts and Figures

Making Comparisons. Study the circle graphs below to help answer the following questions: (a) What percentages of federal government spending went to defense in 1970, 1980, and 1990? (b) What accounts for the higher percentage in 1970? (c) How did the government's spending on interest change from 1970 to 1990? (d) To what do you attribute this change? (e) How did federal spending on grants to states and localities in 1980 compare to its spending in 1990? (f) What impact do you think this spending had on states and localities?

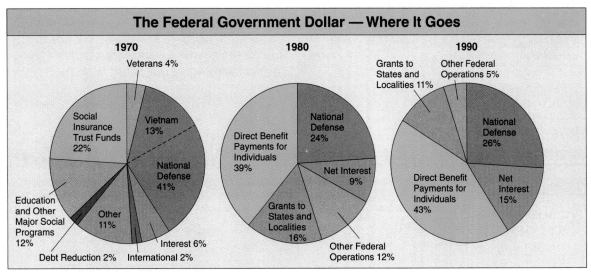

The Federal Government Dollar — Where It Goes

1970
- Veterans 4%
- Social Insurance Trust Funds 22%
- Vietnam 13%
- National Defense 41%
- Education and Other Major Social Programs 12%
- Other 11%
- Debt Reduction 2%
- International 2%
- Interest 6%

1980
- National Defense 24%
- Direct Benefit Payments for Individuals 39%
- Net Interest 9%
- Grants to States and Localities 16%
- Other Federal Operations 12%

1990
- Grants to States and Localities 11%
- Other Federal Operations 5%
- National Defense 26%
- Direct Benefit Payments for Individuals 43%
- Net Interest 15%

Source: *Budget of the United States Government*

MAKING CONNECTIONS
Unit 12

This unit began with the observation that although Americans have the oldest written constitution still in use, the nation remains young in spirit:

As the twentieth century neared its close, the United States remained a nation of experiments.

This conclusion was supported by the three unit themes that are reprinted in **dark type** below. Use the time line and the information in Unit 12 to answer the questions that follow the unit themes.

THEMES IN HISTORY

Using Making Connections: Have students look at the unit themes printed in dark type. Explain that each event on the time line relates to one of these themes. Ask students to decide which events are related to which theme. Students should use events from the time line in their answers and explain how events are related. Have students go back through the text of Unit 12 to find other events related to the unit themes.

1. **Congress passes legislation intended to extend equality of opportunity to all Americans.** SOCIAL CHANGE
   How have laws enacted by Congress since 1950 supplemented Thomas Jefferson's belief in a "natural aristocracy"? (Identifying Assumptions)

2. **Conflicts with other nations create new problems for the United States.** CONFLICT
   What new conflicts arose during the period from 1971 to 1994, and which old conflicts were resolved? (Checking Consistency)

3. **The end of the cold war brought new opportunities and new challenges for the United States.** GOVERNMENT AND POLITICS
   What were some of the questions raised for the United States by the collapse of Soviet power in Eastern Europe? (Recognizing Cause and Effect)

Events in American History

1972 Congress passes the Equal Employment Opportunity Act, guaranteeing equal pay for equal work.

1973 The Rehabilitation Act forbids discrimination against the disabled.

| 1971 | 1974 | 1977 | 1980 |

Events in World History

1975 South Vietnam surrenders to North Vietnam. Phnom Penh, the capital of Cambodia, falls to the Khmer Rouge guerrillas.

1978 Egyptian and Israeli leaders meet at Camp David.

1979 Ayatollah Khomeini deposes the Shah of Iran.

1979 Nicaragua's Sandinista guerrillas overthrow the dictator Anastasio Somoza.

1982 President Reagan and Congress agree to $30 billion in budget cuts.

1987
President Reagan and Gorbachev sign the Intermediate-Range Nuclear Forces (INF) Treaty, reducing the size of the nuclear forces in both countries.

1991
The United States and 27 other nations defeat Iraq in the Persian Gulf War.

1994
President Clinton pushes for health care reform.

| 1983 | 1986 | 1989 | 1992 | 1995 |

1985
Mikhail Gorbachev becomes leader of the Soviet Union.

1989
The Berlin Wall falls; revolution spreads throughout Eastern Europe.

1992
Boris Yeltsin is elected president of Russia.

1993
The Israelis and Palestinians agree to Palestinian self-rule in Gaza and the West Bank town of Jericho.

1994
War continues in Bosnia.

Epilogue: The Mysterious Future

When we look back on the story of America, we feel very wise. In some ways we really are even wiser than William Bradford or Benjamin Franklin or George Washington or Abraham Lincoln.

We know what they did not know. What for us is history, for them would have been prophecy. For we know how it turned out. They had to guess.

We can see how right it was for the Pilgrims to risk the long voyage across the wild ocean. We see how lucky it was that the thirteen little colonies somehow united for independence. We can see how much better the American Revolution would have been fought with a stronger, more unified Continental Army.

We can see how futile were all the "compromises" on slavery before the Civil War. We can see, too, the Civil War toll in blood and hate. We can see that while the Civil War abolished slavery and saved the Union, it cost more than 600,000 lives and created new hates that would not quickly die.

From American history we can learn that the future is always full of surprising secrets. This New World has been such an exciting place because it has been so new. The great achievements of America are mostly things that never before seemed possible.

Which signers of the Declaration of Independence in 1776 could have imagined that their feeble little confederation, in two centuries, would be the world's greatest democracy—a continent-nation of more than 250 million people, the refuge of the world, the strongest nation on earth?

Of those 55 men in Philadelphia struggling in the hot summer of 1787 to agree on how to prevent the colonies from falling apart—how many would have believed that their work would become the longest-lived written constitution in history?

Who would have imagined that a nation of immigrants, the most miscellaneous people on earth, would someday be the most powerful? Or that men and women from the Western Hemisphere, from all over Europe, from Africa and Asia—of many races and religions and traditions—would adopt one language, and become loyal builders of one new nation?

Who would have guessed that out of the American wilderness (still only half explored in 1850) so soon would come men to explore the moon, and then to send marvelously complicated machines into space to photograph and study the planets of our solar system? Or that modern science, which brings us from the whole universe the boundless vistas of the radio-telescope, would discover strange new kinds of knowledge, and keep us ever faithful to the motto, "Toward the Unknown!"

These were some of the happy surprises. But there were others not quite so happy, and to the founders of our nation just as secret.

Who would have guessed that, within less than 200 years, a trackless, half-mapped continent could be crisscrossed by superhighways, defaced by billboards and tin cans? Who would have guessed that Americans would perfect horseless carriages to go a hundred miles an hour—and yet be stuck in traffic jams where they could not even move as fast as a walking horse? Or that ten times as many would be killed by these horseless carriages every year as were killed in all the battles of the American Revolution?

Who would have imagined that the fresh air of a New World would begin to be smoke-filled? Or that the sparkling waters of lakes and rivers would become so darkened and dirtied by factory sewage that even the fish found them unlivable and the birds no longer enjoyed their shores?

Who would have believed that the wonderful American silences—once broken by Indian chants or the songs of birds or the call of the coyote—would be shattered by the roar of speeding jets, lumbering trucks, and ear-jarring motorcycles? Who would have believed that a continent, once frightening by its emptiness, would now terrify people by crowding them together?

Who would have believed that a nation of nations, created by people of all races from everywhere, which had suffered through a bloody war for union and freedom, would see new forms of racism?

Who would have believed that a nation designed to be a refuge for all people from the violence of the Old World could ever be plagued by reckless violence within?

Who would have foreseen that a nation rich in natural resources—in coal, oil, uranium, natural gas, and flowing water—would fear that it might be crippled by a lack of enough energy to run its cars and factories and to warm its houses?

But Americans have always faced hard problems. We, even more than other people, love the adventure of the unexpected. Ours has always been a story of dealing with the unknown, a story of movement and discovery—to America, within America, from America. The future is just as much a mystery story as it ever was.

Americans have been planters in this faraway land, builders of cities in the wilderness, Go-Getters. Americans—makers of something out of nothing—have delivered a new way of life to far corners of the world.

If the future is a mystery story, then, that does not frighten Americans. For we Americans have always lived in the world's greatest treasure house of the unexpected.

130°

PACIFIC OCEAN

WASHINGTON
Seattle
Olympia
Tacoma
Columbia
Spokane
Portland
Salem
Columbia

OREGON

IDAHO
Boise
Snake R.
Pocatello

Calgary
C A N A D A N

110°
100°

Regina

Columbia
Great Falls
Missouri R.
MONTANA
Helena
Butte
Yellowstone

NORTH DAKOTA
Bismarck
Far

40°

CALIFORNIA
Sacramento
San Francisco
Oakland

Reno
Carson City

NEVADA
Humboldt R.

Great
Salt
Lake
Salt Lake
City
Ogden

WYOMING
Casper
Cheyenne

SOUTH DAKOTA
Pierre
Sioux Fa

Missouri
NEBRASKA
Platte R.
Linco

Los Angeles

San Diego

UTAH

Las Vegas

Colorado

R.

ARIZONA

Phoenix

Tucson

Colorado

COLORADO
Denver
Pueblo

R.

Arkansas

KANSA
Wichita

30°

120°

Albuquerque
Santa Fe
Rio Grande

NEW MEXICO

Rio

Pecos

El Paso

Amarillo
OKLA
Oklahoma City

T E X A S
Colorado

Fort Worth

Austin R.

San Antonio

Corpus
Christi

Rio Grande

170°
180°
170°
160°
150°
140°

Cape Prince of Wales
Bering Strait
SEWARD
PEN.
Barrow

BERING
SEA

Nome
Yukon R.

NUNIVAK
ISLAND

Fairbanks

70°

Klondike

160°
KAUAI
NIIHAU

22° 30'

OAHU
Honolulu
Pearl Harbor

157° 30'
MOLOKAI
LANAI
MAUI
KAHOOLAWE

Anchorage

PRIBILOF
ISLANDS

KENAI
PEN.
Seward

ALASKA
PEN.

A L E U T I A N   I S L A N D S

Dutch Harbor

Kodiak

GULF
OF
ALASKA

ALASKA

750 Miles

750 Kilometers

PACIFIC OCEAN

Juneau
Sitka

Ketchikan
Prince Rupert
QUEEN
CHARLOTTE
ISLANDS

PACIFIC

OCEAN

HAWAII

155°

HAWAII
Hilo

20°

100 Miles

100 Kilometers

United States
Political

951

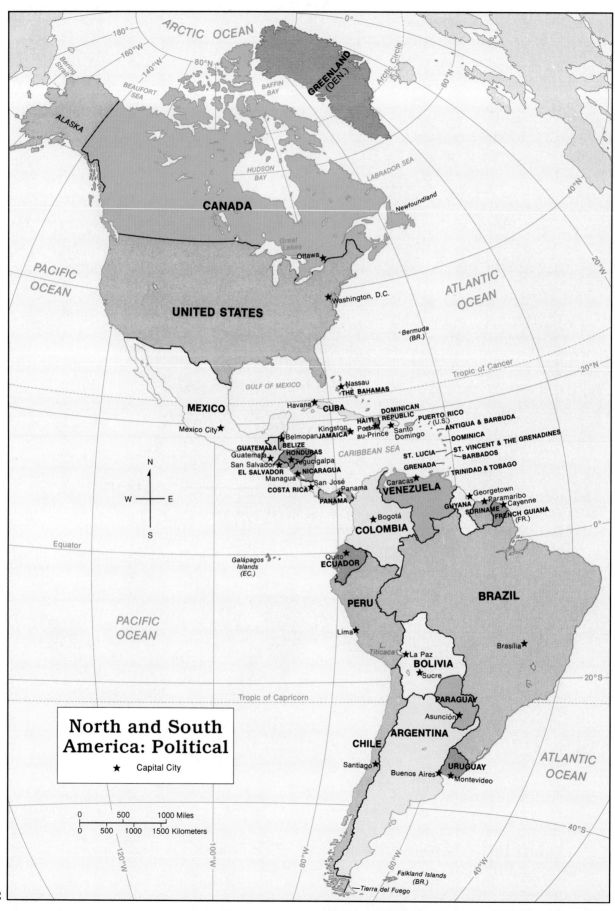

North and South America: Political

★ Capital City

| 0 | 500 | 1000 Miles |
| 0 | 500 | 1000 | 1500 Kilometers |

ARCTIC OCEAN

GREENLAND (DEN.)

ALASKA

BAFFIN BAY

HUDSON BAY

LABRADOR SEA

CANADA

Newfoundland

Great Lakes

Ottawa ★

PACIFIC OCEAN

ATLANTIC OCEAN

UNITED STATES

Washington, D.C. ★

Bermuda (BR.)

Tropic of Cancer

GULF OF MEXICO

Nassau ★
THE BAHAMAS

MEXICO

Havana ★ CUBA

DOMINICAN REPUBLIC

Mexico City ★

HAITI

PUERTO RICO (U.S.)

Kingston Port-
au-Prince Santo
Domingo

ANTIGUA & BARBUDA

Belmopan
GUATEMALA BELIZE
Guatemala HONDURAS
San Salvador Tegucigalpa
EL SALVADOR NICARAGUA
Managua

JAMAICA

DOMINICA

CARIBBEAN SEA

ST. LUCIA

ST. VINCENT & THE GRENADINES

BARBADOS

GRENADA

TRINIDAD & TOBAGO

San José
COSTA RICA Panama
PANAMA

Caracas ★
VENEZUELA

Georgetown
GUYANA Paramaribo Cayenne
SURINAME FRENCH GUIANA (FR.)

Bogotá ★
COLOMBIA

Equator

Galápagos Islands (EC.)

Quito ★
ECUADOR

PERU

BRAZIL

Lima ★

L. Titicaca La Paz ★
BOLIVIA
★ Sucre

Brasília ★

Tropic of Capricorn

PARAGUAY

Asunción ★

CHILE ARGENTINA

Santiago ★

URUGUAY

Buenos Aires ★ ★ Montevideo

ATLANTIC OCEAN

Falkland Islands (BR.)

Tierra del Fuego

PACIFIC OCEAN

N
W E
S

952

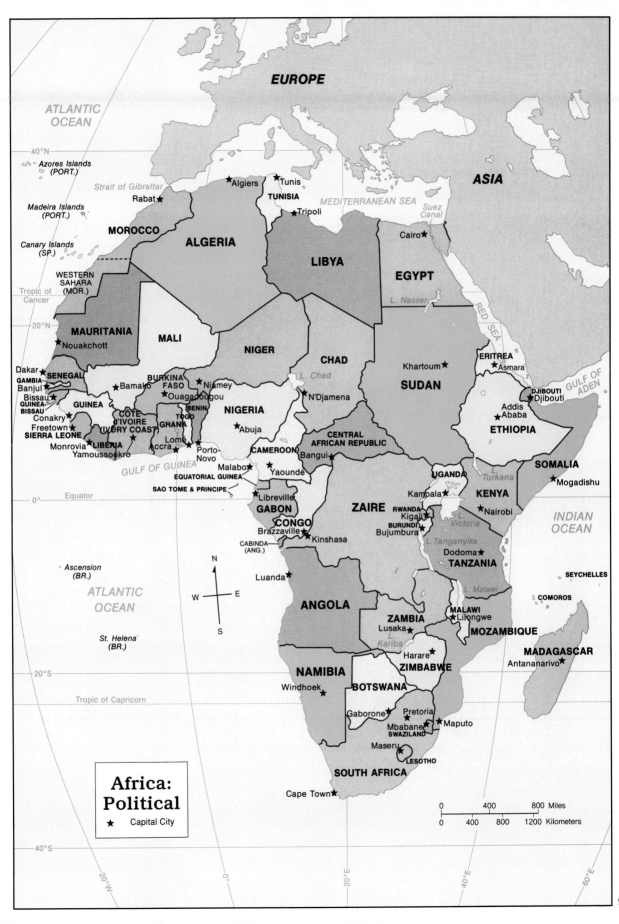

Africa: Political

★ Capital City

953

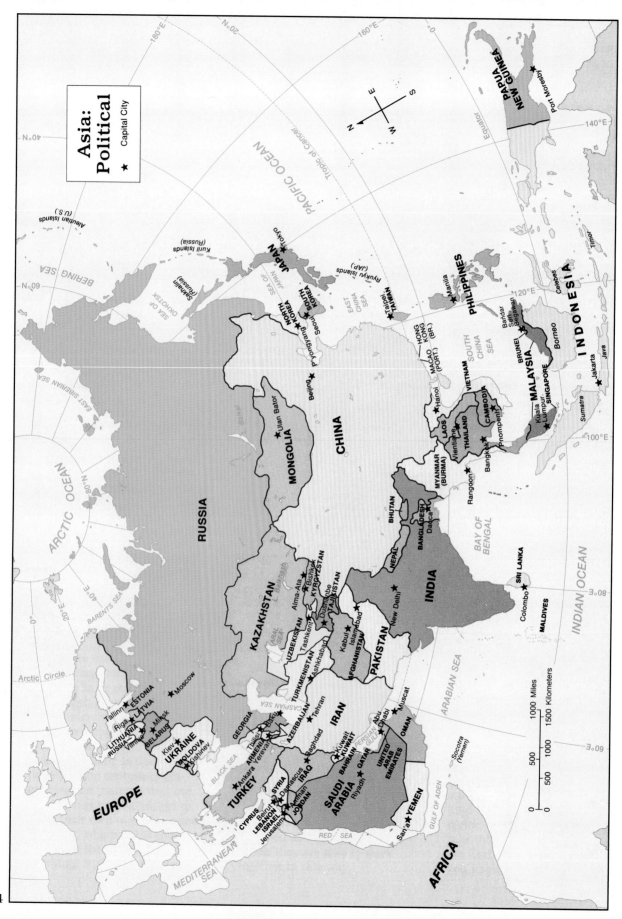

Asia: Political

★ Capital City

N E S W

AFRICA

EUROPE

ARCTIC OCEAN

PACIFIC OCEAN

Aleutian Islands (U.S.)

Kuril Islands (Russia)

Sakhalin (Russia)

BERING SEA

SEA OF OKHOTSK

EAST SIBERIAN SEA

BARENTS SEA

KARA SEA

RUSSIA

★ Moscow

Tallinn ★ **ESTONIA**
Riga ★ **LATVIA**
LITHUANIA
Vilnius ★
RUSSIA
★ Minsk
BELARUS
Kiev ★ **UKRAINE**
MOLDOVA
Kishinev ★

BLACK SEA

Ankara ★ **TURKEY**

CYPRUS
Beirut ★
LEBANON
ISRAEL
Jerusalem ★
Damascus ★ **SYRIA**
Amman ★ **JORDAN**
IRAQ
Baghdad ★

GEORGIA
Tbilisi ★
★ Baku
ARMENIA **AZERBAIJAN**
Yerevan ★

CASPIAN SEA

★ Tehran

IRAN

SAUDI ARABIA
Riyadh ★

Kuwait ★ **KUWAIT**
BAHRAIN ★
QATAR ★
Abu Dhabi ★
UNITED ARAB EMIRATES
Muscat ★ **OMAN**

PERSIAN GULF

YEMEN
San'a ★

RED SEA

GULF OF ADEN

Socotra (Yemen)

ARABIAN SEA

MEDITERRANEAN SEA

KAZAKHSTAN

ARAL SEA

L. Balkhash

Alma-Ata ★
Bishkek ★
KYRGYZSTAN
UZBEKISTAN
Tashkent ★
TAJIKISTAN
Dushanbe ★
TURKMENISTAN
Ashkhabad ★

Kabul ★
AFGHANISTAN
Islamabad ★
PAKISTAN

L. Baikal

★ Ulan Bator

MONGOLIA

CHINA

★ Beijing

NEPAL
★ New Delhi

INDIA

BHUTAN

BANGLADESH
Dacca ★

SRI LANKA
Colombo ★

MALDIVES

BAY OF BENGAL

INDIAN OCEAN

NORTH KOREA
P'yongyang ★
Seoul ★ **SOUTH KOREA**

JAPAN
Tokyo ★

SEA OF JAPAN

EAST CHINA SEA

Ryukyu Islands (JAP.)

TAIWAN
Taipei ★

HONG KONG (BR.)
MACAO (PORT.)

MYANMAR (BURMA)
Rangoon ★

LAOS
Vientiane ★
THAILAND
Bangkok ★
VIETNAM
Hanoi ★
CAMBODIA
Pnompenh ★

SOUTH CHINA SEA

PHILIPPINES
Manila ★

BRUNEI
Bandar Seri Begawan ★
MALAYSIA
Kuala Lumpur ★
SINGAPORE ★

INDONESIA

Borneo

Celebes

Sumatra

Java
Jakarta ★

Timor

PAPUA NEW GUINEA
Port Moresby ★

Equator

Tropic of Cancer

Arctic Circle

40°N 60°N 80°N

180°E 160°E 140°E 120°E 100°E 80°E 60°E 40°E 20°E 0° 20°E

1000 Miles
1500 Kilometers
1000
500
500
0
0

954

Europe: Political

★ Capital City
• Other City

955

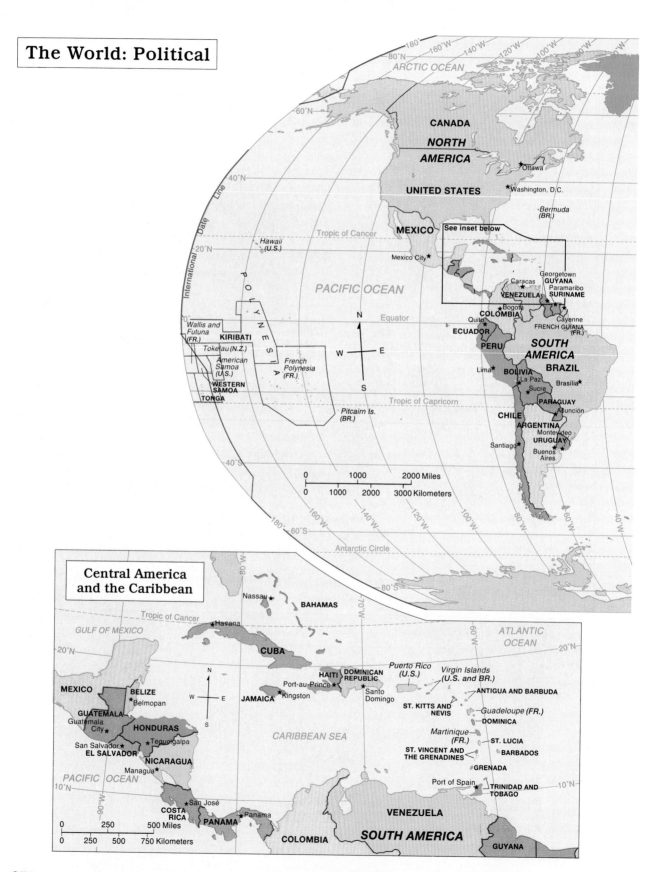

The World: Political

ARCTIC OCEAN

180° 160°W 140°W 120°W 100°W 80°W
80°N
60°N

CANADA

NORTH AMERICA

★Ottawa

40°N

UNITED STATES

★Washington, D.C.

Bermuda (BR.)

Tropic of Cancer

See inset below

MEXICO

20°N

Hawaii (U.S.)

Mexico City★

Georgetown

Caracas★ **GUYANA**
Paramaribo
VENEZUELA **SURINAME**

PACIFIC OCEAN

★Bogotá

COLOMBIA

Quito★ Cayenne
FRENCH GUIANA
(FR.)

P O L Y N E S I A

0° Equator

N

Wallis and Futuna (FR.)

KIRIBATI

ECUADOR

W   E

PERU

SOUTH AMERICA

Tokelau (N.Z.)

American Samoa (U.S.)

French Polynesia (FR.)

S

Lima★ **BOLIVIA**
La Paz
★Sucre

BRAZIL

Brasília★

WESTERN SAMOA

TONGA

Tropic of Capricorn

PARAGUAY

Asunción★

Pitcairn Is. (BR.)

CHILE **ARGENTINA**

Montevideo
URUGUAY

Santiago★ Buenos
Aires★

0	1000	2000 Miles
0	1000 2000	3000 Kilometers

40°S 60°S

180° 160°W 140°W 120°W 100°W 80°W 60°W 40°W

80°S

Antarctic Circle

Central America and the Caribbean

Nassau★

BAHAMAS

Tropic of Cancer

★Havana

GULF OF MEXICO

20°N

CUBA

Puerto Rico (U.S.)

Virgin Islands (U.S. and BR.)

ATLANTIC OCEAN

20°N

HAITI **DOMINICAN REPUBLIC**

MEXICO

BELIZE

★Belmopan

Port-au-Prince★

JAMAICA ★Kingston

Santo
Domingo

ANTIGUA AND BARBUDA

ST. KITTS AND NEVIS

Guadeloupe (FR.)

DOMINICA

GUATEMALA

Guatemala
City★

HONDURAS

★Tegucigalpa

Martinique (FR.)

ST. LUCIA

San Salvador★
EL SALVADOR

NICARAGUA

CARIBBEAN SEA

ST. VINCENT AND THE GRENADINES

BARBADOS

Managua★

GRENADA

PACIFIC OCEAN

10°N

N

W   E

S

Port of Spain **TRINIDAD AND TOBAGO**

10°N

★San José

COSTA RICA

PANAMA ★Panama

VENEZUELA

0	250	500 Miles
0	250 500	750 Kilometers

COLOMBIA **SOUTH AMERICA**

GUYANA

International Date Line

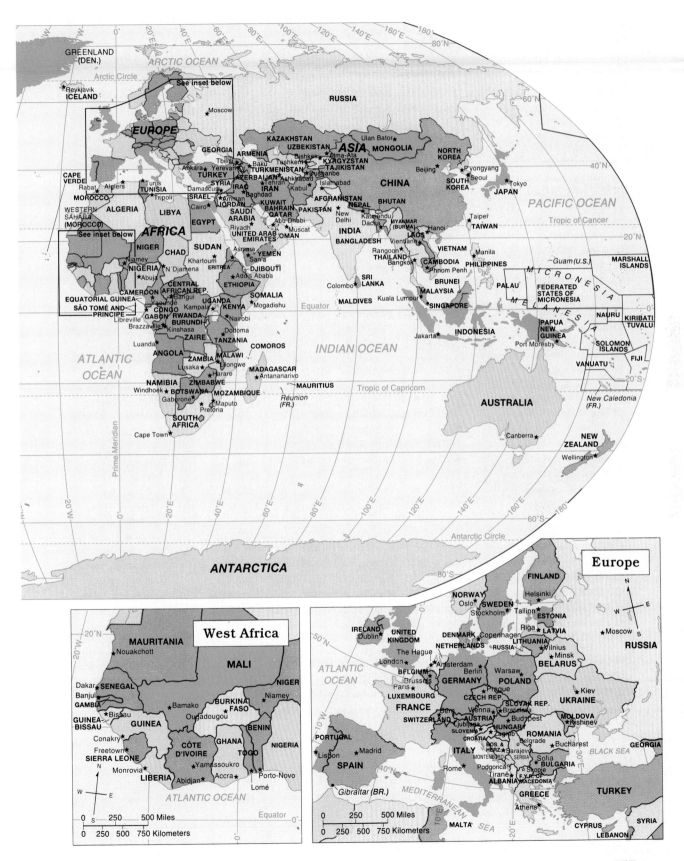

GREENLAND (DEN.)

ARCTIC OCEAN

Arctic Circle

★Reykjavik
ICELAND

RUSSIA

EUROPE

★Moscow

ASIA

CAPE
VERDE

MOROCCO

WESTERN
SAHARA
(MOROCCO)

ALGERIA

TUNISIA

LIBYA

AFRICA

See inset below

NIGER

CHAD

NIGERIA

Abuja

CAMEROON

CENTRAL
AFRICAN REP.

EQUATORIAL GUINEA

SÃO TOMÉ AND
PRINCIPE

CONGO

GABON

ZAIRE

Luanda

ANGOLA

NAMIBIA

Windhoek★

Gaborone

BOTSWANA

SOUTH
AFRICA

Cape Town★

ATLANTIC
OCEAN

Rabat

Algiers

Tunis

Tripoli

EGYPT

Cairo

SUDAN

Khartoum

N'Djamena

Niamey

Bangui

Yaoundé

Libreville

Brazzaville

Kinshasa

Kampala

UGANDA

RWANDA

BURUNDI

TANZANIA

ZAMBIA

Lusaka

ZIMBABWE

Harare

MOZAMBIQUE

Maputo

Pretoria

KAZAKHSTAN

UZBEKISTAN

GEORGIA

ARMENIA

TURKEY

Ankara

Tbilisi

Yerevan

AZERBAIJAN

Baku

TURKMENISTAN

Ashkhabad

Bishkek

Alma-Ata

KYRGYZSTAN

TAJIKISTAN

Dushanbe

Tashkent

MONGOLIA

Ulan Bator

CHINA

Beijing★

NORTH
KOREA

P'yongyang

Seoul

SOUTH
KOREA

Tokyo★

JAPAN

PACIFIC OCEAN

Tropic of Cancer

SYRIA

Damascus

IRAQ

Baghdad

ISRAEL

JORDAN

Amman

SAUDI
ARABIA

Riyadh

KUWAIT

BAHRAIN

QATAR

Abu Dhabi

UNITED ARAB
EMIRATES

OMAN

Muscat

YEMEN

San'a

IRAN

Tehran

AFGHANISTAN

Kabul

Islamabad

PAKISTAN

New
Delhi

NEPAL

Katmandu

BHUTAN

BANGLADESH

Dacca

INDIA

MYANMAR
(BURMA)

Rangoon

LAOS

Vientiane

Hanoi

Taipei★

TAIWAN

THAILAND

Bangkok

CAMBODIA

Phnom Penh

VIETNAM

Manila★

PHILIPPINES

Guam (U.S.)

MARSHALL
ISLANDS

MICRONESIA

SRI
LANKA

Colombo

MALDIVES

Kuala Lumpur

MALAYSIA

SINGAPORE

BRUNEI

PALAU

FEDERATED
STATES OF
MICRONESIA

MELANESIA

NAURU

KIRIBATI

TUVALU

ERITREA

Asmara

DJIBOUTI

Addis Ababa

ETHIOPIA

SOMALIA

Mogadishu

KENYA

Nairobi

Dodoma

Equator

INDONESIA

Jakarta

PAPUA
NEW
GUINEA

Port Moresby

SOLOMON
ISLANDS

VANUATU

FIJI

New Caledonia
(FR.)

INDIAN OCEAN

COMOROS

MALAWI

Lilongwe

MADAGASCAR

Antananarivo

MAURITIUS

Réunion
(FR.)

Tropic of Capricorn

AUSTRALIA

Canberra★

NEW
ZEALAND

Wellington★

Prime Meridian

ANTARCTICA

957

Presidents and Vice-Presidents of the United States

President	Years in office	Party	Born	Died	State Born/Home	Vice-President
1 George Washington	1789–1797		1732	1799	Virginia	John Adams
2 John Adams	1797–1801	Federalist	1735	1826	Massachusetts	Thomas Jefferson
3 Thomas Jefferson	1801–1809	Republican	1743	1826	Virginia	Aaron Burr George Clinton
4 James Madison	1809–1817	Republican	1751	1836	Virginia	George Clinton Elbridge Gerry
5 James Monroe	1817–1825	Republican	1758	1831	Virginia	Daniel D. Tompkins
6 John Quincy Adams	1825–1829	Nat. Rep.	1767	1848	Massachusetts	John C. Calhoun
7 Andrew Jackson	1829–1837	Democratic	1767	1845	S.C./Tenn.	John C. Calhoun Martin Van Buren
8 Martin Van Buren	1837–1841	Democratic	1782	1862	New York	Richard M. Johnson
9 William Henry Harrison	Mar. 1841	Whig	1773	1841	Va./Ohio	John Tyler
10 John Tyler	1841–1845	Whig	1790	1862	Virginia	
11 James K. Polk	1845–1849	Democratic	1795	1849	N.C./Tenn.	George M. Dallas
12 Zachary Taylor	1849–1850	Whig	1784	1850	Va./La.	Millard Fillmore
13 Millard Fillmore	1850–1853	Whig	1800	1874	New York	
14 Franklin Pierce	1853–1857	Democratic	1804	1869	New Hampshire	William R. D. King
15 James Buchanan	1857–1861	Democratic	1791	1868	Pennsylvania	John C. Breckinridge
16 Abraham Lincoln	1861–1865	Republican	1809	1865	Ky./Ill.	Hannibal Hamlin Andrew Johnson
17 Andrew Johnson	1865–1869	Republican	1808	1875	N.C./Tenn.	
18 Ulysses S. Grant	1869–1877	Republican	1822	1885	Ohio/Ill.	Schuyler Colfax Henry Wilson
19 Rutherford B. Hayes	1877–1881	Republican	1822	1893	Ohio	William A. Wheeler
20 James A. Garfield	1881	Republican	1831	1881	Ohio	Chester A. Arthur
21 Chester A. Arthur	1881–1885	Republican	1830	1886	Vt./N.Y.	
22 Grover Cleveland	1885–1889	Democratic	1837	1908	N.J./N.Y.	Thomas A. Hendricks
23 Benjamin Harrison	1889–1893	Republican	1833	1901	Ohio/Ind.	Levi P. Morton
24 Grover Cleveland	1893–1897	Democratic	1837	1908	N.J./N.Y.	Adlai E. Stevenson
25 William McKinley	1897–1901	Republican	1843	1901	Ohio	Garret A. Hobart Theodore Roosevelt
26 Theodore Roosevelt	1901–1909	Republican	1858	1919	New York	Charles W. Fairbanks
27 William Howard Taft	1909–1913	Republican	1857	1930	Ohio	James S. Sherman
28 Woodrow Wilson	1913–1921	Democratic	1856	1924	Va./N.J.	Thomas R. Marshall
29 Warren G. Harding	1921–1923	Republican	1865	1923	Ohio	Calvin Coolidge
30 Calvin Coolidge	1923–1929	Republican	1872	1933	Vt./Mass.	Charles G. Dawes
31 Herbert C. Hoover	1929–1933	Republican	1874	1964	Iowa/Cal.	Charles Curtis
32 Franklin D. Roosevelt	1933–1945	Democratic	1882	1945	New York	John N. Garner Henry A. Wallace Harry S Truman
33 Harry S Truman	1945–1953	Democratic	1884	1972	Missouri	Alben W. Barkley
34 Dwight D. Eisenhower	1953–1961	Republican	1890	1969	Tex./N.Y., Pa.	Richard M. Nixon
35 John F. Kennedy	1961–1963	Democratic	1917	1963	Massachusetts	Lyndon B. Johnson
36 Lyndon B. Johnson	1963–1969	Democratic	1908	1973	Texas	Hubert H. Humphrey
37 Richard M. Nixon	1969–1974	Republican	1913	1994	Cal./N.Y., Cal.	Spiro T. Agnew Gerald R. Ford
38 Gerald R. Ford	1974–1977	Republican	1913		Neb./Mich.	Nelson A. Rockefeller
39 Jimmy (James Earl) Carter	1977–1981	Democratic	1924		Georgia	Walter F. Mondale
40 Ronald Reagan	1981–1989	Republican	1911		Ill./Cal.	George H. W. Bush
41 George Herbert Walker Bush	1989–1993	Republican	1924		Mass./Tex.	J. Danforth Quayle
42 William Jefferson Clinton	1993–	Democrat	1946		Arkansas	Albert Gore, Jr.

The Declaration of Independence

Introduction

We Americans are luckier than most other people because the Founders of our new nation left us a short, clear, and simple list of reasons for the founding. The Declaration of Independence is our nation's birth certificate. It tells us in a few words what were the parent-ideas and hopes out of which the nation was born.

In the following pages we print the Declaration of Independence. We explain why it happened to say what it did, and what it has come to mean to Americans and to people everywhere in the world. The Declaration of Independence, like the Constitution, is a sacred document for Americans. This is because it is a *living* document. Of course it was written by living men in 1776 to suit the needs of American patriots in the Revolution. But it proved to have a life much longer than that of the men who adopted it. It is still very much alive. To understand why and how it lives will help us understand our country, and where it has been going in the centuries since 1776.

Why there had to be a Declaration of Independence, and how it fits into the story of the Revolution, is explained earlier in this book (p. 88). In the following pages we provide in the center column the words of the Declaration precisely as Jefferson, helped by John Adams and Benjamin Franklin, wrote it. These very words were adopted by the Continental Congress in Independence Hall (which we can still visit) in Philadelphia on July 4, 1776. We have left their spelling, their punctuation, and their capitalization precisely as they wrote it. Even if this looks a little odd to us, it will help us remember that the Declaration was written two centuries ago. And this will not get in the way of our understanding.

In *Origins* we give some of the reasons why they wrote those words. In *Afterlife* we see what those words have come to mean in later years.

THE DECLARATION OF INDEPENDENCE

When in the Course of human events, it becomes necessary for one people to dissolve the political bands which have connected them with another, and to assume among the powers of the earth, the separate and equal station to which the Laws of Nature and of Nature's God entitle them, a decent respect to the opinions of mankind requires that they should declare the causes which impel them to the separation.

We hold these truths to be self-evident, that all men are created equal, that they are endowed by their Creator with certain unalienable Rights, that among these are Life, Liberty and the pursuit of Happiness. That to secure these rights, Governments are instituted among Men, deriving their just powers from the consent of the governed, That whenever any Form of Government becomes destructive of these ends it is the Right of the People to alter or to abolish it, and to institute new Government, laying its foundation on such principles and organizing its powers in such form, as to them shall seem most likely to effect their Safety and Happiness. Prudence, indeed, will dictate that Governments long established should not be changed for light and transient causes; and accordingly all experience has shewn, that mankind are more disposed to suffer, while evils are sufferable, than to right themselves by abolishing the forms to which they are accustomed. But when a long train of abuses and usurpations, pursuing invariably the same Object evinces a design to reduce them under absolute Despotism, it is their right, it is their duty, to throw off such Government, and to provide new Guards for their future security. Such has been the patient sufferance of these Colonies; and such is now the necessity which constrains them to alter their former Systems of Government. The history of the present King of Great Britain is a history of repeated injuries and usurpations, all having in direct object the establishment of an absolute Tyranny over these States. To prove this, let Facts be submitted to a candid world.

He has refused his Assent to Laws, the most wholesome and necessary for the public good.

He has forbidden his Governors to pass Laws of immediate and pressing importance, unless suspended in their operation till his Assent should be obtained; and when so suspended, he has utterly neglected to attend to them. He has refused to pass other Laws for the accommodation of large districts of people, unless those people would relinquish the right of Representation in the Legislature, a right inestimable to them and formidable to tyrants only.

He has called together legislative bodies at places unusual, uncomfortable, and distant from the depository of their public Records, for the sole purpose of fatiguing them into compliance with his measures.

He has dissolved Representative Houses repeatedly, for opposing with manly firmness his invasions on the rights of the people.

He has refused for a long time, after such dissolutions, to cause others to be elected; whereby the Legislative powers, incapable of Annihilation, have returned to the People at large for their exercise; the State remaining in the mean time exposed to all the dangers of invasion from without, and convulsions within.

He has endeavoured to prevent the population of these States; for that purpose obstructing the Laws for Naturalization of Foreigners; refusing to pass others to encourage their migrations hither, and raising the conditions of new Appropriations of Lands.

He has obstructed the Administration of Justice, by refusing his Assent to Laws for establishing Judiciary powers.

He has made Judges dependent on his Will alone, for the tenure of their offices, and the amount and payment of their salaries.

He has erected a multitude of New Offices, and sent hither swarms of Officers to harass our People, and eat out their substance.

He has kept among us, in times of peace, standing Armies without the Consent of our legislatures.

He has affected to render the Military independent of and superior to the Civil power.

He has combined with others to subject us to a jurisdiction foreign to our constitution, and unacknowledged by our laws; giving his Assent to their Acts of pretended Legislation:

For Quartering large bodies of armed troops among us:

For protecting them, by a mock Trial, from punishment for any Murders which they should commit on the Inhabitants of these States:

For cutting off our Trade with all parts of the world:

For imposing Taxes on us without our Consent:

For depriving us in many cases of the benefits of Trial by Jury:

For transporting us beyond Seas to be tried for pretended offences:

For abolishing the free System of English Laws in a neighbouring Province, establishing therein an Arbitrary government, and enlarging its Boundaries so as to render it at once an example and fit instrument for introducing the same absolute rule into these Colonies:

For taking away our Charters, abolishing our most valuable Laws, and altering fundamentally the Forms of our Governments:

For suspending our own Legislatures, and declaring themselves invested with power to legislate for us in all cases whatsoever.

He has abdicated Government here, by declaring us out of his Protection and waging War against us.

He has plundered our seas, ravaged our Coasts, burnt our towns, and destroyed the Lives of our people.

He is at this time transporting large Armies of foreign Mercenaries to compleat the works of death, desolation and tyranny, already begun with circumstances of Cruelty & perdify scarcely paralleled in the most barbarous ages, and totally unworthy the Head of a civilized nation.

He has constrained our fellow Citizens taken Captive on the high Seas to bear Arms against their Country, to become the executioners of their friends and Brethren, or to fall themselves by their Hands.

He has excited domestic insurrections amongst us, and has endeavoured to bring on the inhabitants of our frontiers, the merciless Indian Savages, whose known rule of warfare, is an undistinguished destruction of all ages, sexes and conditions.

In every state of these Oppressions We have Petitioned for Redress in the most humble terms: Our repeated Petitions have been answered only by repeated injury. A Prince, whose character is thus marked by every act which may define a Tyrant, is unfit to be the ruler of a free people.

Nor have We been wanting in attentions to our Brittish brethren. We have warned them from time to time of attempts by their legislature to extend an unwarrantable jurisdiction over us. We have reminded them of the circumstances of our emigration and settlement here. We have appealed to their native justice and magnanimity, and we have conjured them by the ties of our common kindred to disavow these usurpations, which, would inevitably interrupt our connections and correspondence. They too have been deaf to the voice of Justice and of consanguinity. We must, therefore, acquiesce in the necessity, which denounces our Separation, and hold them, as we hold the rest of mankind, Enemies in War, in Peace Friends.

We, therefore, the Representatives of the united States of America, in General

Congress, Assembled, appealing to the Supreme Judge of the world for the rectitude of our intentions, do, in the Name, and by Authority of the good People of these Colonies, solemnly publish and declare, That these United Colonies are, and of Right ought to be Free and Independent States; that they are Absolved from all Allegiance to the British Crown, and that all political connection between them and the State of Great Britain, is and ought to be totally dissolved; and that as Free and Independent States, they have full Power to levy War, conclude Peace, contract Alliances, establish Commerce, and to do all other Acts and Things which Independent States may of right do. And for the support of this Declaration, with a firm reliance on the protection of divine Providence, we mutually pledge to each other our Lives, our Fortunes and our sacred Honor.

Button Gwinnett	George Wythe	James Wilson	Wm: Whipple
Lyman Hall	Richard Henry Lee	Geo. Ross	Saml. Adams
Geo Walton	Th: Jefferson	Caesar Rodney	John Adams
Wm. Hooper	Benja. Harrison	Geo Read	Robt. Treat Paine
Joseph Hewes	John Hancock	Tho M: Kean	Elbridge Gerry
John Penn	Thos. Nelson jr.	Wm. Floyd	Step. Hopkins
Edward Rutledge	Francis Lightfoot Lee	Phil. Livingston	William Ellery
Thos. Heyward Junr.	Carter Braxton	Frans. Lewis	Roger Sherman
Thomas Lynch Junr.	Robt. Morris	Lewis Morris	Saml. Huntington
Arthur Middleton	Benjamin Rush	Richd. Stockton	Wm. Williams
Samuel Chase	Benja. Franklin	Jno Witherspoon	Oliver Wolcott
Wm. Paca	John Morton	Fras. Hopkinson	Matthew Thornton
Thos. Stone	Geo Clymer	John Hart	
Charles Carroll of	Jas. Smith	Abra Clark	
Carrollton	Geo. Taylor	Josiah Bartlett	

Note: This text of the Declaration of Independence is taken from the reprint in the Revised Statutes of the United States, corrected by comparison with the version printed in the journal of the Continental Congress. The original manuscript can be seen in the National Archives, Washington, D.C.

ORIGINS

The Preamble. The Declaration of Independence was directed not just to a few insiders— American colonists who wanted their independence—but to the whole world. It had to be plain and simple. The first part therefore had to state the "common sense" of the subject. The opening words of the Declaration, like the opening words of the Constitution, gave the basis for the whole argument. They expressed not only what most Americans believed, but also what would seem "self-evident" (needing no proof) to Britons of goodwill, and to people in France and other countries from whom the Americans wanted help.

Since Jefferson was not aiming to devise a new theory, it is not surprising that he wrote his draft in short order. On June 28, 1776, only about two weeks after he received the assignment, the energetic 33-year-old lawyer from Virginia managed to have his Declaration approved by the Committee and submitted to the Continental Congress. If he had needed a lot of research and reflection, it would have taken him much longer. He did not even need a library. He explained that he had purposely not referred to any books or pamphlets for special arguments. He wrote the Declaration in Philadelphia on a desk in the second-floor parlor of the house of a young German immigrant bricklayer where he was staying. He wanted to be sure that what he was saying simply summed up what educated people already knew from their schoolbooks.

The basis for government described here is precisely what Englishmen had accepted in their Glorious Revolution of 1688. All good Whigs in England still believed those principles. The Englishman John Locke had been the philosopher of that Glorious Revolution. His sacred three purposes of government were life, liberty, and property. Jefferson preferred "Life, Liberty and the pursuit of Happiness."

The List of Grievances. Thomas Jefferson was a lawyer. He had studied law at William and Mary College. He was admitted to the Virginia bar in 1767 and was a successful practicing lawyer until the cause of Independence focused his talents on public issues. One of the main reasons why Jefferson was chosen to write the Declaration was that in 1774 he had written a brilliant *Summary View of the Rights of British America.* This eloquent little pamphlet brought him wide notice both as a learned lawyer and a lively stylist. There he had proven that the Parliament had no authority at all over the colonies. He did concede that the colonists, of their own free will, had submitted to the king as their connecting link with the home country.

And Jefferson was a careful lawyer. This explains why Jefferson's Declaration of Independence makes no mention at all of the British Parliament. On one occasion he mentions that "the present King of Great Britain" (George III) "has combined with *others*" for his nefarious purposes. Those "others" were, of course, the Parliament. But the lawyerly Jefferson would not do them the honor of naming them by name! From a lawyer's point of view the king was to blame, and had to take all the blame for allowing those "others" to oppress the colonies.

The list that Jefferson provides is detailed and technical. The colonists' rights, he says, were the traditional rights of all British subjects. This, of course, prevented the Declaration from having a radical sound. According to Jefferson's Declaration the colonists were now declaring their independence simply to preserve the rights that Britons had fought for and won over the past centuries.

We can already see here the need for compromise among the States, which would appear so plainly in the Constitution. The list of grievances that finally was approved by the Continental Congress was not precisely that which Jefferson included in his draft. Some sentimental members of the Continental Congress removed a few of Jefferson's personal remarks about George III. Out of tenderness to some delegates from the slave states, they also removed Jefferson's bitter attack on slavery and the slave-trade, for which he held the British king responsible.

AFTERLIFE

At the time, to the colonists, Jefferson's legalistic list of grievances seemed the heart of their case. These facts "submitted to a candid world" against the king of England justified the colonies' independence. The Preamble was only the "common sense" basis behind those grievances. In later years, after the United States had fought for and won independence, the facts of that day came to seem less interesting. To understand those facts required an understanding of history, of the sort we have tried to give in this book. Since they were in lawyers' language, they were easy to forget.

The Preamble, by contrast, stated the principles of free government. Jefferson's flowing language could not be forgotten. It is not surprising, then, that in the years since 1776 the Preamble has overshadowed all the rest of the document. Who can forget these words? "We hold these truths to be self-evident, that all men are created equal, that they are endowed by their Creator with certain unalienable Rights, that among these are Life, Liberty and the pursuit of Happiness. That to secure these rights, Governments are instituted among Men, deriving their just powers from the consent of the governed."

These words of the Preamble resound down

the centuries. They have a wonderful ring, but Americans have not always agreed on what they meant.

Elizabeth Cady Stanton and her companions at the women's rights convention at Seneca Falls, New York, in 1848, issued their own "Declaration" modeled on Jefferson's work of 1776. They began "When, in the course of human events . . . " and went on to their own list of "self-evident" truths, and their grievances against man for oppressing woman.

The Civil War would have to be fought to secure agreement on what the Declaration meant when it said that "all men are created equal." When the southern states seceded they, too, declared that they were only following the principles of the Declaration of 1776.

Even today Americans disagree over precisely what a government should do to help Americans in the "pursuit of Happiness." But Jefferson's words in the Declaration of Independence still provide an American creed. We can all agree to this statement of principles. If the words had been more prosaic or more limited, they might not have lived. And we might have lacked the eloquent standard by which we can still judge ourselves.

The Declaration of Independence and the World. Jefferson's words have appealed to freedom-loving people everywhere. No other human document has been so inspiring to people with grievances against their government. The men and women who made the French Revolution of 1789 appealed to the Declaration. English reformers, and Irish rebels against English oppression, appealed to the Declaration. In the early nineteenth century, translated into Spanish, the Declaration inspired colonists in South America to become independent. It was translated into German and Italian to support liberal revolutions in the 1830s and 1840s. It was translated into scores of other languages, and everywhere has encouraged people fighting for freedom, helping them explain their cause to the world.

Jefferson himself knew that his Declaration was a voice for posterity and that it would have an Afterlife without end. He wrote his own epitaph. After a long life of countless achievements, he chose to have it written on his tombstone (along with his recognition as author of the Virginia statue for religious freedom and as father of the University of Virginia) that he was the author of the Declaration of Independence.

The Constitution of the United States

Introduction

These pages give us the text of the Constitution, and they will help us understand why it was written this way, and how it has changed. For Americans, the Constitution is a sacred document. The Constitution itself prescribes that before taking office each American President must "solemnly swear (or affirm) that I will . . . to the best of my Ability, preserve, protect and defend the Constitution of the United States" (Article II, section 1). While the Constitution is our sacred national document, it is not a fossil. It can be changed and has changed. Most of this book could be considered a history of how the Constitution has worked.

We have arranged the following pages on the Constitution to show that the Constitution was a *living* document. In the Convention in Philadelphia in the hot summer of 1787 the Framers had reasons for everything that they said. We can understand these reasons by our study of history. It was written by living people for their living needs. It would be changed slowly over the centuries to meet the needs of other living people, including ourselves.

In the beige sections (*The Text*) we print the Constitution as the Framers approved it on September 15 and signed it in Independence Hall in Philadelphia (a place we can still visit) on September 17, 1787. Their spelling, their punctuation, and their capitalizing of words may look a little odd to us. But we have left the document the way they wrote it, to remind us that it was written a long time ago. This, too, will remind us of the miracle of the survival of our Constitution as the frame of government of a great nation. None of the peculiarities will get in the way of our understanding.

In *Origins* we see some of the reasons that led men of the eighteenth century to write the words as they did. Here we have a glimpse of their arguments, disagreements, and compromises before they settled on the words we now read. All these are explained at greater length in the earlier pages of this book. The references to chapters and sections within chapters appear in brackets: [4:1] is Chapter 4, Section 1.

In *Afterlife* we see how the meaning of the document has changed to suit needs that the Framers never imagined. Some of their words were not clear, and the meanings of some words would change. These changes, too, are described in the earlier pages of this book.

The story of the Constitution itself is one of the most remarkable in all history. Like the life of a person, it is full of surprises—and disappointments. But the story as a whole must make Americans proud. We can still prosper under this Constitution written over two centuries ago.

One of the best features of the document was that it was so short. It is shorter than the Constitution of any of the states. The Framers wanted to provide for the future, but they did not try to second-guess the future. They believed in change—otherwise they would not have dared to start a new nation and write a new constitution. They respected the wisdom of the future. They left plenty of room for future Americans to make this Constitution serve their needs.

The Constitution survives because it is a living document. The Framers intended this Constitution to *live.* We help it live by understanding what they intended, why and how they wanted it to endure, why and how it has been changed, and how it can still be changed. And by seeing its wonderful simplicity and wisdom.

THE CONSTITUTION OF THE UNITED STATES

We the People of the United States, in Order to form a more perfect Union, establish Justice, insure domestic Tranquillity, provide for the common defence, promote the general Welfare, and secure the Blessings of Liberty to ourselves and our Posterity, do ordain and establish this Constitution for the United States of America.

ORIGINS

The Preamble. This is not merely an introduction, but one of the most important passages in the Constitution. It describes both the *basis* of government and the *purposes* of government. The Framers chose their words carefully.

A new basis. The weak Articles of Confederation of 1781 [5:3] had been formed by "Delegates of the States." To make "a more perfect Union," the Constitution of the new nation was now ordained and established by "the People of the United States." To make a fresh start, the voters of the whole country (strictly limited at that time to certain white male property owners) delegated certain powers to the new national government, others to the states.

The purposes. The "in Order to" items were a list of the worries of Americans at the time. They wanted to "establish Justice" (which the British government had denied the colonies). They wanted to "insure domestic Tranquillity" (which Shays's Rebellion in Massachusetts, August 1786–February 1787 [5:3], and other riots had threatened). They wanted better to "provide for the common defence" (the weak Continental Congress had almost lost the Revolution) [4:3]. They wanted to "promote the general Welfare" (till then threatened by inflation and rivalries between the states). They wanted to "secure the Blessings of Liberty" not only to themselves but to their "Posterity" (that's us!),

which required a firm and durable Constitution.

The Framers in the Federal Convention in Philadelphia in August–September 1787 worked over this language for the Preamble. The final form was given by Gouverneur Morris of Pennsylvania, who had signed the Articles of Confederation, had helped manage the troubled finances under the weak Articles, and had good reason to want a strong national government.

AFTERLIFE

The Preamble. While the Federalist Framers thought the meaning of this preamble was clear, it would not be so clear to all later generations. The Civil War would be fought partly over the precise meaning of the words. If the basis of government really was not "the People" of the whole United States but only the states—then what the states had made by coming together they could destroy by seceding. In 1819, Chief Justice John Marshall, drawing on the preamble, declared in *McCulloch* v. *Maryland* [8:2], "The government of the Union . . . is emphatically and truly a government of the people. In form and in substance it emanated from them, its powers are granted by them, and are to be exercised directly on them, and for their benefit." But in the years before the Civil War, John C. Calhoun and other Southern secessionists did not agree.

The Civil War settled that issue.

The Constitution does not define *who* "the People" are. Like much else in the document the meaning of this phrase has changed. At first, "the People" were only white male property own-ers. Then all white males were included. Later black males were added by the 15th Amendment [14:3], then women by the 19th Amendment [22:1], and all citizens 18 years old or older by the 26th Amendment [33:3].

ARTICLE I

Section 1. All legislative Powers herein granted shall be vested in a Congress of the United States, which shall consist of a Senate and House of Representatives.

Section 2. The House of Representatives shall be composed of Members chosen every second Year by the People of the several States, and the Electors in each State shall have the Qualifications requisite for Electors of the most numerous Branch of the State Legislature.

No Person shall be a Representative who shall not have attained to the age of twenty five Years, and been seven Years a Citizen of the United States, and who shall not, when elected, be an Inhabitant of that State in which he shall be chosen.

ORIGINS

The Powers of Government and the Separation of Powers. The plan of the Constitution was wonderfully simple. The Framers believed that there were three main tasks of government: making the laws, enforcing (or "executing") the laws, and interpreting the laws. They described these in the first three Articles. Article I ("All leg-islative Powers") described the Congress. Article II ("The executive Power") described the Presi-dent. Article III ("The judicial Power") described the Supreme Court and other courts.

The Revolution had been fought because Par-liament had tried to tyrannize over the colonies. Now the Framers wanted to make all branches of government efficient, but prevent tyranny by any one of them. Therefore they kept each of these powers separate. Each would check the others, and the people would not have to fear any one.

The Articles of Confederation had provided nothing but a "firm league of friendship" among the sovereign states. There was no exec-utive at all, and there was no national system of courts. Questions had to be decided by approval of at least nine of "the united states in Congress assembled" where each state had one vote.

Legislative Powers. In Article I, the Framers took a bold step to remedy these weaknesses. The new Congress would represent not just the states, but "the People of the several States." And the Framers showed their hope to make a truly representative government by devoting more than half of the entire Constitution to this first Article describing the Congress.

Creating *two* houses of Congress was a cru-cial compromise between the large states (led by Virginia), who wanted members of Congress apportioned entirely by population, and the small states who wanted every state to have a single equal vote (as under the Articles of Con-federation). There was already an example in England of a two-branched Parliament: a "lower" House of Commons, and an "upper" House of Lords. After much discussion and some bitterness, members of the Convention finally agreed to create a House of Representa-tives representing parts of the country accord-ing to their population, and a Senate where each state had an equal vote. Lawmaking powers were divided. The House of Representatives would have greater power over taxation and the ways of spending government money, for money bills had to begin there. The Senate would have greater control over foreign policy, for it had to approve treaties.

AFTERLIFE

Article I which set up the organization and structure of Congress has needed few changes over the years.

The freedom of each state to decide who can vote in federal elections has been limited by amendments to the Constitution. The Supreme Court has interpreted the 14th Amendment's "equal protection" clause as forbidding discriminatory practices by state election officials. The 15th and 19th amendments prohibited denying the franchise because of race, color, or sex. The 26th Amendment prohibited denying the franchise to persons 18 years old or older. The 24th Amendment outlawed the poll tax. It has needed further federal action to enforce the 15th Amendment [29:3, 32:1, and especially 33:1 on the Voting Rights Act of 1965].

Art. I
Sec. 2

Representatives and direct Taxes shall be apportioned among the several States which may be included within this Union, according to their respective Numbers, which shall be determined by adding to the whole Number of free Persons, including those bound to Service for a Term of Years, and excluding Indians not taxed, three fifths of all other Persons. The actual Enumeration shall be made within three Years after the first Meeting of the Congress of the United States, and within every subsequent Term of ten Years, in such Manner as they shall by Law direct. The Number of Representatives shall not exceed one for every thirty Thousand, but each State shall have at Least one Representative; and until such enumeration shall be made, the State of New Hampshire shall be entitled to chuse three, Massachusetts eight, Rhode-Island and Providence Plantations one, Connecticut five, New-York six, New Jersey four, Pennsylvania eight, Delaware one, Maryland six, Virginia ten, North Carolina five, South Carolina five, and Georgia three.

When vacancies happen in the Representation from any State, the Executive Authority thereof shall issue Writs of Election to fill such Vacancies.

The House of Representatives shall chuse their Speaker and other Officers; ● and shall have the sole Power of Impeachment.

ORIGINS

Another bold decision which we see here was to *list* the powers of the Congress (in section 8). These were called the "enumerated powers" of the federal government. The Articles of Confederation had provided no such list and this was one of the reasons for its weakness.

The large states (Virginia again in the lead) wanted Congress to have the power to veto laws passed by the states. But the smaller states were fearful. Instead the delegates to the Convention finally agreed on a list of subjects (in section 10) on which the states were forbidden to pass their own laws. These included foreign policy, currency, and tariffs on imports or exports.

AFTERLIFE

A census of the population has been taken every ten years since 1790. The Congress decides how many members of Congress there will be. Each state is then informed how many representatives it may have on the basis of the census. In *Wesberry* v. *Sanders* (1964) the Supreme Court ruled that congressional districts within a state had to be roughly equal in population [33:1]. Since taxes were also to be apportioned among the states according to the census, the 16th Amendment (ratified in 1913) was required to allow an income tax to be imposed. In 1912 the maximum size of the House was set at 435. According to the census of 1980, after providing for states entitled to only one representative, the ratio is one member for about every 500,000 persons.

● The House "impeaches" and the Senate (sec. 3, pars. 6-7) tries the impeachment [8:3, 14:3, 33:3].

Art. I

Section 3. The Senate of the United States shall be composed of two Senators ■ from each State, chosen by the Legislature thereof, for six Years; and each Senator shall have one Vote.

Immediately after they shall be assembled in Consequence of the first Election, they shall be divided as equally as may be into three Classes. The Seats of the Senators of the first Class shall be vacated at the Expiration of the second Year, of the second Class at the Expiration of the fourth Year, and of the third Class at the Expiration of the sixth Year, so that one third may be chosen every second Year; and if vacancies happen by Resignation, or otherwise, during the Recess of the Legislature of any State, the Executive thereof may make temporary Appointments until the next Meeting of the Legislature, which shall then fill such Vacancies.

No Person shall be a Senator who shall not have attained to the Age of thirty Years, and been nine Years a Citizen of the United States, and who shall not, when elected, be an Inhabitant of that State for which he shall be chosen.

The Vice President of the United States shall be President of the Senate, but shall have no Vote, unless they be equally divided.

The Senate shall chuse their other Officers, and also a President pro tempore, ▲ in the Absence of the Vice President, or when he shall exercise the Office of President of the United States.

The Senate shall have the sole Power to try all Impeachments. When sitting for that Purpose, they shall be on Oath or Affirmation. When the President of the United States is tried the Chief Justice shall preside: And no Person shall be convicted without the Concurrence of two thirds of the Members present.

Judgment in Cases of Impeachment shall not extend further than to removal from Office, and disqualification to hold and enjoy any Office of honor, Trust or Profit under the United States: but the Party convicted shall nevertheless be liable and subject to Indictment, Trial, Judgment and Punishment, according to Law.

AFTERLIFE

■ The 17th Amendment (1913) provided for the election of senators directly by the people instead of by state legislatures [20:2].

▲ The 25th Amendment now provides for filling the Vice-Presidency when the office becomes vacant. Gerald Ford was the first person to be selected by this procedure [33:3].

Art. I   **Section 4.** The Times, Places and Manner of holding Elections for Senators and Representatives, shall be prescribed in each State by the Legislature thereof; but the Congress may at any time by Law make or alter such Regulations, except as to the Places of chusing Senators.

The Congress shall assemble at least once in every Year, and such Meeting ■ shall be on the first Monday in December, unless they shall by Law appoint a different Day.

AFTERLIFE

Under federal law all the states now hold elections for Congress on the first Tuesday after the first Monday in November in even-numbered years.

■ The meeting time of Congress was changed in the 20th Amendment, section 2 [24:1].

Art. I   **Section 5.** Each House shall be the Judge of the Elections, Returns and Qualifications of its own Members, and a Majority of each shall constitute a Quorum to do Business; but a smaller Number may adjourn from day to day, and may be authorized to compel the Attendance of absent Members, in such Manner, and under such Penalties as each House may provide.

Each House may determine the Rules of its Proceedings, punish its Members for disorderly Behaviour, and, with the Concurrence of two thirds, expel a Member.

Each House shall keep a Journal of its Proceedings, and from time to time publish the same, excepting such Parts as may in their Judgment require Secrecy; and the Yeas and Nays of the Members of either House on any question shall, at the Desire of one fifth of those Present, be entered on the Journal.

Neither House, during the Session of Congress, shall, without the Consent of the other, adjourn for more than three days, nor to any other Place than that in which the two Houses shall be sitting.

AFTERLIFE

The right of each house to punish its own members has enabled them to discipline senators and representatives whose activities are judged to be improper. For example, under this clause Senator Joseph R. McCarthy was condemned in 1954, Representative Adam Clayton Powell was denied his seat in 1967 on the charge that he misused government funds, and Senator Herman Talmadge was "denounced" in 1979 for financial irregularities.

Art. I   **Section 6.** The Senators and Representatives shall receive a Compensation for their Services, to be ascertained by Law, and paid out of the Treasury of the United States. They shall in all Cases, except Treason, Felony and Breach of the

Peace, be privileged from Arrest during their attendance at the Session of their respective Houses, and in going to and returning from the same; and for any Speech or Debate in either House, they shall not be questioned in any other Place.

No Senator or Representative shall, during the Time for which he was elected, be appointed to any civil Office under the Authority of the United States, which shall have been created, or the Emoluments whereof shall have been encreased during such time; and no Person holding any Office under the United States, shall be a Member of either House during his Continuance in Office.

Section 7. All Bills for raising Revenue shall originate in the House of Representatives; but the Senate may propose or concur with amendments as on other Bills.

Every Bill which shall have passed the House of Representatives and the Senate, shall, before it become a Law, be presented to the President of the United States; If he approve he shall sign it, but if not he shall return it, with his Objections to that House in which it shall have originated, who shall enter the Objections at large on their Journal, and proceed to reconsider it. If after such Reconsideration two thirds of that House shall agree to pass the Bill, it shall be sent, together with the Objections, to the other House, by which it shall likewise be reconsidered, and if approved by two thirds of that House, it shall become a Law. But in all such Cases the Votes of both Houses shall be determined by yeas and Nays, and the Names of the Persons voting for and against the Bill shall be entered on the Journal of each House respectively. If any Bill shall not be returned by the President within ten Days (Sunday excepted) after it shall have been presented to him, the Same shall be a Law, in like Manner as if he had signed it, unless the Congress by their Adjournment prevent its Return, in which Case it shall not be a Law.

Every Order, Resolution, or Vote to which the Concurrence of the Senate and House of Representatives may be necessary (except on a question of Adjournment) shall be presented to the President of the United States; and before the Same shall take Effect, shall be approved by him, or being disapproved by him, shall be repassed by two thirds of the Senate and House of Representatives, according to the Rules and Limitations prescribed in the Case of a Bill.

AFTERLIFE

Although section 1 grants all legislative power to Congress, all bills must be submitted to the President. The President may then sign the bill and make it a law, or let it become a law without signing it. The President may also refuse to sign and return the bill with his reasons for doing so—that is, "veto" it. The bill can then become law only if each house passes it by a two-thirds majority. A bill sent to the President in the last ten days of a session of Congress does not become law if the President does not sign it. This is called a "pocket veto."

Andrew Jackson was the first president actively to use the veto power. He believed that the President had an equal right with the legislature and the courts to decide what was constitutional. He also thought that the President, as the only person elected by all the people, could veto measures passed by Congress if he disapproved of them even if they were clearly constitutional. Jackson vetoed more bills than all the

Presidents who served before him put together. Among the other active Presidents, such as Lincoln, Theodore Roosevelt, and Wilson, none used the veto power more vigorously than Franklin D. Roosevelt. He vetoed more than 600 bills during his twelve years in office. Congress was able to override his veto only nine times.

Art. I

Section 8. The Congress shall have Power To lay and collect Taxes, Duties, Imposts and Excises, to pay the Debts and provide for the common Defence and general Welfare of the United States; but all Duties, Imposts and Excises shall be uniform throughout the United States;

To borrow Money on the credit of the United States;

To regulate Commerce with foreign Nations, and among the several States, and with the Indian Tribes;

To establish an uniform Rule of Naturalization, and uniform Laws on the subject of Bankruptcies throughout the United States;

To coin Money, regulate the Value thereof, and of foreign Coin, and fix the Standard of Weights and Measures;

To provide for the Punishment of counterfeiting the Securities and current Coin of the United States;

To establish Post Offices and post Roads;

To promote the Progress of Science and useful Arts, by securing for limited Times to Authors and Inventors the exclusive Right to their respective Writings and Discoveries;

To constitute Tribunals inferior to the supreme Court;

To define and punish Piracies and Felonies committed on the high Seas, and Offences against the Law of Nations;

● To declare War, grant Letters of Marque and Reprisal, and make Rules concerning Captures on Land and Water;

ORIGINS

● On letters of marque, see [3:2], page 62.

AFTERLIFE

One of the most disputed of the enumerated powers has been the right of Congress "to regulate Commerce." Exactly what the Framers meant both by "regulate" and by "Commerce" was unclear. In the case of *Gibbons* v. *Ogden* (1824) the Supreme Court laid down rules about a state establishing a monopoly [8:2]. There Marshall also declared that Congress's power over commerce "may very well be restricted to that commerce which concerns more states than one"—that is, "interstate commerce." But Marshall also saw that commercial transactions taking place entirely within a state could influence commerce among the states. Since the late 1930s the Court has followed that line of reasoning to allow Congress a broad power to regulate commerce.

For example, the Court has interpreted the "Commerce" clause in such a way that it not only allows the regulation of railroads, pipelines, and other clearly interstate activities, but also permits minimum wage regulation and prohibitions on child labor. In the case of *NLRB* v. *Jones and Laughlin Corp.* (1937), the Court declared that the Wagner Act [25:4], dealing with the rights of labor to organize and to bargain collectively, was constitutional. Justice Benjamin Cardozo stated that the power to regulate commerce was "as broad as the need that evokes it."

Art. I
Sec. 8

To raise and support Armies, but no Appropriation of Money to that Use shall be for a longer Term than two Years;

To provide and maintain a Navy;

To make Rules for the Government and Regulation of the land and naval Forces;

To provide for calling forth the Militia to execute the Laws of the Union, suppress Insurrections and repel Invasions;

To provide for organizing, arming, and disciplining, the Militia, and for governing such Part of them as may be employed in the Service of the United States, reserving to the States respectively, the Appointment of the Officers, and the Authority of training the Militia according to the discipline prescribed by Congress;

To exercise exclusive Legislation in all Cases whatsoever, over such District (not exceeding ten Miles square) as may, by Cession of Particular States, and the Acceptance of Congress, become the Seat of the Government of the United States, and to exercise like Authority over all Places purchased by the Consent of the Legislature of the State in which the Same shall be, for the Erection of Forts, Magazines, Arsenals, dock-Yards, and other needful Buildings;—And

To make all Laws which shall be necessary and proper for carrying into Execu- ■ tion the foregoing Powers, and all other Powers vested by this Constitution in the Government of the United States, or in any Department or Officer thereof.

AFTERLIFE

■ The meaning of this "necessary and proper" clause (or "elastic clause") was the dividing line between broad and strict constructionists. The first dispute occurred over Alexander Hamilton's proposal for a national bank [6:2]. The Supreme Court under John Marshall in *McCul-*loch v. *Maryland* (1819) agreed with the broad constructionists [8:2]. Since the government was granted wide powers "on the due exercise of which the happiness and prosperity of the nation so vitally depends," Marshall ruled, it "must also be entrusted with ample means for their execution."

Art. I

▲ **Section 9.** The Migration or Importation of such Persons as any of the States now existing shall think proper to admit, shall not be prohibited by the Congress prior to the Year one thousand eight hundred and eight, but a Tax or duty may be imposed on such Importation, not exceeding ten dollars for each Person.

ORIGINS

Absolute prohibitions on Congress.
▲ This clause was inserted to prevent Congress from outlawing the foreign slave trade before 1808.

AFTERLIFE

In 1808 Congress did outlaw the foreign slave trade.

Art. I	The Privilege of the Writ of Habeas Corpus shall not be suspended, unless when
Sec. 9	in Cases of Rebellion or Invasion the public Safety may require it.
	■ No Bill of Attainder or ex post facto Law shall be passed.

ORIGINS

On *habeas corpus*, see [13:1], see page 340.

■ A *bill of attainder* is a legislative act pronouncing an individual guilty of a crime, usually treason, without a trial. It had been used by kings and queens to get rid of personal or political enemies.

An *ex post facto* law is a law passed after the fact, and was a way of punishing people whom the ruling powers disliked, even though they had not violated any existing law.

AFTERLIFE

During the Civil War, Abraham Lincoln suspended the writ of habeas corpus in certain areas [13:1]. When he suspended it in Maryland, Chief Justice Taney ruled in the *Merryman* case (1861) that only Congress had the right to suspend the writ of habeas corpus. Lincoln did not agree and continued to follow his own interpretation of the Constitution.

| Art. I | No Capitation, or other direct, Tax shall be laid, unless in Proportion to the |
| Sec. 9 | Census of Enumeration herein before directed to be taken. |

AFTERLIFE

In *Pollock* v. *Farmers' Loan and Trust Co.* (1895), the Supreme Court ruled that a federal income tax was unconstitutional because it was a direct tax, but not laid in proportion to the census [18:5]. An income tax was made legal by the 16th Amendment (1913).

Art. I	No Tax or Duty shall be laid on Articles exported from any State.
Sec. 9	No Preference shall be given by any Regulation of Commerce or Revenue to the Ports of one State over those of another; nor shall Vessels bound to, or from, one State, be obliged to enter, clear or pay Duties in another.
	No Money shall be drawn from the Treasury, but in Consequence of Appropriations made by Law; and a regular Statement and Account of the Receipts and Expenditures of all public Money shall be published from time to time.
	No Title of Nobility shall be granted by the United States: And no Person holding any Office of Profit or Trust under them, shall, without the Consent of the Congress, accept of any present, Emolument, Office, or Title, of any kind whatever, from any King, Prince or foreign State.
Art. I	**Section 10.** No State shall enter into any Treaty, Alliance, or Confederation; grant Letters of Marque and Reprisal; coin Money; emit Bills of Credit; make any

Thing but gold and silver Coin a Tender in Payment of Debts; pass any Bill of Attainder, ex post facto Law, or Law impairing the Obligation of Contracts, or grant any Title of Nobility.

No State shall, without the Consent of the Congress, lay any Imposts or Duties on Imports or Exports, except what may be absolutely necessary for executing it's inspection Laws: and the net Produce of all Duties and Imposts, laid by any State on Imports or Exports, shall be for the Use of the Treasury of the United States; and all such Laws shall be subject to the Revision and Controul of the Congress.

No State shall, without the Consent of Congress, lay any Duty of Tonnage, keep Troops, or Ships of War in time of Peace, enter into any Agreement or Compact with another State, or with a foreign Power, or engage in War, unless actually invaded, or in such imminent Danger as will not admit of delay.

ARTICLE II

● **Section 1.** The executive Power shall be vested in a President of the United States of America. He shall hold his Office during the term of four Years, and, together with the Vice President, chosen for the same Term, be elected, as follows

ORIGINS

● *"The executive Power."* The Presidency was one of the boldest inventions of the Framers. By creating a strong President, they showed their faith in representative government. They believed that a strong Congress and a strong judiciary would protect the people from any President's misuse of powers. During the Constitutional Convention there was much heated discussion of the problem of the executive. Some, like Roger Sherman of Connecticut, feared a strong President. They wanted him to be nothing but a kind of superpoliceman, who would see that the laws of Congress were enforced. But Gouverneur Morris wanted a President who would be "the guardian of the people, even of the lower classes, against Legislative tyranny," and many others agreed with him. His views finally prevailed.

During the Convention, the draft of this article was revised again and again. Some members, afraid that a single President might become a despot, argued for a three-man executive, one from each part of the country. Some wanted the President to be chosen by the Congress to be sure that he would enforce the will of Congress. The first draft they agreed on provided for a single executive, but had him chosen by the Congress. He was to be elected for a single term of seven years and could not be reelected.

Gradually in the Convention the movement for a strong, independent President made headway. The ingenious device of an electoral college allowed him to be elected, indirectly, by "the People." Then the Convention agreed that the President should be elected for four years with no limit on the number of his terms. More and more powers were given to him, including the power to make treaties (with the advice and consent of the Senate). He was given the power to veto acts of Congress. But his veto could be overridden by a two-thirds vote of both houses. And there was insurance against a despot, for the President could be removed from office "on Impeachment for, and Conviction of, Treason, Bribery, or other high Crimes and Misdemeanors."

The Framers were influenced not only by the fearful example of British tyranny over the colonies, but also luckily by the inspiring example of the heroic leader of the Revolution. "Many of the members cast their eyes toward General Washington as President," Pierce Butler of South Carolina who was at the Convention noted, "and shaped their ideas of the Powers to be given a President, by their opinions of his Virtue."

AFTERLIFE

While the President was given many powers in the Constitution, Article II does not say how the President is to use those powers. Whether the office is weak or strong depends on how the President interprets the Constitution and uses the powers it gives.

The powers of the office have grown, especially under such Presidents as Jackson, Lincoln, Theodore Roosevelt, Wilson, and Franklin D. Roosevelt. As Jefferson's purchase of Louisiana showed, even a President who considered himself a strict constructionist could act in such a way as to enlarge greatly the powers of the office [7:2].

Art. II
Sec. 1

Each State shall appoint, in such Manner as the Legislature thereof may direct, a number of Electors, equal to the whole Number of Senators and Representatives to which the State may be entitled in the Congress: but no Senator or Representative, or Person holding an Office of Trust or Profit under the United States, shall be appointed an Elector.

The Electors shall meet in their respective States, and vote by Ballot for two Persons, of whom one at least shall not be an Inhabitant of the same State with themselves. And they shall make a List of all the Persons voted for, and of the Number of Votes for each; which List they shall sign and certify, and transmit sealed to the Seat of the Government of the United States, directed to the President of the Senate. The President of the Senate shall, in the Presence of the Senate and House of Representatives, open all the Certificates, and the Votes shall then be counted. The Person having the greatest Number of Votes shall be the President, if such Number be a Majority of the whole Number of Electors appointed; and if there be more than one who have such Majority, and have an ▲ equal Number of Votes, then the House of Representatives shall immediately chuse by Ballot one of them for President; and if no Person have a Majority, then from the five highest on the List the said House shall in like Manner chuse the President. But in chusing the President, the Votes shall be taken by States, the Representation from each State having one Vote; a quorum for this Purpose shall consist of a Member or Members from two thirds of the States, and a Majority of all the States shall be necessary to a Choice. In every Case, after the Choice of the President, the Person having the greatest Number of Votes of the Electors shall be the Vice President. But if there should remain two or more who have equal Votes, the Senate shall chuse from them by Ballot the Vice President.

The Congress may determine the Time of chusing the Electors, and the Day on which they shall give their Votes; which Day shall be the same throughout the United States.

AFTERLIFE

▲ The election of 1800 in which Jefferson and Burr each received the same number of electoral votes brought about the replacement of paragraph 3 by the 12th Amendment in 1804 [6:4]. In 1824 the election was thrown into the

House, where John Quincy Adams was chosen over Andrew Jackson [9:1]. Then in 1876, when Hayes defeated Tilden, the question of who was to count the electoral votes became a problem [14:4]. Again and again there have been movements for a constitutional amendment to abolish the electoral college and provide that the President and Vice-President be chosen by a majority of votes cast by citizens throughout the nation. But these movements have been resisted by the smaller and less populous states and others. The "electoral college" survives. The "Electors" meet in their respective state capitals and cast their ballots. The results are sent to Washington and counted in a session of the Congress.

Art. II
Sec. 1

No Person except a natural born Citizen, or a Citizen of the United States, at the time of the Adoption of this Constitution, shall be eligible to the Office of President; neither shall any person be eligible to that Office who shall not have attained to the Age of thirty five Years, and been fourteen Years a Resident within the United States.

In Case of the Removal of the President from Office, or of his Death, Resignation, or Inability to discharge the Powers and Duties of the said Office, the Same shall devolve on the Vice President, and the Congress may by Law provide for the Case of Removal, Death, Resignation or Inability, both of the President and Vice President, declaring what Officer shall then act as President, and such Officer shall act accordingly, until the Disability be removed, or a President shall be elected.

AFTERLIFE

In 1886 Congress enacted a law making the succession pass from the Vice-President to the members of the Cabinet in the order in which their offices were established. In 1947 this was changed. The purpose was to make it more likely that the President would be a person who had held some elective office. The succession now goes to the Speaker of the House, then to the President Pro Tempore of the Senate, and finally to the Cabinet officers. The 25th Amendment, however, makes it highly unlikely that succession will ever go beyond the Vice-President. Section 2 of that amendment provides that whenever a vacancy in the office of the Vice-President exists, the President shall nominate a Vice-President who shall take office with the approval of a majority of the members of Congress.

Art. II
Sec. 1

The President shall, at stated Times, receive for his Services, a Compensation, which shall neither be encreased nor diminished during the Period for which he shall have been elected, and he shall not receive within that Period any other Emolument from the United States, or any of them.

Before he enter on the Execution of his Office, he shall take the following Oath or Affirmation:—"I do solemnly swear (or affirm) that I will faithfully execute the Office of President of the United States, and will to the best of my Ability, preserve, protect and defend the Constitution of the United States."

Art. II   **Section 2.** The President shall be Commander in Chief of the Army and Navy of the United States, and of the Militia of the several States, when called into the actual Service of the United States; he may require the Opinion, in writing, of the principal Officer in each of the executive Departments, upon any Subject relating to the Duties of their respective Offices, and he shall have Power to grant Reprieves and Pardons for Offences against the United States, except in Cases of Impeachment.

AFTERLIFE

This provision insures that the military is clearly under civilian control. During the Civil War President Lincoln [13:1], who greatly enlarged the powers of the Presidency in other ways, played a major role in military affairs. In 1950 President Truman used his powers as Commander in Chief to commit troops to Korea and to remove General MacArthur from command [28:3]. Despite criticism from those who believed this provision did not give the President so much power, Eisenhower, Kennedy, Johnson, and Nixon used it to justify a variety of military moves [32:4].

Art. II
Sec. 2   He shall have Power, by and with the Advice and Consent of the Senate, to make Treaties, provided two thirds of the Senators present concur; and he shall nominate, and by and with the Advice and Consent of the Senate, shall appoint Ambassadors, other public Ministers and Consuls, Judges of the supreme Court, and all other Officers of the United States, whose Appointments are not herein otherwise provided for, and which shall be established by Law: but the Congress may by Law vest the Appointment of such inferior Officers, as they think proper, in the President alone, in the Courts of Law, or in the Heads of Departments.

     The President shall have Power to fill up all Vacancies that may happen during the Recess of the Senate, by granting Commissions which shall expire at the End of their next Session.

Art. II   **Section 3.** He shall from time to time give to the Congress Information of the State of the Union, and recommend to their Consideration such Measures as he shall judge necessary and expedient; he may, on extraordinary Occasions, convene both Houses, or either of them, and in Case of Disagreement between them, with Respect to the Time of Adjournment, he may adjourn them to such Time as he shall think proper; he shall receive Ambassadors and other public Ministers; he shall take Care that the Laws be faithfully executed, and shall Commission all the Officers of the United States.

Art. II   **Section 4.** The President, Vice President and all Civil Officers of the United States, shall be removed from Office on Impeachment for, and Conviction of, Treason, Bribery, or other high Crimes and Misdemeanors.

On the impeachment and trial of Andrew Johnson, and the recommendation that Richard Nixon should be impeached, see [14:3], pages 370–371, and [33:3], page 837.

For additional material on the Presidency, see also Amendments 20, 22, and 25.

ARTICLE III

Section 1. The judicial Power of the United States, shall be vested in one supreme Court, and in such inferior Courts as the Congress may from time to time ordain and establish. The Judges, both of the supreme and inferior Courts, shall hold their Offices during good Behaviour, and shall, at stated Times, receive for their Services, a Compensation, which shall not be diminished during their Continuance in Office.

ORIGINS

● *"The judicial Power."* The Articles of Confederation had provided no system of national courts. The Congress of the Confederation could only appoint special courts to settle disputes between states, and certain cases arising out of naval warfare during the Revolution. Under the Confederation a citizen was judged only by the courts of his state. But, of course, under the Confederation, there was no national system of laws to be interpreted.

Delegates to the Constitutional Convention agreed quickly and unanimously (on June 4, 1787) that a strong new nation, with a Congress empowered to pass many laws, required "that a national Judiciary be established." At first the New Jersey Plan, speaking for the small states, proposed only a "supreme Tribunal" with final powers over state courts and dealing only with federal matters. The compromise in Article III, proposed by James Madison of Virginia and James Wilson of Pennsylvania, created a Supreme Court for the nation, but left the question of lower courts to the future Congress. The belief that there had to be a national system of courts for a strong nation was confirmed when the first Congress met. By the Judiciary Act of 1789, they created a system of lower federal courts. Members of the Convention agreed (see Article VI) that there could not

be a nation without some national system of courts, uniformly interpreting "the supreme Law of the Land" for every citizen.

The last three paragraphs of Article III aimed to protect citizens against the kind of despotic laws or interpretations of the law they had known before the Revolution. The Convention therefore guaranteed trial by jury in criminal cases.

In England over the centuries, tyrants had defined "treason" in any way that suited their purposes. The Framers gave "treason" a narrow and precise definition to protect innocent citizens against their unscrupulous enemies in power. This would encourage citizens to criticize their government without fear of being prosecuted as traitors. Citizens were protected too against "bills of attainder"—the name for laws that had sometimes been passed in England to convict people of crimes of which they had been acquitted or for which they had not been tried. Many supporters of the Constitution believed these safeguards were not enough. Their demands resulted in the "Bill of Rights," the first ten amendments.

The belief of the Framers that "a national Judiciary" was crucial to a new nation was soon to be justified. The Chief Justices of the Supreme Court, beginning with the first, John Jay, would prove effective champions of a national government of uniform laws.

AFTERLIFE

The Judiciary Act of 1789 [6:2] provided for the establishment of "inferior courts." There are now district courts, circuit courts of appeals, and various other federal courts.

The Jeffersonian attempt to change the membership of the courts by impeachment [7:3] was defeated as was the attempt by Franklin D. Roosevelt to change the Court by "packing" it with additional members [24:3].

The creation of national courts to enforce federal laws directly on citizens played an important part in establishing the power of the central government.

Art. III   **Section 2.** The judicial Power shall extend to all Cases, in Law and Equity, arising under this Constitution, the Laws of the United States, and Treaties made, or which shall be made, under their Authority;—to all Cases affecting Ambassadors, other public Ministers and Consuls;—to all Cases of admiralty and maritime Jurisdiction;—to Controversies to which the United States shall be a Party;—to Controversies between two or more States;—between a State and Citizens of another State;—between Citizens of different States;—between Citizens of the same State claiming Lands under Grants of different States, and between a State, or the Citizens thereof, and foreign States, Citizens or Subjects.

In all Cases affecting Ambassadors, other public Ministers and Consuls, and those in which a State shall be Party, the supreme Court shall have original Jurisdiction. In all the other Cases before mentioned, the supreme Court shall have appellate Jurisdiction, both as to Law and Fact, with such Exceptions, and under such Regulations as the Congress shall make.

The Trial of all Crimes, except in Cases of Impeachment, shall be by Jury; and such Trial shall be held in the State where the said Crimes shall have been committed; but when not committed within any State, the Trial shall be at such Place or Places as the Congress may by Law have directed.

AFTERLIFE

The Supreme Court, in *Chisholm v. Georgia* (1793) ruled that a private citizen could bring a lawsuit against a state in a federal court. The 11th Amendment was adopted (1798) to make this impossible in the future.

The rights of individuals charged with crimes were further protected in the Bill of Rights (Amendments 4, 5, 6, 7, & 8) and later Supreme Court decisions [31:1].

Art. III   **Section 3.** Treason against the United States, shall consist only in levying War against them, or in adhering to their Enemies, giving them Aid and Comfort. No Person shall be convicted of Treason unless on the Testimony of two Witnesses to the same overt Act, or on Confession in open Court.

The Congress shall have Power to declare the Punishment of Treason, but no Attainder of Treason shall work Corruption of Blood, or Forfeiture except during the Life of the Person attainted.

AFTERLIFE

For the precedent-setting trial of Aaron Burr on
the charge of treason, see [7:2], page 189.

ARTICLE IV

Section 1. Full Faith and Credit shall be given in each State to the public Acts, ●
Records, and judicial Proceedings of every other State. And the Congress may by
general Laws prescribe the Manner in which such Acts, Records and Proceedings shall be proved, and the Effect thereof.

Section 2. The Citizens of each State shall be entitled to all Privileges and Immunities of Citizens in the several States.

A Person charged in any State with Treason, Felony, or other Crime, who shall
flee from Justice, and be found in another State, shall on Demand of the executive Authority of the State from which he fled, be delivered up, to be removed to
the State having Jurisdiction of the Crime.

No Person held to Service or Labour in one State, under the Laws thereof, ★
escaping into another, shall, in Consequence of any Law or Regulation therein,
be discharged from such Service or Labour, but shall be delivered up on Claim
of the Party to whom such Service or Labour may be due.

Section 3. New States may be admitted by the Congress into this Union; but no ■
new State shall be formed or erected within the Jurisdiction of any other State;
nor any State be formed by the Junction of two or more States, or Parts of
States, without the Consent of the Legislatures of the States concerned as well
as of the Congress.

The Congress shall have Power to dispose of and make all needful Rules and
Regulations respecting the Territory or other Property belonging to the United ▲
States; and nothing in this Constitution shall be so construed as to Prejudice
any Claims of the United States, or of any particular State.

Section 4. The United States shall guarantee to every State in this Union a ○
Republican Form of Government, and shall protect each of them against Invasion; and on Application of the Legislature, or of the Executive (when the Legislature cannot be convened) against domestic Violence.

ORIGINS

Having described the three branches of the new
government—the Congress (legislative), the
Presidency (executive), and the courts (judiciary)—and the relations among these
branches, the Framers had still more to do.
What about the relations between the states?
What about criminals who fled from one state to
another? What about new states? Could they be
carved out of the existing states? How could
new states be admitted to the Union? What was
the central government required to do to preserve representative government in the states?
Did the national government have a duty to prevent invasion into the states?

Article IV aimed to answer these questions. If
the nation was to expand, and yet avoid becoming an empire with colonies, there had to be
some way to add new states. The Articles of

Confederation had made it difficult to add a new state, by requiring that nine of the original states had to agree. Now the Framers wisely provided that new states could be admitted to the Union by the vote of Congress. Some delegates feared what might happen if new states were added endlessly toward the west. Wouldn't the original Atlantic states be overwhelmed? One delegate, Elbridge Gerry of Massachusetts, actually proposed a clause providing that the total number of representatives in the House of Representatives from new states should never be allowed to be greater than the number from the original states. Wiser heads saw that this would produce a nation with second-class citizens. No such clause was adopted. Instead, the Framers decided to allow future Congresses to make the rules.

Delegates saw that Maine and Vermont and the western territories of Georgia, of North Carolina, and of Virginia were being made into states. They feared that some other states might be carved up in the future. These delegates were reassured by the provision that no state could be divided into two, nor joined to another, without the consent of its own legislature.

AFTERLIFE

● Without this clause, the United States would have been merely a league of states. This clause, together with the "supremacy" clause in Article VI, helped weld the nation together, but it also proved to be a basis for many of the legal disputes over "states' rights" before the Civil War.

★ This clause was the basis for the Fugitive Slave Laws [12:1]. The provision became ineffective with the adoption of the 13th Amendment [13:5].

■ This section allowed the United States to grow and to become more than a continental nation [5:3].

▲ It was this clause that allowed Congress to deal with the question of slavery in the territories [8:3, 12:1, 12:2].

○ This section was used in the nineteenth century to deal with labor violence [18:1, 18:3].

ARTICLE V

The Congress, whenever two thirds of both Houses shall deem it necessary, shall propose Amendments to this Constitution, or, on the Application of the Legislatures of two thirds of the several States, shall call a Convention for proposing Amendments, which, in either Case, shall be valid to all Intents and Purposes, as Part of this Constitution, when ratified by the Legislatures of three fourths of the several States, or by Conventions in three fourths thereof, as the one or the other Mode of Ratification may be proposed by the Congress; Provided that no Amendment which may be made prior to the Year One thousand eight hundred and eight shall in any Manner affect the first and fourth Clauses in the Ninth Section of the first Article; and that no State, without its Consent, shall be deprived of its equal Suffrage in the Senate.

ORIGINS

Amendments. What would have happened if the Framers had not provided some way to amend the Constitution? Later generations might have been tempted to abandon the Constitution, and start all over again. Some delegates, like Charles Pinckney of South Carolina, thought their work was nearly perfect. They could imagine only that later generations would try to "undo" their good work. They opposed any scheme for amendments.

But most delegates saw that the Constitution was more likely to survive if it included some way of amendment to suit changing needs. Yet they believed it should not be too easy to amend the Constitution. Otherwise, future generations would not respect the Constitution nor exert the effort needed to make it work. People then might be tempted to treat the Constitution like an ordinary law, easily changed by vote of Congress. Instead, the Framers hoped they were shaping a true "constitution"—the enduring foundation for preserving, making, and changing laws. They dared not leave it only to Congress to decide when an amendment was needed, or to block an amendment. So they provided that (even if two-thirds of Congress did not *propose* an amendment) two-thirds of the states could bring about the calling of a national convention to *propose* amendments. An amendment could then be *adopted* either by three-fourths of the state legislatures or by three-fourths of the state conventions called for that purpose.

To secure majority agreement to this amending clause, still other Compromises were required. One (to reassure the slave states) provided that no amendment affecting the slave trade could be made before 1808. Another (to reassure the small states) provided that without its own consent no state could be deprived of its equal representation in the Senate.

AFTERLIFE

The Constitution has been amended 26 times, but so far there has never been a national convention to suggest amendments. And only in the case of the 21st Amendment has ratification been done by state conventions.

The Constitution has also been changed by interpretations made by the Supreme Court. The Court has been called "a continuing constitutional convention." Its decisions on the commerce clause (above, page 626) have allowed the federal government far-reaching regulatory powers. Its decision in *Brown* v. *Board of Education* (1954) outlawed racial segregation in the classroom [29:3]. In other civil rights cases the Court has given the federal government increasing powers to enforce the equality of rights of all citizens. In *Gideon* v. *Wainwright* (1963) and other cases the Court has enlarged federal protection of the rights of the criminally accused—to have a lawyer, to be informed of their rights, and to be free from "cruel and unusual punishment."

ARTICLE VI

All Debts contracted and Engagements entered into, before the Adoption of this Constitution, shall be as valid against the United States under this Constitution, as under the Confederation.

This Constitution, and the Laws of the United States which shall be made in ● Pursuance thereof; and all Treaties made, or which shall be made, under the Authority of the United States, shall be the supreme Law of the Land; and the Judges in every State shall be bound thereby, any Thing in the Constitution or Laws of any State to the Contrary notwithstanding.

The Senators and Representatives before mentioned, and the Members of the several State Legislatures, and all executive and judicial Officers, both of the United States and of the several States, shall be bound by Oath or affirmation, to support this Constitution; but no religious Test shall ever be required as a Qualification to any Office or public Trust under the United States.

ORIGINS

The Supremacy Clause. Under the Articles of Confederation, the decisions of the Congress of the Confederation were supposed to have the force of "law." But they really had no force at all.

Since there was no federal system of courts, all decisions were left to the state courts. And when a rule of the Confederation Congress conflicted with a state law, the state courts ignored the Confederation's rule and simply enforced their own state law. Now this was changed. Under the Constitution, there would be a national court system. But suppose there was a conflict between a state law and a law passed by the new Congress. Which law should prevail? And who decided?

This was one of the most difficult problems facing the delegates to the Constitutional Convention. Some, including James Madison, wanted a scheme which would give the Congress power to veto conflicting state laws. Naturally the small states objected.

Luckily the proposed New Jersey Plan, speaking for the small states, contained a "supremacy clause" which saved the day. This clause declared that the Constitution, the acts of Congress, and treaties should be the supreme law of all the states. They would be state law just as much as if they had been adopted separately by the state legislatures. When this clause was proposed to the Convention, everybody agreed to it. Then (as we see in Article VI) the Constitution of the United States, the laws of the new federal Congress, and treaties made by the United States would be "the supreme Law of the Land." In the future the Constitution and the laws of the new nation would be enforced, not only by a system of national courts (still to be created), but by the systems of state courts that had been at work since early colonial days. "And the Judges in every State shall be bound thereby, any Thing in the Constitution or Laws of any State to the Contrary notwithstanding."

The Virginia delegation proposed still another way (described here in Article VI) to enforce nationwide respect for the Constitution and laws of the new nation. Simply require all members of state legislatures and all executive and judicial officers of all the *states* (in addition to all officers of the United States) to take an oath or affirmation "to support this Constitution." Then all state officials would be solemnly reminded (under penalty of the criminal laws of perjury) that it was their duty to keep the laws of the new nation supreme! Incidentally the wise Framers took this occasion to make it plain that no official had to believe in God or in any particular religion to make his oath or affirmation binding. They forever banned any "religious Test" for "any Office or public Trust under the United States."

AFTERLIFE

On the repayment of the debt of the Confederation, see [6:2].

● This clause became the basis for the American constitutional system. But the question of who was to decide the powers of the federal government was hotly debated (see [6:4], page 168, Virginia and Kentucky Resolutions; [7:3], page 191, *Marbury* v. *Madison*; [8:2], page 213, *Martin* v. *Hunter's Lessee* and *Cohens* v. *Virginia*; and [9:3], pages 232–233, Calhoun's "Exposition and Protest," nullification, and the Webster-Hayne debate). The Civil War was the final major battle over the question of the supremacy of the federal government.

ARTICLE VII

The Ratification of the Conventions of nine States, shall be sufficient for the Establishment of this Constitution between the States so ratifying the Same.

Done in Convention by the Unanimous Consent of the States present the Seventeenth Day of September in the Year of our Lord one thousand seven hundred and Eighty seven and of the Independence of the United States of America the Twelfth In witness whereof We have hereunto subscribed our Names,

Go. Washington—*Presid! and deputy from Virginia*

NEW HAMPSHIRE	DELAWARE
John Langdon	Geo: Read
Nicholas Gilman	Gunning Bedford jun
MASSACHUSETTS	John Dickinson
Nathaniel Gorham	Richard Bassett
Rufus King	Jaco: Broom
CONNECTICUT	MARYLAND
Wm. Saml. Johnson	James McHenry
Roger Sherman	Dan of St Thos. Jenifer
NEW YORK	Danl. Carroll
Alexander Hamilton	VIRGINIA
NEW JERSEY	John Blair—
Wil: Livingston	James Madison Jr.
David Brearley.	NORTH CAROLINA
Wm. Paterson.	Wm. Blount
Jona: Dayton	Richd. Dobbs Spraight
PENNSYLVANIA	Hu Williamson
B Franklin	SOUTH CAROLINA
Thomas Mifflin	J. Rutledge
Robt Morris	Charles Cotesworth Pinckney
Geo. Clymer	Charles Pinckney
Thos. FitzSimons	Pierce Butler
Jared Ingersoll	GEORGIA
James Wilson	William Few
Gouv Morris	Abr Baldwin

Note: This text of the Constitution of the United States is taken from the "literal print" of the document as reproduced in *The Constitution of the United States: Analysis and Interpretation* (Washington, D.C.: U.S. Government Printing Office, 1964). The original manuscript can be seen in the National Archives, Washington, D.C.

ORIGINS

Ratification. Down to the very last words of the Constitution, the delegates to the Convention showed their boldness and their willingness to learn from the unhappy recent experience of the Articles of Confederation. The Constitutional Convention had been called merely to revise the Articles of Confederation. Under the Articles, no such revision could be made except by unanimous approval of all the state legislatures. Some legalistic delegates believed that the only proper procedure was to send the painfully drawn draft of the new Constitution to the Congress of the Confederation. They could then "recommend" that it be submitted to a convention in each of the states. But how long would be required for this cumbersome procedure?

At the very last minute, just as they were about to adjourn, the delegates took a bolder course. They would submit their work directly and at once to state conventions especially called for the purpose. Then as soon as any *nine* states had adopted the new Constitution it would go into force between them. A few laggards would not be allowed to sabotage the work. The remaining hold-out states would see themselves left in the cold. This final article, like the Preamble with which the Constitution began, showed that the new government owed its powers not to any older document, but directly to "the People of the United States."

For the battle over ratifications, see [5:5].

In Convention Monday, September 17th 1787.

Present The States of New Hampshire, Massachusetts, Connecticut, Mr. Hamilton from New York, New Jersey, Pennsylvania, Delaware, Maryland, Virginia, North Carolina, South Carolina and Georgia.

Resolved,

That the preceeding Constitution be laid before the United States in Congress assembled, and that it is the Opinion of this Convention, that it should afterwards be submitted to a Convention of Delegates, chosen in each State by the People thereof, under the Recommendation of its Legislature, for their Assent and Ratification; and that each Convention assenting to, and ratifying the Same, should give Notice thereof to the United States in Congress assembled. Resolved, That it is the Opinion of this Convention, that as soon as the Conventions of nine States shall have ratified this Constitution, the United States in Congress assembled should fix a Day on which Electors should be appointed by the States which shall have ratified the same, and a Day on which the Electors should assemble to vote for the President, and the Time and Place for commencing Proceedings under this Constitution. That after such Publication the Electors should be appointed, and the Senators and Representatives elected: That the Electors should meet on the Day fixed for the Election of the President, and should transmit their Votes certified, signed, sealed and directed, as the Constitution requires, to the Secretary of the United States in Congress assembled, that the Senators and Representatives should convene at the Time and Place assigned; that the Senators should appoint a President of the Senate, for the sole Purpose of receiving, opening and counting the Votes for President; and, that after he shall be chosen, the Congress, together with the President, should, without Delay, proceed to execute this Constitution.

By the Unanimous Order of the Convention

W. Jackson *Secretary.*   Go. Washington—*Presid.*[t]

AMENDMENT [I.]

Congress shall make no law respecting an establishment of religion, or prohibiting the free exercise thereof; or abridging the freedom of speech, or of the press; or the right of the people peaceably to assemble, and to petition the Government for a redress of grievances.

ORIGINS

The objections to the Constitution raised during the fight over ratification became the first ten amendments, or Bill of Rights [5:5, 6:2]. They limit the powers of the federal government and were born from English and colonial experience with despotic government. Submitted to the states in 1789, ratified in 1791.

The 1st Amendment was intended to insure freedom of religion, speech, press, assembly, and petition in the nation as a whole.

AFTERLIFE

The courts have always had difficulty deciding what limits can be placed on freedom of speech and the press. They have often used a formula first stated by the Supreme Court in *Schenck* v. *United States* (1919). In that case the Court concluded that when there was "a clear and present danger" that words will bring about "substantive evils," speech could be limited. But it is difficult to tell what is a "clear and present danger." And even this doctrine has not been uniformly applied, and speech and the press have sometimes been allowed to be limited for other reasons.

For the Court's application of the provision against the establishment of religion on the question of prayer and Bible reading in schools, see [33:1], page 819.

AMENDMENT [II.]

A well regulated Militia, being necessary to the security of a free State, the right of the people to keep and bear Arms, shall not be infringed.

AMENDMENT [III.]

No Soldier shall, in time of peace be quartered in any house, without the consent of the Owner, nor in time of war, but in a manner to be prescribed by law.

AMENDMENT [IV.]

The right of the people to be secure in their persons, houses, papers, and effects, against unreasonable searches and seizures, shall not be violated, and no Warrants shall issue, but upon probable cause, supported by Oath or affirmation, and particularly describing the place to be searched, and the persons or things to be seized.

ORIGINS

The right to keep and bear arms was insured by the 2nd Amendment.

After the experience with the British before the Revolution [4:1], the 3rd Amendment restricted the government's right to quarter soldiers in private homes.

To prevent searches and arrests without reason by a tyrannical government the 4th Amendment was ratified.

AMENDMENT [V.]

No person shall be held to answer for a capital, or otherwise infamous crime, unless on a presentment or indictment of a Grand Jury, except in cases arising in the land or naval forces, or in the Militia, when in actual service in time of War or public danger; nor shall any person be subject for the same offence to be twice put in jeopardy of life or limb; nor shall be compelled in any criminal case

> to be a witness against himself, nor be deprived of life, liberty, or property, without due process of law; nor shall private property be taken for public use, without just compensation.

ORIGINS

The 5th Amendment was intended to give broad protection to accused persons and to protect the owners of private property from having it taken by the government without the payment of a fair price.

AFTERLIFE

The 5th Amendment is a basic bulwark protecting the rights of individuals in criminal cases. Its provision that no person "shall be compelled in any criminal case to be a witness against himself" has often been used by individuals who do not wish to testify in court or before congressional investigating committees. This is often referred to as "taking the Fifth Amendment." See also the 14th Amendment below.

AMENDMENT [VI.]

In all criminal prosecutions, the accused shall enjoy the right to a speedy and public trial, by an impartial jury of the State and district wherein the crime shall have been committed, which district shall have been previously ascertained by law, and to be informed of the nature and cause of the accusation; to be confronted with the witnesses against him; to have compulsory process for obtaining witnesses in his favor, and to have the Assistance of Counsel for his defence.

ORIGINS

The 6th Amendment attempted to insure that a defendant in a criminal case would receive a fair trial.

AMENDMENT [VII.]

In Suits at common law, where the value in controversy shall exceed twenty dollars, the right of trial by jury shall be preserved, and no fact tried by a jury shall be otherwise re-examined in any Court of the United States, than according to the rules of the common law.

AMENDMENT [VIII.]

Excessive bail shall not be required, nor excessive fines imposed, nor cruel and unusual punishments inflicted.

ORIGINS

The Constitution (Art III, sec. 2, par. 3) guarantees trial by jury in criminal cases. The 7th Amendment extends that guarantee to civil cases.

The 8th Amendment means that the courts should not ask for unreasonable amounts of bail (money paid to secure the release of an arrested person) or fines. The amendment also bars punishments that are cruel and unusual.

AFTERLIFE

In 1972 in *Furman* v. *Georgia* the Supreme Court ruled that the death penalty was unconstitutional in Georgia because it was applied inconsistently—blacks were far more often executed than whites who had committed similar crimes. The Court did not, however, declare that the death penalty itself was necessarily a "cruel and unusual punishment."

AMENDMENT [IX.]

The enumeration in the Constitution, of certain rights, shall not be construed to deny or disparage others retained by the people.

AMENDMENT [X.]

The powers not delegated to the United States by the Constitution, nor prohibited by it to the States, are reserved to the States respectively, or to the people.

ORIGINS

In order to make it clear that the rights listed in the Constitution and its amendments were not the only rights of the people, the 9th Amendment was adopted.

The 10th Amendment made it clear that powers not given to the federal government in the Constitution remained with the states or with the people.

AMENDMENT [XI.]

The Judicial power of the United States shall not be construed to extend to any suit in law or equity, commenced or prosecuted against one of the United States by Citizens of another State, or by Citizens or Subjects of any Foreign State.

ORIGINS

In the case of *Chisholm* v. *Georgia* (1793) the Supreme Court ruled that a state did not have the right to protect itself from being sued by saying that it was a sovereign state and immune from suits by citizens of other states. To give states that right—known as sovereign immunity—this amendment was passed. Submitted to the states in 1794, ratified in 1798.

AMENDMENT [XII.]

The Electors shall meet in their respective states and vote by ballot for President and Vice-President, one of whom, at least, shall not be an inhabitant of the same state with themselves; they shall name in their ballots the person voted for as President, and in distinct ballots the person voted for as Vice-President, and they shall make distinct lists of all persons voted for as President, and of all persons voted for as Vice-President, and of the number of votes for each, which lists they shall sign and certify, and transmit sealed to the seat of the government of the United States, directed to the President of the Senate;—The President of the Senate shall, in the presence of the Senate and House of Representatives, open all the certificates and the votes shall then be counted;—The person having the greatest number of votes for President, shall be the President, if such number be a majority of the whole number of Electors appointed; and if no person have such majority, then from the persons having the highest numbers not exceeding three on the list of those voted for as President, the House of Representatives shall choose immediately, by ballot, the President. But in choosing the President, the votes shall be taken by states, the representation from each state having one vote; a quorum for this purpose shall consist of a member or members from two-thirds of the states, and a majority of all the states shall be necessary to a choice. And if the House of Representatives shall not choose a President whenever the right of choice shall devolve upon them, before the fourth day of March next following, then the Vice-President shall act as President, as in the case of the death or other constitutional disability of the President—The person having the greatest number of votes as Vice-President, shall be the Vice-President, if such number be a majority of the whole number of Electors appointed, and if no person have a majority, then from the two highest numbers on the list, the Senate shall choose the Vice-President; a quorum for the purpose shall consist of two-thirds of the whole number of Senators, and a majority of the whole number shall be necessary to a choice. But no person constitutionally ineligible to the office of President shall be eligible to that of Vice-President of the United States.

ORIGINS

The 12th Amendment was brought about by the election of 1800, when the Democratic-Republicans' presidential candidate Jefferson and vice-presidential candidate Burr each received the same number of electoral votes. To avoid any chance of such an event occurring again, electors were now to vote for President on one ballot and for Vice-President on another [6:4]. For elections in the House and disputed returns see [9:1], pages 223–224, and [14:4], pages 377–379. Submitted to the states in 1803, ratified in 1804.

AMENDMENT [XIII.]

Section 1. Neither slavery nor involuntary servitude, except as a punishment for crime whereof the party shall have been duly convicted, shall exist within the United States, or any place subject to their jurisdiction.

> **Section 2.** Congress shall have power to enforce this article by appropriate legislation.

ORIGINS

The 13th, 14th, and 15th amendments were produced by the Civil War and its aftermath. See [14:2], pages 365 and 368, and [14:3], page 372.

The 13th Amendment abolished slavery [13:3]. Submitted to the states in 1865, ratified in 1865.

AMENDMENT [XIV.]

Section 1. All persons born or naturalized in the United States and subject to the jurisdiction thereof, are citizens of the United States and of the State wherein they reside. No State shall make or enforce any law which shall abridge the privileges or immunities of citizens of the United States; or shall any State deprive any person of life, liberty, or property, without due process of law; nor deny to any person within its jurisdiction the equal protection of the laws.

ORIGINS

In the *Dred Scott* case (1857), Chief Justice Taney had stated that blacks were not citizens when the Constitution was adopted and were not covered by its provisions [12:3]. By the 14th Amendment blacks were made citizens, and the privileges and immunities of citizens of the United States were extended to citizens of the states.

AFTERLIFE

The 14th Amendment is the most important amendment added to the Constitution since the Bill of Rights. The key part is Section 1 which contains the potent, but undefined phrases, "due process of law" and "equal protection of the laws."

Often in the nineteenth and early twentieth centuries the Court used the amendment to protect corporations (which it defined as "persons") from state regulation, but in *Munn v. Illinois* (1877) and other later decisions the right of states and the federal government to regulate wage rates, hours, and other terms of employment was recognized [18:3].

Over time the amendment has been increasingly interpreted to extend the protection of the Bill of Rights to citizens from actions by the states as well as against the federal government. Although in *Plessy v. Ferguson* (1896) [14:5] the Court upheld the "separate but equal" doctrine which legalized racial segregation, that was completely overturned in the series of decisions that culminated in *Brown v. Board of Education* (1954) [29:3]. In such cases as *Gideon v. Wainwright* (1963), *Escobedo v. Illinois* (1964), and *Miranda v. Arizona* (1966) [33:7] the Court greatly enlarged the rights of accused persons in state courts.

[XIV] **Section 2.** Representatives shall be apportioned among the several States according to their respective numbers, counting the whole number of persons in each State, excluding Indians not taxed. But when the right to vote at any elec-

[XIV] tion for the choice of electors for President and Vice President of the United States, Representatives in Congress, the Executive and Judicial officers of a State, or the members of the Legislature thereof, is denied to any of the male inhabitants of such State, being twenty-one years of age, and citizens of the United States, or in any way abridged, except for participation in rebellion, or other crime, the basis of representation therein shall be reduced in the proportion which the number of such male citizens shall bear to the whole number of male citizens twenty-one years of age in such State.

ORIGINS

The fear that Southern states would keep blacks from voting prompted this provision. It provides that a state's representation in Congress may be cut if it denies the right to vote to any group of adult male citizens.

[XIV] **Section 3.** No person shall be a Senator or Representative in Congress, or elector of President and Vice President, or hold any office, civil or military, under the United States, or under any State, who, having previously taken an oath, as a member of Congress, or as an officer of the United States, or as a member of any State legislature, or as an executive or judicial officer of any State, to support the Constitution of the United States, shall have engaged in insurrection or rebellion against the same, or given aid or comfort to the enemies thereof. But Congress may by a vote of two-thirds of each House, remove such disability.

[XIV] ● **Section 4.** The validity of the public debt of the United States, authorized by law, including debts incurred for payment of pensions and bounties for services in suppressing insurrection or rebellion, shall not be questioned. But neither the United States nor any State shall assume or pay any debt or obligation incurred in aid of insurrection or rebellion against the United States, or any claim for the loss or emancipation of any slave; but all such debts, obligations and claims shall be held illegal and void.

[XIV] **Section 5.** The Congress shall have power to enforce, by appropriate legislation, the provisions of this article.

ORIGINS

This clause barred from federal office any former federal or state official who had served the Confederacy in the Civil War—unless Congress removed the ban by a two-thirds vote of each house.

● This section legalized the federal Civil War debt and voided all debts incurred by the Confederate states.

See p. 368 for further discussion of the origin of the 14th Amendment. Submitted to the states in 1866, ratified in 1868.

AMENDMENT [XV.]

Section 1. The right of citizens of the United States to vote shall not be denied or abridged by the United States or by any State on account of race, color, or previous condition of servitude.

Section 2. The Congress shall have power to enforce this article by appropriate legislation.

ORIGINS

The 15th Amendment attempted to insure that blacks would have the vote. Submitted to the states in 1869, ratified in 1870.

AFTERLIFE

The 15th Amendment did not, as it turned out, prevent blacks from being kept from the polls in the South. In the beginning, the Ku Klux Klan and other groups harassed and intimidated them [14:3]. Then a variety of legal tricks was used to deprive them of the vote [25:2]. It has needed strong federal activity to insure their right to vote (see [29:3, 31:4, 32:1] and especially [33:1] on the Voting Rights Act).

AMENDMENT [XVI.]

The Congress shall have power to lay and collect taxes on incomes, from whatever source derived, without apportionment among the several States, and without regard to any census or enumeration.

ORIGINS

In *Pollock* v. *Farmers' Loan and Trust Co.* (1895), the Supreme Court declared that an income tax was unconstitutional. As a result the 16th Amendment was passed [18:3]. Submitted to the states in 1909, ratified in 1913.

AMENDMENT [XVII.]

The Senate of the United States shall be composed of two Senators from each State, elected by the people thereof, for six years; and each Senator shall have one vote. The electors in each State shall have the qualifications requisite for electors of the most numerous branch of the State legislatures.

When vacancies happen in the representation of any State in the Senate, the executive authority of such State shall issue writs of election to fill such vacancies: *Provided,* That the legislature of any State may empower the executive

[XVII] thereof to make temporary appointments until the people fill the vacancies by election as the legislature may direct.

This amendment shall not be so construed as to affect the election or term of any Senator chosen before it becomes valid as part of the Constitution.

ORIGINS

The Framers of the Constitution distrusted "the people" in the mass and tried to restrict their role to electing only the representatives. The dominance of the electoral college by political parties soon gave the people control of presidential elections. But the Senate continued to be elected by the state legislatures, and since wealthy men were often able to use their cash to buy their elections, the Senate became a "rich man's club." This amendment gave the election of senators to the people [20:2]. Submitted to the states in 1912, ratified in 1913.

AMENDMENT [XVIII.]

Section 1. After one year from the ratification of this article the manufacture, sale, or transportation of intoxicating liquors within, the importation thereof into, or the exportation thereof from the United States and all territory subject to the jurisdiction thereof for beverage purposes is hereby prohibited.

Sec. 2. The Congress and the several States shall have concurrent power to enforce this article by appropriate legislation.

Sec. 3. This article shall be inoperative unless it shall have been ratified as an amendment to the Constitution by the legislatures of the several States, as provided in the Constitution, within seven years from the date of the submission hereof to the States by the Congress.

ORIGINS

In the moral fervor of World War I, national prohibition was enacted [22:1]. Submitted to the states in 1917, ratified in 1919.

AFTERLIFE

The "noble experiment" of Prohibition turned out to be a disaster. Millions of Americans became lawbreakers, and criminals took over the liquor trade [22:1].

AMENDMENT [XIX.]

The right of citizens of the United States to vote shall not be denied or abridged by the United States or by any State on account of sex.

Congress shall have power to enforce this article by appropriate legislation.

After World War I, during which the work of women in the war effort had been important and conspicuous, women's suffrage was enacted [22:1]. Submitted to the states in 1919, ratified in 1920.

The suffragists, who worked for the right to vote, had hoped that when women could go to the polls they would improve their chances to be treated equally. But women often failed to vote and did not vote as a bloc [25:3].

AMENDMENT [XX.]

Section 1. The terms of the President and Vice President shall end at noon on the 20th day of January, and the terms of Senators and Representatives at noon on the 3d day of January, of the years in which such terms would have ended if this article had not been ratified; and the terms of their successors shall then begin.

Sec. 2. The Congress shall assemble at least once in every year, and such meeting shall begin at noon on the 3d day of January, unless they shall by law appoint a different day.

ORIGINS

The "Lame Duck" Amendment. A lame duck is an official who continues to serve to the end of his term even though he has not been reelected. Prior to this amendment a President leaving office was a "lame duck" for four months, since he left office on March 4. By pushing back the inauguration to January 20, the amendment shortened the time between when a President was elected (in early November) and when he took office. Submitted to the states in 1932, ratified in 1933.

[XX]

Sec. 3. If, at the time fixed for the beginning of the term of the President, the President elect shall have died, the Vice President elect shall become President. If a President shall not have been chosen before the time fixed for the beginning of his term, or if the President elect shall have failed to qualify, then the Vice President elect shall act as President until a President shall have qualified; and the Congress may by law provide for the case wherein neither a President elect nor a Vice President elect shall have qualified, declaring who shall then act as President, or the manner in which one who is to act shall be selected, and such person shall act accordingly until a President or Vice President shall have qualified.

Sec. 4. The Congress may by law provide for the case of the death of any of the persons from whom the House of Representatives may choose a President whenever the right of choice shall have devolved upon them, and for the case of the death of any of the persons from whom the Senate may choose a Vice President whenever the right of choice shall have devolved upon them.

[XX] **Sec. 5.** Sections 1 and 2 shall take effect on the 15th day of October following the ratification of this article.

Sec. 6. This article shall be inoperative unless it shall have been ratified as an amendment to the Constitution by the legislatures of three-fourths of the several States within seven years from the date of its submission.

AMENDMENT [XXI.]

Section 1. The eighteenth article of amendment to the Constitution of the United States is hereby repealed.

Sec. 2. The transportation or importation into any State, Territory or possession of the United States for delivery or use therein of intoxicating liquors, in violation of the laws thereof, is hereby prohibited.

Sec. 3. This article shall be inoperative unless it shall have been ratified as an amendment to the Constitution by conventions in the several States, as provided in the Constitution, within seven years from the date of the submission hereof to the States by the Congress.

ORIGINS

Disappointment over Prohibition, disgust at the activities of gangsters, and fear that disrespect for this one law would breed disrespect for all laws brought about the repeal of Prohibition in 1933 [24:1]. Submitted to the states in 1933, ratified in 1933.

AMENDMENT [XXII.]

[XXII]
Sec. 1
Section 1. No person shall be elected to the office of the President more than twice, and no person who has held the office of President, or acted as President, for more than two years of a term to which some other person was elected President shall be elected to the office of the President more than once. But this Article shall not apply to any person holding the office of President when this Article was proposed by the Congress, and shall not prevent any person who may be holding the office of President, or acting as President, during the term within which this Article becomes operative from holding the office of President or acting as President during the remainder of such term.

[XXII] **Sec. 2.** This Article shall be inoperative unless it shall have been ratified as an amendment to the Constitution by the legislatures of three-fourths of the several States within seven years from the date of its submission to the States by the Congress.

In 1947 for the first time in 14 years, the Republicans controlled both houses of Congress. Since President Washington there had been an unwritten tradition limiting a President to two terms. To strike at the Democrats and at Franklin D. Roosevelt, who had been elected four times, the Republicans proposed and supported this amendment making the tradition into law [28:2]. Submitted to the states in 1947, ratified in 1951.

AMENDMENT [XXIII.]

Section 1. The District constituting the seat of Government of the United States shall appoint in such manner as the Congress may direct:

A number of electors of President and Vice President equal to the whole number of Senators and Representatives in Congress to which the District would be entitled if it were a State, but in no event more than the least populous State; they shall be in addition to those appointed by the States, but they shall be considered, for the purposes of the election of President and Vice President, to be electors appointed by a State; and they shall meet in the District and perform such duties as provided by the twelfth article of amendment.

Sec. 2. The Congress shall have power to enforce this article by appropriate legislation.

ORIGINS

Since the District of Columbia was not a state, its residents had no vote in presidential elections. This amendment gave them the right to vote. Submitted to the states in 1960, ratified in 1961.

AFTERLIFE

Numerous proposals have been made for an amendment to give the District of Columbia representation in the House and in the Senate, but none has been adopted.

AMENDMENT [XXIV.]

Section 1. The right of citizens of the United States to vote in any primary or other election for President or Vice President, for electors for President or Vice President, or for Senator or Representative in Congress, shall not be denied or abridged by the United States or any State by reason of failure to pay any poll tax or other tax.

Section 2. The Congress shall have power to enforce this article by appropriate legislation.

The "Anti-poll tax" Amendment. The poll tax was a tax everyone had to pay before he or she could vote [25:2, 31:4]. Some southern states used a poll tax as a way to prevent blacks from voting. Submitted to the states in 1962, ratified in 1964.

As a result of this amendment and of the civil rights laws, black registration and voting increased rapidly in the 1960s [32:3]. Blacks elected mayors in many southern cities. Southern political candidates increasingly turned away from white supremacy and tried to win the votes of their black fellow citizens.

AMENDMENT [XXV.]

Section 1. In case of the removal of the President from office or of his death or resignation, the Vice-President shall become President.

Section 2. Whenever there is a vacancy in the office of the Vice-President, the President shall nominate a Vice-President who shall take office upon confirmation by a majority vote of both houses of Congress.

Section 3. Whenever the President transmits to the President pro tempore of the Senate and the Speaker of the House of Representatives his written declaration that he is unable to discharge the powers and duties of his office, and until he transmits to them a written declaration to the contrary, such powers and duties shall be discharged by the Vice-President as Acting President.

Section 4. Whenever the Vice-President and a majority of either the principal officers of the executive departments or of such other body as Congress may by law provide, transmit to the President pro tempore of the Senate and the Speaker of the House of Representatives their written declaration that the President is unable to discharge the powers and duties of his office, the Vice-President shall immediately assume the powers and duties of the office as Acting President.

Thereafter, when the President transmits to the President pro tempore of the Senate and the Speaker of the House of Representatives his written declaration that no inability exists, he shall resume the powers and duties of his office unless the Vice-President and a majority of either the principal officers of the executive department or of such other body as Congress may by law provide, transmit within four days to the President pro tempore of the Senate and the Speaker of the House of Representatives their written declaration that the President is unable to discharge the powers and duties of his office. Thereupon Congress shall decide the issue, assembling within forty-eight hours for that purpose if not in session. If the Congress, within twenty-one days after receipt of the latter written declaration, or, if Congress is not in session, within twenty-one days after Congress is required to assemble, determines by two-thirds vote of both houses that the President is unable to discharge the powers and duties of his office, the Vice-President shall continue to discharge the same as Acting President; otherwise, the President shall resume the powers and duties of his office.

ORIGINS

Americans remembered the problems caused by the incapacity of President Wilson and the deaths in office of eight Presidents and six Vice-Presidents.

The serious illnesses of President Eisenhower were the immediate reason for this amendment. It aimed to avoid a gap in the functioning of the Presidency if the elected President himself was not able to do his job. It also aimed to avoid in the future a situation (like that in the last months of President Wilson) when the President's wife or somebody else close to him might take over his decisions without legal authority. Submitted to the states in 1965, ratified in 1967.

AFTERLIFE

When Vice-President Agnew resigned in 1973, President Nixon nominated Gerald R. Ford to take his place [33:3]. After Ford became President, Nelson Rockefeller was made Vice-President by the procedure described in this amendment [35:1].

AMENDMENT [XXVI.]

Section 1. The right of citizens of the United States, who are 18 years of age or older, to vote shall not be denied or abridged by the United States or any State on account of age.

Section 2. The Congress shall have the power to enforce this article by appropriate legislation.

ORIGINS

During the war in Vietnam, many Americans began to feel that those who were old enough to be drafted and sent off to fight were old enough to vote. Submitted to the states in 1971, ratified in 1971.

AFTERLIFE

As with the 19th Amendment, which gave women the right to vote, the 26th Amendment had no far-reaching effects. Many citizens between 18 and 21 failed to go to the polls to vote.

AMENDMENT [XXVII.]

No law, varying the compensation for the services of the senators and representatives, shall take effect until an election of representatives shall have intervened.

ORIGINS

Congressional pay has been the subject of heated controversy for more than two hundred years. This amendment modified Article I, Section 6, Clause 1. It limits the power of Congress to fix the salaries of its members—delaying the effectiveness of any increase in that pay until after the next regular congressional election. Submitted to the states in 1989, ratified in 1992.

AFTERLIFE

The debate over congressional pay is not likely to end soon. This amendment gives the American people a chance to express their opinion on the subject of a congressional pay increase at the ballot box, before the pay increase becomes law.

Glossary

Abolitionist a person seeking the legal end of slavery in the United States (p. 286)

Abstract Expressionism style of painting dominant from the late 1940s to the early 1960s, in which no attempt was made to reflect objects realistically, and feeling was expressed through the use of color (p. 766)

administration one President's term in office; the officials who do the government's business during the term of the President (p. 166)

admiralty law or courts dealing with cases involving shipping and navigation (p. 65)

advice and consent the power given to the United States Senate by the Constitution to review and approve TREATIES and certain major appointments made by the President (p. 154)

affirmative action steps taken to increase the representation of women and minorities, especially in jobs and higher education, often by the use of timetables or QUOTAS (p. 850)

alien a citizen of a foreign country (p. 167)

Allies in World War I and World War II, the nations fighting against Germany and its associates, including the United States and Great Britain (p. 547)

ambassador a high-ranking diplomatic official representing his or her country in another country (p. 184)

amendment a change in or addition to a legal document, motion, bylaw, law, or constitution (p. 120)

amnesty a government pardon for a group of offenders (p. 362)

anarchy a complete absence of government; lawlessness, disorder, and confusion brought about by the absence of government (p. 116)

Anglo-Saxons the English people, or people of English descent, so called because the Angles, the Saxons, and the Jutes (Germanic tribes) settled in England in the fifth and sixth centuries A.D. (p. 443)

annex to attach new TERRITORY to an existing area, such as a city or country (p. 296)

antebellum before a war; in American history, used to describe the period before the Civil War (p. 207)

antiballistic missile (ABM) a missile capable of destroying BALLISTIC MISSILES in flight (p. 828)

anti-Semitism prejudice against Jews (p. 632)

antitrust opposed to TRUSTS, MONOPOLIES, price-fixing, and other agreements that restrain trade (p. 418)

Appalachia the Appalachian mountain area, especially the region stretching from Pennsylvania to Alabama and Georgia (p. 77)

appeasement the policy of giving in to an aggressor nation in the hope that this will satisfy it and encourage it to stop being aggressive (p. 662)

arbitration the hearing and settling of a dispute by a third person who is not involved in the disagreement (p. 507)

aristocracy a privileged class of persons of high rank, such as the nobility; rule by such a class (p. 151)

armistice a temporary pause, agreed to by both sides, in a war or battle (p. 560)

arsenal a government building or buildings where arms and other war supplies are manufactured or stored; also, the war supplies themselves (p. 675)

ashcan school a group of American artists of the early twentieth century whose work realistically portrayed scenes from everyday city life (p. 530)

assembly line a moving workbench—a procedure in which automobiles or other items being manufactured move past workers and machines and are assembled piece by piece until completed (p. 594)

Atlantic Charter a joint declaration issued by President Franklin D. Roosevelt and British Prime Minister Winston Churchill on August 14, 1941, stating their common aims for the years after World War II: a peaceful world where all people would have the right of self-determination and adequate food and shelter (p. 670)

Atlantic Pact see NATO (p. 717)

automation the automatic performance by a machine of a manufacturing process or other task (p. 761)

Baby boom the rapid growth in the U.S. population between about 1945 and 1960 (p. 751)

balance of power a condition in which two countries or groups of countries are roughly equal in power, and neither can become dominant (p. 540)

balanced budget a BUDGET in which income and expenses are equal (p. 625)

balance of trade the relationship between the value of a nation's EXPORTS and the value of its IMPORTS in a given year. If imports are greater than exports, the balance is *negative*. If exports are greater than imports, the balance is *positive*. (p. 900)

ballistic missile a rocket-powered object, often carrying a nuclear warhead, which is shot into the air and hits its ground target after a free fall (p. 784)

bank holiday a day or several days when banks are closed and depositors cannot withdraw money; especially March 6 to March 10, 1933, when President Franklin D. Roosevelt temporarily closed all the nation's banks (p. 624)

belligerents nations fighting a war, usually after a declaration of war (p. 660)

Bessemer converter a furnace used for changing iron into steel (p. 454)

bilingual able to speak two languages (p. 873)

bill of attainder a legislative act pronouncing an individual guilty of a crime, usually TREASON, without a trial; specifically prohibited by Article I, Sections 9 and 10 of the U.S. CONSTITUTION (p. 974)

Bill of Rights the first ten AMENDMENTS to the U.S. CONSTITUTION (p. 123)

bipartisan supported by two parties; in the United States, supported by both the DEMOCRATIC PARTY and the REPUBLICAN PARTY (p. 719)

Black Codes laws passed, especially by the Southern states after the Civil War, to control the actions and limit the rights of blacks (p. 365)

Black Power a movement among some blacks in the United States in the late 1960s to achieve social, political, and economic equality by rejecting integration and white assistance and attempting to unite all blacks in pursuit of these goals (p. 807)

blitzkrieg a sudden invasion or "lightning war," first practiced by the Germans in World War II (p. 664)

bloody shirt a method of campaigning used by Republicans after the Civil War, when they "waved the bloody shirt" to remind the voters that they had fought the war, freed the slaves, and saved the Union (p. 372)

Bolshevik a member of the group within the Social Democratic party in Russia that favored seizing power by force (and ultimately did so) in the revolution of 1917; in the United States, an extreme left-wing radical (p. 577)

boycott an organized refusal to buy or use a product, or to deal with a company or group of companies, as a protest or as a means of forcing them to take some action (p. 81, 865)

broad construction an interpretation of the U.S. CONSTITUTION that holds that government has the right to do everything necessary and proper to carry out any of the powers granted to it in the Constitution; compare STRICT CONSTRUCTION (p. 157)

budget a detailed prediction of estimated income and expenses for a given period (p. 830, 897)

bureaucracy all the men and women, taken as a group, who run the agencies that do the everyday business of a government (p. 821)

Cabinet the group of advisers to the President that is made up of the heads of the executive departments of the government (State, Defense, Treasury, etc.) as well as certain other important government officials (p. 154)

caravel a fast, maneuverable three-masted sailing ship with a rounded hull, used by Spanish and Portuguese explorers in the late 1400s and early 1500s (p. 12)

carpetbaggers Northerners who went South to acquire wealth or power during RECONSTRUCTION, after the Civil War. They were said to have arrived with no more belongings than they could carry in a carpetbag, an old-fashioned suitcase made of carpeting. The term is sometimes applied to any people who come from outside to interfere in local affairs (p. 372)

casualties in a war or battle, combatants who are killed, wounded, captured, missing in action, or in any way rendered unable to fight (p. 812)

caucus a meeting of the members of a political party or a segment of that party, or of like-minded politicians, to try to reach decisions on matters of concern (p. 223)

census an official counting of a population (p. 153)

charter a legal document issued by a government to define the purposes and privileges of a CORPORATION (p. 40)

Chicano an American of Mexican origin or descent (p. 864)

Christendom collectively, those who believe in Jesus as the Christ (p. 16)

citizen a person who by birth or NATURALIZATION owes loyalty to, and receives the protection of, a nation's government; a resident of a locality, usually having the right to vote (p. 218)

civil liberties certain rights guaranteed to the CITIZENS of a nation; in the United States, especially those rights protected by the BILL OF RIGHTS and the Fourteenth Amendment (p. 566)

civil rights rights guaranteed to CITIZENS by the CONSTITUTION and laws of the nation, especially the rights of minorities to political, social, and economic equality (p. 790)

civil service government jobs for which appointments and promotions are based on merit (often determined by an examination) rather than on political PATRONAGE (p. 460)

clemency leniency or mercy shown toward an enemy, a criminal, or other offender (p. 834)

closed shop a workplace where employees must be LABOR UNION members in order to be hired (compare UNION SHOP) (p. 714)

cloture a procedure for ending a debate or a FILIBUSTER in a legislature or meeting so the question at issue can be brought to a vote (p. 798)

cold war a hostility between nations that stops just short of open war; especially, the relationship of the United States and its free-world allies to the Soviet Union and its Communist allies and satellites in the decades after World War II (p. 707)

collective bargaining negotiations between a group of workers and their employer concerning wages, hours, and working conditions. The group of workers is usually represented in collective bargaining by a LABOR UNION. (p. 634)

colony a land area settled by a group of EMIGRANTS who continue to be subjects of their parent country; a people or TERRITORY that is ruled by another nation (p. 27)

commerce trade; the buying and selling of goods and services (p. 464)

commonwealth the name used instead of *state* by four of the United States (Kentucky, Massachusetts, Pennsylvania, and Virginia); the term used to designate the special status of Puerto Rico in the United States (p. 866)

company town a town built and controlled by a company, or a town that depends on a single company for most of its jobs (p. 455)

concentration camps camps where political opponents or other "enemies" of the state are confined, especially those established by Nazi Germany before and during World War II (p. 658)

confederacy a union, alliance, or league. During the Civil War, the Southern states called their union a confederacy (p. 324)

Congress the legislative branch of the United States government, made up of the SENATE and the HOUSE OF REPRESENTATIVES (p. 121)

conquistadores Spanish word for "conquerers"; especially the Spanish adventurers who explored and conquered a large part of the western HEMISPHERE in the sixteenth century (p. 15)

Constitution the fundamental and supreme law of the United States (p. 104)

containment the United States policy after World War II of trying to keep the Soviet Union from expanding its area of influence and dominance (p. 709)

contraband goods that are illegal to import or export. During the Civil War, Northerners applied the term to slaves who fled the CONFEDERACY for the UNION. (p. 550)

convention a formal meeting of individuals, often delegates or representatives of others, to pursue common interests or goals; especially, a meeting of members of a political party to choose candidates for office and write a PLATFORM (p. 228)

convoy an organized group of merchant and/or passenger ships escorted and protected by naval vessels to ward off attack (p. 562)

corollary a principle that logically adds to or follows from another, as the Roosevelt Corollary was thought to follow from the Monroe Doctrine (p. 542)

corporation a group legally organized to act and to have its own rights separate from those of its members; a company in which the owners hold shares of STOCK and the firm has a separate legal identity from its owners; see JOINT STOCK COMPANY (p. 261)

coup d'etat a sudden move to overthrow an existing government (p. 711)

currency coins and paper bills that serve as money (p. 108)

czar an emperor, king, or supreme ruler; the title of the ruler of Russia before the revolution of 1917 (p. 577)

Daguerreotype (duh–GARE–uh–type) an early form of photograph named after Louis Daguerre (1789–1851), its French inventor (p. 309)

de facto in fact or actuality (rather than by law) (p. 543)

default failure to pay a loan, mortgage, or other debt when it is due (p. 609)

deficit the amount by which money spent is greater than money received (p. 626)

deflation a widespread fall in prices (p. 459)

demilitarized zone an area where, by international agreement, no troops or armaments are allowed (p. 731)

democracy a form of government in which the people rule either directly or through freely elected representatives (p. 555)

Democratic party one of the two major political parties in the United States. It is a descendant of the Republican party established by Thomas Jefferson and James Madison in the early years of the republic (p. 225)

demography the study of human populations and their characteristics (p. 751)

depression a long and severe decline in economic activity. The one that lasted from 1929 to about 1940 is known as the Great Depression. Compare RECESSION. (p. 114)

deregulation the reduction of government control over business and other activities (p. 902)

desegregation the elimination of SEGREGATION (p. 715)

détente a French word meaning relaxing or easing; in diplomacy, used especially to refer to an easing of tensions between nations (p. 829)

dictatorship a government in which one individual (the *dictator*) has absolute authority (p. 657)

diplomacy the art and practice of conducting relations between nations by peaceful means (p. 657)

disarmament the act of getting rid of military weapons (p. 584)

discrimination prejudice for or against someone based on race, religion, sex, or other classification (p. 848)

dividend a payment to a shareholder of a portion of the earnings of a CORPORATION (p. 211)

domino theory the idea that if one nation falls to the Communists, its neighbors will, too—just as a row of standing dominoes will fall if the first in line falls. President Eisenhower and others used this term in referring to the nations of Southeast Asia. (p. 810)

Dust Bowl the area of the United States that became so arid in the 1930s due to lack of rain that the topsoil became dust and in a strong wind blew away (p. 643)

Ecology the science that deals with the relationship of organisms and their environments (p. 803)

electoral college jointly, all the electors chosen by the voters to cast the ballots of the states and the District of Columbia for President and Vice-President (p. 461)

emancipation the act of setting a person or people free (p. 340)

embargo a law or government order prohibiting trade with a foreign company or nation (p. 195)

embassy the building or buildings serving as the headquarters of the AMBASSADOR and other diplomatic personnel of a nation in a foreign country (p. 894)

emigrant a person who leaves one place—usually one country—to settle in another (p. 51)

empire a group of nations ruled by one supreme authority (p. 16)

encomienda a system of labor control in Spanish America, in which Spanish settlers exercised control over groups of American Indians and required those Indians to pay them a tribute in the form of crops or days of labor (p. 27)

entitlements payments from the government to which individuals are legally entitled because of age, unemployment, illness or incapacity, or status as veterans (p. 898)

e pluribus unum the motto of the United States. In Latin it means "one out of (or made from) many." (p. 175)

executive branch the part of the government charged with putting into effect the laws passed by the legislature; made up of the President, Vice-President, CABINET secretaries, and federal departments and agencies (p. 120)

exports goods sent abroad, usually to be traded or sold (p. 79)

ex post facto law a law passed "after the fact" that makes a previous action a crime although it was legal when it took place; specifically prohibited in Article I, Sections 9 and 10 of the U.S. CONSTITUTION (p. 974)

Federal relating to a union of states that recognize a single central government but retain certain powers for themselves (p. 116)

federalism the belief in or advocacy of a FEDERAL system of government; the federal form of government (p. 116)

Federalist party originally, the followers of Alexander Hamilton in the 1790s; believers in a strong central government (p. 158)

Federal Reserve System the nation's central bank; a system of 12 regional banks overseen by a central board in Washington, D.C. (p. 539)

filibuster a tactic that uses endless talk to prevent a vote on pending legislation; also, an illegal military operation by civilians of one country against another (p. 466)

financier a person who makes or oversees transactions involving large sums of money (p. 418)

foreclosure the act of taking possession of a mortgaged property (one against which money has been borrowed) when the debtor can no longer make the required payments (p. 469)

freedom riders people of different races who rode buses throughout the South in 1961 and attempted to force the integration of segregated facilities in public bus stations (p. 790)

free silver the making and issuing of silver coins in a fixed ratio to gold (p. 459)

frigate originally, a three-masted naval warship with 24 to 50 guns; today, a U.S. Navy vessel larger than a destroyer but smaller than a cruiser (p. 168)

frontier the border of a country; the edge of the unknown in a field of knowledge; in the United States, defined by the Bureau of the Census as the edge of settlement beyond which the land is occupied by two or fewer persons per square mile (p. 385)

Gag rule a rule in the HOUSE OF REPRESENTATIVES in 1836 that prevented the discussion of any antislavery petition (p. 295)

G.I. from "Government Issue"; applied to American soldiers in World War II and later wars (p. 712)

G.I. Bill of Rights also simply "G.I. Bill"; legislation, first passed in 1944, to help veterans readjust to civilian life, for example by supporting their college education (p. 712)

Gilded Age the title of a novel by Mark Twain and Charles Dudley Warner, the term is often applied to the gaudy, tawdry years from 1865 to 1900 (p. 436)

glasnost a Russian word meaning a more open society (p. 916)

GNP see GROSS NATIONAL PRODUCT (p. 757)

gold standard a policy under which all paper money legally equals a certain amount of gold, and can be exchanged for that much gold on demand (p. 474)

GOP the REPUBLICAN PARTY, the "Grand Old Party" (p. 730)

grandfather clause laws passed in some Southern states giving the right to vote only to people who had that right on January 1, 1867, and to their descendants. This was a way to keep blacks from voting. (p. 646)

Grangers members of the Patrons of Husbandry, the farmers' league founded in 1867; so called because their lodges were called granges (p. 470)

greenbacks U.S. paper money, so called because of its color (p. 459)

gross national product (GNP) the total value of all the goods and services produced in a nation during a year (p. 757)

guerrilla one who fights by stealth and within small bands that make surprise raids against stronger forces (p. 96)

Habeas corpus, writ of a court order by which a judge may free a person who is being held in jail illegally or without just cause; protected by Article I, Section 9 of the U.S. CONSTITUTION (p. 340)

hacienda Spanish for a large house or estate (p. 28)

hawks people who favor war or warlike policy; used especially during the Vietnam War (p. 813)

hemisphere half of the earth. The *northern* and *southern* hemispheres are separated by the equator; the *eastern* and *western* hemispheres are separated by a MERIDIAN with Europe, Asia, and Africa in one half and the Americas in the other (p. 6)

Hessians German soldiers from the state of Hesse who were hired by the British to fight for them in the American Revolution; sometimes applied to anyone who fights for a foreign country for pay (p. 90)

holding company a company that owns (or "holds") and controls other companies (p. 417)

Hoovervilles the shantytowns built of cartons and wood scraps during the Great Depression of the 1930s; so called after President Herbert Hoover (p. 606)

House of Burgesses the lower house of the legislature in colonial Virginia and Maryland. Virginia's, established in 1619, was the first representative assembly among European settlers in the New World. In England, a *burgess* was a citizen of a borough (or town). (p. 38)

House of Representatives the lower house of the United States Congress, whose members are elected for two-year terms; also, the lower house of most state legislatures (p. 121)

Immigrant a person who enters one country from another country with the intention of settling (p. 437)

immigration the movement of people from other countries into a country (p. 51)

impeach to bring a charge of wrongdoing by a government official before a proper legal body (p. 370)

imperialism the attempt to create an EMPIRE, either directly or through economic or political dominance (p. 515)

imports goods brought into a country from another country, usually to be traded or sold (p. 78)

impound to refuse to spend money that has been APPROPRIATED (set aside) for a specific purpose. In the Budget and Impoundment Act of 1974, Congress prohibited Presidents from impounding money it had voted to appropriate. (p. 879)

impressment the act of forcing a person to serve in the armed forces (p. 194)

inauguration a formal induction into office (p. 179)

indentured servant a person who is required by an agreement to work for another person for a number of years, so called because of the perforation (indenture) that divides the two copies of the agreement (p. 38)

Industrial Revolution the revolution in manufacturing that began in about the middle of the eighteenth century with the introduction of power-driven machinery, and the social and cultural changes that followed (p. 259)

inflation a rapid, widespread rise in prices (p. 459)

initiative the procedure by which, in some states, a certain percentage of the voters can "initiate" or propose a law by PETITION and have it voted on by the people (p. 529)

injunction a court order preventing a certain action (p. 474)

interchangeable parts parts of a certain product that are mechanically produced to be the exact same size, shape, and weight as all similar parts. The use of interchangeable parts makes mass production techniques possible. (p. 264)

interlocking directorates boards of directors of several CORPORATIONS that have some of the same members, so that the businesses are to a degree under the same control; a device often used by FINANCIER J. P. Morgan (1837–1913) (p. 539)

international law the norms of behavior generally agreed to and followed by the nations of the world in their dealings with each other (p. 550)

internment confinement, especially in wartime (p. 677)

interstate between two or more states (p. 524)

iron curtain the line between Soviet-dominated Eastern Europe and the West, so called by Winston Churchill because the Soviets and their SATELLITE NATIONS prevented the free passage of people, information, and ideas across their borders (p. 708)

isolationism a policy of avoiding alliances and other types of involvement in the affairs of other nations (p. 660)

isthmus a narrow strip or neck of land running from one larger land area to another (p. 541)

Jim Crow laws laws in the Southern states in the nineteenth and twentieth centuries that forced the SEGREGATION of the races. The term came from the name of a song in a minstrel show. (p. 379)

jingoism aggressive nationalism (p. 513)

joint stock company a company whose owners hold shares of its STOCK (p. 33)

judicial branch the part of the government that includes courts of law and the administration of justice (p. 120)

judicial review the power of the Supreme Court to declare acts of Congress unconstitutional (p. 191)

junta (HOON—tuh) Spanish for a small group of individuals, often military officers, who rule a country (p. 788)

Keynesian (KANE—zee—uhn) following the economic theories of the English economist John Maynard Keynes (1883–1946) (p. 626)

Know-Nothing party the usual name for the American party, which was formed in 1849; so called because its members were sworn to secrecy, and when asked about the party's activities replied, "I don't know" or "I know nothing about it" (p. 314)

Ku Klux Klan (KKK) a secret society, first formed in the South after the Civil War, whose purpose was to insure white supremacy over blacks. In the 1920s a new Klan was formed, still favoring white supremacy, but opposed also to Jews, Catholics, BOLSHEVIKS, and many other groups they considered "un-American." More recently the Klan has appeared again all over the country to attempt to restore segregation and white supremacy. (p. 374)

Labor union workers organized as a group to seek higher wages, improved working conditions, and other benefits (p. 434)

lame duck an elected official whose term is about to end, and whose successor has been chosen but has not yet taken office; thus, someone who is no longer effective (p. 622)

land-grant colleges colleges that received land from the federal government under the Morrill Act of 1862 for the purpose of providing education in the agricultural and mechanical arts (p. 448)

latitude the angular distance calculated from the center of the earth north or south of the equator as measured in degrees. The North and South poles are each 90 degrees from the equator. All places that are the same distance from the equator in the same direction (north or south) are said to be located on the same PARALLEL, or line of latitude. (p. 5)

legal tender currency that can legally be used to pay a debt (p. 624)

legislative branch the part of the government that has the power to make laws; in the U.S. government, the CONGRESS, consisting of the SENATE and the HOUSE OF REPRESENTATIVES (p. 120)

Lend-Lease the World War II program under which the United States either lent or leased weapons, food, and services to our friends and the nations that would soon become our ALLIES, and especially to Great Britain and the Soviet Union (p. 669)

literacy tests a test of the ability to read and write once used by some Southern states to prevent blacks from voting (p. 647)

lithograph a picture created by a process of treating a stone (*lithos* means stone in Greek) or other flat surface so that certain parts retain ink and repel water; next, the surface is covered with water and is inked. Then a piece of paper is pressed against the stone, picking up color only from the inked areas. (p. *xvi*)

lobby to attempt to influence legislation; also, groups that attempt to do so. So called from the lobby outside a legislative chamber where people can meet their representatives. (p. 528)

lockout during a labor dispute, the closing of a business (by locking the gates) to keep employees from entering (p. 714)

longitude distance east or west of the prime MERIDIAN (the line of 0° longitude, which passes through Greenwich, England), as measured in degrees. The distance around the earth measures 360 degrees, because a degree is by definition 1/360 of the circumference of a circle. (p. 12)

Loyalists colonists who remained loyal to England during the American Revolution; TORIES (p. 87)

lynch to execute someone illegally by hanging, burning, or other means. So named after Colonel Charles Lynch of Virginia, whose informal "court" during the American Revolution was swift to punish LOYALISTS, often by whipping. (p. 578)

Machine see POLITICAL MACHINE (p. 441)

mainstreaming taking the handicapped out of special institutions and bringing them into the mainstream of American education (p. 872)

majority more than half (p. 614)

Manifest Destiny the idea, prevalent especially in the 1840s and 1850s, that it was America's obvious (manifest) and inevitable fate to occupy the entire continent (p. 298)

martial law temporary rule by the military when civil government can no longer keep order (p. 38)

massive retaliation the military policy of the United States announced by Secretary of State John Foster Dulles in January 1954, which threatened to respond to Soviet or Communist Chinese attacks on another country with an immediate all-out strike (p. 731)

Master Race according to Nazi dictator Adolph Hitler (1889–1945), the so-called "pure" Germans who, because of their supposed racial superiority, had the right to conquer and rule other peoples (p. 657)

media the outlets through which information reaches the public, such as television, radio, newspapers, magazines, and books. The word is the plural of *medium.* (p. 530)

mediation the attempt of a neutral third party to settle a dispute (p. 549)

megalopolis a number of cities so close together that they seem to create one giant city (p. 755)

mercantilism the theory that money, especially gold and silver, is what makes a nation powerful. As applied to COLONIES, this meant that they existed only in order to enrich the mother country. (p. 28)

mercenaries people who are paid to fight for a country other than their own (p. 86)

merchant marine a nation's commercial ships (p. 194)

mestizo Spanish for "mixed"; the term is applied to people who have both Spanish and Indian ancestors (p. 30)

metropolitan relating to a large city or urban area (p. 755)

Middle Ages the period in European history dating from approximately the fall of Roman civilization in the fifth century A.D. to the revival of learning during the RENAISSANCE in the fourteenth, fifteenth, and sixteenth centuries (p. 10)

middle passage the sea voyage of black slaves from Africa to the western HEMISPHERE; so called because vessels in the trade made one trip (passage) to the coast of Africa, then the trip across the Atlantic to North or South America, and finally the passage back to their home ports (p. 272)

militarist a person who advocates the predominance of the military (armed forces) and military ideas in a nation or region (p. 671)

military-industrial complex the combination of interests of the armed forces and the industries that supply their needs. The term was used by President Dwight Eisenhower in his 1961 farewell address. (p. 748)

militia all the able-bodied citizens capable of bearing arms (except ministers and members of a few other professions) who in colonial times and for many years thereafter met several times a year for drill and target practice in order to be able to serve as a defense force (p. 90)

monopoly dominance in or control of a market for certain goods or services by a single company or combination of companies; see also TRUST (p. 214)

muckraking investigating and exposing corruption and other illegal activities, especially as done by journalists during the Progressive Era (p. 529)

Mugwump a person who refuses to support his political party, especially the Republicans who worked to defeat James G. Blaine in 1884 (p. 463)

Nationalize to take property, such as land or a business, from its private owners and place it under government control (p. 733)

NATO the North Atlantic Treaty Organization, an alliance formed for mutual defense in 1949 under the North Atlantic Treaty, and now made up of 15 nations stretching from Canada to Turkey (p. 717)

natural aristocracy Jefferson's concept of a democratic ARISTOCRACY of the ablest, most industrious, and best educated, who would run the government (p. 846)

naturalization the granting of full citizenship to a foreigner (p. 181)

neutrality the policy of not taking sides in a dispute or a war (p. 548)

nonintercourse the suspension of trade with another country, especially as decreed by the Nonintercourse Act of 1809, which prohibited trade with Great Britain and France (p. 196)

nonpartisan not influenced by or supporting any political party or belief (p. 527)

nuclear freeze a halt in the manufacture and deployment (putting in place) of nuclear weapons (p. 915)

nuclear power energy produced from a controlled atomic reaction (p. 886)

nullification the declaration of an individual state that an act of the U.S. CONGRESS is null and void. Many Southern states claimed the right to do this in the years before the Civil War. (p. 232)

OPEC the Organization of Petroleum Exporting Countries; a group of oil-producing and exporting countries, first organized in 1960 to protect member nations' interests and control world oil prices (p. 880)

ordinance a government rule or law (p. 111)

organized labor collectively, all workers who are members of LABOR UNIONS (p. 652)

PAC see POLITICAL ACTION COMMITTEE (p. 884)

pacifist a person who is opposed to war, and refuses to fight under any circumstances (p. 553)

parallel an imaginary line of LATITUDE; so called because it runs parallel to the equator (p. 723)

pardon to forgive a punishable offense, and release the offender from further punishment (p. 877)

parity in agriculture, a level of crop prices designed to give farmers the same real income from their crops as they received between 1910 and 1914 (p. 628)

Parliament Great Britain's legislature (p. 61)

partisan devoted to a single political party and its beliefs (p. 837)

patronage the distribution of government jobs to political supporters; see also SPOILS SYSTEM (p. 189)

peculiar institution black slavery in the pre-Civil War South (p. 273)

per capita per person (p. 757)

perestroika a Russian word meaning to restructure the economy, the party, and the government (p. 916)

petition a written request to an individual or group in power (p. 89)

pioneers people who go into unoccupied or little-known regions, or people who explore new areas of knowledge (p. 32)

plantation an early settlement or COLONY; a large agricultural estate in the South, especially before the Civil War (p. 53)

platform a declaration of the principles, beliefs, and aims of a political party, usually adopted during its national CONVENTION. The individual sections of the platform are known as *planks*. (p. 471)

plurality in an election, the largest number of votes, but not a majority (p. 461)

Political Action Committee (PAC) an independent committee set up to receive funds and give them to a political candidate or candidates; legalized by the Federal Election Campaign-funding Reform Act of 1974 (p. 884)

political machine a political organization that works so smoothly and retains control so easily that it seems similar to a machine; found in many American cities in the late 1800s and early 1900s (p. 441)

poll tax a tax that must be paid before one can vote; once used in the South to discourage or prevent blacks from voting, and now prohibited in national elections by the Twenty-fourth Amendment to the U.S. CONSTITUTION (p. 647)

popular sovereignty the idea that the people in an area should decide for themselves the questions that concern them; especially, before the Civil War, that people in a TERRITORY should decide whether or not slavery should exist there (p. 308)

pork barrel federally financed improvement projects, such as dams, canals, and highways, that are designed to benefit a particular locality (p. 884)

preamble an introduction; especially, the opening statements of the Declaration of Independence and the U.S. CONSTITUTION (p. 88)

precedent something that happened or was done before and can now be used as an example to justify or explain similar occurrences or behavior (p. 152)

President the chief executive of a modern republic, especially of the United States (p. 120)

productivity in economics, a measure of the quantity of goods and services produced from a given amount of labor, equipment, land, and time (p. 596)

Prohibition the years from 1920 to 1933, when the Eighteenth Amendment to the U.S. CONSTITUTION was in effect, making it illegal to manufacture, sell, or transport alcoholic beverages in the United States (p. 582)

puppet government a government whose actions are completely controlled by another government, just as a puppet is manipulated by a person (p. 681)

Quarantine in foreign affairs, the isolation of a nation, carried out by refusing to communicate or trade with it and by preventing other nations from doing so (p. 660)

quota a predetermined maximum or minimum number of people who may or should be admitted to a group, institution, or nation (p. 851)

Racism the idea that a person's race determines his or her character or ability, and that one race is superior to others; prejudice against or preference for the members of one race (p. 379)

ratify to give formal approval (p. 121)

ration to limit the amount of something that each person may have. During World War II, such scarce items as sugar, butter, and gasoline were rationed in the United States. (p. 675)

real income the actual purchasing power of a person's income, rather than just the dollar amount (p. 566)

reapportionment the changing of the distribution of seats and the size of election districts for a legislature. Seats in the U.S. HOUSE OF REPRESENTATIVES must be reapportioned every ten years based on the results of the CENSUS. (p. 751)

recall a procedure established in some cities and states by which a percentage of the voters can remove an elected official from office at any time (p. 529)

recession a decline in economic activity, less severe and usually shorter than a DEPRESSION (p. 638)

Reconstruction the period (1867–1877) during which the former states of the CONFEDERACY were ruled by the federal government or by local Republican governments. Reconstruction lasted the full period only for Louisiana, Florida, and South Carolina. (p. 367)

Red a radical, anarchist, or Communist; so called because red was the color of the banner often used by revolutionaries, as in the Russian Revolution of 1917 (p. 579)

referendum a direct popular vote on a proposed new law or change in an existing law (p. 529)

refugee a person who flees from one country or region to seek refuge in another (p. 87)

regulation government control of the operations of business or other activities (p. 590)

Renaissance French for "rebirth"; the age, beginning about A.D. 1300 in Italy and later spreading throughout Europe, when there was a rebirth of art, literature, and learning; any period when there is a lively cultural life, as in the Harlem Renaissance of the 1920s (p. 10)

reparations payments required from a defeated nation for the damages and injuries it caused during a war (p. 568)

representative government a government in which the people are represented by delegates chosen in free elections (p. 38)

republic a form of government in which power is exercised by representatives elected by the people (p. 164)

Republican party Thomas Jefferson's party in the early days of the Republic; later, a new party launched in 1854 with the intent of opposing the spread of slavery into the TERRITORIES (p. 159)

reservations areas set aside (reserved) by the U.S. government for American Indian tribes (p. 386)

reverse discrimination the disadvantages suffered by others as a result of the special opportunities given to minorities in AFFIRMATIVE ACTION programs (p. 851)

revolution a sudden, violent change, especially the overthrow of a government (p. 89)

right-to-work laws laws in some states that forbid businesses to require workers to join a LABOR UNION as a condition of employment (p. 714)

SALT Strategic Arms Limitation Treaties; SALT I, signed in May 1972, and SALT II, signed in June 1979. Both aimed to slow down the nuclear arms race. SALT II was not ratified by the U.S. Senate. (p. 828)

salutary neglect the manner in which England governed the American colonies during much of the late 1600s and early 1700s; especially the policy of weak enforcement of the laws regulating colonial trade (p. 62)

satellite nations nations that are subservient to another nation, especially the nations of Eastern and Central Europe that have been dominated by the Soviet Union since the years of World War II (p. 711)

scalawags an insulting name for white Southerners who were Republicans during RECONSTRUCTION (p. 372)

secession the act of withdrawing formally from a group; the attempt of eleven Southern states to withdraw from the UNION in 1860 and 1861 (p. 237)

sectionalism loyalty to and love of a region, such as the East, the Midwest, or the South (p. 164)

sedition an attempt to incite a rebellion against a national government (p. 167)

segregation separating people according to some standard—in American history, usually race—in schools, housing, industry, and public facilities (p. 379)

Senate the upper house of the U.S. CONGRESS, to which each state elects two members, called senators, for terms of six years each; also, the upper house in *bicameral* state legislatures (legislatures that have two houses) (p. 121)

seniority priority based on higher rank or longer term of service (p. 713)

separate but equal the standard by which the SUPREME COURT approved segregated facilities in *Plessy* v. *Ferguson* (1896). The Court overturned this decision in *Brown* v. *Board of Education* (1954), ruling that separate facilities were unequal. (p. 381)

separation of powers the doctrine that gives the powers of making, enforcing, and interpreting the laws to separate branches of government (LEGISLATIVE, EXECUTIVE, and JUDICIAL) (p. 120)

settlement house a private center providing social services for the poor in a needy neighborhood (p. 445)

sharecroppers farmers who do not own the land they work but pay rent to the owner in the form of a share of the crop they grow (p. 644)

shuttle diplomacy the conduct of international relations by traveling back and forth between two or more nations frequently; first applied to the activities of Henry Kissinger, who was Secretary of State in Richard Nixon's second term as President and Gerald Ford's term as President (p. 889)

sit-down strike a work stoppage in which employees refuse to leave the workplace and occupy it in an attempt to force their employer to come to terms (p. 653)

sit-in a form of protest in which the participants occupy a building or a site in the hope of forcing their opponents to give in to their demands (p. 790)

SMSA Standard Metropolitan Statistical Area; a classification developed by the Office of Management and Budget for planning purposes, used to describe a central town and its outlying areas or a group of towns that make up a dense METROPOLITAN area (p. 754)

social security various programs of the federal government, some paid for by contributions from employers and employees, which provide economic assistance to the disabled, unemployed, and aged, as well as low-cost medical insurance for those over 65 (p. 633)

speakeasy an illegal bar during PROHIBITION (p. 593)

special interest groups groups of people who organize to take action on a particular issue (the environment, gun control, gun owners' rights, farm policy, etc.), hoping to influence public policy on that issue (p. 884)

specie money in the form of coins (p. 157)

speculator a person who gambles by buying or selling something, hoping to make a large profit (p. 110)

sphere of influence an area not within its own borders where the interests of one large nation are considered to be supreme (p. 517)

spoils system the procedure of rewarding political supporters with government jobs; partly abolished on the national level by the Pendleton Civil Service Act of 1883 (p. 230)

Stalwarts conservative Republicans who continued to favor the policies and procedures the party had followed during the Presidency of Ulysses S. Grant— and who especially opposed CIVIL SERVICE reform—in the years after Grant left office in 1877 (p. 460)

standard of living a rough measure of the material well-being of a person or group in a society (p. 757)

staple crop the main agricultural product grown in an area (p. 38)

states' rights the doctrine that seeks to limit the power of the federal government by interpreting the U.S. CONSTITUTION in a way that stresses the retained rights of the states and insists that the central government was granted only limited powers (p. 169)

status quo the way things are at a particular time (p. 207)

stock shares of ownership in a CORPORATION (p. 600)

stockholder the owner of STOCK (p. 419)

Strategic Defense Initiative (SDI) a defensive shield of advanced weapons, some operating in outer space, to make the United States safe from nuclear attack. Sometimes called "Star Wars." (p. 917)

strict construction an interpretation of the U.S. CONSTITUTION that holds that Congress and the President have no power to do anything unless the Constitution grants them that power in so many words; compare BROAD CONSTRUCTION (p. 157)

subpoena a legal order requiring someone or something to appear in court for questioning or inspection (p. 836)

subsidize when the government makes a monetary payment to assist an individual, organization, or cause (p. 802)

suburbs smaller towns surrounding large cities (p. 753)

suffrage the right to vote. The word comes from the Latin *suffragium*, which means "ballot" or "vote." (p. 226)

summit conference a meeting of the heads of state of two or more countries (p. 733)

superpower a nation far more powerful than most others; in the years since World War II, the United States and the Soviet Union (p. 786)

supply-side economics the theory that the government can best stimulate the economy by cutting taxes and encouraging investment in businesses, thus increasing the supply of goods (p. 897)

Supreme Court the highest federal court. Its powers are stated in Article III, of the U.S. CONSTITUTION. (p. 121)

Tactical atomic weapons smaller nuclear weapons, such as artillery shells, designed to be used on a conventional battlefield (p. 800)

tariff a charge placed by the government on certain imported goods (p. 157)

temperance when referring to alcohol, total abstinence from, or prohibition of, intoxicating beverages (p. 279)

tenant farmers farmers who rent the land they work (p. 644)

territory a political division of the United States before it becomes a state; a large area of land (p. 111)

terrorism the use of violence, intimidation, and coercion to achieve an end, to gain publicity for a cause, or to disrupt the normal functioning of society (p. 909)

Third World nations that profess not to be allied with either the Soviets and their SATELLITE NATIONS or the United States and its allies; especially the developing countries of Asia, Africa, and Latin America (p. 893)

Tories Americans who favored the British during the American Revolution; LOYALISTS (p. 87)

totalitarianism a form of rule in which the central government holds absolute control over the lives of its citizens (p. 723)

treason betrayal of one's country by making war on it or purposely aiding its enemies (p. 189)

treaty a formal agreement concluded between two or more countries (p. 13)

trust a MONOPOLY formed by combining the ownership of several formerly separate CORPORATIONS under a board of trustees (p. 417)

Ultimatum a final demand or set of demands, with the threat of serious consequences if the terms are not met (p. 213)

unalienable impossible to give up or surrender (p. 959)

unconditional surrender giving up without any terms or conditions decided upon beforehand (p. 685)

unconstitutional not allowed under the U.S. CONSTITUTION (p. 191)

Underground Railroad the informal network of escape routes and rest stops (stations) in the Northern states, and leading into Canada, by which slaves made their way to freedom (p. 310)

Union the separate states gathered together as the United States; the Northern states during the Civil War (p. 333)

union see LABOR UNION (p. 430)

union shop a business whose employees must join a LABOR UNION, but need not be members when they are hired; compare CLOSED SHOP (p. 714)

urban renewal the attempt to renew large areas of old cities, usually by tearing down old buildings and constructing new ones (p. 802)

utopia an imaginary place where everything is perfect; from two Greek words meaning "no place" (p. 456)

Veto under the U.S. CONSTITUTION, the power of the President to reject an act passed by Congress (p. 368)

viceroy in the Spanish empire, the governor of a COLONY or a province (p. 28)

Viet Cong Vietnamese Communists in South Vietnam who fought against the South Vietnamese government forces and the United States forces in the Vietnam War (p. 787)

War criminals persons who commit acts during wartime that go beyond the bounds of accepted behavior, especially those tried for such acts after World War II (p. 716)

welfare various state and federal programs that aim to provide food, money, medical care, and other help to those in need (p. 372)

Whigs the name taken by the political party that opposed President Andrew Jackson, to imply a similarity to the English Whigs who had struggled against the king in the late 1700s (p. 242)

writ a written court order commanding an individual or organization to do (or stop doing) something (p. 340)

writ of habeas corpus see HABEAS CORPUS (p. 340)

Yellow press newspapers that, in order to attract readers, feature sensational, often distorted stories; especially the Hearst and Pulitzer papers of the late 1890s, which encouraged the United States to fight a war with Spain (p. 511)

Index

A *p* following a page reference indicates an illustration; an *m*, a map; and a *c*, a chart or graph.

A

ABC powers, 544
Abilene, Kansas, 400
Abolition movement, 101–106, 286–288; and *Uncle Tom's Cabin*, 311–312, 311*p*
Abortion, 859, 912, 938
Abstract expressionism, 766, 766*p*, 767*p*
Acheson, Dean, 709, 710*p*, 714
Acid rain, 886
Acoma Indians, 8
Acquired Immune Deficiency Syndrome (AIDS), 936, 936*p*
Act of Toleration, 46
Adam, 110
Adams, Abigail, 97, 97*p*, 149, 178; on slavery, 106; and women's rights, 283–284
Adams, Charles Francis, 307, 507
Adams, John, 75, 81, 84, 99, 99*p*, 106, 176, 180; and appointment of midnight judges, 189–191; Cabinet of, 165–166; death of, 170; in election of 1796, 164–165; in election of 1800, 169; election of as Vice-President, 148; foreign policy of, 166–169; legacy of, 169–170; as member of Continental Congress, 107; as our first minister to England, 114; as President, 165; and rewriting of Declaration of Independence, 88; and voting rights, 227
Adams, John Quincy: on Cuba, 511; and education, 218; in election of 1824, 223–224, 224*p*; in election of 1828, 225; and gag rule, 296; and Indian policy, 234; and Missouri Compromise, 216; national program of, 224–225; as Secretary of State, 212, 213, 217; and Tariff of Abominations, 213, 217, 225
Adams, Samuel: as colonial leader, 80*p*, 81, 82, 84; as member of Continental Congress, 107
Adams-Onís Treaty (1819), 213
Addams, Jane, 444–445, 445*p*, 549*p*, 622, 648; as Anti-Imperialist, 514
Add-a-State Plan, 111, 186
Adjusted Compensation Act (1924), 586
Admiralty Courts, 65–66, 79
Advertising: colonial, 35*p*, 36*p*; and consumer products, 760; discrimination against women in, 856; industry of, 760; negative political, 923; in 1920s, 595–596, 596*p*; in 1950s, 750*p*, 762*p*; for railroad workers, 257*p*; for *Uncle Tom's Cabin*, 311*p*; for western settlement, 270*p*; for western travel, 525*p*
Aeronautics, Bureau of, 667
Affirmative action, 850–851, 853*p*
Afghanistan: Soviet invasion of, 895, 910, 911; Soviet withdrawal from, 921
Africa: and Liberia, 286; and Portugal, 12; and slave trade, 52, 272; in World War II, 680–682
African Americans: in American Revolution, 98; in Civil War, 352, 352*p*; in colonial America, 51; and Declaration of Independence, 106; economic advancement of, 854*p*; education for, 448*p*, 449–450, 853; and equality, 738–742, 850–855; in government, 756, 853, 854; and Jim Crow laws, 380–381; and Ku Klux Klan, 374; migration of, 592, 647*p*, 677, 755–756; and New Deal, 646–649; in 1920s, 592; political power of, 756; in Reconstruction, 367–368, 368*p*; voting rights for, 379–380, 380*p*, 646–

648, 848; in War of 1812, 204; in work force, 654, 855; in World War I, 560*p*, 565–566; in World War II, 676–677, 678. *See also* Civil rights movement; Slavery
Afrika Korps, 681
Agnew, Spiro T., 819, 820*p*; resignation of, 835
Agricultural Acts (1949, 1954), 735
Agricultural Adjustment Act (1933), 628, 644; second (1938), 638
Agricultural Marketing Act (1929), 604, 607
Agriculture, 515; in colonial America, 51; and crop surpluses, 735–736, 735*p*; dry farming in, 404–405; under Eisenhower, 735–736, 735*p*; on Great Plains, 401–406, 402*p*; green revolution in, 903; and migration of farmers, 752–753; in New Spain, 30; and organization of farm laborers, 864*p*, 865–866; output and price of wheat 1867–1900, 477*c*; planting of war gardens, 564; and productivity, 469–470, 470*p*; and sharecropping, 381, 644–645; and use of barbed wire, 404. *See also* Farmers
Aguinaldo, Emilio, 515
AIDS (Acquired Immune Deficiency Syndrome), 936, 936*p*
Airline industry, deregulation of, 902, 902*p*
Airplanes/airpower: and attack on Pearl Harbor, 671–672, 672*p*, 686–687, 687*p*; and Billy Mitchell, 665–667; building of, in 1930s, 666–667; Doolittle's raid on Tokyo, 683; Lindbergh's flight, 593, 594*p*, 666; in World War II, 666–667, 686–688, 687*p*
Air pollution, 758, 803, 803*p*, 886
Air traffic controllers' strike, 903
Alabama: exploration of, 21; Reconstruction government in, 373; secession of, 323; and slavery issue, 216; and voting rights, 227
Alabama claims, 507
Alamo, 294–295
Alamogordo, New Mexico, 698
Alaska: admission to Union, 776; and *Exxon Valdez* spill, 880; oil deposits in, 879, 886; purchase of, 506; sale of coal lands in, 533
Alaska National Interest Lands Conservation Act (1980), 886, 886*p*
Albany, New York, 44–45
Albany Congress (1754), 67–68
Albany Plan of Union, 67–68, 84
Albuquerque, New Mexico, 288
Alcatraz Island, seizure of, 861–862
Alcohol: and election of 1840, 243–244, 243*p*; Lovejoy's campaign against, 287–288; prohibition of, in Georgia, 48; Weld's campaign against, 287. *See also* Prohibition; Temperance movement
Alcott, Bronson, 279–280
Alcott, Louisa May, 280, 338
Aldrich, Nelson W., 532
Aldrin, Edwin E., Jr., 822, 823*p*
Aleutian Islands, in World War II, 683
Alexander VI, Pope, 14
Algeciras (Spain) Conference (1906), 542
Algiers, 181–182, 181*m*
Alien and Sedition Acts (1798), 167–168, 169, 181
Allegiance, Pledge of, 819
Allen, Ethan, 86
Allen, Florence, 651
Allen, Richard, 373*p*

Alliance for Progress, 782
Allison, William, 459
Along This Way (Du Bois), 649
Amalgamated Clothing Workers, 653, 654
Amendments, constitutional: *See* Bill of Rights; *by specific number*
American Colonization Society, 286
American Expeditionary Force (AEF): in World War I, 559–560, 560*p*
American Federation of Labor (AF of L), 433–434, 652
American High School Today, The (Conant), 764
American Independent party: in election of 1968, 819
American Indian Defense Association, 861, 867
American Indian Movement (AIM), 861–863
American Indians: *See* Native Americans
American Liberty League, 631
American Peace Commissioners, 569
American Protective Association, 848
American Red Cross, 338
American Revolution, 93*m*; Battle of Bunker Hill, 86; Battles of Lexington and Concord, 84–85; blacks in, 98; causes of, 56; and *Common Sense*, 86–87; and Declaration of Independence, 88–90; events leading to, 77–84, 85–86; foreign troops in, 86; French aid in, 87–88; heroes of, 218; Loyalists in, 95, 98; medical care in, 97; Olive Branch Petition, 86; purpose of, 846; reasons British lost, 100; soldiers in, 90–92; start of, 85; surrender of British in, 96; Treaty of Paris, 98–200, 99*p*; Washington as commander, 85–86, 91, 92, 94–97, 98; women in, 96*p*, 97–98, 97*p*
Americans with Disabilities Act (1990), 872–873
American System, Clay's, 209–210, 211, 214
American Telephone & Telegraph (AT&T), 763; deregulation of, 902–903
American Tragedy, An (Dreiser), 530
Amherst, Jeffrey, 68, 69
Anasazi Indians, 8
Anderson, Robert, 326
Anderson, Sherwood, 582
Andropov, Yuri K., 911
Andros, Edmund, 65
Anhalt mercenaries, 86
Anian, Strait of, 20
Annapolis (Maryland) meeting, on commerce, 116
Anthony, Susan B., 284*p*, 285, 859–860
Antiballistic missiles (ABMs), 828
Antietam, Battle of, 348–349
Anti-Federalists, 121
Anti-Imperialists, 514–515
Anti-Nebraska party, 314
Anti-Semitism: and Father Coughlin, 632; and World War II, 657, 658, 700. *See also* Jews
Antislavery movement, 105–106, 286–288. *See also* Abolition movement
Antitrust laws, 523–524, 523*p*, 539; and AT&T breakup, 902–903; early, 418, 467; and Roosevelt, 534–535
Antiwar protests, and Vietnam War, 811, 812, 813*p*, 824
Antwerp, Belgium, 689
ANZUS pact, 726
Apache Indians, 288
Apartheid, 922

Apollo 11, 822
Appalachian Regional Development Act (1965), 802
Appeasement, in World War II, 662
Appomattox Court House, 358
Arabic (ship), sinking of, 552
Arabic pledge, 552
Arab oil embargo (1973–1974), 880, 880p
Arabs: *See* Middle East
Arafat, Yasir, 906p, 943
Arawak Indians, 863, 866
Architecture: bridge building, 450–453, 451p; cast-iron buildings, 425–427, 426p; Chicago, 436p, 454; and Civil Works Administration, 629–630; department stores, 453; for garden apartments, 456; hotels in, 229–230, 270, 425, 453; and housing industry, 270–271; skyscrapers in, 453–455, 454p; tenement buildings, 438, 438p, 440, 440p; of Washington, D.C., 177–179, 178p. *See also* Housing
Area Redevelopment Act, 788
Argentina, 682, and Falklands War, 921–922; military aid to, 891
Arias Sanchez, Oscar, 921
Ariel, 109
Aristide, Jean-Bertrand, 869, 942, 942p, 944
Aristocracy: in America in 1790s, 151–152; Jefferson on, 846–847, 874
Arizona, 405; Native Americans in, 8; settlement of, 29, 30, 392; as state, 534; as territory, 353
Arkansas: desegregation in, 739, 850; exploration of, 21; Reconstruction government in, 373
Armenians: ethnic unrest of, 929, 929p
Armies of the Night, The (Mailer), 768
Armistice, for World War I, 560, 577; for Korean War, 731
Arms limitation talks, 892, 911, 916–917
Armstrong, Louis, 592
Armstrong, Neil, 822
Army, U.S.: under Jefferson, 181; Nurses Corps for, 561; Signal Corps for, 665; under Wilson, 553; women in, 676; in World War I, 559–560, 559p
Arnold, Benedict, 86, 96
Arroyo, Martina, 867
Art: Abstract expressionism, 766, 766p, 767p; ashcan school in, 530–531; in colonial America, 60–61, 60p; computer, 842p; Hudson River School, 200, 385p; minimal art, 766; pop art, 766
Arthur, Chester A., 460, 461; and dedication of Brooklyn Bridge, 453; as President, 462–463
Articles of Confederation, 106–107; successes and failures of, 114; weaknesses of, 108–115
Ashcan school of painting, 530–531
Asian Americans, 868, 868p; discrimination of, 848
Assembly line, 594–595, 595p
Astor, John Jacob, 290
Astrolabe, 12, 12p
Astronauts: *See* Space exploration
Atlanta, Georgia, 356; in Civil War, 336p; first black mayor in, 756
Atlantic, Battle of, 680
Atlantic Charter (1941), 670
Atlantic Pact (1949), 718. *See also* North Atlantic Treaty Organization (NATO)
Atomic bomb: development of, 696–698; dropping of, in World War II, 699, 699p;

Manhattan Project, 698; Soviet testing of, 722, 784; U.S. testing of, 784–785. *See also* Hydrogen bomb
Atomic Energy Act (1946), 712–713, 734
Atomic Energy Commission, 713
Atomic power, controlling, 708, 708p, 712–713
Attorney General: and civil rights, 799; and communism, 578–580; first, 153
Attucks, Crispus, 81
Audubon, John James, xvi
Austin, Stephen F., 288
Austin, Texas, lithograph of, 289p
Australian ballot, 528
Austria: pre-World War II, 661–662; in World War I, 548
Austria-Hungary, 547
Automobile(s): advertising, 762p; assembly line in manufacturing, 594–595, 595p; in Great Depression, 606; importance of, 758; in 1920s, 592; sales of, 597c; and suburban life, 757–758
Automobile industry: automation in, 762; model changes in, 762–763; and safety, 803–804
Azerbaijanis: ethnic unrest of, 929, 929p
Azores, 3
Aztecs, 7, 17, 17p

B

B-17 bombers, 666–667, 687–688, 687p
Bañuelos, Romana A., 862
Baby boom, 751, 752p, 808
Backlash, and reverse discrimination, 851–852
Bad Axe, Battle of, 234
Badger, Joseph, xvi
Baer, George F., 522
Baffin Island, 13
Baghdad Pact (1955), 732
Bagot, Charles, 212
Bahamas, 5
Baker, Ray Stannard, 531
Bakke case (1978), 851
Balanced budget, constitutional amendment for, 912
Balanced Budget and Emergency Deficit Control Act (1985), 914
Balboa, Vasco Núñez de, 14–15, 19m
Balfour, Arthur, 585p
Ballinger, Richard A., 533
Balloon frame construction, 270–271
Ballot, 528; development of paper, 227–228
Baltimore (ship), 508
Baltimore, Lord, 58
Baltimore, Maryland, 149, 254, 508; strikes in, 459
Baltimore and Ohio Railroad, 432, 459
Bankhead, John, 645
Bankhead-Jones Farm Tenant Act (1937), 645
Banking: in Civil War, 352–353; under Hamilton's proposal for national, 157; and Jackson, 238–242, 240p, 241p; and *McCulloch* decision, 213; and pet banks, 241; reforms in, under Hoover, 604–606; reforms in, under Roosevelt, 624–625; reforms in, under Wilson, 538–539; and savings and loan crisis, 924
Bank of the United States: first, 157, 171c, 216; second, 210–211, 213, 238–242, 240p
Banneker, Benjamin, 177

Bannock War (1878), 391
Bañuelos, Romana A., 865–866
Bao-Dai, 732
Barbary pirates, 181–182, 189, 192
Barbary States, 181–182
Barkley, Alben W., 719
Barrios, 861, 865
Barron, Captain, 194
Barton, Clara, 338, 338p
Baruch, Bernard M., 565, 708
Batista, Fulgencio, 748
Bauman, Leila T.: painting by, 249p
Bay of Pigs, Cuba, 780
Bear Flag Republic, 301
Beatles, 767
Beauregard, P. G. T., 326
Becknell, William, 289
Beecher, Henry Ward, 316
Beecher's Bibles, 316
Begin, Menachem, 893–894, 894p
Beijing (Peking), China, 528, 828–829, 930
Beirut, Lebanon, 908–909
Belgian War Relief program, 564
Belgium: in World War I, 547–548; in World War II, 665
Belize, 7
Belknap, W. W., 375–376
Bell, Alexander Graham, 427
Bell, John, 322, 323
Belleau Wood, France, 559
Bellow, Saul, 768
Belpre, Ohio, 113
Benson, Ezra Taft, 735
Bent, Charles, 289
Benton, Thomas Hart (painter), xvi; painting by, 575p, 645p
Benton, Thomas Hart (senator), 241
Benton Harbor, Michigan, 754
Bentsen, Lloyd, 929p
Bering Strait, 6
Berle, Adolph A., Jr., 622
Berlin, Germany: blockade of, 717, 717p, 780–781, 911; as divided city, 780; 1953 revolt in, 742; U.S.-Soviet relations over, 746–747; in World War II, 692–694
Berlin Wall: breaching of, 932–933; building of, 781–782, 781p; opening of, 926, 926p
Bernstein, Carl, 833
Bessarabia, in World War II, 663
Bessemer, Henry, 454
Bessemer converter, 429p, 454–455
Bethlehem Iron Company, 428
Bethune, Mary McLeod, 649, 651
Beveridge, Albert J., 509
Biddle, Nicholas, 238–239, 239p, 240
Bierstadt, Albert, xvi; painting by, 526p
Bilingual education, 873–874
Billeting Act (1765), 80
Billion-dollar Congress, 467–468, 474
Bill of Rights (English), 105
Bill of Rights (U.S.), 122, 123, 153
Birney, James G., 286, 297
Birch, William, engraving by, 103p, 117p, 168p
Birmingham, Alabama, 719, 790–791
Bison, 385. *See also* Buffalo
Bissell, George H., 419
Bitter Cry of the Children, The (Spargo), 531
Black, Hugo, 738
Black Americans: *See* African Americans
Black Codes, 365–366
Black Hawk, Chief, 234
Black Manhattan (Du Bois), 649
Blackmun, Harry A., 852, 940

Black Muslims, 806
Black Power, 807–808
Blacks, in Spanish Empire, 15, 28–29
Black Thursday, 601
Black Tuesday, 602
Blackwell, Elizabeth, 285
Blackwell, Emily, 285
Blaine, James G., 376, 461; in election of 1884, 463–464; as Secretary of State, 508
Bland, Richard, 459
Bland-Allison Act (1878), 459, 467
Bleeding Kansas, 315–316, 315p
Blitzkrieg, 664–665, 670
Block, Herbert (Herblock), xvii
Blockade: in Civil War, 337p; in War of 1812, 208; in World War I, 551–552
Blockade runners, 337p
Blood bank, development of first, 676
Bly, Nelly, 511
Board of Trade, 64
Boat people, 891
Bodmer, Karl, xvi
Bogardus, James, 426–427, 453
Boland, Edward P., 907–908
Boland Amendment, 907–908, 918
Bomb: See Atomic bomb; Hydrogen bomb
Bonus Army, 606–607, 642, 643
Bonus Bill of 1816, 211; of 1924, 586
Books: See authors by name; Literature
Boomers, 405–406
Boone, Daniel, 114, 151
Booth, Edwin, 364
Booth, John Wilkes, 364
Borah, William E., 569–570, 663
Border states, in Civil War, 339–340
Bork, Robert, 836, 914–915
Bosch, Juan, 811
Bosnia, 547, 942
Boston (ship), 509
Boston, Massachusetts, 50p, 55, 254; closing of port, 83; desegregation in, 850; ending of siege of, 87; fire of 1872, 376–377p, 377; growth of, 149; immigrants in, 437; settlement of, 41
Boston Associates, 262
Boston Massacre, 81, 82p
Boston Tea Party, 81–83, 83p
Bourke-White, Margaret, xvii
Bowie, James, 294
Boxer Rebellion, 518
Braceros, 865
Braddock, Edward, 68, 94, 149
Bradford, William, 40
Bradley, Omar, 725
Bradstreet, John, 69
Brady, Mathew, xvii, 337; photograph by, 358p, 361p, 372p
Brag boats, 253–254
Brain Trust, 622
Brandeis, Louis D., 539, 919
Braun, Carol Moseley, 854, 859p
Brazil, 14; military aid to, 891; in World War II, 682
Breckinridge, John C., 322
Breed's Hill, 86
Brennan, William, 923, 934
Brent, Margaret, 58
Breyer, Stephen, 940
Brezhnev, Leonid, 828, 892, 911
Briand, Aristide, 609–610
Bridges, building of, 450–453, 451p
Brinkmanship, 731
Bristol, England, 22
Britain, Battle of, 667–668, 668p
British Orders in Council, 193–194, 199

Brittany, France, 22, 688
Brooke, Edward, 756
Brooklyn Bridge, 451–452, 452p
Brooks, Preston S., 316
Brotherhood of Sleeping Car Porters, 677
Brown, Jerry, 936
Brown, John, 316, 316p, 346; raid of, 320–321
Brown, Ronald, 853
Brown, William Wells, 373p
Brown Power movement, 865
Brown v. Board of Education of Topeka, Kansas (1954), 738–739, 852
Brunei, Sultan of, and Iran-contra affair, 919
Brunswick mercenaries, 86
Brussels, Belgium, 689
Bryan, Charles W., 589
Bryan, William Jennings, 475–476, 475p, 535, 923; as Anti-Imperialist, 514; in election of 1896, 476; in election of 1900, 515–516; in election of 1908, 532, 537, religious appeal; as Secretary of State, 542, 551, 552
Bryn Mawr College, 449
Buchanan, James: Douglas break with, 319; in election of 1856, 317; as President, 317–318
Buchanan, Patrick, 937–938
Buddhists, in Vietnam, 787
Budget: congressional powers on, 584–586; federal, 641c, 1928–1940; under Reagan, 898–899; under Roosevelt, 625–626
Budget, Bureau of the, 585
Budget and Accounting Act (1921), 585
Budget and Impoundment Act (1974), 879
Budget deficit: under Clinton, 939; under Ford, 879; under Johnson, 804; under Kennedy, 789; and New Deal, 626, 638, 639; under Nixon, 830; under Reagan, 898, 900
Buell, D.C., 343
Buena Vista, Battle of, 307
Buffalo, 20, 385; killing of, 390–391, 390p
Buffalo, New York: canal between New York City and, 251, 253; Cleveland as mayor of, 463; desegregation in, 850; growth of, 269; immigrants in, 437
Buford (ship), 579
Bulgaria: changes in, 927, 933; and Soviet control, 708; in World War I, 548; in World War II, 690, 693
Bulge, Battle of the, 691
Bull market, 920
Bull Moose party, 535–536
Bull Run (Manassas): first battle of, 335, 341–343; second battle of, 346, 348
Bumaide, Ambrose, 351
Bunche, Ralph, 708
Bunker Hill, Battle of, 85p, 86, 98, 108, 218
Bureau of Corporations, 524
Bureau of Indian Affairs (BIA), 868, 869
Burger, Warren, 829–830, 922
Burger, Warren E., 914
Burgesses, House of, 38, 176, 847
Burgoyne, "Gentleman Johnny," 94
Burma, In World War II, 682
Burnet, David G., 294
Burr, Aaron, 189, 192; conspiracy of, 189; duel with Hamilton, 188–189; in election of 1800, 169; as presiding officer at Chase's trial, 192; treason trial of, 189
Bush, George: 906p, and affirmative action, 853; appointments of, 866; and choice

of Quayle as Vice-President, 922–923; domestic policy under, 924, 939; economy under, 924, 934; in election of 1984, 913; in election of 1988, 922–923, 923p, in election of 1992, 936–938, 937p; and end of cold war, 928; foreign policy under, 924; and Gulf War, 932–933, 932p, 938–940; immigration policy under, 869; inauguration of, 924, 930–931; and midterm elections, 931–932, 940; popularity of, 933–934; relations with Congress, 932–933; and savings and loan crisis, 931; Supreme Court appointments of, 852, 853, 934
Bush, George, Jr., 941p
Business: aid to, under Hoover, 604, 608; and antitrust regulation, 418, 467, 523–524, 534–535, 539, 902–903; under Calvin Coolidge, 590; competition in, post-Civil War, 416–418; corporations in, 261; and growth of mail order, 422–425, 424p; holding companies in, 603, 633; programs for, under Franklin D. Roosevelt, 628–629; and the railroads, 464; regulation of, under Wilson, 539; trusts in, 417–418
Bus transportation: banning of segregated, 790; boycott in Montgomery, 741; issue of school, 850, 851p
Byelorussia, 707, 929, 936

C

Cabinet: creation of, 153–154; and presidential succession, 715
Cabot, John, 15m, 22
Cadiz, 32
Cahokia, 96
Caine Mutiny, The (Wouk), 767
Caisson disease, 451
Cajamarca, Peru, 17–18
Calder, Alexander, sculpture of, 704p
Calhoun, Floride, 231
Calhoun, John C., 200, 306–307; Bonus Bill of, 211; and Compromise of 1850, 307–308; and election of 1824, 223; and nullification, 238; opposition to tariff, 232; and opposition to Wilmot Proviso, 307; proslavery doctrine of, 318; and Secretary of State, 297; on slavery, 234, 272; of Tariff of 1816, 210; as War Hawk, 200
California: admission to Union, 306, 308; conquest of, 301; gold rush in, 305, 305p, 394p; settlement of, 29–30, 291; women suffrage in, 446p
Cambodia, 734, 824, 831; fall of, 889–890; refugees from, 868
Camden, South Carolina, 96
Camelot, Kennedy years as, 774
Campaign finance, need for reform, 879
Camp David talks: between Begin and Sadat, 893–894, 894p; between Khrushchev and Eisenhower, 747
Canada: in American Revolution, 86, 98; boundary with U.S., 162, 212, 301; exploration of, 23–24, 24m; Loyalists in, 98; and Treaty of Paris, 99–100; and War of 1812, 202
Canals, 211, 251, 253, 254m
Canary Islands, 5
Canning, George, 195, 217
Cannon, Joseph G., 533

Capa, Robert, xvii; photograph by, 681p, 686p
Cape Cod, 39
Cape Fear, North Carolina, 22
Cape Hatteras, 22
Cape of Good Hope, 4
Capitalism: Hoover's belief in, 600; labor struggles and, 433. See also Business; Industry
Caplock, 334–335
Caravels, 4, 12
Cárdenas, Lázaro, 659
Caribbean: refugees from, 868–869; U.S. interests in, 506–507. See also Latin America; specific countries
Carlson, Chester F., 761
Carmichael, Stokely, 807
Carnegie, Andrew, 418, 419p, 421, 455; as Anti-Imperialist, 514
Carnegie Endowment for International Peace, 721
Carnegie Steel Company, 418, 456
Carolinas, 84; life in, 54; settlement of, 46. See also North Carolina; South Carolina
Carpenters' Hall, 84
Carpenters' Union, 652p
Carpetbaggers, 372
Carranza, Venustiano, 544
Carson, Kit, 289
Carson, Rachel, 802–803, 808
Carter, James Earl "Jimmy," 854, 876p, 883p, 913; appointments of, 853; cabinet choices of, 882–883, 888; and deregulation, 902; domestic policy of, 882; in election of 1976, 881–882; in election of 1980, 896, 897p; energy policy of, 885, 887–888; environmental policy of, 885–887; foreign policy of, 891–895; and human rights, 891; image of, 887–888, 896; immigration policy of, 869; inaugural address of, 882; inflation under, 884–885; and Iran hostage crisis, 896; and Latin America, 894–895; and Middle East, 893–894; and Native Americans, 862; and Panama Canal Treaties, 892–893; pardon of draft evaders by, 878; relations with Congress, 882–884; and Soviet Union, 892
Carter, Rosalynn Smith, 881, 882–883, 883p
Cartier, Jacques, 19m, 23–24
Casablanca Conference (1943), 684–685
Casey, William, 919, 920
Cass, Lewis, 307
Castillo, Alonso del, 18, 20
Cast-iron buildings, 425–427, 426p
Castlereagh, Lord, 202
Castro, Fidel, 748, 780, 785–786, 867, 869
Catalogs, 422–425, 424p
Catch-22 (Heller), 767
Catcher in the Rye (Salinger), 767
Cathay (China), 5
Catholic church: in California, 291; and discrimination, 849; and education, 788, 801; in election of 1924, 589, 591; in election of 1928, 849; in election of 1928, 589, 591; in election of 1960, 775; and gay and lesbian rights, 870; and Henry VIII, 30; in Montana Territory, 290p; in Oregon country, 290–291; in Philippines, 515; and Quebec Act, 83; school aid and, 788; in Spanish Empire, 28–29, 29p; and Texas settlement, 288; and Treaty of Tordesillas, 13–14

Catlin, George, xvi; painting by, 215p, 235p, 236p, 390p
Cattle drives, 398–399
Cattle ranching: and cowboys, 397–398; and cow towns, 399–400, 400m; and Texas longhorns, 398
Cavazos, Lauro F., 866
Cayuga Indians, 8
Cédras, Raoul, 942p
Census, Bureau of the, 751
Census, in 1890, 442
Centennial Exposition (Philadelphia, 1876), 427
Centerville, 394
Central America: nations of, 907m. See countries by name; Latin America
Central Intelligence Agency (CIA), 715, 733, 837, 878, 907–908, 918
Central Pacific Railroad, 375
Central Powers, in World War I, 547–548, 549–550
Century of Dishonor, A, (Jackson), 391
Chagall, Marc, painting by, 706p
Challenger tragedy, 918, 918p
Chamberlain, Neville, 661, 662, 665
Chambers, Whittaker, 721
Chamorro, Violeta Barrios de, 921
Champlain, Samuel de, 44
Chancellorsville, Battle of, 354
Charbonneau, Toussaint, 187
Charles I (of England), 61
Charles I (of Spain), 16
Charles II (of England), 45, 46, 61, 63–64
Charleston, South Carolina, 251, 254; in 1790, 9, 149; and abolition movement, 296; in American Revolution, 96; life in, 54; and nonimportation agreements, 81
Charlestown, Massachusetts: in American Revolution, 85; settlement of, 41
Charles V (Holy Roman Emperor), 16–17, 21
Charter of Paris for a New Europe, 928
Chase, Salmon P., 353
Chase, Samuel, impeachment trial of, 192
Château-Thierry, 559
Chavez, Cesar, 864p, 865–866
Checks and balances, 120
Chernenko, Konstantin U., 911
Chernobyl, 916
Cherokee Indians, 169, 235–236, 405
Cherry Creek, Colorado, 393
Chesapeake (ship), 194, 204
Chesapeake affair, 194
Chesapeake Bay, 23, 37
Cheyenne Indians, 401
Chiang Kai-shek, 671, 721, 722, 724, 725, 742, 746
Chicago, Illinois, 253, 269, 271, 313; in 1837, 436p; architecture in, 436p, 454; construction in, 271; Democratic convention in 1968, 817–818, 818p; fire in, 376; Haymarket Massacre in, 432; Hull House in, 445–446; and railroad construction, 254; reforms in, 530; smog in, 886; strikes in, 459; suburbs of, 455–456
Chicago, University of, 448; atomic bomb and, 697
Chicago Tribune, Dewey headline in, 720p
Chichén Itzá, Mexico, 7p
Chickamauga Creek, Battle of, 355
Chickasaw Indians, 405
Chihuahua, 188
Child care, as issue, 859
Child labor, 528, 530p, 531, 539, 638
Chile, problems with, 508

China: Boxer Rebellion in, 518; communism in, 722, 722p, 732, 746; under Deng Xiaoping, 922, 930; and Korean War, 723–726; under Mao Zedong, 922; Nixon visit to, 828–829, 829p; Open Door policy in, 517–518, 540; refugees from, 868; repression in, 930–931, 930p; United States relations with, 888; and UN organization, 707
Chinese: discrimination against, 848; as immigrants, 443; as railroad workers, 415p
Chinese Exclusion Act (1882), 444
Chippewa Indians, 863
Chivington, John M., 388
Choctaw Indians, 405
Choris, Louis, lithograph of, 29p
Chrysler Corporation, 653
Churchill, Winston, 577, 665, 667, 669, 684, 685, 693, 710; "iron curtain" speech of, 708–709; and World War I, 552; at Yalta Conference, 691–692, 692p
Church of England, 38–39
Cibola, Seven Cities of, 20
Cincinnati, Ohio, 114, 210, 253, 269, 271
Cisneros, Henry, 865
Citadel Rock, 413p
Cities: company towns, 455, 456p; crime in, 440; garden cities, 455–456; greenbelt communities in, 627; growth of, 269–270, 437–438, 439m, 440–444; immigrants in, 437, 437p; mining, 391–392, 392p, 393–395, 395p; political machines in, 440–442, 463, 527; post-World War I riots in, 578; Progressive reforms in, 527; racial riots in, 807, 807p, 814; and suburbia, 753–755, 754p; tenements in, 438, 438p, 440, 440p
City manager system, 527
Civilian Conservation Corps, 626
Civil Rights Act of 1866, 368, 853; of 1957, 741; of 1960, 741–742; of 1964, 798–799, 800, 852, 854, 857, 872, 873
Civil Rights Act of 1964, 852, 854, 857, 872–873; call for amendment to, on sexual orientation, 870; Title VII of, 858
Civil Rights Act of 1966, 852–853
Civil rights and liberties: Black Codes, 365–366; gag rule, 295–296; internment of Japanese Americans, 677, 678p; and Los Angeles riots, 935; and urban rights, 578; in World War I, 566–567; Zenger case, 60
Civil rights movement: under Eisenhower, 738–742, 739p, 740p, 741p; and election of 1948, 719; under Kennedy, 790–792, 791p; and Lyndon B. Johnson, 798–799, 805p, 806–807, 807p
Civil service: under Arthur, 462–463; reforms in, 460, 527–528; spoils system in, 230, 460
Civil War: attempts to prevent, 324–325; banking system during, 352–353; blacks in, 352, 352p; and border states, 339–340; comparison of North and South, 333–334; draft in, 351–352; from 1861–1865, 342m; from 1863–1865, 353–358, 354m, 356p, 357m, 358p; and emancipation, 340–341; as everybody's war, 337; expectations for short war, 334; in first year, 341–346, 344p, 345m, 347m, 348–349; and Lincoln, 346, 348; Northern leadership, 341, 343; railroads during, 335,

416; secession of South, 323–324; and settlement of *Alabama* claims, 507; start of, 325–326; surrender of Lee in, 358; as war of exhaustion, 335–337; weapons in, 334–335, 335*p*; women in, 337–339, 338*p*, 339*p*

Civil Works Administration (CWA), 629–630, 651

Clark, Champ, 535

Clark, George Rogers, 96, 109, 186

Clark, Tom, 721

Clark, William, 114, 186

Clay, Henry, 100, 223, 309*p*; and American System, 209–210, 214; and Bank of U.S., 238–239; and Compromise of 1850, 307–308; and election of 1840, 243; in election of 1844, 297–298; and nullification, 238; as Secretary of State, 224; as Speaker of the House, 200; and U.S. Bank, 240

Clayton Antitrust Act (1914), 539

Clean Water Restoration Act (1965), 804

Clemenceau, Georges, 567

Clermont (steamboat), 253

Cleveland, Grover: and annexation of Hawaii, 509–510; and dedication of, Brooklyn Bridge, 453; economic policies under, 474–475; in election of 1884, 463–464; in election of 1888, 464–466; in election of 1892, 472; and immigration restrictions, 444; income tax issue, 473–474; and interstate commerce, 464; and labor movement, 472, 474; and Monroe Doctrine, 510; pension veto under, 464; as reformer, 463; second term of, 472–475; and silver issue, 472–473; and tariff issue, 464, 465*p*, 473

Cleveland, Ohio, 253, 269; growth of, 421; immigrants in, 437; suburbs of, 456

Clifford, Clark, 813

Clinton, DeWitt, 204, 251

Clinton, Henry, 95

Clinton, Hillary Rodham, 936, 938*p*

Clinton, William Jefferson "Bill," 906*p*; appointments of, 853, 866, 940; in election of 1992, 936–938, 937*p*, 938*p*; foreign policy under, 942–944; and health care reform, 940–941; immigration policy under, 869; inauguration of, 939; and midterm elections, 941–942; relations with Congress, 939–940; and Supreme Court, 853

Clipper ships, 305–306, 306*p*

Cloture, 798

Coahuila-Texas, 294, 295*p*

Coal mining, 886; and pollution, 713; strikes in, 522, 713

Coast Guard, women in, 676

Cody, William F., 390

Coercive Acts, 83

Coeur d'Alene, Idaho, 472

Cohens v. Virginia (1821), 213

Cold war: beginnings of, 707–711; under Bush, 928; Camp David meeting, 747; and Cuban missile crisis, 785–786, 785*p*; domino theory in, 891; end of, 924–930; under Kennedy, 779–782; under Nixon, 888–889; under Reagan, 911–912; and summit talks, 733–734; and test-ban negotiations, 784–785; trouble spots in 1950s, 746–747, 746*m*

Cole, Thomas, xvi; painting by, 174*p*

Colfax, Schuyler, 375

College of New Jersey (Princeton), 60

Colleges and universities, 281–282; and antiwar movement, 808–809; colonial, 59; for freed blacks, 368; growth of, 447–448

Collier, John, 861

Collins, Michael, 822

Colonial America: collision course with British, 77–84; and Declaration of Independence, 88–90, 89*p*; declaring independence, 84–90; education in, 59–60; ethics makeup of, 51–52, 71*c*; family life in, 58–59; founding, 49*c*; government in, 61–66; industry and trade in, 54–58, 57*m*; journalism in, 60–61; New England, 38–44; New France, 44; New Netherland, 44–45; New Sweden, 45; post-Peace of Paris, 70, 78*m*; proprietary, 46–48; reaction of to British controls, 79; settlement of, 51–52; to 1775, 54*m*; slavery in, 51, 52–53; Virginia, 34–35, 36*p*, 37–38; women in, 58, 59, 59*p*

Colorado, 405; gold rush in, 392–393; populism in, 472; settlement of, 392; women's rights in, 855, 856*p*

Colt, Samuel, 386, 422

Columbia (space shuttle), 913

Columbia River, 187

Columbus, Bartholomew, 4

Columbus, Christopher, 3, 3*p*, 12–16; early experiences, 3–4; voyages of, 4–6, 5*m*

Columbus, Ohio, 113

Comanche Indians, 288

Comic strip, 511–512

Commerce: and Annapolis meeting on regulation of, 116; by colonies, 53–58, 57*m*, 62–64, 81–83; compromise on, in Constitution, 120, 121; department stores, 425–427; dollar diplomacy, 542–543; foreign regulation of interstate, 214, 638; Hamilton and, 157–158; Interstate Commerce Act, 464; Jefferson and, 181–182, 193–196; and Louisiana Purchase, 188; mail-order business, 422–425; Sherman Antitrust Act, 467; transportation developments affect, 254, 257; and War of 1812, 198–200, 207–208; and World War I neutrality, 550, 552. *See also* Trade, foreign

Commerce, U.S. Department of, 534, 600

Commerce and Labor, U.S. Department of, 524

Commission for Relief, 599

Commission on the Status of Women, 856

Commission plan of government, 527

Committee for Industrial Organization (CIO), 652

Committee of Reconstruction, 367

Committee on Equal Employment Opportunity, 790

Committee on Public Information, 566

Committees of Correspondence, 82

Common Market, European, 786, 893

Common Sense (Paine), 86–87, 87*p*

Commonwealth of Independent States, 930

Commonwealth v. Hunt (1842), 431

Communications: deregulation of, 902–903

Communications satellites, development of, 760

Communism: in China, 722, 722*p*, 732, 746, 888; collapse in Eastern Europe, 925–927; and Creel Committee, 577; in Cuba, 864; in Eastern Europe, 708, 710–711, 742, 786; and Henry Wallace, 709–710; in Indochina, 890–891; and

Korean War, 723–726; in Latin America, 895, 907–908; and McCarthy hearings, 723, 736–737, 737*p*; and red scare, 578–580, 578*p*, 579*p*; and Rosenberg trial, 723; and second red scare, 721; in Southeast Asia, 779–780, 779*p*, 890–891; and Truman Doctrine, 709–710

Communist party, in election of 1936, 637

Company towns, 455, 456*p*

Compromise of 1850, 305–312, 309*m*, 313

Computers: advances in, 900–901, 900*p*, 901*p*; and stock market crash of 1987, 920

Comstock, Henry, 394

Comstock Lode, 394

Conant, James Bryant, 764

Concentration camp, in World War II, 658, 658*p*, 694*p*

Concord, Massachusetts, battle at, 84–85, 98; town meeting in, 104

Conda, 336

Conestoga wagon, 51

Confederate States of America, 323–326, 340*m*; compared with Union, 333–334; creation of, 324; women in, 339. *See also* Civil War

Congress (ship), 346

Congress, U.S.: 80th, 714–715, 719–720; and balanced budget, 914; billion-dollar, 467–468; Black Caucus in, 943; and Boland amendment, 907–908, 918; budget powers of, 879; constitutional power of, 121, 169, 185–186, 214; early jobs of, 152–153; effects of 1994 midterm elections on makeup of, 941–942; and gag rule, 295–296; impact of Reconstruction on, 383*c*; and Iran-contra affair, 918–919, 920–921, 920*p*; Library of, 768; and Political Action Committees, 884; Reed Rules in, 466; relations with Bush, 932–933; relations with Carter, 882–884; relations with Clinton, 939–940; relations with Reagan, 896–897; signing of "Southern Manifesto," 739; and special interests, 884; strengthening powers of, 879; and term limits legislation, 932; Watergate hearings in, 879. *See also* House of Representatives, U.S.; Senate, U.S.

Congressional Budget Office (CBO), 879

Congressional Government (Wilson), 536

Congress of Industrial Organization: new members for, 654; origin of, 652–653; and strikes, 653–654

Conkling, Roscoe, 460, 461, 461*p*

Connally, John B., 792

Connecticut: antislavery movement in, 106; colonial government in, 66, 105; industry in, 263; settlement of, 42–43; and voting rights, 227; western claims of, 83, 109

Connecticut Compromise, 118

Connor, Bull, 791

Conquistadores, 15, 17

Conscience Whigs, 307

Conscription: *See* Draft

Conservation: under Franklin D. Roosevelt, 626–627, 627*m*, 643–644; under Johnson, 799; under Theodore Roosevelt, 524–525. *See also* Environment policy

Constitution (ship), 204, 230*p*

Constitution, U.S.: broad versus strict construction of the new, 157; Congress in, 121; and impeachment proceedings,

370–371; as national symbol, 218; necessary and proper clause, 213; President in, 120–121; ratification of, 121–124; Supreme Court in, 121
Constitutional convention, 116–117, 117p; Commercial compromise, 120; delegates to, 117, 118; Great Compromise at, 118; lack of records from, 118; need for compromise, 117–120; Three-fifths compromise at, 118–120
Constitutional-Union party, 322
Constitutions, writing state, 104–105, 372
Consumer goods: in jazz age, 592–593; in 1920s, 595–596, 596p; post-World War II, 713–714, 756, 758–760
Containment, 732, 828–829
Continental Army, 85–86, 91, 92, 94–97, 98, 108
Continental Congress: first, 84; second, 85–86, 87, 88, 89, 89p, 103, 106, 107p
Contras, 907–908
Coolidge, Calvin, 577, 599p; and business, 590; decision not to run in 1928, 590; in election of 1924, 589–590, 589p; and farm problems, 590; foreign policy under, 610–611; and passage of Adjusted Compensation Act, 586; as President, 588–589, 588p; on stock market, 600; as Vice-President, 588
Coolidge, Grace, 588
Cooper, James Fenimore, 227
Cooper, Thomas, 168
Copernicus, 11
Copley, John Singleton, xvi; painting by, 52p
Coral Sea, Battle of the, 683
Corbin, Margaret, 97
Cornell, Alonzo, 460
Cornwallis, Charles, 94, 96, 111
Coronado, Francisco de, 19m, 20
Corporation, 261
Corruption: in election of 1824, 223–224; in election of 1888, 464–465; under Grant, 375–376; under Harding, 586–587, 587p; and Muckrakers, 529–531; and political bosses, 440–441, 527; in Reconstruction government, 373; and Tweed Ring, 376–377
Corsair (yacht), 418
Cortes, Hernando, 17, 19m
Cosmopolitan, 530
Costa Rica, 907; and desire for peace, 921
Cotton: aristocracy and, 152; and depression of 1819, 232; Embargo Act and, 196; and Great Depression, 604, 628; and invention of Cotton gin, 152, 215; and northern textile mills, 260, 261; production of, 327c; role in Civil War, 333; and sharecropping 381; and slavery, 273
Cotton gin, 130, 215
"Cotton Pickers, The" (Homer), 381p
Coughlin, Charles E., 632, 637
Council of Economic Advisers, 713, 789
Council of National Defense, 564
Council on Environmental Quality, 885
Counter-revolutionaries, 907
Courts: See Supreme Court, U.S.; Supreme Court cases
Coventry, England, bombing of, 667
Cowboys, 397. See also Cattle ranching
Cow towns, 399–401, 400m
Cox, Archibald, 835, 836, 922
Cox, James M., 570
Coxey, Jacob, 474, 474p

Cramer, Charles F., 586
Crawford, William H., 223
Crazy Horse, Chief, 389
Credibility gap, 811
Credit, in 1920s, 596
Credit cards, 758
Credit Mobilier scandal, 375
Creek Indians, 159, 405
Creel, George, 566
Creel Committee, 566, 577
Crime: as issue in 1988 election, 929; and Prohibition, 582; Supreme Court approach to, 819, 829
Crisis, The (black journal), 648, 677
Crisis, The, (Paine), 92
Crittenden, John C., 325
Crockett, Davy, 294
Cromwell, Oliver, 61, 62
Cross-staff, 12
Cruise missiles, 892, 911, 940
Cuba: Bay of Pigs invasion, 780; Castro takeover of, 748; missile crisis in, 785–786, 785p, 911; and Ostend Manifesto, 312–313; Platt Amendment, 659; refugees from, 867, 869, 944; reorganization of, 516–517; and Soviet Union, 748; and Spanish American War, 512, 513; under Weyler, 511; in World War II, 682
Cullen, Countee, 649
Cullom, Shelby M., 464
Culp's Hill, 355
Cumberland (ship), 346
Cumberland, Maryland, 251
Cumberland River, 182
Cumberland Road, 251
Currency: See Money and currency
Currier and Ives, xvi–xvii, 326p, 376p, 457p
Curtis, George W., 460, 463
Cushing, Caleb, 505
Custer, George A., 338p, 389
Cutler, Manassah, 112
Czechoslovakia: Communist coup d'etat in, 711; creation of, post-World War I, 567; opposition to Solidarity, 925; pre-World War I, 661–662, 661m; and Soviet domination, 710–711; velvet revolution in, 927; in World War II, 692, 693, 694
Czolgosz, Leon, 521

D

Daladier, Edouard, 662
Dallas, Texas, Kennedy assassination in, 792–793
Dana, Richard Henry, 291
Danish West Indies, 507, 509
Danvers, Massachusetts, 112
Darien, Panama, 14
Dartmouth College, 60
Dartmouth College Case (1819), 213
Daugherty, Harry, 583, 586, 587
Davenport, Iowa, 269
David, 44
Davis, David, 378
Davis, Jefferson, 350, 354, 357; as Confederate president, 339, 342, 346; and opposition to Wilmot Proviso, 307; proslavery doctrine of, 318
Davis, John W., 589, 631
Dawes, Charles G., 589
Dawes, William, 85

Dawes Act (1887), 391
D-Day, 688, 689p
Deadwood, South Dakota, 391, 394
Deane, Silas, 98
Deaver, Michael, 922
Debates: Bush-Clinton-Perot, 938; Carter-Reagan, 896; Kennedy-Nixon, 775–776, 776p; Lincoln-Douglas, 320; Webster-Hayne, 232–234, 233p
Debs, Eugene V., 535, 566, 567p
Debt moratorium, 609
Debts, Hamilton on payment of, 155–157
Decatur, Stephen, 182, 204
Declaration of Independence, 88–90, 89p, 102, 105, 106, 107, 286, 846; signing of, 107–108, 107p
Declaration of Panama, 682
Declaration of Rights and Grievances (Adams), 84
Declaratory Act (1766), 79–80
Deerfield Massacre, 66–67
Defense, U.S. Department of, 715
Deficit, federal: See Budget deficit
Deflation, 459, 624
De Gaulle, Charles, 786
De Grasse, Admiral, 96
De Kalb, Baron, 95
Delaware, 66, 162; approval of Constitution by, 121; in Civil War, 340; colonial government in, 66; end of slavery in, 351; settlement of, 46
Delaware Bay, 23
Delaware Indians, 77
Delaware River, 92
De Lôme, Dupuy, 512
Delta Wedding (Welty), 767
Democratic party: blacks flock to, 637; and civil rights movement, 854; in election of 1852, 310; in election of 1860, 322; F. D. Roosevelt and, 621–622; origin of, 225; rising appeal in cities, 592; splits in 1948, 719; women in 1930s and, 680–681
Demography: 1851–1900, 457c. See also Population
Demonstrations: civil rights, 806; Coxey's army, 474, 474p; in election of 1968, 818p; Shays's Rebellion, 114–115, 116; on Vietnam War, 811–812, 813p; Whiskey Rebellion, 162–164; women in 1970s, 858p. See also Women's suffrage
Dempsey, Jack, 593
Deng Xiaoping, 922, 930–931, 930p
Denmark: and Jay's Treaty, 161–162; neutrality of in World War I, 548; in World War II, 665
Department stores, 425–427, 453
Dependent Pension Act (1890), 467–468
Depression: of 1784, 114–115; of 1877, 459; of 1892, 472, 474. See also Great Depression
Deregulation, 902–903, 902p
Desegregation, 850, 851p; and Civil Rights Act of 1964, 798–799; in 1950s, 738–742; of schools, 738–740
Des Moines, Iowa, 269
De Soto, Hernando, 19m, 20–21
Detroit, Michigan, 77, 253, 269, 527; immigrants in, 437; riots in, 807, 807p
De Vaca, Cabeza, 18, 19m, 20, 21
Developing nations, 893; and Point Four, 711
Dewey, George, 512, 513
Dewey, John, 764

Dewey, Thomas E., 668, 718, 719; in election of 1944, 690–691; in election of 1948, 718–720, 720p
Dewson, Mary (Molly), 650–651, 651p
Dial, 280
Dias, Bartholomew, 4, 15m
Diaz, Justino, 864, 867
Dickinson, Charles, 231
Dickinson, John, 60, 106
Dictionary, Webster's contributions to, 220
Dienbienphu, fall of, 732, 826
Dillon, C. Douglas, 778
Dingley tariff (1897), 532
Direct democracy, 528–529
Direct primary, 527
Discourse of a Discoverie for a New Passage to Catala (Cathay) (Gilbert), 32
Discourse on Western Planting (Hakluyi), 32
Discovery, early voyages of, 3–6, 5m, 12–16, 15m, 22–24
Discrimination: and affirmative action, 851–853; reverse, 851–852. *See also* Equality
Disease: *See* Medicine
District of Columbia, slavery abolished in, 350. *See also* Washington, D.C.
Divorce laws, 285
Dix, Dorothea, 282, 283, 337–338, 855
Dixiecrats, 719
Dodge City, Kansas, 401
Dollar: decline in value of, 900. *See also* Money and currency
Dollar diplomacy, 542–543, 543m, 610
Dominican Republic: under Coolidge, 610; under Johnson, 811; and Roosevelt Corollary, 542
Dominion of New England, 64–65
Domino theory, 810
Doolittle, Amos, engraving by, 74p, 91p
Doolittle, James B., 683
Dorantes, Andrés, 18, 20
Douglas, Stephen A., 309–310, 313p, 315; break with Buchanan, 319; debates with Lincoln, 319–320; in election of 1860, 322, 323; and Freeport Doctrine, 320; and Kansas-Nebraska Act, 313–314, 313p; and Lecompton Constitution, 319
Douglas, William O., 738
Douglass, Frederick, 321, 373p, 646
Downing, Major Jack, 239p
Draft: in Civil War, 351–352; pardoning of evaders, 878; in World War I, 561; in World War II, 669, 675
Drake, Edwin L., 420
Drake, Sir Francis, 31, 32
Dred Scott v. *Sanford* (1857), 317–318
Dreiser, Theodore, 530
Drew, Charles, 676
Drug abuse, 808
Dry farming, 404–405
Dry Valley, Nebraska, 402p
Dubcek, Alexander, 927, 934
Du Bois, W. E. B., 450, 646, 648, 648p, 649
Dukakis, Michael, 923
Duke of York, 46
Dulles, Allen, 780
Dulles, John Foster, 726, 731, 732, 733, 742, 743
Dumbarton Oaks Conference, 707
Dumbbell tenements, 438, 438p, 440, 440p
Dunn, Harvey, painting by, 547p
Dunne, Finley Peter, 513, 530
Durand, Asher, xvi; painted by, 200p
Dust Bowl, 608, 608p, 643

Dust storms, in 1930s, 643
Dutch, in colonies, 44–45, 58
Dutch East Indies, in World War II, 671
Dutch West Indies, 78
Duvalier, "Baby Doc," 868
Duvalier, "Papa Doc," 868
Dyer, Mary, 64

E

Eads, James Buchanan, 450–451
Eagle (lunar module), 822
Eagleton, Thomas F., 832
Eakins, Thomas, xvi
Earl, Ralph, xvi; painting by, 119p
Early Bird (satellite), 760
Early cultures, 6–8, 7p
East Berlin, workers' revolt in, 742. *See also* Berlin, Germany
Eastern Europe: changes in, 925–927; communism in, 742; Soviet domination of, 710–711. *See also countries by name*
Eastern Woodland Indians, 8
East Germany: changes in, 925–927, creation of, 717; mutual recognition of, 888
East India Company, 82–83
Eastman, George, xvii
Eaton, John, as Secretary of War, 231
Eaton, Peggy O'Neale, 231
Ecology, 802–803
Economic and Social Council (UNESCO), 708
Economic Opportunity Act, 799
Economic sanctions: against South Africa, 922
Economic sectionalism, 212
Economy: and Alexander Hamilton, 154–158; and bank issue under Jackson, 238–242, 240p, 241p; under Bush, 924, 934; under Carter, 884–885; and Industrial Revolution, 261; under Johnson, 799, 804; under Kennedy, 788–789; Keynesian approach to, 599, 626, 639, 897; mercantilism, 28, 62; in 1920s, 599; under Nixon, 830; and Panic of 1837, 242–243; and Panic of 1873, 376; post-Revolution, 114–115; post-World War II, 713–714, 713p, 756–757; and problem of Third World debt, 910; under Reagan, 912–914; reforms in, under Roosevelt, 624–626; and stock market crash of 1929, 601–603; and stock market crash of 1987, 919–920, 924; supply-side theory of, 897–898; and Whiskey Rebellion, 162–164; in World War I, 563–564
Economy Act, 626
Edict of Nantes, 51
Edison, Thomas A., 429–430, 763
Education: for African Americans, 449–450; bilingual, 873–874; and busing, 850, 851p; computer skills in, 900p; and desegregation, 738–739, 850; Dewey reforms in, 764; environment statistics, 303c; and equal opportunity, 848, 853; German contributions to, 268; and G.I. Bill of Rights, 712, 764; growth of colleges, 447–448; of handicapped, 872–873; higher, 281–282; for immigrants, 268, 447, 449p; impact of space race on, 745, 764; Jefferson on, 846; under Johnson, 799, 801; under Kennedy, 788; for Native Americans, 235, 873p;

in 1920s, 593; one-room schoolhouse in, 847p; reforms in, 280–281; in South, 214–215; spread of, in 19th century, 446–447, 447p; spread of high school, 763–764; use of mail order catalog in, 425; Wilson reforms in, 537; for women, 282, 283p, 449, 855, 858–859
Edwards, Jonathan, 60
Efficiency experts, 428–429; and labor, 428–429
Egypt: assassination of Sadat, 908; deposing of King Farouk, 742; under Nasser, 733, 742, 743; as part of United Arab Republic, 746; peace negotiations with Israel, 893–894, 894p; relations with Israel, 742, 889; and relations with Soviet Union, 743, 745; and Suez War, 743; and Yom Kippur War, 835, 879, 889
Ehrlichman, John D., 821, 834, 836
Eighteenth Amendment, 582, 850; repeal of, 626
Einstein, Albert, 696–697, 845p
Eisenhower, Dwight D., 689p, 692–694, 777, 780p; Camp David meeting with Khrushchev, 747; as commander of the NATO forces, 718, 719; domestic policy under, 734–737, 738–742; early career, 730; in election of 1952, 729–730, 729p, 731p; in election of 1956, 737–738; farewell address of, 748; foreign policy under, 731–734, 742–748; and Indian policy, 861; and Indochina War aid, 732; and interstate highway system, 757; as leader of NATO forces, 726; and Native Americans, 861; retirement of, 748; as Supreme Commander of the Allied Forces in Western Europe, 688; and Vietnam War, 826–827
Eisenhower Doctrine, 745–746
El Alamein, Egypt, 680
Elderly population: growth of, 756; and Social Security, 633, 721, 736, 788, 801, 883–884, 917; and Townshend Plan, 632
Elders, Joycelyn, 853
Election(s): of 1796, 164–165; of 1800, 169–170, 189; of 1804, 192–193; of 1808, 196; of 1812, 204; of 1816, 209; of 1824, 223–224, 224p, 245c; of 1828, 225, 225p, 227; of 1836, 242, 242p; of 1840, 243–244; of 1844, 297–298; of 1848, 307; of 1852, 310; of 1856, 317; of 1860, 321–324, 324m; of 1864, 356; of 1868, 371–372; of 1872, 375; of 1876, 376–378, 459; of 1880, 460–461, 461p; of 1884, 463–464; in 1888, 459, 464–466, 468, of 1890; of 1892, 472; of 1896, 476, 512; of 1900, 515–516; of 1904, 524; of 1908, 532, 532p; of 1912, 534p, 535–536; of 1916, 553–554, 554p; of 1920, 570; of 1924, 589–590, 589p; of 1928, 590–592, 591p, 849; of 1932, 613–614, 614p; of 1936, 635–637, 635p; of 1940, 668–669; of 1944, 690–691; of 1948, 718–720, 720p; of 1952, 729–730, 729p, 731p; of 1956, 737–738; of 1960, 775–776, 776p, 821, 849; of 1964, 800, 854; of 1968, 813, 817–820, 817p, 818p; of 1972, 830–883, 832p; of 1976, 880–882; of 1980, 896, 897p; of 1984, 913, 913p; of 1988, 922–923, of 1992, 936–938, 937p, 938p; reforms in, 879
Electoral Commission (1877), 378

Electric power, 759, 761; lighting by, 429; public ownership issue, 734–735; in rural America, 645–646
Electronics industry, 763
Elementary and Secondary Education Act (1965), 802
Elevators, 453
Eliot, Charles W., 514
Eliot, John, 90
Eliot, T. S., 582
Elizabeth I (of England), 30, 31–33, 31p, 35
Elizondo, Hector, 867
Elk Hills, California, 587
Ellington, "Duke," 592
Ellison, Ralph, 767, 768p
Ellsberg, Daniel, 831
Ellsworth, Abigail Wolcott, 119p
Ellsworth, Oliver, 118, 119p
Elm Grove, Missouri, 291
El Salvador: civil war in, 907–908; desire for peace, 921; refugees from, 868
Em, David, computer art by, 842p
Emancipation, 340–341
Emancipation Proclamation, 349–350, 350p, 849
Embargo: arms, 660, 662–663; of grain to Soviets, 896; on Japan, 671; Jefferson and, 195–196; Madison and, 199, 202; of oil by Arabs, 835, 880, 880p
Embargo Act (1807), 195–196; repeal of, 196
Emergency Banking Act (1933), 624
Emerson, Ralph Waldo, 233, 279–280, 302
"Empire for Liberty," 111–112, 186
Employers' Liability Act (1906), 524
Employment: discrimination in, 804–805, 857, 872–873; of Puerto Ricans, 863; of women, 857, 859, 860p; in World War I, 465–466; in World War II, 675, 677–678
Employment Act (1946), 713
Employment Services, U.S., 565
Encomienda, 27–28, 27p
Energy, U.S. Department of, 887, 924
Energy policy: under Carter, 885, 887–888; under Eisenhower, 734
Energy problems: and oil shortage of 1973, 879; resources on Indian reservations, 863
England: from civil war to Glorious Revolution, 61–66; and colonial trade, 56, 61–63, 63p; colonies of, 34–35, 37–44; defeat of Spanish Armada, 32; discovery and exploration, 15m, 19m, 22; explorations, 30–33; New England colonies, 38–44, 43m; and Peace of Paris (1763), 70; proprietary colonies, 46–48; takeover of New Netherland, 45; Tudor transformation of, 30; war with France, 66–69. See also Great Britain
English Bill of Rights, 105
English language: debate over, 873–874
English Privy Council, 154
Enrique, 16
Enterprise (aircraft carrier), 629
"Enterprise of the Indies," 4
Entitlements, 898
Environmental impact statements, 885
Environmental policy: under Carter, 885–887, 885p; under Johnson, 802–803; under Nixon, 895. See also Conservation
Environmental Protection Agency (EPA), 885, 898, 899
Equal Employment Opportunity Act (1972), 859

Equal Employment Opportunity Commission (EEOC), 799, 934
Equality: for African-Americans, 738–742, 850–855; among nations, 874; education in, 848; and freedom, 844, 845–850; for gays and lesbians, 869–871, 870p; for immigrants, 848–850; link between freedom and, 844, 845–849; for Mexican Americans, 864–865; for Native Americans, 860–863; for physically disabled, 871–873, 871p; for Spanish-speaking people, 864–867; for women, 855–860
Equal Rights Amendment, 857–858
Era of Good Feelings, 211
Eric, 112
Erie Canal, 251, 253, 261, 266, 267p
Erikson, Leif, 13, 22
Eriksson, Freydis, 13
Ervin, Sam, 833
Ervin Committee hearings, 833–834, 834p
Escobedo v. Illinois (1964), 819
Espionage Act (1917), 566; after World War II, 723
Espy, Michael, 853
Essay on the Duty of Civil Disobedience (Thoreau), 279
Esteban, 18, 20
Estonia, 929, 929p, 936; and Soviet control, 708; in World War II, 663
Ethiopia, Italian invasion of, 658; military aid to, 891
Europe: about 1500, 11m; and Monroe Doctrine, 217; Napoleonic Wars in, 217, 267; wars in, in 1700s, 90. See also countries by name; Eastern Europe; North Atlantic Treaty Organization (NATO); World War I; World War II
European Common Market, 786
European Defense Community, 732
European Recovery Program (ERP), 710–711, 715
European Security Conference (1975), 888, 889
Evans, Oliver, 253
Evans, Walker, xvii
Everett, Edward, 322
Evers, Medgar, 791
Executive Order 8802, 677
Exploration: English, 15m, 19m, 22; French, 15m, 19m, 22–24; Norse, 13; Portuguese, 4, 12; reasons for, 10–12; Spanish, 3–8, 5m, 12–18, 15m, 19m, 20–21. See also Space exploration
Explorer I, 745
Expropriation, 610
Exxon Valdez, 880

F

Factories: in 1920s, 593–595; rise of, 260–262, 260p
Fair Deal, 715, 721
Fair Employment Practices Committee (FEPC), 677
Fair Labor Standards Act (1938), 638–639
Falklands War, 909–910, 922
Fall, Albert B., 583, 587
Fallen Timbers, Battle of, 162
Family life, in colonial America, 58–59
Faneuil, Peter, 56
Faneuil Hall, 56, 61
Farley, James A., 622, 637
Farm Credit Act, 628

Farmers: aid to, under Hoover, 604, 607, 608; economic conditions for, 904p; financial problems of, 468–469; and the Granger laws, 470–471; move of, to cities, 437; New Deal programs for, 638, 643–644; organization of, 469–471; problems of, in 1930s, 643–646; problems of, under Coolidge, 590; programs for, under Franklin D. Roosevelt, 628; push for cheaper money, 459–460; under Reagan, 903–904, 904p; and Shays's Rebellion, 115; and transport of crops in 1790s, 149; and TVA, 626–627. See also Agriculture
Farmers' Alliances, 471
Farmers Castle, 113
Farm laborers: organizing, 864p, 865–866
Farm Security Administration, 645
Farm surplus, 590, 628
Farouk, King, 733, 742
Farragut, David Glasgow, 344–345
Fascism, 632, 656
Faubus, Orval, 739
Faulkner, William, 582, 767–768
Federal Aviation Administration (FAA), 903
Federal Bureau of Investigation (FBI), 831, 837, 878
Federal Crop Insurance Corporation, 638
Federal debt: growing, 913–919. See also Budget deficit
Federal Deposit Insurance Corporation (FDIC), 624, 927, 931
Federal Election Campaign–funding Reform Act (1974), 879
Federal Emergency Relief Act (1933), 629, 644
Federal Farm Board, 604
Federal Farm Loan Act (1916), 539
Federal Hall, 153p
Federal Home Loan Bank Act (1932), 608
Federal Housing Administration (FRA), 627
Federal Indian Claims Commission, 863
Federalism, 125c
Federalist Papers, 122–123, 122p
Federalist party, 158, 161; and Alien and Sedition Acts, 167–169; in election of 1800, 169; end of, 167, 211; on French Revolution, 161; and Hartford Convention, 208–209; opposition of, to Louisiana Territory, 192; and patronage, 189–191; protest of, on Louisiana Purchase, 188
Federalists (supporters of Constitution), 121
Federal Reserve Act (1913), 538–539, 605, 624
Federal Reserve Board, 590, 898
Federal Reserve Notes, 539
Federal Reserve System, 898, 920
Federal Trade Commission, 539, 590
Federal Trade Commission Act (1914), 539
Federal Writers' Project, 649
Federation of Organized Trades and Labor Unions, 434
Feke, Robert, xvi
Feliciano, José, 867
Feminine Mystique, The (Friedan), 855–856
Ferdinand, King of Spain, 14, 17
Ferguson, Miriam A. ("Ma"), 590
Fermi, Enrico, 697, 698
Ferraro, Geraldine, 913, 913p
Ferrer, José, 867
Fetterman, W. J., 388
Field, Cyrus W., 259
Fifteenth Amendment, 374, 382, 382p, 646, 782, 849

Figueroa, José, 867
Fiji Islands, in World War II, 683
Filibuster, 466
Filipinos in America, 643, 865
Fillmore, Millard: in election of 1852, 310; in election of 1856, 317; foreign policy under, 505; as President, 309
Financier, The (Dreiser), 530
Finland: immigrants from, 58; and World War I debt, 586, 609; in World War II, 663, 664
Finney, Charles Grandison, 279
Fireside chats, Roosevelt's, 624, 637
Firestone Rubber Company, 654
First Amendment, 819
Fisk University, 368
Fitch, John, 149
Fitzgerald, F. Scott, 582
Fitzhugh, George, 272
Fitzpatrick, Daniel, xvii
Five Power Treaty (1922), 584
Flag, adoption of first, 218
Flappers, 593, 593p
Flexible response, 782
Florida, 70; acquisition of West, 184; discovery of, 18; exploration of, 21; Jackson's invasion of East, 206–207; Reconstruction government in, 373; secession of, 323; Seminole Indians in, 234–235; settlement of, 29; Spanish cession of, 212–213; in War of 1812, 206–207
Flying Cloud (ship), 306
Following the Color Line (Baker), 531
Food Administration, 564, 565p
Food Security Act (1985), 903–904
Foote, A. H., 343
Foraker Act (1900), 517
Forbes, Charles R., 586, 587
Forbestown, California, 396p
Force Bill (1833), 238
Ford, Gerald, 876p; domestic policy under, 878–879; economic policy under, 879–880, 898; in election of 1976, 880; foreign policy under, 878, 889, 890; pardoning of Nixon by, 877–878, 878p; and selection of Vice-President, 877; succession to Presidency, 877
Ford, Henry, 549, 549p, 594–595, 643, 762
Fordney-McCumber tariff (1922), 585
Foreign affairs: *See Presidents by name*
Foreign aid: and Alliance for Progress, 782; and Eisenhower Doctrine, 745–746; and Marshall Plan, 710–711, 715; Peace Corps, 782–783; and Truman Doctrine, 709–710
Forest reserves, 525, 534. *See also* Conservation
Formosa: *See* Taiwan (Formosa)
Forts: Dearborn, 202; Donelson, 343, 344; Duquesne, 68; Frontenac, 69; Frye, 113; Harmar, 113; Henry, 343; Jackson, Treaty of, 206; Kearney, Nebraska, 400; Mandan, 186; McHenry, 205; Moultrie, 235; Pitt, 69, 77; Sumter, 325–326, 326p; Ticonderoga, 86, 98
Fort Washington, Ohio, 114, 159
Forty-ninth parallel, in Rush-Bagot Agreement, 212
Foster, John, woodcut by, 43p
Fourdrinier, Pierre, 84p
Four Freedoms speech, 669
Four Power Treaty (1921), 584
Fourteen Points, 555–556, 567
Fourteenth Amendment, 368–369, 374, 382, 634, 738, 849, 859

France, 547; aid to colonies, 87–88; and Algeciras Conference, 542; colonial settlements of, 44, 69m; discovery and exploration, 15m, 19m, 22–23; and Indochina War, 731–732; issuance of imperial decrees, 193–194; under Napoleon, 182–183, 185, 193; and NATO, 786; naval war with, 167; in 1930s, 610; and Open Door policy in China, 517; and Peace of Paris (1763), 70; recognition of U.S. by, 108; relations with under Adams, 166–168; relations with under Washington, 159–161; and Suez War, 743; and UN organization, 707; war with England, 66–69; and Washington Conference, 584; in World War I, 558, 558p; and World War II, 662, 665, 681, 685, 686, 688
Francis Ferdinand, Archduke, 547
Francis I (King of France), 22, 23
Franco, Francisco, 659, 660
Frankenthaler, Helen, 766; painting by, 767p
Frankfurter, Felix, 622
Franklin, Benjamin, 68, 70, 79, 89p, 99, 99p, 165, 218; and Albany Plan, 67; as delegate to Constitutional Convention, 118; inventions of, 60; as member of Continental Congress, 102, 107; and rewriting of Declaration of Independence, 88; and taxation, 80
Franklin, William Temple, 99p
Freake, family portrait, 59p
Fredericksburg, Virginia, 351
Freedmen's Bureau, 367–368
Freedom: and Bill of Rights, 123, 153; link between equality and, 844, 845–849; as national slogan, 218; and state constitutions, 104–105. *See also* Equality
Freedom marchers, 791
Freedom of Information Act (1966), 878
Freedom riders, 790
Freeport Doctrine, 320
Free silver issue, 459, 467; and election of 1896, 475–476; and election of 1900, 515; and gold crisis, 472–473; Populists and, 471
Free-Soil party, 307, 308p; and Lecompton Constitution, 319
Fremont, John C., 301, 317, 340
French and Indian War (1754–1763), 68–69, 70
French Revolution, 158, 159, 160–161, 177, 184
Freud, Sigmund, 764
Friedan, Betty, 855–856, 857
Frolic (ship), 204
From Here to Eternity (Jones), 767
Frontier: *See* Western settlement
Frost, Robert, 777
Fuchs, Klaus, 722, 723
Fugitive Slave Act (1850), 308, 309, 310
Fulbright, J. William, 811, 827
Fuller, Margaret, 280
Fulton, Robert, 214, 253
Fundamentalists, 765, 923
Fundamental Orders of Connecticut, 43

G

G–7 meeting, 887
Gaddis, John, painting by, 351lp
Gadsden, James, 312
Gadsden Purchase, 301, 302p, 312
Gagarin, Yuri, 784

Gag rule, 295–296
Gallatin, Albert, 181, 192, 196
Gallipolis, Ohio, 114
Galloway, Joseph, 84
Galveston, Texas, city government in, 527
Gambling casinos, 863
Gandhi, Mahatma, 279, 740
Garden cities, 455–456
Garden Cities of Tomorrow (Howard), 456
Garfield, James A., 375, 461; assassination of, 462; election of, 460–461, 461p; as President, 461–462
Garner, John Nance, 613, 614p, 635
Garrison, William Lloyd, 287, 324
Gates, Horatio, 96
Gay and lesbian rights, 869–871, 870p
Gaza Strip, 743, 943
Gemayel, Amin, 909
Gemayel, Bashir, 908
General Accounting office, 585
General Assembly (UN), 707
General Electric Company (GE), 654, 763
General Motors Corporation, 603, 653
Geneva, Switzerland: and arbitration over Alabama claims, 507; Indochina conference in (1962), 779; summit meetings in, 733–734, 916
Gent, "Citizen" Edmond, 160
George II (of England), 47
George III (of England), 81, 86, 87, 88, 98, 114
Georgia: colonial government in, 66; exploration of, 21; life in, 54; Reconstruction government in, 373; secession of, 323; settlement of, 46, 47–48, 48p; western claims of, 109
Germain, Lord George, 94, 95
German Americans, 51, 266–269, 566; discrimination against, 848
German Confederation, 267–268
German Revolution, 268
Germany, 547–548; aggression of, in 1930s, 661–662, 661p; and Algeciras Conference, 542; division of, 715–716; and Open Door policy in China, 517; post-World War II division of, 727m; resentment of Versailles Treaty, 657; reunification of, 927–928, 927p, rise of Hitler, 657–658; and Samoa, 508; split of, post-World War II, 715–716; surrender of, in World War II, 694–695; in World War I, 548, 550, 551–552, 554–555, 558, 559–560; in World War II, 658–659, 661–663, 664–665, 667–668, 670, 675, 679–682, 685–690, 691–694
Germany, Federal Republic of: *See* West Germany
Gerrard, Forrest J., 862, 869
Gerry, Elbridge, 107, 166; as member of Continental Congress, 107; mission of, to France, 166
Gettysburg Address, 355
Gettysburg, Battle of, 354–355
Ghana, independence of, 738
Ghent, Treaty of (1814), 207, 209, 210
Ghost towns, 391
G.I. Bill of Rights, 712, 764
Giants in the Earth (Rölvaag), 396
Gibbons v. *Ogden* (1824), 214
Gideon v. *Wainwright* (1963), 819
Gilbert, Sir Humphrey, 19m, 32
Gilbert Islands, 682, 683, 695, 696
Ginsburg, Douglas H., 915, 923
Ginsburg, Ruth Bader, 940
Glasnost, 916, 925
Glass-Steagall Act (1933), 624

Glendive, 401
Glidden, Joseph G., 404
"Glorious Revolution," 61, 65, 88
Glover, John, 92, 94
Goddard, John, 61
Goddard, Robert H., 743–744
Godey's Lady's Book, 285
Golan Heights: Israeli annexation of, 908
Gold (currency), 157, 241, 515; Civil War greenbacks and, 353; F. D. Roosevelt and, 624–625; Grover Cleveland and, 474; issue in 1896 election, 475–476; Nixon and, 830; and Sherman Silver Purchase Act, 472–473. *See also* Money and currency
Goldberg, Rube, 756
Gold mining, 391–393, 393*m*
Gold Reserve Act (1934), 624
Gold rush, in California, 305, 305*p*
Gold standard, 474
Goldwater, Barry, 800, 809, 838, 854
Gompers, Samuel, 433, 514, 565, 652
Gonzales, Rodolfo "Corky," 865
Good Neighbor policy, 659
Goodnight, Charles, 398
Gorbachev, Mikhail S., 915, 916–917, 916*p*, 925, 928–929; overthrow of, 930
Gore, Albert, Sr., 739
Gore, Albert, Jr., 937, 937*p*, 938*p*
Gore, Tipper, 938*p*
Gorgas, William, 541*p*
Gorges, Sir Ferdinando, 44
Gorman, Albert, 473
Gottlieb, Adolph, 766; painting by, 772*p*
Government: African Americans in, 649, 853, 854; in colonial America, 61–66; progressive reforms in, 527–529; women in, 650–651. *See also* State government
Government Contracts Act (1936), 634
Governor: colonial, 63–64; in early state constitutions, 105
Graham, Billy, 764–765, 765*p*
Grand Canyon of the Yellowstone, The (Moran), xvii
Grandfather clause, 646, 648
Granger laws, 470–471
Granges, 469–470
Grant, Ulysses S., 343, 344, 355, 357, 461; Cabinet of, 376–377; in Civil War, 333*p*, 372*p*; and corruption, 375–376; and dedication of St. Louis Bridge, 451; in election of 1868, 371–372; in election of 1872, 375; and Panic of 1873, 376
Grapes of Wrath, The (Steinbeck), 643
Gray, Robert, 187
"Great American Desert," 187, 385, 398. *See also* Great Plains
Great and General Court, 41
Great Britain: and American Declaration of Independence, 88–90; and American Revolution, 84–88; versus Argentina, 909–910; and Canadian boundary claims, 162; and *Chesapeake* affair, 194–195; and Common Market membership, 786; control of seas by, 195–197; and financial panic of 1837, 242; imports from 1763–1776, 101*c*; and impressment of American seamen, 194; and independence of Ghana, 738; and Indian uprisings, 201; issuance of Orders in Council, 193–194; and Jay's Treaty, 161–162; land claims of, 114, 196; and Monroe Doctrine, 217; in 1930s, 610; and Open Door policy in

China, 517; and Oregon Territory, 298, 298*m*; reasons for loss of American Revolution, 100; relations with, under Washington, 159; relations with colonies, 77–84; rule of Palestine, 742–743; and Rush-Bagot Agreement, 212; and Samoa, 508; seizure of American ships by, 161; and settlement of *Alabama* claims, 507; and Suez War, 743; and Tariff of 1816, 210; and Texas question, 296–297; and Treaty of Ghent, 207, 210; and Treaty of Washington, 507; and *Trent* affair, 343; and UN organization, 707; and War of 1812, 202–208, 203*m*; war with France, 161; and Washington Conference, 584; in World War I, 548, 550, 551, 555, 558; in World War II, 661, 662, 667–670, 681, 687; at Yalta Conference, 691–692, 692*p*
Great Compromise, 118
Great Depression: beginning of, 606; in Germany, 657; impact of, on foreign affairs, 609; life in, 604*p*; Roosevelt's programs for, 622–631
Great Divide, 187
Greater East Asia Co-Prosperity Sphere, 670
Great Lakes, 44, 212
Great Meadows, 67
Great Plains, 385–386; and buffalo slaughter, 390–391, 390*p*; cattle ranching on, 396–401, 397*p*, 399*p*, 400*m*; farming on, 401–406, 402*p*; Indians of, 8, 385–391, 387*p*, 388*m*, 390*p*; precipitation in, 386*m*; vegetation in, 386*m*
Great Salt Lake, 294
Great Seal of the United States, 104*p*
Great Society, 801–804, 811
Greece: civil war in, 709; and Truman Doctrine, 709–710; and World War II, 662
Greek-Turkish Aid bill (1947), 709
Greeley, Horace, 280, 324, 349, 375
Green, William, 632, 652
Greenbacks, 353, 459
Greenbelt communities, 627
Greene, Catherine Littlefield, 215
Greene, Nathanael, 96, 215
Greenland, 13; and World War II, 670
Green Mountain Boys, 86
Green revolution, 903
Greenville, Treaty of (1795), 162
Greer (ship), 670
Grenada, United States invasion of, 909–910, 910*p*
Grenville, George, 77–78, 79
Griggs v. *Duke Power Co.* (1971), 852
Grimké, Angelina, 286
Grimké, Sarah, 286
Griquet Harbor, 22
Gross National Product (GNP), 757
Gruening, Ernest, 809
Guadalcanal: Battle for, 683–684; fall of, 695
Guadalupe Hidalgo, Treaty of (1848), 301–302
Guadeloupe, 70
Guam, 16, 513
Guanahani, 5
Guatemala, 7; desire for peace, 921; refugees from, 868
Guerrière (ship), 204
Guffey-Snyder Coal Act (1935), 634
Guggenheim, Daniel, 533
Guide to Confident Living (Peale), 764
Guiteau, Charles, 462

Gulf of St. Lawrence, 23
Gulf War, 931, 932–933, 932*p*
Gun manufacturer, 263–264
Gunpowder, 47
Gutenberg, Johann, 11

H

Habeas Corpus, writ of, 340
Habib, Philip, 908
Haciendas, 28
Hacker, Andrew, 790
Hag, Prescott Farnsworth, 443
"Hail, Columbia," 167
Haiphong Harbor, North Vietnam, 824
Haiti: overthrow of Aristide, 869; refugees from, 865, 868–869, 869, 944; return of Aristide, 869, 942, 942*p*, 944; slave revolt in, 184–185
Hale, Sarah Josepha, 285
Haldeman, H. R., 821, 834, 836, 836*p*
Halduyt, Richard, 32
Half-breeds, 461
Halfway houses, 872
Hamilton, Alexander, 117, 122, 158*p*, 169, 176; at Annapolis meeting, 116; and banking issue, 213; duel with Burr, 188–189; as Federalist, 158; on interpretation of Constitution, 157; as Secretary of Treasury, 153, 154–158; and Washington's Farewell Address, 164; and whiskey tax, 162–163
Hamlet, The (Faulkner), 767
Hampton Institute, 368
Hancock, John, 89, 107, 122
Hancock, Winfield Scott, 459, 461
Handicapped: and equality, 871–873, 871*p*
Hanna, Mark, 476
Hanson, Ole, 578
Harding, Warren G.: Cabinet of, 583–584; and corruption, 586–587, 587*p*; death of, 586; domestic policy under, 570, 583*p*, 584–586, 599; economic policy under, 586; foreign policy under, 584
Hardwick, Senator, 578
Harian, John Marshall, 380
Harlem Renaissance, 649
Harmar, Josiah, 159
Harnly, Perkins, painting by, 847*p*
Harpers Ferry, Virginia, 320–321
Harper's New Monthly Magazine, 285
Harper's Weekly, 377, 378*p*
Harriman, E. H., 523
Harrington, Michael, 790
Harris, Patricia Roberts, 853–854
Harrison, Benjamin: and antitrust regulation, 467; in election of 1888, 464–465; in election of 1892, 472; foreign policy under, 508
Harrison, Peter, 42
Harrison, William Henry, 204, 242*p*, 296; and Battle of Tippecanoe, 201; in election of 1836, 242; in election of 1840, 243–244, 243*p*; inauguration of, 244*p*
Hart, Gary, 913, 914
Harte, Bret, 396
Hartford, Connecticut, settlement of, 42
Hartford Convention, 208–209, 208*p*
Harvard College, 59, 282, 443, 447, 848
Hasenfus, Eugene, 918, 919, 920
Hassam, Childe, xiv; painting by, 502*p*
Hastic, William H., 649
Hathaway, Rufus, painting by, 56*p*
Haugen, Representative, 590
Havel, Vaclav, 906*p*, 927, 934

Hawaii: admission to Union, 776; American traders in, 505; annexation of, 505, 509, 510; Japanese attack on, 671–672, 672p
Hawley-Smoot Tariff Act (1930), 604
Hay, John, 513, 518, 541
Hayes, Rutherford B., 376; and civil service reform, 460; and Compromise of 1877, 378–379; and ending of Reconstruction, 379; as President, 459
Haymarket Massacre, 432
Hayne, Robert Y., 232–234, 233p
Health: See Medicine
Health, Education, and Welfare (HEW), U.S., Department of, 736
Health care reform: Clinton's efforts in, 940
Healy, G. P. A., painting by, 233p
Hearst, William Randolph, 512, 535
Heart Is a Lonely Hunter, The (McCullers), 767
Held, John, Jr., drawing by, 577p, 593p
Helena, Montana, 394, 395p, 401
Heller, Joseph, 767
Helms, Richard, 833
Helsinki Agreements on Human Rights, 888–889, 891
Hemingway, Ernest, 582
Hendrick, Burton J., 531
Henri, Robert, 530
Henry, Patrick, 82, 84, 122
Henry, Prince, the Navigator, 12
Henryetta, Oklahoma, Great Depression in, 606
Henry VII (of England), 22, 30
Henry VIII (of England), 30
Hepburn Act (1906), 524
Herblock (Herbert Block), xvii
Herjulfson, Bjarni, 13
Hermitage, The, 242
Hessian mercenaries, 86, 94
Higginson, Francis, 55
Highway Safety Act (1966), 804
Hill, Anita, 934, 934p
Hill, James J., 523
Hill, Thomas, xvi
Hillman, Sidney, 653
Hillsdale, 401
Hinduism, 765
Hines, Earl "Fatha," 592
Hippies, 808–809, 808p
Hiroshima, Japan, 699
Hispanics, 864; education of, 853; in government, 865–866
Hispaniola, 5, 14
Hiss, Alger, 721, 821
History of the Great American Fortunes (Myers), 531
History of the World (Raleigh), 32
Hitler, Adolf, 656p, 681, 685, 688, 707; and anti-Semitism, 657; early aggression under, 661–662; rise of, 657–658; suicide of, 695; in World War II, 664–670, 670
Hobby, Oveta Culp, 736
Ho Chi Minh, 731–732, 826p
Hodel, Donald P., 862
Hodges, Courtney, 689
Hogue, Alexander, painting by, 608p
Holding companies, 603, 633
Holland: See Netherlands
Homelessness, 872p
Home Owners Loan Corporation, 627
Homer, Winslow, painting by, 331p, 360p, 381p
Homestead, Pennsylvania, 432–433, 455, 456p

Homestead Act (1862), 403–404, 405
Homestead Strike, 472
Honduras, 7, 907; desire for peace, 921
Honecker, Erich, 926
Hong Kong: refugees from, 868
Hooker, Fighting Joe, 354
Hoover, Herbert, 583; and beginning of Great Depression, 606–608; beliefs of, 600; domestic programs under, 603–608; early career, 599–600; economic program of, 600, 603–606; in election of 1928, 590–592, 591p; in election of 1932, 613–614; and Food Administration, 564; inauguration of, 599p; Latin American policy of, 659; as leader of Belgium Commission for Relief, 599; limitations of, 608–609; as Secretary of Commerce, 590, 600; and stock market crash, 601–603, 602p; and unemployment, 606–609; at Washington Conference, 585p
Hoover, J. Edgar, 831
Hoover, Lou Henry, 591p
Hoover flag, 613
Hoovervilles, 606
Hope, 38
Hopi Indians, 8
Hopkins, Harry, 622, 629, 631, 644
Hopper, Edward, xvi
Horseshoe Bend, Battle of, 206
Hotels, 229–230, 270, 425, 453
House, Edward, 554
House of Representatives, U.S., 721, 821; constitutional powers of, 121; early jobs of, 153; and impeachment, 370, 836; under Madison's leadership, 153, 155; under Speaker Cannon, 533; under Speaker Reed, 466, 466p. See also Congress, U.S.; Senate, U.S.
House Un-American Activities Committee (HUAC), 721, 821
Housing, 788; balloon frame construction, 270–271, 403; colonial, 166p; in Levittown, 754p; New Deal programs for, 627–628; sod, 402, 402p; tenement, 438, 438p, 440, 440p. See also Architecture
Housing Act (1961), 788
Housing and Urban Development (HUD), U.S. Department of, 802
Housing and Urban Development Act (1965), 802
Housing industry, 270–271
Houston, Sam, 295
Howard, Charles, 653
Howard, Ebenezer, 456, 627
Howard, O. O., 391
Howard University, 368
Howe, William, 86, 92, 95, 98, 100
Hudson, Henry, 44–45
Hudson River, 92, 188, 251
Hudson River School, 200p, 385p, xvi
Hudson's Bay Company, in Oregon, 290
Huerta, Victoriano, 543–544
Hughes, Charles Evans, 553–554, 583, 638
Hughes, Langston, 649
Huguenots, 44, 51
Hull, Cordell, 622, 659
Hull House, 445
Human rights: issue of, 889, 891
Humphrey, Hubert H., 798, 800, 826; in election of 1960, 775; in election of 1968, 817–820, 817p
Hungary: changes in, 925–927, 932–933; 1956 revolt in, 742, 742p, 925; and

Soviet control, 708; in World War I, 548; in World War II, 693
Huron Indians, 67–68
Hussein, King, of Jordan, 746, 908
Hussein, Saddam, 931, 931p, 932, 933
Hutchins, Robert Maynard, 764
Hutchinson, Anne, 42
Hydrogen bomb: controlling use of, 731; Soviet explosion of, 745; testing of, 731. See also Atomic bomb; Atomic power, controlling

I

IBM: See International Business Machines (IBM)
ICBMs (intercontinental ballistic missiles), 784
Iceland, and World War II, 670
Ickes, Harold L., 622, 629
Idaho, 405; mining in, 395; populism in, 472; settlement of, 392; and women's rights, 855
Iliff, John Wesley, 397–398
Illegal aliens: problem of, 869
Illinois: coal mining in, 522; Mormons in, 293; move of Lovejoy to, 287–288; and railroad construction, 254; and voting rights, 227
Illinois River, 182
Immigration: and arrival in New York City, 265p; of Asian refugees, 865; and assimilation, 449p, 477; of Chinese, 443p; in cities, 437, 437p; and education, 268; of German, 266–268; and Industrial Revolution, 265–266; and inequality, 848–849; of Irish, 266; and Know-Nothing party, 314–315; of Latin American refugees, 865–866; and literacy test, 443–444; and machine politics, 441–442; and McCarran-Walter Act, 723; and naturalization acts, 167, 181; new waves of, 868–869; oldcomers versus newcomers, 443; origins, 277c; reform in, 869; restrictions on, 443–444; and union membership, 654; of women, 437p
Immigration Act of 1924, 580; of 1965, 802
Immigration and Naturalization Service, 866
Immigration Reform and Control Act (1986), 869
Immigration Restriction League, 443, 444, 580, 848
Impeachment: of Andrew Johnson, 370–371, 371p; and Nixon, 836–837; of Samuel Chase, 192
Imperial decrees: and Alabama claims, 507; and Alaska, 506–507; and China, 517–518; in Far East, 505–506; and Hawaii, 505, 509–510; and Mexico, 507–509; of Napoleon, 193–194; and South America, 510; and Spanish-America War, 510–517
Imperialism, 505
Imperial Presidency, 896
Impressment, of sailors, 161, 162, 194, 204
Incas, 7
Income, median family, 749c
Income tax: under Hoover, 604; under Johnson, 799; under Kennedy, 789; post-World War I, 585–586; post-World War II, 714–715; under Reagan, 914; and Sixteenth Amendment, 474, 534; and Wilson-Gorman tariff, 473–474; and World War II, 679

Indentured servants, 38, 52
Independence Hall, 116, 117p
Indiana: as territory, 192; and voting rights, 227
Indian Affairs, Bureau of (BIA), 861
Indian power, 861–863
Indians: See Native Americans
Indian Self-Determination and Education Act (1975), 862
Indochina: end of war in, 890–891; U.S. policy in, 825–827; war in, 731–732
Industrial Revolution, 259–265; and agriculture, 269, 404–405, 422; and factory system, 260–263; and interchangeable parts, 263–264; and mass production, 264–265; and slavery, 275–276; and transportation, 261, 413–416; and women, 263, 283
Industrial Workers of the World (IWW), 566
Industry: advances in, 427–430; and automation, 761–762; decline of smokestack, 899–900; Hamilton on, 157–158; and New Deal, 628–629; post-World War I, 585; in World War I, 564–565; in World War II, 675–676
Inflation, 459; under Carter, 884–885; under Ford, 879, 881; under Johnson, 804; under Kennedy, 788–790; under Nixon, 830, 879
Influence of Sea Power upon History, The (Mahan), 508–509
Initiative, 529
Intelligence Oversight Board, 878
Inter-American Conference in Uruguay (1933), 782
"Interchangeable" System, 264
Integration: See Desegregation
Interior, U.S. Department of, for Indian Affairs, 862–863
Interlocking directorates, 539
Intermediate-Range Nuclear Forces (INF) Treaty, 917, 927–928
Internal Security Act, 723
International Bureau of American Republics, 508
International Business Machines (IBM), 763
International Court of Justice, 708
International Ladies Garment Workers Union, 654
International Women's Day, 858p
Internment, for Japanese Americans, 677, 678p
Interstate commerce, regulation of, 214
Interstate Commerce Act (1887), 464
Interstate Commerce Commission, 524, 533, 902
Interstate Highway System, 757, 758m
Intolerable Acts (1774), 83
Invisible Man (Ellison), 767
Iran: hostage crisis in, 894, 895p, 896; and Iran-contra affair, 918–919, Iraq invasion of, 908; Israeli bombing of, 908; under Khomeini, 887, 894; overthrow of shah, 887, 894; Soviet troops in, 709
Iran-Iraq war, 908, 921
Iraq: and Arab nationalism, 746; and Eisenhower Doctrine, 746; invasion of Iran, 908; Israeli bombing of, 908; seizure of Kuwait, 931–933; and Suez War, 743
Irish, 51
Irish-Americans, 266; discrimination against, 848
Iron curtain speech of Churchill, 708–709
Iron manufacture, 428–429
Iron stove, 51

Iroquois Indians, 67–68
Iroquois League, 8
Isaac, 102
Isabella, Queen of Spain, 4, 6, 14, 17
Isolationists, and World War II, 660–661
Israel: annexation of Golan Heights by, 908, 908p; bombing of Iraq by, 908; invasion of Lebanon by, 908; and Iran-contra affair, 919; peace agreement with Jordan, 943; peace treaty with Egypt, 894p; post-World War II, 742–743; recognition of, 893–894; relations with Egypt, 889; in Suez War, 743; UN creation of, 743; and Yom Kippur War, 889
Italian immigrants: discrimination against, 848
Italy: invasion of Ethiopa, 658; in 1930s, 610; and Washington Conference, 584; in World War I, 548; in World War II, 685–686
Iwo Jima, 696

J

Jackson, Andrew, 222p, 230p, 296; and banking, 238–242, 240p, 241p; career and character of, 229–230, 231; domestic policy under, 231–242; in East Florida, 206–207, 212–213; in election of 1824, 223, 224; in election of 1828, 225, 225p; inauguration of, 226; Indian policy of, 234–236, 237p; Kitchen Cabinet of, 231; and nullification controversy, 236–238; and Peggy Eaton affair, 231; and voting rights issue, 226–227; in War of 1812, 206–207
Jackson, Helen Hunt, 391
Jackson, Henry, 745
Jackson, Jesse, 913, 914, 923, 928–929, 928p
Jackson, Mahalia, 791
Jackson, Rachel, 231
Jackson, Thomas J. (Stonewall), 342–343, 354, 355
Jackson, William Henry, photograph by, 412p
Jakes, Milos, 927
James, Duke of York, 45–46
James, William, as Anti-imperialist, 514
James I (of England), 35, 39
James II (of England), 61, 64–65, 88
James River, 346
Jamestown, 21, 35, 36p, 37–38, 51, 52
Japan: aggression in 1930s, 610, 612–613, 613p, 659, 663; annexation of Korea in 1910, 723; "Humiliation Day" in, 580p; industrial advances in, 901; and Open Door policy in China, 517; Perry in, 505, 505p, 506p; and Russo-Japanese War, 540; and Washington Conference, 584; as world power, 893; in World War I, 548; and World War II, 670–672, 682–685, 682p, 695–696, 699
Japanese-American Commercial Treaty (1911), 663
Japanese Americans: discrimination against, 848; immigration restrictions on, 580; World War II internment of, 677, 678p, 849
Jaruzelski, Wojciech, 925
Jarvis, John Wesley, painting by, 87p
Jaworski, Leon, 836
Jay, John, 99, 99p, 122, 161, 165
Jay's Treaty (1794), 161–162, 192

Jazz Age, life in, 592–596
Jefferson, Thomas, 54, 82, 122, 158p, 176, 179p, 847, 927; on aristocracy, 846–847, 874; as author of Declaration of Independence, 88–90, 105, 106, 846, 846p; and banking issue, 213; birthday celebration of, 234; Cabinet of, 181; death of, 170; early career of, 847; in election of 1796, 164–165; in election of 1800, 169; in election of 1804, 192; foreign policy under, 151–182, 181m, 193–196, 193p; inauguration of, 179–181; on interpretation of Constitution, 157; as member of Continental Congress, 107; as minister to France, 114, 160; and Missouri Compromise, 216; and Northwest Ordinance, 111; as President, 177, 179; as Secretary of State, 154, 156, 160–161; on slavery, 179, 286; and Supreme Court, 189–192; and western expansion, 182–189
Jellicoe, Sir John, 562
Jenney, William Le Baron, 454
Jericho, 943
Jervis, John Bloomfield, 256
Jews: and anti-Semitism, 632, 657, 658, 700; discrimination against, 848, 849; in World War II, 657, 658, 700
Jim Crow laws, 380–381
John II (King of Portugal), 4, 13
Johns Hopkins University, 448
Johnson, Andrew, 370p; assassination attempt on, 364; character of, 365; impeachment of, 370–371, 371p; and Reconstruction, 365–369, 365p
Johnson, Eliza, 365
Johnson, Governor (of North Carolina), 64
Johnson, Hugh, 628–629
Johnson, Lady Bird, 778p, 792
Johnson, Lyndon B., 739, 778p, 792, 797p, 868; and civil rights, 741, 798–799, 804–808, 805p, 807p, 854; decision not to seek reelection, 814; domestic policy of, 798–800, 801p; early career, 797–798; in election of 1960, 775; in election of 1964, 800, 854; fall of, 813–814; and Great Society programs, 801–804, 811; and Native Americans, 861; and Panama riots, 892; as space enthusiast, 784; succession to Presidency, 793p, 798; and Supreme Court, 853; and Vietnam War, 809–813, 810m, 827–828
Johnson, William Samuel, 118
Johnston, Albert Sidney, 344
Johnston, Frances Benjamin, photograph by, 448p
Johnston, Joseph E., 341, 344, 345, 346, 357
Joint Committee of Fifteen, 367
Joint stock company, 33, 261
Jonathan, 48
Jones, Bobby, 593
Jones, James, 767
Jones, John Paul, 218
Jones, Samuel M. "Golden Rule," 527
Joplin, Scott, 538
Jordan: driving out of PLO, 908; and Eisenhower Doctrine, 746; under King Hussein, 746, 908; peace agreement with Israel, 943; and Suez War, 743
Jordan, David Starr, 514
Joseph, Chief, 389, 389p
Journalism, 191; in colonial America, 60; and muckrakers, 529–531; role of women in, 280; and World War I propa-

ganda, 566; and yellow press, 511–512. *See also* Magazines; Newspapers
Judicial review, 191
Judiciary Act (1789), 153, 191
Judiciary Act (1801), 189–190; repeal of, 190
Julia, 116
Julia, Raul, 867
Julia Frances, 12
Jungle, The (Sinclair), 524
Justice, U.S. Department of: and affirmative action, 851–852

K

Kahn, Florence, 651
Kanagawa, Treaty of (1854), 505
Kansas, 405; bleeding, 315–316, 315*p*; and Lecompton Constitution, 318–319; and slavery issue, 313, 315–316; as territory, 313, 315–316
Kansas City, Missouri, reform movement in, 530
Kansas-Nebraska Act (1854), 313–314, 314*m*
Kaskaskia, Illinois, 96
Kaskaskia River, 182
Kearny (ship), 670
Kearny, Stephen, 301
Kefauver, Estes, 737, 739
Kelley, Oliver H., 469
Kellogg, Frank, 609–610, 610*p*
Kellogg-Briand Pact (1929), 609–610, 609*p*, 612
Kemble, Edward, cartoon by, 468*p*
Kennan, George F., 709, 711
Kennedy, Anthony M., 915, 923
Kennedy, Edward M., 896, 915
Kennedy, Jacqueline, 774, 774*p*, 778*p*, 792
Kennedy, John F., 774, 774*p*, 778*p*, 780*p*, 874; appraisal of, 793–794; assassination of, 792–793; in Berlin, 782; Cabinet of, 777–778; and civil rights movement, 790–792, 791*p*; and cold war, 779–782, 787*p*; debate with Nixon, 775–776, 776*p*; domestic policy under, 788–792; early career of, 776–777; in election of 1960, 775–776, 776*p*, 821, 849; foreign policy under, 779–788; funeral of, 794*p*; Grand Design of, 786; inaugural address of, 777; inauguration of, 776*p*; and Vietnam War, 786–788, 827
Kennedy, Joseph P., 776–777, 778*p*
Kennedy, Robert, 778; assassination of, 817; as Attorney General, 790; in election of 1968, 813
Kennedy, Rose, 778*p*
Kent State University, antiwar violence at, 824
Kentucky: in Civil War, 340; settlement of, 151; and slavery issue, 215, 351; as state, 151
Kentucky Resolutions (1798), 169, 232, 234
Keppler, J., xvii; lithograph by, 442*p*, 465*p*, 514*p*
Kerensky, Alexander, 577
Kerosene, 419
Kesey, Ken, 872
Key, Francis Scott, 205
Keynes, John Maynard, 599, 626, 897, 898
KGB, 911
Khmer Rouge, 826, 889–890, 891
Khomeini, Ayatollah Ruhollah, 887, 894

Khrushchev, Nikita, 733, 743, 747; and Kennedy, 780–781, 784
Killian, James R., Jr., 745
Killing Fields, The, 890
Kindergarten, 268
King, Coretta Scott, 805*p*
King, Martin Luther, Jr., 649, 741*p*, 756, 765, 790–791, 806, 913; assassination of, 814, 817, 819; early career, 740; and nonviolence, 740–741
King, Rodney, 935
King, Rufus, 209
King George's War (1744–1748), 70
King's College (Columbia), 60, 116
King's Mountain, South Carolina, 96
King William's War (1689–1697), 70
Kino, Eusebio Francisco, 29
Kirghiz: ethnic unrest of, 929
Kissinger, Henry, 828, 888–889, 889*p*
Kitchen Cabinet, 231
Kleindienst, Richard, 834
Klerk, F. W. de, 943
Kline, Franz, 766
Knight, E. C., Company, 467
Knights of Labor, 433, 469
Knights of the Black Cross, 374
Knights of the Rising Sun, 374
Knights of the White Camellia, 374
Know-Nothing party, 314–315, 848
Knox, Frank, 663
Knox, Henry, 154
Knox, Philander C., 542
Kohl, Helmut, 927, 927*p*, 928, 934, 935, 935*p*
Kooning, Willem de, xvi, 766
Koop, C. Everett, 873, 936
Korea: civil war in, 723–724; crisis in North, 942; immigrants from, 848, 868; Soviet attack on airliner of, 911–912
Korean War, 677, 723–726, 725*m*, 729; peace negotiations, 731
Kosciusko, Thaddeus, 95
Krenz, Egon, 926
Ku Klux Klan, 373–374, 374*p*, 849; post-World War I, 580, 589, 591, 849; post-World War II, 715
Ku Klux Klan Acts (1870–1871), 374
Kuwait, 923; Iraqi seizure of, 931–933
Kwajalein Island, 696

L

Labor (land measure), 288
Labor, U.S. Department of, 534
Labor force: and affirmative action, 851–853, 853*p*; African Americans in, 855; changes in, 764; and Coxey's Army, 474, 475*p*; and deregulation, 902–903; and efficiency experts, 428–429; under Eisenhower, 736; in factory system, 262–263; and length of workday, 243, 539; and minimum wages, 634–635; and mobilization for World War II, 675–676, 678; and New Deal, 633–663; post-World War I, 577–578; post-World War II, 713–714, 713*p*; under Reagan, 903; and reverse discrimination, 851–852; and steel industry, 789; women in, 263, 431*p*, 634, 654, 654*p*, 857, 859, 860*p*, 875*c*, 901; in World War I, 565–566; in World War II, 679
Labor unions: for air traffic controllers, 903; American Federation of Labor, 433–434, 652; and bomb scares, 578, 579*p*; and collective bargaining, 634;

and Congress of Industrial Organization, 652–654; decline in membership, 903; early trade unions, 430–432; early violence, 432–433; growth of, 430–432; Knights of Labor, 433; membership in, 655*c*; and organization of farm laborers, 865–866; organizing farm laborers, 861–863, 862*p*; and passage of North American Free Trade Agreement (NAFTA) treaty, 939–940; retraining programs of, 899*p*; strikes by, 459, 472, 522, 578, 653–654, 653*p*, 713, 903; and Taft-Hartley Act, 714, 720. *See also specific unions*
Labrador, 13
Lafayette, Marquis de, 95, 96, 218
La Follette, Belle Case, 528*p*
La Follette, Robert M., 527–528, 528*p*, 534, 555, 589–590
La Follette Seamen's Act (1915), 539
Laika, 744–745
Lake Champlain, 205
Lake Forest, Illinois, 456
Lake of the Woods, Minnesota, 212
Lancaster Turnpike, 251
Land, Edwin H., 761
Land grants, to railroads, 413, 413*m*, 415
Landon, Alf, 635, 637
Land Ordinance (1785), 111, 112
Land speculation, post-Revolution, 110–111
Lange, Dorothea, xvii, photograph by, 604*p*, 605*p*, 644*p*
Language: debate on English as official, 873–874
Lansing, Robert, 552
Laos, 779–780, 779*p*, 890–891; refugees from, 868
Laramie, 401
Larimer, William, 393
Laser, 763
Last Chance Gulch, 391, 394
Lateen sail, 12, 13*p*
Latin America: and Alliance for Progress, 782; under Coolidge, 610–611; and Dollar diplomacy, 542–543, 543*m*; and Eisenhower, 747–748; and formation of Organization of American States, 508; Good Neighbor policy toward, 659; under Hoover, 611–612; under L. B. Johnson, 811; and Monroe Doctrine, 217, 510; and Panama Canal treaties, 892–893, 892*p*; and problem in Chile, 508; and problem of Third World debt, 910; Reagan policy in, 907–908, 921; refugees from, 868–869; and Roosevelt Corollary, 452, 542, 592, 611; Sanchez peace plan in, 921; and World War II, 682. *See also specific country*
Latvia, 929, 929*p*; and Soviet control, 708; in World War II, 663, 936
Laud, William, 40
Laurens, Henry, 99*p*
Law: colonial, 62; granger, 470–471; in mining fields and towns, 394–395
Law, Bernard, Cardinal, 873
Lawrence, James, 204
Lawrence, Kansas, 316
Leadville, 394
League of Nations, 569; Harding's disinterest in, 584; as ineffective, 612; Japanese withdrawal from, 659; U.S. opposition to, 569–570
League of United Latin American Citizens, 861, 865
Lease, Mary Elizabeth, 471–472, 471*p*

Lebanon, 908–909; and Eisenhower Doctrine, 746; hostages in, 919; and Middle East conflict, 908–909; 1956 civil war in, 746; and Suez War, 743
LeClerc, General, 185
Lecompton Constitution, 318–319
Lee, Charles, 166
Lee, Jason, 290
Lee, Richard Henry, 107
Lee, Robert E., 335, 341, 346; as general in Civil War, 348, 348p, 354, 355, 358; and John Brown's raid, 321; surrender of, 358
Lemke, William, 637
Lend-Lease Act (1941), 669
L'Enfant, Pierre-Charles, 177
Leni, 44
Lenin, V. I., 577
Leopard (ship), 194
Letter of marque, 62, 63
Levittown, Pennsylvania, 754p
Lewis, John L., 652–654, 652p
Lewis, Meriwether, 114, 186
Lewis, Sinclair, 582
Lewis and Clark expedition, 186–187, 187m; journals of, 188p
Lexington (ship), 683
Lexington, Battle of, 84–85, 98
Leyte Gulf, Battle of, 696, 697p
Liberator, The, 287
Liberty, as national slogan, 218
Library of Congress, 205, 768
Libya: and explosion of PAN AM flight 103, 921; under Qaddafi, 878–879, 879, 919; U.S. bombing of, 917
Lie, Trygve, 708
Lieberman, Joshua Loth, 764
Life among the Paiutes, Their Wrongs and Claims (Winnemucca), 391
Light bulbs, 429
Liliuokalani, Queen, 509–510
Lincoln, Abraham, 320p, 322p, 349, 361p; assassination of, 363–364; call for troops, 333; career of, 323; and Civil War, 339–340, 346, 348; debates with Douglas, 318–319, 320, 775; in election of 1860, 322–324; in election of 1864, 356; and emancipation, 340–341, 349–350, 350p; and Fort Sumter, 325–326; funeral of, 364p; inauguration of, 325, 332; Reconstruction plan of, 361–363; and slave issue, 323, 349; and Trent affair, 343
Lincoln, Tad, 361p
Lindbergh, Anne Morrow, 611
Lindbergh, Charles, 611, 663; in Mexico, 611p; New York-Paris flight of, 593, 594p, 666
Lippmann, Walter, 614
Lisbon, Portugal, 3
Literacy test, 443–444, 647
Literature: Harlem Renaissance in, 649; in 1920s, 581–582; post-World War II, 767–768; and slave issue, 311, 311p; and Transcendentalists, 279–280
Lithuania, 929, 929p, 936–937; and Soviet control, 708; in World War II, 663
Little Rock, Arkansas: school segregation in, 739–740, 741p, 850
Little Round Top, 355
Little Theater movement, 445
Little Women (Alcott), 280
Livingston, Robert, 183–184, 186, 214
Llama, 8
Llewellyn Park, New Jersey, 455–456
Lloyd George, David, 567

Locke, John, 46, 103
Lodge, Henry Cabot, Sr., 466, 509, 570, 570p, 585p
Lodge, Henry Cabot, Jr., 775
Lôme, Dupuy de, 512
London Company, 35, 39
London Conference (1930), 610
Lone Star Republic, 294–295
Long, Huey, 632, 633, 637
Long Island, Battle of, 100
Longshoremen's Union, 434
Lon Nol, General, 890
Lookout Mountain, Battle of, 355
Lords Commissioners of Trade and Plantations, 65–66
Lords of Trade, 63–64
Los Angeles, California: Mexican Independence Day parade in, 849p; race riots in, 935; reform movement in, 530; smog in, 886
Losantville, Ohio, 113
Losing Battles (Welty), 767
Lost Colony, 33
Louisbourg, 44, 67, 69
Louisiana, 70; Reconstruction government in, 373; secession of, 323
Louisiana Purchase, 182–186, 183m; exploration of, 186–188, 187m
Louisiana Territory, 70; explored, 186–187; French settlements before 1763, 69m; Pinckney's Treaty, 162; purchased, 185–186
Louisville, Kentucky, 269
Louis XIV (of France), 61, 182
Louis XVI (of France), 88, 160
Lovejoy, Elijah Parish, 287–288, 287p
Lowden, Frank, 583
Lowell, A. Lawrence, 581
Lowell, Francis Cabot, 261–263
Loyalists: in American Revolution, 95, 98; and Treaty of Paris, 100
Lujan, Manuel, Jr., 866
Luks, George, 530
Lumber industry, 403p, 404
Lusitania (ship), 552, 553p
Luxembourg, in World War II, 665
Lyman, Phineas, 98
Lynch, Charles, 578
Lynching, 578, 715
Lynn, Massachusetts, settlement of, 41

M

MacArthur, Douglas, 695–696, 695p, 724–726
MacCready, Paul, Jr., 902
Macdonough, Thomas, 206, 207
Macedonia (ship), 204
MacFarlane, Robert, 918
Machine politics: and immigrants, 443; reform of, 527
Machinery Hall, 427
Machine tools, 427–428
Machu Picchu, 8p
Mackay, John W., 394
Macmillan, Harold, 747
Macon's Bill No. 2, 199
Madeira Islands, 3
Madero, Francisco, 543
Madison, Dolley, 205
Madison, James, 117, 118, 122, 176, 191, 199p; and Bill of Rights, 153; as delegate to Constitutional Convention, 118; domestic policy of, 211; in election of

1808, 196; in election of 1812, 205; on estate government, 103; foreign policy under, 199; and impressment of American seamen, 194; on interpretation of Constitution, 157; as leader in House of Representatives, 153, 155; and message of 1815, 209–210; on payment of debt, 155; as Secretary of State, 181, 196; and voting rights, 227; and War of 1812, 199, 202, 205
Magazines: and women's rights, 285. See also Journalism; Newspapers
Magellan, Ferdinand, 15–16, 15m
Maginot line, 664, 665
Magna Carta, 105
Mahan, Alfred Thayer, 508–509, 509p, 510
Mailer, Norman, 768
Mail order, growth of, 422–425, 424p
Mail system: development of national, 257–259; issuance of postal stamps, 259; and mail order catalogs, 422–425, 424p; rural, 259; in 1790, 151
Maine: border disputes with Canada, 301; as free state, 216; industry in, 262; settlement of, 44; temperance in, 582; and voting rights, 227
Maine (ship), 512
Mainstreaming, 872–873
Malay peninsula, in World War II, 671
Malaysia: refugees from, 868
Malcolm X, 806, 807
Mallorca, 29
Malvinas (Falkland Islands), 922; battles of, 335, 341, 346–348
Manchester, Ohio, 114
Manchuria, Japanese invasion of, 659
Mandela, Nelson, 922, 943–944, 944p
Manhattan, 44–45. See also New York City
Manhattan Project, 698
Manifest destiny, 298
Mankiller, Wilma, Chief, 863p
Mann, Horace, 281
Manned Spacecraft Center (Houston, Texas), 822
Mann-Elkins Act (1910), 533
Mansion, The (Faulkner), 767
Manuel I (King of Portugal), 15–16
Manufacturing: See Industry
Mao Zedong, 722, 922
Mapmaking, early, 13, 14m
Marblehead regiment, 92, 94
Marbury, William, 191
Marbury v. Madison (1803), 191–192
Marcos, Fray, 20
Marcy, William L., 312
Margin loans, 600
Mariana Islands, in World War II, 695
Marie Antoinette, 160
Mariel Boat Lift, 867p
Marietta, Ohio, 113
Marin, Luis Muñoz, 866
Marines, U.S.: in Grenada invasion, 909–910, 910–911; landing of, at Veracruz, 544; in Lebanese conflict, 909, 909p; and Somoza, 895; women in, 676
Marion, Francis "Swamp Fox," 96
"Marseillaise," 161
Marshall, George, 710p; and European Recovery Program (ERP), 710–711, 715; as Secretary of State, 709, 710; and voting rights, 227
Marshall, John, 167, 169, 189, 190p, 231; as Chief Justice, 189–192, 213–214, 235–236; mission of, to France, 166
Marshall, Thurgood, 738–739, 790, 807–808, 853, 934

Marshall Islands, in World War II, 683, 695, 696
Marshall Plan, 710–711, 715
Martin, E. Hall, painting by, 393*p*
Martineau, Harriet, 262, 263
Martinique, 70
Martinsburg, West Virginia, strike in, 459
Martin v. *Hunter's Lessee* (1816), 213
Martin v. *Wilks* (1989), 852
Mary I (of England), 32
Mary II (of England), 61, 65–66, 88
Maryland: in Civil War, 339–340; colonial government in, 66; end of slavery in, 351; payment of debt, 155; settlement of, 46; and western land claims, 109–110, 111, 118
Mason, George, 122
Mason, James M., 343
Massachusetts: industry in, 262, 263; and ratification of Constitution, 122; and Shays's Rebellion, 115; start of American Revolution in, 84–85; state government in, 104; and voting rights, 227; western land claims of, 83, 109
Massachusetts Bay Colony, 40–41; colonial government in, 55; colonial resistance in, 82–83; and colonial trade, 64; education in, 59
Massachusetts Centinel, 124*p*
Mass production, 264–265
Mathew (ship), 22
Matsu, 746
Mauldin, Bill, xvii
Mauro, Fra: map drawn by, xxm
Mayas, 7
Mayflower (ship), 39
Mayflower Compact, 40
Mayor-council form of government, 527
McAdoo, William, 563–564, 589
McAuliffe, A. C., 691
McAuliffe, Christa, 918
McCarran Internal Security Act (1950), 723
McCarran-Walter Act (1952), 723
McCarthy, Eugene, 813, 817
McCarthy, Joseph, 736–737, 737*p*, 777, 778, 823, 826
McCauley, Mary (Molly Pitcher), 97
McClellan, George, 343, 345, 346, 348, 356
McClure's Magazine, 529, 530
McCoy, Joseph G., 399
McCullers, Carson, 767
McCulloch v. *Maryland* (1819), 213
McDowell, Irvin, 341–342
McDuffie Act (1934), 696
McGovern, George, 832–833, 832*p*, 890
McHenry, James, 165
McKay, Donald, 306
McKay, Douglas, 734
McKinley, William, 621; assassination of, 521; in election of 1890, 468; in election of 1896, 476, 512; in election of 1900, 515–516; foreign policy under, 516–518, 517*m*; and Spanish American War, 512–513
McKinley Tariff (1890), 466–467, 473
McLoughlin, John, 290
McMahon, Thomas, 653
McNamara, Robert S., 777–778, 782, 811, 812, 813
McNary, Charles, 590, 669
McNary-Haugen bill, 590
Mead, Margaret, 857
Meade, George Gordon, 354
Meat Inspection Act (1906), 524
Mechanics' institutes, 281
Medford, Massachusetts, settlement of, 41

Medicaid, 801, 872
Medicare, 801, 801*p*, 872
Medicine: advances in, 901; in American Revolution, 97; and building Panama Canal, 541–542; in Civil War, 338–339; in Colonial America, 58; development of blood banks, 676; impact of disease on Native Americans, 17, 27–28, 77; and Medicare, 801, 801*p*, 872; in 1920s, 593; and trench warfare, 557; and women's rights, 285; in World War II, 699–700; and yellow fever, 516, 542
Meese, Edwin, 919, 920, 922, 928
Mein Kampf (My Struggle) (Hitler), 657
Mellon, Andrew, 583, 585–586, 603
Member of the Wedding, The (McCullers), 767
Memphis, Tennessee, 269
Mencken, H. L., 581
Mental illness: and equality, 872; reforms in treating, 282
Mentally retarded: education of, 872
Mercantilism, 28, 62, 70
Mercenaries, in American Revolution, 86, 90
Merchant marine, growth of, 194; British, 204; in World War I, 562*p*; in World War II, 675
Meredith, James, 790, 807
Merrimac (ship), 345–346
Merrimack Manufacturing Company, 262*p*
Mestizos, 30
METO (Middle East Treaty Organization), 732
Metternich, Prince, 268
Mexican Americans, equality for, 864–865; after World War I, 590; as migrant workers, 643; in New Mexico, 384; unions for, 654
Mexican G.I. Forum, 865
Mexican War (1846–1848), 299–301, 299*m;* treaty ending, 301–302
Mexico: Aztecs in, 7–8, 17, 17*p;* discovery of, 18, 20; Good Neighbor Policy toward, 659; Mayans in, 7–8, 7*p;* and Napoleon ill, 507; policy toward, under Coolidge, 610–611; policy toward, under Wilson, 543–544; and Texas settlement, 294–295; and western settlement, 287–289, 291; and World War II, 682; and Zimmermann note, 555
Meynall, Godfrey, painting by, 55*p*
Miami, Florida: gay and lesbian rights in, 870
Miami (Indian) Confederacy, 162
Miami River, 182
Michigan, lumber industry in, 404
Middle class: anxious, 936
Middle Colonies, economy of, 58
Middle East: and Arab oil embargo, 880, 880*p;* assassination of Sadat, 908; and creation of Israel, 742–743; and Eisenhower Doctrine, 745–746; and Gulf War in, 938–940, 939*p;* Gulf War in, 432*p*, 931, 932–933; Iran hostage crisis in, 894, 895*p*, 896; Iran-Iraq war in, 921, 923–924, 924*p;* and Iraq seizure of Kuwait, 938–940; Iraq seizure of Kuwait, 931–933; Lebanese conflict in, 924; Lebanese crisis in, 908–909, 909*p;* and oil shortage of 1973, 879; and Organization of Petroleum Exporting Countries (OPEC), 880; Palestine Liberation Organization in, 893; Palestinian issue in, 743, 894, 906*p*, 908*p;* peace negotiations in, 893–894, 894*p,*

906*p*, 943, 943*p;* problems in Iran, 887, 894–895, 919; and recognition of Israel, 893–894; religious conflict in, 893, 908; Soviet invasion of Afghanistan, 895, 910, 911, 921; and Suez War, 743; and terrorism, 916–917, 916*p;* in World War II, 880; and Yom Kippur War, 879, 889
Middle passage, 55*p*, 292
"Midnight judges," 190
Midway, Battle of, 683
Migrant workers, 643, 861–862
Mikoyan, Anastas, 747
Miles City, 401
Military ballooning, 665
"Military-industrial complex," 748
Militia, and Whiskey Rebellion, 163
Miller, Alfred Jacob, xvi
Miller, Dorie, 676
Miller, William, 800
Millerites, 279
Milwaukee, Wisconsin, 268; immigrants in, 437
Miner, Thomas W., 587
Minimum-wage, 528, 634, 638–639, 721, 736, 788
Mining, of silver and gold, 391–396, 392*p*, 393*p*, 394*p*, 395*p*
Mining Act (1866), 395
Mining frontier, significance of, 395–396, 395*m*
Minneapolis, Minnesota, 269; reform movement in, 530
Minnesota: Indian land claims in, 869; lumber industry in, 404; settlement of, 396
Minutemen, in American Revolution, 85
Minutemen missiles, 784
Miquelon Island, 70
Miranda v. *Arizona* (1966), 819
Missiles: antiballistic, 828; cruise, 911, 940; development of, 743–744; under Kennedy, 783–784; Minutemen, 784; Pershing 11, 911; Pershing II, 911; Polaris, 784. *See also* Rockets
Missions, building of, 28–30, 29*p*, 290–291, 290*p*
Mississippi: exploration of, 21; Native American Indians in, 8, 10; Pinckney's Treaty in, 162; Reconstruction in, 365, 367, 373; secession of, 323; and Spanish land claims, 114; as territory, 192
Mississippi River: and Civil War, 341; control of, 183–184, 186; exploration of, 21, 44, 188; and Louisiana Purchase, 182, 183*m;* Pinckney's Treaty and, 162; and St. Louis Bridge spanning, 450–451; Spanish closing of, 114; and transportation, 149, 251; and U.S. boundaries, 99, 186
Missouri: and "Bleeding Kansas," 316; in Civil War, 333, 340; and Dred Scott, 318; and Lecompton Constitution, 319; and Mormons, 283; and slavery issue, 215–216, 287, 350–351
Missouri Compromise, 214–216, 216*m*, 313, 325
Mitchell, Billy, 665–667, 666*p*, 672, 744
Mitchell, John (Attorney General), 833, 834, 836
Mitchell, John (labor leader), 522
Mitchell, Maria, 285
Mitterand, François, 911
Moffett, William A., 667
Mohawk Indians, 8
Molasses Act (1733), 78

Moley, Raymond, 622, 624
Molly Maguires, 432, 432p
Mondale, Walter F.: in election of 1976, 881–882; in election of 1984, 913, 913p
Money and currency: in Civil War, 353; creation of Federal Reserve notes, 539; and deflation after Civil War, 459; and gold standard, 474, 830; greenbacks as, 353, 459; issuance of state, 210; post-Revolution, 114–115, 115p; problems with paper, 115; reform in, under Wilson, 538; under Roosevelt, 624–625; and Shays's Rebellion, 114–115, 115p; and silver coinage, 459, 467, 471; silver versus gold standard in, 475–476; under Wilson, 538. See also Economy
Monitor (ship), 345–346
Monmouth, New Jersey, 95, 97
Monongahela River, 113
Monopolies: See Antitrust laws
Monroe, James, 176, 186; domestic policy under, 217; and economic sectionalism, 212; in election of 1816, 209; and Era of Good Feelings, 211; foreign policy of, 212–213, 217; inauguration of, 211; and Indian policy, 234; as minister to France, 166, 184; as minister to London, 194; and Monroe Doctrine, 217; and voting rights, 227
Monroe Doctrine, 217; Roosevelt Corollary to, 452, 542, 592, 611; and Venezuela boundary dispute, 510
Montana, 405; mining in, 395; settlement of, 392; as territory, 353
Montcalm, Marquis de, 68, 69
Montgomery, Bernard, 681, 691
Montgomery, Richard, 86
Montgomery bus boycott, 741
Montgomery Ward Company, 422–424, 603
Monticello, 180, 180p
Montoya, Joseph, 865
Montpelier, Vermont, 199
Moon exploration, 784, 822, 823p
Moral Majority, 765
Moreno, Rita, 867
Morgan, Daniel, 96
Morgan, J. P. & Co., 539, 601
Morgan, J. Pierpont, 418–419, 418p, 421, 474, 523, 526, 533, 578
Morgenthau, Henry, Jr., 622
Mormons, 293–294, 405
Morocco, 181–182, 181m
Morrill, Justin S., 448
Morrill Act (1862), 448
Morris, Gouverneur, 60, 109, 117
Morris, Robert, 107, 156p
Morrow, Dwight W., 611
Morse, Jedidiah, 220, 220p
Morse, Samuel F. B., xvii, 259; painting by, 220p, 264p
Morse, Wayne, 809
Morton, Ferdinand Joseph La-Menthe, 592
Moses, Grandma, xvi
Mossadegh, Mohammad, 733
Motherwell, Robert, 766
Mott, Lucretia, 284, 855
Mountain men, 289–290
Mount Suribachi, in World War II, 696
Mount Vernon, 151p
Movies, in 1920s, 592
Muñoz Marín, Luis, 863
Muckrakers, 529–531
Mugwumps, 463
Muhammad, Elijah, 806
Muir, John, 526p

Munchukuo, 612
Munich Agreement, 662
Munn v. Illinois (1876), 470–471
Munsey's (magazine), 530
Murfreesboro, Tennessee, 351
Music, in 1920s, 592, 593; ragtime, 538p; rock 'n'roll, 766–767
Muskie, Edmund, 832
Muskingum River, 113
Muslims, 10; Black, 806–807; in Iran, 893
Mussolini, Benito, 610, 656, 659, 662, 685–686, 695
Mutual assured destruction (MAD), 783–784
Myers, Gustavus, 531
Myers, Myer, 61
My Lai, South Vietnam, 813

N

Nader, Ralph, 803, 808
Nagasaki, 699, 699p
Nagy, Imre, 925–926
Naked and the Dead, The (Mailer), 768
Nantucket, 57
Nantucket Sound, 23
Napoleon Bonaparte, 167, 202; downfall of, 205; dream of, 182–183; empire of, 195m; and relations with U.S., 199; and sale of Louisiana, 185
Napoleonic Wars, 217, 267
Napoleon III, 507
Naragansett Bay, 23
Narragansett Indians, 863
Narváez, Pánfilo, 18, 19m
Nasser, Gamal Abdel, 733, 742, 743
Nast, Thomas, xvii, 377; cartoon by, 378p, 466p
Natchez Indians, 8
National Aeronautics and Space Administration (NASA), 745
National Association for the Advancement of Colored People (NAACP), 446, 648, 808, 934
National Association of Colored Women, 446
National Council of Negro Women, 649
National Defense Education Act (1958), 745, 799
National Environmental Policy Act (1970), 885
National Guard: mobilization of, in Mexican Revolution, 544; in World War I, 561
National Housing Act, 627
National Industrial Recovery Act (1933), 628
Nationalism, 198, 218, 220, 224–225
National Labor Relations Act (1935), 634
National Labor Relations Board (NLRB), 634, 652, 654
National Liberation Front (NLF), 787
National Organization for Women (NOW), 856, 857
National Origins Act (1924), 580
National Recovery Administration (NRA), 628–629, 632
National Republican party, 225–226; renaming of, as Whigs, 242–243
National Security Act (1947), 715
National Security Council, origin of, 715, 716
National Socialist (Nazi) party, 657–658, 590
National Trades Union, 431
National War Labor Board, 565
National Woman Suffrage Association, 855

National Youth Administration (NYA), 631, 649
Native Americans: between 1850–1900, 407c; aid to, 868; and American Indian Movement, 868–869; and Andrew Jackson, 234–236, 237p; and Battle of Tippecanoe, 201; in Central America, 7, 17–18, 17p, 18p, 25c; and colonial settlers, 37–38, 40, 47, 77; and Deerfield Massacre, 66–67; education of, 853, 873p; equality for, 860–863; and French and Indian War, 68–69; impact of disease on, 17, 27–28, 77; in North America, 6, 8, 9m, 10, 10p; and purchase of Manhattan, 44–45; and reservations, 387–388, 388m; and Spanish Empire, 27–29, 27p, 28m; termination and relocation of, 861; war and resettlement, 385–391, 385p, 387p, 388m, 389p; and western settlement, 66–67, 113, 159, 162, 163m, 288–289, 291–292; women leaders of, 863p; in World War II, 861, 867–868
NATO: See North Atlantic Treaty Organization (NATO)
Natural resources, 359c
Naturalization Act, 167
Navaho Indians, 288
Navigation Acts (1660, 1963), 56, 58, 62, 64, 66, 78, 79, 84
Navy, U.S.: in Civil War, 335–336, 337p, 345–346; creation of first American, 86; and Iran-Iraq war, 924p; under Jefferson, 181; under John Adams, 167; under Theodore Roosevelt, 504p, 508, 509, 540, 541; in War of 1812, 202, 204, 207; under Wilson, 553; women in, 561, 676; and World War I, 553, 562; in World War II, 683
Navy Department, creation of, 167
Nebraska, 405; and Kansas-Nebraska Act, 313–314, 314m; and slavery issue, 313; sod houses in, 402, 402p
Negative ads, 923
Neptune's Car (ship), 306; advertisement for, 306p
Netherlands: colonies of, 44–45; and oil shortage, 879; trade with colonies, 62; in World War I, 548; in World War II, 665
Neumann, John von, 761
Neutrality: in World War I, 660; in World War II, 659–661, 660p, 663, 667
Neutrality Act, 1937, 663; 1939, 663, 667
Nevada, 405; populism in, 472; as state, 353
New American System of Manufacture, 422
Newark, New Jersey, riots in, 807
New Bedford, Massachusetts, 57
New Deal: appraisal of, 639–640; and black Americans, 646–649; and conservation, 643–644; end of, 637–638; failures of, 648–649; and farmers, 643–644; first, 622–631; second, 631–639; under Truman, 715; and women, 649–651
New England, 34, 202, 207–208; colonial education, 59–60; Dominion of, 64–65; Hartford Convention, 208; industry and trade in, 55–56, 56m, 258–265; life in, 55; opposition in War of 1812, 207–208; settlement of, 38–44, 43m
New England Primer, 425
Newfoundland, 13, 22, 23, 70, 669
New France, 44, 69m
"New Frontier," Kennedy's, 788–790
New Guinea, in World War II, 683

New Hampshire: colonial government in, 66; and ratification of Constitution, 122–123

New Haven Colony, 43

New Jersey, 202, 323; as colony, 46, 58, 60, 64–65; and election of 1864, 356; land claims of, 118; ratifies Constitution, 122; in Revolution, 94; settlement of, 46

New Jersey Plan, 118

Newlands Reclamation Act (1902), 524

New Left, 809, 812

Newman, Barnett, 766

New Mexico: conquest of, 301; establishment of, 21; Native Americans in, 8; settlement of, 29, 30, 288–289; as state, 534

New Nationalism, 533–536

New Negro Movement, 649

New Netherland, settlement of, 44–45

New Orleans, 44, 149, 159, 184p, 251; Battle of, 206–207, 206p, 209, 222, 223; and Burr conspiracy, 189; capture of, in Civil War, 344–345; immigrants in, 437

Newport Harbor, 23

New Spain, 21. See Spanish Empire

Newspapers: in colonial America, 60; comic strip in, 511–513; coverage of Civil War, 337; coverage of World War I, 676–677; and Pentagon Papers, 812, 831; and Watergate investigation, 833; and yellow press, 511–512, 513. See also Journalism

New Sweden, settlement of, 45

New York (city), 251, 253; African Americans in, 854; Boss Tweed in, 373, 376–377, 378p, 441; building Brooklyn Bridge in, 451–452, 452p; Central Park in, 456; docks in, 533p; gay and lesbian rights in, 870, 871; Great Depression in, 606; Herald Square in, 430p; immigrants in, 437, 438p; Puerto Ricans in, 866–867, 866p; and purchase of Manhattan, 44–45; in 1790s, 149; skyscrapers in, 454p; smog in, 886; tenements in, 438, 440

New York (state), 58; exploration of, 23; land claims of, 118; and non-importation agreements, 81; and privateers, 62–63; and ratification of Constitution, 122–123; and Roosevelt as governor of, 621; and voting rights, 227; and western settlement, 83

Nez Percé Indians, 389

Ngo Dinh Diem, 787–788

Nguyen, Jean, 868

Niagara, New York, 77

Niagara Movement, 450, 648

Nicaragua: civil war in, 894–895, 907–908, 918; Coolidge policy in, 610; desire for peace, 921; and Iran-contra affair, 918–919; refugees from, 868

Nicholas II, of Russia, 577

Nickelodeon, 592

Nihilism, 765

Nimitz, Chester, 683

Niña (ship), 4

Nine Power Treaty (1992), 584, 612

Nineteenth Amendment, 582, 649, 855

Nixon, Richard M., 765p, 783; appointments of, 866; Cabinet of, 821; debates with Kennedy, 775–776, 776p; domestic policy under, 829–830; early career of, 820–821; economic policy under, 830, 879; in election of 1960, 775–776;

in election of 1968, 819–820; in election of 1972, 830–833; energy policy under, 880, 886; environment under, 885; Ford's pardon of, 877–878, 878p; foreign policy under, 888–889; foreign visits of, to Beijing and Moscow, 747, 747p, 828–829, 829p; and health care reform, 940; inauguration of, 820p; and Indian policy, 868; as member of House Un-American Activities Committee, 721; and Native Americans, 861; pardon of, 877–878, 878p; resignation of, 816p, 837–838, 838p; and resignation of Agnew, 835; in Senate, 729; and space exploration, 821–822, 823p; Supreme Court appointments by, 914; as Vice-President, 737, 747; and Vietnam War, 822, 824–829, 889–890; and Watergate, 833–837, 837p, 879; and women's rights, 858

Nobel Prize: to Desmond Tutu, 925; to Martin Luther King, Jr., 805; to Theodore Roosevelt, 540; to writers, 768

Non-importation agreements, 81

Non-Importation Association, 84

Nonintercourse Act (1809), 196, 199

Nonviolence movement: and Chavez, 861–862; and Martin Luther King, 740–741

Noriega, Manuel, 931

Normandy invasion, 688–689, 690p

Norris, Frank, 530

Norse discoveries, 13

North, Lord, 81, 82, 96

North, Oliver, 919

North American Free Trade Agreement (NAFTA), 939–940

North Atlantic Treaty Organization (NATO), 730, 736, 786, 911, 935; admission of West Germany, 717–718, 718m; creation of, 717–718, 718m; under Kennedy, 786

North Bend, 114

North Carolina: antislavery movement in, 106; exploration of, 22–23; as Lost Colony, 33; ratification of Constitution in, 123; Reconstruction government in, 373; western claims of, 109

North Carolina White Brotherhood, 374

North Dakota, 405

Northern Securities Company, 523–524

North Korea, 724; crisis in, 942. See also Korean War

North Platte, Nebraska, 400

North Vietnam, 732; Cambodian attack on, 889; victory of, 890, 890p. See also Vietnam War

Northwest Ordinance (1787), 111–112, 112m, 215

Northwest Territory, 113p

Norway: neutrality of in World War I, 548; in World War II, 665

Novello, Antonio C., 866

Nuclear materials: disposal of, 885, 924

Nuclear power, 886–887, 927–928, 931; accident at Three Mile Island, 887p; and Chernobyl explosion, 916

Nullification controversy, 169, 232, 236–238

Nuremberg trials, 716

Nye, Gerald P., 660

O

Oberlin College, 282

O'Brien, Lawrence, 833

O'Connor, Rachel, 275

O'Connor, Sandra Day, 852, 914, 921, 922

Octopus, The (Norris), 530

Ogallala, Nebraska, 400

Oglala Sioux Pine Ridge Reservation, 862

Oglethorpe, James, 47

Ohio: coal mining in, 522; early settlement of, 112–114; education in, 282; Indians in, 113; Kent State incident, 824; and railroad construction, 254; suffrage in, 227; and women's rights, 284

Ohio Company, 112–114

"Ohio Gang," 583–584, 586

Oil: and Arab embargo, 880, 880p; early developments in, 419–422; and Exxon Valdez spill, 880; and inflation, 879; and offshore deposits, 734; and OPEC, 880, 887; and Persian Gulf crisis, 921; and production of crude petroleum, 435c, and second oil shock, 887

O'Keeffe, Georgia, xvi

Okies, 643, 645

Okinawa, in World War II, 696

Oklahoma, 405; exploration of, 21; Indian reservations in, 405–406; and Sooners, 406, 406p

Old Colonial System, 661

Oldenburg, Claes, 766

O'Leary, Hazel, 853

Olive Branch Petition, 86

Oliver, "King," 592

Olmsted, Frederick Law, 455–456

Olympic games in Moscow, 895

Omaha, Nebraska, 269, 271

One Flew Over the Cuckoo's Nest (Kesey), 872

Oneida Indians, 8

O'Neill, Eugene, 582

Onondaga Indians, 8

OPEC: See Organization of Petroleum Exporting Countries (OPEC)

Open Door policy in China, 517–518, 540

Operation Bootstrap, 866

Operation Desert Shield (1990–1991), 933

Operation Desert Storm (1991), 933

Operation Just Cause (1989), 931

Operation Paperclip, 744

Opium War (1839–1842), 505

Order of the Star–Spangled Banner, 315

Orders in Council, 193, 202

Oregon: border settlement, 298, 298m; claimed by U.S., 187; joint occupation, 212; Nez Percés in, 389; settlement of, 290–291; and Wilmot Proviso, 306–307

Oregon Trail, 290, 291

Oregon Trail, The (Parkman), 290

Organization of American States, 508, 938

Organization of Eastern Caribbean States, 910

Organization of Petroleum Exporting Countries (OPEC), 880, 887

Orlando, Vittorio, 567

Origin of Species, The (Darwin), 923

Osceola, Chief, 234–235, 236p

Ostend Manifesto, 312–313

Ostfriesland (ship), 666

O'Sullivan, John L., 298

Oswald, Lee Harvey, 792

Other America, The (Harrington), 790

Otis, Elisha Graves, 453

Ottawa Indians, 77

Outcault, Richard F., 512

Overman Act (1918), 565

P

Pacific Fur Company, 290
Pacific Ocean, discovery of, 15, 16; and Lewis and Clark expedition, 187; World War II in, 670–672, 682–684, 695–696
Packaging industry, 759–760
PACs (political action committees), 884
Pactomania, 732
Page, Walter Hines, 550
Pago Pago, Samoa, 508
Pahlavi, Mohammad Reza, 887, 894
Paine, Thomas, 86–87, 87p, 92
Paiute Indians, 391
Palestine, British rule of, 742–743; and creation of Israel, 743; Palestine question, 894, 908–909; and Suez War, 743. See also Middle East
Palestine Liberation Organization (PLO), 893, 894, 908, 917, 943
Palestinian revolt, 921
Palmer, A. Mitchell, 578
Palmer, William C., painting by, 642p
Palos, Spain, 4
Pamlico Sound, North Carolina, 23, 37
Panama, 509; economic sanctions on, 931; exploration of, 14, 15; settlement in, 14; United States invasion of, 931
Panama, Declaration of, 682
Panama Canal: building of, 541–542; treaties on, 892–893, 892p
Panay (gunboat), 659
Panic: of 1837, 242–243, 253, 431; of 1873, 376; of 1907, 525–526
Panmunjom, North Korea, 731
Paris, Peace of, 70, 78m, 1763
Paris, Treaty of (1783), 98–100, 99p
Parker, Alton B., 524
Parker, Theodore, 279
Parkman, Francis, 290
Parks, Rosa, 740, 756
Parliament, British, 78–79, 81
Passamaquoddy Indians, 863
Patch, A. M., 689
Patent, 39
Paterson, William, 118
Pathet Lao, 826, 890, 891
Patronage: See Civil service
Patrons of Husbandry, 469
Patten, Mary Brown, 306
Patton, George, 689, 691
Paul, 50
Pawtucket, Rhode Island, 260
Payment-in-kind (PIK), 903
Payne-Aldrich Tariff (1909), 532–533, 537–538
Peace Corps, 782–783, 783p
Peace of mind (Lieberman), 764
Peace of soul (Sheen), 764
Peace Ship, 549p
Peale, Charles Willson, 218, xvi; painting by, 94p
Peale, Norman Vincent, 764
Pearl Harbor, 686; Japanese attack on, 671–672, 672p
Peenemünde, Germany, 744
Peffer, Senator, 405
Pemberton, John C., 355
Peña, Federico, 865, 866
Pendergast, Tom, 707
Pendleton, George H., 462
Pendleton Act (1883), 462
Peninsular campaign, 346, 347m
Penn, William, 46–47, 46p

Pennsylvania: antislavery movement in, 106; in Civil War, 354–355; coal mining in, 522; colonial government in, 66; industry in, 210; ratification of Constitution by, 121–122; in Revolution, 92, 95, 97, 106; settlement of, 46–47; Whiskey Rebellion, 162–164
Pennsylvania Rock Oil Company, 419
Penobscot Indians, 863
Pensacola, Florida, 207, 212
Pentagon Papers, 732, 831
People's Republic of China: See China
Perceval, Spencer, 202
Perestroika, 916, 928
Perkins, Frances, 622, 623p, 651
Perot, H. Ross, 937, 938, 939
Perry, Matthew C., 505, 505p
Perry, Oliver Hazard, 204
Pershing, John J., 544, 559, 665–667
Pershing II missiles, 911
Persian Gulf, 924p; troubles in, 920p, 921
Personal Liberty laws, 310
Peru, Incas in, 7–8, 8p, 17–18, 18p
Pesticides, 802–803
Pet banks, 241
Petersburg, Battle of, 335, 355–356, 356p
Philadelphia, Pennsylvania, 58, 103p, 251; Constitutional Convention in, 116–117, 117p; corruption in, 441; growth of, 149; and non-importation agreements, 81; reform movement in, 530; in 1790s, 149; unions in, 430
Philadelphia and Reading Coal and Iron Company, 522
Philip II (of Spain), 31–32
Philippine Commission, 515
Philippines: independence of, 696; Magellan's exploration of, 16; mutual defense treaty with, 726; refugees from, 868; and Spanish American War, 513–515; in World War II, 671, 682, 696
Phnom Penh, Cambodia, 890
Phonograph, 429–430, 592
Phony War, 664–665
Photography, in Civil War, 337, 358p, 361p, 372p
Physically disabled: equality for, 871–873, 871p
Pickens, Andrew, 96
Pickens, Horace, xvi
Pickering, Timothy, 165, 188
Pickett, George, 355
Pierce, Franklin: in election of 1852, 310; and expansion, 312–313; foreign policy under, 505; inauguration of, 311–312
Pigafetta, Antonio, 16
Pike, Zebulon, 114, 188
Pikes Peak, 188
Pilgrim's Progress (Bunyan), 529
Pinchot, Gifford, 525, 533
Pinckney, C. C., 166, 169, 192, 196
Pinckney, Thomas, 162, 165
Pinckney's Treaty (1795), 162
Pine Bluffs, 401
Pine Ridge Reservation, 869
Pingree, Hazen S., 527
Pinta (ship), 4
Pit, The (Norris), 530
Pitcher, Molly, 92
Pitt, William, 68, 70
Pittsburgh, Pennsylvania, 253, 269, 441; industry in, 210; strikes in, 459
Pittsburg Landing, 343–344
Pizarro, Francisco, 17–18, 19m, 21
Plantations, 51, 54, 271–272, 273p, 276p
Platt, Orville H., 517

Platt Amendment, 517, 659
Plattsburg, New York, 205
Plessy v. Ferguson (1896), 380, 738
Plumber and Sanitary Engineer, The, 439
Plumbers, and Watergate, 831–832, 833
Plymouth Colony, 40, 55
Pocahontas, 37, 37p
Poindexter, John, 919, 920, 921
Point Four program, 711
Poland: post-World War I, 662p; post-World War II, 664p; pre-World War II, 661–662, 661m; Solidarity in, 911, 924–925, 925p; and Soviet control, 708, 710–711; under Walesa, 925, 925p; in World War II, 663, 689–690, 693
Polaris missile, 784
Polish immigrants: discrimination against, 848
Political Action Committees (PACs), 884
Political machines, 440–442, 463, 527
Political parties: conventions for, 229–230; and nomination process, 228; and patronage, 190; in post-Reconstruction South, 381–382; rise of, 158–259. See also by name
Polk, James K: in election of 1844, 297; and Mexican War, 299–300
Pollock, Jackson, xvi, 766; painting by, 766p
Pollock v. Farmers Loan and Trust Co. (1895), 473–474
Pollution: and nuclear power, 803p. See also Air pollution; Water pollution
Polo, Marco, 12
Ponce de León, Juan, 18, 19m
Pontiac's Conspiracy, 77
Pony Express, 353
Poor, Salem, 98
Pop art, 766
Pope, John, 344, 346, 348
Popular sovereignty, 313, 315
Population: aging of, 756; and baby boom, 751, 752p, 808; colonial, 5 1; growth of, 202; growth of western, 405–406, 405m; of Native Americans, 25c, 407c; post-World War II growth and shift in, 751 756, 753m, 769c; by region, 221c; of slaves, 327c
Populist party: in election of 1892, 472; formation of, 471–472; and social reforms, 527–531
Pork barrel projects, 883
Porter, Katherine Anne, 767
Port Hudson, 355
Port Moresby, in World War II, 683
Portugal, discovery and exploration, 3, 4, 12, 13–14
Postage stamps, issuance of first, 259
Postmaster General, 153
Post Office Department, 259
Post road, 257
Potomac, 204
Potsdam Conference, 715–716
Pottawatomie Creek massacre, 316, 321
Poverty: and the Great Society, 801–804, 811; under Kennedy, 789–790; in 1960–1985, 795c
Powell, Lewis F., Jr., 914, 922
Power of Positive Thinking, The (Peale), 764
Powhatan, Chief, 8
Prague, Czechoslovakia, 692, 693, 694
Prejudice: and labor movement, 654; post-World War I, 580. See also Anti-Semitism; Racism
Presbyterian, 536
Prescott, William, 86

Presidency: Imperial, 896; Teflon, 917–920
President, U.S.: constitutional powers under, 120–121; and executive privilege, 835; and lame duck amendment, 622–623; power of, under Jackson, 241–242; selection of, 169
Presidential Succession Act (1947), 715
Presley, Elvis, 767
Press, freedom of, 60. *See also* Journalism; Newspapers
Princeton, Battle at, 94
Prince William Sound, 880
Principall Navigations, Voiages and Discoveries of the Engish Nation (Hakluyt), 32
Privacy Act (1974), 878
Privateers: American, 86, 161; British, 63p; colonial, 62–63; and War of 1812, 204
Proclamation of Neutrality (1793), 161
Proclamation Line of 1763, 77
Proclamation of Amnesty and Reconstruction (1863), 362
Profiles in Courage (Kennedy), 777
Prohibition, 582, 850; repeal of, 626
Propaganda, in World War I, 566
Proprietary colonies, 46–48
Ptolemy, 4
Public assistance, 633
Public domain, 111
Public land, sale of, 533
Public school movement, 281
Public Utility Holding Company Act (1935), 633
Public works: under Adams, J. Q., 224; under Franklin Roosevelt, 626–627, 629–631; under Hoover, 606; Truman and, 721
Public Works Administration (PWA), 629
Pueblo Indians, 8, 10p, 21, 289
Puerto Ricans, 654, 863–864, 863p, 866–867, 866p
Puerto Rico: and Foraker Act, 517; Operation Bootstrap in, 863, 866; recent issues in, 866–867; in recent times, 863–864, 863p; U.S. acquisition of, 513
Pulaski, Count Casimir, 95
Pulitzer, Joseph, 511–512
Pullman, George M., 455
Pullman Company, 677
Pullman Strike (1894), 433, 474
Pure Food and Drug Act (1906), 524
Puritans, settlement of, in New England, 38–44
Putnam, Israel, 112, 113, 218
Putnam, Rufus, 112

Q

Qaddafi, Muammar el-, 878–879, 917, 919
Quakers, 42, 46–47, 64, 118
Quayle, J. Danforth, 922–923, 923p, 938
Quebec, Canada, 23, 44, 67; fall of, 68–69
Quebec Act (1 774), 83–84
Queen Anne's War (1702–1713), 70
Queen's College (Rutgers), 60
Quitrent, 46
Quota systems, 851

R

Rabin, Yitzhak, 943
Racial discrimination, post-World War II, 715
Racial segregation, and World War II, 676–677

Racism, 850–855, 935; and anti-Semitism, 632, 657, 658, 700; and fear of foreigners, 500; and immigration, 443; and internment of Japanese Americans, 677, 678p; and Jim Crow laws, 380–381; and Ku Klux Klan, 373–374, 374p, 580, 589, 591, 715, 849; and treatment of German Americans, 566
"Radical" Republicans: *See* Reconstruction
Radio: F. D. Roosevelt on, 623; Harding on, 583p; in 1920s, 592
Railroads: in 1850s, 254–257, 256m; and business, 464; and cattle ranching, 398; and Chinese workers, 415p; in Civil War, 335, 416; growth of, 412p, 413, 413p; and interstate commerce, 464; land grants to, 413, 413m, 415; and settlement of Great Plains, 403, 403p, 404; and standard gauge, 415–416; and steam, 257; strikes in, 459; and time zones, 415; transcontinental, 375, 413, 413p; travel conditions on, 417p; and western settlement, 257
Raincy, Joseph, 373p
Raleigh, Sir Walter, 32–33; and son, 33p
Ramona (Jackson), 391
RAND (Research and Development) Corporation, 793
Randolph, A. Philip, 677, 791
Randolph, Edmund, 87, 118, 153
Randolph, John, 201, 225
Rappites, 279
Rationing, in World War I, 560, 564; in World War II, 675
Reagan, Ronald, 819; and affirmative action, 852; appointments of, 866; attempted assassination of, 897; conservative image of, 896; domestic policy under, 898–899, 913; economic policy under, 897–898, 912–914; and education, 923; in election of 1976, 880–881; in election of 1980, 896, 897p; in election of 1984, 913–915, 913p; farm programs under, 903–904; foreign policy under, 907–912, 909p, 921–922; and Grenada invasion, 910–911; and immigration policy, 868, 869; inauguration of, 896–897; and Indian policy, 869; and labor relations, 903; and Native Americans, 862–863; political style of, 896–897; relations with Congress, 896–897; space exploration under, 913; and Star Wars, 917; Supreme Court appointments of, 852, 914–915, 915p; tax reform under, 914; as Teflon President, 917–920
Recall, 529
Recession(s): in 1974, 898; of 1981, 899p; in 1982, 898; of 1990, 934
Reconstruction: Black, 369–375; evaluation of, 381–382; impact on congressional representation, 383c; under Johnson, 365–369, 365p; Lincoln's plan for, 361–362; military, 369–371; myths of, 372–373; radical, 361–362; Wade-Davis plan for, 362–363
Reconstruction Finance Corporation, 608
Recycling, 885p
Red Jackets, 374
Red scare: first, 578–580, 578p, 579p; second, 721
Reed, Thomas B., 466, 466p
Reed, Walter, 516, 542
Reforms: in campaign finance, 879; in cities, 527; consumer, 524; in education, 280–282, 446–450; in government,

528–529; in immigration, 869; for mentally ill, 282; and muckrakers, 529–531; need for health care, 940–941; role of women in, 444–446, 855; and settlement houses, 445–446; in state government, 527–528; and temperance movement, 287–288, 446, 528, 582; and voting rights, 446; and women's rights, 283–285, 855–860, 856p, 858p, 859p, 860p
Regionalism: and population growth, 221c
Rehabilitation Act (1973), 871
Rehnquist, William H., 852, 914, 922
Religion: in colonial America, 38–42, 46–47, 51; and First Amendment rights, 819; and Northwest Territory, 112; in postwar America, 764–765; revival meetings, 279, 280p; and slavery, 275
Remington, Frederic, painting by, 399p
Renaissance, 10–11
Reno, Janet, 940, 940p
Rensselaer Polytechnic Institute, 281–282
Reparations, and World War I, 568, 586
Report on a National Bank, 157
Report on Manufactures, 157–158
Report on the Public Credit, 155–157
Republican party (Jefferson), 159, 180; and Alien and Sedition Acts, 167–169; and Chase impeachment, 192; end of, 211; and Louisiana Purchase, 188; patronage issue in 1801, 189–191
Republican party (modern): and civil rights movement, 854; in election of 1856, 317; in election of 1860, 322, 325; in election of 1952, 729–730, 729p; founding of, 314; Johnson, Andrew, and, 365–369
Research and development, 763; of atomic energy, 713; by Edison, 429–430
Resettlement Administration, 627, 645
Reuben James (ship), 670
Revels, Hiram, 373p
Revenue Act (1935), 633
Revenue Act (1962), 789
Revere, Paul, 51–52, 52p, 61, 85
Reverse discrimination, 851–852
Reykjavik, Iceland, 916–917
Rhee, Syngman, 724
Rhode Island: antislavery movement in, 105, 106; colonial government in, 66, 105, 116; industry in, 263; land claims of, 118; ratification of Constitution in, 123; settlement of, 41–42; and Shays's Rebellion, 115
Rhode Island University (Brown), 60
Rhodes, John, 838
Richardson, Elliot, 831, 831p, 836
Richmond, Virginia, 322; affirmative action in, 852; in Civil War, 334, 341, 346, 348, 355, 358p; Liberation Day in, 366p
Richmond v. Croson (1989), 852
Ridgway, Matthew B., 725
Rifle, 334–335, 335p
Right-to-life movement, 859
Riis, Jacob, xvii, 531; photograph by, 438p, 447p, 449p, 531p
Rio Grande, 20, 299
Rivera, Chita, 867
Riverside, Illinois, 455–456
Rivlin, Alice Mitchell, 879
Roads: in 1960s, 803p; and American System, 211; building of, 149, 150m, 757, 758m, 759p in 1800; interstate system, 757, 758m; under Johnson, 799, 802; post, 257; and safety, 804; turnpikes,

251; and western settlement, 290, 291–293, 292m
Roanoke Island, 32–33
Robertson, Pat, 923
Rochambeau, General, 96, 185
Rochester, New York, 269
Rock Creek, 401
Rockefeller, John D., 416–418, 421–422, 448, 449, 578
Rockefeller, Nelson A., 775, 819, 877, 877p, 878
Rockets: race for, 744–745; V–1, 688; V–2, 688, 744. See also Missiles
Rock 'n'roll music, 766–767
Rock oil, 420. See also Oil industry
Rock River, 401
Rocky Mountains, 212; exploration of, 187, 289–290
Roebling, Emily Warren, 453
Roebling, John, 451–452, 451p
Roebling, Washington, 452–453
Roebuck, Alvah Curtis, 425
Roe v. Wade (1971), 859
Rogers, Will, 621
Rolfe, John, 37–38
Rölvaag, Ole, 396
Roman Catholics: See Catholic church
Romania: changes in, 934; and Soviet control, 708; and World War 11, 662, 663, 690, 693
Romans, Bernard, engraving by, 85P
Rommel, Erwin, 680–681, 685, 688
Roosevelt, Eleanor, 642, 643, 649, 650, 650p, 856
Roosevelt, Franklin D., 619, 620p, 635, 640p; appraisal of New Deal, 639–640; as Assistant Secretary of Navy, 599; and Brain Trust, 622; death of, 694; early career of, 621–622; in election of 1932, 613–614, 614p; in election of 1936, 635, 635p; in election of 1940, 668–669; in election of 1944, 690–691; and end of New Deal, 637–638; and FBI, 878; fireside chats of, 624, 637; first New Deal under, 622–631; Indian New Deal under, 861; and midterm election of 1934, 630–631; opposition to, 631–632; prewar foreign affairs, 657–664; relations with Congress, 639; second New Deal, 631–639; and Supreme Court, 632, 634–635, 637–638; use of radio by, 636p, 637; and World War II, 664–672; at Yalta Conference, 691–692, 692p
Roosevelt, Theodore, 440, 510, 521p, 541p, 848; and antitrust movement, 523–524; as Assistant Secretary of Navy, 512–513; and conservation, 524–525; decision not to run for third term, 532; early career of, 440, 463; and economic policy, 525–526; in election of 1900, 515–516; in election of 1904, 524; in election of 1912, 534p, 535–536; foreign policy under, 540–542; and immigration restrictions, 444, 848–849; and labor, 522; and New Nationalism, 533–534; as reform President, 524, 526–527; and Rough Riders, 513; as Secretary of Navy, 509; square deal under, 521–527; versus Taft, 534–535; and World War I, 552–553
Roosevelt Corollary to the Monroe Doctrine, 452, 542, 592, 611
Root-Takahira Agreement (1908), 540–541
Rosenberg, 723, Ethel
Rosenberg, Julius, 723

Rosenman, Samuel, 622
Rosie the Riveter, 678
Ross, Neille T., 590
Rothko, Mark, 766
Rough Riders, 513
Rough Riders, The (Roosevelt), 513
Rowan, Carl, 790
Roxbury, Massachusetts, 41
Royal colony, 38
Ruby, Jack, 792
Rural Electrification Administration, 645646
Rural Free Delivery (RFD), 259
Rush, Richard, 212
Rush-Bagot Agreement (1817), 212
Rusk, Dean, 777, 809, 812
Russell, Richard, 854
Russia: allied intervention in, 577; 1917 revolution in, 577; and Open Door policy in China, 517; and Russo-Japanese War, 540; in World War I, 547. See also Soviet Union
Russo-japanese War, 540
Rustin, Bayard, 791
Ruth, George Herman "Babe," 593
Ryder, Albert Pinkham, xvi

S

Sacajawea, 187
Sacco, Nicola, 580–581, 581p
Sadat, Anwar el-, 893–894, 894p; assassination of, 908
St. Augustine, Florida, 29
St. Clair, Arthur, 159
Saint Dominique, 184
St. Ignatius Mission, 290P
St. John's Newfoundland, 24
St. Lawrence River, 44, 68
St. Leger, Lieutenant Colonel, 94–95
St. Louis, Missouri, 251, 253, 269; and Mississippi River Bridge, 450–451; strikes in, 459
St. Marks, 212
St. Paul, Minnesota, 269
St. Pierre Island, 70
Saipan, 696
Salem, Massachusetts, 55; in 1790s, 149
Salem, Peter, 98
Salinger, J. D., 767
SALT talks, 828, 892, 911
Salutary neglect, 62
Samoa, 508; in World War II, 683
Sampson, Deborah, 97
Sanchez, Oscar Arias, 921
San Diego, California, 291; mission at, 29
Sandinistas, 895, 907
Sandino, César Augusto, 895
SSan Francisco, California, 291, 707; gay and lesbian rights in, 870; mission and presidio at, 29, 29p; reform movement in, 530; segregation in, 848; and seizure of Alcatraz Island, 861–862; UN conference in, 721
San Gabriel, California, 29
San Jacinto, Battle of, 295
San Luis Obispo, California, 29
San Salvador, 5
Santa Anna, Antonio Lopez de, 294, 295
Santa Clara, California, 29
Santa Fe, New Mexico, 21, 29, 188, 288, 289
Santa Maria (ship), 4, 5
Santiago, Battle of, 513

Sarajevo, 547
Saratoga, Battle of, 94–95
Sargent, John Singer, painting by, 570p
Satellites, earth, 745, 760, 784
Satellite nations, Communist, 693–694
Saturday Night Massacre, 835–836
Saudi Arabia, and Gulf War, 932,939–940, 939p; and Iran-contra affair 919
Savannah, Georgia, 48p; in American Revolution, 96; in Civil War, 357
Savings and loans crisis, 924
Savo Island, Battle of, 684
Scalawags, 372
Scalia, Antonin, 914
Scandals: See Corruption
Schechter v. United States (1935), 632, 633
Schlafly, Phyllis, 858
Schlesinger, James R., 838
School prayer, 938
Schools: See Education
Schurz, Carl, 268, 268p, 460, 463
Schuyler, Nebraska, 400
Science, in colonial America, 60
Scientific management, 428–429, 594
Scopes, John T., 923
Scotch-Irish, 51
Scots, 51
Scott, Dred, 317–318, 320
Scott, Hugh, 837, 838
Scott, Winfield, 236, 300, 310, 341, 346
SCUD rockets, 933
Sears, Richard, 425
SEATO: See Southeast Asia Treaty Organization (SEATO)
Second Reconstruction, 852–853
Secretariat (UN), 708
Secret ballot, 528
Sectionalism, 198
Securities and Exchange Commission (SEC), 625, 633, 920, 927
Security Council (UN), 707–708
Sedan, France, 559
Sedition Act (1798), 167, 192, 566, 723
Sedition Act (1918), 566
Segregation: black revolt of 1960s, 790, 791, 804–805; of blacks, 379–381; and Civil Rights Act of 1964, 798–799; equality and, 850–851; fight against, in 1950s, 738–742; in Little Rock, 740p, 850; Supreme Court on, 848, 850; in World War II, 676–677
Selective Service Act (1917), 561
Selma (Alabama) march, 806
Seminole Indians, 234–235, 405
Senate, U.S.: cloture in, 798; constitutional powers of, 121, 154; direct election of members, 529; early jobs of, 153, 154; Ervin hearings in, 833–834; filibuster in, 446; and impeachment, 370–371; McCarthy hearings in, 736–737, 737p; and ratification of Panama Canal treaties, 893; and SALT II treaty, 892; and Supreme Court appointments, 915, 934; and Versailles Treaty, 569–570, 707. See also Congress, U.S.; House of Representatives, U.S.
Seneca Falls Convention, 284, 855
Seneca Indians, 8, 77
Separation of powers, 120
Separatists, 39
Sequoya, 235
Serbia, in World War I, 547
Serra, Father Junípero, 29–30
Servicemen's Readjustment Act (1944), 712
Settlement houses, 445–446, 447p
Seventeenth Amendment, 529

Seward, William H., 308; assassination attempt on, 364; and expansion, 506, 507; and Trent affair, 343
Sexual harassment, 934
Seymour, Horatio, 371–372
Shafter, W. R., 513
Shahn, Ben, xvii; paintings by, 581*p*, 845*p*
Shaker Heights, Ohio, 456
Shakers, 279
Shakespeare, William, 32
Shame of the Cities, The (Steffens), 529, 530
Shanghai, China, 612
Sharecropping, 381, 644–645
Share the Wealth Program, 632
Sharon, 50
Sharpsburg, Virginia, 348
Shaw (ship), 672*p*
Shawnee Indians, 77, 162
Shays, Daniel, 115, 163
Shays's Rebellion, 114–115
Sheen, Fulton J., 764
Shepard, Alan B., 784
Sheridan, Philip, 356
Sherman, John, 467, 468
Sherman, Roger, 107, 118
Sherman, William T., 337, 343, 356–358, 386, 388, 392, 451
Sherman Antitrust Act (1890), 467, 474, 523–524, 536, 539
Sherman Silver Purchase Act (1890), 467, 468, 472–473; repeal of, 473, 474
Shiite Muslims, 917
Shiley, S. B., painting by, 429*p*
Shiloh, Battle of, 344, 344*p*
Shiner, Michael, 243
Shinn, Everett, painting by, 441
Shipbuilding, in Portugal, 12
Shopping centers, 592
Shoshone Indians, 187
Shriver, Sargent, 832
Shuttle diplomacy, 889
Sidney, Nebraska, 400
Siegfried line, 691
Sihanouk, Norodom, 889–890, 891
Silent majority, 819
Silent Spring (Carson), 802
Silicon Valley, 900–901
Silliman, Benjamin, Jr., 420
Silver City, 394
Silver coinage, 459, 467, 471
Silver mining, 393–394, 394*m*
Simplified Practice, Office of, 600
Simpson, Jerry, 472
Sims, William S., 562
Sinclair, Upton, 524
Singapore, in World War II, 682
Sioux Indians, 863
Sirhan, Sirhan, 817
Sit-down strikes: in civil rights movement, 739, 790; in labor actions, 653, 653*p*
Sitting Bull, Chief, 389
Six Day War, 943
Sixteenth Amendment, 474, 534
Skelton, Martha Wayles, 180
Skyscrapers, 453–455, 454*p*
Slater, Samuel, 259–260, 263
Slavery: and Abraham Lincoln, 349; in colonial America, 38, 52–53; and Compromise of 1850, 307–309; conditions in, 273–275, 274*p*, 287; and cotton plantation, 271–272, 276*p*; ending, 350–351; and gag rule, 295–296; and Missouri Compromise, 216, 216*m*; and Northwest Ordinance, 215; profits in, 214–215; revolts in, 232, 236, 273–

274; in Spanish Empire, 28–29; and three-fifths compromise, 118–220; and western settlement, 302, 314; and Wilmot Proviso, 306–307
Slavery As It Is (Weld), 287, 311
Slave trade, 52, 55*p*, 272
Slidell, John, 343
Sloan, John, 530; painting by, 576*p*
Slums, in cities, 438
Smet, Pierre de, 290–291
Smibert, John, xvi, 61
Smith, Alfred E., 589, 590–592, 591*p*, 613, 631, 849
Smith, Bessie, 592
Smith, Howard, 857
Smith, Hyrum, 293
Smith, Jedediah, 98
Smith, Jesse, 586
Smith, John, 37
Smith, Joseph, 293
Smith, William (Uncle Billy), 420
Smith College, 449
Smithsonian Institution, 744
Smog, 886
Smokestack industries: decline of, 899–900
Smuggling, 62, 66
Snyder Act (1924), 861
Sobell, Morton, 723
Social classes, in 1790s, 151–152; in early America, 151–152
Socialist party, 566–567, 567*p*, 636, 677
Social Security: under Carter, 882; under Eisenhower, 736; under Kennedy, 788; and Medicare/Medicaid, 801; under Reagan, 917; under Roosevelt, 633, 638; under Truman, 721
Social Security Act (1935), 633, 638
Society of the White Rose, 374
Soil Bank plan, 735
Soil Conservation and Adjustment Act (1936), 634, 638, 643–644
Soil Erosion Service, 643
Soldiers: in American Revolution, 85–86, 90–92, 91*p*, 92–97, 98, 108; in Civil War, 335. *See also* Army, U.S.; Marines, U.S.
Solidarity, 911, 924–925, 925*p*, 931–932, 936
Solomon Islands, 682
Somalia: crisis in, 942–943
Somoza, Anastasio, 894–895, 907
Sonar, 678
Sons of Liberty, 79
Sooners, 406, 406*p*
Souter, David, 934
South: antislavery movement in, 286; plantations in, 51, 54, 271–272, 273*p*, 276*p*; post-Reconstruction, 381–382; slavery in, 271–276
South Africa: apartheid in, 922; democracy in, 943–944, 944*p*
South America: *See* Latin America; *specific countries*
South Carolina: and nullification controversy, 236–238; and ratification of Constitution, 122–123; and Reconstruction, 365, 373; secession of, 323; and shelling of Fort Sumter, 325–326, 326*p*; state government in, 372–373; tariff opposition in, 231–232; western claims of, 109
South Dakota, 405
Southeast Asia, communism in, 779–780, 779*p*
Southeast Asia Treaty Organization (SEATO), 732

Southern Christian Leadership Conference (SCLC), 790–791
Southern Manifesto, 739
South Korea, 724, 732. *See also* Korea; Korean War
South Vietnam, 732, 890*p*; collapse of, 890. *See also* Vietnam; Vietnam War
Soviet Union: under Andropov, 911; and arms control, 892; and Berlin blockade, 717, 780–781; blockage of atomic bomb control, 708; breakup of, 869; under Brezhnev, 828, 892, 911; changes in, 928–929; under Chernenko, 911, 915; and cold war, 708–709, 733–734; and Cuba, 748, 785–786, 785*p*; and domino theory, 891; and Eastern Europe, 708; economic problems in, 928–929, ethnic unrest in, 929–930; explosion of atomic bomb, 722; explosion of hydrogen bomb, 745; German invasion of, in World War II, 670; *Glasnost/Perestroika* in, 916; under Gorbachev, 916–917, 925, 928–929; and Gulf War, 932–933; and human rights issues, 891–892; invasion of Afghanistan, 895, 911, 921; and Iran, 709; under Khrushchev, 733, 743, 744–745, 780–782, 785–786; and Korean War, 723–726, 725*m*; Nixon visit to, 828–829; relations with Egypt, 743, 745; relations with United States, 891–892, 893, 910–911, 915–916; under Stalin, 658, 663, 691–692, 692*p*, 694, 733; and UN organization, 707; in World War II, 681–682, 689–690; at Yalta Conference, 691–692, 692*p*; under Yeltsin, 929. *See also* Russia
Soyer, Isaac, painting by, 598*p*
Space exploration: and *Challenger* disaster, 918, 918*p*; under Kennedy, 784; moon exploration, 822, 823*p*; under Nixon, 821–822, 823*p*; under Reagan, 912–913; Russian, 744–745; and Titan 34D, 918; U.S., 745
Spain: cession of Florida, 212–213; claim to Pacific Northwest, 213; colonial empire of, 27–30, 27*p*, 28*m*, 29*p*; and control of Mississippi, 114; defeat of Armada, 32; discovery and exploration, 3–8, 5*m*, 12–18, 15*m*, 19*m*, 20–21, 31–32; fascism in, 659; land claims of, 114; neutrality of in World War I, 548; and Ostend Manifesto, 312–313; Pinckney's Treaty with, 162; relations with, under Washington, 159; and Treaty of Paris, 99
Spanish-American War, 511*m*, 548–549; causes of, 511–512; fighting of, 513; outcomes of, 513–517; U.S. preparation for, 512–513
Spanish Armada, 32
Spanish borderlands, 28*m*, 29–30
Spanish Empire: colonial government in, 28–29; control of Indians in, 27–28, 27*p*; results of the Spanish conquests, 30; settling the Spanish borderlands, 29–30
Spanish missions, 28, 29, 29*m*
Spanish-speaking people, 849*p*, 860–865; bilingual education for, 873; equality for, 864–867. *See also groups by name*
Spargo, John, 531
Spaulding, Elizabeth Hart, 290
Spaulding, Henry H., 290
Specie Circular, 241
Spheres of influence, 517*m*

Spirit of St. Louis (airplane), 594*p*
Spoils system, 230, 460
Sports, in 1920s, 593
Springfield, Illinois, race riot in, 648
Sputnik I, 744, 745*p*, 764
Sputnik II, 744
Squanto, 40
Square Deal, 521–527
Stagecoach, 149
Stagflation, 884, 897
Stalin, Josef, 658, 694, 733, 915; and
  World War II, 663; at Yalta Conference,
  691, 692, 692*p*
Stalingrad, Battle of, 682, 685
Stalwarts, 460, 461
Stamp Act (1765), 78–79, 79*p*; repeal of,
  79, 80
Stamp Act Congress, 79
Standard gauge railroad, 415–416
Standard Metropolitan Statistical Areas
  (SMSAs), 754, 755*m*
Standard Oil Company, 421–422, 421*p*,
  464, 467
Standard Oil Trust, 417
Standish, Miles, 40
Stanford, Leland, 448
Stanton, Edwin M., 370
Stanton, Elizabeth Cady, 284, 284*p*, 285,
  855
Stark (frigate), 921
"Star-Spangled Banner," 205, 209
Starving Time, 37
Star Wars weapons, 917
Stassen, Harold, 718
State Department, U.S., 153
State government: after Reconstruction,
  372–373; post-Revolution, 103–106;
  progressive reforms in, 527–528; rela-
  tionship with national government,
  108–109, 121
States' Rights Democrats, 719
Steamboat, 149, 253–254, 255*p*
Steel industry, 429*p*; and skyscraper con-
  struction, 454–455, 454*p*
Steffens, Lincoln, 529, 530
Steinbeck, John, 643
Stephenson, George, 416
Stevens, Thaddeus, 362, 367*p*, 369, 370*p*,
  374
Stevenson, Adlai, 786, 792; in election of
  1952, 729–730; in election of 1956,
  737–738
Stewart, A. T., 426
Stewart's Cast Iron Palace, 425–426, 426*p*
Stimson, Henry, 610, 611, 612, 663
Stock market: boom, in 1920s, 600, 601*p*;
  under Coolidge, 590; crash of 1929,
  601–603, 602*p*; crash of 1987, 924;
  regulation of, 625
Stonewall Rebellion, 871
Storey, Moorfield, 648
Story of Life Insurance, The (Hendrick), 531
Stowe, Harriet Beecher, 311, 311*p*, 312,
  391
Strait of Magellan, 16
Strategic Arms Limitation Treaties (SALT I
  and II), 892, 911
Strategic defense initiative, 917
Strikes, labor, 472, 522, 578, 653–654,
  653*p*, 713, 864*p*, 903
Strip mining, 886
Stuart, Gilbert, xvi, 218; painting by, 199*p*
Student Nonviolent Coordinating Committee
  (SNCC), 808–809
Students for a Democratic Society (SDS),
  809

Stuka bombers, 665*p*
Sturtevant, Julian, 281
Stuyvesant, Peter, 45
Submarines: nuclear, 784; in World War I,
  550, 551–552, 551*p*, 555, 562; in
  World War II, 669, 670, 680
Suburbs: blacks in, 756–757; growth of,
  456; movement to, 753–755, 754*p*; and
  need for automobile, 757–758
Sudetenland, 662
Suez Canal, 678, 743
Suez War, 743
Suffrage: *See* Voting rights
Sugar Act (1764), 77–78, 82
Sullivan, Louis, 436
Summer Freedom Project, 805
Summit meetings: in Geneva, 733–734,
  916; in Reykjavik, 916–917; in Wash-
  ington, D.C., 916*p*
Sumner, Charles, 316–317, 362, 506–507
Sumter, Fort, 325–326, 326*p*
Sunbelt, shift of population to, 752
Superconductivity, 901
Supply-side economics, 897–898
Supreme Council of the Indies, 28
Supreme Court, U.S.: and affirmative ac-
  tion, 851–853; appointment of Thurgood Marshall to, 807–808; under Burger, 829–830; under Bush, 852, 934;
  and civil rights, 738–739, 741, 848,
  850, 852–853; under Clinton, 940;
  constitutional powers of, 121, 191; and
  executive privilege, 837–838; and
  Franklin Roosevelt, 632, 634–635,
  637–638; under Hughes, 638; and Jim
  Crow laws, 380–381; and judicial review, 191; under Marshall, 189–192,
  213–214, 235–236; on mentally ill,
  872; and midnight judges, 189–191;
  under Reagan, 852, 914–915, 915*p*;
  under Rehnquist, 852, 922; salary of
  Justices, 375; under Taft, 536; under
  Taney, 318; under Warren, 738–739,
  741, 819–820
Supreme Court cases: *Bakke* decision
  (1978), 851; *Brown v. Board of Education of Topeka, Kansas* (1954), 738–
  739, 852; *Cohens v. Virginia* (1821),
  213; *Commonwealth v. Hunt* (1842),
  431; *Dartmouth College* case (1819),
  213; *Dred Scott v. Sanford* (1857), 317–
  318; *Escobedo v. Illinois* (1964), 819;
  Gibbons v. Ogden (1824), 214; *Gideon
  v. Wainwright* (1963), 819; *Griggs v.
  Duke Power Co.* (1971), 852; *Marbury v.
  Madison* (1803), 191–192; *Martin v.
  Hunter's Lessee* (1816), 213; *Martin v.
  Wilks* (1989), 852; *McCulloch v. Maryland* (1819), 213; *Miranda v. Arizona*
  (1966), 819; *Munn v. Illinois* (1876),
  470–471; *Plessy v. Ferguson* (1896),
  380, 738; *Pollock v. Farmers' Loan and
  Trust Co.* (1895), 473–474; *Richmond v.
  Croson* (1989), 852; *Roe v. Wade*
  (1971), 859; *Schechter v. United States*
  (1935), 632, 633; *Ward's Cove Packing
  Co. v. Antonio* (1989), 852; *Weber*
  (1979), 851; *Webster v. Reproductive
  Health Services* (1992), 859; *Worcester
  v. Georgia* (1832), 235
Supreme Headquarters, Allied Powers in
  Europe (SHAPE), 718
Surratt, John, 364
Surratt, Mary E., 364
Sussex (ship), sinking of, 552
Sussex pledge, 552

Sutter, John, 291
Sutter's Mill, 305, 305*p*
Sweden: colonies of, 45; and Jay's Treaty,
  161–162; neutrality of In World War I,
  548
Swimmer, Ross, 862–863
Switzerland, neutrality of in World War I,
  548
Symington, Stuart, in election of 1960, 775
Syria: and Middle East conflict, 908; as
  part of United Arab Republic, 746; and
  Suez War, 743; willingness to negotiate,
  943; and Yom Kippur War, 835, 879,
  889
System of Screw Threads and Nuts (Sellers),
  428

T

Taft, Robert, 711, 714, 714*p*, 718, 729
Taft, William Howard, 532; and anti-trust
  law, 534; in election of 1908, 532,
  532*p*; in election of 1910, 534; in
  election of 1912, 535–536; foreign pol-
  icy under, 542–543; and immigration
  restrictions, 444; and Philippines, 515;
  as President, 532; and reform, 532–
  534; as Supreme Court Chief Justice,
  536; U.S. treaty with, 732
Taft-Hartley Act (1947), 714, 719–720, 721
Taiwan (Formosa): 722, 724, 746; immigrants from, 868; U.S. treaty with, 732
Talleyrand, Charles-Maurice de, 166–167
Tammany Hall, 376, 463, 613
Tampico, Mexico, 544
Taney, Roger B., 241, 318, 318*p*, 340
Taos, New Mexico, 289
Tarbell, Ida, 529–530, 529*p*
Tariff(s): of 1816, 210; of abominations,
  225, 231–232; under Cleveland, 464,
  465*p*; Dingley, 532; Fordney-McCum-
  ber, 585; Hamilton's plan for, 157–158;
  Hawley-Smoot, 604; McKinley, 466–
  467, 473; Payne-Aldrich, 532–533,
  537–538; Underwood-Simmons, 538
Tavernier, Jules, painting by, 387*p*
Tax: on tea, 82–83; on whiskey, 162–164.
  See also Income tax
Tax reform: under Reagan, 914
Tax Reform Act (1986), 914
Taylor, Frederick W., 428–429, 594
Taylor, Glenn H., 719
Taylor, Zachary, 299; and Compromise of
  1850, 309; death of, 309; and election
  of 1848, 307; as general, 300
Teapot Dome affair, 587
Tecumseh, 201, 204
Tecumseh Confederation, 201, 201*m*
Teflon president, 917
Teheran: student seizure of United States
  embassy in, 895*p*
Telegraph, 259, 353
Telephones: affect rural life, 753; and AT&T
  breakup, 902–903; tapping by FBI, 831
Television: Bush-Clinton-Perot debate on,
  938; Carter-Reagan debate on, 896;
  close captioning of programs on, 871–
  872; coverage of Vietnam War, 809,
  813, 814; in election of 1948, 720;
  Ervin Committee hearings on, 834–835;
  evangelists on, 764–765; granting of
  pardon to Nixon on, 877; and Kennedy
  assassination, 792, 794*p*; Kennedy-
  Nixon debates on, 775–776, 776*p*;
  McCarthy hearings on, 736–737, 737*p*;

news coverage on, 760–761; Nixon resignation on, 838; spread of, 760–761, 769c
Teller Amendment, 516
Temperance movement, 287–288, 446, 528, 582. See also Alcohol
Tenements, 438, 438p, 440, 440p
Tennessee, 351; Reconstruction in, 373; and slavery issue, 215
Tennessee Coal and Iron Company, 526
Tennessee Pale Faces, 374
Tennessee Valley Authority (TVA), 626–627, 627m, 631, 668, 721, 734–735
Tenskwatawa (The Prophet), 201
Tenure of Office Act (1867), 370
Termination, Indian policy, 861
Terrorism, 909, 909p, 918, 921, 943; and bomb scares, 578, 579p; and Ku Klux Klan, 373–374, 374p, 580, 589, 591, 715
Test-ban treaty, 784–785, 786
Tet offensive, 812–813, 827
Texas: annexation of, 296–298; Coahuila, 294, 295m; Lone Star Republic, 294–295; secession of, 323; settlement of, 29, 30, 288, 289p; U.S. claim to, 213
Texas longhorns, 398
Textile Workers Union, 653
Thailand: refugees from, 868; in World War II, 671, 682
Thieu, Nguyen Van, 890
Third parties: in election of 1936, 636–637; in election of 1948, 719. See specific parties
Third World, 893; debts in, 910
Thirteenth Amendment, 351, 365, 374, 849
Thomas, Clarence, 853, 934, 934p
Thomas, Norman, 636
Thomson, Charles, drawing by, 104p
Thoreau, Henry David, 279–280, 740
Three-fifths compromise, 118–120
Three Mile Island nuclear power plant, 887, 887p
Thurmond, J. Strom, 719, 720
Tiananmen Square, 930–931, 930p
Tijerina, Reis Lopez, 865
Tilden, Samuel J., 376–377
Tillman, Ben, 475
Time zones, standard, 415
Tippecanoe, Battle of, 201
Titan, The (Dreiser), 530
Titan 34D, 918
Tito, Marshal, 709
Titusville, Pennsylvania, 420
Tobacco, 77, 176; colonial trade and, 53–54; and economy of South, 261; and Embargo Act, 196; Indian use of, 10; in Virginia, 38
Tocqueville, Alexis de, 249, 269
Tofft, Peter Peterson, painting by, 290p
Tojo, Hideki, 671, 716
Tokyo, Japan, raid on, 683
Toledo, Ohio, 269
Tomb of the Unknowns, 912
Tombstone, Arizona, 391
Tompkins, Sallie, 339p
Tonkin Gulf Resolution (1964), 809–810
Tordesillas, Treaty of (1493), 13–14
Tories: See Loyalists
Touré, Sékou, 782
Touro Synagogue, 42, 42p
Toussaint L'Ouverture, Pierre Dominique, 184–185
Tower, John, 919
Town, The (Faulkner), 767
Town meetings, 196

Townsend, Francis, 632, 633, 637
Townsendites, 632
Townshend, Charles, 80–81
Townshend Acts (I 767), 80–81
Trade, foreign: 1800–1812, 197c; British attempt to control colonial, 77–84; colonial, 55–57, 56m, 57m, 62–63, 63p; embargo against Haiti, 869; 1865–1915, 519c, and regulation of interstate commerce, 214; U.S. deficit in, 899–900; and passage of North American Free Trade Agreement (NAFTA) treaty, 939–940; in World War I, 552. See also Tariff(s)
Trade Expansion Act (1962), 786
Trading with the Enemy Act (1917), 566
Transcendentalists, 279–280
Transcontinental railroad, 375
Transjordan: See Jordan
Trans-Mississippi West, in Civil War, 353
Transportation: in 1790, 149, 150m; in 1800s, 251, 252m, 253–257, 254m, 256m; Calhoun's Bonus Bill, 211; and clipper ships, 305–306, 306p; and regulation of interstate commerce, 214; by wagon trains, 305. See also specific means
Travis, William B., 294
Treason, and Aaron Burr, 189
Treasury Department, 153, 154–158
Trent affair, 343
Trenton, Battle of, 94
Triangular trade, 57, 57m
Tripartite Security Treaty (1940), 726
Tripoli, 181m, 182
Trollope, Anthony, 270
Trollope, Mrs., 279
Truman, Harry S, 710p; attempt to extend New Deal, 715; and Berlin blockade, 717, 717p; and civil rights policy, 849; and decision to use bomb, 699; early career of, 707; in election of 1944, 690–691; in election of 1948, 718–720, 720p; Fair Deal under, 721; firing of MacArthur, 725–726; foreign policy under, 707–711; and health care reform, 940; and Korean War, 723–726; and labor, 713–714; and racial segregation, 677; and red scare, 721; and return of U.S. troops, 711–712; veto of McCarran Act, 723; and World War II, 696
Truman Doctrine, 709–710, 715
Trumbull, John, xvi, 218; painting by, 107p
Trusts, 417–418, 468p
Truth, Sojourner, 284–285, 285p
Tsongas, Paul, 936
Tubman, Harriet, 310, 310p
Tudors, 30
Tugwell, Rexford G., 622, 645, 866
Tulagi, Solomon Islands, 683, 684
Tunis, 181m, 182
Tunisia, 681, 685
Turkey, 37, 732; in NATO, 718; in World War I, 548
Turner, Benjamin, 373p
Turner, Frederick Jackson, 442
Turner, Nat, 236, 273, 646
Turnpikes, 251. See also Roads
Tuskegee Institute, 449
Tutu, Desmond, 922, 922p, 925, 925p
Tutuila, Samoa, 508
Twain, Mark, 394, 396, 514
Tweed, William, 373, 376–377, 378p
Tweed Ring, 376–377, 441
Twelfth Amendment, 169, 223, 378

Twentieth Amendment, 622
Twenty-fifth Amendment, 835, 877
Twenty-first Amendment, 626
Twenty-fourth Amendment, 788, 848
Twenty-second Amendment, 715, 748
Twenty-sixth Amendment, 833
Two-plus-four talks, 928
Two Years Before the Mast (Dana), 291
Tydings-McDuffie Act (1934), 660
Tyler, John, 296; in election of 1840, 243–244; and foreign policy under, 505; as President, 296; and Texas question, 296–297
Typographical Union, 653

U

U-2 flights, 747, 783, 785p
Ukraine, 689, 707, 929
"Ultra," 667–668, 679
Uncle Tom's Cabin (Stowe), 311–312, 311p, 391
Underground Railroad, 310
Underwood, Oscar, 535, 537–538
Underwood-Simmons Bill (1913), 538
Unemployment: from 1920 to 1933, 615c; in 1980s, 899, 899p; of blacks, 855; in Great Depression, 606–607; New Deal programs for, 629–630, 631, 635. See also Labor force
Unemployment insurance, 633
Uniformity system, 264
Union, as national slogan, 218
Union of Russian Workers, 579
Union Pacific Railroad, 375
Union party: in 1864 election, 365; in 1936, 637
Unions: See Labor unions and unions by name
United Arab Republic, 746
United Auto Workers, sit-down strike, 653p
United Farm Workers Organizing Committee, 865
United Mine Workers, 522, 652
United Nations: and creation of Israel, 743; and Cuban missile crisis, 785–786; and disarmament negotiations, 784–785; East and West Germany in, 888; elections in Cambodia, 891; and Gulf War, 931, 932–933; issue of China as member of, 724; and Korean War, 723–726, 731; and Lebanese crisis, 908–909; member nations of, 874; organization and function, 707–708; and the Peace Window, 706p; and Soviet invasion of Afghanistan, 895; and Suez War, 743; and trade embargo against Haiti, 869; and Yom Kippur War, 888
United Nations Relief and Rehabilitation Administration (UNRRA), 708
United States (frigate), 204
United States Colored Volunteers, 352
United States Sanitary Commission, 338–339
United States Steel, 418–419, 526, 590, 603, 653, 789; strike against, 578
University of Chicago, 448
University of Pennsylvania, 60
Unsafe at Any Speed (Nader), 803
Up from Slavery (Washington), 449
Utah: settlement of, 293–294; and women's suffrage, 446, 855
Uzbeks: ethnic unrest of, 929, 929p

V

V-1 flying bombs, 688
V-2 rockets, 688, 744
Vachon, John, photograph by, 639p
Vallard, Nicolas, map made by, 24m
Valley Forge, Pennsylvania, 95, 95p, 97
Valparaiso, Chile, 508
Van Buren, Martin, 239p, 242p; in election of 1836, 242; in election of 1840, 243–244; and election of 1844, 297; in election of 1848, 307; Presidency of, 242–243; as Secretary of State, 231; and Texas question, 296
Vance, Cyrus, 891, 894
Vandalia, Illinois, 251
Vanzetti, Bartolomeo, 580–581, 581p
Vasco de Gama, 15m
Vassar, Matthew, 449
Vassar College, 285, 449
Vaux, Calvert, 455–456
V-E (Victory in Europe) Day, 694–695
Venezuela, boundary dispute with, 510; as member of OPEC, 880
Veracruz, Mexico, 544
Vergennes, 99, 100
Verrazzano, Giovanni da, 19m, 22–23, 23p
Versailles Treaty (1919), 567–570, 568m, 584, 586
Vesey, Denmark, 232, 236, 646
Vespucci, Amerigo, 13, 15m
Veterans: from Civil War, 464, 467–468; and G.I. Bill of Rights, 712, 764; post-World War I, 586; from Vietnam, 871
Veto, use of, in UN Security Council, 707
Vice-President, selection of, 169
Vichy French, 681
Vicksburg, Mississippi, 344, 351; siege of, 353–354
Vienna, Austria: 1961 conference in, 780, 781; arms reduction talks in, 917; 1979 SALT II conference, 892
Viet Cong, 787, 810, 812–813. See also Vietnam War
Viet Minh, 732, 787
Vietnam: division of, 732; post-World War II liberation of, 731; refugees from, 496p, 814p, 868, 891; veterans from, 871
Vietnam Veterans' Memorial, 911–912, 912p
Vietnam War: and antiwar movement, 811, 812, 813p, 824; clemency for draft evaders, 878; under Eisenhower, 826–827; under Johnson, 827–828; under Kennedy, 786–788, 827; under Nixon, 822, 824–829; and peace negotiations, 824–825, 888; troops in, 801p, 825p, 839c; United States demand for MIA report, 911–912; victory of North, 890, 890p
Vikings: See Norse discoveries
Villa, Pancho, 544
Vincennes (ship), 921
Vincennes, Indiana, 201
Vineyard Sound, 23
Virginia: antislavery movement in, 106; colonial government in, 38, 66, 176; colonial life in, 38, 54; colonial resistance in, 82–83; Native Americans in, 37–38; payment of debt, 155; and ratification of Constitution, 122–123; Reconstruction in, 373; settlement of, 34–35, 36p, 37–38; and voting rights, 227; western land claims of, 83, 109, 111, 118
Virginia, C.S.S. (ship), 346

Virginia City, Nevada, 391, 393–394
Virginia Company, 35, 38
Virginia dynasty, 176
Virginia Plan, 118
Virginia Resolutions, 169, 232
Virgin Islands, 507, 715
Visscher, John, engraving by, 34p
VISTA (Volunteers in Service to America), 799
Vittoria (ship), 16
Volcker, Paul, 898
Von Arnim, General, 685
Von Braun, Wernher, 744
Von Steuben, Baron, 95
Voting, 815c; development of paper ballot, 227–228
Voting rights: for 18-year-olds, 833; for African Americans, 848; for blacks, 379–380, 380p, 646–648; colonial, 58; widening of, 226–227; for women, 58, 446, 446p, 520p, 529, 582, 855, 856p
Voting Rights Act (1965), 805–806, 848, 854

W

Wabash River, 182
Wade-Davis bill, 362–363
Wage-price controls and guidelines, 679, 734, 788–789, 804, 830
Wagner Act (1931), 623p, 634, 638, 652
Wagner-Steagall Act (1937), 627
Wagon trains, 291–293
Wake Island, in World War II, 683
Walden Pond, 279
Waldseemüller, Martin, 13; map made by, 14m
Walesa, Lech, 925, 925p
Wallace, George C., 791, 819; and civil rights, 806; in election of 1972, 832
Wallace, Henry A., 662, 669, 710, 711, 719, 720
Wallace, Henry C., 583
Walls, Josiah T., 373p
Wall Street, 553; bombing, 579p; 1929 stock market boom and crash, 600–603; 1987 crash of, 919–920; and Panic of 1907, 525–526; and reforms under Wilson, 538. See also Stockmarket
Waltham, Massachusetts, 263; and factory system, 261–262
Wanghia, Treaty of (1844), 505
Ward, A. Montgomery, 422–424, 423p
Ward, Robert DeCourcy, 443
War Department, creation of, 153–154
Ward's Cove Packing Co. v. Antonio (1989), 852
War Hawks, 200–202
Warhol, Andy, xvi, 766
War Industries Board, 564–565
War of 1812, 182, 199–202, 203m, 204–209; and Andrew Jackson, 206–207; battles in, 202, 203m, 204; British offensive in, 204–206; declaration of, 202; New England opposition to, 207–209; opposition to war, 208; and Treaty of Ghent, 207–208; as unavoidable, 202
War on Poverty, 802
War Powers Act (1973), 879
Warren, Charles, 443
Warren, Earl, 718, 719, 738, 819–820
Warren, Mercy Otis, needlepoint by, 60p
Warren Commission, 792

Warsaw Pact, 925, 927, 932, 935
Washington, Booker T., 449–450, 646
Washington, D.C.: in 1826, 226p; design of, 177–179, 178p; destruction of, in War of 1812, 205, 205p, 206; march on, 791–792, 791p; selection of site for, 155–156
Washington, George, 54, 58, 67, 116, 122, 176, 213, 405; Cabinet of, 153–154; as chairman of Constitutional Convention, 118; as commander of Continental Army, 85–86, 91, 92, 94–97, 94p, 98, 108; death of, 58; domestic policy under, 162–164, 251; election of, as President, 148; Farewell Address, 164, 218; first Cabinet of, 153–155; foreign policy under, 159–162; legacy of, 218; personal prestige of, 152; and postal service, 257; as President, 152; return to Mount Vernon, 165; and slavery, 286; support of Hamilton's economic plan, 159
Washington, James, 338p
Washington, Treaty of (1871), 507
Washington Conference (1921), 584, 585p
Washington Monument, 309
Washington Summit (1987), 916p
Wasp (ship), 204
Waste Land, The (Eliot), 582
Watergate Affair, 833–837; Ervin Committee hearings on, 833–834, 834p; and Ford's pardon of Nixon, 877–878; hearings on, 879; impact of, on government, 878–879; and impeachment hearings, 836–837; and Nixon resignation, 837–938; and pardoning of Nixon, 877–878; plumbers and, 831, 832, 833; and Saturday Night Massacre, 835–836; Senate investigation of, 833–835, 836p
Water pollution, 803
Water Quality Act (1965), 804
Watertown, Massachusetts, 41
Watkins, Carleton, photograph by, 525p
Watson, Tom, 472
Watt, James, 862, 869
Watts (Los Angeles) riots, 806
Wayne, Anthony, 162, 164p
We (Lindbergh), 593
Weaver, James B., 472
Weaver, Robert C., 790, 802, 853
Weber, Brian, 851
Weber, Max, painting by, 618p
Weber case (1979), 851
Webster, Daniel, 222, 232–234, 233p, 296
Webster, Noah, 220
Webster-Ashburton Treaty (1842), 296, 301
Webster-Hayne debate, 232–234, 233p
Webster v. Reproductive Health Services (1992), 859
Weems, Parson, 218
Weinberger, Caspar, 898
Weir, John Ferguson, painting by, 410p
Weld, Theodore Dwight, 286, 311
Welfare programs: growth of, 855; in post-Civil War South, 372–373; provided by Social Security Act, 633
Welles, Gideon, 346
Wellesley College, 449
Wells-Barnett, Ida B., 446
Welty, Eudora, 767
Wesleyan College, 282
West, Benjamin, xvii; painting by, 99p
West Bank, of Jordon River, 743
Western settlement: in 1750s, 67; and California, 291; and Civil War, 353; Clay's interest in, 200–201; disappearance of